MOUNCE'S

COMPLETE EXPOSITORY DICTIONARY *of* OLD & NEW TESTAMENT WORDS

WILLIAM D. MOUNCE

GENERAL EDITOR

D. MATTHEW SMITH
ASSOCIATE EDITOR

MILES V. VAN PELT
ASSOCIATE EDITOR

ZONDERVAN

Mounce's Complete Expository Dictionary of Old and New Testament Words

Requests for information should be addressed to:
Zondervan, *3900 Sparks Dr. SE, Grand Rapids, Michigan 49546*

Library of Congress Cataloging-in-Publication Data

Mounce, William D.
Mounce's complete expository dictionary of Old and New Testament words / William D. Mounce, general editor.
p. cm.
Includes index.
ISBN 978-0-310-24878-1
1. Bible—Dictionaries. 2. Hebrew language—Dictionaries—English. 3. Greek language, Biblical—Dictionaries—English. I. Title: Complete expository dictionary of Old and New Testament words. II. Mounce, William D.
BS440.M63 2006
220.3—dc22 2006005245

Interior design: William D. Mounce
Typeset: Stonehaven, Inc.

Printed in China

21 22 23 24 25 26 27 28 29 30 /TRM/ 31 30 29 28 27 26 25 24 23 22 21 20 19 18 17 16

For my sons,

Tyler and Hayden

whom God called to himself at an early age,

blessed them with spiritual sensitivity beyond their years,

and in whatever they do, will be ministers of their Lord,

"proclaiming the excellencies of him who called them

out of darkness into his marvelous light."

My son, if your heart is wise,
my heart too will be glad. (Prov. 23:15)

Sons are a heritage from the Lord,
children a reward from him.
Like arrows in the hands of a warrior
are sons born in one's youth.
Blessed is the man
whose quiver is full of them. (Ps. 127:3-5)

General Editor
William D. Mounce

Zondervan Editor
Verlyn D. Verbrugge

Associate Editors
D. Matthew Smith
Miles V. Van Pelt

Contributors

Corey L. Abney
William D. Barker
Denny Burk
Kevin Roy Burris
Kevin Carroll
Micah Daniel Carter
Brian C. Gault
Mark Gignilliat
Wendy Wilcox Glidden
Robert Andrew Gowins
Mattie Green Greathouse
Fredrick T. Greco
Daniel M. Gurtner
James M. Hamilton Jr.
Justin K. Hardin
Tim Hegg
Joseph Douglas Hillrich
Paul Norman Jackson
Ryan Jackson
Barry C. Joslin
Myron C. Kauk
Edward W. Klink III
Joshua Knott
John David Laing
Stefana Dan Laing
Darian Lockett
Phillip Marshall
G. D. Mason III
R. Kelvin Moore
David Scott Morlan
Robert H. Mounce
Ronald A. Osborne
David S. Parks
Jonathan T. Pennington
Seth Michael Rodriquez
Elizabeth Shively
Gregory Scott Smith
Joel Allen Troxler Jr.
Andy Williams
W. Stephen Williams
Stephen Witmer
Jonathan Worthington

Contents

Introduction

When God chose to reveal himself and his will, he usually did so with words. And what precious words they are. Because every word is "breathed out by God" (2 Tim. 3:16), "every word of God proves true" (Prov. 30:5). While words have meaning primarily in the context of sentences and paragraphs, we still tend to cling to individual words. They guide us; they help us; sometimes they tease us when their meanings are elusive and flexible, especially when they come from other languages and from people immersed in different cultures. *Mounce's Expository Dictionary* (*MED*) will help you learn the meaning of the words God has used.

What are the distinctives of this book? (1) The integration of Old and New Testament words. The OT was written primarily in Hebrew, with parts in Aramaic; the NT is in Greek. But because the Old and New Testaments are one revelation, these words are tied together and can only be explained together. You cannot understand the NT concept of "mercy" (GK *1799*) without understanding the OT word *heṣed* (GK 2876).

(2) Words are defined in biblical context. As I discuss in "How to Do Word Studies" (pages xvii-xxx), words have "bundles of meanings." They have a range of meanings, and it is the context of the sentence primarily that determines what any one word means in any one verse. While looking at the meaning of the parts of a word (its "etymology") can be interesting, the meaning of many words has moved beyond the sum of its parts. And apparent etymologies can be deceptive; a "butterfly" is not a dairy product with wings.

(3) The "Golden Nugget." Whenever possible, we have tried to give you something special, something that makes for a good illustration; "Paul tells Timothy not to become entangled in civilian affairs (2 Tim. 2:4); the word 'entangled' is used elsewhere of a rabbit entangled in a briar bush." We have also tried to list those most familiar verses; "This is the same word that Jesus uses when he says, 'For God so loved the *world* that he gave his only Son' (Jn. 3:16)."

(4) *MED* is not keyed to just one English translation but works with many, ranging from the King James Version to present-day translations.

(5) *MED* uses two numbering systems, one developed by Edward W. Goodrick and John R. Kohlenberger III ("GK"), and the older system developed by James Strong ("S"). While the latter is better known, the former is more complete and ties *MED* in with many of the best study tools.

(6) Hebrew and Greek words are organized around the English words generally used to translate them, and all Hebrew and Greek words are given in their original script as well as in English transliteration. While you can enjoy learning some aspects of the original languages, you do not need to have a working knowledge of Greek and Hebrew to use this book. (If you have not studied Hebrew or Greek, I would encourage you to read "How to Do Word Studies," pages xvii-xxx.)

(7) There are actually three dictionaries in this book. The first is the main set of word studies, organized by their English translation. It includes all Greek words occuring ten times or more, all Hebrew words occuring fifty times or more, and other words occuring less if they are theologically or exegetically significant (excluding some proper nouns, adverbs, conjunctions, and particles). The second is a Hebrew-English dictionary alphabetized by Hebrew order, cross-referenced to the first part. We have included all Hebrew words that occur fifty times or more, and any theologically significant word that occurs fewer times (excluding proper nouns, adverbs, conjunctions, and particles). Frequencies

are taken from John Kohlenberger's list. The third is a Greek-English dictionary alphabetized by Greek order, also cross-referenced to the first part. It includes all the Greek words that occur in the NT. Frequencies are taken from the GNT-T module of the Accordance software program, which I developed.

(8) *MED* has an effective and accurate cross-reference system. If a Hebrew or Greek word is translated basically by one English word, it will be discussed at that location. If, however, a Hebrew or Greek word is translated by multiple English words, we have chosen one English word and there you will find the primary discussion. If you go to the other English words, there will be a short definition and a cross-reference to the main article. If a translation uses an English word that is generally not used by the other translations, there will just be a cross-reference, such as, "Longsuffering, see *patience*."

(9) Under every English entry we list first the OT Hebrew words (if applicable) and then the NT Greek words (again, if applicable). Within each of these categories words are generally sorted by verb, noun, adjective, adverb, and then other forms. If you are studying the actual Hebrew or Greek word, you can also locate them in the second or third dictionary. There you will see the full range of meanings for that word, and can then follow the cross-references to the fuller discussion in the first part of *MED*.

(10) The articles are written in such a way that if you want to do further study, you can move smoothly to other major word studies. For Hebrew words we recomend the five volume *New International Dictionary of Old Testament Theology and Exegesis*, edited by Willem A. VanGemeren (Zondervan, 1997). For Greek words we highly recommend the *New International Dictionary of New Testament Theology: Abridged Edition*, by Verlyn D. Verbrugge (Zondervan, 2000). This is an abridgment of the excellent three-volume *New International Dictionary of New Testament Theology*, edited by Colin Brown (Zondervan, 1978). If you want to venture more deeply into Greek beyond word studies, being able to use it without spending years in all the detailed work, may I recommend my own *Greek for the Rest of Us* (Zondervan, 2003).

I have spent much of my professional life writing books so that people can understand their New Testaments better. I am glad to have completed this trilogy: *Mounce's Complete Expository Dictionary of Old and New Testament Words*, *The Interlinear for the Rest of Us*, and *Greek for the Rest of Us*. My special thanks to the forty-two Ph.D. students and scholars who wrote these articles, the three assistant editors without whose work this book could not have been finished in my lifetime (Verlyn Verbrugge, Miles Van Pelt, Matt Smith), and to my father, Robert Mounce, who shared much of the burden. Thanks to Jack Kuhatschek, the Zondervan editor who first approached me about the project and provided invaluable assistance in defining the basic approach of the book, to my friends Ed and Tacie Taylor of Stonehaven, and special thanks to my wife Robin and our three children, Tyler, Kiersten, and Hayden, who patiently waited for me to finish reading "one more article" before resurfacing for the evening.

May God richly bless you as you strive to know him and his Word better.

Bill Mounce
February, 2006

Abbreviations

BDAG	*A Greek-English Lexicon of the New Testament and Other Early Christian Literature*
ESV	English Standard Version
GK	Goodrick/Kohlenberger numbers (Greek in italics, Hebrew in roman)
Gr.	Greek
Heb.	Hebrew
KJV	King James Version
LXX	Septuagint (the Greek translation of the OT)
NASB	New American Standard Bible
NIDOTTE	*New International Dictionary of Old Testament Theology and Exegesis*
NIDNTT-A	*New International Dictionary of New Testament Theology: Abridged Edition*
NIV	New International Version
NT	New Testament
OT	Old Testament
RSV	Revised Standard Version
S	Strong's number (Greek in italics, Hebrew in roman)

Hebrew Verbal Stems

Q	Qal	P	Piel	H	Hiphal	Hit	Hitpael	Qp	Qal passive
N	Niphal	Pu	Pual	Ho	Hophal	Hi	Hithpael		

Books of the Bible

Gen.	Genesis	Isa.	Isaiah	Rom.	Romans
Exod.	Exodus	Jer.	Jeremiah	1 Cor.	1 Corinthians
Lev.	Leviticus	Lam.	Lamentations	2 Cor.	2 Corinthians
Num.	Numbers	Ezek.	Ezekiel	Gal.	Galatians
Deut.	Deuteronomy	Dan.	Daniel	Eph.	Ephesians
Jos.	Joshua	Hos.	Hosea	Phil.	Philippians
Jdg.	Judges	Joel	Joel	Col.	Colossians
Ruth	Ruth	Amos	Amos	1 Thess.	1 Thessalonians
1 Sam.	1 Samuel	Obad.	Obadiah	2 Thess.	2 Thessalonians
2 Sam.	2 Samuel	Jon.	Jonah	1 Tim.	1 Timothy
1 Ki.	1 Kings	Mic.	Micah	2 Tim.	2 Timothy
2 Ki.	2 Kings	Nah.	Nahum	Tit.	Titus
1 Chr.	1 Chronicles	Hab.	Habakkuk	Phlm.	Philemon
2 Chr.	2 Chronicles	Zeph.	Zephaniah	Heb.	Hebrews
Ezr.	Ezra	Hag.	Haggai	Jas.	James
Neh.	Nehemiah	Zech.	Zechariah	1 Pet.	1 Peter
Est.	Esther	Mal.	Malachi	2 Pet.	2 Peter
Job	Job	Matt.	Matthew	1 Jn.	1 John
Ps.	Psalms	Mk.	Mark	2 Jn.	2 John
Prov.	Proverbs	Lk.	Luke	3 Jn.	3 John
Eccl.	Ecclesiastes	Jn.	John	Jude	Jude
Song.	Song of Solomon	Acts	Acts	Rev.	Revelation

Hebrew Transliterations

Consonants			Vowels		
א	Alef	ʾ	בַ	Pathach	*a*
ב	Bet	*b*	בֶ	Seghol	*e*
ג	Gimel	*g*	בִ	Hireq	*i*
ד	Dalet	*d*	בָ	Qamets Hatuf	*o*
ה	He	*h*	בֻ	Qibbuts	*u*
ו	Waw	*w*			
ז	Zayin	*z*	בָ	Qamets	*ā*
ח	Het	*ḥ*	בֵ	Tsere	*ē*
ט	Tet	*ṭ*	בֹ	Holem	*ō*
י	Yod	*y*	בָה	Qamets He	*â*
כ ך	Kaf	*k*	בֵי	Tsere Yod	*ê*
ל	Lamed	*l*	בִי	Hireq Yod	*î*
מ ם	Mem	*m*	בוֹ	Holem Waw	*ô*
נ ן	Nun	*n*	בוּ	Shureq	*û*
ס	Samek	*s*			
ע	Ayin	ʿ	בֲ	Hateph Pathach	*ª*
פ ף	Pe	*p*	בֱ	Hateph Seghol	*ᵉ*
צ ץ	Tsade	*ṣ*	בֳ	Hateph Qamets	*ᵒ*
ק	Qof	*q*			
ר	Resh	*r*	בְ	Vocal Shewa	*ᵉ*
שׂ	Sin	*ś*			
שׁ	Shin	*š*			
ת	Taw	t			

Greek Transliterations

α	Alpha	*a*	ρ	Rho	*r*
β	Beta	*b*	σ, ς	Sigma	*s*
g	Gamma	*g*	τ	Tau	*t*
δ	Delta	*d*	υ	Upsilon	*y* or *u*
ε	Epsilon	*e*	φ	Phi	*ph*
ζ	Zeta	*z*	χ	Chi	*ch*
η	Eta	*ē*	ψ	Psi	*ps*
θ	Theta	*th*	ω	Omega	*ō*
ι	Iota	*i*			
κ	Kappa	*k*	γγ		*ng*
λ	Lambda	*l*	γκ		*nk*
μ	Mu	*m*	γξ		*nx*
ν	Nu	*n*	γχ		*nch*
ξ	Xi	*x*			
ο	Omicron	*o*	ῥ		*rh*
π	Pi	*p*	῾		*h*

Two Ways to Use This Book

English Only

There are two basic ways to use this book. The most common way for people who do not know Greek and Hebrew is to work purely from the English. You are reading a verse, you see an English word, and you want to know what the Greek or Hebrew behind the English word means.

In many cases this will work fine. For example, you want to know what "prophet" means. You go to the first of the three dictionaries in this book, find the entry "PROPHET," and you can read the entry for the Hebrew *nābîʾ* and the Greek *prophētēs*. If you want to learn about "Propitiation," you can read about the verb *hilaskomai* or the noun *hilasmos*.

However, what if you want to learn about "Purpose"? There are three Greek nouns that we list under this entry: *boulē*, *eudokia*, and *prothesis*. As you will learn in the next section ("How to Do Word Studies"), these three Greek words have some overlap in meaning, but each one has its own range of meanings. In other words, *boulē* may have a meaning that *prothesis* doesn't, and vice versa. If you don't know the Greek (or Hebrew) word behind the specific English word in the specific verse you are studying, you wouldn't know which set of definitions apply in your situation.

Greek and Hebrew Tools

There is another way to do word studies based on the actual Greek or Hebrew word that has been translated in your specific verse, and you don't have to know Greek or Hebrew to do it. I would highly recommend doing your word studies this way. *If you are going to do biblical word studies, you should be studying the actual words God used*, and God didn't speak in English back then.

In my book the *Interlinear for the Rest of Us*, it is easy to look up a verse, find the English word, and under it you will see its "GK number." Use this number to look up the word in the Hebrew-English or the Greek-English dictionaries in this book, see the basic range of meanings, and if the word is discussed in more detail in the first dictionary in this book, it will be cross-referenced.

For example, you are reading Acts 2:23. Here is the Reverse Interlinear:

This	man was	handed	over to you	by	God's	set	purpose
τοῦτον ←		ἔκδοτον ←		↱	⌊τοῦ θεοῦ⌋	ὡρισμένῃ	⌊τῇ βουλῇ⌋
r.asm		a.asm			d.gsm n.gsm	pt.rp.dsf	d.dsf n.dsf
4047		1692		1087	3836 2536	3988	3836 1087

Under the word "purpose" you see that it is Greek word 1087. (You will quickly learn that word 3836 is the definite article ["the"], which is often untranslated, and the second word is the one you are looking for.) If you know Greek, you will recognize that the Greek word is βουλῇ and it is a noun, dative singular feminine. You go to the Greek-English dictionary, read the article, and see that it is cross-referenced to "purpose." Now when you come to "PURPOSE" in the first dictionary, you know that the word you are studying is βούλη (*boulē*), GK *1087* (S *1012*). Its GK number is *1087*, and its Strong number is *1012*. There are also computer programs that provide this same information, and I will discuss this in the next section.

There is no Hebrew counterpart to the Reverse Interlinear, so for the OT you will have to use a computer program or an exhaustive concordance.

This second way of doing word studies requires one extra step, but you are assured that you are then studying the correct Greek or Hebrew word. This is by far the better way to study God's words.

How to Do Word Studies

(The following discussion is drawn from my text, *Greek for the Rest of Us*. It centers on Greek, but there is a discussion of Hebrew word studies at the end.)

Words have a "semantic range." "Semantic" refers to a word's meaning; "semantic range" refers to the range of possible meanings a word possesses. Think of all the ways we use the word "run."

> I scored six runs today.
> Could you run that by me again?
> My computer runs faster than yours!
> He runs off at the mouth.
> I left the water running all night.
> He ran to the store.
> The car ran out of gas.
> The clock ran down.
> Duane ran for senate.
> Her nose ran.
> I ran up the bill.

In describing this concept to students I prefer the phrase "bundle of meanings." A word usually does not possess just one meaning; it has different meanings, hence "bundle."

This is true in any language. For example, the semantic range of the preposition ἐν (*en*) is quite large. Just look at how it is used in the following verses, all from Matthew. (All translations are from the RSV; the format is that of a standard interlinear.)

Matt. 1:20 τὸ γὰρ **ἐν** αὐτῇ γεννηθὲν ἐκ πνεύματός ἐστιν ἁγίου.
the for *in* her conceived of spirit is holy
for that which is conceived *in* her is of the Holy Spirit

Matt. 2:1 Τοῦ ... Ἰησοῦ γεννηθέντος **ἐν** Βηθλέεμ ... **ἐν** ἡμέραις Ἡρῴδου
the Jesus was born *in* Bethlehem *in* days of Herod
Jesus was born *in* Bethlehem … *in* the days of Herod.

Matt. 3:9 καὶ μὴ δόξητε λέγειν **ἐν** ἑαυτοῖς
and not presume to say *in* yourselves
and do not presume to say *to* yourselves

Matt. 3:11 Ἐγὼ ... ὑμᾶς βαπτίζω **ἐν** ὕδατι
I you baptize *in* water
I baptize you *with* water.

Matt. 4:23 θεραπεύων πᾶσαν νόσον καὶ πᾶσαν μαλακίαν **ἐν** τῷ λαῷ.
healing every disease and every infirmity *in* the people
healing every disease and every infirmity *among* the people

Matt. 5:34 μὴ ὀμόσαι ὅλως· μήτε **ἐν** τῷ οὐρανῷ, ὅτι θρόνος ἐστὶν τοῦ θεοῦ
not swear at all either *in* the heaven for throne it is of the God
Do not swear at all, either *by* heaven, for it is the throne of God.

Languages are not codes. There is not a one–to–one correspondence between languages, and this applies especially to vocabulary. Rarely if ever can you find one word in one language that corresponds exactly to another word in another language, especially in its semantic range. English has no single word that matches the range of meanings for *en*. The semantic range of a Greek and English word may overlap, but they are not identical.

So how do we translate the Bible when we do not have English words that correspond exactly to the Greek? We have to interpret, which is why all translation is interpretive; no Bible translation is neutral. For example, in 1 Tim. 6:13-14 Paul writes,

> In the presence of God who gives life to all things, and of Christ Jesus who in his testimony before Pontius Pilate made the good confession, I *charge* you to keep the commandment unstained and free from reproach until the appearing of our Lord Jesus Christ. (RSV)

The Greek word behind "charge" is *parangellō*, which means "to command, insist, instruct, urge." Quite a wide range of meanings for which there is no single counterpart in English. The translator must decide whether Paul is "commanding" Timothy (who is a member of his inner circle, fully trusted, and probably his best friend) or "urging" him. This is an interpretive decision that must be made by the translator. The RSV chose "charge," the NLT "command," and the NKJV rightly (in my opinion) selected "urge."

But let's say that you want to know what Paul means when he "charges" Timothy to keep the commandment unstained. It doesn't do any good to look up the English word "charge," because "charge" can't mean "urge" (and "urge" can't mean " charge"). If you really want to decide for yourself what Paul is saying, you have to know the Greek word behind the English, learn its semantic range, and see the decision faced by the translators.

How do you do this? There are four steps. 1. Decide what English word to study. 2. Identify the Greek word. 3. Discover its semantic range. 4. Look for something in the context that helps determine what the biblical author meant by this word in this particular verse.

Step 1. Choose the English Word

Rom. 10:9-10 is one of the most succinct and crucial passages in the Bible on the nature of salvation (ESV translation).

> If you confess with your mouth that Jesus is Lord and believe in your heart that God raised him from the dead, you will be saved. For with the heart one believes and is justified, and with the mouth one confesses and is saved.

The key term in the entire passage is what? It's "Lord," isn't it? The essence of salvation is the confession, "Jesus is Lord," accompanied with the acceptance of the resurrection. So what does "Lord" mean?

This is actually the first step in doing a word study: you've decided on a significant word. If you try to do word studies on every word you read, not only will you run out of time, but you'll get bored. So how do you pick the right words? There is not a clear-cut answer to this question, but here are some suggestions.

- Look for *repeated* words. This normally indicates a recurring theme, and perhaps the central theme in the passage. This includes the use of synonyms.

- Look for *theological* terms. This will be more obvious in teaching passages (e.g., in Paul) than in narrative (e.g., in the gospels).
- Sometimes a verse will "hang" on a word. It is a word that is central to the meaning of the verse, and without it the sentence will not make sense. In Rom. 10:9 it is "Lord."
- As you compare translations, you may find a significant word that is translated *differently* among the different translations.

What do you think "Lord" means? Let's find out.

2. Identify the Greek Word

It may be at this point your search is done. You may look up the English word "Lord," and there is only one Greek word translated "Lord." But what if there is more than one Greek word translated as "Lord"? You could read all the entries and have a basic understanding of what the "word group" means. But if you want more, you need to know which specific Greek word lies behind the English word in this specific verse. How do you do this?

Interlinear for the Rest of Us

There are several tools that will show you the Greek behind the English. You will excuse me if I am a little biased, but my favorite is a book I wrote, *The Interlinear for the Rest of Us* (Zondervan, 2006, originally entitled, *The NIV English-Greek New Testament: A Reverse Interlinear*, Zondervan, 2000). The whole point behind this book is to give people who do not know Greek access to the Greek words behind the English, the Greek word's parsing, and its GK number.

I created the term "reverse interlinear" because the book does one thing significantly different from standard interlinears. Most interlinears keep Greek word order and include a word-for-word English translation under each Greek word. Because English word order is often fundamentally different from Greek, the interlinear English translations generally do not make sense. *IRU* keeps the English word order and alters the Greek to match the English text of the NIV. This way you can read the English and drop down to the Greek whenever you wish.

If you look up Rom. 10:9 in *IRU*, here is what you will find.

9 That	if	you	confess	with	your	mouth,		"Jesus is
ὅτι	ἐὰν	→	ὁμολογήσῃς	ἐν	σου	⌊τῷ	στόματι⌋	Ἰησοῦν
cj	cj		v.aas.2s	p.d	r.gs.2	d.dsn	n.dsn	n.asm
4022	1569		3933	1877	5148	3836	5125	2652

Lord,"	and	believe	in	your	heart		that	God		raised
κύριον	καὶ	πιστεύσῃς	ἐν	σου	⌊τῇ	καρδίᾳ⌋	ὅτι	⌊ὁ	θεὸς⌋	ἤγειρεν
n.asm	cj	v.aas.2s	p.d	r.gs.2	d.dsf	n.dsf	cj	d.nsm	n.nsm	v.aai.3s
3261	2779	4409	1877	5148	3836	2840	4022	3836	2536	1586

The inflected form is κύριον, it is a noun (see the "n" in "n.asm"), and its GK number is *3261*. The conversion chart at the back of *IRU* tells you its Strong's number is *2962*.

Software

Another easy way to get at the Greek behind the English is to use a good software program. There are several I could use as illustrations, but my favorite is Accordance (Macintosh computers only). If you have purchased the appropriate modules (NIV-G/K, NAS95S, or KJVS), you simply find a verse and move the cursor over the English word. The Greek word behind the English, its definition, GK number, and lexical form (in Greek and transliteration) appear in the amplify window.

If you use a Microsoft Windows computer, there are several good options. BibleWorks is especially good for showing you the original languages, as long as you use the KJV and/or the NASB texts with codes. Zondervan's new Pradis also does an excellent job.

Concordances

You could also find the Greek word behind the English the old fashioned way, using an exhaustive concordance. Let's do this using the NIV text and the *NIV Exhaustive Concordance*.

What is a *concordance*? A concordance is a book that lists all the words in the Bible in alphabetical order, and under each word shows you the verses in which that word occurs. So, for example, if you looked up "love," you would find that the word occurs 551 times in 505 verses.

What is an *exhaustive* concordance? It is a concordance that lists *every* word in the Bible and lists *every* verse in which each word occurs. There are shorter concordances, published as separate books or in the back of your Bible, but they do not show every word, and usually do not show you every verse in which the words occur. The serious student needs a serious concordance. Get an exhaustive.

But many exhaustive concordances give you one more invaluable piece of information. They show you the GK (or Strong's) number of the Greek word used in the sentence. So let's say you want to find the Greek word behind the English word "love" in Matt. 19:19, "You shall love your neighbor as yourself." Look up the word "love" in *The NIV Exhaustive Concordance* and look through the entries until you find Matt. 19:19. This concordance lists the entry as, "and '**l** your neighbor as yourself.'" (The editor made a decision as to which words to the left and the right of the selected word to include, and also abbreviated "love" to "**l**" and bolded it. This is standard practice.) If you look to the right of the entry, you will see that "love" in this verse translates the Greek word with the GK number, "*26*."

This is the key piece of information for word studies. If you wish, you can go to the back of the concordance and look up the number in the Greek lexicon (not the Hebrew, which is the first of the three dictionaries in the back of this concordance). There you will find that the dictionary form of the Greek word *26* is ἀγαπάω, which is transliterated as *agapaō*. This step is not always crucial for word studies, but you may enjoy knowing the information.

If you use the KJV, there are several exhaustive concordances available. In my opinion, the best is the *Strongest Strong's,* not because Zondervan (my publisher) published it, but because it is the best. They worked from the best English KJV text, and they provide the best helps in the back of the book. The original Strong's concordance is published by several publishers, as is Young's. There is an exhaustive concordance for the NASB and the RSV as well. Most use Strong's numbers; the *NIV Exhaustive* and I use the GK numbers (and there are conversion charts in the back so you can move from GK to Strong and back again).

Step 3. Discover its Semantic Range

Before you can discover what the word means in a particular context, you have to learn its range of meaning, its "semantic range." As I have been saying, we are looking for the semantic range of the Greek word, not the English, since they are almost always (if not always) different. So we are going to learn the semantic range of the Greek word *kyrios*.

This is where the Hebrew-English and Greek-English dictionaries in *MED* come into play. Each entry shows you the entire semantic range of the Hebrew or Greek word. Here is the entry for κύριος:

> **[3261]** κύριος *kyrios* 717x *a lord, master,* Matt. 12:8; *an owner, possessor,* Matt. 20:8; *a potentate, sovereign,* Acts 25:26; *a power, deity,* 1 Cor. 8:5; *the Lord, Jehovah,* Matt. 1:22; *the Lord* Jesus Christ, Matt. 24:42; Mk. 16:19; Lk. 10:1; Jn. 4:1; 1 Cor. 4:5; freq.; κύριε, a term of respect of various force, *Sir, Lord,* Matt. 13:27; Acts 9:6, et al. freq. [2962]. See *Lord.*

You can see the range of meaning, running from a term of polite address, to a servant's respectful address to his master, to a term for deity. This word is discussed in *MED* under the English translation "Lord" in the first part of this book.

Let me introduce you to another marvelous tool. It used to be called an "Englishman's Concordance." The new one by John Kohlenberger is titled *The Greek-English Concordance to the New Testament* (Zondervan, 1997), and especially if you read the NIV, this is the one to use. With this text you look up a Greek word based on its lexical form (or GK number), and you can see every place the Greek word occurs in the NT, *but the verses are listed in English.*

There is a considerable difference between this type of concordance and others. In a regular concordance, if you look up "Lord," the entries list all the places where the English word "Lord" occurs. However, there may be several different Greek words that are translated "Lord," and *kyrios* may not always be translated with "Lord." For example, *sarx* is translated in Galatians by the NIV as "body" (1x), "flesh" (1x), "human effort" (1x), "illness" (2x), "man" (1x), "no one" (1x), "ordinary way" (2x), "outwardly" (1x), "sinful nature" (7x), and "that nature" (1x). (In some of these occurrences, *sarx* was combined with another word when translating.)

But with an "Englishman's" concordance, you know you are looking at every place the same Greek word occurs, regardless of how it is translated. (In a regular Greek concordance, the verses would be in Greek.) As you scan through the entries, you can see how the NIV has translated *kyrios*.

There are also specific books that help you see the semantic range of a word and, to a greater or lesser degree, will tell you more about the word, especially its usage throughout the Bible and other ancient writings. My favorite one-volume word study book (after *MED*, of course) is Verlyn D. Verbrugge's *New International Dictionary of New Testament Theology: Abridged Edition*. It lists words alphabetically and by their GK number, and the discussion is excellent. Verbrugge's work is an abridgment of the three-volume set, *New International Dictionary of New Testament Theology,* edited by Colin Brown. This too is an excellent discussion of the words in the NT that often moves, as the name implies, into the word's theological significance; however, it is generally too advanced for many people. Zondervan published a fourth volume that contains all the indexes.

Geoffrey W. Bromiley's one volume *Theological Dictionary of the New Testament: Abridged in One Volume* is, as the name says, an abridgment of the multi-volume *Theological Dictionary of the New Testament,* edited by Kittel and Friedrich. We affectionately call Bromiley's abridgment *Little Kittel* or *Kittelbits.* Whatever its name, Bromiley did a masterful job of cutting out discussion that is mostly irrelevant for most people. It lists words alphabetically based on their transliteration. But be sure to use the index; it doesn't discuss every Greek word, and you could spend a long time looking for an entry that isn't included. The full multi-volume series of *Theological Dictionary of the New Testament,* while it looks good on your shelf, is of little value for most people.There are also multi-volume word studies by Wuest (*Word Studies in the Greek New Testament*), Vincent (*Word Studies in the New Testament*), and Robertson (*Word Pictures in the New Testament*).

If the word is an important theological term, it may be discussed in reference works like the *Evangelical Dictionary of Theology* (rev. ed.), edited by Walter A. Elwell (Baker, 2001). This is a marvelous book, and everyone ought to have a copy of it for their study. (I don't say that very often.)

4. Context

Once you have located the Greek word and learned its semantic range, it is time to decide what it means in the particular verse you are studying. The question is, how do you decide?

In short, the answer is "context." You look for something in the immediate context that gives a clue as to the precise meaning of the word. I like to think in terms of a series of concentric circles. The word in the verse is the smallest circle. The next circle out is the verse, then the paragraph, the book, etc. The point is that you look for something in the verse that will define the word. If there isn't anything, then look at the paragraph. If there is nothing to help you in the paragraph, go to the book as a whole. But you want to stop as soon as you can. The further you go out from the center, the less assuredness you have that you are defining the word properly. But if you have to keep going out from the center, then you have to.

Why do you want to stop as soon as possible? Because different people can use the same word differently. Even the same person can use the same word differently in different contexts, as our previous example of *sarx* in Paul shows. Paul and James use "justify" in significantly different ways, even though they both mention Abraham and the same verse in Habakkuk (discussed below).

I saw a sign the other day that said: "GO CHILDREN SLOW," where each word was stacked above the next. One of the sillier signs I have ever seen, it seemed to me. What does it mean? Does it mean, "Go, the children are slow," or, "Go children, but slowly," or, "Go slow, there are children." Obviously, it is the latter, but why is it obvious? Because we understand the sign within its *context* of being a road sign, and we probably notice that we are driving through a neighborhood full of children. And yet, in order to get to this understanding, we had to alter the word order and recognize that there is a grammatical error in the sign ("slow" should be "slowly" since it is an adverb).

Another good one is, "Speed radar controlled." Silly sign #2. The radar doesn't control my speed. My foot does. (Of course, it could be argued that the threat of a ticket proven by a radar gun is the ultimate cause of my speed.) How about the most common sign, "Stop." Shouldn't it be "Stop and then go"? And my other favorites from New England: "Lightly salted"; "Blind drive"; "Thickly settled."

The point is that common sense tells us these signs are to be understood within their context. The same is true for word studies. How does the context help us decided what a word means? Let's look at some examples as we move out from the center of the concentric circles.

Verse. 1 Thess. 4:3. "For this is the *will* of God, your sanctification." What is God's will for your life? To be sanctified; to be holy.

Paragraph. 1 Tim. 2:14-15. "and Adam was not deceived, but the woman was deceived and became a transgressor. Yet woman will be *saved* through bearing children, if she continues in faith and love and holiness, with modesty" (RSV). What does "saved" mean? V 14 suggests we are dealing with spiritual salvation ("transgressor") and not physical safety.

Book. 1 Tim. 1:10. At the end of a list of sins, Paul states that these are "contrary to *sound* doctrine." What is "*sound* doctrine"? Most translations miss the fact that the word is a medical metaphor meaning "healthy," and that it contrasts with the heresy being spread in Ephesus, which Paul elsewhere describes as sick and morbid (1 Tim. 6:4), infectious abrasions (1 Tim. 6:5) spreading like gangrene (2 Tim. 2:17). Sound doctrine is that which is opposed to the false teaching.

New Testament. In Rom. 4:2-3 (ESV) Paul says,

> For if Abraham was justified by works, he has something to boast about, but not before God. For what does the scripture say? "Abraham believed God, and it was counted to him as righteousness."

("Justify" and "righteous" are the same concept.) What does "justification" mean? How are we justified? If you look at Jas. 2:21-24 (ESV) you will see that he says,

> Was not Abraham our father *justified by works* when he offered up his son Isaac upon the altar? You see that faith was active along with his works, and faith was completed by his works; and the Scripture was fulfilled that says, "Abraham believed God, and it was counted to him as righteousness"—and he was called a friend of God. You see that a person is *justified by works* and not by faith alone.

As you look at the whole of the NT a fuller picture emerges as to the meaning of "justification." Paul is discussing how justification is granted; James is discussing how justification is shown to have occurred. What at first appears to be a contradiction are actually complementary teachings.

Bible. Acts 4:8. "Then Peter, *filled* with the Holy Spirit, said to them, 'Rulers of the people and elders ....'" But I thought Peter was filled at Pentecost (Acts 2:4). What does "filled" mean in v 8? If you look through Acts you will see this statement of "filling" repeated, always followed by mention of what the person said or did. But if you look at the book of Judges in the OT, you will see the same metaphor used the same way of the Spirit possessing the person in a powerful but temporary way in order to accomplish a specific task. While the Holy Spirit comes in his fullness at a believer's conversion, Luke uses the terminology of Judges to describe a work of the Holy Spirit in which he grips a person in a special way to enable that individual to say or do something special.

As you continue out to the outer circles, be careful. Once you get out of the Bible and are looking at how the word is used in secular thought, it becomes more and more likely that the words are going to be used differently. And especially if you are looking at how the word was used five hundred years before the writing of the NT, you must recognize that words can totally change their meaning over this time span. For example, a century ago, if you were to "skim" a book, this meant you would read it carefully. "To prevent" was "to go before," which obscures Paul's meaning in the KJV of 1 Thess. 4:15.

> For this we say unto you by the word of the Lord, that we which are alive and remain unto the coming of the Lord shall not *prevent* them which are asleep.

The dead in Christ will go *first.*

References from texts outside the Bible can sometimes give us helpful illustrations. For example, Paul tells Timothy not to become "entangled" in civilian affairs (2 Tim. 2:4). The verb *emplekō* (*1861*) can mean much more than "to be involved" (contra the NIV), and this unfortunate translation has caused unnecessary grief for many pastors who were forced by their churches to have little or no contact with secular society, including a second job. (The blame for this does not lie with the NIV but with the unfortunate and unbiblical notion that a church must keep its pastor poor—but I digress.) *emplekō* means "to be involuntarily interlaced to the point of immobility, be entangled; to become involved in an activity to the point of interference with other activity or objective" (BDAG, 324). The word is used by Hermes (*Similitudes*, 6.2.6-7) of a sheep and by Aesop (74) of hares caught in thorns. These make great illustrations, but it is dangerous to define a biblical word based on them since they are so far removed from the biblical writer.

So let's get back to our word study on "Lord" in Rom. 10:9. Is there anything in the immediate context that will help us define the confession "Jesus is Lord" more precisely? The connection between the confession and belief in Jesus' resurrection suggests "Lord" means much more than "sir"; someone raised from the dead is more than a "sir."

As you move out into the paragraph, in v 12 Paul says that Jesus is "Lord of all," asserting his universal lordship. It is especially significant that in v 13 Paul quotes Joel 2:32, because in its OT context Joel is speaking of Yahweh, God. Douglas Moo writes, "In the OT, of course, the one on whom people called for salvation was Yahweh; Paul reflects the high view of Christ common among the early church by identifying this one with Jesus Christ, the Lord" (*The Epistle to the Romans,* Eerdmans, 1996, page 660).

In Rom. 1:4 Paul states that Jesus "was declared to be the Son of God in power according to the Spirit of holiness by his resurrection from the dead, Jesus Christ our Lord," connecting Jesus' lordship with his resurrection as in 10:9 and with his identification as the Son of God. As we see who Jesus is as Lord, we see that he is also God's Son. As God's Son, the OT references to God can be applicable to Jesus. It is a small step from this to agreeing with Thomas' confession: "My Lord and my God!" (Jn. 20:28).

As you expand further out into the NT, we find similar confessions: "at the name of Jesus every knee should bow, in heaven and on earth and under the earth, and every tongue confess that Jesus Christ is Lord, to the glory of God the Father" (Phil. 2:10-11, NIV; cf. 1 Cor. 12:3).

Salvation requires having a correct understanding of who Jesus is, and that understanding causes you to submit to his lordship. Jesus was raised from the dead, he was raised to a position of lordship over all, and in his lordship we see that he is in fact the Son of God. Christianity is grounded in the historical event of the incarnation, death, and resurrection of Jesus Christ. Who we are as disciples is intimately tied up with who he is as Lord, our Lord and our God. This is what "Lord" means in Rom. 10:9.

Septuagint

As you get further into word studies beyond this book, you will often see writers paying special attention to how a word is used in the Septuagint, often abbreviated LXX. This is the Greek translation of the Hebrew Scriptures that was probably started about 250 B.C. and finished somewhere around the time of Christ. There are certain words that are important in the OT, especially theological words. When the Septuagint was translated, the translators chose a Greek word for each of these Hebrew words. When it comes to defining these Greek words in the NT, it is the word's background in the OT via the Septuagint that is the most important background in defining the Greek word, not its general usage in the first century.

For example, how was the LXX to translate the Hebrew word *hesed*, which describes God's love for his covenantal people, when there is no such word in Greek? When the LXX translators finally settled on *eleos*, *eleos* automatically carried the specific meaning of *ḥesed* into the use of *eleos* in the NT. This is our earlier illustration that you must know the meaning of the OT word *ḥesed* in order to understand the NT idea of mercy.

Given the fact that *kyrios* is used by the LXX to translate *YHWH*, "Yahweh," it is hard for me to imagine that the Jewish Paul meant anything less than confessing the deity of Christ in Rom. 10:9.

Cognates

A cognate is a word that is related to another and actually shares the same root. In English, the words "prince" and "princess" share the same root, although their specific forms are altered because they are masculine and feminine gender, respectively.

Sometimes Greek cognates have similar meanings. However, at other times there are definite nuance differences between cognates. For this reason it is important not to assume that all cognates have the same meaning, and when doing a word study try to stick to your specific word. But if you can't get a clear meaning, then look at the cognates and see if they are used with the same or with different meanings as the word you are studying.

Common Mistakes

Before ending this discussion of word studies, I must cover common mistakes made in doing word studies. For a more detailed discussion of these issues you can read *Exegetical Fallacies* by D. A. Carson (Baker, 1991).

Anachronism

The first is the bad habit of defining a Greek word using an English word derived from that Greek word. My favorite example is when someone talks about the "power" of God, and adds that this word "power" is *dynamis*, from which we get our word "dynamite," and then goes on to say God's power is dynamite. This is backwards and wrong. English wasn't a language until the second millenium A.D. Regardless of where our words came from, the definitions don't work backwards. Supposedly there is a reason that a specific Greek word was used as the basis of an English word, but as the years go by that English word can take on a meaning totally different from its Greek origin. God's power is never pictured in Scripture as something that blows rocks apart.

Etymological Fallacy

"Etymology" refers to how the word was created. What would you say if a pastor or Bible study leader told you that the "butterfly" is an animal made of butter that can fly? Or perhaps that a pineapple is a type of apple grown on pine trees? After the laughter died down, and if the speaker were serious, you would point out that this is not what the word means. The etymology, the pieces that were originally used to make up the word, does not define the word today, any more than a butterfly is a milk by-product. (I doubt "butterfly" actually is derived from "butter" and "fly," but it makes for a memorable example.)

The worst example I know of is the Greek word for "repent," *metanoeō,* which some people define as "to change your mind," but not necessarily your behavior. "Repentance," they say, "involves an intellectual shift in understanding, but repentance does not require a change of action." They often base their position on the meaning of the two parts that were used to create *metanoeō*; *meta* means "after," which implies change, and *nous* means "mind"; hence, repentance means to change your mind but not necessarily your behavior. Certainly, *metanoeō* can mean "to regret" (cf. Lk. 17:3-4; 2 Cor. 7:9-10), but the NT's understanding of repentance is not drawn from the etymology of one word but from the biblical *concept* of repentance, especially from the background of conversion in the OT. See the article on *metanoeō* in Bromiley's *Theological Dictionary of the New Testament: Abridged,* where he writes, "The concept of conversion stresses positively the fact that real penitence involves a new relation to God that embraces all spheres of life and claims the will in a way that no external rites can replace.... It means turning aside from everything that is ungodly" (pp. 640, 641).

Is it ever the case that a word carries the meaning of its parts? Sure. *eiserchomai* is made up of the preposition *eis*, meaning "into," and *erchomai*, meaning "to go." *eiserchomai* means "to go into." But it is not the word's etymology that determines its meaning. Because context makes it clear that *eiserchomai* to mean "to go into," we can see it has retained the meaning of its etymological parts.

It is also true that some prepositions (*ek, kata, apo, dia, syn*) have what is called a "perfective" function. When added to a word they can intensify its meaning. *esthiō* means "I eat"; *katesthiō* means "I devour." Some perfective forms, however, have lost this intensified nuance, and the compound form has the same basic meaning as the simple word. For example, Paul tells Timothy that the teaching of the opponents in Ephesus produces only "speculations," *ekzētēsis*. It is difficult to determine whether Paul intended the intensified "extreme speculations" (or perhaps "useless speculations"), or just "speculations," which is the meaning of the simple *zētēsis* ("investigation, controversy, debate"). As always, context is the guide as to whether or not the intensified meaning is present.

Connected to the etymological fallacy is the fact that words change their meaning over the years. Just think of the lyrics to the old song that ends, "We'll have a gay old time," or the KJV use of "prevent" in 1 Thess. 4:15 (cited above). What a word meant when it was first created, or what it meant a thousand years ago, may be at best irrelevant today. A word's meaning today is seen in how it is used today, not in how it used to be used.

- "Hussy" is from the Middle English word "huswife," meaning "housewife."
- "Enthusiasm" meant to be inspired or possessed by a god.
- "Nice" originally meant "foolish" in Middle English (from the Latin *nescire,* "to be ignorant").
- "Gossip" is from *godsib,* a word that refered to godparents, and came to be used of the type of chatter that stereotypically occurs at christenings (see *God, Language*

and Scripture by Moisés Silva, Zondervan, 1995). Today, when I preach about gossip, christenings are nowhere in my mind, and its etymology is irrelevent in an attempt to define the Bible's prohibition of slander.

Words have a range of meaning, but that range is not determined by the parts that made up the word or even by how it was used hundreds of years earlier.

A Few Other Errors

Don't put too much weight on a word, thinking that the word, all by itself, is full of meaning. Granted, there are a few technical terms that have a specific meaning in almost any context. But for the most part, we do not communicate with individual words but with phrases, sentences, and paragraphs. Focus your study on the larger unit, hesitating to place too much emphasis on an individual word.

Linked to this is the fact that theological concepts are larger than a word. Regardless of how many times you have heard the word *agapē* defined as the sacrificial love of the unlovely, the kind of love that is bestowed on the undeserving, that simply is not what the word in and of itself means. It is not the word that conveys this meaning, but it is the concept of biblical love as illustrated by God that infuses *agapē* with this particular meaning in the biblical context.

Hebrew Words

Hebrews poses its own challenges to doing word studies. Here is a little bit of Hebrew that may help.

Roots and stems. Many nouns and verbs share the same consonants. For example,

melek	king	➢	*mālak*	to reign
dābār	word	➢	*dābar*	to speak
mišpāṭ	judgment	➢	*šāpaṭ*	to judge

Notice how each pair shares a common set of consonants and related definitions. The reason for this relationship is due to the fact that they share a common root. It is important to understand the distinction between a root and those words derived from that root. It is a distinction between root and stem.

Hebrew roots are typically composed of three consonants. *A root represents the origin or simplest form from which any number of Hebrew words are derived.* From a root, therefore, any number of nouns or verbs may be derived. *A stem is the most basic form of any word derived from a root.*

For example, from the root *mlk* comes the nouns *melek* (king), *malkâ* (queen), and *malkût* (kingdom), and the verb *mālak* (to reign, be king). Once again, notice how each different word shares a common set of consonants and related definitions. This relationship is based on the sharing of a common root.

Word studies, cognate words, and cognate languages. Word studies will often take these related forms into consideration. The meaning of many Hebrew words is clear. However, the meaning of some words is less clear, and writers will often turn to related Hebrew words to help determine the meaning of these words.

If related Hebrew words do not help, writers will often resort to looking at related or cognate languages (e.g., Akkadian, Arabic, Aramaic, Egyptian, Ugaritic) in order to determine what a particular Hebrew word may mean. The further we move away from Hebrew, the less certain we are of the meaning of the Hebrew word.

Person, gender, and number. In English, a verb by itself does not have person, gender, or number (e.g., "study"). (Greek verbs, likewise, do not designate gender.) It must be supplied by the addition of a personal pronoun (e.g., "she studied"). However, in Hebrew, most verbs have person, gender, and number. These verbal characteristics are indicated by certain patterns of inflection. For example, the verb *kātab* means "he wrote" and the verb *kātbâ* means "she wrote." The different ending indicates person, gender, and number.

Even though most Hebrew verbs are capable of indicating person, gender, and number by themselves, verbs may also occur with independent personal pronouns. For example, *kātabtî* and *ʾanî kātabtî* are both translated "I wrote." Because Hebrew verbs by themselves indicate person, gender, and number, the addition of an independent personal pronoun such as *ʾanî* typically expresses some type of emphasis.

Here's the point. If you are using a tool such as a software program like Accordance to look at a Hebrew word, you will quickly notice that when you move the cursor over what appears to be a single word, the software is telling you the one form is actually multiple words. In fact, a single cluster of Hebrew letters, something that looks like a single word to most of us, may in fact represent an entire clause consisting of multiple lexical items or words. For example, the single Hebrew construction *wayyeʾehābehā* (e.g., Gen. 24:67) actually consists of three different lexical items. The initial letter (*w*) is the Hebrew conjunction translated "and." The last letter (*h*) is a third person, feminine singular, suffix translated "her." The middle section of this Hebrew construction (*yʾhb*) contains a verb that we can translate as "he loved." When we put it all together, this single Hebrew construction represents an entire English clause translated "and he loved her." This example represents a common feature of the Hebrew language. That is, Hebrew nouns and verbs can take a number of prefixes (such as conjunctions, prepositions, or the definite article) and/or suffixes (such as pronominal suffixes with objective or possessive translation values) that have their own distinct lexical values.

Doing Hebrew Word Studies

John Kohlenberger has written an excellent interlinear, *The Interlinear NIV Hebrew-English Old Testament* (Zondervan, 1979). This can help you find the Hebrew word behind the English, but because of the issues I have been raising, this may not be the best choice for you.

You can use an exhaustive concordance that lists the number of the Hebrew word at the end of the entry, as we learned in Greek. Some of the software programs also give you access to the Hebrew behind the English.

If you want to do serious word study, we are pleased to have the five-volume *New International Dictionary of Old Testament Theology and Exegesis,* edited by Willem A. VanGemeren (Zondervan, 1997). VanGemeren organized the Hebrew words based on their GK number, so once you have the number it is easy to find the word. This is as advanced as you will need, and it is a trustworthy resource. You can also use Kohlenberger's *The English-Hebrew Concordance to the Old Testament* (Zondervan, 1998) that, like its Greek counterpart, will list in English every verse that uses a specific Hebrew word, in order to discover the word's semantic range. *The Theological Wordbook of the Old Testament,* edited by R. Laird Harris, Gleason L. Archer Jr., and Bruce K. Waltke (Moody, 1980), is not as detailed but may be helpful.

Verbal Stems

The following is a little more advanced, but it does explain some of the abbreviations in the Hebrew-English dictionary in this book such as "P" and "N." In the Hebrew verbal system, there are seven major stems: the Qal, Niphal, Piel, Pual, Hiphil, Hophal, and Hithpael. The Qal stem is the basic or simple verbal stem. From the Qal stem all other verbal stems are formed. Verbal stems tell us two things about the action or meaning of a verb: the type of verbal action and the voice of verbal action.

In Hebrew, there are three basic categories of verbal action: *simple* action (e.g., to break), *intensive* action (e.g., to smash into pieces), and *causative* action (e.g., to cause to break). There are also three basic categories of verbal voice: *active, passive,* and *reflexive.* With the reflexive voice, the subject of the verb is both doing and receiving the action of the verb. In the example "David dressed himself," David is both performing and receiving the verbal action. Understanding the basic significance of a verbal stem is necessary if you are going to follow the discussion in a commentary or even some word studies.

1. Qal. The Qal is the simple or basic verbal stem. Qal verbs are active in voice, though a few passive forms do exist. The Qal stem also exhibits the simple or unnuanced type of action. For example, "he heard."

2. Niphal. The Niphal stem is used to express simple action with either a passive or reflexive voice. In other words, whatever a verb means in the Qal stem, it becomes passive or reflexive in the Niphal stem. An example of a translated Niphal verb is "he was heard" (passive) or "he heard himself" (reflexive).

3. Piel. The Piel stem is sometimes used to express an intensive type of action with an active voice. In other words, the simple action of the Qal stem will take on some type of intensive nuance in the Piel stem. For example, a verb meaning "he broke" in the Qal stem can mean "he smashed into pieces" in the Piel stem.

4. Pual. The Pual is the passive form of the Piel. The Pual stem, therefore, is used to express an intensive type of action with a passive voice. For example, the Piel verb meaning "he smashed into pieces" would be translated in the Pual stem as "he (it) was smashed into pieces."

5. Hiphil. The Hiphil stem is used to express causative action with an active voice. For example, a Qal verb meaning "he was king" or "he reigned" would be translated "he caused to reign" or "he made (someone) king" in the Hiphil stem.

6. Hophal. The Hophal is the passive form of the Hiphil. The Hophal stem, therefore, is used to express causative action with a passive voice. For example, the Hiphil verb translated "he made (someone) king" would be translated "he was made king" in the Hophal stem.

7. Hithpael. The Hithpael stem is used to express an intensive type of action with a reflexive (or sometimes passive) voice. For example, a Qal verb meaning "he hid" would be translated "he hid himself" in the Hithpael stem.

	simple	*intensive*	*causative*
active	Qal	Piel	Hiphil
passive	Niphal	Pual	Hophal
reflexive	Niphal	Hithpael	

Verbal stems and verbal meaning. Many verbs in Hebrew are "regular." That is to say, their meanings follow the pattern summarized above when they appear in the different stems. For example, a Hebrew verb in the Qal meaning "to break" will mean "to smash into pieces" in the Piel stem. In this and many other instances, the relationship between the meanings of a verb in different stems is apparent in light of the discussion above.

However, the meaning of a verb in the Qal may be significantly different when that same verb appears in another stem. For example, the verb *bārak* means "to kneel" in the Qal, but in the Piel stem it means "to bless." Always consult a dictionary to be certain of a verb's meaning in a given stem.

ABANDON

Old Testament

Verb: עָזַב (*ʿāzab*), GK 6440 (S 5800), 214x. *ʿāzab* is used most often for the action of "abandonment" and can refer to the abandonment of land because of exile (Lev. 26:43; Isa. 18:6; 32:14; cf. Isa. 60:15; Jer. 49:25; Ezek. 36:4). It can also mean setting a person, particularly a prisoner, free from captivity (2 Chr. 28:14; Ps. 10:14; 16:10). Sometimes it refers simply to a person leaving behind his cloak (Gen. 39:15), his family, flocks, or herds (Gen. 50:8).

God as the subject of this verb abandons the apostate nation (Jer. 12:7), the king (2 Chr. 32:31), Zion (Isa. 60:15), or (allegedly) the psalmist (Ps. 71:11). But more common is the negation of the verb with respect to God, indicating that he *will not forsake* or abandon his people (Gen. 28:15; Deut. 31:6, 8), despite the fact that his people have frequently abandoned the Lord (Jdg. 2:12–13; 1 Ki. 19:10; 2 Ki. 21:22), his covenant (Jer. 22:9), the law (2 Chr. 12:1), and statutes (1 Ki. 18:18).

This verb is used over 100x in the OT to denote an act of breaking a covenant with God (Deut. 29:25; Jer. 2:13, 17, 19; 22:9; Dan. 11:30). When covenant curses are unleashed by God, he abandons his people (Isa. 54:7–8), yet his abandonment is temporary.

New Testament

Verb: ἀφίστημι (*aphistēmi*), GK *923* (S *868*), 14x. *aphistēmi* generally means to "leave, depart" in a physical sense. It can also express various forms of apostasy, such as Paul's teaching that in later times "some will *abandon* the faith" (1 Tim. 4:1; cf. Heb. 3:12). See *leave*.

Verb: ἐγκαταλειπω (*enkataleipō*), GK *1593* (S *1459*), 10x. This verb means to separate connection with someone or something by leaving, to "forsake, abandon, desert." See *forsake*.

ABASE

See *humble*.

ABBA

New Testament

Noun: ἀββά (*abba*), GK *5* (S *5*), 3x. *abba* is an Aramaic word that means "father"; it is a term of endearment used within the family circle (not unlike our word "dad"); its degree of familiarity toward God was unknown in Judaism. Jesus uses this term in reference to his heavenly Father in his prayer in Gethsemane (Mk. 14:36). Paul uses this term twice in his letters, both times with reference to what the Spirit inspires us do when we become believers in Jesus and so become children of God: we begin to cry out to God as "Abba, Father" (Rom. 8:15; Gal. 4:6).*

ABDOMEN

Old Testament

Noun: בֶּטֶן (*beṭen*), GK 1061 (S 990), 72x. The basic sense of *beṭen* seems to be the hollow or inside of something. It is used in several ways in the OT, referring to the belly or abdomen, the reproductive organs (of men or women), and the womb. See *womb*.

ABHOR

Old Testament

Verb: שָׂנֵא (*śānēʾ*), GK 8533 (S 8130), 148x. Usually translated "to hate," *śānēʾ* refers to varying levels of dislike toward someone or something. See *hate*. This abhorrence can be toward another man or woman. For example, Jacob has an aversion for his wife Leah (Gen. 29:31).

ABIDE

New Testament

Verb: μένω (*menō*), GK *3531* (S *3306*), 118x. The basic sense of *menō* is "to remain, stay, abide." See *remain*.

ABILITY

Old Testament

Noun: דַּעַת (*daʿat*), GK 1981 (S 1847), 88x. Derived from the verb *yādaʿ* (GK 3359, "to know"), *daʿat* means "knowledge" in all spheres of life. It can also denote any special ability one has. See *knowledge*.

Noun: חַיִל (*ḥayil*), GK 2657 (S 2428),

246x. The basic sense of *ḥayil* is "power, strength, or capability." It is also used to describe persons who have a special skill or ability. In Gen. 47:6, Pharaoh asks Joseph to put in charge of his livestock men of *ḥayil* ("men of special ability") from among the Israelites. See *strength*.

New Testament

Verb: δύναμαι (*dynamai*), GK *1538* (S *1410*), 210x. *dynamai* communicates ability or capability of doing something. See *can*.

Noun: δύναμις (*dynamis*), GK *1539* (S *1411*), 119x. *dynamis* essentially means "power," but it can also denote acts of power ("miracles") or a person's "ability." See *power*.

Adjective: δυνατός (*dynatos*), GK *1543* (S *1415*), 32x. *dynatos* denotes what is possible or what one has the power to do. See *possible*.

(BE) ABLE

New Testament

Verb: δύναμαι (*dynamai*), GK *1538* (S *1410*), 210x. *dynamai* communicates ability or capability of doing something. See *can*.

Verb: ἰσχύω (*ischyō*), GK *2710* (S *2480*), 28x. In the NT, *ischyō* primarily means "to be strong, powerful, mighty." Sometimes it simply means "to be able." See *be strong*.

ABOLISH

New Testament

Verb: ἀναιρέω (*anaireō*), GK *359* (S *337*), 24x. *anaireō* means "to take away, abolish." See *take away*.

Verb: καταργέω (*katargeō*), GK *2934* (S *2673*), 27x. *katargeō* means "to release, destroy, nullify, cause something to be useless." See *destroy*.

ABOMINATION

Old Testament

Noun: תּוֹעֵבָה (*tôʿēbâ*), GK 9359 (S 8441), 118x. Regularly translated "detestable thing, repulsive thing, abomination," *tôʿēbâ* generally denotes persons or actions that are morally or religiously offensive, especially to God. Idolatry, for example, is an abomination to the Lord (Deut. 7:25; 32:6; Jer. 16:18; Mal. 2:11). See *detestable*.

New Testament

Noun: βδέλυγμα (*bdelygma*), GK *1007* (S *946*), 6x. *bdelygma* describes that which is reprehensible or detestable to God, an "abomination." In the NT it usually refers to some sort of idolatry. Specifically, "the *abomination* that causes desolation," a term that derives from Dan. 12:11 (LXX), refers to that which desecrates God's temple and Jerusalem and leads to their destruction (Mt. 24:15; Mk. 13:14).

Jesus explains to the Pharisees that the sin of self-justification, which is highly valued among humans, is an abomination to God (Lk. 16:15). The whore of Babylon, who is associated with blasphemy and filth, is the source of such abomination (Rev. 17:4–5). The names of those exhibiting this characteristic will not be found in the book of life (21:27). See *NIDNTT-A*, 91-92.*

ABOUND

New Testament

Verb: περισσεύω (*perisseuō*), GK *4355* (S *4052*), 39x. *perisseuō* means "to abound, be in abundance, overflow." Jesus announces that unless one's righteousness "abounds" more than that of the Pharisees, the kingdom of heaven cannot be entered (Mt. 5:20). It is a radical statement, and only a heart changed by the grace of God can bring about a righteous life. Mark records the woman who gave all she had versus those that gave out of their "abundance" (cf. Lk. 12:15). In Acts 16:5, the church "grew" in numbers (cf. also Phil. 1:9).

Paul writes that the truth of God "abounds" (Rom. 3:7), as does God's grace (Rom. 5:15). The Colossians "abound" in gratitude (Col. 2:7). The spread of God's grace results in thanksgiving that "*overflows* to the glory of God" (2 Cor. 4:15; cf. Eph. 1:8). Hope "*overflows* by the power of the Holy Spirit" (Rom. 15:13), as should the work that is done for the Lord (1 Cor. 15:58). The Thessalonians are urged to "abound" in love (1 Thess. 3:2; 4:1, 10). Both the sufferings of Christ as well as the comfort and help through Christ are "abundant" (2 Cor. 1:5). Likewise, the "ministry of righteousness "*overflows* with glory" in contrast to the ministry of condemnation (2 Cor. 3:9). In 2 Cor. 8–9, on Paul's collection for the impoverished Christians in Jerusalem, believers ought "to *abound* in this gracious work" (2 Cor. 8:7; 9:8b; cf. 9:12–13).

ABOUT TO

New Testament

Verb: μέλλω (*mellō*), GK *3516* (S *3195*), 109x. *mellō* is generally translated "about to, going to, intend to," as in Mt. 20:17, "As Jesus *was about to* go up to Jerusalem, he took the twelve disciples aside by themselves" (NASB). In Jn. 6:15, the Jewish people "were intending to" make Jesus their king. It is important to note, however, that for the most part, *mellō* speaks of events that are inevitable. Whenever the term is used, there is a notion of certainty accompanying it; for example, both Paul and Peter use *mellō* when speaking of "the glory that *is about to be* revealed" (Rom. 8:18; 1 Pet. 5:1). John writes in Rev. 17:8, "The beast, which you saw, once was, now is not, and *will* come up out of the Abyss and go to his destruction." Paul says in 1 Thess. 3:4, "In fact, when we were with you, we kept telling you that we *would be* persecuted."

The above examples demonstrate that *mellō* communicates true intention or inevitability rather than wishful thinking. This is especially true concerning the fulfillment of prophecy in the gospels and Acts. When the disciples ask Jesus about future events that are to be fulfilled, there is no doubt that they will occur (Mk. 13:4, "Tell us, when will these things happen? And what will be the sign that they *are about to be* fulfilled?"). Matthew quotes Jesus as saying, "In the same way the Son of Man *is going to* suffer at their hands" (Mt. 17:12; see also 17:22; Lk. 9:44). The suffering of the Messiah was prophesied in the OT; therefore, Jesus and the disciples use *mellō* when speaking of the certainty of his suffering, as in Acts 26:22–23, "I am saying nothing beyond what the prophets and Moses said *would* happen—that the Christ would suffer and, as the first to rise from the dead, *would* proclaim light to his own people and to the Gentiles."

ABSTAIN FROM

New Testament

Verb: ἀπέχω (*apechō*), GK *600* (S *566*, *567*, *568*), 19x. *apechō* means "to abstain from." Paul encourages the Thessalonians to "abstain from sexual immorality" (1 Thess. 4:3) and "every kind of evil" (5:22), and Peter instructs Christians to "abstain from worldly desires" (1 Pet. 2:11). The Jerusalem Council decides that Gentile believers should "abstain from" things polluted by or sacrificed to idols (Acts 15:20, 29). Legalists in Ephesus were requiring that people "abstain from" certain foods (1 Tim. 4:3). *apechō* can also mean "to be far" (see *[be] far*) or "to receive in full" (see *receive in full*).

ABUNDANCE

Old Testament

Noun: רֹב (*rōb*), GK 8044 (S 7230) 150x. *rōb* denotes a multitude or an abundance. It is probably derived from the verb *rābâ*, which means to become numerous, much, or great. In about one-third of the word's occurrences, it is used (adverbially) with a preposition and means "in abundance" or "abundantly/greatly. See *many*.

ACCEPT

Old Testament

Verb: לָקַח (*lāqaḥ*), GK 4374 (S 3947), 967x. The basic meaning of *lāqaḥ* is "to take, grasp." The meaning is often simply to "take into/by the hand." See *take*.

Verb: רָצָה (*rāṣâ*), GK 8354 (S 7521), 52x. *rāṣâ means* "to be pleased, accept, delight in." See *(be) pleased*.

New Testament

Verb: παραλαμβάνω (*paralambanō*), GK *4161* (S *3880*), 49x. *paralambanō* means "to take, receive, accept." See *take*.

Verb: προσλαμβάνω (*proslambanō*), GK *4689* (S *4355*), 12x. *proslambanō* means "to accept, take aside, welcome." In Thessalonica, Paul's enemies round up or take aside some scoundrels from the marketplace to create a scene (Acts 17:5). Peter takes Jesus aside so as to rebuke him for speaking of his coming death (Mt. 16:22; Mk. 8:32). This verb can also denote welcoming a person into one's home (Acts 18:26; Phlm. 17) as well as welcoming strangers (Acts 28:2). An important use is the notion of accepting all believers, whether they are considered weak or strong, into Christian fellowship, for Christ himself has accepted all of us (Rom. 14:1, 3; 15:5). See *NIDNTT-A*, 327-28.

Verb: χωρέω (*chōreō*), GK *6003* (S *5562*), 10x. *chōreo* means "to accept, hold, have room for." This verb occurs in a variety of contexts. (1) Of objects, food is "accepted" into the stomach before being expelled (Mt. 15:17), and the house in which Jesus is teaching can no longer "accept, hold" more people (Mk. 2:2). The ritual water jugs "hold" twenty to thirty gallons of water, which Jesus turns into wine (2:6). The entire world, by John's estimation, cannot "hold" all the books if every miracle of Jesus were recorded (21:25).

(2) Of people, Jesus admonishes his hearers to "accept" his teaching about marriage and divorce (Mt. 19:11–12). Jesus tells his Jewish listeners that though they claim to be children of Abraham, they are ready to kill him since his word "finds no acceptance" in them (Jn. 8:37). Paul admonishes the Corinthians to "make room" for him in their hearts (2 Cor. 7:2a), for he has not taken advantage of anyone. Peter explains that the reason Jesus is delaying his return is because he is patiently giving sinners a longer chance to "accept" repentance so as to not perish (2 Pet. 3:9). See *NIDNTT-A*, 616.*

ACCEPTABLE, ACCEPTED

Old Testament

Noun: רָצוֹן (*rāṣôn*), GK 8356 (S 7522), 56x. *rāṣôn* denotes three different ideas in the OT: favor (see *favor*), acceptance, or will (see *please*). It is attributed most often to God (39x) and occurs most frequently in Proverbs (14x), Psalms (13x), and Leviticus (7x).

rāṣôn is used frequently with reference to an acceptable sacrifice to God, particularly in worship. It is the only sense of *rāṣôn* used in Leviticus (7x). Sacrifices may or may not be "acceptable" or "accepted" (Lev. 1:3; 19:5; 22:19, 20, 21, 29; 23:11; Isa. 56:7; 60:7), and so may the sacrificer (Lev. 22:19; 23:11), gifts (Exod. 28:38), and days (Isa. 58:5). The prayer of the psalmist is that his words and meditation may "be pleasing" in God's sight (Ps. 19:14). In Proverbs, God "delights" in accurate weights (Prov. 11:1), the blameless (11:20), truthful men (12:22), and the prayer of the upright (15:8), and a king "delights" in a wise servant (14:35).

New Testament

Adjective: εὐάρεστος (*euarestos*), GK *2298* (S *2101*), 9x. *euarestos* means "pleasing, acceptable." See *pleasing*.

ACCESS

New Testament

Noun: προσαγωγή (*prosagōgē*), GK *4643* (S *4318*), 3x. *prosagōgē* means "access." All three uses occur in Paul's letters and refer to Jesus. Through Jesus we gain "access" into God's forgiving grace (Rom. 5:2). Furthermore, through Jesus all human beings, whether Jew or Gentile, can gain "*access* to the Father by one Spirit" (Eph. 2:18), "*approaching* God with freedom and confidence" (3:12).*

ACCOMPANY

New Testament

Verb: ἀκολουθέω (*akoloutheō*), GK *199* (S *190*), 90x. *akoloutheō* occurs mostly in the gospels and Acts. Its basic meaning is "to follow" (Mt. 4:25) or "to accompany" (8:10). See *follow*.

ACCOMPLISH

New Testament

Verb: ποιέω (*poieō*), GK *4472* (S *4160*), 568x. This verb, generically translated as "to do," has a wide range of meanings, such as "to make, cause to happen, accomplish." See *do*.

ACCURSED

New Testament

Noun: ἀνάθεμα (*anathema*), GK *353* (S *331*) 6x. *anathema* means "curse, accursed, condemned (eternally)." See *curse*.

ACCUSE, ACCUSATION

New Testament

Verb: ἐγκαλέω (*enkaleō*), GK *1592* (S *1458*), 7x. *enkaleō* means "to accuse." Most uses of this word occur in connection with the riot in Ephesus (Acts 19:38, 40) and with Paul's arrest in Jerusalem and his trial in Caesarea (23:28–29; 26:2, 7). The only other occurrence is in Rom. 8:33, where Paul reaches his triumphant conclusion concerning life in Christ and his Spirit. He begins with this rhetorical question: "Who *will bring any charge* [accusation] against those whom God has chosen?" His implied answer is clear: no one can, for since Christ has died and risen again and is interceding for us, no one can condemn us, and nothing can separate us from his love (8:34–35, 38–39).*

Verb: κατηγορέω (*katēgoreō*), GK *2989* (S *2723*), 23x. *katēgoreō* means "to bring charges against, accuse" someone. Paul uses this word in a nonlegal sense in writing of the Gentiles who fulfill the requirements of the law: "their thoughts now *accusing*, now even defending them" (Rom. 2:15). But for the most part, *katēgoreō* functions in a legal framework. For example, "the Pharisees and the teachers of the law were looking for a reason to *accuse* Jesus" (Lk. 6:7). *katēgoreō* is used several times to refer to the charges brought against Paul by the Jews (Acts 22:30; 24:2; 25:5; 28:19). Formal accusation was done before a judge or political official. The chief priests accused Jesus before Pilate (Mk. 15:3–4).

One must note that no criminal code existed for the non-Roman citizen tried in Jerusalem. Consequently, the governor was given liberty to make his own judgments. Typically, the Roman governor would not carry out death sentences simply for the violation of some religious regulation. It wasn't until religious matters became political that a governor might impose a death sentence on the accused. This is why Pilate asks Jesus, "Are you the King of the Jews?" (Mk. 15:2). He is concerned about the political impact Jesus might have on Rome.

Lastly, *katēgoreō* signifies the accusations made at the last judgment. Moses, not Jesus, will accuse the Jews because of their unbelief (Jn. 5:45–46). They have denied the law of Moses, which bears witness to Christ. See *NIDNTT-A*, 297.

Noun: αἰτία (*aitia*), GK *162* (S *156*), 20x. *aitia* is the basis for some action or the legal basis for a charge—a "reason, cause, basis, charge." See *reason*.

ACCUSER

See *devil*.

ACKNOWLEDGE

Old Testament

Verb: יָדַע (*yādaʿ*), GK 3359 (S 3045), 956x. *yādaʿ* expresses a wide range of meanings connected to the idea of "knowing" or "understanding." See *know*.

Verb: נָכַר (*nākar*), GK 5795 (S 5234), 44x. *nākar* (which occurs mostly in the Hiphil form) refers to general knowing, such as the basic awareness of another's existence or the acknowledgment of who a person is. See *recognize*.

New Testament

Verb: ἐπιγινώσκω (*epiginōskō*), GK *2105* (S *1921*), 44x. *epiginōskō* can mean to "know, perceive, recognize, understand." See *know*.

Verb: ὁμολογέω (*homologeō*), GK *3933* (S *3670*), 26x. *homologeō* means "to acknowledge, confess [especially confess faith]," also "to promise."

The most basic meaning of this verb is to solemnly "promise" to do something. Herod uses this verb when he "promises" with an oath to give to Herodias's daughter whatever she wants (Mt. 14:7). More pointedly, Stephen describes God as preparing to fulfill what he "promised" to Abraham (Acts 7:17).

From this basic meaning, *homologeō* comes also to mean the act of publicly acknowledging someone or something. Christ promises to "acknowledge" before the Father all who "acknowledge" him before other people (Mt. 10:32; Lk. 12:8; cf. Rev. 3:5). John describes the one who "acknowledges" the Son as having the Father also (1 Jn. 2:23). Similarly, the Jews decided that anyone bold enough to publicly "acknowledge" Jesus as the Christ would be cast out of the synagogue (Jn. 9:22), a fact that frightened many Pharisees from making such a confession (12:42).

homologeō also takes on itself the meaning of a confession of faith. Thus, John the Baptist publicly confesses a religious fact, that he is not the Christ (Jn. 1:20); believers can confess that they are strangers and pilgrims on earth (Heb. 11:13), and they confess the name of Christ as a sacrifice of praise (13:15). This confessional use of *homologeō* becomes in itself an act of faith as described by Paul in Rom. 10, when he states that confessing with the mouth that Jesus is Lord, together with believing in one's heart about the resurrection, brings about salvation (Rom. 10:9–10). This is undoubtedly what Paul refers to as "the good *confession*" that leads to eternal life in Timothy (1 Tim. 6:12).

Finally, *homologeō* can sometimes describe the public acknowledgment of one's sins (1 Jn. 1:9), knowing that our faithful God will forgive those sins . See *NIDNTT-A*, 410-11.

ACQUIRE

Old Testament

Verb: עָשָׂה (*ʿāśa*), GK 6913 (S 6213), 2632x. The verb *ʿāśâ* has the basic meaning "to do, make," appears in numerous contexts, and is used in a variety of ways. See *make*.

ACT

New Testament

Verb: πράσσω (*prassō*), GK *4556* (S *4238*), 39x. *prassō* has a basic meaning of "to do, act, practice" something. See *do*.

ADAM

Old Testament

Noun: אָדָם (*ʾādām*), GK 132, 134 (S 120, 121), 558x. The basic meaning and most common translation of *ʾādām* is "man." But *ʾādām* is used 12x as the proper name "Adam," mostly in Gen. 2–4. See *man*.

New Testament

Noun: Ἀδάμ (*Adam*), GK *77* (S *76*), 9x. Adam obviously means "*Adam*," the first human being whom God created. His name occurs in Luke's genealogy of Jesus (Lk. 3:38), and Jude defines Enoch as "the seventh [generation] from Adam" (Jude 14). In 1 Tim. 2:13–14, Paul reflects on the creation of Adam and Eve and notes that Eve was the first one to sin.

In the rest of the references to Adam in the NT, he is much more than just the first human being; he is the progenitor of the entire human race and the one who has passed down sin and death to all of his descendants (Rom. 5:14). Note too in Rom. 5:12, 15–17, 19, many of the references to "one man" apply to Adam; the rest of the references to "one man" apply to Jesus Christ, who by his sacrifice has undone the disastrous effects of Adam's sin. Thus, in 1 Cor. 15:45, Jesus Christ is called "the last Adam." One of the most blessed passages of Scripture, therefore, is 15:22: "For as in *Adam* all die, so in Christ all will be made alive." This does not mean that everyone will be saved; rather, Paul is saying that just as all of those who are in Adam are subject to physical, spiritual, and eternal death because of his sin, so all of those who are in Christ will escape the judgment of eternal death and receive instead the gift of eternal life.*

ADD

Old Testament

Verb: יָסַף (*yāsap*), GK 3578 (S 3254), 213x. The basic meaning of *yāsap* is "to add" or, by extension, "to do something again." Rachel names her son Joseph (*yôsēp*) because she requests, "May the LORD *add* to me another son" (Gen. 30:24). The priest is to "add firewood" to the altar of sacrifice every morning (Lev. 6:12). The firstborn of animals is to be dedicated to the Lord, but can be redeemed by giving its worth in money, to which the owner "must *add* a fifth to its value" (Lev. 27:13). God *adds* fifteen years to Hezekiah's life (2 Ki. 20:6, cf. Isa. 38:5).

Sometimes *yāsap* conveys the sense of "surpass." Solomon's wisdom is "greater *by far*" than any who have come before him (Eccl. 2:9, cf. 1:16), and the wisdom and wealth of Solomon *far exceeds* the report given to the queen of Sheba (1 Ki. 10:6). In a negative sense, *yāsap* is used of sin piled on sin (1 Sam. 12:19; Jer. 45:3).

yāsap in the sense of "add" has its opposite in "subtract" (*gāraʿ*). The two terms are used in the repeated covenant formula, "do not *add* to what I command you and do not subtract from it" (Deut. 4:2; cf. 12:32; Rev. 22:19). In the same way, God's works endure forever—"nothing can be *added* to it and nothing taken from it" (Eccl. 3:14).

yāsap is also found in the common oath formula: "May the LORD deal with me, *be it ever so severely*" (Ruth 1:17)—lit., "thus may the LORD do to me and thus may he *add more*." This standard oath formula (1 Sam. 3:17; 20:13; 2 Sam. 3:35; 19:13; 1 Ki. 2:23; 20:10; 2 Ki. 6:31) is probably a shortened form of "may he add the curses of the covenant on me if I fail to complete my vow."

yāsap may also convey the sense of "increase." In a series of blessings the psalmist prays, "May the LORD make you *increase*, both you and your children" (Ps. 115:14), which parallels the prayer of Moses: "May the LORD, the God of your fathers, *increase* you a thousand times and bless you as he has promised!" (Deut. 1:11). According to Proverbs, those who are generous will themselves *increase* (Prov. 11:24; cf. 22:9; 29:7), and one who learns to listen will gain even more wisdom (1:5; cf. 9:9).

yāsap regularly conveys the meaning "continue to do" or "do again," and with a negative, "to discontinue." Thus Pharoah sins *again* (Exod. 9:34), suggesting a repetitive habit of sin that evidences his hardened heart (v. 35). Our word is also used of Israel, who "once again … did evil in the eyes of the LORD" (Jdg. 3:12; cf. 10:6; Ps. 78:17; Hos. 13:2). The use of *yāsap* denotes a pattern and highlights the wayward heart of God's chosen nation. But the faithfulness of God is also signaled by *yāsap*, for in the time of restoration he will act on behalf of his people, and "*once more* the humble will rejoice in the LORD; the needy will rejoice in the Holy One of Israel" (Isa. 29:19). See *NIDOTTE*, 2:476-79.

New Testament

Verb: προστίθημι (*prostithēmi*), GK *4707* (S *4369*), 18x. *prostithēmi* means "to add, increase." Jesus asks the important question: "Who of you by worrying can add a single hour to his life?" (Mt. 6:27; Lk. 12:25). But if we seek first God's kingdom and his righteousness, then the other things we need in life "will be added" to us as well (Mt. 6:33; Lk. 12:31). In Lk. 17:5, the disciples ask Jesus, "Increase our faith."

prostithēmi is used frequently in Acts to refer to the continuing number of disciples who are being "added" to the church (Acts 2:41, 47; 5:14; 11:24). And in a theological argument in Galatians, Paul mentions that "the law was added because of transgressions" until Christ should come (Gal. 3:19); by this Paul is stressing that through the law of Moses we come to a knowledge of our sin (cf. Rom. 3:20), which in turn drives us to search for a Redeemer, Jesus Christ. Thus, the law leads us to Christ.

ADEQUATE

New Testament

Adverb: ἱκανός (*hikanos*), GK *2653* (S *2425*), 39x. *hikanos* conveys the idea that something is adequate or large enough in its quantity or quality and may best be translated "sufficient, deserve, adequate." See *sufficient*.

ADMONISH

New Testament

Verb: νουθετέω (*noutheteō*), GK *3805* (S *3560*), 8x. *noutheteō* means "to admonish." Part of the task of the leadership in the church is to admonish believers to live in the way God wants them to live. Paul does this himself (Col. 1:28), and he expects leaders in the church to do the same (1 Thess. 5:12). In fact, all Christians have a role to "teach and *admonish* one another with all wisdom" (Col. 3:16; cf. Rom. 15:14). *noutheteō* also means "to warn" (see *warn*).

ADONAI

See *Lord.*

ADOPTION

New Testament

Noun: υἱοθεσία (*huiothesia*), GK *5625* (S *5206*), 5x. *huiothesia* means "adoption." All uses of this term in the NT are in Paul's letters, and all refer not to earthly adoption but to becoming adopted children of God. Jesus is the natural, eternal Son of God; human beings become children of God by virtue of spiritual adoption. In Rom. 9:4, Paul acknowledges that the Jewish people, during the time of the OT, were adopted as God's children (cf. Exod. 4:22, "Israel is my firstborn son"). But now adoption as children of God takes place through Jesus Christ (Gal. 4:5; Eph. 1:5), by the power of the Holy Spirit (Rom. 8:15). Note, however, that we still await the final fulfillment of our adoption (8:23), which will not occur until the return of Jesus Christ.

While the term *huiothesia* is not used elsewhere in the NT, the concept of becoming children of God certainly is, especially in the writings of John. Note Jn. 1:12: "Yet to all who received him [Jesus], to those who believed in his name, he gave the right to become children of God" (cf. also 1 Jn. 3:1–2).*

ADORN

New Testament

Verb: κοσμέω (*kosmeō*), GK *3175* (S *2885*), 10x. *kosmeō* means "to adorn, decorate, make attractive." It can describe a state of beauty or the process of decorating something to make it beautiful. The temple is described as adorned with beautiful stones (Lk. 21:5), and the foundations of the wall of the new Jerusalem are similarly described as being adorned with many beautiful stones (Rev. 21:19). In some cases, the beauty is merely superficial. For example, Jesus criticizes the scribes and Pharisees because they "decorate" (KJV: "garnish") the tombs of their righteous ancestors and prophets while behaving like the ones who brought about their deaths (Mt. 23:29). Several NT authors use *kosmeō* to describe a woman adorning herself to heighten her beauty (1 Tim. 2:9; 1 Pet. 3:5; Rev. 21:2). Drawing on the same meaning, though more figuratively, Paul speaks of making the gospel attractive (Tit. 2:10). See also *put in order* and *trim*. See *NIDNTT-A*, 315-16.

ADULTERY

New Testament

Verb: μοιχεύω (*moicheuō*), GK *3658* (S *3431*), 15x. *moicheuō* is always translated "to commit adultery"; for a discussion of this verb, see *commit adultery*.

ADVERSARY

Old Testament

Noun: צַר (*ṣar*), GK 7640 (S 6862), 433x. *ṣar* comes from the root *ṣrr*, which means "to be hostile." It can be translated "enemy, foe, adversary." See *enemy.*

ADVICE

Old Testament

Noun: עֵצָה (*ʿēṣâ*), GK 6783 (S 6098), 87x. *ʿēṣâ* has two basic, though closely related, meanings: "counsel, advice" (see *counsel*) and "plan, purpose" (see *plan*).

ADVISE

Old Testament

Verb: יָעַץ (*yāʿaṣ*), GK 3619 (S 3289), 80x. *yāʿaṣ* carries the two basic meanings of "to counsel, advise" (Num. 24:14; 2 Sam. 17:11) and "to plan, purpose" (Isa. 7:5; 14:24), though the verb seems to carry the former nuance more frequently. Also related to this former meaning is "to consult, to receive counsel" (2 Chr. 10:8; 25:17). See *counsel.*

ADVOCATE

New Testament

Noun: παράκλητος (*paraklētos*), GK *4156* (S *3875*), 5x. *paraklētos* is used 5x in the NT, all of them in the writings of John. It is often translated as "counselor, helper, advocate." See *counselor.*

AFFAIR

Old Testament

Noun: דָּבָר (*dābār*), GK 1821 (S 1697), 1455x. *dābār* means "word, report, command," but can also signify a "thing, matter, affair." See *word.*

AFFAR

See *far.*

AFFECTION

New Testament

Noun: σπλάγχνον (*splanchnon*), GK *5073* (S *4698*), 11x. *splanchnon* refers to a feeling of "affection, tenderness, compassion, pity." Technically, this noun refers to the intestines (see its use in Acts 1:18). This is the area of the body from which Greeks thought emotions of compassion and tenderness, even love, originated. Just as the English use of "heart" can refer to much more than the muscle that pumps blood throughout the body, so the Gk. *splanchnon* can refer to a range of tender emotions instead of just the bowels or intestines. Paul writes of his "heart" in his account to Philemon about Onesimus (Phlm. 7, 12, 20). John similarly writes of the false profession of one who closes up "affection" or "pity" to one's brother (1 Jn. 3:17).

Most uses of *splanchnon* occur in Paul's letters (8x). He tells the Corinthians that he has not withheld his "affection" from them, even though they have withheld their "affection" from him (2 Cor. 6:12). He tells the Philippians that he longs for them with the "*affection* of Christ" (Phil. 1:8). Titus is described similarly as having "great *affection*" for the Corinthians (2 Cor. 7:15) because of the way in which they received him. This type of affection is more than mere fondness, for the one with feelings in the *splanchnon* is tender (Phil. 2:1) and compassionate (Col. 3:12). Finally, God himself is described as giving to his people the knowledge of salvation because of his "affection" for us (Lk. 1:78). See *NIDNTT-A*, 535-36.*

AFFLICT, AFFLICTED, AFFLICTION

Old Testament

Verb: עָנָה (*ʿānâ*), GK 6700 (S 6031), 79x. *ʿānâ* can denote humbling in a positive sense (i.e., repentance and contrition) or with connotations of violence (i.e., affliction and oppression). It is used in parallelism with words like *kātat*, "to crush" (Ps. 94:5), *nāgaš*, "to oppress" (Isa. 53:7) and *nāgaʿ*, "to strike, hit, wound" (Isa. 53:4).

Forms of *ʿānâ* that are pleasing to God include fasting and prayer (Lev. 16:31; 23:27; Ps. 35:13). The psalmist is thankful for affliction, testifying that it leads to obedience (Ps. 119:67, 71, 75; cf. 2 Cor. 7:9–10). Isaiah's Suffering Servant is afflicted by God (Isa. 53:4, 7; cf. 53:10).

God warns his people not to oppress the vulnerable, such as widows and orphans (Exod. 22:22–23). *ʿānâ* is used in reference to rape (Jdg. 20:5; 2 Sam. 13:12, 14, 22; Lam. 5:11) and consensual encounters in which a woman's virginity is lost (Deut. 21:14; 22:24, 29). It describes the treatment of the Hebrews at the hands of the Egyptians (Exod. 1:11–12). Although the Israelites face many enemies in their history, their *ʿānâ* is usually attributed to God, who punishes them by the hand of enemy nations (1 Ki. 8:35; 2 Ki. 17:20; Ps. 90:15; Nah. 1:12). See *NIDOTTE* 3:449-52.

Verb: רָעַע (*rāʿaʿ*), GK 8317 (S 7489), 95x. *rāʿaʿ* expresses the quality or state of being evil or causing evil. It may be translated as "to be evil, afflict." See *evil.*

Adjective: עָנִי (*ʿānî*), GK 6714 (S 6041), 80x. *ʿānî* describes one who has been humbled or afflicted by circumstances, and who, because of current disability, finds himself or herself dependent on others for life's necessities. See *poor.*

New Testament

Noun: θλίψις (*thlipsis*), GK *2568* (S *2347*), 45x. *thlipsis* is a cognate of the verb *thlibō* (see *persecute*). It denotes the results of being squeezed or put into a narrow place—hence, "trouble, affliction, distress." See *trouble*.

AFFORD

Old Testament

Verb: נָשַׂג (*nāśag*), GK 5952 (S 5381), 50x. *nāśag*, usually translated "to overtake," generally denotes the action of catching someone or something from behind. See *overtake*.

The phrase *nāśag yād* (lit., "a hand will overtake") is a Hebrew idiom used 12x (e.g., Lev. 14:22, 30, 31, 32; 1 Sam. 14:26; Ezek. 46:7) with the sense of a person's ability to obtain a particular item, especially material wealth. The NIV usually translates this phrase "he can afford" and often indicates what an Israelite should offer as a sacrifice. For example, if an Israelite "cannot afford" to sacrifice two doves, he should bring flour (Lev. 5:11).

AFRAID

Old Testament

Verb: חָתַת (*ḥātat*), GK 3169 (S 2865), 55x. *ḥātat* is a verb that means "to be discouraged, dismayed, afraid, terrified." See *(be) discouraged*.

Adjective: יָרֵא (*yārēʾ*), GK 3710 (S 3373), 63x. *yārēʾ* typically describes the subject as one who is a "fearer" of God and denotes the sense both of awe and of worship. See *fear*.

(BE) AFRAID

Old Testament

Verb: יָרֵא (*yārēʾ*), GK 3707 (S 3372), 317x. *yārēʾ* denotes both a sense of terror and a sense of awe and worship. It is commonly translated "be afraid, revere, worship." See *fear*.

New Testament

Verb: φοβέω (*phobeomai*), GK *5828* (S *5399*), 95x. *phobeomai* is used in two main senses in the NT. It means to be "frightened, alarmed," or to "respect, stand in awe of" someone. See *fear*.

AFTER

Old Testament

Noun: אַחֲרִית (*ʾaḥªrît*), GK 344 (S 319), 61x. *ʾaḥªrît* in its most basic sense denotes "that which comes after." Specifically it may describe what follows temporally, that is, the "cessation, end" of an event or the final "outcome." The word may also mean "after" in a logical sense, as in Prov. 23:32, which describes the "aftereffects" of drunkenness as the bite of a serpent. See *end*.

AFTERWARD

New Testament

Adjective: ὕστερος (*hysteros*), GK *5731* (S *5305*, *5306*), 12x. *hysteros* means "later, afterward," though it is often used as an adverb meaning "finally." It occurs primarily in a comparative or superlative sense. See *later*.

AGAIN

New Testament

Adverb: ἄνωθεν (*anōthen*), GK *540* (S *509*), 13x. *anōthen* can mean "from above" or "again." See *from above*.

AGAINST

Old Testament

Verb: קָרָא (*qārāʾ*), GK 7925 (S 7122), 136x. The primary meaning of *qārāʾ* is "to meet, encounter, happen." The infinitive form of this verb became so common (used 119x) that it also functioned as a preposition meaning "against" or "toward." See *meet*.

AGE

New Testament

Noun: αἰών (*aiōn*), GK *172* (S *165*), 122x. *aiōn* can indicate "prolonged time, eternity, an age, a time of the world." The English word "eon" is derived from this word. The prophets predicted the sufferings of the Messiah, fulfilled in Jesus, and his return "*long ago* through his holy prophets" (Acts 3:21). When Jesus restored sight to a blind man, the healed man declared, "never *since the world began* [lit., "from *aiōn*"] has it been heard that anyone opened the eyes of a person born blind" (Jn. 9:32).

aiōn can represent an "age." In the parable of the sower, Jesus speaks of a group of seeds choked out by "the cares of this *world*" (Mk. 4:19). The gospel Paul proclaims is that God's wisdom is not like the wisdom of "this age," but is "God's wisdom, secret and hidden, which God decreed *before the ages* for our glory" (1 Cor. 2:7). Similarly, the mystery of Christ crucified for the salvation of the world and of his residence within the faithful is "the mystery that has been hidden *throughout the ages* and generations" (Col. 1:26). Jesus promises a reward for anyone who gives up everything for his sake both in this age, and "in the *age* to come," he or she will receive eternal life (Mk. 10:29–30).

One frequent idiomatic usage of this word is an expression that literally translates, "unto the ages" or "unto the ages of the ages." In our Bibles, this is usually translated "forever" (e.g., Lk. 1:33; Jn. 6:51) or "forever and ever" (e.g., Heb. 13:21). God the Father is eternal, and that attribute is reported in the NT to extend to Christ: "Jesus Christ is the same yesterday, today, and *forever*" (Gal. 1:5; Heb. 13:8). See *NIDNTT-A*, 25-27.

Noun: γενεά (*genea*), GK *1155* (S *1074*), 43x. *genea* is used of a "race" of people, those living at the same time ("generation"), or the time in which a generation lives ("age"; Acts 14:6; 15:21). See *generation.*

AGITATE

New Testament

Verb: σαλεύω (*saleuō*), GK *4888* (S *4531*), 15x. *saleuō* means essentially to "shake, wave." But it can also be used of emotional agitation (Acts 2:25; 17:13). See *shake.*

AGREE

New Testament

Verb: συμφωνέω (*symphoneō*), GK *5244* (S *4856*), 6x. *symphoneō* means "to agree." This verb usually denotes an agreement among people, such as the workers in the vineyard who all "agree" to work for a denarius per day (Mt. 20:2, 13), or Ananias and Sapphira who "have agreed" to test the Spirit by lying about the sale of their property (Acts 5:9). In Acts 15 James gives a speech at the council in Jerusalem that endorses the principle that Gentiles do not need to be circumcised to be saved; "the words of the prophets *agree* with this" (15:15).

Jesus says in Mt. 18:19 that "if two of you on earth *agree* about anything you ask for, it will be done for you by my Father." This verse must not be taken out of context as if God is some sort of cosmic vending machine; rather, it is set in the context of judicial matters of the church (cf. 18:15–18), that God endorses decisions made by leaders within his church.

AIR

Old Testament

Noun: שָׁמַיִם (*šāmayim*), GK 9028 (S 8064), 421x. *šāmayim* is an important and frequent word in the Bible and plays a key role in many central texts from Genesis through Revelation. The wide variety of meanings for this word fall into two main categories: the sky, atmosphere, or space; and the dwelling place of God. See *heaven, heavens*.

ALARM

New Testament

Noun: φόβος (*phobos*), GK *5832* (S *5401*), 47x. *phobos* in the NT can mean "fear, fright, alarm," but it can also describe a healthy awe and respect for God. See *fear*.

ALAS

Old Testament

Interjection: הוֹי (*hôy*), GK 2098 (S 1945), 51x. *hôy* is an onomatopoeic particle that is often translated "woe, alas." See *woe*.

New Testament

Interjection: οὐαί (*ouai*), GK *4026* (S *3759*), 47x. *ouai* is an onomatopoeic word; the sound of the word suggests its meaning, such as the English "bang" or "ouch." See *woe*.

ALIEN

Old Testament

Noun: גֵּר (*gēr*), GK 1731 (S 1616), 92x. *gēr* is a sojourner or alien in a land. Sojourners are not like foreigners visiting some other country; rather, they have settled in the land for some time and live there, even though they are not native to that area. Abraham was a sojourner in Hebron (Gen. 23:4), Moses in Midian for forty years (Exod. 2:22), Elimelech and his family in Moab (Ruth 1:1), and the Israelites in Egypt (Exod. 6:4; 22:20).

According to God's law, aliens in the midst of Israel must be assisted and protected by Israelites (Exod. 22:21; Jer. 7:6), they have right to material access (e.g., gleaning, Lev. 19:10), and they may participate in religious observances (tithe, Deut. 14:29; Sabbath, Deut. 5:14; the Sabbath year, Lev. 25:6; and cities of refuge, Num. 35:15). The identity of God's people as aliens themselves in Egypt provides a powerful metaphor for the pilgrimage of life (cf. Exod. 23:9). "Hear my prayer, O Lord, and give ear to my cry; do not hold your peace at my tears. For I am your passing guest, an *alien*, like all my forebears" (Ps. 39:12).

The *gēr* reminds Israel that that the earth belongs to the Lord. "The land shall not be sold in perpetuity, for the land is mine; with me you are but *aliens* and tenants" (Lev. 25:23). See *NIDOTTE*, 1:836–39.

Adjective: זָר (*zār*), GK 2424 (S 2214), 70x. In most instances, *zār* modifies a noun and means "strange, foreign, alien" or, by extension, "unauthorized, illegitimate." In other instances, the adjective can function like a noun and mean "alien, foreigner." See *foreigner, foreign*.

New Testament

Noun: παρεπίδημος (*parepidēmos*), GK *4215* (S *3927*), 3x. While *parepidēmos* is, strictly speaking, an adjective, in the NT it is used as a noun meaning "stranger" or "alien." See *strange(r)*.

Noun: πάροικος (*paroikos*), GK *4230* (S *3941*), 4x. *paroikos* is a resident foreigner or more generally a stranger. See *strange(r)*.

Adjective: ξένος (*xenos*), GK *3828* (S *3581*), 14x. *xenos* denotes something "strange" or unusual (outside of one's experience), a person who is unknown, or a person from another place. See *strange(r)*.

ALIVE

New Testament

Verb: ζάω (*zaō*), GK *2409* (S *2198*), 140x. The basic sense of *zaō* is "to live, be alive" and has several nuances in the NT. See *live*.

ALL

Old Testament

Noun: כֹּל (*kōl*), GK 3972 (S 3605), 5415x. *kōl* means "whole, all, every." When *kōl* is followed by a plural word, it is usually translated as "all": "you will eat dust *all* the days of your life" (Gen. 3:14). When it is followed by an indefinite singular (e.g., without the article), it is often translated "every": "Then God said, 'I give you *every* seed-bearing plant on the face of the whole earth'" (Gen. 1:29). *kōl* is used with *bāśar* ("flesh") to mean "everyone": "God saw how corrupt the earth had become, for *all the people* on earth [KJV, "all flesh"] had corrupted their ways" (Gen. 6:12).

kōl may also stand by itself to denote "everything." In such a case, the context determines the scope of the word: "Not one of *all* the LORD's good promises to the house of Israel failed; *every one* was fulfilled" [KJV, "all came to pass"] (Jos. 21:45). God is not like the pagan gods, for he is "the Maker of *all things*, including Israel, the tribe of his inheritance" (Jer. 10:16).

kōl, meaning "whole, complete," is used to describe the devotion God requires of those who are his covenant people: "Love the LORD your God with *all* your heart and with *all* your soul and with *all* your strength" (Deut. 6:5, cf. Lk. 10: 27). Since God is the only God (Deut. 6:4), there is no reason to divide one's covenant loyalty—one's entire life must be devoted to him. See *NIDOTTE*, 2:657-58.

Noun: כֹּל (*kōl*), GK 10353 (S 3606), 105x. *kōl* is the Aramaic equivalent of the Heb. *kōl* (GK 3972) and has essentially the same meaning: "every, whole, all." When *kol* is accompanied with a plural noun, it means "all" (e.g., Dan. 5:8, 19). When it is found with an indefinite singular noun (i. e., without the article), it means "every" (e.g., 4:12; 6:26).

New Testament

Adjective: ἅπας (*hapas*), GK *570* (S *537*), 34x. *hapas* expresses the wholeness of the object it describes, the fullness of a group; it sometimes occurs alone as a pronoun meaning "everyone." Originally it was a strengthened form of *pas*, the usual word for "all" (see *all*), and was used when the preceding word ended in a vowel.

In Lk. 3:21 "all" the people were baptized, in contrast to the response later given in 8:37, when "all" the people asked Jesus to leave (cf. 19:37, 48; 23:1; Acts 25:24). Satan tempts Jesus with all of his power and authority (Lk. 4:6). *hapas* is used in 21:4 to describe sacrificial giving: "These people gave their gifts out of their wealth; but she out of her poverty put in *all* she had to live on."

hapas is used as a pronoun in Lk. 5:26: "*Everyone* was amazed and gave praise to God" (cf. 7:16).

In a world of selfish ambition, Christians are challenged by Acts 2:44, where Luke writes, "All who believed were together and had *all* things in common." See *NIDNTT-A*, 441-42.

Adjective: ὅλος (*holos*), GK *3910* (S *3650*), 109x. *holos* means "whole, all." Rather than being a word for distributive completeness (e.g., "all the people"), *holos* usually denotes undistributive wholeness. See *whole*.

Adjective: πᾶς (*pas*) GK *4246* (S *3956*), 1243x. *pas* generally means "each, every" in the singular, "all" in the plural. In Gal. 5:14 the emphasis of *pas* in the singular lies on the sum total of the law ("the *entire* law"), in contrast to the smaller subdivisions within it; the summary of this law is the command to love one's neighbor. This command ironically occurs in Lev. 19:18b—in the heart of the law. This stress on love as a *summary* of the law derives from Jesus (Mt. 22:37–40). Paul reinforces it later (Rom. 13:8–10; cf. Jas. 2:8).

Likewise, the emphasis in *pas* in the plural is not so much on each individual within the group as on the group as a whole. For example, in 1 Cor. 15:22 Paul writes, "For as in Adam *all* die, so in Christ *all* will be made alive." His emphasis here is on two "all" groups: the "all" group that dies because of Adam's sin (i.e., every single human being) and the "all" group that lives in Christ (i.e., those who believe in him). In a similar vein Paul writes in 2 Cor. 5:14–15: "For Christ's love compels us, because we are convinced that one died for *all*, and therefore *all* died. And he died for *all*, that those who live should no longer live for themselves but for him who died for them and was raised again." Christ's love extends to the entire human race, but not every individual accepts the Lord by faith and lives in and for him.

Paul uses *pas* to endorse the Jewish understanding of monotheism, i.e., just one God, who has no rivals and has total dominion over *all* creation (1 Cor. 8:6; also see Rom. 11:36). The same concept is abundantly clear in what appears to be an early Christian hymn that is saturated with various forms of *pas* (Col. 1:15–20). Jesus is the "firstborn of *all* creation" (1:15); "through him *all things* were created" (1:16ab); "he himself is before *all things*" (1:17a); "*all things* hold together in him" (1:17b); "he is the head of the body—the church, and the beginning, the firstborn from the dead so that *in everything* he might have supremacy" (1:18); "for God was pleased to have *all* his fullness dwell in him" (1:19); "and through him to reconcile to himself *all things*" (1:20). Paul delivers this poetic praise to Christ because many in Colosse were fearing the influence of astral hosts, terrestrial spirits, and underworld powers. At the heart of this false teaching was the idea that Jesus was just an insignificant subset of all God's creation and thus no more powerful than the angels they used to call upon for protection. But to Paul Jesus is the exalted Lord, Creator, sustainer, and goal of the universe, preeminent in everything, and infinitely superior to all earthly authorities or heavenly angelic powers.

Just before ascending to the Father after the resurrection, Jesus proclaimed, "*All* authority in heaven and on earth has been given to me" (Mt. 28:18). Even though the power and evil of Rome and the Jewish authorities raised their ugly heads and struck Jesus down, and even though there exists uninterrupted flexing of evil muscle against his church even to this day, eventually "at the name of Jesus *every* knee should bow ... and *every* tongue confess that Jesus Christ is Lord, to the glory of God the Father" (Phil. 2:10–11). See *NIDNTT-A*, 441-42.

ALLELUIA

New Testament

Interjection: ἀλληλουϊά (*hallēlouia*), GK *252* (S *239*), 4x. *hallēlouia* means "Hallelujah, Alleluia." See *Hallelujah*.

ALLOCATE

Old Testament

Verb: נָפַל (*nāpal*), GK 5877 (S 5307), 435x. *nāpal* generally indicates the simple action of falling. See *fall*. Sometimes it can indicate the sense of "allocating" of the promised land to the tribes of Israel (Jos. 13:6, "allocating" in the sense of *causing* a certain territory *to fall* to a particular tribe).

ALLOT, ALLOTMENT

Old Testament

Verb: חָלַק (*ḥālaq*), GK 2745 (S 2505), 55x. *ḥālaq* is translated "divide, share, allot." A wise servant "shares" his inheritance with others (Prov. 17:2; cf. Jos. 18:2; 22:8; 1 Chr. 24:4–5). See *divide*.

Noun: חֹק (*ḥōq*), GK 2976 (S 2706), 131x. *ḥōq* is derived from the related verb *ḥāqaq*, which means "to cut in, inscribe, decree" and denotes something that is limited or restricted. Most frequently *ḥōq* refers to the prescribed law of God (see *decree*). Less frequently, it expresses a fixed quantity or some sort of limit. Pharaoh's priests receive a regular "allotment" of food so they are not forced to sell their land (Gen. 47:22), and the excellent wife provides a "portion" of food for her servants (Prov. 31:15).

ALLOW

New Testament

Verb: ἐάω (*eaō*), GK *1572* (S *1439*), 11x. *eaō* means "to let, allow." See *let*.

Verb: ἐπιτρέπω (*epitrepō*), GK *2205* (S *2010*), 18x. *epitrepō* essentially means "to let, permit, allow." See *permit*.

ALMIGHTY

Old Testament

Noun: צָבָא (*ṣābāʾ*), GK 7372 (S 6635), 479x. *ṣābāʾ* appears to come from a military context and bears both a general and specific meaning in the OT.

(1) Approximately 200x in the OT, *ṣābāʾ* refers to those who participate in warfare and/or comprise an army (Gen. 21:22; 1 Sam. 17:55; 2 Sam. 2:8). Related to this, at times *ṣābāʾ* designates the wandering tribes of Israel (Exod. 6:26; 12:17, 41; Num. 10:14), probably because the Israelites are like a war camp, marching to and fro as God leads them. Beyond the usage related to human armies, the created elements in the heavens are at times called the *ṣābāʾ* (Gen. 2:1; Deut. 4:19; Ps. 33:6; Isa. 40:26). These occurrences are frequently translated as "starry host" or "host of heaven," but it is not entirely clear whether these elements are the planets and stars or angels. At times, in light of the close association of angels and stars in the ancient world, both may be meant. Again, this usage of *ṣābāʾ* is related to the military notion in that this heavenly host comprises part of God the King's entourage and at times fights on his behalf (Jdg. 5:20; cf. Jos. 10:12–14).

(2) From the latter usage derives the OT's other important function of *ṣābāʾ*. About 279x, *ṣābāʾ* occurs as part of a sig-

nificant and exalted title for God (1 Sam. 1:3; Ps. 24:10; Isa. 6:5). "The LORD (Yahweh) of hosts" appears frequently in Isaiah, Jeremiah, and Zechariah (but not once in the Pentateuch), and the phrase seems to have taken on a technical usage meaning "the LORD all-powerful," hence the expression "the LORD Almighty." While this designation has military overtones, it emphasizes especially God's sovereignty over the entire world. The title is important in the later OT period as Israel faces many powerful nations and their gods. God's people are exhorted to entrust themselves to their God, who as the Almighty will deliver them.

Martin Luther picks up on this powerful title for God in his famous hymn, "A Mighty Fortress is Our God." Facing many conflicts and fears himself, Luther encourages his fellow Christians with these lines about the one who is our help: "Dost ask who that may be? Christ Jesus, it is he, *Lord Sabaoth* his name, from age to age the same, and he must win the battle." See *NIDOTTE*, 3:733-35.

Noun: שַׁדַּי (*šadday*), GK 8724 (S 7706), 48x. *šadday* constitutes a name or title for God in the OT. However, both its origin and its original meaning are unknown. The translation "Almighty" comes to us from the LXX, where oftentimes it is rendered with the Greek word *pantokratōr*, meaning "Almighty" or "Omnipotent One."

The first occurrences of *šadday* appear in connection with the patriarchs and the patriarchal promises (Gen. 17:1; 28:3; 35:11; 43:14; 48:3). In these contexts (as well as Exod. 6:3 and Ezek. 10:5), the title appears as *ʾēl šadday* (*ʾēl* is GK 446) or "God Almighty." It was not until the time of Moses that God chose to reveal his covenant name, "Yahweh" (יהוה, GK 3378), to his people, "I appeared to Abraham, to Isaac and to Jacob as *God Almighty*, but by my name Yahweh [the LORD] I did not make myself known to them." It is a favorite title of God in the book of Job. In fact, of the 48x this word occurs in the Hebrew Bible, it appears 31x (65 percent) in Job.

In addition to its association with the patriarchal promises, *šadday* is associated with the Day of the Lord in the prophets (Isa. 13:6; Joel 1:15). It also suggests power (Ezek. 1:24; 10:5; Ps. 68:14), protection (Ps. 91:1), and the force of life (Job 33:4). Perhaps it was these realities that caused the psalmist to reflect, "The one who dwells in the protective covering of the Most High will rest in the shadow of the *Almighty*" (Ps. 91:1).

New Testament

Noun: παντοκράτωρ (*pantokratōr*), GK *4120* (S *3841*), 10x. *pantokratōr* is a compound of the two Greek words meaning "all" and "power"—thus either "the Almighty" or "the all-powerful One." It is used only of God in the NT. Though a popular title for God in the LXX, *pantokratōr* is used only once outside of Revelation (2 Cor. 6.18), where Paul quotes 2 Sam. 7:8, 14 ("says the Lord Almighty"). In Rev. 1:8; 4:8; 11:17; 15:3; 16:7, 14; 19:6, 15; 21:22 it is often part of the fuller title "the Lord God, the Almighty." This title serves to describe the immense greatness of God, who has power over all creation. It also stands in contrast to the Roman emperor, who saw himself as the most powerful person in the world. See *NIDNTT-A*, 317.*

ALMS

New Testament

Noun: ἐλεημοσύνη (*eleēmosunē*), GK *1797* (S *1654*), 13x. Generally, *eleēmosunē* indicates either (1) the act of giving to the needy or poor (Mt. 6:2, 3, 4; Lk. 11:41; Acts 9:36; 10:2), or (2) the actual gifts or alms themselves (Acts 3:2, 3, 10; 10:4). See *gift*.

ALONE

Old Testament

Noun: בַּד (*bad*), GK 963 (S 905), 161x. *bad* means "alone, only." When God observes Adam at the time of his naming the animals, God says, "It is not good for the man to be *alone*" (Gen. 2:18); note that this is the only thing before the fall of which God says, "This is not good." As a result, God creates the woman to be a "helper suitable for him" (see *helper*). When the Israelites are in the desert, God tests them to see what is in their hearts and feeds them with manna, "to teach you that man does not live on bread *alone* but by every word that comes from the mouth of the Lord" (Deut. 8:3). When human beings sin, ultimately sin is against God "only" (Ps. 51:4).

When used of God, *bad* expresses the incomparability of God vis-à-vis the other so-called gods. The Lord is separate from all other gods; he "*alone* [is] the Most High over all the earth" (Ps. 83:18; cf. Isa. 37:16, 20); "*besides* him there is no other" (Deut. 4:35). He "alone" does wondrous deeds (Ps. 72:18), and "only" his righteousness counts (72:16). "His name *alone* is exalted" (148:13). Note that *bad* occurs with respect to God only as he compares with other gods; the OT does not use this term for God as he is in himself; when the OT wants to stress the oneness of God, it uses *ʾeḥad*. This latter word can include the notion of plurality, which is not implied in *bad* (see comments on *one*). See *NIDOTTE*, 1:600–602.

New Testament

Adjective: μόνος (*monos*), GK *3668* (S *3441*), 44x. *monos* means "only, alone" and has several nuances. See *only*.

Adverb: μόνον (*monon*), GK *3667* (S *3440*), 70x. *monon* is typically used as a marker of limitation and means "only, alone." See *only*.

ALPHA, OMEGA

New Testament

Noun: ἄλφα (*alpha*), GK *270* (S *1*), 3x. *alpha* means "Alpha."

Noun: Ὠ (*O*), GK *6042* (S *5598*), 3x. *O* means "Omega."

These two words appear only together in the NT, in three places in the book of Revelation: 1:8; 21:6; 22:13. *alpha* is the first letter of the Greek alphabet, and *O* is the last letter (in the Greek NT the *O* is never spelled out as *ōmega,* as *alpha* is spelled out). John, the writer of the book of Revelation, stresses that Jesus is the beginning of all things (he was there when creation took place, cf. Jn. 1:1–3), and he is the one who will bring history to an end by his return (cf. Rev. 22:20). This "bookend" view of Jesus links with the significance of the other two phrases used along with the Alpha and Omega phrase: "the Beginning and the End" (Rev. 21:6; 22:13) and "the First and the Last" (Rev. 1:17; 2:8; 22:13).

ALTAR

Old Testament

Noun: מִזְבֵּחַ (*mizbēaḥ*), GK 4640 (S 4196), 403x. Related to the verb *zābaḥ* ("to sacrifice"), the noun *mizbēah* refers to a place of sacrifice, an "altar." The first altar mentioned in Scripture is built by Noah after the flood (Gen. 8:20). Abraham builds an altar at various places in the promised land where the Lord appears to him (Gen. 12:7–8; 13:18; 22:9). Altars are sometimes built and named to commemorate significant events (Gen. 35:1, 7; Jdg. 6:24).

Following the Exodus, God instructs the people of Israel to build altars of earth or of uncut stone (Exod. 20:24–25). For the tabernacle Moses is to build an altar of wood overlaid with bronze for the sacrifices (27:1–7) and an altar of wood overlaid with gold for burning incense (30:1–8). Solomon later builds a bronze-plated altar for the temple that is twenty cubits square (2 Chr. 4:1). The main altar in the temple had horns on it, though their practical significance is not fully understood (see *horn*).

Throughout the OT, altars become an important part of Israelite worship, and not just the altar in the temple. Note, for example, the altar to the Lord that Elijah rebuilds on Mount Carmel and where the Lord answers his sacrifice with fire from heaven (1 Ki. 18:30–38)—though this sort of altar tends to be the exception (cf. Deut. 12:1–14). Esp. after the time of Solomon, any solitary "altar" other than the altar in the temple is generally associated with idolatry (e.g., 2 Ki. 17:9–11; 23:5–9). After the exile, the first thing the returned exiles do is to rebuild the altar to the Lord on the site of the destroyed temple (Ezr. 3:2–3).

The Israelites are not to worship at pagan altars but rather must destroy them (Deut. 12:2–3). Nevertheless, Jeroboam I sets up a rival altar at Bethel (1 Ki. 12:23–33), and many kings of Judah and Israel are guilty of worshiping at the altars of foreign gods. The kings of Judah who fear and worship the Lord are often praised for tearing down these altars (2 Chr. 34:4, 7; see also *high place*). See *NIDOTTE*, 2:888–908.

New Testament

Noun: θυσιαστήριον (*thysiastērion*), GK *2603* (S *2379*), 23x. *thysiastērion* denotes an "altar." Biblical literature reserves this term exclusively for the altar of God (for pagan altars *bōmos* [GK *1117*] is used). It can refer to the altar of incense (Lk. 1:11) and the altar of burnt offering (1 Cor. 9:13) in the Jerusalem temple and to other altars of God in the OT (Rom. 11:3; Jas. 2:21). In the NT it is used primarily of the golden altar that is before the throne of God in heaven (Rev. 6:9; 8:3, 5; 9:13; 11:1; 14:18; 16:7). Metaphorically, Heb. 13:10 uses *thysiastērion* in reference to the sacrifice of Christ. This draws attention to the fact that the cross of Christ is the fulfillment of the OT sacrificial system, especially the sacrifice offered on the Day of Atonement (see *atonement*). See *NIDNTT-A*, 254-57.

ALWAYS

Old Testament

Noun (used as adv.): תָּמִיד (*tāmîd*), GK 9458 (S 8548), 104x. As an adverb, *tāmîd* describes that which is "lasting" or something done "continually." "Put the bread of the Presence on this table to be before me *at all times*" (Exod. 29:30). "Aaron is to tend the lamps before the LORD from evening till morning, *continually*" (Lev. 24:3). Thus, the word can describe both an action done repeatedly (often according to a schedule) as well as something that is ongoing without interruption.

As an adjective, *tāmîd* denotes the characteristic of continuance, as the *regular* offerings in the tabernacle and temple (e.g., the daily burnt offering, Exod. 29:42; the continual burning of incense, 30:8; the daily grain offering, Num. 4:16). So common is the use of *tāmîd* to describe the daily offerings that, following the exile, the word itself stands alone to denote the morning and evening burnt offerings (Dan. 8:11, 13; 11:31; 12:11). As an adjective, *tāmîd* can also describe the general characteristic of a person's duties, as "men will be *regularly* employed" (Ezek. 39:14).

When used to describe God and his actions, *tāmîd* emphasizes divine faithfulness. Thus, the walls of Jerusalem are *constantly* before the Lord, meaning that he never ceases to protect his holy city (Isa. 49:16). Indeed, Isaiah foresees a time when the gates of Jerusalem will *continually* be open (60:11), meaning that the city will dwell in perfect peace and security without fear of any enemy. Similarly, David prays that God's *continual* love and truth would be his protection (Ps. 40:11).

Even as God is faithful, so those who belong to him are to be characterized by faithfulness. Hosea enjoins his readers to "return to your God; maintain love and justice, and wait for your God *always*" (Hos. 12:6). The psalmist encourages *continual* praise to be in one's mouth (Ps. 34:1; 71:6) and to "hope *continually* in the Lord" (Ps. 71:14). See *NIDOTTE*, 4:302-5.

(BE) AMAZED

New Testament

Verb: ἐκπλήσσω (*ekplēssō*), GK *1742* (S *1605*), 13x. This word means "to be amazed, greatly astonished." It most often describes the reaction of those who heard Jesus' teaching. These people included the crowds (Mt. 7:28; 13:54; 22:33; Mk. 1:22; 6:2; 11:18; Lk. 4:32); Jesus' disciples, "astonished" at his words regarding the difficulty of the rich entering heaven (Mt. 19:25; Mk. 7:37; 10:26); Mary and Joseph, "astonished" at finding Jesus in the temple

(Lk. 2:48); and the disciples and the crowd, "amazed" at the greatness of God after Jesus' exorcism of an evil spirit (Lk. 9:43). Its only use outside the gospels describes Sergius Paulus being amazed at the teaching about the Lord (Acts 13:12), an amazement that results in faith. See *NIDNTT-A*, 175.*

Verb: ἐξίστημι (*existēmi*), GK *2014* (S *1839*), 17x. *existēmi* carries two distinct but related meanings. It can mean confusing, astounding, or terrifying. It's secondary meaning is to be out of one's senses.

In most instances, this word denotes amazement or astonishment, as the crowds "were amazed" at Jesus' miraculous healings and exorcisms (Mt. 12:23; Mk. 2:12). Jesus' disciples were "terrified" at his authority over the storm (Mk. 6:51) and "stunned" at the women's news about his resurrection (Lk. 24:22). The teachers in the temple were amazed at the young Jesus' understanding (2:47). The crowds in Jerusalem were amazed at those speaking in tongues at Pentecost (Acts 2:7, 12). In Samaria Simon the magician amazed the crowds with his powers (8:9, 11), then was himself amazed at Philip's miracles. Saul's conversion to Christianity (9:21) and the descent of the Holy Spirit on Gentiles (10:45) drew stunned amazement from Jewish believers in Damascus and Joppa, respectively, while Peter's miraculous escape drew astonishment from believers in Jerusalem (Acts 12:16).

existēmi also means "to drive out of one's wits, be out of one's mind." Jesus' family accused him of being "beside himself" (KJV) or "out of his mind" (NIV) (Mk. 3:21), and Paul remarks that his evangelism team is "*out of our mind* … for the sake of God," regarding the strength of their convictions about salvation (2 Cor. 5:13). See *NIDNTT-A*, 175-76.

Verb: θαυμάζω (*thaumazō*), GK *2513* (S *2296*), 43x. *thaumazō* denotes "to be amazed, wonder, marvel." In classical Greek, this verb occasionally carried overtones of fear. In the NT this verb does not necessarily involve an element of fear, although occasionally fear can be deduced according to its context, such as at Jesus' calming of the storm (Mt. 8:27; Lk. 8:25), the disciples' reaction to Jesus' sudden post-resurrection appearance in the upper room (Lk. 24:41), and the reaction to Peter and John's healing of a crippled beggar (Acts 3:12).

Its usual meaning is "surprise, wonder." In the gospels, Jesus was twice "astonished," once at the remarkable faith of the centurion (Mt. 8:10; Lk. 7:9), the other at the lack of faith of the people of Nazareth (Mk. 6:6). A crowd was amazed at Jesus' performance of an exorcism (Mt. 9:33; Lk. 11:14), while skeptical and critical onlookers accused Jesus of exorcising by the help of Beelzebub. The crowds are amazed at his healings (Mt. 15:13; Jn. 7:21), exorcisms (Mk. 5:20; Lk. 9:43), and teaching (Lk. 4:22; Jn. 7:15). Great amazement occurs in the disciples at the cursing of the fig tree (Mt. 21:20), at finding Jesus conversing with a Samaritan woman (Jn. 4:27), by Pilate at Jesus' refusal to defend himself (Mt. 27:14), and at Jesus' quick death (Mk. 15:44).

Outside the Gospels, the Sanhedrin was amazed by the scriptural knowledge and courage of the "unschooled" Peter and John (Acts 4:13). Paul expresses amazement at the fickleness of the Galatians (Gal. 1:6). John writes that believers should not be amazed at the world's hatred (1 Jn. 3:13). In Revelation, John is awestruck by the vision of the woman on the beast (Rev. 17:6), while in the same vision, the world is amazed at the beast (13:3, 17:7–8) and worships it. See *NIDNTT-A*, 240-41.

AMBITION

New Testament

Noun: ἐριθεία (*eritheia*) GK *2249* (S *2052*), 7x. *eritheia* means "selfish ambition." This term is sometimes included in a list of human vices (2 Cor. 12:20; Gal. 5:20; cf. Rom. 2:8). For this reason Paul instructs the Philippians to "do nothing of selfish ambition" (Phil. 2:3). James too warns against this vice (Jas. 3:14, 16).

AMEN

New Testament

Adverb: ἀμήν (*amēn*), GK *297* (S *281*), 129x. *amēn* is a transliteration of the Heb. word *ʾāman*, which means "to show oneself dependable, know oneself to be secure, have faith." In general *amēn* means "certain[ly]" or "true[ly]."

In the NT *amēn* is primarily a strong affirmation of what is stated. In the Gospels *amēn* is found only in the mouth of Jesus, generally in the phrase, "Amen, I say to you" Sometimes *amēn* is translated with "truly" (9:27) or "in truth" (4:24). John uses a double *amēn* 25x, either for liturgical reasons or to emphasize the *amēn*. By using *amēn* to introduce his words, Jesus labels them as certain and reliable and makes them binding on himself and on his hearers.

The term *amēn* appears in other NT writings at the close of prayers and doxologies in order to strengthen and confirm them (Rom. 1:25; 9:5; Eph. 3:21; Heb. 13:21). In the NT letters it is assumed that the congregation will answer with an "amen" (Rom. 15:33; Gal. 6:18; Rev. 1:7). According to Rev. 3:14, Christ calls himself "the Amen" and affirms that he is "a faithful and true witness." Even today we use the term "amen" to close our prayers, because we know the one to whom we pray and we are aware of his faithfulness to his glory and our good. See *NIDNTT-A*, 40-41.

AMONG

Old Testament

Noun: קֶרֶב (*qereb*), GK 7931 (S 7130), 227x. The basic meaning of *qereb* is "inner parts." *qereb* is parallel to "heart" in Isa. 16:11: "My heart laments for Moab like a harp, my *inmost being* for Kir Hareseth." See *inner parts*.

New Testament

Adjective: μέσος (*mesos*), GK *3545* (S *3319*), 58x. *mesos* is a fluid word. It has two basic meanings: one that refers to a "middle" position spatially or temporally, and a second that have the nuance of "among," without reference to the actual center. See *middle*.

ANATHEMA

See *curse*.

ANCESTOR

New Testament

Noun: πατήρ (*patēr*), GK *4252* (S *3962*), 413x. *patēr* refers to a male parent (e.g., Mk. 9:24) or often to one's ancestors (Mt. 3:9; Jn. 4:12; Acts 7:4, 11, 12, 14). See *father*.

ANCIENT

Old Testament

Noun: עוֹלָם (*ʿôlām*), GK 6409 (S 5769), 439x. *ʿôlām* means "ancient, eternal, forever, everlasting." See *eternal*.

Noun or Adjective: קֶדֶם (*qedem*), GK 7710 (S 6924), 61x. This word originally meant "in front of" or "before" and came to denote "east" (see *east*). But this word is also used temporally to mean "ancient" or "long ago" (Deut. 33:15, 27; 2 Ki. 19:25; Neh. 12:46; Ps. 44:1; 74:2; Prov. 8:22–23; Isa. 23:7; 37:26; Hab. 1:12). Such an indication of time serves as a reference to different points in Israel's history of salvation. "I remember the days *of long ago*; I meditate on all your works" (Ps. 143:5; cf. 78:2; Mic. 7:20). See *NIDOTTE*, 3:872–74.

New Testament

Adjective: ἀρχαῖος (*archaios*), GK *792* (S *744*), 11x. *archaios* refers to the long-standing age of something or someone and can describe something that is old or that pertains to a time long ago. It is derived from the verb *archō* (see *begin*).

In the gospels, Jesus speaks of the law given in days of old (Mt. 5:21, 27, 33; KJV, "of old time"; NIV, "long ago"). Some people during Jesus' ministry believed him to be "a prophet of long ago" (Lk. 9:8, 19), who had risen from the dead. Satan is referred to as the "*ancient* serpent" (Rev. 12:9; 20:2), while Mnason of Cyprus was a disciple of long standing (Acts 21:16; NIV, "early disciple"). *archaios* also refers to the age of the world (2 Pet. 2:5; cf. Acts 15:7; 15:21). Finally, Paul encourages Christians that being in Christ makes them a new creation, which means the "old things" in their lives (i.e., the things in life before Christ) have passed away and all things are made new (2 Cor. 5:17). See *NIDNTT-A*, 74-76.*

ANGEL

Old Testament

Noun: אֱלֹהִים (*ʾelōhîm*), GK 466 (S 430), 2602x. *ʾelōhîm* is a name for "God," but it can also mean "gods, judges, angels." See *God*.

Noun: מַלְאָךְ (*malʾāk*), GK 4855 (S 4397) 213x. Like *angelos* in the NT, there are two primary uses of *malʾāk* in the OT: "messenger" (see *messenger*) and angel. These two uses are divided about evenly in the OT.

(1) *malʾāk* is used to denote angels who are heavenly beings. They are messengers sent from God himself. Their appearance is a revelation of the supernatural world in the earthly realm. As members of the court of God, angels serve and praise him (Job 1:6; cf. Ps. 103:20; 148:2; Isa. 6:2–3). He is their Creator. They witnessed the creation of the world (Job 38:7), but as created beings they are not without fault (Job 4:18; cf. 15:15). They can be mediators of revelation from God (Zech. 1:9, 11–19; 2:2–5; cf. Ezek. 40:3). They were instrumental in saving events of the exodus and the conquest of Canaan (e.g., Exod. 23:20; Jos. 2:1–4). They sometimes rescued the Israelites from invading armies (2 Chr. 32:21) and also individuals from danger (Ps. 91:11–12). The OT describes special kinds of angels: cherubim, who exhibit both human and animal characteristics (Gen. 3:24; Ezek. 1:5–12), and seraphim, who have six wings (Isa. 6:2).

(2) One special angel often sent by God is called "the *angel* of the Lord." He is a heavenly being given a particular task by God. At times it is difficult to distinguish between God himself and his angel, because he speaks with the word "I" as he brings a message from God (Gen. 16:7–14; Exod. 14:19; Num. 22:22; Jdg. 6:11–24; 2 Ki. 1:3–4). Some scholars view this angel as the preincarnate Christ appearing as a human messenger. If this is not correct, the angel is certainly a proleptic type of the Messiah.

Modern culture's fascination with angels is, for the most part, foreign to the OT perspective, for angels were only witnesses to something much greater—God himself. See *NIDOTTE*, 2:941–43.

New Testament

Noun: ἄγγελος (*angelos*), GK *34* (S *32*), 175x. *angelos* means "angel, messenger." Similar to *malʾāk* in the OT, there are two primary uses of this word in the NT.

(1) *angelos* can refer to a human messenger serving as an envoy (see *messenger*).

(2) *angelos* refers especially to nonmaterial, spiritual beings—a transcendent power who carries out various missions or tasks for God ("Then an *angel* of the Lord appeared to him" Lk. 1:11; cf. Acts 5:19; Gal. 4:14). The NT also makes distinctions between good and evil angelic beings or spirits; note Jesus' words in Mt. 25:41 ("the eternal fire prepared for the devil and his *angels*") or Peter's words in 2 Pet. 2:4 ("For God did not spare *angels* when they sinned"). *angelos* can also be found in the multitudes surrounding the throne of God, who are a part of the heavenly world (Rev. 5:11) and who act out God's will and judgment (1:1; 7:1).

(3) Our culture has a strong interest in angels for their own sake. It is important for Christians to realize that angels in the Bible are always witnesses for God and do not draw attention to themselves. They bring messages from God (Lk. 1:26–33). They praise God (2:13–14; Heb. 1:6; Rev. 5:11–12). They serve God's people on his behalf (Mt. 4:11; Heb. 1:14). They protect and care for God's people (Mt. 18:10; Lk. 4:10; Acts 12:7–10). They sometimes give specific guidance to God's people (Acts 8:26; 27:23–24). They are also involved in the punishment of God's enemies (Rev. 14:17–16:21). All of God's creation is to serve God alone and to witness to his greatness and glory. See *NIDNTT-A*, 8-9.

ANGER

Old Testament

Verb: כָּעַס (*kāʿas*), GK 4087 (S 3707), 55x. *kāʿas* denotes the idea of provoking one to anger and may be translated "to anger, irritate." This term commonly conveys the anger of God against his people, usually for idolatry (e.g., 1 Ki. 14:9, 15; 2 Ki. 22:17); it occurs most often in Deuteronomy to Kings. Deut. 4:25 proclaims, "After you have had children and grandchildren and have lived in the land a long time—if you then become corrupt and make any kind of idol, doing evil in the eyes of the LORD your God *and provoking him to anger....*" The term is also used to mean "anger" (Neh. 4:1) or even "jealousy" (Ps. 78:58). Ezekiel proclaims, "Then my wrath against you will subside and my *jealous anger* will turn away from you; I will be calm and no longer angry" (16:42).

All parents experience *kāʿas* when they are provoked to anger by disobedient children. In the same way, we can provoke God to anger when we are lured away by sin and modern forms of idolatry. 1 Ki. 16:13 states, "Because of all the sins Baasha and his son Elah had committed and had caused Israel to commit, so that they provoked the LORD, the God of Israel, to anger by their worthless idols." See *NIDOTTE*, 2:684-86.

Noun: אַף (*ʾap*), GK 678 (S 639), 277x. The noun *ʾap* literally means "nose" or, in the plural, "face" or "nostrils" (see *nose*), but it is often used figuratively for "anger." Because the nose commonly reflected intense anger—a flaring and snorting of the nostrils—*ʾap* is often used to convey anger.

(1) About 80x in the OT and always in connection with God, *ʾap* is used with the verb "burn" (*ḥārâ*) in the expression (lit.), "his nose became hot," which in context means "his anger was kindled" (Exod. 4:14; Deut. 13:18; cf. Deut. 32:22; see *burn*). "Therefore the anger of the Lord was kindled against his people, and he struck out his hand and struck them" (Isa. 5:25). In such instances, it almost always occurs in the context of disobedient Israel (Num. 12:9; Jos. 7:1; Jdg. 2:20; Isa. 5:24–25; Hos. 8:5), who has begun to follow after foreign gods (Deut. 6:15; 7:4; 29:27; 31:17; Jos. 23:16). Job 4:9 describes God's righteous anger against sinners: "At the breath of God they are destroyed; at the blast of his *anger* they perish." Ps. 18:8 states even more vividly that "smoke rose from his [God's] nostrils." Most of the time, however, these phrases are translated with words such as "fury." Thus in Ps. 78:49 the NIV translates the phrase "hot anger" (cf. Num. 22:22; 2 Ki. 23:26).

(2) When *ʾap* is linked with the word "slow" (*ʾārēk*), the figurative sense can mean "slow to anger." This phrase is used, in fact, many times to characterize God's loving patience. Thus, the psalmist says: "The Lord is gracious and compassionate, slow to anger and rich in love" (Ps. 145:8; cf. Exod. 34:6; Num. 14:18; Neh. 9:17; Ps. 86:15; 103:8; 145:8; Prov. 14:29; 15:18; 16:32; 19:11; 25:15; Jer. 15:15; Joel 2:13; Jon. 4:2; Nah. 1:3). See *NIDOTTE*, 1:462-65.

Noun: חֵמָה (*ḥēmâ*), GK 2779 (S 2534), 125x. The basic meaning of *ḥema* is "anger, wrath," though in certain contexts it may mean "poison, venom." See *poison*.

As an intense emotion of hot displeasure, the most common use of *ḥēma* describes the fury or rage of God or of his people. This word is found mostly in poetic and prophetic literature. Ezekiel speaks of the "heat" of his spirit, which is descriptive of his righteous anger against the Israelites for their sin (Ezek. 3:14). People express anger (2 Sam. 11:20; 2 Ki. 5:12; Dan. 11:44). Jacob waits for the "fury" of Esau to subside (Gen. 27:44). King Xerxes seethes with anger when Queen Vashti refuses to come at his command (Est. 1:12; 2:1), and Haman is full of "rage" when Mordecai refuses to bow down to him (3:5, 9). Proverbs speaks about the damage caused by the anger or fury of people

(Prov. 6:34; 15:18; 19:19; 22:24; 27:4; 29:22).

In contrast to human anger, God's anger is righteous because it is incited when the Israelites sin against him (Lev. 26:28; 2 Ki. 22:13, 17; Ps. 90:7). God causes Israel to be defeated by enemies because of his anger toward them (2 Chr. 28:9; Isa. 42:25), but his anger can also be restrained or turned away from his people (Num. 25:11). Ultimately, God will burn with great "fury" against his enemies (Zech. 8:2). See *NIDOTTE*, 2:170-71.

New Testament

Noun: θυμός (*thymos*), GK *2596* (S *2372*), 18x. *thymos* is generally used to refer to "anger, rage, fury." See *wrath*.

Noun: ὀργή (*orgē*), GK *3973* (S *3709*), 36x. *orgē* signifies "anger, wrath." Depending on the context, the term emphasizes either emotional anger or retributive wrath. In the former sense, it can refer to a person who is angry, such as Jesus' anger at the lack of concern and legalism of the Jewish leaders (Mk. 3:5). In several places the NT instructs believers not to be given to anger (Eph. 4:31; Col. 3:8; 1 Tim. 2:8).

More often, however, *orgē* signifies God's indignation directed at wrongdoing (e.g., Rom. 1:18). When God cut off a generation from entering the Promised Land, it was an oath he made "in wrath" (Heb. 3:11; 4:3). Paul equates God's wrath with his vengeance, "Do not take revenge, my friends, but leave room for God's *wrath*, for it is written: 'It is mine to avenge; I will repay,' says the Lord" (Rom. 12:19). Paul speaks of those who heap up their sins, saying that "the *wrath* of God has come upon them at last" (1 Thess. 2:16; cf. Rom. 1:18). Governing authorities are temporal conduits of divine retribution (Rom. 13:1). "The *wrath* of God" remains on those who do not believe in the Son (Jn. 3:36). Paul writes that "God's *wrath* comes on those who are disobedient" (Eph. 5:6; cf. Col. 3:6). God "stores up his *wrath*" for those who are unrepentant and saves it for a "day of *wrath*," when it will be visited on the same (Rom. 2:5). But Christians are not destined for such an end, "For God did not appoint us to suffer *wrath* but to receive salvation through our Lord Jesus Christ" (1 Thess. 5:9). See *NIDNTT-A*, 416-17.

ANGRY

Old Testament

Verb: חָרָה (*hārâ*), GK 3013 (S 2734), 93x. *hārâ* literally means "to burn," but in most occurrences it is used figuratively for enflamed rage (i.e., "to burn with anger"). Often the word "nostril" (*ʾap*) is used in tandem with *hārâ* because the nose commonly reflects intense anger (i.e., flaring or snorting of the nostrils; see Num. 22:22; 2 Ki. 23:26). When *hārâ* is used of God, it almost always refers to his fury against disobedient Israel (Num. 12:9; Jos. 7:1; Jdg. 2:20; Isa. 5:24–25; Hos. 8:5), especially in response to their following after foreign gods (Deut. 6:15; 7:4; 29:27; 31:17; Jos. 23:16).

In the OT, the portrayal of human anger is sometimes viewed negatively, as when Cain becomes enraged because God does not accept his offering (Gen. 4:5–6; cf. Ps. 37:1, 7–8). In other contexts, anger appears as an appropriate response, as when Moses comes down from the mountain with the two tablets and sees Israel's dancing and worshiping the golden calf: "his anger *burned* and he threw the tablets out of his hands, breaking them to pieces at the foot of the mountain" (Exod. 32:19).

ANGUISH

See *trouble*.

ANIMAL

Old Testament

Noun: בְּהֵמָה (b^e*hēmâ*), GK 989 (S 929), 190x. The noun b^e*hēmâ* can be translated "beast, animal, cattle" and is distinguished in the OT from birds, fish, and reptiles (1 Ki. 4:33). The term denotes four-footed animals, and it can refer to wild (Jer. 7:33) or domesticated animals, especially cattle (Gen. 34:23; Ps. 8:7). Several laws are given in the OT that govern humanity's relationship with four-footed animals, including laws relating to idolatry (Deut. 4:17), sexual behavior (Exod. 22:19), and diet (Deut. 14:4–8).

b^e^hēmâ were created on the sixth day just prior to Adam (Gen. 1:24–26), were named by Adam in the Garden (Gen. 2:20), entered the ark (Gen. 7:2, 8, 14, 21, 23), and were among those God remembered when he promised never again to destroy the world by a flood (Gen. 8:1). God provides food for the animals (Ps. 104:14) and they belong to him (50:10).

It is also significant, though not surprising, that over half of the biblical references to "animals" are found in the Pentateuch alone (103x), where God gives many regulations concerning the animals that were to be offered in sacrifice.

Noun: חַיָּה (*ḥayyâ*), GK 2651 (S 2416), 96x. Based on the verb "to be alive" (*ḥāyâ*, GK 2649), *hayyâ* is a generic term for all kinds of animals (Gen. 1:28, 30; Lev. 11:2), though usually of nondomesticated, land animals (e.g., Gen. 1:24). *ḥayyâ* is often found together with "birds of the air" (e.g., 1 Sam. 17:46; Ps. 79:2; Ezek. 29:5). Regularly *ḥayyâ* is made more specific with the addition of the words "the land," "the field," or "evil" to denote "wild animals": "And God said, 'Let the land produce living *creatures* according to their kinds: livestock, creatures that move along the ground, and *wild animals* [beast of the earth, KJV], each according to its kind.' And it was so" (Gen. 1:24); "The man gave names to all the cattle, and to the birds of the sky, and to every *beast* of the field" (2:20); "For thus says the Lord GOD, 'How much more when I send my four severe judgments against Jerusalem: sword, famine, *wild beasts* and plague to cut off man and beast from it!'" (Jer. 27:6). Indeed, wild beasts are used by God as a means of enacting his righteous wrath against sin (Ezek. 14:15, 21; 34:5; Hos. 2:12; 13:8; cf. Ps. 22:12–13).

By contrast, all of God's creation is called to give him praise: "Praise the LORD from the earth, you great sea creatures … wild animals and all cattle, small creatures and flying birds…. Let them praise the name of the LORD!" (Ps. 148:7–13). See *NIDOTTE*, 2:113-15.

New Testament

Noun: θηρίον (*thērion*), GK *2563* (S *2342*), 46x. *thērion* refers to wild "animals" or "beasts." See *beast*.

ANNIHILATE

Old Testament

Verb: שָׁמַד (*šāmad*), GK 9012 (S 8045), 90x. *šāmad* (occurring mostly in the Heb. Hiphil verb form) means "to destroy, exterminate," or "annihilate" and expresses the partial or complete destruction of a group of people. See *destroy*.

ANNOUNCE

Old Testament

Verb: שָׁמַע (*šāmaʿ*), GK 9048 (S 8085), 1165x. *šāmaʿ* means "to hear, listen, pay attention to, perceive, obey, proclaim, announce." See *hear*.

New Testament

Verb: ἀναγγέλλω (*anangello*), GK *334* (S *312*), 14x. *anangellō* means "to tell, proclaim." See *tell*.

Verb: καταγγέλλω (*katangellō*), GK *2859* (S *2605*), 18x. *katangellō* means "to proclaim, announce, make public." See *proclaim*.

Verb: κηρύσσω (*kēryssō*), GK *3062* (S *2784*), 61x. *kēryssō* means to "preach, proclaim, tell, announce a message." See *preach*.

ANNUL

New Testament

Verb: ἀθετέω (*atheteō*), GK *119* (S *114*), 16x. *atheteō* means "to reject, set aside, nullify, annul." See *reject*.

ANOINT

Old Testament

Verb: מָשַׁח (*māšaḥ*), GK 5417 (S 4886), 70x. The basic meaning of *māšaḥ* is to "rub" with a liquid (see *rub*). In this nontechnical sense, the word is used of such things as painting a house (Jer. 22:14), rubbing a shield with oil (2 Sam. 1:21; Isa. 21:5), or using oil as a cosmetic lotion (Amos 6:6). As a technical term, however, *māšaḥ* means "to anoint," and this meaning accounts for the majority of uses of this verb in the OT.

Religious objects such as the tabernacle and its entire contents—such as the altar of burnt offering and the basin with its stand—are anointed with oil at the time of their dedication (Exod. 40:9–11). Jacob anoints the rock at Bethel on which he has slept (cf. Gen. 31:13). Four other passages refer to wafers being "*spread* with oil" as a regular ritual (Exod. 29:2; Lev. 2:4; 7:12; Num. 6:15).

The rest of the uses of *māšah* have people being anointed, which signifies their undertaking special responsibilities in the nation of Israel. Those anointed are priests (e.g., Exod. 30:30), kings (e.g., 1 Sam. 16:12–13; Ps. 89:20), and (in one passage) a prophet (1 Ki. 19:16). The anointed person has been set apart for special service to God and through the anointing receives empowerment for that service (Isa. 61:1 relates this to the power of God's Spirit). Biblical writers draw special attention to the anointing of a king when there is either a change in dynasty (e.g., 2 Ki. 9:3, 6) or when there are other contenders to the throne (1 Ki. 1:34, 39, 45).

Of special significance is the concept of the anointed Son of David, the Messiah (*māšîaḥ*, "anointed one," GK 5431, which derives from *māšaḥ*). Prophets (1 Chr. 16:22; Ps. 105:15), priests (Lev. 4:3), and kings (1 Sam. 24:6; 26:11; Ps. 2:2) are all called by this term in the OT. *māšîah* carries over into the NT into the ministry of Jesus "Christ" (*christos*, a word derived from the Gk. verb *chriō*, "to anoint" [see *Christ*]; cf. the connection between Isa. 61:1 and Lk. 4:18). See *NIDOTTE*, 2:1123–27.

New Testament

Verb: ἀλείφω (*aleiphō*), GK *230* (S *218*), 9x. *aleiphō* means "to anoint." About half of the uses of this verb in the NT have to do with the anointing of Jesus: by the sinful woman in Lk. 7:38, 46 and by Mary in Jn. 12:3 (cf. 11:2). After Jesus' death, the women purchase oil so that they may "anoint" Jesus' body on the day after the Sabbath (Mk. 16:1). Anointing oneself with oil can also be a sign of contrition (Mt. 6:17). The final two occurrences of this verb concern anointing the sick. James instructs elders to pray over the sick and "anoint [them] with oil in the name of the Lord" (Jas. 5:14); this follows the example of the disciples when they were sent out on their mission by Jesus (Mk. 6:13).*

Verb: χρίω (*chriō*), GK *5987* (S *5548*), 5x. *chriō* means "to anoint." Four of the uses of this verb refer to the anointing of Jesus. In Heb. 1:9, the author quotes from Ps. 45:7 but applies *chriō* to Jesus as God's Son. In Lk. 4:18, Jesus reads from Isa. 61:1 and applies it to himself, that the Spirit "has anointed" him to preach the good news to the poor. In an early Christian prayer in Acts 4:27 and in a message by Peter in 10:38, Jesus was "anointed" by God (the Holy Spirit) to his ministry on our behalf (that anointing took place at his baptism; e.g., Lk. 3:21–22).

The final occurrence of *chriō* is in 2 Cor. 1:21–22, where Paul writes that God "has anointed us, set his seal of ownership on us, and put his Spirit in our hearts." John uses the corresponding noun *chrisma* (GK *5984*) to refer to an "anointing" we have from the Holy One, which remains in us and teaches us all things (1 Jn. 2:20, 27; cf. Jn. 14:26; 16:13).*

ANOINTED ONE

Old Testament

Noun: מָשִׁיחַ (*māšîaḥ*), GK 5431 (S 4899), 38x. *māšîaḥ* means "anointed one"; it is the Heb. word from which we derive the word "Messiah." There are three categories of people in the OT that receive this designation: high priest (Lev. 4:3, 5, 16; 6:22), prophet (Ps. 105:15, in parallel with "prophets"), and king (2 Sam. 22:51). By far the majority of references are to the last of these, the king. David, for example, though he has already been anointed king, will not take action against Saul because he is "the Lord's anointed" (1 Sam. 24:6; 26:9, 11, 23; 2 Sam. 1:14, 16). This "anointed" king receives special protection (Ps. 20:6; 84:9) and kindness (18:50) from the Lord.

The focus of *māšîaḥ* as a term for the king is not on his power or his royal status, but on the fact that he has been chosen by God to fulfill tasks that the Lord has given. It is with this in mind that Isaiah is able to call Cyrus the Lord's "anointed" (Isa. 45:1).

As God's revelation progresses in the OT, *māšîah* takes on the added nuance of an eschatological "Anointed One," who will appear in the last days. This person is clearly evident in Dan. 9:25–26, and the NT sees Jesus Christ and the fulfillment of the *māsîaḥ* (cf. Jn. 1:41; see Christ). Then, as the early Christians look back at various OT passages, they begin to understand "the Anointed One" in Ps. 2:2 as a messianic reference fulfilled in Jesus Christ (note especially Acts 4:25–26). It is interesting to observe that all three categories of "anointed ones" in the OT are all applied to Jesus in the NT: "prophet" (Mt. 21:11; Jn. 6:14; 7:40), "priest" (Heb. 3:1; 4:14–16; 8:1), and "king" (Mt. 27:11, 37, 42; Rev. 17:14; 19:16). See *NIDOTTE*, 2:1123–27.

New Testament

Noun: Χριστός (*Christos*), GK *5986* (S *5547*), 529x. *Christos* means "Messiah, anointed one, Christ." See *Christ*.

ANOTHER

Old Testament

Adjective: אַחֵר (*ʾaḥēr*), GK 337 (S 312), 166x. *ʾaḥēr* is formed from the verb אָחַר, *ʾāḥar* (GK 336), "to delay" or "to detain someone." Thus, *ʾaḥēr* may originally have had the sense of "one who comes after," which evolved in meaning to "other" or "another." It is often used in this common sense: "he waited seven *more* days" (Gen. 8:10, "he stayed yet *other* seven days," KJV); "*another* place" (Num. 23:13); "*another* generation" (Jdg. 2:10). Frequently, *ʾaḥēr* is used to denote "other gods," i.e., false gods (66x). For example, the first commandment is, "You shall have no *other* gods before me" (Exod. 20:3). So often is *ʾaḥēr* used in connection with false gods, that it can also be used by itself to denote pagan deities: "I am the LORD; that is my name! I will not give my glory to *another* or my praise to idols" (Isa. 42:8).

It was for this reason that the Hebrew scribes were concerned that they not mistake the word *ʾaḥēr* for the word *ʾeḥād*, "one," and vice versa. Since the Hebrew letters "dalet" and "resh" are similar in appearance (ד / ר) and since only this letter distinguished the words "other" and "one," a small mistake in the stroke of the letter could be disastrous. For example, if the wrong letter were written in Exod. 34:14 it would read, "Do not worship the one God…" when the text actually states, "Do not worship any *other* gods…." This may be partially why Jesus reminds us that even the smallest stroke of the sacred text is of great importance (Mt. 5:18). See *NIDOTTE*, 1:360-61.

New Testament

Adjective: ἄλλος (*allos*), GK *257* (S *243*), 155x. *allos* means "other" or "another." See *other*.

Adjective: ἕτερος (*heteros*), GK *2283* (S *2087*), 98x. *heteros* means "other" or "another." See *other*.

ANSWER

Old Testament

Verb: עָנָה (*ʿānâ*), GK 6699 (S 6030), 316x. The basic meaning of *ʿānâ* is "to answer, reply, respond." It often indicates a verbal answer and is frequently accompanied by the verb *ʾāmar* ("to say, speak"), as in Gen. 23:5, "The Hittites answered (*ʿānâ*) and said (*ʾāmar*) to Abraham, 'Sir, listen to us'" (cf. Gen. 18:27). The same expression, influenced by the Gk. version of the OT, is found throughout the Greek NT. This verb is used frequently in the book of Job to introduce the speakers (e.g., 3:2; 4:1;5:1).

ʿānâ can also refer to nonverbal responses. God tells Israel, "When you march up to attack a city, make its people an offer of peace. If they *accept* [lit., "if they answer peaceably"] and open their gates, all the people in it shall be subject to forced labor and shall work for you" (Deut. 20:10–11).

Similarly, the Lord announces to his people, "In the time of my favor I *will answer* you, and in the day of salvation I will help you" (Isa. 49:8). Elsewhere, God responds nonverbally to David with fire (1 Chr. 21:26) and to Moses with thunder (Exod. 19:19). By contrast, when the Lord refuses to answer, that is a sign of his displeasure (1 Sam. 14:37; Ps. 18:41).

In the Psalms, *ʿānâ* is often used when God is petitioned (Ps. 55:2; 69:13). David writes, "*Answer* me when I call to you, O my righteous God" (4:1; cf. 13:3). God often answers with salvation, as in 20:6, "Now I know that the Lord saves his anointed; he *answers* him from his holy heaven with the saving power of his right hand" (cf. 118:21).

ʿānâ can also be used in a legal sense, meaning "to testify." The ninth commandment asserts, "You shall not *give* false testimony against your neighbor" (Exod. 20:16). Furthermore, 23:2 declares, "Do not follow the crowd in doing wrong. When you *testify* in a lawsuit, do not pervert justice by siding with the crowd." See *NIDOTTE*, 3:447–49.

New Testament

Verb: ἀποκρίνομαι (*apokrinomai*), GK *646* (S *611*), 231x. *apokrinomai* means "to answer, reply," and is used almost exclusively in the gospels and Acts. The gospel writers seem to rely on the meaning of the word as it was used in the LXX ("to answer and say"), which explains the common repetition of "he answered and said" (e.g., Mt. 16:2; Mk. 7:6; Lk. 19:40; Jn. 9:25). The verb almost always introduces direct speech, and in most cases reflects a response to a conversation or a situation (e.g., Mt. 3:15; 4:4) or to a specific question (e.g., 16:16).

Outside the Gospels and Acts, *apokrinomai* only occurs in Col. 4:6 and Rev. 7:13. Paul writes in Col. 4:6, "Let your conversation be always full of grace, seasoned with salt, so that you may know how to *answer* everyone." This passage is set in the context of how to deal with "outsiders" who presumably either challenge the Christian faith or have questions about it. We must always be ready to speak up for what we believe.

Verb: φημί (*phēmi*), GK *5774* (S *5346*), 66x. *phēmi* means "to say, declare, answer, reply." See *say*.

ANTICHRIST

New Testament

Noun: ἀντίχριστος (*antichristos*), GK *532* (S *500*), 5x. *antichristos* means "antichrist." While there are references in the gospels to "false Christs and false prophets" (Mt. 24:24; Mk. 13:22), only John actually uses the word *antichristos*. The prefix "anti" before "Christ" denotes either someone who is "against" Christ or someone who claims to be a messiah "instead of" Christ; both of these essentially mean the same thing. "Many *antichrists*" were around in John's day (1 Jn. 2:18); they began in the church but then left it. They taught false teachings about Christ—in John's day, they denied that Jesus came in the flesh (2:22; 4:2–3; 2 Jn. 7). But anyone in any era who teaches doctrines about Christ that are not in conformity with Scripture follows this spirit of the antichrist.*

ANXIETY

New Testament

Noun: μέριμνα (*merimna*), GK *3533* (S *3308*), 6x. *merimna* is a "care, anxiety, concern" that can easily (though not necessarily) distract a believer. See *concern*.

APOSTLE

New Testament

Noun: ἀπόστολος (*apostolos*), GK *693* (S *652*), 80x. *apostolos* broadly refers to a "messenger, delegate," or "sent one." In classical Greek, *apostolos* referred to a person of merit sent as an envoy or on behalf of a master in an administrative role. John uses the term in a similar way, applying it to any messenger without the specific idea of an office with special status (Jn. 13:16). In contrast, in Luke *apostolos* is used almost solely as a designation for the Twelve (except in Lk. 11:49 and Acts 14:14; in the latter, Luke identifies both Barnabas and Paul as apostles). For Luke, the apostles are God's messengers or delegates who have unique status among the fledgling churches. Every important decision is made by the apostles, and no independent authority is found outside of this unique group of leaders. Matthew and Mark use *apostolos* rather sparingly when referring to the Twelve (Mt. 10:2; Mk. 3:14; 6:30).

Within Paul's letters, where the term is found more frequently than in any other part of the NT, *apostolos* does not refer to the Twelve alone but more generally to an honored group of believers with special status as God's messengers or envoys (e.g., Paul identifies both Peter and Barnabas as apostles, Gal. 1:18–19; 2:1, 9, 13). Paul's understanding of *apostolos* and its distinguishing features are as follows: (a) The call to apostleship is not initiated by the human agent but by God in Jesus Christ alone (Gal. 1:1) and comes about through meeting the risen Lord (1 Cor. 9:1; 15:7; Gal. 1:16). (b) Suffering is a mark of apostleship (1 Cor. 4:9–13; 2 Cor. 4:7–12; 11:23–29). (c) Like the OT prophets, apostles have special insight into the mysteries of God (1 Cor. 4:1). (d) Apostolic authority is not the result of inherent quality in the office holder but is a function of the gospel's own power to convict and communicate truth (Rom. 15:18; 2 Cor. 4:2).

Without doubt, the technical use of *apostolos* in the NT canon varies between different books and must be treated carefully as one seeks to define this term clearly. It should be stated, however, that the overall thrust of the word in Pauline and Lukan usage is that of an emissary of God, similar to the prophets of the OT, with special authority and status in Christ for the sake of the gospel.

(BE) APPALLED

Old Testament

Verb: שָׁמֵם (*šāmēm*), GK 9037 (S 8074), 92x. *šāmēm* is used in two distinct but related ways. It can mean "to be desolate, deserted, lay waste" or it can point to the response to such desolation and mean "to shudder, be horrified, be appalled." As to the second usage, it denotes the reaction of people to the desolation caused by divine judgment on themselves (Ps. 40:15; 143:4) or others (Lev. 26:32; Jer. 2:12; Job 17:8). In these cases, it is translated "to shutter, be horrified, be appalled." Isaiah prophesies that people will be appalled at the appearance of God's servant because he will be marred more than any man (52:14). See *desolate*; also see *NIDOTTE*, 4:167-71.

APPAREL

See *clothes.*

APPEAL

New Testament

Verb: ἐπικαλέω (*epikaleō*), GK *2126* (S *1941*), 30x. *epikaleō* means "to call on someone" or even "to appeal to someone for help." See *call.*

APPEAR

Old Testament

Verb: רָאָה (*rāʾâ*), GK 8011 (S 7200 and 7202), 1,311x. *rāʾâ* is the most frequent Heb. verb for "seeing," encompassing a variety of actions including physical, visionary, and mental. See *see.*

New Testament

Verb: ἐφίστημι (*ephistēmi*), GK *2392* (S *2182*), 21x. *ephistēmi* means "to appear," often with the idea of suddenness. It is a favorite word of Luke, who uses it 19x. It can refer to manifestations of the supernatural, such as angels (Lk. 2:9), but also of a human being arriving (2:38). Since appearances of someone or something imply proximity, the word can connote nearness either in distance (4:39, "he *bent over* her") or in time (2 Tim. 4:6, "the time of my departure *is at hand*").

Sometimes an appearance can "close in on" a person unexpectedly (Lk. 21:34). Violence can also accompany *ephistēmi* (see Acts 17:5; KJV uses "assaulted"). Paul uses *ephistēmi* to illustrate the suddenness of the second coming (1 Thess. 5:3, "destruction *will come on* them suddenly"). As a natural consequence of the meaning of *ephistēmi*, it also gained the idea of being prepared, expecting the unexpected (2 Tim. 4:2, "Preach the Word; *be prepared* in season and out of season"). The preacher must always be vigilant for opportunities to proclaim the Word and to be prepared to do it when the opportunity arises. See *NIDNTT-A*, 202-4.

Verb: ἵστημι (*histēmi*), GK *2705* (S *2476*), 154x. The basic sense of *histēmi* is "to set" or "stand." It has a variety of nuances in the NT, one of which is "to appear." See *stand.*

Verb: ὁράω (*horaō*), GK *3972* (S *3708*), 454x. *horaō* is the most frequently used word for seeing in the NT. It can also mean "appear, perceive, consider" (i.e., a more mental seeing). See *see.*

Verb: φαίνω (*phainō*), GK *5743* (S *5316*), 31x. *phainō* refers to objects coming into sight (i.e., appearing) and to bright objects shining their light (cf. Rev. 8:12; 18:23; 21:23). (1) Its more common use is of something coming into sight and being noticed. It is used of angels, stars, weeds, and even Jesus "appearing" in people's sight (Mt. 1:20; 2:7, 13, 19; 13:26; Mk. 16:9). As lightening begins from one side of the sky and "is visible" all across to the other, so also at the end will "the sign of the Son of Man *appear*" so that all will see Jesus in his power and great glory (Mt. 24:27, 30). *phainō* can be used of people's opinions, as in "What do you *think*?" (Mk. 14:64; cf. Lk. 24:11). *phainō* is also used of the way in which people present themselves so as to be noticed. Pharisees and hypocrites want to "appear" before people as pious, praying and fasting like good believers (Mt. 6:5, 16). This causes them to "appear" on the outside as beautiful and righteous, while inwardly they are corrupt, lawless, and full of death (23:27).

(2) *phainō* also denotes light that "shines." The uses of *phainō* here are all metaphorical. John the Baptist is like a "burning and *shining* lamp" (Jn. 5:35), and believers are to "*shine* as lights in the world" by being "children of God without blemish in the midst of a crooked and twisted generation" (Phil. 2:15). The OT prophetic word is to be held to as "a lamp *shining* in a dark place" (2 Pet. 1:19). As is common in the Bible, light and darkness can refer to morality. Therefore, good (i.e., God's purpose in Christ) triumphs over evil just as "light *shines* in the darkness, and the darkness has not overcome it" (Jn. 1:5). The light of Jesus' love is "already *shining*" as the darkness of hate is passing away (1 Jn. 2:8); therefore believers are to walk in the light of the love in which Jesus walked. The light of Jesus is his glory, giving his brilliance "as the sun *shining* in its power" (Rev. 1:16). See *NIDNTT-A*, 587.

Verb: φανερόω (*phaneroō*), GK *5746* (S *5319*), 49x. *phaneroō* denotes the act of making visible or disclosing that which is not readily seen—"to show, appear, reveal." In several places it refers to the appearing of Jesus—in his incarnation (1 Tim. 3;16; 1 Jn. 1:2; 3:8), after his resurrection (Mk. 16:12, 14; Jn. 21:1), and at his second coming (Col. 3:4; 1 Jn. 2:28; 3:2). Someday we ourselves will appear before the judgment seat of Christ (2 Cor. 5:10).

Paul refers to God's word as "the mystery that has been kept hidden for ages and generations, but is now *disclosed* to the saints" (Col. 1:26). For him, the fullness of the gospel has finally been revealed in Christ. He writes, "But now a righteousness from God, apart from law, *has been made known*, to which the Law and the Prophets testify" (Rom. 3:21). Every believer is to be a walking billboard for Christ. Paul again writes, "But thanks be to God, who always leads us in triumphal procession in Christ and through us *spreads* everywhere the fragrance of the knowledge of him" (2 Cor. 2:14; 4:11). The fullness of God's disclosure to humankind was Jesus Christ (1 Tim. 3:16). John invites all believers to share in God's initiative and writes, "This is how God *showed* his love among us: He sent his one and only Son into the world that we might live through him" (1 Jn. 4:9; cf. 1:2; 2:28; 3:2). See *NIDNTT-A*, 202-4.

APPEARANCE

Old Testament

Noun: מַרְאֶה (*mar'eh*), GK 5260 (S 4758), 103x. *mar'eh* refers both to prophetic "visions" and to outward "appearances."

(1) God often reveals his messages to his servants through visions, and sometimes the word used is *mar'eh*. God comforts Jacob in "a *vision* in the night," encouraging him to go to Egypt where God promises to fulfill some of his promises (Gen. 46:2). God gives prophets visual images: "The Spirit lifted me up between earth and heaven and brought me in *visions* of God to Jerusalem" (Ezek. 8:3; cf. 1:1). Many of these images are emotionally charged: "So I was left alone and saw this great *vision*, and no strength was left in me" (Dan. 10:7).

(2) *mar'eh* more commonly refers to outward appearances. It is used to describe the appearance of animals (cows, Gen. 41:4), objects (temple basins, Exod. 38:8), events (God's presence coming as fire, Num. 9:16), skin (disease, Lev. 13:3ff.), strange phenomena (the burning bush, Exod. 3:3; the glory cloud, Num. 9:15; flashes of lightening, Ezek. 1:14), and people (Song 2:14b; 5:15). Rebekah was (lit.) "good of *appearance* exceedingly" (Gen. 24:16), and Joseph was "beautiful of *appearance*" (39:6). But the suffering Messiah "has no *appearance* that we should desire him" (Isa. 53:2). While humans favor people for their *mar'eh*, God does not: "But the LORD said to Samuel, 'Do not look on his *appearance* or on the height of his stature, because I have rejected him. For the LORD sees not as man sees: man looks on the outward *appearance*, but the LORD looks on the heart'" (1 Sam. 16:7). We too should learn to see the inside of a person, not the outside appearance. See *NIDOTTE*, 3:1012-1013.*

New Testament

Noun: σχῆμα (*schēma*), GK *5386* (S *4976*), 2x. *schēma* means "form, outward appearance, figure." See *form*.

APPEASE

Old Testament

Verb: כָּפַר (*kāpar*), GK 4105 (S 3722), 102x. *kāpar* is generally translated "to atone, wipe clean, appease." While scholars debate whether the root meaning of this verb is "to cover," "to ransom," or "to wipe clean/purge," it is the latter meaning that seems most appropriate in the OT. It can also mean "appease." See *atone*.

New Testament

Verb: ἱλάσκομαι (*hilaskomai*), GK *2661* (S *2433*), 2x. *hilaskomai* means "to atone, have mercy on, to make atonement for, propitiate," and refers in the NT to the atoning work of Christ whereby he propitiate God's anger. See *atone, make atonement*.

APPETITE

New Testament

Noun: κοιλία (*koilia*), GK *3120* (S *2836*), 23x. The basic meaning of *koilia* is "body-cavity"; it is often translated "stomach, belly, womb, appetite." See *stomach*.

APPOINT

Old Testament

Verb: עָמַד (*ʿāmad*), GK 6641 (S 5975), 524x. *ʿāmad* has the basic meaning "to stand" but includes multiple nuances depending on the context in which it occurs. When it means "to appoint," it has the idea of causing someone to stand. See *stand*.

Verb: פָּקַד (*pāqad*), GK 7212 (S 6485), 304x. While *pāqad* has a wide range of meaning, it basically expresses the action of overseeing an individual for a particular purpose, such as counting the people (see *count*). In a causative sense, *pāqad* means "to cause to oversee" and is often translated "to appoint," an action performed by kings (Jer. 41:2), Pharoah (Gen. 41:34), and God (Jer. 1:10).

New Testament

Verb: καθίστημι (*kathistēmi*), GK *2770* (S *2525*), 21x. *kathistēmi* denotes "to appoint, put in charge." It is sometimes used for the appointing of a person to an office or position, such as deacons (Acts

6:3), elders (Tit. 1:5), and the high priest (Heb. 5:1). See *put in charge*.

Verb: ὁρίζω (*horizo*), GK *3988* (S *3724*), 8x. *horizō* means "to appoint, set." Six of its occurrences are in Luke and Acts. Its only use with a human subject is the statement that "the disciples, each according to his ability, *decided* to send help to the brothers and sisters living in Judea" (Acts 11:29).

Among the other uses, God is explicitly the subject six times. Peter says, "This man [Jesus] was handed over to you in God's *set* purpose and foreknowledge" (Acts 2:23). Peter also says, "he [Jesus] is the one *appointed* by God as judge of the living and the dead" (10:42). Likewise Paul in his speech at the Areopagus said that God "*determined* the times set for them [people] and the exact places where they should live" (17:26). Later in the same speech, Paul says that God "has set a day when he will judge the world with justice by the man he has *appointed*" (17:31). Paul's last use of the word is in his description of Jesus as "the *appointed* Son of God" (Rom. 1:4). The author of Hebrews writes, "Again God *set* a certain day" (Heb. 4:7).

In Lk. 22:22 God is not explicitly mentioned as the subject in this verse or its context, but he should be understood as the agent of the action in Jesus' statement that uses a passive voice: "The Son of Man will go as it has been *appointed*."

It is worth emphasizing that our Father has "appointed or set" about the events in the world and in our lives. Furthermore, of the seven occurrences with God as explicit or implicit subject, Jesus is the object five times (Lk. 22:22; Acts 2:23; 10:42; 12:26, 31; Rom. 1:4) and is in view a sixth time (Heb. 4:7). Therefore, not only has God appointed the events of this world, he has first and foremost appointed his Son to accomplish redemption on our behalf. See *NIDNTT-A*, 418.*

Verb: ποιέω (*poieō*), GK *4472* (S *4160*), 568x. This verb, generically translated as "to do," has a wide range of meanings, such as "to appoint" someone to a task. See *do*.

Verb: προχειρίζω (*procheirizō*), GK *4741* (S *4400*), 3x. *procheirizō* means "to choose, appoint." See *choose*.

Verb: τίθημι (*tithēmi*), GK *5502* (S *5087*), 100x. The basic meaning of *tithēmi* is "to put, lay something down." It can also mean "to appoint." See *put*.

APPOINTED TIME

Old Testament

Noun: מוֹעֵד (*mô*ʿ*ēd*), GK 4595 (S 4150), 223x. *mô*ʿ*ēd* is often used in cultic contexts, such as "the Tent of *Meeting*" (see *meeting*). In places, it also denotes the appointed times of Israel's pilgrimage feasts (Exod. 13:10; Lev. 23:2, 4, 44; Num. 9:2; 10:10; 29:39). In noncultic contexts, it is commonly used of a different sort of appointed time, such as the promise that Sarah will bear a son "at this *time* next year" (Gen. 17:21).

New Testament

Noun: καιρός (*kairos*), GK *2789* (S *2540*), 85x. *kairos*, like *chronos*, can be used as a temporal indicator, such as a particular season ("it was not the *season* for figs," Mk. 11:13). But unlike *chronos*, which is more focused on chronological time, *kairos* is time as significant events. See *time*.

APPORTION

Old Testament

Verb: חָלַק (*ḥālaq*), GK 2745 (S 2505), 55x. *ḥālaq* is translated "divide, share, allot." A wise servant "shares" his inheritance with others (Prov. 17:2; cf. Jos. 18:2; 22:8; 1 Chr. 24:4–5). See *divide*.

APPREHEND

New Testament

Verb: καταλαμβάνω (*katalambanō*), GK *2898* (S *2638*), 15x. *katalambanō* can mean "to catch, obtain, seize, overtake." See *catch*.

APPROACH

Old Testament

Verb: בּוֹא (*bô*ʾ), GK 995 (S 935), 2592x. *bô*ʾ is the fourth most common verb in the OT. It denotes motion toward a specific goal, such as "to go, arrive, enter a house, come." It expresses a variety of motions. See *come.*

Verb: נָגַשׁ (*nāgaš*), GK 5602 (S 5066), 125x. *nāgaš* is synonymous with *qārab* (GK 7928, "come near, offer") and denotes "to be near, come into close proximity to an object." Isaac requests of Jacob: "*Come near* so I can touch you, my son" (Gen. 27:21). *nāgaš* can also have a causative sense, "to bring near": "Then he said, "My son, *bring* me some of your game to eat" (27:25).

Often *nāgaš* is used in the context of drawing near to someone of rank. In restoring the covenant blessings to Israel, Jeremiah announces: "I will bring him near [*qārab*] and he will *come close* [*nāgaš*] to me, for who is he who will devote himself to *be close* [*nāgaš*] to me?' declares the LORD," NIV ("and he shall *approach* unto me: for who is this that engaged his heart to *approach* unto me? saith the LORD," KJV, Jer. 30:21).

This sense of drawing near to someone of venerable position is emphasized in the repeated use of *nāgaš* for the work of the priests in serving God at the altar (Exod. 19:22; 28:43; Ezek. 44:13). Here we find the means by which fallen humanity is able to draw near to the infinitely holy God, through his appointed priests who are made holy (symbolized by their sacred garments), and who are, therefore, able to draw near to God on behalf of the people. "Bring the grain offering made of these things to the LORD; present it to the priest, who shall *take it to* the altar" (Lev. 2:8). Yet the worshiper himself must draw near to God with a pure heart (cf. Jas. 4:8). Isaiah rebukes Israel because "these people *come near* to me with their mouth and honor me with their lips, but their hearts are far from me" (Isa. 29:13). The ability of the Israelites to draw near to God through the agency of the priest sets the background for the ultimate priestly work of Jesus, through whom we draw near to God: "Therefore he is able also to save forever those who draw near to God through Him, since He always lives to make intercession for them" (Heb. 7:25; cf. 10:22). See *NIDOTTE*, 3:29-30.

Verb: קָרַב (*qārab*), GK 7928 (S 7126), 280x. The basic meaning of *qārab* is "to draw near" or, in a causative sense, "to bring near." This basic meaning may denote physical or spatial proximity as well as nonphysical. When Moses approaches the burning bush, God warns him: "Do not come any closer" (NIV; "Draw not nigh hither," KJV, Exod. 3:5).

In some cases, *qārab* essentially means "to come." Moses commands Mishael and Elzaphan to remove the stricken Nadab and Abihu: "*Come here*; carry your cousins outside the camp, away from the front of the sanctuary" (Lev. 10:4; cf. Num. 31:48; Jon. 1:6). An event in time may "draw near": "When the time drew near for Israel to die, he called for his son Joseph" (Gen. 47:29). A special use of *qārab* relates to sexual relations. "No one is to *approach* any close relative to have sexual relations. I am the LORD" (Lev. 18:6; cf. 20:16; Gen. 20:4; Isa. 8:3).

"To draw near" may have the purpose of paying close attention to what is being said: "Come near, you nations, and listen; pay attention, you peoples!" (Isa. 34:1; cf. 48:16; Deut. 5:27). It may also take on a technical sense of engage in battle: "When you *march up* to attack a city, make its people an offer of peace" (NIV), "When thou comest nigh unto a city to fight against it" (KJV; Deut. 20:10; cf. Jos. 8:51; 1 Sam. 17:48; 1 Ki. 20:29). Likewise, *qārab* is used in the technical sense of coming before leaders to obtain a legal decision (Num. 27:1–2, 36; Jos. 17:4).

Theologically, the most significant use of *qārab* is in its connection with the service of the tabernacle or temple, as describing the priest who is able to *approach* the holy things, or of one who *brings near* his offering. Indeed, the common term for those things dedicated for sacrifice, *qorbān* (GK 7933), "offering," is derived from this verb. Thus, *qārab* is used extensively throughout Leviticus in connection with the priestly service and sacrifices: "*Bring* Aaron and his sons to the entrance to the Tent of Meeting and wash them with water" (Exod. 40:12); "Speak to the Israelites and say to them: 'When any of you brings (*qārab*) an offering (*qorbān*) to the LORD" (Lev. 1:2). Yet the common person may not approach the altar, and thus the priest must *offer* ("bring near") the sacrifice (e.g., Lev. 7:8).

This repeated use of *qārab* in connection with the sacrificial service highlights the significant point that the sacrifices were the means by which people could draw near to God. The foreigner, who has no part in the sacrifices of Israel, is "far off." Only when he joins the people of God may he "come near": "An alien living among you who wants to celebrate the LORD's Passover must have all the males in his household circumcised; then he may *take part* [then let him come near, KJV] like one born in the land" (Exod. 12:48). Based on this fact, Paul describes the Gentiles who were "far off" as having now been "brought near": "But now in Christ Jesus you who once were far away have been brought near through the blood of Christ" (Eph. 2:13). The message of "drawing near" to God so carefully revealed in the tabernacle and temple service is fulfilled in the sacrifice of the Messiah. See *NIDOTTE*, 3:976-78.

New Testament

Verb: ἐγγίζω (*engizō*), GK *1581* (S *1448*), 42x. *engizō* means "to approach, come near." Most of its occurrences are in the gospels. See *come near*.

Verb: προσέρχομαι (*proserchomai*), GK *4665* (S *4214*), 86x. *proserchomai* simply means "to approach, come to," though it sometimes carries significant theological meaning with reverential overtones.

(1) *proserchomai* generally refers to physical movement toward something. For example, after Jesus' temptation, the angels "come to" him (Mt. 4:11). In another place, Peter is "approached" by tax collectors (17:24). Often people "come to" or "approach" Jesus (4:3; 8:2, 5, 25; 9:14, 18:21) to ask for favor such as healing, often within the context of faith (8:2, 5; 9:20, 28). After the transfiguration, Jesus comes to the three disciples and comforts them in their fear (17:7). This verb can also denote "coming to" a city, such as Capernaum (Mt. 17:24). In Acts, Stephen recounts how Moses "approached" (with awe and fear) the burning bush (Acts 7:31; cf. 8:29; 9:1; 12:13; 18:2; 23:14).

(2) Several times in the NT letters, *proserchomai* has the idea of "coming to" or "approaching" the Father and/or the Son in a reverential sense, as in 1 Pet. 2:4: "And you *come to* him, the living Stone—rejected by men but chosen by God." The writer of Hebrews is fond of this verb (7x), and most uses convey this reverential overtone. Whereas in the OT, the high priest could only "approach" the Most Holy Place once each year, now all believers without exception may "*come to* God through Christ" and find salvation (7:25). The author exhorts believers to come to God the Father through the Son also to receive mercy and find grace (4:16). Those who draw near to God's presence under the new covenant (10:22) have their sins forgiven and have God's law written on their hearts. But when they approach God, they must do so in faith (11:6).

APPROVE

New Testament

Verb: δοκιμάζω (*dokimazō*), GK *1507* (S *1381*), 22x. *dokimazō* means to "test, discern, approve." See *test*.

APTITUDE

Old Testament

Noun: חָכְמָה (*hokmâ*), GK 2683 (S 2451), 153x. *hokmâ* has a wide variety of meanings, covering both physical skill and intellectual wisdom. It can be translated as "wisdom, aptitude, experience, good sense, skill." See *wisdom*.

ARABAH

Old Testament

Noun: עֲרָבָה (*ʿarābâ*), GK 6858 (S 6160), 60x. *ʿarābâ* conveys a dry, desolate, wilderness area, similar to a desert, and may be translated as "plains" or "desert." The historical books of the Bible use this term to refer to the "plains of Moab," a low, dry, desolate area just north of the Dead Sea on the eastern side of the Jordan River. This was the "death valley" of the biblical lands. It was there that Moses instructed the people after the forty years in the wilderness (Num. 22:1; Deut. 1:1–2).

Theologically, the prophets use *ʿarābâ* to describe the desolation that results from a reversal of the covenant blessing (Isa. 33:9; Zech. 14:10). It also appears in the context of the promised restoration of covenant blessing: "The desert and the parched land will be glad; the *wilderness* will rejoice and blossom" (Isa. 35:1). See *NIDOTTE*, 3:526.

ARGUE

Old Testament

Verb: יָכַח (*yākaḥ*), GK 3519 (S 3198), 59x. *yākah* has a broad range of meaning, but it generally carries the sense of arguing a case or issuing judgment with the intent to correct. It is often translated "rebuke," "correct," "judge," "punish," or "argue," and is found most frequently in legal contexts (especially in Job [17x]) and in the wisdom instruction of Proverbs (10x). See *rebuke*.

New Testament

Verb: διαλέγομαι (*dialegomai*), GK *1363* (S *1256*), 13x. *dialegomai* means "to reason, argue, prove, persuade." See *reason*.

Verb: διαλογίζομαι (*dialogizomai*), GK *1368* (S *1260*), 16x. *dialogizomai* means "to discuss, consider, argue" about something. See *consider*.

ARGUMENT

New Testament

Noun: διαλογισμός (*dialogismos*), GK *1369* (S *1261*), 14x. *dialogismos* can refer to a discussion or personal thoughts, or even an argument between two parties. See *thought*.

ARISE

Old Testament

Verb: קוּם (*qûm*), GK 7756 (S 6965), 627x. The general range of meanings for *qûm* includes "to stand up, arise, get up (in the morning)." It can also mean "to raise up, confirm something, establish." See *rise*.

ARK

Old Testament

Noun: אֲרוֹן (*ʾarôn*), GK 778 (S 727), 202x. Often translated "ark, box, chest," the noun *ʾarôn* bears distinct though related meanings in secular and cultic contexts.

(1) In secular contexts, it refers to a box for carrying the dead (i.e., a coffin, Gen. 50:26) or a money chest (2 Ki. 12:10).

(2) Its more common use is in Israel's worship, where it denotes the "*ark* of the covenant." The Lord empowers a craftsman named Bezalel, who makes "the *ʾarôn* of acacia wood—two and a half cubits long, a cubit and a half wide, and a cubit and a half high" (Exod. 37:1). The ark is a chest in which the stone tablets of the Ten Commandments, the "Testimony," are placed (Exod. 25:16; 40:3, 20). Its cover is called the "mercy seat," on which two cherubim are stationed. There God's presence will manifest itself, and he will commune with his people (Exod. 25:21–22). As noted in Num. 7:89, "When Moses entered the Tent of Meeting to speak with the LORD, he heard the voice speaking to him from between the two cherubim above the atonement cover on the *ʾarôn* of the Testimony. And he spoke with him" (Num. 7:89). The ark is placed in the tabernacle's Most Holy Place, behind the inner veil (Exod. 26:33–34), and is anointed by Moses (Exod. 30:26). Because God's presence cannot be taken lightly, access to the *ʾarôn* is severely restricted (Lev. 16:2; Jos. 3:3–4). It is there that the blood of atonement is applied and forgiveness granted (Lev. 16).

The ark has rings into which poles are inserted so that it can be carried without being touched (Exod. 35:12). The Kohathite clan is responsible for caring for the

ʾ*ᵃrôn* (Num. 3:31), and when the ark is in transit, Aaron and his sons cover it with the tabernacle's inner veil (Num. 4:5). Joshua takes it into the promised land, and when it is carried by the priests as they cross the Jordan River, the waters miraculously stop in a way reminiscent of the Red Sea experience (Jos. 3:13–17; cf. Exod. 14–31). It is carried ahead of the Israelites at the miraculous battle against Jericho (Jos. 6:4), and the penitent Joshua worships God before it: "Then Joshua tore his clothes and fell facedown to the ground before the ark of the LORD, remaining there till evening. The elders of Israel did the same and sprinkled dust on their heads" (Jos. 7:6).

The ark is kept for a time at the Lord's tabernacle in Shiloh (1 Sam. 4:3–6), but God allows it to be captured by the Philistines when the disloyal Israelites take it into battle (4:11). After placing the ʾ*ᵃrôn* in the temple of their god Dagon, the Philistines find the Dagon idol fallen prostrate before it in a miraculous act of reverence (4:21–5:4), which ultimately leads to their sending the ark back to the Israelites (6:8).

God's presence above the ʾ*ᵃrôn* renders it so sacred that the seemingly well-intentioned Uzzah is struck dead for touching it (2 Sam. 6:6–7). Amidst great acclamations of the Israelites, King David eventually brings the ark to Jerusalem (2 Sam. 6:15–17). He becomes disturbed that he lives in a palace of cedar "while the ark of God remains in a tent" (2 Sam. 7:2). Yet Solomon his son is the one who builds the temple into which the ark is finally placed (1 Ki. 8:3–7). Despite the intriguing plot portrayed in the 1981 motion picture *Indiana Jones: Raiders of the Lost Ark*, there has been no evidence of the ark since its mention by Josiah, king of Judah, who reigned from ca. 639–608 B.C. (2 Chr. 35:3; cf. Jer. 3:16). It may have been taken off to Babylon during the raids on Jerusalem that climaxed in the destruction of the temple in 586 B.C. (cf. 2 Ki. 24:13; 25:13–16; 2 Chr. 36:7, 18).

In Rev. 11:19, John refers to an ark in the heavenly temple: "Then God's temple in heaven was opened, and within his temple was seen the ark of his covenant. And there came flashes of lightning, rumblings, peals of thunder, an earthquake and a great hailstorm."

ARM

Old Testament

Noun: זְרוֹעַ (*zᵉrôaʿ*), GK 2432 (S 2220), 91x. *zᵉrôaʿ* denotes the arm or forearm. It is used to denote the literal arm of a person (Gen. 49:24; Isa. 9:20) and sometimes, by extension, the *shoulder* (of an animal offering in Num. 6:19; Deut. 18:3). Since the arm can be viewed as the seat of strength, it can be used metaphorically to refer to someone's *strength* or *power* (1 Sam. 2:31), especially God's power (Ps. 44:4; 79:11; 89:11). Or it may refer to someone's lack of strength (note how 2 Chr. 32:7 refers to human power as an "arm of flesh," which is weak compared with God's ability to help Israel). Finally, and most prominently, the OT uses the expression "with a mighty hand and an outstretched *arm*" to describe God's great act of delivering Israel from Egypt by working powerful miracles and bringing judgment on the enemy (Exod. 6:6; Deut. 4:34; 5:15). See *NIDOTTE*, 1:1146-47.

New Testament

Noun: βραχίων (*brachiōn*), GK *1098* (S *1023*), 3x. *brachiōn* means "arm." The OT frequently refers to the mighty arm of God, which acted in history to save his people. The three uses of this noun in the NT all refer to the same concept. In Jn. 12:38 John refers to Jesus' fulfillment of Isa. 53:1. In Acts 13:17, Paul reminds his audience about how God led his people out of Egypt "with a powerful *arm*." And in Lk. 1:51, in Mary's song, she reflects on how Israel's God "has performed mighty deeds with his *arm*."*

ARMOR

Old Testament

Noun: כְּלִי (*kᵉlî*), GK 3998 (S 3627), 325x. *kᵉlî* is a noun denoting a variety of equipment, tools, containers, etc., used in a given activity or occupation. The use of this noun to refer to such a large number of different objects is comparable to the English noun "thing." See *thing*.

ARMY

Old Testament

Noun: חַיִל (*ḥayil*), GK 2657 (S 2428), 246x. The basic sense of *ḥayil* is "power, strength, or capability." In military contexts, *ḥayil* can refer to an "army" of fighting men (e.g., Pharaoh's army in Exod. 14:4, 9, 17, 28). See *strength*.

Noun: צָבָא (*ṣābā*ʾ), GK 7372 (S 6635), 479x. *ṣābā*ʾ appears to come from a military context and bears both a general and specific meaning in the OT. As to the former, approximately 200x in the OT, *ṣābā*ʾ refers to those who participate in warfare and/or comprise an army (Gen. 21:22; 1 Sam. 17:55; 2 Sam. 2:8). Sometimes this army is celestial. See *Almighty*.

New Testament

Noun: στράτευμα (*strateuma*), GK *5128* (S *4753*), 8x. *strateuma* means "army." In contrast to the OT, which has over 700 references to words for "army" and where there are numerous wars and battles, the NT has relatively few such references. Jesus uses *strateuma* in his parable of the wedding banquet (Mt. 22:7). Luke uses it in a reference to Herod and his army who mock Jesus (Lk. 23:11), and for the troops in Jerusalem who rescue Paul from the rioters there (Acts 23:10, 27). The other four references to *strateuma* are in Revelation, where war occurs in the end times (Rev. 9:16; 19:14, 19).*

AROMA

Old Testament

Noun: רֵיחַ (*rēaḥ*), GK 8194 (S 7381), 58x. *rēaḥ* denotes an aroma, scent, or fragrance.

(1) In common usage, it can refer to the fragrance of perfume (Song 1:1), the scent of vines (2:13), the odor of garments (4:11), or the smell of one's breath (7:8).

(2) *rēaḥ* occurs most commonly in the technical, cultic expression *rēaḥ hannîḥōaḥ* (43x), often translated "a pleasing aroma" and always associated with a sacrifice offered to God. After Noah made a sacrifice to God, "The LORD smelled the *pleasing aroma*" (Gen. 8:21).

(a) Scholars debate the precise meaning of *rēaḥ hannîḥōaḥ*. In view of texts like 1 Sam. 26:19, where David pleads with Saul to accept an offering to sooth his wrath (with a form of the verb *rîaḥ*, "to smell"), some hold that the expression carries a sense of propitiation. Other texts suggest it may (also?) indicate that the sacrifice is legitimate. The numerous texts in Lev. can be read in this way (cf. Lev. 2:12; 3:16; 8:21, 28; 23:13).

Regardless of the exact meaning of *rēaḥ hannîḥōaḥ*, when a sacrifice is offered from an upright heart, it pleases God and he accepts it willingly. When, however, the sacrifice is performed as a mere outward act and not as an expression of one's life worship to God, he is not pleased. Thus he warns Israel, "I will turn your cities into ruins and lay waste your sanctuaries, and I will take no delight in the *hannîḥōaḥ* of your offerings" (Lev. 26:31). The repentant David clearly recognizes the heart of biblical worship (Ps. 51:16–17): "You do not delight in sacrifice, or I would bring it; you do not take pleasure in burnt offerings. The sacrifices of God are a broken spirit; a broken and contrite heart, O God, you will not despise."

(b) Significantly, the NT applies the Gk. equivalent found throughout the LXX for *hannîḥōaḥ* (= *osmē euōdias*) to the ultimate sacrifice of Jesus Christ. "Just as Christ loved us and gave himself up for us as *a fragrant offering* and sacrifice to God" (Eph. 5:2). See *NIDOTTE*, 3:1070-73.

New Testament

Noun: εὐωδία (*euōdia*), GK *2380* (S *2175*), 3x. *euōdia* means "aroma, fragrance." See *aroma* (in the comments on *osmē*) for discussion on *euōdia*.

Noun: ὀσμή (*osmē*), GK *4011* (S *3744*), 6x. *osmē* means "aroma, odor." It occurs once in the gospel of John (for the "fragrance" of Mary's perfume, Jn. 12:3); the rest of its uses are in Paul's letters. Twice Paul couples this word with *euōdias* (lit., "aroma of fragrance," i.e., "a fragrant aroma"), which is the phrase used frequently in the OT for offerings as they ascend to God as a sweet smell (e.g., Gen. 8:21; Lev. 1:9, 13, 17; Num. 28:2, 6, 8; etc.). God would smell an offering and be pleased with it. With this background, the sacrifice of Christ is seen as "a fragrant offering" (Eph. 5:2), acceptable to God for the sins of all people. Paul uses this same terminology to refer to the generous gift the Philippians sent Paul—"a fragrant offering, an acceptable sacrifice pleasing to God" (Phil. 4:18).

The idea of *osmē* as a life-giving or death-giving force is prominent in 2 Cor. 2:14–16. The message that Paul brings concerning Christ "spreads everywhere the fragrance of the knowledge of him." Missionaries are to God "the aroma [*euōdia*] of Christ," and their message has a double effect on those who listen: To those who accept Christ, it is a "fragrance of life"; to those who reject Christ, it is "the smell of death." That is, no one stands in neutral territory when hearing the saving message about the Lord Jesus Christ. See *NIDNTT-A*, 420.

AROUND

Old Testament

Adjective and Adverb: סָבִיב (*sābîb*), GK 6017 (S 5439), 334x. *sābîb* as an adverb means "around" and as an adjective denotes one's "surroundings." As an adverb, it often means simply "around," as when Saul's army encamped "around" him (1 Sam. 26:5, 7) or the wall Ezekiel sees "around" the temple (Ezek. 40:5; Ezekiel uses this word well over 100x). This adverb often relates to God's encircling and protective care of his people (e.g., Ps. 34:7; 125:2; Zech. 2:5). In fact, Satan complains to God that the Lord has "put a hedge around" Job, thus protecting him from evil happenings (Job 1:10).

As a adjective, *sābîb* refers to the courtyard "surrounding" the tabernacle (Exod. 38:20), the "surrounding" pasturelands of a town (Jos. 21:42), and even "the surrounding nations" (1 Ki. 4:31; Neh. 6:16). See *NIDOTTE*, 3:219–20.

AROUSE

Old Testament

Verb: עוּר (*ʿûr*), GK 6424 (S 5782), 80x. *ʿûr* means "to awaken, arouse from sleep," or (in a causative sense) "to rouse someone or something, incite." This verb finds a particularly important role in the matter of prayer and worship. In life's struggles, it may seem that God is inactive, passive, or even indifferent. Thus, the downtrodden soul cries out to God that he should "wake up." See *awake*.

New Testament

Verb: κινέω (*kineō*), GK *3075* (S *2795*), 8x. *kineō* means "to move, stir, arouse." See *move*.

ARRANGE

Old Testament

Verb: עָרַךְ (*ʿārak*), GK 6885 (S 6186), 75x. *ʿārak* denotes the action of arranging an object in a particular way or arranging objects in a specific order to produce a desired effect. A common use of *ʿārak* is "to arrange" a table for a banquet, which the NIV translates as "to prepare" a table (Ps. 23:5), "to spread" a table (78:19; Isa. 65:11; Ezek. 23:41), and "to set" a table (Prov. 9:2; Isa. 21:5). *ʿārak* is found most frequently in three contexts: war, words, and worship.

(1) Regarding war, *ʿārak* denotes the action of arranging armies for battle. The NIV translates this use of *ʿārak* in various ways: e.g., "drew up their battle lines" (Gen. 14:8), "took up battle positions" (Jdg. 20:20), "took up their positions" (Jdg. 20:22), "deployed their forces" (1 Sam. 4:2), and "drawing up their lines" (1 Sam. 17:21). In this context, *ʿārak* appears 9x with the infinitive *liqraʾt*, "to meet" (1 Sam. 4:2; 17:2, 21; 2 Sam. 10:9, 10, 17; 1 Chr. 19:10, 11, 17) with the sense "to draw up in battle array to meet" their opponent, often rendered "to deploy/array against" their opponent.

(2) Words are frequently "arranged" in

order to present an argument. Job declares, "Behold now, I have *prepared* my case, I know that I will be in the right" (Job 13:18), and, "I would *state* my case before him" (23:4). Later Elihu points out to Job the difficulty of presenting a case to God because of our ignorance, for "we cannot *draw up our case* from the face of darkness" (37:19; cf. 32:14; 33:5). Elsewhere, God declares that he will rebuke Israel and "state the case" before their eyes (Ps. 50:21). Interestingly, the arranging of words in order to present an argument seems to be used of prayer in Ps. 5:3[4], though the object is not explicit: "in the morning I will *arrange* [my prayer] to you and watch."

(3) As to worship, *ʿārak* describes the arranging of objects for the purpose of worship. Wood is "arranged" on an altar for the fire of sacrifice by Abraham during the offering of Isaac (Gen. 22:9) and by Elijah in the contest on Mount Carmel (1 Ki. 18:33; cf. Lev. 1:7). In tabernacle worship, the cultic objects on the table are to be "arranged" (Exod. 40:4), as are the bread (40:23; Lev. 24:8) and the lamps (Lev. 24:3, 4; cf. Ps. 132:17). In the sacrificial system, the pieces of the animal are to be "arranged" over the wood for the burnt offering (Lev. 1:8, 12; 6:5). The specific arrangement of these objects in the OT paints a picture of orderly worship.

(4) Another sense of *ʿārak* is arrangement for the sake of comparison. While it is used for the comparison of things (e.g., Job 28:17, 19), its theologically significant use describes the incomparability of God. The psalmist proclaims, "Many, O LORD my God, are the wonders you have done and your thoughts toward us; there is not one *comparing* to you" (Ps. 40:5; cf. 89:6; Isa. 40:18). See *NIDOTTE*, 3:535-37

ARREST

New Testament

Verb: ἐπιβάλλω (*epiballō*), GK *2095* (S *1911*), 18x. *epiballō* means "to lay on, arrest, sew on." See *lay on*.

Verb:ἐπιλαμβάνομαι (*epilambanomai*), GK *2138* (S *1949*), 19x. *epilambanomai* can mean "to seize, take hold, catch." See *seize*.

Verb: κρατέω (*krateō*), GK *3195* (S *2902*), 47x. *krateō* means "to arrest, seize, hold, grasp." The gospel writers use it a technical term for seeking to arrest someone, such as John the Baptist (Mt. 14:3; Mk. 6:17), Jesus (Mk. 12:12; 14:1, 44, 46), and Paul (Acts 24:6). Elsewhere, Lk. 24:16 uses *krateō* to indicate the disciples' eyes being "held" so they could not recognize Jesus, and in Acts 2:24 *krateō* describes what death could not do, namely, "hold" Jesus. The word also carries such nuances as "holding fast" (Mt. 7:3–4; 2 Thess. 2:15; Heb. 4:14), "holding" a teaching (2 Thess. 2:15; Rev. 2:14–15), "holding firm" to the faith we profess (Heb. 4:14), "holding on" to a possession (Rev. 2:25), and even "forgiving" sins (Jn. 20:23). See *NIDNTT-A*, 317.

Verb: πιάζω (*piazō*), GK *4389* (S *4084*), 12x. *piazō* means "to arrest, catch." John uses this verb for some of the attempts to seize Jesus before his actual arrest in Gethsemane (Jn. 7:30, 32, 44; 8:20; 10:39; 11:39). In the last chapter of this gospel, this verb is used for a miraculous "catch" of fish (Jn. 21:3, 10). Luke uses it for the arrest of Peter in Acts 12:4), and Paul uses it for his attempted arrest in Damascus shortly after his conversion (2 Cor. 11:32).

Verb: συλλαμβάνω (*syllambanō*), GK *5197* (S *4815*), 16x. *syllambano* conveys the basic idea of bringing together or gathering and is translated "arrest, seize, capture, conceive." In the context of Jesus calling his first disciples, Luke recalls the reaction of Peter and his fishing partners to the quantity of fish they had caught. He writes, "For he and all his companions were astonished at the catch of fish they had *taken*" (Lk. 5:9; also v. 5). In the context of his arrest, Jesus asks, "Am I leading a rebellion ... that you have come out with swords and clubs to *capture* me?" (Mk. 14:48; cf. Mt. 26:55; Lk. 22:54; Jn. 18:12). Luke also uses *syllambanō* in the birth narratives of John the Baptist and Jesus. The angel of the Lord comforts Mary with his announcement, "Do not be afraid, Mary, you have found favor with God. You *will be with child* and give birth to a son, and you are to give him the name Jesus" (Lk. 1:31; cf. vv. 24, 36; 2:21). This same idea is used to describe the process of temptation that gives birth to sin. James writes, "But each one is tempted when, by his own evil desire, he is dragged away and enticed. Then, after desire has *conceived,* it gives birth to sin; and sin, when it is full-grown, gives birth to death" (Jas. 1:14–15). See *NIDNTT-A*, 543.

ARRIVE

Old Testament

Verb: בּוֹא (*bôʾ*), GK 995 (S 935), 2592x. *bôʾ* is the fourth most common verb in the OT. It denotes motion toward a specific goal, such as "to go, arrive, enter a house, come." It expresses a variety of motions. See *come.*

Verb: נָגַע (*nāgaʿ*), GK 5595 (S 5060), 150x. The verb *nāgaʿ* means "to touch physically," but its various nuances include "to touch, strike, reach, arrive." See *reach.*

New Testament

Verb: ἔρχομαι (*erchomai*), GK *2262* (S *2064*), 632x. *erchomai* usually means "come, arrive." See *come.*

Verb: καταντάω (*katantaō*), GK *2918* (S *2658*), 13x. *katantaō,* derived from the prefix *kata* ("down") and the verb *antaō* ("to meet"), means literally "to come down to meet." Its usage in the NT is much broader than this etymology would suggest, however, and is best rendered "arrive." *katantaō* possesses the idea of hitting the target or reaching a final goal. The verb is only found in Acts and Paul.

While *katantaō* can indicate the physical arrival of individuals (Acts 16:1; 18:19; 18:24; 20:15; 21:7; 25:13; 27:12; 28:13), it is also used theologically of the arrival of God's promises realized in the resurrection of Jesus (Acts 27:7–8). Paul writes that the failures of Israel in the desert have been written for those "on whom the fulfillment of the ages *has come*" (1 Cor. 10:11). Paul asks sarcastically if the word of God arrived only among the spiritual elite in Corinth when it is obvious that it had not (14:36). Paul believes each member of the church must edify the body until it arrives at the unity of faith and of the knowledge of the Son of God (Eph. 4:13). Finally, the ultimate hope for Christians is not living in a disembodied existence in heaven, as has been espoused in much of Western Christianity, but rather the arrival of the resurrection of the dead (Phil. 3:11). See *NIDNTT-A*, 294-95.*

Verb: παραγίνομαι (*paraginomai*), GK *4134* (S *3854*), 37x. *paraginomai* means "to come, arrive." See *come.*

ARROW

Old Testament

Noun: חֵץ (*ḥēṣ*), GK 2932 (S 2671), 55x. Literally, *ḥēṣ* refers to an "arrow." Many uses of this term are of actual arrows shot by a bow. For example, Jonathan shoots arrows beyond his son in order to signal to David that he must leave the territory (1 Sam. 1:20–22). It was not unusual in the ancient world to dip the point of the arrow in poison (see Job 6:4). Sometimes arrows were used for casting lots in order to determine how one should act (cf. Ezek. 21:21).

ḥēṣ has various metaphorical uses. Lightning flashes are called "arrows" from God (Ps. 18:14; 77:18). Job likens his afflictions to "arrows" from God (Job 6:4; 34:6). The words of the wicked are also compared to arrows (Ps. 64:3; Prov. 25:18; Jer. 9:7). Just as arrows can kill or inflict damage from a great distance, so words can hurt the human soul and kill the human spirit. In Ps. 91:5, *ḥēṣ* is parallel to "terror" in the night.

Positively, sons are compared to arrows in one's quiver (Ps. 127:4); in the ancient world, the bow and arrow was a masculine symbol. Similarly, the servant of the Lord is compared to "a polished arrow" that has been hidden in God's quiver (Isa. 49:2). See *NIDOTTE*, 2:242–43.

ARTICLE

Old Testament

Noun: כְּלִי (*k*^{e}*lî*), GK 3998 (S 3627), 325x. *k*^{e}*lî* is a noun denoting a variety of equipment, tools, containers, etc., used in a given activity or occupation. The use of this noun to refer to such a large number of different objects is comparable to the English noun "thing." See *thing*.

ASCEND

Old Testament

Verb: עָלָה (*ʿālâ*), GK 6590 (S 5927), 894x. *ʿālâ* typically means "to go up, ascend," and sometimes "to exalt." Since the Holy Land is very hilly, there were many occasions when people had to go up in order to get somewhere (e.g., to Bethel, Gen. 35:1, 3). As the Israelites anticipate the fight for the promised land, God tells them to "go up" and take possession of it (Deut. 1:21).

Although *ʿālâ* is not inherently a theological term, it often appears in highly significant contexts. Moses "ascends" to the Lord at Sinai, but the people were forbidden to do so on pain of death (Exod. 19:3, 24). Later, when Moses receives the stone tablets of the covenant and finds the people worshiping a golden calf, he says, "You have sinned a great sin. But now I will *go up* to the Lord; perhaps I can make atonement for your sin" (32:30). Moses then "goes up" the mountain to intercede on the people's behalf.

God is not a part of this world; the fact that his worshipers ascend to holy places underscores his otherness. Since Jerusalem and the temple are built on a mountain, one "ascends" to God in order to worship him. "Who may *ascend* the hill of the Lord? And who shall stand in his holy place? Those who have clean hands and pure "(Ps. 24:3–4). In fact, almost all ancient worship was done on high places, so that it involved an ascent on the part of the worshiper. There are many accounts of individuals *going up* to the Lord (or the temple) to worship. Hannah "goes up" to the house of God (1 Sam. 1:7), receives a blessing and the promise of a child, whom she then returns to God's service. Samuel, her son, "goes up" to the high places to worship God (1 Sam. 9:13–14), as does Hezekiah (2 Ki. 19:14; 20:5) and Josiah (2 Ki. 23:2). With great irony, the princes and leaders of Judah "go up" to the gates of the temple to condemn Jeremiah to death for prophesying God's word (Jer. 26:10).

God himself ascends at times, especially when his people have won a victory through his help (Ps. 47:5; cf. 68:18). Thus, he is greatly "exalted" (47:9). When God declares his intent to deliver his people from Egypt, he states, "I know their sufferings, and I have come down to deliver them from the Egyptians, and to *bring them up* out of that land to a good and broad land, a land flowing with milk and honey" (Exod. 3:7–8). God brings them up metaphorically, up from slavery to a place where they can know him and worship him, and be with him (Exod. 3:12). See *NIDOTTE*, 3:402–4.

New Testament

Verb: ἀναβαίνω (*anabainō*), GK *326* (S *305*), 82x. *anabainō* generally means to "go up, ascend, come up." (1) It is most often used in the gospels and Acts when describing someone's travel. For example, Jesus went up to a mountain to pray (Mt. 14:23), Joseph went up from Galilee (Lk. 2:4), and two men went up to the temple (Lk. 18:10). The Gospel writers often speak of "going up" to Jerusalem, since it was located on one of the highest elevations in Palestine. In the book of Revelation *anabainō* is used when John was caught up into heaven (Rev. 4:1), when angels ascend from the east (7:2), when believers' prayers ascend to God (8:4), when the beast and the Antichrist come up from the sea (13:1) and the abyss (11:7), and when the smoke of God's judgment goes up forever and ever (14:11; 19:3).

(2) *anabainō* carries theological significance when used of Jesus ascending to heaven. For example, Jesus says in Jn. 3:13, "No one has ever *gone* into heaven except the one who came from heaven —the Son of Man." Peter's sermon at

Pentecost argues that even David did not ascend into heaven after his death, because Ps. 110 was fulfilled in Jesus (Acts 2:34). The apostle Paul, after citing Ps. 68, states that only Jesus has ascended into heaven because he is the only one who has descended (Eph. 4:8–10). Jesus' descent reveals the Father's love for us; Jesus' ascent reveals his power and kingship.

Another theologically significant occurrence of *anabainō* is found in Jn. 1:51, when Jesus says to Nathanael, "I tell you the truth, you shall see heaven open, and the angels of God *ascending* and descending on the Son of Man." The fact that the angels ascend first means that they begin their journey on the stairway to heaven from the earth; thus, we can be sure they are with us now, sent to minister on our behalf (cf. Heb. 1:14). Note that this vision is consistent with Jacob's vision in Gen. 28:11–15.

ASHAMED

Old Testament

Verb: בּוֹשׁ (*bôš*), GK 1017 (S 954), 125x. *bôš* has the basic meaning "to feel ashamed, put to shame." It often denotes a feeling of embarrassment, humiliation, or failure, or a sense of rejection and abandonment by a friend or deity.

In the OT, shame occurs on a personal, corporate, and national level. It can be active (causing disgrace or behaving shamefully) or passive (to be ashamed or put to shame), as a distressing or humiliating condition coming on a person that must be endured. Shame is perceived as such in the context of a community; behavior deemed unacceptable by communal standards is considered shameful or disgraceful. References occur in a communal and household context, referring specifically to children (Prov. 10:5; 17:2; 19:26; 29:15), a wife (12:4), and a servant (14:35). Interestingly, it should be noted that shame does not refer primarily to sexual shame. The sole usage of *bôš* in this context is found in Gen. 2:25, where Adam and his wife feel no shame, despite their nakedness.

The psalmist often asks for God's continuing presence and assistance so as not to be put to shame (e.g., Ps. 25:2, 20). In these contexts, shame results when a person's trust or confidence has been disappointed ("May those who hope in you not be disgraced," 69:6; also Isa. 49:23). Conversely, prayers to God asking that he put enemies to shame occur in Ps. 31:17, 35:4, 35:26; 40:14; 71:13; and the prophetical books. This pattern appears in Ps. 119 where David pleads with God: "I hold fast to your statutes, O LORD; do not let me be put to shame" (Ps. 119:31); he then requests, "May the arrogant be put to shame for wronging me without cause" (119:78). In 129:4, those who hate Zion must be ashamed because they have failed in their expectation of victory over Israel.

Ps. 97:7 mentions the kind of shame felt by "all who worship images." Their trust in idols is brought to shame because heaven, earth, and all peoples can clearly see the power of the true God. This idea is most common in Jeremiah and Isaiah. Shame takes on a spiritual sense in the context of Israel's idolatrous behavior. Israel has committed spiritual adultery against God and, therefore, will be disappointed, distressed, and disgraced by her behavior. She has acted shamefully; therefore, she is rightly shamed (Isa. 1:29; Ezek. 36:32; Hos. 10:6). Isaiah focuses more on the shamefulness and absurdity of idolatry (Isa. 42:17; 44:9–11), while Jeremiah focuses on Israel's unfaithfulness to God through idolatry and foreign alliances (Jer. 2:26; 9:19; 22:22; 48:13; also Isa. 20:5; 30:5). Such trust in foreign alliances causes disgrace when these alliances fail to save from destruction; Israel compounds her guilt by feeling no shame for her sin (Jer. 6:15; 8:12). Furthermore, the idolatrous foreign nations are shamed by their own false gods that cannot save (Jer. 46:24; 48:13, 20, 39; 49:23; 50:2, 12). Punishment for sin negatively affects the natural productivity of the land, bringing a "shameful harvest" to the farmers (Jer. 12:13; 14:3–4; Hos. 13:15; Joel 1:11).

New Testament

Verb: ἐπαισχύνομαι (*epaischynomai*), GK *2049* (S *1870*), 11x. *epaischynomai* means "to be ashamed, embarrassed, fearful of ridicule" because of one's actions or beliefs. Note that this verb generally does not carry the connotation of being ashamed of the wrong things one has done (although it does carry this nuance in Rom. 6:21).

This verb usually occurs in reference to both belief in Christ and his word (Mk. 8:38; Lk. 9:26), where Jesus states that if anyone is too embarrassed to confess him before men, he will be "ashamed of them when he comes in his Father's glory." Conversely, Paul insists that he is not ashamed of the gospel of Christ (Rom. 1:16), and he instructs believers not to be ashamed of testifying about Christ to a watching world (2 Tim. 1:8). This sense of embarrassment is the type that comes when one is associated with something that is not popular or "proper." Paul uses this verb to praise Onesiphorus because he was not too embarrassed by Paul's chains to help him (2 Tim. 1:16). The answer for being so ashamed is faith, as Paul says, "I am not ashamed, because I know whom I have believed" (2 Tim. 1:12).

Not being ashamed is even ascribed to God. The author of Hebrews describes God as "not ashamed" to be the God of his people, even though they are sinful and in need of mercy (Heb. 11:16). Even more significant, Jesus is not ashamed to call them his brothers (2:11). See *NIDNTT-A*, 22-23.*

Verb: καταισχύνω (*kataischynō*), GK *2875* (S *2617*), 13x. *kataischynō* means "to embarrass, be ashamed, disappoint." See *embarrass*.

ASK

Old Testament

Verb: שָׁאַל (*šāʾal*), GK 8626 (S 7592), 176x. *šāʾal* is often translated "ask" or "inquire." It is used to ask for a drink (Jdg. 5:25), to be in someone's presence (Jdg. 4:20; cf. Gen. 26:7), to ask for a song (Ps. 137:3), and to inquire about the fate of person (Num. 27:21; cf. Jdg. 18:5). Hannah names her son Samuel, because she "has asked" the Lord for him (1 Sam. 1:20). The Lord gives Israel a king because they have asked for one (1 Sam. 12:13; cf. 8:10; Jdg. 1:1). He appears to Solomon and tells him to ask for whatever he wants (1 Ki. 3:5). Job laments that if one where to ask the animals regarding his tragedy, they would answer that it is the Lord's doing (Job 12:7).

In prophetic literature, Ahaz tries the patience of God because he refuses to "ask" the Lord for a sign (Isa. 7:10–11). The Lord, speaking through his prophet Jeremiah, tells Judah to "stand at the crossroads and look; *ask* for the ancient paths, *ask* where the good way is, and walk in it, and you will find rest for your souls" (Jer. 6:16). The Lord is angry when his people act without asking him for direction first (Isa. 30:2; cf. Hos. 4:10). However, it is important theologically to know that God reveals himself even to those who do not know how to ask for him (Isa. 65:1 "I revealed myself to those who did not *ask* for me; I was found by those who did not seek for me"). God's salvation is always by grace and not by anything we can do or *ask*.

New Testament

Verb: αἰτέω (*aiteō*), GK *160* (S *154*), 70x. *aiteō* generally means "to ask, request, demand." On a human level, such asking is usually made of a superior (Mt. 27:20; Acts 9:2). Most often, however, it is used in passages that address prayer to God (also a superior!), such as Mt. 21:22, "If you believe, you will receive whatever you *ask* for in prayer." In its simplest form, Jesus says, "Ask and it will be given to you" (Mt. 7:7). Most uses of *aiteō* occur in the gospels (e.g., Mt. 6:8; 7:7–11; Mk. 11:24; Lk. 11:9–13; Jn. 16:23–26). In prayer, we are to trust that God is a loving, caring Father who delights in giving what we ask for.

James uses the word five times in his letter, most notably in Jas. 4:2–3: "You have not because you ask not. You ask and do not receive, because you ask with wrong motives." James also uses *aiteō* to emphasize that asking for the things that God has promised us (such as wisdom) must be done without doubting that God will indeed fulfill his promises (1:5–6). The apostle John too uses this verb 4x in 1 Jn. 5:14–16, where he emphasizes that when we ask God for anything, it must be "according to his will."

While *aiteō* is most often used in reference to a petition, it is also used in reference to a requirement or demand. In these cases, the verb is usually spoken by a superior to a subordinate person. The jailer in Philippi, for example, "*called for* lights" when he heard Paul's voice after the earthquake. Note too what Jesus says in Lk. 12:48: "to whom much is given, much will be *required*." This helps to understand Paul's message in 1 Cor. 1:22, that "the Jews *require* a sign." They ask for such a sign from the God, as it were calling him to answer their resumptive demands. See *NIDNTT-A*, 23.

Verb: ἐπερωτάω (*eperōtaō*), GK *2089* (S *1905*), 56x. *eperōtaō* means "to ask a question, to question, interrrogate someone." Generally speaking, this verb is a synonym for *erōtaō* (GK *2263*), having for the most part the same meaning. Whereas *erōtaō* is the preferred word for "ask" used by John, *eperōtaō* is the common word used by Mark (25x). For example, Mark uses this verb when Jesus asks the disciples who the people say that he is (Mk. 8:29), when the disciples ask Jesus why they could not cast out demons (9:28), and when Jesus asks the demon-possessed boy's father how long he had been afflicted (9:21).In Matthew and Luke, these 2 vbs. are equally divided.

eperōtaō can also be used in a narrower sense of questioning someone as a part of an interrogation, such as Pilate's interrogation of Jesus (Mt. 27:11; Mk. 15:2, 4), the high priest's interrogation of Jesus (Mk. 14:60), and the Pharisees' interrogation of the blind man's parents (Jn. 9:19). See *NIDNTT-A*, 209-10.

Verb: ἐρωτάω (*erōtaō*), GK *2263* (S *2065*), 63x. *erōtaō* means "to ask a question, inquire," or "to request" something be done. It is commonly used to describe what someone does when seeking information.

The disciples ask Jesus questions about the meaning of his teachings, e.g., when they do not understand his parables (Mk. 4:10), when they do not know why a man was born blind (Jn. 9:2), or when they do not know what Christ means when he says that they will not see him in a little while (16:19). Jesus uses this manner of questioning in order to teach the disciples, asking them, "Who do people say the Son of Man is?" (Mt. 16:13). *erōtaō* is especially used by John in his gospel. There is often introduces a doubting, probing question, such as when John the Baptist is questioned by the Levites (Jn. 1:19) as to whether he is Elijah (Jn. 1:21) and why he baptizes if he is not the Christ (1:25).

erōtaō is also used for making a request. This is most clearly seen in Acts, where 12 of the 13 uses of this verb are requests rather than questions seeking information. For example, a beggar asks Peter and John for money (Acts 3:3), those with Cornelius ask Peter to remain with them (10:48), and the Jews request Paul to be brought before the Sanhedrin (23:20). When Jesus' disciples become frustrated with the Canaanite woman's pleas, they "urge" Jesus to send her away. See *NIDNTT-A*, 209-10.

Verb: παρακαλέω (*parakaleō*), GK *4151* (S *3870*), 109x. *parakaleō* variously means "to ask, summons, exhort, comfort, or encourage" (see *exhort, comfort*). Within the Synoptic Gospels, *parakaleō* means "to ask, implore, summons." The contexts of this imploring are often the needy who come to Jesus with their requests (Mt. 8:5, 31; 18:29; Lk. 15:28).

Verb: πυνθάνομαι (*pynthanomai*), GK *4785* (S *4441*), 12x. *pynthanomai* means "to ask." This verb tends to be used in a situation where information is being sought, such as Herod asking where the Israel's Messiah would be born (Mt. 2:4) or a blind man asking what the commotion was all about (Lk. 18:38). In Acts, this verb is mostly used for questions being asked in a legal setting, such as the Sanhedrin questioning Peter and John (Acts 4:7) or the Roman commander asking who Paul was and what he had done to cause such a riot (21:33; cf. 23:19–20).

Noun: δέομαι (*deomai*), GK *1289* (S *1189*), 22x. *deomai* is a general word for prayer where a request is being made, either of a person or of God. It can be translated as "to pray, beseech, ask, beg, plead."

ASLEEP

New Testament

Verb: κοιμάω (*koimaō*), GK *3121* (S *2837*), 18x. *koimaō* refers to the act of falling sleeping, or, euphemistically, to death. See *fall asleep*.

ASS

See *donkey*.

ASSEMBLE

Old Testament

Verb: אָסַף (*ʾāsap*), GK 665 (S 622), 200x. In varying contexts, *ʾāsap* can mean "to gather, assemble, take away, or bring up the rear." When *ʾāsap* is used reflexively, it means "to assemble." See *gather*.

Verb: קָבַץ (*qābaṣ*), GK 7695 (S 6908), 127x. The verb *qābaṣ* means "to gather, assemble" and can denote the gathering of any of a number of items. See *gather*.

New Testament

Verb: συνάγω (*synagō*), GK *5251* (S *4863*), 59x. *synagō* has the basic meaning "to gather together." It is often used in agricultural contexts of harvesting or gathering crops. See *gather*.

Verb: συνέρχομαι (*synerchomai*), GK *5302* (S *4905*), 30x. *synerchomai* means "to assemble, come together, gather." (1) This verb can refer to the "assembling" of a group of people. Multitudes "gather" around Jesus because of his overwhelming popularity (Mk. 3:20). In contrast, the religious leaders "assemble" in order to try Jesus before the high priest (Mk. 14:53). John speaks of "the temple, where all the Jews *come together*" (Jn. 18:20). After the resurrection, the disciples "meet together" with Jesus and ask him about the restoration of the kingdom of Israel (Acts 1:6). In Acts, crowds "gather" to hear the apostles (2:6; 5:16; 10:27; 16:13; 19:32; 28:17).

(2) *synerchomai* is also used of a group of believers "coming together" for worship. Paul has no praise for the Corinthians as they assemble for the Lord's Supper (1 Cor. 11:17, 18, 20, 27), for they are divided and self-centered. Thus he instructs them, "When you *come together* to eat, wait for each other" (11:33–34).

(3) *synerchomai* can be used to refer to those who travel together (Jn. 11:33; Acts 9:39; 10:23, 45; 11:12; 15:38; 21:16). Lk. 23:55 refers to the group of women who traveled with Jesus. When the apostles are seeking a twelfth man to replace Judas Iscariot, one of the requirements is that the replacement has to "*have been with* us the whole time the Lord Jesus went in and out among us" (Acts 1:21).

(4) *synerchomai* can also refer to becoming one flesh through marriage (Mt. 1:18).

ASSEMBLY

Old Testament

Noun: עֵדָה (*ʿēda*), GK 6337 (S 5712), 171x. *ʿēdâ* means a gathering of people (for worship or legal matters) or a herd or swarm of animals. See *community*.

Noun: עַם (*ʿam*), GK 6639 (S 5971), 1869x. *ʿam* can refer to military troops (Num. 20:20; Jos. 8:1) or to a general assembly of people (Ruth 4:9; 1 Sam. 10:17). Especially in the plural, this word is often used to refer to the "nations" of the world (Ps. 18:47; 45:5; Isa. 12:4; 63:3). But most frequently *ʿam* denotes a large group of people united by a familial relationship. See *people*.

Noun: קָהָל (*qāhāl*), GK 7736 (S 6951), 123x. *qāhāl* describes the gathering of a great body of people for civil, religious, or other occasions.

(1) *qāhāl* sometimes denotes the assembly of God's people for a variety of civil reasons. For example, they assemble to hear the Song of Moses (Deut. 31:30), to

see Solomon crowned as king (1 Chr. 29:1), to receive a blessing from Solomon (1 Ki. 8:14, 22, 55; 2 Chr. 6:3), and to hear Ezra's comments about mixed marriages (Ezr. 10:1, 8, 12, 14). Certain situations could exclude people from the general community God's people (Deut. 23:1–3). At times *qāhāl* can denote the entire Israelite community (Gen. 28:3; 35:11; 48:4), where God's people are called "the assembly of the Lord" (Deut. 23:2–4; Mic. 2:5; 1 Chr. 28:8) or "the Lord's assembly" (Num. 16:3; cf. 20:4). This is the predominant use of *qāhāl.*

(2) *qāhāl* sometimes refers specifically to the assembly of God's people who gather to worship and praise God on special religious occasions (see Ps. 107:32; 149:1; Joel 2:16). At the coronation of Solomon, "the whole assembly" praises the Lord God (1 Chr. 29:20). Hezekiah gathers the people together at the rededication of the temple, where they bring sacrifices and thank offerings (2 Chr. 29:23, 28, 31). During the time of Nehemiah, "the whole company" that have returned from the exile celebrate the Feast of Tabernacles (Neh. 8:17).

(3) There is, however, also a more generic use of *qāhāl*, which denotes any assembly of people. David uses *qāhāl* to describe an assembly of wretched people: "I abhor the *qāhāl* of evildoers and refuse to sit with the wicked" (Ps. 26:5). Solomon uses it to talk about "the company of the dead" (Prov. 21:16). Ezekiel uses *qāhāl* to describe a "mob" of people who will wreak havoc on God's people (Ezek. 16:40; 23:46–47). See *NIDOTTE*, 3:888–92.

New Testament

Noun: συναγωγή (*synagōgē*), GK *5252* (S *4864*), 56x. *synagōgē* denotes what is brought together or assembled, an "assembly, congregation, synagogue." See *synagogue.*

Noun: ἐκκλησία (*ekklēsia*), GK *1711* (S *1577*), 114x. *ekklēsia* is derived from *ekklēsia* ("to call out"), so the church is the "called-out ones" of God. In its secular use *ekklēsia* refers to the gathering of the competent citizens of a city-state to order to decide issues regarding laws, office appointments, and public policy. But the prototype of the NT *ekklēsia* lies not in Greco-Roman history but in the assembly of God's people in the OT (cf. Acts 7:38), which developed into the Jewish synagogue as the gathering of the community of God. But while the *ekklēsia* may find its roots in the synagogue, it is not a subset of it but becomes the new term used for the gathering of various groups of Christian believers. See *church.*

ASSIGN

New Testament

Verb: μερίζω (*merizō*), GK *3532* (S *3307*), 14x. *merizō* means "to divide, assign." See *divide.*

ASSURANCE

New Testament

Noun: παρρησία (*parrēsia*), GK *4244* (S *3954*), 31x. *parrēsia* generally means "confidence" and is used mostly with reference to one's speech. It can also reflect the positive assurance of how a situation will turn out (e.g., 2 Cor. 7:4; cf. Phil. 1:20; Col. 2:15). See *confidence.*

ASTONISH, ASTOUND

New Testament

Verb: ἐκπλήσσω (*ekplēssō*), GK *1742* (S *1605*), 13x. This word means "to be amazed, greatly astonished." See *amazed.*

Verb: ἐξίστημι (*existēmi*), GK *2014* (S *1839*), 17x. *existēmi* carries two distinct but related meanings. Usually it means "to astound, terrify" someone. See *amazed.*

Verb: θαυμάζω (*thaumazō*), GK *2513* (S *2296*), 43x. *thaumazō* denotes "to be amazed, astonished, wonder, marvel." See *amazed.*

ATONE

Old Testament

Verb: כָּפַר (*kāpar*), GK 4105 (S 3722), 102x. *kāpar* is generally translated "to atone, wipe clean, appease." While scholars debate whether the root meaning of this verb is "to cover," "to ransom," or "to wipe clean/purge," it is the last one that seems most appropriate in the OT.

(1) When *kāpar* is used in verses not connected with Israel's sacrificial system, it has the nuance of wiping something clean or appeasing someone. Jacob attempts to appease Esau's anger (i.e., to wipe the anger off his face) by the enormous gift he has sent on ahead of his actual encounter with him (Gen. 32:20). Similarly, a wise man knows how to wipe away a king's wrath (Prov. 16:14).

(2) In Israel's religious ceremonies other than the Day of Atonement, *kāpar* usually refers to God's wiping away our sins through various sacrifices (cf. Lev. 1:4; 4:20, 26, 31). Note especially the parallel lines of Jer. 18:23: "Do not *forgive* their crimes or *blot out* their sins from your sight." To forgive sins is to blot them out and wipe them clean. As Ps. 65:3 attests, when we come to God overwhelmed by our sins, God wipes them clean (KJV, "will purge them away"; NIV "forgave"; cf. 78:38).

(3) As described in Lev. 16 (*kāpar* occurs 16x), the Day of Atonement was a day of purging sins from the holy sanctuary. All throughout the year, the priest sprinkled the blood of sacrificial animals in front of the curtain of the sanctuary (e.g., 4:6) and thus symbolically transferred the sins of God's people into his Holy Place. By the end of the year, that place was, as it were, filled up with all their sins. Something had to be done in order to "clean house"; this was the purpose of the Day of Atonement. Note how in the final stage of this ceremony, the sins of God's people were placed on the head of the live goat, who then carried them far away into the desert, never to be seen again. There was now "room" for another year's worth of sin in the Most Holy Place. Jesus, of course, has by his sacrifice taken away our sins once for all (Heb. 9–10). See *NIDOTTE*, 2:699–702.

New Testament

Verb: ἱλάσκομαι (*hilaskomai*), GK *2661* (S *2433*), 2x. *hilaskomai* means "to atone, have mercy on, to make atonement for, propitiate."

(1) Since this verb occurs only 2x in the NT, we need to get some understanding of its meaning from how it was used in the LXX. There God is always the subject of this verb; half of its occurrences mean primarily "to forgive" (e.g., 2 Ki. 5:18; Ps. 25:11; Dan. 9:19); the other half speak of God's turning aside his anger against his people (e.g., Exod. 32:14; Ps. 78:38).

(2) In Lk. 18:13, the tax collector asks God to "have mercy" on him, a sinner. He wants his sins forgiven by God's grace and wants to be reconciled with God.

(3) In Heb. 2:17, Jesus is identified with the high priest of the OT, who used blood from various sacrifices in order to turn God's anger away from his people so that their sins might be atoned for, wiped out, and thus forgiven (cf. Lev. 4:20, 26, 31, 35).

ATONEMENT, ATONEMENT COVER, ATONING SACRIFICE

Old Testament

Noun: כַּפֹּרֶת (*kappōret*), GK 4114 (S 3727), 27x. Generally translated "atonement cover, mercy seat," *kappōret* almost exclusively occurs in Exod. 25 and 37 (in the building of the ark of the covenant) and in Lev. 16. The word describes the golden cover placed on the ark of the covenant; on it were two cherubim, whose outstretched wings formed the earthly throne of Yahweh. Because he "lived" there, the Most Holy Place had to be filled with a cloud of incense on the Day of Atonement, lest the high priest see God and die as a result. All forgiveness and purging of sin, of course, is possible only because of the forgiving grace and mercy of God.

New Testament

Noun: ἱλασμός (*hilasmos*), GK *2662* (S *2434*), 2x. *hilasmos* refers to "an atoning sacrifice, propitiation." This word occurs only in 1 Jn. 2:2 and 4:10. Jesus is himself the sacrifice that atones for sin (see *atone*). Our sins have destroyed our relationship with God, but the shed blood of Jesus purifies us from all sin and restores us to fellowship with God (1 Jn. 1:6–7). We should never forget that the root of our reconciliation with God is his incredible love, expressed when he sent his Son to be that atoning sacrifice.

Noun: ἱλαστήριον (*hilastērion*), GK *2663* (S *2435*), 2x. *hilastērion* means "atonement cover, sacrifice of atonement," or "that which propitiates or expiates." In the LXX, it is used almost exclusively for the atonement cover (*kappōret*) placed on top of the ark of the covenant.

(1) In Heb. 9:5, *hilastērion* corresponds to the OT use, that is, the atonement cover on top of the ark. That is where God dwelt in all his glory.

(2) The other use of *hilastērion* is in Rom. 3:25, where Paul writes that God has presented Jesus as a "place of atonement." This word must relate first to its OT usage, so that Jesus is the person/place where God passes over our sins without punishing them because of Christ's sacrifice. What the atonement cover meant in the Most Holy Place for the removal of sins in the OT ritual on the Day of Atonement, Christ now occupies that place. He is also the One in whom God lives in the flesh, and he is the One through whom God's wrath against sin (Rom. 1:18) is placated so that a renewed relationship between God and his people occurs. See *NIDNTT-A*, 269-70.

When we put these two Greek nouns together along with the verb *hilaskomai* (see *atone*), we see that Jesus is represented in the NT as the priest who does the atonement sacrifice (*hilaskomai*), as the One who is himself the sacrifice of atonement (*hilasmos*), and as the place where atonement occurs (*hilastērion*). Everything we need for forgiveness, for the removal of God's anger, and for reconciliation with him can be found in Jesus.

ATTACK

Old Testament

Verb: לָחַם (*lāḥam*), GK 4309 (S 3898), 171x. *lāḥam* means "to fight, battle, attack." See *fight*.

New Testament

Verb: καταλαμβάνω (*katalambanō*), GK *2898* (S *2638*), 15x. *katalambanō* can mean "to catch, obtain, seize, overtake." See *catch*.

ATTEMPT

New Testament

Verb: πειράζω (*peirazō*), GK *4279* (S *3985*), 38x. *peirazō* has several basic usages, most of which revolve around either "to tempt" or "to test." But it sometimes means "attempt, try." See *tempt*.

ATTEND TO

Old Testament

Verb: פָּקַד (*pāqad*), GK 7212 (S 6485), 304x. While *pāqad* has a wide range of meaning, it basically expresses the action of overseeing an individual for a particular purpose, such as counting the people (see *count*). When oversight leads to an appropriate response on behalf of the superior to the actions or situation of the subordinate, *pāqad* may be translated "to attend to" or "to visit" and regularly takes God as the subject. When God "visits," he often brings divine blessing with a deep sense of care (see *visit*).

New Testament

Verb: προσκαρτερέω (*proskartereō*), GK *4674* (S *4342*), 10x. *proskartereo* is "to attend to, devote oneself to" with regularity. Its verbal form is *kartereō*, which comes from the root *kratos*, "strength." While both vbs. connote remaining strong or being steadfast, *proskartereō* emphasizes duration of activity. In a nonreligious sense, it shows constant, enduring action. It is used of servants who were permanent attendants to Cornelius (Acts 10:7). Simon Magus attends to Philip by following him in ministry (8:13), rulers are to attend to their governing duties (Rom. 13:6), and the disciples keep a boat *ready* for Jesus to use as needed (Mk. 3:9).

In religious contexts, *proskartereō* denotes constancy and perseverance. This is true of the early church's practice of temple attendance (Acts 2:46), ministry of the word (6:4), and devotion to the apostle's teaching and fellowship (2:42). *proskartereō* is most frequently applied to the proper performance of prayer. The disciples (6:4) and women (1:14) of the early church devote themselves steadfastly to prayer. In like manner, Paul exhorts believers to be constant and steadfast in prayer (Rom. 12:12; Col. 4:2). See *NIDNTT-A*, 290.*

AUTHORITY

New Testament

Noun: ἐξουσία (*exousia*), GK *2026* (S *1849*), 102x. *exousia* means "authority, power, right," and the word is used in a variety of different contexts.

(1) God is the ultimate source and possessor of all authority. Some authority God reserves exclusively for himself, to which Jesus alludes when Luke records him saying, "It is not for you to know the times and the seasons which the Father has set by his own authority" (Acts 1:7). Jesus instructs people to fear God, for God has authority to cast a person into hell (Lk. 12:5). Paul likens God's authority to that of a potter over his clay (Rom. 9:21). God has authority over calamity (Rev. 16:9). Those who worship God and his Son ascribe authority to him (Jude 25; Rev. 12:10).

(2) God has granted authority to Jesus. The Father gave Jesus "authority to make judgment" (Jn. 5:27), and he gave him authority over all flesh (Jn. 17:2). The resurrected Christ proclaims that all authority in heaven and on earth has been given to him (Mt. 28:18).

God also grants authority to human and angelic beings. Paul insists that no authority—in the sense of human institutions—exists except what comes from God, and that resisting God-ordained authority amounts to resisting God (Rom. 13:1–2). Pilate says to Jesus that he has authority to release or crucify him, and Jesus retorts that he has no authority over him except what comes from above (Jn. 19:10–11). In other words, God has given Pilate authority to crucify Jesus. Angels possess authority over various things, such as calamity (Rev. 14:18; cf. 18:1).

(3) As God, Jesus exercises the divine authority, and he is head over every authority (Col. 2:10). Jesus taught with authority (Mt. 7:29). The Son of Man has authority on earth to forgive sin, a power that belongs solely to God (Mt. 9:8). The chief priests and elders of the people inquire regarding the nature and origin of Jesus' authority (Mt. 21:23), but Jesus refused to disclose that information to them. Jesus personally claimed the authority to lay down his life and the authority to take it up again (Jn. 10:18).

As God, Jesus also distributes authority to whomever he pleases. He grants authority to those who receive him by faith to become children of God (Jn. 1:12). Jesus gave the disciples authority over unclean spirits (Mt. 10:1). Luke adds that Jesus gave the disciples authority to "trample over serpents and scorpions" (Lk. 10:19), giving the seed of the woman victory over the seed of the serpent (Gen. 3:15). Paul possesses apostolic authority from the Lord (2 Cor. 10:8; 13:10). Jesus will give authority over the nations to those who overcome (Rev. 2:26).

(4) Set in opposition to the authority of God is the authority claimed by the devil and his minions. Even this power, however, derives from almighty God, who uses his enemies to accomplish his purposes (Rev. 6:8; 9:3; 13:5, 7; 17:12). When tempting Jesus, Satan offered him authority over all the kingdoms of the world (Lk. 4:5–6), but Jesus refused to take the bait, knowing that through his cross and resurrection he would gain authority over all. Jesus told the Jewish religious leaders that the "authority of darkness" belongs to them only temporarily during the time of his trial and crucifixion (Lk. 22:53). Jesus commissioned Saul/Paul to turn the Gentiles from darkness to light and from the authority of Satan to God (Acts 26:18). Jesus will someday destroy every demonic authority (1 Cor. 15:24), and he has already been seated over every demonic authority (Eph. 1:21). For other references to satanic authority and to demonic beings as "authorities," see Eph. 2:2; 3:10; 6:12; Col.

1:13, 16; 2:15; 1 Pet. 3:22; Rev. 13:2, 4, 12; 17:13).

(5) *exousia* is sometimes used with reference to various types of divinely ordained human authority enforced by civil law—such as authority to govern, to own property, or to regulate the peace (Rom. 13:3–6). Referring to his superiors, the centurion says to Jesus, "I am a man under authority" (Mt. 8:9). The scribes and chief priests want to hand Jesus over to "the authority of the governor" (Lk. 20:20). Saul had authority from the chief priests to bind Christians (Acts 9:14; 26:10, 12). The owner of a field has authority over it (Acts 5:4). In the church, because of the watching angels, women are to demonstrate their submission to male headship by having a sign of authority on their heads—that is, they are to reject the urge to usurp male authority (1 Cor. 11:10). See *head*.

(6) *exousia* can also refer to human rights or ability to exercise self-control, as in Paul's statement regarding "*control* over [one's] own will" (1 Cor. 7:37). Paul also uses the term with reference to Christian liberty, or freedom, when he warns the Corinthians not to allow their authority to cause the weak to stumble (8:9), when he speaks of the "right" to eat or drink (9:4) and the "right" to take a wife (9:5), and when he speaks of the "right" to refrain from working (9:6; cf. also 9:12, 18; 2 Thess. 3:9). Those who worship God and are cleansed by the blood of Christ have "the right" to the tree of life in that they have access to it through the work of the lamb (Rev. 22:14).

(7) Simon the magician wanted to purchase from the apostles "the power" to bestow the Holy Spirit through the laying on of hands (Acts 8:18–19), but access to such authority cannot be bought or sold. *exousia* is also used with reference to power that harms people (Rev. 9:10, 19). See *NIDNTT-A*, 191-92.

AVENGE

Old Testament

Verb: גָּאַל (*gāʾal*), GK 1457 (S 1350), 104x. *gāʾal* means variously "to ransom, redeem, function as a kinsman-redeemer." But it can also mean "avenge." If a person was killed, either intentionally or unintentionally, it was the duty of the closest relative (usually a son) to "avenge" (*gāʾal*) the shedding of this blood (Num. 35:6–34; Deut. 19:1–13). The killer could flee to a city of refuge for temporary protection, but he could keep that protection only if the homicide was unintentional (as determined by a court hearing). Note the intersection here between private and public justice.

Verb: נָקַם (*nāqam*), GK 5933 (S 5358), 35x. *nāqam* means "to avenge, take vengeance, punish."

Noun: נָקָם (*nāqām*), GK 5934 (S 5359), 17x. *nāqām* means "vengeance."

Noun: נְקָמָה (*nᵉqāmâ*), GK 5935 (S 5360), 27x. *nᵉqāmâ* means "vengeance." While vengeance often has negative connotations in our society, in the OT it has a positive thrust. Of all the uses of these words in the OT, God is the subject about 85 percent of the time (see, e.g., Ps. 94:1; Nah. 1:2). Taking vengeance is his prerogative (Deut. 32:35). When God does avenge something, however, it does not derive from a desire to even a score because of outrage or anger (as so often happens in human vengeance; cf. Ps. 44:16; Lam. 3:60; Ezek. 25:15); rather, it arises out of his sense of justice (e.g., 32:41, 43; 2 Ki. 9:7; Ezek. 24:14, 17), especially to stand up for the defenseless who have no ability to stand up for themselves. It is a punitive retribution that comes from the hand of the sovereign Lord. When the injustice and suffering that have happened to the righteous are avenged, the righteous rejoice (Ps. 58:10).

It is true that God's vengeance is often directed toward the enemies of his people, such as Babylon (Isa. 47:3), Egypt (Jer. 46:10), and Assyria (Nah. 1:2) because of their intense cruelty toward others and their lust for power. Through such acts of vengeance God delivers his people (Isa. 59:17; 61:2; Jer. 51:36). But God will also take vengeance against his own people if they break his covenant (Lev. 26:25; Jer.

5:9, 29; 9:9). His vengeance on his own people is disciplinary, with a goal of restoring his people to being "a city of righteousness" (see Isa. 1:24–26).

It is in this light that we must understand the prayers for vengeance by certain psalmists (the so-called imprecatory psalms). They are not calls for destruction for destruction's sake; rather, they are calls for God to exercise justice on the earth and for God to keep his word. See *NIDOTTE*, 3:154–56.

New Testament

Verb: ἐκδικέω (*ekdikeō*), GK *1688* (S *1556*), 6x. *ekdikeō* means "avenge, seek justice, punish."

Noun: ἐκδίκησις (*ekdikēsis*), GK *1689* (S *1557*), 9x. *ekdikēsis* means "vengeance, punishment, justice."

The verb *ekdikeō* is used 2x in the parable of the unjust judge, where a widow is seeking justice for her legitimate cause but finds the judge unresponsive to her plea (Lk. 18:3, 5). Jesus uses her persistence as an example of persistence in prayer, and he assures us that God will indeed "bring about justice [*ekdikēsis*] for his chosen ones" (18:7, 8).

Paul uses *ekdikeō* in his warning to Christians not to seek revenge against others, but to leave that up to the Lord (Rom. 12:19). As he does so, he quotes a familiar OT proverb, "Vengeance [*ekdikēsis*] is mine, says the Lord" (see also Heb. 10:30).

The martryred believers in Revelation cry out to the Lord to "avenge" their blood against those who have persecuted them (Rev. 6:10). And in 19:2, John hears a voice in heaven stating that such vengeance is beginning. Likewise, Jesus uses *ekdikēsis* to refer to the "punishment" that will come on the ungodly (Lk. 21:22; see also 2 Thess. 1:8).

Finally, earthly authority figures do have a right to mete out earthly punishment. Peter notes how God has appointed kings and governors for the "punishment" (*ekdikēsis*) of those who do wrong (1 Pet. 2:14). And in the church, Paul notes that as pastor of his churches, he stands ready to "punish" (*ekdikeō*) the Corinthians for their recalcitrance in following the paths of false teachers (2 Cor. 10:6).

AWAIT

New Testament

Verb: μένω (*menō*), GK *3531* (S *3306*), 118x. The basic sense of *menō* is "to remain, stay." It can also mean "to await, wait for." See *remain*.

Verb: προσδέχομαι (*prosdechomai*), GK *4657* (S *4327*), 14x. *prosdechomai* means "to receive, welcome" (see *welcome*), and "to wait for, expect something" in the sense of looking forward to. See *wait for*.

AWAKE

Old Testament

Verb: עוּר (*ʿûr*), GK 6424 (S 5782), 80x. *ʿûr* means "to awaken, arouse from sleep," or (in a causative sense) "to rouse someone or something, incite." The psalmist speaks of one awaking from a dream (Ps. 73:20) and Zechariah is awakened from his prophetic vision "as a man is wakened from his sleep" (Zech. 4:1). While people may rouse themselves from sleep, they are unable to arouse themselves from the sleep of death (Job 14:12).

Though this is the basic and literal meaning of the verb, it is used more commonly in a figurative way. Inanimate objects are awakened and stirred into action. The eagle stirs up her nest (Deut. 32:11); Abishai awakens (raises) his spear (2 Sam. 23:18; cf. 1 Chr. 11:11, 20); the coals of a fire are stirred (Hos. 7:4); an idol of stone is called upon to "wake up!" (Hab. 2:19); the bow is *uncovered* for battle, (Hab. 3:9); harp and lyre are *awakened* for music (Ps. 57:8; 108:2).

ʿûr is used several times in the Song of Songs with reference to love. Three times the daughters of Jerusalem are admonished, "Do not *arouse* or *awaken* love until it so desires" (2:7; 3:5; 8:4). The meaning is that love, as a personified emotion, should not be coerced. Love has its own schedule.

ʿ*ûr* portrays God's active hand in history. Far from being removed from the events of the world, God is carefully bringing about his sovereign design. Thus, he stirs up leaders such as Tiglath-Pileser (Tilgath-pilneser, KJV), the king of Assyria, against the tribes in the Transjordan (1 Chr. 5:26). He arouses the Babylonians against Jerusalem (Ezek. 23:22), and then he incites the Medes against Babylon (Isa. 13:17; Jer. 50:9, 11; 51:11).

All of these military missions that God orchestrates are done in accordance with his plan for Israel. Her disobedience is punished as promised, but God remains faithful to her. Thus God stirs up Cyrus in order to allow the Jewish exiles to return to Judah and to facilitate the rebuilding of the temple (Isa. 45:13; 2 Chr. 36:22; Ezr. 1:1). He arouses Zerubbabel and Joshua through the prophets Haggai and Zechariah to complete the construction of the temple (Hag. 1:14). He also awakens the discouraged exiles, restoring them to the land and preparing them as agents of judgment against the nations (Joel 3:7).

ʿ*ûr* finds a particularly important role in the matter of prayer and worship. In life's struggles, it may seem that God is inactive, passive, or even indifferent. He appears to be asleep (even though it is certain that "he who watches over Israel will neither slumber nor sleep," Ps. 121:4). The downtrodden soul cries out to God that he should "wake up" and become active in bringing help and salvation. We find this theme primarily in the Psalms. David cries for God's help against his enemies: "Arise, O LORD, in your anger; rise up against the rage of my enemies. *Awake*, my God; decree justice" (Ps. 7:6). God's people, beset by troubles and overrun by the ungodly, cry out for help: "Awake, O Lord! Why do you sleep? *Rouse yourself*! Do not reject us forever" (Ps. 44:23). The individual, wrongly accused, pleads for God's assistance: "I have done no wrong, yet they are ready to attack me. *Arise* to help me; look on my plight!" (Ps. 59:4). These "wake up" prayers should not be construed as a lack of faith, but rather, just the opposite. So close is the relationship between God and his children that they are permitted to express to him their frustration with the inequities of life. See *NIDOTTE*, 3:356-60.

New Testament

Verb: ἐγείρω (*egeirō*), GK *1586* (S *1453*), 144x. In the transitive (active) sense *egeirō* means to "waken, lift up, stimulate." In the intransitive (passive) sense it conveys "to get up, rise up." See *raise*.

AWE

New Testament

Noun: φόβος (*phobos*), GK *5832* (S *5401*), 47x. *phobos* in the NT can mean "fear, fright, alarm," but it can also describe a healthy awe and respect for God. See *fear*.

AX

Old Testament

Noun: בַּרְזֶל (*barzel*), GK 1366 (S 1270), 76x. *barzel* is first found in Gen. 4:22, where Tubal-Cain is said to have "forged all kinds of tools out of bronze and iron." *barzel* can also mean "ax" (2 Ki. 6:5; Eccl. 10:10). See *iron*.

BAAL

Old Testament

Noun: בַּעַל (*baʿal*), GK 1251 (S 1167, 1168), 161x. *baʿal* means "lord" or "master" in the sense of a ruler or owner. As wives were considered property to be owned in the ancient world, the "husband" could also be referred to as *baʿal* (Exod. 21:22; 2 Sam. 11:26; Prov. 31:11) and the verb *baʿal* (related to this noun) communicates the idea of marriage or rulership (Deut. 21:13; Isa. 54:1). Note that this verb applies marriage imagery to the relationship between God and his people (Isa. 54:5; Jer. 3:14; Hos. 2:18; Jer. 31:32).

baʿal is used primarily with reference to the Canaanite storm god, Baal. As the pagan god who was thought to send rain and nurturing weather for crops, he was also known as the god of fertility. Archaeological discoveries represent Baal with exaggerated genitalia. The OT consistently treats Baal as an object of scorn, whose powers as a god are outclassed by God (2 Ki. 1:2–6). The story of Elijah's showdown with the prophets of Baal on Mount Carmel serves to ridicule the powerless prophets of Baal and their false god. When the people see that the Israelite God has answered Elijah's prayer by fire, they cry out, "The LORD—he is God! The LORD—he is God" (1 Ki. 18:39).

When the Lord is depicted riding on the clouds or in control of the storm, this is a direct affront to those who believe Baal is master of the storm (Ps. 18:12–14; Dan. 7:13; Nah. 1:3). God's people, whom he calls "a thriving olive tree," provoke him to anger by "burning incense to Baal." Since Baal is god of the storm, it is striking to see God's judgment against the "tree": "with the roar of a mighty storm he will set it on fire, and its branches will be broken" (Jer. 11:16–17). Baal worship was the popular religion of Canaan and proved a constant problem for Israel (Jdg. 10:10; 1 Sam. 12:10; 1 Ki. 16:31; 2 Ki. 21:3; Jer. 12:16).

Just as the verb *baʿal* applied the image of marriage to the relationship between God and his people, worshiping foreign gods was sometimes referred to as prostitution (Jer. 2:2, 20, 23–25; Hos. 2:8, 10–13). This bears particular importance since worship of Baal may have involved sexual rituals. It is helpful to think of the implications of how a relationship with God, like any healthy marriage, requires fidelity, trust, and honesty. In the same way that the Israelites were commanded to purify the land of Canaan by removing its pagan influences, Christians should seek to confront the pagan influences of culture with the truth of the gospel. See *NIDOTTE*, 1:681–83.

BABE

See *infant*.

BAD

Old Testament

Verb: רָעַע (*rāʿaʿ*), GK 8317 (S 7489), 95x. *rāʿaʿ* expresses the quality or state of being evil or causing evil. It may be translated as "to be evil, afflict." See *evil*.

Adjective or Noun: רַע (or רָע) (*raʿ* [or *rāʿ*]), GK 8273 (S 7451), 312x. In most contexts, *raʿ* is translated "evil, wicked" (e.g., Gen. 13:13). As an adjective, *raʿ* gives a negative or inferior quality to the word it modifies. It describes something as corrupt, base, or bad. See *evil*.

New Testament

Adjective: κακός (*kakos*), GK *2805* (S *2556*), 50x. *kakos* conveys the idea of something that is "evil, bad, wicked, wrong." See *evil*.

Adjective: πονηρός (*ponēros*), GK *4505* (S *4190*, *4191*), 78x. The adjective *ponēros* basically means "bad, wicked, evil." See *evil*.

BADNESS

Old Testament

Noun: חָמָס (*ḥāmās*), GK 2805 (S 2555), 60x. *ḥāmās* denotes the idea of sinful violence and may be translated as "violence, wrong." It also describes the general injustice or badness observed in society. See *violence*.

BANDIT

New Testament

Noun: λῃστής (*lēstēs*), GK *3334* (S *3027*), 15x. *lēstēs* denotes one who is a "robber" or a political rebel ("insurrectionist"). See *robber*.

BANISH

Old Testament

Verb: חָרַם (*ḥāram*), GK 3049 (S 2763), 50x. *ḥāram* has the basic meaning "to destroy, banish, or devote to the ban." It describes the consecration of someone or something as a permanent offering to God. See *destroy*.

Verb: נָדַח (*nādaḥ*), GK 5615 (S 5080), 51x. *nādaḥ* generally has two distinct but related meanings: "to banish, cast out" and "to stray" (see *stray*).

Most often, *nādaḥ* means "to banish, cast out," with the common referent being the exile of Israel. The theme of exile is important especially to the prophets, who recognize that God has scattered (i.e., banished) Israel from the land because of their disobedience to the covenant (Jer. 8:3; 24:9; 27:10, 15; Ezek. 4:13; Dan. 9:7; cf. Jer. 50:17). They also recognize, however, that the Lord will ultimately restore his people by bringing them back to the land in order to serve him in peace and prosperity (Jer. 46:28; Mic. 4:6; Zeph. 3:19).

Even before Israel enters into the land of Canaan, Moses acknowledges that Israel will experience both the blessings and curses of Deut. 27:9–28:68, curses that include the exile (30:1). But he too understands that when they return to the Lord, he will restore them to relationship and will circumcise their hearts so that they will love the Lord completely and will live (30:6).

Verb: שָׁלַח (*šālaḥ*), GK 8938 (S 7971), 847x. Generally translated "to send," *šālaḥ* usually refers to a human or divine person sending an object away from the subject for some purpose. In certain forms, this verb can carry the negative nuance of dismissal. For example, the Lord banishes (i. e., sends away) Adam and Eve from the Garden of Eden (Gen. 3:23). See *send*.

BANK (OF A RIVER)

Old Testament

Noun: יָד (*yād*), GK 3338 (S 3027), 1627x. *yād* usually refers to a human hand, although occasionally it has additional meanings such as the bank of a river (Exod. 2:5; Lev. 25:47; Num. 13:29; Deut. 2:37; Jer. 46:6; Dan. 10:4). See *hand*.

Noun: שָׂפָה (*śāpâ*) GK 8557 (S 8193), 178x. *śāpâ* often denotes the physical "lip(s)" of a person (Num. 30:7, 13; Song 4:3, 11; 5:13). When used metaphorically, this word can be translated as "shore" (on the seashore, Gen. 22:17; Exod. 14:30) or "bank" (of a river, Gen. 41:3, 17; Exod. 2:3). See *lip*.

BANQUET

New Testament

Noun: δεῖπνον (*deipnon*), GK *1270* (S *1173*), 16x. *deipnon* means "supper, banquet" and refers to the main meal in biblical times. In addition, it can refer to a more formal eating occasion, a "banquet." See *supper*.

BAPTISM, BAPTIST

New Testament

Noun: βάπτισμα (*baptisma*), GK *967* (S *908*), 20x.

Noun: βαπτιστής (*baptistēs*), GK *969* (S *910*), 12x.

These two nouns are mentioned most clearly concerning the ministry of John, who is called "the Baptist" (*baptistēs*, i.e., the one who baptizes). John's baptism was a "baptism of repentance for the forgiveness of sins" (Mk. 1:4). It marked the turn (repentance) of a Jew to God and anticipated the messianic baptism with Spirit and fire, assuring the penitent one a place in the kingdom of God (Mt. 3:11). Since the earliest use of *baptisma* is for the baptism of John, this word may have been coined by John's disciples; more likely, however, this term is a Christian innovation that referred back to John's baptism, but also included Jesus' understanding of baptism. See *baptize* for more details.

Noun: βαπτισμός (*baptismos*), GK *968* (S *909*), 4x. *baptismos means* "baptism, washing." In Col. 2:12 Paul refers to having been "buried with [Christ] in baptism" (cf. Rom. 6:4, where Paul uses *baptisma* for this same concept). Heb. 6:2 mentions that one of the teachings in which new believers are instructed is "about baptisms" (the plural may refer to proselyte baptism, John the Baptist's baptism, and Christian baptism). See *wash, washing*.

BAPTIZE

New Testament

Verb: βαπτίζω (*baptizō*), GK *966* (S *907*), 77x. (1) The verb *baptizō* literally means "to put or go under water," although it has several different senses. It is used in the NT to describe a ceremonial washing for the purpose of sanctification (Mk. 7:4; Lk. 11:38). Usually this type of "baptism" is connected to the ritual washing rooted in Israelite tradition, as in Heb. 9:10, where it refers to the purification of a person. It is also used in the NT to describe the use of water in a rite for the purpose of establishing or renewing a relationship with God. It is in this way that the act of baptizing became a technical term in the NT (see *baptism*).

(2) The first person who did baptizing in the NT was John the Baptist, the one whose task was to prepare the way for Jesus and his ministry. He baptized people in the Jordan River, teaching "a baptism of repentance for the forgiveness of sin" (Mk. 1:4). His baptism was not, however, linked with the reception of the Holy Spirit (Mt. 3:11; Acts 19:1–7). Jesus himself insisted that he be baptized by John, primarily to identify with his people and to symbolize that he was taking upon himself the sins of humankind (Mt. 3:13–16). When Jesus began his ministry, he did not baptize people himself; rather, he delegated this to his disciples (Jn. 4:1–2). After his resurrection and prior to his ascension, Jesus instructed his disciples with the Great Commission, to go and make disciples of all nations, "baptizing them in the name of the Father and of the Son and of the Holy Spirit" (Mt. 28:19).

In the early church baptism accompanied the proclamation of the gospel from the beginning of the church's mission (Acts 2:37–41). It required repentance (2:38) and was administered in the "name of Jesus" (22:16). Baptism is one of the two main sacraments adopted by all branches of Christianity. One of the debated issues is whether there is a second baptism of the Holy Spirit, separate from water baptism (see especially 8:12–17; 10:44–48; 19:1–7).

(3) Paul explains that the importance of being "baptized into Christ" is related to our being relationally "in Christ" (Gal. 3:26–27). By being baptized into Christ the believer is baptized "into his death" (Rom. 6:3–4); it relates us to Christ's redemptive act. In this way, baptism into Christ is baptism into the church, for to be "in Christ" is to be a member of the body of Christ (1 Cor. 12:13; Gal. 3:27–29). Thus, Christian baptism is an end-time event whereby a believer is linked to Christ's redemptive act accomplished in the past and life with Christ in the kingdom of God promised in the future. See *NIDNTT-A*, 85-86.

BARE

See *naked.*

BARRACKS

New Testament

Noun: παρεμβολή (*parembolē*), GK *4213* (S *3925*), 10x. *parembolē* is a barracks or fortified camp. In Acts, it refers to the barracks or headquarters of the Roman troops in Jerusalem (Acts 21:34, 37; 22:24; 23:10, 16, 32). See *camp.*

BARREN

New Testament

Noun and Adjective: ἔρημος (*erēmos*), GK *2245* (S *2048*), 48x. In the NT, *erēmos* is used both as an adjective and a noun. As an adjective, it can mean "barren" or "desolate." Paul uses *erēmos* in Gal. 4:27 (quoting Isa. 54:1) to refer to a "barren" woman; this is the only use in the NT with this sense. See *desolate.*

BASE

Old Testament

Noun: אֶדֶן (*ʾeden*), GK 149 (S 134), 58x. *ʾeden* means "base." Almost all of the uses of this noun are in the building of the tabernacle. Since the tabernacle is a portable structure that can be set up wherever the Israelites camp, the post frames that form the overall structure have to be inserted into "bases," made of silver (e.g., Exod. 26:19, 21) or bronze (27:10–11). The Merarites are in charge of transporting these bases during a time of travel (Num. 3:36–37; 4:31–32). In Job 38:6, this word is used in a building metaphor for God's creation of the universe.

BASIS

New Testament

Noun: αἰτία (*aitia*), GK *162* (S *156*), 20x. *aitia* is the basis for some action or the legal basis for a charge—a "reason, cause, basis, charge." See *reason.*

BATHE

Old Testament

Verb: רָחַץ (*rāḥaṣ*), GK 8175 (S 7364), 72x. *rāḥaṣ* denotes the cleansing of an object, body part, or entire person for the purposes of sacrifice, priestly service, or cultural etiquette. It may be translated as "wash, bathe, cleanse." See *wash*.

BATTLE

Old Testament

Verb: לָחַם (*lāḥam*), GK 4309 (S 3898), 171x. *lāḥam* means "to fight, battle, attack." See *fight*.

Noun: מִלְחָמָה (*milḥāmâ*), GK 4878 (S 4421), 319x. *milḥāmâ* means "battle, war, fighting." See *war*.

New Testament

Noun: πόλεμος (*polemos*), GK *4483* (S *4171*), 18x. *polemos*, from which we get our word "polemical," is the word for a conflict, up to and including "battle" or "war." *polemos* can refer to an epic battle of apocalyptic-sized proportions (Rev. 16:14; 20:8), a skirmish of 30,000 troops (Lk. 14:31), or a "fight" within the body of Christ (Jas. 4:1). The fact that the same word is used of Armageddon as of "fights" within the body of Christ not only demonstrates its range of meaning but also show that such "fights" are serious business.

When used of epic battles and wars, God's people will hear about wars and rumors of wars, but these things should come as no surprise (Mt. 24:6; Mk. 13:7; Lk. 21:9). The faith of OT believers helped them become mighty in such battles (Heb. 11:34), and faith should likewise strengthen us in our battles of life.

Revelation is replete with epic battles with Satan and his armies of evil (Rev. 9:7, 9) against the two witnesses (11:7), Michael and his angels (12:7), the woman and her offspring (12:17), the saints (13:7), God Almighty (16:14), and the rider on the white horse and his army (19:19; 20:8). See *NIDNTT-A*, 481-83.

BE

Old Testament

Verb: הָיָה (*hāyâ*), GK 2118 (S 1961), 3562x. *hāyâ* means "to be, become, come to pass." This verb rarely functions as a simply copula verb, stating "x is y." In most such phrases in Hebrew, there is no expressed verb (though cf. Gen. 2:25; 3:1). One of the most frequent uses of this verb is to move historical narrative along; this is often translated in the KJV "and it came to pass," though most modern translations leave this usage untranslated. The verb can also denote that the word of the Lord has come to a particular prophet (lit., e.g., "the word of the Lord was to me" in Jer. 1:4, 11; Ezek. 12:1). In a covenant formula, God says to his people, "I will be your God" (Exod. 6:7), sometimes followed by "you will be my people" (Jer. 7:23). On the meaning of God's self revelation as "I am who I am," see discussion of the name of God as Yahweh (see *Lord*). See *NIDOTTE*, 1:1022–26.

New Testament

Verb: γίνομαι (*ginomai*), GK *1181* (S *1096*), 669x. *ginomai* means "to be, become." It has various nuances relating to being and manner of being. See *become*.

Verb: εἰμί (*eimi*) GK *1639* (S *1510*), 2462x. *eimi* means "to be." This verb is often used as a simple copula verb, joining two things together in the sense of "x is y" (e.g., "you are the light of the world, Mt. 5:14; "God is love," 1 Jn. 4:8, 16). There are many times, however, when this verb is not present but is understood. For example, the early Christian confession that "Jesus is Lord" (Rom. 10:9) does not have the verb "is" (cf. KJV, "if thou shalt confess … the Lord Jesus").

One of the most debated uses of this verb is in the saying of Jesus in the upper room regarding the bread, "This is my body," and regarding the wine in the cup, "This is my blood" (Mt. 26:26, 28). Since *eimi* has a wide variety of nuances from identity to representation, the expression has been interpreted to mean that the bread actually is the body of Christ, or that the bread represents the body of Christ (in the same sense that we may say of an item in a picture, "This is a house," when what we mean is, "This is a picture of or this represents a house"). This issue cannot be decided on the basis of the meaning of the verb *eimi*.

The most significant expression using *eimi* is the one on the mouth of Jesus, "I am" (e.g., Jn. 8:58), along with his many "I am" sayings, such as "I am the light of the world," 8:12). On this expression, see *I*.

Verb: ὑπάρχω (*hyparchō*), GK *5639* (S *5224*, *5225*), 60x. *hyparchō* is a multifaceted term ranging in meaning from the verb "to be," to being used as the noun for "possessions" (i.e., to describe things *being* at one's disposal; see *possess, possessions*), to being translated as "exist" (see *exist*).

Acts uses *hyparchō* extensively to describe people "being" a certain nationality, such as Greek (Acts 16:3), Jewish (16:30), or Roman (16:37). It is used to attribute certain qualities to individuals, such as "being" lame (3:2), "being" full of the Spirit (7:55), "being" baptized (8:16), and "being" children of God (17:29), and it is used of God "being" Lord of heaven and earth (17:24; cf. 21:20; 22:3; 27:13). *hyparchō* is used in a theologically significant sense in Phil. 2:6, which explains the nature of Jesus, "who, *being* in very nature God, did not consider equality with God something to be grasped." Those who "are" children of God are instructed to follow Jesus' example and consider others more important than themselves (Phil. 2:4–5).

BEAR

Old Testament

Verb: נָשָׂא (*nāśā'*), GK 5951 (S 4984), 659x. *nāśā'* means "to lift, raise high, bear, carry." It occasionally means "to forgive" (i.e., "to carry away"). See *lift*.

New Testament

Verb: βαστάζω (*bastazō*), GK *1002* (S *941*), 27x. *bastazō* simply means "to carry, bear" something. Metaphorically, people can carry burdens, hardships, and even the marks of Jesus (Gal. 6:17). See *carry*.

BEAR (SINS)

New Testament

Verb: ἀναφέρω (*anapherō*), GK *429* (S *399*), 10x. *anapherō* is used 2x in the NT with the meaning "to bear," referring to sins. Both times it refers to Christ's bearing the sins "of many" (Heb. 9:28) "in his body on the tree" (1 Pet. 2:24). The idea is that Christ has "borne" the penalty of sin on himself (cf. Isa. 53:11, 12; Mk. 10:45). *anapherō* can also mean "to offer up a sacrifice" (see *offer up*) or "lead up" (see *lead up*).

BEAR A CHILD

Old Testament

Verb: יָלַד (*yālad*), GK 3528 (S 3205), 492x. *yālad* means "to beget, give birth, bear a child." See *give birth*.

New Testament

Verb: γεννάω (*gennaō*), GK *1164* (S *1080*), 97x. *gennaō* means "to give birth, bear a child" (of the mother) or "to father" (of the father). See *give birth*.

BEAR WITH

New Testament

Verb: ἀνέχομαι (*anechomai*), GK *462* (S *430*), 15x. *anechomai* means "to bear with, endure, tolerate, put up with" something or someone. See *endure*.

BEAST

Old Testament

Noun: בְּהֵמָה (*bᵉhēmâ*), GK 989 (S 929), 190x. The noun *bᵉhēmâ* can be translated "beast, animal, cattle." See *animal*.

Noun: חַיָּה (*ḥayyâ*), GK 2651 (S 2416), 96x. Based on the verb "to be alive" (*ḥāyâ*, GK 2649), *ḥayyâ* is a generic term for all kinds of animals (Gen. 1:28, 30; Lev. 11:2), though usually of nondomesticated, land animals (e.g., Gen. 1:24, "wild animals"). See *animal*.

New Testament

Noun: θηρίον (*thērion*), GK *2563* (S *2342*), 46x. *thērion* refers to wild "animals" or "beasts." Jesus was with the wild animals during his forty days in the wilderness (Mk. 1:13). In his vision prior to meeting Cornelius, Peter sees wild beasts, which he had previously considered unclean (Acts 11:6). The word refers to the "snake" or "creature" that hung from Paul's hand in Acts 28:4–5. Looking back to the OT, the writer of Hebrews relates that even if an "animal" were to touch Mount Sinai, it would be stoned (Heb. 12:20). "Animals" can be tamed, but the tongue cannot (Jas. 3:7). Wild beasts are used as an instrument of death as part of the fourth seal in Revelation 6:8.

Most uses of *thērion* (38 out of 45) are in Revelation, where the word refers to "the beast" who is the agent of Satan. He has the features of all four beasts of Dan. 7 (Rev. 13:1–2) and comes from the abyss just as they do (Rev. 11:7; see Dan. 7:3), which points to the fulfillment of this OT prophecy. The dragon (Satan), the beast, and the false prophet form an unholy union in Revelation, which is a caricature of the Trinity. The beast resembles the dragon and does whatever the dragon does or arouses him to do (Rev. 13:1–4; 19:19–21; 20:7–10). A second beast, the image of the first, looks like a lamb but speaks like a dragon (13:10, 14). This second beast, who is later called the false prophet, deceives people, causes them to worship the first beast, and forces them to receive the mark of the beast on the hand or forehead (13:11–18; 14:9, 11). Not only is the union of the dragon, beast, and false prophet a false trinity, but also the beast is a parody of Jesus. Just like Jesus, he has global authority, receives worship, and recovers from a fatal wound (13:1–8). But unlike Jesus, the beast is destined for shame and defeat as he, along with his cohorts, will be captured and thrown into the lake of fire (19:19–20; 20:10). See *NIDNTT-A*, 249.

BEAT

Old Testament

Verb: נָכָה (*nākâ*), GK 5782 (S 5221), 501x. The verb *nākâ* generally means "to strike down, destroy, hit, kill." It can denote a light striking of one's hands (i.e., a clap, 2 Ki. 11:12). It may also express a severe beating that stops short of death (Deut. 25:2–3) or a strike that causes death (Jos. 10:26). In Exod. 2:11–13, *nākâ* is used in three different ways: Moses sees an Egyptian beating a Hebrew (v. 11), kills the Egyptian (v. 12), and later sees two Hebrews fighting (v. 13). See *strike*.

New Testament

Verb: δέρω (*derō*), GK *1296* (S *1194*), 15x. *derō* originally meant to flay or skin, but it came to mean "to beat, strike" in the NT period. This type of beating occurs with varying degrees of severity, but does not result in death. It was part of the physical suffering of Christ before his crucifixion (Lk. 22:63; Jn. 18:23).

Being beaten on account of identification with and bearing witness to Christ is also a mark of the saints. Through a parable, Jesus speaks of the beating of the servants whom God sent before him as messengers to Israel (Mt. 21:35; Mk. 12:3, 5; Lk. 20:10–11). Toward the end of his ministry, Jesus predicts that among other persecutions to be suffered for his sake, his followers will be "beaten in the synagogues" (Mk. 13:9). This prediction came to fruition as early Christians were beaten by the Jews (Acts 5:40; 22:19) and civil magistrates (16:37). Far from discouraging them, however, being beaten for Christ's sake caused these early Christians to rejoice at being considered worthy to suffer for his name (cf. 5:41).

Paul speaks hypothetically of a man who strikes Christians in the face as part of a systematic abuse of their person (2 Cor. 11:20). Jesus refers to the beating of unfaithful servants in one of his parables; "those who knew the master's will but did not get ready" will be beaten with many stripes; whereas "those who did not know" will be beaten with few (Lk. 12:47–48).

Finally, Paul uses this word to speak of the discipline of the Christian life, when he compares the Christian's self-discipline like that of a great fighter who does not waste energy beating the air but brings his body under his control (1 Cor. 9:26). See *NIDNTT-A*, 357-58.*

Verb: τύπτω (*typtō*), GK *5597* (S *5180*), 13x. *typtō* means "to beat, strike." Several uses of this verb have to do with the beating of Christ during his trial (Mt. 27:30; Mk. 15:19) or beatings that occur in the book of Acts (Acts 18:17; 21:32; 23:2–3). In Lk. 6:29, Jesus instructs us, "If someone strikes you on the one cheek, turn to him the other also" (Lk. 6:29). In the parable of the Pharisee and the tax collector, the latter "beats his breast and says, 'God, be merciful to me, a sinner'" (18:13). The only nonphysical use of this verb is in 1 Cor. 8:12, where Paul warns strong Christians about sinning against Christ by "wounding" the conscience of weaker believers.

BEATING

New Testament

Noun: πληγή (*plēgē*), GK *4435* (S *4127*), 22x. *plēgē* can denote a beating or wound, but it is most closely associated with the plagues in Egypt. It sometimes indicates an intense physical beating that does not lead to death (Lk. 10:30; 12:48; 2 Cor. 6:5; 11:23). See *plague*.

BEAUTIFUL

New Testament

Adjective: καλός (*kalos*), GK *2819* (S *2566, 2570*), 101x. *kalos* denotes the quality of an object or action that is beautiful, ordered, or virtuous and may be translated as "beautiful, good." Jesus commented that the stone of the temple were "beautiful" (Lk. 21:5) and that the woman who anointed her with perfume had done a "beautiful thing" (Mt. 26:10; Mk. 14:6). See *good*.

BECOME

Old Testament

Verb: הָיָה (*hāyâ*), GK 2118 (S 1961), 3561x. *hāyâ* means "to be, become, come to pass." See *be*.

New Testament

Verb: γίνομαι (*ginomai*), GK *1181* (S *1096*), 669x. *ginomai* means "to be, become." It has various nuances relating to being and manner of being and has no unique religious or theological meaning. It is one of the most fluid words in the NT. It is sometimes used simply as a synonym to the verb *eimi*, "to be."

ginomai is used frequently in combination with *kai* ("and") in order simply to move a story along throughout the NT, especially in narrative texts (the bulk of the occurrences are in the Gospels and Acts): "and it *happened* that," or "*and it came to pass*" (KJV). This literally copies a unique style in Hebrew historical writing and is often left untranslated in modern English versions of the Bible.

ginomai can refer to the initial experience of life, as in "being born" or "being produced." Jesus stupefies and angers his Jewish audience by saying, "Before Abraham *was* [i.e., *was born*], I am" (Jn. 8:58). In this sense there never was a time when Jesus was not, so *ginomai* does not apply to Jesus when one considers his deity; on the other hand, he *did come to be* as a human being through the line of David according to the flesh (Rom. 1:3). Jesus was a real, live, flesh-and-blood human as much as he was God. Jn. 1:14 provides a theological perspective on the beginning of Jesus' ministry on earth by saying simply, "The Word *became* flesh, and dwelt among us."

Paul uses *ginomai* to assist in the communication of the real "state of affairs" of his missionary team's mode of operation in their midst. He says in effect in 1 Thess. 1:5, "Our gospel *did not materialize* or *operate* among you in word only, but also in power and by the Holy Spirit, and in much conviction, just as you know what sort of men *we proved to be* among you." Thus, *ginomai* can go beyond the idea of *being* to describe *character* or *effect*. See *NIDNTT-A*, 106-7.

Verb: καθίστημι (*kathistēmi*), GK *2770* (S *2525*), 21x. *kathistēmi* has a variety of nuances of NT. It is used for the appointing of a person to an office or position, such as deacons (Acts 6:3), elders (Tit. 1:5), and the high priest (Heb. 5:1). See *put in charge*.

But *kathistēmi* can also have the meaning of "make, become something, appear as." James warns of being too fond of the world. "Anyone who chooses to be a friend of the world *becomes* an enemy of God"

(Jas. 4:4), It is also used to contrast Adam and Christ in Rom. 5:19: "For just as through the disobedience of the one man the many *were made* sinners, so also through the obedience of the one man the many *will be made* righteous." Adam's rebellion against God brought sin and death to all people, but through Jesus Christ he has brought righteousness and life to all who belong to him. Christ has reversed the devastating effects of Adam's sin through his perfect obedience. See *put in charge.*

BECOME GREATER

New Testament

Verb: αὐξάνω (*auxanō*), GK *889* (S *837*), 21x. *auxanō* means "to grow, increase, become greater." See *grow.*

BED

New Testament

Noun: κράβαττος (*krabbatos*), GK *3187* (S *2895*), 11x. *krabbatos* is associated with one who is paralyzed, lame, or bedridden because of physical infirmities. See *mat.*

BEFORE

Old Testament

Adjective: רִאשׁוֹן (*riʾšôn*), GK 8037 (S 7223), 182x. As an adjective, *riʾšôn* describes what is first in a series or rank. In terms of time, *riʾšôn* can convey the meaning "previously, in a former time." See *first.*

New Testament

Adverb: πρῶτον (*prōton*), GK *4754* (S *4412*), 58x. The adv. *prōton* often refers to something that is *temporally* prior to something else (cf. Jn. 15:18, where it has the sense "before"). Jesus commands in Mt. 5:24 that one should "first" be reconciled to one's brother and then present one's offering. See *first.*

BEG

New Testament

Noun: δέομαι (*deomai*), GK *1289* (S *1189*), 22x. *deomai* is a general word for prayer where a request is being made, either of a person or of God. It can be translated as "to pray, beseech, ask, beg, plead."

BEGET

See *give birth.*

BEGIN

Old Testament

Verb: חָלַל (*ḥālal*), GK 2725 (S 2490), 135x. *ḥālal* refers either to making something impure ("to defile"; see *defile*), or it can have a more neutral, "to begin, proceed."

When *ḥālal* means "to begin, proceed," it refers to the inception of an activity (e.g., calling on the name of God, Gen. 4:26; planting a vineyard, Gen. 9:20; or eyes starting to become weak, 1 Sam. 3:2). When Joshua takes command of Israel after Noah's death, the Lord says: "Today I will *begin* to exalt you in the eyes of all Israel, so they may know that I am with you as I was with Moses" (Jos. 3:7).

New Testament

Verb: ἄρχω (*archō*), GK *806* (S *757, 756*), 86x. *archō* has two different meanings in the NT: "to rule" (see *rule*) and "to begin." It can indicate the beginning of an action, such as speaking (Mt. 11:7, 20; 26:22; Mk. 5:20, Acts 2:4; 11:15; Lk. 3:8; 4:21; 7:15, 24, 49), thinking (Lk. 5:21) preaching (Mt. 4:17), teaching (Mk. 8:31), beating (Mt. 24:49), building (Lk. 14:30), washing (Jn. 13:5), picking (Mt. 12:1), eating (Acts 27:35), and leaving (Jn. 8:9). John the Baptist warns Jews not even to begin to say they are in right standing with God because of their relationship with Abraham (Lk. 3:8). The prodigal son began to be in need during a famine.

archō indicates the beginning of the coming of the Son of Man (Lk. 21:26), the beginning of speaking in tongues (Acts 2:4; 11:15), and Peter's beginning to sink when he focuses on the waves rather than Jesus (Mt. 14:30). Jesus teaches that as one considers the financial cost before building a structure, so also one should consider the cost before beginning to follow him (Lk. 14:31–33). *archō* also indicates starting points, such as the beginning of Jesus' preaching ministry (Mt. 4:17), the beginning of his passion predictions (Mt. 16:21), the beginning of his sharing of the gospel from the Scriptures (Lk. 24:27 cf. Acts 8:35), the beginning of judgment (1 Pet. 4:17), and the beginning of the church of Jesus Christ (Acts 1:22). See *NIDNTT-A*, 74-75.

BEGINNING

Old Testament

Noun: רֹאשׁ (*rōʾš*), GK 8031 (S 7218), 600x. The primary meaning of *rōʾš* is "head" (see *head*), but it also has a number of metaphorical meanings. For example, *rōʾš* can be translated as "beginning." Exod. 12:2 refers to the beginning of months (NIV, the *first* month). In Prov. 8:23, Wisdom is personified as having been brought forth from the beginning (of time). *rōʾš* also refers to the beginning of a watch (Jdg. 7:19; Lam. 2:19). In the prophet Isaiah, God contrasts himself with the idols of the nations, for only the Lord can declare things from the *beginning*, before they happen (40:21; 41:4, 26).

Noun: רֵאשִׁית (*rēʾšît*), GK 8040 (S 7225), 51x. *rēʾšît* indicates the "beginning" of something, such as "the *beginning* of wisdom" (Prov. 1:7) or knowledge (3:9), and "*the beginning* of sin" (Mal. 1:13). *rēʾšît* marks the beginning and end of the year (Deut. 11:12). It can also mean "firstfruits" (see *firstfruits for the connection here)*.

Rarely is rēʾšît used by itself with no other noun. The two most common passages are Gen. 1:1, which simply says "in *the beginning* God created the heavens and the earth." The other passage is a description of God in Isa. 46:9–10: "I am God, and there is none like me. I make the end known from *the beginning*, from ancient times, what is still to come." The uniqueness of this construction seems to point to the uniqueness of the event: in the beginning; God created, but he did so with the end in view. Furthermore, the beginning of creation is characterised elsewhere in Scripture as *ex nihilo*; in other words, God created at the beginning of time out of nothing, by his sheer power alone (cf. Ps. 33:6, 9; Heb. 11:3).

Adjective: רִאשׁוֹן (*riʾšôn*), GK 8037 (S 7223), 182x. As an adjective, *riʾšôn* describes what is first in a series or rank. In terms of time, *riʾšôn* can convey the meaning "previously, in a former time." See *first*.

New Testament

Noun: ἀρχή (*archē*), GK *794* (S *746*), 55x. Similar to the verb *archō* (see *begin*), *archē* means both "beginning" and "ruler" (see ruler). The double meaning of this Gk. word is derived from the idea that something long ago put the world into motion and established the rules by which the world itself is obligated to obey. This philosophy explains why *archē* is used in the NT to denote both the beginning of something (Jn. 1:1, "In the "beginning" was the Word"; cf. 1:2; 1 Jn. 1:1; 2:7, 13, 14, 24) and the person or thing that exercises authority over others ("When you are brought before synagogues, *rulers* and the authorities, do not worry," Lk. 12:11; cf. 20:20).

archē can indicate beginning. Concerning the issue of divorce, Jesus concedes that Moses permitted it but that it was "not this way from *the beginning*" (Mt. 19:8) because "at the *beginning* the Creator made them male and female" (19:4; cf. Mk. 10:6). Jesus warns his disciples that when other people start claiming to be the Messiah and when there are wars, rumors of wars, numerous famines, and earthquakes, "all these are the *beginning* of birth pains" (Mt. 24:8; Mk. 13:8, 19). Mark titles his gospel "the beginning of the gospel about Jesus Christ, the Son of God" (Mk. 1:1; cf. 1 Jn. 3:11; 2 Jn. 5), while Luke writes his gospel based on the testimony of those who were with Jesus "from the beginning" (Lk. 1:2).

The beginning of Jesus' miracle ministry occurs at a wedding in Cana (Jn. 2:11; cf. 16:4). Jesus knows from the beginning that many people will reject him (Jn. 6:64; cf. 15:27; 2 Pet. 3:4). Satan is a murderer from the beginning (Jn. 8:44; cf. 1 Jn. 2:24, "the devil has been sinning from *the beginning*"). In Acts *archē* refers to the birth of the church on the day of Pentecost (11:15; cf. 26:4). Just as Melchizedek was "without beginning" in that he had no genealogy, so too Jesus has no beginning or end, giving him the rightful title of "priest forever" (Heb. 7:3; cf. 5:12: 6:1).

BEHAVE

New Testament

Verb: ἀναστρέφω (*anastrephō*), GK *418* (S *390*), 9x. *anastrephō* can mean "to turn back," but it has a related meaning "to conduct oneself, behave" in a certain way. See *live*.

Verb: περιπατέω (*peripateō*), GK *4344* (S *4043*), 95x. Literally, *peripateō* means "to walk around" (Mt. 9:5; 11:5; Jn. 6:66; Rev. 2:1; see *walk*). Figuratively, the NT uses *peripateō* to refer to the way believers behave or conduct daily life (Mk. 7:5; Eph. 2:2; 2 Cor. 5:7; Gal. 5:16). Some translations use "live" for this meaning (see *live*).

BEHOLD

Old Testament

Interjection: הִנֵּה (*hinnēh*), GK 2180 (S 2009) 1061x.

Interjection הֵן (*hēn*), GK 2176 (S 2005 and 3860), 107x. *hinnēh* and *hēn* represent two different ways of spelling the same interjection or particle. This word is commonly used to denote surprise (Gen. 29:25), awe (Exod. 3:2), unease (Jer. 1:6), or praise (Ps. 119:40). Used at the beginning of statements, it draws attention (as in "Behold," "Look at this!" or "Pay attention to this!") to something such as a promise or a threat (Gen. 28:15; 1 Sam. 2:31), a necessary fact (Ps. 33:18), an important event (Ruth 1:15; Ps. 7:14; Amos 7:8), or a significant attribute (Jdg. 6:15; Jer. 1:6). About half of the uses of these two particles are left untranslated in the NIV. It is often placed within a statement before a specific word or idea in order to gain the attention of the reader (Gen. 28:12; 1 Ki. 3:21). On many occasions, God uses these words in order to highlight a promise or threat. A common use of *hinnēh* is in a direct summons, often by God. The person shows his willingness ("Here I am") before the Lord by literally saying, "Behold me!" (Gen. 22:1; Exod. 3:4; 1 Sam. 3:4; Isa. 6:8). See *NIDOTTE*, 4:1032–33.

New Testament

Verb: θεάομαι (*theaomai*), GK *2517* (S *2300*), 22x. *theaomai* means "to see, behold, observe." See *see*.

Interjection: ἰδού (*idou*), GK *2627* (S *2400*), 200x. *idou* ("look, behold") is derived from the aorist principal part of the verb *horaō*. See *look*.

BEING

Old Testament

Verb: נֶפֶשׁ (*nepeš*), GK 5883 (S 5315), 757x. *nepeš* has a wide range of meaning; the basic meaning is "breath," but it can also mean "soul, life, entire being." See *soul*.

BELIEF

See *faith*.

BELIEVE

Old Testament

Verb: אָמַן (*ʾāman*), GK 586 (S 539), 97x. *ʾāman* means "to believe, trust." In its participial form it has the nuance of "trustworthy, faithful" and can also be used to express the type of support a guardian might provide for a child (Num. 11:12; Ruth 4:16; 2 Sam. 4:4; Isa. 49:23).

ʾāman addresses the nature of God and his word as being faithful and true. God is "the *faithful* God, keeping his covenant of love" (Deut. 7:9). Moreover, the Lord "is *faithful* to all his promises" (Ps. 145:13). Because God is faithful, so is what he speaks: "The statutes of the Lord are trustworthy" (Ps. 19:7). Because God expects his people to look to him for guidance in life characteristics, God also expects faithfulness and integrity from his people (cf. 1 Sam. 2:35; Ps. 101:6; Isa. 1:26). Moses, for example, was "*faithful* in all [God's] house" (Num. 12:7).

The most common usage of *ʾāman* connotes belief, recognizing that something is true. When Jacob's sons tell their father that Joseph is still alive and that he is ruler of Egypt, Jacob is stunned; "he does not *believe* them" (Gen. 45:26; cf. Exod. 4:1, 8; 1 Ki. 10:7; 2 Chr. 32:15; Isa. 53:1). But the full biblical concept of believing in both the OT and NT is not merely acknowledging something to be true, nor is it the popular notion of belief that implies little more than having a deep emotional resonance with something. The biblical concept of believing involves action. "Abram believed the LORD, and he credited it to him as righteousness," for his "believing" involved doing (Gen. 15:6; see the argument of James in Jas. 2:20–24). At least twice before this pronouncement from God, Abraham left his "comfort-zone" to obey God (Gen. 12:1–4; 13:14–18), and later he was willing to sacrifice his son Isaac (Gen. 22). Abraham's basic faith was in God himself as the faithful, covenant Lord.

ʾāman also involves trusting that God is powerful enough to accomplish his word and that what he says is absolute truth and certainty. "And when the Israelites saw the great power the LORD displayed against the Egyptians, the people feared the LORD and *put their trust in him* and in Moses his servant" (Exod. 14:31; cf. Num. 14:11; Deut. 1:32; Ps. 78:22, 32, 37). A key story here is that of King Jehoshaphat, when he faces the threat of Moab and Ammon. The king assures the people that the Lord will fight for them, provided they have faith: "*Have faith* in God and you will *be upheld*; *have faith* in his prophets and you will be successful" (2 Chr. 20:20). God then destroys the enemy nations gathered against his people.

It is from this same root that we get the word "amen" (GK 589; see Num. 5:22; Deut. 27:15–26; 32:20; 1 Chr. 16:36; Ps. 72:29). Rather than being a perfunctory reply to an agreeable statement, "amen" means "so let it be established" or "let it be so." Like the idea of faith in general, "amen" is to be followed by a commitment to enact it: "At this the whole assembly said, 'Amen,' and praised the LORD. And the people did as they had promised" (Neh. 5:13). To amen the Lord's commandments is not just to say they are good ideas. It is to say, "I commit myself to obeying them." See *NIDOTTE*, 1:427–33.

New Testament

Verb: δοκέω (*dokeō*), GK *1506* (S *1380*), 62x. *dokeō* means "to think, believe, suppose." See *think*.

Verb: πιστεύω (*pisteuō*), GK *4409* (S *4100*), 241x. *pisteuō* generally means "to believe, be convinced of something," and in a more specific way "to have faith" in God or Christ. It can also mean "to entrust something to someone."

(1) *pisteuō* can mean "to believe, be convinced of something" (Mt. 8:13; Jn. 9:18; 11:27; Acts 15:11; Rom. 6:8; 14:2; 1 Jn. 5:1). Before healing a group of blind men, Jesus asks them if they believe he is able to do it (Mt. 9:28). Martha is convinced that Jesus is the Christ (Jn. 11:27), and Jesus' disciples finally believe that God sent him (Jn. 16:27, 30; 17:8). *pisteuō* is used to express the central convictions of the Christian faith, as in the assertion, "We believe that Jesus died and rose again and so we believe that God will bring with Jesus those who have fallen asleep in him" (1 Thess. 4:14).

In particular, *pisteuō* is used to mean "to be convinced of" what is spoken or written (Mt. 24:23, 26; Mk. 16:14; Jn. 4:21; 4:53; 8:46; Acts 24:14; 1 Cor. 15:11). Mary is blessed because she believes what the Lord said will be accomplished for her (Lk. 1:45). To believe Jesus' words is to believe the one who sent him (Jn. 5:24) and to believe the witness of the OT Scriptures (5:46–47). After the resurrection, the disciples remember and believe the Scriptures and the words Jesus spoke while he was with them (Jn. 2:22). People respond to hearing the gospel message by believing it (Acts 4:4; 8:12).

pisteuō also means "to accept as true" what someone says. Jesus rebukes the chief priests and elders for not believing John the Baptist, while tax collectors and prostitutes believed him (Mt. 21:25, 32).

Abraham believed God and it was credited to him as righteousness (Rom. 4:3; Gal. 3:6; Jas. 2:23). Someone can believe God and still not possess saving faith, since even the demons believe God (Jas. 2:19). This indicates that to believe is not simply to give mental assent, but to turn one's whole being over to God.

(2) *pisteuō* can also mean "to have faith in" or "trust in" God (Jn. 14:1; Acts 16:34; Rom. 4:17; Tit. 3:8). Those who believe in God have their faith credited to them as righteousness (Rom. 4:5, 24). Often *pisteuō* means "to have faith or trust in" Jesus (Mt. 18:6; Jn. 2:23; 4:39; Acts 5:14; 9:42; Phil. 1:29; 1 Jn. 3:23) and so to receive eternal life (Jn. 3:16; 6:40; Acts 16:31; 1 Jn. 5:13). Believing in Jesus also leads to justification (Rom. 10:4, 10; Gal. 2:16), forgiveness of sin (Acts 10:43), and receiving the promises of God (Gal. 3:22). Those who believe in Jesus become children of God (Jn. 1:12), never thirst (Jn. 6:35), are filled with the Spirit (Jn. 7:38–39), and move from darkness into light (Jn. 12:46). Jesus said, "The work of God is this: to believe in the one he has sent" (6:29).

There is a correlation between seeing and believing. Many people do not believe even though they have seen Jesus (Jn. 6:36). Thomas says that he will not believe that the other disciples have seen Jesus unless he sees him. When Jesus appears to Thomas and he finally confesses belief, Jesus responds by saying, "Blessed are those who believe without seeing" (Jn. 20:25, 29; see also 1 Pet. 1:8).

There is also a correlation between hearing and believing in that believing is the expected response to hearing the gospel (Jn. 4:39, 41, 42; Acts 11:21; 14:1; Rom. 10:14–17). Jesus calls for a response of belief to his preaching when he says, "The time has come, the kingdom of God is near. Repent and *believe* the good news" (Mk. 1:15). Consequently, rather than call God's people "Christians," the NT often simply calls them "those who believe" or "believers" (Acts 2:44; 4:32; 15:5; 21:25; 22:19; Rom. 4:11; 1 Cor. 14:22; 1 Thess. 1:7). Jesus says that everything is possible for those who believe, because of the power of the God in whom he believes (Mk. 9:23; 11:23, 24).

(3) *pisteuō* can also mean "to commit or entrust something to someone." If someone has not been faithful in handling worldly wealth, no one will "trust" him with true riches (Lk. 16.11). Jesus did not entrust himself to those who seemed to believe in him at the Passover feast (Jn. 2:24). The Jews had been entrusted with the words of God in the OT Scriptures (Rom. 3.2). Paul sees the gospel as having been entrusted to him by God for him to preach to the Gentiles (1 Cor. 9:17; Gal. 2:7; 1 Thess. 2:4; 1 Tim. 1:11; Tit. 1:3). See *NIDNTT-A*, 462-66.

BELLY

Old Testament

Noun: בֶּטֶן (*beṭen*), GK 1061 (S 990), 72x. The basic sense of *beṭen* seems to be the hollow or inside of something. It is used in several ways in the OT, referring to the belly or abdomen, the reproductive organs (of men or women), and the womb. See *womb*.

New Testament

Noun: κοιλία (*koilia*), GK *3120* (S *2836*), 23x. The basic meaning of *koilia* is "body-cavity"; it is often translated "stomach, belly, womb, appetite." See *stomach*.

BELOVED

Old Testament

Noun: דּוֹד (*dôd*), GK 1856 (S 1730), 61x. *dôd* sometimes denotes a close male relative, such as an "uncle" or "cousin"; it also means "beloved." Of the 61x it occurs, 39x occur in Song of Songs, the majority of which refers to the "beloved" (the male party in this song). The Shulammite woman describes the man in her life asm her "lover." The word sometimes refers to sexual passion, as illustrated by the harlot's request in Prov. 7:18, "Come, let's drink deep of love till morning; let's enjoy ourselves with love!" (Prov. 7:18).

dôd is also translated "uncle" 11x in the

OT. Although this seems completely disjointed from the other uses, one must note that it is used in the context of an individual sleeping with one's own aunt. If this occurs, the person doing so "has dishonored his uncle" (Lev. 20:20). *dôd* also occurs in Levitical law to describe a provision whereby an uncle or blood relative may redeem a family member sold into slavery (25:47–49). The expression "son of a *dôd*" probably designates a male paternal cousin (Lev. 25:49; Jer. 32:8–9, 12). Note that the daughters of Zelophehad married their relatives/cousins (Num. 36:11–12).

New Testament

Adjective: ἀγαπητός (*agapētos*), GK *28* (S *27*), 61x. *agapētos* is an adjective meaning "beloved, dear," though it often functions as a noun with the idea "dear friend." It comes from a group of words that means "love." Two related ideas are communicated by this word.

(1) The first idea pertains to the special bond that exists between the one who gives love (the lover) and the one who is loved (*agapētos*). This is most clearly seen in the gospels where they describe God the Father's intimate relationship with Jesus, his "beloved" son. At his baptism a voice from heaven calls Jesus "my Son, *whom I love*" (Mt. 3:17; KJV, "my *beloved* Son"). *agapētos* here details the intimate relationship between the Father and the Son, not merely that the Son is loved. The Synoptic Gospels go on to use the expression "beloved Son" to speak of the loving activity to be accomplished through the Son. As Mk. 12:6 explains in the parable of the tenants, "He had one left to send, a *beloved* son. He sent him last of all."

(2) The second idea focuses more specifically on the person or party receiving the love. The term appears frequently in the NT letters with two general uses. (a) It can be used to address specific individuals ("our *beloved* Barnabas and Paul," Acts 15:25; "Greet my *beloved* Epaenetus," Rom. 16:5; NIV has "*dear friend(s)*" here). (b) But it can also address an entire group. This use of *agapētos* is normally synonymous with the church, which has been chosen by God and has become his dear children through the Son ("To all in Rome who are *loved* of God" Rom. 1:7; "but as my *beloved* sons I warn you" 1 Cor. 4:14; "Therefore, my *dear* brothers, stand firm." 1 Cor. 15:58). Frequently *agapētos* will begin a sentence by calling to all who are "dearly beloved" (1 Pet. 2:11; 1 Jn. 2:7; Jude 3; NIV "dear friends"). Just as Jesus was in a special, loving relationship with the Father, so also are we who are his church. We are God's "beloved, dear children." See *NIDNTT-A*, 5-7.

BEND

Old Testament

Verb: דָּרַךְ (*dārak*), GK 2005 (S 1869), 63x. *dārak* denotes the activity of walking on a path (Deut. 1:36; Jos. 14:9; Hab. 3:19), treading on a winepress (Neh. 13:15; Isa. 16:10), or bending a bow (Ps. 7:12; Lam. 2:4; Jer. 50:29),

(BE) BENEFICIAL

New Testament

Verb: συμφέρω (*sympherō*), GK *5237* (S *4851*), 15x. *sympherō* has both a positive and a comparative nuance: "it is beneficial" and "it is better." Jesus indicates, for example, that "it is better for you to lose one part of your body" than to have your whole body be condemned in hell (Mt. 5:29–30; cf. 18:6). In Jn. 11:50, the high priest unwittingly makes a prediction about the benefit of the death of Christ when he insists to the Jewish council that "it is better for you that one man to die for the nation."

In 1 Cor. 6:12; 10:23, Paul cites a common maxim that "everything is permissible," but he follows it up with a states that "not everything is beneficial." Heb. 12:10 tells us that God disciplines us "for our good." And in Jn. 16:7, Jesus assures his disciples that it is "for their good" that he is going away, because then he will send the Holy Spirit to them.

BESEECH

New Testament

Noun: δέομαι (*deomai*), GK *1289* (S *1189*), 22x. *deomai* is a general word for prayer where a request is being made, either of a person or of God. It can be translated as "to pray, beseech, ask, beg, plead."

BEST

Old Testament

Noun: חֵלֶב (*ḥēleb*), GK 2693 (S 2459), 92x. *ḥēleb* usually denotes the literal body fat of a human or, more commonly, an animal. Since the fat of an animal seems to be considered a special portion in the ancient world, this word comes to be used figuratively for the "best" part of something. Thus, *ḥēleb* can mean the choicest part of an animal (Num. 18:29–30, 32), the highest quality wheat (Deut. 32:14; Ps. 81:16; 147:14), or the finest of olive oil or wine (Num. 18:12). Its use in the phrase the "best of the land" (Gen. 45:18) is similar to the English expression "the cream of the crop." See *fat*.

BESTOW

Old Testament

Verb: נָתַן (*nātan*), GK 5989 (S 5414), 2014x. *nātan* is a high frequency verb in the OT and bears a wide range of meanings, some of which are "to give, present, allow, permit, surrender, deliver, set, put, place." It is sometimes used of a less tangible act of "granting," or "bestowing" a blessing, as in Gen. 28:4. See *give*.

BETRAY

Old Testament

Verb: בָּגַד (*bāgad*), GK 953 (S 898), 49x. *bāgad* means "to be unfaithful, betray." See *(be) unfaithful*.

New Testament

Verb: παραδίδωμι (*paradidōmi*), GK *4140* (S *3860*), 119x. *paradidōmi* signifies "to hand over, deliver up, betray, pass down." In the NT it has a wide variety of meanings, both negative and positive. See *hand over*.

BETTER

New Testament

Adjective: κρείττων (*kreittōn*), GK *3202* (S *2908, 2909*), 19x. *kreittōn* means "better." Found mainly in the book of Heb., it is always used as a comparative adjective. It can convey the idea of someone having a higher rank or status. Christ is "much *superior*" to the angels (Heb. 1:4). Jesus is the mediator of a "*better* covenant" (8:6; cf. 7:19, 22; 12:24), founded on "*better* promises" (8:6). His sacrifice is "better" than the sacrifices of the old covenant (9:23). God has planned something "better" for us than for the OT saints by themselves (11:40).

kreittōn can also refer to something being more useful or advantageous. Paul says to be with Christ is "far better" than to remain in the flesh (Phil. 1:23).

BEWAIL

New Testament

Verb: πενθέω (*pentheō*), GK *4291* (S *3996*), 10x. *pentheō* means "to mourn, grieve, bewail." This word is used in contexts of mourning over disasters or grieving the loss of someone. See *mourn*.

BEWARE

New Testament

Verb: φυλάσσω (*phylassō*), GK *5875* (S *5442*), 31x. *phylassō* means to "guard" physically or to "keep" in the sense of observing. People are encouraged to guard themselves (i.e., beware) against such things as covetousness (Lk. 12:15). See *guard*.

BEYOND

Old Testament

Noun: עֵבֶר (*ʿēber*), GK 6298 (S 5676), 90x. *ʿēber* means "side," but many times it is translated as the preposition "beyond." See *side*.

BEYOND MEASURE

New Testament

Adverb: περισσοτέρως (*perissoterōs*), GK *4359* (S *4056*), 12x. *perissoterōs* describes an action as being "exceedingly, beyond measure, more than what would be expected." See *exceedingly*.

BID

See *order.*

BIND

Old Testament

Verb: אָסַר (*ʾāsar*), GK 673 (S 631), 73x. The most basic meaning of *ʾāsar* is "to bind, tie up." Animals may be tied to something for a particular function. Horses and donkeys may be "tethered" to keep them in place (2 Ki. 7:10), cows may be "hitched" to a cart in order to pull it (1 Sam. 6:7, 10), and chariots may be "made ready" in the sense of hitching the horses to it (Gen. 46:29). More figuratively, *ʾāsar* is used in Num. 30 (10x) in the sense of being "bound" or "obligated" by an oath, vow, obligation, promise, or pledge (e.g., 30:2, 6, 7).

But most frequently, *ʾāsar* means "to tie up" in the sense of limiting freedom. This meaning is found in the Samson narrative in Judg. 15-16, where *ʾāsar* is used more than in any other OT book. In this story, Delilah entices Samson to tell her how he might be "tied up" and subdued (Jdg. 16:6, 10, 13), but Samson misleads Delilah by saying that he will lose his strength if he is "tied" with seven fresh thongs (16:7) or with new ropes (16:11). When Delilah "ties" Samson with these fetters, they do not hold him (16:8, 12). Finally Samson gives away his secret, and the Philistines gouge out his eyes, "binding" him with bronze shackles (16:21).

Zedekiah, Judah's last king, also suffers Samson's fate and is "bound" with bronze shackles (Jer. 39:7). Jeremiah is "bound" in chains with the rest of the exiles (Jer. 40:1). *ʾāsar* also may be used in the sense of being imprisoned. The chief cupbearer and baker are put into the jail where Joseph "is imprisoned" (Gen. 40:3, 5; cf. 39:20), and when Joseph comes to power, he requires that one of his brothers "be confined" to prove that they are honest men (Gen. 42:19) after he "confined" all of them for three days (42:16).

In an eschatological sense, the OT teaches that God will set "the ones being imprisoned" free (Ps. 146:7; Isa. 49:9; 61:1), a promise that Jesus ultimately fulfills (Lk. 4:17-20). See *NIDOTTE*, 1:472-73

New Testament

Verb: δέω (*deō*), GK *1313* (S *1210*), 43x. *deō* means to "tie up, bind" someone or something. It is used in a parable of Jesus about tying up a strong man (Mt. 12:29) and in an agricultural context of tying up weeds (13:20). It is also used of prisoners (14:3; Acts 9:2), animals (Mt. 21:2), angels (Rev. 9:14), and even Satan (20:2). *deō* could be done with ropes or even with chains (Mk. 5:3). The wrapping of corpses also falls under the idea of *deō* (Jn. 11:44). A bound person is not necessarily immobile, since Jesus could move around after he was bound (Mt. 27:2, "They *bound* him [and] led him away").

In a spiritual sense, *deō* refers to physical ailments, especially when they arise out of demonic influence (Lk. 13:16) or of the impediments to spiritual influences (2 Tim. 2:9, "God's word is not *chained*"). The Holy Spirit can also bind someone in the sense of compelling that person to do something (Acts 20:22). Covenants, especially marriage covenants, were considered binding, that is, exclusive until death (Rom. 7:2); in fact the word itself can mean to be married (1 Cor. 7:27, "Are you *married?* Do not seek a divorce").

Mt. 16:19 and 18:18 ("Whatever you *bind* on earth *will be bound* in heaven.") contain the most perplexing uses of *deō*. "Binding and loosing" was a technical term in rabbinic Judaism for the authority given to rabbis for teaching and exercising discipline. The binding and loosing authority of Peter, and subsequently of the church, involves the ability to admit or refuse admission to individuals into the visible covenant community based on their doctrinal orthodoxy. Such admission or refusal reflects a higher spiritual authority. Expulsion from the church indicates the judgment of God's people that a professing believer is in fact not a believer. See *NIDNTT-A*, 131.

BIRD

Old Testament

Noun: עוֹף (*ʿôp*), GK 6416 (S 5775), 71x. *ʿôp* denotes both clean and unclean fowl or birds; occasionally it also means "winged insects." It is a collective singular, which means that in the singular it can refer to more than one bird.

When *ʿôp* stands alone, various kinds of birds are in view. Different terms are used to distinguish these various birds (eagles, vultures, kites, ravens, etc., see Lev. 11:13–19). When winged insects are in view, *ʿôp* is modified by a term that means "swarming things" (see 11:20). For the regulations regarding which birds and "swarming winged things [insects]" are clean and which are unclean, see 11:13–23.

God created these creatures (Gen. 1:20) and so they are good. Some of the *ʿôp* can be used as sacrificial animals (Gen. 8:20; Lev. 1:14), and the Israelites are permitted to eat certain birds and insects (Lev. 11:21; Deut. 14:20). A relatively common battle image is that of slain corpses being devoured by birds of prey (Deut. 28:26; 1 Sam. 17:44, 46; Ps. 79:2; Jer. 19:7; cf. Rev. 19:17–18, 21). In some prophetic passages, birds are used in similes or metaphors (e.g., Isa. 16:2; Hos. 9:11). See *NIDOTTE*, 3:354–55.

New Testament

Noun: πετεινόν (*peteinon*), GK *4374* (S *4071*), 14x. *peteinon* refers to a wild or domestic bird and are often used in the NT as illustrations. They serve as examples of the providential care of the heavenly Father for his creation (Mt. 6:26). Jesus contrasts the birds, who have nests, with his own homeless wandering (8:20). The evil one is likened to birds devouring seed sown next to the path in the parable of the sower (13:4, 19). Birds are also used to illustrate the growth of the kingdom (13:32). Peter sees birds of the air among the other beasts in his vision of the unclean things he is commanded to eat (Acts 10:12; 11:6). Paul lists birds among the images worshiped instead of the glory of the incorruptible God (Rom. 1:23). James states that while birds can be controlled, the tongue cannot be made to obey (Jas. 3:7, 8). See *NIDNTT-A*, 457.

BIRTH PANGS

New Testament

Verb: ὠδίνω (*ōdinō*), GK *6048* (S *5605*), 3x. *odinō* means "to have birth pangs." Paul uses this verb to describe the intense pain he feels in his heart as he "births" a new church (Gal. 4:19). In the case of the churches in Galatia, because they have drifted far away from the teachings of Paul, he feels he will have to painfully give birth to them all over again. Note how in 1 Thess. 2:7 Paul continues the mothering metaphor in reference to his care for the churches he has started (cf. also 2 Cor. 11:28). Paul also uses *odinō* in Gal. 4:27 in a quotation from the OT. This verb likewise occurs in Rev. 12:2 in the vision John has of the glorious woman about to give birth to Christ and his church (but Satan is ready to attack the child).*

Noun: ὠδίν (*ōdin*), GK *6047* (S *5604*), 4x. *ōdin* means "birth pangs." Peter uses this noun when he talks about the resurrection of Christ, when God "freed him from the agony of death" (Acts 2:24). The other three uses of this noun are also set in the context of resurrection—not of Jesus' resurrection but of the resurrection at the last day, when the renewal of all things will take place. Just prior to this amazing event, there will be a time of "great tribulation," which Jesus compares to the intense labor pains of a woman just before her joy at experiencing the birth of her child (Mt. 24:8; Mk. 13:8). Paul too uses this metaphor to describe the coming destruction of the world that will happen just before the day of the Lord comes, and he emphasizes that those who do not know Jesus as their Savior will not escape this time of destruction (1 Thess. 5:1–2).*

BISHOP

New Testament

Noun: ἐπίσκοπος (*episkopos*), GK *2176*

(S *1985*), 5x. *episkopos* means “overseer, bishop.” See *overseer.*

BLASPHEME

New Testament

Verb: βλασφημέω (*blasphēmeō*), GK *1059* (S *987*), 34x. *blasphēmeō* means “to slander, blaspheme, insult,” especially with regard to speech.

Scripture uses *blasphēmeō* in various ways, almost all of which have a direct or indirect reference to God: e.g., slander directed toward the Word (Tit. 2:5), Moses (Acts 6:11), God’s angels (2 Pet. 2:10–12; Jude 8–10), the person of God (Acts 6:11; Rev. 13:6; 16:11, 21), and his name (Rom. 2:24; 1 Tim. 6:1; Rev. 16:9). Blasphemy against God is a sin against his majesty and detracts from his holiness. The gospels indicate that Christians can slander Christ by doubting him (Mk. 15:29; Lk. 22:64–65; 23:39). Any act of disobedience is considered blasphemy because it resists God’s will and damages the reputation of the faith (Rom. 2:24; 1 Tim. 6:1; Tit. 2:5; Jas. 2:7). The willful, conscious, and intentional rejection of the gift of salvation is blasphemy against the Holy Spirit and is the only sin that cannot be forgiven (Mt. 12:32; Mk. 3:29).

This concept is decidedly Jewish. The Jews accused Jesus of blasphemy when he forgave sins and thus assumed messianic rights and authority that they regarded as belonging to God alone (Mk. 2:7). In the first century blasphemy was still a capital offense, and the sentence of death imposed on Jesus was in part for this sin. However, the Bible teaches that the ones who are truly guilty of slander are those who deny the claims of Christ and mock him (see Mt. 27:39–40). *blasphēmeō* is a willful, deliberate, and conscious effort to slap God in the face. God regards this sin seriously. See *NIDNTT-A*, 95-96.

BLASPHEMY

New Testament

Noun: βλασφημία (*blasphēmia*), GK *1060* (S *988*), 18x. This noun is used to denote the violation of the glory, majesty, and power of God and may be translated “blasphemy” or “mockery.” This term describes a violation of God himself (Rev. 13:6) and his angels (2 Pet. 2:10–12; Jude 8–10).

blasphēmia is also associated with false witness, wounding a reputation by evil reports and evil speaking (Mk. 7:22; Eph. 4:31; Col. 3:8; 1 Tim. 6:4). Theologically, the term conveys a consistent rejection of the movement and power of the Holy Spirit; such an action that cannot be forgiven because it involves a hardened rejection of the salvation of God (Mt. 12:32). See *NIDNTT-A*, 95-96.

BLAZE

Old Testament

Verb: בָּעַר (*bāʿar*), GK 1277 (S 1197), 60x. Generally translated “to burn, light a fire, set ablaze, flare up, consume with fire,” *bāʿar* can refer to a literal burning of fire or to a figurative “burning,” be it of desire or anger.

BLESS

Old Testament

Verb: בָּרַךְ (*bārak*), GK 1385 (S 1288), 327x. *bārak*, usually translated “to bless,” indicates the action of pronouncing good things upon the recipient. It is found most frequently in Genesis (76x), as God blesses patriarchs and they bless others; in Deuteronomy (40x), with respect to blessings that result from covenant obedience; and in Psalms (76x), as people return blessing to God in worship. When God blesses, it is not an impotent wish but the empowering and transforming word that accomplishes its purpose. To pronounce a blessing carries a sense of inevitability such that, once it has been uttered, it cannot be retracted (Gen. 27:38). However, the OT does not portray a blessing as magical, but as a prayer offered to a sovereign God.

(1) *Source of blessing*. Blessing comes from God. While sometimes implied rather than stated, God is the ultimate source of blessing in the OT. Consequently, either God or an agent of God’s blessing (frequently patriarchs or priests) is the subject

of *bārak* over 100 times. God blesses Adam, Noah, Abram (Gen. 12:2–3), Sarah (17:16), Ishmael (17:20), Isaac (25:11), Laban (30:27), Jacob (32:29), the people of Israel (Deut. 2:7), Samson (Jdg. 13:24), Job (Job 42:12), the righteous (Ps. 5:13), and those who fear God (115:13). As agents of God's blessing, Isaac blesses (Gen. 27:27), Jacob blesses (49:28), Moses blesses (Exod. 39:43), Aaron blesses (Lev. 9:22), Joshua blesses (Jos. 14:13), Eli blesses (1 Sam. 2:20), kings bless (2 Sam. 13:25), and Ezra blesses (Neh. 8:6).

(2) *Substance of blessing.* At the heart of God's blessing is God's presence (Gen. 26:3, 24). Num. 6:24-26, perhaps the most important blessing in the OT, refers to God's presence with the metaphor of his face: "May God *bless* you ... may God make his face shine on you ... may God lift up his face upon you." God's presence also implies God's protection (cf. Gen. 12:3), such that Balaam, a pagan diviner, could bless God's people even though he was paid by the king of Moab to curse them (Num. 22-24, *bārak* occurs 14x). The blessing of God's presence also highlights the relationship between God and his covenant people. With a holy God in their midst, God's people are either blessed as a result of their obedience (Deut. 7:12-15; 28:1-14) or cursed as a result of their disobedience (Deut. 28:15-68). God's blessing, particularly to the patriarchs, often includes the promise of offspring (Gen. 1:28; 9:1; 12:2; 22:17; 26:4; 28:3; Deut. 7:13; Jos. 17:14; Ps. 107:38), so that barrenness becomes a disgrace in the OT. The promises of land and of other types of material prosperity (Gen. 24:35; 26:3; 39:5; Deut. 2:7; 12:7; 15:4) are also frequently a part of God's blessing.

(3) *Pattern of blessing.* In the OT, we see God's character as he determines to bless his creation and an undeserving and often rebellious people. God establishes this pattern of blessing as he blesses the birds and fish in Gen. 1:22, "And God *blessed* them, saying" and continues with his first words to humankind in Gen. 1:28, "And God *blessed* them, and said to them, 'Be fruitful and multiply'" (cf. Gen. 5:2). God even blesses the Sabbath itself (Gen. 2:3). After the fall, the increase of wickedness on the earth, and the punishment of the flood, God starts again and reissues the blessing of Gen. 1:28 to Noah in 9:1. After the rebellion of the Tower of Babel and God's subsequent punishment, God blesses again—this time Abram (Gen. 12:2) with a promise that in Abram, "all the families of the ground will *be blessed*" (Gen. 12:3 cf. 18:18; 22:18; 26:4; 28:14).

(4) *Uses of blessing.* God's blessing can be pronounced as with Melchizedek's blessing in Gen. 14:19, "Blessed be Abram by God Most High" (cf. Jdg. 17:2; Ruth 2:20; 3:10) or with the prayer of the psalmist, "May the Lord bless you from Zion" (Ps. 128:5; cf. 134:3). Other times, God's blessing is merely acknowledged as with Laban's recognition of Abraham's servant's blessed status (Gen. 24:31; cf. 24:35). Blessing is so central to the life of God's covenant people that "May God bless you" becomes a greeting (Ruth 2:4; cf. 1 Sam. 15:13). In 2 Ki. 10:15 *bārak* is translated "greet" or "salute."

(5) *Blessing as worship.* As God blesses humanity, so also do we bless God in worship. The formula "Blessed be God" is found throughout Scripture (Gen. 9:26; 24:27; Exod. 18:10; Ruth 4:14; 1 Sam. 25:32; 1 Ki. 1:48; 8:15; 8:56; 1 Chr. 16:36; 2 Chr. 6:4; Ezek. 7:27) and appears most notably in the OT book of worship, Psalms (28:6; 31:21; 41:14; 72:18; 89:53; 106:48; 124:6; 135:21; 144:1). The Psalms also call others to bless God (e.g., Ps. 103, 7x). The NIV almost exclusively translates *bārak* "praise" when it refers to blessing God (72x; 3x it is translated as "extol"). These two senses of *bārak* (to praise God and to bless others) are seen clearly in 2 Chr. 31:8 when Hezekiah and his officials "*praised* God and *blessed* his people Israel" (cf. 1 Sam. 25:32-33; Ps. 134:2–3). See *NIDOTTE,* 1:757-67.

New Testament

Verb: εὐλογέω (*eulogeō*), GK *2328* (S

2127), 41x. *eulogeō* means "to bless, praise, thank" someone. This notion of praise and blessing is used in various relationships in the NT.

(1) God and Jesus bless people (e.g., at Jesus' ascension, Lk. 24:50), especially by giving them salvation (Acts 3:26; Gal. 3:9). At final judgment, the king will welcome those on his right, "Come, you who *are blessed* by my Father; take your inheritance, the kingdom prepared for you since the creation of the world" (Mt. 25:34). Paul speaks of "the God and Father of our Lord Jesus Christ, who has *blessed* us in Christ with every spiritual blessing in the heavenly places" (Eph. 1:3). God's blessing is to give his people spiritual blessings in life here and now and eventually welcome them into his eternal kingdom. When Elizabeth cries out to Mary, "*Blessed* are you among women, and *blessed* is the child you will bear!" (Lk. 1:42), she is indicating how much God has blessed Mary is in being chosen as the mother of the Christ child.

(2) We can bless God. When we do so, we "praise" him for who he is, for what he has done, and for what he will do. When Zechariah is allowed to speak after John is born, the first thing he does is "praise" God for keeping his promises to Abraham and raising up a horn of salvation (Lk. 1:64, 68). Simeon likewise praises God when he sees the baby Jesus (2:28), as do the disciples after Jesus ascends into heaven (24:53). Paul, using an adjective related to this verb, says in Eph. 1:3, "*Blessed* [*eulogētos*, GK *2329*] be the God and Father of our Lord Jesus Christ"; here he is praising and thanking God for the blessings he has given to us. Furthermore, when we "bless" God and Jesus (Mt. 21:9; Mk. 11:9; Lk. 19:38; 24:53), we are expressing our gratitude. We should note too that while God's blessing of his creation adds substantively to them, our blessing of God adds nothing to him.

(3) People can also bless one another. For example, Melchizedek "blessed" Abraham as he returned from war (Heb. 7:1, 6–7), and Jacob "blessed" the sons of Joseph upon his death (11:21). Blessing on such occasions may involve material blessings, but they also involve an attitude of human kindness and acceptance. Disciples not only have the responsibility to bless other Christians, but even their enemies who actively curse them (Lk. 6:27–28; Rom. 12:14; 1 Cor. 4:12; 1 Pet. 3:9).

(4) *eulogeō* can also refer to the act of blessing and giving thanks before a meal (Mt. 14:19; 26:26; Mk. 6:41; 8:7; Lk. 24:30), which Jesus does before multiplying the food for the hungry crowd. He also blesses the bread in the upper room (Mt. 26:26). We follow his example when at mealtime and the Lord's Supper we express thanks and praise God as the one who makes it possible for us to enjoy nourishment and salvation (1 Cor. 10:16; cf. 1 Tim. 4:4–5). See *NIDNTT-A,* 216-18.

BLESSED

New Testament

Adjective: εὐλογητός (*eulogētos*), GK *2329* (S *2128*), 8x. *eulogētos* means "blessed, praised." In Mk. 14:61, the high priest asks Jesus, "Are you the Christ, the Son of the *Blessed One*?" In Jewish circles by this time, since there was reticence to speak the name of God, God was given the title of "the Blessed One." In Lk. 1:68, Zechariah begins his song this way: "*Blessed* be the Lord, the God of Israel" (for this use of *eulogētos*, see *bless*, Heb. *barāk*, GK *1385*, sec. [5]; note how the NIV here uses "praise"). All the rest of the uses of *eulogētos* in the NT are in NT letters and are in the same vein as Lk. 1:68, that God is to be blessed or that praise is bestowed on the Lord (see Rom. 1:25; 9:5; 2 Cor. 1:3; 11:31; Eph. 1:3; 1 Pet. 1:3).*

Adjective: μακάριος (*makarios*), GK *3421* (S *3107*), 50x. There are two major ways *makarios* may be taken in the NT. First, a *makarios* individual is "happy" or "fortunate" because of life's circumstances. Paul says that the widow who remains unmarried is "happier" remaining as she is (1 Cor. 7:40), and, in a somewhat ironic sense, Paul declares that he is "fortunate" to make his defense in chains before King Agrippa (Acts 26:2).

Second, *makarios* conveys the idea of being especially favored: "blessed, happy, or privileged." This is particularly true of the individual who receives divine favor, as in the blessings cited in the Sermon on the Mount in Mt. 5:3–11. The message of joy is brought to the poor: "Blessed are the poor in spirit, for theirs is the kingdom of heaven" (Mt. 5:3). The poor, though weak and powerless now, are, in the end, "privileged" because of God's favor toward them. Mary is proclaimed "blessed" because she believed the report of Gabriel (Lk. 1:45). Likewise those who persevere in trial (Jas. 1:12; 1 Pet. 3:14; 4:14) and those who are doers of the word (Mt. 24:46; Lk. 12:43; Jas. 1:25; see also Jn. 13:17) find God's favor. In most of these contexts, *makarios* takes the form of a pronouncement. That is, though the present situation of those facing trials is difficult, they are encouraged by the prospect of future consolation and reward ("blessing") from God and thus are able to face the present with courage and hope. See *NIDNTT-A*, 352-53.

BLESSING

Old Testament

Noun: בְּרָכָה (*b^e^rākâ*), GK 1388, (S 1293), 71x. *b^e^rākâ*, usually translated "blessing," denotes the pronouncement of good things on the recipient or the collection of those good things themselves. The NIV also translates *b^e^rākâ* as "gift" (1 Sam. 25:27; 2 Ki. 5:15; 18:17; 20:20), "present" (30:26), "peace" (2 Ki. 18:31), "generous" (Prov. 11:25), and "good" (Isa. 65:8). *b^e^rākâ*, a noun related to the verb *bārak*, "to bless," is found most frequently in Genesis (16x), Deuteronomy (12x), and Psalms (9x).

b^e^rākâ first occurs in the OT when God calls and blesses Abram (Gen. 12:1-3). In the midst of this blessing, God declares that Abram "will be a *blessing*" (12:2). How? Abram and, by implication, his descendants are to be a blessing to the nations through the promise that in Abram, "all the families of the earth will be blessed" (12:3; cf. Isa. 19:24; Zech. 8:13). God will bless the world through his people. Ultimately, God fulfills this promise to Abram by sending Christ as Abram's seed (Mt. 1:2).

God's blessing brings righteousness (Ps. 24:5), life (Ps. 133:3), and salvation (Ps. 3:8). It is the opposite of cursing (Ps. 109:17), though the two are closely related. God turns Balaam's curse into a blessing for Israel (Num. 22-24; cf. Deut. 23:6; Neh. 13:2), and God curses Israel's blessing because of their disobedience (Mal. 2:2). In the OT, prosperity (Deut. 16:17; 2 Sam. 7:29; Prov. 10:22) and descendants (Ps. 37:26) are often the substance of blessing. God abundantly blesses his people with "showers of *blessing*" (Ezek. 34:26; cf. Ps. 84:6) to the extent that blessings can "overflow" (Mal. 3:10). God's people should earnestly seek God's blessing.

Blessings are passed on from generation to generation, usually pronounced by a father on a son. Isaac unknowingly pronounces blessing on Jacob (Gen. 27:12, 35, 36, 38, 41), and Jacob passes the blessing on to his sons (49:25, 26, 28). Moses blesses the tribes of Israel with a blessing before his death (Deut. 33:1), and God pours out his blessing on Jacob's descendents (Isa. 44:3).

Within the context of the Mosaic covenant, blessings result from a life of covenant obedience to God (Exod. 32:29; Deut. 11:26-29; 28:2) such that a faithful man (Prov. 28:20), those who rebuke the wicked (Prov. 24:25), and the righteous (Prov. 10:6-7) will receive blessing.

New Testament

Noun: εὐλογία (*eulogia*), GK *2330* (S *2129*), 16x. In its most general sense, *eulogia* means "speaking well." Rom. 16:18 reflects this meaning ("By smooth talk and *flattery* they deceive the minds of naive people"); in this case the good words are false and meant to deceive. But for the most part, *eulogia* is a NT word that derives its meaning primarily from the influence of the OT rather than its Greek etymology. The word is used to refer to the blessings God bestows on others as well as the blessings and praise he receives.

(1) Blessing God involves both words and thoughts that magnify, honor, and praise God's being, nature, and attributes (Rev. 5:12–13; 7:12). Such praises are acts of worship. Saying a blessing or offering thanks for food and participating in the Lord's Supper are examples of responding to God's blessing by offering a blessing (1 Cor. 10:16).

(2) *eulogia* also refers to the benefit of a blessing received (Rom. 15:29). Blessings come from God in both the realm of the natural (Heb. 6:7) and the supernatural (1 Pet. 3:9). The ultimate blessing is salvation (Gal. 3:14; Eph. 1:3). Blessings are unavailable to the unreceptive (Heb. 12:16–17), whether offered by God or by people.

(3) People also have the capacity and responsibility to bless others; in 2 Cor. 9:5–6 Paul uses *eulogia* 4x for the "generous gift" he is collecting for fellow believers in Jerusalem. Blessing others is especially important because of the human tendency to degrade others (Jas. 3:10).See *NIDNTT-A,* 216-18.*

BLIND

New Testament

Adjective: τυφλός (*typhlos*), GK *5603* (S *5185*), 50x. *typhlos* describes a person who is "blind." It is used in the NT in two basic but related senses: to be physically blind and unable to see the world around oneself, and to be metaphorically or figuratively blind, namely, without understanding.

The overwhelming majority of occurrences of *typhlos* are found in the gospel narratives (42x), and 36x in the NT this word refers to literal, physical blindness. A person can be *typhlos* from birth (Jn. 9:20), without apparent cause, or as a result of God's judgment (Acts 13:11). In NT times those who are *typhlos* have no other resort but to beg (e.g., Bartimaeus in Mk. 10:46).

Because of this great hardship and the inability to receive help from any other regular source, the blind often come to Jesus begging for mercy (Mt. 9:27; 20:30). Jesus heals them and alludes to the prophecy in Isa. 35:5 where the coming of the messianic age coincides with the blind receiving their sight (Mt. 11:2–5). In Jn. 9, the literal *typhlos* of the man born blind is blended with the figurative *typhlos* of the Jews. There is further irony in the Jews being referred to as *typhlos* (Jn. 9:39), for it was a matter of pride to them that they were the teachers and guides to the blind (Rom. 2:19). Jesus directly confronts the Jews with their *typhlos* of unbelief, declaring that they are blind guides of the blind (Mt. 15:14). See *NIDNTT-A*, 566-67.

BLOOD

Old Testament

Noun: דָּם (*dām*), GK 1947 (S 1818), 361x. *dām* means "blood." In the OT it is used broadly both in the context of sacrifice and as a metaphor for concepts like murder, judgment, impurity, covenant, and family relationships.

(1) "The shedding of blood" is an expression for physical harm and usually *murder* (Gen. 9:6; 37:22; Lev. 17:4; Ezek. 22:9; 39:19; 1 Sam. 25:31; 2 Ki. 3:23), which is sometimes avenged (Num. 35:27).

(2) *dām* is at times used in the sense of *judgment*, as when the waters in Egypt are turned into blood as the first of the series of plagues (Exod. 7:19; cf. Ezek. 5:17).

(3) Blood is regularly shed during *sacrifices* (Exod. 23:18; 34:25; Lev. 4:7; 7:14) and is often associated with cleansing, consecration, and atonement for sin. The altar of the priests is consecrated with *dām* (Lev. 8:14–15, 23–30).

(4) *dām* is considered *impure*, and contact with it defiles and pollutes. Menstruation, for example, causes a woman to be ceremonially unclean (Lev. 15:19). God does not allow Israel to consume the *dām* of a live animal "because the life of every creature is its blood" (Lev. 17:14; cf. 3:17;

7:26–27; 17:10). Those who do are to be cut off from the community.

(5) *dām* is an important element in *covenant* contexts. When Moses sprinkles blood on the Israelites, he declares, "This is the blood of the covenant [*dām berît*] that the LORD has made with you" (Exod. 24:8). During the Last Supper, Jesus uses this precise expression when describing the bread and wine as his body and blood (Mt. 26:28; cf. Zech. 9:11).

(6) Blood is sometimes a sign of a close *familial relationship* (2 Chr. 19:10). More commonly, though, family ties are expressed by someone being of the same "bone" (*ʾeṣem*) and "flesh" (*bāśār*) (cf. Gen. 2:23; Jdg. 9:2).

New Testament

Noun: αἷμα (*haima*), GK *135* (S *129*), 97x. *haima* is the standard Greek term for "blood." It occurs in its literal sense in such verses as Jn. 19:34, where the soldiers pierce the side of Jesus, "bringing a sudden flow of blood and water" (cf. Mk. 5:25; Acts 15:20).

haima is used extensively in contexts relating to killing and death. Jesus warns an expert in the law that "this generation will be held responsible for the blood of all the prophets" (Lk. 11:50); Paul acknowledges before the crowd that he stood by giving his approval when "the blood of your martyr Stephen was shed" (Acts 22:20); the chief priests refused the money returned by Judas because it was "blood money" (Mt. 27:6); and the souls under the altar ask the Sovereign Lord, "How long [will it be] until you judge the inhabitants of the earth and avenge our blood?" (Rev. 6:12). Revelation uses *haima* in connection with death in such phrases as "blood of the Lamb" (12:11); "blood of your saints and prophets" (16:6); "blood of prophets" (18:24); "blood of his servants" (19:2).

haima is used metaphorically in a number of ways. In Acts 5:28 the apostles are brought before the Sanhedrin and charged with determining to make the religious leaders of the Jews "guilty of this man's blood"—i.e., his death (also Mt. 27:25, where the crowd before Pilate assumes the responsibility for Jesus' death saying, "Let his blood be on us and on our children!"). *haima* is also used in combination with "flesh" to refer to the natural state of human existence (1 Cor. 15:50; "flesh and blood cannot inherit the kingdom of God;" cf. Jn. 1:13 where the NIV translates *haima* with "natural descent.")

Of special interest is the sacrificial nature of the *haima* of Christ. Paul encourages the Ephesian elders to shepherd the church that Christ "bought with his own blood" (Acts 20:28). Foreshadowing this great truth, Moses sprinkled the scroll and all the people with "the blood of calves" (Heb. 9:19). And Peter speaks of "the precious blood of Christ, a lamb without blemish or defect" (1 Pet. 1:19). Central to NT teaching on the sacrificial death of Christ is the fact that for the believer, it results in justification ("we have been justified by his blood," Rom. 5:9), redemption ("we have redemption through his blood," Eph. 1:7), reconciliation ("making peace through his blood," Col. 1:20), forgiveness ("without the shedding of blood there is no forgiveness," Heb. 9:22), holiness ("Jesus also suffered outside the city gate to make the people holy through his own blood," Heb. 13:12), purification ("the blood of Jesus, his Son, purifies us from all sin," 1 Jn. 1:7), and freedom from sin ("to him who loves us and has freed us from our sins by his blood," Rev. 1:5). Little wonder that the four living creatures fall down before the Lamb and cry, "You are worthy … because you were slain, and with your blood you purchased men for God" (Rev. 5:9).

BLOT OUT

New Testament

Verb: ἐξαλείφω (*exaleiphō*), GK *1981* (S *1813*), 5x. *exaleiphō* means "to blot out, wipe out." In Peter's message to the people gathered in the temple after the healing of the crippled man, he exhorts the crowd: "Repent, then, and turn to God, so that your sins may be *wiped out*" (Acts 3:19). Paul indicates in Col. 2:14 that this blotting out of our sins has taken place through the cross of Christ. The promise God gives to those who overcome in the church of Sardis is that their names "will never *be blotted out* ... from the book of life" (Rev. 3:5).

Two other uses of this verb are not connected with sin. God promises that in the new heaven and the new earth, he "*will wipe away* every tear" from the eyes of his children (Rev. 7:17; 21:4).*

BLOW

Old Testament

Verb: תָּקַע (*tāqaʿ*), GK 9546 (S 8628), 70x. *tāqaʿ* is used to describe such actions as blowing, thrusting, or clapping (see also *clap, thrust*).

tāqaʿ is used to indicate the blowing of a horn. Gideon instructs his men to follow his lead by *blowing* their trumpets after he *blew* his trumpet (Jdg. 7:18, 20; cf. 3:27; 6:9; Num. 10:8; Isa. 18:3; Ezek. 7:14; Hos. 5:8). The sounding of a trumpet in a city can be cause for rejoicing as a new king is crowned (1 Ki. 1:34, 39), but it can also cause the occupants of a city to tremble (Amos 3:6) because it signals an alarm (Joel 2:1, "*Blow* the trumpet in Zion; sound the alarm on my holy hill"; cf. 2:15; Jdg. 7:22; Jer. 4:5). The sounding of a ram's horn also calls God's people to special days of worship (Ps. 81:3).

BOARD

Old Testament

Noun: קֶרֶשׁ (*qereš*), GK 7983 (S 7175). 51x. In most cases, *qereš* refers to the upright wooden frames of the tabernacle. The word is translated in English in various ways, including "frame" or "board." See *frame*.

BOAST

Old Testament

Verb: הָלַל (*halāl*), GK 2146 (S 1984), 146x. *halāl* means "to praise, boast, exult." Personal *halāl* (boasting) can take place because of one's unscrupulous activities (Ps. 52:1; Prov. 20:14; 25:14); if we do boast, we should do so only in the Lord (Jer. 9:23–24). See *praise*.

New Testament

Verb: καυχάομαι (*kauchaomai*), GK *3016* (S *2744*), 37x. *kauchaomai* means "to boast, brag, rejoice." This verb is used almost exclusively by Paul in the NT (34x). It does not necessarily have a negative connotation, as might be implied by the translation "brag." Its range of meaning includes both boasting in something and rejoicing (Rom. 5:2) or glorying (1 Cor. 1:31) in something. Whether the verb describes a positive or negative activity depends on the object of the boasting.

Paul uses it generally in a positive sense when he (or someone else) boasts or rejoices in the Lord (2 Cor. 10:17), in Christ (Gal. 6:14), in his own weakness (2 Cor. 11:30), or in the hope of glory (Rom. 5:2–3). Paul can even use the verb to describe the proper pride he takes in the fruit he has seen in the Corinthian church (2 Cor. 7:14), as long as it is within proper limits (10:13).

This verb denotes the negative sense of bragging or prideful boasting when it describes those who boast not in God but in themselves or their own ability (1 Cor. 4:7)—whether in the wisdom of the Greeks (1 Cor. 1:29) or in the Jews' ability to keep the law as a means of relating to God (Rom. 2:17, 23). The verb carries with it an emphasis of trusting in something, as implied by James, who criticizes those who think that they can do anything without God (Jas. 4:16). The clear contrast between good boasting and bad boasting occurs in Gal. 6, where Paul rebukes the Judaizers for boasting in circumcision (Gal. 6:13) and describes his own proper boasting in Christ (6:14). See *NIDNTT-A*, 298-99.

Noun: καύχημα (*kauchēma*), GK *3017* (S *2745*), 11x. *kauchēma* is a "boast," an object of "pride," or a thing boasted about (Rom. 4:2). This noun describes the result of boasting and is closely related to the verb *kauchēma* (GK *3016*); thus, it carries the same positive or negative connotation as this verb, depending on the context.

Paul sums up the Corinthians' lack of

grief and pride in the face of sexual immorality as their "boast" (1 Cor. 5:6). Elsewhere, if Abraham were able to rely on himself and his works for justification, that would be his reason for boasting (Rom. 4:2). But *kauchēma* can also be used in a neutral fashion, describing the pride one feels in oneself without comparing oneself to others (Gal. 6:4). Finally, *kauchēma* is more often used in a positive sense, for the pride one has in the inner growth of believers (2 Cor. 5:12), the boasting on the day of the Lord Jesus that Paul will do regarding those whom he has led to Christ (2 Cor. 1:14), a boast of joy in Christ Jesus (Phil. 1:26), and a boast of hope because of the faithfulness of Christ (Heb. 3:6). See *NIDNTT-A*, 298-99.

Noun: καύχησις (*kauchēsis*), GK *3018* (S *2746*), 11x. *kauchēsis* refers to the act of boasting, distinguished from the result of such action, as is the meaning of *kauchēma* (GK *3017*). It can be negative or positive (e.g., having a sense of legitimate "pride" in a person or "glorying" in God). *kauchēsis* can be evil (Jas. 4:16), forbidden (Rom. 3:27), or the unstoppable result of the truth of Christ (2 Cor. 11:10), depending on the context and content of the boast. On one occasion, Paul uses *kauchēsis* to describe the "talking like a fool" he did in order to make a point to the Corinthian church (2 Cor. 11:17).

Paul also uses *kauchēsis* to describe his act of taking pride in fellow believers (1 Cor. 15:31; 2 Cor. 7:4, 14; 8:24) and his act of glorying in the Lord Jesus Christ in his service to God (Rom. 15:17), before fellow believers (2 Cor. 1:12), and in view of the hope of Christ's return (2 Thess. 2:19). See *NIDNTT-A*, 298-99.*

BOAT

New Testament

Noun: πλοῖον (*ploion*), GK *4450* (S *4143*), 67x. *ploion* denotes a "boat" or "ship." In classical Greek, this word is used for a small sailing craft, a fishing boat, or a vessel of war. In the NT, all but three of its uses occur in the gospels and Acts. Since four of the disciples had been fishermen before Jesus called them and since much of his ministry was around the Sea of Galilee, a variety of boats for sailing or fishing appear in the gospels. In Acts, we read of boats that were used on the Mediterranean Sea for transporting people and goods (e.g., Acts 20:13; 21:2; 27:2).

Only James uses *ploion* for illustrative purposes: "Or take ships as an example. Although they are so large and are driven by strong winds, they are steered by a very small rudder wherever the pilot wants to go" (Jas. 3:4). He compares the rudder of a ship to the power of the human tongue, a tiny organ in our body that can do tremendous good or harm and can steer a relationship in one direction or another.

BODY

New Testament

Noun: σάρξ (*sarx*), GK *4922* (S *4561*), 147x. *sarx* literally means "flesh." However, the use of *sarx* within the NT is quite diverse. In the NIV, for example, it is translated 20x as "body." See *flesh*.

Noun: σῶμα (*sōma*), GK *5393* (S *4983*), 142x. *sōma* can refer to the living bodies of animals (Jas. 3:3), but usually it refers to human beings (Mt. 5:29; 6:22; 26:12; Mk. 5:29, 14:8; Rom. 1:24). Greek philosophy set a course of dualism that the Bible does not recognize, i.e., that the body and the soul are separate entities. This led to a general depreciation of the body as compared to the soul. This misunderstanding is what plagued the Corinthians, who viewed things done in the body, such as joining sexually with a prostitute, as inconsequential for maintaining spiritual vitality and purity. Lying with a prostitute was no different from eating a bowl of stew—both were bodily functions. Paul would have none of it as he unmistakably drew the conclusion that whatever you subject your body to, you are at the same time involving the Holy Spirit, who lives in your body (1 Cor. 6:18–20). Thus, in Paul's writings especially, *body* takes on the idea of *person*.

Paul's theology of humanity is drawn

from the OT, which sees people as basically *psychē* (soul)/*sōma* (body) units (cf. Gen. 2:7). It is more correct, therefore, to say that a person *is* a body rather than *has* a body. In one place Paul appears not to abide by this concept, but there is a good explanation. In 1 Thess. 5:23, Paul says, "May God himself, the God of peace, sanctify you through and through. May your whole spirit, soul, and *body* be kept blameless at the coming of our Lord Jesus." Just as we should not make a sharp distinction between the four elements "heart, soul, mind, and strength" in Mk. 12:30, you likewise cannot make a division here; Paul is merely giving further emphasis to the completeness of sanctification.

It is important, however, to distinguish between the physical and the spiritual. This is possible without creating any kind of unbiblical dualism. Paul told Timothy, "Bodily exercise profits little," (1 Tim. 4:8). By this statement he means that attending to the spiritual aspect of life is infinitely more important than the physical. In 1 Cor. 15, rather than divide body and soul, Paul speaks of two kinds of bodies—heavenly bodies and earthly bodies (15:40). A heavenly body and its characteristics can be seen in Jesus' resurrected body (cf. Phil. 3:20–21), which was fitted for heaven—no longer subject to decay, disintegration, or death. While Jesus appears in the upper room without using the door, he invites his disciples to touch him, and he eats with them—things associated with a body (Lk. 24:36–43). Where Paul parts ways with Greek philosophy is that at death there is not a spirit or soul escaping the body to return to its origin. The NT does not teach the "immortality of the soul" in that sense. Rather, it stresses the resurrection of the body (1 Cor. 15:42–44; cf. Jn. 5:28–29, 1 Thess. 4:13–18). What continues at death is the "I," the *person*, who will survive death through the creative act of God that initially gave us life to begin with (1 Cor. 15:38, 42, 44).

Finally, *sōma* goes beyond the individual to refer to the collective whole, such as the concept of "the *body* of Christ," which represents the church (Rom. 12:5; 1 Cor. 12:27; Eph. 4:12). It is important that this body function as a unity (1 Cor. 12:13–27). This image is striking insofar as it depicts Jesus as the head of this body (Eph. 4:15–16). Connected to this corporate expression is the celebration of the Lord's Supper among the body of believers, where eating the bread is symbolic of the body of Christ. This "interim time celebration" reflects on Jesus' offering his body as the supreme sacrifice in his crucifixion (Mt. 26:26–29; 1 Cor. 11:23–26). See *NIDNTT-A*, 551-52.

BOLDNESS

New Testament

Noun: παρρησία (*parrēsia*), GK *4244* (S *3954*), 31x. *parrēsia* generally means "confidence" and is used mostly with reference to one's speech. As such, it refers to *clarity of speech* or *boldness*. See *confidence.*

BOND

New Testament

Noun: δεσμός (*desmos*), GK *1301* (S *1199*), 18x. *desmos* can refer to either literal chains, such as those of a prisoner, or figurative chains, that which hinders or obstructs. See *chain.*

BONDSERVANT

See *servant.*

BONES

Old Testament

Noun: עֶצֶם (*ʿeṣem*), GK 6795 (S 6106), 126x. The Hebrew word *ʿeṣem* means "bones." In the Bible, bones are often considered the seat of physical strength and good health. When people are under physical or emotional distress, their bones are said to be in pain or distress (Job 33:19), in agony (Ps. 6:3), out of joint (22:15), weak/consumed (31:11), wasting away (32:3), or without soundness or rest (38:4). To have one's bones broken is to be under the discipline of the Lord (51:8), while God protects the bones of the righteous so that not one of them will be broken (34:19–20).

In Ezekiel, the valley of dry bones

represents the national death of Israel brought about by her exile, but the divine spirit/wind/breath will bring them back to life and restore them to glory (Ezek. 37:1–14). Finally, the expression "flesh and bone" ("flesh and *blood*" in NIV) refers to a kinship relationship, notably between the first man and woman as the divinely-ordained pattern for marriage (Gen. 2:23) and between more distant relations (Gen. 29:14; Jdg. 9:2). See *NIDOTTE*, 3:499-501.

BOOK

Old Testament

Noun: סֵפֶר (*sēper*), GK 6219 (S 5612), 191x. *sēper* means "book, scroll." It essentially denotes a written document, whether it is a legal deed ("*certificate* of divorce," Deut. 24:1; Isa. 50:1; a "*deed* of purchase," Jer. 32:11), a letter (1 Ki. 21:8, 9, 11), or a book (e.g., "the *Book* of the Covenant," Exod. 24:7). At the time of the OT, "books" were written on papyrus or leather and rolled up as a "scroll" (Jer. 36:2, 10–16).

Several significant books are noted in the OT. "The Book of the Law" is the document that Moses presents to the people shortly before his death (Deut. 29:21; 30:10; 31:24, 26), which serves as a guide to his successor, Joshua (Jos. 1:8; 23:6; 24:26). This book is rediscovered and read during the time of King Josiah (2 Ki. 22:8, 11) and again during the time of Ezra (Neh. 8:1–8). Kings carefully recorded their histories "in the *book* of the annals of the kings of Israel" (e.g., 1 Ki. 15:7, 23, 31; 2 Ki. 14:15, 18, 28). The record of what Nahum wrote is called "the *book* of the vision of Nahum" (Nah. 1:1). Most important is "the *book* of life" (Ps. 69:28), from which the psalmist wants the wicked to be blotted out. While this is the only occurrence of this phrase in the OT (cf. Phil. 4:3; Rev. 3:5; 20:12, 15), presumably this is the same "book" that Moses refers to in Exod. 32:32–33; only unrepentant sinners are not included in that book. See *NIDOTTE*, 4:1292.

New Testament

Noun: βιβλίον (*biblion*), GK *1046* (S *975*), 34x. Our English word "Bible" is derived from this Greek word, which refers to a "book, scroll, writing." Though it may sometimes refer to a codex or book, the imagery of Rev. 6:14 requires this word to refer often to a scroll, for John sees the sky split "like a *scroll* when it is rolled up." A *biblion* was usually made of animal hide (vellum or parchment) or papyrus, a writing material made from strips of papyrus reeds that have been split and laid vertically, another layer placed horizontally, and then pressed together.

Often *biblion* refers to a scroll containing the Heb. Scriptures, as in the famous passage where Jesus reads and then expounds on the "scroll" of Isaiah (Lk. 4:17, 20). But *biblion* may also refer to smaller documents, such as a certificate of divorce (e.g., Mt. 19:7). Paul requests of Timothy that he bring his "*scrolls*, especially the parchments" (2 Tim. 4:13). John refers to his own gospel as a *biblion* (Jn. 20:30) and notes that the world cannot contain all the "books" required to record all of Jesus' actions (21:25). The law of Moses is also referred to in the NT as a *biblion* (Gal. 3:10; Heb. 9:19).

In the NT, *biblion* appears most often in Revelation. John is commanded to write in a *biblion* what he sees (Rev. 1:11; cf. 20:7, 9, 10, 18, 19). In ch. 5, John sees God sitting on a throne, holding a "scroll" with seven seals—no one is able to open the scroll except the Lion of the tribe of Judah. After opening the scroll he receives the praise of the four living creatures and the twenty-four elders (5:8–9). The "book of life" also features prominently in this book (13:8; 17:8; 20:12; 21:27). See *NIDNTT-A*, 94.

Noun: βίβλος (*biblos*), GK *1047* (S *976*), 10x. *biblos* refers to a "book, scroll, writing" (cf. the English word "Bible"; see also *biblion*). *biblos* is used 5x in the NT to refer to sections of the OT: the "*book* of Moses" (Mk. 12:26); "the *book* of the words of Isaiah the prophet" (Lk. 3:4); "the *book* of the Psalms" (Lk. 20:42; Acts 1:20); "the *book* of the prophets" (Acts

7:42). Matthew refers to the beginning section of his gospel as "the *book* of the genealogy of Jesus Christ" (Mt. 1:1). Acts 19:19 mentions "books" of magic being burned by those in Ephesus who formerly practiced magic but were converted through Paul's ministry. Finally, *biblos* is used 3x for the "*book* of life," in which are written the names of all who will be saved (Phil. 4:3; Rev. 3:5; 20:15). See *NIDNTT-A*, 94.*

BOOTY

Old Testament

Noun: שָׁלָל (*šālāl*), GK 8965 (S 7998), 74x. *šālāl* usually designates the plunder taken in war. It is closely related to the verb *šālal*, "to plunder, spoil." However, whereas the verb *šālal* stresses the act of plundering, the noun *šālāl* denotes the results of plundering, i.e., the spoil or booty. See *plunder*.

BORDER

Old Testament

Noun: גְּבוּל (*g*ᵉ*bûl*), GK 1473 (S 1366), 241x. *g*ᵉ*bûl* can mean either "border" (a boundary line between two areas) or "territory" (the area within borders). It is difficult to know which meaning is intended. For example, 2 Chr. 9:26 states that the realm of Solomon's authority reached "as far as the *border/territory* of Egypt." As people approach a border, they also approach a new territory, and vice versa. In such instances it is not wise to be dogmatic about one meaning or the other.

*g*ᵉ*bûl* can apply to a nation (Gen. 47:21), a tribe (Jos. 18:11), a city (1 Sam. 6:12), or even personal property (1 Chr. 4:10). Naturally, the word is found most often in texts that describe the borders of Israel and its tribes, namely Num. 34, Jos. 13–19, and Ezek. 47–48. The borders of other nations are also mentioned in the OT, such as Moab (Num. 33:44) and Edom (Num. 20:23). God is the one who has established the borders of Israel (Exod. 23:31). Furthermore, he has established the borders of the sea (Ps. 104:9; Jer. 5:22).

In the OT period, as in modern times, people were highly concerned with borders, and boundary markers were used not only in Israel (Deut. 19:14) but in other nations of the ancient Near East. The Hittites had officers responsible for maintaining the nation's divinely protected borders. In Israel, God himself watches over the borders of each family, and particularly those of widows (Prov. 15:25). Condemnation comes on those who dare change the borders that God has established (Deut. 27:17; Hos. 5:10). See *NIDOTTE*, 1:802-804.

Noun: פֵּאָה (*pē*ʾ*â*), GK 6991 (S 6285), 86x. *pē*ʾ*â* can be translated as "side, boundary, border, edge." See *side*.

Noun: קָצֶה (*qāṣeh*), GK 7895 (S 7097), 92x. *qāṣeh* is derived from the verb *qāṣâ*, which means "to cut off," and refers to the point where something is cut off, i.e., its edge or end. When it refers to the edge of a country, "border" is a good translation (Exod. 16:35). See *end*.

New Testament

Noun: ὅριον (*horion*), GK *3990* (S *3725*), 12x. *horion* means "region, vicinity." See *region*.

BORN

Old Testament

Verb: יָלַד (*yālad*), GK 3528 (S 3205), 499x. The verb *yālad*, which appears most frequently in the biblical genealogies, has the general meaning "to give birth." The precise meaning of this verb, however, depends on the particular Hebrew verb form in which it occurs. In one form (Niphal), *yālad* can refer to the child's being born. See *give birth*.

New Testament

Verb: γεννάω (*gennaō*), GK *1164* (S *1080*), 97x. *gennaō* means "to give birth, bear a child" (of the mother) or "to father" (of the father). See *give birth*.

BOTH

New Testament

Adjective: ἀμφότεροι (*amphoteroi*), GK *317* (S *297*), 14x. *amphoteroi* means "both," sometimes "all." It is used to refer to two objects or two individuals, such as both wine and skins (Mt. 9:17), wheat and weeds (13:30), and debtors (Lk. 7:42). Paul says that two groups, Jews and Gentiles, have "both" been made one through the work of Christ (Eph. 2:14, 16, 18). Luke uses *amphoteroi* to mean "all" in Acts 19:16; 23:8.

BOTHER

New Testament

Verb: παρέχω (*parechō*), GK *4218* (S *3930*), 16x. *parechō* means "to provide, bother." Most of the uses in the gospels mean "to bother." Jesus wonders why his disciples are bothering the woman who has just anointed him with perfume (Mt. 26:10; Mk. 14:6). In two of Jesus' parables, a man sleeping with his family does not want to be bothered by someone knocking at his door (Lk. 11:7), and an unjust judge does not want a widow bothering him (18:5). See *provide*.

BOUNDARY

Old Testament

Noun: גְּבוּל (*g^ebûl*), GK 1473 (S 1366), 241x. *g^ebûl* can mean either "border" (a boundary line between two areas) or "territory" (the area within a border). It is difficult to know which meaning is intended. See *border*.

Noun: חֹק (*ḥōq*), GK 2976 (S 2706), 131x. *ḥōq* is derived from the related verb *ḥāqaq*, which means "to cut in, inscribe, decree" and denotes something that is limited or restricted. Most frequently *ḥōq* refers to the prescribed law of God (see *decree*). Less frequently, it expresses a fixed quantity or some sort of limit. For example, God promises a future day in which Israel's "boundary" will be extended (Mic. 7:11). In nature God sets a "boundary" for the waters or seas (Job 26:10; 38:10; Prov. 8:29).

Noun: פֵּאָה (*pēʾâ*), GK 6991 (S 6285), 86x. *pēʾâ* can be translated as "side, boundary, border, edge." See *side*.

BOW

Old Testament

Noun: קֶשֶׁת (*qešet*), GK 8008 (S 7198), 76x. *qešet* denotes the "bow" (Gen. 48:22; Jos. 24:12; 1 Sam. 2:4; 2 Sam. 1:22; 2 Ki. 9:24; 1 Chr. 5:18; 12:2; Jer. 50:14; Hos. 1:7) or sometimes "archers" (Jer. 4:29). This instrument was considered a crucial weapon for ancient armies since it was effective from a great distance. They were made from a number of different materials: wood, horns of animals, tendons, and even metal (2 Sam. 22:35; Ps. 18:35). From ancient sources we know bows could be either simple or compound.

The bow is also a symbol of strength. Because the Lord remained with him, Joseph's "bow remained steady" (Gen. 49:24; cf. Job 29:20; 1 Sam. 2:4). The breaking of the bow represents the breaking of a person's power or an army's strength (Ps. 37:15). The Lord could break the bow of his own people or that of enemy nations (Ps. 76:3; Jer. 49:35).

To "break/abolish the bow" means to banish war and establish peace (Ps. 46:9; Hos. 2:18; Zech. 9:10). There is evidence to suggest that the breaking of bows was a way of making a treaty between warring parties. This is interesting with regard to the rainbow—which is shaped like a bow—that God set in the clouds after the flood (Gen. 9:13–16; cf. Ezek. 1:28). The rainbow reveals God's glory and serves as a reminder of his power to judge as well as to restore. It also serves as a reminder to God of his promise never to destroy the world again with a flood. See *NIDOTTE*, 3:1004-5.

BOW DOWN

Old Testament

Verb: הָוָה (*hāwâ*), GK 2556 (S 2331), 173x. *hāwâ* essentially means "to bow down." This action may be directed either to a human being or to a divine being. It may be a mere greeting, but it can also indicate submission or "worship." See *worship*.

Verb: נָפַל (*nāpal*), GK 5877 (S 5307), 435x. *nāpal* generally indicates the simple action of falling. See *fall*. One significant usage of *nāpal* is "to fall on one's face" (22x). This idiomatic expression for self-humiliation before a superior is occasionally translated "to bow down" by the NIV (e.g., 1 Ki. 18:7). While this expression is used to show respect to other people (e.g., Ruth 2:10; 2 Sam. 9:6), it is often used in the worship of God. Abraham "*falls* on his face" when God is establishing the covenant with him (Gen. 17:3); Aaron and Moses "*fall* on their faces" before the glory of Yahweh in the tent of meeting (Num. 20:6); and Ezekiel "*falls* on his face" before the glory of God revealed in a vision (Ezek. 1:28).

New Testament

Verb: πίπτω (*piptō*), GK *4406* (S *4098*), 90x. *piptō* means "to fall, collapse, bow down." See *fall*.

BOWL

New Testament

Noun: φιάλη (*phialē*), GK *5786* (S *5357*), 12x. *phialē* means "bowl." All of the occurrences of this noun are in Revelation, and all but one refer to the "bowls of God's wrath" poured out on the sinful world (e.g., Rev. 15:7; 16:1–17). In 5:8, by contrast, the four living creatures and the twenty-four elders hold "golden bowls full of incense, which are the prayers of the saints." These passages challenge us to ask ourselves which bowl applies to us.

BOX

Old Testament

Noun: אֲרוֹן (*ʾᵃrôn*), GK 778 (S 727), 202x. Often translated "ark, box, chest," the noun *ʾᵃrôn* bears distinct though related meanings in secular and cultic contexts. In secular contexts, it refers to a box for carrying the dead (i.e., a coffin, Gen. 50:26) or a money chest (2 Ki. 12:10). See *ark*.

BOY

Old Testament

Noun: יֶלֶד (*yeled*), GK 3529 (S 3206), 89x. *yeled* refers in almost all cases to a male "child" of various ages; hence, "boy, young man." See *child*.

Noun: נַעַר (*naʿar*), GK 5853 (S 5288), 240x. The meaning of *naʿar* falls into two main categories. (1) It can refer to a male child, "a boy." The emphasis in this case is on youth, but with a wide range of possibilities. It may refer to an infant (Exod. 2:6), a weaned child (1 Sam. 1:24), or a young man of marriageable age (Gen. 34:19). Joseph is still considered a "boy" at age seventeen (Gen. 37:2), and Absalom is considered a "boy" by his father David even though he is old enough to usurp the kingship and lead a military campaign against his father (2 Sam. 18:5, similar, perhaps, to how a father or mother will consider even a grown man to be "my baby"). Benjamin, the youngest of Jacob's sons, is still considered a "boy" (Gen. 44:30–34) at a time when he has ten sons of his own (46:21). In contrast to the other Heb. word for "boy" (*yeled*), *naʿar* seems to stress an attitude of care and concern rather than a biological relationship.

(2) *naʿar* can also be a title, emphasizing subordination of rank. In this sense, it may refer to a personal servant (2 Ki. 4:12), a household steward (2 Sam. 16:1), a military aide (Exod. 33:11), or an armor bearer (1 Sam. 14:1, 6). Sometimes these "servants" are of significant rank and responsibility themselves, such as the "foreman" who supervises Boaz's harvesters (Ruth 2:5) or Ahab's "young officers" (1 Ki. 20:14–19). In these cases, the point emphasized is their relationship to a superior.

BRAG

New Testament

Verb: καυχάομαι (*kauchaomai*), GK *3016* (S *2744*), 37x. *kauchaomai* means "to boast, brag, rejoice"; it has both a positive and negative sense. See *boast*.

BRANCH

Old Testament

Noun: קָנֶה (*qāneh*), GK 7866 (S 7070), 62x. In its most basic sense, *qāneh* refers to the generic reeds or rushes found in the watery areas of the ancient Near East (Job 40:21; Isa. 19:6; 35:7). It also refers frequently to the *branches* of the candlesticks of the tabernacle in Exodus (Exod. 25:31–33; 35–36; 37:17–19, 21–22). See *reed*.

New Testament

Noun: κλάδος (*klados*) GK *3080* (S

2798), 11x. *klados* is a "branch." It can refer to the literal branches of plants (Mt. 13:22; 21:8) and sometimes to new growth on a tree (Mt. 24:32, referring to the new "twigs" that come out in the spring). Jesus used *klados* in his kingdom parables to describe the small beginnings and mighty consummation of the kingdom of God (Mt. 13:22; Mk. 4:32; Lk. 13:19). A significant use of this noun occurs in Rom. 11, where Paul teaches that the covenant community, true Israel, is broader than the Jews had imagined. Unbelieving Jews had been removed to make room for believing Gentiles. Since the root of that community is holy, so are "the branches" who make it up (11:16). But the new branches are not inherently better than the old, for as Paul reminds them: "Do not boast over those branches. If you do, consider this: You do not support the root, but the root supports you" (11:18) Thus, there is unity in God's one people of all ages, supported by the Root. See *NIDNTT-A*, 127-28.

BRASS, BRAZEN

Old Testament

Noun: נְחֹשֶׁת (*nᵉḥōšet*), GK 5733 (S 5178), 139x. *nᵉḥōšet* refers either to copper or to bronze. Copper was mined "out of the hills" (Deut. 8:9) and was then combined with another metal to make bronze, an alloy containing about 5 to 10 percent of tin. When the KJV translation was being worked on, the word "brass" referred to all copper alloys. See *bronze*.

BREAD

Old Testament

Noun: לֶחֶם (*lechem*), GK 4312 (S 3899), 340x. In the OT, *lechem* means either "bread" in particular or "food" in general. As "bread" it can refer to a baked product produced from cereal grain, being translated "bread" or "loaf (of bread)." But since bread was one of the most important foods in the ancient world, *lechem* is often used as a synonym for "food."

Originally, the Israelites made bread from barley flour mixed with broad beans and lentils. Later, wheat bread became more common, but only the wealthy could afford it. Both forms of bread were baked on a griddle (Lev. 2:5) or in clay ovens (Hos. 7:4, 6–7). The flat loaves were about an inch thick and up to twenty inches in diameter.

lechem is full of symbolic imagery in the OT. In the Israelite sacrificial system, flour or bread could be given as a gift in the grain offering (Lev. 2). The twelve loaves of "the bread of the Presence" were placed on a special table in the sanctuary and represented the tribes of Israel (Exod. 25:30; 1 Chr. 28:16). Special attention was paid to "unleavened bread" at the time of the Passover (bread made without yeast), which symbolized the removal of impurities from the people (see *yeast*). See *NIDOTTE*, 2:789-92.

New Testament

Noun: ἄρτος (*artos*), GK *788* (S *740*), 95x. *artos* means "bread" (Mt. 4:4; Mk. 6:38; Jn. 6:9, 13) or more generally "food" (Lk. 15:17; 2 Thess. 3:8). Its first sense is physical bread, such as Jesus used to feed the crowds (Mk. 6:38; Jn. 6:11).

But *artos* also can carry a metaphorical sense. When Paul instructs the Thessalonians to earn their own living, he does so by saying literally that they are to "eat their own bread" (2 Thess. 3:12). Jesus use of *artos* in the fourth petition of the Lord's Prayer (Mt. 6:11) is symbolic of all of life's basic necessities.

Similar to its use in the LXX (Exod. 12:8, 11, 34, 39; 13:3–10), *artos* is full of symbolic imagery. Just as bread was an offering to God, so also Christ, who called himself "the bread that came down from heaven" (Jn. 6:31, 41), became an offering to God on behalf of the world (cf. Jn. 3:16). It is in this sense that the "bread" of the last supper, the Eucharist, represents the body of Christ; and our partaking of that bread represents our participation in his death (1 Cor. 10:16–17; 11:23-26). It is important that when we do partake in the "bread" at the Lord's Supper, we are humbled by his sacrifice and celebratory of his victory. See *NIDNTT-A*, 74.

(UNLEAVENED) BREAD

Old Testament

Noun: מַצָּה (*maṣṣeh*), GK 5174 (S 4682), 53x. Usually translated "unleavened bread," *maṣṣeh* is bread made without yeast. The earliest use of *maṣṣeh* in the Scriptures is Gen. 19:3, when Lot unknowingly entertains angels in his home. This type of bread is quick to prepare and is therefore commonly made for unexpected guests.

The Feast of Unleavened Bread immediately follows Passover and is celebrated for seven days, although the two festivals are often referred to as one (Exod. 12:17; 23:15). The significance of *maṣṣeh* in the Passover celebration is explained in Deut. 16:3, "... for seven days eat unleavened bread, the bread of affliction, because you left Egypt in haste—so that all the days of your life you may remember the time of your departure from Egypt." The haste with which the Israelites left Egypt will remind them that the exodus was not their plan and fulfillment, but God's.

In the temple, both grain offerings and fellowship offerings consisted of unleavened bread (Lev. 2:4, 5; 7:12). See *NIDOTTE*, 2:1065-68.

BREADTH

Old Testament

Noun: רֹחַב (*rōḥab*), GK 8145 (S 7341) 103x. *rōḥab* refers to the "width" of an object or an area, and "breadth" is an appropriate translation when an area is large. The word often occurs in connection with the word "length" and, occasionally, with the word "height." See *wide, width*.

BREAK

Old Testament

Verb: שָׁבַר (*šābar*), GK 8689 (S 7665), 148x. *šābar* can variously mean "to break, break down, break up."

(1) God is often the subject of *šābar*, and the common reference is to his judgmental, punitive activity. Usually this judgment is against those not in covenant with him, as in Jer. 28:2: The God of Israel says: "I will *break* the yoke of the king of Babylon." But Israel can also be the object of God's breaking. For example, God commands Jeremiah to break a jar to depict what is about to happen to Judah (19:10). Earlier, God declares through Hosea: "In that day I will *break* Israel's bow in the Valley of Jezreel" (Hos. 1:5). In addition, *šābar* often denotes the liberation of God's people from bondage to a foreign nation. "Son of man, I have *broken* the arm of Pharaoh king of Egypt" (Ezek. 30:21).

In five instances where God is the subject of *šābar*, the object is the idiomatic phrase, "the staff [supply] of your bread," as in "I/He has *broken* the staff of your bread" (Lev. 26:26; Ps. 105:16; Ezek. 4:16; 5:16; 14:13). Some scholars suggest that the phrase indicates one form of God's retributive justice, depriving people of what they consider essential for their diet. The staff describes some piece of wood that is used to carry the food or from which food is suspended to protect it from animals.

(2) *šābar* can express the action of a human subject. After Israel's sin with the golden calf, for example, Moses "breaks" the stone tablets containing the Ten Words (Exod. 32:19). In many other texts, Israel destroys pagan idols (2 Ki. 11:18; 2 Ki. 18:4; 2 Chr. 14:3; Jer. 43:13). "Under [Josiah's] direction the altars of the Baals were torn down; he cut to pieces the incense altars that were above them, and smashed the Asherah poles, the idols and the images. These he broke to pieces and scattered over the graves of those who had sacrificed to them" (2 Chr. 34:4).

(3) In several instances, *šābar* is connected with the heart. A person's heart can be broken because of abuse (Ps. 69:20) or sin (51:17). And God can be "broken" as a result of the disloyalty of his people's hearts: "Then in the nations where they have been carried captive, those who escape will remember me—how I have been broken by their adulterous hearts, which have turned away from me, and by their eyes, which have lusted after their idols" (Ezek. 6:9).

(4) Lastly, *šābar* refers to what is not to be done to the Passover sacrifice (Exod. 12:46; Num. 9:12): No bone is to be broken. This finds prophetic fulfillment in the sacrifice of Christ, whose bones also are not broken (Jn. 19:30). See *NIDOTTE*, 4:38-39.

New Testament

Verb: ἐπιβάλλω (*epiballō*), GK *2095* (S *1911*), 18x. *epiballō* can means "to break over, down," such as waves "breaking over" a boat (Mk. 4:37) or Peter "breaking down" and weeping (Mk. 14:72). *epiballō* can also mean "lay on, arrest, sew" (see *lay on*).

Verb: κλάω (*klaō*), GK *3089* (S *2806*), 14x. *klaō* means to "break, break off into pieces." In the NT it always occurs in reference to bread. In the first century, the common practice was to break bread with one's hands rather than slicing it with a knife. Jesus broke the bread to feed the multitudes (Mt. 14:19). Paul broke bread on the boat as he headed to Rome (Acts 27:35). Early Christians often had meals together, expressed by breaking bread (Acts 2:46; 20:11).

klaō takes on religious significance when Jesus broke bread with his disciples in the upper room (Lk. 22:19). This event was not intended to be a one-time experience, for he commanded his disciples to keep doing it in remembrance of him. As time passed, the breaking of bread became synonymous with the Lord's Supper. Paul argues that the breaking of bread with other believers is a "participation in the body of Christ" (1 Cor. 10:16). And since the risen Christ also broke bread with his disciples before the ascension (Lk. 24:30), the breaking of bread in the Lord's Supper may also have served to them as a reminder that their Lord was now risen (Lk. 24:35; Acts 10:41). So should it for us—a reminder of Jesus' death and resurrection. See *NIDNTT-A*, 307.

Verb: λύω (*lyō*), GK *3395* (S *3089*), 42x. *lyō* means "to loose, untie" (see *loose*), but also "break, destroy." In Acts 27:41, the stern of the ship is "broken to pieces" in the high seas. In Rev. 5:2, no one is found worthy to "break" the seals of the scroll.

Figuratively, *lyō* has a variety of nuances with this meaning. Paul uses this verb to indicate the destruction of the dividing wall between Jews and Gentiles that came about through the death of Christ (Eph. 2:14). It is also found in connection with breaking the laws of Judaism. Christ warns those who are not faithful. "Anyone who *breaks* one of the least of these commandments and teaches others to do the same will be called least in the kingdom of heaven" (Mt. 5:19). It is important to note the strictness that Christ imposed on the law. He applies it to one's inner attitudes as well as to outward acts (Mt. 5:27-32). Consequently, everyone is in need of forgiveness for *breaking* one of the least of these commandments. *lyō* is also used to speak of breaking the Sabbath: "For this reason the Jews tried all the harder to kill him; not only was he *breaking* the Sabbath, but he was even calling God his own Father, making himself equal with God" (Jn. 5:18).

lyō is twice used with reference to destroying the temple (Mk. 14:58; Jn. 2:19). In both instances, Jesus alludes to the destruction of his body.

BREATH

Old Testament

Verb: נֶפֶשׁ (*nepeš*), GK 5883 (S 5315), 757x. *nepeš* has a wide range of meaning; the basic meaning is "breath," but it can also mean "soul, life, entire being." See *soul*.

Noun: הֶבֶל (*hebel*), GK 2039 (S 1892), 73x. *hebel* literally means "breath," but in the OT it occurs only 3x with this sense. For example, Isa. 57:13 states, "When you cry out for help, let your collection of idols save you! The wind will carry all of them off, a *mere breath* will blow them away" (see also Ps. 62:9–10; Prov. 21:6). In most OT instances, the noun functions metaphorically (see *vanity*).

Noun: רוּחַ (*rûaḥ*), GK 8120 (S 7307), 378x. While *rûaḥ* has a wide range of meanings in the OT, its basic sense is that of "wind" or "breath." See *wind.*

New Testament

Noun: πνεῦμα (*pneuma*), GK *4460* (S *4151*), 379x. Similar to *rûaḥ* in the OT, *pneuma* can mean "air in movement." In Jn. 3:8 Jesus uses *pneuma* twice: once for "wind" or "air" and once for the "Spirit" ("the *wind* blows where it chooses ... so it is with everyone born of the *Spirit*"). *pneuma* can also mean that which animates or gives life to the body (Mt. 27:50) or the human spirit in general (Jas. 2:26). *pneuma* can also refer to evil and good "spirits" as well as the "Holy Spirit." See *spirit*.

BRIDE

New Testament

Noun: νυμφη (*nymphē*), GK *3811* (S *3565*), 8x. *nymphē* means " bride" or "daughter-in-law." John the Baptist uses *nymphē* to say, "I am not the Christ but am sent ahead of him. The *bride* belongs to the bridegroom" (Jn. 3:29). In describing the destruction of "Babylon," John states that "voice of bridegroom and bride will never be heard in you again" (Rev. 18:23). In describing how some families will be divided against each other as a result of choosing, or not choosing, to follow Jesus, he says, "They will be divided, father against son and son against father, mother against daughter and daughter against mother, mother-in-law against *daughter-in-law* and *daughter-in-law* against mother-in-law (Mt. 10:35; Lk. 12:53).

nymphē is used in the Revelation to describe the church and the glorious love relationship that exists between Christ and his church. One of the angels says to John, "Come, I will show you the *bride*, the wife of the Lamb" (Rev. 21:9). Elsewhere the imagery is mixed as John describes all the people of God as "the Holy City, the new Jerusalem, coming down out of heaven from God, prepared as a *bride* beautifully dressed for her husband" (21:2). The final call by the Spirit to the *nymphē* is to "Come!" (22:17). See *NIDNTT-A*, 396-397.*

BRIDEGROOM

New Testament

Noun: νυμφίος (*nymphios*), GK *3812* (S *3566*), 16x. *nymphios* is typically translated "bridegroom." When Jesus goes to the wedding in Cana in Galilee and turns the water into wine, the master of the banquet "calls the *bridegroom* aside" to praise him for his generous provision (Jn. 2:9). In describing the destruction of "Babylon," John states that "voice of *bridegroom* and bride will never be heard in you again" (Rev. 18:23).

John the Baptist compares himself to "the friend who attends the *bridegroom*," that is, the person who helps to arrange the marriage. But then he emphasizes that he is not the Christ and that "the bride [the church] belongs to the *bridegroom* [Jesus]" (Jn. 3:29). Jesus uses the imagery of a bridegroom to explain why his disciples do not fast. "How can the guests of the *bridegroom* mourn while he is with them? The time will come when the *bridegroom* will be taken from them; then they will fast" (Mt. 9:15; cf. Lk. 5:34). In explaining the needs for disciples to be prepared for Jesus' return, Jesus says, "The kingdom of heaven will be like ten virgins who took their lamps and went out to meet the *bridegroom*" (Mt. 25:1). See *NIDNTT-A*, 396-97.

BRING

Old Testament

Verb: בּוֹא (*bôʾ*), GK 995 (S 935), 2592x. *bôʾ* is the fourth most common verb in the OT. It denotes motion toward a specific goal, such as "to go, arrive, enter a house, come." It expresses a variety of motions. This verb can also be used in the sense of "causing something to go or come," that is, "to bring something or someone." See *come.*

Verb: נָגַשׁ (*nāgaš*), GK 5602 (S 5066), 125x. *nāgaš* denotes "to be near, come into close proximity to an object." Isaac requests of Jacob: "*Come near* so I can touch you, my son" (Gen. 27:21). *nāgaš* can also have a causative sense, "to bring near": "Then he said, "My son, *bring* me some of your game to eat" (27:25). See *approach.*

New Testament

Verb: ἄγω (*agō*), GK *72* (S *33, 71*), 67x. In its most basic NT sense, *agō* means "to bring, lead, go." See *lead.*

Verb: προσφέρω (*prospherō*), GK *4712* (S *4374*), 47x. *prospherō* has a general meaning "to bring" a person or an object to someone; in a religious sense, it means "to bring an offering, offer." The religious sense predominates in the LXX, and this meaning carries over into the NT, especially in Hebrews (Heb. 5:1, 3, 7; 8:3–4; 9:7, 9, 14, 25, 28; 10:1, 2, 8, 11, 12; 11:4 17) but also in the gospels (Mt. 5:23–24; Mk. 1:24).

The gospels and Acts also frequently use *prospherō* in the more common sense. The sick (Mt. 4:24) and little children (19:13) are "brought" to Jesus. Jesus is "brought" to Pilate for trial (Lk. 23:14). The soldiers who crucify Jesus "offer" him vinegar (Lk. 23:36), and Simon "offers" to buy the apostolic power for money (Acts 8:19).

Heb. 12:7 uses *prospherō* in the sense of "to deal with" or "behave toward." This sense occurs only here in the NT but is evidenced in other early Greek literature. See *NIDNTT-A*, 254-57.

Verb: φέρω (*pherō*), GK *5770* (S *5342*), 66x. *pherō* has the basic meaning "to bring, carry, present," but it has a wide range of figurative meanings, such as "to endure, sustain." (1) In the gospels, *pherō* is frequently used to describe the literal act of bringing or carrying something from one place to another, such as bringing the sick and demon-possessed to Jesus for healing (Mk. 1:32; 2:3; 7:32; 8:22). The head of John the Baptist "was presented" to Herod on a platter (Mt. 14:11). Simon was forced "to carry" the cross of Christ (Lk. 23:26), and Nicodemus "brought" one hundred pounds of spices to prepare the body of Jesus for burial (Jn. 19:39). At times, Jesus commands that something "be brought" to him, such as five loaves and two fish (Mt. 14:18), a demonized boy (17:17), a colt (Mk. 11:2), a denarius (12:15), and fish (Jn. 21:10).

(2) In a figurative sense, accusations can be "brought" forward before a court: "What accusation do you *bring* against this man?" (Jn. 18:29). Believers are exhorted to look ahead to the grace that "will be brought" to them at the revelation of Christ (i.e., the second coming; 1 Pet. 1:13). (a) In addition, in 2 Pet. 1:21 *pherō* takes on the meaning of someone "being moved" or "borne along." Fisherman Peter was familiar with the idea of a boat "being moved along" by the wind (cf. Acts 27:15, 17), so he could understand how those who penned the Scriptures were "carried along" by the Holy Spirit. (b) *pherō* can mean "to bear" something in the sense of "to put up with, endure," such as the "vessels of wrath" (Rom. 9:22). In Heb. 12:20, the Israelites could not "bear" (endure) the command of the Lord from the mountain. In 13:13, the writer encourages believers to "endure" any reproach for Christ. (c) In 2 Pet. 1:18, *pherō* is used of a word that was "brought" from heaven by God to Peter, James, and John at the transfiguration of Christ (cf. 2 Pet. 1:17). (d) *pherō* can also mean "to bear" in the sense of bearing fruit, especially spiritual fruit (Mk. 4:8; Jn. 12:24; 15:2, 4, 5, 8, 16). (e) In Heb. 1:3, *pherō* has the meaning of "sustain." Christ "bears/sustains" all creation by the word of his power.

BRING ABOUT

New Testament

Verb: κατεργάζομαι (*katergazomai*), GK *2981* (S *2716*), 22x. *katergazomai* means "to bring about, produce." This word occurs mainly in the writings of Paul. He says that "law *brings about* wrath" (Rom. 4:15), but "suffering *produces* perseverance" (Rom. 5:3). Similarly, James says "the testing of your faith *produces* perseverance" (Jas. 1:3). The world's light momentary troubles "are bringing about" an eternal weight of glory (2 Cor. 4:17).

BRING FORTH

New Testament

Verb: τίκτω (*tiktō*), GK *5503* (S *5088*), 18x. The basic meaning of *tiktō* is "to give birth, bring forth." See *give birth*.

BRING IN

New Testament

Verb: εἰσάγω (*eisagō*), GK *1652* (S *1521*), 11x. *eisagō* means "to bring in." Joseph and Mary "bring" the child Jesus into the temple (Lk. 2:27). After Jesus is betrayed, he "is brought" into the high priest's house (22:54). After he is blinded, Saul "is brought" into Damascus (Acts 9:8). It is alleged that Paul has brought Greeks into the temple, thereby violating its sanctity (21:28–29). When God "*brings* the firstborn into the world," he commands the angels to worship him (Heb. 1:6).

BRING NEAR

Old Testament

Verb: קָרַב (*qārab*), GK 7928 (S 7126), 280x. The basic meaning of *qārab* is "to draw near" or, in a causative sense, "to bring near." This basic meaning may denote physical or spatial proximity as well as nonphysical. See *bring*.

BRING OUT

Old Testament

Verb: יָצָא (*yāṣāʾ*), GK 3655 (S 3318), 1076x. *yāṣāʾ* most frequently means "to go out, come out, bring out." See *go out*.

BRING UP

Old Testament

Verb: עָלָה (*ʿālâ*), GK 6590 (S 5927), 894x. *ʿālâ* typically means "to go up, ascend," sometimes "to exalt, bring up." Although it inherently is not a theological term, it often appears in highly significant contexts. See *ascend*.

New Testament

Verb: ἀνάγω (*anagō*), GK *343* (S *321*), 23x. *anagō* means "to bring, lead up." Jesus is "led up" by the Spirit to be tempted in the wilderness (Mt. 4:1). Peter is "brought up" to an upper room where Dorcas has died (Acts 9:39). God "brought up" Jesus from the dead (Heb. 13:20; cf. Rom. 10:7). It is used once to describe the "bringing" of an offering (Acts 7:41). *anagō* is also a technical term meaning "to put out to sea, sail." See *sail*.

BROAD

Old Testament

Noun: רֹחַב (*rōḥab*), GK 8145 (S 7341) 103x. *rōḥab* refers to the "width" of an object or an area, and "breadth" is an appropriate translation when an area is large. The word often occurs in connection with the word "length" and, occasionally, with the word "height." See *wide, width*.

BRONZE

Old Testament

Noun: נְחֹשֶׁת (*nᵉḥōšet*), GK 5733 (S 5178), 139x. *nᵉḥōšet* refers either to copper or to bronze. Copper was mined "out of the hills" (Deut. 8:9) and could then be combined with another metal to make bronze, an alloy containing about 5 to 10 percent of tin. When the KJV translation was being worked on, the word "brass" referred to all copper alloys, and so "brass" was used extensively to translate *nᵉḥōšet*.

Bronze is a strong, virtually indestructible, metal (Jer. 1:18; 15:12), which has several uses in the OT period. Texts from the ancient Near East inform us that many everyday items were bronze, such as bowls, pots, and plows. It could also be polished to a shine and be used as a mirror (Exod. 38:8; cf. Dan. 10:6).

Bronze, as a strong metal, plays a significant part in warfare. It was used for helmets and armor (1 Sam. 17:5–6, 38), weapons (1 Sam. 17:6; 2 Sam. 21:16), and chains to bind prisoners (2 Ki. 25:7). Additionally, bronze was carried off as the spoils of war (Jos. 6:19, 24). This metal was used extensively in the construction of the Jewish tabernacle and temple. In the tabernacle, the basin, utensils, clasps, sockets, and pegs were all made of bronze. The altar was also bronze plated (Exod. 26:11, 37; 27:2, 6, 19; 30:18; 38:3). Likewise, Solomon's temple had a bronze altar, pillars, basins, and utensils (1 Ki. 7:14–16, 38; 1 Chr. 18:8). When the ark was brought up to Jerusalem, bronze cymbals were among the instruments used in the celebration (1 Chr. 15:19). Another familiar cultic use was the bronze serpent fashioned by Moses in the desert (Num. 21:9), which was later used for idolatrous practices (2 Ki. 18:4).

Metaphorically, bronze describes something hard or stubborn. As an act of God's judgment, the sky will "become bronze" instead of releasing rain (Deut. 28:23), and the stubborn and rebellious Israelites are compared to bronze and iron (Jer. 6:28). *n^eḥōšet* is synonymous with the word *n^eḥûšâ* (GK 5703), which occurs 9x in the OT. See *NIDOTTE*, 3:88-89.

BROOK

Old Testament

Noun: נַחַל (*naḥal*), GK 5707 (S 5158), 137x. *naḥal* refers to a dry river bed or wadi. Usually, however, it refers to the raging water that fills a wadi, turning it into a fast flowing river. See *river*.

BROTHER

Old Testament

Noun: אָח (*ʾāḥ*), GK 278, (S 251), 629x. *ʾāḥ* denotes a "brother" or one who is close in some type of human relationship. It can even denote treaty partners.

(1) This noun refers most frequently to blood brothers (Cain and Abel, Gen. 4:2; Jacob and Esau, Gen. 25:26; Judah and his brothers, Gen. 44:14; Moses and Aaron, Exod. 4:14) and half brothers (Joseph and his brothers, Gen. 37:2; Abimelech and his seventy brothers, Jdg. 9:3; Solomon and Adonijah, 1 Ki. 1:10). The OT places emphasis on the special relationship between brothers. Within the many OT brother narratives are stories of intense hatred and jealousy, such as Cain and Abel (Gen. 4:2–26) and Jacob and Esau (Gen. 25:24–34; 27:1–28:9; 33:1–17). However, God shows his disapproval for such animosity in this relationship: Cain is cursed after he murders Abel (Gen. 4:10–12), and Jacob does not fully become Israel until after he is reconciled to Esau (Gen. 35:10; cf. 32:28; 33:4).

(2) Other familial relationships are also described by *ʾāḥ*. Abraham and Lot, uncle and nephew, are referred to as brothers (Gen. 14:12, 14, 16). In several places, especially laws dealing with family matters, *ʾāḥ* denotes kinsmen (Lev. 19:17; 25:25; Deut. 15:12; 17:15). It is also used in a more extended sense to describe members of the same tribe (Levites, Num. 16:10; Judahites, 2 Sam. 19:12).

(3) Rarely, *ʾāḥ* is used to denote treaty partners. This can be between kings (Solomon and the king of Tyre, 1 Ki. 9:13) or between nations (Israel and Edom, Num. 20:14; Deut. 2:4, 8; Obad. 10).

(4) Finally, Deut. uses *ʾāḥ* in laws denoting the relationships of the covenant community. These laws require compassion and concern for fellow Israelites and citizens as brothers. The laws extend even to those who are poor (15:1-11) or not directly known (22:1-4). See *NIDOTTE*, 1:345-48.

New Testament

Noun: ἀδελφός (*adelphos*), GK *81* (S *80*) 343x. *adelphos* ("brother") has a wide range of uses in the NT; a closely related word (*adelphē*) means "sister." (1) It denotes first of all a sibling from the same parents (Mt. 1:2, 11; 4:18, 21). Even Jesus had brothers and sisters (Mk. 6:3), though some argue that these are step-brothers and step-sisters or close relatives (such as cousins). Paul, however, understands James, the head of the Jerusalem church, to be Jesus' brother (Gal. 1:19).

(2) *adelphos* can also refer to a fellow member or an associate of a person. Under this definition, three nuances emerge. (a) This brother can be one who shares a belief system. Jesus points to his disciples and says, "Whoever does the will of my Father who is in heaven, he is my *brother* and sister and mother" (Mt. 12:50). This usage of *adelphos* to describe one person's spiritual relationship with another person carries over into the early church (Acts 6:3, 9:30; 10:23; Rom. 8:29; 1 Cor. 5:11; Eph. 6:23; 1 Tim. 6:2; Rev. 1:9; 12:10). *adelphos* thus indicates membership in the Christian community (Rom. 16:23; 1 Cor.

1:1, 16:12; 2 Cor. 1:1; Phil. 2:25; Col. 1:1, 4:7, 9; 1 Thess. 3:2; Phlm. 1; 1 Pet. 5:12; 2 Pet. 3:15). Since both men and women were involved in the early church, we must usually understand the plural of *adelphos* as "brothers and sisters."

(b) *adelphos* can indicate a person's ethnic relationship, somewhat like the English "compatriot" (Acts 2:29; 3:17, 21). These compatriots killed the Messiah in ignorance, not realizing his true identity.

(c) *adelphos* is sometimes used in the simple sense of *neighbor*, as in Mt. 5:22 ("Anyone who is angry with his brother") and Lk. 6:41–42 ("Why do you look at the speck that is in your brother's eye?").

One of the challenging areas of translation is how to handle the masculine form of this word, which sometimes is generic and includes both brothers and sisters. Sometimes its generic meaning is obvious, and translation philosophy will dictate whether to say "brother" or perhaps "brother and sister." For example, 1 Jn. 5:16: "If anyone sees his *brother* committing a sin not leading to death, he shall ask, and God will give him life" (ESV); "If you see a *Christian brother or sister* sinning in a way that does not lead to death, you should pray, and God will give that person life" (NLT); "If anyone sees his *fellow Christian* committing a sin not resulting in death, he should ask, and God will grant life to the person" (NET). Other times it is more difficult and hence more interpretive, such as in Jas. 3:1: "Not many of you should presume to be teachers, my *brothers*" (NIV); "Dear *brothers and sisters*, not many of you should become teachers in the church" (NLT). See *NIDNTT-A*, 15-16.

BUILD (UP)

Old Testament

Verb: בָּנָה (*bānâ*), GK 1215 (S 1129), 377x. *bānâ* means "to build" or "to fashion."

(1) God is the first person in the Bible to "build" something. In Gen. 2:22, he takes a rib from Adam and "builds" or "fashions" it into a woman. Amos 9:6 says that God builds his upper chambers in the heavens, and the Psalms often speak of God's building Zion (Ps. 51:18; 102:16) and his temple (78:69).

(2) Two of the main objects in the OT said to be built are cities and altars. Gen. 11 depicts God's judgment on a proud people who, in defiance of God, build a city and a tower. The building of "high places" for idolatrous worship is also condemned (2 Ki. 17:9). The temple in Jerusalem is one of the central building projects in the Bible, and the story of David's desire to build it and of Solomon's successful completion of it is told at great length in Samuel, Kings, and Chronicles (cf. Ps. 89:4; 1 Ki. 6–9; 11:38; Amos 9:11).

Rebuilding is also a significant part of the prophetic promises of restoration to the land (cf. Isa. 58:12; 61:4), and *bānâ* occurs frequently in Ezra and Nehemiah, both of which deal with rebuilding Jerusalem after return from exile. The promise of the prophets is that the cities of Judah will be rebuilt after exile (Jer. 1:10; cf. 42:10).

(3) The idea of "building" may be used metaphorically in the OT. In Gen. 16:2 and 30:3, Sarah thinks she will be "built up" through Hagar's child. The same sense appears in Deut. 25:9, where the laws of levirate marriage dictate that a man should "build up" the house of his dead brother through impregnating his widow with a child. In 1 Sam. 2.35, God promises to build an enduring house for his faithful priest, and in 2 Sam. 7:27 God promises to build a house for David. Here again, God's activity of "building" is a metaphor for his giving of many descendants. In Ps. 28:5, building up and tearing down is used metaphorically for God's blessing or cursing of people. See *NIDOTTE*, 1.677-79.

New Testament

Verb: κατασκευάζω (*kataskeuazō*), GK *2941* (S *2680*), 11x. The basic meaning of *kataskeuazō* concerns preparation (e.g., Mt. 11:10), although the vast majority of the NT usage means to build something. In Heb. 3:3 Jesus is pictured as greater than

Moses, "just as *the builder* of a house has greater honor than the house itself." God is the architect of the covenants (3:4, "God is the *builder* of everything"), of which Christ is both the fulfillment and hope. The arrangement of the furniture in the Tent of Meeting was "set up" as a shadow of the Holy Place in heaven (9:2), "arranged" for atonement and worship (9:6) and prefiguring the work of Christ. Similarly, Noah is pictured as preparing for the future saving work of God (11:7, "Noah ... built an ark"; cf. 1 Pet. 3:20). Noah's building the ark depicts both divine sovereignty and human responsibility in the unfolding drama of salvation. See *NIDNTT-A*, 296.

Verb: οἰκοδομέω (*oikodomeō*), GK *3868* (S *3618*), 40x. In the gospels *oikodomeō* often has the normal meaning of building a physical structure, such as a house (Mt. 7:24, 26), watchtower (21:33), tomb (Mt. 23:29), town (Lk. 4:29), synagogue (7:5), or barn (12:18). However, it can also refer to Jesus' "rebuilding" of his own body through resurrection (Jn. 2:19–22) and to his "building" of his church (Mt. 16:18).

This latter use may explain the striking development of the word in Acts and the rest of the NT: *oikodomeō* becomes a significant metaphor for the mutual encouragement and strengthening of the people of God. Acts 9:31 notes that the early church was "built up" or "strengthened" by the Holy Spirit (cf. 20:32). Paul describes his own ministry as one of "building" (Rom. 15:20). In 1 Cor. 3 and 2 Cor. 7 Paul actually conceives of himself as master builder building the church, which is a temple of God (cf. 1 Pet. 2:5). However, though Paul lays the foundation, he does not see himself alone in this occupation of building. His concern is that Christians will building upon the foundation with proper materials and will "build up" their fellow believers in love (1 Cor. 8:1; 10:23; 14:4, 17; 1 Thess. 5:11). The KJV translation "edify" is a good one for *oikodomeō* since "edify" itself means to "build up." See *NIDNTT-A*, 402-3.

BUILDING (UP)

New Testament

Noun: οἰκοδομή (*oikodomē*), GK *3869* (S *3619*), 18x. *oikodomē* can mean either "a building" or "building up, edification." In other words, it can refer to a physical structure or to the process of building the structure. The former sense is found in Mk. 13:1–2, where Jesus' disciples marvel at the temple buildings (cf. Mt. 24:1). In 1 Cor. 3:19, Paul refers to the Corinthian church as God's "building," and in 2 Cor. 5:1 he calls the resurrection body a "building from God." Eph. 2:21 further develops the metaphor that God's people are a temple-building.

The latter sense of "building up" or edifying is frequent in the NT. Paul claims that God has given him authority to build up the church (2 Cor. 10:8; 13:10) and says that everything he does is for the "edification" of the Corinthian church (2 Cor. 12:19). Paul longs for all believers to seek in all they do to build up their fellow believers (Rom. 14:19; 15:2; 1 Cor. 14:3, 5, 12, 26). Though God gifts leaders to build up his people (Eph. 4:12), he wants *all* Christians to build up other believers through love (Eph. 4:16, 29). See *NIDNTT-A*, 402-403.*

BULL

Old Testament

Noun: בָּקָר (*bāqār*), GK 1330 (S 1241), 183x. *bāqār* refers to domesticated cattle (e.g., bulls, cows, and calves). In the ancient world, cattle were a measure of one's wealth. Larger cattle were deemed more valuable than smaller animals. See *cattle*.

Noun: פַּר (*par*), GK 7228 (S 6499), 133x. Generally translated "bull," a *par* is the prominent type of male bovine used for sacrifice, especially for the burnt offering to atone for sin in general (Num. 7), the sin offering to atone for unintentional sins (Exod. 29:14; but cf. Lev. 4:1–3 with 4:27–28, 32), and the peace offering for continual fellowship with God (Exod. 24:5). In Lev. 16:11 the *par* is used as the sacrificial animal for the sin offering of the high priest and his family on the Day of Atonement. Only after this sacrifice can he go before the Lord on behalf of the people by sacrificing one goat for the sin offering and sending a second goat—laden with the confessed sins of Israel—into the desert as the scapegoat. See *NIDOTTE*, 3:670-72.

Noun: שׁוֹר (*šôr*), GK 8802 (S 7794), 79x. Technically, *šôr* may refer to a male or female cow, but in the OT it primarily refers to the bull (though see Lev. 22:28). These bulls are valuable primarily because of their value in work (Deut. 15:19; 22:10). Although they can become valuable sources of meat (Lev. 14:4; 22:28; 1 Sam. 14:34), the *šôr* is more of a "work-horse," while another type of bull (*par*) is the animal most often used for sacrifice. See *NIDOTTE*, 4.72-73 (also see 3:670-72).

BURN

Old Testament

Verb: בָּעַר (*bāʿar*), GK 1277 (S 1197), 60x. Generally translated "to burn, light a fire, flare up, set ablaze, consume with fire," *bāʿar* can refer to a literal burning of fire or to a figurative "burning," be it of desire or anger.

(1) In many contexts *bāʿar* refers to a literal lighting or burning of fire (Exod. 3:2–3; 22:5; Lev. 6:5; Num. 11:1, 3; Deut. 4:11; 5:23; 9:15; Jdg. 15:5; Ezek. 5:2). God commands Israel not to light a fire on the Sabbath day (Exod. 35:3).

(2) Often *bāʿar* is used figuratively for the enlivening of personal emotion. (a) It can refer to a person's burning desire to speak, as when the psalmist declares, "My heart grew hot within me, and as I meditated, the fire "burned"; then I spoke with my tongue" (Ps. 39:3; cf. Jer. 20:9). In a similar way, *bāʿar* may also be used to describe the heightening of human passion or emotion in a negative sense. For instance, Hosea speaks of the faltering moral condition in Israel and Judah: "They are all adulterers, burning like an oven. ... Their passion smolders all night; in the morning it *blazes* like a flaming fire" (Hos. 7:4, 6; cf. Isa. 9:18).

(b) *bāʿar* can also be used figuratively of the enflaming of God's wrath in response to those who rebel against his rule. The prophets speak of the Lord's righteous anger in this way: "See, the Name of the LORD comes from afar, with *burning* anger and dense clouds of smoke; his lips are full of wrath, and his tongue is a consuming fire" (Isa. 30:27; cf. 2 Sam. 22:9; Ps. 18:8; Jer. 4:4; Lam. 2:3). The psalmist inquires how long the Lord's anger will burn before his people are restored (Ps. 79.5; 89.46), but he also declares his persevering trust in God's goodness (Ps. 79:13). Significantly, in the first of the royal psalms (Ps. 2:12), God's people are instructed to "Kiss [i.e., pay homage to] the Son, lest he be angry and you be destroyed in your way, for his wrath *can flare up* in a moment. Blessed are all who take refuge in him." It is those who "kiss the Son" by acknowledging his Lordship who will not come to ruin but will instead be upheld by his goodness. See *NIDOTTE*, 1:683-90.

Verb: חָרָה (*ḥārâ*), GK 3013 (S 2734), 93x. *ḥārâ* literally means "to burn," but it is used almost exclusively in a figurative sense for enflamed rage (i.e., "to burn with anger"). See *angry*.

Verb: שָׂרַף (*śārap*), GK 8596 (S 8313), 117x. The *śārap* is one of many Heb. words meaning "to burn." It is always used of a literal burning, such as the burning of idols (Exod. 32:20), cities (Jos. 6:24), a door (Jos. 9:52), a scroll (Jer. 36:27–29, 32), and chariots (Jos. 11:6). Burning was often used as a tactic in war, especially if there was any fear that a people might return to a city to live (Jos. 6:24; Jdg. 9:52; 2 Ki. 25:9).

Unlike *qāṭar*, *śārap* is rarely used for the "burning" of sacrifices, although it is used in Lev. 4:12 when the Lord commands Moses to burn the remains of a bull sacrificed as a sin offering. The burning of a red heifer was intended to produce ashes for purification (Lev. 19:5, 8). Moreover, this term is used for pagan ceremonies, as when sons were sacrificed to Molech (Jer. 7:31; 19:5).

Verb: קָטַר (*qāṭar*), GK 7787 (S 6999),

115x. *qāṭar* means "to burn" and is used almost exclusively in a sacrificial context (the only exception is Song 3:6). This word is used either of burning incense (Exod. 30:7–8) or of offering a variety of other sacrifices to the Lord (29:13; Lev. 1:9; 2:2; 3:5; 4:10; 7:5). God's law states clearly that only the priests are allowed to burn incense and other sacrifices before the Lord (Num. 16:40; 1 Chr. 23:13).

All too often in the history of God's people, however, they burn their own incense on high places rather than going to the temple (2 Ki. 12:3; 14:4; 15:4) or even burn incense to foreign gods (1 Ki. 22:43: Jer. 1:16; 44:3, 5; Hos. 2:15). Even Solomon is criticized for burning incense on the high places (1 Ki. 3:3). King Uzziah becomes a leper when he attempts to enter "the temple of the LORD to *burn incense* on the altar of incense" (2 Chr. 26:16, 18–19). See *NIDOTTE*, 3:913–16.

New Testament

Verb: καίω (*kaiō*), GK *2794* (S *2545*), 11x. *kaiō* means "to burn." It can mean "to light" a lamp, but the emphasis in this term is on keeping something burning (Mt. 5:15; Lk. 12:35). It can be used figuratively to refer to an emotional experience (e.g., "burning hearts," Lk. 24:32). *kaiō* can also have the connotation of being completely consumed, "to burn up," such as those who do not remain in Christ are like dried up branches that are thrown into the fire and "consumed" (Jn. 15:6). John refers to "the lake that burns with fire and sulfur" (Rev. 19:20; 21:8).

Verb: κατακαίω (*katakaiō*), GK *2876* (S *2618*), 12x. *katakaiō* means "to burn," with the implication of being completely consumed. It is a compound word; *kata* (GK *2848*) is an emphatic form that intensifies the more general *kaiō* (GK *2794*), "to burn." This verb is often associated with the judgment that will take place at the end of the age. The wheat will be gathered but the chaff "will be burned with unquenchable fire" (Mt. 3:12; cf. 13:30, 40). On the last day, the quality of a Christian's work will be tested through fire; those works not based on sound doctrine will be "burned up" (1 Cor. 3:15). Fire is also used as a symbol for God's judgment in Rev. 8:7; 17:16; 18:8.

BURNT OFFERING

Old Testament

Noun: עֹלָה (*ʿōlâ*), GK 6592 (S 5930), 286x. *ʿōlâ* is derived from the verb *ʿālâ*, which means "to go up." Presumably, this is related to the way the smoke of the burnt offering goes up as a fragrance before God (Lev. 1:9, 13, 17). Specifically, *ʿōlâ* refers to one of the five regular offerings prescribed in Leviticus (1:1–17). This offering is unique in that it is entirely consumed by fire (sometimes it is called "the holocaust," which means "entirely burned") whereas only a portion of the other offerings is burned. Bulls, male sheep and goats, or birds can be used for burnt offerings. These animals must be without blemish. After they are killed, their blood is sprinkled against the altar and the entire animal is burned on the altar. Part of the purpose of this offering is "to make atonement for" the person who is offering the animal (1:4; cf. also 9:7). Note too that on the Day of Atonement, some of the sacrifices offered are "burnt offerings" (16:3, 5, 24), so the burnt offering plays an important role in purging sin from the nation.

The first reference to *ʿōlâ* appears in Gen. 8:20, where Noah offers burnt offerings to God after the flood. Abraham is about to offer Isaac as a "burnt offering" until God substitutes a ram (22:13). Jephthah vows to make a burnt offering of whatever comes out first to meet him from battle (Jdg. 11:31). His daughter comes out to meet him and it is said that he does as he has vowed (11:39), though the exact implication of his vow is debated.

It is important to note that burnt offerings in and of themselves as rituals do not please the Lord (see, e.g., Ps. 50:7–11; Isa. 1:11; Jer. 6:20). God's acceptance of such offerings is linked with whether the offerer is the kind of person whom the Lord accepts. The true sacrifices of God are "a broken spirit" and "a contrite heart" (Ps.

51:17). At times the wickedness of the whole nation makes the entire sacrificial system unacceptable (see Jer. 6:20; Amos 5:22).

BURY

Old Testament

Verb: קָבַר (*qābar*), GK 7699 (S 6912), 133x. *qābar* is most naturally translated "to bury" and is always used in reference to human beings.

In the OT, a proper burial was viewed as a form of honor and divine blessing (see *bury*). Bodies were buried in caves (Gen. 25:9), graves (Gen. 50:1), and sepulchers (Jdg. 8:32). In the ancient world, not to be buried was considered a shameful thing (cf. 2 Ki. 9:10; Jer. 8:2; 16:4, 6). In fact, in the Bible we see a sort of hierarchy of burial types; the most desirable was burial in the family tomb (2 Ki. 15:7, 38). Of lesser value was burial in any tomb (e.g., 1 Ki. 13:29–31), being covered over with stones in a pit (cf. 2 Sam. 18:17), and the least desirable was no burial at all but rather being exposed to scavenger birds and animals (cf. Deut. 28:26; Jer. 16:4).

One law revealed by God that governed burial had implications for Jesus' caretakers, "If a man … is put to death and his body is hung on a tree, you must not leave his body on the tree overnight. Be sure to him on that same day, because anyone who is hung on a tree is under God's curse" (Deut. 21:22–23; see Gal. 3:13). See *NIDOTTE*, 3:865–68.

New Testament

Verb: θάπτω (*thaptō*), GK *2507* (S *2290*), 11x. *thaptō* means simply "to bury." In the NT, this term is used exclusively for the burial of the dead (Mt. 8:21, 22; 14:12; Lk. 9:59, 60; 16:22; Acts 2:29; 5:6, 9, 10). That Jesus was buried after his death became a standard part of the earliest gospel traditions handed down by the apostles: "For what I received I passed on to you as of first importance: that Christ died for our sins according to the Scriptures, that he *was buried*, that he was raised on the third day according to the Scriptures" (1 Cor. 15:4). See *NIDNTT-A*, 239.*

BUY

Old Testament

Verb: קָנָה (*qānâ*), GK 7864 and 7865 (S 7069), 91x. *qānâ* appears to bear two distinct meanings in the OT: "to buy, purchase, redeem," and also "to create" (see *create*).

qānâ is most often found in contexts where an acquisition is made. The word is used to refer to the purchase of land (Gen. 25:10; 33:19; 47:20; 2 Sam. 24:21–24; Jer. 32:43; Ruth 4:5), supplies (2 Ki. 12:12; 2 Chr. 34:11), and slaves (Gen. 39:1; Exod. 21:2; Lev. 25:44–45). *qānâ* is also used in redemptive contexts, such as Exod. 15:13, "In your unfailing love you will lead the people you have *redeemed*" (i.e., "purchased"). Asaph writes, "Remember the people you *purchased* of old, the tribe of your inheritance, whom you redeemed—Mount Zion, where you dwelt" (Ps. 74:2). See *NIDOTTE*, 3:940–42.

New Testament

Verb: ἀγοράζω (*agorazō*), GK *60* (S *59*), 30x. The word means (lit.) "to buy, purchase something in the *agora*" (i.e., the marketplace). In the NT, however, it usually means to buy in general, regardless of the location. Thus, *agorazō* is most often used in the ordinary commercial sense to describe the purchase of some commodity, such as a field (Mt. 13:44; 27:7), a precious pearl (13:46), food (14:15), oil (25:9–10), cloth (Mk. 15:46), spices (16:1), or oxen (Lk. 14:19). In a few NT uses, *agorazō* is also used metaphorically to describe the redemption of Christians: as a master pays for a slave, so Christ's blood has paid for the sin of those who believe in him, so that we "have been bought at a price" (1 Cor. 6:20; 7:23; cf. 2 Pet. 2:1; Rev. 5:9; 14:3–4). See *NIDNTT-A*, 12-13.

CALAMITY

Old Testament

Noun: רָעָה (*rāʿâ*), GK 8288 (S 7465), 354x. At the heart of *rāʿâ*, lies the idea of badness, whether physical or moral. When used in the physical sense, it is often translated "calamity, disaster, harm, trouble." See *evil*.

CALCULATE

Old Testament

Verb: חָשַׁב (*ḥāšab*), GK 3108 (S 2803), 124 x. *ḥāšab* is most often translated as "think" or "plan" (see *think, plan*). One use of this word is in reference to mathematical computations and can also be translated as "count," "calculate," and "value."

CALL

Old Testament

Verb: קָרָא (*qārā*ʾ), GK 7924 (S 7121), 739x. *qārā*ʾ is the most common verb in Heb. that means "to call, summon, proclaim." The basic meaning of this verb is to draw attention to oneself by using one's voice. It is often accompanied by a corresponding verb "to hear" or "to answer."

(1) The first use of this verb in the OT means "to call, name." "God *called* the light 'day' and the darkness 'night'" (Gen. 1:5). In Gen. 2:19–20, Adam "names" the animals, and in 2:23, he "calls" Eve "woman." And after Adam and Eve sin, "God *called* to the man, 'Where are you?'" (3:9). These uses illustrate some of the most common meanings of *qārā*ʾ.

(2) One of the more important uses of *qārā*ʾ is with God as the subject, calling various people into his service. God calls Abraham into his service (see Isa. 51:2), Israel (41:9; 42:1), Cyrus (45:3), and Eliakim (22:20). And when he calls someone, he expects that person to answer to his call; anything less is disobedience. This use can be compared to the contemporary notion of a person being called by God to teach and preach his Word.

(3) Conversely, *qārā*ʾ is also often used of people calling on the Lord. About the time of the birth of Seth, people "began *to call* on the name of the Lord" (Gen. 4:26). When Abraham left his home country, traveled to Canaan, and built an altar, he "*called* on the name of the Lord" (12:8). A frequent comment in the Psalms is "I call(ed) on you, O God" (e.g., Ps. 17:6; 18:3, 6; 30:8; 55:16). For the most part, the Lord responds to these verbal requests, though at times a psalmist may feel silence from the Lord (e.g., 22:2). When people do not call on the name of the Lord, it concerns him deeply (e.g., Isa. 43:22).

(4) In the prophets, *qārā*ʾ is an expression used for a servant of God who "proclaims" his will (e.g., 1 Ki. 13:32; Isa. 40:2; 58:1; Jer. 2:2; 11:6; Zech. 1:14). Jonah, for example, was called by God to "go to the great city of Nineveh and *preach* against it" (Jon. 1:2). After his attempt to run away, this is precisely what Jonah does do (3:2). See *NIDOTTE*, 3:971–74.

New Testament

Verb: βοάω (*boaō*), GK *1066* (S *994*), 12x. *boaō* means "to cry out, call loudly." Each of the gospels quotes at least part of Isa. 40:3 to describe John: "A voice of one *calling* in the desert, 'Prepare the way of the Lord, make straight paths for him.'" (Mt. 3:3; Mk. 1:3; Lk. 3:4; Jn. 1:23). These uses recall the idea of a herald making an announcement (also Acts 17:6; possibly 25:24). In Gal. 4:27, in a quote from Isa. 54:1, *boaō* heralds good news, but the verb also includes the idea of shouting in joyful exuberance. A similar use but with fear instead of joy is the account of Philip in Samaria, when evil spirits "shrieked" as they came out of many people (Acts 8:3).

While the previous occurrences describe a general announcement or cry, the following uses of *boaō* have a specific audience in mind. Twice citizens "call out" or "complain" to a public official (Acts 17:6; 25:24). Elsewhere *boaō* denotes begging or pleading. The object of the pleading is God or Jesus in four of these occurrences. For example, Jesus "cries out" to God on the cross, saying, "My God, my God, why have you forsaken me" (Mk. 15:34, a quote from Ps. 22:1). In Lk. 9:38 and 18:38 Jesus hears the cry of a person and performs a miracle for them. Similarly, in Lk. 18:7 Jesus says that God will listen to his chosen ones who "cry out" to him. The common thread in these examples is that God listens when people cry out to him. Christians need not offer up expertly composed and theologically insightful prayers in order to be heard; rather, we simply need to cry out to our Father. As the psalmist says of God, "O you who hears prayer" (Ps. 65:2). See *NIDNTT-A*, 96-97.

Verb: ἐπικαλέω (*epikaleō*), GK *2126* (S *1941*), 30x. *epikaleō* is a compound verb formed from the preposition *epi* ("on, upon") and the verb *kaleō* ("to call"). The resulting verb means "to call on someone" or even "to appeal to someone for help." The majority of occurrences fall within this range.

Peter in his Pentecost message quotes from the prophet Joel: "Everyone who *calls on* the name of the Lord will be saved" (Acts 2:21; see also 9:14, 21; 22:16; Rom. 10:12; 2 Tim. 2:22). Some NT books use this verb to express the idea of calling on Jesus with the idiomatic phrase "*call(s) on* the name of the Lord" (Rom. 10:13; 1 Cor. 1:12). Jesus is the addressee when *epikaleō* is used in the sense of praying (Acts 7:59). This verb is also used of Paul calling on God as his witness (2 Cor. 1:23) and the act of Christians calling on God the Father (1 Pet. 1:17). When Paul appeals his imprisonment to Caesar, he uses this verb (Acts 25:11, 12, 21, 25; 26:32; 28:19).

A special use of *epikaleō* in the passive is to identify someone: "Joseph *called* Barsabbas" (Acts 1:23); "John also *called* Mark" (12:12). This is the case in Hebrews, which states that "God is not ashamed *to be called* their God" (Heb. 11:16), and also, "my name [the Lord] *is called on* them" (i.e., "they are called by my name"; Acts 15:17; also Jas. 2:7). See *NIDNTT-A*, 285-86.

Verb: καλέω (*kaleō*), GK *2813* (S *2564*), 148x. *kaleō* means "to call, invite, summon." It is used mainly in three ways in the NT. (1) *kaleō* can express the ordinary idea of an audible call to someone to get their attention or invite a person to join a group. This usage is particularly prevalent in narrative literature. Herod "called" the Magi to himself (Mt. 2:7). Mark writes that Jesus' mother and brothers "called him" to meet with them (Mk. 3:31). Luke writes of a Pharisee who "invited" Jesus to dine with him (Lk. 7:39). In the parable of the dinner guests, *kaleō* is used in its participial form to denote the dinner guests, "those who were called" (Lk. 14:7ff.).

(2) The second notion is that of God or Jesus doing the calling. This moves from the simple idea of inviting or summoning to a more theological meaning of *kaleō*. This idea is first seen when Matthew quotes Hos. 11:1, where God says, "Out of Egypt I called my son" (Mt. 2:15). When Jesus began his ministry, he "called" his disciples (4:21; Mk. 1:20). This was a call to physically come to Jesus, but the more important element was a spiritual call, which the disciples heeded. The spiritual sense of calling is clear in Jesus' statement, "I did not come to *call* the righteous, but sinners" (Mk. 2:17; Lk. 5:32). While the idea of spiritual calling is not prevalent in the gospels and Acts, it is highly developed in Paul's writings. When God calls, it is a call that roots in predestination and ends in glorification (Rom. 8:29–30; 1 Pet. 5:10). God calls us by his grace (Gal. 1:6) into his fellowship (1 Cor. 1:9). But his calling is not only to salvation; it is also to a life of serving him and our fellow believers (7:15; Eph. 4:1, 4; 1 Thess. 2:12; 4:7; 2 Tim. 1:9).

(3) An additional, relatively frequent use of *kaleō* is to express the idea of naming something, e.g., the angel of Lord told Zechariah that his son would be "called" John, and he told Joseph that Mary's baby would be "called" Jesus (Lk. 1:13, 31). See *NIDNTT-A*, 285-86.

Verb: λέγω (*legō*), GK *3306* (S *3004*, *2036*, *2046*), 2353x. Usually translated as "say," *legō* sometimes has the notion of "to call" someone by some specific name or attribute. See *say*.

Verb: φονέω (*phoneō*), GK *5888* (S *5455*), 43x. *phoneō* means "to call out, call to, make a noise." Several times in the NT it is used for calling out a question (Acts 10:18) or, more commonly, a statement or command. For example, Jesus "cried out" on the cross, "My God, My God, why have you forsaken me" (Mt. 27:47), and "Father, into your hands I commit my spirit" (Lk. 23:46). Paul "called out" to the jailer, "Don't harm yourself, we are all here" (Acts 16:28). Luke uses it when Jesus "called out" to a crowd, "he who has ears to hear, let him hear" (Lk. 8:8). These last two examples are somewhere between an interjection and a command. Elsewhere *phoneō* occurs in the context of more clear-cut commands, as when Jesus commands a dead girl to rise (Lk. 8:54) and an angel commands the one with the sickle to reap the earth's harvest (Rev. 14:18).

An additional nuance of *phoneō* is to "summon, invite" others. This meaning occurs frequently in the NT; e.g., "do not *invite*" (Lk. 14:12), he "called the bridegroom" aside (Jn. 2:9), and Cornelius "called/summoned" two of his servants and a devout soldier (Acts 10:7; cf. also Mk. 9:35; 10:49; Lk. 16:2; 19:15).

Lastly, the meaning of *phoneō* is so broad that in addition to its use with human subjects, it is also used of a cock "crowing" (Mt. 26:34, 74, 75; Mk. 14:30, 72; Lk. 22:34, 60, 61; Jn. 13:38) and of an evil spirit "shrieking" as it comes out of a person (Mk. 1:26). See *NIDNTT-A*, 597.

CALL ON

New Testament

Verb: ἐπικαλέω (*epikaleō*), GK *2126* (S *1941*), 30x. *epikaleō* means "to call on someone" or even "to appeal to someone for help." See *call*.

CALL OUT

Old Testament

Verb: זָעַק (*zāʿaq*), GK 2410 (S 2199), 73x. *zāʿaq* means "to cry out, call out, summon," often to the Lord. See *cry out*.

CALLED

New Testament

Adjective: κλητός (*klētos*), GK *3105* (S *2822*), 10x. This adjective is part of the same word group as the verb *kaleō* (see *call*). It denotes someone or something that has been called. All of its uses in the NT denote someone who has been called by God. "You are called of Jesus Christ" (Rom. 1:6); "to those who have been called" (Jude 1); "with him will be the called, chosen, and faithful" (Rev. 17:14; also Mt. 22:14; Rom. 1:7; 8:28; 1 Cor. 1.2; 1:24). The only use of this adjective in a more specific context is to describe Paul as one "called" to be an apostle (Rom. 1:1; 1 Cor. 1:1). See *NIDNTT-A*, 285-86.*

CALLING

New Testament

Noun: κλῆσις (*klēsis*), GK *3104* (S *2821*), 11x. This noun belongs to the group of words related to the verb *kaleō* (see *call*). *klēsis* is a call or calling. All of its occurrences refer to the action that God takes to summon people to himself. This is explicitly the case when Paul writes about "the *calling* of God" (Rom. 11:29; Phil. 3:14), "his (God's) *calling*" (Eph. 1:18; 2 Thess. 1:11; also 2 Pet. 1:10), and "holy *calling*" (2 Tim. 1:9; cf. Heb. 3:11). Elsewhere, *klēsis* is used without modifiers to describe God's calling in the life of a Christian. Good examples of this are the commands to "remain in the *calling* in which you were called [*kaleō*]" (1 Cor. 7:20), and to "walk in a manner worthy of your *calling*" (Eph. 4:1, 4; also 1 Cor. 1: 26). See *NIDNTT-A*, 285-86.*

CALVARY

See *skull*.

CAMEL

Old Testament

Noun: גָּמָל (*gāmāl*), GK 1695 (S 1581), 54x. This noun means "camel." The camel is especially suited for life in dry and sparse climates. This made it an ideal beast of burden and essential for developing long-distance trade routes (Gen. 37:25; cf. 1 Ki. 10:2). *gāmāl* were used for transportation (Gen. 24:61–64; Isa. 21:7; 30:6) as well as for warfare. They were even known for their speed (1 Sam. 30:17). They were kept as livestock and constituted an important token of wealth (Gen. 12:16; 30:43; Job 1:3; 42:12), both because they were intrinsically valuable and because they were typically used to transport one's possessions (Gen. 24:10, 32; Jdg. 8:21, 26; 2 Chr. 9:1).

The camel plays an important role in the story of Abraham's procuring of a daughter for Isaac (Gen. 24:10–64). They also served to display Abraham's wealth and to test Rebekah's character. Watering these animals was hard work. The effect of God's curse upon the camels of the Egyptians indicates both the thoroughness of his judgment (1 Sam. 15:3) as well as the fact that the curse affected the national economy (Exod. 9:3; cf. Zech. 14:14–15). See *NIDOTTE*, 1:873-74.

New Testament

Noun: κάλημος (*kalēmos*), GK *2823* (S *2574*), 6x. *kalēmos* means "camel." All uses of this word occur in the gospels. John the Baptist wore clothes made of "camel's hair" (Mt. 3:4; Mk. 1:6). In Mt. 19:24; Mk. 10:25; Lk. 18:25, Jesus says that "it is easier for a *camel* to go through the eye of a needle than for a rich man to enter the kingdom of God." This is simply hyperbole on the part of Jesus to stress how easy it is for those who are wealthy to cling to their riches. There is no small door in the city gates through which a camel may squeeze; that is religious "urban myth." Finally, Jesus accuses the Pharisees of straining out a gnat but swallowing a camel—that is, they are quick to worry about the minutiae of the law of God but ignore the weightier matters, like "justice, mercy and faithfulness" (Mt. 23:24).

CAMP

Old Testament

Verb: חָנָה (*ḥānâ*), GK 2837 (S 2583), 143x. *ḥānâ* generally means "to pitch camp, set up camp, encamp."

(1) This verb can denote the encamping of military units (Jdg. 11:20) or of nomadic peoples, such as the patriarchs. "So Isaac moved away from there and *encamped* in the Valley of Gerar and settled there" (Gen. 26:17). In Num. alone the verb occurs 74x, the high frequency arising from the attention given to the travels of God's people from place to place in the wilderness. Multiple factors come into play in choosing a campsite, including availability of water (Jos. 11:5) and lines of natural defense to provide protection (1 Sam. 26:3). For the Israelites in the wilderness, however, they set up camp wherever the cloud of God comes to rest (Num. 9:15–22).

During Israel's journey to the promised land, their camp is organized in a square, with the tabernacle in the center (cf. Num. 1:47–2:34; 3:14–16; 10:11–28). Three tribes are arranged on each of the four sides of the tabernacle, with special positioning given to the Levites (those who minister to God). The tabernacle serves as the focal point of the camp, thus giving due stress to the presence and holiness of God in their midst. Significantly, all ceremonially unclean and ritually impure individuals are kept "outside of the camp" so as to maintain a level of holiness, a principle similar to Paul's urging the Corinthians to remain pure because they are the temple of God (1 Cor. 6:19).

(2) In several texts, *ḥānâ* is used metaphorically. The prophet Nahum pictures the guardsmen of Nineveh as locusts "encamped" on stone walls for protection against the cold of the night (Nah. 3:17). In a different context, the encroaching evening is portrayed as the day settling down (lit., "encamping") for the night (Jdg. 19:9). See *NIDOTTE*, 2:192-96.

Noun: מַחֲנֶה (*maḥ^{a}neh*), GK 4722 (S 4264), 215x. Deriving from the verb *ḥānâ*, "to set up a camp, encamp," *maḥ^{a}neh* means "camp." It usually signifies a temporary residence composed of tents (Gen. 32:1), but it can also refer to the group of individuals encamped together, whether military or civilian. In the OT, the term most frequently occurs in the narratives associated with the period prior to Israel's settlement in Canaan.

(1) *maḥ^{a}neh* is most often associated with a war camp, whether of Israel (Jos. 9:6; 2 Sam. 1:2; 2 Ki. 3:24) or of other nations (Jdg. 7:9, 11, 21; 1 Sam. 14:21). *maḥ^{a}neh* can also carry the meaning of a war camp on the move, in other words, an army (1 Sam. 17:1; 28:1; 2 Ki. 3:9). It can even be defined as a battlefront (1 Ki. 22:34). In view of the surpassing power

and faithfulness of God, the psalmist declares, "Though an *army* encamp against me, my heart will not fear; though war arise against me, yet I will be confident" (Ps. 27:3).

The motif of a war camp also describes the living conditions of the Israelites as they travel from Egypt to Canaan under the direction of God. Along with the glory cloud is the ark of the covenant and the tabernacle, all of which represent the presence and power of the God of war in their midst (cf. Num. 10:35). Consequently, the *maḥ*[a]*neh* has to be kept holy, that is, set apart, and no ceremonially unclean or ritually impure individual can dwell within the camp (e.g., Num. 5:2). So symbolically, to be "outside the camp" is to be distant from God.

(2) There are a few instances where *maḥ*[a]*neh* refers to the camp of God's heavenly army. When Jacob sees the messengers of God, he declares, "This is the *camp* of God!" and then names the place Mahanaim ("two camps") (Gen. 32:2). Similarly, Joel 2:11 declares, "The LORD utters his voice before his army, for his *forces* are exceedingly great." This latter reference is designed to stress the extent to which God's wrath will be displayed during the great Day of the Lord.

(3) Lastly, *maḥ*[a]*neh* may possibly be found in the Song 6:13, where the singers proclaim, "Come back, come back, O Shulammite; come back, come back, that we may gaze on you! Why would you gaze on the Shulammite as on the dance of *maḥ*[a]*nāyim*?" The NIV translates *maḥ*[a]*nāyim* as the place name "Mahanaim," but others suggests the form is merely the dual of *maḥ*[a]*neh* and that the phrase means "the dance of two war camps." In this latter interpretation, the point of the metaphor would be that the Shulammite spellbinds her watchers in the same way one is awed by the movement of two armies engaged in battle. See *NIDOTTE*, 2:918-19.

New Testament

Noun: παρεμβολή (*parembole*), GK *4213* (S *3925*), 10x. *parembolē* is a barracks or fortified camp. In Acts, it refers to the barracks or headquarters of the Roman troops in Jerusalem (see *barracks*).

More importantly, the author of Hebrews uses *parembolē* in the phrase "outside the camp" to identify the believer with Christ in his rejection by the Jews. He first refers to the sin offering, which was to be burned outside the Israelite camp (13:11), and compares this to Jesus' being crucified "outside the gate in order to sanctify the people through his own blood" (cf. 13:12). Therefore, he exhorts his audience to "go to [Christ] outside the camp, bearing abuse for him" (13:13). Camp is also used figuratively in Hebrews to refer to the people in an armed camp; thus, an army (11:34).

Finally, John pictures the church as "the *camp* of God's people, the city he loves." Though it is surrounded by an innumerable multitude of enemies, God protects it by consuming all of the enemies with fire from heaven (Rev. 20:9). See *NIDNTT-A*, 481-83.*

CAN

New Testament

Verb: δύναμαι (*dynamai*), GK *1538* (S *1410*), 210x. *dynamai* communicates ability or capability of doing something.

(1) God *can* do whatever he pleases. He is able to raise up children for Abraham from stones if he wants to (Mt. 3:9). No one is able to do what Jesus does unless God is with him (Jn. 3:2; cf. 9:33). God is able to establish believers (Rom. 16:25; cf. Jude 24) and to do more abundantly than we ask or think (Eph. 3:20). Christ Jesus is able to subject all things to himself. God alone is able to save and destroy (Jas. 4:12; cf. Mt. 10:28).

(2) God also gives ability to his people to act through his power. He will not allow persons to be tempted beyond what they "are able" to bear, but with the temptation he will make a way out so that they "will be able" to endure (1 Cor. 10:13). Christians are to clothe themselves with the armor of God so that they will be able to

take a stand against the forces of evil arrayed against us (Eph. 6:11). Since Jesus suffered when he was tempted, he is able to help us as we are being tempted (Heb. 2:18). He is able to save to the uttermost those who come to God through him (7:25). The implanted word is able to save souls (Jas. 1:21).

(3) Often *dynamai* is accompanied with a negative. When it is, it communicates things that cannot (i.e., are not able to) happen. For example, unless people are born again from above, they are not able to enter the kingdom of God (Jn. 3:3, 5). People are not able to come to Jesus unless they are drawn by the Father (6:44). People are unable to make one hair white or black (Mt. 5:36). Those who are in the flesh and without the Spirit are not able to submit to the law (Rom. 8:7), nor can they please God (8:8). The natural man is not able to understand the things of the Spirit (1 Cor. 2:14). Good trees are not able to produce bad fruit, and vice versa (Mt. 7:18). No one is able to say that Jesus is Lord except by the Holy Spirit (1 Cor. 12:3). Jesus is not able to deny himself (2 Tim. 2:13). A city set on a hill cannot be hidden (Mt. 5:14). And, most important, nothing will ever be able to separate believers from the love of God that is revealed in Christ Jesus (Rom. 8:39). See *NIDNTT-A*, 154-55.

CANDLE, CANDLESTICK

New Testament

Noun: λύχνος (*lychnos*), GK *3394* (S *3088*), 14x

Noun: λυχνία (*lychnia*), GK *3393* (S *3087*), 12x. These two words are used for a lamp or light (*lychnos*) and the implement (*lychnia*) on which the lamp is placed. See *lamp, lampstand.*

CAPABILITY

Old Testament

Noun: חַיִל (*ḥayil*), GK 2657 (S 2428), 246x. The basic sense of *ḥayil* is "power, strength, or capability." It is also used to describe persons who have a special skill or ability. In Gen. 47:6, Pharaoh asks Joseph to put in charge of his livestock men of *ḥayil* ("men of special ability") from among the Israelites. See *strength.*

CAPSTONE

New Testament

Noun: γωνία (*gōnia*), GK *1224* (S *1137*), 9x. *gōnia* essentially means "corner" and refers to the inside or outside "corner" of a structure. See *corner.*

CAPTAIN

See *commander.*

CAPTURE

Old Testament

Verb: לָכַד (*lākad*), GK 4334 (S 3920), 121x. *lākad* generally means "to capture, seize, take captive." It can be used actively (i.e., "to catch, capture," Num. 21:32; Deut. 2:34; Jos. 10:42; Jdg. 7:24; 15:4; Ps. 35:8; Amos 3:4, 5), passively (i.e., "to be seized," 1 Ki. 16:18; Isa. 23:13; Jer. 6:11; 38:28; 48:1, 41; 51:56; Ezek. 7:26), or reflectively (i.e., "to cling to each other," Job 38:30; 41:17).

(1) In the OT, *lākad* is most often associated with the capturing and/or seizing involved in military action. The verb is used of the taking of cities (Jos. 8:21), territory (Dan. 11:8), and captives (Jdg. 7:25; 8:12; 2 Sam. 8:4). In the context of God's war of judgment, the setting apart of the Israelite Achan is also viewed as a capturing of the guilty (Jos. 7:14–18).

(2) In other contexts, sin is pictured as a net that "entangles" (*lākad*) its prey. The nations are caught in the trap that they themselves set (Ps. 9:15), and the wicked will be caught and kept for divine judgment (Isa. 8:15; 24:18). Prov. 5:22 states plainly the ultimate plight of man without God: "His own iniquities *will capture* the wicked, and he will be held with the cords of his sin."

Verb: לָקַח (*lāqaḥ*), GK 4374 (S 3947), 967x. The basic meaning of *lāqaḥ* is "to take, grasp." The meaning is often simply to "take into/by the hand." *lāqaḥ* is also used to describe taking something as one's own possession. See *take.*

Verb: תָּפַשׂ (*tāpaś*), GK 9530 (S 8610),

65x. *tāpaś* conveys the seizing or grasping of an object or person, usually with a degree of force, and may be translated as "take hold of, seize." In some contexts, it may be translated "captured." See *seize*.

CARE

Old Testament

Verb: דָּרַשׁ (*dāraš*), GK 2011 (S 1875), 164x. *dāraš* means "to seek, search for, strive after" an object. " It can have relational connotations, even meaning "to care." See *seek*.

Verb: פָּקַד (*pāqad*), GK 7212 (S 6485), 304x. While *pāqad* has a wide range of meaning, it basically expresses the action of overseeing an individual for a particular purpose, such as counting the people (see *count*). When oversight leads to an appropriate response on behalf of the superior to the actions or situation of the subordinate, *pāqad* may be translated "to attend to" or "to visit" and regularly takes God as the subject. When God "visits," he often brings divine blessing with a deep sense of care (see *visit*).

Noun: מִשְׁמֶרֶת (*mišmeret*), GK 5466 (S 4931), 78x. *mišmeret* derives from the verb *šāmar*, "to keep, watch, guard," and denotes the regular responsibility or duty to care for or guard an object. Sometimes the guarded object is a general reference to God's law, but usually it refers to a specific object, and often that object is cultic in nature (i.e., used in worship). See *duty*.

New Testament

Noun: μέριμνα (*merimna*), GK *3533* (S *3308*), 6x. *merimna* is a "care" or "concern" that can easily (though not necessarily) distract a believer. See *concern*.

CARE ABOUT

New Testament

Verb: μέλει (*melei*), GK *3508* (S *3199*), 10x. *melei* occurs in the NT only in an impersonal form; its basic meaning is "to care about, be concerned for someone or something." Paul, for example, asks rhetorically whether God is concerned solely about oxen when he established the law regarding muzzling (1 Cor. 9:9). The idea presented by *melei* of concern for the well-being of another can be seen in Jesus' concern for the poor (Jn. 12:6). Similarly, the disciples ask Jesus if he does not care for them because he is sleeping in the boat with a storm raging around them (Mk. 4:38), and Gallio "does not care" that the Greeks take Sosthenes out and beat him (Acts 18:17).

The idea of being concerned for someone or something can also lead to placing value on them, as when the hireling is distinguished from the shepherd because he does not care for the sheep (Jn. 10:13). In a more generic sense, *melei* can reflect the preference one has for something, e.g., when the Pharisees and the Herodians describe Jesus as not placing one man above another (Mt. 22:6; Mk. 12:14). Martha also uses *melei* to refer to Jesus' involvement (or lack thereof) in her cause (Lk. 10:40). The slave is called not to be concerned about or bothered by the fact that he does not have freedom (1 Cor. 7:21). Perhaps the fullest statement about the nature of *melei* is Peter's use of this word to encourage believers to cast all their anxieties on God, because "he *cares* for you" (1 Pet. 5:7). See *NIDNTT-A*, 364.*

CARNAL

See *worldly*.

CARRY

Old Testament

Verb: בּוֹא (*bô*ʾ), GK 995 (S 935), 2592x. *bô*ʾ is the fourth most common verb in the OT. It denotes motion toward a specific goal, such as "to go, arrive, enter a house, come." It expresses a variety of motions. This verb can also be used in the sense of "causing something to go or come," that is, "to bring or carry something or someone." See *come.*

Verb: נָשָׂא (*nāśā*ʾ), GK 5951 (S 4984), 659x. *nāśā*ʾ means "to lift, raise high, bear, carry." It occasionally means "to forgive" (i.e., "to carry away"). See *lift*.

New Testament

Verb: βαστάζω (*bastazō*), GK *1002* (S

941), 27x. *bastazō* means "to carry, bear" something. It is used of carrying physical burdens, such as a jar (Mk. 14:13), a coffin (Lk. 7:14), luggage (Lk. 10:4), a money bag (Jn. 12:5), a cross (19:17), or a body (20:15). *bastazō* can also refer euphemistically to childbirth and childrearing (Lk. 11:27, "Blessed is the mother who *gave* you *birth*") and of toleration (Rev. 2:2, "You cannot *tolerate* wicked men"). It also refers to carrying spiritual burdens (cf. Mt. 8:17).

Sometimes *bastazō* is idiomatic, referring to carrying something that cannot literally be carried, such as work and heat (Mt. 20:12), emotional distress (Jn. 16:12), God's name (Acts 9:15), the requirements of the law as a yoke (Acts 15:10), and hardships (Rev. 2:3). One of the more difficult uses of this verb in the NT occurs in Gal. 6:17, where Paul declares, "I *bear* on my body the marks of Jesus." In some sense Paul did have scars similar to Christ's injuries when he was severely beaten (cf. 2 Cor. 11:25) but here *bastazō* is probably best understood as referring to suffering for the gospel in general. See *NIDNTT-A*, 91.

Verb: φέρω (*pherō*), GK *5770* (S *5342*), 66x. *pherō* has the basic meaning "to bring, carry, present," but it has a wide range of figurative meanings, such as "to endure, sustain." See *bring*.

CARRY OFF

New Testament

Verb: αἴρω (*airō*), GK *149* (S *142*), 101x. *airō* can mean to "lift up, take up/away, carry off, remove." See *lift up*.

CARRY THROUGH

New Testament

Verb: διαφέρω (*diapherō*), GK *1422* (S *1308*), 13x. The transitive form of *diapherō* generally means "to carry through or across, spread out." It derives from *dia* ("through") and *pherō* ("to carry"). It is used in this way several times in the NT. For example, Jesus, in his cleansing of the temple, did not allow "anyone to *carry* merchandise *through* the temple courts" (Mk. 11:16). Luke emphasizes how "the word of the Lord *spread through* the whole region" by the ministry of Paul and Barnabas (Acts 13:49; cf. also 27:27).

The intransitive form is usually translated "to have value, be valuable, differ, be different." See *have value*.

CASE

Old Testament

Noun: דָּבָר (*dābār*), GK 1821 (S 1697), 1455x. *dābār* means "word, report, command," but can also signify a "thing, matter, affair." See *word*.

Noun: רִיב (*rîb*), GK 8190 (S 7379), 62x. *rîb* (related to the verb *rîb*, usually translated "contend") indicates an argument or conflict with another individual. There may be "strife" among humans (e.g., Gen. 13:7), which the book of Proverbs tells us repeatedly to avoid (Prov. 17:1, 14). Among the legal codes in the OT, *rîb* may be translated "lawsuit" (e.g., Exod. 23:2; Deut. 17:8; cf. 2 Sam. 15:1–6) or "dispute" (e.g., Deut. 19:17; 21:5; 25:1), in which a priest, judge, or king will render a decision. It may be in this legal sense, particularly in the prophetic literature, that God brings a "case" against his people for breaking the covenant (Hos. 4:1; Mic. 6:2), which ultimately results in exile. By way of contrast, in the exilic literature God's people long for him to plead their "case" (e.g., Ps. 43:1; Lam. 3:58; Mic. 7:9) and deliver them from wicked men. As Israel calls on Yahweh to defend them in exile, so Israel is called upon to defend the "cause" of the needy, widows, and orphans (Exod. 23:6; Prov. 23:11; Isa. 1:23). See *NIDOTTE*, 3:1105-6

CAST

Old Testament

Verb: יָצַק (*yāṣar*), GK 3668 (S 3332), 53x. *yāṣa* is best translated as "pour," though it is used 15x in the context of metal casting (Exod. 25:12; 38:27; 1 Ki. 7:23–24). See *pour*.

New Testament

Verb: βάλλω (*ballō*), GK *965* (S *906*), 122x. The basic meaning of *ballō* is "to throw" something, but it also carries the idea of allowing something to lie as it falls. See *throw.*

CAST OUT

Old Testament

Verb: נָדַח (*nādaḥ*), GK 5615 (S 5080), 51x. *nādaḥ* generally has two distinct but related meanings: "to banish, cast out" and "to stray." See *banish, stray*.

New Testament

Verb: ἐκβάλλω (*ekballō*), GK *1675* (S *1544*), 81x. *ekballō* means "to drive out, expel, eject." It often indicates a violent expulsion, especially of demons. See *drive out*.

CATCH

Old Testament

Verb: חָזַק (*ḥāzaq*), GK 2616 (S 2388), 290x. *ḥāzaq* can describe the severity of an impersonal force. For instance, we read that the famine is *strong* on all the land (Gen. 41:57; cf. 47:20). Absalom's head is *strong* in the oak, and we read that his head "caught hold" (KJV) or "got caught" (NIV) (2 Sam. 18:9). See *strong.*

New Testament

Verb: ἁρπάζω (*harpazō,* GK *773* (S *726*), 14x. *harpazō* means "to snatch, catch." It generally connotes a forceful and/or violent seizing (e.g., Mt. 11:12). See *snatch.*

Verb: καταλαμβάνω (*katalambanō*), GK *2898* (S *2638*), 15x. *katalambanō* can mean "to catch, obtain, seize, overtake." In the middle voice it means "to grasp, understand." In the NT, this verb can indicate the assault of evil (Mk. 9:18; Jn. 12:35; 1 Thess. 5:4), though it is important to realize that evil can never extinguish good, in the same sense that darkness can never distinguish light (Jn. 1:5; these were the days before people knew about a "black hole," which can swallow up even light!). In a more positive framework, this verb indicates grasping hold of Christ (1 Cor. 9:24; Phil. 3:12–13; cf. Rom. 9:30). In Eph. 3:18 Paul calls believers to seek to understand the breadth and depth of God's love. See *NIDNTT-A*, 327-28.

Verb: πιάζω (*piazō*), GK *4389* (S *4084*), 12x. *piazō* means "to arrest, catch." See *arrest*.

Verb: συλλαμβάνω (*syllambanō*), GK *5197* (S *4815*), 16x. *syllambano* conveys the basic idea of bringing together or gathering and is translated "arrest, seize, capture, conceive." See *arrest.*

CATTLE

Old Testament

Noun: בְּהֵמָה (*bᵉhēmâ*), GK 989 (S 929), 190x. The noun *bᵉhēmâ* can be translated "beast, animal, cattle." See *animal.*

Noun: בָּקָר (*bāqār*), GK 1330 (S 1241), 183x. *bāqār* refers to domesticated cattle (e.g., bulls, cows, and calves) and is distinguished from *ṣōʾn* (see *flock*), which connotes smaller domesticated animals (such as sheep and goats). The word *ʿēder* ("flock, herd") is also used to designate a herd of cattle, though it is most often used of smaller domesticated animals.

In the ancient world, cattle were a measure of one's wealth. For instance, the Hebrew word *miqneh* means "property," but it is used most often of "livestock." Abraham is wealthy in "sheep and *cattle*" (Gen. 24:35, cf. 13:2–7), along with silver, gold, and servants. Regarding Isaac the text records: "He had so many flocks and *herds* and servants that the Philistines envied him" (26:14). Larger cattle are deemed more valuable than smaller animals. *bāqār* are valuable spoils in war (Num. 31:33; 1 Sam. 27:9). Those who know the God of Israel are reminded that the increase in cattle is the result of God's faithfulness (Gen. 24:35; 30:30; Job 42:12).

Since *bāqār* are of high economic value, they also figure significantly into the sacrificial system (see, e.g., Lev. 1:2). Only the unblemished male of the herd or flock can be used for the burnt offering, which is entirely consumed on the altar (1:3; 23:18). Likewise, only an unblemished male of the herd or flock is to be used in the sin offering (4:3, 14; 9:2: 16:3). For the peace or fellowship offering, either an unblemished male or female from the herd or flock can be offered (3:1; 22:21).

Of course, *bāqār* may also denote draught animals, primarily for plowing or pulling carts (1 Sam. 6:7–12). Moreover, *bāqār* are also a source of meat and milk (1 Ki. 4:23; 1 Chr. 12:40). The Mosaic legislation presumes that the common person will eat meat of the herd (Deut. 14:4). See *NIDOTTE*, 1:707-10.

Noun: מִקְנֶה (*miqneh*), GK 5238 (S 4735), 76x. *miqneh* describes livestock, including pack animals, cattle, sheep, and goats. Since among nomadic peoples livestock constitute their primary source of wealth, it is understandable how *miqneh* comes to have the meaning "livestock." See *livestock*.

CAUSE

Old Testament

Noun: רִיב (*rîb*), GK 8190 (S 7379), 62x. *rîb* (related to the verb *rîb*, usually translated "contend") indicates an argument or conflict with another individual. As Israel calls on Yahweh to defend them in exile, so Israel is called upon to defend the "cause" of the needy, widows, and orphans (Exod. 23:6; Prov. 23:11; Isa. 1:23).See *case*.

New Testament

Noun: αἰτία (*aitia*), GK *162* (S *156*), 20x. *aitia* is the basis for some action or the legal basis for a charge—a "reason, cause, basis, charge." See *reason*.

Verb: ποιέω (*poieō*), GK *4472* (S *4160*), 568x. This verb, generically translated as "to do," has a wide range of meanings, including the idea of "creating" the world. See *do*.

CAUSE OF SIN

New Testament

Noun: σκάνδαλον (*skandalon*), GK *4998* (S *4625*), 15x. *skandalon* is something that leads a person to sin or to fall away from faith (see also *obstacle, offense*). Initially it referred to a stick used as the trigger of an animal trap, reflected in Rom. 11:9 (quoting Ps. 69:22), "May their table become a snare and a trap, a *stumbling block* and a retribution for them." However, the prevalent imagery in the NT is of something that causes a person to lose his or her footing and fall. Jesus warns about the things from the world that inevitably cause people to sin (Mt. 18:7). See *NIDNTT-A*, 526-27.

CAUSE TO SIN

New Testament

Verb: σκανδαλίζω (*skandalizō*), GK *4997* (S *4624*), 29x. In the active voice *skandalizō* means "to lead someone to sin or to fall away" from faith (see also *offend*). Jesus warns about people who would cause a little child to sin, and then about body parts that might cause a person to sin (Mt. 18:6, 8–9). Causing someone to sin brings such serious judgment that it is better to be drowned or to mutilate yourself (18:8). While the metaphor is not meant to be taken literally, it is true that it is better to go into heaven maimed than to hell whole. Everything that causes sin will be taken out of the kingdom of God (13:41).

In the passive voice, *skandalizō* means "to be led into sin" or "to fall away from faith." Those who receive the gospel with joy but have no firm root fall away from faith once trouble or persecution comes (Mk. 4:17). Jesus says that those who do not fall away on account of him are blessed (Mt. 11:6). He later warns that many will fall away because of persecution at the end of the age (24:10). Just before being arrested, Jesus tells his disciples that they will all fall away because of him later that night (26:31), but Peter vows he will never fall away (v. 33). See *NIDNTT-A*, 526-27.

CEASE

Old Testament

Verb: הָלַךְ (*hālak*), GK 2143 (S 1980), 1554x. *hālak* describes motion, primarily of humans, and is usually translated "walk, go, come." In certain cases it may describe when something "ceases" (goes away): rain (Song 2:11), dew (Hos. 6:4), wind (Ps. 78:39), and even human life ("to go the way of all the earth," e.g., Jos. 23:14). See *go*.

Verb: חָדַל (*ḥādal*), GK 2532 (S 2308), 55x. *ḥādal*, most often translated "stop" in the NIV, generally indicates the simple cessation of action. See *stop*.

Verb: שָׁבַת (*šābat*), GK 8697 (S 7673), 71x. The primary sense of *šābat* is the cessation of activity. After the flood, God promises that while the earth remains, the seasonal and daily patterns of nature will not "cease" (Gen. 8:22). In the new covenant, Yahweh promises that the seed of Israel will never "cease" to be a people (Jer. 31:36). After the Israelites enters the promised land, the manna that sustained them during their wilderness wanderings "stops" on the same day that they begin to eat from the land of Canaan (Jos. 5:12). Work (Exod. 5:5; 2 Chr. 16:5; Neh. 6:3) and joyous celebration (Isa. 24:8; Jer. 48:33; Lam. 5:14) may "stop." Egypt's proud strength will "come to an end" (Ezek. 30:18), and so will Judah's (33:28).

Often activity does not cease on its own, but someone causes it to cease. In the prophets in particular, God causes activity to cease. God declares that he will "put an end" to the arrogance of the proud (Isa. 13:11; Ezek. 7:24). In Hosea, God will "put an end" to the kingdom of Israel (Hos. 1:4). In Jeremiah, he will "bring an end" to the sounds of joyous weddings as he brings about the exile (Jer. 7:34; 16:9). In Ezekiel, God asserts that he will "stop" Israel from their spiritual prostitution (Ezek. 16:41; 23:27).

šābat, related to the noun *šabbāt* ("Sabbath)," appears 13x in connection with Sabbath observance, and the verb *šābat* is regularly translated "to rest" in these instances (see *rest*).

New Testament

Verb: παύω (*pauō*), GK *4264* (S *3973*), 15x. pauō means "to stop, finish." See *stop*.

CEDAR

Old Testament

Noun: אֶרֶז (*ʾerez*), GK 780 (S 730), 73x. *ʾerez* denotes a "cedar" tree, a tree that made Lebanon famous (1 Ki. 4:33; Ps. 92:12; Isa. 2:13). This tree is a huge, flat-topped evergreen tree that can grow to heights of a hundred feet (cf. 2 Ki. 19:23), with a trunk circumference up to forty to fifty feet. According to Ezek. 31:3–5, it has beautiful branches and towers higher than the other trees of the forest. The wood of a cedar tree is considered a luxury (Isa. 9:10). David (2 Sam. 5:11) and Solomon (1 Ki. 5:6, 8, 10; 9:9–20) import cedar wood from Lebanon for their palaces and for the Lord's temple, and cedar is also used in building ships (Ezek. 27:5).

In addition to its purposes for building, cedar wood is also linked with hyssop in two cleansing rituals: in the sacrifice of the red heifer (Num. 19:6) and in the purification after leprosy (Lev. 14:4, 6, 49–52). Perhaps cedar is used in these rituals because of its aromatic qualities. In Ps. 29:5, the strength of the cedar tree points out the power of the Lord, for by his mere voice he is able to break "the cedars of Lebanon." They belong to him (104:16), and another psalmist calls on them, along with fruit trees and all nature, to praise the Lord (148:9). When God comes in judgment on evil kings, he will destroy their "*cedar* beams" (Jer. 22:7, 14–15). See *NIDOTTE*, 1:510–11.

CELEBRATE

New Testament

Verb: εὐφραίνω (*euphrainō*), GK *2370* (S *2165*), 14x. *euphrainō* conveys the basic idea of a created state of joy or euphoria and may be translated as "rejoice, gladden, celebrate." See *rejoice*.

CELESTIAL

See *heavenly*.

CENTURION

New Testament

Noun: ἑκατοντάρχης (*hekatontarchēs*), GK *1672* (S *1543*), 20x. *hekatontarchēs*, found only in Matthew and Luke-Acts, is the technical term for a "centurion," a commander of one hundred Roman soldiers. It literally means "commander of 100." The Romans deployed troops in legions (6,000 soldiers each), which consisted of 10 regiments of 600 (called a *speira*), which in turn consisted of 6 divisions of 100 men, with a centurion in charge of each division of 100. In almost every occurrence of the word, centurions are portrayed in a positive light. For instance, a centurion and his division come to Paul's aid against a Jewish mob (Acts 21:32), a centurion listens and defends Paul's claim of Roman citizenry (22:25, 26), and an initially obstinate centurion named Julius winds up trying to save Paul's life (27:1, 6, 11, 31, 43).

It is a *hekatontarchēs* who picks up on the fact that Jesus is no common criminal, saying, "Truly this was the Son of God!" (Mt. 27:54) or, in Luke's gospel, "Surely this man was innocent" (Lk. 23:47). When the gospel spread powerfully to the Gentiles in Acts, Luke focuses in on the conversion of a God-fearing centurion named Cornelius (Acts 10:22). Perhaps the most exemplary use of *hekatontarchēs* occurs in Mt. 8:5–13 and the parallel account in Lk. 7:1–6. Here a Gentile centurion has the faith that Israel lacks. He recognizes that just as his division follows his authoritative commands, so healing comes, and disease flees, at the authoritative pronouncement of Jesus Christ. Thus, it is of a Gentile centurion that Jesus says, "Truly, I tell you, with no one in Israel have I found such faith." See *NIDNTT-A*, 481-83.

CERTAINTY

New Testament

Noun: παρρησία (*parrēsia*), GK *4244* (S *3954*), 31x. *parrēsia* generally means "confidence" and is used mostly with reference to one's speech. It can also carry the meaning of the *certainty* of an outcome. See *confidence*.

CESSATION

Old Testament

Noun: אַחֲרִית (*ʾaḥᵃrît*), GK 344 (S 319), 61x. *ʾaḥᵃrît* in its most basic sense denotes "that which comes after." Specifically it may describe what follows temporally, that is, the "cessation, end" of an event or the final "outcome." See *end*.

CHAIN

New Testament

Noun: ἅλυσις (*halysis*), GK *268* (S *254*), 11x. *halysis* means "chain." Chains were used to no avail to bind those who were demon-possessed (Mk. 5:3–4; Lk. 8:29). Peter was freed from his chains after an angel appeared to him in prison (Acts 12:6–7); it was normal in Roman imprisonment for the prisoner to be chained to a soldier, as is the case here with Peter. On several occasions Paul was arrested and bound with chains (21:33; 28:20); he even refers to himself as "an ambassador in chains" (Eph. 6:20). In an emotionally powerful statement, Paul calls on God to show mercy to the household of Onesiphorus, "because he often refreshed me and was not ashamed of my chains" (2 Tim. 1:16). John has a vision of an angel with a "great chain" (Rev. 20:1), which is used to bind Satan.*

Noun: δεσμός (*desmos*), GK *1301* (S *1199*), 18x. *desmos* can refer to either literal chains, such as those of a prisoner, or figurative chains, that which hinders or obstructs.

(1) In the literal sense, Luke 8:29 refers to a man with an unclean spirit who, though chained hand and foot and kept under guard, received power from the demon to break his "chains" (Lk. 8:29). Likewise in Acts 16:26, an earthquake shakes the prison in which Paul is being held, so that "everybody's *chains* came loose" (cf. Acts 20:23; 23:29; 26:29, 31; Heb. 11:36). In several of these usages, *desmos* can be translated as "imprisonment," referring to the place where chains hold prisoners (see also Phil. 1:7; 1:13, 14, 17; Col. 4:18; 2 Tim. 2:9; Phlm. 10, 13). Jude refers to rebellious angels who have been "bound with everlasting *chains* for judgment on the great Day" (Jude 6). These chains are a sort of metaphorical chain that keeps these angels in check until judgment.

(2) *desmos* can also refer to that which holds a person in bondage. In Mk. 7:35, a

literal translation reads, "the *chain/bond* of his tongue was loosened." Similarly, in Luke 13:10–17, a woman crippled for eighteen years by a sickness stands before Jesus, and he heals her. Jesus refers to her as being "loosed from this *bond*" (11:16 KJV).

CHANGE

New Testament

Verb: στρέφω (*strephō*), GK *5138* (S *4762*), 21x. *strephō* means "to turn, return, change." See *turn*.

CHANGE ONE'S MIND

Old Testament

Verb: נָחַם (*nāḥam*), GK 5714 (S 5162), 108x. *nāḥam* bears two distinct but related meanings in the OT: "to comfort, console" (see *comfort*) and "to relent, repent, change one's mind, be grieved."

nāḥam denotes repentance or a change of mind. Of these occurrences, the most theologically significant relate to a shifting of the divine countenance. God relents from destroying Israel after the golden calf (Exod. 32:12, 14). He is grieved that he made Saul king (1 Sam. 15:11). And in accordance with his promise, he replaces judgment with grace when people repent of their sins and turn back to him (Jer. 18:7–10; cf. 8:6; 31:19). God's changing of his mind takes place in the temporal sphere of creation and is related to his providence. As such, it is a real changing of the mind. At the same time, however, God's eternal decrees and immutable will never come into conflict with his providential interaction with creation. The full reality of both aspects of God's being and action need be affirmed.

CHARGE

New Testament

Noun: αἰτία (*aitia*), GK *162* (S *156*), 20x. *aitia* is the basis for some action or the legal basis for a charge—a "reason, cause, basis, charge." See *reason*.

Verb: κατηγορέω (*katēgoreō*), GK *2989* (S *2723*), 23x. *katēgoreō* means "to bring charges against, accuse" someone. For the most part, this word functions in a legal framework. For example, this term is used several times to refer to the charges brought against Paul by the Jews (Acts 22:30; 24:2; 25:5; 28:19). See *accuse*.

CHARIOT

Old Testament

Noun: רֶכֶב (*rekeb*), GK 8207 (S 7393), 120x. The basic meaning of *rekeb* is "chariot," but it is also used of the chariot horse (2 Sam. 8:4) or the chariot driver (10:18). The lack of chariots was a military disadvantage to Israel from the Exodus (Exod. 14) through the period of the conquest (Jos. 14:16–18) and up to the time of the judges (Jdg. 1:19; 4:3). King David first introduced the chariot to the armies of Israel (2 Sam. 8:4), and they became plentiful during the reign of King Solomon (1 Ki. 10:26). However, the people of Israel were not to trust in chariots (Ps. 20:7; Isa. 31:1), but in the Lord, for "the *chariots* of God are tens of thousands and thousands of thousands" (Ps. 68:17; cf. 2 Ki. 6:17). One of these divine chariots carried Elijah into heaven (2:11–12).

On three occasions, *rekeb* is also used for an upper millstone (see *millstone*).

CHARITY

See *love*.

CHARM

Old Testament

Noun: חֵן (*ḥēn*), GK 2834 (S 2580), 69x. *ḥēn* describes that which is favorable or gracious. It is used 11x with the nuance of "charm." See *favor*.

CHASTE

See *pure*.

CHASTEN

See *teach*.

CHERUB, CHERUBIM

Old Testament

Noun: כְּרוּב (*k^erûb*), GK 4131 (S 3742), 91x. Outside the Bible, a related Akkadian form of this word was used both for priestly intercessors and for winged throne-bearers of a deity. Similarly, in the OT, the *k^erûbîm* (pl. of *k^erûb*) are often portrayed as winged creatures that are closely associated with the Lord's presence. All of the 91 OT references to *k^erûbîm* occur in contexts related to the Most Holy Place or theophanic appearances. They typically show up where humanity enjoys a level of extraordinary communion with God (cf. Exod. 25:22; Num. 7:89).

k^erûbîm first appear in Gen. 3:24 as beings guarding "the way to the tree of life" in the garden sanctuary of God. In the tabernacle narrative (Exod. 25:1–22), two cherubim are crafted and placed atop the mercy seat, from which the divine glory speaks to Israel (Exod. 25:18–20; cf. Heb. 9:5). They are formed of gold, face each other, and bear wings spreading upward that overshadow the atonement slate on top of the ark of the covenant. God is said to be enthroned between them (1 Sam. 4:4; 2 Sam. 6:2; 2 Ki. 19:15; 1 Chr. 13:6; Ps. 80:1; 99:1; Isa. 37:16) or to mount them and fly (2 Sam. 22:11; Ps. 18:10). It is therefore likely that their outstretched wings symbolize their flight and serve as a seat for the throne of God.

In Solomon's temple, these same figures are in the inner sanctuary and are made of olive wood overlaid with gold (1 Ki. 6:23–28; 8:6–7). Their image is carved on walls around the temple (inner and outer rooms; 1 Ki. 6:29, 32, 35; 7:29, 36; 2 Chr. 3:7) and woven into some of the curtains of the tabernacle (Exod. 26:1, 31). They also figure prominently in Ezekiel's temple visions, where in wall reliefs, carvings, statues, or woven work they signify the divine presence (cf. especially Ezek. 10 and 41).

That the *k^erûbîm* figure so prominently in the outer hangings of Israel's sanctuary is a sign of the divine presence within. It seems that not only are they representative of the presence of the enthroned God but more specifically of the presence of God enthroned among his people.

CHEST

Old Testament

Noun: אֲרוֹן (*ʾ^arôn*), GK 778 (S 727), 202x. Often translated "ark, box, chest," the noun *ʾ^arôn* bears distinct though related meanings in secular and cultic contexts. In secular contexts, it refers to a box for carrying the dead (i.e., a coffin, Gen. 50:26) or a money chest (2 Ki. 12:10). See *ark*.

CHIEF

Old Testament

Noun: אַיִל (*ʾayil*), GK 380 (S 352), 171x. *ʾayil* literally means "ram" (see *ram*), but can also be used figuratively for "chief, ruler, leader" (see Exod. 15:15; Ezek. 31:11; 32:21). In Ezek. 34:17, the Lord states that he will judge the shepherds of Israel for scattering the flock and allowing them to fall pray to predators. The Lord will judge between the sheep and the rams (i.e., the leaders), promising to install a Davidic shepherd over his flock in their place. Echoes of this passage in both the NT gospels and letters make clear that both these writers understand this Ezek. reference to be a messianic prophecy fulfilled in Christ, the good shepherd (cf. Lk. 15:3–7; Jn. 10:1–18; Heb. 13:20; 1 Pet. 2:25). See *NIDOTTE*, 1:372-78.

Noun: רֹאשׁ (*rōʾš*), GK 8031 (S 7218), 600x. The primary meaning of *rōʾš* is "head" (see *head*), but it also has a number of metaphorical meanings. For example, *rōʾš* can be translated as "leader" or "chief." See *leader*.

Noun: שַׂר (*śar*), GK 8569 (S 8269) 421x.

Noun: נָשִׂיא (*nāśîʾ*), GK 5954 (S 5387) 130x.

Noun: אַלּוּף (*ʾallûp*), GK 477 (S 441) 60x.

These terms are a number of overlapping nouns in the OT that refer to leaders, chiefs, and officials of various sorts. They need to be translated differently according to the context in Israel's history. See *leader* for a thorough discussion.

New Testament

Noun: ἄρχων (*archōn*), GK *807* (S *758*), 37x. *archōn* is part of an extensive group of *arch-* words with meanings related to the ideas of beginning, cause, and thereby, rule and authority. See *ruler.*

Adjective: πρῶτος (*prōtos*), GK *4754*,

4755 (S *4413*), 97x. *prōtos* signifies that a thing is "first" in a sequence or in prominence. see *first.*

CHIEF PRIEST

New Testament

Noun: ἀρχιερεύς (*archiereus*), GK *797* (S *749*), 122x. In the singular, *archiereus* refers to the high priest, the leader of the priestly group of Israel. In the plural it denotes all the ruling priests. See *high priest.*

CHILD, CHILDREN

Old Testament

Noun: בֵּן (*bēn*), GK 1201 (S 1121), 4941x. *bēn* has a wide variety of nuances in the OT, one of which is "child." See *son.*

Noun: יֶלֶד (*yeled*), GK 3529 (S 3206), 89x. *yeled* refers in almost all cases to a male "child" (only in Exod. 21:4 does it clearly mean children of both genders; cf. also 1 Sam. 1:2). It can even refer to the offspring of animals (Isa. 11:7). A *yeled* may range in age from an infant (Exod. 2:3; Ruth 4:16; 1 Sam. 12:15) to young boys (Gen. 21:8) to teenagers (Gen. 37:30; 2 Ki. 2:23) to fully-grown adults (1 Ki. 12:8; Dan. 1:4, 10). In most cases, a *yeled* is not married (but cf. Ruth 1:5),

Figuratively, *yeled* is used of the nation of Israel as God's "child" (Jer. 31:20). Note, however, that this is not the word used in the common phrase "the children of Israel" (for this, see *bēn*, "son," GK 1201). But *yeled* is the word that is used for the coming deliverer of God's people in Isa. 9:6, whose name is called "Wonderful Counselor, Mighty God, Everlasting Father, Prince of Peace." Note too that a city that is filled with "*boys* and girls playing in the streets" is a symbol of peace and God's blessing (Zech. 8:5). See *NIDOTTE,* 2:455–60.

Noun: נַעַר (*naʿar*), GK 5853 (S 5288), 240x. The meaning of *naʿar* falls into two main categories. It may refer to a male child of almost any age or to a servant. See *boy.*

New Testament

Noun: νήπιος (*nēpios*), GK *3758* (S *3516*), 15x. In the NT *nēpios* refers to a "young child, infant." See *infant.*

Noun: παιδίον (*paidion*), GK *4086* (S *3813*), 52x. *paidion* is a diminutive form of *pais* ("child"; GK *4090*) and is restricted to young children. See *little child.*

Noun: τέκνον (*teknon*), GK *5451* (S *5043*), 99x. *teknon* is the general term for a "child" (Mt. 7:11; 21:28), but can also be used of "descendants" (27:25; Lk. 3:8; 16:25; Rom. 9:8). In a figurative sense it can mean someone who is close and dear but without any blood relationship.

Children are instructed to be obedient: "*Children*, obey your parents in the Lord, for this is right" (Eph. 6:1). When children do obey their parents in the Lord, they receive promises of a better and longer life (6:3). Paul then instructs fathers: "Do not exasperate your *children*; instead, bring them up in the training and instruction of the Lord" (6:4).

Jesus uses *teknon* to describe his paternalistic desires for Israel: "O Jerusalem, Jerusalem, you who kill the prophets and stone those sent to you, how often I have longed to gather your *children* together, as a hen gathers her chicks under her wings, but you were not willing" (Mt. 23:37).

teknon is a common colloquialism used to address an individual. When Jesus is speaking to a group of adults, he can refer to them as children: "*Children*, how hard it is to enter the kingdom of God" (Mk. 10:24). Jesus speaks to the paralytic he is about to heal as "my *child*" (Mt. 9:2; Mk. 2:5). *teknon* can also describe our position with God the Father upon conversion: "Yet to all who received him, to those who believed in his name, he gave the right to become *children* of God—children born not of natural descent, nor of human decision or a husband's will, but born of God" (Jn. 1:12).

Spiritually speaking, *teknon* can describe the spiritual relationship between such people as Paul and Timothy (1 Cor. 4:17; 1 Tim. 1:2, 18; 2 Tim. 1:2; 2:1), Titus

(Tit. 1:4), Onesimus (Phlm. 10), as well as with his congregations (1 Cor. 4:14; 2 Cor. 6:13; Gal. 4:19). John speaks of his church fellowships with the same degree of endearment (3 Jn. 4). Rev. speaks of followers of the false teachers as their "children" (Rev. 2:23). See *NIDNTT-A*, 558.

Noun: υἱός (*huios*), GK *5626* (S *5207*), 377x. Similar to the use of *ben* in the OT, *huios* describes the son of human parents, though it can also refer more generally to offspring and descendents. It is not limited to the male gender but often has the nuance of "child." See *son*.

CHOOSE

Old Testament

Verb: בָּחַר (*bāḥar*), GK 1047 (S 977), 172x. *bāḥar* means "to choose, select, prefer." While this word has secular uses, it is also intimately linked with God's election of Israel as a nation and of individuals within the nation (although note that other words also speak of the concept of election, such as "know, separate, establish, call").

(1) In secular uses, *bāḥar* has a wide variety of uses, such as choosing wives (Gen. 6:2), choosing a town to live in (Deut. 23:16), and choosing stones to put in a sling (1 Ki. 18:23). It is frequently used for a select number of soldiers as "*chosen* men" (Exod. 17:9; 1 Sam. 13:2; 24:2; 1 Chr. 19:10).

(2) In religious uses, the psalmist "would choose" to be a doorkeeper in God's house rather than to live a wicked life (Ps. 84:10). The psalmist of Ps. 119 has "*chosen* the way of truth" and God's precepts (119:30, 173). It is much better "to *choose* understanding rather than silver" (Prov. 16:16) and a good name than great riches (22:1).

(3) About 60 percent of the uses of *bāḥar*, however, have God as the subject. (a) Prior to Israel's entry into Canaan, God indicates he "will choose" a place to put his Name where the nation can worship him (Deut. 12:5; 14:23–25; 16:6–7, 11). This place is Jerusalem, where Solomon builds the temple, and the entire nation is instructed to worship there. This is "the city the Lord *has chosen* out of all the tribes of Israel" (2 Chr. 12:13). In Ps. 132:13, this is phrased as God's choosing of Zion.

(b) God also "*chose* David his servant and took him from the sheep pens" to be ruler over his people (Ps. 78:70). Although Saul was God's first "chosen" king (1 Sam. 10:24), because of his disobedience the Lord rejected him and chose David in his place. Solomon recalls this choice of God in his dedicatory prayer for the recently built temple (1 Ki. 8:16; 2 Chr. 6:6).

(c) God also decided on the family line he chose to be the official high priests of his people (Num. 16:5, 7), which ended up being the line of Aaron/Eleazer (17:5; cf. 1 Sam. 2:28). Along with this choice was that of the entire tribe of Levi to be his special ministers (cf. 1 Chr. 15:2; 2 Chr. 29:11).

(d) The main use of this verb however, is for God's choice of Israel as his elect nation. The Lord did not choose them because they were any better than any other people; rather, he chose them because of his unmerited love and his faithfulness to the promises of Abraham, Isaac, and Jacob (Deut. 7:6–7). Over and over in the psalms and prophets, God reaffirms his election of Israel / Jacob (e.g., Ps. 47:4; 135:4; Isa. 41:8; 44:1–2; Ezek. 20:4). The purpose for this choosing is not simply blessing, but that God's people can be a light to the nations (e.g., Gen. 12:1–3; Isa. 43:10). The NT affirms this goal of election even more strongly for the church, his "chosen people" (1 Pet. 2:9–10).

Verb: לָקַח (*lāqaḥ*), GK 4374 (S 3947), 967x. The basic meaning of *lāqaḥ* is "to take, grasp." The meaning is often simply to "take into/by the hand." *lāqaḥ* is also used to describe taking something as one's own possession as well as to choose a wife for oneself. See *take*.

New Testament

Verb: βούλομαι (*boulomai*) GK *1089* (S *1014*), 37x. *boulomai* describes the desire or intention of a person to do something, to have something, or to obtain a result. See *want*.

Verb: ἐκλέγομαι (*eklegomai*), GK *1721* (S *1586*), 22x. *eklegomai* means "to choose, set apart, elect." It sometimes refers to decisions made by people. Mary chose the better thing than Martha by sitting at Jesus' feet and listening to his teaching (Lk. 10:42). When eating at the home of a Pharisee, Jesus noticed that the guests chose the seats of honor (Lk. 14:7). This verb also denotes the action of the church to choose people for service (Acts 1:24; 6:5; 15:22, 25).

But *eklegomai* can also signify the electing activity of God according to his divine purpose and grace. Jesus is God's chosen one, for at his transfigutation God said, "This is my Son, my Chosen One; listen to him!" (Lk. 9:35). Jesus chose the twelve disciples (Lk. 6:13; Jn. 6:70; 13:18; 15:16, 19; Acts 1:2). God's sovereign purpose is manifest in his choosing of believers before the creation of the world (Eph. 1:4) and his preservation of those whom he has chosen through the days of tribulation (Mk. 13:20). His sovereign grace is apparent in that his choosing runs contrary to human wisdom and expectation. He has chosen what is foolish to shame the wise, what is weak to shame the strong, and what is lowly and despised so that no one can boast (1 Cor. 27–28; see also Jas. 2:5). See *NIDNTT-A*, 173-75.

Verb: προχειρίζω (*procheirizō*), GK *4741* (S *4400*), 3x. *procheirizō* means "to choose, appoint." It is derived from the preposition *pro* ("before") and the noun *cheir* ("hand"), so that the general idea is to handpick or designate someone for a task or post. It occurs only in Acts, where it describes Jesus as "appointed" by the Father for us (Acts 3:20), and Paul as someone whom God "chose" when he was on the road to Damascus (22:14; 26:16). It is important to note that the subject of this verb in all cases is God the Father. Furthermore, the objects—namely, Jesus and Paul—are appointed in order to bring salvation to people. Both of these observations certify that God is the one who appoints the events of this world and our lives, and his appointments are made so that those who don't know him will come to know him. See *NIDNTT-A*, 501.*

CHOSEN

New Testament

Adjective: ἐκλεκτός (*eklektos*), GK *1723* (S *1588*), 22x. *eklektos* is the quality of being "chosen, elected, set apart," with the biblical implication that God is the one who chooses. Jesus said, "Many are called, but few are chosen" (Mt. 22:14).

Used as a noun, *eklektos* refers to the body of believers as God's "chosen ones" or "the elect." Thus, it has a corporate rather than individual sense (though it is used once to refer to an individual, Rom. 16:13). The church's experience of salvation rests in the sovereign decision of God from beginning to end. God will indeed "bring about justice for his chosen ones" (Lk. 18:7), and no one can bring a charge against them (Rom. 8:33). They will display God's praises for bringing them out of darkness into light (1 Pet. 2:9).

Divine election is the basis for calling the church to be holy (Col. 3:12). In Matthew and Mark, it is the basis for the assurance of surviving the end-time tribulations. The days of tribulation will be cut short so that the elect will survive them (Mt. 24:22). False christs and prophets will try but fail to deceive the elect (v. 24). At the very end of the age Jesus will return to gather his elect to himself (v. 31). Paul too writes of his ministry for the sake of the elect (Tit. 1:1; 2 Tim. 2:10).

eklektos can also refer to Jesus as the Chosen One (Lk. 23:35). Even though he was a living stone rejected by most people, he is chosen by God (1 Pet. 2:4, 6). It is on Jesus as the cornerstone that the church, made up of living stones chosen by God, is built. Throughout the NT, the designation of the church as the elect of God is a pastoral teaching, often found in contexts where people are suffering or struggling to keep the faith. The comfort of this teaching is that there is a surety to our salvation because it is grounded in God's sovereign actions. His work on behalf of his people will be accomplished no matter what the outward circumstances may indicate to the contrary. See *NIDNTT-A*, 173-75.

CHRIST

New Testament

Noun: Χριστός (*Christos*), GK *5986* (S *5547*), 529x. *Christos* means "Messiah, anointed one, Christ." Its root is the verb *chriō*, which in Greek meant "to smear, rub, spread." In the LXX, because of the connection with "rubbing or smearing oil," the term was associated with "one who had been anointed, or set apart, for a special task." In the Hebrew Bible, the "anointed ones" were the king and the high priest, occasionally a prophet (all three offices are associated with Jesus; cf. Jn. 6:14; Heb. 9:11; Rev. 19:16). In later Jewish writings in Greek, *Christos* came to mean "the Messiah." Thus, it came into extensive usage as the NT designation for Jesus. The transliterated word *Messias* occurs 2x in the NT, translated in each case as *Christos* (Jn. 1:41; 4:25).

Matthew uses *Christos* with the definite article to demonstrate that Jesus is the expected, "end-time," messianic figure (Mt. 2:4). These references served as powerful touchstones for Matthew's Jewish audience. Peter's confession at Caesarea Philippi, "You are the *Christos*, the Son of the living God" (16:16), draws on God's promise to David of an unending heir to his throne (2 Sam. 7:14). This era would be initiated by a figure who would actualize the promise of the end-time reign of David's line. By the first century, Jews for the most part expected the Messiah to be like David, who would triumph in the last days by defeating and expelling the occupying Roman army. But Jesus did not posture himself in this warlike manner, at least not in the physical sense. He enters Jerusalem riding a donkey, not on a great white stallion waving a sword over his head (Mt. 21:1–11). At his arrest, instead of seeking physical protection, he has Peter sheath his sword and then reminds Peter of his divine mission (Jn. 18:11).

According to the NT, Jesus as the Christ fulfilled Israel's expectation of a deliverer *from their sins*. His violent death on the cross in Paul's mind serves as a powerful signal of God's purpose and control and thus becomes the central focus of first-century messianic preaching (1 Cor. 15:1–7). Far from collapsing a movement, Jesus' death and resurrection form the nucleus for its undying success. Jesus understands his death as a "must" (e.g., Mk. 8:31). He faithfully fulfills what he was anointed to do, for Luke tells us that after the Transfiguration, "Jesus resolutely set out for Jerusalem" (Lk. 9:51).

NT preaching, especially among Jews, focuses on presenting Jesus as the *Christos*: "Philip went down ... and proclaimed *the Christ* there" (Acts 8:5). When Paul preached, he first demonstrated from the OT what sort of *Christos* was to be expected, and then came with his clincher: "This Jesus I am proclaiming to you is *the Christ*" (17:2–3). Paul anguishes over the fact that his Jewish brothers do not acknowledge Christ (Rom. 9:1–5). To Paul it is both a disaster and totally unbelievable.

Paul's writings are saturated with the term *Christos* as a name (Rom. 5:6; 1 Cor. 1:6, 13, 17; Eph. 2:5; Phil. 1:15; 2 Thess. 3:5; 1 Tim. 5:11). Paul writes Galatians because false teachers known as the Judaizers are threatening to pervert "the gospel of *Christ*" (Gal. 1:7). Paul's favorite phrase to describe the Christian's new relationship to the Lord is "in *Christ*" (2 Cor. 5:17; Eph. 1:3–14; Phil. 3:8–9). Other NT authors also use *Christos* as a name (Heb. 3:14; 9:28; 1 Pet. 4:13; 2 Jn. 9; Rev. 20:4). The final book in the NT is known as the "Revelation of Jesus Christ." See *NIDNTT-A*, 610-12.

CHRISTIAN

New Testament

Noun: χριστιανός (*Christianos*), GK *5985* (S *5546*), 3x. *Christianos* means "Christian." Strange as it may seem, this word occurs only 3x in the NT. The followers of Jesus were called "Christians" first in Antioch (Acts 11:26—probably meaning "one who is associated with Christ"). In 1 Pet. 4:16, Peter implies that being a Christian in his day meant that one would suffer. Agrippa has a somewhat sarcastic reply to Paul when the latter challenges whether or not the governor believes the prophets: "Do you think that in such a short time you can persuade me to be a *Christian*" (Acts 26:28). What, then, were Christians called in the NT era? They were called either people "of the Nazarene sect" (Acts 24:5, since Jesus was "Jesus of Nazareth") or those who "belonged to the Way" (9:2; 19:9, 23; 22:4; 24:22).

CHURCH

New Testament

Noun: ἐκκλησία (*ekklēsia*), GK *1711* (S *1577*), 114x. *ekklēsia* is derived from *ekklēsia* ("to call out"), so the church is the "called-out ones" of God. In its secular use *ekklēsia* refers to the gathering of the competent citizens of a city-state in order to decide issues regarding laws, office appointments, and public policy. But the prototype of the NT *ekklēsia* lies not in Greco-Roman history but in the assembly of God's people in the OT (cf. Acts 7:38), which developed into the Jewish synagogue as the gathering of the community of God. In these gatherings the great stories of salvation history were regularly rehearsed and the wonderful promises of God to Israel recounted (cf. Num. 14:7–9). But while the *ekklēsia* may find its roots in the synagogue, it is not a subset of it but becomes the new term used for the gathering of various groups of Christian believers.

It is noteworthy that the only occurrences of *ekklēsia* in the gospels are in Mt. 16:18 and 18:17. Jesus promises to build his church, and he instructs his followers to practice discipline in the church. Luke uses this word only in Acts.

ekklēsia is basically a Pauline term (more than half of its NT uses are in his letters). Paul never thinks of the church as a physical structure but as a dedicated group of disciples of Jesus Christ (cf. Phlm. 2; also Col. 4:15), whom he has purchased with his blood (cf. Rev. 5:9). The apostle sees the church as a new race, which he lists it alongside Jews and Greeks in 1 Cor. 10:32; it is sufficiently equipped with leadership and gifts to fulfill God's purposes on earth (12:28); and it is the avenue through which the wisdom of God is made known (Eph. 1:22).

The writer of Hebrews uses the phrase "church of the firstborn" to refer to believers in general who make up this body—the redeemed whose names are written in heaven (Heb. 12:23). James sees the church as a source of divine healing during times of illness through the prayers of local ministers (Jas. 5:14). John uses the term throughout Rev. 2-3 in the letters to the seven "churches." These were actual churches in Asia Minor at the end of the first century, but they also serve as models of various churches today. See *NIDNTT-A*, 170-73.

CIRCUMCISE

Old Testament

Verb: מוּל (*mûl*), GK 4576 (S 4135), 31x. *mûl* occurs in the first six books of the Bible and in Jeremiah, and all occurrences deal with circumcision--either physical circumcision or heart circumcision.

(1) Circumcision involved the cutting the foreskin of the male sexual organ. In the ancient world, the Western Semites and the Egyptians practiced a form of circumcision (a slitting of the foreskin); Israel was unique in cutting off the foreskin completely as a commanded religious ritual. The Philistines and Mesopotamians were termed "uncircumcised."

After God entered into a formal covenant relationship with Abraham in Gen. 17, as a sign of that covenant God commands that every male in his household be circumcised (Gen. 17:9–13), so that the covenant can be "in your flesh." Every male subsequently born in his household is to be circumcised at eight days old (Gen. 17:12; Lev. 12:3). Any male not circumcised is to be "cut off" from God's people (Gen. 17:14). In other words, as a sign that God has made (lit., "cut") his covenant with his people, all males must have the foreskin cut off. Anyone who does not obey this command will be cut off from the people. See *make a covenant*.

(2) The OT also knows a spiritual meaning to circumcision. Only those who humble themselves before God, offer sacrifices for sins (Lev. 26:41), and so pledge loyalty to the covenant are truly circumcised to the Lord (Jer. 4:4; cf. 9:25; Ezek. 44:9). Thus, through Moses God calls his people to circumcise their hearts to him (Deut. 10:16). Since human beings cannot do this in our own power, God himself promises to circumcise their hearts (Deut. 30:6).

New Testament

Verb: περιτέμνω (*peritemnō*), GK *4362* (S *4059*), 17x. *peritemnō* means "to circumcise." This verb literally means to "cut around." Thus, it refers to the act of cutting around the foreskin of the male sexual organ in order to remove it.

(1) John the Baptist (Lk. 1:59), Jesus (Lk. 2:21), and Paul (Phil. 3:5) were all circumcised on the eighth day after birth. Paul personally circumcised Timothy as an adult since his Greek father apparently had not allowed him to be circumcised as an infant (Acts 16:3).

(2) The NT church experienced a debate on whether all believers, Jew and Gentile, had to be circumcised in order to be saved. Some believers who had formerly been Pharisees insisted on this (Acts 15:1, 5); Paul taught it was not necessary, and he argued vehemently against it in some of his letters (Rom. 4:1–12; Gal. 5:1–12; Phil. 3:2–11; Col. 2:11–12). The end result of a meeting of the apostles and elders in Jerusalem was that circumcision was not a requirement. Paul's main concern was that if circumcision were required, soon the entire burden of the law would be required for Christians; such thinking would jeopardize his gospel of salvation by grace alone, received through faith (cf. Eph. 2:8). See *NIDNTT-A*, 456.

Noun: περιτομή (*peritomē*), GK *4364* (S *4061*), 36x. *peritomē* means "circumcision." This noun means literally the act of cutting around (the foreskin).

(1) This noun is occasionally used as a euphemism either for the Jews (Gal. 2:7–9; Eph. 2:11) or for those early believers who held that circumcision was a requirement for a person to become a Christian (Acts 10:45; 11:2; Gal. 2:12). Paul, however, insists that those who worship by the Spirit of God, glory in Jesus, and put no confidence in the flesh are the true circumcision (Phil. 3:3). On the controversy in the early church on whether circumcision was required for believers, see the discussion above under *peritemnō*.

(2) Like Jeremiah, Paul held that the only true circumcision is the circumcision of the heart (Rom. 2:28–29), a work that only the Spirit can do and is thus equivalent to redemption (cf. Col. 2:11–12). For Christians, baptism has replaced circumcision as a sign of faith and the covenant.

CISTERN

Old Testament

Noun: בּוֹר (*bôr*), GK 1014 (S 953), 65x. *bôr*, often translated as "pit," can also mean "well, dungeon, cistern, grave." See *pit*.

CITY

Old Testament

Noun: עִיר (*ʿîr*), GK 6551 (S 5892), 1087x. *ʿîr* refers to any permanent settlement. Normally it refers to walled settlements and some believe that to be considered an *ʿîr*, fortification is necessary. However, it seems that the word is also used to refer to unwalled settlements. Deut. 3:5 refers to both "fortified cities" and "cities of the open country" (cf. 2 Ki. 17:9, where *ʿîr* seems to be a general term for any settlement).

"The cities of Judah" is a common phrase in the OT (Isa. 40:9). The size of an *ʿîr* ranges from very small (sometimes translated as "town," Gen. 19:20) to very large (Jon. 3:3). Normally, however, the size of an ancient city is smaller than what we consider a "city" today. In fact, one scholar has suggested that *ʿîr* be translated as "town" in most places except where it refers to extremely large cities such as Nineveh or Babylon.

Cities can be fortified (Num. 13:28), besieged (Isa. 1:8), forsaken (Jer. 4:29), and ruined (Deut. 13:16). They may contain gates (Jdg. 16:2), defensive walls (Jos. 6:5), houses (Lev. 25:29), squares (Jdg. 19:15), and towers (Jdg. 9:51). In ancient Israel, the elders of the city were the ruling authorities (Deut. 21:19; Ruth 4:2).

Aside from referring to cities as a whole, *ʿîr* can also refer to a part of a city. For example, 2 Ki. 10:25 refers to the inner shrine of the temple of Baal by using the phrase "the city of Baal's temple." Not surprisingly, Jerusalem is the most common city referred to in the OT and is sometimes spoken of in descriptive ways, such as the city of David (Isa. 22:9), the city of God (Ps. 87:3), or the holy city (lit., "the city of holiness," Neh. 11:1). See *NIDOTTE*, 3:396-99.

New Testament

Noun: πόλις (*polis*), GK *4484* (S *4172*), 163x. In the NT, *polis* refers mainly to a place of human inhabitation such as a "city, town, village." This is in marked contrast to the use of *polis* in classical Gk., where it often refers to the political entity of a city or a larger region (city-states). This broader use of *polis* can be seen in the English adjective *political*, used to describe events and matters related to governing.

The NT avoids this earlier use of *polis*, preferring to refer to governments by such terms as "king" (1 Pet. 2:13) or "authorities" (Rom. 13:1). Thus, *polis* designates villages or towns such as Nazareth (Mt. 2:23; Lk. 1:26; 2:4, 39) and Bethany (Mt. 11:30). The designation of Bethany as a *polis* points to the NT's lack of distinction between "city" proper and "village" (*polis*) because Bethany is called a *poliș* (GK *3267*) in Mk. 8:23. Most significantly, Jerusalem is portrayed as "the holy *city*" (Mt. 4:5; 27:53; see also Rev. 11:2; 20:9). This concrete use of *polis*, as opposed to a more abstract and political use, accounts for the fact that most uses of this term in the NT are in the Synoptics and Acts (117x). *polis* can also describe the inhabitants of a place (Mt. 8:34; 21:10; Mk. 1:33).

The other main sense in which *polis* is used is to describe the heavenly "city" to which believers are headed, the heavenly Jerusalem. Thus, almost all uses of *polis* outside of the Gospels and Acts are in Revelation (27x) and the passages in Hebrews (4x) that describe the everlasting city whose maker is God (Heb. 11:16), the city that is to come (13:14) and that is to descend out of the heavens (Rev. 21:2). See *NIDNTT-A*, 483-84.

CLAN

Old Testament

Noun: מִשְׁפָּחָה (*mišpāḥâ*), GK 5476 (S 4940), 304x. The noun *mišpāḥâ* designates a subgroup of a larger division, and is, therefore, variously translated as "clan, family, people" as well as "kind, kingdoms, nation." The KJV uses "family, kindred, kind." See *kind*, *nation*.

In the Pentateuch, *mišpāḥâ* often denotes a subdivision of *šēbeṭ* ("tribe," e.g., Jdg. 21:24) or *maṭṭeh* (also "tribe," e.g., Num. 36:6). *mišpāḥâ* has a wider range of meaning than the English word "family" usually implies. "Family" in the sense of one's immediate or close relatives is usually designated in Hebrew by *bēt ʾāb*, "father's house" (e.g., Gen. 12:1; 24:23; 28:21) or simply by *bēt*, "house" (e.g., Gen. 12:17; 14:14). Thus, in searching for the guilty one who brought God's displeasure on Israel at the conquest of Ai, the tribe/clan (*šēbeṭ*) of Judah is first designated, then the family (*mišpāḥâ*) of the Zerahites, then the household (*bēt*) of Zabdi. The household of Zabdi is further examined, and Achan, himself the father of children, is found to be the guilty one (Jos. 7:16–18). See *NIDOTTE*, 2:1139-42.

CLAP

Old Testament

Verb: תָּקַע (*tāqaʿ*), GK 9546 (S 8628),

70x. *tāqaʿ* is used to describe such actions as blowing, thrusting, or clapping (see also *blow, thrust*). *tāqaʿ* is used to indicate the clapping of hands. For example, Nahum writes that people will "clap" their hands in joy when Assyria is destroyed (Nah. 3:19). The psalmist calls all nations to "clap their hands" and shout aloud to the God of all the earth (Ps. 47:1).

CLEAN

Old Testament

Adjective: טָהוֹר (*ṭāhôr*), GK 3196 (S 2889), 96x. *ṭāhôr* means "clean, pure" and is used in a material or *natural* sense, as well as in both a ritual and ethical sense. In the *natural* sense, *ṭāhôr* describes the "pure" gold of the furnishings of the tabernacle, such as the ark (Exod. 25:11), the mercy seat (25:17), the table (25:24), various vessels (25:29), the lampstand (25:31), the plate (28:36), and the incense altar (30:3). Garments for Aaron are made with cords as of pure gold (39:15). Likewise, the appliances of the temple are made of pure gold (1 Chr. 28:17), as are its inner decorations (2 Chr. 3:4) and Solomon's throne (9:17).

The Lord promises cleansing in a number of key passages in Ezekiel: "I will sprinkle *clean* water on you, and you will be clean; I will cleanse you from all your impurities and from all your idols" (Ezek. 36:25; cf. vv. 23, 33); "I will show you how to distinguish between the unclean and the *clean*" (44:23).

That such cleansing is not just intended for the people of God as a group but for the individual as well is demonstrated by Ps. 51, where David, after his sin with Bathsheba, cries out: "Wash away all my iniquity" (51:2); "Cleanse me with hyssop, and I will be clean" (51:7); and "Create in me a *pure* heart, O God" (51:10). See *NIDOTTE*, 2:338-53; 4:477-86.

New Testament

Adjective: καθαρός (*katharos*), GK *2754* (S *2513*), 27x. Similar to the verb *katharizō* (see *cleanse*), *katharos* ("clean, pure") conveys three different senses. First, in a natural or material sense, *katharos* describes something as being free from that which defiles: a clean cup (Mt. 23:26), clean linen (Mt. 27:59; Rev. 15:6), clean water (Heb. 10:22), pure gold (Rev. 21:18). A person who has bathed is said to be "clean all over" (Jn. 13:10).

Second, *katharos* relates to traditional ceremonial distinctions between clean and unclean, pure and defiled. Paul uses *katharos* in this sense when he declares that "all food is clean" (Rom. 14:20). Here he certainly does not mean that all food is free from physical dirt, but that all foods are ceremonially clean and thus are able to be eaten.

Third, closely connected to the previous notion of ritual purity, *katharos* can refer to an individual who is free from moral guilt. In this sense one is "morally pure." Jesus washes his disciples' feet demonstrating how they are now in fact morally clean (Jn. 13:10, 11) through the words that he has spoken to them (Jn. 15:3). Jesus announces that the morally pure in heart will see God (Mt. 5:8). Furthermore, Paul professes his moral integrity: "I am innocent (*katharos*) of the blood of all men" (Acts 20:26; see also 18:6). Similarly, the notion of moral uprightness may be expressed by relating "purity" as a characteristic of the heart (1 Tim. 1:5; 2 Tim. 2:22; 1 Pet. 1:22) and the conscience (1 Tim. 3:9; 2 Tim. 1:3). See *NIDNTT-A*, 278-279.

CLEANSE

Old Testament

Verb: טָהֵר (*ṭāhēr*), GK 3197 (S 2891), 94x. *ṭāhēr* is normally rendered "to cleanse, purify, consecrate." It often appears in cultic contexts and refers to physical, ritual, and ethical cleansing or purification. This verb and its derivatives are most frequently used with reference to the purification necessary to restore to a state of purity someone who has contracted ritual impurity (Lev. 22:4–7; for the opposite of *ṭāhēr*, see *ṭāmēʾ*). Because of the separation between "holy" and "common" (see Lev. 10:10), God requires his people to observe purification rites when they come into his presence for worship. Ritual purity is intended to teach God's holiness and moral purity. Purification rituals, therefore, prepare individuals to approach God (Exod. 19:10; Num. 8:15; see *sanctify*).

Often "cleansing" is accomplished by physically removing objects of defilement. This may involve washings (a man who has a discharge waits seven days, then washes his clothes and bathes in order to be clean, Lev. 25:13), offerings (after the birth of a child a mother has to wait a certain period and then brings certain offerings to be cleansed "from the flow of her blood," 12:7–8), or other procedures (a "leprous" man who has been healed must go through an elaborate ceremony to be declared clean, 14:4–20; a "leprous" house that is "purified" goes through a similar process, 14:48–53). The ultimate cleansing is the Day of Atonement, which requires blood as the purifying agent: "He shall sprinkle some of the blood on it with his finger seven times to *cleanse* it and to consecrate it from the uncleanness of the Israelites" (Lev. 16:19).

It is important to note, however, that it is not the ritual purification by the officiating priest that ultimately imparts purity. Individuals are cleansed by the forgiveness that comes from God. Only he can cleanse. Prov. 30:12 speaks of "those who are pure in their own eyes and yet are not cleansed of their filth" (see also Job 4:17). Ultimately, the Lord promises: "I will *cleanse* them from all the sin they have committed against me and will forgive all their sins of rebellion against me" (Jer. 33:8).

Verb: כָּבַס (*kābas*), GK 3891 (S 3526), 51x. *kābas* means "to clean, cleanse, wash," usually by treading, kneading, or beating. In contrast to *rāḥaṣ*, which is used of washing the human body, *kābas* is never used of bodily cleansing and almost always refers to the washing of clothes. See *wash*.

Verb: רָחַץ (*rāḥaṣ*), GK 8175 (S 7364), 72x. *rāḥaṣ* denotes the cleansing of an object, body part, or entire person for the purposes of sacrifice, priestly service, or cultural etiquette. It may be translated as "wash, bathe, cleanse." See *wash*.

New Testament

Verb: καθαρίζω (*katharizō*), GK *2751* (S *2511*), 31x. In the NT *katharizō* ("make clean, cleanse") takes on three distinct nuances. First, the term can refer in a general sense to making something physically clean. Jesus speaks of the Pharisees making the outside of a cup or dish "clean" (Mt. 23:25, 26; Lk. 11:39). Second, *katharizō* is used in the sense of "healing" a disease that has made a person ceremonially unclean, specifically leprosy. In Mt. 8:2–3 Jesus "cleanses" a leper from his defiling skin disease and in this sense heals him (see also 10:8). In the parallel account of the healing of the leper the NIV translates *katharizō* as "cured" ("cleansed" KJV) in Mk. 1:42 (see also Mt. 11:5; Lk. 7:22). Thus in these contexts cleansing is akin to healing.

Finally, *katharizō* may refer to purification through ritual cleansing. Here the OT notion of clean and unclean animals is given a new meaning in Acts 10:15: "Do not call anything impure that God has made clean" (see also Mk. 7:19; Acts 11:9). Furthermore, the ceremonial notion of ritual purification (deriving from the OT priestly cult) may take on a moral sense where cleansing denotes repentance (Jas. 4:8: "Wash your hands, you sinners, and purify your hearts, you double-minded") or spiritual purification from sin (Tit. 2:4; Heb. 9:14; 1 Jn. 1:7, 9).

CLIFF

Old Testament

Noun: סֶלַע (*selaʿ*), GK 6152 (S 5553), 58x. *selaʿ* denotes a piece of geographic terrain usually characterized as a "cliff" or steep "rock" face found on a mountain. See *rock*.

CLING

Old Testament

Verb: דָּבַק (*dābaq*), GK 1815 (S 1692), 55x. *dābaq* denotes the basic action of one object or person adhering or clinging to another. It takes both people and physical objects as its subject, but never God.

(1) When *dābaq* takes a physical object as its subject, it carries the sense of two things sticking together, and the subject is frequently a part of the human body (see Job 41:17, 23 as exceptions). In a display of courage in a time of exhaustion, one of David's mighty men struck down the Philistines until he was weary and his hand "clung" to the sword (2 Sam. 23:10, NIV translates "froze"). As an expression of despair and physical agony, the psalmist declares that his bones "cling" to his flesh (Ps. 102:5; cf. Job 19:20). The expression "the tongue *clinging* to the roof of one's mouth" may be used to indicate a person's silence (Job 29:10; Ps. 137:6; Ezek. 3:26) or thirst (Lam. 4:4). In Ps. 22:15, this expression indicates thirst, and the expression lies behind Jesus' cry on the cross, "I thirst" (Jn. 19:28).

(2) When *dābaq* takes a person as its subject, sometimes mere physical proximity is signified. Boaz instructs Ruth to "stay here" with his maids as they glean in the field (Ruth 2:8, 21; cf. 2:23). In certain contexts, *dābaq* occurs in a form that conveys the notion of "to pursue, overtake." Laban "overtakes" Jacob in Gilead (Gen. 31:23), and the Israelites "pursue" the Philistines in battle after the Philistines flee (1 Sam. 14:22).

But more often when *dābaq* takes a person as its subject, much more than mere physical proximity is implied. In these instances, devotion and affection are communicated along with physical proximity, as one person "clings" to another. As marriage is established in the creation account, the OT teaches, "For this reason a man shall leave his father and his mother and *cling* to his wife, and they shall become one flesh" (Gen. 2:24). Outside of marriage, Ruth "clings" to Naomi after Orpah leaves (Ruth 1:14), and the men of Judah "remain steadfast" to their king when Israel does not (2 Sam. 20:2).

In this sense of devotion, affection, and physical proximity, Moses and Joshua repeatedly urge Israel to "cling" to God (Deut. 10:20; 11:22; 13:4; 30:20; Jos. 22:5; 23:8; NIV translates "hold fast") because the Israelites are so prone to worship other gods. Perhaps because of the frailty associated with human clinging, *dābaq* never takes God as its subject, but Yahweh's covenant faithfulness is expressed through *ḥesed* instead. See *NIDOTTE*, 1:910-12.

Verb: לָכַד (*lākad*), GK 4334 (S 3920), 121x. *lākad* generally means "to capture, seize, take captive." It can be used actively (i.e., "to catch, capture," Num. 21:32; Deut. 2:34; Jos. 10:42; Jdg. 7:24; 15:4; Ps. 35:8; Amos 3:4, 5), passively (i.e., "to be seized," 1 Ki. 16:18; Isa. 23:13; Jer. 6:11; 38:28; 48:1, 41; 51:56; Ezek. 7:26), or reflectively (i.e., "to cling to each other," Job 38:30; 41:17). See *capture*.

New Testament

Verb: ἅπτω (*haptō*), GK *721* (S 680, *681*), 39x. At its most basic level *haptō* means "to make close contact with something, touch something." But it can also mean "to cling to, take hold of something." See *touch*.

Verb: κολλάω (*kollaō*), GK *3140* (S *2853*), 12x. *kollaō* means to "join, unite closely." It can also mean "cling, stick to"; for example, "the dust that *clings* to our feet" (Lk. 10:11). Elsewhere Paul challenges his readers to "*cling to* what is good" (Rom. 12:9). See *join*.

CLOAK

New Testament

Noun: ἱμάτιον (*himation*), GK *2668* (S *2440*), 60x. *himation* is sometimes used of "clothing" in general, but more frequently of the outer "robe" or "cloak." See *clothes*.

CLOTHE

Old Testament

Verb: לָבַשׁ (*lābaš*), GK 4252 (S 3847), 112x. *lābaš* is the most common word in the OT for "to clothe, put on clothes." God clothes Adam and Eve with skins (Gen. 3:21), Rebekah puts Esau's clothes on Jacob in order to deceive Isaac (27:15), people can be clothed with sackcloth (Jon. 3:5;

Est. 4:1), and Esther puts on fine linen, or perhaps royal robes (Est. 5:1; cf. Jer. 4:30; Ezek. 9:2; Dan. 10:5).

Clothing can be used as a sign of rank. Hence, David's daughters indicate their royalty (and virginity) by what they wear (2 Sam. 13:18). When Pharaoh elevates Joseph, he not only gives the young Hebrew his signet ring and a gold necklace, but also "dresses" him in robes of fine linen.

lābaš can also refer to abstract qualities. Jerusalem "*puts on* garments of splendor" (Isa. 52:1), and God "puts on" righteousness and garments of vengeance (59:17). The psalmist writes, "The Lord reigns, he is *robed* in majesty; the Lord is *robed* in majesty and is armed with strength" (Ps. 93:1). Job uses the imagery of clothing to describe his pursuit of righteousness and justice: "I *put on* righteousness as my *clothing*; justice was my robe and my turban" (Job 29:14).

People may "put on" salvation (2 Chr. 6:41; Isa. 61:10) and strength (Isa. 52:1), but they may also "put on" negative qualities such as shame (Ps. 35:26) and cursing (109:18). See *NIDOTTE, 2:757-59.*

New Testament

Verb: ἐνδύω (*endyō*), GK *1907* (S *1746*), 27x. *endyō* means "to put something on, wear." It is generally used of clothes, though there are also many metaphorical uses. See *put on.*

Verb: περιβάλλω (*periballō*), GK *4314* (S *4016*), 23x. *periballō* means "to wear, clothe, dress." See *wear.*

CLOTHES, CLOTHING

Old Testament

Noun: בֶּגֶד (*beged*), GK 955 (S 899), 216x. *beged* is a general term for "clothing, garments" of any kind. It is used in Num. 4:6–13 for various cloths used as coverings in the tabernacle, but most references are to human clothing.

(1) *beged* is used for the robes of the priests (Exod. 28:2–4) and kings (1 Ki. 22:10), but also for the clothes of a widow (Gen. 38:14) or a prisoner (2 Ki. 25:29). It can reveal something about an individual. For example, torn clothing can symbolize grief (Gen. 37:29; 2 Sam. 1:11; 3:31; 2 Ki. 22:11; Ezr. 9:3, 5). A garment with red stains can symbolize that an individual has been in a battle (cf. Isa. 63:1–3). It is possible for a garment to be ritually unclean (Lev. 11:25, 28; 13:47–59). God also commands that the "*cloak* of a widow" cannot be taken as a pledge for an unpaid debt (Deut. 24:17).

(2) Certain types of people wore special clothing. Chief among these are the special "sacred *garments*" of the high priest (Exod. 28:2–4; 29:21, 29; 31:10; 35:19; Num. 20:26, 28). Kings too often wore "royal *robes*" (1 Ki. 22:10, 30). At a time of a royal wedding, the groom's clothing was sometimes perfumed (Ps. 45:8).

(3) Clothing can be used in symbolic ways for spiritual realities. After their sin in the garden of Eden, Adam and Eve sewed fig leaves to cover their nakedness and to attempt to hide their sin from God. Isaiah writes that "all our righteous acts are like filthy *rags*" (Isa. 64:5). As sinners, we are unable to clothe ourselves to stand clean in God's presence, as Joshua the high priest discovers in Zech. 3. He is dressed in "filthy *clothes*" (3:3), which represent the sins of the people. But the angel commands that these be taken off him and instead he be given new clothing; "so they put a clean turban on his head and put *clothes* on him" (3:5).

beged can also a metaphor for God's actions on behalf of his people. Since his people are unable to save themselves, God goes to work destroying the enemies of God's people and staining his clothes blood-red (Isa. 63:1–5). Following this, clothing becomes a symbol of the joy of God's salvation. The phrase "*garments* of salvation" speaks of the fullness of God's deliverance and blessing (Isa. 61:10). The phrase "*garments* of splendor" signifies the royal and holy status of God's people (52:1). See *NIDOTTE*, 1:595–97).

New Testament

Noun: ἱμάτιον (*himation*), GK *2668* (S *2440*), 60x. *himation* is sometimes used of "clothing" in general (Lk. 23:34; Jas. 5:2), but more frequently of the outer "robe" or "cloak" (Mt. 5:40). A woman was healed when she touched Jesus' clothes (Mk. 6:56). Most uses of this word are in the gospels and Acts.

Jesus says, "And if anyone would sue you and take your tunic [*chitōn*, GK *5945*), let him have your *cloak* as well" (Mt. 5:40). The *chitōn* was the inner garment worn next to the body for which someone could sue. However, Mosaic law forbade the taking of the outer tunic, the *himation* (Exod. 22:26; Deut. 24:13). Jesus' disciples must be willing to forgo their rights in their service to Christ. Peter insists that outer clothing is not nearly as important as the inner beauty of a gentle and quiet spirit (1 Pet. 3:3–4)—a message appropriate to our generation.

Clothing is often used in symbolic ways. White clothing is associated with Jesus at the transfiguration (Mt. 17:2), the elders around the throne of God (Rev. 4:4), and the redeemed (3:4–5, 18). New clothing is compared to the newness of Jesus' message (Mt. 9:16). Conversely, people tore their clothes in response to blasphemy (Mt. 26:65; Acts 14:14), and Paul shook out his clothes to protest Jewish rejection of the gospel (Acts 18:16). See *NIDNTT-A*, 270.

CLOUD

Old Testament

Noun: עָנָן (*ʿānān*), GK 6727 (S 6051), 87x. *ʿānān* is consistently translated "cloud," sometimes "mist." Occasionally this noun is used of rain clouds (Gen. 9:13–16; Ezek. 1:28) and of incense smoke (Lev. 16:13). But by far its most frequent usage is for "the pillar of *cloud*" that leads the Israelites in the desert (Exod. 33:9–10; Neh. 9:12, 19) and later the cloud that descends on the temple at its dedication (2 Chr. 5:13–14). This cloud is a form of theophany (i.e., an appearance of God); it represents the majesty and mystery of the Lord, who is not to be seen by human eyes (see Exod. 24:15–18; Ps. 97:2; Ezek. 1:4). Several of the prophets use this word as one of the major elements that describe the day of the Lord (see Ezek. 30:3; Joel 2:2; Zeph. 1:15).

There are also metaphorical uses of *ʿānān*. The people of Israel are compared to clouds because their loyalty is transitory (Hos. 6:4; 13:3). As a figure for something enormous, Ezekiel speaks of the power of Gog as "a *cloud* covering the land" (Ezek. 38:9). As a picture of impenetrability, a mass of clouds signifies the distance that the exiles feel between themselves and God: "You have covered yourself with a *cloud* so that no prayer can get through" (Lam. 3:44).

New Testament

Noun: νεφέλη (*nephelē*), GK *3749* (S *3507*), 25x. *nephelē* is usually translated "cloud." Sometimes this term refers to a natural phenomenon in the sky that can help predict the weather (Lk. 12:54). But interestingly, the vast majority of its NT occurrences are in passages with eschatological overtones. A voice speaks from the cloud at Jesus' transfiguration (Mt. 17:5). Jesus ascends in a cloud after his resurrection (Acts 1:9) and the Son of Man will return on a cloud (Mt. 24:30; Mk. 13:26; Rev. 1:7; 14:14–16). Believers will be caught up to meet Jesus in the clouds (1 Thess. 4:17). The mighty angel comes from heaven wrapped in a cloud (Rev. 10:1), and the two prophets in Revelation are caught in a cloud after their resurrection (11:12).

In an attempt to call the people to perseverance, Paul reminds the Corinthians that the Jewish people of the exodus were under the miraculous cloud of God's presence, and yet when they sinned God punished them. So too the Corinthians will face judgment for their sins if they remain in them.

In an interesting twist of imagery, false teachers in the early church are compared to "waterless clouds," denying people the very thing they appeared to bring (Jude 12). See *NIDNTT-A*, 79.

CLUB

New Testament

Noun: ξύλον (*xylon*), GK *3833* (S *3586*), 20x. *xylon* means "tree, club, wood, stocks." It refers to living or dead wood or anything made of wood. See *tree*.

COAST

Old Testament

Noun: גְּבוּל (g^e*bûl*), GK 1473 (S 1366), 241x. g^e*bûl* can mean either "border" (a boundary line between two areas) or "territory" (the area within a border). It is difficult to know which meaning is intended. When it refers to the borders of the sea (Ps. 104:9; Jer. 5:22), it can denote the coastline. See *border*.

COCK

New Testament

Noun: ἀλέκτωρ (*alektōr*), GK *232* (S *220*), 12x. *alektōr* means "rooster, cock." See *rooster*.

COIN

New Testament

Noun: δηνάριον (*dēnarion*), GK *1324* (S *1220*), 16x. The *dēnarion* was a Roman silver coin worth about one worker's average daily wage. See *denarius*.

COLLAPSE

New Testament

Verb: πίπτω (*piptō*), GK *4406* (S *4098*), 90x. *piptō* means "to fall, collapse, bow down." See *fall*.

COLT

New Testament

Noun: πῶλος (*pōlos*), GK *4798* (S *4454*), 12x. *pōlos* means "colt." All uses of this noun are in the story of Jesus' triumphal entry into Jerusalem on a donkey (Mt. 21:1–9; Mk. 11:1–10; Lk. 19:29–38; Jn. 12:12–15). This story is important not only because through this event Jesus is fulfilling Scripture (Zech. 9:9), but also because it visibly demonstrates the nature of Jesus' kingdom, namely, that his kingdom is characterized by peace and humility (for a donkey was a domestic animal, not a war animal like a horse).

COLUMN

Old Testament

Noun: עַמּוּד (*ʿammûd*), GK 6647 (S 5982), 112x. *ʿammûd* means "pillar, post" and refers to a columnar support for a structure, whether literal or metaphorical, or to a column-like image, such as a funnel cloud. It can also denote vaporous columns of smoke, fire, and cloud (Num. 12:5; Deut. 31:15). See *pillar*.

COME

Old Testament

Verb: בּוֹא (*bôʾ*), GK 995 (S 935), 2592x. *bôʾ* is the fourth most common verb in the OT. It denotes motion toward a specific goal, such as "to go, arrive, enter a house, come." For example, "God *came* to Abimelech in a dream" (Gen. 20:3); "the spies *entered* the promised land" (Num. 13:27), and "Samuel got up and *went* to Eli" (1 Sam. 3:6). The verb *hālak* (GK 2143), "to walk, go," is a synonym.

bôʾ is used metaphorically of death, in the expression "go to the fathers" (Gen. 15:15). It is also used idiomatically of sexual relations, in the expression, "he *went* into her" (Gen. 16:4, "He slept with Hagar, and she conceived…," NIV; "And he *went in* unto Hagar, and she conceived…," KJV). The metaphor "go in the days" means "advanced age." For example, in Gen. 24:1, "Abraham was now old and *well advanced in years*" is literally translated "he went in the days." In covenantal contexts, the blessings of the covenant *come* upon those who obey, but the curses *come* upon those who rebel and disobey (Deut. 28:2, 15). Thus, *bôʾ* may have the sense of "to happen, occur," as in Isa. 42:9, "the former things *have taken place*" (KJV, "… have come to pass").

This verb can also be used in the sense of "causing something to go or come," that is, "to bring something or someone." God fashioned Eve "and he *brought* her to the man" (Gen. 2:22). The noble woman "is like the merchant ships, *bringing* her food from afar" (Prov. 31:14). This causative aspect of *bôʾ* takes on particular theological significance when God is the subject.

He is the one who promises to *bring* the Israelites to the promised land (Deut. 4:38) in fulfillment of his oath to the fathers (6:10). When Israel comes into the land by God's faithful care, she is to *bring* her offerings to the designated place (12:10–11) as an expression of worship and thankfulness to God. Her military victories are not her own; they belong to God. Israel thus finds her rest in the land because of God's faithfulness *to bring* her there (12:9). In this way, the land of promise stands metaphorically as the rest of faith (Heb. 4:1–11). As Israel trusts in God, it is God who fulfills his promises to her and *brings* her to the place of rest.

Perhaps most significant is the use of *bô*ʾ to describe God's own *coming* into the world. He *comes* enshrouded in thick clouds to Mount Sinai (Exod. 19:9; 20:20), from where he *comes* with his myriad of thousands to fight for Israel (Deut. 33:2–5; Hab. 3:3). Throughout Israel's history, the "name of the LORD" *comes* to fight for her (Isa. 30:27), assuring her of the final victory (Ps. 96:13; 98:9). In the final day, God *will come* to judge the evildoers (Isa. 66:15) and to *bring back* his people from the ends of the earth (40:9–11). In this eschatological victory, the Redeemer *comes* to Zion and *causes* Israel *to return* in faithfulness to him (59:20–21, cf. Rom. 11:26).

The "coming" of God into the sphere of human history thus stands as the centerpiece of redemption. From earliest times, the promise of the one who would come summarizes the reign of God among men (Gen. 49:10, "The scepter will not depart from Judah, nor the ruler's staff from between his feet, *until he comes*," NIV; "until Shiloh *come*," KJV). Ezekiel speaks of the "coming one" (Ezek. 21:27) and Zechariah promises that "your king *comes* to you, righteous and having salvation, gentle and riding on a donkey" (Zech. 9:9). The hope of final redemption awaits the coming of God as the Messiah.

Since God is true, his words never fail. When *bô*ʾ is used in connection with God's word or purpose, it means "to come to pass, come true." Manoah asks the angel of the Lord, "What is your name, so that we may honor you when your word *comes true*?" (KJV, "comes to pass," Jdg. 13:17). In the same way, the words of God's prophet *come to pass* (Jer. 32:24), for they are the words of God himself. See *NIDOTTE*, 1:615-18.

Verb: הָלַךְ (*hālak*), GK 2143 (S 1980), 1554x. *hālak* describes motion, primarily of humans, and is usually translated "walk, go, come." See *go*.

New Testament

Verb: ἔρχομαι (*erchomai*), GK *2262* (S *2064*), 632x. *erchomai* usually means "come, arrive." Only rarely is it used to express "go" or "going," since other words are used for this purpose (see, e.g., Mt. 13:36; Mk. 1:14; Jn. 21:3). It usually refers to an individual's physically arriving at a location; for this reason the vast majority of its uses are in the gospels, Acts, and the travel sections of NT letters.

But *erchomai* can also be used in reference to "coming to" his senses (Lk. 15:17) or to the illness of a woman "becoming" worse (Mk. 5:26). Furthermore, this verb can refer to a prophetic event such as the wrath of God, conveying imminence and/or certainty (1 Thess. 1:10). Then the time "had fully come," God sent his Son into this world (Gal. 4:4). *erchomai* is also used when speaking of an appearance, especially a coming of Jesus. John makes note of the appearance of the Messiah among us (Jn. 7:31; 1 Jn. 5:6; Jude 14), and the expression "the Coming One" is used as a messianic title (Mt. 11:3; Heb. 10:37). But note too that "the antichrist is coming" (1 Jn. 2:18).

Verb: ἥκω (*ēkō*), GK *2457* (S *2240*), 26x. *ēkō* means "to come" or "to have come." It often has a future nuance ("will come"). It is, in this sense, different from *erchomai*, which is used much more frequently in the NT.

ēko refers often to something that will happen in the future, especially in Matthew—the coming of the kingdom of God, future salvation, and judgment. When teaching the disciples about the kingdom, Jesus says, "Many *will come* from the east and the west and will take their places ... in the kingdom of heaven" (Mt. 8:11). Future tribulations "will come" (23:36; 24:50; cf. 2 Pet. 3:10), and after the gospel is preached everywhere, "the end *will come*" (Mt. 24:14). The usage in Matthew contrasts with the verb in Mk. 8:3, where "have come" relates to the present, "If I send them home hungry, they will collapse on the way, because some of them *have come* a long distance." In Luke, both senses are used (see Lk. 12:46; 13:29, 35; 15:27; 19:43).

In the gospel of John, Jesus speaks of his hour, which "*has* not yet *come*" (Jn. 2:4), of those who "will come" to him for salvation (Jn. 6:37), and of "his coming" from the Father (Jn. 8:42; 1 Jn. 5:20). In Revelation, *ēkō* refers explicitly to things that are to come, such as the return of Christ (Rev. 2:25; 3:3, 9). In 15:4 "all nations *will come* and worship" the Lord. In 18:8 it refers the future fall of Babylon.

Verb: παραγίνομαι (*paraginomai*), GK *4134* (S *3854*), 37x. *paraginomai* means "to come, arrive." Most of the uses of this verb are in narrative parts of the NT. Wise men come from the east (Mt. 2:1), John the Baptist comes to the desert (3:1), and Jesus comes to John to be baptized (3:13). Luke uses *paraginomai* in both his gospel and in Acts as a verb for travel, such as the apostle Paul arriving in various places in his journeys (Acts 13:14; 14:27; 15:4; 17:10; 24:17). Paul reports in 2 Tim. 4:16 that when he stood before Caesar at his first defense, no one "came" to support him. The author of Hebrew refers to the fact that "Jesus came as high priest of the good things that are already here" (Heb. 9:11).

Interjection: δεῦτε (*deute*), GK *1307* (S *1205*), 12x. *deute* is an interjection that signifies "Come." It can be used with either a positive or a negative connotation.

Jesus uses *deute* as an invitation to come to him—inviting his would-be disciples (Mt. 4:19; Mk. 1:17; cf. Jn. 21:12), those who are weary and need rest (Mt. 11:28), or those on his right hand who are ready to enter the kingdom (25:34). The angel at the empty tomb invites the women to "*come* and see the place where he lay" (28:6). The Samaritan woman said to the people of her town, "*Come*, see a man who told me everything I ever did" (Jn. 4:29).

deute is also used by the tenants in the parable of the vineyard as they plot to kill the master's son: "*Come*, let's kill him, and the inheritance will be ours" (Lk. 12:7; cf. Mt. 21:38). Its only use outside the gospels is Rev. 19:17, where the invitation is given: "*Come,* gather together for the great supper of God."

COME DOWN

New Testament

Verb: καταβαίνω (*katabainō*), GK *2849* (S *2597*), 81x. *katabainō* means "to come down, go down, descend." This verb is most often found in the gospels and Acts and generally retains its spatial meaning. It is in contrast to *anabainō*, which means "to go up." This verb is used of Jesus and/or his disciples "*coming down* from the mountain" (Mt. 8:1; Mk. 9:9; Lk. 6:17). The mocking crowds urge Jesus to "*come down* from the cross" (Mt. 27:40, 42; Mk. 15:30, 32). Zacchaeus "came down" from a perch in a tree (Lk. 19:5–6). The verb is used in the account of Peter getting out of the boat (Mt. 14:29), of Capernaum's "descent into Hades" (Mt. 11:23), and of a "descent from Jerusalem" (Mk. 3:22; Lk. 2:51; 10:30; Acts 8:15; 25:7). Since Jerusalem is at a high elevation, leaving that city meant that one would "descend" (Acts 14:25; 16:8; 18:22).

katabainō is also used of a descent from heaven by the angel in Mt. 28:2 (cf. Jn. 1:51), of the Son of Man (see Jn. 3:13), of the bread that has "*come down* out of heaven" (Jn. 6:33, 38, 41, 42, 50, 51, 58), of the Holy Spirit's descent as a dove in Mt. 3:16 (Mk. 1:10; Lk. 3:22; Jn. 1:32), and of a great wind descending on the sea of Galilee (Lk. 8:23). In Peter's vision, an object like a sheet "comes down" (Acts 10:11).

In the NT letters, Paul uses *katabainō* only to refer to Christ's "descent" to earth in the incarnation (Eph. 4:9–10; cf. also Rom. 10:7) or in the second coming (1 Thess. 4:16). James speaks of the gifts that are "*coming down* from the Father of Lights" (Jas. 1:17). See *NIDNTT-A*, 340.

Verb: κατέρχομαι (*katerchomai*), GK *2982* (S *2718*), 16x. *katerchomai* means "to come down, go down, land (at a seaport; see *land*)." This verb usually refers to going from a place of higher elevation to lower elevation, e.g., coming down from a mountain (Lk. 9:37). It was necessary for Jesus to "come down" from Nazareth to Capernaum since the latter is located along the Sea of Galilee (Lk. 4:31). *katerchomai* is also used in a figurative sense when James says that worldly wisdom does not "*come down* from above" (Jas. 3:15).

COME NEAR

Old Testament

Verb: קָרַב (*qārab*), GK 7928 (S 7126), 280x. The basic meaning of *qārab* is "to come, draw near" or, in a causative sense, "to bring near." This basic meaning may denote physical or spatial proximity as well as nonphysical. See *bring*.

New Testament

Verb: ἐγγίζω (*engizō*), GK *1581* (S *1448*), 42x. *engizō* means "to approach, come near." Most of its occurrences are in the gospels. Sometimes it simply means that Jesus and his disciples are approaching a particular city (Mt. 21:1; Lk. 7:12). But it can also denote the nearness of events or people (e.g., feasts, harvest, Judas, a commander; see Mt. 21:34; Lk. 22:1; 22:47; Acts 21:33). It is often used with reference to the kingdom of heaven, which Matthew describes as being "at hand" (KJV) or "near" (Mt. 3:2; 4:17; 10:7). It likewise refers to impending spiritual events, such as the hour of betrayal (26:45) and Israel's redemption (Lk. 21:28).

engizō also occurs in the NT letters. Here it sometimes refers to the second coming (Jas. 5:8), the day of the Lord (Rom. 13:12; Heb. 10:25), and the end of the age (1 Pet. 4:7). Behind this verb stands God's promises in the OT and his preparation for those promises (see especially Isa. 46:13, where Isaiah indicates that God's righteousness and salvation are near). James commands his audience, "*Come near* to God and he will *come near* to you" (Jas. 4:8), and the writer of the Hebrews notes that through Jesus, we can now draw near to God (Heb. 7:19; cf. 10:19–22).

COME OUT

Old Testament

Verb: יָצָא (*yāṣāʾ*), GK 3655 (S 3318), 1076x. *yāṣāʾ* most frequently means "to go out, come out, bring out." See *go out.*

New Testament

Verb: ἐκπορεύομαι (*ekporeuomai*), GK *1744* (S *1607*), 33x. *ekporeuomai* means "to come, go out." Jesus said that it is what "comes out" of a person's mouth that makes him or her unclean (Mt. 15:11, 18). The Spirit "goes out" from the Father (Jn. 15:26). Paul commands the Ephesians not to let any "unwholesome talk come out of [their] mouths" (Eph. 4:29). The river of the water of life "flows" or "comes out" from the throne of God and of the Lamb (Rev. 22:1).

Verb: ἐξέρχομαι (*exerchomai*), GK *2002* (S *1831*), 218x. *exerchomai* means to "go out, come out." See *go out.*

COME THROUGH

New Testament

Verb: διερχομαι (*dierchomai*), GK *1451* (S *1330*), 43x. *dierchomai* means "to come or go through, pass through." See *go through.*

COME TO

New Testament

Verb: προσέρχομαι (*proserchomai*), GK *4665* (S *4334*), 86x. *proserchomai* simply means "to approach, come to," though it sometimes carries significant theological meaning with reverential overtones. See *approach.*

COME TO PASS

Old Testament

Verb: הָיָה (*hāyâ*), GK 2118 (S 1961),

3561x. *hāyâ* means "to be, become, come to pass." See *be*.

COME TOGETHER

New Testament

Verb: συνέρχομαι (*synerchomai*), GK *5302* (S *4905*), 30x. *synerchomai* means "to assemble, come together, gather." See *assemble*.

COME UPON

New Testament

Verb: ἐπιπίπτω (*epipiptō*), GK *2158* (S *1968*), 11x. *epipiptō* can mean "to come upon, fall upon, embrace." In the NT *epipiptō* is used only in respect to persons. It indicates embracing in Lk. 15:20 and Acts 20:37. This describes John's reclining on Jesus at the Last Supper (Jn. 13:25) and can have the sense of "to press upon" (as in Mk. 3:10). It is a favorite word in Acts for the Holy Spirit descending on people (Acts 8:16; 10:44; 11:15). Metaphorically, *epipiptō* can refer to being "gripped" or "seized" by fear (Lk. 1:12; Acts 19:17). See *NIDNTT-A*, 461-62.

COMFORT

Old Testament

Verb: נָחַם (*nāḥam*), GK 5714 (S 5162), 108x. *nāḥam* bears two distinct but related meanings in the OT: "to comfort, console" and "to relent, repent, change one's mind, be grieved" (see *change one's mind*).

Isaac is comforted after his mother's death (Gen. 24:67), and David comforts Bathsheba after the death of their firstborn child (2 Sam. 12:24). For suffering Israel, the opening scene of Isa. 40 declares, " 'Comfort, comfort my people,' says the LORD" (Isa. 40:1). After years of pain and punishment for sin, God returns with words of hope and comfort.

Most often, God is of the one who does the comforting, and *nāḥam* is used in contexts that describe God as gracious, compassionate, slow to anger, and abounding in love (Joel 2:13; Jon. 4:2). Ultimate comfort comes solely from the gracious hand of God.

New Testament

Verb: παρακαλέω (*parakaleō*), GK *4151* (S *3870*), 109x. *parakaleō* variously means "to ask, summons, exhort, comfort, or encourage" (see *ask*, *exhort*).

parakaleō sometimes refers to comfort. This is displayed most directly in 2 Cor. 1:1–6, where the verb occurs 4x alongside the noun *paraklēsis*, which also occurs 4x. Echoing in some sense the Isaianic comfort of Isa. 40:1, Paul encourages the believers of Corinth in the comfort given to them by Christ. Though suffering, they have not been forgotten by the God of all comfort.

Noun: παράκλησις (*paraklēsis*), GK *4155* (S *3874*), 29x. *paraklēsis* carries the idea of consolation, comfort, or encouragement.

Paul's second letter to Corinth is colored with words of comfort, containing eleven instances of *paraklēsis*, which is over a third of the total occurrences in the NT. In Lk. 2:25 Simeon is described as one awaiting the *paraklēsis* of Israel. In Acts the believers look for encouragement or comfort from one another (Acts 13:15; 15:31). The source of all comfort is the Holy Spirit (Acts 9:31). This association of comfort with the Holy Spirit is evident in Jesus' reference to the Spirit as the *paraklētos*, "the comforter" (KJV, see Jn. 14:26; 15:26; 16:13–14).

COMING

New Testament

Noun: παρουσία (*parousia*), GK *4242* (S *3952*), 24x. *parousia* indicates one's arrival (1 Cor. 16:17), as when Titus arrives in Macedonia (2 Cor. 7:6). It can also mean being present; Paul writes that his being present with the Philippians will increase their joy (Phil. 1:26). "In person," Paul is criticized as being unimpressive (2 Cor. 10:10).

For the most part, however, *parousia* has a technical meaning, referring to Jesus' second coming at the end of time. In secular thought, a *parousia* was the coming of an important person, such as a king or emperor, or even the appearing of a god. This may form some of the backdrop to *parousia* being used of the second coming (Mt. 24:3, 27, 37, 39; 1 Cor. 15:23).

Jesus teaches that his coming will be as sudden as a lightening flash (Mt. 24:27). Life will be going on in a normal fashion and the coming of the Lord will be unexpected (Mt. 24:37-41). His teachings conclude with a warning to "keep watch, because you do not know on what day your Lord will come." Paul continues this emphasis on the suddenness of Jesus' return (1 Thess. 4:15; 5:4) and stresses the importance of living blameless lives until that "coming" (5:23). Much of the teaching about Jesus' *parousia* is done with an eye to how we must live in anticipation of this most assured future event.

The Thessalonian church fell into controversy over the *parousia* of the Lord. As the coming of the Lord delayed and Christian believers began to die, the Thessalonians became concerned. Paul makes it clear that when Jesus returns, those who have died will rise first and then will be followed by those who are still alive (1 Thess. 4:15); this is the "rapture." Because of a delay, the Thessalonians are also concerned that they may have missed the coming of the Lord (2 Thess. 2:1–2). Paul clarifies that the lawless one's *parousia* (i.e., the "coming" of the Antichrist) will occur prior to Jesus' coming (2 Thess. 2:8–9). Some Thessalonians were also quitting their jobs, possibly because they expected the coming of the Lord soon (3:10); Paul insists that if they do not work, the church should not care for them (1 Thess. 5:14; 2 Thess. 3:6–12).

James also addresses the delay in the expected "coming" of the Lord (5:7–8). Believers are to be patient, just as a farmer waits for his crop, "for the *coming* of the Lord is at hand." Peter writes that God does not consider length of time as perhaps people do, and that Jesus delays because "he is patient with you, not wanting anyone to perish, but everyone to come to repentance" (2 Pet. 3:8–9).

Biblical teaching about the end times have the purpose of encouraging disciples to have hope during hardship, to witness to others, and to live righteously, for they can know with absolute assuredness when he does return, evil will be punished and righteousness will be rewarded. See *NIDNTT-A*, 440-41.

COMMAND

Old Testament

Verb: אָמַר (*ʾāmar*), GK 606 (S 559), 5316x. *ʾāmar* is the most common verb in the OT for "to say, utter." See *say*. It is also used to indicate a command or an instruction. Joshua did as the Lord "instructed" by hamstringing the horses and burning the chariots (Jos. 11:9). Job 36:8 states, "He makes them listen and *commands* them to repent of their evil." See *say*.

Verb: צָוָה (*ṣāwâ*), GK 7422 (S 6680), 496x. This verb is used to denote the issuing of an authoritative statement and means "to command, order." When used negatively, it can be translated as "to forbid." *ṣāwâ* is common in Exodus through Deuteronomy with the giving of the Mosaic law. Joshua and Jeremiah frequently use this verb when making reference to this legislation, "Remember the word which Moses the servant of the Lord commanded you" (Jos. 1:13). God is the most common subject of this verb (about 280x) and Moses is the next most common subject (about 85x). When God is the subject, there can be a close connection between his commands and his creative power. In Ps. 148:5 it is written, "Let them praise the name of the Lord, for he commanded and they were created" (see also Isa. 45:12). See *NIDOTTE*, 3:776-80.

New Testament

Verb: διαστέλλω (*diastellō*), GK *1403* (S *1291*), 7x. *diastellō* means "to command, order" with authority. Jesus commands people who have seen him heal not to tell anyone (Mk. 5:32; 7:36). The disciples are commanded not to tell what they have seen at the Transfiguration (9:9), and God commanded the Israelites not to touch Mount Sinai while he was present (Heb. 12:20). See *warn*.

Verb: διατάσσω (*diatassō*), GK *1411*

(S *1299*), 16x. *diatassō* means "to command, direct, order." This verb is sometimes used by military and governmental officials. Tax collectors, employed by the state, are to collect no more than they are "commanded" (Lk. 3:13). Paul came into contact with a Jew named Aquila, who had recently fled (with his wife Priscilla) from Rome, "because Claudius had *ordered* all the Jews to leave Rome." The word is used in military contexts for the soldiers carrying out their orders to take Paul to Antipatris in Acts 23:31, and Felix's orders to the centurion guarding Paul to keep him in custody but give him some liberty (24:23). In other words, *diatassō* denotes a command given from an authority.

In Mt. 11:1, Matthew records, "When Jesus had finished *instructing* his twelve disciples, he went on from there to teach and preach in their cities" (ESV). The context is Jesus' issuing commands (see Mt. 10:5, where a different verb is used). *diatassō* as an authoritative order is also seen in the references to Jesus' "ordering" food to be brought to a recovering child (Lk. 8:55), servants' obedience to their master's "orders" (Lk. 17:9, 10), and Moses' specific "commands" for how the tent of witness was to be built (Acts 7:44).

For Paul, *diatassō* describes the "commands" or "rules" he has laid down in the churches (1 Cor. 7:17) or will lay down when he visits (11:34). A good example is the command for a collection for the saints in Jerusalem to be taken by both the Corinthians and the Galatians (16:1), and Paul's direction regarding church government guidelines (Tit. 1:5). Such commands are just as binding as the "commands" God gave concerning pastoral pay (1 Cor. 9:14), or the Mosaic law "commanded" through (or by) angels (Gal. 3:19). See *NIDNTT-A*, 557.

Verb: ἐντέλλω (*entellō*), GK *1948* (S *1781*), 15x. *entellō* means "to command, order, instruct." This verb is sometimes used for what Moses "commanded" God's people in the OT (Mt. 19:7; Jn. 8:5). Jesus commands his disciples in the Great Commission to teach all people everything that Jesus taught them (Mt. 28:20). Jesus instructed the disciples during his time on earth (Acts 1:2). Joseph instructed the Israelites to take his bones back to Canaan (Heb. 11:22). See *NIDNTT-A*, 426-30.

Verb: ἐπιτάσσω (*epitassō*), GK *2199* (S *2004*), 10x. *epitassō*, similar to *diatassō*, means "to order, command." The verb is used of Jesus' authoritative commands issued to demons to flee (Mk. 1:27; 9:25; Lk. 4:36; 8:31), as well as his commands given to the wind and the waves to be still (Lk. 8:25). This verb is also used in a more secular fashion in the context of Herod's "orders" for the head of John the Baptist (Mk. 6:27), and Ananias's "orders" to strike Paul on the mouth (Acts 23:2).

Philemon is most helpful in terms of defining *epitassō* as an authoritative order. In Phlm. 8 Paul says, "Therefore, although in Christ I could be bold and order [*epitassō*] you to do what you ought to do, yet for love's sake I prefer to appeal [*parakalō*; see *exhort*] to you—I, Paul, an old man and now a prisoner also for Christ Jesus" (NIV). Paul is well within his rights as an apostle to authoritatively command (*epitassō*) Philemon, but he chooses something equally authoritative but less caustic. See *NIDNTT-A*, 557.

Verb: κελεύω (*keleuo*), GK *3027* (S *2753*), 25x. *keleuō* means "to order, command." In the NT, it denotes a specific verbal order given by a person of superior rank or status. The command is usually terse and followed by strict obedience. See *order*.

Verb: παραγγέλλω (*parangellō*), GK *4133* (S *3853*), 32x. *parangellō* means "to command, order" with authority, such that the person is obligated to obey. Demons are commanded to leave the human body (Lk. 8:29; Acts 16:18), people who have seen a healing are commanded to be quiet (Lk. 8:56), the apostles are commanded not to leave Jerusalem until the Holy Spirit is sent (Acts 1:4), the Sanhedrin commands the apostles not to preach about Jesus (5:28), the Judaizers "insist" that believers follow the Mosaic law (15:5), God commands all people to repent (17:30), and Paul commands that Timothy stop the false teachers (1 Tim. 1:3). See *NIDNTT-A*, 964-65.

Verb: προστάσσω (*prostassō*), GK *4705* (S *4367*), 7x. *prostassō* means "to command," with an emphasis on specific instructions, such as those issued by the angel to Joseph (Mt. 1:24), Moses' instructions concerning the healing of a leper (Mt. 8:4), the Lord's command to Peter about what he is to say to Cornelius (Acts 10:33), and God's command that everyone must repent (17:26).

Verb: συντάσσω (*syntassō*), GK *5332* (S *4929*), 3x. *syntassō* means "to command something" specifically, such as the disciples following Jesus' instructions (Mt. 21:6; 26:19; cf. 27:10).*

COMMANDER

New Testament

Noun: χιλίαρχος (*chiliarchos*), GK *5941* (S *5506*), 21x. *chiliarchos* is the technical term used to refer to a commander of a *speira* (see *centurion* for comments on the division of a Roman army). These commanders were high up the military ladder, over thousands of troops. They were invited to Herod's infamous birthday banquet (Mk. 6:21), one was required to go with his troops to accompany the Jewish authorities in arresting Jesus (Jn. 18:12), they followed in the train of Agrippa and Bernice (Acts 25:23), and they join the ranks of influential leaders who will flee the divine wrath alongside of kings (Rev. 6:15; 19:18).

chiliarchos is used 16x to refer to Claudius Lysias (Acts 21–23). When Claudius heard of rioting in Jerusalem, he quickly came and arrested Paul for troublemaking (21:31, 32, 33), although he have Paul the freedom to make a public defense outside the barracks (21:37). Claudius then ordered a centurion to flog information out of Paul, but quickly regretted his decision when informed that Paul was a Roman citizen and therefore illegally arrested (22:24, 26, 27, 28, 29). In the end, Claudius had to protect Paul from the violent Jewish mob by ordering a huge escort to take him by night to Felix (23:15, 17, 18, 19, 22). Felix listened to Paul's testimony and defense and then told the Jews he would wait for Claudius Lysias to come and help sort things out. See *NIDNTT-A*, 606-7.

COMMANDMENT

Old Testament

Noun: דָּבָר (*dābār*), GK 1821 (S 1697), 1455x. *dābār* means "word, report, command," but can also signify a "thing, matter, affair." See *word*.

Noun: מִצְוָה (*miṣwâ*), GK 5184 (S 4687), 184x. *miṣwâ* means "command, commandment, order" and usually denotes the commands of God (Num. 15:39; Deut. 4:2; 1 Ki. 18:18), though it is also used of human commands (Isa. 29:13; Jer. 35:14–18) and the commands of kings (1 Ki. 2:43; 2 Ki. 18:36; Est. 3:3; Neh. 11:23). Obedience to God's commands brings blessing and disobedience brings curses (Deut. 11:26–28; cf. Gen. 3:16–19; 6:22; Lev. 10:1–2; 1 Sam. 13:13–14). See *NIDOTTE*, 2:1070-71.

New Testament

Noun: διάταγμα (*diatagma*), GK *1409* (S *1297*), 1x. The NT's only use of *diatagma* occurs with respect to Pharaoh's edict to kill all the Hebrew baby boys (Heb. 11:23).

Noun: ἐντολή (*entolē*), GK *1953* (S *1785*), 67x. *entolē* means "commandment."

(1) The majority of uses of this word refer to various laws of the OT (Heb. 9:19), especially the Ten Commandments (Mk. 10:19). Jesus sums up the entire OT law (see *law*) by citing two texts of the OT: Deut. 6:5 and Lev. 19:18 (see Mt. 22:36–40).

(2) In the gospel of John and in 1-2 John, Jesus gives a new *entolē*: to love one another (Jn. 13:34; 1 Jn. 4:21; 2 Jn. 6). Yet this command is really an old one, since it was from the beginning. Jesus' other *entolē* is that we must believe in the name of the Son of God (1 Jn. 3:23). Seen from this

standpoint, the choice to believe in Jesus is not an invitation; it is a command. If we choose not to do so, we are being disobedient. See *NIDNTT-A*, 187-89.

COMMEND

New Testament

Verb: συνίστημι (*synistēmi*), GK *5319* (S *4921*), 16x. *synistēmi* means "to commend, hold together." This verb is especially used by Paul in 2 Corinthians, where the issue of commendation is prominent. While in 2 Cor. 12:11 Paul suggests that in his so-called "fools' speech" (11:1–12:10) he has been commending himself (cf. also 3:1; 5:12), this is not what he really wants to do; in fact, he insists that the only commendation that is worth anything is that which comes directly from the Lord (10:12, 18), not from one's boastful self. In Rom. 16:1, Paul writes a commendation for Phoebe to the Romans, probably because she is the one who will be carrying Paul's letter to Rome; typically in the ancient world, such a letter of endorsement was sent along with someone who was unknown to a group.

In two other important uses of this verb, in Rom. 5:8 Paul stresses how God "has commended" or "demonstrated" his own love for us in that while we were yet sinners, Christ died for us. In Col. 1:17, Paul emphasizes that this entire universe would fall apart if it were not for Christ, because "in him all things hold together."

COMMENDATION

New Testament

Noun: ἔπαινος (*epainos*), GK *2047* (S *1868*), 11x. *epainos* denotes the approval or recognition that is offered to an object worthy of such designation and is best translated as "praise, commendation." See *praise*.

COMMIT

New Testament

Verb: παρατίθημι (*paratithēmi*), GK *4192* (S *3908*), 19x. *paratithēmi* means "to set before, commit." See *set before*.

Verb: ποιέω (*poieō*), GK *4472* (S *4160*), 568x. This verb, generically translated as "to do," has a wide range of meanings, including the idea of "creating" the world. See *do*.

COMMIT ADULTERY

New Testament

Verb: μοιχεύω (*moicheuō*), GK *3658* (S *3431*), 15x. *moicheuō* is always translated "to commit adultery," unlike *porneuō*, which means to indulge in any kind of illegitimate sexual intercourse (see *commit sexual immorality*). In the NT, *moicheuō* is always used when the seventh commandment is recited, "Do not commit adultery" (Exod. 20:14, Deut. 5:18). In fact, *moicheuō* occurs most frequently in reference to this commandment (Mt. 5:27, 19:18; Mk. 10:19, Lk. 18:20; Rom. 13:9; Jas. 2:11). Notice also that Jesus equates lustful intentions with the actual deed of adultery, as in Mt. 5:28, "But I tell you that anyone who looks at a woman lustfully *has already committed adultery* with her in his heart."

Another prominent usage of *moicheuo* is found in Jesus' teaching on divorce. Jesus says, "Anyone who divorces his wife and marries another woman *commits adultery*, and the man who marries a divorced woman *commits adultery*" (Lk. 16:18). Jesus stated that divorce is permissible only in the case of *porneia*, that is, sexual immorality (Mt. 19:9; see the discussion of the "exception clause" under *sexual immorality*). Without some legitimate occurrence of *porneia*, whoever divorces his spouse "causes her *to become an adulteress*" (Mt. 5:32), and whoever marries someone who has been divorced commits adultery as well. See *NIDNTT-A*, 375-76.

COMMIT SEXUAL IMMORALITY

New Testament

Verb: πορνεύω (*porneuō*), GK *4519* (S *4203*), 8x. The word group to which *porneuō* belongs generally relates to any kind of sexual immorality or fornication (KJV) (see *sexual immorality*). *porneuo* as a verb means primarily to "commit sexual immorality," and it can include "adultery."

This verb is only found in 1 Cor. (3x) and Rev. (5x).

Paul urges the Corinthians to flee from sexual immorality because "he who *sins sexually* sins against his own body," which is the temple of the Holy Spirit (1 Cor. 6:18-19). Reminding them of the consequences of committing sexual immorality, Paul states, "We should not *commit sexual immorality*," as some of the Israelites did and were punished by God (1 Cor. 10:8 (2x); cf. Num. 25:1–9).

John also refers to the Num. 25 event in Rev. 2:14, where he records Christ's message to the church of Pergamum: "I have a few things against you: You have people there who hold to the teaching of Balaam, who taught Balak to entice the Israelites to sin by eating food sacrificed to idols and by *committing sexual immorality.*" Christ rebukes the church at Thyatira for tolerating a woman named Jezebel, who "by her teaching … misleads my servants into *sexual immorality*" (Rev. 2:20).

Finally, *porneuo* describes the effects of the great prostitute Babylon on the inhabitants of the earth. John writes that "with her the kings of the earth *committed adultery* and the inhabitants of the earth were intoxicated by the wine of her adulteries" (Rev. 17:2; cf. 18:3, 9). In the end, Babylon will be "thrown down with violence, and will be found no more" (18:21), to the praise of heaven. See *NIDNTT-A*, 485-86.*

COMMON

New Testament

Adjective: κοινός (*koinos*), GK *3123* (S *2839*), 14x. The basic meaning of *koinos* is "common" and can refer to objects held in "common," or it can convey the sense of "profane, impure." The term is logically paired with the notion of "holy" (see *holy*), much like the antithetical pair "clean" (*kathartos*) and "unclean" (*akathartos*). In Mk. 7:2, 5 Jesus declares that impurity is a matter of the thoughts and intents of the heart, not externals such as dirt or unclean foods. In Peter's vision in Acts 10, *koinos* is used to describe the unclean creatures set before him (14, 28; 11:8). In these examples the ritual sense of the word is apparent, while in Revelation 21:27 those who are "impure" are such in a moral sense. See *defile*.

koinos also describes the possessions of the first disciples that were held in "common" (Acts 2:44; 4:32). It likewise refers to the common faith or salvation held among believers (Tit. 1:4, cf. Jude 3). See *NIDNTT-A*, 310-312.

COMMUNION

New Testament

Noun: κοινωνία (*koinōnia*), GK *3126* (S *2842*), 19x. *koinōnia* generally means "fellowship, communion, participation, sharing." See *fellowship*.

COMMUNITY

Old Testament

Noun: עֵדָה (*ʿēdâ*), GK 6337 (S 5712), 171x. *ʿēdâ* means a gathering of people (for worship or legal matters) or a herd or swarm of animals, such as bees (Jdg. 14:8). The swarming imagery can be transferred to people as well, in the sense of mobs, troops, or hordes. Most occurrences of this word are in Exodus to Numbers, where it denotes the "community" or "assembly" of Israel.

The "herd of bulls" in Ps. 68:30 is not a group of cattle but rather a metaphor for those who trample others in their pursuit of wealth and war booty. Of people, *ʿēdâ* refers to both good and bad groups. The worshiping "community" at Passover was a *ʿēda* (Exod. 12:3), as is the community that witnesses Aaron's ordination (Lev. 8:3). God's wrath falls on the whole community of Israel when Achan sins and takes the devoted things (Jos. 22:20).

The main distinction between *ʿēdâ* and *qāhāl* (GK 7736), for the most part, is that *ʿēdâ* are Israelites gathered *for a specific goal* while *qāhāl* means a more general gathering of all Israel. The psalmist refers to all peoples who will appear before God for judgment as *ʿēdâ*. "Let the *assembly* of the peoples be gathered around you, and over it take your seat on high." (Ps. 7:7). See *NIDOTTE*, 3:326–28.

Noun: קָהָל (*qāhāl*), GK 7736 (S 6951), 123x. *qāhāl* describes the gathering of a great body of people for civil, religious, or other occasions. See *assembly*.

COMPANY

Old Testament

Noun: רֹאשׁ (*rōʾš*), GK 8031 (S 7218), 600x. The primary meaning of *rōʾš* is "head" (see *head*), but it also has a number of metaphorical meanings. For example, *rōʾs* can also be translated as "company," meaning a division or part of something. In military language, Gideon divided his army into three *companies* (Jdg. 7:16, 20), Saul divided his people into three *divisions* (*companies* in KJV, 1 Sam. 11:11), and the Philistine raiding parties went out in three *detachments* (*companies* in KJV, 1 Sam. 13:17). In Gen. 2:10, the main river in Eden was said to divide into four *headwaters*.

COMPARE

Old Testament

Verb: מָשַׁל (*māšal*), GK 5439 (S 4911), 17x. *māšal* bears two distinct meanings in the OT: "to compare, liken, be like" and "to quote (a proverb)" (see *quote*). *māšal* is sometimes a verb of comparison, denoting equality in some aspect or nature. When referring to humanity, Job compares himself to dust and ashes (Job 30:19), the psalmist compares human beings without God's word to those who go down to the pit (Ps. 28:1; 143:7) and pompous men to beasts (49:12, 20), and Isaiah compares kings to weak people (Isa. 14:10). In a more positive statement, Isaiah makes it emphatically clear that no one can be compare to the Lord. In God's own words, "To whom would you *liken* me that we may be compared?" (46:5).

New Testament

Verb: ὁμοιόω (*homoioō*), GK *3929* (S *3666*), 15x. *homoioō* means "to make like something, liken, compare." See *like, liken*.

COMPASSION

New Testament

Noun: ἔλεος (*eleos*) GK *1799* (S *1656*), 27x. *eleos* is used to express "mercy or compassion" for those in need. See *mercy*.

Noun: σπλάγχνον (*splanchnon*), GK *5073* (S *4698*), 11x. *splanchnon* refers to a feeling of "affection, tenderness, compassion." See *affection*.

(HAVE) COMPASSION

New Testament

Verb: σπλαγχνίζομαι (*splanchnizomai*), GK *5072* (S *4697*), 12x. *splanchnizomai* means "to have compassion for someone, show compassion." This verb carries the idea of being moved in the inner parts of the body. The ancients thought of the inward parts of the body (i.e., the entrails) as being the seat of emotions. In English we usually refer to the "heart," but we also talk of a person having "visceral" feelings; note how true compassion can affect us in the pit of our stomachs.

splanchnizomai occurs only in the Synoptic Gospels and describes the compassion Jesus had for those he saw in difficulty. Jesus is filled with compassion for those who are without a shepherd (Mt. 9:36; Mk. 6:34) or without food (Mt. 15:32; Mk. 8:2). Compassion causes him to heal the sick (Mt. 14:14), including lepers (Mk. 1:31), to give sight to the blind (Mt. 20:34), and to raise a widow's son from the dead (Lk. 7:13). The father of a demon-possessed child calls on Jesus to show compassion for his son and do whatever he can (Mk. 9:22).

splanchnizomai can move beyond compassion into the realm of mercy or pity. The verb is used in this fashion in three parables: the initial pity of the master on the unjust servant (Mt. 18:27), the Samaritan on the injured man (Lk. 10:33), and the father on the returning prodigal son (15:20). See *NIDNTT-A*, 535-36.*

COMPEL, COMPELLED

New Testament

Verb: ἀναγκάζω (*anankazō*) GK *337* (S *315*), 9x. *anankazō* means "to compel, be compelled." Paul admits that when he was a persecutor of the church, he tried to compel or force Christians to blaspheme by confessing Jesus as the Christ (Acts 26:11; such a statement would be considered blasphemous by the Jewish leaders). Paul himself felt compelled to appeal to Caesar since he was not receiving justice during his imprisonment in Caesarea. This verb becomes important in the churches in Galatia since some there were compelling new believers to be circumcised (Gal. 2:14; 6:12). But Paul cites the precedent of Titus, who was not compelled by the leaders in Jerusalem to be circumcised (2:3).

Verb: συνέχω (*synechō*), GK *5309* (S *4912*), 12x. *synechō* has a variety of meanings. Paul uses this verb in 2 Cor. 5:14 when he writes about what "compels" him to spread the gospel, namely, "the love of Christ"—probably a combination of his love for Christ and Christ's love for him (cf. also his total "devotion" in Acts 18:5). See *suffer*.

Noun: ἀνάγκη (*anankē*), GK *340* (S *318*), 17x. *anankē* carries the meaning of necessity, compulsion, pressure, or even calamity and distress. See *necessary*.

COMPLETE

Old Testament

Verb: כָּלָה (*kālâ*), GK 3983 (S 3615), 207x. Often rendered "to complete, finish, destroy," *kālâ* expresses the basic idea of bringing a process to completion. The process may involve adding something until an object is full or an activity complete, or it may involve taking something away until there is nothing left (see *destroy*).

Some of the activities that are brought to completion include speaking (Gen. 17:22), drinking (Gen. 24:19), harvesting (Ruth 2:21), offering (1 Sam. 13:10), eating (1 Ki. 1:41), and building (2 Chr. 8:16). Significantly, in these contexts it is not merely that a person comes to a certain point in the middle of a project or activity and stops but that he or she has carried out the job in full. Thus Naomi declares that Boaz will not rest "until he *has finished* the matter" (Ruth 3:18). There is a sense, then, that *kālâ* means "to bring to perfection," but "perfection" here means only "completion" and not "without error." *kālâ* does not address the question of errors.

Verb: תָּמַם (*tāmam*), GK 9462 (S 8552), 64x. *tāmam* is used for a wide range of ideas having to do with ending, completion, or even destruction. See *end*.

Noun: כֹּל (*kōl*), GK 3972 (S 3605), 5415x. *kōl* means "whole, all, every." It can mean "whole, complete" and be used to describe the devotion God requires of those who are his covenant people (Deut. 6:5). See *all*.

New Testament

Verb: ἐπιτελέω (*epiteleō*), GK *2200* (S *2005*), 10x. *epiteleō* means "to complete, bring to completion." Paul must first "complete" his trip to Jerusalem before heading to Rome and Spain (Rom. 15:28). He encourages the Corinthians to "complete" their collection for the saints that they began (2 Cor. 8:6, 11). This verb can also be used regarding spiritual matters. Paul challenges the Galatians not to "complete" their salvation through the flesh (Gal. 3:3). He tells the Philippian church that God saved them and he will "bring to completion" their salvation (Phil. 1:6). The Corinthians are encouraged to "bring holiness to completion" by making a clean break from their past (2 Cor. 7:1).

Verb: πίμπλημι (*pimplēmi*), GK *4398* (S *4130*), 24x. *pimplēmi* means "to fill, fulfill, complete" and is used in literal and figurative ways. See *fill*.

Verb: τελέω (*teleō*), GK *5464* (S *5055*), 28x. The basic meaning of *teleō* is "to finish, complete." It is used several times in the Gospels for completing a task. See *end*.

Verb: τελειόω (*teleioō*), GK *5457* (S *5048*), 23x. *teleioō* refers to attaining an end or purpose, in the sense of being complete or perfect. It also refers to completing an activity, both in the sense of "to finish" (e.g., "After the Feast *was over*," Lk. 2:43) and "to accomplish, fulfill." See *end*.

COMPLETENESS

Old Testament

Noun: שָׁלוֹם (*šālôm*), GK 8934 (S 7965), 237x. *šālôm* is one of the most important words in the OT. In addition to "peace," this word can be translated as "prosperity, well-being, health, completeness, safety." See *peace*.

COMPLETION

Old Testament

Noun: אַחֲרִית (*ʾaḥarît*), GK 344 (S 319), 61x. *ʾaḥarît* in its most basic sense denotes "that which comes after." Specifically it may describe what follows temporally, that is, the "completion, end" of an event or the final "outcome." See *end*.

CONCEAL

Old Testament

Verb: כָּסָה (*kāsâ*), GK 4059 (S 3680), 153x. This word is predominately used with the literal sense "to cover." In other contexts, it can denote "conceal, hide" and even "forgive." See *cover*.

Verb: סָתַר (*sātar*), GK 6259 (S 5641), 82x. The verb *sātar* means "to hide, conceal, keep secret." See *hide*.

New Testament

Verb: κρύπτω (*kryptō*), GK *3221* (S *2928*), 18x. *kryptō* means "to conceal, hide." See *hide*.

CONCEIVE

See *give birth*.

CONCERN

New Testament

Noun: μέριμνα (*merimna*), GK *3533* (S *3308*), 6x. *merimna* is a "care, anxiety, concern" that easily distracts. For Paul, his "*merimna* for all the churches" falls under his list of trials that make him qualified to be an apostle (2 Cor. 11:28). How should believers handle concerns and anxieties? Listen to Peter: "Humble yourselves, therefore, under the mighty hand of God so that at the proper time he may exalt you, casting all your *anxieties* on him, because he cares for you" (1 Pet. 5:6–7, ESV). Putting these two verses together, even holy pastoral concerns are to be cast on Jesus.

A use of *merimna* that is *not* an example for us occurs in the parable of the sower. In explaining the parable, Jesus says, "As for what was sown among thorns, this is the one who hears the word, but the *cares* of the world and the deceitfulness of riches choke the word, and it proves unfruitful" (Mt. 13:22, ESV). Lost humanity is preoccupied with this life and with the deceitfulness of wealth, both of which keep the Word of God from taking root in our hearts (Mt. 13:22; Mk. 4:19; Lk. 8:14). Related to this parable is Jesus' exhortation to believers not to be "weighed down with dissipation, drunkenness and the *anxieties* of life" (Lk. 21:34 ESV). Note that these worries can weigh heavy on believers, and with disastrous consequence, unless we are wary of them.

In sum, *merimna* itself is neutral. But two things are clear. The first is that the worries of the world exist and threaten to hinder the believer in walking with the Lord. Second, even spiritual worries must be willingly and consistently laid at the cross of Christ. See *NIDNTT-A*, 364.*

Noun: σπουδή (*spoudē*), GK *5082* (S *4710*), 12x. *spoudē* means "earnestness, eagerness, concern." See *earnestness*.

CONCERNED

New Testament

Verb: μέλει (*melei*), GK *3508* (S *3199*), 10x. *melei* occurs in the NT only in an impersonal form; its basic meaning is "to care about, be concerned for someone or something." See *care about*.

Verb: μεριμνάω (*merimnaō*), GK *3534* (S *3309*), 19x. *merimnaō* means "to worry, be concerned about something." See *worry*.

CONDEMN, BE CONDEMNED

Old Testament

Verb: אָשַׁם (*ʾāšam*), GK 870 (S 816), 35x. *ʾāšam* means "to be guilty, be condemned." See *(be) guilty*.

New Testament

Verb: κατακρίνω (*katakrinō*), GK *2891* (S *2632*), 18x. *katakrinō* means "to condemn, judge someone guilty." It involves passing judgment or condemnation on someone (or something) because of a declaration of guilt.

In John's gospel, Jesus asks the woman caught in adultery if anyone remains "to condemn" her, that is, to pronounce her guilty of violating the law; he then declares that he does not condemn her either (Jn. 8:10–11). Jesus himself knows that he will soon be condemned by the chief priests and scribes as a necessary part of his work as Redeemer (Mt. 20:18; Mk. 10:33). This becomes evident in Jesus' trial, where the Sanhedrin condemns Jesus for blasphemy (Mk. 14:64), an act of condemnation so manifestly unjust that it causes Judas to return the thirty pieces of silver for which he betrayed Jesus (Mt. 27:3).

Christ tells the unrepentant Jews that the men of Nineveh and the Queen of Sheba will rise up in the judgment and "condemn" them because the Jews did not respond to the one greater than Jonah and Solomon (Mt. 12:41–42; Lk. 11:31–32). Most significantly, *katakrinō* is used of God's condemnation of sin (Rom. 8:3), the unbeliever (Mk. 16:16), the world (1 Cor. 11:32; Heb. 11:7), and Sodom (2 Pet. 2:6). A glorious element in the gospel is that no one can condemn believers who have been bought by Christ (Rom. 8:34).

Condemnation can come from within as well as without, such as when a hypocrite condemns himself for judging another person, and when someone eats food because of a lack of faith (Rom. 14:23). See *NIDNTT-A*, 318-19.*

CONDEMNATION

New Testament

Noun: κρίμα (*krima*), GK *3210* (S *2917*), 27x. *krima* refers to the act of "judgment" or its consequences (e.g., "punishment, condemnation"). See *judgment*.

Noun: κρίσις (*krisis*), GK *3213* (S *2920*), 47x. *krisis* is the most common noun in the NT carrying the meaning of "judgment." Sometimes it connotes "condemnation." See *judgment*.

CONDEMNED

New Testament

Noun: ἀνάθεμα (*anathema*), GK *353* (S *331*) 6x. *anathema* means "curse, accursed, condemned (eternally)." See *curse*.

CONDUCT

Old Testament

Noun: דֶּרֶךְ (*derek*), GK 2006 (S 1870), 712x. *derek* may be translated in numerous ways, both literal and metaphorical, including "way, road, path, journey, conduct." See *way*.

New Testament

Verb: ἀναστρέφω (*anastrephō*), GK *418* (S *390*), 9x. *anastrephō* can mean "to turn back," but it has a related meaning "to conduct oneself, live" in a certain way. See *live*.

Noun: ἀναστροφή (*anastrophē*), GK *419* (S *391*), 13x. *anastrophē* means one's "manner of life" or simply "conduct." See *way of life*.

CONFESS

Old Testament

Verb: יָדָה (*yādâ*), GK 3344 (S 3034), 111x. *yādâ* means "praise, (give) thanks, confess." The core meaning of this verb is to express acknowledgment of some sort, such as confession of sin. See *praise*.

New Testament

Verb: ἐξομολογέω (*exomologeō*), GK *2018* (S *1843*), 10x. *exomologeō* is closely related to *homologeō* (GK *3933*), especially with respect to the meaning "to confess." It can also mean "to profess, praise." On three occasions, *exomologeō* refers to confessing sins. John instructs those who come to him for baptism to confess their sins (Mt. 3:6; Mk. 1:5); those in Ephesus who formerly practiced sorcery and magic come and confess them (Acts 19:18); and James urges believers to confess their sins to one another and to pray for one another for healing (Jas. 5:16).

exomologeō can also describe the confession or profession of something other than sins, as when Paul describes looks ahead to the day when every being will profess Christ as Lord (Rom. 14:11; Phil.

2:11). This type of profession may have the connotation of praise: Jesus "praises" the Father for hiding the truth from the wise and revealing it to children (Mt. 11:25; Lk. 10:21), and Paul describes God as being "praised" among the Gentiles (Rom. 15:19).

Beyond this, in Lk. 22:16, *exomologeō* describes Judas' agreement or consent to take money in order to betray Jesus. See *NIDNTT-A*, 410-11.*

Verb: ὁμολογέω (*homologeō*), GK *3933* (S *3670*), 26x. *homologeō* means "to acknowledge, confess [especially confess faith]," also "to promise." See *acknowledge*.

CONFIDENCE

New Testament

Noun: παρρησία (*parrēsia*), GK *4244* (S *3954*), 31x. *parrēsia* generally means "confidence" and is used mostly with reference to one's speech. As such, it refers to *clarity of speech* or *boldness*. It can also carry the meanings of the *certainty* of an outcome and the *confidence* to approach God.

(1) *parrēsia* is used most commonly to connote clarity and forthrightness of speech. Jesus spoke *plainly* about his impending suffering (Mk. 8:32; cf. Jn. 10:24; 11:14), that is, without ambiguous or metaphorical language (Jn. 16:25, 29; 18:20). *parrēsia* can also carry the nuance of making a full disclosure (Jn. 7:4), even making something public (Jn. 7:26; 11:54): "But no one would say anything *publicly* about him for fear of the Jews" (Jn. 7:13; cf. 11:54).

(2) *parrēsia* can refer to the confidence one has in speaking, especially with respect to proclaiming the gospel (cf. Acts 2:29; 4:13, 29, 31; Phlm. 8; Acts 28:31; 2 Cor. 3:12; Eph. 6:19).

(3) *parrēsia* can also reflect the positive outcome of a situation (2 Cor. 7:4; cf. Phil. 1:20; Col. 2:15): "Those who have served well gain an excellent standing and great *assurance* in their faith in Christ Jesus" (1 Tim. 3:13 cf. Heb. 3:6; 4:16).

(4) Finally, *parrēsia* is a quality or attitude a believer should possess when approaching God (Eph. 3:12): "In him and through faith in him we may approach God with freedom and *confidence*" (Heb. 4:16; cf. 10:19, 35; 1 Jn. 2:28; 3:21; 4:17; 5:14). See *NIDNTT-A*, 441.

CONFIDENT EXPECTATION

New Testament

Noun: ἐλπίς (*elpis*), GK *1828* (S *1680*), 53x. The majority of the NT writers invest *elpis*, "hope," with the nuance of "confident expectation" or "solid assurance." See *hope*.

CONFINE

Old Testament

Verb: אָסַר (*ʾāsar*), GK 673 (S 631), 73x. The most basic meaning of *ʾāsar* is "to bind, tie up." But this verb also may be used in the sense of being imprisoned. The chief cupbearer and baker are put into the jail where Joseph "is confined" (Gen. 40:3, 5; cf. 39:20). See *bind*.

CONFIRM

New Testament

Verb: μαρτυρέω (*martyreō*), GK *3455* (S *3140*), 76x. *martyreō* means to "confirm, testify" to something from firsthand experience. See *testify*.

CONFUSE

See *embarrass*.

CONFUSION

Old Testament

Noun: הָמוֹן (*hāmôn*), GK 2162 (S 1995), 82x. *hāmôn* expresses a quality of immensity or magnitude, whether it bears an emotive, audible, or spatial reference. It is translated with words like "confusion, tumult, noise, abundance, army, hordes." See *hordes*.

CONGREGATION

New Testament

Noun: συναγωγή (*synagōgē*), GK *5252* (S *4864*), 56x. *synagōgē* denotes what is brought together or assembled, an "assembly, congregation, synagogue." See *synagogue*.

CONQUER

See *overcome*.

CONSCIENCE, CONSCIOUSNESS

New Testament

Noun: συνείδησις (*syneidēsis*), GK *5287* (S *4893*), 30x. *syneidēsis* means "conscience." In the OT, the conscience is often correlated with the heart, where it functions to bring individuals to repentance, but it does not seem to serve that function in the NT.

(1) In the NT, the conscience is that part of the mind that performs moral judgments and ethical evaluations; it refers to one's moral sensibilities. Thus, it can refer to one's ethical reflection regarding one's own actions (much in line with the modern English usage) as well as one's ethical reflection regarding the actions of others (something foreign to common English usage). Paul appeals to this moral judgment of the conscience in his discussion of natural law. The conscience evaluates the moral quality of one's thoughts with regard to the moral law that is written on the hearts of everyone, even of the Gentiles, who do not have the written revelation of Torah (Rom. 2:15).

A "clear" or "good" conscience serves as something akin to a character witness for its possessor before God, others, and even oneself. Thus, Paul can say that his "*conscience* testifies" that he has acted in holiness and sincerity (2 Cor. 1:12). Likewise, he and his companions commend themselves "to everyone's *conscience* in the sight of God" (2 Cor. 4:2; 5:11). In his defense before Felix, Paul claims that he strives always "to keep my *conscience* clear before God and man" (Acts 24:16), and before the Sanhedrin, Paul claims that he has fulfilled his duty to God "in all good *conscience* to this day" (23:1). In similar fashion, Peter claims that a clear conscience will cause those who speak maliciously against the good behavior of his hearers to be ashamed (1 Pet. 3:16).

A good conscience also produces good actions. In 1 Tim. 1:5, Paul claims that love comes in part from a good conscience, and he appears to tie deep faith with a clear conscience as well (3:9). Submission to the governing authorities is motivated by one's conscience (i.e., it is the right thing to do) as well as by fear of punishment (Rom. 13:5). The writer of Hebrews also ties a clear conscience to ability to perform good deeds (Heb. 9:14; 13:18).

(2) A "bad" conscience can serve to indict its possessor before God, others, and oneself and leads to sinful activity. Those who do not believe have corrupt "minds and *consciences*" (Tit. 1:15). Those who have "seared *consciences*" seek to cause others to sin by distorting the gospel. The most common way was to add legal requirements to the gospel of salvation—either dietary or ceremonial in nature (see, e.g., 1 Tim. 4:2–3). Paul instructs his readers to bear with those who are of "weak *conscience*" (1 Cor. 8:7, 10, 12; 10:28–29). See *NIDNTT-A*, 545.

CONSECRATE

Old Testament

Verb: טָהֵר (*ṭāhēr*), GK 3197 (S 2891), 94x. *ṭāhēr* is normally rendered "to cleanse, purify, consecrate." It often appears in cultic contexts and used to refer to physical, ritual, and ethical cleansing or purification. See *cleanse*.

Verb: קָדַשׁ (*qādaš*), GK 7727 (S 6942), 171x. *qādaš* describes the state of the sacred realm. Negatively, it represents that which is distinct from the common or profane. It is usually translated "make holy" (NIV), "sanctify," or "dedicate." It is used to describe the state or action of consecration in the rituals of the Levites. See *sanctify*.

New Testament

Verb: ἁγιάζω (*hagiazō*), GK *39* (S *37*), 28x. *hagiazō* is usually rendered "make holy, sanctify, consecrate." In the NT this verb expresses the action of including a person or a thing in the sphere of what is holy in either a ritual (ceremonial) and moral sense. See *make holy*.

Adjective: ἅγιος (*hagios*), GK *41* (S *40 & 39*), 233x. In general, two facts stand out in the NT regarding *hagios* ("holy, consecrated"). First, God and what is associated with him is declared as "holy."

Second, the proper sphere of the holy in the NT is not the priestly or ritual but the prophetic. See *holy*.

CONSENT

Old Testament

Verb: אָבָה (*ʾābâ*), GK 14 (S 14), 54x. *ʾābâ* means "to will, be willing, consent." See *(be) willing*.

CONSIDER

Old Testament

Verb: נָבַט (*nābaṭ*), GK 5564 (S 5027), 70x. As with other Hebrew words used to denote "seeing," *nābaṭ* may refer to physical sight, mental activities, or the way in which God and humans relate. See *look*.

Verb: רָאָה (*rāʾâ*), GK 8011 (S 7200 and 7202), 1,311x. *rāʾâ* is the most frequent Heb. verb for "seeing," encompassing a variety of actions including physical, visionary, and mental. See *see*.

New Testament

Verb: διαλογίζομαι (*dialogizomai*), GK *1368* (S *1260*), 16x. *dialogizomai* means "to discuss, consider, argue" about something. See *discuss*.

Verb: ἡγέομαι (*hēgeomai*), GK *2451* (S *2233*), 28x. *hēgeomai* means "to consider, think, regard." Strange as it may seem, the participle form of this verb (*hēgoumenos*) is variously translated as "ruler, leader" (Mt. 2:6; Lk. 22:26; Acts. 7:10; 15:22; Heb. 13:7, 17, 24) and "chief" speaker (Acts 14:12). Thus, the verb at times carries the connotation of leadership or rule. So when Paul says, for instance, that he "*thought* it necessary" to urge a group to visit the church at Corinth in order to make arrangements for the gift they were to give the saints, included is an element in which the authority of the apostolic office is being invoked (2 Cor. 9:5).

Elsewhere, however, *hēgeomai* denotes what people ought "to consider" or "think" about themselves or others. In Phil. 2:3, Paul urges his readers to "*consider* others better than themselves," which means they are to act in such a way that others may see an attitude of humility. Interestingly, the same word is used of Christ in his consideration of equality with God as something that should not be grasped (2:6); such consideration is determinative for action or inaction. When Paul says that he considers his past as loss in comparison with the wonderful knowledge of Christ, he knows that there is no question regarding which is better (3:7–8).

Paul's exhorts believers not to "regard" as an enemy but to warn as a brother (2 Thess. 3:15) those who are not following through on their Christian responsibility to work. Also, he exhorts believers to "hold" in high honor those who work for the church (1 Thess. 5:13). Christians should "consider" it joy when they face trials, since this gives them an opportunity to grow in their faith (Jas. 1:2). See *NIDNTT-A*, 230.

Verb: κατανοέω (*katanoeō*), GK *2917* (S *2657*), 14x. Although *katanoeō* is sometimes translated as "consider, perceive, look," these English words do not communicate the depth of knowledge presumed by this verb It is best understood as a focusing of one's complete attention on something. This meaning clarifies James's point regarding the ridiculous nature of one who listens to the word of God but does not do what it says—he is like a man who "examines" his face in a mirror and then immediately forgets what he looks like (Jas. 1:23). Abraham "*faced the fact* that his body was as good as dead" (Rom. 4:19), and Peter is said to have "looked" carefully into the sheet that came down from heaven (Acts 11:6). Paul and his companions, when in danger at sea, "*saw* a bay with a sandy beach" on which they could run their ship aground (Acts 27:39); *katanoeō* implies that they put some thought into alternatives before acting on their plan.

The use of *katanoeō* in the NT sometimes involves a drive toward spiritual growth or insight. For example, Jesus tells his followers to "consider" how God takes care of the ravens and the lilies in an effort to aid the development of their faith (Lk. 12:24–27). He also warns against the lack of attention paid to the log in one's own eye while "concentrating on" the speck in a brother's eye (Mt. 7:3; Lk. 6:41). Luke claims that Jesus "perceived" (NIV, "saw through") the attempt of the spies to trap him with the question of paying taxes (Lk. 20:23). It was not until Moses "looked more closely" at the burning bush that he heard the Lord's voice (Acts 7:31). Ultimately, this kind of consideration will lead to action. Thus, the writer to the Hebrews tells his readers to "*fix your thoughts* on Jesus" and to "*consider* how we may spur one another on toward love and good deeds" (Heb. 3:1; 10:24). See *NIDNTT-A*, 394-96.

Verb: κρίνω (*krinō*), GK *3212* (S *2919*), 114x. *krinō* essentially means "to consider, decide, judge," though it has a variety of nuances. See *judge*.

Verb: λογίζομαι (*logizomai*), GK *3357* (S *3049*), 40x. The basic meaning of *logizomai* has to do with counting or thinking (see also *think, regard as*). It is also used for crediting something for or against someone (see *credit*). Paul "considers" (or holds) that a person is justified by faith apart from works of the law (Rom. 3:28). Believers are to "consider themselves" dead to sin and alive to God in Jesus Christ (6:11). Present suffering "is not considered" to be worthy of comparison to future glory (8:18). Paul "does not consider himself" to have taken hold of the perfection for which Jesus Christ took hold of him (Phil. 3:13). See *NIDNTT-A*, 338-39.

Verb: ὁράω (*horaō*), GK *3972* (S *3708*), 454x. *horaō* is the most frequently used word for seeing in the NT. It can also mean "appear, perceive, consider" (i.e., a more mental seeing). See *see*.

CONSIST

See *be*.

CONSOLATION

New Testament

Noun: παράκλησις (*paraklēsis*), GK *4155* (S *3874*), 29x. *paraklēsis* carries the idea of consolation, comfort, or encouragement. See *comfort*.

CONSTANTLY

Old Testament

Noun (used as adv.): תָּמִיד (*tāmîd*), GK 9458 (S 8548), 104x. As an adverb, *tāmîd* describes that which is "lasting" or something done "constantly." The word can describe both an action done regularly (often according to a schedule) as well as something that is ongoing without interruption. See *always*.

CONSULT

Old Testament

Verb: יָעַץ (*yāʿaṣ*), GK 3619 (S 3289), 80x. *yāʿaṣ* carries the two basic meanings of "to counsel, advise" (Num. 24:14; 2 Sam. 17:11) and "to plan, purpose" (Isa. 7:5; 14:24), though the verb seems to carry the former nuance more frequently. Also related to this former meaning is "to consult, to receive counsel" (2 Chr. 10:8; 25:17). See *counsel*.

CONSUME

Old Testament

Verb: אָכַל (*ʾākal*) GK 430 (S 398), 820x. The basic meaning of *ʾākal* is "to eat," but it often means "to consume, devour." See *eat*.

Verb: כָּלָה (*kālâ*), GK 3983 (S 3615), 207x. Often rendered "to complete, finish, destroy," *kālâ* expresses the basic idea of bringing a process to completion. In contexts where *kālâ* denotes completion by subtraction, the verb often expresses the notion of using up, destroying, or consuming. See *destroy*.

CONTAIN

See *accept*.

CONTAINER

New Testament

Noun: σκεῦος (*skeuos*), GK *5007* (S *4632*), 23x. *skeuos* refers to an "instrument, container" (e.g., a "jar"). See *instrument*.

CONTEMPT

Old Testament

Noun: חֶרְפָּה (*ḥerpâ*), GK 3075 (S 2781), 73x. The meaning of *ḥerpâ* is "disgrace, insult, reproach, contempt." *ḥerpâ* can refer to general suffering or humiliation (1 Sam. 11:2; Neh. 2:17; Ps. 69:20), shameful behavior (Gen. 34:14), or slanderous and condemning speech poured out on someone (Neh. 5:9; Job 16:10; Isa. 51:7–8).

CONTEND

Old Testament

Verb: יָכַח (*yākaḥ*), GK 3519 (S 3198), 59x. *yākaḥ* has a broad range of meaning, but it generally carries the sense of arguing a case or issuing judgment with the intent to correct. It is often translated "rebuke," "correct," "judge," "punish," or "argue," and is found most frequently in legal contexts (especially in Job [17x]) and in the wisdom instruction of Proverbs (10x). See *rebuke.*

Verb: רִיב (*rîb*), GK 8189, (S 7378), 72x. *rîb* denotes the action of entering into an argument, conflict, or lawsuit with another person. People may "quarrel" with one another (e.g., Gen. 26:20-22), but often the quarrel involves God. When the Israelites "quarrel" with Moses and test God by demanding water in the desert (Exod. 17:2), Moses commemorates the rebellion by naming that place "Me*rib*ah" (17:7; cf. Ps. 95:8-9). A theme central to the book of Job is that Job "contends" with God (e.g., Job 40:2), seeking to know God's case against him (e.g., 10:2, using the nominal form of *rib*). When a case or a cause is the object of *rîb*, the NIV may translate the verb as "plead" (e.g., Ps. 43:1), "defend" (e.g., 74:22), "present" (e.g., Prov. 18:17), or "take up" (e.g., 22:23; 23:11). So Ps. 43:1 reads, "Vindicate me, O God, and *plead* my cause against an ungodly nation. ..."

Particularly in prophetic literature, as God accuses his people of breaking the covenant, he "contends" with Israel in a covenant lawsuit (Jer. 2:9; Hos. 2:4; cf. Mic. 6:1). In the OT, there is a formal covenant lawsuit format that is derived from the covenant form. The first formal covenant lawsuit is delivered by Moses (Deut. 32) and the last one by Stephen (Acts 7); interestingly, after both of these lawsuits are delivered, the one who delivered the lawsuit dies. The OT holds out the promise that God will not "contend" forever (Isa. 57:16; cf. Ps. 103:9) against his people. See *NIDOTTE,* 3:1105-6.

New Testament

Verb: διακρίνω (*diakrinō*), GK *1359* (S *1252*), 19x. *diakrinō* means "to judge, distinguish, evaluate." When applied to oneself, it can mean to "doubt" or "waver." See *judge.*

CONTINUALLY

Old Testament

Noun (used as adv.): תָּמִיד (*tāmîd*), GK 9458 (S 8548), 104x. As an adverb, *tāmîd* describes that which is "lasting" or something done "continually." The word can describe both an action done regularly (often according to a schedule) as well as something that is ongoing without interruption. See *always.*

CONTINUE

New Testament

Verb: ἐπιμένω (*epimenō*), GK *2152* (S *1961*), 16x. *epimenō* means "to stay, remain, continue." See *stay.*

CONTRADICT

New Testament

Verb: ἀντιλέγω (*antilegō*), GK *515* (S *483, 471*), 11x. *antilegō* means "to speak against, contradict" someone. It sometimes has the notion "to rebel" verbally. See *speak against.*

CONTRIBUTION

Old Testament

Noun: תְּרוּמָה (*t*[e]*rûmâ*), GK 9556 (S 8641), 76x. *t*[e]*rûmâ* can be translated as "offering, portion, gift, contribution." See *offering.*

CONTRITION

Old Testament

Verb: עָנָה (*ʿānâ*), GK 6700 (S 6031), 79x. *ʿānâ* can denote humbling in a positive sense (i.e., repentance and contrition) or with connotations of violence (i.e., affliction and oppression; see *afflict*). Forms of *ʿānâ* that are pleasing to God include fasting and prayer (Lev. 16:31; 23:27; Ps. 35:13).

CONVERT

See *turn.*

CONVICT

See rebuke.

CONVINCE

New Testament

Verb: πείθω (*peithō*), GK *4275* (S *3982*), 52x. *peithō* means "to persuade, convince." In the NT, it has a wide range of application. Paul, for example, uses this word to refer to his own personal convictions about the work of God, that nothing can separate us from the love of Christ (Rom. 8:38) and that God will complete his good work of salvation in us (Phil. 1:6). See *persuade.*

Verb: πιστεύω (*pisteuō*), GK *4409* (S *4100*), 241x. *pisteuō* generally means "to believe, be convinced of something," and in a more specific way "to have faith" in God or Christ. It can also mean "to entrust something to someone." See *believe.*

COPPER

Old Testament

Noun: נְחֹשֶׁת (*n^e^ḥōšet*), GK 5733 (S 5178), 139x. *n^e^ḥōšet* refers either to copper or to bronze. Copper was mined "out of the hills" (Deut. 8:9) and was then combined with another metal to make bronze, an alloy containing about 5 to 10 percent of tin. See *bronze.*

COPY

New Testament

Noun: ὑπόδειγμα (*hypodeigma*) GK *5682* (S *5262*), 6x. *hypodeigma* means "example, copy" (see *example*). The writer to the Hebrews demonstrates how the worship patterns of the Israelites in the desert under the leadership of the high priest serve as "a copy and shadow of what is in heaven" (Heb. 8:5; see also 9:23). Jesus is the fulfillment of these shadows and copies.

CORNER

Old Testament

Noun: כָּנָף (*kānāp*), GK 4053 (S 3671), 111x. *kānāp* has the basic meaning of a wing, such as the wing of a bird. A number of verses refer to the "*wings* of the earth," meaning the extremities of the earth (Job 37:3; 38:13; Isa. 24:16; "the four *corners* of the earth," Isa. 11:12). See *wing.*

Noun: קֶרֶן (*qeren*), GK 7967 (S 7161), 76x. This word refers primarily to the horn of an animal, but *qeren* can also be understood as "point, corner," such as the "*horns* of the altar" (Exod. 29:12). See *horn.*

New Testament

Noun: γωνία (*gōnia*), GK *1224* (S *1137*), 9x. *gōnia* essentially means "corner" and refers to the inside or outside "corner" of a structure. An outside corner can imply a public setting (Mt. 6:5), and an inside corner a private, hidden setting (Acts 26:26). *gōnia* is used in Revelation to refer to the far extremities or horizons ("the four corners") of the earth (Rev. 7:1; 20:8). When accompanied with the word *kephalē* ("head"), *gōnia* is used figuratively to refer to Jesus Christ as the "head of the corner, cornerstone, capstone" (Mt. 21:42; Mk. 12:10; Lk. 20:17; Acts 4:11; 1 Pet. 2:7). This stone was the most important stone in a building, a sort of anchor stone. It may refer to a stone that occupies the corner where two walls meet. Some, however, argue it refers to the wedge-shaped stone piece that stands at the highest point of an archway; were that stone to fall, the entire door would collapse. The five NT figurative uses of this expression all quote Ps. 118:22. See *NIDNTT-A*, 119.*

CORNERSTONE

New Testament

Noun: γωνία (*gōnia*), GK *1224* (S *1137*), 9x. *gōnia* essentially means "corner" and refers to the inside or outside "corner" of a structure. See *corner.*

CORRECTION

Old Testament

Noun: מוּסָר (*mûsār*), GK 4592 (S 4148), 50x. *mûsār* is used for personal instruction or correction and may be translated as "instruction, discipline, correction."

It is used 31x in Proverbs. The translation "correction" or "discipline" is determined by the context. See *instruction*.

CORRUPT, CORRUPTION

Old Testament

Verb: שָׁחַת (*šāḥat*), GK 8845 (S 7843), 152x. In various contexts, *šāḥat* can broadly mean "to corrupt, destroy, ruin, spoil, wipe out." It denotes the corrupting or destroying of a wide variety of physical things, including eyes (Exod. 21:26), vineyards (Jer. 12:10), buildings (Lam. 2:6), crops (Jdg. 6:4), trees (Deut. 20:19–20), semen (Gen. 38:9), and kings (1 Sam. 26:15). It is also used to describe the corruption of morals (Prov. 6:32; Deut. 4:16; 31:29). This type of moral corruption is what prompts God to send the flood (Gen. 6:11–12). David associates *šāḥat* with the fool who denies the existence of God and does abominable deeds (Ps. 14:1). See *destroy*.

Adjective or Noun: רַע (or רָע) (*raʿ* [or *rāʿ*]), GK 8273 (S 7451), 312x. In most contexts, *raʿ* is translated "evil, wicked" (e.g., Gen. 13:13). As an adjective, *raʿ* gives a negative or inferior quality to the word it modifies. It describes something as corrupt, base, or bad. See *evil*.

New Testament

Verb: φθείρω (*phtheirō*) GK *5780* (S *5351*), 9x. *phtheirō* means "to corrupt, destroy."

Verb: διαφθείρω (*diaphtheirō*) GK *1425* (S *1311*), 6x. *diaphtheirō* means "to corrupt, destroy."

Noun: φθορά (*phthora*) GK *5785* (S *5356*), 9x. *phthora* means "corruption, destruction."

Adjective: φθαρτός (*phtharos*) GK *5778* (S *5349*), 6x. *phtharo* means "corruptible, perishable."

Corruption is first of all an element of the natural world ever since the sin of Adam and Eve (Rom. 8:21). It is an integral ingredient of the old self (Eph. 4:22; 2 Pet. 1:4; 2:19), the sinful nature, and those who live out of that nature are headed for "destruction" (Gal. 6:8; 2 Pet. 2:12; Jude 10). The teaching of the Scriptures, however, is that we can escape this corruption by being born again of imperishable seed, through the living and abiding word of God (1 Pet. 1:23; cf. 1 Cor. 15:33–34).

It is a sad fact that by acting in a divisive manner in the church, it is possible to "corrupt/destroy" the church (1 Cor. 3:17). False teachers are "men of corrupt mind," who can also do great damage to the church of God (1 Tim. 6:5). It is Paul's fear that in Corinth the minds of true believers might "be corrupted" by the false teachers in their midst (2 Cor. 11:3). The end result for those who either live corrupt lives or who seek to destroy the church will be destruction by God (Rev. 11:18; 19:2). See *NIDNTT-A*, 588–89.

COT

New Testament

Noun: κράβαττος (*krabbatos*), GK *3187* (S *2895*), 11x. *krabbatos* is associated with one who is paralyzed, lame, or bedridden because of physical infirmities. See *mat*.

COUNCIL

New Testament

Noun: συνέδριον (*synedrion*), GK *5284* (S *4892*), 22x. *synedrion* can mean a "governing board, council," "an official session of a council," or, more specifically, "the high council in Jerusalem." See *Sanhedrin*.

COUNSEL

Old Testament

Noun: עֵצָה (*ʿēṣâ*), GK 6783 (S 6098), 87x. *ʿēṣâ* has two basic, though closely related, meanings: "counsel, advice" and "plan, purpose" (see *plan*).

The meaning "counsel, advice" is common throughout the OT. Kings in the ancient world had highly respected counselors who offered advice on legal affairs, war plans, etc. (2 Sam. 16:23; 2 Ki. 18:20; Isa. 19:11). Often it was a sage (Jer. 18:18) or the elders (Ezek. 7:26; 2 Chr. 10:8) who gave counsel to the king.

The themes of seeking wise counsel and avoiding evil counsel are common, both for kings and for the average Israelite.

King Rehoboam foolishly listens to the *ʿēṣâ* of his younger counselors instead of the wisdom of his elders (1 Ki. 12:8) and suffers the consequences. Ps. 1:1 blesses the person who does not walk in the "*counsel* of the wicked" (cf. Job 21:16), and Isa. 47:13 taunts those who have received "counsel" from astrologers. The truly wise individual will seek good "counsel" (Prov. 12:15; 20:18) from godly individuals. The OT affirms that God is the one who gives counsel to humans (Ps. 73:24; 107:11; Isa. 11:2 says that the "spirit of counsel" will rest on the coming Messiah) and that, unlike earthly kings, God needs the counsel of no one (Isa. 40:13).

Verb: יָעַץ (*yāʿaṣ*), GK 3619 (S 3289), 80x. Like the related noun *ʿēṣâ*, "counsel, plan," *yāʿaṣ* carries the two basic meanings of "to counsel, advise" (Num. 24:14; 2 Sam. 17:11) and "to plan, purpose" (Isa. 7:5; 14:24), though the verb seems to carry the former nuance more frequently. Also related to this former meaning is the meaning "to consult, to receive counsel" (2 Chr. 10:8; 25:17). In the OT, kings and their counselors are often engaged in giving or receiving counsel.

Often, the noun *ʿēṣa* and verb *yāʿas* are conjoined in a single Heb. idiom, so that one "counsels a counsel" (2 Sam. 16:23; 1 Ki. 1:12; 12:13), or "purposes a purpose" (Isa. 19:17), or "plans a plan" (Jer. 49:30; Isa. 14:26). The participial form of the verb is frequently used to mean "counselor" (2 Sam. 15:12; Isa. 1:26; 9.6; 41:28; Prov. 11:14). Moses' father-in-law, Jethro, counsels Moses wisely (Exod. 18:19) and strikingly; God himself counsels his people (Ps. 16:7; 32:8). In one of the great OT prophecies of the future Messiah, Isaiah prophesies the coming of one whose name will be called "Wonderful *Counselor*, Mighty God, Eternal Father, Prince of Peace" (Isa. 9.6). See *NIDOTTE,* 2.490-92.

New Testament

Noun: βουλή (*boulē*), GK *1087* (S *1012*), 12x. *boulē* describes the free decision of the will, by way of purpose, plan, or counsel. See *will.*

COUNSELOR

Old Testament

Verb: יָעַץ (*yāʿaṣ*), GK 3619 (S 3289), 80x. *yāʿaṣ* carries the two basic meanings of "to counsel, advise" (Num. 24:14; 2 Sam. 17:11) and "to plan, purpose" (Isa. 7:5; 14:24), though the verb seems to carry the former nuance more frequently. The participial form of the verb is frequently used to mean "counselor" (2 Sam. 15:12; Isa. 1:26; 9:6; 41:28; Prov. 11:14). See *counsel.*

New Testament

Noun: παράκλητος (*paraklētos*), GK *4156* (S *3875*), 5x. *paraklētos* is used 5x in the NT, all of them in the writings of John. The Greek word literally means "one who is called to someone's aid." Various translations have been given to summarize the term: "counselor, helper, advocate," or simply transliterated as "Paraclete."

paraklētos was used in pre-Christian Greek literature to mean "one who appears in another's behalf ("mediator, intercessor"). It bears a similar sense in the NT. When Jesus makes clear to his disciples that he is to be leaving them, he encourages them by revealing that they will not be all alone: "I will ask the Father, and he will give you another *Counselor* to be with you forever" (Jn. 14:16). This Counselor, also called the "Holy Spirit," "will teach you all things and remind you of everything I have said to you" (14:26). As the "Spirit of truth," he will testify about the Father (15:26). The fact that he is about to depart is an advantage, Jesus claims, for the Counselor can only come when Jesus has left (16:7). In 1 Jn. 2:1 the Counselor is mentioned again—this time as an "advocate" to the Father on our behalf for the occasions when we sin.

John's depiction of the third person of the Trinity, though unique in the NT, is helpful for its portrayal of the Spirit's intimate role as "another" Jesus. Jesus himself describes the Counselor as "another helper" (Jn. 14:16). As Christians, we can feel confident that Christ will never leave us; the sending of the Counselor makes that clear. See *NIDNTT-A*, 436-37.*

COUNT

Old Testament

Verb: חָשַׁב (*ḥāšab*), GK 3108 (S 2803), 124 x. *ḥāšab* is most often translated as "think" or "plan" (see *think*, *plan*). One use of this word is in reference to mathematical computations and can also be translated as "count," "calculate," and "value."

Verb: סָפַר (*sāpar*), GK 6218 (S 5608), 107x. *sāpar* means "to count, tell, declare." Note the relationship between these meanings in that the English "recount" means "tell."

(1) *sāpar* is the verb God uses when he tells Abraham to "count" the stars; when Abraham is unable to do so, God tells him that that is how numerous his descendants will eventually become (Gen. 15:6; 16:10). Nor can he "count" the grains of sand on the seashore (32:12). In Israel's determination of the annual festival days for each year, they are to "count off" from the Passover (Lev. 23:15–16; cf. also 25:8; Deut. 16:9). David, much to God's displeasure, counts the number of fighting men in Israel (1 Chr. 21:2).

(2) But more frequently the verb means "to tell." It can denote telling something on a merely human level. Joseph "tells" his dreams to his father and brothers (Gen. 37:9–10). The Israelites are to "tell" their children and grandchildren about the exodus (Exod. 10:2). Hamaan "tells" his wife and friends about what happened at the dinner with Esther and the king (Est. 6:13). The false prophets of Jeremiah's day tell each other their dreams (Jer. 23:27–28, 23).

(3) Far more important, however, are the uses of *sāpar* in the Psalms. The psalmist vows to "tell" others of all God's wonders (Ps. 9:1) and to "declare" his praises (9:14). Ps. 78 is a powerful psalm about telling the wonderful deeds of God from one generation to the next (78:1, 3, 4, 6; cf. 79:13). The psalmist calls on God's people to declare and proclaim what the Lord has done (96:3; 118:17). In addition to words, nature itself (the heavens) "declare" the glory of God (19:1). See *NIDOTTE*, 3:284–85.

Verb: פָּקַד (*pāqad*), GK 7212 (S 6485), 304x. While *pāqad* has a wide range of meaning, it basically expresses the action of overseeing an individual for a particular purpose. Since the verb carries the idea of "oversight," the person of higher position or rank usually serves as the subject of *pāqad* while a subordinate is the object. Half of its appearances in the OT occur in two books: Numbers (103x) and Jeremiah (49x).

In the sense of oversight, *pāqad* is used most frequently in the sense of a superior counting someone in his charge during a census. The NIV generally translates this use "to count" or "to number." This sense occurs primarily in the context of military censuses for the inspection of troops in preparation for battle (though occasionally censuses are for tax purposes, see Exod. 30:12; 38:25). As a result, the NIV occasionally translates this use of *pāqad* as "to muster": Joshua "musters" the people before Ai (Jos. 8:10); Saul "musters" them at Bezek (1 Sam. 11:18); and David "musters" the people with him (2 Sam. 18:1). It seems likely that David's census in 2 Sam. 24 is military in nature, provoking Yahweh's wrath because David is trusting in military force rather than in God himself.

The censuses of Num. 1-4 and 26 (in which *pāqad* appears 95x) are clearly military censuses. God commands Moses to take a census of the men of Israel who are twenty years old and able to go out to war. Then he says, "You and Aaron shall *number* them to their armies" (1:3), perhaps implying not just counting but an actual assembling of the Israelites into military formation. Later, the Levites are not "counted" among the other tribes that form the army (1:47, 49; 2:33) but in a separate census (4:34-49, *pāqad* is used 17x) because their purpose is not to fight but to serve in the tabernacle (1:50). After the initial conquest fails and Israel wanders in the desert for forty years, God commands a census of the new generation (26:2; cf. 1:3) in preparation for Joshua to lead this second generation of Israelites into the promised land.

When oversight leads to an appropriate response on behalf of the superior to the actions or situation of the subordinate, *pāqad* may be translated "to attend to" or "to visit" and regularly takes God as the subject (see *visit*). *NIDOTTE*, 3:657-63

Noun: מִסְפָּר (*mispār*), GK 5031 (S 4557), 134x. *mispār* means "number," the result of what happens when someone has "counted" or "listed" something. See *number*.

New Testament

Verb: κρύπτω (*kryptō*), GK *3221* (S *2928*), 18x. *kryptō* means "to conceal, hide." See *hide*.

COUNTENANCE

Old Testament

Noun: פָּנֶה (*pāneh*; occurs only in plural, פָּנִים [*pānîm*]), GK 7156 (S 6440), 2126x. In the OT, *pāneh* basically refers to the front side of something or someone, typically the head or the face. When God shows favor to his people, he makes his face shine on them (Num. 6:25) and he turns his countenance toward them (Num. 6:26). See *face*.

New Testament

Noun: πρόσωπον (*prosōpon*), GK *4725* (S *4383*), 76x. *prosōpon* essentially means "face." It commonly refers to the face or countenance of a person, but it is also found in a number of different expressions. See *face*.

COUNTRY

New Testament

Noun: χώρα (*chōra*), GK *6001* (S *5561*), 28x. The basic sense of *chōra* is an area or space. Although in classical Greek the word usually refers to relatively small spaces (e.g., a soldier's "station"), in the NT it refers to relatively large areas, such as a cultivated field, a region, or a country.

(1) Jesus tells his disciples that the "fields" are white with harvest (Jn. 4:35; cf. Jas. 5:4). In one of his parables, Jesus refers to the "field" of a rich man, meaning all his cultivated property (Lk. 12:16). The word can also refer to the broader areas where fields are located, i.e., the "countryside" as opposed to the city (Lk. 21:21).

(2) More generally, *chōra* refers to regions or territories. In Mk. 6:55, the people run about the whole "district" and brought the sick to Jesus. Most often *chōra* has a political aspect to it, such as the "regions" of Judea and Samaria (Acts 8:1), the "country" of the Gerasenes (Mk. 5:1; Lk. 8:26), and the Phrygian and Galatian "region" (Acts 16:6). In Mt. 4:16, *chōra* is picked up from Isa. 9:2, where Isaiah is referring to people who live in the territories of Zebulun and Naphtali. In Acts 27:27 *chōra* is translated as "land" in most versions, but it can also be understood as "country" (see KJV). See *NIDNTT-A*, 616.

COUNTRYSIDE

New Testament

Noun: ἀγρός (*agros*), GK *69* (S *68*), 36x. *agros* can refer to arable "land" or the "countryside." See *field*.

(HAVE) COURAGE

New Testament

Verb: τολμάω (*tolmaō*), GK *5528* (S *5111*), 16x. *tolmaō* means "to dare, have courage." See *dare*.

COURAGEOUS

Old Testament

Verb: חָזַק (*ḥāzaq*), GK 2616 (S 2388), 290x. *ḥāzaq* can describe the severity or strength of an impersonal force. At some points it is interpreted to mean being courageous. So the KJV translates the word in Jos. 23:6, "Be ye therefore very courageous" (cf. the NIV, "Be very strong"; cf. also 1 Chr. 19:13; 2 Chr. 19:11; Ezr. 10:4; Ps. 27:14; Isa. 41:6). See *strong*.

COURT

Old Testament

Noun: חָצֵר (*ḥāṣēr*), GK 2958 (S 2691), 192x. *ḥāṣēr* probably comes from a root that means "surround" and, drawing from this basic meaning, refers to a courtyard or a village (see *village*). A courtyard differs from a field in that it is surrounded by a fence, a wall, or buildings (cf. Exod. 8:13, "the frogs died in the houses, *courts*, and fields"). In 2 Sam. 17:18 we read of a well in the courtyard of a personal house.

More often, *ḥāṣēr* refers to the court of the tabernacle (Exod. 27:9) or to one of the temple courts (1 Chr. 28:12). The tabernacle court measures 50 by 100 cubits with a height of 5 cubits (Exod. 27:18). The temple has two courts (2 Chr. 33:5): an inner court surrounding it (1 Ki. 6:36; 7:12, probably also known as "the court of the priests" 2 Chr. 4:9), and an "outer court" (Ezek. 10:5, possibly also known as "the great court," 1 Ki. 7:12). It is difficult to know exactly how they all relate to one another. Similarly, Xerxes' palace in Persia has an inner and an outer court (Est. 4:11, 6:4).

For the OT saint, there is no better place to be than in the temple courts: "better is a day in your *courts* than a thousand elsewhere" (Ps. 84:10; cf. v. 2). See *NIDOTTE*, 2:249-250.

New Testament

Noun: βῆμα (*bēma*), GK *1037* (S *968*), 12x. *bēma* typically signifies a "judgment seat," that is, an official's place or seat of authority from which he exercises judgment. A contemporary eqivalent is a courtroom setting, where a judge sits behind "the bench" in order to exercise authority and issue judgment. This explains the NIV's use of "court" for *bēma* (Acts 18:12, 16–17; 25:6, 10, 17). The KJV generally uses "judgment seat."

Jesus is tried before Pilate, who brings Jesus out and sits down "on the *judge's seat*" (Jn. 19:13) to hear the accusations of the Jewish priests and elders. From this *bēma*, Pilate addresses the crowds (Mt. 27:19). In the same manner, the Jews bring Paul before the *bēma* of Gallio (Acts 18:12, 16–17) to be tried. Festus also commands that Paul appear before him at the *bēma* in Caesarea (Acts 25:6, 17), again as a result of the instigation and accusations of the Jewish leaders. Acts 25:10 clearly demonstrates that the *bēma* was a place of trial and judgment, as Paul said, "I stand at Caesar's *judgment seat*, where I ought to be judged" (KJV).

Paul uses *bēma* twice to indicate the place of *divine* judgment. In view of our tendency to wrongfully judge one another, Paul warns in Rom. 14:10 that "we will all stand before God's *judgment seat*." Perhaps Paul has in mind the words of Jesus regarding our coming judgment (Mt. 7:1–2). In 2 Cor. 5:10 Paul remnds his readers that we "must all appear before the *judgment seat* of Christ," where we will be held accountable "for the things done while in the body, whether good or bad." Notice especially the emphasis on Christ's deity as Paul uses *bēma* with reference first to God (Rom. 14:10), then to Christ in the context of divine judgment (2 Cor. 5:10; cf. also Mt. 25:31–46; Jn. 5:22–29).

There are two unique meanings to *bēma* in the NT. This noun is used once to express a unit of measurement (Acts 7:5—here translated as "a foot of ground," i.e., a very small area). And *bēma* is used once as "throne," where Herod sits to deliver a public address (Acts 12:21). The setting does not allow for "judgment seat," especially since Herod is there in all his "royal robes." See *NIDNTT-A*, 93.*

COURTYARD

New Testament

Noun: αὐλή (*aulē*), GK *885* (S *833*), 12x. *aulē* means "courtyard" or "palace." It is used mainly for an open area, sometimes enclosed by walls (Mt. 26:58, 69; Mk. 14:54, 66; Lk. 22:55; Jn. 18:15; Rev. 11:12). In Jn. 10:1, 6 *aulē* refers specifically to a fold for sheep. The word came to be used for an entire building complex, e.g., a house or palace (Mt. 26:3; Mk. 15:16; Lk. 11:21).*

COUSIN

Old Testament

Noun: דּוֹד (*dôd*), GK 1856 (S 1730), 61x. *dôd* sometimes denotes a close male relative, such as an "uncle" or "cousin"; it also means "beloved." See *beloved*.

COVENANT

Old Testament

Noun: בְּרִית (*b^e^rît*), GK 1382 (S 1285), 287x. *b^e^rît* means "covenant, treaty." The ancient world, like the modern world, was filled with treaties or covenants among people groups, often as military alliances. This analogy was used to describe God's entering into a relationship with his people. See *NIDOTTE*, 1:747–54. See also *treaty*.

Most uses of *b^e^rît* in the OT are the covenants that God made with his people. The first is the Noahic covenant after the Flood, where God promised not to destroy the earth again (Gen. 9:9–17). In the covenant established with Abraham (Gen. 15:18; 17:1–19), God promised to make his name great and to give him a descendant, from whom a great nation would arise. In both of these covenants, God established the terms, and he was the one who vowed to keep a series of promises.

In the covenant at Mount Sinai, the LORD also sets the terms (his law), but he calls on the Israelites to agree to those terms (Exod. 24:1–8). As his covenant people, they promise to obey his revealed laws. Note too how God lives among his people in "the ark of the covenant" (Num. 10:33). The promise God makes to have a descendant of David on the throne is also called a "covenant" (2 Sam. 23:5; 2 Chr. 13:5; 21:7; Ps. 89:3–4).

But God's people do not keep his covenant; they break it again and again. Therefore, through Jeremiah God promises to make a new covenant with his people (Jer. 31:31–34), a covenant that they will not break. By his incredible grace, he will forgive their sins and iniquities. This covenant the NT sees as fulfilled in Jesus Christ (Lk. 22:20; Heb. 8:8; 9:15; 12:28).

New Testament

Noun: διαθήκη (*diathēkē*), GK *1347* (S *1242*), 33x. *diathēkē* can mean "covenant, testament, will." The majority of the occurrences of this word are in quotations from or allusions to the OT. In fact, the very term "NT" (*kainē diathēkē*) contains this word. It is also used for one's last will and testament. See *testament*.

Jesus is the mediator of the new covenant (Heb. 8:6; 12:24). The blood he shed on Calvary and symbolized in the cup of the Lord's Supper is "the blood of the new covenant" (Lk. 22:20; 1 Cor. 11:25). Both Paul in 2 Cor. 3 and the writer to the Hebrews in Heb. 8:6–10:18 demonstrate various ways in which this new covenant is superior to the old. It has better promises, and its glory will never fade. See *NIDNTT-A*, 134-36.

(MAKE A) COVENANT

Old Testament

Verb: כָּרַת (*kārat*), GK 4162 (S 3772), 289x. *kārat* broadly means "to cut (objects), exclude and/or destroy, make a covenant." While these three basic meanings seem divergent, they are closely linked together around the notion of cutting. See also *cut*; *exclude*.

The majority of the uses of *kārat* have to do with making (cutting) a covenant, either between human beings (Gen. 21:27, 32; Jos. 9:11, 15) or between God and his people (Exod. 34:10; Deut. 4:23). Two different backgrounds have been suggested for this use of the word relative to covenants/treaties. Most scholars relate it to a rite of ratification for a covenant, in which the parties to the covenant walked through dismembered parts of a sacrificed animal (see Gen. 15:9–10, 17; Jer. 34:18–20). The tacit announcement made through this event is: "Let it be done to me as has been done to this beast if I fail to keep my pledge of covenant loyalty." Other scholars have noted how many ancient treaties were cut into pieces of stone, so that there was a permanent record of the treaty. Usually two copies were made—one for each member in the party, to store in their respective temples. Many today consider the two tablets of the law that God gave Moses to store in the ark to be these two copies. See *NIDOTTE*, 4:1290-91.

COVER

Old Testament

Verb: כָּסָה (*kāsâ*), GK 4059 (S 3680), 153x. This word is predominately used with the literal sense "to cover." In other contexts, it can denote "conceal, hide" and even "forgive."

(1) In general, *kāsâ* simply means "to cover," including the idea of covering oneself with clothing (2 Ki. 19:1–2; Isa. 37:2). Water "covered" the earth during the flood (Gen. 7:19–20; Ps. 104:6, 9). During the Exodus, frogs and locusts "covered" Egypt and water "covered" the armies of Pharaoh (Exod. 8:2; 10:5, 15; 14:28). *kāsâ* implies completeness or thoroughness as in Num. 22:5, where the Israelites are said to "*cover* the face of the land" or in the promise that "the earth will be filled with the knowledge of the glory of the LORD, as the waters *cover* the sea" (Hab. 2:14; cf. Isa. 11:9).

(2) In some cases, covering is used to conceal something (Gen. 9:23; 18:17; Jdg. 4:18–19) or to protect something (e.g., 1 Ki. 1:1, where David is given clothes to keep warm). The concealment can be negative if it is used with reference to one's own sin; e.g., hiding sin is the opposite of confessing (Ps. 32:5; Prov. 28:13). Concealment can also be for protection. In the Most Holy Place, incense is burned so that the atonement cover will be concealed (Lev. 16:13). In Isa. 51:16, the Lord declares, "I have put my words in your mouth and *covered* you with the shadow of my hand." In a time of great distress, the psalmist takes refuge in the Lord: "Rescue me from my enemies, O LORD, for I *hide* myself in you" (Ps. 143:9). The glory cloud that covered the tabernacle represented the presence of God and was intended to conceal his awesome holiness from the people for their own protection (Num. 9:15–16; 17:7). Similarly, in the NT, believers lives are "hidden with Christ in God" (Col. 3:3).

(3) *kāsâ* can also convey the idea of forgiveness. When God "hides" sin, he makes it completely invisible and casts it into the depths of the sea (cf. Mic. 7:19). In Ps. 32:1, *kāsâ* occurs as a parallel expression for *nāśā*ʾ ("to forgive," GK 5951): "Blessed is he whose transgressions are forgiven, whose sins are *covered*." Neh. 4:5 uses "to cover" as a parallel expression for "to blot out": "Do not *cover up* their guilt or blot out their sins". Where *kāsâ* connotes "forgiveness," it is God who does the covering. "You forgave the iniquity of your people and *covered* all their sins" (Ps. 85:2). And in human relations, love is so important, since "love covers all wrongs" (Prov. 10:12; cf. 17:9). See *NIDOTTE*, 2:674–78.

(TO BE) COVERED

New Testament

Verb: γεμω (*gemō*), GK *1154* (S *1073*), 11x. *gemō* conveys the passive idea of being filled to capacity and may best be translated as "full" or "covered." See *(to be) full.*

COVET

New Testament

Verb: ἐπιθυμέω (*epithymeō*), GK *2121* (S *1937*), 16x. *epithymeō* means "to desire earnestly, long for something, lust, covet." It has both negative and positive connotations, but it always describes the inner motivation. See *desire.*

COVETOUSNESS

New Testament

Noun: πλεονεξία (*pleonexia*), GK *4432* (S *4124*), 10x. *pleonexia* means "greed, covetousness." See *greed.*

COW

Old Testament

Noun: בָּקָר (*bāqār*), GK 1330 (S 1241), 183x. *bāqār* refers to domesticated cattle (e.g., bulls, cows, and calves). In the ancient world, cattle were a measure of one's wealth. Larger cattle were deemed more valuable than smaller animals. See *cattle.*

COWORKER

New Testament

Noun: συνεργός (*synergos*), GK *5301* (S *4904*), 13x. This word means "coworker, fellow worker, assistant." See *fellow worker*.

CREATE

Old Testament

Verb: בָּרָא (*bārā'*), GK 1343 (S 1254), 48x. *bārā'* means "to create." While there is some scholarly difference of opinion about the meaning of this verb, it is fair to say that it occurs exclusively with God as the subject or the implied agent of creation. Creating is only something that God does.

(1) *bārā'* is used 5x in Gen. 1 (1:1, 21, 27[3x]; cf. 2:3–4; 5:1–2; 6:7) for the great creative act of God "in the beginning." While the expression "out of nothing" does not appear here (but cf. Heb. 11:3), most scholars accept this as the nuance behind the creation story, namely, that God did not use any previously made material in order to create "the heavens and the earth" (an expression that denotes all of reality). Because God has created everything, all things belong to him; he is the sovereign Creator and Lord. Several passages in the Psalms (e.g., Ps. 89:12; 104:30; 148:5) and many in Isaiah (e.g., Isa. 40:26, 28; 42:5; 45:18) affirm the same thing.

(2) But God's creation is not limited to physical stuff; he also created a people for himself, the nation of Israel, whom he created for his own glory (Isa. 43:1, 7; Mal. 2:10). This theme carries over into the NT in the creation of "the one new man" in Christ Jesus (Eph. 2:15; see discussion of *ktizō*, GK 3231).

(3) God's creative activity does not end with creation in Genesis. He remains the Creator. Since the world he created has been soiled by sin, God promises that the day will come when "I will create new heavens and a new earth" (Isa. 65:17), which includes a new Jerusalem (65:17–25) and a new humanity. This, too, is a NT theme (cf. 2 Pet. 3:13; Rev. 21:1).

(4) Finally, the verb *bārā'* can also be applied to more abstract concepts. Isa. 45:8, for example, indicates that God "creates" and rains down righteousness and salvation. In fact, 45:7 indicates that God "creates evil." The word for "evil" used here does mean that God is the originator and author of moral evil and sin; rather, it denotes "disaster"; that his, God creates events that can serve as warnings of and as judgments upon his people, and indeed on the entire human race. Once again, this is a demonstration that God is ultimately in charge of all that he has made; he is sovereign over all the events of history. See *NIDOTTE*, 1:728–35.

Verb: קָנָה (*qānâ*), GK 7864, 7865 (S 7069), 91x. *qānâ* appears to bear two distinct meanings in the OT: "to buy, purchase, redeem" (see *buy*); also "to create."

There are several places in the OT where *qānâ* means "create" (e.g., Ps. 139:13). Upon giving birth to Cain, Eve said, "With the help of the LORD I have *brought forth* a man" (i.e., "created," Gen. 4:1). When Melchizedek blessed Abram, he said, "Blessed be Abram by God Most High, *Creator* of heaven and earth" (i.e., "possessor," Gen. 14:19; see also 14:22; Deut. 32:6). In Deut. 32:6, Moses says to Israel, "Is this the way you repay the LORD, O foolish and unwise people? Is he not your Father, your *Creator*, who made you and formed you?" Wisdom states, "The LORD *brought me forth* as the first of his works, before his deeds of old" (Prov. 8:22).

New Testament

Verb: κτίζω (*ktizō*), GK *3231* (S *2936*), 15x. In the NT, *ktizō* ("to create") is used exclusively of God's creative activity. It may refer to God's activity in relation to the physical world (Rom. 1:25; Rev. 10:6; cf. Mk. 13:19), food (1 Tim. 4:3), people (Mt. 19:4; 1 Cor. 11:9), and all things (Eph. 3:9; Col. 1:16; Rev. 4:11). *ktizō* is also used of God's creative activity (Eph. 2:10) in forming the new self in believers (Col. 3:10), which is "*created* after the likeness of God" (Eph. 4:24). Moreover, through the cross of Christ, God brought about reconciliation in the human race and "created" one new man out of Jew and Gentile (Eph. 2:15). See *NIDNTT-A*, 321-23.*

Verb: ποιέω (*poieō*), GK *4472* (S *4160*), 568x. This verb, generically translated as "to do," has a wide range of meanings, including the idea of "creating" the world. See *do*.

CREATION

New Testament

Noun: καταβολή (*katabolē*), GK *2856* (S *2602*), 11x. *katabolē* literally means "something thrown down." Most often it is translated "creation" or "foundation."

(1) Of the occurrences of *katabolē* in the NT, only once does the phrase "of the world" not immediately follow it. The phrase "foundation/creation of the world" is a fixed expression for the point from which historical dates are reckoned. These phrases have several uses. It is used to speak of God's election of his people (Mt. 25:34; Eph. 1:4). Revelation uses the expression to emphasize the eternal state of the condemned (Rev. 13:8; 17:8). It can speak of a historical failure for which judgment is rendered (Lk. 11:50; Heb. 4:3). Finally, it emphasizes the unique and central position of Christ in the history of salvation (Mt. 13:35, citing Ps. 78:2; Jn. 17:24; Heb. 9:26; 1 Pet. 1:20). In all these uses this phrase is always associated with a statement about humanity's destiny and implies a connection with God's foreknowledge.

(2) Only in Heb. 11:11 is the term *katabolē* not followed by "of the world." In context the noun means something like the ability to sow a seed. The emphasis is on the "creation" of life, although the context makes clear that it is not without God's powerful assistance, for this verse is in the "faith" chapter in Hebrews. The use of *katabolē* in the NT is a powerful reminder that all things are rooted in the sovereign plan of God. See *NIDNTT-A*, 291.*

Noun: κτίσις (*ktisis*), GK *3232* (S *2937*), 19x. The noun *ktisis* refers either to the act of creation (Rom. 1:20) or to that which God has created (Rom. 1:25; 2 Pet. 3:4; Rev. 3:14). It encompasses both inanimate creation (Rom. 8:19–22) and animate creatures (Col. 1:23) such as people (Mk. 10:6). Only in 1 Pet. 2:13 does *ktisis* perhaps refer to a "human institution" created by human beings, but even here the sense seems to be that God has established these institutions.

God has revealed himself clearly to all people through what can be seen in creation (Rom. 1:20), but people have turned from the obvious self-revelation of God to worship the creation as if it were the Creator (Rom. 1:25). Creation is seen as groaning in pain (probably a reference the reality of death and natural disasters) and longs to be set free from this bondage of decay (Rom. 8:19–22). This will occur at the end of time when God creates a new heaven and a new earth, in which righteousness dwells (cf. 2 Pet. 3:10–13).

Through the work of Christ, believers are made into a new creation (2 Cor. 5:17), and only this matters in comparison to human distinctions such as circumcision (Gal. 6:15).

In the great Christ-hymn in Col. 1, Jesus is proclaimed as the "image of the invisible God, the firstborn of all creation" (Col. 1:15). This does not mean that Jesus was a created being (see *firstborn*), but rather that he existed before creation and as such is supreme "over all creation" (NIV). Paul is alluding to the rights of primogeniture in which the firstborn son holds special and unique privileges. See *NIDNTT-A*, 321-23.

CREDIT

New Testament

Verb: λογίζομαι (*logizomai*), GK *3357* (S *3049*), 40x. The basic meaning of *logizomai* has to do with counting or thinking (see also *think, consider, regard as*). It is sometimes used for crediting something for or against someone (e.g., 2 Cor. 5:19). Paul uses *logizomai* to declare that God "credits" (or counts) faith as righteousness. We can picture faith being set down as a mark on the credit side of a ledger for righteousness, rather than the debit side. This is the doctrine of justification by faith (see Rom. 4). Paul demonstrates that this teaching is not a new idea but has its roots in the OT, where Abraham believed God and it "was credited" to him as righteousness (Gen. 15:6 in Rom. 4:3; see also Gal. 3:6; Jas. 2:23). This stands in contrast to crediting wages to someone who has worked to earn them (Rom. 4:4). Just as with Abraham, faith is credited as righteousness to anyone who does not attempt to earn them but rather trusts God to give it for him by his grace (v. 5). See *NIDNTT-A*, 338-39.

CRIPPLED

New Testament

Adjective: ἀδύνατος (*adynatos*), GK *105* (S *102*), 10x. *adynatos* means (lit.) "not able," but in Acts 14:8 it means one who is physically unable to walk—a "crippled" person. See *impossible*.

Adjective: χωλός (*chōlos*), GK *6000* (S *5560*), 14x. *chōlos* is someone who is "lame" or "crippled." See *lame*.

CROP

Old Testament

Noun: פְּרִי (*p^eri*), GK 7262 (S 6529), 119x. *p^erî* means "fruit, crops, produce." See *fruit*.

New Testament

Noun: καρπός (*karpos*), GK *2843* (S *2590*), 66x. *karpos* refers to the natural product of a living being. In the literal sense, it is used of "fruit" born by trees (Mt. 12:33) or vines (21:41) and of "crops" of grain from the ground (Jn. 12:24). See *fruit*.

CROSS

New Testament

Noun: σταυρός (*stauros*), GK *5089* (S *4716*), 27x. *stauros* means "cross." There are three related ideas that are communicated by the *stauros* word group. (1) The most basic meaning of *stauros* is a pole placed in the ground that was used for capital punishment. It was made of wood and dropped into a hole dug into the ground so that it could stand in an upright position. A crosspiece was usually attached to its upper part so that it looked like a "T." Thus, when the gospels refer to the events of Jesus' death (Mt. 27:40; Jn. 19:25; Phil. 2:8), the "cross" is the physical pole on which Jesus was crucified.

(2) From the perspective of the NT a cross is much more than a wooden pole for capital punishment. *stauros* sometimes means the death of Jesus. His death on a cross is one of the most important elements in the Christian faith. Paul can even speak of the message he preaches as "the message of *the cross*" (1 Cor. 1:18; cf. Gal. 5:11; 6:12). Christ's death on a cross gives life to those who believe in him. That message is a message of saving reconciliation (Rom. 1:16). See also *crucify*.

(3) Finally, the NT applies *stauros* metaphorically to all followers of Christ. Jesus declares in the gospels that the way of Christ, the way of the "cross," is also the way for all Christians as we take up our cross and follow him (Mt. 10:38; Lk. 9:23; 14:27). These sayings of Jesus implore Christians to bear the cost of Christian discipleship and be willing to sacrifice ourselves in service to him and to others. This message is as pertinent to us today as it was to the disciples in Jesus' day. We too have a "cross" to bear in our faithful and obedient life and witness. See *NIDNTT-A*, 537-39.

CROSS OVER

Old Testament

Verb: עָבַר (*ʿābar*), GK 6296 (S 5674), 553x. *ʿābar* occurs frequently in the OT with a variety of nuances. It is predominantly used in a spatial sense of crossing over (Gen. 31:21), passing by (31:52), or passing through (Exod. 30:12). For the most part, human beings are the subject of this verb as they move from one place to another, such as the Israelites "crossing" the Jordan into the promised land (Deut. 3:18, 21, 25; Jos. 1:2, 11, 14; 2:23). In a temporal sense, *ʿābar* refers to the passage of time (Gen. 50:4). Those who die are said euphemistically to pass away (Ps. 37:36; Job 33:18). The verb can be used with God as the subject, such as his glory passing in front of Moses at Sinai (Exod. 33:22; 34:6) and similarly in front of Elijah (1 Ki. 19:11).

ʿābar sometimes has covenantal overtones. It is used for passing between the dismembered animal pieces in a covenant inauguration ceremony (Gen. 15:17; Jer. 34:18–19). In addition, it is used both for act of entering into a covenant (Deut. 29:12; Jos. 7:15) and for violating the commandment (Num. 14:41; Jdg. 2:20; Hos. 6:7).

The causative (Hiphil) stem of *ʿābar* can be used of giving something over as a sacrifice (Exod. 13:12), especially of giving over children to Molech and causing them to pass through the fire (Lev. 18:21; 2 Ki. 16:3). It is used when God caused wind to blow over the earth after the Flood (Gen. 8:1) and when a person causes a sound or voice to be heard (Exod. 36:6; Lev. 25:9; 2 Chr. 30:5; 36:22). It is also used of God's forgiving sin and causing it to pass away (Job 7:21; Mic. 7:18).

There are other specialized uses of *ʿābar*. It can be used of making a proclamation and causing it to pass through the land (Ezek. 1:1), of becoming angry (Ps. 78:59), and of being overcome by wine (Jer. 23:9). See *NIDOTTE*, 3:314–16.

CROW

New Testament

Verb: φονέω (*phoneō*), GK *5888* (S *5455*), 43x. *phoneō* means "to call out, call to, make a noise." This noise can be the noise of a bird, such as a crow. See *call*.

CROWD

Old Testament

Noun: הָמוֹן (*hāmôn*), GK 2162 (S 1995), 82x. *hāmôn* expresses a quality of immensity or magnitude, whether it bears an emotive, audible, or spatial reference. It is translated with words like "confusion, tumult, noise, abundance, army, hordes." See *hordes*.

New Testament

Noun: ὄχλος (*ochlos*), GK *4063* (S *3793*), 175x. *ochlos* describes a large "crowd" or "multitude" of people. "When Jesus saw the *crowd* around him, he gave orders to cross to the other side of the lake" (Mt. 8:18). When Jesus heals a demon-possessed man, the Bible tells us, "All the *people* were astonished" (Mt. 12:23). "Large *crowds* from Galilee, the Decapolis, Jerusalem, Judea, and the region across the Jordan followed him" (Mt. 4:25; cf. Acts 5:16). In Revelation, *ochlos* denotes that great "multitude" that no one can number (Rev. 7:9; 19:1, 6).

ochlos can also be used to describe a group of people who have become unruly and out of control: "… the violence of the mob was so great [Paul] had to be carried by the soldiers" (Acts 21:35; cf. Jn. 7:49).

ochlos is also used as a "number" that can be quantified. "So the word of God spread. The number of disciples in Jerusalem increased rapidly, and a large *number* of priests became obedient to the faith" (Acts 6:7; cf. 11:24; 19:26). Upon converting so many, we later read, "Barnabas and Saul met with the church and taught great *numbers* of people" (Acts 11:26). See *NIDNTT-A*, 425.

Noun: πλῆθος (*plēthos*), GK *4436* (S *4128*), 31x. *plēthos* denotes the number or quantity of an object and is best translated "number, crowd, multitude." See *number*.

CROWN

New Testament

Noun: στέφανος (*stephanos*), GK *5109* (S *4735*), 18x. There are three related ideas communicated with the word *stephanos*. It can refer to a physical crown or wreath worn by someone of high status. In the Greco-Roman world, a crown (often a woven wreath) was given as a sign of honor to people of high status. One such group of admired people was the victors of athletic games. Paul picks up on this usage to contrast perishable athletic crowns with the imperishable reward of obedience to Christ (1 Cor. 9:25; 2 Tim. 4:8; cf. the verb *stephanoō* ["to crown"] in 2 Tim. 2:5). Besides athletes, notable public servants and high-ranking officials were also given crowns as a sign of honor—a usage reflected in Rev. 4:4, 10; 6:2; 12:1; 14:14. This same sense is used in a mocking way by the soldiers who make a *stephanos* of thorns (along with a purple robe) for Jesus (Mt. 27:29; Mk. 15:17; Jn. 19:2, 5). For the NT writers, there is a great irony here, for Jesus is in fact the true King of kings.

The other two ideas communicated by *stephanos* are metaphorical. It can refer to an adornment or source of pride. In Phil. 4:1 and 1 Thess. 2:19 *stephanos* is used in the sense of "to be proud of." Paul speaks of his spiritual children in Philippi and Thessalonica as his joy and crown before God (cf. the gray head as a "crown of glory" in Prov. 16:31).

stephanos can also mean "prize, reward." In Jas. 1:12 the "crown of life" (i.e., eternal life) is given to the one who perseveres under trial, and in 1 Pet. 5:4, faithful shepherd-elders are promised an unfading "crown of glory" (i.e., eternal honor). Similarly, in Rev. 2:10 the crown of life" is promised to those who overcome tribulation. In each instance the emphasis is on "of life" and "of glory." The crown or reward is in fact the life or the glory promised. The use of *stephanos* in such phrases heightens the drama and paints a wonderful word picture of the beauty of one who has faithfully and painfully endured and now stands on the victor's platform with joy. See *NIDNTT-A*, 540.

CRUCIFY

New Testament

Verb: σταυρόω (*stauroō*), GK *5090* (S *4717*), 46x. *stauroō* means "to crucify." (1) Paul speaks of Christ's manner of death as being "crucified" (1 Cor. 1:23; 2:2). Most uses of this verb are in the latter chapters of each of the gospels, as the religious leader cry out, "Crucify him!" (Mt. 27:22–23) and then lead Jesus how "to be crucified."

(2) But "to crucify" means more than simply the way Jesus died, for it bears the theological message implied by his death. Paul summarizes his preaching in Corinth as "Christ crucified" (1 Cor. 1:23; 2:2). To the Gentiles, this was foolishness, for who would want to believe in someone who had suffered the form capital punishment saved for the worst of criminals (1:18, 23)? To the Jews, it was a stumbling block, for hanging on a cross meant one was experiencing the curse of God (cf. Gal. 3:13).

In Col. 2 Paul describes further the cosmic significance of Christ's having been "crucified." God has now "cancelled the written code, with all its regulations, that was against us and that stood opposed to us; he took it away, nailing it to the cross" (2:14). That is, Christ's crucifixion was a public declaration of the cancellation of our sins and the end of all claims to legalism. It was not just the cross, but Christ's death upon it, that Paul proclaims. Moreover, by his cruficixion, Christ broke the curse that was upon us for our disobedience to God's law (Gal. 3:10–13). See also *cross*.

(3) Finally, in Gal. 5:24, Paul calls on all believers to "crucify the sinful nature"; that is, we must put to death the works of the flesh in us and live by the power of the Spirit, who wants to work his fruit in our lives.

CRY

Old Testament

Verb: בָּכָה (*bokâ*), GK 1134 (S 1058), 114x. *bokâ* has the basic meaning "to weep," but can be translated with other terms such as "sob, mourn, wail, cry." See *weep*.

New Testament

Verb: κλαίω (*klaiō*), GK *3081* (S *2799*), 40x. *klaiō* means "to weep, mourn" because of grief. In the NT, this verb expresses violent emotions brought about by various circumstances that cause sorrow. See *weep*.

CRY OUT

Old Testament

Verb: זָעַק (*zāʿaq*), GK 2410 (S 2199), 73x. *zāʿaq* means "to cry out, call out, summon," often to the Lord. It is similar in pronunciation to and is a synonym of *ṣāʿaq* (GK 7590).

(1) For the most part, *zāʿaq* refers to a cry in time of need or distress. The Israelites "cry out" to God during the time of slavery in Egypt (Exod. 2:23). On various occasions during the period of the judges,

the people "cry out" to the Lord in their distress (Jdg. 3:9; 6:6; 10:10; 1 Sam. 7:7–8). And when people cry out to the Lord, he comes to their aid and delivers them (Ps. 22:5; 107:13, 19). Hosea admonishes the Israelites because they are not crying out to the Lord but are merely wailing and gashing themselves instead (Hos. 7:14). Other prophets state that when God's people have rejected him and turned aside to idols, if and when they do cry out to him, he will not hear (Isa. 57:13; Jer. 11:11–12).

(2) But it is not only the Israelites as a nation who cry out. Tamar cries out after she has been raped (2 Sam. 13:17). The Philistines cry out because of God's judgment (Isa. 14:31). The sailors on the boat that is carrying Jonah to Tarshish cry out in fear during the fierce storm (Jon. 1:5). Later, the king of Assyria issues a proclamation (i.e., cries out, 3:7), calling his nation to repent in sackcloth and ashes.

(3) *zā*ʿ*aq* can also mean "to summon aid," such as what both Barak (Jdg. 4:10) and Gideon (6:34) do as they begin the battle. Likewise, Saul "summons" the Israelites soldiers to attack the Philistines (1 Sam. 14:20). See *NIDOTTE*, 2:1131–32.

Verb: צָעַק (*ṣā*ʿ*aq*), GK 7590 (S 6817), 55x. *ṣā*ʿ*aq* means "to cry out," usually for help in a desperate situation, especially one of injustice and suffering. It is frequently used for the Israelites crying out during their time of slavery to the Egyptians (Num. 20:16; Deut. 26:7; Neh. 9:27). It is also used as a cry of distress to God in a crisis (Exod. 14:15; 15:25; Ps. 34:17; 77:1; 107:6, 28; 2 Chr. 13:14). Such a cry can, however, also be made to idol gods (Isa. 46:7).

In addition, this verb can be used for a human cry of lament. Esau "cries out" to his father when he realizes his brother has tricked him. A prophet cries out because he has lost his axe head and it was borrowed (2 Ki. 6:5). Jeremiah expects the Ammonites to cry out in pain when their time of destructions comes (Jer. 49:3). Very important in biblical history is the fact that the blood of Abel cries out from the ground against his brother Cain (Gen. 4:10); Cain receives a strong rebuke from the Lord. But as Heb. 12:24 points out, the blood of Jesus "speaks a better word" than Abel's blood, since the blood of crucified Jesus cleanses us from all sin. See *NIDOTTE*, 3:827–30.

Verb: רָנַן (*rānan*), GK 8264 (S 7442), 53x. *rānan* generally denotes the action of shouting or singing for joy, though there are several instances in which joy may be absent. For example, God's people "cry out" in distress (Lam. 2:19) and in yearning (Ps. 84:2), and Wisdom "cries aloud" in the streets (Prov. 1:20; cf. 8:3). See *sing*.

New Testament

Verb: βοάω (*boaō*), GK *1066* (S *994*), 12x. *boaō* means "to cry out, shout, call loudly." See *call*.

Verb: κράζω (*krazō*), GK *3189* (S *2896*), 55x. *krazō* means "to shout, cry out." Such shouting can be in hostility, anguish, joyful elation, or urgent authoritative testimony. See *shout*.

CUBIT

Old Testament

Noun: אַמָּה (ʾ*ammâ*), GK 564 (S 520), 249x. ʾ*ammâ* means "cubit." It is the basic unit of measurement in the OT, much like the modern foot or meter. The measurements of Noah's ark (Gen. 6:15–16), the tabernacle (Exod. 25–27), Solomon's temple and palace (1 Ki. 6, 7), and Ezekiel's visionary temple (Ezek. 40–43) are all given in cubits. Measurements of more common items are also given in cubits: Og's bed is 9 x 4 cubits (Deut. 3:11), Goliath is 6.5 cubits tall (1 Sam. 17:4, a "span" is half a cubit), and Haman's gallows are 50 cubits high (Est. 5:14; 7:9).

A cubit is the length of a person's forearm—specifically, from the tip of the fingers to the tip of the elbow. Thus, a cubit measures about 18 to 21 inches (45 to 53 cm). Since the length from fingertip to elbow differs from person to person, standard lengths of a cubit are used in Bible times in professional construction works such as a temple or tomb. During the OT period, there seems to have been different standard lengths for the cubit. Deut. 3:11 mentions a "cubit of a man," 2 Chr. 3:3 describes Solomon's temple using a "former" cubit, and Ezek. 40:5 defines a cubit as "a cubit and a handbreadth." Based on archaeological findings, there seems to have been two standard lengths in use during the OT period, a short cubit of 17.7 inches (45 cm) and a long cubit of 20.7 inches (52.5 cm). A modern equivalent for biblical cubits can be estimated by multiplying cubits by 1.5 to get feet, or by 0.5 to get yards or meters. See *NIDOTTE*, 1:421-24.

CUP

New Testament

Noun: ποτήριον (*potērion*), GK *4539* (S *4221*), 31x. *potērion* means a "cup," often used as the object of the verb "to drink" (see *drink*). Sometimes this word is used literally, as in giving a cup of cold water to a needy individual (Mk. 9:41). Jesus refers to the normal activities of cleaning the outside of a cup and then drinking from it as on object lesson to identify the location of the sins of greed and self-indulgence, which are fixed inside the heart (Mt. 23:25–26).

But more often, *potērion* is used symbolically. Isa. 51:17, 22 gives the origin of drinking a cup of judgment of God's wrath against sin. For those who have rejected Christ and persecuted his followers, God is preparing a cup of his fury for them to drink because of their sins (Rev. 16:19; 18:6). But this meaning is also what lies behind the question Jesus poses in Jn. 18:11: "Shall I not drink the cup the Father has given me?" The same idea is behind the horrific inner turmoil of Jesus as he asks the Father, "Take this cup from me!" (Mk. 14:36). The cup represents the judgment that God meted out to Jesus on the cross because of our sins. He did not cheerfully welcome this cup of extreme suffering, but he firmly set his course to go to Jerusalem to endure it. In a different nuance, martyrs partake of the cup of Christ in death (Mt. 20:23; Mk. 10:39).

potērion is also used in the language of the Eucharist (Mk. 14:23). The cup here refers to the new covenant (see Lk. 22:20b; 1 Cor. 11:25a). Christians are invited to share in the cup of thanksgiving as we celebrate the Lord's Supper in the family of faith (1 Cor. 10:16; 11:25-28). Partaking of this cup requires reflecting on the death of Christ, celebrating new life in him, examining one's spiritual life, and anticipating Jesus' second coming. See *NIDNTT-A*, 460-61.

CURE

Old Testament

Verb: רָפָא (*rāpā'*), GK 8324 (S 7495), 69x. *rāpā'* conveys the process of restoring or making whole the health of an individual. See *heal*.

New Testament

Verb: ἰάομαι (*iaomai*) GK *2615* (S *2390*), 26x.

Verb: θεραπεύω (*therapeuō*) GK *2543* (S *2323*), 43x. These two words meaning "to heal, cure" are used interchangeably in the NT.

CURSE

Old Testament

Verb: אָרַר (*'ārar*), GK 826 (S 779), 63x. *'ārar* means "to curse." Cursing is intended either as a judgment for misdeeds or as a deterrent to disobedience (Mal. 2:2; 3:9). Though the term can be synonymous with the term *qālal*, it has a more restricted range of meaning (note that nearly two-thirds of the uses of this word are in the Pentateuch).

'ārar is the term used throughout the highly charged curses of the creation narrative. The Lord curses Satan for deceiving Eve (Gen. 3:14–15). He curses creation itself because of Adam's disobedience, and he curses Cain for his fratricide (3:16–17; 4:11). Noah is designated as the one who will reverse the effects of the curse, "He will comfort us in the labor and painful toil of our hands caused by the ground the LORD *has cursed*" (5:29). Yet, even though

the earth has been destroyed, sin remains a problem (cf. 11:1–9); the curse continues. The Lord then offers the ultimate solution through the seed of Abraham (12:3). As Paul recognizes in Gal. 3:10–14, only in Christ is the curse finally removed.

The highest concentration of *ʾārar* usages in the OT occurs in Deut., where the theme of blessing and cursing is an important part of the Mosaic covenant (Deut. 27:15–26; 28:16–19; cf. Ps. 30:19). The list of curses in Deut. corresponds to ancient treaties where the less powerful are bound in allegiance to the great kings with the threat of curses for their disobedience (cf. Jer. 11:3; Mal. 1:14). Curses could be invoked by God or others (Gen. 9:25; Exod. 22:28; 1 Sam. 14:24). The effectiveness of the curse is generally based on the standing of the individual who makes it. A curse becomes more serious when it is undertaken "before the Lord" (Jos. 6:26). The idea here is like the contemporary idea that an oath is more significant if it is made while placing one's hand on the Bible. See *NIDOTTE*, 1:524–26.

Verb: קָלַל (*qālal*), GK 7837 (S 7043), 82x. *qālal* means "to curse," though it is also used to express mitigation, such as water "receding" after the flood (Gen. 8:8, 11) or the burden Moses carried as the judge of the Israelites that needed to be "lightened" (Exod. 18:22; cf. 1 Ki. 12:4; 2 Ki. 10:10; Eccl. 10:10; Jon. 1:5). The term could more generally be used in the context of despising someone or of something being despicable and vile (Gen. 16:4–5; 1 Sam. 2:30; 3:13; Job 40:4; Isa. 23:9; Nah. 1:4).

When *qālal* means "curse," it can be virtually synonymous with *ʾārar* (GK 826), except that it is more often used in the context of people being the agents of cursing (Gen. 8:21; 12:3; Jdg. 9:27; Eccl. 7:21–22; 10:20); sometimes this takes the nuance of blasphemy (Lev. 24:11, 14, 15). The curse could have deadly effect (2 Ki. 2:24; cf. Prov. 30:10), though one uttered without good cause is doomed to be ineffective (1 Sam. 17:43; 2 Sam. 16:12; Prov. 26:2).

There is a degree of flexibility attached to the curse. When Jacob seems uncomfortable with the idea of deceiving his father and possibly incurring a curse, Rebekah responds with, "My son, let *the curse* fall on me" (Gen. 27:13). See *NIDOTTE*, 3:926–27.

New Testament

Noun: ἀνάθεμα (*anathema*), GK *353* (S *331*) 6x. *anathema* means "curse, accursed, condemned (eternally)." This word is used for something or someone doomed to eternal destruction. The related word *anathēma* (GK *356*) simply means a consecrated gift or votive offering (its only use is Lk. 21:5). Both of these words are linked in the Heb. word *ḥerem* (GK 3049 and 3051; see *curse*, OT). The word *anathema* progressed through "a thing devoted to evil" to "a thing accursed" and eventually applied to individuals and the judicial wrath (divine curse) of God.

Paul uses *anathema* in Rom. 9:3 to indicate separation from Christ. The term does not indicate reprimand intended as discipline but being given up to eternal, divine condemnation. In Gal. 1:8–9 Paul uses *anathema* to declare emphatically and categorically that the gospel he preaches is the one and only way to salvation and that to preach or teach otherwise is to invalidate and nullify the death of Christ. Anyone doing so will be eternally condemned (cf. also 1 Cor. 16:22). The final use of this word (in 1 Cor. 12:3) creates difficulties for interpreters, since one might question how anyone could say "Jesus is cursed." Perhaps this is something a demon might drive a person to say, and Paul is suggesting that believers need to be free in their lives from all influence of heathenism. See *NIDNTT-A*, 44-45.*

CURTAIN

Old Testament

Noun: יְרִיעָה (*y^eriʿâ*), GK 3749 (S 3407), 54x. *y^eriʿâ* generally refers to the goat-hair fabric that makes up one of the layers of material used for the tabernacle

(Exod. 26:7). The same term can refer to a tent that contains the ark of the covenant (2 Sam. 7:2). It can also refer to a private dwelling (Jer. 4:20). It is used metaphorically in the Psalms to describe God stretching "out the heavens like a tent" (Ps. 104:2). See *NIDOTTE*, 2:542.

Noun: פָּרֹכֶת (*pārōket*), GK 7267 (S 6532), 25x. All occurrences of *pārōket* in the OT refer to the "inner curtain" before the Most Holy Place; 25 refer to the curtain in the tabernacle and one to the curtain in Solomon's temple (2 Chr. 3:14). It is also called the "veil of the covenant" or "curtain of the Testimony" (Lev. 24:3) and "the curtain of the Holy [Place]" (4:6).

The *pārōket* is made of high quality material with images of cherubim, the guardians of God's sacred presence, woven into it. Its location at the center of the tabernacle and temple indicate that it is the most sacred of the various curtains. The form itself may derive from an Akkadian noun *parakku*, meaning "curtain," most likely from the Akkadian verb *parku*, "to spread open, lay across" perhaps in a prohibitive manner—i.e., "to shut off, block."

CUSTOM

Old Testament

Noun: חֻקָּה (*ḥuqqâ*), GK 2978 (S 2708), 104x. The feminine noun *ḥuqqâ,* derives from the verb *ḥāqaq*, "to cut in, inscribe, decree," is related to its masculine counterpart, *ḥōq*, though the two nouns never appear together (see *decree*). *ḥuqqâ* also occurs in cultic contexts, where the NIV translates "regulations." There are "regulations" for Passover (Exod. 12:43; Num. 9:3, 12, 14), the altar (Ezek. 43:18), and the house of God (44:5). When *huqqâ* is used for the practices of Israel's surrounding nations, the NIV, NASB, and KJV translate "customs" (Lev. 18:30; 20:23; Jer. 10:3).

New Testament

Noun: ἔθος (*ethos*), GK *1621* (S *1485*), 12x. *ethos* is the tendency or convention by which things are done, a "habit" or "custom." This word can describe a regular practice or general personal habit, such as that fact that Jesus habitually went to the Mount of Olives (Lk. 22:39) or that some believers did not meet regularly with the church (Heb. 10:25). More frequently in the NT, *ethos* indicates a formal custom that is usually regulated by some religious tradition (Lk. 1:9; 2:42; Jn. 19:40; Acts 21:21), most often the Mosaic tradition (Acts 6:14; 15:1 ["manner" (KJV)]; 26:3; 28:17), although *ethos* is also sometimes used of the Roman political-religious practices (Acts 16:21; 25:16). See *NIDNTT-A*, 162-63.*

CUT

Old Testament

Verb: כָּרַת (*kārat*), GK 4162 (S 3772), 289x. *kārat* broadly means "to cut (objects), exclude and/or destroy, make a covenant." While these three basic meanings seem divergent, they are closely linked together around the notion of cutting. See also *make a covenant*; *destroy*.

This verb is sometimes used for physical cutting, such as cutting down a tree (Deut. 19:5; 20:19–20; Isa. 44:14; Jer. 10:3). It occurs once for cutting off the foreskin in the act of circumcision (Exod. 4:25). In obedience to God's command to get rid of idols in the promised land, the Israelites cut down the Asherah poles (Jdg. 6:26; 2 Ki. 18:4).

New Testament

Verb: ἐκκόπτω (*ekkoptō*), GK *1716* (S *1581*), 10x. *ekkoptō* means "to cut down, off." It is used when referring to "cutting down" a tree, particularly a tree that does not bear fruit (Mt. 3:10; 7:19; Lk. 3:9; 13:7, 9) or "cutting off" a branch (Rom. 11:22, 24). Jesus refers to "cutting off" body parts that cause sin (Mt. 5:30; 18:8). Paul also uses the term with respect to "removing" an opportunity from his opponents (2 Cor. 11:12).*

CUT OFF

New Testament

Verb: ἀφαιρέω (*aphaireō*), GK *904* (S *851*), 10x. *aphaireō* means "to cut off." The ear of a servant of the high priest is "cut off" by one of Jesus' disciples (Mt.

26:51; Mk. 14:47; Lk. 22:50). John says the servant's name was Malchus and the disciple was Peter (see Jn. 18:10, which uses *apokoptō*, GK 644, "to cut off"). *aphaireō* can also mean "to take away." See *take away*.

DAGGER

Old Testament

Noun: חֶרֶב (*ḥereb*), GK 2995 (S 2719), 413x. *ḥereb* describes a "sword," a common weapon of war, although it is sometimes translated as "knife, dagger" (Jos. 5:2; 2 Sam. 20:8). See *sword*.

DAILY

Old Testament

Noun: (used as adv.): תָּמִיד (*tāmîd*), GK 9458 (S 8548), 104x. As an adverb, *tāmîd* describes that which is "lasting" or something done "continually." The word can describe both an action done regularly (often according to a schedule). As an adjective, *tāmîd* is used for the *regular* or *daily* offerings in the tabernacle and temple. See *always*.

Adverb: יוֹמָם (*yômām*), GK 3429 (S 3119), 53x. *yômām* derives from the Heb. *yôm* ("day") and denotes a present period of time and may be translated "daily" or "by day." The term is significant in the Exodus narrative, where Yahweh is said to have gone before his people in a pillar of cloud *by day* (Exod . 13:21–22), which marked the daily occurrence of the leading of God. It is repeated in later texts that reflect on the same event (Num. 9:21; 10:34; 14:14; Deut. 1:33; Neh. 9:12, 19; Ps. 78:14). The term also occurs commonly in the phrase "day and night" to convey the sense of continuous activity (cf. Lev. 8:35; Num. 9:21; Deut. 28:66). Jos. 1:8 describes the activity of one fully devoted to God: "Do not let this Book of the Law depart from your mouth; meditate on it *day and night*, so that you may be careful to do everything written in it. Then you will be prosperous and successful." See *NIDOTTE*, 2:419-424.

DAMN, DAMNATION

See *judge* and *judgment*.

DARE

New Testament

Verb: τολμάω (*tolmaō*), GK *5528* (S *5111*), 16x. *tolmaō* means "to dare, have courage." After Jesus' profound responses to the questions of the scribes, Pharisees, and Sadducees, no one "dares" to ask him any more questions (Mt. 22:46; Mk. 12:34; Lk. 20:40). Similarly, because the disciples know better already, none of them "dares" to ask the man on the shore if he really is Jesus (Jn. 21:12). The only other occurrence of *tolmaō* in the gospels occurs when Joseph of Arimathea "dares" to go to Pilate and ask for Jesus' body (Mk. 15:43).

Paul's use of the term carries much the same nuance, meaning either "to draw up courage" or "to have nerve" to do something. Concerning the courageous kind of "daring," Paul uses the term of a person "daring" to die for a good person (Rom. 5:7) and begs the church not to cause him to have to drum up courage to take on his opponents directly (2 Cor. 10:2). Note too Phil. 1:14, where the comfort of God's sovereignty increases Paul's "daring" in witnessing.

The majority of Paul's uses of *tolmaō* is in a negative context. He himself does "not dare " to speak of anything except what Christ has accomplished (Rom. 15:18), while elsewhere he rebukes the Corinthians, asking how they "dare" to go to court in front of the unrighteous (1 Cor. 6:1). The word occurs most in 2 Corinthians, where the apostle is up against some critics who "have a lot a nerve." Lest he be misunderstood, Paul distances himself from his haughty critics by saying he does "not dare to assert" that he is somehow like them (2 Cor. 10:12).

The final use of *tolmaō* is in Jude 9, where Michael "did not dare" to pronounce a blasphemous judgment but leaves it in the hands of the Lord. See *NIDNTT-A*, 565.

DARKNESS

Old Testament

Noun: חֹשֶׁךְ (*ḥošek*), GK 3125 (S 2822), 80x. Depending on the context, *ḥošek* can represent literal or metaphorical darkness. Even in the creation account where literal darkness is in view, *ḥošek* comes across as ominous (Gen. 1:2). By the hand of Moses, the Lord brings a plague of deep darkness on Egypt (Exod. 10:21–22). When the Lord appears on Mount Sinai, clouds and darkness conceal him (Deut. 4:11; 5:23). Here *ḥošek* represents concealment and mystery rather than any notion of evil.

The use of light and darkness as contrastive metaphors is especially common in poetry. Over half of the occurrences of *ḥošek* occur in Job, Psalms, and Isaiah. Here *ḥošek* represents evil and sin (Isa. 5:20; 59:9), death (Job 10:21; 17:13; 18:18; Ps. 88:12), literal and figurative imprisonment (Ps. 107:10; Isa. 42:7; 49:9), confusion (Job 12:25; Ps. 35:6), and divine punishment (Job 5:14; 15:23, 30). Isaiah makes use of the contrastive metaphors of light and darkness in messianic texts. The coming of the Messiah to "Galilee of the Gentiles" is described as a light dawning in a land of deep darkness (Isa. 9:1–7). Here the darkness symbolizes bondage of sin and the hopelessness of the human condition apart from redemption. When Jesus comes to Galilee and begins his preaching ministry, Matthew reminds the reader that Jesus is fulfilling Isaiah's prophetic words (Mt. 9:1–2). See *NIDOTTE*, 2:312-15

New Testament

Noun: σκοτία (*skotia*), GK *5028* (S *4653*), 16x. *skotia* means "darkness." Except for Jn. 6:17; 20:1, where this word refers to the actual darkness of night or early morning, *skotia* is always used metaphorically in the NT. Jesus uses it to describe times of private teaching with the Twelve, away from the crowds (Mt. 10:27). He also warns against the hypocrisy of the Pharisees, saying that everything spoken in "darkness" will be revealed (Lk. 12:3). Jesus is the light (Jn. 12:35), and he invites people to walk in his light instead of their darkness (Jn. 8:12; 12:46). Those who have hatred in their hearts may think they are in the light, but they are deceived and even blinded (1 Jn. 2:9, 11). This lost and sinful world, characterized by *skotia*, cannot understand the light that has come to illuminate it (Jn. 1:5). Darkness is not a power that is equal to God, for God dispels it. Finally, light and darkness are used to contrast the purity and holiness of God and the wickedness and sinfulness of this world (1 Jn. 1:5). See *NIDNTT-A*, 531-32.*

Noun: σκότος (*skotos*), GK *5030* (S *4655*), 31x. *skotos* denotes the physical state of "darkness" (as in the absence of light). The only use of this word for actual darkness is the darkness that occurred during Jesus crucifixion (Mt. 27:45; Mk. 15:33; Lk. 23:44). Even here it has metaphorical qualities, for at this time the powers of "darkness" seems to achieve the victory (cf. Lk. 22:53).

For the most part, therefore, *skotos* is used in a metaphorical way as referring to "darkness of the mind or spirit." This metaphorical sense of *skotos* is clearly negative. People live in darkness (Isa. 9:2; Mt. 4:16) and cannot avoid the darkness of death (Lk. 1:79). All too often, people "love *darkness* instead of light because their deeds are evil" (Jn. 3:19).

But *skotos* is not a power equal to God. God now causes light to shine in human hearts (2 Cor. 4:6). He "has rescued us from the dominion of *darkness*" (Col. 1:13). He has sent his Son to call people out of the "darkness" and into his wonderful light (1 Pet. 2:9). Once we were darkness, says Paul, but now we are "light in the Lord" (Eph. 5:8). Consequently, we should have nothing to do with "darkness" (5:11); instead, we should wage war against the powers of "darkness" (6:12). For those who give in to sin, "the blackest darkness" is reserved (2 Pet. 2:17; Jude 13). See *NIDNTT-A*, 531-32.

DAUGHTER

Old Testament

Noun: בַּת (*bat*), GK 1426 (S 1323), 587x. *bat* is the common Hebrew noun for one's own daughter (e.g., Gen. 24:24; 29:10; Exod. 21:7; Deut. 16:14; Jos. 15:16; 2 Sam. 6:16). The status of granddaughter is normally expressed as "my son's daughters" (Gen. 46:7) though *bat* alone can also mean "granddaughter" (2 Ki. 8:26). "Daughter of my father" or "daughter of my mother" (Gen. 20:12) designates a half-sister, who, according to the Mosaic legislation (Lev. 18:9, 11; 20:17; Deut. 27:22, cf. Ezek. 22:11), may not be taken in marriage by a close relative. "Uncle's daughter" (Est. 2:7) is a cousin. *bat* is also used simply of women: "The *women* [daughters, KJV] will call me happy" (Gen. 30:13), or young girls: "Like a lily among thorns is my darling among the *maidens* [daughters, KJV]" (Song 2:2). Children, in general, are often designated by the phrase "sons and daughters" (e.g., Gen. 11:11; 37:35; Lev. 10:14), though "sons" meaning "children" may also include daughters (as in the common "children of Israel" = "Israelites," e.g., Exod. 13:2).

While the social status of a daughter in ancient Israel may have been lower than that of a son, in general, daughters were considered valuable and deeply loved by their fathers. The psalmist refers to the blessed lives of both sons and daughters as an indication of God's favor (Ps. 144:12). Nathan uses the metaphor of a father's love for his daughter to indicate deep affection (2 Sam. 12:3). And Mordecai, who apparently had adopted his cousin Esther as his own daughter (Est. 2:7, 15), shows great concern and care for her.

The marriage of a daughter (like a son) was in the hands of her father (Gen. 24:51; 29:19; Exod. 22:17). The bride price was given to the father, but he normally gave it to his daughter as a dowry (Gen. 31:15). The dowry may have even exceeded the bride price (*TWOT*, 1:115).

bat may be used to indicate membership in a group. "Daughters of the Philistines" means "Philistine women" (2 Sam. 1:20). In geographical designations, a "town and its daughters" means "a town and its satellite villages"; "Heshbon and all its *surrounding settlements*" (lit., "her daughters") (Num. 21:25; cf. 1 Chr. 7:29). Hannah pleads to Eli, "Do not take your servant for a wicked woman (lit., "a daughter of Belial," so KJV) (1 Sam. 1:16; cf. 2:12, where Eli's sons are called "wicked men," lit., "sons of Belial").

bat is also used in figurative ways. Gen. 49:22 uses "daughters" to mean "branches." In Eccl. 12:4, "daughters of the song" ("daughters of music," KJV) may simply mean "musical notes." And in Ps. 17:8 (cf. Lam. 2:18), "apple of the eye" is literally "daughter of the eye."

Of particular theological importance is the use of *bat* as a figurative designation for Zion and Jerusalem. This should not be construed as "daughter who belongs to Zion/Jerusalem" but "daughter who is Zion/Jerusalem," where Zion and Jerusalem stand for the whole nation. This metaphor allows the prophets to present the people of God as a woman in the pain of labor, gasping for air and crying out for help (Jer. 4:31, cf. Mic. 4:10). She is vulnerable and needs to be rescued and protected (Isa. 1:8; 52:2; Lam. 2:13). Though God will punish her for her transgressions (Jer. 6:2; Lam. 2:1, 4), yet he will send a Savior to rescue her: "The LORD has made proclamation to the ends of the earth: Say to the Daughter of Zion, 'See, your Savior comes! See, his reward is with him, and his recompense accompanies him' " (Isa. 62:11, cf. Zech. 9:9). Thus, the designation "Daughter of Zion" emphasizes God's tender relationship with Israel and the salvation he promises to her. Then she will rejoice and be glad, celebrating the salvation of her God (Zeph. 3:14; Zech. 2:10). See *NIDOTTE*, 1:779-81.

New Testament

Noun: θυγάτηρ (*thygatēr*), GK *2588* (S *2364*), 28x. *thygatēr* means "daughter." This noun is used most often to refer to the literal female child of a parent, e.g., "the *daughter* of Herodias" (Mt. 14:6). It can also be used to refer to female descendants (Lk. 1:5). *thygatēr* is used in greetings, as though someone were being treated as a daughter (Mt. 9:22; Mk. 5:34; Lk. 8:48). Of particular interest is the term "daughter of Zion" (Mt. 21:5; Jn. 12:15); here *thygatēr* refers to the city of Jerusalem and its inhabitants (cf. Isa. 62:11; Zech. 9:9).

DAWN

Old Testament

Noun: בֹּקֶר (*bōqer*), GK 1332 (S 1242), 213x. *bōqer* can be translated as "morning," though it can also be "dawn" or "daybreak." See *morning*.

New Testament

Adverb: πρωΐ (*prōi*), GK *4745* (S *4404*), 12x. Because *prōi* can designate any time covered in the fourth watch (from 3:00 to 6:00 a.m.), sometimes it refers to very early in the morning, for which we have the phrase "the crack of dawn." See *early; appear.*

DAY

Old Testament

Noun: יוֹם (*yôm*), GK 3427 (S 3117), 2301x. *yôm* is the most common biblical expression of time in the OT. Most of the occurrences are in the sing. (1452x), and the highest frequency of usage is found in Deut. (167x), Gen. (152x), 1 Sam. (150x), Jer. (137x), and Isa. (121x). Although *yôm* has a variety nuances, there are five primary categories that encompass the majority of its occurrences.

(1) The most basic meaning of *yôm* is the period of light in a day and night cycle (i.e., daylight, from sunrise to sunset). In this sense, *yôm* stands in contrast to *laylâ*, "night," as in Gen. 1:5: "God called the light *yôm*, and the darkness he called *laylâ*." Gen. 8:22 declares, "As long as the earth endures, seedtime and harvest, cold and heat, summer and winter, *day* and night will never cease" (cf. also Exod. 24:18, "forty *days* and forty nights"; Ps. 139:12; Isa. 28:19; Amos 5:8).

(2) *yôm* is also, as is "day" in English, the normal designation of a 24-hour period of time. During the time of the flood, we are told that "for forty days the flood kept coming on the earth" (Gen. 7:17). These references help illustrate the fact that every occurrence of *yôm* with a cardinal number (1, 2, 7, 40, etc.; see Lev. 8:35; Num. 10:33; Est. 1:4) or an ordinal number (first, second, third, etc.; Num. 7:18–78 [13x]; 29:12–35 [8x]) indicates a 24-hour period of time. Significantly, the creation account in Gen. 1 commonly uses the construction of *yôm* plus an ordinal number (Gen. 1:5, "And there was evening, and there was morning—the *first day*," etc.) to portray the sequence of God's creative activity. Although wide disagreement is found in regard to interpreting Gen. 1 (from both secular and religious perspectives), in light of the usage and translation of *yôm* plus an ordinal/cardinal number as a literal 24-hour period of time, some argue that there should not be a different meaning assigned to *yôm* in Gen. 1.

(3) *yôm* may also refer to a general, unspecified period of time. The frequent construction of *b*[e]*yôm* + infinitive (60x) means "on the day [when] . . . ," as in Ezek. 20:5–6, "This is what the Sovereign LORD says: *On the day* I chose Israel, I swore with uplifted hand to the descendants of the house of Jacob and revealed myself to them in Egypt. … *On that day* I swore to them that I would bring them out of Egypt into a land I had searched out for them" (cf. 36:33; Lev. 7:36, 38; Num. 9:15; Obad. 11).

(4) *yôm* may also signify a specific point of time or in time. The common construction (350x) of *hāyôm hazzeh* means "this day" or "today." Exod. 13:3 says, "Then Moses said to the people, 'Commemorate *this day*, the day you came out of Egypt" (cf. 12:17; Lev. 16:30; 2 Ki. 19:3). The OT often uses the phrase "in the days of …" to distinguish a particular period of time in history (see Jer. 26:18; cf. Gen. 26:1; 1 Ki. 10:21; Ezr. 4:7). A final example of *yôm*'s designation as a specific point in time is the phrase "the day of the LORD" (16x). This day denotes a coming, eschatological day of judgment, as in Isa. 13:9, "See, the *day of the* LORD is coming—a cruel day, with wrath and fierce anger—to make the land desolate and destroy the sinners within it" (cf. 13:6;

Ezek. 13:5; Joel 1:15; 2:1, 11; 3:4; 4:14; Mal. 3:23).

(5) Finally, the plural *yômîm* in some contexts designates a period of a year or the sense of "annually." In 1 Sam. 27:7 we read, "David lived in Philistine territory *a year* and four months." Deut. 30:20 declares, "For the LORD is your life, and he will give you *many years* in the land he swore to give to your fathers, Abraham, Isaac and Jacob." There is also the sense of "year to year," meaning "annually," as in Exod. 13:10 (in reference to the feast of unleavened bread), "You must keep this ordinance at the appointed time *year after year*" (cf. 1 Sam. 1:21; 20:6).

Adverb: יוֹמָם (*yômām*), GK 3429 (S 3119), 53x. *yômām* derives from the Heb. *yôm* ("day") and denotes a present period of time and may be translated "daily" or "by day." See *daily*.

New Testament

Noun: ἡμέρα (*hēmera*), GK *2465* (S *2250*), 389x. *hēmera* is an indication of time that can refer to either a literal day (24-hour period of time) or a period of time that is unspecified (cf. Heb. *yôm*, 3427). As to the former, *hēmera* is often linked with *nyx* ("night," 23x) to indicate a cycle of time as "night and day" (e.g., Lk. 2:37; cf. Mt. 4:2; Acts 9:24; 1 Thess. 2:9; Rev. 4:8). *hēmera* indicates a literal day when it refers to Jesus' resurrection on the third day (Mt. 16:21; cf. Lk. 9:22) (the Jewish reckoning of days is different from our modern system; any part of a day is counted as an entire day). Probably referring to Hos. 6:2, Paul states that Jesus "was raised on the third day according to the Scriptures" (1 Cor. 15:4). Jesus refers to his resurrection on the third day in literal terms, especially in comparison with the historical account of Jonah: "For as Jonah was three days and three nights in the belly of a huge fish, so the Son of Man will be three days and three nights in the heart of the earth" (Mt. 12:40). Jesus' resurrection on the third day is the foundation for Christian preaching (Acts 10:40).

hēmera most frequently indicates a period of time of unspecified length, as in Mt. 23:30, "the days of our forefathers." In the NT, 49 times we read about "those days" or in "that day"—clearly an unspecified length of time. Also here are such expressions as "in the *time* of Herod" (Mt. 21) or "in the *days* of Jesus' life on earth" (Heb. 5:7).

hēmera can also indicate the time between Christ's first coming and second coming known as the "last days." In these "last days," God will pour out his Spirit (Acts 2:17), but they will be terrible times filled with people who live unrighteous and ungodly lives (2 Tim. 3:1). Nonetheless, "in these last *days* [God] has spoken to us by his Son," who is the perfect image of the Father and the purification for our sins (Heb. 1:2–3).

Finally, *hēmera* is used in an end-time sense to denote future events. Jesus declares in Jn. 6:40, "everyone who looks to the Son and believes in him shall have eternal life, and I will raise him up at the *last day*." This "last day" refers to the time of judgment at the consummation of the ages. This day is the "*day* of judgment" (Mt. 10:15; 11:22, 24; 2 Pet. 2:9; 3:7), which will also be a "*day* of wrath" (Rom. 2:5; Rev. 6:17). Peter and Paul label this as "the *day* of the LORD" (Acts 2:20; 1 Thess. 5:2; 2 Thess. 2:2; 2 Pet. 3:10), in keeping with the teaching they received from the OT regarding the "day of the LORD" (e.g., Isa. 13:6, 9; Ezek. 13:5; Joel 1:15; Zeph. 1:7, 14 [2x]). Paul often prays that his readers will be found blameless and strong on the "*day* of Christ" (1 Cor. 1:8; Phil. 1:6, 10; 2:16). That final *hēmera* will be a "great and glorious *day*" (Acts 2:20), full of the authority and majesty of Jesus Christ our LORD. See *NIDNTT-A*, 232-34.

DAYBREAK

Old Testament

Noun: בֹּקֶר (*bōqer*), GK 1332 (S 1242), 213x. *bōqer* can be translated as "morning," though it can also be "dawn" or "daybreak." See *morning*.

DAY'S WAGE

New Testament

Noun: δηνάριον (*dēnarion*), GK *1324* (S *1220*), 16x. The *dēnarion* was a Roman silver coin worth about one worker's average daily wage. See *denarius*.

DEACON

New Testament

Noun: διάκονος (*diakonos*), GK *1356* (S *1249*), 29x. *diakonos* means "servant, minister." On a few occasions this word means "deacon" (an English word that is derived from this Gk. word). See *servant*.

DEAD

Old Testament

Noun: חָלָל (*ḥālāl*), GK 2728 (S 2491), 94x. *ḥālāl* denotes someone who has been pierced for the purpose of killing or wounding and may be translated as "pierced, wounded, killed." See *pierced*.

New Testament

Adjective: νεκρός (*nekros*), GK *3738* (S *3498*), 128x. *nekros* is used in the NT as an adjective and as a noun. (1) As an adjective, *nekros* pertains to a person or thing being "dead" either physically or spiritually. (a) In the physical sense, *nekros* pertains to a loss of physical life. When Sapphira endorsed her husband's lie, she fell "dead" (Acts 5:10). Eutychus fell from a window and became physically "dead" (20:9). Jesus passed to a state of physical life from physical death, "I was *dead*, and behold I am alive for ever and ever" (Rev. 1:18; cf. 2:8).

(b) In the spiritual sense, *nekros* pertains to being so morally or spiritually bankrupt as to be in effect dead. Persons even though alive are described as "dead" in this sense. "For this son of mine was *dead* and is alive again; he was lost and is found" (Lk. 15:24; cf. 15:32). "You were *dead* in your transgressions and sins" (Eph. 2:1; cf. 2:5; Col. 2:13). Nonpersons or things are also described as "dead" in this sense. Hebrews speaks of "*dead* works" as that which characterizes the pre-Christian life (Heb. 6:1; 9:14). James declares that, "faith without works is *dead*" (Jas. 2:26; cf. 2:17).

(2) As a noun, *nekros* refers to a person who is "dead" either physically or figuratively. Sometimes we can use the word "corpse" as an adequate translation (e.g., Mk. 9:26). (a) In the physical sense, *nekros* refers to one who is no longer physically alive. The term has a literal sense (Lk. 7:15; 1 Thess. 4:16; Heb. 9:17; 11:35; Rev. 20:5). In some contexts, it can refer to all people who have ever died, summarily called "the dead" (Rom. 14:9; 2 Tim. 4:1; 1 Pet. 4:5). Thus, when one is resurrected to life, he is raised up from among those who have died (Mk. 6:14; Lk. 9:7). In this way, Jesus' resurrection is a raising up "from the *dead*" (Mt. 17:9; 28:7; Mk. 9:9; Lk. 24:5, 46; Jn. 2:22; 20:9; 21:14; Acts 3:15).

(b) In the figurative sense, *nekros* is applied to those who are not concerned with the priorities of the kingdom, "Allow the *dead* to bury their own *dead*" (Mt. 8:22; Lk. 9:60; cf. Eph. 5:14). See *NIDNTT-A*, 384-85.

DEAF

New Testament

Noun: κωφός (*kōphos*), GK *3273* (S *2974*), 14x. *kōphos* refers to someone who is either mute or deaf. In some cases *kōphos* means "unable to speak" (Mt. 9:32, 33; 12:22; 15:30, 31; Lk. 1:22; 11:14); in other cases "unable to hear" (Mt. 11:5; Mk. 7:37; 9:25; Lk. 7:22). This word only occurs in the Synoptic Gospels, and, in every occurrence, the biblical writer highlights the miraculous power of Jesus Christ over such disabilities. See *NIDNTT-A*, 326.

DEAR

New Testament

Adjective: ἀγαπητός (*agapētos*), GK *28* (S *27*), 61x. *agapētos* is an adjective meaning "beloved, dear," though it often functions as a noun with the idea "dear friend." See *beloved*.

DEARTH

See *famine*.

DEATH

Old Testament

Noun: מָוֶת (*māwet*), GK 4638 (S 4194), 153x. *māwet* means "death." The OT reveals various facets of the notion about death. (1) Death (at least since the time of Adam and Eve's sin in the garden of Eden) is a part of the reality of what it means to be human. The only two valid options we face in life are "life and *death*" (Deut. 30:15, 19). And death is inevitable for all of us (Ps. 89:48)—the righteous (Num. 23:10) as well as the wicked (Ezek. 18:23).

(2) While death for the righteous can be precious (Ps. 116:15) and even be considered a form of sleep (13:3), for the wicked it can be considered punishment (cf. Deut. 21:22, 26; Ezek. 28:10). The OT does not seem to view death after living a long and full life as an evil thing, only a natural thing. Yet it is possible to "die before your time" (Eccl. 7:17), and that prospect of death, understandably, can bring about feelings of terror (Ps. 55:4) and panic (1 Sam. 5:11).

(3) In some places in the OT, death is considered a place, equivalent to Sheol (e.g., Ps. 89:48; Song 8:6; see *grave*). It is a dusty place (Ps. 22:15) that has many chambers (Prov. 7:27). As one faces death, one feels like a person caught in a trap (Ps. 18:5) or tied up with cords (116:3). And as one enters into its realm, one passes through gates (Job 38:17; Ps. 9:13). While these may be metaphors, they do present a vivid picture of the reality of death.

(4) In the ancient world, anything over which human beings did not have control were seen as gods. Thus, there was the god of the storm, the god of lightning, and the sun god. And there was the god called Death (his name was Mot, using the letters of this Semitic word). Since the Israelites did not believe in other gods, they acknowledged that life and death are in the hands of their sovereign Lord (e.g., 1 Sam. 2:6; see *die*).

(5) While there is no resounding note of victory over death in the OT, the psalmist does believe that God has the power to deliver from death (Ps. 116:8). And when death has occurred, God can redeem people from death (Hos. 13:14). Thus, the rhetorical questions posed by Hosea in this verse resound in the NT as part of the Christian's triumph over death: "Where, O *death*, are your plagues? Where, O grave, is your destruction?" (cf. 1 Cor. 15:54–57). And when the final kingdom of the Lord comes, the Lord God "will swallow up death forever [and] … wipe away the tears from all faces" (Isa. 25:8; cf. Rev. 21:4). See *NIDOTTE*, 2:886–88.

New Testament

Noun: αἷμα (*haima*), GK *135* (S *129*), 97x. *haima* is the standard Greek term for "blood." It is used extensively in contexts relating to killing and death. For example, Jesus warns an expert in the law that "this generation will be held responsible for the blood [death] of all the prophets" (Lk. 11:50; see also Acts 22:20; Rev. 6:12). See *blood*.

Noun: θάνατος (*thanatos*), GK *2505* (S *2288*), 120x. *thanatos* means "death." It is used in the NT to describe physical death (the separation of the soul from the body) and spiritual death (the separation of a human being from God), though these two concepts can be closely linked in Scripture. The term never indicates nonexistence, and the NT never regards *thanatos* as a natural process; rather, it is a consequence and punishment for sin (Rom. 6:23). Sinners alone are subject to death, beginning with Adam (Rom. 5:12, 17), and it was as the bearer of our sin that Jesus died on the cross (1 Pet. 2:24). Since he was without sin, it was our death that he died (cf. Rom. 8:1–2).

The Bible teaches that all human beings are mortal and that our existence is under the shadow of death (Mt. 4:16; Heb. 2:15). All of us will die, because we "all have sinned"; thus, the need for a Savior is universal.

Often in the NT *thanatos* conveys the opposite of *zōē* ("life"), which reflects the idea of eternal happiness and the magnificence of the resurrection. *thanatos* includes exclusion from the kingdom of God through rejection of the Son of God. This death is more than physical as it includes eternal separation from God (see Jn. 8:51; Rom. 6:16, 21, 23; 7:5, 10; 8:2, 6; 2 Cor. 2:16; 3:7; 2 Tim. 1:10; Heb. 2:15; Jas. 5:20; 1 Jn. 3:14; 5:16–17). Spiritual separation is also referred to as the second death in Rev. 2:11; 20:6, 14; 21:8.

Death reigns over what is carnal (Rom. 8:6) and transmits a shadow and darkness (Lk. 1:79). The works of humankind are death from the start (Heb. 9:14), and sinners are already dead (Mt. 8:22; Jn. 5:21; Rom. 7:10, 24). Christ's death is unique in that God made him sin for us so that he died in our place. It is through his death that death itself is destroyed (2 Tim. 1:10; Heb. 2:14). Thus, we can look forward to the resurrection from the dead (1 Cor. 15:21, 55–56; see also *nekros*, "dead"). See *NIDNTT-A*, 236-39.

DEBATE

New Testament

Verb: συζητέω (*syzēteō*), GK *5184* (S *4802*), 10x. *syzēteō* means "to debate, discuss." This verb is used for some of the discussions between the Jewish leaders and Jesus or his followers, most of which take the form of a "debate" (Mk. 8:11; 9:14, 16; 12:28; cf. Acts 6:9; 9:29). The disciples "discuss" among themselves which disciple will betray Jesus (Lk. 22:23).

But not all uses are in a negative setting, for the crowds "discuss" among themselves who this man Jesus is who has such authority over demons (Mk. 1:27). Also, Peter, James, and John "discuss" among themselves after the transfiguration what Jesus could possibly mean by rising from the dead (9:11).

DEBAUCHERY

New Testament

Noun: ἀσέλγεια (*aselgeia*), GK *816* (S *766*), 10x. *aselgeia* means "debauchery, lewdness, sensuality." It occurs most often in vice lists where it is connected to other sexual overindulgences (e.g., Rom. 13:13; 2 Cor. 12:21; 2 Pet. 2:2; probably Gal. 5:19; Eph. 4:19; 1 Pet. 4:3). Jesus identifies *aselgeia* as a vice that destroys from within (Mk. 7:22). According to Peter *aselgeia* was one of the chief sins of Sodom and Gomorrah (2 Pet. 2:7), and the term is also used to characterize paganism (2 Pet. 2:2; Jude 4). See *NIDNTT-A*, 76.

DEBTOR

New Testament

Noun: ὀφειλέτης (*opheiletēs*) GK *4050* (S *3781*), 7x. *opheiletēs* means "debtor" or "one who is obligated" (see obligation). This is the word used in the Lord's Prayer, "Forgive us our debts, as we also have forgiven our debtors" (Mt. 6:12).

DECEIT

New Testament

Noun: δόλος (*dolos*), GK *1515* (S *1388*), 11x. *dolos* means "deceit." Jesus lists "deceit" as one of the sins that come out of the human heart (Mk. 7:22). After seeing Nathanael Jesus says, "There is no *deceit*" in him (Jn. 1:47). Paul and Peter also include "deceit" in their list of vices (Rom. 1:29; 1 Pet. 2:1). Paul says that he has not attempted to "deceive" the Thessalonian church (1 Thess. 2:3; cf. 2 Cor. 12:16). Peter says that Jesus was sinless and "no *deceit* was found in his mouth" (1 Pet. 2:22, quoting Isa. 53:9).

Noun: πλάνη (*planē*), GK *4415* (S *4106*), 10x. *planē* means "error, deception, deceit." See *error*.

DECEIVE

New Testament

Verb: ἐμπαιζω (*empaizō*), GK *1850* (S *1702*), 13x. *empaizō* denotes mocking or making sport of. In the NT it is found exclusively in the Gospels. It sometimes carries the meaning of being tricked or deceived, such as Herod being "outwitted" by the Magi (Mt. 2:16). See *mock*.

Verb: πλανάω (*planaō*), GK *4414* (S *4105*), 39x. In the active voice, *planaō* means "to lead astray, deceive"; in the middle/passive voice, "to wander, go astray." The word occurs in the NT in both a spatial and an ethical sense.

The ethical sense predominates in the NT. It refers to those who wander from the truth (Jas. 5:19) and who try to deceive others (1 Jn. 2:26). The context in which it is used often deals with the end times (Mt. 24:4–5; Rev. 20:8–10). The devil is the deceiver (Rev. 12:9), and there are many who hope to deceive believers (1 Cor. 6:9; 15:33; Gal. 6:7). However, the one deceiving often in turn is deceived (2 Tim. 3:13).

In the spatial sense, it describes OT men of faith, who wander without a home in this world (Heb. 11:38). It is also used to describe sheep who wander from the flock (Mt. 18:4–5), a spatial image with clear ethical implications (1 Pet. 2:25). Note that in the parable of the one hundred sheep, whereas Luke has a "lost" sheep (set in an evangelistic context, Lk. 15:1–7), Matthew records a "wandering" sheep," which is more appropriate to the context of how to minister to church members. See *NIDNTT-A*, 466-67.

DECEPTION

Old Testament

Noun: שֶׁקֶר (*šeqer*), GK 9214 (S 8267), 113x. *šeqer* is derived from the root verb *šāqar*, "to lie, deceive, betray" (only 6x in the OT). The meaning of this word is tied to lies, falsehood and deception. Everything that is a *šeqer* is opposed to truth. See *lie*.

New Testament

Noun: πλάνη (*planē*), GK *4415* (S *4106*), 10x. *planē* means "error, deception, deceit." See *error*.

Noun: ψεῦδος (*pseudos*), GK *6022* (S *5579*), 10x. *pseudos* is typically translated as "lie," but it may also indicate falsehood, deception, or anything counterfeit (e.g., 1 Jn. 2:27). See *lie*.

DECIDE

New Testament

Verb: κρίνω (*krinō*), GK *3212* (S *2919*), 114x. *krinō* essentially means "to consider, decide, judge," though it has a variety of nuances. See *judge*.

Verb: ὁρίζω (*horizo*), GK *3988* (S *3724*), 8x. *horizō* means "to appoint, set, determine" and occurs most often in Luke and Acts. See *appoint*.

DECLARATION

Old Testament

Noun: נְאֻם (*ne*ʾ*um*), GK 5536 (S 5002), 376x. *ne*ʾ*um* is used of an utterance, word or revelation. It is often translated as "oracle" (NIV), "parable" (KJV), "declaration," and "word." See *word*.

DECLARE

Old Testament

Verb: נָגַד (*nāgad*), GK 5583 (S 5046), 371x. *nāgad* means "to tell, declare, report." It normally indicates spoken communication, whether relaying a message or reporting on some situation. See *tell*.

Verb: סָפַר (*sāpar*), GK 6218 (S 5608), 107x. *sāpar* means "to count, tell, declare." See *count*.

New Testament

Verb: ἀναγγέλλω (*anangello*), GK *334* (S *312*), 14x. *anangellō* means "to tell, proclaim." See *tell; report*.

Verb: φημί (*phēmi*), GK *5774* (S *5346*), 66x. *phēmi* means "to say, declare, answer, reply." See *say*.

DECORATE

New Testament

Verb: κοσμέω (*kosmeō*), GK *3175* (S *2885*), 10x. *kosmeō* means "to adorn, decorate, make attractive." See *adorn*.

DECREE

Old Testament

Noun: חֹק (*ḥōq*), GK 2976 (S 2706), 131x. *ḥōq* is derived from the related verb *ḥāqaq*, which means "to cut in, inscribe, decree" and denotes something that is limited or restricted, using "to cut in" in the sense of defining a boundary or drawing a line in the sand. Most frequently *ḥōq* refers to the prescribed law of God, an inscribed boundary for human behavior, but it may also indicate a fixed portion or an actual boundary. *ḥōq* occurs 31x in Psalms and 21x in Deuteronomy.

When *ḥōq* is used in the primary sense of the prescribed law of God, the NIV regularly translates it with "decree" while the NASB and KJV use "statute." The most common verb found in the OT with *ḥōq* is *šāmar*, "to keep" (e.g., Deut. 4:6; 1 Ki. 3:14), commanding God's people to obey his law. The semantic range of *ḥōq* generally overlaps with other law-related words in the OT: *mišpāṭ*, "judgment"; *miṣwâ*, "commandment"; and *tôrâ*, "law"; and it is not uncommon to find various combinations of these words together (e.g., Deut. 6:1; 2 Chr. 19:10). Of the 31x that *ḥōq* is used in the Psalms, it appears 21x in Ps. 119, each time in the primary sense of denoting God's law.

Less frequently, *ḥōq* expresses a fixed quantity or some sort of limit. Pharaoh's priests receive a regular "allotment" of food so they are not forced to sell their land (Gen. 47:22), and the excellent wife provides a "portion" of food for her servants (Prov. 31:15). Israel is forced to make the same "quota" of bricks without straw (Exod. 5:14); Israel's priests receive a "portion" or "share" of the offering (29:28; Lev. 24:9; Num. 18:8, 11, 19); and God promises a future day in which Israel's "boundary" will be extended (Mic. 7:11). In nature God sets a "boundary" for the waters or seas (Job 26:10; 38:10; Prov. 8:29), a "limit" for the rain (Job 28:26), and a "limit" on each one's days (Job 14:5). See *NIDOTTE*, 2:250-51

Noun: חֻקָּה (*ḥuqqâ*), GK 2978 (S 2708), 104x. The feminine noun *ḥuqqâ*, derives from the verb *ḥāqaq*, "to cut in, inscribe, decree," is related to its masculine counterpart, *ḥōq*, though the two nouns never appear together. Like its counterpart, *ḥuqqâ* most frequently indicates the law of God, and the NIV regularly translates these occurrences "decree" while the NASB and KJV use "statute." God's people are called upon to keep his "decrees" in covenant life before a holy God (e.g., Lev. 18:4, 5; 19:19). The meaning of *ḥuqqâ* overlaps in meaning with other OT references to law: *mišpāṭ*, "judgment"; *miṣwâ*, "commandment"; and *tôrâ*, "law"; and these various legal words often appear together with *ḥuqqâ* (e.g., Gen. 26:5; Deut. 8:11; 11:1; 30:10, 16; 1 Ki. 2:3; 6:12; 2 Ki. 17:13, 34; Ezek. 5:6, 7; 44:24).

ḥuqqâ frequently occurs in cultic (i.e., worship) contexts. It appears 23x in combination with *ʿôlām*, "forever," to denote what the NIV translates as a "lasting ordinance" for Israel. "Lasting ordinances" govern religious festivals such as Passover (Exod. 12:14), the Feast of Unleavened Bread (12:17), the Day of Atonement (Lev. 16:29, 31, 34; 23:21), the Feast of Weeks (23:21), and the Festival of Booths (23:41). "Lasting ordinances" also shape temple worship: the Aaronic priesthood (Exod. 29:9), clothing for the Aaronic priesthood (28:43), lamps in the tent of meeting (27:21; Lev. 24:3), and the offering of the firstfruits (Lev. 23:14).

ḥuqqâ also occurs in cultic contexts without being modified by *ʿôlām*, and in these instances the NIV translates "regulations." See *regulations*. See *NIDOTTE*, 2:250-51

Noun: מִשְׁפָּט (*mišpāṭ*), GK 5477 (S 4941), 425x. Generally rendered "justice" or "judgment," *mišpāṭ* carries a legal or judicial connotation, though it is used in variety of ways. The laws given by Moses are described with the plural of *mišpāṭ*, "judgments, decrees" (Exod. 21:1; Deut. 5:1; see *judgment*).

Noun: עֵדוּת (*ʿēdût*), GK 6343 (S 5715), 61x. *ʿēdût*, usually translated "testimony," is closely connected to God's law. In the Pentateuch, this noun describes the two tablets containing the Ten Commandments. Generally, outside the Pentateuch *ʿēdût* is a more generic reference to law (1 Ki. 2:3; 2 Ki. 23:3; 1 Chr. 29:19), perhaps with the physical tablets of the Ten Commandments in the background. In this sense, the plural of *ʿēdût* may be translated "requirements, warnings, regulations, or decrees." See *testimony*.

DEDICATE

Old Testament

Verb: קָדַשׁ (*qādaš*), GK 7727 (S 6942), 171x. *qādaš* describes the state of the sacred realm. Negatively, it represents that which is distinct from the common or profane. It is usually translated "make holy" (NIV), "sanctify," or "dedicate." See *sanctify*.

DEED

Old Testament

Noun: מַעֲשֶׂה (*maʿaśeh*), GK 5126 (S 4639), 235x. *maʿaśeh* is the noun derived from the verb *ʿāśâ* (GK 6913), "to make, do." It therefore denotes that which is "done" or "made." See *work*.

DEFEND

Old Testament

Verb: רִיב (*rîb*), GK 8189, (S 7378), 72x. *rîb* denotes the action of entering into an argument, conflict, or lawsuit with another person. When a case or a cause is the object of *rîb*, the NIV may translate the verb as "plead" (e.g., Ps. 43:1), "defend" (e.g., 74:22), "present" (e.g., Prov. 18:17), or "take up" (e.g., 22:23; 23:11). See *contend*.

New Testament

Verb: ἀπολογέομαι (*apologeomai*), GK *664* (S *621*), 10x. *apologeomai* means "to defend something or someone, including oneself, through speech." The word bears the sense of advocacy and defense, which our word "apologetics" still retains; it often occurs in a legal context.

Because persecution and public trials are inevitable, legal self-defense is inevitable. Thus, Jesus tells his disciples to settle their hearts and not to meditate on how to defend themselves, for the Lord will give them what they need to say at that time (Lk. 12:11; 21:14). Showing Jesus' words to ring true, *apologeomai* as "self-defense" occurs when Paul defends himself before Felix (Acts 24:10), before Festus (25:8), and before Agrippa (26:1–2, 24). In 2 Corinthians, Paul defends himself against his opponents (2 Cor. 12:19). The only example in the NT of defending someone else is Alexander's attempted defense of the Jews during the uprising in Ephesus (19:33).

The only occurrence of *apologeomai* as an action by a thing rather than by a person occurs in Rom. 2:15. Paul says that the Gentiles "show that the work of the law is written on their hearts, while their conscience also bears witness, and their conflicting thoughts accuse or even *excuse* them" (ESV). The word picture is of conflicting thoughts standing up before the heart and conscience, extending their anthropomorphic hands and pleading their case. By way of application, wise is the Christian who targets this courtroom of the heart when he interacts with lost humankind. See *NIDNTT-A*, 63-64.*

DEFILE

Old Testament

Verb: חָלַל (*ḥālal*), GK 2725 (S 2490), 135x. *ḥālal* can refer either to making something impure ("to defile"), or it can have a more neutral meaning "to begin, proceed" (see *begin*).

(1) Often translated "to defile, profane, desecrate," *ḥālal* regularly refers to issues of morality. It can refer to the defiling or profaning of things set apart for God, such as the Sabbath (Ezek. 20:13, 16, 21), the sanctuary (Lev. 21:12), or the land: "I will repay them double for their wickedness and their sin, because they have *defiled* my land with the lifeless forms of their vile images" (Jer. 16:18).

In addition, *ḥālal* can be used for profaning other persons, such as a covenant of friendship ("My companion attacks his friends; he *violates* his covenant; Ps. 55:20) or an oath to God or another person: "When a man makes a vow to the LORD or takes an oath to obligate himself by a pledge, he must not *break* his word but must do everything he said" (Num. 30:2).

(2) More than half of the occurrences of *ḥālal* refer to profaning the name of God (Lev. 18:21; 19:12; 21:6; 22:2). Of course, God's name cannot literally be made unholy, but through profane actions people can disregard the majesty of his supreme

holiness. Thus, in Ezek. 36, the prophet speaks of God's name being profaned among the nations because of Israel's disobedience and their resulting exile: "And wherever they went among the nations they *profaned* my holy name, for it was said of them, 'These are the LORD's people, and yet they had to leave his land' " (Ezek. 36:20). Because God is concerned about the holiness of his name, however, he promises to vindicate his name by bringing the people of Israel back to their land and cleansing them from their uncleanness and by putting his Spirit within them: "Therefore say to the house of Israel, 'This is what the Sovereign LORD says: It is not for your sake, O house of Israel, that I am going to do these things, but for the sake of my holy name, which you have *profaned* among the nations where you have gone" (Ezek. 36:22).

New Testament

Verb: κοινόω (*koinoō*), GK *3124* (S *2840*), 14x. *koinoō* means "to make impure, defile" in a ritual (or ceremonial) sense. It can refer to making individuals (Mt. 15:11, 18, 20) or objects (Acts 21:28) impure in a ritual sense (but see Jesus' reinterpretation of *koinoō* in Mk. 7:15–23). In Peter's account of his vision of the unclean animals, God commands him to no longer call these animals "impure" (Acts 11:9).

DEFILED

Old Testament

Verb: טָמֵא (*ṭāmēʾ*), GK 3237 (S 2930), 88x. *ṭāmēʾ* means to "become ceremonially unclean, defiled." This word and its derivatives are concentrated in certain sections of the OT, especially Leviticus. See *unclean*.

Adjective: טָמֵא (*ṭāmēʾ*), GK 3238 (S 2931), 162x. *ṭāmēʾ* as an adjective denotes that which is "unclean," especially in a ritual context. In most cases, it is a technical term for the state of being ritually "unclean" or "defiled" and thus disqualified from the sphere of the holy (e.g., the temple). See *unclean*.

New Testament

Adjective: ἀκάθαρτος (*akathartos*), GK *176* (S *169*), 32x. *akathartos* pertains to that which may not be brought into contact with what is holy (see *holy*). In this sense it is "impure, unclean," and at times "evil." See *unclean*.

Adjective: κοινός (*koinos*), GK *3123* (S *2839*), 14x. The basic meaning of *koinos* is "common" and can refer to objects held in "common," or it can convey the sense of "impure." See *common*.

DELEGATE

New Testament

Noun: ἀπόστολος (*apostolos*), GK *693* (S *652*), 80x. *apostolos* broadly refers to a "messenger, delegate, or sent one" (see *send*). In classical Greek, *apostolos* referred to a person of merit sent as an envoy or on behalf of a master in an administrative role. John uses the term in a similar general way, applying it to any messenger without the specific idea of an office with special status (Jn. 13:16). In contrast, in Luke *apostolos* is used almost solely as a designation for the Twelve (except in Lk. 11:49 and Acts 14:14; in the latter, Luke identifies both Barnabas and Paul as apostles). Matthew and Mark use it sparingly for the Twelve (Mt. 10:2; Mk. 3:14; 6:30). See *apostle*.

DELIGHT (IN)

Old Testament

Verb: חָפֵץ (*ḥāpēṣ*), GK 2911 (S 2654), 74x.

(1) *ḥāpēṣ* often refers to taking joy or pleasure in something or someone. It is sometimes synonymous with the verbs "to love" and "to be pleased." The Lord *delights* in David (2 Sam. 22:20; Ps. 41:11), Solomon (2 Chr. 9:8), and Jerusalem (Isa. 66:4). He urges the unrepentant to turn to him, because he does not *delight* in the death of the wicked (Ezek. 18:23, 32; 33:11), but he *delights* in showing mercy (Mic. 7:18). God *delights* in "righteous" sacrifice (Ps. 51:19), but he does not *delight* in a sacrifice that is a substitute for, or is void of a relationship with, him

(Ps. 40:6; 51:16; Isa. 1:11; Hos. 6:6). The godly *delight* in the laws of the Lord (Ps. 112:1; 119:35) and choose the things that *please* him (Isa. 56:4). Those who choose the things that are displeasing to him (i.e., sin, evil, wickedness) will be punished (Isa. 65:12; 66:4).

(2) At times, *ḥāpēṣ* denotes the action of seeking or desiring to do what will bring happiness, pleasure, fulfillment, or satisfaction. An English idiom that expresses this meaning of *ḥāpēṣ* is "to have one's heart set on" someone or something. The nominal use can be explained by the expression "the longing of one's heart." It expresses Solomon's desire to build a magnificent temple and royal palace in Jerusalem (1 Ki. 9:1) and Job's sincere desire to present his case before God (Job 13:3). The psalmist desires to do the Lord's will (Ps. 40:8), for there is nothing on earth more desirous (73:25). God's word always accomplishes his desires (Isa. 55:11). The phrase *ḥāpēṣ yhwh* can be translated "the LORD's will" (Jdg. 13:23; 1 Sam. 2:25; Ps. 135:6; Isa. 53:10). See *NIDOTTE*, 2:231-34.

Verb: שָׂמַח (*śāmaḥ*), GK 8523 (S 8055), 156x. *śāmaḥ* can describe both one's feeling of joy and the outward expression of such gladness in the form of rejoicing. It can be translated many ways, including "rejoice, delight, filled with joy, or gladden." See *rejoice*.

Verb: רָצָה (*rāṣâ*), GK 8354 (S 7521), 52x. *rāṣâ means* "to be pleased, accept, delight in." See *(be) pleased*.

Noun: רָצוֹן (*rāṣôn*), GK 8356 (S 7522), 56x. *rāṣôn* denotes three different ideas in the OT: favor (see *favor*), acceptance (see *acceptable*), or will (see *please*). It is attributed most often to God (39x) and occurs most frequently in Proverbs (14x), Psalms (13x), and Leviticus (7x). In Proverbs, God "delights" in accurate weights (Prov. 11:1), the blameless (11:20), truthful men (12:22), and the prayer of the upright (15:8), and a king "delights" in a wise servant (14:35).

New Testament

Verb: ἀγαλλιάω (*agalliaō*), GK *22* (S *21*), 11x. *agalliaō* means "to rejoice greatly, exult, be overjoyed." See *rejoice*.

DELIVER

Old Testament

Verb: יָשַׁע (*yāšaʿ*), GK 3828 (S 3467), 184x. Often translated "to save, rescue, deliver," the basic meaning of *yāšaʿ* is to deliver or save human beings from a time of danger, often from personal enemies or from a time of sickness. See *save*.

Verb: מָלַט (*mālāṭ*), GK 4880 (S 4422), 94x. *mālāṭ* means to "escape, flee to safety," and it may also be translated in the passive "to be delivered, rescued, or saved." Note Ps. 41:4, "Blessed is he who has regard for the weak; the LORD *delivers* him in times of trouble." See *escape*.

Verb: נָצַל (*nāṣal*), GK 5911 (S 5337), 213x. For the most part, *nāṣal* means "save, rescue, deliver, take away." See *save*.

New Testament

Verb: ἀποδίδωμι (*apodidōmi*), GK *625* (S *591*), 48x. *apodidōmi* means "to give (back), deliver, render, hand over, produce." See *give (back)*.

Verb: ῥύομαι (*rhyomai*), GK *4861* (S *4506*), 17x. *rhyomai* means "to rescue, deliver." See *rescue*.

DELIVERANCE

Old Testament

Noun: יְשׁוּעָה (*yᵉšûʿâ*), GK 3802 (S 3444), 78x. *yᵉšûʿâ* generally means "salvation, deliverance, Savior." Even more so than the verb *yāšaʿ* (see *save*), this noun is limited to God as Savior and the deliverance he brings. See *salvation*.

Noun: תְּשׁוּעָה (*tᵉšûʿâ*), GK 9591 (S 8668), 34x. *tᵉšûʿa means* "salvation, deliverance, victory." See *salvation*.

DEMAND

New Testament

Verb: αἰτέω (*aiteō*), GK *160* (S *154*), 70x. *aiteō* generally means "to ask, request, demand." See *ask*.

DEMON

New Testament

Noun: δαιμόνιον (*diamonion*), GK *1228* (S *1140*), 63x. *diamonion* denotes a "demon." Demons are unseen but real beings, intent on opposing God's kingdom and the gospel of Jesus, and on harming people. They are called by various names: evil spirits (Lk. 8:2), unclean spirits (Mk. 1:26), spirits (Mk. 9:20; Lk. 9:39), "spirit of an unclean demon" (Lk. 4:33), and rulers, authorities and powers (Eph. 3:10; 6:12; Col. 2:15). These terms are basically synonymous and are often used interchangeably within a single passage (Lk. 8:2; 9:42). Demons are angels who sinned against God (2 Pet. 2:4), thus losing their position of authority and even "their own dwelling" (Jude 6). They are purely wicked, yet they vary in degrees of wickedness (Mt. 12:45). Their ruler is Satan (Mt. 9:34; 12:24; Mk. 3:22; Lk. 11:15; see *Satan*), and by doing his bidding their activities can be said to be done by Satan himself (Lk. 13:11, 16).

"Demon possession" is a difficult topic (see *diamonizomai*, GK *1227* ("[be] demon-possessed"). Even though demons are said to "go into" a person (Mk. 9:25; Lk. 8:30), a more common phrase is that of the person "having" the demon (Mt. 11:18; Lk. 13:11). Nevertheless, demons can be "cast out of" people (Mt. 7:22; Mk. 3:15), and the idea of inhabitation is certainly pictured in Jesus' parable of the unclean spirits (Mt. 12:43–45). Demons can exert tremendous control over humans; how much control, however, it is difficult to say. Demons can keep a person from performing natural functions (seeing, Mt. 12:22; hearing, Mk. 9:25; speaking, Lk. 11:14; standing straight, Lk. 13:11; moving at all, Mk. 9:18). They can also cause unnatural functions (throwing people to the ground, Lk. 4:35; shaking them violently, Mt. 17:15; tossing them into fire and water, Lk. 9:39; dragging them around against their will and breaking metal chains, Lk. 8:29; causing one man to physically abuse seven, Acts 19:16). Demons can talk through humans (Mk. 1:34; Lk. 4:34, 41; Acts 19:15) and affect peoples' minds, making them of "unsound judgment" (Lk. 8:35; Jn. 8:52; 10:20). Multiple demons can affect a single person at one time (see Lk. 8:2, 30), and they even torment children (Mk. 7:30; Lk. 9:38).

Demons are behind idol worship (1 Cor. 10:20–21; Rev. 9:20; cf. Ps. 106:37) and fortune-telling (Acts 16:16). They lead people against God through miraculous wonders (Rev. 16:14). They attack the truth by perverting sound teaching (1 Tim. 4:1), pervert righteousness through prompting perpetual sin (1 Jn. 5:18–19), and even attempt to hamper evangelism (Acts 16:16). "Bitter jealousy" and "selfish ambition" in the heart can be labeled "from the devil" (Jas. 3:14). Demons are active today, and it is this spiritual world that stands as the primary enemy in the Christian life (Eph. 6:12).

Demons believe there is one God, and they shudder with fear (Jas. 2:19). They know Jesus Christ (Mk. 1:34; Lk. 4:34, 41; Acts 19:15) and are afraid of his power (Lk. 4:34; 8:28). He has all authority over demons (Lk. 4:36) and gives it to his followers (Mk. 3:15; 16:17; Lk. 10:19; Acts 8:7). Even those not directly following Jesus could cast demons out in his name (Mk. 9:38). One characteristic of the kingdom of God is that as it spreads into people's hearts, demons are stripped of their power and forced to leave (Lk. 11:20; Acts 26:18). Through the cross Jesus has triumphed over "powers and authorities" (Col. 2:15), and even now he is destroying "all dominion, authority, and power" (1 Cor. 15:24). Therefore all Christians are to stand in the day of battle in the power of God's armor (Eph. 6:12–13) and to "test the spirits" (1 Jn. 4:1). See *NIDNTT-A*, 120.

DEMON-POSSESSED

New Testament

Verb: δαιμονίζομαι (*daimonizomai*), GK *1227* (S *1139*), 13x. *daimonizomai* refers to the action of demon possession or demon oppression. This word can refer to demon possession in and of itself (Mt. 8:16; Mk. 1:32), or to a demon-induced illness and disability (Mt. 9:32; 12:22; 15:22), or to demon-controlled actions (Mk. 5:16, 18; Lk. 8:36), which can evoke destructive behavior (Mt. 8:28). Since it seems difficult at times to posit degrees of demon possession, it is best to understand *daimonizomai* as sometimes meaning the action of demon *oppression*. This is particularly true for when physical conditions or illnesses are related to demons. Regardless of the nuances of possession (internal) versus oppression (external), the focus of Scripture is clearly on the ability of Jesus to triumph over demons in *all* their manifestations. See *NIDNTT-A*, 120.

DEMONSTRATE

New Testament

Verb: δείκνυμι (*deiknymi*), GK *1259* (S *1166*), 30x.

Verb: ἐνδείκνυμι (*endeiknymi*), GK *1892* (S *1731*), 11x. The basic meaning of both verbs is "to show" something. Especially *endeiknymi* carries the idea of demonstrating through logic or acts. See *show*.

DENARIUS

New Testament

Noun: δηνάριον (*dēnarion*), GK *1324* (S *1220*), 16x. The *dēnarion* was a Roman silver coin worth about one worker's average daily wage. As Mt. 20:2 makes clear, day laborers normally received one *dēnarion* for each day's work. Mk. 14:5 tells how the perfume used to anoint Jesus' feet was worth over 300 denarii—nearly a year's worth of wages. The moneylender in Lk. 7:41 is described as being owed 550 denarii.

One of the most famous NT passages concerning money that uses the term *dēnarion* is Mk. 12:13–17. When questioned by the Pharisees and Herodians concerning paying taxes to Caesar, a question that is relevant both politically and theologically, Jesus first asks to look at a denarius. After showing that Caesar's image is on the denarius, Jesus answers, "Give to Caesar what is Caesar's and to God what is God's" (12:17). In the same way, although we all earn our own wages for each day's work, we too must give to God what is God's. That is, since we bear God's image as human beings, we must give ourselves to God. See *NIDNTT-A*, 536-37.

DENY

New Testament

Verb: ἀπαρνέομαι (*aparneomai*), GK *565* (S *533*), 11x. The verb *aparneomai* essentially means the same as *arneomai* (GK *766*): to "deny, reject, disown." This word occurs only in the gospels, a majority of them in the prediction of Peter's denial (e.g., Mt. 26:34–35): "This very night, before the rooster crows, you will *deny* me three times." Peter responds with the same word, "Even if I have to die with you, I will never *deny* you."

aparneomai also denotes what will happen to those who have denied Christ: "But he who disowns [*arneomai*] me before men will be disowned [*aparneomai*] before the angels of God" (Lk. 12:9). On the judgment day, God will reject all who have rejected him.

Finally, *aparneomai* can denote a positive form of denial. Jesus exhorts all disciples to deny themselves, take up their cross daily, and follow Christ (Mt. 16:24; Mk. 8:34). This is a call to selfless, total commitment to the Lord. In a real sense, we face a double choice: to choose to put our own interests and ourselves first and thus deny the Lord Jesus, or else to deny ourselves and in place of that to choose to live for God. See *NIDNTT-A*, 72.

Verb: ἀρνέομαι (*arneomai*), GK *766* (S *720*), 33x. *arneomai* primarily means "to deny," although its wider range of meaning covers "disown, fail to confess, reject, say 'No,' refuse, renounce."

The basic meaning of *arneomai* is seen in verses like Acts 4:16 (the Sanhedrin cannot "deny" the miracle performed by Peter and John), 2 Pet. 2:1 (the false teachers have introduced destructive heresies "even denying the sovereign Lord"), and

1 Jn. 2:22 (a liar is one who "denies that Jesus is the Christ"). In each case the one who denies adopts a position opposed to the truth. It is the kind of blind allegiance to error that we find in those who have rejected truth and embraced fallacy. It involves both intentionality and self-delusion.

As used in the NT, *arneomai* often has serious theological consequences. In Mt. 10:33 Jesus warns that whoever disowns him before men, he will disown before God the father.

And Paul, quoting from what may be an early Christian hymn, gives notice that "if we disown him [Christ], he will also disown us" (2 Tim. 2:12). Peter's threefold denial of Jesus is recounted in all four gospels (e.g., Mt. 26:72, "He denied it again, with an oath: 'I don't know the man!'"), but fortunately it was followed by remorse and forgiveness. Writing to Timothy, Paul warns of the terrible plight of the last days in which people may be characterized as "having a form of godliness but denying its power" (2 Tim. 3:5). They will claim to know God but "by their actions they deny him" (Tit. 1:16). The plain truth is that "no one who denies the Son has the Father" (1 Jn. 2:23). Truly, denial of Christ and his redemptive work has serious consequences for eternity.

What the believer is called upon to deny is himself. All three synoptists record the stringent requirements laid down by Jesus for those who wold follow him: "If anyone would come after me, he must deny himself and take up his cross daily and follow me" (Lk. 9:23). See *NIDNTT-A*, 72.

DEPART

Old Testament

Verb: גָּלָה (*gālâ*), GK 1655 (S 1540), 187x. *gālâ* has a wide variety of uses in the OT: "to exile, go into exile, expose, depart, reveal, have sexual relations with." See *exile*.

Verb: נָסַע (*nāsaʿ*), GK 5825 (S 5265), 146x. The original meaning of *nāsaʿ* is "to pull out (tent pegs)," from which the sense "set out" or "journey" is derived. See *journey*.

New Testament

Verb: ἀναχωρέω (*anachōreō*), GK *432* (S *402*), 14x. *anachōreō* means "to depart, return." It can refer to simply leaving one place for another place, such as Judas "departing" from the temple to go hang himself (Mt. 27:5). It can also refer to withdrawing from a place as a way of seeking refuge. Joseph, Mary, and Jesus "take refuge" from Herod in Egypt (Mt. 2:14). On several occasions Jesus withdraws alone (Mt. 14:13; Jn. 6:15) or along with others (Mt. 12:15; 15:21; Mk. 3:7). The Magi "return" to their country by a different route after being warned not to go back to Herod (Mt. 2:12).

Verb: ἀφίστημι (*aphistēmi*), GK *923* (S *868*), 14x. *aphistēmi* generally means to "leave, depart" in a physical sense, as when the devil finished tempting Jesus and "*left* him until an opportune time" (Lk. 4:13, cf. 2:27; Acts 12:10). See *leave*.

Verb: καταλείπω (*kataleipō*), GK *2901* (S *2641*), 24x. *kataleipō* is means simply to "leave behind, depart." See *leave behind*.

Verb: μεταβαίνω (*metabainō*), GK *3553* (S *3327*), 12x. *metabainō* means "to leave, depart, pass on," both geographically and metaphorically. See *leave*.

Verb: ὑπάγω (*hypagō*) GK *5632* (S *5217*), 79x. *hypagō* means "to go" in the sense of departing (Mt. 4:10, "*Away* from me, Satan!") or accompanying (5:41, "*Go* with him two miles"). It is used figuratively to refer to dying (Mt. 26:24, "The Son of Man will go just as it is written") or to an outward sign of conversion (Jn. 12:11, "Many of the Jews were going over to Jesus") The phrase, "*Get* behind me" (Mk. 8:33) may reflect the Hebrew idea of both contempt and rejection. Going and bearing fruit are also a part of what it means to be chosen by God (Jn. 15:16, "I chose you and appointed you to go and bear fruit."). Jesus uses the verb often in the gospel of John to refer to "where he is going," namely, to his Father in heaven (8:14; 13:3; 14:4–5, 28).

DEPEND ON

Old Testament

Verb: בָּטַח (*bāṭaḥ*), GK 1053 (S 982), 118x. This word means "to trust, rely on, depend on," with the sense of being completely confident and feeling utterly safe. See *trust*.

DEPENDABLE

New Testament

Adjective: πιστός (*pistos*), GK *4412* (S *4103*), 67x. *pistos* means "faithful, trustworthy, reliable, dependable." See *faithful*.

DEPLOY

Old Testament

Verb: עָרַךְ (*ʿārak*), GK 6885 (S 6186), 75x. *ʿārak* denotes the action of arranging an object in a particular way or arranging objects in a specific order to produce a desired effect. Regarding war, *ʿārak* denotes the action of arranging armies for battle. The NIV sometimes translates this use of *ʿārak* as "deploy their forces" (1 Sam. 4:2). See *arrange*.

Verb: קָרָא (*qārāʾ*), GK 7925 (S 7122), 136x. The primary meaning of *qārāʾ* is "to meet, encounter, happen." It is used in a technical sense for engagement in battle, as in 1 Chr. 19:10. See *meet*.

DEPOSIT

New Testament

Noun: ἀρραβών (*arrabōn*), GK *775* (S *728*), 3x. *arrabōn* is a "pledge or deposit guaranteeing what is to come." A Heb. word that in the OT is used on a purely human level (e.g., Gen. 38:17–20) becomes a transliterated Greek word to describe what God has done for us by his saving grace. See *pledge*.

DEPRIVE

Old Testament

Verb: לָקַח (*lāqaḥ*), GK 4374 (S 3947), 967x. The basic meaning of *lāqaḥ* is "to take, grasp." The meaning is often simply to "take into/by the hand." *lāqaḥ* can also have the meaning "deprive," as Solomon being deprived of his kingdom (1 Ki. 11:34) or Elijah being *taken away from* Elisha (2 Ki. 2:3, 5). See *take*.

DESCEND

New Testament

Verb: καταβαίνω (*katabainō*), GK *2849* (S *2597*), 81x. *katabainō* means "to come down, go down, descend." See *come down*.

DESCENDANT

Old Testament

Noun: זֶרַע (*zeraʿ*), GK 2446 (S 2233), 229x. The noun *zeraʿ* generally means "seed, descendant, offspring." It has various nuances in the OT. See *seed*.

New Testament

Noun: σπέρμα (*sperma*), GK *5065* (S *4690*), 43x. *sperma* means "seed, descendant." As with *zeraʿ* in the OT, *sperma* can mean the children or descendants of an individual. In the Sadducees' story of the woman who married seven brothers, none of these brothers raised up "seed" (i.e., children) through her (Mt. 22:24–25). The Jews considered themselves the seed or descendants of Abraham (Jn. 8:33, 37; 2 Cor. 11:22). One important theme in the NT is that Jesus is a descendant of David (Rom. 1:3; 2 Tim. 2:8). See *seed*.

DESECRATE

Old Testament

Verb: חָלַל (*ḥālal*), GK 2725 (S 2490), 135x. *ḥālal* can refer either to making something impure ("to defile") or it can have a more neutral meaning "to begin, proceed" (see *begin*). In the first usage, it can refer to the defiling or desecrating of things set apart for God, such as the Sabbath, or the very name of God (see *defile*).

DESERT

Old Testament

Noun: מִדְבָּר (*midbār*), GK 4497 (S 4057), 269x. *midbār* is generally translated "desert, wasteland, open country." Some translate the noun simply as "wilderness," but a modifying word like "barren" needs to be added to portray adequately the arid nature of a *midbār*. It is an area that lacks water (Ezek. 19:13; Hos. 13:5), is uninhabited (Job 38:26), and is uncultivated and usually unfruitful (Jer. 2:2; 4:26), though some deserts have enough vegetation for pasturing flocks (1 Sam. 17:28). Away from the safety and light of the inhabited areas of the county, the *midbār* is a place of thick darkness and danger (Jer. 2:31) and is not usually portrayed in a positive light (Song 3:6 is an exception). Jer. 2:6 sums up these aspects well when it describes the desert that the Israelites passed through after the exodus: "a land of wilderness plain and gorges … a land that is dry and dark … a land no one passes through and where no one lives." The only natural inhabitants of the *midbār* are wild animals, such as jackals (Mal. 1:3), ostriches (Lam. 4:3), and donkeys (Job 24:5).

Often *midbār* is connected directly with a place name, such as the desert of Sinai (Exod. 19:1), the desert of Paran (Num. 12:16), and the desert of Maon (1 Sam. 23:24). When the central location is a city—e.g., "the desert of Gibeon" (2 Sam. 2:24)—the phrase may be referring to pasturelands surrounding the city. Within the borders of Palestine, "the desert" sometimes refers specifically to the eastern side of the hill country (Jos. 12:8; 16:1). This area is in the rain shadow of the hills and so receives little rainfall. But *midbār* can also refer to any dry area, such as "the fords of the desert" at the Jordan River, which were surrounded by arid land (2 Sam. 15:28).

Intriguingly, the *midbār* is a place where repeatedly God shows his faithfulness and love to his people (Deut. 32:10; Neh. 9:21; Hos. 2:14). A number of times we are told that God used the desert as a training ground for them (1 Ki. 19:4), such as during the forty years of "wilderness" wanderings (Deut. 8:2), which throughout the OT is considered one of the most important periods in Israel's history (Ps. 78:52; 136:16; Ezek. 20:10–26). Significantly, it was also in the desert region around the Jordan River that John the Baptist took up his ministry of preparation, in fulfillment of the prophesy in Isa. 40:3, "A voice is calling: 'In the desert, clear the way of the LORD' " (cf. Mt. 3:3). See *NIDOTTE*, 4:520-28.

Noun: עֲרָבָה (*ʿarābâ*), GK 6858 (S 6160), 60x. *ʿarābâ* conveys a dry, desolate, wilderness area, similar to a desert, and may be translated as "plains" or "desert." See *Arabah*.

New Testament

Verb: εγκαταλειπω (*enkataleipō*), GK *1593* (S *1459*), 10x. This verb means to separate connection with someone or something by leaving, to "forsake, abandon, desert." See *forsake*.

Noun and Adjective: ἔρημος (*erēmos*), GK *2245* (S *2048*), 48x. In the NT, *erēmos* is used both as an adjective and a noun. As an adjective it usually means "desolate" (see *desolate*). As a noun *erēmos* can refer to any wilderness or uninhabited, lonely region (e.g., Lk. 5:16; 9:12). More often it refers specifically to either the Judean desert or the Arabian desert. The former is where John the Baptist grew up (Lk. 1:80) and exercised his public ministry of baptism (Lk. 3:2). John probably chose the desert as his place of ministry because of the influence of Isa. 40:3, which predicted the return of the Lord from the desert to save his people (Lk. 3:4). The expectation of the Jews that God's salvation would come from the desert may account for the presence of various bands of Jewish patriots who went out into the desert around the time of Jesus (e.g., Acts 21:38).

Jesus himself was led by the Spirit into the Judean desert for forty days (Mt. 4:1), recalling Israel's forty years in the desert. The Gospels emphasize that Jesus succeeded in obeying God where Israel had failed (note that Jesus quotes Deuteronomy each time he is tempted by the devil). The NT frequently refers to Israel's forty years of wandering and rebellion in the desert of Sinai (Jn. 6:31, 49; Acts 7:30, 36, 38, 42; 13:18; 1 Cor. 10:5; Heb. 3:8, 17). See *NIDNTT-A*, 206-7.

DESERTED

Old Testament

Verb: שָׁמֵם (*šāmēm*), GK 9037 (S 8074), 92x. The verb *šāmēm* is used in two distinct but related ways. It can mean "to be desolate, deserted, lay waste" or it can point to the response to such desolation and mean "to shudder, be horrified, be appalled." Two-thirds of the instances of *šāmēm* occur in prophetic passages. It most often means either causing or suffering destruction. Most occurrences denote the resulting state of desolation (see *desolate*).

DESERVE

New Testament

Adverb: ἱκανός (*hikanos*), GK *2653* (S *2425*), 39x. *hikanos* conveys the idea that something is adequate or large enough in its quantity or quality and may best be translated "sufficient, deserve, adequate." See *sufficient*.

DESERVING

New Testament

Adjective: ἄξιος (*axios*), GK *545* (S *514*), 41x. In classical Greek *axios* had to do with tipping or balancing the scales. Such fitness implies worth, and so *axios* came to mean "worthy, deserving." In 1 Tim. 1:15, for example, Paul cites "a trustworthy saying that *deserves* full acceptance." See *worthy*.

DESIGNATE

New Testament

Verb: ὀνομάζω (*onomazō*), GK 3951 (S 3687), 10x. *onomazō* is the verbal form of the noun *onoma* (see *name*). In the Synoptics it occurs in the sense of "to designate." See *name*.

DESIRE

Old Testament

Verb: חָפֵץ (*ḥāpēṣ*), GK 2911 (S 2654), 74x. 1. *ḥāpēṣ* often refers to taking joy or pleasure in something or someone. Elsewhere, this verb denotes the action of seeking or desiring to do what will bring happiness, pleasure, fulfillment, or satisfaction. See *delight*.

Noun: רָצוֹן (*rāṣôn*), GK 8356 (S 7522), 56x. *rāṣôn* denotes three different ideas in the OT: favor (see *favor*), acceptance (see *acceptable*), or will (see *please*). It is attributed most often to God (39x) and occurs most frequently in Proverbs (14x), Psalms (13x), and Leviticus (7x). When *rāṣôn* is used generally for a creature's desire, it is translated as "desires" (Ps. 145:16, 19) or something "wished" for (Est. 1:8).

New Testament

Verb: βούλομαι (*boulomai*) GK *1089* (S *1014*), 37x. *boulomai* describes the desire or intention of a person to do something, to have something, or to obtain a result. See *want*.

Verb: ἐλπίζω (*elpizō*), GK *1827* (S *1679*), 31x. In general *elpizō* means "hope" (see *hope*), though it sometimes denotes "desire, wish." The verb can be used to denote the act of desiring or wishing something where the outcome is uncertain. Herod hoped to see Jesus perform a miracle (Lk. 23:8; cf. a similar use in Acts 24:26). Paul and John often write that they hope to see a person or congregation (e.g., Rom. 15:24; Phlm. 22; 2 Jn. 12; 3 Jn. 14) even though they are sometimes clearly not certain that their plans will work out (1 Cor. 16:7; 1 Tim. 3:14–15). They do realize, however, that they are dependent on God to work out their plans, so they "hope in the Lord" (1 Cor. 16:7; Phil. 2:19, 23)

Verb: ἐπιζητέω (*epizēteō*), GK *2118* (S *1934*), 13x. *epizēteō* means "to look for, desire after, strive for." See *look for*.

Verb: ἐπιθυμέω (*epithymeō*), GK *2121* (S *1937*), 16x. *epithymeō* means "to desire earnestly, long for something, lust, covet." Although its noun form, *epithymia* is most commonly translated as "lust" or "covetousness," the verb *epithymeō* has both negative and positive connotations. It always describes the inner motivation rather than focusing on the object of desire.

In a positive sense, *epithymeō* denotes the earnest longing of the prophets and the righteous to see the messianic fulfillment in Jesus' ministry (Mt. 13:17), the disciples' longing to see one of the days of the Son of Man (Lk. 17:22), and the angels' longing to look into the wonder of salvation (1 Pet. 1:12). It describes the prodigal son's longing to eat the swine's husks (Lk. 15:16) and Lazarus's longing to eat the crumbs from the rich man's table (Lk. 16:21). Jesus tells his disciples that he eagerly desired to eat the Passover with them (Lk. 22:15). Finally, Paul thinks that the desire to be a bishop is a good thing (1 Tim. 3:1), and the writer of Hebrews desires for his correspondents to continue diligently in spiritual growth (Heb. 6:11).

Instances of a more negative use of *epithymeō* as lust or covetousness are found in Mt. 5:28; Acts 20:33; Rom. 7:7, 13; 1 Cor. 10:6; and Jas. 4:2. In Gal. 5:17, the term takes on a more refined theological meaning as Paul teaches the Galatians about the struggle between the flesh and the Spirit, explaining that the flesh "lusts" (KJV) against or desires what is contrary to the Spirit, and the Spirit desires what is contrary to the flesh. See *NIDNTT-A*, 196-197.

Verb: θέλω (*thelō*), GK *2527* (S *2309*), 208x. *thelō* means "to will, want, desire," sometimes with human beings as the subject, sometimes with God as subject. See *will*.

Noun: ἐλπίς (*elpis*), GK *1828* (S *1680*), 53x. The majority of the NT writers invest *elpis*, "hope," with the nuance of "confident expectation" or "solid assurance," though in several places it means simply "desire" or "wish" (Acts 16:19; 27:20; 2 Cor. 10:15), as our common English usage ("I hope the sun will shine tomorrow"). See *hope*.

Noun: ἐπιθυμία (*epithymia*), GK *2123* (S *1939*), 38x. *epithymia* is based on the root word *thymos*, meaning "an urge" or "passion." Stoic philosophers classed *epithymia* along with three other human emotions: fear, pleasure, and grief. These are detrimental to one's ethical life because they conflict with a person's rationality. In Jewish thought the sinful motivation of the heart is to be condemned as strongly as the sinful act itself. *epithymia* thus denotes impulsive sensual desire, contrary to the will and pleasure of God. Sometimes this word appears in more mundane fashion in the NT (e.g., for hunger in Lk. 15:16) or in a positive sense indicating intense longing (1 Thess. 2:17), especially where Paul is torn between a "desire" leaving this life to be with the Lord or to remain for the benefit of the congregation (Phil. 1:23).

Mostly, however, *epithymia* constitutes wrong sensual and sexual desires that are selfish and result in disobedience to God. Willfully disobedient persons are given up by God to the perverse "*desires* of their hearts" (Rom. 1:24). Christians are admonished to change their former sinful behavior, in which (like the heathen) they once followed and performed the lusts of the flesh (Rom. 6:12; 7:7; Eph. 2:3; 4:22; 1 Thess. 4:5; Tit. 3:3; 1 Pet. 1:14; 4:2–3). Salvation entails crucifixion of the "flesh with its passions and *desires/lusts*" (Gal. 5:24; Col. 3:5) and walking in the Spirit (Gal. 5:16) so as to "make no provision for the flesh to perform its *lusts*" (Rom. 13:14). "Covetous desire" for riches can lead people into ruin and destruction (1 Tim. 6:9). Paul admonishes Timothy to "flee youthful *lusts*" (2 Tim. 2:22), warning that in the last days, people will follow the inclinations of their own desires (3:6) and will find teachers according to their own desires (4:3; cf. 2 Pet. 3:3; Jude 16, 18). James explains that each person is enticed by the desires already present in human nature, and once a person is enticed, lust produces sin, which ultimately results in death (Jas. 1:14–15). Finally, John warns that the "*desires* of the flesh and the *lust* of the eyes … are from the world," which is passing away "with its *desires*" (1 Jn. 2:16–17). See *NIDNTT-A*, 196-97.

Noun: εὐδοκία (*eudokia*) GK *2306* (S *2107*), 9x. *eudokia* can mean "good pleasure, purpose; desire." Most of its nine uses in the NT refer to God rather than humans and denote God's good intention or purpose for his people. See *pleasure*.

DESIRE EAGERLY

New Testament

Verb: ζηλόω (*zēloō*), GK *2420* (S *2206*), 11x. *zēloō* means to be "zealous" or "jealous." It is related to the noun *zēlos* ("jealousy, zeal," GK *2419*). In classical Greek this word group sometimes carried a positive sense (eager striving, enthusiasm, or praise) and sometimes a negative sense (jealously, ill will, or envy). The same applies to the NT. Note Paul's challenge, "Follow the way of love and *eagerly desire* spiritual gifts" (1 Cor. 14:1, 12, 39). See *zealous*.

DESOLATE, (BE) DESOLATE

Old Testament

Verb: שָׁמֵם (*šāmem*), GK 9037 (S 8074), 92x. *šāmēm* is used in two distinct but related ways. It can mean "to be desolate, deserted, lay waste" or it can point to the response to such desolation and mean "to shudder, be horrified, be appalled." Two-thirds of the instances of *šāmēm* occur in prophetic passages.

šāmēm most often means either causing or suffering destruction. Most occurrences denote the resulting state of desolation. Jer. compares the desolation of the land of Babylon to an empty pasture in which all of the flock, even the smallest ones, have been dragged away (Jer. 50:45). *šāmēm* is used to describe the result of God's judgment on Israel (Jer. 12:11; Ezek. 6:4; 25:3; 33:28; Amos 7:9; Mic. 6:13) and other foreign nations (Jer. 49:20; Ezek. 29:12; 30:12, 14; 32:15). For Israel, a prophecy of destruction/judgment is frequently followed by a prophecy of hope (Isa. 49:8; Jer. 33:10–11; Amos 9:14). Ezekiel writes that God will cleanse (i.e., forgive) Israel's sins, restore her to her land, and make the desolate land like the garden of Eden (36:33–36).

In a few instances, people are described as desolate (2 Sam. 13:20; Job 16:7; Lam. 1:13,16). Isaiah equates the desolate woman with one who is barren (Isa. 54:1). Also, in a unique but very important way, Daniel uses *šāmēm* to describe the "abomination that desolates" (Dan. 8:13; 11:31; 12:11), a reference that Jesus cites in the NT (cf. Mk. 13:14). See *NIDOTTE*, 4:167-71.

New Testament

Noun and Adjective: ἔρημος (*erēmos*), GK *2245* (S *2048*), 48x. In the NT, *erēmos* is used both as an adjective and a noun. As an adjective, it can mean "barren" or "desolate." Paul uses *erēmos* in Gal. 4:27 (quoting Isa. 54:1) to refer to a "barren" woman; this is the only use in the NT with this sense. The rest of the NT uses of the adjective describe a desolate or secluded place. Jesus foresees that Jerusalem will be judged and left desolate (Mt. 23:38; cf. Acts 1:20). Jesus is said to withdraw to a secluded place to pray after having heard of John the Baptist's death (Mt. 14:13; Mk. 1:35 and Lk. 5:16 show that this practice was not uncommon for Jesus). It is in fact the desolateness of the place that occasions the need for food and Jesus' miraculous feeding of the multitudes (Mt. 14:15ff.).

DESOLATION

Old Testament

Noun: שְׁמָמָה (*šᵉmāmâ*), GK 9039 (S 8077), 56x. *šᵉmāmâ* conveys the divine destruction of peoples, cities, lands, and idols and may be translated "desolate, "desolation, wasteland." The term is found almost exclusively in prophetic texts to describe the state of an object (land, people, city) resulting from a prolonged exile and the removal of covenant blessing (Isa. 6:11; 64:10; Jer. 10:22; Ezek. 6:14). Mic. 7:13 declares, "The earth will become *desolate* because of its inhabitants, as the result of their deeds." The term portrays the sense of permanent and extreme damage, similar to the lingering and deadly effects of radiation from a nuclear accident. This sense is captured by the verb form *šāmēm* (GK 9037), which can mean both "to be desolate" and "to be astonished, horrified." See *NIDOTTE*, 4:167-71.

DESPISE

Old Testament

Verb: מָאַס (*māʾas*), GK 4415 (S

3988a), 74x. *mā'as*, usually translated "to reject" and occasionally "to despise" (usually in noncovenant contexts), expresses the action of rejecting someone or something (see *reject*). For example, Job "despises" his life (Job 7:16, 9:21) and is "despised" by others (19:18); ultimately, Job simply "despises" or "rejects" (42:6; likely he rejects his declaration made in ignorance, see 42:3). Additionally, Israel is encouraged not to "despise" God's discipline (Prov. 3:11; cf. Job 5:17) because the one who ignores discipline "despises" himself (Prov. 15:32).

Verb: קָלַל (*qālal*), GK 7837 (S 7043), 82x. *qālal* means "to curse," though the term can more generally be used in the context of "despising" someone. See *curse*.

Verb: שָׂנֵא (*śānē'*), GK 8533 (S 8130), 148x. Usually translated "to hate," *śānē'* refers to varying levels of dislike toward someone or something (see *hate*). This abhorrence can be toward another man or woman. For example, Jacob despises his wife Leah (Gen. 29:31). God too despises—for example, the routine, religious feasts of his people (Amos 5:21).

New Testament

Verb: ἐξουθενέω (*exoutheneō*), GK *2024* (S *1848*), 11x. *exoutheneō* essentially means "to hold someone in contempt, ridicule, despise" (Rom. 14:3; Gal. 4:14). See *look down on*.

DESTROY

Old Testament

Verb: אָבַד (*'ābad*), GK 6 (S 6), 185x. *'ābad* means "to perish, destroy, demolish, become lost." It has a variety of uses in the OT. See *perish*.

Verb: חָרַם (*ḥāram*), GK 3049 (S 2763), 50x. *ḥāram* has the basic meaning "to destroy, banish, or devote to the ban." It describes the consecration of someone or something as a permanent offering to God.

This word is used most often to designate cities that are to be utterly destroyed. This involves the total annihilation of the human and animal population and the burning of all items not given over in consecration to God. On several occasions, God commands Israel to destroy the cities of Canaan and other neighboring nations (Num. 21:2–3; Deut. 2:34; Jos. 8:26), but there are also instances of foreign nations following the practice (2 Ki. 19:11; 2 Chr. 20:23; Dan. 11:44). Isaiah writes that Yahweh has devoted the foreign nations to the ban (Isa. 34:2). These nations are devoted to the ban because of their sin: prolonged immoral and idolatrous practices and hostility against God and his people (cf. Gen. 15:16; Deut. 7:4–5, 25–26; 9:5).

Certain items, often taken from cities devoted to the ban, are described as *ḥāram* in that they are considered holy to Yahweh. Among these are tithes (Lev. 27:28), the unjust gain of other nations (Mic. 4:13), and treasures (Josh. 6:19). Sometimes the priest's portion of the offering is also described by *ḥāram* (Num. 18:14; Ezek. 44:29).

Both of these nuances are portrayed in Joshua's description of the story of Jericho's fall. God declares Jericho to be a devoted city—all that are in it belong to God. The Israelites are strictly charged to keep themselves from the devoted things of the city (Jos. 6:17-18), and the articles of gold, silver, bronze, and iron are devoted to the treasury of God (6:19). Most of the people follow this order closely (6:21), but Achan takes some of the devoted things (7:1). As a result, God temporarily devotes Israel to the ban (7:11–12) and allows them to be defeated by Ai until Achan is punished and the items he took are destroyed.

ḥāram is occasionally used of punishment on individuals. This punishment can be severe as in an execution (Exod. 22:20) or less severe as in the forfeiture of property (Ezr. 10:8). See *NIDOTTE* 2:276-77.

Verb: כָּלָה (*kālâ*), GK 3983 (S 3615), 207x. Often rendered "to complete, finish, destroy," *kālâ* expresses the basic idea of bringing a process to completion. The process may involve adding something until an object is full or an activity complete (see *complete*), or it may involve taking something away until there is nothing left.

In contexts where *kālâ* denotes completion by subtraction, the verb often expresses the notion of using up, destroying, or consuming. Like grass that "withers" (Isa. 15:6; 32:10), a person's strength (Isa. 49:4) and days can be "spent" (Job 7:6). Both spirit and soul "faint" because of separation from God (Ps. 84:2; 119:81; 143:7). And the violent destruction often associated with war "consumes" both people and land (Deut. 7:22; 1 Sam. 15:18; Jer. 16:4). The Bible teaches that all who forsake the Lord will be consumed (Isa. 1:28), including scorners (Isa. 29:20), the wicked (Ps. 37:20), and all God's enemies (Ps. 18:37). In such destruction, God's wrath is "accomplished" (RSV "completed," Ezek. 5:13; 7:8) both on the nations (Canaanites, Deut. 7:22; Amalekites, 1 Sam. 15:18; and Syrians, 2 Ki. 13:17) and on unfaithful Israel (Jos. 24:20; Jer. 5:3; Ezek. 22:31).

Verb: כָּרַת (*kārat*), GK 4162 (S 3772), 289x. *kārat* broadly means "to cut (objects), exclude and/or destroy, make a covenant." While these three basic meanings seem divergent, they are closely linked together around the notion of cutting. See *exclude*; see also *make a covenant*; *cut*.

Verb: נָכָה (*nākâ*), GK 5782 (S 5221), 501x. The verb *nākâ* generally means "to strike down, destroy, hit, kill." See *strike*.

Verb: שָׁחַת (*šāḥat*), GK 8845 (S 7843), 152x. In various contexts, *šāḥat* can broadly mean "to corrupt, destroy, ruin, spoil, wipe out." It denotes the corrupting or destroying of a wide variety of physical things, including eyes (Exod. 21:26), vineyards (Jer. 12:10), buildings (Lam. 2:6), crops (Jdg. 6:4), trees (Deut. 20:19–20), semen (Gen. 38:9), and kings (1 Sam. 26:15). It is also used to describe the corruption of morals (Prov. 6:32; Deut. 4:16; 31:29). This type of moral corruption is what prompts God to send the flood (Gen. 6:11–12). David associates *šāḥat* with the fool who denies the existence of God and does abominable deeds (Ps. 14:1).

Perhaps because of the variety of ways in which *šāḥat* can be used, the OT incorporates it into passages dealing with divine judgment. It is used of God's judgment against all the earth (Gen. 6:13,17; 9:11,15), nations and cities (Jer. 51:11; Ezek. 26:4), and groups of people (e.g., Exod. 12:23 uses it to describe the messenger who slays the firstborn of Egypt.). Sodom and Gomorrah serve as examples of the severity of this destruction. God rains down fire and brimstone, which overthrows the city and all forms of life within it (Gen. 13:10; 19:13–14, 29; cf. vv. 23–25). However, God never completely destroys his own people. This is partly due to intercession on their behalf (Deut. 10:10) and their repentance (2 Chr. 12:7) but mainly due to his faithful love that does not fail like human love (Hos. 11:9). See *NIDOTTE*, 4:92-93.

Verb: שָׁדַד (*šādad*), GK 8720 (S 7703), 59x. *šādad* generally means "to destroy, devastate." It occurs in passages dealing with violent destruction. For example, the predicted destruction of Jerusalem is compared to the *šādad* that a wolf from the desert would cause (Jer. 5:6). *šādad* can be applied to inanimate objects, as where Hosea predicts how the Lord will destroy Israel's sacred pillars (Hos. 10:2) and Ephraim's fortresses (10:14). More often, however, it is applied to God's judgment on peoples such as the Philistines (Jer. 47:4), Egyptians (Ezek. 32:12), and Babylonians (Ps. 137:8). God will destroy individuals who plot out evil and oppress others (Mic. 2:4; cf. vv. 1–3). Joel also uses *šādad* to describe the calamitous Day of the Lord (Joel 1:15; cf. Isa. 13:6). See *NIDOTTE*, 4:48-49.

Verb: שָׁמַד (*šāmad*), GK 9012 (S 8045), 90x. *šāmad* (occurring mostly in the Heb. Hiphil verb form) means "to destroy, exterminate, or annihilate" and expresses the partial or complete destruction of a group of people. It is closely related to, and often appears with, the root *šḥt*, "to destroy, perish, ruin." In certain contexts, *šāmad* is used with reference to the conquest and complete destruction

(*ʿābad*) of the Canaanites when Israel was commanded to occupy the land of promise. Although *šāmad* can denote human action (2 Sam. 14:7, 11, 16; Est. 3:6, 13; Jos. 7:12), it usually refers to divine action on a nation or other group of people. Many times *šāmad* describes the destruction that God brings on the inhabitants of Canaan (Deut. 2:22; 12:30; 33:27). This destruction, in which God delivered them over to Israel, throws them into confusion, wipes their names from under heaven (7:23–24), and causes a great fear to come upon the people of Canaan (Jos. 9:24). God also promises future judgment against the nations (Jer. 48:8; Zech. 12:9).

Though *šāmad* signifies the complete destruction of the nations, God will not completely destroy his people (Amos 9:8). He knows that Israel will quickly rebel in the promised land and must be destroyed because of it (Deut. 28:20). This destruction involves being scattered among the nations, being made few in number, and being given over to serve other gods. In the end, however, the mercy and compassion of God will triumph as he spares a remnant and brings back a people for himself (Deut. 4:26, 31; cf. 28:15–28). See *NIDOTTE* 4:151-52.

Verb: תָּמַם (*tāmam*), GK 9462 (S 8552), 64x. *tāmam* is used for a wide range of ideas having to do with ending, completion, or even destruction. See *end*.

New Testament

Verb: ἀπόλλυμι (*apollymi*), GK *660* (S *622*), 90x. *apollymi* means "to destroy, perish, lose." See *lose*.

Verb: διαφθείρω (*diaphtheirō*) GK 1425 (S 1311), 6x. *diaphtheirō* means "to corrupt, destroy." See *corrupt, corruption*

Verb: καταλύω (*katalyō*), GK *2907* (S *2647*), 17x. *katalyō* denotes the broad idea of loosening, severing, breaking, or putting down, and may best be translated "destroy" or "abolish." Sometimes the prefix *kata* ("down") combines with a verb to give a more intensive sense, such as "to utterly destroy" (e.g., Mt. 24:2; Lk. 21:6). More common, however, is the basic sense of "to destroy" (Mk. 14:58; Gal. 2:18). Paul uses this sense to contrast the fragility of life with the durability of God's kingdom when he writes, "Now we know that if the earthly tent we live in is *destroyed*, we have a building from God, an eternal house in heaven, not built by human hands" (2 Cor. 5:1). Jesus contrasts his ministry of fulfilling the OT teachings with the idea of invalidating them: "Do not think that I have come to *abolish* the Law or the Prophets; I have not come to *abolish* them but to fulfill them" (Mt. 5:17). The less common meaning of "to lodge" occurs in Lk. 9:12; 19:7. See *NIDNTT-A*, 346-48.*

Verb: καταργέω (*katargeō*), GK *2934* (S *2673*), 27x. *katargeō* means "to release, destroy, nullify, cause something to be useless." In the parable of the fig tree in Lk. 13:7 it has non-metaphorical meaning, namely, "to use up the soil." Most other references are in Pauline texts and bear a theological message.

In Rom. 7:2 *katargeō* is used for the release of someone from an obligation; that is, a woman "is released" from the law of marriage after her husband's death. Similarly, it describes our "release" from the law once we come to serve in the new way of the Spirit (7:6).

Paul also uses *katargeō* to refer to that which causes something to lose its power or effectiveness. "*Will* their lack of faith *nullify* God's faithfulness?" (Rom. 3:3; also see 3:31; 4:14). In a passage that drips with paradox, Paul says that the community of the cross is populated mainly with the "nothings" of this world—the foolish, the weak, and the lowly (1 Cor. 1:26–31). Ironically, God uses these people "to *nullify* the things that are." That is, God uses the "nots" to *nullify* the "ares." Surprisingly, God presents Jesus on the cross as his main "nothing" (see cf. Phil. 2:5–11).

A final nuance of *katargeō* takes on an end-times twist. It goes beyond rendering something ineffective to causing it to come to an end. Building on the last passage, the apostle refers to end-time repercussions for the "wisdom of this age or of the rulers of this age, who *are coming to nothing*" (1 Cor. 2:6). Later, Paul uses it to depict God's "destroying" both stomach and food (6:13) and his "bringing to an end all dominion, authority, and power" (15:24). Rom. 6:6 uses this verb to refer to the "doing away with" our sinful bodies, which amounts to liberation from enslavement to sin. While sin has lost its ability to overpower, it has not lost its ability to deceive. So, the destruction of the flesh is "already" but "not yet" fully realized, which will happen in eternity. The only non-Pauline use of this verb refers to the "destruction" of the devil, the one who has the power of death (Heb. 2:14). See *NIDNTT-A*, 296.

Verb: λύω (*lyō*), GK *3395* (S *3089*), 42x. *lyō* means "to loose, untie" (see *loose*), but also "break, destroy." In Acts 27:41, the stern of the ship is "broken to pieces" in the high seas. See *break*.

Verb: φθείρω (*phtheirō*) GK *5780* (S *5351*), 9x. *phtheirō* means "to corrupt, destroy."

DESTRUCTION

Old Testament

Adjective or Noun: רַע (or רָע) (*ra*ʿ [or *rā*ʿ]), GK 8273 (S 7451), 312x. In most contexts, *ra*ʿ is translated "evil, wicked" (e.g., Gen. 13:13). As a noun, it sometimes denotes destruction (e.g., Deut. 30:15). See *evil*.

New Testament

Noun: ἀπώλεια (*apōleia*), GK *724* (S *684*), 18x. *apōleia* means "destruction, ruin, waste." It refers to either the destruction that one causes or the destruction that one experiences. (1) The term can have the meaning of the destruction that one causes, "destruction, waste." The disciples wonder why the woman anointing Jesus' head would waste such a valuable commodity: "Why this *waste*?" (Mt. 26:8; Mk. 14:3).

(2) *apōleia* can also mean the destruction that one experiences as a result of divine wrath. The broad path leads to this ruined state (Mt. 7:13; cf. 1 Tim. 6:9). It is the certain destiny of false teachers (2 Pet. 2:1, 3; 3:16). The one who metes out this ruin is God himself: "What if God, choosing to show his wrath and make his power known, bore with great patience the objects of his wrath—prepared for *destruction*?" (Rom. 9:22). The betrayer (Judas) was bound for this end (Jn. 17:12). Such destruction is the eternal destiny both of ungodly humans (Acts 8:20; Phil. 3:19; 2 Pet. 3:7) and of the devil and his minions (2 Thess. 2:3; Rev. 17:8, 11). The destruction of the wicked is contrasted with the salvation of God's people: "This is a sign to them that they will be *destroyed*, but that you will be saved—and that by God" (Phil. 1:28; cf. Heb. 10:39). See *NIDNTT-A*, 68.*

Noun: φθορά (*phthora*) GK *5785* (S 5356), 9x. *phthora* means "corruption, destruction." See *corrupt, corruption*.

DETERMINE

New Testament

Verb: διακρίνω (*diakrinō*), GK *1359* (S *1252*), 19x. *diakrinō* means "to judge, distinguish, evaluate." When applied to oneself, it can mean to "doubt" or "waver." See *judge*.

Verb: κρίνω (*krinō*), GK *3212* (S *2919*), 114x. *krinō* essentially means "to consider, decide, judge," though it has a variety of nuances. See *judge*.

Verb: ὁρίζω (*horizo*), GK *3988* (S *3724*), 8x. *horizō* means "to appoint, set" and occurs most often in Luke and Acts. See *appoint*.

Verb: προορίζω (*proorizō*), GK *4633* (S *4309*), 6x. *proorizō* means "to predestine; choose, determine, set apart beforehand." See *predestine*.

Old Testament

Noun: תּוֹעֵבָה (*tô*ʿ*ēbâ*), GK 9359 (S 8441), 118x. Regularly translated "detestable thing, repulsive thing, abomination," *tô*ʿ*ēbâ* generally denotes persons or actions that are morally or religiously offensive, especially to God. Idolatry, for example, is an abomination to the Lord (Deut. 7:25; 32:6; Jer. 16:18; Mal. 2:11).

In the Pentateuch, *tô*ʿ*ēbâ* is often used in the context of Israel's special relationship to God. Accordingly, Israel was to be set apart from the foreign nations who had practiced detestable ways (Lev. 18:26–27; Deut. 7:25–26; 12:31). Thus, forty years after the exodus from Egypt when Israel was preparing finally to enter the promised land, Moses instructed the people: "When you enter the land the Lord your God is giving you, do not learn to imitate the detestable ways of the nations there" (Deut. 18:9).

The covenant relationship between God and Israel becomes pivotal in the prophetic and wisdom literature. Over 40x in Ezek. alone the Lord declares Judah's wickedness as *tôʿēbâ.* Specifically, on account of Judah's blatant idolatry (Ezek. 5:9; 7:20; 11:18, 21; 16:36) and evil deeds (5:11; 6:9, 11; 7:3–4, 8:6–17; 16:43–58; 44:6–7) God declares: "Repent! Turn from your idols and renounce all your detestable practices!" (14:6).

Similarly, some 21x in Prov. the sage declares certain things that the Lord abhors. Prov. 6:16–19 lists seven in a row: "haughty eyes, a lying tongue, hands that shed innocent blood, a heart that devises wicked plans, feet that run rapidly to evil, a false witness that utters lies, and one who nurtures strife among brothers." Other texts stress the abominable nature of dishonesty (11:1), lying lips (12:22), the sacrifices and ways of the wicked (15:8–9), and all who are perverse or arrogant (3:32; 16:5). Even prayer is loathsome when it comes from one who refuses to heed God's law (28:9). See *NIDOTTE*, 5:314-18.

DEVASTATE

Old Testament

Verb: שָׁדַד (*šādad*), GK 8720 (S 7703), 59x. *šādad* generally means "to destroy, devastate." See *destroy.*

DEVIL

New Testament

Noun: διάβολος (*diabolos*), GK *1333* (S *1228*), 37x. *diabolos* is a literal, evil being, viciously opposed to God and to his children (Rev. 12:17). The word means "slanderer" or "accuser." It is sometimes used in this general sense. Paul notes that in the last days people will be "without love, unforgiving, *slanderous*" (2 Tim. 3:3). Likewise, Paul admonishes the older women in the church "not to be *slanderers* or addicted to much wine" (Tit. 2:3; cf. also 1 Tim. 3:11).

However, 33x in the NT *diabolos* refer to a literal, evil being—"the devil" (see *Satan* for his other titles). "The devil" appears to be more of a title for the diabolical creature, while "Satan" is his personal name. Both Jesus and John are clear "the devil" was in the serpent in Eden (Jn. 8:44; Rev. 12:9; 20:2). Various attributes of the devil are brought to the surface in the NT: he is a tempter (Mt. 4:1ff.), a liar and murderer (Jn. 8:44), a betrayer (Jn. 13:2), a perpetual sinner (1 Jn. 3:8), full of hate (1 Pet. 5:8; 1 Jn. 3:10), and conceited (1 Tim. 3:6). Those who live in this same manner are considered "his children" (Jn. 8:44; Acts 13:10; 1 Jn. 3:10).

The works of the devil are always painful and many times subtle. He longs to bring suffering on believers—prison and persecution, "even to the point of death" (Rev. 2:10; 12:17). He is a devious schemer (Acts 13:10; Eph. 6:11; 1 Tim. 3:7; 2 Tim. 2:26), who sneaks enemies of the gospel into the church (Mt. 13:39) and snatches the gospel from some who hear it (Lk. 8:12). He claims to hold all the authority of the kingdoms of the world and is able to give it to whomever he desires (Lk. 4:6), but while he is called "the ruler of this world" (Jn. 16:11) and "the prince of the power of the air" (Eph. 2:2), it is really God who gives the kings and kingdoms their authority (Jn. 19:11; Rom. 13:2; cf. Isa. 37:16; Jer. 18:7–10). His rule is over unbelievers (Acts 10:38; 26:18), holding them in captivity to do his will (2 Tim. 2:26). The devil can prompt people to sin, even people close to Jesus (Jn. 13:2).

But Jesus has appeared in order to "destroy the devil's work" (1 Jn. 3:8), through death destroying even "him who holds the power of death—that is, the devil" (Heb. 2:14; cf. Rev. 12:11). The devil's downfall is so sure that there is already a place prepared for his eternal destruction by fire and sulfur (Mt. 25:41; Rev. 20:10). Believers should exercise self-control and alertness in order to stand against the devil (1 Pet. 5:8). "Resisting" the devil will cause him to flee (Jas. 4:7), and not sinning out of anger will keep the devil from having "a place" in our lives (Eph. 4:27). Putting on "the full armor of God" enables us to take a stand in the face of the schemes of the devil (Eph. 6:11). Jesus' followers are to pray to the Father for deliverance from "the evil one" (Mt. 6:13). Regardless of the devil's claims to his rightful authority, Jesus boldly states after his resurrection from the dead, "All authority in heaven and on earth has been given to me" (Mt. 28:18). See *NIDNTT-A*, 133-34.

DEVOTE TO THE BAN

Old Testament

Verb: חָרַם (*ḥāram*), GK 3049 (S 2763), 50x. *ḥāram* has the basic meaning "to destroy, banish, or devote to the ban." It describes the consecration of someone or something as a permanent offering to God. See *destroy*.

(BE) DEVOTED TO

New Testament

Verb: προσκαρτερέω (*proskartereō*), GK *4674* (S *4342*), 10x. *proskartereo* is "to attend to, devote oneself to" with regularity and steadfastness. For example, the disciples (Acts 6:4) and women (1:14) of the early church devote themselves steadfastly to prayer. See *attend to*.

DEVOTION

New Testament

Noun: εὐσέβεια (*eusebeia*), GK *2354* (S *2150*), 15x. *eusebeia* denotes "godliness" or a life of "devotion to God." See *godliness*.

DEVOUR

Old Testament

Verb: אָכַל (*ʾākal*) GK 430 (S 398), 820x. The basic meaning of *ʾākal* is "to eat," but it often means "to consume, devour." See *eat*.

New Testament

Verb: κατεσθίω (*katesthiō*), GK *2983* (S *2719*), 14x. *katesthiō* means "to devour, eat up." It is a compound word; *kata* (GK *2848*) is an emphatic form that intensifies the more general *esthiō* (GK *2266*), "to eat." This verb can refer to devouring something, as when the birds eat up the seed scattered along the path (Mt. 13:4). It can also carry the meaning of completely destroying something (Rev. 11:5, fire "devouring" enemies; cf. 20:9), wasting something (Lk. 15:30, the father's property), robbing someone (20:47, widows' houses), partisan backbiting (Gal. 5:5), or exploiting someone (2 Cor. 11:20). See also *eat*.

DIE

Old Testament

Verb: מוּת (*mût*), GK 4637 (S 4191, 4192), 854x. *mût* means "to die, put to death, kill." It occurs hundreds of times in the OT for natural death, whether it occurs naturally as a result of old age (Deut. 34:5, 7) or violently as a result of war (2 Sam. 1:4) or some other human activity (1 Ki. 2:25). In the Hiphil verb stem, this word means "to cause to die," in other words, "to kill."

This word first appears in Gen. 2:17, when God says to Adam that if he eats of the tree of knowledge of good and evil, he "*will surely die*." This death involves more than simply physical death, for when Adam and Eve did eat of that tree, they did not die physically on that day, but they did experience the beginning of stages of death (3:19b). In a number of OT passages, death is directly linked with sin (e.g., Ezek. 3:18–20; 18:20). Moreover, the NT makes it plain that Adam died spiritually on the day of his first sin (cf. Rom. 5:12–18). Thus, death is unnatural in the human race in the sense that it was not God's original design for those whom he created in his own image. It is perhaps for this reason that the psalmist says, "It is not *the dead* who praise the LORD" (Ps. 115:17); in the OT the grave is not a place where there is a consciousness of God (see also *grave*).

Life and death are in the hands of the Lord—as Hannah sings in her song, "The Lord *brings death* and makes alive" (1 Sam. 2:6). The writer of Ecclesiastes also acknowledges that there is "a time to be born and a time to die" (Eccl. 3:2), and the Lord is involved in this process. Many times in the OT death comes as a direct result of the judgment of the Lord, either among the enemies of Israel (Isa. 37:36) or among God's people themselves (Jer. 42:22). And while in much of the OT there is little concept of life after death and of the resurrection of the dead, by the time God's progressive revelation reaches the latter parts of the OT, there is a clear reference to a doctrine of the resurrection (see especially Dan. 12:2). Death will be conquered. See also *death*. See *NIDOTTE*, 2:886–88.

Verb: נָפַל (*nāpal*), GK 5877 (S 5307), 435x. *nāpal* generally indicates the simple action of falling. In over one-quarter of its occurrences, *nāpal* occurs in military contexts, simply meaning "to die," but translated "to fall." Deborah's song makes the connection between "falling" and "dying" explicit: Sisera "falls" at Jael's feet, "dead" (Jdg. 5:27, 3x). The phrase "to *fall* by the sword" occurs some 38x in the OT. See *fall*.

New Testament

Verb: ἀποθνῄσκω (*apothnēskō*), GK *633* (S *599*), 111x. The basic sense of this verb is "to die." This dying has at least three different nuances in the NT: physical death, supernatural death, and threatened death. (1) *apothnēskō* can refer to the physical death of living beings on earth. This verb is often used for the cessation of human life (Mt. 9:24; 22:24, 27; Mk. 5:35, 39; 9:26; Lk. 8:42, 52; Rom. 7:2; Phil. 1:21; Heb. 9:27). It is used especially in reference to Christ's death (Rom. 5:8; 14:15; 1 Cor. 15:3; 2 Cor. 5:14; 1 Thess. 5:10; 1 Pet. 3:18). "Pilate was surprised to hear that [Jesus] *was* already *dead*. Summoning the centurion, he asked him if Jesus *had* already *died*" (Mk. 15:44).

(2) Supernatural death is death in a transcendent sense. There are at least three kinds of supernatural deaths: death as a loss of eternal life, death as a believer's mystical union with Christ, and death as a separator from elements other than physical life. (a) In the first sense, death is represented as not receiving eternal life. "For if you live according to the sinful nature, *you will die*" (Rom. 8:13). "I am going away, and you will look for me, and *you will die* in your sin" (Jn. 8:21). "Once I was alive apart from law; but when the commandment came, sin sprang to life and *I died*. I found that the very commandment that was intended to bring life actually *brought death*" (Rom. 7:9–10). (b) In the second sense, believers are described as having died with Christ in a mystical union. "Now if we *died* with Christ, we believe that we will also live with him" (Rom. 6:8; cf. 2 Cor. 5:14; Col. 3:3). (c) In the third sense, death separates someone from a person or a thing. "We *died* to sin" (Rom. 6:2; cf. 7:6). "For through the law I *died* to the law so that I might live for God" (Gal. 2:19). "You *died* … to the basic principles of this world" (Col. 2:20).

(3) Finally, *apothnēskō* also refers to threatened death in the sense that one is faced with the prospect of death or the realization of one's mortality; "to be about to die, face death, be mortal." Paul writes, "I die every day" (1 Cor. 15:31). Paul commends himself as "dying" while yet living (2 Cor. 6:9). The mortality of a priest who "dies" is compared to the immortality of another, even Jesus, who is a priest forever after the order of Melchizedek (Heb. 7:8). See *NIDNTT-A*, 236-38.

Verb: τελευτάω (*teleutaō*) GK *5462* (S *5053*), 11x. *teleutaō* simply means "to come to an end, die." It describes the passing of named people such as Jacob (Acts 7:15), David (2:29), Lazarus (Jn. 11:39), Herod (Mt. 2:19), and the approaching death of Joseph (Heb. 11:22), but also unnamed people such as a ruler's daughter (Mt. 9:18) and the impending death of a centurion's sick servant (Lk. 7:2). Other uses of *teleutaō* for people who died include those in the story of the Sadducees' challenge to Jesus concerning the resurrection (Mt. 22:23), Jesus' description of the worm of hell that "never dies" (Mk. 9:48), and the punishment cited in the OT for reviling one's father and mother (quoted in Mt. 15:4). Note, however, that death magnifies the work of Jesus Christ, since Lazarus and the ruler's daughter were just as dead as either Jacob or David, but the Lord of glory raised them up. See *NIDNTT-A*, 63.

DIFFER

New Testament

Verb: διαφέρω (*diapherō*), GK *1422* (S *1308*), 13x. The intransitive form of *diapherō* means "to have value, be valuable, differ." See *have value*.

DIFFICULT

Old Testament

Verb: פָּלָא (*pālā*ʾ), GK 7098 (S 6381), 71x. In its participle form, *pālā*ʾ means "miracles, wonders," and refers to the extraordinary deeds of God (see *wonders*). Sometimes it points to the wondrous nature of activities or ideas that are beyond one's abilities to do. Cases too "difficult" for local judges are to be taken to the "supreme court" at the central sanctuary (Deut. 17:8), and Moses tells the people that the commandment he proclaims is not "too difficult" for them (Deut. 30:11). Nothing is "too hard" for God to perform (Gen. 18:14; see too Jer. 32:17, 27).

DIGNITY

See *glory*.

DILIGENCE

New Testament

Verb: σπουδάζω (*spoudazō*), GK *5079* (S *4704*), 11x. *spoudazō* generally indicates to strive to give one's best effort to do something. See *make effort*.

Noun: σπουδή (*spoudē*), GK *5082* (S *4710*), 12x. *spoudē* means "earnestness, eagerness, concern." See *earnestness*.

DIRECT

New Testament

Verb: διατάσσω (*diatassō*), GK *1411* (S *1299*), 16x. *diatassō* means "to command, direct, order." See *command*.

DIRECTOR OF MUSIC

Old Testament

Verb: נָצַח (*nāṣaḥ*), GK 5904 (S 5329), 65x. While the noun *nēṣaḥ* most regularly means "duration," the verb bears a similar meaning in only Jer. 8:5, where it refers to "*perpetual* backsliding." In every other occurrence, *nāṣaḥ* designates the activity of oversight or, more commonly, the role of "supervisor."

In the OT, two distinct supervisory activities or roles are designated by *nāṣaḥ*. The first is noted in Ezra, where the Levites are appointed as supervisors of the temple restoration (Ezr. 3:8–9; see also 1 Chr. 23:4; 2 Chr. 2:1, 17; 34:12–13). The second and much more common oversight activity/role is that associated with the music of Israel's worship. The title "director of music" or "choir master" (i.e., the ptc. form of *nāṣaḥ*) is found in roughly one-third of the psalm titles (e.g., Ps. 8; 22; 51; 68; 139; 140) and is additionally mentioned in Hab. 3:19 and 1 Chr. 15:21 in association with the reestablishing of the worship of the true God.

Far from being an afterthought, worshiping God through music was an essential element in Israel's worship, especially when the proper worship of God in the temple was being restored. This made the role of the music supervisor important. In Christian worship services today, the role of the director of music is no less significant, for the singing of praises remains an essential part of worship (Eph. 5:19; Col. 3:16; Jas. 5:13), as we await the day when we will sing with all the saints praises to our God (Rev. 5:9; 14:3; 15:3). "Praise the LORD; sing to the LORD a new song, his praise in the assembly of the saints" (Ps. 149:1). See *NIDOTTE*, 3:138-39.

DIRT

Old Testament

Noun: עָפָר (*ʿāpār*), GK 6760 (S 6083), 55x. *ʿāpār* refers to fine, dry dirt. In Ps. 18:42, David declares that he ground his enemies "like *dust* before the wind." Note that in the Middle East, the ground or dirt is mostly dry dust. See *dust*.

DISAPPEAR

New Testament

Verb: παρέρχομαι (*parerchomai*), GK *4216* (S *3928*), 29x. *parerchomai* means "to pass by or alongside" and is often translated as "pass away, disappear." See *pass by*.

DISAPPOINT

New Testament

Verb: καταισχύνω (*kataischynō*), GK *2875* (S *2617*), 13x. *kataischynō* means "to embarrass, be ashamed, disappoint." See *embarrass*.

DISASTER

Old Testament

Noun: אָוֶן (*ʾāwen*), GK 224 (S 205), 81x. *ʾāwen* refers, in general, to evil, sin, or wickedness. It may also describe the punishment or disaster that befalls those who practice wickedness. See *evil*.

Noun: רָעָה (*rāʿâ*), GK 8288 (S 7465), 354x. At the heart of *rāʿâ*, lies the idea of badness, whether physical or moral. When used in the physical sense, it is often translated "calamity, disaster, harm, trouble." See *evil*.

Adjective or Noun: רַע (or רָע) (*raʿ* [or *rāʿ*]), GK 8273 (S 7451), 312x. In most contexts, *raʿ* is translated "evil, wicked" (e.g., Gen. 13:13). As a noun, it sometimes denotes disaster (e.g., 1 Ki. 5:4; Ps. 140:11; Isa. 3:11; 31:2). See *evil*.

DISBELIEVE

See *(be) unbelieving*.

DISCERN

Old Testament

Verb: בִּין (*bîn*), GK 1067 (S 995), 171x. *bîn* is most commonly found in the wisdom literature, especially Job and Proverbs. It is sometimes used in the general sense of "to know" (Prov. 24:12; Mic. 4:12), but more often refers to a technical, detailed, or specific understanding. Alternate translations such as "perceive, discern" may more readily capture the nuance of the term. See *understand*.

New Testament

Verb: διακρίνω (*diakrinō*), GK *1359* (S *1252*), 19x. *diakrinō* means "to judge, distinguish, evaluate." When applied to oneself, it can mean to "doubt" or "waver." See *judge*.

Verb: δοκιμάζω (*dokimazō*), GK *1507* (S *1381*), 22x. *dokimazō* means to "test, discern, approve." See *test*.

DISCIPLE

New Testament

Noun: μαθητής (*mathētēs*), GK *3412* (S *3101*), 261x. In general *mathētēs* means a "learner, disciple." In the NT this term becomes almost a technical term for the followers of Jesus, though is used also of the followers of John the Baptist, of Moses, and even of the Pharisees.

(1) As did many respected Jewish teachers in NT times, John the Baptist had a loyal following of disciples who remained near him during his imprisonment (Mt. 1:2) and later buried his body (Mk. 6:29). John had taught them to pray (Lk. 11:2) and fast (Mk. 2:18), and they occasionally were engaged in controversy with other Jews (Jn. 3:25). Jesus' first two disciples at one time were among John's disciples (Jn. 1:25–42). The Pharisees likewise had disciples who, on one occasion, were sent to test Jesus (Mt. 22:16). They too fasted, like the disciples of John the Baptist (Mk. 2:18).

(2) The most frequent use of *mathētēs* refers to Jesus' twelve "disciples." Typically in the Jewish world, a disciple would voluntarily join a school or otherwise seek out a master rabbi; however, Jesus seeks out and chooses those whom he wants as his disciples (Mk. 1:17; 2:14; Lk. 5:1–11; cf. Mt. 4:18–21). A dedicated disciple was generally expected someday to become a rabbi himself, yet Jesus teaches his disciples that he will always be their rabbi and they will have a lifetime of discipleship (Mt. 23:8; cf. 10:24–25, 37; Lk. 14:26–27; Jn. 11:16). Jesus' disciples are bound to him and to God's will (Mt. 12:46–50; cf.

Mk. 3:31–45). They are called to a lifetime of work and service (Mt. 16:15–19; Mk. 1:17; Lk. 5:10), including proclaiming the good news of the kingdom (Mt. 10:24–25; 16:24–25; Mk. 6:7-12). But in the NT they characteristically fail to grasp both Jesus' message (Mk. 4:10–11; 10:13–16, 48; 14:47) and the true nature of their own discipleship (Mk. 10:35–45). Later, however, after the outpouring of the Holy Spirit, they become apostles (see *apostle*) and spend their lives in spreading Jesus' kingdom message.

(3) *mathētēs* refers not only to the Twelve but is used of the wider circle of adherents to Jesus' message. Their lives are to be characterized by renunciation (Mt. 23:7–12), humility (18:1–4), poverty (29:23–30), readiness to suffer (10:17–33) and, most important, faith in Jesus (18:5; Jn. 2:11; 6:69; 11:45). See *NIDNTT-A*, 350-52.

DISCIPLINE

Old Testament

Noun: מוּסָר (*mûsār*), GK 4592 (S 4148), 50x. *mûsār* is used for personal instruction or correction and may be translated as "instruction, discipline, correction." It is used 31x in Proverbs. The translation "correction" or "discipline" is determined by the context. See *instruction.*

New Testament

Verb: παιδεύω (*paideuō*), GK *4084* (S *3811*), 13x. *paideuō* means "to teach, educate," but also "to chasten, punish." See *teach.*

DISCLOSE

New Testament

Verb: ἀποκαλύπτω (*apokalyptō*), GK *636* (S *601*), 26x. *apokalyptō* means In general "to reveal, disclose." See *reveal.*

Verb: ἐμφανίζω (*emphanizō*), GK *1872* (S *1718*), 10x. *emphanizō* means "to show or disclose" something previously hidden (Heb. 11:14). See *show.*

Verb: φανερόω (*phaneroō*), GK *5746* (S *5319*), 49x. *phaneroō* denotes the act of making visible or disclosing that which is not readily seen—"to show, appear, reveal." See *appear.*

(BE) DISCOURAGED

Old Testament

Verb: חָתַת (*ḥātat*), GK 3169 (S 2865), 55x. *ḥātat* is a verb that means "to be discouraged, dismayed, afraid, terrified." God frequently encourages his people not to be afraid, nor to be discouraged. "The LORD himself goes before you and will be with you; he will never leave you nor forsake you. Do not be afraid; do not *be discouraged* (Deut. 31:8, Jos. 1:9, 1 Chr. 28:20). God encourages Israel to take possession of the land, "See, the Lord your God has given you the land; go up, take possession, as the LORD, the God of your ancestors, has promised you; do not fear or *be dismayed*" (Deut. 1:21).

In contrast, the enemies of God's people terrify them during periods of weakness and defeat, as when Goliath taunts Israel and Saul and his people were "greatly afraid" (1 Sam. 17:11). Although the Lord sends his people into exile, he will extract vengeance on his enemies. In so doing he comforts his people, "have no fear, my servant Jacob, and do not be *dismayed,* O Israel; for I am going to save you from far away, and your offspring from the land of their captivity" (Jer. 46:27).

Also, God's covenant relationship requires awe, for which the Levites are commended. "My covenant with [Levi] was a covenant of life and well-being, which I gave him; this called for reverence, and he revered me and *stood in awe* of my name" (Mal. 2:5). See *NIDOTTE*, 2:331–32.

DISCOVER

New Testament

Verb: εὑρίσκω (*heuriskō*), GK *2351* (S *2147*), 176x. *heuriskō* means "to find" something either by a purposeful search or accidentally. See *find.*

DISCUSS

New Testament

Verb: διαλογίζομαι (*dialogizomai*), GK *1368* (S *1260*), 16x. *dialogizomai* means "to discuss, consider, argue" about something. It is related to the English word "dialogue" and is used only in the Synoptic Gospels. It describes a kind of thorough consideration of issues that are often of a curious or a spiritual nature. It can refer to a conversation between several parties or to the thoughts of an individual. In both cases, there is an internal aspect to the process. When it refers to an individual, it is often used of deep reflection (lit., thinking in the heart) conveyed by the English "wonder." For example, the Pharisees were wondering in their hearts about Jesus' identity after he proclaimed that the paralytic's sins were forgiven (Mk. 2:6, 8; Lk. 5:21, 22). Mary wondered about the greeting of the angel of the Lord (Lk. 1:29), and the people wondered if John was the Messiah (Lk. 3:15). See also Lk. 12:17; 20:14. See *NIDNTT-A*, 138.

Verb: συζητέω (*syzēteō*), GK *5184* (S *4802*), 10x. *syzēteō* means "to argue, discuss, debate." See *argue*.

DISCUSSION

New Testament

Noun: διαλογισμός (*dialogismos*), GK *1369* (S *1261*), 14x. *dialogismos* can refer to a discussion or personal thoughts, or even an argument between two parties (e.g., the disciples' argument over who would be greatest, Lk. 9:46; see also Phil. 2:14; 1 Tim. 2:8). It is most often used to refer to the internal thoughts of an individual or individuals. In every case, it refers to evil thoughts (Mt. 15:19; Mk. 7:21; Rom. 1:21; Jas. 2:4; see also Lk. 2:35; 1 Cor. 3:20) or to thoughts that are full of doubt (Lk. 24:38; Rom. 14:1). For example, Jesus knew the "thoughts" of the Pharisees, who thought he blasphemed when he told the paralytic his sins were forgiven (Lk. 5:22) and who thought he violated the Sabbath when he healed the man with the shriveled hand (Lk. 6:8). Jesus also knew the "thoughts" of the disciples as they argued about who was the greatest (Lk. 9:47). See *NIDNTT-A*, 138.*

DISEASE, DISEASED

Old Testament

Verb: חָלָה (*ḥālâ*), GK 2703 (S 2470), 75x. *ḥāla* describes a person who is weak, sick, ill, diseased, or wounded; it is also used to describe human frailties. See *weak*.

Noun: נֶגַע (*negaʿ*), GK 5596 (S 5061), 78x. This term generally denotes some form of "plague." It especially applies to the skin diseases that are regulated in Lev. 13–14. See *plague*.

New Testament

Noun: ἀσθένεια (*astheneia*), GK *819* (S *769*), 24x. *astheneia* means "weakness" and can also be used of a physical weakness ("sickness"). See *weakness*.

Noun: νόσος (*nosos*), GK *3798* (S *3554*), 11x. *nosos* is one of the words used to describe a "disease, illness, sickness." It can also refer to a moral sickness, but it is not used this way in the NT.

As Jesus travels from place to place, people "brought to him all who were ill with various *diseases*, those suffering severe pain, the demon-possessed, those having seizures, and the paralyzed, and he healed them" (Mt. 4:24). This healing ministry of Jesus fulfills the prophecy in Isa. 53:4 (see Mt. 8:17). Luke tells us that Jesus also gave his disciples this healing power as well: "When Jesus had called the Twelve together, he gave them power and authority to drive out all demons and to cure *diseases*" (Lk. 19:1). In Acts, we are told that God was so using Paul that "even handkerchiefs and aprons that had touched him were taken to the sick, and their *illnesses* were cured and the evil spirits left them" (Acts 19:11). See *NIDNTT-A*, 393.

DISGRACE

Old Testament

Noun: חֶרְפָּה (*ḥerpâ*), GK 3075 (S 2781), 73x. The meaning of *ḥerpâ* is "disgrace, insult, reproach, contempt." *ḥerpâ* can refer to general suffering or humiliation (1 Sam. 11:2; Neh. 2:17; Ps. 69:20), shameful behavior (Gen. 34:14), or the disgrace of an individual or nation (Ps. 31:12; Prov. 18:3). See *insult*.

DISGUISE

Old Testament

Verb: נָכַר (*nākar*), GK 5795 (S 5234), 44x. *nākar* (which occurs mostly in the Hiphil form) refers to general knowing, such as the basic awareness of another's existence or the acknowledgment of who a person is. In rare instances and forms, *nākar* appears to bear the meaning "make unrecognizable, act as a stranger, disguise oneself." See *recognize*.

DISH

Old Testament

Noun: כַּף (*kap*), GK 4090 (S 3709), 195x. This term is used to denote the "hand" as a part of the body. In ceremonial texts, *kap* often denotes "dishes," probably because the palm of the hand was used to hold or carry such items (cf. Num. 4:7). See *hand*.

DISLIKE

Old Testament

Verb: שָׂנֵא (*śānē'*), GK 8533 (S 8130), 148x. Usually translated "to hate," *śānē'* refers to varying levels of dislike toward someone or something (see *hate*). In Mal. 1:2–3 ("I have loved Jacob, but Esau I have *hated*), the prophet is emphasizing the sovereign choice of God rather than an intense emotion of dislike for Esau.

(BE) DISMAYED

Old Testament

Verb: חָתַת (*ḥātat*), GK 3169 (S 2865), 55x. *ḥātat* is a verb that means "to be discouraged, dismayed, afraid, terrified." See *(be) discouraged*.

DISOBEY

New Testament

Verb: ἀπειθέω (*apeitheō*), GK *578* (S *544*), 14x. *apeitheō* means "to disobey, be disobedient, reject, refuse to believe." This is a compound Greek verb *peithō*, "to trust in, obey," with the prefix *a*, which indicates negation—thus, "disobey." The term is used with reference to all sinners in Rom. 2:8; the wilderness generation in Heb. 3:18; unbelieving Jews in Acts 14:2 and Rom. 15:31; Gentiles in Rom. 11:30 and Heb. 11:31; and the flood generation in 1 Pet. 3:20. Disobedience is identified as toward the Son (Jn. 3:36), the message about Jesus (1 Pet. 2:8), the truth (Rom. 2:8), and the gospel (1 Pet. 4:17). Frequently this term refers more to an inward attitude (heart) that is sometimes outwardly expressed (action). See *NIDNTT-A*, 59, 446-47.

DISOWN

New Testament

Verb: ἀπαρνέομαι (*aparneomai*), GK *565* (S *533*), 11x. The verb *aparneomai* essentially means the same as *arneomai* (GK *766*): to "deny, reject, disown." This word occurs only in the gospels, a majority of them in the prediction of Peter's denial (e.g., Mt. 26:34–35). But there is also a positive form of disowning, namely, disowning one's self (Mt. 16:24). See *deny*.

Verb: ἀρνέομαι (*arneomai*), GK *766* (S *720*), 33x. *arneomai* primarily means "to deny," although its wider range of meaning covers "disown, fail to confess, reject, say 'No,' refuse, renounce." It often carries the nuance of disowning Jesus as the God-sent Messiah (cf. 2 Pet. 2:1; 1 Jn. 2:22–23). See *deny*.

DISPERSE

Old Testament

Verb: פּוּץ (*pûṣ*), GK 7046 (S 6327), 65x. *pûṣ* denotes the act of dispersing an object or group of persons and may be translated "scatter." It often conveys divine judgment. See *scatter*.

DISPUTE

Old Testament

Noun: רִיב (*rîb*), GK 8190 (S 7379), 62x. *rîb* (related to the verb *rîb*, usually translated "contend") indicates an argument or conflict with another individual. Among the legal codes in the OT, *rîb* may be translated "dispute" (e.g., Deut. 19:17; 21:5; 25:1). See *case*.

DISTANT

Old Testament

Verb: רָחַק (*rāḥaq*), GK 8178 (S 7368), 59x. In a general sense meaning "to be far/ distant, remove, send away," *rāḥaq* can be used either to describe the state of a thing ("to be far, at a distance") or to indicate an action ("to go far, make far," i.e., "remove"). See *far*.

Adjective: רָחוֹק (*rāḥôq*), GK 8158 (S 7350), 84x. *rāḥôq* describes something "far, distant." It can be used with the meaning "distant" in a spatial or temporal sense. See *far*.

New Testament

Adverb: μακράν (*makran*), GK *3426* (S *3112*), 10x. *makran* means "to be far away"; it refers primarily to space, but sometimes may refer to time. See *far*.

DISTINGUISH

Old Testament

Verb: נָכַר (*nākar*), GK 5795 (S 5234), 44x. *nākar* (which occurs mostly in the Hiphil form) refers to general knowing, such as the basic awareness of another's existence or the distinguishing of who one person is versus another. See *recognize*.

New Testament

Verb: διακρίνω (*diakrinō*), GK *1359* (S *1252*), 19x. *diakrinō* means "to judge, distinguish, evaluate." When applied to oneself, it can mean to "doubt" or "waver." See *judge*.

DISTRESS

Old Testament

Noun: צָרָה (*ṣrâ*), GK 7650 (S 6869), 70x. *ṣrâ* comes form the root *ṣrh*, which means "to bind, tie up, restrict." Thus, the noun comes to denote a narrow place in life in which one is bound or restricted, i. e., "trouble or distress." *ṣrâ* designates the trials and tribulations experienced in life. These troubles come on the just and unjust alike and reveal much about the character of each. See *trouble*.

New Testament

Verb: ταράσσω (*tarassō*), GK *5429* (S *5015*), 17x. *tarassō* means to "trouble" or "disturb." It is normally used figuratively to describe people's distress at some surprising, exciting, or troubling event. See *trouble*.

Noun: ἀνάγκη (*anankē*), GK *340* (S *318*), 17x. *anankē* carries the meaning of necessity, compulsion, pressure, or even calamity and distress. See *necessary*.

Noun: θλίψις (*thlipsis*), GK *2568* (S *2347*), 45x. *thlipsis* is a cognate form of the verb *thlibō* (see *persecute*). It denotes the results of being squeezed or put into a narrow place—hence, "trouble, affliction, distress." It is used in several ways in the NT. See *trouble*.

DISTRICT

Old Testament

Noun: מְדִינָה (*m^edînâ*), GK 4519 (S 4082), 53x. *m^edînâ* is a "district" or "province" in a kingdom and is mentioned most often in the later periods of OT history. See *province*.

New Testament

Noun: τόπος (*topos*), GK *5536* (S *5117*), 94x. *topos* means "place"; in the plural it can refer to a "region" or "district." See *place*.

DISTURB

New Testament

Verb: ταράσσω (*tarassō*), GK *5429* (S *5015*), 17x. *tarassō* means to "trouble" or "disturb." It is normally used figuratively to describe people's disturbed reactions at some surprising, exciting, or troubling event. See *trouble*.

DIVIDE

Old Testament

Verb: בָּקַע (*bāqaʿ*), GK 1324 (S 1234), 51x. Often translated "to divide, split, tear open, crack open," *bāqaʿ* is frequently used in domestic contexts for activities like splitting wood (Eccl. 10:9), hatching eggs (Isa. 34:15; 59:5), or cracking wineskins (Jos. 9:4; Job 32:19). It is also used for breaching a military line in battle (2 Sam. 23:16; 2 Ki. 25:4; Jer. 39:2; Ezek. 26:10; 30:16; 2 Chr. 21:17) and the horrific practice of ripping open pregnant women (2 Ki. 8:12; 15:16; Amos 1:13).

bāqaʿ is also associated with miraculous openings, such as the dividing of the Red Sea (Exod. 14:16, 21), the splitting of both mountain (Zech. 14:4) and valley (Mic. 1:4) during the eschatological "day of the LORD," and the penetrating of light into darkness during the age of Israel's re-creation/restoration (Isa. 58:8). See *NIDOTTE*, 1:702–4.

Verb: חָלַק (*ḥālaq*), GK 2745 (S 2505), 55x. *ḥālaq* is translated "divide, share, allot." It is used for the dividing of hair in an enacted parable of Ezekiel (Ezek. 5:1) as well as the allotment of good sense to only some in the animal kingdom (Job 39:17; cf. Isa. 34:17).

(1) A wise servant "shares" his inheritance with others (Prov. 17:2; cf. Jos. 18:2; 22:8; 1 Chr. 24:4–5) while God allots to Israel the remotest frontiers (Neh. 9:22; cf. Jos. 14:5; Isa. 53:12; Dan. 11:37). Job believes that even though the wicked seem to win, in due time "the innocent will *divide* their silver" (Job 27:17).

(2) Conversely, the allotment of a nation by an outside power is a sign of judgment (Gen. 49:7; Isa. 33:23; Lam. 4:16; Amos 7:17; Zech. 14:1). David laments that his enemies are dividing his personal garments (Ps. 22:18; cf. Mic. 2:4).

(3) David commands wisely that the allotment of goods for those who have stayed with the supplies should be the same as those who went into battle (1 Sam. 30:24). It is an amazing theological truth that God "has apportioned" the heavens for the benefit of all nations (Deut. 4:19).

New Testament

Verb: διαμερίζω (*diamerizō*), GK *1374* (S *1266*), 11x. *diamerizō* means to "divide, separate something into parts." It may be a cup of wine shared among the disciples at the Last Supper (Lk. 22:17), the goods and possessions the early church divided among those who were in need (Acts 2:45), or the divided tongues as of fire that comes to rest on each believer gathered on the day of Pentecost (Acts 2:3). The Roman soldiers "divide" up Jesus' clothes among them by casting lots, in accordance with the Scriptures (Jn. 19:24; cf. Mt. 27:35; Mk. 15:24; Lk. 23:34).

Metaphorically *diamerizō* can mean "to cause dissension." When responding to the charge that he is casting out demons by demonic powers, Jesus reminds his adversaries that any kingdom "divided" against itself will fall (Lk. 11:17–23). Jesus also states that his coming will not bring peace but "division," even within family groups: "From this time forward, five in one household will be divided, three against two and two against three" (Lk. 12:52; cf. Mt. 10:32–42). Although we are instructed, "If possible, so far as it depends on you, live peaceably with all" (Rom. 12:18), we must also recognize that family divisions in the present point ahead to the judgment that will accompany the return of our Lord (Lk. 12:35–48; cf. Jn. 12:44–50). See *NIDNTT-A*, 363-64.*

Verb: μερίζω (*merizō*), GK *3532* (S *3307*), 14x. *merizō* means "to divide, assign." It is derived from the word *meros* (see *part*), meaning a part of the whole.

In Lk. 12:13 a man asks Jesus to tell his brother "to divide" the inheritance with him. Jesus teaches that a kingdom "divided" against itself cannot stand (Mt. 12:25, 26; cf. Mk. 3:24–26). At the feeding of the five thousand, Jesus divides the fish among all the people (Mk. 6:41). The Roman soldiers "divide" Jesus' clothes by casting lots (Mt. 27:35). Paul wants the single Christians in Corinth to give undivided devotion to the Lord; marriage, he suggests, might divide one's devotion between spouse and the Lord (1 Cor. 7:34, 35). God, who is the ultimate giver of good gifts, "has assigned" to each believer a portion of faith (Rom. 12:3) so that they can serve accordingly in the body of Christ (Rom. 12:4; cf. 1 Cor. 7:17; 2 Cor. 10:13).

merizō is important to a proper understanding of Christology and ecclesiology. Christ is not divided (1 Cor. 1:13). Therefore, those who wear Christ's name must work toward keeping unified in mind and judgment (1 Cor. 1:10; Eph. 4:31). In short, since Christ is not divided, neither should Christians be divided. See *NIDNTT-A*, 363-64.*

Verb: σχίζω (*schizō*), GK *5387* (S *4977*), 11x. *schizō* means "to tear." It can refer to the tearing of fabric, such as an old garment (Lk. 5:36) or a fishing net (Jn.

21:11). It is also used in connection with a *division* that arises between disputing parties (Acts 14:4; 23:7). See *tear*.

DIVISION

Old Testament

Noun: רֹאשׁ (*rōʾš*), GK 8031 (S 7218), 600x. The primary meaning of *rōʾš* is "head" (see *head*), but it also has a number of metaphorical meanings. For example, *rōʾš* can also be translated as "company," meaning a division or part of something. Saul divided his people into three *divisions* (*companies* in KJV, 1 Sam. 11:11). See *company*.

New Testament

Noun: σχίσμα (*schisma*) GK *5388* (S *4978*), 8x. *schisma* means "division, schism." There are two main uses for this noun. (1) On several occasions a division arises among the Jews as to who Jesus really is (Jn. 7:43; 9:16; 10:19). (2) In the church at Corinth, there are divisions among the believers, going along the lines of which human leader they should follow (1 Cor. 1:10). Divisions in the church also surface between the rich and the poor during the celebration of the Lord's Supper and the love feast that precedes it (11:18). But Paul's main instruction to the people there is "that there should be no divisions in the body" (12:25). See *divide*.

DIVORCE

Old Testament

Verb: שָׁלַח (*šālaḥ*), GK 8938 (S 7971), 847x. Generally translated "to send," *šālaḥ* usually refers to a human or divine person sending an object away from the subject for some purpose. In texts related to the marriage covenant, *šālaḥ* often means "to divorce" (Deut. 22:19; Ezr. 10:3). See *send*.

New Testament

Verb: ἀπολύω (*apolyō*), GK *668* (S *630*), 66x. *apolyō* is a compound verb that literally means "to loose away from." In the NT it is frequently translated as "to release, send away" (see *release*). But it also means "to divorce," as when a husband "sends away" his wife, or a wife "sends away" her husband. Joseph initially desires to "send away" Mary when he finds out she is pregnant (Mt. 1:19). In fact, it takes a revelation from the Lord to change his mind (Mt. 1:20ff.).

In Mk. 10:1–12 Jesus gives his teaching about divorce. In the Greco-Jewish culture of first century Palestine, it was considered acceptable for a man to divorce his wife, provided the separation was legal. The exact reasons for an "acceptable" divorce were debated by two schools of thought (the Jewish rabbinic schools of Shammai and Hillel). The school of Shammai interpreted Deut. 24:1ff. to be something explicitly morally shameful, especially adultery. The school of Hillel was much more liberal in its definition, going so far as to include anything which caused annoyance or embarrassment, such as burning her husband's meal, going out uncovered, having bad breath, speaking too loudly in the house, lying with him during her menstrual cycle—or even if he no longer found her attractive.

In Mk. 10:1–12 some Pharisees test Jesus on his view: "Is it lawful for a man to divorce [*apolyō*] his wife?" (Mk. 10:2). When Jesus asks them what the law of Moses commands, they respond with Deut. 24:1, 3. But Jesus responds that this was clearly not God's plan when the marriage union was created in Gen. 2. Instead, the reason why the law contains a provision for divorce is due to sin and hardness of heart. (Note Jesus' exception clause for "marital unfaithfulness" or "fornication" in Mt. 5:32; 19:9) Even though the Jewish law had no provision for a wife to divorce her husband, Jesus applies the same principles to both the husband and the wife. See *NIDNTT-A*, 64.

Verb: ἀφίημι (*aphiēmi*), GK *918* (S *863*), 143x. Depending upon its particular context, *aphiēmi* means to "forgive, release, leave, abandon." In 1 Cor. 7:11–13 it means "to divorce." See *forgive*.

Verb: χωρίζω (*chōrizō*), GK *6004* (S *5563*), 13x. *chōrizō* means "to separate";

in some of its uses it means "divorce." See *separate.*

DO

Old Testament

Verb: עָשָׂה (*ʿāśa*), GK 6913 (S 6213), 2632x. The verb *ʿāśâ* has the basic meaning "to do, make," appears in numerous contexts, and is used in a variety of ways. See *make.*

Verb: פָּעַל (*pāʿal*), GK 7188 (S 6466), 58x. *pāʿal* means "to do, make" and is used primarily in Job and Psalms as a poetic synonym to *ʿāśâ.* Nearly one-third of its uses have God as the subject. It first occurs in the OT during the Song of Moses: "the place, O Lord, you made for your dwelling" (Exod. 15:17).

pāʿal can have human beings as its subject. It can refer to humanity's moral acts, whether positive ("He whose walk is blameless and who *does* what is righteous," Ps. 15:2) or negative ("This is the way of the adulteress: She eats and wipes her mouth and says, 'I've *done* nothing wrong,'" Prov. 30:20). In Psalms, the term is used 18x in the phrase "*workers* of iniquity" or "evildoers" (see also Isa. 31:2; Hos. 6:8; Prov. 10:29). See *NIDOTTE,* 3:646–49.

New Testament

Verb: ἐργάζομαι (*ergazomai*), GK *2237* (S *2038*), 41x. *ergazomai* is derived from *ergon* (work) and means "to work, produce, perform, do" something. See *work.*

Verb: κατεργάζομαι (*katergazomai*), GK *2981* (S *2716*), 22x. *katergazomai* means "to do." This word occurs mainly in the writings of Paul. It is used in a negative sense in Rom. 1:27, that men "*do* shameless acts," and 2:9, "every human being who *does* evil" (cf. 7:15, 17, 20; 1 Cor. 5:3; 1 Pet. 4:3). It is used positively for doing good works in Rom. 7:18; 2 Cor. 12:12; Eph. 6:13. Paul also encourages the Philippians to "work out" (not "work for") their salvation (Phil. 2:12) while God clearly "works" (*energeō,* GK *1919*) to bring about his purposes (2:13). *katergazomai* also means "to bring about, produce" (see *bring about*).

Verb: ποιέω (*poieō*), GK *4472* (S *4160*), 568x. This verb, generically translated as "to do," has a wide range of meanings, such as "to make, cause to happen, accomplish."

(1) *poieō* describes the act of making in the sense of crafting or constructing physical objects. God's hand made the whole of creation (Acts 7:50). Through Jesus God made the world (Heb. 1:2). God made humans male and female (Mk. 10:6). The earth dwellers make an image to the beast (Rev. 13:14). Dorcas made tunics and clothing (Acts 9:39). Moses was to "construct" the tabernacle according to the pattern shown him on the mountain (Acts 7:44). At the transfiguration Peter expresses his desire to make three tents (Mt. 17:4).

(2) *poieō* also describes things done that are not construction projects, i.e., doing deeds. Jesus tells the Jews that if they were truly Abraham's children, they would do the deeds of Abraham. Instead, they show themselves as belonging to the seed of the serpent (and thus they are at enmity with the seed of the woman, Gen. 3:15) as they do the deeds of their father, the devil (Jn. 8:39–41). Joseph did as the angel told him (Mt. 1:24). At points "doing" has specific reference to "doing required deeds," as the one who "does" and teaches the commandments of the law will be called great in the kingdom of heaven (Mt. 5:19). Similarly, in 23:3 Jesus directs his hearers to do whatever the Pharisees teach them to do, but not to imitate what they do.

(3) In some instances *poieō* describes the accomplishment of things that result in a new state. In Eph. 2:15 Paul tells us that God "has made" the two, Jew and Gentile, one new man in Jesus, "making" peace between them. In Jas. 3:18 we read that the fruit of righteousness is sown in peace for those who "make" peace. Jesus tells the disciples he will make them fishers of men (Mt. 4:19). John the Baptist's ministry is to make straight the paths of the Messiah (Mt. 3:3).

(4) Although more commonly commu-

nicating actions of doing or making, *poieō* can also mean "appoint," as when Heb. 3:2 tells us that Jesus "was faithful to the one who *appointed* him." Perhaps Rev. 1:6 fits here as well: Jesus has appointed us kings and priests. See *NIDNTT-A*, 479-80.

Verb: πράσσω (*prassō*), GK *4556* (S *4238*), 39x. *prassō* has a basic meaning of "to do, act, practice" something and often overlaps with *poieō* (GK *4472*). It is often used in negative contexts with actions that are not virtuous and befitting of believers. Note that *prassō* is never used of God's actions. But the word itself is neutral; it does not necessarily denote something negative.

(1) *prassō* is used to denote the collection of taxes or of interest (Lk. 3:13; 19:23). The twelve wondered who would "do" such a thing as betray Jesus (Lk. 22:23). Pilate finds that Jesus "has done" nothing that merits death (23:15; cf. 23:41). In Acts, the people "act" in ignorance (Acts 3:17; cf. 15:29, which as a more positive nuance). In Jn. 3:20 and 5:29, *prassō* is connected with "evil deeds."

(2) In Paul, *prassō* frequently means to do something, which in context is seen to be sinful (Rom. 1:32; 2:1, 2, 3; 13:4; 1 Cor. 5:2; 2 Cor. 12:21; Gal. 5:21). He sometimes uses it parallel with *poieō*, as in Rom. 7:15bc, "for I am not practicing [*prassō*] what I would like, but I am doing [*poieō*] the very thing I hate" (NASB; cf. also 7:19). *prassō* is neutral in 9:11 (cf. 2 Cor. 5:10), and "practicing/doing" the law is contrasted to transgressing the law in Rom. 2:25. It is also used in a positive sense in 1 Cor. 9:17, where it refers to the act of preaching the gospel (cf. Eph. 6:21; Phil. 4:9; 1 Thess. 4:11). See *NIDNTT-A*, 486-87.

DO AGAIN

Old Testament

Verb: יָסַף (*yāsap*), GK 3578 (S 3254), 213x. The basic meaning of *yāsap* is "to add." Sometimes the word conveys the sense of "surpass" or "increase" (cf. Ps. 115:14; Eccl. 2:9; see *add*).

Verb: שָׁכַם (*šākam*), GK 8899 (S 7925), 65x. *šākam* can mean "to rise early in the morning, be eager, or do again and again," though the former meaning is much more common than the others. The meaning "to do again and again" is found in Jer. 11:7, where the Lord states that he has warned his people "again and again" (cf. 25:3, 4, 5, 19; 32:33; 35:14, 15). See *arise early*.

DO GOOD

Old Testament

Verb: יָטַב (*yāṭab*), GK 3512 (S 3190), 117x. *yāṭab* is a verb that means "to do good, go well, please, prosper." It is used in a wide variety of contexts in the OT. This verb is related to the most common adjective in the OT for "good," the word *ṭôb* (GK 3202).

(1) *yāṭab* can be used to denote the basic idea of things "going well" for people. Abram tells Sarai to say she is his sister that it may "go well" with him (Gen. 12:13). Joseph urges Pharaoh's cupbearer to remember him when things "go well" for him (40:14). *yāṭab* is frequently used to describe the prosperity that God's people will have when they enter the land and keep the covenant (e.g., Deut. 4:40; 5:16, 29; 6:3, 18; 12:25, 28; 22:7). Jeremiah instructs God's people to "*reform* your ways" in order that "it *may go well* with you" (Jer. 7:3, 5, 23).

(2) The expression that a thing is good in someone's sight means that the thing in view is pleasing. The proposal that the men of Shechem be circumcised so that they can intermarry with the Israelites (lit.) "*was good* in [Hamor and Shechem's] sight," i.e., they *were pleased* with it (Gen. 34:18). Joseph's plan seems good in the eyes of Pharaoh and his officials (41:37; cf. 45:16; Lev. 10:19–20).

(3) The expression "the heart is *good*" means that a person is happy. In Judg. 18:20 the priest's "heart was *glad*." When Boaz had eaten and drunk, his "heart was *merry*" (Ruth 3:7).

(4) In a causative sense, *yāṭab* can convey the idea that one person has treated another well. Pharaoh treats Abram well

(Gen. 12:16). Joshua alludes to the fact that God has treated the people well (Jos. 24:20). Boaz tells Ruth that her latter kindness is better than what she showed earlier (Ruth 3:10). Indeed, our good God "does good" to those who love him and follow his commandments (Ps. 119:68; 125:4; cf. Jer. 32:40).

(5) In a few instances, the verb communicates the notion that someone is "doing well" at something, e.g., playing an instrument "skillfully" (1 Sam. 16:17; Ps. 33:3; Isa. 23:16). See *NIDOTTE*, 3:353–57.

DO WRONG

New Testament

Verb: ἀδικέω (*adikeō*), GK *92* (S *91*), 28x. *adikeō* is used mostly in Rev. (11x) and in Paul's writings (9x) to denote doing wrong, harming or hurting another, or mistreating someone (committing injustice). Notice that *adikeō* (as well as its cognates) stands in direct contrast to *dikaios* ("just," *1465*) and especially *dikaiosynē* ("righteousness," *1466*).

The primary meaning of *adikeō* is to "do wrong." As Paul stands before his accusers, he defends himself, saying "I have not *done anything wrong* to the Jews" (Acts 25:10), and questions whether or not he has done anything deserving of death (25:11). The angel states to John in Rev. 22:11, "Let him who does wrong continue to do wrong." See also 1 Cor. 6:7, 8; 2 Cor. 7:2, 12a; Gal. 4:12; Col. 3:25 [2x]; and Phlm. 18).

adikeō also refers to the mistreatment or hurt of other people or things. This usage is seen in Stephen's speech before the Sanhedrin as he recounts how Moses "saw one of [his fellow Israelites] *being mistreated* by an Egyptian," which provoked him to kill (Acts 7:24; cf 7:27). Moses also questions why two Israelites would "want to *hurt* each other" (7:26). See also Rev. 2:11: "He who overcomes *will not be hurt* by the second death."

Physical harm or damage is also an aspect of *adikeō*, whether of people (Lk. 10:19; 2 Pet. 2:13; Rev. 11:5 [2x]) or things, such as the earth or sea (Rev. 6:6; 7:2, 3; 9:4). This harm can also be referred to as *injury* (2 Cor. 7:12b; Rev. 9:19).

Finally, *adikeō* is used once as "torment" (Rev. 9:10, "[The locusts] had tails and stings like scorpions, and in their tails they had the power *to torment* people for five months") and once, in the parable of the workers in the vineyard, as "unfair" (Mt. 20:13, "But [Jesus] answered one of them, 'Friend, I am not *being unfair* to you. Didn't you agree to work for a denarius?'"). See *NIDNTT-A*, 17-18.*

DOCTRINE

New Testament

Noun: διδασκαλία (*didaskalia*), GK *1436* (S *1319*), 21x. *didaskalia*, like *didachē*, denotes "teaching" or "doctrine." See *teaching*.

Noun: διδαχή (*didachē*), GK *1439* (S *1322*), 30x. *didachē*, like *didaskalia*, denotes "doctrine, teaching," as well as "instruction." See *teaching*.

DOMINION

Old Testament

Noun: מַלְכוּת (*malkût*), GK 4895 (S 4438), 91x.

Noun: מַמְלָכָה (*mamlākâ*), GK 4930 (S 4467), 117x.

These two nouns are both connected with the *mlk* root and, along with other words, comprise a frequent and important concept in the OT. *malkût* ranges in meaning from an abstract reference to a king's dynasty or power (Num. 24:7; 1 Sam. 20:31) to the more concrete location of a "kingdom, dominion" (2 Chr. 1:1; Neh. 9:35). In this sense of "kingdom," *malkût* overlaps with *mamlākâ*, which is the more frequent term used for "kingdom, dominion" (Gen. 10:10; Ps. 135:11; Jer. 1:10). For a thorough discussion, see *kingdom*.

New Testament

Noun: βασιλεία (*basileia*), GK *993* (S *932*). 162x. In the NT, *basileia* plays a large role. Most English versions consistently translate *basileia* with "kingdom," though at times it would be better understood as "reign" or "rule." Thus, some scholars today prefer to speak of "the rule of God" or even "the dominion of God." See *kingdom*.

Noun: κράτος (*kratos*), GK *3197* (S *2904*), 12x. *kratos* is generally translated "power, strength, might." See *power*.

DONKEY

Old Testament

Noun: חֲמוֹר (*ḥamôr*), GK 2789 (S 2543), 96x. Donkeys, one of the chief beasts of burden in the ancient world (2 Sam. 16:1; Neh. 13:15), are mentioned frequently throughout the OT. They are often listed along with other livestock in order to emphasize great personal wealth (e.g., Gen. 12:16; 24:35; 30:43), and their value is illustrated by the fear of Joseph's brothers that the Egyptians will "take us for slaves with our donkeys" (Gen. 43:18; cf. Num. 16:15). Under the Mosaic law, even the donkey of one's enemy is to be well-treated (Exod. 23:5), and donkeys are given a Sabbath rest together with humans and other livestock (Exod. 23:12; cf. Deut. 5:14).

The donkeys of Jericho are included under the ban and destroyed (Jos. 6:21). Isa. 1:3 compares Israel unfavorably to a donkey, and Jeremiah prophesies that Judah's king will be given the dishonorable burial of a donkey (Isa. 22:19). Zech. 9:9 calls Zion to rejoice in light of the future king who will come mounted on a donkey. This passage is quoted as fulfilled in Matthew's account of Jesus' entry into Jerusalem (Mt. 21:5). See *NIDOTTE*, 2:172-74.

DOOR

Old Testament

Noun: דֶּלֶת (*delet*), GK 1946 (S 1817), 88x. *delet* means "door, gate." For the most part, this noun refers to doors on houses (e.g., Gen. 19:6; 2 Ki. 4:4–5) or on the temple (1 Ki. 6:31–34; 2 Chr. 4:9, 22). Samuel opens the doors of the sanctuary every morning for worship (1 Sam. 3:15; cf. 2 Chr. 29:3); the closing of the doors of the temple indicate the cessation of worship of the Lord (e.g., 2 Chr. 28:24). Just like today, doors in Bible times swung open and shut on hinges (Prov. 26:14), and they could be bolted shut (2 Sam. 13:17–18). In a few cases, *delet* refers to the "gates" of a city (Deut. 3:5; Jdg. 16:3; 2 Chr. 8:5; Ps. 107:16).

Most references in the OT to *delet* are to physical doors and gates. But there are several metaphorical uses of this word. Job wishes that the "door" to his mother's womb had been shut on the day of his birth, so that he would not have been born (Job 3:10). When Job says his "door" was always open to the traveler (31:32), he means that he practiced the type of hospitality typical in the ancient world by welcoming strangers. In 41:14, God asks whether anyone dares to "open the doors [i.e., jaws]" of the mouth of leviathan with its fearsome teeth. According to Ps. 78:23, when God sent manna to his people in the desert, he opened the "doors" of heaven and rained it down.

Noun: פֶּתַח (*petaḥ*), GK 7339 (S 6607), 164x. *petaḥ* means "door" or "entrance." It is used most often in the OT to indicate the entrance to a house or tent (Gen. 18:1, 2, 10; Exod. 33:8; Num. 11:10; 1 Chr. 9:21) or the entrance to a city (2 Sam. 10:8; Gen. 38:14; cf. Jer. 36:10). See *entrance*.

New Testament

Noun: θύρα (*thyra*), GK *2598* (S *2374*), 39x. *thyra* signifies a door, gate or entrance. It can be used in either a literal or a metaphoric sense. *thyra* is used literally as the door of a house (Mt. 6:6), of the temple (Acts 3:2), of a prison (5:19), and of the opening of a cave tomb (Mk. 16:3).

Figuratively, *thyra* has several connotations. It denotes nearness in time or place, "at the door" (Mt. 24:33). It is represents an opportunity for the spread of the gospel; upon arriving at Antioch, Paul reported "how [on their first missionary journey] he had opened the door of faith to the Gentiles" (Acts 14:27; cf. also 1 Cor. 16:9; 2 Cor. 2:12). Furthermore, *thyra* is used to indicate entrance into the kingdom of God (Lk. 13:24). The narrowness of the door refers to the exclusivity of salvation found in Christ. A closed door is symbolic of judgment and loss (cf. Mt. 25:10).

thyra carries even greater meaning as Christ uses it to describe his entrance into the heart of a believer as he knocks upon it: "If anyone hears my voice and opens the *door*, I will come in" (Rev. 3:20). Just as a closed door prevents someone from going into a house, so does a closed heart prevent Christ from entering. When all is said and done, however, God must open a believer's heart to the gospel: "The Lord opened [Lydia's] heart to respond to Paul's message" (Acts 16:14; cf. 14:27). Additionally, *thyra* is used with reference to the door of heaven. Once again, the only entrance is through Christ ("I am the *gate*" said Jesus, "whoever enters through me will be saved" Jn. 10:9). See *NIDNTT-A*, 253-254.

Noun: πύλη (*pylē*), GK *4783* (S *4439*), 10x. *pylē* means "gate, door." See *gate*.

Noun: πυλών (*pylōn*), GK *4784* (S *4440*), 18x. *pylōn* means "gate, door" of a house or city. See *gate*.

DOUBT

New Testament

Verb: διακρίνω (*diakrinō*), GK *1359* (S *1252*), 19x. *diakrinō* means "to judge, distinguish, evaluate." When applied to oneself, it can mean to "doubt" or "waver." See *judge*.

DOVE

New Testament

Noun: περιστερά (*peristera*), GK *4361* (S *4058*), 10x. A dove or pigeon is of the order "Columbiformes." This word occurs only in the gospels. (1) As animals of sacrifice, doves were among the beasts Jesus drove from the temple (Mt. 21:12; Jn. 2:14, 16). Because Joseph and Mary were poor, they were allowed by OT law to offer "a pair of doves or two young *pigeons*" for Mary's cleansing after the birth of Jesus instead of a lamb (Lk. 2:24; cf. Lev. 12:8).

(2) Doves could be used as symbols of purity and innocence. The Holy Spirit descends on Jesus as a dove at his baptism (Mt. 3:17; Mk. 1:10; Lk. 3:22). This signals to John the Baptist that Jesus is the one for whom he has been preparing (Jn. 1:32–34). Jesus urges his disciples to be "as shrewd as serpents and as innocent as *doves*" (Mt. 10:16). See *NIDNTT-A*, 457.

DRAGON

New Testament

Noun: δράκων (*drakōn*), GK *1532* (S *1404*), 13x. *drakōn* occurs only in Revelation as a symbolic representation of Satan. The dragon is explicitly identified as "that ancient Serpent, who is the Devil, or Satan" (Rev. 12:9; also 20:2). This depiction associates him with the OT dragon or sea monster, who represents the enemies of God's people (e.g., Ps. 74:13–14; Isa. 27:1; Ezek. 29:3). In Revelation the dragon is the chief enemy of God and his church, who uses earthly enemies to accomplish his purposes.

The dragon first appears in Rev. 12, where he attempts unsuccessfully to devour the son of a woman who is destined to rule the nations (12:3–4). After warring with Michael and the heavenly angels, the dragon and his demonic angels are thrown down from heaven to earth (vv. 7, 9; also 20:1–3). Angered at his defeat, he persecutes the woman and her offspring, the faithful believers in Jesus Christ (vv. 13, 16–17). The dragon brings forth the beast, which resembles him with seven heads and ten horns and gives him power and authority on the earth (13:1–2, 11). Through the beast, the dragon entices those whose names are not written in the Lamb's book of life to worship both beast and dragon (13:4). The dragon is defeated initially by being cast into the abyss for a thousand years, where his power to deceive the nations is limited (20:2). He is defeated ultimately in a final cosmic battle after which he along with his minions—the beast and false prophet—are thrown into the lake of fire for all eternity. Ultimate victory belongs only to Jesus Christ. See *NIDNTT-A*, 153.

DRAW NEAR

Old Testament

Verb: קָרַב (*qārab*), GK 7928 (S 7126), 280x. The basic meaning of *qārab* is "to come, draw near" or, in a causative sense, "to bring near." This basic meaning may denote physical or spatial proximity as well as nonphysical. See *bring*.

New Testament

Verb: ἐγγίζω (*engizō*), GK *1581* (S *1448*), 42x. *engizō* means "to approach, come near." Most of its occurrences are in the gospels. See *come near*.

Verb: προσέρχομαι (*proserchomai*), GK *4665* (S *4334*), 86x. *proserchomai* simply means "to approach, come to," though it sometimes carries significant theological meaning with reverential overtones. See *approach*.

DRAW UP

Old Testament

Verb: עָרַךְ (*ʿārak*), GK 6885 (S 6186), 75x. *ʿārak* denotes the action of arranging an object in a particular way or arranging objects in a specific order to produce a desired effect. Regarding war, *ʿārak* denotes the action of arranging armies for battle. The NIV sometimes translates this use of *ʿārak* as "drew up their battle lines" (Gen. 14:8) and "drawing up their lines" (1 Sam. 17:21). See *arrange*.

DREAM

Old Testament

Noun: חֲלוֹם (*ḥ*ᵃ*lôm*), GK 2706 (S 2472), 65x. *ḥ*ᵃ*lôm* means "*dream.*" Normally dreams are no more than images and thoughts that play through a person's mind during sleep (Ps. 73:20; Isa. 29:7–8). However, on certain occasions God communicated with someone "in a dream" (Gen. 20:3; 31:10, 24; Num. 12:6; 1 Ki. 3:5), not only revealing himself, but also providing an appropriate explanation or interpretation (Gen. 41:15–16; Dan. 2:1–3, 28).

(1) God used dreams to communicate with many people in the OT. Among his covenant people who received dreams were Jacob (Gen. 31:10, 11), Joseph (37:5–20; 42:9), various prophets of Israel (Num. 12:6), Saul (1 Sam. 28:6, 15), and Solomon (1 Ki. 3:5, 15). But God also appeared to foreigners in dreams: Abimelech (Gen. 20:3), Laban (31:24), an Egyptian cupbearer and baker (40:5–16; 41:11–12), an Egyptian pharaoh (Gen. 41:7), and Nebuchadnezzar (Dan. 2:1–3). Both Joseph and Daniel were promoted to significant positions of leadership based on their God-given ability to interpret dreams.

(2) God used dreams to reveal the future (Gen. 41:25, 32; Dan. 2:28) and to give specific instructions to his appointed leaders (1 Sam. 28:6, 15; 1 Ki. 3:5). Simply having dreams, however, did not make them true. God compared many "dreamers" to diviners, sorcerers, fortunetellers, and liars (Jer. 27:9). He rebuked them for giving false words and "empty consolation" (Zech. 10:2). The Lord is "against those who prophecy lying dreams" (Jer. 23:32), though he used such false prophets and their dreams "to test" the genuineness of his people's love for him (Deut. 13:1–3).

(3) In the OT, dreams were a regular form of communication between God and his people (Num. 12:6). In the last days, however, God will "pour out" his Spirit directly on "all flesh." Then the "sons and daughters" of the people of God "will prophesy," old men will "dream *dreams*," and young men will "see visions" (Joel 2:28). This prophecy foretells Pentecost, the coming of the Holy Spirit on God's people (Acts 2:16ff.). See *NIDOTTE*, 2:153-155.*

DRESS

New Testament

Verb: περιβάλλω (*periballō*), GK *4314* (S *4016*), 23x. *periballō* means "to wear, clothe, dress." See *wear*.

DRINK

Old Testament

Verb: שָׁתָה (*šātâ*), GK 9272 (S 8354), 217x. The basic meaning of *šātâ* is "to drink" and, in the Heb. Hiphil verb stem, "to give drink to, water." (1) As far as drinking is concerned, the subject of the verb is usually people (Gen. 9:21), sometimes animals (Num. 20:19), and God one time (Ps. 50:13, in a rhetorical question). What is drunk may be water, wine, milk, or other liquids. The combination of eating and drinking becomes an expression for a complete meal (1 Ki. 19:6, 8) or even a celebration (Eccl. 2:24; see also *eat*). To "*drink* fermented drink" makes a person "a drunkard" (cf. Ps. 69:12; Isa. 5:22; 24:9; Jer. 25:27).

(2) In terms of watering or giving drink, the object can be plants (Gen. 2:6, 10; Ps. 104:13), animals (Gen. 29:2–3, 7–8; Ps. 104:11), and human beings (Gen. 21:19)—these all need water to survive. Therefore, to give someone a drink is a sign of kindness (Gen. 21:19), compassion (cf. Jer. 16:7), and love (1 Chr. 11:17; perhaps Prov. 25:21–22). The fact that God provides water for his creatures is a sign of his goodness (Ps. 36:8; Isa. 43:20). By contrast, God can also judge people by giving them "poisoned water *to drink*" (Jer. 8:14; 9:15; 23:15) or "wine that makes us stagger" (Ps. 60:3). Human beings can show meanness by giving a thirsty person vinegar to drink (69:21).

(3) In addition to the literal meaning, *šāṯâ* occurs with a number of metaphorical uses. The promised land drinks rain from heaven (Deut. 11:11). Drinking also becomes a figure for sexual activity (Prov. 5:15 in context) or receiving God's punishment (Jer. 25:15–17; 49:12). Being made to drink one's tears is a sign of extreme sorrow and anguish (Ps. 80:5). See *NIDOTTE*, 4:231-34.

New Testament

Verb: πίνω (*pinō*), GK *4403* (S *4095*), 73x. *pinō* means "to drink." It often accompanies the word *esthiō* (see *eat*) (e.g., Mt. 6:25, 31; 24:38; Lk. 10:7; 13:26; 17:8; 1 Cor. 9:4). In order to show that "eating and drinking" have no inherent moral dimension, Jesus observes that John the Baptist, in Nazirite fashion, "came neither eating or drinking" (Mt. 11:18), while he himself came "eating and drinking" (11:19). Yet John was charged with being demon-possessed and Jesus with gluttony and drunkenness. Jesus' enemies show no consistency in the standards by which they criticize others.

In the parable of the rich fool (Lk. 12:19) and in 1 Cor. 15:32, eating and drinking appear as a part of the Epicurean philosophy: "Eat, drink, and be merry, for tomorrow we die." Such an attitude stresses failure to recognize one's responsibility to God. In Lk. 17:27–28, Jesus reminds his hearers that the moral dimension of drinking is connected to judgment.

Jesus uses physical water from a well to invite the Samaritan woman to take a drink of living water (Jn. 4:7, 9, 10, 12, 13, 14). The well water is natural drink, but Jesus is the supernatural drink, from which one will never thirst again. The theme is modified slightly in the bread of life discourse in Jn. 6, in which Jesus warns his disciples that unless they "eat the flesh of the Son of Man and drink his blood," they did not have eternal life (6:53, 54, 56). This must have sounded blasphemous as the Mosaic law outlaws the drinking of blood as well as the eating of meat tainted with blood (Lev. 17:10–14). Thus, to follow Jesus requires great devotion and a willingness to act contrary to popular interpretations of OT law. It is noteworthy that many could not "stomach" this teaching and refused to follow Jesus any longer (Jn. 6:66).

pinō is linked with the theme of Jesus' death. When James and John seek special seats of favor and greatness with Jesus in his kingdom glory (Mk. 10:35–45), Jesus measures their understanding by asking, "Can you drink the cup I drink?" (10:38). He not only quizzes their desire to "drink his death," but he also decrees that they will in fact follow him in death (10:39). Jn. 18:11 also refers to Jesus' agreeing to drink his cup of suffering and death. Paul later uses the expression "drink the cup" in 1 Cor. 11:17–34 for one of the two important elements in observing the Lord's Supper (cf. Mt. 26:27), in which we commemorate Jesus' death.

Finally, Revelation paints some graphic and violent pictures of drinking; anyone who worships the beast "will drink the wine of God's fury" (14:10); punishment is tailored to fit the crime as persecutors who shed the blood of the saints are given "blood to drink as they deserve" (16:6), and "the nations have drunk the maddening wine of her [Babylon the Great's] adulteries" (18:3). See *NIDNTT-A*, 460-61.

DRINK OFFERING

Old Testament

Noun: נֶסֶךְ (*nesek*), GK 5821 (S 5262), 60x. *nesek* refers to a "drink offering." Once (Ps. 16:4) this is an offering of blood (offered to a pagan god); in all other cases where a liquid is specified, it is an offering of wine or other fermented drink. Like the burnt and fellowship offerings, the practice of offering a drink offering (i.e., a libation) predates the tabernacle system (e.g., Gen 35:14). But more than half of the uses of this word are in the book of Numbers (especially Num. 27–28), in the instructions about Israel's daily offerings and feast-day offerings. Perhaps the idea behind offering a libation is to make sure that what is offered to the Lord is a meal complete with meat, grain, and wine.

The notion of a drink offering occurs elsewhere in the OT, but for the most part, these are offered foreign gods (e.g., Jer. 19:13; 32:29; Ezek. 20:28) or on a foreign altar in the temple (2 Ki. 16:13, 15). According to Joel, a famine or plague will cause the drink offering to be removed from Israel because of a lack of wine (Joel 1:9, 13; cf. 2:14); this is a sign of the impending day of the Lord (cf. 1:15; 2:1, 11). See *NIDOTTE*, 3:113–17.

DRIVE

Old Testament

Verb: רָכַב (*rākab*), GK 8206 (S 7392), 78x. *rākab* generally means "to mount or ride (something)," but it can also mean "to drive (something)" and in this sense is most often used of chariots (Gen. 24:61; 41:43;1 Ki. 1:33, 38, 44; Ezek. 23:6, 12, 23; Zech. 1:8). See *ride*.

DRIVE OUT

Old Testament

Verb: יָרַשׁ (*yāraš*), GK 3769 (S 3423), 232x. *yāraš* means "to possess, take possession of (especially by force), drive out, inherit." See *possess*.

New Testament

Verb: ἐκβάλλω (*ekballō*), GK *1675* (S *1544*), 81x. *ekballō* means "to drive out, expel, eject." It often indicates a violent expulsion. The term is used frequently in the NT for the casting out of demons (Mt. 8:16; Mk. 1:34; 6:13: Lk. 11:14). Jesus also uses the term to say that it is better "to expel" the eye than to allow the eye to entice a person to sin (Mk. 9:47).

ekballō can also be used for expelling someone from the community of believers (Lk. 4:29; Jn. 9:34; Acts 13:50; 3 Jn. 10). Interestingly, it is also used to describe the way in which the Spirit of God compelled Jesus to go into the Judean desert to face the temptations of Satan (Mk. 1:12–13). The term's use in this passage implies that after Jesus submitted himself to the Spirit in baptism (Mk. 1:9–11), the Holy Spirit purposefully and aggressively directed Christ to confront and defeat the power of Satan in the temptations in the desert.

DRY UP

Old Testament

Verb: יָבֵשׁ (*yābēš*), GK 3312 (3001), 59x. *yābēš* means "to wither, dry up." See *wither*.

New Testament

Verb: ξηραίνω (*xērainō*), GK *3830* (S *3583*), 15x. *xērainō* denotes the "scorching" or "drying up" of something, usually due to the sun. In Jas. 1:11 the "withering of grass" is compared to the withering of earthly riches. The passive form describes a tree that has dried up or cannot bear fruit (Mt. 21:19, 20; Mk. 11:20, 21).

xērainō is central to the parable of the sower (Mt. 13:6; Mk. 4:6; Lk. 8:6), where this verb denotes the drying up of plants that lack a sufficient root system. As believers, the Lord is our source of strength and nourishment so that we do not dry up spiritually. See *NIDNTT-A*, 399.

DUE

See *owe.*

DUNGEON

Old Testament

Noun: בּוֹר (*bôr*), GK 1014 (S 953), 65x. *bôr*, often translated as "pit," can also mean "well, dungeon, cistern, grave." See *pit*.

DUST

Old Testament

Noun: אֲדָמָה (*ʾᵃdāmâ*), GK 141 (S 127), 222x. *ʾᵃdāmâ* has a variety of nuances in the OT (see *land*). It is used in reference to the covenant promises and warnings about the earth (Exod. 20:12; Deut. 4:40; 2 Ki. 17:23; Amos 7:11, 17), and at times, it designates the inhabited world (Ezek. 38:20; Isa. 24:21). It also refers to various kinds of soil: dust (1 Sam. 4:12), clay (1 Ki. 7:46), and the matter used to form mankind and the animals (Gen. 2:7, 19). See *land*.

Noun: עָפָר (*ʿāpār*), GK 6760 (S 6083), 55x. *ʿāpār* refers to fine, dry dirt. In Ps. 18:42, David declares that he ground his enemies "like *dust* before the wind" (cf. grinding idols to dust in Deut. 9:21 and 2 Ki. 23:6). *ʿāpār* also refers to loose earth, as in Gen. 26:15, where the Philistines fill in all the wells of Abraham with *earth*. At times *ʿāpār* describes things that either contain dust or have the consistency of dust, such as plaster (Lev. 14:41–42, 45), rubble (Neh. 4:10), and ashes (Num. 19:17). Since in the Middle East the ground is composed mainly of dust, *ʿāpār* can also refer to the ground itself: "He brings it down to the earth, he throws it to the *dust*" (Isa. 26:5; cf. Job 19:25, "[my Redeemer] will arise upon the *dust*," i.e., the surface of the earth).

In general, dust is associated with humiliation. The serpent was condemned to "eat *dust*" in Gen. 3:14 (cf. Isa. 65:25; Mic. 7:17). As a sign of lament, people would throw dust on their heads (Jos. 7:6; Job 2:12). "Dust" is also used as a metaphor for absolute destruction (2 Ki. 13:7). In contrast, however, it is also a metaphor for something numerous, as when God tells Abraham that he will make his descendants as numerous "as the *dust* of the earth" (Gen. 13:16).

In one of the most pivotal theological passages of the OT, God created the human race from the dust of the ground (Gen. 2:7; cf. 18:27; Job 10:9; Ps. 103:14; Eccl. 3:20)—that is, the human being is a physical being into whom God breathed the breath of life. Dust is not only the physical origin of the human race but is also now their destiny, for when God removes the breath from a human being, he or she returns to dust (Gen. 3:19; Job 34:15; Ps. 104:29; Eccl. 12:7). Furthermore, *ʿāpār* is used as a metaphor for the grave and the realm of the dead; the dead who "inhabit the *dust*" are called to awake and shout with joy in Isa. 26:19 (cf. Dan. 12:2). See *NIDOTTE*, 3:472-73.

DUTY

Old Testament

Noun: מְלָאכָה (*mᵉlāʾkâ*), GK 4856 (S 4399), 167x. *mᵉlāʾkâ* has the notion of "sending forth one's hand to accomplish a task" or "duty" (cf. Deut. 12:7, 18). See *work*.

Noun: מִשְׁמֶרֶת (*mišmeret*), GK 5466 (S 4931), 78x. *mišmeret* derives from the verb *šāmar*, "to keep, watch, guard," and denotes the regular responsibility or duty to care for or guard an object. Sometimes the guarded object is a general reference to God's law, but usually it refers to a specific object, and often that object is cultic in nature (i.e., used in worship).

mišmeret appears most frequently in Numbers (29x), where it refers almost exclusively to the responsibility for cultic objects. Particular Israelites from the tribe of Levi are responsible for the "care" or "charge" of the tabernacle (Num. 1:53; 31:30, 47) or tent of meeting (18:4), its furnishings (3:8, 31) and structural equipment (3:36), its covering and curtain (3:25), the sanctuary (3:28, 32, 38; cf. Ezek. 44:8), and the altar (Num. 18:5). Though the Levites generally perform the "duties" or "responsibilities" at the tent of meeting (e.g., 3:7; 4:28; 8:26; 18:3), all three uses of *mišmeret* in Leviticus refer not to the "responsibilities" of the tent of meeting but instead to keeping (*šāmar*) the "charge" of Yahweh (Lev. 8:35; 18:30; 22:9).

mišmeret appears 11x with the participle of *šāmar*, "to keep," with the sense of "the ones keeping the charge." "The ones keeping the charge" are responsible for the sanctuary (Num. 3:28, 32, 38; Ezek. 44:8), the tabernacle of God (Num. 31:30, 47), the house of the king (2 Ki. 11:5; 1 Chr. 12:30), the temple (Ezek. 40:45; 44:14), and the altar (40:46).

In a noncultic sense, *mišmeret* may refer to a "guard" in the sense of a military watchman defending Jerusalem (Neh. 7:3), to a "ward" in the sense of a place of confinement that is under guard (2 Sam. 20:3), or to a "guard post" in the sense of the place from which guard is kept (Isa. 21:8).

When *mišmeret* is used more generally as a reference to God's law, it is regularly the object of *šāmar*, "to keep," and is often translated "charge" or "requirements." Abraham keeps God's "charge" (Gen. 26:5), and Moses urges Israel to keep the "charge" of God (Deut. 11:1). David instructs Solomon to keep the "charge" of God by walking in his ways and keeping his decrees, his commandments, his judgments, and his testimonies in order that Solomon will succeed in whatever he does (1 Ki. 2:3). See *NIDOTTE*, 4:182-83.

New Testament

Verb: ὀφείλω (*opheilō*), GK *4053* (S *3784*), 35x. *opheilō* conveys the idea of being in debt or under obligation and may best be translated as "owe" or (as a helping verb) "ought." See *owe*.

DWELL

Old Testament

Verb: גּוּר (*gûr*), GK 1591 (S 1481), 82x. The basic meaning of *gûr* is to "live, settle, dwell." In most instances, this verb refers to someone living outside of their clan, that is, dwelling among people who are not blood relatives. This can be the result of famine or other circumstances beyond the individual's control. As such, *gûr* results in a social status that is often disadvantaged, without the rights and protection of citizenship.

When *gûr* is used to convey its basic meaning "to dwell," it never loses the sense of temporariness. Joseph's brothers explain that they have come to Egypt to "live for a while" (NIV) because of the famine in Canaan, and they request permission to live there (Gen 47:4). Even those who live a long time in one place may still be considered "strangers" (KJV) or "nomads" (NIV) (Jer. 35:7). Jeremiah speaks of the "remnant of Judah" who are intent on *living* (*gûr*) in Egypt, but who will long to return to their homeland (Jer. 44:14). Here, again, *gûr* emphasizes a temporary situation. It is understandable, then, that *gûr* is used of the sojourning of the patriarchs (Gen. 12:10; 32:4; 47:4). The land promised to Abraham and his offspring (Gen. 15) is not yet theirs, and so they reside as foreigners or aliens. Even Abimelech, though recognizing Abraham's wealth and power, still considers him an alien living in the land (21:23). Likewise, the nation of Israel, while in Egypt, *"lived as foreigners"* (NIV), "*sojourned,*" (KJV) (Ps. 105:12, 23).

gûr also describes the dwelling of foreigners within Israel. Oftentimes, it is construed with its corresponding noun *gēr* (GK 1731, "sojourner, alien"), in the sense "to sojourn as an alien." In the majority of cases, the foreigner within Israel dwells among God's people as a resident foreigner. Though they do not have clan identity or inheritance in the land, they are to be treated with justice (Deut. 1:16; Num. 35:15) and provided opportunity to worship (e.g., Passover, Exod. 12:48–49; Day of Atonement, Lev. 16:29; sacrifices, Num. 15:14). There is to be one law for the native born and foreigner (Num. 15:16, 29). This also means that the foreigner who sojourns with Israel is expected to accept the commandments of God as his own and live in accordance with them (Lev. 17:12, 15; 18:26; 24:16, cf. Num. 15:30).

The alien sojourning within Israel is classed together with the widow, orphan, and Levite, all of whom do not hold an inheritance in the land. As such, they are to be cared for and treated as a native born (Lev. 19:33). In addition to the common help they receive within their immediate community, third-year tithes are gathered for their support (Deut. 14:28–29). In Ezekiel's picture of future restoration, the resident foreigner will receive an inheritance in the land along with the native born (Ezek. 47:22–23).

gûr is also used metaphorically to denote the sojourning of God's people. Israel is reminded that she dwells in the promised land as a sojourner, since the land belongs to God (Lev. 25:23). Likewise, all of us find ourselves as sojourners seeking a place to dwell. The psalmist asks the penetrating question, "LORD, who may *dwell* in your sanctuary (tent)? Who may live on your holy mountain?" (Ps. 15:1). The answer is reassuring. Dwelling with God is not a matter of clan identity but is offered to everyone whose "walk is blameless and who does what is righteous" (v. 2). Those who seek God in humble obedience "will never be shaken" (v. 5). See *NIDOTTE*, 1:836-39.

Verb: יָשַׁב (*yāšab*), GK 3782 (S 3427), 1088x. The general meaning of *yāšab* is to "sit, sit down," with the connotations of "live, dwell, remain, settle." See *live*.

Verb: שָׁכַן (*šākan*), GK 8905 (S 7931) 130x. *šākan* has the basic meaning "to live, dwell," and it has several synonyms with which it is sometimes found in close proximity: *yāšab* (GK 3782, "dwell") and *gûr* (GK 1591, "dwell, sojourn," e.g., Jdg. 5:17; Ps. 15:1; Isa. 32:16; Job 29:25). In terms of possible nuances that distinguish these synonyms, *šākan* "reflects dwelling or resting that is consistently more temporary than *yāšab*, while more permanent, perhaps, than *gûr*" (*NIDOTTE,* 4:109–10).

šākan is first found in Gen. 3:24 of the cherubim who are "placed" at the east side of the Garden of Eden. Other examples of its use are: Abram *living* near the trees of Mamre (Gen. 14:13), the descendants of Ishmael *living* in the region from Havilah to Shur (Gen. 25:18), of the glory of God *settling* on Mount Sinai (Exod. 24:16), of the tabernacle (Tent of Meeting) *abiding* within Israel (Lev. 16:16), and of the cloud of the divine presence that *settled* in a location, indicating that Israel should camp there (Num. 9:17). The use of *šākan*, associated with the visible presence of God, has given rise to the postbiblical term *Shekinah* to describe God's presence among human beings.

In nearly one-third of the times *šākan* is used in the OT, God is the subject. He dwells among his people Israel: "I *will dwell* among the sons of Israel, and will not forsake my people Israel." (1 Ki. 6:13, cf. Exod. 29:45–46; Num. 5:3; 35:34; Ezek. 43:7; Zech. 2:10–11; 8:3, 8). He dwells among Israel as an act of his sovereign love and grace and not because of Israel's special character (Deut. 12:5–6), though his presence among his people requires holy living on their part (23:14). A common refrain in Deuteronomy is God's promise to make a place for his name to dwell, to which the Israelites are to bring their sacrifices (12:11, cf. 14:23; 16:2, 6, 11; 26:2).

Thus, God "dwells on Mount Zion" (Isa. 8:18; Joel 3:17, 21), and of the eschatological temple God promises: "This is the place of my throne and the place of the soles of my feet, where I will *dwell* among the sons of Israel forever" (Ezek. 43:7, cf. Zech. 8:3). Zechariah prophecies of the ingathering of the nations to the place of God's dwelling: "Many nations will join themselves to the LORD in that day and will become my people. Then I will *dwell* in your midst, and you will know that the LORD of hosts has sent me to you" (Zech. 2:11; cf. Isa. 56:7). According to the NT, the amazing thing about the incarnation of Jesus is that he came to dwell among us

(Jn. 1:14, which uses a Gk. verb related to this Heb. verb).

Even though God may specify a location for his dwelling, he is not confined to that place. He dwells on a high and holy place, yet also with the contrite and lowly of spirit (Isa. 57:15). Indeed, *šākan* emphasizes a sense of rest, when one settles down after a period of travel. Thus, the contrite and lowly spirit, who seeks the rest of divine companionship, finds it by God's gracious desire to dwell with them. The King takes up his abode in the tent of humankind, and in so doing brings them rest. See *NIDOTTE*, 4:109-11.

New Testament

Verb: κατοικέω [*katoikeō*], GK *2997* (S *2730*), 44x. The verb *katoikeō* means "to inhabit, live, dwell." See *live*.

Verb: σκηνόω (*skēnoō*), GK *5012* (S *4637*), 5x. *skēnoō* means "dwell, live," but it often retains the notion of pitching a tent. In John 1:14 the evangelist says of Jesus: "The Word became flesh and made his dwelling [*skēnoō*, lit., 'tabernacled'] among us." That is, Jesus is the incarnation of the glory of God, dwelling among God's people as God did in the tabernacle (*skēnē*) of the OT. Similarly, Rev. 21:3 says, "Now the dwelling [*skēnē*] of God is with men, and he will live [*skēnoō*] with them" (cf. also 13:6). See also *tabernacle*. See *NIDNTT-A*, 527-28.

DYNASTY

Old Testament

Noun: בַּיִת (*bayit*), GK 1074 (S 1004), 2047x. *bayit* means "house" (see *house*) and bears both literal and figurative meanings in the OT. Significantly, it describes kingship, a royal dynasty, and particularly the "house of David" (2 Ki. 17:21; Isa. 7:2; cf. especially 2 Sam. 7:11–16).

EACH

Old Testament

Noun: כֹּל (*kōl*), GK 3972 (S 3605), 5415x. *kōl* means "whole, all, every." When it is followed by an indefinite singular (e.g., without the article), it is often translated "each, every." See *all*.

New Testament

Adjective: ἕκαστος (*hekastos*), GK *1667* (S *1538*), 82x. *hekastos* means "each" or "every." It most often functions as a pronoun, "each one" or "every one." For example, the Son of Man will reward "each one" according to what he has done (Mt. 16:27). "Each one" of us will have to give an accounting to God (Rom. 14:12). Used most often by Paul (42x [22x in 1 Cor.]), he says "to *each one* is given the manifestation of the Spirit for the common good" (1 Cor. 12:7). *hekastos* is also used as an adjective modifying a noun, e.g., "*each* tree" (Lk. 6:44) or "*each* part" (Eph. 4:16).

Adjective: πᾶς (*pas*) GK *4246* (S *3956*), 1243x. *pas* generally means "each, every" in the singular, "all" in the plural. See *all*.

EACH OTHER

Old Testament

Noun: אָחוֹת (*ʾāḥôt*), GK 295 (S 269), 119x. This noun primarily denotes a blood relative and is used for both a sister (Gen. 4:22) and a half-sister (Gen. 20:15) (see *sister*). But the Hebrew also uses *ʾāḥôt* as part of an idiomatic expression to convey the sense of "each other" or "together." Thus, when the subject is masculine, the idea of "each other" is literally "a man to his brother" (Gen. 37:19, " 'Here comes that dreamer!' they said *to each other*"). Likewise, when the subject is feminine, the idiom is "a woman to her sister." Note Exod. 26:3 where "Join five of the curtains *together*" is literally, "Join five of the curtains, a woman to her sister."

New Testament

Pronoun: ἀλλήλων (*allēlōn*), GK *253* (S *240*), 100x. ἀλλήλων is a reciprocal pronoun that means "each other, one another." See *one another*.

(BE) EAGER

Old Testament

Verb: שָׁכַם (*šākam*), GK 8899 (S 7925), 65x. *šākam* can mean "to rise early in the morning, be eager, or do again and again," though the former meaning is much more common than the others. The meaning "to be eager" appears in Zeph. 3:7, where Jerusalem is said "to be eager" to corrupt all her deeds. See *arise early.*

EAGERNESS

New Testament

Noun: σπουδή (*spoudē*), GK *5082* (S *4710*), 12x. *spoudē* means "earnestness, eagerness, concern." See *earnestness*.

EAR

Old Testament

Noun: אֹזֶן (*ʾōzen*), GK 265 (S 241), 188x. *ʾōzen*, meaning "ear," is used in reference to earrings (Gen. 35:4, Exod. 32:2), which shows someone to be a slave (Exod. 21:6). Tipping the lob of the *ʾōzen* with blood is a Levitical procedure (Lev. 8:23, 24; 14:14, 17, 25, 28), and being tortured by cutting the *ʾōzen* is associated with being taken over by a foreign power (Ezek. 23:25).

Proverbs warns that a person who meddles in a quarrel that is not one's own is like someone who grabs a dog by its ears (Prov. 26:17). *ʾōzen* also indicates the listening function of ears, as in Job 42:5, "My *ears* had heard of you, but now my eyes have seen you." Isaiah envisions a day when Israel's "*ears* will hear a voice behind them saying 'This is the way; walk in it'" (Isa. 30:21). The psalmist asked rhetorically whether God, who has implanted the *ʾōzen* in humans, can hear the cries of his people (Ps. 94:9). David exclaims that Israel hears with their ears of the greatness of the Lord (2 Sam. 7:22). Ultimately is the Lord who "wakens" our ears in order to be taught by him (Isa. 50:4–5).

Proverbs instructs us to turn our ears to wisdom and apply our hearts to understanding (Prov. 2:2; cf. 18:15). The Lord says that ears will tingle when they hear his judgment (1 Sam. 3:11; 2 Ki. 21:12; Jer. 19:3). Jeremiah emphasizes that Israel cannot listen to his words because her *ʾōzen* are uncircumcised (Jer. 6:10).

The Lord too has *ʾōzen*. The psalmist prays that God will answer him and give ear to his prayer (Ps. 17:6; cf. 71:2, "turn your *ears* to me and save me").

New Testament

Noun: ἀκοή (*akoē*), GK *198* (S *189*), 24x. *akoē* can mean "hearing," but it can also refer to the organ of hearing ("ear") or to what is actually heard ("message"). See *hearing*.

Noun: οὖς (*ous*), GK *4044* (S *3775*), 36x. *ous* means "ear." In some passages, the phrase "to reach the ears" simply means "to hear" (Mt. 10:27; Acts 11:22). But nearly half of the uses of this noun are in some form of the expression, "He who has ears, let him hear" (Mt. 11:15; Mk. 4:23; Lk. 8:8; Rev. 2:7, 11, 17, 29). This expression essentially means, "Listen carefully to what I [the Lord Jesus] am saying to you"; since what the Lord has said is now in Scripture, this expression means today that we should pay careful attention to God's Word. By contrast, Jesus strongly criticizes those who refuse "to hear with their ears" (Mt. 13:15; Mk. 8:8; cf. Acts 7:51; 28:27; Rom. 11:8).

Peter cut off the ear of the servant of the high priest in the garden (Lk. 22:50), but Jesus healed it; he also performed the miracle of hearing on a man who could not hear (Mk. 7:33). Paul stresses that the ear is as essential to the human being as the eye is (1 Cor. 12:16). Peter quotes one of the most blessed promises from Psalms, that "the eyes of the Lord are on the righteous and his ears are attentive to their prayers" (1 Pet. 3:12)—one of only two NT passages that refer to the ears of the Lord (cf. Jas. 5:4).

EARLIER

New Testament

Adjective: πρότερος (*proteros*), GK *4728* (S *4387*, *4386*), 11x. *proteros* is a comparative adjective that denotes a period of time preceding another period of time, "earlier, former."

EARLY

Old Testament

Adjective: רִאשׁוֹן (*riʾšôn*), GK 8037 (S 7223), 182x. As an adjective, *riʾšôn* describes what is first in a series or rank. In terms of time, *riʾšôn* can convey the meaning "previously, in a former time." See *first*.

New Testament

Adverb: πρωΐ (*prōi*), GK *4745* (S *4404*), 12x. Because *prōi* can designate any time covered in the fourth watch (from 3:00 to 6:00 a.m.), sometimes it refers to very early in the morning, for which we have the phrase "the crack of dawn" (Mk. 13:35; 15:1; 16:2; Jn. 18:28). *prōi* can also signify a time early enough to be still dark (cf. Mk. 1:35, where "Jesus rose *early in the morning*, while it was still dark, and departed to a deserted place to pray"; cf. Jn. 20:1). On another occasion *prōi* refers to a working day that began early (Mt. 20:1). Finally, in Acts 28:23 Luke recalls that from *morning* until evening, Paul expounded the Scriptures. Here *prōi* is used idiomatically with *hestera* ("evening") meaning that Paul preached "all day."

EARNESTNESS

New Testament

Noun: ζῆλος (*zēlos*), GK *2419* (S *2205*), 16x. In the NT *zēlos* can be either a good thing or a bad thing: "zeal, earnestness" is highly commended whereas "jealousy, envy" is condemned. See *zeal*.

Noun: σπουδή (*spoudē*), GK *5082* (S *4710*), 12x. *spoudē* means "earnestness, eagerness, concern." In the gospels it describes the manner in which someone departs to go somewhere; e.g., concerned not to keep Herod waiting, the daughter of Herodias comes in "with haste" to the king (Mk. 6:25), and Mary "hurries" to a town of Judah (Lk. 1:39). In both instances "concern" is what motivates the haste.

spoudē in the rest of the NT refers to the earnestness and concern with which an action is carried out (see Jude 3). Those with the spiritual gift of leadership are to lead with *spoudē* (Rom. 12:8), and believers should not be lazy but "zealous" in their lives as believers (Rom. 12:11; Heb. 6:11–12). Peter encourages believers to put forth great "effort" to grow in their Christian life (1 Pet. 1:5). Zeal, diligence, and efficiency are the result of having *spoudē*.

spoudē is a commanded virtue for believers. Godly grieving over sin in the Corinthian church produces *spoudē*, and Paul writes the Corinthians to provoke just that (2 Cor. 7:11–12). Even as the church excels in *spoudē* (8:7), Paul wants these believers to be generous so as to prove by their concern for others that their love is "earnest" (8:8). Of course, Paul is only asking the church for what he already practices himself, and so he thanks God, "who put into the heart of Titus the same *concern* I have for you" (2 Cor. 8:16, NIV). See *NIDNTT-A*, 536.*

EARTH

Old Testament

Noun: עָפָר (*ʿāpār*), GK 6760 (S 6083), 55x. *ʿāpār* refers to fine, dry dirt. In Ps. 18:42, David declares that he ground his enemies "like *dust* before the wind." This word also refers to loose earth, as in Gen. 26:15, where the Philistines fill in all the wells of Abraham with *earth*. See *dust*.

Noun: אֶרֶץ (*ʾereṣ*), GK 824 (S 776), 2505x.

Noun: אֲדָמָה (*ʾadāmâ*), GK 141 (S 127), 222x.

These two nouns for "land, earth" often overlap in the OT, yet at times there are some distinctions in meaning. Both words play an important role in OT theology. *ʾereṣ* occurs frequently throughout the OT and has two primary meanings: (a) the earth or land in general, and (b) the land of Israel in particular. *ʾadāmâ* is used in reference to the covenant promises and warnings about the earth (Exod. 20:12; Deut. 4:40; 2 Ki. 17:23; Amos 7:11, 17), and at times, it designates the inhabited world (Ezek. 38:20; Isa. 24:21). See *land*.

New Testament

Noun: γῆ (*gē*), GK *1178* (S *1093*), 250x. The LXX translates both *ʾereṣ* and *ʾadāmâ* with the Greek word *gē* (see *land*). *gē* is also the standard word for "earth, land" in the NT. It occurs especially in the gospels, Acts, and Revelation. *gē* is not nearly as theologically important in the NT as it is in the OT. This is due to the theological shift from an ethnic, land-based people (Israel) to a sojourning remnant consisting of people from all nations (the church). As a result, the vast majority of the occurrences of *gē* in the NT refer simply to geographic space—the land, earth, or soil—on which people travel or in which they live (Mt. 9:26; Mk. 4:1; Lk. 5:3; Jn. 12:24). As in the OT, at times *gē* is combined with "heaven" to refer to all of creation (Mt. 5:18; Rev. 5:3).

There are other times, however, when *gē* is used in a theologically charged way. Taking their cue from the OT and intertestamental literature, NT authors sometimes combine *gē* with heaven to emphasize a contrast or comparison between God's ways and human ways. This is especially prominent in Matthew, but it also occurs in Hebrews (Heb. 8:4–5; 12:25–26), Revelation, and elsewhere. It has a strong and practical application for believers: Christians are to set their minds on things above, not on earthly things (Col. 3:2), and are to live here on earth according to the coming kingdom of heaven (Mt. 4:17; 5:3–11; 6:10). See *NIDNTT-A*, 106.

EARTHQUAKE

New Testament

Noun: σεισμός (*seismos*), GK *4939* (S *4578*), 14x. In most uses *seismos* is an "earthquake." Earthquakes are known throughout the Mediterranean region and particularly in eastern Palestine. Geologically, this is because of the movements of the African and Arabian tectonic plates against the Eurasian plates. Earthquakes in the Bible are often seen as divine acts with theological significance. A violent *seismos* shakes the foundation of the prison holding Paul and Silas; the doors fly open, enabling all the prisoners to escape (though no one does; Acts 16:26).

A *seismos* also occurs in connection with significant events such as the death of Jesus (Mt. 27:54) and his resurrection (28:2). In Revelation, an earthquake announces the opening of sixth seal by Jesus (Rev. 6:12) and the opening of God's heavenly sanctuary (11:19). Earthquakes are among the cataclysmic events that will occur in the days of judgment accompanying the last days (Mt. 24:7; Mk. 13:8; Lk. 21:11; Rev. 8:5; 11:13; 16:18).

In one instance, *seismos* refers to a furious storm on the Sea of Galilee (Mt. 8:24), which Jesus subsequently calms in a dramatic display of his power. See *NIDNTT-A*, 521-522.*

EAST

Old Testament

Noun, Adverb, or Adjective: מִזְרָח (*mizrāḥ*), GK 4667 (S 4217), 74x. This word means "the east," the place from where the sun rises (Exod. 27:13; 38:13; Num. 2:3; Jos. 1:15; Ps. 50:1; 113:3; Isa. 41:25; Mal. 1:11); it is related to the Heb. verb for "to rise, shine." The Heb. sense of direction was oriented towards the east, with the west behind, north to the left, and south to the right. *mizrāḥ* can be used with reference to the east side of something (Num. 32:19; Jos. 4:19; 1 Chr. 4:39) or simply to an eastward direction (Jos. 11:3; 13:32; 16:1; 1 Ki. 7:25; Neh. 3:26; Isa. 46:11).

The vastness of the earth is used to illustrate the extent to which God has dealt with sin: "As far as the east is from the west, so far has he removed our transgressions from us" (Ps. 103:12). The thought is that God has so completely removed our transgressions from us that no matter how far toward the sun one travels, one can never reach the place where the sun rises. The compass is also used to indicate how God will bring complete salvation to his people. He promises to restore them from all parts of the globe, "Do not be afraid, for I am with you; I will bring your children from the east and gather you from the west" (Isa. 43:5–6). See *NIDOTTE, 2:912.*

Noun or Adjective: קָדִים (*qādîm*), GK 7708 (S 6921), 69x. *qādîm* designates the eastward direction. It is commonly used with reference to the "east wind." Similar to how people from New England might refer to a "Northeaster" as a cold and blustery storm with winds coming off the waters of the icy north Atlantic, *qādîm* can speak about a scorching wind that blows in from the desert lands east of the Jordan River. This wind could scorch crops (Gen. 41:6), wither vines (Ezek. 17:10; 19:12), and make for uncomfortable conditions (Jn. 4:8). The Lord, the Creator and Ruler of nature, used the east wind as an instrument to accomplish his purposes. It brought the locusts on Egypt (Exod. 10:13), and with it he divided the Red Sea (14:21). He also used it to feed the Israelites with quail (Ps. 78:26–27). It can be used metaphorically to refer to God's judgment (Ps. 48:8; Isa. 27:8; Jer. 18:17).

qādîm is especially prominent in Ezekiel, where it is used to discuss the new temple and the new land (Ezek. 48:1–32). The temple faces eastward (11:1; 40:6). The glory of the Lord that departed to the east (11:23) will return to the temple through the Eastern Gate (43:1–4). The gate will be shut thereafter because, "the LORD God of Israel has entered by it; therefore it shall be shut" (44:1–2). It will be opened only on the Sabbath, and no one will be allowed to walk through it (44:3–4; cf. 46:12). The ancient Israelites believed that the Messiah would come through this gate. See *NIDOTTE, 3:871-73.*

Noun or Adjective: קֶדֶם (*qedem*), GK 7710 (S 6924), 61x. This word originally meant "in front of" or "before" and came to denote "east"—from the idea of facing (being in front of) the rising sun (Gen. 10:30; 11:2; 12:8; 25:6; 29:1; Num. 23:7). The east was the place where the Garden of Eden was located (Gen. 2:8). Like the entrance to the tabernacle, the entrance to the Garden was on the east side (3:24). The east was known for its learning and wisdom (1 Ki. 4:30) and also for its divination and magic arts (Isa. 2:6).

The east sometimes refers to enemies of Israel (Jdg. 6:3, 33; Isa. 9:12); "the people of the East" are used as instruments of God's judgment on the enemies of his people (Ezek. 25:4, 10). Promises of restoration from exile included promises that the enemies of the east will become plunder for God's people. Those eastern nations that exiled Israel will be punished (Isa. 11:11–14). The "day of the LORD" is to be a time when God will stand to the east of Jerusalem on the Mount of Olives prepared to fight Israel's enemies. The mountain will split and create an east-west pathway that approached the Eastern Gate of the temple, through which the Messiah is expected to pass (Zech. 14:2–5). See *NIDOTTE*, 3:872-74.

New Testament

Noun: ἀνατολή (*anatolē*), GK *424* (S *395*), 11x. *anatolē* indicates the direction east or action that comes from the east. It is translated either "east" or "rising." The meaning "east" comes because that is the direction of the rising of the sun.

The Magi came "from the east" to visit the newborn king of the Jews (Mt. 2:1), because they saw his star "when it rose" (see NIV note on 2:2; cf. 2:9). Jesus prophesies that many followers will come "from the east" and take their places at the feast with Abraham (Mt. 8:11; cf. Lk. 13:29). Speaking of his return, Jesus says that just as lighting comes from the east and goes to the west, so his return will be visible to all (Mt. 24:27). *anatolē* is used in Revelation of angels and kings coming from the east (Rev. 7:2; 16:12) and of the gates of heaven "on the *east*" (21:13). *anatolē* is used metaphorically of John the Baptist, whose ministry will serve as a rising light that prepared the way for Jesus (Lk. 1:78). See *NIDNTT-A*, 50.*

EAT

Old Testament

Verb: אָכַל (*ʾākal*) GK 430 (S 398), 820x. The basic meaning of *ʾākal* is "to eat." When a person or an animal is the subject of the verb, the object is usually food. Eating may take place in a variety of contexts. The combination of "eating and drinking" is an idiom for celebration (Exod. 32:6; Eccl. 2:24), though the phrase can also mean simply having a meal (Gen. 25:34). Eating a meal with someone in ancient culture was a sign of acceptance

(Gen. 26:30; 43:32). Eating in connection with sacrifice has ritual and covenantal significance (Lev. 7:15ff.; Ezek. 18:15), and God gave numerous laws to his people about what they could and could not eat (Lev. 11). Particularly prohibited was the eating of blood (17:10–15). One of God's blessing for his people was to give them "the bread of angels" to eat while in the desert (Ps. 78:24–25). Eating well is a sign of prosperity (Joel 2:26), while not having enough to eat is a sign of poverty (Mic. 6:14) or of God's judgment (Lam. 2:20; 4:5).

When subject of *ʾākal* is other than human beings or animals, or when something other than food is consumed, *ʾākal* takes on metaphorical significance, and the translation is often "consume, devour." Sword, plague, and famine "consume" or "devour" in times of war (Ezek. 7:15). Fire consumes (2 Ki. 1:10). The wicked devour people (Ps. 14:4; 27:2; Prov. 30:14). The activity of an adulteress is described figuratively as eating (Prov. 30:20). On a more positive note, zeal for God's house consumes the psalmist (Ps. 69:9). See *NIDOTTE*, 1:393–97.

New Testament

Verb: γεύομαι (*geuomai*), GK *1174* (S *1089*), 15x. *geuomai* means "to taste, eat, partake of," usually implying enjoyment of the experience. See *taste*.

Verb: ἐσθίω (*esthiō*), GK *2266* (S *2068*), 158x. *esthiō* means "to eat"; it commonly occurs along with *pinō* for eating and drinking—two necessary actions to sustain physical life. *esthiō* mainly refers to that which is taken in through the mouth. Jesus is concerned about such issues since he performs a miracle by taking seven small loaves and two small fish to give 5,000 people "something *to eat*" (Mt. 14:16–21). Eating involves the consumption of all kinds of things, such as "locusts and wild honey" (Mk. 1:6), "manna from heaven" in the desert (Jn. 6:31), "vegetables" (Rom. 14:2b), "meat" (14:21), and even "the flesh of the Son of Man" (Jn. 6:53). While this last reference has ramifications for the Lord's Supper, its context primarily suggests receiving Christ spiritually through faith.

God turns a food eating tradition on its head in Peter's threefold housetop vision (Acts 10). Three times a sheet filled with all kinds of things forbidden on the Jewish menu appears to Peter (cf. Lev. 11), and each time God tells him to "rise, kill, and *eat*" (10:13). God clearly communicates the lesson not only that nothing is off limits for the Jew, but also that Gentiles have equal access to the kingdom. Jesus taught a similar lesson earlier when he declared, "Nothing outside a man can make him 'unclean' by going into him. Rather, it is what comes out of a man that makes him 'unclean'" (Mk. 7:14b–15). Jesus thereby declared all foods clean (7:19), and went on to say that human waste is better than what comes out of a person's heart (see 7:20–23).

The only thing that makes eating a problem is the context in which it occurs or the motives of those involved. In the parable of the rich fool, eating, drinking, and living in merriment and wanton disregard for spiritual things suddenly comes into sharp focus with unexpected death (Lk. 12:19). Some early Christians who were mooching off of the socially responsible members of their community of faith were to be denied something to eat if they did not return to work (2 Thess. 3:10). See *NIDNTT-A*, 210.

Verb: κατεσθίω (*katesthiō*), GK *2983* (S *2719*), 14x. *katesthiō* means "to devour, eat up." See *devour*.

EATING

New Testament

Noun: βρῶσις (*brōsis*), GK *1111* (S *1035*), 11x. This noun can refer either to that which is eaten ("food") or to the act of "eating, consuming." See *food*.

EDGE

Old Testament

Noun: כָּנָף (*kānāp*), GK 4053 (S 3671), 111x. *kānāp* has the basic meaning of a wing, such as the wing of a bird. By extension, it can refer to the edge of something, particularly the skirting or hem of a garment. See *wing*.

Noun: פֵּאָה (*pēʾâ*), GK 6991 (S 6285), 86x. *pēʾâ* can be translated as "side, boundary, border, edge." See *side*.

Noun: פֶּה (*peh*), GK 7023 (S 6310), 498x. *peh* refers to the "mouth" of people or animals as the organ of eating/drinking or of speech. As a metaphor, the "mouth" of the sword is the "edge" of the sword (Gen. 34:26; Jos. 10:28). See *mouth*.

Noun: קָצֶה (*qāṣeh*), GK 7895 (S 7097), 92x. *qāṣeh* is derived from the verb *qāṣâ*, which means "to cut off," and refers to the point where something is cut off, i.e., its edge or end. See *end*.

Noun: שָׂפָה (*śāpâ*) GK 8557 (S 8193), 178x. *śāpâ* often denotes the physical "lip(s)" of a person (Num. 30:7, 13; Song 4:3, 11; 5:13). When used metaphorically, this word can be translated as "shore" (on the seashore, Gen. 22:17; Exod. 14:30) or "edge" (of an object like a curtain, Exod. 26:4, 10). See *lip*.

New Testament

Noun: στόμα (*stoma*), GK *5125* (S *4750*), 78x. The word *stoma* refers to the "mouth," but it can also denote the "edge" of a sword. See *mouth*.

EDIFICATION

New Testament

Noun: οἰκοδομή (*oikodomē*), GK *3869* (S *3619*), 18x. *oikodomē* can mean either "a building" or "building up, edification." See *building*.

EDIFY

New Testament

Verb: οἰκοδομέω (*oikodomeō*), GK *3868* (S *3618*), 40x. In the gospels *oikodomeō* often has the normal meaning of building a physical structure. But in Acts and the rest of the NT, this verb becomes a significant metaphor for the mutual encouragement and strengthening of the people of God. See *build, build up*.

EDUCATE

New Testament

Verb: παιδεύω (*paideuō*), GK *4084* (S *3811*), 13x. *paideuō* means "to teach, educate," but also "to chasten, punish." See *teach*.

(BE) EFFECTUAL

See *work*.

EIGHT

Old Testament

Noun: שְׁמֹנֶה (*šᵉmōneh*), GK 9046 (S 8083), 147x. *šᵉmōneh* means "eight" in the singular and "eighty" in the plural. It can also mean the ordinal numeral "eighth." *šᵉmōneh* can also combine with other numbers: e.g., with *ʾelep* ("thousand," GK 547), it means "eight thousand"; with the number ten, it means "eighteen."

The Feast of Tabernacles was an eight-day festival (Lev. 23:36; Num. 29:35), with both the beginning and ending days being special days without work. Circumcision was to be done when a male child was "*eight* days old" (Gen. 17:12).

Since the number forty represents one generation, the number "eighty" represents two generations. Perhaps it is for this reason that the psalmist of Ps. 90 considers this age to be a good old age, even though life may be filled with many sorrows (Ps. 90:10). And certainly the writer of Proverbs considers it a great blessing not only to have children but also to be able to see our children's children (Prov. 17:6). God wants the great stories of salvation communicated to our children and grandchildren (Exod. 10:2; Ps. 78:1–6). See *NIDOTTE*, 4:174–75.

EIGHTH

Old Testament

Noun: שְׁמֹנֶה (*šᵉmōneh*), GK 9046 (S 8083), 147x. *šᵉmōneh* means "eight" in the singular and "eighty" in the plural. It can also mean the ordinal numeral "eighth." See *eight*.

EIGHTY

Old Testament

Noun: שְׁמֹנֶה (*šᵉmōneh*), GK 9046 (S 8083), 147x. *šᵉmōneh* means "eight" in the singular and "eighty" in the plural. It can also mean the ordinal numeral "eighth." See *eight*.

EJECT

New Testament

Verb: ἐκβάλλω (*ekballō*), GK *1675* (S *1544*), 81x. *ekballō* means "to drive out, expel, eject." It often indicates a violent expulsion, especially of demons. See *drive out.*

ELDER

Old Testament

Verb: זָקֵן (*zāqēn*), GK 2416, 2418 (S 2204, 2205), 206x. *zāqēn* generally means to be old (Gen. 18:11–13; Jdg. 19:17, 20; Job 14:8; Isa. 47:6). See *old.*

(1) In an age when people usually did not live long, becoming old was viewed as a blessing (Prov. 17:6). Unlike many Western cultures today, the elderly were looked on with great respect (Lev. 19:32) and were highly regarded for their wisdom (Ps. 119:100). Thus, *zāqēn* eventually came to be associated with people who served in positions of authority and honor. In this sense the word was commonly used of leaders of a city (Deut. 19:12), who sat in the gate to serve as judges (Deut. 21:2) or witnesses of legal transactions (Ruth 4:2, 4, 9), or of a nation (Gen. 50:7; 1 Ki. 8:1, 3). During the time of the exodus, Moses chose seventy elders to assist in governing Israel (Exod. 24:1).

Less frequently, *zāqēn* is applied to rulers/leaders of households (2 Sam. 12:17), tribes (Deut. 31:28), and regions (Jdg. 11:5–11). The verb can also be used of councilors (1 Ki. 12:6; 8, in which old age is implied; Job 12:20; Ezek. 7:26) and prominent priests (2 Ki. 19:2; see also Isa. 37:2; Jer. 19:1)

(2) The principle title for church leaders in the NT—*presbyteros*, "elder"—is the same word used in the Greek OT (the Septuagint) to translate *zāqēn*. When referring to persons of authority within the community, *zāqēn* always pointed to male leaders. The Bible of the early church was the Septuagint, and early Christian congregations, predominantly Jewish, were direct extensions of the OT community of faith. The data suggest that NT elders would naturally have been men. For further reading, see *NIDOTTE* 1:1134–37.

New Testament

Noun and Adjective: πρεσβύτερος (*presbyteros*), GK *4565* (S *4245*), 66x. *presbyteros* means "older" and, when used with the definite article, is a common term for older men as well as for the leaders ("elders") in the synagogue and the church.

(1) *presbyteros* can simply mean older (Lk. 15:25; Jn. 8:9; Acts 2:17; 1 Tim. 5:1; Tit. 2:2) in contrast to younger people (Acts 2:17) or to people living long ago (Heb. 11:2). In its feminine form it is used of "older women" (1 Tim. 5:2). In the ancient world, an older person was usually respected and thus had much to offer in terms of leadership.

(2) *presbyteros* is often used for the past leaders of Judaism ("Why do your disciples break the tradition of the *elders*?"; Mt. 15:2; Mk. 7:3) and of the current leaders of a city (Lk. 7:3). This term commonly refers to the official leaders of Judaism (Mt. 28:12; Lk. 7:3; Acts 4:5; 23:14), often combined with the chief priests and scribes (Mt. 16:21; 21:23; 26:3) as part of the Sanhedrin.

(3) *presbyteros* is also a title of leadership in the church (Acts 11:30; 15:2, 4, 6, 22, 23; 16:4; 1 Pet. 5:1). Paul's practice from the earliest days was to appoint elders in the young churches (Acts 14:23; Tit. 1:5), following the pattern of the synagogue; this is evident in many churches, such as Ephesus (Acts 20:17) and Jerusalem (21:18). The basic requirements for an elder are cited in 1 Tim. 3:1–7; 5:17–20; Tit. 1:5–9. It seems that *presbyteros* and *episkopos* ("overseer") refer to the same office (cf. Acts 20:1; 1 Tim. 3:1–2; Tit. 1:5-7); the fact that these two words can be used interchangeably demonstrates the relatively young age of church structure in the NT.

Church elders are to be honored, which includes both respect and remuneration (1 Tim. 5:17). Charges against an elder may not be accepted without adequate witnesses (5:19). They are to be appointed slowly; the sins of some are evident, but others are not. Likewise, the good deeds of some are quickly evident (1 Tim. 5:24–25). Elders provide basic oversight of the church, specifically in teaching (3:2), and they are to pray for the sick (Jas. 5:14). Younger people must submit to their leadership (1 Pet. 5:5).

(4) The author of 2 and 3 John refers to himself as *presbyteros*. It most likely refers to a person of spiritual maturity and renown, but possibly one of age as well.

(5) *presbyteros* also occurs repeatedly in Revelation of the twenty-four "elders" around God's throne (Rev. 4:4). These elders fall down before the Lord God Almighty and worship him (4:10; 11:16; 19:4). They give instructions to John (5:5–14), have a position of great importance (7:11), and have insights into some of the mysterious things that John sees (7:13–14). See *NIDNTT-A*, 488-90.

ELECT

New Testament

Verb: ἐκλέγομαι (*eklegomai*), GK *1721* (S *1586*), 22x. *eklegomai* means "to choose, set apart, elect." See *choose*.

Adjective: ἐκλεκτός (*eklektos*), GK *1723* (S *1588*), 22x. *eklektos* is the quality of being "chosen, selected, set apart," with the biblical implication that it is God who chooses. See *chosen*.

EMBARRASS, (BE) EMBARRASSED

New Testament

Verb: ἐπαισχύνομαι (*epaischynomai*), GK *2049* (S *1870*), 11x. *epaischynomai* means "to be ashamed, embarrassed, fearful of ridicule" because of one's actions or beliefs. See *ashamed*.

Verb: καταισχύνω (*kataischynō*), GK *2875* (S *2617*), 13x. *kataischynō* means "to embarrass, be ashamed, disappoint, humiliate." Both Paul (Rom. 9:33; 10:11) and Peter (1 Pet. 2:6) use it to describe the state that believers in Christ will never experience because they have put their trust in Christ. When used in this way, *kataischynō* has a legal aspect—that believers in Christ will not be condemned because they trust in Christ.

kataischynō used in a related manner to refer to the shame that a person experiences because one has no evidence to substantiate his or her claims. Paul does not want to be embarrassed when he arrives in Corinth with some Macedonians. But if the Corinthians have not participated significantly in Paul's collection for the poor Christians in Jerusalem, he will in fact be embarrassed of his strong confidence that they would participate (2 Cor. 9:4). Elsewhere, the detractors of Christians will be ashamed for their slander by the good behavior of Christians (1 Pet. 3:15), and Christian hope will never "disappoint" or disgrace the believer by proving false (Rom. 5:5).

kataischynō can also be used in the sense of humiliating or embarrassing someone (1 Cor. 11:22; 2 Cor. 7:14) or dishonoring something (1 Cor. 11:4–5). While such humiliation or dishonor may come as a result of wrong actions, there are also times when God in Jesus Christ works his victory to the shame and disgrace of his enemies (Lk. 13:17; 1 Cor. 1:27). See *NIDNTT-A*, 22-23.*

EMBRACE

New Testament

Verb: ἐπιπίπτω (*epipiptō*), GK *2158* (S *1968*), 11x. *epipiptō* can mean "to come upon, fall upon, embrace." See *come upon*.

EMMANUEL

KJV and RSV spelling for Immanuel. See *Immanuel*.

EMPTY

New Testament

Adjective: κενός (*kenos*), GK *3031* (S *2756*), 18x. *kenos* means "empty, empty-handed," and by extension, "vain, useless, futile." In the literal sense, *kenos* occurs in Mk. 12:3 and Lk. 20:10–11 where, in the parable of the vineyard, the master's servants are sent back empty-handed by the vineyard tenants (cf. also Lk. 1:53). Most other occurrences of *kenos* are in the writings of Paul. Generally it refers figuratively to things such as the empty words of paganism (Eph. 5:6), empty deceit (Col. 2:8), futile preaching (1 Cor. 15:10, if the resurrection is not true), and work that is in vain (1 Cor. 15:58). Paul uses *kenos* to indicate that under certain conditions things such as grace (2 Cor. 6:1), mission work (1 Thess. 3:5), and even his own service as an apostle (Gal. 2:2; Phil. 2:16) can be in vain or ineffective. See *NIDNTT-A*, 299-300.

EMPTY-HANDED

New Testament

Adjective: κενός (*kenos*), GK *3031* (S *2756*), 18x. *kenos* means "empty, empty-handed," and by extension, "vain, useless, futile." See *empty*.

ENCAMP

Old Testament

Verb: חָנָה (*ḥānâ*), GK 2837 (S 2583), 143x. *ḥānâ* generally means "to pitch camp, set up camp, encamp." It is used especially of the encamping of military units (Jdg. 11:20) or of nomadic peoples, such as the patriarchs. See *camp*.

ENCOUNTER

Old Testament

Verb: קָרָא (*qārāʾ*), GK 7925 (S 7122), 136x. The primary meaning of *qārāʾ* is "to meet, encounter, happen." See *meet*.

ENCOURAGEMENT

New Testament

Noun: παράκλησις (*paraklēsis*), GK *4155* (S *3874*), 29x. *paraklēsis* carries the idea of consolation, comfort, or encouragement (see *comfort*). In Acts the believers look for encouragement or comfort from one another (Acts 13:15; 15:31). The source of all comfort and encouragement is the Holy Spirit (Acts 9:31). This association with the Holy Spirit is clearly evident through Jesus' reference to the Spirit as the *paraklētos*, "the comforter" (see Jn. 14:26; 15:26; 16:13–14).

END

Old Testament

Verb: שָׁבַת (*šābat*), GK 8697 (S 7673), 71x. The primary sense of *šābat* is the cessation of activity. Often activity does not cease on its own, but someone causes it to cease. In the prophets in particular, God declares that he will "put an end" to the arrogance of the proud (Isa. 13:11; Ezek. 7:24). In Hosea, God will "put an end" to the kingdom of Israel (Hos. 1:4). In Jeremiah, he will "bring an end" to the sounds of joyous weddings as he brings about the exile (Jer. 7:34; 16:9). See *cease*.

Verb: תָּמַם (*tāmam*), GK 9462 (S 8552), 64x. This verb is used to describe a wide range of ideas having to do with completion, exhaustion, or ending.

(1) *tāmam* is used with reference to the completion of a specific work or of written or spoken words: "Moses *finished* writing the words of this Torah" (Deut. 31:24); "the words of Job are *ended*" (Job 31:40). The work on the temple "was completed" (1 Ki. 6:22).

(2) Some things come to an end, or cease, such as years (Gen. 47:18) and days of mourning (Deut. 34:8). Conversely, the "years [of God] *will* never *end*"(Ps. 102:27)—i.e., he is eternal.

(3) In other contexts, *tāmam* communicates the exhaustion or completion of an allotted number or fund of resources. When money runs out, it is gone: all Egypt's money "is spent" (Gen. 47:15). When the wilderness generation is all dead, all the men "are gone" or "have perished" (Deut. 2:16). In fact, there are numerous places where this verb denotes something that about to perish or to be destroyed (see, e.g., Jer. 14:15; 27:8; 44:12, 18, 27). See *NIDOTTE*, 4:306–8.

Noun: קֵץ (*qēṣ*), GK 7891 (S 7093), 67x. *qēṣ* generally bears one of three distinct but related meanings: "end," "limit," and at times "boundary."

(1) In Gen. 6:13 *qēṣ* refers to the "end" of life. It often appears in the context of divine judgment: "God said to Noah, 'I am going to put an *end* to all people, for the earth is filled with violence because of them.'" Likewise, the prophet declares to those with abundant treasures: "your *end*

has come, the time for you to be cut off" (Jer. 51:13).

The translation "end" also captures the frequent temporal sense of the term *qēṣ*: "After forty days [at the *end* of forty days] Noah opened the window he had made in the ark" (Gen. 8:6; cf. Est. 2:12). At least 26 of the 67 occurrences of *qēṣ* bears a temporal reference. The temporal sense of the term is taken up figuratively by the prophets to signify the eschaton, the end time, of human history (Dan. 8:17, 19; 11:40; 12:4, 6; see also Ezek. 7:2–3). The prophets envision an end of wrongdoing (Ezek. 21:25, 29), just as they expect a time of peace without *end* (Isa. 9:7).

(2) *qēṣ* is rendered "limit" in Ps. 119:96 (NIV) and refers to the threshold of perfection, and in Job 6:11 it denotes the "end" or "limit" of human endurance.

(3) Finally, *qēṣ* may refer to the "remotest" part of a country (2 Ki. 19:23) but is rarely used of spatial boundaries (but see Jer. 50:26).

Noun: אַחֲרִית (*ʾaḥᵃrît*), GK 344 (S 319), 61x. *ʾaḥᵃrît* in its most literal sense denotes "that which comes after." Specifically it may describe what follows temporally, that is, the "cessation, end" of an event or the final "outcome." The noun derives from the verb *ʾāḥar*, which refers to occasions of staying behind, delaying, or waiting.

(1) *ʾaḥᵃrît* can refer to the "end," temporally, referring to what comes in the future. For example, God makes known "the *end* from the beginning" (Isa. 46:10), and "surely there is a *future*, and your hope will not be cut off" (Prov. 23:18, NRSV). The noun may also refer to the good things that come "after" God's testing (Deut. 8:16; Job 42:12).

(2) *ʾaḥᵃrît* may convey the notion of "cessation" or conclusion of an event or action. Balaam, relenting from his desire to curse Israel, says, "Let me die the death of the righteous, and may my *end* be like theirs!" (Num. 23:10). Likewise *ʾaḥᵃrît* describes the "outcome" of a court case (Prov. 25:8). The word may also mean "after" in a logical sense, as in Prov. 23:32, which describes the "aftereffects" of drunkenness as the bite of a serpent (also the "aftereffects" of promiscuity is bitterness, 5:4). In Ps. 109:13 and Dan. 11:4 *ʾaḥᵃrît* refers to "posterity" (as children or descendants coming afterwards).

Finally, the phrase *ʾaḥᵃrît hayyāmîm* ("end of days"), in a technical sense, expresses future time (Ezek. 38:16; Dan. 2:28; 10:14; Hos. 3:5; see also Isa. 2:2; Mic. 4:1). For some, this phrase designates those "latter days" when the final judgment is to come.

Noun: קָצֶה (*qāṣeh*), GK 7895 (S 7097), 92x. *qāṣeh* is derived from the verb *qāṣâ*, which means "to cut off," and refers to the point where something is cut off, i.e., its edge or end. This noun occurs only in the singular, but at times, it is translated as a plural to communicate the correct English nuance (e.g., Prov. 17:24, "the eyes of the foolish are on the *ends* of the earth"). It can refer to the edge of numerous geographical areas, such as a city (1 Sam. 9:27), a river (Jos. 3:8), a camp (Num. 11:1), a valley (Jos. 15:8), a hill (Jos. 18:16), or a wilderness area (Exod. 13:20).

Even the heavens and the earth have an end (Ps. 19:6). Often the phrase "the *end* of the earth" means the remote places of the world, seen from the vantage point of the land of Israel (Isa. 49:6), but it can also mean the world's farthest reaches (cf. "the *ends* of the world," Ps. 19:4). When the reference is to the edge of a country, "border" is a good translation (Exod. 16:35), and when it refers to the edge of a lake or sea, "shore" may be used (Jos. 15:2). Jos. 15:5 refers to the end of the Jordan River, meaning the place where it empties into the Dead Sea, so "mouth" is also used in some translations.

qāṣeh is used in connection with smaller items as well, such as a pile of grain (Ruth 3:7), a curtain (Exod. 26:5), or a staff (Jdg. 6:21). If a group of items has "no end," then there is an abundance of them (Isa. 2:7). At times, totality is referred to by the phrase "from *end* to *end*" (i.e., "from one end to the other end," Gen. 47:21). *qāṣeh* can also refer to a section of something (19:4). Taking something from the "end" of a group can refer to taking it from among the group (47:2). In addition to these spatial uses, it can be used temporally in reference to the end of a certain period of time (8:3). See *NIDOTTE*, 3:956-59.

New Testament

Verb: τελειόω *(teleioō)*, GK *5457* (S *5048*), 23x. *teleioō* refers to attaining an end or purpose, in the sense of being complete or perfect. It can take several different but related meanings. It refers to completing an activity, both in the sense of "to finish" (e.g., "After the Feast *was over*," Lk. 2:43) and "to accomplish, fulfill" (e.g., "if only I may finish the race and complete the task the Lord Jesus has given me" [Acts 20:24; see also Jn. 4:34; 5:36; 17:4]). Often the aspect of "to accomplish" specifically refers to the object of bringing something to its designed goal (i.e., "perfection," see Heb. 12:23). Jn. 19:28 is a good example of the interrelation of these terms: "Later, knowing that all was now completed (*teleō*), and so that the Scripture would be fulfilled (*teleioō*), Jesus said, 'I am thirsty.' "

teleioō occurs frequently in Hebrews where it conveys the notion of "make perfect," often with ritual (or ceremonial) overtones. Christ, our high priest, is "perfected" through suffering (Heb. 2:10) and made eternally "perfect" (7:28); he is differentiated from the priests of the old covenant. God's love reaches "perfection" when believers obey God's word: "if anyone obeys his word, God's love is truly *made complete* in him" (1 Jn. 2:5; cf. 4:12, 17, 18).

Verb: τελέω (*teleō*), GK *5464* (S *5055*), 28x. The basic meaning of *teleō* is "to finish, complete."

(1) It is used several times in the Gospels for finishing a task (e.g., Jesus finished teaching, Mt. 7:28; 11:1). In Matthew *teleō* marks the ending of each of Jesus' five discourses and the resumption of narrative. In 17:24 the verb is used in the rare instance of paying what is due (see also Rom. 13:6). Luke uses the verb in the sense of "accomplish" or "complete" (Lk. 12:50) and specifically of the words of the prophets being accomplished or fulfilled (18:31; 22:37; see Jn. 19:28; Acts 13:29). Significantly, Jesus cried out from the cross in Jn. 19:30: "It is finished." These words are a triumphant cry of victory in the hour of apparent defeat—the price for sin had been paid and redemption was accomplished.

(2) *teleō* also refers to keeping or fulfilling the law (Rom. 2:27, see Jas. 2:8, NIV "keep the royal law") and gratifying the desires of the flesh (Gal. 5:16, NIV; NASB, "carry out"). And the verb appears eight times in Revelation, where it refers to the completion of a testimony in 11:7, the completion of God's wrath in 15:1 (see 15:8), the end of the thousand-year reign (20:3, 5, 7), and the fulfillment of God's words (10:7; 17:17).

Noun: τέλος (*telos*), GK *5465* (S *5056*), 40x. *telos* can refer to the end result or ultimate fate. Paul speaks of the life or death alternatives facing individuals as the final result or goal of one's conduct (Rom. 6:21–22; see also Heb. 3:14; 6:11; 1 Pet. 1:9, 4:17). The word appears in Revelation in the phrase "beginning and *end*." This theologically rich phrase articulates the power of God (Rev. 21:6) and Christ (22:13), denoting both extremes of beginning and end along with everything temporally and spatially in between. God is the Creator and Perfecter of all things, so also is the exalted Christ (see 1:17; 2:8), thus in 2:26 Jesus calls the church to hold fast to the "end."

In the end-time discourses of the Gospels, Jesus uses *telos* as a technical term for the end of the world (Mt. 24:6; Mk. 13:7; Lk. 21:9; see also the phrase *eis telos*, "to the end," in Mt. 10:22; 24:13). Paul also uses *telos* as an end-time term. In 1 Cor. 10:11 he uses the phrase "the fulfillment of the ages," which refers to living in the last days. In 15:24 *telos* refers to the conclusion of the end-time events, the point at which Christ hands over the kingdom to the Father. A similar use is found in 1 Pet. 4:7: "The end of all things is near." "End" here does not denote merely the cessation of movement but rather the consummation or goal of the process in which final meaning and intentions are realized.

Adjective: τέλειος (*teleios*), GK *5455* (S *5046*), 19x. *teleios* conveys a range of meanings: "perfect, mature, complete." It can refer to something of the highest standard (i.e., "perfect" Jas. 1:4a, 17, 25), to a fully "mature" adult (Eph. 4:13), or fully developed, "perfect," or "complete" in a moral sense (Mt. 5:48; Jas. 1:4b; 3:2). Connected to the theological idea of *telos*, *teleios* conveys the sense of something reaching its end and therefore its "completion" or "perfection." This is not the idea of ethical perfection by degrees, but rather a sense of undivided wholeness of heart before God, and this by promise of God. The notion of "perfection" in contemporary English conveys the idea of "sinlessness" but *teleios* refers to "completion" without reference to fault or sin. For something to be "perfect" means to fulfill its ultimate design. For example, a chair is "perfect" if it has four legs and can support a person, thus fulfilling the purpose for which it was designed. See *NIDNTT-A*, 559-60.

ENDEAVOR

See *make effort.*

ENDUE

See put on.

ENDURANCE, ENDURE

Old Testament

Verb: עָמַד (*ʿāmad*), GK 6641 (S 5975), 524x. *ʿāmad* has the basic meaning "to stand" but includes multiple nuances depending on the context in which it occurs. The idea of standing firm gives the notion of enduring. See *stand.*

New Testament

Verb: ἀνέχομαι (*anechomai*), GK *462* (S *430*), 15x. *anechomai* means "to bear with, endure, tolerate, put up with" something or someone." The KJV translates it as "forbear" or "suffer." When the object of *anechomai* is personal, it means to put up with or tolerate an individual. In the gospels, Jesus exclaims in frustration, "O unbelieving generation . . . how long shall I *put up with* you?" (Mt. 17:17; Mk. 9:19; Lk. 9:41). The proconsul Gallio refused to *tolerate* the Jews and their accusations against Paul (Acts 18:14). Twice Paul exhorts believers to "bear with" one another in the sense of being patient with one another, overlooking differences through love and forgiveness. This mutual forbearance is essential in the church in order to promote peace and unity within the church body (Eph. 4:2; Col. 3:13). Several times in 2 Cor. 11, Paul makes a sarcastic play on this word, asking the Corinthians to "*put up with* a little" foolishness from him as he defends himself and his apostleship (2 Cor. 11:1, 4). While they will "tolerate" fools who enslave, exploit and abuse them (vv. 19–20), ironically, they will not bear with Paul, who has never wronged them.

anechomai can also apply to teachings. The author of Hebrews pleads with his readers to bear with his exhortation (Heb. 13:22), while Paul warns Timothy that in latter days, sound teaching will not be tolerated or endured (2 Tim. 4:3).

Finally, *anechomai* has the sense of suffering persecution, as in the case of the Thessalonian church (2 Thess. 1:4), whom Paul commends for "the persecutions and trials you are *enduring*," and in Paul's own case, in which, as an apostle, he *suffers* persecution without retaliating (1 Cor. 4:12). See *NIDNTT-A*, 51.*

Verb: ὑπομένω (*hypomenō*), GK *5702* (S *5278*), 17x. *hypomenō* may be rendered positively as "endure, stand firm, persevere." The term is used in the NT in its literal sense in Lk. 2:43: "the boy Jesus *stayed behind* in Jerusalem," and in Acts 17:14 "Silas and Timothy *stayed* at Berea." *hypomenō* can also refer to maintaining a conviction or action in the face of opposition and thus "endure" or "stand firm." As a weight-lifter bears up under the weight of the bar, one bears up under trouble or affliction (Mt. 10:22; 24:13; Rom. 12:12). The individual who stands firm in trial is blessed (Jas. 1:12; 5:11), and enduring suffering for doing what is right brings God's commendation (1 Pet. 2:20). Finally, the preeminent example of standing fast under opposition and persecution is Jesus, "the author and perfecter of our faith, who for the joy set before him *endured* the cross.... Consider him who *endured* such opposition from sinful men, so that you will not grow weary and lose heart" (Heb. 12:2–3).

Verb: φέρω (*pherō*), GK *5770* (S *5342*), 66x. *pherō* has the basic meaning "to bring, carry, present," but it has a wide range of figurative meanings, such as "to endure, sustain." See *bring*.

Verb: μακροθυμέω (*makrothymeō*), GK *3428* (S *3114*), 10x.

Verb: μένω (*menō*), GK *3531* (S *3306*), 118x. The basic sense of *menō* is "to remain, stay." See *remain*.

Noun: μακροθυμία (*makrothymia*), GK *3429* (S *3115*), 14x.

These two words are normally translated as some form of "patience, endurance." See *patience, (be) patient*.

Noun: ὑπομονη (*hypomonē*), GK *5705* (S *5281*), 32x. *hypomonē* refers to perseverance in the face of hostile forces. Job, for example, manifested great endurance in the midst of his afflictions from Satan (Jas. 5:11). This characteristic is pleasing to God: "To those who by *persistence* in doing good seek glory, honor, and immortality, he will give eternal life" (Rom. 2:7). Here *hypomonē* can be understood either in an active (steady persistence in doing good) or a passive (patient endurance under difficulties) sense. *hypomonē* in a passive sense is used in Rom. 12:12, where it is connected with persecution: "Be joyful in hope, *patient* in affliction, faithful in prayer" (see also 1 Thess. 1:3: "endurance inspired by hope"). The connection with hope sets *hypomonē* in the context of end-time expectation where believers endure to the end because of their hope in the Lord's coming. *hypomonē* is not only a characteristic of hope, but of love (1 Cor. 13:7) and the service of Christian workers (1 Tim. 6:11; 2 Tim. 3:10). Furthermore, *hypomonē* itself produces character (Rom. 5:3–5; Jas. 1:3–4; 2 Pet. 1:6) and is associated with the virtue of patience (Col. 1:11; Jas. 5:7–11). See *NIDNTT-A*, 581-82.

ENEMY

Old Testament

Verb: אֹיֵב (*ʾōyēb*), GK 367 (S 341), 285x. *ʾōyēb* is a personal or national "enemy." It occurs in parallel with ptc. forms of the verb *śānēʾ*, "to hate" (e.g., Lev. 26:17; Num. 10:35; 2 Sam. 22:18; Ps. 21:8; 68:1; 83:2). It describes the enemies of Israel (Deut. 20:1, 23; Jos. 10:13; 21:44; 1 Sam. 4:3; Jer. 18:17; Lam. 1:5) and God's enemies (Num. 10:35; 2 Sam. 12:14; Ps. 68:1; 92:9; Isa. 1:24), which are usually the same. Protection from an *ʾōyēb* is a theme in blessings and covenants (Gen. 22:17; 49:8; Exod. 23:22, 27; Lev. 26:7-8; Deut. 28:7; 33:27), while falling to an *ʾōyēb* is a theme in curses (Lev. 26:16-17, 25, 38–39; Deut. 28:25). The people of God are to treat even their enemies well (Exod. 23:4; Prov. 24:17). The psalmist prays for protection against and vengeance on *enemies* (Ps. 25:2; 31:15; 35:19; 64:1; 139:19; 143:12).

While the *ʾōyēb* is often vague and unidentifiable in the Psalms and may sometimes seem supernatural, there are no clear instances of *ʾōyēb* referring to Satan in the OT.

Noun: צַר (*ṣar*), GK 7640 (S 6862), 433x. *ṣar* comes from the root *ṣrr*, which means "to be hostile." It can be translated "enemy, foe, adversary."

ṣar occurs 17x in parallelism with *ʾōyēb*, "enemy" (e.g., Deut. 32:27; Ps. 13:4; 27:2; Isa. 1:24; 9:11; Lam. 1:5; 2:4). Like *ʾōyēb*, *ṣar* occurs in parallel with forms of the verb "to hate," *śānēʾ* (Deut. 32:41; Ps. 44:7,10; 89:23). *ṣar* is used of Israel's enemies collectively (Deut. 32:27; 2 Sam. 24:13; Jer. 30:16), of the Egyptians who pursued Israel into the Red Sea (Ps. 106:11), and of Haman, the notorious enemy of the Jews in Persia (Est. 7:6). It is not used in reference to Satan.

New Testament

Noun: ἐχθρός (*echthros*), GK *2398* (S *2190*), 32x. In NT teaching, your *echthros* is someone who opposes you. The hostile behaviors described by this word includes hatred (Lk. 6:27), persecution (Mt. 5:44), and bodily harm (Rev. 11:5). A child of God may *have* enemies but is not to *be* an enemy toward another person. Rather, believers are instructed to love and pray for their enemies (Mt. 5:44), provide food and drink for them (Rom. 12:20), and lend freely to them (Lk. 6:35). Those who have not been reconciled to the Father through his Son, Jesus Christ, are enemies of God (Rom. 5:10; Phil. 3:18; Col. 1:21), as are those who maintain friendship with the world (Jas. 4:4). *echthros* is also used to describe both Satan and death (Mt. 13:39; Lk. 10:19; 1 Cor. 15:26). Deliverance from both human and supernatural enemies comes from the Lord (Lk. 1:71, 74; 10:19). See *NIDNTT-A*, 221.

ENLIGHTEN

New Testament

Verb: φωτίζω (*phōtizō*), GK *5894* (S *5461*), 11x. *phōtizō* means "to give light, enlighten." See *(give) light*.

(HAVE) ENOUGH

Old Testament

Verb: שָׂבַע (*śāba*ʿ), GK 8425 (S 7646), 97x. The verb *śāba*ʿ means "to be satisfied, have enough, be filled," generally of food rather than drink. See *(be) satisfied*.

New Testament

Adverb: ἱκανός (*hikanos*), GK *2653* (S *2425*), 39x. *hikanos* conveys the idea that something is adequate or large enough in its quantity or quality and may best be translated "sufficient, deserve, adequate." See *sufficient*.

(BE) ENSLAVED

New Testament

Verb: δουλεύω (*douleuō*), GK *1526* (S *1398*), 25x. *douleuō* means "to serve, be enslaved," especially in the capacity of a slave. See *serve*.

ENTER

Old Testament

Verb: בּוֹא (*bô*ʾ), GK 995 (S 935), 2592x. *bô*ʾ is the fourth most common verb in the OT. It denotes motion toward a specific goal, such as "to go, arrive, enter a house, come." It expresses a variety of motions. See *come*.

New Testament

Verb: εἰσέρχομαι (*eiserchomai*), GK *1656* (S *1525*), 194x. *eiserchomai* is a compound of *eis* ("into") and *erchomai* ("come, go") and is most frequently translated "to go into, enter." It is used often of the physical realm, such as a person entering a house (Mk. 7:24), a city (Acts 11:20), the Most Holy Place (Heb. 9:25), or a church (Jas. 2:2). For this reason, its most frequent occurrence is in the gospels and Acts.

But *eiserchomai* is also used of the spiritual realm. Demonic spirits can enter into human beings (Mk. 9:25; Lk. 8:30) or even into swine (Mk. 5:12–13). Satan entered Judas (Lk. 22:3). Sin entered the world through Adam's sin in the Garden of Eden (Rom. 5:12). Jesus commands his disciples, "Pray that you will not enter into temptation" (22:40, 46). When one is born again and lives a humble, God-glorifying life, one enters the kingdom of God/heaven (Mt. 7:21; 19:24; Mk. 10:15; Jn. 3:5). God's ultimate goal for us is to enter into eternal rest (Heb. 3:11, 18; 4:11).

Verb: εἰσπορεύομαι (*eisporeuomai*), GK *1660* (S *1531*), 18x. *eisporeuomai* means "to enter, go in." Jesus says that nothing that "*enters* a man from the outside" makes him unclean (Mk. 7:15, 18–19). It is hard for the rich to "*enter* the kingdom of God" (Lk. 18:24). Saul was "*going into* house after house" attempting to destroy the church (Acts 8:3). Many "go in" to see Paul when he is under house arrest in Rome (28:30).

ENTERTAIN

New Testament

Verb: ξενίζω (*xenizō*), GK *3826* (S *3579*), 10x. *xenizō* generally means "to entertain, show hospitality," though it can also mean "to be surprised, to be strange" (see *strange, be strange*). The writer of Heb. 13:2 instructs us: "Do not forget to entertain strangers, for by so doing some people have *entertained* angels without knowing it." Hospitality was an important characteristic in both church and secular society. Peter "stayed as a guest" with Simon the Tanner (Acts 10:6, 18, 23, 32; cf. 21:16). Publius welcomed Paul and his traveling companions "to his home and for three days *entertained* us hospitably" (Acts 28:7). See *NIDNTT-A*, 398-99.

ENTIRE

Old Testament

Noun: כֹּל (*kōl*), GK 3972 (S 3605), 5415x. *kōl* means "whole, all, every." See *all*.

ENTRANCE

Old Testament

Noun: פֶּתַח (*petaḥ*), GK 7339 (S 6607), 164x. *petaḥ* means "door" or "entrance." It is used most often in the OT to indicate the entrance to a house or tent (Gen. 18:1, 2, 10; Exod. 33:8; Num. 11:10; 1 Chr. 9:21) or the entrance to a city (2 Sam. 10:8; Gen. 38:14; cf. Jer. 36:10).

petaḥ is also used metaphorically or figuratively. In the Psalms, for example, a *petaḥ* is personified as praising God by welcoming the King of glory (Ps. 24:7, 9: "Lift up you heads, O you gates! And be lifted up, you everlasting *petaḥ*! And the King of glory will come in."). In Ezek. 8:8, the prophet Ezekiel has a vision of a *petaḥ* through which he is able to see all the wicked and detestable things done by Israel (cf. Ezek. 8:14, 10:19). In Genesis, Cain gives a less honorable gift to the Lord than his brother, Abel. The Lord warns Cain that sin is crouching at the *petaḥ* of his life and desires to dominate him (Gen. 4:7). In the next verse (v. 8), Cain falls victim to sin and murders his brother. Because of our human nature, sin is always at our *petaḥ*, but by the power of the Spirit we can learn to master it before it is too late (cf. Gal. 5:16–26).

ENTRUST

New Testament

Verb: πιστεύω (*pisteuō*), GK *4409* (S *4100*), 241x. *pisteuō* generally means "to believe, be convinced of something," and in a more specific way "to have faith" in God or Christ. It can also mean "to entrust something to someone." See *believe*.

ENVY

New Testament

Verb: ζηλόω (*zēloō*), GK *2420* (S *2206*), 11x. *zēloō* means to be "zealous" or "jealous." It is related to the noun *zēlos* ("jealousy, zeal," GK *2419*). In classical Greek this word group sometimes carried a positive sense (eager striving, enthusiasm, or praise) and sometimes a negative sense (jealously, ill will, or envy). The same applies to the NT. Note the text, "Love does not *envy*" (1 Cor. 13:4). See *zealous*.

Noun: ζῆλος (*zēlos*), GK *2419* (S *2205*), 16x. In the NT *zēlos* can be either a very good thing or a very bad thing: "zeal, earnestness" is highly commended whereas "jealousy, envy" is condemned. See *jealousy*.

Noun: φθόνος (*phthonos*), GK *5784* (S *5355*), 9x. *phthonos* means "envy." This quality in a person is never regarded favorably in the NT. Pilate know that it was because of "envy" that the chief priests and the leaders of the people were attempting to destroy Jesus (Mt. 27:18; Mk. 15:10). The writers of the NT letters frequently include "envy" in a series of sins to be avoided (Rom. 1:29; Gal. 5:21; Tit. 3:3; 1 Pet. 2:1; cf. 1 Tim. 6:4).

EPHOD

Old Testament

Noun: אֵפֹד (*ʾēpōd*), GK 680 (S 646), 49x. *ʾēpōd* is usually simply transliterated into English as "ephod." This term is used in three different ways in the OT. (1) It refers to a special garment worn by the high priest on his shoulder (see Exod. 28; 39), bound by rings to the breastplate and made of colorful linen and yarn. It contained two stones on which were engraved the names of the tribes of Israel. Thus, in his official duties, Aaron bore on the ephod "the names on his shoulder as a memorial before the Lord" (28:12).

(2) The second meaning of *ʾēpōd* is a simple linen garment worn by Samuel (1 Sam. 2:18) or other priests; David had access to one and used it to aid him in making important decisions while running away from Saul (1 Sam. 23:9; 30:7)—perhaps because it was worn during a time when Urim and Thummim were used to determine God's will.

(3) *ʾēpōd* can also be an independent object used for divination (perhaps related to an idol). Gideon made an ephod that eventually became an idol for worship (Jdg. 8:23–27; cf. also 17:5; 18:14–20). Hosea relates this term to an idol (Hos. 3:4).

EPISTLE

New Testament

Noun: ἐπιστολή (*epistolē*), GK *2186* (S *1992*), 24x. Most frequently *epistolē* is translated as "letter" or "epistle." See *letter*.

ERR

New Testament

Verb: πλανάω (*planaō*), GK *4414* (S *4105*), 39x. In the active voice, *planaō* means "to lead astray, deceive"; in the middle/passive voice, "to wander, go astray." See *deceive*.

ERROR

New Testament

Noun: πλάνη (*planē*), GK *4415* (S *4106*), 10x. *planē* means "error, deception, deceit." Literally, the word denotes something that has wandered from its path (the English word "planet" derives from this word). The vestiges of the literal meaning can be seen in phrases such as "the error of his way" (Jas. 5:20).

However, in all NT occurrences the word refers figuratively to moral (Rom. 1:27) or spiritual (1 Jn. 4:6) deception or error. Paul's appeal for maturity is so that people no longer be deceived by "error" (Eph. 4:14; cf. 2 Pet. 2:18; 3:17; Jude 11). Paul's appeal to the Thessalonians does not stem from "error" (1 Thess. 2:3). *planē* can refer to an attempt to lead others into deception (Mt. 27:64). In the last days, God will send a "strong delusion," "a working of error," so that people will believe the Antichrist (2 Thess. 2:11). See *NIDNTT-A*, 466-67.*

ESCAPE

Old Testament

Verb: בָּרַח (*bāraḥ*), GK 1368 (S 1272), 63x. Like the Heb. verb *rûs*, *bāraḥ* is translated as "flee, escape." In general *bāraḥ* implies a secret, clandestine escape or flight. See *flee*.

Verb: מָלַט (*mālāṭ*), GK 4880 (S 4422), 94x. *mālāṭ* means to "escape, flee to safety," and it may also be translated in the passive "to be delivered, rescued, saved." It is used mostly by the prophets and often stresses human action in contrast to the deliverance of the LORD.

(1) *mālāṭ* is used to command or compel someone to flee from danger and escape to safety. At the destruction of Sodom and Gomorrah, the angels command Lot and his family to flee for their lives into the mountains in order to escape the wrath and judgment of God (Gen. 19:17–22).

(2) Elsewhere, *mālāṭ* emphasizes the escape or flight from enemies, especially in battle (1 Ki. 20:20; Jer. 41:15). This sense is seen clearly in the story of David's escape from Saul (1 Sam. 19:10–18 [5x]).

(3) Finally, *mālāṭ* can connote the salvation or deliverance that Yahweh provides, as in Ps. 41:4, "Blessed is he who has regard for the weak; the LORD *delivers* him in times of trouble." The LORD will "rescue" his people (Isa. 31:5) and they "will be *delivered*" (Dan. 12:1). An important text in this usage of *mālāṭ* is Joel 2:32, "And everyone who calls on the name of the LORD *will be saved*" (cf. Paul's use of this text in Rom. 10:13).

Verb: נוּס (*rûs*), GK 5674 (S 5127), 160x. Usually translated "flee," *rûs* refers to the escape or flight from impending danger, whether physical, spiritual, or moral. See *flee*.

New Testament

Verb: φεύγω (*pheugō*), GK *5771* (S *5343*), 29x. *pheugō* primarily means "to flee, escape, elude, run off/away." It occurs most frequently in the Gospels (17x). See *flee*.

ESCORT

New Testament

Verb: καθίστημι (*kathistēmi*), GK *2770* (S *2525*), 21x. *kathistēmi* denotes "to put in charge." In the NT, this word has nuances of meanings. It can signify leading or bringing; in Acts 17:15, a group of men escort Paul. See *put in charge*.

ESTABLISH

Old Testament

Verb: כּוּן (*kûn*), GK 3922 (S 3559), 219x. *kûn* means "to establish, prepare, provide." (1) When human beings are the subject of this verb, they provide or prepare things for other people. Joseph's brothers "prepare" their gifts for the governor of Egypt, who is actually their brother Joseph (Gen. 43:25). Solomon "prepares" the inner sanctuary of the temple to receive the ark of the covenant (1 Ki. 6:19). The families of the warriors surrounding David "provide" supplies for them (1 Chr. 12:39). In other uses, biblical writers acknowledge that through the help of the Lord, our ways "will be established" and secure (Ps. 90:17; 119:133).

(2) Far more frequently, however, God is the subject of this verb God has "established" or founded the earth (Ps. 119:90; Isa. 45:18; Jer. 33:2). He has also "set in place" the moon and the stars (8:3). Because the world has been "established" by God, it cannot be moved (93:1; 96:10). Moreover, God has also "formed" his special people (Deut. 32:6) and securely "established" the city of Jerusalem (Ps. 48:8; 87:5).

(3) *kûn* is also one of the vbs. that refer specifically to God's establishment of his covenant, especially with David. God "*will establish* the throne of [David's] kingdom forever" (2 Sam. 7:12–13; cf. Ps. 98:4, 37; Isa. 9:6). Moreover, when God restores the fortunes of Judah after the exile, God promises that "their community *will be established* before me" (Jer. 30:20). And in the even more distant future, God promises, "the mountain of the Lord's temple *will be established* as chief among the mountains" (Isa. 2:2; Mic. 4:1). All this comes about because of God's faithfulness to his promises. See *NIDOTTE*, 2:615–17.

Verb: נָטַע (*nāṭaʿ*), GK 5749 (S 5193). 59x. *nāṭaʿ* broadly means "to plant, fix, establish" and can be used both of literally planting things and of figuratively establishing a people. See *plant*.

Verb: נָצַב (*nāṣab*), GK 5893 (S 5324), 74x. *nāṣab* conveys the act of standing or the setting up an object and may be translated as "to stand, set." Genesis uses the term to convey the activity of setting up or establishing altars or monuments (Gen. 21:28; 33:20; 35:14, 20). The term also conveys the establishment by God of the boundaries of creation (Ps. 74:17) and his righteous rule (Ps. 82:1; Isa. 3:13). See *stand*.

Verb: קוּם (*qûm*), GK 7756 (S 6965), 627x. The general range of meanings for *qûm* includes "to stand up, arise, get up (in the morning)." It can also mean "to raise up, confirm something, establish." See *rise*.

New Testament

Verb: ἵστημι (*histēmi*), GK *2705* (S *2476*), 154x. The basic sense of *histēmi* is "to set" or "stand." It has a variety of nuances in the NT, one of which is "to establish." See *stand*.

Verb: στηρίζω (*stērizō*), GK *5114* (S *4741*), 13x. *stērizō* means "to strengthen, fix something in place, establish." See *strengthen*.

ESTEEM

See *regard*.

ETERNAL

Old Testament

Noun: עוֹלָם (*ʿôlām*), GK 6409 (S 5769), 439x. *ʿôlām* means "ancient, eternal, forever, everlasting." (1) The idea of time extending into the distant past *and* future develops into the abstract sense of "eternity" and is typically oriented around events or things that are very old. For example, Joshua exhorts the people of Israel before his death saying, "Thus says the LORD, the God of Israel: *Long ago* your ancestors lived beyond the Euphrates … and served other gods" (Jos. 24:2). Distant times can be the past of one's own life (Ps. 77:5) or the distant future (Exod. 15:18). When used to modify a noun, *ʿōlām* can mean "ancient." For example, Prov. 22:8 and 23:10 warn against moving an "*ancient* boundary stone"; the psalmist describes the gates of Jerusalem as "ancient" (Ps. 24:7); Isaiah predicts the restoration of "*ancient* ruins" (Isa. 58:12; 61:4); Moses exhorts the people to remember the "days *of old*, consider the years long past" (Deut. 32:7).

(2) The use of *ʿôlām* particularly in reference to God illustrates his faithfulness, trustworthiness, and goodness. God's mercy and love originate in "ancient" times (Ps. 25:6). God's word is "eternal" (Isa. 40:8), his covenant faithfulness and commitment to his people is "eternal" (1 Chr. 16:34; 2 Chr. 20:21; Ps. 89:2; 100:5; 103:17). His creation is firmly established as a reflection of his own care and goodness, and for it he merits praise (Ps. 148). God is to be praised from the farthest time in the past to the farthest time in the future (41:13); after all, "from *everlasting* to *everlasting* you are God" (90:2).

God is addressed as "the *Ancient* One" or "the *Ancient* of Days" (Dan. 7:9). He is an "eternal" light for his people (Isa. 60:19). God keeps his covenants "forever": with creation (Gen. 9:12, 16), with Abraham (17:7, 13, 19), with David (2 Sam. 7:13; Isa. 55:3). He also requires certain perpetual observances from his people: circumcision (Gen. 17:13), keeping the Sabbath (Exod. 31:16), the bread of the Presence (Lev. 24:8), and the observance of Passover (Exod. 12:14, 17).

(3) One difficult passage to understand is Eccl. 3:11. "God has set *eternity* in to the hearts of men; yet they cannot fathom what God has done from beginning to end." It is particularly odd in light of the fact that the Hebrew understanding of eternity was measured against the "present" (either time long ago, or time yet to come in the future). The implication, however, loses no effect: though humans have an innate sense of life beyond our own, we cannot understand the greatness and eternity of God himself, nor of the scope of his creativity, nor of the way in which he will bring time to a close. See *NIDOTTE*, 3:345–51.

New Testament

Adjective: αἰώνιος (*aiōnios*), GK *173* (S *166*), 71x. This adjective typically functions in three settings: the eternity of God and the divine realm; the blessings of salvation; and everlasting conditions that have neither beginning nor end. Forty-three times *aiōnios* is linked with "life," particularly in John's writings.

(1) The only place where *aiōnios* describes God himself as eternal is Rom. 16:26. However, his glory and Spirit are eternal (Heb. 9:13; 1 Pet. 5:10), and he himself is immortal (1 Tim. 6:16). Jesus is the source of "*eternal* salvation" (Heb. 5:9), delivering the righteous from "eternal" fire and judgment (Mt. 18:8; 25:41; 2 Thess. 1:9; Heb. 6:2; Jude 7). There is only one sin that will never be forgiven (i. e., "an *eternal* sin"), namely, blasphemy against the Holy Spirit (Mk. 3:29–30).

(2) One of the great blessings of salvation is "*eternal* life." This is the gift of God for anyone who believes in Jesus (e.g., Jn. 3:16; 1 Tim. 1:16; 6:12; Rom. 2:7; 5:21). Such life originates with God, and we receive it only by his grace. The rich young man who asked Jesus how to obtain eternal life was pointed first to the commandments (indicating the need for righteousness), then to the "impossible" act of faith of selling everything and following him—impossible for a human being, but entirely possible for God (Mt. 19:16; Mk. 10:11).

(3) God's kingdom is eternal, having

neither beginning nor end (2 Pet. 1:11). Those who believe receive an "*eternal* inheritance" (Heb. 9:15). The resurrected body will also be eternal, dwelling forever in heaven (2 Cor. 5:1ff.). See *NIDNTT-A*, 25-27.

ETERNITY

New Testament

Noun: αἰών (*aiōn*), GK *172* (S *165*), 122x. *aiōn* can indicate "prolonged time, eternity, an age, a time of the world." See *age*.

EVALUATE

New Testament

Verb: διακρίνω (*diakrinō*), GK *1359* (S *1252*), 19x. *diakrinō* means "to judge, distinguish, evaluate." When applied to oneself, it can mean to "doubt" or "waver." See *judge*.

EVANGELIST

New Testament

Noun: εὐαγγελιστής (*euangelistēs*), GK *2296* (S *2099*), 3x. *euangelistēs* means "evangelist," and it only occurs 3x in the NT. Even though Philip was originally chosen in the early church to minister to widows (Acts 6), he eventually becomes an "evangelist" (Acts 21:8). In 8:4–25, he evangelizes Samaria, and in 8:26–40, he leads the Ethiopian eunuch to salvation in Christ and baptizes him. Paul commissions Timothy with doing "the work of an *evangelist*" (2 Tim. 4:5). In Paul's listing of the various ministry gifts in the church, one of them is the gift of "evangelist" (Eph. 4:11). While all believers are called upon the share their faith and in that sense "evangelize," there is a gift of special empowerment whereby God blesses their evangelistic work with the fruit of conversions.*

EVANGELIZE

New Testament

Verb: εὐαγγελίζω (*euangelizō*), GK *2294* (S *2097*), 54x. Generally, *euangelizō* simply means "to bring a message, announce good news" (1 Thess. 3:6, Rev. 10:7). See *preach*.

EVENING

Old Testament

Noun: עֶרֶב (*ʿereb*), GK 6847 (S 6153), 134x. *ʿereb*, meaning "evening, twilight," normally refers to the time of day at about sundown. According to Jer. 6:4, this is the time when daylight is fading and shadows grow long. Only rarely does this word refer to the night (e.g., Job 7:4). Evening and morning constitute each day of creation (cf. Gen. 1:5), which suggests that in Heb. thought a day begins in the evening. The evening sacrifice takes place at this time (1 Chr. 16:40; 2 Chr. 31:3), as does the lighting of the lamps (Exod. 30:8). Esp. the Passover sacrifice must be killed "at twilight" (Deut. 16:6), because that is the time when the original lambs were killed in Egypt (Exod. 12:6). A prayer in the evening is also like "the *evening* sacrifice" before God (Ps. 141:2). Ceremonial uncleanness generally lasts until evening (Lev. 11:24) or the end of the day.

Daily activity is carried on from morning until evening, such as Moses' judging the people (Exod. 18:13–14), Ruth's gleaning in the field (Ruth 2:17), or the Israelites' seeking direction from the Lord (Jdg. 20:23, 26). At dusk, the women go out to draw water (Gen. 24:11). In a metaphorical use, one psalmist describes human life as transitory, like grass that "by evening is dry and withered" (Ps. 90:6). But another psalmist writes that although weeping may remain for "a night," joy comes with the morning (30:5). In the coming age, there will be no night, for "when evening comes, there will be light" (Zech. 14:7; cf. Rev. 21:25).

New Testament

Noun: ὀψία (*opsia*), GK *4069* (S *3798*), 15x. *opsia* means "evening." It occurs only in the gospels in connection with various significant events in the life of Jesus that take place in the evening. After Jesus begins to do miracles, as word spreads, many come in the evening to seek healing (Mt. 8:16; Mk. 1:32). On one particular evening Jesus feeds the multitudes (Mt. 14:15), and on another evening the disciples start rowing across the Sea of Galilee, only to encounter a storm (Mk. 4:35; cf. 6:47). Jesus eats the Last Supper with his disciples in the evening (Mt. 26:20; Mk. 14:17), and the very next evening, he was buried in a garden tomb by Joseph of Arimathea (Mt. 27:57). Then, after Jesus' resurrection, he appeared to all his disciples in the evening (Jn. 20:19).

EVENT

New Testament

Noun: ῥῆμα (*rhēma*), GK *4839* (S *4487*), 68x. *rhēma* means a "word" or "matter, event." See *word.*

EVER

Old Testament

Noun (used as adv.): תָּמִיד (*tāmîd*), GK 9458 (S 8548), 104x. As an adverb, *tāmîd* describes that which is "lasting" or something done "continually." The word can describe both an action done regularly (often according to a schedule) as well as something that is ongoing without interruption. See *always*.

EVERLASTING

See *eternal*.

EVERY

Old Testament

Noun: כֹּל (*kōl*), GK 3972 (S 3605), 5415x. *kōl* means "whole, all, every." When it is followed by an indefinite singular (e.g., without the article), it is often translated "every." See *all*.

Particle: כֹּל (*kōl*), GK 10353 (S 3606), 105x. *kōl* is the Aramaic equivalent of Heb. *kōl* and has essentially the same meaning: "every, whole, all." See *all*.

New Testament

Adjective: ἕκαστος (*hekastos*), GK *1667* (S *1538*), 82x. *hekastos* means "each" or "every." See *each*.

Adjective: πᾶς (*pas*) GK *4246* (S *3956*), 1243x. *pas* generally means "each, every" in the singular, "all" in the plural. See *all*.

EVERYONE

New Testament

Adjective: ἅπας (*hapas*), GK *570* (S *537*), 34x. *hapas* expresses the wholeness of the object it describes, the fullness of a group; it sometimes occurs alone as a pronoun meaning "everyone." See *all*.

EVERYTHING

Old Testament

Noun: כֹּל (*kōl*), GK 3972 (S 3605), 5415x. *kōl* means "whole, all, every." When it is followed by an indefinite singular (e.g., without the article), it is often translated "every." *kōl* may also stand by itself to denote "everything." In such a case, the context determines the scope of the word. See *all*.

EVIL

Old Testament

Verb: רָעַע (*rāʿaʿ*), GK 8317 (S 7489), 95x. *rāʿaʿ* expresses the quality or state of being evil or causing evil. It may be translated as "to be evil, afflict." The term can describe a state of being troubled (Gen. 21:11, 12) or angry (Gen. 48:17; Isa. 59:15). Elkanah comforts Hannah, who was distressed over her bareness, with the words, "Hannah, why are you weeping? Why don't you eat? Why are you *downhearted*? Don't I mean more to you than ten sons?" (1 Sam. 1:8). *rāʿaʿ* is often used with the Heb. verb *ṭôb* ("to be good") in order to describe the full range of activity, both *good* and *evil* (i.e., Isa. 41:23; Jer. 10:5). Zephaniah declares, "At that time I will search Jerusalem with lamps and punish those who are complacent, who are like wine left on its dregs, who think, 'The LORD will do nothing, either *good or bad*' (Zeph. 1:12). It is also used in parallel with other terms that describe various degrees of evil (i.e., Num. 16:15; Deut. 26:6; Jer. 23:14). Theologically, the evil implied in *rāʿaʿ* is set in contrast to the activity of keeping the LORD's commands. Ps. 119:115 declares, "Away from me, you *evildoers,* that I may keep the commandments of my God. See *NIDOTTE*, 3:1154-58.

Noun: אָוֶן (*ʾāwen*), GK 224 (S 205), 81x. *ʾāwen* refers, in general, to evil, sin, or wickedness, with the connotations of injustice, deception, falsehood, or emptiness. In Gen. 35:18, as Rachel dies she names her son Ben-*Oni*, "son of *my trouble*." ʾ*āwen* also describes the punishment or disaster that befalls those who practice wickedness. For example, to those who "harbor wicked thoughts" (Jer. 4:14), God sends a voice to pronounce ʾ*āwen* (disaster) in the form of a besieging army (4:15). Notably, one of the six things that the Lord detests is a heart that devises "schemes of ʾ*āwen*" ("wicked schemes," Prov. 6:18). The psalmist complains that his enemy speaks falsely and his heart gathers ʾ*āwen* (*slander* in NIV, Ps. 41:6).

As is evident from these passages in the OT, ʾ*āwen* is something that comes from the heart of human beings. The Lord will not hear the prayer of one who cherishes ʾ*āwen* in his heart (Ps. 66:18), and, in the end, he will destroy the evildoers (lit., the "doers of ʾ*āwen*" (94:16) for their ʾ*āwen* (94:22). Nevertheless, God also shows his great compassion by calling evildoers to repent and offering them mercy and pardon (Isa. 55:7). See *NIDOTTE*, 1:309-15.

Noun: רָעָה (*rāʿâ*), GK 8288 (S 7465), 354x. At the heart of *rāʿâ* lies the idea of badness, whether physical or moral.

(1)When used in the moral sense, *rāʿâ* is often translated "evil, wickedness, wrongdoing." In many instances, it is the direct opposite of the good (see *good, ṭôb*). For example, although Joseph had been sold into slavery by his brothers, he later told them, "You meant it for *evil*, but God meant it for good" (Gen. 50:20). Even King Saul recognized that he had rewarded David with evil (NIV "treated you *badly*"), although David rewarded him with good. Ps. 15:3 tells us that the one who can dwell on God's holy hill is the one who, among other things, does no *wrong* (KJV "evil") to his neighbor.

(2) When used in the physical sense, *rāʿâ* is often translated "calamity, disaster, harm, trouble." In several instances, physical *rāʿâ* comes on those who commit moral evil, as when Moses promises that disaster will fall on Israel because they have done evil in God's eyes (Deut. 31:29). Sometimes in the KJV, *rāʿâ* is translated "evil," but there is no moral connotation in the particular instance (e.g., see Gen. 19:19, where the "evil" that Lot fears will overtake him is really "calamity"). It is in this light that we should read passages such as Jer. 26:19, where God is implicated in the bringing of "evil" on people. This does not mean that God is personally guilty of committing moral evil; rather, he sovereignly and righteously dispenses the judgment of disaster or calamity on a sinful people (see also Jer. 36:36). See *NIDOTTE*, 3:1154-58.

Adjective or Noun: רַע (or רָע) (*raʿ* [or *rāʿ*]), GK 8273 (S 7451), 312x. In most contexts, *raʿ* is translated "evil," as in Ps. 23:4, "Even though I walk through the valley of the shadow of death, I will fear no *raʿ*." Another frequent translation is "wicked," such as Gen. 13:13, "Now the men of Sodom were *wicked* and were sinning greatly against the LORD." Grammatically, *raʿ* is used mainly as an adjective (as in "a *bad* report," Num. 14:37), but it is also used as a noun (e.g., "purge the evil from among you," Deut. 22:24).

(1) When used as a noun, *raʿ* is often found in conjunction with, or in contrast to, *tôb*, "good" (32x). (a) After Adam and Eve ate from the tree of the knowledge of good and evil, Gen. 3:22 states, "And the LORD God said, 'The man has now become like one of us, knowing good and *raʿ*'" (cf. Deut. 1:35, 39). Isaiah laments, "Woe to those who call *raʿ* good and good *raʿ*" (Isa. 5:20). This construction is found twice in the exhortation of Amos 5:14–15: "Seek good, not *raʿ*, that you may live. … Hate *raʿ*, love good."

(b) *raʿ* is also commonly used in the familiar expression "evil in the eyes of the LORD" or "evil in his sight" (59x, mostly in 1–2 Ki. and 2 Chr.). For example, Jdg. 3:7 says, "The Israelites did evil in the eyes of the LORD; they forgot the LORD their God and served the Baals and the Asherahs." Clearly, the use of *raʿ* here indicates a moral deficiency in the Israelites.

(c) A final category of *raʿ* as a noun refers to instances where *raʿ* is translated as "disaster, destruction." Deut. 30:15 says, "See, I set before you today life and prosperity, death and *destruction*." *raʿ* is translated as "disaster" on numerous occasions (1 Ki. 5:4; Ps. 140:11; Isa. 3:11; 31:2), but the most significant instance is perhaps Isa. 45:7, "I form the light and create darkness, I bring prosperity and create *disaster*; I, the LORD, do all these things" (cf. Mic. 1:12).

(2) As an adjective, *raʿ* gives a negative or inferior quality to the word it modifies. (a) Often it describes something as corrupt, base, or bad. For example, when God sent out "an *evil* spirit" to torment Saul (1 Sam. 16:14–16 [3x]; 18:10; 19:9; cf. Jdg. 9:23), and when animals are labeled as "ferocious" (Gen. 37:20, 33), "savage" (Lev. 26:6), and "wild" (Ezek. 5:17; 14:15, 21; 34:25). Arrows are described as "deadly" (Ezek. 5:16), and illnesses are called "severe" (Deut. 28:59). Fish are said to be caught in a "cruel net" (Eccl. 9:12), and Ezekiel warns about the "dreadful judgments" against Jerusalem (Ezek. 14:21). In other contexts, *raʿ* is best translated as "displeasing" (Gen. 28:8; Isa. 29:7), "distressing" (Exod. 33:4), "painful" (Deut. 28:35; Job 2:7), and "harmful" (2 Kings 4:41).

(b) *raʿ* can also describe the inferior, bereft quality of an object or action. So cows are called "ugly" (Gen. 41:3–27 [6x]) because of their gaunt appearance, and decisions are labeled as "undesirable" (Jos. 24:15) and "unfavorable" (Jer. 42:6).

In a text that bears significant theological import, the vision of Jer. 24:2–8, figs are described as "poor" (4x), which in context serves to stress the displeasing nature of the people of Judah in the eyes of God.

Adjective: רָשָׁע (*rāšāʿ*), GK 8401 (S 7563), 264x. As an adjective *rāšāʿ* describes the quality of being wicked, evil, guilty, or unjust. When the adjective is used as a noun, it refers to a wicked, evil, or guilty person. See *wicked*.

New Testament

Noun: ἀδικία (*adikia*), GK *94* (S *93*), 25x. *adikia* is consistently translated as either "unrighteousness" or "iniquity" in the KJV. The NIV, however, offers numerous glosses, such as "evil, wickedness, dishonest, worldly, sin, wrong, wrongdoing." See *unrighteousness*.

Noun: κακία (*kakia*), GK *2798* (S *2549*), 11x. *kakia* means "malice, evil," primarily "wickedness" in quality or baseness. See *malice*.

Adjective: ἀκάθαρτος (*akathartos*), GK *176* (S *169*), 32x. *akathartos* pertains to that which may not be brought into contact with what is holy (see *holy*). In this sense it is "impure, defiled," and at times "evil." See *unclean*.

Adjective: κακός (*kakos*), GK *2805* (S *2556*), 50x. *kakos* conveys the idea of something that is "evil, bad, wicked, wrong"—i.e., a perversion of what pertains to goodness. Generally speaking, it is not a significant term in the NT, for *ponēros* and *harmartia* are usually preferred terms for the expression of evil and personal guilt. *kakos* is the wider term. The presence of *kakos* raises the question of the origin, nature, and purpose of evil in relation to God, man, and providence. Theologians refer to this concept as the question of theodicy. In the NT good and evil are opposites, but they are not equal. Since "God cannot be tempted by evil" (Jas. 1:13), the root of evil cannot lie in God.

The use of *kakos* can be loosely divided into what is morally or ethically evil and what is destructive, damaging, or harmful. People are morally or ethically evil in Mt. 21:41; 24:48; Phil. 3:2; and Rev. 2:2. The same applies to qualities, emotions, deeds, etc. in Jn. 18:23, 30; Rom. 1:30; 3:8; 7:19, 21; 13:4; 14:20; 16:19; 1 Cor. 13:5; 2 Cor. 13:7; 1 Thess. 5:15; 1 Pet. 3:9, 12. Jesus goes so far as to say that the heart is the seat of evil (Mk. 7:21).

Objects, events, and actions are credited with being *kakos* in a destructive or damaging way in various Scriptures (Lk. 16:25; Acts 16:28; 28:5; Tit. 1:12; Rev. 16:2). These two concepts are joined when the love of money (an emotion, 1 Tim. 6:10) and the tongue (destructive object,

Jas. 3:8) are both given credit for being present at the root of *kakos*. See *NIDNTT-A*, 284-85.

Adjective: πονηρός (*ponēros*), GK *4505* (S *4190*, *4191*), 78x. The adjective *ponēros* basically means "bad, wicked, evil." (1) It can be used in the purely physical sense to mean sick or in a bad condition (Mt. 6:23 and Lk. 11:34 speak of a "bad eye" [KJV has "evil eye," but the sense is the physical condition]), or to mean painful or serious (Rev. 16:2 speaks of "painful" sores).

(2) Most commonly, however, *ponēros* bears a strong ethical connotation of something or someone being wicked or evil. Jesus calls the Israelites who oppose him an "evil" generation (Mt. 12:39; 16:4; Lk. 11:29). God shows his marvelous benevolence toward his creatures by causing the sun to rise on both the "evil" and the good (Mt. 5:45) and being kind to the "wicked" (Lk. 6:35). Nonhuman entities in the NT are also called *ponēros*, such as thoughts (Mt. 15:19) and works (Col. 1:21; 2 Tim. 4:18).

(3) When used as a noun, *ponēros* can refer to evildoers (Mt. 5:39, 45), to the preeminently "evil (one)," who is the devil (Mt. 6:13, NIV; 13:19, 38; Jn. 17:15; Eph. 6:16; 1 Jn. 5:18), or simply to "evil" or "evil things" (Lk. 6:45, the "evil man" brings out of his heart "what is evil"; Rom. 12:9, hate "what is evil"). See *NIDNTT-A*, 484-85.

Adverb: κακῶς (*kakōs*), GK *2809* (S *2560*), 16x. The adverb *kakōs* can designate those with physical illness (the "sick") or moral ("wrong, evil") harm. See *sick*.

EVILDOER

New Testament

Noun: ἄδικος (*adikos*), GK *96* (S *94*), 12x. In most contexts, *adikos* may be translated "unjust" or "unrighteous." In some occurrences, however, *adikos* may mean dishonest or untrustworthy (Lk. 16:10–11), evildoer (Lk. 18:11), or ungodly (1 Cor. 6:1). See *unjust*.

EVIL SPEAKING

See *blasphemy*.

EXALT

Old Testament

Verb: גָּדַל (*gādal*), GK 1540 (S 1431), 117x. *gādal* means "to be(come) great, exalted," but it can mean "to make great, exalt" someone or something; in most cases God is the subject of this action. He makes great those whom he wills, and he calls us to "exalt him with thanksgiving" (Ps. 69:30; cf. 70:4; 92:5; 104:1; 126:2; 138:2). See *great, greatness*.

Verb: עָלָה (*ʿālâ*), GK 6590 (S 5927), 894x. *ʿālâ* typically means "to go up, ascend." Although it inherently is not a theological term, it often appears in highly significant contexts. See *ascend*.

Verb: רוּם (*rûm*), GK 8123 (S 7311), 197x. *rûm* means "to lift up, exalt." It can indicate the state of things that are high or exalted, such as God and his throne (Gen. 14:22; Ps. 46:10; Isa. 6:1) as well as the stars (Job 22:12). The psalmist calls the believer to exalt the Lord and his name (Ps. 18:46; 34:3; 57:5; 99:2, 5, 9). See *lift up*.

New Testament

Verb: ἐπαίρω (*epairō*), GK *2048* (S *1869*), 19x. *epairō* means "to look up, lift up," though it has several senses in the NT. See *lift up*.

Verb: μεγαλύνω (*megalynō*), GK *3486* (S *3170*), 8x. The basic meaning of *megalynō* is "to magnify, exalt." See *magnify*.

Verb: ὑψόω (*hypsoō*), GK *5738* (S *5312*), 20x. In the LXX, *hypsoō* is similar to the Hebrew word *rûm*, which means to "lift up, exalt." However, in the NT, *hypsoō* is used almost exclusively in a theological way. It plays a part in two important theological themes: the exaltation of Jesus and God's promise to the humble.

In the gospel of John, Jesus' exaltation (*hypsoō*) is an important part of who Jesus is as the Christ. Jesus often describes his crucifixion as his being "lifted up" (*hypsoō*) on the cross (Jn. 3:14; 8:28; 12:32, 34). This has a powerful double meaning, referring not only to Jesus being lifted up on the cross of wood, but also to his exaltation before all humanity and his coming exaltation in the presence of God. Similarly, in Acts, Jesus' resurrection and exaltation (*hypsoō*) are connected (Acts 2:33; 5:31).

The word *hypsoō* is also used many times in the NT as one of the great promises of God to believers: i.e., in due time, they will be exalted or lifted up. There is one crucial condition for this promise, however: a humbling of oneself. Therefore, the NT often exhorts believers to "humble yourselves before the Lord and he *will lift you up*" (Jas. 4:10; 1 Pet. 5:6). Conversely, those who exalt themselves will be put down by God (Mt. 23:12; Lk. 14:11; 18:14).

These two theological themes are brought together perfectly in the life and death of Jesus. In Phil. 2:5–11, Paul paints a picture of the amazing truth that Jesus, who was himself God, humbled himself completely. As a result, God highly exalted (*hyperypsoō* [GK *5671*], an intensified form of the same word) him. This serves as the model for all believers to humble themselves and to await God's future exaltation. See *NIDNTT-A*, 585-86.

EXALTED

New Testament

Noun: ὕψος (*hypsos*), GK *5737* (S *5311*) 6x.

Adjective: ὑψηλός (*hypsēlos*), GK *5734* (S *5308*), 11x.

These two words carry the idea of high or exalted with both spatial and figurative meanings. See *high, highest*.

EXAMINE

Old Testament

Verb: שָׁמַר (*šāmar*), GK 9068 (S 8104), 468x. Often translated "to keep," the verb *šāmar* bears three distinct but related meanings in the OT: "to guard, tend," "to watch over," and "to preserve" (see *keep*). It is used, for example, of Eli "watching" Hannah's mouth (1 Sam. 1:12) or of Balaam "examining" Israel (Num. 23:12).

New Testament

Verb: ἀνακρίνω (*anakrinō*), GK *373* (S *350*), 16x. *anakrinō* means "to examine, judge, investigate." Luke uses this verb to describe the eagerness with which the Bereans examine the OT Scriptures to ensure Paul is speaking accurately in his daily synagogue presentations (Acts 17:11). Luke also uses this verb as a judicial term. It describes Pilate's "thorough investigation" of Jesus, compelling the governor to agree to have him whipped and released rather than executed (Lk. 23:14). In Acts, Peter and John "are called to account" for their healing a lame beggar (Acts 4:9). Instead of receiving a civic award for the good act, which would ordinarily have happened in the Greco-Roman world, the apostles find themselves on trial. When Herod discovers that Peter, whom he had hoped to execute, has escaped, he "cross-examines" the guards for a suitable explanation (12:19; cf. also 24:8; 28:18).

In Paul's writings, *anakrinō* appears only in 1 Corinthians. In a discussion of the moral implications of believers eating meat bought in the marketplace that had previously been offered to idols, *anakrinō* means "to sift evidence" or "to reach a judgment" (1 Cor. 10:25, 27). If nothing is disclosed about the history of the meat's whereabouts, Paul says they should not to make an issue out of it. But if an unbeliever reveals that the meat had passed before an idol, for the sake of that unbeliever's conscience, Paul instructs the Corinthians not to eat it (10:28–29). The goal in all of this, as in all of life, is to glorify God.

In 1 Cor. 4:3–4, Paul advises his readers that no matter who conducts an "investigation" about his ministry, the only verdict that really counts is God's. With this language Paul contrasts sharply a mere human day in court with the Day of the Lord's judgment, where *anakrinō* finds its ultimate expression. In 2:14–15 the word can best be translated as "spiritually discern." Only a person with spiritual vision can understand how the foolishness of God plus the weakness of God equals the power of God in the death of Jesus on the cross. See *NIDNTT-A*, 318-19.

Verb: δοκιμάζω (*dokimazō*), GK *1507* (S *1381*), 22x. *dokimazō* means to "test, discern, approve." See *test*.

EXAMPLE

New Testament

Noun: τύπος (*typos*), GK *5596* (S *5179*), 15x. *typos* is a "pattern, example, model," taken from the concept of an impression or a mark left behind by something on a surface. This word is used in the NT in a practical and theological sense. The most concrete way in which it is used is of the marks made by the nails in Jesus' body, when Thomas says he will not believe unless he sees the "nail *marks*" (Jn. 20:25). *typos* is also used to describe a summary of a letter written by Claudius Lysias to Felix, translated as either "in the following manner" or "as follows" (Acts 23:25). Similarly, *typos* is the "form" or summary of teaching that Paul entrusts to the Roman Christians (Rom. 6:17).

Because God is not to be copied or imaged, Stephen censures the Jews for having made "forms" (NIV "idols") and worshiping them (Acts 7:43). The precise nature of *typos* as a form or pattern can be seen by the fact that Israel constructed the tabernacle according to the pattern that God had given Moses on Mount Sinai (Acts 7:44; Heb. 8:5).

But *typos* is not limited to a physical form or pattern of things; the NT also uses this word to describe a theological pattern or example. In this sense Adam is a "pattern" of Christ, the one to come (Rom. 5:14), and the people and events of the OT are cited as "examples" to the Corinthians to spur them on to reject evil (1 Cor. 10:6). Paul applies this in a personal context for believers, writing that they are to follow his example (Phil. 3:17) and that he has acted in such a manner to be a "model" to believers in the church (2 Thess. 3:9). One of the roles of an elder is to be an "example" to his flock (1 Pet. 5:3), setting a pattern by doing what is good (Tit. 2:7) and not allowing anything else to interfere with his example (1 Tim. 4:12). In this way, people in the church must emulate the example of the elders by becoming examples themselves to others (1 Thess. 1:7). See *NIDNTT-A*, 565-66.*

Noun: ὑπόδειγμα (*hypodeigma*) GK *5682* (S *5262*), 6x. *hypodeigma* means "example, copy" (see *copy*). We all need examples to show us in concrete ways how God wants us to live. Thus, Jesus himself provides an "example" when he washes his disciples' feet (Jn. 13:15). The prophets of the OT serve as "an example of patience in the face of suffering" (Jas. 5:10; James goes on to cite Job in particular). But examples can also be negative (i.e., examples to avoid), such as the rebellious Israelites in the desert (Heb. 4:11) and the sins of Sodom and Gomorrah that were judged by God (2 Pet. 2:6).

EXCEED

Old Testament

Verb: יָסַף (*yāsap*), GK 3578 (S 3254), 213x. The basic meaning of *yāsap* is "to add." Sometimes the word conveys the sense of "exceed" or "increase" (cf. 1 Ki. 10:6; Ps. 115:14; Eccl. 2:9; see *add*).

New Testament

Verb: περισσεύω (*perisseuō*) GK *4355* (S *4052*), 39x. *perisseuō* means "to abound, overflow, exceed." See *abound*.

EXCEEDINGLY

Old Testament

Noun: מְאֹד (*m*e*ʾōd*), GK 4394 (S 3966), 300x. *m*e*ʾōd* is usually used adverbially, meaning "very, much, greatly, exceedingly." For example, the people of Sodom "were wicked and were sinning against the Lord *exceedingly*" (Gen. 13:13). See *greatly*.

New Testament

Adverb: περισσοτέρως (*perissoterōs*), GK *4359* (S *4056*), 12x. *perissoterōs* describes an action as being "exceedingly, beyond measure, more than might be expected." Paul claims he is more a servant of Christ than others because he has labored exceedingly, was imprisoned more often, and was beaten exceedingly (2 Cor. 11:23; cf. 2 Cor. 12:15; Gal. 1:14; Heb. 2:1; 13:19). In response to his imprisonment, many Christians proclaim the truth of Jesus more courageously and fearlessly (Phil. 1:12). By God's grace Paul acts with exceeding sincerity and holiness toward the Corinthians (2 Cor. 1:12; cf. 7:15), and he writes with "much" love for them (2 Cor. 2:4). Paul is extremely eager to see the faces of the Thessalonians but has been prevented by Satan (1 Thess. 2:17; cf. 2 Cor. 7:13). See *NIDNTT-A*, 454-55.*

EXCEL

See *exceed.*

EXCESS

Old Testament

Noun: יֶתֶר (*yeter*), GK 3856 (S 3499), 97x. *yeter* denotes the remainder, excess, or leftover parts of a whole and may be translated as "remainder, excess." See *remnant*.

EXCLUDE

Old Testament

Verb: כָּרַת (*kārat*), GK 4162 (S 3772), 289x. *kārat* broadly means "to cut (objects), exclude and/or destroy, make a covenant." While these three basic meanings seem divergent, they are closely linked together around the notion of cutting. See also *make a covenant*; *cut*.

This verb occurs frequently with the meaning of excluding, ostracizing, and even destroying and annihilating. The literal meaning here is "to cut off." God gave various laws to his people at Mount Sinai; those who refused to obey these laws could be cut off or excluded from the people (Lev. 7:20, 21, 25). In some cases this might mean mere exclusion from the nation, but in the case of blasphemy as recorded in Lev. 20:17–18, it meant physical death. This notion of death is also prominent in God's promise to "cut off" the nations in the promised land (Deut. 12:29) and later to "cut off" his own people from their land if they disobeyed this law (1 Ki. 9:7). In the Psalms, the wicked are cut off/killed (Ps. 37:9, 22, 28) and their memory is annihilated (34:16).

New Testament

Verb: ἀφορίζω (*aphorizō*), GK *928* (S *873*), 10x. *aphorizō* carries the idea of "to separate, set apart, exclude." It can designate the setting apart of a person for a specific task. Paul was "*set part* for the gospel of God" (Rom. 1:1; cf. Gal. 1:5). See *separate.*

EXCUSE

Verb: ἀπολογέομαι (*apologeomai*), GK *664* (S *621*), 10x. *apologeomai* means "to defend something or someone, including oneself, through speech." The word bears the sense of advocacy and defense, which our word "apologetics" still retains; it often occurs in a legal context. See *defend.*

EXECUTE

See do.

EXHORT

New Testament

Verb: παρακαλέω (*parakaleō*), GK *4151* (S *3870*), 109x. *parakaleō* variously means "to ask, summons, exhort, comfort, or encourage" (see *ask*, *comfort*).

Within Acts and Paul's letters, *parakaleō* often refers to the necessary role of exhortation in the church (1 Cor. 14:30–31). Judas and Silas, for example, exhort and strengthen the church in Antioch with their message (Acts 15:32). Within the Pauline corpus, the exhortative aspects are often, though not exclusively, found at the end of his letters and are preceded by the hortatory formula "let us ..." or the statement "I urge you... ." The latter is found in the familiar exhortation in Rom. 12:1, in which believers are exhorted to offer themselves as living sacrifices of worship to God because of the transforming power of the gospel displayed in Rom. 1–11. Significantly, this example from Rom. 12 emphasizes a fundamental feature of the apostle's exhortation. Paul does not exhort for exhortation's sake alone or because of a Stoic view of virtue for virtue's sake. Rather, Paul always exhorts believers to godly living on the theological basis of God's mercy in Christ. Paul's imperatives flow from his indicatives. Another example is found in Col. 3:1, where Paul states, "Since you have been raised with Christ [indicative, statement of fact], seek those things that are above [imperative]."

EXILE

Old Testament

Verb: גָּלָה (*gālâ*), GK 1655 (S 1540), 187x. *gālâ* has a wide variety of uses in the OT: "to exile, go into exile, expose, reveal, depart, have sexual relations with."

(1) In the law God gives to Israel is a listing of a number of inappropriate sexual relations, for which *gālâ* is used (Lev. 18:6–19). The nuance here is to expose one's nakedness to another person.

(2) Consistent with the notion of exposing is that of revealing something, especially when God reveals something to his people. When the Lord calls the boy Samuel in the middle of the night, he does not recognize the voice, "for the word of the LORD *had* not yet *been revealed* to him" (1 Sam. 3:7). Similarly, the prophet Isaiah writes of a future time "when the glory of the LORD *will be revealed*" (Isa. 40:5).

(3) When Phinehas's wife hears that the ark of God has been captured and that her husband and father-in-law are dead, she gives birth. Just before dying in labor, she names the child Ichabod, because "the glory *has departed* from Israel" (1 Sam. 4:19–22).

(4) One of the most common uses of this verb is in connection with the great low point in Israel's history, the exile. God delivered his people from slavery in Egypt and made them his own people; yet they persevere in sin and rebellion. As a result, "my people *will go into exile* for lack of knowledge" (Isa. 5:13), and "Israel *will surely go into exile*, away from their native land" (Amos 7:11).

Exile came to Israel three times: the first was to Tiglath Pileser III (2 Ki. 15:29) in 734 B.C.; the second to Shalmaneser V (or possibly Sargon II) in 722 B.C. (2 Ki. 17:1–6; 18:9–12); and Judah fell to Nebuchadnezzar (this deportation occurred in three stages: in 605 B.C. [Daniel 1:1]; in 597 B.C. [2 Ki. 24:10–17], and in 586 B. C., when Jerusalem was destroyed [2 Ki. 25:8–21]). Israel's lament for exile is recorded in Psalm 137. God gave hope to his people for a return from exile (Isa. 60:9), and it was during the exile that the majority of the OT was collected, edited, and copied. See *NIDOTTE*, 1:8611–64.

EXIST

New Testament

Verb: ὑπάρχω (*hyparchō*), GK *5639* (S *5224*, *5225*), 60x. *hyparchō* is a multifaceted term ranging in meaning from the verb "to be" (see *be*), to being used as the noun for "possessions" (i.e., to describe things *being* at one's disposal; see *possess, possessions*), to being translated as "exist." In Lk. 7:25, Jesus says that those wearing nice clothes "exist" (NASB, "are found") in palaces, in contrast to John the Baptist, who lived in the desert (cf. also Lk. 9:48; 16:23; 23:50).

EXPECT

New Testament

Verb: προσδέχομαι (*prosdechomai*), GK *4657* (S *4327*), 14x. *prosdechomai* means "to receive, welcome" (see *welcome*), and "to wait for, expect something" in the sense of looking forward to (see *wait for*).

Verb: προσδοκάω (*prosdokaō*), GK *4659* (S *4328*), 16x. *prosdokaō* denotes an expectation or waiting born of either hope or fear. The verb is akin to waiting for something with butterflies in your stomach.

(1) The pagans at Malta expect Paul to swell up and die after a viper bites his hand (Acts 28:6). The hopes and especially the fears of John the Baptist are wrapped up in the answer to his question to Jesus, "Are you the one who is to come, or shall we *look for* another?" (Mt. 11:3; Lk. 7:19, 20). In the parable of the faithful and unfaithful servant, convinced his master has been delayed, the wicked servant is caught off guard by his master's return because he

has not been expecting it (Mt. 24:50; Lk. 12:46). This led to loose living on his part.

(2) The hopeful aspect of *prosdokaō* is evident when the object expected is the new heavens and earth. Of the 16x the word is used in the NT, it occurs outside the gospels and Acts only 3x, all in 2 Pet. 3:12–14. Peter begins by saying that since the entire universe will be destroyed, "what sort of people ought you to be in lives of holiness and godliness, *waiting* … the coming of the day of God, because of which the heavens will be set on fire and dissolved, and the heavenly bodies will melt as they burn! But according to his promise we are *waiting* for new heavens and a new earth in which righteousness dwells. Therefore, beloved, since you are *waiting* for these, be diligent to be found by him without spot or blemish, and at peace" (ESV). *prosdokaō*, in this context, is clearly a hopeful expectation that produces appropriate actions. As we look forward to the new heavens and the new earth, we are motivated to Christian living all the more as the day approaches. See *NIDNTT-A*, 62.

EXPEDIENT

Verb: συμφέρω (*sympherō*), GK *5237* (S *4851*), 15x. *sympherō* has both a positive and a comparative nuance: "it is beneficial" and "it is better." See *(be) beneficial.*

EXPEL

New Testament

Verb: ἐκβάλλω (*ekballō*), GK *1675* (S *1544*), 81x. *ekballō* means "to drive out, expel, eject." It often indicates a violent expulsion, especially of demons. See *drive out*.

EXPERIENCE

Old Testament

Noun: חָכְמָה (*ḥokmâ*), GK 2683 (S 2451), 153x. *ḥokmâ* has a wide variety of meanings, covering both physical skill and intellectual wisdom. It can be translated as "wisdom, aptitude, experience, good sense, skill." See *wisdom*.

EXPOSE

Old Testament

Verb: גָּלָה (*gālâ*), GK 1655 (S 1540), 187x. *gālâ* has a wide variety of uses in the OT: "to exile, go into exile, expose, depart, reveal, have sexual relations with." See *exile*.

EXTERMINATE

Old Testament

Verb: שָׁמַד (*šāmad*), GK 9012 (S 8045), 90x. *šāmad* (occurring mostly in the Heb. Hiphil verb form) means "to destroy, exterminate, or annihilate" and expresses the partial or complete destruction of a group of people. See *destroy*.

EXULT

Old Testament

Verb: הָלַל (*halāl*), GK 2146 (S 1984), 146x. *halāl* means "to praise, boast, exult." See *praise*.

New Testament

Verb: ἀγαλλιάω (*agalliaō*), GK *22* (S *21*), 11x. *agalliaō* means "to rejoice greatly, exult, be overjoyed." See *rejoice*.

EYE

Old Testament

Noun: עַיִן (*ʿayin*), GK 6524 (S 5869), 889x. *ʿayin* means "eye." It can refer to the literal body part, but it appears in many expressions and idioms related to sight—of physical sight occasionally, but more often of metaphorical sight (i.e., attitudes or judgments) or of spiritual sight.

(1) In a literal sense *ʿayin* can refer to the sight organ of humans (1 Ki. 20:38) or of animals (Job 28:7). When used idiomatically, this word is found in such phrases as "to look up" (lit., "to lift the eyes," Gen. 13:14), "in front of" (lit., "before the eyes of," 30:41), "the face of the ground" (lit., "the eyes of the ground," Exod. 10:5), "on the forehead" (lit., "between the eyes," Dan. 8:5), "unaware of" (lit., "away from the eyes of," Num. 5:13), "to be despised" (lit., "to be slight in the eyes of," Gen. 16:5), "to look at the outward appearance" (lit., "to see to the eyes," 1 Sam. 16:7), "good looking" (lit., "with beautiful eyes," 1 Sam. 16:12), and "a proud look" (lit.,

"eyes being high," Prov. 6:17). Being "pleasant to the eye" describes desire (e.g., Gen. 3:6; 1 Ki. 20:6; Lam. 2:4; Ezek. 24:16).

(2) When used metaphorically, *ʿayin* can refer to someone's attitude toward or judgment of a person or situation. During the time of the judges, the Israelites practiced relativism: every man "did what was right in his own eyes," that is, in his own judgment (Jdg. 17:6; 21:25; cf. Gen. 19:8). The faithfulness of Israel's kings was determined by whether they did evil or right according to God's judgment ("in the eyes of the LORD," 1 Ki. 15:34; 2 Ki. 18:3). In one of the most common phrases that includes "eyes," people "find favor in the eyes of" someone (Ruth 2:10; 2 Sam. 16:4).

(3) Because God is a spirit, he does not have physical eyes. When "the eyes of the LORD" are mentioned, it refers to his watchful care of his people (Ps. 34:15) and their possessions (Deut. 11:12), his condemnation toward sin (Amos 9:8), his awareness of and oversight over all things (Prov. 5:21; 15:3), his attentiveness to the prayers of his people (1 Ki. 8:29, 52), and his purity ("Your *eyes* are too pure to look on evil," Hab. 1:13). God's personal presence is expressed to his people as "face to face" (lit., "eye on eye," Num. 14:14). In symbolic (apocalyptic) texts, the eyes in various prophetic visions refer to God's ability to see all things (Ezek. 1:18; 10:12; Zech. 3:9; 4:10; cf. Rev. 4:8).

"Eyes" can refer to human spiritual sight. For example, in the Garden of Eden, Satan uses a desirable idea ("your *eyes* will be opened") so as to make disobedience sound appealing and even proper (Gen. 3:5). Therefore, when Adam and Eve rebel against God, their "eyes" are opened, but it is not as Satan promised. Their eyes are now aware of their separation from God and the shame that comes with it (Gen. 3:7).

In the rest of Scripture, the expression "eyes being open" refers to a good thing: awareness and acceptance of truth. Conversely, "eyes being closed" or "blind" refers to people's hard-hearted rejection of God and his righteousness. Thus God can say to Israel that they "have *eyes* but do not see" (Jer. 5:21; cf. Isa. 6:9–10). Indeed, the eyes of the idolater are "plastered over so they cannot see" that worshiping wood and stone is utter foolishness (Isa. 44:18). Because God is sovereign and just, he himself can blind sinners to the truth (6:10); yet because he is sovereign and merciful, he can "open their eyes" as well (42:7). The believer should therefore cry out, "Uncover my *eyes* that I may see wonderful things from your law" (Ps. 119:18), for "the commands of the LORD are pure, enlightening the *eyes*" (19:8). See *NIDOTTE*, 3:390-395.*

New Testament

Noun: ὀφθαλμός (*ophthalmos*), GK *4057* (S *3788*), 100x. *ophthalmos* means "eye." (1) In the NT can refer to the literal body part (Mt. 18:9) and to physical sight (Jn. 9:6), but it appears most commonly in various expressions and idioms that have to do with other notions of sight, such as metaphorical sight (i.e., attitudes or judgments) or spiritual sight.

(2) Eyes that are physically open must still be spiritually opened in order to see reality, such as who Jesus truly is (the men on the Emmaus road, Lk. 24:31; Gentiles through Paul's preaching, Acts 26:18). Reflecting an OT theme, some did not believe in Jesus because their hearts were divinely hardened and their "eyes" sovereignly blinded so that they could not recognize him (Jn. 12:40; Rom. 11:8).

(3) As in the Heb. conception, "eyes" can be used metaphorically as the playground of spiritual happenings—whether sinful or righteous. Hence eyes that are closed or opened can refer to spiritual rebellion, sin, or submission (Mk. 8:18; 1 Jn. 2:11; Mt. 13:16, respectively). The "*eyes* of the heart" being enlightened refers to the gain of increased hope because of a deeper understanding of one's inheritance in Christ (Eph. 1:18). The eyes can symbolically represent envy (Mt. 20:15; Mk.

7:22) and often signify sexual lust, the eyes being "full of adultery" (2 Pet. 2:14; cf. Mt. 8:19). The eyes may even symbolize a person's rebellious and disobedient way of life: "they had no fear of God before their *eyes*" (Rom. 3:18).

(4) The "eyes of the Lord" are not mentioned nearly as many times in the NT as in the OT, but the concept is nonetheless present. God is the all-seeing judge: "Nothing in all creation is hidden from God's sight. Everything is uncovered and laid bare before the *eyes* of him to whom we must give account" (Heb. 4:13). God is faithful in protecting and punishing: "For the *eyes* of the Lord are on the righteous and his ears are attentive to their prayer, but the face of the Lord is against those who do evil" (1 Pet. 3:12; cf. Ps. 34:12–16). See *NIDNTT-A*, 413-15.

FABLE

See *myth.*

FACE

Old Testament

Noun: פָּנֶה (*pāneh*; occurs only in plural, פָּנִים [*pānîm*]), GK 7156 (S 6440), 2126x. In the OT, *pāneh* basically refers to the front side of something or someone, typically the head or the face.

(1) It can refer to the face of animals (Ezek. 1:10), supernatural creatures (the face of the cherubim over the ark in Exod. 25:20; the seraphim cover their faces in Isa. 6:2), and God (Exod. 33:11, 14). When it refers to the face or front of an object (the visible part), it can be translated "front side, surface" (of the scroll, Ezek. 2:10; of the temple, Ezek. 41:14; of the earth, Gen. 2:6; Isa. 14:21).

(2) The word *pāneh* is used in several metaphorical ways and in a number of idiomatic expressions. The "light of one's face" is a symbol of acceptance and favor (Prov. 16:15 of the king; Num. 6:25 of the Lord). To "turn one's face" is to turn or move in a new direction (Jdg. 18:23), and to "set one's face toward" something can mean to turn toward something or to decide to do something (2 Ki. 12:18; Jer. 42:15 [NIV reads "are determined"]). Sometimes *pāneh* stands for the individual person (2 Sam. 17:11, KJV *in thine own person*, NIV *you yourself*) or for his or her presence (Gen. 27:30; 41:46).

(3) The OT refers to God's *pāneh* in several theologically significant ways. God promises Moses that his face will go with him, meaning that God's "presence" will personally accompany him in Israel's journey to Canaan. Moses recognizes this as evidence that Israel finds favor with God (Exod. 33:15–17; see also Isa. 63:8). When God shows favor to his people, he makes his face shine on them (Num. 6:25) and he turns his face toward them (Num. 6:26). However, when God is displeased with them, he sets his face against them (Lev. 17:10; 26:17), hides his face (Deut. 31:17–18; 32:20; Ps. 30:8), and turns away his face (Ezek. 7:22). See *NIDOTTE*, 3:637-39.

New Testament

Noun: πρόσωπον (*prosōpon*), GK *4725* (S *4383*), 76x. *prosōpon* essentially means "face." (1) It commonly refers to the face or countenance of a person (Mt. 6:16–17; Acts 6:15). Just as in the OT the face can stand for someone's "presence," so also in the NT (e.g., in 1 Thess. 2:17, Paul speaks of how he was taken from the church "in *presence* [lit., 'in face'], not in heart"). As well, *prosōpon* can stand for the whole person, as when Paul prays that "we may see you again" (lit., "we may see your face again," 3:10), or speaks of those who "have not met me personally" (lit., "have not seen my face," Col. 2:1).

(2) There are various expressions involving *prosōpon*. To "fall on one's face" is to display an attitude of humility and subservience (Mt. 26:39; Lk. 5:12), worship (Rev. 7:11), and even fear/reverence (Mt. 17:6; 1 Cor. 14:25), Metaphorically, *prosōpon* can refer to the "surface" of the earth (Lk. 21:35; Acts 17:26 [NIV says "*whole* earth"]) and to the "appearance" of things ("the *appearance* of the sky" in Mt. 16:3, NIV). In 2 Cor. 5:12 *prosōpon* describes the "outward *appearance*,"

and elsewhere of the outer surface of the earth (Lk. 21:35; Acts 17:26).

(3) There is special theological significance attached to *prosōpon* in 2 Cor. 4:6. Paul indicates that just as Moses' face was covered with a veil to hide its decreasing glory, so the hearts of unbelievers are covered when they hear the reading of the old covenant. But when they turn to Jesus Christ, the veil is removed, their hearts are enlightened, and they behold "the light of the knowledge of the glory of God in the *face* of Christ" (4:6). See *NIDNTT-A*, 497-98.

FAIL

Old Testament

Verb: חָדַל (*ḥādal*), GK 2532 (S 2308), 55x. *ḥādal*, most often translated "stop" in the NIV, generally indicates the simple cessation of action. Sometimes the verb is used for the stopping of an action before it ever starts. In this context, *ḥādal* appears frequently when determining whether an action (i.e., listening or engaging in battle) will begin. Ezekiel, for example, must speak God's words to the Israelites whether they listen or "fail" to listen (Ezek. 2:7; cf. 2:5; 3:11). See *stop*.

New Testament

Verb: ἐκπίπτω (*ekpiptō*), GK *1738* (S *1601*), 10x. *ekpiptō* means "to fall, fall off, fail." See *fall*.

FAIN

See *want*.

FAITH

New Testament

Noun: πίστις (*pistis*), GK *4411* (S *4102*), 243x. *pistis* means "belief, trust, confidence," though it can also mean "faithfulness."

(1) Faith can refer to the act of believing (see also *believe*). The NT speaks about faith in God (Mk. 11:22; 1 Thess. 1:8; 1 Pet. 1:21; Heb. 6:1) and faith in Jesus (Acts 3:16; 20:21; 24:24; Gal. 3:26; Eph. 1:15; Col. 1:4; 1 Tim. 3:13). It also simply speaks about "faith" with the unspoken object being understood as Jesus Christ (Rom. 1:8; 1 Cor. 2:5; 15:14, 17). In the gospels, Jesus heals people as an affirmation of their faith and a visual aid of the spiritual healing they experience (Mt. 8:10; 9:2; 15:28; Mk. 5:34; 10:52; Lk. 18:42). In other instances he reprimands people for their lack of faith (Mt. 17:20; Mk. 4:40; Lk. 8:25).

A major theme in Romans and Galatians is that believers are justified by faith and not by works (Rom. 3:28, 30; 4:5, 11, 12, 13, 16; 5:1, 2; 9:30–32; 10:6; Gal. 2:16; 3:8, 9, 11, 12, 14, 22, 24; 5:5; see also Phil. 3:9). Paul shows the proper relationship between faith and works. Righteousness is received by faith from first to last (Rom. 1:17). At the same time, true faith produces obedience (Rom. 1:5; 16:26; see also Gal. 5:6; 1 Thess. 1:3; 1 Tim. 1:5; Tit. 1:1; 1 Pet. 1:5). This is well in line with the exhortation of James that true, saving faith is demonstrated by action (Jas. 2:14, 17, 18, 20). Reflecting these truths, a Reformation saying is that salvation is by faith alone, but not by a faith that is alone.

In one sense, to have faith is equivalent to being a Christian. Paul affirms that "those who are of faith are children of Abraham" (Gal. 3:7). Every Christian is saved by grace through faith as a gift from God, and not as the result of anything they do (Eph. 2:8). Christ dwells in the hearts of believers through faith (Eph. 3:17). Faith gives believers the assurance that they can approach God (Heb. 10:22) and is the means by which God gets them to the finish line of their salvation (1 Pet. 1:5). Faith is part of the armor of God that protects believers against the enemy (Eph. 6:16; 1 Thess. 5:8). Christians are people who "live by faith, not by sight" (2 Cor. 5:7). The writer of Hebrews defines faith as "being sure of what we hope for and certain of what we do not see" (Heb. 11:1) and follows with a list of OT saints who lived that way. Jesus is the author and perfecter of faith (Heb. 12:2).

However, the degree of faith can vary from believer to believer. Faith can be weak (Rom. 14:1), can be possessed in differing measures (Rom. 12:3, 6), and can grow (2 Cor. 10:15; 2 Thess. 1:3). Faith can be tested and needs to be strengthened in the face of trials (1 Thess. 3:2, 5, 6, 7, 10). Faith can be renounced, abandoned, or destroyed (1 Tim. 1:19; 6:10, 21; 2 Tim. 2:18; Rev. 2:13). The testing of faith results in perseverance (Jas. 1:3).

(2) *pistis* can also refer to Christian doctrine or collection of beliefs (Jas. 2.17; Phil. 1:27; 1 Tim. 1:13; Tit. 2:2; Jude 3). The word can also refer to the Christian religion as in Paul's exhortation to the Corinthian Christians to "stand firm in the faith" (1 Cor. 16:13; see also Acts 13:8; 14:22; 2 Cor. 13:5; Gal. 1:23; Phil. 1:25; Col. 2:7; 1 Tim. 3:9; 4:1, 6; 2 Tim. 4:7; Tit. 3:15). As the gospel is preached in the early days of the church, a number of priests become obedient to the faith (Acts 6:7), and churches are strengthened in the faith (Acts 16:5). There is "one hope, one *faith*, one baptism" (Eph. 4:5), and Jesus gives various people in service to the church to build it towards unity in the faith (v. 3). Christians belong to the "household of faith" (Gal. 6:10). The Christian faith rests on the resurrection of Christ and has no validity without it (1 Cor. 15:14, 17).

(3) *pistis* can also denote a conviction or certainty of belief. Jesus says that if someone tells a mountain to be thrown into the sea and has faith that it will happen, then it will (Mk. 11:23). Paul calls this aspect of faith one of the gifts of the Holy Spirit (1 Cor. 12:9; see also 13:2). Similarly, *pistis* can refer to an assurance or proof. God has given assurance that he will send Jesus back to judge the world by raising him from the dead (Acts 17:31).

(4) Finally, *pistis* can mean "faithfulness" or "trustworthiness." Jesus remonstrates with the Pharisees for neglecting justice, mercy and faithfulness (Mt. 23:2). A lack of trusting in people does not nullify the faithfulness of God (Rom. 3:3). Scholars debate whether *pistis* in Rom. 3:22 means "*faith* in Jesus" or "the *faithfulness* of Jesus." Slaves are to show good faith (show that they can be trusted) to their masters (Tit. 2:10). Persecution will call for the faithfulness of the saints (Rev. 13:10) and will require endurance to be faithful to Jesus (Rev. 14:12). Faithfulness is an aspect of the fruit of the Spirit, which is to mark all believers (Gal. 5:22). See *NIDNTT-A*, 462-66.

FAITHFUL

Old Testament

Verb: אָמַן (*ʾāman*), GK 586 (S 539), 97x. *ʾāman* means "to believe, trust." In its participial form it has the nuance of "trustworthy, faithful." See *believe*.

New Testament

Adjective: πιστός (*pistos*), GK *4412* (S *4103*), 67x. *pistos* means "faithful, trustworthy, reliable, dependable." (1) People are labeled "faithful" (1 Cor. 4:17; Eph. 6:21; Col. 1:2, 7; 4:7, 9; 1 Tim. 3:11). Jesus tells a parable about a "faithful" and wise servant (Mt. 25:21, 23). Paul considers himself to be "trustworthy" in his teaching (1 Cor. 7:25). The teaching of the gospel is to be entrusted to "reliable" men (2 Tim. 2:2; see also 1 Cor. 4:2). To be "faithful" in the book of Revelation is to refuse to compromise the Christian faith, even in the face of persecution and martyrdom (Rev. 2:10, 13; 17:14).

(2) Words or sayings too can be called "faithful" (Acts 13:34; Rev. 21:5; 22:6). Note 1 Tim. 1:15: "Here is a *trustworthy* saying that deserves full acceptance: Christ Jesus came into the world to save sinners." There are several such trustworthy sayings in the Pastoral Letters (1 Tim. 3:1; 4:9; 2 Tim. 2:11; Tit. 1:9; 3:8).

(3) God and Jesus are called "faithful" (1 Cor. 1:9; 2 Cor. 1:18; Heb. 2:17; 10:23; 1 Pet. 4:19; Rev. 1:5; 3:14; 19:11). God is faithful even if his people are not (2 Tim. 2:13). He is faithful not to let them be tempted beyond what they can bear (1 Cor. 10:13) and to keep on making them holy until the coming of Christ (1 Thess. 5:24). When we confess our sin, God is faithful and just to forgive us (1 Jn. 1:9).

(4) *pistos* is also used to describe someone who "believes" or "trusts" in Jesus, such as a "believing" master (1 Tim. 6:2). It can be used in the place of a noun to

refer to people who have put their faith in Christ, usually translated as "believers" (Acts 10:45; 16:1, 15; 2 Cor. 6:15; 1 Tim. 4:3; 1 Tim. 4:3, 10, 12; 5:16). Paul calls Abraham a believer because the gospel was preached to him in advance (Gal. 3:9; see Gen. 12:1–3). See *NIDNTT-A*, 462-66.

FAITHFULNESS

Old Testament

Noun: אֱמוּנָה (*ʾemûnâ*), GK 575 (S 530), 127x. *ʾemûna* means "faithfulness, trustworthiness, integrity." Like *ʾemet*, it occurs in the context of moral language (steadfast love, righteousness, justice, etc.) and is used to reveal God's character, often in language of praise. The Song of Moses, for example, exalts God as "a *faithful* God who does not wrong" (Deut. 32:4). Jeremiah also uses this term to exclaim, "Great is your *faithfulness*" (Lam. 3:23). He does so after contemplating the fact that it is God's persevering great love that has kept his people from total destruction. God answers the unfaithfulness of his people with a fresh supply of compassion, as fresh and undiminished as the morning dew.

ʾemûnâ is also a desired human characteristic (see 2 Ki. 12:15; 22:7). This term is the one used in Hab. 2:4, "but the righteous will live by his *faith[fulness]*." The life of the righteous that will survive judgment must be built on faithfulness, trustworthiness, and integrity toward God and others (cf. Rom. 1:17; Gal. 3:11; Heb. 10:38). This characteristic is especially relevant in our society, where truth is considered to be relative and faithfulness is out of fashion.

Noun: אֱמֶת (*ʾemet*), GK 622 (S 571), 127x. *ʾemet* denotes "faithfulness" in the sense of fidelity and trustworthiness, honesty and moral rectitude. It implies absolute reliability and complete integrity. It also denotes "truth" in the sense of an accurate expression of reality, especially as it is opposed to falsehood (Gen. 42:16; Deut. 13:14; 1 Ki. 10:6; 17:24; Prov. 14:25; Jer. 9:5).

Used as an attribute for God, *ʾemet* expresses an essential element of his character. When God reveals himself to Moses on Mount Sinai, he declares, "The LORD, the LORD, the compassionate and gracious God, slow to anger, abounding in love and *faithfulness* [or *truth*]" (Exod. 34:6). The remarkable thing about this revelation is that it occurs just after the Israelites have worshiped the golden calf. Despite their unfaithfulness, God is constant in his love and commitment to them (Neh. 9:33). No wonder the Psalmist is able to say, "Your *faithfulness* reaches to the skies" (Ps. 108:4; cf. 86:15; 115:1; 117:2; 146:6). God is absolutely trustworthy and reliable because he is the God of truth (31:5; 45:4).

The Lord desires his people to emulate his truth or trustworthiness (Jos. 24:14; 1 Sam. 12:24; 1 Ki. 3:6; 2 Ki. 20:3). The psalmist says, "Surely you desire *truth* in the inner parts" (Ps. 51:8). The idea is that God desires the absolute truth of his character to be reflected in his people. "Truth in the inner parts" has to do with integrity, being of the same quality throughout—on the surface as well as underneath. It means that we maintain our standards of behavior both when people are watching and when we are far away from the scrutiny of others. Unfortunately, God's people all too often fail to live in this manner. Hosea, for example, indicates that there is no "faithfulness" in the land (Hos. 4:1).

Adjective: תָּמִים (*tāmîm*), GK 9459 (S 8549), 91x. Most often *tāmîm* describes animals or crops intended for sacrificial offerings as "unblemished" or "whole." The NIV renders *tāmîm* as "faithfulness" in Jos. 24:14; in this sense, it refers to the conduct of the righteous and wise. See *unblemished.*

New Testament

Noun: πίστις (*pistis*), GK *4411* (S *4102*), 243x. *pistis* means "belief, trust, confidence," though it can also mean "faithfulness, trustworthiness." See *faith*.

FALL

Old Testament

Verb: כָּשַׁל (*kāšal*), GK 4173 (S 3782), 65x. *kāšal* conveys the act of stumbling or falling and may be translated "stumble, fall." See *stumble*.

Verb: נָפַל (*nāpal*), GK 5877 (S 5307), 435x. *nāpal* generally indicates the simple action of falling. Ahaziah "falls" through the lattice (2 Ki. 1:2); some of the men of Sodom and Gomorrah "fall" into the tar pits as they flee in defeat (Gen. 14:10); and Eli "falls" backward off his seat and breaks his neck when he hears the ark has been captured (1 Sam. 4:18). The wall of Jericho "fall" flat when the Israelites shout (Jos. 6:20), and Elisha takes Elijah's cloak that "fell" when God took Elijah (2 Ki. 2:13).

Sometimes *nāpal* can indicate intentional falling, such as "dismounting" from a camel (Gen. 24:64) or a chariot (2 Ki. 5:21). *nāpal* is also used for the "casting" of lots (Neh. 10:34[35], "casting" in the sense of *causing to fall*) and for the "allocating" of the promised land to Israel (Jos. 13:6, "allocating" in the sense of *causing* a certain territory *to fall* to a particular tribe).

Another significant usage of *nāpal* for intentional falling is "to fall on one's face" (22x). This idiomatic expression for self-humiliation before a superior is occasionally translated "to bow down" by the NIV (e.g., 1 Ki. 18:7). While this expression is used to show respect to other people (e.g., Ruth 2:10; 2 Sam. 9:6), it is often used in the worship of God. Abraham "*falls* on his face" when God is establishing the covenant with him (Gen. 17:3); Aaron and Moses "*fall* on their faces" before the glory of Yahweh in the tent of meeting (Num. 20:6); and Ezekiel "*falls* on his face" before the glory of God revealed in a vision (Ezek. 1:28).

In over one-quarter of its occurrences, *nāpal* occurs in military contexts, simply meaning "to die," but translated "to fall." Deborah's song makes the connection between "falling" and "dying" explicit: Sisera "falls" at Jael's feet, "dead" (Jdg. 5:27, 3x). The phrase "to *fall* by the sword" occurs some 38x in the OT (e.g., Saul and Jonathan "*fall* by the sword" in 2 Sam. 1:12), frequently in the context of punishment for sin. Moses makes this clear in his warning to first generation Israelites before the attempted conquest, "Because you have turned away from God, he will not be with you and you will *fall* by the sword" (Num. 14:43). Of the thirty-eight occurrences of "to fall by the sword," thirty appear in the prophets, frequently in the sense of punishment for sin. Not only will Israel "*fall* by the sword" because of their evil abominations (Ezek. 6:11, 12), but the nations will also "*fall* by the sword" in judgment (30:5, 6). This mortal use of *nāpal* may explain the connection with the Nephilim (Gen. 6:4; Num. 13:33), perhaps indicating that they are men of violence.

Perhaps the most theologically significant use of *nāpal* is found in the literary climax of Joshua (Jos. 21:45) and then again in Joshua's farewell address (23:14): "Not one word from all the good words that God spoke to the house of Israel *fell*; all came to pass" (lit. trans.). While *nāpal* is usually translated "failed" here, the sense of *nāpal* is that nothing can vanquish the standing of God's word—it bears the full weight of certainty and inevitability (cf. Rom. 8:38-39). See *NIDOTTE*, 3:129-31.

New Testament

Verb: ἐκπίπτω (*ekpiptō*), GK *1738* (S *1601*), 10x. *ekpiptō* means "to fall, fall away, fail." *ekpiptō* derives from *ek* ("out of, away from") and *piptō* ("to fall"). In Acts 12:7, this verb is used literally (chains "fell off" Peter's wrists; cf. similar uses in Acts 27:32; Jas. 1:11; 1 Pet. 1:24). In Acts 27:17, 26, 29, it refers to the storm-tossed ship possibly running aground. The term is used figuratively in Gal. 5:4 and 2 Pet. 3:17 to convey the sense "to lose" one's salvation or "to fall away" from grace. Paul uses *ekpiptō* in Rom. 9:6 to express the fact that the word of God has not "failed" or fallen away from its usefulness. See *NIDNTT-A*, 461-62.*

Verb: πίπτω (*piptō*), GK *4406* (S *4098*), 90x. *piptō* means "to fall, collapse, bow down." It is a common verb in the NT and is most often used in a literal sense. Primarily it denotes unintentional falls, such as houses (Mt. 7:25), birds (10:29), seed (13:4ff.), people (15:14; Acts 20:9), stars (Mt. 24:29), buildings (Lk. 13:4; Heb. 11:30), a stone (Lk. 20:18), cliffs or hills (Lk. 23:30; Rev. 6:16), walls (Heb. 11:30), Babylon (Rev. 14:8, 18:2), and cities (Rev. 16:19). In some cases the literal falling down means to descend from an erect to a prostrate position. Generally this is intentional, such as bowing down before a master (Mt. 18:26), worshiping (Mt. 4:9; Acts 10:25; 1 Cor. 14:25), or showing gratitude or respect (Mk. 5:22; Lk. 17:16; Jn. 11:32).

The term also has figurative uses. The lot "falling" on someone is expressed in Acts 1:26, and fear and darkness also fall on people (Acts 13:11; Rev. 11:11). Though *piptō* does not mean fall as in falling into specific sin, it does convey a deeper meaning such as becoming guilty; that is, falling on the stone in Lk. 20:18 involves the guilt of rejecting Christ. In Rom. 11:11 falling means abandonment by God to guilt. See *NIDNTT-A*, 461-62.

FALL ASLEEP

New Testament

Verb: κοιμάω (*koimaō*), GK *3121* (S *2837*), 18x. *koimaō* refers to the act of falling sleeping, or, euphemistically, to death. Examples of the former include sleeping guards (Mt. 28:13), the disciples' sleeping in the Garden of Gethsemane (Lk. 22:45), the disciples' misunderstanding Jesus' euphemistic use of the term (Jn. 11:12), and Peter's sleeping in prison (Acts 12:6).

When biblical authors want to focus on death as an entrance into the intermediate state and therefore as something temporary, they use *koimaō*. After the tragic stoning of Stephen, Luke tells us that he simply "fell asleep" (Acts 7:60); physical death is not the true end for Stephen. Paul likely has a pastoral motive when he uses *koimaō* in 1 Cor. 7:39; 11:30, where he touches on the "sensitive" topics of the death of a spouse and death as a result of judgment. The bodies of the saints who have "fallen asleep" were raised at the death of Jesus (Mt. 27:52). Jesus says that "our friend Lazarus *has fallen asleep*, but I go to awaken him," before he raises him from the dead (Jn. 11:11).

Paul uses the word extensively in his letters to the Corinthians and Thessalonians concerning the resurrection. In his Corinthian correspondence, Paul argues that if the resurrection of the dead does not exist, "then those also who have *fallen asleep* in Christ have perished. If in this life only we have hoped in Christ, we are of all people most to be pitied. But in fact Christ has been raised from the dead, the first fruits of those who have *fallen asleep*" (1 Cor. 15:18–20, ESV). In this passage, "fallen asleep" pictures death as sleep against the hopeful backdrop of the resurrection. Indeed, many will "fall asleep" before all will be changed at that glorious final trumpet (1 Cor. 15:51). In 1 Thess. 4:13–15 Paul echoes much the same understanding of *koimaō*, still against the backdrop of the resurrection, with the added encouragement to that particular church that those who have "fallen asleep" will precede all the remaining saints in the glorious resurrection day. See *NIDNTT-A*, 279-80.

FALL AWAY

New Testament

Verb: ἀφίστημι (*aphistēmi*), GK *923* (S *868*), 14x. *aphistēmi* generally means to "leave, depart" in a physical sense. It can also express various forms of apostasy, such as the seeds that fall on the rock representing those who receive the message with joy, but having no root "they fall away" in the time of testing (Lk. 8:13). See *leave*.

Verb: ἐκπίπτω (*ekpiptō*), GK *1738* (S *1601*), 10x. *ekpiptō* means "to fall, fall away, fail." See *fall*.

FALL DOWN BEFORE

New Testament

Verb: προσκυνέω (*proskyneō*), GK *4686* (S *4352*), 60x. *proskyneō* means "to fall down and/or worship" someone or something. While it is most often used of people worshiping God, it does not limited bowing down before the God of the Bible. See *worship*.

FALL SHORT

New Testament

Verb: ὑστερέω (*hystereō*), GK *5728* (S *5302*), 16x. *hystereo* conveys the idea of lagging behind or failing to attain a certain standard; thus, "to lack, fall short." See *lack*.

FALL UPON

New Testament

Verb: ἐπιπίπτω (*epipiptō*), GK *2158* (S *1968*), 11x. *epipiptō* can mean "to come upon, fall upon, embrace." See *come upon*.

FALSE PROPHET

New Testament

Noun: ψευδοπροφήτης (*pseudoprophētēs*), GK *6021* (S *5578*), 11x. *pseudoprophētēs* (a combination of the word *prophētēs*, "prophet," and the prefix *pseudo*, "false") refers to someone who falsely claims to be God's prophet, or one who utters false prophecies.

Such false prophets existed in OT times (Lk. 6:26) and during the NT period (Acts 13:6; 2 Pet. 2:1; 1 Jn. 4:1). Jesus warns that many false prophets will arise among his people throughout history (Mt. 7:15; 24:11, 24; Mk. 13:22), and the book of Revelation speaks of a final false prophet who will appear at the end of the age (Rev. 16:13; 19:20; 20:10). See *NIDNTT-A*, 499-500.*

FALSEHOOD

Old Testament

Noun/Adverb: שָׁוְא (*sawʾ*), GK 8736 (S 7723), 54x. *sawʾ* denotes ineffectiveness or falseness and may be translated as "vain, worthless, false." The term describes the futility of certain things or activities. See *worthless*.

Noun: שֶׁקֶר (*šeqer*), GK 9214 (S 8267), 113x. *šeqer* is derived from the root verb *šāqar*, "to lie, deceive, betray" (only 6x in the OT). The meaning of this word is tied to lies, falsehood and deception. Everything that is a *šeqer* is opposed to truth. See *lie*.

New Testament

Noun: ψεῦδος (*pseudos*), GK *6022* (S *5579*), 10x. *pseudos* is typically translated as "lie," but it may also indicate falsehood, deception, or anything counterfeit (e.g., 1 Jn. 2:27). See *lie*.

FAME

Old Testament

Noun: שֵׁם (*šēm*), GK 9005 (S 8034), 864x. While *šēm* is used many times in Scripture for no more than a person's given name, in the context of the ancient Near East it also conveys much more, such as "reputation, fame" (see *name*).

FAMILY

Old Testament

Noun: מִשְׁפָּחָה (*mišpāḥâ*), GK 5476 (S 4940), 304x. The noun *mišpāḥâ* designates a subgroup of a larger division, and is, therefore, variously translated as "clan, family, people" as well as "kind, kingdoms, nation." See *clan, kind, nation*.

New Testament

Noun: γένος (*genos*), GK *1169* (S *1085*), 20x. *genos* means "family," referring to a small group of relatives. Members of the high-priestly family examine Peter and John (Acts 4:6). Stephen relates how Pharaoh was introduced to "Joseph's family" (Acts 7:13). *genos* can also mean "offspring" (see *offspring*), "people" (see *people*), or "kind" (see *kind*).

Noun: οἶκος (*oikos*), GK *3875* (S *3624*), 114x. *oikos* sometimes refer to ancestral family lineage, such as "the house of Israel," "the house of Jacob," or "the house of Judah" (Lk. 1:33; Acts 7:42; Heb. 8:8, 10). The Christian community is seen as the "family" of God (Eph. 4:17). See *house*.

FAMINE

Old Testament

Noun: רָעָב (*rāʿāb*), GK 8280 (S 7457), 101x. *rāʿāb* means "famine, hunger, starvation." Life in the ancient Near East was unpredictable, and people faced drought and famine with some regularity (e.g.,

Gen. 12:10; Ruth 1:1; 1 Ki. 18:2; Neh. 5:3); however, people in relationship with the Lord did not have to fear famine. Early and latter rains were promised as a sign of obedience to the covenant (Deut. 11:13–17). When Pharaoh dreamed of a famine, a warning sent by God, and through Joseph's interpretation Egypt was able to prepare, so that God spare the lives of Joseph's family (Gen. 41). When Solomon prayed at the dedication of the temple, he instructed people to repent if there was no rain and to return to the Lord (1 Ki. 8:37).

Judgment comes on Israel for their idolatry in the form of hunger and famine. In the context of Judah's ongoing sinfulness, the Lord prophesies through Jeremiah: "I will destroy them with the sword, *famine* and plague" (Jer. 14:12). This was fulfilled during the siege of Jerusalem by Nebuchadnezzar. Amos declares a more damaging hunger than lack of food: "The time is coming, says the Lord God, when I will send a *famine* on the land; not a *famine* of bread, or a thirst for water, but of hearing the words of the Lord" (Amos 8:11).

However, those who cry out to the Lord in humility and thanksgiving receive satisfaction, "There he lets the hungry live, and they establish a town to live in; they sow fields and plant vineyards, and get a fruitful yield" (Ps. 107:36–37). God describes true worship as the activities of removing the sin of oppression, feeding the hungry, and satisfying the needs of the afflicted (Isa. 58:10). See *NIDOTTE*, 3:1133–37.

New Testament

Noun: λιμός (*limos*), GK *3350* (S *3042*), 12x. *limos* can be translated "hunger, famine." It refers to literal hunger or famine, as in Lk. 4:25 (famine in Elijah's time), Lk. 15:14, 17 (parable of the prodigal son), Acts 7:11 (famine in Canaan led Israel to Egypt), Acts 11:28 (Agabus's prophecy), Rom. 8:35 ("Who shall separate us from the love of Christ? Shall … *famine*?"), and 2 Cor. 11:27 ("I have known *hunger* and thirst and have often gone without food").

In keeping with this meaning, *limos* is one of the signs of distress during the end times, as in Jesus' Mount Olivet discourse: "There will be *famines* and earthquakes in various places" (Mt. 24:7; Mk. 13:8; Lk. 21:11). Moreover, the opening of the fourth seal in Rev. 6:7–8 reveals a rider named Death, who has the power to kill by sword, plague, wild beasts, and famine. Finally, John describes the fall of Babylon as the day her plagues overtake her, namely, "death, mourning, and *famine*. She will be consumed by fire, for mighty is the Lord God who judges her" (Rev. 18:8). There is no figurative use of "famine" in the NT, such as there is in Amos 8:11.*

FAR

Old Testament

Verb: רָחַק (*rāḥaq*), GK 8178 (S 7368), 59x. In a general sense meaning "to be far/distant, remove, send away," *rāḥaq* can be used either to describe the state of a thing ("to be far, at a distance") or to indicate an action ("to go far, make far," i.e., "remove").

(1) In the OT *rāḥaq* is always used in a spatial rather than a temporal sense. Joseph's brothers have not "gone far" before Joseph sends his servant after them (Gen. 44:4). While Pharaoh gives the Israelites permission to go into the barren wilderness, he tells them not to "go very far" (Exod. 8:28). The psalmist complains, "You have *removed* my acquaintances from me" (Ps. 88:8), and Solomon says regarding the adulteress, "*Keep* your path *away* from her" (Prov. 5:8).

(2) *rāḥaq* is also used figuratively. The rod of discipline is said to remove the foolishness bound up in the heart of a child (Prov. 22:15). Eccl. 3:5 refers to "a time to embrace, and a time to be far [i.e., *refrain*] from embracing." Often the figurative use of the word is infused with theological meaning. For example, God can be far from someone (Ps. 22:19, "And you, O Lord, do not *be distant*"; cf. 35:22; 38:21; 71:12). Or conversely, through sin, someone can be far from God (Isa. 29:13, "but their heart is far from me"; cf. Jer. 2:5). To prevent such separation, people must stay

far from sin (Exod. 23:7; Prov. 4:24; Ezek. 43:9). Thankfully, the Scriptures teach that for those of us who repent from sin and turn to God, he "removes" (lit., "makes far") our transgressions as far as the east is from the west (Ps. 103:12). See *NIDOTTE* 3:1099-1103.

Adjective: רָחוֹק (*rāḥôq*), GK 8158 (S 7350), 84x. *rāḥôq* describes something "far, distant." Naturally, its antonym is "near" (1 Ki. 8:46), and often it is used with the preposition "from" (e.g., "from *afar*," Gen. 22:4; "*far* from," Jer. 12:2).

(1) Most commonly, *rāḥôq* is used in a spatial sense. Miriam "stood at a *distance*" to see what would happen to baby Moses (Exod. 2:4), and Prov. says, "A neighbor who is close is better than a brother who is *far away*" (Prov. 27:10). The word can also refer to distant Gentile countries, such as Babylon (2 Ki. 20:14; cf. 1 Ki. 8:41; Isa. 49:1). *rāḥôq* is also used with temporal reference, as when Ezekiel's audience thought he was "prophesying about times *far off*" (Ezek. 12:27; cf. 2 Sam. 7:19; Isa. 37:26). Finally, *rāḥôq* is used in a qualitative sense in Proverb's estimation of the excellent wife: "Her value is *far greater* than jewels" (Prov. 31:10).

(2) *rāḥôq* is used with theological significance in various ways. After God spoke the Ten Commandments, the Israelites "stood at a *distance* while Moses came near the darkness where God was" (Exod. 20:21). Later, Moses and the leaders of Israel were to "worship from *afar*" (Exod. 24:1). Thus, at Sinai the Israelites learn that God's nature demands a distance between themselves and God. At the same time, the commandment of God is "not *far away*" from the Israelites; that is, it is available for them to observe (Deut. 30:11). In a different sense, God can be far from people. He is said to be far from the wicked (Prov. 15:29), and salvation is far from them as well (Ps. 119:155). But when God or his salvation is far from the righteous, we find complaints such as, "Why, O LORD do you stand in the *distance*?" (Ps. 10:1), and, "The words of my groaning are *far away* from my salvation" (Ps. 22:1). In yet another sense, the word is used to portray the transcendence and omnipotence of God: "You understand my thought from a *distance*" (Ps. 139:2; cf. Jer. 23:23). See *NIDOTTE*, 3:1099-103.

New Testament

Adverb: μακράν (*makran*), GK *3426* (S *3112*), 10x. *makran* means "to be far away"; it refers primarily to space, but sometimes may refer to time.

(1) *makran* can refer to a far distance. When Jesus was casting out demons from two men, there was a herd of swine feeding "at a distance" (Mt. 8:30). The father in the parable of the lost son runs to meet his son when he is still "far away" (Lk. 15:20). Conversely, the word is used with a negative to describe something close. The centurion sends friends to Jesus when he is "not far" from his house (Lk. 7:6), and after the resurrection, the disciples were in a boat "not far" from the shore, i. e., only a hundred yards away (Jn. 21:8).

(2) A possible temporal use is found in Acts 2:39, where Peter says God's promise is to those Jews present at Pentecost, to their children, and "to all those *far away*." Peter may be referring to future generations or to people in distant lands, either Diaspora Jews or Gentiles.

(3) *makran* is also used in a spiritual sense. Jesus tells one man, "You are not *far* from the kingdom of God" (Mk. 12:34), and Paul says that God is "not far" from everyone (Acts 17:27). Jesus uses this word in reference to the Gentiles in his message to Paul in Acts 22:21: "I will send you *far away* to the Gentiles"). In fact, in Eph. 2:13, 17, one of the key passages about the relationship between Jewish and Gentile believers, *makran* refers to Gentiles believers as those who were once "far away," but have now been brought near to God by the blood of Christ. See *NIDNTT-A*, 158-59.*

(BE) FAR

New Testament

Verb: ἀπέχω (*apechō*), GK *600* (S *566*, *567*, *568*), 19x. *apechō* means "to be far off," e.g., a boat being some distance from the shore (Mt. 14:24). Jesus rebukes the Pharisees and scribes because their hearts "are far" from God (Mt. 15:8; Mk. 7:6). The prodigal son "is far off" when his father sees him and runs to him (Lk. 15:20). *apechō* can also mean "to abstain from" (see *abstain from*) or "to receive in full" (see *receive in full*).

FARM

See *field.*

FARMER

New Testament

Noun: γεωργός (*geōrgos*), GK *1177* (S *1092*), 19x. *geōrgos* can refer to the owner of a farm or to those who work the farm (a "tenant"). Jesus uses this term in the parable of the tenants for those who have rented the vineyard from the landowner (Mt. 21:33–41; Mk. 12:1–9; Lk. 20:9–16). He also uses metaphorically to refer to God the Father as the owner of a vineyard, the "vinedresser" (Jn. 15:1). Paul compares the Christian minister to a "hard-working farmer" who should receive the first share of his crops (2 Tim. 2:6). According to James, the patience needed in waiting for the coming of the Lord is the same as that required by a farmer waiting for his crops to bear fruit (Jas. 5:7).

FASHION

Old Testament

Verb: בָּנָה (*bānâ*), GK 1215 (S 1129), 377x. *bānâ* means "to build" or "to fashion." God is the first person in the Bible to "build" something. In Gen. 2:22, he takes a rib from Adam and "builds" or "fashions" it into a woman. See *build.*

FAST

New Testament

Verb: νηστεύω (*nēsteuō*), GK *3764* (S *3522*), 20x. *nēsteuō* denotes fasting or abstaining from food. All NT occurrences of this word are found in the Synoptic Gospels and Acts. *nēsteuō* is frequently undertaken as a religious ritual. In the mystery religions, there was a belief that demonic infection could take place through eating and drinking while the soul of a dead person was still near. Consequently, people fasted to avoid such danger. Such superstitions were not, however, a part of the Jewish or Christian world.

A prominent reason for fasting Jews to fast was to display penitential mourning in order to avert God's wrath. In the NT, however, Jesus supports his disciples for not fasting (Mk. 2:18–19). Why should the disciples mourn since the Messiah has come? Yet Jesus is not against all forms of fasting. Before he began his public ministry, he himself went out into the desert and fasted for forty days (Mt. 4:2). There are instances when the local churches prayed and fasted (Acts 13:3; 14:23). Therefore, fasting is still a discipline that may be practiced by God's people. However, the attitude of the heart must be examined, and fasting must be done voluntarily. The Jewish law required only one fast a year, on the Day of Atonement (Lev. 23:27–32).

nēsteuō may never be intended to bring recognition from other people. That is why Christ speaks against fasting as practiced by the hypocrites, for their fasting was to impress others and it had no value (Mt. 6:16–18). The goal is, rather, to humble oneself before God and to seek his face in prayer. *nēsteuō* involves an outward act that expresses an inward humility toward God. Its motive is as important as the act itself. See *NIDNTT-A*, 386-87.

FASTEN

See *look; straight.*

FAT

Old Testament

Noun: חֵלֶב (*ḥēleb*), GK 2693 (S 2459), 92x. *ḥēleb* usually denotes the literal body fat of a human or, more commonly, an animal. It is not clear whether the fatty portions of a beast were considered a delicacy in the ancient world or whether an animal's *ḥēleb* was special in Israel simply because Yahweh deems it so (cf. Num. 18:29–30, 32). What is clear, however, is that *ḥēleb* comes to be used figuratively for the "best" part of something. In other contexts, the noun can refer to a condition of hardness or unresponsiveness.

(1) While *ḥēleb* can describe the "fat" of a human body (Jdg. 3:22; Job 15:27), it usually designates the "fat" of sacrificial animals (Exod. 23:18; 29:13; 1 Sam. 2:15). This meaning is found no less than 45x in Lev. alone! Specifically, the *ḥēleb* of an animal usually designates the "fatty portions" surrounding the kidneys and the intestines, which are to be offered on the fire by the priests (Lev. 3:3–4, 10, 14–16; cf. Exod. 29:22). The cooking of such fat is part of the burnt offering (Lev. 1:8, 12), the peace offering (3:9), the sin offering (4:8–10), and the trespass offering (7:3–4). And like the blood, the "fat" is not to be eaten (3:17; 7:23, 25). Furthermore, while a layperson can participate in the slaughtering of the sacrifice, only the priest can offer the "fat." Thus, the essential focus of the sacrificial rite is not in the slaughtering of the animal but in the priestly offering of the *ḥēleb*. According to Isa. 43:24, God delights in such offerings (cf. Gen. 4:4), and it is clear from elsewhere that to offer the "fat portions" means to offer one's best to God (Num. 18:29–30, 32).

(2) It is probably from the context of Israel's sacrifice that *ḥēleb* comes to be used broadly in the OT for the "best" or "finest" of something. *ḥēleb* can mean the choicest part of an animal (Num. 18:29–30, 32), the highest quality wheat (Deut. 32:14; Ps. 81:16; 147:14), or the finest of olive oil or wine (Num. 18:12). Its use in the phrase the "best of the land" (Gen. 45:18) is similar to the English expression "the cream of the crop." In Ps. 63:5, David's passion to find satisfaction only in God drives him to proclaim, "My soul will be satisfied as with the *richest* of foods; with singing lips my mouth will praise you." David finds life's best in God.

(3) In a few instances in Psalms, *ḥēleb* is used negatively to represent the condition of a callous, dull, or unresponsive heart (Ps. 17:10; 73:7). "[The arrogant man] is insensitive as the fat of his heart, but I delight in your law" (119:70).

FATHER

Old Testament

Noun: אָב (*ʾāb*), GK 3 (S 1), 1210x. Usually translated "father," *ʾāb* is an honorary title applied most usually to the head of household but also to various authority figures.

(1) *ʾāb* most often denotes the biological male parent (Gen. 4:20; Jdg. 14:10; Prov. 23:22), but it can also refer to a grandfather (Gen. 28:13; 32:9) or even a more distant ancestor (1 Ki. 15:11; 19:4). Ancient Israel was a tribal society in which the household was the fundamental social unit. The head of the family was the father, and thus Israel is often called a patriarchal society. On many civil issues, the father has the authority to act without reference to the judges (Deut. 21:15–17; Jdg. 6:30–31). The father is responsible for teaching his children about God and his commands. Abraham, for example, is to teach his children to keep God's ways so that God will fulfill his promises to them (Gen. 18:19; cf. Deut. 6:6–9). In order to preserve the sacred traditions and the continuity of the covenant community, God also calls fathers to answer their children's questions regarding their divinely shaped heritage (Exod. 12:26–27; 13:14–15; Deut. 6:20–25; Jos. 4:6–7, 21–23). Significantly, the father's performance of his discipling duty is directly linked to Israel's continual possession of the promised land (Deut. 4:9; 6:7; 11:19). The father's great responsibility accords him the right to receive honor (Exod. 20:12; Deut. 5:16) and obedience (Prov. 1:8; 15:20) from his children. While the positive performance of his duties brings blessing, his sin can negatively influence his children, resulting in divine punishment for generations to come (Exod. 20:5; Deut. 5:9)

(2) Intriguingly, *ʾāb* is often used to portray the unique relationship between God and Israel. As father of his people, God bought and constituted Israel (Deut. 32:6). He blesses Israel (Jer. 3:19), leads them in the safe path (Jer. 31:9), and redeems them (Isa. 63:16) as his covenant

son. God is also described as the father of the Davidic king who represents the nation (2 Sam. 7:14; Ps. 2:7; 89:26). Just as an earthly father deserves to receive honor, so God is worthy of honor and respect from his people (Mal. 1:6). However, his fatherly care and authority are often ignored by rebellious, faithless, and disobedient sons (Isa. 1:2; 30:9). Fortunately, as Father, God cannot forever abandon his sons and will ultimately remember and redeem them (Isa. 64:8 with v. 9 and 65:8–10,17–25).

(3) Similar to the use of *ʾāb* for head of household, the noun can also refer to the head of an extended family or clan (Jos. 14:1; 19:51; 1 Chr. 5:13, 15).

(4) Finally, *ʾāb* is used as a title of respect toward authorities such as masters (2 Ki. 5:13), priests (Jdg. 17:10), prophets (2 Ki. 2:12), counselors (Gen. 45:8), and kings (1 Sam. 24:11). See *NIDOTTE*, 1:219-23.

New Testament

Verb: γεννάω (*gennaō*), GK *1164* (S *1080*), 97x. *gennaō* means "to give birth, bear a child" (of the mother) or "to father" (of the father). See *give birth*.

Noun: ἀββά (*abba*), GK *5* (S *5*), 3x. *abba* is an Aramaic word that means "father"; it is a term of endearment used within the family circle (not unlike our word "dad"). See *abba*.

Noun: πατήρ (*patēr*), GK *4252* (S *3962*), 413x. *patēr* refers to a male parent (e.g., Mk. 9:24) or one's ancestors (e.g., Mt. 3:9; Jn. 4:12; Acts 7:4, 11, 12, 14) or as a term of respect for an older man (Acts 7:2). It is also used to refer to God, who is the Father of all believers (Mt. 5:16) and of Jesus (Mt. 7:21; Mk. 11:10; Lk. 1:32). Jesus' words in Mt. 12:50 are significant: "For whoever does the will of my Father who is in heaven, he is my brother and sister and mother." In creating a new "family" of believers, Jesus recognizes that his followers will be mothers, brothers, and sisters to each other, but he reserves the role of "father" for God alone (cf. Mt. 23:9). In Mk. 14:36, Jesus refers to God as "Abba" (a corresponding Aramaic word) and *patēr* (cf. Rom. 8:15; Gal. 4:6). God's paternal relationship with his people implies that they should be like him—there should be a "family resemblance" (Mt. 5:48; cf. Jn. 8:39).

A major theme in the gospel of John is that God, who is preeminently the Father of Jesus (e.g., Jn. 3:35; 5:17–18; 17:1), has worked through Jesus so that men and women can now also know him as their Father (cf. 1:12–13 and 20:17). Jesus compares human fathers to God as the perfect Father (Lk. 11:11–13), and God's identity as Father stands behind the famous parable of the prodigal son in Lk. 15.

Though stressing the validity of the fifth commandment to honor one's father and mother (Mt. 15:4; 19:19), Jesus also recognizes that his claims on those who follow him will sometimes cause fractures even in father-son relationships (Mt. 10:35–37). "Father" is also used metaphorically in the NT in several striking ways. Jesus accuses his opponents in Jn. 8:44, who want to kill him, of having the devil as their father. Paul identifies himself as the spiritual father of his converts (1 Cor. 4:15; cf. Phil. 2:22; 1 Thess. 2:11) and encourages believers to relate to older men as fathers (1 Tim. 5:1). See *NIDNTT-A*, 445-46.

FAVOR

Old Testament

Noun: חֵן (*ḥēn*), GK 2834 (S 2580), 69x. *ḥēn*, which is cognate to the verb *ḥānan* ("show mercy, favor, be gracious") describes that which is favorable or pleasing, and especially the favorable disposition of one person toward another.

(1) Most uses of *ḥēn* occur in the idiomatic phrase, "to find favor in someone's eyes" (53x). This expression highlights an important cultural reality of ancient Israel, as well as the ancient Near East, that favor is expressed in one's countenance. Even the word "face" (*pānîm*) is sometimes translated "favor" (Ps. 119:58, KJV; Dan. 9:13, NIV). This explains the metaphor of God turning his face toward his people (Ps. 25:16; 86:16; 119:132, cf. Num. 6:26),

as well as hiding his face from those who refuse to turn from their sin (Deut. 31:17–18; 32:20; Jer. 33:5; Mic. 3:4). Yet God, in his abundant mercy, remains faithful to his promises, for he sends his Spirit to renew the wayward people and bring them back within his favor (see Ezek. 39:29).

Thus, to "find grace in God's eyes" is to receive his gift of acceptance and favor. We first encounter this in the story of Noah: "But Noah found *favor* in the eyes of the Lord" (Gen. 6:8). Moses also found favor with God (Exod. 33:12), and he pleads with God that such *favor* might continue (33:13). Indeed, it is on the basis of having found *favor* in God's eyes that Moses intercedes for the people (34:9).

(2) The same metaphor is used of interpersonal relationships. Abraham implores the visitors who arrive at his tent: "If I have found *favor* in your eyes, my lord, do not pass your servant by" (Gen. 18:3). Jacob sends his gifts to Esau in hopes of finding "favor" in his eyes, that is, of being graciously received (33:8–9). Joseph finds "favor" in the eyes of Potiphar (39:4), and Joseph's brothers seek to find "favor" in his eyes (47:25; see also similar expressions for David with Jonathan, 1 Sam. 20:3; Ruth with Boaz, Ruth 2:10; and Esther with Xerxes, Est. 7:3). In a negative sense, Deut. 24:1 speaks of a wife who has "become displeasing" to her husband (lit., "she does not find *favor* in his eyes") because of "something indecent," resulting in divorce.

In a number of cases, God sovereignly changes the disposition of people in order to further his plans. Of Joseph we read: "The LORD was with him; he showed him kindness and granted him *favor* in the eyes of the prison warden" (Gen. 39:21). Likewise, God made the Egyptians "favorably disposed" toward the Israelites just before the exodus (Exod. 3:21; 11:3; 12:36) so that they plundered the Egyptians.

(3) Setting aside the times *ḥēn* is used idiomatically for "finding favor in someone's eyes," it is used 11x to describe charm (either positively or negatively), including the lure of a harlot (Nah. 3:4), the demeanor of those who are wise (Prov. 1:9; 3:22), feminine beauty ("a *graceful* deer," Prov. 5:19; cf. 31:30), a "kind-hearted" woman (11:16), and "gracious" speech (Prov. 22:11, Eccl. 10:12; see also uses in 17:8; 22:1; Eccl. 9:11).

(4) In the five remaining independent occurrences of *ḥēn*, Ps. 84:11 combines *ḥēn* with "honor" (*kābôd*) as the gift of God: "The Lord bestows *favor* and honor." In Ps. 45:2, the royal groom is lauded as "the most excellent of men and your lips have been anointed with *grace*, since God has blessed you forever," describing the gracious words by which he will lead the people as their king. Zech. 4:7 has a double use of *ḥēn*, which points to the finished temple as a clear demonstration of God's power and grace. In 12:10, the prophet foresees the time when God will pour out on the house of David and the inhabitants of Jerusalem a spirit of "grace" and supplication. See *NIDOTTE*, 2:203–6.

Noun: רָצוֹן (*rāṣôn*), GK 8356 (S 7522), 56x. *rāṣôn* denotes three different ideas in the OT: favor, acceptance (see *acceptable*), or will (see *please*). It is attributed most often to God (39x) and occurs most frequently in Proverbs (14x), Psalms (13x), and Leviticus (7x).

The sense of *rāṣôn* as "favor" signifies a kind regard or special status usually bestowed by a superior. The NIV often translates this sense as "favor" or "favored," but also as "goodwill" (Prov. 11:27; 14:9) and "pleasure" (Ps. 51:18; Prov. 16:13; Mal. 2:13). Favor is something commonly bestowed by God, though it is also associated with kings (Prov. 16:13; 16:15; 19:12). Divine favor is associated with blessing (Deut. 33:23) and protection (Ps. 5:12; 51:18), and lasts a lifetime (30:5). Recipients of divine favor include the one who finds wisdom (Prov. 8:35), the one who seeks good (11:27), the upright (14:9), a good man (12:2), and the one who finds a wife (18:22). In the OT, there is a time of divine favor (Ps. 69:13; Isa. 49:8) and the year of God's favor (Isa. 61:2). Jesus explains that the year of God's favor is fulfilled in his ministry (Lk. 4:17–21; cf. Isa. 61:1–2).

New Testament

Noun: χάρις (*charis*), GK *5921* (S *5485*), 155x. *charis* is "grace, favor" the acceptance of and goodness toward those who cannot earn or do not deserve such gain. See *grace.*

FAVORED

New Testament

Adjective: μακάριος (*makarios*), GK *3421* (S *3107*), 50x. There are two major ways *makarios* may be taken in the NT. One who is *makarios* can be "happy" or "fortunate" because of life's circumstances or because of divine favors bestowed on him or her (cf. the Beatitudes). See *blessed.*

FEAR

Old Testament

Verb: יָרֵא (*yārē*ʾ), GK 3707 (S 3372), 317x. *yārē*ʾ denotes both a sense of terror and a sense of awe and worship. It is commonly translated "be afraid, fear, worship." God appears as the most common object of the verb, and the context determines whether the term is best understood as *terror* or *awe/reverence.* The polarity of this term is vividly demonstrated in Jonah 1, where the *terror* of the sailors (Jon. 1:5, 10) turns to *worship* after the storm is calmed (v. 16). Each of these aspects is evident in other biblical texts.

(1) We see fear as terror in Adam and Eve, who fear God after they have sinned (Gen. 3:10); in Moses, who fears after he commits murder (Exod. 2:14); and in Gideon, who fears the household of his father (Jdg. 6:27). In this sense, fear exhibits certain negative connotations and is something to be avoided.

(2) Fear as reverence and worship is commanded as the proper covenantal response to the Lord. Deut. 10:12–13 states: "And now, O Israel, what does the LORD your God ask of you but to *fear* the LORD your God, to walk in all his ways, to love him, to serve the LORD your God with all your heart and with all your soul, and to observe the LORD's commands and decrees that I am giving you today for your own good?" Fearing God is set in parallel with obedience to the commands (Deut. 5:29), walking in the ways of God (8:6), doing his commands (6:24), and listening to his voice (13:4), and it is set as the means by which God blesses his people (6:2). This fear of God is learned from hearing his word (4:10) and is central to the spiritual vitality of the king as leader of the people (17:19).

The fear of God is central to the acquisition of wisdom in Proverbs (Prov. 1:7 cf. Job 28:28). In this sense, fear is a positive quality and something to be pursued in the life of the believer. Ultimately, our fear is to be transformed into worship when its right and proper object is God. See *NIDOTTE*, 2:527-33.

Adjective: יָרֵא (*yārē*ʾ), GK 3710 (S 3373), 63x. *yārē*ʾ typically describes the subject as one who is a "fearer" of God and denotes the sense both of awe and of worship. It may be translated "fearing, being afraid, or reverent." It is a technical term denoting "God-fearer" in later wisdom and prophetic texts (Job 1:1; Ps. 22:23, 24; 31:19; 145:19; Eccl. 8:13). This concept finds NT application in Acts 10:2, 22, 35; 13:16, 26 in the term "God fearers." While God is the standard object of this fear, individuals can also fear an oath (Eccl. 9:2), a king (Dan. 1:10), the commandments (Prov. 13:13), and the very name of God (Mal. 4:2). See *NIDOTTE*, 2:527-533.

New Testament

Verb: φοβέω (*phobeomai*), GK *5828* (S *5399*), 95x. *phobeomai* is used in two main senses in the NT. It means to be "frightened, alarmed," or to "respect, stand in awe of" someone. The first sense is common throughout the NT, and the objects of fear are numerous: angels (Mt. 28:5; Lk. 2:9–10), Jesus (Mt. 14:27; 27:54), the crowds (14:5; 21:26, 46), political leaders (2:22), John the Baptist (Mk. 6:20), the elements of nature (Mt. 14:30), and Paul

(Acts 9:26). One of Jesus' most memorable teachings on fear comes in Mt. 10:28, where he tells his hearers not to fear those who can kill the body, but rather to fear God, who can destroy both soul and body in hell. Here God is to be feared because of his power to judge and punish. Paul sometimes mentions his own "fear" or "worry" for the congregations to whom he writes (2 Cor. 11:3; 12:20; Gal. 4:11) and these passages function as powerful appeals to those congregations to continue walking with God. An anxious fear of people or circumstances is not good, however. Heb. 11:23, 27 suggests that trusting in God conquers such fear (cf. Heb. 13:5–6). In 1 Jn. 4:17–18, the author asserts that love for God and others conquers fear of future judgment.

In most cases where God is the object of "fear," the sense seems to be more of "awe" or "respect" than terror or alarm. The centurion Cornelius is described as a man who fears God (Acts 10:2, 22; cf. 10:35; 13:16, 26), and fear of God is commended and commanded throughout the NT (Col. 3:22; 1 Pet. 2:17; Rev. 11:18; 14:7; 15:4; 19:5). Paul suggests that fear of God is necessary for those who are conceited (Rom. 11:20). See *NIDNTT-A*, 591-92.

Noun: φόβος (*phobos*), GK *5832* (S *5401*), 47x. *phobos* in the NT can mean "fear, fright, alarm," but also "awe." Jesus occasions fright and alarm in the course of his ministry, both among his disciples (Mt. 14:26) and others (Lk. 5:26). The presence of angels almost invariably evokes a terrifying reaction of "fear," as we see in the shepherds on the fields of Bethlehem (Lk. 2:9). John mentions that the crowds, Joseph of Arimathea, and Jesus' disciples were in "fear" of the Jewish leaders (Jn. 7:13; 19:38; 20:19). We in fact derive our English word "phobia" from *phobos*.

But *phobos* can also mean "awe," and the early church as described in Acts can aptly be referred to as a "fearful" church, for they are characterized by a continual "awe" of God's presence and power among them (Acts 2:43; 5:5; 9:31; 19:17). Paul encourages believers to have a proper fear of God (Rom. 3:18; 13:7). The fear of the Lord's coming to judgment and our standing before him to give account of our lives serves as a powerful motivation for Paul to keep preaching the gospel of salvation (2 Cor. 5:11). Moreover, fear of the Lord is a powerful means of producing holiness in the life of the believer (2 Cor. 7:1; Eph. 5:21; Phil. 2:12; 1 Tim. 5:20). In the NT, an undue fear creates bondage (Heb. 2:15; 1 Jn. 4:18), but proper fear of God promotes holiness (1 Pet. 1:17). See *NIDNTT-A*, 591-92.

(BE) FEARFUL

New Testament

Verb: ἐπαισχύνομαι (*epaischynomai*), GK *2049* (S *1870*), 11x. *epaischynomai* means "to be ashamed, embarrassed, fearful of ridicule" because of one's actions or beliefs. See *ashamed.*

FEAST

Old Testament

Noun: חַג (*ḥag*), GK 2504 (S 2282), 62x. Translated either as "religious feast" or "festival," *ḥag* describes an annual pilgrimage festival as opposed to the weekly and monthly celebrations of Sabbath and New Moon (2 Chr. 8:13). Each year, every Israelite male was to come to the Lord's sanctuary for the Feast of Tabernacles, the Passover, and the Feast of Weeks (Deut. 16:16). These festivals were times of rejoicing (Deut. 16:14; 2 Chr. 30:21; Ezr. 6:22; Isa. 30:29) and sacrificing (Ezr. 3:4; Ezek. 45:23). No worshiper was to come before the Lord empty-handed (Exod. 23:15). The prophets foresaw a day when all nations would celebrate these feasts before the Lord (Zech. 14:16). See *NIDOTTE*, 2:20-21.

New Testament

Noun: δεῖπνον (*deipnon*), GK *1270* (S *1173*), 16x. *deipnon* means "supper, banquet, feast" and refers to the main meal in biblical times. The more formal meaning of "feast" was well known in the OT. See *supper*.

Noun: ἑορτή (*heortē*), GK *2038* (S *1859*), 25x. *heortē* always denotes Jewish feasts or pilgrimage festivals in the NT, such as the Feast of the Passover (Lk. 2:41), the Feast of Unleavened Bread (Lk. 22:1), and the Feast of Tabernacles (Jn. 7:2). Jesus and his disciples celebrated the feasts (Jn. 2:23; 5:1; 7:10, 14). More than half of the occurrences of *heortē* are found in John (Jn. 12:12; 13:1), where the beloved disciple demonstrates that the OT feasts find their true significance in Christ (7:37).

There is only one usage of *heortē* outside of the gospels (Col. 2:16). Here Paul teaches that believers are free to eat, drink, and celebrate feast days without condemnation. But they must always remember that these feasts are "a shadow of the things that were to come" and that Christ fulfilled these feasts (2:17). See *NIDNTT-A*, 192-94.

FEEBLE

See *weak.*

FEED

Old Testament

Verb: רָעָה (*rāʿâ*), GK 8286 (S 7473), 167x. *rāʿâ* means "to shepherd, tend, feed graze." This verb can thus be used for sheep feeding or grazing in a pasture. See *shepherd.*

New Testament

Verb: βόσκω (*boskō*) GK *1081* (S *1006*), 9x. *boskō* means "to feed." All of the uses of this verb are in the gospels. In all except two instances it refers to the feeding of pigs (Mt. 8:30, 33; Mk. 5:11, 14; Lk. 8:32, 34; 15:15). In Jn. 21:15, 17, Jesus instructs Peter to "feed my lambs/ sheep." Jesus is here restoring Peter to his place of leadership after his denials of Jesus during his trial.*

FEET

New Testament

Noun: πούς (*pous*), GK *4546* (S *4228*), 93x. *pous* often refers to the physical "feet" of human beings (Mt. 10:4; Acts 14:8), animals (Mt. 7:6), Jesus in a vision (Rev. 1:15, 17), angelic beings (10:2; 19:10; 22:8), and one of the beasts of Revelation (13:2). In 10:1, *pous* means the legs of the angel, since they are likened to fiery pillars.

Jesus' example of washing the disciples' feet (Jn. 13:5–14) pictures true servanthood (by one who is Lord and Master). Paul describes the worthy widow who serves the Lord as one known for "washing the feet of the saints" (1 Tim. 5:10).

In the NT, to fall at the feet of someone is an act of reverence and fear (Acts 10:25; Rev. 1:17; 19:10; 22:8), of prayerful pleading (Mk. 5:22), or of gratitude (Lk. 17:16). To be or sit at the feet of a teacher is an expression of discipleship (Lk. 10:39; Acts 22:3).

God promises that one day all of Christ's enemies will be made a footstool "for his feet" (1 Cor. 15:25, 27; Eph. 1:22; Heb. 1:13; cf. Ps. 110:1; Heb. 10:13); this is a picture of the ancient victor who shows the finality of his victory and dominion by placing his foot on the neck of the foe he has thrown down (cf. Jos. 10:24).

FELLOW

See *man.*

FELLOW SERVANT

New Testament

Noun: σύνδουλος (*syndoulos*), GK *5281* (S *4889*), 10x. *syndoulos* means "fellow servant, fellow slave" (see the parable in Mt. 18:28–33; cf. also 24:49). Paul refers to those who have partnered with him in the gospel as "fellow servants," including Epaphras (Col. 1:7) and Tychicus (Col. 4:7). The idea is that both Paul and his fellow servants have a common master and common task to fulfill, namely, the carrying out of the gospel of Jesus Christ in faithfulness. When John mistakenly begins to worship the angel who is showing him visions, John is told that that they are "fellow servants" (Rev. 19:10; 22:9). See also *servant*. See *NIDNTT-A*, 151-53.

FELLOW SLAVE

New Testament

Noun: σύνδουλος (*syndoulos*), GK

5281 (S *4889*), 10x. *syndoulos* means "fellow servant, fellow slave." See *fellow servant*; see also *servant*.

FELLOW WORKER

New Testament

Noun: συνεργός (*synergos*), GK *5301* (S *4904*), 13x. This word means "coworker, fellow worker, colaborer, assistant." It derives from *ergon* ("work") and *syn* ("with"). Its use in the NT is exclusively Pauline (except for 3 Jn. 8). *synergos* describes Paul's own sense of call to join both with God in his work (as 1 Cor. 3:9, along with Apollos; also 2 Cor. 1:24) and with his missionary partners, whom he sometimes describes as fellow workers "in Christ." Those workers included Aquila, Priscilla, and Urbanus (Rom. 16:3); Timothy (Rom. 16:21), also described as "our brother and God's fellow worker" (1 Thess. 3:2); Titus (2 Cor. 8:23); Epaphroditus (Phil. 2:25); Epaphras (Col. 4:11); Clement, Euodia, and Syntyche (Phil. 4:3); Justus (Col. 4:11), Mark, Aristarchus, Luke, and Demas (Col. 4:11; Phlm. 24); and Philemon (Phlm. 1). See *NIDNTT-A*, 205-6.*

FELLOWSHIP

New Testament

Noun: κοινωνία (*koinōnia*), GK *3126* (S *2842*), 19x. *koinōnia* generally means "fellowship, communion, participation, sharing." It can refer to the mutual interests and sharing of members in the community of faith, the church. This mutual sharing is seen in the description of the newly founded church in Acts 2:42, in which one of the four patterns of discipleship is the early Christians' continuing together in *koinōnia.* In the context of the early church in Acts, such sharing involved not only associating with each other, but also sharing food and other necessities of life.

Paul uses this word most often (13x). He too uses it for the sharing of material things—it is one of the words he uses for his collection of funds for the poor saints in Jerusalem (Rom. 15:26; 2 Cor. 8:4; 9:13). Such sharing requires a mindset that esteems others over oneself (Phil. 2:1). Paul also uses *koinōnia* to refer to the intimate fellowship shared between the believing community and Jesus Christ (1 Cor. 1:9). In other contexts, he speaks of his *koinōnia* in the sufferings of Christ (Phil. 3:10), the fellowship of the Spirit (2 Cor. 13:13), the participation in the body and blood of Christ in the Eucharistic celebration (1 Cor. 10:16), and the sense of "partnership" that Paul and the Philippians had in spreading the gospel (Phil. 1:5; note that they helped fund Paul's mission work, 4:14–19; cf. also Phlm. 6). By contrast, we should have no fellowship with darkness (2 Cor. 6:14).

John uses *koinōnia* to refer to the Christian fellowship we have with one another (1 Jn. 1:3, 7). This fellowship is centered in and based on our common fellowship with the Father and his Son, Jesus (1:3, 6). See *NIDNTT-A*, 310-12.*

FELLOWSHIP OFFERING

Old Testament

Noun: שֶׁלֶם (*šelem*), GK 8968 (S 8002), 87x. *šelem* is the word used for the fellowship offering or the peace offering, one of the required sacrifices of the Israelites. The name tells us something about nature of this offering: the person or community offering this sacrifice to God was in a positive, covenant-keeping relationship with him and God's people enjoyed all the fullness of his peace (Lev. 3; 7:11–34).

The *šelem* was a voluntary sacrifice and was often used to express thanksgiving to God or to demonstrate the fulfilling of a vow (Lev. 3; 7:11–34). Such an offering was unique because part of it was sacrificed to God and part of the meat of the sacrifice was eaten by the one making the sacrifice. Thus, the peace offering also indicated a positive relationship and the joys of communion between God and the one(s) making the sacrifice. The peace offering is a clear demonstration of God's desire to be in covenant relationship with his people. It looks forward to the ultimate sacrifice of Christ that provides us reconciliation with God.

FEMALE SLAVE

Old Testament

Noun: אָמָה (*ʾāmâ*), GK 563 (S 519), 56x. *ʾāma* frequently translates as "maidservant" or "slave girl" (Gen. 20:17), but may also be translated simply as "servant." See *servant*.

FESTIVAL

Old Testament

Noun: חַג (*ḥag*), GK 2504 (S 2282), 62x. Translated either as "religious feast" or "festival," *ḥag* describes an annual pilgrimage festival as opposed to the weekly and monthly celebrations of Sabbath and New Moon (2 Chr. 8:13). See *feast*.

FETTER

New Testament

Noun: δεσμός (*desmos*), GK *1301* (S *1199*), 18x. *desmos* can refer to either literal chains, such as those of a prisoner, or figurative chains, that which hinders or obstructs. See *chain*.

FEW

Old Testament

Noun: מְעַט (*meʾaṭ*), GK 5071 (S 4592), 101x. *meʾaṭ* conveys the small amount of something and may be translated as "little" or "few." See *little*.

New Testament

Adjective: ὀλίγος (*oligos*), GK *3900* (S *3641*), 40x. *oligos* typically denotes a small number, a small amount of something, or shortness in size or time. There is significant overlap with *mikros* (see *small*).

(1) *oligos* often refers to a small number and is often translated "few." In Mt. 9:37, Jesus laments that though "the harvest is plentiful, the workers are *few*." The young boy in Mt. 15:34 brings "seven loaves and *a few* small fish" (cf. Mk. 8:7). Those who are "faithful with *a few* things" will be given more (Mt. 25:21, 23). Peter tells us that only eight were saved from the flood, that is, "a few" (1 Pet. 3:20). This word can also be used in connection with forgiveness and love for Christ (Lk. 7:47).

(2) *oligos* can also refer to a "short" time. Agrippa sarcastically asks Paul whether in a "short amount of time" he thinks he can make Agrippa a Christian (Acts 26:28, 29; cf. Heb. 12:10; Rev. 12:12; 17:10). James tells his readers that life is like a vapor, which, from an eternal perspective, is gone in "a little while" (Jas. 4:14). This term can also be negated, as in Acts 14:28: "They remained *no small time* with the disciples."

(3) *oligos* can also refer to something on a small scale, such as a disturbance (Acts 12:18). Paul states that he has written before "briefly" (Eph. 3:3; cf. 1 Pet. 5:12). Only a "small" amount of gain results from bodily discipline (1 Tim. 4:8). See *NIDNTT-A*, 369-70.

FIDELITY

See *faith*.

FIELD

Old Testament

Noun: שָׂדֶה (*śādeh*), GK 8441 (S 7704), 329x. The basic meaning of *śādeh* is a field. It can be used for any number of activities, including farming (Gen. 37:7; Ruth 2:8–9), pasturing a flock (Gen. 34:5; Exod. 9:3), hunting (Gen. 27:5), or engaging in battle (Jdg. 9:42–44; 1 Sam. 4:2; 2 Sam. 18:6). A *śādeh* is often cultivated, but it can also be a wild place (2 Ki. 4:39), where "the beasts of the field" live (i.e., wild animals, Deut. 7:22; 1 Sam. 17:44; cf. Song 2:7).

In the Bible, fields can be bought, sold, or given away (Gen. 23:11, 13; Ruth 4:5), but coveting your neighbor's field is forbidden by the law of Moses (Deut. 5:21). Often *śādeh* is used for rural areas, the "countryside" as opposed to urban areas (Deut. 28:3, 16; 1 Sam. 27:5). Sometimes it indicates the land or territory belonging to a certain nation or tribe, such as the "*land* of Moab" (lit., "fields of Moab," Ruth 1:1; cf. 1 Sam. 6:1). In one instance, it refers to the *mainland* section of the city of Tyre as opposed to its fortified island (Ezek. 26:6, 8). *śādeh* is synonymous with *śāday* (GK 8442), which is simply a different form of the word sometimes used in poetic passages. See *NIDOTTE*, 3:1217-19.

New Testament

Verb: χωρίον (*chōrion*), GK *6005* (S *5564*), 10x. *chōrion* means "place, field." See *place*.

Noun: ἀγρός (*agros*), GK *69* (S *68*), 36x. *agros* can refer to arable "land" or the "countryside." (1) In most of its occurrences, *agros* refers to a cultivated field, such as where "good seed" can be sown (Mt. 13:24) as well as trees planted (13:31; Mk. 11:8). Jesus symbolically uses *agros* in the parable of the weeds to represent the world (Mt. 13:38, "*the field* is the world"). *agros* can also refer to a wild field (6:28, "See how the lilies of *the field* grow"). A "field" is also used for pasturing animals (Lk. 15:15; 17:7) and even as burial grounds (Mt. 27:7, "they bought the *field* of the potter as a burial place for foreigners"). (2) *agros* sometimes refers to rural areas in contrast to cities or villages and can be translated "countryside" (Mk. 5:14; 6:36, 56; 15:21). See *NIDNTT-A*, 13.

Noun: χώρα (*chōra*), GK *6001* (S *5561*), 28x. The basic sense of *chōra* is an area or space; in the NT it refers to large areas, such as a cultivated field, a region, or a country. See *country*.

FIFTH

Old Testament

Noun: חָמֵשׁ (*ḥāmēš*), GK 2822 (S 2568), 508x. *ḥāmēš* means "five" in the singular and "fifty" in the plural. It can also mean the ordinal numeral "fifth." See *five*.

FIFTY

Old Testament

Noun: חָמֵשׁ (*ḥāmēš*), GK 2822 (S 2568), 508x. *ḥāmēš* means "five" in the singular and "fifty" in the plural. It can also mean the ordinal numeral "fifth." See *five*.

FIG TREE

New Testament

Noun: συκῆ (*sykē*), GK *5190* (S *4808*), 16x. *sykē* means "fig tree" and in some cases "fig (fruit)." All of the NT uses of this noun are symbolic in nature except for Jesus' seeing Nathanael under the fig tree (Jn. 1:48–50). The cursing of the *sykē* (Mt. 21:18–22; Mk. 11:12–14, 20–25) comprises the only destructive miracle performed by Christ. This parabolic miracle depicts the pending judgment of Israel. (Note that the OT sometimes pictures God's people as a fig tree; cf. Jer. 24; Hos. 9:10.) Luke's gospel does not contain the cursing of the *sykē* but rather an equivalent parable. Lk. 13:6 depicts a fig tree in a vineyard. The tree represents Israel, which despite the efforts of the vinedresser fails to produce fruit. The vineyard owner has expected figs for three years, but to no avail. The vinedresser intercedes and asks for another year, stating that if the tree fails to produce this time, he will cut it down.

sykē as it appears in Mt. 24:32–33; Mk. 13:28; and Lk. 21:29 symbolizes the growth of the fig tree as the approaching time of harvest. The allusion is to Jesus' gathering of believers and the coming judgment. See *NIDNTT-A*, 542.

FIGHT

Old Testament

Verb: לָחַם (*lāḥam*), GK 4309 (S 3898), 171x. *lāḥam* means "to fight, battle, attack." It is most often used in contexts where armies battle each other (Num. 21:23; Jos. 10:5; 1 Sam. 17:9, 19, 32–33).

The most theologically significant uses occur when God fights for Israel (Exod. 14:14, 25; Deut. 1:30; 20:4; Neh. 4:14). When the Israelites take the promised land, the one who does the fighting on their behalf is the Lord their God (Jos. 10:14; 23:3). But the Lord does not fight for Israel simply because they are his people; in fact, if the Israelites are not serving the Lord according to his law, he actually fights against them, as Jeremiah points out (Jer. 21:5). Isaiah too describes a time when God fights *against* Israel: "they rebelled and grieved his Holy Spirit. So he turned and became their enemy and he himself *fought* against them" (Isa. 63:10). Zechariah speaks of a coming day when the Lord will fight once more against the nations who have attacked Israel (14:3). See *NIDOTTE*, 2:785–89.

New Testament

Noun: πόλεμος (*polemos*), GK *4483* (S *4171*), 18x. *polemos*, from which we get our word "polemical," is the word for a "fight," up to and including "battle" or "war." See *battle*.

FIGHTING

Old Testament

Noun: מִלְחָמָה (*milḥāmâ*), GK 4878 (S 4421), 319x. *milḥāmâ* means "battle, war, fighting." See *war*.

FIGURE

New Testament

Noun: σχῆμα (*schēma*), GK *5386* (S *4976*), 2x. *schēma* means "form, outward appearance, figure." See *form*.

Noun: τύπος (*typos*), GK *5596* (S *5179*), 15x. *typos* is a "pattern, example, model," taken from the concept of an impression or a mark left behind by something on a surface. See *example*.

FILL

Old Testament

Verb: מָלֵא (*mālēʾ*), GK 4848 (S 4390), 252x. *mālēʾ* broadly means "to fill, be full, be fulfilled" and can carry either a spatial or temporal sense.

(1) Spatially, the term depicts the filling of things with certain objects. For example, Jer. 16:18 depicts the land as being filled with idols, and Jos. 3:15 speaks of the Jordan banks being full of water. Similarly, the glory of the Lord can fill a place such as the tabernacle (Exod. 40:34), the temple (1 Ki. 8:10), or the earth (Hab. 2:14). Jer. 23:24 speaks of the Lord himself filling heaven and earth. See also *full*.

(2) Temporally, this verb refers to the completion of a particular period of time. The death of a particular individual can be spoken of as his or her days being fulfilled (2 Sam. 7:12). It can also refer to the keeping or fulfilling of a vow (Jer. 44:25). Most importantly, the Lord has fulfilled and will fulfill all that he has promised (1 Ki. 8:15; Ps. 20:5).

New Testament

Verb: πίμπλημι (*pimplēmi*), GK *4398* (S *4130*), 24x. *pimplēmi* means "to fill, fulfill" and is used in literal and figurative ways.

(1) In a literal sense, *pimplēmi* can describe boats that were filled with the miraculous catch of fish (Lk. 5:7), the wedding hall filled with guests (Mt. 22:10), and the sponge filled with sour wine (Mt. 27:48).

(2) Equally literal but in a spiritual sense, is a believer being filled with God's Spirit. Luke often uses this terminology. It means that the person is controlled and empowered by the Holy Spirit, receiving a sudden burst of the Spirit's inspiring power; this filling is often connected with speaking or prophesying as a fulfillment of God's promise in Joel for the outpouring of the Spirit (Joel 2:28; Acts 2:17). John the Baptist was filled with the Holy Spirit from his mother's womb, meaning he would be prophetic his whole life (Lk. 1:15). Elizabeth was filled with the Holy Spirit (1:41) and gave prophetic utterance (1:42–45). Zechariah was filled with the Holy Spirit and prophesied (1:67). All the believers were filled with the Holy Spirit on Pentecost and began to speak in unlearned human languages (Acts 2:4). These events are similar to those in the OT, such as when the Spirit rushed on Samson and he killed the lion (Jdg. 14:6), on Gideon and he went to war (6:34), and on Saul and he prophesied (1 Sam. 10:10).

Even after people are permanently filled with the Spirit at conversion, the Spirit can again fill them in the sense that he possesses and empowers them in a special way for a temporary, specific task, such as when Peter spoke to the Sanhedrin (Acts 4:8) and the church prayed for boldness (4:31). Paul is filled with the Spirit (9:17) and almost immediately begins to testify (9:20). He is later filled with the Spirit again and denounces Elymas the magician (13:9).

(3) Related to the above is the use of *pimplēmi* to describe people who are over-

taken with sudden, powerful emotions. Everyone in the synagogue in Nazareth is filled with wrath in response to the teaching of Jesus (Lk. 4:28). After Jesus heals a paralytic, all in the house are filled with fear (5:26). The scribes and the Pharisees are filled with anger in response to Jesus' healing of the man with the withered hand on the Sabbath (6:11). In response to the healing of the lame man at the beautiful gate, all the people are filled with wonder and amazement (Acts 3:10). The Jewish leadership is filled with jealousy in response to the success of the apostles (5:17). The Jews of Pisidian Antioch are likewise filled with jealousy after a crowd gathers to hear Paul (13:45). When the riot breaks out in Ephesus, the city is filled with confusion (19:29).

(4) *pimplēmi* can also communicate that an allotted period of time has been completed. The time of Zechariah's priestly service "was completed" (Lk. 1:23). The time for Elizabeth to give birth was filled (1:57)—also the days for Mary (2:6). The days were filled for Jesus to be circumcised on the eighth day (2:21). The time for the purification of Mary and Jesus "was completed" (2:22). Eight times between Lk. 1:15 and 2:22, Luke uses *pimplēmi* to emphasize that the fullness of time has come for the Messiah to arrive on the scene.

(5) On one occasion *pimplēmi* points to either typological or predictive fulfillment (or both): Everything that is written will be fulfilled in the days of vengeance (Luke 21:22). See *NIDNTT-A*, 469-71.

Verb: πληρόω (*plēroō*), GK *4444* (S *4137*) 86x. Generally meaning "to fill, fulfill," *plēroō* is used both spatially and figuratively in the NT.

Infrequently, *plēroō* means "to fill (something), make (something) full" in a spatial sense. For example, nets are filled with fish (Mt. 13:48), and the upper room is filled with the presence of God (Acts 2:2). Most often this verb means "to fulfill," especially to fulfill the Scriptures (see *fulfill*).

FILLED, (BE) FILLED

Old Testament

Verb: שָׂבַע (*śābaʿ*), GK 8425 (S 7646), 97x. The verb *śābaʿ* means "to be satisfied, have enough, be filled," generally of food rather than drink. See *(be) satisfied.*

New Testament

Adjective: πλήρης (*plērēs*), GK *4441* (S *4134*), 16x. *plērēs* means to be "full, filled," sometimes with the nuance of being complete. See *full.*

FILTHINESS

See *debauchery.*

FINALLY

New Testament

Adjective: ὕστερος (*hysteros*), GK *5731* (S *5305, 5306*), 12x. *hysteros* means "later, afterward," though it is often used as an adverb meaning "finally." It occurs primarily in a comparative or superlative sense. See *later.*

FIND

Old Testament

Verb: מָצָא (*māṣāʾ*), GK 5162 (S 4672), 457x. *māṣāʾ* generally means "to find," though it can also mean "to come upon, meet, reach." It often is paired with the verb *bāqaš* ("to seek"). This verb is used when Noah's dove was unable to find a place to land (Gen. 8:9) and when Lot's visitors were blinded and unable to find the door (19:11).

māṣāʾ is frequently used in an abstract sense when referring to "finding" favor in the eyes of God (Gen. 6:8) or of another person (Gen. 18:3; 32:5; 47:25). This verb indicates human rank, as the one in whose eyes a person finds favor is usually superior to him or her (e.g., 1 Sam. 16:22; 20:3). This expression is often used as a prayer or a request. *māṣāʾ* can also be used for trouble that finds Israel (Jdg. 6:13), to God's search for Adam's helpmate (Gen. 2:20), and to God's search for fifty righteous men in the city of Sodom (18:26).

Some of the most theologically profound uses of *māṣāʾ* are in texts that refer to "finding" God. For example, Deut. 4:29 states, "If from there [i.e., exile] you seek the LORD your God, you will *find* him." Similarly, Isa. 55:6 asserts, "Seek the LORD while he may *be found*." But if God's people are not in a relationship with him, they may seek him but they will not find him (Hos. 5:6; Amos 8:12).

māṣāʾ can sometimes have the meaning "to catch," as in Jer. 50:24 ("I set a trap for you, O Babylon, and you were *caught* before you knew it"; cf. Exod. 22:2; Prov. 6:30–31). In other contexts, it is best translated "reach" (Job 7:11) or "overtake" (Ps. 21:8; 116:3; 119:143).

New Testament

Verb: εὑρίσκω (*heuriskō*), GK *2351* (S *2147*), 176x. *heuriskō* means "to find" something either by a purposeful search or accidentally. In Mt. 7:7, Jesus' famous admonition is "seek, and you shall find"—a "finding" that is without question purposeful (cf. Lk. 11:9; Jn. 10:9). Sometimes a purposeful search results in not finding what is sought (Jn. 7:34; Acts 5:22: Rev. 9:6). But *heuriskō* can also indicate an unexpected finding (Mt. 18:28; 27:32; Acts 13:6).

Likewise, *heuriskō* can denote an intellectual discovery that results from reflection, observation, examination, or investigation. In one of the most introspective passages in the Bible, Paul "discovers" the principle that while he wishes to do good, evil is all too often present in him (Rom. 7:21). Another example of intellectual discovery has to do with judicial finding (Lk. 23:2; Jn. 18:38). *heuriskō* can also refer to obtaining a state or condition. Such is the meaning in Heb. 9:12, "he entered the Most Holy Place once for all by his own blood, having *obtained* eternal redemption" (cf. Mt. 10:39; Lk. 1:30). See *NIDNTT-A*, 219-20.

FINE FLOUR

Old Testament

Noun: סֹלֶת (*sōlet*), GK 6159 (S 5560), 53x. *sōlet* describes finely ground flour. See *flour*.

FINISH

Old Testament

Verb: כָּלָה (*kālâ*), GK 3983 (S 3615), 207x. Often rendered "to complete, finish, destroy," *kālâ* expresses the basic idea of bringing a process to completion. The process may involve adding something until an object is full or an activity complete (see *complete*).

Verb: תָּמַם (*tāmam*), GK 9462 (S 8552), 64x. *tāmam* is used for a wide range of ideas having to do with ending, completion, or even destruction. See *end*.

New Testament

Verb: παύω (*pauō*), GK *4264* (S *3973*), 15x. pauō means "to stop, finish." See *stop*.

Verb: τελέω (*teleō*), GK *5464* (S *5055*), 28x. The basic meaning of *teleō* is "to finish, complete." It is used several times in the Gospels for finishing a task. Significantly, Jesus cried out from the cross in Jn. 19:30: "It is finished." See *end*.

Verb: τελειόω (*teleioō*), GK *5457* (S *5048*), 23x. *teleioō* refers to attaining an end or purpose, in the sense of being complete or perfect. It also refers to completing an activity, both in the sense of "to finish" (e.g., "After the Feast *was over*," Lk. 2:43) and "to accomplish, fulfill." See *end*.

FIRE

Old Testament

Noun: אֵשׁ (*ʾēš*), GK 836 (S 784, 800), 376x. *ʾēš* is a common word for "fire." There are some references to fire for ordinary purposes, such as cooking (Exod. 12:8; 2 Chr. 35:13) and heating (Isa. 44:16b). It was also used for smelting ore and shaping metal (Isa. 54:16; Ezek. 22:20). Military campaigns sometimes ended with burning a city with fire (e.g., *ʾēš* is used in 2 Chr. 36:19; see also 1 Ki. 9:16). And many of the sacrifices commanded by God were offered by fire (Lev. 1:7; 4:12; 6:9).

ʾēš is often related to God's revelation of himself and our worship of him. In Gen. 15:17 a flaming fire is a sign of God's presence in the covenant ceremony with Abraham. The Lord appears to Moses in a bush of "flaming fire" (Exod. 3:2), Ezekiel's first vision is dominated by fire (Ezek. 1:26–27), and Elijah calls down fire from heaven to demonstrate that the Lord is God (1 Ki. 18:38–39). This last reference may refer to "lightning." While the Israelites were in the desert, God's presence was seen at night by a "pillar of fire" (13:21–22; Deut. 1:33).

The fire of the Lord can symbolize both judgment and cleansing. Concerning judgment, Sodom and Gomorrah were ravished by fire (Gen. 3:24), Aaron's sons were consumed by fire (Lev. 10:1–2), Korah's supporters who opposed Moses were destroyed by fire (Num. 16:35), and Ezekiel saw an angelic being scatter coals of fire over disobedient Jerusalem (Ezek. 10:2). As for cleansing, Mal. 3:2 refers to the Lord's coming as a refiner's fire, Isaiah was purified by a burning coal (Isa. 6:6–7), and Eleazar the priest told Israel, "Gold, silver, bronze, iron, tin, lead and anything else that can withstand fire must be put through the fire, and then it will be clean" (Num. 31:22–23). See *NIDOTTE*, 1:532–37.

New Testament

Noun: πῦρ (*pyr*), GK *4786* (S *4442*), 71x. *pyr* means "fire." In the NT, *pyr* can signify natural combustion, supernatural punishment, or figuratively the presence of God. (1) In the sense of natural combustion, *pyr* is an important element used in a variety of ways, such as for warmth or to get rid of undesirable material (e.g., Mt. 13:40; Lk. 22:55; Jn. 15:6). One demoniac fell "into the *fire* or into the water" (Mt. 17:15; cf. Mk. 9:22; Acts 28:5). This sense of "fire" is also used in metaphor (Rev. 3:18) as well as in comparisons (Acts 2:3).

(2) In several places, *pyr* is used metaphorically. Jesus talks of the "fire" of discord (Lk. 12:49). In Rev. 3:18, he counsels the believers in Laodicea to buy gold refined in the fire (a reference to the precious treasures of God and his Word). Note also a related metaphorical use of the verb "to burn" in Lk. 24:32.

(3) *pyr* can sometimes refer to supernatural combustion. In this sense, the "fire" is heavenly in origin and nature. For the most part, this kind of fire appears in the NT as a means used by God to execute judgment. In the past, it was the instrument of God's judgment on Sodom, where fire destroyed the city and everything in it (Lk. 17:29; cf. 9:54). In the last judgment, God will use fire: "The first angel sounded his trumpet, and there came hail and *fire* mixed with blood" (Rev. 8:7; cf. 13:13; 20:9). This is also fire that God uses to punish sinners, "where 'their worm does not die, and the *fire* is not quenched.' Everyone will be salted with fire" (Mk. 9:48). This judgment of fire is in fact eternal in duration, "It is better for you to enter life maimed or crippled than to have two hands or two feet and be thrown into eternal *fire*" (Mt. 18:8; cf. 25:41; Jude 7). Fire burns in hell (Mt. 5:22; 18:9; Mk. 9:47–48), in a lake of fire (Rev. 20:14–15). Some see the fire of hell as a literal fire; others see it as figurative of painful eternal punishment and separation from God. This fire of hell is also pictured in certain parables and allegories (e.g., Mt. 3:10; 7:19; Lk. 3:9).

(4) Finally, *pyr* is sometimes used to symbolize the presence of God. Such is the case in Moses' burning bush (Acts 7:30). When John saw the throne of God in his vision, he saw seven "blazing" lamps before the throne (Rev. 4:5). Fire is also connected to the presence of the Holy Spirit (Acts 2:3). In at least two places fire represents the reception of the Holy Spirit (Mt. 3:11; Lk. 3:16). See *NIDNTT-A*, 505-6.

FIRST

Old Testament

Adjective: אֶחָד (*ʾeḥād*), GK 285 (S 259), 976x. *ʾeḥād* means "one, first, other." It can translated either as the ordinal numeral ("the *first* day," Gen. 1:3) or the cardinal numeral ("he took *one* of the man's ribs," 2:21). See *one*.

Adjective: רִאשׁוֹן (*riʾšôn*), GK 8037 (S

7223), 182x. As an adjective, *riʾšôn* describes what is first in a series, as in months (Gen. 8:13), twins (Gen. 25:25), miraculous signs (Exod. 4:8), battles (Jud. 20:39), tablets taken up to God by Moses (Exod. 34:1), and so on. It may also describe what is first in time: "So they moved out for the *first time* according to the commandment of the LORD through Moses" ("And they first took their journey...," KJV). *riʾšôn* may also denote first in rank. A list of princes are given in Est. 1:14 and described as "*highest* in the kingdom" ("sat the first in the kingdom," KJV).

In terms of time, *riʾšôn* can convey the meaning "previously, in a former time." Isaiah notes that "*In the past* he [God] humbled the land of Zebulun and the land of Naphtali" (Isa. 9:1). The cupbearer in Pharoah's prison was to be restored to his position and would "put Pharaoh's cup in his hand, just as you *used* to do when you were his cupbearer" ("after the former manner when thou wast his butler," KJV; Gen. 40:13). The idea of the "old days" is represented by *riʾšôn* in the sense of "first days": "Do not say, 'Why were the *old* days better than these?' For it is not wise to ask such questions" (Eccl. 7:10). The "former days" are in contrast to the "latter days," which are yet in the future (Deut. 4:30, 32).

riʾšôn is sometimes paired with *ʾaḥᵃrôn* ("last") to form a merism. A merism is a literary device in which polar terms are used together to describe totality. Thus, "first and last" means "the only one." God says through the prophet Isaiah, "I am the *first* and I am the last; apart from me there is no God" (Isa. 44:6; cf. 41:4; Rev. 1:8). See *NIDOTTE*, 3:1025-27.

New Testament

Adverb: πρῶτον (*prōton*), GK *4754* (S *4412*), 58x. The adv. *prōton* often refers to something that is *temporally* prior to something else (cf. Jn. 15:18, where it has the sense "before"). Jesus commands in Mt. 5:24 that one should "first" be reconciled to one's brother and then present one's offering. One must "first" bind the strong man before he can plunder the strong man's house (Mk. 3:27). The gospel is the power of God for salvation to the Jew "first" and then to the Gentile (Rom. 1:18).

In addition to its temporal meaning, *prōton* is used to indicate a priority of importance. Something that is more important is "first." Jesus tells his followers to "seek *first* the kingdom" of God—in other words, to place God's kingdom as their highest priority (Mt. 6:33; 2 Pet. 1:20; 3:3).

Finally, *prōton* can also indicate the first item in a list, as is common in modern English. God appointed in the church first apostles, second prophets, third teachers, etc. (1 Cor. 12:28). This does not refer to the order in which God appointed these functions, or to their relative importance, for Paul makes the point in 1 Cor. 12 that all parts of the body are equally necessary and important. Rather, he simply uses "first ... second ... third" to mark off each item in his list (cf. Heb. 7:2; Jas. 3:17). See *NIDNTT-A*, 501-2.

Adjective: πρῶτος (*prōtos*), GK *4754, 4755* (S *4413*), 97x. *prōtos* signifies that a thing is "first" in a sequence or in prominence. It functions in the NT both as an adjective and (in the neut. sing.) as an adverb. Being the "first" in a sequence can pertain to time (Lk. 11:26; Phil. 1:5), number (Lk. 2:2; Heb. 10:9), or space (Heb. 9:2, 6, 8). *prōtos* is sometimes used in enumerations. Paul says that "in the church God has appointed *first of all* apostles, second prophets, third teachers," etc. (1 Cor. 12:28). Being the first in prominence can refer to things or to persons. In Mt. 22:38, Jesus expounds what is "the first and greatest commandment." In Mt. 10:2, Simon Peter is singled out as the "first" in prominence of the twelve apostles. As an adverb, *prōtos* also signifies *degree*, "in the first place, above all, especially." In this sense, Jesus commands, "Seek *first* the kingdom of God" (Mt. 6:33). See *NIDNTT-A*, 501-2.

FIRSTBORN

Old Testament

Noun: בְּכֹר (*bᵉkōr*), GK 1147 (S 1060), 120x. *bᵉkōr* means "firstborn" and usually refers to male offspring (Gen. 10:15; 22:21; 27:19; 41:51). For a father, it refers to the first evidence of his procreative strength (49:3); for a mother, to that which first opens her womb (Exod. 13:2; Num. 3:12).

The OT accords significant place to the firstborn male descendent (Num. 3:11–13). Double portions of the inheritance are given to the firstborn coupled with all the blessings of receiving the birthright (especially observed in Jacob and Esau, Gen. 25:31–34). Reuben, Jacob's firstborn, should have enjoyed special honor, but he and his next two brothers, Simeon and Levi, forfeit their right to the blessing by acting wickedly (Gen. 49:3–12). Judah, Jacob's fourth born, thus receives the firstborn blessing (49:8–12), and his line ultimately gives rise to the Messiah (Mt. 1:1–17; cf. Gen. 49:10; Num. 24:17; Ps. 2:6–9; 72:8–11; 60:7; 108:8). In line with this last note, the succession of royal dynasties takes place through the firstborn (2 Chr. 21:3).

Especially significant is the status given to the nation of Israel as God's firstborn (Exod. 4:22-23). Israel belongs to God, and the firstborn status is accorded not on the basis of her own intrinsic qualities but on the divine and gracious initiative of God (4:22; Jer. 31:9). The theological theme of the death and resurrection of the firstborn throughout the OT is significant (e.g., Exod. 13:2, 11–16; Num. 8:15–18). This theme carries significant theological weight in our understanding of Jesus as firstborn, coupled with the significance of his death and resurrection for both Israel and the nations (Zech. 10:12).

New Testament

Noun: πρωτότοκος (*prōtotokos*), GK *4758* (S *4416*), 8x. The Greek term for "firstborn" (*prōtotokos*) in the NT has both a literal and metaphorical meaning. The former is evident where Jesus is referred to as the firstborn son of Mary (Lk. 2:7). Figuratively, *prōtotokos* points to someone having special status. For example, the description of Christ as the firstborn of all creation (Col. 1:15; cf. Heb. 1:6) refers not to his temporal beginnings but to his supremacy and honor. This is also the sense when Jesus is portrayed as "the firstborn among the dead" (Col. 1:18; cf. Rev. 1:5) and the "firstborn among many brothers" (Rom. 8:29). The church is described as firstborn (in the pl.) in Heb. 12:23, referring to the unique status of the church as coheirs with Christ, God's firstborn (1:6; cf. chs. 1–2).

FIRSTFRUITS

Old Testament

Noun: רֵאשִׁית (*rēʾšît*), GK 8040 (S 7225), 51x. *rēʾšît* indicates the "beginning" of something (see *beginning*). But another common use of this noun is for "the firstfruits" that the Israelites are expected to give to the Lord (see Lev. 2:12; 18:12; 2 Chr. 31:5). This offering is, in other words, one to be given to the Lord at the "beginning" of the harvest. God expects his share from the first, not from the scraps of leftovers at the end. In fact, the entire nation of Israel is designed to be "the *firstfruits* of [the LORD's] harvest," that is, the firstfruits of human beings belonging to God, from which many more would be added from the nations (cf. Amos 6:1).

New Testament

Noun: ἀπαρχή (*aparchē*), GK *569* (S *536*), 9x. *aparchē* means "firstfruits." Since the time of the OT the Israelites were to bring the first part of a harvest as a gift to the Lord (Exod. 23:19; Neh. 10:35). By doing so they acknowledged that the harvest was provided by God and that their act of bring the firstfruits expressed faith that the rest of the harvest would follow.

aparchē is used figuratively by NT writers. Israel was and continues to be part of God's salvation history; they were his original people. "If the dough offered as *firstfruits* is holy, so is the whole lump, and if the root is holy, so are the branches" (Rom. 11:16). The first converts of a particular region are called "firstfruits" (16:5; 1 Cor. 16:15; cf. 1 Thess. 2:13). In a more general sense, Christians are the "firstfruits," who are important in God's new created order. Speaking of God, Jas. 1:18 says, "Of his own will he brought us forth by the word of truth, that we should be a kind of *firstfruits* of his creatures" (cf. Rev. 14:4).

In Rom. 8:23, Paul reverses the OT use of *aparchē* by describing Christians (and not God) as the ones who receive the "firstfruits" of the Spirit. The Spirit is the first installment of God's assured final redemption of the body. In a similar end-time context, Paul speaks of Christ's resurrection as the "firstfruits" of the final resurrection of the dead (1 Cor. 15:20, 23). Thus, the hope of the believer's resurrection from the dead is as assured as Christ's own resurrection, since Christ's resurrection is the *aparchē* of the resurrection to be realized at the consummation of the ages. See *NIDNTT-A*, 58.*

FISH

New Testament

Noun: ἰχθύς (*ichthys*), GK *2716* (S *2486*), 20x. This word means "fish." Jesus calls at least seven fishermen to be a part of his closest friends (Mt. 4:18–22; Jn. 21:1–2). It is noteworthy that from the outset, their calling is linked to their charge to be "fishers of men" (Mt. 4:19, albeit using the word *halieus*, "fisherman"). Thus, Jesus desires that a large harvest of people be pulled into the boat as the disciples journey through the world (cf. Lk. 5:6–10): "They caught such a large number of fish that their nets began to break" (v. 6; cf. also Jn. 21:11).

Jesus teaches a lesson about provision in the separate feedings of the five thousand (Mk. 14:17, 19) and the four thousand (Mt. 15:36), where fish and bread are miraculously multiplied. His provision for his people is extended as he instructs Peter to fetch a coin from the mouth of the first fish he catches to pay the temple tax, thus avoiding disloyalty to the temple at this time (17:27). Jesus also uses a fish in contrast to a snake when teaching a lesson on the overwhelming graciousness of the heavenly Father (7:1).

Even though no NT writer refers to this imagery, the early church used fish and fishing in its art and literature. The church, for example, is a boat wherein one finds safety and salvation. It is regularly pointed out that the Greek capitals ΙΧΘΥΣ is an acronym standing for "Jesus Christ, God's Son, Savior." See *NIDNTT-A*, 276-77.

FIVE

Old Testament

Noun: חָמֵשׁ (*ḥāmēš*), GK 2822 (S 2568), 508x. *ḥāmēš* means "five" in the singular and "fifty" in the plural. It can also mean the ordinal numeral "fifth." *ḥāmēš* can combine with other numbers: e.g., with *ʾelep* ("thousand," GK 547), it means "five thousand"; with the number ten, it means "fifteen."

When Abraham was "bargaining" with God about the fate of Lot and the cities of Sodom and Gomorrah, he began with "fifty" righteous people and moved down to ten (Gen. 18:20–33). The most important use of "fifty" is the year of Jubilee, described in Lev. 25; on that year (the year after seven units of seven years each), the Israelites were to redistribute the land to the original owners, thereby keeping poverty in check and the rich from oppressing fellow-Israelites who were poor. Since five is half of ten (the numbers of fingers), this number occurs frequently in the building of the temple, where five items (e.g., stands) were placed on the south side of a temple room and five on the north side (1 Ki. 7:38–40; 2 Chr. 4:6–8).

New Testament

Adjective: πέντε (*pente*), GK *4297* (S *4002*), 38x. *pente* is the cardinal number "five." It is a routine counting number, so its appearance in the NT is not surprising and need not carry any symbolic meaning. The five loaves feed thousands (Mt. 14:17, 19; 16:9). Paul prefers to speak five intelligible words rather than ten thousand words in an unknown tongue (1 Cor. 14:19). The Samaritan woman at the well had five former husbands (Jn. 4:18). Elizabeth hid herself for five months after John's conception (Lk. 1:24). The locusts tormented those who did not have God's seal on their foreheads for five months (Rev. 9:5, 10).

Since all four Gospels recount the feeding of the five thousand, ten of the thirty-eight NT uses of *pente* enumerate the five loaves in these parallel accounts (Jn. 6:9, 13). Jesus also commonly (15x in the gospels) uses groups of five in his parables and sayings, such as five foolish and five wise virgins (Mt. 25:2), five talents (Mt. 25:15, 16, 20), five sparrows (Lk. 12:6), a family of five (Lk. 12:52), five yoke of oxen (Lk. 14:19), and five brothers (Lk. 16:28). See *NIDNTT-A*, 451.

FIX

New Testament

Verb: στηρίζω (*stērizō*), GK *5114* (S *4741*), 13x. *stērizō* means "to strengthen, fix something in place, establish." See *strengthen*.

FLARE UP

Old Testament

Verb: בָּעַר (*bāʿar*), GK 1277 (S 1197), 60x. Generally translated "to burn, light a fire, set ablaze, flare up, consume with fire," *bāʿar* can refer to a literal burning of fire or to a figurative "burning," be it of desire or anger.

FLEE

Old Testament

Verb: בָּרַח (*bāraḥ*), GK 1368 (S 1272), 63x. Like the Heb. verb *rûs*, *bāraḥ* is translated as "flee, escape." Perhaps the difference between the two words used in the OT is that *bāraḥ* implies a secret, clandestine escape or flight, whereas *rûs* implies an open, visible flight or escape. The surreptitious flight implied in *bāraḥ* is evident when Rebekah compels Jacob to flee from Esau to her brother Laban in Haran of Aram (Gen. 27:43; Hos. 12:12) and when Moses flees from Pharaoh and goes to live in Midian (Exod. 2:15). Similarly, Jonah flees from the presence of the LORD and heads to Tarshish (Jon. 1:3, 10; 4:2), and David flees for his life from Saul (1 Sam. 19:12). Each of these instances demonstrates the secretive aspect of *bāraḥ*. Finally, the psalmist asked the LORD rhetorically, "Where can I go from your Spirit? Where can I *flee* from your presence?" (Ps. 139:7). Since God is everywhere, there is no place that one can flee from his presence or escape his judgment.

Verb: נוּס (*rûs*), GK 5674 (S 5127), 160x. Usually translated "flee," *rûs* refers to the escape or flight from impending danger, whether physical, spiritual, or moral (e.g., Joseph flees from the sexual advances of Potiphar's wife, Gen. 39:12–18 [4x]). By far its most common usage is flight from physical danger: King Rehoboam flees for his life from the Israelites who seek to dethrone him or kill him (1 Ki. 18:12; cf. 2 Chr. 10:18); "a person who has killed someone accidentally may *flee*" to a city of refuge from the kinsman-redeemer (Num. 35:11–32); warriors flee from their pursuing enemies (Gen. 14:10; Jos. 8:20); and people flee in fear from natural disasters resultant of God's judgment (Num. 16:34; Zech. 14:5).

Finally, *rûs* is also used to declare that the enemies of God will flee from his people because of his presence in them. Moses exhorts the Israelites: "The LORD will grant that the enemies who rise up against you will be defeated before you. They will come at you from one direction but *flee* from you in seven" (Deut. 28:7). This is exactly what happens (e.g., see Jer. 46:5, 21; 48:6, 44; 49:8, 24, 30; 50:16).

New Testatment

Verb: φεύγω (*pheugō*), GK *5771* (S *5343*), 29x. *pheugō* primarily means "to flee" (e.g., "flee to the mountains," Mt. 24:16; cf. Mk. 13:14, Lk. 21:21), but also can mean "to escape" (Mt. 2:13; Acts 27:30; Heb. 11:34), "elude" (Rev. 9:6), and "run off/away" (Mt. 8:33; cf. Mk. 5:14, Lk. 8:34). *pheugō* occurs most frequently in the Gospels (17x).

Both Jesus and John warn people to "*flee* from the coming wrath" (Mt. 3:7; 23:33; Lk. 3:7). As Jesus sends out the

Twelve to minister in his name, he instructs them to flee to other cities to continue ministry if they experience persecution from those who reject their message (Mt. 10:23). In Jn. 10, Jesus teaches that his sheep will *run away* from false shepherds because they do not recognize their voices (Jn. 10:5). In contrast to the good shepherd, hired hands will *run away* when danger threatens the flock (Jn. 10:12). The good shepherd, however, will never flee and abandon his sheep, regardless of the danger (Jn. 10:11). When Jesus was arrested in Gethsemane, "all the disciples deserted him and *fled*" (Mt. 26:56; cf. Mk. 14:50). Similarly, "the women went out and *fled* from the tomb" once they saw the vision of an angel, because they were bewildered and afraid (Mk.16:8).

Paul uses *pheugō* to command his readers to "*flee* from sexual immorality" (1 Cor. 6:18) and to "*flee* from idolatry" (1 Cor. 10:14). He also exhorts Timothy, his son in the faith, to "*flee* the evil desires of youth, and pursue righteousness, faith, love and peace" (2 Tim. 2:22) and to *flee* from unrighteousness completely (1 Tim. 6:11).

Finally, James encourages his readers to "submit yourselves, then, to God. Resist the devil, and he will *flee* from you" (Jas. 4:7). See *NIDNTT-A*, 588.

FLESH

Old Testament

Noun: בָּשָׂר (*bāśār*), GK 1414 (S 1320), 270x. *bāśār*, usually translated "flesh" or "meat," generally refers to the muscular structure of an animal and can, by extension, refer to the human body (sometimes referring to the physical aspect as opposed to the spiritual), human relations, humankind, and all living creatures. *bāśār* occurs most frequently in Leviticus (61x) and Genesis (33x), and the Pentateuch accounts for more than half of its occurrences. See also *meat*.

As flesh, *bāśār* is used in reference to human "flesh" with Moses' leprous hand (Exod. 4:7), Naaman's leprosy (2 Ki. 5:10, 14), and with the Levitical prescriptions for leprosy in general (17x in Lev. 13). In Ezekiel, God promises to replace Israel's heart of stone with a heart of "flesh" (Ezek. 11:19). God's covenant with Abraham is in his "flesh" (Gen. 17:13), as Abraham and his entire clan are to be circumcised in the "flesh" of the foreskin as a sign of the covenant (Gen. 17:11; cf. 17:14, 23, 24, 25; Lev. 12:3). *bāśār* is also used for the human "body" in general, which has discharges (Lev. 15:2, 3, 19), feels pain (Job 14:22; cf. 7:5), is not to be cut or tattooed (Lev. 19:28), and must be bathed (14:9; 15:13, 16; 16:4, 24, 26, 28; 17:16; 22:6).

bāśār, "flesh," may be used with *ᶜeṣem*, "bone," to describe the physical body (Job 2:5; 10:11; 19:20; Ps. 102:5[6]). But "bone and flesh" together are also used as a formula for blood relations (Gen. 29:14; Jdg. 9:2; 2 Sam. 5:1; 19:13–14), translated idiomatically "flesh and blood" by the NIV. When God presents Eve to Adam, Adam exclaims that Eve is "bone of my bone and *flesh* of my *flesh*" (Gen. 2:23), thus establishing the reason why a man shall leave his family and become one "flesh" with his wife (2:24).

The phrase *kāl bāśār*, "all flesh," appears forty-one times and generally refers to all humankind (Deut. 5:26) and may even include animals in some instances (e.g., Num. 18:15). God instructs Noah to build the ark because he is going to destroy "all flesh" through the flood (Gen. 6:12, 13, 17; cf. 7:21) and to take two of "every living thing" on the ark to preserve life (6:19; cf. 7:16; 8:17). After the flood, God establishes a covenant with Noah and "all flesh" that a flood will never again destroy the earth (9:11, 15, 16, 17). But in the last days, God will execute judgment on "all flesh" with fire and the sword (Isa. 66:16) before "all flesh" finally bows before him (66:23). Ultimately, "all flesh" is fleeting and temporal (40:6), in contrast to God's word, which is eternal (40:8). See *NIDOTTE*, 1:777-78.

New Testament

Noun: σάρξ (*sarx*), GK *4922* (S *4561*), 147x. *sarx* literally means "flesh." However, the use of *sarx* within the NT is quite diverse. Of the 147x *sarx* occurs, Paul employs it the most (91x). The NIV reflects the diverse usage of *sarx*, by offering translations such as "flesh" (33x), "sinful nature," (23x), "body" (20x), "human" (3x), and "people" (3x).

sarx has a number of basic usages.

(1) It can refer simply to the physical material that covers the bones of a human or animal body, such as in Paul's famous phrase, "thorn in my *flesh*" (2 Cor. 12:7; cf. also Lk. 24:39; 1 Cor. 15:39; Rev. 19:18, 21).

(2) It may also refer to a person's "body" (Acts 2:26, 31; 1 Cor. 6:16; 2 Cor. 12:7; Col. 2:5). In Eph. 5:29, Paul argues that a husband is to take care of his wife as he would take care of his own "body." The writer of Hebrews applies this sense to Jesus, who opened up our way to God through his "body" and the blood he shed for our sins (Heb. 10:20). This sense may also be observed in the "one flesh" marital union, where two bodies become one in sexual relations (Mt. 19:5; Mk. 10:8; cf. 1 Cor. 6:12–17).

(3) *sarx* may refer also "human nature" in general (Lk. 3:6; 2 Cor. 4:11; Acts 2:31). The incarnation of the Son of God uses this sense of *sarx* when John declares that "the Word became *flesh* and made his dwelling among us" (Jn. 1:14). This is to say, the Son of God became a man, or human person (cf. Phil. 2:5–11). Jesus shared in our "humanity" in order that he might free us from power of sin and death (Heb. 2:14).

(4) *sarx* may also indicate physical ancestry or human genealogy (Rom. 9:3; Gal. 4:23). For example, Paul declares that Jesus was a descendant of David according to "human lineage" (Rom. 1:3; cf. Mt. 1:1–16).

(5) Often, *sarx* reflects more than mere earthly existence and is conceptually conjoined with the principles of this world. Those who are "wise according to the flesh" (1 Cor. 1:26) are not in the sphere of God's salvation but in the sphere of the principles of this world (Eph. 2:11–12). It follows that Paul expressly pits life lived in the Spirit against a life lived in the flesh (Rom. 8:4; see 1 Pet. 2:11).

Paul's theological usage of *sarx* indicates that the flesh is a willing instrument of sin. This sense is observed especially in Rom. where *sarx* denotes humanity encompassed by the power of sin as demonstrated in self-sufficient independence of God (Rom. 6:19; 7:5; 18, 25; 8:3–9). *sarx*, therefore, is a sphere of activity demarcated by sin over against the sphere of God's Spirit (Rom. 8:4–5). Thus, in some cases, *sarx* indicates the "sinful nature" (Gal. 5:13; Col. 2:11). See *NIDNTT-A*, 517-19.

FLESHLY

New Testament

Adjective: σαρκικός (*sarkikos*), GK *4920* (S *4559*), 7x. *sarkikos* means "worldly, fleshly." See *wordly*.

FLOCK

Old Testament

Noun: מִקְנֶה (*miqneh*), GK 5238 (S 4735), 76x. *miqneh* describes livestock, including pack animals, cattle, sheep, and goats. Since among nomadic peoples livestock constitute their primary source of wealth, it is understandable how *miqneh* comes to have the meaning "livestock." See *livestock*.

Noun: צֹאן (*ṣōʾn*), GK 7366 (S 6629), 274x. Often translated "sheep, lambs, goats," *ṣōʾn* is commonly used to refer to flocks of sheep. It has both a literal and a metaphorical meaning in the OT (see *sheep*). Especially noteworthy is the use of this word as an expression of one's devotion to God. The firstborn of the flock belong to God, as is clear in Exod. 13:12: "You are to give over to the LORD the first offspring of every womb. All the firstborn males of your livestock belong to the LORD." See *firstborn*.

FLOUR

Old Testament

Noun: סֹלֶת (*sōlet*), GK 6159 (S 5560), 53x. *sōlet* describes finely ground flour. According to some, this flour was obtained by using the inner kernel of the wheat (as opposed to the whole kernel and bran). Others have suggested that *sōlet* describes the finely ground flour (or dust) that remained after the general grinding of wheat. Either way, *sōlet* clearly denotes flour that was less common than *qemaḥ* ("meal") and, therefore, more expensive (2 Ki. 7:1). When baked, it produced a bread of finer texture.

Abraham instructs Sarah to bake bread of *sōlet* to offer to his guests (Gen. 18:6). *sōlet* is used for the bread of Solomon's royal table (1 Ki. 4:22), and Ezekiel chastises Israel because even though she is given the finest of provisions, including *sōlet*, she offers them to pagan deities (Ezek. 16:13, 19).

sōlet is used most often in connection with various offerings prescribed in the Mosaic legislation (e.g., grain offerings, Lev. 2:1–2, 4–5, 7; Num. 15:1–3; thank offering, Lev. 7:12; completion of a Nazirite vow, 14:10, 21; Num. 6:15; Festival of Weeks offering, Lev. 23:17; Bread of the Presence, 24:5–9; dedication of the altar, Num. 7:10ff.). In some cases, those unable to afford the more expensive animal sacrifices are allowed to substitute a grain offering of *sōlet* (Lev. 5:11; 14:21).

Since *sōlet* is the flour used for the finest bread and since the offerings of Israel are presented to their divine king, it is understandable why it is deemed appropriate for the grain offerings. Moreover, its fine consistency reinforces the lesson that offerings to God are to be one's best and pure—unmixed and unblemished. In this way, the offerings reflect the worshiper's heart. See *NIDOTTE*, 3:269-70.

FOE

Old Testament

Verb: אֹיֵב (*ʾōyēb*), GK 367 (S 341), 285x. *ʾōyēb* is a personal or national "enemy or foe." See *enemy*.

Noun: צַר (*ṣar*), GK 7640 (S 6862), 433x. *ṣar* comes from the root *ṣrr*, which means "to be hostile." It can be translated "enemy, foe, adversary." See *enemy*.

New Testament

Noun: ἐχθρός (*echthros*), GK *2398* (S *2190*), 32x. In NT teaching, your *echthros* is someone who opposes you. The hostile behaviors described by this word includes hatred (Lk. 6:27), persecution (Mt. 5:44), and bodily harm (Rev. 11:5). A child of God may *have* enemies but is not to *be* an enemy toward another person. See *enemy*.

FOLLOW

Old Testament

Verb: בּוֹא (*bôʾ*), GK 995 (S 935), 2592x. *bôʾ* is the fourth most common verb in the OT. It denotes motion toward a specific goal, such as "to go, arrive, enter a house, come." It expresses a variety of motions. See *come*.

Verb: הָלַךְ (*hālak*), GK 2143 (S 1980), 1554x. *hālak* describes motion, primarily of humans, and is usually translated "walk, go, come." It is also used in a metaphorical sense to describe actions or the process of living, especially following or walking in the ways of the Lord. See *go*.

New Testament

Verb: ἀκολουθέω (*akoloutheō*), GK *199* (S *190*), 90x. *akoloutheō* occurs mostly in the gospels and Acts. Its basic meaning is "to follow" (Mt. 4:25) or "to accompany" (1 Cor. 10:4). In some instances *akoloutheō* has the nuance of becoming a disciple (see 4:20, "they left their nets and *followed* him"). Jn. 10 uses the verb a number of times to describe the response of Christ's sheep to various voices: they "*follow* him because they know his voice" (Jn. 10:4), "they will never *follow* a stranger" (v. 5), and they "follow" Christ because he knows them and they listen to his voice (v. 27). Thus following is not only a description of movement, but it is also a metaphor of salvation. To follow Christ means to accompany him, to learn from him, and to respond to his voice. See *NIDNTT-A*, 28-29.

FOLLOW AFTER

Old Testament

Verb: רָדַף (*rādap*), GK 8103 (S 7291),

144x. *rādap* means "to pursue, follow after, persecute." See *pursue*.

FOOD

Old Testament

Noun: לֶחֶם (*leḥem*), GK 4312 (S 3899), 340x. In the OT, *lechem* means either "bread" in particular or "food" in general. See *bread*.

New Testament

Noun: ἄρτος (*artos*), GK *788* (S *740*), 97x. *artos* means "bread" or more generally "food." See *bread*.

Noun: βρῶμα (*brōma*), GK *1109* (S *1033*), 17x. In the Synoptic Gospels, *brōma* refers to physical consumption of food (Mt. 14:15; Mk. 7:19; Lk. 3:11; 9:13). In Jn. 4, however, Jesus uses the disciples' desire that he eat some food to illustrate what his followers should truly hunger for—doing the will of God: "My *food* is to do the will of him who sent me and to finish his work" (Jn. 4:34). An all-consuming desire to do God's will should be just as natural as the desire to satisfy physical hunger. Interestingly, earlier in Jn. 4, Jesus offered the Samaritan woman "living water" (see *water*) to drink that would quench thirst forever (vv. 13–14), thus serving up the same lesson.

Paul's uses the word literally in Rom. 14:15, 20, in a section on eating "food" sacrificed to idols. Paul's bottom line is that "all food is clean" (v. 20) and suitable for eating, but what is more important is maintaining brotherly love. Nothing physical should stand in the way of positive, loving relationships in the church (cf. also 1 Cor. 8:8, 13). *brōma* is used in the literal sense as part of a popular Corinthian slogan in 1 Cor. 6:13: "Food is for the stomach and the stomach is for food." Dealing with the problem of sexual immorality, Paul attacks the Corinthians' misguided notion that there was no essential difference in eating a bowl of stew and consorting with a prostitute in the temple of Aphrodite.

Paul contrasts *brōma* with "milk" in 1 Cor. 3:2. Because Paul's initial message to the Corinthians consisted of the full disclosure of the word of the cross, his *brōma* at that time was no different from his milk. But as believers grow in their faith, they can go begin to understand deeper truths of God's Word, which Paul seems to call here "solid food." See *NIDNTT-A*, 98-99.

Noun: βρῶσις (*brōsis*), GK *1111* (S *1035*), 11x. This noun can refer either to that which is eaten ("food") or to the act of "eating, consuming." In the former sense, *brōsis* refers to the food or "meal" that Esau accepted as payment for his inheritance rights (Heb. 12:16). Jesus presents his body in a figurative sense as "food" (*brōsis*) that is to be eaten by faith (Jn. 4:32; 6:27, 55). In the latter sense, Paul writes that "the kingdom of God is not a matter of *eating* and drinking" (Rom. 14:17; cf. 1 Cor. 8:4; 2 Cor. 9:10; Col. 2:16). In Mt. 6:19–20, *brōsis* is often rendered as "rust" (i.e., that which consumes or corrodes metal). But *brōsis* is more likely used here as a general term for "consuming," which could have been done by a variety of insects. See *NIDNTT-A*, 98-99.*

Noun: τροφή (*trophē*), GK *5575* (S *5160*), 16x. *trophē* means "food." Food is a necessary part of our daily lives (Mt. 3:4; Jn. 4:8; Acts 27:33, 34, 36). Yet, according to Jesus, we must never forget that "life is more important than food" and clothing (Mt. 6:25; cf. Lk. 12:23). Nevertheless, if we see a fellow believer who lacks "food," God expects us to give him or her assistance (Jas. 2:15). The writer to the Hebrews uses this noun in a metaphorical sense, when he calls learning the deeper truths of God's Word as getting "solid food" (Heb. 5:12, 14).

FOOL

Old Testament

Noun: כְּסִיל (*k*[e]*sîl*), GK 4067 (S 3684), 70x. *k*[e]*sîl* refers to a "fool, a stupid or shameless person." The noun is used solely of humanity and found only in the wisdom literature of the OT (Ps., 3x; Prov., 49x; Eccl., 18x). Prov. describes the *k*[e]*sîl* as not only one who hates knowledge (Prov. 1:22) and takes no pleasure in understanding (18:2), but also as one who displays a defective moral character: he takes sport in doing mischief (10:23) and displays dishonor (3:35).

The meaning of *k^esîl* is clarified in light of the words with which it is frequently paired. *k^esîl* is contrasted with *ḥ^akāmîm*, "(the) wise," (Prov. 3:35; 10:1; Eccl. 2:14–16; 4:13); *nābôn*, "(those who are) discerning" (Prov. 14:33; 17:10, 24); and *ʿārûm*, "(the) prudent, cunning" (12:23; 13:16; 14:8). It is synonymous with *baʿar*, "(the) stupid" (Ps. 49:10; 92:6) and *sākāl*, "(the) fool" (Eccl. 10:2–3, 12–15). In Prov., *k^esîl* is closely associated with *ʾiwwelet*, "folly." The fool feeds on folly (Prov. 15:14) so that his heart proclaims it (15:2) and his mouth spouts it out (12:23). God's people are warned about being *k^esîl* because foolishness causes one to repeat mistakes (26:11, "as a dog returns to its vomit"), brings strife (18:6), and ultimately destroys the fool (18:7; Eccl. 10:12). See *NIDOTTE* 2:678-80.

New Testament

Noun/Adjective: ἄφρων (*aphrōn*), GK *933* (S *878*), 11x. As an adjective, *aphrōn* means "foolish, senseless," but it is often used as a noun to mean "fool." Whereas the root *phrōn* indicates wisdom, reason, or insight, the prefix *a* indicates a lack of wisdom, reason, or insight. It is important to note that *aphrōn* does not indicate a lack of knowledge but an inability to use it correctly.

The Bible portrays foolishness as the lack of a proper fear of God and understanding of his will; thus, Paul writes, "Do not be *foolish*, but understand what the will of the Lord is" (Eph. 5:17). In 2 Cor. 11:16, 19; 12:6, 11, Paul argues that if it were appropriate to foolishly boast in human accomplishments, he could boast more than all men. However, he chooses not to be a fool but to boast only in his weakness. Elsewhere he writes that the foolish person does not understand how God works in resurrecting the body (1 Cor. 15:36). Fool also receive instruction from those who know God's law, but they do not obey it (Rom. 2:20, cf. vv. 17–24). Jesus declares that those who value outward purity over inward purity (Lk. 11:40) and the rich man who stores up earthly treasures instead of heavenly treasures (12:20) are both fools. Peter writes that doing good puts to silence the ignorance of the foolish (1 Pet. 2:15). See *NIDNTT-A*, 380-381.*

Noun/Adjective: μωρός (*mōros*), GK *3704* (S *3474*), 12x. *mōros* means "fool" when used as a noun, "foolish" when used as an adjective. The prefix *mōr-* denotes foolishness or stupidity. *mōros* is used in LXX to describe the people of Israel when they act in contrast to what they know about their God (Deut. 32:6). In the NT *mōros* is often contrasted with wisdom (*phronimos)*. Foolishness often denotes not only simple stupidity, but ignorance of and willful rebellion against God and his will.

(1) Jesus uses *mōros* to describe those who disobey God's will and, as a result, will be severely judged. The person who listens to Jesus' words and does them is wise; he is like a man who builds his house on the solid rock foundation (Mt. 7:24–25). But the foolish person is the one who listens to Jesus' words but does not do them; he is like a foolish man who builds his house on a foundation of sand, a house that will be destroyed by the storms (7:26–27). This stands as Jesus' conclusion to his Sermon on the Mount, urging disciples not only hear but also to obey.

In discussing the needs of true kingdom people to move beyond the external religiosity of the Jewish leaders, Jesus uses *mōros* to stress that the commandment "You shall not murder" is broken by the attitude of hate that eventually might lead to murder. "Whosoever shall say to his brother, 'Raca' [a term of contempt similar to saying 'idiot, imbecile'], shall be in danger of the council: but whosoever shall say, 'Thou *fool*,' shall be in danger of hell fire" (Mt. 5:22, KJV).

Jesus also uses *mōros* in his parable of the ten virgins. The five who bring enough oil, who are prepared to wait for Jesus' return, are wise; those who are not prepared are "fools" and will pay the consequences (Mt. 25:2–3, 8). Pharisees and scribes who are blinded by outward rituals and symbols are also fools (23:17).

(2) Paul uses *mōros* to describe the distance that exists between the world's wisdom and God's. The difference is so great that "God's foolishness" (if he were foolish, which he is not) is wiser than human wisdom (which is not wise) (1 Cor. 1:25); this is by God's design (1:27). In fact, the distance is so great that the wisdom of God as seen in the cross is foolishness (the related noun *mōria*) to the unbelieving world but the power of God to those who are being saved (1:18). Indeed, the non-disciple can't even understand the spiritual things of God (2:14) because they are folly (*mōria*) to him. Consequently, true disciples must become "fools" in the eyes of the world so they can be truly wise (3:18).

In an apparently sarcastic vein, Paul compares the "foolish" apostles to the arrogantly "wise" Corinthians (1 Cor. 4:10). He also warns Timothy and Titus to stay away from the "foolish" controversies of their opponents (2 Tim. 2:23; Tit. 3:9). See *NIDNTT-A*, 380-81.*

FOOLISH

New Testament

Noun/Adjective: ἄφρων (*aphrōn*), GK *933* (S *878*), 11x. As an adjective, *aphrōn* means "foolish, senseless," but it is often used as a noun to mean "fool." See *fool*.

Noun/Adjective: μωρός (*mōros*), GK *3704* (S *3474*), 12x. *mōros* means "fool" when used as a noun, "foolish" when used as an adjective. See *fool*.

FOOT

Old Testament

Noun: פַּעַם (*paʿam*), GK 7193 (S 6471), 118x. The sense of "time" conveyed by *paʿam* is no doubt related to its root, meaning the "foot" or the "sole of the foot." Like the sound of footsteps or the beating of the foot to keep time, *paʿam* usually connotes time as a succession of repeated events. See *time*.

Noun: רֶגֶל (*regel*), GK 8079 (S 7272), 251x. In the OT *regel* signifies the foot (Gen. 24:32; 43:24) or the leg (Isa. 7:20; metaphorically the legs of a table in Exod. 25:26). The expression "from the head to the (soles of the) feet" (and vice versa) signifies "all over the body" (Deut. 28:35 and Isa. 1:6 refer to sores all over the body). To wash the feet of a visitor was a sign of hospitality (Gen. 18:4; 19:2; 24:32) and, at times, of servanthood (1 Sam. 25:41; cf. Jesus' act of washing the disciples' feet in John 13).

When in the presence of the holiness of God, it seems that one's feet were in some sense defiling or unclean (could this be a euphemism?); consequently, the seraphim of Isaiah's vision had to cover their feet in God's presence (Isa. 6:2), and the priests had to wash their feet before entering to serve in the tabernacle (Exod. 30:19, 21; 40:31).

Finally, sometimes *regel* is used euphemistically for the genitalia. When someone "covers his feet" he is relieving himself (Jdg. 3:24; 1 Sam. 24:3). Concerning the woman who gives birth, Deut. 28:57 refers literally to "what comes from between her feet," which is to say what comes from her reproductive area. See *NIDOTTE*, 3:1048-49.

New Testament

Noun: πούς (*pous*), GK *4546* (S *4228*), 93x. *pous* usually means "foot, feet." See *feet*.

FOOTSTOOL

New Testament

Noun: ὑποπόδιον (*hypopodion*) GK *5711* (S *5286*), 7x. *hypopodion* means "footstool." In Jas. 2:3 this noun occurs in James's criticism of a sad situation in the early church, namely, that some church members are treating visitors from the poorer classes in a prejudicial manner, asking them to stand over to one side or even "sit on the floor by my footstool"; wealthy visitors, by contrast, are given special seats of honor (see 2:1–7). The remaining occurrences of this noun allude to OT passages, either to Ps. 110:1 ("Sit at my right hand until I make your enemies a footstool for your feet," see Lk. 20:43; Acts 2:35; Heb. 1:13; 10:13) or to Isa. 66:1 ("Heaven is my throne, and earth is my footstool," see Mt. 5:35; Acts 7:49).*

FORBEAR

See *endure.*

FORBID

Old Testament

Verb: צָוָה (*sāwâ*), GK 7422 (S 6680), 496x. This verb is used to denote the issuing of an authoritative statement and means "to command, order." When used negatively, it can be translated "forbid." See *command, commandment*.

New Testament

Verb: κωλύω (*kōlyō*), GK *3266* (S *2967*), 23x. *kōlyō* means "to hinder, stop, forbid, oppose." It is found most often in the writings of Luke. See *hinder*.

FORCES

Old Testament

Noun: חַיִל (*hayil*), GK 2657 (S 2428), 246x. The basic sense of *ḥayil* is "power, strength, or capability." In military contexts, *hayil* can refer to an "army" of fighting men (e.g., Pharaoh's forces in Exod. 14:4, 9, 17, 28). See *strength*.

FOREIGN(ER)

Old Testament

Adjective: זָר (*zār*), GK 2424 (S 2214), 70x. In most instances, *zār* modifies a noun and means "strange, foreign, alien" or, by extension, "unauthorized, illegitimate." In other instances, the adjective can function like a noun and mean "stranger, foreigner."

(1) *zār* most commonly refers to something or someone as *strange* or *foreign*. Nadab and Abihu, for example, offered strange or unauthorized fire before God and were judged accordingly (Lev. 10:1–2). Similarly, the Scriptures command God's people not to follow after "foreign" gods (Ps. 44:22; 81:9; Jer. 2:25; 3:13; 5.19). God's restorative work in Zion is also viewed as "strange" or extraordinary (Isa. 28:21).

(2) *zār* can also be used as a substantive for those who were not Israelites but foreigners or strangers (Isa. 1:7; 25:5; 61:5; Jer. 51:51; Ezek. 11:9; 28:7, 10; 30:12; Obad. 11; Lam. 5:2; cf. 2 Ki. 19:24). The prophet Jeremiah, for example, anticipates a day after Jerusalem's destruction that God's people will ask, "Why has the LORD our God done all this to us?" To this God responds curtly, "As you have forsaken me and served foreign gods in your own land, so now you will serve *foreigners* in a land not your own" (Jer. 5:19). In Joel 3:17, God promises that he will again dwell in Zion, that Jerusalem will once again be holy, and that *foreigners* will never again pass through it. See *NIDOTTE*, 1:1142-43.

New Testament

Noun: πάροικος (*paroikos*), GK *4230* (S *3941*), 4x. *paroikos* is a resident foreigner or more generally a stranger. See *strange(r)*.

Adjective and Noun: ἀλλότριος (*allotrios*), GK *259* (S *245*), 14x. *allotrios* is used to describe a thing that is not one's own or a person not from one's own people group. See *other*.

Adjective: ξένος (*xenos*), GK *3828* (S *3581*), 14x. *xenos* denotes something "strange" or unusual (outside of one's experience), a person who is unknown, or a person from another place. See *strange(r)*.

FOREKNOW, FOREKNOWLEDGE

New Testament

Verb: προγινώσκω (*proginōskō*) GK *4589* (S *4267*), 5x. *proginōskō* means "to foreknow."

Noun: πρόγνωσις (*prognōsis*) GK *4590* (S *4268*), 2x. *prognōsis* means "foreknowledge." Two occurrences of the verb *proginōskō* refer to human knowledge, namely, that someone "has known" some person or some Christian teaching "for a long time" (Acts 26:5; 2 Pet. 3:17). The other three uses of the verb and the two uses of the noun refer to divine foreknowledge. Peter in his Pentecost message indicates that Jesus was delivered over to his enemies "by God's set purpose and foreknowledge" (Acts 2:23). In fact, Jesus was divinely "chosen" to this task "before" the creation of the world (1 Pet. 1:20). Peter also states that believers "have been chosen according to the foreknowledge of God" (1 Pet. 1:2). Paul emphasizes the same message, that "those God foreknew he also predestined to be conformed to the image of his Son" (Rom. 8:29; cf. also 11:2). We serve a God who knows all things and acts in accordance with his will.*

FOREST

Old Testament

Noun: יַעַר (*ya*ʿ*ar*), GK 3623 (S 3293), 56x. *ya*ʿ*ar* is the general term for a forest. However, it does not always refer to areas covered with tall trees; it can also refer to areas covered with shrubs and bushes.

(1) Whatever the vegetation, a *ya*ʿ*ar* is a place that is uninhabitable and dangerous. After the conquest of the promised land, the tribe of Ephraim goes to Joshua complaining that they need more land. Joshua's advice is to clear away the forests in their territory in order to create more space (Jos. 17:15). Incidentally, the "forest of Ephraim," where David's men fight against Absalom (2 Sam. 18:6), may not have been located within the territory of Ephraim but rather on the other side of the Jordan. The dangerous nature of a forest is illustrated by the fact that "the *forest* consumed more people that day than the sword" (2 Sam. 18:8). Among the dangers of the forest are the wild animals that live there ("the beasts of the *forest*," Mic. 5:8). Lions, bears, and wild boars are specifically mentioned (Jer. 12:8; 2 Ki. 2:24; Ps. 80:13). Forest fires pose another danger and are used in prophetic passages to illustrate God's judgment (Jer. 21:14).

(2) The forest also has benefits such as lumber (Deut. 19:5). Unfortunately, even this benefit is used for a wicked purpose when the people use wood from the forest to make idols (Jer. 10:3).

(3) In spite of their dangers and drawbacks, forests contain an aspect of glory and prosperity (Isa. 10:18, "the splendor of his *forest*"). Solomon himself cultivates a forest (Eccl. 2:6) and builds "the house of the *forest* of Lebanon," which is probably a luxurious reception hall (1 Ki. 7:2). Ezekiel foretells a day when all the dangers of the forest will be removed and people can sleep there in safety (Ezek. 34:25). See *NIDOTTE*, 2:492-94.

FORETELL

New Testament

Verb: προλέγω (*prolegō*), GK *4625* (S *4302*, *4277*, *4280*), 15x. *prolegō* refers to saying something in advance of an event. See *say before*.

FOREVER

Old Testament

Noun: אֹרֶךְ (ʾ*ōrek*), GK 802 (S 753), 95x. ʾ*ōrek* means length and is used with reference to either space or time. Normally "*length* of days" refers to a long earthly life (Job 12:12; Prov. 3:2, 16). This phrase is used in connection with "eternity" (Ps. 21:4; Lam. 5:20), though at times it can carry the meaning "forever" (Ps. 93:5). See *length*.

Noun: עוֹלָם (ʿ*ôlām*), GK 6409 (S 5769), 439x. ʿ*ôlām* means "ancient, eternal, forever, everlasting." See *eternal*.

New Testament

Adjective: αἰώνιος (*aiōnios*), GK *173* (S *166*), 71x. This adjective typically functions in three settings: the eternity of God and the divine realm; the blessings of salvation; and everlasting conditions that have neither beginning nor end. See *eternal*.

FORGET

Old Testament

Verb: שָׁכַח (*śākaḥ*), GK 8894 (S 7911), 102x. *śākaḥ* means "to forget" and refers to any failure to remember someone or something that was once known. Its most common use is in reference to Israel's covenantal unfaithfulness—i.e., the failure of the people of Israel to remember the LORD their God.

(1) At times *śākaḥ* describes a simple failure to remember past experiences or previous knowledge. In times of famine, for example, previous good harvests are forgotten (Gen. 41:30).

(2) But *śākaḥ* most frequently refers to Israel's past, present, or future failures to remain loyal to their covenant with the LORD. Forgetting the LORD is manifested in worshiping idols (Deut. 4:23), trusting in oneself (Deut. 8:11), and worshiping foreign gods (e.g., Baal and Ashtoreth, 1 Sam. 12:9-10).

(a) Significantly, Israel's worship calendar is designed specifically to protect against this sin of forgetfulness. The Passover celebration is instituted for all generations so that the people will remember their deliverance from Egypt by the mighty hand of the Lord (Deut. 12, especially vv. 14, 17, 26-27). Similarly, the Feast of Tabernacles is instituted to help the people remember God's covenant faithfulness and deliverance through the desert (Lev. 23:42–43).

(b) Although God's people often forget their covenant commitments to him, it is clear that God never forgets his commitments to his people. When under divine judgment or when suffering unjustly, Israel often cries out to God, urging him not to forget them and his covenant with the patriarchs. This is the basis for Moses' intercession on behalf of the people of Israel when the Lord is ready to destroy them (Exod. 33:10, cf. Deut. 9:26–29). So, too, Hannah asks God to remember her and "not forget" her by opening her womb (1 Sam. 1:11; cf. Ps. 10:12). Though the oppressed may feel as if the Lord has forgotten them (Ps. 42:9–10; Isa. 49:14), ultimately, hope is found in God alone (Ps. 42:11), who will indeed show himself faithful by remembering Israel (Isa. 49:15).

New Testament

Verb: ἐπιλανθάνομαι (*epilanthanomai*) GK *2140* (S *1950*), 8x. *epilanthanomai* means "to forget." This verb is used both on the human level and with respect to God. (1) On the human level, on one of their journeys, the disciples "forget" to take food along (Mt. 16:5; Mk. 8:14), which becomes a teaching moment for Jesus. James compares a person who listens to God's Word but does not keep it to someone who looks at oneself in a mirror and immediately goes away and forgets what he or she looks like (Jas. 1:24). The author of Hebrew instructs us not to "forget to entertain strangers" (i.e., visitors in our midst, Heb. 13:2) and not to "forget to do good and to share with others" (13:16). Paul, however, tells us something that we should "forget," namely, things we have done in the past (which we cannot change anyway); instead, we should press forward in our service to Christ (Phil. 3:13).

(2) Jesus points out that the smallest details of what happens on this earth, such as what happens to two sparrows, is "not forgotten by God" (Lk. 12:6). Similarly, God "will not forget" our work and the love we have shown to others (Heb. 6:10).*

FORGIVE

Old Testament

Verb: חָנַן (*ḥānan*), GK 2858 (S 2603), 77x. The primary meaning of *ḥānan* is "to show mercy, favor, be gracious" toward someone. It can also have the nuance of "to forgive." See *show mercy, favor*.

Verb: כָּסָה (*kāsâ*), GK 4059 (S 3680), 153x. This word is predominately used with the literal sense "to cover." In other contexts, it can denote "conceal, hide" and even "forgive." See *cover*.

Verb: נָשָׂא (*nāśā'*), GK 5951 (S 4984), 659x. *nāśā'* means "to lift, raise high, bear, carry." It occasionally means "to forgive" on the part of God (i.e., "to carry away sin"). See *lift*.

New Testament

Verb: ἀφίημι (*aphiēmi*), GK *918* (S *863*), 143x. Depending upon its particular context, *aphiēmi* means to "forgive, leave, abandon." It is found predominantly in the synoptic gospels (130x; 47x in Matthew), where in narrative sections it usually denotes the process of leaving one place and going somewhere else. In 1 Cor. 7:11–13 this verb means "to divorce." In non-narrative sections of the gospels, *aphiēmi* often means "to forgive" (45x), usually the forgiveness of sins (Mk. 2:5), debts (Mt. 6:12) or trespasses (Mk. 11:25–26); see *forgiveness* (under the related noun *aphesis*).

Verb: χαρίζομαι (*charizomai*), GK *5919* (S *5483*), 23x. *charizomai* means "to give graciously," but it can also mean "to forgive." See *give*.

FORGIVENESS

New Testament

Noun: ἄφεσις (*aphesis*), GK *912* (S *859*), 17x. In contrast to the verb *aphiēmi* (see *forgive*), of the 17x that *aphesis* appears in the NT, it primarily carries the sense of "forgiveness" (15x). Only twice does *aphesis* denote a "release" from captivity (Lk. 4:18). *aphesis* almost always refers to divine forgiveness, and its meaning is usually clarified by adding "of sins." In conjunction with Isa. 61:1, Lk. 4:18 uses *aphesis* in the sense of release, which contextually is also the forgiveness of sins. In Eph. 1:7; Col. 1:14, Paul defines redemption as specifically related to "*the forgiveness* of sins." Similarly, Matthew, in the context of the Lord's Supper (Mt. 26:28), speaks of "*the forgiveness* of sins" as the result of the pouring out of Jesus' blood for many. In Peter's preaching on Pentecost, he proclaimed "*forgiveness of your sins*" in the name of Jesus Christ (Acts 2:38; cf. 5:31; 10:43; 13:38; 26:18).

According to Mk. 10:15 (where the word "ransom" is used), the preaching of Jesus reaches its zenith in the forgiveness of sins. Sin has destroyed the relationship between God and human beings. The cross of Christ is God's means of removing this fissure. Without the shedding of his blood "there is no forgiveness" (Heb. 9:22; 10:18). The forgiveness of sins is a central feature of the Christian message and witness, standing at the heart of the gospel. Also, the divine initiative in the forgiveness of sins creates a forgiving spirit in the life of the Christian. As Christ forgave us, so should we forgive others (Mt. 5:38–48; Rom. 12:19–21).

Although Paul does not use these terms very often, he sees the forgiveness of sins not only as the removal of past guilt but the total deliverance from the power of sin and restoration to fellowship with God. These concepts are seen most clearly in Paul's doctrine of justification (e.g., Rom. 3:21–28; 4:22) and reconciliation (2 Cor. 5:14–21). That a believer is "in Christ" reflects the fact that a believer is a pardoned sinner (Rom. 8:1) in God's end-time new creation (2 Cor. 5:17). The task of proclaiming the forgiveness of sins is given to the church symbolized anew in each observance of the Lord's Supper (1 Cor. 11:26) and in announcing the message of reconciliation (2 Cor. 5:18–21). The validity of forgiveness is found in the authority of Christ alone as given to the church (Mt. 18:18; Jn. 20:23). See *NIDNTT-A*, 80-82.

FORM

Old Testament

Verb: יָצַר (*yāṣar*), GK 3670 (S 3335), 63x. *yāṣar* principally means "to form" or "to make," and it emphasizes the shaping or forming of an object. For example, an idol is pictured as being fashioned by hammers in Isa. 44:9–12, and elsewhere in the prophets *yāṣar* is used in connection with a potter's shaping of vessels (Isa. 29:16; Jer. 18:2, 4, 6; Zech. 11:13).

When *yāṣar* is applied to God, it usually refers to his creative activity. In Gen. 2:7–9 it describes God's creative work of forming man and beasts from the dust of the earth. Isa. 64:8 speaks of God as the one who forms human beings in the womb (Jer. 1:5) and also forms his people as a nation (Isa. 43:7; 44:2, 24).

yāṣar can also refer to God's preordained purposes in the sense that he frames or fashions something in his mind. Thus, 2 Ki. 19:25 states, "Have you not heard? Long ago I ordained it. In days of old I *planned* it; now I have brought it to pass" (see also Ps. 139:16; Isa. 37:26; 46:11; Jer. 18:11).

Noun: דְּמוּת (*d^e^mût*), GK 1952 (S 1823), 25x. *d^e^mût* denotes a likeness between two things. It is frequently used in the visions of Ezekiel (Ezek. 1:10, 13, 16, 22, 26, 28) to describe, for example, the form of the creatures the prophet sees. See *likeness.*

New Testament

Noun: μορφή (*morphē*) GK *3671* (S *3444*), 3x. *morphē* means "form, nature." These three occurrences have to do with Jesus. When Jesus came into this world as a baby, he retained his "very nature" as God (Phil. 2:6), but he also took on "the very nature of a servant" (2:7, that is, a human nature whose goal was to do his Father's will). These are critical texts in our doctrine of the Incarnation, that Jesus was fully God and fully human at the same time. He was not human on the outside and divine on the inside; he was not God and only appeared to be human, nor the reverse. The Incarnation, that God "became flesh," is not only the greatest miracle but also the greatest mystery of our faith.

Then, after Jesus resurrection, he had the ability to disguise himself and appear "in a different form" to his followers (Mk. 16:14; cf. Lk. 24:13–32).*

Noun: σχῆμα (*schēma*), GK *5386* (S *4976*), 2x. *schēma* means "form, (outward) appearance, figure." In classical Greek this word typically meant form or figure, though could also mean appearance as opposed to reality. In the NT, the word occurs only 2x. Paul uses *schēma* to submit that the "world in its present *form* is passing away" (1 Cor. 7:31), which shows the temporariness of things in the present world. In Phil. 2:7 he uses the term to present Jesus as "being found in *appearance* as a man." This does not mean that Jesus only appeared as a human being but really wasn't. Rather, his figure was truly that of a human being, though in essence he was on an equality with God. See *NIDNTT-A*, 548.

Noun: τύπος (*typos*), GK *5596* (S *5179*), 15x. *typos* is a "pattern, example, model," taken from the concept of an impression or a mark left behind by something on a surface. See *example.*

FORMER

Old Testament

Adjective: רִאשׁוֹן (*riʾšôn*), GK 8037 (S 7223), 182x. As an adjective, *riʾšôn* describes what is first in a series or rank. In terms of time, *riʾšôn* can convey the meaning "previously, in a former time." See *first.*

New Testament

Adjective: πρότερος (*proteros*), GK *4728* (S *4386*, *4387*), 11x. *proteros* is a comparative adjective that denotes a period of time preceding another period of time, "earlier, former." *proteros* appears both as an adjective (Eph. 4:22; Heb. 10:32; 1 Pet. 1:14) and an adverb (Jn. 7:50; Heb. 7:27). Paul says in Gal. 4:13, "it was because of an illness that I *first* preached the gospel to you." See *NIDNTT-A*, 501-2.

FORNICATION

New Testament

Verb: πορνεύω (*porneuō*), GK *4519* (S *4203*), 8x. The word group to which *porneuō* belongs generally relates to any kind of sexual immorality or fornication (KJV). See *commit sexual immorality.*

Noun: πορνεια (*porneia*), GK *4518* (S *4202*), 25x. The word group to which *porneia* belongs generally relates to any kind of illegitimate sexual intercourse—that is, sexual immorality or fornication (KJV). See *sexual immorality.*

FORNICATOR

New Testament

Noun: πόρνος (*pornos*), GK *4521* (S *4205*), 10x. *pornos* generally refers to any kind of illegitimate sexual intercourse (see also *prostitute*), but in most scriptural contexts, it carries the sense of one who is sexually immoral (a fornicator or whoremonger, KJV). See *sexual immorality.*

FORSAKE

Old Testament

Verb: עָזַב (*ʿāzab*), GK 6440 (S 5800), 214x. *ʿāzab* is used often for the action of "abandonment" of the promised land and God's forsaking of his people because of exile (Lev. 26:43; Isa. 18:6; 32:14; cf. Isa. 60:15; Jer. 49:25; Ezek. 36:4). This verb is commonly negated with respect to God, indicating that he *will not forsake* or abandon his people (Gen. 28:15; Deut. 31:6, 8), despite the fact that his people have forsaken him. See *abandon.*

New Testament

Verb: ἐγκαταλειπω (*enkataleipō*), GK *1593* (S *1459*), 10x. This verb means to separate connection with someone or something by leaving, to "abandon, forsake, desert" (2 Cor. 4:9; 2 Tim. 4:10, 16; Heb. 10:25). It signifies the promises of God never to "forsake" his people (Heb. 13:5) or to "abandon" his Messiah to the grave (Acts 2:27, 31). The use of this term in divine promises brings into sharp relief the calamity of Christ's suffering on the cross when he cried, "My God, my God, why have you *forsaken* me?" (Mt. 27:46; Mk. 15:34).

In Rom. 9:29, *enkataleipō* resembles *kataleipō* in signifying "to leave over" in the sense of causing something to remain in existence (cf. *kataleipō* in Rom. 11:4; Heb. 4:1). See *NIDNTT-A*, 331-33.*

FORTHWITH

See *immediately.*

FORTUNATE

New Testament

Adjective: μακάριος (*makarios*), GK *3421* (S *3107*), 50x. There are two major ways *makarios* may be taken in the NT. One who is *makarios* can be "happy" or "fortunate" because of life's circumstances or because of divine favors bestowed on him or her (cf. the Beatitudes). See *blessed.*

FORTY

Old Testament

Noun: אַרְבַּע (*ʾarbāʿ*), GK 752 (S 702, 706), 455x. *ʾarbāʿ* means "four" in the singular and "forty" in the plural. It can also mean the ordinal numeral "fourth." See *four.*

New Testament

Adjective: τεσσεράκοντα (*tesserakonta*), GK *5477* (S *5062*), 22x. *tesserakonta* is the word for "forty." The man who was healed in Acts 3:1–10 was "more than *forty* years old" (Acts 4:22), his age emphasizing the reality of the healing. This word is also used with other numbers, such as the 144,000 in Rev. 7:4, the "*forty* and six years" (46 years) that it took to build the temple (Jn. 2:20), and the fact that Paul received "*forty*-minus-one" (i.e., 39) lashes on five occasions (2 Cor. 11:24).

Forty is an important number in biblical history. The rebellious Exodus generation saw the works of God for forty years (Heb. 3:10; cf. Acts 7:36, 42), and God was angry with them for forty years (Heb. 3:17). As a result they faced his wrath. When Jesus went out into the desert after his baptism, he fasted for forty days and forty nights (Mt. 4:2; cf. Mk. 1:13; Lk. 4:2). After his resurrection, he appeared to the disciples over a period of forty days (Acts 1:3). Some have suggested that while *tesserakonta* certainly can refer to forty literal days, its frequency of usage may be intended to indicate an approximate but completed length of time.

FOUL

See *unclean.*

FOUNDATION

New Testament

Noun: θεμέλιος (*themelios*), GK *2529* (S *2310*), 15x. *themelios* refers to the supporting groundwork or base of a building or city, suggesting the permanence and strength of what is built on it. Jesus calls people to be like the man who built the foundation of his house on rock so that it would stand firm against the floods (Lk. 6:48, 49).

(1) *themelios* is used only metaphorically by Paul. In preaching the gospel to establish the church, he "laid a foundation as an expert builder" (1 Cor. 3:10). He identifies that foundation as Jesus himself (v. 11) and warns that those who build on it must take great care in their work since they will be held accountable by God (v. 12). Through association with Christ, apostles, prophets, and even the church

itself are given the label of *themelios*. Because they bear Jesus' authentic message, the apostles and prophets are called the foundation of the church, with Jesus as the cornerstone (Eph. 2:20). Even in the midst of apostasy, "the firm foundation of God [i.e., true believers who have not gone astray] stands" (2 Tim. 2:19).

(2) This word also refers to the fundamental elements of the Christian faith. The writer of Hebrews calls his readers to "move on to maturity, not laying again a foundation of repentance … and of faith in God" (Heb. 6:1).

(3) Finally, *themelios* refers to the foundations of the new Jerusalem. Abraham "was looking forward to the city that has foundations, whose designer and maker is God" (Heb. 11:10). In Revelation, the twelve foundation stones of the city wall of the new Jerusalem are precious stones (Rev. 21:14, 19a, b).

With the image of a foundation, the Bible gives us a built-in illustration for the solid groundwork upon which our lives, our church, and our service for Christ are to be built. Without the proper foundation, even the most impressive building—and the most outwardly impressive person, congregation, or ministry—will collapse. See *NIDNTT-A*, 242-43.

Noun: καταβολη (*katabolē*), GK *2856* (S *2602*), 11x. *katabolē* literally means "something thrown down." It is most frequently translated "creation, foundation." See *creation*..

FOUNTAIN

New Testament

Noun: πηγή (*pēgē*), GK *4380* (S *4077*), 11x. *pēgē* usually refers to a well or spring of water (Jn. 4:6 [2x]; Jas. 3:11; Rev. 8:10; 14:7; 16:4), though it can include any flow of liquid. See *spring*.

FOUR

Old Testament

Noun: אַרְבַּע (*ʾarbāʿ*), GK 752 (S 702, 706), 455x. *ʾarbāʿ* means "four" in the singular and "forty" in the plural. It can also mean the ordinal numeral "fourth." *ʾarbāʿ* can combine with other numbers: e.g., with *ʾelep* ("thousand," GK 547), it means "four thousand"; with the number ten, it means "fourteen."

"Four" is a common number in the Bible, just as it is in our society. There are four points of the compass (east, south, west, north), four winds (Dan. 8:8), four corners in a house (Job 1:19), four corners of the earth (Isa. 11:12), and the four spirits of heaven (Zech. 6:5). The expression "three, yes four" (e.g., Prov. 30:15, 18, 21, 24, 29; Amos 1:3, 6, 9, etc.) is a means of building a climax through poetic symmetry.

Perhaps more important than "four" is the plural "forty." During the flood it rained forty days and forty nights. The nation of Israel spent forty years in the desert (Exod. 16:35; Num. 32:13). Moses was on Mount Sinai forty days and forty nights (Exod. 24:18; 34:28; Ps. 95:10). Elijah traveled forty days and forty nights to Horeb on the strength of the food God provided for him. The expression "the land had peace for forty years" suggests a generation of peace (Jdg. 3:11; 5:31; 8:28). The 480 years mentioned in 1 Ki. 6:1 probably means twelve generations. This symbolism of forty carries over into the NT (e.g., Mt. 4:2; Acts 1:3).

New Testament

Adjective: τέσσαρες (*tessares*), GK *5475* (S *5064*), 41x. *tessares* simply means the number "four." It is used both literally and symbolically.

(1) In a numeric sense, the paralytic was carried by four men (Mk. 3:2). Lazarus had been in the tomb four days, hence the objection that there would surely be a foul odor if the tomb were opened (Jn. 11:17). When Jesus' garments are divided four ways, it implies that there were four soldiers (19:23). Four squads of soldiers arrest Peter (Acts 12:4; cf. 21:9, 23; 27:49).

(2) *tessares* can also used in a symbolic sense, usually in connection with the idea of "the *four* corners of the earth" (Rev. 20:8) or related phrases, such as "the *four*

winds" (Mt. 24:31). Both phrases mean "from all over the earth." That is, the elect will be gathered from all over the earth, Jew and Gentile. In this sense, it is prophetic (cf. Isa. 11:12).

Sometimes *tessares* is both numeric and symbolic. For example, in Acts 10:11, the four corners of the sheet in Peter's vision refers to the actual corners of the sheet, but they may also be symbolic since the sheet is part of a vision given to the apostle. In Rev. 4:6, John sees four living creatures, but they are symbolic in the context of this book (cf. also 7:1–2). See *NIDNTT-A*, 562.

FOURTH

Old Testament

Noun: אַרְבַּע (*ʾarbāʿ*), GK 752 (S 702, 706), 455x. *ʾarbāʿ* means "four" in the singular and "forty" in the plural. It can also mean the ordinal numeral "fourth." See *four*.

Adjective: רְבִיעִי (*rᵉbîʿî*), GK 8055 (S 7243), 55x. *rᵉbîʿî* means the ordinal number "fourth"; it can also mean "quarter." On "the *fourth* day" of creation, God made the sun, moon, and stars (Gen. 1:14–19). In the history of the kings, the writers will sometimes refer to some significant event that took place "in the *fourth* year of" a particular king (e.g., Solomon begins building the temple, 1 Ki. 6:1; Jehoiakim burns the scroll of Jeremiah, Jer. 36:1). The dynasty of Jehu will sit on the throne of Israel "to the *fourth* generation" (2 Ki. 10:30; 15:12), while God promises that David's descendants will reign forever (2 Sam. 7:12–16). Several of the offerings required by the Lord use "a *quarter* of a hin of water" (Num. 15:4–5) or oil (28:5, 7). During the time of Nehemiah when the people come together to confess their sins, "a quarter" of the day is spent listening to the law of God and "another *quarter* in confessing and in worshiping the Lord their God" (Neh. 9:3).

New Testament

Adjective: τέταρτος (*tetartos*), GK *5480* (S *5067*), 10x. *tetartos* means "fourth." It can be used in the marking of time, such as the "*fourth* watch of the night" (Mt. 14:25; Mk. 6:48; i.e., 3-6 am). In Acts 10:30, *tetartos* means "on the fourth day ago." *tetartos* is also used to identify something in a group, such as the fourth creature (Rev. 4:7; cf. 6:7), the fourth angel (Rev. 8:12; cf. 16:8), the fourth seal (Rev. 6:7), and the fourth foundation stone of the heavenly city (Rev. 21:18). It is also used to delineate one-fourth (i.e., one quarter) of the earth (Rev. 6:8).*

FRAGRANCE

Old Testament

Noun: רֵיחַ (*rēaḥ*), GK 8194 (S 7381), 58x. *rēaḥ* denotes an aroma, scent, or fragrance. In common usage, it can refer to the fragrance of perfume (Song 1:1), the scent of vines (2:13), the odor of garments (4:11), or the smell of one's breath (7:8). Its technical, cultic expression is in the phrase *hanniḥōaḥ* (43x), often translated "a pleasing aroma" See *aroma*.

FRAME

Old Testament

Noun: קֶרֶשׁ (*qereš*), GK 7983 (S 7175). 51x. In most cases, *qereš* refers to the upright wooden frames of the tabernacle. These wooden frames are described in detail in Exod. 26:15–29 and 36:20–34. They are made of acacia wood, covered with gold, and connected to one another by crossbars. Gold rings hold the crossbars in place. They measure ten cubits long and one and a half cubits wide, but no thickness is recorded. They have two projections (i.e., tenons) at the bottom, which fit into two silver bases. The word is translated in English in various ways, including "frame" or "board."

Aside from referring to the frames of the tabernacle, the word is used in Ezek. 27:6 to refer to some part of the ships of Tyre, but the exact feature is uncertain. Although "small room," "cabin wall," and "mast" have all been suggested, many versions translate the word "deck." The ivory mentioned in the verse would have been inlaid into the wood of the *qereš*. See *NIDOTTE*, 3:995-96.

FREE

New Testament

Verb: λύω (*lyō*), GK *3395* (S *3089*), 42x. *lyō* means "to loose, untie," but also "break, destroy" (see *break*). In the NT, it is both literally and metaphorically. Metaphorically, *lyō* has a sense of setting free. For example, God sets free a crippled woman bound by Satan (Lk. 13:16). Spiritually, *lyō* is used for being set free from sin: Jesus Christ "loves us and has *freed* us from our sins by his blood" (Rev. 1:5). See *loose*.

Adjective: ἐλεύθερος (*eleutheros*), GK *1801* (S *1658*), 23x. *eleutheros* denotes the state of being "free" or "independent." In classical Gk., this adjective was used for a person with the full rights of citizenship in society. The NT adapts this idea of political freedom in its use of *eleutheros*, for its primary meaning is of a person who is not a slave. Paul uses this adjective 16x, often in a direct contrast to a slave. Paul reminds the Galatians and Colossians that there is neither "slave nor *free*" in Christ (Gal. 3:28; Col. 3:11). Regardless of one's societal or cultural status before becoming part of the body of Christ, "whether Jews or Greeks, slaves or *free*" (1 Cor. 12:13), all believers are baptized into the same body and same Spirit. A practical result of this is that the reward one receives from the Lord is not dependent on the status of being free (Eph. 6:8).

Paul emphasizes the contrast of freedom with slavery in his allegory of the difference between Sarah and Hagar (Gal. 4:22–31); the key distinction here is that freedom is a spiritual reality. The Pharisees insist before Jesus that they do not need to be made free, for they have never been slaves of anyone (Jn. 8:33). But Jesus emphasizes that true freedom comes from being set free by him as God's Son (8:36).

This does not mean that being free results in complete independence from others in the body of Christ; in fact, the opposite is true. Paul himself asserts that though he is "*free* and belongs to no person," he nevertheless makes himself a "slave to everyone, to win as many as possible" (1 Cor. 9:19). One is always free in one sense and a slave in another, Paul points out. Before being set truly free by Christ, a person is a slave to sin and "*free* from the control of righteousness" (Rom. 6:20); afterward, one is freed from sin and a slave to Christ (1 Cor. 7:22).

A second, related sense of *eleutheros* is freedom from subjection, especially from authority or law. In this manner Paul can speak of the freedom of a widow from the bond of marriage after the death of her husband (Rom. 7:23; 1 Cor. 7:23). See *NIDNTT-A*, 180-82.

FREEDOM

New Testament

Noun: ἄφεσις (*aphesis*), GK *912* (S *859*), 17x. In contrast to the verb *aphiēmi* (see *forgive*), of the 17x that *aphesis* appears in the NT, it primarily carries the sense of "forgiveness" (15x). Only twice does *aphesis* denote a "release" or "freedom" from captivity (Lk. 4:18). See *forgiveness*.

Noun: ἐλευθερία (*eleutheria*), GK *1800* (S *1657*), 11x. *eleutheria* refers to "freedom, the state of being free." It describes the state of a person who is no longer enslaved by an oppressive force. The primary sense of freedom in the NT is freedom from the bondage of sin. Sin is a bondage into which we have been thrust by the fall, a bondage that affects the entire creation. So Paul describes the "glorious freedom" into which the creation itself is brought when it is liberated from the curse of sin (Rom. 8:21). In a similar fashion, James describes the law itself as something that gives freedom, as a person looks intently into the law and does it (Jas. 1:25). The law is liberating because those who follow it are freed from the bondage of sin. As a result, even the judgment of the law is a judgment that gives freedom (2:12).

The experience of freedom is not something we can bring to ourselves; rather, it is the work of the triune God. In order to possess freedom, Paul says, Christ has set us free (Gal. 5:1). Freedom is not to be found in the absence of God or his commands; rather, it exists where the Spirit of God is (2 Cor. 3:17). Those who think freedom can be found apart from God are deceived, for anyone who promises such freedom not only cannot provide it to others, but they do not even have freedom themselves (2 Pet. 2:19). In fact, Paul says, those who are not in Christ would prefer that believers be enslaved than to have freedom (Gal. 2:4). This is a result of the very purpose of freedom, which is not to be able to do "whatever one wants," but is in reality the freedom from the incapacitating effects of sin. True freedom is not for oneself or for one's own needs; rather, true freedom is the freedom to obey God and to serve others (1 Cor. 10:29; Gal. 5:13; 1 Pet. 2:16). See *NIDNTT-A*, 180-82.*

FRESH

See *new*.

FRIEND

Old Testament.

Noun: רֵעַ (*rēaʿ*), GK 8276 (S 7453), 188x. *rēaʿ* is primarily translated as "neighbor, other, friend." See *neighbor*.

New Testament

Noun and Adjective: φίλος (*philos*), GK *5813* (S *5384*), 29x. *philos* originally was an adjective meaning "dear" or valuable," but eventually became the standard noun for "friend" or "relative."

Leaders slander the name of the Lord by calling him "a glutton and a drunkard, a *friend* of tax collectors and sinners" (Mt. 11:19; Lk. 7:34). Jesus, however, did not hesitate to adopt that title. "Friends" can be distinct from family: "Then Jesus said to his host, 'When you give a luncheon or dinner, do not invite your *friends*, your brothers or relatives'" (Lk. 14:12). They can be separate from neighbors: "Then he calls his *friends* and neighbors together and says, 'Rejoice with me; I have found my lost sheep'" (Lk. 15:6). In speaking of the high cost of following him, Jesus speaks of betrayal by family and friends: "You will be betrayed even by parents, brothers, relatives and *friends*, and they will put some of you to death" (Lk. 21:16).

Jesus uses *philos* to describe the sacrificial aspects of friendship: "Greater love has no one than this, that he lay down his life for his *friends*" (Jn. 15:13). James uses this term to remind the people of the affection that God had for Abraham: "'Abraham believed God, and it was credited to him as righteousness,' and he was called God's *friend*" (Jas. 2:23).

philos is used to describe a disciple's passage from being an enemy of God to being his friend. A disciple comes to Jesus as a sinner, but because of Jesus' love he or she becomes his friend (Jn. 15:13). Not only do Jesus' followers becomes friends of Jesus (Lk. 12:4; Jn. 15:14–15) just like Abraham, but also friends with one another (3 Jn. 14).

When the object of friendship is bad, so is that friendship. "Anyone who chooses to be a *friend* of the world becomes an enemy of God" (Jas. 4:4). John uses *philos* in a technical sense in the shout of the Jewish leaders to Pilate: "If you let this man go, you are no *friend* of Caesar" (Jn. 19:12). It was the goal of every Roman political leader to become a "friend of Caesar," and this desired title is a powerful tool used by Jesus' enemies at his trial to make sure they get a conviction and the death sentence. See *NIDNTT-A*, 590-91.

Adjective: γνωστός (*gnōstos*), GK *1196* (S *1110*), 15x. *gnōstos* means "known" or "able to be know," i.e., "intelligible." "Known" people can be considered "friends." See *known*.

FRIGHT

New Testament

Noun: φόβος (*phobos*), GK *5832* (S *5401*), 47x. *phobos* in the NT can mean "fear, fright, alarm," but it can also describe a healthy awe and respect for God. See *fear*.

FROM ABOVE

New Testament

Adverb: ἄνωθεν (*anōthen*), GK *540* (S

509), 13x. *anōthen* can mean "from above" or "again."

(1) James uses this word to emphasize that "every good and perfect gift is from above," especially true wisdom, coming down to us from the Father (Jas. 1:18; 3:15, 17). We can only receive wisdom as a gift from God through his Spirit (cf. 1 Cor. 2:6–16).

(2) The most significant use of *anōthen* occurs in Jn. 3:3, 7, when Jesus tells Nicodemus that he must be "born again" (or does it mean "born from above"?). We really do not need to choose between these two options, for when we are born from above (i.e., born of the Spirit of God), we experience rebirth (i.e., we are born again). The ambiguity in the word beautifully covers both concepts. See *NIDNTT-A*, 56.

FRUIT

Old Testament

Noun: פְּרִי (*p*ᵉ*rî*), GK 7262 (S 6529), 119x. *p*ᵉ*rî* means "fruit, crops, produce." The literal meaning of this noun may refer to the produce of any crop-bearing plant (Gen. 1:11), including trees, vines, and grain (Deut. 7:13). Every tree has been created to yield its own "fruit with seed in it" (Gen. 1:11–12). *p*ᵉ*rî* is likewise used for the forbidden "fruit" that Adam and Eve eat in Gen. 3:2–3, 6. When the Israelites enter the promised land of Canaan, they can look forward to eating "the fruit of the land" (Deut. 1:25), and God will bless "the crops of your land" (7:13). Conversely, if they rebel against the Lord in that land, he will curse their "crops" (28:18).

*p*ᵉ*rî* also may refer to the offspring of animals or humans (Deut. 7:13, "the fruit of your womb"; 28:4. "the young of your livestock"). Interestingly, the word for "children" in Ps. 127:3 is "the fruit of the belly," which in context appears to refer to what comes from the father, not the mother (cf. also Mic. 6:7). Metaphorically, *p*ᵉ*rî* refers to the consequences of one's actions (Prov. 1:31; 31:16; Mic. 7:13). See *NIDOTTE*, 3:676–80.

New Testament

Noun: καρπός (*karpos*), GK *2843* (S *2590*), 66x. *karpos* refers to the natural product of something that is alive. In the literal sense, it is used of "fruit" born by trees (Mt. 12:33) or vines (21:41) and of "crops" of grain from the ground (Jn. 12:24). It is also used of the offspring of human beings (Lk. 1:42).

Metaphorically, *karpos* can refer to the natural product of a spiritual being, whether it be praise as the fruit of righteous lips (Heb. 13:15), converts as the results of ministry (Rom. 1:13), or "the *fruit* of the Spirit" (Gal. 5:22–23), which stands in contrast to the works of the sinful nature. Note that Paul does not refer to the "fruits" of the Spirit, but the "fruit," which suggests that all of the nine characteristics listed must be present in our lives as a homogeneous whole. Fruit is an organic metaphor; that is, the fruit must be growing in our lives, though it does take constant nourishment from Christ and his Word for this to occur. The Spirit is available to help his fruit ripen in our lives.

In a significant passage on discipleship, Jesus tells his disciples that those who do not bear fruit will be taken away to be burned, but those that do bear fruit will be pruned to produce even greater fruit. Disciples cannot bear fruit apart from abiding in Christ; good trees produce good fruit (Mt. 7:17). This is especially significant because God the Father is glorified by disciples bearing spiritual fruit and so proving to be his disciples (Jn. 15:2, 4, 8). Note too that just as a bad tree produces bad fruit (Mt. 7:16–20), so bad people produce bad results in their lives (Rom. 6:21–22). See *NIDNTT-A*, 289-290.

FULFILL

Old Testament

Verb: שָׁלֵם (*šālēm*), GK 8966 (S 7999), 116x. *šālēm* means "to repay, reward, fulfill, be at peace." It is used in a variety of contexts. See *repay*.

Verb: מָלֵא (*mālē*ʾ), GK 4848 (S 4390), 252x. *mālē*ʾ broadly means "to fill, be full, be fulfilled" and can carry either a spatial or temporal sense. Especially the temporal meaning designates something fulfilled. See *fill.*

New Testament

Verb: πίμπλημι (*pimplēmi*), GK *4398* (S *4130*), 24x. *pimplēmi* means "to fill, fulfill" and is used in literal and figurative ways. See *fill.*

Verb: πληρόω (*plēroō*), GK *4444* (S *4137*) 86x. Generally meaning "to fill, fulfill," *plēroō* is used both spatially and figuratively in the NT. See *fill.*

Most often in the NT, *plēroō* is used metaphorically, with reference to the fulfillment of the Scriptures and eschatological time.

(1) Throughout the Gospels and Acts, the OT is portrayed as finding its fulfillment in Jesus (Mt. 26:56; Lk. 24:44; Acts 13:27; Jn. 12:38). Similarly, Mark speaks of Jesus' initiating the eschatological age of Israel's kingdom expectations (Mk. 1:15).

Significantly, *plēroō* should not always be equated with direct prophetic fulfillment. In Mt. 3:15, for example, Jesus' baptism fulfills "all righteousness," but this is not to be understood in the context of prediction. Neither should Jesus' claim that he fulfills the Law and the Prophets (5:17) be understood in the limited sense of prediction and fulfillment. Rather, in eschatological contexts like these, *plēroō* is best regarded as portraying Jesus as the one to whom the entire OT points and the one for whom Israel longs (cf. Lk. 24:44).

(2) Paul considers love to be the fulfillment of the law (Gal. 5:14; cf. Rom. 13:8). He also speaks of fulfilling the preaching of Christ in the eastern part of the Roman empire (Rom. 15:19), which suggests that the apostle's mission was to help complete the work begun by Christ (cf. Col. 4:17). Similar to John's call to be filled with the joy of Jesus (Jn. 15:11; 16:16; 17:13), Paul also exhorts his audience to be filled with the fruit of righteousness and the Spirit (Eph. 5:18; Phil. 1:11). This "filling" is tied to the displacement of competing traits or realities (e.g., sorrow) that rival the centrality of Christ and all the benefits of one's union with him (e.g., joy, righteousness, the Spirit).

Verb: τελέω (*teleō*), GK *5464* (S *5055*), 28x. The basic meaning of *teleō* is "to finish, complete." *teleō* also refers to keeping or fulfilling the law (Rom. 2:27, see Jas. 2:8, NIV "keep the royal law").

Verb: τελειόω (*teleioō*), GK *5457* (S *5048*), 23x. *teleioō* sometimes refers to completing an activity, both in the sense of "to finish" (e.g., "After the Feast *was over*," Lk. 2:43) and "to accomplish, fulfill" (see Acts 20:24; also Jn. 4:34; 5:36; 17:4). See *end.*

FULFILLMENT

New Testament

Noun: πλήρωμα (*plērōma*), GK *4445* (S *4138*), 17x. *plērōma* describes that which fills, the fullness of something, or what is brought to completion. See *fullness.*

FULL

Old Testament

Adjective: מָלֵא (*mālēʾ*), GK 4849 (S 4392) 61x. *mālēʾ* generally means "full" and describes fullness of state or quality. The good corn in Joseph's dream is described as full (i.e., ripe) (Gen. 41:7), and when the Lord blesses his people, their barns will be full of all provisions (Ps. 144:13). When the Syrians flee before God, the road is full of the belongings they leave behind (2 Ki. 7:15). God promises his people through Ezekiel that the future holds a time when the cities ruined by the Babylonians will "be full of flocks of people."

New Testament

Adjective: πλήρης (*plērēs*), GK *4441* (S *4134*), 16x. *plērēs* means to be "full, filled," sometimes with the nuance of being complete. (1) *plērēs* describes something as being full. After the feeding of the five and four thousand, the baskets of leftovers were full (Mt. 14:20; 15:37). At the riot in Ephesus, the men of the city are described as "full of wrath" (Acts 19:28). John seeks for his audience to receive a "full reward" (2 Jn. 8). Jesus is "*full* of grace and truth" (Jn. 1:14). Some people are "*full* of leprosy" (Lk. 5:12), "*full* of good works" (Acts 9:36), and "*full* of every deceit and all villainy" (13:10).

(2) This word is often used with respect to the Holy Spirit. People are described as "*full* of the Holy Spirit"; this seems to designate an ongoing experience rather than a sudden burst of the Spirit's power (Luke uses the verb *pimplēmi* [see *fill*] to describe the sudden filling of the Spirit). Jesus returned from the Jordan after his baptism "*full* of the Holy Spirit" (Lk. 4:1). The church is directed to seek deacons who are "*full* of the Spirit and wisdom" (Acts 6:3). Stephen is "a man *full* of faith and the Holy Spirit" (6:5) and "*full* of grace and power" (6:8). As he dies, Stephen is "*full* of the Holy Spirit" (7:55). Barnabas, too, is described as "a good man and *full* of the Holy Spirit and faith" (11:24).

(3) *plērēs* is also used in the natural world to designate a completed growth cycle. After the first blade, then the ear, and finally comes "full" grain in the ear (Mk. 4:28). See *NIDNTT-A*, 469-71.

(TO BE) FULL

New Testament

Verb: γέμω (*gemō*), GK *1154* (S *1073*), 11x. *gemō* conveys the passive idea of being filled to capacity or overburdened and may best be translated as "full" or "covered." Well over half of its uses are in Revelation. John uses this term to describe several aspects in the throne room of God. Regarding the four winged creatures he writes, "In the center, around the throne, were four living creatures, and they were *covered* with eyes, in front and in back" (Rev. 4:6b, also v. 8a). In 5:8 he describes the filled capacity of golden bowls: "Each one had a harp and they were holding golden bowls *full* of incense, which are the prayers of the saints." Later on he sees "seven golden bowls *filled* with the wrath of God, who lives for ever and ever" (15:7; also 17:3–4; 21:9).

In other uses, Jesus accuses the Pharisees and teachers of the law with being filled with hypocrisy and charges, "You clean the outside of the cup and dish, but inside they are *full* of greed and self-indulgence" (Mt. 23:25b; Lk. 11:39; also Mt. 23:27). Paul quotes Ps. 10:7 in his discussion of sin as regards both Jew and Gentile: "Their mouths are *full* of cursing and bitterness" (Rom. 3:14). See *NIDNTT-A*, 104.*

FULLNESS

New Testament

Noun: πλήρωμα (*plērōma*), GK *4445* (S *4138*), 17x. *plērōma* describes that which fills, the fullness of something, or what is brought to completion.

(1) In several instances *plērōma* describe the absolute wholeness, the fullness, of the deity. Thus, we have all received grace upon grace from the fullness of Jesus (Jn. 1:16). In Christ, God was "pleased to have all his *fullness* dwell" (Col. 1:19); indeed, "in him all the *fullness* of the Deity lives in bodily form" (2:9). Knowing Christ is, for Paul, for the purpose of being filled to "all the *fullness* of God" (Eph. 3:19). This is the goal of the discipling ministry of the church, that people might become mature, "attaining to the whole measure of the *fullness* of Christ" (4:13).

(2) Occasionally *plērōma* communicates the completion of a specified amount, such as the "fullness" of the Jews (Rom. 11:12) and the "fullness" of the Gentiles (11:25). Along these lines is the completion of the ordained amount of time before the coming of the Messiah, so that "when the time had *fully* come, God sent forth his Son" (Gal. 4:4). There seems to be an already/not yet aspect to this "fullness of time," for on the one hand the "fullness of time" has been reached at the coming of Messiah into the world, but on the other hand the "fullness of time" in Eph. 1:10 points to the consummation of all things.

(3) *plērōma* can have figurative uses. For example, it can denote that which sums up something, as in Rom. 13:10, where Paul writes that "love is the *fulfillment* of the law." Another such reference is to the

church as Christ's body, "the *fullness* of him who fills everything in every way" (Eph. 1:23).

(4) *plērōma* can also be synonymous with the adjective *plērēs* (see *full*) and mean something like "full, whole," as when the baskets of leftovers are described as "full" (Mk. 6:43). Similarly, Paul states that he expects to come to the Romans "in the *full measure* of the blessing of Christ" (Rom. 15:29). The fullness of the earth belongs to the Lord (1 Cor. 10:26, taken from Ps. 24:1). See *NIDNTT-A*, 469-471.

FURNISHING

Old Testament

Noun: כְּלִי (*kᵉlî*), GK 3998 (S 3627), 325x. *kᵉlî* is a noun denoting a variety of equipment, tools, containers, etc., used in a given activity or occupation. The use of this noun to refer to such a large number of different objects is comparable to the English noun "thing." See *thing*.

FURY

Old Testament

Noun: אַף (*ʾap*), GK 678 (S 639), 277x. The noun *ʾap* literally means "nose" or, in the plural, "face" or "nostrils" (see *nose*), though it is often used figuratively for "anger, fury" (see *anger*).

Noun: חֵמָה (*hēmâ*), GK 2779 (S 2534), 125x. The basic meaning of *hēma* is "anger, wrath." Its most common use describes the fury or rage of people or of God. See *anger*.

New Testament

Noun: θυμός (*thymos*), GK *2596* (S *2372*), 18x. *thymos* is generally used to refer to "anger, rage, fury." See *wrath*.

FUTILE

New Testament

Adjective: κενός (*kenos*), GK *3031* (S *2756*), 18x. *kenos* means "empty, empty-handed," and by extension, "vain, useless, futile." See *empty*.

FUTILITY

Old Testament

Noun: הֶבֶל (*hebel*), GK 2039 (S 1892), 73x. *hebel* literally means "breath," but in the OT it occurs only 3x with this sense (see *breath*). The word occurs 38x in Ecclesiastes alone (including at least once in each of the twelve chapters except ch. 10), where it usually denotes the meaninglessness or futility of life. See *vanity*.

Noun/Adverb: שָׁוְא (*sawʾ*), GK 8736 (S 7723), 54x. *sawʾ* denotes ineffectiveness or falseness and may be translated as "vain, worthless, false." The term describes the futility of certain things or activities. See *worthless*.

GAIN

New Testament

Verb: κερδαίνω (*kerdainō*), GK *3045* (S *2770*), 17x. This verb denotes the activity of gaining, profiting, or winning and is best translated "win, gain." See *win*.

Verb: ὠφελέω (*ōpheleō*), GK *6067* (S *5623*), 15x. *ōpheleō* denotes the basic idea of benefiting through a particular condition or situation, hence, "to gain, profit, value." See *gain*.

GAINSAY

See *speak against*.

GARMENT

Old Testament

Noun: בֶּגֶד (*beged*), GK 955 (S 899), 216x. *beged* is a general term for "clothing, garments" of any kind. See *clothing*.

New Testament

Noun: ἱμάτιον (*himation*), GK *2668* (S *2440*), 60x. *himation* is sometimes used of "clothing" in general, but more frequently of the outer "robe" or "cloak." See *clothes*.

Noun: χιτών (*chitōn*), GK *5945* (S *5509*), 11x. *chitōn* means "garment, tunic." It was the article of clothing worn next to the skin by both men and women. Jewish law allowed a person to sue for another's tunic (cf. Mt. 5:40), but not the outer garment, which was required to keep a person warm on cold nights.

All except one use of this noun (in Jude 23) occur in the narrative literature of the NT. When Jesus sends out the twelve, they are not to take an extra "tunic" along (Mt. 10:10; Mk. 6:9; Lk. 6:29; 9:3). During the trial of Jesus, the high priest tears his "garments" when he thinks Jesus is blaspheming (Mt. 14:63). The soldiers at Jesus crucifixion cast lots for Jesus "garments" (Jn. 19:23). Dorcas, whom Peter raises from the dead, had sewn "tunics" and other clothes for needy people (Acts 9:39).

GARNISH

See *adorn.*

GATE

Old Testament

Noun: דֶּלֶת (*delet*), GK 1946 (S 1817), 88x. *delet* usually means "door." Only occasionally does it refer to the "gate" of a city (Deut. 3:5; 2 Chr. 8:5; Ps. 107:16). See *door*.

Noun: שַׁעַר (*šaʿar*), GK 9133 (S 8179), 373x. The *šaʿar* often denotes a "gate" used to control access to a walled city. Depending on its size, a city could have more than one gate. The gates were made of wood and sometimes reinforced by a metal covering and iron bars (Neh. 3:3; Ps. 107:16; Isa. 45:2). This was the strategic center of an ancient city; once the gates were broken down, the city lost its key defenses. In Deuteronomy "to live in your town" is (lit.) "to live in your gates" (e.g., Deut. 14:21, 27–29; 15:7, 22). Thus, when Samson carries away the gates of Gaza, he is leaving the city defenseless (Jdg. 16:2–3); the rest of a city's defenses are then useless (cf. Isa. 24:12).

The city gate held an important social and administrative role in the culture of ancient cities. Prov. 31:23 refers to the city gate as a place where the respected elders congregate; 1 Ki. 22:10 records the kings of Israel and Judah sitting on their thrones at the gate of Samaria. Deut. 21:19 notes that justice was dispensed at the city gate (see also Prov. 22:22; Amos 5:15). Boaz transacted his legal business for purchase the property of Naomi in the town gate (Ruth 4:1, 10–11). Furthermore, prophets often addressed the people of a given city at the gate (2 Ki. 7:1; Jer. 17:19–20).

Also important are the gates of the temple. The psalmist invites people to "enter his *gates* with thanksgiving and his courts with praise." The Lord loves "the *gates* of Zion" (87:2), and these gates are invited to lift up their heads in order to welcome the King of glory (24:7, 9). In Ps. 118:19–20, which was presumably sung as the Israelites ascended the Temple Mount on one of the feast days, these gates are called "the gates of righteousness." When entering through these gates, God's people gain access to him.

Finally, *šaʿar* is sometimes used metaphorically to speak of death. When one dies, he passes through "the gates of death/Sheol" (Ps. 107:18; Isa. 38:10). See *NIDOTTE*, 4:208–11.

New Testament

Noun: πύλη (*pylē*), GK *4783* (S *4439*), 10x. *pylē* means "gate, door." The term usually refers to the gate of a city, temple, or prison. In the literal sense, *pylē* in the NT refers to a city gate (Lk. 7:12, Acts 9:24; 16:13), the Jerusalem gate outside of which Jesus suffered (Heb. 13:12), a temple gate (Acts 3:10), and a prison gate (12:10).

Matthew uses *pylē* in two significant passages. In Mt. 7:13–14, Jesus encourages his followers not to take the easy way in order to find true life, but to enter through "the narrow gate," for that is the one that leads to life. In 16:18 Jesus refers to the "gates of Hades," reflecting the common ancient idea that the underworld was secured by strong gates that prevented either escape or assault by outsiders. In this verse Jesus is assuring his followers that the church will never succumb to Hades; that is, it will never die out. See *NIDNTT-A*, 505.

Noun: πυλών (*pylōn*), GK *4784* (S *4440*), 18x. *pylōn* means "gate, door." The term usually refers to the gateway of a city (Acts 14:13) or a house (Mt. 26:71; Lk. 16:20; Acts 10:17; 12:13–14). It is especially prominent in the description of the gates of the new Jerusalem (Rev. 21:12–13, 21, 25; 22:14). See *NIDNTT-A*, 505.*

GATHER

Old Testament

Verb: אָסַף (*ʾāsap*), GK 665 (S 622),

200x. In varying contexts, *ʾāsap* can mean "to gather, assemble, take away, or bring up the rear."

Sometimes *ʾāsap* means to gather things or people. It often refers to the careful process of reaping the harvest, as when Ruth asks for permission to collect the leftover grain after the reapers had garnered the fields (Ruth 2:7; see also Exod. 23:10, 16; Isa. 17:5). Similarly, *ʾāsap* can refer to the collection and storage of food, which is what God commands Noah to do before the flood (Gen. 6:21). People are also gathered (Gen. 29:22; 42:17; Jos. 2:18). The king of Assyria thinks he will gather up all the earth as a man gathers abandoned eggs (Isa. 10:14).

When *ʾāsap* is used reflexively, it means "to assemble." Both humans (Gen. 49:1; Ezr. 3:1; 9:4) and animals (Gen. 29:3; Num. 11:22) gather themselves together. In this light, *ʾāsap* can be used to refer to death and burial: "gathered to one's people" (Gen. 25:17; 35:29), "gathered to their fathers" (Jdg. 2:10), "gathered to one's grave" (2 Chr. 34:28), and simply "gathered" (Num. 20:26). See also *remove, rear guard.*

Verb: קָבַץ (*qābaṣ*), GK 7695 (S 6908), 127x. The verb *qābaṣ* means "to gather, assemble" and can denote the gathering of any of a number of items. For example, humans gather grain (Gen. 41:35, 48), plunder (Deut. 13:16), and money (2 Chr. 24:5). People often gather themselves together (i.e., assemble) for a common cause such as war (1 Sam. 7:5; 28:4; 29:1; Jos. 10:6) or a religious ceremony (1 Ki. 18:19, 20; 2 Ki. 10:18; Joel 2:16).

qābaṣ is used to describe God's gathering of people or nations. Most of the occurrences deal with his gathering of his people Israel back to the land from which they were taken (Deut. 30:3–4; Isa. 43:5; 54:7; 56:8; Jer. 31:8, 10; Mic. 2:12; 4:6). Isaiah compares this process to a shepherd who gathers his lambs to gently carry and lead them (Isa. 40:11). However, God will also gather the nations to witness Israel's temporary judgment (Ezek. 16:37) and to experience their own permanent judgment (Isa. 66:18; Joel 4:2). Though the nations think they are assembling to defile Zion, God is actually gathering them as sheaves to the threshing floor. He will then empower "the daughter of Zion" to beat the nations into many pieces and to take all their wealth for God (Mic. 4:12; cf. vv. 11, 13). See *NIDOTTE* 3:862-65.

New Testament

Verb: συνάγω (*synagō*), GK *5251* (S *4863*), 59x. *synagō* has the basic meaning "to gather together." It is often used in agricultural contexts of harvesting or gathering crops (e.g., Mt. 3:12; 13:30; 25:24; Lk. 12:17–18) and can also refer to the gathering of fish in nets (Mt. 13:47). Since harvesting is a biblical metaphor for mission work, this word is also used in that connection (Jn. 4:36). The word can also describe the gathering of crowds around Jesus (e.g., Mt. 13:2; Mk. 4:1). In Mt. 18:20 if two or three "gather together" in Jesus' name (presumably to confront a sinning brother), Jesus promises to be in their midst.

The word is used in Acts for the gathering of the early Christian communities (e.g., Acts 4:31; 11:26; 14:27; 15:30; 20:7–8; cf. 1 Cor. 5:4). God's new people "gather" just as his people Israel "gathered" in assembly (e.g., Num. 1:18; 8:9 in the LXX). The word "synagogue" used throughout the NT to describe Jewish places of meeting is a noun closely related to the verb "to gather" (cf. Mt. 4:23; Lk. 4:15–16).

synagō is also sometimes used in the context of end-time events. It describes both the gathering of armies for the climactic final battle (Rev. 16:14, 16; 19:19; 20.8). It is also used of God's "harvesting" of people at the end of time and separating believers from unbelievers (Mt. 3:12; 25:32). See *NIDNTT-A*, 543-44.

Verb: συνέρχομαι (*synerchomai*), GK *5302* (S *4905*), 30x. *synerchomai* means "to assemble, come together, gather." See *assemble.*

GAZE

Old Testament

Verb: חָזָה (*ḥāzâ*), GK 2600 (S 2372), 68x. *ḥāzâ* means "to see, observe, gaze"; it is a broad word, having a variety of nuances. See *see*.

New Testament

Verb: ἀτενίζω (*atenizō*), GK *867* (S *816*), 14x. *atenizō* means "to look with intensity, stare, gaze." See *look straight*.

GENERATION

Old Testament

Noun: דּוֹר (*dôr*), GK 1887 (S 1755), 167x. *dôr* signifies a "generation" of people and is widely used throughout the OT. For the most part, a generation is considered to be about forty years. The whole point of God's having the Israelites wander in the desert for forty years is so that "the whole generation" that had rebelled against the Lord would die in the desert (Num. 32:13; cf. Ps. 78:8).

dôr is often used in pairs (74x); for example, after God declares to Moses that he is "I AM WHO I AM" (Exod. 3:14), he adds, "This is my name to be remembered from generation to generation" (3:15). This expression denotes an unending period of time. When used in the plural, the expression "your generations" means "for generations to come," which likewise speaks of the indefinite future (37x; e.g., Lev. 23:14, 21, 31).

Isa. 51 gives a good example of how *dôr* may be used with regard to the future or to the past. Through his exhortation of the remnant who "pursue righteousness" (Isa. 51:1), God looks to the future and declares, "But my righteousness will last forever, my salvation through all generations" (lit., "to generations of generations," Isa. 51:8; cf. 60:15). The next verse looks to the past with the expressions "generations of old" (51:9).

It is not necessary for God to make a new covenant with each generation. In fact, when God makes a covenant, he makes one that spans generations: to Noah (Gen. 9:12), to Abraham (17:7, 9); to Israel (Deut. 7:9), and to David (Ps. 89:4). It is probably for this reason that God expects parents to pass on the faith from one generation to the next—a responsibility that has never ceased for God's people. Ps. 71 shows us a person who has been brought up in the Lord. His love for the Lord is such that he pleads with God, "Even when I am old and gray, do not forsake me, O God, till I declare your power to the next generation, your might to all who are to come" (71:18; cf. 78:1–6). In a later psalm, David says of God's great love and mighty works: "One generation will commend your works to another; they will tell of your mighty acts. They will speak of the glorious splendor of your majesty, and I will meditate on your wonderful works" (145:4–5).

New Testament

Noun: γενεά (*genea*), GK *1155* (S *1074*), 43x. *genea* in a general sense denotes one's own kind. It is used of a "race" of people, those living at the same time ("generation"), or the time in which a generation lives ("age"; Acts 14:6; 15:21).

Matthew uses *genea* to describe the successive members of a particular family or genealogy (Mt. 1:17). Mary glorifies God for being favorable toward her: "For he has been mindful of the humble state of his servant. From now on all *generations* will call me blessed" (Lk. 1:48). The apostle Paul declares that God had revealed the "mystery of Christ, which was not made known to men in other *generations* as it has now been revealed by the Spirit to God's holy apostles and prophets" (Eph. 3:4–5).

However, many times when *genea* is used, it is done so with a sense of disgust and contempt. Jesus asks, "To what can I compare to this *generation*?" (Mt. 11:16). When the Pharisees and teachers ask Jesus for a miracle for them, he responds, "A wicked and perverse *generation* asks for a miraculous sign!" (Mt. 12:39). In the same breath, Jesus declares, "The men of Nineveh will stand up at the judgment with this *generation* and condemn it, for they repented at the preaching of Jonah, and now one greater than Jonah is here" (Mt. 12:41). The generation to whom Jesus was referring would later be called wicked (Mt. 12:45), perverse (17:17), sinful (Mk. 8:39), and unbelieving (9:19). Such was his rebuke that Jesus declared, "Therefore this *generation* will be held responsible for the blood of all the prophets that has been shed since the beginning of the world" (Lk. 11:50).

Because of the flexibility of the word's meaning, Mt. 24:34 becomes a difficult passage to interpret. "Truly, I say to you, this *generation* will not pass away until all these things take place." It can be referring to the generation of those living at the time when "these things" begin to take place, or it can refer to the Jewish nation.

Later usage is somewhat limited in the NT. We see Peter boldly preaching a message of repentance and pleading with the people, "Save yourselves from this corrupt *generation*" (Acts 2:40). Paul exhorts the church in Philippi to "do everything without complaining or arguing, so that you may become blameless and pure, children of God without fault in a crooked and depraved *generation*, in which you shine like stars in the universe" (Phil. 2:14–15). See *NIDNTT-A*, 104-5.

GENTILE

Old Testament

Noun: גּוֹי (*gôy*), GK 1580 (S 1471), 567x. *gôy* is commonly understood as "nation" (e.g., Egypt, Exod. 9:24). In the Exodus God promises to make the Hebrews a great nation (Exod. 32:10). But *gôy* does not always refer to a political kingdom; it can refer more generally to groups of people (non-Jews), thus meaning "Gentiles" or in some contexts "pagans" (with their gods, Isa. 37:12). See *nation*.

New Testament

Noun: ἔθνος (*ethnos*), GK *1620* (S *1484*), 162x. *ethnos* appears in the NT with two meanings, "nation" and "Gentile." In the latter sense, it refers specifically to all non-Jews, that is, to people groups foreign to Israel—specifically those groups that do not profess faith in the God of Israel (Mt. 10:18; Acts 11:1; 14:5). By extension, *ethnos* also sometimes refer to non-Israelite Christians. In this sense Paul writes, "Not only I but all the churches of the *Gentiles* are grateful to them" (Rom. 16:4). Paul is outraged by Peter's refusal to eat with such Gentile brothers: "Before certain men came from James, he used to eat with the Gentiles" (Gal. 2:12; cf. Eph. 3:1). See also *nations*. See *NIDNTT-A*, 161-62.

GENTLENESS

New Testament

Noun: πραΰτης (*prautēs*), GK *4559* (S *4240*), 11x. *prautēs* means "gentleness, humility." Gentleness is first of all a notable characteristic of Jesus (2 Cor. 10:1); twice in Matthew Jesus is called "gentle" (using the corresponding adjective *praus*; see Mt. 11:29; 21:5). Gentleness means to approach others (including one's enemies) in a humble and caring spirit, not using force to get one's way. Gentleness is something that should characterize Christians (Eph. 4:2; Col. 3:12; 1 Pet. 3:15). It is included as one of the nine aspects of the fruit of the Spirit in our lives (Gal. 5:23) and is part of how wisdom from above goes to work in our lives (Jas. 3:13). See *NIDNTT-A*, 487–88.

GET

Old Testament

Verb: לָקַח (*lāqaḥ*), GK 4374 (S 3947), 967x. The basic meaning of *lāqaḥ* is "to take, grasp." The meaning is often simply to "take into/by the hand." *lāqaḥ* is also used to describe taking something as one's own possession. See *take*.

Verb: נָחַל (*nāḥal*), GK 5706 (S 5157), 59x. In addition to meaning "to inherit," *nāḥal* can be translated as "to possess, take possession, get." See *inherit*.

New Testament

Verb: κερδαίνω (*kerdainō*), GK *3045* (S *2770*), 17x. This verb denotes the activity of gaining, profiting, or winning and is best translated "win, gain." See *win*.

Verb: λαμβάνω (*lambanō*), GK *3284* (S *2983*), 258x. *lambanō* conveys the basic idea of acquiring or obtaining something and may best be translated as "take, seize, receive, get." See *take.*

GET BACK

New Testament

Verb: ἀπολαμβάνω (*apolambanō*), GK *655* (S *618*), 10x. *apolambanō* means "to receive, get back, be repaid," generally from another individual. See *receive.*

GET INTO (A BOAT)

New Testament

Verb: ἐμβαίνω (*embainō*), GK *1832* (S *1684*), 16x. *embainō* means "to get into." In the NT, it is used only of getting or stepping into a boat. Jesus and his disciples used boats for transportation (Mt. 8:23; 9:1; 14:22; 15:39; Mk. 5:18; 6:45; 8:10, 13; Lk. 8:22; 8:37; Jn. 6:17), teaching (Mt. 13:2; Mk. 4:1; Lk. 5:3), and fishing (Jn. 21:3). On one occasion a crowd "got into" some boats to search for Jesus (Jn. 6:24).*

GET UP

Old Testament

Verb: קוּם (*qûm*), GK 7756 (S 6965), 627x. The general range of meanings for *qûm* includes "to stand up, arise, get up (in the morning)." It can also mean "to raise up, confirm something, establish." See *rise.*

New Testament

Verb: ἀνίστημι (*anistēmi*), GK *482* (S *450*), 108x. *anistēmi* depicts someone getting up from a reclined position, "to stand up, get up," including being raising from the dead. It occurs most frequently in the Gospels and Acts. It can be used simply to denote the act of getting up from a seated or reclined position, such as when Jesus calls Matthew, "and Matthew *got up* and followed him" (Mt. 9:9; cf. Mk. 1:35; 14:57, 60; Lk. 4:16; 11:7). In Lk. 5:25, Jesus heals the crippled man: "Immediately he *stood up* in front of them, took what he had been lying on and went home praising God." It is also used of "raising up children" for a dead brother in the sense of "to cause to be born" (Mt. 22:24), and also can be used in the sense of "to appear" or "to come." In Mt. 12:41, "the men of Nineveh will *rise up* at the judgment with this generation and condemn it." An enemy "rises up" against someone in Mk. 3:26; Acts 5:36; 6:9.

anistēmi is also used of one who is raised from the dead. In Mk. 5:42 Jesus heals the daughter of Jairus; "immediately the girl *stood up* and walked around." In the account of the rich man and Lazarus, Abraham says, "If they do not listen to Moses and the Prophets, they will not be convinced even if someone *rises* from the dead."

anistēmi is used in relation to the NT doctrine of the resurrection of the dead ("the dead are *raised up*"). In the Gospels, Jesus announces his resurrection to the disciples in Mk. 8:31: "He then began to teach them that the Son of Man ... must be killed and after three days *rise again*" (see also 9:9, 10, 31; 10:34). In Lk. 24:46, Jesus recalls that the OT Scriptures teach about the death and the resurrection of the Messiah, that God would "raise up" Jesus Christ. John records Jesus' promise that those who belong to him will be "*raised up* on the last day" (Jn. 6:39, 40, 44, 54). See *NIDNTT-A*, 48-49.

GIFT

Old Testament

Noun: בְּרָכָה (b^e*rākâ*), GK 1388, (S 1293), 71x. b^e*rākâ*, usually translated "blessing," denotes the pronouncement of good things on the recipient or the collection of those good things themselves. The NIV also translates b^e*rākâ* as "gift" (1 Sam. 25:27; 2 Ki. 5:15; 18:17; 20:20) or "present" (30:26). See *bless, blessing.*

Noun: מִנְחָה (*minḥâ*), GK 4966 (S 4503), 211x. The basic idea conveyed by this word is "gift." *minḥâ* can designate an offering in general or, more specifically, a "grain offering." See *grain offering.*

Noun: קָרְבָּן (*qorbān*), GK 7933 (S 7133), 80x. *qorbān* means "offering, gift"; it is one of the most general terms for an offering to the Lord in the OT. See *offering.*

Noun: תְּרוּמָה (t^e*rûmâ*), GK 9556 (S 8641), 76x. t^e*rûmâ* can be translated as "offering, portion, gift, contribution." See *offering*.

New Testament

Noun: δωρεά (*dōrea*), GK *1561* (S *1431*), 11x. *dōrea* conveys the idea of a "gift" or present that is unwarranted and received without merit. Paul brings emphasis to the unmerited aspect of salvation by writing, "For if the many died by the trespass of the one man, how much more did God's grace and the *gift* that came by the grace of the one man, Jesus Christ, overflow to the many!" (Rom. 5:15; cf. "*gift* of righteousness" in v. 17). In Eph. 3:4, Paul refers to his own reception of God's gift in Christ: "I became a servant of this gospel by the *gift* of God's grace given me through the working of his power" (cf. 4:7). When Jesus is talking with the Samaritan woman at the well, he offers himself to her as "the gift of God," the living water that keeps on giving (Jn. 4:10).

dōrea also refers to what is given as a result of salvation through the work of the Holy Spirit. Peter declares, "Repent and be baptized, every one of you, in the name of Jesus Christ for the forgiveness of your sins. And you will receive the *gift* of the Holy Spirit" (Acts 2:38; 8:20; 10:45; 11:17; cf. Heb. 6:4). Unmerited gifts from God should evoke the greatest response of gratitude in the hearts of those who receive them: "Thanks be to God for his indescribable *gift*" (2 Cor. 9:15). See *NIDNTT-A*, 157.*

Noun: δῶρον (*dōron*), GK *1565* (S *1435*), 19x. *dōron* basically means a "gift" or "present"; most frequently it denotes an "offering" to God (Mt. 5:23–24; 23:18–19[2x]; Heb. 5:1; 8:3–4; 9:9; 11:4) or the temple (Lk. 21:1, 4). It is most commonly linked with *prospherō* (see *bring*) as its direct object, and this construction likely infers the OT sacrificial system (see also *sacrifice*, *thyō*). In Jewish society such gifts were usually given through the priesthood (Heb. 5:1; 8:3–4). Although a *dōron* was offered to God, Jesus questioned its sincerity and integrity when it is offered with a wrong motive or at the expense of proper obedience (Mt. 15:5).

A *dōron* can also be a gift between people—once used as an expression of mutual celebration (Rev. 11:10) and once as an expression of honor (Mt. 2:11b, speaking of the Magi at their meeting with the infant Jesus).

Perhaps the most important occurrence of *dōron* is in Eph. 2:8: "For it is by grace you have been saved, through faith—and this is not from yourselves, it is the *gift* of God." Clearly, the context of this verse shows that this *dōron* from God—our salvation—is unearned and undeserved, in order that God alone might receive the glory and praise (Eph. 1:4–14). See *NIDNTT-A*, 157.

Noun: ἐλεημοσύνη (*eleēmosynē*), GK *1797* (S *1654*), 13x. Generally, *eleēmosynē* indicates either (1) the act of giving to the needy or poor (Mt. 6:2, 3, 4; Lk. 11:41; Acts 9:36; 10:2), or (2) the actual gifts or alms (Acts 3:2, 3, 10; 10:4). *eleēmosynē* is closely related to *eleos* (see *mercy*) in that it represents a gift of mercy or compassion. Typically, the KJV translates *eleēmosynē* as "alms" or "almsdeeds," whereas the NIV translates the word according to its context (e.g., Acts 3:10, "the same man who used to sit *begging* at the temple gate called Beautiful"). In most instances, this word occurs in the plural.

eleēmosynē is mostly used to demonstrate that concern for the welfare of others in need should be a characteristic of Christ's followers (cf. Mt. 25:34–46; Gal. 1:10). In the Sermon on the Mount Jesus instructs his followers how they should offer their gifts for the needy (Mt. 6:2–4)—a sharp contrast to the self-serving hypocrisy of the Pharisees. See *NIDNTT-A*, 179-80.*

Noun: εὐλογία (*eulogia*), GK *2330* (S *2129*), 16x. In its most general sense, *eulogia* means "speaking well." The word is especially used for the blessings God bestows on others as well as the blessings and praise he receives. See *blessing*.

Noun: χάρισμα (*charisma*), GK *5922*

(S *5486*), 17x. *charisma* means "gift, spiritual endowment." It refers to that which is freely and graciously given by God regardless of its kind, physical or spiritual. Paul views deliverance from mortal danger a *charisma* in 2 Cor. 1:11. In Rom. 1:11, Paul hopes to share words of hope and comfort with the Romans. *charisma* is equated with eternal life or redemption in 5:15–16; 6:23. God's "gifts" can never be revoked (11:29).

All but one occurrence of *charisma* appear in Paul's letters, 1 Pet. 4:10 being the only non-Pauline reference. But that verse matches thematically with Paul's use of the word in Rom. 12 and 1 Cor. 12—namely, *spiritual gifts* provided by God's generosity on certain individuals, intended to benefit others. A sample list of such gifts is given in Rom. 12:5–8 and 1 Cor. 12:7–11, 28–31. Timothy received a *charisma* by the laying on of hands and is exhorted to fulfill zealously his God-given duties (1 Tim. 4:14; 2 Tim. 1:6). Paul even attributes his ability to maintain a celibate life as a charismatic endowment (1 Cor. 7:7). See *NIDNTT-A*, 601-4.*

GIRL

Old Testament

Noun: בַּת (*bat*), GK 1426 (S 1323), 587x. *bat* is the common Hebrew noun for one's own daughter (e.g., Gen. 24:24; 29:10; Exod. 21:7; Deut. 16:14; Jos. 15:16; 2 Sam. 6:16). But it has a variety of other nuances, including girl, granddaughter, and even woman. See *daughter*.

Noun: נַעֲרָה (*na*ᶜ*ᵃrâ*), GK 5855 (S 5291), 76x. *na*ᶜ*ᵃrâ* denotes a "girl" from infancy to adolescence. It is most commonly translated "young girl" and typically describes a girl who has come of age to be married but is not married (2 Ki. 5:2). "Now bands from Aram had gone out and had taken captive a young girl from Israel" (2 Ki. 5:2). The emphasis seems to be on the youth and vitality of the girl. Frequently, the word does have the nuance of "servant girl" or "maid" (Gen. 24:61; Exod. 2:5; Ruth 3:2).

While this is the most common rendering of the word, it is not the only usage. As a young widow, Ruth is also called by this designation: "Through the offspring the Lord gives you by this young woman, may your family be like that of Perez whom Tabor bore to Judah" (Ruth 4:12). Even more unusual, the Levite's concubine is called a *na*ᶜ*ᵃrâ* (Jdg. 19:3), as is the woman whom Amos mentions. "Father and son use the same girl and so profane my holy name" (Amos 2:7). Virginity was not requisite for such a designation, but many such girls maintained their virginity until they were married (Gen. 24:14; Jdg. 21:12; Est. 2:2), or they suffered terrible consequences such as death by stoning (Deut. 22:24; cf. 22:15–29, where the word occurs 14x). See *NIDOTTE*, 3:125–27.

New Testament

Noun: παιδίσκη (*paidiskē*), GK *4087* (S *3814*), 13x. *paidiskē* is the diminutive form of the word for "girl," used in the NT always for a "servant girl." See *servant girl*.

GIVE

Old Testament

Verb: נָתַן (*nātan*), GK 5989 (S 5414), 2014x. *nātan* is a high frequency verb in the OT and bears a wide range of meanings, some of which are "to give, present, allow, permit, surrender, deliver, set, put, place."

nātan can communicate the action of "giving." The giver may be a person, an inanimate object (land and trees "yield" fruit), or God. God "sends" the plagues (Exod. 9:23); he "gives" the rain (Lev. 26:4; Deut. 11:14), grass for cattle (Deut. 11:15), and life (Jer. 45:5). The verb may express the physical handing over of a present, reward, or person (e.g., wives for the Benjamites, Jdg. 21:22; the restitution required by the guilt offering, Lev. 5:16).It may also be used of the less tangible act of "giving," "granting," or "bestowing" a blessing, as in Gen. 28:4. See also *set*, *make*.

New Testament

Verb: δίδωμι (*didōmi*), GK *1443* (S *1325*), 415x. This common verb conveys the basic idea of a transaction or transferring an object and is usually translated "give, grant, yield, permit."

Most of the uses of this verb simply denote some transaction of giving, especially in the narrative portions of the Bible. In the Sermon on the Mount, for example, Jesus instructs his disciples to "give to the one who asks" (Mt. 5:42) and to "ask and it will be given to you" (7:7); its most familiar use is probably the fourth petition of the Lord's Prayer, "Give us today our daily bread" (6:11).

Theologically, John describes the supreme divine transaction in Jn. 3:16: "For God so loved the world that he *gave* his one and only Son, that whoever believes in him shall not perish but have eternal life." Jesus is an active participant here, for he "gave" his life for us on the cross (Gal. 1:4; 1 Tim. 2:6; Tit. 2:14). Not only has God given us his Son, but he has also given us his Spirit (Rom. 5:5; 2 Cor. 1:22; 5:5; Eph. 1:17), including the Spirit's gifts (Rom. 12:6; 1 Cor. 12:7). In terms of spiritual blessings, the apostles never tire of mentioning how God has given us his grace (Rom. 12:3; 1 Cor. 1:4; 3:10; 2 Tim. 1:9) and eternal life (Jn. 10:28–29; 1 Jn. 5:11). Close to 90 percent of uses of *didōmi* in the NT letters have God as their subject; thus, Christianity is a religion of receiving gifts from God that we cannot earn ourselves. In response, God wants us to give ourselves to him in love and service (cf. 2 Cor. 8:5). We should note too that the time will come when we have to "give" account of our lives to God (Rom. 14:12).

In a context of prayer, the believers in Jerusalem ask God to grant Peter and John special power and boldness in the proclamation of the Gospel, "Now, Lord, consider their threats and *enable* your servants to speak your word with great boldness" (Acts 4:29). In his parable of the sower, Jesus describes the fruit producing qualities of the word of God in terms of the yielding or *giving* of seed and writes, "Still other seed fell on good soil. It came up, grew and *produced* a crop, multiplying thirty, sixty, or even a hundred times" (Mk. 4:8; cf. v. 7). May our lives be those of yielding fruit to God up to a hundredfold. See *NIDNTT-A*, 157.

Verb: χαρίζομαι (*charizomai*), GK *5919* (S *5483*), 23x. *charizomai* means "to give, forgive." It is related to the noun *charis* ("grace"; GK 5921). While in Acts 25:11, 16 this verb means simply handing someone over to the authorities (Acts 25:11, 16), for the most part *charizomai* refers to the giving of a gift that is unattainable, unrequested, or even undeserved. Jesus, for example, "gives" sight to the blind (Lk. 7:21), Pilate gives the prisoner Barabbas freedom (Acts 3:14), and God gives his promised inheritance to Abraham (Gal. 3:18). In many instances the gift are much more than could ever be expected. God "freely gives" believers the Spirit along with his gifts (1 Cor. 2:8). In addition to the gift of salvation, God "graciously *gives* to us all things" (Rom. 8:32).

charizomai can also mean "to forgive." On these occasions it appears in the context of debt—whether monetary debt (Lk. 7:42–43), the sin of offending a person (2 Cor. 2:7, 10), or the debt of transgression against God (Col. 2:13; 3:13). The idea conveyed in these contexts is that the one to whom the debt is owed "gives" the cancellation of the debt, so that it is "forgiven." The recipient does not earn that gracious gift. Paul urges Christians to "forgive" one another, both because of "tenderheartedness" and because of what God has done for us in Jesus Christ (Eph. 4:31–32). God is motivated to "give" gracious gifts only by his own gracious desires and not by a third party (Acts 27:24; Rom. 8:32; 1 Cor. 2:12; Phil. 1:29).

On only one occasion can it be argued that someone has actually earned from God a gift: God "gave" (*charizomai*) to Jesus "the name that is above every name" because Jesus was obedient to his death on the cross (Phil. 2:8–9). How great is Jesus, the Lord of glory, and how gracious is the Father for freely canceling our debts and giving us all things in Christ! See *NIDNTT-A*, 601-4.

GIVE (BACK)

New Testament

Verb: ἀποδίδωμι (*apodidōmi*), GK *625* (S *591*), 48x. *apodidōmi* means "to give (back), deliver, render, hand over, produce." It can also mean "to repay, reward, reimburse" (see *repay*). It is composed of the preposition *apo* ("away from," which denotes separation or movement away from something) and the verb *didōmi* ("to give").

apodidōmi can indicate a simple giving or handing over of something, as when Jesus gives the scroll back to the synagogue attendant (Lk. 4:20). In this sense, it also describes Pilate's handing over of Jesus' body to Joseph (Mt. 27:58).

apodidōmi is used in the common expression of giving an account for one's actions or behavior (Lk. 16:2; Acts 19:40; Heb. 13:17; 1 Pet. 4:5), as when one must give an account on the day of judgment (Mt. 12:36). Similarly, the word may be translated "to testify" or to "give witness" to (Acts 4:33).

In agricultural contexts, *apodidomi* describes the production of harvest (used figuratively in Heb. 12:11) or a tree's yielding of fruit (Rev. 22:2).

GIVE BIRTH

Old Testament

Verb: יָלַד (*yālad*), GK 3528 (S 3205), 499x. The verb *yālad*, which appears most frequently in the biblical genealogies, has the general meaning "to give birth." The precise meaning of this verb, however, depends on the particular Hebrew verb form in which it occurs. In one form, *yālad* refers to a mother's giving birth (Hebrew Qal), whereas in another it refers to the role of the father in "begetting" or having sired a child (Hiphil). *yālad* can refer to the child's being born (Niphal) or to the helpful role of the midwife in the birthing process (Pi'el). One other form of *yālad* always refers to someone's birthday—literally, the day on which the person was "begotten" (Hophal). According to this snapshot of the biblical usage of *yālad*, at least four people might be involved in the birth of a child.

However, the OT's use of *yālad* also makes it clear that God alone is the author of life and the only one who ultimately provides the barren with children (Gen. 29:31; 30:22; 1 Sam. 1:1–28). It is within this context that Abraham and Sarah are called to trust in God for a child in spite of their extreme old age (Gen. 17:1–21). As children of the father of all those who have faith (Rom. 4:16), we can follow Abraham's example and trust God even when our circumstances seem contrary to his promises, for indeed, with God all things are possible (Mt. 19:26).

New Testament

Verb: γεννάω (*gennaō*), GK *1164* (S *1080*), 97x. *gennaō* means "to give birth" (of the mother) or "to father" (of the father); it has both literal and figurative uses.

gennaō is used of the father's role in procreation in Matthew's genealogy (Mt. 1), translated in older English as "begat." As to the mother's role, when Elizabeth is about to deliver John the Baptist, Luke writes, "When it was time for Elizabeth to have her baby, she *gave birth* to her son" (Lk. 1:57). *gennaō* can also refer to conception. When Joseph is struggling with the miraculous conception of his fiancée, Mary, an angel of the Lord appears to him and says, "Joseph son of David, do not be afraid to take Mary home as your wife, because what *is conceived* in her is from the Holy Spirit" (Mt. 1:20).

John uses *gennaō* in some of his references to the spiritual realm when he speaks of "children *born* not of natural descent, nor of human decision or a husband's will, but *born* of God" (Jn. 1:13). Nicodemus misunderstands Jesus' call to be born again and asks, "How can a man *be born* when he is old?" (3:4a). To press the point, Nicodemus states, "Surely he cannot enter a second time into his mother's womb *to be born*!" (3:4b). Jesus insists he is speaking of being born of water and Spirit, probably referring to John's baptism of cleansing and the later regenerative outpouring of God's Holy Spirit.

In speaking to believers, John writes, "We know that anyone *born* of God does not continue to sin; the *one who was born* of God [probably a reference to Jesus as God's Son] keeps him safe, and the evil one cannot harm him" (1 Jn. 5:18; cf. 2:29; 3:9; 4:7; 5:1, 4). *gennaō* is also used in the context of giving birth to an attitude. "Don't have anything to do with foolish and stupid arguments, because you know they *produce* quarrels" (2 Tim. 2:23). Paul uses this verb to present himself as the spiritual father of the Corinthians (1 Cor. 4:15) and Philemon (Phlm. 12). See *NIDNTT-A*, 105.

Verb: τίκτω (*tiktō*), GK *5503* (S *5088*), 18x. The basic meaning of *tiktō* is "to give birth, bring forth." In the NT, it is used in both a literal and figurative sense.

(1) *tiktō* can literally mean "to give birth, to bear," especially in referring to physical human birth. "A woman *giving birth* to a child has pain because her time has come" (Jn. 16:21; cf. Lk. 1:57; Gal. 4:27; Rev. 12:2, 4, 5, 13). This is the term used of Jesus' mother Mary: "She *will give birth* to a son, and you are to give him the name Jesus" (Mt. 1:21; cf. 1:23, 25; 2:2; Lk. 1:31; 2:6, 7, 11).

(2) But *tiktō* can have the figurative meaning of causing something "to come into being, bring forth, produce." In Heb. 6:7, the ground is personified as that which produces vegetation. Likewise, James personifies sinful desires that bring forth spiritual death, "Then, after desire has conceived, it *gives birth* to sin; and sin, when it is full-grown, *gives birth* to death" (Jas. 1:15). See *NIDNTT-A*, 563.*

GIVE DRINK TO

Old Testament

Verb: שָׁתָה (*šātâ*), GK 9272 (S 8354), 217x. The basic meaning of *šātâ* is "to drink" and, in the Heb. Hiphil verb stem, "to give drink to, water." See *drink*.

GIVE HONOR

New Testament

Verb: δοξάζω (*doxazō*), GK *1519* (S *1392*), 61x. *doxazō* means "to glorify, give honor to, praise." See *glorify*.

GIVE LIFE

New Testament

Verb: ζῳοποιέω (*zōopoieō*), GK *2443* (S *2227*), 11x. The basic sense of *zōopoieō* is "to cause to live, make alive, give life to." It is used in a spiritual sense of God, Christ, or the Spirit giving life to someone: "For just as the Father raises the dead and *gives them life*, even so the Son *gives life* to whom he is pleased to give it" (Jn. 5:21). "The Spirit *gives life*" (6:63). See also Rom. 4:17; 8:11; 1 Cor. 15:22, 45; 2 Cor. 3:6; 1 Pet. 3:18.

In two instances, *zōopoieō* refers to things or words that are able to impart life. "Is the law, therefore, opposed to the promises of God? Absolutely not! For if a law had been given that could *impart life*, then righteousness would certainly have come by the law" (Gal. 3:21). "What you sow does not *come to life* unless it dies" (1 Cor. 15:36). See *NIDNTT-A*, 226-228.*

GIVE THANKS

New Testament

Verb: εὐχαριστέω (*eucharisteō*), GK *2373* (S *2168*), 38x. *eucharisteō* means "to thank, give thanks." See *thank*.

GIVE TO DRINK

New Testament

Verb: ποτίζω (*potizō*), GK *4540* (S *4222*), 15x. *potizō* means "to give to drink, cause one to drink, give water." It is used with reference to giving animals water to drink (Lk. 15:13) and offering Jesus sour wine while he was on the cross (Mt. 27:48; Mk. 15:36).

The word is used symbolically in NT passages that address a display of Christian kindness toward those in need (Mt. 10:42; 25:35, 37, 42; Mk. 9:41); in the poor to whom a drink is given, Christ is encountered. Note too the strategy that Paul adapts from the OT in order to disarm our enemies: "If your enemy is hungry, feed him; if he is thirsty, give him something to drink" (Rom. 12:20). Paul also uses *potizō* when he speaks of Christian ministry in 1 Cor. 3:6–8: "I planted the seed, Apollos *watered* it, but God made it grow. So neither he who plants nor he who *waters* is anything, but only God, who makes things grow." Paul uses *potizō* earlier in this chapter to speak of the Corinthian's spiritual immaturity: "I gave you milk *to drink*, not solid food, for you were not ready for it" (3:2).

The verb is elsewhere used to describe the Christian's baptism by the Holy Spirit into the body of Christ, "For we were all baptized by one Spirit into one body—whether Jews or Greeks, slave or free—and we were all given the one Spirit *to drink*" (12:13). A final use of *potizō* is found in Rev. 14:8, when the nations of the earth are "made to drink" the wine of the adulteries of the harlot Babylon.*

GLADDEN

Old Testament

Verb: שָׂמַח (*śāmaḥ*), GK 8523 (S 8055), 156x. *śāmaḥ* can describe both one's feeling of joy and the outward expression of such gladness in the form of rejoicing. It can be translated many ways, including "rejoice, delight, filled with joy, or gladden." See *rejoice*.

New Testament

Verb: εὐφραίνω (*euphrainō*), GK *2370* (S *2165*), 14x. *euphrainō* conveys the basic idea of a created state of joy or euphoria and may be translated as "rejoice, gladden, celebrate." See *rejoice*.

GLADNESS

Old Testament

Noun: שִׂמְחָה (*śimḥâ*), GK 8525 (S 8057), 94x. Depending on the context, *śimḥâ* can be translated "joy, rejoicing, gladness, pleasure," or "happiness." See *joy*.

New Testament

Noun: χαρά (*chara*), GK *5915* (S *5479*), 59x. As an antonym of grief and sorrow (Jn. 16:20), *chara* denotes "joy, happiness, gladness." See *joy*.

GLOAT

Old Testament

Verb: שָׂמַח (*śāmaḥ*), GK 8523 (S 8055), 156x. *śāmaḥ* can describe both one's feeling of joy and the outward expression of such gladness in the form of rejoicing. It can be translated many ways, including "rejoice, delight, filled with joy, or gladden." When *śāmaḥ* denotes the rejoicing of the psalmist's enemies, it is sometimes translated "gloat" (Ps. 30:1; 35:19, 24, 26; 38:16). See *rejoice*.

GLORIFY

New Testament

Verb: δοξάζω (*doxazō*), GK *1519* (S *1392*), 61x. *doxazō* means "to glorify, give honor to, praise." (1) To give "glory" to God is to "glorify" him. Our behavior may cause other to "glorify" God (Mt. 5:18). When the people in Jesus' day saw the miracle he performed on the paralytic, they "*praised* God, who had given such authority to men" (9:8). According to Paul, even our physical body can "glorify" or "honor" God (1 Cor. 6:20).

(2) John particularly uses *doxazō* to refer to the manner in which God was glorified in Jesus and the way in which Jesus glorified God (Jn. 12:28; 13:32; 17:1). Moreover, Jesus looked ahead to that special time when God would glorify him through his cross (Jn. 12:23; 17:4) and especially his resurrection and ascension (12:16). Linked to this is the time when God's chosen people will be "glorified," presumably at Jesus' second coming (Rom. 8:29–30).

(3) Christians are to "glorify" God by lives of obedience (2 Cor. 3:18; cf. Rom. 1:21). In so doing we reflect in our lives the glory of God. The goal is so that when others see our good deeds, they too will glorify God and praise him, perhaps by becoming believers (Mt. 5:16; 1 Pet. 2:12). A unique emphasis in Luke is that when people "glorify God," they do so by telling others about the things they have seen and heard about what God and his Son Jesus have done (Lk. 2:20; 5:25–26; 7:16; 18:43;

23:47; Acts 11:18). See *NIDNTT-A*, 150-51.

GLORY

Old Testament

Noun: כָּבוֹד (*kābôd*), GK 3883 (S 3519), 200x. The basic meaning of *kābôd* is "glory" or "honor." Such honor or glory can be associated with dignity, wealth, or high position. It involves respect or reverence from others; sometimes it refers to an object as being worthy of respect.

God has crowned humanity with "honor" or "dignity" (Ps. 8:5), which entails rule over God's creation (see vv. 6–8). Commonly the dignity denoted by *kābôd* is exhibited in external splendor, such as wealth (Gen. 31:1; Hab. 2:9). Other examples include the priests, whose garments signify the position of "honor" that they occupy (Exod. 28:2, 40), and the honor exhibited in military success (Ps. 21:5). *kābôd* also carries a more theological sense when used in connection with God's high position over his creation (Ps. 57:5, 11; 108:5, 113:4; 138:5). In this way *kābôd* can denote the heavenly honor that awaits the faithful (Ps. 73:24) or the place of God's presence.

kābôd is frequently connected with the ideas of respect or reverence. It can be applied to individuals (e.g., David, 1 Chr. 17:18) as well as to people in general (Prov. 20:3). However, it is especially applied to God in the OT. Often *kābôd* denotes the result of an action. In this sense verbs like "tell" and "sing" can describe modes of ascribing respect or reverence to God, usually in public worship. The common expression in the psalms, "the glory of God," should be understood in this way (Ps. 29:2; 66:2; 79:9; 96:8).

kābôd is also associated with an object of respect. Only two or three times the object involves humanity, as when God's people exchange their honor for false gods (Jer. 2:11; Ps. 106:20). More common is the technical use of *kābôd* for God's visible presence. The normal use of the expression "the glory of the LORD" is a technical designation for the Lord's manifest presence with his people. The term first appears in Exod. 16:7, where the manifest glory of God accompanies Israel during the wilderness period. Although the last reference in the Pentateuch is Deut. 5:24, the technical sense of God's presence is not limited to that time: God's presence is to continue through sacrificial worship (Exod. 29:43; 40:34; Lev. 9:6; 1 Ki. 8:11; Ps. 63:2). In 1 Sam. 4:21–22, the loss of the ark of God to the Philistines signified that God's "glory" or presence departed from Israel.

In reference to God, the *kābôd* or "the glory of the LORD" refers to the reality of his presence as the supreme ruler of his people manifested in power, splendor, and holiness (Isa. 3:8). This is consistent with Exod. 24:17, where the appearance of the "glory of the LORD" was like a consuming fire; this explains why Moses could not enter the tent in 40:34. Hence, this is called the "glory of the LORD" because it reveals his person and dignity. The proper response to such revelation is to give him "honor" or "glory." In this way, the "glory of the LORD" is essentially a name for God (Isa. 11:10; 24:23; 35:2; 60:1–2; Zech. 2:5).

In the last days a full manifestation of *kābôd* was expected in order to bring salvation to Israel (Isa. 60:1–2; Ezek. 39:21–22) and to convert the nations (Zech. 2:5–11). See *NIDOTTE*, 2:577-587.

Noun: תִּפְאֶרֶת (*tipʾeret*), GK 9514 (S 8597), 51x. *tipʾeret* means "glory, splendor, honor." Human beings are able to do various things in order to display different forms of glory. King Artaxerxes uses a 180-day celebration in order to show off the "splendor and glory of his majesty" (Est. 1:4). Solomon overlays the temple with precious stones for splendor (2 Chr. 3:6). Aaron and his sons have special garments to give them "dignity and honor" (Exod. 28:2, 40). Human beings can wear "fine jewelry" to make themselves look beautiful (Ezek. 16:12, 17). Even something like "gray hair" for elderly people can be considered "a crown of splendor" (Prov. 16:31). But note too that God can take all of that away in an instant (Isa. 3:18; Ezek. 16:39; 23:26).

The OT especially emphasizes the glory and splendor of the Lord. The psalmist declares the "splendor" of the Lord all day long (Ps. 71:8). Majesty, strength, and "glory" are in the sanctuary of the Lord. The temple itself, the dwelling place of God, is "holy and glorious" (Isa. 64:11). God grants his salvation to Zion, "his splendor to Israel" (46:13). He guides his people in order to make for himself "a glorious name" (63:14). And in the promised coming days, "the Lord will be your everlasting light, and your God will be your glory" (60:10).

New Testament

Noun: δόξα (*doxa*), GK *1518* (S *1391*), 166x. *doxa* can be translated as "glory, honor, splendor." (1) Occasionally *doxa* simply denotes the "honor" an earthly person receives for how he or she lives. A person can do or say something simply in order to gain personal honor or praise (Jn. 7:18; 12:43).

(2) *doxa* can also designate earthly "splendor." Satan showed to Jesus at his temptations "all the kingdoms of the earth and their *splendor*" (Mt. 4:8). Jesus referred in his Sermon on the Mount to "Solomon in all his *splendor*" (6:29; KJV "glory"). The bright light that blinded Paul on the road to Damascus, brighter than the noonday sun, exuded "brilliance" (Acts 22:11).

(3) But the vast majority of uses of *doxa*, like *kābôd* in the OT, are related to God and his glory. God is the "*glorious* Father" (lit., "Father *of glory*," Eph. 1:17), the "God *of glory*" (Acts 7:2). When Jesus came into this world, he bore "the *glory* of the One and Only" God (Jn. 1:14). *doxa* describes God and his dwelling (1 Cor. 15:40), angelic beings (Lk. 2:9; Heb. 9:5; Rev. 18:1), the gospel of salvation (1 Tim. 1:11), humans involved in transcendent circumstances (i.e., Moses, 2 Cor. 3:7–11, 18), or even humans in the next life (Col. 3:4). When Jesus Christ returns again, his appearing will be "glorious" (Tit. 2:13).

(4) Because God is so glorious, it is only natural that his people want to ascribe "glory" to him (2 Cor. 4:15; Eph. 3:21). For this reason, there are many *doxo*logies (ascriptions of glory to God) in the NT (e.g., Rom. 11:33–36; Gal. 1:5; 2 Pet. 3:18; Rev. 5:12–13). Furthermore, every part of our lives should reflect the fact that the glorious God lives in us—even our eating and drinking (1 Cor. 10:31). See *NIDNTT-A*, 150-51.

Noun: καύχησις (*kauchēsis*), GK *3018* (S *2746*), 11x. *kauchēsis* refers to the act of boasting. It can be negative or positive (e.g., having a sense of legitimate "pride" in a person or "glorying" in God). See *boast*.

GO

Old Testament

Verb: בּוֹא (*bôʾ*), GK 995 (S 935), 2592. *bôʾ* is the fourth most common verb in the OT. It denotes motion toward a specific goal, such as "to go, arrive, enter a house, come." It expresses a variety of motions. See *come*.

Verb: הָלַךְ (*hālak*), GK 2143 (S 1980), 1554x. *hālak* describes motion, primarily of humans, and is usually translated "walk, go, come." It can, however, describe the "crawl" of a snake (Gen. 3:14), the "prowling" of jackals (Lam. 5:18), the "floating" of the ark (Gen. 7:18), or even the "running" of a river (Gen. 2:14). In certain cases *hālak* may describe when something ceases (goes away): rain (Song 2:11), dew (Hos. 6:4), wind (Ps. 78:39), and even human life ("to go the way of all the earth," e.g., Jos. 23:14).

hālak is also used in a metaphorical sense to describe actions or the process of living. Even as life is viewed as progress on a "path" (*derek*, e.g., Ps. 1:6; Job 8:19; Prov. 3:6), so *hālak* describes the events and actions that occur on life's journey. David says, "Even though I *walk* through the valley of the shadow of death, I will fear no evil, for you are with me" (Ps. 23:4). To "walk through the valley of the shadow of death" conveys life in its most difficult moments, when the presence of

God becomes all the more precious. Similarly, Isaiah encourages those who "*walk* in darkness" to trust in God (Isa. 50:10).

Oftentimes, *hālak* describes one's actions with reference to God's covenant standards. Thus, one may walk in obedience or disobedience. (Note the rabbinic term *halakah* to describe "how one should walk [live].") The Sabbath regulation is given to Israel with regard to gathering manna. They are to gather sufficient manna on Friday so as not to gather it on the Sabbath: "In this way I will test them and see whether they will *follow* my instructions" ("whether they will *walk* in my law, or no," KJV) (Exod. 16:4). Those who are part of God's covenant people demonstrate their faithfulness to God by walking according to his statutes (e.g., Lev. 18:3; Deut. 30:16; 1 Ki. 2:3; 11:38; Ezek. 11:20). Such obedience brings God's promised blessings (Lev. 26:3; cf. Gen. 18:19). In contrast, disobedience is described as "not walking" according to God's commandments (1 Ki. 9:6; 11:33; 2 Ki. 17:8; Jer. 44:10; Ezek. 5:6), and such unfaithfulness brings God's judgment.

In the OT, the way of the Lord (righteousness) is made known to his people through the light of his revelation: "Show me your ways, O LORD, teach me your paths" (Ps. 25:4), and particularly through his established instructions (laws): "Blessed are they whose ways are blameless, who *walk* according to the law of the LORD" (Ps. 119:1). When God's way is made known, it becomes the responsibility of his people to walk in it: "Teach me your way, O LORD, and I will *walk* in your truth; give me an undivided heart, that I may fear your name" (Ps. 86:11). Yet to walk in God's ways requires constant dependence on him, for each step along the path of righteousness requires his direction: "Show me the way I should *go*, for to you I lift up my soul" (Ps. 143:8). Thus, the life ("walk") of the righteous is one of humble dependence on God, for it is a journey traveled together with him: "He has shown you, O man, what is good. And what does the LORD require of you? To act justly and to love mercy and to *walk* humbly with your God" (Mic. 6:8). See *NIDOTTE*, 1:1032-35.

New Testament

Verb: ἄγω (*agō*), GK *72* (S *71*, *73*), 67x. In its most basic NT sense, *agō* means "to bring, lead, go." See *lead*.

Verb: ἀπέρχομαι (*aperchomai*), GK *599* (S *565*), 117x. *aperchomai* means "to go away, withdraw," though it can also simply mean "to go." See *go away*.

Verb: ἔρχομαι (*erchomai*), GK *2262* (S *2064*), 632x. *erchomai* usually means "come, arrive," sometimes it can mean "go." See *come*.

Verb: πορεύομαι (*poreuomai*), GK *4513* (S *4198*), 153x. *poreuomai* can be translated "go, travel, walk." It is a common term in the NT to refer to physical motion from one place to another (e.g., Lk. 2:3, "And everyone *went* to his own town to register," cf. 7:8, 11, 50; 17:19; Jn. 4:50). In Jn. 8:11 Jesus tells the woman caught in adultery, "*Go* now and leave your life of sin." The hope of all believers is that Jesus will "*go* and prepare a place for you" (14:3; cf. Acts 1:10, 11).

While *poreuomai* itself is not a significant theological term, it becomes important when one understands that the Christian life is not one to be lived standing still. Motion is vital to living as Christ commands. With the emphasis on the action of making disciples, the risen Jesus instructs his followers: "Therefore *go* and make disciples of all nations, baptizing them in the name of the Father, the Son, and the Holy Spirit" (Mt. 28:19; cf. Mk. 16:15). See *NIDNTT-A*, 485.

Verb: ὑπάγω (*hypagō*) GK *5632* (S *5217*), 79x. *hypagō* means "to go" in the sense of departing (Mt. 4:10) or accompanying (5:41, "*Go* with him two miles"). See *depart*.

GO AHEAD

New Testament

Verb: προάγω (*proagō*), GK *4575* (S *4254*), 20x. *proagō* means "to go ahead" of someone. The star that the wise men saw in the east "went ahead of them" (Mt. 2:9) and directed them to the manger. On several occasions, the people go on ahead of Jesus on land as he is crossing the lake, so that when he disembarks, they are already waiting for him (14:22; 21:9; Mk. 6:45).

One of the most poignant uses of the verb is in Mk. 10:32. Immediately after Jesus' third prediction of his death in Jerusalem, he walks so fast that he "goes far ahead" of his disciples, so eager he is to get to Jerusalem in order to accomplish his life's task. After Jesus' resurrection, he tells his disciples that he "will go ahead" of them into Galilee, and they will see him there (14:28; cf. 16:7; Mt. 26:32; 28:7).

In a more negative usage, 2 Jn. 9, John warns against deceivers who "run ahead" in their doctrine and do not continue in the true teachings about Jesus.

GO AROUND

Old Testament

Verb: סָבַב (*sābab*), GK 6015 (S 5437), 163x. *sābab* is generally translated "surround, go around, turn." See *surround*.

GO ASTRAY

Old Testament

Verb: תָּעָה (*tāʿâ*), GK 9494 (S 8582), 51x. *tāʿâ* may be translated as to "go astray, stray, lead astray, wander, stagger." OT authors use this verb in reference to physical roaming (Exod. 23:4); wandering as a result of intoxication (Isa. 28:7; NIV "staggering"; cf. 19:14); mental, moral, or spiritual wandering (Ps. 95:10); and ethical wandering (Ezek. 44:10). By their prophecies and worship of false gods, false prophets lead the people astray (Jer. 23:13, 32; Mic. 3:5). Ps. 58:3 records that "even from birth the wicked *go astray.*" By contrast, the devoted psalmist insists that "I have not *strayed* from your precepts" (Ps. 119:176).

Isa. 53:6 records the most familiar use of *tāʿâ*. In what has been called the final "Servant of the Lord" passage (52:13–53:12), Isaiah prophesies that in the coming messianic age, "we all, like sheep, have *gone astray*, each of us has turned to our own way; and the Lord had laid on him the iniquity of us all." Whereas in the past, "my people have been lost sheep; their shepherds have *led them astray*" (Jer. 50:6), in the future, "the people of Israel will no longer *stray* from me.... They will be my people, and I will be their God" (Ezek. 14:11). See *NIDOTTE, 4:319-20.*

New Testament

Verb: πλανάω (*planaō*), GK *4414* (S *4105*), 39x. In the active voice, *planaō* means "to lead astray, deceive"; in the middle/passive voice, "to wander, go astray." See *deceive*.

GO AWAY

New Testament

Verb: ἀπέρχομαι (*aperchomai*), GK *599* (S *565*), 117x. *aperchomai* means "to go away, withdraw," though it can also simply mean "to go." It is used mostly in the Gospels and Acts.

In its basic sense, *aperchomai* means to move from one point to another. In Mt. 8:18, Jesus orders the disciples "to depart" and go to the other side of the lake (see also Mt. 9:7; 13:25; Mk. 5:30; Lk. 1:38; 5:25; Jn. 4:8; 6:1; Acts 9:17). In Lk. 8:39b, after the demon-possessed man was healed, "the man *went away* and told all over town how much Jesus had done for him." Jesus uses this verb twice in Jn. 16:7 when he explains, "It is for your good that I *am going away*. Unless I *go away*, the Counselor will not come to you; but if I go, I will send him to you." Here he is speaking of his impending death and resurrection.

aperchomai can also mean simply "to go." Mk. 6:36 records the words of the disciples, "Send the people away so that they can *go* to the surrounding countryside and villages and buy themselves something to eat" (cf. Mt. 8:33; 28:10; Mk. 4:24; Jn. 4:28; 11:54). In such cases, the verb is followed by the location where one was to go, such as "to the mountain," "to the city," "to the house."

In the NT letters, *aperchomai* typically retains this general sense. In Rom. 15:28, Paul tells the Roman church, "So after I have completed this task . . . I *will go* to Spain and visit you on the way." Similarly, in Gal. 1:17, Paul tells the Galatians "I *went* immediately into Arabia and later returned to Damascus." (cf. Jas. 1:24). Jude 7 uses *aperchomai* to refer to Sodom and Gomorrah and the cities around them who "*went* after strange flesh." Here this word denotes how the people of these cities indulged themselves in sexual immorality. John uses *aperchomai* metaphorically to refer to the "passing away" of the first heaven and earth (Rev. 21:1). Death, mourning, crying, and pain have all "passed away" as well (21:4).

aperchomai can also refer metaphorically to someone "going away from Jesus," as in Jn. 6:66. The many who withdrew from Jesus did not simply change their location but refused to believe and instead abandoned him. This is confirmed two verses later when Peter utters the wonderful confession, "Lord, to whom *shall* we *go*, you have words of eternal life" (Jn. 6:68; cf. 12:19).

GO DOWN

Old Testament

Verb: יָרַד (*yārad*), GK 3718 (S 3381), 382x. This common verb means "to go down, come down, descend, bring down."

(1) The basic meaning of this verb is for a person going down some terrain. For example, Pharaoh's daughter goes down to the Nile River to bathe (Exod. 2:5). After Moses has gone up Mount Sinai to hear God's instructions, he then "goes down" against to the people (32:15), sometimes at the direct command of God (19:21). Since towns were often built in valleys, people usually had to "go down" into the town (1 Sam. 9:25; 27; 23:4; 2 Ki. 2:2).

(2) Theologically, this word can be used to describe God's going down to earth, usually with some specific purpose in mind. For example, he "comes down" to see what is going on at Babel when a tower is being built (Gen. 11:5). He "comes down" in order to save his people, to rescue them from their slavery in Egypt (Exod. 3:8). He "descends" on Sinai and manifests his glory to the people of Israel and to Moses (Exod. 19:11).

That God *descends* to visit the earth emphasizes the fact that he is high and exalted, transcendent over the world; that he *descends* emphasizes his desire to be in relationship with his creation. God descends to meet with Moses: "Whenever Moses went out to the tent [of meeting] . . . the pillar of cloud would *descend* and stand at the entrance of the tent, and the LORD would speak with Moses" (Exod. 33:8–9).

(3) The Lord's descent from on high is also prominent in those places in the prophets that refer to the day of the Lord, often with ominous foreboding of judgment. For example, God prophesies against Tyre, "I *will bring* you *down* with those who *go down* to the pit (Ezek. 26:20). Micah testifies that the Lord "will come down" and tread the high places of the land (Mic. 1:3). According to Isaiah, "the LORD Almighty *will come down* and do battle on Mount Zion" (Isa. 31:4). The psalmist prays that God will "*bring down* the nations" (Ps. 56:7). See *NIDOTTE*, 2:534–35.

New Testament

Verb: καταβαίνω (*katabainō*), GK *2849* (S *2597*), 81x. *katabainō* means "to come down, go down, descend." See *come down*.

Verb: κατέρχομαι (*katerchomai*), GK *2982* (S *2718*), 16x. *katerchomai* means "to come, go down." See *come down*.

GO IN

New Testament

Verb: εἰσπορεύομαι (*eisporeuomai*), GK *1660* (S *1531*), 18x. *eisporeuomai* means "to enter, go in." See *enter*.

GO OUT

Old Testament

Verb: יָצָא (*yāṣāʾ*), GK 3655 (S 3318), 1076x. *yāṣāʾ* most frequently means "to go out, come out, bring out." Most of the uses of this verb have a literal meaning. It is first used in Gen. 2:10 in reference to the river that "came out" or "flowed out" of Eden. *yāṣāʾ* is used when the animals "came out" of the ark (9:10), when Goliath "went out" of the Philistine camp (1 Sam. 17:4), and when Moses spoke of the need for an unclean man to "go outside" the camp (Deut. 23:10).

But there are also a number of figurative uses. For example, *yāṣāʾ* can refer to the departing of a human soul at death (Gen. 35:18) or to deep-seated discouragement (Gen. 42:28, "Their hearts *sank* [*went out*] and they turned to each other trembling and said, 'What is this that God has done to us?'"). It is also used when speaking of the close of a year (Exod. 23:16), the premature birth of a child (Exod. 21:22), and the future blessing of Abraham's descendants (Gen. 17:6, "kings *will come* from you").

When applied to God, *yāṣāʾ* often refers to the Lord's "going out" to assist his people (Exod. 11:4; Jdg. 5:4). Moreover, the Lord brings his people out of the land of Egypt (Exod. 3:10; Num. 20:16; Jer. 7:22). It is also used of things that proceed or "go out" from the Lord, such as his justice (Isa. 45:23), his wisdom (Isa. 51:4), his salvation (Isa. 51:5), his word (Isa. 55:11), his hand (Ruth 1:13), and even his wrath (Num. 16:46)

Finally, *yāṣāʾ* can relate God's abandonment of his people (Ezek. 10:18, "Then the glory of the LORD *departed* [*went out*] from over the threshold of the temple and stopped above the cherubim").

New Testament

Verb: ἐκπορεύομαι (*ekporeuomai*), GK *1744* (S *1607*), 33x. *ekporeuomai* means "to come, go out." See *come out*.

Verb: ἐξέρχομαι (*exerchomai*), GK *2002* (S *1831*), 218x. *exerchomai* means to "go out, come out." It is often used in narrative passages (especially in the gospels and Acts) that speak of a person going away from a place or from another person's presence (Mt. 8:28; Lk. 5:8). It can also be used in reference to a specific act, such as going out to preach (Mk. 6:12) or to work (Mt. 13:3). Sometimes it is used when referring to something that goes out of a person, such as rumors, statements, thoughts, or even demons (Mt. 15:18–19; 12:43; Mk. 1:26). When the church is in view (especially in the NT letters), *exerchomai* refers to the Word of God going out to the world (1 Thess. 1:8), the people of God coming out from unbelievers (2 Cor. 6:17), and the false teachers going out from the church to demonstrate their apostasy (1 Jn. 2:19).

In Jn. 8:42, Jesus uses *exerchomai* to tell the Jews that he came from God. He says, "If God were your Father, you would love me, for I *came from* God and now am here. I have not come on my own; but he sent me." John highlights this unique relationship between the Father and the Son throughout his gospel, demonstrating both Jesus' divine nature and his mission; therefore, anyone who embraces Jesus as Savior must first recognize his sovereign position as one who has proceeded from the Father.

GO THROUGH

New Testament

Verb: διέρχομαι (*dierchomai*), GK *1451* (S *1330*), 43x. *dierchomai* means "to go or come through, pass through." This verb occurs primarily in the gospels and Acts, where it often means "to move through an area." In Mt. 12:43, "when an evil spirit comes out of a man, it *goes through* arid places"; in 19:24 Jesus speaks of a camel "going through" the eye of a needle. In Lk. 4:30, even though Jesus angers the crowd in Nazareth, "he *walks right through* the crowd" and goes on his way. In 5:15, the word about Jesus "spreads through" the region, and in 9:6, the disciples "go through" the villages, preaching and healing. Philip preaches the gospel to all the cities he "passes through" (Acts 8:40). In 1 Cor. 10:1 Paul recalls that the people of Israel "*passed through* the sea." *dierchomai* is used of Jesus as the eternal high priest who has "*passed through* the heavens" (Heb. 4:14).

In a few instances, *dierchomai* can mean to go through an obstacle in the sense of "to penetrate." For example, in Lk. 2:35 Simeon takes Jesus in his arms as an infant and prophesies that, among other things, a sword will "pierce" Mary's own soul too. In Rom. 5:12 Paul says, "death *came* to all men" as a result of the sin of Adam.

GO UP

Old Testament

Verb: עָלָה (*ʿālâ*), GK 6590 (S 5927), 894x. *ʿālâ* typically means "to go up, ascend." Although it inherently is not a theological term, it often appears in highly significant contexts. See *ascend*.

New Testament

Verb: ἀναβαίνω (*anabainō*), GK *326* (S *305*), 82x. *anabainō* generally means to "go up, ascend, come up." See *ascend*.

GO WELL

Old Testament

Verb: יָטַב (*yāṭab*), GK 3512 (S 3190), 117x. *yāṭab* is a verb that means "to do good, go well, please, prosper." It is used in a wide variety of contexts in the OT. See *do good*.

GOAT

Old Testament

Noun: עֵז (*ʿēz*), GK 6436 (S 5795), 74x. The meaning of *ʿēz* as "goat" overlaps significantly with that of *śāʾîr*, also "goat," and the two words show up in the same contexts. *ʿēz* refers to the goat as a sacrificial animal, which was to be without defect in order to be acceptable before God (Lev. 22:19; Deut. 17:1). In contexts related to the weaving of material, *ʿēz* is best rendered "goat hair." The Israelites spun goat hair to create eleven curtains that served as a tent over the tabernacle (Exod. 26:7; 36:14; cf. 25:4; 35:23, 26). See *NIDOTTE*, 3.362.

Noun: צֹאן (*ṣōʾn*), GK 7366 (S 6629), 274x. Often translated "sheep, lambs, goats," *ṣōʾn* is commonly used to refer to flocks of sheep. It has both a literal and a metaphorical meaning in the OT. See *sheep*.

Noun: שָׂעִיר (*ṣāʿîr*), GK 8538 (S 8163), 52x.

Noun: שָׂעִיר (*ṣāʿîr*), GK 8539 (S 8163), 2x. *ṣāʿîr* almost always means "(hairy) goat," though 3x the word operates as an adjective meaning "hairy" (see *hairy*). The most common use of this word is in reference to "goats"—i.e., the "hairy ones."

(1) In the ancient world, the veneration of goats was common in some forms of pagan worship (Lev. 17:7; 2 Chr. 11:15); in such contexts, some prefer to translate *ṣāʿîr* as "goat idol."

(3) But *ṣāʿîr* appears most often in contexts of Israel's sin offering, the purpose of which is to atone for any unintentional sins against God. These offerings have specific guidelines, which are outlined extensively in Lev. and Num. (Lev. 4:1–35; 5:1–13; Num. 15:24; cf. Lev. 10:16; Num. 7:1–89). Although a bull is to be sacrificed as a sin offering for the people (Lev. 4:1–21), a male goat (or a female lamb) can substitute for those who cannot afford a bull (4:32–35).

In the history of Israel, probably the clearest indication of the people's repentance and spiritual renewal to worship God is seen in their reinstitution of the sin offering, as was done during the reign of King Hezekiah when seven male goats were offered for the kingdom, the sanctuary, and Judah (2 Chr. 29:21, 23). Similarly, when Ezra brings back the exiles from Babylon, they resume their worship of God by dedicating twelve male goats as a sin offering, one for each of the twelve tribes of Israel (Ezr. 6:17; 8:35). Ezekiel's vision of the restored temple includes the performance of sin offerings (Ezek. 43:22, 25; 45:23).

Perhaps the most important day in Israel's calendar year is the Day of Atonement, when atonement is made for the people's sins. The priests take two male goats, one for a sin sacrifice and one as a scapegoat. After the first goat is sacrificed, the priest lays his hands on the second goat and confesses Israel's sins; then the goat is then set free into the desert (Lev. 16:1–22; cf. Num. 29:12–40). In the NT we learn of the priestly ministry of Jesus Christ, who fulfills the Day of Atonement by offering himself as the sacrifice once for all for our sins (see especially Heb. 4:14–10; 8:1–10:18). See *NIDOTTE*, 3:727-33.

GOAT HAIR

Old Testament

Noun: עֵז (*ʿēz*), GK 6436 (S 5795), 74x. The meaning of *ʿēz* as "goat" overlaps significantly with that of *śāʾîr*, also "goat." In contexts related to the weaving of material, *ʿēz* is best rendered "goat hair." See *goat*.

GOD

Old Testament

Noun: אֵל (*ʾēl*), GK 446 (S 410), 242x. *ʾēl* is one of the two main Heb. words for "God." (1) It is used mainly with reference to the one and only true God of Abraham, Isaac, and Jacob—"Yahweh," the covenant God of Israel, the Creator of heaven and earth. *ʾēl* is often compounded with place or descriptive names: *Bet-el* ("house of God"), *El-Elyon* ("God Most High"), *El-Olam* ("Everlasting God"), and (perhaps most familiar) El-Shaddai ("God Almighty"). *ʾēl* is also found in names such as "Immanu*el*" (Isa. 7:14, meaning "God with us"). It is also a part of the new name given Jacob in Gen. 32:28, namely, "Isra*el*" (meaning "one who strives with God"), the name also adopted by God's chosen people.

(2) But *ʾēl* is sometimes used to designate "gods" of other nations, as in Exod. 15:11, "Who is like you among the *gods*?" The Lord asserts in Isa. 43:10, "Before me there was no *god* formed."

(3) As with *ʾelôhîm* (GK 466), the phrase "sons *of God*" with *ʾēl* can refer to angels (cf. Ps. 29:1 [but see #4, below]; see also 89:6).

(4) *ʾēl* can also designate "might," as when the psalmist calls for the "sons of the mighty" (KJV, NASB, NIV) to ascribe strength to the Lord (Ps. 29:1 [but this expression here could refer to angels, see #3, above]). This word is appropriately translated "Mighty One" in Jos. 22:22. The term is also used with reference to the "*mighty* leaders" in the grave—i.e., dead rulers—in Ezek. 32:21.

(5) Sometimes the word connotes "strength, power." For instance, this term is used when we read, "It is in my *power* to do you harm" (Gen. 31:29), and "there will be no *strength* in your hand" (Deut. 28:32). Many scholars today, however, consider this a separate Heb. word that is also spelled *ʾēl*. See *NIDOTTE*, 1:398–403.

Noun: אֱלֹהִים (*ʾelōhîm*), GK 466 (S 430), 2602x. *ʾelōhîm* is a name for "God," but it can also mean "gods, judges, angels."

(1) The predominant usage of *ʾelōhîm* is to refer to God, the one true and living God. Over two thousand times in the OT, *ʾelōhîm* is used to designate the God who created everything, pledged himself to Abraham, brought the Israelites out of Egypt and into the promised land, judged them when they broke the covenant, sent them into exile, and orchestrated the return from exile. All along, he sustained a remnant who hoped that the seed of the woman would come and reverse the curses God had announced at the fall, save Israel by judging her enemies, and reign righteously for the benefit of all nations. *ʾelōhîm* itself is a plural word, but it always takes a singular verb, which probably suggests that the plural is an intensification of the word, showing the exclusivity of the Lord God. Many orthodox scholars in previous centuries have seen in this phenomenon a hint of the Trinity, though this is now considered uncertain.

(2) At points it is clear that *ʾelōhîm* refers to other "gods" besides the Lord God. "I know that the Lord is greater than all the *gods*" (Exod. 18:11). "The Lord your *God*, he is *God* of *gods*" (Deut. 10:17). About one-tenth of the uses of *ʾelōhîm* in the OT have this meaning. Similarly, this word is sometimes used in conjunction with the name of a specific god other than the Lord, such as Dagon (1 Sam. 5:7), Chemos (Judg. 11:24), Baal (1 Ki. 18:24), or Ashtoreth (11:33).

(3) In some instances, *ʾelōhîm* may mean "judges" because such individuals are divine representatives or because they reflect divine power. "If the thief is not found, let the owner of the house draw near to the *judges*" (Exod. 22:8). The KJV

translates ʾ^{e}*lōhîm* in 1 Sam. 2:25 as "judge," but NIV and NASB render the term "God."

(4) In other instances, ʾ^{e}*lōhîm* seems to refer to superhuman beings in general—angels, divine ones. The Heb. of Ps. 8:5 literally reads, "You caused him to lack a little from *God*"; the Greek translation of the OT renders this, "You made him for a certain while lower than *angels*" (cf. Heb. 2:6–7). The KJV renders ʾ^{e}*lōhîm* here "angels"; the NIV translates "heavenly beings"; the NASB translates "God." Another text where *angels* may be in view is Ps. 97:7, "All who worship images are put to shame, those who boast in idols—worship him, all you *gods*!" (NIV). The phrase "sons of *God*" also seems to refer to angels, though this is debatable (see Gen. 6:2, 4; Job 1:6; 2:1; 38:7).

(5) On a few occasions human beings are compared to ʾ^{e}*lōhîm*: Moses (Exod. 4:16; 7:1), Samuel (1 Sam. 28:13; NIV has "spirit" here, referring to the deceased Samuel), and possibly the messianic King (Ps. 45:6; cf. Heb. 1:8). See *NIDOTTE*, 1:405–6.

Noun: אֱלוֹהַּ (ʾ^{e}*lôah*), GK 468 (S 433), 976x. ʾ^{e}*lôah* means "God." In contrast to the other words for God in the OT (ʾ*ēl*, GK 446; ʾ^{e}*lōhîm*, GK 466), this one appears almost exclusively in the book of Job. Some consider ʾ^{e}*lôah* to be the singular form of ʾ^{e}*lōhîm*, which is a plural noun (but it always takes a singular verb when referring to the God of Israel).

Elsewhere in the OT, the psalmist asks, "For who is *God* besides the Lord?" (Ps. 18:31). And God asks through Isaiah, "Is there any *God* besides me? No, there is no other Rock; I known not one" (Isa. 44:8). Israel's God is indeed unique. In several other places, ʾ^{e}*lôah* is appropriately placed in lowercase "god," since it refers to other possible gods (2 Chr. 32:15; Dan. 11:37–39; Hab. 1:11). See *NIDOTTE*, 1:405–6.

Noun: אֱלָהּ (ʾ^{e}*lāh*), GK 10033 (S 426), 96x. ʾ^{e}*lāh* is an Aramaic word (several sections of the OT are written in Aramaic rather than Hebrew: Ezr. 4:8–6:18; 7:12–26; Jer. 10:11; Dan. 2:4–7:28). This word is related to the Heb. singular noun ʾ*el* (GK 446) and plural noun ʾ^{e}*lōhîm* (GK 466), both of which mean "God."

ʾ^{e}*lāh* is used both for the true "God" of Israel and for "gods" of other nations. Both uses occur together in Dan. 3:28, "Blessed be the *God* of them, of Shadrach, Meshach and Abednego...who did not serve or worship any *god* except their own *God*." See other words in this section on *God* for further discussion on the God of the Scriptures.

Proper Noun: יָהּ (*yāh*), GK 3363 (S 3050), 49x.The Hebrew name *yhwh* or "Yawheh," commonly translated into English as "the LORD," is the most frequently appearing name for God in the OT (almost 7000x). See *Lord*.

New Testament

Noun: θεός (*theos*), GK *2536* (S *2316*), 1317x. As a general term, *theos* means "god." It is a word used for any being, real or imagined, whom people acknowledge as a "god." Paul noticed an altar in Athens with the inscription, "TO AN UNKNOWN *GOD*" (Acts 17:23). In his witness to the Gentiles, he preached against "man-made *gods*" (19:26).

But the vast majority of times in which *theos* occurs in the NT, it refers to the Lord God. It sometimes refers to "the *God* of Abraham, Isaac and Jacob, the *God* of our fathers" (Acts 3:13). This ownership extends into the NT as God sent Jesus into this world to save it from spiritual bondage and to establish the church, the new "Israel of God" (Gal. 6:16). God is God of the NT as well as the OT. Unfortunately, some see the God of the OT as a harsh, judgmental judge, while the God of the NT is a tender, loving, compassionate grandfatherly figure into whose lap you can crawl. The truth is—God is both in both. Note, for example, the theme of Deuteronomy as love, while in Acts 5:1–11, God hurls a couple of judgmental thunderbolts at Ananias and Sapphira. Lydia, Barnabas, and Luke worship the same God as Miriam, Deborah, and Jeremiah.

theos is one, he is only, and he is unique (Mt. 23:9; Rom. 3:20; 1 Cor. 8:4, 6; Gal. 3:20). Jesus casts his lot for this concept when he pledges his allegiance to God by quoting the Shema: "Hear, O Israel, the Lord your *God* is one Lord" (Mk. 12:29–30; cf. Deut. 6:4). Moreover, God is "holy" (Lev. 19:1–2; 1 Pet. 1:16; Rev. 4:8), "perfect" (Mt. 5:48), "faithful" (Rom. 3:3; 1 Cor. 1:9), the ultimate "promise keeper" (Rom. 9:6–8), a constant "teller of the truth" (Tit. 1:2; Heb. 6:18), "wise" (Rom. 16:27), "invisible" (Col. 1:15–16), "immortal" (1 Tim. 1:17), "blessed" (6:15–16), "totally righteous" (2 Cor. 5:21), and "love" (1 Jn. 4:8). But while God maintains his transcendence (sovereign sway and ultimate control) over all the creation, he is also immanent (in our midst), intimately involved with his creation. Jesus describes *theos* as personal, compassionate, and tender, with a love that extends far beyond the abilities of the most loving human father (Mt. 7:7–12).

Jesus claimed a "oneness" with *theos* not only as his unique, sinless Son, but also as *theos* himself: "Anyone who has seen me has seen the Father" (Jn. 14:9). In fact, Peter calls Jesus Christ "our *God* and Savior" (2 Pet. 1:1). Jesus saw himself in a special Father-Son relationship, as did other NT writers revealed in the oft-repeated phrase, "the God and Father of our Lord Jesus Christ" (Rom. 15:6; 2 Cor. 1:3; Eph. 1:3; Col. 1:3; 1 Pet. 1:3). The unique relationship Jesus shared with *theos* is best seen in the Garden of Gethsemane and on the cross of Golgotha. *God* did not intervene when Jesus was tormented with the reality of sacrificial crucifixion (Mk. 14:32–42). While Jesus prayed for an alternative, he was totally committed to his Father's will (vv. 35–36).

theos is also seen as the one who will bring history to a close. One of the most important themes in Revelation is "worship." John envisions many scenes with God majestically enthroned, receiving the praise of all the inhabitants of heaven (4:8). *God* will vindicate the Lamb and his church (Rev. 5; 14) and preside at the judgment and the final consignment to hell of Satan and all his disciples (20:7–15). See *NIDNTT-A*, 243-48.

GODLESS

New Testament

Adjective: ἀσεβής (*asebēs*), GK *815* (S *765*), 9x. *asebēs* means "ungodly, godless, wicked." See *ungodly*.

GODLINESS

New Testament

Noun: εὐσέβεια (*eusebeia*), GK *2354* (S *2150*), 15x. *eusebeia* occurs in the NT only in the Pastoral Letters (10x) and 2 Peter (4x), and in a statement of Peter recounted in Acts 3:12. In these contexts, *eusebeia* refers to a particular manner of life in which the believer is devoted to God. Thus, Paul exhorts believers to train themselves for "godliness" (1 Tim. 4:7), even to an extent that it requires a strenuous pursuit (6:11). The goal of such training is far more valuable than physical training (4:8).

The chief means of training oneself in godliness is sound instruction (1 Tim. 6:3) and knowledge of the truth (Tit. 1:1), especially knowledge of God (2 Pet. 1:3). While *eusebeia* leads to a life of contentment and gain (1 Tim. 6:6), it is an end in itself, not a means. Peter, for example, is shocked when the onlookers suppose that it is his own godliness that gave him the power to heal the lame man (Acts 3:12), and Paul rebukes those who use godliness as a mere means to obtain wealth (1 Tim. 6:5). One might be able to put on a show of godliness (2 Tim. 3:5), but such a show is without the true transforming power of the gospel, described by Paul as the mystery of godliness (1 Tim. 3:16). This is because *eusebeia* is but one in a series of Christian virtues that are indicative of the renewed life. It stands between the personal virtues of knowledge, self-control, and perseverance (2 Pet. 1:6), and the community virtues of brotherly kindness and love (1:7). Godly believers are encouraged to pray for those in authority (1 Tim. 2:2), because the world around them is not eternal, but what is truly lasting is to live lives marked by godliness. See *NIDNTT-A*, 520-21.

GOING TO

New Testament

Verb: μέλλω (*mellō*), GK *3516* (S *3195*), 109x. *mellō* is generally translated "about to, going to, intend to." See *about to*.

GOLD

Old Testament

Noun: זָהָב (*zāhāb*), GK 2298 (S 2091), 392x. *zāhāb* denotes the precious metal "gold." Its first reference occurs in Gen. 2:11–12, prior to the fall, where we read of "*gold* in the land of Havilah." While not much is known about how gold was mined or crafted in the OT, we do know it was hammered (Exod. 25:18; 39:3) and cast (37:13). Presumably much of the hammered gold was a form of gold leaf. Gold shekels were used as currency (see 1 Chr. 21:25).

(1) Gold is considered a precious metal and symbol of wealth (see Gen. 13:2; 24:35; Num. 22:18; 24:13; Prov. 22:1; Eccl. 2:8; Isa. 2:7; 60:9). A finely adorned person would wear gold jewelry (Gen. 41:42; Prov. 25:12; Jer. 4:30). It was used in the manufacture of symbols of royal power, including a scepter (Est. 4:11), a crown (2 Sam. 12:30), and overlay for the throne (1 Ki. 10:18). Many of the references to gold in the OT occur in the stories of the building of the tabernacle (Exod. 25–40) and the temple (1 Ki. 6–7; 2 Chr. 3–4) and the accoutrements for Israel's worship. Even the high priest's turban had a gold plate affixed to it, engraved with the words "HOLY TO THE LORD" (Exod. 28:36). Unfortunately, gold could also be used in the manufacture of idol gods, such as the golden calf (32:31; cf. Deut. 29:17). Gold could also used to seal an alliance with a more powerful king, in order to keep that enemy nation from invading (e.g., 1 Ki. 15:18). Gold items were, of course, a frequent element in the spoils of war (2 Sam. 8:7; 1 Ki. 14:26).

(2) Gold has metaphorical uses in the OT. A good reputation is far more valuable than silver or gold (Prov. 22:1). Devotion to the God's law, which bestows life and joy, is more precious than the finest gold (Ps. 19:10; 119:72, 127). Yet gold cannot buy wisdom (Job 28:17; cf. 28:28). And gold can easily become the object of one's misplaced confidence (Job 31:24). Gold has the power to corrupt (e.g., Achan's sin in Jos. 7). No amount of gold can protect us if we are out of sorts with God (Lam. 4:1; Ezek. 7:19; Zeph. 1:18). In another metaphorical use, the process of refining gold becomes a symbol of God's testing of the human heart (Prov. 17:3) and his purifying power in our lives (Mal. 3:2–3).

New Testament

Verb: χρυσοῦς (*chrysous*), GK *5997* (S *5552*), 18x. *chrysous* means "gold, golden." Except for one use in 2 Tim. 2:20 and two in Heb. 9:4 (referring to the "golden" altar of incense and the "golden" jar of manna), all uses of *chrysous* are in Revelation. There are references to "golden" lampstands (Rev. 1:12, 20), crowns "of gold" (4:4; 14:14), "golden" bowls of incense (5:8) or of wrath (15:7), and a "golden" altar (8:3; 9:13). Gold is frequently noted in this book to emphasize the preciousness of heaven.

Noun: χρυσός (*chrysos*), GK *5996* (S *5557*), 10x.

Noun: χρυσίον (*chrysion*), GK *5992* (S *5553*), 12x. The two words chrysos and chrysion are used interchangeably in the NT. They denote the precious metal "gold," which is often associated with other materials of great value, such as incense and myrrh (Mt. 2:11) or silver and costly stones (1 Cor. 3:12; Rev. 18:16). Gold was used as a currency (Acts 3:6) and made into idols (Acts 17:29), jewelry (1 Tim. 2:9), and other articles of value. Gold symbolizes great value and is used in 1 Pet. 1:7 as a standard of comparison to show the surpassing value of the Christian faith. In fact, salvation cannot be purchased by silver or gold but can only be accomplished through the sacrifice of Christ (1:18). Also symbolically, the heavenly, new Jerusalem will be a city of gold, to show both its beauty and its incredible value (Rev. 21:18, 21). See *NIDNTT-A*, 614.

GOLGOTHA

See *skull*.

GOOD

Old Testament

Noun: טוֹבָה (*tôbâ*), GK 3208 (S 2896), 67x. *tôbâ* is the noun related to the adjective *tôb* and means "good, prosperity." Joseph acknowledges to his brothers that what they intended for evil, "God intended for good" (Gen. 50:20). Indeed, the psalmist proclaims that apart from the Lord, "I have no good thing" (Ps. 16:2), and the Lord crowns our year "with good things" (65:11). After the dedication of the temple, Solomon and all Israel praised God "for all the good things the Lord had done" for them (1 Ki. 8:66). These passages remind us that whatever blessings we have received in life, we must attribute them to the goodness of the Lord.

Goodness in the OT is generally linked with material things. God promises to his people just before entering Canaan that he "will grant [them] abundant prosperity"—in giving them children, livestock, and food (Deut. 28:11). Later, Jeremiah promises that after the exile is over, God "will give them all the prosperity" he promised them. Yet the writer to Ecclesiastes warns us that mere prosperity is insufficient; we need also to have a relationship with and depend on the Lord in order "to enjoy prosperity" (Eccl. 6:3, 6). And just as prosperity can be given, it can also be taken away in judgment (see Lam. 3:17). The psalmist of Ps. 106:4–5 says it all: "Remember me, O Lord … that I may enjoy the prosperity of your chosen ones, that I may share in the joy of your nation and join your inheritance in giving praise."

Adjective: טוֹב (*tôb*), GK 3202 (S 2896), 530x. This adjective means good or well; it describes goodness, beauty, and moral uprightness. Throughout the process of creating, God declared all that he made "good" (Gen. 1:31). The entire creation is inherently valuable, it is well done, and God is satisfied with what he has made. Elsewhere, in terms of beauty, Rebekah is "*fair* to look upon," (Gen. 24:16), as is David (1 Sam. 16:12).

God warns against intentionally denying goodness and calling evil things good: "You who call evil *good* and *good* evil, who put darkness for light and light for darkness, who put bitter for sweet and sweet for bitter!" (Isa. 5:20–24). They will be consumed as in a fire. Micah declares, "He has showed you, O man, what is good. And what does the LORD require of you? To act justly and to love mercy and to walk humbly with your God" (Mic. 6:8, NIV). In Proverbs, the "child" is admonished to "walk in the way of the *good*, and keep to the paths of the just. For the upright will abide in the land, and the innocent will remain in it" (Prov. 2:20–21). Also, "a *good* name is *better* than fine perfume" (7:1).

God himself is good, as is testified numerous times in Scripture, especially in the Psalms. "You, O Lord, are *good* and forgiving, abounding in steadfast love to all who call on you" (Ps. 86:5; also 100:5, 106:1, 107:1, 118:1; 145:9). God is good to Israel, to those who are pure in heart (73:1; cf. Ezr. 3:11). Because the Lord is his shepherd, David feels confident that "*goodness* and love will follow me all the days of my life" (Ps. 23:6). See *NIDOTTE*, 2:353–57.

New Testament

Adjective: ἀγαθός (*agathos*), GK *19* (S *18*), 102x. *agathos* means "good," though its connotations overlap with *kalos* ("beautiful") and *chrēstos* ("kind").

(1) The nature of good is by definition theocentric, for the triune God defines what is good. Only God is good (Mt. 19:17). Jesus is addressed as "*good* teacher" (Mk. 10:17), and he is referred to as the "high priest of the *good things* that are already here" (Heb. 9:11). Good gifts given by God in Mt. 7:11 is equivalent to

the Holy Spirit in Lk. 11:13. The abounding of God's truth to his glory is good (Rom. 3:7–8). God's will is good (12:2), and he works all things together for good for those who love him (8:28). The work God does in believers is a good work (Phil. 1:6).

God's goodness overflows: every good and perfect thing comes from God (Jas. 1:17). Paul calls the law and the commandment good (Rom. 7:12), and the writer of Hebrews says the law has a shadow of the good things to come (Heb. 10:1).

(2) God's choice of people is not based on good things they do (Rom. 9:11). In fact, Paul contends that "nothing *good*" lives with him (7:18) and that he is unable to do the good he wants to do (7:19). Nevertheless, Paul insists he has a good conscience (Acts 23:1; 1 Tim. 1:5), and he urges Timothy to hold to the same (1 Tim. 1:19). Salvation is what provides this good conscience to Christians (1 Pet. 3:21).

Good soil in the parable means a good heart receptive to the gospel (Lk. 8:8, 15). A contrast between those who are and are not God's people can be seen in the contrast between good and evil people (Mt. 5:45; 22:10; cf. 7:18). The brood of vipers (i.e., the seed of the serpent, Gen. 3:15) cannot do good (12:34–35).

(3) Wisdom from God bears good fruit (Jas. 3:17), and good people—that is, people who are submitted to God—produce good fruit, which symbolize good deeds (Mt. 3:10; 7:17). Good men have a good treasure from which they bring forth good deeds (Lk. 6:45), as they imitate good (3 Jn. 11). Those who inherit eternal life will have done good things as evidence of their salvation (Jn. 5:29; Rom. 2:7, 10; Eph. 2:10). Paul promises that these good deeds will be rewarded (Eph. 6:8). The author of Hebrews prays for God to equip his audience with everything good that they might do his will (Heb. 13:20–21). God's grace abounds to empower good deeds (2 Cor. 9:8; cf. Phil. 2:13). To do good is to faithfully do what God expects (Mt. 25:21, 23; faithfulness = "good" in Lk. 19:17)

God redeems his people and purifies them so they will be "zealous for good works" (Tit. 2:14). They must therefore devote themselves to good deeds (3:14), unlike the Cretian false teachers, whose sinful conduct made them unfit for any good work (1:16). God-breathed Scripture equips the man of God for good works (2 Tim. 3:16–17), and sharing the faith leads to an understanding of every good thing we have in Christ (Phil. 1:6). Paul commands the Romans to be joined to the good (Rom. 12:9), and they are to overcome evil with good (12:21), to not allow good to be blasphemed (14:16), to build up their neighbors for their good (15:2), and to be "wise as to what is good and innocent as to what is evil" (16:19). Paul commands the Galatians to do good to all, especially believers (Gal. 6:9), and he prays that the Colossians will bear fruit in good works (Col. 1:10). Rather than being consumed with their appearance, women are to clothe themselves with good deeds (1 Tim. 2:9–10), like Tabitha, who was full of good works (Acts 9:36; cf. the instructions for widows in 1 Tim. 5:9–10). Those who are taught are to share all good things with their instructors (Gal. 6:6).

(4) Those in authority are servants of God for good (Rom. 13:4). "Good things" describes prosperity (Lk. 12:19; 16:25). Joseph of Arimathea is described as a good man (Lk. 23:50), as is Barnabas (Acts 11:24). See *NIDNTT-A*, 3-4.

Adjective: καλός (*kalos*), GK *2819* (S *2566*, *2570*), 101x. *kalos* denotes the quality of an object or action that is beautiful, ordered, or virtuous and may be translated as "beautiful, good." It designates something as being good in terms of its outward appearance or in the sense of useful or excellent.

In the gospels, that which is authentic in the kingdom of God is designated as "good fruit" (Mt. 3:10; 7:15–20) and "good seed" (13:24, 27, 37–38). Those who belong to the kingdom of God demonstrate their "good works" as light shining before the whole world. Jesus states, "In the same way, let your light shine before men, that they may see your *good* deeds and praise your Father in heaven" (Mt. 5:16). Paul summarizes the internal struggle faced by every believer in pleasing God according to his will when he states, "For I have the desire to do what is *good*, but I cannot carry it out.... When I want to do *good*, evil is right there with me" (Rom. 7:18, 21). Those things that are ordered and oriented to Jesus Christ and the gospel are described as "good," such as works (1 Tim. 5:10, 25; 6:18; Tit. 2:7, 14; 3:8, 14), prayer (1 Tim. 2:3), the law (Rom. 7:16; 1 Tim. 1:8), doctrine (1 Tim. 4:6), and God's creation (4:4). See *NIDNTT-A*, 286-87.

Adverb: καλῶς (*kalōs*), GK *2822* (S *2573*), 37x. *kalōs* conveys the goodness or appropriateness of an activity or action and may best be translated as "well, good, right." This word is frequently used in the gospels to indicate that someone has spoken rightly or accurately (e.g., Mk. 7:6; 12:32; Lk. 20:39). Paul uses this word to comment on the quality of the faith of the Galatian church that existed before the influence of the false teachers: "You were running a *good* race. Who cut in on you and kept you from obeying the truth?" (Gal. 5:7; cf. 1 Jn. 2:8). Jesus compares the person who hears and obeys the words of God to a wise builder who builds his house on a rock: "When a flood came, the torrent struck that house but could not shake it, because it was *well* built" (Lk. 6:48). Paul links the beneficial leadership qualities of those overseeing the church to their ability to lead at home with these words, "He must manage his own family *well* and see that his children obey him with proper respect" (1 Tim. 3:4). This term also describes the appropriate response that one should have for the inspired Word of God. Peter writes, "And we have the word of the prophets made more certain, and you will do *well* to pay attention to it, as to a light shining in a dark place, until the day dawns and the morning star rises in your hearts" (2 Pet. 1:19). See *NIDNTT-A*, 286-87.

GOOD NEWS

New Testament

Noun: εὐαγγέλιον (*euangelion*), GK *2295* (S *2098*), 76x. *euangelion* is the "good news" about the salvation God has provided through Jesus Christ. See *gospel*.

GOODNESS

New Testament

Noun: χρηστότης (*chrēstotēs*), GK *5983* (S *5544*), 10x. *chrēstotēs* means "kindness, goodness" and is used especially of God. This word occurs only in Paul's letters. See *kindness*.

GOODWILL

Old Testament

Noun: רָצוֹן (*rāṣôn*), GK 8356 (S 7522), 56x. *rāṣôn* denotes three different ideas in the OT: favor, acceptance (see *acceptable*), or will (see *please*). It is attributed most often to God (39x) and occurs most frequently in Proverbs (14x), Psalms (13x), and Leviticus (7x). The sense of *rāṣôn* as "favor" signifies a kind regard or special status usually bestowed by a superior. The NIV often translates this sense as "favor" or "favored," but also sometimes as "goodwill" (Prov. 11:27; 14:9). See *favor*.

GORGE

Old Testament

Noun: נַחַל (*naḥal*), GK 5707 (S 5158), 137x. *naḥal* refers to a dry river bed or wadi. Since it can refer to the dry river bed itself, by extension it also can be used to describe a valley or gorge. See *river*.

GOSPEL

New Testament

Noun: εὐαγγέλιον (*euangelion*), GK *2295* (S *2098*), 76x. *euangelion* is the "good news" about the salvation God has provided through Jesus Christ. The gospel is "the power of God for the salvation of everyone who believes" (Rom. 1:16). In addition, it has to do with the fulfillment of the OT promise of the coming kingdom of

God. For this reason, Jesus announces, "the time has come, the kingdom of God is near. Repent and believe the *good news*" (Mk. 1:15). Jesus' preaching is associated with healings, which are proof of the good news that the kingdom of God has arrived (Mt. 4:23; 9:35; 24:14). The NT speaks of the gospel in a way that describes its benefits: it is "the gospel of God's grace" (Acts 20:24), "the gospel of salvation" (Eph. 1:13), "the gospel of peace" (6:19), and the gospel that holds out hope (Col. 1:23). The gospel is worth dying for (Mk. 8:35; 10:29).

The gospel is intended to be preached in order to announce God's salvation in Christ and to elicit a response from those who hear it (Mt. 26:13; Mk. 1:14; 1 Cor. 9:14a; 2 Cor. 2:12; 1 Thess. 2:9). It is to be preached to all nations (Mt. 24:14; Mk. 13:10; 16:15; Acts 15:7; Rev. 14:6). Accordingly, Paul's calling is to preach the gospel to the Gentiles (Rom. 1:1, 9; 15:16, 19; Gal. 2:7; Eph. 3:6–7; 1 Thess. 2:4). At times he refers to "my gospel," which is the message of Christ's death and resurrection that God has entrusted him to preach (Rom. 2:16; 16:25; 2 Cor. 4:3; 1 Thess. 1:5; 2 Tim. 2:8), as opposed to the "different gospel" of false teachers (2 Cor. 11:4; Gal. 1:6, 7, 11; 2:2).

Paul sometimes uses *euangelion* to denote the work of evangelism (1 Thess. 3:2). He suffers for the gospel (1 Cor. 9:12; 2 Tim. 1:8; see also Phil. 1:12) and becomes all things to all people for the sake of the gospel (1 Cor. 9:23). People give service to the work of the gospel (2 Cor. 8:18; Phil. 1:5; 2:22; 4:3, 15).

euangelion also sometimes refers to the subject matter of the gospel (2 Cor. 4:4; Phil. 1:7; 1 Thess. 2:2, 8, 9; 2 Thess. 2:14). Paul reminds the Corinthians of the content of the gospel he preached to them: Christ died, was buried, and was raised on the third day (1 Cor. 15:1, 2; see also 2 Tim. 2:8). The content of the gospel is truth (Gal. 2:5; Col. 1:5) and is meant to be confessed (2 Cor. 9:13), and those who don't obey it will be punished (2 Thess. 1:8; 1 Pet. 4:17). Through the gospel message, the Gentiles become part of the people of God (Eph. 3:6). By contrast, most Jews do not receive the "good news" but reject Christ, in fulfillment of OT prophecy (Isa. 53:1 in Rom. 10:16).

The word *euangelion* was not invented by the gospel writers but was already in use in the Roman world, *euangelion.* It referred to an announcement of "glad tidings" regarding a birthday, rise to power, or decree of the emperor that was to herald the fulfillment of hopes for peace and well-being in all the world. Mark redefines this concept of "glad tidings" by introducing his gospel with the phrase, "the beginning of the good news of Jesus Christ," implying that it is really the birth and subsequent actions of Jesus that will change the face of the world in a cosmic way that no earthly king could ever do. Jesus Christ, the Son of God, brings true and lasting well-being and peace to the world, in fulfillment of OT hope. See *NIDNTT-A*, 213-15.

GOVERN

Old Testament

Verb: שָׁפַט (*šāpaṭ*), GK 9149 (S 8199), 204x. *šāpaṭ* means "to judge, govern." This word has both human beings and God as the subject. See *judge*.

GOVERNOR

New Testament

Noun: ἡγεμών (*hēgemōn*), GK *2450* (S *2232*), 20x. *hēgemōn*, "ruler, leader," communicates the general idea of ruler (Mt. 2:6; Mk. 13:9; 1 Pet. 2:14), though it is often more specifically a title for various Roman officials (Mt. 27:2; Lk. 20:20; Acts 23:24; 26:30). See *ruler*.

GRACE

Old Testament

Noun: חֵן (*ḥēn*), GK 2834 (S 2580), 69x. *ḥēn* describes that which is favorable or gracious, especially the favorable disposition of one person toward another. See *favor*.

New Testament

Noun: χάρις (*charis*), GK *5921* (S *5485*), 155x. *charis* is "grace, favor"—the acceptance of and goodness toward those who cannot earn or do not deserve such gain. As in the OT, "finding *favor* in the presence of God" (Lk. 1:30) means that God has an attitude of kindness toward someone, wishing to prosper them. Being "highly favored" highlights God's decision to bless and use that person for his good purpose (of Mary, Lk. 1:28; even of Jesus, 2:52; cf. also Stephen, Acts 6:8). Paul acknowledges that God's "grace" has called and equipped him to be the authoritative apostle of Christ's gospel (Rom. 15:15).

Jesus' mission to the world is seen as the appearance of "*grace* and truth" (Jn. 1:14, 17), even "*grace* upon *grace*" (1:16). The gospel of Jesus Christ can rightfully be called "the word of his *grace*" (Acts 14:3; 20:32) and "the gospel of the *grace* of God" (20:24), and being sent out to preach the gospel is seen as "being handed over to the *grace* of God" (14:26; 15:40).

In the NT, God's grace manifests itself most clearly in the sacrificial, substitutionary death of Jesus Christ (Rom. 3:24–26; Heb. 2:9). By nature gifts of grace cannot be earned (Rom. 11:6), for a gift earned is the opposite of a gift of grace (4:4). Grace, Christ, and salvation are so connected that those who attempt to earn righteousness have "fallen away from the *grace*" (Gal. 5:4; cf. 2:21). Salvation is "by *grace* through faith, and not of yourselves; it is the gift of God" (Eph. 2:8).

The undeserved blessings of grace are numerous. Jesus gave up the riches of heaven, making himself poor so as to make sinful humans rich—that is "grace" (2 Cor. 8:9)! Every step of God's salvation (from eternity past to the everlasting future) is accomplished through grace: his precreational choosing of the elect in Christ (Eph. 1:4–6), his inner call to the gospel (2 Tim. 1:9), his regeneration of dead sinners (Eph. 2:5), his gift of saving faith (Acts 18:27), his redemption of sinners (including justification, Tit. 3:7; forgiveness of sins, Eph. 1:7), his sanctification of believers (2 Cor. 9:8; 2 Thess. 2:16–17), his preservation of the saints (1 Cor. 1:4, 8), and his glorification of believers (1 Cor. 15:57; 2 Thess. 1:12). God saves "in order that in the coming ages he might show the surpassing richness of his *grace* in kindness on us in Christ Jesus" (Eph. 2:7).

Grace is a new domain in which and by which Christians live (Rom. 15:15; 16:20). In this realm sin no longer rules (6:14). By his grace, God affects Christians' personal lives, giving them the ability to obey the gospel from the heart (Rom. 6:17), the ability to work hard (1 Cor. 15:10), and an increase of joy in severe trials (2 Cor. 8:1–2). God graciously affects Christians' interpersonal relations, giving them care in their hearts for others (2 Cor. 8:16) and different spiritual gifts that cause the body of Christ to function together (Rom. 12:6). The believer is motivated to show practical grace to others. Jesus applies *charis* (translated "credit," "benefit," or "thanks") to the act of doing something kind for someone who has not earned and does not deserve it (Lk. 6:32–34). The Christian knows that no matter the level of suffering or weakness in life, Christ's grace toward them is sufficient (2 Cor. 12:9), allowing them to "approach the throne of *grace* with confidence in order that we may receive mercy and find *grace* to help us in our time of need" (Heb. 4:16). Dependence on Christ's power and grace causes an overflow of thanksgiving (2 Cor. 4:15). See *NIDNTT-A*, 601-4.

(TO BE) GRACIOUS

Old Testament

Verb: חָנַן (*ḥanan*), GK 2858 (S 2603), 77x. The primary meaning of *ḥānan* is "to show mercy, favor, be gracious" toward someone. See *show mercy, favor*.

GRAIN

New Testament

Noun: σῖτος (*sitos*), GK *4992* (S *4621*), 14x. *sitos* means "wheat, grain." See *wheat*.

GRAIN OFFERING

Old Testament

Noun: מִנְחָה (*minḥâ*), GK 4966 (S

4503), 211x. The basic idea conveyed by this word is "gift." *minḥâ* can designate an offering in general or, more specifically, a "grain offering." It can also refer to a present from one person to another to honor them (1 Ki. 10:25; 2 Ki. 20:12; Ps. 45:12), or a tribute given to kings or nations (Jdg. 3:15, 17–18; 2 Sam. 8:2; Ps. 72:10; Hos. 10:6). Jacob sends a "gift" to mollify his brother Esau (Gen. 32:13, 18). Joseph's brothers bring gifts to him from Canaan to merit his favor (43:11; cf. 2 Ki. 8:8–9).

A *minḥâ* can denote an "offering" of any type. Gen. 4:3–4 uses the term with reference both to Cain's offering of "the fruits of the soil" and to the firstborn of Abel's flock (cf. 1 Chr. 16:29; Ps. 96:8; Zeph. 3:10; Mal. 3:3–4). But *minḥâ* is used most often with reference to the "grain offering" (Exod. 29:41; Lev. 6:14–15, 20–21; Num. 8:8; 2 Ki. 16:13, 15; Ezek. 45:24; Amos 5:22). The regulations for this offering are described in Lev. 2:1–16. It can be given in many forms: sifted flour, baked, or prepared on a griddle or pan. Grain offerings must always contain salt (Lev. 2:13); this reminds the Israelites of God's enduring relationship with them (Num. 18:19; 2 Chr. 13:5).

The grain offering was a regular part of the burnt offering given daily at the tabernacle as a pleasing aroma to God (Num. 28:4–8; Exod. 29:41; 2 Ki. 16:15; Neh. 10:33). It reminded the Israelites of God's divine provision, and it reminded God of his commitment to his people. Even in the OT, God does not desire legalistic adherence to perfunctory ceremonies. When the heart of the worshiper is not right before God, the sacrifice is meaningless and detestable (Isa. 1:13; Amos 5:22; Mal. 1:10; 2:12–13). Jesus highlights the priority of this relationship over religious practice in Mt. 5:23–24, "Therefore, if you are offering your gift at the altar and there remember that your brother has something against you, leave your gift there in front of the altar. First go and be reconciled to your brother; then come and offer your gift."

In Isa. 66:20, we see a prophetic use of *minḥâ* that looks forward to the mission outreach among the Gentiles. When God's glory is proclaimed among the nations, people will be brought from these nations and be presented to the Lord "as an *offering*." And these people, in turn, will present to the Lord in his temple their own "grain offerings." See *NIDOTTE*, 2:978-90.

GRANDCHILD

Old Testament

Noun: בֵּן (*bēn*), GK 1201 (S 1121), 4941x. *bēn* has a wide variety of nuances in the OT, one of which is "grandchild." See *son*.

GRANDDAUGHTER

Old Testament

Noun: בַּת (*bat*), GK 1426 (S 1323), 587x. *bat* is the common Hebrew noun for one's own daughter (e.g., Gen. 24:24; 29:10; Exod. 21:7; Deut. 16:14; Jos. 15:16; 2 Sam. 6:16). But it has a variety of other nuances, including girl, granddaughter, and even woman. See *daughter*.

GRANT

Old Testament

Verb: נָתַן (*nātan*), GK 5989 (S 5414), 2014x. *nātan* is a high frequency verb in the OT and bears a wide range of meanings, some of which are "to give, present, allow, permit, surrender, deliver, set, put, place." It is sometimes used of a less tangible act of "granting," or "bestowing" a blessing, as in Gen. 28:4. See *give*.

New Testament

Verb: δίδωμι (*didōmi*), GK *1443* (S *1325*), 415x. This common verb conveys the basic idea of a transaction or transferring an object and is usually translated "give, grant, yield, permit." See *give*.

GRASP

Old Testament

Verb: אָחַז (*ʾāḥaz*), GK 296 (S 270), 63x. This verb conveys the general sense of *grasping* or *taking hold of* an object or *being taken hold of* by an object, person, or emotion (see Jdg. 1:6; Num. 31:30; Ruth 3:15; 1 Chr. 13:9). See *seize*.

Verb: חָזַק (*ḥāzaq*), GK 2616 (S 2388), 290x. *ḥāzaq* can describe the severity or strength of an impersonal force. In some cases it means "to seize, grasp." For example, Moses grasps the snake (Exod. 4:4). See *strong*.

Verb: לָקַח (*lāqaḥ*), GK 4374 (S 3947), 967x. The basic meaning of *lāqaḥ* is "to take, grasp." The meaning is often simply to "take into/by the hand, grasp." See *take*.

Verb: תָּפַשׂ (*tāpaś*), GK 9530 (S 8610), 65x. *tāpaś* conveys the seizing or grasping of an object or person, usually with a degree of force, and may be translated as "take hold of, seize." See *seize*.

New Testament

Verb: καταλαμβάνω (*katalambanō*), GK *2898* (S *2638*), 15x. *katalambanō* can mean "to catch, obtain, seize, overtake." In the middle voice it means "to grasp, understand." See *catch*.

Verb: κρατέω (*krateō*), GK *3195* (S *2902*), 47x. *krateō* means "to arrest, seize, hold, grasp." See *arrest*.

GRASS

New Testament

Noun: χόρτος (*chortos*), GK *5965* (S *5528*), 15x. *chortos* usually refers to green grass standing in a field (i.e., wild grass; Jn. 6:10). It can also refer to hay (1 Cor. 3:12) or the early stage of the stalks of a plant (Mt. 13:26; Mk. 4:28). Jesus orders the multitude to sit down on "the grass" (Mt. 14:19); Mark adds that the grass is "green" (Mk. 6:39). In Revelation, after the first trumpet blows, a third of the earth with its trees and green grass will be burned up (Rev. 8:7). The locusts are told not to harm the grass of the earth, but rather "only those people who did not have the seal of God on their foreheads" (9:5).

chortos can be used as an illustration of that which is temporary. If God governs something as minor as the grass of the field, how much more important are believers in his eyes (Mt. 6:30; Lk. 12:28). *chortos* is temporary and cannot stand the test of fire (1 Cor. 3:12), and it will pass away (Jas. 1:10, 11; 1 Pet. 1:24).*

GRAVE

Old Testament

Noun: בּוֹר (*bôr*), GK 1014 (S 953), 65x. *bôr*, often translated as "pit," can also mean "well, dungeon, cistern, grave." See *pit*.

Noun: קֶבֶר (*qeber*), GK 7700 (S 6913), 67x. Often translated "tomb" or "grave," a *qeber* is a natural cave or a hewn-out cavity used as a burial site. While *qeber* is sometimes used metaphorically (Ps. 5:9; Ezek. 37:12), in most cases it refers to the literal resting place of a dead body (Jdg. 8:32; 2 Ki. 13:21). Burial with one's own family and in one's own land was important to Israelites (Gen. 50:5). To die and be buried far from one's family was considered a divine punishment (1 Ki. 13:22). As the Lord began to fulfill his promises to Abraham, the patriarch purchases his first parcel of land in Canaan, the *qeber* of his wife, Sarah (Gen. 23:20). Jacob's insistence to be buried in Canaan rather than Egypt testifies to the fact that he believes Canaan will once again be his family's home (Gen. 50:5, 13; cf. Exod. 13:19).

Noun: שְׁאוֹל (*šeʾôl*), GK 8619 (S 7585), 65x. *šeʾôl* refers to the place known as "Sheol." It is used with reference to the "grave" or the "netherworld," the dwelling place of the dead. Descriptions of this place are not always consistent and are somewhat enigmatic. The term can simply refer to death (1 Sam. 2:6; Job 7:9; Ps. 88:3; Isa. 38:10). It is generally a place of despair and hopelessness (Gen. 42:38; Ps. 18:5; Ps. 49:14–15; 88:3–5) and is thought to be located beneath the surface of the earth (Gen. 37:35; Ezek. 32:27), which, along with its association with death (Gen. 3:19), probably explains why it is thought of as a place of dust (Job 17:16).

šeʾôl is personified as a terrifying enemy. It "enlarges its appetite and opens its mouth without limit; into it will descend their nobles and masses with all their brawlers and revelers" (Isa. 5:14). It snatches people away (Job 24:19), sets snares (Ps. 18:5), and entangles victims in its cords (116:3). It wields irresistible power over every human (89:48) and is viewed as a place where existence is reduced to almost nothing.

Isa. 14:9–11 vividly depicts the arrival of the king of Babylon in this horrible place. The rulers of the earth point out that he has "become weak," just as they are (v. 10). The lavish splendor of this great king has been reduced to the equalizing decay of death (v. 11). In contrast to the view of some cultures of the ancient world, *šeʾôl* is not a place where life continues in a different state. According to Ecclesiastes, "in the *grave*, where you are going, there is neither working nor planning nor knowledge nor wisdom" (Eccl. 9:10).

Despite its terrible power, *šeʾôl* is no obstacle for God. He can deliver his people from the grave (Ps. 16:10; 49:14; 56:13; 86:13) and offer hope beyond what can be expected from the gods of wood and stone. "But your dead will live; their bodies will rise. You who dwell in the dust, wake up and shout for joy. Your dew is like the dew of the morning; the earth will give birth to her dead" (Isa. 26:19; cf. Dan. 12:2; 1 Cor. 15:51–55). See *NIDOTTE*, 4:6-7.

New Testament

Noun: ᾅδης (*hadēs*), GK *87* (S *86*), 10x. *hadēs* is found in the NT only in Matthew, Luke, Acts, and Revelation. In Acts 1:27, 31 *hadēs* occurs in a quote from Ps. 16, where the Heb. word Sheol ("grave") occurs. See above; see also *hell*.

Noun: μνημεῖον (*mnēmeion*), GK *3646* (S *3419*), 40x. *mnēmeion* means "grave, tomb." All of its occurrences are found in the gospels plus one in Acts (Acts 13:29). It comes from the Greek root *mnē*, which essentially means "remember." More than half of the references in the NT are to Jesus' tomb (e.g., Mt. 27:60; Mk. 15:46; Lk. 23:55; Jn. 19:41; Acts 13:29). It is also used for the tombs where the demoniac roamed (Mk. 5:2) and Lazarus's grave (Jn. 11:17, 31, 38; 12:17). Jesus rebuked the Pharisees, calling them unmarked graves (Lk. 11:44). He spoke of the resurrection of the dead, saying that everyone in the tombs will hear his voice and rise (Jn. 5:28–29). Matthew records that after Jesus' death, the graves broke open (Mt. 27:52), and after his resurrection, holy people left their tombs and came into Jerusalem, appearing to many people (27:53). See *NIDNTT-A*, 239.

GRAZE

Old Testament

Verb: רָעָה (*rāʿâ*), GK 8286 (S 7473), 167x. *rāʿâ* means "to shepherd, tend, feed graze." This verb can thus be used for sheep feeding or grazing in a pasture. See *shepherd*.

GREAT

Old Testament

Noun: רֹב (*rōb*), GK 8044 (S 7230) 150x. *rōb* denotes a multitude or an abundance. It is probably derived from the verb *rābâ*, which means to become numerous, much, or great. Ps. 33:16 states, "The king is not victorious by the *multitude* of an army, nor will a war-hero be saved by an *abundance* of strength." Since *rōb* is often used to modify another noun, it can be translated as an adjective. For example, Ps. 33:16 can also be translated using the phrases "by a *great* army" and "by *great* strength." See *many*.

Adjective: גָּדוֹל (*gādôl*), GK 1524 (S 1419), 527x. *gādôl* means "great, large." It is used to describe the size of things such as the "great" creatures of the sea (Gen. 1:21), the "vast" desert of Sinai (Deut. 1:19), the "great" Nile River (Gen. 15:18), the "great" size of an army (2 Ki. 7:6), the great strength of God (Gen. 4:37), the great size of Abram's nation (Gen. 12:2), the great fire of the LORD (Gen. 18:16), and the great pestilence God sent against Israel (Jer. 21:6).

Greatness can also be ascribed to abstract things, such as God's "mighty" judgments (Exod. 6:6) and a "great" victory (Jdg. 15:18; 1 Sam. 19:5). The status of Joseph in the house of Potiphar was "great" (Gen. 39:9). Human sinfulness can also be "great" (Exod. 32:21), and God's people sometimes commit "great" blasphemies (Neh. 9:26).

Finally, greatness is ascribed to God in various ways. Many times God (Deut. 7:21; 10:17; Dan. 9:4) and the Lord (Exod. 18:11; Ps. 48:1; 95:3; 96:4; 135:5; 145:3) are called "great." Moreover, many of God's characteristics are great, such as his name (Ps. 76:1; 99:3), power (Exod. 32:11), kindness (1 Ki. 3:6), glory (Ps. 21:5), and wrath (Jer. 32:37). See *NIDOTTE*, 1:823–27.

Adverb: הַרְבֵּה (*harbēh*), GK 2221 (S 7235), 50x. *harbēh* means "many, great." See *many*.

New Testament

Adjective: μέγας (*megas*), GK *3489* (S *3173*), 243x. *megas* means "great, loud, large" and is found throughout the NT. Revelation accounts for almost one-third of its occurrences. It can have a general meaning of something that exceeds the norm and sometimes is used in a context of theological significance.

(1) *megas* can simply refer to something that exceeds the norm. For example, the shepherds in Lk. 2:10 rejoice with "great" joy. The NT also speaks of a "great" storm (Mt. 8:26) and "great" faith (Mt. 15:28). Jesus cries out with a "loud" voice (Lk. 23:46), as do demons (8:28) and those who are healed (17:15). People can be "greatly" astounded (Mk. 5:42; Lk. 19:37; 23:23; Acts 7:60; 19:34; 23:9). The stone at the tomb was "great" (Mk. 16:4). "Great" signs and wonders are done at the hands of the apostles (Acts 4:33; 6:8; 8:13), signifying the Lord's presence and power. Likewise, "great" fear can fall on a people as a result of judgment (5:5, 11). Paul can speak of his "great" sorrow because of the present unbelief of the Jewish nation (Rom. 9:2).

(2) The witness of God is "great" (1 Jn. 5:9). Paul writes that the mystery of Christ and the church is "great" (Eph. 5:32), as is the mystery of godliness (1 Tim. 3:16). Christ Jesus is the "great" God and Savior (Tit. 2:13). In Hebrews, Jesus is the "great" high priest and "great" *s*hepherd (Heb. 4:14; 10:21; 13:20).

The Sermon on the Mount teaches that to be "great" in the kingdom one must keep and teach the commandments of God. True "greatness" is ascribed to those who serve (Lk. 22:27). This word also refers to great things that will occur in the end times. There will be "great" earthquakes and signs (Lk. 21:11) and distress (21:13). Many cosmic signs and wonders will accompany the "great" Day of the Lord (Acts 2:20; Jude 6). The tribulation is "great" (Rev. 7:14; cf. Mt. 24:14), as is the Day of Judgment (6:17). Often the Lord's voice is "great" or "loud" (Rev. 1:10; 5:2; 7:2; 10:3; 11:15; 16:1; 21:3). See *NIDNTT-A*, 359.

Adjective: πολύς (*polys*), GK *4498* (S *4118*, *4119*, *4183*), 416x. *polys* is used to designate a large quantity ("many") or size ("great/large"). See *many*.

(BE) GREAT

Old Testament

Verb: גָּדַל (*gādal*), GK 1540 (S 1431), 117x. *gādal* means "to be(come) great, exalted; to make great, exalt, magnify." The greatness can be that of quantity or quality.

(1) In a stative sense, *gādal* means "to be great" and can refer either to persons or things (e.g., an outcry to the Lord, Gen. 19:13; a feast, Gen. 21:8; riches and wisdom, 1 Ki. 10:23; God's love, Num. 14:19). King David praises God for his greatness: "You are great, O LORD, for there is none like you" (2 Sam. 7:22; cf. 1 Sam. 12:24; Ps. 35:27: 40:17; 70:5; 104:1; Mic. 5:3; Mal. 1:5).

(2) When used of children, *gādal* simply means that they are weaned and have grown up (Gen. 21:8, 20; Exod. 2:10).

(3) *gādal* can also mean to make great or to magnify someone or something, and in most cases God is the subject of the magnifying action. In fulfilling his purposes on earth, he makes great those whom he wills (Jos. 3:7; 1 Sam. 2:21; 2 Sam. 5:10; 1 Ki. 1:37, 47), all the while magnifying his own perfect work (1 Sam. 12:24;

Ps. 126:2, 3; Joel 2:21). If God were to exalt anything or anyone over himself, he would be an idolater! The proper human response to God's work in history, therefore, is to join him in that which he is most passionate about—magnifying God: "I will praise God's name in song and *magnify* him with thanksgiving" (Ps. 69:30; cf. 70:4; 92:5; 104:1; 126:2; 138:2).

God's passion to preserve and display his greatness is highlighted in an intriguing way in three key passages that contain *gādal*. In Gen. 12:2–3 God promises that he will make Abra(ha)m great and that through the patriarch's offspring, blessing, the reversal of the curse in Gen. 3, will spread to the world. This promise is then restated and clarified to King David, where the Lord pledges to make David's name great and to establish the Davidic dynasty forever (2 Sam. 7:12–29; cf. 1 Chr. 17). Finally, the prophet Micah declared that a King from Bethlehem will one day "stand and shepherd his flock in the strength of the LORD, in the majesty of the name of the LORD his God. And they will live securely, for then his *greatness* will reach to the ends of the earth" (Mic. 5:4). This offsping, this Shepherd King, is Jesus the Messiah, whose greatness spans the universe and who therefore deserves to be *magnified* among his people (Mt. 28:18–20; cf. Rom. 12:1–6).

GREATER

New Testament

Adjective: μείζων (*meizōn*), GK *3505* (S *3183, 3187*), 48x. *meizōn* is the comparative adjective of *megas* (see *great*) and can also be used in the superlative sense (see *greatest*). Jesus states that John is *greater* than all others born of women (Mt. 11:11). He rebukes the Pharisees, "You blind fools! Which is *greater*: the gold, or the temple that makes the gold sacred?" (23:17). Likewise, no commandment is "greater" than loving God and neighbor (Mk. 12:31). The Samaritan woman questions Jesus, "Are you *greater* than our father Abraham?" (Jn. 4:12; cf. 8:53). Jesus' ministry is *greater* than John the Baptist's (5:36). Likewise, no servant is *greater* than his master (13:16). Jesus declares that, "the Father is *greater* than I" (14:28; 15:20). This does not suggest inequality in the Trinity, but rather expresses a willing subordination of the Son to the will of the Father. For Paul, prophecy is *greater* than speaking in tongues (1 Cor. 14:5). In 1 John, "God is *greater* than our hearts" (1 Jn. 3:20), and the witness of God is "greater" than the witness of humankind (1 Jn. 5:9). *meizōn* can also mean "older," as in the case of Esau (Rom. 9:12).

Adjective: περισσότερος (*perissoteros*), GK *4358* (S *4055*), 7x. *perissoteros* describes an object or person as either "greater" or "more" than what would be considered normal.

John the Baptist is "greater than" a prophet in that he has prepared the way for the King of Israel (Mt. 11:9; cf. Lk. 7:26). Jesus instructs his disciples to fear God, who can kill "more than" the body by also throwing one into hell (Lk. 12:4). *perissoteros* describes the severe punishment of hypocritical religious leaders (Mk. 12:40; cf. Lk. 20:47). Luke uses this as a reminder that of those who have been given much, even more will be asked in return (Lk. 12:48; cf. 2 Cor. 10:8). Jesus tells an inquirer that he is not far from the kingdom because he understands that loving God and one's neighbor is more important than any religious ceremony (Mk. 12:33). God chooses to swear on himself in order to demonstrate his "great" willingness to prove the unchangeable nature of his promises (Heb. 6:17). By God's grace Paul has labored more than the other apostles (1 Cor. 15:10). Paul commands the Corinthians to welcome a repentant sinner back into their community so that he will not experience greater sorrow (2 Cor. 2:7; cf. 1 Cor. 12:23–25). See *NIDNTT-A*, 454-55.*

GREATEST

New Testament

Adjective: μείζων (*meizōn*), GK *3505* (S *3183, 3187*), 48x. *meizōn* is the comparative adjective of *megas* (see *great*) and means "greater" (see *greater*), but it can also be used in the superlative sense ("greatest"). In Mt. 18:1ff., the disciples ask Jesus as to who "is the *greatest*" in the kingdom (cf. 23:11; Mk. 9:34; Lk. 9:46; 22:24, 26); Jesus tells them that true greatness involves humility, brokenness, and sacrifice. John the Baptist is "the greatest" of all those born of women (Lk. 7:28). Paul states that love is the "greatest" of the three abiding virtues (1 Cor. 13:13).

GREATLY

Old Testament

Noun: מְאֹד (*me*ʾ*ōd*), GK 4394 (S 3966), 300x. *me*ʾ*ōd* is usually used adverbially, meaning "very, much, greatly, exceedingly." On the sixth day of creation, the Lord surveyed what he had made and proclaimed it "*very* good" (Gen. 1:31). By contrast, the people of Sodom "were wicked and were sinning against the Lord *exceedingly*" (Gen. 13:13). In Ps. 47:9, the Lord is described in praise as "*greatly* exalted." Occasionally the word is used as a noun, in which case it means "power, might." One of the two greatest commandments, as identified by Jesus in the gospels, comes from Deut. 6:5, where Israel is commanded to give the Lord unswerving loyalty by "loving the Lord your God with all your heart, soul, and *strength*" (see also 2 Ki. 23:25, which cites Deut. 6:5). See *NIDOTTE*, 2:824-27.

New Testament

Adverb: σφόδρα (*sphodra*), GK *5379* (S *4970*), 11x. *sphodra* is an adverb that increases the intensity of the accompanying verbal concept. For example, when the wise men saw the star, they were not only happy, but "exceedingly" happy (Mt. 2:10). When the disciples saw Jesus transfigured, they were not just frightened, but "terrified" (17:6; cf. 27:34). When Jesus told his disciples that one of them would betray him, they were "very" sad (26:22). In the expansion of the NT church, it increased "rapidly" (Acts 6:7).

GREED

New Testament

Noun: πλεονεξία (*pleonexia*), GK *4432* (S *4124*), 10x. *pleonexia* means "greed, covetousness." This term is a common component in the lists of vices that a Christian should avoid (Mk. 7:21; Rom. 1:29; Eph. 5:3; Col. 3:5). According to 2 Pet. 2:3, greed is a characteristic of false prophets, who are out to exploit people for their own monetary advancement. Paul expressly disavows greed as a motivation for his ministry (1 Thess. 2:5; cf. also the related verb *pleonekteō*, "to exploit," in 2 Cor. 7:2; 12:17–18). In fact, all believers should "guard against all kinds of *greed*" (Lk. 12:15). And in our giving, we should give freely and willingly, not with a grudging desire to keep for ourselves (2 Cor. 9:5, "not grudgingly given").

While *pleonexia* usually denotes a desire for material possessions, the NT often associates this monetary desire with sexual immorality. For example, in Eph. 4:19 greed is a characteristic of "sensuality" ("lasciviousness" [KJV]); in Eph. 5:3 and Col. 3:5, it is associated with "sexual immorality" ("fornication" [KJV]); and in Mk. 7:21 and 2 Pet. 2:14, it is closely associated with adultery. Thus, the desire for someone else's property is not so different from the desire for someone else's spouse or other kinds of illicit sexual behavior. See *NIDNTT-A*, 468.*

GREEKS

New Testament

Noun: Ἕλλην (*Hellēn*), GK *1818* (S *1672*), 25x. *Hellēn* communicates three ideas, all related to the Greek or Gentile world. (1) At its most basic level, *Hellēn* designates a person of Greek language or culture. Paul calls himself a debtor to both Greeks and barbarians (Rom. 1:14), as if the former were of the cultured sort whereas the barbarians were not. Even cultured Romans, who had an interest in the Greek culture that preceded them, considered themselves under this term.

(2) In a *cultural* sense *Hellēn* refers to all persons who came under the influence

of Greek culture, as distinguished from Israel's culture. Since Greek culture so dominated NT times, the term can refer to most individuals living in that era. The term "Hellenism" comes from *Hellēn*. Concepts like polytheism fall under the rubric of Hellenism. In Jn. 7:35 the Jews speak of the Greeks in this capacity.

(3) From *religious* perspective, *Hellēn* was understood as anyone who was a non-Jew. As far as the Jews were concerned, a person was either a Jew or a Gentile/Greek. Paul clearly has those two worlds in mind when he discusses religious things ("but to those whom God has called, both Jews and Greeks," 1 Cor. 1:24). For Paul, the phrase "Jews and Greeks" can stand for all of humanity (Col. 3:11). Although the OT shows God's relationship to the Jews, the NT brings both "Jews and Greeks" into this relationship ("to the Jew first, and also to the Greek," Rom. 1:16). Through Christ all Christians, no matter their cultural background, are a new people of God; differences of origin are removed (Gal. 3:28). All cultures that have been baptized into Christ have been baptized into "one body" (1 Cor. 12:13). Being a Jew or a Greek belongs to our pre-Christian days, which must be put away along with all its evil characteristics (Col. 3:3, 11). See *NIDNTT-A*, 182-83.

GREET

New Testament

Verb: ἀσπάζομαι, *aspazomai*, GK *832* (S *782*), 59x. *aspazomai* means "to greet, welcome." It occurs only 13x in the gospels and Acts. When Mary meets Elizabeth at her house, she "greets" her warmly (Lk. 1:40). When Jesus sends his disciples out on their mission, they are to give a greeting to whatever house they enter, wishing them "peace" (Shalom). If a welcome is not reciprocated, they are to leave, shaking the dust off their feet (Mt. 10:12). *aspazomai* can be used either at the beginning (Mk. 9:15) or at the end of a meeting (Acts 20:1).

aspazomai is most commonly used in the NT letters as a way to greet various churches and individuals (Rom. 16:3–16, 21-23; 1 Cor. 16:19–20; 2 Cor. 13:12–13). The greeting between believers often included an embrace and a "holy kiss" (Rom. 16:16; 1 Cor. 16:20; 2 Cor. 13:12; 1 Thess. 5:26; 1 Pet. 5:14). *aspazomai* is used once in a theological context by the author of Hebrews, who wrote in Heb. 11:13, "All these people were still living by faith when they died. They did not receive the things promised; they only saw them and *welcomed* them from a distance." The verb here means to express happiness about the arrival of something.

GREETING

New Testament

Noun: ἀσπασμός (*aspasmos*), GK *833* (S *783*), 10x. *aspasmos* signifies a salutation or greeting. It can describe a greeting given in person (like the one given by Gabriel to Mary in Lk. 1:29 or Mary's greeting to Elizabeth in 1:41, 44). The scribes and Pharisees loved to receive greetings in the marketplace (Mt. 23:7).

aspasmos is also used in written salutations, such as: "I, Paul, write this greeting in my own hand" (1 Cor. 16:21; Col. 4:18; 2 Thess. 3:17). Note Paul's emphasis on his personally writing the greeting. In the first century, Paul used a skilled secretary (the technical word is an *amanuensis)* to write the basic content of his letters. But the phrase "in my own hand" is like a personal signature. The recipients of his letters know that the contents of the letter are authentically from their apostle. And his own personal *aspasmos* most likely includes his closing greeting, also probably written in his own hand: "Grace be with you." Paul's letters are not some mass mailing with little real care as to who is receiving them. On the contrary, his greeting indicates a genuine concern for the recipients. See *NIDNTT-A*, 216-218.

GRIEF

New Testament

Noun: λυπή (*lypē*), GK *3383* (S *3077*), 16x. *lypē* denotes "grief, sorrow, pain," the result that comes from the action of the verb *lypē* (see *grieve*). It can be physical pain that comes from childbirth (Jn. 16:21), emotional pain that comes from relational difficulties (e.g., those experienced by Paul and the Corinthian church, 2 Cor. 2:1), or an unpleasant mixture of the two that results from either discipline (Heb. 12:11) or persecution (1 Pet. 2:19).

lypē links pain with the grief that follows, e.g., when Jesus uses a woman's physical pain in childbirth to describe the sorrow that the church will experience from his absence (Jn. 16:20, 22). *lypē* has a deep effect on people, including heaviness of heart (Jn. 16:6; Rom. 9:2), distress (2 Cor. 2:3), or even weariness (Lk. 22:45). Grief can even affects relationships, and because of that people may be "reluctant" to give to others (2 Cor. 9:7). It is possible for grief to overwhelm someone (Phil. 2:7); thus, Paul exhorts Christians to forgive and comfort each other (2 Cor. 2:7). But one of the great blessings of the gospel is that God can even use the believer's sorrow to his or her own spiritual good, bringing repentance out of grief (2 Cor. 7:10). See *NIDNTT-A*, 344.*

GRIEVE

Old Testament

Verb: נָחַם (*nāḥam*), GK 5714 (S 5162), 108x. *nāḥam* bears two distinct but related meanings in the OT: "to comfort, console" (see *comfort*) and "to relent, repent, change one's mind, be grieved." This verb is especially applied to God's changing his mind (see *change one's mind*).

New Testament

Verb: λυπέω (*lypeō*), GK *3382* (S *3076*), 26x. *lypeō* means "to grieve, feel sorrow or pain." This verb refers to the emotional or mental state that results from any situation of grief, such as pain or distress.

Paul uses *lypeō* five times in 2 Cor. 2, in which he describes the sadness that has come on him and the church because of sin. Paul regrets that he caused the Corinthians to sorrow when he last saw them (2 Cor. 2:2), and he determines not to grieve over them when he should rejoice (2:3). Grief is often the result of emotional pain, e.g., when the disciples grieve at Jesus' impending departure (Jn. 16:20), when Peter is struck by Jesus' repeated questioning of his love (Jn. 21:17), or even when the rich young ruler is disturbed by the command of Jesus to sell all he has (Mt. 19:22; Mk. 10:22). Herod experiences grief as a result of his rash promise to the daughter of Herodias (Mk. 14:9), and *lypeō* also describes the distress of the brother who observes another eating meat sacrificed to idols (Rom. 14:15). *lypeō* is the mixture of fear, sadness, and concern that comes on the disciples when Jesus states that one of them will betray him (Mt. 26:22; Mk. 14:19).

But Christians need not feel overwhelmed by grieving. Peter writes to those who grieve as a result of suffering and persecution, yet at the same time they greatly rejoice (1 Pet. 1:6). Elsewhere, Paul describes the makeup of a Christian as one who grieves at present difficulties, yet inwardly rejoices (2 Cor. 6:10).

Finally, one use of *lypeō* serves as proof of the personality of the Holy Spirit, who is said to grieve at the sins of Christians (Eph. 4:30). See *NIDNTT-A*, 344.

Verb: πενθέω (*pentheō*), GK *4291* (S *3996*), 10x. *pentheō* means "to mourn, grieve, bewail." This word is used in contexts of mourning over disasters or grieving the loss of someone. See *mourn*.

GROUND

Old Testament

Noun: אֲדָמָה (*ʾᵃdāmâ*), GK 141 (S 127), 222x. *ʾᵃdāmâ* has a variety of nuances in the OT (see *land*). It is used in reference to the covenant promises and warnings about the earth (Exod. 20:12; Deut. 4:40; 2 Ki. 17:23; Amos 7:11, 17). It can mean also cultivatable ground in particular as compared to desert or barren lands (Gen. 2:5; Zech. 13:5). It is the *ʾᵃdāmâ* that is cursed by God after the fall (Gen. 3:17). Thus, in this earthly realm, all of humanity's labor—not only agricultural—is now subjected to difficulty and futility.

New Testament

Noun: γῆ (*gē*), GK *1178* (S *1093*), 250x. *gē* is the standard word for "earth, land, soil" in the NT. It occurs especially in the gospels, Acts, and Revelation. See *earth*.

GROW

New Testament

Verb: αὐξάνω (*auxanō*), GK *889* (S *837*), 21x. *auxanō* means "to grow, increase, become greater." In Mt. 6:28 and Mk. 4:8, it refers (in a parable) to the natural growth of plants. Luke adds that as a boy Jesus "grows up" (Lk. 2:40). John uses *auxanō* on the lips of John the Baptist: "He must *become greater*, I must become less," (Jn. 3:30). As the forerunner of Christ, he will recede into the background since the promised one has arrived (cf. Isa. 40:3).

In Acts, Luke tells us that the "Word of God *increased*" or "*spread*" (Acts 6:7; 12:24; 19:20). The missionary endeavor instituted by Christ (in Acts 1:8) has increased throughout the known world. Stephen reflects that the people of Israel "*increased* in number" when they were slaves in Egypt (7:17).

In the NT letters, Paul notes that though he planted and Apollos watered, God is the one who brought about growth (1 Cor. 3:6, 7). The church grows both numerically and spiritually. This finds expression in a growth in personal and corporate righteousness, as well as an increase in one's faith (2 Cor. 9:10; 10:15). The body of Christ "grows" (Eph. 4:15) and bears spiritual fruit (Col. 1:6), "*growing* in the knowledge of God" (Col. 1:10). Peter echoes this same theme, likening the new believer to newborn babies: "Like newborn babies, crave pure spiritual milk, so that by it you may in your salvation" (1 Pet. 2:2). This kind of growth in spiritual maturity is linked to growth in knowledge of doctrine and the things of God (2 Pet. 3:18).

Verb: πληθύνω (*plēthynō*), GK *4437* (S *4129*), 12x. *plēthyno* means "to increase, grow, multiply." See *increase*.

GRUMBLE

New Testament

Verb: γογγύζω (*gongyzō*), GK *1197* (S *1111*), 8x. *gongyzō* means "to grumble, murmur." Human beings have an amazing capacity to grumble when they see something as unfair or when things don't go their way. The Israelites grumbled in the desert after the exodus, and God judged them (1 Cor. 10:10). In the parable of the workers in the vineyard, those who worked all day for the same wages as those who worked one hour "began to grumble against the landowner" (Mt. 20:11). On several occasions the Jewish leaders began to grumble about things Jesus said or did (Lk. 5:30; Jn. 6:41, 43; 7:32). Even followers of Jesus sometimes grumbled against him (Jn. 6:61). But such grumbling is sin, for it does not accept what comes from the hand of our good God. Thus, using the noun related to this verb (*gongysmos*), both Paul and Peter instruct believers to live our Christian lives without grumbling or complaining (Phil. 2:14; 1 Pet. 4:9). See *NIDNTT-A*, 111.

GUARANTEE

New Testament

Noun: ἀρραβών (*arrabōn*), GK *775* (S *728*), 3x. *arrabōn* is a "pledge or deposit guaranteeing what is to come." A Heb. word that in the OT is used on a purely human level (e.g., Gen. 38:17–20) becomes a transliterated Greek word to describe what God has done for us by his saving grace. See *pledge*.

GUARD

Old Testament

Verb: שָׁמַר (*šāmar*), GK 9068 (S 8104), 468x. Often translated "to keep," the verb *šāmar* bears three distinct but related meanings in the OT: "to guard, tend," "to watch over," and "to preserve" (see *keep*). For example, it is used of guarding against intruders (Gen. 3:24; 1 Sam. 26:15; Song 5:7; Isa. 21:11).

Verb: נָצַר (*nāṣar*), GK 5915 (S 5341), 63x. *nāṣar* generally indicates the action of carefully watching over a particular object so that the object is preserved or protected. It may be translated "to keep, guard, watch, protect." God "preserves" the faithful (Ps. 31:23) and "guards" their lives (Prov. 24:12) from trouble (Ps. 32:7), from violent men (140:1, 4), and from the plot of their enemies (64:1). See *keep*.

Noun: מִשְׁמֶרֶת (*mišmeret*), GK 5466 (S 4931), 78x. *mišmeret* derives from the verb *šāmar*, "to keep, watch, guard," and denotes the regular responsibility or duty to care for or guard an object. Sometimes the guarded object is a general reference to God's law, but usually it refers to a specific object, and often that object is cultic in nature (i.e., used in worship). See *duty*.

In a noncultic sense, *mišmeret* may refer to a "guard" in the sense of a military watchman defending Jerusalem (Neh. 7:3), to a "ward" in the sense of a place of confinement that is under guard (2 Sam. 20:3), or to a "guard post" in the sense of the place from which guard is kept (Isa. 21:8).

New Testament

Verb: γρηγορέω (*grēgoreō*), GK *1213* (S *1127*), 22x. *grēgoreō* means "to keep watch over, guard" something. It carries the idea of vigilance in the face of something impending. See *watch*.

Verb: προσεχω (*prosechō*), GK *4668* (S *4337*), 24x. *prosechō* means "to guard, watch out, pay attention," usually with a warning implication. Jesus instructs his disciples to watch out for false prophets (Mt. 7:15) and to be on guard for the influence of the Pharisees (16:6, 11; Lk. 12:1; cf. 20:46). In the Pastoral Letters, Paul instructs Titus to "pay no attention" to Jewish myths (Tit. 1:14; cf. 1 Tim. 1:4). In Acts 20:28, Paul instructs the elders of Ephesus to "watch over themselves and all the flock," because apostasy will come in their midst.

In a more positive sense, Lydia opened her heart to "pay attention and respond" to Paul's message (Acts 16:14). Timothy must "devote himself" to the public reading of Scripture (1 Tim. 4:13). In fact, we all must pay close attention to the message of Christ so that we do not drift away from it (Heb. 2:1; cf. 2 Pet. 1:19).

Verb: φυλάσσω (*phylassō*), GK *5875* (S *5442*), 31x. *phylassō* means to "guard" physically or to "keep" in the sense of observing (see *keep*). It often indicates a careful and constant guarding of someone or something of importance. It is most often applied to guarding prisoners (Lk. 8:29; Acts 12:4; 23:35; 28:16), but is also used of guarding personal property such as flocks (Lk. 2:8), a palace (11:21), and garments (Acts 22:20).

Spiritually, Paul exhorts Timothy to guard the deposit of faith in a careful, constant manner through the help of the Holy Spirit (1 Tim. 6:20; 2 Tim. 1:12, 14). People are also encouraged to guard themselves (i.e., beware) against certain things: covetousness (Lk. 12:15), idols (1 Jn. 5:21), the error of lawlessness (2 Pet. 3:17), and those who seek their harm (2 Tim. 4:15). Paradoxically, Jesus says that whoever wishes to guard his life eternally must lose it and not be preoccupied with seeking to keep it safe on earth (Jn. 12:25).

God also guards his people in a careful, constant way. Just as God guarded Noah from the flood and brought him safely to dry land (2 Pet. 2:5), Jesus guarded his apostles while he is on earth with them (Jn. 17:12). He promises to keep believers safe from the evil one (2 Thess. 3:3) and to present them blameless in the last day (Jude 24).

Noun: ὑπηρέτης (*hypēretēs*), GK *5677* (S *5257*), 20x. *hypēretēs* denotes those who serve in a subordinate position, such as "guards" or "officials" under orders. See *official*.

GUEST

New Testament

Verb: ἀνάκειμαι (*anakeimai*), GK *367* (S *345*), 14x. The image that *anakeimai* captures is that of a person lying outstretched on a couch in front of a low table. When several people do that, they are considered "dinner guests." See *recline*.

GUILT

Old Testament

Noun: עָוֹן (*ʿāwōn*), GK 6411 (S 5771), 233x. *ʿāwōn* is usually translated "sin, guilt, wickedness, iniquity" and is one of the three primary words for sin in the OT, an offense against God that ranges from willful rebellion to unintentional sins (see *sin*).

GUILT OFFERING

Old Testament

Noun: אָשָׁם (*ʾāšām*), GK 871 (S 817), 47x. *ʾāšām* is a "guilt offering," one of the main offerings discussed in Leviticus (see Lev. 5:14–6:6; cf. also Ezr. 10:19), but it can also be a more general word for "penalty" (e.g., Lev. 5:5, 6). The "guilt offering" was used "as a penalty" for an unintentional sin, and the animal offered was to be a ram without defect. The sin offering was also used "as a penalty" to atone for sin, but in this case *ʾāšām* is not considered a guilt offering. The *ʾāšām* offering was also used after a person who had a skin disease was declared clean (14:12–28) and for certain sexual sins (19:21–22). This same noun is used by the Philistines after they captured the ark of the covenant but then decided to send it back after a plague broke out in their midst; they accompanied the ark with "a guilt offering" (1 Sam. 6:3–4, 8, 17). Most important, this noun is used in connection with the Servant of the Lord in Isa. 53:10, that "the Lord makes his life a guilt offering"; in Christian typology, this refers to the sacrifice of Jesus Christ on the cross. See *NIDOTTE*, 1:557–66.

GUILTY

Old Testament

Adjective: רָשָׁע (*rāšāʿ*), GK 8401 (S 7563), 264x. As an adjective *rāšāʿ* describes the quality of being wicked, evil, guilty, or unjust. When the adjective is used as a noun, it refers to a wicked, evil, or guilty person. See *wicked*.

New Testament

Adjective: ἔνοχος (*enochos*), GK *1944* (S *1777*), 10x. *enochos* means "guilty, subject to, liable for, worthy of." In classic Greek this adjective means "be subject to" and was frequently used as a procedural legal term. As such, *enochos* in a forensic sense denotes the connection of a person either with his crime or his punishment. In a similar vein, *enochos* occurs four times in Mt. 5:21–22, each in respect to a different court before which an accused must appear and plead his case.

Mt. 26:66 and Mk. 14:64 both use *enochos* to pronounce the death sentence at the trial of Christ ("he is *worthy* of death"). Jas. 2:10 uses *enochos* to indicate guilt for sin and the corresponding obligation to punishment on that account. In 1 Cor. 11:27 Paul uses this word to indicate that someone who does not properly discern the body of Christ in the Lord's Supper becomes "guilty of" sinning against Christ. See *NIDNTT-A*, 186-87.

(BE) GUILTY

Old Testament

Verb: אָשַׁם (*ʾāšam*), GK 870 (S 816), 35x. *ʾāšam* means "to be guilty, be condemned." Sin against God was an ongoing problem in the Israelite community, as it continues to be for us. Note that such guilt is not primarily a feeling; in fact, guilt can be present even if an individual is not aware of having done anything against God's law (Lev. 5:2–4, 17), and such guilt must still be dealt with (5:5; cf. Num. 5:5–6). Isaiah insists that all people on earth must "bear their guilt" (Isa. 24:6; cf. Hos. 10:2). If, however, we take refuge in the Lord, we "will not be *condemned*." He is our only hope.

Verb: חָטָא (*ḥāṭāʾ*), GK 2627 (S 2398), 240x. The verb *ḥāṭāʾ* carries the basic meanings of "to miss (the mark)" and by extension "to sin, be guilty." See *sin*.

HABIT

New Testament

Noun: ἔθος (*ethos*), GK *1621* (S *1485*), 12x. *ethos* is the tendency or convention by which things are done, a "habit" or "custom." See *custom*.

HADES

New Testament

Noun: ᾅδης (*hadēs*), GK *87* (S *86*), 10x. *hadēs* is found in the NT only in Matthew, Luke, Acts, and Revelation, though the idea is also found in other texts (1 Pet. 3:19; 4:6). It is conceived as an underground prison with locked gates to which Christ holds the key (Mt. 16:18; Lk. 16:23; Acts 2:27, 31; Rev. 1:18). *hadēs* is a temporary place that will give up its dead at the general resurrection (Rev. 20:13–14). See *hell*.

HAIR

New Testament

Noun: θρίξ (*thrix*), GK *2582* (S *2359*), 15x. *thrix* means "*hair*." On at least two occasions, Jesus' feet were washed and dried by a woman's "*hair*" (Lk. 7:36, 44; Jn. 11:2). Peter reminds us that we should spend more time working on inner beauty than fussing with our hair and fine jewelry (1 Pet. 3:3).

Jesus says that the Father values his children to the extent that "even the hairs of your head are all numbered" (Mt. 10:30; Lk. 12:7). Despite persecution that is certain to come for believers, Jesus offers a promise of protection, that "not a *hair* of your head will perish" (Lk. 21:18; cf. Acts 27:34; a proverbial expression found in the OT, 1 Sam. 14:45; 2 Sam. 14:11; 1 Ki. 1:52). Because two verses (Lk. 21:16) earlier Jesus shows that there will be Christian martyrs, "perish" must refer to spiritual fate; Jesus' protection keeps them not from death but from hell. Jesus' white hair in Rev. 1:14 symbolizes his wisdom and dignity (cf. Dan. 7:9).

HAIRY

Old Testament

Adjective: שָׂעִיר (*ṣāʿîr*), GK 8537 (S 8163), 3x. *ṣāʿîr* almost always means "(hairy) goat," but in a few instances it operates as an adjective meaning "hairy"––e.g., Esau's appearance (Gen. 27:11, 23; cf. Dan. 8:21). This may be the base meaning for word for it came to be applied almost solely for the goat," that is, a long, shaggy-haired animals (see *goat*).

HALF

Old Testament

Noun: חֲצִי (*ḥᵃṣî*), GK 2942 (S 2677), 125x. *ḥᵃṣî* means "half"; occasionally it can be translated "middle," as in "the middle of the night" (Jdg. 16:3; Ruth 3:8; lit., "the half of the night"). Many of the references to "half" are references to the "*half-tribe* of Manasseh," which (along with Reuben and Gad) settled east of the Jordan River (Num. 34:13–15). In Solomon's famous legal decision regarding a child disputed between two prostitutes, he suggests cutting him "in two and giv[ing] *half* to the one and *half* to the other" (1 Ki. 3:25); in this way he determines the true mother. During the time of Nehemiah, in order to protect the workers on the walls, "*half* of the men" did the construction and "the other *half* were equipped with spears, shields, bows and armor" (Neh. 4:16, 1). Isaiah mocks those who take a piece of wood, use "one half" to make a fire for cooking and the other "half" to make a god in order to worship it (Isa. 44:16, 19). Probably the most puzzling use of *ḥᵃṣî* is Daniel's reference to "time, times and *half* a time" (Dan. 12:7). See *NIDOTTE*, 2:244–46.

HALL

Old Testament

Noun: אֵילָם (*ʾêlām*), GK 395 (S 361), 61x. The *ʾêlām* is the first section of the interior of a king's palace (1 Ki. 7:6–8) or temple (7:12, 19, 21). It is translated variously as "vestibule, porch, entrance hall, portico" (7:19; 2 Chr. 3:4). See *portico*.

HALLELUJAH

New Testament

Interjection: ἀλληλουϊά (*hallēlouia*), GK *252* (S *239*), 4x. *hallēlouia* means "Hallelujah, Alleluia." This word is a transliteration of a Hebrew expression that means "Praise Yah," that is, "Praise Yahweh [the Lord]" (the Heb. expression occurs in, e.g., Ps. 116:19; 117:1–2). In the NT *hallēlouia* occurs only in Rev. 19 in the triumphant song of praise that comes from "a great multitude in heaven" (19:1, 3, 4, 6) as they sing about God's reign and prepare for the wedding of the Lamb.

HALLOW

See *make holy.*

HAND

Old Testament

Noun: יָד (*yād*), GK 3338 (S 3027), 1627x. *yād* usually refers to a human hand, although occasionally it has additional meanings such as a memorial or monument (1 Sam. 15:12; 2 Sam. 18:18; Isa. 56:5) or the bank of a river (Exod. 2:5; Lev. 25:47; Num. 13:29; Deut. 2:37; Jer. 46:6; Dan. 10:4). *yād* can also indicate that something is situated "near to" or "beside" a particular site or location (Jos. 15:46; 1 Sam. 4:18; 2 Sam. 15:2; 18:4; 2 Chr. 21:16; Ezek. 48:1). *yād* is also used with special and unusual meanings in a number of phrases in the OT.

yād is one of several terms in the Bible that refer to the hand or a part of the arm. There are other Hebrew terms for the palm of the hand and the right hand, but the word the Bible uses most frequently to refer to the hand is *yād* (over 1600 occurrences). In ancient Mesopotamia, "the hand" could refer to the wrist or the lower arm, and *yād* can also be used this way in the Bible (Gen. 24:22).

In the OT, the hand is a symbol of authority and control, and thus it can represent stewardship and personal responsibility (Gen. 41:35; 1 Sam. 17:22; 1 Ki. 14:27; 1 Chr. 25:2; 26:28; 29:8; 2 Chr. 12:10; 26:11; Est. 2:3, 8, 14; Ps. 95:7; Job 12:9–10). Lifting up or offering the *yād* came to be shorthand for taking a vow or making a pledge (Lev. 6:2 [5:21 in Heb.]; Ps. 106:26). From the power of a benevolent hand come care and provision for others (Ps. 123:2; 95:7). As a symbol of power, *yād* can also refer to military strength (Jdg. 3:10, 30; 4:24; 6:2; 1 Sam. 18:17, 21; 23:17; 1 Ki. 11:26–27; 2 Ki. 8:20, 22; 13:5; 2 Chr. 21:8, 10; Neh. 13:21; Dan. 8:25; Zech. 14:13). For this reason, "to lay hands on someone" can mean to arrest or assassinate that person (Est. 2:21; 3:6; 6:2; 9:2), and "to give the hand" to a person or to God denotes personal allegiance (1 Chr. 29:24) or submission (2 Chr. 30:8). In the context of misused power or jurisdiction, a hand can represent abuse, manipulation, forced labor, or oppression (Exod. 18:10; Jdg. 1:35; 2 Ki. 17:7). A "short hand" or "being short-handed" signifies impotence or the inability to take action (2 Ki. 19:26; Isa. 37:27; 59:1; cf. Deut. 32:36). By contrast, a strong or mighty hand indicates sovereignty and capability (Jos. 4:24; Isa. 66:4). Not surprisingly, therefore, it is "by a mighty hand" that God brings Israel out of Egypt (Exod. 13:3, 14, 16).

Although the *yād* of God is frequently referred to in the OT with many of the meanings discussed above, it is used especially in two additional ways. (1) The hand of the Lord is often said to bring miracles (Isa. 41:2) or to pass judgment (Exod. 9:3; Deut. 2:15; Jdg. 2:15; Job 19:21). Thus, the hand of God represents his power, sovereignty, mercy, provision, and justice. At times the hand of the Lord is said to be "against" a person or kingdom (Ruth 1:13; 1 Sam. 5:6, 9; 7:13; 12:15). When the hand of God is "heavy," God's judgment is severe (2 Sam. 5:11). At other times, the hand of God is "good," bringing blessings (Ezr. 8:22; Neh. 2:18). (2) The Bible speaks of the hand of God "coming upon" certain individuals. In such cases, that hand represents the presence of the Spirit of the Lord upon an individual, and frequently prophecy or visions occur as a result (2 Ki. 3:15; 2 Chr. 30:12; Isa. 25:10; Ezek. 1:3; 3:22; 8:1; 37:1; 40:1).

In Exod., there is sometimes a special relationship between a person's hand and God's intervention in human circumstances: when either Moses or Aaron raises his hand, God miraculously defeats the enemies of Israel through plague, the parting and closing of waters, or battle (Exod. 8:6; 10:22; 14:21, 27; 17:10–13).

Perhaps the most striking example of

the symbolism and meaning of the hand is found in the OT's use of *yād* in connection with consecration and ordination. The transference of leadership involves "the laying on of hands" (Deut. 34:9), and "the filling of hands" refers to consecration and ordination (Exod. 29:9; 32:29; Lev. 8:33; Num. 3:3). Specifically, "to fill the hands" of a priest means to ordain him to serve the Lord. This imagery implies that the priest cannot properly serve God or his people without first being filled with the presence, authority, and care of God. From God's hands to the hands of his priests are transferred his holiness, power, authority, personal liability, stewardship, responsibility, and compassion In light of the priesthood of all believers (1 Pet. 2:4–9), we should recognize the importance of this OT concept. We cannot minister unless God fills our hands. We must trust that even as we are in the very hands of the great Shepherd (Ps. 95:7), so he is filling and equipping our hands "with everything good that [we] may do his will, working in us that which is pleasing in his sight, through Jesus Christ, to whom be glory forever and ever. Amen" (Heb. 13:20–21).

Noun: כַּף (*kap*), GK 4090 (S 3709), 195x. This term is used to denote the "hand" as a part of the body and specifically refers to the palm of the hand (Gen. 40:11, 21; Exod. 4:4; Lev. 14:15; 1 Sam. 5:4; 2 Sam. 18:12; Job 9:30; Isa. 28:4; Dan. 10:10). It is virtually synonymous with *yād* (GK 3338), except that whereas both terms can refer to "power," *kap* more specifically refers to one's "grasp" or "grip" (Jdg. 6:13–14; 1 Sam. 4:3; 2 Sam. 19:9; Ps. 71:4; Isa. 38:6). To "save Israel out of Midian's hand" (Jdg. 5:14) means to save the people out of Midian's "power." When people "strike *hands*" together in pledge, they make a solemn agreement (Prov. 6:1; 17:18), similar to our shaking hands on a deal. People also work with their hands (Ps. 9:16; Prov. 31:13).

Idiomatically, *kap* conveys the idea "feet" or "hollow" (Gen. 8:9; Deut. 28:35 [lit. "hand/palm of the foot"]). In Numbers, *kap* is used with reference to ceremonial "dishes," probably because the palm of the hand was used to hold or carry such items (cf. Num. 4:7; 7). *kap* can also be used to express approximate measurement or quantity (Deut. 2:5; 1 Ki. 17:12). The imagery of unclean or bloody hands was applied to sin (Ps. 24:4; 26:6; 73:13; Isa. 59:3); conversely, a person who has lived a godly life can claim "innocent/clean *hands*" (Ps. 24:4; 26:6; 73:13). Stretching out or lifting up one's hands to the Lord means approaching him in prayer (1 Ki. 8:22, 38; Job 11:13; Ps. 91:12; Isa. 1:15). Finally, in order to praise God, people will often "clap their hands" (2 Ki. 11:12; Ps. 47:1). See *NIDOTTE*, 2:686-87.

New Testament

Noun: χείρ (*cheir*), GK *5931* (S *5495*), 177x. Commonly *cheir* refers to the "hand" as a part of the body (Mt. 12:10; Acts 12:7). (1) Many times it is used in the practice of "the laying on of hands," as when someone is commissioned for ministry (Acts 6:6; 13:3; 1 Tim. 5:22), someone prays for, blesses, or heals another (Mt. 9:18; 19:13, 15), or the apostles convey the Holy Spirit (Acts 8:17, 19).

(2) *cheir* also occurs in several expressions. "By/through the hands of" means "through [the agency of] someone" (Mk. 6:2; Acts 5:12). "The work of one's hands" refers to something that someone has made (idols in Acts 7:41; Rev. 9:20; God's creation in Heb. 1:10).

(3) In addition, the NT gives significance to God's hand as a symbol of divine power, ascribing to his hand the mighty works of creation (Acts 7:50; Heb. 1:10), of providential care and protection (Lk. 1:66; 23:46; Jn. 10:29), of miracles by the apostles (Acts 4:30), and of salvation (4:28: "your *power*", NIV; "your hand", KJV). Remarkably, what Jesus asserts of the Father in Jn. 10:29 (that "no one can snatch [the sheep] out of the Father's *hand*"), he asserts of himself in 10:28 ("no one can snatch them out of my *hand*"). See *NIDNTT-A*, 604.

HAND OVER

Old Testament

Verb: סָגַר (*sāgar*), GK 6037 (S 5462), 91x. *sāgar* broadly means "to shut something up" and is most frequently used of doors and gates (e.g., Gen. 19:6; Jdg. 3:23; Eccl. 12:4; Isa. 24:10). It can also have an extended meaning used in a military sense of handing or giving over—that is, the idea of surrounding a foe, shutting them in, and forcing them to surrender (e.g., Deut. 23:15; 32:30; Jos. 20:5). See *shut*.

New Testament

Verb: ἀποδίδωμι (*apodidōmi*), GK *625* (S *591*), 48x. *apodidōmi* means "to give (back), deliver, render, hand over, produce." See *give (back)*.

Verb: παραδίδωμι (*paradidōmi*), GK *4140* (S *3860*), 119x. *paradidōmi* signifies "to hand over, deliver up, betray, pass down." In nonbiblical Greek, *paradidōmi* refers to all aspects of deliberately giving over, including betraying. As a legal term, it is used of bringing someone before the court as well as delivering up a prisoner.

In the NT, *paradidōmi* has a wide spectrum of uses. The most prevalent meaning is to deliver up to judgment and death. John the Baptist experienced this when he was imprisoned (Mt. 4:12). Jesus warns his followers, "You will be *handed over* to be persecuted and put to death" (Mt. 24:9). He also predicts that brothers "will hand over" brothers to death (Mk. 13:12). Jesus' own betrayal by Judas uses this word: "The Son of Man is going *to be betrayed* into the hands of men" (Mt. 17:22). Jesus is then delivered up to the Gentiles (20:19), to Pilate (27:2), and to crucifixion (26:2). Note that Jesus allows himself to be delivered up into the hands of sinful men. He reminds the disciples at his arrest, "Do you think I cannot call on my Father, and he will at once put at my disposal more than twelve legions of angels?" (Mt. 26:53). His arrest is not happening outside of his sovereign control. He willingly goes to the cross for the salvation of sinners.

Additionally, *paradidōmi* can indicate deliverance to something other than a human court. "Therefore God *gave* them *up* in the sinful desires of their hearts to sexual impurity for the degrading of their bodies with one another" (Rom. 1:24) It is also used of excommunication as Paul delivers men over to Satan (1 Cor. 5:5; 1 Tim. 1:20). Moreoever, *paradidōmi* can describe the giving up of one's life (Jn. 19:30), including Christ's giving himself up for us: "The life I live in the body, I live by faith in the Son of God, who loved me and *gave himself* for me" (Gal. 2:20).

paradidōmi can also have the meaning of allowing something to be done, such as the ripening of fruit (Mk. 4:29). It can denote the sovereignty given to Jesus by his Father: "All things have been *given* to me by my Father" (Mt. 11:27). Moreover, it can represent being placed under the protective power of something: Paul and Barnabas "had been *commended* to the grace of God for the work they had now completed" (Acts 14:26). The term is often used in connection with handing down tradition and teaching (Mk. 7:13; Acts 6:14; 2 Pet. 2:21; Jude 3), including the Christian message: "For what I received *I passed on* to you as of first importance: that Christ died for our sins according to the Scriptures … (1 Cor. 15:3). See *NIDNTT-A*, 435-36.

HAPPEN

Old Testament

Verb: קָרָא (*qārāʾ*), GK 7925 (S 7122), 136x. The primary meaning of *qārāʾ* is "to meet, encounter, happen." See *meet*.

New Testament

Verb: τυγχάνω (*tynchanō*), GK *5593* (S *5177*), 12x. *tynchanō* usually designates what might "happen" or how something might "turn out." In Heb. 8:6, the author stresses that the ministry of Jesus "has turned out" superior to that of the OT. In 11:35, those who are persecuted "happen" to gain a better resurrection than those heroes of faith who have escaped their enemies with powerful miracles. When accompanied with the Gk. word ei ("if"), this verb gives the nuance of "perhaps" (lit., "if perchance things turn out"; 1 Cor. 15:37; cf. 16:6).

HAPPINESS

Old Testament

Noun: שִׂמְחָה (*śimḥâ*), GK 8525 (S 8057), 94x. Depending on the context, *śimḥâ* can be translated "joy, rejoicing, gladness, pleasure," or "happiness." See *joy*.

New Testament

Noun: χαρά (*chara*), GK *5915* (S *5479*), 59x. As an antonym of grief and sorrow (Jn. 16:20), *chara* denotes "joy, happiness, gladness." See *joy*.

HAPPY

New Testament

Adjective: μακάριος (*makarios*), GK *3421* (S *3107*), 50x. There are two major ways *makarios* may be taken in the NT. One who is *makarios* can be "happy" or "fortunate" because of life's circumstances or because of divine favors bestowed on him or her (cf. the Beatitudes). See *blessed*.

HARDEN

Old Testament

Verb: חָזַק (*ḥāzaq*), GK 2616 (S 2388), 290x. *ḥāzaq* can describe the severity or strength of an impersonal force. In several instances it refers to God's "making strong" (i.e., hardening) the heart of Pharaoh (Exod. 4:21; 7:13, 22; 8:19; 9:12, 35; 10:20, 27; 11:10; 14:4, 8, 17). See *strong*.

HARLOT

New Testament

Noun: πόρνη (*pornē*), GK *4520* (S *4204*), 12x. *pornē* identifies a person as a "prostitute" ("harlot" or "whore," KJV); it belongs to a word group that denotes various forms of sexual deviance. See *prostitute*.

HARM

Old Testament

Verb: נָגַע (*nāgaʿ*), GK 5595 (S 5060), 150x. The verb *nāgaʿ* means "to touch physically," but its various nuances include "to touch, strike, reach, arrive." See *strike*.

New Testament

Verb: ἀδικέω (*adikeō*), GK *92* (S *91*), 28x. *adikeō* is used mostly in Rev. (11x) and in Paul's writings (9x) to denote doing wrong, harming or hurting another, or mistreating someone (committing injustice). See *do wrong*.

HARVEST

New Testament

Verb: θερίζω (*therizō*), GK *2545* (S *2325*), 21x. *therizō* ("reap, harvest") is an agricultural term that is used in a literal sense for the collection of a cultivated crop from a field. Jesus uses the verb in this sense when he illustrates how God cares for the birds of the air: "Look at the birds of the air; they do not sow or reap or store away in barns, and yet your heavenly Father feeds them" (Mt. 6:26). James describes the activity of hired day-laborers as "mowing" or "harvesting" (Jas. 5:4).

The term may also be used figuratively to refer to the gaining of a specific result. This meaning is seen in a general sense in the parable of the talents (Mt. 25:24, 26) and pounds (Lk. 19:21–22). More specifically, *therizō* may convey the sense of conversion. In Jn. 4:36 the reaper "harvests the crop for eternal life;" and within the same context Jesus tells his disciples that "others have done the hard work, and you have reaped the benefits of their labor" (4:37–38). Paul uses the term in this figurative sense to describe the right he and other have for material support from their churches in light of their spiritual investment in them (1 Cor. 9:11); and proverbially: "Whoever sows sparingly will also reap sparingly, and whoever sows generously will also reap generously" (2 Cor. 9:6; see also Gal. 6:7–9).

Finally, *therizō* may refer figuratively to final judgment: "Put in your sickle and reap, for the hour to reap has come, because the harvest of the earth is ripe" (Rev. 14:15–16).

Verb: συνάγω (*synagō*), GK *5251* (S *4863*), 59x. *synagō* has the basic meaning "to gather together." It is often used in agricultural contexts of harvesting or gathering crops. See *gather*.

Noun: θερισμός (*therismos*), GK *2546* (S *2326*), 13x. *therismos* ("harvest") denotes the time or act of harvesting or reaping a cultivated crop. As with *therizō*, *therismos* may be used in a literal or figurative sense. Jesus uses the term in referring to a literal time of harvest (Mt. 13:30), but even here in the parable of the weeds the harvest referred to is a figurative harvest (13:39), alluding to the final judgment when the righteous (wheat) and wicked (weeds) will be finally separated. This represents one of the two major figurative uses of *therismos*, namely, an image depicting the final judgment. *therismos* in this sense is also seen in the image of winnowing grain in Mt. 3:12 and the parable of the seed growing in secret (Mk. 4:29). The other common figurative use of *therismos* develops the idea of potential fruit in the Christian mission. Humans, prepared by God for reception of the gospel, are compared to a crop ready for harvest (Mt. 9:37–38; Lk. 10:2; see also Jn. 4:36–38). See *NIDNTT-A*, 248-49.

HASTEN

Old Testament

Verb: מָהַר (*māhar*), GK 4554 (S 4116), 81x. *māhar* generally means "to hurry" in the sense of moving quickly (Gen. 18:6; 19:22; 1 Sam. 4:14; Jer. 9:17; Nah. 2:6). With a negative, *māhar* means to procrastinate (e.g., 2 Chr. 24:5). See *hurry*.

HATE

Old Testament

Verb: שָׂנֵא (*śānēʾ*), GK 8533 (S 8130), 148x. Usually translated "to hate," *śānēʾ* refers to varying levels of dislike toward someone or something.

(1) In the OT, the verb frequently denotes the ill will felt by a human being. It carries a wide range of meaning in expressing this hatred. (a) This abhorrence can be toward another man or woman. For example, Jacob has an aversion for his wife Leah (Gen. 29:31). *śānēʾ* often refers to varying levels of hatred toward the enemies of God. "Do I not *hate* those who *hate* you, O LORD, and abhor those who rise up against you?" (Ps. 139:21).

(b) It can denote ill will towards actions or ideas. For example, *śānēʾ* may signify something that should be avoided, such as serving as a guarantor for a debt (Prov. 11:15). It can also characterize the opposition of nations against Zion (Isa. 66:5). The sage bemoans hatred toward the poor (Prov. 19:7). It may also be used to express the annoyance of a neighbor: "Seldom set foot in your neighbor's house—too much of you, and he will *hate* you" (Prov. 25:17).

(2) In the OT, the verb is commonly used with God as the subject. (a) God directs his hate against actions and ideas. For example, God hates divorce (Mal. 2:16). He hates the practices of heathens (Deut. 12:31). He hates Israel's feast days while injustice remains: "I *hate*, I despise your religious feasts; I cannot stand your assemblies" (Amos 5:21): He hates sin: "There are six things the LORD *hates*, seven that are detestable to him" (Prov. 6:16).

(b) God also directs *śānēʾ* against people: "I have loved Jacob, but Esau I have *hated* (Mal. 1:2–3). In context, the prophet is emphasizing the sovereign choice of God rather than an intense emotion of dislike for Esau.

(c) God also can be the recipient of hatred (see Exod. 20:5; Deut. 5:9; 2 Chr. 19:2).

(3) The OT often pairs the verb *śānēʾ* with its antithesis, love. (a) It can characterize one's emotions toward various objects. For example, "the LORD loves righteousness and hates wickedness" (Ps. 45:7). The psalmist says, "I hate and abhor falsehood but I love your law" (119:163). There is "a time to love and a time to hate" (Eccl. 3:8).

(b) It can also denote the intensity of these emotions. *śānēʾ* indicated the passion Ammon had for his sister, Tamar. Originally, he loved her (2 Sam. 13:1). But after he raped her, "Amnon *hated* her with intense hatred. In fact, he *hated* her more than he had loved her" (2 Sam. 13:15). See *NIDOTTE*, 3:1256-60.

New Testament

Verb: μισέω (*miseō*), GK *3631* (S *3404*), 40x. *miseō* denotes hating or having malicious feelings toward things or people. In the NT, this verb can have both positive and negative connotations. Christ commends the church of Ephesus for hating the works of the Nicolaitans (Rev. 2:6). Paul characterizes his battle with the flesh by stating, "I do not understand what I do. For what I want to do I do not do, but what I *hate* I do" (Rom. 7:15). Christ also is praised for hating wickedness (Heb. 1:9). Furthermore, Christ declares the cost of discipleship, "If anyone comes to me and does not *hate* his father and mother, his wife and children, his brothers and sisters–yes, even his own life–he cannot be my disciple" (Lk. 14:26). He is not teaching to abhor one's parents but emphasizing that love for Christ must be far greater than love for family.

But *miseō* is also used to harbor malicious feelings toward others. Christ warns, "Everyone who does evil *hates* the light" (Jn. 3:20). He warns the disciples that they will be hated for his name's sake (Mt. 10:22). It is even a blessing to receive such treatment (Lk. 6:22). Christ commands his followers not to hate their enemies, but rather to love them (Mt. 5:43–44). This serves as a sign of discipleship. John writes, "Anyone who claims to be in the light but hates his brother is still in the darkness" (1 Jn. 2:9). *miseō* can also signify being indifferent to (as Christ warns of the impossibility of serving two masters in Lk. 16:13).

Finally, Paul employs *miseō* in his citation of Mal. 1:2–3: "Jacob I loved, but Esau I hated" (Rom. 9:13). It is crucial to understand *miseō* in light of Rom. 9:12 and the preceding quotation from Gen. 25:23. In this passage, God is speaking of two nations. The meaning of Rom. 9:13 relates to God's covenantal dealings with these nations: Israel (Jacob) and Edom (Esau). God's choice of Jacob and his rejection of Esau have nothing to do with emotional feelings toward the two historical individuals, but refer rather to his sovereign choice of two nations in the plan of salvation. See *NIDNTT-A*, 373-74.

HAVE

New Testament

Verb: ἔχω (*echō*), GK *2400* (S *2192*), 708x. *echō* means "to have, possess." It has a broad range of meaning in the NT. (1) *echō* is used in verbal equations signifying possession and relationship. During a stinging rebuke, Jesus reminds some of his opponents that they said John "*had* a demon" (Mt. 11:18). The NIV translates *echō* as "possessed" in Mk. 3:22 in reference to the charge against Jesus as "*possessed* by Beelzebub" and later as "*having* an unclean spirit" (3:30). In this category the word also describes various relationships: regarding physical assistance, "I *have* no one to help me into the pool" (Jn. 5:7); regarding marriage, "I *have* no husband," (Jn. 4:17; cf. 1 Cor. 7:2); regarding children, "Abraham *had* two sons" (Gal. 4:22); regarding paternity, the Jews said, "We *have* one Father, God" (Jn. 8:41); and regarding one's ultimate allegiance, "Masters … you know that you also *have* a Master in heaven" (Col. 4:1).

(2) *echō* is also used to exemplify the relationship with God that salvation produces. Having salvation not only creates the possibility of meaningful horizontal human relationships, but more importantly the critical vertical relationship we enjoy with the Father. In fact, it is having a relationship with the entire Trinity. Standing in a personal relationship with the Jesus of Scripture through the ministry of the Holy Spirit John stresses that we "have" the Father (1 Jn. 1:1–3, 4:13–16). This theme is expressed in a slightly different way as "having" the Spirit of God (Rom. 8:9), which is synonymous with being led by the Spirit (8:14). Corinthian Christians slowly grasped the fact that their bodies "templed" the Holy Spirit, which "they *have* from God" (1 Cor. 6:19). Later, Paul

exclaims that the Spirit is a treasure they "have" in earthen vessels (2 Cor. 4:7); moreover, once our bodies have run their course and died, "we *have* a building from God, a house not built with hands, eternal in the heavens" (5:1).

Perhaps the most pointed personal use of *echō* is found in Rom. 5:1, where Paul says that those who have been justified by faith "*have* peace with God." Similarly, in Eph. 3:12 *echō* denotes that "we *have* the boldness and access with confidence through faith in him." This news is titanic for the Gentiles who once were uncircumcised and cut off from God, but now have equal and unending benefits. See *NIDNTT-A*, 221-23.

HAVE SEXUAL RELATIONS WITH

Old Testament

Verb: גָּלָה (*gālâ*), GK 1655 (S 1540), 187x. *gālâ* has a wide variety of uses in the OT: "to exile, go into exile, expose, depart, reveal, have sexual relations with." See *exile*.

HEAD

Old Testament

Noun: פָּנֶה (*pāneh*; occurs only in plural, פָּנִים [*pānîm*]), GK 7156 (S 6440), 2126x. In the OT, *pāneh* basically refers to the front side of something or someone, typically the head or the face. See *face*.

Noun: רֹאשׁ (*rōʾš*), GK 8031 (S 7218), 600x. The primary meaning of *rōʾš* is "head" (it is translated this way over 300x in the OT). When used in this primary sense, it most commonly refers to the heads of people (Gen. 40:16–17; Lev. 24:14), but it can also refer to the heads of animals (Exod. 12:9; Lev. 1:4), statues or idols (1 Sam. 5:4), and other creatures (cherubim in Ezek. 10:1, 10; Leviathan in Job 41:7 and Ps. 74:14).

In addition to this primary and literal sense, *rōʾš* has a number of metaphorical meanings. See *leader*, *top*, *beginning*, *company*. See *NIDOTTE*, 3:1015-20.

New Testament

Noun: κεφαλή (*kephalē*), GK *3051* (S *2776*), 75x. *kephalē* means "head." It can be used literally or figuratively. (1) *kephalē* is used literally to refer to the head of a human or animal. Those who fast are to put oil on their heads and wash their faces so that they do not appear to be fasting (Mt. 6:17). Unlike foxes and birds, the Son of Man has nowhere to lay his head (Mt. 8:20). Throughout the passion of Jesus, there are several references to his head. Mary of Bethany pours expensive perfume on Jesus' head (Mt. 26:7). A short time later, a crown of thorns is jammed onto his head, he is struck on the head (Mt. 27:29, 30), and finally as he hangs on the cross a sign is placed over his head (Mt. 27:37). The dragon and beast of Revelation both have seven heads and ten horns, looking back to the features of the beasts of Dan. 7 (Rev. 12:3; 13:1; 17:3, 7, 9).

(2) *kephalē* is used in figures of speech. It is used as a synechdoche, in which the part represents the whole. Upon having his message rejected by the Jews Paul cries, "Your blood be on your own heads!" (Acts 18:6), the reference to the head signifying the destruction of the whole person. God numbers the hairs of our head (Mt. 10:30), which represents his care for our entire being. The word is also used metaphorically when Paul illustrates the interdependence of believers when he says, "The head cannot say to the body 'I don't need you' " (1 Cor. 12:21).

(3) *kephalē* is used figuratively to mean the uppermost or chief part of something. It can refer to a "leading" or "capital" city (Acts 16:12) or the "capstone" of a building (Mt. 21:42). The NT quotes Ps. 118:22 several times when speaking of those who reject Jesus: the stone that the builders rejected has become the "chief" cornerstone (Mk. 12:10; Lk. 20:17; Acts 4:11; 1 Pet. 2:7).

(4) *kephalē* is also used figuratively to mean a higher position of authority. Jesus is the head over every power and authority in the universe (Eph. 1:22; Col. 2:10). Moreover, Jesus is the head of the church, which is his body (Eph. 1:22; 4:15; Col. 1:18; 2:19). Paul speaks of the husband as

the head of his wife as Christ is the head of the church (1 Cor. 11:3; Eph. 5:23). In 1 Cor. 11:3–15 Paul shifts back and forth from a figurative to a literal use of *kephalē*. Figuratively, God is the head of Christ, who is the head of man, who is the head of his wife (v. 3; also vv. 4b, 5b). Paul exhorts the Corinthian women to honor their husbands by following the custom of showing respect for a superior by wearing head coverings (vv. 5–7). Even though this is not the practice of our day, the principle remains: a wife must honor her husband just as he honors Christ and as Christ honors God. Whereas 1 Cor. 11:3–15 deals with how a wife should act towards her husband as her head, Eph. 5:23–33 discusses how a husband as head should act towards his wife. Here, the model is of the head, Christ, who acts sacrificially for the good of his body, the church. This suggests that a husband's headship is not to follow the model of a CEO but of a head and body relationship, where the husband takes sacrificial action to nurture his wife into Christian maturity. See *NIDNTT-A*, 302-5.

HEADWATER

Old Testament

Noun: רֹאשׁ (*rō'š*), GK 8031 (S 7218), 600x. The primary meaning of *rō'š* is "head" (see *head*), but it also has a number of metaphorical meanings. For example, in Gen. 2:10, the main river in Eden was said to divide into four *headwaters*. See *company*.

HEAL

Old Testament

Verb: רָפָא (*rāpā'*), GK 8324 (S 7495), 69x. *rāpā'* conveys the process of restoring or making whole the health of an individual and may be translated as "heal." It is often used in the sense of healing or restoring with regard to covenant blessing (Gen. 20:17; Exod. 15:26; Deut. 7:12–15). Exod. 15:26 states, "If you listen carefully to the voice of the LORD your God and do what is right in his eyes, if you pay attention to his commands and keep all his decrees, I will not bring on you any of the diseases I brought on the Egyptians, for I am the LORD who *heals* you." This sense of restoration is also applied to the land (2 Chr. 7:14; cf. Deut. 29:22). God also heals his people of their sin and apostasy (Jer. 3:22; Hos. 14:3), especially after a time of extended judgment (Isa. 6:10; Jer. 30:17). Isa. 30:26 states "The moon will shine like the sun, and the sunlight will be seven times brighter, like the light of seven full days, when the LORD binds up the bruises of his people and *heals* the wounds he inflicted." Speaking prophetically of Jesus and the4 Servant, Isaiah writes, "But he was wounded for our transgressions; he was crushed for our iniquities; upon him was the chastisement that brought us peace, and with his stripes we are *healed*" (Isa. 53:5). See *NIDOTTE*, 3:1162-73.

New Testament

Verb: ἰάομαι (*iaomai*) GK *2615* (S *2390*), 26x.

Verb: θεραπεύω (*therapeuō*) GK *2543* (S *2323*), 43x. These two words meaning "to heal, cure" are used interchangeably in the NT. Sometimes they refer to healing by ordinary medical means through a physician (Lk. 8:43), but for the most part they speak of miraculous healing through touch, command, or exorcism—the healings that Jesus and, later, his disciples performed.

Healing formed an integral part of Jesus' ministry. His work consisted chiefly of teaching and healing, often done together (Mt. 4:23–24; Lk. 9:2). His miraculous healings often followed teaching about the kingdom of God, as a demonstration of the in-breaking of the kingdom, as well as of Jesus' messianic status. As the Messiah and as God incarnate, Jesus exercised authority over illnesses and demonic forces, which bound and incapacitated people in various ways (cripples, Mt. 9:35; Acts 4:14; hunchback, Lk. 13:14; hemorrhage, Lk. 8:43; deafness and blindness, Mt. 12:22, 14:14; 15:30; Mk. 1:34; demonic afflictions, Lk. 6:18; 8:2; Acts 10:38; epilepsy, Mt. 17:18; leprosy, Lk. 17:15). As Jesus sent out bands of disciples to carry the gospel of the kingdom of God, he also empowered them to heal and cure diseases and to cast out demons (Mt. 10:1–8; Mk. 6:13; Lk. 10:9). Their mission was precisely the same as his: "preach the kingdom of God and to heal (*iaomai*) the sick" (Lk. 9:2).

Healing is sometimes associated with the faith of the ones needing healing (Mt. 8:8, centurion; Mt. 15:28, Syro-Phoenician woman), though not always (e.g., Lk. 22:51). As some required physical healing, others required spiritual healing (Mt. 13:15; Lk. 7:7; Jn. 12:40; Acts 28:27). In the growth and expansion of the early church, some had a gift of healing (Acts 5:16, 8:7; 1 Cor. 12:9), but the power to do so came from Jesus and the Holy Spirit (cf. Lk. 9:1ff.; Acts 9:34). See *NIDNTT-A*, 259-60.

Verb: σῴζω (*sōzō*), GK *5392* (S *4982*), 106x. *sōzo* means "to save," "to rescue," or "to heal." For the most part, this verb is used for our being spiritually saved from sin. See *salvation*. But in some instances the verb means to heal a person from an illness. This meaning occurs especially in the Gospels and occasionally in Acts to refer to the miraculous healings and deliverances that Jesus and his apostles performed. For example, the woman with the bleeding problem wanted to touch Jesus' garment in order to "be healed." After the miracle took place and the woman came forward, Jesus said to her, "Take heart, daughter . . . your faith has healed you" (Mt. 9:21–22). In Lk. 8:26–39, Jesus healed a demoniac (see especially 8:37). In Acts 4:9, Peter healed a cripple. Jas. 5:15 also seems to use this meaning of *sōzō*. See *NIDNTT-A*, 549-551; *TDNT-A*, 1132-1140.

HEALTH

Old Testament

Noun: שָׁלוֹם (*šālôm*), GK 8934 (S 7965), 237x. *šālôm* is one of the most important words in the OT. In addition to "peace," this word can be translated as "prosperity, well-being, health, completeness, safety." See *peace*.

(BE) HEALTHY

New Testament

Verb: ὑγιαίνω (*hygiainō*), GK *5617* (S *5198*), 12x. *hygiainō* means "to be healthy, sound," depending on the context. When it refers to people, the word is generally translated as "to be healthy." The healed centurion's servant was found in "good health" (Lk. 7:10), the prodigal son was received back home "safe and *sound*" (15:27), and John prays for Gaius to be "in good health" (3 Jn. 2). Jesus uses the physical sense of the term to prove a spiritual point, saying, "Those who *are well* have no need of a physician, but those who are sick" (Lk. 5:31).

In Paul's writings, *hygiainō* refers exclusively to doctrine, which is "sound." Wicked people follow and teach things different than, or contrary to, "*sound* doctrine" (1 Tim. 1:10; cf. also 6:3; 2 Tim. 4:3). Paul exhorts Timothy and Titus time and time again to follow the pattern of "*sound* teaching" that he has laid out (2 Tim. 1:13), to hold firm in the word to be able to instruct others in "*sound* doctrine" (Tit. 1:9; 2:1–2), and to rebuke false teaching in order to produce people "sound" in the faith (1:13). In other words, *hygiainō* shows the constant need of believers to preserve "sound" doctrine. In today's day, where so many cringe at the word "doctrine," not only are they to have it but to pour effort into keeping it "sound." *hygiainō* is the call to study, learn, and read widely in intellectual honesty as a vital part of living in the kingdom. See *NIDNTT-A*, 568.

HEAR

Old Testament

Verb: שָׁמַע (*šāmaʿ*), GK 9048 (S 8085), 1165x. *šāmaʿ* means "to hear, listen, pay attention to, perceive, obey, proclaim, announce." Primarily it means "to hear sounds with the ear"; when the mind is also engaged, it means "to listen," as when Sarah listened at the entrance of the tent (Gen. 18:10). Rahab had heard about the Israelites and hide the spies because of her reverence for the Lord (Jos. 2:10–11).

šāmaʿ can also mean "to perceive, understand." The great call to worship and identity of Israel as God's people begins with *šāmaʿ* and is generally called the "Shema": "Hear, O Israel: the LORD is our God, the LORD alone. You shall love the LORD your God with all your heart, and with all your soul, and with all your might" (Deut. 6:4–5). When God wearies of Israel's persistent sin, he highlights the distinction between hearing and understanding: "Tell the people, 'Be ever *hearing*, but never understanding; be ever seeing, but never perceiving'" (Isa. 6:9). This lack of spiritual perception is a mark of God's judgment on Israel's sin: they are called to hear and obey, but fail to understand.

šāmaʿ may also function as a call to address an assembled community. The heavens and the earth "hear" as witnesses for God against his rebellious people (Isa. 1:2) in the same way that the heavens and earth were witnesses to the covenant (Deut. 4:26). The prophets commonly state, "*Hear* the word of the LORD" in order to announce a divine message to Israel (Isa. 28:14; Jer. 7:2; Ezek. 6:3).

šāmaʿ also implies acting on what one heard, as when Moses "listens" to his father-in-law and does everything he suggests (Exod. 18:24). Prov. 13:1 contrasts the wisdom of a child who listens and applies what he has heard to the foolish one, who ignores instruction. That God hears and acts distinguishes him from idols: if the people refuse to obey the Lord, he will scatter them from the land, and "there you will serve gods made by human hands, objects of wood and stone that neither see, nor *hear*, nor eat, nor smell. From there you will seek the LORD your God, and you will find him if you search after him with all your heart and soul. ... Then in the latter days you will return to the Lord your God and *obey* him" (Deut. 4:27–29).

God hears as well, and his hearing implies his acting on the cries that come before him. God "hears" (and answers) prayers. "I cried to him with my mouth, and high praise was on my tongue. If I had cherished iniquity in my heart, the Lord would not have *listened*. But truly God has *listened*; he has attended to the voice of my prayer" (Ps. 66:17–19). Often *šāmaʿ* appears in the Psalter: "*Hear* my prayer" (e.g., Ps. 4:1; 39:12; 30:10; 61:1; 64:1; 102:1; 119:149). But there is a profound warning to those who cry out to God without repentance for their sin: "See, the LORD's hand is not too short to save, nor his ear too dull *to hear*. Rather, your iniquities have been barriers between you and your God, and your sins have hidden his face from you so that he does not *hear*" (Isa. 59:1–2).

New Testament

Verb: ἀκούω (*akouō*), GK *201* (S *191*), 428x. *akouō* is the common term for "to hear." The word has at least five nuances in the NT: literal hearing, legal hearing, learning hearing, obedient hearing, and understanding hearing .

(1) Literal "hearing" is to exercise the human faculty of hearing. In this sense, *akouō* is used both without and with a direct object. In the former, Jesus pronounces a blessing on those who get to hear him: "Blessed are your eyes because they see, and your ears because they *hear*" (Mt. 13:16; cf. 13:13–15; Mk. 7:37; Lk. 7:22; Acts 28:26). For examples of *akouō* with direct objects see Mt. 11:4; 13:17; Mk. 14:64; Lk. 7:22; 15:25; Jn. 5:25, 28; Acts 9:7; 1 Jn. 1:1, 3.

(2) "Legal hearing" means to hear a legal case, "to grant a hearing." In this sense, Nicodemus asks the question, "Does our law condemn anyone without first *hearing* him to find out what he is doing?" (Jn. 7:51). Agrippa expresses the same with regard to Paul, "I would like to *hear* this man myself" (Acts 25:22).

(3) "Learning hearing" is to receive news or information about something, "to learn about." In this sense, Jesus "learns" about John the Baptist's death, "When Jesus *heard* what had happened" (Mt. 14:13). Likewise, Jesus says, "Everyone

who *listens* to the Father and learns from him comes to me" (Jn. 6:45).

(4) "Obedient hearing" is to give careful attention to so as "to heed, obey." In this sense, the divine command is to heed Jesus' words: "This is my Son, whom I love; with him I am well pleased. *Listen* to him!" (Mt. 17:5; cf. Lk. 9:35; Acts 3:22). Abraham says, "They have Moses and the Prophets; let them *listen* to them" (Lk. 16:29; cf. 16:31). Jesus says that true disciples do not heed those who do not speak for God; "the sheep did not *listen* to them" (Jn. 10:8).

(5) "Understanding hearing" is to hear and "understand" a message. When people speak in foreign languages in the assembly, they are not understood by those in attendance; "For anyone who speaks in a tongue does not speak to men but to God. Indeed, no one *understands* him; he utters mysteries with his spirit" (1 Cor. 14:2). Likewise, "With many similar parables Jesus spoke the word to them, as much as they could *understand*" (Mk. 4:33). The Judaizers had heard the law, but they had not understood it: "Tell me, you who want to be under the law, are you not *aware* of what the law says?" (Gal. 4:21). In this sense, Jesus speaks of those who can physically hear the sound of his voice but who do not understand what he is saying; "though hearing, they do not *hear* or understand" (Mt. 13:13). See *NIDNTT-A*, 29-31.

HEARING

New Testament

Noun: ἀκοή (*akoē*), GK *198* (S *189*), 24x. *akoē* can mean "hearing," but it can also refer to the organ of hearing ("ear") or to what is actually heard ("message").

In emphasizing the importance of all the parts of the body (i.e., the church), Paul asks, "If the whole body were an eye, where would be the *sense of hearing*?" (1 Cor. 12:17). Jesus quotes Isa. 6:9, "*You will be ever hearing* but never understanding; you will be ever seeing but never perceiving" (Mt. 13:14; cf. Acts 28:26). When Jesus heals a man who is deaf, Mark writes, "the man's *ears* were opened" (Mk. 7:35). The philosophers in the Athenian marketplace report about Paul's teaching, "You are bringing some strange ideas to our *ears*" (Acts 17:20; cf. 2 Tim. 4:3). Matthew comments on the reports that were spreading about Jesus and writes, "*News* about him spread all over" (Mt. 4:24; cf. 14:1; 24:6; Mk. 1:28; 13:7). In a similar vein Paul writes, "Faith comes from hearing *the message*, and *the message* is heard through the word of Christ" (Rom. 10:17). See *NIDNTT-A*, 29-31.

HEARKEN

See *hear*.

HEART

Old Testament

Noun: לֵב (*lēb*), GK 4213 (S 3820), 854x. *lēb*, often translated "heart," denotes the seat of emotion (1 Sam. 2:1), desire (Ps. 37:4), thought (Gen. 6:5), and decision (1 Chr. 12:38). The Lord repeatedly calls his people to love and trust him with *all* their hearts, indicating that the *lēb* can be divided (Deut. 6:5; Prov. 3:5). In fact, many things can fill or dwell in the *lēb*, including pride (Obad. 3), pain (Gen. 6:6; Isa. 65:14), idols (Ezek. 14:4), joy (Ps. 4:7), wisdom (Exod. 28:3; Prov. 14:33), and the word of God (Deut. 30:14; Ps. 119:11).

The idiom "to say in his *lēb*" is sometimes translated "to think" (Ps. 35:25; Zeph. 1:12). Plans are made in the *lēb* (Gen. 27:41; 1 Chr. 17:2), and it is the place where commitments are determined, kept, or broken (Deut. 30:17; 2 Chr. 16:9; Prov. 23:19; Dan. 10:12; Mal. 2:2). When God's children rebel against him, he calls on them to turn their hearts back to him (Joel 2:12). Significantly, the inner recesses of hearts and minds are never beyond God's reach. He knows what is in the *lēb* (2 Chr. 6:30) because he can see directly into it (1 Sam. 16:7). God can turn hearts to himself (1 Ki. 8:58); he can move the hearts of his people (Ezr. 1:5) as well as the hearts of foreign kings to carry out his will (Ezr. 1:1).

A hardened *lēb* is one that is faithless and obstinately opposed to God and his ways (1 Sam. 6:6; Ps. 95:8; Ezek. 3:7). To accomplish his purposes, God sometimes hardens hearts (Deut. 2:30; Jos. 11:20), most notably that of Pharaoh (Exod. 14:4, 8). God also takes hearts of stone and replaces them with hearts of flesh (a heart transplant!) (Ezek. 11:19; 36:26). Jeremiah prophesies that in the new covenant, during the age of restoration, the Lord will give his people undivided hearts (Jer. 32:39) with his law written on them (31:33), and he will keep these hearts from straying from him again (32:40). See *NIDOTTE* 2:749-54.

Noun: לֵבָב (*lēbāb*), GK 4222 (S 3824), 252x. *lēbāb* is a synonym of *lēb* (GK 4213) and means "heart, mind." There is essentially no difference in nuance between these two words; *lēb* occurs more than twice as often in the OT. Thus, for a discussion of the meaning of these two words in the OT, see *lēb*.

New Testament

Noun: καρδία (*kardia*), GK *2840* (S *2588*), 156x. *kardia* denotes the "heart." The metaphorical use of this word dominates in the NT, just as it does the OT. *kardia* covers the whole range of activities that go on within one's inner self, including thinking (Mk. 2:6,8), grieving (Jn. 16:6), rejoicing (Jn. 16:22), desiring (Rom. 1:24), understanding (Eph. 1:18), and decision-making (2 Cor. 9:7). While people may be deceived by their own hearts and the deceitful hearts of others (Jas. 1:26), and while sin and evil reside in the human heart (Rom. 1:21; Jas. 3:14), before the Lord the heart is an open book. He knows our hearts (Lk. 9:47; 16:15), tests them (1 Thess. 2:4), searches them (Rom. 8:27; Rev. 2:23), strengthens them (1 Thess. 3:13), and reveals their motives (1 Cor. 4:5).

The center of one's spiritual life is in the *kardia*, where there may be temptation (Jn. 13:2), devotion (Lk. 12:34), faith (Rom. 10:9), or doubt (Lk. 24:38). Paul teaches that salvation is a matter of the heart (Rom. 10:9–10), but the human heart by itself cannot accomplish it (Eph. 2:8). The Lord must open the *kardia*, enabling a person to respond to his grace (Acts 16:14). The Spirit then comes to reside in the *kardia* (2 Cor. 1:22; Gal. 4:6). There can still be struggles in the *kardia*, since Peter exhorts believers to set apart Christ as the Lord of their hearts (1 Pet. 3:15), and the author to the Hebrews warns his audience not to harden their hearts as their forefathers had done (Heb. 3:8, 12). Acknowledging that there are many things vying for control of our hearts, Paul instructs (with an imperative command) believers to "let the peace of Christ rule in your hearts" (Col. 3:15). See *NIDNTT-A*, 288-89.

HEAVEN(S)

Old Testament

Noun: שָׁמַיִם (*šāmayim*), GK 9028 (S 8064), 421x. "Heaven" is an important and frequent word in the Bible and plays a key role in many central texts from Genesis through Revelation. The wide variety of meanings for *šāmayim* fall into two main categories: the sky, atmosphere, or space; and the dwelling place of God.

(1) In the first classification, *šāmayim* is quite fluid. It can refer to the place of meteorological phenomena such as rain, snow, frost, dew, hail, thunder, wind, and clouds (e.g., Gen. 8:2; Isa. 55:9–11; Job 38:29; Deut. 33:13; Jos. 10:11; 1 Sam. 2:10; Zech. 6:5; Ps. 147:8), as well as the place of astronomical elements like the stars, sun, and moon (Gen. 15:15; Deut. 4:19; Job 9:8–9; Ps. 8:3). Flying creatures are frequently called "the birds of the *šāmayim*" (Gen. 1:26; Deut. 28:26; 1 Ki. 16:4; Ps. 8:8), and many signs and wonders appear in the *šāmayim* (Isa. 50:3; Ezek. 32:7; Joel 2:10).

(2) In the second meaning, *šāmayim* often refers to the invisible and separate dwelling place and presence of God. God abides above the created heavens of the sky, yet even the highest heavens cannot contain him (1 Ki. 8:27). He abides there, sees all things, and reveals himself from

there (Gen. 28:12, 17; 1 Ki. 8:30; Job 22:12; Ps. 14:2). God speaks, listens, and answers from heaven (Gen. 21:17; Exod. 20:22; Ps. 20:6). In heaven are the temple and throne of God (Ps. 11:4; 103:19; Isa. 66:1). Occasionally, the OT also speaks of angels residing in heaven (Gen. 21:17; 1 Ki. 22:19; cf. Job 1–2; Ps. 103:20–21). Especially in the later OT texts, God is regularly referred to as the "God of heaven" (2 Chr. 36:23; Ezr. 1:2; cf. Tob. 7:12).

While these two poles of meaning are distinct, they are nevertheless closely connected. Some texts hint at both senses and in this way carry a double meaning. For example, God promises bread will rain "from heaven" (Exod. 16:4), and judgment comes in the form of God throwing hailstones "from heaven" (Jos. 10:11). These uses indicate both the physical origin of the material (the sky) *and* the divine source of the bread and hailstones (God in heaven).

A frequent and important use of *šāmayim* is in conjunction with "earth." Because the universe is understood to consist of two fundamental parts—heaven and earth—the OT often uses the phrase "heaven and earth" to refer to God's creation in totality (Gen. 1:1; 14:19; 2 Ki. 19:15; Ps. 115:15; Jer. 10:11). This use of *šāmayim* focuses on the "sky, atmosphere" aspect of the word. Alternatively, *šāmayim* and earth are also often paired together when *šāmayim* is used as a reference to God's dwelling. Thus, we read that "the heavens are the LORD's heavens, but the earth he has given to the sons of men" (Ps. 115:16). In this sense, *šāmayim* and earth serve as a contrasting pair. This theme of the distinction between God's ways (those of heaven) and humanity's (those of the earth) weaves its way throughout the OT and into the NT.

One of the most important things to understand about *šāmayim* is that in the OT heaven is not generally regarded as the location of deceased believers. Instead, Sheol is the place of postmortem existence for all people (see *grave*). This fact, however, does not diminish the importance of *šāmayim* in the OT. Indeed, as a fundamental part of God's creation and as a reference to God's presence, *šāmayim* is crucial to OT theology. These truths are relied upon and expanded in the fuller revelation of the NT. See *NIDOTTE*, 4:160-66.

New Testament

Noun: οὐρανός (*ouranos*), GK *4041* (S *3772*), 273x.

Adjective: οὐράνιος (*ouranios*), GK *4039* (S *3770*), 9x. Coming from the same worldview as the OT, the NT authors frequently employ terms for heaven. *ouranos* is used in a variety of ways in the NT. At times it simply denotes the "sky" (Mt. 16:3; Mk. 13:25). God is said to be the creator of heaven and earth (Acts 4:24; 14:15; 17:24; Rev. 10:6; 14:7) and to dwell there (Mt. 5:34; Acts 7:49; Heb. 8:1; Rev. 4). There are angels in heaven who are messengers and servants of God (Mt. 18:10; Mk. 12:25; 13:32; Eph. 3:15; Rev. 12:7; 19:1), and from heaven Jesus will return with his angels (Mt. 24:31; 1 Thess. 4:16; Rev. 19:11f.). There is a heavenly tabernacle and heavenly Jerusalem (Gal. 4:26; Heb. 12:22; Rev. 3:12; 11:19; 21:2–22). People lift their eyes to heaven (Mk. 6:41; Lk. 18:13; Jn. 17:1; Acts 1:11; 7:55), and the Christian's citizenship is said to be in heaven (Phil. 3:20), along with his or her treasures and rewards (Mt. 5:12; 6:20; Lk. 5:23; 1 Pet. 1:4).

ouranos occurs most frequently in Matthew (82x) and Revelation (52x).*ouranos*, especially in conjunction with earth, proves to be an important theme in Matthew and is often found in the phrase "the kingdom of (the) heaven(s)" (Mt. 3:2; 13:24; 25:1). Similarly, Matthew often speaks of the believer's Father in heaven (5:16; 10:32; 18:19) and the heavenly (*ouranios*) Father (5:48; 15:13; 23:9). In Revelation, we are given an extensive picture of heaven, where the slain Lamb reigns and is worshiped by his saints (Rev. 4:2ff.). The cataclysmic events depicted in Revelation all stem from God's initiative in heaven and have their effect on earth (5:13; 8:10; 10:1).

The concept of heaven that develops throughout Christian history has often missed the mark of the Bible's teaching. While heaven is important in NT theology, the goal of God's redemption is *not* a disembodied heavenly experience (as many hymns teach). Instead, all of creation itself is awaiting redemption (Rom. 8:19–22), and the consummation of God's work will be a new creation, a new heaven and earth (Isa. 65:17; 2 Pet. 3:13; Rev. 21:1). Indeed, the great hope of the gospel is summed up in Jesus' exemplary prayer: "Your kingdom come, your will be done, on earth as it is in *heaven*" (Mt. 6:10). See *NIDNTT-A*, 421-24.

HEAVENLY

New Testament

Adjective: οὐράνιος (*ouranios*), GK *4039* (S *3770*), 9x. *ouranios* is related to *ouranos*, which means "heaven" (see *heaven, heavens*). Matthew often speaks of the believer's Father in heaven (Mt. 5:16; 10:32; 18:19) and the heavenly (*ouranios*) Father (5:48; 15:13; 23:9)—phrases that are synonymous.

Adjective: ἐπουράνιος (*epouranios*), GK *2230* (S *2032*), 19x. *epouranios* refers to heavenly things and is found most commonly in Paul and in Hebrews (Eph. 1:3, 20; Heb. 3:1). Frequently, *epouranios* things (such as the *epouranios* image, body, city, and sanctuary) are contrasted with their earthly counterparts (1 Cor. 15:40–49; Heb. 8:5; 11:16). See *heaven, heavens*.

(BE, MAKE) HEAVY

Old Testament

Verb: כָּבֵד (*kābēd*), GK 3877 (S 3513), 114x. *kābēd* generally means "to honor." It can also mean, by extension, "be heavy" or "unresponsive." See *honor*.

New Testament

Noun: λυπή (*lypē*), GK *3383* (S *3077*), 16x. *lypē* denotes "grief, sorrow, pain," the result that comes from the action of the verb *lypeō* (see *grieve*). See *grief*.

HEIGHT

Old Testament

Noun: גִּבְעָה (*gibʿâ*), GK 1496 (S 1389), 66x. Regularly translated "hill, hilltop, height," *gibʿâ* refers to a rise in the land's terrain smaller than a mountain. See *hill*.

HEIGHTS

Old Testament

Noun or Adjective: מָרוֹם (*mārôm*), GK 5294 (S 4791), 54x. *mārôm* is used either as a noun, meaning "heights," or as an adjective, meaning "high." It derives from and is used in ways similar to the Hebrew verb *rûm*, which means "to lift up, exalt" (see *lift up*).

mārôm occurs most frequently in Isaiah (16x) and Psalms (13x). At times, it refers simply to high places, such as mountains or hills (2 Ki. 19:23; Prov. 8:2; 9:3, 14). But more often it is used with the important meaning of the place where God dwells (Job 25:2; Ps. 92:8; 93:4; Isa. 33:5; Obad. 3; Mic. 6:6). In this sense, *mārôm* is often connected closely with heaven (Job 16:19; Ps. 102:19; 148:1; see *heaven, heavens*).

Alternatively, *mārôm* can have a negative sense of those who do something in a self-exalting way (e.g., "with high eyes") and therefore, proudly (Ps. 56:2; 2 Ki. 19:22; Isa. 37:23). This human self-exaltation is condemned by God, for he alone is the Exalted One. Instead, humans are to humble themselves and await the consummation of God's exaltation and victory. See *NIDOTTE*, 3:1078-80.

HEIR

New Testament

Noun: κληρονόμος (*klēronomos*), GK *3101* (S *2818*), 15x. *klēronomos* refers to an "heir." It is used literally of someone who is expected to receive an inheritance after the death of his father (Mt. 21:38; Mk. 12:7; Lk. 20:14) and of a son who is an heir (Gal. 4:1). By extension, Abraham is called the heir of the world (Rom. 4:13–14).

Christ, God's Son, is heir of all things

(Heb. 1:2), not in the sense that he will acquire his inheritance through the death of someone, but simply that he possess all things. Jesus holds the place of supremacy in the universe.

Christians are the heirs of God (Heb. 6:17) because they are children of God (Gal. 4:7), if indeed they suffer with Christ so that they too can be glorified with him (Rom. 8:17). Gentiles are included as heirs according to the promise, and as such are considered descendants of Abraham (Gal. 3:29). Believers are heirs of the kingdom (Jas. 2:5) and of eternal life (Tit. 3:7). Because Noah believed God and built the ark, he became an heir of the righteousness that comes by faith (Heb. 11:7). See *NIDNTT-A*, 308-10.*

HELL

New Testament

Noun: γέεννα (*geenna*), GK *1147* (S *1067*) 12x.

Noun: ᾅδης (*hadēs*), GK *87* (S *86*), 10x. The concept of a place of punishment after death ("hell") is not particularly clear until the time of the NT.

In the OT conception, Sheol is the place of the dead for all people, both righteous and unrighteous. In Jesus' teaching, however, we find mention of a place of postmortem punishment in contrast with a place of reward (often "heaven"). In the NT there is some distinction between *geenna* and *hadēs*; later Christian reflection fleshes out these ideas and generally combines the ideas of *geenna* and *hadēs* into that of hell.

hadēs is found in the NT only in Matthew, Luke, Acts, and Revelation, though the idea is also found in other texts (1 Pet. 3:19; 4:6). It is conceived as an underground prison with locked gates to which Christ holds the key (Mt. 16:18; Lk. 16:23; Acts 2:27, 31; Rev. 1:18). *hadēs* is a temporary place that will give up its dead at the general resurrection (Rev. 20:13–14).

Unlike *hadēs*, which is used in Classical Greek and the LXX, *geenna* comes about later as a translation from the Hebrew and Aramaic phrase referring to a desecrated valley south of Jerusalem (Hinnom Valley). In NT usage it refers to an eternal, fiery abyss of punishment where both body and soul are judged (Mt. 5:22, 29–30; Mk. 9:43; Lk. 12:5). This is likely the same thing as the lake of fire mentioned in Revelation. Assuming this connection, *geenna* is distinguished from *geenna* in that at the final judgment, Satan, Death, and even Hades will be cast into this abyss (Rev. 19:20; 20:10, 14–15).

Jesus' strong language about hell, especially in Matthew, does not sit well on the modern ear. Nevertheless, the point of all such exhortations is to invite people soberly to seek God who graciously offers them his kingdom and eternal life. See *NIDNTT-A*, 16, 102.

HELP

Old Testament

Verb: עָזַר (*ʿāzar*), GK 6468 (S 5826), 82x. *ʿāzar* means "to help." This help can be any sort of help, such as when the Gibeonites ask Joshua for "help" against the five kings of the Amorites (Jos. 10:6), the Arameans come to "help" Hadadezer (2 Sam. 8:5), and the many warriors come to David's side to "help" him (1 Chr. 12:19, 21, 22). Ahaz king of Judah thinks that the gods of Damascus will "help" him win battles (2 Chr. 28:23).

But in the vast majority of occurrences of *ʿāzar*, the helper is the Lord, the God of Israel. When Samuel defeats the Philistines at Mizpah, he sets up a stone and calls it "Ebenezer" (which means "stone of helping"), saying, "Thus far has the Lord *helped* us" (1 Sam. 7:12). When God's people are faced with danger, they cry out: "*Help* us, O Lord our God, for we rely on you" (2 Chr. 14:11; cf. Ps. 30:10; 79:9). This can be a cry from an individual (109:26; 119:86) or a community. While the help of God often seems to imply military assistance against an enemy army (e.g., Isa. 41:10–16), in Isa. 44:2 *ʿāzar* appears to be more spiritual blessings (cf. especially 44:3). In Ps. 10:14 we read of the God who is "the *helper* of the fatherless." The confession of the believer should be at all times: "Surely God is my *help*; the Lord is the one who sustains me" (Ps. 54:4). See *NIDOTTE*, 3:378–79.

HELPER

Old Testament

Noun: עֵזֶר (*ʿēzer*), GK 6469 (S 5828), 21x. *ʿēzer* means "helper." Two-thirds of the uses of this noun have God as the designated helper, for he has the ability to save and deliver. "I lift up my eyes to the hills—where does my *help* come from? My *help* comes from the Lord, the Maker of heaven and earth" (Ps. 121:1–2; cf. 124:8). Three times in Ps. 115 the psalmist says, "Trust in the Lord—he is their *help* and shield" (115:9–11). All believers should wait in hope for the Lord, for he is "our *help* and our shield" (33:20). The three uses of *ʿēzer* in Deut. 33 (vv. 7, 26, 29) all suggest that *ʿēzer* is a word with strong military overtones.

With so many references to God as our helper, it is obvious that an *ʿēzer* is in no way inferior to the one who receives help. This is important because this is the word that God uses in Gen. 2:18, when he says about Adam, "It is not good for the man to be alone. I will make a *helper* suitable for him." God then forms Eve as his *ʿēzer*. According to God's design, therefore, the man and the woman, the husband and the wife, have been designed by God to stand together and help each other fight the battles of life. And God is there as the divine *ʿēzer* to fight with them. Note too that there is a feminine noun related to this noun (*ʿezrâ*, GK 6476), which is used exclusively in the Psalms for God's help of his people (e.g., Ps. 22:19; 38:22; 40:13, 17). See *NIDOTTE*, 3:378–79.

New Testament

Noun: παράκλητος (*paraklētos*), GK *4156* (S *3875*), 5x. *paraklētos* is used 5x in the NT, all of them in the writings of John. It is often translated as "counselor, helper, advocate." See *counselor*.

Noun: συνεργός (*synergos*), GK *5301* (S *4904*), 13x. This word means "coworker, fellow worker, assistant." See *fellow worker*.

HEM

Old Testament

Noun: כָּנָף (*kānāp*), GK 4053 (S 3671), 111x. *kānāp* has the basic meaning of a wing, such as the wing of a bird. By extension, it can refer to the edge of something, particularly the skirting or hem of a garment. See *wing*.

HERD

Old Testament

Noun: בָּקָר (*bāqār*), GK 1330 (S 1241), 183x. *bāqār* refers to domesticated cattle (e.g., bulls, cows, and calves). In the ancient world, cattle were a measure of one's wealth. Larger cattle were deemed more valuable than smaller animals. See *cattle*.

Noun: עֵדָה (*ʿēdâ*), GK 6337 (S 5712), 171x. *ʿēdâ* means a gathering of people (for worship or legal matters) or a herd or swarm of animals. See *community*.

HERE

Old Testament

Adverb: הֵנָּה (*hēnnâ*), GK 2178 (S 2008), 51x. *hēnnâ* is an adverb meaning "here," usually in the sense of "in this place," though it sometimes can mean "now." Joseph as ruler in Egypt demands that his brother Benjamin must "come *here*" before he will give his family more food (Gen. 42:15). Joshua invites the Israelites to "come *here* and listen to the words of the LORD your God" (Jos. 3:9). In a proverb similar to the parable of Jesus in Lk. 14:7–11, Solomon writes: "Do not exalt yourself in the king's presence, and do not claim a place among great men. It is better for him to say to you, 'Come up *here*,' than for him to humiliate you before a nobleman" (Prov. 25:6–7). In a few instances there are double uses of this word to signify "*here* and *there*" (1 Ki. 20:40), "*to the right* and *to the left*" (2 Ki. 2:8, 14), or "*back* and *forth*" (4:35). In a more metaphorical use of the concept of place, Jer. 51:64 says, "The words of Jeremiah end *here*."

This adverb does on occasion have a nuance of time rather than place. In Moses' intercessory prayer to God, he says, "You have pardoned them from the time they left Egypt until *now*" (Num. 14:19). The meaning of the name Ebenezer is given as, "Thus *far* [Until *now*] has the Lord helped us" (1 Sam. 7:12). The psalmist writes, "Since my youth, O God, you have taught me, and to *this day* I declare your marvelous deeds" (Ps. 71:17).

HERITAGE

Old Testament

Noun: נַחֲלָה (*nah^elâ*), GK 5709 (S 5159), 222x. In addition to "inheritance," *nah^ela* can be translated as "heritage" and "possession." See *inheritance*.

HIDDEN

New Testament

Adjective: κρυπτός (*kryptos*), GK *3220* (S *2927*), 17x. *kryptos* describes something that is "secret" or "hidden." See *secret*.

HIDE

Old Testament

Verb: כָּסָה (*kāsâ*), GK 4059 (S 3680), 153x. This word is predominately used with the literal sense "to cover." In other contexts, it can denote "conceal, hide" and even "forgive." See *cover*.

Verb: סָתַר (*sātar*), GK 6259 (S 5641), 82x. The verb *sātar* means "to hide, conceal, keep secret." When humanity is the subject, *sātar* often refers to hiding oneself or others for the sake of protection from life-threatening situations. David hides himself because Saul is seeking his life (1 Sam. 20:5, 19, 24). Similarly, Elijah hides from Ahab (1 Ki. 17:3), and God conceals Baruch and Jeremiah from Jehoiakim (Jer. 36:19, 26). Moses hides his face because he is afraid to look at God (Exod. 3:6), and God hides the upright from the plots of the wicked (Ps. 17:8; 31:20; 64:2).

People also try to hide sin, i.e., to keep it secret from God and other people. This is often true of adultery (Num. 5:13), secret plots of evil (Isa. 29:14–15), and even presumptuous sins (Ps. 19:13). It is possible to hide such sin from other human beings (1 Sam. 20:2) but not from God (Job 34:22; Jer. 16:17; 23:24).

Though people cannot hide themselves or their sins from God, he can remain hidden from them (Job 34:29; Isa. 45:15). He also hides information (Prov. 25:2) and wisdom (Deut. 29:29; Job 28:21). Therefore, special divine revelation is necessary for us to know how to behave and walk in life (Job 3:23; Ps. 119:19).

Finally, in the OT, God often hides his face. This idiom signifies that God's wrath is against his people as a result of their breach of covenant (Deut. 31:17, 18; Isa. 59:2; Mic. 3:4). Fortunately, this wrath is only temporary; God will not forever hide his face from the prayers of the righteous (Ps. 27:9; 69:17; 102:2; 143:7). See *NIDOTTE* 3:301-3.

Noun: עוֹר (*ʿôr*), GK 6425 (S 5785), 99x. *ʿôr* is used to designate both human (55x) and animal (44x) skin. See *skin*.

New Testament

Verb: κρύπτω (*kryptō*), GK *3221* (S *2928*), 18x. *kryptō* means "to conceal, hide." Jesus uses the term in its most natural sense in Mt. 5:14, "A city on a hill cannot *be hidden*." Just as you cannot make a huge city invisible, so you cannot avoid being a visible witness if you are truly in Christ. Likewise, Paul says that sins and good deeds "cannot be hidden" (1 Tim. 5:25).

In two separate parables, *kryptō* is used in this same natural sense to refer to something buried underground (Mt. 13:44; 25:18, 25). The word is used of Jesus' hiding himself from the crowds (Jn. 8:59; 12:36), the baby Moses hidden by his parents (Heb. 11:23), and people of the earth hiding themselves in caves (Rev. 6:15–16). A slightly nuanced use of *kryptō* refers to when people lack understanding of a prophecy or parable, that such a truth is "hidden" from them (Mt. 11:25; 13:35; Lk. 18:34; 19:42).

A final, and unique, use of the term Paul's comment: "For you have died, and your life *is hidden* with Christ in God" (Col. 3:3). The focus here is on the security of the life to come and the urgency of holy living, for believers are "hidden" safely with the Almighty. *kryptō* also sheds light on Christ's role as mediator. If our life was not "concealed" in Jesus Christ and if we were to approach a holy God without being "hidden" in Christ, who could stand in his presence? See *NIDNTT-A*, 319-21.

HIGH

Old Testament

Noun or Adjective: מָרוֹם (*mārôm*), GK 5294 (S 4791), 54x. *mārôm* is used either as a noun, meaning "heights," or as an adjective, meaning "high." It derives from and is used in ways similar to the Hebrew verb *rûm*, which means "to lift up, exalt" (see *lift up*).

New Testament

Noun: ὕψος (*hypsos*), GK *5737* (S *5311*) 6x.

Adjective: ὑψηλός (*hypsēlos*), GK *5734* (S *5308*), 11x.

Adjective: ὕψιστος (*hypsistos*), GK *5736* (S *5310*) 13x. The related words *hypsēlos* and *hypsos* carry the idea of high or exalted with both spatial and figurative meanings. In several verses these words are used spatially to describe a "high mountain" (Mt. 4:8; 17:1; Mk. 9:2; Rev. 21:10) or wall (Rev. 21:12). At other times, these terms are used figuratively to denote the dwelling place of God "on high" (Lk. 1:78; 24:29; Heb. 1:3) and the place to which Jesus ascended after his resurrection (Eph. 4:8; Heb. 7:26). Both the spatial and figurative uses overlap in meaning in that the "high mountain" has symbolic or figurative overtones while at the same time God's dwelling place was considered to be spatially located above "in the heights." In a different kind of usage, these words occasionally have a negative connotation, referring to human pride (Rom. 11:20; 12:16) or a high position as opposed to a humble attitude (Jas. 1:9).

The superlative form of *hypsos* is the adjective *hypsistos*, meaning "highest" or when referring to God, "Most High." Four times *hypsistos* is used in words of praise to God "in the highest" (Mt. 21:9; Mk. 11:10; Lk. 2:14; 19:38). Its other nine occurrences are all used as a descriptive name for God as the "Most High God" (Mk. 5:7; Lk. 8:28; Acts 16:17; Heb. 7:1) or simply, "the Most High" (Lk. 1:32, 35, 76; 6:35; Acts 7:48). This title for God is most common in Luke and Acts and is related to another name for God common in the later OT books: the "God of heaven" (Ezr. 1:2; Neh. 1:4; Dan. 2:8; Jon. 1:9). To call God "the Most High" emphasizes that, contrary to all other gods that humans create, the God and Father of Jesus Christ is the only true reigning God. There is nothing or no one greater than he, and therefore, humans are called to humble themselves before him. For those who walk humbly and righteously before the Most High God, there is the incredible promise that they will become the children of the Most High (Lk. 6:35). See *NIDNTT-A*, 585.

HIGH PLACE

Old Testament

Noun: בָּמָה (*bāmâ*), GK 1195 (S 1116), 106x. *bāmâ* literally refers to a high place such as a mountain top (Amos 4:13). As such, on a few occasions God's riding on the "heights" of the earth means his supremacy over all things (Deut. 32:13; Isa. 58:14).

For the most part, however, the *bāmâ* is associated with higher elevations as cultic places of worship (though a *bāmâ* did not have to be on a higher elevation; cf. "the shrines at the [city] gates" in 2 Ki. 23:8). Certainly before the time of the building of the temple, "high places" (such as those at Gibeon and in Samuel's home town) were used in the worship of the Lord (1 Sam. 9:16–24; 1 Ki. 3:4–5). Up to the time of Josiah, these high places seem to have been tolerated as long as they were used for the worship of Israel's God (2 Ki. 14:4; 15:4; 23:8–9, 12–15). In the OT, however, most of the high places are associated with pagan worship, whether by pagan nations or even by God's people (e.g., 2 Ki. 21:3; Jer. 7:31). As early as Lev. 26:30, God announces his intention to destroy the high places, and the prophets regularly denounce them (Ezek. 6:3, 6; Hos. 10:8). God wants us to worship him in the way he instructs in his Word, not the way we think suits our idea of who God is (see especially Jn. 4:21–24). See *NIDOTTE*, 1:670.

HIGH PRIEST

New Testament

Noun: ἀρχιερεύς (*archiereus*), GK *797* (S *749*), 122x. In the singular, *archiereus* refers to the one priest selected each year, often through political connections, to officiate over the sacrificial ritual in the temple and to preside over the Sanhedrin (see *Sanhedrin*). The most important duty of this priest was to enter the Most Holy Place on the Day of Atonement, one of the three most important days of the Jewish calendar (Lev. 16). On this day, after having made atonement for himself, he went behind the veil and made atonement for all Israel. He alone was able to stand in the presence of God. Picking up on this theme, Hebrews describes Jesus as the ultimate and final high priest (Heb. 7–8) as well as the ultimate and final sacrifice, who accomplished "eternal redemption" in contrast to the annual redemption of the Day of Atonement. Outside of Hebrews *archiereus* is used in the singular a number of times in reference to Caiaphas (Mt. 26:3; Jn. 18:13; Acts 4:6).

In the plural *archiereus* denotes the ruling priests of Israel, which was the group of priests from whom the singular high priest was chosen each year. This use of *archiereus* is often combined with scribes (Mt. 2:4; 16:21; 20:18; Mk. 8:31; 10:33; Lk. 9:22; 23:10), elders (Mt. 16:21; 27:13; Mk. 8:31; 14:43; Lk. 9:22; 22:52; Acts 4:23; 25:15), and Pharisees (Mt. 21:45; Jn. 7:32, 45; 11:47, 57). These leaders felt threatened by the mission and ministry of Jesus. These priests were economically dependent on the temple and the sacrificial system and were in positions of significant power. Therefore, Jesus' cleansing of the temple (Mt. 21:12–13; Lk. 19:45–46), his declaration that he would tear down the temple (Jn. 2:19–22), and his statement that he came to "fulfill the Law and the Prophets" (Mt. 5:17) threatened these priests. See *NIDNTT-A*, 260-62.

HILL

Old Testament

Noun: גִּבְעָה (*gibʿâ*), GK 1496 (S 1389), 66x. Regularly translated "hill, hilltop, height," *gibʿâ* refers to a rise in the land's terrain smaller than a mountain. The noun *gibʿâ*, along with two other words ("turban" and "cup/bowl"), may come from a root that means "convex." Moses goes to the top of a hill while Joshua fights the Amalekites (Exod. 17:9–10), and the house of Abinadab was located on a hill (1 Sam. 7:1). A number of times, specific hills are named, such as the hill of foreskins (Jos. 5:3), the hill of Moreh (Jdg. 7:1), the hill of Hakilah (1 Sam. 23:19), the hill of Ammah (2 Sam. 2:24), or the hill of Jerusalem (Isa. 10:32). The term is used as a proper name for the city of Gibeah (*gibʿâ*), which was probably located on top of a hill (cf. Jos. 24:33; Jdg. 19–20; 1 Sam. 10:26).

The hills were created by God at the beginning of time (Job 15:7; Prov. 8:25), and so are sometimes described as "ancient/everlasting" (Gen. 49:26; Deut. 33:15). In poetic texts, *gibʿâ* is often parallel with the term *har*, "mountain" (Ps. 72:3; Song 2:8; see *mountain*), or associated with it (Ps. 148:9; Isa. 40:4). However, unlike *har*, which can refer to a range of mountains, *gibʿâ* refers only to individual hills. Many times the term is used to refer to a place of idolatrous worship (Deut. 12:2; Hos. 4:13). The Israelites worshiped idols "on every high *hill* and under every luxuriant tree" (2 Ki. 17:10; Jer. 2:20; cf. Ezek. 20:28). See *NIDOTTE*, 1:805.

New Testament

Noun: ὄρος (*oros*), GK *4001* (S *3735*), 63x. *oros* can refer to an individual mountain, a mountain range, or even a mere hill. See *mountain*.

HINDER

New Testament

Verb: κωλύω (*kōlyō*), GK *3266* (S

2967), 23x. *kōlyō* means "to hinder, stop, forbid, oppose." It is found most often in the writings of Luke. From a personal point of view, hindering relates primarily to people. Children are hindered from coming to Jesus (Mt. 19:14; Mk. 10:14), soldiers are hindered from killing the apostle Paul (Acts 27:43), and Paul is hindered from going to Rome (Rom. 1:13). One of the charges brought against Jesus was that he "opposed" payment of taxes to Caesar (Lk. 23:2).

Elsewhere, *kōlyō* relates to various sorts of hindrances to preaching the gospel (Acts 16:6; Rom. 1:13; 1 Cor. 14:39; 1 Thess. 2:16; 3 Jn. 10). Both Paul and Luke see the ultimate origin of such hindrances for Christians as coming from God himself, not from circumstances. In Acts 8:36; 10:47, *kōlyō* is used with respect to there being no hindrance to baptism, and this word became a technical term later in church history for either refusing or not refusing baptism. See *NIDNTT-A*, 326.

HIT

Old Testament

Verb: נָכָה (*nākâ*), GK 5782 (S 5221), 501x. The verb *nākâ* generally means "to strike down, destroy, hit, kill." See *strike*.

New Testament

Verb: πατάσσω (*patassō*), GK *4250* (S *3960*), 10x. *patassō* is one of several NT words meaning "to strike, hit." It can be used literally or figuratively. See *strike*.

HITCH

Old Testament

Verb: אָסַר (*ʾāsar*), GK 673 (S 631), 73x. The most basic meaning of *ʾāsar* is "to bind, tie up." Animals may be tied to something for a particular function. Horses and donkeys may be "tethered" to keep them in place (2 Ki. 7:10), cows may be "hitched" to a cart in order to pull it (1 Sam. 6:7, 10), and chariots may be "made ready" in the sense of hitching the horses to it (Gen. 46:29). See *bind*.

HITHER

See *here*.

HOIST UP

See *lift up*.

HOLD

New Testament

Verb: κατέχω (*katechō*), GK *2988* (S *2722*), 17x. *katechō* means "to hold to, restrain." It can refer to preventing someone from doing something, "hold back" (e.g., the people try to "keep" Jesus from leaving them, Lk. 4:42), Paul wants to "hold on to" Onesimus and keep him with him (Phlm. 13), and God is "restraining" or "holding back" the man of lawlessness (2 Thess. 2:6, 7). *katechō* can also refer to rendering something ineffective, "hold down" (e.g., wicked men "suppress" the truth, Rom. 1:18). It can also refer to "holding fast" to one's beliefs (Lk. 8:15; 1 Cor. 11:2; 15:2; 1 Thess. 5:21; Heb. 3:6, 14; 10:23) or "holding on" to something in the sense of possessing it (1 Cor. 7:30; 2 Cor. 6:10).

Verb: κρατέω (*krateō*), GK *3195* (S *2902*), 47x. *krateō* means "to arrest, seize, hold, grasp." See *arrest*.

Verb: χωρέω (*chōreō*), GK *6003* (S *5562*), 10x. *chōreo* means "to accept, hold, have room for." See *accept*.

HOLD FAST

Old Testament

Verb: דָּבַק (*dābaq*), GK 1815 (S 1692), 55x. *dābaq* denotes the basic action of one object or person adhering or clinging to another. It takes both people and physical objects as its subject, but never God. See *cling*.

HOLD IN CONTEMPT

New Testament

Verb: ἐξουθενέω (*exoutheneō*), GK 2024 (S *1848*), 11x. *exoutheneō* essentially means "to hold someone in contempt, ridicule, despise" (Rom. 14:3; Gal. 4:14). See *look down on*.

HOLD TOGETHER

New Testament

Verb: συνίστημι (*synistēmi*), GK *5319* (S *4921*), 16x. *synistēmi* means "to commend, hold together." See *commend*.

HOLINESS

Old Testament

Noun: קֹדֶשׁ (*qōdeš*), GK 7731 (S 6944), 470x. *qōdeš* connotes the concept of "holiness," i.e., the essential nature of that which belongs to the sphere of the sacred and is distinct from the common or profane. This distinction is evident in Lev. 10:10, where the Lord commands: "You must distinguish between the holy and the common, between the unclean and the clean." Here *qōdeš* is set in opposition to what, in essence, is "common" or "profane." In Ezek. 22:26 God condemns the wicked priests because they "do violence to my law and profane my holy things; they do not distinguish between the holy and the common; they teach that there is no difference between the unclean and the clean; and they shut their eyes to the keeping of my Sabbaths, so that I am profaned among them."

God himself is *qōdeš* in both power and character. He is totally good and entirely without evil. He is separate from sinful humankind because of his transcendent holiness. Because of that holiness, those who participate in the priestly functions of Israel are to be holy. Lev. 19:2 records God's command: "Be holy because I, the Lord your God, am holy," a statement often quoted in the OT (Lev. 11:44–45; 20:7; see also 1 Pet. 1:16) and one that forms the basis of the Holiness Code (Lev. 17–26). Humankind is made in the image of God and is capable of reflecting the divine likeness. As God reveals himself to be ethically holy, he calls individuals to a holiness resembling his own.

Though the sphere of the holy is conceptually distinct from the "common" or "profane" world, it can, nevertheless, operate within the world as long as its integrity is strictly maintained. The maintenance of the purity of the "holy" is the primary function of the Israel's priesthood. God chooses to dwell in the temple and, therefore, Israel must guard the purity of holiness, the characteristic of God's essential nature. Even before the establishment of the Levitical system this principle is recognized (see Exod. 3:5).

HOLY

Old Testament

Adjective: קָדוֹשׁ (*qādôš*), GK 7705 (S 6918), 117x. Generally *qādôš* is translated as "holy," "holy one," or "saint." It describes that which is by nature sacred or that which has been admitted to the sphere of the sacred by divine rite. It describes, therefore, that which is distinct or separate from the common or profane.

qādôš is usually an attribute of God. The title "the Holy One of Israel" (NIV and KJV) is applied to God numerous times in the OT, but is especially frequent (26x) in the prophecy of Isaiah (Isa. 1:4; 5:19, 24; 10:20; 12:6; 17:7; 29:19; 30:11, 12, 15; 31:1; 37:23; etc.). *qādôš* casts the sinfulness of Isaiah's day in sharp contrast to God's moral perfection (Isa. 30:11) and expresses God's absolute separation from evil (Isa. 17:7). God is intrinsically holy and calls his people to be holy, providing himself as the standard of holiness (Lev. 19:2). Because God is holy, he is free from the moral imperfections and frailties common to human beings (Hos. 11:9) and, therefore, is faithful to his promises (Ps. 22:3–5). This aspect of God's character forms the basis of Habakkuk's hope that his people will not perish (Hab. 1:12).

The distinction between the spheres of the sacred and of the profane forms the basis for the ethical aspects of the concept of holiness. Because God is holy, the Israelites cannot serve him when they persist in their idolatrous practices (Jos. 24:19). They are to be separate from all that is unholy (Lev. 11:44–45; Deut. 14:21). Stipulations are imposed on them so that they will not engage in practices common to other peoples (Lev. 19:2; Lev. 20:7; Num. 15:40). Their call to holiness is due to the fact that they have become God's possession by virtue of his separating them from the nations (Lev. 20:26; Deut. 7:6; 14:2; 26:19).

By far, the most frequent occurrences of the *qdš* word group (see also *sanctify*, *holiness*) appear in the priestly legislation of the OT (Exod. 25–Num. 10; Ezek. 40–48). In these contexts, everything that belongs to the realm of the cult is holy, including the dimensions of space (temple), time (e.g., feasts and festivals, New Moons, Sabbaths, Year of Jubilee), objects (e.g., the furnishings of the temple, pure foods), and people (e.g., priests, the high priest). The believer is called to reflect God's holiness throughout the OT (cf. Lev. 17-26), a call echoed also in the NT: "But just as he who called you is holy, so be holy in all you do for it is written: 'Be holy, because I am holy' " (1 Pet. 1:15–16; see also, Mt. 5:48; Eph. 1:4; Heb. 12:14). See *NIDOTTE*, 3:875-87.

New Testament

Verb: ἁγιάζω (*hagiazō*), GK *39* (S *37*), 28x. *hagiazō* is usually rendered "make holy, sanctify, consecrate." See *make holy*.

Adjective: ἅγιος (*hagios*), GK *41* (S *40* & *39*), 233x. In general, two facts stand out in the NT regarding *hagios* ("holy, sacred"). First, God and what is associated with him is declared as "holy." God is specifically described as holy (Jn. 17:11; 1 Pet. 1:15–16; Rev. 4:8; 6:10), and Christ is called holy in the same sense as God (Rev. 3:7; cf. 1 Jn. 2:20). God's name is holy (Lk. 1:49), as is his covenant (Lk. 1:72), his angels (Mk. 8:38; Lk. 9:26; Acts 10:22; Jude 14; Rev. 14:10), his attendants (Eph. 2:19; Col. 1:12; 1 Thess. 3:13; Rev. 18:20), the prophets (Lk. 1:70), and the Scriptures (Rom. 1:2; 7:12). Jesus is addressed as "the Holy One of God" by an unclean spirit (Mk. 1:24; Lk. 4:34), by the angel Gabriel (Lk. 1:35), and by Simon Peter (Jn. 6:69). He is called God's "holy servant" (Acts 4:27; cf. 3:14). Here reference to "holy" means belonging to and authorized by God and thus, resisting Jesus is equivalent to resisting God.

Second, the proper sphere of the holy in the NT is not the priestly or ritual but the prophetic. The sacred no longer belongs to things, places, or rites, but to manifestations of life produced by the Spirit. In Paul's letters those who name Jesus as their Lord are called *hagioi*, "saints." This is not primarily an ethical expression but is parallel to being "called" (Rom. 1:7; 1 Cor. 1:2), "chosen" (Rom. 8:33; Col. 3:12), and "faithful" (Col. 1:2). It implies association with the Holy Spirit. Christ is the one in whom believers become holy to the true God (see 1 Cor. 6:11). The power to do so comes from the risen Christ, who operates according to the Spirit of holiness (Rom. 1:4). In these cases holiness refers to a relationship with God that is not mediated through ritual (ceremonial) observance but through the leading of the Holy Spirit (Rom. 8:14). Spiritual worship is the offering of oneself as a living, holy sacrifice, acceptable to God (Rom. 12:1).

Noun: ἁγιασμός (*hagiasmos*), GK *40* (S *38*), 10x. *hagiasmos* ("holiness, sanctification, consecration") is generally used in the NT the moral sense, referring to the process (or the final result of that process) of making pure or holy. It is like a growing fruit that results in eternal life (Rom. 6:19–22; see 1 Thess. 4:3–7). An essential aspect of sanctification is love for all the saints (Eph. 1:15). Both Christ (1 Cor. 1:30) and the Spirit (2 Thess. 2:13; 1 Pet. 1:2) are agents of "sanctification," without which the author of Hebrews says none will see the Lord (Heb. 12:14).

Adjective: ὅσιος (*hosios*), GK *4008* (S *3741*), 8x. This rare word in the NT occurs five out of eight times in quotations from the OT and is usually rendered "holy." In classical usage *hosios* often distinguished between what is "holy" according to God's law from that which is "holy," or lawful, in human law (*dikaios*; see *righteous*). In Acts 2:27 and 13:35 (quoting Ps. 16:10) Luke refers to God's promise to save his "Holy One" from decay, a promise not fulfilled in David but in Christ's resurrection from the dead. Jesus, as high priest, is completely *hosios* in that he is utterly sinless and totally pure (Heb. 7:26). God is called *hosios* in two quotations from the OT. In Rev. 15:3–4 (quoting Ps. 145:17) it is God alone who is *hosios*, as is stated in

Rev. 16:5 (quoting Deut. 32:4): "You are just in these judgments, you who are and who were, the Holy One, because you have so judged."

HOLY DAY

See *feast.*

HOLY PLACE

Old Testament

Noun: מִקְדָּשׁ (*miqdāš*), GK 5219 (S 4720), 75x. *miqdāš* comes from the Hebrew root *qdš*, which is a term for distinction between the sacred and profane. Translated variously as "sanctuary, shrine, holy place," *miqdāš* most often refers to Israel's sanctuary of worship, wherein offerings and sacrifices are made to the Lord (e.g., Exod. 15:17; 25:8; Lev. 16:33; 21:12). See *sanctuary.*

HOME

See *house.*

HONEY

Old Testament

Noun: דְּבַשׁ (*d^e^baš*), GK 1831 (S 1706), 54x. *d^e^baš* refers to bees' honey (Jdg. 14:8–9) and perhaps also to a sweet syrup made of boiled-down fruit (other ancient Near Eastern sources suggest this). It is valued as a sweetener (Ezek. 3:3) and as a trade commodity (27:17), but it must not be used in a sacrifice (Lev. 2:11, perhaps because the sugar in it may cause fermentation). It is frequently used as one element in a gift (Gen. 43:11; 2 Sam. 17:29; Jer. 41:8). For the most part, honey seems to have been wild (e.g., Deut. 32:13; 1 Sam. 14:25–29; Ps. 81:16), but since in the days of Hezekiah it was given to the Lord as part of a tithe (2 Chr. 31:5), there may have also been domesticated honey.

Nearly half of the occurrences of *d^e^baš* in the OT are variations on the phrase, "a land flowing with milk and honey" (Exod. 3:8; Num. 13:27; Deut. 11:9; Jos. 5:6), which is figurative language for the fertile land of Canaan, a land where both animals and agriculture are productive. Because honey is so sweet to the taste, it becomes a metaphor for anything that is sweet, such as the ordinances of the Lord (Ps. 19:10; 119:103; Ezek. 3:3), pleasant words from one's mouth (Prov. 16:24), and wisdom (24:13–14). See *NIDOTTE*, 1:916–17.

HONOR

Old Testament

Verb: כָּבֵד (*kābēd*), GK 3877 (S 3513), 114x. *kābēd* generally means "to honor." It has the basic meaning of "weight." It can also mean, by extension, "be heavy" or "unresponsive." In a literal sense, the term can refer to something that is heavy. Eli was an old and "heavy" person (1 Sam. 4:18; 2 Sam. 14:26; cf. Prov. 27:3). As wealth is measured in possessions, the rich are literally "heavy" with their belongings. This may be how the concepts of heaviness and honor became related.

In a metaphorical sense, heaviness can express sluggishness or unresponsiveness. Pharaoh's heart "was unresponsive" to God and his will (Exod. 7:14; 8:11, 28). "Heavy ears" cannot hear God's commandments (Isa. 6:10; cf. 59:1). *kābēd* can refer to something as serious as God's judgment (Exod. 9:3; 1 Sam. 5:6, 11; Ps. 32:4) or something as burdensome as oppression from rulers or famine (Gen. 12:10; 1 Ki. 12:10; Neh. 5:18). The grievous nature of sin is expressed with this term (Gen. 18:20; Isa. 1:4; 24:20). The psalmist says, "My guilt has overwhelmed me like a burden too *heavy* to bear" (Ps. 38:4). When *kābēd* is used of a group, it means numerous or abundant (Exod. 8:24; 12:38 ; Num. 22:15).

Just as the entourage of the wealthy can be "heavy" with their possessions, the prestige of their riches contribute weightiness or importance to their character, that is, honor (Gen. 13:2). "To honor" means to esteem highly (Isa. 43:4) or consider someone or something as worthy of respect, reverence, and awe. Children are commanded to "honor" (lit., "make heavy") their parents (Exod. 20:12); prophets could receive honor from the people of God (1 Sam. 9:6). Honor is improper if it exceeds that given to God (1 Sam. 2:29–30) or is directed to one's self (Prov. 12:9). When the Lord gets honor for himself, he causes people to acknowledge the unequaled value of his character (Exod. 14:4, 17–18). In this sense, the term is often translated "glory." The Lord is unique among other gods because they cannot match his powerful deeds. For this reason, the nations come and "bring glory" to God. In other words, they honor him and acknowledge him as supremely valuable (Ps. 86:8–10). The word for "glory" (*kābôd*, GK 3883) comes from this root; see *glory*. See *NIDOTTE,*

Noun: כָּבוֹד (*kābôd*), GK 3883 (S 3519), 200x. The basic meaning of *kābôd* is "glory" or "honor." See *glory*.

Noun: תִּפְאֶרֶת (*tipʾeret*), GK 9514 (S 8597), 51x. *tipʾeret means* "glory, splendor, honor." See *glory*.

New Testament

Verb: τιμάω (*timaō*), GK *5506* (S *5091*), 21x. *timaō* means "to honor, hold in esteem, place value on someone or something." The verb includes showing respect to all people in general (1 Pet. 2:17) and recognizing those with specific status or needs (1 Tim. 5:3). This act of honor can be shown in practical and concrete ways, as when the people of Malta provide for Paul and his shipmates in response to Paul's healing them (Acts 28:10). The most common example of *timaō* is the honor that one should pay to one's parents (i.e., the fifth commandment; see Mt. 15:4; 15:6; 19:19; Mk. 7:10; 10:19; Lk. 18:20; Eph. 6:2). When Judas is given thirty silver coins to betray Christ, it is an example of *timaō* being used for setting a price or value (Mt. 27:9).

The NT makes clear, however, that it is not sufficient outwardly to show honor to God, for Jesus confronts those who honor him with their lips but not their hearts (Mt. 15:8; Mk. 7:6). The most visible way to honor the Father is to honor the Son (Jn. 5:23; 12:26). Finally, Jesus provides the ultimate example of what it means to show honor, because he truly honors the Father (8:49). See *NIDNTT-A*, 564-65.

Noun: δόξα (*doxa*), GK *1518* (S *1391*), 166x. *doxa* can be translated as "glory, honor, splendor." See *glory*.

Noun: τιμή (*timē*), GK *5507* (S *5092*), 41x. *timē* is the amount at which something is "valued," its "price," or it can mean "honor, respect." See *value*.

HONORABLE

New Testament

Adjective: τίμιος (*timios*), GK *5508* (S *5093*), 13x. *timios* refers to something that is considered "valuable, precious, honorable." See *valuable*.

HOPE

New Testament

Verb: ἐλπίζω (*elpizō*), GK *1827* (S *1679*), 31x. In general *elpizō* means "hope," though it sometimes denotes "desire, wish" (see *desire*). In several places, NT writers quote OT passages about hoping in the Lord, which essentially means trusting in the Lord (Mt. 12:21; Rom. 15:12). According to Paul, we should never put our hope or trust in wealth (1 Tim. 6:17).

The most important sense of this verb is the firm conviction that because of Jesus' resurrection from the dead, we can have confidence as we face the future (Rom. 8:24–25; 1 Cor. 15:19). This sense of confident expectation (Heb. 11:1)is used when the NT writers speak about hoping in God (1 Tim. 4:10) or in Jesus (1 Pet. 1:13). See *NIDNTT-A*, 183-85.

Noun: ἐλπίς (*elpis*), GK *1828* (S *1680*), 53x. The majority of the NT writers invest *elpis*, "hope," with the nuance of "confident expectation" or "solid assurance," though in several places it means simply "desire" or "wish" (Acts 16:19; 27:20), as our common English usage ("I hope the sun will shine tomorrow"). This predominant understanding of hope is based on the OT, where hope is essentially synonymous with "trust": to hope in the Lord is to trust in the Lord (cf. Rom. 15:13). When Paul says in Rom. 5:2 that Christians "rejoice in the hope of the glory of God," he obviously does not intend for hope to mean merely "wish." Only a confident expectation produces joy; wishing for something one is not sure to receive produces anxiety rather than joy. As Paul goes on to write, Christian hope is a hope that will never disappoint us (Rom. 5:5).

Hope is directed toward the future. Once we have received what we have hoped for, hope ceases (Rom. 8:24). Thus, the ultimate focus of Christian hope, according to the NT, is the return of Jesus Christ (Tit. 2:13), the resurrection from the dead (Acts 23:6), God's ultimate salvation of his people, and the resultant eternal life in a restored creation (Rom. 8:20–21; Gal. 5:5; Eph. 1:18; Tit. 1:2; 3:7). At that point, we will live in eternal glory, centered in Jesus Christ himself, "the hope of glory" (Col. 1:27; 1 Tim. 1:1).

Christian hope is strengthened by the Scriptures (Rom. 15:4), by the work of Jesus (1 Pet. 1:3, 21), and by God's present gift of the Spirit to believers (Rom. 5:5). God wants us to wear hope around our heads as a helmet (1 Thess. 5:8) and to be ready at all times to share our hope with others (1 Pet. 3:15). By contrast, those who do not have God in their lives are without hope (Eph. 2:12). See *NIDNTT-A*, 183-85.

HORDES

Old Testament

Noun: הָמוֹן (*hāmôn*), GK 2162 (S 1995), 82x. *hāmôn* expresses a quality of immensity or magnitude, whether it bears an emotive, audible, or spatial reference. It is translated with words like "confusion, tumult, noise, abundance, crowd, hordes."

hāmôn can indicate immensity of emotion, sound, size, etc. "Though a whole band of shepherds is called together against him, he is not frightened by their shouts or disturbed by their clamor" (Isa. 31:4). "I saw great confusion just as Joab was about to send the king's servant and me" (2 Sam. 18:29). Jeremiah speaks of the "noise of the enemy chariots and the rumble of their wheels" (Jer. 47:3), of "idolatrous commotion on the hills" (3:23). Isaiah uses *hāmôn* to describe the voice of God (though rarely is this word used of God): "At the thunder of your voice, the peoples flee" (Isa. 33:3).

hāmôn most commonly describes a multitude of people—usually soldiers. Isaiah speaks of Israel's enemies becoming as dust in the wind and the "ruthless hordes like blown chaff" (Isa. 29:5). Ezekiel also uses *hāmôn* to describe how "Pharaoh and his all his hordes will be laid among the uncircumcised" (Ezek. 32:32). God tells Habakkuk how he is raising up the Babylonians, who will sweep across the earth in fear and dread: "Their hordes advance like a desert wind and gather prisoners like sand" (Hab. 1:9).

HORN

Old Testament

Noun: קֶרֶן (*qeren*), GK 7967 (S 7161), 76x. This word refers primarily to the horn of an animal, but *qeren* can also be understood as "point, corner," such as the "*horns* of the altar" (Exod. 29:12).

(1) *qeren* primarily refers to the horns of various animals, such as the ram (Gen. 22:13) and wild oxen (Ps. 22:21), even the tusks of an elephant (Ezek. 27:15). Because animal horns could be turned into horns, *qeren* can be used of the instrument. "When you hear them sound a long blast on the *trumpets*, have all the people give a loud shout; then the wall of the city will collapse and the people will go up, every man straight in" (Jos. 6:5). *qeren* can also be used of vessels (1 Sam. 16:1).

(2) The most frequent use of this word is for the "*horns* of the altar," that is, the horn-like projections at the four corners of the altar of the Lord. Atoning blood was applied to these horns (Lev. 4:7, 18, 25; 16:18). Prominent people who felt threatened for their lives would cling to the horns of the altar as a plea for mercy (1 Ki. 1:50–51; 2:28).

(3) The animal horn can be used as a metaphor to describe "might, power, strength." "Moab's *horn* is cut off, her arm is broken" (Jer. 48:25). "In majesty he [the members of the tribe of Joseph] is like a firstborn bull, his *horns* are the *horns* of a wild ox" (Deut. 33:17). This metaphor

appears in the Psalms, where the psalmist affirms that the Lord is his shield and "the *horn* of my salvation" (Ps. 18:2; cf. 2 Sam. 22:3). The idea of lifting up one's horn is a symbol of triumph or sometimes arrogance (Ps. 75:4–5, 10; 89:17, 24; 92:10), whereas the cutting of a horn is a symbol of humiliation and defeat (75:10; Jer. 48:25; Amos 3:14). See *NIDOTTE. 3:990-992.*

New Testament

Noun: κέρας (*keras*), GK *3043* (S *2768*), 11x. In classical Gk., *keras* is the ordinary word for the horn of an animal. In Assyrian and Babylonian history, *keras* came to portray the strength of gods and humans. Royalty and religious heads wore double-horned head garb, much like the gods. Alexander the Great was referred to as "The Horned One."

In Lk. 1:69, Zechariah's song praising Jesus' coming birth uses *keras* to apply the Messiah's "saving power" referred to in Ps. 18:2. "Raising up the horn of salvation" communicates a dramatic increase in power (cf. Deut. 33:17). Several OT passages point to the coming of the Messiah by depicting the horn of David as exalted (e.g., Ps. 89:24; 132:17).

All other uses of *keras* occur in Revelation. Horns appear on the Lamb of God (Rev. 5:6), on the golden altar (9:13), but also on the unholy trinity, namely, Satan's great red dragon (12:3), and on two of his four beasts (13:1, 11; 17:3, 7, 12, 16). Apocalyptic literature featured the horned lamb or ram as a messianic conqueror who leads God's people to victory (*1 Enoch* 90:9-12). John initially pictured Jesus as a sacrificial lamb in Jn. 1:29, "Behold, the Lamb of God, who takes away the sin of the world." But when the image of Jesus as a lamb resurfaces in Rev. 5:6, the horned lamb is the warrior Messiah who will destroy his enemies. He is equipped with seven horns, stressing the Lamb's immeasurable and unmatched strength. Part of the irony projected in John's vision is that the sacrificial lamb and the military lamb are one and the same, communicating God's mercy and justice. While Satan and his evil representatives (depicted as horrific, fearsome beasts) have power, they are decisively no match for the totally eclipsing power of the Lamb when they finally "lock horns" in the final battle of Armageddon (16:13–17). See *NIDNTT-A*, 301-2.*

HORRIFIED

Old Testament

Verb: שָׁמֵם (*šāmēm*), GK 9037 (S 8074), 92x. The verb *šāmēm* is used in two distinct but related ways. It can mean "to be desolate, deserted, lay waste" or it can point to the response to such desolation and mean "to shudder, be horrified, be appalled." As to the second usage, it denotes the reaction of people to the desolation caused by divine judgment on themselves (Ps. 40:15; 143:4) or others (Lev. 26:32; Jer. 2:12; Job 17:8). See *appalled.*

HORSE

Old Testament

Noun: סוּס (*sûs*), GK 6061 (S 5483), 138x. Inhabitants of the OT world used the horse for riding, for transporting goods, and, by the wealthy, for hunting. But the majority of the references to *sûs* occur in military contexts, in which the *sûs* was seen as an animal of war—sometimes with soldiers riding on horses (Exod. 15:1; Ezek. 38:15) and sometimes with horses pulling chariots (Jos. 11:4; 1 Ki. 20:21). In contrast, the prophet Zechariah prophesies that the Messiah will come riding on a humble donkey (9:9–10), an animal of peace. As a further indication of peace, Zechariah prophesies that when the Messiah comes, he will abolish both "the chariots from Ephraim and the *war-horses* from Jerusalem" (Zech. 9:9–10).

Scholars believe the horse originally came from Central Asia and South Russia. Evidence indicates the introduction of the horse into the Middle East occurred over four thousand years ago. Although first mentioned in Gen. 47:17, the horse did not become common in Israel until the time of David and Solomon (c. 1000 – 922 BC). Solomon possessed twelve thousand horses and fourteen hundred chariots (2 Chr. 1:14). Because the Mosaic law prohibited the breeding of horses (Deut. 17:16), Solomon imported them from Egypt (2 Chr. 1:16). 2 Chr. 1:7 lists the price of a horse in Solomon's day as 150 shekels of silver. Yet David indicates correct priorities in Ps. 20:7: "Some trust in chariots and some in *horses*, but we trust in the name of the Lord our God." See *NIDOTTE*, 3:234-36.

New Testament

Noun: ἵππος (*hippos*), GK *2691* (S *2462*), 17x. In ancient times, the "horse" was a common animal for use, among other things, by armies in war. In the OT the horse was a symbol of power (Job 39:19–25). Sometimes horses symbolized a resource that might be relied upon instead of on God's power (Ps. 147:10; Hos. 1:7). In the NT, 15 of the 16 occurrences of *hippos* occur in Revelation. In most of these, each horse accompanies a destructive power stronger than human beings (Rev. 6:2–8; 9:1ff.). Images of power are added together to reinforce the image of power. Grasshoppers are like horses with heads like lions (Rev. 9:7–10).

When Jesus enters Jerusalem before his death and resurrection, he does so on a donkey (Mk. 11:1–11), not on a horse, thus rejecting the notion that he is coming for a military victory. But in Rev. 19:11–21, which depicts his second coming, he is riding a white horse of victory.

In Jas. 3:3, the powerful and resistant human tongue is compared to a horse that must be controlled with bridle and bit.

HOSANNA

New Testament

Interjection: ὡσαννά (*hōsanna*), GK *6057* (S *5614*), 6x. *hōsanna* is the shout that the people make as Jesus enters Jerusalem during his triumphal entry (Mt. 21:9, 15; Mk. 11:9–10; Jn. 12:13). This word is actually a Hebrew word that occurs in Ps. 118:25, where it is translated "save us." Psalm 118 was a typical psalm of hope and triumph that pilgrims to Jerusalem sang as they climbed their way up the road to Jerusalem and then into the temple during Passover week. This word takes on added meaning, of course, when it is sung to Jesus as he goes up to Jerusalem and within a week is crucified for the salvation of his people.*

HOST

Old Testament

Noun: צָבָא (*ṣābāʾ*), GK 7372 (S 6635), 479x. *ṣābāʾ* appears to come from a military context and bears both a general and specific meaning in the OT. As to the latter, *ṣābāʾ* occurs about 280x as part of a significant and exalted title for God (1 Sam. 1:3; Ps. 24:10; Isa. 6:5). "The LORD (Yahweh) of hosts" appears frequently in Isaiah, Jeremiah, and Zechariah. While this designation has military overtones, it emphasizes especially God's sovereignty over the entire world. See *Almighty*.

New Testament

Adjective: ξένος (*xenos*), GK *3828* (S *3581*), 14x. Usually *xenos* denotes something "strange" or unusual or a person who is unknown, but in one text is used as a noun to denote a "host," one who shows "hospitality" (Rom. 16:23). See *strange(r)*.

HOUR

New Testament

Noun: ὥρα (*hōra*), GK *6052* (S *5610*), 106x. *hōra* communicates a period of time. It is normally taken to mean "hour." Three related ideas are communicated by this word.

(1) *hōra* can in a general sense simply refer to an undefined period of time in a day. Mk. 11:11 describes how when Jesus entered Jerusalem it was already late in the day (lit., "the *hour* was already late"). In Mt. 24:44 Jesus says to "be ready, because the Son of Man will come at an *hour* when you do not expect him."

(2) The Romans divided the daylight time into "twelve hours" (Jn. 11:9). *hōra* can be used to refer to one of these divisions of a day, such as the "sixth hour" (noon) or the "ninth hour" (3:00 p.m.) (Acts 10:3, 9). If something occurs for the approximate length of one of these time

periods, it lasts about an hour (Lk. 22:59); Sapphira came to see Peter "about three *hours*" after her husband's death (Acts 5:7). Rev. 9:15 lists four general time divisions: year, month, day, and *hōra*. This word can also define a segment of a "very short time," as in Rev. 18:10: "In one *hour* your doom has come."

(3) Since *hōra* can designate a specific point in time, the term can also be used to designate a point of time as an occasion for an event. It can refer to the exact "moment" that something takes place (Mt. 8:13) or the special character of the time when something occurs (Lk. 10:21). The NT places stress on particular points in Jesus' life in which things happen to or through Jesus that reveal his majesty and authority (Lk. 7:21–23). This is especially clear in the gospel of John. For John, the entire redemptive act of Jesus—his arrest, death, resurrection, and return to the Father—is his special "hour" or "time" (Jn. 2:4; 13:1).

The time of Christ's redemptive act on our behalf points to another specific point in time that the church awaits: "the last hour" (Jn. 16:2, 32; 1 Jn. 2:18; Rev. 3:10), where Jesus returns to judge the world and collect his own. As Christians, we celebrate the sacred hour in which Christ died on our behalf, but we also await the coming time when we will be with him forever. It is for this reason that we must do as Paul says, "The *hour* has come for you to wake up from your slumber because our salvation is nearer now than when we first believed" (Rom. 13:11). See *NIDNTT-A*, 625-26.

HOUSE

Old Testament

Noun: בַּיִת (*bayit*), GK 1074 (S 1004), 2047x. *bayit* means "house" and bears both literal and figurative meanings in the OT.

(1) Frequently, *bayit* refers to a private dwelling for an individual or family. (a) Most often, it refers to the abode of a common person ("house," Jos. 2:19) or royalty ("palace," 2 Sam. 7:1; cf. *hêkāl*, "temple"). The structures are built of various materials such as wood, stone, or ivory (Deut. 20:15; 22:18; 1 Ki. 2:36; Ps. 127:1) and often include a roof supported in such a way that one can walk on it (2 Sam. 11:2; cf. Jos. 2:6–8). *bayit* can also refer to the dwelling of undomesticated animals, such as a wild donkey (Job 39:6), a hyrax (Prov. 30:6), or even a spider's web (Job 8:14).

(b) *bayit* is also used for temples, the earthly dwelling places of god(s)—e.g., of the Philistine god Dagon in Ashdod (1 Sam. 5:2) and of God in Shiloh (Jdg. 18:31) or in Jerusalem (1 Ki. 6:5). The presence of the Lord at the temple is no guarantee of safety for a people who practice idolatry, a reminder frequently revisited by the prophets (Isa. 1:10–17; Jer. 7:1–15; 26:4–6; Amos 5:21–27). This is underscored by Ezekiel's vision of the glory of God departing from the temple (Ezek. 10:1–22; 11:22–23). The Lord's abode in heaven was also called a *bayit* (Ps. 36:8).

(2) *bayit* can also be used figuratively for the members of one's family or household. Among one's "house" are included servants (Gen. 7:1; 17:27; cf. Jos. 7:14) and both immediate (Deut. 25:9) and extended family (2 Sam. 3:6). Pharaoh's court is called a *bayit* (Gen. 50:4). Significantly, *bayit* describes kingship, a royal dynasty, and particularly the "house of David" (2 Ki. 17:21; Isa. 7:2; cf. especially 2 Sam. 7:11–16).

In 2 Sam. 7 is a wordplay on these two meanings of the term *bayit*. In 7:1-2, David is distraught that he lives in a "palace" (*bayit*) while God lives in a "tent" (*yᵉrîʿâ*). Though David wants to build a palace (*bayit*) for God, God says that "the LORD himself will establish a house" (*bayit*) for David (7:11). The former refers to an earthly temple, while the latter refers to the eternal Davidic kingship. In the NT, an angel announced that Jesus is the heir to the throne of David (Lk. 1:32).

New Testament

Noun: οἶκος (*oikos*), GK *3875* (S *3624*), 114x.

Noun: οἰκία (*oikia*), GK *3864* (S *3614*), 93x. In the legal terminology of prebiblical Greek, *oikos* was distinct from *oikia*, the former referring to property left by a person after death and the latter referring only to a dwelling or house. By the time of the NT the terms are practically synonymous and most commonly denote a place where a person lives either literally (Mt. 2:11; 7:24–27; 9:7; Mk. 7:30) or figuratively in the sense of a family grouping (Mt. 13:57; Mk. 6:4; Jn. 4:53; 1 Cor. 1:16; 2 Tim. 1:16; 4:19). It is used in other ways as well.

(1) *oikos* can refer to the temple in Jerusalem (*oikos theou* "house of God"; Mk. 2:26; 11:17; Jn. 2:16–17; cf. Acts 7:47).

(2) *oikos* can refer to ancestral family lineage, such as "the house of Israel," "the house of Jacob," or "the house of Judah" (Lk. 1:33; Acts 7:42; Heb. 8:8, 10). This is a common usage in the OT.

(3) *oikos* is also used of the Christian community as the "house of God" (Heb. 3:2–6; 10:21; 1 Pet. 4:17; see *bayit*). It can refer to the "family" of God (Eph. 4:17) and is explicitly linked with the church (1 Tim. 3:15). This is partially because the earliest and most basic unit of Christian groups met in private homes (Acts 11:14; 16:15, 31, 34; 18:8; 1 Cor. 1:16; 2 Tim. 1:16; 4:19).

(4) A Christian's body is seen as a temple (*oikos*) of the Holy Spirit (1 Cor. 6:19; cf. 3:16). See *NIDNTT-A*, 404-5.

HOUSEHOLD GODS

Old Testament

Noun: תְּרָפִים (*t^e^rāpîm*), GK 9572 (S 8655), 15x. *t^e^rāpîm*, a plural noun, refers to pagan "idols," often translated as "household gods." See *idol*.

HOUSEHOLDER

See *owner*.

HUMAN BEING

New Testament

Noun: ἄνθρωπος (*anthrōpos*), GK *476* (S *444*), 550x. *anthrōpos* means "man, human being, mankind." See *man*.

HUMANITY

Old Testament

Noun: אָדָם (*ʾādām*), GK 132, 134 (S 120, 121), 558x. The basic meaning and most common translation of *ʾādām* is "man." Unlike *ʾîš*, which carries not only the sense of "man" but also of "male," *ʾādām* may be used by the OT writers to describe humanity as a whole—men, women, and children. See *man*.

HUMANKIND

New Testament

Noun: ἄνθρωπος (*anthrōpos*), GK *476* (S *444*), 550x. *anthrōpos* means "man, human being, mankind." See *man*.

Noun: οἰκουμένη (*oikoumenē*), GK *3876* (S *3625*), 15x. This noun is used in the NT to refer to the "inhabited earth" rather than the whole globe. It can also denote the human race. See *world*.

HUMBLE

Old Testament

Verb: עָנָה (*ʿānâ*), GK 6700 (S 6031), 79x. *ʿānâ* can denote humbling in a positive sense (i.e., repentance and contrition) or with connotations of violence (i.e., affliction and oppression; see *afflict*). Forms of *ʿānâ* that are pleasing to God include fasting and prayer (Lev. 16:31; 23:27; Ps. 35:13).

Adjective: עָנִי (*ʿānî*), GK 6714 (S 6041), 80x. *ʿānî* describes one who has been humbled or afflicted by circumstances, and who, because of current disability, finds himself or herself dependent on others for life's necessities. Since *ʿānî* describes someone who is lowly, it also describes the coming Messiah (Zech. 9:9). See *poor*.

New Testament

Verb: ταπεινόω (*tapeinoō*), GK *5427* (S *5013*), 14x. *tapeinoō* conveys various shades of meaning; "level," "humble" (socially, politically, economically), "make small," and "be obedient." The NIV renders *tapeinoō* as "humble" or "make low" ("abase," KJV), and in a general sense of causing something to be at a lower point. Luke refers to the one preparing the way of the Lord as making every mountain and hill level or *low* (Lk. 3:5). Furthermore, Paul uses *tapeinoō* in the sense of "humble means"; the NIV renders the sense correctly: "I know *what it is to be in need*" (Phil. 4:12).

In all the other NT occurrences, the word refers either to the loss of prestige or status ("to be humiliated, abased") or to the lowering of one's estimation of oneself ("to become humble in attitude"). Jesus warns of this first type of humilation: "For everyone who exalts himself will be humbled, and he who humbles himself will be exalted" (Lk. 18:14, see also Jas. 1:9–10). In the second sense, Christ humbled himself by taking on the form of a servant (Phil. 2:8), and Paul, who worked with his hands, voluntarily humbled himself (2 Cor. 11:7). Here the humiliation, especially that of Christ, is a reversal of status. Christ, who is worthy of the name above all names, humbles himself to the point of death upon a cross. Furthermore, 1 Pet. 5:6, quoting Prov. 3:34, concisely conveys this second sense of *tapeinoō* in the NT as a command: "Humble yourselves, therefore, under God's mighty hand, that he may lift you up in due time." Here the end-time reality of God's care and provision for the humble is stressed. In a similar context Luke tells of the sinner who goes away forgiven because he has humbled himself (Lk. 18:14), and Matthew records Jesus' teaching that the one who humbles himself like a little child will be great in the kingdom (Mt. 18:4; see also 23:12). See *NIDNTT-A*, 555-56.

HUMILIATE

New Testament

Verb: καταισχύνω (*kataischynō*), GK *2875* (S *2617*), 13x. *kataischynō* means "to embarrass, be ashamed, disappoint." See *embarrass*.

Verb: ταπεινόω (*tapeinoō*), GK *5427* (S *5013*), 14x. In several NT occurrences, *tapeinoō* refers either to the loss of prestige or status ("to be humiliated, abased") or to the lowering of one's estimation of oneself ("to become humble in attitude"). See *humble*.

HUMILITY

New Testament

Noun: πραΰτης (*prautēs*), GK *4559* (S *4240*), 11x. *prautēs* means "gentleness, humility." See *gentleness*.

HUNDRED

Old Testament

Noun: מֵאָה (*mēʾā*), GK 4395 (S 3967), 583x. *mēʾā* means "hundred" in the singular and "two hundred" in the plural. Accompanied with other cardinal numbers, it can be used to designate any number of hundred, such as "three *hundred*" (Jdg. 8:4), "four *hundred*" (1 Sam. 25:13), etc. *mēʾā* is used frequently in genealogies (e.g., Gen. 5; Ezr. 2; Neh. 7), in the numbering of the Israelites (Num. 1–2; 26), and in the measurements of Ezekiel's temple (Ezek. 42; 48). For items that one expects to find in small quantities, *mēʾâ* expresses a large number—see, e.g., Prov. 17:10: "A rebuke impresses a man of discernment more than a *hundred* lashes a fool" (cf. also Eccl. 6:3; 8:12). See *NIDOTTE*, 2:827–29.

New Testament

Adjective: ἑκατόν (*hekaton*), GK *1669* (S *1540*), 17x. *hekaton* is the cardinal number "one hundred." Almost half of its uses in the NT are part of a compound cardinal number, like 120 (Acts 1:15), 144 (Rev. 21:17), 153 (Jn. 21:11), and 144,000 (Rev. 7:4; 14:1, 3).

hekaton often indicates a large amount of something, like a hundredfold yield of seed (Mt. 13:8, 23; Mk. 4:8, 20) or a flock of a hundred sheep (Mt. 18:12; Lk. 15:4). But *hekaton* can also indicate comparative smallness, as it does in Jesus' parable of the unmerciful servant. In this parable a debt of one hundred denarii is as nothing compared to a debt of ten thousand talents (Mt. 18:24, 28). A further example of this use can be seen in Mk 6. Here the disciples direct the five thousand people to sit in groups of hundreds before Jesus miraculously feeds them all.

In Jn. 19:39, the KJV and NASB translate *hekaton* literally as a "hundred pounds," but the NIV translates it "seventy-five pounds." The reason for the differing translations is that the Roman pound of which this verse speaks weighed around twelve ounces, only three-quarters the weight of a contemporary pound. Thus, while "hundred" is more literal, "seventy-five" conveys the amount of the unit more clearly to readers unaware of the metrological difference.*

HUNGER

Old Testament

Noun: רָעָב (*rāʿāb*), GK 8280 (S 7457), 101x. *rāʿāb* means "famine, hunger, starvation." See *famine*.

New Testament

Noun: λιμός (*limos*), GK *3350* (S *3042*), 12x. *limos* can be translated "hunger, famine." See *famine*.

HUNGRY

New Testament

Verb: πεινάω (*peinaō*), GK *4277* (S *3983*), 23x. *peinaō* means "to hunger, be hungry." For most occurrences in the NT, this verb is used literally. After fasting forty days, Jesus was hungry (Mt. 4:2), which indicates that he was genuinely human. When the disciples plucked grain on the Sabbath, they were hungry (12:1). Paul knew what it was like to be well fed or hungry (Phil. 4:12; cf. 1 Cor. 4:11). One of the questions that will be asked of God's people on the Day of days is whether we have provided food for those among the least of God's children who do not have enough to eat (Mt. 25:35–44).

In addition to physical hunger, *peinaō* can signify a hunger that is spiritual. The term expresses a passionate longing for something that, if unavailable, would result in death. Jesus promises blessings to those who "hunger and thirst for righteousness" (Mt. 5:6). He also promises to meet our spiritual needs: "I am the bread of life. He who comes to me will never go hungry" (Jn. 6:35). See *NIDNTT-A*, 448-49.

HURRY

Old Testament

Verb: מָהַר (*māhar*), GK 4554 (S 4116), 81x. *māhar* generally means "to hurry" in the sense of moving quickly (Gen. 18:6; 19:22; 1 Sam. 4:14; Jer. 9:17; Nah. 2:6). With a negative, *māhar* means to procrastinate (e.g., 2 Chr. 24:5).

(1) With regards to time, *māhar* implies quickness or suddenness. For instance, Isaac expresses surprise that Esau (actually, Jacob) has completed his hunt so quickly (Gen. 27:20; see also Exod. 2:18; 1 Sam. 28:20). God promises to assist Israel in the conquest of Canaan, but it will be a controlled conquest. It will be quick in the sense that it is sure to succeed (Deut. 9:3).

(2) The Bible frequently portrays hurrying in a negative light. *māhar* can denote Israel's rapid descent into apostasy (Exod. 32:8; see also Ps. 16:4, "who *run* [KJV, "*hasten*"] after other gods"; 106:13, "they *soon* forgot."). It can describe those who rush into evil (Prov. 1:16; 6:18; Isa. 59:7). It can also refer to undesirable character qualities, such as being impetuous (Prov. 7:23, "like a bird *darting* into a snare"; see also Hab. 1:6), hasty, perhaps in the sense of being frivolous (Prov. 25:8), rash (Eccl. 5:1; see also Isa. 32:4), or fearful (Isa. 35:4, "say to those with *fearful* hearts"; *māhar* may be used here on account of the rapid heartbeat that often accompanies fear).

(3) *māhar* is also often used with respect to God. The Psalms call on God to provide quick answers to prayer (Ps. 69:18; see also 102:2; 143:7). Moreover, God's judgment is swift (Jer. 48:16; Zeph. 1:14). God warns his people of swift judgment if they are unfaithful to the covenant (Deut. 4:26; 7:4; 28:20; Mal. 3:5). At the same time, God will restore his people swiftly if they are penitent (Isa. 49:17).

For further reading, see *NIDOTTE*, 2:857–59.

Verb: רוּץ (*rûṣ*), GK 8132 (S 7323), 104x. *rûṣ* conveys the basic sense "to run, make haste by running." See *run*.

HURT

See *do wrong*.

HUSBAND

Old Testament

Noun: אִישׁ (*'îš*), GK 408 (S 376), 2188x. The most basic and frequent meaning of *'îš* in the OT is "man" (NIV = 612x) or, in the plural, "men" (NIV = 523x). A secondary meaning for *'îš* is "husband" (NIV = 64x), as in Gen. 3:16. See *man*.

New Testament

Noun: ἀνήρ (*anēr*), GK *467* (S 435), 216x. *anēr* generally means a "man" as opposed to a woman and is also the word for "husband." See *man*.

HUSBANDMAN

Noun: γεωργός (*geōrgos*), GK *1177* (S *1092*), 19x. *geōrgos* can refer to the owner of a farm or to those who work the farm (a "tenant"). See *farmer*.

HYPOCRISY

New Testament

Noun: ὑπόκρισις (*hypokrisis*) GK *5694* (S *5272*), 6x. *hypokrisis* means "hypocrisy." Hypocrisy is pretending to act one way while secretly acting in a different (often the opposite) way. For example, Jesus' enemies pretend they want to learn something from Jesus by asking him a question, but their true intent is to find a reason to arrest him and put him on trial (Mk. 12:15; cf. Mt. 23:28). Jesus calls this sort of hypocrisy "the yeast of the Pharisees" (Lk. 12:1). In the early church, when Peter, Barnabas, and others first eat with Gentiles and then, because some visitors arrive from Jerusalem, pull themselves away from the Gentiles our of fear, Paul calls that "hypocrisy" (Gal. 2:13). We must in fact do all we can to live honestly and not be filled with "hypocrisy" (1 Pet. 2:1; cf. 1 Tim. 4:2). It is interesting to note that this and related words originally come from the theater, from Greek words that mean to act.*

HYPOCRITE

New Testament

Noun: ὑποκριτής (*hypokritēs*), GK *5695* (S *5273*), 17x. *hypokritēs* means "hypocrite," a person who pretends to be something he or she is not. A *hypokritēs* was originally an actor who replied back to the chorus in Greek plays, turning speeches into dialogue. From this general meaning of an actor on a stage, *hypokritēs* was later applied to someone who acted in real life or who pretended to be something that he was not, especially in the moral aspects of life.

In the NT, *hypokritēs* is used exclusively in the Synoptic Gospels, most often in Matthew (13x). Jesus is the only one to use the word. In his Sermon on the Mount, Jesus urges his disciples to be true to their profession of faith and not to put up false pretenses. They are not to be "hypocrites" in their giving (Mt. 6:2), prayer life (6:5), or fasting (6:16). Jesus is especially critical of those Jews, including the teachers of the law and the Pharisees, who pretend to be close to God when in reality they were far from him. Jesus applies the prophetic judgment of Isa. 29:13 to them (Mt. 15:7; cf. Mk. 7:6); in Mt. 23 he pronounces a series of woes on them for their hypocrisy. They are hypocrites because they prevent others from entering the kingdom of heaven (23:13), they only pretend to be concerned about conversion (23:15), they are overly diligent about the minute things of the law while neglecting the weightier matters (23:23), they obsess about what can be observed while neglecting inner reality (23:25; 23:27), and they venerate the tombs of the prophets while being sons of those who murdered the prophets (23:29).

Jesus confronts these hypocrites with the fact that they are unable to understand what is truly important, such as the meaning of Jesus' presence (Lk. 12:56) or the substance of the Sabbath laws (Lk. 13:15). This inability to distinguish between pretense and reality causes the hypocrite to judge others of crimes of which the hypocrite himself is guilty (Mt. 7:5; Lk. 6:42). Because Jesus points out the duplicity of the hypocrites, they want to entrap and defeat him (Mt. 22:18). Ultimately, the hypocrite cannot be saved by his pretending, but their place will be in hell (24:51). See *NIDNTT-A*, 581.*

I (AM)

New Testament

Pronoun: ἐγώ (*egō*) GK *1609* (S *1473*), 2666x. *egō* means "I." The most significant usage of this pronoun is in the expressions of Jesus that begin with "I am" (*egō eimi*; see also be, GK *1639*). In Jn. 8:58, in response to the exclamation, "You are not yet fifty years old … and you have seen Abraham!" Jesus replies, "I tell you the truth … before Abraham was born, I am." Through this statement Jesus links himself with Yahweh, the covenant God of the OT, who revealed himself as the great "I am" (Exod. 3:14b; see *Lord*).

Jesus uses this same expression several other times; our English translations often obscure that simple expression "I am" by translating it, "It is I." For example, when Jesus comes to his disciples walking on the water during a storm, the disciples are frightened because they think they are seeing a ghost. But Jesus says to them, "Take courage! It is I" (lit., "I am"; Mt. 14:27; Mk. 6:50). Jesus is here asserting that he has the same power over the wind and the waves that the Lord manifests in the OT (e.g., Ps. 104:3–4; 107:27). In Mk. 13:6, Jesus warns his followers against imposters who will come claiming to be the Messiah; they will say, "I am he," but once again the expression is "I am." Only Jesus has the right to use these words. At his examination before the Jewish Council, when Jesus is asked point blank, "Are you the Christ, the Son of the Blessed One?" he replies, "I am"—words that are considered blasphemy since Jesus applies the "I am" of the OT to himself here (Mk. 14:61–62). Finally, after his resurrection, when the disciples again think they are seeing a ghost, this time at an appearance of the risen Savior, he says to them, "It is I myself" (lit., "I am, myself," Lk. 24:39).

Since Jesus applies *egō eimi* to himself so consistently, he probably has this in mind as well when he expresses about himself in John's gospel: "I am the bread of life" (Jn. 6:35); "I am the light of the world" (8:12); "I am the gate" (10:7, 9); "I am the good shepherd" (10:11); "I am the resurrection and the life" (11:25); I am the way and the truth and the life" (14:6); and "I am the vine" (15:1). See *NIDNTT-A*, 164–65.

IDOL

Old Testament

Noun: אֱלִיל (*ʾelîl*), GK 496 (S 457), 20x. *ʾelîl* frequently translates as "idol" but it can be translated as "image" and "worthless." This noun communicated to the Hebrews that any god other than the LORD is worthless. Lev. 26:1 records the word's initial use in the OT with, "Do not make *idols* … for yourselves." Although unclear, the root meaning of this word may be "to be weak, deficient." In contrast to the omnipotence of the Lord, other gods are weak. The Lord created the heavens, while all the gods of other nations are worthless idols (cf. Ps. 96:5). Such idols tremble before the Lord (Isa. 19:1). Isaiah describes the people of Judah and Samaria as "kingdoms of *the idols*" (10:10–11). He preaches that when God's day of judgment comes, individuals will throw "their *idols* of silver and gold" to the rodents and bats (2:20). The prophet predicts that one day the *ʾelîl* will totally disappear (2:18). See *NIDOTTE*, 1:411.

Noun: גִּלּוּלִים (*gillûlîm*), GK 1658 (S 1544), 48x. *gillûlîm* is one of about ten words for "idol" in the OT. The noun, always plural, can also be translated as "logs, blocks, shapeless things." Some scholars speculate that *gillûlîm* comes from the Heb. word for "dung, manure." Thus, *gillûlîm* ("idols") are as worthless as dung.

The author of 1 Kings praises King Asa of Judah for removing "all the *idols*" that his father (Abijam) had made (1 Ki. 15:12). He later gives a scathing criticism of King Ahab of Israel: "Ahab … did more to provoke the Lord, the God of Israel, to anger than all the kings of Israel who were before him" (16:33). Ahab's persistent pursuit of *gillûlîm* prompts the writer's unparalleled criticism in 21:26.

Ezekiel uses *gillûlîm* 39x in his attack on Judah's idolatry. For example, God says to Ezekiel, "Son of man, these men have taken their *idols* into their hearts, and set the stumbling block of their iniquity before their faces. Should I indeed let myself be consulted by them?" (Ezek. 14:3). Ezekiel insists that the worship of *gillûlîm* constitutes the inhabitants of Jerusalem's most despicable sin (6:13; 14:3) and has led to their exile in Babylon. See *NIDOTTE*, 1:864-65.

Noun: צֶלֶם (*ṣelem*), GK 7512 (S 6754), 15x. *ṣelem* "means idol, image." In some cases, it refers to pagan idols (e.g., Num. 33:52; 2 Ki. 11:18; 2 Chr. 23:17). See *image*.

Noun: תְּרָפִים (*t^erāpîm*), GK 9572 (S 8655), 15x. *t^erāpîm*, a plural noun, refers to pagan "idols," often translated as "household gods." This word is somewhat ambiguous in the OT, since it is used in a variety of contexts.

(1) According to Gen. 31:19, "when Laban had gone to shear his sheep, Rachel stole her father's *household gods*" (cf. 31:34–35). These items seemed important to Rachel, since Laban wanted them back, but Rachel was sitting on them and deceived her father by pretending she was having her period and could not get up. Some scholars hold that possessing these images entitled the owner to the legal rights of inheritance.

(2) In Jdg. 17:5; 18:14, 17–20, these images appear to be connected with a worship setting, for they are linked with an ephod, a carved image, and a cast idol (cf. also 2 Ki. 23:24; Hos. 3:4). The Jewish historian Josephus (born AD 37) wrote of the common practice of Mesopotamians carrying their *t^erāpîm* with them as they traveled (*Ant.* 18.9.5).

(3) But some *t^erāpîm* could also be large, since Michal hid one in David's bed to make it appear as if he was sleep there while, in fact, he had escaped (1 Sam. 19:11–17).

(4) In at least two places, it appears as if *t^erāpîm* could be used for divination (1 Sam. 15:23; Ezek. 21:21)—a specific practice condemned by the Lord in his law (Deut. 18:10–12, 20–21).

(5) In any case, the OT mocks the *t^erāpîm*. Rachel's sitting on them during a menstrual period would render them unclean. To use them like a bunch of rags as a lump in a bed shows what they are best useful for. And the prophet Zechariah specifically cites the *t^erāpîm* as deceitful: "The *idols* speak deceit; diviners see visions that lie; they tell dreams that are false; they give comfort in vain" (Zech. 10:2). As with other words for "idol" in the OT, this one too is incompatible with Israel's God. Is it any wonder that when Jacob returns to Bethel, where he first met the Lord God, he is told, "Get rid of the foreign gods you have with you, and purify yourselves" (Gen. 35:2)? See *NIDOTTE, 4:339.**

New Testament

Noun: εἴδωλον (*eidōlon*), GK *1631* (S *1497*), 11x. An *eidōlon* is an "image" or "idol" that represents a false god. The NT writers emphasize the futility of idols when compared to the living God (1 Thess. 1:9). Note how an *eidōlon* is fashioned by human hands (Acts 7:41), is mute (1 Cor. 12:2), and cannot see, hear, or walk (Rev. 9:20). These NT Scriptures echo Isaiah's satirical, but serious, condemnation of idol worship in Isa. 44. In keeping with this tradition, the Jews abhorred idols (Rom. 2:20). While the NT writers do not attribute power to an *eidōlon*, Paul teaches that worship offered to idols is truly being offered to demons (1 Cor. 10:19–21).

Believers must have nothing to do with idols (2 Cor. 6:16; 1 Jn. 5:21). *eidōlon* occurs in NT teachings in connection with meat that has been sacrificed to idols (Acts 15:20; 1 Cor. 8:4,7; 10:19). Also occurring in these discussions is the word *eidōlothytos*, a compound word that comes from *eidōlon* + *thyō* ("to sacrifice"), meaning "food sacrificed to idols" (Acts 15:29;

21:25, 1 Cor. 8:1, 4, 7, 10; 10:19; Rev. 2:14, 20). See *NIDNTT-A*, 163-64.*

IDOLATER, IDOLATRY

New Testament

Noun: εἰδωλολάτρης (*eidōlolatrēs*) GK *1629* (S *1496*), 7x. *eidōlolatrēs* means "idolater."

Noun: εἰδωλολατρία (*eidōlolatria*) GK *1630* (S *1497*), 4x. *eidōlolatria* means "idolatry." Idolatry is not limited to the worship of false images, but it is placing anything or anyone before God as the object of allegiance and devotion. Idolatry was a constant temptation in the early church, since many new believers had only recently come out of paganism. This word often appears in a list of sins of the human nature (Gal. 5:20; Col. 3:5; 1 Pet. 4:3); thus, there are admonitions to "flee from idolatry" (1 Cor. 10:14; cf. 10:7). The NT is forthright that "no idolaters" can enter the kingdom of God (6:9; Eph. 5:5; Rev. 21:8; 22:15), nor should believers have intimate contact with idolaters (1 Cor. 5:10–11).*

(BE) IGNORANT

New Testament

Verb: ἀγνοέω (*agnoeō*), GK *51* (S *50*), 22x. *agnoeō* means to be ignorant of something, not know something, or not understand something. The disciples do not understand Jesus' saying about his coming passion but are afraid to inquire further (Mk. 9:32; Lk. 9:45). Paul uses a negative with this verb on several occasions when he writes that he does not want his readers to be uninformed about something important (Rom. 1:13; 11:25; 1 Cor. 10:1; 1 Thess. 4:13); on other occasions Paul asks a rhetorical question with this verb, "Do you not know … ?" (Rom. 6:3; 7:1).

In 1 Tim. 1:13, Paul pleads ignorance regarding his persecution of Christians in his early years. He insists that if that phase of his life had not been done in ignorance, he would not have received the mercy and been appointed to his present ministry. This is not to say, however, that ignorance is an excuse for sin or serves to protect one from guilt. On the contrary, specific OT sacrifices were required for sins committed in ignorance (see Lev. 4:2, 22, 27). Paul himself needed God's forgiving mercy for his persecuting days.

Ignorance carries a largely negative connotation. It stifles intellectual, spiritual, and physical growth. *agnoeō* can refer to a disobedient state in which the individual is unteachable (Acts 13:27; Rom. 10:3; cf. Heb. 5:12) and turns away from the revelation of God in Christ (1 Cor. 14:38). See *NIDNTT-A*, 11-12.

ILL

Old Testament

Verb: חָלָה (*ḥālâ*), GK 2703 (S 2470), 75x. *ḥāla* describes a person who is weak, sick, ill, diseased, or wounded; it is also used to describe human frailties. See *weak*.

ILLNESS

New Testament

Noun: ἀσθένεια (*astheneia*), GK *819* (S *769*), 24x. *astheneia* means "weakness" and can also be used of a physical weakness ("sickness"). See *weakness*.

Noun: νόσος (*nosos*), GK *3798* (S *3554*), 11x. *nosos* is one of the words used to describe a "disease, illness, sickness." See *disease*.

ILLUSTRATION

New Testament

Noun: παραβολή (*parabolē*), GK *4130* (S *3850*), 50x. A "parable" is a story from everyday life used to illustrate a moral or religious truth. It is the primary method Jesus used to teach about the kingdom of God. In addition, the author of Hebrews refers to OT ceremonial practice as a *parabolē* (Heb. 9:9, the NIV translates "illustration"). See *parable*.

IMAGE

Old Testament

Noun: אֱלִיל (*ʾelîl*), GK 496 (S 457), 20x. The noun frequently translates as "idol" but can be translated as "image" and "worthless." See *idol*.

Noun: דְּמוּת (*demût*), GK 1952 (S 1823), 25x. *demût* denotes a likeness between two things. It is closely associated with the word *ṣelem* ("image") in Gen. 1:26. See *likeness*.

Noun: צֶלֶם (*ṣelem*), GK 7512 (S 6754), 15x. *ṣelem* "means idol, image." It has at least two major uses in the OT. (1) *ṣelem* sometimes refers to an image as a representation of a god, a man-made idol. God commands his people to destroy all the idols that they find in the land of Canaan (Num. 33:52). But the Israelites themselves begin to serve idols, and several times in their history at a time of national revival, the people smash pagan altars and "idols" (2 Ki. 11:18; 2 Chr. 23:17). Yet they revert back to idolatry, and many prophets speak out against "detestable *idols*"(Ezek. 7:20; cf. 16:17; Amos 5:26).

(2) But *ṣelem* can also mean something made in the likeness of something else. The Philistines, for example, make "models" of gold rats and tumors when they return the stolen ark to Israel (1 Sam. 6:5, 11). When Seth is born, he is made in Adam's own "image" (Gen. 5:6). And this is also the word used for human beings created "in the *image* of God": "So God created man in his own *image*, in the *image* of God he created him, male and female he created them" (Gen. 1:27; cf. 1:26; 9:6). While that *ṣelem* is not specifically defined, it does not appear to mean a physical likeness between human beings and God; rather, it is a moral and spiritual likeness. In contrast to animals, human beings can develop a relationship with God and can worship him. Moreover, the image of God is probably linked with God's command to the first man and woman: "Be fruitful and increase in number; fill the earth and subdue it. Rule over the fish of the sea and the birds of the air and over every living creature that moves on the ground" (1:28). The concept may also be relational: men and women have the unique ability to image God to one another as well as to image God back up to God. See *NIDOTTE, 3:810.*

New Testament

Noun: εἴδωλον (*eidōlon*), GK *1631* (S *1497*), 11x. An *eidōlon* is an "image" or "idol" that represents a false god. See *idol*.

Noun: εἰκών (*eikōn*), GK *1635* (S *1504*), 23x. *eikōn* means "image, likeness." It generally refers to something shaped to resemble something else, such as Caesar's portrait on the coin (Mt. 22:20). *eikōn* also can refer an idol. Sinful humanity "exchanged the glory of the immortal God for *images* made to look like mortal man and birds and animals and reptiles" (Rom. 1:23). The second beast will make "an image" of the first beast that was wounded by the sword but lived (Rev. 13:14–15). The saints who die during the great tribulation because they have not worshiped the "image" of the beast will reign with Christ in the millennium (Rev. 20:4).

In a figurative sense, *eikōn* is used for the law as only a shadow, and not the reality, of the good things to come in Christ Jesus (Heb. 10:1).

eikōn is also used to identify Christ as the perfect representation or likeness of God (2 Cor. 4:4; Col. 1:15). In kind, it is used to refer to the "image" of God in the Christian (1 Cor. 11:7), who is being transformed into the perfect "likeness" of Christ (Rom. 8:29; 2 Cor. 3:18). At some future date, we will bear the perfect "likeness" of the Son (1 Cor. 15:49). See *NIDNTT-A,* 164.

Noun: ὁμοίωμα (*homoiōma*), GK *3930* (S *3667*), 6x. *homoiōma* has two basic meanings. It can refer to "a similarity, a likeness," and to "an image" of something else. See *likeness*.

IMITATE, IMITATOR

New Testament

Verb: μιμέομαι (*mimeomai*) GK *3628* (S *3401*), 4x. *mimeomai* means "to imitate."

Noun: μιμητής (*mimētēs*) GK *3629* (S *3402*), 6x. *mimētēs* means "imitator." In the early church, many new believers needed models to show them how to live a redeemed lifestyle, since up to that time their lives were shaped by a pagan culture.

John informs his audience, "Do not imitate what is evil but what is good" (3 Jn. 11). The author of Hebrews suggests that believers use their leaders as "examples" (Heb. 13:7; cf. 6:12). Paul acknowledges that the Thessalonians have used Paul and company as their examples (1 Thess. 1:6; 2 Thess. 3:7, 9. In fact, Paul does not hesitate to instruct his churches to "imitate" him (1 Cor. 4:16; 11:1). But Paul says this only because he feels deeply that he himself is following the example of Christ the Lord (11:1; Eph. 5:1).

IMMANUEL

New Testament

Noun: Ἐμμανουήλ (*Emmanouēl*), GK *1842* (S *1694*), 1x. This word occurs only once in the NT: "The virgin will be with child and will give birth to a son, and they will call him 'Immanuel'—which means, 'God with us'" (Mt. 1:23). Matthew is quoting from Isa. 7:14 and 8:8 where the Hebrew *ʿimmānû ʾēl* literally means "God [is] with us." In Isaiah it refers to a child not yet born, promising that by the time he is born and able to know right from wrong, God will provide deliverance for his people. Matthew uses the name with respect to Jesus, who is the incarnation of God living among people. As God with us, Jesus came to "save his people from their sins" (1:21). See *NIDNTT-A*, 185.

IMMEDIATELY

New Testament

Adverb: εὐθέως (*eutheōs*), GK *2311* (S *2112*), 36x. The primary meaning of *eutheōs*, like *euthys*, is "immediately," although the NIV also translates it as "quickly" (Mt. 13:5), "right away" (Lk. 21:9), "soon" (3 Jn. 14), "suddenly" (Acts 12:10), "as soon as" (17:10), and "now" (Lk. 17:7). *eutheōs* most frequently denotes the immediate connection of events. For example, Peter and Andrew (as well as James and John), leave all they have and immediately follow Jesus right after he calls them (Mt. 4:22). After Peter denies Jesus the third time, "immediately a rooster crowed" (Mt. 26:74; cf. Jn. 18:27, "at that moment" a rooster crowed).

eutheōs also occurs in the context of healing, as when a man is "immediately cured of his leprosy" by Jesus (Mt. 8:3) and Aeneas "immediately" gets up after Peter heals him (Acts 9:34). The word can also denote something that is done without delay. For example, after Jesus walked on the turbulent water to the disciples' boat, "immediately the boat reached the shore" where it was heading (Jn. 6:21). Also, James stated that the one who merely hears the word but does not do what it says is like a man who looks into a mirror, but once he leaves, he "immediately forgets what he looks like" (Jas. 1:24; cf. Acts 17:14; 22:29; Gal. 1:16).

Adverb: εὐθύς (*euthys*), GK *2317* (S *2117*), 59x. *euthys*, like *eutheōs*, primarily means "immediately." It is usually considered in the category of time. Of its 51 occurrences in the NT, Mark uses 41 of them. This gives a sense of urgency and immediacy to the actions of Jesus. The other uses are also in the gospels (with one exception being in Acts 10:16).

euthys, when translated as "immediately," can mean either the immediate occurrence of events connected to each other (Mk. 5:29, 42) or an action/response given without delay (1:42; 2:8). It is also translated in the NIV as "at once" (Mt. 13:20; Mk. 1:12; Jn. 13:32), "as soon as" (Mt. 3:16; Mk. 1:29; Jn. 13:30), "quickly" (Mt. 13:21; Mk. 1:28), "shortly" (Mk. 11:3), "right away" (Mt. 21:3), and as "sudden" (Jn. 19:34). See *NIDNTT-A*, 282-83.

Adverb: παραχρῆμα (*parachrēma*), GK *4202* (S *3916*), 18x. *parachrēma* means "immediately." Except for Mt. 21:19–20 (in the cursing of the fig tree, which dries up "immediately"), Luke is the only NT writer to use this adverb. He points out how several of Jesus' miracles happen "immediately" (Lk. 4:39; 5:25; 8:44, 47, 55; 13:13; 18:43). The same thing happens in Acts (3:7), though in three cases the miracles are miracles of judgment (5:10;

12:23; 13:11). In Philippi, an earthquake "immediately" opens the doors of a prison (16:26), but by the end of the evening, the jailer and his family are "immediately" baptized (16:33).

IMMORALITY

Old Testament

Verb: זָנָה (*zānâ*), GK 2388 (S 2181), 60x. *zānâ* broadly refers to illicit or illegitimate sexual misconduct. The most common translation of this word in the NIV is "to commit prostitution, prostitute oneself." It often refers to the physical action of sexual immorality. See *prostitute*.

IMPLORE

New Testament

Verb: παρακαλέω (*parakaleō*), GK *4151* (S *3870*), 109x. *parakaleō* variously means "to ask, summons, exhort, comfort, or encourage" (see *exhort, comfort*). Within the Synoptic Gospels, *parakaleō* means "to ask, implore, summons." The contexts of this imploring are often the needy who come to Jesus with their requests (Mt. 8:5, 31; 18:29; Lk. 15:28).

IMPOSSIBLE

New Testament

Adjective: ἀδύνατος (*adynatos*), GK *105* (S *102*), 10x. *adynatos* means (lit.) "not able," but it has a variety of nuances. In Acts 14:8 it means one who is physically unable to walk, that is, a "crippled" person. In Rom. 15:1, it denotes those who are "weak" as opposed to those who are strong, spiritually speaking. The "weak in faith" are generally those who have only recently come to salvation in Christ or those who have not grown in their knowledge of God and his Word. For the rest of the occurrences of this work, *adynatos* means "impossible."

It is important to note the grammatical structure of those verses where *adynatos* means "impossible." Either expressed or implied in the sentence is the party *for whom* something is impossible, followed by *an infinitive* that expresses the deed that is impossible. For example, Jesus uses *adynatos* in response to the disciples' question, "Who can then be saved?" He answers, "With man this is impossible, but with God all things are possible" (Mt. 19:26, ESV; cf. Mk. 10:27; Lk. 18:27). That is, it is impossible *for a sinful human being* (the person) *to save himself or herself* (the infinitive). It is, however, is possible *for God* by his grace *to save* human beings, provided that we respond to his merciful offer in faith. In a similar manner, in Rom. 8:3, Paul notes that it is "impossible" *for the law* (the agent) *to make anyone spiritually righteous* (the infinitive); for that reality, we depend on God actions in Christ.

The author of Hebrews uses *adynatos* four times. Most noteworthy is Heb. 6:18, where the author says it is "impossible" *for God to lie* (note the same structure). God is unable to do anything that is contradictory to his unchangeable character, especially when he has uttered an oath that he will not change his word. Similarly, it is "impossible" for the blood of bulls and goats to take away sin (Heb. 10:4), and it is "impossible" for a believer to please God without faith (Heb. 11:6).

The most problematic verse is Heb. 6:4, where the writer says it is "impossible" that those who have tasted of the gift of salvation and of God's Word, if they then fall away, be renewed to repentance. In terms of the structure of *adynatos* phrases, it is legitimate to ask, "For whom is it impossible?" Since being renewal to repentance is not contrary to the character of God, we certainly *cannot* take the position that it is impossible *for God* to renew them to repentance. Note that this would go contrary to the statement of Jesus in Mt. 19:26 (see above). Thus, we must take the position that it is impossible *for us as human beings* to draw such people back to the faith. The reason why this is impossible is not stated. Perhaps what the writer means is the often observed phenomenon that those who have once been within the realm of God's grace, if they sour on the Christian faith and turn their backs on God, are the most difficult to draw back to him. But while "with man this is impossible ... with God all things are possible." See *NIDNTT-A*, 154-55.*

IMPRISON

Old Testament

Verb: אָסַר (*ʾāsar*), GK 673 (S 631), 73x. The most basic meaning of *ʾāsar* is "to bind, tie up." But this verb also may be used in the sense of being imprisoned. The chief cupbearer and baker are put into the jail where Joseph "is imprisoned" (Gen. 40:3, 5; cf. 39:20). In an eschatological sense, the OT teaches that God will set "the ones being imprisoned" free (Ps. 146:7; Isa. 49:9; 61:1), a promise that Jesus ultimately fulfills (Lk. 4:17-20). See *bind.*

IMPURE

Old Testament

Verb: טָמֵא (*ṭāmēʾ*), GK 3237 (S 2930), 88x. *ṭāmēʾ* means to "become ceremonially unclean, defiled." This word and its derivatives are concentrated in certain sections of the OT, especially Leviticus. See *unclean.*

Adjective: טָמֵא (*ṭāmēʾ*), GK 3238 (S 2931), 162x. *ṭāmēʾ* as an adjective denotes that which is "unclean," especially in a ritual context. In most cases, it is a technical term for the state of being ritually "unclean" or "defiled" and thus disqualified from the sphere of the holy (e.g., the temple). See *unclean.*

New Testament

Noun: ἀκαθαρσία (*akatharsia*), GK *174* (S *167*), 10x. *akatharsia*, a derivative of *akathartos*, can refer to anything that is filthy or dirty ("uncleanness"), or figuratively to a state of moral corruption ("impurity"). See *unclean.*

Adjective: ἀκάθαρτος (*akathartos*), GK *176* (S *169*), 32x. *akathartos* pertains to that which may not be brought into contact with what is holy (see *holy*). In this sense it is "impure, unclean," and at times "evil." See *unclean.*

Adjective: κοινός (*koinos*), GK *3123* (S *2839*), 14x. The basic meaning of *koinos* is "common" and can refer to objects held in "common," or it can convey the sense of "impure." See *common.*

IMPURITY

Old Testament

Noun: טֻמְאָה (*ṭumʾâ*), GK 3240 (S 2932), 36x. *ṭumʾâ* means "uncleanness, impurity." See *unclean, uncleanness.*

IMPUTE

See *credit.*

INCENSE

Old Testament

Noun: קְטֹרֶת (*qᵉṭōret*), GK 7792 (S 7004), 60x.

(1) Generally meaning "incense," *qᵉṭōret* most commonly refers to a scented mixture that is burned during Israel's worship, usually to God but at times to pagan deities.

(a) A special incense mixture is to be burned on an altar located near the ark of the covenant within the tabernacle (Exod. 30:1–10, 27; Num. 4:16; 1 Chr. 6:49). This *qᵉṭōret* consists of several ingredients, which God details to Moses in Exod. 30:34–35: "Take fragrant spices—gum resin, onycha and galbanum—and pure frankincense, all in equal amounts, and make a fragrant blend of *incense*, the work of a perfumer. It is to be salted and pure and sacred."

On at least two occasions, the incense appears to have served as a protective screen. In Lev. 16:12–13, Aaron is to take the incense with him into the Most Holy Place so that he will not die (cf. Exod. 30:6). Incense is used again in Num. 16:47–48 to provide protection: "The plague had already started among the people, but Aaron offered the *incense* and made atonement for them. He stood between the living and the dead, and the plague stopped."

(b) By waving handheld censers filled with burning incense, the Israelite priests also appear to use *qᵉṭōret* as a common offering in Israel's worship (cf. Num. 16:7).Unfortunately, it is sometimes misappropriated. For example, the "unholy fire" offered by Nadab and Abihu is related to the misuse of *q^e^ṭōret* (Lev. 10:1). Similarly, in Ezekiel's vision of the pagan practices going on within the Jerusalem temple, the seventy elders are each waving censers from which "a fragrant cloud of *incense* was rising" (Ezek. 8:10–11).

(2) In a few instances, *q^e^ṭōret* signifies the burning of sacrifices. The psalmist declares, "I will sacrifice fat animals to you and an *offering* of rams; I will offer bulls and goats" (Ps. 66:15). Similarly, Isaiah writes (1:13), "Stop bringing meaningless offerings! Your *incense* is detestable to me."

(3) In one instance, *q^e^ṭōret* is used figuratively to refer to a person's prayers, which are said to be like incense before God. "May my prayer be set before you like *incense*, may the lifting up of my hands be like the evening sacrifice" (Ps. 141:2). See *NIDOTTE*, 3:913-16.

INCITE

Old Testament

Verb: עוּר (*ʿûr*), GK 6424 (S 5782), 80x. *ʿûr* means "to awaken, arouse from sleep," or (in a causative sense) "to rouse someone or something, stir up, incite." Far from being removed from the events of the world, God is carefully bringing about his sovereign design. Thus, he "stirs up" leaders such as Tiglath-Pileser, the king of Assyria, against the tribes in the Transjordan (1 Chr. 5:26). He also arouses the Babylonians against Jerusalem (Ezek. 23:22). See *awake*.

INCREASE

Old Testament

Verb: יָסַף (*yāsap*), GK 3578 (S 3254), 213x. The basic meaning of *yāsap* is "to add." Sometimes the word conveys the sense of "surpass" or "increase" (cf. Ps. 115:14; Eccl. 2:9). See *add*.

Verb: רָבָה (*rābâ*), GK 8049 (S 7235), 229x. *rābâ* typically refers to an increase in quantity, as in Gen. 7:17, where the flood waters "*increased* as they lifted the ark high above the earth." One of God's central purposes in history was to create a people who would represent him in the world, and so God charges Adam to "be fruitful and *multiply*" (Gen. 1:28), and he promised Abraham that he would "multiply" his offspring like the stars in the sky and the sand on the seashore (Gen. 22:17).

rābâ can also be used when speaking of an increase in frequency or number of a variety of things. For instance, Israel "multiplies transgression" (Amos 4:4) and God "increasingly pardons" (Isa. 55:7). God promises to "multiply" his signs and wonders in Egypt until Pharaoh finally lets the Israelite nation go (Exod. 7:3).

Infrequently, *rābâ* is used metaphorically. It is used to speak of long life ("I shall *multiply* my days as the sand," Job 29:18), of Job sinning against God ("To his sin he adds rebellion; scornfully he claps his hands among us and *multiplies* his words against God," 34:37), having many children ("they *had many* wives and sons," 1 Chr. 7:4; lit., "they multiplied wives ands sons"), and a lioness nourishing her cubs ("she *reared* her cubs," Ezek. 19:2). See *NIDOTTE*, 3:1037–41.

New Testament

Verb: αὐξάνω (*auxanō*), GK *889* (S *837*), 21x. *auxanō* means "to grow, increase, become greater." See *grow*.

Verb: πληθύνω (*plēthynō*), GK *4437* (S *4129*), 12x. *plēthyno* means "to increase, grow, multiply." This verb was used in the LXX in God's command to the human race to "be fruitful and *multiply*" (Gen. 1:22, 28). It is also used in Gen. 22:17, where God tells Abraham that he will surely "multiply" his seed, a passage quoted in Heb. 6:14. Similarly, in Acts 7:17, Stephen uses *plēthyno* to describe the rapid growth of Israel in Egypt (cf. Exod. 1:7). Note too how "the word of God grew and *multiplied*" (Acts 12:24). In this vein, the NT uses *plēthynō* to describe the growth of the church ("the number of the disciples *increased* rapidly," 6:7; cf. 6:1; 9:31).

Speaking figuratively, Paul tells the Corinthians that God will supply and *multiply* their "seed," that is, the monetary resources of the saints given to help those in need (2 Cor. 9:10). *plēthynō* also occurs for "the *increase* of wickedness" in Jesus' Olivet Discourse (Mt. 24:12). Three times this verb occurs in the greeting of a letter: twice, "May grace and peace *increase* to you" (1 Pet. 1:2; 2 Pet. 1:2), and once, "May mercy, peace, and love *increase* to you" (Jude 2). See *NIDNTT-A*, 468-69.*

Verb: προστίθημι (*prostithēmi*), GK *4707* (S *4369*), 18x. *prostithēmi* means "to add, increase." See *add*.

INDEPENDENT

New Testament

Adjective: ἐλεύθερος (*eleutheros*), GK *1801* (S *1658*), 23x. *eleutheros* denotes the state of being "free" or "independent." See *free*.

INFANT

New Testament

Noun: νήπιος (*nēpios*), GK *3758* (S *3516*), 15x. In the NT *nēpios* refers to a "young child, infant." The noun is used three main ways in the NT. (1) It is used to picture immaturity. In 1 Cor. 3:1, Paul responds to a report from some insiders in Corinth by pointing out that there are Christians who, long after they receive Christ, prove themselves unable to receive solid knowledge of the Scripture, mature theological dialogue, and seasoned Christian behavior. Christians must grow in their faith so that they can handle deeper truths without choking (cf. also Heb. 5:13). In 1 Cor. 13:11, Paul uses *nēpios* four times to contrast infancy with adulthood. In chs. 12-14, where he deals with the friction existing between the "tongue-speakers" and "those who prophesied," he reveals that "the more excellent way" is the practice of love (12:31b). Just as he pointed out in 2:6 that the wisdom for the mature will not be grasped by those who demonstrate childish self-centeredness, here Paul insists that being *nēpios* stands in contrast with the goal of mature adulthood.

Paul paints a similar picture in Eph. 4:14: "Then we will no longer be *nēpios*, tossed back and forth by the waves, and blown here and there by every wind of teaching and by the cunning and craftiness of men in their deceitful scheming." Christians who advance from the stages of *nēpios* can develop loving relationships and can more easily detect false teachers and their poisonous messages.

(2) Jesus uses *nēpios* in a positive sense. During a prayer, he thanks the Father for revealing truth to the "childlike" and hiding it from those who think themselves "so wise and clever" (Mt. 11:25). In this context, Jesus aligns *nēpios* with the concept of humility and thus in direct conflict with pride. In 21:16, on Palm Sunday the leading priests and the teachers of the law express indignation as they observe children "praising God for the Son of David." Jesus replies that the praise of children and "infants" fulfills the Scriptures (Ps. 8:2). Here again he uses the term positively to demonstrate that these particular young children have been taught by God to praise him, in contrast to those adults who are missing the wonder and importance of Jesus' mission.

(3) Finally, *nēpios* can fall under the definition of "one who is not yet of legal age," that is, a "minor" (Paul applies this to covenant history in Gal. 4:1, 3). See *NIDNTT-A*, 385-86.

INFIDEL

See *unbeliever.*

INFIRMITY

See *disease.*

INFORM

New Testament

Verb: κατηχέω (*katēcheō*), GK *2994* (S *2727*), 8x. *katēcheō* is used in two senses in the NT: telling about something and instructing someone in the Christian faith. See *instruct*.

INHABITED EARTH

New Testament

Noun: οἰκουμένη (*oikoumenē*), GK *3876* (S *3625*), 15x. This noun is used in the NT to refer to the "inhabited earth" rather than the whole globe. See *world.*

INHERIT

Old Testament

Verb: יָרַשׁ (*yāraš*), GK 3769 (S 3423), 232x. *yāraš* means "to possess, take possession of (especially by force), drive out, inherit." See *possess*.

Verb: נָחַל (*nāḥal*), GK 5706 (S 5157), 59x. In addition to meaning "to inherit," *nāḥal* can be translated as "to possess, take into possession, get." A few instances of this verb deal with individual issues of inheritance (such as including male and female slaves as inherited property, Lev. 25:44–46; Jephthah's half-brothers disinheriting him, Jdg. 11:2). Note this proverb: "A good man *leaves an inheritance* for his children" (Prov. 13:22).

But for the most part, *nāḥal* refers to inheriting the promised land (Exod. 32:13). God promises the Hebrews that he will go before them in the conquest and destroy their enemies in the land of Canaan in order that they might "inherit" the land (Exod. 23:30). Each tribe and each clan within a tribe received their *nāḥal* when Joshua divided up the land after the conquest (Jos. 14:1; 16:4; 19:9). In two passages, God promises that his people will "inherit" or "possess" all the nations (Ps. 82:8; Isa. 14:2).

The OT also speaks of less tangible things than physical property as that which a person can inherit. The psalmist in Ps. 119:111 speaks of inheriting God's statutes. In Proverbs, "the wise inherit honor" (Prov. 3:35), but "the simple inherit folly" (14:18). See also *inheritance*. See *NIDOTTE* 3:77-81.

New Testament

Verb: κληρονομέω (*klēronomeō*), GK *3099* (S *2816*), 18x.*klēronomeō* means "to inherit." Whereas in the OT inheriting often refers to receiving earthly goods after the death of one's father, the only time it has this meaning in the NT is when OT stories are being referenced (see Gal. 4:30; Heb. 12:17).

Used theologically, the NT speaks of the disciple inheriting salvation (Heb. 1:14), which is equated with entering (Mt. 25:34) or inheriting the kingdom of God (1 Cor. 6:9–10; 15:50; Gal. 5:21) and eternal life (Mt. 19:29; Lk. 18:18). Disciples who are meek—which should be true of all disciples—will receive the opposite of what the world expects of those who are meek, which is the inheritance of the entire world (Mt. 5:5). Segments of Judaism believed that they could do certain things in order to inherit eternal life (Mk. 10:17; Lk. 10:25); Jesus goes on to stress that a relationship with him is the first and most important thing. Peter tells the people, "Do not repay evil with evil or insult with insult, but with blessing, because to this you were called so that you may inherit a blessing" (1 Pet. 3:9).

The promise of God is, "To him who is thirsty I will give to drink without cost from the spring of the water of life. He who overcomes will inherit all this, and I will be his God and he will be my son" (Rev. 21:6–7, NIV). That is the inheritance that awaits us. See *NIDNTT-A*, 308-10.

INHERITANCE

Old Testament

Noun: נַחֲלָה (*naḥᵉlâ*), GK 5709 (S 5159), 222x. In addition to "inheritance," *naḥᵉla* can be translated as "heritage" and "possession."

(1) *naḥᵉlâ* connotes anything that may be passed on as an inheritance. Rachel and Leah ask, "Do we still have any share in the *inheritance* of our father's estate?" (Gen. 31:14). Job granted his three daughters a share in his inheritance along with his seven sons (Job 42:12–15). Solomon speaks of "houses and wealth" as the inheritance one might received from one's parents (Prov. 19:14).

(2) For the most part, however, *naḥᵉlâ* has a theological meaning in the OT. First and foremost, God gives the promised land to the Israelites as their "inheritance" (Deut. 19:10, 14; 20:16; Jos. 11:23). Most of the uses of this noun in Num., Deut., and Jos. use this noun in this way. Since the land belongs ultimately to God (several passages actually describe the land as the Lord's "inheritance"; see Exod. 15:17;

1 Sam. 26:19; 2 Sam. 20:19; Jer. 2:7), he prescribes that each parcel of land is to stay within a particular family or clan in perpetuity (cf. Jos. 13–19). It is on the basis of this command of God that Naboth refuses to sell his vineyard to Ahab (1 Ki. 21:3–4). Only the Levites are not to receive any land inheritance; their inheritance is "all the tithes in Israel" (Num. 18:20–26). In another passage, God reveals himself as the Levites' "inheritance" (Deut. 18:1-2).

(3) But *naḥ*^{e}*lâ* also expresses the relationship between the Israelites and God. God takes the Hebrews as his own "inheritance" or "possession" (Deut. 32:8–9; 1 Sam. 10:1). "For you [God] singled them [the Hebrews] out from all the nations of the world to be your own inheritance" (1 Ki. 8:53; cf. Isa. 19:25). In return, the Hebrews understand that they are God's most prized "possession." Jeremiah reminds his hearers of the uniqueness of this relationship: "He who is the portion of Jacob is not like these [pagan idols], for he is the maker of all things, including Israel, the tribe of his *inheritance*—the Lord Almighty is his name" (Jer. 10:16). When the Israelites rebel against God and prove odious to him, God says he will reject his house and abandon his "inheritance" (12:7–9). But the prophets and psalmists plead upon the fact that a *naḥ*^{e}*lâ* is permanent in order to ask the Lord God to restore Israel to himself (Deut. 9:26, 29; Ps. 94:14; Joel 2:17). See *NIDOTTE* 3:77–81.

New Testament

Noun: κληρονομία (*klēronomia*), GK *3100* (S *2817*), 14x. *klēronomia* refers to an "inheritance," which in the OT could be land (Acts 7:5; Heb. 11:8). In the gospels, this term is used 4x for what is available to divide after someone's death (Mt. 21:38; Mk. 12:7; Lk. 12:13; 20:14).

The inheritance of the Christian, however, is salvation (Acts 20:32; Eph. 1:18; Heb. 9:5), which is given not by law (Gal. 3:18) but by faith. This inheritance is the reward of the believer (Col. 3:24; Eph. 5:5), "imperishable, undefiled, and unfading, kept in heaven for you" (1 Pet. 1:4). The Holy Spirit himself is the "deposit guaranteeing our *inheritance* until the redemption of those who are God's possession" (Eph. 1:14). See *NIDNTT-A,* 308-10.

Noun: κλῆρος (*klēros*), GK *3102* (S *2819*), 11x. In the NT *klēros* usually designates the casting of lots, but in a more general sense it can also mean the "allotment" or "inheritance" that one receives (Col. 1:12). See *lot*.

INIQUITY

Old Testament

Noun: עָוֹן (*ʿāwōn*), GK 6411 (S 5771), 233x. *ʿāwōn* is usually translated "sin, guilt, wickedness, iniquity" and is one of the three primary words for sin in the OT, an offense against God that ranges from willful rebellion to unintentional sins (see *sin*).

New Testament

Noun: ἀδικία (*adikia*), GK *94* (S *93*), 25x. *adikia* is consistently translated as either "unrighteousness" or "iniquity" in the KJV. The NIV, however, offers numerous glosses, such as "evil, wickedness, dishonest, worldly, sin, wrong, wrongdoing." See *unrighteousness*.

Noun: ἀνομία (*anomia*), GK *490* (S *458*), 15x. *anomia means lawlessness, a violation of law.* See *wicked*.

INMOST BEING

Old Testament

Noun: קֶרֶב (*qereb*), GK 7931 (S 7130), 227x. The basic meaning of *qereb* is "inner parts." *qereb* is parallel to "heart" in Isa. 16:11: "My heart laments for Moab like a harp, my *inmost being* for Kir Hareseth." See *inner parts*.

INNER PARTS

Old Testament

Noun: קֶרֶב (*qereb*), GK 7931 (S 7130), 227x. The basic meaning of *qereb* is "inner parts" (both of humans and animals) and, by extension, "interior." When combined with the preposition "in" or "from," *qereb* means "within, in the midst of," or "from the midst of," and this is the most common use of the word in the OT (198x).

qereb describes the entrails of sacrificial animals, of which specific commands are given in the sacrificial laws: "Then take all the fat around the *inner parts*, the covering of the liver, and both kidneys with the fat on them, and burn them on the altar" (Exod. 29:13). Regarding the burnt offering: "He is to wash the *inner parts* and the legs with water, and the priest is to bring all of it and burn it on the altar" (Lev. 1:13). In some cases (e.g., the fellowship offering, the sin offering, the guilt offering), the fat surrounding the inner parts is removed and burned on the altar (Lev. 3:3, 9, 14; 4:8; 7:3), creating a burst of flames upward, a picture of ascending to the Most High.

When *qereb* is used of the inner parts of a human, it may describe the core of one's life: "Then he [Elijah] stretched himself out on the boy three times and cried to the LORD, "O LORD my God, let this boy's life return to him [come into him again, KJV, lit., 'be upon his inward parts']!" (1 Ki. 17:21; cf. Zech. 12:1). *qereb* is parallel to "heart" in Isa. 16:11: "My heart laments for Moab like a harp, my *inmost being* for Kir Hareseth." Since *qereb* describes the inner organs where the heart resides (cf. 1 Sam. 25:37), it also denotes the place of emotions (Ps. 39:3; 55:5; 109:22) and one's will (Jer. 31:33). Moreover, one's deepest feelings reside in the "spirit within" (KJV; Isa. 26:9; "spirit," NIV).

Likewise, the inner parts may contain wickedness (Jer. 4:14), destruction (Ps. 5:9), and deceit (Prov. 26:24). Only the cleansing work of divine renewal is able to overcome the sinfulness of a person's inner being. Thus David, overwhelmed by his sin, prays: "Create in me a pure heart, O God, and renew a steadfast spirit within me [lit., 'in my inward parts']" (Ps. 51:10). See *NIDOTTE*, 3:978-79.

INNOCENCE

Old Testament

Noun: צְדָקָה (*ṣᵉdāqâ*), GK 7407 (S 6666), 159x. *ṣᵉdāqa* generally means "righteousness, justice, innocence." Like the noun *ṣedeq*, "righteousness," this noun also describes the state or quality of that which accords with some recognized standard, not always expressed in the context. See *righteousness*.

New Testament

Noun: δικαιοσύνη (*dikaiosynē*), GK *1466* (S *1343*), 92x. *dikaiosynē* can mean "righteousness, innocence, justice, justification." This word is prominent in Paul's letters, containing 58 of the 91 occurrences (64%). See *righteous, righteousness*.

INNOCENT

Old Testament

Adjective: צַדִּיק (*ṣaddîq*), GK 7404 (S 6662), 206x. *ṣaddîq* is generally rendered "righteous, innocent, just." Similar to the nouns *ṣᵉdāqâ* and *ṣedeq*, this adjective describes those who act in such a way that their behavior accords with some standard. In general, this word describes as "righteous" persons rather than an abstract concept like the law. See *righteous*.

New Testament

Adjective: ἁγνός (*hagnos*), GK *54* (S 53), 8x. *hagnos* means "pure, innocent." See *pure*.

Adjective: δίκαιος (*dikaios*), GK *1465* (S *1342*), 79x. *dikaios* means "righteous, innocent, just, upright." This adjective follows many of the characteristics of the Heb. word *ṣaddîq*; see *righteous, righteousness*.

INQUIRE

Old Testament

Verb: דָּרַשׁ (*dāraš*), GK 2011 (S 1875), 164x. *dāraš* means "to seek, search for, inquire after" an object. See *seek*.

Verb: שָׁאַל (*šāʾal*), GK 8626 (S 7592), 176x. *šāʾal* is often translated "ask" or "inquire." It is used to ask for a drink (Jdg. 5:25), to be in someone's presence (Jdg. 4:20; cf. Gen. 26:7), to ask for a song (Ps. 137:3), and to inquire about the fate of person (Num. 27:21; cf. Jdg. 18:5). See *ask*.

New Testament

Verb: ἐρωτάω (*erōtaō*), GK *2263* (S *2065*), 63x. *erōtaō* means "to ask a question" or "to request" something be done. See *ask*.

INSECT

Old Testament

Noun: עוֹף (*ʿôp*), GK 6416 (S 5775), 71x. *ʿôp* denotes both clean and unclean fowl or birds; occasionally it also means "winged insects" (see especially Lev. 11:20). See *bird*.

INSIGHT

New Testament

Noun: σύνεσις (*synesis*), GK *5304* (S *4907*), 7x. *synesis* refers to spiritual "understanding, insight." See *understanding*.

INSIGNIFICANT

New Testament

Adjective: μικρος (*mikros*), GK *3625* (S *3298*), 46x. *mikros* is the antonym of *megas* ("great") and means "small, little, insignificant." See *small*.

INSTEAD

New Testament

Adverb: μᾶλλον (*mallon*), GK *3437* (S *3123*), 81x. *mallon* is a comparative adverb that means "rather, instead, more." See *rather*.

INSTRUCT

Old Testament

Verb: אָמַר (*ʾāmar*), GK 606 (S 559), 5307x. *ʾāmar* is the most common verb in the OT for "to say, utter." See *say*. It can also be used to indicate a command or an instruction. Joshua did as the Lord "instructed" by hamstringing the horses and burning the chariots (Jos. 11:9). Job 36:8 states, "He makes them listen and *commands* them to repent of their evil."

Verb: לָמַד (*lāmad*), GK 4340 (S 3925), 87x. *lāmad* is one of the twelve words used in the OT for teaching or instructing. See *teach*.

New Testament

Verb: διατάσσω (*diatassō*) GK *1411* (S *1299*), 16x. *diatassō* means "to command, give specific instructions," with varying degrees of authority. See *command, commandment*.

Verb: διδάσκω (*didaskō*), GK *1438* (S *1321*), 97x. *didaskō* means "to teach, instruct" and is the action performed by a *didaskalos* (see *teacher*). See *teach*.

Verb: ἐντέλλω (*entellō*), GK *1948* (S *1781*), 15x. *entellō* means "to command, order, instruct." See *command, commandment*.

Verb: κατηχέω (*katēcheō*), GK *2994* (S *2727*), 8x. *katēcheō* is used in two senses in the NT: telling about something and instructing someone in the Christian faith. Luke uses both meanings, while Paul uses exclusively the meaning of religious instruction.

Luke wrote his gospel so that Theophilus would be certain of what he had been "taught" (NIV) or "instructed" (KJV) (Lk. 1:4). The sense here is unclear, but the interpretation explains the purpose of Luke's gospel as to either reinforce the faith in which Theophilus has already been instructed or to serve as a demonstration of the truth of what had been reported to him. Paul is told that "reports" concerning him have reached the zealous Jews in Jerusalem, who were "informed" that his teachings are contrary to the law of Moses (Acts 21:21, 24). In Acts 18:25, Apollos has some knowledge of the tenets of the gospel, but his knowledge is incomplete, so that Aquila and Priscilla "instruct" him more fully.

Paul uses *katēcheō* for instruction in the law (Rom. 2:18) and instruction in the gospel through intelligible words (in contrast to unintelligible tongues, 1 Cor. 14:19). He makes an early reference to the Christian teaching office by commenting on the obligations of a pupil to the one "instructing" him in the faith to share all good things (Gal. 6:6). This usage was retained by the church to describe the process whereby a baptismal candidate (catechumen) was instructed (catechized) in the rudiments of Christianity, the systematized format being known in English as a "catechism." See *NIDNTT-A*, 297.*

Verb: παραγγέλλω (*parangellō*) GK *4133* (S *3853*), 32x. *parangellō* means "to instruct," sometimes with authority. Jesus gives instructions to the Twelve (Mt. 10:5) and to the crowd to sit down (15:35). Paul gives instructions to the Thessalonians (1 Thess. 4:11) and to Timothy about widows (1 Tim. 5:7). See *NIDNTT-A*, 964-65.

Verb: προστάσσω (*prostassō*), GK *4705* (S *4367*), 7x. *prostassō* means "to command," with an emphasis on specific instructions. See *command, commandment*.

Verb: συντάσσω (*syntassō*), GK *5332* (S *4929*), 3x. *syntassō* means "to command something" specifically, such as the disciples following Jesus' instructions (Mt. 21:6; 26:19). See *command, commandment*.

INSTRUCTION

Old Testament

Noun: מוּסָר (*mûsār*), GK 4592 (S 4148), 50x. *mûsār* is used for personal instruction or correction and may be translated as "instruction, discipline, correction." It is used 31x in Proverbs. Prov. 1:8 states "Hear, my son, your father's *instruction*, and do not forsake your mother's teaching." The translation "correction" or "discipline" is determined by the context. Prov. 22:15 states "Foolishness is bound up in the heart of a child; the rod of *discipline* will remove it far from him." Theologically, it is through the mouth of the prophets that rebellious Israel is rebuked for her unwillingness to hear and obey the *instruction* of God. This reoccurring theme is captured in Jeremiah by the question " 'Will you not receive *instruction* by listening to my words?' declares the LORD" (Jer. 35:13b; see also 5:3; 7:28; 17:23; 32:33; 35:13). With regard to children, effective parenting requires a balance of *instruction* and *correction*. See *NIDOTTE*, 2:479-82.

Noun: תּוֹרָה (*tôrâ*), GK 9368 (S 8451), 223x. Generally rendered "law, regulation, instruction, teaching," *tôrâ* was originally used to describe the instructions for conduct that God gave his people; eventually other meanings developed for this word. See *law, teaching*.

New Testament

Noun: διδαχή (*didachē*), GK *1439* (S *1322*), 30x. *didachē*, like *didaskalia*, denotes "doctrine, teaching," as well as "instruction." See *teaching*.

INSTRUMENT

Old Testament

Noun: כְּלִי (*kᵉlî*), GK 3998 (S 3627), 325x. *kᵉlî* is a noun denoting a variety of equipment, tools, containers, etc., used in a given activity or occupation. The use of this noun to refer to such a large number of different objects is comparable to the English noun "thing." See *thing*.

New Testament

Noun: σκεῦος (*skeuos*), GK *5007* (S *4632*), 23x. *skeuos* refers to an "instrument, container" (e.g., a "jar"). (1) *skeuos* can refer to a literal vessel such as what one might find in a house (Mt. 12:29; Mk. 3:27), to merchandise for sale (Mk. 11:16), to valued worldly possessions (Lk. 17:31), to a vessel of sour wine (Jn. 19:29), to the objects used in Levitical worship (Heb. 9:21), and to objects made of precious woods and metals (Rev. 18:12).

(2) Figurative uses include Paul's reference to himself as God's chosen "vessel" or "instrument" (Acts 9:15), his comparison of the glory of the gospel of Jesus Christ within believers to a treasure within a "clay vessel" (2 Cor. 4:7), and his exhortation to the Thessalonians to exert control over their own "body" in holiness and honor (1 Thess. 4:4).

The most puzzling use of *skeuos* occurs in 1 Pet. 3:7, where Peter refers to the wife as a "weaker *vessel*." Regardless of Peter means here, women are to be honored, wisely understood, and respected in the relationship. The details may be difficult to sort out, but the message is clear.

The most significant use of *skeuos* is in Rom. 9:21–23 (see also 2 Tim. 2:20–21). In defense of his statement in Rom. 9:18 that God loved Jacob and hated Esau, Paul says in 9:21–23, "Has the potter no right over the clay, to make out of the same lump one *vessel* for honored use and another for dishonorable use? What if God, desiring to show his wrath and to make known his power, has endured with much patience *vessels* of wrath prepared for destruction, in order to make known the riches of his glory for *vessels* of mercy, which he has prepared beforehand for glory" (ESV). In this use of *skeuos*, the apostle is helping his objectors to know their place before God by comparing them to a created household container. But he is also driving home the point that just as people manufacture one container for serving fine beverages and another for a mop bucket, so God is within his rights as Creator to choose some and reject others. See *NIDNTT-A*, 300-301.

INSULT

Old Testament

Noun: חֶרְפָּה (*ḥerpâ*), GK 3075 (S 2781), 73x. The meaning of *ḥerpâ* is "disgrace, insult, reproach, contempt." *ḥerpâ* can refer to general suffering or humiliation (1 Sam. 11:2; Neh. 2:17; Ps. 69:20), shameful behavior (Gen. 34:14), slanderous and condemning speech (Neh. 5:9; Job 16:10; Isa. 51:7–8), or the disgrace of an individual or nation (Ps. 31:12; Prov. 18:3). Reproach can often serve as part of God's judgment (Ps. 79:4; Ezek. 5:15; Mic. 6:9–16), and the removal of reproach can be a result of God's gracious ending of judgment (Isa. 25:8; Joel 2:19; Zeph. 3:18). More often than not, such reproach is brought on Israel because of its sin and idolatry (Ps. 44:13; Ezek. 5:5–17; 22:4).

ḥerpâ causes contempt and scorn to fall on the innocent (cf. Isa. 51:7–8). Goliath slandered Israel in 1 Sam. 17 because of his unjustified intent to treat them with scorn. The giant insulted "the armies of Israel," but by doing so he was also insulting and pouring shame on the name and reputation of the God of Israel's army (1 Sam. 17:45). David knew that Goliath's words were meant not only to taunt Israel, but also to proclaim that the Philistine idols were greater than Israel's God. Just as the Philistine god, Dagon, had fallen and was decapitated before the presence of God (1 Sam. 5:1–5), so Goliath would fall and be decapitated before the living God, as David defended the name and reputation of Yahweh from the slanderous insults of Goliath and his pagan idols.

New Testament

Verb: βλασφημέω (*blasphēmeō*), GK *1059* (S *987*), 34x. *blasphēmeō* means "to slander, blaspheme, insult," especially with regard to speech. See *blaspheme*.

Verb: ὀνειδίζω (*oneidizō*), GK *3943* (S *3679*), 9x. *oneidizō* is used for the insults heaped on Christ on the cross and for similar insults that can be heaped on us as believers. See *reproach*.

Noun: ὀνειδισμός (*oneidismos*), GK *3944* (S *3680*), 5x. *oneidismos* means "reproach, insult." See *reproach*.

INSURRECTIONIST

New Testament

Noun: λῃστής (*lēstēs*), GK *3334* (S *3027*), 15x. *lēstēs* denotes one who is a "robber" or a political rebel ("insurrectionist"). See *robber*.

INTEGRITY

Old Testament

Noun: אֱמוּנָה (*ʾemûnâ*), GK 575 (S 530), 127x. *ʾemûna* means "faithfulness, trustworthiness, integrity." See *faithfulness*.

INTELLECT

New Testament

Noun: νοῦς (*nous*), GK *3808* (S *3563*), 24x. *nous* refers to the "mind, intellect, understanding," that is, the part of the human system that initiates thoughts and designs. See *mind*.

INTELLIGENT

New Testament

Adjective: φρόνιμος (*phronimos*), GK *5861* (S *5429*), 14x. One who is *phronimos* is "wise, intelligent" in a prudent or shrewd way, acting in a way that is appropriate for the circumstance or situation. See *wise*.

INTEND

Old Testament

Verb: בָּקַשׁ (*bāqaš*), GK 1335 (S 1245), 225x. *bāqaš* refers to a search for, or a striving after, someone or something. It can also mean to intend (often something bad). See *seek*.

New Testament

Verb: βούλομαι (*boulomai*) GK *1089* (S *1014*), 37x. *boulomai* describes the desire or intention of a person to do something, to have something, or to obtain a result. See *want*.

INTEND TO

New Testament

Verb: μέλλω (*mellō*), GK *3516* (S *3195*), 109x. *mellō* is generally translated "about to, going to, intend to." See *about to*.

INTERCEDE

Old Testament

Verb: פָּלַל (*pālal*), GK 7137 (S 6419), 84x. *pālal* means "to pray, intercede." The Heb. language contains at lease twelve words for "pray" and "prayer," *pālal* being the most common one. See *pray*.

INTERCESSION

Old Testament

Noun: תְּפִלָּה (*tᵉpillâ*), GK 9525 (S 8605), 77x. *tᵉpillâ* is a common word in the OT for "prayer, intercession, petition"; it is related to the verb *pālal* (GK 7137; see *pray*). See *petition*.

INTERROGATE

New Testament

Verb: ἐπερωτάω (*eperōtaō*), GK *2089* (S *1905*), 56x. *eperōtaō* means "to ask a question" or "to question, interrogate someone." See *ask*.

INTREAT

See *ask*.

INTRUST

See believe.

INVESTIGATE

New Testament

Verb: ἀνακρίνω (*anakrinō*), GK *373* (S *350*), 16x. *anakrinō* means "to examine, judge, investigate." See *investigate*.

INVITE

New Testament

Verb: καλέω (*kaleō*), GK *2813* (S *2564*), 148x. *kaleō* means "to call, invite, summon." See *call*.

Verb: φονέω (*phoneō*), GK *5888* (S *5455*), 43x. *phoneō* means "to call out, call to, make a noise." It can also mean "to invite." See *call*.

IRON

Old Testament

Noun: בַּרְזֶל (*barzel*), GK 1366 (S 1270), 76x. *barzel* is first found in Gen. 4:22, where Tubal-Cain is said to have "forged all kinds of tools out of bronze and iron." Iron from ore deposits is attested in the third millennia BC. Iron is introduced into Palestine in the twelfth century, apparently in connection with the appearance of the Philistines. Since they have metallurgy expertise, which they keep as a military secret, their weapons are superior (1 Sam. 13:19). Israelites with iron farm implements are dependent on the Philistines for sharpening and repair (1 Sam. 13:20–22).

Iron is used for many implements and tools: for weapons (1 Sam. 17:7), stone cutting (Deut. 27:5), wood cutting (2 Ki. 6:5–6), and farming (2 Sam. 23:7). It is used for reinforcement (Jos. 17:16; Jdg. 1:19), for city gates (1 Chr. 22:3) and defensive structures (Deut. 33:25; Isa. 45:2). *barzel* can also mean "ax" (2 Ki. 6:5; Eccl. 10:10).

The strength of iron over softer metals offers significant advantages in certain applications and also makes *barzel* a ready metaphor for strength as well as for hardship, difficulty, and stubbornness. Used as a metaphor in the list of covenant curses (Deut. 28:23, cf. Lev. 26:19), Israel's rebellion against the covenant will result in the land becoming as hard as iron. Moreover, disobedience will bring subjugation to the nations as though in an iron yoke (Deut. 28:48). Likewise, Jeremiah makes a yoke of iron to symbolize the unbreakable strength of the Babylonians (Jer. 28:13–14).

Israel is pictured as having a neck of iron, meaning she is unwilling to submit to God and trust in him (Isa. 48:4). *barzel,* and particularly the smelting process that produces it, is used metaphorically of tribulation and subjugation. Thus Israel, in the exodus, comes out of the "iron-smelting furnace" of Egypt (Deut. 4:20; 1 Ki. 8:51;

Jer. 11:4). Ezekiel uses the metaphor of the smelting furnace to picture the coming wrath of God against wayward Israel: "As men gather silver, copper, *iron*, lead and tin into a furnace to melt it with a fiery blast, so will I gather you in my anger and my wrath and put you inside the city and melt you" (Ezek. 22:20).

But *barzel* also constitutes a positive metaphor for strength. Judah will be fortified with horns of iron and hooves of bronze to pulverize her enemies (Mic. 4:13), and the prophet Jeremiah is strengthened as a city fortified with iron (Jer. 1:18). "Iron sharpens iron" (Prov. 27:17) pictures the wisdom of one person to sharpen that of another. As a picture of strength, the psalmist represents Zion's enthroned King as ruling with a rod of iron, with which he smashes his enemies like clay pots (Ps. 2:9). Thus, God's power is invincible. See *NIDOTTE*, 1:741-43.

IRRITATE

Old Testament

Verb: כָּעַס (*kāʿas*), GK 4087 (S 3707), 55x. *kāʿas* denotes the idea of provoking one to anger and may be translated "to anger, irritate." See *anger*.

ISRAEL

New Testament

Noun: Ἰσραήλ (*Israēl*), GK *2702* (S *2474*), 68x. *Israel* is a transliteration of a Hebrew name. Jacob's name was changed to "Israel" after he wrestled with God (Gen. 32:28)—a verse that explains the name as one who struggles (*śārâ*) with God (*ʾel*).

In the NT *Israēl* is used in at least two ways. (1) It denotes the group of people who practiced the religion of the OT and in particular obeyed the law of Moses. In the first century ethnic Israelites made up a large part of this group, but many other nations were represented. Most of these other people were God-fearing proselytes (Acts 2:10; 13:42; 16:14). In particular, many women were converts, as men were less willing to fully convert because of the requirement of circumcision, though they often followed the rest of the Torah. Some scholars estimate that as many as one in ten inhabitants in some parts of the Mediterranean world of the first century were Israelites or proselytes. In this sense, Israel's worship was centered around the temple in Jerusalem and its leadership was dominated by ethnic Israelites. Uses that emphasize Israel as the ethnic people of God include Mt. 2:6.

(2) Paul makes a somewhat controversial claim when he writes, "not all who are descended from *Israel* belong to *Israel*, and not all are children of Abraham because they are his offspring" (Rom. 9:6–7). Elsewhere he writes, "For neither circumcision counts for anything, nor uncircumcision, but a new creation. And as for all who walk by this rule, peace and mercy be upon them, and upon the *Israel* of God" (Gal. 6:15–16). Many believe Paul is redefining what it means to be "Israel," a theological move paralleled by the term "Jew" in Rom. 2:28–29: "For no one is a Jew who is merely one outwardly, nor is circumcision outward and physical. But a Jew is one inwardly, and circumcision is a matter of the heart, by the Spirit, not by the letter" (ESV). See *NIDNTT-A*, 272-76.

IVORY

Old Testament

Noun: שֵׁן (*šēn*), GK 9094 (S 8127), 55x. *šēn* denotes a "tooth" or (in the plural) the "teeth" of animals and humans (see *tooth*). Sometimes, this word refers to "ivory," specifically, that which comes from the teeth of an elephant. In buildings, certain things were inlaid with ivory (the throne in 1 Ki. 10:18; beds in Amos 6:4; the entire palace in 1 Ki. 22:39). God threatens to destroy the ivory-adorned houses of the wealthy who oppress the poor in Israel (Amos 3:15).

JAIL

New Testament

Noun: φυλακή (*phylakē*), GK *5871* (S *5438*), 47x. *phylakē* denotes a "prison" or "jail." Frequently in Acts, for example, the apostles were put into jail overnight (e.g., Acts 5:19, 22, 25; 16:23–24). See *prison*.

JAR

New Testament

Noun: σκεῦος (*skeuos*), GK *5007* (S *4632*), 23x. *skeuos* refers to an "instrument, container" (e.g., a "jar"). See *instrument*.

JEALOUS

New Testament

Verb: ζηλόω (*zēloō*), GK *2420* (S *2206*), 11x. *zēloō* means to be "zealous" or "jealous." It is related to the noun *zēlos* ("jealousy, zeal," GK *2419*). In classical Greek this word group sometimes carried a positive sense (eager striving, enthusiasm, or praise) and sometimes a negative sense (jealously, ill will, or envy). The same applies to the NT. See *zealous*.

JEALOUSY

New Testament

Noun: ζῆλος (*zēlos*), GK *2419* (S *2205*), 16x. In the NT *zēlos* can be either a very good thing or a very bad thing: "zeal, earnestness" is highly commended whereas "jealousy, envy" is condemned. The Sadducees are jealous of Peter (Acts 5:17) and the Jews are jealous of Paul (Acts 13:45). Jealousy shows up frequently in the vice lists of the NT (e.g., Rom. 13:13; 2 Cor. 12:20; Gal. 5:20), and the NT writers particularly urge that it not occur within the church (1 Cor. 3:3; Jas. 3:14, 16). See also *zeal*. See *NIDNTT-A*, 224.

JESUS

New Testament

Noun: Ἰησοῦς (*Iēsous*), GK *2652* (S *2424*), 917x. The name *Iēsous* is the Greek translation of the Hebrew name "Joshua." Two OT figures named Joshua provide intriguing foreshadowings of Jesus Christ. First is Moses' godly successor, who led Israel through the Jordan River and into the promised land of Canaan (see the relationship between these two in Heb. 4:6–11). Second is the high priest at the time of Israel's return from exile: Zech. 3:8 states that this Joshua (or "Jesus" in the Greek translation of the OT) is a symbol of the coming Messiah.

The name *Iēsous* was common among Jews at the time of Jesus Christ and prior to the first century (for other individuals named Joshua/Jesus, see, e.g., Neh. 3:19; possibly Mt. 27:16f; Lk. 3:29; Col. 4:11). The personal name given to Jesus is an especially appropriate one for the Messiah to bear since its Hebrew antecedent, Joshua, means "The LORD [Yahweh] is salvation." The words of the angel to Joseph in Mt. 1:21 emphasize this very point: "And she will bear a Son; and you shall call his name Jesus, for it is he who will save his people from their sins."

There is power in the name of Jesus. When Peter and John stood before the authorities and were told to account for the healing of the crippled man, Peter said boldly, "Salvation [also healing] is found in no one else, for there is no other name under heaven given to men by which we must be saved" (Acts 4:12). The writers of the book of Hebrew instructs us to fix our eyes on Jesus, "the apostle and high priest whom we confess" and "the author and perfecter of our faith" (Heb. 3:1; 12:2). He is the mediator of the new covenant (12:24). See *NIDNTT-A*, 267.

JEW(S)

Old Testament

Adjective: יְהוּדִי (*yᵉhûdî*), GK 3374 (S 3064), 76x. *yᵉhûdî* means "of Judah, Judahite" and is used substantively to mean "Jew." This word did not come into widespread use until about the time of the exile. During much of the OT God's people were known as "Israelites" (i.e., descendants of Israel). After the northern kingdom was destroyed and only those living in the area of Judah remained, over time God's people became known as "people of Judah" or "Judahites" (e.g., 2 Ki. 16:6; 25:25). Thus, in the exilic and postexilic books of Nehemiah, Esther, Jeremiah, and Zechariah, the common term for God's people becomes "the Jews" (e.g., Neh. 2:16; Est. 3:4, 6, 10; Jer. 40:11–12; Zech. 8:23). This applies both to God's people living in Judah and to his people living in Babylon and elsewhere (i.e., in the Diaspora). This term has remained with this nation of people to the present day.

New Testament

Noun: Ἰουδαῖος (*Ioudaios*), GK *2681* (S *2453*), 194x. *Ioudaios* comes from the word group related to the terms "Jews" and "Judeans." This term has three related ideas.

(1) *Ioudaios* can designate the *physical* or *ethnic* designation of a person, "Judean" or "Jew." This sense is both geographic and cultural; for example, a person can be a Judean and not actually live in the land of Judea, but their ethnic identity remains "Judean" (Acts 22:3). They are "Judean" in the sense of their birth or nationality (Jn. 4:9; Acts 18:2; Rom. 2:9). There is also a physical location known as "Judea." Since Jerusalem set the standard to Israel's tradition and since Jerusalem was in "Judea," *Ioudaios* normally implies conformity to culture and practices as found in the OT. Note too how John writes that Jesus and his disciples came into the land of the "*Judean* countryside" (Jn. 3:22).

(2) *Ioudaios* can also designate the *religious* adherence of a person—"Jew." The term denotes not only those who have grown up as Jews but also the people who turn to Judaism and live according to "*Jewish* customs" (Gal. 2:14; Tit. 1:14), regardless of their ethnic background. In this sense the "Jews" are to be distinguished from the "Greeks" in biblical times (see *Greek*).

(3) In NT times Christianity was seen as a subgroup of Judaism or a Jewish sect. The fact that the Christian Bible contains both the OT and NT makes this apparent. In Acts 18:14–15, for example, Gallio tells Paul and his opponents not to bother him with a squabble over things between "Jews." In other words, Gallio saw both Paul the Christian and the Jews in Corinth as part of the same religion.

But there were obvious differences between Judaism and the emerging Christian movement. In the NT, it becomes clear that a true descendant of Abraham (i.e., a true Jew) should recognize and accept Jesus as Lord (Jn. 8:33–42). The gospels show the intensity that developed as Christianity defined itself as centered on Christ, who is the fulfillment of Jewish belief and practice (Mt. 5:17). No matter what our ethnic identity, all people can become "children of Abraham" (Gal. 3:7). We are all to be as Paul teaches us in Gal. 3:9: "those who have faith (in Christ) are blessed along with Abraham, the man of faith." See *NIDNTT-A*, 272-76.

JOIN

New Testament

Verb: κολλάω (*kollaō*), GK *3140* (S *2853*), 12x. *kollaō* means to "join, unite closely." It is used frequently in reference to a person uniting or associating with other people. The degree to which two entities come together varies on the circumstances. Paul tries to join the disciples in Jerusalem (Acts 9:26) but is not successful. *kollaō* can also mean "cling, stick to"; for example, "the dust that *clings* to our feet" (Lk. 10:11). Paul challenges his readers to "*cling to* what is good" (Rom. 12:9). In Lk. 15:15, *kollaō* signifies selling one's services, "The prodigal son *hired* himself *out* to a foreign citizen." It can also depict the building of a pile, "her sins *piled up* to heaven" (Rev. 18:5).

kollaō is also used for the intimacy of the marriage relationship. Jesus describes that relationship in this way: "For this reason a man will leave his father and mother and *be united* to his wife, and the two will become one flesh" (Mt. 19:5) He goes on to warn that "what God has joined together [using a different verb here], let no man separate" (Mt. 19:6). This alludes to the binding nature of marriage, finding its origin at creation (Gen. 2:24). It must be preserved from defilement.

When *kollaō* is used in reference to God's activity, the relationship is one of spiritual intimacy. The believer's spiritual union with God is one of permanence and closeness. For this reason Paul warns the Corinthian believers not to unite themselves with a prostitute, or they will become one with her, just as a husband becomes one with his wife. He reminds them that they are to be one with God: "But he who *unites himself* with the Lord is one with him in spirit" (1 Cor. 6:16–17). This serves as a reminder that God is married to his covenant people. If they indulge in immorality, they will defile the sanctity of such a relationship. They are to remain pure as they await the return of Christ, their bridegroom. See *NIDNTT-A*, 313.

JOURNEY

Old Testament

Verb: נָסַע (*nāsaʿ*), GK 5825 (S 5265), 146x. The original meaning of *nāsaʿ* is "to pull out (tent pegs)," from which the sense "set out" or "journey" is derived. The translation of this verb as "to break camp" (Deut. 1:7, NIV) captures the sense.

nāsaʿ describes the journeys of Abraham (Gen. 12:9; 20:1) and Jacob (33:17; 33:5, 16, 21; 46:1) in the Genesis narrative. Since they are nomads living in tents, *nāsaʿ* appropriately describes their sojourning as strangers in a land they do not yet possess (cf. Heb. 8:11–16). Similarly, this verb is used for the journeys of Israel.

The book of Numbers utilizes *nāsaʿ* 89x in mapping the travels of Israel through the desert on their way to the promised land. As they head toward the Red Sea, the angel of God and the pillar of cloud, who have been *traveling* at their lead, move behind them to act as their rear guard (Exod. 14:19). And so it is throughout the journeys of Israel: when the cloud moves on, the Israelites *set out*, and when the cloud remains, they camp (Exod. 40:36; Num. 9:17). Moreover, God designs a specific order in which the tribes are to travel on their journey. With Judah are Issachar and Zebulun, who *set out* first. Then comes Reuben with Simeon and Gad, followed by the Levites, who carry the ark and all of the parts of the tabernacle. Third to *set out* is Ephraim with Manasseh and Benjamin, and finally Dan, with Asher and Naphtali (Num. 2:9–31). According to the signal of the trumpet blasts, the Israelites are to set out in this divine order (Num. 10:5–6), with the very presence of God in their midst. Moses offers a prayer for the journey each time the Israelites break camp: "Whenever the ark *set out*, Moses said, "Rise up, O LORD! May your enemies be scattered; may your foes flee before you" (Num. 10:35).

nāsaʿ is also used in a causative sense, as when God "*let loose* the east wind from the heavens" (NIV; "caused an east wind to blow in the heavens," KJV), and brought quail to Israel in the desert (Ps. 78:26; cf. Num. 11:31). God can also cause Sennacherib to *break camp* ("departed," KJV) and retreat from his attack on Israel (2 Ki. 19:36).

The journeys of Israel on her way to the promised land form a useable metaphor for Isaiah as he foretells the coming restoration of God's chosen people: "Look upon Zion, the city of our festivals; your eyes will see Jerusalem, a peaceful abode, a tent that will not be moved; its stakes will never *be pulled up*, nor any of its ropes broken" (Isa. 33:20). With the King residing in her city, Israel's journeys will be over. See *NIDOTTE*, 3:117-19.

Noun: דֶּרֶךְ (*derek*), GK 2006 (S 1870), 712x. *derek* may be translated in numerous ways, both literal and metaphorical, including "way, road, path, journey, conduct." See *way*.

New Testament

Noun: ὁδός (*hodos*), GK *3847* (S *3598*), 101x. *hodos* is basically a "road" or "path" on which one travels, or the act of traveling. It can also mean "the way" of life. See *way*.

JOY

Old Testament

Noun: שִׂמְחָה (*śimḥâ*), GK 8525 (S 8057), 94x. Depending on the context, *śimḥâ* can be translated "joy, rejoicing, gladness, pleasure," or "happiness." It can be expressed by singing (Gen. 31:27; 2 Chr. 23:18; Ps. 137:3), shouting (Ezr. 3:12,13; Isa. 16:10; Jer. 31:7; 48:33), dancing (1 Chr. 15:29; Jer. 31:13), and playing musical instruments (1 Sam. 18:6; 1 Ki. 1:40), but it is also a matter of the heart (Prov. 12:20; Song 3:11; Isa. 30:29; Jer. 15:16; Ezek. 36:5).

Weddings and harvest time epitomize joy in Israel, and therefore they are common images throughout the Scriptures, especially in the Hebrew prophets (Isa. 9:3; Jer. 7:34; 16:9; 25:10). Apart from the Day of Atonement, Israel's feasts and festivals are also times of joy and celebration (Num. 10:10; 2 Chr. 30:21, 23, 26; Neh. 8:17).

The Psalms are full of joyful praise and thanksgiving. The Lord has clothed the psalmist with joy (30:11) and filled his heart with joy (4:7), which is found in the presence of the Lord (21:6). Joy belongs to the righteous (68:3; 97:11).

According to the prophets, messianic hope brings *śimḥâ*. Just before Isaiah foretells the birth of the Wonderful Counselor (Isa. 9:6), he prophesies that God will magnify the joy of his people (Isa. 9:3). Indeed, the Lord will crown his people with *śimḥâ ʿôlām* ("everlasting joy"; Isa. 51:11). Though they may have suffered, the Lord promises future joy (Isa. 51:3; Zech. 8:19; Zeph. 3:17). See *NIDOTTE*, 3:1251-54.

Verb: שָׂמַח (*śāmaḥ*), GK 8523 (S 8055), 156x. *śāmaḥ* can describe both one's feeling of joy and the outward expression of such gladness in the form of rejoicing. It can be translated many ways, including "rejoice, delight, filled with joy, or gladden." See *rejoice*.

New Testament

Noun: χαρά (*chara*), GK *5915* (S *5479*), 59x. As an antonym of grief and sorrow (Jn. 16:20), *chara* denotes "joy, happiness, gladness." It can refer to feelings and can result from circumstances (Jn. 16:21), but for the believer, it is continual because of our relationship with Christ (1 Pet. 1:8).

The first use of *chara* in the NT describes the joyful response of the Magi when they saw the star that led them to Christ (Mt. 2:10). This is an emphatic construction of *chara* along with the related verb *chairō* (see *rejoice*), thus expressing the overwhelming nature of their joy. So from the beginning of the NT, Jesus is a source of joy for those who find him. Jesus teaches that there is joy in heaven whenever a sinner repents and returns to the Father (Lk. 15:7, 10). His incarnation and death on the cross were fulfilled with the joy of this redemption and reconciliation in mind (Heb. 12:2).

chara is one of the elements in the fruit produced by the Spirit in our lives (Gal. 5:22). With joy, believers pray (Phil. 1:4), give thanks (Col. 1:11), receive the Word of God (1 Thess. 1:6), and welcome fellow believers (Phil. 2:29).

The NT authors emphasize that the joy of the Lord transcends all earthly circumstances and that Christian joy is actually proven through hardship (2 Cor. 7:4; 8:2; 1 Thess. 1:6; Heb. 10:34). According to James, believers should consider trials a joy, because they lead to deeper faith and maturity (Jas. 1:2). Though Paul wrote his letter to the Philippians from prison, in the midst of personal suffering, he maintains the steadfast joy that he instructs the Philippian believers to maintain (Phil. 1:25; 2:2; 4:1). He also emphasizes in his letters that the work of ministry, however difficult or dangerous, is a joy (2 Cor. 1:24; 2:3; 1 Thess. 2:19–20; 3:9). See *NIDNTT-A*, 599-600.

JUDGE

Old Testament

Verb: יָכַח (*yākaḥ*), GK 3519 (S 3198), 59x. *yākaḥ* has a broad range of meaning, but it generally carries the sense of arguing a case or issuing judgment with the intent to correct. It is often translated "rebuke," "correct," "judge," "punish," or "argue," and is found most frequently in legal contexts (especially in Job [17x]) and in the wisdom instruction of Proverbs (10x). See *rebuke*.

Verb: שָׁפַט (*šāpaṭ*), GK 9149 (S 8199), 204x. *šāpaṭ* means "to judge, govern." In the OT human beings are the subject of this verb 60 percent of the time (mostly in narrative passages and some in the prophets;

the other 40 percent God is the subject (mostly in the Psalms and prophets).

(1) One of the main duties of a king and other national leaders is to establish or maintain justice, especially for the poor and needy (Lev. 19:15; Deut. 1:16; Ps. 72:4; Prov. 29:14). If a king fails to do this, he is severely rebuked (Ps. 82:2–3; Isa. 1:23; Jer. 5:28). This is one key characteristic of the coming messianic king (Isa. 11:3–4).

The ruler of the people is also expected to settle legal disputes among the people. This was one of the tasks of Moses (Exod. 18:13, 16), and after it apparently became too overwhelming, he appointed assistants to help in judging such cases (18:22, 26; Deut. 1:16). Occasionally the entire assembly of God's people are to enter into the process of judging (Num. 35:24). In the period of the eschatological temple, Ezekiel sees the priests functioning in this capacity (Ezek. 44:24). When judges are performing their duties, they must be aware of the fact that they are judging for the Lord; thus, "Let the fear of the LORD be upon you" (2 Chr. 19:6–7).

Occasionally *šāpaṭ* can be used not for judging specifically in legal disputes but as a general term for ruling or governing (e.g., 1 Ki. 3:9; 2 Chr. 1:10–11; Dan. 9:12). This is probably the general meaning of the word during the time of "the judges" (e.g., Jdg. 4:4; 10:2–3, 8–9; 15:20; Ruth 1:1; 1 Sam. 7:6).

(2) Many of the same nuances of human judging apply to divine judging. The Lord God is the divine ruler over all the earth (1 Chr. 16:33; Ps. 96:13; 98:9). And as the sovereign ruler, he is the divine "*Judge* of the earth" (Ps. 94:2; Isa. 33:22). In contrast to human judges, who all too often judge unfairly and in their own interest (Isa. 1:23), God "*defends* the cause of the weak and the fatherless" (Ps. 82:3; 10:18). He judges with righteousness, truth, and equity (96:13; 98:9; Isa. 11:3–4; cf. Gen. 18:25; Ps. 7:11; 9:4, 8).

Because God's judgment is always righteous, it is within his right to judge and punish earthly judges who do not follow his law or his principles in their capacity as rulers and judges (Jer. 5:28–29; Ezek. 7:3, 8; Ezek. 34:17–21). The OT also looks forward to the day of the Lord, in which God will sit to "*judge* all the nations on every side" (Joel 3:12). This day, of course, has a messianic message, for the NT makes it plain that Jesus himself is the one who "will judge the world with justice" (Acts 17:31; cf. 2 Tim. 4:1; 1 Pet. 4:5). See *NIDOTTE*, 4:213–20.

Noun: אֱלֹהִים (*ʾelōhîm*), GK 466 (S 430), 2602x. *ʾelōhîm* is a name for "God," but it can also mean "gods, judges, angels." See *God*.

New Testament

Verb: ἀνακρίνω (*anakrinō*), GK *373* (S *350*), 16x. *anakrinō* means "to examine, judge, investigate." See *investigate*.

Verb: διακρίνω (*diakrinō*), GK *1359* (S *1252*), 19x. *diakrinō* means "to judge, distinguish, evaluate" (Mt. 16:3; 1 Cor. 4:7; 11:29; Jas. 2:4). When applied to oneself, it can mean to "doubt" or "waver" (see Mt. 21:21; Mk. 11:23; Acts 10:20; Rom. 4:20; 14:23; Jas. 1:6; Jude 22). Peter, for example, is told to go with the men from Cornelius without "doubting" (NIV, "hesitating," Acts 10:20). This "hesitation" arose from Peter's state of mind in which he distinguished between Jew and Gentile (Acts 10:28). He knows that the place he will visit will be filled with ritually unclean Gentiles. But he must put out of his mind such ethnic divisions and ritualistic cleanliness requirements and consider all persons clean (10:34–35). James instructs his readers to ask for wisdom in faith, without "doubting" (Jas. 1:6). One sign of saving faith is to resist making "distinctions" between the rich and the poor (Jas. 2:4); to make distinctions shows a lack of true faith.

The notion of distinguishing is clearly seen in Paul's discussion of eating meat sacrificed to idols. Paul says that for believers, all foods are clean; there is no distinction between clean and unclean foods (Rom. 14:14a, 20a). Those who doubt are condemned because they make this distinction in an attempt to retain ritual purity and thereby rely on law rather than grace (14:20–24). The concept of distinguishing is likewise present in Paul's discussion of Abraham's faith regarding God's ability to give him a son from Sarah even though both were aged (Rom. 4:20). But Abraham "did not doubt"; he believed God would give him a son by Sarah (Rom. 4:21).

diakrinō is used in a technical legal sense in Paul's exhortation for believers to refrain from suing one another. He suggests there should be people in the church who can "judge a dispute" between believers (1 Cor. 6:5). See *NIDNTT-A*, 138.

Verb: κρίνω (*krinō*), GK *3212* (S *2919*), 114x. *krinō* essentially means "to consider, decide, judge," though it has a variety of nuances. It can refer to making a simple *distinction* between one day and another (Rom. 14:5). It is also used in the sense of passing judgment on the lives and actions of people in order to influence or control them. In Mt. 7:1, some form of *krinō* occurs four times: "Do not *judge*, or you too *will be judged*. For in the same way *you judge* others, *you will be judged*." The lesson is not that a person should not judge, because how would a person know who the "dogs" and the "pigs" are without exercising some degree of *discretion*? But we must not judge self-righteously or hypocritically. Thus, Jesus goes on to instruct the accuser to first remove the beam from his own eye in order to see the speck in his brother's eye (7:5). There is humor in Jesus' suggesting we try to see through a log on our own eye in order to remove sawdust from someone else's eye. James warns about unauthorized judging or critical speech, which results from double-mindedness (Jas. 4:11–12; see also 1 Cor. 4:5; Col. 2:16).

Judgments can appropriately be made as a result carefully inspecting a situation and taking various factors into account. For example, Jews demanding circumcision for Gentile created a severe threat to the purity of the gospel Paul preached. This precipitated the Jerusalem Conference, where the church leaders "considered" this issue carefully. James reached a "judgment" (Acts 15:19) after hearing from all parties involved by making a careful inspection of Scripture and probing all the facts. His decision helped create a situation where Paul's mission to the Gentiles could advance with the backing of predominant Jewish leadership in Jerusalem.

krinō also surfaces in situations where conclusions are reached as a result of deep thought and contemplation. For example, having made what is known as a "painful visit" to the Corinthians, Paul "decides" not to make another one (2 Cor. 2:1). Instead, he sends them what is known as the letter of tears (cf. 2:4; 7:8–9).

The law court provides the last context in which *krinō* is used. Paul views the church as a human court charged with policing its own spiritual issues (1 Cor. 5). In the case where a young Christian man is involved in an illicit sexual relationship, Paul says, "I have already *judged* him who has so committed this" (v. 3). While he calls for the expulsion of this man four times in thirteen verses, he is chiefly concerned with his restoration, since the ultimate day of judgment is coming (v. 5). Paul also indicates his right and the church's to carry out such action (vv. 12–13). Similarly in the next chapter, Paul points out the error of one Christian's suing another in a pagan law court (6:1–11). Settling an issue among themselves or suffering injustice are the only two options Paul grants them (6:4–7). Of course God is the ultimate tribunal as he will administer final judgment (Jn. 5:30; 8:16, 50; Rev. 6:10). See *NIDNTT-A*, 318-19.

Noun: κριτής (*kritēs*), GK *3216* (S *2923*), 19x. *kritēs* is a "judge," a person who passes judgment. Most commonly, it refers to a judge in the same manner that our society does, especially in the sense of the black-robed judge over criminal trials.

Jesus warns his listeners that the *kritēs*, by his authority, has the ultimate power to cast them into prison (Mt. 5:25; Lk. 12:58).

Such a person is invested with authority (e.g., the Roman governors Gallio [Acts 18:15] and Felix [24:10]) and can be unjust (Lk. 18:2, 6). There is also a sense in which a *kritēs* is one who has moral authority to judge others, as do the judges of Israel (Acts 13:20), including those who see and rebuke hypocrisy (Mt. 12:27; Lk. 11:19). A person can also be self-appointed *kritēs*, judging in matters that he ought not (Jas. 2:4; 4:11).

In spite of the fact that Christ refused to be drafted as a *kritēs* in squabbles over inheritance (Lk. 12:14), he is the most significant *kritēs* of all—the judge of the living and the dead (Acts 10:42). This is fully consistent with the Lord being the righteous judge of all (2 Tim. 4:8; Heb. 12:23), who is the very giver of the law (Jas. 4:12). This should make believers careful about their judgments and actions, for they must someday stand before the one who will judge all the judgments of others (Jas. 5:9). See *NIDNTT-A*, 318-19.*

JUDGE GUILTY

New Testament

Verb: κατακρίνω (*katakrinō*), GK *2891* (S *2632*), 18x. *katakrinō* means "to condemn, judge someone guilty." See *condemn*.

JUDGMENT

Old Testament

Noun: מִשְׁפָּט (*mišpāṭ*), GK 5477 (S 4941), 425x. Generally rendered "justice" or "judgment," *mišpāṭ* carries a legal or judicial connotation, though it is used in variety of ways. It is often found in the context of some sort of dispute, whether between two differing human parties or between God and Israel.

The laws given by Moses are described with the plural of *mišpāṭ*, "judgments, decrees" (Exod. 21:1; Deut. 5:1). For the Israelites to act in a just way entails observing God's ordinances in civil cases. These laws are fixed and should be used without partiality because justice belongs to God (Lev. 18:4; 19:37; Deut. 1:17; Ezr. 7:10). Within the Psalter, God's justice is cause for praise and hope (Ps. 7:6; 9:4; 10:5; 19:9; 25:9; 36:6; 97:2; see especially Ps. 119). See *justice*.

New Testament

Noun: κρίμα (*krima*), GK *3210* (S *2917*), 27x. *krima* refers to the act of "judgment" or its consequences (e.g., "punishment, condemnation"). (1) Paul uses this noun to describe the mystery of the mind of God, how "unsearchable [are] his *judgments*" because the wisdom and knowledge that God uses to make judgments is so beyond mere humans (Rom. 11:33). That does not mean that humans are totally unable to understand God's judgment, for Paul also says that God's judgment is according to truth (2:2) and is sure (2:3). In fact, there is a human parallel to the divine judgment, in that decisions of law courts were also called *krima* (1 Cor. 6:7). *krima* is not limited to a human legal context either, for Jesus warns the disciples that they will be judged with the "judgment" by which they judge others (Mt. 7:2), and James states that teachers will receive a stricter "judgment" because of their position (Jas. 3:1).

(2) *krima* also refers to the results of judging. Jesus describes his purpose for coming into the world as one of bringing judgment, a judgment that is a blessing to some ("so the blind will see") and a punishment or condemnation of others ("those who see will become blind") (Jn. 9:39). Those who prey on the weak will receive a severe judgment (Mk. 12:40; Lk. 20:47). The crucifixion endured by the thief is described as his (and Jesus') judgment (Lk. 23:40), a "sentence to death" (24:20). Such punishment or condemnation can be the result of any one of a manifold expressions of sin, including rebellion against God (Rom. 13:2), slander (Rom. 3:8), misuse of the Lord's Supper (1 Cor. 11:29), pride (1 Tim. 3:6), or teaching false doctrine (Gal. 5:10). The judgment for personal sin is a result of the "judgment" that entered the world through Adam's first sin (Rom. 5:16).

Furthermore, *krima* can also be used for

the final eternal judgment of God (Heb. 6:2) that will come on all creatures (Acts 24:25), starting with God's people (1 Pet. 4:17) and resulting in the damnation of those who have rejected the faith (1 Tim. 5:12), oppose God (2 Pet. 2:3; Jude 4), and persecute his people (Rev. 18:20). See *NIDNTT-A*, 318-19.

Noun: κρίσις (*krisis*), GK *3213* (S *2920*), 47x. *krisis* is the most common noun in the NT carrying the meaning of "judgment." *krisis*, like its related word *krima*, refers to the determination resulting from the act of judging, usually done by one in authority. *krisis* can refer to a judgment passed on temporal matters by a person of authority (Mt. 5:21–22), or a verdict passed on eternal matters by the coming of Jesus Christ (Jn. 3:19).

Most often, *krisis* refers to the judgment of the final day, when all will rise and everything will be made known (Mt. 10:15; 11:22, 24; 12:41–42). This final judgment is the last determination concerning all people (Heb. 9:27). Because of this, *krisis* sometimes refers in a negative sense to the judgment passed on all who disbelieve and disobey God—a condemnation or damnation (Mt. 23:33; Jn. 5:29). Furthermore, judgment is the possession of Jesus Christ, committed to him by the Father (Jn. 5:22, 27), and Christ's judgment is just and right (Jn. 5:30). In the same way, the judgment of God is described as righteous (2 Thess. 1:5); the judgment of human beings should be no different (Jn. 7:24).

Because of the righteous nature of judgment by God and Christ, *krisis* can also have the positive meaning of justice, i.e., judgment that is a blessing to the nations (Mt. 12:20). This was a blessing denied to Christ (Acts 8:33) and to many Jews (Lk. 11:42) by the scribes and Pharisees, who left undone the weightier matters of the law. See *NIDNTT-A*, 318-19.

JUDGMENT SEAT

New Testament

Noun: βῆμα (*bēma*), GK *1037* (S *968*), 12x. *bēma* typically signifies a "judgment seat," that is, an official's place or seat of authority from which he exercises judgment. A contemporary eqivalent is a courtroom setting. See *court*.

JURISDICTION

See *authority*.

JUST

Old Testament

Adjective: צַדִּיק (*ṣaddîq*), GK 7404 (S 6662), 206x. *ṣaddîq* is generally rendered "righteous, innocent, just." Similar to the nouns *ṣᵉdāqâ* and *ṣedeq*, this adjective describes those who act in such a way that their behavior accords with some standard. In general, this word describes as "righteous" persons rather than an abstract concept like the law. See *righteous*.

New Testament

Adjective: δίκαιος (*dikaios*), GK *1465* (S *1342*), 79x. *dikaios* means "righteous, innocent, just, upright." This adjective follows many of the characteristics of the Heb. word *ṣaddîq*; see *righteous, righteousness*.

JUSTICE

Old Testament

Noun: מִשְׁפָּט (*mišpāṭ*), GK 5477 (S 4941), 425x. Generally rendered "justice" or "judgment," *mišpāṭ* carries a legal or judicial connotation, though it is used in variety of ways. It is often found in the context of some sort of dispute, whether between two differing human parties or between God and Israel.

Within the Psalter, God's justice is cause for praise and hope (Ps. 7:6; 9:4; 10:5; 19:9; 25:9; 36:6; 97:2; see especially Ps. 119). This theme of the absolute justice of God is an important one in the book of Job, where one of Job's main arguments against his "friends" is that God cannot pervert justice (Job 8:3; 9:19). God confirms this sentiment at the end of the book when he states that justice is one of his chief characteristics (40:8).

The term *mišpāṭ* is found most often in prophetic literature and is used in a striking way in Isa. 40–55, where *mišpāṭ* is tied to God's sovereign execution of world affairs. His people cry out for justice (Isa. 40:27), and in 42:1–4 God proclaims that his servant will bring justice not only to suffering Israel but also to the nations. God's justice is always perfect, even when his plan baffles human understanding.

Noun: צֶדֶק (*sedeq*), GK 7406 (S 6664), 123x. Usually rendered "righteousness, justice, rightness," the noun *ṣedeq* generally describes the state or quality of that which accords with some recognized standard (not always expressed). It can be God's law or natural law or some other assumed standard. See *righteousness*.

Noun: צְדָקָה (*s^e^dāqâ*), GK 7407 (S 6666), 159x. *ṣ^e^dāqa* generally means "righteousness, justice, innocence." Like the noun *ṣedeq*, "righteousness," this noun also describes the state or quality of that which accords with some recognized standard, not always expressed in the context. See *righteousness*.

New Testament

Noun: δικαιοσύνη (*dikaiosynē*), GK *1466* (S *1343*), 92x. *dikaiosynē* can mean "righteousness, innocence, justice, justification." This word is prominent in Paul's letters, containing 58 of the 91 occurrences (64%). See *righteous, righteousness*.

Noun: κρίσις (*krisis*), GK *3213* (S *2920*), 47x. *krisis* is the most common noun in the NT carrying the meaning of "judgment." Sometimes it connotes "justice." See *judgment*.

JUSTIFICATION

New Testament

Noun: δικαιοσύνη (*dikaiosynē*), GK *1466* (S *1343*), 92x. *dikaiosynē* can mean "righteousness, innocence, justice, justification." This word is prominent in Paul's letters, containing 58 of the 91 occurrences (64%). See *righteous, righteousness*.

JUSTIFY

New Testament

Verb: δικαιόω (*dikaioō*), GK *1467* (S *1344*), 39x. *dikaioō* means "to declare righteous, justify." This word is prominent in Paul's letters, containing 27 of the 39x (about 70%). See *righteous, righteousness*.

KEEP

Old Testament

Verb: נָצַר (*nāṣar*), GK 5915 (S 5341), 63x. *nāṣar* generally indicates the action of carefully watching over a particular object so that the object is preserved or protected. It may be translated "to keep, guard, watch, protect." *nāṣar* shares the same meaning as the much more common verb *šāmar* and appears with *šāmar* 12x (Deut. 33:9; Ps. 12:8; 105:45; 119:34; 140:5; Prov. 2:8, 11; 4:6; 5:2; 13:3; 16:17; 27:18). *nāṣar* occurs most frequently in Psalms (24x) and Proverbs (18x).

The objects that *nāṣar* takes provide insight into the verb's meaning. Proverbs teaches, "He who *tends* the fig tree will eat its fruit" (Prov. 27:18). In the restoration Israel is commanded to "guard" the fortress (Nah. 2:1), and those who stand such a post are called "watchmen" (Jer. 31:6; cf. 2 Ki. 17:9; 18:8, "towers of *watchmen*").

But such physical objects are not usually governed by *nāṣar*. More frequently, *nāṣar* directs the conduct of God's people by imploring them to "keep" God's covenant (Deut. 33:9; Ps. 25:10). In keeping the covenant, Israel is not only to "keep" God's laws, testimonies, decrees, precepts, and commands (Ps. 78:7; 105:45; 119:2, 22, 33, 34, 56, 69, 100, 115, 129, 145), but also they are to "keep" the commands of parents (Prov. 6:20), sound wisdom and discretion (3:21), instruction (4:13), and knowledge (5:2). God's people must "guard" their mouth (13:3), their heart (4:23), and the path they take (16:17) because doing so will preserve their lives. Israelites are to "keep" their tongue from evil (Ps. 34:13), and they pray that God will "keep watch" over their lips (141:3). In short, keeping the covenant requires a careful guarding of all of one's life.

Ultimately, Israel's covenant keeping is in response to the character of the LORD. In the great statement of God's character in Exod. 34:6–7, God is described as the one "*keeping* covenant love (*ḥesed*) to thousands." God is the "watcher" of all people (Job 7:20), but he "watches over" his vineyard (i.e., Israel) in a special way to protect it from harm (Isa. 27:3). God "preserves" the faithful (Ps. 31:23) and "guards" their lives (Prov. 24:12) from trouble (Ps. 32:7), from violent men (140:1, 4), and from the plot of their enemies (64:1). See *NIDOTTE* 3:147-48.

Verb: שָׁמַר (*šāmar*), GK 9068 (S 8104), 468x. Often translated "to keep," the verb *šāmar* bears three distinct but related meanings in the OT: "to guard, tend," "to watch over," and "to preserve."

(1) *šāmar* is regularly used in the sense of "tending, guarding, taking care." The first occurrence of this verb has this sense: God placed the man/Adam "into the Garden of Eden to cultivate it and *to keep* it" (Gen. 2:15; cf. 3:24). *šāmar* is used in a similar sense to describe God's watch-care over Israel, "Behold, he who *keeps* Israel will neither slumber nor sleep" (Ps. 121:4). It is used of tending to a flock (Gen. 30:31) and a house (2 Sam. 15:16; Ps. 15:16) and of guarding against intruders (Gen. 3:24; 1 Sam. 26:15; Song 5:7; Isa. 21:11).

(2) In other contexts, *šāmar* denotes "watching over" or giving attention to something. (a) It is used generally of Eli "watching" Hannah's mouth (1 Sam. 1:12) or of Balaam "examining" Israel (Num. 23:12).

(b) But it may also be used of "heeding" (i.e., "watching over" or "observing") a covenant. "God said to Abraham, 'Now as for you, you shall *keep* my covenant' " (Gen. 17:9). *šāmar* expresses the careful devotion and action that is necessary in order to fulfill the covenant obligations. It is used in Gen. 18:19 to signify the need for spiritual and physical obedience to the covenant: "For I have chosen him, so that he may command his children and his household after him to keep the way of the LORD." Those who claim allegiance to God are "to observe" all that he has commanded (Exod. 20:6; Lev. 18:26; Deut. 26:16; Ezek. 11:20).

(c) Similarly, *šāmar* is used of the attitude of reverence or the careful paying attention to something (2 Sam. 11:16; Ps. 31:6; Hos. 4:10; Zech. 11:11). When *šāmar* is used in conjunction with another verb, it can mean to do the stated action with care. Balaam responds to Balak concerning the thwarting of the curses, "He replied, 'Must I not *be careful* to speak what the LORD puts in my mouth?' " (Num. 23:12). In addition, *šāmar* can express the fulfilling of an obligation (Jdg. 1:24).

(3) *šāmar* is also used to communicate the idea of preserving or retaining. After Joseph shared his vision with Jacob and his brothers, "his brothers were jealous of him, but his father *kept* the saying in mind" (Gen. 37:11). Accordingly, "the lips of the priest should *preserve* knowledge" (Mal. 2:7). In Job 2:6 God gives Satan freedom to persecute Job, but Satan must "spare" his life. Similarly, Prov. 13:3 states, "The one who guards his mouth *preserves* his life." Grain is preserved (Gen. 41:35), money is protected (Exod. 22:7), food is set aside (1 Sam. 9:24), and fury is sustained (Amos 1:11).

New Testament

Verb: τηρέω (*tēreō*), GK *5498* (S *5083*), 70x. *tēreō* conveys the idea of watching over something closely or guarding—"to keep, obey; guard, protect." Sometimes it can simply denote guards, such as the one guarding at the tomb of Jesus (Mt. 28:4) or the act of guarding apostles in a prison (Acts 12:5–6; 16:23).

More often, however, *tēreō* denotes keeping the commandments of the OT or the teachings of Christ. Jesus says to the rich young man, "If you want to enter life, keep the commandments" (Mt. 19:17; cf. Jn. 8:51–52; 6:16; Acts 15:5). The OT teaches that one who "loves" God is also one who remains obedient to his commands. Jesus makes this point by declaring to his disciples, "If you love me, you will *obey* what I command" (cf. Mt. 28:20; Jas. 2:10).

Obedience is the authenticating mark of a true believer. John writes, "We know that we have come to know him if we *obey* his commands.... But if anyone *obeys* his word, God's love is truly made complete in him" (1 Jn. 2:3–5; cf. 1 Tim. 6:14; Heb. 5:9). The reward of such obedience carries eternal weight. Paul instructs us to "keep the unity of the Spirit" (Eph. 4:3). Regarding his own life he writes, "I have fought the good fight. I have finished the race, I *have kept* the faith. Now there is in store for me the crown of righteousness" (2 Tim. 4:7–8; cf. 1 Pet. 1:4).

Jesus is involved in keeping his children safe from the evil one (1 Jn. 5:18) and in keeping a place in heaven for us (1 Pet. 1:4). By contrast, God did not "spare" the wicked angels when they sinned but cast them out (2 Pet. 2:4). See *NIDNTT-A*, 562-63.

Verb: φυλάσσω (*phylassō*), GK *5875* (S *5442*), 31x. *phylassō* means to "guard" physically or metaphorically (see *guard*) or to "keep" in the sense of observing. It can denote a careful observance of divine or human law. Jesus uses *phylassō* in this way when he speaks to the rich young ruler of keeping the commandments (Mt. 19:20; Mk. 10:20; Lk. 18:21). It is also used of keeping various laws and decisions (Acts 7:53; 16:4; 21:24–25; Rom. 2:26; Gal. 6:13; 1 Tim. 5:21). Finally, Jesus says the one who keeps God's word will be blessed (Lk. 11:28), but the one not keeping his word, i.e., not believing in him, will be judged (Jn. 12:47). See also *guard*.

KEEP WATCH

New Testament

Verb: γρηγορέω (*grēgoreō*), GK *1213* (S *1127*), 22x. *grēgoreō* means "to keep watch over, guard" something. It carries the idea of vigilance in the face of something impending. See *watch*.

KILL

Old Testament

Verb: הָרַג (*hārag*), GK 2222 (S 2026), 167x. *hārag* can variously mean "to kill, murder, slaughter, massacre." *hārag* most often denotes intentional killing, as in the case of Cain and Abel (Gen. 4:8). However, it can also refer to unintentional killing (Exod. 21:12–14). It is not the word used in the sixth commandment (see *murder, slaughter*).

Numerous times in the OT God kills people in judgment: the firstborn children of Egypt (Exod. 4:23; 13:15), those who mistreat the widow and orphan (Exod. 22:22–24), and even his own people when they sin (Ps. 78:31, 34). In the same manner, God sometimes commands men to kill other humans as part of his judgment: Moses and the sons of Levi kill Israelites who stand against the Lord after the golden calf incident (Exod. 32:27), and the judges of Israel kill those who yoke themselves to Baal of Peor (Num. 25:5). Such instances do not violate the commandment against murder, for the humans are operating as divine agents of judgment against wickedness in direct accord with God's verbal mandate.

God uses hail to kill vines and frost to kill sycamores (Ps. 78:47). *hārag* is also used of men killing animals (Balaam threatens his donkey, Num. 22:29; men kill oxen, Isa. 22:13), and animals killing humans (lions, 2 Ki. 17:25; viper, Job 20:16).See *NIDOTTE*, 1:1055-57.

Verb: מוּת (*mût*), GK 4637 (S 4191, 4192), 854x. *mût* means "to die, put to death, kill." See *die*.

Verb: נָכָה (*nākâ*), GK 5782 (S 5221), 501x. The verb *nākâ* generally means "to strike down, destroy, hit, kill." See *strike*.

Verb: שָׁחַט (*šāḥaṭ*), GK 8821 (S 7819), 81x. *šāḥaṭ* means "to slaughter, kill."

The verb is most often used in the context of ritualistic animal or human sacrifice. The traditional rabbinic interpretation for *šāḥaṭ* proposes that it originally referred to the first step in the sacrificial process, namely, slitting the throat (see Mish. *Hullin* 1–3). In Lev., *šāḥaṭ* is used for a variety of sacrifices: burnt offerings (1:5), peace offerings (3:2), sin offerings (4:4), and guilt offerings (7:2). The OT also uses *šāḥaṭ* to refer to the ritualistic sacrificing of people (e.g., Isa. 57:5; Ezek. 16:20–21; 23:39), including Abraham's offering of

Isaac on Mount Moriah (Gen. 22:10). See also *slaughter*. See *NIDOTTE*, 4:77-80.

New Testament

Verb: ἀναιρέω (*anaireō*), GK *359* (S *337*), 24x. *anaireō* means "to kill, put to death." James, the brother of John, was "killed" with the sword (Acts 12:2). Paul had actually participated in "putting to death" many Christians before his conversion (26:10). Jesus will "kill" the lawless one with the "breath of his mouth" (2 Thess. 2:8). *anaireō* can also mean "to take away, abolish"; See *take away*.

Verb: ἀποκτείνω (*apokteinō*), GK *650* (S *615*), 74x. *apokteinō* essentially means "to deprive of life, put to death, kill." This killing may refer to physical life or to spiritual life. Both senses are used in Mt. 16:28, "Do not be afraid of those who *kill* the body but cannot *kill* the soul." (1) In the bodily sense, "Herod wanted to *kill* John" (Mt. 14:5). Jesus would be "killed" by those who crucified him (Mt. 17:23; Mk. 8:31; 9:31; Lk. 9:22).

(2) In the spiritual sense, sin "kills" those it touches. Paul personifies the power of sin in this way: "For sin, seizing the opportunity afforded by the commandment, deceived me, and through the commandment *put* me *to death*" (Rom. 7:11). When sinful humans come into contact with God's law, "the letter *kills*, but the Spirit gives life" (2 Cor. 3:6). Christ's cross "puts to death" the hostility that existed between Jews and Gentiles (Eph. 2:16). See *NIDNTT-A*, 63.

Verb: θανατόω (*thanatoō*), GK *2506* (S *2289*), 11x. *thanatoō* conveys the termination of physical life and may best be translated "kill" or "put to death." See *put to death*.

Verb: θύω (*thyō*), GK *2604* (S *2380*), 14x. The root of *thyō* carries the meaning of "to sacrifice" a burnt offering. A derived meaning is simply "to kill." See *sacrifice*.

KILLED

Old Testament

Noun: חָלָל (*ḥālāl*), GK 2728 (S 2491), 94x. *ḥālāl* denotes someone who has been pierced for the purpose of killing or wounding and may be translated as "pierced, wounded, killed." See *pierced*.

KILLING

New Testament

Noun: αἷμα (*haima*), GK *135* (S *129*), 97x. *haima* is the standard Greek term for "blood." It is used extensively in contexts relating to killing and death. For example, Jesus warns an expert in the law that "this generation will be held responsible for the blood [killing] of all the prophets" (Lk. 11:50; see also Acts 22:20; Rev. 6:12). See *blood*.

KIND

New Testament

Noun: γένος (*genos*), GK *1169* (S *1085*), 20x. *genos* means "kind." The NT refers to different "kinds" of fish (Mt. 13:47), spirits (Mk. 9:29), tongues (1 Cor. 12:10, 28), and languages (1 Cor. 14:10). *genos* can also mean "offspring" (see *offspring*), "family" (see *family*), or "people" (see *people*).

Noun: φύσις (*physis*), GK *5882* (S *5449*), 14x. *physis* means "nature, natural condition, kind." See *nature*.

Adjective: χρηστός (*chrēstos*) GK *5982* (S *5543*), 7x. *chrēstos* means "kind." This adjective refers first of all to God, who is "kind to the ungrateful and wicked" (Lk. 6:35). In fact, his being "kind" to all people is intended to lead them to repentance (Rom. 2:4). Once we have become children of God, we continue to experience God's kindness or goodness (1 Pet. 2:3). Then, as a result of and in imitation of our loving God, God calls us to "be kind and compassionate to one another" (Eph. 4:32). See *kindness*.

KIND(S)

Old Testament

Noun: מִשְׁפָּחָה (*mišpāḥâ*), GK 5476 (S 4940), 304x. The noun *mišpāḥâ* designates a subgroup of a larger division, and is, therefore, variously translated as "clan, family, people" as well as "kind, kingdoms, nation." See *clan, nation*.

That *mišpāḥâ* can designate constituent parts of larger groupings is demonstrated by its use to denote "kinds" of animals. When the animals come out of the ark (Gen. 8:19), they do so "one *kind* after another" (NIV), "after their *kinds*" (KJV). This use of *mišpāḥâ* to identify constituent parts is also seen in Jer. 15:3, "I will send four *kinds* of destroyers against them," declares the LORD, "the sword to kill and the dogs to drag away and the birds of the air and the beasts of the earth to devour and destroy."

KINDLE

New Testament

Verb: ἅπτω (*haptō*), GK *721* (S 680, *681*), 39x. At its most basic level *haptō* means "to make close contact with something, touch something." But it can also mean "to cling to, take hold of something." See *touch*.

KINDNESS

Old Testament

Noun: חֶסֶד (*ḥesed*) GK 2876 (S 2617), 249x. *ḥesed* is one of the richest, most theologically insightful terms in the OT. It denotes "kindness, love, loyalty, mercy." See *love*.

New Testament

Noun: χρηστότης (*chrēstotēs*), GK *5983* (S *5544*), 10x. *chrēstotēs* means "kindness, goodness" and is used especially of God. This word occurs only in Paul's letters.

(1) *chrēstotēs* is a characteristic of God. It denotes the kindness and good favor that he shows to believers. Paul reminds those who think that they are beyond judgment that it is only God's kindness and patience that forestall his judgment (Rom. 2:4). But a time will come when the *chrēstotēs* of God will no longer be provided to those who do not continue in their faith, regardless of what they presume their position to be (11:22 [3x]). The kindness of God is expressed primarily in Christ (Eph. 2:7) and was manifested to people in his appearance as Savior (Tit. 3:4).

(2) As a result of receiving the *chrēstotēs* of God, believers are to clothe themselves with *chrēstotēs* (Col. 3:12), to such an extent that it characterizes them even in the midst of trials and persecution (2 Cor. 6:6). Believer are able to exhibit *chrēstotēs* because of the work of the Spirit in their lives, for *chrēstotēs* is one of the aspects of the fruit of the Spirit (Gal. 5:22). Because unbelievers are without the Spirit, Paul can say that no one among them manifests *chrēstotēs* (Rom. 3:12). See *NIDNTT-A*, 609-10.*

KINDRED

Old Testament

Noun: מִשְׁפָּחָה (*mišpāḥâ*), GK 5476 (S 4940), 304x. The noun *mišpāḥâ* designates a subgroup of a larger division, and is, therefore, variously translated as "clan, family, people" as well as "kind, kingdoms, nation." The KJV uses "family, kindred, kind." See *clan*, *kind*, *nation*.

KING

Old Testament

Noun: מֶלֶךְ (*melek*), GK 4889 (S 4428 and 4429), 2513x. Words with the Heb. *mlk* root comprise an incredibly frequent and important concept in the OT. The most common of all these related terms is the basic noun *melek*. Occurring more than 2500x, it conveys a variety of meanings. It is not a technical term but refers to a large assortment of leader-types, from an emperor to the kings of Israel and Judah down to tribal and city leaders. It is one of many terms in the OT for *leaders* (see *leader*). Of course, frequently *melek* is best translated with English "king." Several OT texts teach that the king of Israel is adopted as God's son (Ps. 2:7; 45:7; 110:1).

One of the key uses of *melek* in the OT is for God as King. The two main books of the Bible in which this concept occurs is the book of Psalms and Isa. 40–44. The psalmists frequently address Israel's God as "my *King* and my God" (Ps. 5:2; 44:4; 84:3). The Lord Almighty is "the *King* of glory" (24:7–10), who sits enthroned on high (2:4; 22:3; 29:10; 99:1; 113:5; Isa. 40:22). God is "the *King* over all the earth" (Ps. 47:2, 7), and to him we should sing praises. He is also "the King above all gods" (95:3), and before him we should worship and bow down. Isaiah acknowledges "the LORD Almighty" as "Israel's *King* and Redeemer" (Isa. 44:6) and "Israel's Creator, your *King*" (43:15). See *NIDOTTE*, 2:956-65.

Noun: נָשִׂיא (*nāśîʾ*), GK 5954 (S 5387) 131x. There are a number of overlapping nouns in the OT that refer to leaders, chiefs, and officials of various sorts (see *leader* for a thorough discussion). One of these is *nāśîʾ*, which Ezekiel uses frequently as a royal title rather than the more common *melek*, "king" (Ezek. 12:10; 19:1). The prophet also uses *nāśîʾ* to describe the coming Davidic ruler who will shepherd the restored flock of Israel (Ezek. 34:24; 37:25).

New Testament

Noun: βασιλεύς (*basileus*), GK *995* (S *935*). 115x. *basileus* means "king, ruler." These terms relate to the idea of kingship and kingdom (see also the word *basileia* under *kingdom*) and make up an important theme throughout the NT. Building on the same theme in the OT, Jesus proclaims the kingdom of God as his primary message (Mt. 4:17; Mk. 1:15; Lk. 4:43), implying that he is the King of that kingdom. The book of Revelation likewise describes Jesus as "*King* of *kings* and Lord of lords" (17:14; 19:16; cf. 1:5) and promises that faithful disciples will reign with Christ eternally (5:10; 20:4; 22:5).

In the LXX, the noun *basileus* and the verb *basileuō* are used with reference to a large assortment of human kings as well as God. This is also true in the NT, though earthly kings are often depicted negatively and God as king is emphasized. Herod, Pilate, and many others are portrayed as those who set themselves against God's kingdom (Mt. 2:1–18; Acts 12:1; 2 Cor. 11:32), while Jesus' actions and teaching show him to be the true king (Mt. 11:2–6; 12:28; Lk. 4:16–27). Several NT authors use elevated language to describe God as king (Mt. 5:35; Lk. 19:38; Jn. 12:13; 1 Tim. 1:17; Rev. 17:14). Interestingly, in John the term *basileus* is reserved solely for Jesus (16x). See *NIDNTT-A*, 87–91.

Verb: βασιλεύω (*basileuō*), GK *996* (S *936*) 21x. *basileuō* means "to rule, reign."

KINGDOM

Old Testament

Noun: כִּסֵּא (*kissēʾ*), GK 4058 (S 3676 and 3678), 135x. For the most part, *kissēʾ* means denotes a "throne"—either an earthly throne or God's heavenly throne. God is the one who establishes and overthrows "thrones," that is, kingdoms or dynasties (2 Sam. 3:10; 1 Ki. 9:5; Dan. 5:20; Hag. 2:22). See *throne*.

Noun: מַלְכוּת (*malkût*), GK 4895 (S 4438), 91x.

Noun: מַמְלָכָה (*mamlākâ*), GK 4930 (S 4467), 117x. Words with the Heb. *mlk* root comprise a frequent and important concept in the OT. The term *malkût* ranges in meaning from an abstract reference to a king's dynasty or power (Num. 24:7; 1 Sam. 20:31) to the more concrete location of a "kingdom" (2 Chr. 1:1; Neh. 9:35). In this sense of "kingdom," *malkût* overlaps with *mamlākâ*, which is the more frequent term used for "kingdom, dominion" (Gen. 10:10; Ps. 135:11; Jer. 1:10). Both terms are flexible and distinctions are not always maintained, but in some cases there is a difference (1 Chr. 29:30).

The idea of king and kingdom is important in the OT for several reasons. First, the Davidic dynasty was a crucial stage in Israel's history and one to which the subsequent OT literature looks back as foundational. Second, kingship becomes important for Israel's future hopes as the people look for a messianic figure in David's line who will consummate God's kingdom. Third, God himself is often called a king, and his kingship is emphasized especially in Psalms, Isaiah, Jeremiah, and Zechariah.

The kingdom of God serves well as an overarching theme for understanding and communicating the foundational ideas of the whole Bible. It is the purple thread that weaves its way throughout Scripture as a unifying theme. Beginning with the vision of God enthroned in his heavenly court and ordaining Adam as his royal vice-regent on earth, the theme of God's kingdom is manifest throughout the OT, breaks forth in Jesus' ministry, and awaits its fulfillment at the return of Christ. See *NIDOTTE*, 2:956-65.

New Testament

Noun: βασιλεία (*basileia*), GK *993* (S *932*). 162x. In the NT, *basileia* plays a greater role than its Hebrew counterpart did in the OT. As in the OT, *basileia* can be used abstractly to refer to royal power or kingship, while at other times the geographical sense of "area of rule" is emphasized. Most English versions consistently translate *basileia* with "kingdom," though at times it would be better understood as "reign" or "rule." Thus, some scholars today prefer to speak of "the rule of God" or even "the empire of God."

The kingdom is central to Jesus' ministry and message. The theology of the *basileia* of God (often "kingdom of heaven" in Matthew) can be summed up under the rubric "already, not yet." That is, Jesus teaches that the kingdom has already come in his own person, yet it awaits fulfillment at the end of this age. In the meanwhile, Jesus reveals the workings and demands of God's kingdom, often in the form of parables (Mt. 13:24–52). God's *basileia* has radical and unexpected ethics that are consistently counterintuitive to our human nature (see the Sermon on the Mount, Mt. 5–7).

Even though the proclamation of the kingdom is central to the OT as well as Jesus' ministry, it is often overshadowed in Christian teaching by the message of individual forgiveness of sins. This overshadowing has occurred because we tend to read the NT letters as if personal reconciliation is the crucial issue. However, even though the word *basileia* does not occur as frequently in the letters as in the gospels, the message of Christ's kingdom is still central there as it is in the preaching of the early church (cf. the sermons in Acts). The foundational proclamation "Jesus is Lord" is at its core a proclamation of Jesus' present kingship and his coming kingdom when he returns (cf. 1 Cor. 11:26; see *Lord*). See *NIDNTT-A*, 87-91.

KINGSHIP

Old Testament

Noun: מַלְכוּת (*malkût*), GK 4895 (S 4438), 91x.

Noun: מַמְלָכָה (*mamlākâ*), GK 4930 (S 4467), 117x.

These two nouns are both connected with the *mlk* root and, along with other words, comprise a frequent and important concept in the OT. *malkût* ranges in meaning from an abstract reference to a king's dynasty or power (Num. 24:7; 1 Sam. 20:31) to the more concrete location of a "kingdom" (2 Chr. 1:1; Neh. 9:35). In this sense of "kingdom," *malkût* overlaps with *mamlākâ*, which is the more frequent term used for "kingdom or dominion" (Gen. 10:10; Ps. 135:11; Jer. 1:10). For a thorough discussion, see *king*.

KNEE

New Testament

Noun: γόνυ (*gony*), GK *1205* (S *1119*), 12x. The basic meaning of *gony* is "knee." In the NT it usually occurs as the direct object of a verb where the whole expression may be translated as "to kneel/fall before" (lit., "to place the knee," Mk. 15:19; Lk. 22:41; Acts 7:60, 9:40, 20:36, 21:5), "to bend the knee, bow" (Rom. 11:4; Eph. 3:14), or "to fall on one's knees" (Lk. 5:8).

Referring to Isa. 45:23, Paul describes a time when God's universal lordship over all creation will be recognized, symbolized by the fact that everyone's knee will bow before the Lord and everyone's tongue will make the proper confession that Jesus is Lord (Phil. 2:10) or will simply confess to God (Rom. 14:11). In Heb. 12:12, the author calls for the weak knees (and the feeble arms) to be strengthened, which is a metaphor for enduring God's loving, fatherly discipline so as to grow into maturity and walk on the level path. See *NIDNTT-A*, 111.*

KNIFE

Old Testament

Noun: חֶרֶב (*ḥereb*), GK 2995 (S 2719), 413x. *ḥereb* describes a "sword," a common weapon of war, although it is sometimes translated as "knife, dagger" (Jos. 5:2; 2 Sam. 20:8). See *sword.*

KNIT TOGETHER

See *unite.*

KNOW

Old Testament

Verb: בִּין (*bîn*), GK 1067 (S 995), 171x. *bîn* is most commonly found in the wisdom literature, especially Job and Proverbs. It is sometimes used in the general sense of "to know" (Prov. 24:12; Mic. 4:12), but more often refers to a technical, detailed, or specific understanding. See *understand.*

Verb: יָדַע (*yādaʿ*), GK 3359 (S 3045), 956x. *yādaʿ* expresses a wide range of meanings connected to the idea of "knowing" or "understanding." In general, the epistemology of the OT is far more holistic than that of Western philosophy. Thus, knowledge gained through sensory experience and that which comes through intellectual apperception are not distinguished categorically; rather, both are viewed as valid and necessary aspects of knowledge acquisition.

(1) *yādaʿ* is often paired with verbs of perception, sometimes used idiomatically, to denote the process of gaining knowledge. Thus, in legal matters, a witness who has "seen or *learned*" something is obligated to testify (Lev. 5:1). To "see and *know*" may simply mean "to know" something (cf. Deut. 4:35; 1 Sam. 12:17; 14:38; 2 Sam. 24:13; Isa. 41:20). In the same way, *yādaʿ* is coupled with *šāmaʿ* ("to hear," GK 9048) in Ps. 78:3, "what we have heard and *known*, what our fathers have told us" (cf. also Deut. 9:2; Neh. 6:16; Isa. 33:13; Jer. 5:15). In some cases, *yādaʿ* seems to denote the mental synthesis of facts gleaned through sensory experience. Describing God's knowledge in human terms, Exod. 3:7 reads, "The LORD said, 'I have indeed seen the misery of my people in Egypt...and I am *concerned* about their suffering'" ("I *know* their sorrows," KJV). Indeed, the piling up of similar verbs in Isa. 40:21 indicates the manner in which a number of terms overlap to express the concept of "knowing."

(2) Consequently, the eyes and ears are considered essential for the mind (heart) to acquire knowledge. "But to this day the LORD has not given you a mind [heart] that *understands* or eyes that see or ears that hear" (Deut. 29:3; cf. Isa. 6:10). Thus, eyes that are closed or blind (Isa. 32:3–4; 44:18) fail to know the truth, while eyes that are open gain true knowledge (Gen. 3:7; Num. 24:15; 1 Ki. 8:29, 52; Ps. 119:18; Isa. 42:7). One comes to know God by seeing and experiencing his works. Having experienced God's hand against Egypt, Israel is to rehearse his wonders in each generation, "that you may *know* that I am the LORD" (Exod. 10:2; cf. 16:12; 18:11; Deut. 4:35).

For the Hebrew, the heart (*lēb*, GK 4213) was the place of cognitive activity, for the ability "to *know*" is related to one's heart (Prov. 27:23; Eccl. 7:22; 8:5; Isa. 42:25; 51:7; Jer. 12:3). When Pharaoh's heart was hardened, he failed to "take to heart" (i.e., understand or acknowledge) the reality of the situation (Exod. 7:22). This same expression is used with *yādaʿ* in Deut. 4:39, "*Acknowledge* and take to heart this day that the LORD is God in heaven above and on the earth below. There is no other" ("*know*... and consider in thine heart," KJV, cf. also Isa. 42:25).

(3) Ultimately, all of humanity's knowledge is a gift from God (Prov. 1:7), but this does not negate the effort needed to acquire knowledge. One must search out the truth (Eccl. 7:25), test it against the facts (Jer. 6.27), and weigh the evidence (Gen. 8:11). This is particularly emphasized in the wisdom literature, where one must strive for wisdom and understanding regardless of what it may cost (Prov. 4:7). Yet by ourselves we cannot attain true knowledge (see Job 28:13; cf. 28:23), for true knowledge is bound up in a relationship with

God: "The fear of the LORD is the beginning of knowledge" (Prov. 1:7; cf. 2:5). Those who fear the Lord walk in his ways (Deut. 6:2; 10:12; 31:12), and it is in this relationship of trust and obedience that true knowledge is found, for God knows all things (Job 37:16; Ps. 139:1–6; 147:5) and he sovereignly reveals the truth (Jer. 16:21; Ps. 25:4; 119:66). It is the fool who declares "there is no God" (Ps. 14:1; 53:1).

(4) That *yādaʿ* includes a sense of relationship is evident, for the verb expresses sexual intimacy within the marriage covenant: "Adam *lay with* [lit., *knew*] his wife Eve, and she became pregnant" (Gen. 4:1; cf. also 1 Sam. 1:19). In a more general sense of relationship, *yādaʿ* can describe friendship (Job 19:13) or even an acquaintance (Gen. 29:5).

This use of *yādaʿ* to denote relationship may also describe the proper relationship of partners within a covenant. Thus, when *yādaʿ* is found within covenant contexts of the OT, it describes covenant relationship rather than mere cognitive activity. When Pharaoh declares "I do not *know* the LORD" (Exod. 5:2), he is declaring that he has no covenant obligation to him. The same may be said of the Pharaoh who "*knew* not Joseph" (Exod. 1:8, KJV; NIV, "*know about* Joseph," is interpretative). Conversely, David admonishes Solomon: "And you, my son Solomon, *acknowledge* the God of your father, and serve him with wholehearted devotion and with a willing mind" (1 Chr. 28:9). In similar covenant language, the Lord declares regarding Israel: "You only *have I chosen* [lit., *known*] of all the families of the earth; therefore I will punish you for all your sins" (Amos 3:2). Within covenant contexts, "to *know* the Lord" means "to acknowledge the covenant relationship" one has with him (Hos. 6:6). When the new covenant is established with Israel, "they will all *know* me, from the least of them to the greatest" (Jer. 31:34), meaning that Israel will live in covenant faithfulness to God. Likewise, when God *knows* Israel (Deut. 9:24; Hos. 5:3–4; 13:5), it means that he has entered into a covenant relationship with her as a husband to his wife (Jer. 31:32; Ezek. 16:32).

It is in light of this covenant relationship that Israel's unfaithfulness is seen, for she has worshiped gods she did not "know" (i.e., with whom she had no covenant relationship, Deut. 13:2, 6, 13; 28:64) and has committed spiritual adultery: "they do not *acknowledge* the Lord" (Hos. 5:4; cf. Isa. 1:21; Ezek. 6:9; 16:32), and there is no "knowledge of God in the land" (KJV, Hos. 4:1). The prophet's message, then, is that Israel should "*acknowledge* the Lord" (6:3). Indeed, in fulfilling her covenant obligations, Israel is to "make known" God's words and deeds "so that the nations may *know* me" (Ezek. 38:16; cf. 2 Ki. 19:19; Isa. 11:9; 12:4–5; Ezek. 39:7). See *NIDOTTE*, 2:408–14.

New Testament

Verb: γινώσκω (*ginōskō*), GK *1182* (S *1097*), 222x. *ginōskō* means "to know, understand, recognize." It has a variety of nuances. It can mean "to learn" or "to possess factual knowledge." For example, Paul tells the Ephesian Christians that he is sending Tychicus to tell them how he is doing, that they may "know" how he is (Eph. 6:22; see also Mt. 6:3; Mk. 15:10; Jn. 19:14; Rom. 6:6; Phil. 4:5; Col. 4:8; Jas. 5:20; 2 Pet. 1:20).

It can also refer to learning something by observation or noticing something. For example, when Jesus was twelve years old and his parents took him to Jerusalem, they did not "know" he was not with them on the return trip to Galilee (Lk. 2:43). When Paul spoke before the Sanhedrin, he came to "know" (i.e., notice, realize) that some of them were Pharisees and some were Sadducees, and this observation provided him an avenue to introduce confusion into the meeting of his accusers (Acts 23:6; see also Lk. 1:22; Jn. 4:53; Acts 19:34; 21:24).

ginōskō can also refer to a kind of mental assent—to know God and his will is to acknowledge the claim he has on one's own life (and to agree with that claim). It is to take God's law and apply it to one's own life in experience/obedience (Rom. 1:32; 2:18; 7:1; 1 Cor. 8:2–3; cf., Jn. 7:49). Paul utilizes a play on words in Rom. 1 when he says that some "know" God's just judgment (1:32), but they do not wish to "know" God (1:28). That is, the heathen have a knowledge of God that makes no difference in their activity; they have an intellectual awareness of his existence and perhaps even a belief that he exists, but they do not have a personal or intimate knowledge of him and do not have faith in him (Rom. 1:21–28). Thus, there is a sense in which true knowledge (of God) leads to action in keeping with obedience (2 Cor. 10:3–6).

John especially has a rich view of what it means to "know." When Jesus says he knows his sheep and he knows the Father, he is speaking of an intimate relationship that involves deep feelings of love (Jn. 10:14–15). Such a relationship leads to obedience on our part (10:27). "Those who say, 'I *know* him,' but do not do what he commands are liars" (1 Jn. 2:4; cf. 3:6). In fact, Jesus defines eternal life as "knowing God and Jesus Christ," which involves both faith in him and love for him (Jn. 17:3). By contrast, John makes it plain that the world "does not know" God (Jn. 17:25; 1 Jn. 3:1). See *NIDNTT-A, 107-10.*

Verb: ἐπιγινώσκω (*epiginōskō*), GK *2105* (S *1921*), 44x. *epiginōskō* can mean "to know, perceive, recognize, understand."

epiginōskō can have just the basic meaning "to know" and as such is synonymous with *ginōskō* ("to know," GK 1182), insofar as *ginōskō* is often used for a general, basic, or earthly knowledge (2 Tim. 1:18; 3:1). The uses of *epiginōskō* in Mk. 6:33, 54; Lk. 23:7; Acts 22:24; 23:28; 28:1 refer to merely recognizing someone or finding out some information.

There are other places, however, where *epiginōskō* conveys a deeper sense of knowing as suggested by the prefix *epi-* (and therefore is different from *ginōskō*). However, it is the context that confirms *epiginōskō* is used with this deeper sense of knowing rather than merely being assumed. When Jesus tells the paralytic his sins are forgiven, he "perceives" that the scribes are thinking he has blasphemed; he knows their thoughts (Mk. 2:8). Jesus also proclaims that false prophets "will be recognized" by the fruit they produce (7:16, 20), which involves spiritual perception. This sort of knowledge is implied in Jesus' reference to the intimate and exclusive knowledge between the Son and the Father—"no one *knows* the Son except the Father, and no one *knows* the Father except the Son" (Mt. 11:27). When the woman with the issue of blood is healed, Jesus "realizes" that power has gone out from him (Mk. 5:30). In his teaching on John the Baptist, Jesus proclaims that Elijah has already come, but the people have not "recognized" John for who he truly is (Mt. 17:12). In the Emmaus story, the disciples are prevented from "recognizing" Jesus until the moment he breaks the bread (Lk. 24:16, 31).

In the NT letters, *epiginōskō* is often used for what people should understand or realize. Unbelievers should be able to "understand" God's righteous decree that sinners deserve death (Rom. 1:32). Believers will "fully know" at the return of Jesus (1 Cor. 13:12), and believers also should be able to "*understand* God's grace in all its truth" (Col. 1:6). Peter refers to knowing the way of righteousness (2 Pet. 2:21). See *NIDNTT-A, 107-10.*

Verb: ἐπίσταμαι (*epistamai*), GK *2179* (S *1987*), 14x. In classical Gk., *epistamai* often refers to knowing on the basis of either observation or inner awareness. In the NT, this word seems to be used in a more general sense for an awareness of a situation. This usage is most prominent in Acts. For example, Demetrius, in addressing the craftsmen who helped build shrines to Artemis, claims that they "know" it is a profitable business (Acts 19:25). Apollos is described as only "knowing" (i.e., being aware) about John's baptism. Peter refers to elements either in Jewish tradition or in

Christian ministry that people are well aware of (Acts 10:28; 15:7). Paul's defenses of his ministry to the Gentiles before the elders of the Ephesian church (Acts 20:18), before the crowd at Jerusalem (22:19), before Felix (24:10), and before Festus and Agrippa (26:26) all make use of this term as awareness.

There are at least two instances in which *epistamai* refers to a lack of knowledge about the future (Heb. 11:8; Jas. 4:14). This verb is also used to clarify or expand the meaning of *oida* (another Gk. word for "know"). In Peter's denial, he claims that he knows nothing about what those who accuse him of being with Jesus are talking about (Mk. 14:68; cf. 1 Tim. 6:4; Jude 10). Thus, *epistamai* can refer to a level of understanding beyond mere intellectual awareness, but this is not always the case. See *NIDNTT-A*, 199.

Verb: οἶδα (*oida*), GK *3857* (S *1492*), 318. *oida* is the most common word for "know, understand" in the NT. There is little difference between *ginōskō* (GK *1182*) and *oida* in NT usage as they are often used synonymously and merely reflect the speaker's preference for one word rather than the other (e.g., Mt. 16:3 compared to Lk. 12:56).

oida can mean simply "to know," such as when Jesus "drove out many demons, but he would not let the demons speak because they *knew* who he was" (Mk. 1:34). It can indicate a deeper awareness of someone or something, as when Peter denies knowing Jesus at his trial (Mt. 26:72). It can carry the nuance of knowing in the sense of having ability: "If anyone does not *know* how to manage his own family, how can he take care of God's church?" (1 Tim. 3:5). *oida* can also mean to come to know something in the sense of recognizing or experiencing something: "If you give thanks with your spirit, how can anyone in the position of an outsider say 'Amen' to your thanksgiving when he does not *know* what you are saying?" (1 Cor. 14:16). See *NIDNTT-A*, 402.

KNOWLEDGE

Old Testament

Noun: דַּעַת (*daʿat*), GK 1981 (S 1847), 88x. Derived from the verb *yādaʿ* (GK 3359, "to know"), *daʿat* means "knowledge" in all spheres of life. (1) Its first occurrence is in Gen. 2:9, 17, in which Adam and Eve are prohibited from eating of "the tree of the *knowledge* of good and evil." This first mention of *daʿat* in the Bible pertains to moral knowledge. Traditionally, this tree has been understood as a revelation of the clear distinction between good and evil, which the first pair would have known either through their obedience or their disobedience.

(2) Our word, however, describes *"knowledge"* in the many spheres of human existence. Thus, *daʿat* is used of the technical "abilities" or "skills" of the craftsmen who constructed the tabernacle and temple (Exod. 31:3; 35:31; 1 Ki. 7:14). It may also describe "knowledge" in general (Job 34:35; 35:16; Dan. 1:4). Manslaughter is identified as being done "unintentionally" (i.e., "without *knowledge*"; Deut. 4:42; 19:4; Jos. 20:3, 5, "unawares," "ignorantly," "unwittingly," KJV). *daʿat* also denotes common sense, or knowledge derived from obvious, observable facts. For instance, Isaiah mocks the idolator who lacks "knowledge," for from the same piece of wood he builds a fire to cook his food, and fashions an idol to worship (Isa. 44:19, cf. Jer. 10:14; 51:17). This term also describes knowledge gained through learning, for a teacher imparts knowledge to students (Eccl. 12:9), and it was the responsibility of the priests in Israel to give knowledge to the people (Mal. 2:7).

(3) Our knowledge of God results from God's own self-revelation. The creation itself displays knowledge of God's existence and power (Ps. 19:1–2; cf. Rom. 1:20). Moreover, he gives knowledge of himself to individuals through visions (Num. 24:16), through his commandments (Ps. 119:66), and by his Spirit (Isa. 11:2). Having sovereignly chosen Israel as his people (Deut. 10:15; Amos 3:2), God

reveals himself to them in the context of a covenant relationship. Israel's knowledge of God is therefore more than a cognitive exercise. Israel is to have a knowledge of God (note the use of *yādaʿ* "to know" describing the intimate relationship of marriage) manifested through her covenant faithfulness to him, and when she acts in disobedience, she has failed to "acknowledge" him as she should (Hos. 4:1, 6; 6:6). Her refusal to act in faithfulness to the covenant results in her exile (Isa. 5:13, "for lack of *understanding*," NIV; "because they have no *knowledge*," KJV).

God is the only one who has all knowledge, and no one is able to teach him anything (Job 21:22; Isa. 40:14; Ps. 94:10; 139:6, 17–18). He is therefore the true source of all knowledge, a storehouse of wisdom and understanding to those who fear him (Isa. 33:6). False teachers and prophets claim to give knowledge, but they actually dispense nonsense (Isa. 44:25; 47:10). Those who truly know God defend "the cause of the poor and needy" (Jer. 22:16).

(4) As one would expect, *daʿat* is particularly emphasized in the wisdom literature (Job, 10x; Prov., 39x; Eccl., 7x). Here, *daʿat* is used as a close synonym to a number of other words, including *ḥākma=*, "wisdom" (GK 2683); *mûsār*, "discipline" (GK 4592); *tᵉbûnâ*, "understanding" (GK 9312); *ʿārmâ*, "prudence" (GK 6893); and *mᵉzimâ*, "discretion" (GK 4659). It is impossible to give distinct meanings to each of these terms, for together they describe the wise person in contrast to the fool. It is important, however, to note that in the wisdom literature, true knowledge is the possession of those who "fear the Lord" (i.e., those who obey him, Deut. 6:2; 10:12; Ps. 128:1). Indeed, "the fear of the LORD is the beginning of knowledge" (Prov. 1:7) and procures "the knowledge of the Holy One" (9:10). It is in this relationship of obedience to God that one gains knowledge from him (2:5–6; cf. 1:29; Eccl. 2:26), and such knowledge, which is of highest value (Prov. 20:15), brings honor (14:18), strength (24:4–5), success (22:12), and protection (Eccl. 7:12). Those who possess such knowledge are careful with their words (Prov. 5:2; 10:14; 12:23; 15:2, 7; 17:27; cf. Jas. 3:2). They constantly seek to acquire more knowledge (Prov. 15:14; 18:15; 22:17), and learn even from being corrected or rebuked (12:1; 19:25; 21:11). See *NIDOTTE,* 2:409–14.

New Testament

Noun: γνῶσις (*gnōsis*), GK *1194* (S *1108*), 29x. *gnōsis* means "knowledge," and it has a rich meaning in the NT. All but six of its occurrences are in the letters of Paul (though see also *ginōskō*, "to know," for more on the biblical message about this word group).

Knowledge begins with God, and that knowledge contains deep riches (Rom. 11:33). Moreover, in Jesus, God's Son, "are hidden all the treasures of wisdom and knowledge" (Col. 2:3). Paul considers "the surpassing greatness of *knowing* Christ Jesus" as the most important thing in the world to him (Phil. 3:8). And God uses us to impart that knowledge to others as we spread his Word abroad (2 Cor. 2:14).

Furthermore, God wants us to "grow in the grace and knowledge of our Lord and Savior Jesus Christ" (2 Pet. 3:18; cf. 1:5–6). To this end the Spirit gives, as one of his gifts, the gift of "knowledge" (1 Cor. 12:8; 13:2; 14:6). That knowledge is for the mature Christians to instruct others so that they too may grow (Rom. 15:14). Unfortunately, however, Christians sometimes use this knowledge to fill themselves with pride and even look down on those who have not sufficiently grown in their faith and knowledge (1 Cor. 8:1, 7, 10–11).

As the NT church developed, this attachment to *gnōsis* became even more of a problem, so much so that Paul refers to "the opposing ideas of what is falsely called *knowledge*" (1 Tim. 6:20). This appears to have been the beginning of the Christian heresy known as Gnosticism, in which people began to center their faith not on Christ as the Savior of all but on a secret body of knowledge that excluded all but a small inner circle of initiated Christians. See *NIDNTT-A, 107-10.*

Noun: ἐπίγνωσις (*epignōsis*), GK *2106* (S *1922*), 20x. *epignōsis* means "knowledge, understanding." Paul links *epignōsis* with faith when he proclaims that "through the law comes *knowledge* of sin" (Rom. 3:20), that the zeal of the Jewish leaders is not based on "knowledge" (10:2), and that God hands people over to their sins because they do not have a "*knowledge* of God" (1:28). He also prays that the love of his readers may abound "in *knowledge* and depth of insight" (Phil. 1:9) and that they will have "a full understanding" of what they have in Christ (Phlm. 6). In all of these cases, the knowledge spoken of has a close connection to true faith; it does not refer to mere intellectual assent.

In the some of the later NT writings, *epignōsis* appears to function in a more technical way as Christian knowledge or saving knowledge. In the pastoral letters, Paul frequently refers to the "*knowledge* of the truth" (1 Tim. 2:4; 2 Tim. 2:25; 3:7; Tit. 1:6), which is contrasted with another form of so-called knowledge taught by the false teachers in Ephesus. Paul claims that God desires "all men to be saved and to come to a *knowledge* of the truth" (1 Tim. 2:4), and links this knowledge of the truth to repentance (2 Tim. 2:25).

Likewise, Peter ties *epignōsis* to a full knowledge of Jesus Christ and of God (2 Pet. 1:2, 8; 2:20). This noun is also used in Hebrews to refer to "*knowledge* of the truth" (10:26). See *NIDNTT-A, 107-10.*

KNOWN

New Testament

Adjective: γνωστός (*gnōstos*), GK *1196* (S *1110*), 15x. *gnōstos* means "known" or "able to be know," i.e., "intelligible." "Known" people can be considered "friends."

The most common meaning of *gnōstos* is something that is "known." The Roman Jews want to hear from Paul, "for we *know* [lit.., it is *known* by us] that people everywhere are talking against this sect" (Acts 28:22; cf. also 1:19; 4:10; 9:42; 19:17). It can also mean "notable" (KJV) or "outstanding" (NIV, 4:16). Used as a noun it can mean "friend." At the cross, "Jesus' *friends*, including the women who followed him from Galilee, stood at a distance watching" (Lk. 23:49, NLT; cf. also 2:44; Jn. 18:15–16).

In its only use outside the gospels and Acts, *gnōstos* carries the idea of "knowable": "What may be *known* about God" (NIV) has been made plain by God in the things he has created (Rom. 1:19). See *NIDNTT-A*, 107-10.

Adjective: φανερός (*phaneros*), GK *5745* (S *5318*), 18x. *phaneros* means "obvious, known, plain." See *obvious*.

LABOR

Old Testament

Noun: עֲבוֹדָה (*ʿᵃbôdâ*), GK 6275 (S 5656), 145x. In the early use of *ʿᵃbôdâ* in the Pentateuch, it describes the physical labor of Jacob to Laban as the bride price, but there are other uses in the OT as well. See *work*.

New Testament

Noun: κόπος (*kopos*), GK *3160* (S *2873*), 18x.

Verb: κοπιάω (*kopiaō*), GK *3159* (S *2872*), 23x. In the NT, the *kopos* word group is used in three main ways: it refers to hard manual labor (like the farmer in 2 Tim. 2:6) or to working to physically exhaustion (cf. Jn. 4:6); Paul often uses it to refer to Christian ministry; and with the verb *parechō* ("to offer, supply, give"), it means "to trouble or bother" someone (i. e., giving someone a "hard" time).

(1) In Jesus' teaching on the lilies of the field, he notes that they do not toil (Mt. 6:28; Lk. 12:27). The disciples are exhausted from fishing all night (Lk. 5:5). Manual labor can earn money to be given to those in poverty (Eph. 4:28). Paul works hard to earn a living so as not to burden any of the churches to whom he ministers (Acts 20:35; 1 Cor. 4:12; 1 Thess. 2:9; 2 Thess. 3:8).

(2) The second usage yields fruitful lessons for practical ministry. Jesus combines

the sense of manual labor with a reference to ministry by his metaphor of reaping a harvest (Jn. 4:38). The Ephesian church has remained faithful in working for Christ and has not "wearied" despite hardships borne for his sake (Rev. 2:2–3).

Paul refers to the difficult and exhausting work of ministry performed by others as well as by himself. In Rom. 16:6, 12, Paul commends four women (Mary, Tryphaena, Tryphosa, and Persis) who "*worked very hard* in the Lord." After commending the Thessalonians for their "*labor* of love" (1 Thess. 1:3), he admonishes them to respect those who "*work hard* among them" (5:12). He tells Timothy that those "whose *work* is preaching and teaching" are doubly worthy of honor (1 Tim. 5:17; cf. 1 Cor. 16:16). One of the hallmarks of Paul's Christian ministry was hard work to the point of physical exhaustion (2 Cor. 6:5), which he performed joyfully. Paul strove for godliness (1 Tim. 4:10) and worked harder than any who had been before him (1 Cor. 15:10; 2 Cor. 11:23).

(3) The third meaning Jesus uses in reference to the sinful woman who anointed him (Mt. 26:10; Mk. 14:6), and in his parables about the persistent widow who incessantly "troubles" the unjust judge (Lk. 18:5) and of the neighbor already in bed who does not wish to be "disturbed" (Lk. 11:7). Finally (and poignantly), Paul demands, "Let no one cause me *trouble*," since his body bore the marks of Jesus (Gal. 6:17).

(4) *kopos* carries theological meaning as an antonym for end-time hope; that is, God's people look forward to a time of rest, when their labors and earthly striving will cease (Rev. 14:13). Jesus calls to himself all those who are "*weary* and burdened," to whom he will give rest (Mt. 11:28). In the end, believers will receive an eternal reward for their toil carried out on behalf of God's kingdom. Paul expresses this thought in conjunction with the idea that his (and other Christians') labor for the Lord is not in vain (1 Cor. 3:8; 15:58; Gal. 4:11; Phil. 2:16; 1 Thess. 3:5). See *NIDNTT-A*, 313-14.

LABORER

New Testament

Noun: ἐργάτης (*ergatēs*), GK *2239* (S *2040*), 16x. This word refers to someone who does something, a "worker or laborer." See *worker*.

LACK

New Testament

Verb: ὑστερέω (*hystereō*), GK *5728* (S *5302*), 16x. *hystereo* conveys the idea of lagging behind or failing to attain a certain standard; thus, "to lack, fall short." Theologically, *hystereō* can describe the spiritual condition of the sinner in light of God's standard, as Paul writes: "For all have sinned and *fall short* of the glory of God" (Rom. 3:23). Regarding the goal of salvation, the author of Hebrews warns, "Therefore, since the promise of entering his rest still stands, let us be careful that none of you be found to have *fallen short* of it" (Heb. 4:1; cf. 12:15). The sense of lacking something is evident in the command of Jesus to the rich young ruler: "Jesus looked at him and loved him. 'One thing you *lack*,' he said. 'Go, sell everything you have and give to the poor, and you will have treasure in heaven. Then come, follow me'" (Mk. 10:21; cf. Mt. 19:20). Paul uses *hystereō* to contrast the difficulty of his ministry experience with the reality of his contentment in Christ and writes, "I have learned the secret of being content in any and every situation, whether well fed or hungry, whether living in plenty or in *want*" (Phil. 4:12b). See *NIDNTT-A*, 584-85.

LACK OF FAITH

New Testament

Noun: ἀπιστία (*apistia*), GK *602* (S *570*), 11x. *apistia* is a "lack of faith, unbelief," the negated form of the noun *pistia* ("belief, faith"). See *unbelief*.

LACKING

New Testament

Verb: ὑστέρημα (*hysterēma*) GK *5729* (S *5303*), 9x. *hysterēma* means "something that is lacking," either on a physical level or a spiritual level. Paul knows, for example, that the Christians in Jerusalem are going through difficult times, and that what they are lacking he hopes to supply from a collection of money taken from the Gentile churches (2 Cor. 8:14; 9:12). Paul is refreshed when visitors come from Corinth, since they fill him in on the details of what is going on in that city ("supply what is lacking," 1 Cor. 16:17). Paul writes to the Thessalonians because he wants to "supply what is lacking in [their] faith" (1 Thess. 3:10). Most challenging to interpreters is Col. 1:24, where Paul writes that through his suffering, he fills up "in my flesh what is still lacking in regard to Christ's afflictions"; whatever the precise nuance may be, Paul clearly sees that his sufferings are linked with the sufferings of Christ.

LAKE

New Testament

Noun: λίμνη (*limnē*), GK *3349* (S *3041*), 11x. *limnē* denotes a "lake, pond." It is typically a body of water smaller than that associated with *thalassa* (see *sea*). It is related to the word *limēn*, which is a harbor or haven. The concept may be that *limnē* describes bodies of water in which a boat is always close to land or, in other words, near a safe haven. In the NT only Luke and Revelation use this noun; other books appear not to distinguish between an inland lake and open sea. Luke uses *limnē* to describe Genessaret (5:1, 2), a body of water described as *thalassa* in Mt. 14:34 and Mk. 6:53. In Revelation *limnē* is used of the "lake of fire" in which Satan, the beast, and the false prophet will be thrown on the day of the Lord (Rev. 19:20; 20:10ff.). See *NIDNTT-A*, 338.

LAMB

Old Testament

Noun: כֶּבֶשׂ (*kebeś*), GK 3897 (S 3532), 107x. A *kebeś* is a young "lamb"; in most instances in the OT it is used as a sacrificial animal. The most common sheep in Israel are the fat-tailed Awassi. These sheep are a little over two feet tall at their shoulders and full-grown males weigh approximately 130–200 pounds.

(1) As to sacrificial contexts, Moses instructs that the Passover lamb (*śeh*, GK 8445) must be taken from a flock of *kebeś* (Exod. 12:3–5). Two of these "lambs" are to be offered on the altar every day, one in the morning and one in the evening (29:38–39; Num. 28:3–8). This is Israel's regular burnt offering, which makes the Tent of Meeting holy so that God can dwell among the people (Exod. 29:42–46). A *kebeś* can be offered as a sin offering (Lev. 5:6–7), which though unable to take away sins (Rom. 3:25; Heb. 10:4), nevertheless results in atonement and forgiveness (Lev. 5:6, 10). A *kebeś* can also be offered for purification (12:6–8). They are offered at the dedication of the altar (Num. 7:11, 15, 23) and in association with the various offerings of the seventh month (Num. 29).

Lambs are also offered in association with Solomon's ascension to the throne (1 Chr. 29:21–22), Hezekiah's restoration of worship at the temple (2 Chr. 29:20–21), Josiah's renewal of the covenant (34:31; 35:7), and Ezra's return from exile (Ezr. 8:35). In Ezekiel's visions of the eschatological temple, lambs are likewise offered (Ezek. 46:4).

(2) In nonsacrificial contexts, Job refers to the warmth that comes from the fleece of sheep (Job 31:20; cf. Prov. 27:26). Jeremiah likens himself to a lamb led to the slaughter as he speaks of those who are persecuting him (Jer. 11:19). Hosea likens God's people to a lamb in the Lord's pasture (Hos. 4:16). Isaiah uses the image of grazing lambs to depict the desolation of Judah—cultivated fields will become like a pasture for grazing animals (Isa. 5:17); when the shoot of Jesse ushers in the final days of peace, this prophet envisions that Òthe wolf will live with the *lamb*" (11:6). See *NIDOTTE*, 3:728.

Noun: צֹאן (*ṣōʾn*), GK 7366 (S 6629), 274x. Often translated "sheep, lambs, goats," *ṣōʾn* is commonly used to refer to flocks of sheep. It has both a literal and a metaphorical meaning in the OT. See *sheep*.

New Testament

Noun: ἀρνίον (*arnion*), GK *768* (S *721*), 30x. *arnion* refers to a "lamb" or young "sheep." All uses of this word except for Jn. 21:15, where Jesus refers to his followers as "lambs," are in Revelation. In Rev. 13:11, the beast coming out of the sea has "two horns like a lamb." All other uses of *arnion* in this book refer metaphorically to Jesus. Given the multiple references to the "blood of the Lamb" (e.g., 7:14; 12:11) and the "Lamb who was slain" (e.g., 5:12; 13:8), the author appears to be drawing on the OT imagery of sacrifice.

In several places, the use of *arnion* to refer to Jesus creates strikingly paradoxical results. In Rev. 5:5–6, the author is told to behold "the Lion of the tribe of Judah"; when John does so, he sees "a *Lamb*, looking as if it had been slain." Further striking uses of the word include references to the "wrath of the Lamb" (6:16) and the Lamb who is a shepherd (7:17). In several places in this book, praises are sung to this worthy Lamb (5:12; 12:11; 15:3). See *NIDNTT-A*, 41.

LAME

New Testament

Adjective: παραλυτικός (*paralytikos*), GK *4166* (S *3885*), 10x. *paralytikos* is an adjective that denotes someone who is "lame" or "paralytic." See *paralytic*.

Adjective: χωλός (*chōlos*), GK *6000* (S *5560*), 14x. *chōlos* is someone who is "lame" (Mt. 11:5; 15:30, 31; 21:14; Lk. 7:22; 14:13, 21; Jn. 5:3; Acts 14:8; Heb. 12:13) or "crippled" (Mt. 18:8; Mk. 9:45; Acts 3:2; 8:7), either as a birth defect (Acts 14:8) or by some other means.

Christ shows great compassion to those afflicted by disease and maladies of various degrees. It is important to note that he never healed anyone as a means of bringing glory to himself. To the contrary, when Jesus healed the lame and crippled, people praised God (see Mt. 15:31; Acts 8:7). Such is also the case when the residents of Lystra saw a man "*lame* from birth" healed by Paul (Acts 14:8–11). Likewise, Jesus did not heal people in order to draw the praise of religious leaders or the religious community. In fact, everywhere Jesus went, he drew criticism from the religious establishment (Mt. 21:14).

In NT times the lame or crippled were typically reduced to pleading for charity (see Acts 3:2–10); there were no government programs for the handicapped. Jesus gives the responsibility to care for such people to his followers. He makes it clear that the compassion they demonstrate should never be carried out with reciprocity in mind, but rather so that their reward may be realized in eternity. When hosting a banquet, we should not invites friends and family; rather, "invite the poor, the crippled, the *lame*, the blind, and you will be blessed. Although they cannot repay you, you will be repaid at the resurrection of the righteous" (Lk. 14:12–14).

Heb. 12:13 appears to use a lameness as a figure of speech for those who are not yet able to spiritually walk on their own. See *NIDNTT-A*, 615-16.*

LAMP, LAMPSTAND

New Testament

Noun: λύχνος (*lychnos*), GK *3394* (S *3088*), 14x

Noun: λυχνία (*lychnia*), GK *3393* (S *3087*), 12x. These two words are used for a lamp or a light (*lychnos*) and the implement (*lychnia*) on which the lamp is placed to illuminate its surroundings. Jesus says that people do not "light a lamp and put it under a basket, but on the lampstand, and it gives light to all who are in the house" (Mt. 5:15). *lychnos* and *lychnia* usually describe the light and witness of the gospel and often stand in contrast to darkness, which represents sin, evil, and the world of Satan.

A person's association with the light of a lamp keeps him in good spiritual health. Jesus tells us to be ready and keep our lamps lit, so as not to be caught in darkness (Lk. 12:35; cf. also Mt. 6:22).

The lamp also represents the witness of

the gospel in the midst of a dark world. Jesus calls John the Baptist "a burning and shining lamp" (Jn. 5:35). We are enjoined to pay attention to the words of the prophets, "as to a lamp shining in a dark place" (2 Pet. 1:19). In the new Jerusalem, Jesus himself will be the lamp that dispels the darkness for God's people (Rev. 21:23; 22:5).

In Revelation, the seven churches are symbolically called "the seven lampstands" (Rev. 1:20; also 2:1), and the two witnesses are called "the two lampstands" (11:4). These designations point back to Zech. 4, where the "lampstand" stands for the witnessing presence of God's Spirit within Israel. Now the Spirit-empowered church, rather than Israel, is the lampstand. Jesus threatens to remove the lampstand, or the witness, from the church at Ephesus unless they repent (Rev. 2:5); i.e., it will be as if their light is hidden under a basket rather than placed on the lampstand (see Mt. 5:15). See *NIDNTT-A*, 346.

LAND

Old Testament

Noun: אֶרֶץ (*ʾereṣ*), GK 824 (S 776), 2505x. *ʾereṣ* occurs frequently throughout the OT and has two primary meanings: (a) the earth or land in general; and (b) the land of Israel in particular.

(1) From Gen. 1:1 on, *ʾereṣ* is often combined with heaven to refer to all of God's creation (cf. the phrase "heaven and earth"). In a similar way, heaven and *ʾereṣ* can be contrasted, with the heavens as God's abode and the earth as humanity's dwelling (Ps. 115:16). In fact, God has put humanity on the *ʾereṣ* to be its stewards (Gen. 2:15). Related to this, we find that *ʾereṣ* can refer not only to the physical globe but also to all the inhabitants of the earth. The OT offers an eschatological hope that God's salvation and glory will eventually cover the whole earth (Ps. 22:27; Isa. 52:10; 62:11; Jer. 16:19).

(2) The significance of *ʾereṣ* in the OT is highlighted in that the "land" of Israel is one of the most important elements in God's covenant with his people. God promises (Gen. 12:7; 15:18–21) and gives (Exod. 6:8; 34:10–11; Deut. 1:8) the *ʾereṣ* to his chosen ones. He also warns them of their future rejection and tells them that they will be removed—even vomited (Lev. 18:24)—from the *ʾereṣ* if they are disobedient and unfaithful to their covenant with him (Lev. 26:32–39; Deut. 28:63). When the Israelites are exiled and lose their land, this loss symbolizes the broken covenant between God and Israel. However, God's grace is multiplied in that even in the midst of this judgment, he again promises the *ʾereṣ* to a remnant of his people (Lev. 26:40–45; Deut. 30:1–4; Jer. 32:36–44; Amos 9:14–15). The NT understands this promise as fulfilled in Jesus Christ and his body, the church. See *NIDOTTE*, 1:518-24.

Noun: אֲדָמָה (*ʾadāmâ*), GK 141 (S 127), 222x. *ʾadāmâ* ("land, ground") does not occur nearly as frequently as the other word for "land" (*ʾereṣ*), but it often has the same meaning. *ʾadāmâ* is used in reference to the covenant promises and warnings about the earth (Exod. 20:12; Deut. 4:40; 2 Ki. 17:23; Amos 7:11, 17), and at times, it designates the inhabited world (Ezek. 38:20; Isa. 24:21). But *ʾadāmâ* communicates some nuances that are not found in *ʾereṣ*. *ʾadāmâ* refers to various kinds of dirt: dust (1 Sam. 4:12), clay (1 Ki. 7:46), and the matter used to form mankind and the animals (Gen. 2:7, 19; note the close connection with the name of man, Adam). Also, *ʾadāmâ* can mean cultivatable land in particular as compared to desert or barren lands (Gen. 2:5; Zech. 13:5). It is the *ʾadāmâ* that is cursed by God after the fall (Gen. 3:17). Thus, in this earthly realm, all of humanity's labor—not only agricultural—is now subjected to difficulty and futility. See *NIDOTTE*, 1:269-74.

Noun: שָׂדֶה (*śādeh*), GK 8441 (S 7704), 329x. The basic meaning of *śādeh* is a field. Sometimes it is used to indicate the land or territory belonging to a certain nation or tribe, such as the "*land* of Moab" (lit., "fields of Moab," Ruth 1:1; cf. 1 Sam. 6:1). See *field*.

New Testament

Verb: κατέρχομαι (*katerchomai*), GK *2982* (S *2718*), 16x. *katerchomai* is a nautical technical term meaning "to land," in the sense of arriving at a seaport. Paul "*lands* at Caesarea" (Acts 18:22; cf. 21:3, 27:5). *katerchomai* also means "to come down, go down" (see *come down*).

Noun: γῆ (*gē*), GK *1178* (S *1093*), 250x. *gē* is the standard word for "earth, land, soil" in the NT. It occurs especially in the gospels, Acts, and Revelation. See *earth*.

Noun: χώρα (*chōra*), GK *6001* (S *5561*), 28x. The basic sense of *chōra* is an area or space; in the NT it refers to large areas, such as a cultivated field, a region, or a country. See *country*.

LANDOWNER

New Testament

Noun: οἰκοδεσπότης (*oikodespotēs*), GK *3867* (S *3617*), 12x. *oikodespotēs* means the "master, owner of a house, landowner." See *owner*.

LANGUAGE

Old Testament

Noun: לָשׁוֹן (*lāšôn*), GK 4383 (S 3956), 117x. *lāšôn* literally means "tongue," the physical organ of speech or eating/drinking (Jdg. 7:5; Lam. 4:4). By extension, it can refer to that which proceeds from the mouth, namely, a person's *language* (Gen. 10:5; Deut. 28:49; Est. 1:22) or *speech* (Ps. 55:9 NIV). See *tongue*.

Noun: שָׂפָה (*śāpâ*) GK 8557 (S 8193), 178x. *śāpâ* often denotes the physical "lip(s)" of a person (Num. 30:7, 13; Song 4:3, 11; 5:13), but it can also mean that which proceeds from the lips, such as a person's *language* (Gen. 11:1a, 6–7, 9; Ps. 81:5; Isa. 19:18). See *lip*.

New Testament

Noun: γλῶσσα (*glōssa*), GK *1185* (S *1100*), 50x. *glōssa* means the physical "tongue," but it can also mean "language." See *tongue*.

Noun: φωνή (*phōnē*), GK *5889* (S *5456*), 139x. *phōnē* signifies at least three ideas in the NT depending on context: "sound, voice, language." See *sound*.

LARGE

Old Testament

Adjective: גָּדוֹל (*gādôl*), GK 1524 (S 1419), 527x. *gādôl* means "great, large." See *great*.

New Testament

Adverb: ἱκανός (*hikanos*), GK *2653* (S *2425*), 39x. *hikanos* conveys the idea that something is adequate or large enough in its quantity or quality and may best be translated "sufficient, deserve, adequate." See *sufficient*.

Adjective: μέγας (*megas*), GK *3489* (S *3173*), 243x. *megas* means "great, loud, large" and is found throughout the NT. See *great*.

Adjective: πολύς (*polys*), GK *4498* (S *4118*, *4119*, *4183*), 416x. *polys* is used to designate a large quantity ("many") or size ("great/large"). See *many*.

LASCIVIOUS

New Testament

Noun: ἀσέλγεια (*aselgeia*), GK 816 (S 766), 10x. *aselgeia* means "debauchery, lewdness, sensuality." See *debauchery*.

LAST

Old Testament

Adjective: אַחֲרוֹן (*ʾaḥarôn*), GK 340 (S 314), 51x. *ʾaḥarôn* denotes the sequential placement of objects, persons, events, or periods of time and may be translated as "last" or "latter." The term frequently occurs in the historical books in the phrase "first and *last*" to convey the totality or duration of time covered during the events described (e.g., 2 Chr. 9:29; 12:15; 16:11). It also conveys the idea of "west, western" (cf. Deut. 11:24; 34:2). Theologically, this same phrase occurs in Isaiah, where God uses it to communicate the totality of his rule over all he has created: "I, the LORD—with the first of them and with the *last*—I am he" (Isa. 41:4; 44:6; 48:12). This same reality is expressed in Rev. 22:13: "I am the Alpha and the Omega, the First and the *Last*, the Beginning and the End" (see also 1:8). See *NIDOTTE*, 1:360-61.

New Testament

Adjective: ἔσχατος (*eschatos*), GK *2274*

(S *2078*), 52x. Although *eschatos* is sometimes used in the NT in a spatial sense ("the *ends* of the earth," Acts 1:8; 13:47) or in a quantitative sense (e.g., "the *last* penny," Mt. 5:26; Lk. 12:59; "the *last* seat," Lk. 14:9–10; "the *end* of the procession," 1 Cor. 4:9), it is most commonly used to refer to time. In this sense *eschatos* often designates the final item in a series of actions or events, such as the last day of the Feast of Tabernacles (Jn. 7:37).

In theological contexts *eschatos* is often used to designate the future of God's kingdom that is fully realized in Jesus' second coming, the resurrection from the dead, and his just judgment of humankind. Thus, theologians use the term "eschatology" to designate the study of "the last times." In this sense *eschatos* can refer specifically to Jesus' return on "the last day" or more generally to the period of time between his first and second coming, "Long ago, at many times and in many ways, God spoke to our fathers by the prophets, but in these *last* days he has spoken to us by his Son" (Heb. 1:2, ESV). With the coming of the Holy Spirit, Peter recognizes the prophetic fulfillment of Joel 2:28–32: "in the *last* days it shall be, God declares, that I will pour out my Spirit on all flesh."

Paul also reminds Timothy that the "last days" (i.e., the period before Christ's second coming) will be marked by many difficult trials (2 Tim. 3.1–9; cf. 2 Pet. 3:3; 1 Jn. 1:18; Jude 18). On the "last day," however, Jesus, the "*last* Adam" (1 Cor. 15:45), will raise up his people from the dead (Jn. 6:39–40, 44, 54), thus destroying death (1 Cor. 15:26); those who have rejected Jesus will be condemned (Jn. 12:48). This reality is why Jesus has the authority to claim, as God did in Isa. 1:17; 2:8; 22:13, that he is "the first and the *last*" (Rev. 1:17; 2:8; 22:13). See *NIDNTT-A*, 211-12.

LATER

New Testament

Adjective: ὕστερος (*hysteros*), GK *5731* (S *5305*, *5306*), 12x. *hysteros* means "later, afterward," though it is often used as an adverb meaning "finally." It occurs primarily in a comparative or superlative sense.

(1) In the comparative it denotes a time subsequent to a previous point in time (Mt. 25:11; Mk 16:14; Jn. 13:26; Heb. 12:11). Matthew, for example, makes it clear that Jesus is tempted by Satan only *after* he has fasted in the desert for forty days and nights (Mt. 4:2), thus highlighting the intensity of Satan's first temptation to turn the stones into loaves of bread.

(2) In the superlative, *hysteros* states a final occurrence in a series of events and is thus most often translated "finally" (Mt. 21:37; 22:27; 26:60; Lk. 20:32; probably 1 Tim. 4.1). In the parable of the tenants (Mt. 21:33–46), for example, the owner (God) of the vineyard (Israel) sends several groups of servants (the prophets) to collect his fruit (God's possession). After each group has been killed by the wicked tenants, the owner *finally* sends his Son (Jesus), but the tenants kill even him. Here the superlative is used to emphasize the climactic nature of God's sending his own Son. This parables stirs up the anger of religious leaders (Mt. 21:45–46). See *NIDNTT-A*, 584-85.

LAW

Old Testament

Noun: תּוֹרָה (*tôrâ*), GK 9368 (S 8451), 223x. Generally rendered "law, regulation, instruction, teaching," *tôrâ* was originally used to describe the instructions for daily conduct that God gave his people; eventually other meanings developed for this word. See also *teaching*.

(1) In Exod. through Deut., *tôrâ* covers a wide spectrum of regulations: from specific regulations about sacrifices (Lev. 6:9), food laws (11:46), skin conditions (14:32), etc., to a summary word for the entire revelation that Moses received on Mount Sinai ("the Book of the Law," Deut. 28:61; cf. Jos. 8:31). These laws regulate every aspect of Israelite life, from food to offerings to social interactions to warfare. It is impossible to divide these neatly into categories such as ceremonial, civil, and

moral, since the OT does not make such distinctions and various types of laws are all intertwined. All of Israelite life is religiously oriented; the Lord is God of every aspect of life and has something to say about every human activity.

(2) Several psalms extol the beauty of God's law (e.g., Ps. 1; 19; 119). God's law is something to love, since it comes from a loving God. True Israelites found the law liberating, not confining. Any negative statements relative to the law in the OT concern abuses of it, not the law itself. On *tôrâ* as a gracious gift from God, see Deut. 4:1–8.

(3) In Ps. 78:1, the word *tôrâ* covers not only the commands, regulations, and instructions of the Lord but also the historical review of Israel's past—that is, the narrative portions of the Pentateuch. Ezra's reading of the *tôrâ* most likely involved the entire Pentateuch (Neh. 8:3). From understanding God's past actions with and for his people, we learn his will for our own lives today. See *NIDOTTE* 4:893-98.

New Testament

Noun: νόμος (*nomos*), GK *3795* (S *3551*), 194x. *nomos* means "law." This word has a variety of nuances in the NT.

(1). *nomos* can refer to the first five books of the OT—that is, the Torah or the Pentateuch. This is its meaning in the phrase "the Law and the Prophets" (Mt. 5:17; Jn. 1:17; Rom. 3:21). But by extension, it sometimes refers to the entire OT revelation (see Jn. 10:34, where Jesus quotes Ps. 82:6 as part of "the law"; cf. also Rom. 3:19; 1 Cor. 14:21).

(2) *nomos* can also refer specifically to the legal parts of the OT, the composite body of rules, regulations, and commands God gave to his people (Jn. 7:19; Acts 15:5). Keeping the laws revealed by God, however, is not a pathway to being saved (Acts 15:1, 5); we are saved by grace, not by works (Eph. 2:8–10). Paul wrote especially Romans and Galatians because he knew of people who taught that a person could be justified by keeping the law (Rom. 3:28; Gal. 2:16).

(3) Even though the law cannot save us, the law itself is still good, because it has come from God (Rom. 7:7–12; 1 Tim. 1:8). But in our weakened human condition, rather than enlightening us on how to serve God, the law often ends up only revealing our sin (Rom. 3:20). In fact, the law can even increase our sin because of our innate human tendency to rebel against God (Rom. 5:20). This is why Paul can call it "the *law* of sin and death" (Rom. 8:2).

(4) Jesus himself perfectly kept the law and so was sinless (Heb. 4:15; 1 Pet. 2:22). His righteousness is imputed to us by faith when we believe (Rom. 3:22; 2 Cor. 5:21), so that "the righteous requirements of the law [are] fully met in us" (Rom. 8:4; see *righteous, righteousness*). Through his accursed death on the cross he paid the wages for human sin—death (Rom. 6:23; Gal. 3:13)—so that we can now live freely in newness of life.

(5) Even though we do not have to keep God's law in order to be saved, true believers attempt, to the best of their ability with the help of the Holy Spirit, to obey the law. This is the message of James, that faith without works (of the law) is dead (Jas. 2:14–26). But this is also the message of Paul, who asks: "Shall we sin because we are not under *law* but under grace? By no means!" (Rom. 6:15). See *NIDNTT-A*, 389-93.

LAWFUL

New Testament

Verb: ἔξεστι (*exesti*), GK *2003* (S *1832*), 31x. *exesti* is an impersonal verb that means "it is lawful, it is permitted." The term occurs primarily in the Gospels and Acts (26 of 31 times) to signify what is right, what is permitted, or what is proper. The term figures prominently in the disputes between Jesus and the Jewish religious authorities as to what is and is not in keeping with Jewish law (Mt. 12:2, 4, 10, 12; 19:3; 22:17; Mk. 2:24, 26; Lk. 6:2, 4; Jn. 5:10). *exesti* is also used with respect to Roman law (Acts 16:21; 22:25). Paul quotes *exesti* as a slogan of libertarian members of the Corinthian church (1 Cor. 6:12; 10:23). This verb can also denote the idea of something being within the range of possibility (Acts 2:29). See *NIDNTT-A*, 191-92.

LAWLESS, LAWLESSNESS

New Testament

Noun: ἀνομία (*anomia*), GK *490* (S *458*), 15x. *anomia means lawlessness, a violation of law.* See *wicked.*

Adjective: ἄνομος (*anomos*), GK *491* (S *459*), 9x. Literally both words mean "absence of law."

(1) *anomia* is the opposite of righteousness (2 Cor. 6:14; 2 Pet. 2:8; cf. 1 Tim. 1:9), and God hates it (Heb. 1:9). Jesus, the sinless Son of God, was put to death by "lawless men" (Acts 2:23); from this we learn that we can expect that those who dedicate their lives to wickedness will have no use for those who try to live holy lives. Toward the end of human history, lawlessness will increase (Mt. 24:12) and the antichrist, "the lawless one," will be revealed (2 Thess. 2:3, 7).

(2) If it were not for God's grace, our lives would be filled with increasing lawlessness (Rom. 6:19; cf. Mt. 23:28). The wicked will not enter God's eternal kingdom (Mt. 7:23; 13:41). But the blessed news of the Bible is that God promises to forgive the wicked things we do (Rom. 4:7) and to remember them no more (Heb. 10:17). This he does through the redemptive power of Jesus Christ (Tit. 2:14).

(3) Paul uses *anomos* four times in 1 Cor. 9:21 to refer to Gentiles (those to whom God had not revealed his law and hence are "without the law"); in Paul's ministry to them, he did not insist they had to keep the OT law in order to be saved. See *NIDNTT-A*, 389-93.

LAWSUIT

Old Testament

Noun: רִיב (*rîb*), GK 8190 (S 7379), 62x. *rîb* (related to the verb *rîb*, usually translated "contend") indicates an argument or conflict with another individual. Among the legal codes in the OT, *rîb* may be translated "lawsuit" (e.g., Exod. 23:2; Deut. 17:8; cf. 2 Sam. 15:1–6). See *case.*

LAY

See *put; put on.*

LAY DOWN

New Testament

Verb: τίθημι (*tithēmi*), GK *5502* (S *5087*), 100x. The basic meaning of *tithēmi* is "to put, lay something down." Jesus, for example, lay down his life. See *put.*

LAY ON

New Testament

Verb: ἐπιβάλλω (*epiballō*), GK *2095* (S *1911*), 18x. *epiballō* means "to lay on, arrest, sew on." The most common use of the verb refers to "laying on hands" in the sense of "arresting" or "seizing" (Mt. 26:50; Mk. 14:46; Lk. 20:19; 21:12; Jn. 7:30, 44; Acts 4:3; 5:18; 12:1; 21:27). It is also used in the sense "laying down" cloaks (Mk. 11:7) and "laying on a restraint" (1 Cor. 7:35). A derived meaning is in Jesus' words: "No one *sews* [*lays on*] a piece of unshrunk cloth on an old garment" (Mt. 9:16; cf. Lk. 5:36). *epiballō* can also mean "break over or down" (see *break over, down*).

LAY WASTE

Old Testament

Verb: שָׁמֵם (*šāmēm*), GK 9037 (S 8074), 92x. The verb *šāmēm* is used in two distinct but related ways. It can mean "to be desolate, deserted, lay waste" or it can point to the response to such desolation and mean "to shudder, be horrified, be appalled." Two-thirds of the instances of *šāmēm* occur in prophetic passages. It most often means either causing or suffering destruction. Most occurrences denote the resulting state of desolation. See *deslolate.*

LEAD

New Testament

Verb: ἄγω (*agō*), GK *72* (S *71*, *73*), 67x. In its most basic NT sense, *agō* means "to bring, lead, go." Most occurrences are located in the gospels and Acts.

(1) The basic sense of *agō* is to be led or

brought from one place to another. In Mt. 21:7, the disciples "lead" the donkey and colt to Jesus. In Lk. 4:40, the sick are "brought" to Jesus for healing (cf. 18:40; cf. Jn. 9:13; Acts 9:27). Paul tells Timothy to get Mark and "bring" him (2 Tim. 4:11). In Acts 8:32, the eunuch cites the OT prophet Isaiah, "he was *led* as a sheep to the slaughter." Like a lowly sacrificial lamb, Jesus was "led away" to the cross to die for the sins of the world, as Isaiah had promised hundreds of years earlier.

Acts 13:23 records the words of Paul, "God has *brought* to Israel a Savior, Jesus." This is a theologically significant usage, as it denotes the leadership of the Father over the Son in the divine plan of redemption. In 1 Thess. 4:14, Paul reminds the church that as Jesus rose from the grave, so all who have died "will also be *brought* with him" at the second coming.

(2) *agō* can also mean "to be led away" into custody. This term is used both of Jesus (Lk. 22:54; Jn. 7:45) and of his followers (Mt. 10:18; Mk. 13:11; Acts 6:12; 18:12). Prisoners "are transported" from one place to another (Jn. 18:28; Acts 21:34; 23:31).

(3) Believers can also be "led" in a spiritual sense. They "are led" to repentance by God's kindness (Rom. 2:4). The author of Hebrews writes that God the Father "*brings* many sons to glory" (Heb. 2:10). Such leading is by the indwelling Spirit of God (Rom. 8:14; Gal. 5:18). Conversely, others "are led" astray from the truth (2 Tim. 3:6) and into sin (cf. 1 Cor. 12:2). In addition, Jesus "was *led* by the Spirit" into the desert (Lk. 4:1), and shortly after "was led" by Satan to Jerusalem (4:9).

(4) Finally, *agō* can simply mean "to go," in the sense of moving from one place to another. In Mt. 26:46 Jesus exhorts his disciples, "*Let us go*" (cf. Jn. 11:16).

LEAD ASTRAY

Old Testament

Verb: תָּעָה (*tāʿâ*), GK 9494 (S 8582), 51x. *tāʿâ* may be translated as to "go astray, stray, lead astray, wander, stagger." See *go astray*.

New Testament

Verb: πλανάω (*planaō*), GK *4414* (S *4105*), 39x. In the active voice, *planaō* means "to lead astray, deceive"; in the middle/passive voice, "to wander, go astray." See *deceive*.

LEAD AWAY

New Testament

Verb: ἀπάγω (*apagō*), GK *552* (S *520*), 15x. *apagō* means "to lead away." The basic idea is that of leading from one place to another (e.g., leading an animal to water, Lk. 13:15). It is used most often in the NT as a legal technical term, i.e., to lead a person from one point to another in legal proceedings. Jesus is "led" to Caiaphas (Mt. 26:57), Pilate (27:2), and finally to be crucified (27:31; cf. Acts 12:19). Jesus says his followers will also be "brought before" the authorities for his name's sake (Lk. 21:12). Jesus also uses *apagō* to refer to the roads that "lead" to life (Mt. 7:14) or to destruction (7:13). Paul says that the Corinthians were at one time "led astray" by idols (1 Cor. 12:2).

LEAD OUT

New Testament

Verb: ἐξάγω (*exagō*), GK *1974* (S *1806*), 12x. *exagō* means "to lead out." The soldiers lead Jesus out to crucify him (Mk. 15:20). The shepherd leads out the sheep, calling them by name (Jn. 10:3). God led Israel out of Egypt (Acts 13:17; Heb. 8:9) with Moses as his appointed leader (Acts 7:36, 40). An angel of the Lord leads the apostles out of prison (5:19; cf. 12:17).

LEAD UP

New Testament

Verb: ἀνάγω (*anagō*), GK *343* (S *321*), 23x. *anagō* means "to bring, lead up." See *bring up*.

Verb: ἀναφέρω (*anapherō*), GK *429* (S *399*), 10x. *anapherō* means "to lead, take up." Jesus "leads" Peter, James, and John up the mountain to witness his transfiguration (Mt. 17:1; Mk. 9:2). Jesus was "taken up" into heaven (Lk. 24:51). It can also mean "to offer up a sacrifice" (see *offer* *up*) or "to bear, take up," referring to sins (see *bear [sins]*).

LEADER

Old Testament

Noun: אַיִל (*ʾayil*), GK 380 (S 352), 171x. *ʾayil* literally means "ram" (see *ram*) but can also be used figuratively for "ruler, leader, chief." See *chief.*

Noun: מֶלֶךְ (*melek*), GK 4889 (S 4428 and 4429), 2513x. Occurring more than 2500x, *melek* conveys a variety of meanings. It is not a technical term but refers to a large assortment of leader-types, from an emperor down to tribal and city leaders. It is often translated "king." See *king*.

Noun: רֹאשׁ (*rōʾš*), GK 8031 (S 7218), 600x. The primary meaning of *rōʾš* is "head" (see *head*), but it also has a number of metaphorical meanings. For example, *rōʾš* can be translated as "leader" or "chief." It denotes leaders in general (Exod. 18:25; Num. 14:4 [KJV reads *captain*]; 25:4; Jos. 23:2), those who have high social standing in a community (Isa. 9:14–15), and leaders of specific units of people, such as families and clans (Exod. 6:14; Num. 7:2), the tribes of Israel (Num. 1:16; 32:28; Deut. 1:15; 1 Sam. 15:17), and military units (David's thirty chief men in 2 Sam. 23:13; the title of chief in 1 Chr. 11:6).

Noun: שַׂר (*śar*), GK 8569 (S 8269) 421x.

Noun: נָשִׂיא (*nāśîʾ*), GK 5954 (S 5387) 130x.

Noun: אַלּוּף (*ʾallûp*), GK 477 (S 441) 60x.

There are a number of overlapping nouns in the OT that refer to leaders, chiefs, and officials of various sorts. These assorted terms need to be translated differently according to the context in Israel's history.

(1) For example, when the usage refers to the time when Israel and her neighbors were primarily semi-nomadic tribes, "chieftain" and "tribal chief" are the most appropriate expressions. For this type of leader the OT most frequently uses the term *ʾallûp* (Gen. 36:15; 1 Chr. 1:51). A similar term is *nāśîʾ*, which is used more frequently and refers to leaders, heads, or chiefs of clans or tribes. The *nāśîʾ* are the representatives of the twelve tribes of Israel in political and religious affairs (Num. 1:16, 44; 25:14; 36:1; Jos. 9:15). Ezekiel uses *nāśîʾ* frequently as a royal title rather than the more common *melek*, "king" (Ezek. 12:10; 19:1). The prophet also uses *nāśîʾ* to describe the coming Davidic ruler who will shepherd the restored flock of Israel (Ezek. 34:24; 37:25).

(2) The most common of these related terms is *śar*. At times this word refers to tribal chieftains or leaders (Num. 21:18; Jdg. 5:15; 1 Sam. 22:2). Yet at other times the context requires the word to be understood as a nobleman or courtier (Jer. 26:11, 21; 2 Chr. 31:8). *śar* can also communicate the idea of head or official in a profession such as "chief jailer" (Gen. 39:21), "chief butler" (40:2), "chief baker" (40:2), or "chief of the eunuchs" (Dan. 1:7). Quite frequently *śar* (and less often, *nāśîʾ*) is translated into English with the term "prince." This can be misleading if this English word is understood to mean only the son of a king. Instead, *śar* indicates more broadly a leader among people in various capacities and situations.

Some of the most theologically significant uses of *śar* are found in Isaiah and Daniel. In Dan. 10:13, 21 and 12:1, the angel Michael is called a "chief prince" (*śar*) who fights on behalf of Israel against his counterpart, the "prince" (*śar*) of Persia (10:20). In the vision of Dan. 8, a wicked king arises, destroys many, and even attempts to oppose the "prince of princes" (using *śar*), but he is ultimately broken (see especially Dan. 8:23–25). This grand figure—the "prince of princes"—is identified in the NT as Jesus and is called the "prince of peace" in the great prophetic passage of Isa. 9:6, "For to us a child will be born, to us a son will be given; and the government will be upon his shoulders, and his name will be called 'Wonderful Counselor, Mighty God, Everlasting

Father, *Prince* of Peace.' " See *NIDOTTE*, 1:406-10, 3:171-72, and 4:1294-95.

New Testament

Noun: ἄρχων (*archōn*), GK *807* (S *758*), 37x. *archōn* is part of an extensive group of *arch-* words with meanings related to the ideas of beginning, cause, and thereby, rule and authority. See *ruler.*

Noun: ἡγεμών (*hēgemōn*), GK *2450* (S *2232*), 20x. *hēgemōn*, "ruler, leader," communicates the general idea of ruler (Mt. 2:6; Mk. 13:9; 1 Pet. 2:14), though it is often more specifically a title for various Roman officials (Mt. 27:2; Lk. 20:20; Acts 23:24; 26:30). See *ruler*.

LEARN

Old Testament

Verb: לָמַד (*lāmad*), GK 4340 (S 3925), 87x. *lāmad* is one of the twelve words used in the OT for teaching or instructing (see *teach*). But the same word can also be used for learning (i.e., the notion of accepting instructions; cf. Isa. 29:24). When it means instruction, only human beings are the subjects. God cannot learn, as Job acknowledges (Job 21:22).

New Testament

Verb: μανθάνω (*manthanō*), GK *3443* (S *3129*), 25x. *manthanō* means "to learn." Sometimes it describes the mere acquisition of factual data, but other times context shows that the person is called not only to know but then to obey what they had learned. Learning in the NT frequently focuses on the gospel and the teachings of the apostles.

(1) Learning is an important aspect of discipleship (the word disciple, *mathētēs*, is derived from this verb). It involves not only exposure to information but also comprehension (Mt. 9:13; cf. Jn. 6:45). Information apart from understanding is of little use (2 Tim. 3:7). What is to be learned is the gospel itself (Rom. 16:17) as conveyed through the teachings of the apostles (1 Cor. 4:6; cf. 14:35; Eph. 4:20; Phil. 4:9; Col. 1:7; 1 Tim. 2:11; 2 Tim. 3:14) and prophecy (1 Cor. 14:31). In addition to the gospel, one can learn from Jesus about the kingdom of God (Mt. 11:29), or the lesson taught by a fig tree (Mt. 24:32; Mk. 13:28). One can also learn a Christian character trait by experience (Phil. 4:11; cf. 1 Tim. 5:4; Tit. 3:14; Heb. 5:8).

(2) Some Jews marveled that Jesus had "such learning without having studied" (Jn. 7:15), and Paul was treated differently when his centurion captors learned he was a Roman citizen (Acts 23:27; cf. Gal. 3:2; Rev. 14:3). See *NIDNTT-A*, 350-52.

LEARNING

New Testament

Noun: γράμμα (*gramma*), GK *1207* (S *1121*), 14x. Usually translated "writing, letters," *gramma* can refer to the letters of the alphabet (Gal. 6:11), written information (Acts 28:21), a debtor's bill (Lk. 16:6), or learning in general (Jn. 17:5; Acts 26:24). See *write, writing*.

LEAST

New Testament

Adjective: ἐλάχιστος (*elachistos*), GK *1788* (S *1646*), 14x. *elachistos* can mean the lowest in class or status, or convey the idea of having little importance or significance.

(1) *elachistos* can refer to the lowest in class or status (or even size, cf. Jas. 3:4). For example, Bethlehem, in the land of Judah, is "by no means *least* among the rulers of Judah" (Mt. 2:6; cf. 25:40, 45). Paul feels that he is "the least" of all of the apostles (1 Cor. 15:9) and "*least* of all God's people" (Eph. 3:8), indicating how he truly sees himself, especially given his history of persecuting the church before his conversion. Paul is not dealing with an unrelenting sense of guilt that is not absolved by God's forgiveness and grace (1 Cor. 15:10–11), but he is acknowledging the sin of his life before his conversion. In our Christian activities, we must minister to "the least of these brothers of mine" (Mt. 25:40, 45).

(2) In his teaching about anxiety and worry (Lk. 12:26), Jesus tells the crowd that worry produces nothing: "Since you cannot do this *very little* thing, why do you worry about the rest?" We cannot

accomplish even the smallest thing by worrying or by anxiety; rather, we must trust God in all matters—both the biggest and the *elachistos*. Lk. 16:10 and 19:17 stress the importance of being faithful in the things that seem "unimportant."

(3) Finally, Mt. 5:19 uses *elachistos* twice. In 5:19a, Jesus speaks of the *least* of the commandments in the law. Here this adjective carries the meaning of one commandment being less important than the other. Yet in 5:19b, Jesus says that any who annuls or breaks even "one of the *least* commandments" will be regarded as "least" in the kingdom of heaven.

LEATHER

Old Testament

Noun: עוֹר (*ʿôr*), GK 6425 (S 5785), 99x. *ʿôr* is used to designate both human (55x) and animal (44x) skin. Animal skins (leather) were used as coverings for the ark of the covenant and other furniture of the tabernacle, along with the sacred utensils (Num. 4:6ff.). See *skin*.

LEAVE

Old Testament

Verb: חָדַל (*ḥādal*), GK 2532 (S 2308), 55x. *ḥādal*, most often translated "stop" in the NIV, generally indicates the simple cessation of action. Occasionally, *ḥādal* indicates that one's presence ceases and may be translated "to leave." Israel (Exod. 14:12) and Job (Job 7:6) both plead, "*Leave* me alone," and the trees and vine of Jotham's parable ask whether they should "leave" their current situation for another (Jdg. 9:9, 11, 13). See *stop*.

Verb: נוּחַ (*nûaḥ*), GK 5663 (S 5117), 140x. The most basic idea of the verb *nûaḥ* is the action of one object coming to rest, roosting, or landing on another object or in a specific location. See *rest*.

Frequently the object does not come to rest on its own but is caused to rest or be placed in a particular location by someone else (104x). In these instances *nûaḥ* may be translated "set," "put," "place," or even "leave." When Joseph is in power in Egypt, he commands his brothers to "leave" one of the brothers with him as they return to Canaan (Gen. 42:33), and God "leaves" nations in the land of Canaan after the conquest to test Israel (Jdg. 3:1; cf. Jdg. 2:23; Jer. 27:11). See *set*.

Verb: נָסַע (*nāsaʿ*), GK 5825 (S 5265), 146x. The original meaning of *nāsaʿ* is "to pull out (tent pegs)," from which the sense "set out" or "journey" is derived. See *journey*.

Verb: עָזַב (*ʿāzab*), GK 6440 (S 5800), 214x. *ʿāzab* is used most often for the action of "abandonment" (see *abandon*). Sometimes it refers simply to a person leaving behind his cloak (Gen. 39:15), his family, flocks, or herds (Gen. 50:8).

New Testament

Verb: ἀφίημι (*aphiēmi*), GK *918* (S *863*), 143x. Depending upon its particular context, *aphiēmi* means to "forgive, release, leave, abandon." See *forgive*.

Verb: ἀφίστημι (*aphistēmi*), GK *923* (S *868*), 14x. *aphistēmi* generally means to "leave, depart" in a physical sense, as when the devil finished tempting Jesus and "*left* him until an opportune time" (Lk. 4:13, cf. 2:27; Acts 12:10).

aphistēmi is also used to express various forms of apostasy. The seeds that fall on the rock are those who receive the message with joy, but having no root "they fall away" in the time of testing (Lk. 8:13). Paul teaches that in later times "some will *abandon* the faith" (1 Tim. 4:1; cf. Heb. 3:12).

Other uses of *aphistēmi* include Paul's desire for the Lord to "take away" the thorn in his flesh (2 Cor. 12:8); Judas the Galilean, who "*led* a band of people in revolt" (Acts 5:37); John Mark's desertion of Paul (15:38); and the forsaking of wickedness as counseled in 2 Tim. 2:19, "Everyone who confesses the name of the Lord must *turn away* from wickedness." See *NIDNTT-A*, 82.*

Verb: μεταβαίνω (*metabainō*), GK *3553* (S *3327*), 12x. *metabainō* means "to leave, depart, pass on," usually indicating a person or a group of people going away from one geographical place to another.

For example, after Jesus heals the demoniacs in the region of the Gadarenes, the people come down and beg him "to leave" their neighborhood (Mt. 8:34, NRSV). Jesus leaves one region and goes to another to heal, teach, and proclaim his message (Mt. 11:1; 12:9; 15:29). Jesus' brothers admonish him saying, "*Leave* here [Galilee] and go to Judea so that your disciples may also see the works you are doing" (Jn. 7:3). Jesus instructs the seventy not to "move about" from house to house (Lk. 10:7), and *metabainō* is used to indicate Paul's departure from the synagogue in Corinth (Acts 18:7) and his determination to preach exclusively to the Gentiles.

But three occurrences of *metabainō* indicate more than geographical motion. Jesus promises, "Anyone who hears my word and believes in him who sent me has eternal life, and does not come under judgment, but *has passed* from death to life" (Jn. 5:24). In 1 Jn. 3:14, the children of God know "that [they] *have passed* from death to life" and are confident in their new position as God's children on the evidence of the love they have for others. The use of *metabainō* in Jn. 13:1 strategically moves the narrative from a focus on the works and teachings of Jesus, to the culmination of Jesus' purpose on earth, his death and resurrection. Jesus recognized that his "hour had come *to depart* from this world and go to the Father." That departure entails his death on the cross and his resurrection, securing the salvation of anyone who believes to likewise depart from death to life. See *NIDNTT-A*, 42-43.

LEAVE BEHIND

New Testament

Verb: καταλείπω (*kataleipō*), GK *2901* (S *2641*), 24x. *kataleipō* is a compound form of *leipō*, "to leave," with the preposition *kata* ("down, behind"). It means simply to "leave behind." In the NT, *kataleipō* can refer to leaving someone or something behind (Mt. 21:17; Lk. 15:4). In this sense, Jesus and Paul quote Gen. 2:24 that a man will "leave" his father and mother to be united to his wife (Mt. 19:5; Mk. 10:7; Eph. 5:31). The term can also signify "to depart" from a place with the implication of finality (Mt. 4:13; Heb. 11:27; 2 Pet. 2:15). On at least two occasions *kataleipō* means "to leave over" in the sense of causing something to remain in existence. In this sense, the writer of Hebrews speaks of a "promise" that "still stands" (Heb. 4:1). Likewise, God "leaves over" or "reserves" a remnant for himself (Rom. 11:4). See *NIDNTT-A*, 331-33.

LEAVEN

New Testament

Noun: ζύμη (*zymē*), GK *2434* (S *2219*), 13x. *zymē* means "yeast, leaven." See *yeast*.

LEFT

Old Testament

Verb: שָׁאַר (*šāʾar*), GK 8636 (S 7604), 133x. Only in rare instances does *šāʾar* mean "to remain" or "to be left" (e.g., 1 Sam. 16:11). More often the term refers to survival, as in Noah and his family surviving the flood (Gen. 7:23). See *survive*.

Noun and Adjective: שְׂמֹאל (*śᵉmōʾl*), GK 8520 (S 8040), 54x. *śᵉmōʾl* is usually employed to denote the "left, left side, left hand." Sometimes when used alone, it can means "[to go] to the left/north" (Gen. 13:9; 2 Sam. 14:19; Isa. 30:21). As Heb. directions were oriented toward the east, facing the sunrise (instead of the north as in many contemporary cultures), north was to the person's left. For this reason the term is occasionally used to designate the geographical direction "north" (Gen. 14:15; 1 Ki. 7:39; 2 Chr. 3:17; 2 Chr. 4:6–8; Job 23:9; Ezek. 16:46). *śᵉmōʾl* can also simply refer to the left side (Exod. 14:22, 29; Jos. 19:27; Jdg. 16:29; 1 Ki. 7:49).

When "left" is used together with "right," it can figuratively refer to obediently following God. The Israelites are commanded to follow his commands, not turning "to the right or to the left" (Deut. 5:32; 17:11, 20; Jos. 1:7). In other places, this expression means "straight" ahead, without distractions (Num. 20:17; 1 Sam. 6:12). Such language provides us with a determined sense of focus. Runners who have their eyes fixed on the finish line never stop to take in the sights along the way (cf. Prov. 4:25–27; cf. Phil. 3:13–14).

Since the right hand was a symbol of strength in the ancient world, the left hand could be a symbol of weakness. God's right hand delivered the Israelites from Egypt, "Your right hand, O LORD, was majestic in power. Your right hand, O LORD, shattered the enemy" (Exod. 15:6). Consequently, *ś^e^mōʾl* is never used with reference to God. The "left" could even be associated with evil, as in Eccl. 10:2: "The heart of the wise inclines to the right, but the heart of the fool to the left." The blessing given from Jacob's left hand was a lesser blessing than what was given by his right hand (Gen. 48:13–14).

The left hand, however, could also be presented in a positive or neutral light. Warriors who were left-handed or ambidextrous were especially dangerous as they could deliver an attack from an unexpected direction. Ehud the Benjamite assassinated Eglon with a surprise attack from his left hand (Jdg. 3:21). David's mighty men were "armed with bows and were able to shoot arrows or to sling stones right-handed or left-handed" (1 Chr. 12:1–2). Both hands are lifted in praise to the Lord (Ps. 63:4), and both are used in his service in the tabernacle (Lev. 14:15, 26).

(BE) LEFT

Old Testament

Verb: יָתַר (*yātar*), GK 3855 (S 3498), 106x. *yātar* means "to remain, be left, survive." See *remain*.

LEFT OVER

New Testament

Verb: περισσεύω (*perisseuō*), GK *4355* (S *4052*), 39x. *perisseuō* means "to abound, be in abundance, overflow." It is used for what was "left over" after feeding the five thousand (Mt. 15:37; Lk. 9:17). See *abound* for more on this verb

Adjective: λοιπός (*loipos*), GK *3370* (S *3062*), 55x. In its most generic sense, *loipos* means "remaining" or "left over." See *remaining*.

LEG

Old Testament

Noun: רֶגֶל (*regel*), GK 8079 (S 7272), 251x. In the OT *regel* signifies the foot (Gen. 24:32; 43:24) or the leg (Isa. 7:20; metaphorically the legs of a table in Exod. 25:26). See *foot*.

LENGTH

Old Testament

Noun: אֹרֶךְ (*ʾōrek*), GK 802 (S 753), 95x. *ʾōrek* means length and is used with reference to either space or time. When the measurements of an object are provided, its *ʾōrek* is always longer than or equal to its width. Thus, the tabernacle's table is two cubits long and one wide (Exod. 25:23), and its altar is a perfect square, five cubits long and five cubits wide (Exod. 27:1). In addition to the tabernacle and its objects (Exod. 25–27, 36–38), the word is used to describe Noah's ark (Gen. 6:15), Solomon's temple (1 Ki. 6:2–3, 20), Ezekiel's visionary temple (Ezek. 40–43), and the future division of the promised land (Ezek. 45, 48). The word is also used in Gen. 13:17, where God tells Abraham to "explore the *length* and breadth of the land."

With reference to time, the word is commonly used in the expression "*length* of days" (Deut. 30:20), which is related to another common expression, "prolong your days" (cf. Deut. 30:18, where the verb "prolong" is from the same root, *ʾrk*). Normally "*length* of days" refers to a long earthly life (Job 12:12; Prov. 3:2, 16). This phrase is used sparingly to denote "eternity" and "everlastingness" (Ps. 21:4; Lam. 5:20), though at times it can carry the meaning "forever" (Ps. 93:5). Thus, although Ps. 23:6 literally reads "I will dwell in the house of the Lord for a *length* of days," many translations read "forever." But since "all the days of my life" is mentioned in the first part of the verse, the psalmist may mean "for the *rest* of my life." Prov. 25:15 teaches that a wise person deals with people using "a *length* of anger," meaning that a wise person is patient and it takes a long time for him to become angry. See *NIDOTTE*, 1:517-18.

LET

New Testament

Verb: ἐάω (*eaō*), GK *1572* (S *1439*), 11x. *eaō* means "to let, allow." Jesus will not "let" a demon to speak about his identity (Lk. 4:41). At one time, God "*let* all nations walk in their own ways" (Acts 14:16). The Spirit will not "allow" Paul and his companions to go into Bithynia to do mission work (16:7); the reason is not given, but Paul trusts that this reflects God's will. God will not "let" believers be tempted beyond what they are able to bear (1 Cor. 10:13).

Verb: ἐπιτρέπω (*epitrepō*), GK *2205* (S *2010*), 18x. *epitrepō* essentially means "to let, permit, allow." See *permit*.

LETTER

New Testament

Noun: ἐπιστολή (*epistolē*), GK *2186* (S *1992*), 24x. Most frequently *epistolē* is translated as "letter" or "epistle." It refers to written communication between parties. Letters were an important part of the NT world. They were especially important to the apostle Paul, for he communicated with his churches via letters to encourage them, to further instruct them, to warn them, and to answer questions they posed to him (1 Cor. 7:1). He also communicated with individuals such as Timothy, Titus, and Philemon. Paul expects his letters to be read aloud in the churches. In a letter to the Colossians he writes, "After this letter has been read to you, see that it is also read in the church of the Laodicians and that you in turn read the letter from Laodicea" (Col. 4:16; see also 1 Thess. 5:27; 2 Thess. 2:15).

But letters were also used by governing officials to engage in government business. Saul, for example, had letters from the high priest that authorized him to persecute believers in Damascus (Acts 9:2; 22:5). Luke comments about a letter written by Claudius Lysias, a Roman centurion, to Governor Felix: "He wrote a letter as follows: Claudius Lysias, To His Excellency, Governor Felix: Greetings" (Acts 23:25). Note the difference in style from our usual letter-writing practices. An ancient letter begins with the writer's name; this is followed by the addressee and a word of greeting. If any date is attached to the letter, it was put at the very end, after closing greetings.

Paul also uses *epistolē* in a figurative sense in 2 Corinthians, "You yourselves are our letter, written on our hearts, known and read by everybody. You show that you are a letter from Christ, the result of our ministry" (2 Cor. 3:2–3). When people see believers, they should be able to see/read Christ in us. See *NIDNTT-A*, 199-200.

LETTERS

New Testament

Noun: γράμμα (*gramma*), GK *1207* (S *1121*), 14x. Usually translated "writing, letters," the noun *gramma* can refer to the letters of the alphabet (Gal. 6:11), written information (Acts 28:21), a debtor's bill (Lk. 16:6), or learning in general (Jn. 17:5; Acts 26:24). See *write, writing*.

LEWDNESS

New Testament

Noun: ἀσέλγεια (*aselgeia*), GK 816 (S 766), 10x. *aselgeia* means "debauchery, lewdness, sensuality." See *debauchery*.

LIABLE

New Testament

Adjective: ἔνοχος (*enochos*), GK *1944* (S *1777*), 10x. *enochos* means "guilty, subject to, liable for, worthy of." See *guilty*.

LIAR

New Testament

Noun: ψεύστης (*pseustēs*), GK *6026* (S *5583*), 10x. *pseustēs* is always translated as "liar" and is found most frequently in John's writings (7x). Jesus calls the devil "a *liar* and the father of lies" (Jn. 8:44), and all who lie belong to him (i.e., the Pharisees) and oppose sound doctrine (1 Tim. 1:10). In contrast to the Pharisees, who claim to know God but do not, Jesus proclaims, "Though you do not know him, I know him. If I said I did not, I would be a *liar* like you" (Jn. 8:55).

John emphatically declares that if anyone (like the Pharisees) does not believe God—that is, believe in his Son—he makes God out to be a liar because he rejects the truthfulness and authority of God as well as the testimony of his Son (1 Jn. 5:10). John also stated, "If we claim we have not sinned, we make [God] out to be a *liar*" because we have rejected his provision of Jesus Christ for our sins (1 Jn. 1:10). Thus, since God is true, John asked, "Who is the *liar*? (1 Jn. 2:22). His answer includes those who hate their brothers (1 Jn. 4:20), do not obey the commands of Christ (1 Jn. 2:4), and deny that Jesus is the Christ (1 Jn. 2:22). Paul's judgment is fitting: "Let God be true and every man a *liar*" (Rom. 3:4). See *NIDNTT-A*, 619-20.

LIE

Old Testament

Noun: שֶׁקֶר (*šeqer*), GK 9214 (S 8267), 113x. *šeqer* is derived from the root verb *šāqar*, "to lie, deceive, betray" (only 6x in the OT). The meaning of this word is tied to lies, falsehood and deception. Note 1 Sam. 15:29, which uses the verb form rather than the noun: "He who is the Glory of Israel *does not lie* or change his mind; for he is not a man, that he should change his mind." *šeqer* occurs most frequently in Jer. (37x), Ps. (22x), and Prov. (20x). Jeremiah writes of the false prophets who spread lies among God's people and lead them away from the LORD (Jer. 23:14–32 [5x]), and Prov. consistently contrasts truth with *šeqer* (Prov. 12:17, 19, 22; 14:5).

Everything that is a *šeqer* is opposed to truth and consequently opposed to God. Illustrative of this is the ninth commandment: "You shall not give *false* testimony against your neighbor" (Exod. 20:16). Similarly, anyone who gives false testimony is a liar (Deut. 19:18). In the strongest terms, the godly sage claims that God hates every *šeqer* (Prov. 6:17; 12:22) and that the righteous should also (13:5). Accordingly, the psalmist declares to God, "I gain understanding from your precepts; therefore I hate every *wrong* path" (Ps. 119:104).

New Testament

Verb: ψεύδομαι (*pseudomai*), GK *6017* (S *5574*), 12x. *pseudomai* means "to lie." It is used most frequently in Paul's writings, as he often writes to assert that the things he is saying are true: "I speak the truth in Christ—I *am* not *lying*, my conscience confirms in the Holy Spirit" (Rom. 9:1; cf. 2 Cor. 11:31, Gal. 1:20, 1 Tim. 2:7). For Paul, lying is a mark of the old nature and must be put off: "Do not *lie* to each other, since you have taken off you old self with its practices" (Col. 3:9).

Lying does not come from God but from the devil, the father of lies (cf. Jn. 8:44). In contrast, the writer of Hebrews declares that "it is impossible for God *to lie*" (Heb. 6:18), for "God is light, and in him is no darkness at all" (1 Jn. 1:5). Consequently, "if we claim to have fellowship with him [who is light] yet walk in darkness, we *lie* and do not live by the truth" (1 Jn. 1:6). Therefore, *pseudomai* is in direct opposition to the very nature of God and must not characterize those who believe in him.

Lying sometimes ends with dreadful consequences. For example, Ananias and Sapphira deceitfully bring a monetary offering to the apostles for distribution among the needy, but they keep for themselves some of the proceeds from a piece of land they have sold. Peter confronts Ananias and asks him, "How is it that Satan has so filled your heart that you have *lied* to the Holy Spirit and have kept for yourself some of the money you received for the land?" (Acts 5:3). Peter concludes that Ananias has "not *lied* to men but to God" (Acts 5:4). Although the consequences for lying will not always be as severe as it was for Ananias and Sapphira (i.e., death, Acts 5:5, 10), lying does not honor God and always hurts others as well as ourselves. See *NIDNTT-A*, 619-20.

Noun: ψεῦδος (*pseudos*), GK *6022* (S *5579*), 10x. *pseudos* is typically translated as "lie," but it may also indicate falsehood, deception, or anything counterfeit (e.g., 1 Jn. 2:27). *pseudos* is often set in contrast to the truth (see *alētheia*, *237*, under *truth*).

John declares to his readers, "I do not write to you because you do not know the truth, but because you do know it and because no *lie* comes from the truth" (1 Jn. 2:21). A *pseudos* originates with Satan, not with God. John proclaims about the devil that "when he *lies*, he speaks his native language, for he is a liar and the father of lies" (Jn. 8:44). The works of Satan will be evident in the last days, "displayed in all kinds of *counterfeit* miracles, signs and wonders," and many will "believe the *lie*" (2 Thess. 2:9, 11). In light of this, God's judgment is seen clearly in turning people over to their lusts, especially when they "exchange the truth of God for a *lie*" and refuse to worship him in favor of lesser things (Rom. 1:25).

Since we are members of Christ's body, Paul instructs us to "put off *falsehood*," in order to demonstrate that we are of God and not Satan. Those who practice falsehood are counted with the sinners who remain outside of the gates of heaven (Rev. 22:15), for "nothing impure will ever enter it, nor will anyone who does what is shameful or *deceitful*, but only those whose names are written in the Lamb's book of life" (Rev. 21:27; cf. 14:5). See *NIDNTT-A*, 619-20.*

LIE DOWN

Old Testament

Verb: שָׁכַב (*šākab*), GK 8886 (S 7901), 213x. *šākab* means "lie down, rest, sleep." There are a variety of nuances to this verb, all of which revolve around the idea of lying down.

(1) *šākab* can simply mean to spend the night (Jos. 2:1) and to lie down and sleep (Gen. 19:4; Lev. 14:47; Jos. 2:8; Ps. 3:5; 4:8). Samuel has a visitation from the Lord while he is lying down in his bed (1 Sam. 3:2–6, 9). According to the Teacher, however, it is possible to be lying down but yet have a mind that "does not *rest*" (Eccl. 2:23; cf. Job 7:4).

(2) Since a dead person is lying down as if in sleep, this verb is sometimes used for death (e.g., Ps. 41:8; Ezek. 32:19, 21, 27–32). Job expects, for example, that he "will soon *lie down* in the dust" (Job 7:21; cf. 3:13). It is clear that in Isa. 14:8 the kings of the nations who are "lying down" are deceased. "To *rest* with one's fathers" means to be buried in the family grave (1 Ki. 1:21; 2:10; 11:43; etc. [frequently in Kings and Chronicles]).

(3) Equally important is the use of the verse for having sexual relations (similar to our expression, "sleeping with someone"). God's law outlines numerous improper occasions for sexual relations with the expression "lying with someone" (Lev. 15:20, 24, 26; 20:11–13; Deut. 27:20–23). This phrase can denote rape (Gen. 34:2; Deut. 22:25). In Gen. 19:23, 33 it is used for the incestuous relations between Lot and his daughters. It is significant that in almost all occurrences of this meaning, *šākab* denotes improper sexual relationships; for appropriate sexual relations between husband and wife, the common verb to use is *yādaʿ* (GK 3359, "to know," e.g., Gen. 4:1). See *NIDOTTE*, 4:100–102.

New Testament

Verb: κατάκειμαι (*katakeimai*), GK *2879* (S *2621*), 12x. *katakeimai* means "to lie down." This term can simply imply "lying down" in the sense of resting from activity, but when used this way in the NT this verb refers to someone who is sick—e.g., Simon's mother-in-law is "lying in bed" with a fever (Mk. 1:30; cf. 2:4; Lk. 5:25; Jn. 5:3; 5:6; Acts 9:33; 28:8). *katakeimai* also means "to recline" for a meal (see *recline*).

Verb: κεῖμαι (*keimai*), GK *3023* (S *2749*), 24x. *keimai* means "to lie, lie down." It is used in a literal sense for a person "lying down" (Mt. 28:6; Lk. 2:12, 16) or an object that is "laid" on something (Mt. 3:10; 5:14). The baby Jesus is "lying" in a manger (Lk. 2:12, 16). It can also have the figurative meanings such as "to be appointed" or "destined" (Lk. 2:34; Phil. 1:16; 1 Thess. 3:3), "to be laid down" (1 Tim. 1:9), or "to lie under the control of" (1 Jn. 5:19). The foundation of the church has been "laid down," namely, Jesus Christ (1 Cor. 3:11).

LIFE

Old Testament

Verb: חָיָה (*ḥāyâ*), GK 2649 (S 2421, 2425), 283x. *ḥāyâ* indicates "life" or "having life" and is the generic term for "life" or "to live" in the OT (Gen. 5:3–30; 11:11–26; cf. Num. 4:19). It refers to one's own life (12:13; 42:2, 18, Isa. 55:3), the life of one's parents (Jos. 2:13), and of the lives of others.

(1) Joshua spares the life of Rahab (Jos. 6:25), God preserves Caleb's life (14:10), and Noah preserves the lives of animals in the ark (Gen. 6:19). Jeremiah tells Zedekiah that if he will surrender to the king of Babylon, his *ḥāyâ* will be spared and Jerusalem will not be destroyed (Jer. 38:17; cf. Exod. 1:16). God instructs his people to "give ear and come to me; hear me, that your soul *may live*" (Isa. 55:3). God is so powerful that no one can see him "and live" (Exod. 33:20), yet Scripture also shows that while God can take away *ḥāyâ* (2 Ki. 5:7), he also has the power to give it (Num. 21:8; 2 Ki. 8:1, 5). The Lord tells Abimelech that he will continue to live because he has not sinned against God's prophet (Gen. 20:6; cf. Lev. 25:36).

(2) *ḥāyâ* is also used indicate preservation of live ("let live"). For example, God sends Joseph to Egypt years before the great famine so that he can "preserve for you for a remnant on earth and to save your *lives* by a great deliverance (Gen. 45:7; cf. 12:13; 47:25; 50:20; Num. 31:18, Jos. 9:20; also cf. Num. 22:33, of saving the life of a donkey). Although scattered throughout the world, Scriptures assures that a remnant of Israel will remember God "and live" (Zech. 10:9). See also *revive*.

Verb: נֶפֶשׁ (*nepeš*), GK 5883 (S 5315), 757x. *nepeš* has a wide range of meaning; the basic meaning is "breath," but it can also mean "soul, life, entire being." See *soul*.

Noun: חַי (*ḥay*), GK 2644 (S 2416), 140x. *ḥay* indicates life or the state of living as contrasted with death.

(1) The psalmist declares that he will praise God as long as he has "life" (Ps. 63:4). Solomon writes that there is nothing better for a person than to rejoice in the Lord and "to do good in their life" (Eccl. 3:12). Jonah, by contrast, declares twice that it would have been better for him to be dead than to be alive (Jon. 4:3, 8).

(2) *ḥay* is also used in various usages of the theologically intriguing formula "as surely as I *live*." This formula suggests that if what is promised does not come true, then death should come on the one who has spoken the false promise. Boaz swears "as surely as the Lord lives" to assure Ruth that he will marry her if a nearer kinsman is unwilling to do so (Ruth 3:13). Saul swears that "as the LORD lives," he will not harm his son Jonathan (1 Sam. 14:39; cf. 1 Ki. 1:29; Hos. 4:15; Jer. 4:2; Dan. 12:7). God even uses the formula in various places in the OT (e.g., Deut. 32:40, "As surely as I *live* forever"; cf. Num. 14:21; Isa. 49:18; Jer. 22:24; Ezek. 5:11; Zeph. 2:9). While it may seem unusual for God to use an oath, it demonstrates his great love and compassion for his people that he will communicate to them in the language they best understand.

Noun: רוּחַ (*rûaḥ*), GK 8120 (S 7307), 378x. While *rûaḥ* has a wide range of meanings in the OT, its basic sense is that of "wind" or "breath" (see *wind*). This latter sense naturally gave rise to "breath" as a sign of life, and hence *rûaḥ* also means "spirit" or "life." See *spirit*.

New Testament

Noun: ἀναστροφή (*anastrophē*), GK *419* (S *391*), 13x. *anastrophē* means one's "manner of life" or simply "conduct." See *way of life*.

Noun: βίος (*bios*), GK *1050* (S *979*), 10x. *bios* denotes the course of one's "life" or the "material possessions, property" by which that life subsists (1 Jn. 3:17). Paul uses this term to describe life in general (1 Tim. 2:2; 2 Tim. 2:4). Note how in 1 Jn. 2:16 translations are split between "the pride of life" (KJV, NASB) and "pride of possessions" (NRSV, NLT); the NIV attempts to incorporate both ideas by translating the phrase "boasting of what he has and does." In Lk. 15:12, 30, the prodigal son receives and squanders the inheritance of his father's "property" (KJV has "living" here).

In several NT instances of the word *bios*, both ideas—life and possessions—are apparent. For example, in Lk. 8:14, *bios* clearly means "life," but the word is used in a context in which life is characterized by worries concerning riches and pleasures. One of the clearest examples in the NT where the meanings overlap is the account of the poor widow who offered two copper coins. Here the KJV implies this overlap in meaning by stating that she offered "all her living" (Mk. 12:44; Lk. 21:4)—"material possessions" on the concrete level but "life" in general on the abstract level. See *NIDNTT-A*, 94-95.*

Noun: ζωή (*zōē*), GK *2437* (S *2222*), 135x. *zōē* mean "life." In the NT this word refers sometimes to present existence (Lk. 16:25; Acts 8:33; 17:25; Rom. 8:38) and sometimes to eternal life in the future (Mt. 7:14; 19:16; Mk. 10:30).

"Life" is an especially important theme in the gospel of John. John emphasizes in his gospel that future, eternal life may be experienced *in the present* through Jesus: "I tell you the truth, whoever hears my word and believes him who sent me has eternal life and will not be condemned; he has crossed over from death to life" (Jn. 5:24; cf. 11:25–26; 1 Jn. 3:14). John's purpose in writing his gospel is in fact to produce eternal life in its readers (Jn. 20:31). Paul agrees with John that eternal life can be entered upon in the present (Rom. 6:4; 8:6, 10), though for Paul (as for John) full life is still future. Consummated life will be a resurrected body in the new creation (2 Cor. 5:4). The book of Revelation powerfully depicts the new creation as a place where the redeemed may eat freely of the tree of life (Rev. 22:2, 14) and drink of the water of life (22:17).

Throughout the NT, Jesus Christ is closely associated with eternal life. He is the "bread of life" (Jn. 6:35, 48), "the way and the truth and the life" (14:6), "the author of life" (Acts 3:15), and the life of believers (Col. 3:4), and he has the power of an "indestructible life" (Heb. 7:16). Jn. 6:68 says that Jesus has the words of eternal life, and Jn. 17:2 says that Jesus has the authority to grant eternal life.

The opposite of life, of course, is death. Death comes as the wages of sin (Rom. 6:23). But because Jesus gave his life on the cross and came back to life in the resurrection, we who join with Jesus in his death and resurrection have life hidden with Christ in God (Col. 3:3) and have our names written in the Lamb's book of life (Rev. 20:15; 21:27). See *NIDNTT-A*, 226-28.

Noun: ψυχή (*psychē*), GK *6034* (S *5590*), 103x. In contrast to the classical Greek idea of soul as an entity separate and distinct from the body, the NT word *psychē* finds its definition in the OT understanding of *nepeš*, translated "life, breath, soul." The NT understanding of *psychē* encompasses the whole person. For example, 1 Pet. 3:20 uses *psychē* to refer to the "persons" rescued from the flood. In 2 Pet. 2:14 we read of unsteady "persons" who are easily enticed, and *psychē* appears in Rev. 18:13 among the goods for which merchants traded with Babylon, meaning "human lives." Herod sought to kill the *psychē*, the "life," of the boy Jesus.

In Mt. 6:25, Jesus teaches a lesson about the value of the kingdom of God, and in so doing illustrates the connectedness of the soul and body. "Therefore I tell you, do not worry about your *psychē* [life], what you will eat or what you will drink, or about your body, what you will wear. Is not *psychē* [life] more than food and the body more than clothing?" The assumption here is that the *psychē* is in need of food and drink, in the same way that the body is in need of clothing.

Like the Hebrew *nepeš*, the *psychē* is both the vital source of life in a person and the seat of the will or mind. Eutychus fell asleep while listening to Paul speak and fell three stories to his death. However, "Paul went down, and bending over him took him in his arms, and said, 'Do not be alarmed, for his *psychē* [life] is in him'" (Acts 20:10). Paul serves God "with my *psychē*" by proclaiming the gospel (Rom. 1:9), and later exhorts "every *psychē* [person] to be subject to the governing authorities" (Rom. 13:1). In Philippians, he instructs believers to live their lives worthily of Christ, so that they will "stand firm in one spirit, striving side by side with one *psychē* [mind] for the faith of the gospel" (Phil. 1:27–28).

psychē is also the seat of the emotions. For example, when Paul and Barnabas preach the gospel and great numbers of people, both Jews and Greeks, become believers, "the unbelieving Jews stirred up the Gentiles and poisoned their *psychē* [minds] against the brothers" (Acts 14:1–2). In Jesus' parable about the rich fool who hoards his food, the man says to his *psychē* (himself), "*Psychē*, you have ample goods laid up for many years; relax, eat, drink, be merry'" (Lk. 12:19). There is a profound warning in this parable. "But God said to him, 'You fool! This very night your *psychē* [life] is being demanded of you.'" (Lk. 12:20–21).

One of the most riveting exhortations Jesus gives to humanity includes the following: "Those who find their *psychē* [life] will lose it, and those who lose their *psychē* [life] for my sake will find it" (cf. Mt. 10:37–39). Here is the cost of what it means to follow Jesus Christ. We may either pursue our own *psychē*, and in so doing lose the true life that only comes from Jesus Christ. Or, by choosing to follow Jesus and subjecting all needs and desires of the *psychē* to the lordship of the crucified one, our *psychē* finds fulfilment in communion with its Creator, Sustainer, and Redeemer. See *NIDNTT-A*, 620-23.

LIFT

Old Testament

Verb: נָשָׂא (*nāśā*ʾ), GK 5951 (S 4984), 659x. *nāśā*ʾ means "to lift, raise high, bear, carry." It occasionally means "to forgive" on the part of God (i.e., "to carry away sin").

(1) *nāśā*ʾ is something that people can do. They may lift or raise their voice, as when Hagar lifts her voice and weeps over the impending death of her son (Gen. 21:16); God hears her cries and intervenes. Others also lift their voices in anguish: when Jacob kisses Rachel (Gen. 29:11),when the Israelites cry out under God's judgment (Jdg. 2:4), and when the men of Israel weep over the loss of Benjamin (21:2). The third commandment ("You shall not take the name of the LORD in vain") is literally, "You shall not *bear* the name of the Lord for what is worthless." Similarly, one may lift his or her "soul" (see *nepeš*, GK 5883) to the Lord in worship and petition (Ps. 25:1; 86:4; 143:9). One may also life up one's hands in prayer and praise to God (63:4). However, if one lifts up one's own head, *nāśā*ʾ connotes pride and arrogant independence from God (Jdg. 8:28; Job 10:15; Ps. 82:2, Zech. 1:21).

(2) *nāśā*ʾ is also a divine activity. In Isa. 46:3, the Lord carries his people, in marked contrast with idols, which must be carried. "Listen to me, O house of Jacob ... you whom I have upheld since you were conceived, and have *carried* since your birth." The suffering servant of Isaiah will "take up" our infirmities and carry our sorrows (53:4).

When the Lord passes before Moses, he proclaims, "The LORD, the LORD, a God merciful and gracious, slow to anger, and abounding in steadfast love and faithfulness, keeping steadfast love for the thousandth generation, *forgiving* iniquity and transgression and sin" (Exod. 34:6–8, cf. also Num. 14:18). When the psalmist confesses his sin and does not hide his iniquity, he says: "I will confess my transgressions to the LORD, and you *forgave* the guilt of my sin" (Ps. 32:5). Once a year a scapegoat would "carry away" the sins of the people of Israel (Lev. 16:22). In Isa. 53:12, the suffering servant is the only person who "bears" the sin of another person. This servant shares undeservedly and at great personal pain the sins and sorrows of others. As a result, he will make many righteous, and receive great honor and reward. See *NIDOTTE*, 3:160–63.

New Testament

Verb: ἐγείρω (*egeirō*), GK *1586* (S *1453*), 144x. In the transitive (active) sense *egeirō* means to "waken, lift up, stimulate." In the intransitive (passive) sense it conveys "to get up, rise up." See *raise*.

LIFT UP

Old Testament

Verb: רוּם (*rûm*), GK 8123 (S 7311), 197x. *rûm* means "to lift up, exalt."

(1) It can refer to lifting up or moving things higher, such as stones (Jos. 4:5), sacrifices (Num. 15:20; Ezek. 45:13), voices (Gen. 39:15; 2 Ki. 19:22), or hands (Gen. 41:44).

(2) *rûm* can also indicate the state of things that are high or exalted, such as God and his throne (Gen. 14:22; Ps. 46:10; Isa. 6:1) as well as the stars (Job 22:12). The psalmist calls the believer to lift high the Lord and his name (Ps. 18:46; 34:3; 57:5; 99:2, 5, 9).

(3) Additionally, *rûm* can be used metaphorically to refer to a proud and arrogant attitude. This is the meaning when *rûm* (or a related form) is combined with heart (Deut. 8:14; Ezek. 31:10) and eyes (2 Ki. 19:22; Ps. 131:1). God is opposed to all such pride and will judge it (Prov. 6:16–17; Ps. 18:27). Instead, all people should lift up or exalt God, who alone is worthy of the highest place. For those who are humble, who are not *rûm* of heart but dependent on him, God promises to give strength and to lift them up over their enemies with blessings and victory (Ps. 37:34). This lifting up is often described with the word picture of a horn, a symbol of strength: God will lift up (*rûm*) the horn of those who trust in him (1 Sam. 2:1, 10; Ps. 92:10). See *NIDOTTE*, 3:1078-80.

New Testament

Verb: αἴρω (*airō*), GK *149* (S *142*), 101x. *airō* can mean to "lift up, take up/away, carry off, remove." This verb can be used literally. The crowds cried out to "take Jesus away" and crucify him (Jn. 19:15). The disciples "picked up" twelve baskets of leftover from the feeding miracle (Mt. 14:20). Jesus' enemies "took up" stones to stone him (Jn. 8:59). Agabus "took" Paul's belt, tied his own hands and feet, and prophesied (Acts 21:11).

But *airō* also has a more figurative sense. Jesus "looked upward" (lit., "lifted up his eyes"; Jn. 11:41), a mighty angel "raised" his hand in oath (Rev. 10:5), and the believers "lifted up" their voices in prayer (Acts 4:24). Jesus willingly gives his life for the salvation of the world: "No one *takes* [my life] from me, but I lay it down of my own accord" (Jn. 10:17–18). Through his death, Jesus "has taken away" our sin (Col. 2:14). In Mt. 21:43, Jesus warns that the kingdom will be "taken away" from those who reject the Messiah. Finally, Jesus encourages the weary and heavy-laden with the invitation and promise: "*Take* my yoke upon you, and learn from me; for I am gentle and humble in heart, and you will find rest for your souls." (Mt. 11:28). See *NIDNTT-A*, 21-22.

Verb: ἀναλαμβάνω (*analambanō*), GK *377* (S *353*), 13x. *analambanō* means "to take up, lift up." See *take up*.

Verb: ἐπαίρω (*epairō*), GK *2048* (S *1869*), 19x. *epairō* means "to look up, lift up," though it is used in several senses: in a natural sense, it means "to look up"; in a religious sense, it denotes prayer, blessing, or hope; and in a secular sense, it means "to raise up" in opposition or exalting oneself in pride.

(1) *epairō* can simply mean to lift up one's eyes, as when Jesus "looked up and saw a great crowd," whom he then fed (Jn. 6:5), or when the disciples "looked up" after the transfiguration and saw only Jesus

(Mt. 17:8). In Acts 27:40, the sailors in the storm, as they sense land, "hoist up" the foresail.

(2) In a religious sense, Paul desires "that in every place the men should pray, *lifting up* holy hands without anger or argument" (1 Tim. 2:8). Jesus led his disciples out "as far as Bethany, and, *lifting up* his hands, he blessed them" (Lk. 24:50). When Jesus returns, those who love him and wait expectantly for him are to "stand up and *raise* your heads, because your redemption is drawing near" (Lk. 21:28).

(3) In the final nuance of *epairō*, Judas "lifted up" his heel against Jesus (Jn. 13:18). Paul's ministry aims to destroy "arguments and every proud obstacle *raised up* against the knowledge of God" (2 Cor. 10:5). Paul later rebukes the Corinthian church, which rejects his ministry, charging them with putting up with those who "make slaves of you, or prey upon you, or take advantage of you, or *pushes himself forward*" (11:20). See *NIDNTT-A*, 21-22.

Verb: ὑψόω (*hypsoō*), GK *5738* (S *5312*), 20x. In the LXX, *hypsoō* is similar to the Hebrew word *rûm*, which means to "lift up, exalt." However, in the NT, *hypsoō* is used almost exclusively in a theological way. For example, one of the great promises of God to believers is that in due time, they will be exalted or lifted up. There is one crucial condition for this promise, however: a humbling of oneself. Therefore, the NT often exhorts believers to "humble yourselves before the Lord and he *will lift you up*" (Jas. 4:10; 1 Pet. 5:6). See *exalt*.

LIGHT

Old Testament

Noun: אוֹר (*ʾôr*), GK 240 (S 216), 120x. *ʾôr* is generally used literally of "*light*" and sometimes of "lightning" (Job 36:30, 32; 37:3; Hos. 6:5). While many uses of this word simply refer to daylight (e.g., 1 Sam. 14:36; 2 Ki. 9:7), *ʾôr* is also used in several significant figurative ways.

(1) Light is an important concept in the OT. It is dependent on God and has come into existence only by his power. God's first creative act was to form light out of chaos. The initial creation account in Gen. 1:1 left the earth "formless and empty" (1:2). Into that formlessness God brought order, beginning with, "Let there be light" (1:3). Light is the first thing that the Bible records as being good (1:4). Additionally, God separated the light from the darkness (1:4). God's light offered order to a disorderly universe.

(2) Light is ultimately a divine quality; it is part of who God is. God "wraps himself in light as with a garment" (Ps. 104:2). Moreover, in a more personal sense, "the Lord is my light and my salvation" (Ps. 27:1); he is also "the light of Israel" (Isa. 10:17). Darkness is generally associated in the Scriptures with evil, but God promises to "turn darkness into light" (42:16). Isaiah also prophesies of the coming Messiah, that he will be a great "*light*" shining in a land of great darkness (9:2) and a "*light*" to the nations (42:6; 49:6). In the age to come, the glory of the Lord will shine (60:1–3) eternally (60:19-20).

(3) The OT authors use light to represent the quality of life that is pleasing to God. To obey God means to "walk before God in the light of life" (Ps. 56:13). Believers pray for God to let his "*light*" and truth guide them (43:3). Moreover, God's Word serves as a "lamp to my feet and a light to my path" (119:105). In God's light our lives become filled with light (36:9). Ps. 97:11 parallels "light ... upon the righteous" with "joy on the upright in heart." We should then heed the exhortation of the prophet: "Come, O house of Jacob, let us walk in the light of the Lord" (Isa. 2:5). See *NIDOTTE*, 1:324-29.

New Testament

Verb: ἅπτω (*haptō*), GK *721* (S 680, *681*), 39x. At its most basic level *haptō* means "to make close contact with something, touch something." But it can also mean "to light [a lamp]" (Lk. 8:16; 11:33; 15:8). See *touch*.

Noun: φῶς (*phōs*), GK *5890* (S *5457*),

72x. *phōs* identifies both the source of light such as the sun, fire, or lamp (Lk. 22:56; Acts 16:29; Rev. 22:5) and the light itself (Acts 9:3; 12:7). It is often used metaphorically, especially in John's writings.

The light/dark contrast is basic to biblical theology. "For God, who said, "Let *light* shine out of darkness," has shone in our hearts to give the light [*phōtismos*, GK *5895*] of the knowledge of the glory of God in the face of Jesus Christ." (2 Cor. 4:6, ESV). Jesus is "the *light* of the world" (Jn. 8:12; cf. 1:4, 5, 7, 8, 9), as are his true disciples (Mt. 5:14).

Biblical passages often use an interplay between physical and spiritual light. "Jesus answered, 'Are there not twelve hours of daylight? A man who walks by day will not stumble, for he sees by this world's *light*. It is when he walks by night that he stumbles, for he has no *light*" (Jn. 11:10–11).

"Light" can be used virtually as a name of Jesus (cf. Jas. 1:17). "And this is the judgment: the *light* has come into the world, and people loved the darkness rather than the *light* because their deeds were evil. For everyone who does wicked things hates the *light* and does not come to the *light*, lest his deeds should be exposed. But whoever does what is true comes to the *light*, so that it may be clearly seen that his deeds have been carried out in God" (Jn. 3:19–21, ESV). Light reveals, and therefore Jesus is the ultimate light (revelation) of God (2 Cor. 4:6; Heb. 1:3). Paul preaches that "the Christ must suffer and that, by being the first to rise from the dead, he would proclaim *light* both to our people and to the Gentiles" (Acts 26:23).

Light describes how disciples are to live. "The night is nearly over; the day is almost here. So let us put aside the deeds of darkness and put on the armor of *light*" (Rom. 13:12, NIV). "Formerly you were darkness, but now you are *light* in the Lord; walk as children of *light*" (Eph. 5:8). The "light/darkness" theme clearly illustrates that God expects his children to be fundamentally different from the world. "For all of you are sons of *light*, sons of the day. We are not of the night or of the darkness" (1 Thess. 5:5). Moreover, we are to testify to others about the light God has brought into this world: "But you are a chosen people ... a people belonging to God, that you may declare the praises of him who called you out of darkness into his wonderful *light*" (1 Pet. 2:9, NIV). See *NIDNTT-A,* 597-98.

LIGHT (A FIRE)

Old Testament

Verb: בָּעַר (*bāʿar*), GK 1277 (S 1197), 60x. Generally translated "to burn, light a fire, set ablaze, flare up, consume with fire," *bāʿar* can refer to a literal burning of fire or to a figurative "burning," be it of desire or anger.

(GIVE) LIGHT

New Testament

Verb: φωτίζω (*phōtizō*), GK *5894* (S *5461*), 11x. *phōtizō* means "to give light, enlighten." The root of this verb is *phōs* ("light," GK *5890*). It denotes the action of making visible things that are not seen. While the metaphor of giving light to a darkened place is physical, it carries moral connotations (e.g., of searching for holiness, Lk. 11:36). In 1 Cor. 4:5 this metaphor is spiritual, in that the final judgment will bring the hidden purposes of each person's heart to light. Moreover, Jesus Christ has abolished death in his resurrection and "has brought to light" both life and immortality through the gospel (2 Tim. 1:10). In fact, one purpose of this gospel is to "bring to light" God's previously unknown plan—that in Jesus Christ people have confident access to God (Eph. 3:9)..

Giving light can be synonymous with giving understanding. It is used of revealing God's eternal plan in Christ (Eph. 3:9), of coming to salvation defined as "being enlightened" (Heb. 6:4; 10:32), and of receiving a deepened understanding of God's will (Eph. 1:18).

The light given can also refer to a visual display of glory. The coming of heavenly glory (of an angel of God, Rev. 18:1; of

God himself, 21:23; 22:5) is depicted as a brilliant light. In the new Jerusalem the redeemed from every nation will not need light from a lamp or the sun, because the glory of the Lord God "will give light" to them." See *NIDNTT-A*, 597-98.

LIGHTEN

Old Testament

Verb: קָלַל (*qālal*), GK 7837 (S 7043), 82x. *qālal* means "to curse," though it is also used to express mitigation, such as the burden Moses carried as the judge of the Israelites that needed to be "lightened" (Exod. 18:22). See *curse*.

LIGHTNING

Old Testament

Noun: אוֹר (*ʾôr*), GK 240 (S 216), 120x. *ʾôr* is generally used literally of "*light*" and sometimes of "lightning" (Job 36:30, 32; 37:3; Hos. 6:5). See *light*.

LIKE, LIKEN

Old Testament

Verb: אָהַב (*ʾahab*), GK 170 (S 157), 217x. *ʾahab* is defined as "to love" or "to like." This verb is used to describe a variety of relationships in the OT. See *love*.

New Testament

Verb: ὁμοιόω (*homoioō*), GK *3929* (S *3666*), 15x. *homoioō* means "to make like something, liken, compare." This term also appears in contexts of Jesus' teaching in parables and similes about the kingdom of heaven (Mt. 13:24; 18:23; 22:2) and about kingdom ethics (Mt. 7:24–26; Lk. 6:47–49). Jesus instructs his followers not to"be like" the pagans in repetitive, babbling prayers (Mt. 6:8). The author of Hebrews explains about Christ's suffering, "It was necessary for him to *be made like* his brothers in every way," so that through his human experience of suffering and temptation, Christ is able to mercifully intercede for humans and help those who are tempted (Heb. 2:17–18). The emphasis in Hebrews is on Jesus' "likeness in every way" to humans, that is, his full humanity as opposed to an angelic nature, which could not suffer (2:14–16).

Adjective: ὅμοιος (*homoios*), GK *3927* (S *3664*), 45x. *homoios*, meaning "like," is heavily used in Jesus' teaching in parables, through the formula, "The kingdom of heaven is *like*" yeast, a mustard seed, a pearl, or a treasure (Mt. 13:31ff.; Lk. 13:18ff.). It is used in other similes offered by Jesus as teaching tools for kingdom principles. In Revelation, John uses *homoios* repeatedly to describe his amazing visions (Rev. 1:13, 15; 3:3ff.). A few contexts bear some theological nuances. Jesus' ethical teaching affirms the first great commandment, but he adds a second, which is "*like* the first," thereby associating the love of neighbor with love for God (Mt. 22:39). In a polemical and apologetic encounter with the Athenians, Paul insists (against the people's idolatrous beliefs) that "the divine being is not *like* gold or silver or stone" (Acts 17:29). Finally, John exclaims that at Jesus' appearing, "we will be *like* him," righteous, holy, and pure (1 Jn. 3:2).

(BE) LIKE

Old Testament

Verb: מָשַׁל (*māšal*), GK 5439 (S 4911), 17x. *māšal* bears two distinct meanings in the OT, one of which is "to compare, liken, be like." See *compare*.

LIKEN

Old Testament

Verb: מָשַׁל (*māšal*), GK 5439 (S 4911), 17x. *māšal* bears two distinct meanings in the OT, one of which is "to compare, liken, be like." See *compare*.

LIKENESS

Old Testament

Noun: דְּמוּת (*d^emût*), GK 1952 (S 1823), 25x. *d^emût* denotes a likeness between two things.

(1) *d^emût* can be used in a simple comparison, as in the lies of the wicked are "in the *likeness* of the venom of a snake" (Ps. 58:4). It can also indicate an image or pattern: "He [King Ahaz] saw an altar in Damascus and sent to Uriah the priest a *sketch* of the altar, with detailed plans for its construction" (2 Ki. 16:10). Additionally, *d^emût* is used to describe a shape or

figure: "Below the rim, *figures* of bulls encircled it" (2 Chr. 4:3). It can even denote audible similarities. "Listen, a noise on the mountains, in the *likeness* of a great multitude" (Isa. 13:4).

(2) *d^emût* is frequently used in the visions of Ezekiel (Ezek. 1:10, 13, 16, 22, 26, 28): "In the fire was what looked like four living creatures. In appearance their *form* was that of a man" (1:5; cf. 8:2). Notice that Ezekiel does not claim to have seen God; he has seen only the likeness of God. Daniel (Dan. 10:16) and John (Rev. 1:13) both share similar experiences.

(3) One of the more theologically important uses of *d^emût* is its association with the word *ṣelem* ("image").Then God said, "Let us make man in our image [*ṣelem*], in our likeness [*d^emût*], and let them rule over the fish of the sea and the birds of the air, over the livestock, over all the earth, and over all the creatures that move along the ground" (Gen. 1:26). The creation account affirms that humans as male and female are made in the likeness of God (5:1). There is much debate regarding the meaning behind the resemblance. One likely possibility is that *d^emût* explains what it means to be in the *ṣelem* of God. A particular way that this is manifested is in the function of dominion held by humankind. Just as God rules over creation, we too share in the exercise of his sovereignty. See *NIDOTTE*, 1:967-72.

New Testament

Noun: εἰκών (*eikōn*), GK *1635* (S *1504*), 23x. *eikōn* means "image, likeness." It generally refers to something shaped to resemble something else. See *image*.

Noun: ὁμοίωμα (*homoiōma*), GK *3930* (S *3667*), 6x. *homoiōma* has two basic meanings. (1) It can refer to "a similarity, a likeness." In Rom. 6 Paul describes what happens to people spiritually when they become Christians, of which water baptism is a symbol. We are buried with Jesus in his death. Paul concludes, "If we have been united with him in the *likeness* of his death, we will certainly also be united with him in his resurrection" (Rom. 6:5). Death reigned over people whose sin was not "like that" of Adam, i.e., was not a transgression of a specified law (5:14). (2) *homoiōma* also refers to having a similar image or likeness. Idol gods are made "to look like" animals and humans (Rom. 1:23). In Revelation, locusts "*looked like* horses prepared for battle" (Rev. 9:7).

homoiōma is theologically important in the first sense because it describes the incarnation of Jesus. Jesus was fully human and fully divine. Paul writes that "what the law was powerless to do ... God did by sending his own Son in the *likeness* of sinful man to be a sin offering" (Rom. 8:3). Later he writes that Jesus "made himself nothing, taking the very nature of a servant, being made in human *likeness*" (Phil. 2:7). By taking on the likeness of humanity, Jesus took on more than mere human appearance. He became perfectly and therefore uniquely human as God intended humanity to be. Although he resisted temptation to sin (Heb. 4:15) as a perfect Lamb of God (Jn. 1:29), he went to the grave bearing the sin of all humans (Gal. 3:13; Phil. 2:8). He rose from the grave exerting power over sin and death and making salvation available to all (Rom. 6:5; Phil. 2:9–11). See *NIDNTT-A*, 409-10.*

LIKEWISE

New Testament

Adverb: ὁμοίως (*homoiōs*), GK *3931* (S *3668*), 30x. *homoiōs* means "likewise, similarly." Peter affirms he will never deny Jesus but is be willing to die for him, and "all the disciples said *likewise*" (Mt. 26:35). In the Golden Rule, we must "likewise" treat others as we would like to be treated (Lk. 6:31). After the illustration of neighborly conduct through the parable of the good Samaritan, Jesus instructs the scribe to "go and do *likewise*" (Lk. 10:37). In Jn. 5:19, Jesus likens his own ministry with the work of God.

This word is also used for some ethical implications for marriage. Both Paul and Peter teach about mutuality and reciprocity between spouses. Paul advises the husband to perform his marital duty to his wife, and "*likewise* the wife to her husband" (1 Cor. 7:3; cf. also v. 4). Here the mutuality and reciprocity of the sexual relationship is emphasized for the purpose of thwarting Satan in the area of immorality. Peter teaches about the marital relationship in the context of submission in order to give a good witness. He begins with a general instruction to submit ourselves to every authority," following Christ's example. After addressing slaves (1 Pet. 2:18–25), Peter appeals to wives, saying "wives, *in the same way*, be submissive to your own husbands," in order to model Christ's example to unbelievers (1 Pet. 3:1). Reciprocally, husbands are enjoined to "*likewise* be considerate … and treat them [wives] with respect" (1 Pet. 3:7). Later, Peter instructs young men to "*likewise* submit to elders," as elders serve the church by shepherding it (1 Pet. 5:5). See *NIDNTT-A*, 409-10.

LIMIT

Old Testament

Noun: חֹק (*ḥōq*), GK 2976 (S 2706), 131x. *ḥōq* is derived from the related verb *ḥāqaq*, which means "to cut in, inscribe, decree" and denotes something that is limited or restricted. Most frequently *ḥōq* refers to the prescribed law of God (see *decree*). Less frequently, it expresses a fixed quantity or some sort of limit. For example, in nature God sets a "boundary" for the waters or seas (Job 26:10; 38:10; Prov. 8:29), a "limit" for the rain (Job 28:26), and a "limit" on each one's days (Job 14:5).

Noun: קֵץ (*qēṣ*), GK 7891 (S 7093), 67x. *qēṣ* generally bears one of three distinct but related meanings: "end," "limit," and at times "boundary." See *end*.

LIP

Old Testament

Noun: שָׂפָה (*śāpâ*) GK 8557 (S 8193), 178x.

(1) *śāpâ* is commonly used to denote the physical "lip(s)" (Num. 30:7, 13; Song 4:3, 11; 5:13). By extension, it can refer to the mouth as the organ of speech (see Ps. 51:15; Eccl. 12:10, where "lips" and "mouth" are parallel terms), or to that which proceeds from the lips, namely, a person's *language* (Gen. 11:1a, 6–7, 9; Ps. 81:5; Isa. 19:18) or *speech* (Prov. 16:27 NIV; 22:11 NIV; Isa. 33:19). For metaphorical uses of this word, see *shore*.

(2) Almost half the occurrences of *śāpâ* (86x) are found in the poetic and wisdom books of Job, Psalms, and Proverbs. In these books, this word often stands for one's speech or verbal communication and regularly has negative connotations. For example, in Proverbs *śāpâ* is often described as perverse/corrupt (4:24; 19:1), flattering or smooth (7:21), lying (10:18; 12:22; 17:7), sinful (12:13), a burning fire (16:27), and wicked (17:4). Conversely, the *śāpâ* (lips or speech) of the wise is described in positive terms (truthful in 12:19, gracious in 22:11, having knowledge in 20:15).

(3) In Isa. 29:13, *śāpâ* is used in connection with hypocrisy among God's people. Here God draws a sharp contrast between their lips and their hearts, indicating that the people of Israel know how to speak as if they are devoted to God, when in truth their hearts are far away. Jesus picks up this theme to describe the unbelieving Jews of his day (Mt. 15:7–9; Mk. 7:6–7).

LISTED

Old Testament

Noun: מִסְפָּר (*mispār*), GK 5031 (S 4557), 134x. *mispār* means "number," the result of what happens when someone has "counted" or "listed" something. See *number*.

LISTEN

Old Testament

Verb: שָׁמַע (*šāmaʿ*), GK 9048 (S 8085), 1165x. *šāmaʿ* means "to hear, listen, pay attention to, perceive, obey, proclaim, announce." See *hear*.

LITTLE

Old Testament

Noun: מְעַט (*meʾaṭ*), GK 5071 (S

4592), 101x. *m*e'*at* conveys the small amount of something, usually an object such as food (Gen. 43:11), persons (Deut. 7:7; Jer. 42:2), and time (Isa. 26:20; Hos. 1:4); it may be translated as "little" or "few." The word occurs with high frequency in historical, poetic, and prophetic texts. The term is used in Deut. 7:7 to emphasize the divine motive behind the Lord's choosing of his people, not because they "were more numerous than other peoples, for you were the *fewest* of all peoples." In a world where bigger is better, it is good to know that God is sometimes more interested in the "little guy." See *NIDOTTE*, 2:1016-17.

New Testament

Adjective: μίκρος (*mikros*), GK *3625* (S *3398*), 46x. *mikros* is the antonym of *megas* ("great") and means "small, little, insignificant." See *small*.

Adjective: ὀλίγος (*oligos*), GK *3900* (S *3641*), 40x. *oligos* typically denotes a small number, a small amount of something, or shortness in size or time. See *few*.

LITTLE CHILD

New Testament

Noun: παιδίον (*paidion*), GK *4086* (S *3813*), 52x. *paidion* is a diminutive form of *pais* ("child"; GK *4090*) and is restricted to young children of either gender (Mt. 14:21)—e.g., the newborn Jesus (Lk. 1:59) and Moses (Heb. 11:23), the young child Jesus (Mt. 2:8), the Syrophoenician's child (Mk. 7:26–17), and demon-possessed child (Mk. 9:24).

Jesus often uses little children as an illustration. When the disciples are arguing about who is greatest in the kingdom of heaven, Jesus places a child in their midst and instructs them that they must "change and become like *little children*" in order to enter the kingdom (Mt. 18:1–5). When they try to stop children coming to Jesus, he says, "Let the *little children* come to me and do not hinder them, for to such belongs the kingdom of heaven" (19:14). He also uses children as an example of humility, of the last being first in God's kingdom (Mk. 9:37).

Jesus uses *paidion* as a term of endearment for his disciples (Jn. 21:5), John uses it of Christians (1 Jn. 2:14, 18), and Paul encourages the Corinthians not to be "like *children*" in their thinking (1 Cor. 14:20). See *NIDNTT-A*, 427-29.

LIVE

Old Testament

Verb: גּוּר (*gûr*), GK 1591 (S 1481), 82x. The basic meaning of *gûr* is to "live, settle, dwell." By and large, this verb refers to someone living outside of their clan, that is, dwelling among people who are not blood relatives. It almost always has the sense of temporariness. See *dwell*.

Verb: הָיָה (*ḥāyâ*), GK 2649 (S 2421, 2425), 283x. *ḥāyâ* indicates "life" or "having life" and is the generic term for "life" or "to live" in the OT (Gen. 5:3–30; 11:11–26; cf. Num. 4:19). See *life*.

Verb: יָשַׁב (*yāšab*), GK 3782 (S 3427), 1088x. The general meaning of *yāšab* is to "sit, sit down," with the connotations of "live, dwell, remain, settle."

(1) A person may sit on a chair, on a throne (2 Ki. 11:19; Neh. 2:6; Jer. 33:17), in the entrance to a tent (Gen. 18:1), in the dust (Isa. 47:1), or in a community of people (Ps. 1:1).

(2) *yāšab* can also mean "to live" in a house (Gen. 38:11; Jos. 2:15; cf. Prov. 21:19) as the place of one's residence.

(3) But this verb is also used for a person who stays in a locality for a longer period of time. In such cases it means "to settle, dwell." For example, Lot "settles" among the cities of the plain (Gen. 13:12), but after the destruction of Sodom and Gomorrah, he goes to "live" in mountains around Zoar (19:30). When the Israelites cross over the Jordan and take over the promised land, Moses promises that they "will live [there] in safety" (Deut. 12:10; cf. 11:31). After the exile and the return to Canaan, the people once again "live" there (Neh. 7:73; 11:1–4). Sometimes Bible translators use the word "residents" for "those who live in" a particular locality.

(4) God, too, has a place of residence. Usually the OT speaks of God as "enthroned" (Ps. 2:4; 22:3) or dwelling in heaven (2 Chr. 6:21, 30). But God does have an earthly dwelling of sorts, for even though he is transcendent, he is said to be enthroned "between the cherubim" above the ark of the covenant (1 Sam. 4:4, 2 Sam. 6:2; Isa. 37:16). See *NIDOTTE*, 2:550–51.

Verb: שָׁכַן (*šākan*), GK 8905 (S 7931) 130x. *šākan* has the basic meaning "to live, dwell, settle." In nearly one-third of the times this verb is used in the OT, God is the subject. See *dwell*.

New Testament

Verb: ἀναστρέφω (*anastrephō*), GK *418* (S *390*), 9x. *anastrephō* can mean "to turn back," but it has a related meaning "to conduct oneself, live" in a certain way. In a literal sense, when the servants of the high priest went to retrieve the apostles from the Jerusalem prison and did not find them, they "went back" and reported what they found.

But for the most part, *anastrephō* has a spiritual meaning. Paul asserts to the Corinthians by his testimony of conscience, "that we *have behaved* in the world with holiness and godly sincerity" (2 Cor. 1:12). This stands in contrast to his description in Eph. 2:3, where the apostle notes that "all of us once *lived* among [the disobedient] in the passions of our flesh." Paul catalogues high moral expectations for the conduct of believers, particularly those who hold office so that they may "know how people ought *to conduct themselves* in the household of God" (1 Tim. 3:15). All believers should "live" their lives here on earth as strangers in reverent fear (1 Pet. 1:17); we should "*live* honorably in every way" (Heb. 13:18). See *NIDNTT-A*, 49-50.

Verb: ζάω (*zaō*), GK *2409* (S *2198*), 140x. The basic sense of *zaō* is "to live, be alive." This "living" has at least three distinct referents in the NT.

(1) *zaō* can mean to live physically, often in contrast to physical death (e.g., Acts 22:22; Rom. 7:1; 1 Cor. 7:39; Phil. 1:22). Other texts use this verb to signify the divine power to create physical life in the present realm. In this sense, Jesus has power to give over physical death, "My daughter has just died. But come and put your hand on her, and she will *live*" (Mt. 9:18; cf. Mk. 5:23; Jn. 4:50). This same life-giving power is evident in the apostles' ministries (Acts 9:41; 20:12). *zaō* is also used to describe Jesus' resurrection life, for the disciples "heard that Jesus *was alive*" (Mk. 16:11). The angels at Jesus' tomb query, "Why do you look for the *living* among the dead?" (Lk. 24:5; cf. 24:23). According to the apostles, Jesus was raised to physical life from physical death: "After his suffering, he showed himself to these men and gave many convincing proofs that he *was alive*" (Acts 1:3; cf. 25:19; Rom. 14:9a; 2 Cor. 13:4; Rev. 1:18b; 2:8).

(2) *zaō* can also mean to live in a transcendent, spiritual sense. This spiritual life is realized in two realms: in the present world and in the glory of the life to come. (a) In the present world, the Spirit causes those who listen to the voice of the Son of God to enjoy new, eternal life already now (Jn. 5:25; 11:26). Likewise, those who accept Jesus are no longer dead but alive: "In the same way, count yourselves dead to sin but *alive* to God in Christ Jesus" (Rom 6:11; cf. Rom. 8:13; Gal. 2:19–20). This life enjoyed in the present is accomplished through the presence of the "Spirit" (Gal. 5:25). (b) This eternal life in the present will issue forth into physical resurrection life, for "when the dead will hear the voice of the Son of God [they] … will live" (Jn. 5:25). In John, this future blessed life that the believer will enjoy is a continuation of one's present life, "I am the resurrection and the life. He who believes in me *will live*, even though he dies" (Jn. 11:25; cf. 6:51, 58; 14:19). Paul envisions the same reality, "He died for us so that, whether we are awake or asleep, we may *live* together with him" (1 Thess. 5:10). At times, *zaō* occurs with respect to various items that offer and effect life in his people: "*living* oracles" (Acts 7:38), "*living*

word of God" (1 Pet. 1:23; cf. Heb. 4:12), "*living* way" (Heb. 10:20), "*living* hope" (1 Pet. 1:3), "*living* bread" (Jn. 6:51a).

(3) Lastly, *zaō* can mean to conduct one's life according to a particular pattern of behavior. Paul once "lived" according to the dictates of the Pharisees (Acts 26:5). The conduct of one's life can have a moral quality, either good or evil. With respect to evil conduct, the prodigal son was "*living* immorally" as he squandered his father's wealth (Lk. 15:13). Paul asks, "How shall we who died to sin still *live* in it?" (Rom. 6:2). With respect to good conduct, there are those "who desire to *live* in a godly manner" (1 Tim. 3:12). The grace of God teaches people "to *live* sensibly, righteously and godly in the present age" (Tit. 2:12). See *NIDNTT-A*, 226-28.

Verb: κατοικέω [*katoikeō*], GK *2997* (S *2730*), 44x. The verb *katoikeō* means "to inhabit, live, dwell," with an emphasis on living in a place for some time, perhaps even permanently. It is comprised of two parts: *kata* meaning "down," and *oikeō*, meaning "to make a home in." The first part of the word, *kata*, adds a sense of permanence, just as "down" does in the English phrase "to settle down."

(1) Abraham "settled down" in Haran before God resettled him in Canaan (Acts 7:4); when he arrived, he "dwelt permanently" in tents (Heb. 11:9). After returning from Egypt, Joseph and Mary "settled down" in Nazareth (Mt. 2:23), and after leaving Nazareth, Jesus "lived" in the town of Capernaum (Mt. 4:13).

In several passages, reference is made to "those who *live* in Jerusalem" (Lk. 13:4; Acts 2:14). In addition to a city, a person can also be said to live in a province, such as Judea (Acts 11:29) or Asia (Acts 19:10). On an even larger scale, Revelation refers many times to "those who *live* on the earth" (Rev. 3:10; 6:10; cf. 17:2, "*inhabitants* of the earth").

(2) There are also spiritual uses of *katoikeō*. Demons can "take up residence" in a person (Mt. 12:45). Christ can live in a person as well, as when Paul prays for the Ephesian Christians that "Christ *settle down permanently* in [their] hearts through faith" (Eph. 3:17). God does not "live" in temples or other man-made structures (Acts 7:48; 17:24). Deity does permanently resides in Christ: "in Christ all the fullness of Deity *lives* in bodily form" (Col. 2:9; cf. 1:19). Finally, Peter tells us that righteousness will be a permanent aspect of the new heavens and new earth (2 Pet. 3:13). See *NIDNTT-A*, 404-5.

Verb: περιπατέω (*peripateō*), GK *4344* (S *4043*), 95x. Literally, *peripateō* means "to walk around" (Mt. 9:5; 11:5; Jn. 6:66; Rev. 2:1; see *walk*). Figuratively, the NT uses *peripateō* to refer to the way believers behave or conduct daily life (Mk. 7:5; Eph. 2:2; 2 Cor. 5:7; Gal. 5:16). Some translations use "live" for this meaning.

Used figuratively, *peripateō* can express the consistent behavior of someone's life. The word is used with regard to walking according to the traditions of the elders (Mk. 7:5) and Jewish customs (Acts 21:21). This use especially describes the kind of behavior that should mark the lives of Christians. Believers used to walk according to their passions and according to the world (Eph. 2:2; Col. 3:7). However, through the power of Jesus they can now walk in a new life (Rom. 6:4). As a result, believers walk according to the Spirit and not the flesh (Rom. 8:4; Gal. 5:16). They are to "*behave* decently" and not indulge the passions (Rom. 13:13), to "*walk* by faith, not by sight" (2 Cor. 5:7), to "do" the good works that God has created ahead of time for them to do (Eph. 2:10), to "*live* a life worthy of their calling" (Eph. 4:1; 1 Thess. 4:1), and to "*live* a life of love" (Eph. 5:2). Once someone has received Jesus Christ, he or she is to continue to walk in him (Col. 2:6). See *NIDNTT-A*, 453-54.

Verb: σκηνόω (*skēnoō*), GK *5012* (S *4637*), 5x. *skēnoō* means "dwell, live," though it often retains the notion of pitching a tent. In Rev. 12:12 is simply refers to those who "live" in heaven. See *dwell*.

LIVESTOCK

Old Testament

Noun: בְּהֵמָה ($b^e hēmâ$), GK 989 (S 929), 190x. The noun $b^e hēmâ$ can be translated "beast, animal, cattle." See *animal*.

Noun: מִקְנֶה (*miqneh*), GK 5238 (S 4735), 76x. *miqneh* is derived from the verbal root *qānâ* ("to buy") and is bound up with the idea of possessions acquired or purchased. In the biblical text, *miqneh* describes livestock, including pack animals, cattle, sheep, and goats. Since among nomadic peoples livestock constitute their primary source of wealth, it is understandable how *miqneh* comes to have the meaning "livestock."

miqneh is regularly found in notices of economic wealth: "Abram had become very wealthy in *livestock* and in silver and gold" (Gen. 13:2; cf. 26:14; 36:7; Jos. 22:8; 2 Chr. 32:29; Job 1:3; Eccl. 2:7). Thus, the plague of hail that kills the *miqneh* of the Egyptians (Exod. 9:22–25) is a significant blow to their economy. In contrast, the livestock of the Israelites (and those Egyptians who heed the warning) are spared (Exod. 9:20, 26). The psalmist emphasizes this theme by picturing Israel as a flock under God's care: "But he brought his people out like *a flock*; he led them like sheep through the desert. He guided them safely, so they were unafraid" (Ps. 78:52–53). See *NIDOTTE*, 2:1089-92.

LIVING

Old Testament

Noun: חַיָּה (*ḥayyâ*), GK 2651 (S 2416), 96x. Based on the verb "to be alive" (*ḥāyâ*, GK 2649), *ḥayyâ* is a generic term for all kinds of living animals (Gen. 1:28, 30; Lev. 11:2), though usually of nondomesticated, land animals (e.g., Gen. 1:24, "wild animals"). See *animal*.

Adjective: חַי (*ḥay*), GK 2645 (S 2416), 146x. *ḥay* describes something as living, having movement, or showing vigor.

(1) *ḥay* is used of animals when God created the world (Gen. 1:20, 21, 24) and of human beings when God made Adam a living creature (2:7). Adam's helpmeet was named Eve because she is the mother of "all *the living*" (3:20). Abraham gives everything he owns to Isaac, but while he is still living, he gives gifts to his other children as well (25:6). Aaron helps to atone for the sin of Israel and stops the spread of a deadly plague by taking hold of a censer, lighting incense in it, and standing "between the dead and the living" (Num. 16:46). The psalmist declares that he walks before the LORD "in the land of the living" (Job 28:13; Ps. 116: 9; cf. Ruth 2:20).

(2) Israel is in awe of God's presence because they know that listening to the voice of "the living God" puts their mortal lives in danger (Deut. 5:26). Likewise, David is angry that Goliath is not in awe of Israel's God and asks, "Who is this uncircumcised Philistine, that he should defy the armies of the *living* God" (1 Sam. 17:26, 36). David knows that his God is the living God and will therefore act to make things right. That is why he also writes, "My soul thirsts for God, for the *living* God" (Ps. 42:2; cf. 84:2). It is important theologically to know that God is indeed the *living* God, who is active in history. While God demonstrates this in the OT by intervening on behalf of Israel, it is by invading history on the first Christmas that he proves himself to be a *living* God.

LIVING CREATURE

New Testament

Noun: ζῷον (*zōon*), GK *2442* (S *2226*), 23x. *zōon* signifies a "living creature." In the NT, "living creatures" are of two sorts. (1) The first kind is an animal, either wild or domesticated. *zōon* refers to the "animals" offered in the sacrificial system of the OT (Heb. 13:11). Blasphemers are compared to "unreasoning animals" (1 Pet. 2:12; Jude 10). (2) *zōon* may also signify a supernatural creature. This term is used of the four "living" creatures before God's throne in Revelation (Rev. 4:6–9; cf. 5:6, 8, 11, 14; 6:1, 3, 5–7; 7:11; 14:3; 15:7; 19:4). These creatures resemble the fantastic creatures described in Ezek. 1:5. See *NIDNTT-A*, 226-28.*

LOAF

Old Testament

Noun: כִּכָּר (*kikkār*), GK 3971 (S 3603), 68x. *kikkār* has the basic meaning of a "round disk" and can refer to a disk of metal (see *talent*), a round loaf of bread, or a circular area of land (see *plain*). A *kikkār* of bread is a round loaf used for daily sustenance (Jdg. 8:5; 1 Sam. 2:36; Jer. 37:21) and also for religious practices (Exod. 29:23; 1 Sam. 10:3). A loaf of bread can also be used as part of a celebration, as when David gives a loaf of bread to everyone present when he brings the ark into Jerusalem (1 Chr. 16:3). See *NIDOTTE*. 2:636-37.

New Testament

Noun: ἄρτος (*artos*), GK *788* (S *740*), 97x. *artos* means "bread" or more generally "food." See *bread*.

LONG

Old Testament

Noun: אֹרֶךְ (*ʾōrek*), GK 802 (S 753), 95x. *ʾōrek* means length and is used with reference to either space or time. See *length*.

LONG AGO

Old Testament

Noun or Adjective: קֶדֶם (*qedem*), GK 7710 (S 6924), 61x. This word originally meant "in front of" or "before" and came to denote "east" (see *east*). But this word is also used temporally to mean "ancient" or "long ago." See *ancient*.

LONGSUFFERING

See *patience*.

LOOK

Old Testament

Verb: חָזָה (*ḥāzâ*), GK 2600 (S 2372), 68x. *ḥāzâ* means "to see, observe, gaze"; it is a broad word, having a variety of nuances. See *see*.

Verb: נָבַט (*nābaṭ*), GK 5564 (S 5027), 70x. As with other Hebrew words used to denote "seeing," *nābaṭ* may refer to physical sight, mental activities, or the way in which God and humans relate.

(1) Whether of physical sight or of mental activity, *nābaṭ* usually has a directional aspect: someone directs his or her physical sight or mental attention toward something else for a specific reason. Of physical sight, Abraham "looks up" at the sky because the number of stars represents the number of his promised offspring (Gen. 15:5), and the sinful Israelites "look at" the bronze snake in order to be healed (Num. 21:9). Of mental activity, this word can refer to actions such as discernment (23:21), paying attention (Ps. 94:9), and deep consideration (1 Sam. 16:7; Ps. 74:20; 119:6, 15). God commands his people to "look to" or "consider" Abraham and Sarah, "the rock from which you were cut," so as to see the faithfulness of the promise-keeping God (Isa. 51:1–2).

(2) God directs his sight and, therefore, his attention toward humankind (Ps. 33:13). Nothing in all the earth escapes his sight (Job 28:24), and his "looking" causes the earth to tremble because of his glory (Ps. 104:31–32). God "looks down" from on high at humans to judge them (Isa. 18:4), yet he also "*looks down* … to hear the groans of prisoners and release those condemned to death" (Ps. 102:20). Revealing his own desires God says, "And to this one I *will look*: to the poor and broken spirit that is trembling at my word" (Isa. 66:2b). Believers cry for God's forgiving look: "Do not be exceedingly angry, O LORD, and do not remember iniquity forever. Please *look*, we are all your people" (Isa. 64:9). Many people throughout history have not "looked to" God, but on the day of the Lord, they "*will look* on him whom they pierced," and they will mourn (Zech. 12:10). Believers, however, trust in God, for "those who *look to* him also shine, and their faces are not ashamed" (Ps. 34:4–5). See *NIDOTTE*, 3:8-10.*

Verb: רָאָה (*rāʾâ*), GK 8011 (S 7200 and 7202), 1,311x. *rāʾâ* is the most frequent Heb. verb for "seeing," encompassing a variety of actions including physical, visionary, and mental. See *see*.

Interjection: הִנֵּה (*hinnēh*), GK 2180 (S 2009) 1061x.

Interjection הֵן (*hēn*), GK 2176 (S 2005

and 3860), 107x. *hinnēh* and *hēn* represent two different ways of spelling the same interjection or particle. See *behold.*

New Testament

Verb: βλέπω (*blepō*), GK *1063* (S *991*), 133x. *blepō* is a general word meaning "to see," but it can also mean "to look at, watch." See *see.*

Verb: κατανοέω (*katanoeō*), GK *2917* (S *2657*), 14x. Although this term is sometimes translated as "consider, perceive, look," these English words do not communicate the depth of knowledge presumed by the word. See *consider*.

Interjection: ἴδε (*ide*), GK *2623* (S *2396*), 29x. *ide* means "see!" or "look!" This word is actually the aorist imperative of the verb *horaō* ("to see"; GK *3972*). It is used when addressing a group of people: to draw attention to something (Mt. 25:20; Mk. 2:24; Gal. 5:2) or to take notice of the unexpected (Jn. 3:26; 7:26). *ide* is also used to point to a place or individual to say "here it is" (e.g., "*see* the place where they laid him," Mk. 16:6).

Interjection: ἰδού (*idou*), GK *2627* (S *2400*), 200x. *idou* ("look, behold") is derived from the aorist principal part of the verb *horaō* and, with *kai idou* ("and behold!"), is often used to attract attention to something surprising or new (Mt. 12:2; Mk. 2:24), whether in the proclamation of salvation (Lk. 2:34) or the fulfillment of a promise (Mt. 12:41; Mk. 14:41–42; Jn. 4:35). It is often associated with the working of a miracle or otherwise displaying something of divine origin (cf. Mt. 27:51). There is no exact English equivalent, and translation often depends on the context. If the writer is drawing attention to something that can be seen, "Look" can be used. If attention is drawn to a miraculous event, the older English "Lo" or "Behold" still functions well. See *NIDNTT-A*, 413-15.

LOOK AFTER

New Testament

Verb: ἐπισκέπτομαι (*episkeptomai*), GK *2170* (S *1980*), 11x. *episkeptomai* means "to visit, take care of." Most often, it means to visit with a heart for the welfare of others, for the sake of Christ. It is no surprise that "episcopal" was retained in English to refer to pastors who "visit" and "take care of" their flock.

At times the verb denotes a hospital or prison visit (Mt. 25:36, 43; Acts 7:23), but can also refer to serving widows (cf. *serve* [*diakoneō*]) and taking care of orphans (Jas..1:27). Clearly, *episkeptomai* means more than just casually stopping by. Accordingly, the apostles choose men full of wisdom and the Spirit to do just that concerning the needy (Acts 6:3), and it was this verb that was the motive behind Paul's second missionary journey (15:36). The verb is quoted in Heb. 2:6 from Ps. 8:4: "What is man that you are mindful of him, the son of man that you *care* for him?" (NIV).

When Christ is the one "visiting," the verb takes on a redemptive significance. James, at the Jerusalem council, says that the fallen booth of David was rebuilt at the "visitation" of Christ to the Gentiles (Acts 15:14). Zechariah recognizes that the birth of Jesus is the visitation of God to his people that will bring promised redemption (Lk. 1:68, 78), just as the crowds at Nain recognized that God had indeed "visited" his people in Jesus Christ because they saw him raise the dead. *episkeptomai*, used in this redemptive-historical sense, is pregnant with the "Immanuel principle"—namely, God's promise that "I will be their God, and they will be my people" (Jer. 31:33; Ezek. 37:27; 2 Cor. 6:16; Heb. 8:10). See *NIDNTT-A*, 198.

LOOK AT

New Testament

Verb: βλέπω (*blepō*), GK *1063* (S *991*), 133x. *blepō* is a general word meaning "to see," but it can also mean "to look at, watch." See *see*.

Verb: ἐμβλέπω (*emblepō*), GK *1838* (S *1689*), 11x. Most of the time, *emblepō* describes a person looking specifically at someone or something. The prefix *em-* usually adds a note of intensity. John "stares" at Jesus before proclaiming, "Behold, the Lamb of God" (Jn. 1:36).

Jesus tells his disciples to "look at" (and learn from) the birds so as to be comforted in God's providence (Mt. 6:26). Jesus "looks directly at" his listeners when he tells them that God can do even the impossible (Mt. 19:26; Mk. 10:27). As Jesus rebukes the unbelievers through his parable of the wicked tenants, he "looks directly at them" and applies Ps. 118 to their situation (Lk. 20:17). At Jesus' trial, the woman "looks directly" at Peter and asks if he is a disciple of Jesus (Mk. 14:67). Jesus "*looks straight* at Peter" when the rooster's crow signals his prophesied denial of Christ (Lk. 22:61). The disciples "stare" into heaven at Jesus' ascension (Acts 1:11)

When Jesus heals the blind man, he can see (Mk. 8:25). There may not be a heightened sense of intensity in this usage, in Jesus looking at Peter in Jn. 1:42, or Paul not being able to see after his encounter with Jesus on the road to Damascus (Acts 22:11). See *NIDNTT-A*, 96.*

LOOK DOWN ON

New Testament

Verb: ἐξουθενέω (*exoutheneō*), GK *2024* (S *1848*), 11x. *exoutheneō* essentially means "to hold someone in contempt, ridicule, despise" (Rom. 14:3; Gal. 4:14), although it can also refer to expressions of that contempt as well, as in the ridicule Christ suffered at the hands of Herod (Lk. 23:11). This verb is used by Peter in his quotation of Ps. 118:22 about the stone that was "rejected" becoming the capstone (Acts 4:11). Paul was idiomatically accused of being a poor speaker who "amounted to nothing" (2 Cor. 10:10). One issue that arose in the church at Corinth was that of believers suing one another. Paul criticized the Corinthians for going before unbelievers for judgment. He maintained that the most "insignificant" believer was well equipped to make such judgments (1 Cor. 6:4). See *NIDNTT-A*, 191.

LOOK FOR

Old Testament

Verb: בָּקַשׁ (*bāqaš*), GK 1335 (S 1245), 225x. *bāqaš* refers to looking for or a striving after someone or something. See *seek*.

New Testament

Verb: ἐπιζητέω (*epizēteō*), GK *2118* (S *1934*), 13x. *epizēteō* means "to look for, desire after, strive toward, hope for." The prefix *epi-* generally adds a note of intensity. When Jesus hides himself from the people, they look for him (Lk. 4:42). Herod searches for Peter when he escapes from prison, and not finding him kills the guards (Acts 12:19). The Roman proconsul is "looking" to hear (i.e., desiring to hear) the Word of God (Acts 13:7), and the Pharisees "look for" miraculous signs (Mt. 12:39).

In the NT letters, *epizēteō* refers not only to the searching, but to the actual striving after something that has not yet been obtained. Israel sought earnestly for God's election (Rom. 11:7). People can strive to attain gifts (Phil. 4:17) and even salvation (Rom. 11:7). Christians should "look for" the heavenly land (Heb. 11:14) and for "the city that is to come" (13:14). See *NIDNTT-A*, 224-25.

Verb: προσδοκάω (*prosdokaō*), GK *4659* (S *4328*), 16x. *prosdokaō* denotes an expectation or waiting born of either hope or fear. See *expect*.

LOOK STRAIGHT

New Testament

Verb: ἀτενίζω (*atenizō*), GK *867* (S *816*), 14x. *atenizō* means "to look with intensity, stare, gaze." All uses of this verb except for 2 Cor. 3:7, 13 are in the writings of Luke. After Jesus reads from Isa. 61 in the synagogue, he sits down in silence and "all the eyes in the synagogue *look straight* at him" (Lk. 4:20). Stephen "gazes" at the glory of God just before his martyrdom (Acts 7:55). Cornelius "stares" at the angel who is visiting him and asks, "What is it, Lord?" (10:4). When Elymas attempts to keep the proconsul from believing the gospel, Paul "*looks straight* at him" and pronounces a curse on him (13:9). Paul uses *atenizō* to picture the way in which the Israelites "were not able to *look intently* into the face of Moses" as it reflected the glory of the Lord under the old covenant (2 Cor. 3:7, 13). See *NIDNTT-A*, 79.

LOOK UP

New Testament

Verb: ἀναβλέπω (*anablepō*), GK *329* (S *308*), 25x. The root *blepō* means "to see, look." When *ana* (a preposition meaning "up") is prefixed to a verb, it sometimes carries the idea of upward motion, as is the case here. (1) Persons with their eyes fixed elsewhere "look up" so as to see what is around them (Lk. 21:1). The women walking to Jesus' grave "look up" to see that the rock has been rolled away from the tomb (Mk. 16:4). (2) People can also look up so as to see something above them. Jesus looks up toward heaven to pray (Mt. 14:19; Mk. 7:34), and he looks up into a tree to see Zacchaeus (Lk. 19:5). (3) The most significant use of *anablepō* is when those who are blind "receive sight," that is, "look up" to see their surroundings for the first time (Mt. 20:34; Mk. 10:51). Indeed, an important aspect of Jesus' mission is to cause lame to walk, the deaf to hear, and the blind to "look up" (Lk. 7:22). After Saul has been blinded by the bright light sent from heaven, Jesus himself tells Ananias to pray for Saul so that he can "look up," in his case "receive his sight again" (Acts 9:12, 17–18). Something like scales fall from Saul's eyes, and he reflects that "at that moment I looked up at him" (22:13; NIV, "I *was able to see* him"). See *NIDNTT-A*, 96.

Verb: ἐπαίρω (*epairō*), GK *2048* (S *1869*), 19x. *epairō* means "to look up, lift up," though it has several senses in the NT. See *lift up*.

LOOSE

New Testament

Verb: λύω (*lyō*), GK *3395* (S *3089*), 42x. *lyō* means "to loose, untie," but also "break, destroy" (see *break*). In the NT, it is both literally and metaphorically. Literally, John the Baptist acknowledges his unworthiness before the Lord when he announces: "He is the one who comes after me, the thongs of whose sandals I am not worthy to untie" (Jn. 1:27). *lyō* can also denote unwrapping, as in the case of Lazarus's grave clothes being removed or untied from around him (Jn. 11:44).

Metaphorically, *lyō* has a sense of setting free, untying, or loosing. God sets free a crippled woman bound by Satan (Lk. 13:16). When Jesus heals a deaf and dumb man, his "ears were opened, his tongue *was loosed* and he began to speak plainly" (Mk. 7:35). Paul uses *lyō* in reference to being set free from marriage. He exhorts, "Do not seek to *be free*" (1 Cor. 7:27). Spiritually, *lyō* is used for being set free from sin: "Jesus Christ "loves us and has *freed* us from our sins by his blood" (Rev. 1:5). It can also describe being released from death. God has delivered Jesus, "freeing him from the agony of death, because it was impossible for death to keep its hold on him" (Acts 2:24).

Lastly, *lyō* denotes the authority given to Peter, as well as to all disciples of the Lord, to admit others into the kingdom, based on the knowledge of the truth about Christ (Mt. 16:19; 18:18) "I tell you the truth, whatever you bind on earth will be bound in heaven, and whatever you *loose* on earth *will be loosed* in heaven." See *NIDNTT-A*, 346-48.

LORD

Old Testament

Noun: אָדוֹן (*ʾādôn*), GK 123 (S 113), 773x. *ʾādôn* is used with reference to "the Lord" and to people of high rank (especially superiors and persons of authority). *ʾādôn* was commonly pronounced in place of the covenant name of Israel's God, Yahweh (יהוה [GK 3378]). The specific form of that vocalization is *ʾᵃdōnāy* ("my Lord"), a plural noun with a first person singular suffix. This practice became so well established that the Greek translators of the Heb. Bible rendered "Yahweh" with the Greek equivalent of Lord (*kyrios*). English translations usually signify Yahweh as "Lord" by placing the letters "ord" in small caps: "LORD." The commandment not to take the Lord's name in vain, however, does not necessarily prohibit its pronunciation as Scripture is read, nor does the prohibition against blaspheming the name (Lev. 24:15–16) prevent any and every use of it.

(1) In addition to its use as the substitute pronunciation for the divine name Yahweh (GK 3378), *ʾᵃdōnāy* also appears as a title for Yahweh approximately 442x (GK 151) in the Hebrew Bible. When it appears in this context, it is normally translated "Lord," but may also be understood as "Master" or "my Master."

(2) About 30x the word *ʾādôn* addresses God as "Lord," as in Ps. 8:1, 9: "O LORD, our *Lord*, how majestic is your name in all the earth." Isaiah frequently calls God "The *Lord*, the LORD Almighty" (Isa. 3:1; 10:3). When Joshua sees the captain of the Lord's army, he addresses him as "my *Lord*" (Jos. 5:14; cf. Ps. 110:1).

(3) This word also refers to various human beings addressed as "lord" or "master." Joseph is the "master" of Pharaoh's household (Gen 45:8). A "husband" (even a wicked one) can be addressed with this word (Jdg. 19:26). Elijah the prophet is likewise called "lord" (1 Ki. 18:7). Uriah calls both King David and his army commander Joab *ʾādôn* ("master" and "lord" in NIV of 2 Sam. 11:11). In fact, anyone with a position of leadership or authority can be addressed by this term. At the same time, to call someone "my lord" is sometimes merely a title of respect for someone (e.g., Gen. 24:18; 32:5; 1 Ki. 18:7).

(4) Similar to other biblical names, *ʾādôn* appears in Heb. royal personal names: *Adoni*jah, *Adoni*kam, and *Adoni*ram; it also appears in the names of some pagan rulers, such as *Adoni*-Zedek (Jos. 10:1, 3) and *Adoni*-Bezek (Jdg. 1:5–7, "lord of Bezek," the Canaanite king of Bezek).

Noun: אֲדֹנָי (*ʾᵃdōnāy*), GK 151 (S 136), 442x. *ʾᵃdōnāy* means "Lord." In addition to its use as the substitute pronunciation for the divine name Yahweh (see discussion of GK 3378), *ʾᵃdōnāy* also appears as an independent title for Israel's God. When it appears in this context, it is normally translated "Lord," but it may also be understood as "Master" or "my Master."

Proper Noun: יהוה (*yhwh*), GK 3378 (S 3068/3069), 6829x.

Proper Noun: יָהּ (*yāh*), GK 3363 (S 3050), 49x. The Hebrew name *yhwh* or "Yahweh," commonly translated into English as "the LORD," is the most frequently appearing name for God in the OT (almost 7000x). It appears in every OT book except Ecclesiastes, Song of Songs, and Esther. This name is often referred to as the Tetragrammaton because of the four (*tetra*) letters (*grammaton*) used in its Hebrew spelling. There is also an alternate, short form of the divine name (*yāh*) that appears nearly 50x, mostly in the book of Psalms (43x); it is best known from the Hebrew expression "Hallelu-*yah*" (translated, "Praise *the LORD*").

The modern spelling and pronunciation "Yahweh" merely represents our best, educated guess as to what the original pronunciation might have been. This is due to the fact that biblical Hebrew was originally written without vowels, and in Hebrew the vowels would show us the precise pronunciation and meaning of the name. The problem is compounded by the fact that the pronunciation of this name ceased from the Hebrew (Masoretic) reading tradition in order to avoid misuse in connection with the third commandment (Exod. 20:7; Deut. 5:11). That is, when the Jews were reading the Hebrew text and came to *yhwh*, instead of saying "Yahweh" they would say the Hebrew word "Adonai" (*ʾᵃdōnāy*, GK 151, which means "Lord").

In terms of the origin and significance of the divine name, three texts from Exodus are especially important. (1) The first is Exod. 3:13–15. Here, the divine name is given for the first time in the context of Israel's imminent deliverance from Egypt. The revelation of the name is related to the statement, "I AM WHO I AM" (v. 14), where Moses is commanded to tell the Israelites that "I AM has sent me." Then, in verse 15, the divine name "Yahweh" is connected to the God of the patriarchs where it is stated that this name, "Yahweh," is his "eternal name." The connection between "I AM" and "Yahweh" is one of verbal person. "I AM" is the first person form of the verb "to be" (*hāyâ*; GK 2118; see *be*), while "Yahweh" represents the third person form of the same verb, perhaps "HE IS" or "HE WILL BE."

(2) In Exod. 6:2–8, the significance of the divine name resurfaces. In verses 2–3 it is stated, "God also said to Moses, 'I am the LORD [Yahweh], I appeared to Abraham, to Isaac and to Jacob as God Almighty, but by my name the LORD [Yahweh] I did not make myself known to them.'" This text also connects the fulfillment of the patriarchal promises (vv. 4, 7–8) with the deliverance of the nation of Israel from Egypt (vv. 5–6) and concludes with the statement, in verse 8, "I am the LORD" or "I am Yahweh."

(3) The texts from Exodus 3 and 6 record the origin of the divine name and locate its significance in the fulfillment of the patriarchal promises through Israel's deliverance from Egypt. The third text is Exod. 34:5–7. Here, in a remarkable display of the divine glory, God *himself* "proclaimed his name" while passing in front of Moses. This proclamation is to be understood as an exposition of the significance or character of the divine name. What does the divine name mean? It is written, "The LORD [Yahweh], the LORD [Yahweh], the compassionate and gracious God, slow to anger, abounding in love and faithfulness, maintaining love to thousands, and forgiving wickedness, rebellion and sin. Yet he does not leave the guilty unpunished; he punishes the children and their children for the sin of the fathers to the third and fourth generation." According to these verses, the divine name is God's covenant name and represents his steadfast determination to maintain the covenant relationship with his people.

In subsequent biblical history, the divine name, "Yahweh," is referred to as "the Name" (Lev. 24:11) or, more passionately, as "this glorious and awesome name" (Deut. 28:58). With reference to the eschatological city of God, the prophet Ezekiel records that its name will be, "THE LORD IS THERE" or "Yahweh is there." In light of the origin, significance, and use of the divine name in the OT, Jesus' statement in Jn. 8:58, "before Abraham was born, *I am*," clearly identifies Jesus as God, the God of the patriarchs and the deliverer of Israel, Yahweh himself (Exod. 3:14). See *I (am)*.

New Testament

Noun: δεσπότης (*despotēs*), GK *1305* (S *1203*), 10x. *despotēs* is similar in meaning to *kyrios* ("lord"), though it occurs far less often. The nuance of *despotēs* emphasizes the right and power to command. See *master*.

Noun: κύριος (*kyrios*), GK *3261* (S *2962*), 717x. *kyrios* means "master, lord, sir" as well as "Lord." Most of its occurrences are in Luke's two works (210x) and Paul's letters (275x). The most plausible reason for this is that Luke wrote for, and Paul wrote to, people whose lives were dominated by Greek culture and language. *kyrios* occurs over 9,000x in the LXX, 6,000 of which replace the Hebrew proper name for God, Yahweh.

In the secular sense, *kyrios* in the NT is translated as the "master" of a slave (Mt. 10:24–25; Eph. 6:5), "owner" (Mt. 15:27; Gal. 4:1), or "employer" (Lk. 16:3, 5). The husband is characterized as *kyrios* with respect to his wife (1 Pet. 3:6; cf. Gen. 18:12, where "master" is *kyrios* in the LXX). By this Peter makes his point that Sarah thought of her husband respectfully. *kyrios* may also communicate politeness as in Mt. 18:21–22; 25:20–26; Acts 16:30, translated with the term of address "sirs." This word is also used to address heavenly beings such as angels (Rev. 7:14).

God is consistently depicted as *kyrios*, especially when the NT author is quoting an OT passage that uses *kyrios* for Yahweh (Rom. 4:8; 9:28–29; 10:16). Many OT formulas surface in the phrases "the hand of the *Lord*" (Lk. 1:66), "the angel of the *Lord*" (Mt. 1:20), "the name of the *Lord*" (Jas. 5:10), "the Spirit of the *Lord*" (Acts

5:9), and "the word of the *Lord*" (Acts 8:25). The prophetic formula, "says the Lord," also emerges from the OT (Rom. 14:11; 1 Cor. 14:21; 2 Cor. 6:17). Jesus also reflects his adoption of OT patterns when he refers to his Father as the "*Lord* of heaven and earth" (Mt. 11:25) and as "the *Lord* of the harvest" (Mt. 9:38).

The earliest Christian confession is that "Jesus is Lord." This was the climax of Peter's speech on Pentecost (Acts 2:36); by making this confession a person is saved (Rom. 10:9–10). Jesus is Lord whether he is on earth (Mt. 7:21; 21:29–30) or exalted in heaven (1 Cor. 16:22; Rev. 22:20). By confessing Jesus as *Lord*, the Christian community was also recognizing that he has dominion over the world. As a result of Jesus' sovereignty, one day every created being will acknowledge what the insignificant, persecuted community at Philippi confesses in its worship: "Jesus Christ is *Lord*" (Phil. 2:11).

Presently, all powers on earth and in heaven are subject to Jesus and must serve him, for he has been elevated to the position of *kyrios* (Eph. 1:20–21; 1 Pet. 3:22). John envisions him as the ruler over all the kings of the earth—"King of kings and *Lord* of lords" (Rev. 17:14; 19:15–16). The Roman emperor was called "king of kings" because he presided over the vassal kings of the empire, but how puny and conceited in light of the absolute sovereignty of the Lamb, the true *Lord* of lords. NT writers found their evidence for Jesus' lordship in Ps. 110:1, the most quoted psalm in the NT (see Mt. 22:44; 26:64; Acts 2:34; Eph. 1:20; Heb. 1:3, 13). This royal psalm speaks of the *kyrios* being seated at Yahweh's right hand in a rank of power, as demonstrated by the subjugation of his enemies. This is where Jesus currently abides, for the benefit of the church. See *NIDNTT-A*, 323-25.

LOSE

New Testament

Verb: ἀπόλλυμι (*apollymi*), GK *660* (S *622*), 90x. *apollymi* means "to destroy, perish, lose."

(1) In some texts *apollymi* denotes the idea of "destroying" or "ruining" something. In this sense, there are two distinct nuances. (a) To cause destruction, "to destroy, ruin." *apollymi* sometimes means to cause someone or something to be destroyed. It can refer to physical destruction in the sense of killing (Mt. 2:13; 12:14; Mk. 3:6; 9:22; 12:9). It can also signify the destruction meted out in divine judgment (Jas. 4:12; Jude 5). According to Matthew, the destruction of divine judgment is realized in hell: "Be afraid of the One who can *destroy* both soul and body in hell" (Mt. 10:28).

(b) To experience destruction, "to perish." Objects can perish (Mt. 9:17; Mk. 2:22; Lk. 5:37), as well as people. The Greek middle voice sometimes indicates physical death. The disciples used this word when they thought they would drown, "Lord, save us, we are *perishing*!" (Mt. 8:25; cf. Mk. 4:38; Lk. 8:24). Jesus warns, "All who draw the sword will *die* by the sword" (Mt. 26:52). It can also signify the destruction meted out in divine judgment: "None of them has *perished* except the son of destruction" (Jn. 17:12; cf. 10:28). The "perishing" destiny is set in contrast to eternal life: "For God so loved the world that he gave his one and only Son, that whoever believes in him shall not *perish* but have eternal life" (Jn. 3:16).

(2) A second meaning is to fail to obtain what one expects or anticipates, "to lose." "I tell you the truth, he will certainly not *lose* his reward" (Mt. 10:42; cf. Mk. 9:41; 2 Jn. 8).

(3) Finally, *apollymi* can mean "to lose" something that one already has or to be separated from a normal connection. In this sense, Jesus uses the verb in a parable, "Or suppose a woman has ten silver coins and *loses* one" (Lk. 15:8). Jesus warns: "It is better for you to *lose* one part of your body than for your whole body to be thrown into hell" (Mt. 5:29). Likewise, Jesus says, "Whoever finds his life will *lose* it, and whoever *loses* his life for my sake will find it" (Mt. 10:39; cf. 16:25;

Mk. 8:35; Lk. 9:24; 17:33; Jn. 12:25). See *NIDNTT-A*, 68.

LOST

Old Testament

Verb: אָבַד (*ʾābad*), GK 6 (S 6), 185x. *ʾābad* means "to perish, destroy, demolish, become lost." It has a variety of uses in the OT. See *perish*.

LOT

Old Testament

Noun: גּוֹרָל (*gôrāl*), GK 1598 (S 1486), 77x. *gôrāl* is usually translated "lot." It refers to an item that was thrown or dropped for the purpose of decision-making.

It is not known how the casting of lots was accomplished, but possibly different techniques were employed in various places and situations. Lots were cast to determine who would serve as fighting men (Jdg. 20:9) and as priests in the temple (1 Chr. 24:5), to discover a guilty person (Jon. 1:7), to settle disputes (Prov. 18:18), and to divide the spoils of a military victory (Obad. 11; Nah. 3:10). David writes, "They divide my garments among them and cast *lots* for my clothing" (Ps. 22:18), a prophecy later fulfilled at the time of Jesus' crucifixion (Jn. 19:24).

Although the practice of casting lots may appear to be a reliance on chance, the OT makes it clear that God is sovereign over the lots. "The *lot* is cast into the lap, but its every decision is from the LORD" (Prov. 16:33). Therefore, God's will was often discovered through the casting of lots (Lev. 16:8–10), and the elders of Israel depended on this practice when they divided the land of Palestine among the tribes (Jos. 14–19).

The last time lots are cast in the Bible is in finding a replacement apostle for Judas; that lot chooses between Joseph called Barsabbas and Matthias, and God picks Matthias (Acts 1:26). Some argue that with the coming of the Holy Spirit in Acts 2, his guidance replaced the lot as the means of determining God's will.

Noun: חֵלֶק (*ḥēleq*), GK 2750 (S 2506), 66x. *ḥēleq* means "share, portion," but also "lot, inheritance." See *share*.

New Testament

Noun: κλῆρος (*klēros*), GK *3102* (S *2819*), 11x. In the NT *klēros* usually designates the casting of lots, but in a more general sense it can also mean the "allotment" or "inheritance" that one receives (Col. 1:12). God promises Paul a "place" among those who are sanctified when he called him on the road to Damascus (see Acts 26:18).

Casting lots was common in the ancient world, and in a general sense it is analogous to our "drawing straws" for decision-making. Such casting of lots was often associated with seeking the will of the gods. Roman soldiers divided up Jesus clothes by casting lots (Mt. 27:35; Mk. 15:24; Lk. 23:34; Jn. 19:24; cf. Ps. 22:18). Among the Jewish people, however, casting lots was a biblical method of seeking God's preordained plan. In the OT the high priest prayerfully used Urim and Thummim to determine God's will (e.g., Exod. 28:30; Lev. 8:8; Deut. 33:8). At the beginning of Acts, the eleven apostles cast lots between Joseph Barsabbas and Matthias to find a replacement for Judas Iscariot (Acts 1:26). The lots were cast in the context of prayer: "You, Lord, who know the hearts of all, show which one of these two you have chosen to take the place in this ministry and apostleship" (Acts 1:24–25a). The lot fell on Matthias. See *NIDNTT-A*, 309-310.

LOUD

New Testament

Adjective: μέγας (*megas*), GK *3489* (S *3173*), 243x. *megas* means "great, loud, large" and is found throughout the NT. See *great*.

LOVE

Old Testament

Verb: אָהַב (*ʾahab*), GK 170 (S 157), 217x. *ʾahab* is defined as "to love" or "to like." This verb is used to describe a variety of relationships in the OT.

(1) *ʾahab* can be used to describe the

marital relationship between a man and a woman. Moses writes of the love of Isaac and Rebekah: "Isaac brought her into the tent of his mother Sarah, and he married Rebekah. So she became his wife, and he loved her" (Gen. 24:67). The culture of the OT was such that women were, at times, given to men in marriage. Love was not a prerequisite for such an event to take place (29:30). But true love could develop. The majority of uses of love in the Song of Songs have the female as subject, expressing love for a male.

Occasionally the word may be used to describe the act of making love, both within the law and outside of the law. The case of Isaac and Rebekah mentioned above probably involves intimate relations. The writer of 1 Kings, however, describes Solomon's love, many of whom were concubines: "But King Solomon loved many foreign women" (1 Ki. 11:1). These relationships were essentially political in nature, not emotional, and they certainly violated the spirit of Gen. 2:24.

(2) *ʾahab* can also describe the special love that exists between parents and their children. God recognizes the great love Abraham has for Isaac: "Take your son, your only son, Isaac, whom you love, and go to the region of Moriah" (Gen. 22:2). In the context of parental love, however, love can also be divided. Isaac and Rebekah have sons, Esau and Jacob: "Isaac … loved Esau, but Rebekah loved Jacob" (25:28). Similarly regarding Jacob, when his ten sons come to Egypt and unwittingly stand before Joseph, he questions them about their father and brother. They tell him of their aged father and describe their brother as "the only one of his mother's sons left, and his father loves him" (Gen. 44:20). Note too that extended families can also experience such love, for in Ruth 4:15 we read about the love that a daughter-in-law expresses to her mother-in-law.

(3) *ʾahab* likewise describes the deep love that friends can have for each other. This is not sexual in nature, but attests to the deep abiding love that only God can provide. This is the love that Saul has for David (1 Sam. 16:21) and that David shares with Jonathan (18:1, 3). This can be called a familial or brotherly love.

(4) *ʾahab* is also used with nonpersonal objects, such as love for: Jerusalem (Ps. 122:6; Isa. 66:10), special food items (Gen. 27:4, 9, 14), discipline and knowledge (Prov. 12:1), a long life (Ps. 34:12), sleep (Prov. 20:13), sin (17:19), pleasure (21:17), wine and oil (21:17), money (Eccl. 5:10), and even (indirectly) death (Prov. 8:36). Prominent in Proverbs is the love of wisdom, personified as a woman (Prov. 4:6; 8:17, 21).

(5) The most important uses of *ʾahab*, however, are in the religious sphere, being used 32x of God's love. Of these, two are of God's love for Jerusalem (Ps. 78:68; 87:2). It is used 7x of God's loving righteousness, judgment, etc., and 23x of his loving Israel or particular individuals. On the other hand, ʾaḥab is used 19x of human love for God, including loving his name, law, precepts, etc. Many of these occur in Deut. (e.g., 5:10; 6:5; 7:9; 10:12) or in contexts that appear to depend on this OT book (e.g., Jos. 22:5; 23:11; 1 Ki. 3:3; Neh. 1:5).

Chief among these human uses is, of course, what is called the Shema (Deut. 6:4–5), which is equivalent to Israel's confession of faith: "Hear, O Israel: The Lord our God, the Lord is one. Love the Lord your God with all your heart and with all your soul and with all your strength." Even today this is cited regularly in Jewish synagogues. Jesus picks up this text as "the first and greatest commandment" of the law of Moses, and he adds to it a second commandment like the first, which contains another use of *ʾahab* (Lev. 19:18), "Love your neighbor as yourself" (see Mt. 22:37–40). These two commands summarize the entire law of God.

Why should Israel love the Lord their God? First and foremost is the fact that God is the only God there is, so any religious feelings must be directed to him alone. Moreover, this God has been active in the lives of his people, rescuing them from slavery in Egypt. Hence, love for God is a grateful response to his actions on their behalf (see especially Deut. 11:1–12). Such love is expressed in obedience to his law (10:12–13; cf. Exod. 20:6). Even that obedience requires the involvement of God in their lives (30:6); we cannot obey him in our own strength. It is for this reason that God's people actually love his law (e.g., Ps. 119:113, 119, 127).

As far as God's own love itself is concerned, *ʾahab* and the figure of marriage point behind the covenant to its motive and origin in the innermost personal being of God. His love for a special people is astounding—something unique in the ancient world, where the notion of God's love refers only to love of the gods for the king, not for the common people. In Hos. 11:1 the OT comes close to saying that God is love. Note too that God's love for Israel is not based on any attractive feature of the nation, for they were often rebellious; rather, that love lies deep within his own being. Nevertheless, Israel can lay claim to that love because of God's faithfulness expressed by his oath (Deut. 7:6–11).

In response to Israel's sin, God's love is expressed in judgment and forgiveness. Yet God's punishment of sin does not contradict his love; rather, it was because he loves so much that he takes Israel's sin seriously (cf., e.g., the "therefore" in Amos 3:2). As Prov. 3:12 states, "the Lord disciplines those he loves, as a father the son he delights in," and note that God is Israel's Father (see Isa. 63:16; Jer. 31:9). But God's severe discipline is never separated from tenderness (cf. Hos. 11:9). That God continues to love his stiff-necked people is almost beyond human comprehension. See *NIDOTTE*, 1:277–99.

Noun: חֶסֶד (*ḥesed*) GK 2876 (S 2617), 249x. *ḥesed* is one of the richest, most theologically insightful terms in the OT. It denotes "kindness, love, loyalty, mercy," most poignantly employed in the context of relationship between God and humans as well as between one human and another—the former relationship using the word three times as often as the latter.

ḥesed describes the special relationship God has with his covenantal people, and as such can be a difficult word to translate because it is so specific: "steadfast love" (ESV, RSV); "loyal love" or "covenant faithfulness" (NET); "unfailing love" (NLT); "loving-kindness" (KJV). In the context of human relationships, "kindness" characterizes familial relationships (Gen. 20:13), friendships, and the relationship of a king to his subjects (1 Ki. 2:7). David and Jonathan's covenant binds them together with the expectation of showing mutual kindness to one another, even at the expense of other relationships (1 Sam. 20:8).

The Lord rebukes Israel because they have not shown faithfulness or "loyalty," and there is no knowledge of God in the land (Hos. 4:1). Micah recounts the requirements of the Lord, "He has told you, O mortal, what is good; and what does the Lord require of you but to do justice, and to love *kindness*, and to walk humbly with your God?" (Mic. 6:8). God requires such fidelity and kindness because he himself is kind and has shown kindness to his people.

Lot acknowledges the *ḥesed* shown to him by the two angelic beings who spared his life from the destruction of Sodom and Gomorrah (Gen. 19:19). The Psalms effusively proclaim the steadfast love of God (e.g., Ps. 31:7, 32:10; 57:3; 59:10; 94:18; 143:12). God's abiding love stabilizes (Ps. 94:18, "When I thought, 'my foot is slipping,' your *steadfast love*, O LORD, held me up") and sustains life (119:88, "In your *steadfast love* spare my life, so that I may keep the decrees of your mouth").

God's great self-disclosure, when allowing his glory to pass before Moses, includes *ḥesed*. "The LORD, the LORD, a God merciful and gracious, slow to anger, and abounding in *steadfast love* and faithfulness, keeping *steadfast love* for the thousandth generation, forgiving iniquity and transgression and sin, yet by no means clearing the guilty" (Exod. 34:6–8). The defining characteristic of God in covenantal relationship with his people is that he shows "kindness" to them. His wrath is short in contrast to his love: "For a brief moment I abandoned you, but with great compassion I will gather you. In overflowing wrath for a moment I hid my face from you, but with everlasting *love* I will have compassion on you, says the LORD, your Redeemer" (Isa. 54:7–8).

ḥesed defines God's rule: "Righteousness and justice are the foundation of your throne; *steadfast love* and faithfulness go before you" (Ps. 89:14). In light of all that Micah prophesies in judgment of Israel's sin, he concludes in worshipful wonder, "Who is a God like you, pardoning iniquity and passing over the transgression of the remnant of your possession.... You will cast all our sins into the depths of the sea. You will show faithfulness to Jacob and unswerving *loyalty* to Abraham, as you have sworn to our ancestors from the days of old" (Mic. 7:19–20). See *NIDOTTE*, 2:211–18.

New Testament

Verb: ἀγαπάω (*agapaō*), GK *26* (S *25*), 143x. *agapaō* is one of four Gk. verbs meaning "to love." In secular Greek especially before the time of Christ, it was a colorless word without any great depth of meaning, used frequently as a synonym of *erōs* (sexual love) and *phileō* (the general term for love). If it had any nuance, it was the idea of love for the sake of its object. Perhaps because of its neutrality of meaning and perhaps because of this slight nuance of meaning, the biblical writers picked *agapaō* to describe many forms of human love (e.g., husband and wife, Eph. 5:25, 28, 33) and, most importantly, God's undeserved love for the unlovely. In other words, its meaning comes not from the Greek but from the biblical understanding of God's love.

A biblical definition of love starts with God, never with us (1 Jn. 4:9–10). God is love itself; it is his character that defines love. Because he is love (4:8, using the related noun *agapē*), he acts with love toward an undeserving world (Jn. 3:16; 1 Jn. 3:1, 16), to save them from their sins and reconcile them to himself (Rom. 5:8). The pure and perfect love of God is typified in the love relationship between God the Father and God the Son, which Jesus shows to his disciples (Jn. 17:26).

In response, people are to love God. "Dear friends, let us love one another, for love comes from God. Everyone who loves has been born of God and knows God. Whoever does not love does not know God, because God is love" (1 Jn. 4:7–8). They are in fact to love God above everything else, which is the greatest commandment (Mk. 12:30, 33), and then to love one another (Mt. 19:19; 22:39; Mk. 12:31; Rom. 13:8; 1 Jn. 3:11, 23), especially their spiritual family (Gal. 6:10; 1 Jn. 2:10).

If a person loves God, he or she will also love other people (Gal. 5:6; 1 Thess. 3:6; 1 Jn. 4:20). Loving the other person is an outflow of God's love for you ("A new command I give you: Love one another. As I have loved you, so you must love one another," Jn. 13:34; cf. 15:12; 1 Jn. 4:11) and sums up the entire law (Rom. 13:7; Gal. 5:14) and is the "royal law" (Jas. 2:8). "Anyone who does not do what is right is not a child of God; nor is anyone who does not love his brother" (1 Jn. 3:10). Our love toward Christ is demonstrated by our obedience to his teachings (Jn. 14:21, 15, 21, 23; 15:10; 1 Jn. 2:5; 5:3; 2 Jn. 6). In return, this obedience invokes the blessing, of God's love for us (Jn. 14:21). No wonder that love stands at the head of the list of the fruits of the Spirit (Gal. 5:22) and is the greatest of all that will last for eternity (1 Cor. 13:13, both using the noun *agapē*).

But disciples are not only to love God and fellow believers; they are to love all people (1 Cor. 16:14; 1 Thess. 3:12; 2 Pet. 1:7) as especially their enemies. "But I tell you: Love your enemies and pray for those who persecute you" (Mt. 5:44; cf. Lk. 6:35).

The very foundation of salvation is grounded in the realization that God's unmerited love toward us is greater than any other power—including death (Rom. 8:37–39; 1 Cor. 15:55–57). See *NIDNTT-A*, 5-7.

Verb: φιλέω (*phileō*), GK *5797* (S *5368*), 25x. *phileō* is the common word in classical Gk. for showing love, affection, hospitality, etc. It comes into English in many words such as "*Phil*adelphia" (the "city of brotherly love"). To make firm distinctions between *phileō* love and *agapaō* love is incorrect, for the meanings of the two words overlap. The word can also mean "kiss."

phileō is used in the Bible to describe the tender affection that God the Father has toward his Son, Jesus Christ: "For the Father *loves* the Son and shows him all he does" (Jn. 5:20). But it is also used for our love for God. Jesus uses *phileō* to warn those who have more affection for family than for him: "Anyone who *loves* his father or mother more than me is not worthy of me; anyone who *loves* his son or daughter more than me is not worthy of me" (Mt. 10:37). Paul warns the Corinthians, "If anyone does not *love* the Lord—a curse be on him" (1 Cor. 6:22).

phileō can also be used for relationships among human beings, whether in a positive or negative framework. Of Lazarus, Jesus was told, "Lord, the one *you love* is sick" (Jn. 11:3; cf. v 36). Judas "kisses" as the sign of betrayal (Mt. 26:48; Mk. 14:44; Lk. 22:47). Paul uses *phileō* to speak of the love that God's people have toward one another: "Greet those who *love* us in the faith" (Tit. 3:15). John uses the word to describe the framework in which God chastens his children: "Those whom I *love* I rebuke and discipline" (Rev. 3:19).

phileō can even be used of love for non-human things. John uses *phileō* to describe ungodly people who "*love* and practice falsehood" (Rev. 22:15) Hypocrites "*love* to pray standing in the synagogues and on the street corners to be seen by men" (Mt. 6:5).

Love is one of the characteristics that separate disciples from the world. If a disciple loves his life in the sense of desperately hanging on to it, he will ironically lose that which he loves; but if a disciple hates his life (i.e., gives it up for Christ), then he will keep his life for all eternity (Jn. 12:25). If disciples were still of this world, the world "would love" them; but because Jesus chose them out of the world, they are hated (15:19). But the wonderful news is that God the Father himself loves those who love Jesus and believe that he came from God (16:27).

In Jn. 21:15–27, some people make a distinction between the two words for love, *agapaō* and *phileō*. But these words do not have distinctly separate meanings, and John is famous for using virtual synonyms without any difference in meaning; he often switches between words merely for the sake of variety. Also, it makes no sense for Jesus to switch meanings from *agapaō* to *phileō* in the third question since Peter has been answering with *phileō*. Jesus' threefold question is meant to balance Peter's threefold denial at the time of Jesus' trial. The fluctuation of synonyms is also seen in the words for "feed"/"tend" and "lambs"/"sheep." See *NIDNTT-A*, 590-91.

Noun: ἀγάπη (*agapē*), GK *27* (S *26*), 116x. *agapē* signifies the true and pure love of God to his dear Son (Jn. 17:26), to his people (Gal. 6:10), and to a depraved humanity that is in rebellion against him (Jn. 3:16; Rom. 5:8). In fact, the Bible declares that the very nature of God can be defined as love (1 Jn. 4:8, 16). We can see that God is love, regardless of our situation in life; Heb. 12:6 explains that even though we may be under the correction of God, the correction is always guided by love. It is the love of God that prompts our obedience to him. Jesus told his disciples, "Whoever has my commandments and obeys them, he is the one who loves me. He who loves me will be loved by my Father, and I too will love him and show myself to him" (Jn. 14:21, using the related verb *agapaō*).

agapē encompasses the mind, emotions, and will of the individual because it comes from God. As such, we are to live the life of love as demonstrated by the Lord Jesus Christ himself (Eph. 5:2). Paul tells us, "The fruit of the Spirit is love" (Gal. 5:22); it is only by the indwelling of the Holy Spirit of God that we can internalize and realize the love that God has for us. This type of godly love compels us to look for unmet needs among our fellow human beings. It is godly compulsion (2 Cor. 5:14), which brings us to a point where the world no longer sees us, but rather Christ in us. This idea prompted the translators of the KJV to translate *agapē* as "charity" (see, e.g., 1 Cor. 13). Derived from the Latin word *caritas*, charity is characterized in the KJV as an out-showing of God's love and benevolence toward humanity. Further examination of 1 Cor. 13 reveals an inseparable relationship between faith, hope, and love (1 Cor. 13:13), yet the apostle affirms the supremacy of love. John explains that as the love of the church increases, God will strengthen the hearts of those in the church so that they "will be blameless and holy in the presence of our God and Father when our Lord Jesus comes with all his holy ones" (1 Thess. 3:13).

God's people are exhorted to be cautious where they place their love. "Do not love the world or anything in the world. If anyone loves the world, the love of the Father is not in him. For everything in the world—the cravings of sinful man, the lust of his eyes and the boasting of what he has and does—comes not from the Father but from the world" (1 Jn. 2:15). Paul warns young Timothy that "the love of money is a root of all kinds of evils," and as a result "some have wandered away from the faith and pierced themselves with many pangs" (1 Tim. 6:10).

agapē is also used to describe an early Christian "love feast" or fellowship meal. Paul links this meal with the Lord's Supper (1 Cor. 11), but eventually it become a celebration all its own (Jude 12; 2 Pet. 2:13). The meal was significant to the life of the church insofar as it typified what the church represented. It was the church's direct response to the command of the Lord Jesus Christ to love one another. This *agapē* served to undergird the *koinōnia* (see *fellowship*) that the church experienced.

Lastly, *agapē* is a beautiful word picture of sacrificial love. It is expressed in the fact that "while we were still sinners, Christ died for us" (Rom. 5:8). As such, *agapē* can be defined as unmerited and unwavering love. God is the originator of this love, and it can only be experienced by one who truly knows God and has received his Son as Lord and Savior. The ultimate expression of God's unmitigated love is the Lord Jesus Christ on Calvary's cross. See *NIDNTT-A*, 5-7.

LOYALTY

Old Testament

Noun: חֶסֶד (*hesed*) GK 2876 (S 2617), 249x. *hesed* is one of the richest, most theologically insightful terms in the OT. It denotes "kindness, love, loyalty, mercy." See *love*.

LUST

New Testament

Verb: ἐπιθυμέω (*epithymeō*), GK *2121* (S *1937*), 16x. *epithymeō* means "to desire earnestly, long for something, lust, covet." It has both negative and positive connotations, but it always describes the inner motivation. See *desire*.

Noun: ἐπιθυμία (*epithymia*), GK *2123* (S *1939*), 38x. *epithymia* denotes "impulsive, sensual desire," contrary to the will and pleasure of God. See *desire*.

MAD

See *angry*.

MAGISTRATE

New Testament

Noun: στρατηγός (*stratēgos*), GK *5130* (S *4755*), 10x. *stratēgos* denotes one who has military authority or influence. It is derived from two Greek words: *stratos* ("army") and *agō* ("to lead"). Hence, the word literally means "to lead an army."

In secular Greek, *stratēgos* refers to the highest official in a Gk. city, that is, a "magistrate." Half of the word's uses in the NT center around Paul and Silas's ministry in Philippi (Acts 16:20–38). When Paul exorcises the demon from the girl who could predict the future, her owners have Paul and Silas brought "before the *magistrates*," who have them stripped, beaten, and thrown into prison. But when it is reported to the magistrates that Paul and Silas are Roman citizens, they become alarmed and release them.

stratēgos is also used for the "commander" of the temple guard (Lk. 22:4–5; Acts 4:1; 5:25, 26). See *NIDNTT-A*, 481-83.*

MAGNIFY

Old Testament

Verb: גָּדַל (*gādal*), GK 1540 (S 1431), 117x. *gādal* means "to be(come) great, exalted," but it can mean "to make great, magnify" someone or something; in most cases God is the subject of the magnifying action. He makes great those whom he wills, and he calls us to "magnify him with thanksgiving" (Ps. 69:30; cf. 70:4; 92:5; 104:1; 126:2; 138:2). See *great, greatness*.

New Testament

Verb: μεγαλύνω (*megalynō*), GK *3486* (S *3170*), 8x. The basic meaning of *megalynō* is "to magnify, exalt." While this word can be used on a simply human level (e.g., the apostles are "highly regarded" by the people [Acts 5:13] and Paul hopes that his "activity among you will greatly expand" [2 Cor. 10:15]), this word is especially used for magnifying the name of the Lord. Mary magnifies the Lord in her "Magnificat" (Lk. 1:46), and the people in the house of Cornelius speak in tongues and "praise God" (Acts 10:46). In Ephesus, because of the successful ministry of Paul, the "name of the Lord Jesus was held in high honor" (Acts 19:15). And in Philippi, Paul writes that his main goal in whatever happens to him is that "Christ will be exalted in my body" (Phil. 1:20).

MAID

Old Testament

Noun: נַעֲרָה (*naʿarâ*), GK 5855 (S 5291), 76x. *naʿarâ* denotes a "girl" from infancy to adolescence. It is most commonly translated "young girl," but can also mean maiden. See *girl*.

MAIDSERVANT

Old Testament

Noun: אָמָה (*ʾāmâ*), GK 563 (S 519), 56x. *ʾāma* frequently translates as "maidservant" or "slave girl" (Gen. 20:17), but may also be translated simply as "servant." The ancient world was a world filled with slavery. Slavery was not based on racial identity; rather, people generally became slaves as a result of being prisoners of war or because of economic poverty.

Several prominent OT people had maidservants: Sarah (Gen. 21:10), Leah (30:3), and Job (Job 19:15). Exod. 2:5 records one of the most recognizable passages of "maidservant." After Pharaoh's daughter noticed the unusual sight of a basket floating on the Nile River, she sent her "maidservant" to get it.

God was concerned for the physical well-being of maidservants and gave various protections for them in his law (Exod. 20:10; 21:7, 20, 26; Lev. 25:6). God would not allow an Israelite to enslave permanently a fellow Israelite, male or female (Deut. 15:12–15), unless that person asked voluntarily to become a servant (15:16–17).

Another major nuance to *ʾāma* is as a title of deference and humility. On a human level, Abigail refers to herself before David as "your *servant*" (1 Sam. 25:24, 25, 28). Similarly, Ruth addresses Boaz in her night encounter as "your *servant*" (Ruth 3:9). On a spiritual level, the devout Hannah calls herself "your *servant*" in her prayer to God for a child (1 Sam. 1:11). In doing so, she expresses her total dependence on the Lord for fulfilling her desire. See *NIDOTTE, 1:418-21*.

Noun: שִׁפְחָה (*šiphâ*), GK 9148 (S 8198), 63x. This feminine noun is generally translated "servant" or "maidservant."

It is related to a verb meaning "to pour" (*šāpak*, GK 9161); the word picture is that of maidservant pouring water over the hands of her mistress. It is nearly synonymous with *ʾāmâ* (GK 563), which is also a female slave. Some have suggested that *šipḥâ* is used when the person is viewed as a possession and a worker, while *ʾāmâ* is used to emphasize her feminine qualities such as her need for protection or her sexual attractiveness. In any case, *ʾāmâ* is the preferred word in legal texts and *šipḥâ in historical narrative (48x).*

Frequently, the OT associates *šipḥâ* with *ʾebed* ("servants"). Laban gives a *šipḥâ* (named Zilpah) to his daughter Leah and another *šipḥâ* (named Bilhah) to his daughter Rachel, evidently as a wedding gift (Gen. 29:24, 29). In general OT writers use this term as personal maids to married women. Like *ʾāmâ*, *šipḥâ* can be used as a title of deference and humility. Abigail uses both words as she addresses David as "your servant" (e.g., *ʾāma* in 1 Sam. 25:28; *šipḥâ* in 25:27; both in 25:41). Interestingly, Hannah uses *ʾāma* when she addresses God in prayer (1:11) and *šipḥâ* when she addresses Eli (1:18). If there is any difference, *ʾāma* stresses a bit more the personal relationship between the woman and the one whom she is addressing.

Prophesying the removal of formal distinctions (age, gender, race, social status), Joel 2:28–29 records an important use of *šipḥâ*: "And afterward, I will pour out my spirit on all people. Your sons and daughters will prophesy, your old men will dream dreams, your young men will see visions. Even on my servants, both men and women (*šipḥâ*), I will pour out my spirit in those days." See *NIDOTTE*, 4:211-13.

Noun: παιδίσκη (*paidiskē*), GK *4087* (S *3814*), 13x. *paidiskē* is the diminutive form of the word for "girl," used in the NT always for a "servant girl." See *servant girl.*

MAKE

Old Testament

Verb: יָצַר (*yāṣar*), GK 3670 (S 3335), 63x. *yāṣar* principally means "to form" or "to make." See *form*.

Verb: נָתַן (*nātan*), GK 5989 (S 5414), 2014x. *nātan* is a high frequency verb in the OT and bears a wide range of meanings, some of which are "to give, present, allow, permit, surrender, deliver, set, put, place, make." When used with the meaning "make," *nātan* expresses how God will make children as officials over the leaders of Israel (Isa. 3:4); he will make Jerusalem a ruin (Jer. 9:11) and an object of scorn (Ezek. 22:4). See also *give, set*.

Verb: עָשָׂה (*ʿāśâ*), GK 6913 (S 6213), 2632x. The verb *ʿāśâ* has the basic meaning "to do, make," appears in numerous contexts, and is used in a variety of ways. The essential nuance of this verb is some sort of activity, and the context of each passage determines what that activity is.

(1) *ʿāśâ* often refers to God's act of creation. "God saw all that he had *made*" (Gen. 1:31). "The serpent was craftier than any beast God had *made*" (3:1). "In six days the LORD *made* heaven and earth" (Exod. 20:11). "May you be blessed of the LORD, who *made* heaven and earth" (Ps. 115:15). In contrast to *bāraʾ* (GK 1434, see *create*), which is only used of God and never indicates any substance from which God has created something, *ʿāśâ* can indicate something from which God made something (e.g., Eve from a rib of Adam made as "a helper suitable for him," Gen. 2:18).

(2) God does many things in addition to creation. He "made" garments of skin for Adam and Eve (Gen. 3:21). He "performed" many signs and wonders in Egypt, which led to the exodus (Deut. 11:3; Ps. 106:21). In fact, his right hand "does" many mighty things (Ps. 118:15–16). In fact, "our God ... *does* whatever pleases him" (115:3).

(3) *ʿāśa* can also designate the manufacturing of objects. For example, "Noah opened the window of the ark he had *made*" (Gen. 8:6). "You have taken away my gods which I *made*" (Jdg. 18:24).

(4) *ʿāśa* can be used with reference to

the preparation of food or sacrifices. Abraham gave the calf to the servant and he quickly "prepared" it (Gen. 18:7). Gideon "prepared" a young goat (Jdg. 6:19).

(5) The verb can also be used to describe acquisition(s). Israel "will acquire" (lit., make) strength (Num. 24:18). "I *acquired* [lit., made, appointed] men and women singers" (Eccl. 2:8). The wicked "acquire" deceptive wages (Prov. 11:18).

(6) In some constructions, what is made is not material but a new state of affairs. "Let him *make* peace with me" (Isa. 27:5). "Joshua *made* war with all these kings" (Jos. 11:18).

(7) *ʿāśâ* often communicates the simple doing or performing of an action. Israel is "to keep and *do*" all the commandments (Deut. 15:5). "Woe to those who are stubborn, declares the LORD, who *do* counsel, but not mine" (Isa. 30:1).

With more than 2600 occurrences of *ʿāśa*, its range of meaning and nuance extend in many directions. See *NIDOTTE*, 3:645–52.

Verb: פָּעַל (*pāʿal*), GK 7188 (S 6466), 58x. *pāʿal* means "to do, make" and is used primarily in Job and Psalms. See *do*.

Verb: שִׂים (*śîm*), GK 8492 (S 7760), 588x. *śîm* generally denotes the action of putting or placing an object or person in a particular location. It is usually translated "put," "set," or "place" (see *put*). Sometimes *śîm* indicates the "putting" of a person or object into a new setting or for a special purpose that implies some sort of transformation. For example, in a humorous twist, Jehu destroys Baal worship and "makes" the pillar of Baal into a latrine (2 Ki. 10:27). God determines the function of the sand and "makes" the sand a boundary for the sea (Jer. 5:22). God promises that he will "make" a great nation out of Ishmael (Gen. 21:18).

Verb: שִׁית (*šît*), GK 8883 (S 7896), 86x. *šît* means "make, put, set." It is a virtual synonym of *śîm* (GK 8492; see *put*) and has many of the same nuances. It is sometimes used for placing something or someone in a particular place (e.g., Gen. 48:17; Exod. 33:4; Ruth 4:16). It is also used for setting or applying one's heart to something (Exod. 7:23; Prov. 22:17; 24:32; Jer. 31:21). Some scholars hold that *šît* was eventually replaced by *śîm* as the more common word for "put, set, place, set." Note that *šît* tends to occur in more poetic passages rather than in narrative passages. For example, while *śîm* occurs 583x in the OT, it occurs only 36x in the Psalms, whereas of the 83x that *šît* occurs, 30x are in the Psalms.

The first occurrence of this verb is in Gen. 3:15, where God promises to "put" enmity between the seed of the serpent and the seed of the woman, with the latter eventually emerging victorious. Hannah sings, "The foundations of the earth are the LORD's; upon them he *has set* the world" (1 Sam. 2:8). In a similar vein, David sings in Ps. 8:6 that God has "*put* everything under" the feet of humankind. In Ps. 110:1, a verse that is quoted frequently in the NT as a messianic psalm, the psalmist writes: "The LORD says to my Lord, 'Sit at my right hand until I *make* your enemies a footstool for your feet." In another psalm, the psalmist recalls God's promise in 2 Sam. 7:11b–16, "The Lord swore an oath to David ... 'One of your own descendants I will *place* on your throne'" (Ps. 132:11; cf. God's message to Jeroboam in 1 Ki. 11:34 about Solomon, "I *have made* him ruler all the days of his life for the sake of David, my servant"). Finally, Isaiah sings an eschatological song about Jerusalem: "We have a strong city; God *makes* salvation its walls and ramparts" (Isa. 26:1).

New Testament

Verb: ποιέω (*poieō*), GK *4472* (S *4160*), 568x. This verb, generically translated as "to do," has a wide range of meanings, such as "to make, cause to happen, accomplish." See *do*.

MAKE A NOISE

New Testament

Verb: φονέω (*phoneō*), GK *5888* (S *5455*), 43x. *phoneō* means "to call out, call to, make a noise." See *call*.

MAKE ATTRACTIVE

New Testament

Verb: κοσμέω (*kosmeō*), GK *3175* (S *2885*), 10x. *kosmeō* means "to adorn, decorate, make attractive." See *adorn*.

MAKE CLEAN

New Testament

Verb: καθαρίζω (*katharizō*), GK *2751* (S *2511*), 31x. In the NT *katharizō* ("make clean, cleanse") takes on three distinct nuances. First, the term can refer in a general sense to making something physically clean. Second, it can denote healing, especially from leprosy. Finally, it can refer to purification through ritual cleansing; this last meaning can also take on the sense of moral cleaning. See *cleanse*.

MAKE EFFORT

New Testament

Verb: σπουδάζω (*spoudazō*), GK *5079* (S *4704*), 11x. *spoudazō* generally indicates to "strive" or to "give one's best effort" to do something. It can be used of physical activities; Paul made every effort to return to Thessalonica (1 Thess. 2:17). But it is especially used of putting forth effort for God-glorifying, spiritual activities. Christians are enjoined to strive for unity in the church (Eph. 4:3). Paul uses this word to express his eagerness to help the poor (Gal. 2:10). Timothy was commanded to do his best in his labors in the Word (2 Tim. 2:15). The author of Hebrews instructs his readers to make every effort to enter spiritual rest (Heb. 4:11), though God is the one who will ultimately bring them into that rest. Believers are to develop Christian virtues to "*be all the more eager* to make your calling and election sure" (2 Pet. 1:10), even though salvation is not of works, but of grace. These uses highlight the fact that while God brings about all the results in salvation, he still lays responsibilities on his people. See *NIDNTT-A*, 536.

MAKE EXCUSES

New Testament

Verb: παραιτέομαι (*paraiteomai*), GK *4148* (S *3868*), 12x. *paraiteomai* denotes either "to make a request" or, in the negative, "to make excuses, reject" something. See *request*.

MAKE HOLY

Old Testament

Verb: קָדַשׁ (*qādaš*), GK 7727 (S 6942), 171x. *qādaš* describes the state of the sacred realm. Negatively, it represents that which is distinct from the common or profane. It is usually translated "make holy" (NIV), "sanctify," or "dedicate." See *sanctify*.

New Testament

Verb: ἁγιάζω (*hagiazō*), GK *39* (S *37*), 28x. *hagiazō* is usually rendered "make holy, sanctify, consecrate." In the NT this verb expresses the action of including a person or a thing in the sphere of what is holy in either a ritual (ceremonial) and moral sense. Thus "to make holy" is to set apart individuals or objects for special use by God. Both individual Christians (1 Cor. 6:11) and the church as a whole (1 Cor. 1:1; Eph. 5:26) are sanctified or set apart for such service to God. The Christian is sanctified by Christ's sacrifice (1 Cor. 1:30; Heb. 10:10), by the truth (Jn. 17:19), and by the Holy Spirit (Rom. 15:16). In Paul's judgment, a non-Christian marriage partner does not profane the Christian. Rather, the non-Christian partner is sanctified by the Christian, just as the children of the marriage are also sanctified (1 Cor. 7:14).

hagiazō also appears in the Lord's Prayer, "*hallowed* be your name" (Mt. 6:9; Lk. 11:2). This expression (perhaps based on an ancient Aramaic prayer) means not only to treat God and his name with reverence and honor but also to glorify him by obeying his commands. *hagiazō* is also used in the sense of "reverence," specifically setting apart Jesus in our lives as Lord and honoring him as such (1 Pet. 3:15).

MAKE IMPURE

New Testament

Verb: κοινόω (*koinoō*), GK *3124* (S *2840*), 14x. *koinoō* means "to make impure, defile" in a ritual (or ceremonial) sense. See *defile*.

MAKE KNOWN

New Testament

Verb: γνωρίζω (*gnōrizō*), GK *1192* (S *1107*), 25x. While related to the verb *ginōskō* ("to know"; see *know*), *gnōrizō* means "to make something known, tell." In some uses of this verb, Paul simply mentions something that he making known or telling his audience (e.g., 1 Cor. 12:3; 2 Cor. 8:1). In 1 Cor. 15:1, he is "reminding" the Corinthians of the core message of the gospel—Jesus' death and resurrection.

But *gnōrizō* is also used to convey some important theological truths. One of the central tasks of Jesus was to "make known" to us everything that he learned from the Father (Jn. 15:15; cf. 17:26). In fact, we would know nothing about God if he had not first of all made it known to us in various ways through revelation. Thus, as Paul says, God "has made known to us the mystery of his will" (Eph. 1:9; cf. 3:3, 5; Col. 1:27). Or, as Peter quotes from Ps. 16, God "*has made known* to [us] the paths of life" (Acts 2:28). The responsibility the Lord gives us, then, is to "*make known* the mystery of the gospel" to those who do not know it (Eph. 6:19; cf. Gal. 1:11). See *NIDNTT-A*, 107-10.

MAKE LOW

New Testament

Verb: ταπεινόω (*tapeinoō*), GK *5427* (S *5013*), 14x. *tapeinoō* conveys various shades of meaning; "make humble" (socially, politically, economically), "make small," and "be obedient." The NIV sometimes renders *tapeinoō* as "make low." See *humble*.

MAKE PUBLIC

New Testament

Verb: καταγγέλλω (*katangellō*), GK *2859* (S *2605*), 18x. *katangellō* means "to proclaim, announce, make public." See *proclaim*.

MAKE TO DRINK

Old Testament

Verb: שָׁקָה (*šāqâ*), GK 9197 (S 8248), 62x. *šāqâ* occurs almost exclusively in the causative Hebrew stem, "to make to drink, to water." It often occurs in close proximity to the active stem of the verb *šātâ*, "to drink" (GK 9272). In several passages, God is the one who gives water to drink. In Gen. 2:6, 10, he "waters" the ground in the Garden of Eden with a mist and a river, and in the creation (Ps. 104:11), God gives animals water to drink. In a negative sense, as part of his judgment on his people, God makes his people "eat bitter food and *drink poisoned water"* (Jer. 23:15). In the final cup of his wrath, all nations will be made to drink it (25:15, 17).

People also can give something to drink. In Genesis, Lot's daughters make a decision to give their father alcohol to drink to get him drunk, so that they may conceive children by him (21:32–34). In 21:19, Hagar gives her son Ishmael a drink after God has provided water; in 24:14, 18–19, Rebekah gives Eliezer's camels water to drink (cf. similarly 29:2–3, 7–8; Exod. 2:16–17, 19). Moses makes the Israelites drink water into which he has ground the remains of the golden calf (Exod. 32:20). A person under persecution is given vinegar to drink (Ps. 69:21), but Solomon recommends that we give our enemies water to drink if they are thirsty (Prov. 25:21). Metaphorically, a person in sorrow is made to drink tears by the bowlful (Ps. 80:5). See *NIDOTTE, 4:231-34*.

MALE

Old Testament

Noun: אִישׁ (*ʾîš*), GK 408 (S 376), 2188x. The most basic and frequent meaning of *ʾîš* in the OT is "man" (NIV = 612x) or, in the plural, "men" (NIV = 523x). Only rarely is *ʾîš* translated as "male" (see Gen. 7:2 [2x]; 17:27). See *man*.

Noun: זָכָר (*zākār*), GK 2351 (S 2145), 82x. *zākār* specifically means "male," in contrast to the general translation "man" as with *ʾîš* and *ʾādam* (see *man*). *zākār* indicates the male offspring of humans

(Lev. 12:2; Isa. 66:7; Jer. 20:15) and animals (Exod. 13:12). The noun is prominent in the distinction of animals for sacrifice (Exod. 12:5; Lev. 1:3, 10; 22:19), which are almost always *zākār* (though see Lev. 3:1, 6, where the sacrifice can be either male or female).

zākār shares a significant place in the creation of man in Gen. 1:27, which says, "So God created man (*ʾādam*) in his own image, in the image of God he created him; *male* (*zākār*) and female he created them" (cf. Gen. 5:2).

Finally, *zākār* is often set in contrast to *nᵉqēbâ* ("female, woman"), as in Deut. 4:16, "[Do not] make for yourselves an idol, an image of any shape, whether formed like a *man* or a woman." Another contrast is found in Lev. 12, where the ceremonial uncleanness of a woman who gives birth to a *zākār* is half as long (12:2) as one who gives birth to a *nᵉqēbâ* (12:5). Similarly, the redemption price for a *zākār* is twice as much as that for a *nᵉqēbâ* (20:2–7). The distinction between *zākār* and *nᵉqēbâ* is not one of intrinsic human value but of the social status of men and women in the times the biblical author was writing.

New Testament

Noun: ἄρσην (*arsēn*), GK *781* (S *730*), 9x. *arsēn* means "male" in contrast to female. When Gen. 1:27 is quoted in the NT, that "God made them male and female," Jesus uses *arsēn* (Mt. 19:4; Mk. 10:6). Similarly, the quote from Exod. 13:2, 12 in at the time of Jesus' circumcision uses this term (Lk. 2:23). Paul uses this word 3x for homosexual activity in Rom. 1:27. In Rev. 12:5, 13 *arsēn* refers to the birth of a "male child" who was pursued by the dragon.

One of the most significant uses of *arsēn* is in Gal. 3:28, where Paul emphasizes that in Christ there is "neither Jew nor Greek, slave nor free, male nor female, for you are all one in Christ Jesus." In the church of God, when dealing with salvation, there are no barriers—a message highly needed in our world with its gender, ethnic, economic, political, and social barriers. See *NIDNTT-A*, 73.*

MALICE

New Testament

Noun: κακία (*kakia*), GK *2798* (S *2549*), 11x. *kakia* means "malice, evil, wickedness," primarily in quality or baseness. Much of the NT views *kakia* as a force that breaks or destroys fellowship (Rom. 1:28–29; Tit. 3:3). *kakia* denotes a single sin in Acts 8:22, but it must be repented of. Christians are to put off *kakia* (Eph. 4:31; Col. 3:8; Jas. 1:21; 1 Pet. 2:1). See *NIDNTT-A*, 284-85.

MAN

Old Testament

Noun: אָדָם (*ʾādām*), GK 132, 134 (S 120, 121), 558x. The basic meaning and most common translation of *ʾādām* is "man." Unlike *ʾîš*, which carries not only the sense of "man" but also of "male," *ʾādām* may be used by the OT writers to describe humanity as a whole—men, women, and children. When used in this generic sense it is commonly translated "men," "people," or "mankind." *ʾîš* and *ʾādām* sometimes occur in parallel clauses, as in Isa. 2:9, "So *ʾādām* will be brought low, and *ʾîš* humbled" (cf. Isa. 5:15). The difference, however, is that *ʾādām* is typically used when the biblical writer wants to indicate humanity as a whole, while *ʾîš* is used to refer to an individual man or a group of individuals.

(1) Of all the occurrences of *ʾādām* in the OT, 132 are found in Ezek., normally in the LORD's designation for the prophet, "son of *man*" (cf. Dan. 8:17 for a messianic emphasis for this phrase). *ʾādām* is likewise frequent in the Ps. (62x), Prov. (45x), and Eccl. (49x). Not surprisingly, *ʾādām* is used often in Gen. (especially chs. 1–11, 46x), which tell the story of the human race from our first parents in the Garden of Eden until the flood, which wiped humanity off the face of the earth (except for Noah and his family). Gen. 12–50 only use *ʾādām* once, in reference

to Ishmael, whom God said would be "a wild donkey of a *man*" (Gen. 16:12).

(2) ʾ*ādām* is used 12x as the proper name "Adam." Until Gen. 2:20, ʾ*ādām* simply refers to "the man," until the LORD determined that "for ʾ*ādām* no suitable helper was found." Aside from the uses of ʾ*ādām* as a personal name in Gen. (3:17; 3:20–21 [2x]; 4:1, 25; 5:1–5 [4x]), only in 1 Chr. 1:1 and Hos. 6:7 does ʾ*ādām* to refer to the first man, the husband of Eve (cf. Deut. 4:32, where the NIV translates ʾ*ādām* with "mankind," although the reference could be to the first male). While some biblical scholarship rejects the historicity of an actual person called Adam, the NT clearly refers to him as the first man created by God (Lk. 3:38; Rom. 5:12–21; 1 Cor. 15:22; 1 Tim. 2:13–14). Notice also the theological significance of the historicity of Adam in 1 Cor. 15:45–49 (cf. Rom. 5:12–21). If Adam did not exist in reality, then the Scriptures cannot be trusted ("so it is written") and Jesus Christ—as well as the salvation he has provided through his death—is rendered meaningless.

(3) The Bible is clear that ʾ*ādām* is created in the image of God. Gen. 1:27 says, "So God created ʾ*ādām* in his own image, in the image of God he created him; male and female he created them" (cf. Gen. 1:26; 9:6). Gen. 5:1–2 reiterates this point: "When God created ʾ*ādām* , he made him in the likeness of God. He created them male and female and blessed them. And when they were created, he called them ʾ*ādām*." Notice that God creates the human race as male and female and calls them collectively ʾ*ādām*. Although Adam was formed from the dust of the ground (Gen. 2:7) and Eve was made from one of Adam's ribs, they are both created in the image and likeness of God.

Even though humankind has been created in God's likeness, there is obviously a significant distinction between God and man. The Bible says in 1 Sam. 15:29, "He who is the Glory of Israel does not lie or change his mind; for he is not an ʾ*ādām*, that he should change his mind." Regardless of how humanity, as made in the image of God, reflects certain characteristics and attributes of God, we must not project our own fallen characteristics on the Creator, the "Glory of Israel." In contrast to the nature of God, ʾ*ādām* is frail and full of unrighteousness. The writer of Eccl. declares, "There is not a righteous ʾ*ādām* on earth who does what is right and never sins" (Eccl. 7:20). Nevertheless, God loves humanity, and his care for us is beyond comprehension. The psalmist marveled, "What is ʾ*îš* that you are mindful of him, the son of ʾ*ādām* hat you care for him?" (Ps. 8:4; cf. 144:3).

Noun: אִישׁ (ʾ*îš*), GK 408 (S 376), 2188x.

(1) The most basic and frequent meaning of ʾ*îš* in the OT is "man" (NIV = 612x) or, in the plural, "men" (NIV = 523x). Only rarely is ʾ*îš* translated as "male" (see Gen. 7:2 [2x]; 17:27; see also *zākār*), but it almost always signifies a person of the masculine gender. For this reason, ʾ*îš* is naturally placed opposite of ʾ*iššâ*, "woman/wife." While the general, more inclusive word for "man" is *zākār*, ʾ*îš* on rare occasion also carries this meaning (NIV translates as "people" 16x; e.g., see Exod. 10:7; Deut. 27:14; 1 Sam. 5:9; Jer. 18:11).

(2) A secondary meaning for ʾ*îš* is "husband" (NIV = 64x), as in Gen. 3:16, where the LORD describes to Eve the results of her disobedience: "Your desire will be for your *husband*, and he will rule over you'" (cf. Gen. 3:6; Num. 5:12–31; Deut. 24:1–4). Notice also that the secondary meaning for ʾ*iššâ* is "wife."

(3) ʾ*îš* is used in connection with general, nondescript words, such as "each" (NIV = 160x), "one" (106x), "anyone" (29x), "everyone" (18x), and "someone" (12x). For example, Isa. 53:6 states, "We all, like sheep, have gone astray, *each* of us has turned to his own way; and the LORD has laid on him the iniquity of us all." Similarly, Lev. 24:15 asserts, "If *anyone* curses his God, he will be held responsible."

(4) ʾ*îš* is often joined with other words to designate vocations or abilities. For

example, "a man who knew game" was a "hunter" (Gen. 25:27); "a man who draws a sword," a "swordsman" (2 Ki. 3:26); "a man of war," a "soldier" (1 Sam. 16:18; cf. Num. 31:28); and "a man who tills the soil," a "farmer" (Zech. 13:5). A similar common construction with *ʾîš* defines a person of certain ethnicity, such as an "Israelite" (*ʾîš yiśrāʾēl*, lit., "a man of Israel" [20x], Num. 25:8–14 [3x]), the "Gileadites" (Jdg. 12:4), the "Moabites" (Jdg. 3:29), and a "Benjamite" (1 Sam. 4:12). *ʾîš* also occurs frequently in the phrase "*man* of God" (i.e., "godly man" or, more likely, "man sent by God" or "man with the authority of God" = a prophet). The phrase occurs 76x, mostly in 1–2 Ki., and in all but 29 of the instances it refers to a specific individual, namely, Moses (6x), Samuel (4x), David (3x), Elijah (7x), and Elisha (29x).

(5) Finally, the LORD is not an *ʾîš*, although sometimes he and his actions are described anthropomorphically (i.e., in human terms). For example, God is designated a "warrior" (Exod. 15:3; cf. Isa. 42:13) and a "husband" (Hos. 2:2–16). Nevertheless, God says of himself in Hos. 11:9, "I am God, and not *ʾîš* —the Holy One among you." Similarly, under the direction of the LORD, the prophet Balaam declares to Balak, "God is not a *man* that he should lie, nor a son of man that he should change his mind" (Num. 23:19; cf. Job 9:32). In other words, while humankind is created in God's image, there is a qualitative difference between God and us. The Creator/creature distinction must be maintained.

Noun: גֶּבֶר (*geber*), GK 1505 (S 1397), 66x. Usually translated as "man," *geber* occurs most frequently in Job (15x), Ps. (10x), Prov. (8x), and Jer. (9x). Its close relationship to the verb *gbr* ("to be strong, mighty," suggests that *geber* directly refers to a "strong" or "mighty" man (Jer. 30:6; cf. Isa. 22:17). The "strength" found in *geber* is not only physical strength—in contrast with that of women and children (see Exod. 10:10–11; Num. 12:37; Jer. 30:6; 31:22; 41:16; 43:6; 44:20)—but also spiritual strength, as in Ps. 34:8, "Taste and see that the LORD is good; blessed is the *geber* who takes refuge in him" (cf. Ps. 18:25; 40:4; 128:4; Prov. 24:5).

Noun: זָכָר (*zākār*), GK 2351 (S 2145), 82x. *zākār* specifically means "male," in contrast to the general translation "man" as with *ʾîš* and *ʾādām* (see *man*). *zākār* can refer to male humans or animals. See *male*.

New Testament

Noun: ἀνήρ (*anēr*), GK *467* (S *435*), 216x. *anēr* generally means a "man" as opposed to a woman (e.g., Mt. 14:21; 1 Cor. 11:3–15); it is also the word for "husband" (e.g., Mk. 10:2; Rom. 7:2–3; Eph. 5:22–25, 28, 33). Occasionally it can mean simply "adult male" (e.g., 1 Cor. 13:11) or even "human being" (Lk. 5:8; Jas. 1:20).

In Acts we find 14x a combination of *anēr* with *adelphos* ("brother"). This expression is always in the plural, as part of direct address (e.g., Acts 2:37; 13:15, 26, 38; 22:1). The apostles use this expression to address fellow adult Jews (see *brother*).

The leadership of the Christian community was composed chiefly of males, and Jesus chose only men to be in his closest circle of disciples; they received this honored position to fulfill God's plan to have men reflect the "glory of Christ" (cf. 1 Cor. 11:7). The sequencing of God – Christ – man – woman is not intended to weave any kind of inferiority into the relationships (11:3–15). Each one is the head of the following without assuming preferential status. When Paul parallels *anēr* and Christ in Eph. 5:25, 28, he is stressing that the man/husband imitate Christ by loving his wife in the same way as Christ loves the church. This means he should love her with sincere devotion even if it means laying down his life for her. Paul's focus is on the husband's responsibility as he fulfills his God-granted role in the husband/wife relationship.

anēr appears in the Pastoral Letters as

part of the qualification lists for bishops (1 Tim. 3:2), deacons (3:12), and elders (Tit. 1:6). The exact expression is that he is to be a "one-woman man" (or "one-wife husband"). Probably Paul is requiring the man to be faithful in marriage, and uses an rather unusual expression to covney his meaning. Others think that Paul is prohibiting having a concubine or mistress in addition to a wife. Many Greeks and Romans purchased female prostitutes and kept them as mistresses outside of the home. They did not regard such a practice as adultery or polygamy. Demosthenes said, "Men had prostitutes for pleasure, mistresses for daily needs, and wives for the bearing of children." Paul, as would any Jew, sees this common practice of maintaining concubines as the same as polygamy and therefore as constituting another marital relationship. Leaders in the church must be free from this type of behavior. See *NIDNTT-A*, 52.

Noun: ἄνθρωπος (*anthrōpos*), GK *476* (S *444*), 550x. *anthrōpos* means "man, human being, mankind." *anthrōpos* is significantly different from God, as in Mk. 10:27, "With *man* this is impossible, but not with God; all things are possible with God" (cf. Mk. 10:9; Jn. 10:33; Acts 5:29). *anthrōpos* is also distinct from angels (1 Cor. 4:9; 13:1) and animals (Mt. 12:12; 1 Cor. 15:39). Although *anthrōpos* is grammatically masculine, it often refers to humanity collectively, including both men and women. In this sense, *anthrōpos* is gender-neutral noun. Referring to general humanity, a familiar construction to designate something to be in "human" terms is *kata anthrōpō* (e.g., Rom. 3:5; 1 Cor. 3:3; 9:8; 15:32; Gal. 1:11; 3:15; 1 Pet. 4:6).

Nevertheless, *anthrōpos* may also refer to a particular individual, and in each instance the person is male: Matthew (Mt. 9:9), John the Baptist (11:8), Judas (Mt. 26:24), Nicodemus (Jn. 3:1), Stephen (Acts 6:13), and Adam (Rom. 5:12, 19). Therefore, whenever *anthrōpos* refers to a specific individual, it may be understood as a synonym for *anēr* ("man," *467*) or *arsēn* ("male," *781*). In fact, *anthrōpos* is sometimes used interchangeably with *anēr* (Acts 15:25–26; Jas. 1:7–8).

Jesus is called *anthrōpos* to designate his humanity apart from his divinity, as in 1 Tim. 2:5, "For there is one God and one mediator between God and men, the *man* Christ Jesus." Not only does this refer to Jesus Christ as a specific man, but it also places emphasis on his humanity. Paul emphasizes Jesus as *anthrōpos* when he writes that Jesus "made himself nothing, taking the very nature of a servant, [and was] made in *human* likeness" (Phil. 2:7). Jesus designates himself as "the Son of Man [*anthrōpos*]," a messianic designation that Jesus claims for himself, cf. Dan. 7:13), as in Lk. 19:10, "For the Son of Man came to seek and to save what was lost." This construction occurs 82 times in the NT, all of which are in the gospels except for Acts 7:56, "[Stephen] said, 'I see heaven open and the Son of Man standing at the right hand of God.' "

Although through Adam all of humanity became sinners, Christ is the "new man" through whom we can find freedom and forgiveness from God. Paul said, "For since death came through a *man*, the resurrection of the dead comes also through a *man*" (1 Cor. 15:21; see also the interplay of Adam and Christ as *anthrōpos* in Rom. 5:12–19). By virtue of our faith relationship with Jesus Christ, our old *anthrōpos* ("self") is taken off and we put on a new *anthrōpos* ("self"; Eph. 4:22–24; Col. 3:9), in order that we might walk in the new life of righteousness and holiness. See *NIDNTT-A*, 52-53.

MANAGER

New Testament

Noun: οἰκονόμος (*oikonomos*), GK *3874* (S *3623*), 10x. *oikonomos* often refers in the NT to a "household manager" or "steward" entrusted with the responsibility of running a household (Lk. 12:42; 16:1, 3, 8; Gal. 4:2). It is from this word that we derive our English word "economy." The term appears in Rom. 16:23 of Erastus, who is said to be the city "treasurer" of Corinth.

oikonomos is transferred to the religious realm in the NT in several striking ways: (1) Paul refers to himself as an *oikonomos* who has been entrusted with the mysteries of God (1 Cor. 4:1–2); (2) Tit. 1:7 calls the "overseer" of a congregation God's *oikonomos*; (3) 1 Pet. 4:10 calls all believers to be "stewards" of God's manifold grace as they serve one another, each in unique ways. All three of these uses presuppose an image of the church as a "household." Such an image is natural since the early church met in homes and referred to its members as "brother" and "sister." The idea is that Paul, the leaders of the churches, and all the members are to manage carefully the responsibilities and skills entrusted to them for the good of the others. See *NIDNTT-A*, 403-4.*

MANIFEST

Verb: φανερόω (*phaneroō*), GK *5746* (S *5319*), 49x. *phaneroō* denotes the act of making visible or disclosing that which is not readily seen—"to show, appear, reveal." See *appear*.

MANKIND

New Testament

Noun: ἄνθρωπος (*anthrōpos*), GK *476* (S *444*), 550x. *anthrōpos* means "man, human being, mankind." See *man*.

MANNA

New Testament

Noun: μάννα (*manna*), GK *3445* (S *3131*), 4x. All of the references to *manna* in the NT are allusions to the food provided for the Israelites in the desert. The word itself is a transliteration of the Heb. *man hûʾ* (lit., "what is it," the question that the Israelites asked on the first day when this substance appeared on the ground; see Exod. 16). Jesus indicates to the Jewish leaders that he is greater than Moses, for whereas Moses only provided the people physical manna (and, in fact, God was the provider; see Jn. 6:31, 49, 58), Jesus himself is "the bread that has come down from heaven," and if we partake of him, we receive eternal life. In the discussion in Hebrews about the ark of the covenant, the writer notes that one of the things it contained was "the gold jar of manna" (Heb. 9:4). In Rev. 2:17, Jesus promises to the church at Pergamum that those who overcome will be given "some of the hidden manna"; that is, they will be partaking of the heavenly feast prepared for all God's children (cf. Rev. 19).*

MANY

Old Testament

Noun: רֹב (*rōb*), GK 8044 (S 7230) 150x. *rōb* denotes a multitude or an abundance. It is probably derived from the verb *rābâ*, which means to become numerous, much, or great. Ps. 33:16 states, "The king is not victorious by the *multitude* of an army, nor will a war-hero be saved by an *abundance* of strength." Since *rōb* is often used to modify another noun, it can be translated as an adjective. For example, Ps. 33:16 can also be translated using the phrases "by a *great* army" and "by *great* strength." Similarly, Ezek. 27:16 refers to Tyre's "*abundance* of products," which can be translated, "*many* products." In about one-third of the word's occurrences, it is used (adverbially) with a preposition and means "in abundance" or "abundantly/greatly."

rōb is used in a variety of situations and an appropriate translation depends to a large degree on the context. Often the word can be translated "many" (Est. 5:11) or "great" (1 Sam. 1:16). The KJV prefers to use "multitude" or "abundance" in a majority of cases, and "great number" and "large quantities" occur a few times in the NIV. Another possible translation is "numerous" as in 1 Sam. 13:5, "as *numerous* as sand on the seashore" (lit., "like sand that is on the seashore in *abundance*"). The OT notes in several places that Solomon made cedars "*plentiful*" in Jerusalem (1 Ki. 10:27; 2 Chr. 1:15; 9:27). More technical terms can be used in certain cases, such as in Jdg. 6:5 ("locusts in *abundance*") and 2 Chr. 14:15 ("sheep in *abundance*"), which the NIV translates "*swarms* of locusts" and "*droves* of sheep" respectively. See *NIDOTTE*, 3:1034-35.

Adverb: הַרְבֵּה (*harbēh*), GK 2221 (S 7235), 50x. *harbēh* means "many, great." It has the same middle consonants as, and is thus related to, the word *rōb*, which also means "many." *harbēh* is used mostly in narrative passages, though it does occur 15x in Ecclesiastes (e.g., "of making many books there is no end, and much study wearies the body," Eccl. 12:12). This word can function as the subject of a sentence ("many fell and died," 2 Sam. 1:4) or the object of a verb ("David took a great quantity of bronze," 8:8). The word can intensify a verbal action, as in Neh. 2:2 ("I was greatly afraid") and in 1 Sam. 26:21 ("I have erred greatly"). In one important passage, God comes to Abraham in a vision and reveals himself as "your shield, your very great reward" (Gen. 15:1), which in context suggests that God is the one on whom Abraham must depend in order to receive protection and his reward of numerous offspring. The psalmist in Ps. 130:7 confesses that with the Lord is unfailing love "and great redemption"; that promise of a full redemption still stands for all who trust in the Lord. See *NIDOTTE*, 3:1037–41.

New Testament

Adjective: πολύς (*polys*), GK *4498* (S *4118*, *4119*, *4183*), 416x. *polys* is used to designate a large quantity ("many") or size ("great/large"). In addition, over 50x it is used either as a comparative ("someone *greater than* Jonah or Solomon," Mt. 12:41–42) or a superlative ("*most* of his miracles," 11:20). Also, sometimes *polys* is not so much making a comparison as it is describing a large number ("a *very large* crowd," Mt. 21:8; cf. Mk. 4:1) or explaining a further progression of something ("avoid godless chatter because it will lead to *more and more* ungodliness," 2 Tim. 2:16; cf. Acts 13:31; 24:4; 25:14; 2 Tim. 3:9).

One of the most important uses of *polys* (and especially its plural with the article, *hoi polloi*) occurs in Rom. 5:15–21, where Paul draws a contrast between "the one" and "the many." "The many" here has the nuance of "all in a group," for just as "the many/all" became sinners through the one man Adam and hence are subject to death, so also through the one man Jesus, the offer of salvation by grace goes out to "the many." The Adam-Christ parallel is all-encompassing, though Paul is careful not to suggest that the same number who are dead in Adam will be saved in Christ, but only those who have a relationship with Jesus by faith. "The many" who are saved in Christ is a more limited number than "the many" who are condemned in Adam.

In Mt. 22:14, Jesus says that "*many* are invited, but few are chosen." Here *polloi* is used without the article and refers to the fact that while the offer of salvation goes out to many, many people, not everyone accepts the offer; only a minority ends up believe in Jesus and so receive salvation.

MARANATHA

New Testament

Expression: μαράνα θά (*marana tha*), GK *3448* (S *3134*), 1x. This term only occurs once in the NT (1 Cor. 16:22), though the idea occurs elsewhere. *marana tha* is a transliteration of an Aramaic phrase that can be translated (depending on how it is divided) as either "The Lord has come" (maran-atha) or "O Lord, come" (marana-tha). Because this Aramaic term is included in a letter written to a congregation that is primarily Gentile and Greek-speaking, this suggests that *marana tha* comes from a liturgical prayer spoken in the very early days of the church, when it was exclusively Aramaic-speaking. In those first days, the Christians were looking for the fulfillment of the angels' promise in Acts 1:11, and they undoubtedly prayed for it to occur. Thus, it is most likely that the prayer form of this Aramaic phrase is the correct one. And it is interesting that in the last book of the NT to be written, in the second to the last verse of the last chapter, this same prayer is included, though in its Greek form: *erchou kyrie Iesou* ("Come, Lord Jesus,"

Rev. 22:20). That should still be our prayer; we should always be living in expectation of the return of our Lord, Jesus Christ.*

MARKETPLACE

New Testament

Noun: ἀγορά (*agora*), GK *59* (S *58*), 11x. The *agora* primarily denotes a financial "marketplace" where commodities and money changed hands. In the NT world, however, the *agora* was also a place where ideas were exchanged—where both social and political interaction took place, much like a "public square" or "town hall" today. When the NT writers mention the *agora*, the emphasis is usually not on the commercial transactions of the location but rather on its social and political activities.

In terms of social activities, the *agora* was the place where children would play and taunt (Mt. 11:16; Lk. 7:32); where people stood around, presumably waiting for a job offer (20:3); where the sick congregated to beg for healing from Jesus (Mk. 6:56); where Paul went in Athens to discuss the Christian faith with those who assembled there (Acts 17:17); and where the Jewish leaders often congregated in order to flaunt their social standing (Mk. 7:4) and where they loved to be greeted with titles of respect (Mt. 23:7; Mk. 12:38; Lk. 11:43; 20:46). The political activity of the *agora* is demonstrated by the fact that after Paul healed the demon-possessed slave girl in Philippi, he and Silas were dragged to the *agora* to be tried by the magistrates (Acts 16:19). See *NIDNTT-A*, 12-13.*

MARRY, MARRIAGE

Old Testament

Verb: לָקַח (*lāqaḥ*), GK 4374 (S 3947), 967x. The basic meaning of *lāqaḥ* is "to take, grasp." The meaning is often simply to "take into/by the hand." "Taking" in the sense of acquiring something is combined with that of selection or choosing when *lāqaḥ* is used to denote the legal arrangement of marriage, especially in the Pentateuch. "To take a wife" or "to take a woman as a wife" is usually translated by the NIV with the simple verb "to marry." See *take*.

New Testament

Verb: γαμέω (*gameō*), GK *1138* (S *1060*), 28x.

Noun: γάμος (*gamos*), GK *1141* (S *1062*), 16x. *gameō* means "to marry, celebrate a wedding, have sexual relations." *gamos* means "wedding, marriage, consummation of marriage, wedding feast." *gameō* (Mk. 6:17; Lk. 14:20) and *gamos* (Jn. 2:1–2) can be used without any theological connotation. The importance of marriage is clearly presupposed in the NT. It is based on God's commandment as told in the creation story (Gen. 2:24; Mt. 19:4–5; Mk. 10:6–7; 1 Cor. 6:16; Eph. 5:31). Although the NT often looks on marriage from the husband's point of view (as the head, cf. 1 Cor. 11:3; Eph. 5:23), the OT traditions are so transcended that the husband's special rights fall away and the shared life of husband and wife stands in the foreground (1 Cor. 7:3; Eph. 5:21–33; Col. 3:18–19).

(1) Jesus takes a strong stand on the sacred nature of marriage in the Sermon on the Mount. Speaking on the seventh commandment ("you shall not commit adultery"), Jesus, the second Moses, likewise prohibits adultery (Mt. 5:31–32). Although Deut. 24:1 in principle permits divorce, Jesus also prohibits divorce (Mk. 10:2–12), granting it only on the grounds of the immoral spouse (Mt. 5:32; 19:9).

(2) The NT portrays *gamos* as symbolic for a person's relationship with God. In Mt. 22:1–4 Jesus uses a royal wedding feast as a parable, portraying the concept of the end-time feast (cf. Isa. 25:6) where the Messiah joins his people. The prophetic picture of *gamos* represents the relationship between God and Israel (cf. Hosea). Earthly marriage will be superseded by the union of God with his people (cf. Mk. 12:24–25). Paul also sees marriage as a picture of our relationship with God. In Rom. 9:25 he quotes Hos. 2:23 so as to show how those who were "not loved" and "not my people" (the names of Hosea's

children), that is, the Gentiles, can be included in the people of God. Paul describes *gamos* as a "mystery" and uses it to illustrate the relationship of Christ and the church (Eph. 5:32). Christ's faithfulness to the church is the primary example of how both husband and wife should be faithful to one another (Eph. 5:21–22, 25–29).

(3) The picture of marriage also lies behind the expression "adulterous generation" (Mt. 12:39; 16:4; Mk. 8:38). Marital unfaithfulness is often used in the OT as a picture of idolatry (i.e., going after false gods; see *adultery*). Jesus is probably alluding to the people's attitude to God in this expression. The NT uses the human race's most intimate relationship, marriage, to show how intimate the relationship should be between God and his people. See *NIDNTT-A*, 100-102.

MARVEL

New Testament

Verb: θαυμάζω (*thaumazō*), GK *2513* (S *2296*), 43x. *thaumazō* denotes "to be amazed, astonished, wonder, marvel." See *amazed*.

MASSACRE

Old Testament

Verb: הָרַג (*hārag*), GK 2222 (S 2026), 167x. The verb *hārag* can variously mean "to kill, murder, slaughter, massacre." *hārag* most often denotes intentional killing, as in the case of Cain and Abel (Gen. 4:8). However, it can also refer to unintentional killing (Exod. 21:12–14). It is not the word used in the sixth commandment (see *murder*; also *slaughter*, *kill*).

MASTER

Old Testament

Noun: אָדוֹן (*ʾādôn*), GK 123 (S 113), 774x. *ʾādôn* is used with reference to "the Lord" and to people of high rank (especially superiors and persons of authority). See *Lord*.

New Testament

Noun: δεσπότης (*despotēs*), GK *1305* (S *1203*), 10x. *despotēs* is similar in meaning to *kyrios* ("lord"), though it occurs far less often. The nuance of *despotēs* emphasizes the right and power to command. In several cases *despotēs* refers to God or Jesus. God is addressed in prayer as *despotēs* (Lk. 2:29; Acts 4:24; Rev. 6:10) and Jesus is the *despotēs* in 2 Tim. 2:21; 2 Pet. 2:1 and Jude 4.

In addition to referring to God or Jesus, *despotēs*, like *kyrios*, can be used to speak of human masters or lords (1 Tim. 6:1–2; Tit. 2:9; 1 Pet. 2:18). This word is reflected eventually in the English word "despot." However, this is a classic example of the importance of recognizing how words can change meaning over time. The negative and harsh connotations of the English "despot" are not found in the Greek *despotēs*, nor should they be read back into the NT usage. See *NIDNTT-A*, 130.

Noun: κύριος (*kyrios*), GK *3261* (S *2962*), 717x. *kyrios* means "master, lord, sir" as well as "Lord." See *Lord*.

Noun: οἰκοδεσπότης (*oikodespotēs*), GK *3867* (S *3617*), 12x. *oikodespotēs* means the "master, owner of a house." See *owner*.

Noun: ῥαββί (*rhabbi*), GK *4806* (S *4461*), 15x. The term *rhabbi* can mean "master, sir" or remain transliterated as "rabbi." See *rabbi*.

MAT

New Testament

Noun: κράβαττος (*krabbatos*), GK *3187* (S *2895*), 11x. *krabbatos* is found only in the gospels and Acts. In every case it is associated with one who is paralyzed, lame, or bedridden because of physical infirmities. The Lord or an apostle cures those who are bedridden. Typically, such mats are small enough to be carried with ease (Mk. 2:12; 6:55; Jn. 5:8–11; Acts 5:15; 9:33). They usually incorporate a wooden frame capable of supporting an adult's weight.

MATTER

Old Testament

Noun: דָּבָר (*dābār*), GK 1821 (S 1697), 1455x. *dābār* means "word, report, command," but can also signify a "thing, matter, affair." See *word.*

New Testament

Noun: πρᾶγμα (*pragma*), GK *4547* (S *4229*), 11x. *pragma* generally refers to something about which an author is already speaking. For instance, when Paul enters the fray of an issue in the Corinthian church, he refers to "this dispute" (lit., "this thing," 1 Cor. 6:1). When James is discussing evil practices, he refers to "every vile practice" (lit., "every vile thing," Jas. 3:16). As Luke undertakes to write his gospel, he begins by noting that "many have undertaken to draw up an account of the *things* that have been fulfilled among us" (Lk. 1:1). Therefore *pragma* can be translated as "matter, thing, dispute, practice," etc., depending on what is being spoken of in context. See *NIDNTT-A*, 486-87.

Noun: ῥῆμα (*rhēma*), GK *4839* (S *4487*), 68x. *rhēma* means a "word" or "matter, event." See *word.*

MATURE

New Testament

Adjective: τέλειος (*teleios*), GK *5455* (S *5046*), 19x. *teleios* conveys a range of meanings: "perfect, mature, complete." In Eph. 4:13 it refers to a fully "mature" adult. See *end.*

MEANINGLESSNESS

Old Testament

Noun: הֶבֶל (*hebel*), GK 2039 (S 1892), 73x. *hebel* literally means "breath," but in the OT it occurs only 3x with this sense (see *breath*). The word occurs 38x in Ecclesiastes alone (including at least once in each of the twelve chapters except ch. 10), where it usually denotes the meaninglessness or futility of life. See *vanity.*

MEASURE

Old Testament

Verb: מָדַד (*mādad*), GK 4499 (S 4058), 52x. *mādad* conveys the basic activity involved in the determination of the measurement of an object and is translated "measure." It is used 35x in Ezek. 40–42 to describe the measuring of portions in the temple. The term also represents the power (Isa. 40:12) and omnipresence of God, as in Isa. 40:12: "Who has *measured* the waters in the hollow of his hand, or with the breadth of his hand marked off the heavens?" Theologically, the term is used in Jer. 31:37, where the extent of Yahweh's judgment is declared, "If the heavens above can be *measured,* and the foundations of the earth searched out below, then I will also cast off all the offspring of Israel for all that they have done." See *NIDOTTE*, 2:850-51.

New Testament

Verb: μετρέω (*metreō*), GK *3582* (S *3354*), 11x. *metreō* means "to measure" and is used in two senses. (1) It can refer to taking the measurements of an object. The new Jerusalem is measured with a measuring rod (Rev. 21:15, 16, 17). John is told to measure the inner court of the temple but not the outer court (11:1–2). The word is used figuratively in 2 Cor. 10:12, where Paul states that a group of people were measuring themselves by one another.

(2) *metreō* can also refer to measuring something out for someone (i.e., apportioning). In this sense, the word only occurs in what many scholars think is a common proverb in Jesus' day: "With the measurement you *use*, it *will be measured* to you." A looser translation has been proposed: "The measure you *give* is the measure you *get*." Figuratively, this refers to judging (Mt. 7:2), listening to Jesus' teaching (Mk. 4:24), and giving (Lk. 6:38). See *NIDNTT-A*, 368.*

Noun: μέτρον (*metron*), GK *3586* (S *3358*), 14x. *metron* refers either to a "standard of measurement" (such as a measuring rod) or to a "measured quantity." (1) *metron* denotes a "*measuring rod* of gold" in Rev. 21:15, which is used to measure the new Jerusalem. This is reminiscent of Ezek. 40-42, where the temple is measured with a "measuring reed." Speaking figuratively, Jesus states that whatever standard of measurement people use in their judgments, that same measurement will be used against them (Mt. 7:2).

(2) Jesus encourages people to give by promising that those who give will receive "a good *measure,* pressed down, shaken together, overflowing; for with the *measure* you use, it will be measured back to you" (Lk. 6:38). In Mt. 23:32, Jesus gives the scribes and Pharisees over to their sins by telling them, "Fill up the *measure* of the sin of your forefathers."

It is interesting to note that Greek philosophers used *metron* when discussing the ultimate standard by which all things are measured. Some believed that this absolute measure can be determined by human beings, but Plato taught that the "measure of all things" is in the gods. See *NIDNTT-A*, 368.

MEASUREMENT

Old Testament

Noun: מִדָּה (*middâ*), GK 4500 (S 4060), 55x. *middâ*, derived from the verb *mādad* ("to measure"), means a "measurement"; it can refer to both spatial and temporal measurements. Most of its uses in the OT refer to measurements of length, such as the measurements in Ezekiel's visionary temple (Ezek. 40) and the measurements of the tabernacle's curtains (Exod. 26:2, 8). A "cord of measurement" and a "reed of measurement" (i.e., a "measuring line" and a "measuring rod," respectively) were both used in OT times to measure various objects and distances (Jer. 31:39; Ezek. 40:3; 42:16–19). In the book of Nehemiah, various people are described as repairing a "measurement" or "section" of the wall (Neh. 3:11, 19–21, 24, 27, 30; translated "piece" in the KJV). When used with reference to a man, his "measurement" is his height or stature (Num. 13:32; 1 Chr. 11:23; 20:6; Isa. 45:14). In one instance, the word is used to refer to a robe, possibly because a robe was essentially a "measure" of cloth (Ps. 133:2).

middâ is also used figuratively to refer to the vast extent of God's knowledge (Job 11:9) and to a length of time, "the measurement of my days" (Ps. 39:4). See *NIDOTTE*, 2:850-51.

MEAT

Old Testament

Noun: בָּשָׂר (*bāśār*), GK 1414 (S 1320), 270x. *bāśār*, usually translated "flesh" or "meat," generally refers to the muscular structure of an animal and can, by extension, refer to the human body (sometimes referring to the physical aspect as opposed to the spiritual), human relations, humankind, and all living creatures. *bāśār* occurs most frequently in Leviticus (61x) and Genesis (33x), and the Pentateuch accounts for more than half of its occurrences.

When referring specifically to the muscular structure of an animal, the NIV uses the translation "meat." Often this translation is used in the context of cultic sacrifice. Israel is to eat the "meat" of the Passover lamb (Exod. 12:8, 46), and Aaron and his sons are to eat the "meat" of the ram during the ordination ceremony (Exod. 29:31, 32, 34). Leviticus gives specific instructions for eating the "meat" of the sacrifice of the peace offering (Lev. 7:15, 17, 18, 19 (3x), 20, 21), and Eli's wicked sons take the "meat" of the sacrifice before the fat is burned (1 Sam. 2:13, 15 (2x); cf. Lev. 7:29-34). As a sign that it is indeed God speaking to Gideon, fire consumes the "meat" from the sacrifice of a young goat that Gideon is instructed to place on a rock (Jdg. 6:19, 20, 21).

But "meat" is also used in noncultic contexts. After God delivers Israel from Egypt, the Israelites grumble that they ate "meat" in Egypt, but are starving in the desert (Exod. 16:3). In addition to the daily "manna," God also provides "meat" in the wilderness (Exod. 16:8, 12), specifically quail. About a year later, the rabble among Israel begin to desire other "meat" (Num. 11:4), which God provides for them for a month (Num. 11:13 (2x), 18 (3x), 21, 33). Moses instructs that when Israel enters the promised land, they may eat as much "meat" as they want (Deut. 12:15, 20 (3x)), though they must not eat the blood of the "meat," for the life is in the blood (Deut.

12:23, 27; cf. Lev. 17:11, 14). See also *flesh.*

New Testament

Noun: βρῶμα (*brōma*), GK *1109* (S *1033*), 17x. In the Synoptic Gospels, *brōma* refers to physical consumption of food (Mt. 14:15; Mk. 7:19; Lk. 3:11; 9:13). It can refer to food in general or meat in particular. See *food.*

MEDIATOR

New Testament

Noun: μεσίτης (*mesitēs*), GK *3542* (S *3316*), 6x. This noun derives from the Gk. adjective *mesos*, which means "in the middle." Thus, a *mesitēs* is someone who mediates a disagreement between two parties in order to reach a common understanding. We still use the word "mediator" and "mediate" today for the moderation of disputes.

(1) The most famous mediator of the OT was Moses, who stood between God and the people, sometimes bringing God's message to the Israelites (see Gal. 3:19–20), sometimes bringing Israel's complaints or sins before God. But there is no word in Hebrew for either "mediate" or "mediator."

(2) The NT calls Jesus a *mesitēs* between God and us in 1 Tim. 2:5. We need someone to stand between God and us and to reconcile us to God (see *reconciliation*). This mediator is Jesus; he himself said no one can come to the Father except through him (Jn. 14:6). The writer to the Hebrews calls Jesus "the *mediator* of a new covenant" (Heb. 9:16; 12:24; cf. 8:6). While the notion of standing between God and us is present here, these passages take on an additional meaning. The *mesitēs* Jesus guarantees our salvation, since the blood he shed on Calvary is the blood of the sinless Son of God, it was shed once-for-all, and God accepted it in the heavenly Holy Place. See *NIDNTT-A*, 365.

MEEK

See *gentleness.*

MEET

Old Testament

Verb: מָצָא (*māṣāʾ*), GK 5162 (S 4672), 457x. *māṣāʾ* generally means "to find," though it can also mean "to come upon, meet, catch." See *find.*

Verb: קָרָא (*qārāʾ*), GK 7925 (S 7122), 137x. The primary meaning of *qārāʾ* is "to meet, encounter, happen." It is a byform (a word spelled two ways) with *qārâ* (GK 7936), "to encounter, happen."

qārāʾ can denote a meeting of guests, as when Abraham welcomes visitors to his tent: "Abraham looked up and saw three men standing nearby. When he saw them, he hurried from the entrance of his tent to *meet* them and bowed low to the ground" (Gen. 18:2). *qārāʾ* can also signify events that may happen on a journey: "But Jacob did not send Benjamin, Joseph's brother, with the others, because he was afraid that harm might *come* to him" ("mischief *befall* him," KJV; 42:4, cf. v. 38; cf. 44:29 which uses *qārâ*). Moreover, *qārāʾ* may speak of any event that happens, whether planned or not, e.g., war (Exod. 1:10), divine judgment (Lev. 10:19; Jer. 44:23), finding something (Deut. 22:6), being afraid (Job 4:14). *qārāʾ* is used in a technical sense for engagement in battle: "Joab saw that there were battle lines in front of him and behind him; so he selected some of the best troops in Israel and *deployed* them ["put them in array," KJV] against the Arameans" (1 Chr. 19:10; cf. Num. 21:33; Deut. 2:32; 29:7; 1 Sam. 4:1; 2 Sam. 18:6).

The infinitive form of this verb became so common (used 119x) that it also functioned as a preposition meaning "against" or "toward": "The Egyptians were fleeing *toward* (against, KJV) it, and the LORD swept them into the sea" (Exod. 14:27, cf. Jdg. 14:5).

qārāʾ may also be used of the divine-human encounter. When Moses meets with Pharaoh to seek the release of the Israelites, he states that "the God of the Hebrews has *met* with us" (Exod. 5:3; cf. 3:18 where *qārâ* is used). Indeed, bringing Israel to Mount Sinai is for the purpose of meeting with God: "Then Moses led the people out of the camp *to meet* with God, and they stood at the foot of the mountain" (Exod. 19:17). The divine encounter is combined with the use of *qārā*ʾ in battle engagement by the prophet Amos. God is coming as a warrior to enact his judgment on wayward Israel and thus he proclaims: "Therefore this is what I will do to you, Israel, and because I will do this to you, prepare to *meet* your God, O Israel" (Amos 4:12). See *NIDOTTE*, 3:974-75.

New Testament

Verb: ὑπαντάω (*hypantaō*), GK *5636* (S *5221*), 10x. *hypantao* is used only in the gospels and Acts and is normally translated "to meet, oppose," designating an encounter with either a friend or foe.

(1) Whe two people meet, they often engage in conversation, such as when the resurrected Jesus meets the two women who have seen the empty tomb and instructs them not to fear, but to tell his disciples to find him in Galilee (Mt. 28:9). When a nobleman, who has gone to Jesus to heal his son, is returning home, he is met by his servants, who inform him that the son has been miraculously cured (Jn. 4:51). In Jesus' triumphal entry into Jerusalem, he is met by the crowds who have heard of the amazing miracle of the raising of Lazarus (Jn. 12:18; cf. 11:20, 30). This meeting with Jesus results in worship: "Hosanna! Blessed is he who comes in the name of the Lord, even the King of Israel" (Jn. 12:13).

(2) Occasionally, *hypantao* denotes a confrontation with an enemy. Thus, the verb is translated "oppose" in Lk. 14:31 to refer to a king meeting head-to-head in battle against another king. A spiritual battle occurs when Jesus is met by a man possessed by many demons, which Jesus then casts into a herd of pigs (Mt. 8:28; Mk. 5:2; Lk. 8:27). Similarly in Acts 16:16, after Paul and his companions are *met* by the girl with a spirit of telling the future, Paul casts the spirit out of her in the name of Jesus Christ (Acts 16:18). See *NIDNTT-A*, 294-95.*

MEETING

Old Testament

Noun: מוֹעֵד (*môʿēd*), GK 4595 (S 4150), 223x. *môʿēd* variously denotes a "meeting, appointed time, appointed season."

(1) *môʿēd* most frequently occurs in Exod. (38x), Lev. (49x), and Num. (65x), and the dominant use is in connection with the cult. Most often, it identifies the Tent of *Meeting*, the central focus of Israel's worship and the place where the nation meets God (Exod. 27:21; 28:43; 40:1–2; 29:44; Lev. 1:1; 3:2; 6:16; 15:29; Num. 2:2; 4:4; 8:19; 16:18; 31:54; cf. Lam. 2:6). In places, it also denotes the appointed times of Israel's pilgrimage feasts (Exod. 13:10; Lev. 23:2, 4, 44; Num. 9:2; 10:10; 29:39). These religious festivals occur yearly and are designed to nurture community and fellowship, to educate and communicate the faith to each generation, and to establish a standard in the practice and performance of the nation's religious faith.

(2) In noncultic contexts, *môʿēd* displays a broad range of meanings. The noun is commonly used of a determined time, such as the promise that Sarah will bear a son "at this *time* next year" (Gen. 17:21). Occasionally, the specific time is linked with a specific place, as when Jonathan departs "to the field for his *meeting* with David" (1 Sam. 20:35). *môʿēd* is also used of a community assembly or council (Num. 16:2). Finally, God places the celestial bodies in the sky to mark the "seasons" of the year (Gen. 1:14; Ps. 104:19), the shifting of which is evident even to the birds (Jer. 8:7).

MEMBER

New Testament

Noun: μέλος (*melos*), GK *3517* (S *3196*), 34x. *melos* can be translated "member, part, limb." In its only gospel reference, Jesus stresses the seriousness of single-minded, single-eyed commitment through deliberate exaggeration (Mt. 5:29–30). Lopping off or popping out any offending *melos* of the body is better than having the whole person thrown into hell.

Paul extends this idea by encouraging the Roman Christians not to offer certain parts of their bodies as a convenient playground for sin (Rom. 6:13, 19), and he refers to a certain law that is at work in our "members" (i.e., every aspect of our being), "waging war against the law of my mind" (7:5, 23). While these members are not in and of themselves sinful, they provide avenues of sinful expression.

Many occurrences of *melos* appear in Paul's discussions about the importance of all parts of the body of Christ and using all the gifts of the Spirit (Rom. 12:3–8;1 Cor. 12:13–27: "As it is, there are many *parts*, but one body" (1 Cor. 12:20). While each part is individual and fulfills a certain function, all the parts form a unified whole (12:27). Thus, diversity, accountability, and unity should all exist in a Christian congregation (also see Eph. 4:25; 5:30). The parts are networked in such as way that they all suffer when one suffers and they all rejoice when one is honored (1 Cor. 12:26).

James identifies the tongue as the most strident body "part" (Jas. 3:5–6). Although relatively small, it has vast potential for inflicting massive damage on the body—that is, the church. How difficult it is for someone in his or her own power to tame the body part known as the tongue! But through God's help, we can. See *NIDNTT-A*, 361.

MEMORIAL

Old Testament

Noun: יָד (*yād*), GK 3338 (S 3027), 1627x. *yād* usually refers to a human hand, although occasionally it has additional meanings such as a memorial or monument (1 Sam. 15:12; 2 Sam. 18:18; Isa. 56:5). See *hand*.

(HAVE) MERCY

Old Testament

Noun: חֶסֶד (*ḥesed*) GK 2876 (S 2617), 249x. *ḥesed* is one of the richest, most theologically insightful terms in the OT. It denotes "kindness, love, loyalty, mercy." See *love*.

New Testament

Verb: ἐλεέω (*eleeō*), GK *1796* (S *1653*), 28x. *eleeō* describes the emotional response and resulting action after encountering the suffering or affliction of another: "to have mercy, feel sorry for, have pity." It is used particularly of God's mercy: giving undeserved kindness or forgiveness to those who do not deserve it.

God ultimately and explicitly demonstrates his mercy before (and to) the world through the ministry and death of Jesus. The ultimate expression of his mercy triumphing over judgment is the death of Jesus, which secures the final salvation of everyone who believes (Rom. 11:30–31). Through his mercy he offers this salvation to sinners—even to one who feels himself as the chief of sinners (1 Tim. 1:13, 16). This gracious offer includes Gentiles (1 Pet. 2:10), who had been passed over in the old covenant.

In the gospels, hurting people frequently cry out to Jesus for mercy—"*have mercy* on us" (Mt. 9:27; 20:30; Mk. 10:47–48)—and they receive it. In turn, Jesus expects us to show mercy to our needy fellow human beings (cf. Rom. 12:8): "Shouldn't you have *had mercy* on your fellow servant just as I had on you?" (Mt. 18:33; cf. 5:7). Mercy is a requisite quality of those who belong to God. It compels Paul's ministry, for God has called him to a ministry through his mercy (2 Cor. 4:1). See *NIDNTT-A*, 179-80.

Verb: ἱλάσκομαι (*hilaskomai*), GK *2661* (S *2433*), 2x. *hilaskomai* means "to atone, have mercy on, to make atonement for, propitiate," and refers in the NT to the atoning work of Christ. In Lk. 18:13, the tax collector asks God to "have mercy" on him, a sinner. He wants his sins forgiven by God's grace and wants to be reconciled with God. See *atone*.

Noun: ἔλεος (*eleos*) GK *1799* (S *1656*), 27x. *eleos* is used to express "mercy" or "compassion" for those in need. It occurs frequently in the NT as an attribute of God and describes his relationship to humankind. This *eleos* was promised to the patriarchs (Lk. 1:72) and is displayed, for example, in God's "great *mercy*" to Elizabeth in giving her a child (1:58). Zechariah celebrates the role of his son as the one who will prepare the way for the Messiah, "because of the tender *mercy* of our God" (1:78). Paul speaks of God as "rich in *mercy*, because of the great love with which he loved us" (Eph. 2:4; cf. Rom. 9:23). God's mercy is "one of the weightier matters of the law" (Mt. 23:23). His wisdom, the "wisdom from above," is "full of *mercy* and good fruit" (Jas. 3:17).

God's *eleos* is seen in his concern for our salvation. Paul reminds Titus that salvation is not by works but "according to [God's] own *mercy*" (Tit. 3:5), and Peter tells his readers that we are born again "according to his great *mercy*" (1 Pet. 1:3). Jude writes of "the *mercy* of our Lord Jesus that leads to eternal life" (Jude 21). God's mercy is for those who fear him (Lk. 1:50), so believers are counseled to draw near to the throne of grace in order to "receive *mercy* and find grace to help in time of need" (Heb. 4:16).

Since God is merciful, he in turn desires his followers to show mercy in their relationships with others. God desired *eleos* more than sacrifice (Mt. 9:13). The best example in the NT of mercy on a human level is seen in the reaction of the good Samaritan to the one who fell into the hands of robbers on his way to Jericho (Lk. 10:30–37). "The one who had *mercy* on him" bandaged his wounds, took him on his donkey to an innkeeper, and paid for his care. Jesus' admonition was, "Go and do likewise" (v. 37). The outstanding negative example is the servant who was forgiven a great debt he owed, but then refused to forgive a small debt owed to him. His master's response was, "should not you have had *mercy* [the corresponding verb *eleeō*; see above] on your fellow servant, as I had *mercy* on you?" (Mt. 18:33). The connection between mercy and forgiveness is then made explicit: "So also my heavenly Father will do to every one of you, if you do not forgive your brother from your heart" (18:35). One way in which disciples are to have mercy on someone is to forgive.

eleos occurs often in connection with "grace" and/or "peace" (Gal:6:16; 1 Tim. 1:2; 2 Tim. 1:2; 2 Jn. 3; Jude 2). Mercy can be defined as God's goodness to those in need; grace is God's goodness to those who do not deserve it. See *NIDNTT-A*, 179-80.

MERCY SEAT

Old Testament

Noun: כַּפֹּרֶת (*kappōret*), GK 4114 (S 3727), 27x. Generally translated "atonement cover, mercy seat," the noun *kappōret* almost exclusively occurs in Exod. 25 and 37 (in the building of the ark of the covenant) and in Lev. 16. See *atonement cover*.

New Testament

Noun: ἱλασμός (*hilasmos*), GK 2662 (S 2434), 2x. *hilasmos* refers to "an atoning sacrifice, propitiation." This word occurs only in 1 Jn. 2:2 and 4:10. See *atonement*.

MESSAGE

New Testament

Noun: ἀκοή (*akoē*), GK *198* (S *189*), 24x. *akoē* can mean "hearing," but it can also refer to the organ of hearing ("ear") or to what is actually heard ("message"). See *hearing*.

Noun: λόγος (*logos*), GK *3364* (S *3056*), 330x. *logos* means "word, message, report." See *word*.

MESSENGER

Old Testament

Noun: מַלְאָךְ (*malʾāk*), GK 4855 (S 4397) 213x. Like *angelos* in the NT, there are two primary uses of *malʾāk* in the OT: "messenger" and "angel" (see *angel*). These two uses are divided about evenly in the OT.

malʾāk can simply designate a messenger or ambassador in human affairs who speaks and acts in the place of the one who has sent him. "The *messengers* returned to Jacob" with word about Esau (Gen. 32:6). "Moses sent *messengers* from Kadesh to the king of Edom" (Num. 20:14). Joshua sent "messengers" into Achan's tent to verify that he had sinned against God and taken spoil from battle (Jos. 7:22). Elisha sent a messenger to tell the leper Naaman to wash seven times in the Jordan (2 Ki. 5:10). God also can send out selected individuals as his messengers, such as the prophet Haggai (Hag. 1:13) or even a priest (Mal. 2:7). In Mal. 3:1, the messenger promised by the Lord who will prepare the way of the Lord ultimately refers to John the Baptist as the forerunner of the Messiah. See *NIDOTTE*, 3:941–43.

New Testament

Noun: ἄγγελος (*angelos*), GK *34* (S *32*), 176x. *angelos* means "angel, messenger." Similar to *malʾāk* in the OT, there are two primary uses of this word in the NT. (1) It can refer to a human messenger serving as an envoy. Jesus used "messengers" during his earthly ministry (Lk. 9:52). God used John the Baptist as a "messenger" to prepare the way for Jesus (Mt. 11:10; Mk. 1:2). Paul's thorn in the flesh was a "*messenger* of Satan" (2 Cor. 12:7). (2) But its more common meaning is "angel." See *angel*.

Noun: ἀπόστολος (*apostolos*), GK *693* (S *652*), 80x. *apostolos* broadly refers to a "messenger, delegate, or sent one" (see *send*). In classical Greek, *apostolos* referred to a person of merit sent as an envoy or on behalf of a master in an administrative role. John uses the term in a similar general way, applying it to any messenger without the specific idea of an office with special status (Jn. 13:16). In contrast, in Luke *apostolos* is used almost solely as a designation for the Twelve (except in Lk. 11:49 and Acts 14:14; in the latter, Luke identifies both Barnabas and Paul as apostles). Matthew and Mark use it sparingly for the Twelve (Mt. 10:2; Mk. 3:14; 6:30). See *apostle*.

MESSIAH

New Testament

Noun: Χριστός (*Christos*), GK *5986* (S *5547*), 529x. *Christos* means "Messiah, anointed one, Christ." See *Christ*.

MIDDLE

Old Testament

Noun: חֲצִי (*ḥᵉṣî*), GK 2942 (S 2677), 125x. *ḥᵃṣî* means "half"; occasionally it can be translated "middle," as in "the middle of the night" (Jdg. 16:3; Ruth 3:8; lit., "the half of the night"). See *half*.

New Testament

Adjective: μέσος (*mesos*), GK *3545* (S *3319*), 58x. *mesos* is a fluid word. It has two basic meanings: one that refers to a "middle" position spatially or temporally, and a second that have the nuance of "among," without reference to the actual center.

(1) *mesos* often refers to the middle or center position. For example, at Herod's birthday celebration, the daughter of Herodias dances "in the midst" of the partygoers (Mt. 14:6). When Jesus calls a child to himself as an object lesson, the child was "set *in the midst of* them," in a place where the disciples can all see. In Lk. 5:19, a paralyzed man is lowered through a roof and is placed into "the *middle* of the crowd, right in front of Jesus." Note also Mk. 6:47, "the *middle* of the lake." Temporally, *mesos* can be translated "midnight" (lit. "in the *middle* of the night," Mt. 25:6; Acts 27:27) or "noon" (Acts 26:13).

(2) *mesos* does not have to mean the absolute center. Rather, it can imply being the center of attention (see Lk. 6:8 for a clear example; Jn. 20:19, 26; Acts 4:7). In this sense it is translated "among," as in Mt. 10:16, "I am sending you out like sheep *among* wolves" (cf. 13:25, 49). In Lk. 8:7, the seed falls "*among* the thorns." Jesus lives and performs miracles while living "*among* the people of Israel" (Acts 2:22; cf. also 1 Cor. 5:2; 6:5; 1 Thess. 2:7; 2 Thess. 2:7; Rev. 2:1).

MIDST

Old Testament

Noun: קֶרֶב (*qereb*), GK 7931 (S 7130), 227x. The basic meaning of *qereb* is "inner parts." When combined with the preposition "in" or "from," *qereb* means "within, in the midst of," or "from the midst of," and this is the most common use of the word in the OT (198x). See *inner parts*.

New Testament

Adjective: μέσος (*mesos*), GK *3545* (S *3319*), 58x. *mesos* is a fluid word. It has two basic meanings: one that refers to a "middle" position spatially or temporally, and a second that have the nuance of "among," without reference to the actual center. See *middle*.

MIGHT, MIGHTY

Old Testament

Noun: אֵל (*ʾēl*), GK 445, 446 (S 410), 242x. *ʾēl* is one of the two Heb. words for "God." But occasionally this word can also mean "might, mighty." See *God*.

Noun: גְּבוּרָה (*gᵉbûrâ*), GK 1476 (S 1369), 62x. The basic sense of *gᵉbûrâ* is "strength, power, might." With respect to the kings of Israel, it regularly refers to what their power produced (1 Ki. 15:23; 16:5, 27). Ultimately, all power belongs to the Lord (1 Chr. 29:11). See *strength*.

Noun: עֹז (*ʿōz*), GK 6437 (S 5797), 76x. The primary sense of *ʿōz* is "strength, might, power." For example, David danced before the ark of the covenant with all his might (2 Sam. 6:14). Most commonly, *ʿōz* is used to describe God's power or might. See *power*.

Adjective: חָזָק (*ḥāzāq*), GK 2617 (S 2389), 57x. The basic sense of the adjective *ḥāzāq* is "mighty, strong, powerful." See *strong*.

New Testament

Noun: δύναμις (*dynamis*), GK *1539* (S *1411*), 119x. *dynamis* essentially means "power," but it can also denote acts of power ("miracles") or a person's "ability." See *power*.

Noun: ἰσχύς (*ischys*), GK *2709* (S *2479*), 10x. *ischys* means "strength, power, might." See *strength*.

Noun: κράτος (*kratos*), GK *3197* (S *2904*), 12x. *kratos* is generally translated "power, strength, might." See *power*.

Adjective: δυνατός (*dynatos*), GK *1543* (S *1415*), 32x. *dynatos* denotes what is possible or what one has the power to do. See *possible*.

Adjective: ἰσχυρός (*ischyros*), GK *2708* (S *2478*), 29x. The adjective *ischyros* means "strong, mighty, powerful." See *strong*.

MILLSTONE

Old Testament

Noun: רֶכֶב (*rekeb*), GK 8207 (S 7393), 120x. The basic meaning of *rekeb* is "chariot" (see *chariot*). On three occasions (Deut. 24:6; Jdg. 9:53; 2 Sam. 11:21), it is used for an upper "millstone."

MIND

Old Testament

Noun: לֵב (*lēb*), GK 4213 (S 3820), 854x. *lēb*, often translated "heart" or "mind," denotes the seat of emotion (1 Sam. 2:1), desire (Ps. 37:4), thought (Gen. 6:5), and decision (1 Chr. 12:38). See *heart*.

Noun: לֵבָב (*lēbāb*), GK 4222 (S 3824), 252x. *lēbāb* is a synonym of *lēb* (GK 4213) and means "heart, mind." See *heart*.

Noun: מַחֲשָׁבָה (*maḥᵃšābâ*), GK 4742 (S 4284), 56x. This noun is best translated "plans" or "thoughts" and can describe the plans of either individuals or God. The basic meaning of this word is captured in the contemporary question, "What's on your *mind*?" See *plan*.

New Testament

Verb: φρονέω (*phroneō*), GK *5858* (S *5426*), 26x. *phroneō* means "to think, set one's mind on something, have in mind." See *think*.

Noun: διάνοια (*dianoia*), GK *1379* (S *1271*), 12x. *dianoia* denotes the "mind, thought, understanding." Its usage in the NT appears to be distanced from the Hellenistic Gk. understanding of *nous* (see *mind*) and is connected more closely with one's heart (Heb. 8:10; 10:16) than with a rational principle.

In his summary of the law, Jesus says that individuals should love the Lord (among other things) "with all your *minds*" (Mt. 22:37; Mk. 12:30; Lk. 10:27). In Mary's song, God is described as scattering those who are proud in their minds (Lk. 1:51; NIV "inmost thoughts"). *dianoia* represents a spiritual consciousness or disposition that can be either positive (e.g., "prepared … for action" in 1 Pet. 1:13; "wholesome" in 2 Pet. 3:1) or negative (e.g., "darkened" in Eph. 4:18; "hostile" in Col. 1:21). When used in a negative sense, it refers to the thoughts of the mind that are centered in the sinful nature (Eph. 2:3). When used in a positive sense, *dianoia* is that ability of Christians to discern God's will and work in the creation. It is given by God's Spirit and can even be described as enlightened (1 Jn. 5:20; cf. 1 Cor. 2:12; 2 Cor. 4:6; Eph. 4:17). See *NIDNTT-A*, 394-96.*

Noun: νοῦς (*nous*), GK *3808* (S *3563*), 24x. *nous* refers to the "mind, intellect, understanding," that is, the part of the human system that initiates thoughts and attitudes. Paul arrays the *nous* against the flesh in Rom. 7:23a: "But, I see another law in my members warring against the law of *my mind*." In Paul's theology "the mind" is that aspect of our being where spiritual development occurs. Believers have "*the mind* of Christ" (1 Cor. 2:16). Thus, for the Christian who daily jousts with sin, the battle is won or lost in the mind, not in the physical members.

Going a step further, the word also refers to "understanding." Jesus opens "the minds" of his disciples in a post-resurrection discussion because of their obvious surprise as to how his whole ministry fulfills OT prophecy (Lk. 24:45). Paul speaks of a peace that "surpasses all *understanding*" (Phil. 4:7). Speaking in tongues evades comprehension also because Paul says "the mind" is not operative during the experience of this gift (1 Cor. 14:14), and he "would rather speak five *intelligible* [mind-produced] words to instruct others than ten thousand words in a tongue" (14:19).

It requires special "insight" to "calculate the number of the beast, for it is a man's number … 666" (Rev. 13:18). This alludes to Dan. 12:10, which refers to the knowledge of the end times that God will grant his people. John calls his readers to exercise extreme caution and divinely guided wisdom in interpreting this number. In the main passage where Paul discusses the two events that will precede the Lord's return (a general apostasy and the appearance of the lawless one), he uses *nous* in the phrase "not losing their *composure*" in light of uncertainty and false teachings (2 Thess. 2:2).

nous also can refer to "a way of thinking," as in Rom. 12:2: "the renewing of your mind." Paul uses it in Ephesians to refer to the futile "thinking" of the Gentiles (Eph. 4:17) and to spur Christians to adopt new attitudes in their "minds" (4:23). Minds can be depraved or corrupt (Rom. 1:28; 1 Tim. 6:5; 2 Tim. 3:8), puffed up (Col. 2:18), or unclean (Tit. 1:15). Paul encourages the family of faith to be "of the same mind" (1 Cor. 1:10). This stresses the importance of a Christian mindset, which includes the ability to distinguish what is good and right from what is evil and wrong. See *NIDNTT-A*, 394-96.

Noun: ψυχή (*psychē*), GK *6034* (S *5590*), 103x. *psychē* has a wide variety of meaning in the NT, being shaped by the Heb. word *nepeš*. Among other things, it means "life, soul, person, mind." See *life*.

MINISTER

Old Testament

Verb: שָׁרַת (*šārat*), GK 9250 (S 8334), 98x.*šārat* denotes "to minister, serve, officiate" and is used of the "serving" performed by royal household workers (2 Sam. 13:17; also 1 Ki. 10:5) or by court officials and public servants (1 Chr. 27:1; 28:1; Est. 1:10). This verb is to be differentiated from *ʿābad*, "to serve," which is used of general work common to all, especially slaves or servants.

(1) Normally, *šārat* refers to the service given to or for individuals of status or import. For example, Joseph "served" Potiphar (Gen. 39:4); Elisha had a servant (2 Ki. 4:43); the sons of Ahaziah's relatives attended Ahaziah (2 Chr. 22:8); and a number of personal attendants ministered to King Xerxes (Est. 2:2).

(2) The most common use of *šārat* is in the context of Israel's worship of God

(Num. 16:9; Deut. 10:8; Ezek. 44:15–16). It frequently denotes those bearing the special role of "ministering" before God or his people (on God's behalf). These individuals are normally part of the Levitical priesthood (e.g., Aaron, Exod. 28:35; the other Levites, 1 Chr. 16:4, 37), though this is not always the case (e.g., Samuel, 1 Sam. 2:11, 18; 3:1).

(3) A number of times in the OT, the ptc. form of the verb *šārat* is used as a noun for a person engaged in service and is translated as "minister" or "servant." For example, Joshua is Moses' servant (Exod. 24:13; 33:11; Num. 11:28; Jos. 1:1), and the angels are servants of God (Ps. 103:21; 104:4). See also *official*.

New Testament

Noun: διάκονος (*diakonos*), GK *1356* (S *1249*), 29x. *diakonos* means "servant, minister." See *servant*.

Noun: ὑπηρέτης (*hypēretēs*), GK *5677* (S *5257*), 20x. *hypēretēs* designates someone in a subordinate, serving role, such as a guard (Mt. 5:25; 26:58; Mk. 14:54, 46). The translators of the KJV often translate this word as "minister": "And he closed the book, and he gave it again to the *minister*, and sat down" (Lk. 4:20; NIV "attendant"). See a similar use in Acts 13:5, where the KJV calls Mark a "minister" (NIV "helper").

MINISTRY

See *service*.

MIRACLE

Old Testament

Verb: פָּלָא (*pālā*ʾ), GK 7098 (S 6381), 71x. In its participle form, *pālā*ʾ means "miracles, wonders," and refers to the extraordinary deeds of God. God is going to smite Egypt with mighty miracles (Exod. 3:20), and as he takes the people into the land, he will do wonders before them (Jos. 3:5). See *wonders*.

New Testament

Noun: δύναμις (*dynamis*), GK *1539* (S *1411*), 119x. *dynamis* essentially means "power," but it can also denote acts of power ("miracles") or a person's "ability." See *power*.

Noun: σημεῖον (*sēmeion*), GK *4956* (S *4592*), 77x. A σημεῖον is a "sign" that marks or distinguishes something. It is also used of a miraculous indicator, often a "miracle." See *sign*.

Noun: τέρας (*teras*), GK *5469* (S *5059*), 16x. *teras* means "wonder, miracle, miraculous occurrence." See *wonder*.

MIRACULOUS SIGN

Old Testament

Noun: אוֹת (ʾ*ôt*), GK 253 (S 226), 79x. ʾ*ôt* refers to a "sign" or symbol that communicates meaning; it can be used of supernatural signs (i.e., miracles) from God. See *sign*.

MISS (THE MARK)

Old Testament

Verb: חָטָא (*ḥāṭā*ʾ), GK 2627 (S 2398), 240x. The verb *ḥāṭā*ʾ carries the basic meanings of "to miss (the mark)" and by extension "to sin, be guilty." See *sin*.

MIST

Old Testament

Noun: עָנָן (ʿ*ānān*), GK 6727 (S 6051), 87x. ʿ*ānān* is consistently translated "cloud," sometimes "mist." See *cloud*.

MISTREAT

New Testament

Verb: ἀδικέω (*adikeō*), GK *92* (S *91*), 28x. *adikeō* is used mostly in Rev. (11x) and in Paul's writings (9x) to denote doing wrong, harming or hurting another, or mistreating someone (committing injustice). See *do wrong*.

MOB

Old Testament

Noun: קָהָל (*qāhāl*), GK 7736 (S 6951), 123x. *qāhāl* describes the gathering of a great body of people for civil, religious, or other occasions. See *assembly*.

New Testament

Noun: ὄχλος (*ochlos*), GK *4063* (S *3793*), 175x. *ochlos* describes a large "crowd" or "multitude" of people. Sometimes it denotes an unruly crowd, a "mob." See *crowd*.

MOCK

New Testament

Verb: ἐμπαιζω (*empaizō*), GK *1850* (S *1702*), 13x. *empaizō* denotes mocking or making sport of. In the NT it is found exclusively in the Gospels. It carries the meaning of being tricked or deceived, such as Herod being "outwitted" by the Magi (Mt. 2:16). In Lk. 14:29, the Lord declares that a person who lays a foundation for a tower but is unable to complete it will be subject to "ridicule."

The eleven other instances of *empaizō* refer to the mocking of Christ. Predicting his death, Jesus asserts that the religious authorities in Jerusalem will "turn him over to the Gentiles to be *mocked* and flogged and crucified" (Mt. 20:19). And so it was. Prior to his crucifixion, the governor's soldiers "twisted together a crown of thorns and set it on his head. They put a staff in his right hand and knelt in front of him and *mocked* him. 'Hail, king of the Jews!'" (27:29). Even "the chief priests, the teachers of the law and the elders *mocked* him" (27:31) while he was hanging on the cross. Note the unjust treatment shown toward Christ but also his willingness to suffer in this way. He is not some first-century revolutionist. Rather, he is the eternal Son of God, who has legions of angels at his disposal, but he does nothing to defend himself (Mt. 26:53). What a great price he willingly pays to bring salvation to us. See *NIDNTT-A*, 411.

MOCKERY

New Testament

Noun: βλασφημία (*blasphēmia*), GK *1060* (S *988*), 18x. This noun is used to denote the violation of the glory, majesty, and power of God and may be translated "blasphemy" or "mockery." See *blasphemy*.

MODEL

New Testament

Noun: τύπος (*typos*), GK *5596* (S *5179*), 15x. *typos* is a "pattern, example, model," taken from the concept of an impression or a mark left behind by something on a surface. See *example*.

MONEY

Old Testament

Noun: כֶּסֶף (*kesep*), GK 4084 (S 3701), 403x. *kesep* refers to "silver" or "money." See *silver*.

New Testament

Noun: ἀργύριον (*argyrion*), GK *736* (S *694*), 20x. *argyrion* means "silver" or the "money" made from it (since hard currency in antiquity was often composed of silver). The two meanings are virtually interchangeable (similar to the American five-cent coin, which is often called a "nickel" because of the primary metal of its composition). For example, when Peter claims to have no "silver," he is saying that he has no money (Acts 3:6). Similarly, Paul uses "silver and gold" as a synonym for money in general, regardless of its metal composition (Acts 20:33). Peter's message in 1 Pet. 1:18 is especially potent, for he stresses that our salvation was not purchased with "*silver* or gold," but "with the precious blood of Christ." Salvation is literally priceless.

When the NT writer leaves the amount of *argyrion* unspecified, most English translations choose "money" (Mt. 25:18, 27; 28:12, 15; Mk. 14:11; Lk. 9:3; 19:15, 23; 22:5; Acts 7:16). But when *argyrion* is accompanied by a specific number, most translations state the number with the words "silver coin(s)" or "piece(s) of silver" (Mt. 26:15; 27:3, 6, 9; Acts 19:19 [NIV: "drachma"]).

In Mt. 27:5, the text does not specify an amount, but it is implied from earlier in the account; consequently, some translations choose "money" (NIV) while others choose "pieces of silver" (KJV, NASB): "And throwing down the *pieces of silver* into the temple, [Judas] departed, and he went and hanged himself" (ESV). A similar divergence in translation occurs in Acts 8:20, where most translations choose "money," although the NASB and NRSV choose "silver." "May your *silver* perish with you, because you thought you could obtain the gift of God with money!" (ESV). See *NIDNTT-A*, 68-69.*

MONTH

Old Testament

Noun: חֹדֶשׁ (*ḥōdeš*), GK 2544 (S 2320), 283x. *ḥōdeš* means "new moon" and thus "month," since the Hebrew month was regulated by the phases of the moon. It is derived from the verb *ḥādaš* ("make new, restore, renew"), corresponding to the fact that the month begins at the appearance of the new moon, the thin crescent visible at sunset. In the majority of its occurrences, *ḥōdeš* refers to one of the twelve months of the calendar year, most often with a number identifying it. *ḥōdeš* and *yeraḥ* ("month") are sometimes used synonymously (1 Ki. 6:38, 40).

In Israel's early history, Canannite designations were apparently used for the months of the year. Four such designations are found in the OT: Passover occurs in the month of Abib (Exod. 13:4; 23:15; 34:18; Deut. 16:1), the second month is Ziv (1 Ki. 6:1), Ethanim is the seventh month (1 Ki. 8:2), and Bul, the eighth month (1 Ki. 6:38). Following the exile, Babylonian names were used (and remain in use in the modern Jewish calendar), of which seven remain in the biblical text: Nisan, the first month (Neh. 2:1, Est. 3:7), Sivan, the third month (Est. 8:9), Elul, the sixth month (Neh. 6:15), Kislev, the ninth month (Zech. 7:1), Tebeth, the tenth month (Est. 2:16), Shebet, the eleventh month (Zech. 1:7), and Adar, the twelfth month (Est. 3:7). Most often, however, the Hebrew Scriptures reference the month by an ordinal, e.g., first month, second month, etc., without adding names (cf. Gen. 8:14). Indeed, it appears that in an attempt to diminish the syncretism of moon worship in which Israel becomes entangled (2 Ki. 23:5) and which is strictly forbidden by God (Deut. 4:19; 17:2–3), the pagan month names are increasingly viewed as pejorative. By the time of Chronicles, all twelve months are designated by ordinal numbers only, without any mention of the foreign month names (1 Chr. 27:1–15). No month names are found in the NT.

ḥōdeš is sometimes paired with *rōʾš* ("head") with the meaning "beginning of the month." The first day of each month is to be celebrated with burnt offerings presented to God (Num. 28:11; cf. 1 Chr. 23:31; Ezr. 3:5; Neh. 10:33), together with blowing trumpets (Num. 10:10; Ps. 81:3). During the united monarchy, the New Moon is a significant festival (1 Sam. 20:5, 18, 24), and in the time of Amos, may have even grown to be regarded as a Sabbath (Amos 8:5). The Mosaic legislation, however, never presents the New Moon as a Sabbath nor as a sacred assembly. In fact, its two requirements (burnt offerings and blowing of trumpets) only involve the priests. Ezekiel foresees the celebration of the New Moon festival in the millennial temple (Ezek. 46:1, 6). In Isaiah's denunciation of Israel's abuse of their appointed times, he groups the New Moon festival with the appointed feasts (Isa. 1:14).

The marking of each new month appears to have been for the purpose of maintaining the festival calendar. The yearly festivals (as well as the weekly Sabbath) are called "sacred assemblies" (Lev. 23). See *NIDOTTE*, 2:38-39.

New Testament

Noun: μήν (*mēn*), GK *3604* (S *3375*), 18x. *mēn* means "month." Since the Jewish nation based it years on the lunar year, for the most part this noun refers to a time period of about twenty-eight days. For example, Elizabeth secluded herself "for five months" when she found out she was pregnant in her old age (Lk. 1:24). In "her sixth month," the angel Gabriel came to visit Mary (1:26, 36), and Mary stayed with Elizabeth "for three months" (1:56) and left just before the birth of John the Baptist. In Rev. 11:2 and 13:5 there is a reference to "forty-two months," which is equivalent to three and a half years, exactly half of the seven-year tribulation period. Only in Gal. 4:10 does this noun have a somewhat different meaning: "You are observing special days and months and seasons and years." In this letter, Paul is criticizing a reversion to Jewish ways by the Christians in Galatia; since the Jews regularly observed the "new moon," these believers apparently felt it was necessary to observe this "monthly" event.

MONUMENT

Old Testament

Noun: יָד (*yād*), GK 3338 (S 3027), 1627x. *yād* usually refers to a human hand, although occasionally it has additional meanings such as a memorial or monument (1 Sam. 15:12; 2 Sam. 18:18; Isa. 56:5). See *hand*.

MOON

New Testament

Noun: σελήνη (*selēnē*), GK *4943* (S *4582*), 9x. *selēnē* means "moon," and in the NT it is always accompanied by some reference to the sun (see *sun*). *selēnē* is used primarily in those passages of the NT that refer to the coming final days of tribulation, when "the sun will be darkened, and the moon will not give its light" (Mt. 24:29; Mk. 13:24; cf. Lk. 21:25) or "the moon [will be turned] to blood" (Acts 2:20; Rev. 6:12; cf. 8:12). A verb related to this noun (*selēniazomai*) does occur in Mt. 4:24; 17:15; both passages reflect the popular ancient notion that demon-possession is somehow connected with the moon (cf. our English word "lunacy").

The reference in Rev. 12:1–2 to the woman who is clothed with the sun, has the "moon" under her feet, and has a crown of twelve stars, suggests power and authority. Noteworthy especially is the fact that in the new Jerusalem, there will be no need for either the sun or the "moon," because the glory of God is its light and the Lamb is its lamp (Rev. 21:23). Physical light gives way to the eternal light of God. See *NIDNTT-A*, 522.

MORE

Old Testament

Adjective: אַחֵר (*ʾaḥēr*), GK 337 (S 312), 166x. *ʾaḥēr* is formed from the verb אָחַר, *ʾāḥar* (GK 336), "to delay" or "to detain someone." Thus, *ʾaḥēr* may originally have had the sense of "one who comes after," which evolved in meaning to "other" or "another." It is often used in this common sense: "he waited seven *more* days" (Gen. 8:10). See *another*.

New Testament

Adjective: περισσότερος (*perissoteros*), GK *4358* (S *4055*), 7x. *perissoteros* describes an object or person as either "greater" or "more" than what would be considered normal. See *greater*.

Adverb: μᾶλλον (*mallon*), GK *3437* (S *3123*), 81x. *mallon* is a comparative adverb that means "rather, instead, more." See *rather*.

MORNING

Old Testament

Noun: בֹּקֶר (*bōqer*), GK 1332 (S 1242), 213x. *bōqer* means "morning," though it can also be "dawn" or "daybreak." The noun normally denotes the end of night and the breaking through of daylight (Ruth 2:7). In the Heb. method of counting time, it is the second part of a day (the first part being "evening" [*ʿereb*, GK 6847]; see Gen. 1:5, 8, 13). Morning is the time when the important elements of a day's activity usually begin (e.g., 19:27; 22:3; 31:55; Exod. 7:15). In Israelite worship there were two main offerings, a "*morning* offering" and an evening offering (Exod. 29:39; 1 Chr. 16:40).

Morning is often a good time for prayer according to the Psalms. "In the morning" David lays his requests before the Lord (cf. also 88:13). The author of Ps. 46, gripped by fear, firmly holds to the belief that "God shall help her, and that *right early*" (46:5; lit., "at the turn of the morning"). The last hours of the night are the coldest and the darkest. Hence, the idea of *bōqer* in this psalm communicates that God will assist the psalmist in the time of his greatest need. As a result, morning light becomes a symbol of hope and help from the Lord. "Weeping may last for a night, but joy comes in the *morning*" (30:5). Since morning can be a refreshing time, Hosea writes that God's "love is like the morning mist, like the morning dew" (Hos. 6:4). See *NIDOTTE, 1:710-20.*

New Testament

Adverb: πρωΐ (*prōi*), GK *4745* (S *4404*), 12x. Because *prōi* can designate any time covered in the fourth watch (from 3:00 to 6:00 a.m.), sometimes it refers to very early in the morning, for which we have the phrase "the crack of dawn." See *early*.

MORTAL

New Testament

Adjective: θνητός (*thnētos*), GK *2570* (S *2349*), 6x. *thnētos* is an adjective related to the verb "to die" (*thnēskō*) and means "mortal." Paul is the only NT author who uses this word. He makes an important point that as a result of our association with Adam and his sin (cf. Rom. 5:12), our bodies are now "mortal" (6:12). But we have the assurance that if the Lord Jesus Christ is living in us, what is mortal will someday be swallowed up by immortality (see Rom. 8:11; 1 Cor. 15:53–54; 2 Cor. 5:4). Since we can be certain of the fulfillment of that promise, our lives are affected in the here and now, so that sin should not reign in our mortal bodies; rather, the life of Jesus should be apparent in us in the way we live our day-to-day lives (Rom. 6:12; 2 Cor. 4:11). See *NIDNTT-A*, 236–38.*

MOST HIGH

New Testament

Adjective: ὕψιστος (*hypsistos*), GK *5736* (S *5310*) 13x.. This is a superlative form of adjective *hypsos* ("high"). Four times *hypsistos* is used in words of praise to God "in the highest" (Mt. 21:9; Mk. 11:10; Lk. 2:14; 19:38). Its other nine occurrences are all used as a descriptive name for God as the "Most High God" (Mk. 5:7; Lk. 8:28; Acts 16:17; Heb. 7:1) or simply, "the Most High" (Lk. 1:32, 35, 76; 6:35; Acts 7:48). See *high, highest*.

MOTHER

Old Testament

Noun: אֵם (*ʾēm*), GK 562 (S 517), 220x. Normally translated "mother," the noun *ʾēm* usually represents one who has given birth to another, whether the offspring is human or animal. It can also denote various other authoritative roles.

(1) *ʾēm* us ually denotes the biological female parent of humans (Gen. 20:12; Exod. 2:8; Ps. 113:9) and animals (Exod. 22:30; Lev. 22:27; Deut. 22:6–7), but it can also refer to a more distant ancestor (1 Ki. 15:10; Ezek. 16:3). Thus, Eve is called the mother of all living things (Gen. 3:20). Though Israel was a patriarchal society, mothers had significant social and spiritual importance within the home and community. Children should seek to honor, please, and obey their mother as well as their father (Exod. 20:12; Deut. 5:16; Prov. 15:20; 19:26). Indeed, respecting one's mother is the first charge given to describe what it means to be holy as God is holy (Lev. 19:2–3). Both the father and mother are given responsibility to teach the truths of God to their children (Prov. 1:8; 6:20), the lasting benefits of which are stressed when Prov. notes that King Lemuel's parental instruction was first given him by his mother (Prov. 31:1–9). In legal texts, the mother's presence is sometimes required alongside the father's in cases involving the children (Deut. 21:18–21; 22:15–21), and not infrequently in the OT, mothers are portrayed as exercising significant domestic influence (e.g., Rebekah, Gen. 27; Micah's mother, Jdg. 17)—even as queen mothers (Bathsheba, 1 Ki. 1:11–31; Athaliah, 2 Ki. 11:1–3).

(2) Occasionally, *ʾēm* is used figuratively as a title of authority. Deborah, a judge and leader, is called "a mother in Israel" (Jdg. 5:7). Abel, a city known of old for its council, is also given the same title (2 Sam. 20:18–19; cf. Jer. 50:12). *ʾēm* can also provide a pictorial analogy for the comfort, security, and love of God (Ps. 131:2; Isa. 66:13). Importantly, however, while many maternal metaphors are used to describe the Lord, he is never directly called "mother." See *NIDOTTE*, 1:219-23, 418.

New Testament

Noun: μήτηρ (*mētēr*), GK *3613* (S *3384*), 83x. *mētēr* often refers in the NT to one's biological mother (Mt. 20:20) and in this sense, often to Mary the mother of Jesus (Mt. 1:18; Jn. 2:1ff; Acts 1:14). From the cross Jesus establishes a new mother-son relationship between the beloved disciple and Mary (Jn. 19:26–27). One of the most touching scenes in the Gospels comes when Jesus raises the only son of a widow from the dead, and then gives "him back to his mother" (Lk. 7:15). The fifth commandment, to honor one's father and mother, is repeated often in the NT (e.g., Lk. 18:20; Eph. 6:2), as is Gen. 2:20, which suggests that marriage requires a man to "leave his father and his mother" (Mk. 10:7; Eph. 5:31). Though Jesus urges that children must honor their father and mother, he also quotes Mic. 7:6 to show that commitment to him must exceed commitment to one's family of natural descent, and may well cause divisions within families (Mt. 10:34–37). Mothers can play an important role in the training and education of children (2 Tim. 1:5; cf. Prov. 1:8).

A new, spiritual use of *mētēr* appears in the gospels, where Jesus suggests that those who hear his word and do it are his mothers and brothers (Lk. 8:20–21). This application of kinship language to the community of believers also appears in Paul (Rom. 16:13; 1 Tim. 5:2). "Mother" appears in Gal. 4:26, where the church as Jerusalem is called the spiritual mother of believers. *mētēr* also appears in Rev. 17:5, where Babylon is said to be "the mother of harlots and of the abomination of the earth." See *NIDNTT-A*, 368-69.

MOUNT

Old Testament

Verb: רָכַב (*rākab*), GK 8206 (S 7392), 78x. *rākab* generally means "to mount or ride (something)," but it can also mean "to drive (something)" and in this sense is most often used of chariots (Gen. 24:61; 41:43;1 Ki. 1:33, 38, 44; Ezek. 23:6, 12, 23; Zech. 1:8). See *ride*.

MOUNTAIN

Old Testament

Noun: הַר (*har*), GK 2215 (S 2022), 558x. *har* can be translated as "mountain, hill, hill country." It often refers simply to an elevation of land such as Gilead (Deut. 3:12), the hills west of Jericho (Jos. 2:15), or "the *hill country* of Ephraim" (Jdg. 2:9). It can also refer to a larger hill or mountain, such as Mount Hermon (Deut. 3:8) or Mount Carmel (1 Ki. 18:19), or an even greater mountain such as Mount Sinai (Exod. 19:11). The flood was so extensive that it covered all the high "mountains" (Gen. 7:19).

The Hebrews viewed *har* in a manner unique from other parts of the natural world. They suggest permanence and durability. Several passages speak of "the ancient mountains" (Gen. 49:6; Hab. 3:6). "As the *mountains* surround Jerusalem, so the Lord surrounds his people both now and forevermore" (Ps. 125:2). Even if the unimaginable happened, that of the *har* falling into the heart of the sea, God nevertheless remains the Hebrews' refuge and strength (Ps. 46:1–2). In other words, while we may look to the hills for a sense of security and comfort, our help ultimately "comes from the Lord, the Maker of heaven and earth" (Ps. 121:1–2). The mountains remain part of creation (Ps. 65:6; 90:2; Prov. 8:25; Amos 4:13), while God is Creator, eternally God. This stands in contrast to much of the rest of the ancient world, which saw the mountains as the unique abode of the gods (cf. Isa. 14:13).

har often has theological overtones. The Hebrews associate two of God's most important revelations with a mountain. God gave the Hebrews the Mosaic law on "*Mount* Sinai." Then, "*Mount* Zion" becomes the place where the Lord puts his name (Exod. 15:17). Thus, Zion is considered "my holy *hill/mountain*" (Ps. 2:6; 87:1), and it is the place where he has chosen to reign (68:16). Those who have clean hands and a pure heart, i.e., those devoted to the Lord, have the right to "ascend *the hill* of the Lord" (24:3) and to worship him there. The day is coming when "many peoples will come and say, 'Come, let us go up to the *mountain* of the Lord, to the house of the God of Jacob" in order to learn his ways (Isa. 2:3; Mic. 4:2). See *NIDOTTE*, 1:1051-55.

New Testament

Noun: ὄρος (*oros*), GK *4001* (S *3735*), 63x. *oros* can refer to an individual mountain (Jn. 4:20), a mountain range (Mt. 24:16), or even a mere hill (5:14), such as "the *Mount* of Olives" (24:3; Acts 1:12). Jesus' famous Sermon on the Mount (Mt. 5:1), in which he instructs his disciples about life in the kingdom, is traditionally viewed as taking place on the low hills on the northern side of the Sea of Galilee. Since Moses received instruction in covenant law from God on Mount Sinai (cf. Acts 7:30, 38), some argue that Matthew is portraying Jesus in Mt. 5–7 as a new Moses. There are other significant events in Jesus' life that take place on a mountain or hill. He goes to a mountain to pray (Mt. 14:23), to call the Twelve (Mk. 3:13), to work a miracle (Jn. 6:3–14), to be transfigured (Mt. 17:1; cf. 2 Pet. 1:18), and to give the Great Commission (2:16–20).

oros is occasionally used symbolically. It can symbolize a challenging barrier to overcome by faith (Mt. 17:20; 1 Cor. 13:2). Jesus' disciples are the light of the world, and as such are to shine into the darkness of the world, just as a "city on a *hill* cannot be hidden" (Mt. 5:14). And, as in the OT, the most significant mountain of all is "*Mount* Zion," which in the NT is a symbol of the eternal kingdom of our Lord (Heb. 12:22; Rev. 14:1).

MOURN

Old Testament

Verb: בָּכָה (*bokâ*), GK 1134 (S 1058), 114x. *bokâ* has the basic meaning "to weep," but can be translated with other terms such as "sob, mourn, wail, cry." See *weep*.

New Testament

Verb: κλαίω (*klaiō*), GK *3081* (S *2799*), 40x. *klaiō* means "to weep, mourn" because of grief. In the NT, this verb expresses violent emotions brought about by various circumstances that cause sorrow. See *weep*.

Verb: πενθέω (*pentheō*), GK *4291* (S *3996*), 10x. *pentheō* means "to mourn, grieve, bewail." This word is used in contexts of mourning over disasters or grieving the loss of someone. Mourning is often associated with weeping. While in classical Greek usage, *penthos* was a passion that a wise person must intentionally avoid, in the NT mourning is encouraged in contexts of sorrow over grievous sin and is acceptable and appropriate in cases of overwhelming disasters.

Mourning over the loss of a person is expressed, often through tears (Mt. 9:15; Mk. 16:10). The mention of mourning in the Beatitudes has end-time significance: those mourning now will be comforted in the kingdom of heaven (Mt. 5:4), whereas those laughing now will mourn and wail later (Lk. 6:25). Paul and James encourage Christians to grieve over their sins, leading to godly sorrow, contrition, and repentance. Mourning is always appropriate with respect to grievous sin, which stains the church community (1 Cor. 5:2; 2 Cor. 12:21). James admonishes sinning Christians to "grieve, mourn, and wail" over their sins (Jas. 4:9). When Babylon is destroyed for her lack of repentance, those who profited from her business stand afar off and "mourn" her demise as well as their own loss of business (Rev. 18:11, 15, 19). See *NIDNTT-A*, 451.*

MOUTH

Old Testament

Noun: פֶּה (*peh*), GK 7023 (S 6310), 498x.

(1) *peh* refers to the "mouth" of people or animals as the organ of eating/drinking or of speech. As a metaphor, it refers to *the opening* of things like a cave (Jos. 10:18, 22, 27), sack (Gen. 42:27) or well (Gen. 29:2). The "mouth of the sword" is the edge of the sword (Gen. 34:26; Jos. 10:28); during the time of the conquest, Israel put certain enemies to the edge of the sword—an idiomatic expression for putting to

death (Jos. 6:21; 8:24; 10:28). Sometimes "mouth" stands for what comes out of one's mouth, such as someone's word (Joseph in Gen. 41:40; Joshua in Jos. 1:18), command (God in Num. 20:24; 22:18; 27:14), or testimony (witnesses in Num. 35:30; Deut. 17:6). In Jos. 1:8, to let the book of the law not depart from your *mouth* was one way of securing a life of obedience and blessing from the Lord.

(2) The Lord's *peh* is described in the OT as powerful and accomplishing great things. In contrast to the dumb (or mute) idols (Ps. 115:5), the God of Israel, by his mouth, actually communicates to his people (Deut. 8:3; Isa. 40:5; 48:3). By his word of his mouth the Lord created the universe (Ps. 33:6). See *NIDOTTE*, 3:583-84.

New Testament

Noun: στόμα (*stoma*), GK *5125* (S *4750*), 78x. The word *stoma* refers to the "mouth" of humans (Mt. 5:2; Lk. 1:64), creatures (a fish, Mt. 17:27), and even figuratively of God ("man shall live ... by every word that proceeds from the *mouth* of God," Mt. 4:4). In addition, *stoma* is used metaphorically in the expression "mouth of the sword," which means "*edge* of the sword" (Lk. 21:24; Heb. 11:34; cf. Gen. 34:26). Furthermore, sometimes *stoma* stands for the thing spoken by the mouth, as in "the *testimony* (lit. "the mouth") of two or three witnesses" (Mt. 18:16), or Jesus' promise, "I will give you *words* [lit. a mouth] and wisdom" (Lk. 21:15). In keeping with certain OT passages, note the expression, "by the mouth of," which means to speak *through* someone (Lk. 1:70; Acts 1:16; cf. 2 Chr. 36:21, 22; Ezr. 1:1).

The NT often describes the mouth in terms of how believers and unbelievers use it in speaking. In Romans, the mouths of the wicked/sinners are full of cursing and bitterness (Rom. 3:14) and have been stopped and shut up under the law in judgment (3:19). In the gospels, Jesus asserts that the mouth reveals the overflow of the heart (Mt. 12:34) and that what comes out of the mouth is what makes the person unclean (because it comes from the heart, 15:11, 17, 18). We as Christians can use our mouths in productive ways: as we confess that Jesus is Lord unto salvation (Rom. 10:8–10); we glorify God "with one mouth" (a sign of unity, confessing the same things, 15:6); nothing unwholesome should come from our mouths but only what is edifying (Eph. 4:29); and out of the believer's mouth should come only blessing, not both blessing and cursing (Jas. 3:10).

Finally, it is of some interest that 22 of the 78 uses of *stoma* occur in Revelation. In this book, the power of God's enemies is commonly represented by what they do with their mouths (Rev. 12:15; 13:5, 6; 16:13), but in contrast God's agents fight for divine victory by the power of their mouths (2:16; 9:17, 18, 19; 11:5; 12:16; 19:15, 21).

MOVE

Old Testament

Verb: נָסַע (*nāsaʿ*), GK 5825 (S 5265), 146x. The original meaning of *nāsaʿ* is "to pull out (tent pegs)," from which the sense "set out" or "journey" is derived. See *journey*.

New Testament

Verb: κινέω (*kineō*), GK *3075* (S *2795*), 8x. *kineō* means "to move, stir, arouse." About half of the uses of this word refer to the arousal of a crowd, such as the crowd of enemies around the cross of Jesus who were "shaking their heads" and hurling insults at him (Mt. 27:39; Mk. 15:29). A crowd of the enemies of the Christian movement also becomes aroused in Jerusalem when Paul arrives and visits the temple (Acts 21:30; cf. 24:5). On a more positive note, Paul preaches before the Areopagus that all human beings "live and move and have their being" in the Creator God, because he has breathed into us the breath of life (17:28).

MULTIPLY

Old Testament

Verb: רָבָה (*rābâ*), GK 8049 (S 7235),

229x. *rābâ* typically refers to an increase in quantity. See *increase*.

New Testament

Verb: πληθύνω (*plēthynō*), GK *4437* (S *4129*), 12x. *plēthyno* means "to increase, grow, multiply." See *increase*.

MULTITUDE

Old Testament

Noun: רֹב (*rōb*), GK 8044 (S 7230) 150x. *rōb* denotes a multitude or an abundance. It is probably derived from the verb *rābâ*, which means to become numerous, much, or great. See *many*.

New Testament

Noun: ὄχλος (*ochlos*), GK *4063* (S *3793*), 175x. *ochlos* describes a large "crowd" or "multitude" of people. See *crowd*.

Noun: πλῆθος (*plēthos*), GK *4436* (S *4128*), 31x. *plēthos* denotes the number or quantity of an object and is best translated "number, crowd, multitude." See *number*.

MURDER

Old Testament

Verb: הָרַג (*hārag*), GK 2222 (S 2026), 167x. *hārag* can variously mean "to kill, murder, slaughter, massacre." *hārag* most often denotes intentional killing, as in the case of Cain and Abel (Gen. 4:8). However, it can also refer to unintentional killing (Exod. 21:12–14). It is not the word used in the sixth commandment (see *murder, slaughter*).

New Testament

Verb: φονεύω (*phoneuō*), GK *5839* (S *5407*), 12x. *phoneuō* means "to murder." Most of the uses of this verb occur in quotations from the sixth commandment, "Do not murder" (Exod. 20:13; see Mt. 5:21; 19:18; Mk. 10:19; Lk. 18:20; Rom. 13:9; Jas. 2:11). In both the OT and NT, God is against the willful destruction of human life. Jesus criticizes the Pharisees for being like those ancient Israelites who "murdered the prophets" (Mt. 23:31, 35). James takes his audience to task for this sin as well (Jas. 4:2; 5:6).*

MURMUR

New Testament

Verb: γογγύζω (*gongyzō*), GK *1197* (S *1111*), 8x. *gongyzō* means "to grumble, murmur." See *grumble*.

MUST

New Testament

Verb: δεῖ (*dei*), GK *1256* (S *1163*), 101x. *dei* occurs frequently in the NT, especially in Luke. It has a basic meaning of something being "necessary." The concept of *dei* plays a distinct role in three contextual areas: eschatological-apocalyptic expectation, the salvation history interpretation of Jesus, and the context of the Christian life.

(1) *dei* is found in prophetic passages. When speaking of things to come, Jesus himself notes that such things as earthquakes, famines, wars, and great distress "are necessary" (Mk. 13:7; cf. Mt. 24:6; Lk. 21:9). In the same context he says that the gospel "must" be preached to the entire world before the end will come (Mt. 24:14; Mk. 13:10). In Rev. 1:1, John writes of "what *must* soon take place," (cf. 22:6). In addition, there are enemies of God that must be killed (11:5); and in 20:3, Satan is thrown into the abyss for a thousand years, after which he "must" be set free for a short time. Paul, too, uses *dei* in this eschatological sense. In 1 Cor. 15:25 he states that Christ "*must* reign until he has put all his enemies under his feet" (cf. also 15:53; 2 Cor. 5:10).

(2) The gospels tell us that throughout Jesus' life, many things "*had* to happen," given that he had come to save the world. John writes that Jesus "*had* to go through Samaria" in order to meet the woman at the well (Jn. 4:4ff.). Jesus "must" do the works of God (9:4). According to Mt. 16:21, "Jesus began to explain to his disciples that he *must* go to Jerusalem and suffer many things," including dying. In other words, in order for the plan of salvation to be worked out, certain things *had to occur*, and *dei* plays an important role in conveying this idea. This was the plan of the triune God, and it could in no way be

thwarted. Note Mt. 26:54, where Jesus says, "But how then would the Scriptures be fulfilled that say it "must" happen this way?"

This divine plan of salvation is a theological emphasis of Luke. The life, death, and resurrection of this Jewish rabbi, Jesus of Nazareth, was the ordained plan of God. Jesus knew his mission was to preach the gospel, to be killed, and to be resurrected in order to fulfill OT prophecy and the plan of salvation in history (Lk. 4:43; 9:22; 13:33; 17:25; 22:37; 24:7, 26, 44; Acts 1:16; 17:3).

(3) This divine necessity includes events in our lives as well. John records Jesus' exchange with Nicodemus in which he said, "You *must* be born again" (Jn. 3:7). Acts 4:12 (cf. 16:30–31) states that people can be saved only through Jesus: "Salvation is found in no one else, for there is no other name under heaven given to men by which we *must* be saved." One "must" obey God rather than men (5:29). Paul's life was ordained by this divine necessity as well (9:6, 16; 27:24). *dei* can also refer simply to those things that should happen because they are fitting (1 Cor. 8:2; Eph. 6:20; Col. 4:6; 1 Thess. 4;1; 2 Thess. 3:7; 2 Tim. 2:6), required (1 Tim. 3:2; Heb. 11:6), or necessary to bring about a certain result (1 Cor. 11:19). See *NIDNTT-A*, 121-22.

Noun: ἀνάγκη (*anankē*), GK *340* (S *318*), 17x. *anankē* carries the meaning of necessity, conpulsion, pressure, or even calamity and distress. See *necessary*.

MUSTER

Old Testament

Verb: פָּקַד (*pāqad*), GK 7212 (S 6485), 304x. While *pāqad* has a wide range of meaning, it basically expresses the action of overseeing an individual for a particular purpose. In this sense, *pāqad* is used most frequently in the sense of a superior counting someone in his charge during a census. The NIV sometimes translates this use "to muster": Joshua "musters" the people before Ai (Jos. 8:10); Saul "musters" them at Bezek (1 Sam. 11:18); and David "musters" the people with him (2 Sam. 18:1). See *count*.

MUTE

New Testament

Noun: κωφός (*kōphos*), GK *3273* (S *2974*), 14x. *kōphos* is the term for someone who is either mute or deaf. See *deaf*.

MUZZLE

New Testament

Verb: φιμόω (*phimoō*), GK *5821* (S *5392*), 7x. *phimoō* means "to be quiet, speechless, muzzled." It has the idea of restraint, either imposed externally or internally. See *quiet*.

MYSTERY

New Testament

Noun: μυστήριον (*mystērion*), GK *3696* (S *3466*), 28x. *mystērion* denotes a "mystery, secret," or something "unknown." In the NT it most often refers to the mystery that Christians now know and which differentiates a Christian from unbelievers. Jesus summarizes this as follows, "The knowledge of the mysteries of the kingdom of heaven has been given to you, but not to them" (Mt. 13:11). *mystērion* is modified in a number of different ways: "the mystery of the kingdom of God (Mk. 4:11); "the mystery of Christ" (Eph. 3:4; Col. 4:3); "the mystery of the gospel" (Eph. 6:19); "the mystery of God" (1 Cor. 2:1; 4:1; Rev. 10:7) "the mystery of God, namely Christ" (Col. 2:2); "God's *secret* wisdom" (1 Cor. 2:7); "the mysteries of the faith" (1 Tim. 3:9); and "the mystery of godliness" (1 Tim. 3:16).

Each of these uses of *mystērion* refers to the same basic idea, which can be summarized as knowledge and understanding (in a spiritual sense) of the life, death, and resurrection of Jesus the Christ. Learning and understanding this mystery does not come via human intellectual or philosophical achievement. The only way to grasp it is through revelation from God. Paul affirms this in the phrase "the mystery made known to me by revelation" (Eph. 3:3; the mystery here is the inclusion of the Gentiles with the Jews to make one new man), which he in turn was appointed by God to make known to others (Col. 1:26–27). Moreover, what God reveals is not secret facts or information, but Jesus Christ. Col. 2:2 says, "the *mystery* of God, namely, Christ, in whom are hidden all the treasures of wisdom and knowledge." Similarly, 1 Cor. 2:1b–2 states, "I [Paul] did not come with eloquence or superior wisdom proclaiming to you the *mystery* of God. For I judged to know nothing among you except Jesus Christ, and him crucified." Again, Paul writes, "this *mystery* is great, but I am speaking in reference to Christ and the church" (Eph. 5:32).

While *mystērion* usually refers to Christian mystery, it can be used in other contexts. Note these expressions: "all *mysteries* and all knowledge" (1 Cor. 13:1), "the *mystery* of lawlessness" (2 Thess. 2:7), "the *mystery* of the seven stars … and the seven golden lampstands" (Rev. 1:20), and "the *mystery* of Babylon" (17:5). See *NIDNTT-A*, 378-80.

MYTH

New Testament

Noun: μῦθος (*mythos*) GK *3680* (S *3454*), 5x. *mythos* means "myth." The noun occurs only in the Pastoral Letters and in 2 Pet. 1:16. Paul warns against those who spend their time speculating not on the truths of God's Word but "on myths and endless genealogies" (1 Tim. 1:4; 2 Tim. 4:4). Thus, he admonishes Timothy and Titus to have nothing to do with them; they are a waste of time and do not help a person grow spiritually (1 Tim. 4:7; Tit. 1:14). The myths were probably stories created around a little-known person in the OT (hence, "genealogies") upon which the false teachers based their heretical teachings that put law above grace and faith.*

NAKED

Old Testament

Noun: עֶרְוָה (*ʿerwâ*), GK 6872 (S 6172), 54x. *ʿerwâ* conveys the general state of being uncovered and exposed, usually in the sense of nakedness. The term is best translated "naked" or "nakedness" and comes from the verb *ʿārâ*, which means "to make bare." Leviticus 18 uses the term 32x as an expression for "sexual relationships" (e.g., 32:6, 7; 20:11). The term is also used to describe *nakedness* in the sense of exposed genitals (Gen. 9:22–23), unprotected land (Gen. 42:9), indecent activity (Deut. 24:1), and the shame associated with covenant infidelity (Deut. 28:48; Mic. 1:11). Ezekiel declares, "Then I will hand you over to your lovers, and they will tear down your mounds and destroy your lofty shrines. They will strip you of your clothes and take your fine jewelry and leave you *naked* and bare" (Ezek. 16:39). The contemporary cliché "caught with your pants down" captures the sense of this term when it is used to denote one's shame. See *NIDOTTE*, 3:527-30.

New Testament

Adjective: γυμνός (*gymnos*), GK *1218* (S *1131*), 15x. *gymnos* means to be "naked, without clothes." It is related to our word "gymnasium," since in ancient Greece athletes were usually naked. It can be used literally, as in the biblical mandate to help a brother or sister *without clothes* (Jas. 2:15). At the final judgment, God receives those saints who clothed the needy and connects helping the poor with service to himself (Mt. 25:40).

gymnos can also function figuratively, as when Paul uses it to mean "being without an immortal body." In eternity believers will not be bodiless souls, but will be clothed with new, spiritual bodies (2 Cor. 5:3). It also means "to be exposed morally before God." Everything in creation is naked, in the sense of being laid bare or exposed before the God to whom we must give account (Heb. 4:13). Nakedness can also represents spiritual poverty (cf. the church at Laodicea; Rev. 3:17). In the wake of his imminent return, Jesus warns us to keep our garments on so as not to go about naked and exposed (16:15). The background of this is Adam and Eve's nakedness before God in the face of judgment (Gen. 3:10). This foreshadows the necessity of being clothed with the garments of Christ's righteousness so as not to stand naked and unprotected before God at the final judgment. See *NIDNTT-A*, 116-17.

NAME

Old Testament

Noun: שֵׁם (*šēm*), GK 9005 (S 8034), 864x. While *šēm* is used many times in Scripture for no more than a person's given name, in the context of the ancient Near East it also conveys much more. Names represented people in much the same way that idols were thought to represent the false gods. A name was a point of access, and naming and/or having knowledge of a name was thought to give one person power over another. The third commandment (Exod. 20:7) may be addressing this ancient Near Eastern philosophy.

(1) Hebrew names were sometimes considered reflective of character and/or destiny. There are numerous instances in the OT of etymological explanations designed to do this, though they are not necessarily related to the initial naming event or circumstances. Abraham (Gen. 17:5), Sarah (17:15) and Israel (32:28) are examples of people whose names God changed to reflect either a transformation in their relationship with him or a prophetic notion of his plans for them. The simple fact that God renames them indicates his lordship and dominion over them. God has given humankind dominion over creation, which Adam first exercised when God brought every creature to him to receive its name (2:19).

(2) At times, the ideas of reputation, fame, and memorial are also included in *šēm*. Having "a good name" is a way of saying that a person has a reputation of integrity (Prov. 22:1). God will give Abraham (Gen. 12:2) and David (2 Sam. 7:9) great names, which means that they will be remembered with honor and their legacies and descendants will be great. After a person dies, he continues on in this life by memory and reputation. This is why it was so tragic to die without having children (Deut. 25:6–7; 2 Sam. 18:18; Isa. 56:5) and why it was potentially dangerous to have only daughters (Num. 27:4).

(3) There are many names ascribed to the Lord in the OT, a number of which proclaim his divine attributes (Gen. 16:13; 22:14; Exod. 15:26; Isa. 11:10; Jer. 23:6). Several examples of attributive names are found in messianic texts (Isa. 7:14; 8:8; 9:6). Yahweh, the Lord's personal and covenantal name, is introduced in Exod. 3, when the Lord encounters Moses at the burning bush. This name derives from the Hebrew verb meaning "to be," thus emphasizing the Lord's self-existence and self-revelation.

"The name of the LORD," the *šēm yhwh*, embodies the power of the Lord. His people find safety in that name (Prov. 18:10). The name of the Lord is to be praised (Ps. 7:17; 135:1; Joel 2:26), called upon (Gen. 12:8; Joel 2:32; Zeph. 3:9), exalted (Isa. 24:15), trusted (Ps. 20:7; Zeph. 3:12), or feared (Ps. 102:15; Isa. 59:19). To speak in the name of the Lord is to speak with his authority (Exod. 5:23; Deut. 18:20; Jer. 30:9). See *NIDOTTE*, 4:147-51

New Testament

Verb: λέγω (*legō*), GK *3306* (S *3004*, *2036*, *2046*), 2353x. Usually translated as "say," *legō* sometimes has the notion of "naming" someone by some specific name. See *say*.

Verb: ὀνομάζω (*onomazō*), GK *3951* (S *3687*), 10x. *onomazō* is the verbal form of the noun *onoma* (see the noun). In the Synoptics it occurs in the sense of "to designate." Jesus appoints the Twelve and then "names" them apostles (Mk. 3:14; Lk. 6:13). In a similar fashion, Jesus "names" Simon, Peter (Lk. 6:14). Because one's name is wrapped up with one's person, the verb can also be used in the sense of "to claim, invoke." For example, the sons of Sceva "name" the name of Jesus in order to try and cast out demons (Acts 19:13).

Elsewhere the verb retains its sense of "to designate," but it can sometimes be translated "proclaim." For example, Paul seeks to evangelize where Christ has not been "named" or proclaimed, so as to avoid building on someone else's foundation (Rom. 15:20). Likewise, whoever "names" the name of the Lord must depart from iniquity (2 Tim. 2:19). Paul tells the Corinthians not to associate with anyone who "names" himself a brother but continues in sin (1 Cor. 5:11).

Paul says Christ is seated "far above all rule and authority and power and dominion, and above every name that *is named*, not only in this age but also in the one to come (Eph. 1:21, ESV)." As Jesus' worth is infinitely greater than any other, so his name is above every other name. In 3:15 ("from whom every family in heaven and on earth *is named*"), while the exact nuance here may be difficult to determine, Paul does imply that every family is known by or originated in the creative act of the Father. See *NIDNTT-A*, 411-13.

Noun: ὄνομα (*onoma*), GK *3950* (S *3686*), 231x. The use of *onoma* in the NT includes identifying people and place names, the idea of reputation (Rev. 3:1), and the authority by which an act is accomplished (Acts 3:6; 4:18). The plural form of *onoma* can be used synonymously with people, echoing the idea that the name represents the essence of a person (Rev. 3:4; 11:13).

(1) There are a few examples of renaming in the NT. Christ changes Simon's name to Peter (Jn. 1:42) and gives new names to the sons of Zebedee (Mk. 3:17). Those who overcome will be given new names (Rev. 2:17).

(2) Christ came to reveal God's name (Jn. 17:6), which the Father glorified (12:28). The revelation of God's name is the revelation of himself (17:26). Jesus protected his disciples through the power of the Father's name, which appears to be spiritual protection, rather than physical (17:11,12). Jesus told his disciples that their names were written in heaven (Lk. 10:20).

(3) Believers are baptized into the name of Jesus (Acts 19:5; 1 Cor. 1:13–15), meaning that they identify with him in his death and resurrection, and they publicly declare their allegiance to Christ. The apostles healed in the name of Jesus (Acts 3:6; 4:10), taught in his name (5:28) and were persecuted on account of *the Name* (Mt. 10:22; Acts 5:41).

(4) Jesus' name, which means *the Lord is salvation*, is used in the NT in much the same way that "the name of the LORD (*yhwh*)" was used in the OT (Phil. 2:9–10). Jesus told his disciples to present their requests in his name, so that they would receive and their joy would be complete (Jn. 16:24). Praying in the name of Jesus is an acknowledgement of his authority and lordship, and salvation is only found through believing in Jesus' name (Acts 10:43; Rom. 10:13; 1 Jn. 2:12). The hope of eternal life and the experience of abundant life are found in his name (Jn. 20:31). See *NIDNTT-A*, 411-413.

NATION

Old Testament

Noun: גּוֹי (*gôy*), GK 1580 (S 1471), 567x. *gôy* is commonly understood as "nation" (e.g., Egypt, Exod. 9:24). In the Exodus God promises to make the Hebrews a great nation (Exod. 32:10). But *gôy* does not always refer to a political kingdom; it can refer more generally to groups of people (non-Jews), thus meaning "Gentiles" or in some contexts "pagans" (with their gods, Isa. 37:12). See *nation*.

In one of the Isaiah's Servant Songs, the Lord explains to his Servant the vast extend of his salvation: "It is too light a thing that you should be my Servant to raise up the tribes of Jacob and to bring back the preserved people of Israel; I will make you as a light for the *nations*, that my salvation may reach to the end of the earth" (Isa. 49:6). Of course, Jesus Christ is this Servant who brings salvation to all peoples, thus fulfilling the divine promise to Abraham that all nations will be blessed through his seed (Gen. 18:18; cf. Gal. 3:16). Although the Bible assumes a special relationship between Israel and God, the promise of salvation is extended to all the nations through faith in Christ: "Behold, my servant, whom I uphold, my chosen, in whom my soul delights; I have put my Spirit upon him; he will bring forth justice to the *nations*" (Isa. 42.1; cf. Gen. 12.1–3; Ezek. 25.11; Gal. 3:13–16). See *NIDOTTE*, 4:966-97.

Noun: עַם (*ʿam*), GK 6639 (S 5971), 1869x. *ʿam* can refer to military troops (Num. 20:20; Jos. 8:1) or to a general assembly of people (Ruth 4:9; 1 Sam. 10:17). Especially in the plural, this word is often used to refer to the "nations" of the world (Ps. 18:47; 45:5; Isa. 12:4; 63:3). But most frequently *ʿam* denotes a large group of people united by a familial relationship. See *people*.

New Testament

Noun: ἔθνος (*ethnos*), GK *1620* (S *1484*), 162x. *ethnos* appears in the NT with two meanings, "nation" and "Gentile." In the former sense, it signifies a body of persons united by kinship, culture, and common traditions, such as the Israelite nation, "the Jewish people" (Acts 10:22; cf. Jn. 18:35), or to a Gentile nation, as in "*nation* will rise against *nation*" (Mt. 24:7). The term has special significance for the church's mission because of its appearance in the Great Commission: "Therefore go and make disciples of all *nations*" (Mt. 28:19). In this text, Jesus' command is not to disciple every "nation" in the sense of geopolitical states, but in the sense of every single people group in the world. See *NIDNTT-A*, 161-62. See also *Gentile*.

Noun: φυλή (*phylē*), GK *5876* (S *5443*), 31x. *phylē* refers to a "tribe" or to a larger unit such as a "nation" or "people." See *tribe*.

NATION

Old Testament

Noun: מִשְׁפָּחָה (*mišpāḥâ*), GK 5476 (S 4940), 304x. The noun *mišpāḥâ* designates a subgroup of a larger division, and is, therefore, variously translated as "clan, family, people" as well as "kind, kingdoms, nation." See *clan, kind*.

mišpāḥâ does indeed denote nations. The covenant promises made to Abraham include a blessing on all peoples (Gen. 12:3, cf. 28:14 and the parallel use of *goyim* in 18:18; 22:18; 26:4): "all *peoples* on earth will be blessed through you" ("in thee shall all *families* of the earth be blessed," KJV). One distinguishing characteristic of sub-groupings among the world's population is language. Thus, Gen. 10:5 reports, "From these the maritime peoples (*gôyim*, GK 1580) spread out into their territories by their *clans* (*mišpāḥâ*) within their nations (*gôyim*), each with its own language" ("every one after his tongue, after their *families*, in their nations" KJV).

Israel's distinction from the nations is based entirely on God's sovereign election (Deut. 7:7–9). "You only have I chosen of all the *families* of the earth; therefore I will punish you for all your sins" (Amos 3:2; cf. Deut. 7:6; 14:2; 32:8). In the eschatological reign of the Messiah, all the nations who waged war against Israel will be called to celebrate the Feast of Tabernacles in Jerusalem. Those who refuse will be punished with draught: "If any of the *peoples* (*mišpāḥâ*) of the earth do not go up to Jerusalem to worship the King, the LORD Almighty, they will have no rain" (Zech. 14:17). See *NIDOTTE*, 2:1139-42.

NATURAL CONDITION

New Testament

Noun: φύσις (*physis*), GK *5882* (S *5449*), 14x. *physis* means "nature, natural condition, kind." See *nature*.

NATURE

New Testament

Noun: μορφή (*morphē*) GK *3671* (S *3444*), 3x. *morphē* means "form, nature." See *form*.

Noun: φύσις (*physis*), GK *5882* (S *5449*), 14x. *physis* means "nature, natural condition, kind." This term was used widely in classical Greek. For example, Aristotle considered *physis* as the original substance of the elements. Homer and Pindar used *physis* to reflect "external form." The Stoics, who believed that humans should live by following nature, used *physis* to describe a god of the universe.

Josephus used the term almost synonymous with "character."

In the NT, the meaning and usage of *physis* is comparable to the various usages in the ancient Greek-speaking world. It occurs frequently in Paul's writings. In Rom. 11 Paul describes the "wild olive tree" (Gentile Christians) and the "natural branches" (Jews). He suggests that the wild olive tree will be removed from the tree that it belongs to "by nature" and be grafted into a tree that it does *not* belong to "by nature." (Rom. 11:21, 24). His point is that there is no advantage for branches grafted in over those that belonged to the tree by nature.

physis can also describe the normal arrangement of the created order, especially regarding the differences between the sexes. The term describes homosexual relations as "unnatural" or "contrary to *nature*" (Rom. 1:26). Rom. 2:14 says that a form of moral law is found in "nature" (pagans following the "law" by nature). The natural order of hair length is the focus in 1 Cor. 11:14, where *physis* is a teacher showing us what is appropriate (this passage has a variety of interpretations). The distinction between our weak mortal nature and the divine essence is presupposed in 2 Pet. 1:4. James uses *physis* to mean "kind [of animal]" (Jas. 3:7). *physis* means birth (family lineage) in Gal. 2:15 and refers to those who are Jews "by nature [i.e., birth]," yet who also realize that to be a true child of God requires faith in Jesus Christ (cf. 2:16). See *NIDNTT-A*, 595-96.

NEAR

Old Testament

Verb: נָגַשׁ (*nāgaš*), GK 5602 (S 5066), 125x. *nāgaš* denotes "to be near, come into close proximity to an object." Isaac requests of Jacob: "*Come near* so I can touch you, my son" (Gen. 27:21). See *approach*.

Adjective: קָרוֹב (*qārôb*), GK 7940 (S 7138), 75x. *qārôb* is widely used in historical, poetic and prophetic texts and is best translated "near." The term stems from the verb *qārab* ("to draw near"). In common use, *qārôb* denotes the nearness of objects, such as cites (Gen. 19:20), people (Deut. 21:6), kings (2 Sam. 19:43), and lands (2 Chr. 6:36). Deut. 4:7 speaks of the nearness of Yahweh to his people as a witness to the nations, "What other nation is so great as to have their gods *near* them the way the LORD our God is near us whenever we pray to him?" Theologically, *qārôb* denotes the nearness of God and his works of salvation (see Ps. 34:18; 75:1; 119:151; Isa. 50:8; 56:1; Jer. 23:23) to his people. It is also the preferred term for the prophets who announce the nearness of the coming "day of the LORD" (Isa. 13:6; Ezek. 30:3; Joel 1:15; 2:1; 3:14; Obad. 15; Zeph. 1:7, 14). The nearness of the second coming of Christ in today's world captures the sense of this term. See *NIDOTTE*, 3:976-978.

New Testament

Adverb: ἐγγύς (*engys*), GK *1584* (S *1451*), 31x. *engys* means "nigh" or "near to"; it can have either a spatial or a temporal meaning in Greek, just as it does in English. (1) It may refer to time, meaning "near" ("summer is *near*," and "the son of man is *near*," Mt. 24:32–33; cf. Rev. 1:3; 22:10). These temporal instances are sometimes translated more freely into English. Thus, in Jn. 2:13 Jesus went up to Jerusalem "when it was *almost time* for the Jewish Passover" (NIV, cf. Jn. 6:4; 7:2; 11:55; see also Heb. 6:8; 8:13).

(2) *engys* can also denote a spatial relationship. In Acts 9:28, for example, the town Lydda was physically near the city of Joppa (see also Lk. 19:11; Jn. 3:23; 6:19). As above, *engys* can be translated more loosely, as in Jn. 6:19, where Jesus, as he walked on the water, was "*approaching* the boat" (NIV; see also 11:18). *engys* may also be used figuratively with this meaning. Paul speaks of the unity of Jews and Gentiles in Christ by affirming that those who were far off (Gentiles) "have been brought *near*" through Christ (Eph. 2:13, 17; see also Rom. 10:8; 13:11).

(3) In a theological sense, *engys* takes on a significant meaning that stems from

the OT, denoting either God's *soon* coming kingdom (Isa. 13:6; cf. Mt. 4:17; Rev. 1:3) or his *close presence* among his people (see e.g., Ps. 34:18). *engys* in Phil. 4:5 has an important theological message After instructing Euodia and Syntyche to agree "in the Lord," Paul tells the Philippians that their gentleness toward one another must be obvious to all, because "the Lord is near." Here the phrase can denote either a temporal sense ("the Lord's coming is near") or a spatial sense ("the Lord is now among his people," cf. Ps. 145:18). Because the Holy Spirit is a sign of the reality of God's presence among his people, the spatial sense cannot be ruled out. At the same time, however, a common motivation to live in unity as God's people is the imminent return of the Lord. In Paul's mind, both meanings are probably valid. Believers, through their relationships with each other, must indicate clearly to all people that the Lord has come to dwell among his people and will soon return as judge. That reality must shape our lives. See *NIDNTT-A*, 158.

Preposition: πλησίον (*plēsion*), GK *4446* (S *4139*), 17x. While *plēsion* is usually an adverb (see *neighbor*), in one instance it is a preposition meaning "near": "Now he had to go through Samaria, so he came to a town in Samaria called Sychar, *near* the plot of ground Jacob had given to his son Joseph" (Jn. 4:4).

NECESSARY

New Testament

Verb: δεῖ (*dei*), GK *1256* (S *1163*), 101x. *dei* occurs frequently in the NT, especially in Luke. It has a basic meaning of something being "necessary." See *must*.

Noun: ἀνάγκη (*anankē*), GK *340* (S *318*), 17x. *anankē* carries the meaning of necessity, compulsion, pressure, or even calamity and distress. In terms of necessity or a ccompulsory need, Lk. 14:18 says, "The first said, 'I have just bought a field, and I *must* go and see it.'" In his teaching on the civil government, Paul says, "Therefore, *it is necessary* to submit to the authorities, not only because of possible punishment, but also because of conscience" (Rom. 13:5). Paul also speaks of one who "is under no *compulsion*" (1 Cor. 7:37). In Phlm. 14 and 2 Cor. 9:7, constraint is contrasted with the Christian acting freely. Similarly, Jude writes, "I felt I *had* [lit., I felt the *anankē*] to write and urge you to contend for the faith" (Jude 3).

anankē can also refer to distress or tribulation. In Lk. 21:23 Jesus prophesies of Jerusalem's destruction (c. A.D. 70): "There will be great *anankē* in the land and wrath against this people." Paul also speaks of distress in 1 Cor. 7:26: "Because of the present *anankē*, I think that it is good for you to remain as you are" (see also 2 Cor. 6:4; 12:10; 1 Thess. 3:7).

Finally, *anankē* can denote something that *must* and *will* occur in the course of God's divine plan of salvation. In Mt. 18:7 Jesus says, "Woe to the world because of the things that cause people to sin! Such things *must* come, but woe to the man through whom they come!" In 1 Cor. 9:16 Paul says, "I am *compelled* to preach. Woe to me if I do not preach the gospel!" (KJV has "for *necessity* is laid upon me"). The writer of Hebrews states that in light of the coming of Christ, since there was a change in the priesthood, there "had" to be a change in the law (Heb. 7:12). Death must necessarily occur (see 9:16), and in 9:23, "It was *necessary*, then, for the copies of the heavenly things to be purified with these (earthly) sacrifices." In 7:27, Jesus, the great and final High Priest, "does not *need* to offer sacrifices day after day, first for his own sins, and then for the sins of the people." He is the great High Priest, and his sacrifice for sins is once for all time. See *NIDNTT-A*, 43-44.*

NEED

New Testament

Noun: χρεία (*chreia*), GK *5970* (S *5532*), 49x. *chreia* refers to a necessity one has for something: e.g., John's need for baptism (Mt. 3:14), the need of the sick for a doctor (Mk. 2:17), or the need of David and his companions for food (Mk. 2:25; cf. Acts 20:34). Being "in need" often refers in the NT to lack of basic, physical necessities (Rom. 12:13; Phil. 4:16). In Acts, the early church shared together as anyone "had need" (Acts 2:45; 4:35). For Paul, mutual dependence and sharing of basic needs are a crucial part of being the body of Christ (1 Cor. 12:21). Paul assures God's people that God will meet all of their needs (Phil. 4:19). But sometimes meeting those needs depends on the "haves" within the church, for "if anyone has material possession and sees his brother in *need* but has no pity on him, how can the love of God be in him?" (1 Jn. 3:17). See *NIDNTT-A*, 608.

NEEDY

Old Testament

Noun: אֶבְיוֹן (*ʾebyôn*), GK 36 (S 34), 61x. Among the terms in the Heb. language used to designate the "poor" or the "needy," *ʾebyôn* is consistently used to describe the physical poverty of those who are destitute. The OT has much to say about providing for the needy. For example, the law of Moses instructs the people: "Do not take advantage of a hired man who is poor and *needy*, whether he is a fellow Israelite or a Gentile living in one of your towns" (Deut. 24:14; cf. 15:4–11). In fact, one of the indications of rebellion against God is disregard or oppression of the poor. Thus the prophet Amos confronts Israel since "they sell the righteous for silver, and the *needy* for a pair of sandals" (Amos 2:6; cf. 4:1; 5:12; 8:4, 6; see also Isa. 14:30; Jer. 2:34–37; 5:28; Ezek. 22:29).

As a result, God promises to turn Israel's feasts into mourning and their songs into lamentation on the great Day of the Lord (Amos 8:10). He also pledges to protect, raise up, and deliver the humble and needy (1 Sam. 2:8; Isa. 29:19; 41:17; Jer. 20:13; 22:16), a truth that plays a significant role within the Psalms (see, e.g., Ps. 9:19; 12:6; 35:10; 69:34; 70:6; 72:4, 12–13; 82:4; 86:1; 107:41; 109:16, 22, 31; 112:9; 113:7; 132:15; 140:13).

The Lord is committed to defending the poor and destitute, and Christians in the twenty-first century must be intentional toward this end. Prov. 14:31 reminds us that "the one who oppresses the poor shows contempt for their Maker, but whoever is kind to the *needy* honors God." Thus, as Christians we are to cast our eyes on the downtrodden and will then be able to say with Job: "Have I not wept for those in trouble? Has not my soul grieved for the *poor*?" (Job 30:25), and "I was a father to the *needy*; I took up the case of the stranger" (29:16). Such a practical concern begins with seeing the needs of those in the family of God (Gal. 6:10), but then also extends to all those in need, to the glory of God (see especially Mt. 25: 34–36, 40). See *NIDOTTE*, 1.228-32.

Adjective: עָנִי (*ʿānî*), GK 6714 (S 6041), 80x. *ʿānî* describes one who has been humbled or afflicted by circumstances, and who, because of current disability, finds himself or herself dependent on others for life's necessities. See *poor*.

NEIGHBOR

Old Testament

Noun: רֵעַ (*rēaʿ*), GK 8276 (S 7453), 188x. *rēaʿ* is primarily translated as "neighbor" or "friend." It describes individuals living in close geographical proximity one to another. "You shall not give false testimony against your neighbor" (Exod. 20:16), nor does God want us to covet anything that belongs to our "neighbor" (20:17). Moses gives various agricultural warnings about how to relate to one's neighbor and his property (Deut. 19:14; 23:24–25). Solomon warns, "He who despises his neighbor sins" (Prov. 14:21).

In some cases, *rēaʿ* means no more than another person. At the building of the Tower of Babel, for example, the builders "said to each other, 'Come, let's make bricks'" (Gen. 11:3; cf. also Jon. 1:7). Later on, however, when God confused their language, they could not "understand each other" (Gen. 11:7).

rēaʿ is also translated "friend," which is an intimate word. "The Lord would speak to Moses face to face, as a man speaks with his friend" (Exod. 33:11). Job typifies what true friendship is when he writes, "My intercessor is my friend as my eyes pour out tears to God; on behalf of a man he pleads with God as a man pleads for his friend" (Job 16:20–21). Solomon writes, "A friend loves at all times" (Prov. 17:17). He later warns, however, "A man of many friends may come to ruin" (18:24).

Jeremiah's usage of *rēaᶜ* is, perhaps, the strongest. In speaking of Israel, the Lord says, "But you have lived as a prostitute with many lovers—would you now return to me?" (Jer. 3:1). Jeremiah later uses *rēaᶜ* to liken Israel to an unfaithful spouse. "But like a woman unfaithful to her husband, so you have been unfaithful to me, O house of Israel" (Jer. 3:20). Jeremiah lived in selfish times not unlike our own, in which no one could trust either "friend" or brother (9:4–5). See *NIDOTTE*, 3:1144–49.

New Testament

Adverb: πλησίον (*plēsion*), GK *4446* (S *4139*), 17x. *plēsion* is used to describe "neighbors," individuals who live in close proximity to one another. The first appearance of this word is in Lev. 19:18: "Do not seek revenge or bear a grudge against one of your people, but love your neighbor as yourself. I am the LORD." While this OT Scripture appears to be limited to "one of your people," the LXX established much broader interpretive boundaries to include those individuals outside of one's own people.

Jesus restates the spirit of this verse several times when he says disciples should love their neighbor (Mt. 5:43) as they love themselves (19:19). This in fact is the second half of the greatest commandment. We are to love God, but if we love God we will of necessity love our neighbor (22:39; Mk. 12:31, 33; Lk. 10:27). As such, it is the fulfillment of the OT law (Rom. 13:9–10; Gal. 5:14; Jas. 2:8). In an attempt to justify himself, a lawyer asks Jesus "Who is my neighbor?" (Lk. 10:29), to which Jesus responds with the parable of the Good Samaritan. The point is that your neighbor is anyone in need whom you can help (Lk. 10:36).

In modern Western culture the translation "neighbor" may be too restrictive as it suggests the people living in the house on either side of your home. The biblical "neighbor" is anyone with whom you come in contact, with whom you can speak truth (Eph. 4:25) and build up (Rom. 15:2), but not judge (Jas. 4:12) or mistreat (cf. Acts 7:27). See *NIDNTT-A*, 471-72.*

NET

New Testament

Noun: δίκτυον (*diktyon*), GK *1473* (S *1350*), 12x. *diktyon* means "net," particularly one used for fishing. This word occurs only in the gospels. When Jesus calls Peter and Andrew, they leave "their nets" and follow him (Mt. 4:20). Jesus asks Peter to go to deep water and let down his "nets"; they catch so many fish their nets begin to break (Lk. 5:4–7). After his resurrection, Jesus appears to some of his disciples and asks them to cast their "net" on the right side of the boat. They catch so many fish that they are unable to haul their "net" into the boat, but have to drag it ashore (Jn. 21:6–11).

NETHERWORLD

Old Testament

Noun: שְׁאוֹל (*šeʾôl*), GK 8619 (S 7585), 65x. *šeʾôl* refers to the place known as "Sheol." It is used with reference to the "grave" or the "netherworld." See *grave*.

NEW

Old Testament

Adjective: חָדָשׁ (*ḥādāš*), GK 2543 (S 2319), 53x. *ḥādāš* denotes the state of being different, new, and superior to a previous state. The term is best translated as "new." The phrase "There is nothing *new* under the sun" (Eccl. 1:9) captures the meaning of this word. A variety of objects or persons are connected with this term, such as kings (Exod. 1:8), a wife (Deut. 24:5), gods (Jdg. 5:8), and swords (2 Sam. 21:16).

Of special theological significance is the reference to the "new covenant" in Jer.

31:31 and its NT use in Heb. 8:8–12. In addition, the phrase "new things" is a repeated motif in Isa. 42:9, 10; 43:19; 48:6, and suggests a future expression of renewal and salvation for God's people common in the prophetic literature. This same emphasis is given in 65:17 and 66:22, which refer to the "*new* heavens and the *new* earth," a phrase that gains apocalyptic meaning in 2 Pet. 3:13 and Rev. 21:1–4. Ezekiel mentions the divine initiative where God himself gives his people a *new* spirit and a *new* heart (see Ezek. 11:19; 18:31; 36:26). Clearly, this term is significant as it points to Jesus Christ, who fulfills the OT anticipation of "new" with regard to the history of redemption. See *NIDOTTE*, 2:30-37.

New Testament

Adjective: καινός (*kainos*), GK *2785* (S *2537*), 42x. *kainos* means "new" in contrast to something old, such as the new covenant in contrast to the old (Lk. 22:20; 1 Cor. 11:25; 2 Cor. 3:6; Heb. 8:8). It can also carry the idea of "new" in the sense of "unused," as in "*new* wineskins" that can hold new wine (Mt. 9:17; Mk. 2:22; Lk. 5:38) or a "*new* tomb" (Mt. 27:60). Finally, it can means "new" in the sense of unknown or strange, such as a "*new* teaching" (Mk. 1:27; Acts 17:19).

Before the time of biblical Greek, *kainos* had a distinctive meaning from its synonym *neos* (GK *3742*) in that *neos* meant new in time and *kainos* referred to something new in the sense of unused. However, in NT Greek there is some overlap in the meanings of the two words so that you cannot assume the older distinction is still present. The "*new* covenant" phrase, for example, is referred to by both *kainos* (Heb. 9:15) and *neos* (12:24).

In speaking of "the *new* covenant" Jesus says, "The cup is the *new* covenant in my blood" (1 Cor. 11:25). Just as "*new* wine" is placed into "*new* wineskins," so also Jesus' teaching requires new forms that are different from those of Judaism (Lk. 5:37–38). Christians look forward to "a *new* heaven and a *new* earth" (2 Pet. 3:13) and the "*new* Jerusalem" (Rev. 3:12). We are a "*new* creation" when we become believers in Christ (2 Cor. 5:17; Gal. 6:15). A "*new* song" is sung in heaven, "Worthy are you to take the book and break its seals" (Rev. 5:9). The "new" command given by Jesus to his disciples is that they should love just as he loved them (Jn. 13:34). This new command is also old because it has been God's command all along (Mt. 22:36-40; cf. Lev. 19:18; Deut. 6:5). This commandment is thus both new and old (1 Jn. 2:7). See *NIDNTT-A*, 280–82.

Adjective: νέος (*neos*), GK *3742* (S *3501*), 24x. *neos* is an adjective describing the age of something, referring to its newness or youth. It is applied to wineskins (Mt. 9:17), to wine itself (Lk. 5:39) and to the "*new* covenant" (Heb. 12:24). With reference to people, *neos* is used comparatively to show someone as younger than another (Lk. 15:12; 1 Tim. 5:11, 14) or superlatively for the youngest of a group (Lk. 22:26). It can also simply refer to an earlier point in someone's life (Jn. 21:18). Although grammatically *neos* is an adjective, it sometimes functions in the NT as a noun, as in Acts 5:6, "The *young men* came forward." Interestingly, in classical Greek, *neos* applied to people between the ages of 20 and 30, an age most people today would consider to be adult.

Paul uses *neos* to describe our new natures (Col. 3:10, "Put on the *new* self"). He also uses it of the church and its need to maintain purity from sin (1 Cor. 5:7, "Get rid of the old yeast that you may be a *new* batch without yeast."). In this passage he reminds the Corinthian church of the Jewish custom of preparing for the Passover by removing yeast from their houses. In a similar fashion, he charges the church to remove sin from its midst, sanctifying itself for the day when the Lamb will return. See *NIDNTT-A*, 385.

NEW MOON

Old Testament

Noun: חֹדֶשׁ (*ḥōdeš*), GK 2544 (S 2320), 283x. *ḥōdeš* means "new moon" and thus "month," since the Hebrew month was regulated by the phases of the moon.

It is derived from the verb *ḥādaš* ("make new, restore, renew"). See *month.*

NIGH

New Testament

Adverb: ἐγγύς (*engys*), GK *1584* (S *1451*), 31x. *engys* means "nigh or near to"; it can have both a spatial and a temporal meaning in Greek, just as it does in English. See *near.*

NIGHT

Old Testament

Noun: לַיְלָה (*laylâ*), GK 4326 (S 3915), 234x. *laylâ* means "night" and is often used with "day" to indicate a twenty-four-hour period (Isa. 28:19). The expression "night and day" represents the normal Jewish order of thinking (Est. 4:16; cf. Gen. 1:5, 8), though the expression "day and night" is more common; the expression generally means "continually." For example, "May your eyes be open toward this temple day and *night*, this place of which you said you would put your Name there" (2 Chr. 6:24). God promises to continually guard his vineyard: "I, the Lord, watch over it; I water it continually. I guard it day and *night* so that no one may harm it" (Isa. 27:3).

The Egyptians dreaded darkness because they believed the sun went home. But the Hebrews understood darkness simply as a part of God's ordained time. God has created *laylâ* just as he did the day (Gen. 1:4, 5), and both day and night belong to him (Ps. 74:16). He provides food for animal during the *laylâ* (Ps. 104:20–22). Not only should individuals not fear the night (91:5–6), God often manifests himself during a "*night* vision" (cf. Gen. 46:2; Zech. 1:8; cf. Mic. 3:5–7). God's proposal to Solomon to "ask for whatever you want me to give you" comes during the night (1 Ki. 3:5). Daniel receives the interpretation of King Nebuchadnezzar's dream during the night (Dan. 2:19).

It is true that there are negative things associated with the night. For example, during the night deviant behavior can occur, such as the prowling of the promiscuous woman (Prov. 7:9) and theft (Obad. 5). Night can also be a time of anxiety (Ps. 42:3) and anguish (22:1–2). But while OT writers do associate fear with the night (91:5), they also know that God is at work as much in the night as in the day. God delivers Hezekiah and the southern kingdom of Judah from the Assyrian army (185,000 men) of King Sennacherib during the night (2 Ki. 20:35). The exodus is God's greatest act of deliverance in the OT; the author of Deuteronomy reminds the Hebrews that the glorious act occurred during the night (Deut. 16:1). Thus, God has power over the darkness, and nothing can be hidden from him (Ps. 139:11–12). See *NIDOTTE*, 2:795.

New Testament

Noun: νύξ (*nyx*), GK *3816* (S *3571*), 61x. *nyx* is most often used when referring to "night," the opposite of day. Jesus fasted forty days and forty nights (Mt. 4:2), Peter denied Jesus the same night Jesus was betrayed (Mt. 26:34; Mk. 14:30), and the soldiers took Paul to Antipatris at night (Acts 23:31). The Roman world divided the night into four watches (cf. Mt. 14:25). Night was often a time for divine activity, when angels visited people (Acts 5:19; 12:6–7) or God came to them in dreams (Mt. 2:12, 22).

This term is used figuratively as well, referring primarily to this present evil age (Rom. 13:12). The people of the world "belong to the night," while the people of God are "sons of the light and sons of the day" (1 Thess. 5:5). The meaning of "night," therefore, intersects with the meaning of "darkness" (see *darkness*). Paul concludes that God's people are to be "alert and self-controlled," since "those who sleep, sleep at night, and those who get drunk, get drunk at night" (1 Thess. 5:6–7). Jesus refers to a coming time of night, when his people cannot work (Jn. 9:4). By this expression he may be referring to the time of age of the antichrist, when opportunities to witness for him will be all but impossible. But note, too, that when the new heaven and the new earth arrive, "there will be no more night" (Rev. 22:5).

NILE

Old Testament

Noun: יְאֹר (y^e'$\bar{o}r$), GK 3284 (S 2975), 64x. y^e'$\bar{o}r$ is a loanword from the Egyptian name for the Nile River (Gen. 41:1; Exod. 1:22; 2:3) and its tributaries (when used in the plural, Exod. 8:1; Isa. 7:18; Ezek. 30:12). Egyptian life depended on the Nile for its very life. But God showed at the time of the exodus that he is greater than the Nile, since he turned its waters into blood (Exod. 7:17–24), and he can even dry up its waters (Isa. 19:5–9; Zech. 10:11).

By derivation, y^e'$\bar{o}r$ can designate other "rivers" (Isa. 33:21; Zech. 10:11) such as the Tigris (Dan. 10:4; 12:5). Job uses y^e'*or* to describe humanity's ability to cut rock channels (Job 28:10). In a land often plagued with drought, Isaiah used y^e'*or* (in the plural) to describe the Lord's bountiful blessings: "The Lord … will be like a place of broad *rivers*" (Isa. 33:21). See *NIDOTTE, 3:48.*

NINE

Old Testament

Noun: תֵּשַׁע (*tēšaʿ*), GK 9596 (S 8672), 58x. *tēšaʿ* means "nine" in the singular and "ninety" in the plural. It can also mean the ordinal numeral "ninth." *tēšaʿ* can also combine with other numbers: e.g., with *ʾelep* ("thousand," GK 547), it means "nine thousand"; with the number ten, it means "nineteen." Undoubtedly the most significant use of this number is in the story of Abraham. When he is "ninety-nine" (lit., "ninety and nine") years old, God appears to him and confirms his covenant with him. God also instructs him about his covenant sign and seal that all males should be circumcised (Gen. 17:1, 24). Sarah at that time is "ninety" years old (17:17). Shortly thereafter, God appears again to tell them that within a year, they will finally become the parents of the promised son Isaac (18:1–15).

NINETY

Old Testament

Noun: תֵּשַׁע (*tēšaʿ*), GK 9596 (S 8672), 58x. *tēšaʿ* means "nine" in the singular and "ninety" in the plural. It can also mean the ordinal numeral "ninth." See *nine.*

NINTH

Old Testament

Noun: תֵּשַׁע (*tēšaʿ*), GK 9596 (S 8672), 58x. *tēšaʿ* means "nine" in the singular and "ninety" in the plural. It can also mean the ordinal numeral "ninth." See *nine.*

New Testament

Adjective: ἔνατος (*enatos*), GK *1888* (S *1766*), 10x. *enatos* means "ninth." It is usually used to refer to the "*ninth* hour," three in the afternoon in Jewish reckoning. During the crucifixion of Christ, darkness comes from the sixth to the ninth hour (Mt. 27:45). It is about the "*ninth* hour" when Jesus cries out, "My God, my God, why have you forsaken me?" (Mt. 27:46). Peter and John go to pray at the temple at "the *ninth* hour" (Acts 3:1). Cornelius has his vision at "the *ninth* hour" (Acts 10:3, 30).

NOISE

Old Testament

Noun: הָמוֹן (*hāmôn*), GK 2162 (S 1995), 82x. *hāmôn* expresses a quality of immensity or magnitude, whether it bears an emotive, audible, or spatial reference. It is translated with words like "confusion, tumult, noise, abundance, army, hordes." See *hordes.*

Noun: קוֹל (*qôl*), GK 7754 (S 6963), 505x. *qôl* generally means "voice, sound, noise." See *voice.*

NORTH

Old Testament

Noun and Adjective: צָפוֹן (*ṣāpôn*), GK 7600 (S 6828), 153x. This word is the geographical designation for "north" (1 Ki. 7:25; Ps. 89:12; Amos 8:12). It may take its origin from the mountain named Saphon, which forms the northern border of Syria-Palestine (Jdg. 12:1; Jos. 13:27; Isa. 14:3).

ṣāpôn sometimes refers to the north side of something (Exod. 26:20, 35; 27:11;

Lev. 1:11; Num. 34:7, 9; Jos. 15:11; 2 Ki. 16:14; Ezek. 42:1) or to a northerly direction (Jos. 19:27; Jer. 3:12; Ezek. 42:1). The term occurs with other directional terms (south, east, and west) to indicate vast areas of land (Gen. 13:14; 28:14; Deut. 3:27). Restoration from every direction underscores the extent of God's actions for his people (Ps. 107:3; Isa. 43:5–6). No matter how far or in what direction they have been cast out in exile, God promises to bring his people back to the land of promise.

Because of the geographical features of the Near East, Israel was usually attacked from the north (e.g., Assyria, Babylon) or from the south (e.g., Egypt). With the sea to the west, the Jordan River and desert to the east, as well as deep ravines on both sides that made east-west travel difficult, the best approach to Jerusalem was always from the north or the south. The north especially became associated with Israel's enemies—Assyria, Babylon, or even the Seleucid kings (Isa. 14:31; Jer. 1:13–15; Dan. 11:6–44; Zeph. 2:13). Some of these enemies carry significance for the eschatological battle envisioned by the prophets (e.g., Ezek. 38:15; 39:2; Joel 2:20). The term can also refer to the northern portion of the divided kingdom of Israel, which was destroyed by the Assyrians in 721 B.C. (Jer. 3:12).

The wind from the north was known to be cool, to bring rains, and to clean the air (Job 37:21–22; Prov. 25:23). In Ps. 48:2, Mount Zion is compared with Mount Zaphon, which may refer to the mythological home of Baal and the purported location of the council of the gods (cf. Isa. 14:3, where "mountain" is *ṣāpôn*). The idea is that God's dwelling is unsurpassed in praise, beauty, security, and righteousness. See *NIDOTTE*, 2:834-47.

Noun and Adjective: שְׂמֹאל (*śᵉmōʾl*), GK 8520 (S 8040), 54x. *śᵉmōʾl* is usually employed to denote the "left, left side, left hand." Sometimes when used alone, it can means "[to go] to the left/north," because of the ancient world's orientation to the east. See *left*.

NOSE

Old Testament

Noun: אַף (*ʾap*), GK 678 (S 639), 277x. The noun *ʾap* literally means "nose" or, in the plural, "face" or "nostrils," though it is often used figuratively for "anger" (see *anger*). In its common usage, *ʾap* refers to the nose as an organ for breathing (Isa. 2:22) or smelling (Ps. 115:6), but it is also a place for ornamental rings (Gen. 24:47) or for rings or hooks for holding beasts captive (e.g., crocodiles, Job 40:24; swine, Prov. 11:22). The Lord gave Adam life by breathing into his nostrils (Gen. 2:7).

NOSTRILS

Old Testament

Noun: אַף (*ʾap*), GK 678 (S 639), 277x. The noun *ʾap* literally means "nose" or, in the plural, "face" or "nostrils" (see *nose*), though it is often used figuratively for "anger" (see *anger*).

NOT KNOW (UNDERSTAND)

New Testament

Verb: ἀγνοέω (*agnoeō*), GK *51* (S *50*), 22x. *agnoeō* means to be ignorance of something, not know something, or not understand something. See *be ignorant*.

NOTICE

Old Testament

Verb: נָכַר (*nākar*), GK 5795 (S 5234), 44x. *nākar* (which occurs mostly in the Hiphil form) refers to general knowing, such as the basic awareness of another's existence or the taking notice of who a person is. See *recognize*.

NOW

Old Testament

Adverb: הֵנָּה (*hēnnâ*), GK 2178 (S 2008), 51x. *hēnnâ* is an adverb meaning "here," usually in the sense of "in this place," though it sometimes can mean "now." See *here*.

New Testament

Adverb: ἄρτι (*arti*), GK *785* (S *737*), 36x. In classical Greek *arti* is used to describe the immediate past, "just" (see

Mt. 9:18; Rev. 12:10 for a possible carry-over from classical to the NT). In the NT it mostly indicates the present time, "immediately, now" (cf. *nyn*).

Jesus is baptized because it is "now" time to fulfill all righteousness (Mt. 3:15; cf. 26:29). A man whose vision Jesus restores says, "Whether he is a sinner or not, I don't know. One thing I do know. I was blind but *now* I see!" (Jn. 9:25). It is a theological reality that "*now* we see but a poor reflection as in a mirror" but that one day Christians will see the Savior face to face (1 Cor. 13:12). The contrast here is between the now and the final future, when Jesus returns again. Peter encourages believers that "though you have not seen him, you love him; and even though you do not see him *now*, you believe in him and are filled with an inexpressible and glorious joy" (1 Pet. 1:8). See *NIDNTT-A*, 282-83.

Adverb: νῦν (*nyn*), GK *3814* (S *3568*), 147x. *nyn* indicates the "present time, now." It is mostly used in narrative (e.g., "Then Peter came to himself and said, '*Now* I know without a doubt that the Lord sent his angel,'" Acts 12:11; cf. 7:4; Mt. 27:42; Lk. 16:25; Jn. 4:18; 12:27; 13:31; 16:29). Paul states in Rom. 8:22, "we know that the whole creation has been groaning as in the pains of childbirth right up to *the present*" (cf. Mt. 24:21; Mk. 13:19; Phil. 1:5).

Understanding *nyn* is important theologically because it is used to reveal the current status of a Christian's relationship with God. This comes through one of the most blessed phrases in the Bible, "but now." The full implication of the gospel was hidden for ages, *but now* it is revealed that through Jesus Christ the promises are given to the Gentiles along with Israel (Eph. 3:5). Therefore, those in Christ are "now" lights in the Lord (Eph. 5:8). Paul explains that even as Gentiles were once enemies of God *but now* receive mercy because of Israel's rejection of the Messiah, so Israel is now disobedient so that they may now receive the same mercy offered to the Gentiles (Rom. 11:30–32). Similarly, 1 Pet. 2:10 assures that, "once you were not a people, *but now* you are the people of God; once you had not received mercy, b*ut now* you have received mercy" (cf. 2:25, "for you were like sheep going astray, *but now* you have returned to the Shepherd and Overseer of your souls"). Christians are called to a holy life because of the grace "now" revealed through the appearing of the Savior (2 Tim. 1:10). Those in Jesus Christ are now justified by his blood and also now have received reconciliation (Rom. 5:9, 11). See *NIDNTT-A*, 282-283.

Adverb: νυνί (*nyni*), GK *3815* (S *3570*), 20x. *nyni* is an emphatic form of *nyn*, although both have the same meaning, "now." Paul wants the brothers and fathers to listen to his defense "now" (Acts 22:1; cf. Acts 24:13; Rom. 15:23, 25). In 1 Cor. 5:11 he says that he is "now" writing to the Corinthians so that they do not associate with the sexually impure.

Paul writes of several theological truths that were to be enjoyed *now* by those who are in Christ. He often introduces these with one of the most exciting expressions a Christian will ever hear: "but now." If Christ had not been raised from the dead, we would be of all people most miserable, *but now* Christ has been raised from the dead (1 Cor. 15:20). The entire human race is under sin, *but now* a way of getting right with God has been revealed in Christ (Rom. 3:21). Christians are "now" released from the law (Rom. 7:6; cf. 7:17), are "now" free from the power of sin (Rom. 6:22), and are now arranged in the body of Christ in a way that pleases God (1 Cor. 12:18; 13:13; 2 Cor. 8:11, 22). Freedom from death and sin means that we are now slaves of Christ Jesus (Phlm. 9; cf. 11). Paul encouraged the Ephesians in Eph. 2:13, "*But now* in Christ you who sometimes were far off are made near by the blood of Christ" (cf. Heb. 8:6; 9:26). See *NIDNTT-A*, 282-83.*

NULLIFY

New Testament

Verb: ἀθετέω (*atheteō*), GK *119* (S *114*), 16x. *atheteō* means "to reject, set aside, nullify, annul." See *reject*.

Verb: καταργέω (*katargeō*), GK *2934* (S *2673*), 27x. *katargeō* means "to release, destroy, nullify, cause something to be useless." See *destroy*.

NUMBER

Old Testament

Noun: מִסְפָּר (*mispār*), GK 5031 (S 4557), 134x. *mispār* means "number," the result of what happens when someone has "counted" or "listed" something. One of the most important elements in the OT world was to know the number of fighting men that a nation had. That is why God had his people numbered in the desert (Num. 1; 2 Chr. 26:11–15). But since any battle belonged to the Lord (see *war*), God was not pleased with David when set out to find his "*number* of the fighting men" (2 Sam. 24:9; 1 Chr. 21:5), for he was beginning to think that winning battles was determined by the numbers game.

God is someone who deals with large numbers. "He determines the *number* of the stars and calls them each by name" (Ps. 147:4). His understanding, too, has "no *limit*" (147:5). The Lord has created a vast ocean, "teeming with creatures beyond *number*" (104:25). God is indeed great; "the *number* of his years is past finding out" (Job 36:26). And in his promise to his people, "the *number* of the Israelites will be like the sand on the seashore, which cannot be measured or counted" (Hos. 1:10). See *NIDOTTE*, 2:1008–9.

Verb: פָּקַד (*pāqad*), GK 7212 (S 6485), 304x. While *pāqad* has a wide range of meaning, it basically expresses the action of overseeing an individual for a particular purpose. In this sense, *pāqad* is used most frequently in the sense of a superior counting someone in his charge during a census. The NIV generally translates this use "to count" or "to number." See *count*.

New Testament

Noun: ἀριθμός (*arithmos*), GK *750* (S *706*), 18x. *arithmos* means "number" or a numerical total. This word often precedes the headcount of a large crowd of people or angels: four hundred (lit., "a *number* of men, about four hundred," Acts 5:36), five thousand (Jn. 6:10; Acts 4:4), one hundred forty-four thousand (Rev. 7:4), thousands upon thousands (5:11), and two hundred million (9:16). Most of these uses of *arithmos* indicate an approximation as indicated by the Greek *hōs*, "about" (cf. Acts 5:36 above). In Acts, Luke often uses *arithmos* to indicate the rapid growth of the church. In these instances, he explains that the church grew by "a *great* number" of people without designating a specific quantity (Acts 11:21; cf. 6:7; 16:5). Similarly, *arithmos* can indicate a quantity so large that it is uncountable, like the number of grains of sand of the sea (Rom. 9:27; Rev. 20:8). Revelation contains the majority of the NT occurrences of *arithmos* (10 of 18 uses); five of these uses describe the much-debated "number" of the beast, 666 (Rev. 13:17, 18[3x]; 15:2).

Occasionally, for the purposes of a smoother translation, an exact English equivalent for the word *arithmos* will not appear in the translation. For example, in Lk. 22:3 the more literal translation of the KJV ("being of the *number* of the twelve") and NASB ("belonging to the *number* of the twelve") is translated by the NIV as simply "one of the Twelve." (Cf. the NIV for Jn. 6:10 and Acts 5:36, which also omit the word "number.") See *NIDNTT-A*, 70-71.*

Noun: ὄχλος (*ochlos*), GK *4063* (S *3793*), 175x. *ochlos* describes a large "crowd" or "multitude" of people. Sometimes it is used as a "number" of people who can be quantified. See *crowd*.

Noun: πλῆθος (*plēthos*), GK *4436* (S *4128*), 31x. *plēthos* denotes the number, amount, or quantity of an object and is best translated "number, crowd, multitude." Luke uses this word frequently to refer to a group of people, whether believers (Acts

4:32; 6:2, 5; 15:12) or unbelievers (Lk. 8:37; Acts 14:4). For example, at Jesus triumphal entry, a "crowd" of disciples began to shout joyfully in praise to God. *plēthos* can also be used to refer to a large quantity of fish (Lk. 5:6), sticks (Acts 28:3), and angels (Lk. 2:13).

In a theological context, the author of Hebrews reflects on the immeasurability and extent of God's promise to the patriarchs: "And so from this one man, and he as good as dead, came descendants as *numerous* as the stars in the sky and as countless as the sand on the seashore" (Heb. 11:12; cf. Gen. 15:5; 22:17; 26:4; Exod. 32:13). The extent of the believer's love for one another is measured in this same way. Peter writes, "Above all, love each other deeply, because love covers over a *multitude* of sins" (1 Pet. 4:8). See *NIDNTT-A*, 468.

NUMEROUS

Old Testament

Noun: רֹב (*rōb*), GK 8044 (S 7230) 150x. *rōb* denotes a multitude or an abundance. It is probably derived from the verb *rābâ*, which means to become numerous, much, or great. In a passage like 1 Sam. 13:5, which lit. translated reads "like sand that is on the seashore in *abundance*," *rōb* can be rendered "as *numerous* as sand on the seashore." See *many*.

OATH, (TAKE AN) OATH

Old Testament

Verb: שָׁבַע (*šāba*ʿ), GK 8678 (S 7650), 186x. *šāba*ʿ means "to swear, take an oath." See *swear*.

New Testament

Noun: ὅρκος (*horkos*), GK *3992* (S *3727*), 10x. *horkos* denotes the confirmation or guarantee before a witness of the truthfulness of one's words, that is, an "oath." Herod swore an oath to his wife's daughter that he would give her whatever she asked for (she ended up asking for the head of John the Baptist; Mt. 14:7, 9; Mk. 6:26). Jesus confirms the OT prohibition against swearing false oaths (cf. Lev. 19:12; Deut. 23:21) and reapplies it in his day: "Again, you have heard that it was said to the people long ago, 'Do not break your oath, but keep the *oaths* you have made to the Lord.' But I tell you, Do not swear at all" (Mt. 5:33; cf. Jas. 5:12). Peter swore an oath before Jesus' enemies that he did not know Jesus (Mt. 26:72). Theologically, the fact of the reliability of God's oath grounded in his unchangeable nature has implications for salvation. Hebrews declares, "Because God wanted to make the unchanging nature of his purpose very clear to the heirs of what was promised, he confirmed it with an *oath*" (Heb. 6:16–17; cf. Lk. 1:73; Acts 2:30). See *NIDNTT-A*, 407-8.*

OBEDIENCE

New Testament

Noun: ὑπακοή (*hypakoē*), GK *5633* (S *5218*), 15x. *hypakoē* denotes "obedience." Obedience for a Christian is doing what God has commanded us to do.

(1) The theme of obedience runs throughout Romans. Paul seeks to bring about "the *obedience* of faith" among all the Gentiles for the sake of God's name (Rom. 1:5), which should probably be understood in the widest sense possible—responding in faith (and not via law) is the obedience God requires, and faith itself shows itself in obedience. Adam's disobedience has made us sinners; Christ's obedience makes many righteous (5:19). Romans 6 presents two options based on whom we obey, either slaves of sin leading to death, or slaves of obedience leading to righteousness (6:16). Paul later states that Christ is bringing about through him "the *obedience* of the Gentiles" (15:18), adding that the report of the "obedience" of the Romans has gone out widely (16:19). The letter concludes with the statement that according to the command of the eternal God, the mystery that was kept hidden has been manifested through the prophetic writings for the "*obedience* of faith" (16:26)—that is, the call on people to respond obediently in faith and for that faith to show itself in obedient lives.

(2) Elsewhere in the NT, Titus is stirred

up in love for the Corinthians at the memory of their obedience (2 Cor. 7:15). Every thought is to be taken captive and made obedient to Christ (10:5). Paul speaks of the obedience of the Corinthians becoming complete (10:6). Paul is sure that Philemon will be obedient (Phlm. 21) in that he will do what Paul requests. Peter writes that believers are foreknown by God and sanctified by the Spirit for obedience to Christ (1 Pet. 1:2). He urges his audience to be "children of *obedience*" (1:14), and he states that their souls have been purified through the obedience of the truth (1:22).

(3) Jesus himself learned obedience through what he suffered, not in the sense that he stopped disobeying and started obeying but in the sense that he learned obedience by being obedient (Heb. 5:8). Experiencing a truth often makes it a richer experience than merely knowing the truth. Because Jesus was perfectly obedient, he has become the source of eternal salvation for those who obey him (5:9). See *NIDNTT-A*, 578.*

OBEY

Old Testament

Verb: שָׁמַע (*šāmaʿ*), GK 9048 (S 8085), 1165x. *šāmaʿ* means "to hear, listen, pay attention to, perceive, obey, proclaim, announce." See *hear*.

Verb: שָׁמַר (*šāmar*), GK 9068 (S 8104), 468x. Often translated "to keep," the verb *šāmar* bears three distinct but related meanings in the OT: "to guard, tend," "to watch over," and "to preserve" (see *keep*). It is especially used with idea of "obeying, heeding, keeping a covenant. "God said to Abraham, 'Now as for you, you shall *obey* my covenant'" (Gen. 17:9). *šāmar* expresses the careful devotion and action that is necessary in order to fulfill the covenant obligations.

New Testament

Verb: τηρέω (*tēreō*), GK *5498* (S *5083*), 70x. *tēreō* conveys the idea of watching over something closely or guarding—"to keep, obey; guard, protect." See *guard, keep, protect*.

Verb: ὑπακούω (*hypakouō*), GK *5634* (S *5219*), 21x. *hypakouō* means "to obey, do what one is told to do."

(1) The winds and the sea do what Jesus tells them to do (Mt. 8:27; Mk. 4:41; Lk. 8:25). The unclean spirits likewise obey his commands (Mk. 1:27). Jesus explains to the disciples that if they have faith, their commands will be obeyed—even if they were to command a mulberry tree to be uprooted and planted in the sea (Lk. 17:6). Rhoda "came to *answer*" when Peter was knocking at the door (Acts 12:13). Christians are not to obey the desires of their bodies; when our bodies tell us to sin, we must refrain from obeying (Rom. 6:12). Note Paul's principle: "You are slaves to the one whom *you obey*" (Rom. 6:16). Paul commands children "*to obey* [their] parents in the Lord" (Eph. 6:1; Col. 3:20). Slaves likewise are commanded "to obey [their] earthly masters" as they would obey Christ (Eph. 6:5; Col. 3:22). Paul writes that the Philippians have always obeyed him (Phil. 2:12). Paul expects his written instructions to be obeyed (2 Thess. 3:14). Jesus becomes the source of eternal salvation to all those who obey him (Heb. 5:9). Abraham obeyed when he was called to go out to another land (Heb. 11:8), and Sarah obeyed Abraham (1 Pet. 3:6).

(2) At points people are described as becoming obedient to the gospel or to the faith, which mean that they have obeyed the call to repent and believe and submit themselves to the lordship of Christ. "A large number of priests *became obedient* to the faith" (Acts 6:7). "Thanks be to God because you were slaves of sin, but *you obeyed* from the heart the form of teaching to which you were entrusted" (Rom. 6:17). Paul writes in Rom. 10:17 that "not all the Israelites *accepted* the good news." Jesus will deal out retribution to those who do not know God and to those who "do not *obey* the gospel" of Christ (2 Thess. 1:8). See *NIDNTT-A*, 578.*

Verb: φυλάσσω (*phylassō*), GK *5875* (S *5442*), 31x. *phylassō* means to "guard" physically or to "keep" in the sense of obeying. It can denote a careful observance of divine or human law. See *keep*.

OBJECT

Old Testament

Noun: כְּלִי (*kᵉlî*), GK 3998 (S 3627), 325x. *kᵉlî* is a noun denoting a variety of equipment, tools, containers, etc., used in a given activity or occupation. The use of this noun to refer to such a large number of different objects is comparable to the English noun "thing." See *thing*.

OBLIGATE

Old Testament

Verb: אָסַר (*ʾāsar*), GK 673 (S 631), 73x. The most basic meaning of *ʾāsar* is "to bind, tie up." Animals may be tied to something for a particular function. More figuratively, *ʾāsar* is used in Num. 30 (10x) in the sense of being "bound" or "obligated" by an oath, vow, obligation, promise, or pledge (e.g., 30:2, 6, 7). See *bind*.

OBLIGATION

New Testament

Noun: ὀφειλέτης (*opheiletēs*) GK *4050* (S *3781*), 7x. *opheiletēs* means "debtor" or "one who is obligated" (see debtor). Paul feels an "obligation" from within himself to preach the gospel to both Jews and non-Jews (Rom. 1:14). In Gal. 5:3 Paul writes that if any believer feels he must be circumcised, then "he is under obligation to keep the whole law" (Gal. 5:3). As Paul seeks to raise money among the Gentile churches for the impoverished Jews in Jerusalem, he writes that the Gentiles are "under obligation" to share their material blessings with those who have shared with them the spiritual blessing of salvation in Christ (Rom. 15:27).

OBSERVE

Old Testament

Verb: חָזָה (*ḥāzâ*), GK 2600 (S 2372), 68x. *ḥāzâ* means "to see, observe, gaze"; it is a broad word, having a variety of nuances. See *see*.

New Testament

Verb: θεάομαι (*theaomai*), GK *2517* (S *2300*), 22x. *theaomai* means "to see, behold, observe." See *see*.

Verb: φυλάσσω (*phylassō*), GK *5875* (S *5442*), 31x. *phylassō* means to "guard" physically or to "keep" in the sense of observing. It can denote a careful observance of divine or human law. See *keep*.

OBSTACLE

New Testament

Noun: σκάνδαλον (*skandalon*), GK *4998* (S *4625*), 15x. *skandalon* is something that leads a person to sin or to fall away from faith (see also *cause of sin, offense*). Paul directs his reader not to put an obstacle in a brother's or sister's way by flaunting certain actions or attitudes (Rom. 14:13). He also speaks against those who would lead his readers away from sound teaching by putting obstacles in their way (16:17). In Revelation, Jesus chastises the church at Pergamum for allowing those to live in their community who put "stumbling blocks" in the way of others in order to lead them into sin (Rev. 2:14). See *NIDNTT-A*, 526-27.

OBSTINATE

Old Testament

Adjective: חָזָק (*ḥāzāq*), GK 2617 (S 2389), 57x. The basic sense of the adjective *ḥāzāq* is "mighty, strong, powerful." In Ezekiel, the expressions "*ḥāzāq* of heart" (2:4) and "*ḥāzāq* of forehead" (3:7, 8, 9) conjure up images of a heart and forehead as hard or strong as stone. Such phrases are metaphors for people who are obstinate or stubborn. See *strong*.

OBTAIN

New Testament

Verb: εὑρισκω (*heuriskō*), GK *2351* (S *2147*), 176x. *heuriskō* means "to find" something either by a purposeful search or accidentally. It can also mean "to obtain" a state or condition. See *find*.

Verb: καταλαμβάνω (*katalambanō*), GK *2898* (S *2638*), 15x. *katalambanō* can mean "to catch, obtain, seize, overtake." In the middle voice it means "to grasp, understand." See *catch*.

OBVIOUS

New Testament

Adjective: φανερός (*phaneros*), GK

5745 (S *5318*), 18x. *phaneros* means "obvious, known, plain." This adjective stresses what is obvious to human sight. Matthew and Mark use this term in connection with the messianic secret, for Jesus tells certain individuals not to "make plain" or tell others who he is (Mt. 12:15; Mk. 3:12). In spite of this, "Jesus' name had become *well known*" (Mk. 6:14).

In Acts 4:16, the Jewish leaders have to admit that Peter and John have performed a miracle by healing the lame man, for this was "obvious" to everyone living in Jerusalem. Similarly, that Paul's imprisonment was because of Christ became "plain" to the whole palace guard (Phil. 1:13). For those who lead sinful lives, "the acts of the sinful nature are *obvious*" (Gal. 5:19).

In a theological sense, all human beings can know certain things about God from nature, for "what may be known about God is *plain* to them" (Rom. 1:19). When the day of the Lord arrives, the work we have (or have not) done for the Lord will be "*shown* for what it is" (1 Cor. 3:13). And the manner in which we treat others helps us "to *know* who the children of God are and who the children of the devil are" (1 Jn. 3:10). See *NIDNTT-A*, 202–3.

ODOR

Old Testament

Noun: רֵיחַ (*rēah*), GK 8194 (S 7381), 58x. *rēah* denotes an aroma, scent, or fragrance. In common usage, it can refer to the fragrance of perfume (Song 1:1), the scent of vines (2:13), the odor of garments (4:11), or the smell of one's breath (7:8). Its technical, cultic expression is in the phrase *hannîḥōah* (43x), often translated "a pleasing aroma" See *aroma*.

New Testament

Noun: ὀσμή (*osmē*), GK *4011* (S *3744*), 6x. *osmē* means "aroma, odor." See *aroma*.

OFFEND

New Testament

Verb: σκανδαλίζω (*skandalizō*), GK 4997 (S 4624), 29x. *skandalizō* means "to offend, cause shock or anger" (see also *cause to sin*). Jesus tells his disciples to pay the tax so as not to offend the government rulers (Mt. 17:27). The disciples take offense when Jesus calls his body bread and his blood drink and invites people to feast on him (Jn. 6:61). See *NIDNTT-A*, 526-27.

OFFENSE

Old Testament

Noun: פֶּשַׁע (*pešaʿ*), GK 7322 (S 6588), 93x. Usually translated as "rebellion, offense, sin, transgression," the noun *pešaʿ* is one of the three primary words for sin in the OT. See *sin*.

New Testament

Noun: πρόσκομμα (*proskomma*), GK *4682* (S *4348*), 6x. *proskommā* means "stumbling block, offense." See *stumbling block*.

Noun: σκάνδαλον (*skandalon*), GK *4998* (S *4625*), 15x. *skandalon* is something that leads a person to sin or to fall away from faith, particularly offenses caused by Jesus (see also *cause of sin, obstacle*). A crucified Christ is an offense to the Jews (1 Cor. 1:23), because his way of salvation is abhorrent to them and leads them to the sin of unbelief. With regard to receiving the gospel message, Jesus becomes for the Jews like an obstacle over which they lose their footing and fall (Rom. 9:33, 1 Pet. 2:8). See *NIDNTT-A*, 526-27.

OFFER

Old Testament

Verb: קָרַב (*qārab*), GK 7928 (S 7126), 280x. The basic meaning of *qārab* is "to draw near" or, in a causative sense, "to bring near." Theologically, the most significant use of *qārab* is in its connection with the service of the tabernacle or temple, as describing the priest who "brings near, presents, or offers" his offering. Thus, *qārab* is used extensively throughout Leviticus in connection with the priestly service and sacrifices. See *bring*.

New Testament

Verb: παρίστημι (*paristēmi*), GK *4225* (S *3936*), 41x. The root meaning of *paristēmi* is "to stand, place beside." A number of variations of meaning are found in the NT, such as "to offer" something. See *stand.*

Verb: προσφέρω (*prospherō*), GK *4712* (S *4374*), 47x. *prospherō* has a general meaning, "to bring" a person or an object to someone; in a religious sense, it means "to bring an offering, offer." See *bring*.

OFFER UP

New Testament

Verb: ἀναφέρω (*anapherō*), GK *429* (S *399*), 10x. *anapherō* is a technical term meaning "to offer up a sacrifice." Sacrifices were originally offered by high priests (Heb. 7:27a); as the great high priest, Jesus has offered himself as the final sacrifice (7:27b). Believers can now offer sacrifices of praise (13:15) and spiritual sacrifices (1 Pet. 2:5) to God through Christ. Abraham "offered up" his son, Isaac (Jas. 2:21). *anapherō* can also mean "bear," referring to sins (see *bear [sins]*), or "lead up" (see *lead up*).

OFFERING

Old Testament

Noun: אִשֶּׁה (*ʾiššeh*), GK 852 (S 801), 65x. *ʾiššeh* traditionally means "offering made by fire" (Exod. 29:25, 30:20; Num. 29:6) and probably derives from the Heb. word for "fire" (*ʾēš*, GK 836). *ʾiššeh* refers to any offering or portion of an offering that is consumed by fire; it thus emphasizes the manner by which individuals make such sacrifices, i.e., by fire. *ʾiššeh* stressed the death of the sacrificial animal in that sacrifices are to be offered by fire. Except for Jos. 13:14 and 1 Sam. 2:28, all occurrences of this word are in the Pentateuch.

Exod. 29 records the first use of this term in the OT, in the Lord's instruction to Moses regarding the ordination of priests. Part of the ordination ceremony included the sacrifice of a ram as an "offering of fire to the Lord" (29:18). OT authors use *ʾiššeh* in reference to the burnt offering (Lev. 1:9), the cereal or grain offering (Lev. 2:3), the peace offering (Lev. 3:3), the guilt offering (Lev. 7:5), and the consecration offering (Lev. 8:28). *ʾiššeh* occurs 10x in Num. 28–29 in the various regular offerings presented to the Lord on the altar at appointed times. Parts of these offerings were permissible for priests to eat within the tabernacle (e.g., Lev. 10:12–13); that was their stipend, as it were, for assisting the people in the sacrifices (Deut. 18:1; 1 Sam. 2:28). Other parts could be taken home to their families (Lev. 7:30–34).

In addition, OT writers frequently use *ʾiššeh* in connection with a "sweet savor" or a "pleasing aroma" (Lev. 1:9, 13, 17; 2:2, 9; Num. 15:10, 13, 14). See *NIDOTTE*, 1:540-49.

Noun: זֶבַח (*zebaḥ*), GK 2285 (S 2077), 162x. *zebaḥ* is the most common noun for "sacrifice" or offering (e.g., Exod. 3:18; 10:25). See *sacrifice*.

Noun: מִנְחָה (*minḥâ*), GK 4966 (S 4503), 211x. The basic idea conveyed by this word is "gift." *minḥâ* can designate an offering in general or, more specifically, a "grain offering." See *grain offering*.

Noun: קָרְבָּן (*qorbān*), GK 7933 (S 7133), 80x. *qorbān* means "offering, gift." With the exception of 2x in Ezekiel (20:28, where it refers to idolatrous offerings; see also 40:43), this noun occurs exclusively in Leviticus and Numbers. The *qorbān* is often used as one of the most general terms in the OT for an offering to the Lord. This term is applied to burnt offerings (Lev. 1:2), grain offerings (2:1), fellowship offerings (3:1), and sin offerings (4:23), the offering of the firstfruits (23:14), the Passover offering (Num. 9:7), and the offering that concludes the Nazirite vow (6:21). Jesus uses this term (transliterated into Gk.) in his discussion of the legalism of the Pharisees (Mk. 7:11–12).

Noun: תְּרוּמָה (*t^e^rûmâ*), GK 9556 (S 8641), 76x. *t^e^rûmâ* can be translated as "offering, portion, gift, contribution." Biblical authors use this noun as a general term for various offerings. Exod. uses this noun 17x during the construction of the tabernacle. For example, Exod. 25:2–3 calls "an offering" the gold, silver, and bronze materials that God instructs the Israelites to bring in order to build the tabernacle. Ezra refers to the contributions of the Persian king given to rebuild the temple as *t^erûmâ* (Ezr. 8:25). The OT also understands gifts to pagan gods (Isa. 40:20) and the war booty presented to the priests (Num. 31:29) as *t^erûmâ.*

The OT also calls as *t^erûmâ* those parts of sacrifices designated for priests, such as the thigh of the wave offering (Lev. 10:14) as well as a portion of the grain sacrifice (7:14). Exod. 30:13–15 records *t^erûmâ* as the half-shekel required for maintaining service of the tabernacle: "This half shekel is an *offering* to the Lord" (v. 13). Mal. 3:8 records a familiar use of *t^erûmâ*. In response to the question, "Will a man rob God?" God insists that his people have indeed robbed him "in tithes and *offerings*." See *NIDOTTE, 4:335-38.*

New Testament

Noun: δῶρον (*dōron*), GK *1565* (S *1435*), 19x. *dōron* basically means a "gift" or "present"; most frequently it denotes an "offering" to God. See *gift*.

Noun: θυσία (*thysia*), GK *2602* (S *2378*), 29x. *thysia* refers to a "sacrifice" or the actual act of "offering" that sacrifice. See *sacrifice*.

OFFICER

Old Testament

Verb: נָצַב (*nāṣab*), GK 5893 (S 5324), 74x. *nāṣab* conveys the act of standing or the setting up an object and may be translated as "to stand, set." Kings and Chronicles use the term to denote "officers" (lit., "standing ones") who served kings (1 Ki. 4:7; cf. 2 Chr. 8:10). See *stand.*

OFFICIAL

Old Testament

Noun: שַׂר (*śar*), GK 8569 (S 8269) 421x.

Noun: נָשִׂיא (*nāśîʾ*), GK 5954 (S 5387) 130x.

Noun: אַלּוּף (*ʾallûp*), GK 477 (S 441) 60x.

These terms are a number of overlapping nouns in the OT that refer to leaders, chiefs, and officials of various sorts. They need to be translated differently according to the context in Israel's history. See *leader* for a thorough discussion.

New Testament

Noun: ὑπηρέτης (*hypēretēs*), GK *5677* (S *5257*), 20x. *hypēretēs* is a compound word derived from *hypo* ("under") and *eretēs* ("rower"). A literal translation is thus "under-oarsman." The word comes from nautical terminology, but it grew to apply to anyone in a subordinate, serving role, such as an official or guard (Mt. 5:25; 26:58; Mk. 14:54, 46).

Luke speaks of those who were "eyewitnesses and *servants* of the word" in reference to the first generation of believers who had seen and learned from Jesus directly and who exercised authority over the story of Jesus (Lk. 1:2). He calls the "attendant" in the synagogue a *hypēretēs* in 4:20.

John uses *hypēretēs* to describe those under the authority of religious leaders: "So Judas came to the grove, guiding a detachment of soldiers and some *officials* from the chief priests and Pharisees" (Jn. 18:3; cf. "temple guards" in 7:32, 45, 46). One of these officials hits Jesus during his inquisition: "When Jesus said this, one of the *officials* nearby struck him in the face" (18:22).

In Acts, *hypēretēs* describes the secular officials who cannot find the apostles after the angel of the Lord has released them (Acts 5:22, 26). John Mark travels with Paul and Barnabas on the first missionary journey as their "assistant" (13:5). God chooses Paul to be his "servant" before the Gentiles (26:16), a title and function Paul accepts (1 Cor. 4:1).

Each time *hypēretēs* is used, it denotes someone who is under the authority of another. In each instance, the distinguishing characteristic is that of subordination. The apostles consider themselves servants of the Lord Jesus. His lordship is never a matter of question or debate. They maintain this level of subordination all the while ministering, serving, guiding, and leading the people of God. See *NIDNTT-A*, 136-38.

OFFICIATE

Old Testament

Verb: שָׁרַת (*šārat*), GK 9250 (S 8334), 98x. *šārat* denotes "to minister, serve, officiate" and is used of the "serving" performed by royal household workers (2 Sam. 13:17; also 1 Ki. 10:5) or by court officials and designated public servants (1 Chr. 27:1; 28:1; Est. 1:10). See *minister*.

OFFSPRING

Old Testament

Noun: זֶרַע (*zeraʿ*), GK 2446 (S 2233), 229x. The noun *zeraʿ* generally means "seed, descendant, offspring." It has various nuances in the OT. See *seed*.

New Testament

Noun: γένος (*genos*), GK *1169* (S *1085*), 20x. *genos* means "offspring." The term can be used to refer to ancestral descent. In his sermon at the Areopagus, Paul says that humanity is "the offspring of God" (Acts 17:28–29). Jesus says that he is "the offspring of David" (Rev. 22:16). *genos* can also mean "family" (see *family*), "people" (see *people*), or "kind" (see *kind*).

OFTEN

New Testament

Adverb: πολλάκις (*pollakis*), GK *4490* (S *4178*), 18x. *pollakis* is an adverb that means "often." Judas knew that he would find on the Mount of Olives because Jesus "often" went there with his disciples (Jn. 18:22). Paul had planned "many times" to go to Rome but when he wrote Rom. 1:13, he had not yet been able to follow through on these plans. Paul "constantly" experienced a variety of sufferings in his life as a missionary (2 Cor. 11:23, 26, 27).

The most important use of *pollakis* is in Hebrews. The OT sacrifices had to be repeated "again and again" (i.e., some daily, some yearly); by contrast, Jesus' sacrifice on the cross was once for all (Heb. 9:25–26, 10:11).

OIL

Old Testament

Noun: שֶׁמֶן (*šemen*), GK 9043 (8081), 193x. *šemen* is the Hebrew word used in the OT for "oil, olive oil," or wood from an olive tree. This oil had many daily uses in ancient Mesopotamia such as an ingredient for cooking (Exod. 29:23; 1 Ki. 17:12; Hag. 2:12), as fuel for lamps (Exod. 25:6; Lev. 24:2), or as the base for perfumes and ointments (Eccl. 10:1; Est. 2:12). Oil could symbolize the productivity of the land and thus might figure prominently in descriptions of a kingdom's prosperity or of the material blessings given by God (Deut. 8:7–8; Job 29:6; Isa. 41:19). Oil was also often used in the tabernacle, and later in the temple, for consecration rituals or as part of certain offerings to God (Exod. 25:6; 29:7; Lev. 2:1, 6; 14:10). Oil was used in this way probably because of its ability to symbolize the holiness and favor of God, or even to symbolize God's Spirit himself (Gen. 28:16-18; Exod. 29:7; 30:22–32). It is likely that this connection with the Spirit is why Jas. 5:14 tells us that elders are to pray for the sick by anointing them with oil. Using oil when praying for those who are ill symbolizes the healing that only God's Spirit can bring.

New Testament

Noun: ἔλαιον (*elaion*), GK *1778* (S *1637*), 11x. *elaion* is "oil" from the fruit of the olive tree (Lk. 16:6; Rev. 6:6 [which may refer to the olive orchard]; 18:13), used for medicinal (Lk. 10:34), cosmetic (7:46), and religious purposes (Heb. 1:9). Olive oil was also used as fuel in lamps (Mt. 25:3–4, 8).

There is a contrast of two oils in Lk. 7:46. The host neglects his duty of hospitality by not putting *elaion* for refreshment and honor on his guest's head, while the woman lavishes an expensive perfume (*myron*, GK 3693) on Jesus' feet.

Olive oil also accompanies healings in the NT. In this case, the oil is a symbol of God's blessing or work in the healing process (Mk. 6:13; Jas. 5:14). The imagery of oil is dependent on the OT, where it is associated with joy (Isa. 61:3), prosperity (Ps. 128:3–6), and the goodness of God (Ps. 52:8–9). See *NIDNTT-A,* 177-78.*

OINTMENT

New Testament

Noun: μύρον (*myron*), GK *3693* (S *3464*), 14x. *myron* is a precious, strongly scented liquid or gelatinous substance used in the ancient world for a variety of purposes, including burial. See *perfume*.

OLD

Old Testament

Verb: זָקֵן (*zāqēn*), GK 2416, 2418 (S 2204, 2205), 206x.

(1) *zāqēn* generally means to be old (Gen. 18:11–13; Jdg. 19:17, 20; Job 14:8; Isa. 47:6). It is derived from the word *zāqān*, which literally means "bearded" and refers to a man coming into adulthood. In that sense it is used exclusively of men, though it can also refer generically to both men and women (cf. Zech. 8:4, where it refers to women).

(2) In an age when people usually did not live long, becoming old was viewed as a blessing (Prov. 17:6). The elderly were looked on with great respect (Lev. 19:32) and were highly regarded for their wisdom (Ps. 119:100). Thus, *zāqēn* came to be associated with people who served in positions of authority and honor. See *elder*.

New Testament

Adjective: ἀρχαῖος (*archaios*), GK *792* (S *744*), 11x. *archaios* refers to the long-standing age of something or someone and can describe something that is old. See *ancient*.

Adjective: παλαιός (*palaios*), GK *4094* (S *3820*), 19x. *palaios* means "old" and is sometimes contrasted with its antonym, *neos* (see *new*). Jesus uses this word pair in two parables about clothing (Mt. 9:16) and wine/wineskins (9:17; Lk. 5:39) to contrast the period of God's revelation in the OT to that of the NT. In fact, Paul actually uses *palaios* to refer to the "*old* covenant" (2 Cor. 3:14). By contrast, John refers to Jesus' command to his disciples to love one another as an "*old* command" that he offers his readers (1 Jn. 2:7).

Metaphorically, this term can refer to the enduring richness of the Word of God (Mt. 13:52) and to the powerlessness of our old natures (Rom. 6:6, "our *old* self was crucified with him"). Elsewhere Paul commands believers to lay this old self and its attendant sins aside like a garment (Eph. 4:22; Col. 3:9) and clothe themselves in Christian virtue (Eph. 4:24; Col. 3:10). In 1 Cor. 5:7 he uses the Passover practice of purging the house of "old" yeast to speak of purging the church of sin (1 Cor. 5:7–8). See *NIDNTT-A*, 429-430.

OLDER

New Testament

Noun and Adjective: πρεσβύτερος (*presbyteros*), GK *4565* (S *4245*), 66x. *presbyteros* means "older" and, when used with the definite article, is a common term for older men as well as for the leaders ("elders") in the synagogue and the church. See *elder*.

OLIVE

New Testament

Noun: ἐλαιον (*elaion*), GK *1777* (S *1636*), 15x. Every use of *elaion* in the gospels refers to the Mount of Olives (e.g., Mt. 21:1; 26:30; Jn. 8:1). It was a hill east of Jerusalem known for its olive trees. Jesus struggled there intensely as he faced his cross.

Paul uses *elaion* in his discussion of the remnant of Israel in Rom. 11. In a notable comparison he applies different parts of the tree to key figures in the salvation history of God's people. The "root" represents the patriarchs (11:16), the natural branches are the Jewish people, descended naturally from them, and the wild shoots are Gentile Christians grafted into the olive tree "contrary to nature," solely by God's grace. There are two significant aspects of Paul's choice of symbols here. First, the olive tree was the most widely cultivated fruit tree in the Mediterranean basin; conversely, the wild olive tree was notoriously unfruitful. Second, Paul describes here something that was normally *not* done—the process of grafting fruitless shoots from wild trees into cultivated trees—in order to accent the power of God's grace. He highlights here the introduction of God's amazing grace into his mission to the Gentile world. Whoever believes, Jew or Gentile, becomes part of God's tree.

James uses *elaion* as one in a series of comparative illustrations to emphasize that we must stop misusing our tongues when we speak. It is absurd that with the same tongue we praise God and curse God's image-bearers (human beings) (3:9–10). Grapevines do not bear figs and fig trees do not bear olives (3:12). In Rev. 11:4 "two olive trees" stand before the Lord. The emphasis here is on the special anointing oil used by priests in worship. This suggests that these two witnesses are representative of NT spiritual realities, much like Zerubabbel and Joshua represented kingship and priesthood in Zechariah's day (4:14). See *NIDNTT-A*, 177-78.

OLIVE OIL

Old Testament

Noun: שֶׁמֶן (*šemen*), GK 9043 (8081), 193x. *šemen* is the Hebrew word used in the OT for "oil, olive oil," or wood from an olive tree. This oil had many daily uses in ancient Mesopotamia such as an ingredient for cooking (Exod. 29:23; 1 Ki. 17:12; Hag. 2:12), as fuel for lamps (Exod. 25:6; Lev. 24:2), or as the base for perfumes and ointments (Eccl. 10:1; Est. 2:12). See *oil*.

New Testament

Noun: ἔλαιον (*elaion*), GK *1778* (S *1637*), 11x. *elaion* is "oil" from the fruit of the olive tree. See *oil*.

OMEGA

New Testament

Noun: Ὦ (*O*), GK *6042* (S *5598*), 3x. *O* means "Omega." This term appears only in the book of Revelation in conjunction with the word alpha, which means "Alpha." See *Alpha*.

ONCE

New Testament

Adverb: ἅπαξ (*hapax*), GK *562* (S *530*), 14x. *hapax* means "once" in the sense of numbering; or "once" in the sense of uniqueness. (1) In the former sense, certain texts indicate that something occurs only one time. When Paul enumerates his persecutions, he says, "Three times I was beaten with rods, *once* I was stoned, three times I was shipwrecked" (2 Cor. 11:25). Christ's sacrifice is contrasted with those of the OT cult: "Then Christ would have had to suffer many times since the creation of the world. But now he has appeared *once for all* at the end of the ages to do away with sin by the sacrifice of himself" (Heb. 9:26). The emphasis here is a single occurrence (cf. Phil. 4:16; 1 Thess. 2:18; Heb. 9:7, 28; 1 Pet. 3:18).

(2) In the second sense, *hapax* pertains to a single and decisively unique occurrence. "For the worshipers would have been cleansed *once for all*" (Heb. 10:2; cf. 6:4). "I felt I had to write and urge you to contend for the faith that was *once for all* entrusted to the saints" (Jude 3; cf. 5). See *NIDNTT-A*, 57-58.

ONCE FOR ALL

New Testament

Adverb: ἅπαξ (*hapax*), GK 562 (S 530), 14x. *hapax* means "once" in the sense of numbering, or "once" in the sense of uniqueness. See *once*.

ONE

Old Testament

Adjective: אֶחָד (*ʾeḥād*), GK 285 (S 259), 976x. *ʾeḥād* means "one, first, other." It can translate either as the ordinal numeral ("the *first* day," Gen. 1:3) or the cardinal numeral ("he took *one* of the man's ribs," 2:21). It is also used for both sides in the expression "the *one* … the *other*" (e.g., Exod. 18:3–4). "One" can be the first of a series (as in day one of a week or month), or it can indicate one person or thing singled out from a group ("*one* of the men," Gen. 26:10; "*one* of the mountains," 22:2).

There are several important emphases that derive from this word. Abraham was "but one [man]" (Isa. 51:2), yet from him

God made a huge nation. This word can be used to designate corporate solidarity, as when the Israelites accept God's covenant "with *one* voice" (Exod. 24:3). But the fact that the whole world was "*one* people" with "*one* language" and "*one* speech" united them in rebellion against God (Gen. 11:1, 6). The notion of "not *one*" is used in connection with both the universality of human sin (Ps. 14:3) and God's faithfulness ("not *one* word [of God] has failed," 1 Ki. 8:56).

It is important to recognize that the notion of *ʾeḥād* does not signify isolation or aloneness (this is the emphasis of the Heb. word *bad*, GK 963). Note, for example, that when Adam and Eve come together in sexual union, they become "*one* flesh," yet they do not lose their individuality. This concept is important when we look at the *Shema*, Israel's confession of faith: "Hear, O Israel: The Lord our God, the Lord is *one*" (Deut. 6:4). While this verse stresses monotheism (that there is only one God) and the uniqueness of Israel's God, it does not suggest that the Lord God is a solitary, isolated, alone individual. That is, consistent with *ʾeḥād* is the notion that God appears in relationship to himself ("let us make man in our image," Gen. 1:26) or in relationship to "the council of the holy ones" (Ps. 89:7). While this observation does not prove the Trinity in the OT, it is certainly consistent with the notion of God's being more than one person—a doctrine that receives more complete treatment in the NT. See *NIDOTTE*, 1:349–51.

New Testament

Adjective: εἷς (*heis*), GK *1651* (S *1520*, *3391*), 343x. *heis* is the cardinal number "one." It can be used simply to count items, like one talent (Mt. 25:15). It may also be used as the last part of a complex number, like the "forty lashes minus one" that Paul received (2 Cor. 11:24). *heis* is occasionally also used like an ordinal number, as in "the *first* woe" (Rev. 9:12) and the common NT phrase "on the *first* day of the week" (Lk. 24:1; Jn. 20:1; Acts 20:7; 1 Cor. 16:2).

heis is also used to indicate the singularity of something, thus emphasizing that there is but one only. Paul explains that only one runner receives a prize (1 Cor. 9:24) and that the law can be summed up with only one statement (Gal. 5:14). Jesus criticizes the Pharisees for going to great lengths to gain one single convert (Mt. 23:15). He condemns a person who breaks even one of the smallest commandments (Mt. 5:19). It was through only one man (Rom. 5:12, 16, 17) and because of only one sin (5:18) that condemnation befell humanity. Yet Christ was the one—and the only one—who died for all (2 Cor. 5:14); he was the one man through whom many become righteous (Rom. 5:15, 19). According to Paul, a qualification of an elder is that he must be "the husband of *one* wife" (Tit. 1:6). John uses *heis* symbolically to depict the rapidity of Babylon's fall: "in only *one* day" she is overtaken with plagues (Rev. 18:8), and "in only *one* hour" she faces judgment and ruin (18:10, 19).

Many of the NT uses of *heis* refer to the singularity of God—"*one* God" (Rom. 3:30; 1 Cor. 8:4, 6; Gal. 3:20; Eph. 4:6; 1 Tim. 2:5). Many other uses explain the unity of the body of Christ. Paul reminds his readers that they, as participants of the Christian church, are members of "*one* body" (Rom. 12:4, 5; 1 Cor. 10:17; 12:12–20; Gal. 3:28; Col. 3:5; cf. Jn. 17:21–23), and he thus encourages them to be "*one* in spirit" (Phil. 1:27; 2:2). In the church there is only "one" hope, Lord, faith, and baptism" (Eph. 4:4–6). A similar unity results when a man and woman join in marriage to become "*one* flesh" (1 Cor. 6:16; Eph. 5:31).

heis can be used less like a numerical indicator and more like an indefinite pronoun or indefinite article. For example, Matthew uses *heis* to describe "*a* [certain] scribe" (Mt. 8:19) and "*a* man" (19:16 [NIV]). *heis* may also describe "*each* person" (Col. 4:6), "*each one* of you" (Eph.

5:33), "*each* of them" (Acts 21:26), or "anything" (Jn. 1:3 [KJV]). See *NIDNTT-A*, 167-69.

ONE ANOTHER

New Testament

Pronoun: ἀλλήλων (*allēlōn*), GK *253* (S *240*), 100x. ἀλλήλων is a reciprocal pronoun that means "each other, one another." In many occurrences it bears no theologically special meaning. The disciples are filled with fear when Jesus calms the storm, and they say "*to one another*, 'Who then is this? The wind and the sea obey him" (Mk. 4:41). They argue "with one another" who is the greatest (9:34). The shepherds say "to one another" that they should look for the infant Jesus, just as the angels instructed (Lk. 2:15).

However, in Paul's ethics especially, this word represents the significant fact that Christians must not live in isolation but are called to interact with one another. To not interact with fellow believers is to live in defiance of the clear teaching of Scripture.

Paul seeks to be mutually encouraged by the Roman church (Rom. 1:12). We are one body and individually members "of one another" (12:5; Eph. 4:25). We should outdo "one another" in showing honor (Rom. 12:10), live in harmony "with one another" (12:16; 15:5), not pass judgment "on one another" (14:13), not provoke "one another," envy "one another" (Gal. 5:26), lie "to one another" (Col. 3:9), speak evil "of one another" (Jas. 4:11), or grumble "against one another" (Jas. 5:9). Rather, we should: build up "one another" (Rom. 14:19), welcome "one another" (15:7), instruct "one another" (15:14), have the same care "for one another" (1 Cor. 12:25), serve "one another" (Gal. 5:13), bear "one another's" burdens (6:2; Col. 3:13) in love (Eph. 4:2) submit "to one another" (5:21), in humility count "one another" more significant than ourselves (Phil. 2:3), encourage "one another" (1 Thess. 4:18; 5:11), do good "to one another" (1 Thess. 5:15), confess our sins to and pray "for one another" (Jas. 5:16), show hospitality "to one another" (1 Pet. 4:9), and most important, love "one another" (Rom. 13:8; 1 Thess. 3:12; 4:18; 2 Thess. 1:3; 1 Pet. 1:22; 1 Jn. 3:11, 23; 4:7, 11, 12; 2 Jn. 5).

As believers walk in the light of Christ, they have fellowship "with one another" (1 Jn. 1:7). "Be kind *to one another*, tenderhearted, forgiving *each other* just as God in Christ forgave you" (Eph. 4:23; cf. Col. 3:13). What a difference from our preconversion life when we hated "one another" (Tit. 3:3); now we consider how to stir up "one another" to love and do good works (Heb. 10:24).

Paul frequently calls on a church to greet "one another" (Rom. 16:16, 20; 2 Cor. 13:12; also 1 Pet. 5:14).

ONE'S OWN

New Testament

Adjective: ἴδιος (*idios*), GK *2625* (S *2398*), 114x. *idios* meant "peculiar to, particular, or private" in ancient Greek literature. In the NT, its sense is weakened to a possessive, but it appears in an assortment of contexts and meanings, such as "*one's own* ability" (Mt. 25:15), "wages received for *one's own* work" (1 Cor. 3:8; cf. the common idea of rendering to each according to "each one's" work in Mt. 16:17; Rom. 2:6; 2 Cor. 11:15; 2 Tim. 4:14; 1 Pet. 1:17; Rev. 2:23, 20:12–13; 22:12), "*one's own* private interpretation" (2 Pet. 1:20), "*one's own* sheep" (Jn. 10:3–4), or "*each one's* turn" (1 Cor. 15:23). As an adverb *idios* means "by oneself, privately" (Mt. 14:13; 1 Cor. 12:11).

The plural form of the word by itself can mean "one's home or things." It appears twice in Jn. 1:11: "He came to that which was *his own*, but *his own* did not receive him." The first probably refers to the created world while the second refers to the Jewish people, who for the most part rejected him. Later John reports Jesus as "having loved *his own* who were in the world, he loved them to the end" (13:1). Here the word denotes his disciples, a narrower group than "his own" in 1:11. These are his closest friends.

Although the rich young ruler kept the

commandments, he could not give up "his own things" to follow Jesus (Lk. 18:18–27). Immediately following this story Peter said, "Look, we have left *all we had* to follow you!" (v. 28; the NLT translates the word "homes"). Jesus assures them that those who have correctly calculated the cost of discipleship by putting him ahead of everything will receive much in this age and eternal life in the age to come (vv. 29-30). In contrast to the burdens that Christians must share, Paul also points out that each Christian must bear "his own" burden, communicating individual responsibility simultaneously to mutual accountability (Gal. 6:5). See *NIDNTT-A*, 454.

ONLY

Old Testament

Noun: בַּד (*bad*), GK 963 (S 905), 161x. *bad* means "alone, only." See *alone*.

New Testament

Adjective: μόνος (*monos*), GK *3668* (S *3441*), 44x. *monos* means "only, alone" and has several nuances. (1) *monos* can refer to the only entity in a class. For example, Jesus tells Satan that "man does not live on bread *alone*" (Mt. 4:4), and that *only* the Lord God is to be served (4:10). Jesus often retreats to where he can be *alone* (14:23). Reproving one's brother must be done *alone*, that is, in private (18:15). *Only* God can forgive sins (Lk. 5:21); and *only* the Father knows the hour of Christ's second coming (Mt. 24:36).

(2) *monos* can also be used when speaking about God as a person. In 1 Tim. 1:17, he is "the *only* God," and in Jude 25 he is "the *only* God our Savior." God is the only entity in his class; he has no peers (cf. Jn. 5:44; 17:3; Rom. 16:27; 1 Tim. 6:15; Jude 4; Rev. 15:4). *monos* can also be used as a prefix, such as in the significant term "only begotten" (*monogenēs*) in Jn. 3:16, which emphasizes Jesus' uniqueness as the "only begotten Son"; that this does not imply that Jesus was created is reflected in the more modern translations such as "only" or "one and only" (NET).

(3) *monos* can also refer to refer to a select group of two or more. In Mk. 9:2 *monos* refers to Jesus' inner circle—Peter, James, and John. Only one specific group, the priests, could eat the consecrated bread (Mt. 12:4). *monos* can also refer to a specific group of fellow missionaries or a whole church body (Rom. 16:4; 1 Cor. 9:6; 14:36; Phil. 4:15; Col. 4:11). See *NIDNTT-A*, 376-77

Adverb: μόνον (*monon*), GK *3667* (S *3440*), 70x. *monon* is typically used as a marker of limitation and means "only, alone." It can limit the action of a verb, such as in Mt. 9:21, "If I *only* touch his cloak, I will be healed" (cf. 14:36). To the synagogue official Jesus states, "Fear not, *only* believe" (Mk. 5:36; cf. Lk. 8:50). In 1 Cor. 7:39, a woman may "*only* marry in the Lord" if her husband dies (i.e., she must marry be a believer). Paul says that if our hope is limited *only* to the present life and has no appreciation for the doctrine of the resurrection, then we are to be pitied (1 Cor. 15:19; see also Mt. 5:47; 10:42; Acts 18:25; Rom. 3:29; Gal. 1:23; 2:10; 3:2; Phil. 1:27; 2 Thess. 2:7; Heb. 9:10). In Gal. 3:2 Paul *only* wants to find out one thing from the Galatians, whether they received the Spirit via law or faith.

monon can also be used with reference to nouns. In Mt. 8:8, the centurion expresses his faith in Jesus when he asks him to speak *only* a word of healing, and the servant will be healed. In Acts 18:25, Apollos is said to be fervent in spirit and an accurate teacher concerning Jesus, although "he knew *only* the baptism of John." Priscilla and Aquila then take him aside in order to further explain to him the way of God more accurately.

monon is also frequently found as part of the coordinating conjunctions "not *only* … but also" or similar phrases. This is especially common in the NT letters (e.g., Rom. 1:32; 4:12, 16; 4:23–24; 2 Cor. 7:7; 8:10, 19, 21; Eph. 1:21; Phil. 1:21), but is found in the gospels and Acts as well (Mt. 21:21; Jn. 5:18; 17:20; Acts 19:26, 27; 21:13). See *NIDNTT-A*, 376-77.

OPEN

Old Testament

Verb: פָּתַח (*pātaḥ*), GK 7337 (S 6605), 136x.

(1) Generally, *pātaḥ* means "to open" objects that are closed, sealed, or blocked, such as a window (Gen. 7:11; 8:6), a room (Gen. 41:56), a cistern (Exod. 21:33), the heavens (Ezek. 1:1), or a letter (Neh. 6:5). A flower "opens" in bloom (Song 7:13) and farming "opens" the ground (Isa. 28:24). Most frequently, *pātah* is used in the expression "to open one's mouth," a figure for the act of speaking (Isa. 53:7) or for the healing of one unable to speak (Ezek. 38:13).

(2) By extension, *pātaḥ* can also mean "to release" or "to set (something) free," such as a person from prison (Isa. 51:14; cf. Jer. 1:14). In other contexts, it means "to loosen" objects like a saddle from a camel (Gen. 24:32), a sackcloth from one's loins (Isa. 20:3), or armor from one's body (1 Ki. 20:11).

New Testament

Verb: ἀνοίγω (*anoigō*), GK *487* (S *455*), 77x. This word is most common in the NT in the writings of John (Revelation and the Gospel of John). It can simply mean "to open" but elsewhere has the connotation of healing. It can also mean "to reveal" or "to speak."

(1) It is used of the simple opening to disclose the contents of something, e.g., the mouth of a fish to reveal a coin, one's heart (2 Cor. 6:11; cf. Rev. 10:2, 8), or a chest to disclose its treasures: "Then they opened their treasures and presented him with gifts of gold and of incense and of myrrh" (Mt. 2:11).

(2) Frequently *anoigō* depicts a miraculous event, such as the opening of eyes in restoration of sight (Mt. 9:30; 20:33; Jn. 9:10, 14, 17, 21, 26, 30; 10:21; 11:37), of ears to restore hearing (Mk. 7:35), and of the mouth to restore speech (Lk. 1:64). Saul opened his eyes on the Damascus Road but could see nothing after his vision of Christ (Acts 9:8; cf. 9:40). It is used of Jesus' divine ability to do such miracles: "Nobody has ever heard of opening the eyes of a man born blind" (Jn. 9:32). Similarly it is used of Jesus opening things that point to his divine authority, such as opening a scroll (Rev. 5:2; 6:1; 8:1; 20:12) or the Abyss (9:2).

(3) *anoigo* can be used in a revelatory sense, involving the opening of heaven and the Spirit descending on Jesus (Mt. 3:16; cf. Lk. 3:21; Jn. 1:51) "He saw heaven opened and something like a large sheet being let down to earth by its four corners" (Acts 10:11; cf. Rev. 4:1; 11:19; 19:11). *anoigō* is also used for the opening of the heavenly tabernacle (Rev. 15:5).

(4) Similarly, it can refer to opening a door to let someone in (Mt. 25:11; Lk. 12:36; 13:25; Acts 12:14, 16), or a prison to let someone out (Acts 5:19, 23; cf. 12:10; 16:26–27), and sometimes by John as a metaphor for conversion (John 10:3). In Acts 14:27 "[God] had opened the door of faith to the Gentiles" (cf. Acts 26:18), a use particularly seen in Revelation (3:7-8, 20). It can carry the connotation of opportunity, either for ministry ("a great door for effective work has opened to me" (1 Cor. 16:9; cf. 2 Cor. 2:12; Col. 4:3) or conversion ("knock and the door will be opened to you. For ... to him who knocks, the door will be opened" (Mt. 7:7–8; cf. Lk. 11:9–10).

(5) Finally, it can be used in a Hebrew sense of "opening one's mouth" to teach (Mt. 5:2; 13:35) or simply speak (Acts 8:32), as it is often used in the OT (Exod. 4:12, 15; Num. 22:28; Ezek. 3:27). See *NIDNTT-A*, 53-55.

OPENING

Old Testament

Noun: פֶּה (*peh*), GK 7023 (S 6310), 498x. *peh* refers to the "mouth" of people or animals as the organ of eating/drinking or of speech. As a metaphor, it refers to *the opening* of things, such as a cave (Jos. 10:18, 22, 27), sack (Gen. 42:27) or well (Gen. 29:2). See *mouth*.

OPENLY

New Testament

Adverb: φανερῶς (*phanerōs*), GK *5747* (S *5320*), 3x. *phanerōs* denotes the openness or visibility of an activity, hence "openly, publicly." At times, the success of Jesus' ministry necessitated a limited public exposure. Mark comments on one such episode, "As a result, Jesus could no longer enter a town *openly* but stayed outside in lonely places" (Mk. 1:45b). At times, Jesus willingly chose to travel outside of the public eye: "However, after his brothers had left for the Feast, he went also, not *publicly*, but in secret" (Jn. 7:10). Luke uses *phanerōs* to describe the clarity of Cornelius's vision: "One day at about three in the afternoon he had a vision. He *distinctly* saw an angel of God" (Acts 10:3). See *NIDNTT-A*, 202-4.*

OPERATE

New Testament

Verb: ἐνεργέω (*energeō*), GK *1919* (S *1754*), 21x. *energeō* means "to be active, work, operate, do" something.

OPPOSE

New Testament

Verb: ἀνθίστημι (*anthistēmi*), GK *468* (S *436*), 14x. *anthistēmi* means "to oppose, resist." The gospel and its messengers continually face "opposition" (Lk. 21:15; Acts 6:10; 13:8; 2 Tim. 3:8; 4:15). Those who "oppose" the authorities are rebelling against those whom God has appointed (Rom. 13:2). Paul "opposes" Peter when he is in the wrong (Gal. 2:11). Believers are urged to stand firm and "resist" the devil (Eph. 6:13; Jas. 4:7; 1 Pet. 5:9).

Verb: κωλύω (*kōlyō*), GK *3266* (S *2967*), 23x. *kōlyō* means "to hinder, stop, forbid, oppose." It is found most often in the writings of Luke. See *hinder*.

Verb: ὑπαντάω (*hypantao*), GK *5636* (S *5221*), 10x. *hypantao* is used only in the gospels and Acts and is normally translated "to meet, oppose," designating an encounter with either a friend or foe. See *meet*.

OPPRESS

Old Testament

Verb: עָנָה (*ʿānâ*), GK 6700 (S 6031), 79x. *ʿānâ* can denote humbling in a positive sense (i.e., repentance and contrition) or with connotations of violence (i.e., affliction and oppression). See *afflict*.

OPPRESSED

Old Testament

Adjective: עָנִי (*ʿānî*), GK 6714 (S 6041), 80x. *ʿāni* describes one who has been humbled or afflicted by circumstances, and who, because of current disability, finds himself or herself dependent on others for life's necessities. See *poor*.

ORACLE

Old Testament

Noun: נְאֻם (*neʾum*), GK 5536 (S 5002), 376x. *neʾum* is used of an utterance, word or revelation. It is often translated as "oracle" (NIV), "parable" (KJV), "declaration," and "word." See *word*.

New Testament

Noun: λόγιον (*logion*), GK *3359* (S *3051*), 4x. *logion* occurs in the NT only as a plural word. This is an important term picked up from the LXX, where it refers to teachings, oracles, or sayings of the Lord (usually spoken by a prophet). Thus in the NT it refers 2x to the OT revelation of God as the "very words of God" (Rom. 3:2; cf. Acts 7:38). In Heb. 5:12 it refers to the truths about God that are taught to new believers, and in 1 Pet. 4:11 Peter says that the goal of a preacher is to speak "the very words of God." See *NIDNTT-A*, 343.*

ORDER

Old Testament

Verb: צָוָה (*ṣāwâ*), GK 7422 (S 6680), 496x. This verb is used to denote the issuing of an authoritative statement and means "to command, order." See *command, commandment*.

Noun: מִצְוָה (*miṣwâ*), GK 5184 (S 4687), 184x. *miṣwâ* means "command, commandment, order." See *command, commandment*.

New Testament

Verb: διαστέλλω (*diastellō*), GK *1403*

(S *1291*), 7x. *diastellō* means "to command, order" with authority. See *command, commandment.*

Verb: διατάσσω (*diatassō*), GK *1411* (S *1299*), 16x. *diatassō* means "to command, direct, order." See *command.*

Verb: ἐντέλλω (*entellō*), GK *1948* (S *1781*), 15x. *entellō* means "to command, order." See *command, commandment.*

Verb: ἐπιτάσσω (*epitassō*), GK *2199* (S *2004*), 10x. *epitassō*, similar to *diatassō*, means "to order, command." See *command.*

Verb: κελεύω (*keleuo*), GK *3027* (S *2753*), 25x. *keleuō* means "to order, command." In the NT, it denotes a specific verbal order given by a person of superior rank or status. The command is usually terse and followed by strict obedience. Peter requests that Jesus command him to come to him on the water. Jesus simply says, "Come," and Peter quickly obeys (Mt. 14:28). Other commands in Matthew are given by Jesus (8:18; 14:19), Pilate (27:58, 64), and Herod (14:9).

The king in the parable of the unforgiving servant (18:23–35) orders that the unforgiving servant and all that he had be sold (18:25). In Luke, Jesus orders that the blind man be brought to him (18:40). In Acts, *keleuō* is used only by human authorities: the Sanhedrin (4:15), the Ethiopian eunuch (8:38), Gamaliel (5:34), Herod (12:19), the magistrates (16:22), the tribune (21:33, 34; 22:24, 30; 23:10), Ananias (23:3), Felix (23:35), Festus (25:6, 17, 21, 23), and the centurion (27:43). See *NIDNTT-A*, 299.*

Verb: παραγγέλλω (*parangellō*), GK *4133* (S *3853*), 32x. *parangellō* means "to command, order" with authority, such that the person is obligated to obey. See *command, commandment.*

Noun: ἐντολή (*entolē*) GK *1953* (S *1785*), 67x. *entolē* is an authoritative "command, order" from a superior to a subordinate. See *command, commandment.*

ORDINANCE

Old Testament

Noun: חֻקָּה (*ḥuqqâ*), GK 2978 (S 2708), 104x. The feminine noun *ḥuqqâ,* derives from the verb *ḥāqaq*, "to cut in, inscribe, decree," is related to its masculine counterpart, *ḥōq*, though the two nouns never appear together. Like its counterpart, *ḥuqqâ* most frequently indicates the law of God, and the NIV regularly translates these occurrences "decree" while the NASB and KJV use "statute." See *decree.*

OTHER

Old Testament

Noun: רֵעַ (*rēaʿ*), GK 8276 (S 7453), 188x. *rēaʿ* is primarily translated as "neighbor, other, friend." See *neighbor.*

Adjective: אֶחָד (*ʾeḥād*), GK 285 (S 259), 976x. *ʾeḥād* means "one, first, other." It can translated either as the ordinal numeral or the cardinal numeral. It is also used for both sides in the expression "the *one* ... the *other*" (see, e.g., Exod. 18:3–4). See *one.*

Adjective: אַחֵר (*ʾaḥēr*), GK 337 (S 312), 166x. *ʾaḥēr* is formed from the verb אָחַר, *ʾāḥar* (GK 336), "to delay" or "to detain someone." Thus, *ʾaḥēr* may originally have had the sense of "one who comes after," which evolved in meaning to "other" or "another." See *another.*

New Testament

Adjective: ἄλλος (*allos*), GK *257* (S *243*), 155x. *allos* means "other" or "another." In the NT, *allos* is virtually interchangeable with *heteros* (cf. Gal. 1:6–7).

allos can denote "the other" of the same kind. For example, Jesus instructs believers who are struck on the right cheek to offer the "other" cheek also (Mt. 5:39). Jesus restores a man's hand so that it is just like "the other" (12:13). Jesus is crucified along with two "others," who have been convicted of crimes (Jn. 19:18). "*Other* believers" accompany Paul and Barnabas to the Jerusalem Council (Acts 15:2). In John's vision in Revelation, one thing is often followed by another similar to it, like "another" horse (Rev. 6:4), angel (7:2; 8:3; 10:1), sign (12:3; 15:1), beast (13:11), voice (18:4), or book (20:12). John's repeated use of "the other disciple" (Jn. 18:15–16; 20:2–4, 8; 21:8) is probably a modest reference to himself.

allos can also simply denote an alternate choice without the nuance of "the same kind." After being warned of Herod's plan, the Magi return to their home country via "another" route (Mt. 2:12). A scribe confesses to Jesus that there is one God, and no other (Mk. 12:32). Peter proclaims that salvation is found in "no one else" but Jesus (Acts 4:12). Paul warns people in Corinth against those preaching "*another* Jesus" (2 Cor. 11:4 [KJV]).

allos can indicate a different person or group, often one contrasting with or expressing an opinion different from that of the first. Some of the crowd call Jesus a good man, but "others" call him a deceiver (Jn. 7:12). Some of the Pharisees claim that Jesus is not from God because he breaks the Sabbath, but "others" ask how a sinner can perform such miracles (9:16). Some of the crowd state that Jesus is demon-possessed, but "others" argue to the contrary (10:21). Some think that Jesus is John brought back from the dead, "others" that he is Elijah, and still "others" that he is a prophet (Mk. 6:14–15; 8:28). In both Ephesus and Jerusalem, Paul is the subject of riots that cause "some" in the crowd to shout one thing, and "some" another (Acts 19:32; 21:34). See *NIDNTT-A*, 36-37.

Adjective and Noun: ἀλλότριος (*allotrios*), GK *259* (S *245*), 14x. *allotrios* is used to describe a thing that is not one's own or a person not from one's own people group. It may be used simply to refer to someone else's possession, such as another person's property (Lk. 16:12), servant (Rom. 14:4), sins (1 Tim. 5:22), or blood (Heb. 9:25). This last passage stresses the uniqueness of Christ as high priest, for while the OT high priest brought blood not his own into the Most Holy Place, Jesus brought *his own* blood! Paul repeatedly articulates his goal of spreading the gospel where "someone else" has not laid a foundation or has established a sphere of influence (Rom. 15:20; 2 Cor. 10:15–16).

allotrios may also describe that which is strange, foreign, or outside of one's household or people (Mt. 17:25, 26). When referring to a person, especially when used as a noun, it denotes a "stranger." An outsider is often the object of distrust or abuse (Jn. 10:5; Acts 7:6) or is regarded as one who brings hostility (Heb. 11:9, 34). The word "stranger" is often understood in a pejorative sense. See *NIDNTT-A*, 37.*

Adjective: ἕτερος (*heteros*), GK *2283* (S *2087*), 98x. *heteros* means "other" or "another." In the NT, it is virtually synonymous with *allos* (GK *257*; cf. Gal. 1:6–7).

(1) *heteros* is used to indicate "another" thing, often one that is different from something already mentioned. For example, in Stephen's final speech, he recounts the story of Joseph, in which "*another* king" rose to power who, unlike the previous Pharaoh, did not know Joseph (Acts 7:18).

Many NT occurrences of *heteros* are found in Luke's gospel (32x), where the term often indicates a contrast between two kinds of people: one man with a large debt and "another" with a smaller debt (Lk. 7:41); hating one master and loving another (16:13); a man who divorces his wife and marries another (16:18); one who is taken and another who is left (17:34, 35); and one man who is a Pharisee and another who is a tax collector (18:10). Paul also uses *heteros* in this contrasting way. He sets God's law in contrast with "*another* law," the law of sin (Rom. 7:23); he warns against those who preach a Jesus other than the one whom he preached (2 Cor. 11:4); and he chastises the Galatians for turning to "a *different* gospel" (Gal. 1:6).

(2) *heteros* is also used to indicate an additional unspecified amount. In this sense it is often used to finish off a list because it helps to account for anything else that may have been omitted. For example, Matthew describes several kinds

of afflicted people brought to Jesus for healing and then mentions that there were also "many others" besides the ones explicitly mentioned (Mt. 15:30). Similarly, in 1 Tim. 1:9–10, Paul provides a list of those who behave in an ungodly manner. He finishes off the list, "and for *whatever else* is contrary to the sound doctrine" (v. 10). After recording several of John the Baptist's warnings and exhortations (Lk. 3:7–17), Luke explains that John exhorted the people "with many *other* words" (Lk. 3:18). After Jesus' arrest, his captors, in addition to the mocking words "Prophesy! Who hit you?" (Lk. 22:64), also said "many *other* insulting things to him" (22:65).

(3) *heteros* can also refer to "someone else." Paul directs his argument about righteousness to Jews who teach "others" the law (Rom. 2:21). To those in Corinth, Paul offers instruction to those having a dispute with "another" (1 Cor. 6:1) and urges them to seek the good of "others" (1 Cor. 10:24; see also Phil. 2:4). See *NIDNTT-A*, 36-37.

Adjective: λοιπός (*loipos*), GK *3370* (S *3062*), 55x. In its most generic sense, *loipos* means "remaining." It can also refer in a general sense to "other people." See *remaining*.

OUGHT

New Testament

Verb: δεῖ (*dei*), GK *1256* (S *1176*), 101x. *dei* occurs frequently in the NT, especially in Luke. It has a basic meaning of something being "necessary." See *must*.

Verb: ὀφείλω (*opheilō*), GK *4053* (S *3784*), 35x. *opheilō* conveys the idea of being in debt or under obligation and may best be translated as "owe" or (as a helping verb) "ought." See *owe*.

OUTCOME

Old Testament

Noun: אַחֲרִית (*ʾaḥarît*), GK 344 (S 319), 61x. *ʾaḥarît* in its most basic sense denotes "that which comes after." Specifically it may describe what follows temporally, that is, the "cessation, end" of an event or the final "outcome." See *end*.

OUTDOORS, OUTSIDE

Old Testament

Noun: חוּץ (*ḥûṣ*), GK 2575 (S 2351), 164x. *ḥûṣ* refers to that which is "outside." Its usual reference is to a location or position outside, such as the "streets" (which are outside of buildings). Solomon tells us, "Wisdom calls aloud in the streets" (Prov. 1:20; cf. 2 Sam. 1:20; Ps. 18:45; Isa. 5:25).

ḥûṣ can also be used in a broader sense to mean a place outside the walls or boundaries of a city or a camp: "Send away male and female [lepers] alike; send them outside the camp so they will not defile their camp" (Num. 5:3). Joshua kept his word to Rahab and "brought out her entire family and put them in a place outside the camp of Israel" (Jos. 6:23). Several of the Levitical offerings had parts that were to be burned "outside the camp" (Lev. 4:21; 8:17; 9:11). The spring where Abraham's servant met Rebekah was "outside the town" (Gen. 24:11). In some places, *ḥûṣ* refers simply to an "outer" gate (Ezek. 47:2) or wall (41:9).

ḥûṣ is also used to designate those belonging to a different race or clan: "He gave his daughters away in marriage to those outside his clan, and for his sons he brought in thirty young women as wives from outside his clan" (Jdg. 12:9).

New Testament

Adverb: ἔξω (*exō*), GK *2032* (S *1854*), 63x. The most common meaning of *exō* is "outside" or "outdoors." "A crowd was sitting around [Jesus], and they told him, 'Your mother and brothers are *outside* looking for you'" (Mk. 3:32). *exō* is also used to describe the exterior of a place (Lk. 13:33), a city (2 Cor. 5:13), or an object. "Now then, you Pharisees clean the *outside* of the cup and dish, but inside you are full of greed and wickedness" (Lk. 11:39). It can describe the outer part of a building (Jn. 18:16) or cave/tomb: "But Mary stood *outside* the tomb crying" (20:11). Paul uses *exō* to describe a mental condition: "If we are *out of* our mind, it is for the sake of God" (2 Cor. 5:13).

exō can also describe those who are outside a designated group. Jesus speaks in parables so that those "outside" the group of disciples will "see but not perceive" (Mk. 4:11–12). Paul does not judge those "outside" the church (1 Cor. 5:12). Those outside are not allowed into the great city of God because of their unforgiven sin: "*Outside* are the dogs, those who practice magic arts, the sexually immoral, the murderers, the idolaters and everyone who loves and practices falsehood" (Rev. 22:15). Paul's concern for outsiders is such that he exhorts the believer to "make it your ambition to lead a quiet life, to mind your own business and to work with your hands, just as we told you, so that your daily life may win the respect of *outsiders*" (1 Thess. 4:11–12; cf. Col. 4:5).

OUTSTANDING

New Testament

Adjective: γνωστός (*gnōstos*), GK *1196* (S *1110*), 15x. *gnōstos* means "known" or "able to be know," i.e., "intelligible." "Known" people can be considered "friends." See *known*.

OVERCOME

New Testament

Verb: νικάω (*nikaō*), GK *3771* (S *3528*), 28x. *nikaō* means "to overcome, be victorious in a struggle." This verb occurs especially in the writings of John, in the context of struggle—most often in Revelation (17x). In Rev. 2–3, it is used in the promises given to "the one who overcomes," including the right to eat from the tree of life (2:7), freedom from the second death (Rev. 2:11), being dressed in white (3:5), and being like a pillar in the temple of God (3:12). These promises are grounded in the fact that the believer who overcomes is becoming more and more like Christ, who assures his disciples that he has "overcome" the world (Jn. 16:33) and whom John describes as able to open the scroll and its seven seals because "he has overcome" (Rev. 5:5).

Believers are those who have overcome the evil one (1 Jn. 2:13–14), because Christ is in them (4:4). It is precisely because we believe in Christ, the one who has overcome the world, that we can overcome the world (4:4). For this reason, we must have confidence and overcome evil with good (Rom. 12:21). See *NIDNTT-A*, 387.

OVERFLOW

New Testament

Verb: περισσεύω (*perisseuō*), GK *4355* (S *4052*), 39x. *perisseuō* means "to abound, be in abundance, overflow." See *abound*.

OVERPOWER

New Testament

Verb: ἰσχύω (*ischyō*), GK *2710* (S *2480*), 28x. In the NT, *ischyō* primarily means "to be strong, powerful, mighty." Sometimes it means "to overpower" someone. See *be strong*.

OVERSEER

New Testament

Noun: ἐπίσκοπος (*episkopos*), GK *2176* (S *1985*), 5x. *episkopos* means "overseer, bishop." Its two root words (*epi* plus *skopos*) literally refer to someone who "looks over" or "watches over" a group of people. In the NT it is used 4x for those who have been appointed as "overseers" or elders in the church (these two words are essentially synonymous in the NT; see Acts 20:28; Phil. 1:1). In 1 Tim. 3:2 and Tit. 1:7 Paul writes about the qualifications for overseers. In 1 Pet. 2:25, Peter refers to Jesus as "the Shepherd and *Overseer* of your souls." Jesus is, in other words, the chief overseer of our lives; all other church leaders function on his behalf and should use his life as a model (cf. 5:1–4).

OVERTAKE

Old Testament

Verb: דָּבַק (*dābaq*), GK 1815 (S 1692), 55x. *dābaq* denotes the basic action of one object or person adhering or clinging to another. It takes both people and physical objects as its subject, but never God. In certain contexts, *dābaq* occurs in a form that conveys the notion of "to pursue, overtake." Laban "overtakes" Jacob in

Gilead (Gen. 31:23), and the Israelites "pursue" the Philistines in battle after the Philistines flee (1 Sam. 14:22). See *cling*.

Verb: נָשַׂג (*nāśag*), GK 5952 (S 5381), 50x. *nāśag*, usually translated "to overtake," generally denotes the action of catching someone or something from behind. This verb is paired 15x with *rādap*, "to pursue," indicating that overtaking something is often the result of pursuing it (e.g., Gen. 44:4; Exod. 14:9; 15:9; Deut. 19:6; 1 Sam. 30:8; 2 Ki. 25:5; Lam. 1:3; Hos. 2:9).

nāśag is frequently used for one person or group catching up with another at the end of a chase. After Joseph's brothers leave, Joseph sends his steward in pursuit with specific instructions for when he "overtakes" the brothers (Gen. 44:4, 6). The Egyptians pursue Israel after Pharaoh releases them and "overtake" them camping by the sea (Exod. 14:9). Rahab deceives the king of Jericho's men by telling them that Israel's spies have left, but if they pursue them quickly, they can "overtake" them (Jos. 2:5). David inquires of God whether he will "overtake" the band responsible for Ziklag's destruction (1 Sam. 30:8). During the fall of Jerusalem, the Chaldeans "overtake" King Zedekiah in the plains of Jericho (2 Ki. 25:5; cf. Jer. 39:5; 52:8).

Figuratively, individuals may be "overtaken" by a wide variety of things, either bleak or cheerful. The wicked may be "overtaken" by terror (Job 27:20). Israel may be "overtaken" by the sword (Jer. 42:16) or war (Hos. 10:9) because of their sin. Their enemies may prevent righteousness from "overtaking" Israel (Isa. 59:9). Lamentations personifies Judah by stating that all who pursue Judah have "overtaken" her (Lam. 1:3). Jacob laments that his years have not "attained" to the years of his fathers (Gen. 47:9). But when those ransomed by God return to Zion, gladness and joy will "overtake" them while sorrow and sighing will flee (Isa. 35:10; 51:11). In Deuteronomy's covenant blessings and curses, Israel is promised that blessings will "overtake" them if they obey (Deut. 28:2), but curses will "overtake" them if they do not (Deut. 28:15, 45).

The phrase *nāśag yād* (lit., "a hand will overtake") is a Hebrew idiom used 12x (e.g., Lev. 14:22, 30, 31, 32; 1 Sam. 14:26; Ezek. 46:7) with the sense of a person's ability to obtain a particular item, especially material wealth. The NIV usually translates this phrase "he can afford" and often indicates what an Israelite should offer as a sacrifice. For example, if an Israelite "cannot afford" to sacrifice two doves, he should bring flour (Lev. 5:11). See *NIDOTTE*, 3:163-70.

New Testament

Verb: καταλαμβάνω (*katalambanō*), GK *2898* (S *2638*), 15x. *katalambanō* can mean "to catch, obtain, seize, overtake." In the middle voice it means "to grasp, understand." See *catch*.

OWE

New Testament

Verb: ὀφείλω (*opheilō*), GK *4053* (S *3784*), 35x. *opheilō* conveys the idea of being in debt or under obligation and may best be translated as "owe" or (as a helping verb) "ought." NT writers frequently write about what Christians "ought" to do in their service to Christ (e.g., Jn. 13:14; Eph. 5:28; 2 Thess. 1:3; 2:13; Heb. 5:12; 1 Jn. 3:16).

In the parable of the unmerciful servant, Jesus stresses the inappropriate behavior of one who has been forgiven a great debt: "But when that servant went out, he found one of his fellow servants who *owed* him a hundred denarii. He grabbed him and began to choke him. 'Pay back what you *owe* me!'" (Mt. 18:28; cf. Lk. 7:41). Not only are Christians under obligation to God, but they are also under obligation to one another. Paul writes, "Let no *debt remain* outstanding, except the continuing debt to love one another" (Rom. 13:8). This sense of spiritual obligation and indebtedness was the motivation for early believers to share their financial resources with others in need (Rom. 15:27). See *NIDNTT-A*, 424-25.

OWNER

New Testament

Noun: οἰκοδεσπότης (*oikodespotēs*), GK *3867* (S *3617*), 12x. *oikodespotēs* means the "master, owner of a house." It is derived from two different words: *oikos* ("house, dwelling place") and *despotēs* ("master, owner"). This word is used only in the Synoptic Gospels.

The *oikodespotē* hires workers for his fields (Mt. 20:1, 11; cf. 13:27), watches over his house in case of burglary (24:43; Lk. 12:39), opens the door for a friend late at night (Lk. 13:25), and invites people to a great banquet (14:21). It is the *oikodespotēs* who allows the disciples to prepare Jesus' last supper in his home (Mk. 14:14; Lk. 22:11).

Just as a servant is like his "master," so also Jesus' disciples can expect to be maligned as Jesus was maligned (Mt. 10:25). Jesus uses *oikodespotēs* when he says, "Therefore every teacher of the law who has been instructed about the kingdom of heaven is like the *master of a house* who brings out of his storeroom new treasures as well as old" (13:52).

oikodespotēs can also be translated "landowner." In the parable of the vineyard workers, Jesus describes the attitude of the laborers saying, "they began to grumble against the *landowner*" (Mt. 21:33). See *NIDNTT-A*, 130.*

OX

Old Testament

Noun: שׁוֹר (*šôr*), GK 8802 (S 7794), 79x. Technically, *šôr* may refer to a male or female cow, but in the OT it primarily refers to the bull (though see Lev. 22:28). See *bull*.

OXEN

Old Testament

Noun: בָּקָר (*bāqār*), GK 1330 (S 1241), 183x. *bāqār* refers to domesticated cattle (e.g., bulls, cows, and calves). In the ancient world, cattle were a measure of one's wealth. Larger cattle were deemed more valuable than smaller animals. See *cattle*.

PAGAN

Old Testament

Noun: גּוֹי (*gôy*), GK 1580 (S 1471), 567x. *gôy* is commonly understood as "nation" (e.g., Egypt, Exod. 9:24). In the Exodus God promises to make the Hebrews a great nation (Exod. 32:10). But *gôy* does not always refer to a political kingdom; it can refer more generally to groups of people (non-Jews), thus meaning "Gentiles" or in some contexts "pagans" (with their gods, Isa. 37:12). See *nation*.

PAIN

New Testament

Noun: λυπή (*lypē*), GK *3383* (S *3077*), 16x. *lypē* denotes "grief, sorrow, pain," the result that comes from the action of the verb *lypeō* (see *grieve*). See *grief*.

PALACE

Old Testament

Noun: הֵיכָל (*hēkāl*), GK 2121 (S 1964), 80x. *hēkāl* bears three distinct but related meanings in the OT. It can refer to a palace (earthly or heavenly), to the temple itself, or to the main room in the temple (see *temple*). It is used for the palace of King Ahab of Israel (1 Ki. 21:1; cf. Hos. 8:14) and of the king of Babylon (2 Ki. 20:18; cf. Dan. 5:5). Since the Jerusalem temple is thought to be God's palace (Mic. 1:2), it is natural that the same term is used for both.

New Testament

Noun: αὐλή (*aulē*), GK *885* (S *833*), 12x. *aulē* means "courtyard" or "palace." See *courtyard*.

Noun: πραιτώριον (*praitōrion*), GK *4550* (S *4232*), 8x. *praitōrion* means "palace"; it is a transliteration of the Latin word Praetorium (which means "palace, headquarters"). "Palace" was an important word in the OT, for it was the residence of the kings of Israel and Judah. In the NT it is used mostly for the living quarters of a Roman governor; this location comes into prominence especially during the trial of Jesus (Mt. 27:27; Mk. 15:16; Jn. 18:28, 33; 19:9). Later in the NT, when Paul the prisoner is transferred out of Jerusalem and brought to Caesarea, he is "kept under guard in Herod's palace" (Acts 23:35). In Phil. 1:13, Paul uses this word to refer to the Roman soldiers guarding him (the "palace guard").*

PARABLE

Old Testament

Noun: נְאֻם ($n^{e\,\prime}um$), GK 5536 (S 5002), 376x. $n^{e\,\prime}um$ is used of an utterance, word or revelation. It is often translated as "oracle" (NIV), "parable" (KJV), "declaration," and "word." See *word*.

New Testament

Noun: παραβολή (*parabolē*), GK *4130* (S *3850*), 50x. A "parable" is a story from everyday life used to illustrate a moral or religious truth. It is the primary method Jesus used to teach about the kingdom of God: "With what can we compare the kingdom of God, or what *parable* shall we use for it?" (Mk. 4:34). In Mt. 13:24 the kingdom of heaven is "like a man who sowed good seed in his field;" in 13:31 it is like a "mustard seed;" in 13:33 it is like "yeast" that a woman mixes with flour.

Naturally, in a largely agricultural environment, many of Jesus' parables involve such things as sowing seed (Mt. 13:18, 24), planting a field (13:31), making bread (13:33), weeding a field (13:36), planting a vineyard (21:33), building barns (Lk. 12:16), or observing a fig tree (Mt. 24:32).

When asked why he taught in parables, Jesus answers by referring to Isa. 6:9–10, that while the secret of the kingdom of God has been given to the Twelve, "to those on the outside everything is said in parables so that 'they may be ever seeing but not perceiving' " (Mk. 4:11–12). This cryptic response may be eased by observing that the "so that" clause of vs. 12 is perhaps a result clause rather than a purpose clause: Jesus uses parables and as a result people do not understand. Through parables Jesus is able to teach truths to his disciples while at the same time keeping it somewhat hidden from those who don't really care about what he has to say. Nevertheless, even some of his parables are not immediately understood by his disciples: "Explain to us the parable of the weeds in the field," they ask (Mt. 13:36; cf. 15:15).

While Jesus discloses "the secrets of the kingdom of God" to the disciples in parables, still his enemies have a feeling that he is in fact directing his teaching against them. Matthew reports that the chief priests and the Pharisees "knew he [Jesus] was talking about them" (Mt. 21:45; Mk. 12:12).

Although most parables are stories of various length, the term *parabolē* is also used for common aphorisms, such as "Physician, heal yourself!" (Lk. 4:23, NIV calls it a "proverb") and "Can a blind man lead a blind man? Will they not both fall into a pit?" (Lk. 6:39). Jesus refers to his advice about not taking the place of honor at a wedding feast as a *parabolē* (Lk. 14:7ff.). The author of Hebrews refers to OT ceremonial practice as a *parabolē* (Heb. 9:9, the NIV translates "illustration;" and in 11:19 renders the word "figuratively speaking"). See *NIDNTT-A*, 432-34.

PARALYTIC

New Testament

Adjective: παραλυτικός (*paralytikos*), GK *4166* (S *3885*), 10x. *paralytikos* is an adjective that denotes someone who is "lame" or "paralytic." Usually, however, this word functions as a noun. Injuries to the spine, legs, and perhaps hands were a death sentence to many living in NT times. If family members or friends did not care for the individual, they were reliant on the graciousness and generosity of others for the bare necessities of life. These individual were often the recipients of Jesus' mercy and compassion. "News about him spread all over Syria, and people brought to him all who were ill with various diseases, those suffering severe pain, the demon-possessed, those having seizures, and *paralytics*, and he healed them" (Mt. 4:24). *paralytikos* describes the condition of the centurion's servant: "'Lord,' he said, 'my servant lies at home *paralyzed* and in terrible suffering'" (Mt. 8:6).

Eight out of ten times *paralytikos* appears in the NT, it is within the context of an incident of Jesus' preaching ministry in Capernaum (Mt. 9:1–6; Mk. 2:1–10). Large crowds are trying to get into the room where the Lord is teaching. As four men carrying a paralytic approach, they are unable to enter. Out of desperation, they hoist the paralytic onto the rooftop, cut a hole, and lower him down in front of Jesus. The context suggests that there may have been some spiritual aspect to the man's paralysis, for the Lord first says, "Son, your sins are forgiven" (Mk. 2:5), before he ever tells him, "Take your mat and go home" (2:11). See *NIDNTT-A*, 437.*

PARENTS

New Testament

Noun: γονεύς (*goneus*), GK *1204* (S *1118*), 20x. *goneus* is used only in the plural in the NT and means "parents." Nearly a third of its uses occur in the story of the man born blind healed by Jesus, where his parents are interviewed by the Jewish leaders (Jn. 9:18–23). The betrayal of parents by their children will be one aspect of the persecution that followers of Christ will face (Mt. 10:21; Mk. 13:12), while at the same time parents will betray their children (Lk. 21:16). A great reward awaits those who follow Christ at the cost of leaving their parents and other relationships (Lk. 18:29–30). Paul commands children to be obedient to their parents (Eph. 6:1; Col. 3:20) and says that disobedience of parents is one characteristic of a sinful lifestyle (Rom. 1:30; 2 Tim. 3:2).

PART

New Testament

Verb: διαμερίζω (*diamerizō*), GK *1374* (S *1266*), 11x. *diamerizō* means to "divide, separate something into parts." See *divide*.

Noun: μέλος (*melos*), GK *3517* (S *3196*), 34x. *melos* can be translated "member, part, limb." See *member*.

Noun: μέρος (*meros*), GK *3538* (S *3313*), 42x. *meros* has a basic meaning of "a part of a whole," but it can also mean "place, region, share."

(1) *meros* can refer to part of a body (Eph. 4:16), part of a group of people (Acts 23:6, 9), part of a country (i.e., a "region" or "district," Mt. 2:22), part of a discussion (Rom. 15:15), etc. The soldiers divided Jesus' clothes into four "parts" (Jn. 19:23). Ananias and Sapphira brought only part of the money they had received from their property (Acts 5:2). According to Paul, the individual members of the church are all a part of Christ's body (1 Cor. 12:27). The prodigal son asked for his "part" or "share" of the inheritance (Lk. 15:12).

(2) In a related meaning, the word is used in passages referring to eternal destiny: "he will set his *place* with the hypocrites" (Mt. 24:51); "their *part* will be in the lake that burns with fire and sulfur" (Rev. 21:8).

(3) An unusual use of the word occurs in Acts 19:27, where it refers to "a line of business," but in this context it may be referring to the particular business of making images of Artemis as a part of the whole economy of Ephesus. When used with a preposition, *meros* can mean "in part" or "partially"—e.g., "we know in *part*" (1 Cor. 13:9; cf. 2 Cor. 1:14), "in *succession*" (1 Cor. 14:27), "with *regard* to" (Col. 2:16), or "*part by part*" (i.e., "in detail," Heb. 9:5). See *NIDNTT-A*, 364-65.

PARTAKE

New Testament

Verb: γεύομαι (*geuomai*), GK *1174* (S *1089*), 15x. *geuomai* means "to taste, eat, partake of," usually implying enjoyment of the experience. See *taste*.

Verb: μετέχω (*metechō*), GK *3576* (S *3348*), 8x. *metechō* means "to partake, share in." Paul uses this word in 1 Cor. 9:10, 12 when he is arguing that preachers "have" a right to earn their living from preaching the gospel (even though he personally does not take advantage of that option). In the next chapter, Paul uses this same verb both for Christians "partaking" of the one loaf in holy communion and for the impossibility of believers "partaking" both of the table of the Lord and the table of demons (10:17, 21; cf. v. 30). In Heb. 2:14, the author refers to the incarnate Christ as "sharing in" our humanity.

PARTICIPANT

New Testament

Noun: κοινωνός (*koinōnos*), GK *3128* (S *2844*), 10x. This noun conveys the basic idea of one who shares in what is common or shared by all and may best be translated "partner, participant." See *partner*.

PARTICIPATE IN

New Testament

Verb: κοινωνέω (*koinōneō*), GK *3125* (S *2841*), 8x. *koinōneō* means "to share, participate in." See *share*.

PARTICIPATION

New Testament

Noun: κοινωνία (*koinōnia*), GK *3126* (S *2842*), 19x. *koinōnia* generally means "fellowship, communion, participation, sharing." See *fellowship*.

PARTNER

Old Testament

Noun: אָח (*ʾāḥ*), GK 278 (S 251), 629x. *ʾāḥ* denotes a "brother" or one who is close in some type of human relationship. It can even denote treaty partners, though this is rare. It is used, for example, of the relationship between kings (Solomon and the king of Tyre, 1 Ki. 9:13) or between nations (Israel and Edom, Num. 20:14; Deut. 2:4, 8; Obad. 10).

New Testament

Noun: κοινωνός (*koinōnos*), GK *3128* (S *2844*), 10x. This noun conveys the basic idea of one who shares in what is common or shared by all and may best be translated "partner, participant." This sense of "partnership" includes sharing in a secular context, such as the fishing business shared by Peter, James, and John (Lk. 5:10), as well as a ministry context, such as the partnership in ministry that Titus shares with Paul (2 Cor. 8:23; see also Phlm. 17). Paul extends the idea of partnership in ministry to all believers and declares, "And our hope for you is firm, because we know that just as you *share* in our sufferings, so also you share in our comfort" (2 Cor. 1:7). The glory and divine nature of Jesus Christ is also made common ground for the community of faith. Peter writes, "Through these he has given us his very great and precious promises, so that through them *you may participate* in the divine nature and escape the corruption in the world caused by evil desires" (2 Pet. 1:4; also 1 Pet. 5:1). By contrast, Paul warns the Corinthians not to participate with demons by eating meat that has been sacrificed to pagan idols (1 Cor. 10:18, 20). See *NIDNTT-A*, 310-12.

PASS (BY, THROUGH)

Old Testament

Verb: עָבַר (*ʿābar*), GK 6296 (S 5674), 553x. *ʿābar* occurs frequently in the OT with a variety of nuances, though its predominate use is "to cross over" or "pass by, through." See *cross over*.

New Testament

Verb: παράγω (*paragō*), GK *4135* (S *3855*), 10x. *paragō* means "to pass by, away." In narrative parts of the NT, this verb refers to Jesus "passing by" from one place to another and doing such things as calling Matthew as a disciple (Mt. 9:9; Mk. 1:16) or encountering blind men who request healing (Mt. 9:27; Jn. 9:1). In both 1 Cor. 9:31 and 1 Jn. 2:17, the authors refer to the world that "is passing away." But more important than that is the fact that as a result of the coming of Jesus, "the darkness is passing away and the true light is already here" (1 Jn. 2:8).

Verb: παρέρχομαι (*parerchomai*), GK *4216* (S *3928*), 29x. *parerchomai* means "to pass by or alongside" and is often translated as "pass away, disappear."

(1) On a literal level, *parerchomai* means to pass by a specific place. When Jesus' disciples are on the Sea of Galilee, Jesus appears in the dark and is about "to pass by" them (Mk. 6:48). In Mt. 8:28, two demon-possessed men prevent people from going past them the road. Similarly, a blind man sitting beside the road is told that Jesus "is passing by" (Lk. 18:37). In a

figurative sense, Jesus berates the Pharisees because in their self-righteousness they "pass by" justice and the love of God (Lk. 11:42). In Mt. 26:39, Jesus prays, "My Father, if it is possible, may this cup *be taken from* me," (KJV, "pass from me"; cf. 26:42).

(2) *parerchomai* can also denote the passage of time. When time "has passed by," it means it is getting late (see Mt. 14:15 in NIV; cf. also Acts 27:9; 1 Pet. 4:3).

(3) *parerchomai* is also used of something that has come to an end. In this sense, the verb carries the meaning "to disappear." In speaking of the perpetuity of the Mosaic law, Jesus says in the Sermon on the Mount, "I tell you the truth, until heaven and earth *disappear*, not the smallest letter, not the least stroke of a pen, will by any means *disappear* from the Law until everything is accomplished" (Mt. 5:18). Jesus assures his followers that his words are eternal and will thus never "pass away" (24:35; cf. also Mk. 13:30). In 1 Cor. 5:17, in speaking of changes that occur when a person is converted, Paul writes, "Therefore, if anyone is in Christ, he is a new creation; the old *has gone*, the new has come!" (cf. Jas. 1:10). Regarding the destruction of the end times when the Day of the Lord arrives, Peter writes that "the heavens *will disappear* with a roar" (2 Pet. 3:10).

PASS DOWN

New Testament

Verb: παραδίδωμι (*paradidōmi*), GK *4140* (S *3860*), 119x. *paradidōmi* signifies "to hand over, deliver up, betray, pass down." In the NT it has a wide variety of meanings, both negative and positive. See *hand over*.

PASS ON

New Testament

Verb: μεταβαίνω (*metabainō*), GK *3553* (S *3327*), 12x. *metabainō* means "to leave, depart, pass on," both geographically and metaphorically. See *leave*.

PASS THROUGH

New Testament

Verb: διέρχομαι (*dierchomai*), GK *1451* (S *1330*), 43x. *dierchomai* means "to come or go through, pass through." See *go through*.

PASSOVER

Old Testament

Noun: פֶּסַח (*pesaḥ*), GK 7175 (S 6453), 49x. *pesaḥ means* "Passover." It applies primarily to the festival that recalled the event of the exodus, when the angel of death passed over the homes of the Israelites and struck the firstborn son in all Egyptian homes (Exod. 12:43; 34:25). This festival became one of the three annual feast days among the Israelites (Lev. 23:5; Num. 9:2, 4–6, 12–14; Deut. 16:1–2). Joshua celebrated it with the Israelites on the plains of Jericho (Jos. 5:10–11), Hezekiah had a special Passover during his reign (2 Chr. 30:1–18) as did Josiah (35:1–19). This word can also, however, be used more specifically for "the Passover lamb" (Exod. 12:21; 2 Chr. 30:15; 35:13). Both of these uses transfer into the NT word *pascha*. See *NIDOTTE*, 3:642–44.

New Testament

Noun: πάσχα (*pascha*), GK *4247* (S *3957*), 29x. *pascha* is a transliteration of the Aramaic word for the Passover celebration, the Passover meal, or Passover lamb. It is the first of the great pilgrimage festivals (Exod. 23:15) for which Israel assembled in Jerusalem, and it celebrated God's deliverance of Israel from their slavery in Egypt. In Heb. 11:28, *pascha* refers to the original Passover event in Egypt. For this Passover, a lamb was slaughtered, and its blood was applied to the doorposts in obedience and faith that God would spare the firstborn of that household (Exod. 12:21). Thus, *pascha* is connected with slaughter (Mk. 14:12a; Lk. 22:7).

In John's gospel, Jesus is consistently typified as the Passover lamb. For example, he was anointed at Bethany at the same time that the lambs were selected (Mt. 26:6–12), and the interrogation of

Jesus corresponded with "the Day of Preparation" (Jn. 19:14, 31, 42). According to John's timetable, Jesus was crucified at precisely the same time as the Passover lamb was being slain in the temple. Paul appeals to the Corinthian Christians to repent, and he explicitly refers to Jesus' death as "the Passover lamb" slaughtered for the salvation of everyone who believes (1 Cor. 5:7). See *NIDNTT-A*, 442-443.

PASTOR

New Testament

Verb: ποιμήν (*poimēn*), GK *4478* (S *4166*), 18x. A *poimēn* is a "shepherd," a person who tends a flock. In Eph. 4:11, this word is often translated "pastors." The English word "pastor" is derived from the Latin word *pascere*, which means "to feed" (Middle English, *pastour*). See *shepherd*.

PASTURELAND

Old Testament

Noun: מִגְרָשׁ (*migrāš*), GK 4494 (S 4054), 114x. *migrāš* is an open area of land surrounding and belonging to a city or temple. Although many translate it as "pastureland," it more likely means "open space" or "open land." However, because the *migrāš* around the Levitical cities have a radius of over a quarter mile (1,000 cubits, cf. Num. 35:4), it is unlikely that whole area is exclusively open fields. (The KJV consistently translates *migrāš* as "suburbs," which adequately conveys the idea of territory surrounding a city but which unfortunately gives the impression that the area is built up, which is not necessarily the case.)

The boundary of the *migrāš* may have been marked in some way, and the purpose of the open space seems to be to distinguish the city from the territory around it. But it also serves practical purposes, one of which is pastureland. This is its primary function around the Levitical cities, where *migrāš* is most frequently mentioned: "The cities will be theirs to live in, and their *open spaces* will be for their cattle, their livestock, and all their animals" (Num. 35:3; cf. Jos. 21:2ff, 1 Chr. 6:55ff.). Elsewhere, *migrāš* refers to the open spaces around both the temple and the city of Ezekiel's eschatological vision (Ezek. 45:2; 48:17). See *NIDOTTE*, 3:1140.

PATH

Old Testament

Noun: אֹרַח (*ʾōraḥ*), GK 784 (S 734), 59x. Deriving from the verb *ʾāraḥ* ("to journey, wander"), *ʾōraḥ* is translated variously as "path, way, road." It can bear either a literal or a figurative reference.

(1) Only rarely is *ʾōraḥ* used in the literal sense of a physical route from one place to another (e.g., Gen. 49:17; Jdg. 5:6). While the English term "path" may suggest a small, curvy, country trail, *ʾōraḥ* is in no way limited to this meaning. For example, in Isa. 41:3, a divinely appointed conqueror (probably Cyrus) is described as traveling down an *ʾōraḥ*, and it is unlikely that such a person would travel a narrow trail through the wilderness. In such instances, *ʾōraḥ* simply means "route, way," which in context is more than simply a "road."

(2) In most of its occurrences, *ʾōrah* is used figuratively for one's conduct or lifestyle, which can be righteous or wicked. Righteous conduct is described as "the *paths* of life" (Prov. 2:19), "the *paths* of justice" (Prov. 2:8), "the *paths* of the LORD" (Ps. 25:10), and sometimes just "the *path*" (Prov. 15:10; Isa. 30:11). We are told that God will make smooth the paths of all who acknowledge him (Prov. 3:6; cf. Isa. 26:7). In contrast, wicked conduct is called an "evil *path*" (Ps. 119:101) and a "*path* of falsehood" (Ps. 119:104). Such paths are crooked (Prov. 2:15).

Often *ʾōrah* is used interchangeably with *derek*, "way" (Prov. 2:8; 4:14). Surprisingly, *ʾōrah* is used almost exclusively in poetic, rather than narrative, texts (primarily Ps., Prov., and Job). It is used only once in a narrative text (Gen. 18:11), where it is used idiomatically as "the *way* of women," which in context means the ability to bear children. See *NIDOTTE*, 1:511-12.

Noun: דֶּרֶךְ (*derek*), GK 2006 (S 1870),

712x. *derek* may be translated in numerous ways, both literal and metaphorical, including "way, road, path, journey, conduct." See *way*.

New Testament

Noun: ὁδός (*hodos*), GK *3847* (S *3598*), 101x. *hodos* is basically a "road" or "path" on which one travels, or the act of traveling. It can also mean "the way" of life. See *way*.

PATIENCE, (BE) PATIENT

Old Testament

Idiom: אֶרֶךְ אַפַּיִם (*ʾerek ʾappayim*), GK 800, 678 (S 750, 639), 14x. The Heb. expression for "patience" is an idiom that translate literally "long of nose." This characteristic is also translated as "slow to anger" and "longsuffering" (KJV).

(1) In Proverbs, *ʾerek ʾappayim* is an attribute of the wise person (Prov. 19:11). Those who possess patience have great understanding (14:29), the ability to calm a quarrel (15:18), and the means to persuade a king (25:25). Conversely, a person "short of nose" (*qebar ʾappayim*, as in Prov. 14:17) is impatient or quick-tempered (cf. the English idioms "hothead" or "short-fused").

(2) Most often, *ʾerek ʾappayim* occurs as a divine attribute, a characteristic of God. It first occurs in Exod. 34:6, where God proclaims his name to Moses, "The Lord, the Lord, the compassionate and gracious God, slow to anger, abounding in love and faithfulness" (cf. Num. 14:18; Neh. 9:17; Ps. 86:15; 103:8; 145:8; Jer. 15:15; Joel 2:13; Jon. 4:2; Nah. 1:3). God's patience must not be underestimated. Because he is patient with us, he does not treat us as we deserve; thus, we do not perish. Reflecting on these things, the psalmist writes, "The Lord is compassionate and gracious, slow to anger, abounding in love. He will not always accuse, nor will he harbor his anger forever; he does not treat us as our sins deserve or repay us according to our iniquities" (Ps. 103:8–10).

Idiom: אֶרֶךְ־רוּחַ (*ʾerek rûah*), GK 800, 8120 (S 750, 7307, 1x (Eccl. 7:8). Literally "long of spirit." This expression is translated as either "patient in spirit" (NASB, KJV) or simply "patience" (NIV) with the same general meaning as above. See *NIDOTTE* 1:464, 516-17.

New Testament

Verb: μακροθυμέω (*makrothymeō*), GK *3428* (S *3114*), 10x.

Noun: μακροθυμία (*makrothymia*), GK *3429* (S *3115*), 14x.

These words are normally translated as some form of "patience, endurance" (especially Heb. 6:9–15; Jas. 5:7–11; 2 Pet. 3:4–15). From *macros*, "long" (in terms of time), and *thymos*, "the soul" as the seat of feelings and passions (including anger, temper), this word group suggests the same as the Heb., "to be long of feeling, delay one's anger" (as in "longsuffering").

(1) Patience is first of all a quality of God. He shows his patience in that he wishes everyone to repent (2 Pet. 3:9) and be saved (3:15), so that he delays punishment (Rom. 2:4), as in Paul's case (1 Tim. 1:16). God's patience provides the extra time sometimes needed to bring someone to repentance; but when that person fails to repent, the punishment is even greater (cf. Rom. 2:4). God waited "patiently" for the ark to be built despite the world's sin (1 Pet. 3:20), and even now he is "patient" with the vessels of wrath made for destruction (Rom. 9:22)—a patience that shows his mercy. Lk. 18:7, a difficult passage, probably means that God will be patient in hearing the requests of his elect and answer them. God's immeasurable patience with the sinner's debt is the basis for human forgiveness of human sin (cf. Mt. 18:23–35).

(2) This word group is used of human patience as well (Acts 26:3), as when a farmer patiently waits for the crops (Jas. 5:7b) and when the two servants cry out for patience in the parable on forgiveness (Mt. 18:26, 29); here human patience links with Peter's need to forgive seventy-seven times (i.e., an unlimited number; cf. 6:12, 14–15).

(3) Patience is an aspect of the fruit of the Spirit (Gal. 5:22), and the believer should be patient with everyone (Eph. 4:2;

Col. 1:11; 3:12; 1 Thess. 5:14; Heb. 6:12). It characterizes Paul (2 Cor. 6:6; 2 Tim. 3:10), the prophets (Jas. 5:10), and those who through faith and patience inherit the promise (Heb. 6:12). The believer's love is patient (1 Cor. 13:4); Abraham was patient in waiting for God's promise (Heb. 6:15).

(4) The believer should especially be patient while waiting for the Lord's return in the face of suffering (Jas. 5:7–8). Timothy is to preach, rebuke, and exhort in the present hour "with all patience" (2 Tim. 4:2). See *NIDNTT-A*, 787-89.

Noun: ὑπομονη (*hypomonē*), GK *5705* (S *5281*), 32x. *hypomonē* is occasionally used to begin across the sense of patient endurance, as in Rom. 12:12, where it is connected with persecution: "Be joyful in hope, *patient* in affliction, faithful in prayer." See *endurance*.

PATTERN

Old Testament

Noun: דְּמוּת (*d*ᵉ*mût*), GK 1952 (S 1823), 25x. *d*ᵉ*mût* denotes a likeness between two things (see *likeness*). It can also indicate an image or pattern (e.g., 2 Ki. 16:10).

New Testament

Noun: τύπος (*typos*), GK *5596* (S *5179*), 15x. *typos* is a "pattern, example, model," taken from the concept of an impression or a mark left behind by something on a surface. See *example*.

PAY ATTENTION

New Testament

Verb: προσέχω (*prosechō*), GK *4668* (S *4337*), 24x. *prosechō* means "to guard, watch out, pay attention." See *guard*.

PAY BACK

New Testament

Verb: κομίζω (*komizō*), GK *3152* (S *2865*), 10x. *komizō* means "to receive, pay back." See *receive*.

(BE AT) PEACE

Old Testament

Verb: שָׁלֵם (*šālēm*), GK 8966 (S 7999), 116x. *šālēm* means "to repay, reward, fulfill, be at peace." It is used in a variety of contexts. See *repay*.

PEACE

Old Testament

Noun: שָׁלוֹם (*šālôm*), GK 8934 (S 7965), 237x. *šālôm* is one of the most important words in the OT. In addition to "peace," this word can be translated as "prosperity, well-being, health, completeness, safety."

(1) About 25x in the OT *šālôm* is used a specific greeting. David instructs his men to greet Nabal with, "Long life to you! *Good health* to you and your household! And *good health* to all that is yours!" (1 Sam. 25:6, NIV; lit., "A life of *peace* to you and to your house, *peace*, and to all which is to you, *peace*"). Aaron's blessing finishes on a note of *šālôm*, "The Lord bless you and keep you; the Lord make his face shine upon you and be gracious to you; the Lord turn his face toward you and give you *peace*" (Num. 6:24–26). Often, modern Israelis greet one another with saying, *šālôm*.

(2) In other places, *šālôm* has a nuance of greeting but is a stronger word to denote personal well-being, prosperity, or bodily health. For example, in Jer. 6:14; 8:11, the idea of giving a greeting of *šālôm* when there is no *šālôm* means that there is not true well-being, prosperity, or safety among the people. By contrast, in God's ideal kingdom "the mountains will bring prosperity to the people" (Ps. 72:3; cf. v. 8). When the psalmist says there is no "soundness" in his bones (Ps. 38:3), he is probably indicating some physical illness. *šālôm* suggests emotional wellness in Prov. 3:2, for following the path of wisdom will give a person an overall sense of *šālôm*. The wicked, on the other hand, experience no inner sense of "peace" (Isa. 48:22; 57:21; 59:8).

(3) *šālôm* can also denote a setting of positive relations between friends, parties, or even nations. This word is used nearly 60x to refer to the absence of strife. "During Solomon's lifetime Judah and Israel, from Dan to Beersheba, lived in *safety*, each man under his own vine and fig tree" (1 Ki. 4:25). Here, *šālôm* means more than

simply the absence of war, for it also speaks of completeness, wholeness, and harmony. This is the meaning when the biblical writers say in 1 Sam. 7:14, "There was *peace* between Israel and the Amorites." The prayer of God's people for their city and nation is that there may be "peace" (Ps. 122:6–8; 128:6).

(4) On a spiritual level, *šālôm* can also indicate peace with God: "I will listen to what God the Lord will say: he promises *peace* to his people, his saints" (Ps. 85:8). If God's people keep their minds focused on him, the Lord "will keep them in perfect *peace*" (Isa. 26:3). On four occasions, God talks about making a "covenant of peace" either with an individual or a nation (Num. 25:12; Isa. 54:10; Ezek. 34:25; 37:26). All peace comes from the Lord, and he is the foundation of peace (1 Ki. 2:33; Mic. 5:5). This peace comes as a result of restored righteousness (Isa. 32:17; 48:18; 53:5; 60:17). And in a glorious eschatological passage, the prophet Isaiah looks ahead to the birth of that child who will be "Prince of Peace" (Isa. 9:6). This is fulfilled in Jesus Christ, who is "our peace" (Eph. 2:14). See *NIDOTTE 4:118.*

New Testament

Noun: εἰρήνη (*eirēnē*), GK *1645* (S *1515*), 92x. This word, commonly translated "peace" in the NT, has both classical Gk. and Heb. underpinnings. In classical Gk. *eirēnē* describes a situation that results from the cessation of hostilities or war and can also refer to the state of law and order that makes the fruits of prosperity possible. *eirēnē* can also characterize peaceful conduct toward others. The Stoic philosophers, like the ones Paul encountered at the Areopagus in Athens (Acts 17:16–34), introduced the idea of spiritual peace, although in limited references.

The LXX translates Heb. *šālôm* 250x with *eirēnē*. Peace can, ironically, prevail internally even when the violence of war is at its peak externally. Conversely, inner spiritual turmoil can be raging out of control when peaceful conditions prevail in the land. In other words, "peace" is a state of being that lacks nothing and has no fear of being troubled in its tranquility; it is euphoria coupled with security. For more on the OT concept of peace, see *šālôm.*

Matthew, Mark, and Luke echo the OT meaning of peace in their presentation of Jesus. In Luke's birth narrative, the angels' voices explode with praise as they proclaim, "Glory to God in the highest heaven, and *peace* on earth to people he favors!" (Lk. 2:14). This peace is God's favor bestowed on his people. Not all people receive this peace—only those who have been reconciled to God.

eirēnē is also used in greetings and partings to communicate blessings (Mt. 10:13). However, when one is exhorted to "go in peace," it sometimes follows an experience of salvation, such as in the case with the woman who anointed Jesus' feet with oil (Lk. 7:50) and the woman with the issue of blood (8:48). The only place the term occurs in John is in the Farewell Discourses. "Peace" is Jesus' parting gift to his disciples (Jn. 14:27; 16:33; 20:19, 21, 26). In other words, Christ is a mediator of *eirēnē*. The NT depicts Jesus as achieving the highest form of peace for us through his reconciling death on the cross—the ultimate state of well-being (see Eph. 2:14–18).

Paul acknowledges that *eirēnē* is a direct derivative of justification, of "having been made right with God" (Rom. 5:1): "Since we have been declared righteous by faith, we have *peace* with God." Perhaps this is why the noun appears in tandem with "grace" in the introductions of his and other NT letters (Rom. 1:7; 1 Cor. 1:3, 1 Tim. 1:2; 2 Tim. 1:2; Tit. 1:4; Phlm. 3; 1 Pet. 1:2; 2 Jn. 3; Rev. 1:4). This combination of terms demonstrates the wide-ranging scope of salvation.

In a sense, then, *eirēnē* is the opposite of disorder. Paul uses the word in his lengthy marriage chapter in 1 Cor. 7 as the reason why a Christian believer ought to stay in a "mixed marriage" as long as the unbelieving partner desires it (7:15). If the unbelieving partner desires to leave, however, that may achieve the goal of harmony among individuals. Paul uses the same reasoning in 14:33, where order in church meetings is the main subject under discussion. Order, structure, and clear communication will more likely lead to a confession, not confusion. Ultimately, the salvation of the unbelieving partner (ch. 7) or a visitor (ch. 14) is in focus.

eirēnē should also be pursued among people in general. Our peaceful disposition should extend beyond the walls of the church in an attempt to impact outsiders (2 Tim. 2:22). Heb. 12:14 affirms the thought: "Pursue *peace* with everyone, and holiness—without it no one will see the Lord." Jesus said, "Blessed are the *peacemakers* [a compound word using *eirēnē*], because they will be called the sons of God" (Mt. 5:9). Peace starts with God, is revealed most graphically on the cross of Christ, is observed as a chief fruit in the transformed children of God, and is a major spiritual component of the ever-growing kingdom of God. See *NIDNTT-A*, 165-67.

PEACE OFFERING

Old Testament

Noun: שֶׁלֶם (*šelem*), GK 8968 (S 8002), 87x. *šelem* is the word used for the fellowship offering or the peace offering, one of the required sacrifices of the Israelites. The name tells us something about nature of this offering: the person or community offering this sacrifice to God was in a positive, covenant-keeping relationship with him and God's people enjoyed all the fullness of his peace (Lev. 3; 7:11–34). See *fellowship offering*.

PENALTY

Old Testament

Noun: אָשָׁם (*ʾāšām*), GK 871 (S 817), 47x. *ʾāšām* is a "guilt offering," but it can also be a more general word for "penalty." See *guilt offering*.

PENNY

See *denarius*.

PENTECOST

New Testament

Noun: πεντηκοστή (*pentēcostē*), GK *4300* (S *4005*), 3x. *pentēcostē* is, strictly speaking, the ordinal numeral "fiftieth." As used in the NT, it refers to the "fiftieth day" after Passover. In the Jewish liturgical year this was the Feast of Weeks (Deut. 16:10; cf. Lev. 23:15–16) or the Feast of Harvest (Exod. 23:16). In Christian circles this day became known as "Pentecost," the time when the Holy Spirit was poured out on the church to begin God's harvest of both Jews and Gentiles to the Christian faith. This event came as the fulfillment of Jesus' promise to send forth his Spirit upon his church (Lk. 24:49; Jn. 14:25–26; 15:26; Acts 1:8). *pentēcostē* itself is used three times in the NT: Acts 2:1; 20:16; 1 Cor. 16:8; it has become an established day in the Christian liturgical year. See *NIDNTT-A*, 452.

PEOPLE

Old Testament

Noun: אָדָם (*ʾādām*), GK 132, 134 (S 120, 121), 558x. The basic meaning and most common translation of *ʾādām* is "man." Unlike *ʾîš*, which carries not only the sense of "man" but also of "male," *ʾādām* may be used by the OT writers to describe humanity as a whole—men, women, and children. See *man*.

Noun: בֵּן (*bēn*), GK 1201 (S 1121), **4941x**. *bēn* has a wide variety of nuances in the OT; in the plural it often means "people." See *son*.

Noun: עַם (*ʿam*), GK 6639 (S 5971), 1869x. *ʿam* can refer to military troops (Num. 20:20; Jos. 8:1) or a general assembly of people (Ruth 4:9; 1 Sam. 10:17). Especially in the plural, this word is often used to refer to the "nations" of the world (Ps. 18:47; 45:5; Isa. 12:4; 63:3). But most frequently *ʿam* denotes a large group of people united by a familial relationship. The relationship referred to by *ʿam* is always the result of some kind of family tie. In the ancient Near East, identity was shaped primarily by family connection. Through kin and clan one had status and was protected; one was always loyal to one's people. To be cast out from one's *ʿam* was accordingly a severe (and potentially lethal) punishment (Gen. 17:14; Lev. 7:20–27; Ezek. 14:7–9).

The Israelites were considered the *ʿam* of God (Num. 11:29; Deut. 7:6; Jdg. 20:2). They were God's chosen people; they were part of his family. This special status indicated that God would protect the Israelites and look after their well-being. In a sense, they were the "next of kin" of God himself. According to Rom. 9-11, Gentiles who believe in Christ have been specially grafted into the family of God and can rejoice in having a privileged relationship with God because of the work of the Messiah, the firstborn heir of God and the first and greatest brother in the family of God (Rom. 8:29).

New Testament

Noun: γένος (*genos*), GK *1169* (S *1085*), 20x. *genos* means "people" and can be used to denote nationality, e.g., Barnabas was "a native of Cyprus" (Acts 4:36; cf. Mk. 7:26; Acts 18:2, 24). It is used to refer to large groups of people, often to the Jewish race (Acts 7:19; 13:26; 2 Cor. 11:26; Gal. 1:14; Phil. 3:5). Peter applies this term to the church when he says, "you are a chosen people" (1 Pet. 2:9). *genos* can also mean "offspring" (see *offspring*), "family" (see *family*), or "kind" (see *kind*).

Noun: ἔθνος (*ethnos*), GK *1620* (S *1484*), 162x. *ethnos* appears in the NT with two meanings, "nation" and "Gentile." In the latter sense, it refers specifically to all non-Jews, that is, to people groups foreign to Israel—specifically those groups that do not profess faith in the God of Israel (Mt. 10:18; Acts 11:1; 14:5). By extension, *ethnos* also sometimes refer to non-Israelite Christians. See *nations*.

Noun: λαός (*laos*), GK *3295* (S *2992*), 142x. *laos* means the general public or the entire human race. Reflecting OT usage, it is also used in a more specialized way to refer to Israel as the people of God. Building on this OT usage, the NT writers use *laos* to refer to the church, made up of both Jews and Gentiles, as the true people of God.

(1) *laos* can refer to crowds of people or the general public, mostly in the gospels and Acts. John the Baptist directed his preaching to the *laos* who came (Lk. 3:18, 21). Jesus also taught and performed miracles among crowds of people (Mt. 4:23; Lk. 6:17; 7:1; Jn. 8:2). The apostles preached, taught, and performed miracles among the people after Jesus had ascended (Acts 4:1, 2; 5:12, 20, 25; 21:40). In some cases *laos* can signify a distinction between the Jewish leaders and the common people (Mt. 26:5; 27:64; Mk. 4:2; Acts 4:17, 21).

(2) *laos* can mean all people on the earth. In Lk. 2:10 the angel said to the shepherds, "I bring you good news of great joy that will be for all *the people*." Simeon saw the baby Jesus and praised God saying that he had prepared his salvation "in the sight of all *people*," both Gentiles and Jews (Lk. 2:31). Revelation looks to the fulfillment of this inclusive work of salvation as it pictures people from "every tribe, language, *people*, and nation" gathered at the throne of God (Rev. 5:9; 7:9).

(3) Israel is called God's chosen "people" (Acts 3:23; 4:10, 27; Heb. 11:25), reflecting the use of *laos* in the LXX (Exod. 3:7, 10; Lev. 26:12; Isa. 5:13; 40:1). While some texts in Jesus' birth narratives, like the ones above, speak about his coming to save all people, others indicate God's specific purpose to save his people Israel in fulfillment of OT promises (Mt. 1:21; 2:6; Lk. 1:77). Zechariah, the father of John the Baptist, says, "Praise be to the Lord, the God of Israel, because he has come and has redeemed his *people*" (Lk. 1:68). Even though Israel by and large ends up rejecting God's provision for salvation, Paul says that God has not rejected "his people" (Rom. 11:1–2).

(4) Finally, Christians are called the people of God. The prophet Zechariah had looked forward to the day when many nations would become God's people (Zech. 2:11). As his prophecy began to be fulfilled,

the leaders of the Jerusalem church realized that God had begun to gather "a *people* for himself" from among the Gentiles (Acts 15:14). The NT writers then use the "people of God" language that had been applied to Israel in the OT and apply it to the church (see 1 Pet. 2:9–10 and Hos. 1:9–10; 2:23; 2 Cor. 6:16 and Lev. 26:12; Rom. 9:25 and Hos. 2:23; Heb. 2:17; 4:9; 13:12). Finally, we look forward to the day when God will dwell with people from every nation, whether Jew or Gentile, who "will be his *people*, and God himself will be with them and be their God" (Rev. 21:3). See *NIDNTT-A*, 329-30.

Noun: φυλή (*phylē*), GK *5876* (S *5443*), 31x. *phylē* refers to a "tribe" or to a larger unit such as a "nation" or "people." See *tribe*.

PEOPLE(S)

Old Testament

Noun: מִשְׁפָּחָה (*mišpāḥâ*), GK 5476 (S 4940), 304x. The noun *mišpāḥâ* designates a subgroup of a larger division, and is, therefore, variously translated as "clan, family, people" as well as "kind, kingdoms, nation." See *clan*, *kind*, *nation*.

PERCEIVE

Old Testament

Verb: בִּין (*bîn*), GK 1067 (S 995), 171x. *bin* is most commonly found in the wisdom literature, especially Job and Proverbs. It is sometimes used in the general sense of "to know" (Prov. 24:12; Mic. 4:12), but more often refers to a technical, detailed, or specific understanding. Alternate translations such as "perceive, discern" may more readily capture the nuance of the term. See *understand*.

Verb: רָאָה (*rāʾâ*), GK 8011 (S 7200 and 7202), 1,311x. *rāʾâ* is the most frequent Heb. verb for "seeing," encompassing a variety of actions including physical, visionary, and mental. See *see*.

Verb: שָׁמַע (*šāmaʿ*), GK 9048 (S 8085), 1165x. *šāmaʿ* means "to hear, listen, pay attention to, perceive, understand, obey, proclaim, announce." See *hear*.

New Testament

Verb: ἐπιγινώσκω (*epiginōskō*), GK *2105* (S *1921*), 44x. *epiginōskō* can mean to "know, perceive, recognize, understand." See *know*.

Verb: θεωρέω (*theōreō*), GK *2555* (S *2334*), 58x. Most uses of *theōreō* refer to physical sight or watching, but it can also be used for perception and understanding. See *see*.

Verb: κατανοέω (*katanoeō*), GK *2917* (S *2657*), 14x. Although this term is sometimes translated as "consider, perceive, look," these English words do not communicate the depth of knowledge presumed by the word. See *consider*.

Verb: ὁράω (*horaō*), GK *3972* (S *3708*), 454x. *horaō* is the most frequently used word for seeing in the NT. It can also mean "appear, perceive, consider" (i.e., a more mental seeing). See *see*.

PERFECT

Old Testament

Adjective: תָּמִים (*tāmîm*), GK 9459 (S 8549), 91x. Most often *tāmîm* describes animals or crops intended for sacrificial offerings as "unblemished" or "whole." Elsewhere, this word is used to describe God as "perfect" (2 Sam. 22:31), both in terms of his knowledge (Job 37:16) and his law (Ps. 19:8). See *unblemished*.

New Testament

Verb: τελειόω (*teleioō*), GK *5457* (S *5048*), 23x. *teleioō* refers to attaining an end or purpose, in the sense of being complete or perfect. See *end*.

Adjective: τέλειος (*teleios*), GK *5455* (S *5046*), 19x. *teleios* conveys a range of meanings: "perfect, mature, complete." It can refer to something of the highest standard (i.e., "perfect" Jas. 1:4a, 17, 25) or fully developed, "perfect" or "complete" in a moral sense (Mt. 5:48; Jas. 1:4b; 3:2). See *end*.

PERFORM

Old Testament

Verb: עָשָׂה (*ʿāśâ*), GK 6913 (S 6213), 2632x. The verb *ʿāśâ* has the basic meaning "to do, make," appears in numerous contexts, and is used in a variety of ways. See *make.*

New Testament

Verb: ἐργάζομαι (*ergazomai*), GK *2237* (S *2038*), 41x. *ergazomai* is derived from *ergon* (work) and means "to work, produce, perform, do" something. See *work.*

PERFUME

New Testament

Noun: μύρον (*myron*), GK *3693* (S *3464*), 14x. *myron* is a precious, strongly scented liquid or gelatinous substance used in the ancient world for a variety of purposes, including burial. The Greek translation of the OT (LXX) uses *myron* both for the oil with which the priests of the tabernacle were anointed (e.g., Exod. 30:25; Ps. 133:2) and for the ointment used to prepare bodies for burial (2 Chr. 16:14).

In the NT, the gospels recount the story of the woman who anointed Jesus with *myron* as he dined at the house of Simon the leper (Mt. 26:6ff.). Both Mk. 14:3 and Jn. 12:3 further specify that the *myron* was of pure nard, a rare and valuable ointment. The gospels emphasize the costliness of the perfume; in Jn. 12:5 some of those present suggest that the perfume might have been sold for 300 denarii (a denarius was a day's wage) instead of being lavished on Jesus. Rev. 18:13 also indicates its great value, for there *myron* is included among other precious commodities (e.g., gold, silver, pearls, ivory) traded by Babylon. Mk. 14:3 powerfully demonstrates the true extent of the woman's lavish devotion to Jesus: not only did she anoint Jesus with a very precious substance but she used *all* of the *myron* by breaking the vial. Jesus claims that the woman's anointing was done in order to prepare him for burial (Mt. 26:12); in fact Lk. 23:56 records that the women who followed Jesus later prepared spices and *myra* (plural of *myron*) for his dead body after the crucifixion. See *NIDNTT-A*, 532.

PERISH

Old Testament

Verb: אָבַד (*ʾābad*), GK 6 (S 6), 185x. *ʾābad* means "to perish, destroy, demolish, become lost." It has a variety of uses in the OT.

(1) This verb can refer to the physical destruction of things, such as "carved images" (Num. 35:52), "weapons" (2 Sam. 1:27), a lion (Job 4:11), a harvest (Joel 1:11), and even the earth and the heavens (Ps. 102:25–26). In addition, *ʾābad* can refer to the annihilation of people through killing them, such as "the whole royal family" (2 Ki. 11:1), the house of Ahab (9:8), and the prophets and priests of Baal (10:19). God sent the nations against Judah to destroy it (2 Ki. 24:2). In Esther, this word is used for the plot of Haman to "destroy" the Jews (Est. 3:13, 4:7).

(2) *ʾābad* can sometimes be used for the physical death of a single individual. Eccl. 7:15 says, "A righteous man *perishes* in his righteousness." Esther says about the dangerous task that Mordecai asked her to perform: "If I *perish*, I *perish*" (Est. 4:16). According to Prov. 21:28, "a false witness will perish"; so will someone who speaks lies (19:9).

(3) The perishing that takes place through *ʾābad* can also be a spiritual perishing, though one cannot rule out a physical perishing as well. According to the psalmist, "the way of the wicked *will perish*" (Ps. 1:6); does this mean a wicked person will die physically or to be cast out of God's presence? Probably both are involved. Note too Ps. 92:8: "For surely your enemies, O LORD, surely your enemies *will perish*; all evildoers will be scattered." God's people are not exempt from this either, if they fail to obey the Lord their God (see Deut. 30:18).

(4) At times, *ʾābad* is used for the perishing of something that is more abstract. Ezek. 19:5 speaks of hope that is "lost" (KJV) or "unfulfilled" (NIV)—i.e. it has perished (cf. Prov. 11:7). Similarly, Ezek. 12:22 speaks of a vision that has "come to nothing," that is, prophecy has perished. The "memory" of someone can also perish (Job 18:17).

(5) Finally, *ʾābad* is also used to refer to

the "lost" donkeys of Saul's father (1 Sam. 9:3, 20), and to the people of Israel as "lost" sheep (Jer. 50:6). See *NIDOTTE*, 1:223–25.

Verb: תָּמַם (*tāmam*), GK 9462 (S 8552), 64x. *tāmam* is used for a wide range of ideas having to do with ending, completion, or even destruction. See *end*.

New Testament

Verb: ἀπόλλυμι (*apollymi*), GK *660* (S *622*), 90x. *apollymi* means "to destroy, perish, lose." See *lose*.

PERMIT, (TO BE) PERMITTED

New Testament

Verb: δίδωμι (*didōmi*), GK *1443* (S *1325*), 415x. This common verb conveys the basic idea of a transaction or transferring an object and is usually translated "give, grant, yield, permit." See *give*.

Verb: ἔξεστι (*exesti*), GK *2003* (S *1832*), 31x. *exesti* is an impersonal verb that means "it is lawful, it is permitted." See *lawful*.

Verb: ἐπιτρέπω (*epitrepō*), GK *2205* (S *2010*), 18x. *epitrepō* essentially means "to permit, allow, let." The KJV often translates this word "suffer," in the sense of allowing. It is used when asking for permission (Mt. 8:21, "*let* me go and bury my father") or for granting it (Mt. 19:8, "Moses *permitted* you to divorce"). Demons asked Jesus for permission to enter pigs (Lk. 8:32). This verb can also refer to providence (1 Cor. 16:7, "I hope to spend some time with you, if the LORD *permits*"). An interesting, if controversial, occurrence of *epitrepō* occurs in 1 Cor. 14:34 where Paul denies women permission to speak in the church; in 1 Tim. 2:12 he restates it this way: "I do not *permit* a woman to teach or to have authority over a man." See *NIDNTT-A*, 201.

PERSECUTE

Old Testament

Verb: רָדַף (*rādap*), GK 8103 (S 7291), 144x. *rādap* means "to pursue, follow after, persecute." See *pursue*.

New Testament

Verb: διώκω (*diōkō*), GK *1503* (S *1377*), 45x. *diōkō* means to "pursue" (see *pursue*) or, most frequently, "persecute." Persecution is a common companion to those who follow Jesus Christ. In fact, just as the OT prophets were harassed and persecuted for the Lord's sake, so also will the followers of Christ be persecuted (Mt. 5:12; Acts 7:52). Through persecution, believers imitate their Lord (Jn. 5:16; 15:20). Paul, who was himself once a persecutor of those who followed Jesus, asserts that he now receives persecution for the sake of Christ Jesus (Gal. 5:11; 2 Tim. 3:11), as will all who seek to live godly lives (2 Tim. 3:12). When Christians are persecuted, Christ is persecuted as well (Acts 9:4–5), but believers must not compromise the truth of the gospel to avoid persecution (Gal. 6:12). Jesus spoke of the blessed status of those who suffer for righteousness' sake (Mt. 5:10–12). During persecution, believers may rely on the help, strength, and saving power of Jesus Christ (Rom. 8:35–39; 2 Cor. 4:7–12; 12:10). In perspective, God is to be thanked when Christians endure persecution (2 Thess. 1:3–4). See *NIDNTT-A, 148-49*.

Verb: θλίβω (*thlibō*), GK *2567* (S *2346*), 10x. *thlibō* literally denotes pressing, squeezing, or crushing. A multitude forces Jesus to get into a boat that was at hand so that they will not press him (Mk. 3:9). Jesus proclaims that the way that leads to life is "narrow" *or squeezed in*, and few are those who find it (Mt. 7:14).

Figuratively, *thlibō* describes the pressure of worldly persecutions common to all people (1 Tim. 5:10), but it is usually related to the persecutions specific to believers. In the middle of a list of physical afflictions, the author of Hebrews describes the OT saints as "persecuted" for their faith (Heb. 11:37). Paul writes that he and his group have been persecuted for the comfort and salvation of the Corinthians (2 Cor. 1:6); that they are "persecuted" in every way (4:8) and "pressed in" on every side (7:5). Though these persecutions are many and severe, they are to be expected (1 Thess. 3:4). However, God promises relief to believers and vengeance on those by whom they are persecuted when the Lord appears with his angels (2 Thess. 1:6–7). See *NIDNTT-A*, 251-52.*

PERSECUTION

New Testament

Noun: διωγμός (*diōgmos*), GK *1501* (S *1375*), 10x. *diōgmos* is usually rendered "persecution" in the NT, denoting the result of physical or verbal harassment and is associated with the noun *thlipsis* ("oppression, affliction"). The term derives from the verb *diōkō* ("pursue, chase") and literally refers to the result of pursuing, thus "persecution." The context of this persecution can be physical, socioeconomic, or emotional. The origin of the "persecution" can be the world in general (Mt. 13:21; Mk. 4:17) or a specific group (e.g., Acts 13:50, "the Jews"). Jesus warns his disciples that they will experience persecution because they follow him (Mk. 10:30; see also Jn. 15:20, where Jesus says: "If they persecuted me, they will persecute you also"). Acts tells of persecution arising in the early church: "On that day a great persecution broke out against the church at Jerusalem" (Acts 8:1).

Paul encourages the Roman Christians by saying that even persecutions cannot separate the believer from the love of Christ (Rom. 8:35). He shares his own experiences of persecution with the Corinthians (2 Cor. 12:10; see also 2 Tim. 3:11). Significantly, in his commendation of the Thessalonians Paul links the church's growth and perseverance with persecution (2 Thess. 1:4). See *NIDNTT-A*, 148-49.

PERSERVERANCE, PERSEVERE

New Testament

Verb: ὑπομένω (*hypomenō*), GK *5702* (S *5278*), 17x. *hypomenō* may be rendered positively as "endure, stand firm, persevere." As a weight-lifter bears up under the weight of the bar, one perseveres under trouble or affliction (Mt. 10:22; 24:13; Rom. 12:12). See *endure*.

Noun: ὑπομονη (*hypomonē*), GK *5705* (S *5281*), 32x. *hypomonē* refers to perseverance in the face of hostile forces. Job, for example, manifested great perseverance in the midst of his afflictions from Satan (Jas. 5:11). See *endurance*.

PERSON

Old Testament

Verb: נֶפֶשׁ (*nepeš*), GK 5883 (S 5315), 757x. *nepeš* has a wide range of meaning; the basic meaning is "breath," but it can also mean "soul, life, entire being." See *soul*.

New Testament

Noun: ἄνθρωπος (*anthrōpos*), GK *476* (S *444*), 550x. *anthrōpos* means "man, human being, mankind." See *man*.

Noun: ψυχή (*psychē*), GK *6034* (S *5590*), 103x. *psychē* has a wide variety of meaning in the NT, being shaped by the Heb. word *nepeš*. Among other things, it means "life, soul, person, mind." See *life*.

PERSUADE

New Testament

Verb: διαλέγομαι (*dialegomai*), GK *1363* (S *1256*), 13x. *dialegomai* means "to reason, argue, prove, persuade." See *reason*.

Verb: πείθω (*peithō*), GK *4275* (S *3982*), 52x. *peithō* means "to persuade, convince." In the NT, it has a wide range of application. *peitho* often has the meaning of persuading: "But the chief priests and the elders *persuaded* the crowd to ask for Barabbas and to have Jesus executed" (Mt. 27:20). It is used of those who were persuaded to follow revolutionaries such as Theudas and Judas the Galilean (Acts 5:36–37). Paul persuades the believers in Antioch to continue in the grace of God (13:43). *peitho* can also refer to being convinced, as in 2 Tim. 1:5, where Paul was *convinced* of Timothy's sincere faith. It can denote "to win approval," as Paul asked the Galatians, "Am I now trying to *win the approval* of men, or of God?" (Gal. 1:10).

Often the desired outcome of *peithō* is for a person to believe or trust in Christ. While Paul was in Ephesus, "He entered the synagogue and spoke boldly there for three months, arguing and *persuading* about the kingdom of God" (Acts 19:8). In Paul's dialogue with King Agrippa, he was asked, "Do you think that in such a short time you can *persuade* me to be a Christian?" (Acts 26:28). Paul uses this word to refer to his own personal convictions about the work of God, that nothing can separate us from the love of Christ (Rom. 8:38) and that God will complete his good work of salvation in us (Phil. 1:6). See *NIDNTT-A*, 446-48.

PETITION

Old Testament

Noun: תְּפִלָּה (*tᵉpillâ*), GK 9525 (S 8605), 77x. *tᵉpillâ* is a common word in the OT for "prayer, intercession, petition"; it is related to the verb *pālal* (GK 7137; see *pray*). See *petition*.

New Testament

Noun: δέησις (*deēsis*), GK *1255* (S *1162*), 18x. *deēsis* is a "prayer, petition, supplication" based on a person's need—in the NT always addressed to God. See *prayer*.

PHARISEE

New Testament

Noun: Φαρισαῖος (*Pharisaios*), GK *5757* (S *5330*), 98x. This Semitic word literally means "the separated ones." The Pharisees are the members of an influential religious sect in Judaism. Although the concept of *Pharisaios* existed before the time of Jesus, by the first century these people were held in public esteem and were the respected and thus leading religious group within Judaism.

Along with the scribes, these men were experts in interpreting the Scriptures. A Pharisee was to take the pattern of a pious Israelite as established by the scribes and put it into practice as best he could. In this way he had both religious authority (study and practice of the law) and political authority (council members; see Sanhedrin).

The Pharisees are best known for their interaction with Jesus and the early church as recorded in the Gospels and Acts (they are only mentioned outside these books in Paul's self-reference in Phil. 1:5). Jesus criticizes the Pharisees for their lack of spiritual discernment and of religious behavior (Mt. 5:20; 23:1–32). They are his primary debate partners during his earthly ministry (Mt. 9:14; 15:12; Mk. 2:24; Lk. 11:38–39; Jn. 9; cf. Mt. 23) and contribute to his eventual capture and execution (Mt. 12:14; Jn. 18:3). The Pharisees' understanding of God and the law make them blind to the true claim of religious life in Jesus (Jn. 9:39–41). As Jesus warns the disciples not to be like the Pharisees, modern Christians also need to guard so that we do not harden ourselves against Jesus by our own traditions. See *NIDNTT-A*, 587-88.

PIERCE

Old Testament

Noun: חָלָל (*ḥālāl*), GK 2728 (S 2491), 94x. *ḥālāl* denotes someone who has been pierced for the purpose of killing or wounding and may be translated as "pierced, wounded, killed." It can refer to anyone who has been killed (Deut. 21:1–3), but most commonly refers to those who have been slain or wounded in battle. 1 Ki. 11:15 describes a battle report of Solomon, "Earlier when David was fighting with Edom, Joab the commander of the army, who had gone up to bury the *dead*, had struck down all the men in Edom."

ḥālāl is Ezekiel's standard term to describe those slain as a result of the judgment of exile (35x; see, e.g., Ezek. 28:8; 32:22; see also Jer. 9:1; 14:18; 51:49). He confronts the idolatry of Jerusalem and proclaims, "They will know that I am the LORD, when their people lie *slain* among their idols around their altars" (6:13). See *NIDOTTE* 2:151-152.

New Testament

Verb: νύσσω (*nyssō*), GK *3817* (S *3572*), 1x. *nyssō* means "to pierce." While this term occurs only once in the NT, it has important theological implications. In order to make sure that the three individuals hanging on the crosses were dead so they could be taken down before the start of the Sabbath, Pilate gives orders to break their legs in order to hasten death. But Jesus was already dead, so a soldier "pierces" his side with his spear, and out flows "blood and water" (Jn. 19:34). This is a different verb from the quotation of Zech. 12:10 that follows in Jn. 19:36: "They will look on the one they have pierced" (*ekkenteō*, GK *1708*; cf. also Rev. 1:7). This piercing of Jesus may be the event that John has in mind when later, in asserting the full humanity of Jesus in the context of an early Christian heresy, he insists that Jesus came not "by water only, but by water and blood" (1 Jn. 5:6).*

PIG

New Testament

Noun: χοῖρος (*choiros*), GK *5956* (S *5519*), 12x. *choiros* is the word for "pig." This word is used only the Synoptic Gospels. Most of its uses occur in the story of the healing of a demon-possessed man who was living by himself among the tombs. The demons begged Jesus to allow them to enter into some pigs, and Jesus gave them permission—they ended up drowning themselves (Mt. 8:30–32; Mk. 5:11–13; Lk. 8:32–33). There may have been some irony in this story since the pig was an unclean animal and not suitable to be eaten by a kosher Jew.

Luke uses *choiros* also in the story of the lost son, who ended up feeding pigs in order to earn food (Lk. 15:15–16). Since pigs were unclean animals and not allowed in Jewish diet, they appear only in Gentile areas. In his Sermon on the Mount, Jesus offers this proverb: "Do not give dogs what is sacred; do not throw your pearls to pigs" (Mt. 7:6). In other words, we are to value the good gifts that God has given us, especially his salvation and his word.

PIGEON

New Testament

Noun: περιστερά (*peristera*), GK *4361* (S *4058*), 10x. A dove or pigeon is of the order "Columbiformes." See *dove*.

PILLAR

Old Testament

Noun: עַמּוּד (*ʿammûd*), GK 6647 (S 5982), 112x. *ʿammûd* means "pillar, post" and refers to a columnar support for a structure, whether literal or metaphorical, or to a column-like image, such as a funnel cloud.

(1) *ʿammûd* often refers to the pillars that structurally support buildings or rooftops. In the well-known story of Samson's final victory over the Philistines, he destroys the temple and many Philistines by knocking out of place the supporting "pillars" (Jdg. 16:25–30). Pillars are also mentioned in connection with Solomon's palace: "He built the palace of the forest of Lebanon a hundred cubits long, fifty wide, and thirty high, with four rows of cedar columns supporting trimmed cedar *columns*"(1 Ki. 7:2). The Jerusalem temple also includes pillars, two of which are made of bronze (1 Ki. 7:13–22). They are named "Jachin" ("he shall establish") and "Boaz" ("in it is strength"). These *ʿammûd* were majestic in appearance and stand some 27 feet high. Some scholars suggest that the beauty and symbolic names of the pillars represent the presence of the Lord and the permanence of the Davidic house. The Ezek. temple visions also describe pillars (Ezek. 42:6).

(2) In a similar sense, *ʿammûd* can be used figuratively to describe the "supports" of heaven and earth: "When the earth and all its people quake, it is I who hold its *pillars* firm" (Ps. 75:3). "He shakes the earth from its place and makes its *pillars* tremble" (Job 9:6). These texts may be alluding to the universe as the ultimate temple of God (cf. Isa. 66:1).

(3) Lastly, *ʿammûd* can also denote vaporous columns of smoke, fire, and cloud (Num. 12:5; Deut. 31:15). "During the last watch of the night the LORD looked down from the *pillar* of fire and cloud at the Egyptian army and threw it into confusion" (Exod. 14:24). These visual aids are designed to encourage Israel and remind

them of God's presence during their journey. See *NIDOTTE*, 3:432-34.

New Testament

Noun: στῦλος (*stylos*), GK *5146* (S *4769*), 4x. *stylos* means "pillar," a normally cylindrical column that often supports part of a structure. In the NT it is used only figuratively, gathering its imagery from the strength or significance of a pillar. James, Cephas, and John are central to the Jerusalem church, hence "pillars" of the church (Gal. 2:9). Paul writes his first letter to Timothy so that he can have official instructions how people, especially leadership, are to behave in the church. To underscore the significance of the instructions, Paul reminds Timothy that the church is God's household, part of the very structure of the gospel, hence "a pillar" (not "the pillar"; 1 Tim. 3:15). Individually, we become pillars in the temple of God when we conquer, i.e., remain faithful to death (Rev. 3:12). In his apocalypse, John sees an angel come down from heaven, "robed in a cloud, with a rainbow above his head; his face was like the sun, and his legs were like fiery pillars" (NIV, 10:1).*

PIT

Old Testament

Noun: בּוֹר (*bôr*), GK 1014 (S 953), 65x. *bôr*, often translated as "pit," can also mean "well, dungeon, cistern, grave." (1) A *bôr* is essentially a large pit in the ground, dug for the purpose of storing water or food. David, for example, longs for a drink from "the *well* near the gate of Bethlehem" (2 Sam. 23:15). The Israelites, who had water issues during their sojourn in the desert, can look forward in the promised land to drinking water from "*wells* you did not dig" (Deut. 6:11).

(2) A *bôr* can be a dangerous place, however. Gen. 37 records that Joseph's brother throw him into a *bôr*, from which he cannot escape, before they finally sell him as a slave to passing Midianites (37: 22, 24, 28, 29; the NIV translates *bôr* as "cistern"). If a person digs a "pit" and does not cover it, and a neighbor's animal falls into it, the person who dug the well will be held liable for those injuries (Exod. 21:33–34).

(3) Evidently a *bôr* makes an excellent prison as well (Isa. 24:22). After being purchased by the Egyptian Potiphar and accused of attempted rape by Potiphar's wife, Joseph finds himself in a "dungeon" (Gen. 40:15; 41:14). Jeremiah's opponents cast him into a "cistern" and sinks down into the mud, where he is threatened with death (Jer. 38:6–13).

(4) Finally, *bôr* can also be a euphemism for "the grave"; note the parallel of these two words in such passages as Ps. 30:3; Prov. 1:12; Isa. 14:15; Ezek. 31:16. A person who feels he is about to die (for whatever reason) can say, "I am counted among those who go down to the *pit*" (Ps. 88:4). But the psalmist in Ps. 40 turns to the Lord in such a situation, and he is delivered. He praises God that "he lifted me out of the slimy *pit* … and set my feet on a rock and gave me a firm place to stand" (40: 2). See *NIDOTTE*, 1:620-21.

PITCH (A TENT)

Old Testament

Verb: נָטָה (*nāṭâ*), GK 5742 (S 5186), 216x. *nāṭâ* conveys the basic idea of "to stretch, spread out, pitch [a tent], turn." See *stretch out*.

New Testament

Verb: σκηνόω (*skēnoō*), GK *5012* (S *4637*), 5x. *skēnoō* means "dwell, live," though it often retains the notion of pitching a tent. In Jn. 1:14 the evangelist says of Jesus: "The Word became flesh and made his dwelling [*skēnoō*, lit., 'tabernacled'] among us." That is, Jesus is the incarnation of the glory of God, dwelling among God's people as God did in the tabernacle of the OT. Similarly, Rev. 21:3 says, "Now the dwelling [*skēnē*] of God is with men, and he will live [*skēnoō*] with them" (cf. also 13:6). See also *tabernacle*. See *NIDNTT-A*, 527-28.

Noun: φρέαρ (*phrear*), GK *5853* (S *5421*), 7x. *phrear* means "pit, well." This noun is used three times in the gospels to refer to a simple well from which water can be drawn (Lk. 14:5; Jn. 4:11–12). But in Rev. 9:1–2 it refers to the "shaft" of the Abyss, that subterranean abode of demonic agents who threaten the church but who will eventually receive ultimate judgment from God (cf. also 20:1).*

PITY

New Testament

Verb: ἐλεέω (*eleeō*), GK *1796* (S *1653*), 28x. *eleeō* describes the emotional response and resulting action after encountering the suffering or affliction of another: "to have mercy, feel sorry for, have pity." See *mercy*.

Noun: σπλάγχνον (*splanchnon*), GK *5073* (S *4698*), 11x. *splanchnon* refers to a feeling of "affection, tenderness, compassion, pity." See *affection*.

PLACE

Old Testament

Verb: נוּחַ (*nûaḥ*), GK 5663 (S 5117), 140x. The most basic idea of the verb *nûaḥ* is the action of one object coming to rest, roosting, or landing on another object or in a specific location. See *rest*.

Frequently the object does not come to rest on its own but is caused to rest or be placed in a particular location by someone else (104x). In these instances *nûah* may be translated "set," "put," "place," or even "leave." God "sets" Ezekiel in the valley of dry bones (Ezek. 37:1) and commands Moses to "place" manna before God in the ark, which Aaron does (Exod. 16:33, 34). After the exile, perhaps with eschatological implications, God promises to "place" his people in their land (Ezek. 37:14). See *set*.

Verb: נָתַן (*nātan*), GK 5989 (S 5414), 2014x. *nātan* is a high frequency verb in the OT and bears a wide range of meanings, some of which are "to give, present, allow, permit, surrender, deliver, set, put, place." One main usage of *nātan* is the act of "setting" or "placing" something somewhere, such as "*placing*" curses on enemies (Deut. 30:7), God's majesty on the heavens (Ps. 8:1), or God's Spirit on his servant (Isa. 42:1). See *set*.

Verb: שִׂים (*śîm*), GK 8492 (S 7760), 588x. *śîm* generally denotes the action of putting or placing an object or person in a particular location. It is usually translated "put," "set," or "place." See *put*.

Verb: שִׁית (*šît*), GK 8883 (S 7896), 86x. *šît* means "make, put, set." It is a virtual synonym of *śîm* (GK 8492; see *put*) and has many of the same nuances. See *make*.

Noun: מָקוֹם (*māqôm*), GK 5226 (S 4725) 401x. *māqôm* is the general term for "place." It comes from the verb *qûm*, which means "to stand up," and so originally it may have meant the spot where something stands. It can refer to any sort of location. A place can be large, such as a city (Deut. 21:19), a territory (Num. 32:1), a valley (Num. 13:24), or the ocean (Gen. 1:9). It can be small, such as a bed (1 Sam. 3:2, 9), a seat at a table (1 Sam. 20:25), or a spot on a wall where a peg is fastened (Isa. 22:23). A place can be considered holy (Lev. 7:6), narrow (Num. 22:26), clean (Lev. 6:11), or unclean (14:40).

Certain things have their "place," such as idols (1 Sam. 5:3; Isa. 46:7), the ark of the covenant (2 Sam. 6:17; 1 Ki. 8:6–7, 21), the waters of the Jordan River (Jos. 4:18), and even the earth and the sun (Job 9:6; Eccl. 1:5). A person's residence is considered one's "place," whether it is a house or a tent, and the OT often refers to a person leaving his place (Exod. 16:29; Job 2:11; Prov. 27:8) or returning to his place (Num. 24:25; 2 Sam. 19:39). Similarly, God's "place" is in heaven (1 Ki. 8:30; Hos. 5:15), but the tabernacle or temple is referred to as the "place" where God has chosen to put his Name (Deut. 12:5; 1 Ki. 8:29). Thus, the precise referent or meaning for *māqôm* must be determined by the context. See *NIDOTTE*, 3:902-5.

New Testament

Verb: ἵστημι (*histēmi*), GK *2705* (S *2476*), 154x. The basic sense of *histēmi* is "to set" or "stand." It has a variety of nuances in the NT, one of which is "to place." See *stand*.

Verb: τίθημι (*tithēmi*), GK *5502* (S *5087*), 100x. The basic meaning of *tithēmi* is "to put, place, lay something down." See *put*.

Verb: παρίστημι (*paristēmi*), GK *4225* (S *3936*), 41x. The root meaning of *paristēmi* is "to stand, place beside." See *stand*.

Verb: χωρίον (*chōrion*), GK *6005* (S *5564*), 10x. *chōrion* means "place, field." Matthew and Mark both talk about Jesus going to "a place called Gethsemane" (Mt. 26:36; Mk. 14:32). Judas purchases a "field" with his thirty pieces of silver, and this field (called in Aramaic, *Akeldema*, "Field of Blood") was later used for the burial of strangers who died in the Jerusalem area (Acts 1:18–19). Several early Christians sold lands or fields and gave the proceeds to help the entire church (4:34; cf. 5:3, 8).

Noun: μέρος (*meros*), GK *3538* (S *3313*), 42x. *meros* has a basic meaning of "a part of a whole," but it can also mean "place, share." See *part*.

Noun: τόπος (*topos*), GK *5536* (S *5117*), 94x. *topos* means "place"; in the plural it can refer to a "region" or "district."

The most basic meaning of *topos* is that of a designated area. It does not necessarily refer to an inhabited place (e.g., a town or city), but can simply be an area of land marked off or designated by reference. Because of this, *topos* is found most often in the historical narrative portions of the NT: in the Synoptic Gospels (39x), the gospel of John (16x), and Acts (18x).

When describing the characteristics of an area, *topos* sometimes has an accompanying adjective or adjectival phrase: level place (Lk. 6:17), waterless place (Lk. 11:24), or deserted place (Mt. 14:13; Mk. 1:35). Luke can use *topos* as a synonym for a city in the sense of an inhabited place (Acts 16:3–4); in the plural it can denote a Roman province (27:2) or broader region (Mt. 14:35; Lk. 4:37). *topos* is used in every instance where Golgotha is mentioned, being referred to as the "The *Place* of the Skull" (Mt. 27:33; Mk. 15:22; Jn. 19:17).

topos is sometimes used (like the English "place") for a nonphysical designation. It can be a place in Scripture (Lk. 4:17; Rom. 9:26), the "dark *place*" where God's grace breaks in (2 Pet. 1:19), the place of the lampstand of the churches in Revelation (Rev. 2:5), the holy place of the temple (Mt. 24:15), or even the rank of a layman in the church (1 Cor. 14:16). Judas goes to his own place of punishment after killing himself (Acts 1:25), and the rich man describes hell itself is described as a "*place* of torment" by the rich man in the parable (Lk. 16:28).

In a metaphorical sense, believers are urged by Paul not to seek revenge but rather to "leave *room* for God's wrath" (Rom. 12:19). Similarly, he urges his readers not to give any place to the devil but rather to make an end to their anger (Eph. 4:27).

Finally, *topos* can be used of an opportunity or occasion, such as the incompleteness of the old covenant providing a place for the new covenant (Heb. 8:7), and Esau sought a place for repentance but found none (12:17).

PLAGUE

Old Testament

Noun: נֶגַע (*negaʿ*), GK 5596 (S 5061), 78x. This term generally denotes some form of "plague" (cf. Exod. 11:1). *negaʿ* can be used to speak of a physical affliction or used metaphorically to speak of a "disaster" that troubles people (1 Ki. 8:37–38; Ps. 91:10). The root of *negaʿ* is the verb "to strike," with the intention to cause harm or even death. Occasionally, *negaʿ* can refer to a blow (literal or metaphorical) inflicted on one human by another (Deut. 17:8; 2 Sam. 7:14).

negaʿ is used most often with reference to various infectious skin conditions such as ringworm or even leprous diseases (Lev. 13:2–59; 14:32–54; Deut. 24:8). As the ancient world did not fully understand what caused these conditions, they were especially threatening and were often viewed as judgments from God. Although sickness was not always a judgment from God because of sin (cf. Job!), God did use these feared, sometimes irreversible, afflictions "to strike" his enemies: "The LORD *inflicted* serious diseases on Pharaoh and his household because of Abram's wife Sarai" (Gen. 12:17; cf. Exod. 11:1; Ps. 39:10; 89:32). God could also deliver from such disasters and promised ultimately to do so through his Servant, who would be "stricken" for the transgression of his people (Isa. 53:8). See *NIDOTTE*, 3:24-25.

New Testament

Noun: πληγή (*plēgē*), GK *4435* (S *4127*), 22x. *plēgē* can denote a beating or wound, but it is most closely associated with plague. It is used to translate the Hebrew word for the plagues of Egypt (cf. Exod. 11:1; 12:13) and is also used for the plagues in Revelation (Rev. 9:18, 20; 11:6; 15:1, 6, 8; 16:9, 21; 18:4, 8; 21:9; 22:18). These plagues demonstrate the wrath and judgment of God, which finally destroys all those who refuse to repent (9:20; 11:6; 15:1; 18:8). However, God is fully in control (16:9) and is able to deliver his people from the destruction caused by these plagues (18:4). They are promised to the ungodly along with anyone who adds a prophecy to the book (22:18).

In Revelation, *plēgē* also designates the mortal wounds suffered by the beast (Rev. 13:3, 12, 14). Similarly, it refers to the wounds inflicted on Paul and Silas when they are beaten by the Roman authorities in Philippi (Acts 16:23, 33). Finally, *plēgē* can indicate an intense physical beating that does not lead to death (Lk. 10:30; 12:48; 2 Cor. 6:5; 11:23). See *NIDNTT-A*, 357-58.*

PLAIN

Old Testament

Noun: כִּכָּר (*kikkār*), GK 3971 (S 3603), 68x. *kikkār* has the basic meaning of a "round disk" and can refer to a disk of metal (see *talent*), a round loaf of bread (see *loaf*), or a circular area of land. A *kikkār* of land is roughly round in shape and most often flat. Thus, it can be translated "plain," as in 2 Sam. 18:23, "Ahimaaz ran by way of the *plain*." In this sense, the word is most often used to refer to the floor (i.e., "plain") of the Jordan Valley (Gen. 13:10; 19:17; Deut. 34:3; 1 Ki. 7:46). However, in at least one passage, *kikkār* refers to the region surrounding Jerusalem, which is not flat (Neh. 12:28; cf. 3:22). Here it should probably be understood as the "district" or "environs" of Jerusalem. See *NIDOTTE*, 2:636-37.

Noun: עֵמֶק (*ʿēmeq*), GK 6677 (S 6010), 65x. An *ʿēmeq* is a broad U-shaped valley, and thus in a certain sense it can be considered a plain (though it is not as wide as a *ʿēmeq*). See *valley*.

Noun: עֲרָבָה (*ʿărābâ*), GK 6858 (S 6160), 60x. *ʿărābâ* conveys a dry, desolate, wilderness area, similar to a desert, and may be translated as "plains" or "desert." The historical books of the Bible use this term to refer to the "plains of Moab." See *Arabah*.

New Testament

Adjective: φανερός (*phaneros*), GK *5745* (S *5318*), 18x. *phaneros* means "obvious, known, plain." See *obvious*.

PLAN

Old Testament

Verb: חָשַׁב (*ḥāšab*), GK 3108 (S 2803), 124 x. *ḥāšab* is most often translated as "think" or "plan" (see *think*). It is used with reference to both divine and human thinking.

When used of God, it refers to his plans for humanity and his reactions to human activity. Thus, God plans protection for his people (Mic. 4:12), and when they sin, he plans punishment for them (Jer. 8:11). Ultimately, God's plans are too deep for human understanding (Ps. 92:6) and are eternal (33:11). One implication of this word is that God's plan for humanity (and by extension, for individual humans) is thoughtful, intricate, detailed, and intentional. God's choice of individuals for salvation, blessing, or calling is calculated and the result of careful consideration and, perhaps, evaluation. Thus, in the letter that Jeremiah sends to the elders, priests, prophets, and Jews living in exile in Babylon, the promise of restoration after seventy years accompanies the reference to God's plans for them are specific in nature: "'For I know the *ḥāšab* [NIV: "plans"; KJV: "thoughts"] I have for you,' declares the LORD, 'plans for peace and not evil, to give you hope for the future'" (Jer. 29:11).

Verb: יָעַץ (*yāʿaṣ*), GK 3619 (S 3289), 80x. *yāʿaṣ* carries the two basic meanings of "to counsel, advise" (Num. 24:14; 2 Sam. 17:11) and "to plan, purpose" (Isa. 7:5; 14:24), though the verb seems to carry the former nuance more frequently. See *counsel*.

Verb: יָצַר (*yāṣar*), GK 3670 (S 3335), 63x. *yāṣar* principally means "to form" or "to make." It can also mean "to plan." See *form*.

Noun: מַחֲשָׁבָה (*maḥašābâ*), GK 4742 (S 4284), 56x. This noun is best translated "plans" or "thoughts" and can describe the plans of either individuals or God. The term may function adverbially to describe the ingenuity of a plan (Exod. 31:4; 2 Sam. 14:4; Jer. 11:19) or may represent the plan itself (Prov. 16:3). The term also describes the plans of the wicked (Prov. 6:18; Isa. 59:7), which do not last over time (Prov. 15:26). In contrast to the human plans and thoughts, God's plans are vast (Ps. 92:6) and last forever (33:11).

Theologically, the thoughts of God are superior to those of human beings. Isa. 55:9 states, "As the heavens are higher than the earth, so are my ways higher than your ways and my *thoughts* than your *thoughts*." The basic meaning of this word is captured in the contemporary question, "What's on your *mind*?" See *NIDOTTE*, 2:303-10.

Noun: עֵצָה (*ʿēṣâ*), GK 6783 (S 6098), 87x. *ʿēṣâ* has two basic, though closely related, meanings: "counsel, advice" (see *counsel*) and "plan, purpose."

As to its meaning of "plan, purpose," *ʿēṣâ* is closely related to the meaning "counsel, advice" since the counsel one has for a particular situation will often become the plan one draws for the future. In Isa. 5:19, the wicked taunt God by requesting that his "purpose" draw near and come to pass. This introduces a significant theme in the book of Isaiah, which repeatedly emphasizes that the plans of humans will fail (Isa. 8:10; 19:3; 29:15) while the plans of God will inevitably come to pass (Isa. 14:26; 25:1; 46:10; see also Jer. 18:23; 32:19). Indeed, God thwarts "the plans of the nations," but "the plans of the LORD stand firm forever, the purposes of his heart through all generations" (Ps. 33:10–11).

New Testament

Verb: βούλομαι (*boulomai*) GK *1089* (S *1014*), 37x. *boulomai* describes the desire or intention of a person to do something, to have something, or to obtain a result. See *want*.

Verb: προτίθημι (*protithēmi*), GK *4729* (S *4388*), 3x. *protithēmi* means "to plan, present." On a human level, Paul "planned" previously to come to the Romans but was prevented (Rom. 1:13). That is, he was unable to follow through on his intention.

The other two uses of this verb have God as the subject. In Rom. 3:25, Christ is the one whom God "presented" (KJV, "set forth"; ESV, "put forward"). After Paul acknowledges the universality of human sin, he notes God's gift of salvation by grace alone through Christ, whom "God *put forward* as a propitiation by his blood, to be received by faith" (Rom. 3:25, ESV). Note that God did not merely plan to send Jesus, but executed his plan successfully, and Jesus was publicly "presented" as a propitiation (*hilastērion*; see *atonement*) by his blood.

In Eph. 1:9, Paul likewise talks about God's "making known to us the mystery of his will, according to his purpose, which he *set forth* in Christ" (ESV). In context, what has been "set forth" in Christ is the mystery of God's will in presenting Jesus as the one to carry out his plan of salvation. See *NIDNTT-A*, 498.*

PLANT

Old Testament

Verb: זָרַע (*zāraʿ*), GK 2445 (S 2232),

56x. *zāraʿ* refers to the activity of sowing or planting and can bear a literal as well as a metaphorical meaning in the OT. See *sow.*

Verb: נָטַע (*nāṭaʿ*), GK 5749 (S 5193). 59x. *nāṭaʿ* broadly means "to plant, fix, establish" and can be used both literally and figuratively.

(1) The basic sense of the term appears in about half of its occurrences. Because ancient Israel is predominantly an agrarian society, the planting of crops is a familiar scene. What is planted are vines or vineyards (Gen. 9:20; Deut. 20:6; 28:30, 39; Ps. 107:37; Prov. 31:16; Eccl. 2:4; Isa. 37:30; 65:21; Jer. 31:5; Ezek. 28:26; Amos 5:11; 9:14; Mic. 1:6; Zeph. 1:13), gardens in general (Jer. 29:5, 28), and various kinds of trees (Lev. 19:23; Deut. 16:21; cf. fruit trees, Eccl. 2:5; olive trees, Deut. 6:11; Jos. 24:13; tamarisk trees, Gen. 21:33; cedar trees, Isa. 44:14; cf. Ezek. 31:4). Many of these passages also emphasize the result of planting, such as eating, enjoying the fruit, or drinking the wine. Agriculture is an important factor in the religious and covenantal life of Israel. All the feasts are structured around the agricultural calendar. The result of good crops means you are enjoying the blessing of God, while bad crops mean that you are experiencing God's curse (cf. Lev. 26; Deut. 27–28). Furthermore, many of these references, and others below, are included in contexts that also mention the construction of houses or cities, thus tying agriculture to Israel's domestic life.

(2) Figuratively, *nāṭaʿ* refers to God's "planting" or "establishing." God is the one who "planted" the original garden: "Now the LORD God had planted a garden in the east, in Eden" (Gen. 2:8; also planting aloes, Num. 24:6; and cedars, Ps. 104:16). He is the one great Planter in Israel (Jer. 11:17). Speaking of Israel as a "vine," Ps. 80 recounts how God "planted" his people (80:8) with his own hand (80:15). The prophet Isaiah describes Israel as "the garden [lit., planting] of his delight" (Isa. 5:7; see also, 60:21; 61:3).

In keeping with the agricultural figure, God tells Israel that they will be uprooted and exiled from the land because of their rebellion: "This is what the LORD says: I will overthrow what I have built and uproot what I have *planted* throughout the land" (Jer. 45:4; see 24:6). Yet God's ultimate promise of restoring Israel is spoken to David: "I will provide a place for my people Israel and will *plant* them so that they can have a home of their own and no longer be disturbed" (2 Sam. 7:10; Jer. 24:6; 32:41; 42:10; Amos 9:15).

God not only "establishes" or "plants" Israel but the nations (Jer. 1:10; 18:9), the wicked (Jer. 12:2), the heavens (Isa. 51:16), and the ear (Ps. 94:9), and he reestablishes the wasteland (Ezek. 36:36).

(3) Other figurative uses of *nāṭaʿ* include "pitching" tents (Dan. 11:45) and "embedded" (NIV) or "fastened" (KJV) nails (Eccl. 12:11). Finally, Eccl. uses the figure of planting to illustrate the fact there is a time for everything: "a time to be born and a time to die, a time to *plant* and a time to uproot" (Eccl. 3:2). See *NIDOTTE*, 3:94–96.

New Testament

Verb: φυτεύω (*phyteuō*), GK *5885* (S *5452*), 11x. *phyteuō* is an agricultural term that means "to plant." In the NT it is used primarily for the planting a tree or crop, especially in the Gospels (Mt. 21:33; Mk. 12:1; Lk. 13:6; 17:6, 28; 20:9; see also 1 Cor. 9:7). Paul uses the verb in a figurative sense referring to the work of evangelism in contrast to the work of discipleship carried out by Apollos. Paul plants the seed of the gospel and Apollos waters it, but the growth is from God (1 Cor. 3:6–8). *phyteuō* is also used once figuratively in Jesus' critique of the Pharisees in Mt. 15:13: "Every plant that my heavenly Father has not *planted* will be pulled up by the roots." See *NIDNTT-A*, 534-35.*

PLEAD

Old Testament

Verb: רִיב (*rîb*), GK 8189, (S 7378), 72x. *rîb* denotes the action of entering into an argument, conflict, or lawsuit with another person. When a case or a cause is the object of *rîb*, the NIV may translate the verb as "plead" (e.g., Ps. 43:1), "defend" (e.g., 74:22), "present" (e.g., Prov. 18:17), or "take up" (e.g., 22:23; 23:11). See *contend.*

New Testament

Noun: δέομαι (*deomai*), GK *1289* (S *1189*), 22x. *deomai* is a general word for prayer where a request is being made, either of a person or of God. It can be translated as "to pray, beseech, ask, beg, plead."

PLEASE, (BE) PLEASED

Old Testament

Verb: יָטַב (*yāṭab*), GK 3512 (S 3190), 117x. *yāṭab* is a verb that means "to do good, go well, please, prosper." It is used in a wide variety of contexts in the OT. See *do good.*

Verb: רָצָה (*rāṣâ*), GK 8354 (S 7521), 52x. *rāṣâ means* "to be pleased, accept, delight in." It is often used in the context of God's accepting (or not accepting) sacrifices offered to him. A newborn calf, lamb, or goat that is more than eight days old "will be acceptable as an offering" (Lev. 22:27; cf. also 1:4). But if God's people do not offer sacrifices in sincere faithfulness, the Lord "does not accept them" (Jer. 14:10, 12; cf. Mic. 6:7; Mal. 1:8, 10, 13). In other words, what is most acceptable to the Lord are the sacrifices of a broken and contrite heart (Ps. 51:16–17). Moreover, God "takes delight in" those who have integrity (1 Chr. 29:17), in those who fear him (Ps. 147:11), and in his chosen people (Isa. 42:1)—especially after they have gone through the purgation of the exile (Ezek. 20:40–41). See *NIDOTTE*, 3:1185–86.

Noun: רָצוֹן (*rāṣôn*), GK 8356 (S 7522), 56x. *rāṣôn* denotes three different ideas in the OT: favor (see *favor*), acceptance (see *acceptable*), or will. It is attributed most often to God (39x) and occurs most frequently in Proverbs (14x), Psalms (13x), and Leviticus (7x).

rāṣôn sometimes expresses an individual's personal desires, wants, or will. The NIV reserves the translation "will" exclusively for God's will (Ezr. 10:11; Ps. 40:8; 103:21; 143:10). When *rāṣôn* expresses the assertion of one man's will against another, the NIV translates that he did "as he pleased." In this sense, kings often do "as they please" (Neh. 9:37; Dan. 8:4; 11:3, 16, 36), and so does Israel (Neh. 9:24; Est. 9:5; cf. Gen. 49:6). When *rāṣôn* is used generally for a creature's desire, it is translated as "desires" (Ps. 145:16, 19) or something "wished" for (Est. 1:8).

New Testament

Verb: ἀρέσκω (*areskō*), GK *743* (S *700*), 17x. *areskō* means "to please," usually through service, which can be holy or shameful, depending on the state of one's heart. The broad range of use of this verb can be seen by comparing its use in a sensual context (the dance of Herodias's daughter, Mt. 14:6; Mk. 6:22) with its noble and honorable use for soldiers who want to earn the approval of their officers (2 Tim. 2:4).

Concerning the duty of believers, *areskō* is used of both human beings pleasing God or other human beings through service. Focusing on the vertical aspect, Paul says, "I want you to be free from anxieties. The unmarried man is anxious about the things of the Lord, how *to please* the Lord. But the married man is anxious about worldly things, how *to please* his wife, and his interests are divided. ... The married woman is anxious about worldly things, how *to please* her husband" (1 Cor. 7:32–34, ESV). The verb here clearly refers to pleasing through service, with a priority given to pleasing God (see also Rom. 8:8; 1 Thess. 2:4; 4:1).

For Paul, horizontal *areskō* is a plumb line for where the heart is. He says, "We who are strong have an obligation to bear with the failings of the weak, and not to *please* ourselves. Let each of us *please* his neighbor for his good, to build him up. For Christ did not *please* himself" (Rom. 15:1–3, ESV). The believer's goal should not be to please himself or herself by selfish service, but to selflessly serve both God and neighbor. And Paul is only asking what he himself attempts to do, as he says, "Give no offense to Jews or to Greeks or to the church of God, just as I try to *please* everyone in everything I do, not seeking my own advantage, but that of many, that they may be saved" (1 Cor. 10:33, ESV). Yet, when the heart goes awry, even serving others can come from the motive of self-love, and *areskō* becomes a shameful motive (Gal. 1:10). See *NIDNTT-A*, 69.

Verb: εὐδοκέω (*eudokeō*), GK *2305* (S *2106*), 21x. *eudokeō* designates the pleasure a person takes in another person or in doing something. (1) The Father states at Jesus' baptism that he is pleased with his beloved Son (Mt. 3:17). Matthew again indicates the Father's pleasure with Jesus when Isa. 42:1–3 is cited in Mt. 12:18–21. At the transfiguration (17:5), the Father against states that he is pleased with the Son (cf. 2 Pet. 1:17). By way of contrast, God was not pleased with most of the wilderness generation (1 Cor. 10:5), nor is he pleased with those who lack courage (Heb. 10:38).

(2) *eudokeō* also serves to describe pleasure taken in certain actions. For example, in Lk. 12:32 Jesus assures his disciples that their "Father is pleased to give" them the kingdom. God is "pleased to save" those who believe through the foolishness of preaching (1 Cor. 1:21). Also, God was "pleased to reveal" his Son in Paul (Gal. 1:15–16), and he was also pleased for his whole fullness "to dwell" in his Son, Jesus (Col. 1:19). Paul and his coworkers were "pleased to give" not only the gospel but their very selves to the Thessalonian church (1 Thess. 2:8). In Rom. 15:26–27 Paul reports that Macedonia and Achaia were "pleased to contribute" to the poor saints in Jerusalem. Those who "take pleasure" in unrighteousness will be judged (2 Thess. 2:12).

(3) Related to this is a use of *eudokeō* to indicate a preferred choice or state of satisfaction. Paul states that he would "prefer" to be absent from the body and at home with the Lord (2 Cor. 5:8). Because the power of God is manifested in his weakness, Paul can be "well content" with his lack of power (2 Cor. 12:10). Paul was pleased to be left in Athens alone (1 Thess. 3:1). God was not pleased (i.e., his wrath was not propitiated) by the sacrifices offered under the old covenant (Heb. 10:6, 8). See *NIDNTT-A*, 215-16.

PLEASING

Old Testament

Noun: רָצוֹן (*rāṣôn*), GK 8356 (S 7522), 56x. *rāṣôn* denotes three different ideas in the OT: favor (see *favor*), acceptance, or will (see *please*). It is attributed most often to God (39x) and occurs most frequently in Proverbs (14x), Psalms (13x), and Leviticus (7x). *rāṣôn* is used frequently with reference to an acceptable sacrifice to God, particularly in worship. The psalmist prays that his words and meditation may "be pleasing" in God's sight (Ps. 19:14; see *acceptable*).

PLEASURE

Old Testament

Noun: רָצוֹן (*rāṣôn*), GK 8356 (S 7522), 56x. *rāṣôn* denotes three different ideas in the OT: favor, acceptance (see acceptable), or will (see *please*). It is attributed most often to God (39x) and occurs most frequently in Proverbs (14x), Psalms (13x), and Leviticus (7x). The sense of *rāṣôn* as "favor" signifies a kind regard or special status usually bestowed by a superior. The NIV often translates this sense as "favor" or "favored," but sometimes as "pleasure" (Ps. 51:18; Prov. 16:13; Mal. 2:13). See *favor.*

Noun: שִׂמְחָה (*śimḥâ*), GK 8525 (S 8057), 94x. Depending on the context, *śimḥâ* can be translated "joy, rejoicing, gladness, pleasure," or "happiness." See *joy.*

New Testament

Noun: εὐδοκία (*eudokia*) GK *2306* (S *2107*), 9x. *eudokia* can mean "good pleasure, purpose; desire." Most of its nine uses in the NT refer to God rather than humans and denote God's good intention or purpose for his people. Thus, Jesus thanks God that it is his "kind intention" to reveal to infants what he has hidden from the wise (Mt. 11:26; Lk. 10:21). The company of angels in Lk. 2 ascribes glory to God and asks for peace on earth among the people toward whom God is "favorably disposed" (2:14). In the great passage of Ephesians 1 the word is used twice (1:5, 9) with the nuance of "good pleasure": it is according to the *eudokia* of his will that God predestines his children for adoption (1:5), and this kind intention is purposed in Christ (1:9). In Phil. 2:13, God works in believers "for his good pleasure" (NASB, KJV), or "according to his good purpose" (NIV). Finally, in Phil. 1:15, some people are preaching from envy and strife, but some from good intentions.

eudokia is used twice in the NT of the wishes or desires of humans. In Rom. 10:1, Paul affirms that his desire is for the salvation of his fellow Jews. Paul's prayer in 2 Thess. 1:11 is that God would fulfill the Thessalonians' every "desire for goodness." See *NIDNTT-A*, 215-16.*

Adjective: εὐάρεστος (*euarestos*), GK *2298* (S *2101*), 9x. *euarestos* means "pleasing, acceptable." It occurs only in the NT letters, and in general it refers to the goal that should be ours of living so as to please God. In Rom. 12:1, for example, Paul calls on believers to "offer your bodies as living sacrifices, holy and *pleasing* to God" (cf. 14:18; Phil. 4:18). One specific act that "*pleases* the Lord" is for children to obey their parents (Col. 3:20). If we truly want to live as children of light, we will search out "what *pleases* the Lord" (Eph. 5:10; cf. 2 Cor. 5:9). But pleasing God is not possible in our own strength, for the writer of Hebrews offers as a benediction that God himself will equip us with everything good and "work in us what is *pleasing* to him through Jesus Christ" (Heb. 13:21).

PLEDGE

Old Testament

Noun: עֵרָבוֹן (*ʿērābôn*), GK 6860 (S 6162), 3x.

The noun *ʿērābôn* occurs only in Gen. 38:17, 18, 20, where Jacob gives Tamar (his daughter-in-law, whom he does not recognize) a pledge by means of his seal, his cord, and his staff in order to guarantee that he will send a young goat in payment for her services as a prostitute. Tamar keeps this pledge in her possession until she uses them to prove that Jacob is the father of her unborn children. This Heb. word for "pledge" gets transliterated into the NT word *arrabōn*.

New Testament

Noun: ἀρραβών (*arrabōn*), GK *775* (S *728*), 3x. *arrabōn* is a "pledge or deposit guaranteeing what is to come." A Heb. word that in the OT is used on a purely human level (e.g., Gen. 38:17–20) becomes a transliterated Greek word to describe what God has done for us by his saving grace. Just as a down payment for a house today serves as a guarantee that the rest of the payment will come, so God sends his Holy Spirit into the hearts of believers as a deposit, guaranteeing that someday the full inheritance of salvation will be ours (2 Cor. 1:22; 5:5; Eph. 1:14). All Christians should understand that the Holy Spirit, the third person of the Trinity, is living in them and is empowering them to exercise his gifts and to live for God. See also *salvation*. See *NIDNTT-A*, 73.

PLUNDER

Old Testament

Noun: שָׁלָל (*šālāl*), GK 8965 (S 7998), 74x. *šālāl* usually designates the plunder taken in war. It is closely related to the verb *šālal*, "to plunder, spoil." However, whereas the verb *šālal* stresses the act of plundering, the noun *šālāl* denotes the results of plundering, i.e., the spoil or booty. Being plundered is frequently a result of God's judgment (Isa. 8:4; Jer. 50:10), but it can also be the result of unjust oppression (Isa. 10:2). Almost anything can be the plunder of war: garments, gold, silver (Jos. 7:21), women (Jdg. 5:30), ornaments (Jdg. 8:24–25), and flocks and herds (1 Sam. 30:20). Sometimes, an entire city or nation is considered to be *šālāl* (Isa. 8:4; Jer. 50:10; Ezek. 7:21; Zech. 2:9). *šālāl* also denotes part of the reward to be given to the Suffering Servant, who will pour himself out in death (Isa. 53:12). See *NIDOTTE* 4:128-30.

POINT

Old Testament

Noun: קֶרֶן (*qeren*), GK 7967 (S 7161), 76x. This word refers primarily to the horn of an animal, but *qeren* can also be understood as "point, corner," such as the "*horns* of the altar" (Exod. 29:12). See *horn*.

POISON

Old Testament

Noun: חֵמָה (*ḥēmâ*), GK 2779 (S 2534), 125x. The basic meaning of *ḥēma* is "anger, wrath" (see *anger*), though in certain contexts it may mean "poison, venom." Snakes are full of "poison" (Deut. 32:24, 33), and people who lie or incite violence with their words have lips full of "venom" like a snake (Ps. 58:4; 140:3). Job describes his suffering as being shot with arrows full of "poison" (Job 6:4).

POND

New Testament

Noun: λίμνη (*limnē*), GK *3349* (S *3041*), 11x. *limnē* denotes a "lake, pond." It is typically a body of water smaller than that associated with *thalassa* (see *sea*). See *lake*.

POOR

Old Testament

Noun: אֶבְיוֹן (*ʾebyôn*) GK 36 (S 34), 61x. Among the several terms in the Heb. language used to designate the "poor," *ʾebyôn* is consistently used to describe the physical poverty of those who are destitute. The OT has much to say about showing genuine concern for such people (see *needy*).

Adjective: עָנִי (*ʿānî*), GK 6714 (S 6041), 80x. *ʿānî* describes one who has been humbled or afflicted by circumstances, and who, because of current disability, finds himself or herself dependent on others for life's necessities. *ʿānî* is distinguished from *ʾebyôn* ("needy") and *dal* ("impoverished") in that it stresses the disability of the person and thus one's utter need for assistance. *ʿānî* is also distinguished from its close counterpart *ʿānāw* ("humble") in that *ʿānî* "is never linked to deserved poverty but always is used to denote those who were exploited and wrongfully impoverished (Job 24:4; Ps. 37:14; Isa. 32:7)" (see *NIDOTTE*, 3:455). As such, the *ʿānî* is grouped with the resident alien, the widow, and the orphan—all of whom are socially disadvantaged through no fault of their own and are dependent on others for their welfare.

God is the defender of the *ʿānî* (Deut. 10:17–18), and he commands Israel to leave gleanings for their use (Lev. 19:10) as well as the corners of the field so that they might also share in the harvest (Lev. 23:22). Moreover, the *ʿānî* are to receive their wages each day, since they live day-to-day and have no surplus. The employer will answer to God with regard to the wages of the *ʿānî* (Deut. 24:15). God is, therefore, the one who saves the *ʿānî* (2 Sam. 22:28, cf. Ps. 18:27), and he expects his covenant people to be open-handed to those who are needy and afflicted (Deut. 15:11).

Because of God's commitment to the *ʿānî* the prophets likewise exhort the people to deal justly with them (Isa. 10:2; 58:7). Ezekiel characterizes the godly as those who give bread to the hungry, clothe the naked, and do not harm the *ʿānî* by charging them excessive interest (Ezek. 18:17). In contrast, the ungodly are those who do not care for the *ʿānî* (Ezek. 16:49; 22:29; Prov. 14:21; cf. Mt. 25:34–46).

Physical affliction and poverty often have a connection with spiritual affliction. Thus, the one whose soul is afflicted cries out to God for help (Ps. 25:16; 34:6; 69:29). Indeed, God's people are often described as *ʿānî* (e.g., 37:14; 68:10; 72:2, 4, 12, 19) and seek God for their welfare: "I know that the LORD secures justice for the *poor* and upholds the cause of the needy" (140:12).

Since *ʿānî* describes those who are lowly, it also describes the coming Messiah: "See, your king comes to you, righteous and having salvation, *gentle* [*humble,*

KJV] and riding on a donkey, on a colt, the foal of a donkey" (Zech. 9:9). As the humble Servant of the Lord, he identifies with those who are afflicted, for he himself was smitten and judged for the sins of others (Isa. 53). As such, the servant identifies with the *ʿānî* and saves them. See *NIDOTTE*, 3:454-64.

New Testament

Noun: πτωχός (*ptōchos*), GK *4777* (S *4434*), 34x. *ptōchos* can be used both literally, referring to the economically disadvantaged, and figuratively, referring to the one whose vulnerable state leads to total dependence on God. This term is frequently used in the Gospels in this literal sense: namely, those without financial or material means and thus powerless (Mk. 10:21; Mt. 19:21; Rom. 15:26; Gal. 2:10). Judas complains: "Why wasn't this perfume sold and the money given to *the poor*?" (Jn. 12:5). Jesus says that the gift of the poor woman in Mk. 12:41–44 is greater than the gifts of the rich. Similarly, Jesus says the presence of the economically disadvantaged will always be a reality (Mt. 26:11). These references are generally to those who are dependent on others for material support.

At times the *ptōchoi* are not only the victims of adverse economic situations but, because of their vulnerable position, they are persecuted and oppressed; thus, these individuals must have confidence in God alone. They are poor in that they are rejected by the world and despised and thus look to God for final vindication and reward. This sense derives from its OT usage (e.g., Ps. 15:2–5; 24:4; Amos 2:6–7). It is significant that Jesus tells the disciples of John the Baptist that "the good news is preached to the poor" (Mt. 11:5; see also Lk. 4:18; 7:22). Furthermore, Jesus announces that the poor are blessed and that the kingdom of heaven is theirs (Mt. 5:3; Lk. 6:20). This seems to be the way James refers to the poor as well: "Has not God chosen those who are poor in the eyes of the world to be rich in faith and to inherit the kingdom he promised those who love him?" (Jas. 2:5; see also 2:2, 3, 6).

Finally, *ptōchos* may be used in a comparative sense, referring generally to what is of extremely inferior quality In Gal. 4:9 Paul asks, "How is it that you are turning back to those weak and *miserable* principles?" See *NIDNTT-A*, 503-5.

PORCH, PORTICO

Old Testament

Noun: אֵילָם (*ʾêlām*), GK 395 (S 361), 61x. The *ʾêlām* is the first section of the interior of a king's palace (1 Ki. 7:6–8) or temple (7:12, 19, 21). Also spelled *ʾûlām* and deriving from the root *ʾlm*, "to be in front," it is translated variously as "vestibule, porch, entrance hall, portico" (7:19; 2 Chr. 3:4).

It is not exactly clear what the nature and function of the *ʾêlām* are in the palace/temple structure. Its function in the temple probably relates to the fact that a temple is considered the "palace" of the god(s) on earth. The *ʾêlām* may thus be part of the public courts of the temple (1 Ki. 6:36; 7:12), though it is not specifically said to have a doorway. There are two large pillars on either side of its entrance (2 Ki. 7:15–22), each one eighteen cubits high (1 Ki. 7:15; 2 Chr. 3:35). From this data scholars presume that the *ʾêlām* is simply a forecourt before the interior sanctuary.

New Testament

Noun: στοά (*stoa*), GK *5119* (S *4745*), 4x. *stoa* is used in the NT primarily for the portico or porch area of Herod's temple, which was built with many columns; in NT times it is termed "Solomon's Colonnade." Jesus commonly teaches in this area of the temple (Jn. 10:23), for it is an area in which both men and women can walk about. Peter and John likewise teach there (Acts 3:11), and the believers of the early church regularly meet in that area (5:12). In Jn. 5:2, *stoa* refers to a different area in Jerusalem with columns, where Jesus heals a man who has been an invalid for thirty-eight years.*

PORTION

Old Testament

Noun: חֵלֶק (*ḥēleq*), GK 2750 (S 2506), 66x. *ḥēleq* means "share, portion," but also "lot, inheritance." See *share*.

Noun: חֹק (*ḥōq*), GK 2976 (S 2706), 131x. *ḥōq* is derived from the related verb *ḥāqaq*, which means "to cut in, inscribe, decree" and denotes something that is limited or restricted. Most frequently *ḥōq* refers to the prescribed law of God (see *decree*). Less frequently, it expresses a fixed quantity or some sort of limit. Pharaoh's priests receive a regular "allotment" of food so they are not forced to sell their land (Gen. 47:22), and the excellent wife provides a "portion" of food for her servants (Prov. 31:15). Israel's priests receive a "portion" or "share" of the offering (29:28; Lev. 24:9; Num. 18:8, 11, 19).

Noun: תְּרוּמָה (*t*ᵉ*rûmâ*), GK 9556 (S 8641), 76x. *t*ᵉ*rûmâ* can be translated as "offering, portion, gift, contribution." See *offering*.

New Testament

Noun: μέρος (*meros*), GK *3538* (S *3313*), 42x. *meros* has a basic meaning of "a part of a whole," but it can also mean "place, share, portion." See *part*.

POSSESS, POSSESSIONS

Old Testament

Verb: יָרַשׁ (*yāraš*), GK 3769 (S 3423), 232x. *yāraš* means "to possess, take possession of (especially by force), drive out, inherit."

(1) *yāraš* is used in military contexts for gaining control over a certain area by conquering and ousting present inhabitants. Taking this military nuance into consideration, *yāraš* comes to mean dispossess, drive out, or seize. The Lord instructs his people, the Israelites, to "*take possession* of the land" that he swore he would give to Abraham (Deut. 1:8, 21; 2:24). He himself will be giving this land to his people "to possess" (5:31), and he will go before them, enabling them to "drive out" the nations (9:3). Well over half of the uses of *yāraš* concern this event of the conquest of Canaan.

But God reminds his people that they are not free to take whatever land they want. For example, he has given Ar to descendants of Lot "as a possession" (this phrase uses a noun related to *yāraš*), so the Israelites have no right to harass the Moabites (Deut. 2:9; cf. 2:12, 19–22).

(2) In civil matters, *yāraš* came to describe an heir. Thus, Abram complains of having no one to "inherit" his possessions other than his adopted son Eliezer (Gen. 15:3–4). King Ahab, through the scheming of his wife, "takes possession" of Naboth's vineyard (1 Ki. 21:15–19), much to the displeasure of Elijah.

(3) As *yāraš* develops, it takes on spiritual significance. As the Israelites come to understand through the exile that possession of the promised land is dependent on obedience to the Lord, Isaiah prophesies a time when "the people [will be] righteous and they will *possess* the land forever" (Isa. 60:21; cf. 57:13). This same message is reflected in the psalms, that "the meek will inherit the land" (Ps. 37:11); elsewhere this activity is ascribed to "those who hope in the Lord" (37:9), to "the righteous" (37:29), and to those who fear the Lord (25:13). This is the theme Jesus picks up in his third beatitude: "The meek will inherit the earth" (Mt. 5:5). See *NIDOTTE*, 2:547–49.

Verb: נָחַל (*nāḥal*), GK 5706 (S 5157), 59x. In addition to meaning "to inherit," *nāḥal* can be translated as "to possess, take possession, get." See *inherit*.

Noun: אֲחֻזָּה (*ʾ*ᵃ*ḥuzzâ*), GK 299 (S 272), 66x. Derived from the verb *ʾāḥaz*, which means "to grasp, seize, hold," the noun *ʾ*ᵃ*ḥuzzâ* means "property, possession." See *property*.

Over two-thirds of the occurrences of this word are found in Genesis through Joshua, and many of these refer to the land God promised to the Israelites as a possession (Gen. 36:43; Lev. 14:34; 25:24; Num. 35:28; Jos. 22:4, 9, 19). Abraham's acquiring of a burial place (Gen. 23:4, 9, 20; 49:30; 50:13) is viewed as a fulfillment of God's promise. The Levites are to receive no land as a possession, though they do acquire certain cities and their surrounding fields (Lev. 25:33). As far as they are concerned, the Lord is to be their possession (Num. 18:20; Ezek. 44:28). To this end, Ezekiel prophesies concerning the Levites' inheritance (Ezek. 45:7; 48:20, 21, 22). From the biblical perspective, possession is a gift from God.

ʾaḥuzzâ is also used of the Lord's promise to the Messiah that the "ends of the earth" are to be his "possession. The psalmist writes, "Ask of me, and I will make the nations your inheritance, and the very ends of the earth your possession" (Ps. 2:8). Jesus the Christ is the name at which "every knee will bow" and "every tongue confess" in heaven and on earth "that he is Lord" (Phil. 2:10–11).

Noun: נַחֲלָה (*naḥelâ*), GK 5709 (S 5159), 222x. In addition to "inheritance," *naḥela* can be translated as "heritage" and "possession." See *inheritance*.

New Testament

Verb: ἔχω (*echō*), GK *2400* (S *2627*), 708x. *echō* means "to have, possess." It has a broad range of meaning in the NT. See *have*.

Verb: ὑπάρχω (*hyparchō*), GK *5639* (S *5224, 5225*), 60x. *hyparchō* is a multifaceted term ranging in meaning from the verb "to be" (see *be*), to being used as the verb "possess" and the noun "possessions," to being translated as "exist" (see *exist*).

hyparchō is used in Scripture to denote "possessions" or "things being at one's disposal." One's possessions often get in the way of an individual's relationship with Jesus. For example, in Matthew Jesus implores the rich young ruler to sell all of his "possessions," give them to the poor, and follow him (Mt. 19:21; cf. 24:47; 25:14). In fact, Jesus states that no one can be his disciple unless he gives up all his "possessions" (Lk. 14:33). Yet Scripture also teaches that it is not possessions that God desires but our hearts. For example, Zacchaeus promises to give only half of his possessions, but that is nevertheless accepted by God because it came from a heart of gratitude. Likewise, Joanna and Susanna do not sell all their possessions but rather use them in godly fashion to support Jesus' ministry (Lk. 8:3). Some early churches did willfully give up their earthly possessions because of severe persecution, but they did so in favor of a "better and enduring *possession*" (Heb. 10:34).

Noun: βίος (*bios*), GK *1050* (S *979*), 10x. *bios* denotes the course of one's "life" or the "material possessions, property" by which that life subsists (1 Jn. 3:17). See *life*.

POSSIBLE

New Testament

Adjective: δυνατός (*dynatos*), GK *1543* (S *1415*), 32x. *dynatos* denotes what is possible or what one has the power to do (see also *can*). (1) *dynatos* describes what is or is not possible. With people salvation is impossible, but with God "all things are *possible*" (Mt. 19:26). Jesus states that all things are possible to the one who believes (Mk. 9:23). False christs and false prophets will be very convincing, with the result that, if it were possible, they would deceive even the elect (Mt. 24:24). Jesus prays, "My Father, if it is *possible*, let this cup pass from me" (Mt. 26:39), and Mark recounts that he continued with the words, "Abba, Father, everything is *possible* for you. Take this cup from me. But not what I will, but what you will" (Mk. 14:36). The necessity of the atonement is the basis of this verse; if Jesus had to die so that our sins could be forgiven, then the cross was a necessity. But at the same time, "it was *impossible* for death" to hold Jesus (Acts 2:24). God, in other words, ordained both the cross and the resurrection as necessities.

(2) *dynatos* can describe ability. Jesus is described by those on the road to Emmaus as a prophet "*mighty* in word and deed" (Lk. 24:19). Similarly, Stephen describes Moses as "*mighty* in his words and deeds" (Acts 7:22). Apollos is described as "*mighty* in the Scriptures" (18:24). Going

to war, what king will not consider whether he is able to overcome his opponent? (Lk. 14:31). Peter asks, "As for me, how was I *able* to hinder God?" (Acts 11:17). Paul indicates that God wants to make his *power* known (Rom. 9:22).

(3) The adjective *dynatos* also occurs as a noun. Luke depicts Mary exclaiming, "*The Mighty One* has done great things for me" (Lk. 1:49). Festus urges "the ones who are able" (i.e., the leaders) to go with him to Caesarea (Acts 25:5). "The strong" (i.e., those who are capable) are to bear with the weaknesses of the weak (Rom. 15:1). Paul notes that not many Christians in Corinth were among "the influential" in that city (1 Cor. 1:26). See *NIDNTT-A*, 154-55.

POST

Old Testament

Noun: עַמּוּד (*ʿammûd*), GK 6647 (S 5982), 112x. *ʿammûd* means "pillar, post" and refers to a columnar support for a structure, whether literal or metaphorical, or to a column-like image, such as a funnel cloud. See *pillar*.

POUR OUT

Old Testament

Verb: יָצַק (*yāṣar*), GK 3668 (S 3332), 53x. *yāṣa* is best translated as "pour," though it is used 15x in the context of metal casting (Exod. 25:12; 38:27; 1 Ki. 7:23–24). It is used in a religious context with regard to the pouring of ceremonial oil (Gen. 38:1–2; Lev. 8:15). The pouring of oil was symbolic of the anointing of the Holy Spirit for the purpose of serving as priest or king (Exod. 29:7; 1 Sam. 10:1). Theologically, the *outpouring* of the Holy Spirit is associated with the future renewal and restoration of Israel. Isa. 44:3 states, "For I will *pour* water on the thirsty land, and the streams on dry ground; I will *pour out* my Spirit on your offspring, and my blessing on your descendants." See *NIDOTTE* 2:502-3.

Verb: שָׁפַךְ (*šāpak*), GK 9161 (S 8210), 117x. *šāpak* generally means "to pour out, shed, spill, scatter." It can refer to a physical or a metaphorical action.

(1) *šāpak* most frequently denotes the pouring out of the lifeblood of a human being (i.e., "to shed blood"); in such instances, it is often best rendered "to kill" (Deut. 21:7; 2 Ki. 24:4; Ezek. 22:3; cf. Zeph. 1:17). God declares to Noah, "Whoever sheds the blood of man, by man shall his blood be shed, for in the image of God he [i.e., God] made man" (Gen. 9:6). Water too is poured out, as when Moses is instructed to pour water from the Nile on dry ground (Exod. 4:9) and when water is spilled as a libation offering (1 Sam. 7:6; Isa. 57:6). *šāpak* is also used idiomatically in connection with the building of siege ramps, probably because the dirt has to be "poured out" in the construction process (2 Sam. 20:15; Isa. 37:33; Jer. 6:6).

(2) In the metaphorical sense, *šāpak* is used of Israel's pouring out their lust on idols (Ezek. 23:8) and of God's pouring out his wrath on the wicked (Isa. 42:25; Ezek. 22:22; Hos. 5:10; Zeph. 3:8). In a positive sense, Joel prophesies of the day when God will pour out his Spirit on his people (Joel 2:29), the fulfillment of which occurs at Pentecost (Acts 2:1–21, especially v. 17).

New Testament

Verb: ἐκχέω (*ekcheō*), GK *1772* (S *1632*), 16x.

Verb: ἐκχύννομαι (*ekchynnomai*), GK *1773* (S *1632*), 11x. These two related verbs convey the idea of emptying out a container or vessel, that is, "to pour out, shed." *ekcheō* is the typical verb used to describe the pouring out of the Holy Spirit at Pentecost, as Peter declares, "Exalted to the right hand of God, he has received from the Father the promised Holy Spirit and has *poured out* what you now see and hear" (Acts 2:33; also vv. 17–18; 10:45). Moreover, God has "poured out" his love for us through the Holy Spirit (Rom. 5:5; cf. Tit. 3:6). In Rev. 16, this verb is used 9x for the pouring out of the bowls of God's wrath.

ekchynnomai describes the murder or

the shedding of blood of the faithful. Jesus rebukes the Pharisees and declares, "And so upon you will come all the righteous blood that has been *shed* on earth" (Mt. 23:35; cf. Rom. 3:15). Regarding his involvement with the murder of Stephen, Paul testifies, "And when the blood of your martyr Stephen was *shed*, I stood there giving my approval" (Acts 22:20). This verb is especially important theologically, since when Jesus was in the upper room with the disciples, he took a cup, gave it to them, and said, "This is my blood of the covenant, which *is poured out* for many" (Mk. 14:24; cf. Lk. 22:20). See *NIDNTT-A*, 177.

POWER

Old Testament

Noun: אֵל (*ʾēl*), GK 445, 446 (S 410), 242x. *ʾēl* is one of the two Heb. words for "God." But occasionally this word can also mean "power." See *God*.

Noun: גְּבוּרָה (*gᵉbûrâ*), GK 1476 (S 1369), 62x. The basic sense of *gᵉbûrâ* is "strength, power, might." With respect to the kings of Israel, it regularly refers to what their power produced (1 Ki. 15:23; 16:5, 27). Ultimately, all power belongs to the Lord (1 Chr. 29:11). See *strength*.

Noun: זְרוֹעַ (*zᵉrôaʿ*), GK 2432 (S 2220), 91x. *zᵉrôaʿ* denotes the arm or forearm. It is used to denote the literal arm of a person (Gen. 49:24; Isa. 9:20). Since the arm can be viewed as the seat of strength, it is used metaphorically to refer to someone's *strength* or *power* (1 Sam. 2:31), especially God's power (Exod. 6:6; Deut. 4:34; 5:15; Ps. 44:4; 79:11; 89:11). See *arm*.

Noun: חַיִל (*ḥayil*), GK 2657 (S 2428), 246x. The basic sense of *ḥayil* is "power, strength, or capability." See *strength*.

Noun: כֹּחַ (*kōaḥ*), GK 3946 (S 3581b), 126x. The basic sense of *kōaḥ* is "strength, power." It can refer to physical strength or strength in some metaphorical sense. For example, *kōaḥ* refers to the power to produce or reproduce (e.g., Gen. 49:3). It is also used of God's power. See *strength*.

Noun: מַלְכוּת (*malkût*), GK 4895 (S 4438), 91x. *malkût* ranges in meaning from an abstract reference to a king's dynasty or power (Num. 24:7; 1 Sam. 20:31) to the more concrete location of a "kingdom" (2 Chr. 1:1; Neh. 9:35). See *king*.

Noun: עֹז (*ʿōz*), GK 6437 (S 5797), 76x. The primary sense of *ʿōz* is "strength, might, power." David danced before the ark of the covenant with all his *might* (2 Sam. 6:14). The *mighty* scepter of the Messiah will extend from Zion (Ps. 110:2), but the *mighty* scepter of Moab (representative of the enemies of Israel) will be broken (Jer. 48:17). Sometimes in the context of military defense, the word *ʿōz*, used by itself, refers to "ramparts, fortifications, strong refuge" (Prov. 21:22; Amos 3:11). This idea is applied metaphorically to God, who is "my strong tower" (Ps. 61:3) and "my mighty rock and refuge" (Ps. 62:7). Most commonly, *ʿōz* is used to describe God's power or strength. Power belongs to God (62:11); in his kingly role he is declared to be mighty (99:4). No one can know the "power of his anger" (90:11). But for those who trust in him as his people, he is their strength and shield (28:7) and a strong deliverer (lit., "the *strength* of my salvation," 140:7). See *NIDOTTE* 3:365-376.

New Testament

Noun: δύναμις (*dynamis*), GK *1539* (S *1411*), 119x. *dynamis* essentially means "power," but it can also denote acts of power ("miracles") or a person's "ability."

(1) God is the source of all power. In the NT, "power" belongs to the Triune God, who can do as he pleases with his creation (Rev. 11:17). "Power" is sometimes used as a circumlocution for God, as when Jesus says, "You will see the Son of Man seated at the right hand of *The Power*" (NIV: "the Mighty One"; Mt. 26:64; Mk. 14:62). Jesus heals by the power of the LORD (Lk. 5:17), and Paul calls Christ the power of God (1 Cor. 1:24). God wants to put his power on display (Rom. 9:17). Those who worship God and the Lamb ascribe power to them (Rev. 4:11; 5:12; 7:12; 19:1).

Jesus, God's Son, sustains all things "by the word of his power" (Heb. 1:3). When the woman with the flow of blood touched Jesus in faith, Jesus perceived that "power" had gone out from him (Mk. 5:30; cf. a similar use in Lk. 6:19). The apostles point to these powers as God's attestation of Jesus (Acts 2:22). The assembled church possesses the power of the LORD Jesus (1 Cor. 5:4). The Son of Man will come with "*power* and much glory" (Mt. 24:30; 2 Thess. 1:7). Jesus remains a priest forever "by the *power* of his indestructible life" (Heb. 7:16).

The Holy Spirit also has power. When Mary asks how she will conceive, being a virgin, Gabriel tells her, "The Holy Spirit will come upon you, and the *power* of the Most High will overshadow you" (Lk. 1:35). Jesus ministers in "the power of the Holy Spirit" (Lk. 4:14). He promises his disciples that when the Holy Spirit comes upon them, they will "receive *power*" (Acts 1:8). Christians abound in hope by the power of the Holy Spirit (Rom. 15:19).

(2) The "power of God" secures the victory of his kingdom (Rev. 12:10). That kingdom will come "with power" (Mk. 9:1; 1 Cor. 4:20). Jesus rebukes the Sadducees for not knowing the "power of God" when they mock the resurrection (Mt. 22:29). Just as the risen and ascended Jesus lives by the power of God, Christians will be raised by the power of God (1 Cor. 6:14; 2 Cor. 13:4; Eph. 1:19–20). The gospel, whereby God builds the kingdom, is the "power of God for salvation" (Rom. 1:16; 1 Cor. 1:18). Paul's preaching and ministry are by the power of God (1 Cor. 2:4; Eph. 3:7; Col. 1:29), with the result that the Corinthians' faith is in the power of God (1 Cor. 2:5). God's power strengthens and keeps believers (Eph. 3:16, 20; Col. 1:11; 2 Tim. 1:7–8; 1 Pet. 1:5; 2 Pet. 1:3) as a foretaste of the powers of the age to come (Heb. 6:5).

(3) *dynamis* is also used to describe the acts of power (i.e., miracles) done by Jesus (Mt. 11:20, 21, 23). He did not do many "miraculous powers" where faith was lacking (Mt. 13:58). His disciples praised God for the "mighty works" he did (Lk. 19:37). At his resurrection, Jesus is enthroned in power as the messianic King (Rom. 1:4).

Jesus' followers can do "mighty works" in his name (Mt. 7:22). For instance, the casting out of demons is equated with "doing a *mighty work*" (Mk. 9:38–39), and when Jesus sends out the twelve, he gives them "*power* and authority to drive out all the demons and to cure diseases" (Lk. 9:1). Jesus also gives to his people authority "to trample on snakes … and to overcome "all the power of the enemy" (Lk. 10:19); this relates to the victory of the seed of the woman over the seed of the serpent (see Gen. 3:15).

Gabriel promised Zechariah that John the Baptist would go forth in the "spirit and *power* of Elijah" (Lk. 1:17; cf. Mal. 4:5–6). As Jesus departs, he promises his followers that they will be clothed with "power from on high" (Lk. 24:49; cf. Acts 1:8). The powerful ministry of Jesus is then carried forward in his name by the disciples (Acts 3:12, 16; 4:7, 33; 6:8; 8:13; 19:11; Heb. 2:3–4). The "working of miracles" is on Paul's list of gifts of the Spirit (1 Cor. 12:10, 28–29). "Miracles" are among the signs of an apostle (2 Cor. 12:12), though Satan is able to counterfeit these miracles (2 Thess. 2:9).

(4) The "*powers* of the heavens" will be shaken when the Son of Man comes (Mt. 24:29). This refers either to the heavenly bodies—sun, moon, stars—or it refers to powerful demonic beings. For demons as "powers" see Rom. 8:38; 1 Cor. 15:24; Eph. 1:21; 1 Pet. 3:22.

(5) *dynamis* occasionally refers to human ability, whether the "ability" to handle responsibility (Mt. 25:15), or difficulties (2 Cor. 1:8; Rev. 3:8), or financial means (2 Cor. 8:3). Sarah received "power" (i.e., the ability) to conceive (Heb. 11:11). Though people have been sown in weakness, they will be raised in power (1 Cor. 15:43).

(6) The forces of nature also have power, as in the references to the power of a voice (1 Cor. 14:11), the power of fire (Heb. 11:34), and the power of the sun (Rev. 1:16, unless the power is not of the sun but of the shining of Jesus' face). See *NIDNTT-A*, 154-55.

Noun: ἐξουσία (*exousia*), GK *2026* (S *1849*), 102x. *exousia* means "authority, power, right," and the word is used in a variety of different contexts. See *authority*.

Noun: ἰσχύς (*ischys*), GK *2709* (S *2479*), 10x. *ischys* means "strength, power, might." See *strength*.

Noun: κράτος (*kratos*), GK *3197* (S *2904*), 12x. *kratos* is generally translated "power, strength, might." (1) This noun can communicate a sense of sovereign dominion and authority in action. In all but one instance in the NT it refers to the power of Christ or God. God has shown "strength" in scattering the proud (Lk. 1:51). According to the Lord's power the church grew (Acts 19:20). By the working "of his mighty *strength*," God raised Jesus from the dead (Eph. 1:19–20). The armor of God clothes Christians with "his mighty *power*" (Eph. 6:10). Paul prays for the Colossians to be empowered according to God's "glorious *might*" (Col. 1:11). The apostle ascribes eternal "power" to the unique God (1 Tim. 6:16); Peter ascribes the same to Jesus (1 Pet. 4:11) and God (5:11), and Jude does the same in his powerful benediction: "to the only God, our Savior, through Jesus Christ our Lord, be glory, majesty, *power*, and authority, before all time and now and forever. Amen" (Jude 25). In Revelation, John too states that power belongs to Jesus, God, and the Lamb (Rev. 1:6; 5:13).

(2) The one use of *kratos* that does not attribute power to God or Christ is in the statement that the death of Christ nullifies "the one who holds the *power* of death," the devil (Heb. 2:14). See *NIDNTT-A*, 317.

POWERFUL

Old Testament

Adjective: חָזָק (*ḥāzāq*), GK 2617 (S 2389), 57x. The basic sense of the adjective *ḥāzāq* is "mighty, strong, powerful." See *strong*.

New Testament

Adjective: ἰσχυρός (*ischyros*), GK *2708* (S *2478*), 29x. The adjective *ischyros* means "strong, mighty, powerful." See *strong*.

PRACTICE

New Testament

Verb: πράσσω (*prassō*), GK *4556* (S *4238*), 39x. *prassō* has a basic meaning of "to do, act, practice" something. See *do*.

PRAISE, PRAISED

Old Testament

Verb: בָּרַךְ (*bārak*), GK 1385 (S 1288), 327x. *bārak*, usually translated "to bless," indicates the action of pronouncing good things upon the recipient. It is frequently found in the Psalms (76x), as people return blessing to God in worship (where the NIV usually translates the verb as "praise"). See *bless, blessing*.

Verb: הָלַל (*halāl*), GK 2146 (S 1984), 146x. *halāl* means "to praise, boast, exult." *halāl* can take place in a human context, as when Pharaoh's servants praise Sarah to him (Gen. 12:15). Absalom too receives praise for his physical appearance (2 Sam. 14:25). The wife of noble character is praised by her husband and others (Prov. 31:28, 30–31). Personal *halāl* (boasting) can take place because of unscrupulous activities (Ps. 52:1; Prov. 20:14; 25:14), but as Jeremiah insists, we should boast only in the Lord (Jer. 9:23–24).

The majority of uses of *halāl*, however, refer to praise to God. Over half of its occurrences are in the Psalms. God is worthy of praise (Ps. 18:3; 48:1), especially because of his marvelous deeds (78:4), notably his deeds of salvation (148:14). Praise is not just a momentary element in a person's life, for the psalmist say, "I *will praise* the Lord all my life" (146:2). God's people are called to praise him both with songs (149:1) and with a large variety of musical instruments (Ps. 150). And not only should people praise him, the entire creation should join in that praise (148:1–10). That familiar word "Hallelujah" (used, e.g., in Ps. 115–117) is drawn from this verb; it means "Praise the Lord."

Verb: יָדָה (*yādâ*), GK 3344 (S 3034), 111x. *yādâ* means "praise, (give) thanks, confess." The core meaning of this verb is to express acknowledgment of some sort. Sixty percent of its uses occur in the psalms. The psalmists frequently call on the people to "*give thanks* to the Lord, for he is good" (e.g., Ps. 106:1; 107:1; 136:1–3, 26; cf. 1 Chr. 16:34). God's unfailing love to his people never ends. Similarly, the psalmists call on us "to praise the Lord," not only with the voice (Ps. 67:3, 5) but also with musical instruments (33:2; 71:22; 92:1). Ultimately, all praise and thanksgiving must come from the heart (9:1; 28:7). One of the formal ways to thank God is through a *tôdâ* (GK 9343, a "thank offering," a noun related to this verb; see Lev. 7:12–15; Ps. 50:14, 23).

The first use of this verb in the OT is from Leah after the birth of Judah (whose name is derived from this verb). After desperately looking for love from her husband, Jacob, at the birth of her first three children, with the birth of the fourth she decides instead to focus on the one who will never disappoint her: "This time I will praise the Lord" (Gen. 29:35; cf. 49:8). It is significant that it is from this son that our Savior Jesus was born.

This same verb can also mean the acknowledgment of one's sins. God is a God who expects us to "confess" our sins, for he is a God of unfailing love and mercy and will forgive our sins (Lev. 26:40; Ps. 32:5; Prov. 28:13). Involved in that process is "confessing" the name of the Lord (1 Ki. 8:33, 35; 2 Chr. 6:24, 26), that is, acknowledging that from him alone is forgiveness possible. In three important OT passages, this confession of sin involves not only the individual's own sin but especially the sins of the entire people (Ezr. 10:1; Neh. 1:6; 9:2–3; Dan. 9:4, 20). See *NIDOTTE*, 2:405–8.

Noun: תְּהִלָּה (*tᵉhillâ*), GK 9335 (S 8416), 58x. *tᵉhillâ* means "praise." This is the noun related to the verb *halāl* (GK 2146). The vast majority of the uses of *tᵉhillâ* are for praise to God. Isaiah specifically states about the Lord God, "I will not give my glory to another or my *praise* to idols" (Isa. 42:8). Habakkuk announces that God's "glory covered the heavens and his *praise* filled the earth" (Hab. 3:3). Because of what God will do for Jerusalem, he will "make her the *praise* of the earth" (Isa. 62:7; cf. Zeph. 3:20). Other cities and nations will lose the human praise and boasting that has been ascribed to them (Jer. 48:2; 49:25; 51:41).

Understandably, more than half of the occurrences of this word are in the Psalms (which is called in the Heb. by the plural of this noun, *tᵉhillîm*, "praises, hymns"). Praise belongs to God because of all his "praiseworthy deeds" (Ps. 78:4). Praise awaits God (65:1), and we are instructed to praise him with song (149:1) and with our mouths (34:1; 51:15). The psalmist encourages us to "enter his gates with thanksgiving and his courts with *praise*" (100:4). In a society in which we seek praise from our fellow human beings, we should never forget the one to whom all praise belongs first and foremost, the Lord our God. "How pleasant and fitting [it is] to *praise* him" (147:1). See *NIDOTTE*, 1:1035–38.

New Testament

Verb: δοξάζω (*doxazō*), GK *1519* (S *1392*), 61x. *doxazō* means "to glorify, give honor to, praise." See *glorify*.

Verb: ἐξομολογέω (*exomologeō*), GK *2018* (S *1843*), 10x. *exomologeō* means "to confess, profess," and even "to praise." See *confess*.

Verb: εὐλογέω (*eulogeō*), GK *2328* (S *2127*), 41x. *eulogeō* means "to bless, praise, thank" someone. See *bless*.

Noun: ἔπαινος (*epainos*), GK *2047* (S *1868*), 11x. *epainos* denotes the approval or recognition that is offered to an object worthy of such designation and is best translated as "praise, commendation." In two instances, the word denotes praise or commendation that rulers give to law-abiding citizens (Rom. 13:3; 1 Pet. 2:14).

For the most part, however, the fullness of God's work of salvation through Christ is the focus of praise. Paul emphatically declares, "He predestined us to be adopted as his sons through Jesus Christ, in accordance with his pleasure and will—to the *praise* of his glorious grace" (Eph. 1:5–6, cf. 1:12, 14; see also Phil. 1:11). When Christ returns, the refined faith of those who have endured persecution and suffering will be a reason to give praise and glory to God, as Peter writes: "These have come so that your faith … may be proved genuine and may result in *praise*, glory and honor when Jesus Christ is revealed" (1 Pet. 1:7). The primary task of humankind is to give this praise to God (Phil. 4:8) and not oneself (Rom. 2:29; 1 Cor. 4:5). This term reminds the community of faith that the standing ovation goes to God alone. See *NIDNTT-A*, 20-21.*

Noun: εὐλογία (*eulogia*), GK *2330* (S *2129*), 16x. In its most general sense, *eulogia* means "speaking well." The word is especially used for the blessings God bestows on others as well as the blessings and praise he receives. See *blessing*.

Adjective: εὐλογητός (*eulogētos*), GK *2329* (S *2128*), 8x. *eulogētos* means "blessed, praised." See *blessed*.

PRAY

Old Testament

Verb: פָּלַל (*pālal*), GK 7137 (S 6419), 84x. *pālal* means "to pray, intercede." The Heb. language contains at lease twelve words for "pray" and "prayer," *pālal* being the most common verb Most often *pālal* refers to intercessory prayer, such as Solomon's intercessory prayer for his people during the dedication of the temple, Solomon using the word 20x (1 Ki. 8; 2 Chr. 6). Many of the prayers in the OT are "representative prayers"; that is, for the most part, people do not appear to have prayed themselves, but came to a prophet, a priest, or a king and asked them to pray for them. This was, in fact, one of the main roles of the priest, especially on the Day of Atonement (see Lev. 16).

Scholars have suggested numerous possibilities for the origin of *pālal*. Some connect *pālal* with an Arabic word that means "to cut or wound oneself." This would reflect the pagan practice of cutting oneself during worship and illustrates the difference between biblical and pagan prayer (note how cutting oneself is prohibited in the Mosaic law, Deut. 14:1). Some suggest that *pālal* developed from the Heb. word meaning "to fall" (i.e., to fall prostrate before the Lord).

Prayer is powerful. Abraham prays for healing, and his prayer is answered (Gen. 20:7, 17). Moses prays for God's fiery anger to subside, and it does (Num. 11:1–3). Moses intercedes before the Lord after the golden calf incident (Deut. 9:25–28), and the Lord forgives his people. Hannah prays to the Lord for a child, and she receives one (1 Sam. 1:10, 12, 26–27). Both Elisha's and Hezekiah's prayers are answered (2 Ki. 6:17–18; 19:15–19, 35–36). Nehemiah's book is sprinkled with many "arrow prayers to God" (Neh. 1:4; 2:4; 4:9). God's willingness to answer prayers is especially seen during the time of opposition from their enemies. Daniel prays fervently before the Lord, confessing the sins of the people (Dan. 9:4, 20). And Jonah prays to God from inside the fish's belly, and shortly thereafter Jonah is vomited up on dry land a couple days later (Jon. 2:1, 10). See *NIDOTTE,* 3:627-28.

New Testament

Verb: δέομαι (*deomai*), GK *1289* (S *1189*), 22x. *deomai* is a general word for prayer where a request is being made, either of a person or of God. It can be translated as "pray" (Mt. 9:39, KJV), "ask" (Lk. 11:37, NASB), "beseech" (Mt. 9:39, NASB), "beg" (Lk. 9:38), or "plead" (2 Cor. 8:4).

Before being delivered of his demons, the Gerasene demoniac "begs": "Don't torture me!" (Lk. 8:28). After being delivered of his demons he "begs" to go with

Jesus (8:38). A man covered with leprosy falls to the ground and "begs" Jesus for healing (5:12). The father of a demoniac "begs" Jesus to heal his son who is often seized with a spirit, which causes him to scream and throws him into convulsions (9:40).

deomai is used for Jesus' prayer that Peter's faith not fail (Lk. 22:32); Paul's earnest praying, night and day, for the Thessalonians (1 Thess. 3:10); Paul's "appeal" that the Galatians to "become like me!" (Gal. 4:12); our appeal to God to send workers of the harvest (Mt. 9:38); and the appeal that God makes through us to the world, "Be reconciled to God" (2 Cor. 5:20). See *NIDNTT-A,* 129.

Verb: προσεύχομαι (*proseuchomai*), GK *4667* (S *4336*), 85x. *proseuchomai* is the most general word meaning "to pray." Praying was a continual part of Jesus' life, often preceding significant upcoming events (Mt. 14:23; 26:36; Mk. 1:35; Lk. 9:18, 28). This is continued in the NT church's community (Acts 2:42; 6:6; 1 Cor. 11:4) and in Paul's life (Acts 9:11; 13:3; Phil. 1:9; Col. 1:3, 9). It should be the activity of all Christians (Eph. 6:18), who are instructed to "*pray* without ceasing" (1 Thess. 5:17)—even for one's enemies (Mt. 5:44).

Prayer is to be modeled on Jesus' pattern prayer (Lk. 11:1–4), commonly known as the "Lord's Prayer," although of course Jesus would not have prayed this prayer since it involves a confession of sin (Mt. 6:12). Christian prayer is to be significantly different from the world's prayers (6:5–15). It is not done for worldly praise or on the assumption that God can be manipulated with many empty words. It is addressed to God, who is both heavenly and approachable; it is concerned primarily with God and his glory. Even praying for our needs is based on the belief that God can meet our deficiencies; e.g., we cannot withstand the onslaught of temptation by ourselves but need God's intervention.

There are many different ways to pray. Jesus prays for children (Mt. 19:13). Paul intercedes for his churches (2 Thess. 1:11) and asks that others pray for him (2 Thess. 3:1; cf. Heb 13:18). Praying can be communal (Acts 12:12; 1 Cor. 11:4–5) or private (Mt. 6:6; Mk. 1:35). Jesus' command to pray privately (Mt. 6:5–6) is not an injunction against public prayer; it is only an injunction against praying in public places in order to be thought of as very religious.

There are different postures for prayer. While the common Jewish posture was standing, head looking up with arms outstretched (1 Tim. 2:8), Jesus also prays prostrate on his face (Mt. 26:39). According to church tradition, James's nickname was "camel-knees," suggesting constantly praying on his knees. No one position of prayer may be viewed as uniquely "right."

The fact that people pray to both God (Mt. 6:9) and Jesus (Acts 1:24) is part of the proof of Jesus' deity. Stephen does pray to Jesus (Acts 7:60), but the norm is to pray to God the Father (Mt. 6:9). Only once in the NT does this verb seem to suggest praying took place to pagan deities (Mt. 6:7); that is, praying is a uniquely Christian activity.

One of the difficult issues of biblical theology is that of apparently "unanswered" prayer. Jesus teaches, "Therefore I tell you, whatever you ask in prayer, believe that you have received it, and it will be yours" (Mk. 11:24). Prayer also must be done in accordance with God's will, and yet even so Jesus gives tremendous privilege to his followers in prayer. We are to pray constantly and not give up (Lk. 18:1). Prayers must be preceded by requesting forgiveness from those we have sinned against (Mk. 11:25). Fortunately, when believers do not know how to pray, the Holy Spirit intercedes for them with groans too deep for words (Rom. 8:26; cf. Jude 20). This is not a charismatic gift but the joy of every believer. See *NIDNTT-A,* 493-95.

PRAYER

Old Testament

Noun: תְּפִלָּה (t^e*pillâ*), GK 9525 (S 8605), 77x. t^e*pillâ* is a common word in the OT for "prayer, intercession, petition"; it is related to the verb *pālal* (GK 7137; see *pray*).

Most often t^e*pillâ* refers to petitionary prayer. Psalms uses this noun 32x. Five superscriptions specifically list the psalm as a t^e*pillâ* (Ps. 17; 86; 90; 102; 142; cf. also Hab. 3:1). The author of Ps. 4 prays and requests deliverance from his enemies: "Answer me when I call to you, O my righteous God. Give me relief from my distress; be merciful to me and hear my *prayer*" (4:1). The author of Ps. 102 prays and requests God's assistance in regard to unexplained suffering (102:1). The t^e*pillâ* prayer can be a plea for mercy, a cry for help, or a pleading with God; it is never used of a request made from one human being to another. Such prayers are, therefore, always directed to the Lord in heaven (cf. 2 Chr. 6:39; 30:27). Ps. 102:17 gives the assurance connected with a t^e*pillâ*: "He will respond to the *prayer* of the destitute; he will not despise their *plea*." Note too that "the Lord is far from the wicked but he hears the prayer of the righteous" (Prov. 15:29).

Ps. 88 has been called the "gloomiest" song found in the Bible. This psalm has been referred to as the story of Job half-told, i.e., tragedy without compensation. Every line of this psalm reveals the excruciating pain of the writer. Its situation portrays lifelong trouble, perhaps a life-threatening illness. Repeatedly, the author expresses his feeling of being totally overwhelmed by suffering. Having no other alternative, he turns to the Lord in t^e*pillâ*: "May my *prayer* come before you; turn your ear to my cry" (Ps. 88:2);"But I cry to you for help, O Lord; in the morning my *prayer* comes before you" (v. 13). See *NIDOTTE, 4:325.*

New Testament

Noun: δέησις (*deēsis*), GK *1255* (S *1162*), 18x. *deēsis* is a "prayer, petition, supplication" based on a person's need—in the NT always addressed to God. It is not a general word for prayer but specifically a prayer of "supplication," a request for a need—usually an urgent request (1 Tim. 5:5), though not always (Lk. 5:33; Eph. 6:18). In every prayer of Paul for the Philippians, the supplication is accompanied with joy (Phil. 1:4).

deēsis is used for Zechariah's prayer for barren Elizabeth (Lk. 1:13), Anna's prayer for the long-awaited Messiah child (2:37), the Philippians' prayers for Paul (Phil. 1:19), Paul's prayers for Timothy (2 Tim. 1:3), and petitions of Christians for governmental leaders (1 Tim. 2:2). Jesus prayed these kinds of prayers with crying and tears during the days of his flesh (Heb. 5:7). These are the kinds of petitions that all Christians should make known to God (Phil. 4:6; Jas. 5:16), and the Lord's ears are attentive to such prayers (1 Pet. 3:12). See *NIDNTT-A,* 129.

Noun: προσευχή (*proseuchē*), GK *4666* (S *4335*), 36x. *proseuchē* is a general word for "prayer." It is a noun that corresponds to the verb *proseuchomai* (GK *4667*; see *pray*). It can be used for a "place of *prayer*" (Acts 16:13, 16), such as a synagogue or the temple, which is to be "called a house of *prayer*" (Mt. 21:13; Mk. 11:17; Lk. 19:46).

proseuchē is always prayer to a deity; in the NT, it is used for prayers to Jesus (Eph. 1:16–17; Rev. 5:8; 8:3–4) or to God (Rom. 15:30), never to pagan deities. Jesus sometimes spends an entire night "praying to God" (Lk. 6:12), and the apostle Paul likewise is a man of much prayer (Rom. 1:10; Eph. 1:16; 1 Thess. 1:2; Phlm. 4). This noun can refer to prayer as a regular habit (Col. 4:2) or as a single act (Lk. 22:45). The literal phrase "with *prayer* he prayed" in Jas. 5:17 means "he *prayed earnestly*." See *NIDNTT-A,* 493-95.

PREACH

New Testament

Verb: εὐαγγελίζω (*euangelizō*), GK *2294* (S *2097*), 54x. Generally, *euangelizō* means simply "to bring a message, announce good news" (1 Thess. 3:6, Rev. 10:7). However, the word is used primarily in the specialized sense of preaching the gospel, that is, God's message of salvation through Jesus Christ (Lk. 1:19, 20; 9:6; 20:1; Acts 5:42; 8:4, 25, 35; 10:36; 11:20; 13:32; 17:18; Gal. 1:16). Reflecting this usage, *euangelizō* is often translated "to preach the gospel" or "to preach the good news" (our word "evangelize" comes from this word). It differs from *keryssō* ("to preach, proclaim") in that the latter emphasizes the act of proclamation while *euangelizō* stresses the content of what is proclaimed.

John the Baptist preaches the good news (Lk. 3:18). One of the signs that Jesus is the Messiah is that the poor have the good news preached to them (Mt. 11:5); Jesus identifies this preaching as the fulfillment of Isa. 61:1 (Lk. 4:18). Jesus preaches the good news of the kingdom of God (4:43; 8:1), and those who follow him do the same (Acts 8:12). The goal of preaching the gospel is to persuade people to turn to God (14:15, 21).

Paul's life work is to preach the gospel (Rom. 1:15; 15:20; 1 Cor. 1:17; 9:16; Eph. 3:8). He condemns those who preach a gospel different from the gospel of grace that God has called him to preach (Gal. 1:8, 9, 11). Paul uses the related word *proeuangelizomai*, "to preach the gospel beforehand," to indicate that the gospel was preached ahead of time to Abraham when God told him, "All nations will be blessed by you" (Gen. 12:3b, quoted in Gal. 3:8). The preaching of the gospel lies at the center of the entire Bible, whether in OT promise or NT fulfillment. See *NIDNTT-A*, 213-15.

Verb: κηρύσσω (*kēryssō*), GK *3062* (S *2784*), 61x. *kēryssō* means to "preach, proclaim, tell, announce a message." In the NT it is used primarily with two objects: the gospel (Mt. 4:23; 24:14; Mk. 1:14; 16:15; Gal. 2:2; 1 Thess. 2:9) and (Jesus) Christ (Acts 8:5; 1 Cor. 1 19; 15:12; 2 Cor. 4:5; Phil. 1:15). Including these cases, almost all of its occurrences refer to the proclamation of the Christian message (see Mt. 3:1; Mk. 6:12; Acts 10:42; 2 Cor. 1:19; 1 Pet. 3:19). Elsewhere it occurs with such objects as the message of John the Baptist (Lk. 3:3; Jn. 3:1; Acts 10:37), the proclamation by Jews of the law of Moses (Acts 15:21; Rom. 2:21), a message in contrast to the gospel (Gal. 5:11), and an angel declaring the worth and deeds of Jesus in heaven (Rev. 5:2).

Among those who do the "proclaim ing" are John the Baptist (Mt. 3:1), Jesus (4:17), the disciples (Mk. 3:14), a formerly demon-possessed man (5:20), Paul (Acts 19:13), and Timothy (2 Tim. 4:2).

A controversial passage is 1 Pet. 3:18, which says that Jesus "proclaimed to the spirits in prison." This could refer to his universal proclamation of victory to the spirit world or to his preaching through Noah's preaching the gospel in his time. It could also refer to the events of the death and resurrection of Jesus themselves being a message to the spirits in prison. In any case, it cannot refer to a second offer of salvation to those who have died (Heb. 9:27), for this interpretation goes contrary to the entire NT message. See *NIDNTT-A*, 304-6.

PRECIOUS

New Testament

Adjective: τίμιος (*timios*), GK *5508* (S *5093*), 13x. *timios* refers to something that is considered "valuable, precious, honorable." See *valuable*.

PREDESTINE

New Testament

Verb: προορίζω (*proorizō*), GK *4633* (S *4309*), 6x. *proorizō* means "to predestine; choose, determine, set apart beforehand." It is derived from *pro*, meaning "before" or "ahead of," and *orizō*, meaning "to appoint, decide, determine."

God is always the one doing the action of this verb In Peter's Pentecost sermon, he says of those who put Jesus to death that "they did what your power and will *had decided beforehand* should happen" (Acts 4:28). Elsewhere, the word is associated with God's purposes for believers determined ahead of time. God "*predestined* us to be adopted as his sons through Jesus Christ" (Eph. 1:5). Believers receive an inheritance from God because they are "*predestined* according to his purpose" (Eph. 1:11). They are "*predestined* to become conformed to the image of his Son" (Rom. 8:29–30). The hidden wisdom of God that Paul preaches was "*predestined* before the ages for our glory" (1 Cor. 2:7). These eternal purposes of God for every Christian are a foregone conclusion because they are grounded in his predetermined will. This is why the eighteenth-century theologian Jonathan Edwards referred to God's predestining of believers along with his other saving acts listed in Rom. 8:29–30 as links in the "inviolable chain of redemption." Some people struggle with the concept of predestination as it seems to conflict with their supposed personal free will, but the doctrine is clearly taught in Scripture. See *NIDNTT-A*, 492.*

PREFER

Old Testament

Verb: בָּחַר (*bāḥar*), GK 1047 (S 977), 172x. *bāḥar* means "to choose, select, prefer." While this word has secular uses, it is also intimately linked with God's election of Israel. See *choose*.

New Testament

Verb: εὐδοκέω (*eudokeō*), GK *2305* (S *2106*), 21x. *eudokeō* designates the pleasure a person takes in another person or in doing something. See *pleased, pleasure*.

PREPARE

Old Testament

Verb: כּוּן (*kûn*), GK 3922 (S 3559), 219x. *kûn* means "to establish, prepare, provide." See *establish*.

Verb: עָרַךְ (*ʿārak*), GK 6885 (S 6186), 75x. *ʿārak* denotes the action of arranging an object in a particular way or arranging objects in a specific order to produce a desired effect. A common use of *ʿārak* is "to arrange" a table for a banquet, which the NIV sometimes translates as "to prepare" a table (Ps. 23:5). See *arrange*.

New Testament

Verb: ἑτοιμάζω (*hetoimazō*), GK *2286* (S *2090*), 40x. *hetoimazō means* "to prepare" and may be linked with either an impersonal or a personal object. Quoting Isa. 40:3, John the Baptist cries out, "*Prepare* the way of the Lord; make straight his paths" (Mt. 3:3; Mk. 1:3; Lk. 3:4; cf. Lk. 1:17, 76). At the end of Jesus' ministry the disciples "prepare" the Passover meal (Mt. 26:17, 19; Mk. 14:12, 15–16; Lk. 22:8, 9, 12, 13). According to John's gospel, during this meal Jesus assures his disciples that he was going away in order to "*prepare* a place for [them]" (Jn. 14:2–3). And when we think of our own future, we can anticipate someday receiving the glorious things "God *has prepared* for those who love him" (1 Cor. 2:9; cf. Heb. 11:16).

Used with a personal object, *hetoimazō* can mean to prepare someone else or to prepare oneself. In Acts 23:23, for example, the Roman tribune in Jerusalem ordered two of his centurions to prepare two hundred soldiers so as to protect Paul from a secret plot to murder him. In 2 Tim. 2:21, Paul emphasizes how God has cleansed believers and "prepared" them to do good works. As we look ahead to the time of Christ's return, we can eagerly anticipate the time when the bride of Christ will "make herself ready" for the coming wedding of the Lamb (Rev. 19:7; 21:2). See *NIDNTT-A*, 212-13.

Verb: καταρτίζω (*katartizō*), GK *2936* (S *2675*), 13x. *katartizō* means "to restore, put in order, prepare" for a specific purpose. (1) In the gospels, this verb can refer to the "preparation" of fishing nets (Mt. 4:21). It can also mean to put into a proper or suitable condition, as in Lk. 6:40: "A student is not like his teacher, but everyone who is *fully trained* will be like his teacher." In Mt. 21:16, Jesus cites Ps. 8:2, and applies it to the children shouting praises in the temple: "From the lips of children and infants you have *ordained* praise."

(2) *katartizō* occurs more frequently in the NT letters. Paul writes in Rom. 9:22 that some "have been prepared" for utter

destruction. The apostle also uses this verb when he tells the Galatian church that when an individual "is restored," it should be done in a spirit of gentleness (Gal. 6:1). In 1 Cor. 1:10 he appeals to the Corinthians to "agree with one another so that there be no divisions among you and that you may be *perfectly united* in mind and thought." In 2 Cor. 13:11, Paul commands the Christians in Corinth to "aim for perfection" (cf. 1 Thess. 3:10; Heb. 13:21). The Corinthian church, which was so divided, should "put in order" and "mend" their behavior so that they may function properly as the body of Christ.

Verb: κατασκευάζω (*kataskeuazō*), GK *2941* (S *2680*), 11x. The basic meaning of *kataskeuazō* concerns preparation (e.g., Mt. 11:10, "I will send my messenger ahead of you, who *will prepare* your way before you"), although the vast majority of the NT usage means "to build" something. See *build.*

PRESENCE

Old Testament

Noun: פָּנֶה (*pāneh*; occurs only in plural, פָּנִים [*pānîm*]), GK 7156 (S 6440), 2126x. In the OT, *pāneh* basically refers to the front side of something or someone, typically the head or the face. God promises Moses that his face will go with him, meaning that God's "presence" will personally accompany him in Israel's journey to Canaan. See *face.*

New Testament

Noun: παρουσία (*parousia*), GK *4242* (S *3952*), 24x. *parousia* means "coming, presence"; it is especially related to the second coming of our Lord. See *coming.*

PRESENT

Old Testament

Verb: קָרַב (*qārab*), GK 7928 (S 7126), 280x. The basic meaning of *qārab* is "to draw near" or, in a causative sense, "to bring near." Theologically, the most significant use of *qārab* is in its connection with the service of the tabernacle or temple, as describing the priest who "brings near, presents, or offers" his offering. Thus, *qārab* is used extensively throughout Leviticus in connection with the priestly service and sacrifices. See *bring.*

Verb: רִיב (*rîb*), GK 8189 (S 7378), 72x. *rîb* denotes the action of entering into an argument, conflict, or lawsuit with another person. When a case or a cause is the object of *rîb*, the NIV may translate the verb as "plead" (e.g., Ps. 43:1), "defend" (e.g., 74:22), "present" (e.g., Prov. 18:17), or "take up" (e.g., 22:23; 23:11). See *contend.*

New Testament

Verb: παρίστημι (*paristēmi*), GK *4225* (S *3936*), 41x. The root meaning of *paristēmi* is "to stand, place beside." A number of variations of meaning are found in the NT, such as "to present" something. See *stand.*

Verb: προτίθημι (*protithēmi*), GK *4729* (S *4388*), 3x. *protithēmi* means "to plan, present." See *plan.*

Verb: φέρω (*pherō*), GK *5770* (S *5342*), 66x. *pherō* has the basic meaning "to bring, carry, present," but it has a wide range of figurative meanings, such as "to endure, sustain." See *bring.*

Noun: δῶρον (*dōron*), GK *1565* (S *1435*), 19x. *dōron* basically means a "gift" or "present"; most frequently it denotes an "offering" to God. See *gift.*

Noun: ενιστημι (*enistēmi*), GK *1931* (S *1764*), 7x. *enistēmi* denotes "the present" (cf. Heb. 9:9), especially in contrast to the future. One of the key features of the "present" age is that it is filled with evil and wickedness (Gal. 1:4; 2 Tim. 3:1); Paul refers in 1 Cor. 7:26 to "the present crisis," though it is difficult to know exactly what he has in mind by this phrase. Yet Paul also assures us that the "present" time is in the hands of our powerful and loving God, and thus no matter what happens, it cannot separate us from the love of God (Rom. 8:38; cf. 1 Cor. 3:22).

In 2 Thess. 2:2 Paul has to deal with a group who are proclaiming that "the day of the Lord has already come" (i.e., "is already present"). Paul goes on to tell the Thessalonians what two things must yet happen before that day arrives: the coming of the "Man of Lawlessness" (i.e., the Antichrist) and the "Rebellion" (a large movement of people claiming to be Christians away from the faith).

(BE) PRESENT

New Testament

Verb: πάρειμι (*pareimi*), GK *4205* (S *3918*), 24x. *pareimi* derives from the verb *eimi* ("I am") and the prefix *para* ("besides"), yielding the meaning "to be at one's side, be present." In the NT it is used of persons being "present" physically (Jn. 11:28, of Jesus; 2 Cor. 10:2, of Paul) as well as spiritually (1 Cor. 5:3, of Paul). It is used of Peter and his companions who are present before God (Acts 10:33), and by Paul of his accusers, who should have been present in the ongoing legal proceedings against him (Acts 24:19). Paul does not need "to be with" the Galatians in order for them to be zealous for good things (Gal. 4:18; cf. v. 20). A crazed crowd in Thessalonica complains that Paul is causing trouble all over the world and "is now present" (NIV, "here") in their town (Acts 17:6).

pareimi can also be applied to concepts. For example, Paul encourages the church in Colosse that the gospel (Col. 1:6) and truth (2 Pet. 1:12) "are present" with them (Col. 1:6; cf. 2 Pet. 1:12). The writer of Hebrews reminds his readers that discipline is not enjoyable "while being implemented" but produces righteousness and peace at a later time (Heb. 12:11; cf. Jn. 7:6). Moreover, God promises never to leave or forsake his children (Heb. 13:5b); they must be content "in the present time," freed from the love of money (13:5a). See *NIDNTT-A*, 440-41.

PRESENT TIME

New Testament

Adverb: νῦν (*nyn*), GK *3814* (S *3568*), 147x. *nyn* indicates the "present time, now." See *now*.

PRESERVE

Old Testament

Verb: שָׁמַר (*šāmar*), GK 9068 (S 8104), 468x. Often translated "to keep," the verb *šāmar* bears three distinct but related meanings in the OT: "to guard, tend," "to watch over," and "to preserve" (see *keep*). *šāmar* sometimes communicate the idea of preserving or retaining. After Joseph shared his vision with Jacob and his brothers, "his brothers were jealous of him, but his father *kept* the saying in mind" (Gen. 37:11). Accordingly, "the lips of the priest should *preserve* knowledge" (Mal. 2:7). In Job 2:6 God gives Satan freedom to persecute Job, but Satan must "preserve" his life. Similarly, Prov. 13:3 states, "The one who guards his mouth *preserves* his life."

New Testament

Verb: τηρέω (*tēreō*), GK *5498* (S *5083*), 70x. *tēreō* conveys the idea of watching over something closely or guarding—"to keep, obey; guard, protect, preserve." See *guard, keep, protect.*

PRESS

New Testament

Verb: θλίβω (*thlibō*), GK *2567* (S *2346*), 10x. *thlibō* literally denotes pressing, squeezing, or crushing. A multitude forces Jesus to get into a boat that was at hand so that they will not press him (Mk. 3:9). Paul writes that he and his group are "persecuted" in every way (4:8) and "pressed in on every side" (7:5). See *persecute.*

PREVAIL

Old Testament

Verb: חָזַק (*ḥāzaq*), GK 2616 (S 2388), 290x. *ḥāzaq* can describe the severity or strength of an impersonal force. The term can describe the impersonal might of a nation or individual that results in that nation or individual prevailing over others. In Jos. 17:13 the Israelites prevail over their enemies (see also Jdg. 1:28; 2 Sam. 16:21, etc.). The word of the king is strong, and it "prevails against" (KJV) or "overrules" Joab (2 Sam. 24:4). See *strong*.

New Testament

Verb: ἰσχύω (*ischyō*), GK *2710* (S *2480*), 28x. In the NT, *ischyō* primarily means "to be strong, powerful, mighty." Sometimes it means "to prevail" against someone. See *be strong*.

PREVIOUS

Old Testament

Adjective: רִאשׁוֹן (*riʾšôn*), GK 8037 (S 7223), 182x. As an adjective, *riʾšôn* describes what is first in a series or rank. In terms of time, *riʾšôn* can convey the meaning "previously, in a former time." See *first*.

PRICE

New Testament

Noun: τιμή (*timē*), GK *5507* (S *5092*), 41x. *timē* is the amount at which something is "valued," its "price," or it can mean "honor, respect." See *value*.

PRIDE

Old Testament

Noun or Adjective: מָרוֹם (*mārôm*), GK 5294 (S 4791), 54x. *mārôm* is used either as a noun, meaning "heights," or as an adjective, meaning "high." On some occasions, this word denotes "pride." For example, to lift one's eyes "high" means to act with pride (2 Ki. 19:22; Isa. 37:23; cf. Ps. 56:2). See *heights*.

New Testament

Noun: καύχημα (*kauchēma*), GK *3017* (S *2745*), 11x. *kauchēma* is a "boast," an object of "pride," or a thing boasted about. See *boast*.

Noun: καύχησις (*kauchēsis*), GK *3018* (S *2746*), 11x. *kauchēsis* refers to the act of boasting. It can be negative or positive (e.g., having a sense of legitimate "pride" in a person or "glorying" in God). See *boast*.

PRIEST

Old Testament

Noun: כֹּהֵן (*kōhēn*), GK 3913 (S 3548), 750x. *kōhēn* normally means "priest." In the beginning men served as their own priests for sacrifices (Gen. 4:3), but as early as the time of Noah priestly responsibilities came under the patriarchal family head (8:20). The OT records the first priest to be Melchizedek (Gen. 14:18). Other familiar priests include Jethro (Moses' father-in-law, Exod. 3:1), Eli (1 Sam. 1:9), Zadok (2 Sam. 8:17), and Ezekiel (Ezek. 1:3).

The priests became the ministers in charge of sacrifice at Israel's worship centers, particularly the early tabernacle and the later temple. When God organized his people at Mount Sinai, he appointed Moses' brother Aaron and his descendants (of the tribe of Levi) as the legitimate priestly line (Exod. 28:1; 40:12–15; Num. 16:17). Shortly after the completion of the tabernacle, Aaron and his sons were consecrated into the priesthood (Lev. 8–9), and they understood their responsibilities as that of officiating at the new sanctuary (Deut. 18:5).

Mediation between the ordinary and the spiritual worlds constituted the major priestly responsibility (Exod. 28:38; Lev. 10:17; Num. 18:1). Priests were responsible for performing the ritual sacrifices and for bringing the prayers of the people to God. They did not receive any specific area of the promised land as their own, though they were given various cities in which to live.

One unique task of the high priest was to serve as an adviser to the political leader of the people, using the Urim and Thummim (see, e.g., Exod. 28:30; Num. 27:21; 1 Sam. 30:7–8). After the exile, priests were given a major role in teaching the people (Neh. 8:1–8).

There is a theology of the priests that reaches beyond the OT, however, for ideally God wanted all Israelites to serve as priests (Exod. 19:6). This theme is applied in the NT to Christians in Peter's affirmation that believers form "a chosen people, a royal priesthood" (1 Pet. 2:9). After the coming of the Spirit, the NT teaches, therefore, the doctrine of "the priesthood of all believers." We do not need to go to a human priest in order to gain access to God; rather, we all have access to the Father through Jesus, the great high priest (see Heb. 10:19–22). See *NIDOTTE* 2:600-605.

New Testament

Noun: ἱερεύς (*hiereus*), GK *2636* (S

2409), 31x. *hiereus*, which means "priest," is formed from one of the Gk. words for "holy" (*hieros*, GK *2641*; cf. *hieron*, "temple," GK *2639*). In Israel, a priest was someone set apart by God for service in the temple. If *hiereus* is used for a pagan "priest" (Acts 14:13), it refers to someone set apart for service to a god foreign to Israel.

(1) *hiereus* is used most often in the NT for the priests of Israel. Jesus instructs a man he healed of leprosy to go and show himself "to the *priests*" as commanded in the law of Moses (Mt. 8:4). Zechariah, the father of John the Baptist, is a "priest" (Lk. 1:5). Priests take an interest in John the Baptist and ask him who he is (Jn. 1:19). A priest is one of the two men who pass by on the other side of the road and refuse to aid the traveler beaten by the robbers in the story of the good Samaritan (Lk. 10:31). Priests oppose the preaching of Peter and John (Acts 4:1). Some of Jewish priests do, however, become Christians (6:7).

(2) Esp. in the book of Hebrews, *hiereus* refers to Christ (Heb. 5:6; 7:3). Jesus has a permanent priesthood, in the order of Melchidezek (5:6; 7:17, 23). He is without blemish or sin and therefore is able to cleanse our consciences from sin once and for all time (10:14). He enables us to enter God's presence, just as the OT high priest brought Israel into God's presence (10:21–22).

(3) *hiereus* is used 3x in the NT for Christians who have been set apart by God for service to God (Rev. 1:6) and who will reign with him in glory (5:10; 20:6). We form a "holy" or "royal priesthood" (1 Pet. 2:5, 9, using a related word). Seen in this light, we can affirm that the NT teaches "the priesthood of all believers." We do not need a human priest in order to help us get in touch with God; we need only Jesus, God's heavenly-sent high priest. See *NIDNTT-A*, 260-62.

PRINCE

Old Testament

Noun: שַׂר (*śar*), GK 8569 (S 8269) 381x. There are a number of overlapping nouns in the OT that refer to leaders, chiefs, and officials of various sorts (see *leader* for a thorough discussion). *śar* is one of them, and it is often translated into English as "prince." This can be misleading if this English word is understood to mean only the son of a king. Instead, *śar* indicates more broadly a leader among people in various capacities and situations.

New Testament

Noun: ἄρχων (*archōn*), GK *807* (S *758*), 37x. *archōn* is part of an extensive group of *arch-* words with meanings related to the ideas of beginning, cause, and thereby, rule and authority. Beelzebul is called the *archōn* ("prince") of the demons (Mt. 12:24; Mk. 3:22; Lk. 11:15), and Satan the *archōn* of this world (Jn. 12:31; 14:20; 16:11; cf. Eph. 2:2). See *ruler*.

PRINCIPALITY

See *ruler*.

PRISON

New Testament

Noun: φυλακή (*phylakē*), GK *5871* (S *5438*), 47x. *phylakē* denotes a "prison" or "jail." In many cases the word denotes an earthly prison. John the Baptist was put in prison by Herod (Mt. 14:3, 10). The ungrateful servant who had been forgiven went out and found a fellow servant who owed him a pittance and "had the man thrown into prison" (Mt. 18:30). Frequently in Acts, the apostles were put into jail overnight (e.g., Acts 5:19, 22, 25; 16:23–24). Jesus told the people of Smyrna that "the devil is about to cast some of you into prison" (Rev. 2:10). But *phylakē* can also carry spiritual connotations, denoting a place of punishment in hell, "the spirits in prison" (1 Pet. 3:19). Satan himself will be thrown into the bottomless pit, which in Rev. 20:7 is called a "prison." See also *watch*. See *NIDNTT-A*, 594-95.

PRISONER

New Testament

Noun: δέσμιος (*desmios*), GK *1300* (S *1198*), 16x. *desmios* refers to a person who has been arrested and is being held in custody. Barabbas is a prisoner, but he is released on demand of the Jews (Mt. 27:15–16; Mk. 15:6). All of the people in jail with Paul and Silas are "prisoners" (Acts 16:25, 27). Paul is accustomed to being called a prisoner since he has been arrested so many times (23:18; 25:14, 27; 28:17).

desmios refers to one who is bound in the chains of captivity, and so the LXX uses this word group to speak of Israel's relationship with the Lord. God has bound his people to himself with "bonds" of love (Hos. 11:4), yet Israel has rejected God's "bonds" by refusing to serve him (Jer. 2:20). Paul uses *desmios* to speak of his relationship to Jesus Christ. He proclaims himself to be "a *prisoner* of Christ Jesus" (2 Tim. 1:8; Phlm. 1, 9), "a *prisoner* of Jesus Christ for the sake of the Gentiles" (Eph. 3:1; cf. 4:1), and "a *prisoner* in the Lord" (Eph. 4:1). There were also Christian prisoners in the time that Hebrews was written (Heb. 10:34; 13:3). See *NIDNTT-A*, 129-30.*

PRIVILEGED

New Testament

Adjective: μακάριος (*makarios*), GK *3421* (S *3107*), 50x. There are two major ways *makarios* may be taken in the NT. One who is *makarios* can be "happy" or "privileged" because of life's circumstances or because of divine favors bestowed on him or her (cf. the Beatitudes). See *blessed.*

PROCEED

Old Testament

Verb: חָלַל (*ḥālal*), GK 2725 (S 2490), 135x. *ḥālal* refers either to making something impure ("to defile"; see *defile*), or it can have a more neutral, "to begin, proceed." See *begin.*

PROCLAIM

Old Testament

Verb: קָרָא (*qārāʾ*), GK 7924 (S 7121), 739x. *qārāʾ* is the most common verb in Heb. that means "to call, summon, proclaim." The basic meaning of this verb is to draw attention to oneself by using one's voice. See *call.*

Verb: שָׁמַע (*šāmaʿ*), GK 9048 (S 8085), 1165x. *šāmaʿ* means "to hear, listen, pay attention to, perceive, obey, proclaim, announce." See *hear.*

New Testament

Verb: καταγγέλλω (*katangellō*), GK *2859* (S *2605*), 18x. *katangellō* means "to proclaim, announce, make public." This verb and *kērussō* (see *preach*) are used synonymously in Phil. 1:15–17. Both vbs. are used almost exclusively in the NT in reference to the gospel or message about Jesus. The only exception is Paul's commending the Romans because "their faithfulness *is being proclaimed* all over the world" (Rom. 1:8).

Paul is the most common subject of *katangellō* (Acts 13:5; 17:3; 26:23; 1 Cor. 2:1). Jesus (Acts 26:23), the apostles (Acts 4:2) and Barnabas (Acts 13:5) also proclaim the gospel, as did the prophets of the OT (Acts 3:24), a girl freed by Paul from a spirit that enabled her to predict the future (Acts 16:17), and people who proclaim Christ out of selfish ambition (Phil. 1:17).

There is also a wide array of recipients of this proclamation. They include worshipers in the temple (Acts 3:24), attendees of synagogues (17:3, 5), presumably people in the streets (16:17), Athenians at the Areopagus (17:23), Jews and Greeks (26:23), Christians (1 Cor. 2:1), and everyone (Col. 1:28).

Finally, although the proclamation is usually a verbal delivery of the gospel, it is described in 1 Cor. 11:26 as the result of taking communion: "For whenever you eat this bread and drink this cup you *proclaim* the Lord's death until he comes." See *NIDNTT-A*, 7-8.

Verb: κηρύσσω (*kēryssō*), GK *3062* (S *2784*), 61x. *kēryssō* means to "preach, proclaim, tell, announce a message." See *preach.*

PROCRASTINATE

Old Testament

Verb: מָהַר (*māhar*), GK 4554 (S 4116), 81x. *māhar* generally means "to hurry" in the sense of moving quickly (Gen. 18:6; 19:22; 1 Sam. 4:14; Jer. 9:17; Nah. 2:6). With a negative, *māhar* means to procrastinate (e.g., 2 Chr. 24:5). See *hurry*.

PRODUCE

Old Testament

Noun: פְּרִי (*p^erî*), GK 7262 (S 6529), 119x. *p^erî* means "fruit, crops, produce." See *fruit*.

New Testament

Verb: ἀποδίδωμι (*apodidōmi*), GK *625* (S *591*), 48x. *apodidōmi* means "to give (back), deliver, render, hand over, produce." See *give (back)*.

Verb: ἐργάζομαι (*ergazomai*), GK *2237* (S *2038*), 41x. *ergazomai* is derived from *ergon* (work) and means "to work, produce, perform, do" something. See *work*.

Verb: κατεργάζομαι (*katergazomai*), GK *2981* (S *2716*), 22x. *katergazomai* means "to bring about, produce." See *bring about*.

Verb: τίκτω (*tiktō*), GK *5503* (S *5088*), 18x. The basic meaning of *tiktō* is "to give birth, bring forth, produce." See *give birth*.

PROFANE

Old Testament

Verb: חָלַל (*ḥālal*), GK 2725 (S 2490), 135x. *ḥālal* can refer either to making something impure ("to defile") or it can have a more neutral meaning "to begin, proceed" (see *begin*). In the first usage, it can refer to the defiling or profaning of things set apart for God, such as the Sabbath, or the very name of God (see *defile*).

New Testament

Noun: βέβηλος (*bebēlos*), GK *1013* (S *952*), 5x. The basic idea of "profane" is that which is for everyday use, as opposed to "holy," which is what is set aside for God's special use. For example, Ahimelech tells David there is no "ordinary" bread in the temple, only the bread of the Presence, which represents God's holy presence (1 Sam. 21:4). That which is profane is accessible to anyone and can be used without ceremony.

bebēlos occurs in the NT mostly in the Pastoral Letters to describe the false teaching in Ephesus. The condemning function of the law is for the "unholy and *profane*" (1 Tim. 1:9). Timothy is to avoid the false teachers' "*irreverent*, silly myths" (4:7) and their "*irreverent* babble" (6:20; 2 Tim. 2:16). The author of Hebrews describes Esau as "sexually immoral and *godless*" (Heb. 12:16).

The same idea can be conveyed by other words such as *anosios* (GK *495*), a negated form of a word for "holy," used as a synonym of *bebēlos* in 1 Tim. 1:9 and also describes the ungodly people in the last days (2 Tim. 3:2).*

Adjective: κοινός (*koinos*), GK *3123* (S *2839*), 14x. The basic meaning of *koinos* is "common" and can refer to objects held in "common," or it can convey the sense of "profane." See *common*.

PROFESS

New Testament

Verb: ἐξομολογέω (*exomologeō*), GK *2018* (S *1843*), 10x. *exomologeō* means "to confess, profess," and even "to praise." See *confess*.

Verb: ἐπαγγέλλομαι (*epangelomai*), GK *2040* (S *1861*), 15x. *epangelomai* generally means "to promise," though in a couple of places it means "to profess." See *promise*.

PROFIT

New Testament

Verb: ὠφελέω (*ōpheleō*), GK *6067* (S *5623*), 15x. *ōpheleō* denotes the basic idea of benefiting through a particular condition or situation, hence, "to profit, gain, value."

Theologically, Jesus measures the value of personal salvation in contrast with the profit derived from earthly existence by asking, "What *good will it be* for a man if he gains the whole world, yet forfeits his soul?" (Mt. 16:26; cf. Mk. 8:36; Lk. 9:25). Spiritual benefits can only be derived though a life of utter dependence on the Spirit and the Word. Jesus comments, "The Spirit gives life; the flesh *counts* for nothing. The words I have spoken to you are spirit and they are life" (Jn. 6:63). These spiritual benefits cannot be derived from strict adherence to OT practices. Paul emphatically writes, "Mark my words! I, Paul, tell you that if you let yourselves be circumcised, Christ will be of no *value* to you at all" (Gal. 5:2; cf. Rom. 2:25). Paul, in fact, sees no earthly benefit in any earthly pursuits outside of the supreme law of love. He writes, "If I give all I possess to the poor and surrender my body to the flames, but have not love, I *gain* nothing" (1 Cor. 13:3). See *NIDNTT-A*, 626.

PROMISE

Old Testament

Verb: אָמַר (*ʾāmar*), GK 606 (S 559), 5316x. *ʾāmar* is the most common verb in the OT for "to say, utter." See *say*. It is also a term used to indicate something that is promised. Note, for example, 1 Chr. 27:23, "the LORD had promised to make Israel as numerous as the stars in the sky" (cf. Neh. 9:15).

Verb: דָּבַר (*dābar*), GK 1819 (S 1696), 1136x. *dābar* ("say, speak") is used hundreds of times for both the human and the divine activity of speaking, sometimes in the context of making a promise. See *word*.

New Testament

Verb: ἐπαγγέλλομαι (*epangelomai*), GK *2040* (S *1861*), 15x. *epangelomai* generally means "to promise," though in a couple of places it means "to profess." (1) For the most part, biblical promises are centered in a faithful God. Stephen recounts that God promised Abraham to give the land to him and to his seed (Acts 7:5; cf. Heb. 6:13). Paul explains that Abraham was fully convinced that God was able to do what he had promised (Rom. 4:21). He also notes that the law was added because of transgressions until the seed to whom the promise was made should come (Gal. 3:19). The author of Hebrews urges his audience to hold fast to the confession of hope on the basis of the fact that the one who promised, God, is faithful (Heb. 10:23). Sarah is cited as an example of one who considered that the one who had promised was faithful (Heb. 11:11).

(2) But God's promises are not only in the past; they belong to the present and future as well. According to Paul, God, who does not lie, has promised his people eternal life before the ages began (Tit. 1:2; cf. 1 Jn. 2:25). James states that God promises a crown of life (1:12) and a kingdom (2:5) to those who love him. God has also made the end-time, apocalyptic promise that he will one final time shake not only the earth but the heavens as well (Heb. 12:26); this message warns us to get things right with him by faith while there is still time.

(3) *epangelomai* can also be used in a more secular fashion. The chief priests promised Judas money when he offered to betray Jesus (Mk. 14:11). Peter states that the false teachers he is opposing make promises of freedom that they themselves do not experience (2 Pet. 2:19).

(4) *epangelomai* also designates that which is "professed," such as godliness (1 Tim. 2:10) or so-called knowledge (1 Tim. 6:20–21). See *NIDNTT-A*, 194-95.

Verb: ὁμολογεω (*homologeō*), GK *3933* (S *3670*), 26x. *homologeō* means "to acknowledge, confess [especially confess faith]," also "to promise." See *acknowledge*.

Noun: ἐπαγγελία (*epangelia*), GK *2039* (S *1860*), 52x. *epangelia* means a "promise."

(1) The predominant use of *epangelia* in the NT refers to the promises made by God to the patriarchs recorded in the OT, such as the ones Stephen preaches about to his accusers (Acts 7:17). This probably includes both the promise to Abraham that he would have many descendents (e.g., Gen. 12:2; 13:16) and the promise that his descendents would serve a foreign nation for over 400 years and then be delivered (Gen. 15:13; Acts 7:17–37). Paul too refers to a promise in his sermon at Pisidian Antioch—the one given to David, which Paul says is fulfilled in Jesus (Acts 13:22–

23). Paul transitions to his discussion of Jesus' resurrection with the statement that he is proclaiming the good news that God has fulfilled his promise to the fathers by raising Jesus (13:32–33). As Paul later testifies before King Agrippa, he connects the promise made by God to the fathers (26:6) with the resurrection of the dead (26:8). This is similar to John's connection between the promise and eternal life (1 Jn. 2:25).

Paul treats the totality of the promises to Abraham in Rom. 4:13–20, where he summarizes the various promises as making Abraham and his offspring "the heir of the world" (see also Gal. 3:14–29). Paul mentions the OT promises in general in Rom. 9:4, and the specific promise to Abraham regarding his seed Isaac is alluded to in 9:8–9 (cf. Gal. 4:23, 28). All the OT promises are "Yes" in Jesus (2 Cor. 1:20), and Paul urges the Ephesians to remember that though they were once strangers to these promises (Eph. 2:11–12), through his ministry the Gentiles have become partakers of the promise in Christ (3:6). Paul identifies himself as an apostle according to the promise of life in Messiah Jesus (2 Tim. 1:1). Hebrews explores the OT promises and those who lived by them (Heb. 6:12, 15, 17; 7:6; 8:6; 9:15; 11:9, 13, 17, 33, 39).

(2) Several places in the NT identify what God has promised as the end-time gift of the Holy Spirit. In Lk. 24:49 Jesus tells the disciples that he is sending "the promise of the Father" to them, and then in Acts 1:4 this thought is resumed when the disciples are instructed to remain in Jerusalem and await "the promise of the Father." In Acts 2:33 it becomes explicit that in this case "the promise of the Father" is the Holy Spirit as Luke records Peter saying in his Pentecost sermon: "having received *the promise* of the Holy Spirit from the Father, he has poured out this that you see and hear." Paul connects the promise of the Holy Spirit to the blessing of Abraham in Gal. 3:14. Believers are sealed by the Holy Spirit of the promise (Eph. 1:13).

(3) The promises of God are explicitly used to urge righteous living, as when Paul appeals for purity on the basis of God's promises (2 Cor. 7:1). Paul reminds the Ephesians that the command to honor father and mother comes with a promise (Eph. 6:2), and he writes to Timothy that the profit of godliness is that it has the promise of life both now and in the age to come (1 Tim. 4:8). This technique of encouraging perseverance based on God's promises is also exploited by the author of Hebrews (cf. Heb. 4:1; 10:36). Peter assures his readers that God will keep his promise even though some may mock it (2 Pet. 3:4, 9).

(4) The only use of *epangelia* in the NT that does not refer to a promise of God occurs in Acts 23:21, where those seeking to ambush Paul seek a promise from Claudius Lysias, the Roman tribune. See *NIDNTT-A*, 194-95.

PROPERTY

Old Testament

Noun: אֲחֻזָּה (*ʾaḥuzzâ*), GK 299 (S 272), 66x. Derived from the verb *ʾāḥaz*, which means "to grasp, seize, hold," the noun *ʾaḥuzzâ* means "property, possession."

ʾaḥuzzâ is a legal term used of personal property (e.g., land, towns, or homes), especially that which is passed down through one's family by right of inheritance (Gen. 23:20; 47:11; Lev. 14:34; 25:10; Num. 27:7; 32:32; Deut. 32:49; Jos. 21:12; Neh. 11:3). In most cases, the inherited property is land located in Canaan apportioned to individuals (Gen. 17:8; 48:4; 23:4; 49:30; 50:13; Jos. 22:19). Resident aliens (e.g., household slaves) can also be considered "property" that can be inherited (Lev. 25:45–46), but native Israelites are not to be thought of in that way.

Over two-thirds of the occurrences of this word are found in Genesis through Joshua, and many of these refer to the land God promised to the Israelites as a possession (Gen. 36:43; Lev. 14:34; 25:24; Num. 35:28; Jos. 22:4, 9, 19). See *possession.*

New Testament

Noun: βίος (*bios*), GK *1050* (S *979*), 10x. *bios* denotes the course of one's "life" or the "material possessions, property" by which that life subsists (1 Jn. 3:17). See *life.*

PROPHECY

New Testament

Noun: προφητεία (*prophēteia*), GK *4735* (S *4394*), 19x. *prophēteia* is used in same way as the verb *prophēteuō* (GK *4736*; see *prophesy*). A prophecy can be a prediction about the future, but in the majority of its uses it refers to authoritative speech that has its origin with God. It can refer to prophetic words (Rev. 19:10) or activities (11:6).

prophēteia refers to the words of the prophets of the OT (Mt. 13:14, 2 Pet. 1:20) and in the NT church (1 Cor. 14:6), where it is seen as a gift of the Holy Spirit (Rom. 12:6; 1 Cor. 12:10; 13:2; 14:22–25).

Prophecy should be respected, but it should also be tested (1 Thess. 5:20–21; cf. 1 Cor. 14:29–32). That is, while prophecy carries some authority, it is ultimately subject to the authority of the apostles and their writings. The gift of prophecy may never contradict the authoritative Word of God, such as is found in Revelation (1:3; 22:19). See *NIDNTT-A,* 499-501.

PROPHESY

Old Testament

Verb: נָבָא (*nābāʾ*), GK 5547 (S 5012), 115x. *nābāʾ* means "to prophesy, speak (or behave) as a prophet." Such prophesying encouraged the Hebrews to be faithful to the Lord.

(1) Scholars debate where the word *nābāʾ* comes from and present four views. (a) *nābāʾ* means "to announce." Thus, those who deliver *nābāʾ* may be understood as "spokespeople." (b) Some believe *nābāʾ* literally means to "bubble up" or "boil forth." This meaning would be of pouring forth words with passion or under divine inspiration. (c) Others understand *nābāʾ* "to be called." Hence, prophets experience a calling from the Lord. (d) Finally, some interpret *nābāʾ* as deriving from an unknown Semitic root. The fourth group insists that while the root of *nābāʾ* remains a mystery, the function of *nābāʾ* is unambiguous: *nābāʾ* is prophecy from an authorized spokesperson.

(2) Early prophecy in Israel tended to be ecstatic in nature (cf. Saul in 1 Sam. 10:10–31; 19:20–24). The phenomenon of prophesying was not limited to the prophets of the Lord, for at Mount Carmel, 400 prophets of Baal prophesy frantically all day (1 Ki. 19:29). The prophet Micaiah (a true prophet) entered into conflict with 400 false prophets who were encouraging Ahab and Jehosphaphat to go to battle against the king of Aram (1 Ki. 22:1–28). Indeed, Jeremiah and Ezekiel often confronted those who were prophesying out of their own imagination rather than from the Lord (cf. Jer. 14:14–16; Ezek. 13:17). In answer to them, these two prophets were called by God to prophesy against error and for his truth (e.g., Jer. 26:12; Ezek. 11:4; 13:2). The essential nature of a true prophet is one who speaks true things in the name of the Lord (see also *prophet*).

(3) Joel 2:28–29 records a familiar use of *nābāʾ*: "And afterward, I will pour out my Spirit on all people. Your sons and daughters will *prophesy*, your old men will dream dreams, your young men will see visions. Even on my servants, both men and women, I will pour out my Spirit in those days." Peter quotes this passage as fulfilled on Pentecost, when God pours out his Spirit on the church and gives the gifts of tongues and prophecy to the apostles (Acts 2:17–21). See *NIDOTTE*, 4:1067–78.

New Testament

Verb: προφητεύω (*propheteuō*), GK *4736* (S *4395*), 28x. *propheteuō* can mean to predict the future (Mt. 15:7; Mk. 7:6), such as Caiaphas's prophecy that Jesus would die for the nation (Jn. 11:51), but it primarily denotes an authoritative speaking for God. At times it is difficult to tell which of these is being referred to, such as when the two witnesses prophesy for 1,260 days (Rev. 11:3) or the four daughters of Philip the evangelist regularly prophesy (Acts 21:9).

propheteuō can refer to an OT prophet's message (Mt. 11:13; 1 Pet. 1:10; Jude 14). It is also used for inspired speech revealing the meaning of a special historical event (Lk. 1:67; sarcastically used by the soldiers, Mt. 26:68) or to inspired speech by spiritually gifted Christians (1 Cor. 11:4; 14:1, 24). It can be a sign of the presence of the last days (Acts 2:17–18) or the living presence of the Holy Spirit (19:6). There are also those who prophesy falsely, some of whom claim to be Christians (Mt. 7:2). Thus, prophesying in the church must be subject to testing by the body of believers (1 Cor. 14:29–32).

The ability to prophesy is one of the greater gifts of the Holy Spirit (1 Cor. 14:1, 5, 39), since prophecy builds up and strengthens the church (14:3-4), teaches and encourages other believers (14:31), and can convict those outside the church (14:24). See *NIDNTT-A,* 499-501.

PROPHET

Old Testament

Noun: נָבִיא (*nābîʾ*), GK 5566 (S 5030), 317x. Normally *nābîʾ* translates as "prophet," but it may also mean "spokesman" or "speaker."

(1) While scholars debate the derivation of *nābîʾ*, the majority relate the word to *nabʾium* in Akkadian, a passive form that means "the called one." Numerous prophets wrote of this "call" experience (Isa. 6; Jer. 1; Ezek. 2; Amos 7). Although OT writers list Abraham as the first *nābîʾ* (Gen. 20:7), prophetism proper begins with Moses (Deut. 18:15) and continues uninterrupted through the NT (Mt. 21:26). Most biblical readers will recognize the names of Elijah (1 Ki. 18:22) and Elisha (2 Ki. 6:12) in the impressive succession of prophets. Most of the latter books of the OT were named after the prophets who wrote them. On some occasions, a woman could be a prophetess (e.g., Deborah, Jdg. 4:4; Huldah, 2 Ki. 22:14). Historically speaking, a prophecy is a communication from God to the people through a chosen representative, inspired by God's Spirit (cf. 2 Pet. 1:20–21).

(2) OT prophets in general addressed contemporary issues among God's people, such as idolatry (1 Ki. 18:25ff.; Ezek. 8), selfishness on the part of Israel's leaders (Ezek. 34), and issues of social injustice (Amos 5:7–13). They often spoke words of judgment against the people (e.g., Mic. 6), but they also offered hope if the people repented (e.g., 7:8–20; Joel 2:12–14). Sometimes their words looked ahead to the far distant future, to the coming messianic age (e.g., Isa. 53; Dan. 7). Moses in particular prophesied of a coming final prophet (Deut. 18:15–18).

(3) Prophets were prevalent in all ancient Near Eastern society, for kings and rulers often consulted them to determine the will of the gods for various things, such as engaging in battle. The prophet Micaiah and the 400 prophets of Baal had significantly different perspectives on whether Ahab and Jehoshaphat should go to war against the Arameans (1 Ki. 22:1–28). Because of the prevalence of false prophets, it was apparently necessary that "tests" be given to determine who was the true prophet of the Lord. The OT gives at least three such tests. (a) Does a prophecy come true? If it does not, then that prophecy has been uttered by a false prophet (Deut. 18:21–22). (b) Does what the prophet prophesy correspond with the revealed word of God? If it doesn't, that person is a false prophet (13:1–3). (c) Is the prophet living a God-fearing life? If he is living a selfish, godless life, he is a false prophet (Jer. 23:9–18).

(4) We do need to distinguish between individual prophets (some of whom were writing, such as Isaiah, Jeremiah, and Ezekiel, and some of whom were not, such as Nathan and Elijah) and groups of prophets, who formed what appear to be like monastic-like communities (e.g., 2 Ki. 2:3, 5, 7); Elisha led one such community, 2 Ki. 4:1.

In their communities, they probably studied the history of God's revelation and God's will for a moral life; they could *not* have been taught how to prophesy, since prophecy could only be received, not learned. Characteristic of the behavior of these prophets during a time of prophecy was the use of music and ecstatic or frenzied speaking (e.g., 1 Sam. 10:5–6, 9–11). See *NIDOTTE*, 4:1067–78.

New Testament

Noun: προφήτης (*prophētes*), GK *4737* (S *4396*), 144x. A *prophētes* is someone who prophesies, and the related words (see *prophecy*; *prophesy*) carry the same basic meaning. A prophet can predict events beforehand (foretell), but its primary meaning is someone who proclaims the truth with God's authority (tell forth). Unusual are the uses of *prophētēs* to describe a Cretan poet (Tit. 1:12) and Balaam (2 Pet. 2:16).

prophētēs is frequently used to refer to the OT prophets (Acts 3:18; Heb. 1:1; 11:32) and their writings (Mk. 1:2). "The *Prophets*" is a distinct title given to one of the three main sections of the Hebrew Bible (Mt. 5:17; Lk. 24:27, 44). *prophētēs* is a title ascribed to John the Baptist (Lk. 1:76), to Jesus Christ (Mt. 21:11; Jn. 4:44), and to those people in the early church gifted with the spiritual gift of prophecy (Acts 13:1; 1 Cor. 12:28; Eph. 3:5; 4:11). These prophets proclaim messages of encouragement (Acts 15:32), messages to edify disciples (1 Cor. 14:3), and also messages that foretell the future (Acts 21:10–11). The words of these prophets are to be carefully weighed by the congregation (1 Cor. 14:29) because there will always false prophets (Mt. 7:15; 24:11, 24). See *NIDNTT-A,* 499-501.

PROPITIATE, PROPITIATION

New Testament

Verb: ἱλάσκομαι (*hilaskomai*), GK *2661* (S *2433*), 2x. *hilaskomai* means "to atone, have mercy on, to make atonement for, propitiate," and refers in the NT to the atoning work of Christ whereby he propitiate God's anger. See *atone, make atonement*.

Noun: ἱλασμός (*hilasmos*), GK *2662* (S *2434*), 2x. *hilasmos* refers to "an atoning sacrifice, propitiation." This word occurs only in 1 Jn. 2:2 and 4:10. See *atonement.*

Noun: ἱλαστήριον (*hilastērion*), GK *2663* (S *2435*), 2x. *hilastērion* means "atonement cover, sacrifice of atonement," or "that which propitiates or expiates." In the LXX, it is used almost exclusively for the atonement cover (*kappōret*) placed on top of the ark of the covenant. See *atonement.*

PROPOSE

New Testament

Verb: ἵστημι (*histēmi*), GK *2705* (S *2476*), 154x. The basic sense of *histēmi* is "to set" or "stand." It has a variety of nuances in the NT, one of which is "to propose." See *stand.*

PROSPER

Old Testament

Verb: יָטַב (*yāṭab*), GK 3512 (S 3190), 117x. *yāṭab* is a verb that means "to do good, go well, please, prosper." It is used in a wide variety of contexts in the OT. See *do good.*

Verb: צָלַח (*ṣālaḥ*), GK 7503 (S 6743), 55x. *ṣālaḥ means* "to prosper, succeed, be successful." This verb can refer to a vine that "thrives" (Ezek. 17:9) or a weapon that "prevails" (Isa. 54:17). For the most part, however, *ṣālaḥ* refers to human beings who prosper or succeed. When Solomon completed the temple and his palace, "he had succeeded in carrying out all that he had in mind to do" (2 Chr. 7:11). This same king points out that those who hide sin cannot expect to "prosper" (Prov. 28:13).

It is possible to succeed on a purely human level (i.e., to be financially successful); this is something even the wicked can do (Ps. 37:7; Jer. 12:1). But for the most part in the OT, success is impossible without the involvement of the hand of the Lord. The Lord was with Joseph in Egypt and "gave him success" (Gen. 39:2–3, 23). King Uzziah sought the Lord, and as long as he did, "God gave him success" (2 Chr. 26:5). Undoubtedly this is why the psalmist prays in Ps. 118:25, "O Lord, grant us success." Nehemiah feels confident that "the God of heaven will give us success" (Neh. 2:20). The Lord promises too that even though his Servant will suffer and die, he will ultimately "prosper" (Isa. 53:10). The "success" and "prosperity" talked about in these passages is not primarily earthly success, but success in obeying the Lord and is experiencing his daily presence. See *NIDOTTE*, 3:805–5.

PROSPERITY

Old Testament

Noun: טוֹבָה (*ṭôbâ*), GK 3208 (S 2896), 67x. *ṭôbâ* is the noun related to the adjective *ṭôb* and means "good, prosperity." See *good*.

Noun: שָׁלוֹם (*šālôm*), GK 8934 (S 7965), 237x. *šālôm* is one of the most important words in the OT. In addition to "peace," this word can be translated as "prosperity, well-being, health, completeness, safety." See *peace*.

PROSTITUTE

Old Testament

Verb: זָנָה (*zānâ*), GK 2388 (S 2181), 60x. *zānâ* broadly refers to illicit or illegitimate sexual misconduct. The most common translation of this word in the NIV is "to commit prostitution, prostitute oneself." *zānâ* may also include adultery (*nāʾap*, "to commit adultery"; see *adultery*).

(1) *zānâ* often refers to the actual, physical action of sexual immorality or, as a ptc., to the one who has given herself to sexual immorality or prostitution (Gen. 38:24; Lev. 19:29; 21:9; Num. 25:1). Hosea, under God's direction, took for himself a woman given to prostitution and adulterous actions (Hos. 3:3).

(2) The most significant usage of *zānâ* is metaphorical In most cases, the illicit sexual misconduct refers to those who follow after other gods instead of serving the LORD (Exod. 34:15–16; Lev. 20:5–6; Jdg. 8:27, 33; Ps. 106:39). In this sense, those who worship other gods or idols are *unfaithful* to the LORD and will be destroyed (Ps. 73:27). The LORD declared that Israel and Judah have "committed adultery" against him with other gods (Jer. 3:1, 6, 8). Likewise, Ezekiel records the covenantal unfaithfulness of God's people, who "engage in prostitution" with idols (Ezek. 16:15–17; cf. 16:26, 28, 34, 41). Hosea's own relationship with his "unfaithful" wife demonstrates the relationship between the LORD and Israel (Hos. 4:10–18; cf. 5:3; 9:1), as well as the depth of love that God has for his people (Hos. 11) and his intolerance for anything that rivals him in their eyes.

New Testament

Noun: πόρνη (*pornē*), GK *4520* (S *4204*), 12x. *pornē* identifies a person as a "prostitute" ("harlot" or "whore," KJV); it belongs to a word group that denotes various forms of sexual deviance (see *sexual immorality*).

Scripture teaches that Jesus came to "seek and save the lost" (Lk. 19:10), and among those who received his healing and forgiveness were prostitutes. In Jewish law, prostitutes were not included in the community of God, nor were they fit for God's salvation. However, Jesus taught that even prostitutes could enter the kingdom of God on the basis of their faith (Mt. 21:31–32). By way of example, notice that the prostitute Rahab was justified by faith (Heb. 11:31) and "considered righteous for what she did when she gave lodging to the spies" (Jas. 2:25; cf. Jos. 2). Although Jesus made provision for prostitutes to enter into the kingdom of God by faith, by no means did he condone their behavior (cf. Mt. 15:19; Mk. 7:21).

In 1 Corinthian, Paul dealt with numerous issues concerning sexual immorality, such as incest, adultery, and prostitution. Rhetorically, Paul asks if a Christian can join sexually with a prostitute. In response, he declares, "Never! Do you not know that he who unites himself with a *prostitute* is one with her in body?" (1 Cor. 6:15–16). Thus, he commands the Corinthians to "flee from sexual immorality," since sexual immorality is a sin against one's own body, which itself is the temple of the Holy Spirit (6:18–19). Rather, believers should use their bodies to glorify God (6:19b–20).

Finally, Revelation uses *pornē* in a religious or spiritual sense. This word identifies "the great prostitute," who will be condemned and punished for her opposition to God (17:1, cf. 17:15–16). John identifies Babylon (possibly a symbol of Rome) as "the mother of prostitutes" (17:5), "the great prostitute who corrupted the earth by her adulteries" (19:2). In the end, Babylon will be "thrown down with violence" (18:21), to the immense praise of heaven. See *NIDNTT-A*, 485-86.*

PROSPER

Old Testament

Verb: שָׂכַל (*śākal*), GK 8505 (S 7919), 60x. *śākal* means "to be wise, understand, prosper/be successful." See *(be) wise*.

PROTECTION

Old Testament

Noun: צֵל (*ṣēl*), GK 7498 (S 6738), 53x. *ṣēl* means literally "shadow, shade," but it can also be used figuratively for the notion of "protection" or of the "transitory or empty nature" of things. See *shadow*.

PROUD

New Testament

Adjective: ὑψηλός (*hypsēlos*), GK *5734* (S *5308*), 11x. For the most part this word denotes something that is high (e.g., a "high" mountain; see *high, highest*). But in Rom. 11:20 and 12:126 the word is used metaphorically to denote pride or arrogance.

PROVE

Old Testament

Verb: בָּחַן (*bāḥan*), GK 1043 (S 974), 29x. *bāḥan* denotes the divine examination of an individual and may be translated as "test, try, prove." It is common in the poetic and prophetic books of the OT. See *test*.

Verb: נָסָה (*nāsâ*), GK 5814 (S 5254), 36x. *nāsâ* denotes the testing of a person's loyalty or obedience and may be translated "test, prove." This verb is most common in the narrative and poetic books of the OT. See *test*.

New Testament

Verb: διαλέγομαι (*dialegomai*), GK *1363* (S *1256*), 13x. *dialegomai* means "to reason, argue, prove, persuade." See *reason*.

Verb: δοκιμάζω (*dokimazō*), GK *1507* (S *1381*), 22x. *dokimazō* means to "test, discern, approve." See *test*.

PROVERB

New Testament

Noun: παραβολή (*parabolē*), GK *4130* (S *3850*), 50x. While this term usually means "parable," it can also be used for common aphorisms or proverbs, such as "Physician, heal yourself!" (Lk. 4:23, NIV calls it a "proverb"). See *parable*.

PROVIDE

Old Testament

Verb: כּוּן (*kûn*), GK 3922 (S 3559), 219x. *kûn* means "to establish, prepare, provide." See *establish*.

New Testament

Verb: παρέχω (*parechō*), GK *4218* (S *3930*), 16x. *parechō* means "to provide, bother." In Acts the demon-possessed slave girl in Philippi "has provided" much income for her owners (Acts 16:16; cf. also 19:24), and the islanders on Malta show (provide) kindness to the shipwrecked people (28:2). Paul instructs masters to "provide" their slaves with what is right and fair (Col. 4:1). To Titus, Paul gives the instruction to provide an example by doing what is good (Tit. 2:7). Most important is the message in 1 Tim. 6:17, that God "richly provides us with everything for our enjoyment." See *bother*.

PROVINCE

Old Testament

Noun: מְדִינָה (*mᵉdînâ*), GK 4519 (S 4082), 53x. *mᵉdînâ* is a "district" or "province" in a kingdom. Because it derives from the verb *dîn*, "to judge," the noun may have originally carried the meaning "a judicial district." Most of its occurrences are in Esther, referring to the provinces of the Persian empire, but it also occurs in references to Israel's kingdoms. The author of Eccl. states that one should not be surprised to find injustice in the *m^e^dînâ* (Eccl. 5:8). In this instance, the word is probably being used in the sense of "a place of judicial decisions"—i.e., a judicial court, rather than an entire province. However, does denote a province in Eccl. 2:8, where the Teacher refers to "the personal property of kings and provinces."

In the time of the divided monarchy, Ahab's army was led out on one occasion by "the young men of the officials of the *provinces*," implying that Ahab's kingdom was divided into districts (1 Ki. 20:17). The Neo-Babylonian empire was also divided into provinces (Dan. 8:2), and the large Persian empire had 127 provinces during the time of Esther (Est. 1:1). The Persian provinces are also mentioned in Ezr. 2:1; Neh. 1:3; 7:6; 11:3. See *NIDOTTE*, 2:853.

PROVOKE TO ANGER

Old Testament

Verb: כָּעַס (*kāʿas*), GK 4087 (S 3707), 55x. *kāʿas* denotes the idea of provoking one to anger and may be translated "to anger, irritate." See *anger*.

PRUDENT

New Testament

Adjective: φρόνιμος (*phronimos*), GK *5861* (S *5429*), 14x. One who is *phronimos* is "wise, intelligent" in a prudent or shrewd way, acting in a way that is appropriate for the circumstance or situation. See *wise*.

PSALM

Old Testament

Noun: מִזְמוֹר (*mizmōr*), GK 4660 (S 4210), 57x. The noun *mizmōr*, translated "psalm," is related to the verb *zāmar*, "to make music." *mizmōr* occurs exclusively in the book of Psalms and is used only in psalm titles. Of the fifty-seven psalm headings in which it occurs, *mizmōr* occurs 36x with the phrase *l^e^dāwid* ("of David"), 34x with *lam^e^naṣeaḥ* ("for the director of music"; "of David" and "for the director of music" appear together 23x), and 9x with the phrase *leʾāsāp* ("of Asaph").

New Testament

Noun: ψαλμός (*psalmos*), GK *6011* (S *5568*), 7x. The NT church was a singing church (see *sing*). Believers apparently sang newly written songs sung in honor of Christ, but the church did not forget the songs of the OT, namely, the Psalms. There are three specific references to "the book of Psalms" in the NT (Lk. 20:42; 24:44; Acts 1:20), one of which may refer to the entire section of the Heb. Bible known as "the Writings" (Lk. 24:44). In his sermon in Acts 13:33, Paul refers to "the second Psalm" as a messianic psalm. The other three references are to those elements in NT worship where "psalms" were sung, along with hymns and spiritual songs (Eph. 5:19; Col. 3:16; cf. 1 Cor. 14:26). See *NIDNTT-A*, 611.

PUBLICAN

See *tax collector*.

PUBLICLY

New Testament

Adverb: φανερῶς (*phanerōs*), GK *5747* (S *5320*), 3x. *phanerōs* denotes the openness or visibility of an activity, hence "openly, publicly. See *openly*.

PUNISH, PUNISHMENT

Old Testament

Verb: יָכַח (*yākaḥ*), GK 3519 (S 3198), 59x. *yākaḥ* has a broad range of meaning, but it generally carries the sense of arguing a case or issuing judgment with the intent to correct. It is often translated "rebuke," "correct," "judge," "punish," or "argue," and is found most frequently in legal contexts (especially in Job [17x]) and in the wisdom instruction of Proverbs (10x). See *rebuke*.

Verb: נָקַם (*nāqam*), GK 5933 (S 5358), 35x. *nāqam* means "to avenge, take vengeance, punish."

Noun: נָקָם (*nāqām*), GK 5934 (S 5359), 17x.

Noun: נְקָמָה (n^e*qāmâ*), GK 5935 (S 5360), 27x. Both *nāqām* and n^e*qāmâ* mean "vengeance." See *avenge*.

Verb: פָּקַד (*pāqad*), GK 7212 (S 6485), 304x. While *pāqad* has a wide range of meaning, it basically expresses the action of overseeing an individual for a particular purpose, such as counting the people. See *count*.

When oversight leads to an appropriate response on behalf of the superior to the actions or situation of the subordinate, *pāqad* may be translated "to attend to" or "to visit" and regularly takes God as the subject. When God "visits," he may bring divine blessing with a deep sense of care. More frequently, however, God "visits" not to bring divine blessing, but to bring divine judgment in response to human sin. In these instances, *pāqad* is translated "to punish." See *visit*.

Noun: אָוֶן (*ʾāwen*), GK 224 (S 205), 81x. *ʾāwen* refers, in general, to evil, sin, or wickedness. It may also describe the punishment or disaster that befalls those who practice wickedness. See *evil*.

New Testament

Verb: ἐκδικέω (*ekdikeō*), GK *1688* (S *1566*), 6x. *ekdikeō* means "avenge, seek justice, punish." See *avenge*.

Verb: παιδεύω (*paideuō*), GK *4084* (S *3811*), 13x. *paideuō* means "to teach, educate," but also "to chasten, punish." See *teach*.

Noun: ἐκδίκησις (*ekdikēsis*), GK *1689* (S *1557*), 9x. *ekdikēsis* means "vengeance, punishment, justice." See *avenge*.

Noun: κρίμα (*krima*), GK *3210* (S *2917*), 27x. *krima* refers to the act of "judgment" or its consequences (e.g., "punishment, condemnation"). See *judgment*.

PURCHASE

Old Testament

Verb: קָנָה (*qānâ*), GK 7864, 7865 (S 7069), 91x. *qānâ* appears to bear two distinct meanings in the OT: "to buy, purchase, redeem," and also "to create."See *buy*.

New Testament

Verb: ἀγοράζω *agorazō*, GK *60* (S *59*), 30x. The word literally means "to buy, purchase something." See *buy*.

PURE, PURITY

Old Testament

Noun: קֹדֶשׁ (*qōdeš*), GK 7731 (S 6944), 470x. *qōdeš* connotes the concept of "holiness," i.e., the essential nature of that which belongs to the sphere of the sacred and is distinct from the common or profane. See *holiness*.

Adjective: טָהוֹר (*ṭāhôr*), GK 3196 (S 2889), 96x. *ṭāhôr* means "clean, pure" and is used in a material or *natural* sense, as well as in both a ritual and ethical sense. See *clean*.

Adjective: קָדוֹשׁ (*qādôš*), GK 7705 (S 6918), 117x. Generally *qādôš* is translated as "holy," "holy one," or "saint." It describes that which is by nature sacred or that which has been admitted to the sphere of the sacred by divine rite. See *holy*.

New Testament

Noun: ἁγνεία (*hagneia*), GK *48* (S *47*), 2x.

Noun: ἁγνότης (*hagnotēs*), GK *55* (S *54*), 2x. *hagneia* and *hagnotēs* both mean "purity." While the former word seems to apply in the NT specifically to sexual purity (1 Tim. 4:12; 5:2), *hagnotēs* is a more general word for keeping oneself fully devoted to Christ and the Christian way of life (2 Cor. 6:6; 11:3). See *NIDNTT-A*,12.

Adjective: ἁγνός (*hagnos*), GK *54* (S *53*), 8x. hagnos means "pure, innocent." The overwhelming message of the NT is that believers should keep themselves pure; this term should not be limited to sexual purity, as we so often think of the word—though it can have that nuance (cf. Tit. 2:5; 1 Pet. 3:2). When Paul sets as his goal to present the Corinthian church to Christ as a "pure virgin" (2 Cor. 11:2), he is using *hagnos* in the context of the OT, where adultery and prostitution are often used as metaphors for idolatry. When Paul instructs Timothy to keep himself "pure" (1 Tim. 5:22), he is advising him to keep away from any involvement in the sins of others. In fact, if believers want to enjoy the peace of God, they must concentrate their lives (among other qualities) on things that are "pure" (Phil. 4:8–9). Finally, as to the basis of Christian purity, just as our holiness is founded on the fact that God is holy (see holy), so our purity is to be based on the fact that "he is pure" (1 Jn. 3:3). See *NIDNTT-A*, 12.

Adjective: καθαρός (*katharos*), GK *2754* (S *2513*), 27x. *katharos* ("clean, pure") conveys three different senses: a natural sense, a ceremonial sense, and a moral sense. See *clean*.

PURIFY

Old Testament

Verb: טָהֵר (*ṭāhēr*), GK 3197 (S 2891), 94x. *ṭāhēr* is normally rendered "to cleanse, purify, consecrate." It often appears in cultic contexts and used to refer to physical, ritual, and ethical cleansing or purification. See *cleanse*.

New Testament

Verb: ἁγνίζω (*hagnizō*), GK *49* (S *48*), 7x. *hagnizō* has two main uses in the NT. (1) In Jn. 11:55; Acts 21:24; 24:18, the word refers to the idea of ceremonial purity or cleanness, which was an important element in the Jewish liturgical life, accomplished by using special washings and other rites. (2) In three other passages, this verb refers to being fully devoted to following the Christian way of life. A person is purified when he or she obeys the truth (1 Pet. 1:22). James speaks about the important of purifying our hearts (Jas. 4:8). And John talks about purifying ourselves in the same way as God keeps himself pure and holy in all things (1 Jn. 3:3). See *NIDNTT-A*, 12.

PURPOSE

Old Testament

Verb: יָעַץ (*yāʿaṣ*), GK 3619 (S 3289), 80x. *yāʿaṣ* carries the two basic meanings of "to counsel, advise" (Num. 24:14; 2 Sam. 17:11) and "to plan, purpose" (Isa. 7:5; 14:24), though the verb seems to carry the former nuance more frequently. See *counsel*.

Noun: עֵצָה (*ʿēṣâ*), GK 6783 (S 6098), 87x. *ʿēṣâ* has two basic, though closely related, meanings: "counsel, advice" (see *counsel*) and "plan, purpose" (see *plan*).

New Testament

Noun: βουλή (*boulē*), GK *1087* (S *1012*), 12x. *boulē* describes the free decision of the will, by way of purpose, plan, or counsel. In this sense it is closely related to the verb *boulomai*. As with the verb, it is used of both God and human beings.

(1) When *boulē* refers to God (7x), it occurs in three ways. (a) It can describe the "set purpose" or counsel of God for specific events of history. Peter refers to this in his description of the crucifixion of Christ, in which Christ was handed over to the wicked authorities by "God's set *purpose*," distinguished from God's foreknowledge (Acts 2:23). Paul describes how God works out all things "in conformity with the *purpose* of his will" (Eph. 1:11); *boulē* here is distinguished from another word for will (*thelēma*) and means God's decision or counsel resulting from his own free decision. Similarly, Herod and Pilate are described as having done what God determined beforehand would happen as a result of both God's "power and *will*" (Acts 4:28), and this purpose or counsel of God is clearly communicated to the heirs of the promise by means of an oath (Heb. 6:17). (b) Another use of *boulē* with respect to God describes what he desires from us as human beings, namely, obedience to his revealed word. In this way the Pharisees are described as having "rejected God's *purpose* for themselves" (Lk. 7:30), and David "served God's *purpose* in his own generation" (Acts 13:36). (c) Finally, *boulē* describes God's entire plan of salvation, as when Paul declares to the Ephesians that he has not "hesitated to proclaim to you the whole *will* of God" (Acts 20:27).

(2) With reference to the will of human beings, *boulē* can describe a decision or plan reached after collective deliberation,

such as the decision of the Sanhedrin to condemn Christ (Lk. 23:51) or the decision of the sailors on the ship carrying Paul to set sail and the soldiers to kill the prisoners (Acts 27:12, 42). *boulē* can also refer to the motive(s) of humans in coming to a decision, whether unknown to others (Acts 5:38) or known to God (1 Cor. 4:5). See *NIDNTT-A*, 97-98.*

Noun: εὐδοκία (*eudokia*) GK *2306* (S *2107*), 9x. *eudokia* can mean "good pleasure, purpose; desire." Most of its nine uses in the NT refer to God rather than humans and denote God's good intention or purpose for his people. See *pleasure*.

Noun: πρόθεσις (*prothesis*), GK *4606* (S *4286*), 12x. This noun is related to the compound verb *protithēmi* ("to purpose, plan") and means "a purpose, plan, display." It is used four times to denote "the *consecrated* bread" that was in the Holy Place of the tabernacle (Mt. 12:4; Mk. 2:26; Lk. 6:4; Heb. 9:2).

In its other occurrences *prothesis* is used in a personal manner, i.e., of people or God. Paul, for example, writes to Timothy, "you know all about my teaching, my way of life, my *purpose*, faith, patience, love, endurance" (2 Tim. 3:10; cf. Acts 11:23; 27:13). In a number of instances *prothesis* is used of God's "purpose." A well-known example is Rom. 8:28: "And we know that all things work together for good to those who love God, to those who are called according to his *purpose*" (cf. Eph. 1:11; 2 Tim. 1:9). Similarly, it denotes God's "purpose" in choosing Jacob over Esau (Rom. 9:11) and his "eternal *purpose*, which he accomplished in Christ Jesus" (Eph. 3:11). See *NIDNTT-A*, 498.*

PURSUE

Old Testament

Verb: דָּבַק (*dābaq*), GK 1815 (S 1692), 55x. *dābaq* denotes the basic action of one object or person adhering or clinging to another. It takes both people and physical objects as its subject, but never God. In certain contexts, *dābaq* occurs in a form that conveys the notion of "to pursue, overtake." Laban "overtakes" Jacob in Gilead (Gen. 31:23), and the Israelites "pursue" the Philistines in battle after the Philistines flee (1 Sam. 14:22). See *cling*.

Verb: רָדַף (*rādap*), GK 8103 (S 7291), 144x. *rādap* means "to pursue, follow after, persecute." It is commonly used in a military sense, where one party pursues another with harmful intent (Gen. 14:14–15; Exod. 14:4, 8–9, 23; 15:9; Deut. 1:44; Jdg. 7:25; 1 Sam. 17:52; 2 Sam. 20:6–7; Ps. 18:37; Jer. 39:5; Hos. 8:3). In the Exodus, Pharaoh's army "*pursued* the Israelites and overtook them as they camped by the sea" (Exod. 14:9). In some instances, *rādap* refers to the continuation of fighting after an enemy has retreated or is decisively defeated. In these cases, it connotes the complete destruction or utter defeat of the enemy (Jos. 10:10, 19; 11:8; Jdg. 1:6; 1 Ki. 20:20).

When used figuratively, abstractions can replace the parties involved. "He who pursues evil goes to his death" (Prov. 11:19). Especially in the Psalms, *rādap* is personified to describe situations of danger or affliction. Some of these maintain the military imagery of an enemy in pursuit ("O LORD my God, I take refuge in you; save and deliver me from all who *pursue* me,“ Ps. 7:1; cf. 31:15); others pick up the idea of oppression or abuse from sickness or slander (119:86; 143:3). When used positively, *rādap* carries the notion of seeking something zealously like a hunter seeking game (1 Sam. 26:20). "He who pursues righteousness and love finds life, prosperity and honor" (Prov. 21:21). Ps. 23 uses *rādap* to speak of those shepherded by God: "Surely goodness and love *will follow* me all the days of my life, and I will dwell in the house of the LORD forever" (Ps. 23:6). Though *rādap* can also be used in the more neutral sense of "to follow after" (Jdg. 3:28), here it seems to suggest a stronger thrust. God's goodness and love pursues, overtakes, and overwhelms his people.

rādap is also used to express persecution or affliction (Job 19:28; Ps. 69:26; 109:16; 119:86, 157, 161). Given the military imagery this term usually conveys, it may evoke powerful and threatening image. Only God can deliver from this type of persecution (Deut. 30:7; Ps. 119:84; Jer. 15:15, 17:18; 20:11). See *NIDOTTE*, 3:1057–62.

New Testament

Verb: διώκω (*diōkō*), GK *1503* (S *1377*), 45x. *diōkō* means to "pursue" or, more frequently, "persecute" (see *persecute*). Christians should "pursue" hospitality (Rom. 12:13), mutual peace (14:19; Heb. 12:14), holiness (Heb. 12:14), love (1 Cor. 14:1), doing good (1 Thess. 5:15), and righteousness (1 Tim. 6:11). Paul "presses on" toward the prize of the high calling of God in Christ Jesus (Phil. 3:14). The attainment of any of these goals, however, is due to God's mercy (Rom. 9:16). See *NIDNTT-A*, 148-49.

PUT

Old Testament

Verb: נוּחַ (*nûaḥ*), GK 5663 (S 5117), 140x. The most basic idea of the verb *nûaḥ* is the action of one object coming to rest, roosting, or landing on another object or in a specific location. See *rest*.

Frequently the object does not come to rest on its own but is caused to rest or be placed in a particular location by someone else (104x). In these instances *nûaḥ* may be translated "set," "put," "place," or even "leave." God "sets" Ezekiel in the valley of dry bones (Ezek. 37:1) and commands Moses to "place" manna before God in the ark, which Aaron does (Exod. 16:33, 34). After the exile, perhaps with eschatological implications, God promises to "place" his people in their land (Ezek. 37:14). See *set*.

Verb: שִׂים (*śîm*), GK 8492 (S 7760), 588x. *śîm* generally denotes the action of putting or placing an object or person in a particular location. It is usually translated "put," "set," or "place." Sometimes the action of putting an object has a transformational quality to it, which validates the translation "make."

The relationship of persons or objects to the new location in which they have been "placed" involves various prepositions. God "puts" Moses *in* the cleft of the rock when his glory passes by (Exod. 33:22), and he blesses the Israelites as the priests "put" his name *on* them through the Aaronic blessing (Num. 6:27). The Book of the Law is to be "placed" *beside* the ark of the covenant (Deut. 31:26) and Moses "sets" the Torah *before* the Israelites (Deut. 4:44). Jacob "puts" his wives and children *in front of* him when he meets Esau (Gen. 33:2) and "puts" a stone *under* his head to sleep (Gen. 28:11), while Joshua "sets" five thousand men *between* Bethel and Ai in ambush (Jos. 8:12). In this sense, two verses have particular theological significance: Yahweh "places" Adam *in* the garden of Eden (Gen. 2:8), and he says, "*In* Jerusalem I will *put* my name" (2 Ki. 21:4).

śîm is used frequently in the context of setting up cultic objects for worship. As God gives instructions for setting up the tabernacle, *śîm* is used twelve times in connection with the furniture in the tabernacle (Exod. 40:3, 5, 8, 18, 19, 20, 21, 24, 26, 28, 29, 30). But *śîm* is also used to describe the "setting up" of idols for false worship (e.g., Deut. 27:15; Jdg. 18:31).

The verb *śîm* is regularly paired with body parts to express a physical gesture that has a specific meaning. Jacob "places" his *hands* on Joseph's sons' heads to express blessing (Gen. 48:18); Abraham's servant "puts" his *hand* under Abraham's thigh to indicate an oath (Gen. 24:9); Job "puts" his *hand* over his mouth to signify his silence (Job 40:4); and God "lays" his *hand* on the nations to demonstrate his sovereign rule (Ezek. 39:21). Jacob "sets" his *face* toward Gilead, indicating the beginning of a journey (Gen. 31:21), while Ezekiel "sets" his *face* against Israel to express a stance toward Israel's sin (Ezek. 13:17) that God shares (15:7). God "sets" his *eyes* on Israel to signify that he is watching them (Jer. 24:6), and the Israelites are supposed to "take" all of Moses' words to *heart*, indicating a special care and concern for those words (and ultimately obedience, Deut. 32:46).

Sometimes *śîm* indicates the "putting" of a person or object into a new setting or for a special purpose that implies some sort of transformation. The transformation may be one of function. In a humorous twist, Jehu destroys Baal worship and "makes" the pillar of Baal into a latrine (2 Ki. 10:27). God determines the function of the sand and "makes" the sand a boundary for the sea (Jer. 5:22). He also fills a particular time with new meaning as he "sets" an appointed time for the livestock plague in Egypt (Exod. 9:5). Indicating that God's covenant now has a new recipient, God "puts" the everlasting covenant to David (2 Sam. 23:5).

The transformation of function is seen in the appointment to a position. A superior may "set" his subordinate over others, granting a position of authority: Saul "sets" David over the men of war (1 Sam. 18:5) and Absalom "appoints" Amasa over the army (2 Sam. 17:25). Rejecting God as their king, Israel asks Samuel to "appoint" a king for them like the other nations (1 Sam. 8:5). Elsewhere, the change of function may be to "set" the object in the context of a metaphor or simile. The beloved requests to be "put" like a seal on the heart (Song 8:6), and God will "make" Zerubbabel like his signet ring (Hag. 2:23).

The transformation indicated by *śîm* may be a transformation of quality. Yahweh "turns" the sea into dry land so the Israelites can escape the Egyptians (Exod. 14:21). He "turns" rivers into a desert (Ps. 107:33), and the desert into pools of water (107:35). Israel defiles the land with their idolatry and "makes" God's inheritance (i. e., the land) an abomination (Jer. 2:7). God promises that he will "make" a great nation out of Ishmael (Gen. 21:18).See *NIDOTTE* 3:1237-40

Verb: שִׁית (*šît*), GK 8883 (S 7896), 86x. *šît* means "make, put, set." It is a virtual synonym of *śîm* (GK 8492; see *put*) and has many of the same nuances. See *make*.

New Testament

Verb: τίθημι (*tithēmi*), GK *5502* (S *5087*), 100x. The basic meaning of *tithēmi* is "to put, place, lay something down." It can refer to physical objects, such as not putting a lamp under a bowl (Mt. 5:15), placing a body in a tomb (Mk. 6:29), or putting aside a garment (Jn. 13:4). It can also refer to spiritual things, such as the Spirit being put on Jesus (Mt. 12:18) or God's entrusting to us the message of reconciliation (2 Cor. 5:19).

The word has several idiomatic uses. The expression "*put* under your feet" (Mt. 22:44) means to subdue. The phrase "*put* a knee" means to bow (Mk. 15:19) or kneel down (Lk. 22:41). To "*lay up* in one's heart" is to ponder or reflect on something (Lk. 1:66). To "*set* something in one's heart" is to arrive at a decision (Lk. 21:14); "to *set* in the spirit" means to intend (Acts 19:21); "*setting* counsel" is giving advice (27:12).

tithēmi is used in two theologically significant ways. First, it can mean to "appoint" someone to salvation, highlighting God's sovereignty in calling the elect (Jn. 15:16, "You did not choose me, but I chose you and *appointed* you to go and bear fruit"). God has appointed spiritual gifts in the church (1 Cor. 12:28), called individuals to his service in ministry (1 Tim. 1:12), and decreed the final salvation of the elect (1 Thess. 5:9, "God did not *appoint* us to suffer wrath but to receive salvation").

Second, Jesus uses *tithēmi* in the gospel of John to refer to his death. As the good shepherd, he "lays down" his life for his sheep (Jn. 10:11, 15, 17). His sacrifice is a powerful and efficacious atonement for his people. The Father grants to his Son the power to defeat death and to rise again (v. 18, "I have authority to *lay it down* and authority to take it up again"). Jesus' life is not taken from him; rather, he voluntarily "lays it down" as an expression of his love for his friends (15:13-14). See *NIDNTT-A*, 563.

PUT IN CHARGE

New Testament

Verb: καθίστημι (*kathistēmi*), GK *2770* (S *2525*), 21x. *kathistēmi* has a variety of nuances of NT. It can signify leading or escorting; in Acts 17:15, a group of men escort Paul. But its predominant use is for "appointing" a person to an office or "putting a person in charge" of something. This includes appointing people to the positions of deacons (Acts 6:3), elders (Tit. 1:5), and the high priest (Heb. 5:1). It is also used in the parable of the talents for the king's decision to put the owners of ten and five talents to be "put in charge" of many things in the kingdom of heaven (Mt. 25:21, 23; cf. also 24:47). See also *become*.

PUT IN ORDER

New Testament

Verb: καταρτίζω (*katartizō*), GK *2936* (S *2675*), 13x. *katartizō* means "to prepare, put in order, restore" for a specific purpose. See *prepare*.

Verb: κοσμέω (*kosmeō*), GK *3175* (S *2885*), 10x. *kosmeō* means "to adorn, decorate, make attractive" (see *adorn*). But it can also mean "to put in order," as in arranging or organizing a house (Mt. 12:44; Lk. 11:25).

PUT ON

Old Testament

Verb: לָבַשׁ (*lābaš*), GK 4252 (S 3847), 112x. *lābaš* is the most common word in the OT for "to clothe, put on clothes." See *clothe*.

New Testament

Verb: ἐνδύω (*endyō*), GK *1907* (S *1746*), 27x. *endyō* means "to put something on, wear." It is generally used of clothes (Mt. 27:31; Mk. 1:6; Acts 12:21); in Mt. 6:25, Jesus tells us not to be concerned about what we wear.

Many of its NT uses, however, are metaphorical. The Holy Spirit clothes God's people with power (Lk. 24:49). Christians are to be spiritually clothed with Christ (Rom. 13:14), with the new self (Eph. 4:24), with the armor of God (Eph. 6:11; cf. Rom. 13:12), and with Christian virtues (Col. 3:12, "*clothe* yourselves with compassion, kindness, humility, gentleness, and patience"; cf. 1 Thess. 5:8). In 1 Cor. 15:53, Paul uses *endyō* when referring to the resurrection body. We are currently clothed with a perishable, mortal body, but someday in the future, this "perishable must *clothe itself* with the imperishable." That new body will no longer be subject to death. See *NIDNTT-A*, 155-56.

Verb: ἐπιτίθημι (*epithēmi*), GK *2202* (S *2007*), 39x. *epithēmi* means to place or put something on another, such as putting cloaks on the donkey Jesus rode (Mt. 21:7). It is used frequently in the gospels and Acts for the laying on hands—for healing (9:18), blessing (19:13, little children), ordination (Acts 6:6; cf. 1 Tim. 5:22), the impartation of the Holy Spirit (Acts 8:17; 19:6), and sending off missionaries (13:3).

Idiomatically, *epithēmi* can refer to the imposition of a burden (Mt. 23:4), the giving of a name (Mk. 3:16), an attack on someone (Acts 18:10), or the furnishing of provisions (Acts 28:10). Luke uses it as a figure of speech for injuring someone by beating (Lk. 10:30: the phrase "beat him" lit. reads, "laid a wound on him"). See *NIDNTT-A*, 200-201.

PUT OUT TO SEA

New Testament

Verb: ἀνάγω (*anagō*), GK *343* (S *321*), 23x. *anagō* has a technical meaning "to sail, put out to sea." See *sail*.

PUT TO DEATH

Old Testament

Verb: מוּת (*mût*), GK 4637 (S 4191, 4192), 854x. *mût* means "to die, put to death, kill." See *die*.

New Testament

Verb: ἀναιρέω (*anaireō*), GK *359* (S *337*), 24x. *anaireō* means "kill, put to death." See *kill*.

Verb: ἀποκτείνω (*apokteinō*), GK *650* (S *615*), 74x. *apokteinō* essentially means "to deprive of life, kill." See *kill*.

Verb: θανατόω (*thanatoō*), GK *2506* (S *2289*), 11x. *thanatoō* conveys the termination of physical life and may best be translated "kill" or "put to death." Jesus describes the extremes of persecution in the last days by saying, "Brother will betray brother to death, and a father his child; children will rebel against their parents and have them *put to death*" (Mt. 10:21; cf. Mk. 13:12; Lk. 21:16). In a context of encouragement amidst persecution of believers, Paul quotes Ps. 44:22, "For your sake *we face death* all day long; we are considered as sheep to be slaughtered" (Rom. 8:36; cf. also 2 Cor. 6:9). Matthew describes the evil plot of the religious leaders against Jesus in these words, "The chief priests and the whole Sanhedrin were looking for false evidence against Jesus so that they could *put* him *to death*" (Mt. 26:59; cf. 27:1; Mk. 14:55; 1 Pet. 3:18). This death was not the end for Jesus, however, for even though "he *was put to death* in the body," he "was made alive by the Spirit" (1 Pet. 3:18).

But the death signified by this word can also be a metaphorical death. Paul uses this word to describe the normal process of sanctification for all believers when he writes, "For if you live according to the sinful nature, you will die; but if by the Spirit *you put to death* the misdeeds of the body, you will live" (Rom. 8:13; see also 7:13). See *NIDNTT-A*, 236-38.*

PUT TO SHAME

Old Testament

Verb: בּוֹשׁ (*bôš*), GK 1017 (S 954), 125x. *bôš* has the basic meaning "to feel ashamed, put to shame." See *ashamed*.

QUARREL

Old Testament

Verb: רִיב (*rîb*), GK 8189, (S 7378), 72x. *rîb* denotes the action of entering into an argument, conflict, or lawsuit with another person. People may "quarrel" with one another (e.g., Gen. 26:20–22), but often the quarrel involves God. When the Israelites "quarrel" with Moses and test God by demanding water in the desert (Exod. 17:2), Moses commemorates the rebellion by naming that place "Me*rib*ah" (17:7; cf. Ps. 95:8–9). See *contend*.

QUARTER

Old Testament

Adjective: רְבִיעִי (*r^ebîʿî*), GK 8055 (S 7243), 55x. *r^ebîʿî* means the ordinal number "fourth"; it can also mean "quarter." See *fourth*.

QUENCH

New Testament

Verb: σβέννυμι (*sbennymi*), GK *4931* (S *4570*), 6x. *sbennymi* means "to quench." This verb is used on a physical level when the five foolish virgins are concerned that their lamps "will go out" if they do not get more oil (Mt. 25:8). The writer of Hebrews refers to those among God's children who have faced persecution but, by God's power, "quenched the fury of the flames" (Heb. 11:34; cf. Dan. 3).

The other uses of *sbennymi* are metaphorical. Matthew applies the Servant Song of Isa. 42:1–4 to the ministry of Jesus, one feature of which is the fact that he "will not quench" a smoldering wick; that is, Jesus was concerned to bring light and life especially to those in society who are weak and powerless (Mt. 12:20). Elsewhere, Jesus refers to the place of eternal punishment as a place where "the fire is not quenched" (Mk. 9:48). In Paul's discussion of the armor of the believer, the "shield of faith" can "extinguish" all the fiery darts of the devil (Eph. 6:16); through the power of faith, we can deflect the temptations of the evil one. And one of Paul's most important instructions to the believers in Thessalonica is not to "quench the Holy Spirit" (1 Thess. 5:19); that is, we must let the Holy Spirit burn in our hearts and drive us to live and witness for Jesus. See *NIDNTT-A*, 520.

QUESTION

New Testament

Verb: ἐπερωτάω (*eperōtaō*), GK *2089* (S *1905*), 56x. *eperōtaō* means "to ask a question" or "to question, interrrogate someone." See *ask*.

QUICKLY

New Testament

Adverb: ταχέως (*tacheōs*), GK *5441* (S *5030, 5032, 5033*), 15x.

Adverb: ταχύς (*tachys*), GK *5444* (S *5035, 5036*), 13x. Both of these adverbs mean "quickly, soon." Many of its uses are in narrative parts of the NT (e.g., at the time of Jesus' resurrection, the women go "quickly" from the tomb, Mt. 28:7–8; Paul hopes to send Timothy to the Philippians "soon," Phil. 2:19; cf. 2 Tim. 4:9). The father in the parable of the lost son wants the celebration of his returned son to begin "quickly" (Lk. 15:22). James reminds us that "everyone should be quick to learn [and] slow to speak" (Jas. 1:19). Perhaps most important use of *tachys* is the promise of Jesus in Revelation that he is "coming soon" (Rev. 3:11; 22:7, 12, 20). That promise still stands.

QUIET

New Testament

Verb: σιγάω (*sigaō*), GK *4967* (S *4601*), 10x. *sigaō* is used primarily to a person's being quiet or silent. In Luke's gospel, it describes how the disciples keep silent about Jesus' transfiguration, telling no one of the things they have seen (Lk. 9:36; cf. Mt. 17:9); how the crowds around Jesus command a blind man "to be quiet," (Lk. 18:39); and how Jesus' enemies "become silent" at his wise and skillful answer regarding paying taxes to Caesar (Lk. 20:26).

In Acts, *sigaō* is used when Peter insists that the joyful believers "be quiet" so he can tell them how the Lord brought him out of prison (Acts 12:17). Later, the whole assembly in Jerusalem "becomes silent" as they listen to Barnabas and Paul tell them about the miraculous signs and wonders God did among the Gentiles (15:12; see also v. 13).

Finally, in Paul's writings, *sigaō* describes the gospel of Jesus Christ as "the revelation of the mystery *hidden* [NIV; "kept secret" KJV] for long ages past" (Rom. 16:25) but now revealed by God for the obedience of faith from the nations. Paul also uses *sigaō* in his discussion of spiritual gifts in the church. With reference to tongues, Paul states that "if there is no interpreter, the speaker must *keep quiet* in the church and speak to himself and God" (1 Cor. 14:28). With reference to prophecy, "If a revelation comes to someone who is sitting down, the speaker *should stop*" (1 Cor. 14:30, NIV; "hold his peace" KJV). A final use of *sigaō* in Paul's writings has invited much controversy in modern times, as he instructs that "women should *remain silent* in the churches" (1 Cor. 14:34). Paul's language is strong, exhorting his readers that in the churches women are not even permitted to speak but must learn in submission (cf. also 1 Cor. 11:5; 1 Tim. 2:11–12). While Paul allows for women to pray and prophesy (1 Cor. 11:5), speaking and teaching are apparently not allowed. See *NIDNTT-A*, 524-25.*

Verb: σιωπάω (*siōpaō*), GK *4995* (S *4623*), 10x. *siōpaō* means "to be quiet, silent." With one exception (Acts 18:9), it is found only in the gospels. *siōpaō* refers primarily to the silencing of the human voice.

Gabriel informs Zechariah that he will "*be silent* and unable to speak" until the birth of his son John (Lk. 1:20). In contrast, Jesus responds to the Pharisees at his triumphal entry into Jerusalem that if his disciples "*keep quiet*, the stones will cry out" (Lk. 19:40). Also related to the human voice, *siōpaō* describes those who "remain silent" before accusations or questions (Mk. 3:4; 9:4). Notice especially how Jesus "remained silent" before his accusers (Mt. 26:62; Mk. 14:61).

With particular reference to a command to keep silent, people command the blind beggars "to be quiet" as they cry out for Jesus' attention and mercy (Mt. 20:31; Mk. 10:48). In contrast, God exhorts Paul in a vision to "keep on speaking, do not *be silent*" (Acts 18:9). Paul must not be afraid of harm for, God tells him, "I have many people in this city" (18:10).

Perhaps the most significance usage of *siōpaō* is Jesus' command the raging sea,

"Quiet!" (Mk. 4:39, NIV; "Peace!" KJV). This usage indicates not only the deity of Jesus Christ, but also his full and perfect humanity, as one who has dominion over creation ("what manner of man is this?" Mk. 4:41, KJV; cf. Ps. 107:29). See *NIDNTT-A*, 525-26*

Verb: φιμόω (*phimoō*), GK *5821* (S *5392*), 7x. *phimoō* means "to be quiet, speechless, muzzled." It has the idea of restraint, either imposed externally or internally. Probably the most helpful passage in showing the *internal* restraint aspect of *phimoō* is Jesus' parable in Mt. 22:10–12, where the guest who does not have a wedding garment is "speechless," for he does not know how to answer the king. Jesus refutes the Sadducees so soundly that he "silences" them (Mt. 22:34). This is no doubt the force of *phimoō* in 1 Pet. 2:15, where Peter says, "For it is God's will that by doing good you should *silence* the ignorant talk of foolish men." In living out the Christian walk by faith and good deeds and words, we must emulate Jesus Christ, who indeed silenced the ignorant talk of foolish men.

In the case of demons, which are normally neither embarrassed nor silent, Jesus commands them to "be quiet" (Mk. 1:25; Lk. 4:35). Here the verb is being used as a kind of *external* restraint that results in speechlessness. This same sense of external restraint is obvious in 1 Tim. 5:18 where Paul quotes Deut. 25:4 as saying, "'Do not *muzzle* the ox while it is treading out the grain.'" Perhaps the most well-known use of *phimoō* comes from Mk. 4:39, which says, "He got up, rebuked the wind and said to the waves, 'Quiet! *Be still*!' Then the wind died down and it was completely calm" (NIV). The point of *phimoō* is beautiful in its simplicity. At the feet of Jesus Christ, demons, humankind, and even the often tumultuous creation is rendered speechless. See *NIDNTT-A*, 591.

QUOTA

Old Testament

Noun: חֹק (*ḥōq*), GK 2976 (S 2706), 131x. *ḥōq* is derived from the related verb *ḥāqaq*, which means "to cut in, inscribe, decree" and denotes something that is limited or restricted. Most frequently *ḥōq* refers to the prescribed law of God (see *decree*). Less frequently, it expresses a fixed quantity or some sort of limit. For example, Israel is forced to make the same "quota" of bricks without straw (Exod. 5:14).

QUOTE

Old Testament

Verb: מָשַׁל (*māšal*), GK 5439 (S 4911), 17x. *māšal* bears two distinct meanings in the OT: "to compare, liken, be like" (see *compare*) and "to quote (a proverb)." *māšal* sometimes refers to the use of an oft-repeated saying. These proverbs are usually short, pithy statements in which a general truth is applied to a specific situation. For example, God uses a proverb to compare Jerusalem in its adultery to the nations from which she came: "like mother, like daughter" (Ezek. 16:44–45; see also 12:23; 18:2–3; 20:49, 24:3; cf. Num. 21:27). The *māšāl* (i.e., "proverb") can be more lengthy (Ezek. 17:2; cf. vv. 1–10). In a unique usage, because of the horror of Job's calamities, he is ridiculed and abused to the point that he becomes a *māšal* ("byword," NIV) to everyone (17:6). See *NIDOTTE*, 2:1134-36.

RABBI

New Testament

Noun: διδάσκαλος (*didaskalos*), GK *1437* (S *1320*), 59x. *didaskalos* means "teacher" and is the Gk. word used for the Heb. word *rabbi*. See *teacher*.

Noun: ῥαββί (*rhabbi*), GK *4806* (S *4461*), 15x. *rhabbi* can mean "master, sir" or remain transliterated as "rabbi." In Hebrew it literally means "my lord" ("lord" with a lower-case "l" simply means "sir" or "master"). It was originally a proper form of address and came to be used as an honorary title for teachers of the law (Mt. 23:7). It was also used as a technical title for those who had received authority to act as a judge in religious matters. But the word was applied to any respected teacher.

John the Baptist's disciples addressed him as rabbi (Jn. 3:26), as was Jesus: by Nicodemus (Jn. 3:2), Nathaniel (1:49), Peter (Mk. 9:5; 11:21), and Judas (Mt. 26:25, 49; Mk. 14:45). Jesus was called "teacher" or "Lord" more often than "rabbi" (Mt. 13:27; Lk. 5:5; 17:13).

Interestingly, six times in John the term *rhabbi* is explained for the readers (Jn. 1:38; 3:26; 4:31; 6:25; 9:2; 11:8). Thus, although the term was common to Jewish readers, it may not have been in Greek-speaking circles. The abusive use of the honorary term *rhabbi* by the Jewish leaders in Jesus' day may have motivated Jesus to teach his disciples not to use the title for themselves; for as Jesus said: "You have one teacher, and you are all brothers" (Mt. 23:8). Christians today are no different. No matter what our theological training or religious authority (e.g., ordination in professional ministry), we all have only one teacher or *rhabbi* (Jesus Christ), and all of us are brothers and sisters in him. See *NIDNTT-A*, 508.

RACE

New Testament

Noun: γενεά (*genea*), GK *1155* (S *1074*), 43x. *genea* used of a "race" of people, those living at the same time ("generation"), or the time in which a generation lives ("age"). See *generation*.

RAGE

Old Testament

Noun: חֵמָה (*ḥēmâ*), GK 2779 (S 2534), 125x. The basic meaning of *ḥēma* is "anger, wrath." Its most common use describes the fury or rage of people or of God. See *anger*.

New Testament

Noun: θυμός (*thymos*), GK *2596* (S *2372*), 18x. *thymos* is generally used to refer to "anger, rage, fury." See *wrath*.

RAISE

New Testament

Verb: ἐγείρω (*egeirō*), GK *1586* (S *1453*), 144x. In the transitive (active) sense *egeirō* means to "waken, lift up, stimulate." In the intransitive (passive) sense it conveys "to get up, rise up." Note that this word was not used prior to the NT to refer to the resurrection of the dead.

In the active sense *egeirō* depicts the action of getting up, usually after waking up—as in Mt. 1:24 ("Joseph *awoke* from sleep and did as the angel of the Lord commanded him"), 8:26 ("Then [Jesus] *got up* and rebuked the wind and sea"), and 25:7 ("Then all those virgins *rose* and trimmed their lamps").

More importantly, the word can describe people being raised who were known to be dead. After the death of Jairus' daughter (Mk. 5:22–24, 35–43), in a situation that seemed hopelessly irreversible, Jesus took the girl's hand and said, "*Talitha kum*" ("Little girl, I say to you, *get up*!"), an Aramaic phrase translated into Greek by *egeirō*. The idea of the death as sleep reaches back to the OT, for when a prominent character or king dies, he has gone to "sleep with his fathers" (Gen. 47:30; Deut. 31:16; 1 Ki. 1:21; 2:10). While there is no developed doctrine of the resurrection in the OT, it is a clear, audible whisper (see especially Isa. 26:19; Dan. 12:2). For NT writers, however, death is not final. For example, in Jn. 11:11–14 Jesus uses sleep-of-death talk regarding Lazarus; John then uses *egeirō* three times to refer to raising Lazarus (12:1, 9, 17).

The core of *egeirō* has to do with the raising of Jesus from the dead. Except for Phil. 1:17, the letters of the NT never use this verb for anything except the resurrection of Jesus. It becomes a technical term for Paul because it occurs so often in Romans and 1 Corinthians (more than 30x, with a heavy saturation in 1 Cor. 15, the chief passage on the resurrection in the NT). Jesus is the firstfruits of the resurrection, who is thus qualified to raise us from the dead when he returns to this earth (1 Cor. 15:20; 2 Cor. 4:14). God has transferred the power to raise the dead to his Son, who will enact it when he returns (1 Thess. 4:13–18). See *NIDNTT-A*, 159.

RAISE UP

Old Testament

Verb: קוּם (*qûm*), GK 7756 (S 6965), 627x. The general range of meanings for *qûm* includes "to stand up, arise, get up (in the morning)." It can also mean "to raise up, confirm something, establish." See *rise*.

New Testament

Verb: ἀνίστημι (*anistēmi*), GK *482* (S *450*), 108x. *anistēmi* depicts someone getting up from a reclined position, "to stand up, get up," including being raising the dead. See *get up*.

Verb: ἐπαίρω (*epairō*), GK *2048* (S *1869*), 19x. *epairō* means "to look up, lift up, raise up," though it has several senses in the NT. See *lift up*.

RAM

Old Testament

Noun: אַיִל (*ʾayil*), GK 380 (S 352), 171x. *ʾayil* literally means "ram" but can also be used figuratively for "leading man, ruler, leader, chief" (see *chief*).

The ram becomes an important sacrificial animal in the OT especially in the light of the Lord's miraculous deliverance of Isaac in Gen. 22, when Abraham passes the test and is given a ram for the sacrifice in place of Isaac. In the history of Israel, probably the clearest indication of the people's repentance and spiritual renewal to worship God is seen in their reinstitution of the burnt offerings, as was done during the reign of King Hezekiah, when ninety-six rams were offered to the Lord (2 Chr. 29:32). Similarly, when Ezra brings back a group of exiles from Babylon, they resume their worship of God by dedicating as a burnt offering one hundred rams (Ezr. 8:35).

The ram is used for the guilt offering in Lev. 5:18, and the ram skins are used to make a tent covering for the tabernacle (Exod. 25:5; 26:14; 36:19).

RANSOM

Old Testament

Verb: גָּאַל (*gāʾal*), GK 1457 (S 1350), 104x. *gāʾal* means variously "to ransom, redeem, function as a kinsman-redeemer" (see *redeem*). It can also mean "avenge" (see *avenge*).

Verb: פָּדָה (*pādâ*), GK 7009 (S 6299), 60x. The verb *pādâ* means "to redeem, ransom." As with the parallel verb *gāʾal*, the use of this verb for redeeming often involved the exchange of money to buy something back. See *redeem*.

New Testament

Noun: ἀπολύτρωσις (*apolytrōsis*), GK *667* (S *629*), 10x. *apolytrōsis* means "redemption, ransom." In Heb. 9:15 this word is a synonym for *lytron* (see previous word), meaning "ransom." See *redemption*.

Noun: λύτρον (*lytron*), GK *3389* (S *3083*), 2x. *lytron* means "ransom." In both Mt. 20:28 and Mk. 10:45 Jesus says that the Son of Man has come to give his life as a "ransom" for many. In the Roman world, prisoners of war and slaves could be ransomed for a price. Christ has bought us "at a price" (1 Cor. 6:20), the price of his blood. To whom was this price paid? Church theologians have had interesting theories, such as payment to an angry God who demanded blood or to a bloodthirsty devil. But the Bible never says to whom the price was paid, so we should not push the metaphor beyond what Scripture says. Rather, as a thanksgiving response, "glorify God in your body" (1 Cor. 6:20). See also *redemption*.

RATHER

New Testament

Adverb: μᾶλλον (*mallon*), GK *3437* (S *3123*), 81x. *mallon* is a comparative adverb that means "rather, instead, more." It often brings to light some contrast to a preceding phrase. For example, God feeds the birds; "are you not much more valuable than they?" (Mt. 6:26). God clothes the lilies of the field; "will he not much more clothe you?" (6:30). The upshot of the trial of Jesus was that "Pilate released Barabbas instead" (Mk. 15:1). In their statement before the Sanhedrin, Peter and the other apostles reply, "We must obey God rather than men!" (Acts 5:29).

The most important uses of this adverb occur in some of the NT letters. In Paul's comparison of Adam and Christ in Romans 5, he indicates several times "how much more" the work of Christ surpasses the disaster brought about through Adam's sin (Rom. 5:15, 17; cf. 5:9–10). In 11:24, Paul stresses that if God can graft wild branches (Gentiles) into the root (Israel), "how much more readily will these, the natural branches, be grafted into their own olive tree." In 2 Cor. 3:9, 11, Paul stresses "how much more glorious" is the ministry of the new covenant than the old covenant. Similarly, the author of Hebrews emphasizes "how much more" the blood of the eternal Christ will atone for sin in contrast to the blood of bulls and goats on the Day of Atonement (Heb. 9:14). Again, if we submitted to the discipline of earthly fathers for our good, "how much more should we submit to the Father of our spirits and live" (12:9). Finally, in terms of Christian living, Paul's prayer is that we "abound more and more" in the way of the Lord (Phil. 1:9; 1 Thess. 4:1, 10; cf. 2 Pet. 1:10).

RAVINE

Old Testament

Noun: נַחַל (*naḥal*), GK 5707 (S 5158), 137x. *naḥal* refers to a dry river bed or wadi. Since it can refer to the dry river bed itself, by extension it also can be used to describe a valley or ravine. See *river*.

REACH

Old Testament

Verb: בּוֹא (*bôʾ*), GK 995 (S 935), 2592x. *bôʾ* is the fourth most common verb in the OT. It denotes motion toward a specific goal, such as "to go, arrive, enter a house, come." It expresses a variety of motions. See *come*.

Verb: מָצָא (*māṣāʾ*), GK 5162 (S 4672), 457x. *māṣāʾ* generally means "to find," though it can also mean "to come upon, meet, catch." See *find*.

Verb: נָגַע (*nāgaʿ*), GK 5595 (S 5060), 150x. The verb *nāgaʿ* means "to touch physically," but its various nuances include "to touch, strike, reach, arrive."

nāgaʿ sometimes means "to reach or extend." Thus, Jacob's ladder extends to heaven (Gen. 28:12); plants extend to certain geographic boundaries (Isa. 16:8; Jer. 48:32); messages (Jon. 3:6) and trouble (Mic. 1:9) reach people, in the sense of arrival. Figuratively, *nāgaʿ* can show intensity of action, as in 2 Chr. 28:9, when a rage reaches to heaven. See also *touch, strike*.

READ

New Testament

Verb: ἀναγινώσκω (*anaginōskō*), GK *336* (S *314*), 32x. *anaginōskō* means "to read, read aloud." In the NT era it was a common practice to read aloud, even when alone. Usually, reading of the OT Scriptures is meant (cf. Acts 13:27; 15:21). Jesus' custom was to enter the synagogue and read the OT Scriptures aloud (Lk. 4:16). In Mt. 21:42 Jesus asks the chief priests and the Pharisees whether they have ever even "read" the Scriptures (cf. Mt. 12:3; 19:4; Lk. 10:26). Whether he refers to a particular OT passage (Mt. 12:26; 21:16; Mk. 2:25) or to a specific section of the OT (Lk. 6:3), Jesus always engages his opponents (usually the religious leaders) with the Scriptures themselves. This is the basis for his theological argumentation. Paul tells us that there was a veil over the minds of the Jews as they "*read* Moses" (2 Cor. 3:14–15). For the Lord (and for Paul) reading the OT rightly means reading it as a believer in Christ.

The parenthetical note in Mk. 13:14 ("let *the reader* [lit. the one who reads] understand") is likely addressed to the person reading this gospel aloud when the church gathered to worship. In his letters, Paul uses *anaginōskō* to refer both to the reading of a letter (2 Cor. 1:13; 3:2) and to the public reading of his own letters (Col. 4:16; 1 Thess. 5:27). John uses the term in Rev. 1:3 where he says that those who read and hear the words that he is about to write will be blessed. See *NIDNTT-A*, 43.

READY

New Testament

Adjective: ἕτοιμος (*hetoimos*), GK *2289* (S *2092*), 17x. Like its cognate verb *hetoimazō* (see *prepare*), *hetoimos* can describe either impersonal or personal objects. As to impersonal objects, in 2 Cor. 9:5 Paul wants to make sure that the Corinthian contribution for the needy in Jerusalem was "ready" (cf. also Mt. 22:4, 8; Mk. 14:15; Lk. 14:17; Jn. 7:6; 2 Cor. 10:16; 1 Pet. 1:5). In a personal sense, Jesus warns that like the thief who comes unexpectedly in the night, people must be alert and "ready" for the coming of the LORD (Mt. 24:44; Lk. 12:40). In Lk. 22:33, Peter vows that he is "ready" even to go with Jesus to prison and to death.

But being ready is an ongoing status for believers today. In 1 Pet. 3:15, Peter gives instructions regarding suffering for righteousness' sake, telling his readers "always to be *ready* to make a defense to anyone who asks you for a reason for the hope that is in you" (cf. also Tit. 3:1). Readiness is a biblical theme firmly rooted in the Exodus, where the Israelites were to celebrate the Passover with their loins girded, ready to flee Egypt (Exod. 12:11). In the NT this theme of readiness is carried forward in that a spiritual "exodus" has been brought about through Christ. The contemporary Christians should live with an acute sense of readiness, both in terms of sharing the gospel with others and of living a life of holiness in preparation for his coming. See *NIDNTT-A*, 212-213.

REALIZE

New Testament

Verb: γινώσκω (*ginōskō*), GK *1182* (S *1097*), 222x. *ginōskō* means "to know, understand, recognize." It is a rich verb in the NT. See *know*.

Verb: συνίημι (*syniēmi*), GK *5317* (S *4920*), 26x. *syniēmi* means "to understand, realize." See *understand*.

REALLY

New Testament

Adverb: ἀληθῶς (*alēthōs*), GK *242* (S *230*), 18x. *alēthōs* means "truly, surely, really"—an adverb of certainty. See *truly*.

REAP

New Testament

Verb: θερίζω (*therizō*), GK *2545* (S *2325*), 21x. *therismos* ("reap, harvest") is an agricultural term that is used in a literal sense for the collection of a cultivated crop from a field. The term may also be used figuratively to refer to the gaining of a specific result. See *harvest*.

REAR GUARD

Old Testament

Verb: אָסַף (*ʾāsap*), GK 665 (S 622), 200x. In varying contexts, *ʾāsap* can mean "to gather, assemble, take away, or bring up the rear."

In the context of moving, *ʾāsap* means "to bring up the rear" or "to act as a rear guard." The tribe of Dan acts in this capacity as Israel journeys in the wilderness (Num. 10:25), and armed men are to come behind the ark to guard it (Jos. 6:9, 13). Significantly, God promises to come behind his people to protect them from danger (Isa. 52:12; 58:8). See also *gather, remove*.

REASON

New Testament

Verb: διαλέγομαι (*dialegomai*), GK *1363* (S *1256*), 13x. *dialegomai* means "to reason, argue, prove, persuade." Paul customarily reasons on Sabbath days, in the synagogues, to both Jews and Gentiles (Acts 17:2, 17; 18:4, 19; 19:8, 9; 24:12, 25). In these contexts *dialegomai* is carried out primarily through preaching and teaching, often based on Scripture. Such reasoning apparently could go on for quite some time with Paul (20:7, 9). If we are to emulate Paul's preaching and teaching, we must do much more than just talk. *dialegomai* involves preaching and teaching that harnesses reason and logic into a defensive and positive exposition of God's Word to persuade and edify.

In a more negative framework, the disciples "argue" with each other as to who is the greatest (Mk. 9:34). *dialegomai* is also used to describe the "dispute" between Michael and Satan over the body of Moses (Jude 9). See *NIDNTT-A*, 138.

Verb: διαλογίζομαι (*dialogizomai*), GK *1368* (S *1260*), 16x. *dialogizomai* means "to discuss, consider, argue" about something. Sometimes it can denote an inner wondering to oneself about something. See *consider*.

Noun: αἰτία (*aitia*), GK *162* (S *156*), 20x. *aitia* is the basis for some action or the legal basis for a charge—a "reason, cause, basis, charge." One use of *aitia* is causal, indicating the general reason, motivation, or grounds for doing something (Lk. 8:47; Acts 10:21; 28:20; 2 Tim. 1:6, 12; Tit. 1:13; Heb. 2:11). Occasionally, translations may render the literal "what is the reason?" as a simple "why?" (Acts 10:21; cf. 2 Tim. 1:12). In Mt. 19:10, *aitia* describes a "situation" (NIV) or "case" (KJV, NRSV) of a man with his wife.

The second use denotes a legal charge or grounds for an accusation of culpability (Mt. 27:37; Mk. 15:26; Acts 25:18, 27; 28:18). It is in this sense of *aitia* that the NT describes Pilate's lack of legal basis for condemning Jesus (Jn. 18:38; 19:4, 6; Acts 13:28). In several instances, *aitia* has elements of both meanings (i.e., general cause and legal charge), as it is used to describe a general reason for something within the context of legal proceedings (Mt. 19:3; Acts 22:24; 23:28). See *NIDNTT-A*, 24.*

REBEL

New Testament

Verb: ἀντιλεγω (*antilegō*), GK *515* (S *483*, *471*), 11x. *antilegō* means "to speak against, contradict" someone. It sometimes has the notion "to rebel" verbally. See *speak against*.

REBELLION

Old Testament

Noun: פֶּשַׁע (*peša*ʿ), GK 7322 (S 6588), 93x. Usually translated as "rebellion, offense, sin, transgression," the noun *peša*ʿ is one of the three primary words for sin in the OT. See *sin*.

REBUKE

Old Testament

Verb: יָכַח (*yākaḥ*), GK 3519 (S 3198), 59x. *yākaḥ* has a broad range of meaning, but it generally carries the sense of arguing a case or issuing judgment with the intent to correct. It is often translated "rebuke," "correct," "judge," "punish," or "argue," and is found most frequently in legal contexts (especially in Job [17x]) and in the wisdom instruction of Proverbs (10x).

In a legal context, *yākah* can be used for arguing a case. Job longs to speak with the Almighty, to "argue his case" with him (Job 13:3; cf. 16:21; 23:7; 40:2) or to "argue" his ways before God's face (13:15). Abraham "complains" to Abimelech about the well that Abimelech's servants have seized from Abraham (Gen. 21:25). In the context of a covenant lawsuit, God says "Come now, *let us reason together*" (Isa. 1:18) in the sense of presenting the case in court. Elsewhere, God brings a case against his people and "contends" with Israel (Mic. 6:2; cf. Ps. 50:21).

yākaḥ can also be used for rendering judgment. When Laban accuses Jacob of stealing the household idols and searches the camp, Jacob demands that Laban place the idols before their kinsmen, so the kinsmen may "judge" between Jacob and Laban (Gen. 31:37). In the sense of rendering judgment, *yākaḥ* may be found in parallel with *sāpat*, "to judge." God will "judge" (*sāpat*) between the nations and "decide disputes" (*yākaḥ*) for many peoples (Isa. 2:4; cf. 11:3–4; Mic. 4:3). Less frequently, *yākaḥ* may extend beyond rendering judgment to the actual executing of the sentence. God will "punish" or "rebuke" with the rod David's son who sins (2 Sam. 7:14), and God has appointed Babylon to "punish" Israel (Hab. 1:12).

In wisdom instruction, *yākaḥ* often carries the sense of punishment or discipline for the purpose of training or correction, and so may be found in parallel with *yāsar*, "to discipline, chasten" (Ps. 6:1; 38:1; 94:10; Prov. 9:7; Jer. 2:19). Yahweh "disciplines" those he loves as a father disciplines a son (Prov. 3:12). There is no benefit in "rebuking" a mocker (9:7, 8; 15:12), but a wise man will gain knowledge from being "rebuked" (19:25) and will love the one from whom the "rebuke" comes (9:8). See *NIDOTTE*, 2:441-45.

New Testament

Verb: ἐλέγχω (*elenchō*), GK *1794* (S *1651*), 17x. The basic meaning of *elenchō* is "to rebuke" (1 Tim. 5:20). Rebuking can take a number of forms, such as making someone aware of a sin (Mt. 18:15, "Go and *show* him his fault"), exposing sin (Jn. 3:20, "His deeds will be *exposed*"), and/or convincing someone of guilt (Jn. 8:46, "Can any of you *prove* me *guilty* of sin?"). It can also refer to the refutation of false doctrine (Tit. 1:9). Even though we live in an age that values tolerance, the Bible commends rebuke (which entails judgment) as an act of love (cf. Heb. 12:5-6). It is a major pastoral function; one-third of the occurrences of *elenchō* are in the Pastoral Letters. See *NIDNTT-A*, 178-79.

Verb: ἐπιτιμάω (*epitimaō*), GK *2203* (S *2008*), 29x. *epitimaō* generally means "to rebuke." Peter, for example, rebukes Jesus after he outlined his coming passion (Mt. 16:22). NT rebukes are uttered in a variety of contexts and with varying aims. Using rebukes, Jesus demonstrated his divinity and authority over the weather (8:26), demons (17:18), and illnesses (Lk. 4:39). Rebukes can also take the form of a warning (Mt. 12:16) or a stern command (Mk. 3:12). Rebukes are used to stop people from doing something they are currently engaged in (Mt. 19:13) and often to condemn those who are sinning (Lk. 17:3). Rebuking is a major pastoral function (note Paul's instruction in 2 Tim. 4:2, "correct, *rebuke*, and encourage"). God uses pastoral rebukes—along with preaching, correcting, and encouraging—to turn an erring brother back into the right path. See *NIDNTT-A*, 201.

RECEDE

Old Testament

Verb: קָלַל (*qālal*), GK 7837 (S 7043), 82x. *qālal* means "to curse," though it is also used to express mitigation, such as water "receding" after the flood (Gen. 8:8, 11). See *curse*.

RECEIVE

Old Testament

Verb: לָקַח (*lāqaḥ*), GK 4374 (S 3947), 967x. The basic meaning of *lāqaḥ* is "to take, grasp." The meaning is often simply to "take into/by the hand." *lāqaḥ* is also used to describe taking something as one's own possession. See *take*.

New Testament

Verb: ἀναβλέπω (*anablepō*), GK *329* (S *308*), 25x. The root *blepō* means "to see, look." When used with respect to the blind, it has the notion of "receive sight." See *look up*.

Verb: ἀπολαμβάνω (*apolambanō*), GK *655* (S *618*), 10x. *apolambanō* means "to receive, get back, be repaid," generally from another individual. Rewards and punishments (both temporal and eternal) are what people receive in Lk. 16:25; 18:30; 23:41; Rom. 1:27; Col. 3:24; and 2 Jn. 8. To receive in return or to get something back is the idea conveyed in Lk. 6:34 (what someone has borrowed "is repaid"); in 15:27 (the father "receives back" his lost son); and in Gal. 4:5 (believers "receive the full rights" as God's children). See *NIDNTT-A*, 328.

Verb: δέχομαι (*dechomai*), GK *1312* (S *1209*), 56x. *dechomai* essentially means "to receive" something (e.g., money, Phil. 4:18; instructions, Col. 4:10), but it can also mean "to welcome" someone (e.g., Mt. 10:14). To receive Christ is to be welcomed by the Father in perfect unity (10:40). The word is used of ideas that can be accepted as true (11:14). It applies to things that are picked up (Lk. 2:28) or obtained (Acts 22:5). It can denote coming to a place and remaining there (Acts 3:21, "He must *remain* in heaven"). It is used as one step in the transmission of oral tradition (Acts 7:38).

God's grace is something that we "receive"; we are passive and God is active in salvation (2 Cor. 6:1, "We urge you not to *receive* God's grace in vain"). An interesting corollary occurs in Eph. 6:17, in Paul's description of the armor of God. Most likely Paul watched Roman soldiers don their armor during his imprisonment. In fact, the order in which the armor is listed in Eph. 6:12–18 occurs in the order that it was put on. As a Roman soldier put on each piece of armor, his servant stood by holding the helmet. When the soldier was ready, he received the helmet from his servant. Thus Paul writes: "*Take* the helmet of salvation." Again, human passivity and God's activity are stressed. We receive the salvation that God freely and sovereignly gives us. See *NIDNTT-A*, 130-31.

Verb: κομίζω (*komizō*), GK *3152* (S *2865*), 10x. *komizō* means "to receive, pay back." This verb can refer to getting something back that is owned or owed. For example, in the parable of the talents, the master should have "received" his money back with at least the interest it would have earned in the bank (Mt. 25:27; cf. Heb. 11:19). It can also refer to coming into possession of something, often as payment. In a negative sense, those who do wrong will be "paid back" for the wrong they have done (Col. 3:25). Positively, believers "receive" the goal of their faith, the salvation of their souls (1 Pet. 1:9; cf. Eph. 6:8; Heb. 10:36; 1 Pet. 5:4).

Verb: λαμβάνω (*lambanō*), GK *3284* (S *2983*), 258x. *lambanō* conveys the basic idea of acquiring or obtaining something and may best be translated as "take, seize, receive, get." See *take*.

Verb: παραλαμβάνω (*paralambanō*), GK *4161* (S *3880*), 49x. *paralambanō* means "to take, receive, accept." See *take*.

Verb: προσδέχομαι (*prosdechomai*), GK *4657* (S *4327*), 14x. *prosdechomai* means "to receive, welcome" (see *welcome*) and "to wait for, to expect something" in the sense of looking forward to (see *wait for*).

RECEIVE IN FULL

New Testament

Verb: ἀπέχω (*apechō*), GK *600* (S *566, 567, 568*), 19x. *apechō* means "to receive in full." Those who give, pray, or fast in order to be seen by others have already "received their reward in full" (Mt. 6:2, 5, 16). Jesus says that those who choose worldly gratification over a heavenly reward have "received their comfort" (Lk. 6:24). Paul has "received full payment" from the Philippian church (Phil. 4:18). *apechō* can also mean "to abstain from" (see *abstain from*) or "to be far" (see *[be] far*).

RECKON

See *credit*.

RECLINE

New Testament

Verb: ἀνάκειμαι (*anakeimai*), GK *367* (S *345*), 14x. The image that *anakeimai* captures is that of a person lying outstretched on a couch in front of a low table, propped on his left elbow, feet pointed away from the table, and eating with his right hand (Mt. 26:7; Lk. 22:27; Jn. 12:2). Multiple persons at a dinner table would recline such that they could rest their head back on the chest of the person beside them. This image is seen most clearly in Jn. 13:23, when the disciple whom Jesus loved leans back against Jesus' chest in order to ask him who would betray him.

Because of this widespread custom, *anakeimai* can refer to "those who recline," that is, "guests" at a meal (Mt. 22:10–11; Mk. 6:26). See *NIDNTT-A, 310.*

Verb: ἀναπίπτω (*anapiptō*), GK *404* (S *377*), 12x. *anapiptō* refers to the simple action of "sitting down, reclining," normally for a meal time. See *sit down*.

Verb: κατάκειμαι (*katakeimai*), GK *2879* (S *2621*), 12x. *katakeimai* means "to recline" for a meal. It was typical to "sit" during normal meals, but during special meals (e.g., feasts or banquets) the guests usually "reclined" on couches (Mk. 2:15; 14:3; Lk. 5:29; 7:37; 1 Cor. 8:10). When Jesus "reclined" with tax collectors and sinners, this signified that he was willing to accept those despised by society. *katakeimai* also means "to lie down." See *lie down*.

RECOGNIZE

Old Testament

Verb: נָכַר (*nākar*), GK 5795 (S 5234), 44x.

(1) Unlike the verb *yāda*ʿ (GK 3359, see *know*), which normally implies a measure of intimacy or comprehensiveness in one's knowing, *nākar* (which occurs mostly in the Hiphil form) refers only to general knowing, such as the basic awareness of another's existence or the acknowledgment of who a person is. In various contexts, it is best rendered "recognize" (Gen. 27:23), "inspect" (37:32), "acknowledge, take notice" (Ruth 2:10), and "distinguish" (Ezr. 3:13).

(2) In rare instances and forms, *nākar* appears to bear the meaning "make unrecognizable, act as a stranger, disguise oneself." While some scholars see this use as a different verb that uses the same root letters, the use of *nākar* in the story of Joseph's reunion with his brothers in Gen. 42:7-8 makes this unlikely. The verb appears four times and includes both meanings. We are told that Joseph recognizes (*nākar*) his brothers (vv.7-8), but disguises himself and pretended to be a stranger (*nākar*) before revealing his true identity. Joseph is aware of who his brothers are, though he does not know what to expect from them because he does not know them intimately. Indeed, it has been over twenty-five years since they have been together! That *nākar* is used in this single context with both meanings suggests that there is only one Hebrew word. This means that the concept of stranger is related to the kind of knowing described by the verb and demonstrates the lack of intimate knowledge.

New Testament

Verb: ἐπιγινώσκω (*epiginōskō*), GK *2105* (S *1921*), 44x. *epiginōskō* can mean to "know, perceive, recognize, understand." See *know*.

RECONCILE

New Testament

Verb: ἀποκαταλλάσσω (*apokatallassō*), GK *639* (S *604*), 3x. *apokatallassō* means "to reconcile." It appears to have an end-time emphasis. In Col. 1:20, 22, Paul claims that reconciliation between God and human beings is effected by being washed in Christ's blood as shed on the cross. This reconciliation has ramifications for the reconciliation of the entire universe, which has been out of sorts with God since the fall of Adam and Eve and will not be fully restored until the return of Christ (cf. Rom. 8:18–25; Rev. 21:1–5).

In Eph. 2:16, Paul refers to reconciliation on a human level, namely, that of Jews and Gentiles. Such reconciliation also comes by way of the cross, through which Christ put an end to human hostilities and divisions by creating a new humanity (i.e., the body of Christ). All artificial human divisions should cease to exist in the church, and a failure to do so results from a failure to see what Christ and his sacrifice can ultimately do. See *NIDNTT-A*, 292-94.*

Verb: καταλλάσσω (*katallassō*), GK *2904* (S *2644*), 6x. *katallassō* means "to reconcile." It is related to the Greek word, *allassō,* which means "to change, exchange" (6x in the NT: Acts 6:14; Rom. 1:23; 1 Cor. 15:51–52; Gal. 4:20; Heb. 1:12). In classical Gk., *katallassō* usually meant the coming together of two persons after a time of hostility; it was rarely used in a religious sense. This probably derives from the fact that in pagan religions, the human/divine relationship lacked personal involvement and instead required placating the gods. In the NT, however, *katallassō* is a theological term describing the removal of enmity between humans and God (Rom. 5:10 [2x], 2 Cor. 5:18, 19, 20); it occurs only once in reference to human relationships (1 Cor. 7:11, husband/wife; it is significant that marriage is the relationship chosen for the use of this word). In biblical thought, God reconciles humans to himself through the death of his Son (Rom. 5:10; 2 Cor. 5:18–20). See *NIDNTT-A*, 292-94.*

RECONCILIATION

New Testament

Noun: καταλλαγή (*katallagē*) GK *2903*

(S *2643*), 4x. *katallagē* is the word the NT uses for our "reconciliation" with God, which has taken place through Christ's blood (Rom. 5:11). It is therefore a work of God in that he is the one who removes the enmity between himself and humanity (2 Cor. 5:18–19). This divine act does require a response of faith from the human beings. This is why Paul admonishes his readers to "be reconciled to God" (2 Cor. 5:20; see *reconcile*). Reconciliation has been made available to all people because of a rejection of Christ by the majority of Jews (Rom. 11:15). Such removal of enmity between God and the human race should lead to missionary zeal—to our being Christ's ambassadors (2 Cor. 5:20). See *NIDNTT-A*, 292-94.*

REDEEM, REDEMPTION

Old Testament

Verb: גָּאַל (*gāʾal*), GK 1457 (S 1350), 104x. *gāʾal* means variously "to ransom, redeem, function as a kinsman-redeemer." It can also mean "avenge" (see *avenge*).

(1) More than half of the uses of *gāʾal* have a legal sense concerning the redemption of property or persons. God was the owner of the promised land of Canaan, and the family clans were each given a piece of it only as a trust. Thus the land could never be sold permanently; if any land was sold to cover a debt, a *gōʾēl* (often trans. "kinsman-redeemer"; ptc. of *gāʾal*) could "redeem" the land for his unfortunate relative (Lev. 25; book of Ruth). (Note how important extended family relationships are in Bible times.) If no one was able to redeem it (i.e., buy it back), the land would revert to its original owner in the year of Jubilee. Similarly, if a man sold himself into slavery to cover debts, he could be redeemed by a *gōʾēl* or else be set free in the year of Jubilee.

(2) In Psalms and Isaiah, the Lord is a Redeemer, who has come to help his people in their time of need (Ps. 19:14; Isa. 41:14). The background of this use is the Exodus, where God redeemed his enslaved people by a mighty hand and outstretched arm (Exod. 6:6; 15:13; Isa. 51:10). Isaiah prophesies God's promise to redeem his people again, this time from their exile in Babylon (Isa. 35:9–10; 51:11). The spiritual implications of God as Redeemer from Egypt and Babylon are clear: The Lord will redeem us from our slavery to sin and by his love and mercy will give us freedom to serve him (Isa. 63:9). Our new name is: "the Holy People, the Redeemed of the Lord" (Isa. 62:12). We should wear that name humbly. See *NIDOTTE*, 1:791–94.

Verb: פָּדָה (*pādâ*), GK 7009 (S 6299), 60x. The verb *pādâ* means "to redeem, ransom." As with the parallel verb *gāʾal*, redeeming often involved the exchange of money to buy something back.

(1) This verb regularly occurs in cultic contexts about redeeming the firstborn. Yahweh claimed a right to all the firstborn animals and sons (Exod. 13:1–2; 34:19). The background of this ownership is the death of the firstborn in Egypt at the time of the Exodus. But rather than slaughtering all the firstborn animals and sons in sacrifices to the Lord, the Israelites could pay a fee in order to "redeem" them (Exod. 13:13–15; Num. 18:15–17). This redemption of a firstborn son points ahead to God's firstborn (and only) Son, Jesus, who was in fact sacrificed as the price paid for our redemption (cf. 1 Cor. 6:20).

(2) In some complaint psalms, the psalmist cries out to God, "Redeem me" (Ps. 25:22; 119:134). The Lord does indeed rescue his people from serious illness, from enemies, or from sin (31:5; 55:18; 130:8). As with the verb *gāʾal* in some contexts, God redeems his people from the nations so that they can return home (Jer. 31:11). They are "the ransomed of the Lord" (Isa. 35:10; 51:11). See *NIDOTTE*, 3:578–81.

Verb: קָנָה (*qānâ*), GK 7864, 7865 (S 7069), 91x. *qānâ* appears to bear two distinct meanings in the OT: "to buy, purchase, redeem," and also "to create. "See *buy*.

New Testament

Verb: ἐξαγοράζω (*exagorazō*), GK

1973 (S *1805*), 4x. *exagorazō* means "to redeem" or "make the most of."

(1) Paul uses this verb twice in Galatians to refer to the spiritual redemption that Jesus accomplished for us through his death on the cross. Christ's purpose in entering the world at just the right time was to redeem those who were enslaved to sin and the curse of the law (Gal. 4:5; cf. 3:10). How did he do this? By suffering the death of a curse (3:13). In other words, the sinless, uncursed Christ suffered an accursed death (cf. Deut. 21:23) so that he could remove God's curse from us!

(2) In Eph. 5:16 and Col. 4:5 Paul uses *exagorazō* to express the idea of "redeeming the time"—that is, to buy it up intensively or to snap up every opportunity there is to serve Christ and witness for him. See *NIDNTT-A*, 12-13.

Verb: λυτρόω (*lytroō*), GK *3390* (S *3084*), 3x. *lytroō* means "to redeem." In the three occurrences of this verb, only 1 Pet. 1:18–19 mentions an actual payment: We have been redeemed from a futile, sinful life not with gold or silver but with the precious blood of the Lamb of God, who (like the lamb in the Passover) was without blemish or defect (cf. also Isa. 53:7). Obviously the notion of spiritual redemption stands out here, as it does in Tit. 2:14.

The historical background of redemption from slavery in the Exodus and from political subjugation in the return from Babylonian exile stands out in Lk. 24:21, where the two on the road to Emmaus express the hope that Jesus would have redeemed Israel from political subjugation to Rome. While that did not happen, a far more important redemption, spiritual redemption, *did* occur through Jesus' crucifixion (see *exagorazō*). See *NIDNTT-A*, 346.

Noun: ἀπολύτρωσις (*apolytrōsis*), GK *667* (S *629*), 10x. *apolytrōsis* means "redemption, ransom."

(1) In Heb. 9:15 this word is a synonym for *lytron*, meaning "ransom" (see *ransom*): Jesus died as a ransom to set us free from sin. In Heb. 11:35 *apolytrōsis* bears the meaning of release from captivity and torture.

(2) Most occurrences of *apolytrōsis* denote the redemption provided by Christ through his death on the cross (Rom. 3:24; 1 Cor. 1:30). In Eph. 1:7; Col. 1:14, it describes something that believers have right now. But in the remaining uses of this word (Lk. 21:28; Rom. 8:23; Eph. 1:14; 4:30), there is a future aspect to redemption, which we will not experience fully until Jesus returns again. Is our redemption in jeopardy since we do not have it fully right now? Absolutely not, because we have the Holy Spirit as a deposit guaranteeing our final redemption (see *arrabōn*, discussed under *pledge*). See also *salvation*.

Noun: λύτρωσις (*lytrōsis*), GK *3391* (S *3085*), 3x. *lytrōsis* means "redemption." Right after John the Baptist was circumcised and Jesus was already in the womb of his mother, John's father, Zechariah, praised God because he "has made *redemption* for his people" (Lk. 1:68). After Jesus was born and was presented in the temple, Anna saw the baby, gave thanks to God, and spoke about him to all the Jews who were looking for "redemption" (Lk. 2:38). The writer to the Hebrews (9:12) reminds us that by Christ's own blood, he obtained "eternal *redemption*" for us. Redemption begins now and lasts throughout all eternity!

REED

Old Testament

Noun: קָנֶה (*qāneh*), GK 7866 (S 7070), 62x. In its most basic sense, *qāneh* refers to the generic reeds or rushes found in the watery areas of the ancient Near East (Job 40:21; Isa. 19:6; 35:7). However, since the reed was sometimes used for measuring, by extension this word can stand for the measuring reed/rod (Ezek. 40:3, 5; 42:16–17) or the length denoted by the reed/rod—one reed/rod = 6 cubits (Ezek. 40:5, 7). It can also refer to the *stalk* of a plant (Gen. 41:5, 22) and the spice reed calamus (Isa. 43:24; Song 4:14).

Most often (over 20x), *qāneh* refers to the "branches" of the candlesticks of the tabernacle in Exodus (Exod. 25:31–33, 35-36; 37:17–19, 21–22).

In a metaphorical sense, the nation of Egypt is likened to a "reed," meaning that it is a weak support for Israel to depend on (2 Ki. 18:21; Isa. 36:6; Ezek. 29:6). In addition, the compassion and tenderness of the Messiah is portrayed by the fact that "a bruised reed he will not break" (Isa. 42:3). See *NIDOTTE*, 3:942-43.

New Testament

Noun: κάλαμος (*kalamos*), GK *2812* (S *2563*), 12x. *kalamos* means "reed," referring to a kind of tall grass, sometimes with a segmented stalk, that grows in marshy areas. They were known for being easily broken (Mt. 11:7; 12:20; Lk. 7:24). Jesus is handed a reed to imitate a king's staff (Mt. 27:29), which is also used to beat him (27:30; Mk. 15:19). A reed is also used to give Jesus a sponge soaked with sour wine (Mt. 27:48; Mk. 15:36). Reeds are also used for writing (3 Jn. 13) and as measuring rods (Rev. 11:1; 21:15, 16).*

REFINE

Old Testament

Verb: בָּחַן (*bāḥan*), GK 1043 (S 974), 29x. *bāḥan* denotes the divine examination of an individual and may be translated as "test, try, prove." It is common in the poetic and prophetic books of the OT. *bāḥan* may have originated from the world of metallurgy and the practice of refining gold and other precious metals. See *test*.

Verb: צָרַף (*ṣārap*), GK 7671 (S 6884), 34x. *ṣārap* is commonly used to denote the testing or refining of both metals and human beings and may be translated as "test, refine." See *test*.

REFLECT ON

New Testament

Verb: νοέω (*noeō*), GK *3783* (S *3539*), 14x. *noeō* means "to understand, see, reflect on." It is related to the Greek word *nous* ("mind"). See *understand*.

REFRAIN

Old Testament

Verb: חָדַל (*ḥādal*), GK 2532 (S 2308), 55x. *ḥādal*, most often translated "stop" in the NIV, generally indicates the simple cessation of action. Sometimes the verb is used for the stopping of an action before it ever starts. In this context, *ḥādal* appears frequently when determining whether an action (i.e., listening or engaging in battle) will begin. The king of Israel asks the prophets, "Shall I go to war against Ramoth Gilead, or shall I *refrain*?" (1 Ki. 22:6; cf. Jdg. 20:28; 1 Ki. 22:15; 2 Chr. 18:5, 14). See *stop*.

REFRESH

New Testament

Verb: ἀναπαύω (*anapauō*), GK *399* (S *373*), 12x. *anapauō* means "to gain relief by resting," such as to cease from toil. See *rest*.

REFUGE

Old Testament

Noun: עֹז (*ʿōz*), GK 6437 (S 5797), 76x. The primary sense of *ʿōz* is "strength, might, power." Sometimes the word *ʿōz*, used by itself, refers to "ramparts, fortifications, strong refuge" (Prov. 21:22; Amos 3:11). This idea is applied metaphorically to God, who is "my strong tower" (Ps. 61:3) and "my mighty rock and refuge" (62:7). See *power*.

REFUSE TO BELIEVE

New Testament

Verb: ἀπειθέω (*apeitheō*), GK *578* (S *544*), 14x. *apeitheō* means "to disobey, be disobedient, reject, refuse to believe." See *disobey*.

REFUTE

New Testament

Verb: ἐλέγχω (*elenchō*), GK *1794* (S *1651*), 17x. The basic meaning of *elenchō* is "to rebuke" (1 Tim. 5:20). It is also used for refuting false doctrine (Tit. 1:9). See *rebuke*.

REGARD

New Testament

Verb: ἡγέομαι (*hēgeomai*), GK *2451* (S

2233), 28x. *hēgeomai* means "to consider, think, regard." See *consider*.

Verb: λογίζομαι (*logizomai*), GK *3357* (S *3049*), 40x. The basic meaning of *logizomai* has to do with counting or thinking (see also *think, consider*). It is also used for crediting something for or against someone (see *credit*). Uncircumcised people "are regarded" as circumcised if they keep the requirements of the law (Rom. 2:26). The children of promise "are regarded" as Abraham's offspring (9:8). These two thoughts would have been revolutionary to a Jewish person—that circumcision has to do with a divine decision rather than a physical act and that nonethnic Jews could be Abraham's offspring and inheritors of his promise. If someone "regards" a food as unclean, it is unclean for him (Rom. 14:14). Paul wants people to "regard" him and other church leaders as servants of Christ (1 Cor. 4:1). See *NIDNTT-A*, 338-39.

REGENERATION

New Testament

Noun: παλιγγενεσία (*palingenesia*), GK *4098* (S *3824*), 2x. The concept of regeneration in the NT is much larger than this one word, represented by the ideas of "new birth" (Jn. 3:3, 5), being "born anew" (*anagennaō*, GK *335*, 1 Pet. 1:3, 23), "new creation" (2 Cor. 5:17; Gal. 6:15), and others.

Paul tells Titus that God saved us, "not because of works done by us in righteousness, but according to his own mercy, by the washing of *regeneration* and renewal of the Holy Spirit" (ESV, Tit. 3:5). In conversion the believer is made new, brought from death to life (Eph. 2:1, 5), by the power of God's Holy Spirit. In Mt. 19:28, Jesus uses *palingenesia* in a sense close to Stoicism, which taught that the world was periodically destroyed and then created anew, reborn. However, Jesus uses this term merely to refer to the end of this age and the beginning of the next. "I tell you the truth, at the *renewal of all things*, when the Son of Man sits on his glorious throne, you who have followed me will also sit on twelve thrones, judging the twelve tribes of Israel" (NIV; ESV reads "in the new world").

The idea of being "born again" did not originate with the mystery religions, as some claim. It was part of the common parlance of the first century. It appears from Jn. 3:3 that Jesus is the first to use this metaphor in connection with conversion, and it was copied by the mysteries religions to designate initiation into their rites.

REGION

New Testament

Noun: μέρος (*meros*), GK *3538* (S *3313*), 42x. *meros* has a basic meaning of "a part of a whole," but it can also mean "region, place, share." See *part*.

Noun: ὅριον (*horion*), GK *3990* (S *3725*), 12x. *horion* means "region, vicinity." This noun occurs only in narrative literature and is usually used for various regions that Jesus visited, such as Zebulun and Naphtali (Mt. 4:13), Tyre and Sidon (15:22; Mk. 7:24), Decapolis (Mk. 7:31), and Judea (Mt. 19:1; Mk. 10:1). In Mt. 2:16 it refers to the territory around Bethlehem, and in Acts 13:50 it refers to the region around Antioch in Pisidia.

Noun: τόπος (*topos*), GK *5536* (S *5117*), 94x. *topos* means "place"; in the plural it can refer to a "region" or "district." See *place*.

Noun: χώρα (*chōra*), GK *6001* (S *5561*), 28x. The basic sense of *chōra* is an area or space; in the NT it refers to large areas, such as a cultivated field, a region, or a country. See *country*.

REGULAR

Old Testament

Noun (used as adv.): תָּמִיד (*tāmîd*), GK 9458 (S 8548), 104x. As an adverb, *tāmîd* describes that which is "lasting" or something done "continually." The word can describe both an action done regularly (often according to a schedule). As an adjective, *tāmîd* is used for the *regular* or *daily* offerings in the tabernacle and temple. See *always*.

REGULATIONS

Old Testament

Noun: חֻקָּה (*ḥuqqâ*), GK 2978 (S 2708), 104x. The feminine noun *ḥuqqâ*, derives from the verb *ḥāqaq*, "to cut in, inscribe, decree," is related to its masculine counterpart, *ḥōq*, though the two nouns never appear together (see *decree*). *ḥuqqâ* also occurs in cultic contexts, where the NIV translates "regulations." There are "regulations" for Passover (Exod. 12:43; Num. 9:3, 12, 14), the altar (Ezek. 43:18), and the house of God (44:5). When *ḥuqqâ* is used for the practices of Israel's surrounding nations, the NIV, NASB, and KJV translate "customs" (Lev. 18:30; 20:23; Jer. 10:3).

Noun: עֵדוּת (*ʿēdût*), GK 6343 (S 5715), 61x. *ʿēdût*, usually translated "testimony," is closely connected to God's law. In the Pentateuch, this noun describes the two tablets containing the Ten Commandments. Generally, outside the Pentateuch *ʿēdût* is a more generic reference to law (1 Ki. 2:3; 2 Ki. 23:3; 1 Chr. 29:19), perhaps with the physical tablets of the Ten Commandments in the background. In this sense, the plural of *ʿēdût* may be translated "requirements, warnings, regulations, or decrees." See *testimony.*

Noun: תּוֹרָה (*tôrâ*), GK 9368 (S 8451), 223x. Generally rendered "law, regulation, instruction, teaching," *tôrâ* was originally used to describe the instructions for daily conduct that God gave his people; eventually other meanings developed for this word. See *law*.

New Testament

Noun: δικαίωμα (*dikaiōma*), GK *1468* (S *1345*), 10x. *dikaiōma* refers to "regulations, righteous requirements, righteousness," depending on the context. These meanings are, of course, interrelated. *dikaiōma* can represent the righteous deeds required by the ceremonial law (Heb. 9:1, 10) or the moral law (Lk. 1:6; Rom. 1:32; 2:26; 8:4). It can also denote the revealed actions of God (Rev. 15:4) or the "righteous deeds" of the saints, which are represented by the fine linen they wear (19:8).

dikaiōma, as "righteousness," refers to process of justification (see *justification* for related words), i.e., to the imputation of Christ's fulfillment of the righteous requirements of the law to his chosen people. As Paul says in Rom. 5:16–18, "And the free gift is not like the result of that one man's sin. For the judgment following one trespass brought condemnation, but the free gift following many trespasses brought *justification*.... As one trespass led to condemnation for all men, so one act of righteousness leads to *justification* and life for all men" (see *righteousness*). *dikaiōma* and life are what was accomplished by the person and work of Jesus Christ. His "righteousness" reckoned to us is exactly what the saints are said to be clothed with at the wedding feast of the Lamb (Rev. 19:8). See *NIDNTT-A*, 143-47.*

REIGN

Old Testament

Verb: מָלַךְ (*mālak*), GK 4887 (S 4427), 350x.

Words with the Heb. *mlk* root comprise a frequent and important concept in the OT. The verb *mālak* means "to reign as king" or "to be king." The vast majority of references occur with an assortment of human kings (both those of Israel and Judah as well as the kings of the nations around them—e.g., Jos. 13:10; 1 Sam. 13:1; 2 Sam. 5:4–5; 1 Ki. 11:25, 42). But the psalms and the prophets also speak clearly of God's own reigning activity (Ps. 47:7; 93:1; 96:10; 97:1; Isa. 24:23; 52:7; Mic. 4:7). See *king*.

New Testament

Verb: βασιλεύω (*basileuō*), GK *996* (S *936*) 21x. *basileuō* means "to rule, reign." A few of the NT references to this verb are to an earthly king, such as Archelaus (Mt. 2:22; Lk. 19:14, 27). But more frequent is a reference to Jesus as God's promised King in the line of David (Lk. 1:33) and especially to his present reign from heaven (1 Cor. 15:25; Rev. 11:15; 19:6).

But there are several references in the NT to the reigning of Christians, not in their own right but in the power of Jesus.

Jesus has ascended to God's right hand, and we are now sitting with him in the heavenly realms (Eph. 1:20; 2:6; Col. 3:1–3). Thus, while it is true that in this present dispensation, sin and death "reign" (Rom. 5:14, 17, 21), if have received the gift of righteousness from the one man Jesus, grace now "reigns" in us to bring us eternal life (5:15, 21). Thus, Paul is able to exhort, "Do not let sin *reign* in your mortal body" (6:12). In the coming millennial reign of Christ, Revelation makes it clear that believers "will *reign* with him for a thousand years" (Rev. 20:4, 6). And when the new heaven and new earth are brought in by God, all his saints "*will reign* for ever and ever" (22:5).

Noun: βασιλεία (*basileia*), GK *993* (S *932*). 162x. In the NT, *basileia* plays a greater role. Most English versions consistently translate *basileia* with "kingdom," though at times it would be better understood as "reign" or "rule." Thus, some scholars today prefer to speak of "the rule of God" or even "the empire of God." See *kingdom*.

REIMBURSE

New Testament

Verb: ἀποδίδωμι (*apodidōmi*), GK *625* (S *591*), 48x. *apodidōmi* means "to give (back), deliver, render, hand over" (see *give back*). It can also mean "to repay, reward, reimburse." See *repay*.

REJECT

Old Testament

Verb: מָאַס (*māʾas*), GK 4415 (S 3988a), 74x. *māʾas*, usually translated "to reject" and occasionally "to despise," expresses the action of rejecting someone or something. It is often found in a covenant context, where God's people are rejecting him or he is rejecting them.

The OT portrays Israel's sinful and idolatrous ways in terms of rejecting God again and again. First-generation Israelites in the wilderness "reject" the promised land (Num. 14:31; cf. Ps. 106:24) and even "reject" God himself (Num. 11:20). Later, Israel "rejects" God by asking for a king to replace him as their ruler (1 Sam. 8:7; 10:19), even though the office of king was God's plan for Israel (Deut. 17:14-20; Jdg. 17:6; 21:25). Saul, Israel's first king, "rejects" the word of God, so God "rejects" him as king (1 Sam. 15:23, 26). God sends Samuel to anoint David in the place of the "rejected" Saul (16:1). Throughout their history, Israel "rejects" God's law (Isa. 5:24; Jer. 6:19; Amos 2:4), his word (Isa. 30:12; Jer. 8:9), his judgments (Ezek. 5:6; 20:13, 16), and his statutes (20:24).

Since Israel repeatedly rebels against God, God "rejects" Israel (Ps. 78:59). Israel "rejects" the knowledge of God, which leads to their destruction (Hos. 4:6), and they "reject" God's covenant with their fathers (2 Ki. 17:15), which leads God to "reject" Israel by giving them into the hand of plunderers (2 Ki. 17:20). God finally "rejects" Israel through the fall of Jerusalem and the exile.

During the exile, some seem to struggle with God's rejection of Israel. To one psalmist, it appears as if God has "rejected" his anointed (Ps. 89:38[39]), and Jeremiah wonders if God has "rejected" Israel completely (Jer. 14:19). But the exile should not have come as a surprise. The covenant blessings and curses in Leviticus warn that the punishment for "rejecting" God's statutes (Lev. 26:15) would be to have their enemies rule over them (Lev. 26:16-17). But the good news in the midst of the curses is that when Israel is in the exile, God will not "reject" them so as to destroy them completely and break his covenant with them (Lev. 26:44). Rather, God's rejection of his people in the exile is temporary. He has chosen Israel and not "rejected" them (Isa. 41:9). In response to the question whether God has "rejected" his chosen Israel in exile (Jer. 33:24), God says only if his covenant with day and night is broken (33:25) will he "reject" Israel; and since his covenant is unbreakable, he will not reject Israel forever, but will restore it (33:26; cf. 31:37).

In instances other than a covenant context, Job "despises" his life (Job 7:16,

9:21) and is "despised" by others (19:18); ultimately, Job simply "despises" or "rejects" (42:6; likely he rejects his declaration made in ignorance, see 42:3). Additionally, Israel is encouraged not to "despise" God's discipline (Prov. 3:11; cf. Job 5:17) because the one who ignores discipline "despises" himself (Prov. 15:32). Finally, Jesus applies the psalmist's statement "The stone the builders *rejected* has become the capstone" (Ps. 118:22) to himself (Mt. 21:42). See *NIDOTTE*, 2:833-34.

New Testament

Verb: ἀθετέω (*atheteō*), GK *119* (S *114*), 16x. *atheteō* means "to reject, set aside, nullify, annul." Herod did not want to reject his daughter's request (Mk. 6:26). The Pharisees and the lawyers chose to reject God's purpose when they refused to submit to John's baptism (Lk. 7:30). The one who rejects Jesus' disciples rejects Jesus, and the one who rejects Jesus rejects the one who sent him, who is God (Lk. 10:16). Judgment awaits those who rejects Jesus and his word (Jn. 12:48). Paul states that rejecting God's will regarding sexual purity (1 Thess. 4:1–7) means rejecting not man but God (1 Thess. 4:8).

atheteō can also describe the nullification of something that is, was, or appeared to be valid. Jesus accused the Pharisees of "setting aside" the commandment of God by their man-made traditions (Mk. 7:9). Under the old covenant, "setting aside" the law of Moses resulted in death without mercy (Heb. 10:28). Paul argues that he does not "set aside" the grace of God with his law-free gospel (Gal. 2:21). God "brings to nothing" the discernment of the discerning (1 Cor. 1:19); here *atheteō* is parallel with "destroying" the wisdom of the wise. Human covenants that have been ratified cannot be "annulled" (Gal. 3:15). Decisive actions that prove one is not a believer "annul" any prior indications of faith (1 Tim. 5:12). See *NIDNTT-A*, 18.

Verb: ἀπαρνέομαι (*aparneomai*), GK *565* (S *533*), 11x. The verb *aparneomai* essentially means the same as *arneomai* (GK *766*): to "deny, reject, disown." This word occurs only in the gospels, a majority of them in the prediction of Peter's denial (e.g., Mt. 26:34–35). But there is also a positive form of rejecting, namely, rejecting one's own interests and serving Christ instead (Mt. 16:24). See *deny*.

Verb: ἀπειθέω (*apeitheō*), GK *578* (S *544*), 14x. *apeitheō* means "to disobey, be disobedient, reject, refuse to believe." See *disobey*.

Verb: ἀρνέομαι (*arneomai*), GK *766* (S *720*), 33x. *arneomai* primarily means "to deny," although its wider range of meaning covers "disown, fail to confess, reject, say 'No,' refuse, renounce." It often carries the nuance of rejecting Jesus as the God-sent Messiah (cf. 2 Pet. 2:1; 1 Jn. 2:22–23). See *deny*.

Verb: παραιτέομαι (*paraiteomai*), GK *4148* (S *3868*), 12x. *paraiteomai* denotes either "to make a request" or, in the negative, "to make excuses, reject" something. See *request*.

REJOICE, REJOICING

Old Testament

Verb: שָׂמַח (*śāmaḥ*), GK 8523 (S 8055), 156x. *śāmaḥ* can describe both one's feeling of joy and the outward expression of such gladness in the form of rejoicing. It can be translated many ways, including "rejoice," "delight," "filled with joy," or "gladden." *śāmaḥ* is expressed in many ways, including blowing trumpets (2 Chr. 23:13), singing (Ps. 32:11), and dancing (Jer. 31:13). It is often connected with the heart (Ps. 19:8; Prov. 14:10; 15:30; 23:15).

śāmaḥ describes the manner in which the feasts and festivals of Israel are to be celebrated (Lev. 23:40; 2 Chr. 30:25). Moses commands the Israelites to celebrate joyfully (Deut. 16:11, 14).

The Psalms overflow with rejoicing. The psalmist rejoices in the Lord's strength (Ps. 21:1) and in his law (19:8). *śāmaḥ* is the proper response to the works of God (66:6; 92:4; 126:3). The house of the Lord is also a source of rejoicing (122:1). Those who trust in the Lord can rejoice even in the midst of turmoil (46:4). The psalmist prays that all nations will rejoice in the Lord (67:4). When *śāmaḥ* denotes the rejoicing of the psalmist's enemies, it is sometimes translated "gloat" (30:1; 35:19, 24, 26; 38:16).

Though God's people have suffered, the prophets testify to the future *śāmaḥ* that the Lord will bring (Isa. 66:10; Zeph. 3:14). He will give them comfort and *śāmaḥ* instead of grief (Jer. 31:13). When Isaiah prophesies the birth of the Wonderful Counselor, he also prophesies the future rejoicing of his people in their salvation (Isa. 9:3, 6).See *NIDOTTE* 3:1251-1254.

Noun: שִׂמְחָה (*śimḥâ*), GK 8525 (S 8057), 94x. Depending on the context, *śimḥâ* can be translated "joy, rejoicing, gladness, pleasure," or "happiness." See *joy.*

New Testament

Verb: ἀγαλλιάω (*agalliaō*), GK *22* (S *21*), 11x. *agalliaō* means "to rejoice greatly, exult, be overjoyed." This verb seems to carry a more intense meaning than *chairō*, though the terms do overlap, as in Mt. 5:12, "rejoice (*chairō*) and be glad (*agalliaō*)" (cf. also 1 Pet. 4:13; Rev. 19:7).

In the NT *agalliaō* usually denotes a rejoicing that stems from God's end-time act of salvation. This kind of jubilant exultation is foreshadowed in Psalms, where rejoicing over God's past, present, and future acts of salvation involves the entire created order (Ps. 19; 32; 89; 96; 97). While the OT faithful (such as Abraham [Jn. 8:56] and David [Acts 2:26, citing Ps. 16:9]) looked forward with rejoicing to the coming of Christ, those involved in the fulfillment of the Messiah's coming also manifested ecstatic joy. Mary bursts into a song of joy, her spirit "*rejoicing* in God my Savior" (Lk. 1:47; cf. also the related noun *agaliasis* in 1:14, 44). Looking back on John's ministry, Jesus remarks that John brought joy to those who heard his preaching (Jn. 5:35).

The end-time sense of joy is furthered in Jesus' ministry as the kingdom's work progresses. The victory of God's kingdom over Satan occasions Jesus' rejoicing "in the Holy Spirit" (Lk. 10:21). As testimony to the ongoing fulfillment of the kingdom's saving work, Gentile believers (e.g., the Philippian jailer, Acts 16:34) rejoice at receiving God's salvation. The Gentiles addressed by Peter "*greatly rejoice*" (1 Pet. 1:8), despite present sufferings (1:6), in the hope of Christ's future revelation. Finally, all believers may anticipate with jubilation the ultimate end-time fulfillment in the marriage of the Lamb (Rev. 19:7). See *NIDNTT-A*, 4-5.

Verb: εὐφραίνω (*euphrainō*), GK *2370* (S *2165*), 14x. *euphrainō* conveys the basic idea of a created state of joy or euphoria and may be translated as "rejoice, gladden, celebrate." The joyous occasion over the return of the lost son is captured by *euphrainō*. The father in the parable declares, "Bring the fattened calf and kill it. Let's have a feast and *celebrate*. For this son of mine was dead and is alive again: he was lost and is found" (Lk. 15:23–24, 29, 32). God's eschatological victory is an occasion for celebration in Revelation: "Therefore *rejoice*, you heavens and you who dwell in them!" (Rev. 12:12; also 18:20). For Paul, the fulfillment of the patriarchal promises in Christ was cause for celebration. Quoting Deut. 32:43, he writes, "*Rejoice*, O Gentiles, with his people" (Rom. 15:10; Gal. 4:27). Peter makes the resurrection of Christ as predicted in Ps. 16 a cause for celebration. Quoting the psalmist, he declares, "Therefore my heart is *glad* and my tongue rejoices; my body also will live in hope" (Acts 2:26). See *NIDNTT-A*, 220.

Verb: καυχάομαι (*kauchaomai*), GK *3016* (S *2744*), 37x. *kauchaomai* means "to boast, brag, rejoice"; it has both a positive and negative sense. See *boast*.

Verb: χαίρω (*chairō*), GK *5897* (S *5463*), 74x. *chairō* means "to rejoice, be filled with joy" (Jn. 3:29; Acts 8:39). It is the opposite of mourning (Rom. 12:15). It can refer to feelings and can result from specific situations (e.g., Lk. 1:14; 19:6), but for the believer, it is a constant state because of our relationship with Christ (Phil. 4:4; 1 Thess. 5:16).

The first use of *chairō* in the NT describes the reaction of the Magi when they see the star that leads them to Christ (Mt. 2:10). Thus from the beginning of the NT, Christ is a source of joy for all who find him. Christ's earthly work is also a source of rejoicing for the Father, who is presented in Jesus' parables as rejoicing in reconciliation with his lost children (Mt. 18:13; Lk. 15:32).

Christ's disciples rejoice in his miracles (Lk. 19:37) and his resurrection (Jn. 20:20). When they are joyful, and perhaps proud, that the demons have submitted to them, Jesus tells them that their rejoicing should rather be in their salvation (Lk. 10:20).

Paul in his letters teaches that a spirit of rejoicing transcends all earthly circumstances and that Christian joy is actually proven through hardship (2 Cor. 6:10; Col. 1:24). Though he wrote his letter to the Philippians from prison, in the midst of personal suffering, Paul maintains a steadfast spirit of rejoicing (Phil. 1:18; 2:17; 4:10; cf. Acts 16:25). In turn, he instructs the Philippian believers to "rejoice in the Lord." (3:1; 4:4). See *NIDNTT-A*, 599-600.

RELATIVE(S)

Old Testament

Noun: אָח (*ʾāḥ*), GK 278 (S 251), 629x. *ʾāḥ* denotes a "brother" or one who is close in some type of human relationship. It can even denote treaty partners. Abraham and Lot, uncle and nephew, are referred to as brothers (Gen. 14:12, 14, 16). In several places, especially laws dealing with family matters, *ʾāḥ* denotes kinsmen (Lev. 19:17; 25:25; Deut. 15:12; 17:15). It is also used in a more extended sense to describe members of the same tribe (Levites, Num. 16:10; Judahites, 2 Sam. 19:12). See *brother*.

New Testament

Adjective: συγγενής (*syngenēs*), GK *5150* (S *4773*), 11x. *syngenēs* means "relative." It can refer to family relations, such as the relatives of Zechariah and Elizabeth who are so excited that they finally have a baby boy (Lk. 1:58). When Joseph and Mary return from Jerusalem when Jesus is twelve years old, they look for him among the relatives (2:44). Cornelius has called together his relatives and friends to hear what Peter has to say to them.

But in Romans, Paul refers to the entire Jewish nations as "relatives according to the flesh" (Rom. 9:3). He uses this same word in 16:7, 11, 21; here he may also have this same meaning in mind (though he could also be referring to family relation).

RELEASE

Old Testament

Verb: פָּתַח (*pātaḥ*), GK 7337 (S 6605), 136x. Generally, *pātaḥ* means "to open" objects that are closed, sealed, or blocked. By extension, it can also mean "to release" or "to set (something) free," such as a person from prison (Isa. 51:14; cf. Jer. 1:14). See *open*.

New Testament

Verb: ἀπολύω (*apolyō*), GK *668* (S *630*), 66x. *apolyō* is a compound verb that literally means "to loose away from." In the NT it is frequently translated as "to release, send away," though it can also mean "to divorce" (see *divorce*). *apolyō* is used almost exclusively in the Gospels and Acts (only once elsewhere; see Heb. 13:23).

(1) *apolyō* frequently means "to send away" in reference to a group or an individual. For example, Jesus sends the crowds away or sends an individual away (Mt. 14:22; 15:23, 32, 39; Mk. 8:9; Lk. 8:38; 14:4). Also note Acts 13:3, when being sent away has to do with being commissioned and set apart by a church for a specific service or work for the Lord. Once it is used as a euphemism for death (Lk. 2:29).

(2) *apolyō* is also used of being set free, released from a sickness (Lk. 13:12) or from a debt that is owed (Mt. 18:27). In the accounts of the trial of Jesus, Pilate offers

to "set free" one prisoner, in keeping with the custom (Mk. 15:6, 9, 11, 15; Acts 3:13). In Acts, Luke uses *apolyō* when he writes that certain apostles (such as Peter, John, and Paul) were released from prison (Acts 4:21, 23; 5:40; 16:35, 36; 26:32).

Verb: καταργέω (*katargeō*), GK *2934* (S *2673*), 27x. *katargeō* means "to release, destroy, nullify, cause something to be useless." See *destroy*.

Noun: ἄφεσις (*aphesis*), GK *912* (S *859*), 17x. In contrast to the verb *aphiēmi* (see *forgive*), of the 17x that *aphesis* appears in the NT, it primarily carries the sense of "forgiveness" (15x). Only twice does *aphesis* denote a "release" or "freedom" from captivity (Lk. 4:18). See *forgiveness*.

RELENT

Old Testament

Verb: נָחַם (*nāḥam*), GK 5714 (S 5162), 108x. *nāḥam* bears two distinct but related meanings in the OT: "to comfort, console" (see *comfort*) and "to relent, repent, change one's mind, be grieved." This verb is especially applied to God's changing his mind. See *change one's mind.*

RELIABLE

New Testament

Adjective: πιστός (*pistos*), GK *4412* (S *4103*), 67x. *pistos* means "faithful, trustworthy, reliable, dependable." See *faithful*.

RELY ON

Old Testament

Verb: בָּטַח (*bāṭah*), GK 1053 (S 982), 118x. This word means "to trust, rely on, depend on," with the sense of being completely confident and feeling utterly safe. See *trust*.

REMAIN

Old Testament

Verb: יָשַׁב (*yāšab*), GK 3782 (S 3427), 1088x. The general meaning of *yāšab* is to "sit, sit down," with the connotations of "live, dwell, remain, settle." See *live*.

Verb: לִין (*lîn*), GK 4328 (S 3885), 71x. *lîn* usually describes the act of remaining somewhere for the night while on a journey. See *spend the night*.

Verb: שָׁאַר (*šā᾿ar*), GK 8636 (S 7604), 133x. Only in rare instances does *šā᾿ar* mean "to remain" or "to be left" (e.g., 1 Sam. 16:11). More often the term refers to survival, as in Noah and his family surviving the flood (Gen. 7:23). See *survive*.

Verb: יָתַר (*yātar*), GK 3855 (S 3498), 106x. *yātar* means "to remain, be left, survive." It is often used to denote what is left over after something else has happened. For example, "nothing green *remained*" after the plague of locusts (Exod. 10:15). Those who kept some of the manna until the following morning discovered that "the remaining part" was full of maggots (16:19). In the grain offering, part of the offering is burned before the Lord, and "the *rest* of the grain offering belongs to Aaron and his sons" (Lev. 2:3, 10). When God destroyed the Egyptian army in the Red Sea, "not one of them *survived*" (Ps. 106:11).

In 1 Sam. 15:15b, Saul attempts to recover from his incomplete obedience to the Lord's command by explaining, "They spared the best of the sheep and cattle to sacrifice to the Lord your God, but we totally destroyed the *rest*." Depressed Elijah feels that he is the only prophet of the Lord God "left" (1 Ki. 18:22; 19:10, 14). Isaiah emphasizes the offence of those who worship idols by taking a piece of God's creation (a piece of wood), using part of it for fire and for cooking, and then making "the of it … into a god, his idol, bows down to it and worships it" (Isa. 44:16–17).

The best part of *yātar* is that when God allowed his people to go into exile, he promised that a remnant would survive, who would return and rebuild the city of Jerusalem and the surrounding region (Ezek. 12:16; 14:22; cf. Isa. 1:8). See *NIDOTTE*, 2:571-74.

New Testament

Verb: ἐπιμενω (*epimenō*), GK *2152* (S *1961*), 16x. *epimenō* means "to stay, remain, continue." See *stay*.

Verb: μένω (*menō*), GK *3531* (S *3306*), 118x. The basic sense of *menō* is "to remain, stay." In the NT, it can function as a transitive verb (i.e., requires a direct object) or as an intransitive verb (i.e., does not require a direct object) in Greek.

(1) Without a direct object, *menō* signifies a person or a thing "remaining" in the same *place* or *state*. With respect to *place*, a demon-possessed individual was unable "to live" in a house (Lk. 8:27; cf. Lk. 10:7; 19:5; Jn. 8:35). When Jesus was overwhelmed with sorrow at his impending death, he told his disciples to "*Stay* here and keep watch with me" (Mt. 26:38). With respect to *state*, *menō* describes the continuing condition of a person or thing. In this sense, the writer of Hebrews says that Christ "*remains* a priest forever" (Heb. 7:3). Paul encouraged converts to "*remain* in the situation which he was in when God called him" (1 Cor. 7:20, 24). John uses *menō* frequently to describe the perseverance of believers in their relation to Christ, that is, to "remain" or "abide" in him (Jn. 8:31; 15:4–10, 16; 1 Jn. 2:6, 10).

(2) With a direct object, *menō* means "to await, wait for." In this sense, men "awaited" or "waited for" Paul and Luke at Troas (Acts 20:5). In the same chapter, Paul tells the Ephesian elders that bonds and afflictions "await" him in Jerusalem (20:23). See *NIDNTT-A*, 362-63.

REMAINDER

Old Testament

Noun: יֶתֶר (*yeter*), GK 3856 (S 3499), 97x. *yeter* denotes the remainder, excess, or leftover parts of a whole and may be translated as "remainder, excess." See *remnant*.

Noun: שְׁאֵרִית (*šeʾērît*), GK 8642 (S 7611), 66x. *šeʾērît* often refers, in a general sense, to that which is left over from a larger portion (1 Chr. 4:43; 12:38). For example, in Isa. 44:16–17, Isaiah describes a man who uses half a tree for fire to roast meat and then makes an idol with the "remainder" of the tree. For the most part, however, this word means "remnant." See *remnant*.

REMAINING

New Testament

Adjective: λοιπός (*loipos*), GK *3370* (S *3062*), 55x. In its most generic sense, *loipos* means "remaining." It can describe persons or things that "remain" or are "left over" after an action has been taken. In Rev. 8:13, *loipos* refers to the final blasts of the trumpet that follow the first four blasts, "woe to those who dwell on the earth, because of the *remaining* blasts of the trumpet" (cf. Mt. 22:6; 27:49; Rev. 9:20; 11:13). It can also refer to "other people," either those previously mentioned (Acts 2:37) or, more often, an undefined group of people not previously specified (Lk. 8:10; 18:11; Acts 17:9).

loipos is sometimes used as an adverb meaning "from now on, in the future, henceforth" (1 Cor. 7:9; 2 Tim. 4:8) or "in addition, finally" (Phil. 3:1; 4:8). See *NIDNTT-A*, 331-333.

REMEMBER

Old Testament

Verb: זָכַר (*zākar*), GK 2349 (S 2142), 235x. *zākar* means "to remember." Remembering can occur with either God or human beings as the subject. Such memory can trigger many different reactions in the Bible (and in our own personal lives).

(1) With humans as the subject, memory of certain things can bring about pain, such as the exiles remembering what life was like in Jerusalem (Ps. 137:1; Lam. 3:19–20) or the escaped Israelites remembering the good food they ate in Egypt (Num. 11:5). Yet remembering can also have positive results: memory of God's law brings the psalmist comfort (Ps. 119:52), and memory of God's greatness and past assistance helps to quell fear in the believer's heart (Neh. 4:14; Ps. 77:11).

(2) The call for human beings to remember can be a call to action. When God instructs us in his law to "*remember* the Sabbath day" (Exod. 20:8), we are expected not simply to say, "O, today is the Sabbath"; rather, we are to honor that day and "keep it holy." Joseph's request of the cup-

bearer to "remember" him when he was restored to Pharaoh's service was a call to speak a good word to Pharaoh for Joseph's possible release (Gen. 40:14; cf. 41:9). When the Israelites are called to remember what it felt like to be slaves in Egypt, they were to release their own Israelites slaves after a maximum of servitude of six years (Deut. 15:15). Unfortunately, a failure to remember God's kindness can lead to exploitation of the poor and needy (Ps. 119:16).

(3) There are many references in which God is called upon to remember something, and when he does, God goes into action. The rainbow is a natural phenomenon that God will make God "remember" his covenant not to destroy the entire earth again with a flood (Gen. 9:15–16). Moses pleads with God to remember his covenant promises and hence to forgive his people Israel for their sin and rebellion (Exod. 32:13; Deut. 9:27). Hannah pleads with God to remember her by enabling her to get pregnant (1 Sam. 1:11). The psalmist, who feels the people have been rejected by God, asks the Lord to "*remember* the people you purchased of old" and turn back their pain and ruin (Ps. 74:2–3).

By contrast, God's memory can also trigger negative reactions from him. Jeremiah warns God's people that he "will now *remember* their wickedness and punish them for their sins" (Jer. 14:10; cf. 44:21). Ezekiel writes that God will not remember the earlier good deeds of a righteous person if that person begins to do evil (Ezek. 3:20; 18:24; 33:13). Yet for those who repent and turn to him, the Lord is ready to forgive, for "he *remembers* that we are dust" (Ps. 103:14); that is, he remembers our weaknesses and frailty and does not expect perfection from us. See *NIDOTTE*, 1:1100–1106.

New Testament

Verb: μιμνῄσκομαι (*mimnēskomai*), GK *3630* (S *3403*), 23x.

Verb: μνημονεύω (*mnēmoneuō*), GK *3648* (S *3421*), 21x. These two verbs share a common root (*mnē*) and often carry the simple meaning of remembering or recalling to mind (Mt. 16:9; 26:75; 1 Thess. 2:9). Remembering, however, is often more active and effective than the mere recollection of certain data. Remembering should affect one's life significantly, in terms of changing attitudes (Jn. 2:22; 12:16; Eph. 2:11) or taking some action (Rev. 2:5; 3:3). The NT authors frequently exhort believers to remember with prayer and action (Gal. 2:10; 1 Thess. 1:3; Heb. 13:3, 7). Belief and confession can follow remembering (1 Tim. 2:8; Heb. 11:22).

When God *remembers*, there are always consequences, both merciful (Lk. 1:54, 72; 23:42; Acts 10:31) and just (Rev. 16:19; 18:5). When God does *not remember*, this is not forgetfulness, but a choice to not dwell upon or consider someone or something (Heb. 8:12; 10:17). We can praise him that he has chosen not to remember our sins. See *NIDNTT-A*, 371-73.

REMISSION

See *forgiveness*.

REMNANT

Old Testament

Noun: יֶתֶר (*yeter*), GK 3856 (S 3499), 97x. *yeter* denotes the remainder, excess, or leftover parts of a whole and may be translated "remainder, excess." It describes the remains of natural disasters (Exod. 10:5; Joel 1:4), excess of speech (Prov. 17:7), surplus of goods (Job 22:20), an abundance of honor (Gen. 49:3), and a remnant (Jos. 23:12). Jeremiah writes to the exiles in 29:1, "This is the text of the letter that the prophet Jeremiah sent from Jerusalem to the *surviving* elders among the exiles and to the priests...." The term occurs 43x in the statements "the *rest* of the events of ..." in Kings and Chronicles as a reference to the summary of the life of a king.

The term also denotes a "string" or "bowstring" like the one used to bind Samson (Jdg. 16:7–9; see also Job 30:11). The common meal "leftovers" captures the basic sense of this term. See *NIDOTTE*, 2:571-74.

Noun: שְׁאֵרִית (*šeʾērît*), GK 8642 (S 7611) 66x. *šeʾērît* often refers, in a general sense, to that which is left over from a larger portion (1 Chr. 4:43; 12:38). For example, in Isa. 44:16–17, Isaiah describes a man who uses half a tree for fire to roast meat and then makes an idol with the "remainder" of the tree.

The idea of a "remnant" is significant in OT theology. Throughout the OT, God repeatedly acts to save a "remnant" (e.g., Gen. 45:7), even though he brings great judgment on his people (2 Ki. 19:31). *šeʾērît* is used frequently in the OT for those Jews who survived the destruction of Jerusalem by Babylon in the sixth century B.C. Much of that remnant was exiled to Babylon. In 2 Chr. 36:20 we read that Nebuchadnezzar "carried into exile in Babylon the *remnant*, who had escaped from the sword. They became servants to the king and his sons until the kingdom of Persia rose to power."

The prophets promise that God will eventually restore this remnant of the people to the land (e.g., Jer. 23:3). This same verse also prophesies that God will raise up a Davidic king to reign over them (note, however, Jeremiah usually refers to the survivors left behind in Jerusalem as the "remnant" and those taken to Babylon as the "exiles"). Mic. 2:12 speaks of regathering the remnant into the land (cf. Zeph. 2:7, 9). The remnant motif is also significant in the prophetic books of Isaiah and Amos. In Rom. 11, the apostle Paul picks up and develops this OT theology of the remnant. See *NIDOTTE*, 4:11-17.

New Testament

Noun: λεῖμμα (*leimma*), GK *3307* (S *3005*), 1x.

Noun: ὑπόλειμμα (*hypoleimma*), GK *5698* (S *2640*), 1x. Both *leimma* and *hypoleimma* mean "remnant." While the doctrine of the remnant is an important teaching of hope in the OT, it occurs infrequently in the NT. In Rom. 9:27 (which quotes Isa. 10:22), Paul refers to the OT promise of "a remnant," which denotes the small number of God's people who remained faithful to him especially during the exile and the return. In Rom. 9–11, Paul is struggling with the issue of why more Jews have not come to salvation in Jesus, God's sent Messiah. One of his main points is that God's rejection of the Jews has resulted in the message of salvation going out to Gentiles. But in addition to this observation, Paul insists that the doctrine of the remnant now applies to those Jews who have in fact become believers in Jesus (Rom. 11:5) and so form a part of the new Israel of God. See *NIDNTT-A*, 331–33.*

REMOVE

Old Testament

Verb: אָסַף (*ʾāsap*), GK 665 (S 622), 200x. In varying contexts, *ʾāsap* can mean "to gather, assemble, take away, or bring up the rear." Occasionally, *ʾāsap* means "to take away or remove." For example, a man removes a bundle from the ground (Jer. 10:17), Elisha removes leprosy from Naaman (2 Ki. 5:3, 6, 7), and God removes the disgrace of barrenness from Rachel (Gen. 30:23). God also removes peace (Jer. 16:5), wrath (Ps. 85:4), and harvest (Jer. 8:13) from his people. See also *gather, rear guard*.

Verb: סוּר (*sûr*), GK 6073 (S 5493), 300x. *sûr* means "to turn away, remove." See *turn away*.

Verb: רָחַק (*rāḥaq*), GK 8178 (S 7368), 59x. In a general sense meaning "to be far/distant, remove, send away," *rāḥaq* can be used either to describe the state of a thing ("to be far, at a distance") or to indicate an action ("to go far, make far," i.e., "remove"). See *far*.

New Testament

Verb: αἴρω (*airō*), GK *149* (S *142*), 101x. *airō* can mean to "lift up, take up/away, carry off, remove." See *lift up*.

REND

Old Testament

Verb: קָרַע (*qāraʿ*), GK 7973 (S 7167), 63x. Usually rendered "to tear, rend, rip," *qāraʿ* most often refers to the rending of one's garments as a sign of intense grief, particularly in reaction to a disaster, such as Joseph's apparent death (Gen. 37:34) or a defeat in battle (Jos. 7:6). See *tear*.

RENDER

See *give (back)*.

RENEW, RENEWAL

New Testament

Verb: ἀνακαινίζω (*anakainizō*), GK *362* (S *340*), 1x.

Verb: ἀνακαινόω (*anakainoō*), GK *363* (S *341*), 2x. The writer to the Hebrews uses *anakainizō* to talk about the impossibility of bringing "back to repentance" those who have once fallen away from the faith (the meaning of this passage is much debated). Paul uses *anakainoō* to suggest that the Christian life is a lifetime of constant renewal ("we are being renewed day by day," 2 Cor. 4:16), even if our bodies begin to wear out. Moreover, when we become Christians, we are "being renewed in knowledge in the image of [our] Creator" (Col. 3:10).*

Noun: ἀνακαίνωσις (*anakainōsis*), GK *364* (S *342*), 2x. *anakainōsis* means "renewal." In Rom. 12:2, Paul encourages believers "to be transformed by the renewing of [their] mind" (a transformation that takes place at the deepest recesses of the human heart). Such a renewal is impossible without the direct aid of the Holy Spirit (Tit. 3:5).*

RENOUNCE

New Testament

Verb: ἀρνέομαι (*arneomai*), GK *766* (S *720*), 33x. *arneomai* primarily means "to deny," although its wider range of meaning covers "disown, fail to confess, reject, say 'No,' refuse, renounce." It often carries the nuance of renouncing Jesus as the God-sent Messiah (cf. 2 Pet. 2:1; 1 Jn. 2:22–23). See *deny*.

(BE) REPAID, REPAY

Old Testament

Verb: שָׁלֵם (*šālēm*), GK 8966 (S 7999), 116x. *šālēm* means "to repay, reward, fulfill, be at peace." It is used in a variety of contexts.

(1) In a legal context, *šālēm* denotes what was to happen in cases of the destruction or theft of property. There must be restitution; the guilty party must "repay" the value of the destroyed or stolen property, plus more (see Exod. 21:34, 36; 22:1–15). Sometimes the restitution is put in terms of the *lex talionis* ("eye for eye, tooth for tooth," etc., Lev. 24:18, 21). The same usage is related to God, for in terms of ultimate justice, it is his proper responsibility to avenge and "repay" (Deut. 32:35). Through the prophets, God indicates he will repay sinners according to their deeds (Isa. 59:18; 66:6; Jer. 16:18). Most uses of this verb with God as the subject speak of his retribution on his people and/or on their enemies for their sins (but cf. the positive use of "reward" in 1 Sam. 24:20; Prov. 25:22).

(2) *šālēm* is also used for the fulfillment of a vow. The psalmist wants to fulfill the vows he has made to the Lord (Ps. 7:4; 50:14; 116:14, 18). The writer of Eccl. instructs us that it is better not to vow at all than to vow and not fulfill or pay off that vow (5:4–5). The prophet Nahum encourages Judah to "celebrate your festivals … *fulfill* your vows" (Nah. 1:15).

(3) Since *šālēm* is related to the noun for peace (*šālôm*; GK 8934), on a few occasions *šālēm* has the idea of making peace. The Gibeonites, for example, made a treaty of peace with Joshua and the Israelites (Jos. 10:1, 4). Other nations sought peace with the Israelites when they saw they could not defeat them (2 Sam. 10:19; cf. 2 Ki. 22:44). This usage is even referred to the notion of peace with God by one of the friends of Job: "Submit to God and *be at peace* with him" (Job 22:21). See *NIDOTTE*, 4:130–35.

New Testament

Verb: ἀποδίδωμι (*apodidōmi*), GK *625* (S *591*), 48x. *apodidōmi* means "to give (back), deliver, render, hand over" (see *give back*). It can also mean "to repay, reward, reimburse." It is composed of the preposition *apo* ("away from," which denotes separation or movement away from something) and the verb *didōmi* ("to give").

apodidōmi is used in a monetary sense to describe a simple payment or repayment, as when Jesus commands his listeners to hand over to Caesar what is Caesar's (Mt. 22:21). Since Caesar's picture is on the coin, he has a right to that money. It may also describe the payment received for working, as in the parable of the vineyard workers (Mt. 20:8), or a reimbursement for services given, as when the good Samaritan promises to compensate the innkeeper for expenses (Lk. 10:35). Further, *apodidōmi* can specifically refer to the act of paying back an owed debt, as in the parable of the two debtors (Mt. 18:23–35). In this sense of the word, Zacchaeus promises to "pay back" those whom he has cheated (Lk. 19:8).

apodidōmi is used in reference to a reward bestowed for upright conduct. For example, God "rewards" the one who prays and fasts in secret (Mt. 6:6, 18), and he also rewards each for what he or she has done (Mt. 16:27; Rev. 22:12). Similarly, Paul anticipates that God will "award" (NIV) him with the crown of righteousness on the last day (2 Tim. 4:8). Conversely, the repayment one receives may be in the form of retribution, a just repayment for the evil deeds one has committed (2 Tim. 4:14).

Verb: ἀπολαμβάνω (*apolambanō*), GK *655* (S *618*), 10x. *apolambanō* means "to receive, get back, be repaid," generally from another individual. See *receive*.

REPEAT

Old Testament

Verb: שָׁכַם (*šākam*), GK 8899 (S 7925), 65x. *šākam* can mean "to rise early in the morning, be eager, or repeat," though the former meaning is much more common than the others. The meaning "to repeat" is found in Jer. 11:7, where the Lord states that he has repeatedly warned his people (cf. 25:3, 4, 5, 19; 32:33; 35:14, 15). See *arise early*.

REPENT, REPENTANCE

Old Testament

Verb: נָחַם (*nāḥam*), GK 5714 (S 5162), 108x. *nāḥam* bears two distinct but related meanings in the OT: "to comfort, console"(see *comfort*) and "to relent, repent, change one's mind, be grieved." This verb is especially applied to God's changing his mind (see *change one's mind*).

Verb: עָנָה (*ʿānâ*), GK 6700 (S 6031), 79x. *ʿānâ* can denote humbling in a positive sense (i.e., repentance and contrition) or with connotations of violence (i.e., affliction and oppression; see *afflict*). Forms of *ʿānâ* that are pleasing to God include fasting and prayer (Lev. 16:31; 23:27; Ps. 35:13).

Verb: שׁוּב (*šûb*), GK 8740 (S 7725), 1075x. The basic sense of *šûb* is "to turn, return, repent, go/come back." In the moral-spiritual realm, *šûb* can describe the human act of repentance (turning away from sin or idolatry and turning to God). See *turn*.

New Testament

Noun: μετάνοια (*metanoia*), GK *3567* (S *3341*), 22x.

Verb: μετανοέω (*metanoeō*), GK *3566* (S *3340*), 34x. Both noun and verb denote a radical, moral turn of the whole person from sin and to God. The words themselves are derived from *meta* ("after") plus *nous* ("mind, understanding") for the noun or *noeō* ("to perceive, understand") for the verb. However, the meaning of the words in the NT does not reflect this etymology; that is, *metanoeō* does not simply mean "to perceive afterwards."

Furthermore, the use of the verb *metanoeō* in the NT differs from that in the OT, where the word is mostly used in the LXX to mean "to change one's mind" (e.g., Prov. 20:25; Jer. 4:28; the noun is only used once, in Prov. 14:15). In the LXX, the verb *epistrephō* ("to turn, return"; see *turn*) is the word that most frequently translates the Heb. verb *šûb* ("to turn back, return [to God in repentance]"). This usage reflects the OT presupposition of the covenant relationship from which Israel had turned and to which they must return. In Jer. 18:8, *epistrephō* refers to Israel's repentance and *metanoeō* is used for God's change of mind about judging them. In the NT, *metanoeō* essentially supersedes *epistrephō* as the word of choice to denote a turning from sin to God. When *metanoeō* and *epistrephō* appear together in the NT, the former emphasizes the turn from sin and the latter emphasizes the turn to God (see Acts 3:19, 26:20).

Repentance denotes a radical turning from sin to a new way of life oriented towards God. Peter says to Simon the sorcerer in Acts 8:22, "Repent of your wickedness." True repentance is proven by actions and fruitful living (Mt. 3:8; Acts 26:20). Paul expresses anxiety that he might find some in the Corinthian church who have not repented of their former sins (2 Cor. 12:21). Those who experience a plague of fire in the book of Revelation refuse to repent and give glory to God (Rev. 16:9).

Repentance is the appropriate response to the nearness of the kingdom of God. John the Baptist calls people to "repent for the kingdom of heaven is near" (Mt. 3:2). After announcing the arrival of the kingdom, Jesus calls, "Repent and believe in the gospel" (Mk. 1:15). The apostolic preaching in Acts urges people to repent as a response to the death and resurrection of Jesus, and is associated with baptism (Acts 2:38).

Repentance goes hand in hand with the forgiveness of sin when one becomes a Christian. Repentance is for sinners (Lk. 15:7). John the Baptist preached "a baptism of repentance for the forgiveness of sins" (3:3). Jesus told his disciples that "repentance and forgiveness of sins" must be preached to every nation, beginning in Jerusalem (24:47). Peter fulfills this commission by calling his hearers to "repent … and turn to God, so that your sins may be wiped out" (Acts 3:19; also 5:31; 11:18; 21:21). God's patience in holding back judgment is intended to lead people to repentance and a secure salvation (Rom. 2:4; 2 Pet. 3:9). Moreover, repentance should mark the life of the Christian, for Jesus warns the churches in Revelation to repent (Rev. 2:5, 16; 3:3, 19).

An accurate understanding of the use of *metanoeō* and *metanoia* in the NT is essential to grasp the gospel message, because it does not allow for someone to obtain salvation simply by intellectually believing that Jesus is the Son of God without repenting of sins and turning to live for him. See *NIDNTT-A*, 367.

REPLY

Old Testament

Verb: עָנָה (*ʿānâ*), GK 6699 (S 6030), 316x. The basic meaning of *ʿānâ* is "to answer, reply, respond." See *answer*.

New Testament

Verb: ἀποκρίνομαι (*apokrinomai*), GK *646* (S *611*), 231x. *apokrinomai* means "to answer, reply, and is used almost exclusively in the gospels and Acts. See *answer*.

Verb: φημί (*phēmi*), GK *5774* (S *5346*), 66x. *phēmi* means "to say, declare, answer, reply." See *say*.

REPORT

Old Testament

Verb: נָגַד (*nāgad*), GK 5583 (S 5046), 371x. *nāgad* means "to tell, declare, report." It normally indicates spoken communication, whether relaying a message or reporting on some situation. See *tell*.

Noun: דָּבָר (*dābār*), GK 1821 (S 1697), 1455x. *dābār* means "word, report, command," but can also signify a "thing, matter, affair." See *word*.

New Testament

Verb: ἀναγγέλλω (*anangello*), GK *334* (S *312*), 14x. *anangellō* means "to tell, proclaim." See *tell*.

Verb: ἀπαγγέλλω (*apangellō*), GK *550* (S *518*), 45x. *apangellō* means "to report or tell" something; it is similar to *anangellō* in its range of meaning.

In its first occurrence in the NT, *apangellō* is employed in its typical fashion, as Herod says to the Magi, "as soon as you find him, *report* to me" (Mt. 2:8). The verb does not change based on the situation or content being conveyed. The various subjects of *apangellō* include pig herders telling the townspeople about the demoniac (8:33), John's disciples telling John about Jesus (Lk. 7:18), Mary reporting about the empty tomb to the disciples (Mk. 16:10), Peter and John reporting to "their own people" about the chief priests and elders (Acts 4:23), and a jailer telling Paul and Silas that they are free (16:36). The content of the messages conveyed is equally diverse: the location of the baby Jesus (Mt. 2:8), John's burial (14:12), where the disciples should meet the resurrected Jesus (28:10), the results of the disciples' activities (Mk. 6:30), and an announcement that the apostles are not in prison (Acts 5:22).

apangellō can also border on to preach or proclaim; e.g., a servant girl named Rhoda joyously "proclaims" that Peter is at the door (Acts 12:14), Paul "proclaims" that Gentiles should repent and turn to God (Acts 26:20), and John "proclaims" eternal life (1 Jn. 1:2–3). This nuance of *apangellō* is also evident in two quotes from the OT: in Matthew's quote of Isa. 42:1-4 "He [my son] will *proclaim* justice to the nations" (Mt. 12:18); and in Heb. 2:12, a quotation of Ps. 22:22, in which Jesus says, "I will *declare* your [God's] name to my brothers." See *NIDNTT-A*, 7-8.

Noun: λόγος (*logos*), GK *3364* (S *3056*), 330x. *logos* means "word, message, report." See *word*.

REPROACH

Old Testament

Noun: חֶרְפָּה (*ḥerpâ*), GK 3075 (S 2781), 73x. The meaning of *ḥerpâ* is "disgrace, insult, reproach, contempt." Reproach can often serve as part of God's judgment (Ps. 79:4; Ezek. 5:15; Mic. 6:9–16), and the removal of reproach can be a result of God's gracious ending of judgment (Isa. 25:8; Joel 2:19; Zeph. 3:18). More often than not, such reproach is brought on Israel because of its sin and idolatry (Ps. 44:13; Ezek. 5:5–17; 22:4).

New Testament

Verb: ὀνειδίζω (*oneidizō*), GK *3943* (S *3679*), 9x. *oneidizō* is used for the insults heaped on Christ from the robbers who were hanging on crosses with him (Mt. 27:44; Mk. 15:22). In fact, Jesus' very crucifixion can be termed as his bearing "disgrace" (Heb. 13:13). Followers of Jesus should be willing to undergo similar reproaches for his sake; if indeed that does happen to us, we should consider ourselves blessed (Mt. 5:11; Heb. 10:23; Lk. 6:22; 1 Pet. 4:14). See *NIDNTT-A*, 411.

Noun: ὀνειδισμός (*oneidismos*), GK *3944* (S *3680*), 5x. *oneidismos* means "reproach, insult." Many believers in the NT world were persecuted for their faith and were insulted or reproached by their enemies (Heb. 10:33; 11:26; 13:13). This is something that we should be willing to undergo for our Savior (Rom. 15:3). But in all such insults, we should never deservedly be reproached because of some evil thing that we have done (1 Tim. 3:7). See *NIDNTT-A*, 411.*

REPROOF

See *rebuke*.

REPULSIVE

Old Testament

Noun: תּוֹעֵבָה (*tôʿēbâ*), GK 9359 (S 8441), 118x. Regularly translated "detestable thing, repulsive thing, abomination," *tôʿēbâ* generally denotes persons or actions that are morally or religiously offensive, especially to God. Idolatry, for example, is repulsive to the Lord (Deut. 7:25; 32:6; Jer. 16:18; Mal. 2:11). See *destestable*.

REPUTATION

Old Testament

Noun: שֵׁם (*šēm*), GK 9005 (S 8034), 864x. While *šēm* is used many times in Scripture for no more than a person's given name, in the context of the ancient Near East it also conveys much more, such as "reputation, fame" (see *name*).

REQUEST

New Testament

Verb: αἰτέω (*aiteō*), GK *160* (S *154*),

70x. *aiteō* generally means "to ask, request, demand." See *ask*.

Verb: ἐρωτάω (*erōtaō*), GK *2263* (S *2065*), 63x. *erōtaō* means "to ask a question" or "to request" something be done. See *ask*.

Verb: παραιτέομαι (*paraiteomai*), GK *4148* (S *3868*), 12x. *paraiteomai* denotes either "to make a request" or, in the negative, "to make excuses, reject" something.

The enflamed crowd requests Pilate to release Barabbas rather than Jesus (Mk. 15:6; cf. Heb. 12:19). Jesus tells a parable of a great banquet in which the invited guests "make many excuses" not to come (Lk. 14:18–19). Paul will not "refuse" to die if the charges against him are true (Acts 25:11). He instructs Timothy to "reject" (NIV, "refuse") godless myths and old wives' tales in favor of training for godliness (1 Tim. 4:7; 2 Tim. 2:23; cf. 1 Tim. 5:11). Paul also instructs Titus to "reject" (NIV, "have nothing to do") a divisive person who does not respond to repeated warnings (Tit. 3:10; cf. Acts 25:11). Christians ought not to "reject" God when he speaks to us as he did the people of Israel by speaking through Moses (Heb. 1:3; 12:19, 25). See *NIDNTT-A*, 23-24.*

Noun: δέησις (*deēsis*), GK *1255* (S *1162*), 18x. *deēsis* is a "prayer, petition, supplication" based on a person's need—in the NT always addressed to God. See *prayer*.

REQUIRE, REQUIREMENT

Old Testament

Verb: דָּרַשׁ (*dāraš*), GK 2011 (S 1875), 164x. *dāraš* means "to seek, search for, strive after" an object. In some contexts, it can mean to "require" in the sense of obtaining justice. See *seek*.

Noun: עֵדוּת (*ʿēdût*), GK 6343 (S 5715), 61x. *ʿēdût*, usually translated "testimony," is closely connected to God's law. In the Pentateuch, this noun describes the two tablets containing the Ten Commandments. Generally, outside the Pentateuch *ʿēdût* is a more generic reference to law (1 Ki. 2:3; 2 Ki. 23:3; 1 Chr. 29:19), perhaps with the physical tablets of the Ten Commandments in the background. In this sense, the plural of *ʿēdût* may be translated "requirements, warnings, regulations, or decrees." See *testimony*.

RESCUE

Old Testament

Verb: יָשַׁע (*yāšaʿ*), GK 3828 (S 3467), 184x. Often translated "to save, rescue, deliver," the basic meaning of *yāšaʿ* is to deliver or save human beings from a time of danger, often from personal enemies or from a time of sickness. See *save*.

Verb: מָלַט (*mālāṭ*), GK 4880 (S 4422), 94x. *mālāṭ* means to "escape, flee to safety," and it may also be translated in the passive "to be delivered, rescued, or saved." Note Isa. 31:5, "The LORD will "rescue" his people." See *escape*.

Verb: נָצַל (*nāṣal*), GK 5911 (S 5337), 213x. For the most part, *nāṣal* means "save, rescue, deliver, take away." See *save*.

New Testament

Verb: ῥύομαι (*rhyomai*), GK *4861* (S *4506*), 17x. *rhyomai* means "to rescue, deliver." It often occurs in contexts of redemptive-historical deliverance. God rescued Lot (2 Pet. 2:7); a "rescuer" or "deliverer" is promised in Isa. 59:20–21 and quoted by Paul in Rom. 11:26; Zechariah uses the word in recalling what God did for Abraham's seed (Lk. 1:74); and the words of Ps. 22 are quoted in Mt. 27:43, "He trusts in God; let God *deliver* him now, if he desires him."

Mt. 6:13 fuses both a present need of physical and spiritual rescue and a future need for ultimate deliverance and rescue as Jesus teaches his disciples the Lord's Prayer, saying, "And lead us not into temptation, but *deliver* us from the evil one" (NIV). We need to be extricated from evil (or the evil one) on a daily basis, but we also need an ultimate deliverance from evil (or the evil one) in the last day.

The apostle Paul uses *rhyomai* in two distinct ways. (1) Historically, the apostle either recounts his "rescue" from ministerial trials and evil people or requests prayer to be "delivered" from such trials and people (Rom. 15:31; 2 Cor. 1:10; 2 Thess. 3:2; 2 Tim. 3:11; 4:17). In the same vein, Peter says that the Lord knows how to "rescue" the godly from earthly trials (2 Pet. 2:9). (2) Redemptively, Paul uses this verb a number of times. Most uses contain both a present redemptive reality and an ultimate reality. The present reality of redemptive deliverance is highlighted in Col. 1:13 ("for he has *rescued* us from the dominion of darkness and brought us into the kingdom of the Son he loves"), while 1 Thess. 1:10 highlights both the "now" and the "not yet" of redemption in the phrase, "Jesus, who *rescues* us from the coming wrath" (NIV). Paul has the "not yet" in mind when he says to Timothy that "the Lord *will rescue* me from every evil attack and will bring me safely to his heavenly kingdom. To him be glory for ever and ever. Amen" (2 Tim. 4:18, NIV).

Regardless of whether the rescuing is temporal or eternal, it is worth noting that the credit always goes to Almighty God. See *NIDNTT-A*, 510-11.

Verb: σῴζω (*sōzō*), GK *5392* (S *4982*), 106x. *sōzo* means "to save, rescue, heal." For the most part, this verb is used for our being spiritually saved from sin. See *salvation, save* and *heal*. In several incidents, however, this verb denotes rescuing. The disciples were on the Sea of Galilee in a storm, with Jesus sleeping in the boat. As the wind and waves became greater, they woke him and cried out, "Lord, *rescue* us" (Mt. 8:25). Later, in another storm, after Peter received permission to walk to Jesus on the water but then began to sink into the waves, he cried out, "Lord, *rescue* me" (Mt. 14:30). In the raging storm in Acts 27, all those on board had lost "hope of being *rescued*" (27:20). The link between being rescued in these storms and being saved from sin serves as a powerful illustration: Only the Lord is able to save us in our helplessness. See *NIDNTT-A*, 548-51.

RESIDE

New Testament

Verb: κάθημαι (*kathēmai*), GK *2764* (S *2521*), 91x. *kathēmai* can simply mean the literal act of "sitting," but it can also mean "to reside." It sometimes implies note of authority. See *sit*.

RESIST

New Testament

Verb: ἀνθίστημι (*anthistēmi*), GK *468* (S *436*), 14x. *anthistēmi* means "to oppose, resist." See *oppose*.

RESPECT

New Testament

Verb: φοβέω (*phobeomai*), GK *5828* (S *5399*), 95x. *phobeomai* is used in two main senses in the NT. It means to be "frightened, alarmed," or to "respect, stand in awe of" someone. See *fear*.

Noun: τιμή (*timē*), GK *5507* (S *5092*), 41x. *timē* is the amount at which something is "valued," its "price," or it can mean "honor, respect." See *value*.

Noun: φόβος (*phobos*), GK *5832* (S *5401*), 47x. *phobos* in the NT can mean "fear, fright, alarm," but it can also describe a healthy awe and respect for God. See *fear*.

RESPOND

Old Testament

Verb: עָנָה (*ʿānâ*), GK 6699 (S 6030), 316x. The basic meaning of *ʿānâ* is "to answer, reply, respond." See *answer*.

RESPONSIBILITY

Old Testament

Noun: מִשְׁמֶרֶת (*mišmeret*), GK 5466 (S 4931), 78x. *mišmeret* derives from the verb *šāmar*, "to keep, watch, guard," and denotes the regular responsibility or duty to care for or guard an object. Sometimes the guarded object is a general reference to God's law, but usually it refers to a specific object, and often that object is cultic in nature (i.e., used in worship). See *duty*.

REST

Old Testament

Verb: נוּחַ (*nûaḥ*), GK 5663 (S 5117), 140x. The most basic idea of the verb *nûaḥ* is the action of one object coming to rest, roosting, or landing on another object or in a specific location. In these instances, *nûaḥ* is generally translated "to rest" or "to settle." Birds may try to "rest" on sackcloth (2 Sam. 21:10) and locusts "settle" in Egypt during the plagues (Exod. 10:14). After the flood, the ark of Noah "rests" on the mountains of Ararat (Gen. 8:4). Joshua explains that when the soles of the feet of the priests carrying the ark come to "rest" on the Jordan, the Jordan river will part (Jos. 3:13). The spirit of Elijah "rests" on Elisha (2 Ki. 2:15), and when the Spirit "rests" on Israel's seventy elders, they prophesy (Num. 11:25).

Frequently the object does not come to rest on its own but is caused to rest or be placed in a particular location by someone else (104x). See *set*.

nûah may also be used simply to denote cessation of activity. In this sense it is a synonym for *šābat*, "to rest, end" (cf. Exod. 20:11, where *nûaḥ* refers to Gen. 2:3 *šābat*). Job seeks "rest" from turmoil (Job 3:26), and Israel seeks "rest" from their enemies (Est. 9:16), who constantly pursue them (Lam. 5:5). Humanly speaking, the final cessation of activity is the "rest" of death, when all earthly activity ceases (Job 3:13, 17; Isa. 57:2; Dan. 12:13).

The most theologically significant use of *nûah* occurs in the promise that God will give his people rest from all their enemies (Deut. 12:10; Jos. 21:44; 2 Sam. 7:1; 1 Ki. 5:4). In the context of the fulfillment of God's promise, *nûaḥ* not only includes the sense of being put in a place (i.e., the promised land) and the sense of cessation of activity (i.e., defending themselves from their enemies), but it also carries the sense of safety and security. In the OT, God gives his people rest as a temporary and earthly type foreshadowing the believer's final heavenly rest (see Heb. 3:7–4:13). See *NIDOTTE*, 3:56-59.

Verb: שָׁבַת (*šābat*), GK 8697 (S 7673), 71x. The primary sense of the word is the cessation of activity. *šābat*, related to the noun *šabbāt* ("Sabbath")," appears 13x in connection with Sabbath observance, and the verb *šābat* is regularly translated "to rest" in these instances. God blesses and sanctifies the seventh day because it is on that day that he "rested" from the work of creation (Gen. 2:2, 3; cf. Exod. 20:11). When God gives Israel manna in the wilderness, he supplies two-days worth of manna on the sixth day so that Israel can "rest" on the seventh day (Exod. 16:30). Israel is to observe the Sabbath as a sign of the perpetual covenant with the Lord because he "rested" from his creative work on the seventh day (Exod. 31:17; cf. 23:12; 34:21). See also *cease*.

Verb: שָׁכַב (*šākab*), GK 8886 (S 7901), 213x. *šākab* means "rest, lie down, sleep." There are a variety of nuances to this verb, all of which revolve around the idea of lying down. See *lie down*.

Verb: שָׁכַן (*šākan*), GK 8905 (S 7931) 130x. *šākan* has the basic meaning "to live, dwell, settle." In nearly one-third of the times this verb is used in the OT, God is the subject. See *dwell*.

New Testament

Verb: ἀναπαύω (*anapauō*), GK *399* (S *373*), 12x. *anapauō* means "to gain relief by resting," such as ceasing from toil. Similarly it can mean "to rest" in the sense of bringing something to completion.

(1) *anapauō* can be used for physical rest. People can gain relief from a busy time in their lives by resting. After the twelve disciples return from their evangelistic journey, Jesus takes them to a desolate place so they can "rest" (Mk. 6:31). On a later occasion, when Judas comes to betray him, Jesus questions why his disciples are "resting" (i.e., sleeping; Mt. 26:45; Mk. 14:41).

(2) *anapauō* is also used of spiritual refreshment. Jesus says, "Come to me, all who are weary and heavy laden, and I *will give* you *rest*" (Mt. 11:28). The same Spirit who rested on Isaiah (Isa. 11:2) and on Jesus (Lk. 4:18) now rests on believers. This is seen most clearly when believers suffer as Jesus did, for then the Spirit of God comes and "rests" on them (1 Pet. 4:14). Jesus contrasts rest with anxiety about life and fear of being without earthly possessions. While the wealthy farmer thinks he can now rest in Jesus' parable,

Jesus points out that true rest comes from knowing that the Father in heaven cares for you and will provide all that you need (Lk. 12:19; cf. vv. 13-34).

Related here is Paul's appreciation for other believers who "have refreshed" him, such as believers from Corinth (1 Cor. 16:17–18) and Titus (2 Cor. 7:13). Philemon "has refreshed" Paul (Phlm. 7) too, and he asks Philemon to "refresh" him further (Phlm. 20) by obeying his instructions about Onesimus.

(3) In Revelation, *anapauō* and its related noun (*anapausis*) refer to four things: those in heaven never "stop" worshiping (4:8); those in hell will never rest in their torment (14:11); the saints' are called to "*rest* a little longer" (i.e., wait for Christ's return for their vindication, 6:11); those who die in the Lord "*will rest* from their labors" (14:13). See *NIDNTT-A*, 45-46.

RESTORE, RESTORATION

Old Testament

Verb: רָפָא (*rāpāʾ*), GK 8324 (S 7495), 69x. *rāpāʾ* conveys the process of restoring or making whole the health of an individual and may be translated as "heal." It is often used in the sense of healing or restoring with regard to covenant blessing (Gen. 20:17; Exod. 15:26; Deut. 7:12–15). See *heal*.

Verb: שׁוּב (*šûb*), GK 8740 (S 7725), 1075x. The basic sense of *šûb* is "to turn, return, repent, go/come back." Some forms of *šûb* have a causative sense, meaning "to cause to come back, to bring back, to return (something), to restore." For example, God in his compassion promises to *restore* the nation of Judah (Jer. 15:19; 16:15). See *turn*.

New Testament

Verb: ἀποκαθίστημι (*apokathistēmi*), GK *635* (S *600*), 8x. *apokathistēmi* means "to restore." This verb has two main uses in the NT. (1) It is sometimes used in connection with Jesus' miracles, in which Jesus "restores" a person to wholeness (Mt. 12:13; Mk. 3:5; 8:25). (2) *apokathistēmi* also occurs with regard to the hope that Jesus came to restore not just a person's body, but all things. This verb is used to express the hope the disciples had that when Elijah, the forerunner of the Messiah, came, he would "restore all things" (Mt. 17:11; Mk. 9:12). In fact, the last question the disciples ask Jesus before he ascends into heaven is this one: "Are you at this time going to restore the kingdom to Israel" (Acts 1:6). Jesus refuses to speculate on such issues; instead, he instructs his followers to spend their time proclaiming the gospel everywhere. That perspective still stands.

Verb: καταρτίζω (*katartizō*), GK *2936* (S *2675*), 13x. *katartizō* means "to prepare, put in order, restore" for a specific purpose. See *prepare*.

Noun: ἀποκατάστασις (*apokatastasis*), GK *635* (S *600*), 1x. *apokatastasis* occurs only in Acts 3:21, where Peter calls on the people who have gathered after the healing of the crippled man to repent of their sins so that God may send Jesus Christ back to them: "He must remain in heaven until the time comes for God to restore everything, as he promised long ago through his holy prophets." This "restoration" does not mean the conversion of all humanity but the universal renewal of all things at the last day. See *NIDNTT-A*, 62–63.

RESTRAIN

New Testament

Verb: κατέχω (*katechō*), GK *2988* (S *2722*), 17x. *katechō* means "to hold to, restrain." The meaning "restrain" is particularly important in 2 Thess. regarding the man of lawlessness (see *hold*).

RESURRECTION

Old Testament

There is no Heb. word for "resurrection," and there is little in the OT that explicitly describes a doctrine of general resurrection. The only clear passage is Dan. 12:2, where Daniel prophesies a coming time when "multitudes who sleep in the earth will awake: some to everlasting life, others to shame and everlasting contempt." Because the OT contains so little on this subject, the Sadducees in the NT, who believed only the Pentateuch and did not accept the Prophets as God's Word, denied the doctrine of the resurrection (Mt. 22:23; Acts 23:8).

The OT does record three stories of people who were temporarily raised back to life (1 Ki. 17:17–23; 2 Ki. 4:19–37; 13:21); these stories demonstrate that God has the power to raise the dead (see also Ezek. 37:1–14). Using Exod. 3:6 Jesus emphasized the God of the OT as one who champions life beyond death (see Mk. 12:26–27). He also saw a prophecy of his own resurrection in Jon. 1:17; 2:10 (see Mt. 12:39–40), and both Peter and Paul read Ps. 16:10 as a prophecy about Jesus' resurrection (Acts 2:24–32; 13:35–37). See also *raise up*. See *NIDNTT-A*, 46-48.

New Testament

Noun: ἀνάστασις (*anastasis*), GK *414* (S *386*), 42x. *anastasis* means "resurrection."

(1) The predominant meaning of this word in the NT is of the general resurrection of believers at the time of Christ's return (e.g., Jn. 11:24; Acts 24:15; Heb. 6:2). This is the "better resurrection" that all believers look forward to (Heb. 11:35)—that someday we will receive a new body that does not have the imperfections of our present body (cf. Phil. 3:10–11, 20–21). The ancient Greeks, who felt that only the soul was immortal, laughed when Paul preached to them about the resurrection of the body (Acts 17:32); many skeptics feel the same yet today. But the Bible clearly teaches a future time when all people will be raised back to life—some to eternal life, others to eternal judgment (Jn. 5:29).

(2) This coming resurrection is grounded in Christ's resurrection, which (along with his crucifixion) are the saving events of his life (1 Cor. 15:12–20; 1 Pet. 3:21). Jesus' resurrection demonstrates that he indeed is the Son of God (Rom. 1:4). When we believe in Jesus, we become united with him in his death and burial, but also in his resurrection (Rom. 6:5–6); as his resurrection power goes to work in our lives, we are able to die to a life wallowing in sin and instead to live in service to God (6:8–14). According to Jesus' own testimony, he is "the resurrection and the life" (Jn. 11:25). This teaching about Jesus' resurrection and its effect on our lives should fill us with "hope" (1 Pet. 1:3); no one can live a satisfying earthly life without a sense of hope and ultimate purpose.

(3) One of the most controversial uses of *anastasis* in the NT occurs in Rev. 20:5–6, where Christians debate if "the first resurrection" means the rapture or our raised life in Christ at the time of salvation. See *NIDNTT-A*, 48-49.

RETURN

Old Testament

Verb: בּוֹא (*bô'*), GK 995 (S 935), 2592x. *bô'* is the fourth most common verb in the OT. It denotes motion toward a specific goal, such as "to go, arrive, enter a house, come." It expresses a variety of motions. See *come*.

Verb: הָפַךְ (*hāpak*), GK 2200 (S 2015), 94x. *hāpak* is a Heb. term for turning (see *turn*). On some occasions it can mean "return," as when Israel, though being like a burning stick snatched from the fire, still refuses to "return" to the Lord (Amos 4:11).

Verb: שׁוּב (*šûb*), GK 8740 (S 7725), 1075x. The basic sense of *šûb* is "to turn, return, repent, go/come back." Zechariah, for example, holds out God's promise, "*Return* to me and I will *return* to you" (Zech. 1:3). See *turn*.

New Testament

Verb: ἀναχωρέω (*anachōreō*), GK *432* (S *402*), 14x. *anachōreō* means "to depart, return." See *depart*.

Verb: ἐπιστρέφω (*epistrephō*), GK *2188* (S *1994*), 36x. *epistrephō* generally means "to turn, return." See *turn*.

Verb: στρέφω (*strephō*), GK *5138* (S *4762*), 21x. *strephō* means "to turn, return, change." See *turn*.

Verb: ὑποστρέφω (*hypostrephō*), GK *5715* (S *5290*), 35x. *hypostrephō* means "to return." Almost all the uses of this verb are in the narrative parts of Luke and Acts (cf. also Gal. 1:17; Heb. 7:1). Some stories of returning have significant meaning for our lives, such as the shepherds who "returned" from the manger with songs of praise to God because they had seen the Savior (Lk. 2:20), the cured leper who "returned" to Jesus to give thanks (17:15), and the two disciples from Emmaus who "returned" to Jerusalem after the risen Christ had broken bread with them (24:33). Only Peter uses this verb in a warning passage, about those believers who "turn their backs" on the way of righteousness and will thus face judgment (2 Pet. 2:21).

REVEAL

Old Testament

Verb: גָּלָה (*gālâ*), GK 1655 (S 1540), 187x. *gālâ* has a wide variety of uses in the OT: "to exile, go into exile, expose, depart, reveal, have sexual relations with." See *exile*.

Verb: נָגַד (*nāgad*), GK 5583 (S 5046), 371x. *nāgad* means "to tell, declare, report." It normally indicates spoken communication, whether relaying a message or reporting on some situation. It is sometimes used for what God reveals. See *tell*.

New Testament

Verb: ἀνοίγω (*anoigō*), GK *487* (S *455*), 77x. *anoigō* can simply mean "to open" but sometimes has the connotation of healing. It can also mean "to reveal" or "to speak." See *open*.

Verb: ἀποκαλύπτω (*apokalyptō*), GK *636* (S *601*), 26x. *apokalyptō* means in general "to reveal, disclose." It was used in intertestamental literature for someone who "reveals" secrets about other people and thus has difficulty finding friends (Sir 27:16; cf. 1 Macc. 7:31). It is used in the NT (1) as a general term for "to reveal something that is not known," (2) for a special divine revelation, and (3) for the anticipation of a future event such as the final judgment and the return of Christ.

(1) In Simeon's famous prophesy about the baby Jesus, he told Mary that "a sword will pierce even your own soul—to the end that thoughts of many hearts may be revealed" (Lk. 2:35). Jesus comforts his disciples who will face opposition by saying that "there is nothing that will not *be revealed*, or hidden that will not be known" (Mt. 10:26; Lk. 12:2).

(2) In Mt. 11:25, Jesus praises God for hiding himself from the wise and intelligent and "revealing himself" to little children. 11:27 clarifies that it is *through Jesus* that God is revealing himself. In 16:16–17, it is the Father who "reveals" to Peter Jesus' true identity as "the Christ, the Son of the living God" (16:16-17). Paul says that God's righteousness is presently being revealed through the gospel (Rom. 1:17) and that his wrath is also being revealed against human godlessness and wickedness (1:18). The Spirit of God is one of the primary ways in which God "reveals" his glorious plan of salvation (1 Cor. 2:10; Gal. 1:16; Eph. 3:5). Paul is confident that God "will reveal" to his people what is necessary for their good (Phil. 3:15).

(3) Though Jesus has been revealed to his followers in the present, there is coming a day when he will be revealed publicly to all (Lk. 17:30). Elsewhere the NT teaches that at that time, the glory coming to God's people will also be revealed (Rom. 8:18; 1 Pet. 5:1). See *NIDNTT-A*, 60-62.

Verb: φανερόω (*phaneroō*), GK *5746* (S *5319*), 49x. *phaneroō* denotes the act of making visible or disclosing that which is not readily seen—"to show, appear, reveal." See *appear*.

REVELATION

Old Testament

Noun: נְאֻם (*ne'um*), GK 5536 (S 5002), 376x. *ne'um* is used of an utterance, word or revelation. It is often translated as "oracle" (NIV), "parable" (KJV), "declaration," and "word." See *word*.

New Testament

Noun: ἀποκάλυψις (*apokalypsis*), GK *637* (S *602*), 18x. *apokalypsis* means "revelation," something that has been or will be revealed. The English word "apocalypse" comes from this Gk. word. The last book of the Bible takes its name from

John's opening words, which designate the contents of the book as the "*revelation* of Jesus Christ, which God gave him to show his servants" (Rev. 1:1).

The NT teaches that in Christ "the revelation" of the mystery of God's plan to include Gentiles in his people has come to pass (Lk. 2:32; Rom. 16:25; Eph. 3:3). Paul regularly received visions and "revelations" (2 Cor. 12:1, 7; Gal. 1:12; 2:2) and seems to think it normal that God's people will also have revelations (1 Cor. 14:6, 26). Sometimes in the NT, *apokalypsis* simply means insight into God's purposes (Eph. 1:17).

According to the NT writers, the climactic revelation of all time has yet to occur. At the end of time Jesus Christ will be revealed as Lord of the universe (1 Cor. 1:7; 2 Thess. 1:7; 1 Pet. 1:7, 13; 4:13), God's judgment will be revealed (Rom. 2:5), and God's children will be revealed (Rom. 8:19). See *NIDNTT-A*, 60-62.*

REVERE

Old Testament

Verb: יָרֵא (*yārē*ʾ), GK 3707 (S 3372), 317x. *yārē*ʾ denotes both a sense of terror and a sense of awe and worship. It is commonly translated "fear, revere, worship." See *fear*.

REVERENT

Old Testament

Adjective: יָרֵא (*yārē*ʾ), GK 3710 (S 3373), 63x. *yārē*ʾ typically describes the subject as one who is a "fearer" of God and denotes the sense both of awe and of worship. See *fear*.

REVILE

New Testament

Verb: βλασφημέω (*blasphēmeō*), GK *1059* (S *987*), 34x. *blasphēmeō* means "to slander, blaspheme, insult," especially with regard to speech. See *blaspheme*.

REVIVE

Old Testament

Verb: חָיָה (*ḥāyâ*), GK 2649 (S 2421, 2425), 283x. *ḥāyâ* indicates "life" or "having life" and is the generic term for "life" or "to live" in the OT (Gen. 5:3–30; 11:11–26; cf. Num. 4:19). See *life*.

But *ḥāyâ* also indicates revivification. It is an amazing truth that God, who is said to live in a high and holy place, is also with those who are lowly in order to *ḥāyâ* (NIV, "revive") their hearts (Isa. 57:15 "For this is what the high and lofty One says—he who lives forever, whose name is holy: 'I live in a high and holy place, but also with him who is contrite and lowly in spirit, to *revive* the spirit of the lowly and to *revive* the spirit of the contrite"). God also tells Ezekiel to prophesy to the dry bones, "I will make breath enter you and you will come *to life*" (Ezek. 37:5).

REWARD

Old Testament

Verb: שָׁלֵם (*šālēm*), GK 8966 (S 7999), 116x. *šālēm* means "to repay, reward, fulfill, be at peace." It is used in a variety of contexts. See *repay*.

New Testament

Verb: ἀποδίδωμι (*apodidōmi*), GK *625* (S *591*), 48x. *apodidōmi* means "to give (back), deliver, render, hand over" (see *give back*). It can also mean "to repay, reward, reimburse." See *repay*.

Noun: μισθός (*misthos*), GK *3635* (S *3408*), 29x. *misthos* denotes compensation that is either earned or merited and may best be translated as "wage, reward." In some cases, this word simply denotes earthly wages paid for work done (1 Tim. 5:18; Jas. 5:4). But *misthos* is also theologically significant, as in Paul's argument against salvation by works. He writes, "Now when a man works, his *wages* are not credited to him as a gift, but as an obligation" (Rom. 4:4). But, as Paul continues, the one who simply trusts God does not earn righteousness but rather it is simple "counted" to him "as righteousness" (Rom. 4:5).

Jesus uses *misthos* to describe the eternal benefits earned by those who endure persecution and proclaims, "Rejoice and be glad, because great is your *reward* in heaven, for in the same way they persecuted the prophets who were before you"

(Mt. 5:12; also Mt. 10:41–42; Lk. 6:23, 35). Those who remain faithful in their service to Christ will receive an eternal reward (cf. Mt. 20:8; Jn. 4:36; 2 Jn. 8). However, if we want our reward here on earth through actions designed to impress other people, then we forfeit our eternal reward (Mt. 6:1, 2, 5, 16; cf. 2 Pet. 2:15). Paul emphatically states that the only thing that escapes the flames of God's final judgment is that enduring labor built on the foundation of Christ: "If what [a person] has built survives, he will receive his *reward.* If it is burned up, he will suffer loss; he himself will be saved, but only as one escaping through the flames" (1 Cor. 3:14–15). See *NIDNTT-A*, 374-75.

RICH(ES)

Old Testament

Noun: חַיִל (*hayil*), GK 2657 (S 2428), 246x. The basic sense of *ḥayil* is "power, strength, or capability." In contexts where goods or property are in view, *ḥayil* refers to "wealth, riches, substance." See *wealth*; see also *strength*.

New Testament

Verb: πλουτέω (*plouteō*), GK *4456* (S *4147*), 12x. *plouteō* means "to be or get rich, wealthy." The terms for "rich" are used most often to refer to material wealth in the form of money or agriculture, or generally speaking a good, pleasant, fulfilling, and favorable life. In the NT, these terms refer to material possessions and wealthy individuals, such as Joseph of Arimathea (Mt. 27:57), Zacchaeus (Lk. 19:2), the rich young ruler (Lk. 18:23), and those contributing to the temple treasury (Mk. 12:41; Lk. 21:1). Jesus taught parables concerning money management and attitudes to money (most recorded by Luke).

From Jesus' teachings and extending throughout the NT, several principles emerge. Riches can hinder their owner from entering the kingdom of heaven (Mt. 19:23–24; Mk. 10:25; Lk. 18:23–25) and can lead a person to oppress others or neglect the poor (Lk. 16:19ff., the rich man and Lazarus; Jas. 2:6; 5:1ff.). Riches can further greed, focusing a person inward toward oneself and away from God (Lk. 12:16). Riches can bring favor and can be manipulated or used shrewdly for eternal benefits (16:1ff.). They are also fleeting, uncertain, and deceitful, and they can choke the gospel out of our lives, obstructing spiritual depth and maturity (Mt. 13:22; Mk. 4:19; Lk. 8:14; 1 Tim. 6:17). Riches are perishable (Jas. 1:11; Jas. 5:2) and can be utterly lost through God's judgment, as with Babylon in Rev. 18:3–19. The desire for riches leads to temptation and a trap (1 Tim. 6:9). Riches should be shared generously, without thought of repayment, and considered as a gift to God, who will repay generosity (Lk. 14:12; 1 Tim. 6:18).

The concept of "riches" is also used figuratively, especially by Paul. In Ephesians he writes of "the *riches* of God's grace" (Eph. 1:7, 2:7), of his glorious inheritance (1:18), of God's mercy (2:4), and of Christ (3:8). He further refers to "the *riches* of [God's] kindness" in the sense of his graciousness to the unsaved (Rom. 2:4), of God's glory (9:23), of salvation (11:12), of God's wisdom and knowledge (11:33), of the mystery of Christ in us (Col. 1:27), and of complete understanding (2:2). Of course, God is also fully able to supply material needs, "according to his riches in glory" (Phil. 4:19).

The concept of "riches" is significant in two theological contexts, one spiritual and the other referring to end-times. (1) The parable of the rich fool taught the importance of being "*rich* toward God" (Lk. 12:21) and "*rich* in good works" (1 Tim. 6:18). Paul further uses the concept of "rich" as a spiritual indicator, regardless of outward appearance, so that some who believe themselves to be spiritually rich are actually impoverished (1 Cor. 4:8; cf. Rev. 3:17, church of Laodicea, whose enriching will result only from turning to Jesus), while others who are impoverished are spiritually rich (2 Cor. 8:2; Jas. 1:10; 2:5; Rev. 2:9). (2) The end-times sense brings the understanding of a reversal in the kingdom: the hungry are filled while the rich are sent away empty (Lk. 1:53). The only one who is worthy of receiving riches is the Lamb that was slain (Rev. 5:12), who embodies the kingdom reversal in his own incarnation: "For you he impoverished himself, although he was rich, so that through his poverty you might become rich" (2 Cor. 8:9). See *NIDNTT-A*, 472-73.

Noun: πλοῦτος (*ploutos*) GK *4458* (S *4149*), 22x. *ploutos* means "riches, wealth."

Adjective: πλούσιος (*plousios*), GK *4454* (S *4145*), 28x. *plousios* means "rich, "wealthy."

RIDE

Old Testament

Verb: רָכַב (*rākab*), GK 8206 (S 7392), 78x. *rākab* generally means "to mount or ride (something)," but it can also mean "to drive (something)" and in this sense is most often used of chariots (Gen. 24:61; 41:43;1 Ki. 1:33, 38, 44; Ezek. 23:6, 12, 23; Zech. 1:8).

(1) In an age when walking was the most common method of transportation, riding was viewed as a privilege and an honor often reserved for royalty. Horses and chariots were significant militarily offensive weapons, and their use and numbers indicated the strength of the nation using them. The destruction of Pharaoh's army in the Red Sea thus served as a powerful demonstration of the superiority of Israel's God over the gods of Egypt.

Significantly, Israel's king was not allowed to multiply horses for himself (Deut. 17:16). Rather, he had to trust God, who would fight on Israel's behalf (cf. Exod. 14:14; Deut. 1:30). In this light, God is frequently pictured as a warrior who rides the clouds in his heavenly chariot (Deut. 33:26; 2 Sam. 22:11; Ps. 18:10; Isa. 19:1; Hab. 3:8).

(2) *rākab* is sometimes used metaphorically in the OT. (a) Riding is a picture of divine blessing. In Deut. 32:13 "riding on the heights of the land" is one of the blessings that attend both God's election of his people and the faithfulness of God's people (cf. Isa. 58:14). It also can refer to God's testing his people for the purpose of refining them (Ps. 66:12). (b) This metaphor is not reserved exclusively for blessing, however. Sometimes it signifies judgment. For instance, Job complains that God is causing him to ride on the storm (Job 30:22 KJV). Hosea uses the word of Israel's impending captivity at the hand of the Assyrians (Hos. 10:11, "I will drive Ephraim," NIV; "I will make Ephraim to ride," KJV).

(3) Another theologically significant use of *rākab* is found in the messianic prophecy of Zech. 9:9, where God tells Israel that her victorious King will one day come to Zion, meekly "riding on a donkey." The NT shows this prophecy as fulfilled in Jesus' Triumphal Entry (Mt. 21:5; Jn. 12:15).

For further reading, see *NIDOTTE*, 3:1109–14, which deals extensively with chariots.

RIDICULE

New Testament

Verb: ἐξουθενέω (*exoutheneō*), GK *2024* (S *1848*), 11x. *exoutheneō* essentially means "to hold someone in contempt, ridicule, despise" (Rom. 14:3; Gal. 4:14). See *look down on*.

RIGHT

Old Testament

Noun and Adjective: יָמִין (*yamîn*), GK 3545 (S 3225), 140x. *yamîn* denotes the direction "to the right." Abraham says to Lot that if he goes "to the right," Abraham will go to the left. A common phrase in the OT is the command to "turn aside neither to the right nor to the left" (e.g., Deut. 5:32; Jos. 1:7; 1 Sam. 6:12; 2 Sam. 2:19). In terms of the four points of the compass, most of the ancient Near East was oriented to the east. When facing east, south is at one's right hand, and thus *yamîn* regularly means the geographical direction "south" (e.g., 2 Chr. 4:6–8). According to Ps. 89:12, God has created "the north and the south."

As is the case in the world today, most

people in ancient society were right-handed. Thus, the right hand was a symbol of power. The psalms frequently extol "the right hand" of God. Ps. 20:6 refers to "the saving power of his right hand" (cf. 60:5), and 45:5 prays, "Let your right hand display awesome deeds." Note how "the Lord's right hand has done mighty things" (Ps. 118:15–16). When the Lord swears, he does so "by his right hand" (Isa. 62:8). In an important messianic passage, the Lord invites his anointed king "to sit at my right hand until I make your enemies a footstool for your feet" (Ps. 110:1). The NT applies this passage to the ascension of Jesus and his sitting at God's right hand (see under *right*, *dexios*, GK *1288*). See *NIDOTTE*, 2:466–71.

New Testament

Noun: ἐξουσια (*exousia*), GK *2026* (S *1849*), 102x. *exousia* means "authority, power, right," and the word is used in a variety of different contexts. See *authority*.

Adjective: δεξιός (*dexios*), GK *1288* (S *1188*), 54x. *dexios* means "right" as the opposite of left. It is often used in connection with an explicit noun, as in "*right* hand" (Mt. 5:30; Lk. 6:6), "*right* eye" (Mt. 5:29), "*right* cheek' (5:39), "the *right* side of the boat" (Jn. 21:6). Sometimes it occurs without an explicit noun, in which cases it functions as a noun, meaning "right hand" (Mt. 6:3; Rev. 1:17) or "right side" (Mk. 16:5).

Some expressions in Scripture involving the right hand connote more than just the physical right hand. In Gal. 2:9 Paul says, "James, Peter and John gave me and Barnabas the *right hand* of fellowship," which demonstrates a recognition that Paul and Barnabas share in the same grace and apostolic mission as the apostles (the only difference being the ones to whom they direct their ministry).

For 19x in the NT, Jesus is said to have been raised and seated (or exalted) "to the *right hand* of God," that is, to the place of supreme honor and power. This phrase has in mind the promise in Ps. 110:1 ("Sit at my right hand until I make your enemies a footstool for your feet"; see Mt. 22:41–46; Mk. 12:35–37; Lk. 20:41–44 for explicit references to Ps. 110). In his position at God's right hand, Jesus is portrayed as the dispenser of the Holy Spirit on his people (Acts 2:33), as the Prince and Savior who grants repentance and forgiveness (5:31), as the witness to Stephen the martyr (7:55), as the divine intercessor for his people, guaranteeing that they will not be condemned (Rom. 8:34), as the great high priest who has purified us from our sins by offering himself (Heb. 1:3; 8:1; 10:12; 12:2), and as the sovereign Lord to whom all power has been subjected, whether earthly or angelic, whether past or present (Eph. 1:20; 1 Pet. 3:22). Remarkably, the exaltation of Christ into the heavenly realm is said to be something shared in by believers, who have been raised up with him (Eph. 2:6; Col. 3:1). See *NIDNTT-A*, 128-29.

Adverb: καλῶς (*kalōs*), GK *2822* (S *2573*), 37x. *kalōs* conveys the goodness or appropriateness of an activity or action and may best be translated as "well" or "good." See *good*.

RIGHT HAND

New Testament

Adjective: δεξιός (*dexios*), GK *1288* (S *1188*), 54x. *dexios* means "right" as the opposite of left. Sometimes it occurs without an explicit noun, in which cases it can function as a noun meaning "right hand" (Mt. 6:3; Rev. 1:17). See *right*.

RIGHT SIDE

New Testament

Adjective: δεξιός (*dexios*), GK *1288* (S *1188*), 54x. *dexios* means "right" as the opposite of left. Sometimes it occurs without an explicit noun, in which cases it can function as a noun meaning "right side" (Mk. 16:5). See *right*.

RIGHTEOUS, RIGHTEOUSNESS

Old Testament

Noun: צֶדֶק (*sedeq*), GK 7406 (S 6664), 123x. Usually rendered "righteousness, justice, rightness," the noun *ṣedeq* generally describes the state or quality of that which accords with some recognized standard (not always expressed). It can be God's law or natural law or some other assumed standard.

(1) Righteousness is first and foremost a quality ascribed to God (Ps. 35:24, 28; 85:10–13). His actions are right and just. He hates wickedness and loves righteousness (Ps. 45:7; Isa. 11:4–5). He is sometimes addressed as "righteous God" (Ps. 4:1). Jeremiah twice predicts a coming age in which God's name will become known as "The LORD Our Righteousness" (Jer. 23:6; 33:16). And when he comes to judge the world, he will judge it honestly and fairly and in accordance with his holy standard (Ps. 9:8; 98:9).

(2) God wants his people to pattern their lives after him. Therefore, he wants them to live righteous lives, both religiously and morally (Ps. 4:5; 15:2). This applies to the king, whose job it is to promote the righteous laws of God (Ps. 72:1–2; Prov. 25:5). *ṣedeq* especially refers to a need for social justice to be done to the poor, the needy, and the oppressed (Job 29:14; Isa. 1:21). Unfortunately, Israel's leaders often failed in this regard.

(3) But *ṣedeq* can also be synonymous with salvation that comes from Yahweh. Isaiah particularly points this out in the parallel statements: "My *righteousness* draws near speedily; my salvation is on the way" (Isa. 51:5; cf. 62:1). We as human beings cannot fully live up to God's righteous standards. If we are going to be delivered from sin and have a relationship with God, it can only be on the basis of his grace. Those touched by that grace are called "oaks of righteousness" (61:3).

(4) *ṣedeq* can even be applied to inanimate objects. In business transactions, weights and measures that conform to the accepted standard are called "honest." Ps. 119 extols God's law as "righteous" (commanding behavior that is "upright," Ps. 119:62, 144). When a king rules by personified Wisdom, his laws will be "just" or righteous (Prov. 8:15).

Noun: צְדָקָה (*ṣ*^{e}*dāqâ*), GK 7407 (S 6666), 159x. *ṣ*^{e}*dāqa* generally means "righteousness, justice, innocence." Like the noun *ṣedeq*, "righteousness," this noun also describes the state or quality of that which accords with some recognized standard, not always expressed in the context.

(1) *s*^{e}*dāqa* has essentially the same nuances as *ṣedeq*. God is inherently righteous (Ps. 11:7; 112:3); he loves justice (33:5); and all his deeds are always just and right (Ps. 71:24).

(2) God wants us, his people, to act in a right and just manner (Prov. 8:20; Isa. 61:10; Jer. 22:3). He wants us to sow seeds of justice in our lives (Hos. 10:12). Living in righteousness applies especially to how we treat the poor and oppressed (Amos 5:24).

(3) For people seeking justice in the courts, this noun can have a forensic meaning (2 Sam. 15:4). That is why one of the main responsibilities of a king was to maintain justice and righteousness (1 Ki. 10:9)—justice as defined by what God established in his law (Ps. 72:1).

(4) But try as we might, we can never fully live as God wants us to (Isa. 5:7). "All our *righteous acts* are like filthy rags" (64:6). When God saw our hopeless condition, "his own arm worked salvation," and he bestowed righteousness on us (59:16). For the NT, the programmatic verse of the OT is Gen. 15:6: "Abram believed the LORD, and he credited it to him as *righteousness*." When all is said and done, we can only receive righteousness as a gift from God, though what that gift inspires in us is a life of living righteously. And the ultimate fruit of such righteousness in our lives is "peace . . . quietness and confidence forever" (Isa. 32:17).

Adjective: צַדִּיק (*ṣaddîq*), GK 7404 (S 6662), 206x. *ṣaddîq* is generally rendered "righteous, innocent, just." Similar to the nouns *ṣ*^{e}*dāqâ* and *ṣedeq*, this adjective describes those who act in such a way that their behavior accords with some standard. In general, this word describes as "righteous" persons rather than an abstract concept like the law.

(1) As with the two nouns noted above, this adjective describes God as a "righteous" God (Exod. 9:27; Ps. 119:137)—that is, God does what is right and just. His decision to send his sinful people into exile, for example, demonstrates his just and righteous character (Ezr. 9:15; Neh. 9:33; Dan. 9:14).

(2) But more than any word in this group, *ṣaddîq* designates God's people. Beginning with Noah (Gen. 6:9) and especially in Psalms and Proverbs, those who attempt to live a God-fearing life are called "the righteous" (e.g., Ps. 1:5; Prov. 2:20). This does not mean that they are innately righteous (Eccl. 7:20); rather, the Lord has made them his covenant people, and as a result they love him and try to live as he has commanded in his law. They are honest, generous, loyal, merciful, and just. God rewards the righteous and punishes the wicked (Prov. 11:30–31). See *NIDOTTE*, 3:757.

(3) Occasionally this word simply means "innocent" in a legal sense (2 Sam. 4:11; 2 Ki. 10:9). Unfortunately, far too often Israel's leaders deprived the innocent of the justice that they should have expected because of God's law (Prov. 17:15, 26; Isa. 5:23).

New Testament

Verb: δικαιόω (*dikaioō*), GK *1467* (S *1344*), 39x. *dikaioō* means "to declare righteous, justify." This word is prominent in Paul's letters, containing 27 of the 39x (about 70%).

(1) While we tend to justify ourselves before God that we deserve salvation because of our good behavior (cf. Lk. 10:25–29; 16:15), in reality no one is "*justified* by observing the law" (Gal. 2:16; cf. Rom. 3:20) but only by faith in Jesus Christ. This is Paul's core message in Rom. 3:21–28 (see *dikaiosynē*, above). The result of such justification is peace with God (Rom. 5:1) and the assurance that some day we will be glorified (Rom. 8:30).

(2) But what about James, who writes that Abraham "was *considered righteous*" for his deeds (Jas. 2:21) and that "a person *is justified* by what he does and not by faith alone" (2:24)? Does he not contradict Paul? Absolutely not. Paul and James each define faith differently. For James, faith is an intellectual assent to certain teachings, the type of mental activity even demons can perform (2:19). For Paul, however, faith is a personal commitment to Jesus Christ as Savior and Lord (Rom. 10:9), which inevitably leads one to live a life of service to him and right and holy living (Rom. 6). See *NIDNTT-A*, 143-47.

Noun: δικαιοσύνη (*dikaiosynē*), GK *1466* (S *1343*), 92x. *dikaiosynē* can mean "righteousness, innocence, justice, justification." This word is prominent in Paul's letters, containing 58 of the 91 occurrences (64%). It is not inappropriate to say that Paul attempts to answer the question Job asks in Job 9:2: "But how can a mortal be righteous with God?" The main passage in Paul that discusses this question and this word group is Rom. 3.

(1) While it is not stated as frequently as in the OT, the NT affirms the righteous and sinless character of God (see *dikiaios*, below). In Rom. 3:5, Paul affirms "God's righteousness."

(2) Human beings were created in the image of God, which means in part the ability to live righteous, sinless lives (Eph. 4:24). But Adam sinned in the Garden, and through the sin of that one man, all their descendants "were made sinners" (Rom. 5:19). As a result, we are unrighteous and deserve condemnation and death (5:16–18; 6:23).

(3) How can we then get right with God? God has revealed a way: "This *righteousness* from God comes through faith in Jesus Christ to all who believe" (Rom. 3:22). In other words, Jesus, the Righteous One, lived a sinless life (see *law*) and died an atoning death (see *atonement*). He now offers his "righteousness" to us by faith, so that we can be "declared righteous" (see *dikaioō*, above) before his throne. This

process of justification by faith goes all the way to Abraham, who "believed God, and it was credited to him as *righteousness*" (Rom. 4:3, 5, 9; Gal. 3:6). All those, then, who believe in Jesus are credited with righteousness and have Abraham as their father (4:11–12). Keeping the law plays no role in our being counted as righteous in his sight (cf. 10:1–10; Gal. 3:21; Phil. 3:9); rather, God's grace is at work.

(4) But does this mean that obedience to God's law has no role to play in our lives? Absolutely not! Those who have been justified by faith have been set free from sin and thus must offer themselves to God "as instruments of *righteousness*" (Rom. 6:11–14). We find God's will for us described in the inspired Scriptures, through which we receive "training in *righteousness*" (2 Tim. 3:16–17). It is impossible for those who have been born of God not to do what is right (1 Jn. 3:7–10). As Jesus puts it, those who belong to him "hunger and thirst for *righteousness*" (Mt. 5:6).

(5) Finally, there is a future aspect to righteousness. God has set a day when he will judge the world by his standard of righteousness (Acts 17:31). On that day of days, we "will reap a harvest of *righteousness* and peace" (Heb. 12:11) and thus become fully righteous; this is our Christian hope (Gal. 5:5).

(6) In summary, therefore, like salvation (see *salvation*), "righteousness" is a gift that we receive from God when we believe, is a present reality in our lives, and is a future hope toward which we aspire. See *NIDNTT-A*, 143-47.

Noun: δικαίωμα (*dikaiōma*),GK *1468* (S *1345*), 10x. *dikaiōma* refers to "regulations, righteous requirements, righteousness." See *regulations*.

Adjective: δίκαιος (*dikaios*), GK *1465* (S *1342*), 79x. *dikaios* means "righteous, innocent, just, upright." This adjective follows many of the characteristics of the Heb. word *ṣaddîq*; see above.

(1) The NT affirms the righteous and sinless character of God. Jesus addresses God as "righteous Father" (Jn. 17:25), and he himself is called "the Righteous One" (Acts 3:14; 1 Jn. 2:1). The book of Revelation affirms that God is "just" in all his ways (Rev. 15:3) and judgments (16:5, 7; 19:2; cf. 2 Thess. 1:5–6); he is "the righteous Judge" (2 Tim. 4:8).

(2) Like *ṣaddîq* in the OT, *dikaios* sometimes describes those who set as their goal to live a holy, God-fearing, "righteous" life (Mt. 1:19; Lk. 23:50; Acts 10:22; 2 Pet. 2:7–8); some of these NT uses occur in quotations from the OT (e.g., Heb. 10:38 [Hab. 2:4]; 1 Pet. 3:12 [Ps. 34:15]).

(3) But an equally important message in the NT is that "no one is *righteous*" (Rom. 3:10; we are all in need of a Savior in order to bring us to God. That is why Jesus said he did not come "to call the *righteous* but sinners to repentance" (Lk. 5:32). The word "righteous" here describes those, like the Pharisee in Jesus' story (Lk. 18:9–14), who appear righteous on the outside but fail to see the sin within their lives (Mt. 23:28).

(4) But when Jesus says in his parables that "the *righteous* will shine like the sun" (Mt. 13:43) and that "the *righteous* [will go] to eternal life" (25:37), he is referring to those who have received his own righteousness as a gift by faith (see *dikaiosynē*, above). Note that "through the obedience of the one man [Jesus] the many will be made *righteous*" (Rom. 5:19). It is probably this meaning of *dikaios* that James uses when he says "the prayer of a *righteous* man is powerful and effective" (Jas. 5:16). See *NIDNTT-A*, 143-47.

RIGHTEOUS DEEDS

New Testament

Noun: δικαίωμα (*dikaiōma*),GK *1468* (S *1345*), 10x. *dikaiōma* refers to "regulations, righteous requirements, righteousness." See *regulations*.

RIGHTNESS

Old Testament

Noun: צֶדֶק (*ṣedeq*), GK 7406 (S 6664), 123x. Usually rendered "righteousness, justice, rightness," the noun *ṣedeq* generally describes the state or quality of that which accords with some recognized standard (not always expressed). It can be God's law or natural law or some other assumed standard. See *righteousness*.

RING

Old Testament

Noun: טַבַּעַת (*tabbaʿat*), GK 3192 (S 2885), 50x. *ṭabbaʿat* means "ring"; it has two major uses in the OT.

(1) It can denote an official ring-seal of Pharaoh king of Egypt or some other ancient monarch. In appreciation for Joseph's interpretation of Pharaoh's dream as well as for Joseph's bold plan, Pharaoh elevates the Hebrew slave to the second highest position in all of Egypt (Gen. 41). Pharaoh makes this promotion by giving Joseph his "signet ring" (Gen. 41:42). When it is used, a *ṭabbaʿat* made declarations official by its imprint. When the anti-Semite Haman bribes King Xerxes to allow him to destroy the Jews, Xerxes finalizes the arrangement by giving Haman his signet ring (Est. 3:10; cf. also 8:8).

(2) The book of Exodus records the majority of the uses of *ṭabbaʿat* (28x). There it describes the rings that are used to fasten the tabernacle together (Exod. 26:24, 29), to carry the ark (25:12–16), and to fasten the high priest's breastplate to the ephod (28:27–28).

(3) In a relatively minor use, *ṭabbaʿat* is sometimes considered as a piece of jewelry (Num. 31:50; Isa. 3:21). See *NIDOTTE*, 2:338.

RIP

Old Testament

Verb: קָרַע (*qāraʿ*), GK 7973 (S 7167), 63x. Usually rendered "to tear, rend, rip," *qāraʿ* most often refers to the ripping of one's garments as a sign of intense grief, particularly in reaction to a disaster, such as Joseph's apparent death (Gen. 37:34) or a defeat in battle (Jos. 7:6). See *tear*.

RISE

Old Testament

Verb: קוּם (*qûm*), GK 7756 (S 6965), 627x. The general range of meanings for *qûm* includes "to stand up, arise, get up (in the morning)." It can also mean "to raise up, confirm, establish something."

(1) One particularly apt illustration of *qûm* is Ps. 139:2: God knows "when I sit down (or lie down to sleep) and when I *rise up*." *qûm* can also refer to an initiative to action. God's passion for justice is seen in the situations that galvanize him to action. For example, God arises to help the needy (35:2; 44:26–27), to save from evil oppressors (3:7–8), and to deliver from the schemes of the wicked against the righteous (17:13). God promises that he will rise up and cut off the house of the evildoers (Isa. 14:22, 31:2). God arises to judge (Ps. 76:8–9; 82:8); he promises to arise and stand as a witness to testify against the injustice of all nations (Zeph. 3:8). Frequently the psalmists call on God to "arise" and deliver them from their troubles (Ps. 3:7; 7:6; 10:12).

(2) *qûm* connotes arising in the sense of military encounters. God instructs Joshua to "go up" to Ai, because he has given the king and city over to the Israelites (cf. Jos. 8:1–3, 24:9). In Jdg. 4, Deborah commands Barak, "*Get up*! For this is the day on which the LORD has given Sisera into your hand" (4:14, this use of *qûm* appears in Deborah's song in 5:12 as well). When God arises to battle on behalf of his people, his enemies are scattered (Num. 10:35); there is no foe that can threaten him or his power. God arises to terrify the earth in his coming judgment (Isa. 2:19, 21).

(3) *qûm* functions in common legal matters as well. When Abraham purchases a field with a cave in which to bury his wife, Sarah, the *qûm* indicates that the sale is "established" or "made sure" (Gen. 23:17). In a similar vein, when God makes a covenant with human beings, he "establishes" that covenant (e.g., Gen. 9:6; 17:7, 19). A prophet's word may fall to the ground, as in 1 Sam. 3:19, but God's word "stands" forever (Isa. 40:8).

(4) *qûm* can also mean "to survive, continue." The unrighteous and wicked will not "stand" in the judgment; that is, they

will not survive or continue with the righteous (Ps. 1:5). Similarly, Nahum asks in the context of the earth and the heavens trembling violently before God, "Who can *stand* before [the Lord's] indignation? Who can endure the heat of his anger?" (1:6). When Amos sees a vision of how God intends to bring judgment against Jacob, he intercedes crying, "O LORD God, forgive, I beg you! How can Jacob *stand*? He is so small!" (7:2).

(5) There are two occurrences of *qûm* that have strong, eschatological implications. First, in Balaam's oracle, a scepter "will arise" out of Israel and secure its victory over the nations (Num. 24:17). Second, Job 19:25 triumphantly hopes in this fact: "I know my Redeemer lives, and that at the last he *will stand* upon the earth; and after my skin has been thus destroyed, then in my flesh I shall see God." This last use of *qûm* is the language of resurrection in the OT. See *NIDOTTE*, 3:902–5.

RISE EARLY

Old Testament

Verb: שָׁכַם (*šākam*), GK 8899 (S 7925), 65x. *šākam* can mean "to rise early in the morning, be eager, or do again and again," though the former meaning is much more common than the others.

Examples of the meaning "to rise early" are common, in large part because of the practical value of starting a journey or performing other tasks in the cool of the day (cf. *NIDOTTE*, 4:107-8). Abraham rises early in the morning and sets off to sacrifice Isaac (Gen. 22:3). This reflects his obedience to God in the performance of a difficult task. God tells Moses to rise early in order to confront Pharaoh (Exod. 8:20), and Gideon rises early in the morning to check his famous fleece (Jdg. 6:38). According to Jer. 7:13, 25, God himself rises early in the morning to call his people to obedience and to send his prophets to them. Ps. 127:2 warns that it is vain to "rise early" and go to bed late if the Lord does not bless one's work.

RISE UP

New Testament

Verb: ἐγείρω (*egeirō*), GK *1586* (S *1453*), 144x. In the transitive (active) sense *egeirō* means to "waken, lift up, stimulate." In the intransitive (passive) sense it conveys "to get up, rise up." See *raise*.

RISING

New Testament

Noun: ἀνατολή (*anatolē*), GK *424* (S *395*), 11x. *anatolē* indicates the direction east or action that comes from the east. It is translated either "east" or "rising." The meaning "east" comes because that is the direction of the rising of the sun. See *east*.

RIVER

Old Testament

Noun: יְאֹר (*y*ᵉʾ*ōr*), GK 3284 (S 2975), 64x. *y*ᵉʾ*ōr* is a loanword from the Egyptian name for the Nile River. By derivation, it can designate any "river" or "stream."

Noun: נַחַל (*naḥal*), GK 5707 (S 5158), 137x. *naḥal* refers to a dry river bed or wadi that may have a perennial supply of water, but more often one that becomes a raging torrent primarily in the winter (rainy season). Thus, the *naḥal k*ᵉ*rît* (Kerith Ravine), which was to supply water to Elijah, dried up after he proclaimed a cessation of the rain (1 Ki. 17:4–7).

Since *naḥal* can refer to the dry river bed itself (as that from which David selects his stones, 1 Sam. 17:40), by extension it also can be used to describe a valley or ravine (e.g., *valley* of Eschol, Num. 13:23; Zered *valley,* Num. 21:12; Arnon *gorge*, Deut. 2:24; cf. Deut. 8:7). By further extension, this word can describe a tunnel or shaft (Job 28:4).

Usually, however, *naḥal* refers to the raging water that fills a wadi, turning it into a fast flowing river. The Wadi of Egypt (Num. 34:5; Jos. 15:4), identified variously as Wadi el-'Arish or as an arm of the Nile (Shihor/Pelusiac), is called a *naḥal*. *naḥal* also describes the *river* that watered Eden, which divided into four *rivers* (Gen. 2:10–14).

It is understandable, then, how *naḥal*

can be used metaphorically of something that rages like a swiftly flowing stream. Jeremiah prophecies that invading armies will cover the land as an overflowing torrent (Jer. 47:2) and Isaiah describes the wrathful breath of God as a *naḥal*, which appears suddenly and sweeps away those in its path (Isa. 30:28).

In contrast to the destructive aspects associated with *naḥal*, Amos speaks of justice "like a river, righteousness like a never-failing *stream*" (Amos 5:24). Isaiah describes the future peace God will give to Israel as a *naḥal* and the wealth of the nations will flow to her as a "flooding *stream*" (Isa. 66:12). The psalmist alludes to the paradise of Eden when he describes the believer's privilege of feasting and drinking from God's blessings: "They feast on the abundance of your house; you give them drink from your river (*naḥal*) of delights" (Ps. 36:8). Likewise, Ezekiel foresees in the messianic age that the Kidron Valley, long associated with graves and uncleanness, will be filled with torrents of water flowing from the temple mount and thus made holy to God (Ezek. 47:5–19; cf. Jer. 31:40).

Noun: נָהָר (*nāhār*), GK 5643 (S 5104), 119x. *nāhār* means "river"; in most cases it refers to a specific river. It was a *nāhār* that flowed out of the Garden of Eden (Gen. 2:10–14). God promises Abram that he will give him all the land from the *nāhār* of Egypt (the Nile) to the *nāhār* Euphrates (Gen. 15:18). When "the River" is used without further designation, it is generally understood to be the Euphrates (Gen. 31:21; Jos. 24:2, 14; Isa. 7:20), although other times the Tigris is meant (Gen. 2:14). In Ezek. 1:1, 3, the "Kebar *River*" is a canal off a larger river (cf. also the "Ahava *Canal*" in Ezr. 8:15, 21, 31). *nāhār* can also refer to underground "streams" (Job 28:11) or even sea "currents" (Jon. 2:13) or "seas" (Ps. 93:3).

The author of Ps. 46 writes that "there is a *river* whose streams make glad the city of God" (46:4). But Jerusalem does not have such a *nāhār*. Most likely, the word *nāhār* here symbolizes God's presence (cf. Isa. 8:6ff.; 33:21); just as a *nāhār* flowed from the Garden of Eden, so a *nāhār* (i.e., the presence of the Lord) will bless the city of God. The prophet Ezekiel uses a *nāhār* to encourage the exiled Jews of the future blessings of God (Ezek. 47:1–12). The *nāhār* flows from the temple, and the further it flows the deeper it becomes. This tree-lined *nāhār* (47:7) provides life wherever it flows (47:9; cf. Rev. 22:1–2). Since access to water was such a major issue in the ancient world, God's visions for a more glorious future for his people usually include flowing rivers (Isa. 41:18; 43:19–20). By contrast, God's words of judgment often involve drying up rivers (50:2; Ezek. 31:15; Nah. 1:4).

In contrast to pagan myths that deified the waters, in the OT the Lord controls all waters. When the Lord parted the waters of the Jordan River at the time of Joshua (Jos. 3) and when both Elijah and Elisha struck the Jordan with Elijah's mantel and the waters parted (2 Ki. 2:8, 14), the Lord was manifesting himself as victorious over Canaanite river gods. See *NIDOTTE*, 3:46-51.

New Testament

Noun: ποταμός (*potamos*), GK *4532* (S *4215*), 17x. *potamos* is the term for a "river" of any size, from the Euphrates to the Jordan (which at times is only a stream). Paul finds Lydia at a *potamos* (Acts 16:13), and he lists a *potamos* as one of the many dangers that threatened him during his missionary activity (2 Cor. 11:26).

potamos is used of the Jordan River, in which John baptized Jesus (Mt. 3:6; Mk. 1:5). The term also occurs in Matthew's and Luke's version of the parable of the two builders (Mt. 7:24–27; Lk. 6:47–49). The locale of Jesus' sermon near the Sea of Galilee finds a natural setting for this parable. The silty sand surrounding the Sea of Galilee is hard on the surface during the summer months. But wise builders knew they had to dig down as much as ten feet to find the basalt stone bedrock on to build, so that a house could withstand the Jordan's flood waters from the spring rains. Through this parable Jesus challenges his hearers not to trust in the surface righteousness espoused by the scribes and the Pharisees; rather, they should depend on his teachings to be river-proof.

John connects *potamos* with the celebration of the Feast of the Tabernacles (Jn. 7:37–38), a celebration associated with adequate rainfall. To launch the festivities a priest read Zech. 14:16–17 on the first day. After six successive days of marching and pouring water from the Pool of Siloam at the base of the altar, the celebration climaxed with a special water-pouring rite and lighting ceremony. Jesus' words would have made a huge impact as the participants continued to reflect on the symbolic significance of the water and light. While the water stopped flowing until next year's celebration, Jesus said, "If any one of you is thirsty, let him come to me and drink. Whoever believes in me, as the Scripture has said, *streams* of living water will flow from within him." Jesus is probably alluding to those promised spiritual blessings, including the blessing of the arrival of the Spirit, which was still on the horizon.

In the midst of the description of the Parthian invasion in Rev. 9:12–21, John refers to the great river Euphrates. This river served as the traditional division between Roman and Parthian territories. With this geographical reference figuring into end-time destructive events, the reader comes full circle from the creation story in Gen. 2, where the Euphrates is one of the four headwaters that flowed out of the garden of Eden. An important end-time theme is that even though Satan and his evil forces continue to unleash destruction on God's construction, he remains in ultimate control of all history and all outcomes.

Satan as the dragon attempts to vanquish God's people by sending potentially lethal "water like a *river*" from his mouth (Rev. 12:15). But God's creation comes to the rescue and swallows the river (12:16). While Satan's attacks can be physically deadly, they are nonetheless inconsequential with respect to God's ultimate victory over evil.

The last two occurrences of *potamos* in Revelation echo a theme Jesus initiated in Jn. 7:37–38. From the throne of God and of the Lamb flows the "river of the water of life" (Rev. 22:1; cf. Ezek. 47). The new Jerusalem will become the final Eden; paradise, once lost, will be regained. In the original Eden a river flowed from Eden to water the garden. At the beginning of eternity, double-banking the river of life in Rev. 22:2 is the "unguarded" (cf. Gen. 3:24) tree of life producing twelve "kinds" or crops of fruit. That is, abundant fruit watered by the river of the water of life will be available all twelve months, i.e., forever. God's provision will always be available, without interruption. See *NIDNTT-A*, 459.

ROAD

Old Testament

Noun: אֹרַח (*ʾōraḥ*), GK 784 (S 734), 59x. Deriving from the verb *ʾāraḥ* ("to journey, wander"), *ʾōraḥ* is translated variously as "path, way, road." It can bear either a literal or a figurative reference. See *path*.

Noun: דֶּרֶךְ (*derek*), GK 2006 (S 1870), 712x. *derek* may be translated in numerous ways, both literal and metaphorical, including "way, road, path, journey, conduct." See *way*.

New Testament

Noun: ὁδός *hodos*), GK *3847* (S *3598*), 101x. *hodos* is basically a "road" or "path" on which one travels, or the act of traveling. It can also mean "the way" of life. See *way*.

ROBBER

New Testament

Noun: λῃστής (*lēstēs*), GK *3334* (S *3027*), 15x. *lēstēs* denotes one who is a "robber" or a political rebel ("insurrectionist").

This word applies to the men who hung on crosses to the right and left of the Lord Jesus (Mt. 27:38, 44; Mk. 15:27), as well as to those who attacked the man traveling down the road to Jericho in the parable of the Good Samaritan (Lk. 10:30, 36). Jesus uses *lēstēs* to describe the person who would sneak into a sheep pen: "I tell you the truth, the man who does not enter the sheep pen by the gate, but climbs in by some other way, is a thief and a *robber*" (Jn. 10:1, 8). When Jesus becomes angry with the moneychangers in the temple, he justifies his actions by declaring, "My house will be called a house of prayer, but you are making it a 'den of *robbers*'" (Mt. 21:13; cf. Mk. 11:17; Lk. 19:46).

Jesus also uses *lēstēs* as the name for the person who was the leader of a rebellion (Mt. 26:55; Mk. 14:48; Lk. 22:52). John tells us that Barabbas "had taken part in a rebellion" (Jn. 18:40). In the only use outside the gospels, Paul records in his list of sufferings "dangers from *bandits*" (2 Cor. 11:26). See *NIDNTT-A*, 335-36.*

ROBE

New Testament

Noun: ἱμάτιον (*himation*), GK *2668* (S *2440*), 60x. *himation* is sometimes used of "clothing" in general, but more frequently of the outer "robe" or "cloak." See *clothes*.

ROCK

Old Testament

Noun: אֶבֶן (*ʾeben*), GK 74 (S 68), 276x. *ʾeben* means "rock, stone." (1) The rocks or stones denoted by *ʾeben* can be as large as eight to ten cubits in length (1 Ki. 7:10) or small enough to easily throw some distance (2 Sam. 16:6, 13). They can also be large enough to cover a well (Gen. 29:2, 8, 10) or the entrance to a cave (Jos. 10:18, 27). They can be used to sit on (Exod. 17:12) or as a weapon (Exod. 21:18; Num. 35:17, 23), such as a sling (Jdg. 20:16; 1 Sam. 17:40, 49). Stones were used for writing material (Exod. 24:12; 31:18; Deut. 4:13; 5:22) and as vessels or containers (Exod. 7:19).

Frequently stones were piled up as pillars to function as a memorial or witness (Gen. 28:11, 18, 22; 31:45; Deut. 27:2–6; Jos. 4:3–9, 20–21; 1 Sam. 7:12 [Ebenezer]). They were used for building altars (Exod. 20:25; 1 Ki. 18:31–32, 38) and houses or walls (Gen. 11:3; Lev. 14:43; Ezek. 26:12; Hab. 2:11). In a number of instances, idols are described as made from stone (Lev. 26:1; Deut. 4:28; 28:36, 64; 29:17). Weights for scales were commonly made out of stone (Lev. 19:36; Deut. 25:13, 15; Prov. 11:1; 16:11). *ʾeben* is also used in constructions designating precious stones (Gen. 2:12; Exod. 25:7; 28:9–12; 2 Sam. 12:30). Executions were carried out with stones (Lev. 20:27; Deut. 13:10; Jos. 7:25). The Lord executed his judgments by stoning with hailstones (Jos. 10:11).

(2) On a few occasions, *ʾeben* is used metaphorically. It can describe a state of motionlessness (Exod. 15:16) and a condition of strength (Job 6:12). The armor of Leviathan, particularly the part covering his heart, is as hard or strong as stone (Job 41:24). Jerusalem is described as an immovable rock (Zech. 12:3). In several instances, "stone" is applied to the heart as a metaphor for stubbornness or rebellion (1 Sam. 25:37). Ezekiel prophecies about a day when the Lord will remove Israel's heart of stone and replace it with a heart of flesh (Ezek. 11:19; 36:26).

(3) *ʾeben* is used 4x with possible messianic connotations. When combined with the literal sense of stones as building material (cf. Gen. 11:3; Lev. 14:43; 1 Ki. 5:17–18), the Bible records that a certain rock is laid by the Lord in the foundation of Zion that becomes an object of hope (Isa. 28:16). It is a stone previously rejected by the builders but miraculously exalted by the Lord (Ps. 118:22; cf. Zech. 4:7). As a form of judgment, the Lord will become a stone over which the houses of Israel will stumble or fall (Isa. 8:14).

(4) On one occasion "rock of Israel" occurs as a possible name or title for God (Gen. 49:24). This may allude to Jacob's experiences at Bethel.

Noun: סֶלַע (*selaʿ*), GK 6152 (S 5553), 58x. *selaʿ* denotes a piece of geographic terrain usually characterized as a "cliff" or steep "rock" face found on a mountain.

(1) A *sela*ʿ can form caves suitable for dwelling (1 Ki. 19:11; Isa. 7:19; Jer. 16:16; Amos 6:12). In some instances, particular caves or cliffs have taken on names, such as "*sela*ʿ of Etam" (Jdg. 15:8, 11, 13) or "*sela*ʿ of Rimmon" (Jdg. 20:45, 47; 21:13). Such caves are often used for hiding (1 Sam. 13:6; 23:25; Isa. 2:21 [from God's presence]; Jer. 13:4) and are considered to be a stronghold or refuge (Isa. 31:9; 33:16; Jer. 48:28; Obad. 3), or a solid place to stand (Ps. 40:2). A grave or tomb can be carved out of the *sela*ʿ (Isa. 22:16). It is also recorded that offerings or sacrifices (Jdg. 6:20; Isa. 57:5; Ezek. 24:7, 8) and executions (Ezek. 24:7, 8; Ps. 137:9; 141:6) took place on these rocky cliffs.

(2) In Num. 20:1–13 (recounted in Deut. 32:13; Neh. 9:15; Ps. 78:16), *sela*ʿ is used 5x as the designation for the rock Moses struck twice or a second time. This event is similar to the one recorded in Exod. 17:1–7, where Moses strikes the rock for the first time. In the Exodus account, however, the word for rock is *ṣûr* (GK 7446; see below).

(3) As a secure dwelling, *sela*ʿ is used metaphorically for security or safety: "Your dwelling place is *secure*, your nest is set in a *rock*" (Num. 24:21; cf. Isa. 32:2). Jeremiah uses this term as a metaphor for stubbornness, "They made their faces *harder than stone* and refused to repent (Jer. 5:3). Ezekiel uses the designation "bare *rock*" as a place for public spectacle (Ezek. 24:7–8) and subsequently as a metaphor for desolation, "I will scrape away her rubble and make her a bare *rock*" (26:4, 14).

Noun: צוּר (*ṣûr*), GK 7446 (S 6697), 73x. *ṣûr* can be characterized as a large rocky feature of the geographic terrain (1 Chr. 11:15; Jer. 18:14; 21:13).

(1) Literally, *ṣûr* can describe a place suitable for standing (Exod. 17:6; 34:21–22; 2 Sam. 21:10), an altar or place of sacrifice (Jdg. 13:19), something a snake crawls over (Prov. 30:19), a place to hide (Isa. 2:10), or something permanent to write on (Job 19:24). It is also found as a synonym for "mountain" (Job 14:18; 24:8; 28:10), "earth" (Job 18:4), and "rock" (*sela*ʾ, GK 6152; cf. Deut. 32:13). In Exod. 17:1–7, the Lord stands on the *ṣûr* that Moses strikes. The people are delivered from thirst and death as the rock miraculously produces water, a symbol of salvation and God's presence (i.e., rock of salvation; cf. Rev. 22:1–3). In Exod. 33, the rock is a source of refuge, an escape from destruction that would have been caused by God's presence (i.e., rock of refuge). The rock, therefore, has become both a source of provision and a place of protection.

(2) Unlike both ʾ*eben* (GK 74) and *sela*ʾ (GK 6152) discussed above, *ṣûr* is used more often as a metaphor or divine name (44x) than literally (see [3], below). In Ps. 73:26, the psalmist uses this word metaphorically to express his confidence that God is the "*strength* of my heart" (NIV, NASB). In Isa. 51:1, the prophet uses the rock imagery to characterize Abraham as the father of the people of Israel. Accordingly, Abraham is "the rock" from which the people were cut. Also, the Lord will become a rock to stumble over (Isa. 8:14) in judging the house of Israel. In each instance, the common associations of strength, building, and dwelling are used metaphorically.

(3) *ṣûr* is a name or epithet for God, occurring with a number of different expressions. The Lord is the "Rock of salvation" (Deut. 32:15; 2 Sam. 22:47; Isa. 17:10), "the Rock of refuge" (Deut. 32:37; 2 Sam. 22:3; Ps. 62:2, 6–7), "the Rock of strength" (Ps. 31:2). Other defining expressions include the "Everlasting Rock" (Isa. 26:4) and the "Rock that is higher than I" (Ps. 61:2). Lastly, the phrase "Rock of Israel" is a parallel expression for the "God of Israel" (2 Sam. 23:3) and for the "mountain of the Lord" (Isa. 30:29). It should also be noted that *ṣûr* as a divine name is used with moral or ethical connotations. "The Lord is upright; he is my Rock, and

there is no wickedness in him." (Ps. 92:15; cf. Deut. 32:4).

New Testament

Noun: λίθος (*lithos*), GK *3345* (S *3037*), 59x. *lithos* is commonly translated as "stone" or "rock." (1) This natural resource was used for covering tomb entrances (Mt. 27:60, 66; 28:2; Mk. 15:46; 16:3, 4), as building material, especially for the temple (Mk. 13:1, 2; Lk. 21:5, 6; 1 Cor. 3:12), as writing material (2 Cor. 3:7), and as something from which to make an idol (Acts 17:29) or to use as a weapon (Mk. 5:5; Jn. 8:7, 59; 10:31). In Revelation, *lithos* refers to various precious stones (Rev. 4:3; 17:4; 21:11, 19). In Lk. 22:41, a "stone's throw" is used to describe an approximate short distance.

(2) On a number of occasions, *lithos* refers to certain "messianic" stones. The "rejected stone" of Mt. 21:42; Mk. 12:10; Lk. 20:17; Acts 4:11 portrays Jesus as the messianic fulfillment of Ps. 118:22: "the stone the builders rejected has become the capstone." The "stumbling stone" of Rom. 9:32–33 portrays Jesus as the messianic fulfillment of Isa. 8:14; 28:16. In 1 Pet. 2:4–8, Peter combines all of the OT messianic stones. For those who put their faith in Christ, Jesus is the "chosen and precious cornerstone, and the one who trusts in him will never be put to shame" (1 Pet. 2:6; Isa. 28:16). But for those who do not put their faith in Christ, Jesus has become "the stone the builders rejected" (1 Pet. 2:7; cf. Ps. 118:22) and "a stone that causes men to stumble and a rock that makes them fall" (1 Pet. 2:8; Isa. 8:14).

Noun: πέτρα (*petra*), GK *4376* (S *4073*), 15x. *petra* denotes large rock formations. It is a secure place to build a house (Mt. 7:24, 25; Lk. 6:48), a place from which a tomb may be cut out (Mt. 27:60; Mk. 15:46), and a place among which caves are formed (Rev. 6:15, 16). The *petra* can be split by an earthquake (Mt. 27:51) and is not considered a suitable component for fertile soil (Lk. 8:6, 13).

In a wordplay, the name of the apostle Peter (*petros*) derives from *petra* (cf. Jn. 1:42). In Mt. 16:18, it is written, "You are *petros* [Peter] and on this *petra* [rock] I will build my church." Peter here is representative of all the apostles (cf. 18:18), and the NT is clear that the apostles form the foundation of the church (Eph. 2:20; Rev. 21:14).

In 1 Cor. 10:4, the preexistent Christ is described as the "spiritual rock" from which the people of God drank in the wilderness. This no doubt refers to the events of Exod. 17 (see *ṣûr*, GK 7446, above). Jesus is also the messianic rock over which people will stumble (Rom. 9:33; 1 Pet. 2:8; cf. Isa. 28:16).

ROD

Old Testament

Noun: מַטֶּה (*maṭṭeh*), GK 4751 (S 4294), 252x. *maṭṭeh* has two separate, though related meanings: "rod, staff"; and "tribe" (see *tribe*). See *staff*.

Noun: קָנֶה (*qāneh*), GK 7866 (S 7070), 62x. In its most basic sense, *qāneh* refers to the generic reeds or rushes found in the watery areas of the ancient Near East (Job 40:21; Isa. 19:6; 35:7). But since the reed was sometimes used for measuring, by extension this word can stand for the measuring reed/rod (Ezek. 40:3, 5; 42:16–17). See *reed*.

Noun: שֵׁבֶט (*šēbeṭ*), GK 8657 (S 7626), 190x. *šēbet* means "rod, scepter, or tribe." It is a synonym with *maṭṭeh* (GK 4751) and connotes the part of a tree from which a staff or weapon could be made. Leaders were also known as *šēbet*, and those who followed them; hence, they became the tribe.

(1) *šēbet* as "rod, scepter" bears great theological significance, particularly when it depicts the rod of discipline or the scepter of the Messiah. For example, Gen. 49:10 records the blessing of Jacob to his sons. "The *scepter* shall not depart from Judah, nor the ruler's staff from between his feet, until tribute comes to him; and the obedience of the peoples is his." Balaam prophesies, "I see him, but not now; I behold him, but not near—a star shall come out of Jacob, and a *scepter* shall rise

out of Israel" (Num. 24:17). It is possible that the Magi who visited Jesus recognized him by this reference to a star (Mt. 2:2).

The mention of scepter appears in the context of God's anointed one ruling over the nations (Ps. 2:9). His scepter is a "*scepter* of justice" (45:6). God's "rod" and staff comfort the psalmist in 23:4. In Isaiah, the shoot of Jesse will strike the earth "with the *rod* of his mouth" (Isa. 11:4), bringing justice, righteousness, and an end to the oppression of the poor.

(2) Throughout the historical books, *šēbet* means often means "tribe" (about two-thirds of the occurrences of this word; e.g., Gen. 49:28; Deut. 1:15; Jdg. 18:1). But even in these books, when God makes a covenant with David, he promises to punish David's son with "a *rod* of men," though he still refuses to remove his steadfast love from him (2 Sam. 7:14). In Proverbs, the "rod" is used for remedial punishment in a family context (e.g., Prov. 13:24; 22:15; 23:13). See *NIDOTTE*, 4:27–29.

New Testament

Noun: ῥάβδος (*rhabdos*), GK *4811* (S *4464*), 12x. *rhabdos* refers to a "staff, rod, scepter." See *staff*.

(HAVE) ROOM FOR

New Testament

Verb: χωρέω (*chōreō*), GK *6003* (S *5562*), 10x. *chōreo* means "to accept, hold, have room for." See *accept*.

ROOSTER

New Testament

Noun: ἀλέκτωρ (*alektōr*), GK *232* (S *220*), 12x. *alektōr* means "rooster, cock," probably the male chicken that regularly crows an hour or two before dawn (see also Mk. 13:35 for a rooster crowing just after midnight). All of the references to *alektōr* are in the gospel accounts of Peter denying Jesus three times (Mt. 26:34, 74, 75; Mk. 14:30, 68, 72; Lk. 22:34, 60, 61; Jn. 13:38; 18:27).*

ROOT

New Testament

Noun: ῥίζα (*rhiza*), GK *4844* (S *4491*), 17x. In his description of the fig tree that Jesus cursed, Mark uses *rhiza* in its literal sense as the underground segment of a plant: it "withered from the roots" (Mk. 11:20). In the parable of the soils, Jesus mentions how the seed quickly withered because the plants "had no root" (Mt. 13:6; Mk. 4:17; Lk. 8:13); but in his interpretation of the parable, he uses *rhiza* metaphorically to illustrate what happens when faith cannot withstand persecution (Mt. 13:21; Mk. 4:17).

The remaining occurrences of *rhiza* appear in the metaphorical sense referring to something's source or origin. John the Baptist uses the image of an axe put to the root of a tree as a metaphor for coming judgment (Mt. 3:10; Lk. 3:9). Paul uses the figure of the olive tree, its roots and branches, as a metaphor for God's dealing with both Israel and the Gentile nations (Rom. 11:16–18). The term may also be used generally to denote the origin of something: "For the love of money is a root of all kinds of evil" (1 Tim. 6:10), and "See to it that no one misses the grace of God and that no bitter root grows up to cause trouble and defile many" (Heb. 12:15).

Finally, *rhiza* is used in the NT metaphorically to refer to one's descendant. Jesus is "the Root of Jesse," who will come to rule over the nations (Rom. 15:12; quoting Isa. 11:10). This sense is seen too in Revelation 22:16, where Jesus says of himself, "I am the Root and the Offspring of David" (see also 5:5). See *NIDNTT-A*, 127-28.*

RUB

Old Testament

Verb: מָשַׁח (*māšaḥ*), GK 5417 (S 4886), 70x. The basic meaning of *māšaḥ* is to "rub" with a liquid. Its more common meaning, however, is "to anoint." See *anoint*.

RUIN

Old Testament

Verb: שָׁחַת (*šāḥat*), GK 8845 (S 7843), 152x. In various contexts, the verb *šāḥat* can broadly mean "to corrupt, destroy, ruin, spoil, wipe out." It denotes the corrupting or destroying of a wide variety of physical things, including eyes (Exod. 21:26), vineyards (Jer. 12:10), buildings (Lam. 2:6), crops (Jdg. 6:4), trees (Deut. 20:19–20), semen (Gen. 38:9), and kings (1 Sam. 26:15). See *destroy*.

New Testament

Noun: ἀπώλεια (*apōleia*), GK *724* (S *684*), 18x. *apōleia* means "destruction, ruin, waste." See *destruction*.

RULE, RULER

Old Testament

Verb: מָלַךְ (*mālak*), GK 4887 (S 4427), 350x. *mālak* means "to rule as king" or "to be king" and is used with an assortment of human kings as well as for God's own reigning activity (Gen. 36:31; 2 Sam. 2:10; Isa. 52:7). See *king*.

Noun: אַיִל (*ʾayil*), GK 380 (S 352), 171x. *ʾayil* literally means "ram" (see *ram*) but can also be used figuratively for "ruler, leader, chief." See *chief*.

New Testament

Verb: ἄρχω (*archō*), GK *806* (S *757, 756*), 86x. *archō* has two different meanings in the NT: "to rule" and "to begin" (see *begin*). While Gentile rulers "lord it over" those they govern, Jesus, in stark contrast, teaches his followers that the road to greatness is traveled down the path of servanthood (Mk. 10:42, 44). This is the surprising way by which the root of Jesse would begin to rule the nations (Rom. 15:12).

Verb: βασιλεύω (*basileuō*), GK 996 (S 936) 21x. *basileuō* means "to rule, reign." See *reign*.

Noun: ἀρχή (*archē*), GK *794* (S *746*), 55x. Like the verb *archō* (see *begin*), *archē* means both "beginning" (see *beginning*) and "ruler." In this second sense, *archē* means "power, ruler." All the "rulers" of the universe (whether humans or angels) are sustained by and exist for the glory of Jesus (Col. 1:16), who is the head of "every *power*" (2:10). In light of this truth, Christians are instructed to submit to the earthly "rulers" of this world, knowing that they are ultimately under the authority of Jesus and he will judge accordingly (Tit. 3:1). In contrast, Christians are to never submit to demonic rulers. By his victory on the cross, Jesus publicly disarmed these satanic "powers" and authorities (Col. 2:15; cf. 1 Cor. 15:24). Indeed, it is a central truth that no ruler, earthy or demonic, can separate a Christian from Christ's love (Rom. 8:38). See *NIDNTT-A*, 74-76.

Noun: ἄρχων (*archōn*), GK *807* (S *758*), 37x. *archōn* is part of an extensive group of *arch-* words with meanings related to the ideas of beginning, cause, and thereby, rule and authority. *archōn* occurs 450x in the Greek OT (LXX), translating assorted words all of which communicate the idea of an authoritative ruler or leader. Its usage is similar in the NT. It is used for several different types of rulers: rulers over nations (Mt. 20:25; Acts 4:26), synagogue and other Jewish leaders (Mt. 9:18, 23; 23:13, 35; Acts 3:17), and city authorities (Acts 16:19).

The more widespread *archōn* can refer not only to human rulers, but also those in the demonic realm. Beelzebul is called the *archōn* ("prince") of the demons (Mt. 12:24; Mk. 3:22; Lk. 11:15), and Satan the *archōn* of this world (Jn. 12:31; 14:20; 16:11; cf. Eph. 2:2).

In the ancient world, rulers and their policies were a much closer reality for people than they are in our democratic societies. The NT gives great encouragement that despite all sorts of authorities (human and demonic) opposed to the gospel (even to the point of crucifying Christ, 1 Cor. 2:8), Jesus reigns as the *archōn* of all the kings of the earth (Rev. 1:5). See *NIDNTT-A*, 74-76.

Noun: βασιλεία (*basileia*), GK *993* (S *932*). 162x. In the NT, *basileia* plays a greater role. Most English versions consistently translate *basileia* with "kingdom," though at times it would be better understood as "reign" or "rule." Thus, some scholars today prefer to speak of "the rule of God" or even "the empire of God." See *kingdom*.

Noun: βασιλεύς (*basileus*), GK *995* (S *935*). 115x. *basileus* means "king, ruler." These terms relate to the idea of kingship and kingdom (see also the word *basileia* under *kingdom*) and make up an important theme throughout the NT. Building on the same theme in the OT, Jesus proclaims the kingdom of God as his primary message (Mt. 4:17; Mk. 1:15; Lk. 4:43). The book of Revelation likewise describes Jesus as King of kings and Lord of lords (17:14; 19:16; cf. 1:5) and promises that faithful disciples will reign with Christ eternally (5:10; 20:4; 22:5).

In the LXX, the noun *basileus* and the verb *basileuō* are used with reference to a large assortment of human kings as well as God. This is also true in the NT, though earthly kings are often depicted negatively and God as king is emphasized. Herod, Pilate, and many others are portrayed as those who set themselves against God's kingdom (Mt. 2:1–18; Acts 12:1; 2 Cor. 11:32), while Jesus' actions and teaching show him to be the true king (Mt. 11:2–6; 12:28; Lk. 4:16–27). Several NT authors use elevated language to describe God as king (Mt. 5:35; Lk. 19:38; Jn. 12:13; 1 Tim. 1:17; Rev. 17:14). Interestingly, in John the term *basileus* is reserved solely for Jesus (16x).

Noun: ἡγεμών (*hēgemōn*), GK *2450* (S *2232*), 20x. *hēgemōn*, "ruler, leader," communicates the general idea of ruler (Mt. 2:6; Mk. 13:9; 1 Pet. 2:14), though it is often more specifically a title for various Roman officials, such as "governor" (Mt. 27:2; Lk. 20:20; Acts 23:24; 26:30).

RUN

Old Testament

Verb: רוּץ (*rûṣ*), GK 8132 (S 7323), 104x. *rûṣ* conveys the basic sense "to run, make haste by running." Generally the verb is used of humans (e.g., men: Gen. 18:7; 1 Sam. 20:36; women: Gen. 24:20) but not of animals. Only Joel 2:4 ("They have the appearance of horses; they *gallop along* like cavalry" ["and as horsemen, so shall they run," KJV]) and Amos 6:12 ("Do horses run on the rocky crags?") apply the verb to animals.

In a few instances, *rûṣ* conveys a special meaning. In Gen. 41:14, the verb has a causative sense, meaning "cause to run," and implies bringing something in haste: "So Pharaoh sent for Joseph, and he was *quickly brought* from the dungeon." Nah. 2:5 employs the verb in a seldom used form to give the meaning "run back and forth": "The chariots storm through the streets, *rushing back and forth* through the squares" ("jostle one against another," KJV).

rûṣ can also be used metaphorically. One "runs" to accomplish one's heart's desire. Thus, the wicked run to do evil (Prov. 6:18) and "their feet *rush* into sin" (Isa. 59:7). In chastising the returned exiles for not rebuilding the temple, Haggai says that "each of you is *busy* with his own house" ("ye *run* every man unto his own house," KJV; Hag. 1:9). In a positive sense, the joyful bridegroom comes forth from the wedding canopy like a champion rejoicing to run his course (i.e., eager to fulfill his duties as a husband, Ps. 19:5). And the psalmist says: "I *run* in the path of your commands, for you have set my heart free" (Ps. 119:32). Likewise, the righteous find their refuge in God: "The name of the Lord is a strong tower; the righteous *run* to it and are safe" (Prov. 18:10). God's word will accomplish its purpose, and thus it is characterized as running: "He sends his command to the earth; his word *runs* swiftly" (Ps. 147:15). See *NIDOTTE*, 3:1084-85.

New Testament

Verb: τρέχω (*trechō*), GK *5556* (S *5143*), 20x. *trechō* means "to run" in both a physical sense and a figurative sense. (1) In the gospels and Acts, every occurrence of *trechō* refers to literal running. At the crucifixion, one of the bystanders "runs" to fill a sponge with wine vinegar (Mt. 27:48). The followers of Christ run to or from the empty tomb on Easter morning (28:8; Lk. 24:12; Jn. 20:2, 4). In Jesus' earthly ministry, the demoniac runs to

Jesus (Mk. 5:6). In the parable of the lost son, the father of the rebellious son runs to him (Lk. 15:20). This running says much about the fatherhood of God, for in first-century Palestine, older men did not run; it was neither respectable nor proper conduct. The impact of this parable is as much on the father's running in love as on the prodigal's return to seek forgiveness.

(2) *trechō* can also be used in a figurative sense. Paul uses the literal sense in 1 Cor. 9:24 to illustrate running with full effort in the spiritual life. In Rom. 9:16, Paul notes that the election and salvation of God are not conditioned on "the man who wills or the man who *runs*" (i.e., exertion). That is, nothing a person can do will earn or merit the election and salvation of God. Rather, it is entirely by the sovereign mercy and grace of God (9:16b). *trechō* is used several times to picture of the Christian life in the sense of *running* toward a goal (1 Cor. 9:26c; Gal. 2:2; 5:7; Phil. 2:16; Heb. 12:1). Passivity is not a virtue in the Christian life.

RUN AWAY

New Testament

Verb: φεύγω (*pheugō*), GK *5771* (S *5343*), 29x. *pheugō* primarily means "to flee, escape, elude, run off/away." It occurs most frequently in the Gospels (17x). See *flee*.

RUSH

Old Testament

Verb: רוּץ (*rûṣ*), GK 8132 (S 7323), 104x. *rûṣ* conveys the basic sense "to run, make haste by running." See *run*.

SABBATH

Old Testament

Noun: שַׁבָּת (*šabbāt*), GK 8701 (S 7676), 111x. *šabbāt* means "restfulness," but it is usually translated as the word is in Hebrew: "Sabbath." There are several ritually observed rest days noted in the OT: the weekly Sabbath (Exod. 16:23), the Day of Atonement (Lev. 16:31; 23:32), the first day of the Feast of Trumpets (23:24), the first and eighth days of the Feast of Tabernacles (Lev. 23:39), and the sabbatical year (25:4–5),

God values both work and rest. In creation, he commanded the people he made to "fill the earth and subdue it." Yet the reason given for observing the Sabbath rest in Exodus is God's own rest after creation: "In six days the Lord made heaven and earth, the sea, and all that is in them, but rested the seventh day; therefore the Lord blessed the *Sabbath* day and consecrated it" (Exod. 20:11).

Later the people and their slaves are commanded to rest in order to help them remember that they were delivered from Egypt (Deut. 5:15). This command emphasizes the deliverance from slavery rather than creation, but the effect is the same: rest. To cease working requires unique trust in God, particularly in the context of the unruly land of Palestine. Israel's observance of rest serves as both a sign of their covenant with God and as a witness to the other nations (Exod. 31:13, 16–17; Ezek. 20:12, 20). Note the increasing importance theologically of the observance of the Sabbath in Isa. 56:2–7 and 58:13–14.

In the NT, while Jesus attempts to break the legalistic framework that Sabbath observance acquired, he does see the importance of a time of regular rest (Mk. 6:31) and goes himself regularly to the synagogue on the Sabbath (Lk. 4:16). The author of Hebrews sees the invitation to a "Sabbath-rest" as an invitation to cease striving with God and to receive the salvation available by faith in Jesus Christ (Heb. 4).

New Testament

Noun: σάββατον (*sabbaton*), GK *4879* (S *4521*), 68x. *sabbaton* means "Sabbath." It is a transliteration of the Hebrew word *šabbāt* and is related to the verb *šābat*, which is used of God's resting on the seventh day of creation (Gen. 2:2–3).

The concept of the Sabbath is prevalent throughout the OT and NT. Generally speaking, work is prohibited on the Sabbath. Rabbinic works are replete with lists of what is permitted or prohibited on this day. Various unavoidable obligations (mortal danger, helping in the event of severe sickness, childbirth, the preparation and implementation of burnt offerings) supersede the Sabbath law. The Sabbath was a time of celebration at home with feasting, the inviting of guests, and special blessings closing the day. It was also a time for worship in the temple or synagogue (Lk. 4:16; Acts 13:5, 14, 42–44; 14:1; 16:13; 17:2, 16; 18:4; 19:8).

sabbaton in the NT agrees with Jewish usage and is in keeping with what is known from Jewish sources, e.g., priestly work is permitted (Mt. 12:4–5), picking ears of corn is banned (Mk. 2:23–28), helping the sick is allowed only in life or death situations (3:1), the body of Jesus is buried before the Sabbath (15:42), the Sabbath is a day of rest (Lk. 23:56), items are not to be carried (Jn. 5:9–10), circumcision is also permitted (7:22–23), travel is limited (Acts 1:12), and Scripture is read (13:15, 27).

Jesus had repeated conflicts with the Jews over observing the Sabbath. Most of these are over what is and is not permitted. Picking ears of corn (Mt. 12:1–8; Mk. 2:23–28; Lk. 6:1–5) is breaking the law according to the Pharisees, and while Jesus does not challenge the law, he does put forth the concept that human need overrides ritual law. Several conflicts center around Jesus' healing on the Sabbath: the healing of a man with a withered hand (Mt. 12:9–14; Mk. 3:1–6; Lk. 6:6–11), the disabled woman (Lk. 13:10–17), a man crippled for thirty-eight years (Jn. 5:1–9, 16–17; 7:22), and the man born blind (Jn. 9). Jesus insisted that it was always lawful to do good on the Sabbath (Mt. 12:12).

According to Jesus the Sabbath was made for man, not man for the Sabbath (Mk. 2:27–28). That is, in the creation story, God did not create a Sabbath and then create a human being to keep it; rather, he first created a human being, then knowing human beings would need rest, created the Sabbath for their benefit. The Lord wants us to enjoy the day of rest, not be burdened by it. See *NIDNTT-A*, 512-13.

SACRED, SACREDNESS

Old Testament

Adjective: קָדוֹשׁ (*qādôš*), GK 7705 (S 6918), 117x. Generally *qādôš* is translated as "holy," "holy one," or "saint." It describes that which is by nature sacred or that which has been admitted to the sphere of the sacred by divine rite. See *holy.*

Noun: קֹדֶשׁ (*qōdeš*), GK 7731 (S 6944), 470x. *qōdeš* connotes the concept of "holiness," i.e., the essential nature of that which belongs to the sphere of the sacred and is distinct from the common or profane. See *holiness*.

New Testament

Adjective: ἅγιος (*hagios*), GK *41* (S *40* & *39*), 233x. In general, two facts stand out in the NT regarding *hagios* ("holy, sacred"). First, God and what is associated with him is declared as "holy." Second, the proper sphere of the holy in the NT is not the priestly or ritual but the prophetic. See *holy*.

SACRIFICE

Old Testament

Verb: זָבַח (*zābaḥ*), GK 2284 (S 2076), 134x. *zābaḥ* primarily refers to the slaughtering of animals for sacrifice. The first occurrence of this verb is in Gen. 31:54, where Jacob offers a sacrifice to God and shares a meal with Laban, just before they part ways. This is the verb that Moses uses when he asks Pharaoh if the Israelites can go three days into the desert "*to offer sacrifices* to the Lord our God" (Exod. 5:3). Later, "King Solomon and the entire assembly of Israel that had gathered about him were before the ark, *sacrificing* so many sheep and cattle that they could not be recorded or counted" (1 Ki. 8:5). The psalmist calls on the people to "*sacrifice* thank offerings to God" (Ps. 50:14; cf. 107:22; 116:17).

But *zābaḥ* is not a unique word for sacrificing only to the Lord God. This word is used of the nonsacrificial slaughter of animals as well (Deut. 12:15, 21). And it is one of the words frequently used in later OT passages for sacrifices to pagan gods. Ahaz, for example, "*offered sacrifices* to the gods of Damascus" (2 Chr. 28:23). Hosea uses *zābaḥ* in reference to the idolatrous practice of offering sacrifices to the Canaanite deity Baal (Hos. 11:2). Hos. 13:2 uses *zābaḥ* for the hideous practice of human sacrifice. And in two OT passages, this verb is used to note that when sacrifices were made to idols, people were really sacrificing to demons (Deut. 32:17; Ps. 106:37–38). See *NIDOTTE, 1:1066-73.*

Noun: זֶבַח (*zebaḥ*), GK 2285 (S 2077), 162x. *zebaḥ* is the most common noun for "sacrifice" in the OT (e.g., Exod. 3:18; 10:25). There are several types of *zebaḥ* noted. It is used for the sacrifice of a lamb at the time of the exodus (Exod. 12:27). When the Mosaic covenant was ratified, we read, "Then he sent young Israelite men, and they ... sacrificed young bulls as fellowship *offerings* to the Lord" (Exod. 24:5). Also included are the covenant *zebaḥ* (between Jacob and Laban in Gen. 31:54), the regular Passover *zebaḥ* (Exod. 34:25), the annual *zebaḥ* (1 Sam. 1:21), and the thank *zebaḥ* (Lev. 22:29). Most frequently, however, *zebaḥ* is used in connection with the peace or fellowship offering (Lev. 3:1–9; 7:11–21).

zebaḥ is the word that Samuel uses when he encounters King Saul, who has not obeyed orders to destroy all the Amalekites: "Does the Lord delight in burnt offerings and *sacrifices* as much as in obeying the voice of the Lord? To obey is better than *sacrifice*, and to heed is better than the fat of rams" (1 Sam. 15:22). The psalmist exhorts, "Offer right *sacrifices* and trust in the Lord" (Ps. 4:5). At the same time, mere sacrifice does not satisfy the Lord (cf. Isa. 1:11; Jer. 6:20). As David acknowledges about his own sin, "You do not delight in *sacrifice*, or I would bring it .... The *sacrifices* of God are a broken spirit; a broken and contrite heart, O God, you will not despise" (Ps. 51:16–17). Or, as the Lord speaks directly through the words of Hosea, "I desire mercy, not *sacrifice*" (Hos. 6:4). See *NIDOTTE,* 1:1066-73.

New Testament

Verb: θύω (*thyō*), GK *2604* (S *2380*), 14x. The root of *thyō* carries the meaning of "to sacrifice" a burnt offering. Thus, *thyō* came to mean "to offer a ritual sacrifice" of any kind or "to ceremonially kill an animal for sacrifice" to any god (Acts 14:13, 18; 1 Cor. 10:20).

The word is used in the NT specifically to refer to sacrificing the Passover lamb (Mk. 14:12; Lk. 22:7) and hence to the sacrifice of Jesus, our Passover lamb (1 Cor. 5:7). *thyō* is also in two parables for the killing of animals for a banquet (Mt. 22:4) and for celebration at the time of the return of the prodigal son (Lk. 15:23, 27, 30). An angel uses this word to command Peter to "*kill* and eat" the animals he sees in a vision of all kinds of unclean food (Acts 10:13; 11:7). *thyō* is also used simply to refer to the act of killing any animal or humans being (Jn. 10:10). See *NIDNTT-A,* 254-57.*

Noun: θυσία (*thysia*), GK *2602* (S *2378*), 29x. *thysia* can refer to any "sacrifice" (made to any god, Acts 7:41–42) or to the actual "offering" of a sacrifice (Heb. 10:8). This term refers more specifically to the sacrifices offered in the Jewish temple (Lk. 2:24; Heb. 5:1; 7:27). Jesus, however, is God's designated once-for-all sacrifice for sin (Eph. 5:2; Heb. 9:26; 10:12). He also teaches in the gospels that loving one's neighbor is more important than sacrifice (Mk. 12:33), and mercy likewise is more important than sacrifice (Mt. 9:13; 12:7).

thysia is extended to refer to other kinds of Christian offerings, such as a "*sacrifice* of praise" (Heb. 13:15), doing good deeds, and sharing with others (13:16). Paul uses *thysia* for the monetary gifts he has received from the Philippians (4:18). This term extends even further to refer to the entire Christian life as a "spiritual *sacrifice*" (1 Pet. 2:5; cf. Rom. 12:1). Paul's own life is a "sacrifice" of service to the Philippians (2:17). This important shift in meaning helps explain the decentralization of sacrifices from a single place of worship to the human heart. See *NIDNTT-A,* 254-57.

SAFETY

Old Testament

Noun: שָׁלוֹם (*šālôm*), GK 8934 (S 7965), 237x. *šālôm* is one of the most important words in the OT. In addition to "peace," this word can be translated as "prosperity, well-being, health, completeness, safety." See *peace*.

SAIL

New Testament

Verb: ἀνάγω (*anagō*), GK *343* (S *321*), 23x. *anagō* has a technical meaning "to sail, put out to sea." Luke uses this term to describe boats departing from shore. On numerous occasions Paul and his traveling companions "set sail" (e.g., Acts 13:13; 16:11; 18:21; 20:13). *anagō* can also mean "to bring, lead up"; See *bring up*.

SAINT

Old Testament

Adjective: קָדוֹשׁ (*qādôš*), GK 7705 (S 6918), 117x. Generally *qādôš* is translated as "holy," "holy one," or "saint." It describes that which is by nature sacred or that which has been admitted to the sphere of the sacred by divine rite. See *holy*.

New Testament

Noun: ἅγιος (*hagios*), GK *41* (S *34*, *40*), 233x. *hagios* is an adjective that means "holy," but it is used at least 45x as a substantive to designate "saints." Esp. in Paul's letters those who name Jesus as their Lord are called *hagioi* ("saints"; lit., "holy ones"). Paul tells the Ephesians, "you are no longer strangers and aliens, but you are fellow citizens with the saints and members of the household of God" (2:19). It is not that these people are holier than other people; rather, anyone who has been sanctified in Christ Jesus is, by virtue of that fact, "holy." The later practice of the church in naming certain Christians as "Saints" is not reflected in Scripture. See *holy*.

SALT

New Testament

Noun: ἅλας (*halas*), GK *229* (S *217*), 8x. *halas* refers to "salt," but it is used in fairly significant ways. Most of the occurrences of this word have to do with Jesus' statement that "salt is good, but if salt loses it saltiness, how can it be made salty again?" (Mk. 9:50; Lk. 14:34). Salt was used in the ancient world as a preservative, as something to flavor food, and sometimes in small amounts as a fertilizer. If we adopt these first two usages, Christians are to act as preservatives in the world by conforming to kingdom norms, and we are to help make life in this sin-filled world more palatable by our deeds of kindness and love. Christians are "the salt of the earth" (cf. Mt. 5:13).

Ordinary salt (sodium chloride) is a highly stable compound. The only way in which its value (saltiness) can be lost is if it is mixed with other substances. Thus, Jesus is instructing his followers here indirectly not to adopt the ways of the world, which will then make them lose their distinctiveness and unique task in the world of being salt in and to the world.

The final two uses of *halas* in the NT occur in Jesus' final statement in Mk. 9:50 ("Have *salt* in yourselves, and be at peace with each other") and in Col. 4:6 ("Let your conversation be always full of grace, seasoned with salt"). Both of these verses have to do with living a life of peace and harmony with one's fellow believers. In fact, in the ancient world, sometimes when a covenant was sealed between to parties, they would do so around a meal and the expression was used, "they had salt together." A similar usage is reflected in Acts 1:4, which records Jesus' final conversation with his disciples before his ascension. This took place "while he was eating with them," a phrase that literally translates, "while he was having salt together with them." See *NIDNTT-A*, 31-32.*

SALVATION

Old Testament

Noun: יְשׁוּעָה (y^e*šûʿâ*), GK 3802 (S 3444), 78x. y^e*šûʿâ* generally means "salvation, deliverance, Savior." Even more so than the verb *yāšaʿ* (see *save*), this noun is limited to God as Savior and the deliverance he brings.

(1) God, of course, is the one who has brought deliverance to his people from Egypt (Exod. 14:13); as the Song of Moses states, "the LORD ... has become my *salvation*" (15:2). The LORD likewise single-handedly brought deliverance to his people against the Moabites and Ammonites in the days of Jehoshaphat (2 Chr. 20:17).

(2) This noun is used 45x in the Psalms and 19x in Isaiah to proclaim the Lord's salvation of his people. While some of these may have as their background a time of physical danger for God's people, the spiritual implications of this word cannot be denied: "My soul will rejoice in the LORD and delight in his *salvation*" (Ps. 35:9); "surely God is my *salvation*; I will trust and not be afraid" (Isa. 12:2). God challenges his Servant to tell forth the message of his saving power: "How beautiful on the mountains are the feet of those ... who proclaim *salvation*" (Isa. 52:7). This Servant is primarily fulfilled in the beautiful ministry our Savior Jesus Christ, but then also in his servant people (Rom. 10:14–15). See *NIDOTTE*, 2:556–562; *NIDNTT-A*, 548–49.

Noun: תְּשׁוּעָה (*t^e^šû^c^â*), GK 9591 (S 8668), 34x. *t^e^šû^c^a means* "salvation, deliverance, victory." In the narrative portions of the OT, this noun often denotes a battle "victory" that God's people have achieved, but only with the help of the Lord (Jdg. 15:18; 1 Sam. 19:5; 2 Sam. 23:10, 12; 1 Ki. 13:17; 1 Chr. 11:14). This term occurs frequently in the Psalms, where the psalmist acknowledges the Lord's hand in "salvation" (Ps. 37:39) or asks for help from the Lord for "victory" (144:10). To put hope in human beings or even a horse "for deliverance" is senseless (33:17; 146:3), for only the Lord can be our "Savior" (38:22). Isaiah and Jeremiah say it all: "Israel will be saved by the Lord with an everlasting salvation" (Isa. 45:17); "surely in the Lord our God is the salvation of Israel" (Jer. 3:23). Note too the similarity of this word to *y^e^šû^c^â* (see salvation; Savior). See *NIDOTTE*, 2:556–62.

New Testament

Noun: σωτηρία (*sōtēria*), GK *5401* (S *4991*), 46x. *sōtēria* means "salvation."

(1) In the Gospels, *sōtēria* occurs 3x in the song of Zechariah, the father of John the Baptist (Lk. 1:69, 71, 75). Moreover, when Zacchaeus professes his faith in Jesus and offers to change his entire manner of living (yes, that is what salvation implies), Jesus said, "Today *salvation* has come to this house" (Lk. 19:9).

(2) As with the verb *sōzō* (see *save*) the apostle Paul, along with the book of Hebrews, demonstrates a full-orbed view of *sōtēria*. It is a past experience in Eph. 1:13, for the believers in Ephesus "heard the word of truth, the gospel of [their] *salvation*" (cf. Heb. 5:9), and so were saved (cf. Eph. 2:5, 8). In his letter to the Philippian believers, Paul instructs them to "work out your *salvation* with fear and trembling" (Phil. 2:12); that is, live out today in your life what it means that you are God's saved people (cf. Heb. 6:9). And in Rom. 13:11, Paul speaks of salvation as something that will not be completed until the final day: "our *salvation* is nearer now than when we first believed" (cf. 1 Thess. 5:9; Heb. 1:14).

(3) Salvation is something to sing about. This is why in Revelation, several heavenly songs ascribe salvation to God (Rev. 7:10; 12:10; 19:1). Nothing delights God more than to hear his people sing the great salvation songs. See *NIDNTT-A*, 549-51.

SANCTIFICATION

See *holy*.

SANCTIFY

Old Testament

Verb: קָדַשׁ (*qādaš*), GK 7727 (S 6942), 171x. *qādaš* describes the state of the sacred realm. Negatively, it represents that which is distinct from the common or profane. It is usually translated "make holy" (NIV), "sanctify," or "dedicate." A characteristic use of the verb is found in Num. 16:38, where the censers of the

Korahites are considered holy because they are presented before the Lord and "have become holy." They are thus regarded as having entered the sphere of the "holy" by virtue of following Moses' command (16:17) and are granted holiness (i.e., set-apartness) that disallows their being treated in a common way; thus, *qādaš* denotes the sphere of the "holy." In being set apart, these items became a testimony to God's holiness to Israel.

qādaš frequently describes the state or action of consecration in the rituals of the Levites. In Exod. 30:29 the Lord commands Moses to consecrate the utensils of the altar along with the altar itself "so they will be most holy, and whatever touches them will be holy" (cf. 29:37; Lev. 6:18, 27). These items are to be made holy by means of the Lord's "sacred anointing oil," of which the Lord says, "Do not pour it on men's bodies and do not make any oil with the same formula. It is sacred, and you are to consider it sacred" (30:31). Thus, the designations "sacred," "holy," and "consecrated" all convey the idea of separation from a profane status or common use.

Another example is Exod. 19:23, the consecration of Mount Sinai. Establishing boundaries around it served to keep out all who may have profaned God's holy presence.

Finally, the ethical connotations of holiness find their basis in the proscriptions against confusing the spheres of the holy and the common (Lev. 22:32). See *NIDOTTE,* 3:877-887.

New Testament

Verb: ἁγιάζω (*hagiazō*), GK *39* (S *37*), 28x. *hagiazō* is usually rendered "make holy, sanctify, consecrate." In the NT this verb expresses the action of including a person or a thing in the sphere of what is holy in either a ritual (ceremonial) and moral sense. See *make holy*.

Adjective: ἅγιος (*hagios*), GK *41* (S *40* & *39*), 233x. In general, two facts stand out in the NT regarding *hagios* ("holy, sacred"). First, God and what is associated with him is declared as "holy." Second, the proper sphere of the holy in the NT is not the priestly or ritual but the prophetic. See *holy*.

SANCTUARY

Old Testament

Noun: מִקְדָּשׁ (*miqdāš*), GK 5219 (S 4720), 75x. *miqdās* comes from the Hebrew root *qdš*, which is a term for distinction between the sacred and profane. Translated variously as "sanctuary, shrine, holy place," *miqdās* most often refers to Israel's sanctuary of worship, wherein offerings and sacrifices are made to the Lord (e.g., Exod. 15:17; 25:8; Lev. 16:33; 21:12). The building complex of the *miqdās* is comprised of various parts, including the Holy Place and the Most Holy Place. In other contexts, *miqdās* refers to the sacred objects within the sanctuary (Num. 10:21; cf. 3:31–32). It can also denote the precincts within the tabernacle or temple complex (Exod. 25:8; Lev. 21:23; Ps. 73:17; Jer. 51:51). See *NIDOTTE*, 2:1078-87.

SANDAL

New Testament

Noun: ὑπόδημα (*hypodēma*), GK *5687* (S *5266*), 10x. *hypodēma* means "sandal." Half of the uses of this noun occur in references to John the Baptist, who accepted his place as the forerunner of Jesus when he said, "After me will come one who is more powerful than I, whose sandals I am not fit to carry [or untie]" (Mt. 3:11; cf. Mk. 1:7; Lk. 3:16; Jn. 1:27; Acts 13:25). When Jesus sends out his disciples on their mission, he instructs them to take no "sandals" (Mt. 10:10; Lk. 10:4; 22:35). In the parable of the lost son, the loving father puts a ring on his son's hand and "sandals" on his feet (Lk. 15:22). In Stephen's sermon, he tells the story of Moses, who was instructed to take off his "sandals" at the burning bush, because he was standing on holy ground (Acts 7:33).*

SANHEDRIN

New Testament

Noun: συνέδριον (*synedrion*), GK *5284* (S *4892*), 22x. *synedrion* can mean a "governing board, council," "an official session of a council," "the meeting room where the council session takes place," or, more specifically, "the high council in Jerusalem." The term is found only in the narrative sections of the NT (Gospels and Acts) where councils and meetings are described as taking place.

In biblical times the official "Sanhedrin" was a council composed of 71 members, with the Jewish high priest as chairman. This official council included the heads of the priestly families, leaders of the lay aristocracy (the elders), and a number of the scribes. Thus, in the NT the term most often refers to that group that interrogated Jesus (Jn. 11:47) or examined several disciples after Jesus' return to glory (Acts 4; 5:17–41; 6:8–7:60; 22:30–23:10, 20, 28; 24:20).

But *synedrion* can also refer more loosely to any type of "council" meeting, as when Jesus declares that Christians may have to face a council because of their faithful witness to him (Mt. 10:17). Even today Christians face versions of a "council" in their own contexts, whether that be on the mission field in countries that are anti-Christian, or more metaphorically at school or the work place, where peers and colleagues "judge" their lives and faithful witness to Jesus Christ. See *NIDNTT-A*, 544-45.

SATAN

New Testament

Noun: Σατανᾶς (*Satanas*), GK *4928* (S *4567*), 36x. *Satanas* is a Gk. word formed from the Heb. word *śāṭān*, which means "adversary." It is the name given to the ruler of evil spirits. In the NT "Satan" is a personal name for this diabolical creature, while "the devil" is more like a title. Therefore, while Matthew records that "the devil" tempts Jesus in the desert, when Jesus directly addresses the devil, he called him "Satan" (Mt. 4:10). Of its 36x in the NT, 34x refer to this literal, evil being. In the other two places, Jesus called Peter "Satan," not because Satan possesses him, but because through Peter Satan is attempting to thwart Jesus' journey to the cross (Mt. 16:23; Mk. 8:33).

In the book of Job Satan is shown in detail: he is a heavenly being who, at least in OT times, could appear with the angels in God's presence (Job 1:6; 2:1). He can be in only one place at a time (Job 1:7; 2:2), accuses righteous people (1:9–11; see Zech. 3:1), and destroys anything God allows him to destroy (1:12ff; 2:4ff.). These attributes of Satan are reaffirmed in the NT: he is a tempter (1 Cor. 7:5), a liar and murderer (Jn. 8:44), a betrayer (Lk. 22:3), a perpetual sinner (1 Jn. 3:8), an accuser of Christians (Rev. 12:10), full of hate (1 Pet. 5:8; 1 Jn. 3:10), and conceited (1 Tim. 3:6). People who do live that sort of lifestyle—even those who preach a false christ, Spirit, and gospel—are considered Satan's servants (2 Cor. 11:13–15). Satan is also known as the evil one (Mt. 5:37), Beelzebub and the prince of demons (12:24), the dragon and the ancient serpent (Rev. 12:9), the ruler of this world (Jn. 12:31), and the prince of the power of the air (Eph. 2:2).

Satan longs to bring suffering on anyone (Lk. 13:16), especially on believers (Rev. 12:17). He is a devious schemer (2 Cor. 2:11), masquerading as "an angel of light" (11:14), while even snatching the gospel from some who hear it (Mk. 4:15). He has power over unbelievers, though they can be released to the power of God through the preaching of the gospel (Acts 26:18). Satan "casts into the heart" of people the thought to sin (Jn. 13:2; Acts 5:3). He longs to snatch away Jesus' true followers, but he must ask permission before he acts (Lk. 22:31). Even when given permission, Jesus' prayers are effective to restore what Satan attempts to destroy (Lk. 22:32; cf. 1 Cor. 5:5).

Jesus triumphs over Satan in his earthly work, death, resurrection, and ascension (Mt. 12:28–29; Lk. 10:18; Rev. 12:7–12), and Satan's final end is sure (Rev. 20:7–10). But in the interim he is still active, hindering people from going places (1 Thess. 2:18), empowering people to perform signs and wonders that deceive unbelievers (2 Thess. 2:10), guiding young widows away from the church (1 Tim. 5:15), bringing tribulation and slander on Christians through his religious servants (Rev. 2:9), and even being behind governments that persecute Christians (2:13). Yet Satan remains subservient to God. He is even used by God to mete out divine punishment on sinful church members (1 Cor. 5:5; 1 Tim. 1:20) and to keep God's closest servants holy in humility (2 Cor. 12:7).

In the meantime, forgiveness of those who have wronged us can keep us from being "outwitted by Satan" (2 Cor. 2:10–11). A man and wife who give to each other their God-given conjugal rights will help keep Satan from tempting them through their lack of self-control (1 Cor. 7:5). Satan's end is sure, and God will conquer him through Christ's body, the church: "May the God of peace soon crush Satan under your feet" (Rom. 16:20). See *NIDNTT-A*, 133-34.

(BE) SATISFIED, SATISFY

Old Testament

Verb: שָׂבַע (*śāba*ʿ), GK 8425 (S 7646), 97x. The verb *śāba*ʿ means "to be satisfied, have enough, be filled," generally of food rather than drink (see Exod. 16:8; Deut. 8:10; Ruth 2:14; Neh. 9:25; Ps. 37:19; Jer. 44:17; Ezek. 7:19; Joel 2:26). However, it can also refer to realities like the earth being satisfied with water (Job 38:27), trees receiving abundance of water (Ps. 104:16), and animals and living creatures receiving nourishment (Ps. 104:28, 145:16). *śāba*ʿ is often used figuratively to refer to age, as when one is "old and *full* of years" (1 Chr. 23:1).

*śāba*ʿ can be used with spiritual implications as well. The psalmist in a time of spiritual unrest prays to the Lord and admits he will be spiritually "*satisfied* with seeing your likeness" (Ps. 17:15; cf. 63:5). Moses prays in Ps. 90:14 for the Lord to "*satisfy* us in morning with your unfailing love" (cf. 91:16; 103:5). Apart from God, the writer of Ecclesiastes acknowledges that "the eye never *has enough* of seeing" the weariness of this life (Eccl. 1:8). In a negative sense, God's judgment can be expressed by "filling" Jerusalem with bitter herbs (Lam. 3:15). For those who get their neighbors drunk in order to take advantage of them, "they *will be filled* with shame instead of glory" (Hab. 2:16). In Ezek. 39:20, the Lord promises Israel, "At my table you *will eat your fill* of horses and riders," denoting his vengeance against Gog. Moreover, Prov. 27:20 admits that Death (Sheol) and Destruction (Abaddon) "are never *satisfied*," continually requiring more souls (Prov. 27:20), and the haughty man "enlarges his appetite like Sheol, and he is like death, never *satisfied*" (Hab. 2:5). See *NIDOTTE*, 3:1209–14.

New Testament

Verb: χορτάζω (*chortazō*), GK *5963* (S *5526*), 16x. *chortazō* often refers in the NT to the satisfying of one's physical appetite for food (Mt. 14:20; 15:33, 37; Jn. 6:26; Phil. 4:12; Jas. 2:16; Rev. 19:21). In the parable of the rich man and Lazarus, Lazarus longs to be "satisfied" with the crumbs falling from the rich man's table (Lk. 16:21). Similarly, in the parable of the prodigal son, the rebellious son wants to "satisfy" his appetite by eating the pigs' food (Lk. 15:16).

The satisfying of one's physical appetites is sometimes used in the NT as a metaphor for the satisfying of one's spiritual appetites (Mk. 7:27), just as in the OT (e.g., Ps. 63:5, "My soul is satisfied as with marrow and fatness"). When Jesus promises in the Sermon on the Mount that those who "hunger and thirst for righteousness" will be "satisfied" (Mt. 5:6; Lk. 6:21), he powerfully uses physical hunger and thirst as metaphors for spiritual appetites. Importantly, the future tense of Jesus' promise ("*will* be satisfied") points to the end of time and the return of Jesus as the only time when the spiritual appetites of men and women will be fully and lastingly satisfied. The truth that only God can ultimately satisfy spiritual appetites is expressed in the famous words of St. Augustine: "You have made us for yourself, and our hearts are restless until they rest in you" (*Confessions* 1.1). C. S. Lewis articulated the same truth: "If I find in myself a desire which no experience in this world can satisfy, the most probable explanation is that I was made for another world" (*Mere Christianity*). See *NIDNTT-A*, 607-8.

SAVE

Old Testament

Verb: יָשַׁע (*yāšaʿ*), GK 3828 (S 3467), 184x. Often translated "to save, rescue, deliver," the basic meaning of *yāšaʿ* is to deliver or save human beings from a time of danger, often from personal enemies or from a time of sickness.

(1) In a few instances in the OT, this verb has a human being as a subject. Moses rescues the seven daughters of Jethro from shepherds who are trying to take the water that the women have drawn for their sheep (Exod. 2:17). Often in ancient treaties, the parties agree to help save each other from hostile enemies (Jos. 10:6; Jdg. 12:1–3; 2 Ki. 16:7), and soldiers seek to "rescue" each other in order to win in a battle (2 Sam. 10:11).

(2) But the majority of instances of *yāšaʿ* in the OT have God or the Lord as the subject. In the narratives of the Exodus, "the LORD *saved* his people from the hands of the Egyptians" (Exod. 14:30). Once in the land of Canaan, God raised up judges to "save" his people from their enemy nations around them (Jdg. 2:16, 18; 6:14). Even if the actual deliverance comes through a human leader or warrior, the Israelites know that God is ultimately the one who delivers. This theme of the Lord as a God who saves is prominent in the Prophets (Isa. 33:22; 45:17; Jer. 30:10–11) and in the Psalms (Ps. 20:6; 34:6). The psalmists frequently cry out to God for salvation and deliverance from their enemies (Ps. 3:7; 54:1; 109:26; the verb occurs 23x in Psalms in the imperative).

(3) While "spiritual deliverance" is not a prominent topic in the OT per se, the oracles of salvation in the Prophets imply a salvation that is beyond the here and now. For example, when the Lord raises up his righteous Branch, the King who will reign wisely, "Judah will be *saved* and Israel will live in safety" (Jer. 23:6). God, Israel's Savior, will "save" Israel "with an everlasting salvation" (Isa. 45:17). Such passages look ahead to the saving power of Jesus. See also *salvation*.

Verb: מָלַט (*mālaṭ*), GK 4880 (S 4422), 94x. *mālaṭ* means to "escape, flee to safety," and it may also be translated in the passive "to be delivered, rescued, or saved." Note Joel 2:32, "And everyone who calls on the name of the LORD *will be saved.*" See *escape*.

Verb: נָצַל (*nāṣal*), GK 5911 (S 5337), 213x. For the most part, *nāṣal* means "save, rescue, deliver, take away."

(1) Some uses of this word occur on a human level. Reuben is not in favor of what his brothers are doing to Joseph, and his plan is "to *rescue* him from their hands" (Gen. 37:21–22). Jacob prays to "be delivered" from Esau, his estranged brother (32:11).

nāṣal can also indicate the recovery of possessions or objects that have been lost or plundered. Jephthah warns the king of the Ammonites against taking advantage of the Lord's people, inquiring of him, "While Israel lived in Heshbon and its villages … three hundred years, why did you not *recover* [the lands] at that time?" (Jdg. 11:26). When the Amalekites raid Ziklag and plunder David's possessions and take his people as captives, David asks God whether or not to pursue. God's answer was, "Pursue; for you shall surely overtake and shall surely *rescue*" (1 Sam. 30:8). One of the responsibilities of a king is to deliver people from oppression (2 Sam. 14:6).

(2) Most uses of *nāṣal*, however, is deliverance that God performs. No one can "deliver" out of God's hand (Deut. 32:39), for he is all-powerful. His greatest action of deliverance in the OT is his rescuing his people from slavery in Egypt. "I have observed the misery of my people who are in Egypt; I have heard their cry … and I

have come down *to deliver* them from the Egyptians" (Exod. 3:7–8). This deliverance serves as the foundation of Israel's relationship with God and prefigures the deliverance from sin God accomplishes through the death and resurrection of Jesus. The comparison between the Exodus and the cross are striking theologically. God's deliverance is complete—the people never go back to Egypt to serve as slaves. It is unmerited—Israel is chosen and rescued because of God's faithfulness to the promises made to the patriarchs, not because they are worthy or holy. God is the sole actor in both events—he accomplishes salvation exclusively by his own power.

The Lord not only delivers his people as a group, but he also delivers individuals from specific dangers. David, for example, is rescued from wild animals (1 Sam. 17:37) and from the hand of Saul (2 Sam. 12:7). In the Psalter, the Lord is always the one to whom appeal is made for deliverance: from violent people, from liars, or other enemies (e.g., Ps. 7:1; 25:20; 31:15; 59:1; 71:2). The psalmist often praises and thanks God for past deliverances (33:19; 34:4; 35:10; 106:43; 107:6).

(3) The prophetic rebuke of Israel's sin, however, shows deliverance in an ironic light. Instead of delivering his people from their enemies (such as Egypt), God now delivers his unrepentant, sinful people into the hands of their enemies, into exile. "They have become a prey with no one to *rescue*" (Isa. 42:22). Amos declares the irony of Israel's rejection of God by their immoral and wicked behavior: "Hear this word that the LORD has spoken against you, O people of Israel.... As the shepherd *rescues* from the mouth of the lion two legs, or a piece of an ear, so shall the people of Israel who live in Samaria be *rescued*, with the corner of a couch and a part of a bed" (Amos 3:1, 12).

This deliverance to exile is not the final word, however. Ezekiel uses the image of the shepherd to prophecy the profound delight of God's restoring his people from exile: "I *will rescue* them from all the places where they were scattered" (Ezek. 34:12). Jesus alludes to himself as the great deliverer promised in Isa. 61, who has come to fulfill to the uttermost God's deliverance of all people (Lk. 4:16–21). See *NIDOTTE*, 3:141–47.

New Testament

Verb: σῴζω (*sōzō*), GK *5392* (S *4982*), 106x. *sōzo* means "to save, rescue, heal." For the most part, this verb denotes our being spiritually saved from sin, though in some instances the verb means to heal a person from an illness (see *heal*) or to rescue someone from danger (see *rescue*).

(1) The majority of uses of this verb in the NT are about being saved from the guilt and power of sin. Salvation (see *salvation*) takes place in the name of Jesus (a name that is based on the Heb. word *yāšaʿ*; see above): "There is no other name under heaven given to men by which we must *be saved*" (Acts 4:12). God did not send his Son into the world to condemn the world but "to *save* the world through him" (Jn. 3:17).

(2) The most complete teaching about *sōzo* occurs in the letters of Paul. He uses this verb 29x in his letters and with a variety of nuances. In Rom. 8:24, Paul uses the Greek aorist tense (simple past tense) to indicate that when people believed in Jesus, they "were *saved*." In Eph. 2:5, 8, he uses the Greek perfect tense: "By grace you *have been saved*." This particular tense in the Greek language emphasizes a past action that has an ongoing effect in our personal lives. In Rom. 5:9–10, Paul uses the future tense twice to say that believers "*shall ... be saved* from God's wrath through [Christ]," referring to our ultimate salvation on the judgment day. And in 1 Cor. 15:2, Paul uses the present tense, that by the gospel believers "*are being saved*." While we tend to think of salvation as a past event ("When were you saved?"), for Paul salvation involves a past event, a present experience, and a future hope. See *NIDNTT-A*, 549-51.

SAVIOR

Old Testament

Noun: יְשׁוּעָה (y^e*šû*ʿ*â*), GK 3802 (S 3444), 78x. y^e*šû*ʿ*â* generally means "salvation, deliverance, Savior." Even more so than the verb *yāša*ʿ (see *save*), this noun is limited to God as Savior and the deliverance he brings. See *salvation*.

New Testament

Noun: σωτήρ (*sōtēr*), GK *5400* (S *4990*), 24x. Whereas in the OT the noun *yešû*ʿ*a* ("Savior") describes Israel's God, in the NT *sōtēr* becomes a title for Jesus. The angel in Bethlehem announced the birth of a "Savior" in the town of David (Lk. 2:11). The townspeople in Sychar, after meeting Jesus, told the Samaritan woman, "We know that this man really is the *Savior* of the world" (Jn. 4:42). Typical in the NT letters are references to "our *Savior* Jesus Christ" (Tit. 1:4; 2:13; 2 Pet. 3:18). See *save* and *salvation*.

SAY

Old Testament

Verb: אָמַר (ʾ*āmar*), GK 606 (S 559), 5316x. ʾ*āmar* is the most common verb in the OT for "to say, utter, speak."

(1) ʾ*āmar* is used thousands of times for two or more people speaking within a story. For example, the serpent *says* to the woman, "Did God really *say* …" (Gen. 3:1; cf. 1:22; 4:6; 31:8; 44:16; 45:17; Num. 10:29; 22:28; Jos. 10:12; 2 Sam. 2:21; Isa. 49:20; Mal. 1:7). Melchizedek blesses Abram by what he *says*: "Blessed be Abram by God Most High" (Gen. 14:19; cf. 21:12; Exod. 4:1; Jdg. 9:8; Job 3:2). God *speaks* to Abraham not to worry about Hagar and Ishmael (Gen. 21:12). The psalmist describes adversaries of the Lord as those who "*speak* of you with evil intent; your adversaries misuse your name" (Ps. 139:20). Enemies were *saying* to the psalmist all day long, "Where is your God?" (42:10).

(2) ʾ*āmar* can also used to introduce something that is uttered verbally, as in Deut. 27:15b, "Then all the people shall *say*, 'Amen.' " In the story of creations, God *says*, "Let there be light" (Gen. 1:3)—and when God speaks, things happen ("and there was light").

(3) ʾ*āmar* also has a variety of other nuances. The term used in the phrase "say in the heart," which is often translated "think" (e.g., Deut. 8:17–18; see *think*). It also indicates something that is promised (e.g., 1 Chr. 27:23; see *promise*). And it sometimes indicates a command or an instruction (e.g., Jos. 11:9).

Verb: דָּבַר (*dābar*), GK 1819 (S 1696), 1136x. *dābar* ("say, speak") is used hundreds of times for both the human and the divine activity of speaking. See *word*.

New Testament

Verb: λαλέω (*laleō*), GK *3281* (S *2980*), 296x. The dominant word used in the NT for speaking is *legō* (see *say*). *laleō* appears one-tenth as much. See *speak*.

Verb: λέγω (*legō*), GK *3306* (S *3004*, *2036*, *2046*), 2353x. Usually translated as "say," *legō* has at least four distinct nuances in the NT.

(1) *legō* can mean to express oneself orally or in written form, "to say, tell." This is the routine usage of this verb. Often *legō* is used in this sense with an indication of what is said, "he *told* this parable" (Lk. 13:6). At other times there is an indication of the person or thing about which something is said, "they knew he *was talking* about them" (Mt. 21:45).

(2) *legō* can mean to express oneself in a specific way, "to say." In this sense, the "saying" may be a question, answer, command, etc. "Then John's disciples came and *asked* him, 'How is it that we and the Pharisees fast, but your disciples do not fast?'" (Mt. 9:14). "Again he *asked* them, 'Who is it you want?' And they said, 'Jesus of Nazareth'" (Jn. 18:17). "Why do you call me 'Lord, Lord,' and not do what I *tell* you? (Lk. 6:46). *legō* can also signify what is said in written communication (1 Cor. 6:5).

(3) *legō* can mean to inform about or to tell something, that is, "to speak, to report." In this sense, Jesus commands that a miracle not be reported publicly, "Jesus commanded them not to *tell* anyone" (Mk.

7:36; cf. 1:30; 8:30; Lk. 9:31; Acts 1:3; Eph. 5:12; Phil. 3:18).

(4) *legō* can mean to identify in a specific manner, "to name, call." This usage of *legō* involves identifying someone with a name or attribute. In this sense, Jesus asked, "Why do you *call* me good?" (Mk. 10:18). "David *calls* him 'Lord'" (Mk. 12:37). Jesus was known to *call* God his Father (Jn. 5:18). Sometimes the term has the sense of "so-called": "For even if there are so-called gods" (1 Cor. 8:5; cf. Eph. 2:11). See *NIDNTT-A*, 339-43.

Verb: φημί (*phēmi*), GK *5774* (S *5346*), 66x. *phēmi* means "to say, declare, answer, reply." Most uses of this verb are in narrative parts of the NT, especially when there is conversation between two parties—one person asks, and another person "replies" (Mt. 13:28; 25:21; Acts 2:38; 7:2). Paul uses this verb occasionally to make a solemn "declaration," such as "the time is short" (1 Cor. 7:29) or "flesh and blood cannot inherit the kingdom of heaven" (15:50).

SAY BEFORE

New Testament

Verb: προλέγω (*prolegō*), GK *4625* (S *4302*, *4277*, *4280*), 15x. *prolegō* refers to saying something in advance of an event: *pro* is "before" and *legō* is "to say." Thus, the literal rendering is in keeping with the word's etymology, "to say beforehand." Prophetic utterance is a "speaking beforehand" of what will come to pass (Mt. 24:25; Mk. 13:23; Jude 17). For the NT writers, the OT Scriptures were words spoken beforehand by the Holy Spirit—the Scripture had to be fulfilled which the Holy Spirit *spoke long ago* through the mouth of David" (Acts 1:16; cf. Rom. 9:29; Heb. 4:7; 2 Pet. 3:2). In the NT, the verb often carries with it the idea of warning, "I have *warned* you, and I *warn* you again now" (2 Cor. 13:2; cf. Gal. 5:21; 1 Thess. 3:4). See *NIDNTT-A*, 339-343.

SCATTER

Old Testament

Verb: פּוּץ (*pûṣ*), GK 7046 (S 6327), 65x. *pûṣ* denotes the act of dispersing an object or group of persons and may be translated "scatter." The term conveys divine judgment in the scattering of humanity at the Tower of Babel (Gen. 10:18; 11:8–9). Theologically, the verb is used to describe the scattering of God's people by means of the exile (Ezek. 34:6; Jer. 23:3; Zech. 13:7; cf. also Mt. 26:31; Mk. 14:27). This portrayal is first introduced in Deut. 4:27 (see also 28:64; 30:3). The term also conveys the scattering of the pieces of an object that have been smashed by a hammer (Jer. 23:29). Ultimately, the promised restoration or "gathering" of the scattered sheep promised in Deut. 30:1–3 is fulfilled in Christ (Isa. 40:11; Ezek. 34:5; Jn. 10:11; 1 Pet. 5:4). See *NIDOTTE*, 3:585-89.

Verb: פָּרַשׂ (*pāraś*), GK 7298 (S 6566), 67x. *pāraś* broadly means "to spread (something) out" and is used in a variety of contexts (see *spread*). But at times this verb is used in a more chaotic fashion, carrying the idea of "scattering." For instance, sheep can be scattered (Ezek. 34:12). God scatters both people (Ps. 68:15; Ezek. 17:21; Zech. 2:10) and lightning (Job 36:30).

New Testament

Verb: διασπείρω (*diaspeirō*), GK *1401* (S *1289*), 3x.

Verb: διασκορπίζω (*diaskorpizō*), GK *1399* (S *1287*), 9x. Both of these verbs mean "to scatter." *diaspeirō* is the verb from which the word "Diaspora" is derived (the word used for the scattering of the Jews after the exile to Babylon). In the NT, *diaspeiro* is used only for the scattering of Christians that took place after persecution arose against them in Jerusalem (Acts 8:1, 4; 11:19). *diaskorpizō* is used once for the "scattered children of God" (Jn. 11:52), but it is used more often in parables, such as the scattering of seed (Mt. 25:24, 26) or the squandering of wealth (Lk. 15:13; 16:1). It is also used in the quotation of Zech. 13:7 in Mt. 26:31 and Mk. 14:27: "I will strike the shepherd and the sheep of the flock will be scattered."

SCEPTER

Old Testament

Noun: שֵׁבֶט (*šēbeṭ*), GK 8657 (S 7626), 190x. *šēbeṭ* means "rod, scepter, or tribe." See *rod.*

New Testament

Noun: ῥάβδος (*rhabdos*), GK *4811* (S *4464*), 12x. *rhabdos* refers to a "staff, rod, scepter." See *staff.*

SCORCH

New Testament

Verb: ξηραίνω (*xērainō*), GK *3830* (S *3583*), 15x. *xērainō* denotes the "scorching" or "drying up" of something, usually due to the sun. See *dry up.*

SCRIBE

Old Testament

Noun: סֹפֵר (*sōpēr*), GK 6221 (S 5608), 54x. *sōpēr* means "scribe, secretary." This term can describe any sort of official writer. Frequently in the OT we know the names of these people (e.g., Jeremiah's secretary is Baruch, Jer. 36:32; Hezekiah's secretary is Shebna, 2 Ki. 18:37; Isa. 36:3, 22). They must be skilled in writing, and their role is to accurately write down anything that they are told to write down, usually for records' sake.

sōpēr is a title ascribed to Ezra (Ezr. 7:6, 11; Neh. 8:1, 4, 13), who not only knows how to read and write but also how to teach and expound on God's law. Eventually scribes like Ezra copied down the Scriptures, to preserve them from generation to generation. Since accuracy of dealing with God's Word is so important, Jeremiah takes the scribes of his day to task for mishandling the law of God ("the lying pen of the *scribes* has handled it falsely," Jer. 8:8). See *NIDOTTE*, 4:1289–90.

New Testament

Noun: γραμματεύς (*grammateus*), GK *1208* (S *1122*), 63x. A *grammateus* is a teacher of the law, an expert in legal issues, a scribe. "Ezra … was a scribe well versed in the law of Moses that the LORD the God of Israel had given" (Ezr. 7:6). Scribes served to interpret Scripture as well as to equip their students with appropriate methods of interpretation. Their role blossomed during the Exile, at which time they were in charge of the studying, copying, and collating the Hebrew Scriptures.

In contrast with the priesthood (which was hereditary), becoming a scribe was open to anyone. Students sat at the feet of a famous teacher and memorized his teachings. Jesus was addressed as "rabbi" (Mk. 9:5; 10:51; 11:21; 14:45), a title indicating scribal authority, although he was not an accredited scribe. Scribes frequently debated with Jesus (Mk. 2:6, 16; 3:22; 9:11; 12:28, 32, 35). Often in opposing him they inadvertently displayed the profound contrast between their "learnedness" and the "ignorance" of the common people, who believed the words of Jesus and were entering the kingdom of God. Only once does this word occur outside of the gospels and Acts (see "scholar" in 1 Cor. 1:20).

Although Nicodemus was a teacher in Israel and sought counsel from Jesus, he was soundly rebuked for his lack of understanding about the kind of kingdom in which God rules (Jn. 3:4). Jesus underscores the foolishness of those who know the Scriptures but reject him. He says to the crowd, "You search the Scriptures because you think that in them you have eternal life; and it is they that testify on my behalf. Yet you refuse to come to me to have life" (Jn. 5:39–40). See *NIDNTT-A*, 111-13.

SCRIPTURE

New Testament

Verb: γράφω (*graphō*), GK *1211* (S *1125*), 191x. *graphō* generally means "to write" Of the many uses of *graphō* in the NT, over half refer to the Scriptures. The term is used about 70x in an introductory formula—e.g., "as it is written" (cf. Lk. 2:23; Rom. 2:24; 1 Cor. 1:31)—followed by a quotation from the OT. The verb occurs 17x in conjunction with an allusion to the OT rather than a direct quotation (e.g., Acts 13:29). See *write, writing.*

Noun: γραφή (*graphē*), GK *1210* (S *1124*), 50x.

The noun *graphē* is unique in the NT in that it solely refers to the Scriptures of Israel. In the sing., the noun can refer to a specific portion of the Scriptures (Mk. 12:10; Lk. 4:21; Jn. 13:18) or to the Scriptures as a whole (Jn. 20:29), but in the pl., it always refers to the latter (Mt. 21:42; Mk. 14:49; Jn. 5:39; 2 Pet. 3:16).

A theologically significant text that uses both the noun *graphē* (3x) and the verb *graphō* (2x) is Lk. 24:13–49 (cf. vv. 27, 32, 44–46). Jesus considers the Jewish Scriptures (i.e., the OT) to contain three main parts, which he designates as the Law, the Prophets, and the Psalms (24:27; the latter designation is probably shorthand for the entire section of the Writings). Each of these divisions, Jesus says, speak of him (cf. Mt. 5:17). Clearly, the OT anticipates Jesus Christ, who is the ultimate subject matter of Scripture and whose mission, message, and person provide the foundation and lens for understanding the Scriptures. See *NIDNTT-A*, 113-116.

SCROLL

Old Testament

Noun: סֵפֶר (*sēper*), GK 6219 (S 5612), 191x. *sēper* means "book, scroll." It essentially denotes any written document. See *book*.

New Testament

Noun: βιβλίον (*biblion*), GK *1046* (S *975*), 34x. *biblion* refers to a "book, scroll, writing." See *book*.

Noun: βίβλος (*biblos*), GK *1047* (S *976*), 10x. *biblos* refers to a "book, scroll, writing." See *book*.

SEA

Old Testament

Noun: יָם (*yām*), GK 3542 (S 3220), 396x. *yām* means "sea." In the ancient world, the sea was considered a place of chaos and hostility and was often feared as an unruly monster. This background helps to explain why the term comes from a root that means "to roar" (cf. Ps. 98:7).

In the OT, *yām* is used in naming different bodies of water. The Great Sea (also the "western sea"), the Red Sea, and the Dead Sea all play key roles in the biblical narrative (Exod. 13:18; Num. 34:3, 6–7; Deut. 11:24). *yām* is sometimes used to connote a westerly direction because of the location of the Mediterranean Sea with regard to the land of Israel (Gen. 12:8; Exod. 26:22; Jos. 8:9; Isa. 11:14; Ezek. 41:12; Zech. 14:4). The sea can praise the Lord (Ps. 69:34; 96:11), illustrate vast or boundless measurement (Job 11:9; Ps. 139:9; Hab. 2:14), and even symbolize the extent of God's forgiveness: "You will again have compassion on us; you will tread our sins underfoot and hurl all our iniquities into the depths of *the sea*" (Mic. 7:19). *yām* was also used with reference to the cultic vessel that served ceremonially to purify priests serving in the temple (i.e., the "bronze sea"; 2 Ki. 25:13; 1 Chr. 18:8; Jer. 52:17).

In the ancient view of the world, the sea was considered one of the major divisions of the universe (heavens, earth, sea). Whereas the pagan accounts of creation involved a battle between gods to explain the origins of the universe, the God of the OT created the world through the power of his word. In ancient mythology, the sea was referred to as a monster that could only be defeated by the collaboration of several gods. The OT, however, presents the beast of the sea, Leviathan, as entirely subject to the Lord (Job 41:1; Ps. 74:13–14; 104:26; Isa. 27:1). The parting of the Red Sea (Exod. 14:1–31) would have been understood as a further demonstration of God's absolute power and authority. No other God could do what the Lord did (Exod. 15:11). The chaotic and menacing power of the sea, which was reckoned among the most powerful gods of the ancient world, was subject to the command of the sovereign Creator of the universe (Job 9:8; 38:8; Ps. 33:7; 78:13; 89:9; 95:5; Prov. 8:29; Amos 9:6; Jon. 1:11–12). When the Israelites crossed the Jordan to enter the promised land, God repeated this miracle with the Jordan River to remind them of their past and to secure their future (Jos. 3:10–13; Ps. 114:3–7). The God who acted for them in Egypt would fight for his people in Canaan. See *NIDOTTE*, 2:461-46.

New Testament

Noun: θάλασσα (*thalassa*), GK *2498* (S *2281*), 91x. *thalassa* denotes a large body of water, such as a sea or ocean. In Gk. literature it was typically a larger body of water than a *limnē* ("lake"). However, with the exception of Luke, this distinction is not observed in the NT. *thalassa* is used for the Sea of Galilee (Mt. 4:18, 15:29; Mk. 1:16, 7:31; Jn. 6:1; but cf. Luke's use of *limnē* in Lk. 5:1, 2), the Red Sea (Acts 7:36; Heb. 11:29), and the Sea of Tiberias (Jn. 21:1).

Although *thalassa* usually simply denotes a physical body of water, it also has deeper theological significance. In Acts 4:24 it is one part of the tripartite view of the created world: heavens, earth, and sea (cf. Exod. 20:4). Likewise in Revelation it is one of the three parts of the cosmos or created order (Rev. 5:13; 10:6). This imagery draws on the ancient Near Eastern notion that a sea existed above the skies (which was the source of rain) as well as below the earth. In this view of the created world, *thalassa* symbolized chaos and death. The skies and the earth were created out of the sea—order was brought out of chaos (a hint of this is in Gen. 1:1–2). It is especially significant for the biblical worldview that when the new heaven and new earth appear, there will no longer be a *thalassa*, which indicates that all things will be in order, and chaos will no longer exist (Rev. 21:1). Another symbolic use of *thalassa* is the "crystal sea" before the throne of God (4:6; 15:2). See *NIDNTT-A*, 236.

SEAL

New Testament

Verb: σφραγίζω (*sphragizō*), GK *5381* (S *4972*), 15x. *sphragizō* means "to seal." Ancient documents were often sealed using a waxy substance not only to close them up and thereby protect the contents but also to authenticate the document by imprinting the seal (called a bulla) of the writer in the soft wax (cf. Jer. 32:11). This verb is used in both literal and figurative senses.

In a literal sense, Jesus' tomb was "made ... secure by putting a seal on the stone and posting the guard" (Mt. 27:66). This verb is also used in the sense of sealing something in order to make it (temporarily) inaccessible (see Rev. 10:4; 20:3; 22:10).

In a figurative sense, *sphragizō* certifies the truth of something (Jn. 3:33; cf. Rom. 15:28), and particularly the approval of God (Jn. 6:27; Rev. 7:3–5, 8). Paul says that believers "are sealed" with the Holy Spirit as a "deposit guaranteeing what is to come" (2 Cor. 1:22; cf. Eph. 1:13). In addition to marking believers as authentic, the Holy Spirit "*has sealed* [believers] for the day of redemption" (Eph. 4:13). See *NIDNTT-A*, 546-547.*

Noun: σφραγις (*sphragis*), GK *5382* (S *4973*), 16x. The noun *sphragis* is used in the same way as the verb *sphragizō* (see above). A seal in the ancient world established and expressed ownership (Gen. 4:15; Exod. 13:9; Deut. 6:8; Ezek. 9:4; Rev. 9:4; 13:16–17). Cattle or slaves could be marked by a seal as property. Such marks could also be used to convey authority (Gen. 41:42; Isa. 22:22; Est. 3:10).

In the NT, seven seals are found on the heavenly scroll that only Christ is able to open (Rev. 5:1, 2, 5, 9; 6:1, 3, 5, 7, 9, 12; 8:1). His ability to open them symbolizes the authority given to him. Abraham's circumcision is described as "a seal of the righteousness that he had by faith while he was still uncircumcised" (Rom. 4:11). In this case, the *sphragis* is a mark indicating that one authentically belonged to God (cf. also Rev. 7:2; 9:4; 2 Tim. 2:19). Paul also refers to the Corinthians as the "seal of [his] apostleship in the Lord" (1 Cor. 9:2), that is, the authentication and visible evidence of his apostleship. See *NIDNTT-A*, 546-48.*

SEARCH

Old Testament

Verb: בָּקַשׁ (*bāqaš*), GK 1335 (S 1245), 225x. *bāqaš* refers to a search for, or a striving after, someone or something. See *seek*.

Verb: דָּרַשׁ (*dāraš*), GK 2011 (S 1875), 164x. *dāraš* means "to seek, search for, inquire after" an object. See *seek*.

New Testament

Verb: ζητέω (*zēteō*), GK *2426* (S *2212*), 117x. *zēteō* means "to seek, search."

SEASON

Old Testament

Noun: מוֹעֵד (*môʿēd*), GK 4595 (S 4150), 223x. *môʿēd* is often used in cultic contexts, such as "the Tent of *Meeting*" (see *meeting*). In noncultic contexts, it is sometimes used of the celestial bodies that God put into the sky to mark the "seasons" of the year (Gen. 1:14; Ps. 104:19), the shifting of which is evident even to the birds (Jer. 8:7).

Noun: עֵת (*ʿēt*), GK 6961 (S 6256), 296x. *ʿēt* is one of several words in the OT that express time. This word sometimes designate events that occur in a general framework of time. Spring is the time or season when "kings go out to war" (2 Sam. 11:1) and migratory birds "observe the *time* of their migration" (Jer. 8:7). See *time*.

New Testament

Noun: καιρός (*kairos*), GK *2789* (S *2540*), 85x. *kairos*, like *chronos*, can be used as a temporal indicator, such as a particular season ("it was not the *season* for figs," Mk. 11:13). But unlike *chronos*, which is more focused on chronological time, *kairos* is time as significant events. See *time*.

SEATED

New Testament

Verb: κάθημαι (*kathēmai*), GK *2764* (S *2521*), 91x. *kathēmai* can simply mean the literal act of "sitting," but it can also mean "to reside." It sometimes implies note of authority. See *sit*.

SECLUDED

New Testament

Noun and Adjective: ἔρημος (*erēmos*), GK *2245* (S *2048*), 48x. In the NT, *erēmos* is used both as an adjective and a noun. As an adjective, it can mean "barren" or "secluded, desolate" (see *desolate*). Jesus is said to withdraw to a secluded place to pray after having heard of John the Baptist's death (Mt. 14:13; Mk. 1:35 and Lk. 5:16 show that this practice was not uncommon for Jesus). On more than one occasion, Jesus preached in a "solitary" or secluded place (e.g., Mt. 14:13, 15; Mk. 6:32; Lk. 9:12).

SECOND

Old Testament

Adjective: שֵׁנִי (*šēnî*), GK 9108 (S 8145), 156x. *šᵉmōneh* is the ordinal numeral meaning "second." See *two*.

New Testament

Adjective: δεύτερος (*deuteros*), GK *1311* (S *1208*), 43x. *deuteros* means "second." It can refer to the second in a series, such as the "*second* brother" (Mt. 22:26) or the "*second* sign" (Jn. 4:54). It is used in lists, "God has appointed in the church first apostles, *second* prophets, third teachers" (1 Cor. 12:28). It is also used as an adverb to denote a second occurrence: "The voice spoke to him again a *second time*" (Acts 10:15).

SECRET

Old Testament

Verb: סָתַר (*sātar*), GK 6259 (S 5641), 82x. The verb *sātar* means "to hide, conceal, keep secret." See *hide*.

New Testament

Noun: μυστήριον (*mystērion*), GK *3696* (S *3466*), 28x. *mystērion* denotes a "mystery, secret, or something unknown." See *mystery*.

Adjective: κρυπτός (*kryptos*), GK *3220* (S *2927*), 17x. *kryptos* describes something that is "secret" or "hidden." In the NT it can denote something hidden in a spatial or physical sense; e.g., Jesus instructs people to pray in an inner closet "in secret" (Mt. 6:6), and he "spoke openly to the world," not "in secret" (Jn. 18:20). He also said nobody lights a lamp and then "covers" it with a basket (Mk. 4:22; Lk. 8:17; see also Jn. 7:4, 10).

kryptos is most frequently used in a figurative sense to signify the inward part, the heart or spirit of a person. In Rom. 2:16 Paul speaks of God judging the "secrets" of men. In 1 Cor. 4:5 the phrase "*hidden things* of darkness" is equivalent to "the desires of peoples' hearts." Again in the same letter Paul writes about "*secret things* of the heart" (1 Cor. 14:25). Likewise, Peter says that God considers of great worth the "inner self" of a woman whose spirit is gentle and quiet (1 Pet. 3:4).

A particularly important use of this word is in Rom. 2:28–29 in which Paul says that a true Jew is not a Jew outwardly or because of circumcision of the flesh, but "inwardly" (*kryptos*), with circumcision of the heart. This may be a contextual key to interpreting Rom. 9–11. In particular, when Paul says "all Israel will be saved" (11:26), he may be referring not to ethnic Israel, or those people who are Jews according to outward circumcision or formal religion, but to those who are circumcised inwardly/in their hearts, both Jew and Gentile. See *NIDNTT-A*, 319-21.

SECRETARY

Old Testament

Noun: סֹפֵר (*sōpēr*), GK 6221 (S 5608), 54x. *sōpēr* means "scribe, secretary." This term can describe any sort of official writer. See *scribe*.

SECTION

Old Testament

Noun: מִדָּה (*middâ*), GK 4500 (S 4060), 55x. A *middâ*, derived from the verb *mādad*, "to measure," means "size, measurement"; it can refer to both spatial and temporal measurements. See *measurement*. In the book of Nehemiah, various people are described as repairing a "measurement" or "section" of the wall (Neh. 3:11, 19–21, 24, 27, 30).

SEE

Old Testament

Verb: חָזָה (*ḥāzâ*), GK 2600 (S 2372), 68x. *ḥāzâ* means "to see, observe, gaze"; it is a broad word, encompassing a variety of actions including physical, visionary, mental, and spiritual.

(1) *ḥāzâ* can refer to physical sight (e.g., seeing a skilled man, Prov. 22:29; seeing a mysterious fourth man in the fire with Shadrach, Meshach and Abednego, Dan. 3:25). It can refer to mental perception (Job 27:12; Prov. 24:32) or spiritual understanding (Ps. 46:8; Isa. 26:11). In a few key verses *ḥāzâ* carries the nuance of "gazing": astrologers foolishly "gaze at the stars" (Isa. 47:13), a man longingly gazes at his lover (Song 6:13), and the psalmist longs to "gaze upon the beauty of the LORD" (Ps. 27:4). When prophets "see" visions, *ḥāzâ* is often used (Isa. 1:1; Amos 1:1; Mic. 1:1; Hab. 1:1). Even false prophets can "see" visions, but God labels their visions as "empty" (Lam. 2:14) because, instead of showing people God's truth, they show the people only what they want to see (Ezek. 13:6–10).

(2) Because the Lord is righteous and loves justice, "the upright will see (*ḥāzâ*) his face" (Ps. 11:7). And again, "I, in righteousness, will see (*ḥāzâ*) your face" (17:15a). Occasionally, the more common verb for seeing (*rāʿâ*) appears with *ḥāzâ* in the same verse as a synonym. For example, Job asserts that "after my skin has been destroyed, even in my flesh I will see (*ḥāzâ*) God. I myself will see (*ḥāzâ*) him, and my eyes will see (*rāʿâ*), and not a stranger's" (Job 19:26–27). Although the two words are synonyms, *ḥāzâ* seems used more commonly than *rāʿâ* in the context of seeing God's face. See *NIDOTTE*, 2:56-61.*

Verb: נָבַט (*nābaṭ*), GK 5564 (S 5027), 70x. As with other Hebrew words used to denote "seeing," *nābaṭ* may refer to physical sight, mental activities, or the way in which God and humans relate. See *look*.

Verb: רָאָה (*rāʾâ*), GK 8011 (S 7200 and 7202), 1,311x. *rāʾâ* is the most frequent Heb. verb for "seeing," encompassing a variety of actions including physical, visionary, and mental. "Seeing" often pictures how God interacts with humans, how God makes himself known to humans, and how humans then interact with God.

(1) *rāʾa* is the typical word for physical sight (seeing a ram, Gen. 22:13; seeing a king, Jer. 34:3). It also refers to prophetic, visionary sight (Zech. 3:1), and sight into the spiritual realm (seeing an angelic army, 2 Ki. 6:17; seeing God's throne room, Isa. 6:1). This verb is also used of various cognitive activities: mental awareness (Hagar "sees" that she is pregnant, Gen. 16:4), understanding (Israel is to "see" that their motives have been wrong in asking for a king, 1 Sam. 12:17), taking note (God "sees" the distress of Israel, Ps. 106:44), considering (lit., "*See* the work of God; who can make straight what he has made crooked," Eccl. 7:13), inquiring ("Go now, *see* if it is well with your brothers," Gen. 37:14), and choosing (lit., "I have *seen* to myself a king among his sons," 1 Sam. 16:1). *rāʾa* can have the sense of providing. As Abraham leads Isaac to the mountain to sacrifice him, he literally says, "God will *see* to the lamb for the burnt offering, my son" (Gen. 22:8). When God does provide the ram, Abraham calls the mountain, "The LORD will *see*"; that is, God will provide for the needs of his people (22:14).

(2) *rāʾa* has several idiomatic uses. To "see the sun" means to be alive (Eccl. 6:5), and "Come, let us *see* each other's faces" can be a challenge to fight (2 Chr. 25:17). To "see someone's face" refers to coming into that person's presence (Gen. 43:3, 5).

(3) "Seeing" captures the essence of the relationship between God and human beings. (a) God interacts with us through sight. He takes note of what we do; he *saw* just before the flood that the whole earth "was corrupt" (Gen. 6:12). God's "sight" and his subsequent actions are inseparable; God "*sees*, and the nations tremble" (Hab. 3:6). Because God is omnipresent (Jer. 23:24b), he "sees" all things: "Can anyone hide in secret places so that I cannot *see* him?" (Jer. 23:24a); he also sees the tears of his people (Isa. 38:5). As God interacts with humans his sight is an ever-present reality; worship is literally called, "*being seen* at the face of the LORD" (Deut. 31:11; 1 Sam. 1:22).

(b) God reveals himself to humans through sight. Though invisible, God makes himself "seen" in theophanies (the burning bush, Exod. 3:16; the angel of the Lord, Jdg. 6:22; physical form, Gen. 32:30), in prophetic visions (Ezek. 1:1), and in graphic visualizations of his character and attributes so that humans may "see" him. For example, to give a glimpse of his holiness it is said that God's "brightness was like the light; rays flashed from his hand" (Hab. 3:4). To give an indication of his vastness in relation to us, God visually reveals himself by saying that "the clouds are the dust of his feet" (Nah. 1:3). God thereby enables people to "see" him.

(c) Humans interact with God through sight. Because of God's holiness and human sin, the face of God cannot actually be seen by people ("You cannot *see* my face, for man may not *see* me and live," Exod. 33:20; cf. Jdg. 6:22). Yet because of God's mercy, he allows Moses "to see" his back (Exod. 33:23), and God's presence with his people is described in visual terms: "you, O LORD, have been seen face to face" (Num. 14:14). People are to "taste and *see*" the Lord's goodness (Ps. 34:8). To "see" God's goodness is to see his glory (i.e., his sovereign mercy and compassion, Exod. 33:18–19, and his saving power, Num. 14:22). Seeing God's glory causes humble worship (Ezek. 3:23; 44:4). See *NIDOTTE*, 3:1007-1015.*

New Testament

Verb: βλέπω (*blepō*), GK *1063* (S *991*), 133x. *blepō* is a general word meaning "to see." It commonly refers to seeing physical objects (Mt. 15:31; Lk. 7:21; Jn. 9:7). It can also mean "to look at, watch" such as watching a woman with lustful intent (Mt. 5:28) or looking at the "speck" in someone else's eye (Mt. 7:3). In Rev. 5:3–4, no one is able "to looking into" the scroll (Rev. 5:3–4) except the Lamb.

blepō also can refer to the related ideas such as paying attention, being careful, or perceiving such as keeping alert or on guard (Mk. 13:33; also 1 Cor. 1:26; 2 Cor. 10:7; Rom. 7:23; Heb. 2:9)—e.g., " see to it that ..." (Mk. 8:15; Gal. 5:15). *blepō* refers to perceiving spiritual truths In Paul's statement that "[I] *see* in my members another law waging war against the law of my mind and making me captive to the law of sin that dwells in my members" (Rom. 7:23; cf. Heb. 2:9; Rev. 3:18).

blepō and *horaō* (GK *3972*) can be used interchangeably. "Many prophets and righteous men longed to see [*horaō*] what you see [*blepō*] but did not see it [*horaō*]" (Mt. 13:17). It is doubtful there is any significant difference in meaning when Isa. 28:26 is cited, "Seeing [*blepō*] you will see]*blepō*] but never see [*horaō*, i.e., perceive]" (Mt. 13:14; Mk. 4:12; Acts 28:26). See *NIDNTT-A*, 96.

Verb: θεωρέω (*theōreō*), GK *2555* (S *2334*), 58x. Most uses of *theōreō* refer to physical sight. Note that all but four occurrences are in the gospels and Acts. The women "watch" Jesus' crucifixion from a distance (Mt. 27:55). Jesus "sees" a commotion in Jarius's house when he arrives (Mk. 5:38). Sometimes what is seen can be a vision, as when Peter "sees" a large sheet filled with all sorts of clean and unclean animals (Acts 10:11).

In a few places *theōreō* means "perceive." After his disciples return from their mission, Jesus says, "I *saw* Satan fall like lightning from heaven" (Lk. 10:18). When Peter and John boldly proclaim Jesus to the Sanhedrin, the Jewish leaders "*see* the courage" of these two disciples (Acts 4:13). The woman at the well can "see" that Jesus is a prophet (Jn. 4:19). Exhibiting the flexible use of *theōreō*, Paul physically "sees" the idols of the Athenians (Acts 17:16), and he can "perceive" that these are religious people (17:22). This word can also be used of understanding (Heb. 7:4) and even of experiencing something (Jn. 8:51). Jesus is so closely united with God the Father that Jesus can say that whoever "sees" him is actually "seeing" the invisible one who sent him (12:45). See *NIDNTT-A*, 413-15.

Verb: νοέω (*noeō*), GK *3783* (S *3539*), 14x. *noeō* means "to understand, see, reflect on." It is related to the Greek word *nous* ("mind"). See *understand*.

Verb: θεάομαι (*theaomai*), GK *2517* (S *2300*), 22x. *theaomai* means "to see, behold, observe." As with other words for "to see," the specific nuances of each usage come more from an author's use and less from the word itself.

theaomai can be used to refer to simple sight (Mk. 16:11, 14). Sometimes, however, this verb is used of a longer and more intentional look. Hypocrites, the teachers of the law, and the Pharisees want not only to be seen but to be "watched and noticed" for their prayer and good deeds (Mt. 6:1; 23:5). The apostle John seems especially fond of using *theaomai* in its stronger sense. In the prologue to his gospel, he emphasizes how "we *have seen* his glory" (Jn. 1:14). John the Baptist reports how he "has seen" the Spirit descending on Jesus (1:32). Later, in his first letter John emphasizes how they "have looked upon" or "observed" the earthly Jesus (1 Jn. 1:1; 4:14), so that they know that he is real (in contrast to some heretics who were denying the physical Jesus). When John says that no one has ever "*seen* God" (1 Jn. 4:12), he is teaching that even though no one has "observed God by sight," God's life may still be observed in us as we love one another. See *NIDNTT-A*, 413-15.

Verb: ὁράω (*horaō*), GK *3972* (S *3708*), 454x. *horaō* is the most frequently used word for seeing in the NT. Broadly meaning "to see" and reflecting the OT diversity, *horaō* can have many uses. It commonly refers to seeing physical objects (Mt. 28:10; Mk. 8:33; 13:26; Jn. 16:16; Rev. 1:7), but it can also refer to perceiving spiritual truths such as faith, salvation, and the fulfillment of the Scriptures concerning Jesus' resurrection (Mk. 2:5; Lk.

2:30; Acts 26:16–17; Lk. 24:24, respectively). It is used of observing one's surroundings (Mk. 15:39), coming to a realization (Lk. 24:39), taking heed to one's self (Mk. 8:15—"*See* to it that"), and even of taking close consideration to something ("*See* then the kindness and the severity of God," Rom. 11:22; cf. 1 Thess. 5:15). Paul uses this term for the post-resurrection appearances of Jesus (1 Cor. 15:5–8). It is by far the favorite word of John for what he "sees" in the book of Revelation (Rev. 1:2; 5:1; 5:1–2). Reflecting the teaching and vocabulary of the OT, *horaō* is also used of experience (Jesus, the Holy One, "did not *see* corruption" in the grave, Acts 2:27; cf. Ps. 16:10; "by faith Enoch did not *see* death," Heb. 11:5).

horaō and *blepō* ("to see," GK *1063*) can be used interchangeably. When used alone, each word can be used in similar ways. When used in the same verse, *horaō* is used of both physical sight and metaphorical sight, but *blepō* is used only of the physical sight (Mt. 13:17). See *NIDNTT-A*, 413-15.

SEED

Old Testament

Noun: זֶרַע (*zeraᶜ*), GK 2446 (S 2233), 229x. The noun *zeraᶜ* generally means "seed, descendant, offspring." It has various nuances in the OT.

(1) In the physical world, plants and trees bear seeds (Gen. 1:11–12, 29) and thus perpetuate life. God promised after the Flood that as long as this world continues, there will always be "*seedtime* [*zeraᶜ*] and harvest." The word can also be used for male semen, as the seed that impregnates a woman (Lev. 15:16–18).

(2) Far more frequent in the OT are metaphorical uses of this word for "offspring" or "descendants" of an individual. At times *zeraᶜ* designates a single descendant (Gen. 4:25; 1 Sam. 1:11; 2 Sam. 7:12). The first occurrence of its being used this way is perhaps in Gen. 3:15, where God promised to put enmity between "the seed" of the woman and "the seed" of the serpent until such enmity will eventually be resolved in the defeat of the serpent (this was accomplished in the battle of Christ against Satan; see Rev. 12).

(3) In most other cases, however, *zeraᶜ* is used collectively for a whole group of descendants. God promises Abraham that his "seed" (i.e., descendants) will be as numerous as the dust of the earth and the stars in the sky (Gen. 13:16; 15:5; 26:4). The entire nation of Israel, therefore, is frequently called "the seed" of Abraham (Ps. 105:6; Isa. 41:8) or of Jacob (Isa. 45:19). Moreover, what God seeks from his people is "godly offspring" (Mal. 2:15), and he will bless those "descendants [so that they] will inherit the land" (Ps. 25:13; 37:26). Metaphorically, evildoers are called "the offspring of the wicked" (Ps. 37:28; Isa. 14:20).

New Testament

Noun: σπέρμα (*sperma*), GK *5065* (S *4690*), 43x. *sperma* means "seed, descendant."

(1) As with *zeraᶜ* in the OT, *sperma* sometimes designates physical seed that is planted in the ground. Several of Jesus' parables deal with a farmer sowing seed (Mt. 13:3–9, where the verb *sperma* is used [see *sow*], 24–30, 31–32). In Jesus' interpretation of the parable of the sower, the seed is the word of God (Mk. 4:14); God expects his word to take root in us, grow, and produce fruit. In his interpretation of the parable of the weeds, the seed stands for the children of God's kingdom (Mt. 13:37–38), who have to coexist with the wicked while on this earth.

(2) Also with *zeraᶜ* in the OT, *sperma* can mean the children or descendants of an individual. In the Sadducees' story of the woman who married seven brothers, none of these brothers raised up "seed" (i.e., children) through her (Mt. 22:24–25). The Jews considered themselves the seed or descendants of Abraham (Jn. 8:33, 37; 2 Cor. 11:22). One important theme in the NT is that Jesus is a descendant of David (Rom. 1:3; 2 Tim. 2:8).

(3) Paul makes much of the fact that in

God's promise in Gen. 12:7 to give the land of Canaan to Abraham and his seed, the biblical text uses a singular "seed" rather than the plural "seeds." From this Paul argues that ultimately this "seed" refers to Christ; he is the true "*seed* of Abraham" (Gal. 3:16–19). Consequently, if we as believers belong to Christ, then we are "Abraham's *seed*" (Gal. 3:29). Thus, when all is said and done, it is not the Jews who are Abraham's seed but believers in Christ (see Rom. 4:16–18), so that the spiritual promises of the OT belong to us. See also *circumcise, circumcision*. See *NIDNTT-A*, 534-35.

(4) Finally, Paul uses what happens to a seed to illustrate the burial and resurrection of the bodies of believers (1 Cor. 15:44). Just as a seed goes into the earth and "dies," then comes forth as a beautiful plant, looking much different from its seed, so we will someday receive bodies unlike anything we see now—glorious, spiritual bodies.

SEEK

Old Testament

Verb: בָּקַשׁ (*bāqaš*), GK 1335 (S 1245), 225x. The Hebrew word *bāqaš* refers to a search seeking for, or a striving after, someone or something. It is used to describe seeking after an enemy, (Jdg. 4:22) or a home, (Ruth 3:1), to pursuer, (Jos. 2:22), to seek someone's death (Exod. 4:24; Num. 35:23; 1 Sam. 20:1), to harm, Num. 35:23), destroy (Zech. 12:9), to require (Ezek. 3:18), hold accountable (33:8), and even to plead (Est. 4:8). It most commonly refers to seeking after God, and this is normally done through sacrifices and seeking God's word through the prophets. Seeking repentance (Hos. 3:5), righteousness, humility, and proper judgment are part of seeking God; "Seek the LORD, all you humble of the land … , who do his just commands; seek righteousness; seek humility; perhaps you may be hidden on the day of the anger of the LORD" (Zeph. 2:3).

When *bāqaš* (to seek) and *dāraš* (to seek) are used together in a sentence, they are often interchangeable (1 Chr. 16:11; Job 10:6; Isa. 65:1). Sometimes, though, the second word adds intensity and depth to the first (Deut. 4:29; Ps. 24:6). The LORD promised, "You will *seek* me and you will find me, because you will *seek* me with all your heart" (Jer. 29:13). Also, when used together, one can have the nuance of a general seeking or striving while the other's nuance is "inquiring." In 1 Sam. 28:7 Saul said says to his servants, "*Seek* ("strive toward finding") for me a woman who is a medium, and I will go to her and I will *seek* ("inquire") of her." Believers must seek God. Those who do not "*seek* the LORD or *inquire* of him" are unabashedly paired with those who "bow down on the roofs to the hosts of heaven" (worshiping the stars) and those who "swear to the LORD and yet also swear to Molech" (Zeph. 1:5–6). See *NIDOTTE, 1:720-726.** Also *intend, search, look for*

Verb: דָּרַשׁ (*dāraš*), GK 2011 (S 1875), 164x. *dāraš* means "to seek, search for, inquire after" an object. The object of searching may be concrete (a thing) or abstract (an idea).

(1) *dāraš* can simply mean to look for something, such as lost animals (Deut. 22:2), supplies (Prov. 31:13), or information (2 Sam. 11:3). But many times it refers to a search that involves more than eyes and feet, such as a search for justice (Isa. 1:17), God's strength (1 Chr. 16:11), God's great works (Ps. 111:2), good and not evil (Amos 5:14). The one who searches for evil will find it (Prov. 11:27).

(2) In certain contexts, "seek" can mean to "require" in the sense of obtaining justice. The Lord seeks the blood of murderers and those who afflict the poor and weak (Gen. 9:5; Ps. 9:12). He requires an account from those who do not listen to his prophets (Deut. 18:19) and those who delay in fulfilling their vows (Deut. 23:21. The prophet Micah writes: "What does the LORD *seek* from you except to do justice, and to love steadfast love, and to walk humbly with your God" (Mic. 6:6–8).

(3) "To seek" can have relational con-

notations, even meaning "to care." The Lord "seeks" the promised land by preserving it and nourishing it under a watchful eye (Deut. 11:12). Nations call God's people "an outcast ... for whom no one *cares*," yet God will restore healing to such people (Jer. 30:17; cf. Isa. 62:12). Even though David sees no one around him who "*cares for* his soul," he knows that the Lord himself is his "refuge and portion in the land of the living" (Ps. 142:4–5).

(4) "Seek" commonly characterizes the relationship between God and his people. God's people are to seek him (Isa. 55:6), which is done through prayer (Gen. 25:22) and reading Scripture (1 Chr. 15:13). God, in turn, seeks his people (1 Chr. 18:9). He wants us to "search" inside his book and to realize how faithful he is to his promises (Isa. 34:16). Seeking may also be an act of worship, demonstrating reliance on the one you seek (Isa. 31:1). It is thus a great sin to seek anything other than the Lord (e.g., 2 Ki. 1:2–16; 1 Chr. 10:13; Isa. 8:19). But to those who seek God in a right spirit, "with all your heart and with all your soul" (Deut. 4:29), he promises such wonderful benefits as his presence (2 Chr. 15:2), his loyalty (Ps. 9:10), delivery from fears (Ps. 34:4), and life itself (Amos 5:4, 6). See *NIDOTTE*, 1:993-999.*

New Testament

Verb: ζητέω (*zēteō*), GK *2426* (S *2212*), 117x. *zēteō* means "to seek, search." A person can search for physical objects (Mt. 13:45; Lk. 15:8), other people (Lk. 9:9; Mt. 28:5), blessings such as healing (Lk. 5:18; 6:19), and opportunities to do things such as to betray (Mt. 26:16; Lk. 22:6), arrest (Mt. 21:46), and kill (2:13; Mk. 11:18; Acts 21:31). People are to "search for" spiritual principles and realities such as God's kingdom, righteousness, glory, immortality, wisdom, and peace (Mt. 6:33; cf. 7:7–8; Lk. 5:44; 7:18; 11:9–10; 12:31; 1 Cor. 1:22; 1 Pet. 3:11). Christians are not to "seek their own interests" but rather those of Jesus Christ and his servants (Phil. 2:21). Paul seeks for the good for others (1 Cor. 10:33), which is a characteristic of genuine love ("not self-seeking," 1 Cor. 13:5). Regarding prayer, those who "seek" from the Father will find (Mt. 7:7–8). To those who "seek" glory, honor, and immortality, God gives eternal life (Rom. 2:7), and to those "seeking" the kingdom of God and his righteousness, all necessities will be given as well (Mt. 6:33). The majority of Jews in Jesus' and Paul's day were "seeking to establish their own" righteousness (Rom. 10:3b), but they did not obtain it (9:31).

God's purpose in creating humans is "that they would seek God" (Acts 17:27). God himself seeks for things: people who repent (Lk. 13:5–6), worshipers in Spirit and truth (Jn. 4:23), and stewards who are trustworthy, especially in the mysteries of Christ (1 Cor. 4:2). Revealing his truly divine nature and mission, Jesus declares that he is the good shepherd and will bring back the sheep that are not yet in the fold (Jn. 10:14–16); in fact, he himself has come "to seek and to save the lost" (Lk. 19:10). See *NIDNTT-A*, 224-25.

SEEK JUSTICE

New Testament

Verb: ἐκδικέω (*ekdikeō*), GK *1688* (S *1556*), 6x. *ekdikeō* means "avenge, seek justice, punish." See *avenge*.

SEIZE

Old Testament

Verb: אָחַז (*ʾāḥaz*), GK 296 (S 270), 63x. This verb conveys the general sense of *taking hold of* an object or *being taken hold of* by an object, person, or emotion (see Jdg. 1:6; Num. 31:30; Ruth 3:15; 1 Chr. 13:9). Boaz commands Ruth, "Bring me the shawl you are wearing and *hold it out*" (Ruth 3:15). The term can also denote the metaphorical idea of *being taken over* by a feeling or emotion (2 Sam. 1:9; Job 18:20; Isa. 21:3; Jer. 49:24). Ps. 119:53 states, "Indignation *grips* me because of the wicked, who have forsaken your law." Saul's declares to the Israelite soldier, "Stand over me and kill me! I *am in the throes* of death, but I'm still alive" (2 Sam. 1:9). The contemporary idea of *being* *overcome with emotion* captures this sense of the term. See *NIDOTTE*, 1:354-58.

Verb: חָזַק (*ḥāzaq*), GK 2616 (S 2388), 290x. *ḥāzaq* can describe the severity or strength of an impersonal force. In some cases it means "to seize, grasp." For example, Saul seizes the edge of Samuel's robe (1 Sam. 15:27). See *strong*.

Verb: לָכַד (*lākad*), GK 4334 (S 3920), 121x. *lākad* generally means "to capture, seize, take captive." It can be used actively (i.e., "to catch, capture," Num. 21:32; Deut. 2:34; Jos. 10:42; Jdg. 7:24; 15:4; Ps. 35:8; Amos 3:4, 5), passively (i.e., "to be seized," 1 Ki. 16:18; Isa. 23:13; Jer. 6:11; 38:28; 48:1, 41; 51:56; Ezek. 7:26), or reflectively (i.e., "to cling to each other," Job 38:30; 41:17). See *capture*.

Verb: לָקַח (*lāqaḥ*), GK 4374 (S 3947), 967x. The basic meaning of *lāqaḥ* is "to take, grasp." The meaning is often simply to "take into/by the hand." *lāqaḥ* is also used to describe taking something as one's own possession. See *take*.

Verb: תָּפַשׂ (*tāpaś*), GK 9530 (S 8610), 65x. *tāpaś* conveys the sense of seizing or grasping an object or person, usually with a degree of force, and may be translated as "take hold of, seize." The historical and prophetic books use this word in military contexts with the idea of *taking* a city or king by force (1 Sam. 15:8; 2 Ki. 14:13), or in an exilic context with the idea of *being taken* into exile (Jer. 38:23; Ezek. 17:20). In these contexts, the word may be translated "seized" or "captured." Jeremiah declares to King Zedekiah, "All your wives and children will be brought out to the Babylonians. You yourself will not escape from their hands but will *be captured* by the king of Babylon; and this city will be burned down" (Jer. 38:23). Any fisherman knows the experience of forcefully "grabbing" of a fish in order to get it safely in the boat. See *NIDOTTE*, 4:326-27.

New Testament

Verb: ἐπιλαμβάνομαι (*epilambanomai*), GK *2138* (S *1949*), 19x. *epilambanomai* can mean "to seize, take hold, arrest." It conveys the idea of grasping firmly or taking hold tightly and is used in both positive and negative ways. In a positive way, *epilambanomai* is used in Lk. 14:4 of the healing hand of Jesus. It refers to the solid "grasping" of eternal life in 1 Tim. 6:12, 19. Jesus "catches" Peter by the hand as he is about to sink into the water (Mt. 14:31). In Heb. 8:9 (in a quote from Jer. 31:32) God "took hold" of the Israelites by the hand to lead them out of Egypt. Negatively, in Acts 16:19; 18:17; 21:30, 33, it refers to the idea of "arresting" someone and bringing them before the authorities. See *NIDNTT-A*, 328.

Verb: καταλαμβάνω (*katalambanō*), GK *2898* (S *2638*), 15x. *katalambanō* can mean "to catch, obtain, seize, overtake." In the middle voice it means "to grasp, understand." See *catch*.

Verb: κρατέω (*krateō*), GK *3195* (S *2902*), 47x. *krateō* means "to arrest, seize, hold, grasp." See *arrest*.

Verb: λαμβάνω (*lambanō*), GK *3284* (S *2983*), 258x. *lambanō* conveys the basic idea of acquiring or obtaining something and may best be translated as "take, seize, receive, get." See *take*.

Verb: συλλαμβάνω (*syllambanō*), GK *5197* (S *4815*), 16x. *syllambano* conveys the basic idea of bringing together or gathering and is translated "arrest, seize, capture, conceive." See *arrest*.

SELAH

Old Testament

Noun: סֶלָה (*selâ*), GK 6138 (S 5542), 74x. The meaning of this Hebrew word is unknown, though its almost exclusive appearance in the book of Psalms suggests some sort of musical significance. Perhaps the term identifies the type of music played or the way in which the psalm is to be sung. Of the 74x it occurs, 71 are located in the Psalms. The remaining three are in Habakkuk (Hab. 3:3, 9, 11). Of the thirty-nine Psalms that use *selâ*, twenty are attributed to David (e.g., Ps. 4, 9, 24, 39), nine to the sons of Korah (e.g., 44, 46, 47, 48), and seven to Asaph (e.g., 50, 75, 76, 77). This enigmatic term appears only once in some psalms (e.g., 7:5; 20:3; 21:2; 44:8) but multiple times in others (e.g., 3:2, 4, 8; 32:4, 5, 7; 46:3, 7, 11).

SELECT

Old Testament

Verb: בָּחַר (*bāḥar*), GK 1047 (S 977), 172x. *bāḥar* means "to choose, select, prefer." While this word has secular uses, it is also intimately linked with God's election of Israel. See *choose*.

SELL

Old Testament

Verb: מָכַר (*mākar*), GK 4835 (S 4376), 80x. *mākar* means "to sell" and it is used for the selling of entities like birthrights (Gen. 25:31), land (Gen. 47:20), animals (Gen. 21:35), houses (Lev. 25:29), and slaves (Gen. 37:27–28; Ps. 105:17). Because God outlaws permanent slavery among fellow Israelites, he gives laws against the selling of his people (Deut. 15:12; 21:14). Unfortunately, these laws were all too often ignored (e.g., Neh. 5:8; Amos 2:6), probably because the selling of human beings due to war or debt was common in the ancient Near East (e.g., Joel 3:3, 6). And because the land of Canaan belonged to the Lord, the Israelites were not allowed to make any permanent sale of their land (cf. the laws of Jubilee in Lev. 25; Jer. 34:14).

Figuratively, *mākar* is used when Nineveh is accused of "selling" other nations (i.e., betraying, Nah. 3:4) and when Esther speaks of Israel being "sold" into death (Est. 7:4). The most striking figurative use, however, occurs in contexts where God, in fulfillment of his covenant promise not only to bless but also to curse, "sells" his people into the power of their enemies when they refuse to remain loyal to him (Deut. 32:20; Ps. 44:12; Isa. 50:1; Ezek. 30:12). Samuel states, "But they forgot the Lord their God; so he *sold* them into the hand of Sisera, the commander of the army of Hazor" (1 Sam. 12:9). See *NIDOTTE*, 2:937–39.

New Testament

Verb: ἀποδίδωμι (*apodidōmi*), GK *625* (S *591*), 48x. While in the active voice *apodidōmi* means "to give (back), deliver, render, hand over" (see *give back*), in the Gk. middle voice, *apodidomi* means "to sell"—as when Ananias sells land (Acts 5:8), Esau sells his inheritance (Heb. 12:16), and Joseph's brothers sell him into slavery (Acts 7:9). See *NIDNTT-A*, 60.

Verb: πωλέω (*pōleō*), GK *4797* (S *4453*), 22x. *pōleō* means "to sell," that is, to exchange goods or services for money. Buying and selling were ordinary activities in the ancient world. The NT depicts people who sell sparrows (Mt. 10:29; Lk. 12:6), oil (Mt. 25:9), cattle, sheep, and doves (Jn. 2:14), real estate (Acts 4:37; 5:1), and meat (1 Cor. 10:25). Lk. 17:28 implies that since the citizens of Sodom long ago went about selling, a routine activity, they were unaware of the fate that awaited them. That selling is an integral element of a properly functioning society is also implied by Rev. 13:17, which describes the inability to buy or sell for those lacking the number of the beast.

The reasons for selling in the NT range from altruistic beneficence to dishonest greed. The incredible value of salvation is conveyed in the parable of the man who sells all he has to buy a field that contains a hidden treasure (Mt. 13:44). Jesus exhorts his followers to sell all and give the proceeds to the poor so that they may follow him (Mt. 19:21; Mk. 10:21; Lk. 12:33; 18:22). The early church did in fact sell property for the benefit of those in need (Acts 4:34). The selling of property per se was neither a noble nor ignoble activity; one's motivation was more important. For example, both Barnabas (Acts 4:37) and Ananias and Sapphira (5:1) sold property and placed the proceeds at the apostles' feet, yet their fates differed dramatically because of their dissimilar motivations. Buying and selling are also the activities that compel an enraged Jesus to clear the temple (Mt. 21:12; Mk. 11:15; Lk. 19:45; Jn. 2:14, 16). However, once more it is not the simple act of selling, but rather the motivation and location of the selling that

Jesus finds reprehensible. See *NIDNTT-A*, 506-7.

SEND

Old Testament

Verb: שָׁלַח (*šālaḥ*), GK 8938 (S 7971), 847x. Generally translated "to send," *šālaḥ* usually refers to a human or divine person sending an object away from the subject for some purpose.

The object can be inanimate (the Lord sends the plagues, Exod. 9:14) or animate (the Lord sends Nathan the prophet, 2 Sam. 12:1). In certain forms, this verb can carry the negative nuance of dismissal. For example, the Lord banishes (i.e., sends away) Adam and Eve from the Garden of Eden (Gen. 3:23). Similarly, in texts related to the marriage covenant, *šālaḥ* often means "to divorce" (Deut. 22:19; Ezr. 10:3). The NT's understanding of apostle as "one who is sent" by God may have its roots in the OT's description of prophets as "sent ones" (e.g., 1 Ki. 14:6; Isa. 6:8).

New Testament

Verb: ἀποστέλλω (*apostellō*), GK *690* (S *649*), 132x.

Verb: ἐξαποστέλλω (*exapostellō*), GK *1990* (S *1821*), 13x.

Verb: πέμπω (*pempō*), GK *4287* (S *3992*), 79x. Each of these verbs means "to send," although *exapostellō*, a compound form of *ex* and *apostellō*, literally means "to send out," but may also indicate the idea to send *away* (Lk. 1:53; 20:10). *pempō* is virtually synonymous with *apostellō* in meaning and usage. The majority of uses of *apostellō* and *pempō* are in the gospels and Acts.

(1) Both words can denote the process of a human being sending someone somewhere. For example, Herod "sends" *(pempō)* the wise men on to Bethlehem with orders to tell him where the child is (Mt. 2:8), and later he "sends" (*apostellō*) his soldiers to kill all the babies in Bethlehem who were two years old and younger (2:16). In Paul's letters, he frequently refers to sending his associates to different places (*apostellō* in 2 Tim. 4:12; *pempō* in 1 Thess. 3:2; Tit. 3:12). In many cases the authority of the sender is in view.

(2) Far more important are the uses of these verbs when Jesus or God is the sender. Jesus, for example, "sends" his disciples out two by two to do mission work *(apostellō* is used exclusively here; see Mt. 10:5, 16; Lk. 10:1, 3). John the Baptist was sent out by God as a messenger to prepare the way for the Messiah (*apostellō* in Mk. 1:2; Lk. 7:27; in Jn. 1:33, John uses *pempō* for his being sent to baptize). God also sent the angel Gabriel to both Zechariah and Mary with birth announcements (*apostellō* in Lk. 1:19, 26). Moreover, God sent his Son Jesus into the world (*apostellō* in Jn. 17:3, 18, 21; 1 Jn. 4:9–10; *pempō* in Jn. 5:23–24; 6:44; Rom. 8:3). God the Father and God the Son promise to send the Holy Spirit after the latter's departure to the Father's right hand (*pempō* in Jn. 14:26; 15:26; 16:7).

(3) During the time of the NT church, the triune God continued to send people to different places. He "sent" the messengers of Cornelius to Peter (*apostellō* in Acts 10:17, 20); earlier in the story God commanded Cornelius "to send" for Simon Peter in Joppa (*pempō* in 10:5, 32). The church too sent out people on various missions, such as John and Peter being sent to Samaria after the successful mission of Philip (*apostellō* in 8:14). After the Council of Jerusalem, the church "sent" a letter along Judas and Silas as personal emissaries to announce the decisions of the council (*pempō* in 15:25; *apostellō* in 15:27).

(4) Since God is so heavily involved in the sending process in the NT, it seems reasonable to suppose that when Paul says in Rom. 10:15, "And how can they preach unless they are sent [*apostellō*]," Paul is referring to a divine sending. Obviously in Paul's own mission work, he sees himself as being "sent" by Christ (*apostellō* in 1 Cor. 1:17). We should note also that the noun derived from the verb *apostellō* is *apostolos*, and for the most part in the NT, this term has a technical meaning for those specifically designated by God as the foun-

dation of the church (see *apostle*). See *NIDNTT-A*, 64-67.

Noun: ἀπόστολος (*apostolos*), GK *693* (S *652*), 80x. *apostolos* broadly refers to a "messenger, delegate, or sent one." In classical Greek, *apostolos* referred to a person of merit sent as an envoy or on behalf of a master in an administrative role. John uses the term in a similar general way, applying it to any messenger without the specific idea of an office with special status (Jn. 13:16). In contrast, in Luke *apostolos* is used almost solely as a designation for the Twelve (except in Lk. 11:49 and Acts 14:14; in the latter, Luke identifies both Barnabas and Paul as apostles). Matthew and Mark use it sparingly for the Twelve (Mt. 10:2; Mk. 3:14; 6:30). See *apostle*.

SEND AWAY

New Testament

Verb: ἀπολύω (*apolyō*), GK *668* (S *630*), 66x. *apolyō* is a compound verb that literally means "to loose away from." In the NT it is frequently translated as "to release, send away" (see *release*), but also "to divorce. See *divorce.*

SENSELESS

New Testament

Noun/Adjective: ἄφρων (*aphrōn*), GK *933* (S *878*), 11x. As an adjective, *aphrōn* means "foolish, senseless," but it is often used as a noun to mean "fool." See *fool*.

SENSUALITY

New Testament

Noun: ἀσέλγεια (*aselgeia*), GK 816 (S 766), 10x. *aselgeia* means "debauchery, lewdness, sensuality." See *debauchery*.

SEPARATE

New Testament

Verb: ἀφορίζω (*aphorizō*), GK *928* (S *873*), 10x. *aphorizō* is formed from the preposition *apo* ("from, away from") and the verb *horizō* ("to appoint, designate, define"). In classical Greek it was used for marking off the boundaries of one's property by pillars. In the NT it carries the idea of "to separate, set apart, exclude." In Luke's Sermon on the Mount Jesus says, "Blessed are you when men hate you, when they *exclude* you" (Lk. 6:22). In fact, believers are called to "separate" themselves from what is unclean (2 Cor. 6:17).

aphorizō is also used to designate the setting apart of a person for a specific task. Paul was "*set part* for the gospel of God" (Rom. 1:1; cf. Gal. 1:5, where he writes that God "*set [him] apart* from birth"). Similarly, Paul and Barnabas are set apart for the work of evangelism (Acts 13:2). In Antioch Peter separated himself from the Gentiles when a Jewish party from James arrived, thus incurring Paul's displeasure (Gal. 2:12).

At the end of the age there will be a separation of the "wicked from the righteous" (Mt. 13:49), the "sheep from the goats" (25:32). Better to separate oneself now from all that is unclean than face the prospect of a final separation and exclusion from the kingdom. See *NIDNTT-A*, 418.*

Verb: χωρίζω (*chōrizō*), GK *6004* (S *5563*), 13x. *chōrizō* means "to separate, divorce." (1) This verb can indicate a physical separation of persons (Onesimus "*was separated* from" Philemon, Phlm. 15) or places (Paul "left" Athens to go to Corinth, Acts 18:1; cf. also 1:4; 18:2). But this verb more commonly refers to divorce. A husband and wife should form the "one flesh" that God creates in marriage. If they divorce, they are "separating" what God has joined together (Mt. 19:6; Mk. 10:8). Paul also instructs married believers not to "separate" (1 Cor. 7:10–11), though he does allow for an unbelieving spouse to "leave" (7:15).

(2) *chōrizō* is also used of two notions of separation with regards to Jesus Christ. Jesus, "having been *separated* from sinners," is the high priest who is "holy, blameless, pure" and "exalted above the heavens" (Heb. 7:26). Thus, he is "able to save to the uttermost those who are coming through him to God" (7:25). And because this sinless and exalted Jesus is interceding for "God's elect" (Rom. 8:33), there is no one who can "*separate* us from the love of Christ" (8:35). Indeed, nothing

in all of creation is able "to *separate* us from the love of God that is in Christ Jesus our Lord" (8:39). See *NIDNTT-A*, 616–18.*

SERPENT

New Testament

Noun: ὄφις (*ophis*), GK 4058 (S 3789), 14x. *ophis* is translated as "snake, serpent." See *snake*.

SERVANT

Old Testament

Noun: אָמָה (*ʾāmâ*), GK 563 (S 519), 56x. *ʾāma* frequently translates as "maidservant" or "slave girl," but may also be translated simply as "servant." See *maidservant*.

Noun: נַעַר (*naʿar*), GK 5853 (S 5288), 240x. The meaning of *naʿar* falls into two main categories. It may refer to a male child of almost any age or to a servant. See *boy*.

Noun: עֶבֶד (*ʿebed*), GK 6269 (S 5650), 803x. *ʿebed* means "servant" and is used in theologically significant ways in the OT. It can refer to the position of a human being before God, emphasizing the Creator/creature distinction. For example, Israel is a servant of God (Lev. 25:55), as are the prophets (Jer. 7:25); they do what God bids. *ʿebed* is also used as a descriptor of significant figures in the OT who have distinctive roles and offices in the economy of God—e.g., Abraham, Isaac, Jacob (Exod. 32:13; Deut. 9:27), Caleb (Num. 14:29), Moses (the servant par excellence, Deut. 34:5), Joshua (Jos. 24:29), Isaiah (Isa. 20:3), David (1 Sam. 23:10), Israel as a nation (Isa. 41:8), and surprisingly, even Cyrus and Nebuchadnezzar (Isa. 44:28; Jer. 25:9).

The most significant use of *ʿebed* is found in Isa. 40–55. The "servant of the LORD" is the means of God's restoration of both Israel and the nations (49:1–6). In a surprisingly new and unprecedented fashion, God promises to redeem both the nations and Zion by means of the servant who suffers in the place of and on behalf of others (Isa. 53). When referring to "the servant of the Lord," *ʿebed* is always in the sing. up to Isa. 53, but after this key chapter the term is found only in the pl. and may refer to the righteous offspring promised to Isaiah's servant in 53:10. These righteous servants have recognized, in retrospect, the significance of the servant's suffering. They follow the servant in obedience though they suffer as well while awaiting the coming day of vindication (54:17; 57:1; 65:1–25).

Noun: שִׁפְחָה (*šiphâ*), GK 9148 (S 8198), 63x. This feminine noun is generally translated "servant" or "maidservant." See *maidservant*.

New Testament

Noun: διάκονος (*diakonos*), GK *1356* (S *1249*), 29x. *diakonos* means "servant, minister." The idea of one who waits on tables is a part of the conceptual sphere of *diakonos*, but the word includes much more. Paul's description of himself as one who serves often carries the idea of giving himself at great personal cost for the gospel (2 Cor. 6:1–4). Paul, a servant of God, carries out his task of spreading the gospel through enormous sacrifice. This concept of *diakonos* is found also in Paul's claim to be a servant of the new covenant (2 Cor. 3:6), of righteousness (11:15), of Christ (Col. 1:7), of God (2 Cor. 6:4), of the gospel (Eph. 3:7), and of the church (Col. 1:25).

diakonos is also used to describe a particular office in the church ("deacon" in Phil. 1:1; 1 Tim. 3:8, 12). However, it can be used of people serving in some capacity, such as Phoebe (Rom. 16:1; some argue Phoebe has an official title as deaconess), often official capacity, such as Apollos and Paul (1 Cor. 3:5; cf. 3:6; 6:4; Eph. 3:7; Phil. 1:1; Col. 1:23), Tychicus (Eph. 6:21; Col. 4:7), Epaphras (Col. 1:7), and Timothy (1 Tim. 4:6). It is a matter of interpretation as to which category a specific verse belongs.

Secular rulers can also be termed, "God's *servant*" (Rom. 13:4), and demons can conceal themselves as "*servants of righteousness*" (2 Cor. 11:15).

Noun: δοῦλος (*doulos*), GK *1528* (S *1400*, *1401*), 124x. *doulos* refers to a "servant, slave," usually a male slave such as Onesimus (Phlm. 16). Many of Jesus' parables are stories of how "servants" related to their masters (e.g., Mt. 18:23–35; 25:14–30). The ancient world had an economy driven by slavery (people became slaves either as prisoners of war or because of economic debt). Paul calls on slaves to be obedient to their masters, even unmerciful ones (Eph. 6:5; Col. 3:22). Although Paul does not discourage a slave from seeking his freedom (1 Cor. 7:20–24), true freedom is to be found in Jesus Christ (1 Cor. 7:22–24).

doulos is often used metaphorically to describe the sole commitment of one person to another. Prior to faith in Christ, human beings are "slaves to sin" (Jn. 8:34; Rom. 6:16–17, 20), but Jesus Christ sets us free (Jn. 8:35–36). Paul then defines himself as a *doulos* of the gospel (Phil. 2:22) and especially of Jesus Christ (Rom. 1:1; Gal. 1:10; Phil. 1:1). Part of his responsibility in serving Christ is to be a "servant" of the people to whom he ministers (2 Cor. 4:5; cf. 2 Tim. 2:24).

The foundation of our service is the example Jesus Christ has set before us, since he took on himself "the very nature of a *servant*" (Phil. 2:7). The servant image of Isaiah 40-55 is an important backdrop to the role of Christ as a servant. As the servant of Isaiah lived in obedient and selfless devotion to the will of God, which led to his innocent suffering and death on behalf of others and in the place of others (especially Isa. 49-53), so too does Jesus model a life of selfless devotion to the will of the Father, which lead to death, even the death of the cross. See *NIDNTT-A*, 151-53.

SERVANT GIRL

New Testament

Noun: παιδίσκη (*paidiskē*), GK *4087* (S *3814*), 13x. *paidiskē* is the diminutive form of the word for "girl," used in the NT always for a "servant girl." Most occurrences are in narrative literature and refer to literal servant girls (e.g., Mt. 26:69; Mk. 14:66, 69; Acts 12:13; 16:16).

The only occurrences of *paidiskē* with theological significance in the NT are found in Gal. 4:22, 23, 30, 31, in which Paul sets forth the allegory of Hagar and Sarah. Paul compares two covenants here—a covenant of slavery, represented by Abraham's Egyptian "servant girl" Hagar and her son Ishmael, and a covenant of freedom, represented by Abraham's wife Sarah and her son Isaac. Paul's purpose is to counteract the Judaizers' attempt to adding legalistic requirements on the Gentile converts, specifically the rite of circumcision. Those who attempt to add anything to the gospel message of justification by faith alone (see Gal. 1:8–9) place themselves squarely in line with God's severe judgment. See *NIDNTT-A*, 427-29.

SERVE

Old Testament

Verb: עָבַד (*ʿābad*), GK 6268 (S 5647), 290x. The verb *ʿābad* means "to serve" and is used in both secular and religious contexts.

In popular contexts, *ʿābad* refers to work done in the service of something or someone. Examples are Esau's servitude to Jacob (Gen. 25:23) and the assertion in Eccl. that the sleep of one who works is sweet (Eccl. 5:12; cf. also Gen. 14:4; Exod. 1:13; Lev. 25:6; Deut. 20:11).

The act of serving takes on theological significance in the cult of Israel, where *ʿābad* often means "to worship." See *worship*.

Verb: שָׁרַת (*šārat*), GK 9250 (S 8334), 98x. *šārat* denotes "to minister, serve, officiate" and is used of the "serving" performed by royal household workers (2 Sam. 13:17; also 1 Ki. 10:5) or by court officials and public servants (1 Chr. 27:1; 28:1; Est. 1:10). This verb is to be differentiated from *ʿābad*, "to serve," which is used of general work common to all, especially slaves or servants. See *minister*.

A number of times in the OT, the ptc. form of the verb *šārat* is used as a noun for a person engaged in service and is translated as "minister" or "servant." For example, Joshua is Moses' servant (Exod. 24:13; 33:11; Num. 11:28; Jos. 1:1), and the angels are servants of God (Ps. 103:21; 104:4).

New Testament

Verb: διακονέω (*diakoneō*), GK *1354* (S *1247*), 37x. *diakoneō* means "to serve." It carries the basic idea of serving as exemplified in serving at a table (Mt. 8:15; Lk. 4:39; Acts 6:2), serving individuals (Mt. 4:11; Mk. 1:31), or of service to the church (Heb. 6:10).

diakoneō is not limited to "waiting on tables," however. Its basic meaning is applied specifically to the sacrificial work of Jesus in atonement, as well as to the ministry of deacons (1 Tim. 3:10, 13). Jesus' suffering and giving of himself for others is defined as an act of service (Mt. 20:28). In Mk. 10:45, Jesus' *service* is understood more as an act of sacrifice than mere service of a servant. His mission is to give his life sacrificially as a ransom for others. The relationship between this idea of a sacrifice and the "servant" theme of Isaiah 40–55 (especially 53) should be observed.

Christ's life of service becomes the norm for the life of disciples as they serve both Christ and others in humility (Lk. 12:37). See also *servant.*

Verb: δουλεύω (*douleuō*), GK *1526* (S *1398*), 25x. *douleuō* means "to serve, be enslaved," especially in the capacity of a slave or of one in bondage, who acts or conducts himself in total service to another. Jesus instructs us that no one "can *serve* two masters" (Mt. 6:24). One who is a slave is in complete devotion to his or her master. Outside of the sphere of grace, all human beings are "enslaved" to sin (Rom. 6:6; Tit. 3:3; Gal. 4:8–9). Christ redeems his people from the bondage of sin so that we may lead lives of service and abandonment to that one who is worthy of slave-like devotion (Rom. 12:1–11; 1 Thess. 1:9). As we serve Christ, we must take every opportunity to "*serve* one another in love" (Gal. 5:13). And even those who are officially slaves in the ancient world are to "serve" their masters wholeheartedly, as if they are "*serving* the Lord" (Eph. 6:7; 1 Tim. 6:2). See *NIDNTT-A*, 151-53.

Verb: λατρεύω (*latreuō*), GK *3302* (S *3000*), 21x. *latreuō* refers to service or worship that is always religious in nature (Lk. 1:74; Acts 7:7, 42). In the LXX *latreuō* is used exclusively of service to God, often in a cultic setting, e.g.., serving in the temple. The meaning also occurs in the NT. Anna never left the temple, but "worshiped" God night and day (Lk. 2:37). Paul worships God in accordance with his understanding of the OT (Acts 24:14). The only proper object of worship is God (Mt. 4:10; Lk. 4:8).

The major shift that happens with this word in the NT is the decentralization of worship. an activity that before was limited in locale to certain areas such as the temple, now Christians are to do at all times in all places. This is clearly defined by Jesus' comments to the Samaritan woman, although *latreuō* does not occur in this passage: "The hour is coming, and is now here, when the true worshipers will worship [*proskyneō*, GK *4686*] the Father in spirit and truth, for the Father is seeking such people to worship him. God is spirit, and those who worship him must worship in spirit and truth" (Jn. 4:23–24, ESV).

Paul sees his missionary endeavors as service to God (Rom. 1:9; 2 Tim. 1:3). The (true) circumcision are those who "worship" by the Spirit and do not trust in human ritual (Phil. 3:3), who have been set free from dead works to serve the living God (Heb. 9:14), worship accompanied "with reverence and awe" (12:28). In contrast, those who do not respond to what is clear about God in creation "serve" the creature rather than the Creator (Rom. 1:25).

In the NT *latreuō* can still refer to formal religious service in the past (Acts 7:7; Heb. 9:9; 10:2; 13:10), but usually the word refers to personal service to God (Acts 24:14; Rom. 1:9) and as such separates itself from any localized sense. True service to God, true worship, is not something limited to certain times and certain places; it is how the children of God's kingdom live out their lives day in and day out. Someday, in heaven, our entire lives will truly lived in service, in worship, of God. "Therefore they are before the throne of God, and *serve* him day and night in his temple; and he who sits on the throne will shelter them with his presence. … No longer will there be anything accursed, but the throne of God and of the Lamb will be in it, and his servants will *worship* him" (Rev. 7:15; 22:3, ESV). See *NIDNTT-A,* 330-31.

SERVICE

Old Testament

Noun: עֲבוֹדָה (*ᶜᵃbôdâ*), GK 6275 (S 5656), 145x. In the early use of *ᶜᵃbôdâ* in the Pentateuch, it describes the physical labor of Jacob for Laban. Later in the OT it denotes "service" to the tabernacle/temple or to the king. See *work*.

New Testament

Noun: διακονία (*diakonia*), GK *1355* (S *1248*), 34x. *diakonia* means "service, ministry." Acts 6:1–6 provides the primary understanding of *diakonia* in the NT. This group of seven men were chosen to act on behalf of the apostles in carrying out acts of service, namely, the daily distribution of food and the care of widows. These men, however, were not merely "hired hands" but men who performed a spiritual function within the church, which gives us the general sense of "ministry" related to this word. Thus, they were to be men with particular spiritual qualities enabling them to fulfill the services of the church (see also Rom. 12:7).

diakonia is not limited to the specific office of deacon but is the foundation of NT fellowship as believers serve others in the body who are in need (Acts 4:32–37; 2 Cor. 9:13). This type of ministry edifies the entire church (Eph. 4:12). Note too that Paul uses *diakonia* to describe the whole area of God's "ministry" in the OT dispensation versus that in the NT era (2 Cor. 3:7–9). Then he uses this same word more narrowly for his own specific work of proclaiming the gospel of reconciliation to Jew and Gentile (2 Cor. 5:18–21; 6:3; cf. Rom. 11:13; 1 Tim. 1:12; 2 Tim. 4:11). See *NIDNTT-A*, 136-38.

SET

Old Testament

Verb: נוּחַ (*nûaḥ*), GK 5663 (S 5117), 140x. The most basic idea of the verb *nûaḥ* is the action of one object coming to rest, roosting, or landing on another object or in a specific location. See *rest*.

Frequently the object does not come to rest on its own but is caused to rest or be placed in a particular location by someone else (104x). In these instances *nûah* may be translated "set," "put," "place," or even "leave." When Joseph is in power in Egypt, he commands his brothers to "leave" one of the brothers with him as they return to Canaan (Gen. 42:33), and God "leaves" nations in the land of Canaan after the conquest to test Israel (Jdg. 3:1; cf. Jdg. 2:23; Jer. 27:11). God "sets" Ezekiel in the valley of dry bones (Ezek. 37:1) and commands Moses to "place" manna before God in the ark, which Aaron does (Exod. 16:33, 34). After the exile, perhaps with eschatological implications, God promises to "place" his people in their land (Ezek. 37:14).

Verb: נָצַב (*nāṣab*), GK 5893 (S 5324), 74x. *nāṣab* conveys the act of standing or the setting up an object and may be translated as "to stand, set." See *stand*.

Verb: נָתַן (*nātan*), GK 5989 (S 5414), 2014x. *nātan* is a high frequency verb in the OT and bears a wide range of meanings, some of which are "to give, present, allow, permit, surrender, deliver, set, put, place."

One main usage of *nātan* is the act of "setting" or "placing" an object. It is used literally of the act of "setting" celestial bodies in the sky (Gen. 1:17), the law before the people (Deut. 4:8; 11:26), and a king over Israel (1 Sam. 12:13). The verb also communicates the more figurative act of the "putting on" an object such as a ring or a helmet. Figurative uses of the verb include "*placing*" curses on enemies (Deut.

30:7), God's majesty on the heavens (Ps. 8:1), or God's Spirit on his servant (Isa. 42:1). See also *give*, *make*.

Verb: עָרַךְ (*ʿārak*), GK 6885 (S 6186), 75x. *ʿārak* denotes the action of arranging an object in a particular way or arranging objects in a specific order to produce a desired effect. A common use of *ʿārak* is "to arrange" a table for a banquet, which the NIV sometimes translates as "to set" a table (Prov. 9:2; Isa. 21:5). See *arrange*.

Verb: שִׂים (*śîm*), GK 8492 (S 7760), 588x. *śîm* generally denotes the action of putting or placing an object or person in a particular location. It is usually translated "put," "set," or "place." See *put*.

Verb: שִׁית (*šît*), GK 8883 (S 7896), 86x. *šît* means "make, put, set." It is a virtual synonym of *śîm* (GK 8492; see *put*) and has many of the same nuances. See *make*.

New Testament

Verb: ὁρίζω (*horizo*), GK *3988* (S *3724*), 8x. *horizō* means "to appoint, set" and occurs most often in Luke and Acts. See *appoint*.

Verb: ἵστημι (*histēmi*), GK *2705* (S *2476*), 154x. The basic sense of *histēmi* is "to set" or "stand." It has a variety of nuances in the NT. See *stand*.

SET APART

Old Testament

Verb: קָדַשׁ (*qādaš*), GK 7727 (S 6942), 171x. *qādaš* describes the state of the sacred realm. Negatively, it represents that which is distinct from the common or profane. It is usually translated "make holy" (NIV), "sanctify," or "dedicate." That which is holy has been "set apart" to the service of God. See *sanctify*.

New Testament

Verb: ἀφορίζω (*aphorizō*), GK *928* (S *873*), 10x. *aphorizō* carries the idea of "to separate, set apart, exclude." In Luke's Sermon on the Mount Jesus says, "Blessed are you when men hate you, when they *exclude* you" (Lk. 6:22). See *separate*.

Verb: ἐκλέγομαι (*eklegomai*), GK *1721* (S *1586*), 22x. *eklegomai* means "to choose, set apart, elect." See *choose*.

Adjective: ἐκλεκτός (*eklektos*), GK *1723* (S *1588*), 22x. *eklektos* is the quality of being "chosen, selected, set apart," with the biblical implication that it is God who chooses. See *chosen*.

SET ASIDE

New Testament

Verb: ἀθετέω (*atheteō*), GK *119* (S *114*), 16x. *atheteō* means "to reject, set aside, nullify, annul." See *reject*.

SET BEFORE

New Testament

Verb: παρατίθημι (*paratithēmi*), GK *4192* (S *3908*), 19x. *paratithēmi* means "to set before, commit." When Jesus feeds the crowds, he gives the food to his disciples "to set before the people" (Mk. 6:41; 8:6–7; Lk. 9:16; cf. a similar use with food in Acts 16:34; 1 Cor. 10:27). Twice as Paul is leaving his churches to return to Jerusalem, he speaks with them and "*commits* them" to the Lord (Acts 14:23; 20:32; cf. also 2 Tim. 2:2). Its most important theological use is the final saying of Jesus from the cross: "Father, into your hands I *commit* my spirit" (Lk. 23:46).

SET FREE

Old Testament

Verb: עָזַב (*ʿāzab*), GK 6440 (S 5800), 214x. *ʿāzab* is used most often for the action of "abandonment" (see *abandon*). It sometimes mean setting a person, particularly a prisoner, free from captivity (2 Chr. 28:14; Ps. 10:14; 16:10).

Verb: פָּתַח (*pātaḥ*), GK 7337 (S 6605), 136x. Generally, *pātaḥ* means "to open" objects that are closed, sealed, or blocked. By extension, it can also mean "to release" or "to set (something) free," such as a person from prison (Isa. 51:14; cf. Jer. 1:14). See *open*.

SET OUT

Old Testament

Verb: נָסַע (*nāsaʿ*), GK 5825 (S 5265), 146x. The original meaning of *nāsaʿ* is "to pull out (tent pegs)," from which the sense "set out" or "journey" is derived. See *journey*.

SET THE MIND ON

New Testament

Verb: φρονέω (*phroneō*), GK *5858* (S *5426*), 26x. *phroneō* means "to think, set one's mind on something, have in mind." See *think*.

SETTLE

Old Testament

Verb: גּוּר (*gûr*), GK 1591 (S 1481), 82x. The basic meaning of *gûr* is to "live, settle, dwell." By and large, this verb refers to someone living outside of their clan, that is, dwelling among people who are not blood relatives. It almost always has the sense of temporariness. See *dwell*.

Verb: יָשַׁב (*yāšab*), GK 3782 (S 3427), 1088x. The general meaning of *yāšab* is to "sit, sit down," with the connotations of "live, dwell, remain, settle." See *live*.

Verb: נוּחַ (*nûaḥ*), GK 5663 (S 5117), 140x. The most basic idea of the verb *nûaḥ* is the action of one object coming to rest, roosting, or landing on another object or in a specific location. In these instances, *nûaḥ* is generally translated "to rest" or "to settle." Birds may try to "rest" on sackcloth (2 Sam. 21:10) and locusts "settle" in Egypt during the plagues (Exod. 10:14). See *rest*.

Verb: שָׁכַן (*šākan*), GK 8905 (S 7931) 130x. *šākan* has the basic meaning "to live, dwell, settle." In nearly one-third of the times this verb is used in the OT, God is the subject. See *dwell*.

SETTLEMENT

Old Testament

Noun: בַּת (*bat*), GK 1426 (S 1323), 587x. *bat* is the common Hebrew noun for one's own daughter. But it may also be used to indicate membership in a group. In geographical designations, a "town and its daughters" means "a town and its satellite villages"; "Heshbon and all its *surrounding settlements*" (lit., "her daughters") (Num. 21:25; cf. 1 Chr. 7:29). See *daughter*.

SEVEN

Old Testament

Noun: שֶׁבַע (*šebaʿ*), GK 8679 (S 7651), 490x. *šebaʿ* means "seven" in the singular and "seventy" in the plural.

Adjective: שְׁבִיעִי (*šᵉbîʿî*), GK 8668 (S 7637), 98x. *šᵉbîʿî* means "seventh. *šebaʿ* can combine with other numbers: e.g., with *ʾelep* ("thousand," GK 547), it means "seven thousand"; with the number ten, it means "seventeen."

(1) The OT structures days, weeks, and years on the basis of the number seven. God created the world in six days, and then he rested "on the seventh day" (Gen. 2:2). This becomes one "week" (Heb. *šebûʿâ*, GK 8651—also based on the same Heb. root) and it becomes the basic unit of dividing time. To imitate this same pattern, God commands in the ten commandments that human beings should work six days and rest "on the seventh day" (Exod. 20:8–11).

(2) Seven becomes the number of completeness. Jacob has to work for Leah and then Rachel for seven years each (Gen. 29:18, 20, 27, 30). Journeys are often seven days in length (31:23), and the Israelites march around Jericho for seven days (and seven times on the seventh day; Jos. 6:3–4); during that time seven priests blow trumpets. To have a family of seven sons seems to be ideal (2 Sam. 21:9; Job 1:2; 42:13). Pharaoh's dreams deal with two periods of seven—seven lean and fat cows, seven good and worthless heads of grain. Solomon spends seven years building the temple (1 Ki. 6:38), and the celebration at the dedication of the temple goes on for seven days (2 Chr. 7:8–9).

(3) This association of seven with completeness and perfection leads to various laws based on the number seven. For example, blood is sprinkled "*seven* times before the Lord" (Lev. 4:6, 17; cf. 8:11; 16:14, 19). A person with a skin disease is put in isolation for seven days (13:4–5, 21). A woman after her monthly period is unclean for seven days (15:13, 19). Both the Feast of Unleavened Bread and the Feast of Tabernacles are to be celebrated seven days (23:6, 24). The total number of annual feasts for the Israelites is seven

(Lev. 23; Num. 28–29). Every seventh year is to be a year for canceling debts (Deut. 15:1–9), and after "*seven* sabbaths of years—*seven* times *seven* years," the fiftieth year is the so-called year of Jubilee (Lev. 25:8). In the tabernacle, the seven branches of the lampstand most likely represent the tree of life (Exod. 25:31–37). Priests are consecrated in a seven-day ritual (29:35–37).

(4) The number "seventy" (ten times seven) is also a large round number, which also implies completeness. Seventy descendants of Jacob go into Egypt (Gen. 46:27). Moses appoints seventy elders of Israel to assist him in leadership (Exod. 24:1, 9; cf. Num. 11:16, 24–25). The length of our days might reach seventy years (Ps. 90:10), or possibly even eighty (see *eight* for what this number means). And God's punishment of his people in their exile to Babylon is to last seventy years (2 Chr. 36:21; Jer. 25:11–12; 29:10).

New Testament

Adjective: ἑπτά (*hepta*), GK *2231* (S *2033*), 88x. *hepta* is the cardinal number "seven." Although this number often carries a symbolic meaning in the NT, many of its uses are to be understood literally: e.g., Anna's seven years of marriage (Lk. 2:36), the seven men chosen by the early church to meet the material needs of the poor (Acts 6:3; 21:8), the seven brothers who each married the same woman (Mt. 22:25, 26, 28), the possession of a person by seven demons (Mt. 12:45; Lk. 8:2), the seven loaves that Jesus multiplied to feed thousands (Mk. 8:5, 6), forgiveness to be granted seventy times seven (NIV: "seventy-seven") times (Mt. 18:22), the seven baskets of leftovers after the feeding of the four thousand (Mk. 8:8), and the seven churches of Asia (Rev. 1:4, 11). Where symbolism is implied (e.g., the numerous uses of *hepta* in Revelation), the number apparently serves as a symbol for fullness or completion. Note too, of course, that our division of time is established into seven-day units, according to principle of creation in Gen. 1. In Acts 28:14, the phrase "seven days" means "one week" (cf. NIV).

The large majority of the uses of *hepta* in the NT (nearly two-thirds) occur in Revelation. In this apocalyptic genre, the number seven is normally infused with symbolic value. It is used to describe numerous items: lampstands (Rev. 1:12), stars (1:16), angels (1:20), spirits of God (3:1), seals (5:1), trumpets (8:2), heads of a dragon (12:3), plagues (15:1), etc. Many have even argued for a sevenfold structure to the book of Revelation itself. Revelation's extensive use of this symbolic number conveys the message that both judgment and salvation are complete, or at least will be in the final consummation. See *NIDNTT-A*, 204.

SEVENTH

Old Testament

Adjective: שְׁבִיעִי (*šᵉbîʿî*), GK 8668 (S 7637), 98x. *šᵉbîʿî* means "seventh" and is closely related to *šebaʿ* (GK 8679), which means "seven." See *seven*.

SEVENTY

Old Testament

Noun: שֶׁבַע (*šebaʿ*), GK 8679 (S 7651), 490x. *šebaʿ* means "seven" in the singular and "seventy" in the plural. See *seven*.

SEW ON

New Testament

Verb: ἐπιβάλλω (*epiballō*), GK *2095* (S *1911*), 18x. *epiballō* means "to lay on, arrest, sew on." See *lay on*.

SEXUAL IMMORALITY

New Testament

Verb: πορνεύω (*porneuō*), GK *4519* (S *4203*), 8x. For a discussion of the verb that is linked with the word group regarding sexual immorality, see *commit sexual immorality*.

Noun: πορνεία (*porneia*), GK *4518* (S *4202*), 25x. The word group to which *porneia* belongs generally relates to any kind of illegitimate sexual intercourse—that is, sexual immorality or fornication (KJV). This word is found most frequently in the writings of Paul. His overarching conviction is this: "It is God's will that you should be sanctified: that you should avoid *sexual immorality*" (1 Thess. 4:3). *porneia* is the product of the sinful nature (Gal. 5:19). Paul's understanding resonates with the teachings of Christ, who says, "For out of the heart come evil thoughts, murder, adultery, *sexual immorality*, theft, false testimony, slander" (Mt. 15:19; cf. Mk. 7:21). Thus, *porneia* is completely improper for God's holy people, among whom "there must not even be a hint of *sexual immorality*" (Eph. 5:3).

In light of this, Paul strongly exhorts the Corinthian church to deal with the issues of sexual immorality among them (1 Cor. 5:1). His argument is clear: since the body belongs to the LORD, it must not be used for *porneia* (6:13). And since the believer's body is the temple of the Holy Spirit (6:19), Paul commands: "Flee from *sexual immorality*" (6:18). Paul's fervent stand against this sin calls for its eradication from one's life. He concludes to the Colossians: "Put to death, therefore, whatever belongs to your earthly nature: *sexual immorality*, impurity, lust, evil desire and greed, which is idolatry" (Col. 3:5).

porneia is also well known for its inclusion in Jesus' teaching on divorce and remarriage. Jesus' simply states in Mt. 19:9, "I tell you that anyone who divorces his wife, except for *marital unfaithfulness* [fornication, KJV], and marries another woman commits adultery" (cf. 5:32). Jesus appeals to Gen. 2:24 when the Pharisees ask him for his position on divorce, stating that God intended from the beginning that a man has one wife, joined together as one flesh in covenant with God (Mt. 19:4–6). In response to Jesus, the Pharisees invoke Moses' teaching on divorce from Deut. 24:1–4. But Jesus' response to this is that Moses allowed divorce because the people's hearts were hardened, "but from the beginning it was not so" (Mt. 19:8). Finally, Jesus states that divorce is only permissible if *porneia* (sexual immorality) has been involved. Since *porneia* denotes a general sense of sexual immorality and not merely adultery, this is a significant text that enters the discussion of what the Bible permits for divorce and remarriage.

Finally, *porneia* occurs seven times in Revelation. The great prostitute Babylon (see *prostitute*) intoxicates the nations with the "wine of her *adulteries*" (Rev. 17:2; cf. 17:4). The kings of the earth commit adultery with her, and in John's vision, "all the nations have drunk the maddening wine of her *adulteries*" (Rev. 18:3; cf. 14:8). This usage of *porneia* probably refers to a religious or spiritual adultery against God. All who align themselves with the great prostitute Babylon stand in opposition to God and will face justice and punishment along with her (19:2) in the last day. See *NIDNTT-A*, 485-86.

Noun: πόρνος (*pornos*), GK *4521* (S *4205*), 10x. The word group to which *pornos* belongs generally relates to any kind of illegitimate sexual intercourse (see also *prostitute*), but in most scriptural contexts, it carries the sense of one who is sexually immoral (a fornicator or whoremonger, KJV). *pornos* can also indicate an adulterer.

The writer of Hebrews admonishes his readers to "see that no one is *sexually immoral*" (Heb. 12:16), since "without holiness no one will see the Lord" (Heb. 12:14). Moreover, marriage must be honored and "the marriage bed kept pure, for God will judge the adulterer and the *sexually immoral*" (Heb. 13:4). Paul goes so far as to exhort the Corinthians "not to associate with sexually immoral people," especially in the church (1 Cor. 5:9–11). The context of his exhortation here is in response to the news that one of his readers has taken his father's wife sexually—indicating both an adulterous and an incestuous sexual relationship. Paul strongly admonishes the Corinthians not to eat or drink with him and commands them to "expel the wicked man from among you" (1 Cor. 5:13b). In addition, a person who is *pornos* contradicts the sound doctrine of the gospel of God (1 Tim. 1:10–11) and thus has no fellowship with those who walk in holiness.

Paul and John emphasize that those who are *pornos* are among the sinners who have no inheritance in the kingdom of God. Along with murderers and idolaters, John states that "the sexually immoral" will find themselves outside the gates of heaven (Rev. 22:15), whose final "place will be in the fiery lake of burning sulfur" (21:8). Likewise, Paul's teaching is unequivocal, "For of this you can be sure: No *pornos*, impure or greedy person—such man is an idolater—has any inheritance in the kingdom of Christ" (Eph. 5:5; cf. 1 Cor. 6:9–10).See *NIDNTT-A*, 485-486.*

(HAVE) SEXUAL RELATIONS, SEXUAL RELATIONSHIPS

Old Testament

Verb: שָׁכַב (*šākab*), GK 8886 (S 7901), 208x. *šākab* means "rest, lie down, sleep." There are a variety of nuances to this verb, all of which revolve around the idea of lying down, including lying down to have sexual relations (usually improper). See *lie down*.

Noun: עֶרְוָה (*ʿerwâ*), GK 6872 (S 6172), 54x. *ʿerwâ* conveys the general state of being uncovered and exposed, usually in the sense of nakedness. Leviticus 18 uses the term 32x as an expression for "sexual relationships" (e.g., 32:6, 7; 20:11). See *naked*.

SHADE, SHADOW

Old Testament

Noun: צֵל (*ṣēl*), GK 7498 (S 6738), 53x. *ṣēl* means literally "shadow, shade," but it can also be used figuratively for the notion of "protection" or of the "transitory or empty nature" of things.

(1) *ṣēl* refers to the "shadow" or "shade" that is cast by the sun. Jonah, for example, sits in the *ṣēl* of the plant as he waits in vain for the destruction of Nineveh (Jon. 4:5). Some other objects in the OT that produce shadows include roofs (Gen. 19:8), mountains (Jdg. 9:36), vines (Ps. 80:11), clouds (Isa. 25:5), rocks (Isa. 32:2), and trees (Ezek. 17:23).

(2) Often in the OT, especially in the prophetic literature and the Psalms, *ṣēl* is used figuratively in one of two ways. (a) Being covered under the shadow of someone or something symbolizes being concealed and thus safe and protected (Gen. 19:8; Num. 14:9; Jdg. 9:15; Ps. 121:5; Isa. 4:6; 32:2; 49:2; 51:16; Ezek. 17:23; 31:6; Hos. 14:7). The psalmist declares: "How precious is your unfailing love, O God! Both high and low among men find refuge in the *shadow* of your wings" (Ps. 36:7). He also praises God: "Because you are my help, I sing in the *shadow* of your wings" (Ps. 63:7; see also 17:8; 57:1).

The prophet Isaiah, however, clearly recognizes that Israel has not always sought the shadow of God but has instead turned elsewhere for protection: "Ah, stubborn children . . . who set out to go down to Egypt without asking for my direction, to take refuge in the protection of Pharaoh and to seek shelter in the *shadow* of Egypt!" (Isa. 30:1–2; cf. Hos. 4:13). But Isaiah also affirms that God the king will reign in righteousness and will serve as a shelter from Israel's storm, "like a *shade* of a great rock in a weary land" (Isa. 32:1–2). We are also told that God conceals his Servant—whom we know to be Jesus Christ—in the shadow of his hand (49:2; cf. 51:16).

(b) The psalmist laments: "My days are like an evening *shadow*; I wither away like grass" (Ps. 102:11; cf. 1 Chr. 29:15; Job 8:9; 14:2; 17:7; Ps. 109:23; 144:4; Eccl. 6:12; 8:13). Here the lengthening of the evening *ṣēl* represents human mortality or a life that is wasting away. As David confesses to God before his death, "Our days on the earth are like a *shadow*, and there is no abiding" (1 Chr. 29:15).

No matter how many "fountains of youth" in which our health/diet/fitness-crazed culture attempts to bathe people, the fact remains that we cannot turn back the sundial of our mortal lives (2 Ki. 20:9; Isa. 38:8; 2 Cor. 4:16). Yet with the psalmist we have every reason to praise the Lord with great delight because through our Lord Jesus Christ we will always be in safety under the shadow of his wings and will one day experience the completion of the new creation, where there is neither decay nor death (Rev. 21:4). Thus, the psalmist says: "I lift up my eyes to the hills. From where does my help come? My help comes from the LORD, who made the heaven and earth. . . . Behold, he who keeps Israel will neither slumber nor sleep. The LORD is your keeper; the Lord is your *shadow* on your right hand" (Ps. 121:1–5).

SHAKE

New Testament

Verb: σαλεύω (*saleuō*), GK *4888* (S *4531*), 15x. *saleuō* means to "shake, agitate." It is used of the waving motion of reeds in the wind (Mt. 11:7), which Jesus contrasted with the unshakeable nature of John the Baptist's message and character. He did not bend to political pressure or to popular notions of the kingdom. This verb is also used of shaking that takes place in nature, such as earthquakes (Acts 16:26). Similarly, it is used of an event of the end times when heavenly bodies will be shaken (Mt. 24:29). When this occurs, "what is not shaken" (i.e., God's eternal kingdom) will remain (Heb. 12:27).

saleuō can also refer to emotional agitation. In Acts 2:25, quoting Ps. 16:8, God's Word stresses that with God at one's right hand, a believer "is not shaken." In Acts 17:13 the Jews in Thessalonica went to Berea to "agitate" the people and start a riot. Finally, this verb can indicate God's living presence among his people (4:31, "after they prayed, the place where they were meeting *was shaken*"). See *NIDNTT-A*, 514.

SHAME

Old Testament

Verb: בּוֹשׁ (*bôš*), GK 1017 (S 954), 125x. *bôš* has the basic meaning "to feel ashamed, put to shame, shame someone." See *ashamed*.

Noun: עֶרְוָה (*ʿerwâ*), GK 6872 (S 6172), 54x. *ʿerwâ* conveys the general state of being uncovered and exposed, usually in the sense of nakedness. The contemporary cliché "caught with your pants down" captures the sense of this term when it is used to denote one's shame. See *naked*.

SHAMELESS

Old Testament

Noun: כְּסִיל (*kᵉsîl*), GK 4067 (S 3684), 70x. *kᵉsîl* refers to a "fool, a stupid or shameless person." The noun is used solely of humanity and found only in the wisdom literature of the OT. See *fool*.

SHAPE

Old Testament

Noun: דְּמוּת (*dᵉmût*), GK 1952 (S 1823), 25x. *dᵉmût* denotes a likeness between two things. It is frequently used in the visions of Ezekiel (Ezek. 1:10, 13, 16, 22, 26, 28) to describe, for example, the shape or form of the creatures the prophet sees. See *likeness*.

SHARE

Old Testament

Verb: חָלַק (*ḥālaq*), GK 2745 (S 2505), 55x. *ḥālaq* is translated "divide, share, allot." A wise servant "shares" his inheritance with others (Prov. 17:2; cf. Jos. 18:2; 22:8; 1 Chr. 24:4–5). See *divide*.

Noun: חֵלֶק (*ḥēleq*), GK 2750 (S 2506), 66x. *ḥēleq* means "share, portion," and also "lot, inheritance." Most often, the word refers to a "share" of an inheritance. For example, it describes the "share" of the promised land given to each tribe as they enter the land (Jos. 19:9) or after returning from the exile (Isa. 61:7). Since Aaron and the Levites have dedicated themselves to the Lord's service and receive no land, the Lord himself becomes their inheritance: "That is why the Levites have no *share* or inheritance among their brothers; the Lord is their inheritance" (Deut. 10:9; cf. Num. 18:20).

ḥēleq describes every Israelite's unique relationship with the Lord: "God is the strength of my heart and my *portion* forever" (Ps. 73:26), and "You are my *portion*, O Lord" (119:57). In view of the spiritual ramifications of *ḥēleq*, one understands readily why the word became popular in Hebrew personal names: e.g., "Hilkiah" (2 Ki. 18:18) means "The Lord is my *portion*." See *NIDOTTE,* 2:161-63.

Noun: חֹק (*ḥōq*), GK 2976 (S 2706), 131x. *ḥōq* is derived from the related verb *ḥāqaq*, which means "to cut in, inscribe, decree" and denotes something that is limited or restricted. Most frequently *ḥōq* refers to the prescribed law of God (see *decree*). Less frequently, it expresses a fixed quantity or some sort of limit. For example, Israel's priests receive a "portion" or "share" of the offering (Exod. 29:28; Lev. 24:9; Num. 18:8, 11, 19).

New Testament

Verb: κοινωνέω (*koinōneō*), GK *3125* (S *2841*), 8x. *koinōneō* means "to share, participate in." Of the eight occurrences in the NT, three of them refer to Christians sharing with one another in the things needed for the body. Paul considers this as something that all Christians should do (Rom. 12:3; Gal. 6:6), and he himself has experienced this blessing from the Christians in Philippi (Phil. 4:15). One of the motivations for the collection among the Gentiles that Paul took for the Christians in Jerusalem is that Gentiles "have shared in the Jews' spiritual blessings" (Rom. 15:27). An additional spiritual meaning is given in Heb. 2:14, that Christ shared flesh and blood with human beings. Moreover, Christians who are suffering persecution "participate in the sufferings of Christ" (1 Pet. 4:13).

In two negative passages, both Paul and John warn against "sharing in" the sins or wicked works of those who are not believers (1 Tim. 5:22; 2 Jn. 11).*

Verb: μετέχω (*metechō*), GK *3576* (S *3348*), 8x. *metecho* means "to partake, share in." See *partake*.

Noun: κλῆρος (*klēros*), GK *3102* (S *2819*), 11x. In the NT *klēros* usually designates the casting of lots, but in a more general sense it can also mean the "share" or "inheritance" that one receives (Col. 1:12). See *lot*.

Noun: μέρος (*meros*), GK *3538* (S *3313*), 42x. *meros* has a basic meaning of "a part of a whole," but it can also mean "place, share." See *part*.

SHARING

New Testament

Noun: κοινωνία (*koinōnia*), GK *3126* (S *2842*), 19x. *koinōnia* generally means "fellowship, communion, participation, sharing." See *fellowship*.

SHED

New Testament

Verb: ἐκχέω (*ekcheō*), GK *1772* (S *1632*), 16x.

Verb: ἐκχύννομαι (*ekchynnomai*), GK *1773* (S *1632*), 11x. These two related verbs convey the idea of emptying out a container or vessel, that is, "to pour out, shed." See *pour out*.

SHEEP

Old Testament

Noun: כֶּבֶשׂ (*kebeś*), GK 3897 (S 3532), 107x. A *kebeś* is a young "lamb"; in most instances in the OT it is being used as a sacrificial animal. See *lamb*.

Noun: צֹאן (*ṣōʾn*), GK 7366 (S 6629), 274x.

(1) Often translated "sheep, lambs, goats," *ṣōʾn* is commonly used to refer to flocks of sheep—useful animals throughout Israel's history, especially during the patriarchal period (Gen. 46:32). They provide milk (Deut. 32:14), and their wool is used to make tent coverings (Exod. 26:14). A man's wealth is even measured by the number of sheep he has (1 Sam. 25:2). When Israel is faithful to his covenant, God promises to bless them by increasing their flocks (Deut. 7:13).

(2) *ṣōʾn* is also used in the expression of one's devotion to God. The firstborn of the flock belong to God, as is clear in Exod. 13:12: "You are to give over to the LORD the first offspring of every womb. All the firstborn males of your livestock belong to the LORD." Additionally, sheep are often offerings to God. They are included in the Passover celebration (Exod. 12:5) and are sacrificed for burnt offerings (Lev. 1:10),

sin offerings (5:6), guilt offerings (5:15), and peace offerings (3:6).

(3) *ṣōʾn* frequently serves as a metaphor for God's people, as in Ps. 100:3: "Know that the LORD is God. It is he who made us, and we are his; we are his people, the *sheep* of his pasture." This verse suggests that God's people are naïve and in need of divine guidance. The analogy can also describe the sinfulness and frailty of humans: "We all, like *sheep*, have gone astray, each of us has turned to his own way; and the LORD has laid on him the iniquity of us all" (Isa. 53:6).

It is important to see that God stands as the shepherd of his *ṣōʾn*. He is pictured as the good shepherd, the caring king of his people. As David declares, "The LORD is my shepherd, I shall not be in want" (Ps. 23:1). Consequently, God promises to gather his *ṣōʾn* into his arms (Isa. 40:11). This finds fulfillment in the Messiah Jesus, the good shepherd who has laid his life down for his sheep (Jn. 10:11, 14). This imagery is meant to be a source of great comfort for God's children. As God explains, "I will rescue my *flock* from their mouths" (Ezek. 34:10). No danger is too great to stop our good shepherd from bringing deliverance. See *NIDOTTE*, 3:727-32.

New Testament

Noun: προβατον (*probaton*), GK *4585* (S *4263*), 39x. *probaton* denotes sheep and is used both naturally and metaphorically. Most of the "natural" occurrences of this word are in parables that serve as a springboard for the metaphorical (e.g., the parable of the lost sheep in Lk. 15:3–7; Jesus' description of the good shepherd in Jn. 10). Christ often uses this term to highlight the utter dependence of sheep on their shepherd (Mt. 12:11; Lk. 15:4). While it true that we have wandered away from him (1 Pet. 2:25), the shepherd calls us back. We as his sheep know his voice, hear his call, and follow him (Jn. 10:1–11). This notion of God's people as sheep should be of great encouragement to us. We have a good shepherd who watches over us (Jn. 10:14). He even laid down his life for us (Jn. 10:11). Moreover, Christ promises that not a single one of his sheep can be snatched from his Father's hand (Jn. 10:29).

probaton is also applied to the small band of disciples gathered by Christ. In Mt. 26:31, Jesus quotes from Zech. 13:7, "I will strike the shepherd, and the sheep of the flock will be scattered." This prophecy was fulfilled when Jesus was arrested and all the disciples abandoned him. See *NIDNTT-A*, 490.

SHEKEL

Old Testament

Noun: שֶׁקֶל (*šeqel*), GK 9203 (S 8255), 88x. The *šeqel* is the basic unit of weight in the OT, like the modern pound or gram. The word is derived from the verb *šāqal*, which means "to weigh out (something)."

(1) A shekel was used to measure the weight of any type of material. The ingredients of the holy anointing oil are measured in shekels (Exod. 30:23–24); Goliath's bronze armor weighs 5,000 shekels and his iron spear head 600 shekels (1 Sam. 17:5, 7); the golden nails used in the temple weigh a total of 50 shekels (2 Chr. 3:9); and Ezekiel is instructed to eat 20 shekels of food per day while prophesying (Ezek. 4:10).

(2) The most common use of *šeqel* in the OT is in a monetary sense as an amount of silver or gold. Throughout most of the OT period, business transactions involved payment in a certain weight of a valuable metal (most commonly silver). From the Code of Hammurabi (who reigned in Babylon in the 18th century BC), we learn that a hired laborer earned about 10 shekels of silver per year. This helps puts the biblical figures into perspective: if an ox injures a slave, its owner has to pay 30 shekels of silver (Exod. 21:32); part of the booty Achan takes is 200 shekels of silver and a bar of gold that weighs 50 shekels (Jos. 7:21); David buys Araunah's threshing floor and oxen for 50 shekels of silver (2 Sam. 24:24); and Jeremiah pays 17 shekels of silver for a field (Jer. 32:9).

(3) The shekel is such a common unit of measurement that in a number of passages the Hebrew omits the term and merely uses the number (Deut. 22:19, 29; 2 Sam. 21:16; Zech. 11:12–13). Although there are difficulties in determining the weight of the shekel, it seems to have been about 0.4 ounces (11.3 g). A modern equivalent for biblical shekels can be estimated by multiplying shekels by 0.4 to get ounces, by 0.025 to get pounds, by 11.3 to get grams, or by 0.011 to get kilograms. See *NIDOTTE*, 4:235-40.

SHELTER

Old Testament

Noun: צֵל (*ṣēl*), GK 7498 (S 6738), 53x. *ṣēl* means literally "shadow, shade," but it can also be used figuratively for the notion of "protection" or of the "transitory or empty nature" of things. See *shadow*.

SHEOL

Old Testament

Noun: שְׁאוֹל (*šᵉʾôl*), GK 8619 (S 7585), 65x. *šᵉʾôl* refers to the place known as "Sheol." It is used with reference to the "grave" or the "netherworld." See *grave*.

SHEPHERD

Old Testament

Verb: רָעָה (*rāʿâ*), GK 8286 (S 7473), 167x. *rāʿâ* means "to shepherd, tend, feed graze." This verb can thus be used for sheep feeding or grazing in a pasture (Exod. 34:3; 1 Chr. 27:29; Isa. 49:9). This verb is sometimes used with animals other than sheep, such as cows and calves (see Isa. 11:7; 27:10). Nearly half of the occurrences of this verb are in a participle form (*rōʿeh*), which means "one who shepherds" or "a shepherd." Undoubtedly the most significant chapter of the OT that deals with *rāʿâ* is Ezek. 34 (occurs 31x).

(1) When human beings are the subject of this verb, *rāʿâ* means "to feed, tend, shepherd." The first recorded shepherd is Abel (Gen. 4:2), and Abraham too keeps sheep (13:7). But human beings can also be termed "shepherds" in a metaphorical sense, for this term is sometimes applied to the leaders of Israel, such as David (2 Sam. 5:2; 7:7; Ps. 78:72). Using such a term for a king is understandable because shepherds, like kings, were expected to care for their sheep, feed them, and protect them from danger (cf. 1 Sam. 17:34–35). God even calls the Persian king Cyrus "my shepherd" (Isa. 44:28).

Unfortunately, however, on far too many occasions "the shepherds of the people" did not exercise care and concern for God's flock; rather, they took advantage of the sheep and used them for their own purposes, scattering them and destroying them in the process (Jer. 10:21; 23:1–2; Ezek. 34:1–10). Consequently, the Lord pronounces words of judgment against these leaders and promises his people new and better shepherds (Jer. 23:4; Ezek. 34:23; Mic. 5:4).

(2) Perhaps more important in the OT are the references to God as a shepherd. The most familiar psalm in the OT begins, "The LORD is my *shepherd*, I shall not be in want" (Ps. 23:1), and this psalm proceeds with the shepherd theme. In Ps. 80:1 the psalmist invokes the Lord as "O *Shepherd* of Israel." In Isa. 40:10–11, Isaiah prophesies that the sovereign Lord will "tend his flock like a *shepherd*. He gathers the lambs in his arms and carries them close to his heart."

In several significant OT passages, God promises that he will take over the shepherding of his people because of the failure of Israel's shepherd-leaders. Ezekiel, for example, prophesies that God himself will take over shepherding his people (Ezek. 34:11–16); he will eventually "place over them one *shepherd*, my servant David, and he will *tend* them; he will *tend* them and be their *shepherd*" (34:23). In the context of the NT, it becomes plain that this text is messianic, for in various passages in the gospels, Jesus hints that he is this new shepherd of God's people (Mt. 9:36; 26:31; Lk. 15:4–7); in John 10:11, 14 Jesus actually calls himself "the good shepherd." See *NIDOTTE*, 3:1138–43.

New Testament

Verb: ποιμαίνω (*poimainō*), GK *4477* (S

4165), 11x. *pomainō* describes the actions of a shepherd: "to shepherd, tend, feed a flock" (Lk. 17:7; 1 Cor. 9:7). It is also used metaphorically for leading and caring for people from roles of spiritual or governmental leadership. Jesus gives Peter this charge, "*Shepherd* my sheep" (Jn. 21:16). Sheep and flocks are common metaphors for God's people throughout Scripture, and to lead, guide, and protect them is to shepherd them (Acts 20:28; 1 Pet. 5:2). But as in Ezek. 34, it is possible for those called to lead God's people to selfishly take care only of themselves (Jude 12). *pomainō* is also used of Christ's relationship with his own (Mt. 2:6; Rev. 7:17) and of his rule over the nations (Rev. 2:27; 12:5; 19:15). See *NIDNTT-A*, 480-81.*

Noun: ποιμήν (*poimēn*), GK *4478* (S *4166*), 18x. A *poimēn* is a person who tends to a flock. The term is used of actual shepherds who visited the infant Christ in Bethlehem (Lk. 2:8, 15, 18, 20). Elsewhere in the NT *poimēn* occurs only in parables or as a figure of speech.

poimēn is used most commonly to refer to Jesus Christ and his care for his people. He is "that great Shepherd of the sheep" (Heb. 13:20), as well as "the Shepherd and Overseer of your souls" (1 Pet. 2:25). Jesus uses *poimēn* as a self-designation, "I am the good shepherd" (Jn. 10:11, 14). He contrasts his role as a shepherd to that of a hired hand. According to Exod. 22:13, a hired hand was not responsible for the death of an animal under his care. When the time of turmoil came, the hired hand would often flee. But a shepherd stayed and protected his sheep because he had a vested interest in their well-being (cf. 1 Sam. 17:34–35). The same is true of Christ and his concern for his people. His care and love are so great that he has laid down his life for them (Jn. 10:11). As the parable of the lost sheep indicates, he cares deeply for the weakest in the flock (Lk. 15:3–7). In this way, Jesus fulfills those OT prophecies about the coming shepherd for God's flock who will care for his sheep in a way that human leaders have not (Jer. 23:1–6; Ezek. 34).

Finally, just as God acts as the shepherd of his sheep, he has appointed leaders in the church to serve in like manner: "It was he who gave some to be apostles, some to be prophets, some to be evangelists, and some to be shepherds [or pastors] and teachers" (Eph. 4:11). These shepherds are to care for the spiritual welfare of the church (Jn. 21:15–17) as well as to seek those who are lost. The modern day pastor fulfills the biblical concept of shepherd. See *NIDNTT-A*, 480-81.

SHIELD

Old Testament

Noun: מָגֵן (*māgēn*), GK 4482 (S 4043), 63x. *māgēn* is the standard word for a common "shield"—a hard object made of metal, wood, leather, or reed; it could be small or large (full body). In the OT, it has both literal and figurative uses.

(1) The *māgēn* protects a warrior from the offensive blows of an adversary (Jdg. 5:8; 2 Sam. 1:21; 1 Ki. 10:17; 14:26, 27; Isa. 21:5; Jer. 46:3, 9; Ezek. 27:10). The protective scales of the leviathan (crocodile?) are portrayed as tightly fit rows of shields (Job 41:15), and the adorned neck of the beautiful maiden is depicted as a tower decorated with the shields of warriors (Song 4:4). When the Lord is characterized as a warrior in the OT (Exod. 15:3), he is portrayed both as one who wields a shield on behalf of his people (Ps. 35:2) and as one who smashes the shields of the enemy (76:3).

(2) Because the shield is a defensive weapon, it is often used as a metaphor for God's protection. The earliest metaphorical use appears in Gen. 15:1, where the Lord says to Abraham, "Do not fear, Abram. I am your *māgēn*." The significance of this designation appears grounded in the blessing of Abraham by Melchizedek in 14:20: "Blessed be God Most High, who has delivered [*miggēn*] your enemies into your hand." The significance of this metaphor is also connected to the covenant the Lord makes with Abraham in Gen. 15

(cf. Ps. 47:9). Subsequently, *māgēn* as a metaphor for the Lord becomes a standard expression for recognizing and praising him as the protector and refuge of Israel. Note Deut. 32:29, part of Moses' song: "Blessed are you, O Israel! Who is like you, a people saved by the LORD? He is your *shield* and helper and your glorious sword" (Deut. 32:29). David confesses, "As for God, his way is perfect; the word of the LORD is flawless. He is a *shield* for all who take refuge in him" (2 Sam. 22:31). The use of this metaphor is especially common in Psalms (Ps. 3:1; 7:10; 18:2, 20; 28:7; 33:20; 59:11; 84:11; 115:9, 10, 11; 119:114; 144:2). See *NIDOTTE*, 2:846-47.

SHINE

New Testament

Verb: φαίνω (*phainō*), GK *5743* (S *5316*), 31x. *phainō* refers to objects coming into sight (i.e., appearing) and to bright objects shining their light. See *appear*.

SHIP

New Testament

Noun: πλοῖον (*ploion*), GK *4450* (S *4143*), 67x. *ploion* denotes a "boat" or "ship." Almost all uses of this word refer to boats on the Sea of Galilee or the Mediterranean. See *boat*.

SHORE

Old Testament

Noun: קָצֶה (*qāṣeh*), GK 7895 (S 7097), 92x. *qāṣeh* is derived from the verb *qāṣâ*, which means "to cut off," and refers to the point where something is cut off, i.e., its edge or end. When it refers to the edge of a lake or sea, "shore" may be used (Jos. 15:2). See *end*.

Noun: שָׂפָה (*śāpâ*) GK 8557 (S 8193), 178x. *śāpâ* often denotes the physical "lip(s)" of a person (Num. 30:7, 13; Song 4:3, 11; 5:13). When used metaphorically, this word can be translated as "shore" (on the seashore, Gen. 22:17; Exod. 14:30), "bank" (of a river, Gen. 41:3, 17; Exod. 2:3), or the "edge" (of an object like a curtain, Exod. 26:4, 10). See *lip*.

SHORT

New Testament

Adjective: ὀλίγος (*oligos*), GK *3900* (S *3641*), 40x. *oligos* typically denotes a small number, a small amount of something, or shortness in size or time. See *few*.

SHOULD

New Testament

Verb: δεῖ (*dei*), GK *1256* (S *1163*), 101x. *dei* occurs frequently in the NT, especially in Luke. It has a basic meaning of something being "necessary." See *must*.

SHOULDER

Old Testament

Noun: כָּתֵף (*kātēp*), GK 4190 (S 3802), 67x. *kātēp* denotes the area of the shoulder blades (cf. *šᵉkem*, which denotes the neck and shoulder area) and is often translated "shoulder, side, slope" (see *side*). The Levites carry the tabernacle on their shoulders (Num. 7:9; 1 Chr. 15:15), and beasts of burden carry goods on their shoulders (Isa. 30:6, *backs* in NIV). In Isa. 46:7, God compares himself with the false gods, the idols of Babylon, who are carried on the shoulders of people. God, however, is not a god who is carried by people; rather, he is the God who carries his own people. Finally, by extension, *kātēp* is used (in the plural) for the *shoulder pieces* of the priest's garment (Exod. 28:7, 12). See *NIDOTTE*, 2:743-44.

SHOUT

Old Testament

Verb: רָנַן (*rānan*), GK 8264 (S 7442), 53x. The vast majority of uses for *rānan* clearly includes the concept of joy and thus the verb is regularly translated "shout for joy," "sing for joy," or "sing joyfully." In the OT, God is the primary reason why people "shout for joy." See *sing*.

New Testament

Verb: βοάω (*boaō*), GK *1066* (S *994*), 12x. *boaō* means "to cry out, shout, call loudly." See *call*.

Verb: κράζω (*krazō*), GK *3189* (S *2896*), 55x. *krazō* means "to shout, cry out." Such shouting can be in hostility, anguish, joyful elation, or urgent authoritative testimony. (1) *krazō* naturally denotes hostility when on the lips of demons and unclean spirits (Mt. 8:29; Mk. 3:11; 5:5, 7; 9:26; Lk. 9:39; Acts 16:17), the mob at Jesus' "trial" (Mt. 27:23; Mk. 15:13, 14), the mob at the stoning of Stephen (Acts 7:57), the riotous mob in Ephesus (Acts 19:32), and the hostile mob in Jerusalem (21:28, 36). Perhaps a bit of holy hostility can be found in Acts 14:14, when Barnabas and Paul tear their garments and rush into the crowd, "crying out" for them to stop their pagan sacrifices.

(2) *krazō* as a cry of anguish is used of the demon-oppressed who shout to Jesus for healing (Mt. 15:22, 23), blind men who "cry out" to Jesus for sight (Mt. 9:27; 20:30, 31; Mk. 10:47, 48; Lk. 18:39), the disciples who shout to Jesus to save them from a life-threatening storm (Mt. 14:26, 30), maligned laborers (Jas. 5:4), and the pregnant woman in Rev. 12:2. The most poignant examples of *krazō* are the anguished cries of Jesus in Mt. 27:50, Stephen in Acts 7:60, and the martyred saints beneath the altar in Rev. 6:10.

(3) *krazō* as worshipful praise and rejoicing can be found on the lips of the crowds at the triumphal entry (Mt. 21:9, 15; Mk. 11:9) and the multitudes as Jesus drew near the Mount of Olives (Lk. 19:37). When the Pharisees tell Jesus to rebuke his disciples, he replies in 19:40, "I tell you, if these were silent, the very stones *would cry out*" (ESV). It is with the same sense of worshipful urgency that believers "*cry* 'Abba! Father!'" (Rom. 8:15; Gal. 4:6), and the saints of Rev. 7:10 cry out, "Salvation belongs to our God who sits on the throne, and to the Lamb!" *krazō* can also refer to idolatrous praise and worship (Acts 19:28, 34).

(4) Finally, *krazō* denotes authoritative testimony when used of John the Baptist's witness (Jn. 1:15), Jesus' teaching in the temple (7:28), Jesus' testimony that thirst will be quenched in him alone (7:37), and belief in Jesus as belief in the one who sent him (12:44). It is also used of Paul's giving his defense in Acts 23:6 and 24:21, and a prophecy of Isaiah in Rom. 9:27. Such urgent, authoritative testimony can also be seen in Rev. 10:3; 18:2 and in the blessed command to come and gather for the great supper of God in 19:17. See *NIDNTT-A*, 316-17.

SHOW

New Testament

Verb: δείκνυμι (*deiknymi*), GK *1259* (S *1166*), 30x.

Verb: ἐνδείκνυμι (*endeiknymi*), GK *1892* (S *1731*), 11x. The basic meaning of both verbs is "to show" something (Mt. 4:8, "The devil ... *showed* him all the kingdoms of the world"). *deiknymi* is used for *presenting* oneself to a priest (8:4) and for *explaining* things about the future (16:21). It can also refer to supernatural revelation about what the Father will show (Jn. 5:20). James uses the verb as an evidence of genuine faith: "I will *show* you my faith by what I do" (Jas. 2:18), and later, "Who is wise and understanding among you? Let him *show* it by his good life (3:13)." For James, true, saving faith is never divorced from good deeds, though good deeds alone do not save.

Unlike *deiknymi*, *endeiknymi* carries the idea of demonstrating through logic or acts as opposed to simply putting something on display. It carries the idea of a legal presentation of evidence (Rom. 2:15) and of proving a point (9:17). God demonstrates both his wrath (9:22) and his mercy (Eph. 2:7) as he paints the portrait of his glory. *endeiknymi* can be used of a show of emotion or intent (2 Tim. 4:14) or of a demonstration of character (Tit. 2:10). It is also used of a proof of our devotion to God (Heb. 6:10, "God ... will not forget ... the love you have *shown* him"). See *NIDNTT-A*, 122-123.

Verb: ἐμφανίζω (*emphanizō*), GK *1872* (S *1718*), 10x. *emphanizō* means "to show or disclose" something previously hidden (Heb. 11:14). When used passively, it means "to appear" (Mt. 27:53; Heb. 9:24).

It can mean to request something, probably in the sense of revealing a desire (Acts 23:15) or of making a report (23:22). *emphanizō* can be used in a legal context to refer to an indictment (24:1, "They *brought* their *charges* against Paul before the governor"). In Jn. 14 the verb carries the idea of the personal revelation of Christ to his people (14:21, "I too will love him and *show* myself to him"). Judas (not Iscariot) understood the exclusive nature of that revelation (v. 22, "But, LORD, why do you intend to *show* yourself to us and not to the world?"), which should encourage believers as they contemplate the deliberate, sovereign love of God to his people. See *NIDNTT-A*, 185.

SHOW COMPASSION

New Testament

Verb: σπλαγχνίζομαι (*splanchnizomai*), GK *5072* (S *4697*), 12x. *splanchnizomai* means "to have compassion for someone, show compassion." See *compassion, have compassion.*

SHOW HOSPITALITY

New Testament

Verb: ξενίζω (*xenizō*), GK *3826* (S *3579*), 10x. *xenizō* generally means "to entertain, show hospitality," though it can also mean "to be surprised, to be strange" (see *strange, be strange*). See *entertain.*

SHOW MERCY, FAVOR

Old Testament

Verb: חָנַן (*ḥānan*), GK 2858 (S 2603), 77x. The primary meaning of *ḥānan* is "to show favor, be gracious" toward someone. The verb also has the sense of "showing mercy," since often gracious actions are directed toward someone in need. Note how *ḥānan* is regularly paired with words such as *rāḥam* ("to have compassion") and *ḥesed* ("unfailing love, loving-kindness"). Thus, in God's self-revelation to Moses, he declares, "I will have mercy [*ḥānan*] on whom I will have mercy, and I will have compassion *rāḥam* on whom I will have compassion" (Exod. 33:19). Likewise in 2 Ki. 13:23, the notice is given that "the Lord *was gracious* to them and had compassion *rāḥam* and showed concern for them because of his covenant with Abraham, Isaac and Jacob" (see also Isa. 27:11; 30:18; Ps. 55:1; 102:14).

(1) The use of *ḥānan* in the sense of "show mercy" is especially seen in the Psalms, where the psalmist finds himself in great need and pleads for God's mercy. "*Be merciful* to me, Lord, for I am faint" (Ps. 6:2). Indeed, almost half of the uses of *ḥānan* occur in the Psalms (32x), which highlights the fact that the verb often expresses the gracious (and therefore unearned) action of a superior toward someone in need, and specifically of God's favor given to his people. "As the eyes of slaves look to the hand of their master, as the eyes of a maid look to the hand of her mistress, so our eyes look to the LORD our God, till he *shows us his mercy*" (Ps. 123:2). Such a plea for God's favor can also be made on behalf of others. Thus, Isaiah prays, "O LORD, *be gracious to us;* we have waited for you" (Isa. 33:2; see also Ps. 102:13).

(2) This divine showing of mercy includes more than meeting one's immediate needs. It also includes God's companionship, for in his mercy, he extends his friendship to those he calls into a covenant relationship. For instance, in the Priestly Blessing (Num. 6:24–26; cf. Ps. 67:1), the benediction "The LORD make his face shine on you, and *be gracious* to you," is paralleled in the next line by "The LORD lift up his countenance on you, and give you peace." To "lift up one's countenance" means "to smile" (note the opposite in Cain's case, Gen. 4:6, whose countenance had fallen). God smiles on those to whom he extends his grace. It is this covenant relationship that allows God's children to plead for his favor (a recurring theme in the Psalms). "Turn to me and *have mercy* on me, as you always do to those who love your name" (Ps. 119:132). Yet God's willingness to grant his favor does not negate his own justice. Indeed, he may withhold his favor from those who refuse to honor him in obedience, as demonstrated in Isra-

el's history (1 Ki. 8:33; Isa. 27:11; Lam. 4:16). But his mercy is seen in that he remains ready to restore his chosen people by granting forgiveness and favor when they confess their sin and return to him: "Yet the Lord longs *to be gracious* to you; he rises to show you compassion" (Isa. 30:18; cf. 1 Ki. 8:33, 47).

(3) God's mercy toward his people forms the example for how they are to treat each other. Showing favor to the poor and disadvantaged is characteristic of those who honor God. "He who oppresses the poor taunts his Maker, but he who *is gracious* to the needy honors him" (Prov. 14:31; cf. 19:17). Joseph's brothers recognize that their troubles began when they failed to respond when he "pleaded" for mercy (Gen. 42:21). In fact, a characteristic of the wicked is that though they have been "shown mercy," they refuse to deal justly with others (Isa. 26:10). Jesus likewise teaches that God's gracious actions form the paradigm for interpersonal relationship: "Blessed are the merciful, for they shall receive mercy" (Mt. 5:7), and he taught his disciples to pray, "Forgive us our debts, as we also have forgiven our debtors" (Mt. 6:12). See *NIDOTTE,* 2:203–6.

SHREWD

New Testament

Adjective: φρόνιμος (*phronimos*), GK *5861* (S *5429*), 14x. One who is *phronimos* is "wise, intelligent" in a prudent or shrewd way, acting in a way that is appropriate for the circumstance or situation. See *wise.*

SHUDDER

Old Testament

Verb: שָׁמֵם (*šāmēm*), GK 9037 (S 8074), 92x. The verb *šāmēm* is used in two distinct but related ways. It can mean "to be desolate, deserted, lay waste" or it can point to the response to such desolation and mean "to shudder, be horrified, be appalled." As to the second usage, it denotes the reaction of people to the desolation caused by divine judgment on themselves (Ps. 40:15; 143:4) or others (Lev. 26:32; Jer. 2:12; Job 17:8). See *appalled.*

SHUT

Old Testament

Verb: סָגַר (*sāgar*), GK 6037 (S 5462), 91x. *sāgar* broadly means "to shut something up" and is most frequently used of doors and gates (e.g., Gen. 19:6; Jdg. 3:23; Eccl. 12:4; Isa. 24:10). It can also have an extended meaning of "to hand over, give over."

(1) In 2 Ki. 4 shutting a door *sāgar* as a clever device to indicate faith. In verses 4-5 a destitute woman obeys Elisha's command, shutting her door and pouring oil into jars until she has enough to pay off her debts. In verse 21 the Shunamite woman lays her dead son on Elisha's bed, believing he can raise the boy from the dead. As she leaves, she shuts the door. In verse 33 Elisha shuts the door so he can pray, and he does indeed raise the boy to life.

(2) God also shuts doors, usually with some symbolic meaning. He shuts the door of Noah's ark, by which action he ominously announces that the time for judgment has arrived (Gen. 7:16). In Mal. 1:10, God desires the doors of the temple to be shut as an indication of his rejection of Israel. The opening and shutting of the gates in Ezekiel's temple visions indicate that access to God is either open or closed (Ezek. 46:1–2). One gate in Ezekiel's vision was permanently shut. God had passed through it and his presence made that gate holy, so that no one else was permitted to use it (Ezek. 44:1–2).

(3) Doors are not the only things that are shut. Hearts can be closed in rebellion to God (Ps. 17:10). God closes up Adam's side, in the sense of healing him, after he created Eve (Gen. 2:21). God shuts the lions' mouths so that Daniel is not harmed (Dan. 6:23). God opens and closes wombs as he pleases (1 Sam. 1:5–6). Those struggling with difficulties conceiving today can be sure that God's sovereignty is at work in their lives.

(4) *sāgar* can also be used symbolically. Isaiah uses the imagery of an open gate

(i.e. one that is "not shut") to indicate divine authority, in the sense that no one can undo the work of God's anointed servant (Isa. 22:22; see also Isa. 45:1). There are messianic overtones in this verse and Christ echoes these words in Rev. 3:8. In Isa. 60:11, the fact that the gates of Jerusalem will never be shut indicates divine blessing. There is no longer a need for the city to worry about its enemies.

(5) *sāgar* has a variety of other nuances related to shutting something. For instance, the king of Egypt considers Israel to be trapped in the wilderness (Exod. 14:3). A priest must isolate a person with a spot in his skin to protect the community while he determines if it is leprous (Lev. 13:4).

(6) Some meanings of *sāgar* are difficult to relate to the idea of shutting. It is frequently used in a military sense of handing or giving over; the idea of surrounding a foe, shutting them in, and forcing them to surrender may be in mind (e.g., Deut. 23:15; 32:30; Jos. 20:5). It can also be used to denote repairing a breach in a wall, in the sense of closing up a hole (1 Ki. 11:27). In Ps. 35:3, the psalmist asks God to shut the windows of opportunity for his persecutors to hound him. For further reading, see *NIDOTTE*, 3:224–26.

New Testament

Verb: κλείω (*kleiō*), GK *3091* (S *2808*), 16x.

(1) *kleiō* means "to shut (something)." It is generally used for closing physical objects like doors (Mt. 6:6; cf. 2 Ki. 4, in which shutting a door is an indication of faith; see also Mt. 25:10) and gates (Acts 21:30; see also Rev. 21:25). Sometimes *kleiō* can indicate that a door in not just shut, but locked. Lk. 11:7 uses the imagery of a locked door to describe hindrances to prayer that ought to be overcome with persistence; that is, God sometimes tests a believer's faith by not immediately answering. After his resurrection, Jesus is not hindered by locked doors (Jn. 20:19, 26), nor are the apostles (Acts 5:23) when God chooses to deliver them.

(2) Rev. 3:7–8 uses *kleiō* to refer to the sovereign authority of the glorified Christ. He is pictured as sovereignly opening and closing doors, actions that no one can oppose.

(3) *kleiō* is also used of things both immaterial and intangible. Jesus rebukes the Pharisees for denying people (i.e., closing off) access to God's grace through their faithless regulations and traditions (Mt. 23:13). The verb is also used of God's hindering of Satan (Rev. 20:3). This verse reminds us of God's sovereign limiting of both the power and influence of Satan.

(4) An interesting use of *kleiō* is found in 1 Jn. 3:17, where John criticizes those who literally "shut their intestines" (KJV, "bowels of compassion") against a brother in need. To the Greek, the intestines were the center of human emotion, so to shut up one's intestines was to show a lack of compassion. Tangibly expressing love to those who are suffering is a hallmark of Christianity, so much so that John even questions whether those who fail to demonstrate such love truly belong to God. For further reading, see *NIDNTT*, 2:729–34.

SICK

Old Testament

Verb: חָלָה (*ḥālâ*), GK 2703 (S 2470), 75x. *ḥāla* describes a person who is weak, sick, ill, diseased, or wounded; it is also used to describe human frailties. See *weak*.

New Testament

Verb: ἀσθενέω (*astheneō*), GK *820* (S *770*), 33x. *astheneō* means "to be feeble, weak" and is used both of physical weakness and of moral/spiritual weakness. See *weak*.

Adjective: ἀσθενής (*asthenēs*), GK *822* (S *772*), 26x. *asthenēs* generally means "weak" and refers to that which lacks strength or intensity. Sometimes it means "sick." See *weak*.

Adverb: κακῶς (*kakōs*), GK *2809* (S *2560*), 16x. The adverb *kakōs* can designate those with physical illness (the "sick") or moral ("wrong, wicked") harm.

kakōs is used in the idiom "to have *kakōs*" to describe physical illness. "News about him spread all over Syria, and people brought to him all who were *sick* with various diseases ... and he healed them" (Mt. 4:24; cf. 8:16; 14:35; Mk. 1:32, 34; 6:55). It can also denote someone who is suffering "terribly" from some malady (Mt. 15:22; 17:15).

In terms of moral wrong, Jesus uses *kakōs* to describe sinners in his brief parable: "It is not the healthy who need a doctor, but the *sick*" (Mt. 9:12; Mk. 2:17; Lk. 5:31). Jesus asks his accusers, "If I have spoken *wrongly* [i.e., incorrectly], then produce the witness" (Jn. 18:23). Matthew uses this word to speak of the "*wretched* end" of those who fight against God's purposes (Mt. 21:41). Paul uses *kakōs* to describe criticism against an appointed ruler or high priest: "Do not speak *evil* about the ruler of your people" (Acts 23:5). James tells us that we do not receive answers to our petitions from God because we ask "wrongly," i.e., for the wrong reason (Jas. 4:3). See *NIDNTT-A*, 284-85.*

SICKNESS

New Testament

Noun: ἀσθένεια (*astheneia*), GK *819* (S *769*), 24x. *astheneia* means "weakness" and can also be used of a physical weakness ("sickness"). See *weakness*.

Noun: νόσος (*nosos*), GK *3798* (S *3554*), 11x. *nosos* is one of the words used to describe a "disease, illness, sickness." See *disease*.

SIDE

Old Testament

Noun: כָּתֵף (*kātēp*), GK 4190 (S 3802), 67x. *kātēp* denotes the area of the shoulder blades (cf. *šᵉkem*, which denotes the neck and shoulder area). In certain spatial contexts, *kātēp* refers to the side of something, as in the side of the tabernacle where the curtains hang (Exod. 27:14, 15), or the right side of the temple where the door of the middle chamber is located (1 Ki. 6:8). In a geographic setting, it is sometimes translated "slopes," referring to the sides of the mountains or ridges of Israel's land (Jos. 15:8, 10, 11). See *shoulder*.

Noun: עֵבֶר (*ʿēber*), GK 6298 (S 5676), 90x. *ʿēber* means "side," though most occurrences denote some sort of geographical direction. God wrote on "both sides" of the tablets that contained his law (Exod. 32:15), and there were to be three cities of refuge on each "side" of the Jordan (Num. 35:14).

The phrase "the other side of the Jordan" occurs 38x in the OT; while most occurrences refer to the east side of the Jordan (e.g., Jos. 1:14–15; 20:8), in some cases, depending on the perspective, it can refer to the west side of that river (9:1; 22:7). In Deut. 30:13, Moses reminds the people that they have God's Word; it is not "beyond the sea" (i.e., far to the west of the Mediterranean Sea) but is right in their midst. The phrase "beyond the River" means "beyond the Euphrates River," and it always means the land to the west of that river (2 Sam. 10:16); in fact, the official Persian name for the territory that included Canaan was "Beyond the River" (NIV "Trans-Euphrates"; Ezr. 8:36; Neh. 2:7, 9).

Noun: פֵּאָה (*pēʾâ*), GK 6991 (S 6285), 86x. *pēʾâ* can be translated as "side, boundary, border, edge." It occurs frequently as part of the measurements in Exodus in relation to the tabernacle and the courtyard (Exod. 25–27; 38), and in Numbers and Joshua referring to the boundaries of Israel's land in Canaan (Num. 34–35; Jos. 18). Farmers are not to harvest all the way to the "edges" of the fields (Lev. 19:9).

Over half of the occurrences of *pēʾâ* are found in Ezekiel, especially in chs. 47–48, where Ezekiel describes his vision of a man who delineates the boundaries of the lands apportioned to the twelve tribes after their return from exile (47:15–20). Each tribe's lot is described individually (48:1–29), along with the measurements of the gates of the new city, three gates on each of four sides (48:30–35).

An alternative use of *pēʾa* occurs in Leviticus, where it describes the hair that is not to be cut or trimmed at the "edges" of the priests' beards (Lev. 19:27; 21:5) or at the "sides" of their heads (19:27). *pēʾâ* may also refer to the forehead, that is, the front side of the head (Lev. 14:21) and, metaphorically, to punishment by crushing the foreheads and skulls of Moabite enemies (Num. 24:17; Jer. 48:45).

A final reference seems to indicate the opulent lifestyles of the Israelites living in Samaria just before its fall, describing the wealthy as ones who sit "on the *edge* of their beds" (Amos 3:12, NIV; KJV translates "corner"). These beds are later described as inlaid with ivory (Amos 6:4). An alternative interpretation of this verse might indicate, metaphorically, that only the corner of a bed (bits and pieces) will be salvaged after the ravaging attack of an enemy; that is, Israel will not escape unscathed.

Noun: קִיר (*qîr*), GK 7815 (S 7023), 73x. *qîr* means "wall, side." It can refers to the "sides" of the altar (Lev. 1:15; 5:9). See *wall.*

SIGHT

Old Testament

Noun: עַיִן (*ʿayin*), GK 6524 (S 5869), 889x. *ʿayin* means "eye." It can refer to the literal body part, but it appears in many expressions related to sight. See *eyes.*

SIGN

Old Testament

Noun: אוֹת (*ʾôt*), GK 253 (S 226), 79x. *ʾôt* refers to a "sign" or symbol that communicates meaning; it can be used of supernatural signs (i.e., miracles) from God. Nearly half of the uses of this word are in the Pentateuch.

(1) A sign is a communicative device that points to something. It does not have to have a deep spiritual significance, however. For example, *ʾôt* is used for "the mark" God put on Cain (Gen. 4:15). Signs are built into the creation, as the lights in the sky "serve as *signs* to mark the seasons and days and years" (1:14). There were also signs (banners) for each of the tribes of Israel (Num. 2:2).

(2) But many times the *ʾôt* is a significant element in the salvation history of God's people. The covenant(s) God makes with his people are accompanied by signs. The rainbow in the sky is the "sign" (KJV, "token") of the covenant that God will never send another worldwide flood (Gen. 9:12, 13, 17). Circumcision is the sign of the Abrahamic covenant (17:11) that these people belong to the Lord God. The sign God gives to Moses that he will indeed deliver Israel from Egypt is the promise that they would worship the Lord at Horeb (Exod. 3:12). The blood on the doorposts is the sign for the destroyer to pass over Israelite homes (12:13). Remembrance of the Passover is a sign for coming generations (13:9), as is the dedication of the firstborn (13:16). The Sabbath is a sign between Israel and God (31:13; Ezek. 20:12). None of these signs is designed to draw attention to itself but to God's covenant relationship with his people.

(3) Esp. in the historical books, a sign could serve as an authentication that God is acting or certification of the word of a prophet (cf. Ps. 74:9). Gideon asks for a "sign" that God has really been talking with him (Jdg. 6:11). Hezekiah receives a sign that the Lord will indeed heal him (2 Ki. 20:8). The birth of Immanuel is a sign to Ahaz that God will destroy those who are attacking the nation of Judah (Isa. 7:14). The symbolic actions of Ezekiel are a sign to Israel of God's presence in his prophet (Ezek. 4:3).

Sometimes a sign is an extraordinary demonstration of God's power, such as the signs God gave to Moses to convince the people of Israel (Exod. 4:8, 9, 17, 28, 30). In such cases this word is translated as "miraculous sign(s)" (e.g., Exod. 10:1; Neh. 9:10; Ps. 74:9). These especially relate to the "*signs* and wonders" God performed to authorize his demand that Egypt let Israel go, and he hardened Pharaoh's heart so that he could show more signs (Exod. 7:3; 8:23; cf. Deut. 4:34). God expects his people to remember the signs he has shown them (Num. 14:11, 22).

New Testament

Noun: σημεῖον (*sēmeion*), GK *4956* (S

4592), 77x. A σημεῖον is a "sign" that marks or distinguishes something. It is also used of a miraculous indicator, often a "miracle."

(1) On the most basic level, a sign is nothing more than a communicative indicator between persons. Judas gave the sign of the kiss to those who sought to apprehend Jesus (Mt. 26:48). Paul also spoke of the sign of genuineness in all his letters—a greeting in his own hand (2 Thess. 3:17).

(2) Jesus himself is referred to as a sign. The angel gives the shepherds the sign of a baby in newborn clothes in a manger (Lk. 2:12). Simeon tells Mary that her child will be a sign that will be opposed (Lk. 2:34).

(3) Signs are sought as verification of claims being made. The scribes and Pharisees seek a sign from Jesus that will validate his identity as the Messiah (Mt. 12:38; 16:1). In response to this request, Jesus makes reference to their inability to recognize the "signs of the times" (see 5, below), which appears to be his way of identifying himself as the Messiah by pointing to all that is taking place in and through him (Mt. 16:3). John makes this explicit by referring to the miracles of Jesus as "signs" showing him to be the Messiah (cf. Jn. 2:11, 18, 23; 3:2; 4:48, 54; 6:2, 14, 26, 30; 7:31; 9:16; 10:41; 11:47; 12:18, 37; 20:30). Herod, too, is seeking a sign from Jesus, but it seems he is hoping less for verification that Jesus is the Messiah than for a spectacular trick (Lk. 23:8). The sign of Jonah appears to be a cryptic reference to Jesus' death and resurrection, which Jesus offers to an evil and unbelieving generation as verification of his messianic identity (Mt. 12:38–39; 16:1–4).

(4) Signs also serve to demonstrate God's approval of persons or groups. In the longer ending of Mark, miraculous signs are promised to the disciples (Mk. 16:17, 20). These things are then accomplished in Acts. This book itself points to these signs as verifying that the apostles and members of the early church have God's approval (Acts 2:19, 22, 43; 4:16, 22, 30; 5:12; 6:8; 8:6, 13; 14:3; 15:12; cf. Heb. 2:4). Stephen speaks of the signs and wonders done by Moses (7:36). Paul testifies that signs and wonders accompany his ministry (Rom. 15:19; 2 Cor. 12:12), and he recognizes the Jewish desire for divine verification through signs (1 Cor. 1:22).

(5) Signs can indicate progress in salvation history. The disciples ask Jesus for the "sign of his coming," which will signal the "consummation of the age" (Mt. 24:3). Jesus then describes various signs, such as that false christs will do great signs and wonders (24:24). Finally, the sign of the Son of Man will appear in heaven (24:30). Satan will offer counterfeit signs and wonders at the coming of the lawless one (2 Thess. 2:9). See also Rev. 12:1, 3; 13:13–14; 15:1; 16:14; 19:20.

(6) Abraham's circumcision is a sign (Rom. 4:11), indicating his subjection and the subjection of his seed to God. See *NIDNTT-A*, 522-524.

SILENT

New Testament

Verb: σιγάω (*sigaō*), GK *4967* (S *4601*), 10x. *sigaō* is used primarily to a person's being quiet or silent. See *quiet*.

Verb: σιωπάω (*siōpaō*), GK *4995* (S *4623*), 10x. *siōpaō* means "to be quiet, silent." It is found almost exclusively in the gospels. *siōpaō* refers primarily to the silencing of the human voice. See *quiet*.

SILVER

Old Testament

Noun: כֶּסֶף (*kesep*), GK 4084 (S 3701), 403x. *kesep* refers to "silver" or "money." (1) Since silver was commonly used as a medium of exchange in the ancient world, it was used in commercial transactions. For example, a ram could be purchased in Moses' day for two shekels (approx. 0.2 ounces) of *kesep* (Lev. 5:15). There are at least 30 references to "shekels of *silver*" in the OT.

(2) But *kesep* has other uses as well. It is used to make jewelry and ornaments or other precious items, such as Joseph's cup and trumpets (Gen. 44:2; Num. 10:2). In

the donations from the tribes at the dedication of the tabernacle, each tribe brings a "*silver* plate" and a "*silver* bowl" (e.g., Num. 7:13). The common combination of *kesep* and gold (*zahab*) occurs over 95x and refers to all types of valuables. Idols are also made of silver; God demands, "Do not make any gods to be alongside me; do not make for yourselves gods of *silver* or gods of gold" (Exod. 20:23).

(3) Because of the rarity of silver, biblical writers use *kesep* as a metaphor for preciousness. "And the words of the Lord are flawless, like *silver* refined in a furnace of clay, purified seven times" (Prov. 12:6). Speaking of wisdom we read, "For the gain from her is better than gain from *silver* and her profit better than gold" (Prov. 3:14). The process of purifying silver also finds expression as a metaphor for the refining work of God in a person's life: "The crucible for *silver* and the furnace for gold, but the Lord tests the heart"(Prov. 17:3; cf. also Mal. 3:1–3). See *NIDOTTE, 2:683-84*.

New Testament

Noun: ἀργύριον (*argyrion*), GK *736* (S *694*), 20x. *argyrion* means "silver" or the "money" made from it (since hard currency in antiquity was often composed of silver). See *money*.

SIMILAR

New Testament

Verb: ὁμοιόω (*homoioō*), GK *3929* (S *3666*), 15x. *homoioō* means "to make like something, liken, compare." See *like, liken*.

Adjective: ομοιος (*homoios*), GK *3927* (S *3664*), 45x. *homoios* means "like, similar." See *like, liken*.

Adverb: ὁμοίως (*homoiōs*), GK *3931* (S *3668*), 30x. *homoiōs* means "likewise, similarly." See *like, liken*.

SIMILARITY

New Testament

Noun: ὁμοίωμα (*homoiōma*), GK *3930* (S *3667*), 6x. *homoiōma* has two basic meanings. It can refer to "a similarity, a likeness," and to "an image" of something else. See *likeness*.

SIN

Old Testament

Verb: חָטָא (*ḥāṭā᾽*), GK 2627 (S 2398), 240x. The verb *ḥāṭā᾽* carries the basic meanings of "to miss (the mark)" and by extension "to sin."

(1) The former meaning is best illustrated in Jdg. 20:16, "Among all these soldiers there were seven hundred chosen men who were left-handed, each of whom could sling a stone and *not miss*." Furthermore, Prov. 19:2 warns of the consequence of acting in haste: "It is not good to have zeal without knowledge, nor to be hasty and *miss the way*." Job 5:24 says, "You will know that your tent is secure; you will take stock of your property and find nothing *missing*."

(2) The meaning of *ḥāṭā᾽* as "to sin" is closely tied to the former. God says to Abimelech, "Yes, I know you did this with a clear conscience, and so I have kept you from *sinning* against me" (Gen. 20:6). It can refer to a sin against God (Jos. 7:11), but it can also connote sin against a fellow human (1 Sam. 19:4). The mark that is missed is the revealed will of God; to not do what he has said should be done, or vice versa, is to miss God's mark and therefore sin.

In some verb forms, *ḥāṭā᾽* can mean "to cause to sin," as in Exod. 23:33, "Do not let them live in your land, or they *will cause you to sin* against me, because the worship of their gods will certainly be a snare to you." *ḥāṭā᾽* can also refer to the sense of guilt. "The ruthless will vanish, the mockers will disappear, and all who have an eye for evil will be cut down—those who with a word make a man out to *be guilty*" (Isa. 29:20–21; see also Deut. 24:4, "You shall not bring *guilt* upon the land" [RSV]).

Noun: אָוֶן (*᾽āwen*), GK 224 (S 205), 81x. *᾽āwen* refers, in general, to evil, sin, or wickedness. It may also describe the punishment or disaster that befalls those who practice wickedness. See *evil*.

Noun: חַטָּאת (*ḥaṭṭāʾt*), GK 2633 (S 2403), 298x. *ḥaṭṭāʾt* refers both to "sin" and to "the sin offering" in the ceremonial instructions of the law of Moses. References to this term are concentrated in Exodus through Numbers and in Ezekiel. For example, it occurs 19x in Lev. 4—eight of which refer to "sin," the other eleven to "sin offering."

(1) "Sin" can be depicted as a snare with an attractive power or force. This is seen in the reference to sin crouching at Cain's door, lying in wait to overcome him (Gen. 4:7). The idea of sin as a snare can also be seen when Jeroboam's calves are described as "a sin" to the people (1 Ki. 12:30; cf. 13:34). The cords of a person's sin hold one fast (Prov. 5:22).

ḥaṭṭāʾt in the singular can refer to an accumulation of evil deeds. Thus we read in Gen. 18:20 that "*the sin* of Sodom was great." Similarly, Solomon prays for "*the sin* of your people" to be forgiven (1 Ki. 8:34). References like this are common. *ḥaṭṭāʾt* can also refer to individual transgressions (Lev. 4:3).

(2) Along with meaning "sin," *ḥaṭṭāʾt* can be used to for the sacrifice called the "sin offering." In Lev. 4:3 the blameless young bull from the herd is offered as a "sin offering." The focal point of this offering is what is done with the blood. The *ḥaṭṭāʾt* is the primary means of blood atonement under the Mosaic covenant (4:3–12; 8:14–15). As a result of this offering, God's people "will be forgiven" (4:20, cf. also 4:24–26, 29–31, 32–35 etc.). On the Day of Atonement, Aaron is to present a "sin offering" for himself (16:11–14), and then he is to present a "sin offering" for the people (16:15). These actions accomplish atonement for the Most Holy Place, for Aaron, and for the people (16:16–17).

(3) The fact that *ḥaṭṭāʾt* can refer to either sin or sin offering has profound implications for understanding Paul's statement in 2 Cor. 5:21, that the one who knew no sin was made sin for us, that in him we might become the righteousness of God. Did Jesus become *sin*, or did he become a *sin offering*? Given Paul's thorough acquaintance with the OT, perhaps both are implied. See *NIDOTTE*, 2:93–103.

Noun: עָוֹן (*ʿāwōn*), GK 6411 (S 5771), 233x. *ʿāwōn* is usually translated "sin, guilt, wickedness, iniquity" and is one of the three primary words for sin in the OT, an offense against God that ranges from willful rebellion to unintentional sins. *ʿāwōn* usually has an ethical function, but it sometimes is a catch-all word to designate any sin against God. In Lev. 16:21–22, this word functions as the key word in the confession of since, for it is the only term repeated as a summary word for the sins of the people (v. 22). In Ps. 51, David twice asks God to wash away or blot out his "iniquity" (Ps. 51:5, 9), and in 51:5 he acknowledges the root of his "sinfulness" goes back to his birth.

In Exod. 34:6–7, all three primary terms for sin are used in tandem: "The compassionate and gracious God, slow to anger, abounding in love and faithfulness, maintaining love to thousands, and forgiving *wickedness* (*ʿāwōn*), rebellion (*pešaʿ*, GK 7322) and sin (*ḥaṭṭāʾâ*, GK 2632)." In this passage both the totality of rebellion and complete forgiveness are highlighted. In Isa. 53:5–6, the Suffering Servant (Jesus Christ) was "pierced for our transgressions (*pešaʿ*), he was crushed for our *iniquities* (*ʿāwōn*); the punishment that brought us peace was upon him, and by his wounds we are healed. We all, like sheep, have gone astray, each of us has turned to his own way; and the LORD has laid on him the *iniquity* (*ʿāwōn*) of us all." See *NIDOTTE*, 3:351.

Noun: פֶּשַׁע (*pešaʿ*), GK 7322 (S 6588), 93x. Usually translated as "rebellion, offense, sin, transgression," the noun *pešaʿ* is one of the three primary words for sin in the OT. While sin is any act of offense against God, from willful rebellion to unintentional sin, *pešaʿ* normally denotes intentional disobedience, especially against God's law. The prophecy of

Amos makes this clear, as he speaks out first against Judah (Amos 2:4) and then against Israel (2:6). To the latter he declares, "For I know how many are your *offenses* and how great your sins. You oppress the righteous and take bribes and you deprive the poor of justice in the courts" (5:12).

Committing *pešaʿ* may involve social, political, or cultic acts and can occur on an interpersonal level (e.g., Exod. 22:9; Amos 5:12), a political level (1 Ki. 12:19), or a religious level (Isa. 1:2). In all occurrences of *pešaʿ* the common thread is the breach of a covenant responsibility.

To trespass God's instruction is to rebel against God. On the annual Day of Atonement the *pešaʿ* of Israel is atoned (Lev. 16:16, 21). The priest takes two male goats, one for a sin sacrifice and one as scapegoat. After the first goat is sacrificed, the priest lays his hands on the second goat and confesses Israel's sins before letting the goat free into the desert (Lev. 16:1–22; cf. Num. 29:12–40). In the NT we learn of the priestly ministry of Jesus Christ, who has offered himself as the sacrifice once for all for our sins (see especially Heb. 4:14–10; 8:1–10:18). See *NIDOTTE*, 3:706-10.

New Testament

Verb: ἁμαρτάνω (*hamartanō*), GK *279* (S *264*), 43x. The word group to which *hamartanō* belongs gives the sense of missing the mark, losing, or falling short of a goal (particularly a spiritual one), as in Rom. 3:23, "for all *have sinned* and fall short of the glory of God." *hamartanō* is used mostly by Paul (17x) and John (14x).

hamartanō generally refers to sins or sinning against oneself or another person. For example, Jesus teaches that "if your brother *sins*, rebuke him, and if he repents, forgive him. If he *sins* against you seven times in a day, and seven times comes back to you and says, 'I repent,' forgive him" (Lk. 17:3–4; cf. Mt. 18:15–21, Acts 25:8). One can also sin against oneself. In fact, Paul taught that "all other sins a man commits are outside his body, but he who sins sexually *sins* against his own body" (1 Cor. 6:18). Nonetheless, sinning against another believer is a serious offense. Paul states this truth as such: "When you *sin* against your brothers ... you *sin* against Christ" (1 Cor. 8:12). Likewise, *hamartanō* can also describe sins against God, often with consequences (Jn. 5:14; cf. 1 Cor. 15:34). Nevertheless, not all problems or difficulties in life are the result of sinning against God, but may exist to demonstrate the glory of God (Jn. 9:2–3).

Finally, if anyone denies that he or she has sinned, that person makes God out to be a liar (1 Jn. 1:10), "because all *sinned*" as a result of the sinful nature that Adam passes down to humanity (Rom. 5:12). Although sinning against God is the natural result of our fallen nature inherited from Adam, John declares: "No one who lives in [God] *keeps on sinning*. No one who *continues to sin* has either seen him or known him" (1 Jn. 3:6; cf. 3:9). If we are in Christ, we are new creations, no longer living the way we once did (2 Cor. 5:17). The writer of Hebrews asserts the consequences of deliberately sinning: "If we deliberately *keep on sinning* after we have received the knowledge of the truth, no sacrifice for sins is left, but only a fearful expectation of judgment and of raging fire that will consume the enemies of God" (Heb. 10:26). Therefore, "we know that anyone born of God *does not continue to sin*; the one who was born of God keeps him safe, and the evil one cannot harm him" (1 Jn. 5:18). See *NIDNTT-A*, 37-40.

Noun: ἁμαρτία (*hamartia*), GK *281* (S *266*), 173x. *hamartia* is usually translated as "sin" and typically refers to the transgression of the law; note, for example, 1 Jn. 3:4, "Everyone who sins breaks the law; in fact, *sin* is lawlessness." Thus, *hamartia* is used to denote our sin against God. All other words for sin occur noticeably less frequently in the NT. *hamartia* is found most of all in Paul's writings (64x total; 48x in Romans alone). John also uses it frequently (37x), as does the writer of Hebrews (27x).

Apart from the atoning blood of Jesus Christ, *hamartia* results in death: "For the wages of *sin* is death, but the gift of God is eternal life in Christ Jesus our LORD" (Rom. 6:23; cf. Jas. 1:15). Paul writes that "*sin* entered the world through one man, and death through *sin*, and in this way death came to all men, because all sinned" (Rom. 5:12–13). However, "just as *sin* reigned in death, so also grace might reign through righteousness to bring eternal life through Jesus Christ our LORD" (Rom. 5:20–21). Although Jesus Christ was "tempted in every way, just as we are—yet was without *sin*" (Heb. 4:15; cf. 1 Pet. 2:24), "God made him who had no *sin* to be *sin* for us, so that in him we might become the righteousness of God" (2 Cor. 5:21). Only the perfect sacrifice of Jesus' own blood will cleanse us from our sins (Heb. 10:2–22).

The word *hamartia* is thus often used in conjunction with the forgiveness of sins. "If we confess our *sins*, he is faithful and just and will forgive us our *sins* and purify us from all unrighteousness" (1 Jn. 1:9). For this reason, Jesus teaches his followers to pray, "Forgive us our *sins*, for we also forgive everyone who sins against us" (Lk. 11:4). Thus, forgiveness is available to all who humble themselves and confess their sins to God.

Scripture clearly teaches such forgiveness of our sins is to be found only through Jesus Christ and his atoning blood (Mt. 26:28, 1 Cor. 15:3, Gal. 1:4; cf. Acts 4:12). Before Jesus was born, the angel declared to Joseph: "[Mary] will give birth to a son, and you are to give him the name Jesus, because he will save his people from their *sins*" (Mt. 1:21). John calls Jesus "the Lamb of God, who takes away the *sin* of the world" (Jn. 1:29). Lk. 5:20-24 states that Jesus not only physically healed a paralytic, but also forgave his sins, thus declaring that "the Son of Man has authority on earth to forgive *sins*" (Lk. 5:24; cf. Mt. 9:5–6; Mk. 2:7–10). For this reason, Luke concludes that "repentance and forgiveness of *sins* will be preached in his name to all nations" (Lk. 24:47; cf. Acts 13:38).

Regarding life after salvation, John teaches that "no one who is born of God will *continue to sin*, because God's seed remains in him; he cannot go on sinning, because he has been born of God" (1 Jn. 3:9); in other words, *hamartia* must not be the characteristic of a believer's life. One who is truly born again will increase in holiness and godliness, so that sin will become consistently and purposefully less. However, John also declares forthrightly that if anyone does sin, we have an advocate in Jesus Christ, who is "the atoning sacrifice for our *sins*, and not only for ours but also for the *sins* of the whole world" (1 Jn. 2:1–2).

Finally, Paul exhorts us to count ourselves as "dead to *sin* but alive to God in Christ Jesus," and then commands: "Do not let *sin* reign in your mortal body so that you obey its evil desires. Do not offer the parts of your body to *sin*, as instruments of wickedness, but rather offer yourselves to God, as those who have been brought from death to life" (Rom. 6:11–12; cf. Heb. 12:1). Paul concludes that faith, not sin, should reign in us, and "everything that does not come from faith is *sin*" (Rom. 14:23; cf. "all wrongdoing is sin," 1 Jn. 5:17; Jas. 4:17). See *NIDNTT-A*, 37-40.

Noun: παράπτωμα (*paraptōma*), GK *4183* (S *3900*), 19x. *paraptōma* means "trespass, sin, transgression." See *trespass*.

SIN OFFERING

Old Testament

Noun: חַטָּאת (*ḥaṭṭā*ʾ*t*), GK 2633 (S 2403), 298x. *ḥaṭṭā*ʾ*t* refers both to "sin" and to "the sin offering" in the ceremonial instructions of the law of Moses. See *sin*.

SINCERITY

Old Testament

Adjective: תָּמִים (*tāmîm*), GK 9459 (S 8549), 91x. Most often *tāmîm* describes animals or crops intended for sacrificial offerings as "unblemished" or "whole." The KJV renders *tāmîm* as "sincerity" in Jos. 24:14; in this sense, it refers to the conduct of the righteous and wise. See *unblemished.*

SINFUL

New Testament

Noun and Adjective: ἁμαρτωλός (*hamartōlos*), GK *283* (S *268*), 47x. The word group to which *hamartōlos* belongs gives the sense of missing the mark. *hamartōlos* is used as an adjective to mean "sinful" (7x) and as a noun to mean "sinner" (40x).

SINFUL NATURE

New Testament

Noun: σάρξ (*sarx*), GK *4922* (S *4561*), 147x. *sarx* literally means "flesh." However, the use of *sarx* within the NT is quite diverse. In the NIV, for example, it is translated 23x as "sinful nature." See *flesh*.

SING

Old Testament

Verb: רָנַן (*rānan*), GK 8264 (S 7442), 53x. *rānan* generally denotes the action of shouting or singing for joy, though there are several instances in which joy may be absent. For example, God's people "cry out" in distress (Lam. 2:19) and in yearning (Ps. 84:2), and Wisdom "cries aloud" in the streets (Prov. 1:20; cf. 8:3). But the vast majority of uses clearly includes the concept of joy and thus the verb is regularly translated "shout for joy," "sing for joy," or "sing joyfully."

In the OT, God is the primary reason why people "shout for joy." Their joyful shouts may be in response to his presence (e.g., Isa. 12:6; Zech. 2:10) or protection (e.g., Ps. 5:11; 59:16), his acts of redemption (e.g., Ps. 71:23; Jer. 31:7), his victories as the divine warrior (e.g., Ps. 20:5; Zeph. 3:14), his covenant faithfulness (e.g., Ps. 59:16; 90:14), his final judgment at the last day (e.g., Ps. 67:4; 98:8–9), or his daily provision (e.g., Jer. 31:12). In short, God's people shout for joy because of his character, his work in their lives, and his work in history.

The subject of *rānan* is normally the people of God; they are the ones who "shout for joy," typically because of God's character. It is predictable, then, that *rānan* occurs most frequently in Psalms (25x), the OT hymnal. But God's people are not the only subjects of *rānan*. Frequently, inanimate objects in creation are personified to "shout for joy." The heavens (Isa. 44:23), the mountains (Ps. 98:8), the trees (96:12), and even the sunrise and sunset (65:8) all "shout for joy" in giving glory to their creator. See *NIDOTTE 3:1128-32*

Verb: שִׁיר (*šîr*), GK 8876 (S 7891), 87x. *šîr*, usually translated "sing," generally refers to singing praise to God and often occurs in Psalms (27x). God's people are directed to "sing to God" (Ps. 68:4[5], 32[33]) and to "sing to the LORD" (Ps. 96:1, 2). But *šîr* may also refer to singing a love song (Isa. 5:1), funeral songs (2 Chr. 35:25), or songs to entertain (2 Sam. 19:35[36]; Eccl. 2:8).

The participle of *šîr* appears 47x, and the NIV usually translates it "singer" (e.g., 2 Sam. 19:36; 1 Chr. 15:16) or, occasionally, "musician" (e.g., 1 Ki. 10:12; 1 Chr. 6:18). The concentration of this form of the verb in Chronicles (15x), Ezra (6x), and Nehemiah (17x) highlights the emphasis on temple music in these later OT books. See *NIDOTTE* 4:99-100

New Testament

Verb: ᾄδω (*adō*), GK *106* (S *103*), 5x. While the verb "to sing" is a frequently used verb in the OT, *adō* occurs infrequently in the NT (as does another verb "to sing," (*psallō*). Nevertheless, singing is an important element in the NT worship. In both Eph. 5:19 and Col. 3:16, Paul instructs believers to "sing" and make music to the Lord "with psalms, hymns and spiritual songs." Undoubtedly the frequent reference in the NT to joy and rejoicing (see rejoice) involves the use of songs of praise and thanksgiving.

In addition, singing is a part of heaven. The picture presented in Revelation of the four living creatures and the twenty-four elders before the throne is that "they sing a new song" in praise of the Lamb of God, who is worthy to open the seals (Rev. 5:9). In 14:3 the entire 144,000 "sing a new song before the throne" of God. Finally, in 15:3, those who have conquered the beast and its image "sing the song of Moses, the servant of God, and the song of the Lamb." See *NIDNTT-A*, 624.*

Noun: ψάλλω (*psallō*), GK *6010* (S *5567*), 5x. *psallō* means "to sing." In Rom. 15:9 this verb is picked up from the LXX in Paul's quotation of 2 Sam. 22:50 or Ps. 18:49. In Paul's discussion of spiritual gifts in 1 Cor. 14, he insists that both the spirit and the mind should be active in our singing (14:15); it seems apparent from this verse that Paul considers singing to be one of the gifts of the Spirit. Finally, both Paul in Eph. 5:19 and James in Jas. 5:13 encourage Christians to sing and make music in their hearts to the Lord. See *NIDNTT-A*, 611.

SINGER

Old Testament

Verb: שִׁיר (*šîr*), GK 8876 (S 7891), 87x. *šîr*, usually translated "sing," generally refers to singing praise to God and often occurs in Psalms (27x). The participle of *šîr* appears 47x, and the NIV usually translates it "singer" (e.g., 2 Sam. 19:36; 1 Chr. 15:16) or, occasionally, "musician" (e.g., 1 Ki. 10:12; 1 Chr. 6:18). See *sing*.

SINNER

New Testament

Noun and Adjective: ἁμαρτωλός (*hamartōlos*), GK *283* (S *268*), 47x. The word group to which *hamartōlos* belongs gives the sense of missing the mark, losing, or falling short of a goal (particularly a spiritual one, see Rom. 3:23). *hamartōlos* is used as an adjective to mean "sinful" (7x) and as a noun to mean "sinner" (40x). As a noun, the word is mainly in the plural (30x).

When *hamartōlos* is used as an adjective, it can refer to "a *sinful* generation" (Mk. 8:38), "a *sinful* life" (Lk. 7:37), "*sinful* sin" (Rom. 7:13), and "*sinful* men" (Lk. 24:7, 1 Tim. 1:9, Heb. 12:3). Peter once declared himself to be a "*sinful* man" in the presence of Christ (Lk. 5:8).

As a noun, *hamartōlos* most frequently means "sinner." In the gospels, Jesus said, "I have not come to call the righteous, but *sinners* to repentance" (Lk. 5:32; cf. Mt. 9:13, Mk. 2:17). Jesus is accused by the Pharisees to be a "friend of *sinners*" (Mt. 11:19; cf. Mk. 2:15–16), his love for sinners evidenced in the gospels. Paul also declares the love of Christ for sinners in Rom. 5:8: "But God demonstrates his own love for us in this: While we were still *sinners*, Christ died for us." 1 Tim. 1:15 echoes this truth: "Here is a trustworthy saying that deserves full acceptance: Christ Jesus came into the world to save *sinners*" (cf. Lk. 19:10). For this reason, all of heaven rejoices over the sinner who finds repentance (Lk. 15:7, 10). Sinners, therefore, have no excuse for not turning to Jesus. See *NIDNTT-A*, 37-40.

SIR

New Testament

Noun: κύριος (*kyrios*), GK *3261* (S *2962*), 717x. *kyrios* means "master, lord, sir" as well as "Lord." See *Lord*.

Noun: ῥαββί (*rhabbi*), GK *4806* (S *4461*), 15x. The term *rhabbi* can mean "master, sir" or remain transliterated as "rabbi." See *rabbi*.

SISTER

Old Testament

Noun: אָחוֹת (*ʾāḥôt*), GK 295 (S 269), 119x. This noun primarily denotes a blood relative and is used for both a sister (Gen. 4:22) and a half-sister (Gen. 20:15), whether on the father's side or the mother's side. Lev. 18:9 forbids sexual relations with one's sister or half-sister.

But *ʾāḥôt* may also have the more general sense of a kinswoman. Thus, Lev. 18:18 prohibits taking "your wife's sister as a rival wife," where "sister" should most likely be understood as "(female) fellow-citizen" (cf. Num. 25:18; Jer. 22:18). This use of sister to denote group membership may stand behind the NT use of *adelphē*, "sister," to identify women within the believing community (cf. 1 Cor. 7:15; Rom. 16:1; Phlm. 2; cf. 1 Cor. 9:5 where NIV "believing wife" is literally "sister-wife," KJV, "a sister, a wife"). It is also on this basis that Paul can refer to the entire community of believers as "the household of faith" (Gal. 6:10; cf. Eph. 2:19; 1 Tim. 3:15; 1 Pet. 4:17).

In the Song of Songs, the lover refers to his beloved as his sister (Song 4:9, 10, 12; 5:1, 2), with the added words "my bride" in 4:9 and "my darling" in 5:2. In these instances, *ʾāḥôt* functions as a term of endearment. CEV translates *ʾāḥôt* in these passages by "my very own," which gives the proper sense.

The prophets used the metaphor of harlotry to picture spiritual waywardness. Thus, Jer. 3:6–11 refers to Israel and Judah as sisters who both engaged in harlotry. Ezek.23:1–4 also refers to Israel and Judah as evil sisters, but in 16:49–63 he speaks of three sisters: Israel, Judah, and Sodom. By portraying Israel and Judah as sisters with Sodom, the prophet captures the depth of their offenses; their remedy can come only through God's grace. See *NIDOTTE*, 1:351-53.

New Testament

Noun: ἀδελφή (*adelphē*), GK *80* (S *79*), 26x. *adelphē*, "sister," is sometimes used in its normal sense of physical kinship. Jesus' sisters are mentioned several times in the gospels (Mt. 13:56; Mk. 6:3), and it is the son of Paul's sister who alerts Paul to the plot against his life (Acts 23:16). The early church often spread through kinship connections, so it was not uncommon for brothers and sisters to belong to the same gathering of believers (e.g., Rom. 16:15).

The NT also uses *adelphē*, together with other familial terms, in a new way to describe Christians as "brothers" and "sisters." This use of "kinship" language begins with Jesus, who suggests that the one who does the Father's will is his "brother and *sister* and mother" (Mt. 12:50). In Mk. 10:29–30, Jesus promises that those who leave their biological families for his sake will receive a spiritual family (cf. Mk. 3:32, 35). Allegiance to Jesus must take precedence over allegiance to one's family (Lk. 14:26).

Paul and other NT authors pick up Jesus' use of "brother" and "sister" to describe the relationship of Christians to one another (Rom. 16:1; 1 Cor. 7:15; 1 Tim. 5:2; Phlm. 2; Jas. 2:15). One of the most striking examples of this use in Paul is 1 Cor. 9:5, where he insists he has the right, like the other apostles, to have a "sister-wife," by which he means "a believing wife." *adelphē* in 2 Jn. 13 likely refers to a gathered body of believers, the "sister" of another community of believers. See *NIDNTT-A*, 15-16.

SIT

Old Testament

Verb: יָשַׁב (*yāšab*), GK 3782 (S 3427), 1088x. The general meaning of *yāšab* is to "sit, sit down," with the connotations of "live, dwell, remain, settle." See *live*.

New Testament

Verb: κάθημαι (*kathēmai*), GK *2764* (S *2521*), 91x. *kathēmai* can simply mean the literal act of "sitting," but it can also mean "to reside." It sometimes implies note of authority.

(1) In the literal sense, Jesus finds Matthew "sitting" in his tax office (Mt. 9:9). In 13:1 Jesus "is seated" by the sea as he speaks. At the resurrection, the angel "is sitting" on the stone at Jesus' tomb (28:2). To be seated on the ground indicates a humble place in society (cf. Mk. 10:46; Jn. 9:8; Acts 3:10) and often is a mark of abasement, especially if one is seated in sackcloth and ashes (Lk. 10:13). After Jesus heals a demoniac, he is found "seated" at Jesus' feet (Lk. 8:35; see also 18:35). In Jas. 2:3, some church members are given preferential treatment by being seated in the better seats, while others have to sit on the floor.

(2) *kathēmai* can also refer to "residing." In Lk. 21:35 *kathēmai* simply means "dwelling" or "living" on the earth. In Mt. 4:16, Jesus reads from Isa. 9:1–2, which speaks of those who "reside" in darkness. Jesus Christ is the great light who has

come to bring salvation to all who "sit" in spiritual darkness.

(3) The act of being seated can also have a mark of authority. At the renewal of all things, when "the Son of Man sits on his glorious throne," his followers "*will* also *sit* on twelve thrones" (Mt. 19:28). That authority is connected with being seated is evident from the context, for they will "judge the twelve tribes of Israel" (cf. Lk. 22:30). Mt. 22:44 quotes Ps. 110:1 in which God the Father tells the Son "to sit" at his right hand. The idea of Christ being seated in authority at God's right hand is common in the NT, especially in the letters (e.g., Col. 3:1; Heb. 1:13). This usage can apply to earthly rulers as well (Mt. 27:19; Acts 23:3). See *NIDNTT-A*, 280.

Verb: καθίζω (*kathizō*), GK *2767* (S *2523*), 46x. *kathizō* means "to sit." This verb is used most often to refer to the simple act of sitting down (Mt. 5:1; Mk. 9:35; Lk. 4:20). It is also used of the Holy Spirit's coming upon those in the upper room as tongues of fire, and "sitting" or "coming to rest" on each of the followers of Jesus gathered there (Acts 2:3). *kathizō* takes on special significance in the case of Christ when he "sits down" at the right hand of God (Heb. 1:3; 8:1; 10:2; 12:2). His work has been completed and he is now in the special place of honor and authority, a position in which God the Father has placed him (Eph. 1:20; cf. Acts 2:30–35).

kathizō is also used when referring to someone being put in charge of something, e.g., the "appointing" of judges (1 Cor. 6:4). An extension of the meaning "to sit" is "to remain in one place" for an extended time, e.g., Paul "stayed" in Corinth for a year and a half teaching the word of God (Acts 18:11).

SIT DOWN

New Testament

Verb: ἀναπίπτω (*anapiptō*), GK *404* (S *377*), 12x. *anapiptō* refers to the simple action of "sitting down, reclining" (Lk. 14:10; 17:7). This word occurs only the gospels. To feed the multitudes Jesus asks the people to "sit down" on the ground (Mt. 15:35; Mk. 6:40; 8:6; Jn. 6:10). In most contexts this sitting is at formal meal time and means reclining at a table. In the Roman world, people at a banquet usually reclined on low couches with their head toward the table and their feet away from it (Lk. 11:37; 22:14; Jn. 13:12). At other times, the persons are already sitting at a table and this word is used as they recline even more for some purpose (e.g., as John reclines back against Jesus, Jn. 13:25; 21:20). See *NIDNTT-A*, 310.*

SIX

Old Testament

Noun: שֵׁשׁ (*šēš*), GK 9252 (S 8337), 274x. *šēš* means "six" in the singular and "sixty" in the plural. It can also mean the ordinal numeral "sixth." *šēš* can also combine with other numbers: e.g., with *ʾelep* ("thousand," GK 547), it means "six thousand"; with the number ten, it means "sixteen."

The most significant use of the number six in the Bible is based on the fact that there are seven days in a week. Six of those days are intended for our daily work, just as the Lord himself worked six days and then rested on the seventh day (Gen. 1:1–2:3; Exod. 20:8–11; 31:15–17). Similarly, for six years the Israelites could work their land and sow crops, but on the seventh year, the land was to lie fallow (Lev. 25:3). Six of the towns given to the Levites in the land of Canaan were to be "cities of refuge" (three on each side of the Jordan; Num. 35:13, 15). The expression "six, yes seven" in Prov. 6:16 is a means of building a climax through poetic symmetry. When Isaiah is called to be a prophet and sees a vision of cherubim, each one has six wings (Isa. 6:2). See *NIDOTTE*, 4:257–58.

New Testament

Adjective: ἕξ (*hex*), GK *1971* (S *1803*), 13x. *hex* is the cardinal number "six." It may be used to count objects, like six wings (Rev. 4:8) or six jars (Jn. 2:6). It may also be used to specify a unit of time, like six days (Lk. 13:14) or six months (Lk. 4:25; Acts 18:11; Jas. 5:17; "half a year" in some translations). When used with temporal references, *hex* sometimes indicates chronological sequence, like "*six* days later" (Mt. 17:1; Mk. 9:2), or "*six* days before the Passover" (Jn. 12:1). *hex* may also be used to enumerate people, like six brothers (Acts 11:12) or the 276 people on the ship that was wrecked with Paul aboard (27:37).

Like other Greek numbers, *hex* may be used in a construction of a compound cardinal number (e.g., in Jn. 2:20, forty-six, which is lit. "forty and six"). The best known of these compound constructions in the NT in which *hex* is used is the last element in the number of the beast, 666 (Rev. 13:18). Many understand this use to be a *gematria* representing someone's name, perhaps Nero. (*Gematria* is the substitution of numerical values for Hebrew letters in a name, often for the purpose of concealing the identity of the one named). Except for this use, few other NT uses of *hex* have any apparent symbolic significance.*

SIXTH

Old Testament

Noun: שֵׁשׁ (*šēš*), GK 9252 (S 8337), 274x. *šēš* means "six" in the singular and "sixty" in the plural. It can also mean the ordinal numeral "sixth." See *six*.

New Testament

Adjective: ἕκτος (*hektos*), GK *1761* (S *1623*), 14x. *hektos* means "sixth." Most often used to denote the "*sixth* hour," noon in Jewish reckoning (Mt. 20:5; 27:45; Mk. 15:33; Lk. 23:44; Jn. 4:6; 19:14; Acts 10:9). God sends Gabriel to Nazareth in the "*sixth* month" (Lk. 1:26). Elizabeth was "in her *sixth* month" of pregnancy when Gabriel comes to Mary (Lk. 1:36). It is used in Revelation for "the *sixth* seal" (6:12), "the *sixth* angel" (9:13, 14; 16:12), and "the *sixth* carnelian" (21:20).*

SIXTY

Old Testament

Noun: שֵׁשׁ (*šēš*), GK 9252 (S 8337), 274x. *šēš* means "six" in the singular and "sixty" in the plural. It can also mean the ordinal numeral "sixth." See *six*.

SIZE

Old Testament

Noun: מִדָּה (*middâ*), GK 4500 (S 4060), 55x. A *middâ*, derived from the verb *mādad*, "to measure," means "size, measurement"; it can refer to both spatial and temporal measurements. See *measurement*.

SKILL

Old Testament

Noun: חָכְמָה (*ḥokmâ*), GK 2683 (S 2451), 153x. *ḥokmâ* has a wide variety of meanings, covering both physical skill and intellectual wisdom. It can be translated as "wisdom, aptitude, experience, good sense, skill." See *wisdom*.

SKIN

Old Testament

Noun: עוֹר (*ʿôr*), GK 6425 (S 5785), 99x. *ʿôr* is used to designate both human (55x) and animal (44x) skin. When used of human skin, *ʿôr* can simply denote the outer covering of the body (Exod. 34:29; Lev. 13:2; Jer. 13:23; Ezek. 37:6, 8; Mic. 3:3). But *ʿôr* can also be extended to mean the whole body (Job 19:26) or even the whole person (Exod. 22:27). An abnormal skin disease (which includes a broader spectrum than the common term "leprosy" denotes) is considered a serious matter of ceremonial uncleanness and is dealt with in detail in Lev. 13:1–46.

The phrase "skin of the teeth" (Job 19:20, "I have escaped with only the skin of my teeth") probably does not characterize a narrow escape (as in English) but to escape with nothing (where, from Job's perspective, death would have seemed a better alternative). Another phrase found in Job 2:4, "skin for skin," is a merchant's term meaning equivalent worth, much like our English "apples for apples."

Animal skins were used as coverings for the ark of the covenant and other furniture of the tabernacle, along with the sacred utensils (Num. 4:6ff.). Leather from animal hides could also attract "disease" (probably mildew) that would render them unfit for use and require that they be burned (Lev. 13:51–52).

God graciously uses the skins of animals to cover the naked Adam and Eve following their plunge into sin (Gen. 3:21), foreshadowing, perhaps, the hides used to cover the tabernacle where God's way of atonement will be revealed (Exod. 26:14).

New Testament

Noun: σάρξ (*sarx*), GK *4922* (S *4561*), 147x. *sarx* literally means "flesh." However, the use of *sarx* within the NT is quite diverse. In the NIV, for example, it is translated 23x as "sinful nature." See *flesh*.

SKIRT

Old Testament

Noun: כָּנָף (*kānāp*), GK 4053 (S 3671), 111x. *kānāp* has the basic meaning of a wing, such as the wing of a bird. By extension, it can refer to the edge of something, particularly the skirting or hem of a garment. See *wing*.

SKULL

New Testament

Noun: κρανίον (*kranion*), GK *3191* (S *2898*), 4x. *kranion* means "skull." This noun occurs once in each of the four gospels, where the gospel writer indicates that Jesus' death occurred at Golgotha, which is Aramaic for "The Place of the *Skull*" (Mt. 27:33; Mk. 15:22; Lk. 23:33; Jn. 19:17). Since one of the Latin words for "skull" is *calvaria*, this place has also become known as "Calvary."

SKY

Old Testament

Noun: אֹהֶל (*'ōhel*), GK 185 (S 168), 348x. The basic meaning of the word is "tent, dwelling" (see *tent*). But it is used metaphorically for the *sky*, where God pitches a tent for the sun (Ps. 19:4) and for himself (Isa. 40:22).

Noun: שָׁמַיִם (*šāmayim*), GK 9028 (S 8064), 421x. *šāmayim* is an important and frequent word in the Bible and plays a key role in many central texts from Genesis through Revelation. The wide variety of meanings for this word fall into two main categories: the sky, atmosphere, or space; and the dwelling place of God. See *heaven, heavens*.

New Testament

Noun: οὐρανός (*ouranos*), GK *4041* (S *3772*), 273x. Coming from the same worldview as the OT, the NT authors frequently use terms for heaven. *ouranos* is used in a variety of ways in the NT. On a few occasions it simply denotes the "sky" (e.g., Mt. 16:3; Mk. 13:25). See *heaven, heavens*.

SLANDER

New Testament

Verb: βλασφημέω (*blasphēmeō*), GK *1059* (S *987*), 34x. *blasphēmeō* means "to slander, blaspheme, insult," especially with regard to speech. See *blaspheme*.

SLAUGHTER

Old Testament

Verb: הָרַג (*hārag*), GK 2222 (S 2026), 167x. *hārag* can variously mean "to kill, murder, slaughter, massacre." *hārag* most often denotes intentional killing, as in the case of Cain and Abel (Gen. 4:8). However, it can also refer to unintentional killing (Exod. 21:12–14). It is not the word used in the sixth commandment (see *murder*).

hārag frequently specifies killing or slaying with ruthless violence, as in Gen. 34:25–26, where Simeon and Levi avenge the rape of their sister, Dinah. Ruthless killing also occurs in the context of the complete destruction (*herem*) associated with God's wars of judgment: Moses kills the people of Midian (Num. 31:17) and Joshua slaughters the inhabitants of Ai (Jos. 8:24–28). See also *kill*. See *NIDOTTE*, 1:1055-57.

Verb: זָבַח (*zābaḥ*), GK 2284 (S 2076), 134x. *zābaḥ* primarily refers to the slaughtering of animals for sacrifice. See *sacrifice*.

Verb: שָׁחַט (*šāḥaṭ*), GK 8821 (S 7819), 81x. *šāḥaṭ* means "to slaughter, kill." *šāḥaṭ* can be used nonsacrificially. People slaughter animals to use for food (1 Sam. 14:32, 34; Isa. 22:13) or to acquire the blood (Gen. 37:31). *šāḥaṭ* also describes the slaughter of people in war or for revenge (2 Ki. 10:7, 14). See also *kill*. See *NIDOTTE*, 4:77-80.

SLAVE

New Testament

Noun: δοῦλος (*doulos*), GK *1528* (S *1400*, *1401*), 124x. *doulos* refers to a "servant, slave." See *servant*.

SLAY

New Testament

Verb: σφάζω (*sphazō*), GK *5377* (S *4969*), 10x. *sphazō* means "to slay," sometimes even "to murder." It occurs only in 1 John (where it refers to the murder of Abel by Cain; see 1 Jn. 3:12) and in Revelation—especially in reference to the Lamb that "was slain" (Rev. 5:6, 9, 12; 13:8). In 6:9, John sees the souls of martyrs, who "had been slain."

SLEEP

Old Testament

Verb: שָׁכַב (*šākab*), GK 8886 (S 7901), 208x. *šākab* means "rest, lie down, sleep." There are a variety of nuances to this verb, all of which revolve around the idea of lying down. See *lie down*.

New Testament

Verb: καθεύδω (*katheudō*), GK *2761* (S *2518*), 22x. In classical Greek *katheudō* refers only to natural sleep. In the LXX, this verb is never used for death; that use is found in the NT, but it is used sparingly. Matthew uses *katheudō* to describe Jesus sleeping in the stern of the boat in the midst of a vicious storm (Mt. 8:24), but in the next chapter he places the word on Jesus' lips who injects hope into a desperate death scene involving Jairus's daughter: "The girl is not dead, but *asleep*" (Mt. 9:24). Jesus raises her and successfully communicates that death is not final when he is involved.

During Jesus' harrowing episode of spiritual anguish in the Garden of Gethsemane just hours before his crucifixion he finds the disciples "asleep" three separate times (Mk. 14:37, 40, 41). Their being awake will mean support to him in his pain and suffering.

katheudō can also denote spiritual or moral alertness. In reference to the second coming Mark reports: "If he comes suddenly, do not let him find you *sleeping*" (13:36; cf. also Eph. 5:14). Paul actually uses *katheudō* with three nuances in one context. He addresses the theme of spiritual laxity in the face of the return of Christ in 1 Thess. 5:6: "So then, let us not be like others, who are *asleep*, but let us be alert and self-controlled"; normal sleep in 5:7: "For those who *sleep, sleep* at night"; and the sleep of death in 5:10: "He died for us so that, whether we are awake or *asleep*, we may live together with him." See *NIDNTT-A*, 279-80.

SLOW TO ANGER

Old Testament

Idiom: אֶרֶךְ אַפַּיִם (*ʾerek ʾappayim*), GK 800, 678 (S 750, 639), 14x. The Heb. expression for "patience" is an idiom that translate literally "long of nose." This characteristic is sometimes translated "slow to anger." See *patience*.

New Testament

Verb: μακροθυμέω (*makrothymeō*), GK *3428* (S *3114*), 10x.

Noun: μακροθυμία (*makrothymia*), GK *3429* (S *3115*), 14x.

These two words are normally translated as some form of "patience, endurance." See *patience*.

SMALL

Old Testament

Adjective: קָטֹן (*qāṭōn*), GK 7785 (S 6996), 74x. *qāṭōn* means "small" in size or "young" in age. (1) In some uses, *qāṭōn* can refer to size. Moses refers to the moon as "the lesser light" (Gen. 1:16). Each year, Samuel's mother made for him "a *little* robe" and brought it to Shiloh on the annual feast day (1 Sam. 2:19). As Isaiah looks to the eschatological future, he sees a time when things are so peaceful that "a *little* child will lead them" (Isa. 11:6). In several passages, this word is used in the phrase "from *the least* to the greatest" (Jer. 8:10; 42:1, 8; 44:12; cf. also "small and great" in Deut. 1:17; 2 Chr. 15:13; Job

3:19). This phrase can refer to size or significance (i.e., from the common person to the king).

(2) But *qāṭōn* can also refer to age. Benjamin is regularly cited as the "youngest" of Jacob's children (Gen. 42:13, 15, 20; 43:29). When Solomon becomes king and has his night vision from the Lord, he asks for wisdom because "I am only a *little* boy and do not know how to carry out my duties" (1 Ki. 3:7). When referring to age, the phrase "small and great" become "young and old" (1 Sam. 5:9; 30:2; 1 Chr. 15:8). See *NIDOTTE*, 3:910–12.

New Testament

Adjective: μίκρος (*mikros*), GK *3625* (S *3398*), 46x. *mikros* is the antonym of *megas* ("great") and means "small, little." It can be used in such expressions as being "small" in stature (Lk. 19:3), "small" in number (Lk. 12:32) or stature (19:3), or something or someone that is "insignificant" (Mk. 9:42; Rev. 3:8). When used in the phrase, "small and *great*," the expression means "all" (Acts 8:10; Rev. 13:16).

Two uses of *mikros* are unique to the Synoptic Gospels. (1) It is often used of a child (lit., a "little one"; see Mt. 10:42; 18:6, 10, 14). Jesus' teaching has a distinct emphasis on little children not found in other Jewish literature. Lk. 17:2 warns all who might cause a "little one" to stumble. (2) *mikros* expresses "smallness" and "least" as important aspects about the kingdom. Jesus stresses the importance of being "least" in the kingdom (Mt. 11:11). The kingdom is compared to the mustard seed, "the *smallest* seen you plant in the ground" (Mk. 4:31), which grows until it becomes "the largest of all garden plants."

In John, *mikros* most often refers to time ("a little while"). At times, it contains an element of comfort for the disciples (Jn. 16:16–19), in that "in a little while" they will no longer see the Lord (he will be crucified), yet "in a little while" they will see the Lord (he will be resurrected). See *NIDNTT-A* 369-70.

Adjective: ὀλίγος (*oligos*), GK *3900* (S *3641*), 40x. *oligos* typically denotes a small number, a small amount of something, or shortness in size or time. See *few*.

SMELL

Old Testament

Noun: רֵיחַ (*rēaḥ*), GK 8194 (S 7381), 58x. *rēaḥ* denotes an aroma, scent, or fragrance. In common usage, it can refer to the fragrance of perfume (Song 1:1), the scent of vines (2:13), the odor of garments (4:11), or the smell of one's breath (7:8). Its technical, cultic expression is in the phrase *hannîḥōaḥ* (43x), often translated "a pleasing aroma" See *aroma*.

SMELT

Old Testament

Verb: צָרַף (*ṣārap*), GK 7671 (S 6884), 34x. *ṣārap* is commonly used to denote the testing or refining of both metals and human beings and may be translated as "test, refine." Ancient refining techniques required the heating of precious metals to high temperatures, where the base metals or "dross" would either be burned off or skimmed from the top. See *test*.

SMOKE

New Testament

Noun: καπνός (*kapnos*), GK *2837* (S *2586*), 13x. *kapnos* means "smoke." This term is used almost exclusively in the book of Revelation (the only other use is in Acts 2:19, where smoke is one of the signs of the last days when the Spirit is poured out). Smoke is one of the three plagues (Rev. 9:18) and is associated with the torment of those who worship the beast (14:11). *kapnos* is also associated with the glory and power of God in the temple (15:8).

SNAKE

New Testament

Noun: ὄφις (*ophis*), GK *4058* (S *3789*), 14x. *ophis* is translated as "snake, serpent." It can be an actual snake, as in Mt. 7:10 where Jesus asks whether a father would give his son a snake if he has asked for a fish. Jn. 3:14–15 describes the way salvation will be accomplished and applied: "Just as Moses lifted up the *snake* in the desert, so the Son of Man must be lifted up, that everyone who believes in him may have eternal life" (see Num. 21:8–9).

The snake is used figuratively to illustrate certain character traits or qualities. Jesus calls the scribes and Pharisees snakes because their hypocrisy is as poisonous as the venom of a snake (Mt. 23:33). After sending his disciples to preach the gospel to Israel, Jesus tells them to "be as shrewd as *snakes* and as innocent as doves" (Mt. 10:16). The horses with riders who come as part of the sixth trumpet in Revelation have tails like snakes, inflicting deadly injury like the bite of a poisonous snake (Rev. 9:19).

Believers will be given authority over snakes (Lk. 10:19; cf. Mk. 16:18), demonstrating their power through Christ over Satan (who is called "that ancient Serpent" in Rev. 12:9; 20:2) and his agents. The depiction of Satan as a serpent highlights his deceitfulness, pointing back to Gen. 3:1. Satan has deceived God's people from the beginning of time, and he continues to be the great deceiver: "But I am afraid that, just as the *serpent* deceived Eve by his cunning, so your minds will be led astray from a single-hearted and pure devotion to Christ" (2 Cor. 11:3). See *NIDNTT-A*, 425.

SNATCH

New Testament

Verb: ἁρπάζω (*harpazō,* GK *773* (S *726*), 14x. *harpazō* means "to snatch, catch." It generally connotes a forceful and/or violent seizing (e.g., Mt. 11:12). The word is used of burglary (12:29), the action of mobs (Jn. 6:15), animal attacks (10:12), an arrest (Acts 23:10), and the forceful proclamation of sound doctrine (Jude 23).

As a general rule, *harpazō* underscores the power of the snatcher over the snatched. An exception is in Jn. 10:28-29 where Jesus, proclaiming the security of the believer, says, "No one can snatch them out of my hand . . . no one can snatch them out of my Father's hand." Here the strength, purpose, unity, and oneness of Christ and the Father are highlighted as a guarantee of the eternal security of God's elect.

harpazō also describes God's activity in physically and miraculously transporting people from one place to another. "The Spirit of the Lord suddenly *took* Philip *away*," (Acts 8:39). Paul, presumably referring to himself, spoke of a man who "was caught up to the third heaven" in a vision (2 Cor. 12:2). Finally, *harpazō* appears in 1 Thess. 4:17, where Paul predicts that believers who are alive at the second coming "will be caught up" in the clouds." Here *harpazō* magnifies God's might in completing salvation as he reunites his people before Christ. See *NIDNTT-A*, 72-73.

SOB

Old Testament

Verb: בָּכָה (*bokâ*), GK 1134 (S 1058), 114x. *bokâ* has the basic meaning "to weep," but can be translated with other terms such as "sob, mourn, wail, cry." See *weep*.

SOIL

Old Testament

Noun: אֲדָמָה (*ʾadāmâ*), GK 141 (S 127), 222x. *ʾadāmâ* has a variety of nuances in the OT (see *land*). It is used in reference to the covenant promises and warnings about the earth (Exod. 20:12; Deut. 4:40; 2 Ki. 17:23; Amos 7:11, 17), and at times, it designates the inhabited world (Ezek. 38:20; Isa. 24:21). It also refers to various kinds of soil: dust (1 Sam. 4:12), clay (1 Ki. 7:46), and the matter used to form mankind and the animals (Gen. 2:7, 19).

New Testament

Noun: γῆ (*gē*), GK *1178* (S *1093*), 250x. *gē* is the standard word for "earth, land, soil" in the NT. It occurs especially in the gospels, Acts, and Revelation. See *earth*.

SOJOURNER

Old Testament

Noun: גֵּר (*gēr*), GK 1731 (S 1616), 92x. *gēr* is a sojourner or alien in a land. See *alien*.

SOLDIER

New Testament

Noun: στρατιώτης (*stratiōtēs*), GK *5132* (S *4757*), 26x. *stratiōtēs* means "soldier" (Mt. 27:27; 28:12; Mk. 15:16; Lk. 7:8). The centurion who comes to Jesus to request healing for his servant describes himself as someone "with *soldiers* under me" (Mt. 8:9). Soldiers mock, ridicule, and beat Jesus (Lk. 23:36). John uses *stratiōtēs* only to describe those men of the military who are involved in the passion of Christ (Jn. 19:9, 23, 24, 32, 34). In Acts, soldiers arrest (Acts 12:3), guard (12:4), and are chained to Peter (12:6).

Paul uses the illustration of a soldier to describe the hardships that must sometimes be endured by the believer who is living for Christ in the midst of people who despise Christ. "Endure hardship with us like a good *soldier* of Christ Jesus" (2 Tim. 2:16). As a good soldier, Timothy must not be distracted from his primary objective regardless of what happens to him but rather must continue to serve God. See *NIDNTT-A*, 481-83.

SOMEONE ELSE

New Testament

Adjective and Noun: ἀλλότριος (*allotrios*), GK *259* (S *245*), 14x. *allotrios* is used to describe a thing that is not one's own or a person not from one's own people group. See *other*.

SON

Old Testament

Noun: בֵּן (*bēn*), GK 1201 (S 1121), 4941x. *bēn* has a wide variety of nuances in the OT. (1) One of the most often used words in the OT, *bēn* expresses family or hereditary relationship, and particularly "a son" begotten by a father. Sometimes the plural of *bēn* means "male children" (cf. Gen. 5:4, where *bānîm* and *bānôt*, "daughters" are mentioned together), but the plural can also mean children of both genders: "To the woman he said, 'I will greatly increase your pains in childbearing'" (lit., "when you bear children [*bānîm*]," Gen. 3:26). *bēn* can also denote other family relations, such as (a) brother ("your father's sons," Gen. 49:8; "your mother's sons, Jdg. 8:19), (b) grandchildren ("son's sons" or "children's children," Gen. 45:10; Jer. 27:7; Ps. 128:6), (c) nephew ("his brother's son," Gen. 12:5), (d) daughter-in-law ("your sons' wives," Gen. 8:18), and (e) cousin ("son of an uncle," Lev. 25:49). (f) In some cases, *bēn* by itself may denote grandchildren: "Early the next morning Laban kissed his grandchildren and his daughters and blessed them" (Gen. 31:55).

(2) The fact that *bēn* carries the general sense of hereditary relationship, and since the Semitic cultures frequently added the father's name appositionally (*X* son of *Y*) to describe heredity, *bēn* could be used of membership in the extended clan or nation. Thus "sons of Esau" (Deut. 2:4, 12, 22, 29) or "sons of Judah" (Joel 3:6) are tribal designations. Likewise, the frequent expression "Israelites" (NIV) or "*children* of Israel" (KJV) most often denotes the nation of Israel as a whole (e.g., Exod. 13:2; Jos. 13:6; Ps. 148:14), though it can describe Jacob's own sons from whom the 12 tribes descended (e.g., Exod. 28:21). From the time of the divided kingdom, "*children* of Israel" (KJV) or "*people* of Israel" (NIV) may denote the northern ten tribes as distinguished from Judah and Benjamin in the south (e.g., Jer. 32:30, 32).

In a similar way, *bēn* may describe people related to a geographical or physical location. Thus "*men* of Bethlehem" ("*children* of Bethlehem," KJV) (Ezr. 2:21; Jer. 6:1) describe Bethlehemites, and the designation "Babylonians" in Ezek. 23:17 is (lit.) "*children* of Babylon." Likewise, "a servant in my household" (Gen. 15:3) is (lit.) "a *child* [*bēn*] of my house," and the phrase "my people" (Gen. 23:11, NIV), which denotes "countrymen," is (lit.) "*children* of my people" ("*sons* of my people," KJV).

(3) *bēn* may also speak of a membership within a given social or professional group. Thus, "son of perfumers" is a "perfumer" (Neh. 3:8) and a "son of singers" is

a "singer" (Neh. 12:28). In the same vein, those who carry out the priestly duties are "sons of Levi" (Deut. 21:5; Ezr. 8:15) and "sons of Aaron" (Lev. 1:5, 11; 2:2ff.) as well as "sons of Zadok" (Ezek. 40:46; 44:15). In a common use of *bēn*, "sons of the prophets" (1 Ki. 20:35; 2 Ki. 2:3–4; 4:1, 35) most likely denotes those being trained as prophets.

(4) Our word may also be used to classify people according to moral or ethical standards. Eli's sons were called "*sons* of Belial" (1 Sam. 2:11, KJV), which means "wicked men" (NIV). A "valiant man" (1 Sam. 14:52, KJV; "brave man," NIV) is a "*son* of strength," while a murderer is a "*son* of murdering" (2 Ki. 6:32) and robbers are called "*sons* of the band" (2 Chr. 25:13).

(5) The wide use of *bēn* to convey familial and group relationships naturally gave rise to a figurative use of the term. The offspring of animals are also called *bānîm* (whether male or female, Gen. 32:15; 49:11, Zech. 9:9), and *bēn* is used poetically to describe a bough or shoot in Gen. 49:22. An arrow is a "*son* of the bow" (Job 41:20) or "*son* of the quiver" (Lam. 3:13). A fertile hill is called "*son* of oil/fatness" (Isa. 5:1) and sparks are described as "*sons* of fire/flame" (Job 5:7). Description of age can also utilize the word *bēn*. When Joseph is described as "thirty years old" (Gen. 41:46), the Heb. reads "a *son* of thirty years."

(6) The phrase "*sons* of God" in the OT (Gen. 6:2, 4; Job 1:6; 2:1; 38:7; Ps. 29:1; 89:7) may have several meanings. In Job 1:6 and 2:1, "*sons* of God" (KJV; "angels," NIV) appears to describe beings of the heavenly hosts (including Satan) who have access to God's presence. In 38:7, "*sons* of God" ("angels," NIV) are described along with "morning stars" who render praise to God. Likewise, in Ps. 29:1 and 89:7, the phrase seems to describe heavenly beings who render praise to their Creator. The first biblical appearance of "*sons* of God" (Gen. 6:1, 4) has been understood variously as fallen angels, the line of Seth (who cohabited with the line of Cain), dynastic rulers (note "men of renown" in 6:4) who may have ascribed to themselves a divine status, or fallen angels.

(7) An important expression utilizing *bēn* in the OT is "*son(s)* of man," found in its various forms 161x. This use of *bēn* has a unique characteristic; whereas in all other expressions utilizing the word *bēn*, the one following *bēn* is a distinctly different category, in the phrase "*son(s)* of man" the two terms refer to the same entity. Thus, "son of man" is essentially a "human being." Thus, when Ezekiel is repeatedly referred to as "*son* of man" (93x in Ezek.), he stands as the divinely appointed representative and intercessor for the rebellious nation of Israel.

Characteristic of the phrase "*son(s)* of man" in the OT is its description of humanity's alienation from God. It describes fallen human beings as untrustworthy (Num. 23:19), "full of evil" (Eccl. 9:3), and helpless (Ps. 146:3). While "man" was created by God, endowed with his image, "*son* of man" denotes fallen man, conceived in Adam's likeness and an object of God's wrath. It is only therefore by divine mercy that the "*son* of man" would become an object of God's grace and redemption (Ps. 8:4–8; 31:20; 80:17–19; 144:1–3; 145:8–12).

It may well be that the biblical portrayal of Israel as God's son is cast against the backdrop of the "*son* of man" imagery. Israel is God's firstborn son (Exod. 4:22), for God has chosen to redeem Israel out of the nations ("*son[s]* of man"). When Israel acts as a rebellious son, he is punished (cf. Prov. 3:12). But the enduring love of a father to his son is seen in that God remains faithful, affirming his covenant relationship to Israel time and again: "I will lead them beside streams of water on a level path where they will not stumble, because I am Israel's father, and Ephraim is my firstborn *son*" (Jer. 31:9).

The Davidic dynasty carries this same theme, for the Davidic king is described as God's "son": "I will be his father, and he will be my *son*" (2 Sam. 7:14; cf. Ps. 2:1–3). As the anointed king, he represented the nation in the father/son relationship of the covenant. Yet it is in view of the nation's waywardness, and the demise of the Davidic kings, that Isaiah prophesies of a child, "a son," who will fulfill the divinely appointed role of the true anointed (*māšiaḥ*, "messiah") king, for he will be the miraculous counselor, divine warrior, owner of eternity, and the prince of peace (Isa. 9:2–7). Coming as the "last Adam" (1 Cor. 15:45), as the "*Son* of Man," Jesus the Messiah stood as the quintessential Israelite, the Servant of the Lord, and the King of Israel, proving himself to be the eternal "*son* of God" who alone could redeem the sinful human race. See *NIDOTTE*, 1:671–77.

New Testament

Noun: υἱός (*huios*), GK *5626* (S *5207*), 377x. Similar to the use of *ben* in the OT, *huios* describes the son of human parents, though it can also refer more generally to offspring and descendents. It is certainly not limited to the male gender but often has the nuance of "child." This noun has several special uses in the NT.

(1) The "parent to child" relationship is set in a new light by Jesus' call to discipleship. On the one hand, blood relations pale in significance in light of the call of Jesus (Mt. 10:37; Lk. 14:26–27; cf. Mk. 13:12). On the other hand, family relations regain the significance they had been lost by the Pharisees and their legalistic traditions (Mk. 7:9–13). In the NT letters children have a special place in the directions about social and family relationships (Eph. 6:1–4; Col. 3:20–21).

(2) Similar to the OT, the phrase "son of" is important in various theological messages of the NT. Connected to the OT is Jesus' favorite title for himself, "Son of Man." Although this phrase would appear merely to emphasize Jesus' humanity, it is actually a stronger title of divinity than the title "Son of God." The "Son of Man" title goes back to Dan. 7:13–14, and its use portrays Jesus as a person of unique authority (Mk. 2:1–12). Although the term is related to apocalyptic traditions, Jesus puts his own stamp on this expression as the one who treads a path of suffering appointed for him (Mk. 8:31–39; 9:31; 10:33–34).

(3) The title "Son of God," though it certainly evokes a divine understanding, does so by emphasizing the divine relationship between the Father and Jesus the "Son." When Jesus was baptized, a voice came out of heaven, verifying that "You are my Son, whom I love" (Mk. 1:11; Lk. 3:22). Jesus is the true and faithful Son of God, God's "One and Only Son" (Jn. 3:16). Its close connection with the confession of Jesus as Messiah, as well as the title "Son of David," suggests that this sonship refers back to 2 Sam. 7:12, 14 (cf. also Ps. 2:7). Thus, the messianic element in Jesus' preaching is traceable back to the Davidic tradition in the OT. The phrase "Son of God" is the essential confessional phrase of early Christianity, firmly rooted in baptism, preaching, and confessions (Mt. 16:16; Acts 9:20; 13:33; Rom. 1:3–4).

(4) Just as Israel was a "son" to God in its elected status and just as Jesus the "Son" made complete that relationship for all who desire, believers today are called sons and daughters of God. The way to become a child of God is to believe on the name of God's Son Jesus (Jn. 1:12–13). Through the Spirit living within us, we call God "Abba, Father" (Rom. 8:15; Gal. 4:6). The church is to live as a faithful witness to the God of the universe, as obedient children who serve our Father in heaven (1 Pet. 1:14).

(5) The NT also uses *huios* to describe qualities that should characterize God's people. When we are called "sons of the light" (Lk. 16:8; Jn. 12:36), that means we must live as if the light of God's Word and Jesus as the light of the world are living within us. Similarly, we are to be "sons of peace" (Lk. 10:6). By contrast, unbelievers are "sons of disobedience" (Eph. 2:2) and "sons of destruction" (2 Thess. 2:3); in fact, they are "sons of the evil one" (Mt.

13:38). May God give us the grace to be true sons and daughters of the King. See *NIDNTT-A*, 569-78.

SONG

Old Testament

Noun: שִׁיר (*šîr*), GK 8877 (S 7892), 78x. *šîr means* "song." Singing was an important part of Israelite life (see 1 Chr. 16:37–43; 25). Solomon wrote over a thousand songs (1 Ki. 4:32), one of which is undoubtedly the "song of songs" (Song 1:1); David, of course, wrote many songs that are included in the book of Psalms. In fact, nearly half of the occurrences of *šîr* are in titles of the psalms (cf. "a song" in Ps. 30:T; 108:T), and especially "a song of ascents" (120:T; 121:T; etc.). The book of Psalms frequently encourages us to "sing to the Lord a new song" (96:1; 98:1; 149:1; cf. 33:3; 114:9; cf. Isa. 42:19). The "songs of Zion" and the "songs of the Lord" are apparently a category of song that praise God as the God of Zion (Ps. 137:3–4). The "songs of ascent" are most likely a category of song that pilgrims to Jerusalem sang as they climbed the road to Jerusalem and to the temple. See *sing*. See *NIDOTTE*, 4:99–100.

SOON

New Testament

Adverb: ταχέως (*tacheōs*), GK *5441* (S *5030*, *5032*, *5033*), 15x.

Adverb: ταχύς (*tachys*), GK *5444* (S *5035*, *5036*), 13x. Both of these adverbs mean "quickly, soon." See *quickly*.

SORROW

New Testament

Verb: λυπέω (*lypeō*), GK *3382* (S *3076*), 26x. *lypeō* means "to grieve, feel sorrow or pain." See *grieve*.

Noun: λυπή (*lypē*), GK *3383* (S *3077*), 16x. *lypē* denotes "grief, sorrow, pain," the result that comes from the action of the verb *lypeō* (see *grieve*). See *grief*.

SOUL

Old Testament

Verb: נֶפֶשׁ (*nepeš*), GK 5883 (S 5315), 757x. *nepeš* has a wide range of meaning; the basic meaning is "breath," but it can also mean "soul, life, entire being."

(1) *nepeš* is not limited to human beings, for "breath" is something that all living creatures have. God gives life and breath to both humans and animals (Gen. 1:30). God formed "man from the dust of the ground, and breathed into his nostrils the breath of life; and the man became a living *being*" (2:7).

(2) As far as human beings are concerned, the Heb. understanding of *nepeš* encompasses the entire person, body and soul. It is not that a person *has* a soul; rather, a human being *is* a soul. Each individual is accountable for his or her sin, for which God may require that person's *nepeš* (Gen. 9:5). Note Lev. 4:2 ("If a *person* sins") and Ezek. 18:20 ("the *person* who sins shall die." In Ps. 7:2, the psalmist cries out for deliverance lest his enemies "tear *me* [my *nepeš*] like a lion." *nepeš* is so closely identified with the whole person that it can even mean a corpse (Lev. 21:11).

A human *nepeš* can have natural desires such as hunger (Deut. 12:15; 1 Sam. 2:16; Ps. 107:9; Mic. 7:1) and thirst (Isa. 29:8), as well as nonphysical desires. The psalmist pleads, "Do not give me up to the *will* of my adversaries, for false witnesses have risen against me, and they are breathing out violence" (Ps. 27:12, cf. Prov. 13:2). The *nepeš* is also the seat of emotions: Hannah has deep "bitterness of *soul*" (1 Sam. 1:10 cf. also 30:6); Ezekiel has "anguish of *soul*" (Ezek. 27:31).

(3) The relationship between humans and God is often expresses with *nepeš*. For example, "My *soul* yearns for you in the night, my spirit within me earnestly seeks you (Isa. 26:9). Elsewhere, "O God, you are my God, I seek you, my *soul* thirsts for you; my flesh faints for you" (Ps. 63:1). "As a deer longs for flowing streams, so my *soul* longs for you, O God." (42:1). The soul can also be downcast (42:5, 11). Psalm 42 in particular captures the imagery of breath (the deer panting), hunger/thirst, and the living God, who alone can

satisfy. Moreover, when the psalmist wants to sing in praise to God, he encourages himself out: "Praise the Lord, O my *soul*" (103:1–2, 22; 146:1). It is interesting that of all the occurrences of *nepeš* in Psalms (143x), only one does not have a personal possessive pronoun attached to it. Communion with God—from crying out to him to singing his praise—happens from the core of one's being: life and breath, longing, emotions, the will. All of these are involved in the *nepeš*. See *NIDOTTE*, 3:133–34.

New Testament

Noun: ψυχή (*psychē*), GK *6034* (S *5590*), 103x. *psychē* has a wide variety of meaning in the NT, being shaped by the Heb. word *nepeš*. Among other things, it means "life, soul, person, mind." See *life*.

SOUND

Old Testament

Noun: קוֹל (*qôl*), GK 7754 (S 6963), 505x. *qôl* generally means "voice, sound, noise." See *voice*.

New Testament

Noun: φωνή (*phōnē*), GK *5889* (S *5456*), 139x. *phōnē* signifies at least three ideas in the NT depending on context: "sound, voice, language." (1) *phōnē* can refer to an auditory effect, "sound, tone, noise." John uses the term to refer to "the trumpet *blasts*" (Rev. 8:13; cf. 10:7; 14:2; 18:22). Paul has a similar use: "even in the case of lifeless things that make *sounds*" (1 Cor. 14:7). Note also the words of Jesus: "The wind blows wherever it pleases. You hear its *sound*" (Jn. 3:8).

(2) *phōnē* can refer to the faculty of utterance (i.e., "voice"). This usage usually refers to any form of speech, be it natural or supernatural. "One of them, when he saw he was healed, came back, praising God in a loud *voice*" (Lk. 17:15). God's voice was heard in approval of his Son, "And a *voice* from heaven said, 'This is my Son, whom I love; with him I am well pleased'" (Mt. 3:17; cf. Mk. 1:11; Lk. 3:22; 2 Pet. 1:18).

(3) Finally, *phōnē* can refer to a verbal code shared by a community to communicate with one another, that is, a "language." "Undoubtedly there are all sorts of *languages* in the world" (1 Cor. 14:10). Before God enabled Balaam's donkey, the animal was "a beast without *speech*" (2 Pet. 2:15). See *NIDNTT-A*, 597.

(BE) SOUND

New Testament

Verb: ὑγιαίνω (*hygiainō*), GK *5617* (S *5198*), 12x. *hygiainō* means "to be healthy, be sound," depending on the context. See *be healthy*.

SOUND (A TRUMPET)

Old Testament

Verb: תָּקַע (*tāqaʿ*), GK 9546 (S 8628), 70x. *tāqaʿ* is used to describe such actions as blowing, thrusting, or clapping. See *blow*.

New Testament

Verb: σαλπίζω (*salpizō*), GK *4895* (S *4537*), 12x. *salpizō* is a verb that means "to sound a trumpet." All but two occurrences are in Revelation, where this verb refer to the sounding of the seven trumpets (Rev. 8:6, 7, 8, 10, 12, 13; 9:1, 13; 10:7; 11:15). All these trumpet blasts signal judgment coming on those who oppose God and his servants. They signify an intensification of God's judgment already unleashed by the opening of the seals in 6:1–17; 8:1–5. These judgments manifest similarities with the plagues unleashed on the Egyptians during the Exodus.

In the context of providing for the needy, Jesus commands us not to draw attention to ourselves by "announcing [our gifts] with trumpets" (Mt. 6:2); in other words, "do not toot your own horn!" Jesus may be referring to the "shofar" (a ram's horn) temple signal, used when an especially large gift was being given. Jesus warns against the debilitating sin of self-righteousness. The most effective and rewarding gift is provided by us secretly, knowing that God is the one who sees and knows the heart condition of both the humble and the proud.

The final use of *salpizō* occurs in 1 Cor. 15:52: when Jesus returns and the dead are raised, "the trumpet will sound." This final trumpet is noted elsewhere in the NT (see Mt. 24:31; 1 Thess. 4:16, both containing the related noun *salpinx*; see *trumpet*). See *NIDNTT-A*, 514-15.*

SOUTH

Old Testament

Noun and Adjective: יָמִין (*yamîn*), GK 3545 (S 3225), 140x. *yamîn* denotes the direction "to the right." Because most of the ancient Near East was oriented to the east, the direction "south" is at one's right hand, and thus *yamîn* often means "south" (e.g., 2 Chr. 4:6–8). See *right*.

SOW

Old Testament

Verb: זָרַע (*zāraʿ*), GK 2445 (S 2232), 56x. *zāraʿ* refers to the activity of sowing or planting and can bear a literal as well as a metaphorical meaning in the OT.

(1) *zāraʿ* denotes literally the act of planting seed in the fields (Lev. 25:3–4, 11). God commands the Israelites, "For six years you are *to plant* your fields and harvest the crops" (Exod. 23:10). Prior to the Israelites' entering the promised land, God warns them of the consequences of disobedience: "You *will sow* much seed in the field but you will harvest little, because locusts will devour it" (Deut. 28:38). Note that the harvesting of what has been sown is the result of God's blessing (Gen. 26:12).

(2) *zāraʿ* also has a metaphorical meaning. (a) A woman's conceiving of children, for example, is referred to as sowing seed/offspring (Lev. 12:2; Num. 5:28). Furthermore, Yahweh declares that he will plant Israel for himself in the promised land (Hos. 2:23). Kings, too, are said to be planted, only later to be uprooted (Isa. 40:24).

(b) *zāraʿ* can also describe the connection between an act and its consequences (Job 4:8; Ps. 126:5–6; Hos. 10:12). "But he who *sows* righteousness reaps a sure reward" (Prov. 11:18). Or, as Paul correctly points out, "Do not be deceived: God cannot be mocked. A man reaps what he sows" (Gal. 6:7). This principle is commonly referred to as retribution. Every action has consequences, which may be both immediate and eventual. Significantly, the relationship between the original act and consequence is not always one of equality. The one who sows may reap much more than was sown. It is also important to note that God often extends grace to the one who sows. The human race has earned death because of sin (Rom. 6:23), but God offers forgiveness through his Son. Those who trust in Christ for their salvation will not truly reap what they have sown. See *NIDOTTE*, 1:1151-52.

Verb: נָטַע (*nāṭaʿ*), GK 5749 (S 5193). 59x. *nāṭaʿ* broadly means "to plant, sow, fix, establish" and can be used both of literally planting things and of figuratively planting a people. See *plant*.

New Testament

Verb: σπείρω (*speirō*), GK *5062* (S *4687*), 52x. *speirō* means "to sow, sow seed." A farmer normally scattered seed on freshly-plowed fields. This verb is used literally in the parable of the sower (Mt. 13:3–4, 18–19, 24, 31; Mk. 4:3–20; Lk. 8:4–8) as well as in other parables (Mt. 4:30–31; Lk. 19:21–22; cf. Jn. 4:36–37), but figuratively the verb denotes the sowing of God's Word (Mt. 13:19; Mk. 4:13). Paul uses *speirō* metaphorically to refer to the nature of the resurrection body (1 Cor. 15:35–44), to generosity in stewardship (2 Cor. 9:6, 10), and to the law of the end-time harvest (Gal. 6:7–8). See *NIDNTT-A*, 534-35.

SPACE

Old Testament

Noun: מִגְרָשׁ (*migrāš*), GK 4494 (S 4054), 114x. *migrāš* was an open area of land surrounding and belonging to a city or temple. Although many translate it as "pastureland," it more likely means "open space" or "open land." See *pastureland*.

SPARE

New Testament

Verb: φείδομαι (*pheidomai*), GK *5767* (S *5339*), 10x. *pheidomai* means "to spare." Most uses of this verb have a frightening element to them. Twice Peter writes that if God did not "spare" the angels when they sinned or the rebellious people before the flood, he will eventually send the unrighteous into his final judgment (2 Pet. 2:4–5, 9; cf. also Rom. 11:21). Paul predicts a time when "savage wolves" will attach the church and not "spare" the flock (Acts 20:29). But the most blessed use of this verb is about God, "who did not spare his own Son but gave him up for us all" (Rom. 8:32).

SPEAK

Old Testament

Verb: אָמַר (*ʾāmar*), GK 606 (S 559), 5316x. *ʾāmar* is the most common verb in the OT for "to say, speak." See *say*.

Verb: דָּבַר (*dābar*), GK 1819 (S 1696), 1136x. *dābar* ("say, speak") is used hundreds of times for both the human and the divine activity of speaking. See *word*.

New Testament

Verb: ἀνοίγω (*anoigō*), GK *487* (S *455*), 77x. *anoigō* can simply mean "to open" but sometimes has the connotation of healing. It can also mean "to reveal" or "to speak" ("open the mouth"). See *open*.

Verb: λαλέω (*laleō*), GK *3281* (S *2980*), 296x. The dominant word used in the NT for speaking is *legō* (see *say*). *laleō* appears one-tenth as much, mostly in Luke and Paul. In the majority of the texts this verb describes the communication process, such as what his spoken is the gospel (1 Thess. 2:2), words of wisdom (1 Cor. 2:6), the truth (Eph. 4:25), or the word of God (Phil. 1:14). The word can mean "to give forth sounds or tones," as in Rev. 10:3–4: "When he shouted, the voices of the seven thunders *spoke*." Elsewhere, John relates a "voice *speaking* ... as a trumpet" (4:1).

The writer of Hebrews uses the term strikingly as an image of the "sprinkled blood [of Jesus] that *speaks* a better word than the blood of Abel" (Heb. 12:24). What is spoken is one of the sterling qualities of Jesus' death: after Cain killed Abel, the latter's blood cried out from the ground harshly for judgment (Gen. 4:10), but the shedding of Jesus' blood speaks tenderly for forgiveness and reconciliation.

laleō is used in contexts where speech is restored after a muting demon is driven out of a person (Mt. 9:33; 12:22; 15:31; Lk. 11:14). This verb is a key term in 1 Cor. 14, where Paul is discussing the two speaking gifts of tongues and prophecy as well as not permitting women to speak (14:34–35). Paul's goal in both situations, which appear to be sources of contention within the fellowship, is for the building up of the body of Christ. Where this is not achievable, he opts for silence. James links profession and action by indicating that Christians should regulate their conduct, knowing full well that the manner of speaking and acting will both be judged by the law of liberty (Jas. 2:12). See *NIDNTT-A*, 339-43.

Verb: λέγω (*legō*), GK *3306* (S *3004*, *2036*, *2046*), 2353x. Usually translated as "say," *legō* sometimes has the notion of "to speak." See *say*.

SPEAK AGAINST

New Testament

Verb: ἀντιλέγω (*antilegō*), GK *515* (S *483*, *471*), 11x. *antilegō* is a combination of the prefix *anti* ("against") and the verb *legō* ("I say"), making it quite literally "to speak against." *antilegō* denotes vocal rebellion against authority, often translated as "obstinacy" or "rebelliousness." Human hearts will be revealed when they "speak against" Jesus (Lk. 2:34). Ironically, Jesus' claim to kingship is said to be an act of "speaking against" Caesar (Jn. 19:12). In Rom. 10:21, Paul quotes Isa. 65:2, which calls Israel (lit.) the "speaking-against ones," to highlight their vocal rebellion and obstinacy to Yahweh's authority.

Things that are spoken against include the resurrection by the Sadducees (Lk. 20:27), the words of God's chosen representatives (Lk. 21:15; Acts 13:45; 28:19), Christianity as a whole (28:22), and sound doctrine (Tit. 1:9). In Paul's instructions to Christian slaves, he says that they should not "talk back" to their masters (Tit. 2:9). While *antilegō* denotes vocal opposition to authority, it is clear that vocal opposition has deep roots in the hearts of sinful and rebellious humanity. The way the verb is used highlights the reality that "out of the abundance of the heart the mouth speaks" (Mt. 12:34, ESV). See *NIDNTT-A*, 55.*

SPECIES

Old Testament

Noun: כָּנָף (*kānāp*), GK 4053 (S 3671), 111x. *kānāp* has the basic meaning of a wing, such as the wing of a bird. Sometimes it can refer to various species of birds (lit., "bird of every *wing*," Ezek. 17:23; 39:4). See *wing*.

SPEECH

Old Testament

Noun: לָשׁוֹן (*lāšôn*), GK 4383 (S 3956), 117x. *lāšôn* literally means "tongue," the physical organ of speech or eating/drinking (Jdg. 7:5; Lam. 4:4). By extension, it can refer to that which proceeds from the mouth, namely, a person's *language* (Gen. 10:5; Deut. 28:49; Est. 1:22) or *speech* (Ps. 55:9 NIV). See *tongue*.

Noun: שָׂפָה (*śāpâ*) GK 8557 (S 8193), 178x. *śāpâ* often denotes the physical "lip(s)" of a person (Num. 30:7, 13; Song 4:3, 11; 5:13), but it can also mean that which proceeds from the lips, such as a person's *speech* (Prov. 16:27 NIV; 22:11 NIV; Isa. 33:19). See *lip*.

New Testament

Noun: λόγος (*logos*), GK *3364* (S *3056*), 330x. *logos* means "word, message, report, speech." See *word*.

Noun: φωνή (*phōnē*), GK *5889* (S *5456*), 139x. *phōnē* signifies at least three ideas in the NT depending on context: "sound, voice, speech." See *sound*.

SPEECHLESS

New Testament

Verb: φιμόω (*phimoō*), GK *5821* (S *5392*), 7x. *phimoō* means "to be quiet, speechless, muzzled." It has the idea of restraint, either imposed externally or internally. See *quiet*.

SPEND THE NIGHT

Old Testament

Verb: לִין (*lîn*), GK 4328 (S 3885), 71x. *lîn* usually describes the act of lodging for a night while on a journey. It is best understood against the background of the ancient world, in which hospitality was considered a social imperative.

In portraying a night's stay, this verb connotes a brief lodging at the end of the day's journey. Thus, Lot insists that the angels who have come to destroy Sodom must stay under his roof and "spend the night" (Gen. 19:1–3). Eliezar, Abraham's servant, meets Rebecca and inquires of her if there is a room in which he and his companions can "spend the night" (Gen. 24:23). *lîn* may also denote a short stay for several nights (Jdg. 18:2) or even longer (19:4–15). Ruth resolves that wherever Naomi *lodges*, there she will *lodge* as well (Ruth 1:16); yet the idea of temporary lodging is still in view. This gives meaning to Jeremiah's lament: "O Hope of Israel, its Savior in times of distress, why are you like a stranger in the land, like a traveler who *stays only a night*?" (Jer. 14:8).

This sense of "overnight" is how *lîn* is used in connection with sacrificial meat. The Torah forbids the fat of the sacrifice that is offered on the altar to be kept overnight (Exod. 23:18). Likewise, no part of the Passover lamb is to remain until morning (Exod. 34:25; Deut. 16:4). A similar command is given with regard to those executed by hanging—no corpse is to be left hanging overnight, since one executed in this manner is under God's curse, and to leave the corpse exposed desecrates the land (Deut. 21:23; cf. Gal. 3:13).

lîn brings rich theological meaning when it is used poetically by the prophets. In contemplating the chastening of the Lord, the psalmist writes: "For his anger lasts only a moment, but his favor lasts a lifetime; weeping may *remain for a night*, but rejoicing comes in the morning" (Ps. 30:5). In view of God's grace, our sorrow is temporary, merely a nighttime lodger.

The picture of the gracious host who

welcomes the weary traveler is also connected with *lîn*. Proverbs teaches: "He who listens to a life-giving rebuke will *be at home* [abideth, KJV] among the wise" (15:31), meaning that the one who accepts rebuke will be welcome to lodge with the wise. On the journey of life, the fear of the Lord offers the best overnight accommodations. Indeed, "he who dwells in the shelter of the Most High will *rest* in the shadow of the Almighty" (Ps. 91:1). See *NIDOTTE*, 2:796-97.

SPIRIT

Old Testament

Noun: רוּחַ (*rûaḥ*), GK 8120 (S 7307), 378x. While *rûaḥ* has a wide range of meanings in the OT, its basic sense is that of "wind" or "breath" (see *wind*). This latter sense naturally gave rise to "breath" as a sign of life, and hence *rûaḥ* also means "spirit" or "life." This meaning of the term relates to several different ideas in the OT.

(1) Sometimes *rûaḥ* functions to describe the general character of an individual or group, and when used in this way closely resembles the meaning of *nepes* ("soul"), denoting the general personality or disposition of a person. Thus the "*spirit* of the Egyptians" will be demoralized when God punishes her for her idolatry (Isa. 19:3), so that she will have a "*spirit* of dizziness" (19:14, "perverse *spirit*," KJV). In a similar fashion, *rûaḥ* can describe a state of mind or personal attribute: "bitter *spirit*" (Gen. 26:35, grief; Ezek. 3.14, anger), "sullen *spirit*" (1 Ki. 21:5, depression), "shortness of *spirit*" (Exod. 6:9, discouragement; Job 21:4, impatience), or "high *spirit*" (Prov. 16:18, pride) contrasted with "low *spirit*" (16:19, humility). We also find expressions such as "*spirit* of wisdom" (Exod. 28:3; Deut. 34:9) and "*spirit* of justice," (Isa. 28:6).

(2) *rûaḥ* may also describe supernatural or angelic beings, such as the "*spirit* from God" that came on Saul, causing him mental torment (1 Sam. 16:15–16, 23; 18:10), or the "spirit" from the "host of heaven" sent to entice Ahab into battle by confounding the words of the prophets (1 Ki. 22:19f.). The angels are sent as "winds" or "spirits" (KJV) to accomplish God's purposes (Ps. 104:4; cf. Heb. 1:7).

(3) The zenith of spiritual personality is God himself (Isa. 31:3). In the OT we find the expressions "*Spirit* of God" (11x), the "*Spirit* of the LORD" (25x), the "Holy *Spirit*," (3x, Ps. 51:11; Isa. 63:10, 11), and "my *Spirit*" (13x, where the context shows the referent is to God's Spirit). *rûaḥ* in these constructions may sometimes refer simply to the will or power of God (Isa. 40:13), but in the majority of cases it denotes the active presence of God via his Spirit. Thus, the Spirit is sent by the Lord (48:16), and he is placed on individuals (Num. 11:17, 29; Isa. 42:1) or within God's people (Isa. 63:11). In all his activities, he assumes a distinct personality while at the same time being the very presence of God among those with whom he is pleased to dwell.

The opening verses of the Bible show the "Spirit" of God active in the process of creation (Gen. 1:2; cf. Job 33:4; Ps. 104:30). In the unfolding story of the Bible, the *rûaḥ* of God gives wisdom and endows people with abilities for leadership (Num. 11:17, 25) and for craftsmanship (in preparing items for the tabernacle, Exod. 31:2; 35:31), and his presence provides spiritual guidance (Neh. 9:20; Ps. 143:10; Hag. 2:5). God's "Spirit" enables ordinary people to win military battles against formidable foes (Jdg. 6:34; 13:25; 14:6, 19; 15:14; 1 Sam. 11:6). He removes the rebellious heart and replaces it with one that responds in true obedience to God (Ezek. 11:19; 36:26–27). The "Spirit" is the "breath" that brings life to the dead (regeneration), as pictured in Ezekiel's valley of dry bones (Ezek. 37).

The "Spirit" of God also gives divine revelation to prophets (Num. 11:25; 1 Sam. 10:10; Neh. 9:30; Ezek. 11:24; Joel 2:28; Zech. 7:12), and it is by the "Spirit" of God that the true prophet speaks (Ezek. 13:3). The promised Messiah accomplishes his work of redemption through the power of the "Spirit" of God (Isa. 11:2;

42:1; 61:1). The work of this "Spirit" is often pictured as a "filling" or "coming on" a person. Likewise, in the imagery of anointing, the "Spirit" of God is said to be "poured out" on those he endows with his redemptive presence (always of the restoration of Israel as God's covenant nation, Isa. 32:15; 44:3–4; Ezek. 39:29; Joel 2:28). See *NIDOTTE*, 3:1073–78.

New Testament

Noun: πνεῦμα (*pneuma*), GK *4460* (S *4151*), 379x. (1) Similar to *rûaḥ* in the OT, *pneuma* can mean "air in movement." In Jn. 3:8 Jesus uses *pneuma* twice: once for "wind" or "air" and once for the "Spirit" ("the *wind* blows where it chooses ... so it is with everyone born of the *Spirit*").

(2) *pneuma* can also mean that which animates or gives life to the body (Mt. 27:50) or the human spirit in general (Jas. 2:26). It can also refer to the human person insofar as he or she belongs to and interacts with the spiritual realm. In this sense the human spirit is that aspect of a person through which God most immediately encounters him or her (Rom. 8:16; 1 Cor. 2:11; Gal. 6:18), where a person is most immediately open and responsive to God (Mt. 5:3; Rom. 1:9), or where most sensitive to matters of the spiritual realm reside (Mk. 2:8; Jn. 11:33; Acts 17:16).

(3) Beyond a human being, *pneuma* can refer to evil and good "spirits." It was common in NT times for people to view the mysterious powers that afflicted people as evil spirits or demons. The Synoptic Gospels and Acts especially reveal this (Mt. 8:16; Lk. 4:36; Acts 19:12–16). These evil forces are considered to be "personal forces" from the spiritual realm. But the NT never claims that these "evil spirits" are as strong as God; all evil spirits are inferior to God and subject to the power of his "Spirit," often operating through his agents: Christ and the apostles (Lk. 10:17–19; 11:19–20).

(4) Finally, *pneuma* in the NT can refer to the "Holy Spirit." The Holy Spirit first of all filled Jesus and directed him throughout his earthly ministry (Lk. 1:35; 4:1, 14, 18). Then through his supernatural power, the Spirit worked through and directed the apostles (Acts 1:8; 4:8; 13:2, 4, 9; 16:6–7). The Spirit is presented as a powerful force with visible effects (Acts 2–5). In the early church the Holy Spirit was the "*Spirit* of prophecy" (1:16; 4:25), a transforming power in conversion (9:17), and the director of its mission (9:10; 20:28). In Jewish writings the "Spirit of God" often meant the spiritual reality that performed God's work on earth, most notably in creation (Wis. 1:7; 12:1) and prophecy (Sir. 48:12).

The OT stress laid on Isaiah's promise of a Messiah who would have a special endowment of the Spirit (Isa. 61:1–3) and on Joel's prophecy about the pouring out of the Spirit on the godly in the last days (Joel 2:28–29). In the NT that understanding was fulfilled in the arrival of the Holy Spirit on Pentecost (Acts 2:1–36), who gave each believer various spiritual gifts (Rom. 12:6–8; 1 Cor. 12:8–11; 14:26; Eph. 4:11). Yet as Paul makes clear, though there are different kinds of gifts of the Spirit, there is still only one Spirit and one God (1 Cor. 12:4). Even more important, the Holy Spirit also wants to work his "fruit" in our daily lives and enable us to fight against the sins of the flesh (Gal. 5:22–23).

(5) Just as John baptized with water, the one coming after him would baptize with the Holy Spirit (Mt. 3:11; 16). Such imagery describes the type of "Spirit baptism" the believer receives—a baptism of the Spirit prophesied in the OT and fulfilled in the ministry of Jesus. See *NIDNTT-A*, 473-479.

SPIRITUAL

New Testament

Adjective: πνευματικός (*pneumatikos*), GK *4461* (S *4152*), 26x. *pneumatikos*, an adjective formed from *pneuma* conveys the sense of belonging to the spiritual realm and embodying or manifesting the "Spirit." It is almost exclusively used in the Pauline writings. It is can be used as a pure adjective: a "spiritual" something

(Rom. 1:11). It can stand alone and act as a noun and refer to a spiritual "person" (1 Cor. 2:13, 15; 3:1; 14:37). It can also stand alone in a neuter sense and refer to spiritual "things" (Rom. 15:27; 1 Cor. 9:11).

SPIRITUAL ENDOWMENT

New Testament

Noun: χάρισμα (*charisma*), GK *5922* (S *5486*), 17x. *charisma* means "gift, spiritual endowment." See *gift*.

SPLENDOR

Old Testament

Noun: תִּפְאֶרֶת (*tipʾeret*), GK 9514 (S 8597), 51x. *tipʾeret means* "glory, splendor, honor." See *glory*.

New Testament

Noun: δόξα (*doxa*), GK *1518* (S *1391*), 166x. *doxa* can be translated as "glory, honor, splendor." See *glory*.

SPLIT

Old Testament

Verb: בָּקַע (*bākaʿ*), GK 1324 (S 1234), 51x. Often translated "to divide, split, tear open, crack open," *bākaʿ* is frequently used in domestic contexts for activities like splitting wood (Eccl. 10:9), hatching eggs (Isa. 34:15; 59:5), or cracking wineskins (Jos. 9:4; Job 32:19). It is also used for such miraculous openings as the splitting of both mountain (Zech. 14:4) and valley (Mic. 1:4) during the eschatological "day of the LORD." See *divide*.

New Testament

Verb: σχίζω (*schizō*), GK *5387* (S *4977*), 11x. *schizō* means "to tear." It can refer to the tearing of fabric, such as an old garment (Lk. 5:36) or a fishing net (Jn. 21:11). At the time of Jesus' death, Matthew speaks of the "splitting" of stones (Mt. 27:51b). See *tear*.

SPOIL

Old Testament

Verb: שָׁחַת (*šāḥat*), GK 8845 (S 7843), 152x. In various contexts, the verb *šāḥat* can broadly mean "to corrupt, destroy, ruin, spoil, wipe out." It denotes the corrupting or destroying of a wide variety of physical things, including eyes (Exod. 21:26), vineyards (Jer. 12:10), buildings (Lam. 2:6), crops (Jdg. 6:4), trees (Deut. 20:19–20), semen (Gen. 38:9), and kings (1 Sam. 26:15). See *destroy*.

SPREAD

Old Testament

Verb: עָרַךְ (*ʿārak*), GK 6885 (S 6186), 75x. *ʿārak* denotes the action of arranging an object in a particular way or arranging objects in a specific order to produce a desired effect. A common use of *ʿārak* is "to arrange" a table for a banquet, which the NIV sometimes translates as "to spread" a table (Ps. 78:19; Isa. 65:11; Ezek. 23:41). See *arrange*.

Verb: פָּרַשׂ (*pāraś*), GK 7298 (S 6566), 67x.

(1) *pāraś* broadly means, "to spread (something) out" and is used of a variety of things. (a) Hands can be spread out in prayer (Exod. 9:29, 33; 1 Ki. 8:22, 38, 54; Ps. 44:20) or in a plea for help or comfort (Jer. 4:31; Lam. 1:17). Hands can also be extended in generosity (Prov. 31:20) or in greed (Lam. 1:10; the picture here is probably one of grabbing at everything within reach).

(b) Letters can be spread out. Ancient documents were written on scrolls, and when they were read, they were spread out or unrolled. Hezekiah spread out Sennacherib's letter before God as evidence of the Assyrian's blasphemy (2 Ki. 19:14; Isa. 37:14). Hezekiah's act was closely linked to and accompanied by prayer.

(c) Also spread out are wings. *pāraś* is frequently used of the wings of the cherubim in both the Tent of Meeting and the temple, as they extended over the ark of the covenant (Exod. 25:20; 1 Ki. 8:7; 2 Chr. 3:13). The author of 2 Chronicles makes special note of the fact that the cherubim's wings were spread over the width of the Most Holy Place. The verb is also used of birds' wings (Job 39:26). In Jer. 48:40 and 49:22 the swooping and spreading of an eagle's wings is a metaphor of impending judgment.

One of the more perplexing uses of *pāraś* is found in Ruth 3:9, in which Ruth asks Boaz to, "*Spread* the corner of your garment over me." While interpretations of this request have been varied, a literal reading of the text is helpful. Literally she asks, "spread your wing over me," a request for the protections of marriage. Marriage is a covenantal relationship and as Ruth requests marriage, she invokes the covenantal imagery of Deut. 32:11 (see below). Ruth is interested not only in marriage but in incorporation into the covenant people of God.

(d) Other miscellaneous uses of *pāraś* are the spreading of cloths or coverings (Num. 4:6), sails (Isa. 33:23), garments (Jdg. 8:25), tents (Exod. 40:19), nets (Isa. 19:8), and food in the sense of spreading a meal before someone (Lam. 4:4 NIV, "no one *gives* it to them." KJV, "no man *breaketh* it unto them").

(2) God is sometimes the subject of *pāraś*. (a) He spreads out his hands—sometimes in judgment (Isa. 25:11, KJV), dividing Moab as a swimmer parts water with his hands; sometimes as a sign of relationship (Isa. 65:2).

(b) Two of the most beautiful instances of *pāraś* as it is applies to God occur in expressions of his oversight of and provision for his people. Moses speaks of God as spreading his wings like an eagle to protect its young (Deut. 32:11). Just as an eagle overshadows, carries, and protects its young, so God is a powerful, protecting presence for his people. Second, the Psalmist reminds Israel of God's spreading the cloud and pillar of fire over them as they wandered in the desert (Ps. 105:39). The pillar, a visible symbol of God's presence, provided light, shade, direction, and protection for them. See also *scatter*. See *NIDOTTE*, 3:699–700.

SPREAD OUT

Old Testament

Verb: נָטָה (*nāṭâ*), GK 5742 (S 5186), 216x. *nāṭâ* conveys the basic idea of "to stretch, spread out, pitch [a tent], turn." See *stretch out*.

New Testament

Verb: διαφέρω (*diapherō*), GK *1422* (S *1308*), 13x. The transitive form of *diapherō* generally means "to carry through or across, spread out." See *carry through*.

SPRING

New Testament

Noun: πηγή (*pēgē*), GK *4380* (S *4077*), 11x. *pēgē* usually refers to a spring of water (Jn. 4:6 [2x]; Jas. 3:11; Rev. 8:10; 14:7; 16:4), though it can include any flow of liquid. In Mk. 5:29 *pēgē* refers to the woman's *flow* of blood that miraculously stops after the woman touches Jesus' garment.

In Jn. 4:14 Jesus promises the Samaritan woman at Jacob's well [*pēgē*] that the water he will give to this woman will become "a spring of water welling up for eternal life." This offer goes out to everyone through Jesus as the Alpha and Omega in Rev. 21:6: "To him who is thirsty I will give to drink without cost from the *spring* of the water of life." This significant metaphorical usage of *pēgē* stems from the OT (cf. Isa. 55:1; 58:11) and denotes the eternal life that Jesus gives to those who follow him (see also Rev. 7:17). By contrast, unbelievers and heretics are dry "springs," which offer no water. See *NIDNTT-A*, 459.*

STAFF

Old Testament

Noun: מַטֶּה (*maṭṭeh*), GK 4751 (S 4294), 252x. *maṭṭeh* has two separate, though related meanings: "rod, staff"; and "tribe" (see *tribe*). A *maṭṭeh* is a rod or staff (such as a shepherd's staff). The staff with which Moses worked miracles in Egypt and during the exodus was a *maṭṭeh* (cf. Exod. 4:17). Aaron's *maṭṭeh* budded in affirmation of God's choice of him to serve as priest (Num. 17:1–10). Jonathan tasted honey with his *maṭṭeh (1 Sam. 14:27)*.

To break a ruler's staff is to destroy his power. Speaking of Babylon, Isaiah says, "the Lord has broken the staff of the wicked" (Isa. 14:5). In Ps. 110:2, *maṭṭeh* indicates the power and sovereignty with which the Lord establishes the coming messianic kingdom: "The LORD will extend your mighty scepter from Zion; you will rule in the midst of your enemies" (NIV; see also Jer. 48:17). See *NIDOTTE*, 2:924–25.

New Testament

Noun: ῥάβδος (*rhabdos*), GK *4811* (S *4464*), 12x. *rhabdos* refers to a "staff, rod, scepter," possibly made of wood, used in various professions. Shepherds used them to guide and protect their sheep. Travelers used them to assist their walking and to defend themselves. Disciplinarians used them to punish slaves and children who were out of line. Rulers used them to symbolize their authority and power.

In the NT, *rhabdos* is used in four contexts. (1) It is used in the context of travel, referring to the disciples' staffs and the staff on which Jacob rested (Mt. 10:10; Mk. 6:8; Lk. 9:3; Heb. 11:21). (2) It is used metaphorically in the context of discipline, as Paul asked his church if they would rather him come "with a *rod*" (i.e., in punishment) or in gentleness (1 Cor. 4:21). (3) It is used in the context of measurement as the rod with which John symbolically measures the temple (Rev. 11:1).

(4) Lastly and most extensively, *rhabdos* is used in the context of rule and authority. It is used of Aaron's rod that budded in the OT (Heb. 9:4). But this use is primarily reserved for the kingly reign of the Messiah. In the OT (especially in Ps. 2 and 45), the Messiah is viewed as a king who will come to finally conquer all evil with "a *rod* of iron." These images are applied to Jesus Christ: Jesus is the triumphant God whose "scepter" of righteousness will never end (Heb. 1:8); he will have authority with his scepter over all nations (Rev. 12:5), and he will subdue all hostile nations, ruling them in judgment (19:15). This concept of kingly authority is also applied to those who believe in Jesus: "And the one who conquers and does my will to the end, to him I will give to him authority over the nations, and he will rule them with an iron *scepter*" (Rev. 2:26–27a). See *NIDNTT-A*, 508.*

STAGGER

Old Testament

Verb: תָּעָה (*tāʿâ*), GK 9494 (S 8582), 51x. *tāʿâ* may be translated as to "go astray, stray, lead astray, wander, stagger." See *go astray*.

STAND

Old Testament

Verb: נָצַב (*nāṣab*), GK 5893 (S 5324), 74x. *nāṣab* conveys the act of standing or the setting up an object and may be translated as "to stand, set." While "to stand" is more common, Genesis uses the term to convey the activity of setting up or establishing altars or monuments (Gen. 21:28; 33: 20; 35:14, 20; cf. 2 Sam. 18:17–18). The term graphically portrays the parting of the waters of the Red Sea, which literally "stood upright" before all Israel (Exod. 15:8; Ps. 78:13). Kings and Chronicles use the term to denote "officers" (lit., "standing ones") who served kings (1 Ki. 4:7; cf. 2 Chr. 8:10). The term also conveys the establishment by God of the boundaries of creation (Ps. 74:17) and his righteous rule (Ps. 82:1; Isa. 3:13). See *NIDOTTE*, 3:134-36.

Verb: עָמַד (*ʿāmad*), GK 6641 (S 5975), 524x. *ʿāmad* has the basic meaning "to stand" but includes multiple nuances depending on the context in which it occurs.

(1) *ʿāmad* can have a nontheological meaning, such as simply "to stand" on one's feet (Gen. 41:1; Neh. 8:5; Est. 5:2). It may indicate readiness, as a servant stands ready to attend to his or her master (1 Sam. 16:22). Jehoshaphat "appoints" singers to praise the Lord (2 Chr. 20:21; lit., "causes singers to stand to praise the Lord").

(2) A frequent idiom in the OT is to "stand before the LORD," i.e., to be in the Lord's presence (e.g., Gen. 18:22; Deut. 10:8, 10). Those who stand before God are an exclusive group such as prophets and priests, and often the situation requires preparation (e.g., sacrifices or ritual cleansing to atone for sin) for the privilege of such access. Israel and Judah corporately

gather and "stand" before God (Deut. 4:10; 2 Chr. 20:13).

(3) Discriminating between true and false prophets depends on the whether the prophet has "stood" before/in the presence of God. Jeremiah decries false prophets who delude the people, "Who *has stood* in the council of the LORD so as to see and to hear his word? ... But if they *had stood* in my council, they would have proclaimed my words to my people, and they would have turned them from their evil way" (Jer. 23:18, 22).

(4) Sometimes *ʿāmad* has to do with court appearances. The parties involved stand before the judge (Deut. 19:17). And when oppressed people are being falsely accused, God "*stands* at the right hand of the needy one" (Ps. 109:31).

(5) In biblical poetry, the idea of "standing firm" gives the notion of enduring. In contrast with the wicked, God will "endure" forever (Ps. 102:26). God's plans "stand firm" (33:11), his righteousness and praise "endure" (111:3; 112:3), as does the fear of the Lord (19:9). Likewise, God's covenant with Jacob "stands firm" (105:10). See *NIDOTTE*, 3:232–33.

Verb: קוּם (*qûm*), GK 7756 (S 6965), 627x. The general range of meanings for *qûm* includes "to stand up, arise, get up (in the morning)." It can also mean "to raise up, confirm something, establish." See *rise*.

New Testament

Verb: ἵστημι (*histēmi*), GK *2705* (S *2476*), 154x. The basic sense of *histēmi* is "to set" or "to stand." It has a variety of nuances in the NT. Its usage can be divided between those with a direct object and those without a direct object.

(1) With direct object, *histēmi* can mean to cause to be in a place or position, "to set, place." This is the sense in Acts when the apostles were placed before the religious leaders (Acts 5:27; cf. 22:30; Mt. 25:33; 18:2). The verb can also mean to set something forward or propose. The disciples "proposed" two men as a replacement for Judas, from which one was selected (Acts 1:23). Furthermore, it can mean "to establish" something, as when Paul writes that the Israelites tried to establish their own righteousness (Rom. 10:3; cf. Heb. 10:9). Finally when *histēmi* takes an object, it can mean "to make someone stand." Paul writes, "The Lord is able to make him stand" (Rom. 14:4).

(2) Without direct object, *histēmi* can mean cease from movement and to be in a stationary position, "to stand still, to stop." On the road to Emmaus, the two men "*stood still*, their faces downcast" (Lk. 24:17; cf. Mk. 10:49; Lk. 7:14; Rev. 18:17). Sometimes it denotes "to stand, appear." For example, "Jesus *stood* before the governor" (Mt. 27:11; cf. Lk. 21:36; Acts 10:30). Another nuance is to take one's stand in the sense of resisting, as in Paul's instruction in Eph. 6:11: "Put on the full armor of God so that you can *take your stand* against the devil's schemes" (cf. 6:13). Finally, this verb can mean "to stand firm" so as to remain stable: "Stand firm then" (Eph. 6:14; cf. Rom. 14:4; Rev. 6:17).

Verb: παρίστημι (*paristēmi*), GK *4225* (S *3936*), 41x. The root meaning of *paristēmi* is "to stand, place beside." It can mean to "stand near" (Mk. 14:47, 69), to "stand nearby" (Jn. 18:22), or to "stand in one's presence" (Lk. 1:19). A number of variations of meaning are found in the NT. Paul uses this word for that which is "offered" or "presented" to God by the Christian (Eph. 5:27). We must not offer our bodies to sin but to God (Rom. 6:13). Our bodies are to be offered as living sacrifices to God (Rom. 12:1). Christ's death makes it possible for us to be presented holy to God (Col. 1:22). We should present ourselves as ones who have no need to be ashamed to God (2 Tim. 2:15). Luke uses *paristēmi* when he talks of the child Jesus "presented" to the Lord according to the law (Lk. 2:22).

paristēmi can also mean "put at my disposal," in reference to the legion of angels God could have provided Jesus in Gethsemane at the time of his arrest (Mt. 26:53).

It sometimes carries the idea of becoming present (Mk. 4:29)—when the grain is ripe, harvest "has come." It can mean to provide (Acts 23:24) or to hand over, as when Paul is handed over to the governor (Acts 23:33). *paristēmi* can also mean to show oneself (1:3). On occasion it means to prove, as when a case is convincingly presented (24:13). See *NIDNTT-A,* 439.

STAND FIRM

New Testament

Verb: στήκω (*stēkō*), GK *5112* (S *4739*), 10x. *stēkō* means "to stand firm, stand." As used in the gospel of Mark, it simply means physically to stand somewhere (Mk. 3:31; 11:25). But in Paul's letters, this verb has the nuance of "standing firm in the Lord" (Phil. 4:1; 1 Thess. 3:8), especially in the context of false teaching (Gal. 5:1; 2 Thess. 2:15). Paul encourages the Corinthians to "stand firm in the faith" (1 Cor. 16:13), and he is particularly pleased that the Philippian believers "stand firm in one spirit" (Phil. 1:27).

Verb: ὑπομένω (*hypomenō*), GK *5702* (S *5278*), 17x. *hypomenō* may be rendered positively as "endure, stand firm, persevere." It can also refer to maintaining a conviction or action in the face of opposition and thus to "stand firm." The individual who stands firm in trial is blessed (Jas. 1:12; 5:11). See *endure.*

STAND IN AWE

New Testament

Verb: φοβέω (*phobeomai*), GK *5828* (S *5399*), 95x. *phobeomai* is used in two main senses in the NT. It means to be "frightened, alarmed," or to "respect, stand in awe of" someone. See *fear*.

STAND UP

New Testament

Verb: ἀνίστημι (*anistēmi*), GK *482* (S *450*), 108x. *anistēmi* depicts someone getting up from a reclined position, "to stand up, get up," including being raising up the dead. See *get up*.

STAR

New Testament

Noun: ἀστήρ (*astēr*), GK *843* (S *792*), 24x.

Noun: ἄστρον (*astron*), GK *849* (S *798*), 4x. Both of these words for "star" are found in the NT and have no difference in meaning. The less-common *astron* is used exclusively by Luke (Lk. 21:25; Acts 7:43; 27:20) and Heb. (11:12), while *astēr* is used by other NT authors, especially Mt. (5x) and Rev. (11x). As with many other words, *astēr/astron* can be used both literally (referring to actual stars) and figuratively (using the image of a star to communicate something else). In the OT, the literal meaning predominates, while in the NT, figurative meanings occur more frequently.

(1) Literal uses: In Acts 27:20 Paul and his companions are caught in a storm at sea and see "neither sun nor stars" for several days. In Heb. 11:12 (quoting Gen. 15:5) God promises Abraham that his descendants will be as numerous as the stars of heaven. 1 Cor. 15:41 (3x) refers to differing amounts of glory or splendor from the different celestial bodies: the sun, moon, and stars. In such instances, "stars" often includes reference to the planets as well.

The story of the Magi's visit to the child Jesus in Mt. 2:1–12 contains four references to a special star (2:2, 7, 9, 10). This miraculous star (which may have been the conjunction of Jupiter and Saturn in 7 B.C. or a supernova) appear at the birth of Jesus and indicate to the eastern astrologers that a great king has been born.

(2) Figurative uses: The many figurative uses of *astēr* in the NT depend on OT usage as well as Jewish apocalyptic literature from the intertestamental period. (a) Rev. 1-3 refers five times (1:16, 20; 2:1; 3:1) to the "seven stars" that are held in the right hand of the "one like a son of man." In 1:20 we learn that these seven stars are the angels of the seven churches. The number seven is a common symbol of perfection, and the seven stars may also

allude to the seven planets known to the ancient world. In apocalyptic literature there is a close connection between the stars and angels, thus God's people are forbidden to worship the stars (cf. Job 38:7; Acts 7:43), and the falling of stars is often linked to the falling of angels (Rev. 8:10–12; 9:1; 12:4). There are other figurative uses of *astēr* in Rev. 2:28; 12:1; and 22:16.

(b) Because the sun, moon, and stars are thought of as regular and reliable components in the universe (cf. Gen. 1, where God places the sun and moon to faithfully regulate day and night), the malfunctioning of these bodies indicates cataclysmic events. Thus, apocalyptic literature often speaks with shocking language about the darkening of the sun and moon and the falling of the stars from heaven (Mt. 24:29; Mk. 13:24–25; Lk. 21:25; Rev. 6:13). These images refer to the eschatological judgment—both the destruction of Jerusalem in A.D. 70 and the final judgment yet to come at Jesus' return. This type of language is not to be read like a weather report, but with figurative power as when we speak of it raining "cats and dogs." This kind of language refers to a reality but with creative word images, which communicate the power and awe of God's coming judgment. See *NIDNTT-A*, 77-78.

STARE

New Testament

Verb: ἀτενίζω (*atenizō*), GK *867* (S *816*), 14x. *atenizō* means "to look with intensity, stare, gaze." See *look straight*.

Verb: ἐμβλέπω (*emblepō*), GK *1838* (S *1689*), 11x. For the most part, *emblepō* describes a person looking or staring at someone or something. See *look at*.

STARVATION

Old Testament

Noun: רָעָב (*rāʿāb*), GK 8280 (S 7457), 101x. *rāʿāb* means "famine, hunger, starvation." See *famine*.

STATUTE

Old Testament

Noun: חֹק (*ḥōq*), GK 2976 (S 2706), 131x. *ḥōq* is derived from the related verb *ḥāqaq*, which means "to cut in, inscribe, decree" and denotes something that is limited or restricted. Most frequently *ḥōq* refers to the prescribed law of God, an inscribed boundary for human behavior. The NIV regularly translates this word with "decree" while the NASB and KJV use "statute." See *decree*.

Noun: חֻקָּה (*ḥuqqâ*), GK 2978 (S 2708), 104x. The feminine noun *ḥuqqâ*, derives from the verb *ḥāqaq*, "to cut in, inscribe, decree," is related to its masculine counterpart, *ḥōq*, though the two nouns never appear together. Like its counterpart, *ḥuqqâ* most frequently indicates the law of God, and the NIV regularly translates these occurrences "decree" while the NASB and KJV use "statute." See *decree*.

Noun: עֵדוּת (*ʿēdût*), GK 6343 (S 5715), 61x. *ʿēdût*, usually translated "testimony," is closely connected to God's law. In the Pentateuch, this noun describes the two tablets containing the Ten Commandments. Generally, outside the Pentateuch *ʿēdût* is a more generic reference to law (1 Ki. 2:3; 2 Ki. 23:3; 1 Chr. 29:19), perhaps with the physical tablets of the Ten Commandments in the background. In this sense, the plural of *ʿēdût* may be translated "requirements, warnings, regulations, or decrees." However, in the book of Psalms, the NIV reserves the translation of "statutes" for *ʿēdût* (13x) to carry the general sense of the law's regulations. See *testimony*.

STAY

Old Testament

Verb: גּוּר (*gûr*), GK 1591 (S 1481), 82x. The basic meaning of *gûr* is to "live, settle, dwell." By and large, this verb refers to someone living outside of their clan, that is, dwelling among people who are not blood relatives. It almost always has the sense of temporariness. See *dwell*.

Verb: לִין (*lîn*), GK 4328 (S 3885), 71x. *lîn* usually describes the act of staying for the night while on a journey. See *spend the night*.

Verb: שָׁכַן (*šākan*), GK 8905 (S 7931) 130x. *šākan* has the basic meaning "to live, dwell, settle." In nearly one-third of the times this verb is used in the OT, God is the subject. See *dwell*.

New Testament

Verb: ἐπιμενω (*epimenō*), GK *2152* (S *1961*), 16x. *epimenō* means "to stay, remain, continue." (1) In some contexts, it means to remain at or in the same place for a period of time. In Acts 10:48, the household of Cornelius "asked Peter *to stay* with them for a few days" (cf. Acts 21:4, 10; 28:12, 14). Later, Paul "stayed" with Peter for fifteen days (Gal. 1:18).

(2) In other contexts, *epimenō* means to continue or persevere in an activity or state. With respect to an activity, this verb appears with a helping verb that denotes the activity that is continued (Jn. 8:7, "they *kept on* questioning him;" Acts 12:16). With respect to a state, *epimenō* may have a profound theological meaning as to the character of one's life; in Rom. 6:1 Paul asks the rhetorical question, "Should we *continue* in sin?" (cf. 11:23). In a related sense, this verb can refer to Christian perseverance (Rom. 11:22, "provided that you *continue* in his kindness;" Col. 1:23; 1 Tim. 4:16). See *NIDNTT-A*, 362-63.

Verb: μένω (*menō*), GK *3531* (S *3306*), 118x. The basic sense of *menō* is "to remain, stay." See *remain*.

Verb: ὑπομένω (*hypomenō*), GK *5702* (S *5278*), 17x. *hypomenō* is occasionally used in its literal sense of "to stay," as in Lk. 2:43: "the boy Jesus *stayed behind* in Jerusalem," and in Acts 17:14 "Silas and Timothy *stayed* at Berea." See *endure*.

STEAL

New Testament

Verb: κλέπτω (*kleptō*), GK *3096* (S *2813*), 13x. *kleptō* denotes the unlawful taking of property, usually by stealth (Mt. 16:19–20; Jn. 10:10). In several NT passages, the eighth command from the Ten Commandments ("Do not steal") is listed as one of the primary injunctions of the Mosaic law (Mt. 19:18; Mk. 10:19; Lk. 18:20; Rom. 13:9). Paul explains that since stealing was part of a believer's former way of life, the new person in Christ must not steal (Eph. 4:28[2x]). As Paul points out, the hypocrites preach against stealing, yet do it themselves (Rom. 2:21[2x]).

The Pharisees urge Pilate to seal Jesus' tomb lest the disciples come and steal his body (Mt. 27:64). After learning of Jesus' resurrection, the chief priests devise a story accusing the disciples of stealing the body (28:13). See *NIDNTT-A*, 335-36.*

STEWARD

New Testament

Noun: οἰκονόμος (*oikonomos*), GK *3874* (S *3623*), 10x. *oikonomos* often refers in the NT to a "household manager" or "steward" entrusted with the responsibility of running a household. Its meaning easily transferred to the household of God, the church. See *manager*.

STIR

New Testament

Verb: κινέω (*kineō*), GK *3075* (S *2795*), 8x. *kineō* means "to move, stir, arouse." See *move*.

STIR UP

Old Testament

Verb: עוּר (*ʿûr*), GK 6424 (S 5782), 80x. *ʿûr* means "to awaken, arouse from sleep," or (in a causative sense) "to rouse someone or something, stir up, incite." Far from being removed from the events of the world, God is carefully bringing about his sovereign design. Thus, he "stirs up" leaders such as Tiglath-Pileser, the king of Assyria, against the tribes in the Transjordan (1 Chr. 5:26). He also arouses the Babylonians against Jerusalem (Ezek. 23:22). See *awake*.

STOCKS

New Testament

Noun: ξύλον (*xylon*), GK *3833* (S *3586*), 20x. *xylon* means "tree, club, wood, stocks." It refers to living or dead wood or anything made of wood. See *tree*.

STOMACH

New Testament

Noun: κοιλία (*koilia*), GK *3120* (S *2836*), 23x. The basic meaning of *koilia* is "body-cavity"; it is often translated "stomach, belly, womb, appetite." See also *womb*.

(1) *koilia* is used of the human stomach or belly (Mt. 15:17; Rev. 10:9–10) and the whale's belly (Mt. 12:40). Jesus makes it clear that what comes out of the heart is what defiles a person, not the food that goes into the *koilia* from without (Mk. 7:19). Thus, Jesus teaches us that the spiritual condition of the heart determines whether or not someone is clean or unclean.

(2) Since the stomach is the seat of powerful bodily cravings for food, *koilia* is also used metaphorically for excessive human appetite and urges. Paul in Romans warns the church against divisive and selfish people who "are not serving our Lord Christ, but their own appetites" (Rom. 16:18). These people love their own cravings more than they love God, which amounts to idolatry. In Phil. 3:19 he makes this even clearer when he says of the enemies of the gospel that "their god is their *koilia*." See *NIDNTT-A*, 310.

STONE

Old Testament

Noun: אֶבֶן (*ʾeben*), GK 74 (S 68), 276x. *ʾeben* means "rock, stone." See *rock*.

New Testament

Noun: λίθος (*lithos*), GK *3345* (S *3037*), 59x. *lithos* is commonly translated as "stone" or "rock." See *rock*.

STOP

Old Testament

Verb: חָדַל (*ḥādal*), GK 2532 (S 2308), 55x. *ḥādal*, most often translated "stop" in the NIV, generally indicates the simple cessation of action. When God confuses human language and scatters people, they "stop" building the city (Gen. 11:8). When God promises Abraham and Sarah a son, the way of women has "ceased" to be to Sarah (18:11). During the seven years of plenty, Joseph gathers so much grain for Egypt that they "stop" measuring it (Gen. 41:49). In order to show Pharaoh God's power, the seventh plague of thunder and hail "stops" when Moses leaves the city and raises his hands (Exod. 9:33; cf. 9:29, 34). When God shows Amos that he is calling for judgment by fire, Amos responds, "Lord God, please *stop*!" (Amos 7:5).

Sometimes *ḥādal* is used for the stopping of an action before it ever starts. In this context, *ḥādal* appears frequently when determining whether an action (i.e., listening or engaging in battle) will begin. The king of Israel asks the prophets, "Shall I go to war against Ramoth Gilead, or shall I *refrain*?" (1 Ki. 22:6; cf. Jdg. 20:28; 1 Ki. 22:15; 2 Chr. 18:5, 14), and Ezekiel must speak God's words to the Israelites whether they listen or "fail" to listen (Ezek. 2:7; cf. 2:5; 3:11).

Occasionally, *ḥādal* indicates that one's presence ceases and may be translated "to leave." Israel (Exod. 14:12) and Job (Job 7:6) both plead, "*Leave* me alone," and the trees and vine of Jotham's parable ask whether they should "leave" their current situation for another (Jdg. 9:9, 11, 13).

Verb: שָׁבַת (*šābat*), GK 8697 (S 7673), 71x. The primary sense of *šābat* is the cessation of activity. After the Israelites enters the promised land, the manna that sustained them during their wilderness wanderings "stops" on the same day that they begin to eat from the land of Canaan (Jos. 5:12). Work (Exod. 5:5; 2 Chr. 16:5; Neh. 6:3) and joyous celebration (Isa. 24:8; Jer. 48:33; Lam. 5:14) may "stop." Egypt's proud strength will "come to an end" (Ezek. 30:18), and so will Judah's (33:28). See *cease*.

New Testament

Verb: κωλύω (*kōlyō*), GK *3266* (S *2967*), 23x. *kōlyō* means "to hinder, stop, forbid, oppose." It is found most often in the writings of Luke. See *hinder*.

Verb: παύω (*pauō*), GK *4264* (S *3973*), 15x. *pauō* means "to stop, finish." When

Jesus "finished speaking," he asks Peter to row his boat out into the lake (Lk. 5:4; cf. 11:1). When Jesus commands the wind and the waves, they "stop" their raging (8:24). According to the Sanhedrin, the early Christians never "stop teaching and proclaiming the good news" (Acts 5:42), and Paul "never stopped warning" the believers in Ephesus about coming dangers to their faith (20:31). In the NT letters Paul writes that some day tongues "will cease" (1 Cor. 13:8). Note especially that one thing Paul never "stops" doing is to pray for his churches (Eph. 1:16; Col. 1:9).

STOREHOUSE

Old Testament

Noun: אוֹצָר (*ʾôṣār*), GK 238 (S 214), 79x. *ʾôṣār* means "treasure, storehouse, wealth." See *treasure.*

STOREROOM

New Testament

Noun: θησαυρός (*thēsauros*), GK *2565* (S *2344*), 17x. *thēsauros* is a "treasure" or the "storeroom" where treasure is put. The only clear example of this latter usage is Mt. 13:52, where Jesus talks about the person "who brings out of his *storeroom* new treasures as well as old." See *treasure.*

STORM

New Testament

Noun: σεισμός (*seismos*), GK *4939* (S *4578*), 14x. In general *seismos* is an "earthquake," though in one instance, it refers to a furious storm on the Sea of Galilee (Mt. 8:24). See *earthquake.*

STRAIGHT

Old Testament

Adjective: יָשָׁר (*yāšār*), GK 3838 (S 3477), 119x. Often rendered "upright, right, innocent; straight," *yāšār* usually denotes appropriate human conduct with respect to ethical norms and religious values. It also describes the straight, level pathway that believers are to walk. See *upright.*

STRANGE(R)

Old Testament

Noun: גֵּר (*gēr*), GK 1731 (S 1616), 92x. *gēr* is a stranger or alien in a land. See *alien.*

Adjective: זָר (*zār*), GK 2424 (S 2214), 70x. In most instances, *zār* modifies a noun and means "strange, foreign, alien" or, by extension, "unauthorized, illegitimate." In other instances, the adjective can function like a noun and mean "stranger, foreigner." See *foreigner, foreign.*

New Testament

Verb: ξενίζω (*xenizō*), GK *3826* (S *3579*), 10x. *xenizō* generally means "to entertain, show hospitality" (see *entertain*), but it can also mean "to be surprised, to be strange." As Paul preached about Jesus to the Athenians, they responded by saying, "You are bringing some *strange ideas* to our ears" (Acts 17:20). Peter uses *xenizō* to mean "caught off guard": "Dear friends, *do* not *be surprised* at the painful trial you are suffering, as though something strange were happening to you" (1 Pet. 4:12). Peter also used this word in describing how the lost world views those individuals who have received Christ: "They *think* it *strange* that you do not plunge with them into the same flood of dissipation, and they heap abuse on you" (1 Pet. 4:4). See *NIDNTT-A*, 398-99.

Noun: παρεπίδημος (*parepidēmos*), GK *4215* (S *3927*), 3x. While *parepidēmos* is, strictly speaking, an adjective, in the NT it is used as a noun meaning "stranger" or "alien" (1 Pet. 1:1; 2:11; Heb. 11:13). All three uses infer that believers have an alien status as temporary residents of earth; our permanent citizenship is in heaven (cf. Phil. 3:20). This means that we must never become too comfortable with life here on this earth, for it last only a short while; life in the heavenly kingdom is permanent and will last forever. See *NIDNTT-A*, 438.

Noun: πάροικος (*paroikos*), GK *4230* (S *3941*), 4x. *paroikos* is a resident foreigner or more generally a stranger. In Acts 7:6, 29, Stephen uses this term to concretely refer to a person who dwells outside (Gk.

para) of his homeland (*oikos*). But this word can also be used more abstractly, such as when Paul suggests that a person who is not reconciled to God is a *paroikos* to God's covenant family (Eph. 2:19). Peter too uses the word more abstractly by describing believers as *paroikos* because they are "stranger and *aliens* in the world" (1 Pet. 2:11). This is a description of how all of us should see ourselves in relationship to the sinful world around us; we are only passing through on our way to a better homeland. See *NIDNTT-A*, 439.*

Adjective and Noun: ἀλλότριος (*allotrios*), GK *259* (S *245*), 14x. *allotrios* is used to describe a thing that is not one's own or a person not from one's own people group. See *other*.

Adjective: ξένος (*xenos*), GK *3828* (S *3581*), 14x. *xenos* denotes something "strange" or unusual (outside of one's experience), a person who is unknown, or a person from another place.

(1) *xenos* is used as an adjective to describe something odd or strange. Peter exhorts his readers not to "think it *strange*" when they face an ordeal because of their faith (1 Pet. 4:12). The author of Hebrews urges his readers not be lured by "strange" teachings (Heb. 13:9). In Acts 17:18, the philosophers in Athens deride Paul for advocating what they perceived to be "*strange* gods" (KJV, NASB; NIV uses "*foreign* gods").

(2) More commonly in the NT, however, *xenos* functions as a noun to describe someone who is a foreigner or a stranger to a group in question. Sometimes *xenos* denotes a person who is not a citizen, as in the description of the "foreigners" living in Athens (Acts 17:21) or the resident "aliens" buried in the potter's field (Mt. 27:7). With a similar meaning, though more figuratively, Paul explains that Gentiles were once "foreigners" to the Jewish covenants but are now fellow citizens with God's people (Eph. 2:12, 19). The author of Hebrews describes the patriarchs of the faith as "aliens" on the earth (Heb. 11:13). At other times, *xenos* denotes someone who is simply unknown, as when Jesus describes that acts of kindness to a "stranger" are tantamount to kindness to himself (Mt. 25:35, 38, 43, 44). Similarly, John praises Gaius for ministering to those who were "strangers" to him (3 Jn. 5).

(3) In one case in the NT, *xenos* is used as a noun to denote a "host," one who shows "hospitality" (Rom. 16:23). See *NIDNTT-A*, 398-99.*

STRAY

Old Testament

Verb: נָדַח (*nādaḥ*), GK 5615 (S 5080), 51x. *nādaḥ* generally has two distinct but related meanings: "to banish, cast out" (see *banish*) and "to stray."

The meaning "to stray" is applied in both literal and figurative contexts. As to the former, Deut. 22:1 instructs those who see their neighbor's straying ox or sheep not to ignore it but to bring it back to its owner. In a parallel way, God's people are at times referred to as a straying flock, as in Ezek. 34, where the prophet condemns the shepherds of Israel who have not brought back those in Israel who have strayed (34:4). As a result, God, the good shepherd, will seek out his sheep and restore them to the flock (34:16; cf. Ps. 147:2). This text in Ezek. is crucial for understanding the ministry Jesus Christ, who has fulfilled Ezek. 34 by being the good shepherd of his people (Mt. 10:6; 15:24; Jn. 10:1–18).

A similar figurative use of *nādaḥ* is found in contexts that speak of Israel's *turning away* or *straying* from the Lord to follow fleshly pursuits or to worship other gods. In cautioning against the adulteress, for example, the sage warns of her seductive speech, which leads the foolish man astray (Prov. 7:21). The verb also shows up in this sense within Deuteronomy, a book highly focused on Israel's need to be solely devoted to God (cf. e.g., Deut. 4:39–40; 5:6–7; 6:4–5). In 4:15–31, for instance, Moses exhorts Israel not to be *enticed* into worshiping the created order instead of the Creator, for he alone is God. If they stray, the result will only be destruction (4:26–27; for similar uses of *nādaḥ* see 13:5, 10, 13; 30:17). See *NIDOTTE*, 3:34-35.

Verb: תָּעָה (*tāʿâ*), GK 9494 (S 8582), 51x. *tāʿâ* may be translated as to "go astray, stray, lead astray, wander, stagger." See *go astray*.

STREAM

Old Testament

Noun: יְאֹר (*yeʾōr*), GK 3284 (S 2975), 64x. *yeʾōr* is a loanword from the Egyptian name for the Nile River. By derivation, it can designate any "river" or "stream."

Noun: נַחַל (*naḥal*), GK 5707 (S 5158), 137x. *naḥal* refers to a dry river bed or wadi. Usually, however, it refers to the raging water that fills a wadi, turning it into a fast flowing river. See *river*.

New Testament

Noun: ποταμός (*potamos*), GK *4532* (S *4215*), 17x. *potamos* denotes a "river" of any size, from the Euphrates to the Jordan, which at times is only a "stream." See *river*.

STREET

Old Testament

Noun: חוּץ (*ḥûṣ*), GK 2575 (S 2351), 164x. *ḥûṣ* refers to that which is "outside." Its usual reference is to a location or position outside, such as the "streets." See *outside*.

New Testament

Noun: πλατεῖα (*plateia*), GK *4423* (S *4113*), 9x. *plateia* means "street," such as the public streets of a city, where the Pharisees love to be seen (Mt. 6:5), the disciples are to pronounce judgment (Lk. 10:10), and the people bring their sick for healing (Acts 5:15). In the parable of the great banquet, the servants are ordered to go "into the streets and alleys of the town" in order to find anyone to fill the banquet hall (Lk. 14:21). The most significant streets are those of the new Jerusalem, which are made of gold and have the water of life flowing down them (Rev. 21:21; 22:3).

STRENGTH

Old Testament

Noun: גְּבוּרָה (*gebûrâ*), GK 1476 (S 1369), 62x. The basic sense of *gebûrâ* is "strength, power, might." It refers to the strength of animals (the horse in Ps. 147:10; Job 39:19) and human beings (Jdg. 8:21; Ps. 90:10). With respect to the kings of Israel, it regularly refers to what their power produced, namely, the *achievements* of the king (1 Ki. 15:23; 16:5, 27). Ultimately, all power belongs to the Lord (1 Chr. 29:11), and human beings have power only because God gives it to them (29:12). Because God possesses wisdom and power (Job 12:13), no one can overturn what he does (Job 12:14–15). With his might, God will vindicate his people (Ps. 54:1); he will save them to make known his mighty power (Ps. 106:8), resulting in praise to him for his *mighty acts* (106:2). God does not delight in the strength of horses or men's legs, but in the fear of the Lord (147:10–11). See *NIDOTTE*, 1:806-16.

Noun: זְרוֹעַ (*zerôaʿ*), GK 2432 (S 2220), 91x. *zerôaʿ* denotes the arm or forearm. It is used to denote the literal arm of a person (Gen. 49:24; Isa. 9:20). Since the arm can be viewed as the seat of strength, it is used metaphorically to refer to someone's *strength* or *power* (1 Sam. 2:31), especially God's power (Exod. 6:6; Deut. 4:34; 5:15; Ps. 44:4; 79:11; 89:11). See *arm*.

Noun: חַיִל (*ḥayil*), GK 2657 (S 2428), 246x. The basic sense of *ḥayil* is "power, strength, capability."

(1) In military contexts, *ḥayil* can refer to an "army" of fighting men (e.g., Pharaoh's army in Exod. 14:4, 9, 17, 28). Also, the expression "men of *ḥayil*" can be translated "warriors, men of valour/might, valiant men, fighting men" (Jdg. 20:44, 46; 2 Sam. 11:16; 2 Ki. 24:16; Ps. 76:5). The common expression "mighty (one) of *ḥayil*" also refers to warriors and is usually translated in the KJV as "mighty man of valour" and in the NIV as "(best) fighting men" or "mighty warrior" (Jos. 1:14; 6:2;

8:3; 10:7; Jdg. 6:12; 11:1). But a great army is no substitute for fearing the Lord, and being protected by the one whose purposes and plans will always prevail (Ps. 33:16–17).

(2) *ḥayil* is also used to describe persons who have a special skill or ability. In Gen. 47:6, Pharaoh asks Joseph to put in charge of his livestock any "men of *ḥayil*" ("men of special ability") from among the Israelites. In Exod. 18:21, Moses' father-in-law suggests that Moses choose "men of *ḥayil*" ("capable or able men"), who can help him judge the people. The expression "to do/make *ḥayil*" means to grow strong/ do mighty things (NIV) or, in the KJV, to act valiantly (Num. 24:18; 1 Sam. 14:48; Ps. 118:15, 16). The OT praises women who are characterized by *ḥayil*. Ruth is praised as a woman of *noble character* (Ruth 3:11), one who has proven by her character that she is a capable and virtuous wife. The "woman/wife of *ḥayil*" is called "her husband's crown" (Prov. 12:4), and she is described in full detail in Prov. 31:10–31 as industrious, strong, trustworthy, compassionate, and wise. See *NIDOTTE*, 2:116-26.

Note that in contexts where goods or property are in view, *ḥayil* can refer to "wealth, riches, substance." See *wealth*.

Noun: כֹּחַ (*kōaḥ*), GK 3946 (S 3581b), 126x. The basic sense of *kōaḥ* is "strength, power." It can refer to physical strength (Samson's strength in Jdg. 16:5, 6, 9, 15, 17, 19, 30) or strength in some metaphorical sense. For example, *kōaḥ* refers to the power to produce or reproduce (of Behemoth in Job 40:16; of Jacob in Gen. 49:3; of the earth yielding *her crops* [KJV has "her strength"] in Gen. 4:12). It is also used of God's strength. Because power is in God's hand, no one can withstand him (2 Chr. 20:6); he is the one who gives strength to all (1 Chr. 29:12). See *NIDOTTE*, 2:621-31.

Noun: מְאֹד (*meʾōd*), GK 4394 (S 3966), 300x. *meʾōd* is usually used adverbially, meaning "very, much, greatly, exceedingly." Occasionally the word is used as a noun, in which case it means "strength." For example, Deut. 6:5 exhorts Israel to love the Lord their God "with all your heart and with all your soul and with all your *strength*." See *greatly*.

Noun: עֹז (*ʿōz*), GK 6437 (S 5797), 76x. The primary sense of *ʿōz* is "strength, might, power." Most commonly, *ʿōz* is used to describe God's power or strength. See *power*.

New Testament

Noun: ἰσχύς (*ischys*), GK *2709* (S *2479*), 10x. *ischys* means "strength, power, might." In Jesus' exposition of the first of the two greatest commandments, he calls on the faithful to love the Lord with all their "strength" (Mk. 12:30, 33; Lk. 10:27). *ischys* is also used of God's power at work in believers (Eph. 1:19; 6:10) and at his second coming (2 Thess. 1:9), of human strength or ability given by God (1 Pet. 4:11), and of angelic strength (2 Pet. 2:11). In a remarkable attestation to the deity of Jesus Christ, the apostle John records two doxologies in which what is ascribed to God (the Father) is also ascribed to the Lamb, who is Jesus the Son (Rev. 5:12, "Worthy is the Lamb to receive ... *strength*"; 7:12, "Praise and ... *strength* be to our God forever"). See *NIDNTT-A*, 276.*

Noun: κράτος (*kratos*), GK *3197* (S *2904*), 12x. *kratos* is generally translated "power, strength, might." See *power*.

STRENGTHEN

New Testament

Verb: οἰκοδομέω (*oikodomeō*), GK *3868* (S *3618*), 40x. In the gospels *oikodomeō* often has the normal meaning of building a physical structure. But in Acts and the rest of the NT, this verb becomes a significant metaphor for the mutual encouragement and strengthening of the people of God. See *build, build up*.

Verb: στηρίζω (*stērizō*), GK *5114* (S *4741*), 13x. *stērizō* means "to strengthen, fix something in place, establish." It is used in the NT primarily in the sense of being inwardly established or strengthened.

(1) God is able "to strengthen" his followers (Rom. 16:25) and "to establish" hearts blameless (1 Thess. 3:13). Paul prays for God "to establish" the Thessalonians in every good word and work (2 Thess. 2:17), and he promises them that the Lord will "strengthen" them and protect them from the evil one (3:3). Peter too promises his readers that God will "strengthen" them (1 Pet. 5:10). This strengthening that God does is the process of making people spiritually firm in their faith.

Evidence of the tension between divine sovereignty and human responsibility in this area can be seen in the fact that whereas it is God who strengthens, people are also commanded to strengthen themselves and others. Jesus says to Peter, "and you, when you have returned, *strengthen* your brothers" (Lk. 22:32). Paul expresses his desire to impart spiritual gifts to the Romans in order that they may be strengthened (Rom. 1:11). Paul sends Timothy to strengthen the Thessalonians (1 Thess. 3:2). James urges his audience to strengthen their hearts (Jas. 5:8). Peter encourages his readers, even though he considers them established in the truth they have (2 Pet. 1:12). Jesus urges the church in Sardis to strengthen what remains (Rev. 3:2).

(2) On one occasion *stērizō* is used to designate strength of resolve. Jesus (lit.) "*strengthened* his face to go to Jerusalem" (Lk. 9:51).

(3) On another occasion *stērizō* describes something that has been set in place. In the parable of the rich man and Lazarus, Abraham says to the rich man after death, "Between us and you a great chasm *has been fixed*" (Lk. 16:26). See *NIDNTT-A*, 540.

STRETCH OUT

Old Testament

Verb: נָטָה (*nāṭâ*), GK 5742 (S 5186), 216x. *nāṭâ* conveys the basic idea of "to stretch, spread out, pitch, turn." It is often used in the sense of pitching a tent, probably because the skins were spread out before being set up as a dwelling place (Gen. 12:8; 26:25; 1 Chr. 15:10). The Lord "has pitched" the heavens like a tent (Ps. 104:2; Isa. 42:5) and "spread out" his mercy over Joseph during his prison sentence (Gen. 39:21).

To "turn one's ear" toward someone or something is to listen attentively (2 Ki. 19:16; Ps. 17:6; 31:2; 102:2; Isa. 55:3). *nāṭâ* is often used in conjunction with an object such as a hand or staff. The Lord instructs Moses to tell Aaron to "*stretch out* you hand with your staff over the streams and canals and ponds, and make frogs come up on the land of Egypt" (Exod. 8:5; cf. Jos. 8:18–19). When the Lord stretches out his own hand/arm, it was either to deliver his people or judge foreign nations (Exod. 6:6; Deut. 4:34). Interestingly, the power of Egypt is described in terms of Pharaoh's outstretched arm. However, when the Lord stretches out his arm, even the Egyptians will know that he alone is God (Exod. 7:5). Even the purposes of the most powerful ruler on earth are subject to the Sovereign of the universe (Prov. 21:1).

nāṭâ is also used in a moral sense. Proverbs indicates that keeping one's foot from evil means not "swerving" or "turning" to the right or to the left (Prov. 4:27). The term is used along these lines to express the subversion of justice (Exod. 23:2, 6; Deut. 24:17; 1 Sam. 8:3; Prov. 17:23; Amos 2:7–8). Unfaithfulness to the Lord is sometimes characterised as "turning" the heart toward other gods (1 Ki. 11:2–4). To turn one's heart to the Lord is to refocus the center of one's energy and desire toward him. "May he *turn* our hearts to him, to walk in all his ways and to keep the commands, decrees and regulations he gave our fathers" (1 Ki. 8:58; cf. Jos. 24:23; Ps. 44:19). See *NIDOTTE*, 3:91-93.

New Testament

Verb: ἐκτείνω (*ekteinō*), GK *1753* (S *1614*), 16x. *ekteinō* means "to stretch out." Jesus "stretched out" his hands to heal the sick (Mt. 8:3; Mk. 1:41; Lk. 5:13). The man with a shriveled hand "stretched it out" to Jesus and it was healed (Mt. 12:13; Mk. 3:5; Lk. 6:10). Jesus "stretched out his hand" to point to his spiritual family, those who do the will of the Father (Mt. 12:49–50). Peter and John prayed that God would "stretch out" his hand to heal and to perform signs and wonders (Acts 4:30).

STRIFE

Old Testament

Noun: רִיב (*rîb*), GK 8190 (S 7379), 62x. *rîb* (related to the verb *rîb*, usually translated "contend") indicates an argument or conflict with another individual. There may be "strife" among humans (e.g., Gen. 13:7), which the book of Proverbs tells us repeatedly to avoid (e.g., Prov. 17:1, 14). See *case.*

New Testament

Noun: ἔρις (*eris*), GK *2251* (S *2054*), 9x. *eris* occurs only in the letters of Paul. He includes it in various lists of sins and vices (Rom. 1:29; 13:13; Gal. 5:20; 1 Tim. 6:4; Tit. 3:9). Quarreling and strife seem particularly to have been a part of the picture in Corinth, for Paul has to urge them to get rid of such attitudes and to strive instead for love and unity (1 Cor. 1:11; 3:3; 2 Cor. 12:20). While Paul is in prison, he discovers that some of his enemies have been trying to take advantage of his situation and "preach Christ out of envy and rivalry" (Phil. 1:15).*

STRIKE

Old Testament

Verb: נָגַע (*nāgaʿ*), GK 5595 (S 5060), 150x. The verb *nāgaʿ* means "to touch physically," but its various nuances include "to touch, strike, reach, arrive."

nāgaʿ sometimes denotes doing harm or striking. Isaiah prophesies that the Suffering Servant will be stricken by God with extreme physical abuse (Isa. 53:4). In addition, God strikes the Philistines with plagues (1 Sam. 6:9) and grants Satan's request to harm Job with various troubles (Job 1:11; 2:5). Abimelech does not harm Sarah (Gen. 26:11), and the Israelites are not allowed to harm the inhabitants of Gibeon (Jos. 9:19). See also *touch, reach.*

Verb: נָכָה (*nākâ*), GK 5782 (S 5221), 501x. The verb *nākâ* generally means "to strike down, destroy, hit, kill." It can denote a light striking of one's hands (i.e., a clap, 2 Ki. 11:12). It may also express a severe beating that stops short of death (Deut. 25:2–3) or a strike that causes death (Jos. 10:26). In Exod. 2:11–13, *nākâ* is used in three different ways: Moses sees an Egyptian beating a Hebrew (v. 11), kills the Egyptian (v. 12), and later sees two Hebrews fighting (v. 13).

God is often the subject of *nākâ*. He strikes and destroys the world with the flood (Gen. 8:21) and Egypt with wonders and plagues (Exod. 3:20). Because of the sins of Israel, he smites her with disease (Deut. 28:22, 27, 28), crop failure (Amos 4:9; Hag. 2:17), and death (2 Sam. 6:7). Significantly, *nākâ* is an important term in describing afflictions that God will place on the prophesied Messiah. Isaiah prophesies that God will smite the Suffering Servant (Isa. 53:4). Furthermore, God's sword is against his shepherd; he will strike him and scatter the sheep (Zech. 13:7).

nākâ is also used of striking and destroying a city or other groups of people (Gen. 14:7; Deut. 1:4; Jos. 10:40). It is sometimes paired with vbs. similar in meaning such as *ḥāram*, "to destroy utterly" (Deut. 7:2; Jos. 10:28, 35). In these cases, Yahweh's judgment against sin demands that every human being be utterly destroyed and all the precious metals be devoted to God in the sacred treasury. This is the truth of the Israelites' defeat of Ai. They kill all the inhabitants, burn the city, hang the king, and cover his body over with stones in the gate of the city (Jos. 8:24–29). Only the livestock and food stores are enjoyed by the Israelites (Jos. 8:27). See *NIDOTTE* 3:102-5.

New Testament

Verb: δέρω (*derō*), GK *1296* (S *1194*), 15x. *derō* originally meant to flay or skin, but it came to mean "to beat, strike" in the NT period. This type of beating occurs with varying degrees of severity, but does not result in death. See *beat.*

Verb: πατάσσω (*patassō*), GK *4250* (S *3960*), 10x. *patassō* is one of several NT words meaning "to strike, hit." It is often used literally for striking of varying degrees of severity. An angel strikes Peter on the side to wake him up (Acts 12:7). Peter strikes the high priest's servant with a sword; cutting off his ear (Mt. 26:51; Lk. 22:49–50). Moses kills the Egyptian by striking him (Acts 7:24; cf. Exod. 2:12).

In a figurative sense, *patassō* is used of divine action. God strikes Jesus by placing judgment on him in the cross event: "I will strike the shepherd, and the sheep of the flock will be scattered" (Mt. 26:31; Mk. 14:27; cf. Zech. 13:7). The Lord, through an angel, strikes down Herod by causing worms to eat him because he did not give glory to God (Acts 12:23). God empowers the two witnesses to "strike the earth with every kind of plague" (Rev. 11:6). When Christ returns, he will strike down the rebellious nations with the sharp sword of his mouth and rule them with a rod of iron (Rev. 19:15). See *NIDNTT-A*, 357-58.*

Verb: τύπτω (*typtō*), GK *5597* (S *5180*), 13x. *typtō* means "to beat, strike." See *beat*.

STRIVE

Old Testament

Verb: בָּקַשׁ (*bāqaš*), GK 1335 (S 1245), 225x. *bāqaš* refers to a search for, or a striving after, someone or something. See *seek*.

New Testament

Verb: σπουδάζω (*spoudazō*), GK *5079* (S *4704*), 11x. *spoudazō* generally indicates to strive to give one's best effort to do something. See *make effort*.

STRIVE FOR

New Testament

Verb: ἐπιζητέω (*epizēteō*), GK *2118* (S *1934*), 13x. *epizēteō* means "to look for, desire after, strive for." See *look for*.

STRONG, (BE) STRONG

Old Testament

Verb: חָזַק (*ḥāzaq*), GK 2616 (S 2388), 290x.

(1) *ḥāzaq* can describe the severity of an impersonal force. For instance, we read that the famine is *strong* on all the land (Gen. 41:57; cf. 47:20). Absalom's head is *strong* in the oak, and we read that his head "caught hold" (KJV) or "got caught" (NIV) (2 Sam. 18:9). The term can also describe the impersonal might of a nation or individual that results in that nation or individual prevailing over others. In Jos. 17:13 we read that the Israelites grow strong (see also Jdg. 1:28; 2 Sam. 16:21, etc.). The word can describe compelling force used to overpower others (cf. the awful incident in Deut. 22:25). The word of the king is strong, and we read that it "prevails against" (KJV) or "overrules" Joab (2 Sam. 24:4).

(2) At some points *ḥāzaq* is interpreted to mean being courageous. So the KJV translates the word in Jos. 23:6, "Be ye therefore very courageous" (cf. the NIV, "Be very strong"; cf. also 1 Chr. 19:13; 2 Chr. 19:11; Ezr. 10:4; Ps. 27:14; Isa. 41:6). These overtones of courage are also present in the command, "Only be strong lest you eat the blood" in Deut. 12:23, which is commonly translated along the lines of "be sure" (KJV, NIV). Similar to this is the command to Moses that he "strengthen [i.e., encourage] Joshua" (Deut. 3:28; cf. Jdg. 16:28; 2 Sam. 11:25).

(3) In several instances *ḥāzaq* I refers to God's "making strong" (i.e., hardening) the heart of Pharaoh (Exod. 4:21; 7:13, 22; 8:19; 9:12, 35; 10:20, 27; 11:10; 14:4, 8, 17). In some of these texts Pharaoh's heart is the subject—"The heart of Pharaoh was strengthened"—but several of these are followed by the statement "as God had said," indicating that God is bringing his promise (4:21) to pass. We have neither the authority nor the ability to remove the tension between divine sovereignty and human responsibility from the pages of the Bible. God hardens Pharaoh's heart, yet he holds Pharaoh responsible for choosing to reject what Moses has said.

(4) When the priests have not repaired the temple, the text says that they have not made *strong* its breaches (2 Ki. 12:8, 12;

22:5–6). Nehemiah and the people make strong or repair the walls of the city of Jerusalem (Neh. 3:4, 7, 9, 10).

(5) In some cases *ḥāzaq* means "to seize, grasp." Moses grasps the snake (Exod. 4:4). Saul seizes the edge of Samuel's robe (1 Sam. 15:27).

Adjective: חָזָק (*ḥāzāq*), GK 2617 (S 2389), 57x. The basic sense of the adjective *ḥāzāq* is "mighty, strong, powerful."

(1) *ḥāzāq* is used to describe human beings. Moses sent spies to Canaan to determine if the inhabitants were strong (Num. 13:18, 31). God's judgment on Israel is so overwhelming that neither the swift, nor the *strong*, nor the warrior can rely on his own resources to escape it (Amos 2:14).

(2) *ḥāzāq* is also associated with God. About half of its occurrences are found in the expression "a *mighty* hand," and most of these refer to God's mighty hand displayed in delivering Israel from Egypt during the Exodus. Before the Exodus, God proclaimed to Moses that he would bring Israel out "with a mighty hand" (Exod. 3:19; 6:1); after the Exodus, Israel is regularly exhorted to obey God's commands because he delivered them "with a mighty hand" (Exod. 13:9; Deut. 5:15; 6:21). As well, God uses a "mighty arm" to discipline Israel for her apostasy (Jer. 21:5) and a "mighty hand" to rule over them, pour out wrath (Ezek. 20:33), and gather them together from the nations for judgment (20:34).

(3) Sometimes, when describing inanimate things, *ḥāzāq* can be translated in a way that highlights the intensity of that thing. For example, Exod. 19:16 speaks of a very *loud* trumpet blast; 2 Sam. 11:15 of the *fiercest* battle ("the *hottest* battle" in KJV); 1 Ki. 18:2 of a *severe* famine. In Job 37:18 the metal mirror is strong in the sense of being *hard*. In Ezekiel, the expressions "*ḥāzāq* of heart" (2:4) and "*ḥāzāq* of forehead" (3:7, 8, 9) conjure up images of a heart and forehead as hard as stone. Such phrases are metaphors for people who are obstinate and stubborn. See *NIDOTTE*, 2:63-87.

New Testament

Verb: ἰσχύω (*ischyō*), GK *2710* (S *2480*), 28x. In the NT, *ischyō* primarily means "to be strong, powerful, mighty."

(1) It is used in this basic sense to describe prayer (Jas. 5:16, "is powerful" in NIV, "*availeth* much" in KJV) and people (Lk. 16:3, "I am not *strong enough* to dig").

(2) The basic meaning, however, is stretched so that *ischyō* also takes on various metaphorical senses. For example, someone who is powerful in relation to another is said "to prevail over/against them" (Acts 19:16, the demon-possessed man "overpowered" or "prevailed against" the seven sons of Sceva; Rev. 12:8, the dragon did not prevail against Michael the angel). It can also mean simply "to be able," as when Matthew says that "no one *could* pass that way" (Mt. 8:28), when Jesus asked the disciples, "*Could you not* keep watch with me for one hour?" (Mt. 26:40), and when Jesus warns that we must strive to enter the narrow gate because many will try and not *be able* to (Lk. 13:24).

In some passages *ischyō* has the sense of being in possession of one's powers, meaning "to be healthy" (Mt. 9:12, "It is not *the healthy* who need a doctor"). In 5:13 it means "to be useful for something" (salt that loses its saltiness "is no longer *good for anything*").

Finally, *ischyō* can also be used in the sense of "to have meaning, value, or validity," as in Gal. 5:6 ("neither circumcision nor uncircumcision *has any value*") and Heb. 9:17 (a will "never *takes effect* while the one who made it is living"). See *NIDNTT-A*, 276.

Adjective: δυνατός (*dynatos*), GK *1543* (S *1415*), 32x. *dynatos* denotes what is possible or what one has the power to do. See *possible*.

Adjective: ἰσχυρός (*ischyros*), GK *2708* (S *2478*), 28x. *ischyros* means "strong, mighty, powerful." It refers to superhuman beings like God (Rev. 18:8) and angels (Rev. 5:2; 18:2), but it can also refer to human beings (1 Cor. 4:10; Heb. 11:34) and to things like the "boisterous" wind (Mt. 14:30, KJV), a "severe" famine (Lk. 15:14, NIV), or Paul's "forceful" letters (2 Cor. 10:10). In 1 Corinthians Paul remarks that even God's weakness is "more powerful" than human strength; consequently, God is able to choose the weak of the world to shame the "strong" (1 Cor. 1:25, 27). See *NIDNTT-A*, 276.

STUBBORN

Old Testament

Noun: בַּרְזֶל (*barzel*), GK 1366 (S 1270), 76x. *barzel* is first found in Gen. 4:22, where Tubal-Cain is said to have "forged all kinds of tools out of bronze and iron." Israel is pictured as having a neck of iron, meaning she is stubbornly unwilling to submit to God and trust in him (Isa. 48:4). See *iron*.

Adjective: חָזָק (*ḥāzāq*), GK 2617 (S 2389), 57x. The basic sense of the adjective *ḥāzāq* is "mighty, strong, powerful." In Ezekiel, the expressions "*ḥāzāq* of heart" (2:4) and "*ḥāzāq* of forehead" (3:7, 8, 9) conjure up images of a heart and forehead as hard or strong as stone. Such phrases are metaphors for people who are obstinate or stubborn. See *strong*.

STUMBLE

Old Testament

Verb: כָּשַׁל (*kāšal*), GK 4173 (S 3782), 65x. *kāšal* conveys the act of stumbling or falling and may be translated "stumble, fall." It is used frequently in contexts of judgment and is a common term in prophetic texts. Jer. 6:21 states, "I will put obstacles before this people. Fathers and sons alike will *stumble* over them; neighbors and friends will perish" (see also Isa. 3:8; 59:10; Jer. 46:6; Hos. 4:5; Nah. 2:5). In a play on words Jeremiah uses here both the noun form *mikšôl* ("obstacles, stumbling blocks") and the verb form *kāšal* to convey the idea that Israel is stumbling because of her own doing. *mikšôl* is Ezekiel's favorite term for "idol," which ironically becomes the object of Israel's *stumbling* (see Ezek. 21:15; see also 3:20; 7:19; 14:3, 4, 7; 18:30; 44:12). Ezekiel proclaims in 14:3: "Son of man, these men have set up idols in their hearts and put wicked *stumbling blocks* before their faces." Our "stumblings" too are often the result of our own actions. See *NIDOTTE*, 2:733-35.

STUMBLING BLOCK

New Testament

Noun: πρόσκομμα (*proskomma*), GK *4682* (S *4348*), 6x. *proskommā* means "stumbling block, offense." This word has two main uses in the NT. (1) It is used three times in reference to Isa. 8:14, which both Paul and Peter see as fulfilled in the fact that Jews or other people who are being evangelized stumble over the good news about Jesus Christ and him crucified (Rom. 9:32, 33; 1 Pet. 2:8). (2) The other three uses occur in Paul's discussion of Christian freedom (Rom. 14:13, 20; 1 Cor. 8:9), where the apostle instructs "strong" Christians not to insist on their freedom in Christ to such an extent that "weak" Christians (i.e., especially children and new believers) end up following their example, but in doing so feel deeply that they are sinning against Christ. Thus, that exercise of freedom "becomes a stumbling block to the weak."

Noun: σκάνδαλον (*skandalon*), GK *4998* (S *4625*), 15x. *skandalon* is something that leads a person to sin or to fall away from faith. See *obstacle*.

STUPID

Old Testament

Noun: כְּסִיל (*k*^{e}*sîl*), GK 4067 (S 3684), 70x. *k*^{e}*sîl* refers to a "fool, a stupid or shameless person." The noun is used solely of humanity and found only in the wisdom literature of the OT. See *fool*.

(BE) SUBJECT

New Testament

Verb: ὑποτάσσω (*hypotassō*), GK *5718* (S *5293*), 38x. *hypotassō* means "to submit, be subject." See *submit*.

SUBJECT TO

New Testament

Adjective: ἔνοχος (*enochos*), GK *1944* (S *1777*), 10x. *enochos* means "guilty, subject to, liable for, worthy of." See *guilty*.

SUBURBS

Old Testament

Noun: מִגְרָשׁ (*migrāš*), GK 4494 (S 4054), 114x. *migrāš* is an open area of land surrounding and belonging to a city or temple. The KJV consistently translates it as "suburbs," which adequately conveys the idea of territory surrounding a city but which unfortunately gives the impression that the area is built up, which is not necessarily the case. See *pastureland*.

SUBMIT

New Testament

Verb: ὑποτάσσω (*hypotassō*), GK *5718* (S *5293*), 38x. *hypotassō* means "to submit, be subject." *hypotassō* in general communicates some sense of hierarchy. Context must determine, however, whether or not this subordination is required or voluntary, for *hypotassō* is not synonymous with obedience. Children, on course, are expected to obey their parents; Jesus was no exception. Luke clearly accentuates that while Jesus was chiefly submissive to the authority of the Scriptures and his heavenly Father, he was also "subject" to his parents (Lk. 2:51; NIV "obedient"). God expected his Son to obey his parents, and he voluntarily did so.

hypotassō is used when God places everything in *submission* to Christ (1 Cor. 15:27–28; cf. Eph. 1:22; Phil. 3:21; Heb. 2:5, 8). In each instance God initiates the action, and all things are subject to the exalted Christ, including angels, authorities, powers, and death. Through the power given by Christ, demons "submitted" to the disciples in their ministry, and Jesus reminds them that Satan is quickly heading for decisive defeat. The disciples should not, however, rejoice over this submission; rather, they should rejoice that "their names are written in heaven" (Lk. 10:20).

For the most part, the remaining occurrences of *hypotassō* reflect Christian behavior in the context of recognized authority structures. Believers should respectfully "submit to the Father" (Heb. 12:9), dutifully submit to "governing authorities," whether they are secular (Rom. 13:1; 1 Pet. 2:13) or in the family of faith (1 Pet. 5:5). Christian slaves should freely serve their masters (Tit. 2:9), and wives should voluntarily be submissive to their husbands (Eph. 5:24; Col. 3:18; 1 Pet. 3:1, 5).

The most extensive passage on submission in the Christian home is found in Eph. 5:22–33. The idea is grammatically rooted in v. 21, where Paul admonishes all Christians to submit to each other first, thus transmitting the idea of mutuality. When this manner of submission takes place, then our primary responsibilities to each other as Christian brothers and sisters are highlighted before secondary ones are entertained. See *NIDNTT-A*, 583-84.

SUCCEED

Old Testament

Verb: צָלַח (*sālah*), GK 7503 (S 6743), 55x. *sālah means* "to prosper, succeed, be successful." See *prosper*.

(BE) SUCCESSFUL

Old Testament

Verb: צָלַח (*ṣālaḥ*), GK 7503 (S 6743), 55x. *ṣālah means* "to prosper, succeed, be successful." See *prosper*.

SUFFER

New Testament

Verb: βασανιζω (*basanizō*), GK *989* (S *928*), 12x. *basanizō* means to "torment" or "torture." But in the NT, it sometimes means to experience suffering or struggle. For example, the disciples "are buffeted" by the wind and the waves in Mt. 14:24. In 8:6 the "terrible suffering" of the centurion's servant is the result of paralysis. See *torture*.

Verb: ἐπιτρέπω (*epitrepō*), GK *2205* (S *2010*), 18x. *epitrepō* essentially means "to permit, allow, let." The KJV often translates this word, "suffer," in the sense of allowing. See *permit.*

Verb: πάσχω (*paschō*), GK *4248* (S *3958*), 42x. *paschō* means "to suffer." In the NT it refers primarily to the suffering of Christ, such as in the gospel passion predictions (Mt. 16:21; 17:12). In Mark and Luke (Mk. 8:31; 9:12; Lk. 9:22; 17:25) Jesus emphasizes the necessity of the Messiah's suffering in order for him to be glorified (Lk. 24:26, 46).

Several times in the gospels, *paschō* has other referents: a demon-possessed boy "suffers terribly" (Mt. 17:15); Pilate's wife "suffered much" (perhaps referring to the anguish of pangs of conscience) in a dream because of Jesus' innocence (27:19); the woman with the issue of blood had "*suffered* much from many doctors" while trying to cure her affliction (Mk. 5:26). In some places the word can imply death, as when Jesus tells his disciples that he had desired to "eat this Passover with you before I *suffer*" (Lk. 22:15), and Peter writes that "Christ *suffered* once for all (1 Pet. 3:18: NIV "died").

Outside the gospels, *paschō* is also used of Christ's sufferings (Acts 1:3; 3:18; 17:3; Heb. 9:26; 13:12). Paul and Peter focus on suffering as something that naturally befalls a Christian, as it befell Christ. Paul refers to his own suffering for Christ (Phil. 1:29) and for the gospel (2 Tim. 1:12), and even predating Paul's ministry, Jesus told Ananias that it was "necessary that he [Paul] must *suffer* much for my name" (Acts 9:16). Paul mentions the church's sympathetic suffering within itself among its own members (1 Cor. 1:26, "if one part suffers, all parts suffer with [*synpaschō*] it"), and Paul alludes to the mutually borne sufferings between himself and the churches (2 Cor. 1:6, "the same sufferings we suffer"]; see also Phil. 1:29–30).

The church also suffers because of persecution from without (1 Thess. 2:14; Rev. 2:10), suffering for the kingdom of God (2 Thess. 1:5). Jesus' suffering and subsequent glorification provide a motivation and a model for endurance (Phil. 1:29; 1 Pet. 2:20–21) and for godly, upright living (1 Pet. 4:1: "Since Christ *suffered* in his flesh [NIV "body"], arm yourselves with the same attitude, because he who has *suffered* in his flesh [NIV "body"] is done with sin"). The author of Hebrews indicates that Christ's suffering was not only redemptive but also instructive; Christ "learned obedience from that which he *suffered*" (Heb. 5:8). Furthermore, because he suffered when he was tempted, he can help those who are tempted (2:18).

While Peter comforts and encourages those who suffer, he reminds the church that not all suffering is commendable (1 Pet. 4:15), only suffering unjustly or for the sake of righteousness (2:19–23; 3:14, 17; 4:19). Our suffering is not redemptive; that is reserved for Christ's suffering in our place. If we suffer specifically for the sake or name of Christ, we share in the same glory accorded to him after his suffering (5:10): "God . . . called you to his eternal glory in Christ, after you have *suffered* a little while." See *NIDNTT-A*, 443-45.

Verb: συνέχω (*synechō*), GK *5309* (S *4912*), 12x. *synechō* has a variety of meanings. In some places it can denote suffering and distress (see Mt. 4:24; Lk. 4:38; 12:50; Acts 28:8; Phil. 1:23). See *compel.*

SUFFERING

New Testament

Noun: πάθημα (*pathēma*), GK *4077* (S *3804*), 16x. The classical Greek meaning of *pathēma* as "human passions" is used only twice in the NT. Paul refers to "the sinful *passions* aroused by the law" (Rom. 7:5), and in Gal. 5:24, Paul says that Christians have "crucified the flesh with its *passions* and lusts/desires." To speak of lusts of the flesh, Paul usually uses *epithymia* (see *desire*).

Otherwise, the NT uses *pathēma* in its primary meaning of undergoing suffering, mistreatment, or even death. Paul, Hebrews, and Peter speak of the sufferings of Christ (Heb. 2:9–10; 1 Pet. 1:11, 5:1), which overflow into the lives of Christ's followers (2 Cor. 1:5) as they participate or fellowship in his sufferings (2 Cor. 1:7;

Phil. 3:10; 1 Pet. 4:13). This participation produces spiritual fruit in our lives (2 Cor. 1:6) and allows us to share in his glory at the resurrection (Rom. 8:18). Paul speaks of his own sufferings on behalf of the church (2 Tim. 3:11; Col. 1:24) as well as believers' sufferings for the sake of Christ (Heb. 10:32; 1 Pet. 5:9). The ideas of present suffering and future glory are consistently related in these verses: although Christians currently undergo suffering, it cannot compare to the glory that awaits them. See *NIDNTT-A*, 494.

SUFFICIENT

New Testament

Adverb: ἱκανός (*hikanos*), GK *2653* (S *2425*), 39x. *hikanos* conveys the idea that something is adequate or large enough in its quantity or quality and may best be translated "sufficient, deserve, fit." In theological contexts, for example, John the Baptist comments on the inadequacy of his ministry in comparison to that which is yet to come. He declares, "I baptize you with water for repentance. But after me will come one who is more powerful than I, whose sandals I am not *fit* to carry" (Mt. 3:11a). Paul acknowledges his own inadequacies with regards to his ministry and writes, "For I am the least of the apostles and do not even *deserve* to be called an apostle, because I persecuted the church of God" (1 Cor. 15:9; cf. 2 Cor. 2:16). Paul grounds his adequacy for ministry in the sufficiency of God and writes, "Such confidence as this is ours through Christ before God. Not that we are *competent* in ourselves to claim anything for ourselves, but our *competence* comes from God" (2 Cor. 3:5–6). In nontheological contexts, this term can refer to the large quantity of an object such as a "large" sum of money (Mt. 28:12) or a "large" herd of pigs (Lk. 8:32; cf. Acts 9:23). See *NIDNTT-A*, 267-68.

SUMMON

Old Testament

Verb: זָעַק (*zāʿaq*), GK 2410 (S 2199), 73x. *zāʿaq* means "to cry out, call out, summon," often to the Lord. See *cry out*.

Verb: קָרָא (*qārāʾ*), GK 7924 (S 7121), 739x. *qārāʾ* is the most common verb in Heb. that means "to call, summon, proclaim." The basic meaning of this verb is to draw attention to oneself by using one's voice. See *call*.

New Testament

Verb: καλέω (*kaleō*), GK *2813* (S *2564*), 148x. *kaleō* means "to call, invite, summon." See *call*.

Verb: παρακαλέω (*parakaleō*), GK *4151* (S *3870*), 109x. *parakaleō* variously means "to ask, summons, exhort, comfort, or encourage" (see *exhort, comfort*). Within the Synoptic Gospels, *parakaleō* means "to ask, implore, summons." The contexts of this imploring are often the needy who come to Jesus with their requests (Mt. 8:5, 31; 18:29; Lk. 15:28).

Verb: προσκαλέω (*proskaleo*), GK *4673* (S *4341*), 29x. This is a compound verb formed from the preposition *pros* ("to, toward") and the verb *kaleō* ("to call"). Thus, the meaning is "to call to oneself, summon."

The most common use of this word in the NT is when Jesus "calls" his disciples (Mt. 10:1; 15:32; 20:25; Mk. 6:7; 8:1; Lk. 7:18), a child/children (Mt. 18.2; Lk. 18:16), and the crowds (Mk. 7:14; 8:34). It is used instead of the more usual *kaleō* (see *call*) to describe God's calling people to salvation (Acts 2:39) and calling Paul and his companions to preach the gospel in Macedonia (16:10). Likewise, the Holy Spirit calls Barnabas and Saul to their first missionary journey (13:2).

There are others who are the subject of this verb as well. For example, a sick person should "call" for the elders of the church (Jas. 5:14), the proconsul "sends" for Barnabas and Paul (Acts 13:7), Pilate "calls" a centurion to ask him a question (Lk. 23:17), and the disciples "gather together" all the believers to discuss the problem of the uncared-for Greek widows (6:2). See *NIDNTT-A*, 285-86.

Verb: φονέω (*phoneō*), GK *5888* (S

5455), 43x. *phoneō* means "to call out, call to, make a noise." See *call.*

SUN

Old Testament

Noun: שֶׁמֶשׁ (*šemeš*), GK 9087 (S 8121), 134x. *šemeš* simply refers to the "sun." Many of its natural characteristics are noted in the OT: it rises and sets (Ps. 113:3; Eccl. 1:5), shines (2 Ki. 3:22), and causes food to grow (Deut. 33:14). It is used as a marker of time, as in the phrases "when the sun becomes hot" (Exod. 16:21) and "as the sun goes" (i.e., "at sunset," Deut. 23:11, cf. Gen. 15:12). It is also used as a marker of direction in the phrase "toward the sunrise" (Jos. 1:15). The phrase "the entrance of the sun" is also used to refer to the west (Jos. 1:4; Zech. 8:7, "from the western land"). Eccl. uses the phrase "under the sun," which essentially means "in the world" (Eccl. 1:3, 9, 14). Similar phrases are "before the sun," meaning "in public" (Num. 25:4; cf. 2 Sam. 12:11, "before the eyes of this sun"), and "see the sun," meaning "to live and experience life" (Ps. 58:8; Eccl. 6:5).

Archaeology reveals that the sun is commonly depicted in ancient pictures as a winged disc, which provides insight into the phrase "the sun of righteousness rises with healing in its wings" (Mal. 4:2). Not surprisingly, the sun was part of the pantheon of gods in the religions of Egypt, Canaan, and Mesopotamia. Even the Israelites worshiped the sun in their idolatrous practices (2 Ki. 23:5, 11; Ezek. 8:16). However, the OT makes it clear that the sun is under God's control and is no more than a part of his creation. In fact, in Ps. 148:3, the sun is called to worship God. Ps. 104:19 implies that the sun sets at the time that God appoints. God's control is also seen in the many miracles that involve an unusual activity of the sun: the sun stands still for Joshua and the Israelite army (Jos. 10:12–13), it moves backwards for Hezekiah (Isa. 38:8), and in the day of the Lord, "the sun will be turned into darkness" (Joel 2:31). In Ps. 84:11, God is referred to as "a sun and a shield," which some scholars interpret as royal titles.

One unusual use of *šemeš* occurs in Isa. 54:12, where the expression "your suns" is mentioned in connection with "your gates" and "all your walls." Here the term probably refers to round shields that were hung from the wall as part of a city's fortifications (cf. Ezek. 27:11; Song 4:4). See *NIDOTTE*, 4:185-90.

New Testament

Noun: ἥλιος (*hēlios*), GK *2463* (S *2246*), 32x. *hēlios* is the Greek word for "sun." We derive our English word "helium" from this word; the presence of helium on the sun had been inferred in the nineteenth century before it was actually discovered on earth.

The rising or setting of the sun marks the time of day, either evening (Mk. 1:32) or morning (16:2). The expression "the rising of the sun" can refer to the direction "east" (cf. Rev. 16:12, where "the kings from the east" is lit., "kings from the rising of the sun"). The sun belongs to God, and it is his grace that "causes *the sun* to rise on the evil and the good (Mt. 5:45). The powerful brightness and heat of the sun are used as analogies in Jesus' parables (e.g., the parable of the sower, Mt. 13:6) and in the book of James (Jas. 1:11).

The darkening of the sun is one dramatic sign of the coming of the last days in the OT prophets and in the NT (Mt. 24:29; Lk. 21:25; Rev. 6:12). Thus, it is striking that at Jesus' death the sun was darkened (Lk. 23:45), showing that the crucifixion is one indication that the events of Jesus' life were end-time events that anticipated future judgment and resurrection.

The sun's radiant brightness makes it a favorite object of comparison. Jesus says in Mt. 13:43 that "the righteous will shine like *the sun*" in the future kingdom. In his account of the transfiguration, Matthew reports that Jesus' "face shone like *the sun.*" From Paul's story of his conversion (Acts 26:13) and in John's vision (Rev. 1:16), we learn that the resurrected and reigning Christ presently shines like the sun. In fact, Rev. 21:23 and 22:5 show that in the new creation there will be no need for the sun since the Lord God and the Lamb will provide all necessary light. See *NIDNTT-A*, 231-32.

SUPERVISOR

Old Testament

Verb: נָצַח (*nāṣaḥ*), GK 5904 (S 5329), 65x. In almost all occurrences of *nāṣaḥ*, the verb designates the activity of oversight or the role of "supervisor." This term applies especially to music (see *music director*).

SUPPER

New Testament

Noun: δεῖπνον (*deipnon*), GK *1270* (S *1173*), 16x. *deipnon* means "supper, feast, banquet" and refers to the main meal in biblical times, eaten in the evening. This is clear from Lk. 14:12, where a separate term is used for a "luncheon," a meal eaten earlier in the day. *deipnon* can also refer to a more formal meal or eating occasion, a "banquet."

(1) The idea of *deipnon* as a "feast" is well known in the OT. The Israelites had sacred "feasts" that celebrated various aspects of their relationship to God (e.g., the Passover meal in Exod. 12). The joining in table fellowship at these feasts meant sharing in God's blessing. Isa. 25:6–8 even looks forward to an end-time banquet, where God will provide "for all peoples."

(2) It is not surprising that Jesus also instituted a sacred supper with his disciples (Mt. 26:26–29), a meal the church still celebrates today. According to Paul, this sacred supper was called the "Lord's *Supper*" (1 Cor. 11:20). The Lord's Supper is first of all a reenactment and continuation of Jesus' last meal with his disciples before his death. It is also a present participation with the risen Lord (rooted in the disciples post-resurrection meals with Jesus, cf. Lk. 24:30–40; Jn. 21:13; Acts 10:41) and a way to experience communion (*koinōnia*; see *fellowship*) with other believers (1 Cor. 10:16–17). Finally, the Lord's Supper is a hopeful anticipation of a future end-time meal (Mt. 26:29; Rev. 19:9).

Yet the celebration of the Lord's Supper in the church today should never be too far removed from the initial supper Jesus had with his disciples before he died (the Last Supper). For it was there that the importance of the meal is evident. The Lord's Supper signifies the new covenant made possible through Christ's death—a covenant that all may enter through Christ. Paul makes clear that one should approach the Lord's Supper with a sober and penitent heart (1 Cor. 11:28). Yet, the supper is also celebratory, for although it reminds us of the death of Christ on our behalf, it also allows us to join with him in fellowship with God. See *NIDNTT-A*, 123-25.

SUPPLICATION

New Testament

Noun: δέησις (*deēsis*), GK *1255* (S *1162*), 18x. *deēsis* is a "prayer, petition, supplication" based on a person's need—in the NT always addressed to God. See *prayer*.

SUPPOSE

New Testament

Verb: δοκέω (*dokeō*), GK *1506* (S *1380*), 62x. *dokeō* means "to think, believe, suppose." See *think*.

Verb: νομίζω (*nomizō*), GK *3787* (S *3543*), 15x. *nomizō* means "to think, suppose." See *think*.

SURELY

New Testament

Adverb: ἀληθῶς (*alēthōs*), GK *242* (S *230*), 18x. *alēthōs* means "truly, surely, really" —an adverb of certainty. See *truly*.

SURPASS

Old Testament

Verb: יָסַף (*yāsap*), GK 3578 (S 3254), 213x. The basic meaning of *yāsap* is "to add." Sometimes the word conveys the sense of "surpass" or "increase" (cf. Ps. 115:14; Eccl. 2:9; see *add*).

(BE) SURPRISED

New Testament

Verb: ξενίζω (*xenizō*), GK *3826* (S

3581), 10x. *xenizō* generally means "to entertain, show hospitality" (see *entertain*), but it can also mean "to be surprised, to be strange." See *strange(r), be strange*.

SURROUND(ING)

Old Testament

Verb: סָבַב (*sābab*), GK 6015 (S 5437), 163x. *sābab* is generally translated "surround, go around, turn." It is used most often as a verb of motion, as in Gen. 42:24, "[Joseph] *turned away* from them and began to weep." *sābab* is used with reference to the movement of an individuals (1 Sam. 7:16), of a group of people (Jos. 6:3), of a door on a hinge (Prov. 26:14), or even of the wind (Eccl. 1:6). This verb is often used in a military sense (Jos. 6:3, 4, 7; 2 Sam. 5:23; 2 Chr. 21:9; Ps. 118:10–12) or a hostile sense (Jdg. 19:22; Ps. 22:12, 16).

Figuratively, *sābab* is used in a number of ways. It can speak of the reign of one king being "turned over" to another (1 Ki. 2:15; 1 Chr. 10:14), the nation of Israel being "surrounded" by sin (Hos. 7:2), the alteration of one's circumstances (2 Sam. 3:12; Jer. 31:22), the change of place names or personal names (Num. 32:28; 2 Ki. 23:34; 24:17), or the changing of one's mind (1 Ki. 21:4; Ezr. 6:22; Eccl. 7:25).

sābab is sometimes used when divine deliverance or protection is in view. David writes, "You are my hiding place; you will protect me from trouble and *surround* me with songs of deliverance.… Many are the woes of the wicked, but the Lord's unfailing love *surrounds* the man who trusts in him" (Ps. 32:7, 10; cf. "shielded" in Deut. 32:10). See *NIDOTTE*, 3:219–20.

Noun and Adverb: סָבִיב (*sābîb*), GK 6017 (S 5439), 334x. *sābîb* as an adverb means "around" and as an adjective denotes one's "surroundings." See *around*.

SURVIVE

Old Testament

Verb: יָתַר (*yātar*), GK 3855 (S 3498), 106x. *yātar* means "to remain, be left, survive." See *remain*.

Verb: שָׁאַר (*šāʾar*), GK 8636 (S 7604), 133x. Only in rare instances does *šāʾar* mean "to remain" or "to be left" (e.g., 1 Sam. 16:11).

More often the term refers to survival, as in Noah and his family surviving the flood (Gen. 7:23). Individuals survive or fail to survive numerous calamities, including misfortune (14:10), a family feud (32:8), divine wrath (Lev. 26:36, 39), war (Num. 21:35; 2 Ki. 25:21–22), natural death (Ruth 1:3, 5), and fire (Isa. 24:6).

Theologically, throughout the OT *šāʾar* is linked to the theme of the remnant. In Genesis this is seen with Noah and the flood (Gen. 7:23) and the confession of Joseph to his brothers that God has spared him for the sake of the remnant (45:7). God reveals to Elijah that the existence of a remnant of faithful Israelites is possible only on the basis of God's grace (1 Ki. 19:18), and through Isaiah God proclaims that a remnant will remain in spite of Israel's sin (Isa. 37:32). Amos uses *šāʾar* to refer to three groups: (1) a historical group that has survived a catastrophe (Amos 1:8), (2) a faithful remnant that has remained loyal to God (5:15), and (3) the eschatological remnant who will partake in the everlasting kingdom after the restoration of the Davidic kingdom (9:12).

Similar themes can be found throughout the prophetic writings (e.g., Mic. 5:7; Zeph. 2:7; Jer. 24:5; Ezek. 11:16–21; Hag. 1:12). The remnant is a small number who have escaped from danger and is therefore the group of survivors. The threat of punishment is linked to the promise of restoration, and the remnant has their origin in the saving work of God alone. The presence of a remnant attests to the fact that God has not forgotten nor will he forget the covenant made with his people.

SUSTAIN

New Testament

Verb: φέρω (*pherō*), GK *5770* (S *5342*), 66x. *pherō* has the basic meaning "to bring, carry, present," but it has a wide range of figurative meanings, such as "to endure, sustain." See *bring*.

SWARM

Old Testament

Noun: עֵדָה (*ʿēdâ*), GK 6337 (S 5712), 171x. *ʿēdâ* means a gathering of people (for worship or legal matters) or a herd or swarm of animals, such as bees. See *community*.

SWEAR

Old Testament

Verb: שָׁבַע (*šābaʿ*), GK 8678 (S 7650), 186x. *šābaʿ* means "to swear, take an oath." Because the number seven is identical to the verb for "to swear," there is a possible connection between the two, as when Abraham seals an oath by giving seven ewe lambs to Abimelech (Gen. 21:22–34). The concept of making an oath is an assurance that the person will keep his word.

Normally in the OT, God/the gods were involved in the swearing of an oath. "Eli said, 'What was it that [God] told you? Do not hide it from me. May God do so to you and more also, if you hide anything from me of all that he told you'" (1 Sam. 3:17). Oath taking was serious, and there is no biblical option for someone not keeping the oath (cf. Num. 30:2, 9–11). Thus, oaths are used to affirm a statement of fact (1 Sam. 20:3), attest to someone's innocence (Exod. 22:11), confirm a peace treaty (Jos. 9:15), or demonstrate someone's commitment to God (2 Chr. 15:14).

The Lord "swears" in making a covenant (Ps. 89:3; 132:11). When the Lord makes a promise, he swears by himself because there is none greater: "By myself I *have sworn*, says the LORD, that Bozrah shall become an object of horror and ridicule, a waste, and an object of cursing; and all her towns shall be perpetual wastes" (Jer. 49:13)."By myself I *have sworn*, from my mouth has gone forth in righteousness a word that shall not return: 'To me every knee shall bow, every tongue *will swear*'" (Isa. 45:23). Paul may apply this reference to Jesus, that because of his sufferings and his exaltation by God every knee will bow and every tongue *confess* that Jesus Christ is Lord, to the glory of God the Father (Phil. 2:11). See *NIDOTTE*, 4:32–34.

New Testament

Verb: ὀμνύω (*omnyō*), GK *3923* (S *3660*), 26x. *omnyō* conveys the affirmation or denial of one's word or loyalty by an oath before a witness, "to swear." The veracity of one's word is expected for those who belong to the kingdom of God. In contrast to the rabbinic prescriptions for oath keeping, Jesus commands, "But I tell you, Do not *swear* at all: either by heaven, for it is God's throne; or by the earth, for it is his footstool; or by Jerusalem, for it is the city of the Great King" (Mt. 5:34–35; cf. 23:16–22). Peter in his denials of Jesus "swore" to the Jews that he did not know the man standing on trial before Pilate (26:74; Mk. 14:71). James echoes this same emphasis and states, "Above all, my brothers, do not *swear*—not by heaven or by earth or by anything else. Let your 'Yes' be yes, and your 'No,' no, or you will be condemned" (Jas. 5:12). The author of Hebrews grounds the certainty of God's work of salvation in the unchangeable nature of God's oath or promise to Abraham and declares, "When God made his promise to Abraham, since there was no one greater for him to *swear* by, he *swore* by himself, saying, 'I will surely bless you and give you many descendants'" (Heb. 6:13–14; cf. v. 16; 7:20–22). See *NIDNTT-A*, 407-8.

SWORD

Old Testament

Noun: חֶרֶב (*ḥereb*), GK 2995 (S 2719), 413x. *ḥereb* describes a "sword," a common weapon of war, although *ḥereb* is sometimes translated as "knife, dagger" (Jos. 5:2; 2 Sam. 20:8). It consists of a blade and hilt. Jdg. 3:16 describes Ehud's *ḥereb* as a cubit (KJV) in length (about 18 inches) and doubled-edged. It was a straight-bladed instrument. Its first reference is in Gen. 3:24, where cherubim guard the way back to the Garden of Eden with "a flaming *sword*." The OT mentions a *ḥereb* more often than any other weapon.

King Solomon threatens to resolve the dispute between two mothers over one surviving child by dividing the child with a *ḥereb* (1 Ki. 3:24). A *ḥereb* can be used for slashing and cutting; David uses one to decapitate the Philistine Goliath (1 Sam. 17:51). It can also be used for thrusting; King Saul requests that his armor bearer kill him by using a *ḥereb* and "running" (NIV; "thrust" in the KJV) it through him (1 Sam. 31:4). Ezekiel describes God's judgment as the *ḥereb* of the Lord (see "my sword" in Ezek. 21:3; cf. the entire ch.). Biblical writers commonly used *ḥereb* as a symbol for violence and oppression ("if you resist and rebel, you will be devoured by the *sword*," Isa. 1:20). A person who is facing danger from an enemy prays to the Lord, "Deliver my life from the *sword*" (Ps. 22:20). See *NIDOTTE, 2:259-62.*

New Testament

Noun: μαχαιρα (*machaira*), GK *3479* (S *3162*), 29x. The *machaira* is a short sword or dagger (Mk. 14:43) and can be used as a symbol of violence (14:47–48) and martyrdom (Lk. 21:24; Rom. 8:35; Heb. 11:34, 37; Rev. 13:10). Jesus' enemies came to arrest him "*swords* and clubs" (Mt. 26:47).

Jesus' instructions to his disciples that "if you don't have a *sword*, sell your cloak and buy one" (Lk. 22:36), speaking of the need to handle the impending crisis they are about to face. Paul uses *machaira* as a symbol of our ability to defeat Satan using "the *sword* of the Spirit," part of the spiritual armor provided for us by God (Eph. 6:17). Another figurative use of *machaira* is in Heb. 4:12. "For the word of God is living and active, sharper than any two-edged *sword*, piercing to the division of soul and of spirit, of joints and of marrow, and discerning the thoughts and intentions of the heart" (ESV). The gospel penetrates to the deepest parts of the person. See *NIDNTT-A*, 481-82.

SYNAGOGUE

New Testament

Noun: συναγωγή (*synagōgē*), GK *5252* (S *4864*), 56x. *synagōgē* denotes what is brought together or assembled, an "assembly, congregation, synagogue."

As the word suggests, this term applies to the assembly where the Jews met for worship, that is, the synagogue. Luke writes, "Paul entered the *synagogue* and spoke boldly there for three months, arguing persuasively about the kingdom of God" (Acts 19:8; cf. 9:1–2; 18:26; 22:19). In Paul's missionary strategy (cf. "first for the Jew," Rom. 1:16), he always began with the synagogue in each new city he visited (Acts 13:5; 14:1; 17:1, 10). It was customary for Jesus during his earthly ministry to preach in the synagogue of the town or village where he visited: "Jesus went throughout Galilee, teaching in their *synagogues*, preaching the good news of the kingdom, and healing every disease and sickness among the people" (Mt. 4:23; also Mk. 1:39; Lk. 4:15). The term may also refer to a structure or building. Matthew writes, "So when you give to the needy, do not announce it with trumpets, as the hypocrites do in the *synagogues* and on the streets, to be honored by men" (Mt. 6:2).

synagōgē can also describe a Christian gathering or assembly, as in Acts 13:43, "When the *congregation* was dismissed, many of the Jews and devout converts to Judaism followed Paul and Barnabas, who talked with them and urged them to continue in the grace of God" (cf. Jas. 2:2). See *NIDNTT-A*, 543-44.

TABERNACLE

Old Testament

Noun: אֹהֶל (*ʾōhel*), GK 185 (S 168), 348x. Often translated "tent, dwelling," the noun *ʾōhel* typically refers to a portable dwelling used by nomads and armies of the ancient Near East. But its most common use is in the expression "the *Tent* of Meeting," which is the tabernacle, the place where God meets with his people (Lev. 1:1; cf. Exod. 29:42–43; 33:7). See *tent*.

Noun: מִשְׁכָּן (*miškān*), GK 5438 (S 4908), 139x. The Hebrew noun *miškān* derives from the verbal root *škn,* "to dwell," and refers to dwelling places for both people (Num. 16:24; Isa. 32:18) and God, the latter being its most common usage in the OT. Outside the Bible, a cognate Ugaritic form can refer to an abode for the gods.

When used of God's abode, *miškān* refers to the tabernacle or central sanctuary of the Lord, a detailed description of which is found in Exod. 25–40. The tabernacle, also called "the Tent of Meeting" (*miškān môʿēd*), was constructed while the Israel encamped at Mount Sinai (cf. Exod. 38:21; Num. 1:50, 53), after which the Lord took up residence within it (Exod. 40:34–38; cf. Lev. 9:23–24; 16:2; Num. 9:15–23; Ps. 26:8). Israelites were kept away from the *miškān* so as not to defile it (Lev. 15:31), though priests were allowed to enter in order to offer sacrifices (cf. Lev. 17:4).

The OT reveals that God is looking forward to the day when he will establish an everlasting covenant with his people and put his sanctuary among them forever: "My dwelling place [*miškān*] will be with them; I will be their God, and they will be my people" (Ezek. 37:26–27). See *NIDOTTE*, 2:1130-34.

New Testament

Noun: σκηνή (*skēnē*), GK *5008* (S *4633*), 20x. *skēnē* can refer to a "tent" in which nomads, such as Abraham, lived (Heb. 11:9). It is used in the NT to refer to the "three shelters" Peter wanted to put up for Jesus, Moses, and Elijah at Jesus' transfiguration (Mt. 17:4; Mk. 9:5; Lk. 9:33). Most commonly, *skēnē* refers to the tabernacle in the OT (Acts 7:44; Heb. 9:2-3, 21; 13:10). The tabernacle was a portable temple that could be assembled and disassembled for transport. Within the tabernacle, the prototype for the Jerusalem temple, sacrifices were offered and God dwelt with his people.

skēnē is also used for the true tabernacle, which is in heaven (Heb. 8:2). The earthly one built by Moses is "a copy and shadow of what is in heaven" (8:5; cf. Rev. 13:6; 15:5). The author of Hebrews notes that "the way into the Most Holy Place had not yet been disclosed as long as the first tabernacle was still standing" (Heb. 9:8). But when Christ came, he himself was the "greater and more perfect *skēnē*" (9:11). The *skēnē* is an "eternal dwelling" to which one who uses worldly wealth appropriately will be welcomed (Lk. 16:9). See *NIDNTT-A*, 527-28.

TABLE

Old Testament

Noun: שֻׁלְחָן (*šulḥān*), GK 8947 (S 7979), 71x. *šulḥān* is the regular word for a "table." Tables are used for eating, and a table holds the bread of the Presence in the tabernacle (Exod. 25:23–30; 37:10–16) and in the temple (1 Ki. 7:48; 2 Chr. 4:8, 19). This bread was twelve loaves spread out before the Lord, with six loaves on each side of the table (Lev. 24:5–9).

Speaking to her husband regarding the prophet Elisha, a Shunammite woman said, "Let's make a small room on the roof and put in it a bed and a *table*, a chair and a lamp for him" (2 Ki. 4:10). *šulḥān* can also describe a table spread with food for official business (Neh. 5:17) or to represent domestic harmony: "Your wife will be like a beautiful vine within your house; your sons will be like olive shoots around your *table*" (Ps. 128:3). To eat at someone's table indicates acceptance and peace (2 Sam. 9:6–13).

Ps. 23:5 records one of the most familiar uses of *šulḥān*: God himself prepares "a *table* before me in the presence of my enemies." Use in a figurative sense, a lavish "table" set out by personified Wisdom is available for any who wish to partake from it (Prov. 9:2). See *NIDOTTE*, 4:123-24.

New Testament

Noun: τράπεζα (*trapeza*), GK *5544* (S *5132*), 15x. *trapeza* means "table." A table can be used for dining (Mt. 15:27; Mk. 7:28), for changing money (Mt. 21:12; Jn. 2:15), and for religious ritual, such as the table in the tabernacle that held the Bread of the Presence (Heb. 9:2) and the table that held communion (1 Cor. 10:21). In the NT people reclined at a table (Mt. 14:20), so those tables are not very high. The Philippian jailer literally "sets a table" for Paul (Acts 16:34).

trapeza can also stand for what is on the table, primarily food (Lk. 16:21; Rom. 11:9) or the fellowship that takes place at the meal table (cf. 1 Cor. 10:21). The fact that Judas shares fellowship with Jesus at the table in that culture makes his betrayal that much more horrendous (Lk. 22:21). Disciples who stay with Jesus during his trials will in turn be assigned a kingdom and will eat and drink at Jesus' table in the kingdom (Lk. 22:28–30). Jesus points out that while the world says the one who reclines at a table is greater than the servant, he came as a servant (Lk. 22:27); thus, the disciples should willingly serve. Nevertheless, in terms of division of duties, the apostles recognize that it is not a good use of their time to serve at tables but they must be freed up to pray and preach the gospel (Acts 6:2); others are thus appointed to assist the widows in the early church.

The table of demons in 1 Cor. 10:21 refers to the practice of some of the Corinthian Christian's of eating meat with pagans in their temples. Paul makes it clear that this food has been offered to demons and Christians must not participate in demonic rituals (1 Cor. 10:18–20). See *NIDNTT-A*, 123-25.*

TAKE

Old Testament

Verb: בּוֹא (*bôʾ*), GK 995 (S 935), 2592x. *bôʾ* is the fourth most common verb in the OT. It denotes motion toward a specific goal, such as "to go, arrive, enter a house, come." It expresses a variety of motions. This verb can also be used in the sense of "causing something to go or come," that is, "to bring or take something or someone." See *come*.

Verb: לָקַח (*lāqaḥ*), GK 4374 (S 3947), 967x. The basic meaning of *lāqaḥ* is "to take, grasp." The meaning is often simply to "take into/by the hand." Thus "the LORD God *took* the man and put him in the Garden of Eden" (Gen. 2:15). Eve takes the forbidden fruit (Gen. 3:6), Moses takes the staff (Exod. 7:15), Noah takes the dove back into the ark (Gen. 8:9), Joab takes three javelins (2 Sam. 18:14), and so on.

lāqaḥ can also have the meaning "deprive," as Solomon being deprived of his kingdom (1 Ki. 11:34) or Elijah being *taken away from* Elisha (2 Ki. 2:3, 5). The sword *takes away* the life of its victims (Ezek. 33:4, 6; Hos. 13:11), and wine may deprive the people of understanding (Hos. 4:11).

lāqaḥ also carries the sense of "get for oneself," as in the demand of the taskmasters to the Hebrew slaves: "Go and *get* your own straw wherever you can find it" (Exod. 5:11), or the wisdom saying: "Whoever corrects a mocker *invites* insult [*getteth* to himself shame, KJV]" (Prov. 9:7).

lāqaḥ is also used to describe taking something as one's own possession. Thus Jacob is accused of taking the wealth of Laban (Gen. 31:1), and Rachel takes the household gods when she leaves her father's house (Gen. 31:34). Judah gives up ownership of the pledges he gave to Tamar: "Let her *keep* what she has [Let her *take* it to her, KJV], or we will become a laughingstock" (Gen. 28:23). Note Prov. 31:16: "She considers a field and *buys* it [lit., takes it]; out of her earnings she plants a vineyard."

"Taking" in the sense of acquiring something is combined with that of selection or choosing when *lāqaḥ* is used to denote the legal arrangement of marriage, especially in the Pentateuch. "To take a wife" or "to take a woman as a wife" is usually translated by the NIV with the simple verb "to marry": "Abram and Nahor both *married* [And Abram and Nahor *took* them wives, KJV]" (Gen. 11:29). The same terms signal Rebekah's marriage to Isaac: "Isaac brought her into the tent of his mother Sarah, and he *married* Rebekah [and *took* Rebekah, KJV]. So she became his wife" (24:67). (For additional references for *lāqaḥ* meaning "take a wife," cf.

Exod. 6:20, 25; Lev. 20:21; Num. 12:1; Deut. 24:1; Jer. 16:2; 29:6; Hos. 1:2. For *lāqaḥ* in the sense of "choosing" a wife, cf. Jer. 3:14.)

The use of *lāqaḥ* in the sense of choosing and marrying a wife is the same language used when God "takes" Israel as his own people: "I will *take* you as my own people, and I will be your God. Then you will know that I am the LORD your God, who brought you out from under the yoke of the Egyptians" (Exod. 6:7, cf. Deut. 4:20, 34). God is, therefore, represented as the husband, and Israel as his wife. Speaking of the new covenant God says: " 'It will not be like the covenant I made with their forefathers when I *took* them by the hand to lead them out of Egypt, because they broke my covenant, though I was a husband to them,' declares the LORD" (Jer. 31:32, cf. 3:14). Indeed, the entire message of Hosea is shaped by the metaphor of marriage, with Israel as the unfaithful wife. As God's wife, Israel's rebellion is characterized by the prophets as spiritual adultery (Jer. 3:9; 5:7; 7:9; Ezek. 6:9; 16:38). Ultimately, God will remain faithful to his promises: "For I will *take* you out of the nations; I will gather you from all the countries and bring you back into your own land" (Ezek. 36:24).

Verb: שִׂים (*śîm*), GK 8492 (S 7760), 588x. *śîm* generally denotes the action of putting or placing an object or person in a particular location. It is usually translated "put," "set," or "place." As a derivative nuance, the Israelites are supposed to "take" all of Moses' words to *heart*, indicating a special care and concern for those words (and ultimately obedience, Deut. 32:46). See *put*.

New Testament

Verb: λαμβάνω (*lambanō*), GK *3284* (S *2983*), 258x. *lambanō* conveys the basic idea of acquiring or obtaining something and may best be translated as "take, seize, receive, get." Commenting on the Last Supper Matthew writes, "While they were eating, Jesus *took* bread, gave thanks and broke it, and gave it to his disciples, saying, '*Take* and eat; this is my body.' Then he *took* the cup, gave thanks and offered it to them, saying, 'Drink from it, all of you'" (Mt. 26:26–27).

The idea of taking is an active notion. In the parable of the tenants, for example, the wicked farmers "seize" the servants sent to gather the fruit of the vineyard and beat them; when the son comes, they "take" him, throw him out of the vineyard, and kill him (Mt. 21:34–35). This last act, of course, represents what the Jewish leaders did to Jesus. Yet Jesus makes it clear that he was not a passive victim in this process, for he says, "I lay down my life—only *to take* it again. I have authority to lay it down and authority *to take* it *up* again" (Jn. 10:17–18). In order to fulfill his calling, he first had to "*take* the very nature of a servant" (Phil. 2:7) and became a human being.

The idea of receiving is more of a passive notion, though a person still must do his or her part in the receiving. John writes, "Yet to all to *received* [Jesus], to those who believed in his name, he gave the right to become children of God" (Jn. 1:12). That is, we receive Jesus as Savior and Lord. Moreover, we "receive" all sorts of blessings from our Lord through his grace (1:16). For example, believers obtain the gift of the Holy Spirit by faith, "For you did not *receive* a spirit that makes you a slave again to fear, but you *received* the Spirit of sonship" (Rom. 8:15; cf. 1 Cor. 2:12; 2 Cor. 11:4; Gal. 3:2, 14). Paul also comments on what he has acquired from Christ as the basis for his ministry: "Through him and for his name's sake, we *received* grace and apostleship to call people from among all the Gentiles to the obedience that comes from faith" (Rom. 1:5). According to the writer of Hebrews, all of us "*receive* mercy" from God through Christ (Heb. 4:16).

Thus, this one verb describes both sides of the process and is theologically important: God gives, and humans receive. See *NIDNTT-A*, 327-28.

Verb: παραλαμβάνω (*paralambanō*),

GK *4161* (S *3880*), 49x. *paralambanō* means "to take (along), receive, accept." In the gospels and Acts, this word generally means to take someone along with you somewhere (e.g., Mt. 2:13–14, 20–21; 17:1). But the NT letters show more technical theological meanings. In classical Greek *paralambanō* meant to pass on intellectual things, especially between a student and a teacher. The stress there was on the teacher's orally transmitting religious teachings and special rites and secrets. In Judaism the focus was on the material rather than on the teacher. Authority rested in the law, not in the rabbis. Similarly, in his letters Paul refers to passing on to his churches the teachings that he himself first "received" (1 Cor. 11:23; 15:1, 3; Gal. 1:12; Phil. 4:9; 1 Thess. 2:13). In addition, when believers hear the message of salvation, they "accept" the gospel message (Gal. 1:9), "*receive* Jesus as Lord" (Col. 2:6), and "receive" the kingdom of God (Heb. 12:28). See *NIDNTT-A*, 328.

TAKE ASIDE

New Testament

Verb: προσλαμβάνω (*proslambanō*), GK *4689* (S *4355*), 12x. *proslambanō* means "to accept, take aside, welcome." See *accept*.

TAKE AWAY

Old Testament

Verb: אָסַף (*ʾāsap*), GK 665 (S 622), 200x. In varying contexts, *ʾāsap* can mean "to gather, assemble, take away, or bring up the rear." Occasionally, *ʾāsap* means "to take away or remove." See *remove*.

Verb: נָצַל (*nāṣal*), GK 5911 (S 5337), 213x. For the most part, *nāṣal* means "save, rescue, deliver, take away." See *save*.

New Testament

Verb: ἀναιρέω (*anaireō*), GK *359* (S *337*), 24x. *anaireō* means "to take away, abolish." The baby Moses was "taken away" by Pharaoh's daughter, who rescued him from certain death (Acts 7:21). Jesus has "taken away" or "abolished" the first sacrificial system in order to establish the second, his once-for-all sacrifice (Heb. 10:9). *anaireō* can also mean "to kill"; See *kill*.

Verb: ἀφαιρέω (*aphaireō*), GK *904* (S *851*), 10x. *aphaireō* means "to take away." Jesus says to Martha that "Mary has chosen the good portion, which will not be taken away from her" (Lk. 10:42). Alluded to in Isa. 27:9, a major aspect of the new covenant is the "removal" of sins (Rom. 11:27), something that the old sacrificial system was incapable of doing (Heb. 10:4). A strong warning is given to anyone who will "take away" from God's revelation to John (Rev. 22:19). *aphaireō* can also mean "to cut off." See *cut off*.

Verb: ἀφίστημι (*aphistēmi*), GK *923* (S *868*), 14x. *aphistēmi* generally means to "leave" or "depart" in a physical sense. Other uses of this verb include Paul's desire for the Lord to "take away" the thorn in his flesh (2 Cor. 12:8). See *leave*.

TAKE CAPTIVE

Old Testament

Verb: לָכַד (*lākad*), GK 4334 (S 3920), 121x. *lākad* generally means "to capture, seize, take captive." It can be used actively (i.e., "to catch, capture," Num. 21:32; Deut. 2:34; Jos. 10:42; Jdg. 7:24; 15:4; Ps. 35:8; Amos 3:4, 5), passively (i.e., "to be seized," 1 Ki. 16:18; Isa. 23:13; Jer. 6:11; 38:28; 48:1, 41; 51:56; Ezek. 7:26), or reflectively (i.e., "to cling to each other," Job 38:30; 41:17). See *capture*.

TAKE CARE OF

New Testament

Verb: ἐπισκέπτομαι (*episkeptomai*), GK *2170* (S *1980*), 11x. *episkeptomai* means "to look after, visit, take care of." See *look after*.

TAKE HOLD

Old Testament

Verb: אָחַז (*ʾāḥaz*), GK 296 (S 270), 63x. This verb conveys the general sense of *grasping* or *taking hold of* an object or *being taken hold of* by an object, person, or emotion (see Jdg. 1:6; Num. 31:30; Ruth 3:15; 1 Chr. 13:9). See *seize*.

Verb: תָּפַשׂ (*tāpaś*), GK 9530 (S 8610),

65x. *tāpaś* conveys the seizing or grasping of an object or person, usually with a degree of force, and may be translated as "take hold of, seize." See *seize*.

New Testament

Verb: ἅπτω (*haptō*), GK *721* (S 680, *681*), 39x. At its most basic level *haptō* means "to make close contact with something, touch something." But it can also mean "to cling to, take hold of something." See *touch*.

Verb: ἐπιλαμβάνομαι (*epilambanomai*), GK *2138* (S *1949*), 19x. *epilambanomai* can mean "to seize, take hold, catch." See *seize*.

TAKE POSSESSION

Old Testament

Verb: יָרַשׁ (*yāraš*), GK 3769 (S 3423), 232x. *yāraš* means "to possess, take possession of (especially by force), drive out, inherit." See *possess*.

Verb: נָחַל (*nāḥal*), GK 5706 (S 5157), 59x. In addition to meaning "to inherit," *nāḥal* can be translated as "to possess, take possession, get." See *inherit*.

TAKE UP

Old Testament

Verb: עָרַךְ (*ʿārak*), GK 6885 (S 6186), 75x. *ʿārak* denotes the action of arranging an object in a particular way or arranging objects in a specific order to produce a desired effect. Regarding war, *ʿārak* denotes the action of arranging armies for battle. The NIV sometimes translates this use of *ʿārak* as "took up battle positions" (Jdg. 20:20) and "took up their positions" (Jdg. 20:22). See *arrange*.

Verb: רִיב (*rîb*), GK 8189, (S 7378), 72x. *rîb* denotes the action of entering into an argument, conflict, or lawsuit with another person. When a case or a cause is the object of *rîb*, the NIV may translate the verb as "plead" (e.g., Ps. 43:1), "defend" (e.g., 74:22), "present" (e.g., Prov. 18:17), or "take up" (e.g., 22:23; 23:11). See *contend*.

New Testament

Verb: αἴρω (*airō*), GK *149* (S *142*), 101x. *airō* can mean to "lift up, take up/away, carry off, remove." See *lift up*.

Verb: ἀναλαμβάνω (*analambanō*), GK *377* (S *353*), 13x. *analambanō* means "to take up, lift up." It is used first of all for the ascension of Christ, who was "taken up" into heaven (Mk. 16:19; Acts 1:2, 11, 22; 1 Tim. 3:16). It can also refer to taking someone on board a boat (Acts 20:13–14) or taking on oneself the armor of God (Eph. 6:13), especially the shield of faith (6:16). See *NIDNTT-A*, 328.

Verb: ἀναφέρω (*anapherō*), GK *429* (S *399*), 10x. *anapherō* means "to lead, take up." See *lead up*.

TALENT

Old Testament

Noun: כִּכָּר (*kikkār*), GK 3971 (S 3603), 68x. *kikkār* has the basic meaning of a "round disk" and can refer to a disk of metal (a "talent"), a round loaf of bread (see *loaf*), or a circular area of land (see *plain*).

While the talent is the largest unit in the Heb. system of weights, it may derive its name (*kikkār*, "round") from disks of silver and gold bullion. The lampstand in the tabernacle is made of a talent of gold (Exod. 25:39); the king of Rabbah has a golden crown that weighs a talent (2 Sam. 12:30); and King Omri buys the hill of Samaria for two talents of silver (1 Ki. 16:24). Many of the quantities measured in talents in the OT are large: Solomon receives 666 talents of gold each year (1 Ki. 10:14); David prepares 100,000 talents of gold and 1,000,000 talents of silver for the construction of the temple (1 Chr. 22:14); and Haman gives 10,000 talents of silver to King Xerxes to pay for the extermination of the Jews (Est. 3:9). Most often, talents are used as measurements of gold and silver, but bronze and iron are also measured in talents (1 Chr. 29:7).

The weight of a talent is estimated to be 75 pounds (34.3 kg), the amount of weight an average man can comfortably carry. Exod. 38:25–26 makes clear that a talent is 3,000 shekels, which is in agreement with the Phoenician system of weights. However, it is possible that sometimes a talent is understood as 3,600 shekels, following the Babylonian weight system. A modern equivalent for biblical talents can be estimated by multiplying talents by 75 to get pounds or by 34.3 to get kilograms. See *NIDOTTE*, 2:636–38; 4:238-39.

New Testament

Noun: τάλαντον (*talanton*), GK *5419* (S *5007*), 14x. *talanton* means "talent." This word occurs only in the gospel of Matthew: 1x in the parable of the unforgiving servant (who "owed his master ten thousand talents") and 13x in the parable of the talents (25:14–30). While this word has been carried over directly into English to denote the gifts or natural aptitudes that we possess, in NT times a *talanton* was a monetary unit worth well over a thousand dollars in today's currency.

TALK

New Testament

Verb: λέγω (*legō*), GK *3306* (S *3004*, *2036*, *2046*), 2353x. Usually translated as "say," *legō* sometimes has the notion of "to talk." See *say*.

TASK

Old Testament

Noun: מְלָאכָה (m^e*lā᾿kâ*), GK 4856 (S 4399), 167x. m^e*lā᾿ka* has the notion of "sending forth one's hand to accomplish a task" (cf. Deut. 12:7, 18). See *work*.

TASTE

New Testament

Verb: γεύομαι (*geuomai*), GK *1174* (S *1089*), 15x. *geuomai* means "to taste, eat, partake of," usually implying enjoyment of the experience. This verb is used in a literal sense in Mt. 27:34; Lk. 14:24; Jn. 2:9; Acts 10:10; 20:11; 23:14; Col. 2:21. The literal sense of *geuomai* symbolizes partaking in the kingdom of God in the parable of the banquet (Lk. 14:24).

geuomai is also used figuratively. In Heb. 2:9 it refers to Christ's tasting of death on the cross, through which he partook of death for everyone who believes in him. Jesus also refers to the disciples' not tasting death until they see the kingdom of God (Mt. 16:28; Mk. 9:1; Lk. 9:27; Jn. 8:52). One of the most problematic uses of this verb occurs in Heb. 6:4–5, where the author speaks of the impossibility to renew to repentance those who have "*tasted* the heavenly gift" and "*tasted* the goodness of the word of God" (see also *impossible*). Scholars debate as to whether this means such individuals were ever really saved. While this issue may not be definitively settled, it is certain that such people were thoroughly integrated into the Christian community. Finally, in 1 Pet. 2:3, Peter insists that those who have "*tasted* that the Lord is good" (cf. Ps. 34:8) should grow in their knowledge of salvation and God's Word—a reminder to all of us that we may never become stagnant in our faith. See *NIDNTT-A*, 105-6.*

TAX COLLECTOR

New Testament

Noun: τελώνης (*telōnēs*), GK *5467* (S *5057*), 21x. *telōnēs* refers to those who worked for the Roman government levying taxes (the KJV term is "publican"). In the NT, the Jews despised such people for two reasons. (1) They had a reputation for corruption, often levying taxes beyond what was required, thereby hoping to fill their own pockets (Lk. 3:12). (2) The *telōnēs* for Jewish society were themselves Jews who had "sold out" to the Gentile Roman government and thus worked against their own people.

Jesus harnesses this attitude towards tax collectors by saying that if a brother is rebuked for sin by the church and refuses to listen, "let him be to you as a Gentile and a tax collector" (Mt. 18:17, ESV). Jesus is not encouraging anti-tax collector sentiment, but is making a powerful application through a cultural point-of-contact as people who needed to repent and turn to God.

Reflecting this public attitude towards tax collectors, the Pharisees voice their horror that the one who claims to be the Messiah would associates with such as these (Mt. 9:11; 11:19; Mk. 2:16; Lk. 5:30; 7:34; 15:1–2). Yet *telōnēs* were, ironically, some of the first to recognize their spiritual bankruptcy. They came to and believed in Jesus (Mt. 9:10; Mk. 2:15; Lk. 5:29; 7:29; 15:1), just as they had believed John the Baptist (Mt. 21:32; Lk. 3:12). The disciple Matthew, in fact, was called from the tax collector's booth. The grace of God and the biblical significance of *telōnēs* can be summed up in the familiar parable about a certain self-confident Pharisee and a humble *telōnēs*, who went home justified because of his plea for God's mercy (Lk. 18:10–14). See *NIDNTT-A*, 561-62.

TEACH

Old Testament

Verb: לָמַד (*lāmad*), GK 4340 (S 3925), 87x. *lāmad* denotes teaching as well as learning.

(1) *lāmad* is one of the twelve words used for teaching in the OT. It is used with both a human and a divine subject.

(a) Human teachers instruct on a variety of topics, including languages and literature (Dan. 1:4), music and songs (2 Sam. 1:18), the arts of war (Jdg. 3:2), and wailing and lament (Jer. 9:19). They can also train others in all kinds of wickedness (2:33) and idolatry (9:13). The most important teaching by human subjects is the imparting of the Torah. It was a major responsibility of parents in Israel to educate their children in the ways of God. Through Moses God exhorts Israel, "*Teach* them to your children, talking about them when you sit at home and when you walk along the road, when you lie down and when you get up" (Deut. 11:19). Parents are expected to instruct not only by words but also by a life that is consistent with such teaching.

(b) *lāmad* can also be an activity of God. He teaches humankind (Ps. 94:10), instructing them concerning his law (119:12), his will (143:10), and the ways in which they should go (25:4).

(2) When *lāmad* refers to learning, it occurs only with human subjects. God cannot learn, as Job acknowledges (Job 21:22). *lāmad* can carry the meaning of accepting instruction: "Those who are wayward in spirit will gain understanding; those who complain will accept instruction" (Isa. 29:24). It can also indicate training in various skills, including battle (1 Chr. 5:18; Isa. 2:4) and hunting (Ezek. 19:3, 6). Additionally, *lāmad* can signify being trained, as were the sons of Asaph in music (1 Chr. 25:7).

The most important lesson in the OT is associated with knowing Yahweh and fearing him. Moses reminds Israel, "Remember the day you stood before the LORD your God at Horeb, when he said to me, 'Assemble the people before me to hear my words so that they may *learn* to revere me as long as they live in the land and may *teach* them to their children'" (Deut. 4:10). God calls his people to learn his laws, decrees, and statutes (5:1; Ps. 119:7, 71, 73) as well as wisdom (Prov. 30:3) and righteousness (Isa. 1:17). What they learn is meant to affect their entire lives.

God also warns Israel not to learn the practices of their pagan neighbors: "When you enter the land the LORD your God is giving you, do not *learn* to imitate the detestable ways of the nations there" (Deut. 18:9). Significantly, God even offers the possibility of these pagans learning his ways and being numbered among his people (Jer. 12:16). See *NIDOTTE*, 2:801-3.

New Testament

Verb: διδάσκω (*didaskō*), GK *1438* (S *1321*), 97x. *didaskō* means "to teach, instruct" and is the action performed by a *didaskalos* (see *teacher*). This noun refers mainly to the teaching of Jesus and of the early church, including that done by the apostles; the former occurs mostly in the gospels, the latter mostly outside the gospels.

In the gospels, Jesus is usually the subject of *didaskō*: "Jesus went through Galilee *teaching*" (Mt. 4:23); "Every day I was with you *teaching*" (Mk. 14:49); "Lord, *teach* us to pray" (Lk. 11:1); and "All that Jesus began to do and *teach*" (Acts 1:1; also Mt. 5:2; 21:23; Mk. 1:21; 10:1; Lk. 5:3; 23:5; Jn. 6:59; 18:20). Other passages have the apostles and the early church as the subject. For instance, "*teaching* them to obey everything that I commanded you" (Mt. 28:20), "they began *teaching*" (Acts 5:21b), and "which agrees with what I *teach* everywhere in the church" (1 Cor. 4:17; also Acts 4:2; 18; 15:35; Rom. 12:7; Col. 1:28; 2 Tim. 2:2; Heb. 5:12).

In addition to these two categories, there are other subjects for *didaskō*. The chief priests "instruct" the tomb guards to lie about Jesus' resurrection (Mt. 28:15). Jesus speaks of the Holy Spirit "teaching" Christians what to say as they are brought before religious and political leaders (Lk. 12:12). John the Baptist "taught" his disciples how to pray (Lk. 11:1). The Father "taught" Jesus (Jn. 8:28). Nature "teaches" that it is a disgrace for a man to have long hair (1 Cor. 11:14). Paul does not allow women to "teach" men (1 Tim. 2:12). Lastly, in Rev. 2 *didaskō* is used for the teaching of Balak and Jezebel (Rev. 2:14, 20, respectively). See *NIDNTT-A*, 141-42.

Verb: κατηχέω (*katēcheō*), GK *2994* (S *2727*), 8x. *katēcheō* is used in two senses in the NT: telling about something and instructing someone in the Christian faith. See *instruct*.

Verb: παιδεύω (*paideuō*), GK *4084* (S *3811*), 13x. *paideuō* means "to teach, educate," but also "to discipline, punish." It is derived from the root *pais* meaning "child," so that one who taught and disciplined children was a *paidagōgos* (or schoolmaster; cf. Gal. 3:24–25).

In the sense of educational training, Moses was "*educated* in all Egyptian wisdom" (Acts 7:22), and Paul was thoroughly "*educated* in the law of our fathers" (22:3). As a pastor, Timothy is to "*teach* gently those who disagree" with him (2 Tim. 2:25), while the blasphemers Hymenaeus and Alexander require not gentleness but harsh discipline in order to "be taught" their lesson. The grace of God in salvation also "teaches" us to live pious, godly lives (Tit. 2:12).

paideuō is used twice to mean actual punishment, when Pilate declares he will "punish" Jesus, then release him (Lk. 23:16, 22). Paul uses the word to mean severely beaten down: "*beaten* but not killed" (2 Cor. 6:9). He uses *paideuō* in 1 Cor. 11:32 in the context of the Lord's Supper. Those partaking should examine themselves; if they do not, God will judge them by "disciplining" them, but for their good, so that they will not be judged with the rest of the world. The author of Hebrews further weds the idea of instructive punishment with God's fatherly love for his children, asserting, "For whom the Lord loves, he *disciplines*. For what son is not *disciplined* by his father?" (Heb. 12:6–7, 10). Finally, the risen Jesus confirms that "those whom I love I rebuke and *discipline*" (Rev. 3:19). See *NIDNTT-A*, 426-27.*

TEACHER

New Testament

Noun: διδάσκαλος (*didaskalos*), GK *1437* (S *1320*), 59x. *didaskalos* means "teacher" and is the Gk. word used for the Heb. word *rabbi*. This is explicitly stated in Jn. 1:38, which records Andrew and Peter calling Jesus "'*Rabbi*,' which is translated *didaskalos*" (also Mt. 23:8; Jn. 3:2). Likewise it translates the Aramaic word *rabboni* (Jn. 20:16).

The majority of the occurrences of *didaskalos* in the NT refer to Jesus (in the four gospels). While the disciples certainly call him *didaskalos* (Mk. 4:38; 9:38; 13:1; Lk. 7:40; 21:7), many other people use this title for Jesus as well: the Pharisees (Mt. 8:19; 12:38); Pharisees and Herodians (Mt. 22:16); Sadducees (Mk. 12:19); a teacher of the law (Mk. 12:32); Jewish spies (Lk. 20:21); the so-called rich young ruler (Lk. 18:18); tax collectors (Lk. 3:12); Martha (Jn. 11:28); and Jesus himself (Mt. 26:18; Jn. 13:13–14). The use of this title by Jewish religious leaders may not always be sincere. For instance, in Lk. 10:25 an expert in the law comes to test Jesus and calls him *didaskalos*. However, attempts to expose him as a pretender to the title of teacher are unsuccessful and therefore serve to endorse his status as *rabbi* (Mt. 22:46; Mk. 12:34; Lk. 20:39).

The other major category of usage for *didaskalos* is to denote teachers within the church. Acts 13:1 states, "in the church at Antioch there were prophets and *teachers*," and both 1 Cor. 12:28–29 and Eph. 4:11 list "teachers" as gifts to the church (also Heb. 5:12; Jas. 3:1). Paul also describes himself as a *didaskalos* (1 Tim. 2:7; 2 Tim. 1:11).

In addition to these two major categories, *didaskalos* can refer to teachers in the temple (Lk. 2:46), false teachers (2 Tim. 4:3; possibly Rom. 2:20), and Nicodemus as "the teacher of Israel" (Jn. 3:10). See *NIDNTT-A*, 140-41.

TEACHER OF THE LAW

New Testament

Noun: γραμματεύς (*grammateus*), GK *1208* (S *1122*), 63x. A *grammateus* was a "teacher of the law, an expert in legal issues, a scribe." See *scribe*.

TEACHING

Old Testament

Noun: תּוֹרָה (*tôrâ*), GK 9368 (S 8451), 223x. Generally rendered "law, regulation, instruction, teaching," *tôrâ* was originally used to describe the instructions for daily conduct that God gave his people; eventually other meanings developed for this word. See *law*.

In Prov., *tôrâ* means "teaching," as in the phrase, "do not forget my *teaching*" (Prov. 3:1; cf. 6:20). This refers to the everyday guidance parents give to their children as they bring them up in the fear of the Lord. *tôrâ* can also mean teachings derived from the historical narratives of the OT (Ps. 78).

New Testament

Noun: διδασκαλία (*didaskalia*), GK *1436* (S *1319*), 21x. *didaskalia*, like *didachē*, denotes "teaching" or "doctrine," both the content and the act. Content is expressed in Mt. 15:9, when Jesus refers to the "teachings" of the Pharisees as "rules taught by people," and in Col. 2:22, which mentions "commandments and *teachings* of people." The act is expressed in the reference to the gift of "teaching" (Rom. 12:7) and of the elder who works hard at "preaching and *teaching*" (1 Tim. 5:17).

There is an important distinction in the NT between sound doctrine and false doctrine. The majority of occurrences of *didaskalia* are in the context of doctrine of the church or "sound doctrine," e.g., "sound *doctrine*, which conforms to the glorious gospel of the blessed God" (1 Tim. 1:10; also 1 Tim. 4:6, 13, 16; 5:17; 6:1; 2 Tim. 4:3; Tit. 2:7). An additional example that parallels *didaskalia* and *didachē* is "the trustworthy teaching [*didachē*] as it has been taught . . . sound *doctrine* [*didaskalia*]" (Tit. 1:9). Similarly, *didaskalia* refers to the OT in Rom. 15:4. A different label for sound doctrine is "the *doctrine* of God" (Tit. 2:10). Paul also refers to these teachings as "his *teaching*" (2 Tim. 3:10). In contrast, *didaskalia* can refer to false doctrines as in the aforementioned teachings of Pharisees (Mt. 15:9) and of "people" (Col. 2:22), as well as the negative "every wind of *teaching*" (Eph. 4:14). See *NIDNTT-A*, 139-40.

Noun: διδαχή (*didachē*), GK *1439* (S *1322*), 30x. *didachē*, like *didaskalia*, denotes "doctrine, teaching," as well as "instruction"—both the content and the act. Regarding the former, note "the *doctrine* of the Pharisees and Sadducees" (Mt. 16:12), and "they devoted themselves to the *teaching* of the apostles" (Acts 2:42). Examples of the latter are "in his *teaching* he said" (Mk. 4:2) and "unless I speak to you … in *teaching*" (1 Cor. 14:6).

In the four gospels *didachē* almost always signifies Jesus' teaching. For example, "the crowds were amazed at his *teachings*" (Mt. 7:28), "a new *teaching* with authority" (Mk. 1:27), and "My [Jesus'] *teaching* is not my own. It comes from him who sent me" (Jn. 7:16; also Mt. 22:33; Mk. 4:2; 11:18; 12:38). Outside of the gospels, the most prominent use of *didachē* refers to the teaching by Christians of Jesus' gospel. For example, "the proconsul … was amazed at the *teaching* of the Lord" (Acts 13:12), "this new *teaching*" (Acts 17:19), and "the form of *teaching* to which you were entrusted" (Rom. 6:17; also Acts 2:42; 5:28; 2 Tim. 4:2; Heb. 6:2). An example that parallels *didaskalia* and *didachē* is "the trustworthy teaching [*didachē*] as it has been taught ... sound *doctrine* [*didaskalia*]" (Tit. 1:9).

Other uses of *didachē* include "varied and strange *teachings*" (Heb. 13:9) and a number of heretical "doctrines" in Revelation (Rev. 2:14, 15, 24). See *NIDNTT-A*, 139-40.

TEAR

Old Testament

Verb: קָרַע (*qāraʿ*), GK 7973 (S 7167), 63x.

(1) Usually rendered "to tear, rend, rip," *qāraʿ* most often refers to the tearing of one's garments as a sign of intense grief, particularly in reaction to a disaster, such as Joseph's apparent death (Gen. 37:34) or a defeat in battle (Jos. 7:6). Garments are also torn in order to destroy them because of ceremonial contamination (Lev. 13:56).

(2) *qāraʿ* is also used figuratively. For example, in some prophetic texts, God is not satisfied with outward displays of sorrow and thus commands his people to rend their hearts, not their garments (Joel 2:13; cf. Hos. 13:8). The term is also used for the opening of the heavens, where God comes down in judgment (Isa. 64:1). Finally, *qāraʿ* is used for the tearing away of the kingdom from the hands of its ruler (1 Ki. 11:11). See *NIDOTTE*, 3:993.

New Testament

Verb: σχίζω (*schizō*), GK *5387* (S *4977*), 11x. *schizō* means "to tear." It can refer to the tearing of fabric, such as an old garment (Lk. 5:36) or Jesus' clothing (Jn. 19:24), or a fishing net with an enormous catch (Jn. 21:11). Most importantly, *schizō* is describes the miraculous tearing of the curtain of the temple at Christ's death (Mt. 27:51; Mk. 15:38; Lk. 23:45. In the same context Matthew speaks of the "splitting" of stones (Mt. 27:51b). It is also used of heaven being torn open at Jesus' baptism, when John saw "the Spirit descending on him like a dove" (Mk. 1:10).

schizō is also used in connection with the *division* that arises between disputing parties, as it is in Acts 14:4; 23:7. See *NIDNTT-A*, 548.

TEAR OPEN

Old Testament

Verb: בָּקַע (*bākaʿ*), GK 1324 (S 1234), 51x. Often translated "to divide, split, tear open, crack open," *bākaʿ* is frequently used in domestic contexts for activities like splitting wood (Eccl. 10:9), hatching eggs (Isa. 34:15; 59:5), or tearing open wineskins (Jos. 9:4; Job 32:19). See *divide*.

TEARS

New Testament

Noun: δάκρυον (*dakryon*), GK *1232* (S *1144*), 10x. *dakryon* means "tears." A "sinful city woman" wets Jesus' feet with her tears and wipes them with her hair (Lk. 7:38, 44). Paul tells the elders at Ephesus that he has served the Lord and admonished everyone "with tears" (Acts 20:19, 31). He writes to the Corinthians "with many tears" (2 Cor. 2:4) and recalls the tears of Timothy (2 Tim. 1:4). During his earthly life, Jesus prayed "with loud cries and tears" (Heb. 5:7). Esau sought to reclaim his blessing "with tears" (Heb. 12:17). Ultimately, God will one day "wipe away every tear" (Rev. 7:17; 21:4).*

TELL

Old Testament

Verb: נָגַד (*nāgad*), GK 5583 (S 5046), 371x. *nāgad* means "to tell, declare, report." It normally indicates spoken communication, whether relaying a message or reporting on some situation.

(1) *nāgad* is most often used in a direct, nonreligious sense for the communication of human affairs. For example, Ham tells his two brothers about their father's nakedness (Gen. 9:22); Pharaoh asks Abraham why he did not tell him that Sarah was his wife (12:18); Eliezer asks Rebekah: "Please *tell* me, is there room in your father's house for us to spend the night?" (24:23). Almost any kind of reporting can make use of this verb

(2) *nāgad* can also be used for something

that has been revealed by God (e.g., Ps. 147:19; Isa. 43:12; 46:10; Amos 4:13). Joseph tells Pharaoh that in his dream, "God *has revealed* … what he is about to do" (Gen. 41:25). The angel Gabriel come to Daniel to "to *tell* [him] what is written in the Book of Truth" (Dan. 10:21; cf. 11:2). In Ezekiel's vision, the divine messenger tells the prophet to "*describe* the temple to the people of Israel" (Ezek. 43:10).

(3) *nāgad* is also used in the command in the psalms to "proclaim" among the nations what the Lord has done (Ps. 9:11; 64:9; 92:2). This proclamation of our powerful and loving God is not limited to his chosen servants, however, for the very "skies *proclaim* the works of his hands" (19:1; cf. 50:6; 97:6). See *NIDOTTE*, 3:16–18.

Verb: סָפַר (*sāpar*), GK 6218 (S 5608), 107x. *sāpar* means "to count, tell, declare." See *count*.

New Testament

Verb: ἀναγγέλλω (*anangello*), GK *334* (S *312*), 14x. *anangellō* means "to tell, proclaim." In the NT it is used in much the same way as the verbs *kērussō* ("to preach") and *katangellō* ("to proclaim"), but is closest in meaning to the English verbs "to tell" or "to report" (see also *apangellō*, "to report"). Two typical uses are in Acts 14:27 and 15:4, where Paul and Barnabas "report" about their first missionary trip to the church in Antioch and to the leaders of the church in Jerusalem. Similarly, Titus "reports" to Paul about the great care that the Corinthians expressed for Paul (2 Cor. 7:7). Note also Acts 19:18, in which people from Ephesus believed, confessed, and "told of their deeds."

Overlap with the idea of preaching and proclaiming happens when the object of *anangellō* is a Christian message. Therefore, in the NT, its meaning often approaches to preach or proclaim: e.g., "the things which have now been *proclaimed* to you by those who have preached the gospel [*euangalizō*]" (1 Pet. 1:12; also Acts 20:20, 27); or "This is the message we have heard from him and *proclaim* to you: God is light" (1 Jn. 1:5). Likewise, a Samaritan woman says, "When he [the Messiah] comes, he will *proclaim/explain* everything to us" (Jn. 4:25; see also 5:15; 16:14). See *NIDNTT-A*, 7-8.

Verb: ἀπαγγέλλω (*apangellō*), GK *550* (S *518*), 45x. *apangellō* means "to report or tell" something; it is similar to *anangellō* in its range of meaning. See *report*.

Verb: γνωρίζω (*gnōrizō*), GK *1192* (S *1107*), 25x. While related to the verb *ginōskō* ("to know"; see *know*), *gnōrizō* means "to make something known, tell." See *make known*.

Verb: κηρύσσω (*kēryssō*), GK *3062* (S *2784*), 61x. *kēryssō* means to "preach, proclaim, tell, announce a message." See *preach*.

Verb: λεγω (*legō*), GK *3306* (S *3004*, *2036*, *2046*), 2353x. Usually translated as "say," *legō* sometimes has the notion of "to tell." See *say*.

TEMPLE

Old Testament

Noun: בַּיִת (*bayit*), GK 1074 (S 1004), 2047x. *bayit* means "house" (see *house*) and bears both literal and figurative meanings in the OT. The word is sometimes used for temples, the earthly dwelling places of god(s)—e.g., of the Philistine god Dagon in Ashdod (1 Sam. 5:2) and of God in Shiloh (Jdg. 18:31) or in Jerusalem (1 Ki. 6:5).

Noun: הֵיכָל (*hēkāl*), GK 2121 (S 1964), 80x. *hēkāl* bears three distinct but related meanings in the OT. It can refer to a palace (earthly or heavenly), to the temple itself, or to the main room in the temple. Since the Jerusalem temple is thought to be God's palace, it is natural that the same term is used for both.

(1) As a palace, *hēkāl* closely parallels the Hebrew *bayit*, "house," in royal contexts. It is used for the palace of King Ahab of Israel (1 Ki. 21:1; cf. Hos. 8:14) and of the king of Babylon (2 Ki. 20:18; cf. Dan. 5:5). The Lord's heaven is also thought of as a kingly palace (Mic. 1:2).

(2) The *hēkāl* can also refer to the tem-

ple/tabernacle of the Lord in Shiloh, which is associated with the ministries of Eli and Samuel (1 Sam. 1:9; 3:3), or it can point to the temple in Jerusalem, which is its most common referent (2 Ki. 18:16; Isa. 44:28). Through the temple, God dwells with his people (Ps. 138:2). Originally built by King Solomon (2 Chr. 3:17; 4:7–8), Israel's first major temple structure served as the center for Israelite worship until its destruction by the Babylonians in 586 B.C. (Ps. 79:1). The second temple was built around 516 B.C. during the time of Haggai, Zechariah, and Zerubbabel (Ezr. 3–6; Hag. 2:18), and it stood through the time of Jesus until its destruction by the Romans in A.D. 70. The OT also looks ahead to an eschatological temple that will apparently be established by the Messiah (Zech. 6:12–13; cf. Jn. 2:19–22; 1 Cor. 3:16–17; Rev. 21:22).

The palace and temple complex of Solomon comprises a large enclosure and includes buildings and the temple proper and the inner court (1 Ki. 6:36) or upper (KJV, "higher") court (Jer. 26:10). The palace itself lies lower than the temple, but both are located on the eastern hill of Jerusalem. Following the floor plan of most ancient Near Eastern temples, Solomon's temple has a Most Holy Place (in which is placed the ark of the covenant), a Holy Place (in which stands golden tables for the bread of the Presence, lampstands, and an altar of incense), and a portico (or porch) (cf. 1 Ki. 6:17–20).

Temples and palaces in Assyria, Babylon, and Persia were often joined together to facilitate the king's fulfilling of his religious duties and to ensure the favor of the gods. Sometimes such palaces contained exotic gardens (Est. 7:7–8), and were at times used as metaphors for the fortunes of a nation (Ps. 122:7; Jer. 17:27; Amos 2:5). Pagan palaces in the OT include the *hēkāl* of Pharaoh (Gen. 12:15), Nebuchadnezzar (Dan. 1:4), Xerxes (Est. 1:5, 8), and Artaxerxes (Ezr. 4:14). Among the pagan temples mentioned in the OT is the temple in Babylon (Ezr. 5:14).

(3) Finally, *hēkāl* can refer to the main room of the Jerusalem temple (1 Ki. 6:3, 5, 17).

New Testament

Noun: ἱερόν (*hieron*), GK *2639* (S *2411*), 72x. In Greek literature, *hieron* often refers to the general structure of a temple and its shrines. In the LXX it is almost exclusively reserved for pagan shrines (Ezek. 45:9; 1 Chr. 29:4; 2 Chr. 6:13). In the NT, however, *hieron* refers primarily to the Jerusalem temple and only occasionally to temples of pagan deities (cf. "the temple of the great goddess Artemis" in Ephesus [Acts 19:27]).

The Jerusalem temple had a long history stretching back to the time of Solomon, who built it about 1000 B.C. His father David had wanted to build a "house for the Name of the Lord" (1 Chr. 22:8–10; 2 Chr. 6:20), but his son was the one who did the construction. More than 500 years later, Nebuchadnezzar destroyed that temple. It was rebuilt about fifty years later at the time of the return of the exiles, and Herod the Great embarked a rebuilding project in 20 B.C. This is the temple spoken of in the NT.

The Jerusalem temple was comprised of magnificent buildings (Mt. 24:1) built with "massive stones" (Mk. 13:1). It was the center of Jewish religious life, but it was also politicized since it was under the jurisdiction of the high priest and the Sanhedrin, who were political appointees of Rome. Jesus was concerned about unscrupulous economic activity going on in the temple during the Passover Feast and claimed the Jewish leaders were turning it into a "den of thieves," whereas God intended it to be a "house of prayer" (Mt. 21:13; cf. Jn. 2:14–15). Jesus performed miracles there, and children shouted praises to him there (Mt. 21:14–15). Jesus also taught in its courts (Mt. 26:55; Jn. 7:14; 8:20), as the apostles did after him (Acts 2:46; 5:24–25, 42). It was also the scene of confrontations between Paul and his opponents (Acts 21:26–30).

Just before his crucifixion, Jesus predicts the destruction of the temple (Mk.

13:1–4). One of the accusations against him during his trail is a claim that Jesus said he would destroy the temple and rebuild it in three days (Mt. 26:61; 27:40, where *naos* is used, not *hieron*). Jesus himself was not referring to Herod's temple in this statement, however, but to his body (cf. Jn. 2:20–22). In other words, Jesus represents in himself all that the temple was supposed to symbolize, especially since in him all the fullness of Deity lives (cf. Col. 2:9). Indeed, Jesus shows himself to be *greater* than the temple (Mt. 12:6), since three days after his crucifixion he comes back to life. See *NIDNTT-A,* 262-65.

Noun: ναός (*naos*),GK *3724* (S *3485*), 45x. *naos* means "temple" in the NT, though there are various nuances to this word. (1) In the gospels *naos* refers in general to the temple proper, though not the entire temple complex (for which *hieron*, GK *2639*, is used). It took forty-six years for Herod and his successors to (re)build it (Jn. 2:20). Jesus warns against swearing by it (Mt. 23:16–17, 21), and within its precincts he mentions the curious murder of Zechariah, son of Berekiah (23:35). Jesus is accused of saying he was going to destroy the temple and rebuild it in three days (26:61; 27:40; Mk. 14:58; 15:29; Jn. 2:19). Within the temple Zechariah, father of John the Baptist, sees a miraculous vision (Lk. 1:9, 21–22). The veil of the *naos* is torn at Jesus' death (Mt. 27:51; Mk. 15:30; Lk. 23:45), symbolizing direct access for everyone to God. Paul predicts that in last days, the "man of lawlessness," who will work in the power of Satan, will set "himself up in God's *temple*, proclaiming himself to be God" (2 Thess. 2:4, 9).

(2) *naos* can be a pagan temple as well. God is described as living in heaven rather than in "[pagan] *temples* built by hands" (Acts 17:24). Demetrius of Ephesus built "shrines" of Artemis as souvenirs for visitors to Ephesus (19:24).

(3) The Christian church is called a *naos* of God in which his Spirit lives (1 Cor. 3:16–17); in 6:19 Paul applies this metaphor also to the individual Christian's body. Hence, a Christian should have nothing to do with idols (2 Cor. 6:16). It is significant that the term *naos* is used for the church as a temple (rather than *hieron*), for it was particularly in the *naos*, with its Most Holy Place, that the Lord God dwelt. As the *naos* of the Holy Spirit, the Christian community (with the apostles and prophets as the foundation and Christ as the cornerstone) provides a metaphor for Christian unity (Eph. 2:21).

The most profound Christian images for the *naos* are found in Revelation, where those who persevere will be made "a pillar in the *temple* of my God" (Rev. 3:12). Heavenly worshipers are "before the throne of God and serve him day and night in his *temple*" (7:15). The *naos* here is a heavenly sanctuary (11:1–2; cf. 11:19; 15:5–6). Angelic reapers come from it to reap the harvest of the elect and to pour out God's eschatological judgment (14:15, 17; 15:9–16:1; 16:17). In the new Jerusalem there will be no need for a temple in which God can dwell, "because the Lord God Almighty and the Lamb are its *temple*" (21:22). See *NIDNTT-A*, 383-84.

Noun: οἶκος (*oikos*), GK *3875* (S *3624*), 114x. *oikos* sometimes refer to the temple in Jerusalem (*oikos theou* "house of God"; Mk. 2:26; 11:17; Jn. 2:16–17; cf. Acts 7:47). A Christian's body is also seen as an *oikos* of the Holy Spirit (1 Cor. 6:19). See *house*.

TEMPORALITY

Old Testament

Noun: הֶבֶל (*hebel*), GK 2039 (S 1892), 73x. *hebel* literally means "breath," but in the OT it occurs only 3x with this sense (see *breath*). *hebel* often refers to the temporality or futile nature of a thing. The psalmist of Ps. 39:5, for example, acknowledges the brevity and/or temporal nature of life (Ps. 39:5). See *vanity.*

TEMPT, TEMPTATION

New Testament

Verb: πειράζω (*peirazō*), GK *4279* (S *3985*), 38x. *peirazō* has several basic usages. (1) It can refer to being "tempted" to do or think something wrong or contrary to God's will (Gal. 6:1; Jas. 1:13). The participial form of this verb can be translated "tempter" when speaking of Satan (Mt. 4:3; 1 Thess. 3:5). Jesus was "tempted" by Satan in the desert (Mt. 4:1–11; Lk. 4:1–13; Heb. 4:15).

(2) *peirazō* can refer to a testing, such as a testing to discover the genuineness of one's faith (2 Cor. 13:5; Rev. 2:2). When we are tested, God promises to provide a way of escape for us, if only we depend on him (1 Cor. 10:13). On occasion, Jesus puts his disciples to the test (Jn. 6:6). In times past human beings put the triune God to the test (Acts 5:9; 15:10; 1 Cor. 10:9; Heb. 3:8–9). The term also is used for the opponents of Jesus who try to entrap him with trick questions (Mt. 16:1; 19:3; 22:18, 35; Mk. 10:2; 12:15; Jn. 8:6).

(3) *peirazō* is also used to describe an attempt to do something. After Paul's conversion, he "makes an attempt" to associate with the other disciples, but he is unsuccessful because they are afraid of him (Acts 9:26). Paul "tries" to go into Bithynia, but the Spirit will not allow it (Acts 16:7).

God does indeed sometimes put our faith to the test (Heb. 11:17) and at other times allows us to be tested (1 Cor. 10:13), but it is important to note that God himself never tempts us with evil (Jas. 1:13). See *NIDNTT-A,* 449-51.

Noun: πειρασμός (*peirasmos*), GK *4280* (S *3986*), 21x. *peirasmos* shows the same range of meaning as the verb *peirazō* (GK *4279),* referring either to a testing (Gal. 4:14) or a temptation to do something wrong (Mt. 26:41; Lk. 4:13; 1 Tim. 6:9).

Believers are not to be surprised when trials come, but should rather rejoice in that they are sharing in the sufferings of Christ (1 Pet. 4:12–13). The Israelite nation's time in the desert was in reality of time of "testing," to see if they would stay true to God (Heb. 3:8); like the seed sown on the rock that fell away in a time of testing (Lk. 8:13), many of the Israelites failed the test. The disciples stayed with Jesus during his time of trials (Lk. 22:28). Paul's ministry was replete with trials (Acts 20:19), as he himself was a trial to the Galatians because of his physical condition (Gal. 4:14). Peter writes to a community suffering trials because of their faith, rejoicing in their heavenly status even though they may have to suffer for a little while (1 Pet. 1:6); yet God knows how to rescue the godly from trials (2 Pet. 2:9). Jesus will spare the Christians in Philadelphia from *"the hour of trial*" coming on the earth (Rev. 3:10).

After Satan finishes his "tempting" of Jesus, he leaves him for a time (Lk. 4:13). The disciples are to pray so that they not may enter into temptation (Mt. 26:41; Mk. 14:38; Lk. 22:40, 46); in fact, by God's grace, they are able to resist temptation (1 Cor. 10:13). But those desiring to be rich fall into a special set of temptations (1 Tim. 6:9).

Jesus' final phrase in the Lord's Prayer has proven difficult to understand. We are to pray, "And lead us not into *temptation*, but deliver us from evil" (Mt. 6:13; also Lk. 11:4). Yet elsewhere believers are encouraged to rejoice in the midst of trials (Jas. 1:2), knowing that when we persevere, we will receive the crown of life (Jas. 1:12); moreover, James assures us that God does not tempt anyone (Jas. 1:13, using the related verb form). One way of handling the biblical data is to draw a sharp distinction between trials and temptations. God does not induce anyone to sin, and in fact we are to admit our dependence on God as we pray for protection from temptation. However, trials and sufferings will occur so that our faith can be purified, shown to be true—all of which enables us to grow up into Christian maturity. See *NIDNTT-A,* 449-51*

TEN

Old Testament

Noun: עֶשֶׂר (*ʿeśer*), GK 6924 (S 6235), 60x.

Noun: עֲשָׂרָה (*ᶜᵃśārâ*), GK 6927 (S 6235), 65x.

Noun: עֲשֶׂרֶת (*ᶜᵃśeret*), GK 6930 (S 6240), 52x. *ᶜeśer*, *ᶜᵃśārâ* , and *ᶜᵃśeret* are all based on the same Heb. root (*ᶜśr*) and mean "ten." Probably because of ten fingers on the human hand, this number becomes the beginning of the sequence from 10 to 100 to 1000 to 10,000. Added with other numbers, ten can become part of what makes up numbers like fifteen (Ezek. 45:12), seventeen (Jer. 32:9), and ten thousand (Jdg. 4:10).

"Ten" can be used as a round number or as hyperbole. When Jacob charges Laban with changing his wages "ten times" (Gen. 31:7, 41), he is probably not giving an exact count. When Elkanah considers himself as worth more than ten sons to Hannah, this is surely exaggeration (and exasperation) (1 Sam. 1:8). Similarly with Daniel and his three friends, who are found "ten times better than all the magicians" (Dan. 1:20), this is intended as a stock phrase.

"Ten" can also be used as a number of completion. The references to "the *Ten* Commandments" suggest that they serve as a summary of the entire will of God—Moses spends forty days and nights on Mount Sinai, writing "on the tablets the words of the Covenant—the *Ten* Commandments" (Exod. 34:28). Note also the reference to the ten plagues; while the OT does reference exactly ten plagues, the nuance here is that God's judgment on the Egyptians is complete with these ten events. See *NIDOTTE*, 3:552–53.

New Testament

Adjective: δεκα (*deka*), GK *1274* (S *1176*), 25x. *deka* is the cardinal number "ten." In the NT, *deka* often specifies a quantity of people, like ten apostles (Mt. 20:24; Mk. 10:41) or ten lepers (Lk. 17:12, 17). In other instances it specifies a unit of time, like ten days (Acts 25:6). Eight of the NT uses of *deka* describe either the ten-horned dragon (Rev. 12:3) or the ten-horned, ten-crowned beast of the apocalypse (13:1; 17:3, 7, 12, 16). In Revelation, John also uses "ten days" to represent a period of unspecified, yet limited, duration (2:10). Six of the NT uses of *deka* appear in Jesus' parable of the ten minas (pounds), which mentions ten servants, ten minas, and ten cities (Lk. 19:13a, b, 16, 17, 24, 25; cf. also the parable of the ten talents in Mt. 25:28). Jesus uses the number ten in other parables as well, like the ten virgins (Mt. 25:1), the ten thousand warriors (Lk. 14:31), and the ten silver coins (Lk. 15:8).

Occasionally, *deka* is part of the Greek construction of a compound cardinal number that even the most literal English translations render without using the word "ten." For example, Lk. 13:16 refers to "eighteen years" in almost all English translations rather than "ten and eight years." See *NIDNTT-A*, 125.*

TENANT FARMER

New Testament

Noun: γεωργός (*geōrgos*), GK *1177* (S *1092*), 19x. *geōrgos* can refer to the owner of a farm or to those who work the farm (a "tenant"). See *farmer*.

TEND

Old Testament

Verb: נָצַר (*nāṣar*), GK 5915 (S 5341), 63x. *nāṣar* generally indicates the action of carefully watching over a particular object so that the object is preserved or protected. It may be translated "to keep, guard, watch, protect." The objects that *nāṣar* takes provide insight into the verb's meaning. For example, Proverbs teaches, "He who *tends* the fig tree will eat its fruit" (Prov. 27:18). See *keep*.

Verb: רָעָה (*rāᶜâ*), GK 8286 (S 7473), 167x. *rāᶜâ* means "to shepherd, tend, feed graze." This verb can thus be used for shepherds tending sheep. See *shepherd*.

Verb: שָׁמַר (*šāmar*), GK 9068 (S 8104), 468x. Often translated "to keep," the verb *šāmar* bears three distinct but related meanings in the OT: "to guard, tend," "to watch over," and "to preserve" (see *keep*). For example, it is used of tending to a flock (Gen. 30:31) and a house (2 Sam. 15:16; Ps. 15:16).

TENDERNESS

New Testament

Noun: σπλάγχνον (*splanchnon*), GK *5073* (S *4698*), 11x. *splanchnon* refers to a feeling of "affection, tenderness, compassion." See *affection*.

TENT

Old Testament

Noun: אֹהֶל (*ʾōhel*), GK 185 (S 168), 348x.

(1) Often translated "tent, dwelling," the noun *ʾōhel* typically refers to a portable dwelling used by nomads and armies of the ancient Near East, such as the patriarchs (Gen. 12:8; 13:5; 18:1; 31:25), the Israelites of the exodus (Exod. 16:16; 33:10), and the Israelite armies of the early monarchy period (1 Sam. 17:54). Such tents are typically made of goatskins draped over a wooden frame, tied with cords, and secured to the ground with pegs. Beyond this common usage, however, *ʾōhel* bears three specific meanings in the OT.

(2) The most common use of *ʾōhel* is in the expression "the *Tent* of Meeting," which is the tabernacle, the place where God meets with his people (Lev. 1:1; cf. Exod. 29:42–43; 33:7). At times, the tabernacle is specifically designated the "the tent of the LORD" (Exod. 28:43; 1 Ki. 1:39; 2:28; 1 Chr. 9:23).

(3) In some poetic texts, *ʾōhel* designates a common *house* (cf. Ps. 78:51; 91:10; 132:3; Lam. 2:4).

(4) *ʾōhel* is also used metaphorically for the *sky*, where God pitches a tent for the sun (Ps. 19:4) and for himself (Isa. 40:22). See *NIDOTTE*, 1:300-302.

New Testament

Noun: σκηνή (*skēnē*), GK *5008* (S *4633*), 20x. *skēnē* can refer to a "tent" in which nomads, such as Abraham, lived (Heb. 11:9). It is used to refer to the three tents or "shelters" that Peter wants to put up for Jesus, Moses, and Elijah at Jesus' transfiguration (Mt. 17:4; Mk. 9:5; Lk. 9:33). See *tabernacle*.

TENTH

New Testament

Adjective: δέκατος (*dekatos*), GK *1281* (S *1181*, *1182*), 7x. *dekatos* is a "tenth" portion of something or the "tenth" in a series of ten or more items. Four of the seven NT uses of *dekatos* occur in Heb. 7, which describes Abraham's "tithe" to the priest-king Melchizedek (Heb. 7:2, 4, 8, 9; cf. Mt. 23:23; Lk. 11:42, which use the verb *apodekatoō*, "to tithe"). No NT text mentions the tithe as a responsibility of the church; rather, the instructions to the church about giving are less legalistic: God instructs people to give generously out of their poverty (2 Cor. 8:1–5; 9:6), to give in proportion to their income (1 Cor. 16:1–2), and to share possessions generously with those in need (2 Cor. 8–9; Eph. 4:28). One wonders if God would require less than the OT tithe from NT people.

The other NT uses of *dekatos* appear in the routine counting of a fraction, like "a tenth of the city" (Rev. 11:13), or in the numeration of a series, like "the tenth hour" (Jn. 1:39) or the "tenth" of twelve precious stones forming the foundation of new Jerusalem (Rev. 21:20). See *NIDNTT-A*, 125-27.*

(BE) TERRIFIED, TERRIFY

Old Testament

Verb: חָתַת (*ḥātat*), GK 3169 (S 2865), 55x. *ḥātat* is a verb that means "to be discouraged, dismayed, afraid, terrified." See *(be) discouraged*.

New Testament

Verb: ἐξίστημι (*existēmi*), GK *2014* (S *1839*), 17x. *existēmi* carries two distinct but related meanings. Usually it means "to astound, terrify" someone. See *amazed*.

TERRITORY

Old Testament

Noun: גְּבוּל (*g^ebûl*), GK 1473 (S 1366), 241x. *g^ebûl* can mean either "border" (a boundary line between two areas) or "territory" (the area within a border).

It is difficult to know which meaning is intended. See *border*.

TEST

Old Testament

Verb: בָּחַן (*bāḥan*), GK 1043 (S 974), 29x. *bāḥan* denotes the divine examination of an individual and may be translated as "test, try, prove." It is common in the poetic and prophetic books of the OT. The testing of one's heart is used most frequently. Ps. 17:3 states, "Though you *probe* my heart and examine me at night, though you test me, you will find nothing; I have resolved that my mouth will not sin" (cf. Jer. 12:3; 1 Chr. 29:17; Prov. 17:3). The term also conveys the testing of individuals (Job 23:10; Ps. 11:4; 26:2; 66:10) as well as the examination of words (Gen. 42:15–16; Job 34:3).

bāḥan may have originated from the world of metallurgy and the practice of authenticating or refining gold and other precious metals (see also *ṣārap*, GK 7671). Note Jer. 9:7 and Zech. 13:9, which state, "I will refine them like silver and *test* them like gold." *bāḥan* is similar to *nāsâ* ("test, prove," GK 5814) and shares the basic meaning of proving one's obedience or loyalty, especially in the context of a covenant relationship. Abraham demonstrates his loyalty in his actions on Mount Moriah (cf. Gen. 22:1–18). Greek writers of the sixth century BC used the metaphor of a touchstone to convey the idea of the authentication of a person's life. Ancient goldsmiths would rub gold on a particular black stone or "touchstone" to determine its purity. See *NIDOTTE*, 1:636-38.

Verb: נָסָה (*nāsâ*), GK 5814 (S 5254), 36x. *nāsâ* denotes the testing of a person's loyalty or obedience and may be translated "test, prove." This verb is most common in the narrative and poetic books of the OT. Unlike the related terms *bāḥan* ("test," GK 1043) and *ṣārap* ("refine, test," GK 7671), which occur almost exclusively with persons or metals as the object, *nāsâ* allows for both God and individuals as the object of "testing." God refers negatively to the events of the Exodus generation that have made him the object of their testing (cf. Num. 14:22).

This term is central to the theology of the Pentateuch, where the loyalty of Abraham is tested by means of the offering of his son (Gen. 22:1ff.). The loyalty of Israel is tested by means of the revelation and presence of Yahweh at Sinai (Exod. 20:20). God's loyalty or faithfulness toward his own people is tested in the wilderness (15:25; 17:2, 7; Num. 14:22) and becomes a point of theological reflection in later biblical texts (see Deut. 6:16; 33:8; Ps. 95:9; 78:18, 41, 56; 106:14).

Deut. 8:2-3 suggests that the wilderness experience was a test of deprivation intended to teach the people that covenant relationship is more than just depending on God for food; it requires in addition absolute loyalty to his every word. In the ancient Near East, a superior king would measure or *test* for the loyalty of an inferior king or vassal by means of his demonstrated obedience to the stipulation of the treaty. In the new covenant, believers are called to demonstrate loyalty in response to the one who has demonstrated perfect obedience and stands in our place before God. See *NIDOTTE*, 3:111-13.

Verb: צָרַף (*ṣārap*), GK 7671 (S 6884), 34x. *ṣārap* is commonly used to denote the testing or refining of both metals and human beings and may be translated as "test, refine." The term describes metalworkers (Jdg. 17:4; Prov. 25:4) and the idols they make (Jer. 51:17–18; Isa. 46:7). It also refers to the word of God that is proven true, as in Ps. 119:140: "Your promises have been thoroughly *tested*, and your servant loves them" (cf. 2 Sam. 22:31).

People are also *refined* (Jdg. 7:4; Isa. 1:25). *ṣārap* is common in the prophetic books of the OT, where the prophets use the term to describe the exilic experience as the "refining" or "purifying" event for Israel (Ps. 12:6; Isa. 1:25; 48:10; Jer. 9:7; 10:9; Dan. 11:35; Zech. 13:9; Mal. 3:2–3). Ancient refining techniques required the heating of precious metals to high temperatures, where the base metals or "dross" were either burned off or skimmed from the top. The prophet Zechariah declares, "This third I will bring into the fire; I will *refine* them like silver and test them like gold" (Zech. 13:9) See *NIDOTTE,* 3:847-853.

New Testament

Verb: δοκιμάζω (*dokimazō*), GK *1507* (S *1381*), 22x. *dokimazō* means to "test, approve." It carries the idea of a critical examination of something to determine its genuineness.

Believers are to "test" or examine themselves regarding their own faithfulness (1 Cor. 11:28; 2 Cor. 13:5), as well as their work (Gal. 6:4). Peter speaks of the testing of one's faith by fire, resulting in praise and glory at the revelation of Jesus Christ (1 Pet. 1:7). Paul tells us to know the will of God and "approve" it (Rom. 2:18) and to "test" or "discern" what pleases him (Phil. 1:10; Eph. 5:10). Even the spirits should be tested to see if they are of God (1 Jn. 4:1). In sum, Paul encourages us to "*test* everything" (1 Thess. 5:21).

dokimazō can also refer to a conclusion drawn by testing (to prove or approve). The focus of this sense is the result of the examination process. For example, Paul speaks of sending representatives whom he has tested and approved to be true (1 Cor. 16:3; 2 Cor. 8:22). See *NIDNTT-A*, 150.

Verb: πειράζω (*peirazō*), GK *4279* (S *3985*), 38x. *peirazō* has several basic usages, most of which revolve around either "to tempt" or "to test." See *tempt*.

TESTAMENT

New Testament

Noun: διαθήκη (*diathēkē*), GK *1347* (S *1242*), 33x. *diathēkē* can mean "covenant, testament, will." The majority of the occurrences of this word are in quotation from or allusions to the OT. See *covenant*. In fact, the very term "NT" (*kainē diathēke*) comes from this word. The word is also used for one's last will and testament.

The writer to the Hebrews plays with the fact that *diathēkē* can mean last will and testament (Heb. 9:15–23; cf. also Gal. 3:15–18). Just as no last will ever goes into effect until the one who wrote it dies, so the old covenant required a sacrificial death of an animal to put its terms into effect. But while in OT times sacrificial blood had to be shed every year; Jesus' death as the mediator of the new covenant, by contrast, is once for all, and so his covenant is an "eternal covenant" (Heb. 13:20). See *NIDNTT-A*, 134-36.

TESTIFY

New Testament

Verb: διαμαρτύρομαι (*diamartyromai*), GK *1371* (S *1263*), 15x. This is an intensified compound of the verb *martyreō* ("to testify"). (The preposition *dia* is sometimes added to a verb to intensify its original idea.) It means "to testify, give a warning" in the case of important matters and situations of extreme danger.

Accordingly, in the majority of the uses of *diamartyromai*, the reason for testimony or warning is the need for salvation of non-Christians or living rightly as a Christian. A striking example of the former nuance is Lk. 16:19–31, a parable in which a rich man in Hades wants to go back and "strongly *warn*" (16:28) his brothers so that they may be saved. This meaning is also present in Acts 2:40, when Luke writes that Peter "*warned* them and pleaded with them, 'Save yourselves from this corrupt generation'" (also 8:25; 10:42; 18:5; 20:21, 24; 23:11; 28:23). The latter nuance, which is admonishing Christians to live rightly, is seen in those occasions when Paul admonishes Timothy to keep his instructions and to preach the word (1 Tim. 5:21; 2 Tim. 4:1). Elsewhere he tells Timothy to "*warn* them before God against quarreling over words" (2 Tim. 2:14). Also within the semantic range of warning is Paul's statement, "I know that in every city the Holy Spirit *warns* me that prison and hardships are facing me" (Acts 20:23).

Lastly, *diamartyromai* occurs in Heb. 2:6 with a meaning much like the verb *martyromai*, "But there is a place where someone has *testified*," followed by a quotation from Ps. 8. See *NIDNTT-A*, 355-57.

Verb: μαρτυρέω (*martyreō*), GK *3455* (S *3143*), 76x. *martyreō* means to "confirm, testify" to something from firsthand experience. Frequently it is used for general (nonlegal) attestation (Acts 13:22; Rom. 10:2; 2 Cor. 8:3; Gal. 4:15; Col. 4:13; 3 Jn. 3, 6). Although, as the preceding examples indicate, the agent of attestation is often human, it is not restricted to this usage. That which testifies can be God (1 Jn. 5:9), signs and wonders (Acts 14:3), the Spirit (1 Jn. 5:6), an angel sent by Jesus (Rev. 22:16), or the Scriptures (Acts 10:43; Heb. 7:17). In a number of passages it is equivalent to having a good reputation (Acts 6:3; 16:2; 1 Tim. 5:10; 3 Jn. 12). Closely related to the idea of reputation is its use in Heb. 11:2ff., in which certain OT heroes "gained approval" from God.

As with the noun *martyria* (see *testimony*), *martyreō* can be used as a technical term within a legal setting: "Christ Jesus, who while *testifying* before Pontius Pilate" (1 Tim. 6:13; also Jn. 18:23; Acts 26:5). It may also be used with a legal nuance outside of an overtly legal setting; e.g., in Mt. 23:31 Jesus condemns the Pharisees for "testifying" against themselves. Although Jesus does not make this statement in a trial, his rhetoric has juridical overtones. This again is the case again in Jn. 8:13ff., in which the verb "to judge" (*krinō*) is also used, which heightens the legal sense.

The use of legal rhetoric outside of an official trial reflects the close connection between religion and law in much of first-century Judaism. There was a pervasive belief that all people would be held accountable in a cosmic trial to God's law, and thus there were debates among religious leaders such as the Pharisees and the Sanhedrin that were framed in legal terminology. With this foundation, the theological significance of testifying to Jesus is more readily understood. In the passages that use *martyreō* to refer to someone testifying to the gospel, the idea of cosmic, ultimate judgment is not far removed. See *NIDNTT-A*, 355-57.

TESTIMONY

Old Testament

Noun: עֵדוּת (*ʿēdût*), GK 6343 (S 5715), 61x. *ʿēdût*, usually translated "testimony," is closely connected to God's law. In the Pentateuch, this noun describes the two tablets containing the Ten Commandments, so that in Exod. 31:18 God gave Moses "the two tablets of the *testimony*" (cf. 32:15; 34:29). These two tablets, sometimes simply called "the testimony," are to be put in the ark of the covenant (25:16, 21); as a result, the ark is often referred to as the "ark of the *testimony*" (25:22; 30:6; 39:35; Num. 4:5; 7:89). Since the ark (containing the tablets of testimony) is housed in the tabernacle or tent of meeting, these may be referred to as the "tabernacle of *testimony*" (Exod. 38:21; 1:50; 10:11) or the "tent of *testimony*" (Num. 9:15; 17:7-8[22-23]; 18:2). In fact, every occasion of *ʿēdût* in the Pentateuch describes the two tablets, the ark, or the tabernacle (33x in the Pentateuch).

In the remainder of the OT, there remain references to the "ark of the testimony" (Jos. 4:16), to the "tent of testimony" (2 Chr. 24:6), and even once to a copy of the covenant itself (2 Ki. 11:12; cf. 2 Chr. 23:11). But generally, outside the Pentateuch *ʿēdût* is a more generic reference to law (1 Ki. 2:3; 2 Ki. 23:3; 1 Chr. 29:19), perhaps with the physical tablets of the Ten Commandments in the background. In this sense, *ʿēdût* may be translated "requirements," "warnings," "regulations," or "decrees." However, in the book of Psalms, the NIV reserves the translation of "statutes" for *ʿēdût* (13x) to carry the general sense of the law's regulations. Law and *ʿēdût* are closely connected, demonstrated both in the parallelism of Ps. 19:7[8], in which *ʿēdût* and "law" are equated, and in the nine occurrences of *ʿēdût* in Ps. 119, the well-known acrostic poem declaring the wonders of God's law. See *NIDOTTE*, 3:328-29.

New Testament

Noun: μαρτυρία (*martyria*), GK *3456* (S *3141*), 37x. *martyria* is similar to *martyrion* ("testimony") and is used frequently in conjunction with the verb *martyreō* ("to witness"; Jn. 3:11, 32; 5:31ff.; 1 Jn. 5:9, 10; 3 Jn. 12; Rev. 1:2). *martyria* denotes the act of testifying or the content of a certain testimony. The former is exhibited in the statements that John "came for (the purpose of) *testifying*" (Jn. 1:7), and "now when they completed their *testimony*" (Rev. 11:7). The latter use is seen in such statements as, "and this is the *testimony* of John" (Jn. 1:19), and "the word of his *testimony*" (Rev. 12:11).

As with the noun *martys* ("witness"), *martyria* can have a legal meaning, such as in Mk. 14:55ff. and Lk. 22:71, in the accounts of Jesus' trial before the Jewish leadership. However, *martyria* is most frequently employed in the NT in the context of a testimony of or to Jesus or his gospel; e.g., "you people do not accept our *testimony*" (Jn. 3:11) and "your *testimony* about me" (Acts 22:18; also Jn. 1:7; Rev. 1:2; 12:17; 19:10).

Human testimony is mentioned in several passages. Jesus told the Pharisees, "In your own law it is written that the *testimony* of two men is valid" (Jn. 8:17—a reference to Deut. 17:6; 19:15). Paul describes a quote from the poet Epimenides as a *martyria* (Tit. 1:12–13). John contrasts the testimony of God and that of people (1 Jn. 5:9ff.). Also related to human testimony is the use of *martyria* to denote reputation in 1 Tim. 3:7. See *NIDNTT-A*, 355-57.

Noun: μαρτύριον (*martyrion*), GK *3457* (S *3142*), 19x. *martyrion* denotes an action, statement, or thing that serves as a testimony or witness. It is similar to *martyria*, but is less clearly related to legal ideas.

In the NT *martyrion* mostly occurs in the context of testimony to Jesus or God. "You will stand before governors and kings on account of me as a *witness* to them" (Mk. 13:9). "Do not be ashamed of the *testimony* of our Lord" (2 Tim. 1:8; also Mt. 24:14; Acts 4:33; 1 Cor. 1:6; 2:1). *martyrion* refers to an action that provides testimony to Jesus when he healed a man with leprosy and then said, "show yourself to the priest and offer the gift Moses commanded, as a *testimony* to them" (Mt. 8:4; also Mk. 6:11). Paul describes Jesus as "the testimony" (1 Tim. 2:6). Moses also is described as being faithful as a "testimony" (Heb. 3:5).

In addition to these positive connotations, *martyrion* is used in a negative sense in the statement, "their corrosion will be a *testimony* to you" (Jas. 5:3). Last, *martyrion* is used in conjunction with *skēnē* ("tent, tabernacle") in reference to Israel's "tent of *witness*" in the desert (Acts 7:44; Rev. 15:5). See *NIDNTT-A*, 355-57.

Noun: στόμα (*stoma*), GK *5125* (S *4750*), 78x. The word *stoma* refers to the "mouth," but it can also denote the "testimony" of a witness. See *mouth*.

THANK, (GIVE) THANKS

Old Testament

Verb: יָדָה (*yādâ*), GK 3344 (S 3034), 111x. *yādâ* means "praise, (give) thanks, confess." The core meaning of this verb is to express acknowledgment of some sort. See *praise*.

New Testament

Verb: εὐλογέω (*eulogeō*), GK *2328* (S *2127*), 41x. *eulogeō* means "to bless, praise, thank" someone. See *bless*.

Verb: εὐχαριστέω (*eucharisteō*), GK *2373* (S *2168)*, 38x. *eucharisteō* means "to thank, give thanks." It almost exclusively denotes thanksgiving directed toward God, but sometimes indicates thanksgiving between humans (Lk. 17:16; Acts 24:3; Rom. 16:4).

The majority of occurrences of *eucharisteō* describe thanksgiving directed toward God in light of his benefits and blessings. These words of thanksgiving are often found in the introduction of Paul's letters, even when a strong rebuke is about to follow. Paul thanks God for believer's faith and their influence in the world (Rom. 1:8; 2 Cor. 1:11), for the mutual indwelling of faith and love that flows into action (Eph. 1:15–16; Col. 1:3–4; 1 Thess. 1:2–3), for the grace given to the church (1 Cor. 1:4), for sharing in the gospel (Phil. 1:3, 5), for God's work of election (2 Thess. 2:13), and for endurance in hope (1 Thess. 1:2–3). Aside from the introductions of Paul's letters, *eucharisteō* is directed to God as either general praise or praise for specific gifts of grace (1 Cor. 14:18; 2 Cor. 4:15; Col. 1:12; 1 Thess. 2:13). Also, this verb and its corresponding noun are used as thanksgiving doxologies in Revelation (Rev. 4:9; 7:12; 11:17).

eucharisteō is used also in the blessing said before a meal (cf. Mt. 15:36; Mk. 8:6; 1 Cor. 10:30) and is found at the institution of the Lord's Supper (Lk. 22:17, 19; 1 Cor. 11:24). Thus, from the second century on, the "Eucharist" (*eucharistia*, GK 2374; see *thanksgiving*) became the term used for the service of the Lord's Supper.

THANKSGIVING

New Testament

Noun: εὐχαριστία (*eucharistia*), GK *2374* (S *2169*), 15x. *eucharistia* means "thanksgiving." The noun is most often used by Paul in his epistolary thanksgivings, where he emphasizes the posture of gratitude in the life of the church (Phil. 4:6; Col. 2:7; 4:2; 1 Tim. 2:1). The roots of this NT theme derive from Israel's covenantal tradition where thanksgiving and praise were nearly equated as the necessary posture of a people blessed by divine grace (cf. Ps. 34:1; 100:4; Ezr. 3:11). To neglect thankfulness to God is to forget his benefits and fall prey to the antithesis of covenantal faithfulness, namely, idolatry (cf. 1 Cor. 10:1–16).

Thanksgiving is directed toward God for the past (the work of Christ on our behalf; Col. 1:13–14), for the present (as reflected in obedient lives of faith; Rom. 12:1), and for the future (in the hope of the consummation of all God's blessings in Christ; Rev. 11:17). Thanksgiving defines the covenant community as God-centered. See *NIDNTT-A, 220-21.*

THICKET

Old Testament

Noun: יַעַר (*yaʿar*), GK 3623 (S 3293), 56x. *yaʿar* is the general term for a forest. However, it does not always refer to areas covered with tall trees; it can also refer to areas covered with shrubs and bushes. See *forest.*

THIEF

New Testament

Noun: κλέπτης (*kleptes*), GK *3095* (S *2812*), 16x. *kleptes* is a someone who steals, "a thief." Jesus describes the characteristics of such a person: he approaches people's treasure for devious purposes (Lk. 12:33), he breaks in and steals from their homes (Mt. 6:19–20), and he climbs into their sheep pens to steal sheep (Jn. 10:1). Jesus uses *kleptes* to explain that those who came before him and claimed to bring salvation were like "thieves" who came to steal, kill, and destroy (10:8, 10). In contrast, Jesus brings abundant life. Paul lists thieves among those who will not inherit the kingdom of God (1 Cor. 6:10). Judas Iscariot is described as a thief because of his pilfering from the communal moneybag of Jesus and the disciples (Jn. 12:6). Jesus (Mt. 24:43; Lk. 12:39), Paul (1 Thess. 5:2, 4), Peter (2 Pet. 3:10), and John (Rev. 3:3; 16:15) all exhort us to be watchful for the coming of the day of the Lord because it will come as unexpectedly as "a *thief* in the night." See *NIDNTT-A*, 335-36.*

THING

Old Testament

Noun: כְּלִי (*k*^e^*lî*), GK 3998 (S 3627), 325x. *k*^e^*lî* is a noun denoting a variety of equipment, tools, containers, etc., used in a given activity or occupation. *k*^e^*lî* can refer to jewelry (Gen. 24:53), weapons (Gen. 27:3; Deut. 1:41; cf. 1 Sam. 31:4, where "armor-bearer" is literally "one who bears *k*^e^*lî*"), bags (Gen. 42:25), articles of precious metals (Exod. 3:22), stuff (Exod. 22:7), furnishings (Exod. 25:9), pots or jars (Lev. 6:28; Num. 19:17), furniture (Lev. 15:4, 6, 22), leather goods (Num.

31:20), objects made of iron or wood (Num. 35:16, 18), clothing (Deut. 22:5), baskets (Deut. 23:24), a yoke (2 Sam. 24:22), goblets (1 Ki. 10:21), musical instruments (1 Chr. 15:16), boats (Isa. 18:2), etc. The use of this noun to refer to such a wide variety of objects is comparable to the English noun "thing."

Often (107x) *kᵉlî* is used of various implements for service in the tabernacle or temple, but never of the main items in the sanctuary (altar, menorah, table for the Bread of Presence, altar of incense). Rather, *kᵉlî* is used for the equipment necessary for attending to these primary objects (pans, shovels, tongs, snuffers [wick trimmers], etc.).

New Testament

Noun: πρᾶγμα (*pragma*), GK *4547* (S *4229*), 11x. *pragma* generally refers to something about which an author is already speaking. See *matter*.

THINK

Old Testament

Verb: אָמַר (*ʾāmar*), GK 606 (S 559), 5316x. *ʾāmar* is the most common verb in the OT for "to say, utter." See *say*. But this verb can also mean "to think." *ʾāmar* is the term used in the phrase "say in the heart," which is often translated "think" (Deut. 8:17–18, "You may *say* to yourself ..."). The wicked person thinks to himself, "Nothing will shake me; I'll always be happy" (Ps. 10:6, 10, 13). The fool *thinks* in his heart, "There is no God" (14:1). In Isa. 14, a mysterious tyrant "thinks" in his heart, "I will ascend to heaven; I will raise my throne above the stars of God ... I will make myself like the Most High" (Isa. 14:13–14). Solomon writes, "I *thought* in my heart, 'Come now, I will test you with pleasure to find out what is good' " (Eccl. 2:1; cf. 2:15; 3:17–18).

Verb: חָשַׁב (*ḥāšab*), GK 3108 (S 2803), 124 x. *ḥāšab* is most often translated as "think" or "plan" (see *plan*). This word is used in reference to mathematical computations and can also be translated as "count," "calculate," and "value." It is interesting to note that *ḥāšab* is the only Hebrew verb that refers to mathematical computations beyond mere counting. Scholars agree that this mathematical sense is related to its usage with reference to thinking. That is, when *ḥāšab* is used to refer to mental processes, some element of valuation, intentionality, and calculation is present.

Noun: לֵב (*lēb*), GK 4213 (S 3820), 854x. *lēb*, often translated "heart" or "mind," denotes the seat of emotion (1 Sam. 2:1), desire (Ps. 37:4), thought (Gen. 6:5), and decision (1 Chr. 12:38). The idiom "to say in his *lēb*" is sometimes translated "to think" (Ps. 35:25; Zeph. 1:12). See *heart*.

New Testament

Verb: δοκέω (*dokeō*), GK *1506* (S *1380*), 62x. *dokeō* means "to think, believe, suppose." In some cases, this verb simply denotes human thoughts or opinions (e.g., Lk. 1:3; Acts 25:27; 27:13). Jesus on various occasions asks people for their thoughts, often as he introduces a teaching such as a parable (e.g., Mt. 17:25; 18:12; 21:28; 22:17; Lk. 10:36). In Acts 15:22, 25, 28, *dokeō* is used for what "seemed" good to those gathered in Jerusalem as they discussed the difficult issue of the relationship between circumcision and salvation.

But *dokeō* can also have a decidedly negative tone. It can refer to a false assumption (Mt. 6:7; 1 Cor. 3:18); Phil. 3:4) or a false belief (Jn. 5:45). The Jews are warned against thinking (falsely) that salvation comes from physical lineage: "Do not *think* you can say to yourselves, 'We have Abraham as our father'" (Mt. 3:9). In Gal. 2:2, 6, 9, *dokeō* describes human opinion regarding the status of various persons as apostles; in 1 Cor. 8:2 it denotes a lack of knowledge or a false belief or assumption.

This latter sense is apparent in the ancient heresy of Docetism, whose name is drawn from the root of *dokeō*. According to Docetism, Jesus, the Son of God, only appeared to be flesh, but was in actuality a spiritual being. The Scripture are clear, however, that Jesus was a flesh-and-blood being (Jn. 1:14; 1 Jn. 4:2–3); John's writings seem to have been written in the context of the beginnings of this heresy. See *NIDNTT-A*, 149.

Verb: ἡγέομαι (*hēgeomai*), GK *2451* (S *2233*), 28x. *hēgeomai* means "to consider, think, regard." See *consider*.

Verb: λογίζομαι (*logizomai*), GK *3357* (S *3049*), 40x. The basic meaning of *logizomai* has to do with counting or thinking (see also *consider, regard as*). It is also used for crediting something for or against someone (see *credit*). Paul says that when he was a child, he "thought" like a child (1 Cor. 13:11). Believers are to "think" about certain heavenly things (Phil. 4:8). No one should "think" better of himself than is warranted by his words and actions (2 Cor. 12:6). The Roman Christians are not to "think" they will escape God's judgment if they do what they judge others for (Rom. 2:3). Paul does not "think" that any of his adequacy comes from himself; rather it is only from God (2 Cor. 3:5). See *NIDNTT-A*, 338-39.

Verb: νομίζω (*nomizō*), GK *3787* (S *3543*), 15x. *nomizō* means "to think, suppose," and it is used in various situations. For example, in Mt. 5:17, Jesus says, "Do not think I have come to abolish the Law and the Prophets," and in 10:34 he says, "Do not think I have come to bring peace on the earth." Peter chides Simon Magus because "you thought you could buy the gift of God with money" (Acts 8:20). The Philippian jailor was ready to kill himself because "he thought the prisoners had escaped" after an earthquake (16:27). Paul twice presents his thinking on a particular subject in 1 Cor. 7:26, 36, and in 1 Tim. 6:5 he rejects those "who think that godliness is a means to financial gain."

Verb: φρονέω (*phroneō*), GK *5858* (S *5426*), 26x. *phroneō* means "to think, set one's mind on something, have in mind." Paul exhorts his readers to set their minds on things above (Rom. 8:5; Col. 3:2), and notes that setting one's mind on the sinful nature is sin itself (Rom. 8:7). This appears to have been Peter's problem when he confronted Jesus regarding his prophecy of the crucifixion—Peter's mind was not set on the things of God but on the things of man (Mk. 8:33).

Many NT exhortations refer to the way we think, sometimes in a positive framework (Rom. 12:16; 15:5; 2 Cor. 13:11; Gal. 5:10; Phil. 2:2, 5), sometimes in a warning or negative framework (Rom. 8:5; 12:3; Phil. 3:19). In Rom. 15:5, Paul exhorts his readers to "think the same thing" (i.e., manifest "a spirit of unity"). In Phil. 4:2, Paul pleads with Eudoia and Syntyche to "think the same thing in the Lord" (NIV: "*agree with each other* in the Lord"). The inclusion of the words "in the Lord" here most likely refers to the work of the Holy Spirit in unifying the thoughts of believers. Unity and harmony are required of believers—recall that Jesus said that the world will know his disciples by their love for one another (cf. Jn. 13:35), and this is made possible by the renewing work of the Holy Spirit (cf. Rom. 12:2). See *NIDNTT-A*, 593-94.

THIRD

Old Testament

Adjective: שְׁלִישִׁי (*šᵉlîšî*), GK 8958 (S 7992), 71x. *šᵉlîšî* means "third" and is closely related to *šālōš* (GK 8993), which means "three." See *three*.

New Testament

Adjective: τρίτος (*tritos*), GK *5568, 5569* (S *5154*), 56x. *tritos* is the ordinal number "third." Some of its uses simply refer to the third in a series of events (Mt. 22:26; Mk. 12:21; Lk. 12:38; 20:12, 31; Jn. 2:1; Acts 27:19; 1 Cor. 12:28). A related use is the reference to the "third hour" (Mt. 20:3; Mk. 15:25), which the NIV sometimes translates as "nine in the morning" (Acts 2:15) or "nine tonight" (Acts 23:23). *tritos* can also denote the third time an action takes place. In these instances, the third time is also the final time, thus indicating completeness (Mt. 26:44; Mk. 14:41; Lk. 23:22; Jn. 21:14, 17; 2 Cor. 12:14; 13:1). Thirteen occurrences of *tritos* either directly or indirectly refer to the "third day" on which Christ rose again

(Mt. 16:21; 17:23; 20:19; 27:64; Lk. 9:22; 13:32; 18:32; 24:7, 21, 46; Acts 10:40; 1 Cor. 15:4).

Close to half of the NT uses of *tritos* are in Revelation (23x). Most of these express the fraction "one-third" (12x in Rev. 8:7–12; also 9:15, 18; 12:4), while the rest indicate the third item of a series (Rev. 4:7; 6:5; 8:10; 11:14; 14:9; 16:4; 21:19).

Paul refers to the "third heaven" in 2 Cor. 12:2. The meaning of this phrase is debated, but it is probably to be understood as the highest level of heaven, either literally as the zenith of a tripartite division, or metaphorically as the ultimate or fullest expression of paradise. See *NIDNTT-A*, 565.

THIRST

New Testament

Verb: διψάω (*dipsaō*), GK *1498* (S *1372*), 16x. *dipsaō* means "to thirst, be thirsty." Thirst is something that ceases to exist in the eternal heavens (Rev. 7:16), something that provides a present opportunity for Christian service (Mt. 25:37, 42, 44; Rom. 12:20), and a one-word fulfillment of prophecy by Jesus on the cross (Jn. 19:28).

The most familiar and treasured uses of *dipsaō* have more to do with spiritual longing than physical needs. Jesus says, "Blessed are those who hunger and *thirst* for righteousness, for they will be filled" (Mt. 5:6, NIV). As a paraphrase, we might translate, "Blessed are those who thirst for righteous lives just as they do for water [i.e., continually], for God will grant their desire."

Not only does Jesus promise blessedness for thirsting after righteousness, but he tells people exactly where to go to quench their spiritual thirst for eternal life (Jn. 4:13–15; 6:35; 7:37). Unlike perpetual physical thirst, the drink of eternal life quenches one's thirst for eternal life. This thirsting is genuinely quenched here and now by the present gift of eternal life, while the offer stands even unto the end of the age (see Rev. 21:6; 22:17). See *NIDNTT-A*, 448-49.

THIRTY

Old Testament

Noun: שָׁלֹשׁ (*šālōš*), GK 8993 (S 7969), 606x. *šālōš* means "three" in the singular and "thirty" in the plural. See *three*.

New Testament

Adjective: τριάκοντα (*triakonta*), GK *5558* (S *5144*), 11x. *triakonta* means "thirty." Most uses of this adjective are in the parable of the sower, where the good seed produces "thirty, sixty, or even a hundred times" (Mk. 4:8, 20; cf. Mt. 13:8, 23), and in the story of the betrayal of Jesus, where Judas agrees to betray Jesus for "thirty silver coins" (Mt. 26:15; 27:3, 9). Luke notes that when Jesus begins his ministry, he is about "thirty years old" (Lk. 3:23).

THORN

New Testament

Noun: ἄκανθα (*akantha*), GK *180* (S *173*), 14x. *akantha* refers to a thorn tree or bush. Jesus uses the word as he discusses identifying marks of false prophets": "Do people pick grapes from *thornbushes*?" (Mt. 7:16). It also occurs in the warning of Heb. 6:8: "But land that produces *thorns* and thistles is worthless." Here thorns are an illustration of those who have been exposed to the gospel of grace, only to forsake it for one of works. The burning of thorns in an otherwise fertile field illustrates the spiritual danger such individuals are in.

The majority of the occurrences of *akantha* occur in the parable of the sower and in the description of the crown Jesus wore at his crucifixion. In the parable, the thorns represent the one who hears the word but lets the worries of this life and the deceitfulness of wealth choke it (Mk. 4:18–19). As to the crown of *akantha* Jesus was forced to wear, not only was it an instrument of mockery and torture but it also becomes a powerful illustration. Gal. 3:13 tells us that "Christ redeemed us from the curse of the law by becoming a curse for us." In Gen. 3:18 God cursed the ground, telling Adam that it would grow thorns and thistles, making his work more difficult. The fact that Christ wore a crown of *akantha* is an act of God's judgment in which Jesus was subjected to the curse that should have been ours. See *NIDNTT-A*, 27-28.

THOUGHT

Old Testament

Noun: מַחֲשָׁבָה (*maḥ*[a]*šāḇâ*), GK 4742 (S 4284), 56x. This noun is best translated "plans" or "thoughts" and can describe the plans of either individuals or God. See *plan*.

New Testament

Noun: διαλογισμός (*dialogismos*), GK *1369* (S *1261*), 14x. *dialogismos* can refer to a discussion or personal thoughts, or even an argument between two parties.

Noun: διάνοια (*dianoia*), GK *1379* (S *1271*), 12x. *dianoia* denotes the "mind, thought, understanding." See *mind*.

THOUSAND

Old Testament

Noun: אֶלֶף (*ʾelep*), GK 547 (S 505), 496x. *ʾelep* means "thousand." This number can be used in exact numbers (e.g., Exod. 38:25, 26) or in round numbers (e.g., Jdg. 3:29). Obviously, in census lists, this word appears frequently (e.g., Num. 1–2; 26). *ʾelep* can also be applied to money, animals, measures of food, sacrifices, days, proverbs, songs, etc. (cf., e.g., 1 Ki. 4:26, 32).

In some cases, *ʾelep* is used in an hyperbole. When the Israelite women sang, "Saul has slain his *thousands*, and David his tens of *thousands*" (1 Sam. 18:7), the purpose of this song is comparison, not numerical quotient. The psalmist is not speaking in literal language when he writes that in the eternal God's method of keeping time, "a *thousand* years in your sight are like a day" (Ps. 90:4); rather, he is stressing that God is not bound by human time. The fact that God remembers his covenant love "for a *thousand* generations" (Ps. 105:8; cf. Exod. 20:5–6) emphasizes his enduring faithfulness.

No hypothesis has received consensus on the huge numbers of the Israelite nation in the desert after the Exodus. Some consider that since the word *ʾelep* can also mean a "clan" or "unit," we should understand the number in Num. 26:41, for example, to read "45 units, that is, 600 men," rather than 45,600 men. But not all of these numbers will work this way. In any case, the numbers themselves are not the important factor; what is important is that God has been faithful to his promises to Abraham in making this vast nation. See *NIDOTTE*, 1:416–18.

New Testament

Adjective: χιλιάς (*chilias*), GK *5942* (S *5505*), 23x. *chilias* is the cardinal number "one thousand." It is used interchangeably with *chilioi* in the NT, although *chilias* is more than twice as common. *chilias* predominates (19x) in the book of Revelation. Of these occurrences, fifteen describe the 144,000 (twelve groups of 12,000) from the tribes of Israel (Rev. 7:4–8; 14:1, 3). Whenever *chilias* is used in the NT, whether literally or figuratively, it represents a large amount of something.

A thousand is often used as a round number, an estimate, or a symbolic number. All NT uses appear in combination with other numerical terms, to give a multiple of one thousand or a number in which one thousand is part of the total, such as five thousand (Acts 4:4), seven thousand (Rev. 11:13), ten thousand (Lk. 14:31), twelve thousand (Rev. 21:16), twenty thousand (Lk. 14:31), 23,000 (1 Cor. 10:8), and thousands upon thousands (Rev. 5:11). See *NIDNTT-A*, 606-7.*

Adjective: χίλιοι (*chilioi*), GK *5943* (S *5507*), 11x. *chilioi* is the cardinal number "one thousand." It is used interchangeably with *chilias* in the NT, although the latter is more than twice as common. Except for two uses in 2 Pet. 3:8 ("With the Lord a day is like a *thousand* years, and a *thousand* years are like a day"), *chilioi* only appears in Revelation. Six of its uses there describe the thousand-year reign of Christ (Rev. 20:2, 3, 4, 5, 6, 7), otherwise known as the millennium; two occurrences refer to the 1,260 days (11:3; 12:6); and one refers to the distance that blood flows out of a winepress, namely, 1,600 stadia (14:20 [KJV: "furlongs"]). See *NIDNTT-A*, 606-7.*

THREE

Old Testament

Noun: שָׁלֹשׁ (*šālōš*), GK 8993 (S 7969), 606x. *šālōš* means "three" in the singular and "thirty" in the plural.

Adjective: שְׁלִישִׁי (*šᵉlîšî*), GK 8958 (S 7992), 71x. *šᵉlîšî* means "third." *šālōš* can combine with other numbers: e.g., with *ʾelep* ("thousand," GK 547), it means "three thousand"; with the number ten, it means "thirteen."

(1) Along with four and seven, "three" is a "biblical number." That is, it often represents more than simply three items. It is a number of completeness. From the "*three* sons" of Noah, the entire earth is repopulated (Gen. 6:10; 10). When Elijah soaks his offering with water before calling on the name of the Lord, he has four large jars of water filled "three" times (note that four times three equals twelve; 1 Ki. 18:34–35). "*Three* days" without water is about the limit of human endurance (Exod. 15:22; cf. also Est. 4:16). When David has to choose between three punishments from the Lord for his numbering of the people of Israel, he is given "*three* options": he must choose between "*three* years of famine in your land ... or *three* months of fleeing from your enemies ... or *three* days of plague in your land" (2 Sam. 24:12–13).

(2) Three is also a significant number in the civil and ceremonial aspects of the nation of Israel. The tabernacle and temple are both built with three sections: the court, the Holy Place, and the Most Holy Place (Exod. 25–27; 1 Ki. 6). "*Three* times a year all your men must appear before the Lord at the place he will choose" (Deut. 16:16; cf. Exod. 23:14); these are the Feast of Unleavened Bread, the Feast of Weeks, and the Feast of Tabernacles. There is a special tithe that is to be presented "at the end of every *three* years" (Deut. 14:28). The cities of refuge are six in number, three on each side of the Jordan River (19:1–9). In order for a legal conviction to take place, it must be "established by the testimony of two or *three* witnesses" (19:15).

(3) Three can also be a significant number without the actual number being used. For example, the Aaronic blessing has three elements, with the divine name "Yahweh" ("Lord") mentioned in each one (Num. 6:24–26). The seraphs in Isa. 6:1–3 have three sets of two wings, and they call out to each other: "Holy, holy, holy is the Lord Almighty." The universe is structured into three parts: "heaven above ... the earth beneath ... the waters below" (Exod. 20:4; cf. Ps. 96:11; Amos 9:6). Phrases are sometimes repeated three times, in either identical words (e.g., Jer. 7:4) or similar words (e.g., Deut. 6:5; Mic. 6:8).

(4) Thirty is a significant age, especially for those involved in priestly service (Num. 4:23). Both Joseph (Gen. 41:46) and David (2 Sam. 5:4) undertake their most important work at age thirty (as does Jesus; Lk. 3:23). The price of a slave is "thirty shekels" of silver (Exod. 21:32; cf. Zech. 11:12–13; also Mt. 26:15). A typical period of mourning is thirty days (for Moses, Deut. 34:8; for Jacob, however, it was seventy days, Gen. 50:3).

New Testament

Adjective: τρεῖς (*treis*), GK *5552* (S *5140*), 69x. *treis* is the cardinal number "three." It is used to enumerate a variety of items, like three shelters (Mk. 9:5), three loaves of bread (Lk. 11:5), or three gates (Rev. 21:13). Fourteen of the NT occurrences of *treis* refer to the three days between Jesus' crucifixion and resurrection (e.g., Mt. 12:40; 26:61; Mk. 8:31). Aside from these resurrection references, when *treis* specifies a unit of time, like three hours (Acts 5:7), three days (Acts 9:9; 25:1; 28:12; Rev. 11:9, 11), or three months (Lk. 1:56; Acts 7:20; 19:8), the emphasis is that it is a relatively short time period. References to three years (Lk. 4:25; 13:7; Gal. 1:18; Jas. 5:17), however, indicate a relatively long amount of time.

treis can also indicate fullness. An

example of this is found in the teaching that an accusation against a person must be made by "two or *three* witnesses" (Mt. 18:16; 2 Cor. 13:1; 1 Tim. 5:19; Heb. 10:28). The testimony of one is not sufficient; whereas two is enough, three is more than enough as it complies with OT law.

Since many items and events naturally fall into groups of three, there is no reason to read most of the NT uses of *treis* symbolically or with any particular religious import. Occasionally, this word is not translated literally in English. For example, the NIV of Mt. 13:33 translates "a large amount" rather than the exact measurement ("three measures" [KJV] or "three pecks" [NASB]). Similarly, most of the contemporary translations of Jn. 2:6 modernize the KJV's literal "two or three firkins (i.e., measures)" to "twenty or thirty gallons."

One may note that there is no reference in this discussion of "three" to the doctrine of the Trinity (i.e., three persons, one God). While the NT is clear that the Father, the Son, and the Holy Spirit form one holy, triune God (cf. Mt. 28:19), it nowhere actually mentions three persons as part of one Godhead. This doctrine developed as Christians in the second and third century began to reflect on the entire message of the Scriptures. See *NIDNTT-A*, 565.

THREE TIMES

New Testament

Adverb: τρίς (*tris*), GK *5565* (S *5151*), 12x. *tris* is an adverb meaning "three times." Most of its occurrences in the NT relate to Jesus' prediction of Peter's threefold denial of Jesus and the actual event (Mt. 26:34, 75; Mk. 14:30, 72; Lk. 22:34, 61; Jn. 13:38). *tris* also appears twice in the account of Peter's vision of the sheet full of unclean animals (Acts 10:16; 11:10). While defending his apostleship before the Corinthian church, Paul uses *tris* three times to describe his suffering as an apostle: he was beaten with rods three times (2 Cor. 11:25), he was shipwrecked three times (11:25), and he pleaded with God three times to remove the thorn in his flesh (12:8). Though translated as "thrice" in the KJV, contemporary translations use "three times." See *NIDNTT-A*, 565.*

THRICE

See *three times*.

THRONE

Old Testament

Noun: כִּסֵּא (*kissēʾ*), GK 4058 (S 3676 and 3678), 135x.

In a few instances, *kissēʾ* means an ordinary chair or seat (e.g., 2 Ki. 4:10), but in the vast majority of occurrences, this word should be translated "throne." In the ancient world, the throne was an important symbol of superiority and honor, especially for kings. As can be expected, the OT use of *kissēʾ* becomes much more common and important during and after David's reign. Hence, most instances of *kissēʾ* are found in books such as Kings, Chronicles, and Psalms. Often *kissēʾ* is expanded to "royal throne" or "throne of David" (1 Ki. 1:13; 1 Chr. 17:12; 2 Chr. 23:20).

In prophetic literature, the prophets often use *kissēʾ* to refer to the covenant God made with David, both looking back at what was and looking forward in hope for God's restoration of the kingdom in the future (Isa. 9:7; 16:5; Jer. 14:21; 33:17). God is the one who establishes and overthrows "thrones," that is, kingdoms or dynasties (2 Sam. 3:10; 1 Ki. 9:5; Dan. 5:20; Hag. 2:22). According to God's design, the Israelite kings are to uphold God's laws and adjudicate fairly, with the result that their thrones will be a place of justice (Prov. 16:12; 20:8; 29:14).

One of the most important uses of *kissēʾ* refers to God's throne. Several prophets see visions of God sitting on his *kissēʾ* in heaven (1 Ki. 22:19; Isa. 6:1; Ezek. 1:26). God's throne is established on righteousness and justice (Ps. 89:14; 97:2) and will endure for all eternity (Ps. 45:6; Lam. 5:19). These images of God's kingly rule over all the world (see *king*) give hope to the believer (OT and NT) that despite present injustice, suffering, and hardship,

God's perfect kingdom in heaven will eventually spread over all the earth. This understanding of divine rule helps clarify the hope and conflict that arises when Jesus begins preaching that God's kingdom is coming through him! See *NIDOTTE*, 2:672-74.

New Testament

Noun: βῆμα (*bēma*), GK *1037* (S *968*), 12x. *bēma* typically signifies a "judgment seat," that is, an official's place or seat of authority from which he exercises judgment. A contemporary eqivalent is a courtroom setting. On one occasion is denotes a "throne." See *court*.

Noun: θρόνος (*thronos*), GK *2585* (S *2362*), 62x. *thronos* in the NT depends heavily on the OT concept of royal authority. The Heb. *kissē*ʾ, translated in the LXX as *thronos*, communicated the absolute power and authority of kings of the ancient world. According to the OT, the greatest such king is God himself (see *king*), who rules over the entire world from his heavenly *thronos*.

In the NT, *thronos* is used the same way, though with some additional development because of the revelation of God in Jesus Christ. God's throne is said to be in heaven (Mt. 5:34; 23:22), and both Peter and Stephen speak of David and Solomon's thrones (Acts 2:30; 7:49). But most importantly, the NT closely identifies Jesus with God by speaking of Jesus' glorious heavenly throne (Mt. 25:31; Lk. 1:32; Heb. 1:8; 8:1; 12:2; Rev. 22:1, 3). Amazingly, Jesus also promises that his disciples will share in his reign and sit on the twelve thrones of Israel (Mt. 19:28; Lk. 22:30).

Most instances of *thronos* occur in Revelation (47x), especially in chs. 4-5. The picture there is based on Ezekiel and, like the OT, emphasizes God's rule and majesty. As in the other parts of the NT, the glory and throne of God are also Christ's.

The NT (and Revelation in particular) gives the believer great hope because of the reality of God's universal kingdom: his throne is both just and everlasting. But there is an added dimension that also communicates God's tender love toward his own. His throne is also "a throne of grace" (Heb. 4:16), and therefore we can draw near to God "with confidence" that he will meet our needs. See *NIDNTT-A*, 252-53.

THROW

Old Testament

Verb: שָׁלַךְ (*šālak*), GK 8959 (S 7993), 125x. *šālak* generally means "to throw (something)." It used of a wide variety of physical objects (Gen. 21:15; Exod. 1:22; 2 Sam. 11:21; Neh. 13:8; Isa. 2:20; 19:8; Joel 1:7).

(1) A couple of specific instances deserve note. (a) It frequently describes the throwing of a body (e.g., Jos. 8:29; 1 Ki. 13:24–25; Ezek. 16:5; Amos 8:3). In most all cases this is viewed negatively. To have one's corpse exposed for any length of time was considered to be evidence of divine curse (Deut. 21:23). (b) When Elijah throws his cloak around Elisha, there is an implicit call to discipleship (1 Ki. 19:19).

(2) Immaterial objects can also be thrown: for instance, one's soul (a figure of speech for risking one's life, Jdg. 9:17), the schemes of the wicked (Job 18:7), sin (Ezek. 18:3), truth (Dan. 8:12), and iniquity (Mic. 7:19).

(3) God is often either the subject or object of *šālak*. (a) God throws hail (Jos. 10:11; 18:10; Ps. 147:17).

(b) In judgment, God throws Judah and Jerusalem from his presence (2 Ki. 13:23; 24:20). Similarly, he throws the temple (2 Chr. 7:20) and the wicked king Jehoiachin (Jer. 22:28) from his presence. He also throws people aside in his wrath (Ps. 102:11). These judgments are the ultimate punishment for Israel's unfaithfulness to the covenant (cf. Deut. 27-29). The phrase "*thrust* them from his presence" literally means, "he threw them from his face" (see *face*). To be removed from God's face is to be removed from his presence and blessing. Perhaps it is in this light that David prays that he will not be cast from God's presence (Ps. 51:11). The awfulness of this judgment makes us remember the fact that

God hid his face from Jesus during the crucifixion. During those awful hours Jesus, too, was removed from the presence and blessing of God, as he suffered for us.

(c) God also throws aside the wicked nations and their kings—such as the Canaanites from the land (Deut. 29:27), Pharaoh's army into the sea (Neh. 9:11), and the king of Tyre to the earth (Ezek. 28:17; some scholars see this verse as a typological reference to Satan as well).

(4) An interesting use of *šālak* is found in the expression "to throw (something) behind one's back." This almost always signifies contempt. God complains that his people have thrown him behind their backs (1 Ki. 14:9; see also Ezek. 23:35). The wicked also show contempt for God's law by their actions (Neh. 9:26; see also Ps. 50:17). Interestingly, God throws our sin behind his back, showing his contempt for what we have done as he forgives us (Isa. 38:17). The fact that God no longer regards the sin of the believer should be a source of great spiritual comfort. For further reading, see *NIDOTTE*, 4:127–28.

New Testament

Verb: βάλλω (*ballō*), GK *965* (S *906*), 122x. The basic meaning of *ballō* is "to throw" something, but it also carries the idea of allowing something to lie as it falls. Randomness is often implied. It can also mean to lie (Mt. 8:6), be placed (Mk. 7:33), or with liquids, to pour (Mt. 9:17). Jesus uses *ballō* for the idea of "bringing" peace (Mt. 10:34), "scattering" or "planting" seed (Mk. 4:26; Lk. 13:19), and "fertilizing" a vineyard (Lk. 13:8). *ballō* also means to cast lots (Mk. 15:24), to drive out (1 Jn. 4:18, "Perfect love *drives out* fear"), to entice (Rev. 2:14), and to drop (6:13), to hurl (8:5), to fling (12:4), to spew (12:15), and to swing (14:16). While not all of these actions require the use of the hand, many of them do.

THRUST

Old Testament

Verb: תָּקַע (*tāqaʿ*), GK 9546 (S 8628), 70x. *tāqaʿ* is used to describe such actions as blowing, thrusting, or clapping (see also *blow*, *clap*). Ehud *tāqaʿ* (NIV, "plunged") his sword into the belly of Eglon, king of Moab (Jdg. 3:21). This term is also used when Jael picked up a tent peg and a hammer and "drove" (NIV) it through Sisera's temple into the ground (Jdg. 4:21; cf. Gen. 31:25; Jer. 6:3).

THUNDER

New Testament

Noun: βροντή (*brontē*), GK *1103* (S *1027*), 12x. *brontē* means "thunder," though in the NT this rarely refers simply to the meteorological phenomenon. Note that there is no word in either Heb. or Gk. for "weather."

In the OT thunder is closely associated with the voice of God (cf. God's appearance on Mount Sinai in Exod. 19). In Jn. 12:29 a voice coming from heaven is interpreted by the bystanders as either thunder or the voice of an angel. Similarly, in Revelation peals of thunder are often connected with a heavenly voice (Rev. 6:1; 10:3; 10:4; 14:2; 19:6). The other occurrences of *brontē* in Revelation tie together thunder and lightning (4:5; 8:5; 11:19; 16:18) and often earthquakes as well. Together these images communicate great power and inspire awe. Flashes of lightning and peals of thunder accompany the pouring out of God's wrath and the opening of his temple. For ancient and agrarian societies, whose houses and lives were much more exposed to the elements, the reality of thunder, lightning, and earthquakes carried much more weight than they often do for us today.

The only other use of *brontē* in the NT is when Mark explains the nickname given to James and John: "Boanerges . . . Sons of Thunder" (Mk. 3:17). It is not clear why they receive this label, though at least on one occasion they ask if God should pour out fire from heaven on Jesus' opponents (Lk. 9:54). See *NIDNTT-A*, 78-79.

TIE, TIE UP

Old Testament

Verb: אָסַר (*ʾāsar*), GK 673 (S 631), 73x. The most basic meaning of *ʾāsar* is "to bind, tie up." Animals may be tied to something for a particular function. Horses and donkeys may be "tethered" to keep them in place (2 Ki. 7:10). See *bind*.

New Testament

Verb: δέω (*deō*), GK *1313* (S *1210*), 43x. *deō* means to "tie up, bind" someone or something. It is used in a variety of contexts—animals, people, prisoners, and even angels. It can also have spiritual implications. See *bind*.

TIMBER

Old Testament

Noun: עֵץ (*ʿēṣ*), GK 6770 (S 6086), 330x. *ʿēṣ* is the basic word for tree and wood products. It can be translated as "tree, wood, timber." See *tree*.

TIME

Old Testament

Noun: עֵת (*ʿēt*), GK 6961 (S 6256), 296x. *ʿēt* is one of several words in the OT that express time. Others are *zᵉmān* (a near synonym of *ʿēt*), *yôm* ("day," which divides time into regular units), *môʿēd* (of time that is appointed or scheduled), and *paʿam* (which denotes short spaces, or beats, of time).

The ancient Hebrews conceived of time in two ways. Primarily, time was considered an endless cycle of regularly recurring events. This perspective was based on the observation of natural cycles, such as day and night, but also on the sacred calendar of weekly Sabbaths, yearly festivals, sabbatical years, and Jubilees. Within this ongoing cycle of life occur events of unique significance. Individuals have various life spans, and the events of birth, marriage, and death present a more linear sequence of time within the larger cycle. Most significant, however, is the view that God is the Creator and, therefore, the owner of time. The appointed times of the weekly Sabbath, festivals, and Sabbath years, reinforce this concept. Time belongs to him. The Sabbaths are to time what tithes are to possessions.

In the OT, time is primarily viewed in connection with specific events, and *ʿēt* is the common way to express when an event occurs. Thus, we read that the dove returns to the ark (lit.) "at the *time* of evening" (Gen. 8:11), and Jonathan promises to ascertain his father's opinion of David "by this *time* the day after tomorrow" (1 Sam. 20:12). *ʿēt* can also designate events that occur in a general framework of time. Spring is the season or "*time* when kings go out to war" (2 Sam. 11:1) and migratory birds "observe the *time* of their migration" (Jer. 8:7).

ʿēt may also designate general periods of time characterized by a common element. In "*times* of trouble," the Lord is a refuge and a strong tower (Ps. 9:9). He knows the days of those who are blameless, so that they do not wither "in *times* of disaster" (Ps. 37:19). Yet because of Israel's rebellion and obstinate disobedience, God's judgment will come, and the "*time* of trouble for Jacob" (Jer. 30:7) will bring distress as never before.

A common phrase expressing the relationship between time and event is "at that time" (75x). Historical narrative often uses this construction: "Deborah, a prophetess, the wife of Lappidoth, was leading Israel *at that time*" (Jdg. 4:4). This same phrase is used of future events in prophecy. Jeremiah foresees God's blessing on his chosen nation (Jer. 31:1), and Daniel prophecies a time when Michael will arise to deliver Israel from her oppressors (Dan. 12:1). Such prophetic notices remind us that history and the events of our world are ordered by the Almighty. Anything can be "beautiful in its *time*" (3:11), when viewed and accepted within the scope of God's all-encompassing greatness. The relationship between faith and time is nicely expressed by the psalmist: "My *times* are in your hands" (Ps. 31:15). See *NIDOTTE*, 3:563-67.

Noun: פַּעַם (*paʿam*), GK 7193 (S 6471), 118x. The sense of "time" conveyed by *paʿam* is no doubt related to its root, meaning the "foot" or the "sole of the foot." Like the sound of footsteps or the beating of the foot to keep time, *paʿam* usually connotes time as a succession of repeated events.

The first use of *paʿam* in the OT is Gen. 2:23, "The man said, 'This is *now* [lit., this time] bone of my bones and flesh of my flesh.'" The use of *paʿam* here stresses the fact that Adam had named the animals, but found no companion. This time, God's handiwork corresponded to him. In Gen. 18:32, Abraham, aware that his previous requests has pushed the limit, says: "May the Lord not be angry, but let me speak *just once more*."

paʿam can be used with numbers to indicate successive events, such as "three times" (Exod. 23:17) or "seven times" (Lev. 4:6). When *paʿam* is found in the dual form (used in Hebrew to denote things that occur in pairs), it means "twice" (see Gen. 43:10, cf. 27:36; 41:32; Num. 20:11; 1 Sam. 18:11; 1 Ki. 11:9; Nah. 1:9; Job 33:29; Eccl. 6:6). The idiom "like time in time" refers to customary events or things that have usually happened before. After Samson's hair was cut, he awoke and thought, "I'll go out *as before* and shake myself free" (Jdg. 16:20; cf. 20:30–31; 1 Sam. 3:10; 20:25).

In its meaning as "foot," *paʿam* refers to "hoof beats" (Jdg. 5:28), an "anvil" (from the idea of beating, Isa. 41:7), and the feet of the ark (Exod. 25:12; 37:3; 1 Ki. 8:30). *paʿam* can also refer to one's own feet, for the psalmist confesses, "My steps have held to your paths; my *feet* [footsteps, KJV] have not slipped" (Ps. 17:5, cf. 119:133). Feet represent vulnerability, since people are tripped up by their feet. Thus, the enemy lies in wait to snare the feet (Ps. 57:6; 140:4). Proverbs teaches us that "whoever flatters his neighbor is spreading a net for his *feet*" (Prov. 29:5). See *NIDOTTE*, 3:650-51.

New Testament

Noun: αἰών (*aiōn*), GK *172* (S *165*), 122x. *aiōn* can indicate "prolonged time, eternity, an age, a time of the world." See *age*.

Noun: καιρός (*kairos*), GK *2789* (S *2540*), 85x. *kairos*, like *chronos*, can be used as a temporal indicator, whether designating a specific point in time ("at that *time*," Mt. 11:25; 12:1; 13:30; 14:1), the present ("in the present *age*," Mk. 10:30; Lk. 18:30; Rom. 3:26; 8:18; 11:5; 2 Cor. 8:14), or a general period of time, such as a season ("it was not the *season* for figs," Mk. 11:13). But unlike *chronos*, which is more focused on chronological time, *kairos* is time as significant events. This term frequently designates events in salvation history, such as the "time" of the birth of Moses, who led the Exodus from Egypt (Acts 7:20), as well as "the appointed time" for Christ to lead the second "exodus" (Mt. 26:18; cf. Mk. 1:15; Lk. 19:44; Jn. 7:6, 8; Rom. 5:6; Eph. 1:10). Thus, Peter states that the coming of Jesus marked "the time" of which the prophets inquired and predicted (1 Pet. 1:10–12). Furthermore, *kairos* is used to designate the second coming of Christ (1 Tim. 6:15), including the end judgment ("the *time* is near," Rev. 1:3; 11:18; 22:10; cf. Mt. 8:29; Mk. 13:33; 1 Cor. 4:5).

Although the new creation has already been inaugurated through the life of Christ, we are, for "the present," experiencing the sufferings of this day and age (Rom. 8:18). Because we have not yet fully realized the certain hope of our salvation but are still living in these latter, terrible "times" (1 Tim. 4:1; 2 Tim. 3:1), we are experiencing a tension between the "already" (our victory in Christ) and the "not yet" (the final overpowering of Satan). This is why Scriptures instruct us to make the most of every "opportunity" in these present evil days (Eph. 5:16; Col. 4:5). As we do so, we must inform people that "now is the *time* of God's favor, now is the day of salvation" (2 Cor. 6:2). See *NIDNTT-A*, 282-83.

Noun: χρόνος (*chronos*), GK *5989* (S *5550*), 54x. *chronos* usually denotes "time" in the sense of chronological time. It can refer either to a definite period of time ("a forty-year time period" in Acts 13:18; cf. 7:23) or to an indefinite period. In the latter sense the word forms certain idiomatic phrases such as "a long time" (Mt. 25:19; Lk. 8:27; Jn. 5:6; 14:9; Acts 14:28; 18:20; Heb. 4:7); "a short time" (Jn. 7:33; 12:35; Rev. 6:11; 20:3); "as long as" (Mk. 2:19; Rom. 7:1; 1 Cor. 7:38; Gal. 4:1); and "lifetime" (1 Pet. 4:2). Sometimes it even denotes an "opportunity," as in Rev. 2:21: "I gave her time to repent" (see also *kairos* "time" here)

Finally, *chronos* can refer more narrowly to a specific event, albeit sometimes a repeated event ("The unclean spirit had seized him many times," Lk. 8:29). This final usage is most often used in the context of salvation history to refer to the time in which God redeemed his people through Christ. Thus, King Herod was desperate to learn from the wise men "the exact *time*" the star had appeared announcing the birth of Jesus, the true King of Israel (Mt. 2:7, 16). Paul refers to the time of Jesus' coming as the "fullness of the time" (Gal. 4:4 NASB) in order to highlight the fact that God's plan of redemption not only was fulfilled at precisely the right time in history, but also now stands at the climactic focal point of history. Three times the NT uses the phrase (lit.) "in eternity past" (Rom. 16:25; 2 Tim. 1:9; Tit. 1:2), all of which refer to God's eternal plan of salvation that has been revealed in Jesus Christ.

One special use of *chronos* is in Acts 1:7 and 1 Thess. 5:1, where it is used in tandem with its synonym *kairos* ("*times* and dates"), forming an intensive compound basically meaning "the end times" (probably finding its roots in OT passages such as Dan. 2:21; 7:12). Jude 18 similarly refers to the age before Christ's return as "the last *times*" (see also *last*). Thsu, we live "our lives" (lit., our times") between the ages of Christ's first and second comings (1 Pet. 1:17), when we are "strangers in the present world." We must endure hardships and persecutions. On the last day, however, we will experience the fulfillment of salvation through the new creation, which has already been inaugurated through Christ and will in the last day come to fruition (Rom. 8:18–39). See *NIDNTT-A*, 613-15.

Noun: ὥρα (*hōra*), GK *6052* (S *5610*), 106x. *hōra* communicates a period of time. It is normally taken to mean "hour." See *hour*.

TIME TO COME

Old Testament

Noun / Adverb: מָחָר (*māḥār*), GK 4737 (S 4279), 52x. *māḥār* is best rendered "tomorrow" or "time to come." It is used in the phrase in Exod. 13:14, "And it shall be when your son asks you *in time to come,* saying, 'What is this?' " See *tomorrow*.

TITHE

New Testament

Adjective: δέκατος (*dekatos*), GK *1281* (S *1181*, *1182*), 7x. *dekatos* is a "tenth" portion of something, but it is also the word for a "tithe" (see Heb. 7:2, 4, 8, 9). See *tenth*.

TODAY

Old Testament

Noun: יוֹם (*yôm*), GK 3427 (S 3117), 2301x. *yôm* is the most common biblical expression of time in the OT, and it has a variety of nuances. The common construction (350x) of *hāyôm hazzeh* means "this day" or "today." See *day*.

New Testament

Adverb: σήμερον (*sēmeron*), GK *4958* (S *4594*), 41x. This adverb denotes the span of time during a day, from daybreak to evening, and is normally translated "today." The length of time conveyed by the contemporary phrase "sun up to sun down" captures the sense of this term. The term is common in Acts to convey the time of the address of the speaker (Acts 4:9; 20:26; 27:33) and may be used in other contexts to describe the present day (Mt. 16:3; 21:28).

This term is also used theologically to convey the significant present reality of Christ. Heb. 13:8 states "Jesus Christ is the same yesterday and *today* and forever" (cf. Rom. 11:8; 2 Cor. 3:14). He is faithful to his promises, and has been since time immemorial. Moreover, the author of

Hebrews claims the kingship and deity of Christ in the today of his hearers by grounding his claim in the words of Ps. 95:9–11 (cf. Heb. 3:7–11). See *NIDNTT-A*, 282-83.

TOGETHER

Old Testament

Noun: אָחוֹת (*ʾāḥôt*), GK 295 (S 269), 119x. This noun primarily denotes a blood relative and is used for both a sister (Gen. 4:22) and a half-sister (Gen. 20:15) (see *sister*). But the Hebrew also uses *ʾāḥôt* as part of an idiomatic expression to convey the sense of "each other" or "together." See *each other*.

Adverb: יַחְדָּו (*yaḥdāw*), GK 3481 (S 3162), 96x. *yaḥdāw* is related in form to the adv. *yaḥad*, "together, at the same time," and it usually bears the same meaning.

(1) *yaḥdāw* can simply mean "together." This usage denotes two or more people acting together in a variety of ways. For example, it is used of a community exalting God's name together (Ps. 34:3), two men struggling together (Deut. 25:11), and nations consulting together (Isa. 45:21). Though men can act together to add strength and stability (Isa. 41:1; Jer. 3:18), their unity will never be able to thwart the will of God (Jdg. 6:33; Ps. 83:5).

(2) *yaḥdāw* often means "all together" or "all alike." Sometimes it is paired with *kōl*, "all" (Ps. 14:3), and can be used emphatically as when it is placed at the end of a half line in poetic passages (cf. Ps. 35:26; 37:38). This is the case in Isa. 40:5 where "the glory of God will be revealed, and all flesh will see it *together*." See *NIDOTTE*, 2:433-34.

New Testament

Adverb: ὁμοθυμαδόν (*homothymadon*), GK *3924* (S *3661*), 11x. *homothymadon* means "together, unanimous, of one mind." It is made up of *homo* ("same") with *thymos*, ("principle of life, feeling, thought"). Thus, it meant "unanimous," but later it was weakened to mean simply "together."

All but one of its occurrences are found in Acts. In Acts 12:20 it simply indicates that Tyre and Sidon are joined together in their communication with Herod. However, Luke uses *homothymadon* elsewhere to indicate the essential unanimity of the early Christians as opposed to the unanimity of its enemies. The church prays together (1:14; 4:24), fellowships and breaks bread together (2:46; 5:12), and unitedly sends Judas and Silas as messengers (15:25). The crowds of Samaria pay attention to Philip's message with one accord (8:6). Conversely, there is unanimity in the Jewish leaders' stoning of Stephen (7:57), the Jews' attack on Paul (18:12), and the Ephesians' attack on Gaius and Aristarchus (19:29).

The cause of both the early Christians' and their opponents' cohesion is the same: the preaching of Christ as Savior and Lord. While enemies of the gospel are united in an attempt to destroy it, followers of Christ unanimously come together to glorify God. Paul clearly expresses this idea when he wishes for all believers "*with one heart* … [to] glorify the God and Father of our Lord Jesus Christ" (Rom. 15:6). See *NIDNTT-A*, 408-9.*

TOIL

New Testament

Noun: κόπος (*kopos*), GK *3160* (S *2873*), 18x.

Verb: κοπιάω (*kopiaō*), GK *3159* (S *2872*), 23x. In the NT, the *kopos* word group is used in three main ways, all connected with toil and labor. See *labor*.

TOLERATE

New Testament

Verb: ἀνέχομαι (*anechomai*), GK *462* (S *430*), 15x. *anechomai* means "to bear with, endure, tolerate, put up with" something or someone." See *endure*.

TOMB

Old Testament

Noun: קֶבֶר (*qeber*), GK 7700 (S 6913), 67x. Often translated "tomb" or "grave," a *qeber* is a natural cave or a hewn-out cavity used as a burial site. See *grave*.

New Testament

Noun: μνημεῖον (*mnēmeion*), GK *3646* (S *3419*), 40x. *mnēmeion* means "grave, tomb." See *grave*.

TOMORROW

Old Testament

Noun /Adverb: מָחָר (*māḥār*), GK 4737 (S 4279), 52x. *māḥār* is best rendered "tomorrow" or "time to come" and is used extensively in historical, poetic, and prophetic texts with this basic meaning. It occurs frequently in the events leading up to the Exodus (see Exod. 8:10, 23, 29; 9:5, 18; 10:4), where it is used to mark the sequence of events surrounding the plagues. *māḥār* is also used in the phrase in Exod. 13:14, "And it shall be when your son asks you *in time to come,* saying, 'What is this?' " This instructional theme is repeated (see Deut. 6:20; Jos. 4:6, 21; 22:24, 27, 28) in contexts where children are taught to remember the historical events of the Exodus. The meaning is captured in the famous line from the Broadway play *Annie*: "Tomorrow, tomorrow, I love you, tomorrow. You're always a day away!" See *NIDOTTE*, 2:922-23.

New Testament

Adverb: αὔριον (*aurion*), GK *892* (S *839*), 14x. *aurion* can be rendered "tomorrow" or it may simply indicate an indeterminate period of time. Festus assures Agrippa that he will hear Paul's case on "the next day" (Acts 25:22; cf. 4:3, 5; Lk. 10:35; 13:32). Paul states that the resurrection is so vital to the Christian faith that if it were not true, then Christians should adopt the Epicurean philosophy, "Let us eat and drink for *tomorrow* we die" (1 Cor. 15:32).

Jesus uses *aurion* to teach about the emptiness of worry. If God takes care of the grass, which is here today and gone "tomorrow," he will also surely care for his children (Mt. 6:30). Thus Jesus instructs his disciples, "Do not worry about *tomorrow*, for *tomorrow* will worry about itself" (Mt. 6:34; cf. Lk. 13:33). Likewise, Jesus' brother James taught that Christians ought not boast about the future but should rather understand tomorrow in light of God's ultimate will for their lives (Jas. 4:13, 14; cf. Mt. 6:30).*

TONGUE

Old Testament

Noun: לָשׁוֹן (*lāšôn*), GK 4383 (S 3956), 117x.

(1) *lāšôn* literally means "tongue," the physical organ of speech or eating/drinking (Jdg. 7:5; Lam. 4:4). By extension, it can refer to that which proceeds from the mouth, namely, a person's *language* (Gen. 10:5; Deut. 28:49; Est. 1:22) or *speech* (Ps. 55:9 NIV). Sometimes it refers to entities that bear a shape or form similar to the tongue, as in the *wedge* of gold stolen by Achan (Jos. 7:21, 24) or the *bay* or *gulf* of the sea (Jos. 15:5; 18:19; Isa. 11:15).

(2) Over half the occurrences of *lāšôn* (63x) are found in the poetic and wisdom books of Job, Psalms, and Proverbs; such books speak of the wise and foolish in terms of their use of the tongue. In these books, *lāšôn* often stands for one's verbal communication and in the majority of cases connotes harmful or destructive speech. For example, the tongue is characterized as deceitful or false (Ps. 120:2, 3), sharp (like a razor in Ps. 52:4; like a serpent in Ps. 140:4), perverse (Prov. 10:31), sly or backbiting (Prov. 25:23), and smooth (Prov. 6:24). However, the tongue (or speech) of the wise is also described in positive terms, as gentle or soft (Prov. 25:15), wholesome or healing (Prov. 12:18; 15:4), and choice silver (Prov. 10:20). See *NIDOTTE*, 2:820-22.

New Testament

Noun: γλῶσσα (*glōssa*), GK *1185* (S *1100*), 50x. *glōssa* means the physical "tongue," but it can also mean "language."

(1) In Mk. 1:33, 35 Jesus heals a deaf and mute man by placing his fingers in his ears and touching the man's "tongue." The tongue of Zechariah, the father of John the Baptist, was loosed so that he could speak after a period of muteness. Ironically, while the tongue can "practice deceit" and not acknowledge God (Rom. 3:13), eventually

"every *glōssa* will confess to God" (14:11; cf. also Phil. 2:11).

Jas. 3:1–12 is the classic passage in the NT that deals with the importance and difficulty in controlling the tongue. To communicate his point of the potentially destructive power of the tongue in comparison to its relatively small size, James compares the tongue to a bit in a horse's mouth (3:3), a ship's rudder (3:4), and a small spark of fire (3:5). It has the amazing ability to control, constructively or destructively; James goes so far as to say that "no man can tame the tongue" in his or her own strength (3:8; see also 1 Pet. 3:10). John takes it a step further by saying our actions must authenticate what the *glōssa* has proclaimed (1 Jn. 3:18).

(2) *glōssa* also refers to human languages, as in Acts 2:6, "because each one heard them speaking in his own *language*." The book of Revelation uses *glōssa* as a distinctive feature of nations, using "tongue" as a synonym for "tribe, people, and nation" (Rev. 5:9; 7:9; 10:11; 11:9; 13:7; cf. the background to this in Dan. 7:14).

(3) The third major use of *glōssa* in the NT is the whole matter of glossolalia ("speaking in tongues"). *glōssa* can denote here "ecstatic language or ecstatic speech." Paul lists "speaking in different kinds of tongues" and "the interpretation of tongues" as part of his list of representative spiritual gifts in 1 Cor. 12:10, 28, 30. In 1 Cor. 14 we find the classic passage for the unpacking of this spiritual phenomenon. Paul is not speaking of foreign languages as is referred to in Acts 2. He rather is dealing with a special manifestation of the Spirit, which indeed involves the tongue, but what is uttered has no recognizable syntax and apparently is disengaged from the mind. Paul's argues that for this to be a productive, edifying experience for the fellowship, three rules of engagement must prevail: there must not be any more than two or three, they must speak in order, and someone must interpret (14:27). Paul is unmistakably clear as to which gift is most important for the church: "I would rather speak five intelligible words to instruct others than ten thousand words in a tongue" (14:19). Anytime the tongue is used amidst the community of faith, it must be edifying, whether it is a known or an unknown language. See *NIDNTT-A*, 110-11.

TOOTH

Old Testament

Noun: שֵׁן (*šēn*), GK 9094 (S 8127), 55x. *šēn* denotes a "tooth" or (in the plural) the "teeth" of animals and humans. The expression "eye for eye, tooth for tooth" (Exod. 21:24, 27; Lev. 24:20) expresses the fact that punishment must be just and fit the crime committed, not that it should be identical to the crime itself. In Amos 4:6, the judgment of "cleanness of teeth" is an idiom for famine, since not having food results in clean teeth. See also *ivory*. See *NIDOTTE*, 4:190.

New Testament

Noun: ὀδούς (*odous*), GK *3848* (S *3599*), 12x. *odous* means "tooth." Almost all of the uses of this noun in the NT are in two different expressions: "eye for eye, tooth for tooth" (Mt. 5:38, a quote from Exod. 21:24) and "where there will be weeping and gnashing of teeth" (Mt. 8:12; 13:42, 50; 22:13; 24:51; 25:30; Lk. 13:28). Elsewhere in the NT, an epileptic boy "gnashes his teeth" (Mk. 9:18), the crowd at Stephen's sermon "gnash their teeth at him" (Acts 7:54), and the locusts that appeared at the sounding of the fifth trumpet had "teeth … like those of lions" (Rev. 9:8).

TOP

Old Testament

Noun: רֹאשׁ (*rōʾš*), GK 8031 (S 7218), 600x. The primary meaning of *rōʾš* is "head" (see *head*), but it also has a number of metaphorical meanings. For example, *rōʾš* can designate the "top" of a spatial structure. In his dream Jacob sees a vision of the ladder/stairs with its *top* reaching up into heaven (Gen. 28:12). Moses stands at the *top* of the hill while Israel fights the

Amalekites (Exod. 17:9). Balaam speaks of seeing God from the rocky *peaks* (Num. 23:9). In Jer. 22:6, God's word of judgment against the king of Judah is that, though his palace be like the *summit* of Lebanon, it will become desolate and uninhabited if he fails to keep covenant with the Lord.

TORMENT

New Testament

Verb: βασανιζω (*basanizō*), GK *989* (S *928*), 12x. *basanizō* means to "torment" or "torture." In Revelation, this word usually denotes the retributive judgments on impenitent sinners at the close of this age (Rev. 9:5; 11:10; 20:10) as well as the doom that awaits those who worship the beast and his image (14:10). See *torture*.

TORRENT

Old Testament

Noun: נַחַל (*naḥal*), GK 5707 (S 5158), 137x. *naḥal* refers to a dry river bed or wadi. Usually, however, it refers to the raging water that fills a wadi, turning it into a fast flowing river. See *river*.

TORTURE

New Testament

Verb: βασανιζω (*basanizō*), GK *989* (S *928*), 12x. *basanizō* means to "torment" or "torture." This word was originally used to describe the testing of metals, especially gold, and then using torture as a means of trying to extract information from an individual.

In the NT, *basanizō* sometimes means to experience or to cause grievous pain. In Mt. 14:24 it carries the meaning of being tossed or buffeted by the wind as the disciples struggle against the storm. In 8:6 the "terrible suffering" of the centurion's servant is the result of paralysis. In Mk. 5:7 the demon-possessed man calls out to Jesus, "Swear to God that you won't torture me." Rev. 12:2 uses *basanizō* in describing the experience of the mother of Christ as she gave birth.

But *basanizō* can also denote the retributive judgments on impenitent sinners at the close of this age (Rev. 9:5; 11:10) as well as the doom that awaits those who worship the beast and his image (14:10). John also uses this term to describe the horrendous torture in the lake of burning sulphur that awaits Satan and his agents at the end of history (20:10)—a torment that will last "day and night for ever and ever." Such a horrific future for the unbeiever should serve as a catalyst for the Christian to preach the gospel. That torment will be real and the only hope to avoid it is Christ. See *NIDNTT-A*, 87.

TOUCH

Old Testament

Verb: נָגַע (*nāgaʿ*), GK 5595 (S 5060), 150x. The verb *nāgaʿ* means "to touch physically," but its various nuances include "to touch, strike, reach, arrive."

The subject of *nāgaʿ* can be God, people, angels, or things. God's touch melts the land (Amos 9:5) and makes the mountains smoke (Ps. 104:32; 144:5). He touches the mouth of Jeremiah, enabling him to speak God's words (1:9). He touches the hearts of valiant men to cause them to support Saul as king (1 Sam. 10:26). An angel touches Daniel and raises him to his feet (8:18), and another angel makes a coal touch Isaiah's lips (Isa. 6:7). People are commanded not to touch certain things that are either holy to God (Exod. 19:13; Num. 4:15) or unclean (Lev. 15:10–12; Num. 19:16). See also *strike, reach*.

New Testament

Verb: ἅπτω (*haptō*), GK *721* (S 680, *681*), 39x. *haptō* has several uses in the NT. At its most basic level it means "to make close contact with something, touch something." This is clearly seen when a sinful woman lays herself at the feet of Jesus (Lk. 7:38). The Pharisees criticize Jesus for allowing this sinful woman to "touch" him, but Jesus knows her needs and affirms her desire for forgiveness.

haptō can also mean "to cling to, take hold of something." After his resurrection Jesus commands Mary not to "cling to" him, for he had not yet ascended to the Father (Jn. 20:17). Although *haptō* here could mean simply "touch," the context implies a stronger physical action.

haptō can also carry a more active sense. For example, it has the sense of "lighting" a lamp in Lk. 8:16; 11:33; 15:8. It is also used when an action of physical touch is intended to convey a blessing (Mk. 10:13; Lk. 18:15). Similarly, it can designate physical contact with certain things that communicate religious uncleanness (as in Lev. 11:39); some see Paul using this sense of *haptō* in Col. 2:21. *haptō* sometimes has sexual connotations, as in 1 Cor. 7:1(where it perhaps denotes physical intimacy). Finally, its use in 1 Jn. 5:18 suggests physical or spiritual "harm."

The depiction of Jesus "touching" in the Bible reminds us that he was a real person like you and me, a person whom we will one day truly see face to face (Mk. 1:21–34). We will personally meet Jesus, the man with whom all the fullness of God dwelt in bodily form (Col. 1:19; 2:9). See *NIDNTT-A*, 67-68.

TOWARD

Old Testament

Verb: קָרָא (*qārāʾ*), GK 7925 (S 7122), 136x. The primary meaning of *qārāʾ* is "to meet, encounter, happen." The infinitive form of this verb became so common (used 119x) that it also functioned as a preposition meaning "against" or "toward." See *meet*.

TOWN

Old Testament

Noun: עִיר (*ʿîr*), GK 6551 (S 5892), 1087x. *ʿir* refers to any permanent settlement. Normally the size of an ancient city was smaller than what we consider a "city" today. In fact, one scholar has suggested that *ʿîr* be translated "town" in most places except where it refers to extremely large cities such as Nineveh or Babylon. See *city*.

New Testament

Noun: πόλις (*polis*), GK *4484* (S *4172*), 163x. In the NT, *polis* refers mainly to a place of human inhabitation such as a "city, town, village." See *city*.

TRADITION

New Testament

Noun: παράδοσις (*paradosis*), GK *4142* (S *3862*), 13x. *paradosis* is something deliberately given or handed down over an extended period of time; thus, "tradition." The word is a compound of *para* ("beside, near") and *dosis* ("something given").

In the Gospels *paradosis* refers to keeping the traditions of men with the ultimate effect of disobeying the commands of God (Mt. 15:2, 3, 6; Mk. 7:3, 5, 8, 9, 13). Paul writes that before he became a Christian, he was zealous for "the traditions" of his fathers, but Christ set him apart for the preaching of the gospel (Gal. 1:14–15). He also warns against being taken "captive by philosophy and empty deceit, according to human tradition … and not according to Christ" (Col. 2:8).

But traditions are not inevitably bad, for Paul also admonishes believers to maintain the traditions that he has handed down to them in speech and in writing (1 Cor. 11:2; 2 Thess. 2:15; 3:6). These traditions go back to Christ. See *NIDNTT-A*, 435-36.*

TRAIN

Old Testament

Verb: לָמַד (*lāmad*), GK 4340 (S 3925), 87x. *lāmad* is one of the twelve words used in the OT for teaching or instructing. See *teach*. This verb can also signify being trained, as were the sons of Asaph in music (1 Chr. 25:7).

TRAMPLE

Old Testament

Verb: דָּרַךְ (*dārak*), GK 2005 (S 1869), 63x. *dārak* denotes the activity of walking on a path (Deut. 1:36; Jos. 14:9; Hab. 3:19), trampling on a winepress (Neh. 13:15; Isa. 16:10), or bending a bow (Ps. 7:12; Lam. 2:4; Jer. 50:29),

TRANSFIGURE

New Testament

Verb: μεταμορφόω (*metamorphoō*),

GK *3565* (S *3339*), 4x. *metamorphoō* means "to transfigure, transform." Two of its four uses in the NT occur in reference to Jesus' transfiguration, when he was on a high mountain with three of his disciples and "he was transfigured before them" (Mt. 17:2; Mk. 9:2). This event apparently was intended not only to give Peter, James, and John a view of who Jesus truly was—the glorious Son of God, to whom they should listen—but also to encourage Jesus himself as he faced his coming crucifixion in Jerusalem. This transfiguration assured the human Jesus of the glory that awaited him after his cruel death. See *transform*.

TRANSFORM

Old Testament

Verb: הָפַךְ (*hāpak*), GK 2200 (S 2015), 94x. *hāpak* is a Heb. term for turning (see *turn*). On some occasions it can mean "transform," for God has the power to "transform" things from one reality to another. For example, he turns the night into day and the day into night (Amos 5:8), a rock into a spring of water (Ps. 114:8), the sea into dry land (Ps. 66:6), and rivers into blood (Ps. 78:44).

New Testament

Verb: μεταμορφόω (*metamorphoō*), GK *3565* (S *3339*), 4x. *metamorphoō* means "to transfigure, transform." Paul uses this verb in Rom. 12:2, at the beginning of that section of Romans that outlines the practical life of the Christian. We must not conform our lives to the standards of the sinful world around us, as tempting as that may be (since "everyone is doing it"), but we are to "be transformed by the renewing of [our] mind." That is, Christ has come to give us a new way of thinking—not to legalistically follow a fixed set of rules and regulations, but to desire to serve Jesus with all our heart and mind. In 2 Cor. 3:18, after Paul has contrasted the Christian's superior life of the Spirit to the old covenant's life of the letter of the law, he sums it up in this way: "And we … are being transformed into his likeness with ever-increasing glory, which comes from the Lord, who is the Spirit." The goal we should set our eyes on it to be like Jesus. See *transfigure*.

TRANSGRESSION

Old Testament

Noun: פֶּשַׁע (*pešaʿ*), GK 7322 (S 6588), 93x. Usually translated as "rebellion, offense, sin, transgression," the noun *pešaʿ* is one of the three primary words for sin in the OT. See *sin*.

New Testament

Noun: παράβασις (*parabasis*), GK *4126* (S *3847*), 7x. *parabasis* means "transgression," as in breaking a command of God's law (Rom. 2:23; 5:14; Gal. 3:19). Paul emphasizes especially that no transgression is possible if there is no law (Rom. 4:15; cf. also Heb. 2:2). Eve (and Adam too, of course) were both transgressors of God's command in the Garden of Eden (cf. 1 Tim. 2:14). But through the blood of Christ, the mediator of the new covenant, a ransom has been paid that sets us "free from the sins committed under the first covenant" (Heb. 9:16). See *trespass*.

Noun: παράπτωμα (*paraptōma*), GK *4183* (S *3900*), 19x. *paraptōma* means "trespass, sin, transgression." See *trespass*.

TRANSITORINESS

Old Testament

Noun: צֵל (*ṣēl*), GK 7498 (S 6738), 53x. *ṣēl* means literally "shadow, shade," but it can also be used figuratively for the notion of "protection" or of the "transitory or empty nature" of things. See *shadow*.

TRAVAIL

This KJV word is now usually translated "birth pains" or "birth pangs." See *birth pangs*.

TRAVEL

Old Testament

Verb: נָסַע (*nāsaʿ*), GK 5825 (S 5265), 146x. The original meaning of *nāsaʿ* is "to pull out (tent pegs)," from which the sense "set out" or "journey" is derived. See *journey*.

New Testament

Verb: πορεύομαι (*poreuomai*), GK

4513 (S *4198*), 153x. *poreuomai* can be translated "go, travel, walk." See *go*.

TREAD

Old Testament

Verb: דָּרַךְ (*dārak*), GK 2005 (S 1869), 63x. *dārak* denotes the activity of walking on a path (Deut. 1:36; Jos. 14:9; Hab. 3:19), treading on a winepress (Neh. 13:15; Isa. 16:10), or bending a bow (Ps. 7:12; Lam. 2:4; Jer. 50:29),

TREASURE

Old Testament

Noun: אוֹצָר (*ʾôṣār*), GK 238 (S 214), 79x. *ʾôṣār* means "treasure, storehouse, wealth." Job is questioned by God, who is the Creator and knows the "storehouses" of snow and hail (Job 38:22). Solomon stores the wealth that David dedicated for the building and furnishing of the temple in the "treasuries" of the temple (1 Ki. 7:51). During Rehoboam's reign, Shishak king of Egypt "carried off the *treasures* of the temple and the *treasures* of the royal palace" (1 Ki. 14:26). Those who seek the wealth of wisdom are commended, and with it comes material "treasures" or wealth (Prov. 8:17–21). "Better is little with the fear of the LORD than great *wealth* with turmoil" (15:16).

God associates his people's poverty with their lack of generosity toward him. They rob God by denying him their tithes and offerings, dishonoring his commands. But if they will "bring the full tithe into the *storehouse*, so that there may be food in my house ... I will ... open the windows of heaven for you and pour down for you an overflowing blessing" (Mal. 3:8–10). See *NIDOTTE*, 1:487–89.

New Testament

Noun: θησαυρός (*thēsauros*), GK *2565* (S *2344*), 17x. *thēsauros* is a "treasure" or the "storeroom" where treasure is put. Although it can refer to a receptacle in which treasure is stored, the only clear NT example of this is Mt. 2:11, in which the wise men opened their treasures and gave gifts of gold and frankincense and myrrh.

The most common use in the NT is in reference to material riches (Mt. 6:19, 21; 13:44, 52; Lk. 6:45; 12:34, 35; 2 Cor. 4:7; Col. 2:3; Heb. 11:26), such as what someone may find hidden in a field (Mt. 13:44). A person's treasure is a clear indicator of the state of his heart: "For where your *treasure* is, there your heart will be also" (Lk. 12:34).

True disciples store up their treasures in heaven (Mt. 6:20; 19:21; Mk. 10:21; Lk. 12:33; 18:22), where they will have access to them. Treasures become stored up in heaven when disciples use God's wealth to advance his purposes. They may not be able to take the riches with them when they die, but they can send it on ahead.

In Christ "are hidden all the *treasures* of wisdom and knowledge" (Col. 2:3). Moses saw the abuse suffered for Christ as wealth greater "than the *treasures* of Egypt" (Heb. 11:26). Paul affirms that the gospel is a "*treasure* in jars of clay" so that people will see the power of the gospel is from God, not Paul (2 Cor. 4:7). See *NIDNTT-A*, 249-51.

TREATY

Old Testament

Noun: בְּרִית (*b^erît*), GK 1382 (S 1285), 287x. *b^erit* means "covenant, treaty." The ancient world, like the modern world, was filled with treaties or covenants among people groups, often as military alliances. This analogy was used to describe God's entering into a relationship with his people. See also *covenant*. See *NIDOTTE*, 1:747–54.

Treaties in the ancient world were either bilateral or unilateral. Unilateral treaties were imposed by a conquering king on a nation (sometimes called suzerain-vassal treaties), where he set the terms; an example of this type of treaty is the one Nebuchadnezzar king of Babylon imposed on Zedekiah of Judah when he put him on the throne in Jerusalem as a puppet king (Ezek. 17:11–14). Most of the human treaties in the Bible were bilateral, with both sides contributing to the terms and making promises (Gen. 21:27–31; Jos. 9:6–15). The word could even be used for a verbal agreement made between friends, such as between David and Jonathan (1 Sam. 18:3; 23:18).

TREE

Old Testament

Noun: עֵץ (*ʿēṣ*), GK 6770 (S 6086), 330x. *ʿēṣ* is the basic word for tree and wood products. It can be translated as "wood, tree, timber." Biblical authors used *ʿēṣ* in reference to wooden idols (Isa. 44:12–17; Hos. 4:12), timber (Hag. 1:8), paneling (Ezek. 41:16), a vessel, (Lev. 11:32), and a handle (Deut. 19:5).

The OT records numerous types of *ʿēṣ*, including gopher, acacia, cedar, pine, and olive. When used in the generic sense, *ʿēṣ* may refer to any tree (cf. Gen. 1:11–12, 29). God created the Garden of Eden with a bounty of trees (3:8). In the narratives of the Bible, large trees often become boundary markers (e.g., Gen. 13:18; 12:33; 1 Sam. 14:2; 1 Chr. 10:12).

Of special interest in the OT is the Feast of Booths, where the people were instructed to take various tree branches and makes booths for themselves and live in them, to remind themselves how their ancestors lived in tents in the desert (Lev. 23:39–43; Neh. 8:13–18). Many cedars of Lebanon were used in the construction of the temple of Solomon (1 Ki. 5:6–10; 6:15–20).

Trees are also used as a metaphor in the OT. Trees can symbolize people and how they can flourish when "planted in the house of the Lord" (Ps. 92:12–13). The psalmist in Ps. 1 sees the God-fearing person as one who is "like a *tree* planted by streams of water, which yields its fruit in its season" (1:3). Such an individual does not walk in the counsel of the wicked or stand in the way of sinners or sit in the seat of mockers. Isaiah uses the imagery of trees to represent Israel's coming restoration and abundance (Isa. 60:18). The prophet Ezekiel uses a tree-lined river image to encourage the exiled Hebrews of the future blessings of God (Ezek. 47:1–12). Here, trees symbolize tranquility, beauty, and sustenance from the Lord. See *NIDOTTE*, 3:474-482.

New Testament

Noun: δένδρον (*dendron*), GK *1285* (S *1186*), 25x. *dendron* is a generic term for a "tree," but is often used of fruit trees. It is used literally (e.g., Mt. 21:8 regarding tree branches cut for Jesus' triumphal entry"; also Rev. 7:1, 3) and often metaphorically.

The NT employs wide usage of related agricultural terms to focus symbolically on the presence or absence of a relationship with God. Some of the terms are: *phyteia* ("plant,"GK*5884*),*emphytos*("implanted," GK *1875*), *blastanō* ("sprout, shoot forth," GK *1056*), *rhiza* ("root," GK *4844*), *rhizoō* ("take root," GK *4845*), *ekrizoō* ("uproot," GK *1748*), *klados* ("branch," GK *3080*), *klēma* ("branch," GK *3097*), *phyllon* ("leaf," GK *5877*), and *enkentrizō* ("to graft," GK *1596*).

Jesus often uses trees and their fruit to make his point about the need for his disciples to grow in their holiness, i.e., to bear fruit. If the people do not produce fruit in keeping with repentance, "even now the axe is laid to the root of the *trees*. Every *tree* therefore that does not bear good fruit is cut down and thrown into the fire" (Mt. 3:10; Lk. 3:9). In warning against false prophets, Jesus says that we can know their true identity by their fruit. Healthy trees bear healthy fruit, and a diseased tree cannot bear good fruit. Trees that do not bear good fruit will be destroyed (Mt. 7:20; also 12:33; Lk. 6:43–44).

Jesus uses the mustard "tree" as an example of how the kingdom of God starts small but grows larger than any of the garden plants (Mt. 13:32; Lk. 13:19). The image of a large tree with birds roosting in its branches echoes several OT references to a massive kingdom (Ezek. 17:22–24; 31:2–18; Dan. 4:9–27). The fig tree serves as an example of watching the signs of the times for Jesus' return (Lk. 21:29). See *NIDNTT-A*, 127-128.

Noun: ξύλον (*xylon*), GK *3833* (S *3586*), 20x. *xylon* means "tree, club, wood, stocks." It refers to living or dead wood or anything made of wood. In the NT *xylon* is used to denote a weapon (Mt. 26:47; Mk.

14:43), construction material (Rev. 18:12), stocks (Acts 16:24), and Jesus' cross (Acts 5:30; 10:39; 13:29; Gal. 3:13).

The Bible draws attention to three significant trees in the history of salvation. The first is the tree of knowledge of good and evil in Eden (*xylon* is the word used in the LXX in Gen. 2 and 3), whereby the human race was plunged into sin when Adam and Eve partook of the forbidden fruit of that tree. Jesus then bore our sins in his body when he was hung upon "a tree" (1 Pet. 2:24). And in the new heaven and new earth, God will make available to us for all eternity the tree of life (Rev. 2:7; 22:2, 14, 19); the leaves of this tree are for the healing of the nations. See *NIDNTT-A*, 399-400.

TRESPASS

New Testament

Noun: παράπτωμα (*paraptōma*), GK *4183* (S *3900*), 19x. *paraptōma* means "trespass, sin, transgression." Used figuratively, this term means that someone has stepped outside the bounds of God's law. This word derives from *para*, a preposition meaning alongside or outside, and *piptō*, meaning to fall or collapse.

While in classical Greek *paraptōma* meant a mere oversight or unintentional mistake, in the LXX it expresses conscious and deliberate sin against God. In the NT most occurrences of *paraptōma* are in the writings of Paul (e.g., Rom. 4:25; 5:15–18; Eph. 1:7; 2:1, 5), where the term likewise denotes intentional, deliberate sin (except for Rom. 5:20, where it is used of sin as a universal fact). Implicit with this term are the consequences of sin, for when we trespass, we fall from the position established by God. This means, then, that our sin against another person impacts our relationship with God. Jesus uses this word in Mt. 6:14–15 and Mk. 11:25 in reference to our forgiveness of those who sin against us and to God's forgiveness of our sins. See *NIDNTT-A*, 438.

TRIAL

Old Testament

Noun: צָרָה (*ṣārâ*), GK 7650 (S 6869), 70x. *ṣārâ* comes form the root *ṣrh*, which means "to bind, tie up, restrict." Thus, the noun comes to denote a narrow place in life in which one is bound or restricted, i.e., "trouble or distress." *ṣārâ* designates the trials and tribulations experienced in life. These troubles come on the just and unjust alike and reveal much about the character of each. See *trouble*.

New Testament

Noun: πειρασμός (*peirasmos*), GK *4280* (S *3986*), 21x. *peirasmos* shows the same range of meaning as the verb *peirazō* (GK *4279*), referring either to a testing or a temptation to do something wrong. See *temptation*.

TRIBE

Old Testament

Noun: מַטֶּה (*maṭṭeh*), GK 4751 (S 4294), 252x. *maṭṭeh* has two separate, though related meanings: "rod, staff" (see *staff*); and "tribe." Most of the usages of *maṭṭeh* in the OT, especially in the Pentateuch, mean "tribe" (the vast majority of these are in Numbers). In Num. 1:21–47; 12:4–15, for example, all the "tribes" of Israel are mentioned (cf. also 1 Chr. 6:60–80). God specifically mandates that "no inheritance in Israel is to go from *tribe* to *tribe*" (Num. 36:7, 9).

Noun: שֵׁבֶט (*šēbet*), GK 8657 (S 7626), 190x. *šēbet* means "rod, scepter, or tribe." See *rod*.

New Testament

Noun: φυλή (*phylē*), GK *5876* (S *5443*), 31x. *phylē* refers to a "tribe" or to a larger unit such as a "nation" or "people." The nation Israel was divided into twelve tribes, descendants of the twelve patriarchs, and people are often identified with their tribe: Anna was "of the *tribe* of Asher" (Lk. 2:36); Saul was "of the *tribe* of Benjamin" (Acts 13:21), as was Paul (Rom. 11:1; Phil. 3:5); Jesus was from "the *tribe* of Judah" (Heb. 7:14; Rev. 5:5). Most NT usages of *phylē* occur in Revelation, referring literally to the historic tribes of Israel (Rev. 7:4–8)

The phrase "the twelve *tribes* of Israel" applies to the believing community, the true Israel, in Mt. 19:28; Jas. 1:1; Rev. 7:4; 21:12. This phrase often occurs within the context of the end times (Mt. 19:28; Lk. 22:30).

All "the *nations* of the earth" will mourn when they see Jesus return, presumably because there will be no longer time to repent (Mt. 24:30; Rev. 1:7). Ultimately, those who represent God's people worshiping him around the throne are from "every nation, *phylē*, people, and language" (Rev. 7:9; 11:9; 13:7; 14:6). This description communicates that the "new and true Israel" is composed of a complete cross-section of all inhabitants on earth. In John's description of the heavenly Jerusalem, the twelve gates with the names of the twelve tribes of Israel, supported by the twelve foundations representing the twelve apostles, signify the whole regenerate people of God.

Additional NT connections to the OT tribes of Israel appear in Heb. 7:13–14. To show that the new covenant initiated by Jesus, the ultimate and perfect high priest, set aside certain aspects of the old covenant, the writer points out that Jesus emerged from the *phylē* of Judah. Priests were taken from the *phylē* of Levi. Significantly, in the OT it was Judah's descendants who would be rulers not only of the nation Israel but of all nations. Gen. 49:10 is a messianic prophecy concerning this tribe. It was permanently be tied the royal house of David, the representative ruler of God's people. See *NIDNTT-A*, 595.*

TRIBULATION

Old Testament

Noun: צָרָה (*ṣārâ*), GK 7650 (S 6869), 70x. *ṣārâ* comes form the root *ṣrh*, which means "to bind, tie up, restrict." Thus, the noun comes to denote a narrow place in life in which one is bound or restricted, i. e., "trouble or distress." *ṣārâ* designates the trials and tribulations experienced in life. These troubles come on the just and unjust alike and reveal much about the character of each. See *trouble*.

New Testament

Noun: θλίψις (*thlipsis*), GK *2568* (S *2347*), 45x. *thlipsis* is a cognate form of the verb *thlibō* (see *persecute*). It denotes the results of being squeezed or put into a narrow place—hence, "trouble, affliction, distress." It is used in several ways in the NT. See *trouble*.

TRIM

New Testament

Verb: κοσμέω (*kosmeō*), GK *3175* (S *2885*), 10x. *kosmeō* means "to adorn, decorate, make attractive" (see *adorn*). But when used of lamps, this word has the specific idea of trimming the wicks to make the lamp useful (Mt. 25:7).

TROOPS

Old Testament

Noun: עַם (*ʿam*), GK 6639 (S 5971), 1869x. *ʿam* can refer to military troops (Num. 20:20; Jos. 8:1) or to a general assembly of people (Ruth 4:9; 1 Sam. 10:17). Especially in the plural, this word is often used to refer to the "nations" of the world (Ps. 18:47; 45:5; Isa. 12:4; 63:3). But most frequently *ʿam* denotes a large group of people united by a familial relationship. See *people*.

TROUBLE

Old Testament

Noun: עָמָל (*ʿāmāl*), GK 6662 (S 5999), 54x. *ʿāmāl* bears two distinct but related meanings in the OT: "work" and "trouble." *ʿāmāl* comes from the root *ʿml*, which denotes work or labor. The often difficult and toilsome nature of work produces the secondary meaning of "trouble" (see *work*).

ʿāmāl often denotes the trouble and suffering associated with work. Joseph names his son Manasseh, which sounds like the Hebrew word for "forget" because God has caused him to forget the *ʿāmāl* he has suffered (Gen. 41:51). In lamenting his birth, Jer. describes his life as *ʿāmāl* and sorrow (Jer. 20:18). Similarly, Job uses

ʿ*āmāl* to describe the calamitous part of his life (3:10; 7:3).

ʿ*āmāl* also refers to trouble caused by wickedness. Eliphaz tells Job that the godless conceive ʿ*āmāl* and give birth to wickedness (Job 15:35). The lips of the wicked produce ʿ*āmāl* (Ps. 140:9; Prov. 24:2; Isa. 59:4). However, God does not look favorably on a people characterized by such ʿ*āmāl* (Hab. 1:13) and pronounces woe upon them (Isa. 10:1). See *NIDOTTE*, 3:435-37.

Noun: צָרָה (*ṣārâ*), GK 7650 (S 6869), 70x. *ṣārâ* comes form the root *srh*, which means "to bind, tie up, restrict." Thus, the noun comes to denote a narrow place in life in which one is bound or restricted, i. e., "trouble or distress." *ṣārâ* designates the trials and tribulations experienced in life. These troubles come on the just and unjust alike and reveal much about the character of each.

(1) The just see the cause of *ṣārâ* as their own sin (Gen. 42:21; Deut. 31:17, 21) or simply part of God's providential workings meant for their good (Job 5:17–19). They hope and even expect that God will deliver them from *ṣārâ* (1 Sam. 26:24; Ps. 120:1; Isa. 33:2). Though it sometimes seems that God is far off (Ps. 10:1), for the righteous person he is a refuge (Ps. 9:9) and an ever-present help (Ps. 46:1) in *ṣārâ*. He will ultimately respond to the cries of the afflicted; empowering and defending them (Ps. 10:17–18) even to the "depths of the grave" (Jon. 2:2). God liberates his people from the straights of *ṣārâ* (Ps. 25:22).

(2) The wicked's view of *ṣārâ* is markedly different. They have no hope in God and refuse to repent even in *ṣārâ*. Therefore, God will not hear their cries (Job 27:8–9; Isa. 65:13–16; Nah. 1:7–10). See *NIDOTTE*, 3:853-59.

Noun: רָעָה (*rāʿâ*), GK 8288 (S 7465), 354x. At the heart of *rāʿâ*, lies the idea of badness, whether physical or moral. When used in the physical sense, it is often translated "calamity, disaster, harm, trouble." See *evil*.

New Testament

Verb: θλίβω (*thlibō*), GK *2567* (S *2346*), 10x. *thlibō* literally denotes pressing, squeezing, or crushing. It is usually related to the persecutions specific to believers. In the middle of a list of physical troubles, the author of Hebrews describes the OT saints as "persecuted" for their faith (Heb. 11:37). See *persecute*.

Verb: ταράσσω (*tarassō*), GK *5429* (S *5015*), 17x. *tarassō* means to "trouble" or "disturb" by displacing someone or something from its normal state. The idea can clearly be seen in Jn. 5:7, the only nonfigurative use of *tarassō*. Here the people wait for the static water in the pool of Bethesda to be stirred in some way.

Figuratively, *tarassō* denotes spiritual or emotional excitement. In the Gospels, people are troubled by miraculous works of God: Herod at hearing of Christ's birth (Mt. 2:3), Zechariah at seeing an angel (Lk. 1:12), and the disciples at seeing Jesus walking on the water (Mt. 14:26; Mk. 6:50) and the newly risen Jesus (Lk. 24:38). John writes that Jesus himself was troubled at significant points in his ministry: at the lack of faith and hope among the people before he raises Lazarus (Jn. 11:33), at the approaching cross event after the Greeks seek him (12:27), and at his impending betrayal after washing the disciples' feet (13:21).

Jesus promises the apostles that they will be persecuted by the world, but he encourages them not to let their hearts be troubled (Jn. 14:1, 27). Similar admonitions are given to the early church by Paul (Acts 15:24) and Peter (1 Pet. 3:14; cf. Isa. 8:12). At the same time, the world itself is disturbed because of the spread of the gospel (Acts 17:8, 13). See *NIDNTT-A*, 556-57.*

Noun: θλίψις (*thlipsis*), GK *2568* (S *2347*), 45x. *thlipsis* is a cognate form of the verb *thlibō*, which literally means to "press, squeeze, crush" (see *persecute*). The noun denotes the results of being squeezed or put into a narrow place. It is used in three main ways.

(1) The NT speaks of Christ's afflictions. Paul writes that he is "filling up what is lacking in Christ's *afflictions*" (Col. 1:24) for the sake of the church. He also relates believers' troubles to the sufferings of Christ and encourages them that sharing in these afflictions will allow them to share in Christ's comfort and salvation (2 Cor. 1:4; cf. 1:5–8).

(2) It signifies the end-time tribulation prophesied for the church. Quoting Dan. 12:1, Jesus designates the great "tribulation" as a sign of the end of the age (Mt. 24:21) and a precursor to great cosmological changes and the coming of the Son of Man (Mk. 13:24). The great multitude of Rev. 7:14 is made of those "who come out of the great *tribulation*, and they have washed their robes and made them white in the blood of the Lamb."

(3) Implicit in the first two categories is the idea that believers will suffer troubles. These troubles are a necessary part of our experience (Jn. 16:33; Acts 14:22). However, unlike people of the world who fall away when these troubles arise (Mt. 13:21), true believers will persevere through such distress and all other tribulations to be glorified together with Christ (Rom. 8:35; cf. 8:17). Ultimately, God will comfort those who are afflicted and will repay those who afflict them with *thlipsis* (2 Thess. 1:6–7). Therefore, even in the midst of troubles, Christians can respond with joy rather than grief (Rom. 5:3). See *NIDNTT-A*, 251-52.

TRUE

See *truth*.

TRULY

New Testament

Adverb: ἀληθῶς (*alēthōs*), GK *242* (S *230*), 18x. *alēthōs* means "truly, surely, really" —an adverb of certainty. All but three occurrences are in the gospels. In Luke's gospel, this word functions to introduce a solemn pronouncement by Jesus, "Truly I say to you" (9:27; 12:44; 21:3). This appears to be Luke's version of *amēn* (see, e.g., the parallel usage in Mk. 9:1; see *amen*). In the other gospels, this adv. makes a solid affirmation about the nature of Jesus or some other person; e.g., "Surely this is the Prophet who is to come into the world" (Jn. 6:14; cf. also 4:42; 7:26, 40; 8:31); "surely this man was the Son of God" (Mk. 15:39; cf. Mt. 27:54). In 2 Thess. 2:13 *alēthōs* certifies that Paul's preaching was "the word of God."

Adverb: ἀμήν (*amēn*), GK *297* (S *281*), 129x. *amēn* is a transliteration of the Heb. word; in general it means "certain[ly]" or "true[ly]." See *amen*.

TRUMPET

Old Testament

Noun: שׁוֹפָר (*šôpār*), GK 8795 (S 7782), 72x. *šôpār* denotes the curved musical instrument made from a ram's horn (*qeren*, GK 7967). It is technically not a musical instrument, but it was used to signal many events.

The *šôpār* plays an important role in Hebrew history. A blast from the *šôpār* signaled the time for the Israelites to approach Mount Sinai (Exod. 19:16–17) and to celebrate the new moon (Ps. 81:3), the Jubilee year (Lev. 25:9), various feasts (Joel 2:15), or even taking an oath (2 Chr. 15:14). Watchmen were to sound a *šôpār* as a warning for the approach of an enemy (Neh. 4:18; Isa. 18:3) and to summon Israel to war (Jdg. 3:27; 1 Sam. 13:3; Jer. 42:14), to signal an attack (Jos. 6:16; Jdg. 7:18–20), or to call off an attack (2 Sam. 2:28; 18:16). The *šôpār* also assisted in military maneuvers (2 Sam. 2:28; 18:16). Gideon utilized a *šôpār* in the defeat of the Midianites (Jdg. 7:16).

Joshua 6 records the most recognized biblical passage in reference to a *šôpār*. Joshua and the people conquer the walls of Jericho, not with sword or battering ram, but with a *šôpār*: "When the *trumpets* sounded, the people shouted, and at the sound of the *trumpet*, when the people gave a loud shout, the wall collapsed" (Jos. 6:20). The blast of the *šôpār* will also announce the coming of the Day of the Lord (Joel 2:1; Zeph. 1:16; cf. Isa. 27:13; Zech. 9:14). See *NIDOTTE*, 4:68-69.

New Testament

Noun: σάλπιγξ (*salpinx*), GK *4894* (S *4536*), 11x. A *salpinx* is usually translated as "trumpet" or "bugle," referring to a (metal) trumpet or an (animal's) horn. It was probably a straight tube without valves. *salpinx* can indicate the instrument itself or the sound it creates.

Paul urges the Corinthians that just as an indistinct trumpet blast will not call people to battle, so indistinct speech (i.e., uninterpreted tongues as opposed to prophecy) is of little value in public worship. The trumpet blast, like the clear preaching of the word of God, can bring order to chaos, prevent confusion, and call God's people to act for him.

Trumpet blasts are sometimes associated with supernatural events. Jesus' return to earth will be signaled by a *salpinx* (Mt. 24:31). Paul speaks of the last trumpet blast that will signal the resurrection of the dead at the time of Jesus' return (1 Cor. 15:52; cf. Zech. 9:14; see also *sound the trumpet*). Heb. 12:19 refers to the trumpet blast heard from Mount Sinai at the giving of the law (cf. Exod. 19:16, 19; 20:18). The beginning of the revelation to John began with "a loud voice like a *trumpet*" (Rev. 1:10; cf. 4:1). Later in this book, angels blow on trumpets just before disasters strike (8:2, 6, 13; 9:14). See *NIDNTT-A*, 514-15.*

TRUST

Old Testament

Verb: אָמַן (*ʾāman*), GK 586 (S 539), 97x. *ʾāman* means "to believe, trust." In its participial form it has the nuance of "trustworthy, faithful." See *believe*.

Verb: בָּטַח (*bāṭaḥ*), GK 1053 (S 982), 118x. This word means "to trust, rely on, depend on," with the sense of being completely confident and feeling utterly safe (cf. the related noun *beṭaḥ*, GK 1055, which means "safety, security"). Trusting God is one of the fundamental lifestyle characteristics of the people of God.

Throughout the OT, people are encouraged to put their trust in the Lord. "*Trust* in him at all times, O people; pour out your hearts to him, for God is our refuge" (Ps. 62:8; cf. Ps. 4:5; cf. 115:9–11; 125:1; Isa. 26:4). Though there is a place for trusting other people (Prov. 31:11), human relationships should not be the ultimate basis of our confidence. Jeremiah proclaims, "Cursed is the one who trusts in man, who depends on flesh for his strength and whose heart turns away from the LORD.... But blessed is the man who *trusts* in the LORD, whose confidence is in him" (Jer. 17:5, 7). It is part of human nature to rely on ourselves.

The essence of trust is a recognition of who God is and who we are. Those who are wealthy could be tempted to "trust" in money (Prov. 11:28). Those who are politically powerful could "trust" in their social networks (Ps. 146:3). Those who are strong could seek stability on the basis of physical or military might (Deut. 28:52; Jer. 5:17). Intelligent people may be tempted to think that they can make sense of life on their own understanding and intellectual prowess (Prov. 3:5–6; 28:26). It is only when we recognize that all of these things are insufficient that we must look outside of ourselves. To trust God rather than any of these earthly things is to express confidence in his character and to acknowledge that he is more reliable than anything we possess might or attain.

Trusting God means that we lean upon him even when it may invite our own destruction (e.g., 1 Sam. 17; Dan. 3). In a story repeated three times in the OT (2 Ki. 18:17–19:37 [*bāṭaḥ* occurs 9x]; 2 Chr. 32:1–23; Isa. 36:1–37:38 [*bāṭaḥ* occurs 9x]), the Assyrian king Sennacherib threatens Hezekiah and the city of Jerusalem with a challenge to their dependence on the Lord. Sennacherib specifically derides Hezekiah's trust in God for deliverance (2 Ki. 18:30, 35). It is during these moments when we are surrounded with terrifying circumstances that our trust is tested. To rely on God is to acknowledge our helplessness and to resign ourselves to his care—no matter the cost. It is chilling to think of the massacre Sennacherib would have inflicted on Jerusalem if he had the chance. However, when morning came, 185,000 of his men lay dead and God had proved, once again, why he is a God who can be trusted. When we "trust" in him, we will "not be disappointed" (Ps. 22:5). See *NIDOTTE*, 1:644–49.

New Testament

Verb: πιστεύω (*pisteuō*), GK *4409* (S *4100*), 241x. *pisteuō* generally means "to believe, be convinced of something," and in a more specific way "to have faith" in God or Christ. It can also mean "to entrust something to someone." See *believe*.

TRUSTWORTHINESS

Old Testament

Noun: אֱמוּנָה (*ʾemûna*), GK 575 (S 530), 127x. *ʾemûna* means "faithfulness, trustworthiness, integrity." See *faithfulness*.

New Testament

Noun: πίστις (*pistis*), GK *4411* (S *4102*), 243x. *pistis* means "belief, trust, confidence," though it can also mean "faithfulness, trustworthiness." See *faith*.

TRUSTWORTHY

Old Testament

Verb: אָמַן (*ʾāman*), GK 586 (S 539), 97x. *ʾāman* means "to believe, trust." In its participial form it has the nuance of "trustworthy, faithful." See *believe*.

New Testament

Adjective: πιστός (*pistos*), GK *4412* (S *4103*), 67x. *pistos* means "faithful, trustworthy, reliable, dependable." See *faithful*.

TRUTH

Old Testament

Noun: אֱמֶת (*ʾemet*), GK 622 (S 571), 127x. *ʾemet* denotes "faithfulness" in the sense of fidelity and trustworthiness, and "truth." See *faithfulness*.

New Testament

Noun: ἀλήθεια (*alētheia*), GK *237* (S *225*), 109x.

Adjective: ἀληθής (*alēthēs*), GK *239* (S *227*), 26x.

Adjective: ἀληθινός (*alēthinos*), GK *240* (S *228*), 28x.

Perhaps the most common use of the noun *alētheia* and the two corresponding adjectives is to refer to something that is accurate. For example, Paul claims before Festus and Agrippa that what he said regarding Jesus and the resurrection is "the truth" and reasonable (Acts 26:25). Jesus' testimony is true and valid because the Father testifies about him (Jn. 5:31–32; cf. Rev. 21:5; 22:6); our testimony about Jesus is also true (Tit. 1:13; 3 Jn. 12).

But truth is not only in statements. Paul uses that adjective *alēthinos* to describe God himself. The Thessalonians turned from idols in order to "serve the living and *true* God" (1 Thess. 1:9). And because God is true, what God speaks is also truth; "your word is truth" (Jn. 17:17).

Not only is God true, but Jesus is "True" as well (Rev. 19:11). He is "full of grace and *truth*" (Jn. 1:14, 17). In fact, Jesus himself is "truth" (14:6), and if we are his disciples, we will "know the *truth*" (8:32). Jesus is "the *true* vine," through which his followers draw nourishment. John uses the adjective *alēthēs* to denote a spiritual reality about Jesus that is beyond the observable world. Jesus proclaims that his flesh is "*true* food" and his blood is "*true* drink" (Jn. 6:55).

Furthermore, especially in John's writings, the Holy Spirit is referred to as the "Spirit of truth" (Jn. 14:17; 15:26; 16:13; cf. 1 Jn. 4:6; 5:6). The Holy Spirit recalls to our minds the words of Jesus and certifies to our hearts that they are true (15:26). This usage of *alētheia* is also closely associated with John's reference to the Holy Spirit as the *paraklētos* (Jn. 14:16, 26; 15:26; 16:7; see *counselor*). This means that the Holy Spirit is a defense witness for Christians, defending against false accusations and the lies of the enemy by testifying to the truth.

Truth is not only something that we believe; it is also something that we are called upon to speak and even to practice. This connection between truth and action is found throughout the NT. It is implied in Paul's distinctive use of *alētheia* to refer to the gospel he preached ("the truth"), which is in contrast to the preaching of Paul's opponents who sought to repress the truth (2 Cor. 12:6; Gal. 2:5, 14; 1 Tim. 2:7). Paul commends himself and his fellow workers to the scrutiny of his readers in contrast to the false teachers (2 Cor. 4:2) and implies that his challengers will not endure such a test. He has suffered for the gospel, and that suffering testifies to its truth (2 Cor. 6:4–12). Christians are expected to be truthful in this way, being honest and having actions that reflect the commitment to truth (1 Cor. 5:8; Eph. 4:24-25).

The apostle John has a similar emphasis, arguing that Christians should "do the *truth*," emphasizing the concept of living "in the light." John records Jesus saying, "Whoever lives by the *truth* comes into the light, so that it may be seen plainly that what he has done has been done through God" (Jn. 3:21). Similarly, John reminds his readers that those who claim to have fellowship with Christ but continue to walk in darkness "do not live by the *truth*" (1 Jn. 1:6). Thus, there is a close connection between one's knowledge of truth and godly activity; the two cannot be separated. In an age where truth is all too often shaded to obscure falsehood, there is no group of people who should be more dedicated to speaking the truth forthrightly and living by its holy standards than the followers of Jesus (cf. Phil. 4:8). See *NIDNTT-A*, 32-36.

TRY

Old Testament

Verb: בָּחַן (*bāḥan*), GK 1043 (S 974), 29x. *bāḥan* denotes the divine examination of an individual and may be translated as "test, try, prove." It is common in the poetic and prophetic books of the OT. See *test*.

Verb: נָסָה (*nāsâ*), GK 5814 (S 5254), 36x. *nāsâ* denotes the testing of a person's loyalty or obedience and may be translated "test, prove." This verb is most common in the narrative and poetic books of the OT. See *test*.

New Testament

Verb: πειράζω (*peirazō*), GK *4279* (S *3985*), 38x. *peirazō* has several basic usages, most of which revolve around either "to tempt" or "to test." But it sometimes means "attempt, try." See *tempt*.

TUMULT

Old Testament

Noun: הָמוֹן (*hāmôn*), GK 2162 (S 1995), 82x. *hāmôn* expresses a quality of immensity or magnitude, whether it bears an emotive, audible, or spatial reference. It is translated with words like "confusion, tumult, noise, abundance, army, hordes." See *hordes*.

TUNIC

New Testament

Noun: χιτών (*chitōn*), GK *5945* (S *5509*), 11x. *chitōn* means "garment, tunic." See *garment*.

TURN

Old Testament

Verb: הָפַךְ (*hāpak*), GK 2200 (S 2015), 94x. *hāpak* is a Heb. term for turning.

(1) *hāpak* can refer to various forms of divine punishment ("I will wipe out Jerusalem as one wipes a dish, wiping it and *turning* it upside down," 2 Ki. 21:13). Those who go to battle without the Lord's blessing will "turn" in defeat even if they are well armed physically (Ps. 78:9). Jeremiah complains as he sees the destruction of Jerusalem that the Lord "*has turned* his hand against me again and again, all day long" (Lam. 3:3; cf. 4:6).

(2) *hāpak* can also refer to turning something that is good into something that is bad. For example, Amos insists that Israel "*turns* justice into poison and the fruit of righteousness into bitterness" (Amos 6:12; cf. 5:7). People who hide their plans from the Lord "*turn* things upside down, as if the potter were thought to be like the clay" (Isa. 29:16).

(3) *hāpak* also refers to a broken relationship or the refusal to fix a relationship that has already been broken. Job complains that all of his best friends and loved ones "have turned" against him (Job

19:19), and Israel, though being like a burning stick snatched from the fire, still refuses to "return" to the Lord (Amos 4:11). While the Lord has planted Israel as a choice vine of reliable stock, she nevertheless has turned against her Lord and become a corrupt and wild vine (Jer. 2:21).

(4) *hāpak* is used of God's power to "transform" things from one reality to another. The Creator turns the night into day and the day into night (Amos 5:8), a rock into a spring of water (Ps. 114:8), the sea into dry land (Ps. 66:6), and rivers into blood (Ps. 78:44). If Israel persists in unfaithfulness, the Lord warns that he will "*turn* your religious feasts into mourning and all your singing into weeping" (Amos 8:10). Yet, the Lord offers hope that a day is coming when he will "*turn* their mourning into gladness ... and give them comfort and joy instead of sorrow" (Jer. 31:13).

Verb: נָטָה (*nāṭâ*), GK 5742 (S 5186), 216x. *nāṭâ* conveys the basic idea of "to stretch, spread out, pitch [a tent], turn." See *stretch out*.

Verb: סָבַב (*sābab*), GK 6015 (S 5437), 163x. *sābab* is generally translated "surround, go around, turn." See *surround*.

Verb: פָּנָה (*pānâ*), GK 7155 (S 6437), 134x. *pānâ* is most often translated "turn." It is used to indicate a literal turning toward something (Gen. 18:22; 24:49; Exod. 32:15; 1 Ki. 17:2; Isa. 13:14) or a turning away (Gen. 18:22; Exod. 7:22; Jdg. 18:21; 1 Sam. 10:9), both of God and of human beings. It is also used for someone who turns to look at something (Jos. 8:20; 20:40; 2 Chr. 13:14).

The psalmist cries to the Lord, "*Turn* to me and be gracious to me, for I am lonely and afflicted" (Ps. 25:16); "*turn* to me and have mercy on me" (Ps. 86:16a; cf. 119:132). The Lord does turn to Gideon and instructs him to "go in the strength you have and save Israel out of Midian's hand. Am I not sending you?" (Jdg. 6:14).

The Lord instructs his rebellious people to, "*Turn* to me and be saved, all you ends of the earth; for I am God, and there is no other" (Isa. 45:21). The Lord continues to love the Israelites even though they "*turn* to other gods and love the sacred raisin cakes" (Hos. 3:1; cf. Deut. 31:18, Lev. 19:4). God's people are told not to turn to mediums, spiritists, or to any kinds of evil (Lev. 19:31, Job 36:21), or they will be in danger of being cut off from the Lord (Lev. 20:6). Moses is instructed to "make sure there is no man or woman among Israel ... whose heart *turns* away from the Lord our God" (Deut. 29:18). God's people are in danger of destruction if their hearts "turn" away from him and they worship other gods (Deut. 30:17). Zephaniah proclaims, "The LORD has taken away your punishment, he has *turned* back your enemy" (Zeph. 3:15).

Verb: שִׂים (*śîm*), GK 8492 (S 7760), 588x. *śîm* generally denotes the action of putting or placing an object or person in a particular location. It is usually translated "put," "set," or "place" (see *put*). Sometimes *śîm* indicates the "putting" of a person or object into a new setting or for a special purpose that implies some sort of transformation. That transformation may be a transformation of quality. Yahweh "turns" the sea into dry land so the Israelites can escape the Egyptians (Exod. 14:21). He "turns" rivers into a desert (Ps. 107:33).

Verb: שׁוּב (*šûb*), GK 8740 (S 7725), 1075x. The basic sense of *šûb* is "to turn, return, repent, go/come back."

(1) *šûb* is used often in a physical sense for turning back to a point of departure. In the curse, God tells Adam that he will return to the dust (Gen. 3:19); in the covenant ceremony, God tells Abraham that his descendants will come back to Canaan from Egypt (Gen. 15:16). Some forms of *šûb* have a causative sense, meaning "to cause to come back, to bring back, to return (something), to restore." For example, God in his compassion promises to *bring back* the nation of Judah to her land, even after he has uprooted them (Jer. 12:15; see also

15:19; 16:15 for how God will *restore* them).

(2) *šûb* is also used in several important theological senses. In the moral-spiritual realm, *šûb* can describe both the human act of repentance (turning away from sin or idolatry and turning to God) and the human act of apostasy (turning away from God). For example, when God calls for the sinning nation to repent, he says, "Return to me" (Isa. 44:22), "return to the Lord your God" (Hos. 14:1), and "turn from your evil ways" (2 Ki. 17:13). When God accuses Israel of apostasy, he says, "You have *turned* (around) and profaned my name" (Jer. 34:16), and "they have *turned* (or returned) to the sins of their forefathers" (Jer. 11:10).

(3) Finally, God can be the subject of the verb *šûb*. When God's patience has run out, he promises impending judgment and warns, "I have decided and will not *turn back*" (Jer. 4:28). Conversely, when he makes the everlasting covenant with Israel, God also promises that he will never turn away from them but will do them good (Jer. 32:40). Zechariah holds out God's promise, "*Return* to me and I will *return* to you" (Zech. 1:3), and in Hos. 14:4, God says that if Israel returns to the Lord and seeks compassion, then his anger will turn away from them. See *NIDOTTE*, 4:55-59.

New Testament

Verb: ἐπιστρέφω (*epistrephō*), GK *2188* (S *1994*), 36x. *epistrephō* generally means "to turn, return." This verb sometimes indicates a return to a location, as in the LXX, where it describes the dove that did not "return" to Noah (Gen. 8:12; cf. Acts 15:36). It is used in the NT of spirits who "return" to host bodies (Mt. 12:44; Lk. 8:55).

On many occasions, *epistrephō* in the NT describes simple physical turning (e.g., Jn. 21:20, "Peter *turned* and saw the disciple whom Jesus loved"; Rev. 1:12, "I *turned around* to see the voice that was speaking to me"; cf. Mt. 5:30, 8:33, Acts 9:40, 16:18). But equally important are theological uses of this verb Most notably, *epistrephō* can indicate a spiritual and moral turn *from* sinfulness *to* the true God. In other words, it indicates spiritual conversion. Paul writes to the Thessalonians, "you *turned* to God from idols, to serve a living and true God" (1 Thess. 1:9). Paul and Barnabas declare to the crowd in Lystra, "*turn* from these worthless things to the living God" (Acts 14:15; cf. 3:19; 9:35; 11:21; 15:19; 26:18, 20, 27). In 1 Pet. 2:25 the focus is on the one to whom we are to turn: "Now you *have turned* to the Shepherd and Guardian of your souls." *epistrephō* indicates a change in the relationship between God and the sinner because, "when a man *turns* to the Lord the veil is removed" (2 Cor. 3:16).

epistrephō is also used negatively to describe turning away from God. For example, in Gal. 4:9 Paul asks, "How can you *turn again* to the weak and useless spiritual powers of this world?" However, it is every Christian's responsibility to be active in restoring those who have fallen out of fellowship with God. For instance, James reminds us that when we successfully turn ("convert," KJV) a sinner from error, we help to save that person from death and sin (Jas. 5:19–20). Ultimately however, it is God who causes individuals to turn to him. James stated in Acts 15:16 and 15:19 that the Gentiles turned to God because God first turned to them (cf. Mt. 13:15; Mk. 4:12, Lk. 1:16). See *NIDNTT-A*, 200.

Verb: στρέφω (*strephō*), GK *5138* (S *4762*), 21x. *strephō* means "to turn, return, change." Many of its NT uses means physically "to turn around" (Mt. 7:6; 9:22; Lk. 7:9, 44; 9:55; 14:25; 22:61; Jn. 1:38; 20:14, 16). The word occurs 20x in the gospels and Acts and only once elsewhere (Rev. 11:6).

strephō is used figuratively in Mt. 5:39, when Jesus instructs his followers that, rather than seek revenge against our enemies, we should "*turn* … the other cheek." In Acts 13:46, Paul's decides to focus his evangelistic efforts on the Gentiles when he addresses the Jews in Antioch: "Since you reject [the word of God] and do not consider yourselves worthy of eternal life, we now *turn* to the Gentiles." In Rev. 11:6 the two witnesses have the power to "turn the waters into blood."

Twice in the NT *strephō* refers to change of life focus. Jesus says in Mt. 18:3, "I tell you the truth, unless you *change* and become like little children, you will never enter the kingdom of heaven." Furthermore, Stephen states in Acts 7:39, "But our fathers refused to obey him. Instead, they rejected him and in their hearts *turned back* to Egypt." As a result, God "turned away" from Israel and gave them over to worship idols (7:42).

Noun: μετάνοια (*metanoia*), GK *3567* (S *3341*), 22x.

Verb: μετανοέω (*metanoeō*), GK *3566* (S *3340*), 34x. Both noun and verb denote a radical, moral turn of the whole person from sin and to God. See *repent, repentance*.

TURN AWAY

Old Testament

Verb: נָדָה (*nādah*), GK 5615 (S 5080), 51x. *nādah* generally has two distinct but related meanings: "to banish, cast out" (see *banish*) and "to turn away, stray" (see *stray*).

Verb: סוּר (*sûr*), GK 6073 (S 5493), 300x. *sûr* means "to turn away, remove." It is sometimes used for physically turning aside from what one is doing, such as Pharaoh "taking off" his ring and giving it to Joseph (Gen. 41:42) or Moses "turning aside" from his sheep to examine the burning bush (Exod. 3:3–4). When Israel is in the desert, this verb is sometimes used for the cloud "lifting" from the tabernacle (Num. 12:10).

For the most part, however, this verb has to do with the moral or spiritual direction a person is taking. As Moses reviews the incident of the golden calf, he says, "You turned aside quickly from the way that the Lord had commanded you" (Deut. 9:16; cf. Exod. 32:8). A common phrase about the wicked kings of Israel is that they "did not turn away from the sins of Jeroboam" (e.g., 2 Ki. 13:11; 15:9). Occasionally we read about the Lord commanding his people not "to turn aside" either to the right hand or the left; that is, they must keep to the straight path laid out before them (Deut. 5:32; 17:11; Jos. 1:7; 2 Ki. 22:2). They must "turn away from evil and do good" (Ps. 34:14; 37:27). And if God's people have sinned, they must be careful to "take your evil deeds out of my sight" (Isa. 1:16) and "remove all your impurities" (1:25). The sovereign Lord will then, in turn, "remove" the disgrace of his people from all the earth (25:8). In Ezekiel, God promises to "remove the people's heart of stone and give them a heart of flesh" (Ezek. 36:26). Note a most blessed promise that became a reality for Isaiah: When a coal of fire touches his lips, he hears a voice, "Your guilt is taken away and your sin is atoned for" (Isa. 6:7). See *NIDOTTE*, 3:238–39.

New Testament

Verb: ἀφίστημι (*aphistēmi*), GK *923* (S *868*), 14x. *aphistēmi* generally means to "leave, depart" in a physical sense. Other uses of this verb include the forsaking of wickedness as in 2 Tim. 2:19: "Everyone who confesses the name of the Lord must *turn away* from wickedness." See *leave*.

TURN BACK

New Testament

Verb: ἀναστρέφω (*anastrephō*), GK *418* (S *390*), 9x. *anastrephō* can mean "to turn back," but it has a related meaning "to conduct oneself, live" in a certain way. See *live*.

TURN OUT

New Testament

Verb: τυγχάνω (*tynchanō*), GK *5593* (S *5177*), 12x. *tynchanō* usually designates what might "happen" or how something might "turn out." See *happen*.

TWELVE

Old Testament

Noun: עָשָׂר (*ʿāśār*), GK 6925 (S 6240), 205x.

Noun: עֶשְׂרֵה (*ʿeśrēh*), GK 6926 (S 6240), 136x. *ʿāśār* and *ʿeśrēh* are both based on the same Heb. root (*ʿśr*) and mean "ten" (see *ten*), but these two words only occur in combination with other numbers. Most often they are combined with *šᵉnayim* (meaning "two") and thus mean "twelve." As the number twelve, *ʿāśār* occurs 66x and *ʿeśrēh* 36x.

Twelve is an important biblical number It is the number of the tribes of Israel (Gen. 49:28), traced back to the "twelve" sons of Jacob (Gen. 35:22; 42:13). After the Israelites accept all the words of the law of God revealed to Moses, Moses gets up early the next morning, builds an altar, and sets up "*twelve* stone pillars representing the *twelve* tribes of Israel" (Exod. 24:3–4; cf. Jos. 4:3). The tabernacle is surrounded by the "twelve" tribes in a block formation (Num. 2:17–31). Since the tribe of Levi is not counted among these twelve (as the priestly tribe, they live in the middle of the camp; 2:17, 33), the tribe of Joseph is divided into two tribes (Ephraim and Manasseh) in order to maintain twelve tribes.

"Twelve" representatives of the tribes fulfill various functions (Num. 1:44), and the leaders of the tribes offer dedications to the tabernacle on "twelve" days (Num. 7). During the time of David, the priests and the Levites are divided up into twenty-four (12 x 2) orders (1 Chr. 24:6–18), as are the singers (25:6–31). David divides up his army into twelve divisions (27:1–15). The restoration of the "twelve" tribes of the divided kingdom (1 Ki. 11:30) is a feature of postexilic hope (Ezek. 47:13).

The number "twelve" eventually comes to designate God's people in its totality, just as it previously referred to all Israel. In the NT, Jesus selects "twelve" disciples to indicate the formation of a new Israel, and in the book of Revelation the number 144,000 (12,000 x 12) represents the totality of God's people. See *NIDOTTE*, 3:552–54.

New Testament

Adjective: δώδεκα (*dōdeka*), GK *1557* (S *1427*), 75x. *dōdeka* is the cardinal number "twelve." In the NT it is predominantly used (34x) to refer to the twelve disciples, sometimes simply called "the Twelve" (Mt. 10:1; Mk. 3:14; Lk. 9:1; Jn. 6:67; Acts 6:2; 1 Cor. 15:5; Rev. 21:14). It is also used to refer to the twelve tribes of Israel (Mt. 19:28; Jas. 1:1; Rev. 21:12) or the twelve progenitors of those tribes (Acts 7:8). In Rev. 7:5–8, *dōdeka* appears twelve times in the listing of the twelve thousand from each of the tribes.

In the NT, *dōdeka* also has a number of other uses. It is used to count units of time, like hours (Jn. 11:9), days (Acts 24:11), or years (Mt. 9:20; Mk. 5:25, 42; Lk. 2:42). It is used to number things as varied as baskets (Mk. 6:43; 8:19), men (Acts 19:7), or legions of angels (Mt. 26:53). Revelation contains more uses of *dōdeka* than any other NT book, such as twelve stars (Rev. 12:1), gates (21:12, 21), angels (21:12), pearls (21:21), crops (22:2), and foundations (21:14).

The new Jerusalem, the bride of the lamb, is replete with the number twelve: twelve gates, each with an angel and the name of one of the twelve tribes of Israel; twelve foundations with the names of the twelve apostles; 12,000 stadia in length, width, and height. The wall was 144 (12 x 12) cubits thick. See *NIDNTT-A*, 156.

TWENTY

Old Testament

Noun: עֶשְׂרִים (*ʿeśrîm*), GK 6929 (S 6242), 316x. *ʿeśrîm* is the plural of *ʿeśer* ("ten," GK 6924) and means "twenty." It can be combined with other numbers to make such numbers as twenty-seven (Gen. 8:14) and 120 (6:3).

Twenty seems to be a number of responsible adulthood. When the Israelites are numbered in the desert, those who can serve in the military are "*twenty* years old and more" (Num. 1:18, 20, etc.). Later, when the nation rebels against the Lord by refusing to enter the land of Canaan, God declares that all those "*twenty* years old and more" will die in the desert and not enter the promised land.

New Testament

Noun: εἴκοσι (*eikosi*), GK *1633* (S

1501), 11x. *eikosi* means "twenty." It is almost always found in combination with other numbers, e.g., "twenty thousand" (Lk. 14:31) or "a hundred and twenty" (Acts 1:15). (The only exception is in 27:28, "twenty fathoms.") The most common combination forms the number "twenty-four" (Rev. 4:4, 10; 5:8; 11:16; 19:4).

TWILIGHT

Old Testament

Noun: עֶרֶב (*ʿereb*), GK 6847 (S 6153), 134x. *ʿereb*, meaning "evening, twilight," normally refers to the time of day surrounding sundown. See *evening*.

TWO

Old Testament

Noun: שְׁנַיִם (*šᵉnayim*), GK 9109 (S 8147), 769x. *šᵉnayim* means "two."

Adjective: שֵׁנִי (*šēnî*), GK 9108 (S 8145), 156x. *šēnî* is the ordinal numeral meaning "second." *šᵉnayim* can also combine with other numbers: e.g., with *ʾelep* ("thousand," GK 547), it means "two thousand"; with the number ten, it means "twelve." *šᵉnayim* is actually a dual form in Heb.; many Heb. nouns can have this type of ending to indicate a pair (*ʾoznayim* for "two ears"; *ʿēnayim* for "two eyes").

(1) "Two" is not as significant as the numbers three, four, seven, or twelve, but there are various nuances to this number. It occurs in Israel's civil and ceremonial laws. For example, the Ten Commandments came in "two stone tablets" (Exod. 34:1, 29); these tablets are most likely two copies of the same set of laws rather than the covenant law divided up into two sections; both tablets were placed in the ark (1 Ki. 8:9). On the Day of Atonement, the high priest was to "take *two* male goats" and cast lots between them (Lev. 16:5–8, 21). On the cover to the ark of the covenant were "*two* cherubim" (Exod. 25:18–19). One of the options for a sin offering was "*two* doves or *two* young pigeons" (Lev. 5:11; cf. Lk. 2:24).

(2) There are various binary polarities in the OT. For example, note the following pairs: the sun and the moon (Gen. 1:16), husband and wife (2:25), Cain and Abel (4:1–9), male and female (7:9), two wives at odds with each other (30:1; 1 Sam. 1:2), Esau and Jacob (Gen. 25:22–28), and many others. The united kingdom of Israel was divided up into two nations after the death of Solomon (1 Ki. 11:26–12:33).

(3) The ordinal numeral "second" has a number of important uses in the OT as well. At the end of the second month of the second year after the rains came in the days of Noah, the earth was complete dry (Gen. 8:14). Joseph had two sons, Manasseh and the "*second* son," Ephraim (41:52), who receives the greater blessing (48:17–20). On the second month of the second year after the exodus, the Israelites leave Sinai (Num. 1:1). The Lord will "reach out his hand a *second* time to reclaim the remnant" (Isa. 11:11). Jonah runs away from the Lord; but after he is rescued at sea, "the word of the Lord came to Jonah a *second* time" (Jon. 3:1). Note that God is a God who offers second chances (cf. also the "second chance" given to Peter after his denials [Jn. 21:15–18] and Thomas after doubting Jesus' resurrection [20:24–29]).

New Testament

Adjective: δύο (*dyo*), GK *1545* (S *1417*), 135x. *dyo* is the cardinal number "two." Jesus uses two fish to feed five thousand people (Mk. 6:41). The widow gives two copper coins (Mk. 12:42). Two pennies can buy five sparrows (Lk. 12:6). People have two hands, two feet, and two eyes (Mk. 9:43, 45, 47).

Jesus sends out people in pairs (Mt. 21:1; Mk. 6:7; 11:1; 14:13; Lk. 10:1; 24:13; Acts 9:38; 19:22; 23:23), perhaps recalling the Mosaic regulation that an accusation against a person must be made by "*two* or three witnesses" (Mt. 18:16; 26:60; Jn. 8:17; 2 Cor. 13:1; 1 Tim. 5:19; Heb. 10:28). Both Jesus and Paul often juxtapose two seemingly identical things for the purpose of contrast or forcing a choice between the two, such as a man with two sons (Mt. 21:28), two men taken

(Mt. 24:40), and the like (cf. Mt. 27:21; Lk. 7:41; 15:11; 16:13; 18:10; Gal. 4:22, 24; Phil. 1:23). See *NIDNTT-A*, 156.

UGLY

Old Testament

Adjective or Noun: רַע (or רָע) (*ra*ʿ [or *rā*ʿ]), GK 8273 (S 7451), 312x. In most contexts, *ra*ʿ is translated "evil, wicked" (e.g., Gen. 13:13). As an adjective, *ra*ʿ gives a negative or inferior quality to the word it modifies. Thus, cows are called "ugly" (Gen. 41:3–27 [6x]) because of their gaunt appearance. See *evil*.

UNANIMOUS

New Testament

Adjective: ὁμοθυμαδόν (*homothymadon*), GK *3924* (S *3661*), 11x. *homothymadon* means "together, unanimous, of one mind." It is made up of *homo* ("same") with *thymos* ("principle of life, feeling, and thought"). Thus, it meant "unanimous," but later it was weakened to mean "together." See *together*.

UNAUTHORIZED

Old Testament

Adjective: זָר (*zār*), GK 2424 (S 2214), 70x. In most instances, *zār* modifies a noun and means "strange, foreign, alien" or, by extension, "unauthorized, illegitimate." See *foreigner, foreign*.

UNBELIEF

New Testament

Noun: ἀπιστία (*apistia*), GK *602* (S *570*), 11x. *apistia* is a "lack of faith, unbelief," the negated form of the noun *pistia* ("belief, faith"). As such, *apistia* ("unbelief") and *pistia* ("belief/faith") are polar opposites, and they are often contrasted for emphasis. Such an emphatic contrast is evident and intentional in passages like Rom. 3:3; 4:20; 11:20 (in this last one, Paul says, "They were broken off because of their *unbelief*, but you stand fast through faith" (ESV). Here, *apistia* is something that one possesses, whereas at other times it refers to the state one is presently in.

apistia as the state of unbelief is a condition in which people can choose to stay or which they can abandon (Rom. 11:23). The consequences of living in such a state are acting out of ignorance (1 Tim. 1:13), impeding the miraculous (Mt. 13:58; Mk. 6:6), and, at its worst, leading one to reject God and suffer the consequences (Heb. 3:12, 16). While Jesus may very well may intervene with a sharp rebuke against *apistia* (Mk. 16:14), he graciously condescends to human weakness to help those who struggle with a lack of faith (Mk. 9:24). See *NIDNTT-A*, 462-66.*

UNBELIEVING, UNBELIEVER

New Testament

Adjective: ἄπιστος (*apistos*), GK *603* (S *571*), 23x. In one instance *apistos* means "unbelievable, incredible." Before King Agrippa, Paul asks why anyone would think it incredible that God raises the dead (Acts 26.8). Every other use of *apistos* means "faithless" or "unbelieving." This use occurs as an attribute, as when Jesus blames the crowd for being part of a "faithless and perverse generation" after his disciples are unable to cast an evil spirit out of a boy (Mt. 17:17). In addition, Jesus tells Thomas to stop "doubting" and believe (Jn. 20:27). *apistos* is also used in place of a noun to refer to a person who does not believe the gospel message about Jesus, i.e., an "unbeliever" (Lk. 12:46; 1 Cor. 6:6; 10:27; 2 Cor. 4:4; 1 Tim. 5.8; Tit. 1:15). In several places in his letters to the Corinthians, Paul discusses the relationship between unbelievers and believers: believing husbands and wives are to relate in certain ways to unbelieving spouses (1 Cor. 7:12–15); speaking in tongues is a sign not for unbelievers but for believers (1 Cor. 14:22–24); believers are not to be yoked with unbelievers (2 Cor. 6:14–15). See *NIDNTT-A*, 462-66.

UNBLEMISHED

Old Testament

Adjective: תָּמִים (*tāmîm*), GK 9459 (S 8549). 91x. Most often *tāmîm* describes animals or crops intended for sacrificial offerings as "unblemished" or "whole." This term frequently appears in the cultic context of Israel's worship (e.g., Exod.

12:5; Lev. 1:3, 10; 3:1, 6; 4:3). Neither blemished animals nor priests with physical defects are considered fit for sacrifice or service in the temple (Lev. 21:16–23; 22:17–25). Physical wholeness reflects the holiness of God (see 10:3). Figuratively the term refers to wholeness of heart and, as applied to human action or conduct, conveys the notion of walking blamelessly before the Lord (of Noah in Gen. 6:9; of Abraham 17:1; Deut. 18:13). Likewise the NIV renders *tāmîm* as "faithfulness" ("sincerity" KJV) in Jos. 24:14; "honorably" in Jdg. 9:16, 19. In this sense, it refers to the conduct of the righteous and wise: "For the upright will live in the land, and the blameless will remain in it" (Prov. 2:21).

Finally, this term may be used in other contexts as "complete" as in Jos. 10:13 ("full day"), or "perfect." God is described as perfect (2 Sam. 22:31) both in terms of his knowledge (Job 37:16) and his law (Ps. 19:8). See *NIDOTTE*, 4:306-8, 477-86.

UNCIRCUMCISED, UNCIRCUMCISION

New Testament

Noun: ἀκροβυστία (*akrobystia*), GK *213* (S *203*), 20x. *akrobystia* means "uncircumcised" or "uncircumcision." This noun denotes the foreskin and thus means someone who is still has a foreskin.

(1) Just as *peritomē* ("circumcision") sometimes denotes the Jews in the NT, so *akrobystia* sometimes denotes Gentiles (Acts 11:3; Gal. 2:7; Eph. 2:11).

(2) Paul taught that for those who believe in Christ, whether or not they are physically circumcised is irrelevant (1 Cor. 7:18–19; Gal. 5:6; 6:15; Col. 3:11). What counts is our relationship with Jesus Christ by faith (Rom. 3:30) and keeping the commands of God (Rom. 2:25–27; 1 Cor. 7:18–19). For this reason, Abraham is the father not just of Jews but of all believers (Rom. 4:9–12).

UNCLE

Old Testament

Noun: דּוֹד (*dôd*), GK 1856 (S 1730), 61x. *dôd* sometimes denotes a close male relative, such as an "uncle" or "cousin"; it also means "beloved." See *beloved.*

UNCLEAN, UNCLEANNESS

Old Testament

Verb: טָמֵא (*tāmēʾ*), GK 3237 (S 2930), 88x. *ṭāmēʾ* means to "become ceremonially unclean, defiled." This word and its derivatives are concentrated in certain sections of the OT, especially Lev. 10-15 (describing the ritual uncleanness of animals, Lev. 11; aspects of birth, Lev. 12; "leprosy" in people, houses, and fabrics, Lev. 13-14; and emissions and menstruation, Lev. 15). To a lesser extent, the terms are used in Lev. 18-22; Num. 5-9; 18-19; Deut. 12-15; Ezek. 22; 24; 36-37; 39; and 43-44. Animals and foods are considered clean or unclean by assignment in God's law. Persons and objects can become ritually unclean but, through purification rituals, can become clean again. The major bodily impurities causing one to become *ṭāmēʾ* are "leprosy" (i.e., "skin disease"; the Hebrew word *ṣāraʿat* in Lev. 13-14 is apparently not true "leprosy," commonly known today as Hanson's disease), genital discharges, and contamination by a corpse.

Priests and Levites are especially concerned with issues of cleanness and uncleanness. The most severe types of uncleanness are sexual misconduct, idolatry, and murder, all of which defile the temple and the land (sexual misconduct, Lev. 18:24-25; idolatry, 20:3-5; Ps. 106:38; murder, Num. 35:33). The prophets, in denouncing moral uncleanness, use ritual uncleanness figuratively for the wickedness that only God can cleanse. Priests are to teach the distinction between what is clean and what is unclean (Lev. 10:10; cf. Ezek. 22:26; 44:23). The temple is to be guarded against defilement because God is thought to be physically present there (Exod. 25:8; 1 Ki. 8:1-21; Isa. 12:6; Ezek. 8-11; 43:1-12). The high priest Jehoiada stations guards at the temple so that no one who is unclean can enter (2 Chr. 23:19). Under Zedekiah, however, the temple is defiled (2 Chr. 36:14), and because of

Israel's unfaithfulness, the Lord permits his temple to be defiled by the heathen (Ps. 79:1), abominations (Jer. 7:30; 32:34), slayings (Ezek. 9:7), idolatry, adultery, and human sacrifice 23:37-39).

Idolatry causes the entire land to become *ṭāmēʾ* (Ezek. 36:18; cf. Gen. 35:2). It is clear that Israel has defiled herself by idols of her own making (Ezek. 22:4; see also 14:11; 36:25; 37:23), for the Lord inquires of Judah, "How can you say, 'I am not defiled; I have not run after the Baals'?" (Jer. 2:23).

Noun: טֻמְאָה (*ṭumʾâ*), GK 3240 (S 2932), 36x. *ṭumʾâ* means "uncleanness, impurity." Half of the occurrences of this word are in Leviticus, where laws for uncleanness are outlined (especially the uncleanness that results from bodily discharges, Lev. 15:3, 25–26, 30–31). The Day of Atonement is necessary "because of the *uncleanness* and rebellion of the Israelites" (16:16). Ezekiel is concerned in general about the "impurity" of God's people (Ezek. 24:11, 13; 36:17), but through the prophet God promises to cleanse them "from all your impurities" (36:25) and to save them "from all your uncleanness" (36:29; cf. Zech. 13:2). That promise stands yet today, for through Christ God promises to "purify us from all unrighteousness" (1 Jn. 1:10; see *cleanse*).

Adjective: טָמֵא (*ṭāmēʾ*), GK 3238 (S 2931), 87x.

ṭāmēʾ as an adjective denotes that which is "unclean," especially in a ritual context. In most cases, it is a technical term for the state of being ritually "unclean" or "defiled" and thus disqualified from the sphere of the holy (e.g., the temple). Animals (Lev. 11), people (Lev. 13-15), and objects can be *ṭāmēʾ* and so disqualified from temple service (see the verb above). The impurity of *ṭāmēʾ* objects or people can be conveyed by contact: "Anything that an *unclean* person touches becomes *unclean*, and anyone who touches it becomes *unclean* till evening" (Num. 19:22).

For Christians, purity is achieved in Christ: "The blood of goats and bulls and the ashes of a heifer sprinkled on those who are ceremonially unclean sanctify them so that they are outwardly clean. How much more, then, will the blood of Christ, who through the eternal Spirit offered himself unblemished to God, cleanse our consciences from acts that lead to death, so that we may serve the living God" (Heb. 10:13-14). See *NIDOTTE*, 2:365-76; 4:477-86.

New Testament

Noun: ἀκαθαρσία (*akatharsia*), GK *174* (S *167*), 10x. *akatharsia*, a derivative of *akathartos*, can refer to anything that is filthy or dirty ("uncleanness"), or figuratively to a state of moral corruption ("impurity"). The only literal use in the NT is found in Mt. 23:27, where it describes the contents of a tomb as full of "everything unclean." Here Jesus' point is not only that the tomb is full of dirty things but, even more important to an observant Jew, that the contents of a tomb are ceremonially unclean, ritually defiling anyone who touches it. Figuratively, *akatharsia* is often associated with sexual sins. It is used in conjunction with "sexual sin" (2 Cor. 12:21), "sexual immorality" (Gal. 5:19; Eph. 5:3; Col. 3:5), and "sensuality" (Eph. 4:19). It is also used with reference to one's motivation: "For the appeal we make does not spring from error or impure motives (*akatharsia*), nor are we trying to trick you" (1 Thess. 2:3). See *NIDNTT-A*, 278-79.

Adjective: ἀκάθαρτος (*akathartos*), GK *176* (S *169*), 32x. *akathartos* pertains to that which may not be brought into contact with what is holy (see *holy*). In this sense it is "impure, unclean, defiled" and at times "evil." The root *kathartos* means "clean" or "pure," but the *a* prefix denotes its negation, thus "impure, unclean." In the LXX, *akathartos* often translates *ṭāmēʾ* ("unclean, defiled") and its derivatives, denoting impurity in a ritual (ceremonial) sense. The NT conveys this sense of ritual impurity by pairing *akathartos* with *koinos* in Acts 10:14, 28 and 11:8. In Acts 10:14

and 11:8, Peter says he has been faithful not to eat food that is ritually "unclean"; yet in 10:28 he makes the profound theological statement that one may not characterize individuals as either "impure" or "unclean." Paul, quoting from Isa. 52:11, denounces idolatry saying: " 'Therefore come out from them and be separate,' says the Lord. 'Touch no unclean thing, and I will receive you'" (2 Cor. 6:17). Here the "unclean thing" amounts to association with those who worship idols, and this pushes the idea of "impurity" into the moral sphere (an idea already apparent in the prophets).

The moral sense of *akathartos* is common in the NT. Impurity is associated with fornication (Eph. 5:5; Rev. 17:4) and idolatry, as we have just noted. Impurity is also associated with demonic evil. Those afflicted by demons are often described as having an "unclean" or "evil" (*akathartos*) spirit (see, e.g., Mt. 10:1; 12:43; Mk. 1:23, 26; 3:11, 30; 5:2, 8, 13; 6:7; 7:25; 9:25).

UNCLOTHED

New Testament

Adjective: γυμνός (*gymnos*), GK *1218* (S *1131*), 15x. *gymnos* means to be "naked, without clothes." See *naked*.

UNDERSTAND

Old Testament

Verb: בִּין (*bîn*), GK 1067 (S 995), 171x. *bîn* is most commonly found in the wisdom literature, especially Job and Proverbs. It is sometimes used in the general sense of "to know" (Prov. 24:12; Mic. 4:12), but more often refers to a technical, detailed, or specific understanding. It describes a depth of knowledge beyond mere awareness, but does not seem to include a relational aspect (like, e.g., *ydʿ*, GK 3359; see *know*). Thus, alternate translations such as "perceive," "discern," or "gain insight" may more readily capture the nuance of the term.

(1) *bîn* is often used to describe the kind of knowledge God possesses. For example, God has a comprehensive knowledge of the human mind—not only the totality of its contents, but also the way it processes information and the way it works (1 Chr. 28:9; Prov. 24:12). In addition, God's knowledge is independent and self-sufficient (Isa. 40:14). Theological reflection regarding God's knowledge can lend some insight into the meaning of *bîn*, but it would be an overstatement to claim it is a technical word for divine understanding.

(2) *bîn* is also used to describe human perception, knowledge, and skill. For example, the craftsmen who work on the tabernacle (Bezalel, Oholiab, and others) possess this sort of understanding (Exod. 36:1), as does Kenaniah, the Levite in charge of the singing, when David has the ark brought to Jerusalem (1 Chr. 15:22). It is unclear whether the understanding (*bîn*) is the *skill* or the *insight for the administration* or proper use of the skill. *bîn* is also granted to Solomon in order to assist him in leading God's people (see 1 Ki. 3, especially v. 11), and the psalmist asks God for this kind of understanding (Ps. 119:27, 34; cf. Jas. 1:5; 3:17). *bîn* includes moral discernment (Prov. 2:9), wisdom (10:23), patience (14:29), and most importantly, knowledge of God (9:10). Ultimately, it is a gift from God for those who fear the Lord (2:5) and can be gained from reading his word (Neh. 8:8).

Verb: יָדַע (*yādaʿ*), GK 3359 (S 3045), 956x. *yādaʿ* expresses a wide range of meanings connected to the idea of "knowing" or "understanding." See *know*.

Verb: שָׂכַל (*śākal*), GK 8505 (S 7919), 60x. *śākal* means "to be wise, understand, prosper/be successful." See *(be) wise*.

Verb: שָׁמַע (*šāmaʿ*), GK 9048 (S 8085), 1165x. *šāmaʿ* means "to hear, listen, pay attention to, perceive, understand, obey, proclaim, announce." See *hear*.

New Testament

Verb: γινώσκω (*ginōskō*), GK *1182* (S *1097*), 222x. *ginōskō* means "to know, understand, recognize." It is a rich verb in the NT. See *know*.

Verb: ἐπιγινώσκω (*epiginōskō*), GK *2105* (S *1921*), 44x. *epiginōskō* can mean to "know, perceive, recognize, understand." See *know*.

Verb: ἐπίσταμαι (*epistamai*), GK *2179* (S *1987*), 14x. *epistamai* in the NT refers to a general knowledge or understanding of a situation. See *know*.

Verb: καταλαμβάνω (*katalambanō*), GK *2898* (S *2638*), 15x. *katalambanō* can mean "to catch, obtain, seize, overtake." In the middle voice it means "to grasp, understand." See *catch*.

Verb: νοέω (*noeō*), GK *3783* (S *3539*), 14x. *noeō* means "to understand, see, reflect on." It is related to the Gk. word *nous* ("mind"). While in classical Gk. thought the *nous* served as the ordering principle of the cosmos, in ancient Heb. thought the mind is more closely tied to moral and spiritual perception.

In the NT, *noeō* refers to an ability to see and understand God's activity and plan for the created order. Thus, it is linked to the heart and to faith. In John's quotation of Isa. 6:10, *noeō* is linked with the "heart" (*kardia*). Dead hearts cannot see or understand the gospel and, therefore, do not repent and turn to God (Jn. 12:40). Matthew and Mark use *noeō* in a similar way in the Olivet Discourse. They insert the parenthetical "let the reader understand" in order to state that God's end-time work is something that can only be grasped by those who have spiritual insight (Mt. 24:15; Mk. 13:14). The spiritual nature of *noeō* is also seen in Paul's reference that general revelation is enough to make people understand that there is a God (Rom. 1:20), though such understanding is not yet saving faith. By contrast, the writer to the Hebrews states that it is "by faith that we *understand*" that the world was created by God (Heb. 11:3). See *NIDNTT-A*, 394-96.

Verb: οἶδα (*oida*), GK *3857* (S *1492*), 318. *oida* is the most common word for "know, understand" in the NT. See *know*.

Verb: συνίημι (*syniēmi*), GK *5317* (S *4920*), 26x. *syniēmi* means "to understand, realize." Many of the occurrences of the verb in the NT are found in quotations of OT texts (see Mt. 13:14–15; Acts 28:26–27; Rom. 3:11; 15:21). The Synoptic Gospels also use this verb to refer to the disciples' lack of understanding of Jesus' teaching (Mk. 8:17, 21; Lk. 8:10). Likewise, this term describes the Jews' lack of understanding of the gospel message (Acts 28:26–27). Such a lack of understanding is due to sin or hard-heartedness (Mk. 6:52) and is, therefore, punishable. But *syniēmi* is also used to refer to understanding given by God, such as the understanding Jesus' disciples receive from him (Mt. 16:12; 17:13) and the insight he gives the two disciples on the road to Emmaus, Lk. 24:45).

Thus, on the one hand, to understand is a gift from God (Eph. 3:4), but on the other hand, inability to understand or lack of insight is a result of one's disobedience and unfaithfulness (Rom. 1:21–22). See *NIDNTT-A*, 545-46.

UNDERSTANDING

New Testament

Noun: διάνοια (*dianoia*), GK *1379* (S *1271*), 12x. *dianoia* denotes the "mind, thought, understanding." See *mind*.

Noun: ἐπίγνωσις (*epignōsis*), GK *2106* (S *1922*), 20x. *epignōsis* means "knowledge, understanding." See *knowledge*.

Noun: νοῦς (*nous*), GK *3808* (S *3563*), 24x. *nous* refers to the "mind, intellect, understanding," that is, the part of the human system that initiates thoughts and designs. See *mind*.

Noun: σύνεσις (*synesis*), GK *5304* (S *4907*), 7x. *synesis* refers to spiritual "understanding, insight." It is the child Jesus' *synesis* that amazes the crowds when he answers questions in the temple (Lk. 2:47). Paul prays that God will give the Colossians spiritual wisdom and "understanding" (Col. 1:9) so they will walk in a manner worthy of the Lord (Col. 1:10). They will have riches from such *synesis*, which will enable them to know the mystery of Christ (Col. 2:2). Similarly, in Eph. 3:4, Paul suggests that his "*insight* into the mystery of Christ" has come by revelation. Paul encourages Timothy to reflect on his teaching, for in doing so, the

Lord will give him "*insight* into all this" (2 Tim. 2:7). See also Mk. 12:33 and 1 Cor. 1:19.*

(BE) UNFAITHFUL

Old Testament

Verb: בָּגַד (*bāgad*), GK 953 (S 898), 49x. *bāgad* means "to be unfaithful, betray." An "unfaithful" person is someone who has made some promise but has not kept that promise (cf. Ps. 78:57). For example, the Israelites had promised to keep God's law, but in 1 Sam. 14:32–33a, some of them ate meat with blood in it (cf. Gen. 9:4; Deut. 12:16). Thus, Saul says to them, "You have been unfaithful" (1 Sam. 14:33b), and he takes the necessary steps to correct the problem. Some uses of this verb have to do with Israel's unfaithfulness to the Lord in a fashion similar to a wife's unfaithfulness to her husband (Jer. 3:8, 11, 20; 9:2; Hos. 5:7; Mal. 2:11, 14–16)—a common theme in the prophets.

A number of Proverbs have to do with actions of "the unfaithful" (Prov. 11:3, 6; 13:2; 13:15; 21:18; 22:12; 25:19). This verb can also be used for "one who betrays," i.e., a "traitor" (Isa. 21:2; 33:1). See *NIDOTTE*, 1:582–95.

UNGODLY

New Testament

Adjective: ἀσεβής (*asebēs*), GK *815* (S *765*), 9x. *asebēs* means "ungodly, godless, wicked." The term is derived from *a*, which denotes "non" or "un" in English, and *sebō*, a verb meaning "to worship, be devout." This word has two foci in the NT. It can simply mean those who are godless and who fight against the purposes of God (1 Tim. 1:9; 1 Pet. 4:18; 2 Pet. 2:6; 3:7; Jude 4, 15[2x]), including the ungodly people at the time of the flood (2 Pet. 2:5). The second focus is the blessed message that Christ came into this world precisely to die "for the ungodly" (Rom. 5:6; cf. 4:5). See *NIDNTT-A*, 520-21.*

UNITE

New Testament

Verb: κολλάω (*kollaō*), GK *3140* (S *2853*), 12x. *kollaō* means to "join, unite closely." It is used frequently in reference to a person uniting or associating with other people. When *kollaō* is used in reference to marriage or to God's activity, the relationship is one of intimacy. See *join*.

UNIVERSE

New Testament

Noun: κόσμος (*kosmos*), GK *3180* (S *2889*), 186x. In the NT, *kosmos* always means "the world" (except in 1 Pet. 3:3). Even with the sense of "world," there are a number of nuances within this idea. At times *kosmos* indicates the created universe (e.g., Acts 17:24). See *world*.

UNJUST

New Testament

Noun: ἄδικος (*adikos*), GK *96* (S *94*), 12x. In most contexts, *adikos* may be translated "unjust" or "unrighteous." In some occurrences, however, *adikos* may mean dishonest or untrustworthy (Lk. 16:10–11), evildoer (Lk. 18:11), or wicked (1 Cor. 6:9). *adikos* specifically denotes anyone whose actions are incongruous with divine or human law or with that which is just or righteous (see *righteous*). God, however, is not *adikos* in his dealings with human beings (Rom. 3:5; Heb. 6:10). To the contrary, he is just and righteous in all of his actions toward those who are *adikos*. For example, God "sends rain on the righteous and the *unrighteous*" (Mt. 5:45).

Beyond common grace, God has demonstrated his love for us in that while we were still sinners, Christ died for us (Rom. 5:8). Peter declares, "For Christ died for sins once for all, the righteous for the *unrighteous*" (1 Pet. 3:18). Although we deserve punishment for our unrighteous deeds, God has lavished his grace on us in Jesus Christ, giving us the opposite of what we deserve (Rom. 6:23). But those who are not found in Christ will be punished on the day of judgment (2 Pet. 2:9), where "there will be a resurrection of both the righteous and the *wicked*" (Acts 24:15). Emphasizing the judgment of the wicked, Paul rhetorically asked, "Do you not know that the *wicked* will not inherit the kingdom of heaven?" (1 Cor. 6:9). In this light, the writer of Hebrews concludes that without holiness no one will see the LORD (Heb. 12:14). See *NIDNTT-A*, 17-18.*

UNLEAVENED BREAD

Old Testament

Noun: מַצָּה (*maṣṣeh*), GK 5174 (S 4682), 53x.

Usually translated "unleavened bread," *maṣṣeh* is bread made without yeast. See *bread, unleavened.*

(BE) UNRESPONSIVE

Old Testament

Verb: כָּבֵד (*kābēd*), GK 3877 (S 3513), 114x. *kābēd* generally means "to honor." It can also mean, by extension, "be heavy" or "unresponsive." See *honor*.

UNRIGHTEOUS

New Testament

Noun: ἄδικος (*adikos*), GK *96* (S *94*), 12x. In most contexts, *adikos* may be translated "unjust" or "unrighteous." In some occurrences, however, *adikos* may mean dishonest or untrustworthy (Lk. 16:10–11), evildoer (Lk. 18:11), or ungodly (1 Cor. 6:1). See *unjust*.

UNRIGHTEOUSNESS

New Testament

Noun: ἀδικία (*adikia*), GK *94* (S *93*), 25x. *adikia* is consistently translated as either "unrighteousness" or "iniquity" in the KJV. The NIV, however, offers numerous glosses, such as "evil" (Jas. 3:6, the tongue is "a world of *evil*"), "wickedness" (Rom. 6:13), "dishonest" (Lk. 16:8), "worldly" (Lk. 16:9), "sin" (Acts 8:23), "wrong" (2 Cor. 12:13), and "wrongdoing" (1 Jn. 5:17, which unequivocally declares "All *wrongdoing* is sin").

adikia specifically denotes anything that is incongruous with divine or human law—i.e., what is just or righteous (see *righteous*). Paul declares that "the wrath of God is being revealed from heaven against all the godlessness and *wickedness* of men" (Rom. 1:18), and that "all will be condemned who have not believed the truth but have delighted in *wickedness*" (2 Thess. 2:12). Paul defends his conviction of the righteous judgment of God when rhetorically he asks, "If our *unrighteousness* brings out God's righteousness more clearly, what shall we say? That God is unjust in bringing his wrath on us?" (Rom. 3:5, cf. 9:14). Absolutely not, for God is a righteous judge and is just in all of his dealings toward us (Rom. 3:5, Heb. 6:10).

In light of impending wrath and judgment against *adikia*, Paul charged the Romans: "Do not offer the parts of your body to sin, as instruments of *wickedness*, but rather offer yourselves to God, as those who have been brought from death to life" (Rom. 6:13). Paul's rationale for this appeal is rooted in the nature and evidences of salvation, "Everyone who confesses the name of the LORD must turn away from *wickedness*" (2 Tim. 2:19). Nonetheless, on those occasions when we do commit *adikia*, "if we confess our sins, he [God] is faithful and just and will forgive us our sins and purify us from all *unrighteousness*" (1 Jn. 1:9; cf. Heb. 8:12). See *NIDNTT-A*, 17-18.

UNTIE

New Testament

Verb: λύω (*lyō*), GK *3395* (S *3089*), 42x. *lyō* means "to loose, untie," but also "break, destroy" (see *break*). John the Baptist acknowledges his unworthiness before the Lord when he announces: "He is the one who comes after me, the thongs of whose sandals I am not worthy to untie" (Jn. 1:27). *lyō* can also denote unwrapping, as in the case of Lazarus's grave clothes being removed or untied from around him (Jn. 11:44). See *loose*.

UPRIGHT

Old Testament

Adjective: יָשָׁר (*yāšār*), GK 3838 (S 3477), 119x. Often rendered "upright, right, innocent; straight," *yāšār* usually denotes appropriate human conduct with respect to ethical norms and religious values.

(1) The manner in which God rules over his people is just and upright; he does no

wrong (Deut. 32:4; Hos. 14:9). His works are upright (Ps. 111:8), as are his precepts (19:8), his laws (119:137), and his word (33:4). In fact, God himself is upright (92:15; Isa. 26:7).

(2) This word also describes the straight, level pathway that believers are to walk, in contrast to the crooked and uneven way that the wicked follow (Prov. 14:12; 21:2; Jer. 31:9). Those who live in this manner (especially kings) do "what is *right* in the eyes of the Lord" (2 Ki. 15:3, 34; 2 Chr. 34:2). See *NIDOTTE* 2:564-67.

(3) The plural of this word is a term for God's faithful people ("the upright"), who live and act in a morally righteous manner (Ps. 7:10; 107:42; 111:1).

New Testament

Adjective: δίκαιος (*dikaios*), GK *1465* (S *1342*), 79x. *dikaios* means "righteous, innocent, just, upright." This adjective follows many of the characteristics of the Heb. word *ṣaddîq*; see *righteous, righteousness*.

USE

New Testament

Verb: χράομαι (*chraomai*), GK *5968* (S *5530*), 11x. *chraomai* means "to use." This verb occurs in a variety of passage with a variety of nuances. Paul encourages slaves who are able to gain their freedom to "make use" of that opportunity (1 Cor. 7:21). Two chapters later the apostle says that could have earned his living from being an evangelist, but he freely chooses not to "use" that right (9:12, 15). If we "use" the law in a proper manner, the law is good and not a burden (1 Tim. 1:8). Later in this same letter Paul instructs Timothy to "use a little wine" for his stomach's sake" (5:23).

USELESS

New Testament

Adjective: κενός (*kenos*), GK *3031* (S *2756*), 18x. *kenos* means "empty, empty-handed," and by extension, "vain, useless, futile." See *empty*.

UTENSIL

Old Testament

Noun: כְּלִי (*k^eli*), GK 3998 (S 3627), 325x. *k^elî* is a noun denoting a variety of equipment, tools, containers, etc., used in a given activity or occupation. The use of this noun to refer to such a large number of different objects is comparable to the English noun "thing." See *thing*.

UTTER

See *say*.

UTTERANCE

Old Testament

Noun: נְאֻם (*n^eʾum*), GK 5536 (S 5002), 376x. *n^eʾum* is used of an utterance, word, or revelation. It is often translated as "oracle" (NIV), "parable" (KJV), "declaration," and "word." See *word*.

UTTERMOST

Old Testament

Noun: קָצֶה (*qāṣeh*), GK 7895 (S 7097), 92x. *qāṣeh* is derived from the verb *qāṣâ*, which means "to cut off," and refers to the point where something is cut off, i.e., its edge or end. Since even heaven and earth have an end (e.g., Ps. 19:4, 6), the phrase can mean "the uttermost parts" of the earth. See *end*.

VAIN

Old Testament

Noun/Adverb: שָׁוְא (*sawʾ*), GK 8736 (S 7723), 54x. *sawʾ* denotes ineffectiveness or falseness and may be translated as "vain, worthless, false." The term describes the futility of certain things or activities. See *worthless*.

New Testament

Adjective: κενός (*kenos*), GK *3031* (S *2756*), 18x. *kenos* means "empty, empty-handed," and by extension, "vain, useless, futile." See *empty*.

VALIANT

Old Testament

Noun: חַיִל (*ḥayil*), GK 2657 (S 2428), 246x. The basic sense of *ḥayil* is "power, strength, or capability." In military contexts, *ḥayil* can refer to an "army" of fighting men (e.g., Pharaoh's forces in Exod.

14:4, 9, 17, 28). Also, the expression "men of *ḥayil*" can be translated "warriors, men of valor/might, valiant men, fighting men" (Jdg. 20:44, 46; 2 Sam. 11:16; 2 Ki. 24:16; Ps. 76:5). See *strength*.

VALLEY

Old Testament

Noun: גַּיְא (*gayʾ*), GK 1628 (S 1516), 58x. *gayʾ* means "a valley." Since much of Palestine was hill country, there were many valleys. When the Israelites and the Philistines lined up to do battle, there was a valley between them (1 Sam. 17:3). Nearly half of the occurrences of this term have to do with specific valleys, such as "the Valley of Ben Hinnom" (south of Jerusalem, Jos. 15:8; this valley is associated with pagan cult practices; cf. Jer. 7:31–32), "the Valley of Iphtah El" (19:14), and "the Valley of Salt" (1 Chr. 18:12). Leading into Jerusalem was a "Valley Gate" (2 Chr. 26:9; Neh. 3:13).

Several familiar and beloved passages of the OT contain a reference to a valley. For example, in Ps. 23:4 the psalmist says, "Even though I walk through the valley of the shadow of death, I will fear no evil." Isa. 40:4 prophesies the return from exile with these words: "Every valley shall be raised up, every mountain and hill made low." See *NIDOTTE*, 1:852.

Noun: נַחַל (*naḥal*), GK 5707 (S 5158), 137x. *naḥal* refers to a dry river bed or wadi. Since it can refer to the dry river bed itself, by extension it also can be used to describe a valley or ravine. See *river*.

Noun: עֵמֶק (*ʿēmeq*), GK 6677 (S 6010), 65x. An *ʿēmeq* is a broad valley. It comes from a group of words that share the same root and are related to the meaning "deep." Hebrew actually has four words that can be translated "valley." An *ʿēmeq* is a U-shaped valley as opposed to a V-shaped valley (Heb. *gayʾ*), though to some degree those words are synonymous. While an *ʿēmeq* is usually wider than a *gayʾ*, it is narrower than a *biqʿâ*, a broader U-shaped valley, such as the great plain of Babylon. The fourth word is *naḥal*, which means a stream bed.

The floor of an *ʿēmeq* is often covered with rich soil that has been washed down from the hills and is used for growing crops (1 Sam. 6:13). Other uses include warfare (1 Sam. 17:19) and divine judgment (Joel 3:2). Furthermore, an *ʿēmeq* can be a wild place where flowers such as "the lily of the *valleys*" grow (Song 2:1). Numerous specific valleys are mentioned in the OT, including the Valley of Aijalon (Jos. 10:12), the Valley of Elah (1 Sam. 17:2), and the Valley of Rephaim (2 Sam. 5:18, 22). Since an *ʿēmeq* has a wide floor, it can be considered, in a certain sense, to be a plain. Therefore, in 1 Ki. 20:23, the Arameans say, "Their god is a god of the mountains … if we fight them in the *plain* [*mîšôr*] surely we will overpower them," while in verse 28 the man of God reports that the Arameans say, "'The LORD is a god of hills and not a god of the *valleys* [*ʿēmeq*]" There is no contradiction here between "plain" and "valleys;" each describes the same geographic region. See *NIDOTTE*, 3:440.

VALUABLE

New Testament

Verb: διαφέρω (*diapherō*), GK *1422* (S *1308*), 13x. The intransitive form of *diapherō* means "to have value, be valuable, differ." See *have value*.

Adjective: τίμιος (*timios*), GK *5508* (S *5093*), 13x. *timios* refers to something that is considered "valuable, precious, honorable." It can describe things that are valuable or costly as well as people who are honorable. It is most often found in Revelation (5x), in each case referring to costly or precious stones (Rev. 17:4; 18:16; 21:11; 21:19) or wood (18:12). Paul compares the believer's work for the kingdom of God to valuable materials, including "gold, silver, *costly* stones" (1 Cor. 3:12). *timios* is used in a similar sense, especially given the context of the agrarian world of the NT, when James writes about the farmer waiting for his "*valuable* crop" (Jas. 5:7).

timios is not used exclusively of material physical things, however, but can have the connotation of precious or valuable in the sight of the beholder, such as life itself (Acts 20:24), the great promises of God that are so "precious" to the believer (2 Pet. 1:4), and especially the blood of Christ, which is incalculably "precious" (1 Pet. 1:19).

Finally, *timios* can refer to something (or someone) that is so valuable that it is honorable in itself. In this way Gamaliel is an honorable teacher of the law (Acts 5:34), and marriage is to be "*honored* by all" (Heb. 13:4). See *NIDNTT-A*, 564-65.*

VALUE

Old Testament

Verb: חָשַׁב (*ḥāšab*), GK 3108 (S 2803), 124 x. *ḥāšab* is most often translated as "think" or "plan" (see *think*, *plan*). One use of this word is in reference to mathematical computations and can also be translated as "count," "calculate," and "value."

New Testament

Verb: τιμάω (*timaō*), GK *5506* (S *5091*), 21x. *timaō* means "to honor, hold in esteem, place value on someone or something." See *honor*.

Verb: ὠφελέω (*ōpheleō*), GK *6067* (S *5623*), 15x. *ōpheleō* denotes the basic idea of benefiting through a particular condition or situation, hence, "to gain, profit, value." See *gain*.

Noun: τιμή (*timē*), GK *5507* (S *5092*), 41x. *timē* is the amount at which something is "valued," its "price," or it can mean "honor, respect."

Most basically *timē* is the "value" placed on something; it is often put in monetary terms. In this sense the price of blood represented by the thirty silver coins paid to Judas is "blood *money*" (Mt. 27:46), and in Acts the believers sell their homes and lands and bring the "price" they receive to the apostles (Acts 4:34). It is this price that Ananias and Sapphira hold back (5:2–3). When the sorcerers in Ephesus are converted and destroy their scrolls of magic, they calculate the "value" of the scrolls at 50,000 drachmas (19:19).

timē can also represent value beyond strict monetary terms. For example, Paul reminds the Corinthian church that they have been bought by Christ for a "price" (1 Cor. 6:20; 7:23). With respect to a person, *timē* connotes the "honor" or "respect" paid as a result of the value of a person. In this sense Jesus acknowledges that a prophet is not paid honor by his fellow countrymen (Jn. 7:44), and Paul exhorts the believers in Rome to pay "honor" to those to whom "honor" is due (Rom. 13:7)—most specifically by placing the honor of someone else above one's own (12:10). Above all, Jesus Christ is worthy of honor because of the honor given to him by the Father (2 Pet. 1:17) through his suffering and death (Heb. 2:9). As a result, all living creatures give glory and honor to Jesus (Rev. 4:9). See *NIDNTT-A*, 564-65.

(HAVE) VALUE

New Testament

Verb: διαφέρω (*diapherō*), GK *1422* (S *1308*), 13x. The transitive form of *diapherō* generally means "to carry through or across, spread out" (see *carry through*). Most of the uses of this verb are intransitive, which means "to have value, be valuable, differ." Jesus points out on several instances how Christians "have more value" than the birds of the air (Mt. 6:26; 10:31; Lk. 12:7, 24) or sheep (Mt. 12:12). Paul emphasizes how the differing splendor of the stars suggests the gloriouis nature of the resurrection body in contrast to the physical body (1 Cor. 15:41). In Gal. 4:1, he points out that as long as the son of a wealthy landowner is a child, he "is no different" from a slave in terms of his independence; later, however, he becomes the heir, while the slave remains the slave. Paul applies this analogy to God's people in the OT and in the NT eras. See *NIDNTT-A*, 139.

VANITY

Old Testament

Noun: הֶבֶל (*hebel*), GK 2039 (S 1892), 73x. *hebel* literally means "breath" (see *breath*), but in most OT instances, the noun functions metaphorically, usually denoting vanity, futility, and/or temporality. *hebel* occurs 38x in Ecclesiastes alone (including at least once in each of the twelve chapters except ch. 10). There are three basic categories in which *hebel* is used as a metaphor:

(1) First, it refers to the empty false gods worshiped by God's people. "They made me jealous by what is no god and angered me with their *worthless idols*" (Deut. 32:21). "They are *worthless*, the objects of mockery; when their judgment comes, they will perish" (Jer. 51:18).

(2) Second, *hebel* can signify insubstantial or vain human efforts. "I have labored to no purpose; I have spent my strength *in vain* and for nothing" (Isa. 49:4). "Since I am already found guilty, why should I struggle *in vain*?" (Job 9:29).

(3) Third, *hebel* often refers to the temporality or futile nature of a thing. The psalmist acknowledges the brevity of life (Ps. 39:5): "You have made my days a mere handbreadth; the span of my years is as nothing before you. Each man's life is but a *breath*." Meaninglessness and the fleeting nature of life appear evident in other contexts, such as Eccl. 6:12: "For who knows what is good for a man in life, during the few and *meaningless* days he passes through like a shadow?" The writer of Eccl. lists several aspects of life, including personal efforts, joys, and tragedies, all of which are viewed as temporary in nature and value (7:15; 9:9; 11:10). They are all *hebel*. But in contrast to those scholars who believe the author's conclusion is that all of life is meaningless, the context of the book as a whole suggests that the point is that meaning in life cannot be found outside of God. He is the source of all things, and in him alone life finds purpose (cf. 9:7–9; 12:13–14). Apart from God, however, everything ends in futility. See *NIDOTTE*, 1:1005-6.

VARIOUS

New Testament

Adjective: ποικίλος (*poikilos*), GK *4476* (S *4164*), 10x. *poikilos* means "various," usually with the notion of a variety of kinds or forms of things. In the gospels it is used for Jesus' healing power over "various" diseases (Mt. 4:24; Mk. 1:34; Lk. 4:40; cf. Heb. 2:4). Paul uses it in reference to "various kinds" of evil desires or passions that lurk in people's hearts (2 Tim. 3:6; Tit. 3:3). Both James and Peter refer to "various" trials that Christians face in their lives (Jas. 1:2; 1 Pet. 1:6).

VEIL

Old Testament

Noun: פָּרֹכֶת (*pārōket*), GK 7267 (S 6532), 25x. All occurrences of *pārōket* in the OT refer to the "inner veil" before the Most Holy Place; 25 refer to the veil in the tabernacle and one to the veil in Solomon's temple (2 Chr. 3:14).

New Testament

Noun: καταπέτασμα (*katapetasma*), GK *2925* (S *2665*), 6x. Of the various household and cultic curtains in the ancient world, *katapetasma* is used exclusively in temples. This noun may have come from the basic term for curtains (*petasma*) with the prefix *kata* ("down") added to it because it specifically hung downward in temples.

In the Gk. OT *katapetasma* mostly refers to the inner veil between the Most Holy Place and the rest of the temple (see Heb. *pārōket*), as it does in the NT. This is the curtain that is torn at Christ's death (Mt. 27:51; Mk. 15:38; Lk. 23:45), and it functions as a powerful illustration that all believers now have direct access to God; that is, they are priests (so 1 Pet. 2:9) and can enter God's presence through the work of Christ. Furthermore, the author of Hebrews states that the foundational hope held by believers ("anchor of the soul") is based on both Jesus' entering through this veil as our forerunner and his service as our eternal high priest (Heb. 6:19–20; cf. 9:3; 10:20). See *NIDNTT-A*, 295.*

VENGEANCE

Old Testament

Noun: נָקָם (*nāqām*), GK 5934 (S 5359), 17x.

Noun: נְקָמָה (n^e*qāmâ*), GK 5935 (S 5360), 27x. Both *nāqām* and n^e*qāmâ* mean "vengeance." See *avenge*.

New Testament

Noun: ἐκδίκησις (*ekdikēsis*), GK *1689* (S *1557*), 9x. *ekdikēsis* means "vengeance, punishment, justice." See *avenge*.

VENOM

Old Testament

Noun: חֵמָה (*hēmâ*), GK 2779 (S 2534), 125x. The basic meaning of *hēma* is "anger, wrath" (see *anger*), though in certain contexts it may mean "poison, venom." See *poison*.

VERY

Old Testament

Noun: מְאֹד ($m^{e\text{ʾ}}$*ōd*), GK 4394 (S 3966), 300x. $m^{e\text{ʾ}}$*ōd* is usually used adverbially, meaning "very, much, greatly, exceedingly." For example, on the sixth day of creation, the Lord surveyed what he had made and proclaimed it "*very* good" (Gen. 1:31). See *greatly*.

VESSEL

Old Testament

Noun: כְּלִי (k^e*lî*), GK 3998 (S 3627), 325x. k^e*lî* is a noun denoting a variety of equipment, tools, containers, etc., used in a given activity or occupation. The use of this noun to refer to such a large number of different objects is comparable to the English noun "thing." See *thing*.

New Testament

Noun: σκεῦος (*skeuos*), GK *5007* (S *4632*), 23x. *skeuos* refers to an "instrument, container" (e.g., a "jar"). See *instrument*.

VICINITY

New Testament

Noun: ὅριον (*horion*), GK *3990* (S *3725*), 12x. *horion* means "region, vicinity." See *region*.

(BE) VICTORIOUS

New Testament

Verb: νικάω (*nikaō*), GK *3771* (S *3528*), 28x. *nikaō* means "to overcome, be victorious in a struggle." See *overcome*.

VICTORY

Old Testament

Noun: תְּשׁוּעָה (t^e*šûʿâ*), GK 9591 (S 8668), 34x. t^e*šûʿa means* "salvation, deliverance, victory." See *salvation*.

VILLAGE

Old Testament

Noun: בַּת (*bat*), GK 1426 (S 1323), 587x. *bat* is the common Hebrew noun for one's own daughter. But it may also be used to indicate membership in a group. In geographical designations, a "town and its daughters" means "a town and its satellite villages"; "Heshbon and all its *surrounding settlements*" (lit., "her daughters") (Num. 21:25; cf. 1 Chr. 7:29). See *daughter*.

Noun: חָצֵר (*hāṣēr*), GK 2958 (S 2691), 192x. *hāṣēr* probably comes from a root that means "surround" and, drawing from this basic meaning, refers to a courtyard (see *court, courtyard*) or a village. When it refers to a village (Lev. 25:31; Jos. 15:45; Neh. 11:25), it may be due to the fact that many villages in antiquity were arranged with their houses surrounding a central area. The outer wall of each house was then a part of the outer defense of the settlement.

New Testament

Noun: κώμη (*kōmē*), GK *3267* (S *2968*), 27x. *kōmē* means "village." Used only in the gospels and Acts, it refers to a small community or grouping of houses. Jesus does much of his ministry going from "village to village" (Mk. 6:6; cf. Lk. 13:22). Emmaus (Lk. 24:13), Bethlehem (Jn. 7:42), and Bethany (Jn. 11:1) are called "villages."

Noun: πόλις (*polis*), GK *4484* (S *4172*), 163x. In the NT, *polis* refers mainly to a place of human inhabitation such as a "city, town, village." See *city*.

VINE

Old Testament

Noun: גֶּפֶן (*gepen*), GK 1728 (S 1612), 55x. *gepen* denotes a "vine." The vine is a source of fruit as well as wine drink and is used, metaphorically, as a symbol of life and fertility (Num. 6:4; Hab. 3:17; Zech. 8:12).

This agricultural image is widespread in the OT. The Israelites complain after the Exodus because the desert has no vines (Num. 20:5; Deut. 8:8). Each person living under his own vine is a way of speaking about prosperity and stability in the nation. "During Solomon's lifetime Judah and Israel, from Dan to Beersheba, lived in safety, each man under his own vine and fig tree" (1 Ki. 4:25; cf. Mic. 4:4; Zech. 3:10). Conversely, those who are corrupt and who turn away from the Lord's commandments are connected with pagans, "Their vine comes from the vine of Sodom and from the fields of Gomorrah" (Deut. 32:32).

The vine can be used with reference to a fruitful wife (Ps. 128:3) or as a symbol for Israel (Ps. 80:8, 14; Jer. 2:21; Hos. 10:1; 14:7). If God's people to not produce for him proper fruit but instead become "a wild vine" (Jer. 2:21), judgment awaits them (cf. Isa. 5:1–7, which uses *śōrēq*, "choice vine"). God's judgment is sometimes spoken of in terms of destruction or withering of vines (Job 15:33; Ps. 87:47; Isa. 24:7; Joel 1:11–12). Jesus picks up on the imagery of the vine when he proclaims himself to be the ultimate source of life and spiritual growth (Jn. 15:1, 4). "I am the vine; you are the branches. If a man remains in me and I in him, he will bear much fruit; apart from me you can do nothing" (Jn. 15:5). See *NIDOTTE*, 1:888-89.

New Testament

Noun: ἄμπελος (*ampelos*), GK *306* (S *288*), 9x. *ampelos* means "vine." This word is used in three main places of the NT. In the Synoptic Gospels, when Jesus is with his disciples in the upper room, he says during the Last Supper, "I will not drink of this fruit of the vine from now on until that day when I drink it new with you in my Father's kingdom" (Mt. 26:29; Mk. 14:25; Lk. 22:18). Here Jesus is drawing attention to the heavenly banquet that all God's people can look forward to.

In Jn. 15:1, 4–5, Jesus refers to himself as the "vine" and his followers as the branches. In order to retain true life and especially to bear fruit, we must remain attached to this vine. That is, we draw our true, spiritual nourishment only from the Lord.

In Rev. 14:18–19, the process of harvesting grapes from "the vine" and putting them into a winepress becomes a metaphor of the last day, when those who have had no relationship with the Lord will experience his eternal wrath.

VINEYARD

Old Testament

Noun: כֶּרֶם (*kerem*), GK 4142 (S 3754), 94x. A *kerem* is a "vineyard." The vineyard was an important part of life in the ancient world. Noah is the first man recorded to plant a vineyard in the OT (Gen. 9:20). It becomes a symbol for blessing, wealth, joy, and prosperity (Exod. 22:5; Num. 16:14; 1 Sam. 22:7; 2 Ki. 5:26; 18:32; 2 Chr. 26:10; Eccl. 2:4). In addition to being a symbol of wealth, the *kerem* is also a means of social welfare—the ancient equivalent to food stamps! Vineyards were not to be picked clean but were to be left with something for the underprivileged to take for themselves (Exod. 23:11; Lev. 19:10; Deut. 24:21). The firstfruits of the vineyard belong to the Lord (Num. 18:12; Deut. 18:4).

The economic importance of the vineyard is seen when the Israelites claim to be powerless to secure their children from slavery because their vineyards belong to others (Neh. 5:3–5; cf. Prov. 31:16). It is important to keep vineyards cultivated so that the land will not become barren (2 Ki. 25:12; Prov. 24:30–31; Jer. 52:16). Ownership of the land and working it to produce fruit is an essential part of Israel's identity. Naboth, for example, refused to relinquish his vineyard to Ahab because it was the "inheritance of his fathers" (1 Ki. 21:3).

The *kerem* is also an example of God's blessing. "So I gave you a land on which you did not toil and cities you did not build; and you live in them and eat from *vineyards* and olive groves that you did not plant" (Jos. 24;13; cf. Deut. 6:11). The *kerem* can likewise be a sign of judgment, when God gives Israel's vineyards to someone else (1 Sam. 8:14–15; Isa. 61:5) or makes the vineyards unproductive. "A ten-acre *vineyard* will produce only a bath of wine, a homer of seed only an ephah of grain" (Isa. 5:10; cf. Joel 1:11; Amos 4:9; 5:11; Zeph. 1:13). Restoration after exile is spoken of in terms of God giving back or guarding fruitful vineyards (Isa. 27:2–3; Hos. 2:15; Amos 9:14).

The nation of Israel itself is referred to as a vineyard (Isa. 5:7). God lovingly cultivates his people and expects righteous fruit; he is disappointed when they yield only bad fruit (Isa. 5:1–6; cf. Lk. 6:44). See *NIDOTTE*, 2:723-24.

New Testament

Noun: ἀμπελών (*ampelōn*), GK *308* (S *290*), 23x. An *ampelōn* is a "vineyard." The word occurs 22x in the Synoptics, mostly in parables: the parable of the vineyard laborers (Mt. 20:1–16), the parable of the two sons (21:28–32), the parable of the wicked tenants (21:33–44), and the parable of the barren fig tree planted in a vineyard (Lk. 13:6–9). The only other occurrence is in 1 Cor. 9:7, where Paul describes his rights as an apostle to receive income from his work: "Who plants a *vineyard* and does not eat of its grapes?"

Jesus used the vineyard picture both because he lived in an agricultural society and because in the OT, the vine/vineyard was often used as a metaphor for God's people (e.g., Ps. 80:8, 14; Isa. 5:1–7). Thus, especially in the parable of the wicked tenants, Jesus' enemies were able to capture the message Jesus was trying to communicate. Since the tenants (ethnic Israel) rejected the king's servants (the prophets) sent to take account of them and killed the king's son (Jesus) in hopes of keeping the vineyard for themselves, Jesus announced that the vineyard would be given to others (a reference to spiritual Israel, God's true people throughout the ages). See *NIDNTT-A*, 41-42.

VIOLENCE

Old Testament

Noun: חָמָס (*ḥāmās*), GK 2805 (S 2555), 60x. *ḥāmās* denotes the idea of sinful violence and may be translated as "violence, wrong." The term often describes the extreme corporate or individual wickedness of human beings against God or others (see, e.g., Gen. 6:11). Isa. 53:9 states of the suffering servant, "He was assigned a grave with the wicked, and with the rich in his death, though he had done no *violence*." This violence may take the form of murder (Gen. 49:5) or psychological anguish (Ps. 35:11–12).

God uses the violence of other nations as a means of carrying out his judgment (Jer. 13:22). Ezekiel proclaims, "*Violence* has grown into a rod to punish wickedness; none of the people will be left, none of that crowd—no wealth, nothing of value" (Ezek. 7:11). God also takes revenge on those nations who have acted wickedly against his own people (Jer. 13:22).

ḥāmās also describes the general injustice observed in society (Isa. 59:6; Jer. 6:7). The modern equivalent is the found in the cliché "when *bad* things happen to good people." See *NIDOTTE*, 2:177-80.

New Testament

Noun: βία (*bia*), GK *1040* (S *970*), 3x. *bia* means "violence, force." Since violence is such a significant part of the OT scene, it may be surprising that a word like *bia* rarely occurs in the NT. The Sanhedrin does not want use too much "force" against the apostles in Jerusalem because they realize the popularity that the apostles have with the people (Acts 5:26). There is, however, a "violent" mob in Jerusalem that does attempt to lynch Paul (21:35). (The third use of this word is for a violent storm at sea, 27:41.) Yet perhaps it is not surprising that the NT contains little violence, since Jesus came to present a message of peace, humility, and hope.*

VIRGIN

Old Testament

Noun: בְּתוּלָה (b^e*tûlâ*), GK 1435 (S 1330), 50x. This word describes a young woman of marrying age. Occasionally, nothing in the text specifically suggests virginity, and b^{e}*tûlâ* should be understood merely as a "young maiden," usually paired with a "young man" (Ps. 148:12; Jer. 51:22). In most passages, however, virginity is either specified or alluded to. In these instances "virgin" is a proper translation. For example, Rebekah was a b^{e}*tûlâ* "whom no man had known" (Gen. 24:16), and there were four-hundred b^{e}*tûlâ* from Jabesh Gilead who "had not known a man" (Jdg. 21:12). b^{e}*tûlâ* is contrasted with a widow, a divorced woman, a woman "who has been defiled," and a prostitute (Lev. 21:14). In Deut. 22:13–21, the most extensive passage on the b^{e}*tûlâ*, this word refers to the sexual cloth by which one could determine the virginity, or the lack thereof, of the young maiden. The virginity of a young maiden is exalted (cf. Job 31:1), and both parties are severely punished when virginity is lost outside of marriage (cf. Deut. 22:24).

By the time of the prophets, b^{e}*tûlâ* had come to mean unwed sexual purity, and it no longer needed extra qualifiers such as "whom no man had known." Significantly, its primary prophetic use was to express, metaphorically, the status of nations in the eyes of the Lord. The "virginity" of a nation is determined by its idolatry, the spiritual prostitution of that nation. With regard to foreign nations, God ironically labeled them as "virgin" in order to mock their spiritual promiscuity. The Lord calls Sidon and Tyre prostitutes and then calls them a virgin (Isa. 23:12, 15–17). He destroys Babylon for her pride in her idols (Isa. 46–47), but not before mocking her as "O Virgin daughter of Babylon" (47:1; cf. also Jer. 46:11).

Israel is also called "virgin." The Lord describes his nation as prostitutes going after idols (Jer. 5:7). Israel lost her "virginity" to the idols of Egypt and repeated her lewd indecencies with all of the surrounding nations (Ezek. 23:1ff.). After deriding Israel for her promiscuity, the Lord also called her "O Virgin Israel" (Jer. 31:4–21). In this case it is not mockery, for the Lord promises to restore them to their virginity, to "create a new thing" (Jer. 31:21–22). In an act of divine, covenantal mercy, he miraculously turns a prostitute into a virgin. Only the Lord can make one a virgin again, and he promises to do just that through his new covenant (cf. Jer. 31:31ff.) in Jesus Christ.

The famous Isa. 7:14 passage, "the virgin shall conceive and bear a son, and shall call his name Immanuel," uses a different word, *ʿalmâ* meaning "girl" or "young woman". See *NIDOTTE*, 1:781-784.*

New Testament

Noun: παρθένος (*parthenos*), GK *4221* (S *3933*), 15x. In Greek literature outside the NT, *parthenos* generally refers to a young woman of marriageable age with or without a focus on virginity. But in the NT, *parthenos* stresses the one who has never engaged in sexual intercourse. It bears this general meaning in the parable of the ten virgins, though this fact has little bearing on the meaning of the parable (Mt. 25:1, 7, 11). In Acts 21:9 Phillip's unmarried daughters are noted as virgins, perhaps suggesting that as virgins they are better suited to fulfill their function as prophetesses.

The definitive text on virginity in the NT is 1 Cor. 7:25–40. Paul is likely referring here to "marriageable virgin daughters" (7:25, 28, 34). While Jesus was mute on this issue, Paul's reason for insisting that virginity is better than marriage is because a virgin (male or female) can give oneself full to serving the Lord without the encumbrances of home responsibilities. The last two occurrences of *parthenos* in this passage probably refer to engaged virgins who are struggling with whether or not to get married; Paul writes that neither option is inherently sinful (7:36, 37).

parthenos appears as a striking image in Rev. 14:4. John apparently refers to those 144,000 virgins (men?) who, in contrast to the sexually immoral and idolaters, were able to devote themselves entirely to the Lamb of God. They did not allow themselves to be seduced by the great prostitute Babylon. Similarly, Paul hopes to present the church to the returning Lord as a pure *parthenos* (2 Cor. 11:2). This idea stems from the OT picture of God as the husband of the nation of Israel (Isa. 54:5; Jer. 3:14) and from the picture Paul paints of Christ as the husband of the church (Eph. 5:22–32; cf. Rev. 19:7–9; 21:2).

Mary, the mother of Jesus, is described as *parthenos* (Mt. 1:23; Lk. 1:27), but this applies only up to the time of Jesus' birth (cf. Mt. 1:25). This divine conception is in fulfillment of Isa. 7:14. So as to magnify the significance of Mary's state, Luke mentions *parthenos* before Mary's name. While some religious traditions make too much of Mary as "the blessed virgin," others err by slighting her. It is interesting that Paul makes no explicit reference to the virgin birth of Jesus. See *NIDNTT-A*, 438-39.*

VISION

Old Testament

Noun: מַרְאֶה (*marʾeh*), GK 5260 (S 4758), 103x. *marʾeh* refers both to prophetic "visions" and to outward "appearances." See *appearance*.

New Testament

Noun: ὅραμα (*horama*), GK *3969* (S *3705*), 12x. *horama* refers to a "vision." It may be something seen in actual sight or in a dream. This word occurs once in Matthew; the rest are in Acts.

horama is used of the actual sight in the transfiguration (Mt. 17:9), the burning bush (Acts 7:31), and the angel who appears to Cornelius (10:3). The other nine occurrences refer to dreams (either day or night) in which the Lord reveals something special. The state in which these visions appear can vary. Several come in dreams during the night (16:9, 10; 18:9). Peter is praying at about noon when he receives a vision (10:9–10; 11:5). Cornelius's vision comes during full consciousness at three in the afternoon (10:3). Ananias receives a vision from "the Lord," though its time is unspecified (9:10, 12). Peter is visited by an angel at night while in prison, but he isn't sure whether this is real or a vision (12:9).

Similar to the OT, these "visions" instruct people to do what the Lord wants people to do. Ananias (Acts 9:10), Cornelius (10:3), and Peter (10:17, 19; 11:5) are told to meet certain people. Paul is shown the next step he should take so as to regain his sight (9:12) and, in another vision, where to further the spread of the gospel (16:9, 10). Also as in the OT, the Lord uses visions to comfort discouraged people. For example, he assures Paul of the success of the gospel in Corinth through his sufferings (18:9). The gospel will indeed spread, and nothing can stop it. See *NIDNTT-A*, 413-15.*

VISIT

Old Testament

Verb: פָּקַד (*pāqad*), GK 7212 (S 6485), 304x. While *pāqad* has a wide range of meaning, it basically expresses the action of overseeing an individual for a particular purpose, such as counting the people (see *count*).

When oversight leads to an appropriate response on behalf of the superior to the actions or situation of the subordinate, *pāqad* may be translated "to attend to" or "to visit" and regularly takes God as the subject. When God "visits," he may bring divine blessing with a deep sense of care. In fulfillment of his promise, Yahweh "visits" Sarah and she gives birth to Isaac (Gen. 21:1). Joseph trusts that God will "come to the aid" of his brothers (50:24, 25); the Israelites worship in response to hearing that God is "concerned" about them (Exod. 4:31); and the Lord their God will "care" about the remnant of Judah in the restoration (Zeph. 2:7).

More frequently, however, God "visits" not to bring divine blessing, but to bring divine judgment in response to human sin. In these instances, *pāqad* is translated "to punish." While God's authority to punish extends to all nations (Ps. 59:5[6]), the OT focuses primarily on God's punishment of Israel's sin (Jer. 14:10; Hos. 9:9). This is the predominant use of *pāqad* in the Prophets, especially in Jeremiah (32x). In light of various sins listed in Jeremiah, Yahweh repeatedly asks, "Shall I not *punish* them for this?" (Jer. 5:9, 29; 9:8). God will "punish" Israel through the siege of Jerusalem (6:6) and by the sword and famine (11:22). Yet God does not punish arbitrarily as pagan gods do; rather, he "will punish" Israel as their deeds deserve (21:14), according to the covenant stipulations (see Lev. 26; Deut. 28), and because he has chosen Israel (Amos 3:2).

New Testament

Verb: ἐπισκέπτομαι (*episkeptomai*), GK *2170* (S *1980*), 11x. *episkeptomai* means "to look after, visit, take care of." See *look after*.

VOICE

Old Testament

Noun: קוֹל (*qôl*), GK 7754 (S 6963), 505x. *qôl* generally means "voice, sound, noise." It primarily refers to a "sound" produced by the vocal cords, as when Jotham "lifted up his *voice*" in a parable before the men of Shechem in response to Abimelech's conspiracy to be king (Jdg. 9:7). It can refer to the vocal sounds of animals (1 Sam. 15:14) or personified inanimate objects ("the *voice* of your brother's blood cries to me from the ground," Gen. 4:10). The phrase "to lift up the *voice*" can indicate a cry of mourning (Gen. 21:16), a cry of joy (Gen. 29:11), or a cry for help (Gen. 39:14).

qôl also refers generally to other "sounds," such as the noise of thunder (Exod. 9:23), of battle (Exod. 32:17), of weeping (Isa. 65:19), and of water (Ezek. 1:24). Furthermore, *qôl* often represents what was communicated. For example, with reference to an entire spoken word, God says in Gen. 3:17, "Because you listened to the *voice* of your wife." Similarly, *qôl* can denote the entirety of written communication, as in 2 Ki. 10:6, "Then he wrote a letter the second time to them, saying, 'If you are mine, and if you will listen to my *voice*.'"

Theologically, *qôl* is significant in passages relating to prophecy. The prophets proclaim God's voice on earth, operating as his mouthpieces (Exod. 3:18; 4:1; 7:1; cf. Deut. 18:18–19; Isa. 50:10). The crashing "sound" of thunder and the piercing "sound" of the trumpet portray God's sovereign power and authority when he speaks and/or delivers (Exod. 19:5; 1 Sam. 12:14–18). Note too that when God speaks with his voice, he speaks with authority, and we and human beings must obey (Deut. 27:10; 28:1–2; 30:2, 8; "obey" translates "listen to the voice"). If we do not listen to his voice and instead refuse to obey the Lord, we can expect judgment (28:15, 45, 62). See *NIDOTTE*, 3:898–902.

New Testament

Noun: φωνή (*phōnē*), GK *5889* (S *5456*), 139x. *phōnē* signifies at least three ideas in the NT depending on context: "sound, voice, language." See *sound*.

VOW

Old Testament

Noun: נֶדֶר (*nēder*), GK 5624 (S 5088), 60x. *nēder* represents either the result of making a vow or the actual thing offered to "fulfill a *vow*" (this latter expression occurs 15x). Biblical writers always use this term in reference to a vow made to a deity and never for a vow between people.

nēder can used for a verbal promise of obedience (Gen. 28:20), for a nazirite vow of separation (Num. 6:2, 5), or for an offer of some specific sacrifice to the Lord (Lev. 22:18–25). *nēder* occurs as a type of peace offering in Lev. 7:16 and as a type of thank offering in Ps. 116:17–18. Ps. 22:25 uses *nēder* in reference to praising the Lord for answered prayer. A person can vow himself for service or be vowed for service (Lev. 27:2ff.). Since the vow is a serious matter, the writer of Ecclesiastes makes it plain that it is better not to vow at all than to make a vow and then not fulfill it (Eccl. 5:4).

The Bible does not limit *nēder* by gender, for both men and women can make a vow (Num. 30:2–14). While God accepts the offerings that his people have vowed, Ps. 50:7–14 clearly indicates that God does not receive a *nēder* as food, as the heathen nations taught. Accompanied by joy (Nah. 1:15) and/or singing (Ps. 61:8), the Hebrews fulfill their vows as tangible expressions of love and devotion. See *NIDOTTE*, 3:42.

WAGE

New Testament

Noun: μισθός (*misthos*), GK *3635* (S *3408*), 29x. *misthos* denotes compensation that is either earned or merited and may best be translated as "wage, reward." See *reward*.

WAIL

Old Testament

Verb: בָּכָה (*bokâ*), GK 1134 (S 1058), 114x. *bokâ* has the basic meaning "to weep," but can be translated with other terms such as "sob, mourn, wail, cry." See *weep*.

New Testament

Verb: κλαίω (*klaiō*), GK *3081* (S *2799*), 40x. *klaiō* means "to weep, mourn" because of grief. In the NT, this verb expresses violent emotions brought about by various circumstances that cause sorrow. See *weep*.

WAIT FOR

New Testament

Verb: μένω (*menō*), GK *3531* (S *3306*), 118x. The basic sense of *menō* is "to remain, stay." It can also mean "to await, wait for." See *remain*.

Verb: προσδέχομαι (*prosdechomai*), GK *4657* (S *4327*), 14x. *prosdechomai* means "to receive, welcome" (see *welcome*), and "to wait for, expect something" in the sense of looking forward to it. It has a secular meaning of waiting for an order from the governor to bring Paul in for questioning (Acts 23:21). But several NT uses have a rich theological nuance of awaiting something that God will do or bring, and it is thus intimately connected with faith. It is an expectation or a longing for God to bring something that has been promised. God's people wait for the coming kingdom (Mk. 15:43; Lk. 23:51), the consolation of Israel (Lk. 2:25), the redemption of Israel (2:38), the resurrection (Acts 24:15), the return of Christ (Tit. 2:13), and even the "mercy of our Lord Jesus Christ" that will "bring you to eternal life" (Jude 21).

Verb: προσδοκάω (*prosdokaō*), GK *4659* (S *4328*), 16x. *prosdokaō* denotes an expectation or waiting born of either hope or fear. See *expect*.

WAKE, WAKE UP

Old Testament

Verb: עוּר (*ʿûr*), GK 6424 (S 5782), 80x. *ʿûr* means "to awaken, arouse from sleep," or (in a causative sense) "to rouse someone or something, incite." This verb finds a particularly important role in the whole matter of prayer and worship. In life's struggles, it may seem that God is inactive, passive, or even indifferent. Thus, the downtrodden soul cries out to God that he should "wake up." See *awake*.

New Testament

Verb: γρηγορέω (*grēgoreō*), GK *1213* (S *1127*), 22x. *grēgoreō* means "to keep watch over, guard" something. It is also used as a warning "to wake up," as Jesus' warning to the church in Sardis, which had lost its vigilance (Rev. 3:2–3). See *watch*.

WAKEN

New Testament

Verb: ἐγείρω (*egeirō*), GK *1586* (S *1453*), 144x. In the transitive (active) sense *egeirō* means to "waken, lift up, stimulate." In the intransitive (passive) sense it conveys "to get up, rise up." See *raise*.

WALK

Old Testament

Verb: דָּרַךְ (*dārak*), GK 2005 (S 1869), 63x. *dārak* denotes the activity of walking on a path (Deut. 1:36; Jos. 14:9; Hab. 3:19), treading on a winepress (Neh. 13:15; Isa. 16:10), or bending a bow (Ps. 7:12; Lam. 2:4; Jer. 50:29), and may be translated "march, walk, tread, bend." The noun form *derek* is commonly translated "way, path." The forcefulness of the term is evident in the stomping of grapes and the pulling of a bow. This term is used in connection with two occupational groups, the "winetreaders" and the "archers." A lifestyle of obedience requires an intentional or forceful *walking*. See *NIDOTTE*, 1:989-93.

Verb: הָלַךְ (*hālak*), GK 2143 (S 1980), 1554x. *hālak* describes motion, primarily of humans, and is usually translated "walk, go, come." It is also used in a metaphorical sense to describe actions or the process of living, especially following or walking in the ways of the Lord. See *go*.

New Testament

Verb: περιπατέω (*peripateō*), GK *4344* (S *4043*), 95x. Literally, *peripateō* means "to walk around" (Mt. 9:5; 11:5; Jn. 6:66; Rev. 2:1). Figuratively, the NT uses *peripateō* to refer to the way believers behave or conduct daily life (Mk. 7:5; Eph. 2:2; 2 Cor. 5:7; Gal. 5:16). Some translations use "live" for this meaning. See *live*.

(1) Literally, *peripateō* means "to walk around, follow." Only the Synoptic Gospels and Revelation use the word in this way. Jesus asks whether it is easier to say that someone's sins are forgiven or to tell him to get up and "walk" (Mt. 9:5). Because of the presence of the kingdom of God, the lame walk (Mt. 11:5; 15:31; Acts 3:8–9). After hearing a hard teaching from Jesus, many people no longer "follow" him (Jn. 6:66). Believers must be on their guard because the devil "prowls about" looking for someone to devour (1 Pet. 5:8). Jesus "walks" among the seven churches of Revelation (Rev. 2:1).

(2) In his gospel and letters, John uses *peripateō* not just literally but figuratively as well to signify the trajectory of a person's life. The Word is always associated with light. Jesus said, "I am the light of the world. Whoever follows me will never *walk* in darkness, but will have the light of life" (Jn. 8:12; see also 11:9, 10; 12:35). In his letters, John makes the same association, exhorting his readers to walk in light rather than in darkness (1 Jn. 1:6, 7; 2:11). Believers are to follow in the footsteps of Jesus, walking the way he walked (1 Jn. 2:6). Accordingly, they are to walk in the truth (2 Jn. 4; 3 Jn. 3–4), to walk in obedience to God's commands (2 Jn. 6a), and to walk in love, which is the essence of obedience (v. 6b). See *NIDNTT-A*, 453-54.

Verb: πορεύομαι (*poreuomai*), GK *4513* (S *4198*), 153x. *poreuomai* can be translated "go, travel, walk." See *go*.

WALL

Old Testament

Noun: חוֹמָה (*ḥômâ*), GK 2570 (S 2346), 133x. *ḥômâ* means "wall." The majority of uses of this word refer to the fortified walls of cities in the ancient Near East (cf. Deut. 3:5). Walls were built to protect cities from invaders (much of Neh. 3–6 is about the rebuilding of the walls of Jerusalem), and the challenge of an army was either to scale the wall to get into the city or to break down those walls (2 Sam. 20:15; 2 Ki. 14:13). Well-fortified cities sometimes had two walls (e.g., 2 Chr. 32:5). Archers (cf. 2 Sam. 11:24) and watchmen (cf. Isa. 62:6) patrolled the walls in order to protect a city. Some people lived in houses built into the city wall (Jos. 2:15). Only rarely does this word refer to the wall of a residence (e.g., Lam. 2:7) or the walls surrounding the temple (Ezek. 40:5).

But the concept of a protective wall serves also as a spiritual metaphor. In the song that Isaiah writes for Judah's future, he refers to "a strong city; God makes salvation its *walls* and ramparts" (Isa. 26:1). Similarly, "you will call your *walls* salvation and your gates praise" (60:18). Salvation, in other words, is that which protects us from the onslaughts of the enemy (cf. Eph. 6:17). In Zech. 2:5, God promises protection for his people by being "a *wall* of fire around" them. In an opposite metaphor, Isaiah writes that Israel's sin "will become for you like a high *wall*, cracked and bulging" (Isa. 30:13); in other words, through our sin we are like dilapidated walls, exposing our vulnerability to the enemy. When God's judgment comes on a people, he often focuses it with an attack on city walls (Amos 1:7, 10, 14; Jer. 49:27; Ezek. 26:4, 9–10). See *NIDOTTE*, 2:49–50.

Noun: קִיר (*qîr*), GK 7815 (S 7023),

73x. *qîr* means "wall, side." *qîr* has a broader range of meaning than *ḥômâ* (GK 2570), for while the latter is predominantly used for the walls of a city, *qîr* also refers also to the walls of residential structures (Lev. 14:37; 2 Ki. 20:2; Isa. 38:2), vineyards (Num. 22:25), and the temple (1 Ki. 6:5, 15, 16, 27). It can also refers to the "sides" of the altar (Lev. 1:15; 5:9). Jeremiah expresses pain in the "walls" of his heart over the coming destruction of Jerusalem (Jer. 4:19). Ezekiel frequently uses this noun for one of his visionary sign acts of digging through the wall of the inner court of the temple (Ezek. 8:7–8; 12:5, 7; 13:12–15); later he uses this term for the walls of his visionary temple (41:5–25).

WANDER

Old Testament

Verb: תָּעָה (*tāʿâ*), GK 9494 (S 8582), 51x. *tāʿâ* may be translated as to "go astray, stray, lead astray, wander, stagger." See *go astray*.

New Testament

Verb: πλανάω (*planaō*), GK *4414* (S *4105*), 39x. In the active voice, *planaō* means "to lead astray, deceive"; in the middle/passive voice, "to wander, go astray." See *deceive*.

WANT

New Testament

Verb: βούλομαι (*boulomai*) GK *1089* (S *1014*), 37x. *boulomai* describes the desire or intention of a person to do something, to have something, or to obtain a result. This includes choice, purpose, or intention and desire or longing. This verb occurs in the NT regarding both the actions of God and of people.

(1) When used of people, *boulomai* refers to their action to bring about either godly or sinful desires. Examples of people who take action because of godly desires include: Joseph, who did not divorce Mary publicly because he did not "*want* to expose her to public disgrace" (Mt. 1:19); Apollos, who went to Achaia because he "wanted" to go (Acts 18:27); the centurion who prevented the soldiers from killing all the prisoners in the shipwreck because he "*wanted* to spare Paul's life" (Acts 27:43); and John's intention to visit with his addressees face to face (2 Jn. 12). Ungodly desires can cause people to act as well: Pilate releases Barnabas because he "*wants* to satisfy the crowd" (Mk. 15:15; cf. Jn. 18:39); the Sanhedrin is furious with Peter and John and "*want* to put them to death" (Acts 5:33); and those who "*want* to get rich" take actions that cause them to fall into temptation (1 Tim. 6:9).

In addition to describing what a person wants, *boulomai* can also refer to the actual act of planning something. Paul writes to the Corinthians that he "*planned* to visit you first so that you might benefit twice," (2 Cor. 1:15; cf. also 1:17; Peter and John are accused of intending to bring guilt on the Sanhedrin (Acts 5:28). This type of intention can bring about actual results—either practical (e.g., Jas. 3:4), or moral and spiritual (e.g., 4:4). But the key to *boulomai* is the intention, not the result; what one purposes or wills may not come to pass (cf. Acts 12:4 in the context of the story).

(2) *boulomai* also applies to God. The author of Hebrews speaks of God's "wanting" to make clear his purpose to the heirs of the promise, and then fulfilling that intention by confirming the promise with an oath (Heb. 6:17). Intentional acts of the will are also applied the Son (Mt. 11:27; Lk. 10:22) and the Spirit (1 Cor. 12:11). With respect to God, *boulomai* expresses God's intention and purpose as well as his ability to fulfill his intention, especially with respect to salvation. It is Jesus Christ who "*chooses* to reveal him" (Mt. 11:27; Lk. 10:22), it is God who "chooses" to give new birth to sinners by the power of his word (Jas. 1:18), it is God who "desires" salvation for his people (2 Pet. 3:9), and it is God who "wills" the atoning work of Christ (Lk. 22:42). See *NIDNTT-A*, 97-98.

Verb: θέλω (*thelō*), GK *2527* (S *2309*), 208x. *thelō* means "to will, want, desire," sometimes with human beings as the subject, sometimes with God as subject. See *will*.

WAR

Old Testament

Noun: מִלְחָמָה (*milḥāmâ*), GK 4878 (S 4421), 319x. *milḥāmâ* means "war, battle, fighting." The OT world (as is our own) was filled with wars and fighting; even our own world. The typical time to start a war in the ancient world was in the springtime (2 Sam. 11:1). Deut. 20 contains a series of regulations that God gives his people about going into war or battles. A common expression scholars have given to this sort of fighting is "holy war."

A central teaching in the OT is that "the Lord is a *warrior*" (lit., "man *of war*," Exod. 15:3; cf. Isa. 42:13). When his people fight, it is the Lord who provides the victory because "the *battle* is not yours, but God's" (2 Chr. 20:15). This truth is evident over and over in the books of Joshua and Judges, where Israel's ability to win battles is dependent on whether the Lord is fighting for them (e.g., the battle won by Gideon in Jdg. 7) or against them (as at Ai, Jos. 7). Similarly in battles between individuals, David defeats Goliath because he comes "in the name of the Lord Almighty" (1 Sam. 17:45) and knows that "the battle is the Lord's" (17:47).

The psalmists sing praise to their warrior God. David acknowledges that the Lord "trains my hands for *battle*" (Ps. 18:34; cf. v. 39; 144:1) and that "the Lord is strong and mighty, the Lord is mighty in *battle*" (24:8). And if God should so decide, he can make "*wars* to cease to the ends of the earth" (46:9). The prophets make it plain that if God's people become disobedient to him and serve other gods, the Lord will "pour out on them his burning anger, the violence of *war*" (Isa. 42:15; cf. Jer. 6:23). Yet both Isaiah and Micah look ahead to that glorious messianic age when people "will beat their swords into plowshares and their spears into pruning hooks. Nation will not take up sword again nation, nor will they train for *war* anymore" (Isa. 2:4; Mic. 4:3). See *NIDOTTE*, 2:785–89.

New Testament

Noun: πόλεμος (*polemos*), GK *4483* (S *4171*), 18x. *polemos*, from which we get our word "polemical," is the word for a conflict, up to and including "battle" or "war." See *battle*.

WARN, WARNING

Old Testament

Noun: עֵדוּת (*ʿēdût*), GK 6343 (S 5715), 61x. *ʿēdût*, usually translated "testimony," is closely connected to God's law. In the Pentateuch, this noun describes the two tablets containing the Ten Commandments. Generally, outside the Pentateuch *ʿēdût* is a more generic reference to law (1 Ki. 2:3; 2 Ki. 23:3; 1 Chr. 29:19), perhaps with the physical tablets of the Ten Commandments in the background. In this sense, the plural of *ʿēdût* may be translated "requirements, warnings, regulations, or decrees." See *testimony*.

New Testament

Verb: διαμαρτύρομαι (*diamartyromai*), GK *1371* (S *1263*), 15x. This is an intensified compound of the verb *martyreō* ("to testify"). It means "to testify, warn" in the case of important matters and situations of extreme danger. See *testify*.

Verb: διαστέλλω (*diastellō*) GK *1403* (S *1291*), 7x. *diastellō* means "to command with authority" (see command, commandment). But it can also mean "to warn," as when Jesus warns his disciples against the yeast of the Pharisees (Mk. 8:15).

Verb: νουθετέω (*noutheteō*), GK *3805* (S *3560*), 8x. *noutheteō* means "to warn." As Paul makes plain in his farewell speech to the elders of Ephesus, one important aspect of his ministry was to "warn" believers of the dangers of heresy and of falling away from the faith (Acts 20:31). He himself had to warn the Corinthians (1 Cor. 4:14) and the Thessalonians (2 Thess. 3:15; cf. 1 Thess. 5:14) of this danger. *noutheteō* also means "to admonish" (see *admonish*).

Verb: προλέγω (*prolegō*), GK *4625* (S

4302, *4277*, *4280*), 15x. *prolegō* refers to saying something in advance of an event. It sometimes has the nuance of "to warn." See *say before*.

WARRIOR

Old Testament

Noun: גִּבּוֹר (*gibbôr*), GK 1475 (S 1368), 159x. *gibbôr* means "warrior, mighty one, powerful one." It is often used of those who have strength that surpasses ordinary strength. It can be used of animals, such as the lion who is "mighty among beasts" (Prov. 30:30), but it is usually used of personal beings. Nimrod was "a mighty warrior on the earth" (Gen. 10:8–9). Gideon is called "mighty warrior" (Jdg. 6:12). David has many soldiers, but only some of them fit into the category of "mighty warrior" (2 Sam. 23:8–9, 16–17, 22). The "fighting men" of the two and a half tribes east of the Jordan are supposed to cross over the Jordan to help their compatriots (Jos. 1:14); in such cases, however, this word does not mean someone of extraordinary strength but is used as a mere euphemism for "warrior."

Another important usage for this verb is its application to God. Ps. 24:8 extols "the Lord strong and mighty, the Lord mighty in battle." Isaiah gives the title of "Mighty God" to the coming child-king (Isa. 9:6). Jeremiah addresses Israel's God in prayer as "O great and powerful God, whose name is the Lord Almighty" (Jer. 32:19; cf. Deut. 10:17; Neh. 9:32). See *NIDOTTE*, 1:806–15.

Noun: חַיִל (*ḥayil*), GK 2657 (S 2428), 246x. The basic sense of *ḥayil* is "power, strength, or capability." In military contexts, *ḥayil* can refer to an "army" of fighting men (e.g., Pharaoh's forces in Exod. 14:4, 9, 17, 28). Also, the expression "men of *ḥayil*" can be translated "warriors, men of valor/might, valiant men, fighting men" (Jdg. 20:44, 46; 2 Sam. 11:16; 2 Ki. 24:16; Ps. 76:5). See *strength*.

WASH, WASHING

Old Testament

Verb: כָּבַס (*kābas*), GK 3891 (S 3526), 51x. *kābas* means "to clean, cleanse, wash," usually by treading, kneading, or beating. In contrast to *rāḥaṣ*, which is used of washing the human body, *kābas* is never used of bodily cleansing and almost always refers to the washing of clothes.

(1) Literally, *kābas* refers to the washing of garments (Gen. 49:11; Lev. 6:27). Such garments were not generally washed with soap but instead were pounded, treaded, or kneaded on wet stones in cold water; thus, *kābas* communicates the idea of "treading down" or "subjugating." This washing most often (28x) refers to clothing that is ceremonially unclean (Exod. 19:10; Lev. 11:25; 14:8; 15:5; 16:26, 28; Num. 8:7; 19:7, 8, 10, 19, 21). Of the 51 occurrences of the root word *kbs*, all but 9 occur in the Pentateuch (2 Sam. 19:24; 2 Ki. 18:17; Ps. 51:2, 7; Isa. 7:3; 36:2; Jer. 2:22; 4:14; Mal. 3:2). Thirty-one of the 42 remaining occurrences appear in Lev. 13 (test for leprosy), 14 (law of cleansing a leper), and 15 (instructions for cleansing).

kābas is also translated "washerman's" or "fuller's" in four passages (2 Ki. 18:17; Isa. 7:3; 36:2; Mal. 3:2). In 2 Sam. 19:24, it describes the daily, physical condition of Saul's son Mephibosheth as he awaits the return of King David.

(2) Figuratively, *kābas* refers to the "washing" away of sins (Ps. 51:2; Jer. 2:22), which only God can do. Human iniquities cannot be cleansed or "washed away" by human works and/or actions.

(3) The NT parable of the good Samaritan (Lk. 10:25–37) illustrates well the dynamics of the commandments concerning *kābas*. Both the priest and the Levite were concerned with ceremonial purity, thus avoiding contact with the "beaten man." Such contact would have made them unclean and required them to *kābas*, "to wash their garments," in order to be reinstated into their official roles.

Verb: רָחַץ (*rāḥaṣ*), GK 8175 (S 7364), 72x. *rāḥaṣ* denotes the cleansing of an object, body part, or entire person for the purposes of sacrifice, priestly service, or cultural etiquette. It may be translated as "wash, bathe, cleanse." The book of Leviticus instructs the people regarding the laws of clean and unclean, where washing is a means of maintaining covenant cultic purity (Lev. 15: 5, 6, 7, 8, 10, 21, 22, 27; cf. Exod. 29:4). The term is significant especially in Leviticus 16, where instructions for washing are given for the high priest and those participating in the Day of Atonement (see vv. 4, 24, 26, 28). *rāḥaṣ* is used in contexts where the holiness of God is both present and intended to remain. Isaiah speaks of a day when God himself will *wash* a remnant in Jerusalem for himself (Isa. 4:4). This event climaxes in Christ, who takes up the role of the high priest and *washes* believers by his own blood (Heb. 9:11–14). See *NIDOTTE*, 3:1098-99.

New Testament

Verb: ἀπολούω (*apolouō*), GK *666* (S *628*), 2x. *apolouō* means "to wash." This verb is used once in a reference to Paul's washing away of sins; this was symbolized by baptism, which took place at the time of his conversion (Acts 22:16). *apolouō* is also used for a similar washing that took place when the Corinthians became believers (1 Cor. 6:11).

Verb: λούω (*louō*), GK *3374* (S *3068*), 5x. In Acts 9:37; 16:33 this verb refers to physical washing. But Heb. 10:22 tells us that when we come to God through Christ, our hearts are sprinkled to cleanse us from a guilty conscience, and our bodies are "washed with pure water," presumably baptism, which symbolizes God's forgiveness of our sins.

Verb: νίπτω (*niptō*), GK *3782* (S *3538*), 17x. *niptō* denotes the activity of general and religious washing and may best be translated as "wash." The sense of general washing is evident in the miracle of the man born blind. Jesus commands him to go and "*wash* in the Pool of Siloam ... the man went and *washed*, and came home seeing" (Jn. 9:7). A group of Pharisees criticize Jesus' disciples for not practicing the cultural norm of washing before a meal: "Why do your disciples break the tradition of the elders? They don't *wash* their hands before they eat" (Mt. 15:2; Mk. 7:3–4).

In a religious context, Jesus washes the feet of his disciples as an act of humble servitude. In John's account, Jesus "poured water into a basin and began to *wash* his disciples' feet, drying them with the towel that was wrapped around him." Then Jesus discussed with his disciples the meaning of what he had done in this washing (Jn. 13:5–11). Theologically, it symbolizes the humility and the sacrifice that Christ would soon demonstrate on the cross, where sins replace feet as the object of washing. Later in the NT church, Paul commends those widows who have "*washed* the feet of the saints" (1 Tim. 5:10) in their service to others. See *NIDNTT-A*, 388-89.

Noun: βαπτισμός (*baptismos*), GK *968* (S *909*), 4x. *baptismos means* "baptism, washing." Twice in the NT *baptismos* refers to ceremonial washings of Jewish rituals: to "washing of cups, pitchers and kettles" (Mk. 7:4) and to "various ceremonial washings" of the OT law (Heb. 9:10). See *baptism*.

Noun: λουτρόν (*loutron*), GK *3373* (S *3067*), 2x. *loutron* means "washing." This word for washing refers to the cleansing that Jesus performs on the church through his sacrifice on Calvary, whereby we are washed clean and pure (Eph. 5:26). In Tit. 3:5, Paul refers to this as "the washing of rebirth."

WASTE

New Testament

Noun: ἀπώλεια (*apōleia*), GK *724* (S *684*), 18x. *apōleia* means "destruction, ruin, waste." See *destruction*.

WASTELAND

Old Testament

Noun: מִדְבָּר (*midbār*), GK 4497 (S 4057) 269x. *midbār* is generally translated "desert, wasteland, open country." Some translate the noun simply as "wilderness," but a modifying word like "barren" needs to be added to portray adequately the arid nature of a *midbār*. See *desert*.

Noun: שְׁמָמָה (*šᵉmāmâ*), GK 9039 (S

8077), 56x. *šᵉmāmâ* conveys the divine destruction of peoples, cities, lands, and idols and may be translated "desolate, "desolation, wasteland." See *desolation*.

WATCH

Old Testament

Verb: נָצַר (*nāṣar*), GK 5915 (S 5341), 63x. *nāṣar* generally indicates the action of carefully watching over a particular object so that the object is preserved or protected. It may be translated "to keep, guard, watch, protect." God is the "watcher" of all people (Job 7:20), but he "watches over" his vineyard (i.e., Israel) in a special way to protect it from harm (Isa. 27:3a, c). See *keep*.

Verb: שָׁמַר (*šāmar*), GK 9068 (S 8104), 468x. Often translated "to keep," the verb *šāmar* bears three distinct but related meanings in the OT: "to guard, tend," "to watch over," and "to preserve" (see *keep*). It is used, for example, of Eli "watching" Hannah's mouth (1 Sam. 1:12) or of Balaam "examining" Israel (Num. 23:12).

New Testament

Verb: βλέπω (*blepō*), GK *1063* (S *991*), 133x. *blepō* is a general word meaning "to see," but it can also mean "to look at, watch." See *see*.

Verb: γρηγορέω (*grēgoreō*), GK *1213* (S *1127*), 22x. *grēgoreō* originally came from a verb that meant to wake someone up. In the NT it means "to keep watch over, guard." It carries the idea of vigilance in the face of something impending (Mt. 24:42, "*Keep watch*, because you do not know on what day your LORD will come"). Thus, *grēgoreō* is the command given to believers regarding the second coming, to "be alert" (Mk. 13:33; Lk. 12:37). It is sometimes associated with prayer in the gospels (Mt. 26:41), possibly because of the expectation of a reply. It also carries the idea of wakefulness when drowsiness is the tendency (Mk. 14:37).

Elsewhere in the NT Paul used *grēgoreō* in warnings to the Ephesian elders to "be on guard" against the insidious nature of false doctrine (Acts 20:31), in encouragements to persevere (1 Cor. 16:13), and as a metaphor for being physically alive (1 Thess. 5:10, "whether we are *awake* or asleep"). *grēgoreō* is a necessary element of resisting the devil (1 Pet. 5:8, "Be self-controlled and *alert*. Your enemy the devil prowls around like a roaring lion looking for someone to devour."). It is used as a warning to the church in Sardis to wake up or it will lose its position (Rev. 3:2-3). See *NIDNTT-A*, 116.

Verb: θεωρέω (*theōreō*), GK *2555* (S *2334*), 58x. Most uses of *theōreō* refer to physical sight or watching, but it can also be used for perception and understanding. See *see*.

Noun: φυλακή (*phylakē*), GK *5871* (S *5438*), 47x. *phylakē* mostly denotes a "prison" or "jail" (see *prison*), but it also can refer to a "watch" of the night. The Roman military divided the night into four *watches*, in order to provide rotating guards throughout the night (Mt. 14:25). This helped prevent guards from falling asleep on duty. This fact makes the suggestion that the guards at the tomb of Jesus had fallen asleep highly unlikely (Mt. 28:13). Luke also uses *phylakē* for the activity of the shepherds of Bethlehem "keeping watch" over the flocks at night (Lk. 2:8).

WATCH OUT

New Testament

Verb: προσέχω (*prosechō*), GK *4668* (S *4337*), 24x. *prosechō* means "to guard, watch out, pay attention." See *guard*.

WATER

Old Testament

Verb: שָׁתָה (*šātâ*), GK 9272 (S 8354), 217x. The basic meaning of *šātâ* is "to drink" and, in the Heb. Hiphil verb stem, "to give drink to, to water." See *drink*.

Noun: מַיִם (*mayim*), GK 4784 (S 4325), 585x. In the OT *mayim* simply means "water." But "water" was a significant element of life in the ancient world and is used in a wide variety of ways.

mayim is primarily important because it is vital for all life. The *mayim* that God provided by rain was always highly esteemed (Deut. 11:11; 1 Ki. 18:41–45). Water was viewed as a precious gift from God turning the dead earth into a fertile land by means of a surging spring of *mayim*, just as the abundance of water characterizes the garden of Eden (Gen. 2:10–14). God's provision of *mayim* to the Israelites (Exod. 17:6) was celebrated time and again in Jewish tradition.

mayim can also denote a negative, sometimes even demonic, dimension of reality. Bodies of "water" were viewed as powerful forces that God could use to annihilate his adversaries (Exod. 14–15; cf. Ezek. 26:19–20). The greatest of these was the flood at the time of Noah (Gen. 6–8).

mayim in the ancient world was also the primary means of washing. The priests and Levites washed themselves with *mayim* as part of the consecration rites before performing their ceremonial duties (Exod. 29:4; Num. 8:5–22), as did the high priest on the Day of Atonement (Lev. 16:4, 24). Even the ordinary Israelite was to use *mayim* for ceremonial washing (12:1–8; 14:8–9; 15:1; Num. 19:11–12). The prophets used the concept of washing and *mayim* to foretell the final future of their nation, when an eschatological sprinkling of God's purifying water would cleanse both land and people and God would put a new Spirit in their hearts (Isa. 44:3; Ezek. 36:25–32; Zech. 13:1). The symbolism of water in the OT is equally powerful. We too have been washed and made clean (see NT words on *water*, *wash*). See *NIDOTTE*, 2:929-34.

Verb: שָׁקָה (*šāqâ*), GK 9197 (S 8248), 62x. *šāqâ* occurs almost exclusively in the causative stem, "to make to drink, to water." See *make to drink*.

New Testament

Verb: ποτίζω (*potizō*), GK *4540* (S *4222*), 15x. *potizō* means "to drink, cause one to drink, give water." See *give to drink*.

Noun: ὕδωρ (*hydōr*), GK *5623* (S *5204*), 76x. The NT use of *hydōr* is similar to the OT use of *mayim*. Water was an important commodity to any community (Mk. 9:41). It is needed for drinking and for cleansing (cf. Lk. 7:44; cf. Jn. 13:5). The preciousness of *hydōr* and its vital necessity for life has given the word several metaphorical uses.

(1) As in the OT, *hydōr* in the NT is often linked to the spiritual domain. Angelic and demonic powers shelter under the "waters" (Rev. 16:5). The healing power of springs or brooks was common in NT times (Jn. 5:4, 7). Water was used for ceremonial preparation to symbolize spiritual cleansing (Mt. 23:25–26; Mk. 7:3–4; Jn. 2:6). Although Jesus absolves his disciples from the Jewish prescription of ceremonial hand-washing before and after meals (Mt. 15:1–20), water was still considered a significant element of purification in the baptismal practice of John the Baptist and was important in the early church (Mt. 28:19; cf. 1 Cor. 10:1–2; Eph. 5:26; Heb. 10:22) (see *baptism*).

(2) The writings of John emphasize especially the Christological and spiritual aspects of *hydōr*. Jesus washes his disciples' feet as an example for them to follow (Jn. 13:1–17). Jesus offers the Samaritan woman water that will well up within her to eternal life (4:10–15). He lets anyone who is thirsty come to him for drink, and from that person will flow "streams of living water" (7:37–38), which is the Holy Spirit (7:39; cf. 20:19–22). The Lamb leads us to springs of living water (Rev. 7:17). For all who believe and are baptized, the river of the water of life is already flowing now, without any cost (Rev. 21:6; 22:17). For the Christian, water still symbolizes the cleansing that has been given to us through Jesus Christ. See *NIDNTT-A*, 568-69.

WAVER

New Testament

Verb: διακρίνω (*diakrinō*), GK *1359* (S *1252*), 19x. *diakrinō* means "to judge, distinguish, evaluate." When applied to oneself, it can mean to "doubt" or "waver." See *judge*.

WAY

Old Testament

Noun: אֹרַח (*ʾōraḥ*), GK 784 (S 734), 59x. Deriving from the verb *ʾāraḥ* ("to journey, wander"), *ʾōraḥ* is translated variously as "path, way, road." It can bear either a literal or a figurative reference. See *path*.

Noun: דֶּרֶךְ (*derek*), GK 2006 (S 1870), 712x. *derek* may be translated in numerous ways, both literal and metaphorical, including "way, road, path, journey, conduct." The most common of these is "way," with the idea of a well-worn path or a road. After Sarai abuses Hagar and expels her, the angel of the Lord finds Hagar on the "way" or "road" to Shur (Gen. 16:7). Moses requests permission from the King of Edom to travel along the "road" of the King's Highway, a major thoroughfare that ran north and south in Transjordan (Num. 20:17).

But in the majority of OT passages, *derek* is used figuratively to denote the course of a person's life, often in connection with moral action and character. Essential here is the covenant overtone; one's path in life or spiritual journey begins with the Lord, the covenant God. The first occurrence of this meaning is Gen. 18:19, where the Lord determines to reveal his plan about Sodom and Gomorrah to Abraham, since God had chosen him "so that he will direct his children and his household after him to keep *the way* of the Lord by doing what is right and just." Just before arrival at Mount Sinai, Jethro tells Moses to get some help in governing the people, and to "teach them the decrees and laws, and show them *the way* to live" (Exod. 18:20). A prominent theme in Deuteronomy is the imagery of a journey as a metaphor for covenant obedience (Deut. 5:33; 11:22). After Joshua succeeds Moses, the Lord promised to make Joshua's "way" successful if he meditates on the book of the law night and day (Jos. 1:8).

There is, however, more than one way to travel, more than one road to walk. Ps. 1 promises that a person who does not stand in the "way" of sinners will be blessed. In contrast, Ps. 1:6 reminds readers that the "way" of the wicked will perish. Crucial to following in the desired way is God's law and not our own thinking, for "there is a *way* that seems right to a man, but in the end it leads to death" (Prov. 14:12). Prov. 22:6 records another familiar use of *derek*: "Train up a child in the *way* he should go, and when he is old he will not depart from it." See *NIDOTTE, 1:989-993.*

New Testament

Noun: ὁδός (*hodos*), GK *3847* (S *3598*), 101x. *hodos* is basically a "road" (Acts 8:26) or "path" (Mt. 13:4) on which one travels, or the act of traveling (Lk. 11:6). When Jesus sends the disciples to proclaim the kingdom of God, he tells them: "Take nothing for the *journey*" (Mt. 10:10; Lk. 9:3).

Nearly half (46x) the occurrences of this word are figurative in meaning, focusing on the course one takes in life. Jesus speaks of the "road" to life: the gate that leads to it is small, and the "road" itself is small, while the "way" to destruction is through a wide gate and the "way" itself is broad. Many go to destruction; few travel to life (Mt. 7:13–14). There are thus, in life, only two possible roads to travel; there is no third option! Ultimately Jesus is "the way" (Jn. 14:6; Acts 18:25–26; Heb. 10:20) to life as God intends it to be lived. He is also the one who will "guide our feet into the *path* of peace" (Lk. 1:79; cf. Rom. 3:17).

Christianity itself came to be described as "the Way" (Acts 9:2; 19:9, 23; 22:4; 24:14). Sometimes modifiers are added, such as "the *way* of truth" (2 Pet. 2:2), "of righteousness" (Mt. 21:32; 2 Pet. 2:21), and "of salvation" (Acts 16:17). The "most excellent *way*" is the way of love (1 Cor. 12:31). When we fall short of living according to this way, repentance is required (Jas. 5:19–20).

The metaphor of walking in the newness of life (Rom. 6:4), walking by the Spirit (Gal. 5:16, 25), walking in love (Eph. 5:2), and walking in him (Col. 2:6) is consistent with and builds on the idea of Christianity as "the Way." See *NIDNTT-A*, 401-2.

WAY OF LIFE

New Testament

Noun: ἀναστροφή (*anastrophē*), GK *419* (S *391*), 13x. *anastrophē* is a combination of the verb *strephō* ("to turn") and the prefix *ana* ("up, back, again"). Thus, the term literally means "a turning upside down, turning back." Ancient Greeks used this term to describe soldiers who turned back their path from battle and retreated. While older translations like the KJV rendered *anastrophē* as "conversion," this term is now properly understood to indicate a "manner of life" or simply "conduct." The meaning of words can change over time.

Paul compares his "way of life" when he was in Judaism (Gal. 1:13) to his way of life after Jesus was revealed to him (Gal. 1:15–16; cf. Phil. 3:7–9). He exhorts believers to put off the old self, which was a part of their "way of life" before they knew Jesus, and to put on the new nature, which is created after the likeness of God in righteousness and holiness (Eph. 4:22–23). Peter encouragea wives to have a pure and godly "way of life" so that they may win over those who refuse to accept the gospel (1 Pet. 3:1–2, 16; cf. 1:15). Christians should avoid an empty "life" that characterizes dead religion (1 Pet. 1:18), and instead strive toward a "way of life" that proceeds from humble wisdom (Jas. 3:13). Paul encourages Timothy to be an example of a godly "life" regardless of his young age (1 Tim. 4:12; cf. 2 Pet. 2:7, 12; 3:11). In summary, believers are to be holy in every aspect of their life (1 Pet. 1:15).

A holy life is not one to be lived in isolation as many attempt to do in Western Christianity today. God-honoring Christian lives must be within the encouraging confines of the body of Christ. This truth explains why Scripture exhorts Christians both to remember examples of godly lives of individuals in the past and to imitate their faith in the present (Heb. 13:7). See *NIDNTT-A*, 49-50.*

WEAK

Old Testament

Verb: חָלָה (*ḥālâ*), GK 2703 (S 2470), 75x. *ḥāla* describes a person who is weak, sick, ill, diseased, or wounded; it is also used to describe human frailties. It is the word that Samson used on four occasions to describe what would happen to him if the Philistines were to discover his secret. "I'll become as weak as any other man" (Jdg. 16:7, 11, 13, 17).

ḥāla is most often translated as "ill," such as when Joseph is told, "Your father is ill" (Gen. 48:1). God had forgiven David for his sin (2 Sam. 12:13), yet his sin still carried grievous consequences. "After Nathan had gone home, the Lord struck the child that Uriah's wife had borne to David, and he became ill." It is also the word Daniel uses to describe his physical condition following the various visions given to him by God: "I, Daniel, was exhausted and lay ill for several days" (Dan. 8:27). Sometimes this sickness may end in death (cf. the "diseased" feet of Asa in 1 Ki. 15:23–24).

In the ancient world, most diseases were ascribed to demons or evil spirits. The Hebrews repudiated this notion, ascribing both sickness and health to the actions of the Lord (cf. Deut. 32:39). Even the land can be described as "afflicted" by the Lord (29:22). If the people, however, remain faithful to the Lord, none of the diseases that happened to the Egyptians will occur among his people (Exod. 15:26; see also *heal*).

New Testament

Verb: ἀσθενέω (*astheneō*), GK *820* (S *770*), 33x. *astheneō*, similar to its noun counterpart *astheneia*, means "to be feeble, weak," and is used both of physical weakness and of moral/spiritual weakness.

Jesus uses *astheneō* when he sends out his disciples on their mission: "Heal the *sick*" (Mt. 10:8). John applies the word frequently to the sick in general (Jn. 5:3; 6:2) and to specific individuals, such as an "invalid" (5:7) and Lazarus (11:1–3, 6). Similarly, Paul uses this verb to describe the sickness of Epaphroditus (Phil. 2:26–27) and Trophimus (2 Tim. 4:20).

But equally important is the use of *astheneō* is for weakness of faith. Abraham at age ninety-nine did not weaken in his faith when God came to him with his renewed promise of a son (Rom. 4:19). On several occasions Paul uses this verb for those who are weak in faith with respect to eating meat sacrificed to idols (14:1–2; 1 Cor. 8:11–12). And in his boisterous dealings with the Corinthians, Paul makes several comments about his weakness (2 Cor. 11:21, 29; 12:10; 13:3–4). Moreover, in Paul's discussion of the law, he notes how the law was powerless since it was "weakened by the sinful nature" (Rom. 8:3). See *NIDNTT-A*, 76-77.

Adjective: ἀσθενής (*asthenēs*), GK *822* (S *772*), 26x. *asthenēs* generally means "weak" and refers to that which lacks strength or intensity. It is the opposite of power and vitality. The precise nuance, however, varies with the context.

(1) In Mt. 25:43–44; Lk. 9:2; Acts 5:15–16, this word simply denotes those who are physically sick and in need of attention, especially healing.

(2) In the midst of instructions for Christian household behavior, Peter uses *asthenēs* to refer to the wife as being the "weaker" partner in the marriage relationship (1 Pet. 3:7). This likely refers to the wife's physical weakness, not weaker spiritual capacities.

(3) When Jesus encountered extreme mental, physical, and spiritual pressure in the Garden of Gethsemane, he desired the disciples to stay awake and pray so they would not fall into temptation. Jesus' reason is that "the spirit is willing, but the body is *asthenēs*" (Mk. 14:38). In other words, *asthenēs* describes the condition of the body that can in some degree determine how the spirit functions.

(4) Paul often plays with the spiritual applications of *asthenēs*. In 1 Cor. 1:25, the *asthenēs* of God "is stronger than man's strength." *asthenēs* here refers specifically to Jesus' death on the cross, which the Jews saw as pitiful weakness. Ironically, the Jews demanded powerful signs and expected a sword-swinging Messiah, not one humiliated and hanging in shame on a criminal's cross. What the Jews interpreted as sublime *asthenēs*, God presented as the greatest display of his power—the exact opposite of their expectation. Consistent with Paul's argument, he says that God, in turn, chose the "weak things" of the world in order to shame the strong (1 Cor. 1:27).

(5) Later in 1 Corinthians in the context of whether a Christian should eat food sacrificed to idols, Paul uses *asthenēs* to refer to the spiritually immature (1 Cor. 8:7, 9, 10). Paul concludes that concern for a fellow believer who is *asthenēs* takes priority over exercising one's liberty. The idea of a believer being weak spiritually may account for Paul's admonition in 1 Thess. 5:14 to "help the weak" (though this use may refer instead to physical weakness).

(6) Paul uses *asthenēs* in Rom. 5:6 to refer to our *powerless*, unredeemed state: "when we were still *asthenēs*, Christ died for the ungodly." This refers to our inability to wage war against sin and its power. All of humanity has been *asthenēs* at one time; many still are. Living under the law, which also is *asthenēs*, we will not find the strength there to conquer sin (Gal. 4:9; Heb. 7:18). That can be found only by living in the power of the Spirit. See *NIDNTT-A*, 76-77.

WEAKNESS

New Testament

Noun: ἀσθένεια (*astheneia*), GK *819* (S *769*), 24x. *astheneia* means "weakness" and can be used of a physical weakness ("sickness") or of a weakness in the sense of a limitation or inadequacy. This noun is formed from two parts: *a* ("without") and *sthenos* ("strength"); thus, one who has *astheneia* is one "without strength."

astheneia is used generally of physical illnesses (Lk. 5:15; Acts 28:9), such as Lazarus's illness that eventually led to his death (Jn. 11:4). In Lk. 13:11–12, it is used specifically of a woman who is "crippled."

astheneia is also used of weakness in general, such as the inherent weakness of the human body in comparison to the resurrection body (1 Cor. 15:43). Paul initially preached to the Corinthians "in *weakness*, and in fear and in much trembling" so that their faith would rest not in human wisdom but in God's power (1 Cor. 2:3). Paul is forced to use human concepts in explaining the believer's enslavement to righteousness, and he admits he is speaking in human terms, i.e., "on account of the *weakness* of your flesh" (Rom. 6:19). Jesus, our high priest, because he himself was fully human, is able to sympathize with our "weaknesses" (Heb. 4:15; cf. 5:2). The heroes of the faith were made strong out of their weakness (11:34).

There are times in the life of the believer that human frailty and weakness are the instruments through which God is glorified (2 Cor. 10:5, 9). Paul writes, "That is why, for Christ's sake, I delight in *weakness*, in insults, in hardships, in persecutions, in difficulties. For when I am weak, then I am strong" (12:10). See *NIDNTT-A*, 76-77.

WEALTH

Old Testament

Noun: אוֹצָר (*ʾôṣār*), GK 238 (S 214), 79x. *ʾôṣār* means "treasure, storehouse, wealth." See *treasure*.

Noun: חַיִל (*ḥayil*), GK 2657 (S 2428), 246x. The basic sense of *ḥayil* is "power, strength, or capability." In contexts where goods or property are in view, *ḥayil* refers to "wealth, riches, substance." When Jacob's sons Levi and Simeon destroyed the city of Shechem, "they carried off all their wealth" (Gen. 34:29). In Deuteronomy, God reminds Israel that their own hands ultimately cannot produce "wealth"—that belongs to the Lord (Deut. 8:17–18). See also *strength*.

New Testament

Verb: πλουτέω (*plouteō*), GK *4456* (S *4147*), 12x. *plouteō* means "to be or get rich, wealthy." The terms for "rich" are used most often to refer to material wealth in the form of money or agriculture, or generally speaking a good, pleasant, fulfilling, and favorable life.

Noun: πλοῦτος (*ploutos*) GK *4458* (S *4149*), 22x. *ploutos* means "riches, wealth."

Adjective: πλούσιος (*plousios*), GK *4454* (S *4145*), 28x. *plousios* means "rich, "wealthy."

WEAR

New Testament

Verb: ἐνδύω (*endyō*), GK *1907* (S *1746*), 27x. *endyō* means "to put something on, wear." It is generally used of clothes, though there are also many metaphorical uses. See *put on*.

Verb: περιβάλλω (*periballō*), GK *4314* (S *4016*), 23x. *periballō* means "to wear, clothe, dress." Literally, it means "to throw something around oneself." All of the uses of this verb are in narrative literature or in Revelation. Jesus instructs us not to be concerned about what to "wear" (Mt. 6:31). The young man at the empty tomb was "dressed in a white robe" (Mk. 16:5). John tells us that Jesus' enemies "clothed him in a purple robe" in order to mock him (Jn. 19:2). People in Revelation are "clothed" in various ways, such as white robes (Rev. 7:9, 13; cf. 3:18; 4:4), a cloud (10:1), sackcloth (11:3), the sun (12:1), and fine linen (19:8). Each of these descriptions has its own symbolic significance.

WEDDING

New Testament

Verb: γαμεω (*gameō*), GK *1138* (S *1060*), 28x.

Noun: γάμος (*gamos*), GK *1141* (S *1062*), 16x. *gameō* means "to marry, celebrate a wedding, have sexual relations." *gamos* means "wedding, marriage, consummation of marriage, wedding feast." See *marry*.

WEEP

Old Testament

Verb: בָּכָה (*bokâ*), GK 1134 (S 1058), 114x. *bokâ* has the basic meaning "to weep," but can be translated with other terms such as "sob, mourn, wail, cry."

Hagar begins to sob as she anticipates Ishmael's death (Gen. 21:16). Abraham mourns over Sarah (23:2), Jacob mourns for Joseph (37:35), and Israel mourns for Aaron (Num. 20:29). Weeping is associated with a person's death as well as serves as an expression of grief, personal or national distress (Ezr. 3:12; 10:1), repentance, or remorse. The Israelites wail to Moses, complaining about their lack of food (Num. 11:4, 10, 13, 18, 20). Samson's wife sobs reproachfully to persuade Samson to reveal the answer to his riddle (Jdg. 14:16), persisting in her crying all seven days of the wedding feast (Jdg. 14:17). *bokâ* is often associated with tears (Job 31:38; Jer. 50:4; Lam. 1:16), sitting on the ground (Neh. 1:4; Ezr. 8:14), fasting (1 Sam. 1:7; 2 Sam. 1:12, 12:21; Ps. 69:10; Zech. 7:3), tearing of garments (2 Ki. 22:19; Job 2:12), and covering of heads (2 Sam. 15:30). Rachel weeps inconsolably for her children (Jer. 31:15). The Israelites weep in exile in Babylon as they remember Zion, their home (Ps. 137:1). Solomon teaches that there is an appropriate time for both weeping and laughter (Eccl. 3:4).

Prophetic literature promises a future time when those who "go out *weeping*, carrying seed to sow," will return joyfully (Ps. 126:6). A time of the Lord's favor will come when those living in Jerusalem "will *weep* no more," because God will answer their prayers (Isa. 30:19). Finally, pilgrims who process through the arid Valley of Baca ("weeping") make it a "place of springs"—i.e., an oasis—through the blessings of God (Ps. 84:5–6).

The ancient rites of mourning and weeping are not necessarily tied into this word. *bokâ* is simply part of the stock vocabulary used to express grief, often associated with other symbolic gestures such as tearing one's clothes and sitting in ashes. From a biblical-theological perspective, weeping is a result of the fall and the introduction of pain and death. Ultimately, however, in the new heavens and new earth, there will no longer be any cause for weeping (Rev. 21:4).

New Testament

Verb: κλαίω (*klaiō*), GK *3081* (S *2799*), 40x. *klaiō* means "to weep, mourn" because of grief. In the NT, this verb expresses violent emotions brought about by various circumstances that cause sorrow. Certain believers weep over Paul's leaving for Jerusalem (Acts 21:19). Paul weeps over the enemies of Christ (Phil. 3:18). The widow at Nain mourns the death of her son (Lk. 7:13). Mary cries at the tomb of Jesus on Easter morning (Jn. 20:11, 13, 15). *klaiō* can also be understood as wailing (as in Rev. 18:9, where the kings of the earth wail over the fall of Babylon).

klaiō is also used to teach a lesson on the brevity of earthly suffering. In Lk. 6:17, Jesus declares, "Blessed are you who weep now, for you will laugh." He later warns, "Woe to you who laugh now, for you will mourn and weep" (6:25). He is declaring that his followers will suffer only for a time. Although we may weep in this life, we will not in eternity. One other note of significance, tears of joy are never mentioned in the NT. See *NIDNTT-A*, 306-7.

WELCOME

New Testament

Verb: ἀσπάζομαι, *aspazomai*, GK *832* (S *782*), 59x. *aspazomai* means "to greet, welcome." See *greet*.

Verb: δέχομαι (*dechomai*), GK *1312* (S *1209*), 56x. *dechomai* essentially means "to receive" something, but it can also mean "to welcome" someone (e.g., Mt. 10:14). See *receive*.

Verb: προσδέχομαι (*prosdechomai*), GK *4657* (S *4327*), 14x. *prosdechomai* means "to receive, welcome," and "to wait for, expect something" (see *wait for*). It can mean "to receive" in the sense of to welcome someone in a friendly manner. Jesus is accused by the Jewish leadership of welcoming or receiving sinners (Lk. 15:2; cf. 12:36). Paul asks the Roman church to "welcome" their sister Phoebe

(Rom. 16:2) and the Philippians to "welcome" Epaphroditus (Phil. 2:29). In Heb. 11:35, the author speaks of women "who *received* back their dead, raised to life again." The same author also uses this verb to speak of accepting something willingly, such as the seizure of one's property and belongings (10:34). He encourages his readers to persevere amidst their trials for the sake of the gospel.

Verb: προσλαμβάνω (*proslambanō*), GK *4689* (S *4355*), 12x. *proslambanō* means "to accept, take aside, welcome." See *accept*.

WELL

Old Testament

Noun: בּוֹר (*bôr*), GK 1014 (S 953), 65x. *bôr*, often translated as "pit," can also mean "well, dungeon, cistern, grave." See *pit*.

Adjective: טוֹב (*tôb*), GK 3202 (S 2896), 530x. This adjective means good or well; it describes goodness, beauty, and moral uprightness. See *good*.

New Testament

Noun: πηγή (*pēgē*), GK *4380* (S *4077*), 11x. *pēgē* usually refers to a well or spring of water (Jn. 4:6 [x2]; Jas. 3:11; Rev. 8:10; 14:7; 16:4), though it can include any flow of liquid. See *spring*.

Adjective: ὑγιής (*hygiēs*), GK *5618* (S *5199*), 11x. *hygiēs* describes things that are or have been made well or whole. It almost always refers to the effects of Jesus' healing power. Jesus makes the lame well (Mt. 15:31; cf. Jn. 5:6, 9, 11, 14, 15; Acts 4:10; cf. 3:6), and he *heals* the woman with a flow of blood (Mk. 5:34). Several times in the gospels Jesus makes people well on the Sabbath (Mt. 12:13; Jn. 5:6; 7:23).

Used figuratively *hygiēs* can describe the "wellness" or "soundness" of something, such as words. In Tit. 2:8 Paul instructs Titus to show in his teaching "integrity, dignity, and *sound* speech that cannot be condemned." See *NIDNTT-A*, 568.*

Adverb: καλῶς (*kalōs*), GK *2822* (S *2573*), 37x. *kalōs* conveys the goodness or appropriateness of an activity or action and may best be translated as "well" or "good." See *good*.

WELL-BEING

Old Testament

Noun: שָׁלוֹם (*šālôm*), GK 8934 (S 7965), 237x. *šālôm* is one of the most important words in the OT. In addition to "peace," this word can be translated as "prosperity, well-being, health, completeness, safety." See *peace*.

WELL PLEASED

New Testament

Verb: εὐδοκέω (*eudokeō*), GK *2305* (S *2106*), 21x. *eudokeō* designates the pleasure a person takes in another person or in doing something. See *pleased, pleasure*.

WEST

Old Testament

Adjective: אַחֲרוֹן (*ʾaḥ*[a]*rôn*), GK 340 (S 314), 51x. This adjective denotes the sequential placement of objects, persons, events, or periods of time and may be translated as "last" or "latter." It also conveys the idea of "west, western" (cf. Deut. 11:24; 34:2). See *last*.

WHEAT

New Testament

Noun: σῖτος (*sitos*), GK *4992* (S *4621*), 14x. *sitos* means "wheat, grain." Most uses of this noun are in parables of Jesus, such as the parable of the wheat and the weeds (Mt. 13:24–30) and the parable of the rich fool (Lk. 12:13–20).

In two different places in the NT, however, *sitos* is used as a metaphor of the resurrection. Jesus says that a "kernel of wheat" must die first before it can sprout to abundant new life (Jn. 12:24). Paul makes a similar statement in 1 Cor. 15:36–37, and something (such as a seed of wheat) does not come to life unless it first dies. In Lk. 22:31, Jesus uses the threshing process to tell Peter that Satan had asked to sift him "as wheat."

WHITE

New Testament

Adjective: λευκός (*leukos*), GK *3328* (S *3022*), 25x. *leukos* means "white"; it is derived from a root that means "bright, radiant." This word occurs only in the gospels, Acts, and Revelation, and nearly all of its uses are symbolic. The two exceptions are Mt. 5:36 ("And do not swear by your head, for you cannot make even one hair white or black") and Jn. 4:35 ("I tell you, open your eyes and look at the fields! They are white for harvest").

Most of the symbolic uses of *leukos* refer to a color associated with heaven and relate to white clothing, as in the descriptions of the transfiguration of Jesus (Mt. 17:2), the post-resurrection appearances of angels (28:3; Acts 1:10), and the elders, residents, and martyrs of heaven in the Revelation (Rev. 3:4–5; 4:4; 7:9). Even the horse on which Jesus rides as coming conqueror is white (19:11), as is the throne of God (20:11). The victorious Christ is described as having a white head and white hair (1:14)—imagery that is closely associated with the "Ancient of Days" in Dan. 7:9.

Bright white is the color of God, and it symbolizes his holiness and purity. John specifically defines the meaning of the white of the saints: "Fine [bright white and clean] linen stands for the righteous acts of the saints" (19:8). While we today have available to us all sorts of whitening agents for getting things bright and clean, it was difficult in the ancient world to get something bright white, especially once it had become soiled and dirty. That's why God's people need to given new, clean, white garments to wear (cf. Mt. 22:11; Rev. 3:18; 6:11; 7:9).

WHOLE

Old Testament

Noun: כֹּל (*kōl*), GK 3972 (S 3605), 5415x. *kōl* means "whole, all, every." It can mean "whole, complete" and be used to describe the devotion God requires of those who are his covenant people (Deut. 6:5). See *all*.

Adjective: תָּמִים (*tāmîm*), GK 9459 (S 8549), 91x. Most often *tāmîm* describes animals or crops intended for sacrificial offerings as "unblemished" or "whole." See *unblemished*.

Particle: כֹּל (*kōl*), GK 10353 (S 3606), 105x. *kōl* is the Aramaic equivalent of Heb. *kōl* and has essentially the same meaning: "every, whole, all." See *all*.

New Testament

Adjective: ὅλος (*holos*), GK *3910* (S *3650*), 109x. *holos* means "whole, all." Rather than being a word for distributive completeness (e.g., "all the people," though this expression does occurs with this adjective; cf. Acts 2:47), *holos* usually denotes undistributive wholeness. That is, expressions such as "with the whole heart" (Mt. 22:37; Lk. 10:27), "the whole world" (Mt. 16:26; Mk. 14:9; Rom. 1:8; 1 Jn. 2:2; 5:19; Rev. 12:9), "the whole law" (Mt. 22:40; Gal. 5:3), and "the whole body" (Lk. 11:34, 36; 1 Cor. 12:17; Jas. 2:3) abound with this adjective. If we "gain the whole world" but lose our soul, we have gained nothing (Mt. 16:26). If the "whole body" were one organ (such as an eye or ear), it could not function; there must be variety of parts (symbolizing the variety of gifts of the Spirit in the church; 1 Cor. 12:17). If we keep "the whole law" but stumble in just one commandment, we are guilty of being lawbreakers, for the law is an undivided unity (Jas. 2:10). One of the most blessed uses of this word is in 1 Jn. 2:2: Jesus "is the atoning sacrifice for our sins, and not only for ours but also for the sins of the whole world." This does not mean that everyone will be saved, but that the blood of Christ is sufficient for the sins of all who believe.

Adjective: ὑγιής (*hygiēs*), GK *5618* (S *5199*), 11x. *hygiēs* is describes things that are or have been made well or whole. See *well*.

WICKED, WICKEDNESS

Old Testament

Noun: אָוֶן (*ʾāwen*), GK 224 (S 205), 81x. *ʾāwen* refers, in general, to evil, sin, or wickedness. It may also describe the punishment or disaster that befalls those who practice wickedness. See *evil*.

Noun: עָוֹן (*ʿāwōn*), GK 6411 (S 5771),

233x. *ʿāwōn* is usually translated "sin, guilt, wickedness, iniquity" and is one of the three primary words for sin in the OT, an offense against God that ranges from willful rebellion to unintentional sins (see *sin*).

Noun: רָעָה (*rāʿâ*), GK 8288 (S 7465), 354x. At the heart of *rāʿâ*, lies the idea of badness, whether physical or moral. See *evil*.

Adjective or Noun: רַע (or רָע) (*raʿ* [or *rāʿ*]), GK 8273 (S 7451), 312x. In most contexts, *raʿ* is translated "evil." Another frequent translation is "wicked" (e.g., Gen. 13:13). See *evil*.

Adjective: רָשָׁע (*rāšāʿ*), GK 8401 (S 7563), 264x. As an adjective *rāšāʿ* describes the quality of being wicked, evil, guilty, or unjust. When the adjective is used as a noun, it refers to a wicked, evil, or guilty person. More than 70 percent of the time it is found in the wisdom and poetic books of Job, Psalms, and Proverbs, books that commonly use *rāšāʿ* in describing both wicked character and practice. In Psalms and Proverbs especially, *rāšāʿ* is the opposite of *ṣaddîq* (see *righteous*). Evil (or calamity) will slay "the wicked," who hate the righteous (Ps. 34:21). The wicked do not seek God, nor do they have room for him in their thinking (Ps. 10:4). They do not fear God (Ps. 36:1) and are considered enemies of the Lord (37:20). The OT states that the wicked will perish and vanish away (Ps. 37:20), will be driven away or brought down (Prov. 14:32), are brought to ruin by God (Prov. 21:12), and will in a little while be no more (Ps. 37:10). See *NIDOTTE*, 3:1201-4.

New Testament

Noun: ἀδικία (*adikia*), GK *94* (S *93*), 25x. *adikia* is consistently translated as either "unrighteousness" or "iniquity" in the KJV. The NIV, however, offers numerous glosses, such as "evil, wickedness, dishonest, worldly, sin, wrong, wrongdoing." See *unrighteousness*.

Noun: ἄδικος (*adikos*), GK *96* (S *94*), 12x. In most contexts, *adikos* may be translated "unjust" or "unrighteous." In some occurrences, however, *adikos* may mean dishonest or untrustworthy (Lk. 16:10–11), evildoer (Lk. 18:11), or wicked (1 Cor. 6:9). See *unjust*.

Noun: ἀνομία (*anomia*), GK *490* (S *458*), 15x. *anomia means lawlessness, a violation of law.* See *wicked.*

Noun: κακία (*kakia*), GK *2798* (S *2549*), 11x. *kakia* means "malice," primarily "wickedness" in quality or baseness. See *malice*.

Adjective: ἄνομος (*anomos*), GK *491* (S *459*), 9x. Literally both words mean "absence of law." See *lawless, lawlessness*.

Adjective: ἀσεβής (*asebēs*), GK *815* (S *765*), 9x. *asebēs* means "ungodly, godless, wicked." See *ungodly*.

Adjective: κακός (*kakos*), GK *2805* (S *2556*), 50x. *kakos* conveys the idea of something that is "evil, bad, wicked, wrong." See *evil*.

Adjective: πονηρός (*ponēros*), GK *4505* (S *4190*, *4191*), 78x. The adjective *ponēros* basically means "bad, wicked, evil." See *evil*.

WIDE, WIDTH

Old Testament

Noun: רֹחַב (*rōḥab*), GK 8145 (S 7341) 103x. *rōhab* refers to the "width" of an object or an area, and "breadth" is an appropriate translation when the area is large. Naturally the word often occurs in connection with the word "length" and, occasionally, with the word "height."

When specified, an object or an area's *rōḥab* is either smaller than or equal to its length. Thus, Noah's ark is 300 cubits long and 50 cubits wide (Gen. 6:15), and the tabernacle's incense altar is a cubit long and a cubit wide (Exod. 30:2). The word is used to describe the measurement of various objects, such as buildings (1 Ki. 7:2), rooms (1 Ki. 6:20), walls (Ezek. 42:10), and curtains (Exod. 26:2). Areas that are described in terms of their measurement using the term *rōḥab* include courtyards (Exod. 27:18; Ezek. 40:47) and territories of land (Ezek. 45:1ff.). The word most frequently occurs in passages that describe the tabernacle (Exod. 25–27; 36–37) or the temple, including both Solomon's temple (1 Ki. 6; 2 Chr. 3) and Ezekiel's visionary temple (Ezek. 40–43).

Metaphorically, *rōḥab* is used to describe how God gave Solomon "*breadth* of heart like sand on the seashore" (1 Ki. 4:29), which from the context seems to mean that God gave him insight into many areas of study. "Breadth" is also a good translation for *rōḥab* in Gen. 13:17 ("the length and *breadth* of the land") and Isa. 8:8 ("the *breadth* of your land"). Job 37:10 refers literally to "the width of the waters," which has been translated "*expanse/breadth* of the waters" or "the *broad* waters." When discussing the "width" of a wall, "*thickness*" is an appropriate translation (Ezek. 40:5). See *NIDOTTE*, 3:1090-1092.

WIDOW

Old Testament

Noun: אַלְמָנָה (*ʾalmānâ*), GK 530 (S 490), 55x. The *ʾalmānâ* holds a special place in the OT. While some widows could return to their father's house (Gen. 38:11) or remarry via the law of the levirate marriage (Ruth 4:10), most occurrences of this word refer to widows who are left destitute. Interestingly, *ʾalmānâ* never occurs in Ruth; she is called "Mahlon's wife" or "the wife of the dead man."

Since Israelite women depended on their husbands for provision and protection, the *ʾalmānâ* was left poor and vulnerable, with little or no means of sustaining herself. The Lord, the defender (Ps. 68:5) and sustainer (146:9) of widows, commands that his people leave behind remnants of the olive and grape harvests for their gleaning (Deut. 24:20–21). Anyone who withholds justice from a widow is cursed (Deut. 27:19). As the prophets present their cases against faithless Israel, oppressing widows is one of the sinful charges (Isa. 1:23; 10:2; Mal. 3:5). The *ʾalmānâ* is often mentioned along with aliens and orphans as the trio of God's special concern (Deut. 10:18; 24:17; 26:12–13; Ps. 94:6; Jer. 7:6; 22:3; Ezek. 22:7; Zech. 7:10). See *NIDOTTE*, 1:413-15.

New Testament

Noun: χήρα (*chēra*), GK *5939* (S *5503*), 26x. *chēra* is a feminine noun, always referring to a widow, a woman whose husband has died. As in the OT, this represents a disadvantaged and vulnerable class of people. Jesus chooses this culturally familiar image to teach his disciples about persistence in prayer (Lk. 18:1–8). On another occasion, observing the generosity of a poor widow in the temple, Jesus used the opportunity to teach his disciples about giving (Mk. 12:41–44; Lk. 21:1–4). When warning his disciples about the teachers of the law, Jesus specifically cites their mistreatment of widows as one of their most serious sins (Mk. 12:40; Lk. 20:47).

The controversy that erupted in the early church over the treatment of widows, and the timely and sincere manner in which it was resolved, demonstrate the early church's concern for the care of widows (Acts 6:1–6). Dorcas was especially gifted at that ministry (9:39, 41). Later, Paul gives guidelines for the care of widows (1 Tim. 5:3–16), instructing believers "to learn first of all to live out godliness at home" by caring for the widows in their own family circles (5:4). Those who do not care for their own families have denied the faith (5:8). Widows without families are those in genuine need of the church's care (5:3, 5, 16). He also endorses remarriage for widows (1 Cor. 7:8; 1 Tim. 5:14). James defines the care of widows and orphans as "pure worship" (1:27). The Lord is still the sustainer of the widow (Ps. 146:9), with the hands and feet of Christ's body carrying out this precious ministry. See *NIDNTT-A*, 605.

WIFE

Old Testament

Noun: אִשָּׁה (*ʾiššâ*), GK 851 (S 802), 781x. In the broadest sense of the word, *ʾiššâ* simply means "woman" or "wife." See *woman*.

New Testament

Noun: γυνή (*gynē*), GK *1222* (S *1135*),

215x. *gynē* refers in the first place to an adult female person, a "woman," but it also means "wife." See *woman*.

WILD

Old Testament

Noun: שָׂדֶה (*śādeh*), GK 8441 (S 7704), 329x. The basic meaning of *śādeh* is a field. A *śādeh* is often cultivated, but it can also be a wild place (2 Ki. 4:39), where "the beasts of the field" live (i.e., wild animals, Deut. 7:22; 1 Sam. 17:44; cf. Song 2:7). See *field*.

WILDERNESS

Old Testament

Noun: מִדְבָּר (*midbār*), GK 4497 (S 4057) 269x. *midbār* is generally translated "desert, wasteland, open country." Some translate the noun simply as "wilderness," but a modifying word like "barren" needs to be added to portray adequately the arid nature of a *midbār*. See *desert*.

Noun: עֲרָבָה (*ʿarābâ*), GK 6858 (S 6160), 60x. *ʿarābâ* conveys a dry, desolate, wilderness area, similar to a desert, and may be translated as "plains" or "desert." See *Arabah*.

New Testament

Noun and Adjective: ἔρημος (*erēmos*), GK *2245* (S *2048*), 48x. In the NT, *erēmos* is used both as an adjective and a noun. As an adjective it usually means "desolate" (see *desolate*). As a noun *erēmos* can refer to any wilderness or uninhabited, lonely region (e.g., Lk. 5:16; 9:12). See *desert*.

WILL

Old Testament

Verb: אָבָה (*ʾābâ*), GK 14 (S 14), 54x. *ʾābâ* means "to will, be willing, consent." See *(be) willing*.

Noun: רָצוֹן (*rāṣôn*), GK 8356 (S 7522), 56x. *rāṣôn* denotes three different ideas in the OT: favor (see *favor*), acceptance (see *acceptable*), or will. It is attributed most often to God (39x) and occurs most frequently in Proverbs (14x), Psalms (13x), and Leviticus (7x). *rāṣôn* sometimes expresses an individual's personal desires, wants, or will (see *please*).

New Testament

Verb: βούλομαι (*boulomai*) GK *1089* (S *1014*), 37x. *boulomai* describes the desire or intention of a person to do something, to have something, or to obtain a result. See *want*.

Verb: θέλω (*thelō*), GK *2527* (S *2309*), 208x. *thelō* means "to will, want, desire." It can be broken down into two main categories: the act of willing or desiring as performed by a person, and the act performed by God. This distinction is blurred when it is used in the context of Jesus.

(1) The following examples are all with human subjects. "Rachel did not *want* to be comforted" (Mt. 2:18). "If someone *wants* to sue you and take your tunic, let him have your cloak as well" (5:40). "Herodias ... *wanted* to kill [John]" (Mk. 6:19). "[Peter] became hungry and *wanted* something to eat" (Acts 10:10). "I [Paul] do not *want* you to be unaware, brothers" (Rom. 1:13). "I have much to write you, but I do not *want* to do so with pen and ink" (3 Jn. 13). In such cases the meaning is simply to want or desire something.

But *thelō* can be also used with human subjects in the context of deeper theological issues. Possibly the best-known example is Paul's discussion of his own desires in Rom. 7:15ff., in which he uses *thelō* six times. The opening line is, "What I do, I do not understand. For what I do not *desire*, this I do." Human willing sometimes expresses faith; e.g., in Lk. 18:41 a blind man says that he "wants" Jesus to heal him, to which Jesus replies, "Receive your sight, your faith has healed you." Other such uses are Jesus' statement that Jerusalem is "not willing" to be cared for by him (13:34) and his censure of the Jewish leaders, "You do not *want* to come to me so that you might have life" (Jn. 5:40).

(2) *thelō* also signifies the desire of God or Jesus, which almost always has a theological nuance. God "*desires* all people to be saved and to come to the knowledge of the truth" (1 Tim. 2:4). Our prayers should be conditioned with, "If the Lord *wills*, we will live and do this or that" (Jas. 4:15).

An important topic to mention when thinking about "the will of God and of human beings" is the way in which they intersect. This has been one of the great areas of debate and dissension in the history of the church. Jesus said, "If anyone chooses to do God's *will*" (Jn. 7:17). This reflects the reality that human will is not entirely consumed by God's will or action. At some level, people choose whether or not to do God's will. This point is also reflected in the "Lord's Prayer" ("Your *will* be done on earth as it is in heaven," Mt. 6:10; this vs. uses the noun *thelēma*), and in Jesus' prayer in the garden of Gethsemane, in which he asks to be delivered from the cross, but says "not my *will* but yours be done" (Mt. 26:39). In both cases the implication is that humans do not automatically do God's will.

However, there are also passages such as Rom. 9 that clearly articulate the sovereign will of God. Paul writes, "Therefore God has mercy on whom he *wants* to have mercy and hardens whom he *wants* to harden" (Rom. 9:18). Similar acknowledgment of God's sovereign will is seen in Paul's statement, "I will come to you very soon if the Lord *is willing*" (1 Cor. 4:19; also 1 Cor. 12:18; 1 Cor. 15:38). A passage that connects divine and human will is Phil. 2:13, in which Paul writes, "It is God who works in you to *will* and to act according to his good purpose." In summary, God is sovereign and his will is accomplished, but in some sense each of us chooses to follow him or to rebel against him. See *NIDNTT-A*, 241-42.

Noun: διαθήκη (*diathēkē*), GK *1347* (S *1242*), 33x. *diathēkē* can mean "covenant, testament, will." The majority of the occurrences of this word are in quotation from or allusions to the OT. See *covenant*. In fact, the very term "NT" (*kainē diathēke*) comes from this word. The word is also used for one's last will and testament. See *testament*.

Noun: θέλημα (*thelēma*), GK *2525* (S *2307*), 62x. *thelēma* refers to the "will," both in the sense of what one desires to happen as well as the act itself of desiring something.

(1) The most common use of *thelēma* in the NT refers to the *thelēma* of God. Jesus says that those who do God's will are his brother, sister, and mother (Mk. 3:35). God calls the believer to live in accordance with his will in all things, beginning with the believer's new birth (Jn. 1:13), growth and maturity in the Christian life (Col. 4:12), and even life in the face of suffering (1 Pet. 3:17). Believers must conform the their entire lives to God's will (Rom. 12:2) and avoid carrying out the will of the body and the mind (Eph. 2:3).

The *thelēma* of God manifests itself in believers in their being sanctified (1 Thess. 4:3), in thankfulness (1 Thess. 5:18), and in resting and receiving God's promises (Heb. 10:36). In the same way, believers show their commitment to Christ as his servants by doing the *thelēma* of God sincerely from the heart (Eph. 6:6). Furthermore, Paul understands that his mission to the church is dependent on God's *thelēma*, for his very apostleship is a calling in accordance with that will (cf. 1 Cor. 1:1; 2 Cor. 1:1; Eph. 1:1; Col. 1:1). He is also submissive to God's will as he conducts his missionary service (cf. Rom. 12:10; 15:32).

(2) *thelēma* also occurs with respect to the human will, especially in contrast to God's will. Jesus in the garden of Gethsemane prays that the Father's will, not his will, be done (Lk. 22:42). Pilate delivers Jesus up to the will of the Jewish mob, who prefer that Barabbas be released (Lk. 23:25). Perhaps the most striking distinction between the divine *thelēma* and the human *thelēma* is with respect to the Scriptures themselves. Peter states that the Scriptures were not written by the will of human beings but through God's will (2 Pet. 1:21). See *NIDNTT-A*, 241-42.

(BE) WILLING

Old Testament

Verb: אָבָה (*ʾābâ*), GK 14 (S 14), 54x. *ʾābâ* means "to will, be willing, consent." While this verb strictly speaking has a positive meaning, in all but one instance (Isa. 1:19), the passages in which it occurs contain a negative, so that the verb came to mean "to be unwilling, refuse." David, for example, "was unwilling" (i.e., "refused") to drink the water from Bethlehem that his soldiers brought to him (2 Sam. 23:16–17; 1 Chr. 11:18–19). At the end of his final battle, Saul's armor-bearer "refuses" to kill Saul even though the king has asked him to (1 Sam. 31:4). Even though Jehoram king of Judah worshiped idols, "the Lord was not *willing* to destroy the house of David" because of his covenant with David (2 Chr. 21:7). At the same time, however, God is angry with his people when they "refuse" to listen to and obey him (Ps. 81:11; Isa. 28:12; 30:9, 15; 42:24; Ezek. 3:7; 20:8).

WIN

New Testament

Verb: κερδαίνω (*kerdainō*), GK *3045* (S *2770*), 17x. This verb denotes the activity of gaining, profiting, or winning and is best translated "win, gain." Jesus contrasts the pursuit of eternal life with the futility of preserving one's earthly existence by asking, "What good will it be for a man if he *gains* the whole world, yet forfeits his soul?" (Mt. 16:26; Mk. 8:36; Lk. 9:25). Jesus compares the stewardship of having served God to the best of one's ability to what one may gain from properly invested coins: "The man who had received the five talents went at once and put his money to work and *gained* five more" (Mt. 25:16, 17, 20, 22). Paul uses *kerdainō* to describe his evangelistic efforts: "Though I am free and belong to no man, I make myself a slave to everyone, to *win* as many as possible (1 Cor. 9:19, 20). For Paul, there is no earthly pursuit of greater honor than that of knowing Christ: "What is more, I consider everything a loss compared to the surpassing greatness of knowing Christ Jesus my Lord, for whose sake I have lost all things. I consider them rubbish, that I may *gain* Christ..." (Phil. 3:7). See *NIDNTT-A*, 302.

WIND

Old Testament

Noun: רוּחַ (*rûaḥ*), GK 8120 (S 7307), 378x. While *rûaḥ* has a wide range of meanings in the OT, its basic sense is that of "wind" or "breath." This latter sense naturally gave rise to "breath" as a sign of life, and hence *rûaḥ* also means "spirit" or "life" (see *spirit*). Since our word relates to that which is unseen (air), its focus is on the visible effect of an invisible force.

(1) As "wind," the *rûaḥ* dries up the waters of the flood (Gen. 8:1), separates the chaff from the wheat (Ps. 1:4; 83:13), brings on clouds and storms (148:8; Isa. 32:2; Jon. 1:4), and shakes the trees of the forest (Isa. 7:2). To us, the invisible wind is an unpredictable, uncontrollable force, but the Scriptures assert that the wind is controlled by God and does his bidding (Amos 4:13). Indeed, in the language of theophanies, the divine warrior "rides on *the wind*" (Ps. 18:10; 104:3). God directs the wind to remove the plague of locust from Egypt (Exod. 10:19) and to bring quail to the Israelites in the desert (Num. 11:31). Often, the scorching wind from the desert, usually referred to as the "east wind," is a sign of divine judgment and punishment. It is an "east *wind*" that smites the sea, drying the ground, so that Israel can escape from Egypt (Exod. 14:21). Divine judgment is compared to the hot "east *wind*" that shatters boats (Ps. 48:7; Ezek. 27:26), scatters objects in its path (Jer. 18:17), and parches the fertile soil (Ezek. 17:12; 19:10). In contrast, the wind from the west brings refreshment and deliverance (Jer. 18:17; Hos. 13:15).

Since *rûaḥ* describes "wind," it is also used for the four compass points, which is the meaning of "to every *wind*" (i.e., "to every direction," Ezek. 5:10–12) as well as "the four winds" (Jer. 49:36; Ezek. 37:9; Zech. 2:6, i.e., "from all directions").

Since the wind (*rûaḥ*) cannot be gathered or stored (cf. Prov. 27:16) and since it comes and goes without warning, the word gains the sense of "futile, empty, transitory." For example, idols are "*wind* and emptiness" (Isa. 41:29). The one who seeks for an enduring purpose in life by storing up the transitory events of life is said to be "chasing after the *wind*" ("vexation of *spirit*," KJV; see Eccl. 1:14, 17; 2:11, 17, 26; 4:4, 6, 16; 6:9). Likewise, "inheriting the *wind*" (Prov. 11:29) means that one inherits nothing. Describing false prophets, Jeremiah writes: "The prophets are but *wind* and the word is not in them" (Jer. 5:13). "Full of hot air" is a modern equivalent

(2) *rûaḥ* also denotes "breath," both of humans (Isa. 42:5; 57:16) and animals (Gen. 6:17; 7:15, 22). Breath indicates life (Gen. 6:17; Ezek. 37:5–14), and lack of breath is the sign of death (Ps. 146:4; Eccl. 12:7). Indeed, *rûaḥ* is regularly paired with *n*^{e}*šāma* ("breath," GK 5972), portraying the breathing process as the essential indicator of life (Gen. 7:22; Isa. 42:5; Job 27:3). In the creation of the human race, it is God's own breath (*n*^{e}*šāma*) that gives life to the man (cf. Gen. 2:7), and thus the breath (life) in humankind is always seen as a gift of the Creator (Job 27:3; 33:4; Ps. 104:29). When *rûaḥ* describes the "breath of God," itself, however, it denotes the force of God's power, usually in judgment against the wicked (2 Sam. 22:16; Ps. 18:15; Job 4:9). See *NIDOTTE*, 3:1073–78.

WINE

Old Testament

Noun: יַיִן (*yayin*), GK 3516 (S 3196), 141x. *yayin* means "wine." It occurs in the OT in various settings and with both literal and figurative meanings. (1) For the most part, *yayin* is fermented juice that comes from grapes. But there are some occasions in which this term refers to unfermented grape juice. When Isaiah says that "no one treads out *wine* at the presses" (Isa. 16:10), the *yayin* here must refer to grape juice before it has become fermented (cf. also Jer. 48:33). In Jer. 40:10, 12, *yayin* is a euphemism for freshly harvested grapes.

(2) But for the most part, *yayin* is something that can make a person drunk. Noah became drunk on *yayin* (Gen. 9:21, 24), and after Aaron's sons had offered strange fire on the altar of the Lord, God commanded, "You and your sons are not to drink *wine* or other fermented drink whenever you go into the Tent of Meeting" (Lev. 10:9). It is perhaps for this reason that the Recabites refused all wine (Jer. 35:5–8, 14). Hosea writes that *yayin* takes away understanding from God's people (Hos. 4:11), and Isaiah writes about those stay up late and get inflamed with wine (Isa. 5:11–12).

(3) Nevertheless, the Bible does not endorse teetotalism. God in his goodness has provided "*wine* that gladdens the heart of man, oil to make his face shine" (Ps. 104:15; cf. Isa. 55:1; Zech. 10:7). Wine is one of the elements on Lady Wisdom's table (Prov. 9:2, 5). Wine appears to have been a common drink in Israelite society (1 Sam. 10:3; 16:20; 1 Chr. 9:29; 12:40; 27:27), and only drunkenness was condemned (Prov. 23:29–35).

(4) Wine becomes a symbol of God's judgment. Through Jeremiah God promises to "fill with drunkenness all who live in this land" and smash them without pity (Jer. 13:12–14). A few chapters later the Lord speaks through the prophet: "Take from my hand this cup filled with the *wine* of my wrath and make all the nations to whom I send you drink it" (25:15–16; cf. Ps. 75:8). This symbolism is picked up in Rev. 14:10; 16:19. See *NIDOTTE*, 2:439–41.

New Testament

Noun: οἶνος (*oinos*), GK *3885* (S *3631*), 34x. In the OT, *oinos*, the fruit of the vine, is a regular and important part of culture and symbolizes fertility and well-being. Its misuse is also a potential source of numerous evils (e.g., Prov. 20:1; 23:31–35). Similarly, in the NT, the vine and vineyards appear frequently in Jesus' parables (Mt. 20:1–16; Jn. 15:1–11), yet drunkenness is forbidden (Eph. 5:18), and addiction to wine is unacceptable in an elder or deacon (1 Tim. 3:3, 8; Tit. 2:3).

For the most part in the NT, *oinos* is used literally, but occasionally it has symbolic meanings. In 1 Tim. 5:23, Paul exhorts Timothy to drink a little wine for his stomach's sake, and wine is a means of healing in Lk. 10:34. John the Baptist abstains from drinking wine, perhaps following a Nazirite vow (Lk. 1:15). However, Jesus, like most people, likely drank wine, as can be seen by the exaggerated accusation that he was a "glutton and a drunkard" (Mt. 11:18–19), used by his opponents to mean that he did not fast nor abstain from wine (9:14–17; Mk. 2:18–22; Lk. 5:33–38). Additionally, Jesus' first miracle was turning water into wine (Jn. 2:1–11).

Symbolically, *oinos* is used negatively in Revelation, referring to the wine and cup of God's wrath (14:10; 16:19; 19:15) and to the debauched ways of Babylon (14:8). Positively, *oinos* serves as a token of hope for the coming celebration for all believers at Jesus' return. A picture of this coming new age is given in the creation of wine at the wedding in Cana (Jn. 2:1–11) and in Jesus' promise that he will not drink wine again until the great feast when the kingdom of God comes in all its fullness (Mt. 26:29; Mk. 14:25). See *NIDNTT-A*, 41-42.

WINESKIN

New Testament

Noun: ἀσκός (*askos*), GK *829* (S *779*), 12x. *askos* refers to a leather bag used to hold wine. This term is used only in a parable in the Synoptic Gospels where Jesus says that new wine must not be put into old "wineskins" but into new ones (Mt. 9:17; Mk. 2:22; Lk. 5:37–38). Wine that is still fermenting will burst the old leather skins, which can be quite hard and brittle, unlike the fresh skins, which are still pliable.

WING

Old Testament

Noun: כָּנָף (*kānāp*), GK 4053 (S 3671), 111x. *kānāp* has the basic meaning of a wing, such as the wing of a bird. In Gen. 1:21, God creates "every *winged* bird according to its species." Specifically, the wings of the ostrich, falcon, dove, eagle, and stork/heron are mentioned in the OT (Job 39:13, 26; Ps. 68:13; Ezek. 17:3; Zech. 5:9). Elsewhere *kānāp* refers to various species of birds ("bird of every *wing*," Ezek. 17:23; 39:4) and to birds in general ("any possessor of *wing*," Prov. 1:17).

Heavenly creatures, namely cherubim and seraphim, also have wings. The wings of cherubim are depicted in the images on the ark of the covenant and in the Most Holy Place of the temple (Exod. 25:20; 1 Ki. 6:27). The real cherubim wings are seen by Ezekiel in his visions (Ezek. 10:21; cf. Ps. 18:10), and the wings of the seraphim are seen by Isaiah (Isa. 6:2).

By extension, *kānāp* can refer to the edge of something, particularly the skirting or hem of a garment. In 1 Sam. 15:27, Saul tears the *edge* of Samuel's robe, and in Num. 15:38, God instructs the Israelites to put tassels on the *edges* of their garments. In Hag. 2:12, the prophet discusses carrying holy meat in the *skirt* of a garment. A number of verses refers to the "*wings* of the earth," meaning the extremities of the earth (Job 37:3; 38:13; Isa. 24:16; "four *corners* of the earth," Isa. 11:12).

Figuratively, *kānāp* is used in the rich metaphors "under his *wing*" and "in the shadow of your *wings*" (Ruth 2:12; Ps. 17:8; 91:4). Derived from the image of a bird with its young, *kānāp* signifies protection, care, tenderness, and love (Ps. 36:7). In fact, this image is used twice in the OT as a metaphor for marriage: Ruth 3:9, "spread out your *wing* over your maidservant;" and Ezek. 16:8. (In both instances, *kānāp* may be referring to the "wing" or skirt of a garment.) Other vivid metaphors are "spread his *wings*," depicting swift, unhindered action (Deut. 32:11; Jer. 48:40; 49:22), and "in its *wings*," depicting an accompanying quality (Mal. 4:2, "healing in its *wings*"). See *NIDOTTE*, 2:670-71.

WIPE CLEAN

Old Testament

Verb: כָּפַר (*kāpar*), GK 4105 (S 3722), 102x. *kāpar* is generally translated "to atone, wipe clean, appease." While scholars debate whether the root meaning of this verb is "to cover," "to ransom," or "to wipe clean/purge," it is the last one that seems most appropriate in the OT. See *atone*.

WIPE OUT

New Testament

Verb: ἐξαλείφω (*exaleiphō*), GK *1981* (S *1813*), 5x. *exaleiphō* means "to blot out, wipe out."

WISDOM

Old Testament

Noun: חָכְמָה (*ḥokmâ*), GK 2683 (S 2451), 153x. *ḥokmâ* has a wide variety of meanings, covering both physical skill and intellectual wisdom. It can be translated as "wisdom, aptitude, experience, good sense, skill."

(1) The prideful Assyrians boasted of their military skill (Isa. 10:13). Such skill is manifested in technical work, such as the women with *ḥokmâ* who make furnishings for the tabernacle (Exod. 35:26) and the vestments for the priests (28:3). *ḥokmâ* can be understood as political shrewdness, such as when a woman of Tekoa assists Joab in quelling a revolt against King David led by Sheba (2 Sam. 20:22). An able leader is filled with administrative "wisdom" (Deut. 34:9).

(2) But the majority of the usages of *ḥokmâ* refer to intellectual wisdom. Wisdom is coupled with such qualities as understanding (Prov. 10:23) and knowledge (2:10). Wisdom has its source in God and in the fear of the Lord. Job asks, "From where, then, does *wisdom* come? And where is the place of understanding?" (Job 28:20), and then answers, "God understands the way to it, and he knows its place" (28:23). The psalmist writes, "The fear of the Lord is the beginning of *wisdom*" (Ps. 111:10). As to its entry in human beings, it finds its seat in the heart (see Ps. 90:12; Prov. 2:10; 14:33). Such wisdom involves not just knowledge, but especially life skills. "Wisdom is found in those who take advice" (Prov. 13:10). The books of Job, Proverbs, Ecclesiastes, and Song of Songs are sometimes called "Wisdom Literature."

(3) By far the most exalted view of wisdom is found in Prov. 8, where *ḥokmâ* is personified in a hymn that links wisdom closely with the Lord God. Even before creation took place, wisdom was already there in the heart of God and was involved in the creative process (Prov. 8:22–31). She was "the craftsman at [the Creator's] side" (8:30). Such speculations became increasingly important in Jewish thinking between the time of the OT and NT, producing the two books of the Apocrypha called The Wisdom of Solomon and The Wisdom of Jesus Son of Sirach. See *NIDOTTE*, 2:130-34; 4:1276–85.

New Testament

Noun: σοφία (*sophia*), GK *5053* (S *4678*), 51x. *sophia* is a word meaning "wisdom." It denotes the capacity to not only understand something (Acts 7:22) but also to act accordingly (Col. 1:9; 4:5). It is the latter that separates wisdom from knowledge.

There is a natural wisdom; Moses was instructed in "the *wisdom* of Egypt" (Acts 7:22). But there is also a special wisdom that can come only from God, especially through the Holy Spirit. The seven men chosen to help the apostles were "full of the Spirit and *wisdom*" (Acts 6:3), and believers receive God's wisdom through the Spirit (1 Cor. 2:5–16). There is also a false wisdom, but it is of no value (Col. 2:23).

God's wisdom stands in marked contrast to the world's wisdom, which is ultimately doomed to destruction. This is especially true in preaching: "For Christ did not send me to baptize but to preach the gospel, not with words of *wisdom* [i.e., the world's wisdom] lest the cross of Christ be emptied of its power. For the word of the cross is foolishness to those who are perishing, but to us who are being saved it is the power of God. For it is written, 'I will destroy the *wisdom* of the wise, and the discernment of the discerning I will thwart" (1 Cor. 1:17–19, ESV). This is why the proclamation of the gospel must not be done in lofty words of worldly wisdom but in the simple proclamation of a crucified Jesus (1 Cor. 2:1–2).

Wisdom is an attribute of God (Rom. 11:33; 1 Cor. 1:21; Eph. 3:10) and a possession of Jesus (Mt. 13:54; Lk. 2:52; 1 Cor. 1:30; Col. 2:3; Rev. 5:12). Wisdom is personified in the NT (Mt. 11:19; Lk. 7:35; 11:49) just as it is in the OT (Prov. 8:12–36). Wisdom is a gift from God (Eph. 1:17; Jas. 1:5) and specifically can be a spiritual gift (1 Cor. 12:8). Paul's prayer for the Colossians is that they may be filled with "a knowledge of God's will through all spiritual *wisdom*" so that they may walk in a manner worthy of him, bearing fruit, and being strengthened (Col. 1:9–11); wisdom is, therefore, part of the believer's spiritual growth (Col. 1:28). It is a way of living (Col. 3:16; Jas. 3:13–17); it is practical rather than speculative. See *NIDNTT-A,* 533-34.

Noun: σοφός (*sophos*), GK *5055* (S *4680*), 20x. The natural meaning of *sophos* applies to one who knows how to do something skillfully, such as a master builder (1 Cor. 3:10) or an arbitrator of disputes (1 Cor. 6:5). It is true that a certain amount of wisdom can be gained through intelligence and experience (Mt. 11:25; Rom. 1:14; 1 Cor. 1:19–20, 26–27; 1 Cor. 3:20), but to be truly wise, one must use that wisdom in the service of God. Paul uses *sophos* with both meanings in 1 Cor. 3:18: "*wise* by the standards of this age" is the trained kind of wisdom; "so that he may become *wise*" is the divine kind of wisdom (cf. Lk. 10:21; 1 Cor. 1:20, 25–27).

sophos is also used of God (Rom. 16:27) or of the wisdom that comes from God (Mt. 23:34). Divine wisdom can be seen in one's actions (Rom. 16:19; Eph. 5:15; Jas. 3:13). God's wisdom is to characterize the life of a disciple: "Look carefully then how you walk, not as unwise but as *wise*" (Eph. 5:15). See *NIDNTT-A,* 533-34.

WISE, SKILLFUL

Old Testament

Adjective: חָכָם (*ḥākām*), GK 2682 (S 2450), 138x. This adjective may be translated as "shrewd, crafty, intelligent, prudent, clever" or "cunning" (2 Sam. 13:3).

The majority of the usages of *ḥākām* refer to the intellectual aspect of wisdom. "Let the *wise* listen and add to their learning" (Prov. 1:5). After interpreting Pharaoh's dreams, Joseph counseled Pharaoh to "look for a … wise man and put him in charge of the land of Egypt" (Gen. 41:33). Pharaoh appointed Joseph to this position because of Joseph's *ḥākām* (Gen. 41:39). A wise person conforms to the word of God (Deut. 4:6).

But *ḥākām* also refers to being skillful in technical work. Weavers, sailors (Ezek. 27:8), shipbuilders (Ezek. 27:9), metal (goldsmiths, Jer. 10:9) and wood workers (of the Tabernacle and furniture, Exod. 35:10) were considered wise. And the wise person could accomplish numerous tasks simultaneously, including being a good parent and a philosopher. The wise person oftentimes possessed administrative skills (1 Ki. 5:21). The *ḥākām* woman from Tekoa demonstrated wisdom by handling the touchy issue of King Solomon and his son Absalom's absence in a delicate manner (2 Sam. 14:2). See *NIDOTTE* 2:130-134.

New Testament

Adjective: φρόνιμος (*phronimos*), GK *5861* (S *5429*), 14x. One who is *phronimos* is "wise, insightful" in a prudent or shrewd way, acting in a way that is appropriate for the circumstance or situation. This term is used in parables to describe the "wise man" who builds his house on the rock (Mt. 7:24), the "wise" virgins who have enough oil (25:1–9), and the "*wise* and faithful servant" who is ready for the coming of his master (24:45). Paul uses irony to show that the Corinthians may think they are wise but are not (1 Cor. 4:10; 2 Cor. 11:19), although in 1 Cor. 10:15 he affirms them that they are "sensible" people and can judge for themselves as to what he is saying.

Disciples are to be "as *shrewd* as snakes and as innocent as doves" (Mt. 10:16). Jesus is not directing the disciples here to do evil, but he is calling them to be wise and careful as they go about serving Christ in the world (cf. also Lk. 16:8–9). Paul does not want the believers to "be *wise* in your own conceits" (Rom. 11:25, ESV; "so that you may not be *conceited*," NIV). The inclusion of the Gentiles into God's kingdom has come about because God has sent a partial hardening on the Jewish nation, not because the Gentiles are better people; hence, their is no room for their boasting. See *NIDNTT-A*, 593-94.

(BE) WISE

Old Testament

Verb: שָׂכַל (*śākal*), GK 8505 (S 7919), 60x. *śākal* means "to be wise (Prov. 15:24), understand (Isa. 41:20), prosper/be successful (1 Sam. 18:5, 14–15)." Human beings have a great desire to learn and to gain understanding. This is what the serpent took advantage of in the Garden of Eden, because he knew that Adam and Eve had an insatiable "desire for *gaining wisdom*" (Gen. 3:6).

As Adam and Eve discovered, however, in our own natural selves we cannot gain true understanding (Ps. 14:2; 36:3; 53:2). That is because the ultimate source of all true wisdom and insight is the Lord God (Ps. 119:99; Isa. 52:13; Jer. 3:15; Dan. 1:17) or those whom he has commissioned to instruct us (Prov. 1:3; Dan. 9:22, 25). But once God's people have this wisdom and understanding, they are able to "ponder" what God has done (Ps. 64:9) and then to communicate it to others (32:8). When we gain such wisdom, we become able to focus on the results of such understanding, such as living a wise and prudent life (Prov. 15:24), gaining true knowledge (21:11), speaking in a God-glorifying manner (16:23), and gaining success in life (17:8). Those who do not depend on the Lord, however, "will not prosper" (Jer. 10:21). See *NIDOTTE*, 3:1243.

WISH

Old Testament

Noun: רָצוֹן (*rāṣôn*), GK 8356 (S 7522), 56x. *rāṣôn* denotes three different ideas in the OT: favor (see *favor*), acceptance (see *acceptable*), or will (see *please*). It is attributed most often to God (39x) and occurs most frequently in Proverbs (14x), Psalms (13x), and Leviticus (7x). When *rāṣôn* is used generally for a creature's desire, it is translated as "desires" (Ps. 145:16, 19) or something "wished" for (Est. 1:8).

New Testament

Verb: ἐλπίζω (*elpizō*), GK *1827* (S *1679*), 31x. In general *elpizō* means "hope" (see *hope*), though it sometimes denotes "desire, wish." See *desire*.

Noun: ἐλπίς (*elpis*), GK *1828* (S *1680*), 53x. The majority of the NT writers invest *elpis*, "hope," with the nuance of "confident expectation" or "solid assurance," though in several places it means simply "desire" or "wish" (Acts 16:19; 27:20; 2 Cor. 10:15), as our common English usage ("I hope the sun will shine tomorrow"). See *hope*.

WITHDRAW

New Testament

Verb: ἀπερχομαι (*aperchomai*), GK *599* (S *565*), 117x. *aperchomai* means "to go away, withdraw," though it can also simply mean "to go." See *go away*.

WITHER

Old Testament

Verb: יָבֵשׁ (*yābēš*), GK 3312 (3001), 59x. *yābēš* means "to wither, dry up." Things dry up because of lack of moisture, and thus it is possible for grass (Ps. 90:6), vines (Joel 1:12), and streams (1 Ki. 17:7) to dry up. This verb is sometimes used to demonstrate God's great power over all creation by drying up massive amounts of water: after the flood (Gen. 8:7, 14), the Red Sea at the time of the exodus (Jos. 2:10), and the Jordan as the Israelites were ready to cross over (4:23). At his appearance, the top of Mount Carmel withers (Amos 1:2).

God's message of judgment can come in small events, such as with withering of Jeroboam's hand (1 Ki. 13:4) and the drying up of the vine that was sheltering Jonah (Jon. 4:7). But God can use also his withering power over much larger things. He also has the ability to withhold rain, causing drought and famine (Ezek. 19:12; Amos 4:7). He can also "dry up" of the water supplies of Egypt (Isa. 42:15) and Babylon (Jer. 50:38).

But just as God demonstrates his sovereignty over water by drying it up, he is also sovereign to bring life to things that are dried. In one of the most powerful images of the Bible, God demonstrates his power over death and his will to bring salvation when he restores the "dry" bones in Ezekiel's vision to living, breathing people. "Prophesy to these bones and say to them: O *dry* bones, hear the word of the Lord.... I will cause breath to enter you and you shall live" (Ezek. 37:4–5). See *NIDOTTE*, 2:393–94.

New Testament

Verb: ξηραίνω (*xērainō*), GK *3830* (S *3583*), 15x. *xērainō* denotes the "scorching" or "drying up" of something, usually due to the sun. In Jas. 1:11 the "withering of grass" is compared to the withering of earthly riches. See *dry up*.

WITHIN

Old Testament

Noun: קֶרֶב (*qereb*), GK 7931 (S 7130), 227x. The basic meaning of *qereb* is "inner parts." When combined with the preposition "in" or "from," *qereb* means "within, in the midst of," or "from the midst of," and this is the most common use of the word in the OT (198x). See *inner parts*.

WITNESS

Old Testament

Noun: עֵד (*ʿēd*), GK 6332 (S 5707), 69x. *ʿēd*, usually translated "witness," is a legal term that derives from a verb meaning "to repeat, do again." In the OT, a witness is someone who is able to repeat to others something he has observed firsthand. His testimony is legal and is used to confirm a fact.

ʿēd is found in the context of legal transactions and agreements. "Witnesses" confirm Boaz's redemption of Ruth (Ruth 4:9, 10, 11) and Jeremiah's purchase of the field, symbolizing God's promise of restoration (Jer. 32:10, 12, 25, 44). A heap of stones serves as a "witness" to the covenant between Jacob and Laban (Gen. 31:44, 48), and the tribes of Reuben and Gad (and the half tribe of Manasseh) erect an altar as they settle the promised land in order to serve as a "witness" to the unity of Israel despite the geographic divide caused by the Jordan River (Jos. 22:27, 28, 34).

But *ʿēd* is found more commonly among judicial proceedings. Deuteronomy requires the testimony of more than one "witness" to establish guilt (Deut. 19:15), especially in capital cases (17:6; cf. Num. 35:30), in which the "witnesses" are to cast the first stones (Deut. 17:7). God's love for truth and justice is displayed in the OT demand for witnesses to be faithful (Prov. 14:5) and truthful (14:25). The ninth commandment forbids bearing false "witness" (Exod. 20:16; cf. 23:1; Deut. 5:20). Elsewhere, the law requires that the defendant's penalty be meted out to the "witness" if the witness is found to be false (Deut. 19:16–19). Yahweh hates a false "witness" (Prov. 6:19) who mocks justice (19:28), speaks deceit (12:17), and lies (14:5). A false "witness" will not go unpunished (19:5, 9), but will perish (21:28).

God, who sees all things, is the ultimate witness. He is the "true and faithful witness" (Jer. 42:5), convicting people of their sin (Jer. 29:23; Mal. 3:5) and confirming their integrity (1 Sam. 12:5; Job 16:19).

New Testament

Verb: μαρτυρέω (*martyreō*), GK *3455* (S *3140*), 76x. *martyreō* means to "confirm, testify" to something from firsthand experience. See *testify*.

Noun: μαρτυρία (*martyria*), GK *3456* (S *3141*), 37x. *martyria* is similar to *martyrion* ("testimony") and is used frequently in conjunction with the verb *martyreō* ("to witness"). See *testimony*.

Noun: μαρτύριον (*martyrion*), GK *3457* (S *3142*), 19x. *martyrion* denotes an action, statement, or thing that serves as a testimony or witness. See *testimony*.

Noun: μάρτυς (*martys*), GK *3459* (S *3144*), 35x. A *martys* is one who provides personal testimony or verification.

(1) *martys* is sometimes used of a legal proceeding as well as nonlegal proceedings that nevertheless carry legal connotations. Examples of the former are the statement of the high priest that there was no more need for "witnesses" against Jesus (Mk. 14:63), and Acts 7:58, which recounts that "the witnesses" against Stephen laid their coats at the feet of Saul. Jesus and Paul both teach the practice of having two or three witnesses to provide testimony in disputes (Mt. 18:16; 2 Cor. 13:1; 1 Tim. 5:19). This principle is drawn from Deut. 19:18.

(2) The most prevalent use of *martys* in the NT, however, does not relate to disputes or legal proceedings, but to testimony or affirmation of the truth that someone makes. The majority of these occurrences refer to witnesses to Jesus Christ or his gospel. For example, "you are witnesses of these things" and "a witness of Christ's sufferings" (Lk. 24:48; 1 Pet. 5:1). The idea of witnesses is crucial in the book of Acts, which often mentions Christians as those who give testimony to Jesus' life, death, and resurrection (Acts 1:8, 22; 2:32; 3:15; 10:39; 13:31; 22:15). Among its many occurrences in Acts is the important and well-known statement of Jesus: "You will receive power when the Holy Spirit comes on you and you will be my *witnesses* in Jerusalem, in all Judea, in Samaria, and to the end of the earth" (Acts 1:8).

A theme sometimes associated with Christian witness is its divine appointment. This is evident not only in Acts 1:8 but also in 26:16, where Paul recounts God as saying that he appointed Paul "as a *witness*" (see also 10:41). The ultimate witness to the good news is Jesus himself: "Jesus Christ, the faithful *witness*, the firstborn from the dead and the ruler of the kings of the earth" (Rev. 1:5).

(3) As the church grew and persecution persisted, *martys* also came to be used as a technical term for a Christian put to death because of the faith. The first use of *martys* in this way is in Acts 22:20, which says "the blood of your *witness/martyr* Stephen was shed."

(4) There are a number of other noteworthy uses of this word. It is used to make oaths before God, as when Paul says, "God is my witness" (Rom. 1:9; also Acts 2:32; 5:32; 2 Cor. 1:23; 1 Thess. 2:10). *martys* is used in Rev. 11:3 for the two eschatological witnesses to Jesus. It can also denote other members of the kingdom of heaven who are "witnesses" to the life of Christians (2 Tim. 2:2; Heb. 12:2). See *NIDNTT-A*, 355-57.

WOE

Old Testament

Interjection: הוֹי (*hôy*), GK 2098 (S 1945), 51x. *hôy* is an onomatopoeic particle that is often translated "woe, alas." It expresses personal pain and anguish because of some present or impending situation. After the death of the man of God from Judah, another prophet places the man in his own tomb and cries, "*Oh*, my brother" (1 Ki. 13:30). Perhaps it could better be translated, "Ooooooo, my brother." One can hear the cries of anguish in this word. Isaiah too cries out in personal anguish, "*Ah*, sinful nation, a people loaded with grief" (Isa. 1:4). A similar-sounding word with the same meaning is *ʾôy* (GK 208).

Most of the uses of *hôy* are for impending disaster, not present anguish (note that all such uses are in the prophetic books). In such cases it is often translated "alas" (e.g., Jer. 22:18) or "woe to" (e.g., Isa. 5:8, 11, 18; 18:1; 28:1; Ezek. 13:3, 18). But it is not improper to say that this word here depicts the future sounds of agony that will be made by those on whom the predicted "woe" will soon occur. See *NIDOTTE*, 4:1032.

New Testament

Interjection: οὐαί (*ouai*), GK *4026* (S *3759*), 47x. *ouai* is an onomatopoeic word; the sound of the word suggests its meaning such as "bang" or "ouch." *paristēmi* can be an expression of intense sorrow or pain. "Alas" for the women who are pregnant or have newborns in the last days (Mt. 24:19). "Woe" to Judas for betraying Jesus (26:24).

ouai is also used as a statement of condemnation of a person or group. "*Woe* to Bethsaida," for if the miracles that were done there had been done in Sidon and Tyre, those pagans would have repented (Mt. 11:21). The "woes" are opposites of blessings and express the judgment of God (Lk. 6:20–23, compared with 6:24–26; cf. also Mt. 23; Rev. 8:13; 9:12; 18:10, 16, 19).

ouai is also used figuratively in a special sense of burden felt by Paul for his obligation to preach the gospel: "Yet when I preach the gospel, I cannot boast, for I am compelled to preach. *Woe* to me if I do not preach the gospel!" (1 Cor. 9:16, NIV).

All uses of *ouai* express an intensity of emotion. In Scripture, Christians express both strict condemnation (Jude 11) and intense sorrow for the unbeliever (Rom. 9:2–3). See *NIDNTT-A,* 421.

WOMAN

Old Testament

Noun: אִשָּׁה (*ʾiššâ*), GK 851 (S 802), 781x. In the broadest sense of the word, *ʾiššâ* simply means "woman" or "wife." (1) According to Gen. 2, woman was created after the man: "Then the Lord God made a woman from the rib he had taken out of the man, and he brought her to the man" (Gen. 2:22). This passage asserts a direct association between this man (*ʾîš*) and the woman (*ʾiššâ*). Adam leaves no doubt about this association by proclaiming, "She shall be called woman, for she was taken out of man" (2:23). The emphasis in this earliest passages focuses on the personhood of the two—not their functionality as a family unit.

(2) The next statement in Gen. 2 shows the importance and permanence of the marriage relationship as between a man and his *ʾiššâ* (which now means "wife"): "For this reason a man will cleave his father and mother and be united to his wife, and they will become one flesh" (2:24). Note that this new family unit is now stronger than the relationship of parent and child. Moreover, ideally there should be no secrets between husband and wife, for Adam and his wife were naked before each other (2:25; this is prior to their fall into sin).

(3) OT society was a male-dominated society. For example, few commands are addressed exclusively to women, even in the sexual realm (see, e.g., Lev. 18:23; 20:16). Presumably this is because for the most part, women had no independent access to men outside their immediately families. But the law did offer specific protections for women; an *ʾiššâ* was not even supposed to be coveted (Exod. 20:17; Deut. 5:21).

(4) The nation of Israel is occasionally considered, by analogy, as the Lord's *ʾiššâ* (see Isa. 54:6; Jer. 3:20; Ezek. 16:23). These passages portray the nation as an adulterous wife, whom the Lord is about to divorce for her unfaithfulness. Nevertheless, as Hos. 1–3 points out, the Lord does retain his love for his wife and, in the end, calls his people back to himself.

(5) There are several unusual occurrences of *ʾiššâ* in the OT. (a) In Lam. 2:20 we read one of the few times when an ʾišša denotes a mother. The people say, "Look, O Lord, and consider: Whom have you ever treated like this? Should women eat their offspring, the children they have cared for?" (b) *ʾiššâ* is not exclusively used to describe a human woman. It is sometimes used to refer to livestock. As Noah enters the ark, for example, God tells him what to take along with him "seven of every kind of clean animal, a male and its mate" (Gen. 7:2). (c) In a most unusual

passage centering on *ʾiššâ*, the writer of Proverbs outlines the characteristics of the "wife/woman of noble character" (Prov. 31:10). This woman stands out uniquely as a woman with initiative, involved in her home and family and also in the business world. It is also said about her, "A woman who fears the Lord is to be praised" (31:30). This use is especially important because many other references to *ʾiššâ* in Proverbs are pejorative (e.g., "immoral woman," 6:24; "quarrelsome wife," 27:15; but cf. also "kindhearted woman," 11:16; "wise woman," 14:1). See *NIDOTTE*, 1:537–40.

Noun: בַּת (*bat*), GK 1426 (S 1323), 587x. *bat* is the common Hebrew noun for one's own daughter (e.g., Gen. 24:24; 29:10; Exod. 21:7; Deut. 16:14; Jos. 15:16; 2 Sam. 6:16). But it has a variety of other nuances, including girl, granddaughter, and even woman. See *daughter*.

New Testament

Noun: γυνή (*gynē*), GK *1222* (S *1135*), 215x. *gynē* refers in the first place to an adult female person, a "woman," including virgins (e.g., Mt. 9:20; 13:33; 27:55; Lk. 1:42). Luke is a champion of women, making reference to thirteen women mentioned nowhere else in the NT. For instance, traveling along with the disciples were some women (whom he names) who had been cured of evil spirits and diseases (Lk. 8:2–3). The NT is replete with examples of women being highly esteemed alongside their male counterparts even though the culture at best relegated women to second-class citizenship.

Evenhanded treatment emerges in the company of Jesus. As well as teaching his disciples, he addressed doctrinal and personal issues with the Samaritan woman at the well (Jn. 4:4–30). This amazed the disciples as some rabbis held that to talk too much to a woman, even one's wife, was a waste of time, unnecessarily distracting a man from the study of the law. Jesus also rebuked Martha, who criticized her sister, Mary, for learning at the feet of Jesus (Lk. 10:41–42). In the story of Jesus and the adulterous woman, this woman probably thought she would not emerge from the situation alive as the law of Moses prescribed death for adultery (Jn. 7:53–8:11). But Jesus sidestepped the legal rules of the law in order to forgive her. He placed extraordinary high value on women by recognizing their intrinsic worth as individuals, by ministering to them, and by according them dignity in his ministry.

gynē also denotes a "wife." Paul uses the word 21x in his important chapter dealing with marriage in 1 Cor. 7. *gynē* appears with *anēr* (see *man, husband*) in the qualifications equation pertaining to elders and deacons being the *husband* of but one *wife* (1 Tim. 3:2, 12; Tit. 1:16). In an extended passage, Paul calls on wives to submit to their husbands and on husbands to love their wives, just as Christ loved the church—with a sacrificial love (Eph. 5:22–33; cf. Col. 3:18–4:1). Paul had an exalted view of marriage.

Lastly, *gynē* can also refer to a newly married woman, i.e., a bride. Jerusalem is depicted as "the bride, the *wife* of the Lamb" in Rev. 21:9 (see also 19:7). It is used in the angel's instructions to Joseph when he discovered Mary was pregnant before they were married: "Do not be afraid to take Mary home as your *wife*" (Mt. 1:20). In none of the instances in the NT is *gynē* a negative or inferior term.

Regarding the role of women in the contemporary church, a complication in understanding the NT is the double meaning of *gynē* as "woman" and "wife." In passages such as 1 Cor. 14:34–34 and 1 Tim. 2:11–15, for example, is Paul's issue here how men and women are to relate in the church, or how husbands and wives are to relate in the home? These issues are still being debated. See *NIDNTT-A*, 117-18.

WOMB

Old Testament

Noun: בֶּטֶן (*beṭen*), GK 1061 (S 990), 72x. The basic sense of *beṭen* seems to be the hollow or inside of something. It is used in several ways in the OT, referring to the belly or abdomen, the reproductive organs (of men or women), and the womb.

(1) Sometimes *beṭen* refers to the belly or abdomen of a woman or man. Num. 5:21 speaks of the *abdomen* of the woman suspected of adultery, and Jdg. 3:21–22 describes how Ehud's sword went into Eglon's belly. As well, it often refers to a woman's womb, as when Samson was called to be a Nazirite from the womb (Jdg. 13:5, NIV "from *birth*"), when Job describes how he came naked from the womb (Job 1:21), and when the psalmist confesses his dependence and trust in God from the womb (Ps. 22:9–10; 71:6). In this respect, Ps. 132:11 is interesting because, while women typically are described as having the "fruit of the womb" (meaning "children," Gen. 30:2; Deut. 7:3), here it is the fruit of David's *beṭen* (his belly or body) that is promised to have an everlasting throne. Sometimes the KJV translates *beṭen* as *body* in the expression "fruit of the body" (Deut. 28:4, 11, 18, 53); however, the NIV has "fruit of the womb" in these passages.]

(2) In a metaphorical sense, *beṭen* may refer to the inner being of a person (Prov. 18:8; 22:18), and as an architectural term in 1 Ki. 7:20, it refers to a rounded projection on the pillars of a building (NIV has *bowl-shaped part*).

(3) The word *beṭen* is used in some theologically significant ways. First, the OT indicates that the sinfulness of humanity stretches back to the time of child's existence in the womb; as Ps. 58:4 notes, the wicked are wayward and speak lies from the womb (KJV "as soon as *they are born*"). Second, Job 15:35 likens the godless person's plotting of evil to a pregnancy, during which they conceive trouble, give birth to evil, and have "wombs" that fashion deceit (cf. the similar image in Jas. 1:13–15). Finally, Isaiah uses the imagery of the *beṭen* to describe God's special care for his covenant people. It is God who has formed Jacob in the womb (Isa. 44:2, 24), who upholds his people from the womb (46:3), and who will not forget them in the same way that a nursing woman cannot forget her nursing child and fail to have compassion on the son of her womb (49:15). See *NIDOTTE*, 1:650-51.

New Testament

Noun: κοιλία (*koilia*), GK *3120* (S *2836*), 23x. The basic meaning of *koilia* is "body-cavity"; it is often translated as "stomach, belly, womb, appetite." See also *stomach*.

On occasion this noun refers to the woman's womb or uterus (Lk. 1:41–42, 44; 23:29). The expression "from the womb" simply means "from birth" (Lk. 1:15; Acts 3:2; 14:8; Gal. 1:15). This is the same word Nicodemus uses when he asks Jesus, "How can a man be born when he is old? Surely he cannot enter a second time into his mother's *womb* to be born!" (Jn. 3:4). See *NIDNTT-A*, 310.

WONDER

New Testament

Verb: διαλογίζομαι (*dialogizomai*), GK *1368* (S *1260*), 16x. *dialogizomai* means "to discuss, consider, argue" about something. Sometimes it can denote an inner wondering to oneself about something. See *consider*.

Verb: θαυμαζω (*thaumazō*), GK *2513* (S *2296*), 43x. *thaumazō* denotes "to be amazed, astonished, wonder, marvel." See *amazed*.

WONDERFUL, WONDERS

Old Testament

Verb: פָּלָא (*pālāʾ*), GK 7098 (S 6381), 71x. (1) In its participle form, *pālāʾ* means "miracles, wonders," in reference to the extraordinary deeds of God. God is going to smite Egypt with his wonders (Exod. 3:20), and as he takes the people into the land, he will do wonders before them (Jos. 3:5). The psalmist often sings the wondrous works of God (e.g., Ps. 9:1; 26:7; 40:5; 71:17). The backside of the wonderful nature of God's works is that if his people break the covenant, God will make the plagues against them "wonderful" (Deut. 28:59).

(2) At points *pālāʾ* refers to the wondrous nature of a person, object, or activity. For example, when lamenting Jonathan's death, David declares, "Your love for me was more *wonderful* than the love of women" (2 Sam. 1:26), by which David proclaims the brotherly affection and righteous fellowship the two have enjoyed with each other. Only by ignoring the canonical context of this statement can this verse be hijacked by advocates of homosexuality. David is a man after God's own heart, and Lev. calls lying with a man as one lies with a woman an abomination (Lev. 18:22). What is in view here is a righteous fellowship between like-minded, God-fearing men who are married to women.

(3) In other contexts, *pālāʾ* points to the wondrous nature of activities or ideas that are beyond one's abilities to do or grasp. In Prov. 30:18–19, for instance, the sage speaks of four things that are "too amazing" for him fully to comprehend: "the way of an eagle in the sky, the way of a snake on a rock, the way of a ship on the sea, and the way of a man with a girl." Cases too wonderful (i.e., difficult) for local judges are to be taken to the "supreme court" at the central sanctuary (Deut. 17:8), and Moses tells the people that the commandment he proclaims is not too difficult for them (Deut. 30:11). It seemed beyond Amnon's abilities to do anything to Tamar (2 Sam. 13:2). Nothing is "too hard" for God to perform (Gen. 18:14; see too Jer. 32:17, 27).

(4) *pālāʾ* can also refer to fulfilling (NIV) or accomplishing (KJV) a vow (Lev. 22:21; cf. also 27:2; Num. 6:2; 15:3, 8).

New Testament

Noun: τέρας (*teras*), GK *5469* (S *5059*), 16x. *teras* means "wonder, miracle, miraculous occurrence." Although it is distinct from "signs," in every instance *teras* occurs alongside of "sign," forming a kind of idiom (e.g., Mt. 24:24; Mk. 13:22; Jn. 4:48; Acts 2:19; 22, 43; Rom. 15:19; 2 Cor. 12:12). The ability to perform "signs and wonders" comes from a supernatural power, such as God (through an apostle), but it can also come from the evil one (see Mt. 24:24; Mk. 13:22; 2 Thess. 2:9).

"Signs and wonders" are designed for one major purpose: to confirm the authenticity of the wonder worker (Acts 2:22). So then, the author of Hebrews can say that God bore witness to his great salvation through signs and wonders (Heb. 2:4), such as those found in the gospels and Acts. Yet note too that while a *teras* can create awe (Acts 2:43), it still takes the Spirit to change someone's heart. Not everyone in the NT who saw or benefited from a wonder came to saving faith, especially since some wonders came through demonic powers. That is, signs and wonders are no substitute for spreading the good news of the gospel of Jesus Christ. They never were, and they never will be. See *NIDNTT-A*, 562.

WOOD

Old Testament

Noun: עֵץ (*ʿēṣ*), GK 6770 (S 6086), 330x. *ʿēṣ* is the basic word for tree and wood products. It can be translated as "wood, tree, timber." See *tree*.

New Testament

Noun: ξύλον (*xylon*), GK *3833* (S *3586*), 20x. *xylon* means "tree, club, wood, stocks." It refers to living or dead wood or anything made of wood. See *tree*.

WOODS

Old Testament

Noun: יַעַר (*yaʿar*), GK 3623 (S 3293), 56x. *yaʿar* is the general term for a forest. However, it does not always refer to areas covered with tall trees; it can also refer to areas covered with shrubs and bushes. See *forest*.

WORD

Old Testament

Verb: דָּבַר (*dābar*), GK 1819 (S 1696), 1136x.

Noun: דָּבָר (*dābār*), GK 1821 (S 1697), 1454x.

The verb *dābar* ("say, speak") and the noun *dābār* ("word") are both used hundreds of times for the human and the divine activity of speaking. The verb occurs in speaking in dialog within a narrative (Gen. 8:15, "Then God *spoke* to Noah"; Gen. 21:1; 27:6; 44:6–7; 32:20; Exod. 6:10, 12, 13; 32:7; Lev. 6:19). It is also is used in the formula found numerous times in the prophets, "The Lord *has spoken*" (Isa. 1:2; 24:3; 40:5; 58:14; Jer. 13:15; Joel 3:8; Obad. 18; Mic. 4:4; cf. Isa. 21:17).

(1) Joseph "spoke" harshly to his brothers in Egypt at first (Gen. 42:7) but later spoke a kind word to them (50:19; cf. 37:4, "when his brothers saw that their father loved him more than any of them, they hated him and could not *speak* a kind word to him"). Jonathan "spoke" well of David to Saul in hopes of tempering his father's murderous desires toward David (1 Sam. 19:4).

(2) It is a central theological imperative that God's people use their speech in such a way that reflects the *dābar*/*dābār* of God. God threatens judgment on Israel because her "lips have spoken lies and your tongue mutters wicked things" (Isa. 59:3). In Isa. 58:13 one honors the Sabbath by refusing to speak empty *dābār* (NIV "idle words"). In Deuteronomy God's word is a promise: "May the LORD, the God of your fathers, increase you a thousand time and bless you as he has *spoken*" (Deut. 6:3; 9:3; 11:25; 18:2; 26:18; 27:3; 29:13; cf. Gen. 28:15; 1 Ki. 8:24).

(3) Proverbs states that a "word" (*dābār*) fitly "spoken" (*dābar*) is like apples of gold in settings of silver (Prov. 25:11). The psalmist writes that he who "speaks" the truth from his heart does what is right (Ps. 15:2), which stands in contrast to someone who "speaks" with his neighbors nicely to their face while at the same time holding malice in his heart against them (28:3). There should be integrity in our speech, such as when the psalmist speaks vows when he is in trouble and later fulfills his word after God rescues him (66:13–14). Prov. 16:13 states that "kings take pleasure in honest lips; they value a man who *speaks* the truth." God declares through Isaiah that the one who "speaks" what is right finds refuge with the Lord (Isa. 33:15–16).

(4) Zechariah is instructed to proclaim that the Lord "says" that he is a very jealous for Jerusalem and Zion (Zech. 1:14). We are reminded that true prophets speak the word of the Lord regardless of the kind of response they receive (Jer. 25:3: "the *dābār* of the Lord has come to me and I *have spoken* to you again and again, but you have not listened"). Israel is instructed to listen to the *dābār* that the prophets speak in his name (Deut. 18:19); however, the prophet is in mortal danger if he speaks his own *dābār* in place of God's work (18:20). Nevertheless, all humanity will be held responsible to God because his word is not secret and the truth of his work has been made manifest to all creation (Isa. 45:19; cf. Rom. 1:20). See *NIDOTTE*, 1:912-15.

Noun: נְאֻם ($n^{eʾ}um$), GK 5536 (S 5002), 376x. $n^{eʾ}um$ is used of an utterance, word, or revelation. It is often translated as "oracle" (NIV), "parable" (KJV), "declaration," and "word." This term refers to the "oracles" of Balaam (Num. 24:3, 4), the last "words" of David (2 Sam. 23:1), and, most commonly, a "declaration" of the Lord (especially in prophetic literature; cf. Num. 14:28; Isa. 14:22; 37:34; Ezek. 13:7; 16:58; Hos. 2:16; Joel 2:12).

(1) The $n^{eʾ}um$ of the Lord is proclaimed through his prophets (e.g., Zech. 1:1) and refers to actions he hates (Zech. 8:17, " 'Do not plot evil against your neighbor, and do not love to swear falsely. I hate all this,' $n^{eʾ}um$ of the LORD"; cf. Amos 6:8) and actions he honors (1 Sam. 2:30, "but now $n^{eʾ}um$ of the LORD ... those who honor me I will honor"). The Lord's word can be either judgment (Isa. 1:24; 14:22; Jer. 48:15; 49:5; Nah. 2:13; Amos 3:13; Obad. 8; Zeph. 1:2; 12:1–2) or reconciliation (Isa. 56:8). While the $n^{eʾ}um$ of the Lord is filled with hope, it also reveals the stain of sin that cannot be easily washed away (Jer. 2:22: " 'Although you wash yourself with soda and use much soap, the stain of your

guilt is still before me,' *n*^{e}*'um* of the Sovereign LORD").

(2) Amos warns that days are coming when God will send a famine through the land, not of food or lack of water but of "the word of the LORD" (Amos 8:10). People will go from sea to sea searching for words from the Lord but will not find it (8:12). Therefore, when one hears a message from the Lord, there is no guarantee it will come again at a later time. We must respond to God's word while it is still available.

New Testament

Noun: λόγος (*logos*), GK *3364* (S *3056*), 330x. *logos* means "word, message, report" and sometimes even "deed." It has similar meanings as *dābār* in the OT.

(1) The NT uses *logos* to express many forms of communication, both verbal and physical. This flexibility has its root in the use of *logos* in Greco-Roman literary culture, where it could stand on its own for the spoken word, "a message," as well as what one does, "a deed." The term is used by Paul to refer to all human speech (1 Cor. 1:5). It can be used for any statement (Mt. 5:37), question (Mt. 21:24), prayer (Mk. 14:39), or manner of presentation (1 Cor. 2:4).

(2) It is not surprising to find that the NT uses *logos* to mean Jesus himself. The Synoptic Gospels identify Jesus' preaching as the proclamation of the "*logos* of God," reminiscent of the OT use of the prophetic "word" ("*word* of the kingdom," Mt. 13:19; "*word* of God," Lk. 5:1). But in Jn. 1:1, the *logos* is not only from God, but *is* God. According to John, this *logos* was in the beginning, was with God, and was God himself. As the *logos*, God himself (Jn. 1:1–2) in his divine glory assumes the flesh of humanity in historical time and space (1:14–15). Jesus, the *logos*, signifies the presence of God in the flesh. No religious or philosophical parallel to Jesus the *logos* has been found. The *logos* from God is his own Son (Jn. 3:16). Jesus is the fullness of God (Col. 1:19; 2:9).

(3) Paul calls the "message" that is to be proclaimed in the churches the "*word* of God" (1 Cor. 14:36; 1 Thess. 2:13). Like the prophetic "word" in the OT, this proclamation comes from God. But even more, this "word" is focused directly on the revelation of the Son of God (Gal. 1:1, 15–16), with a focus on "the *message* of the cross" (1 Cor. 1:18). As the author to Hebrews explains, in the past God spoke his "word" through the OT prophets, but now he has spoken through his Son, Jesus Christ, the final "Word" of God (Heb. 1:1–4).

(4) It common for modern Christians to use the term "word" as a synonym for the Bible. While there is no NT usage of *logos* for the written OT (the more typical word to use was *nomos*, "law"), the term does fit well the proclamation of the Bible. Like Paul and the author of Hebrews, when we read the Bible Christians are reading a message from the prophets and the apostles, as well as the final message of Jesus himself. This message of the "word," therefore, carries the authoritative and living voice of God. That these "words" can be written is especially prominent in Revelation (see Rev. 22:7, 9, 10, 18, 19). See *NIDNTT-A*, 339-43.

Noun: ῥημα (*rhēma*), GK *4839* (S *4487*), 68x. *rhēma* means a "word" or "matter." It has at least two distinct uses in the NT. (1) It may refer to something that is said, "a word, saying, expression, or statement of any kind." Although *rhēma* overlaps semantically with *logos* even in the LXX (Exod. 24:27–28; 2 Sam. 14:20–21), the terms in the NT can have distinct nuances depending on context. "Whereas *logos* often designates the Christian proclamation as a whole, *rhēma* usually relates to individual words and utterances" (*NIDNTT-A,* 509). "Man does not live on bread alone, but on every *word* that comes from the mouth of God" (Mt. 4:4; cf. 12:36; 18:16; 26:75; 27:14; Mk. 9:32; 14:72).

(2) *rhēma* may also refer to an event that can be talked about, "a thing, object, matter." This use of *rhēma* follows the

Hebrew way of speaking. Luke says that "throughout the hill country of Judea people were talking about all these *things*" (Lk. 1:65). "For *nothing* is impossible with God" (1:37). Luke also uses the term to refer to an event, "Let's go to Bethlehem and see this *thing* that has happened" (2:15). See *NIDNTT-A*, 509-10.

WORK

Old Testament

Noun: עָמָל (*ʿāmāl*), GK 6662 (S 5999), 54x. *ʿāmāl* bears two distinct but related meanings in the OT: "work" and "trouble." *ʿāmāl* comes from the root *ʿml*, which denotes work or labor. The often difficult and toilsome nature of work produces the secondary meaning of "trouble" (see *trouble*).

ʿāmāl sometimes refer to work itself. Eccl. contains almost all the instances in this category (22x). It portrays all the *ʿāmāl* of a person's life to be vanity or meaningless (1:2–3). It is ceaseless (4:8) and as hopeless as chasing after the wind (4:4). Without God, we as human beings eventually hate the fruits of our *ʿāmāl* because we realize it will ultimately be taken from us and given to another (2:18–22). Only the person who is good in God's sight can gain enjoyment from his *ʿāmāl* (2:24; cf. vv. 25–26). See *NIDOTTE*, 3:435-37.

Noun: מְלָאכָה (*m^e^lāʾkâ*), GK 4856 (S 4399), 167x. *m^e^lāʾkâ* has the notion of "sending forth one's hand to accomplish a task" (cf. Deut. 12:7, 18). In the OT, it is most often used in connection with work in the tabernacle or temple, or involving sacred objects. This aligns with the general meaning of *malʾāk*, which most often describes skilled labor in contrast to common labor. Thus, Bezalel was filled with "skill, ability and knowledge in all kinds of *crafts*" (Exod. 31:3; 35:21, 31), and Huram was skilled in all kinds of "bronze *work*" (1 Ki. 7:14). It took men of wisdom to complete the "work" of constructing the tabernacle (Exod. 36:4, 8) and temple (1 Chr. 28:21)—including skills in stone, wood, metals (Exod. 31:4, 5; 35:33; 38:24; 1 Ki. 7:14, 22), and textiles (Exod. 35:35).

Likewise, the service of the priests in the sanctuary (especially in Chronicles) uses this word. The "task" of guarding the entrance of the temple (1 Chr. 9:19), the "work" of providing music (9:33), and the general priestly "duties" of the temple "service" (1 Chr. 28:13) are all represented by *m^e^lāʾka*.

Since Chronicles uses *ʿ^a^bôdâ* ("work," GK 6275) to mean "sacred service" (cf. also Exod. 35:24; 36:1, 3), the two-word combination *m^e^leʾket ʿ^a^bôda* (lit., "duty of work") refers to "work of sacred service" relating to the sanctuary (1 Chr. 9:13, 19). In Lev. and Num., however, the same two-word combination means "regular work" ("servile work," KJV) or the work by which one makes a living. Such "regular work" is prohibited on the weekly and festival Sabbaths (Lev. 23:7–8, 21, 25, 35–36; Num. 28:18, 25–26; 29:1, 12, 35). This follows the pattern established by God in the creation week, who finished his "work" of creating in six days and ceased from his "work," resting on the seventh day (Gen. 2:2). In each repetition of the weekly Sabbath command, that which is prohibited is *m^e^lāʾka* (Exod. 20:10; 31:14; 35:2; Lev. 23:3; Deut. 5:14), or the work for which one is compensated. The Sabbath commandment, therefore, has this primary lesson to teach: though we will never fully complete our labors (for there is always more to be done), we may rest in the reality that God has finished his work. This foreshadowed the completed work of redemption accomplished by Jesus for his people, so that our rest is in what *he* has finished, not what we have completed (cf. Heb. 4:6–11). See *NIDOTTE*, 2:943–46.

Noun: מַעֲשֶׂה (*maʿ^a^śeh*), GK 5126 (S 4639), 235x. *maʿ^a^śeh* is the noun derived from the verb *(âśâ* (GK 6913), "to make, do." Thus, it denotes that which is "done" or "made."

maʿ^a^śeh is commonly used of a person's actions. Abimelech tells Abraham, "You have done *things* to me that should not be done" (Gen. 20:9). *ma^caśeh* can also denote one's common work or occupation. For example, the forced labor of the Israelites in Egypt is called their "work" (Exod. 5:4, 13). *maᶜᵃśeh* may be used of one's occupation: Joseph's brothers as shepherds (Gen. 46:33; 47:3), or those who made the tabernacle furnishings as "skilled craftsman" (Exod. 26:1, 31; cf. 27:16, "*work* of an embroiderer"). One's common "work" (occupation) is what is done for the six days of the week and from what one ceases on the Sabbath (23:12; note that a different word, *mᵉlāʾkâ*, GK 4856, is used in 20:9–10; see comments on that term). The common phrase "the *work* of your hands" may also refer to one's daily labors, which, for those who are obedient, God blesses (Deut. 14:29; 15:10; 16:15; 24:19; 28:12; 30:9; Ps. 90:17). The author of Ecclesiastes, however, reminds us that our daily work is not the basis for our ultimate and lasting joy (Eccl. 2:11).

In other texts, however, the phrase "the *work* of your hands" is often connected with making idols (18x, e.g., Deut. 31:29; 2 Ki. 19:18; Ps. 115:4; Isa. 2:8; Jer. 25:6-7,14), for since idols are the "work" of man's hands, they are less than man and unable to help him (cf. Jer. 10:8ff.). In contrast are the "works" of God's hands, for they are holy and evoke awe (Isa. 29:23), and they declare his glory (Ps. 19:1; 102:25). While idolaters rejoice in the "work" of their hands (i.e., their idols), the psalmist declares: "For you make me glad by your deeds, O Lord; I sing for joy at the *works* of your hands" (92:4; 143:5). Indeed, the "works" of God's hands are "faithful and just" (111:7). While all of God's "works" are awesome (66:3) and without parallel (86:8), he is kind in all his "works" (145:17, "loving toward all he has made," NIV). In a more specific sense, the "*work* of God's hands" is the establishment of his covenant people in accordance with his faithful promises (138:8; Isa. 60:21; 64:8). Indeed, the tablets of the covenant are thus described by Moses: "The tablets were the *work* of God; the writing was the writing of God, engraved on the tablets" (Exod. 32:16).

In an ethical sense, one's "works" may be judged as evil (Exod. 23:24) or as good (Prov. 31:31). In this regard, God rewards a person "according to what he has done" (Ps. 62:12; cf. Rom. 2:6; 2 Cor. 5:10; Rev. 2:23). See *NIDOTTE*, 3:550–51.

Noun: עֲבוֹדָה (*ᶜᵃbôdâ*), GK 6275 (S 5656), 145x. In the early use of *ᶜᵃbôdâ* in the Pentateuch, it describes the physical labor of Jacob to Laban as the bride price, first for Leah, and then Rachel (Gen. 29:27; 30:26), as well as the toil of the Israelites while enslaved in Egypt (Exod. 1:14; 2:23; 5:9, 11). While *ᶜᵃbôda* is used elsewhere in the OT of common labor or work (e.g., 1 Ki. 12:4; 1 Chr. 4:21; Ps. 104:23), the majority of its occurrences (97x) relate in some way to the tabernacle or temple, either to their construction or to the sacred "service" and worship rendered therein. In describing the sacred activities of the tabernacle, Numbers regularly uses *ᶜᵃbôda* as a general term describing the "*work* of the tabernacle or Tent of Meeting" ("*service* of the tabernacle," KJV; Num. 3:7; 4:23; 16:9; 18:4). While *ᶜᵃbôda* can bear this general sense in the later books of the Bible (e.g., Ezek. 44:14; Neh. 10:32; especially Chr.), *ᶜᵃbôda* is connected specifically to the various "duties" allotted to the priestly families (1 Chr. 6:32, 48; 9:13, 19; 23:24, 32; 24:3; 2 Chr. 8:14), indicating the close association between *ᶜᵃbôda* and the sacred services of the temple. This use of *ᶜᵃbôda* reminds us that what was to characterize worship as God ordained it was "service" or work dedicated to him, not merely ceremony.

The fact that *ᶜᵃbôda* is so often used in the OT to describe the activities associated with the tabernacle and temple explains why an explanatory word was needed with *ᶜᵃbôda* in order to describe ordinary work or labor. Thus, throughout the Pentateuch, labor that is prohibited on the weekly and festival Sabbaths is designated as *mᵉle)ket ᶜᵃbôda*, "regular work" ("servile *work*," KJV). The addition of *mᵉleʾket* (see GK

4856) distinguishes *ᶜᵃbôda* from its commonly used sense of "service in the tabernacle or temple." Thus, what was prohibited on the Sabbath days was laboring in one's normal occupation (Lev. 23:7–8, 21, 25, 35–36; Num. 28:18, 25–26; 29:1, 12, 35). It is not as though one's "regular *work*" is somehow "unholy" and must be suspended on the Sabbath. Rather, resting from one's labors reminds one that in the end, all of one's needs are supplied by the Almighty, even the physical ability to return to one's regular work.

In Ezek. 29:18, *ᶜᵃbôda* is used in the sense of "*service* to the king," and in this case, of a military *campaign* ("great *service*," KJV). See *NIDOTTE*, 307–9.

New Testament

Verb: ἐνεργέω (*energeō*), GK *1919* (S *1754*), 21x. *energeō* means "to be active, work, operate, do" something. This word constitutes the basis of the English word "energy." This word is most often used in the NT to denote supernatural powers, whether godly or demonic. It denotes the power of God to resurrect (Mt. 14:2; Mk. 6:14). Note Paul's comment in Eph. 1:19–20, that he desires the church to know God's power, which is "like … his mighty strength, which he *worked/exerted* in Christ when he raised him from the dead." God is at work in the church through spiritual gifts (1 Cor. 12:6, 11). *energeō* also denotes God's power to effect salvation and spiritual growth in individual believers (2 Cor. 1:6; Eph. 3:20; 1 Thess. 2:13; Phil. 2:13) and to empower apostolic ministry so that the church can fulfill its evangelistic mandate (Gal. 2:8).

Demonic powers are also at work in the world, such as sinful passions working in our bodies (Rom. 7:5), the spirit at work in the sons of disobedience (Eph. 2:2), and the secret power of lawlessness (2 Thess. 2:7).

Other forces that have *energeō* include death (2 Cor. 4:12); faith, which is energized by love (Gal. 5:6); and the prayer of a righteous person, which works powerfully (Jas. 5:16). See *NIDNTT-A*, 205-6.

Verb: ἐργάζομαι (*ergazomai*), GK *2237* (S *2038*), 41x. *ergazomai* is derived from *ergon* (work) and means "to work, create, produce, perform, process, do" something. In many of its NT uses, it simply means doing something, as Jesus says of the woman who anointed his feet, "She *has done* a beautiful thing to me" (Mk. 14:6); or when Jesus says to some persons, "Get away from me, you *workers* of lawlessness" (NIV, "evildoers," Mt. 7:23); or on the contrary, while Paul says, "while we have opportunity, let us *do* good to all" (Gal. 6:10). In Jn. 6:30, it has the sense of performing something, as the crowds, wanting another miracle, ask Jesus, "What will you *perform*?"

It is natural for *ergazomai* to refer to gainful employment, involvement in a trade, and manual labor (Mt. 21:28; 1 Cor. 4:12; Eph. 4:28). It is used when Paul admonishes the Thessalonians to continue working diligently in their regular wage-earning jobs, issuing the famous and pointed mandate, "Whoever does not work, let him not eat" (2 Thess. 3:10). Paul provided himself to the Thessalonians as an example of hard and diligent work, in order not to burden the churches for financial sustenance (Acts 18:3; 2 Thess. 3:8–13). This was Paul's practice despite the fact that he had an apostolic right to be paid by those for whom he worked (1 Cor. 4:12; 9:6, 19). In this vein, Paul considered evangelistic ministry as work, a valid occupation like other jobs (16:10).

Jesus considered his earthly ministries as the work of salvation, stating, "My Father always *works*, and I *am working*" (Jn. 5:17). Additionally, he enjoined his disciples to "*do* the works of the One who sent me while it is day; for the night comes when no one can *work*" (Jn. 9:4). Paul encourages the Colossians, "Whatever you do, *do* it [NIV work at it] with all your soul" (Col. 3:23). James gives *ergazomai* a spiritual meaning with the sense of "producing," "For the human anger does not *work/produce/ result in* the righteousness of God" (Jas. 1:20); later, James writes

that when Christians show favoritism among themselves, they "*work* sin" (2:9). See *NIDNTT-A*, 205-6.

Noun: ἔργον (*ergon*), GK 2240 (S 2041), 169x. *ergon* means "a work," "a deed," "achievement," "action," "thing," or "matter." In the gospels, *ergon* mostly carries an ethical meaning. The gospel writers speak of good works (Mt. 5:16; also Acts 9:36), including a beautiful act or gesture (Mk. 14:6); and evil works (Lk. 11:48; Jn. 3:19–20). Self-righteous works are also mentioned negatively (Mt. 23:3–5). While the gospel writers used *ergon* to describe Jesus' miraculous works (Mt. 11:2; Lk. 24:19), John accords them theological significance (Jn. 5: 36; 7:3, 21; 15:24). The works validate Jesus' claims about himself and point to the Father who sent him. His works are intended to draw faith responses from those who witness them (Jn. 14:11). Consequently, in the preaching of the early church, Jesus was remembered as one who was powerful in word and deed (Lk. 24:19; Acts 7:22).

In John's gospel, good works are associated with light. These works are done through God (Jn. 3:21; 9:3). Even Jesus' works are done by the Father, through Jesus (Jn. 14:10). Evil works are associated with darkness and with the devil (Jn. 7:7, 8:4). When asked by some, "What must we do to work the works of God?" Jesus replied, "This is the work of God; to believe in the one he has sent" (Jn. 6:28–29). Jesus considers his own task of salvation as work given to him by the Father (Jn. 4:34; 5:36; 9:4), work which he willingly did in his earthly ministry (Jn. 17:4), and which he completed on the cross (Jn. 19:30).

In the Pauline letters (primarily Romans and Galatians), works take on a wholly negative meaning when used in conjunction with the law, since those works will not lead to justification, and will not produce a righteousness that saves (Rom. 3:20, 27; Gal. 2:16). David predicted and Abraham exemplified that justification is by faith, apart from works of the law (Rom. 3:28; 4:3, 6). Paul opposes faith and works to one another (Rom. 9:32; Gal. 3:2, 5, 10; also 5:19). Despite his negative view of works of righteousness, which cannot save, Paul does encourage good works that constitute the fruit of a redeemed life (Rom. 13:3; 2 Cor. 9:8, Eph. 2:10; Phil. 1:6; Col. 1:10; 1 Tim. 2:10; 5:10; 6:18; 2 Tim. 2:21; 3:17; Tit. 2:7, 14), while abhorring evil works, reminiscent of the past, sinful life (Eph. 5:11; Col. 1:21), including "deeds of darkness" (Rom. 13:12; 2 Tim. 4:18). Paul also refers to ministerial service as work. He asks the Corinthians, "Are you not my work in the Lord?" (1 Cor. 9:1), and refers also to other believers' work for the Lord (1 Cor. 15:58; 16:10; Phil. 2:30; 2 Thess. 1:11). He encourages Timothy to continue to "do the work of an evangelist" (2 Tim. 4:5), and the Ephesians to continue in their "works of service" for the edification of the church body (Eph. 4:12).

James also has much to say about works. Although his writings are sometimes seen as contradictory to Paul's, especially in verses like 2:24, "You see that a person is justified by works, not by faith alone," James did not refer to works of righteousness, which cannot save. Rather he referred to empty religion, which was devoid of fruit, that is, "Faith without works is dead" (2:26). In the case of Abraham, James explains that "his faith worked together with his works" (2:22).

In Hebrews, the works of God are mentioned in the sense of God's creation (Heb. 1:10) and God's deeds of power in the life of Israel (Heb. 3:9; 4:4), despite which Israel was unfaithful to her God. The author also encourages the believers to "spur one another to good works" (Heb. 10:24), while warning against "works of death" (Heb. 6:1; 9:14).

Finally, the NT generally maintains that there will be a final judgment for all people based upon their works. Paul teaches this (1 Cor. 3:13–15; 2 Cor. 11:15), as do Peter (1 Pet. 1:17) and John (Rev. 18:6; 20:12–13; 22:12). Notably, the risen Jesus

assessed the deeds of each of the seven churches of the Revelation, writing to virtually every one, "I know your *deeds*," whether commendable (Ephesus, 2:2; Thyatira, 2:19) or reprehensible (Laodicea, 3:15). See *NIDNTT-A*, 205-206.

WORKER

New Testament

Noun: ἐργάτης (*ergatēs*), GK *2239* (S *2040*), 16x. *ergatēs* refers to someone who does something, a "worker or laborer." In the NT it sometimes refers to an employee (those unfairly unpaid in Jas. 5:4; vineyard workers in Mt. 20:1ff; the silversmiths and other tradesmen of Ephesus in Acts 19:25). Three times *ergatēs* is used of evildoers or workers of deceit (Lk. 13:27; 2 Cor. 11:13; Phil. 3:2).

Regarding work in the kingdom of God, Jesus comments that "the harvest was plentiful but the *workers* were few" (Mt. 9:37–38; Lk. 10:2). The commissioning of the disciples (Mt. 10:10; Lk. 10:7) is accompanied by Jesus' reminder that "the *worker* is worthy of his wages," indicating that their evangelistic mission is to be considered work and recognized as such by those in each visited town (cf. also 1 Tim. 5:18). Paul exhorts Timothy to work hard and diligently, correctly handling the word of truth, so that he might be "approved, a *workman* who does not need to be ashamed" (2 Tim. 2:15). See *NIDNTT-A*, 205-6.

WORLD

New Testament

Noun: κόσμος (*kosmos*), GK *3180* (S *2889*), 186x. In classical Greek and the LXX, *kosmos* communicated the idea of order and adornment, and from this it developed into the basic term for the cosmos or the universe. The OT conception of the created world or *kosmos* was very different from the Greek notion, however. There, creation is never seen as a separate entity controlled by an all-embracing order (*kosmos*) as in Greek thought. Instead, the universe, usually described with the phrase "heaven and earth," is always understood in its relationship to its Creator, God.

In the NT, *kosmos* always means "the world" except in 1 Pet. 3:3, where it is used with the older sense of "adornment." Even with the sense of "world," there are a number of nuances within this idea. At times *kosmos* indicates the created universe (Acts 17:24), yet at other times, the sphere of human life and humanity itself (Mt. 4:8; Mk. 8:36; Jn. 3:19; 2 Cor. 5:19). In John and Paul especially, the latter meaning of *kosmos* is predominant. The world is the place where God has come to do his redeeming and transforming work. In this sense, *kosmos* often has a negative connotation. This world is equated with this passing, evil age, which is opposed to God (1 Cor. 3:18–19; Eph. 2:2; cf. Rom. 12:2). A fundamental part of Christ's work on the cross was defeating the elements of this world (Col. 2:8–20).

Over half of the NT's occurrences of *kosmos* occur in John's gospel (78x) and epistles (24x). There it plays an important role in John's theology. The *kosmos* resists the very God who created it and his Son (Jn. 1:9–11; 7:7); consequently, this world is ruled by the evil one (12:31; 16:11). Therefore, while Christians continue to live in this *kosmos*, they must maintain purity and refrain from being caught up in this world's systems (17:15–17; 1 Jn. 2:15; cf. Phil. 2:15; Jas. 1:27; 4:4). But the superabundant grace and power of God are shown in that despite this opposition and corruption, "God so loved the *world* that he gave his only Son, that whoever believes in him should not perish but have eternal life" (Jn. 3:16). See *NIDNTT-A*, 315-16.

Noun: οἰκουμένη (*oikoumenē*), GK *3876* (S *3625*), 15x. *oikoumenē* is used in the NT to refer to the "inhabited earth" rather than the whole globe. Jesus states in Mt. 24:14 that the gospel will be preached in all the "inhabited earth" before the coming of the end, and Caesar took a census of all the "inhabited earth" (Lk. 2:1). In Acts 11:28 Agabus predicts that a great famine will come over "the whole world" (and he

obviously is not referring to Antarctica or South America!). In Acts 17:6 the Christians are somewhat hyperbolically accused of having upset the "whole world" (cf. Acts 19:27; see 24:5 for more hyperbole).

A closely related meaning of *oikoumenē* is "humankind." In Acts 17:31, Paul proclaims at the Areopagus that there is coming a day when God will judge all "humankind" in righteousness. In Rev. 12:9 Satan is said to be the one who deceives all the "inhabitants" of the earth. The only NT use of *oikoumenē* that does not refer to the *present* inhabited world is Heb. 2:5, which instead refers to "the world to come." See *NIDNTT-A*, 405.

WORLDLY

New Testament

Adjective: σαρκικός (*sarkikos*), GK *4920* (S *4559*), 7x. *sarkikos* means "worldly, fleshly." In 1 Cor. 3:3, because the Corinthian believers are dividing the church over matters such as human leaders and perhaps over income levels, Paul charges them with acting in a "worldly" manner. Elsewhere Paul refers to "worldly" wisdom (2 Cor. 1:12) and "the weapons of the *world*" (10:4). Peter exhorts believers to abstain from "sinful" desires (1 Pet. 2:11). This adjective is related to the noun *sarx* (GK *4922*), which can mean "flesh" or "sinful human nature" (see *flesh*). God wants us to live by the power of his Spirit instead.

WORRY

New Testament

Verb: μεριμνάω (*merimnaō*), GK *3534* (S *3309*), 19x. *merimnaō* means "to worry, be concerned about something." It most frequently refers to an unhealthy and unproductive concern or worry about events and circumstances. This is especially true of a focus on physical and temporary matters rather than spiritual matters.

merimnaō occurs 6x in the Sermon on the Mount in Matthew 6 and 3x in the Sermon on the Plain in Luke 6, as Jesus explains the futility of such worry for one's life (Mt. 6:25), time (6:27, 34), clothes (6:28), and even what one will eat (6:31). Such a focus is not only a wasted effort on something that one cannot change (cf. Lk. 12:25), but it leads to unhealthy anxiety. Martha is an example of this, as her worry for so many things leads to criticism of others (10:41). Likewise, Paul exhorts the Philippians to not worry about anything, but instead to present requests to God by prayer (Phil. 4:6).

merimnaō can also focus on something that is unnecessary, as when Jesus advises his disciples not to worry about what they are to say before synagogue authorities to whom they must respond (Mt. 10:19; Lk. 12:11). Jesus is not advising them to empty their heads purposefully, but rather not to be focused on the form and exact content of what they speak. Finally, while *merimnaō* can be a focus of concern on even good things, such as marriage, with the result that one's work for the Lord could suffer (1 Cor. 7:32–34), it can also be a legitimate concern for others and their well-being (1 Cor. 12:25; Phil. 2:20). See *NIDNTT-A*, 364.

Noun: μέριμνα (*merimna*), GK *3533* (S *3308*), 6x. *merimna* is a "care, anxiety, concern" that can easily (though not necessarily) distract a believer. See *concern*.

WORSE

New Testament

Adjective: χείρων (*cheirōn*), GK *5937* (S *5501*), 11x. *cheirōn* is a comparative adjective meaning "worse." Jesus uses it the parable of patching a new piece cloth on an old garment, which will shrink and simply make the hole even "worse" than before (Mt. 9:16; Mk. 2:21); that is, the kingdom Jesus is bringing in cannot simply be patched onto the old way of doing things. Several other occurrences stress that after encountering Jesus, those who eventually reject his message end up in a "worse" condition than they were before they heard the gospel (Jn. 5:14; 1 Tim. 5:8; Heb. 10:29; 2 Pet. 2:20; cf. 2 Tim. 3:13); seen from this perspective, it is a frightening thing to be presented with the gospel—

especially for those who end up rejecting it.

WORSHIP

Old Testament

Verb: הָוָה (*hāwâ*), GK 2556 (S 2331), 173x. *hāwâ* essentially means "to bow down." This action may be directed either to a human being or to a divine being. It may be a mere greeting, but it can also indicate submission or "worship." It is the external action of an internal attitude.

(1) In terms of other humans, people bow down before others for various reasons: to greet strangers (Gen. 18:2), to acknowledge authority (1 Sam. 24:18), to pay honor or homage (2 Sam. 1:2; cf. Est. 3:2), and even to beg (1 Sam. 2:36). Bowing low to the ground can even take place within family circles (Gen. 33:3; 48:12; 50:18–20).

(2) But more important is the religious exercise of bowing down. *hāwâ* is used in this manner about 110x, of which more than half refer to bowing down before heathen gods (e.g., 2 Chr. 25:14; 33:3; Isa. 44:15; Jer. 16:11). God's people, of course, are commanded not to worship and bow down to idol gods (Exod. 20:5; 34:14). Instead, the psalmist calls on them to "*worship* the Lord in the splendor of his holiness" (Ps. 29:2; 96:9). He exhorts us, "Come, let us bow down in *worship*; let us kneel before the Lord our God" (Ps. 95:6). We must "exalt the Lord our God and *worship* at his footstool/mountain" (99:5–6). True worship is often accompanied by praise (1 Chr. 29:20; 2 Chr. 29:28–30). Isaiah prophesies that the glorious day is coming when people from foreign nations "will come and *worship* the Lord on the holy mountain of Jerusalem" (Isa. 27:13; cf. 66:23; Zeph. 2:11). We should note that in all these instances of true worship, the focus is on the Lord, never on the one leading in worship or any other human being; he is the only one worthy of true worship. See *NIDOTTE*, 2:42–44.

Verb: יָרֵא (*yārēʾ*), GK 3707 (S 3372), 317x. *yārēʾ* denotes both a sense of terror and a sense of awe and worship. It is commonly translated "fear, revere, worship." See *fear*.

Verb: עָבַד (*ʿābad*), GK 6268 (S 5647), 290x. *ʿābad* means "to serve" and is used in both secular and religious contexts (see *serve*).

The act of serving takes on theological significance in the cult of Israel, where *ʿābad* often means "to worship." At age fifty, a Levite could no longer perform cultic service (Num. 8:25), and Isaiah speaks of sacrificial worship to God as *ʿābad* (Isa. 19:21). Serving God and worshiping him overlap significantly in the OT (Exod. 3:12; Mal. 3:18). It is in this light that the Israelites are commanded not to serve foreign gods (Deut. 4:19; 5:9). Worship belongs to God alone and is evidence of the Israelites' covenantal faithfulness (Exod. 4:23; Deut. 6:13; 1 Sam. 7:3; Ps. 100:2; Jer. 2:20).

New Testament

Verb: λατρεύω (*latreuō*), GK *3302* (S *3000*), 21x. *latreuō* refers to service or worship that is always religious in nature (Rom. 1:25; Acts 7:7, 42). See *serve*.

Verb: προσκυνέω (*proskyneō*), GK *4686* (S *4352*), 60x. *proskyneō* means "to fall down and/or worship" someone or something. While it is most often used of people worshiping God, it does not limited bowing down before the God of the Bible.

In classical Greek and even in some NT passages, *proskyneō* was used of the adoration of idol gods, the falling down and prostration of oneself in reverence (see, e.g., Acts 7:43). It sometimes denotes specifically false worship, especially in Revelation. The recipients of pagan obesiance include the dragon (Rev. 13:4), demons (9:20), and the image of the beast (13:15). *proskyneō* can also be used for prostrating oneself before another human being, such as the servant in the parable of the unforgiving servant falling on his knees before his master, asking for more time to repay his debt (Mt. 18:26). Cornelius too, a man who revered God, fell at Peter's feet in reverence; Peter objected.

But for the most part in the NT, *prosky-*

neō refers to worship addressed to God or to Jesus Christ. Jesus warns Satan, "Worship the Lord your God, and serve him only" (Mt. 4:10). A part of the conversation Jesus has with the Samaritan woman in John 4 revolves around the right place and the correct way to "worship" God (4:20-24, where this verb is used nine times). Jesus insists that true worship only occurs in the inner attitude is appropriate: "in spirit and in truth" (4:24). The elders in the heavenly throne room fall down and worship God, who is sitting on the throne (Rev. 4:10; 5:14).

What these various meanings create, then, is ambiguity in some of the uses of *proskyneō* in the Gospels. When the wise men come and worship the baby Jesus (Mt. 2:2, 11), do they see themselves as falling down before Immanuel, God in human flesh, or as merely giving obesiance to a human "king of the Jews"? When sick people "kneel before" Jesus (e.g., Mt. 8:2; 9:18), do they see him as a human miracle-worker or as the great divine Healer? Yet regardless of how Jesus is viewed by those who come to him for help, there is no doubt that the gospel writers themselves see Jesus as the Son of God. Note especially the use of *proskyneō* as an outward expression of faith in Jn. 9:38, where the man born blind says, "Lord, I believe," and he worships Jesus (Jn. 9:38). Worship is the appropriate response of a believing heart that adores God. See *NIDNTT-A*, 496-497.

Verb: σέβω (*sebō*), GK *4936* (S *4576*), 10x. *sebō* means "to worship." It is used twice in the gospels (Mt. 15:9; Mk. 7:7) where the OT is quoted; in these cases it refers straightforwardly to the worship of God. All other NT uses of the word are in Acts. In 18:13 it is used of the worship of God and in 19:27 of the worship of the pagan goddess Artemis. Elsewhere in Acts *sebō* describe Gentiles who "worship" or "fear" God of the Jews and who are thus affiliated with a synagogue (13:43, 50; 16:14; 17:4, 17; 18:7). These Gentiles are called "God-fearers." Since these people appreciated the Jewish religion but did not want to undergo circumcision in order to become full-fledged Jews, they were a ripe mission field for the apostle Paul, who showed them how they could become members of God's new covenant people through faith in Jesus Christ. See *NIDNTT-A*, 520-21.*

WORTHLESS

Old Testament

Noun: אֱלִיל (*ʾelîl*), GK 496 (S 457), 20x. The noun frequently translates as "idol" but can be translated as "image" and "worthless." See *idol*.

Noun: הֶבֶל (*hebel*), GK 2039 (S 1892), 73x. *hebel* literally means "breath" (see *breath*), but in most OT instances, the noun functions metaphorically, usually denoting vanity, futility, and/or temporality. When it refers to idols gods, it carried the notion of "worthless" (see Deut. 32:21; Jer. 51:18; see *vanity*).

Noun/Adverb: שָׁוְא (*sawʾ*), GK 8736 (S 7723), 54x. *sawʾ* denotes ineffectiveness or falseness and may be translated as "vain, worthless, falsehood." The term describes the futility of certain things or activities (Ps. 127:1–2; Job 7:3; 15:31), the prohibition of giving false testimony (Deut. 5:20; cf. Exod. 20:16; 23:1; Job 31:5), the false visions of lying prophets (Ezek. 13:6–9; 21:29), and the ineffectiveness of idolatry (Ps. 31:6; Jer. 18:15). Of theological interest is Exod. 20:7, where the third commandment states "You shall not *misuse* the name of the LORD your God" (lit. "you shall not lift up … to *falsehood*"). While this command may concern the use of God's name in oaths (cf. Deut. 6:13; 10:20), it also corresponds to the empty or fraudulent representation of the name or reputation of God. See *NIDOTTE*, 4:53-54.

WORTHY

New Testament

Verb: ἀξιόω (*axioō*), GK *546* (S *515*), 7x. *axioō* means "to be worthy, consider [something] worthy." The Roman centurion did not "consider [himself] worthy" to have Jesus come to his house (Lk. 7:7). Paul prays for the Thessalonians, that God may "count [them] worthy of his calling" (2 Thess. 1:11). Elders who serve well "are worthy of double honor" (1 Tim. 5:17). And, above all, Jesus "has been found worthy of greater honor than Moses," since he is not just God's servant but God's Son (Heb. 3:3).

Adjective: ἄξιος (*axios*), GK *545* (S *514*), 41x. In classical Greek *axios* had to do with tipping or balancing the scales. When two entities are compared and found of equal weight, they are "fitting." Since fitness implies worth, *axios* came to mean "worthy, deserving." "A worker is worthy of his wages" (1 Tim. 5:18). The prodigal son considered himself no longer worthy to be called his father's son (Lk. 15:19–21). Occasionally context calls for a slightly different translation; e.g., Mt. 3:8, "Produce fruit *in keeping with* repentance"; Rom. 8:18, "Our present sufferings are not *worth comparing*" with the glory that will be revealed in us; 1 Cor. 16:4, "If *it seems advisable* for me to go also"; 2 Thess. 1:3, "We ought always to thank God for you, brothers, and *rightly so*."

axios often carries the meaning of "deserving" something. For example, the Jewish elders sent to Jesus by the Roman centurion pleaded earnestly that "this man *deserves* that Jesus heal his servant" (Lk. 7:4); in 1 Tim. 1:15 Paul cites "a trustworthy saying that *deserves* full acceptance." By contrast, some things are not deserved. For example, in Acts 25:25 Felix tells King Agrippa that he has found [in Paul's case] "nothing *deserving* of death."

axios is also found several times in the great scenes of exaltation in Revelation. "You are *worthy* to take the scroll and to open its seals, because you were slain, and with your blood you purchased men for God," sing the four living creatures and the twenty-four elders about Jesus, the Lamb (Rev. 5:9). Then they are joined by a countless throng of angels and together they cry out, "*Worthy* is the Lamb who was slain" (5:12). See *NIDNTT-A*, 56-57.

Adjective: ἔνοχος (*enochos*), GK *1944* (S *1777*), 10x. *enochos* means "guilty, subject to, liable for, worthy of." See *guilty*.

Adverb: ἀξίως (*axiōs*), GK *547* (S *514*), 6x. *axiōs* is often used in connection with conduct befitting a true believer. Paul urges the believers at Ephesus to "live a life *worthy* of the calling" they have received (Eph. 4:1). Colossian Christians are to "live a life *worthy* of the Lord" (Col. 1:10), and Thessalonian believers are to "live lives *worthy* of God" (1 Thess. 2:12).

WOUND(ED)

Old Testament

Verb: חָלָה (*ḥālâ*), GK 2703 (S 2470), 75x. *ḥāla* describes a person who is weak, sick, ill, diseased, or wounded; it is also used to describe human frailties. See *weak*.

Noun: חָלָל (*ḥālāl*), GK 2728 (S 2491), 94x. *ḥālāl* denotes someone who has been pierced for the purpose of killing or wounding and may be translated as "pierced, wounded, killed." See *pierced*.

New Testament

Noun: πληγή (*plēgē*), GK *4435* (S *4127*), 22x. *plēgē* can denote a beating or wound, but it is most closely associated with the plagues in Egypt. In Revelation, it designates various plagues, but also the mortal wounds suffered by the beast (Rev. 13:3, 12, 14). See *plague*.

WRATH

Old Testament

Noun: חֵמָה (*ḥēmâ*), GK 2779 (S 2534), 125x. The basic meaning of *ḥēma* is "anger, wrath." Its most common use describes the fury or rage of people or of God. See *anger*.

New Testament

Noun: θυμός (*thymos*), GK *2596* (S *2372*), 18x. *thymos* is generally used to refer to "wrath, anger, rage, fury." *thymos* occasionally designates the wrath or fury of God. Those who follow evil instead of doing good will experience that wrath (Rom. 2:8). Revelation describes God's wrath being poured out on the earth (Rev. 14:19; 15:1, 7; 16:1).

Elsewhere in the NT *thymos* refers to human anger while *orgē* designates God's anger or wrath. People became "furious" at the preaching of Jesus (Lk. 4:28) and of Paul (Acts 19:28). Moses acted without fear of the king's "anger" (Heb. 11:27). *thymos* is included in catalogues of sinful behavior that will keep people out of the kingdom of God, in contrast to the holy conduct that should characterize believers (2 Cor. 12:20; Gal. 5:20; Eph. 4:31; Col. 3:8). The word also describes extremely passionate feeling (Rev. 14:8; 18:3). See *NIDNTT-A*, 253.

Noun: ὀργή (*orgē*), GK *3973* (S *3709*), 36x. *orgē* signifies "anger, wrath." Depending on the context, the term emphasizes either emotional anger or retributive wrath. See *anger*.

WREATH

New Testament

Noun: στέφανος (*stephanos*), GK *5109* (S *4735*), 18x. There are several related ideas communicated with the word *stephanos*. One of these is the physical crown or wreath worn by someone of high status. In the Greco-Roman world, a crown (often a woven wreath) was given as a sign of honor to people of high status, such a winning athletes (cf. 1 Cor. 9:25; 2 Tim. 4:8). See *crown*.

WRITE, WRITING

Old Testament

Verb: כָּתַב (*kātab*), GK 4180 (S 3789), 225x. *kātab* generally means "to write." Though the term occurs in a general way throughout the OT, its significance is most stressed in contexts that emphasize the necessity of preserving the word of the Lord for the sake of future generations. Within the Pentateuch the activity of writing is significant, for by it the foundational covenant principles are given to the people. God himself writes on the tablets of stone (Exod. 31:18; Deut. 4:13), and Moses is told to write down all the events that have transpired (Exod. 17:14; 24:4). Clearly, the writings are important for the stability of God's people. God's acts and commandments are written down so that future generations will have a written record of God's mighty acts and of his covenant obligations given to his people. (This is observed especially in Deut.)

The OT prophets continue to stress the necessity of writing for the benefit of God's people (Hab. 2:2). In covenant renewal ceremonies, both Joshua and Samuel write God's directives down for the purpose of preserving the word of the Lord for the people (Jos. 8:32; 1 Sam. 10:25). Isaiah is told to write things in a book for the sake of a perpetual witness of the things to come (Isa. 8:1; 30:8), and a similar command is given to Jeremiah (Jer. 30:2; 36:6). In the new covenant the law will be written by God on the hearts of humankind (31:33).

New Testament

Verb: γράφω (*graphō*), GK *1211* (S *1125*), 191x. *graphō* generally means "to write" and is attested as early as Homer with reference to the act of scratching or engraving. Jesus writes in the sand (Jn. 8:6, 8); Zechariah writes his son's name on a tablet (Lk. 1:63); Paul writes sentences in his own hand (Gal. 6:11); letters of commendation are written to churches (Acts 18:27); and letters are written to governors or to the emperor (23:25; 25:26). Though *graphō* almost always denotes the act of manual writing, Paul does use the verb to describe the dictation of his letters.

Significantly, of the many uses of *graphō* in the NT, over half refer to the Scriptures. The term is used about 70x in an introductory formula—e.g., "as it is written" (cf. Lk. 2:23; Rom. 2:24; 1 Cor. 1:31)—followed by a quotation from the OT. The verb occurs 17x in conjunction with an allusion to the OT rather than a direct quotation (e.g., Acts 13:29).

Noun: βιβλίον (*biblion*), GK *1046* (S *975*), 34x. *biblion* refers to a "book, scroll, writing." See *book*.

Noun: βίβλος (*biblos*), GK *1047* (S *976*), 10x. *biblos* refers to a "book, scroll, writing." See *book*.

Noun: γράμμα (*gramma*), GK *1207* (S *1121*), 14x.

Usually translated "writing, letters," the noun *gramma* can refer to the letters of the alphabet (Gal. 6:11), written information (Acts 28:21), a debtor's bill (Lk. 16:6), or learning in general (Jn. 17:5; Acts 26:24). *gramma* is also used twice for the Scriptures, once for the writings of Moses (Jn. 5:47) and once for the Scriptures as a whole (2 Tim. 3:15). In the latter text, *gramma* is modified by the term "holy."

Interpreting Paul's contrast of *gramma* with *pneuma*, "Spirit," in 2 Cor. 3:6 is one of the more difficult problems in Pauline study: "the letter kills but the Spirit gives life." If Paul is not denigrating the OT as Scripture (which is unlikely), what does he mean? Most likely the apostle is using eschatological language to compare and contrast life lived under the old economy (which ultimately lead to death—i.e., Israel's exile) versus life lived in the age of the Spirit, the new creation. In the age of fulfillment, the Scriptures themselves have not changed but the new context in which Scripture is read and applied has changed! God's action in Jesus Christ through the Spirit makes life possible in a way the old order without the Spirit could not. Note too that we must always join together the Word and the Spirit, for the Spirit speaks through the Word.

WRONG

Old Testament

Noun: חָמָס (*ḥāmās*), GK 2805 (S 2555), 60x. *ḥāmās* denotes the idea of sinful violence and may be translated as "violence, wrong." See *violence*.

New Testament

Adjective: κακός (*kakos*), GK *2805* (S *2556*), 50x. *kakos* conveys the idea of something that is "evil, bad, wicked, wrong." See *evil*.

Adverb: κακῶς (*kakōs*), GK *2809* (S *2560*), 16x. The adverb *kakōs* can designate those with physical illness (the "sick") or moral ("wrong, wicked") harm. See *sick*.

WRONGDOING

Old Testament

Noun: רָעָה (*rāʿâ*), GK 8288 (S 7465), 354x. At the heart of *rāʿâ*, lies the idea of badness, whether physical or moral. See *evil*.

New Testament

Noun: ἀδικία (*adikia*), GK *94* (S *93*), 25x. *adikia* is consistently translated as either "unrighteousness" or "iniquity" in the KJV. The NIV, however, offers numerous glosses, such as "evil, wickedness, dishonest, worldly, sin, wrong, wrongdoing." See *unrighteousness*.

YAHWEH

Old Testament

Proper Noun: יהוה (*yhwh*), GK 3378 (S 3068/3069), 6829x. The Hebrew name *yhwh* or "Yawheh," commonly translated into English as "the LORD." See *Lord*.

YEAR

Old Testament

Noun: יוֹם (*yôm*), GK 3427 (S 3117), 2301x. *yôm* is the most common biblical expression of time in the OT, and it has a variety of nuances. The plural *yômîm* in some contexts designates a period of a "year" or the sense of "annually." In 1 Sam. 27:7 we read, "David lived in Philistine territory *a year* and four months." See *day*.

Noun: שָׁנָה (*šānâ*), GK 9102 (S 8141), 878x. Of the many times *šānâ* is found in the OT, the majority may be understood in accordance with our modern usage. God created the sun and moon "in order to mark seasons and days and *years*" (Gen. 1:14). Thus, *šānâ* references the years of one's life (Gen. 5:3), the years of a king's reign (2 Ki. 13:1), and the yearly cycle of Israel's festivals (Exod. 12:2; 23:14; Lev. 23:41). God, however, is not subject to time; thus, "you remain the same, and your *years* will never end" (Ps. 102:27).

The month in which the exodus occurred was, from that point on, to be reckoned as the first month of the year in Israel's festival calendar (Exod. 12:2). The Sabbatical year (every seventh year), however, along with the Jubilee year (the fiftieth year following seven Sabbatical years) was reckoned from the seventh month, with the Jubilee year beginning on the Day of Atonement, the 10th day of the seventh month (Lev. 25:1–12). The primary characteristics of the Jubilee year were those of liberty (slaves set free) and restoration (ownership of the land returned to its ancestral owner). Thus, the Jubilee afforded the word *šānâ* a metaphorical nuance relating to the final day of God's judgment of the nations and the restoration of Israel. Isaiah speaks of the "year of retribution": "For the LORD has a day of vengeance, a year of retribution, to uphold Zion's cause" (Isa. 34:8). And Jeremiah writes: "Not even a remnant will be left to them, because I will bring disaster on the men of Anathoth in the year of their punishment" (Jer. 11:23).

Regarding the eschatological Jubilee, Isaiah speaks of the "year of the LORD's favor" (Isa. 61:2; cf. Lk. 4:18–19) and the "year of my redemption" (Isa. 63:4). This use of *šānâ* is therefore parallel in meaning to the use of "day" in the phrase "the day of the LORD" (e.g., Isa. 13:9; Ezek. 13:5; Joel 2:1; Obad. 15; Zeph. 1:14; Mal. 4:5). See *NIDOTTE*, 4:191-93.

New Testament

Noun: ἐνιαυτός (*eniautos*), GK *1929* (S *1763*), 14x. *eniautos* means "year." The term normally refers to the period of one calendar year, e.g., "Caiaphas, who was high priest that *year*" (Jn. 18:13), "for a whole *year*" Barnabas and Saul met with the church in Antioch (Acts 11:26), or "only once a *year*" did the high priest enter the Most Holy Place (Heb. 9:7). *eniautos* can also refer to a more general time frame, e.g., "to proclaim the *year* of the Lord's favor" (Lk. 4:19). *eniautos* may refer to "sabbatical *years*" or "the *Year* of Jubilee" (Lev. 25) in Gal. 4:10.

Noun: ἔτος (*etos*), GK *2291* (S *2094*), 49x. *etos* commonly refers to a calendar year. It can be used for someone's age (Jairus' daughter was twelve years old, Mk. 5:42), or for any other length of time measured in years (Anna the prophetess lived with her husband seven years before he died, Lk. 2:36). Years were commonly measured with reference to imperial rulers and other leaders. Thus, Luke records the year in which John's prophetic ministry began by noting that it was the "fifteenth year of the reign of Tiberius Caesar" (Lk. 3:1).

etos enters into theological discussion in two important areas. First, especially debated by Bible scholars is the notion of the "thousand years" (millennium) in Rev. 20 in the timeline of God's total plan of salvation. Second, it is difficult for human beings to understand the notion of time/years relative to God's sense of time, for "with the Lord a day is like a thousand *years*, and a thousand *years* are like a day" (2 Pet. 3:8). Moreover, the Lord remains the same, and his "*years* will never end."

YEAST

New Testament

Noun: ζύμη (*zymē*), GK *2434* (S *2219*), 13x. *zymē* means "yeast, leaven." In the NT this word is used literally, as the leavening agent in bread, and metaphorically, as a potent agent for multiplying good or evil. Jesus uses the physical properties of *zymē* to symbolize the growth of the kingdom of heaven and the spread of the gospel throughout the world (Mt. 13:33; Lk. 13:21).

Yeast is a type of fungus, and its activity is essentially a spoiling agent in food. Thus Jesus uses this word to symbolize the hypocrisy and corrupt teaching of the Pharisees and Sadducees (Mt. 16:6, 11, 12; Mk. 8:15; Lk. 12:1). Thoroughly removing the yeast from one's house was a familiar activity in the NT Jewish world (Feasts of Passover and Unleavened Bread) and provided an apt illustration of ridding oneself of sin and the polluting effects of the world (1 Cor. 5:6–8; Gal. 5:9). See *NIDNTT-A*, 226.*

YIELD

Old Testament

Verb: נָתַן (*nātan*), GK 5989 (S 5414),

2014x. *nātan* is a high frequency verb in the OT and bears a wide range of meanings, some of which are "to give, present, allow, permit, surrender, deliver, set, put, place." When the verb is used with an inanimate object, it sometimes means "yield" (land and trees "yield" fruit). See *give.*

New Testament

Verb: δίδωμι (*didōmi*), GK *1443* (S *1325*), 415x. This common verb conveys the basic idea of a transaction or transferring an object and is usually translated "give, grant, yield, permit." See *give.*

YOUNG

Old Testament

Adjective: קָטֹן (*qāṭōn*), GK 7785 (S 6996), 74x. *qāṭōn* means "small" in size or "young" in age. See *small.*

New Testament

Adjective: νέος (*neos*), GK *3742* (S *3501*), 24x. *neos* is an adjective describing the age of something, referring to its newness or youth. See *new.*

YOUNG MAN

Old Testament

Noun: בָּחוּר (*bāḥûr*), GK 1033 (S 970), 50x. *bāḥûr* means "young man." Most occurrences of this noun occur in prophetic passages that speak of the destruction of various classes of society, such as the rich and the poor, the young men and the maidens (e.g., Jer. 51:22). Since they are the ones who normally make up the army (cf. Prov. 20:29), this word is sometimes used for "able troops" (2 Chr. 13:3). The *bāḥûr* represent the hope for the next generation, so their destruction threatens the continuity of God's people. In some prophetic passages, however, the young men do represent hope. For example, in Joel 2:28, the prophet's vision is for the outpouring of the Spirit in which "young men will see visions" (cf. Acts 2:17). Zechariah foresees a time when God's people will sparkle in his land; "grain will make young men thrive, and new wine the young women" (Zech. 9:16–17). See *NIDOTTE*, 1:634–35.

Noun: יֶלֶד (*yeled*), GK 3529 (S 3206), 89x. *yeled* refers in almost all cases to a male "child" of various ages; hence, "boy, young man." See *child.*

Noun: נַעַר (*na*ʿ*ar*), GK 5853 (S 5288), 240x. The meaning of *na*ʿ*ar* falls into two main categories. It may refer to a male child of almost any age or to a servant. See *boy.*

New Testament

Noun: νεανίσκος (*neaniskos*), GK *3734* (S *3495*), 11x. *neaniskos* means "young man." It refers to various people in the NT who are probably in their twenties or thirties, such as the rich young man who came to Jesus with a question about eternal life (Mt. 19:20, 22), the young man whom Jesus raised to life at Nain (Lk. 7:14), and the nephew of Paul who warned the Roman commander about the plot against Paul (Acts 23:18, 22). In Mk. 16:5 it refers to the angel at the tomb who apparently looked like a young man, and in 14:51 for the young man who ran away naked during the night of Jesus' arrest. In Acts 2:17 Peter asserts the fulfillment of Joel 2:28 that the Spirit will enable "young men [to] see visions," and twice John mentions that he is writing his letter to "young men" (1 Jn. 2:13–14).

YOUNG WOMAN

Old Testament

Noun: בְּתוּלָה (*b*ᵉ*tûlâ*), GK 1435 (S 1330), 50x. This word describes a young woman of marrying age. See *virgin.*

Noun: נַעֲרָה (*na*ʿᵃ*râ*), GK 5855 (S 5291), 76x. *na*ʿᵃ*râ* denotes a "girl" from infancy to adolescence. It is most commonly translated "young girl." See *girl.*

YOUTH

Old Testament

Noun: נַעַר (*na*ʿ*ar*), GK 5853 (S 5288), 240x. The meaning of *na*ʿ*ar* falls into two main categories. It may refer to a male child of almost any age or to a servant. See *boy.*

ZEAL

New Testament

Noun: ζῆλος (*zēlos*), GK *2419* (S *2205*),

16x. In the NT *zēlos* can be either a good thing or a bad thing: "zeal, earnestness" is highly commended whereas "jealousy, envy" is condemned. *zēlos* as "zeal" is a positive quality. Jesus' actions in the temple are explained by his zeal for his Father's house (Jn. 2:17). Paul commends Israel for having a zeal for God (Rom. 10:2; cf. Phil. 3:6) and rejoices at the zeal of the Corinthians both for him (2 Cor. 7:7, 11) and for the ministry of giving financially (2 Cor. 9:2). In fact, Paul claims that he himself is jealous of the Corinthians with a godly jealousy (2 Cor. 11:2)! Even more strikingly, Heb. 10:27 implies that God himself is zealous in his fury at his enemies. See also *jealousy*. See *NIDNTT-A*, 224.

ZEALOUS

New Testament

Verb: ζηλόω (*zēloō*), GK *2420* (S *2206*), 11x. *zēloō* means to be "zealous" or "jealous." It is related to the noun *zēlos* ("jealousy, zeal," GK *2419*). In classical Greek this word group sometimes carried a positive sense (eager striving, enthusiasm, or praise) and sometimes a negative sense (jealously, ill will, or envy). The same applies to the NT.

(1) The NT uses *zēloō* in a positive sense. Paul is deeply concerned about the church of Corinth and declares, "I am *jealous* for you with a godly jealousy [*zēlos*]" (2 Cor. 11:2). Just as a husband is appropriately jealous if his wife flirts with another man, so Paul is jealous because the Corinthians, whom he intended to present to Christ "as a pure virgin," were going astray after false prophets and apostles. *zēloō* can also refer to eagerly desiring something, as Paul challenges, "Follow the way of love and *eagerly desire* spiritual gifts" (1 Cor. 14:1, 12, 39). Note too what Paul wrote about good zeal in Gal. 4:18, "It is fine *to be zealous*, provided the purpose is good."

(2) But elsewhere in the NT, *zēloō* is linked with harmful intent. It can denote envy: "Love does not *envy*" (1 Cor. 13:4). It can mean covet: "You kill and *covet*, but cannot have what you want" (Jas. 4:2). The Jews who caused Paul problems in Thessalonica were "jealous" of him (Acts 17:5). Lastly, Paul warns the church of Galatia to be cautious of those who stress circumcision, for they have set their hearts on them. "They are *zealous* to win you over, but for no good. What they want is to alienate you from us, so that you may be *zealous* for them" (Gal. 4:17). See *NIDNTT-A*, 224.

Scripture Index

Genesis

Leviticus

Numbers

Deuteronomy

Joshua

Judges

Ruth

I Samuel

2 Chronicles

Psalms

Proverbs

Ecclesiastes

Song of Songs

Isaiah

Jeremiah

Lamentations

Ezekiel

Daniel

Mark

Luke

Acts

Romans

I Corinthians

2 Corinthians

Galatians

Ephesians

Philippians

2 Timothy

Titus

Philemon

Hebrews

James

I Peter

2 Peter

1 John

2 John

3 John

Jude

Revelation

Hebrew-English Dictionary

The first number in bold brackets is the Goodrick-Kohlenberger number. Following it is the Hebrew word, its transliteration, frequency (i.e., the number of times it occurs in the Old Testament) followed by an "x," and then its definition. The final smaller number in brackets is the corresponding Strong's number (e.g., [2]); if there is no corresponding Strong's number, then there are double asterisks ([**]). If the lexical form listed by Kohlenberger is slightly different from that listed by Strong, and if they are still the same word, then an asterisk follows the Strong's number.

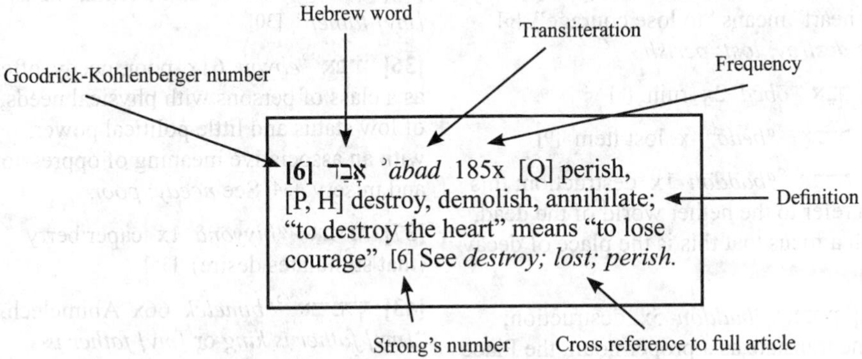

This dictionary includes most of the Hebrew words that occur in the Hebrew OT, except for many place names and personal names. Hebrew frequencies are notoriously difficult to determine because of how Hebrew words are formed. These frequencies are taken from John Kohlenberger's *The Hebrew English Concordance to the Old Testament*. The definitions are also from John (used with permission).

Hebrew words are used in different "stems," and the meaning of the word can vary, sometimes considerably, depending on which stem is used. The letters used in the definitions indicate stem:

Q	Qal
Qp	Qal passive
P	Pie
Pu	Pual
N	Niphal
H	Hiphal
Hit	Hitpael
Ho	Hophal
Hi	Hithpael

For fuller definitions, I recommend the five volume, *New International Dictionary of Old Testament Theology and Exegesis*, edited by Willem A. Van Gemeren (Zondervan, 1997).

[3] אָב *ʾāb* 1,210x father, grandfather, forefather, ancestor; (pl.) ancestors (of both genders); by extension: originator, founder (of a city or profession); a title of respect referring to humans or god. The "house of a father" is a subdivision of a clan [1] See *father.*

[4] אֵב *ʾēb* 2x new (plant) growth, shoot [3]

[6] אָבַד *ʾābad* 185x [Q] perish, [P, H] destroy, demolish, annihilate; "to destroy the heart" means "to lose courage" [6] See *destroy; lost; perish.*

[7] אֹבֵד *ʾōbēd* 2x ruin [8]

[8] אֲבֵדָה *ʾᵃbēdâ* 4x lost item [9]

[9] אֲבַדֹּה *ʾᵃbaddōh* 1x destruction; this can refer to the nether world of the dead, with a focus that this is the place of decay [10]

[11] אֲבַדּוֹן *ʾᵃbaddôn* 5x destruction; some translate as a proper noun, the Place of Destruction (the realm of the dead); see also 9 [11]

[12] אַבְדָן *ʾabdān* 1x destruction [12]

[13] אָבְדָן *ʾobdān* 1x destruction [13]

[14] אָבָה *ʾābâ* 54x [Q] to be willing, consent, yield; with the negative, to be unwilling, refuse [14] See *consent; will; (be) willing.*

[15] אֵבֶה *ʾēbeh* 1x papyrus or reed (boat) [16]

[16] אֲבוֹי *ʾᵃbôy* 1x sorrow (uneasiness); some parse as an interjection: woe! [17]

[17] אֵבוּס *ʾēbûs* 3x manger [18]

[18] אִבְחָה *ʾibḥâ* 1x slaughter [19]

[19] אֲבַטִּיחַ *ʾᵃbaṭṭaîaḥ* 1x melon [20]

[20] 1 אָבִי *ʾābî* 1x Oh, that! [15*]

[24] אֲבִיאֵל *ʾᵃbîʾēl* 3x Abiel, "*[my] father is God [El]*" [22]

[26] אָבִיב *ʾābîb* 8x (month of) Abib, the first month of the Canaanite calendar equal to Nisan (March-April); head (of grain), already ripe but still soft [24]

[28] אֲבִיגַיִל *ʾᵃbîgayil* 17x Abigail, "*[my] father rejoices* or *father [cause] of joy*" [26]

[31] אֲבִיָּה *ʾᵃbiyyâ* 28x Abijah, "*[my] father is Yahweh*" [29]

[32] אֲבִיָּהוּ *ʾᵃbiyyāhû* 2x Abijah, "*[my] father is Yahweh*" [29]

[33] אֲבִיהוּא *ʾᵃbîhûʾ* 12x Abihu, "*he is [my] father*" [30]

[36] אֶבְיוֹן *ʾebyôn* 61x poor, needy, often as a class of persons with physical needs, of low status and little political power, with an associative meaning of oppression and misery [34] See *needy; poor.*

[37] אֲבִיּוֹנָה *ʾᵃbiyyônâ* 1x caper berry (that stimulates desire) [35]

[43] אֲבִימֶלֶךְ *ʾᵃbîmelek* 66x Abimelech, "*[my] father is king* or *[my] father is Molech*" [40]

[44] אֲבִינָדָב *ʾᵃbînādāb* 11x Abinadab, "*[my] father is generous* or *[my] father is Nadab*" [41]

[45] אֲבִינֹעַם *ʾᵃbînōʿam* 4x Abinoam, "*[my] father is graciousness*" [42]

[46] אֲבִינֵר *ʾᵃbînēr* 1x Abner, "*[my] father is Ner [a lamp]*" [74]

[48] אֲבִיעֶזֶר *ʾᵃbîʿezer* 7x Abiezer, "*[my] father is help*" [44]

[49] אֲבִי עֶזְרִי *ʾᵃbî ʿezrî* 3x Abiezrite, "*of Abiezer*" [33*]

[51] אָבִיר *ʾābîr* 6x mighty, powerful; (as a divine title) the Mighty One [46]

[52] אַבִּיר *ʾabbîr* 17x mighty, powerful; this can refer to strong animals, social leaders, and angelic beings [47]

[53] אֲבִירָם *ʾᵃbîrām* 11x Abiram, "*[my] father is exalted*" [48]

[54] אֲבִישַׁג *ʾᵃbîšag* 5x Abishag, "*[my] father strays*" [49]

[57] אֲבִישַׁי *ʾᵃbîšay* 19x Abishai, "*[my] father is Jesse* or *father exists*" [52]

[59] אֶבְיָתָר *ʾebyātār* 30x Abiathar, "*[my] father gives abundance* or *the father is preeminent*" [54]

[60] אָבַךְ *ʾābak* 1x [Ht] to roll upward, to be borne along [55]

[61] אָבַל 1 *ʾābal* 32x [Q, Ht] to mourn, lament, grieve, [H] cause to mourn; mourning can be the emotion or attitude of sorrow, as well as the active observation of mourning rites and ceremonies; see also 63 [56]

[62] אָבַל 2 *ʾābal* 7x [Q] to dry up, lie parched [56]

[63] אָבֵל 1 *ʾābēl* 8x mourning, grieving, weeping [57 & 59*]

[65] אֵבֶל *ʾēbel* 24x ceremony of mourning, period of mourning; a mourning ceremony was a ritual for burial of the dead, with distinctive clothing, music, behaviors, and a set time period for the ritual, generally a longer period for more important people [60]

[66] אֲבָל *ʾᵃbāl* 11x but; however, surely, indeed [61]

[67] אֻבָל *ʾubāl* 3x canal [180*]

[68] אָבֵל בֵּית מַעֲכָה *ʾābēl bêt maʿᵃkâ* 4x Abel Beth Maacah, "*meadow of the house of Maacah [oppression]*" [62]

[74] אֶבֶן *ʾeben* 276x stone, rock, natural or shaped, sometimes of specific size for use in a balance scale; a "precious stone" is a gem or jewel; by extension: hailstone. Rock is a title of God, with a focus of strength and stability, a place of refuge [68] See *rock; stone.*

[75] אֶבֶן הָעֵזֶר *ʾeben hāʿēzer* 3x Ebenezer, "*stone of help*" [72]

[77] אַבְנֵט *ʾabnēṭ* 9x (linen) sash, wrapped around the waist [73]

[78] אָבְנַיִם *ʾobnayim* 2x potter's wheel; delivery stool [70*]

[79] אַבְנֵר *ʾabnēr* 62x Abner, "*[my] father is Ner [a lamp]*" [74]

[82] אֶבֶץ *ʾebeṣ* 1x Ebez [77]

[83] אִבְצָן *ʾibṣān* 2x Ibzan, "*swift*" [78]

[84] אָבַק *ʾābaq* 2x [N] to wrestle (with) [79]

[85] אָבָק *ʾābāq* 6x fine dust, powder [80]

[86] אֲבָקָה *ʾᵃbāqâ* 1x spice (scented powders) [81]

[87] אָבַר *ʾābar* 1x [H] to take flight, soar upward [82]

[88] אֵבֶר *ʾēber* 3x feather, wing; other sources: the strong joint of the body to the wing, "pinion," with the associative meaning of strength that can bring freedom [83]

[89] אֶבְרָה *ʾebrâ* 4x feather, pinion, wing; in some contexts may have the associative meaning of protection [84]

[90] אַבְרָהָם *ʾabrāhām* 175x Abraham, "*father of many*" [85]

[91] אַבְרֵךְ *ʾabrēk* 1x Make way!; others: Kneel down! or Watch out! [86]

[92] אַבְרָם *ʾabrām* 61x Abram, "*exalted father*" [87]

[93] אַבְשַׁי *ʾabšay* 6x Abishai, "*[my] father is Jesse* or *father exists*" [52]

[94] אַבְשָׁלוֹם *ʾabšālôm* 109x Absalom, "*father is peace*" [53*]

[97] אֲגַג *ʾᵃgag* 8x Agag, "[poss.] *violent*" [90]

[98] אֲגָגִי *ʾᵃgāgî* 5x Agagite, "*of Agag*" [91]

[99] אֲגֻדָּה *ʾᵃguddâ* 4x bunch, bundle; group, band; cord, bands; foundation, structure [92]

[100] אֱגוֹז *ʾᵉgôz* 1x nut tree [93]

[102] אֲגוֹרָה *ʾᵃgôrâ* 1x fee, payment, a piece of precious metal used as a medium of exchange (but not a minted coin) [95]

[103] אֵגֶל *ʾēgel* 1x drop (of dew) [96*]

[106] 1 אֲגַם *ʾagam* 9x swamp, pond, marsh (with reeds) [98]

[108] אָגֵם *ʾāgēm* 1x sick, grieved [99]

[109] אַגְמוֹן *ʾagmôn* 5x reed; cord (made of reeds) [100]

[110] אַגָּן *ʾaggān* 3x (large and deep) bowl, goblet [101]

[111] אֲגַף *ʾagap* 7x troop, band [102*]

[112] אָגַר *ʾāgar* 3x [Q] to gather (in) [103]

[113] אֲגַרְטָל *ʾagarṭāl* 2x dish; in context made of precious metals [105]

[114] אֶגְרֹף *ʾegrōp* 2x fist (the hand clenched to strike) [106]

[115] אִגֶּרֶת *ʾiggeret* 10x letter, document [107]

[116] אֵד *ʾēd* 2x stream, fresh water that moves from a higher to lower place; in some contexts this may be an artesian spring [108]

[117] אָדַב *ʾādab* 1x [H] to grieve [109]

[121] אֱדוֹם *ʾedôm* 104x Edom, referring to a person and his ancestral territory S.E. of the Dead Sea, "*red*" [123]

[122] אֲדוֹמִי *ʾadômî* 12x Edomite, "*of Edom*" [130*]

[123] אָדוֹן *ʾādôn* 774x lord, master, supervisor, one who has authority over another; husband; owner; the Lord, (with Yahweh [3378]) Sovereign. "Lord of lords" means the highest power or authority; see also 151 [113] See *Lord; master.*

[128] אוֹדוֹת *ʾōdôt* 11x on account of, because of, for the reason that [182]

[129] אַדִּיר *ʾaddîr* 27x mighty, noble, majestic, splendid; (n.) any powerful or awesome person: noble, believer, elite soldier; (as a divine title) the Mighty One, with a focus on the power and splendor of God [117]

[131] אָדֵם *ʾādēm* 10x [Q] be ruddy; [Pu] be dyed red [119*]

[132] 1 אָדָם *ʾādām* 546x man, human being; humankind, people, often in contrast to animals; "son of man" means a human being (Nu 23:9), but often assumes messianic significance (Ps 8) [120] See *Adam; humanity; man; people.*

[134] 3 אָדָם *ʾādām* 12x Adam, "*[red] earth* or *[ruddy] skin color*" [121] See *Adam; humanity; man; people.*

[137] אָדֹם *ʾādōm* 9x red; ruddy (skin) [122]

[138] אֹדֶם *ʾōdem* 3x ruby [124]

[140] אֲדַמְדָּם *ʾadamdām* 6x reddish, reddish-white [125]

[141] 1 אֲדָמָה *ʾadāmâ* 222x earth, the entire surface of the place where humans dwell, as well as smaller regions: land; with a focus on the elements of the earth: ground, soil, dust. A "man of the soil" is a farmer; "fruit of the soil" are crops [127] See *dust; earth; ground; land; soil.*

[144] אַדְמָה *ʾadmâ* 5x Admah, "*[red] earth*" [126]

[145] אַדְמוֹנִי *ʾadmônî* 3x red; ruddy (skin) [132 & 726*]

[149] אֶדֶן *ʾeden* 58x base, footing, pedestal [134]

[151] אֲדֹנָי *ʾadōnāy* 442x the Lord, (with Yahweh [3378]) Sovereign, a title of the one true God, with a focus on his majesty and authority; see also 123 [136] See *Lord.*

[153] אֲדֹנִיָּה *ʾadōniyyâ* 7x Adonijah, "*[my] lord is Yahweh*" [138]

[154] אֲדֹנִיָּהוּ *ʾadōniyyāhû* 19x Adonijah, "*[my] lord is Yahweh*" [138]

[158] אָדַר *ʾādar* 3x [N] to prove oneself majestic, powerful; [H] to make glorious, make powerful [142]

[159] אֶדֶר *ʾeder* 2x splendor, handsomeness, of obvious quality [145]

[160] אֲדָר *ʾadār* 8x Adar, "[poss.] *dark, clouded*" [143]

[163] אֲדַרְכֹנִים *ʾadarkōnîm* 2x darics, Persian gold coins [150*]

[167] אֶדְרֶעִי *ʾedreʿî* 8x Edrei, "*strong*" [154]

[168] אַדֶּרֶת *ʾadderet* 12x cloak, royal robe, (hairy) garment [155]

[170] אָהַב *ʾāhab* 217x [Q] to love, like, be a friend; [N] to be loved; [P] be a lover, an ally; love can refer to friendship, familial love, romantic love, or covenant loyalty [157] See *like; love.*

[171] אֹהַב *ʾōhab* 2x love; something loved [159]

[172] אֹהַב *ʾahab* 2x lover (negative); loving, charming (positive) [158]

[173] 1 אַהֲבָה *ʾahabāh* 33x love; friendship, familial love, romantic love, or covenant loyalty [160]

[177] אֲהָהּ *ʾahāh* 15x Ah!, Oh!, Alas!; an exclamation of emphasis, surprise, or sorrow [162]

[179] אֵהוּד *ʾēhûd* 9x Ehud, "*united*" [164]

[180] אֱהִי *ʾehî* 3x Where? [165]

[182] 1 אָהַל *ʾāhal* 3x [Q, P] to pitch a tent [167]

[183] 2 אָהַל *ʾāhal* 1x [H] to be bright [166]

[185] 1 אֹהֶל *ʾōhel* 348x tent, tent-dwelling; by extension: home, dwelling place, a permanent dwelling; family group. "The Tent of Meeting" was the worship tent built before the Temple [168] See *sky; tabernacle; tent.*

[188] אָהֳלָה *ʾāhºlâ* 5x Oholah, "*she who has a tent*" [170]

[189] אֲהָלוֹת *ʾahālôt* 2x aloes; an aromatic wood from India [174]

[191] אָהֳלִיבָה *ʾāhºlîbâ* 6x Oholibah, "*my tent is in her*" [172]

[193] 1 אֲהָלִים *ʾahālîm* 2x aloes [174]

[195] אַהֲרוֹן *ʾahªrôn* 347x Aaron [175]

[196] אוֹ *ʾô* 320x or, or if, whether [176]

[197] אַו *ʾaw* 1x crave [176]

[199] 1 אוֹב *ʾôb* 1x wineskin, bag, a leather bag of goatskin turned inside out to hold fluids [178]

[200] 2 אוֹב *ʾôb* 16x medium, spiritist, one who communicates with and conjures ghosts or spirits [178]

[202] אוּד *ʾûd* 3x burning stick [181]

[203] 1 אָוָה *ʾāwâ* 26x [P, Ht] to crave, desire, yearn for, long for [183]

[204] 2 אָוָה *ʾāwâ* 1x [Ht] to run a line, measure [184]

[205] אַוָּה *ʾawwâ* 7x wanting, craving; earnestness [185]

[208] אוֹי *ʾôy* 24x Woe! Alas! [188]

[210] אוֹיָה *ʾôyâ* 1x Woe!, Alas! [190]

[211] 1 אֱוִיל *ʾewîl* 25x foolish; (n.) a fool [191]

[214] 1 אוּל *ʾûl* 1x belly, sometimes referring to the whole body [193]

[216] אֱוִלִי *ʾewilî* 1x foolish, without understanding [196]

[218] 2 אוּלַי *ʾûlay* 45x what if, perhaps, maybe; this is in an expression of hope, pleading, or fear [194]

[219] 1 אוּלָם *ʾûlām* 19x but, however, on the other hand, nevertheless [199]

[222] אִוֶּלֶת *ʾiwwelet* 25x foolishness, folly; in some contexts this may refer to thoughtless speech [200]

[224] 1 אָוֶן *ʾāwen* 81x evil, wickedness, iniquity; evildoer; an unfavorable circumstance: calamity, trouble, injustice; this can also refer to idols, with a focus that they are morally evil [205] See *disaster; evil; punishment; sin; wicked, wickedness.*

[226] 1 אוֹן *ʾôn* 12x power, strength, vigor, manhood; wealth [202]

[230] אוֹנִי *ʾônî* 1x mourning [205*]

[232] אוֹנָן *ʾônān* 8x Onan, "*powerful, intense*" [209]

[233] אוּפָז *ʾûpāz* 2x Uphaz [210]

[234] 1 אוֹפִיר *ʾôpîr* 13x Ophir [211]

[236] אוֹפַן *ʾôpan* 35x wheel (of a vehicle) [212]

[237] אוּץ *ʾûṣ* 10x [Q] to be in haste, be eager; to press (for an answer); to be small, narrow; [H] to urge, insist upon [213]

[238] אוֹצָר *ʾôṣār* 79x treasury, storehouse, storeroom, storage vault [214] See *storehouse; treasure; wealth.*

[239] 1 אוֹר *ʾôr* 45x [Q] to shine, be bright; [H] to give light, make shine, brighten; [N] to be resplendent with light, shine on; the fig. extension "to make the face shine" is to establish favorable circumstance, peace and relief from trouble [215]

[240] 2 אוֹר *ʾôr* 120x light, contrasted with darkness; by extension: brightness; lightning; daylight, sunshine; the fig. extension "light of the face" is a positive, happy attitude, resulting from relief from trouble [216] See *light; lightning.*

[241] 1 אוּר *ʾûr* 6x light; east [the region of light], the direction of the sunrise [217]

[242] 2 אוּר *ʾûr* 7x Urim, devices used by the high priest to make God's will known, possibly related to radiating or reflecting light [224*]

[243] 3 אוּר *ʾûr* 4x Ur [218]

[245] 1 אוֹרָה *ʾôrâ* 3x light, morning light; happiness, serenity, cheerfulness [219]

[246] 2 אוֹרָה *ʾôrâ* 1x herb, mallow; a tasty, edible plant [219]

[247] אוּרִי *ʾûrî* 7x Uri, "*Yahweh is [my] flame, light*" [221]

[249] אוּרִיָּה *ʾûriyyâ* 36x Uriah, "*Yahweh is [my] flame, light*" [223]

[252] אוּת *ʾût* 4x [N] to consent, agree [225]

[253] 1 אוֹת *ʾôt* 79x sign, mark, symbol, a signal or event that communicates; a supernatural event or miracle as a sign from God [226] See *miraculous sign; sign.*

[255] אָז *ʾāz* 141x then, at that time, meanwhile [227]

[257] אֵזוֹב *ʾēzôb* 10x hyssop [231]

[258] אֵזוֹר *ʾēzôr* 14x garments that are wrapped: belt, sash, loincloth [232]

[260] אַזְכָּרָה *ʾazkārâ* 7x memorial offering, memorial portion; the portion of the meal burnt as a token of honor to the Lord [234]

[261] אָזַל *ʾāzal* 5x [Q] to go about, go away; disappear [235]

[263] 1 אָזַן *ʾāzan* 41x [H] to listen, pay attention, give ear [238]

[264] 2 אָזַן *ʾāzan* 1x [P] to ponder, give serious thought, an extension of weighing and testing on scales [239]

[265] אֹזֶן *ʾōzen* 188x ear: the organ for hearing; by extension: listening, and hence, responding, obeying. "To be in the ear" shows close proximity; "to reveal to the ear" means "to inform" [241] See *ear.*

[266] אָזֵן *ʾāzēn* 1x equipment, tools, specifically a digging tool [240]

[272] אֲזִקִּים *ʾaziqqîm* 2x chains, which in context refer to manacles or wrist cuffs [246]

[273] אָזַר *ʾāzar* 17x [Q] to gird up, belt on; [P] to gird someone; [N, Ht] to gird oneself; the action of wrapping a belt or sash around the waist; by extension "to take action" of various kinds: working, providing, going to battle [247]

[274] אֶזְרוֹעַ *ʾezrôaʿ* 2x arm, with the associative meaning of power and potency [248]

[275] אֶזְרָח *ʾezrāḥ* 17x native-born [249]

[277] 1 אָהּ *ʾāh* 2x Alas!, Oh! [253]

[278] 2 אָח *ʾāḥ* 629x brother; by extension: family, kinsman, relative (of either gender); a term of endearment; anyone of the same race or large social group: countryman; associate. "Each to his brother" is usually translated "to each other" or "one to another." [251] See *brother; partner; relatives.*

[279] אָח *ʾaḥ* 3x firepot [254*]

[280] אֹחַ *ʾōaḥ* 1x a howling animal: jackal, hyena, eagle owl [255]

[281] אַחְאָב *ʾaḥʾāb* 92x Ahab, "*brother of father*" [256]

[285] אֶחָד *ʾeḥād* 976x one; a certain one; first [259] See *first; one; other.*

[286] אָחוּ *ʾāḥû* 3x reeds [260]

[288] 1 אַחֲוָה *ʾaḥ^a^wâ* 1x brotherhood, community [264]

[289] 2 אַחֲוָה *ʾaḥ^a^wâ* 1x what is said, declaration [262]

[294] אָחוֹר *ʾāḥôr* 41x back (of the body), rear, hindquarters; backward, from behind; west, as a compass point, because east (the direction of the sunrise) is the direction of orientation [268]

[295] אָחוֹת *ʾāḥôt* 119x sister, by extension: half-sister, any female blood-relative; a term of endearment. "Each to her sister" is a marker of reciprocal reference: one to another [269] See *each other; sister; together.*

[296] 1 אָחַז *ʾāḥaz* 63x [Q] grasp, seize, hold; [Qp] to be fastened; [N] to be caught, acquire [270] See *grasp; seize; take hold.*

[297] 2 אָחַז *ʾāḥaz* 3x [Q] to attach, cover, panel; [Ho] be attached; [P] to cover [270]

[298] אָחָז *ʾāḥāz* 42x Ahaz, "*he has grasped*" [271]

[299] אֲחֻזָּה *ʾ^a^ḥuzzâ* 66x property, possession [272] See *possess, possessions; property.*

[301] אֲחַזְיָה *ʾ^a^ḥazyâ* 7x Ahaziah, "*Yahweh has upheld*" [274]

[302] אֲחַזְיָהוּ *ʾ^a^ḥazyāhû* 31x Ahaziah, "*Yahweh has upheld*" [274]

[308] אֲחִיָּה *ʾ^a^ḥiyyâ* 18x Ahijah, "*[my] brother is Yahweh*" [281]

[309] אֲחִיָּהוּ *ʾ^a^ḥiyyāhû* 5x Ahijah, "*[my] brother is Yahweh*" [281]

[313] אֲחִיטוּב *ʾ^a^ḥîṭûb* 15x Ahitub, "*[my] brother is goodness*" [285]

[314] אֲחִילוּד *ʾ^a^ḥîlûd* 5x Ahilud, "*[my] brother is born*" [286]

[316] אֲחִימֶלֶךְ *ʾ^a^ḥîmelek* 18x Ahimelech, "*[my] brother is king*" [288]

[318] אֲחִימַעַץ *ʾ^a^ḥîmaʿas* 15x Ahimaaz, "*[my] brother is fury*" [290]

[324] אֲחִיקָם *ʾ^a^ḥîqām* 20x Ahikam, "*[my] brother stands*" [296]

[330] אֲחִיתֹפֶל *ʾ^a^ḥîtōpel* 20x Ahithophel, "[poss.] *[my] brother is in the desert* or *[my] brother is foolishness*" [302]

[332] אַחֲלַי *ʾaḥ^a^lay* 2x Oh that!; If only! [305]

[334] אַחְלָמָה *ʾaḥlāmâ* 2x amethyst (exact identification uncertain) [306]

[336] אָחַר *ʾāḥar* 17x [Q] to remain, stay on; [P] to detain, delay, slow down; [H] to take longer (than a set time), come late [309]

[337] 1 אַחֵר *ʾaḥēr* 166x other, another, different; next, additional, more, extra [312] See *another; more; other.*

[339] אַחַר *ʾaḥar* 714x (temporal) after, afterward, later, some time later; (spatial) back, behind, following [310]

[340] אַחֲרוֹן *ʾaḥ^a^rôn* 51x (temporal) next, later, last, end; (spatial) at the back, behind, west, as a compass point, because east (the direction of the sunrise) is the direction of orientation [314] See *last; west.*

[343] אַחֲרַי ʾ*aḥ^aray* 1x in the end, afterward [310*]

[344] אַחֲרִית ʾ*aḥ^arît* 61x (spatial) the far side, the other side; (temporal) at the last, at the end, (in days) to come [319] See *after; cessation; completion; end; outcome.*

[345] אֲחֹרַנִּית ʾ*^aḥōrannît* 7x backwardly, by turning around, in turning back [322]

[346] אֲחַשְׁדַּרְפָּן ʾ*^aḥašdarpān* 4x satraps, an administrative governor of a Persian province [323]

[347] אֲחַשְׁוֵרוֹשׁ ʾ*^aḥašwērôš* 31x Ahaseurus, Xerxes [325]

[350] אֲחַשְׁתְּרָן ʾ*^aḥašt^erān* 2x royal, belonging to the king and used in the king's service [327]

[351] 1 אַט ʾ*aṭ* 5x (adv.) gently, meekly, slowly [328]

[353] 1 אָטָד ʾ*āṭād* 4x thornbush [329]

[355] אֵטוּן ʾ*ēṭûn* 1x linen, possibly red in color [330]

[356] אִטִּים ʾ*iṭṭîm* 1x spirits of the dead [328*]

[357] אָטַם ʾ*āṭam* 8x [Q] to stop up (one's ears); to hold (one's tongue); [Qp] to be narrow [331]

[358] אָטַר ʾ*āṭar* 1x [Q] to close [332]

[360] אִטֵּר ʾ*iṭṭēr* 2x hindered on the right hand, (thus) left-handed; other sources: ambidextrous [334]

[361] אֵי ʾ*ê* 38x where?, which way? [335*]

[362] 1 אִי ʾ*î* 36x island; coastland; distant shores [339]

[363] 2 אִי ʾ*î* 3x hyena, jackals; some understand this to be a spirit or demon [338]

[365] 4 אִי ʾ*î* 2x Woe! [337]

[366] אָיַב ʾ*āyab* 1x [Q] to be an enemy, be hostile towards [340]

[367] אֹיֵב ʾ*ōyēb* 285x enemy, foe [341] See *enemy; foe.*

[368] אֵיבָה ʾ*êbâ* 5x hostility, enmity [342]

[369] אֵיד ʾ*êd* 24x disaster, calamity, destruction [343]

[370] 1 אַיָּה ʾ*ayyâ* 4x black kite; falcon; vulture [344]

[372] אַיֵּה ʾ*ayyēh* 44x Where? [346]

[373] אִיּוֹב ʾ*iyyôb* 58x Job, "*where is my father,* [or perhaps] *Where is my father, O God?*" [347]

[374] אִיזֶבֶל ʾ*îzebel* 22x Jezebel, "[poss.] *unhusbanded, unexalted*" [348]

[375] אֵיךְ ʾ*êk* 61x How? Why?; How! Also! [349]

[376] אִי־כָבוֹד ʾ*îkābôd* 2x Ichabod, "*where is the glory?*" [350]

[377] אֵיכָה ʾ*êkâ* 17x how?, where?; how! (in lament) [349]

[378] אֵיכֹה ʾ*êkōh* 1x Where? [351]

[379] אֵיכָכָה ʾ*êkākâ* 4x How? [349]

[380] 1 אַיִל ʾ*ayil* 171x ram, a male sheep generally more aggressive and protective of the flock; by extension: leading man, ruler [352] See *chief; leader; ram; ruler.*

[381] 2 אַיִל ʾ*ayil* 5x oaks; or any large, mighty tree without reference to a specific species [352]

[382] 3 אַיִל ʾ*ayil* 20x projecting wall; jamb [352]

[384] אֱיָל ʾ*^eyāl* 1x strength [353]

[385] אַיָּל ʾ*ayyāl* 12x deer, young stag [354]

[387] אַיָּלָה ʾ*ayyālâ* 10x deer, doe [355 & 365*]

[389] אַיָּלוֹן ʾ*ayyālôn* 10x Aijalon, "*place of the deer*" [357]

[394] אֱיָלוּת ʾᵉyālût 1x Strength, Power, a title of the one true God, with a focus that he is potent to help [360]

[395] אֵילָם ʾêlām 61x portico, porch, hall [361] See *hall; porch; portico.*

[396] אֵילִם ʾêlim 6x Elim, "*big trees*" [362]

[398] אָיֹם ʾāyōm 3x fearful; majestic, with an implication that this majesty instills awe that borders on fear [366]

[399] אֵימָה ʾêmâ 17x terror, dread, fear [367]

[401] 1 אַיִן ʾayin 789x there is no, not, none, without [369]

[402] 2 אַיִן ʾayin 17x where (from)? [370]

[403] אִין ʾîn 1x there is not [371]

[406] אֵיפָה ʾêpâ 40x ephah (dry measure, about three-fifths of a bushel (22 liters); also a large basket of unspecified measure; "ephah and ephah" means "two differing measures," as a measure that is not standardized [374]

[407] אֵיפֹה ʾêpōh 10x where? [375]

[408] 1 אִישׁ ʾîš 2,188x man, sometimes in contrast to woman, human, sometimes in contrast to animal (without gender distinction); by extension: husband, in contrast to wife; (p.) each, every, someone, a certain one, anyone, whoever. This word is often used in phrases meaning "one of a kind," so a "man of war" is a soldier; a "man of bow" is an archer, etc. [376] See *husband; male; man.*

[410] אִישׁ־בֹּשֶׁת ʾîš-bōšet 11x Ish-Bosheth, "*man of shame*" [378]

[413] אִישׁוֹן ʾîšôn 4x pupil, the black center of the eyeball, formally, "the little man (of the eye)," often translated as "the apple of the eye," an idiom of care and love [380]

[415] אִיתוֹן ʾîtôn 1x entrance [2978*]

[418] אִיתָמָר ʾîtāmār 21x Ithamar, "[poss.] *[is]land of palms; [father] of Tamar*" [385]

[419] 1 אֵיתָן ʾêtān 13x ever-flowing, of a stream that is always filled with water; by extension: never-failing, steady, established, eternal [386]

[420] 2 אֵיתָן ʾêtān 8x Ethan, "*long lived, ever-flowing [streams]*" [387]

[421] אַךְ ʾak 161x but, surely, only, however [389]

[423] אַכְזָב ʾakzāb 2x deceptive, deceitful, referring to a stream or a person [391]

[425] אַכְזָר ʾakzār 4x deadly, ruthless, fierce, heartless [393]

[426] אַכְזָרִי ʾakzārî 8x cruel, merciless [394]

[427] אַכְזְרִיּוּת ʾakzᵉriyyût 1x cruelty [395]

[428] אֲכִילָה ʾᵃkîlâ 1x food [396]

[429] אָכִישׁ ʾākîš 21x Achish, "*the king gives*" [397]

[430] אָכַל ʾākal 820x [Q] to eat; [N] to be eaten; [Pu] be consumed, be destroyed; [H] to give to eat, feed; from the base meaning of eating food is the fig. extension of consuming and destroying something [398] See *consume; devour; eat.*

[431] אֹכֶל ʾōkel 39x food; a general word for food as anything edible [400]

[433] אָכְלָה ʾoklâ 17x what is consumed, food, fuel [402]

[434] 1 אָכֵן ʾākēn 18x Surely! Truly!, an exclamation to emphasize the unexpected [403]

[436] אָכַף ʾākap 1x [Q] to drive, press hard [404]

[437] אֶכֶף ʾekep 1x hand, with a focus that this part of the body that can exert pressure or press hard [405]

[438] אִכָּר *ʾikkār* 7x farmer, people who work in fields and vineyards [406]

[440] 1 אַל *ʾal* 730x no, not [408]

[445] 4 אֵל *ʾēl* 5x power [410] See *God; might, mighty; power.*

[446] 5 אֵל *ʾēl* 237x God, the Mighty One, as a title of majesty and power, often used in combination with other titles; also any false god, gods; any person who is strong and capable: mighty one [410] See *God; power.*

[447] 6 אֵל *ʾēl* 9x these [411]

[448] אֶל *ʾel* 5,513x to, toward; in, into; with regard to [413]

[449] אֵל אֱלֹהֵי יִשְׂרָאֵל *ʾēl ʾelōhê yiśrāʾēl* 1x El Elohe Israel, "*God, the God of Israel*" [415]

[453] אֶלְגָּבִישׁ *ʾelgābîš* 3x hail(stone) or clump of ice [417]

[454] אַלְגּוּמִּים *ʾalgûmmîm* 3x algum (wood); a transliteration of the Hebrew, the exact identification of which is uncertain [418]

[457] 1 אָלָה *ʾālâ* 8x [Q] to utter a curse, swear an oath; [H] to bind under oath, take an oath [422]

[458] 2 אָלָה *ʾālâ* 1x [Q] to mourn, wail [421]

[460] 4 אָלָה *ʾālâ* 34x curse, oath; sworn agreement; public charge [423]

[461] 1 אֵלָה *ʾēlâ* 13x oak, terebinth, or any species of large tree [424]

[462] 2 אֵלָה *ʾēlâ* 13x Elah, "*species of a mighty tree*" [425]

[464] אַלָּה *ʾallâ* 1x oak, or any species of large tree [427]

[465] אֵלֶּה *ʾēlleh* 746x these [428]

[466] אֱלֹהִים *ʾelōhîm* 2,602x God (plural of majesty: plural in form but singular in meaning, with a focus on great power); gods (true grammatical plural); any person characterized by greatness or power: mighty one, great one, judge [430] See *angel; God; judge.*

[467] אִלּוּ *ʾillû* 2x if [432]

[468] אֱלוֹהַּ *ʾelôah* 59x God; god; idol; see also 430 [433] See *God.*

[471] 1 אֵלוֹן *ʾēlôn* 10x great tree, large tree of an unspecified species [436]

[473] 1 אַלּוֹן *ʾallôn* 8x oak tree, large tree of an unspecified species [437]

[476] 1 אַלּוּף *ʾallûp* 9x close friend, partner, ally, companion [441]

[477] 2 אַלּוּף *ʾallûp* 60x chief, leader [441] See *chief; leader; official.*

[480] אָלַח *ʾālaḥ* 3x [N] to be, become (morally) corrupt, a fig. extension of milk turning sour, not found in the OT [444]

[482] אֱלִיאָב *ʾelîʾāb* 21x Eliab, "*God [El] is [my] father*" [446]

[487] אַלְיָה *ʾalyâ* 5x fat tail (of a sheep) [451]

[488] אֵלִיָּה *ʾēliyyâ* 8x Elijah, "*Yahweh is [my] God*" [452]

[489] אֵלִיָּהוּ *ʾēliyyāhû* 63x Elijah, "*Yahweh is [my] God*" [452]

[491] אֱלִיהוּא *ʾelîhûʾ* 7x Elihu, "*Yahweh is [my] God*" [453]

[496] אֱלִיל *ʾelîl* 20x idols, images, gods [457] See *idol; image; worthless.*

[497] אֱלִימֶלֶךְ *ʾelîmelek* 6x Elimelech, "*God [El] is [my] king*" [458]

[499] אֱלִיעֶזֶר *ʾelîʿezer* 14x Eliezer, "*God [El] is [my] help*" [461]

[502] אֱלִיפַז *ʾelîpaz* 15x Eliphaz, "*God [El] is fine gold* or *God crushes*" [464]

[509] אֶלְיָקִים *ʾelyāqîm* 12x Eliakim, "*God [El] establishes*" [471]

[513] אֶלְיָשִׁיב *ʾelyāšîb* 17x Eliashib, "*God [El] restores*" [475]

[514] אֱלִישָׁמָע *ʾelîšāmāʿ* 16x Elishama, "*God [El] has heard*" [476]

[515] אֱלִישָׁע *ʾelîšāʿ* 58x Elisha, "*God [El] is [my] salvation*" [477]

[518] אַלְלַי *ʾallay* 2x Woe!, What misery!, Alas! [480]

[519] 1 אָלַם *ʾālam* 8x [N] to be silenced, be speechless [481]

[520] 2 אָלַם *ʾālam* 1x [P] to bind [481]

[522] אִלֵּם *ʾillēm* 6x mute, unable to speak [483]

[523] אַלְמֻגִּים *ʾalmuggîm* 3x almugwood; a transliteration of the Hebrew, the exact identification of which is uncertain [484]

[524] אֲלֻמָּה *ʾalummâ* 5x sheaf [485]

[527] 1 אַלְמָן *ʾalmān* 1x widowed (one forsaken) [488]

[528] 2 אַלְמָן *ʾalmān* 1x stronghold [488]

[529] אַלְמֹן *ʾalmōn* 1x widowhood [489]

[530] אַלְמָנָה *ʾalmānâ* 55x widow [490] See *widow.*

[531] אַלְמָנוּת *ʾalmānût* 4x widowhood [491]

[532] אַלְמֹנִי *ʾalmōnî* 3x a certain so-and-so, whoever, wherever, with a focus that this is not named or spoken out loud [492]

[540] אֶלְעָזָר *ʾelʿāzār* 72x Eleazar, "*God [El] is a help*" [499]

[544] 1 אָלַף *ʾālap* 4x [Q] to learn, become familiar with; [P] to teach, instruct [502]

[545] 2 אָלַף *ʾālap* 1x [H] to increase by thousands, produce in abundance [503]

[546] 1 אֶלֶף *ʾelep* 7x cattle herd; oxen [504]

[547] 2 אֶלֶף *ʾelep* 496x thousand [505]

[548] 3 אֶלֶף *ʾelep* 12x by extension from "thousand," this refers to any large unit or group: (family) clan, (military) unit [505]

[552] אָלַץ *ʾālaṣ* 1x [P] to prod, urge, a fig. extension of pressing one object hard against another, not found in the OT [509]

[554] אַלְקוּם *ʾalqûm* 1x army [510]

[555] אֶלְקָנָה *ʾelqānâ* 20x Elkanah, "*God [El] has possessed*" [511]

[561] אִם *ʾim* 1,070x if, whether, or; whenever, as often as [518]

[562] אֵם *ʾēm* 220x mother, grandmother, ancestress; by extension: a term of endearment; caregiver; fork (in a road) [517] See *mother.*

[563] אָמָה *ʾāmâ* 56x slave woman; female servant, maidservant [519] See *female slave; maidservant; servant.*

[564] 1 אַמָּה *ʾammâ* 249x cubit (measurement of length, from the elbow to end of fingers, about 18 to 22 inches [about half a meter]); an unspecified unit of time [520] See *cubit.*

[569] אֻמָּה *ʾummâ* 3x tribe, clan [523]

[570] 1 אָמוֹן *ʾāmôn* 2x craftsman [539 & 527 & 525]

[571] 2 אָמוֹן *ʾāmôn* 17x Amon, "*trustworthy*" [526]

[573] 1 אֵמוּן *ʾēmûn* 2x faithful [529]

[574] 2 אֵמוּן *ʾēmûn* 6x faithful, trustworthy [529]

[575] אֱמוּנָה *ʾemûnâ* 49x faithfulness, steadiness, trustworthiness [530] See *faithfulness; integrity; trustworthiness.*

[576] אָמוֹץ *ʾāmôṣ* 13x Amoz, "*strong*" [531]

[579] אַמִּיץ *ʾammîṣ* 6x strong, mighty, brave [533]

[580] אָמִיר *ʾāmîr* 2x branch [534]

[581] 1 אָמַל *ʾāmal* 16x [Qp] to be weak-willed; [Pul] to wither, languish, fade away [535]

[583] אֻמְלַל *ʾumlal* 1x faint, fading away [536]

[584] אֲמֻלָל ʾ*amělāl* 1x feeble, fading [537]

[586] 1 אָמַן ʾ*āman* 97x [N] to be faithful, be trustworthy, be established; [H] to believe, trust, have confidence [539] See *believe; faithful; trust; trustworthy.*

[587] 2 אָמַן ʾ*āman* 9x [Q] to nurse, nurture, care for; be a trustee, be a guardian; [Qp, N] to be nurtured, cared for [539 & 541]

[588] אָמָּן ʾ*ommān* 1x craftsman [542]

[589] אָמֵן ʾ*āmēn* 30x amen, surely; truth [543]

[590] אֹמֶן ʾ*ōmen* 1x faithfulness [544]

[591] 1 אֲמָנָה ʾ*amānâ* 2x binding agreement, trustworthy agreement [548]

[593] 1 אָמְנָה ʾ*omnâ* 2x really, truly, indeed [546]

[594] 2 אָמְנָה ʾ*omnâ* 1x bringing up, caring, tending, fostering [545]

[595] אֹמְנָה ʾ*ōmenâ* 1x doorpost [547]

[596] אַמְנוֹן ʾ*amnôn* 27x Amnon, "*trustworthy*" [550]

[597] אָמְנָם ʾ*omnām* 9x indeed, truly, assuredly [551]

[598] אֻמְנָם ʾ*umnām* 5x really, indeed; used in interrogative sentences [552]

[599] אָמֵץ ʾ*āmēṣ* 41x [Q] to be strong, courageous; [P] to strengthen, support, establish; harden; [Ht] to persist, determine [553*]

[600] אָמֹץ ʾ*āmōṣ* 2x powerful, strong [554]

[601] אֹמֶץ ʾ*ōmes* 1x strength [555]

[602] אַמְצָה ʾ*amṣâ* 1x strength [556]

[604] אֲמַצְיָה ʾ*amaṣyâ* 9x Amaziah, "*Yahweh is powerful*" [558]

[605] אֲמַצְיָהוּ ʾ*amaṣyāhû* 31x Amaziah, "*Yahweh is powerful*" [558]

[606] 1 אָמַר ʾ*āmar* 5,316x [Q, H] to say, speak, think (say to oneself); [Qp, N] to be said; note the many contextual renderings in the NIV [559] See *command; instruct; say; speak; think; utter.*

[607] 2 אָמַר ʾ*āmar* 2x [Ht] to boast [559]

[608] אֹמֶר ʾ*ōmer* 5x saying, word [562]

[609] 1 אֵמֶר ʾ*ēmer* 48x word, saying [561]

[611] 1 אִמֵּר ʾ*immēr* 1x fawn, lamb [561]

[612] 2 אִמֵּר ʾ*immēr* 8x Immer, "*lamb*" [564]

[614] אִמְרָה ʾ*imrâ* 37x word, saying, utterance [565]

[616] אֱמֹרִי ʾ*emōrî* 87x Amorite, "[poss.] *hill dwellers; westerners*" [567]

[621] אֶמֶשׁ ʾ*emeš* 5x last night; yesterday (evening) [570]

[622] אֱמֶת ʾ*emet* 127x faithfulness, reliability, trustworthiness; truth, what conforms to reality in contrast to what is false; "the book of truth" is a reliable book, referring to heavenly scroll detailing future things [571] See *faithfulness; truth.*

[623] אַמְתַּחַת ʾ*amtaḥat* 15x sack [572]

[625] אָן ʾ*ān* 42x how long?; where? [575]

[626] אָנָּא ʾ*onnāʾ* 7x I ask you!, O! (preceding a request) [577]

[627] 1 אָנָה ʾ*ānâ* 3x [Q] to mourn, lament, groan [578]

[628] 2 אָנָה ʾ*ānâ* 4x [P] to make happen; [Pu] to befall, have happen to; [Ht] to pick a quarrel against [579]

[629] אָנָּה ʾ*onnâ* 6x I ask you!, O! (preceding a request) [577]

[631] אָנוּשׁ ʾ*ānûš* 8x incurable, beyond cure; despairing [605*]

[632] 1 אֱנוֹשׁ ʾ*enôš* 42x man, humankind, mortal, with an emphasis on frailty; "a man of peace" is a "friend" [582]

[633] 2 אֱנוֹשׁ ʾ*enôš* 7x Enosh, "*[mortal] man*" [583]

[634] אָנַח ʾ*ānaḥ* 13x [N] to groan, moan [584]

[635] אֲנָחָה ʾ*anāḥâ* 11x groaning, sighing [585]

[638] אֲנִי ʾ*anî* 874x I [589]

[639] אֳנִי ʾ*onî* 7x ships, fleet of ships [590]

[640] אֲנִיָּה ʾ*aniyyâ* 2x lamentation, mourning [592]

[641] אֳנִיָּה ʾ*oniyyâ* 31x ship, trading ship; (pl.) fleet of ships [591]

[643] אֲנָךְ ʾ*anāk* 4x plummet, weight for a plumb line [594]

[645] אָנַן ʾ*ānan* 2x [Htpol] to complain [596]

[646] אָנַס ʾ*ānas* 1x [Q] to compel; "there is no compelling" means "to allow" [597]

[647] אָנַף ʾ*ānap* 14x [Q] to be, become angry; [Ht] to feel angry [599]

[649] אֲנָפָה ʾ*anāpâ* 2x heron, an unclean bird [601]

[650] אָנַק ʾ*ānaq* 4x [Q, N] to groan, lament, sigh [602]

[651] 1 אֲנָקָה ʾ*anāqâ* 4x groaning, sighing [603]

[652] 2 אֲנָקָה ʾ*anāqâ* 1x gecko [604]

[653] אָנַשׁ ʾ*ānaš* 1x [N] be ill, sickly [605]

[654] אָסָא ʾ*āsāʾ* 58x Asa, "[poss.] *healer; myrtle*" [609]

[655] אָסוּךְ ʾ*āsûk* 1x small (oil) jar, flask [610]

[656] אָסוֹן ʾ*āsôn* 5x serious injury, harm [611]

[657] אֵסוּר ʾ*ēsûr* 3x bindings, chains, fetters, shackles [612]

[658] אָסִיף ʾ*āsîp* 3x (Feast of) Ingathering; harvest (from a threshing floor and winepress before the rainy season) [614]

[659] אָסִיר ʾ*āsîr* 12x prisoner, captive [615]

[660] 1 אַסִּיר ʾ*assîr* 4x captive, prisoner [616]

[662] אָסָם ʾ*āsām* 2x barn, storehouse [618]

[665] אָסַף ʾ*āsap* 200x [Q] to store, gather, harvest; [Qp] to be a victim; [N] to be gathered, assembled; [P] to be a rear guard, to bring in, gather; [Pu] to be gathered, collected; [Ht] to assemble; [H] to bring together [622] See *assemble; gather; rear guard; remove; take away.*

[666] אָסָף ʾ*āsāp* 46x Asaph, "*gatherer*" [623]

[667] אָסֹף ʾ*āsōp* 3x storehouse, storeroom [624*]

[668] אֹסֶף ʾ*ōsep* 3x harvest (of fruit), gathering [625]

[669] אֲסֵפָה ʾ*asēpâ* 1x gathering (prisoners); imprisonment [626]

[670] אֲסֻפָּה ʾ*asuppâ* 1x collection (of sayings) [627]

[671] אֲסַפְסֻף ʾ*asapsup* 1x rabble, collection (of grumblers) [628]

[673] אָסַר ʾ*āsar* 73x [Q] to bind, tie up; to obligate; [Qp] to be confined, be bound; [N] to be tied, be kept in prison; [Pu] to be captured, be taken prisoner [631] See *bind; confine; hitch; imprison; obligate; tie, tie up.*

[674] אִסָּר ʾ*issār* 11x pledge, a binding obligation [632]

[676] אֶסְתֵּר ʾ*estēr* 55x Esther, "[Persian] *star* [poss.] *Ishtar*" [635]

[677] 1 אַף *ʾap* 134x how much (better, worse; more, less); really, truly; too, also, even more [637]

[678] 2 אַף *ʾap* 277x nose (representing the face or some part of the face); "hot of nose" signifies anger; "long of nose" signifies patience; "high of nose" signifies arrogance [639] See *anger; fury; nose; nostrils; patience, (be) patient; slow to anger.*

[679] אָפַד *ʾāpad* 2x [Q] to fasten [640]

[680] 1 אֵפֹד *ʾēpōd* 49x ephod, a garment of a priest used for adornment and as an aid in priestly service [646*]

[682] אֲפֻדָּה *ʾapuddâ* 3x skillfully woven covering [642]

[683] אַפֶּדֶן *ʾappeden* 1x palace tent, royal tent [643]

[684] אָפָה *ʾāpâ* 13x [Q] to bake; [N] to be baked [644]

[685] אֹפֶה *ʾōpeh* 11x baker [644*]

[686] אֵפוֹא *ʾēpôʾ* 15x then, so then [645]

[689] אָפִיל *ʾāpîl* 1x late-ripening, late in the season [648]

[692] 1 אָפִיק *ʾāpîq* 18x stream, water channel; valley, ravine, the deepest part of a valley flowing with water [650]

[693] 2 אָפִיק *ʾāpîq* 1x mighty, strong [650]

[694] אֹפֶל *ʾōpel* 9x darkness, the absence of light, often with the associative meaning of gloom, despair; shadows [652]

[695] אָפֵל *ʾāpēl* 1x dark, gloomy [651]

[696] אֲפֵלָה *ʾapēlâ* 10x the dark, darkness, with the associative meaning of mental gloom and despair [653]

[698] אֹפֶן *ʾōpen* 1x (right) time; aptly [655]

[699] אָפֵס *ʾāpēs* 5x [Q] to come to an end, cease [656]

[700] אֶפֶס *ʾepes* 43x ends (of the earth); no, nothing; however, but, only, yet [657]

[701] אֹפֶס *ʾōpes* 1x an extremity of the body, which in context wades through shallow water: ankles, or possibly soles of the feet [657*]

[703] אֶפַע *ʾepaʿ* 1x worthless [659]

[704] אֶפְעֶה *ʾepʿeh* 3x snake, variously identified as an adder or viper [660]

[705] אָפַף *ʾāpap* 5x [Q] to surround, entangle, engulf [661]

[706] אָפַק *ʾāpaq* 7x [Ht] to control oneself, restrain oneself; to feel compelled [662]

[707] אֲפֵק *ʾapēq* 9x Aphek, "*stronghold*" [663]

[709] אֵפֶר *ʾēper* 22x ashes, dust [665]

[710] אֲפֵר *ʾapēr* 2x headband [666]

[711] אֶפְרֹחַ *ʾeprōaḥ* 4x young (of a bird), chick [667]

[712] אַפִּרְיוֹן *ʾappiryôn* 1x carriage; other sources: sedan chair, litter, or palanquin, a vehicle carried on poles by porters [668]

[713] אֶפְרַיִם *ʾeprayim* 180x Ephraim, "*doubly fruitful*" [669]

[716] 1 אֶפְרָתָה *ʾeprātâ* 3x Ephrathah, "*fruitful land*" [672]

[718] אֶפְרָתִי *ʾeprātî* 5x Ephraimite, "*of Ephraim*" [673]

[720] אֶצְבַּע *ʾeṣbaʿ* 31x digit appendage of hand or foot: finger, toe; "four fingers" is a measurement of width (Jer 52:21) [676]

[721] 1 אָצִיל *ʾāṣîl* 1x far corner, the remote areas of the earth [678]

[722] 2 אָצִיל *ʾāṣîl* 1x leader, with an implication of being noble and distinguished [678]

[723] אַצִּיל *ʾaṣṣîl* 3x joint (of shoulder or wrist); "a cubit of the joint" (Eze 41:8) is an unknown length, translated as a "long cubit" [679]

[724] אָצַל *ʾāṣal* 5x [Q] to turn aside; to take away; [N] to be smaller [680]

[725] 1 אֵצֶל *ʾēṣel* 61x beside, near, at the side [681]

[731] אֶצְעָדָה *ʾesʿādâ* 2x armlet, armband; an ornamental chain worn on the wrist or the ankle [685]

[732] אָצַר *ʾāṣar* 5x [Q] to store up; [N] be stored; [H] to be in charge of a storeroom [686]

[734] אֶקְדָּח *ʾeqdāḥ* 1x sparkling jewel; some sources: beryl stone [688]

[735] אַקּוֹ *ʾaqqô* 1x wild goat [689]

[736] אֲרָא *ʾărāʾ* 1x Ara [690]

[737] אֶרְאֵל *ʾerʾēl* 1x brave man, hero [691]

[738] אֲרִאֵל *ʾărîʾēl* 2x best man, warrior [739*]

[741] אָרַב *ʾārab* 41x [Q] to lay in wait against, hide in ambush; [P] to ambush, waylay; [H] to set an ambush [693]

[743] אֶרֶב *ʾereb* 2x cover, hiding place, lair; hiding place (for an ambush) [695]

[744] אֹרֶב *ʾōreb* 2x trap, intrigue [696]

[746] אַרְבֶּה *ʾarbeh* 24x locust, mature locust [697]

[747] אָרְבָּה *ʾorbâ* 1x cleverness; other sources: nimble movements (of the hands), perhaps some concrete survival skill, such as swimming [698*]

[748] אֲרֻבָּה *ʾărubbâ* 9x floodgate; window; nest (nesting hole) [699]

[752] 1 אַרְבַּע *ʾarbaʿ* 455x four, (pl.) forty; fourth, fortieth [702 & 706*] See *forty; four; fourth.*

[755] אָרַג *ʾārag* 14x [Q] to weave, spin (a web) [707]

[756] אֶרֶג *ʾereg* 2x weaver's loom, weaver's shuttle [708]

[760] אַרְגְּוָן *ʾargᵉwān* 1x purple (yarn) [710]

[761] אַרְגַּז *ʾargaz* 3x chest (containing objects); other sources: saddlebag [712]

[763] אַרְגָּמָן *ʾargāmān* 38x purple (yarn) [713]

[768] אָרָה *ʾārâ* 2x [Q] to gather, pick (fruit) [717]

[774] אֻרְוָה *ʾurwâ* 4x (animal) stall, pen, stable [220* & 723]

[775] אָרוּז *ʾārûz* 1x tight, solid [729*]

[776] אֲרוּכָה *ʾărûkâ* 6x healing, health; repair [724]

[778] אֲרוֹן *ʾărôn* 202x ark, chest, box; coffin [727*] See *ark; box; chest.*

[779] אֲרַוְנָה *ʾărawnâ* 9x Araunah, "*strong*" [728]

[780] אֶרֶז *ʾerez* 73x cedar; other sources: fir [730] See *cedar.*

[781] אַרְזָה *ʾarzâ* 1x beam of cedar; other sources: paneling (made of fir) [731]

[782] 1 אָרַח *ʾāraḥ* 7x [Q] to go, travel; (ptcp.) traveler, wanderer; (ptcp.pl.) caravans [732]

[784] אֹרַח *ʾōraḥ* 59x road, way, path, thoroughfare; by extension: way of life, manner of conduct; "the way of a woman" means "childbirth" [734] See *path; road; way.*

[785] אֹרְחָה *ʾōrḥâ* 4x caravan [736]

[786] אֲרֻחָה *ʾăruḥâ* 6x allowance, provision; portion [737]

[787] אֲרִי *ʾărî* 34x (the African) lion, with the associative meanings of strength, fierceness, and sometimes nobility; sometimes fig. of people who are destructive [738]

[789] 1 אֲרִיאֵל *ʾărîʾēl* 3x altar hearth [741]

[790] 2 אֲרִיאֵל *ʾărîʾēl* 4x Ariel, "*lioness of God [El]*" [740]

[793] 1 אַרְיֵה *ʾaryēh* 44x (the African) lion [744]

[799] אָרַךְ *ʾārak* 35x [Q] to be, become long; [H] to lengthen, to have a long (life) [748]

[800] אָרֵךְ *ʾārēk* 15x slow (to anger), patient, long-suffering [750] See *patience, (be) patient; slow to anger.*

[801] אֹרֶךְ *ʾārōk* 3x length (spatial and temporal) [752]

[802] אֹרֶךְ *ʾōrek* 95x length (spatial and temporal) [753] See *forever; length; long.*

[806] אֲרָם *ʾarām* 129x Aram [758]

[810] אַרְמוֹן *ʾarmôn* 33x fortress, citadel, palace, stronghold, a military defensive building usually small of base but many floors high [759]

[811] אֲרָמִית *ʾarāmî* 5x in Aramaic [762* & 7421*]

[812] אֲרַמִּי *ʾarammî* 12x Aramean [761]

[815] 1 אֹרֶן *ʾōren* 1x pine tree; other sources: laurel, sweet laurel, fir, cedar [766]

[817] אַרְנֶבֶת *ʾarnebet* 2x rabbit; other sources: hare [768]

[818] אַרְנוֹן *ʾarnôn* 25x Arnon [769]

[821] אָרְנָן *ʾornān* 12x Araunah, "*strong*" [771]

[822] אַרְפָּד *ʾarpād* 6x Arpad [774]

[823] אַרְפַּכְשַׁד *ʾarpakšad* 9x Arphaxad [775]

[824] אֶרֶץ *ʾereṣ* 2,505x world, earth, all inhabited lands; parts of the earth, land (in contrast to water), ground, soil; country, region, territory; "heaven and earth" means the totality of creation; "the ends of the earth" means "a very distant place" [776] See *earth; land.*

[826] אָרַר *ʾārar* 63x [Q] to curse, place a curse; [Qp] to be cursed, be under a curse; [N] to be cursed; [P] to bring a curse; [Ho] to bring a curse upon one [779] See *curse.*

[827] אֲרָרַט *ʾarārat* 4x Ararat [780]

[829] אָרַשׂ *ʾāraś* 11x [P] to betroth, pledge to marriage; [Pu] to be betrothed, be pledged to be married [781]

[830] אֲרֶשֶׁת *ʾarešet* 1x request, desire [782]

[831] אַרְתַּחְשַׁסְתְּא *ʾartaḥšastʾ* 9x Artaxerxes [783]

[836] 1 אֵשׁ *ʾēš* 376x fire, flame; lightning [784 & 800*] See *fire.*

[844] אֶשֶׁד *ʾāšed* 7x slopes, mountain slopes [794*]

[846] אַשְׁדּוֹד *ʾašdôd* 17x Ashdod, "[perhaps] *fortress*" [795]

[847] אַשְׁדּוֹדִי *ʾašdôdî* 5x from Ashdod [796]

[850] אֲשֵׁדָה *ʾēšdāt* 1x mountain slope [799]

[851] אִשָּׁה *ʾiššâ* 781x woman, in contrast to man; wife, in contrast to husband; "to take a woman" means "to marry" [802] See *wife; woman.*

[852] אִשֶּׁה *ʾiššeh* 65x offering made by fire [801] See *offering.*

[854] אֱשׁוּן *ʾešûn* 1x approach (of darkness) [380*]

[855] אַשּׁוּר *ʾaššûr* 151x Asshur, Assyria [804]

[859] אָשְׁיָה *ʾošyâ* 1x tower [803*]

[861] אֲשִׁישׁ *ʾāšîš* 1x man [808]

[862] אֲשִׁישָׁה *ʾašîšâ* 4x cake of raisins, made of dried, compressed grapes; used as food and as an offering [809]

[863] אֶשֶׁךְ *ʾešek* 1x testicle [810]

[864] 1 אֶשְׁכּוֹל *ʾeškôl* 9x cluster of grapes [811]

[865] 2 אֶשְׁכּוֹל *ʾeškôl* 4x Eshcol, "*[grape] cluster*" [812]

[868] אֶשְׁכָּר *ʾeškār* 2x gifts; payment [814]

[869] אֶשֶׁל *ʾešel* 3x tamarisk tree [815]

[870] אָשַׁם *ʾāšam* 35x [Q] to be guilty; to be in a state of liable for a wrongdoing, with an implication of that one will suffer or be punished for the guilt; [N] to be suffering; [H] to declare guilty [816]

[871] אָשָׁם *ʾāšām* 47x guilt offering, atoning sacrifice; guilt, penalty [817]

[872] אָשֵׁם *ʾāšēm* 2x guilty, bearing guilt [818]

[873] אַשְׁמָה *ʾašmâ* 19x guilt, guiltiness [819]

[874] אַשְׁמוּרָה *ʾašmûrâ* 7x watch of the night (middle or last) [821]

[875] אַשְׁמָן *ʾašmān* 1x strong one [820]

[876] אֶשְׁנָב *ʾešnāb* 2x lattice, a barred or grated window [822]

[879] אַשָּׁף *ʾaššāp* 2x enchanter, conjurer, one of the profession of the secret arts, in communication with the dead [825]

[880] אַשְׁפָּה *ʾašpâ* 6x quiver (for arrows) [827]

[882] אֶשְׁפָּר *ʾešpār* 2x cake of dates [829]

[883] אַשְׁפֹּת *ʾašpōt* 7x ash heap; Dung (Gate) [830]

[884] אַשְׁקְלוֹן *ʾašqᵉlôn* 12x Ashkelon [831]

[886] 1 אָשַׁר *ʾāšar* 6x [Q] to walk (straight); [P] to lead, guide; reprove; [Pu] to be guided [833]

[887] 2 אָשַׁר *ʾāšar* 10x [P] to call blessed, pronounce happy, speak well of; [Pu] to be blessed; in some contexts, to give a blessing is to act kindly and impart benefits to the one being blessed; to be blessed implies the happy state that results [833]

[888] אָשֵׁר *ʾāšēr* 43x Asher, "*Happy One!*" [836]

[889] אֲשֶׁר *ʾᵃšer* 5,496x (rel.) who, which, what; (c.) that, in order that, so that [834]

[890] אֶשֶׁר *ʾešer* 2x fortune, blessedness, happiness [835]

[891] אֹשֶׁר *ʾōšer* 1x fortune, blessedness, happiness [837]

[892] אָשֻׁר *ʾāšur* 9x steps, tracks [838]

[895] אֲשֵׁרָה *ʾᵃšērâ* 40x Asherah (pagan god), Asherah pole [842]

[897] אַשְׁרֵי *ʾašrê* 44x blessed!, happy!, a heightened state of happiness and joy, implying very favorable circumstances, often resulting from the kind acts of God [835*]

[899] אָשַׁשׁ *ʾāšaš* 1x [Htpol] to fix in one's mind [377*]

[906] 1 אֵת *ʾēt* 10,937x usually not translated: marks the direct object [853]

[907] 2 אֵת *ʾēt* 934x with, to, upon, beside, among, against [854]

[908] 3 אֵת *ʾēt* 5x plowshare, mattock [855]

[910] אָתָה *ʾātâ* 21x [Q] to come; [H] to bring [857]

[911] אַתָּה *ʾattâ* 745x you, your, yourself [859]

[912] אָתוֹן *ʾātôn* 34x female donkey [860]

[916] אַתִּיק *ʾattîq* 5x gallery, porch; other sources: street, passage [862]

[917] אַתֶּם *ʾattem* 283x you (all), yours, yourselves [859]

[919] אֶתְמוֹל *ʾetmôl* 8x yesterday; (adv.) before, formerly, lately, in the past [865]

[921] אֶתְנָה *ʾetnâ* 1x payment (of a prostitute) [866]

[924] אֶתְנַן *ʾetnan* 11x wages, payment (of a prostitute) [869]

[928] -בְּ *bᵉ-* 15,552x in, on, among, over, through, against; when, whenever; a spatial, temporal, or logical marker to show relationship of objects, words, and phrases [**]

[929] בִּאָה *biʾâ* 1x entrance [872*]

[930] בָּאַר *bāʾar* 3x [P] to make plain, make clear, expound [874]

[931] 1 בְּאֵר *beʾēr* 39x well, a shaft in the ground for extraction of water; pit, a depression in the earth with no focus on water [875]

[936] בְּאֵר לַחַי רֹאִי *beʾēr lahay rōʾî* 3x Beer Lahai Roi, "*well that belongs to the Living One seeing me*" [883]

[937] בְּאֵר שֶׁבַע *beʾēr šebaʿ* 34x Beersheba, "*seventh well*" [884]

[944] בָּאַשׁ *bāʾaš* 17x [Q] to stink, smell; [N] to become a stench; [H] to make a stench, to cause a bad smell; [Ht] to make oneself a stench [887]

[945] בְּאֹשׁ *beʾōš* 3x stench, stink [889]

[946] בְּאֻשׁ *beʾuš* 2x bad (putrid) fruit, rotten grapes [891*]

[947] בָּאְשָׁה *boʾšâ* 1x weeds, a plant of no value, variously identified [890]

[949] בָּבָה *bābâ* 1x apple (of the eye), eyeball, formally, "little child of the eye," a term of endearment [892]

[951] בָּבֶל *bābel* 262x Babel, Babylon, "*gate of god[s]; [Ge 11:9] confused*" [894]

[953] בָּגַד *bāgad* 49x [Q] to be unfaithful, be faithless; to betray, act treacherously [898]

[954] 1 בֶּגֶד *beged* 2x treachery [899]

[955] 2 בֶּגֶד *beged* 216x clothing, garment, cloak, robe [899] See *clothing; garment.*

[956] בֹּגְדוֹת *bōgedôt* 1x treachery [900]

[957] בָּגוֹד *bāgôd* 2x unfaithful, pertaining to being adulterous, with the implication that the actions were deceptive and treacherous [901]

[963] 1 בַּד *bad* 161x part, member, limb; alone, apart, only; in addition to [905] See *alone; only.*

[964] 2 בַּד *bad* 41x pole, bar [905]

[965] 3 בַּד *bad* 23x formally, a "(cut) piece (of a garment)," likely linen of the flax plant [906]

[966] 4 בַּד *bad* 3x boasting, idle talk [907]

[967] 5 בַּד *bad* 2x false prophet, with a focus on empty, idle talk [907]

[968] בָּדָא *bādāʾ* 2x [Q] to choose; to make up, devise [908]

[969] בָּדַד *bādad* 3x [Q] to be alone, isolated [909]

[970] בָּדָד *bādād* 11x alone, by oneself, apart [910]

[974] בְּדִיל *bedîl* 5x tin, an inexpensive metal that could be used as a medium of exchange; "a stone of tin" is "a plumb line and weight" [913]

[975] בָּדִיל *bādîl* 1x impurities, slag, the dross of the smelting process, used as a figure of moral and ceremonial impurities [913*]

[976] בָּדַל *bādal* 42x [N] separate oneself, be expelled; [H] to separate, sever completely, distinguish between [914]

[977] בָּדָל *bādāl* 1x piece (of an ear) [915]

[978] בְּדֹלַח *bedōlaḥ* 2x aromatic resin; some sources: bdellium-gum (an aromatic, yellowish gum) [916]

[980] בָּדַק *bādaq* 1x [Q] to repair, mend [918]

[981] בֶּדֶק *bedeq* 10x breach (of a temple or a ship) [919]

[983] בֹּהוּ *bōhû* 3x emptiness, desolation, a void associated with chaos; "empty and void" is a state of total chaos [922]

[984] בְּהוֹן *behôn* 2x thumb, big toe [931*]

[985] בַּהַט *bahaṭ* 1x porphyry (or some other precious stone) [923]

[986] בָּהִיר *bāhîr* 1x bright, brilliant [925]

[987] בָּהַל *bāhal* 39x [N] to be terrified, alarmed, dismayed, bewildered; [P] to make afraid, terrify; to make haste; [Pu] to be hastened, made to hurry; to cause terror; to cause to hurry [926]

[988] בֶּהָלָה *behālâ* 4x sudden terror; misfortune [928]

[989] בְּהֵמָה *bᵉhēmâ* 190x beast, animal, livestock, herds, cattle [929] See *animal; beast; cattle; livestock.*

[990] בְּהֵמוֹת *bᵉhēmôt* 1x behemoth; sources variously identify as hippopotamus, crocodile, elephant; the plural form may indicate this is the ultimate creature, a composite description of the strongest attributes of the animal kingdom [930]

[991] בֹּהֶן *bōhen* 14x thumb, big toe [931]

[993] בֹּהַק *bōhaq* 1x harmless rash [933]

[994] בַּהֶרֶת *baheret* 12x spot, bright spot (on the skin) [934*]

[995] בּוֹא *bôʾ* 2,592x [Q] to come, go; [H] to bring, take; [Ho] to be brought [935] See *approach; arrive; bring; carry; come; enter; follow; reach; return; take.*

[996] 1 בּוּז *bûz* 14x [Q] to despise, scorn, deride [936]

[997] 2 בּוּז *bûz* 11x contempt [937]

[999] בּוּזָה *bûzâ* 1x contempt [939]

[1003] בּוּךְ *bûk* 3x [N] to wander around, mill about; to be bewildered [943]

[1005] 2 בּוּל *bûl* 1x piece of wood, in context likely referring to a block of wood that has been crafted into an idol [944]

[1006] 3 בּוּל *bûl* 1x produce; in context produce as a gift or tribute [944]

[1008] בּוּס *bûs* 12x [Q, P] to trample down; loathe; [Htpol] to kick about; [Ho] to be trodden down [947]

[1009] בּוּץ *bûṣ* 8x fine linen; white linen [948]

[1011] בּוּקָה *bûqâ* 1x pillage, that which is made desolate and emptied [950]

[1012] בּוֹקֵר *bôqēr* 1x herdsman, usually a shepherd [951]

[1013] בּוּר *bûr* 1x [Q] to conclude [952]

[1014] בּוֹר *bôr* 65x pit, well, cistern; dungeon; a cistern is usually a shaft in the ground, hewn out of soft stone and plastered to hold water [953] See *cistern; dungeon; grave; pit; well.*

[1017] 1 בּוֹשׁ *bôš* 125x [Q] to be put to shame, be ashamed, be disgraced; [Htpolal] to feel ashamed; [H] to bring shame, to cause disgrace, act shamefully [954*] See *ashamed; feel ashamed; put to shame; shame.*

[1018] 2 בּוֹשׁ *bôš* 2x [Polal] to be delayed, be long [954*]

[1019] בּוּשָׁה *bûšâ* 4x shame [955]

[1020] בַּז *baz* 25x plunder, loot, despoiling [957]

[1021] בָּזָא *bāzāʾ* 2x [Q] to divide, likely referring to the washing out of rivers by force of the waters [958]

[1022] בָּזָה *bāzâ* 44x [Q] to despise, scorn, ridicule, show contempt for; [Qp] to be despised; [N] to be despised, be contemptible; [H] to cause to despise [959 & 960* & 5240*]

[1023] בִּזָּה *bizzâ* 10x plunder, booty, spoils [961]

[1024] בָּזַז *bāzaz* 43x [Q] to plunder, loot, carry off spoils; [Qp, N, Pu] to be plundered [962]

[1025] בִּזָּיוֹן *bizzāyôn* 1x disrespect, contempt [963]

[1027] בָּזָק *bāzāq* 1x flashes of lightning, lightning [65]

[1029] בָּזַר *bāzar* 2x [Q] to distribute; [P] to scatter [967]

[1031] בָּחוֹן *bāḥôn* 1x tester of metals, assayer [969]

[1032] בַּחוּן *baḥûn* 1x siege tower, a moveable military engine used to attack a walled city [971*]

[1033] 1 בָּחוּר *bāḥûr* 50x young man, able (fighting) man; bridegroom [970]

[1035] בְּחוּרוֹת *bᵉḥûrôt* 2x youth, as a state of being [979]

[1036] בְּחוּרִים *bᵉḥûrîm* 1x youth [980]

[1040] בָּחִיר *bāḥîr* 13x chosen one, one preferred or selected by God with an implication of receiving special favor [972]

[1041] 1 בָּחַל *bāḥal* 1x [Q] to detest, disdain, feel an attitude of loathing [973]

[1043] בָּחַן *bāḥan* 29x [Q] to test, try, probe, examine; [Qp, N, Pu] to be tested; to test and learn the genuineness of an object, fig. of assaying a metal to determine its purity or nature [974] See *prove; refine; test; try.*

[1046] 2 בֹּחַן *bōḥan* 1x tested (stone) [976]

[1047] 1 בָּחַר *bāḥar* 172x [Q] to choose, select, desire, prefer; [Qp, N] to be chosen, choice, the best, preferred [977] See *choose; prefer; select.*

[1051] בָּטָא *bāṭāʾ* 4x [Q, P] to speak thoughtlessly, to speak rashly, recklessly [981]

[1053] 1 בָּטַח *bāṭaḥ* 118x [Q] to trust, rely on, put confidence in; [Qp] to be confident; [H] to lead to believe, make trust [982] See *depend on; rely on; trust.*

[1054] 2 בָּטַח *bāṭaḥ* 1x [Q] to stumble, fall to the ground [982]

[1055] 1 בֶּטַח *beṭaḥ* 42x safety, security [983]

[1057] בִּטְחָה *biṭḥâ* 1x trust, confidence [985]

[1058] בַּטֻּחָה *baṭṭuḥâ* 1x security, safety [987*]

[1059] בִּטָּחוֹן *biṭṭāḥôn* 3x confidence, hope [986]

[1060] בָּטַל *bāṭal* 1x [Q] to cease (activity) [988*]

[1061] 1 בֶּטֶן *beṭen* 72x inmost part, viscera: abdomen, belly, stomach, womb; by extension: the inner person, the heart, the seat of emotion, thought, and desire [990] See *abdomen; belly.*

[1062] 2 בֶּטֶן *beṭen* 1x Beten, "*womb, bowels*" [991]

[1063] בָּטְנָה *boṭnâ* 1x pistachio nut [992*]

[1065] בִּי *bî* 12x O!, please! [994]

[1067] בִּין *bîn* 171x [Q] to understand, discern, realize; be prudent; [N] to be discerning, be understanding; [Pol] to care for; to have skill, insight; to instruct, explain; [Htpolel/Htpolal] to look closely, consider with full attention, ponder [995] See *discern; know; perceive; understand.*

[1068] בַּיִן *bayin* 408x between; separate from; whether ... or [996*]

[1069] בִּינָה *bînâ* 38x understanding, insight, discernment, good sense, wisdom, usually referring to the wisdom that responds to the Lord and his instruction [998]

[1070] בֵּיצָה *bêṣâ* 6x egg [1000]

[1072] בִּירָה *bîrâ* 18x citadel, fort, palatial structure [1002]

[1074] 1 בַּיִת *bayit* 2,047x house, home; of royalty: palace; of deity: temple; a specific part of a house: room; place; by extension: household, family, clan, tribe [1004] See *dynasty; house; temple.*

[1075] 2 בַּיִת *bayit* 3x between; among; at a crossroads [996*]

[1078] בֵּית־אֵל *bêt-ēl* 71x Bethel, "*temple [house] of God [El]*" [1008]

[1095] בֵּית־הַלַּחְמִי *bêt-hallaḥmî* 4x the Bethlehemite, "*of Bethlehem*" [1022]

[1103] בֵּית־חוֹרוֹן *bêt-ḥôrôn* 14x Beth Horon, "*house of Horon* or *site of ravine*" [1032]

[1107] בֵּית לֶחֶם *bêt leḥem* 41x Bethlehem, "*house of bread;* [poss.] *temple [house] of Lakhmu*" [1035]

[1121] בֵּית פְּעוֹר *bêt pe*ʿ*ôr* 4x Beth Peor, "*house of Peor*" [1047]

[1126] בֵּית־שְׁאָן *bêt-š*e*ʾān* 9x Beth Shan, "*site [house] of Shan [repose]*" [1052]

[1127] בֵּית שֶׁמֶשׁ *bêt šemeš* 20x Beth Shemesh, "*temple [house] of Shemesh*" [1053]

[1131] בִּיתָן *bîtān* 3x dwelling place, of royalty: palace, with a possible focus on the inner parts of the palace complex [1055]

[1132] בָּכָא 1 *bākāʾ* 4x balsam tree; some sources: baka-shrub [1057]

[1134] בָּכָה *bākâ* 114x [Q] to weep, wail, cry, sob, mourn; [P] to weep for, mourn for; this can refer to ritual mourning as well as personal sorrow [1058] See *cry; mourn; sob; wail; weep.*

[1135] בֶּכֶה *bekeh* 1x weeping [1059]

[1136] בִּכּוּרָה *bikkûrâ* 4x early ripened fruit, usually ripening in June (late fruit ripens in August) [1063 & 1073*]

[1137] בִּכּוּרִים *bikkûrîm* 17x firstfruits, first ripened produce [1061*]

[1140] בְּכִי *b*e*kî* 29x weeping [1065]

[1142] בְּכִירָה *b*e*kîrâ* 6x first born (daughter) [1067]

[1143] בְּכִית *b*e*kît* 1x mourning, weeping [1068]

[1144] בָּכַר *bākar* 4x [P] bear early fruit; give the rights of the firstborn; [Pu] be made a firstborn (dedication); [H] to bear one's first child [1069]

[1145] בֵּכֶר *bēker* 1x young bull camel [1070*]

[1147] בְּכֹר *b*e*kōr* 120x firstborn, first male offspring (human or animal), the oldest son, with associative meanings of honor, status, prominence, and privileges of inheritance to the firstborn; by extension: one in a special relationship with God [1060*] See *firstborn.*

[1148] בְּכֹרָה *b*e*kōrâ* 10x birthright, rights of the firstborn [1062]

[1149] בִּכְרָה *bikrâ* 1x young cow-camel (having given birth to her first calf) [1072]

[1153] בַּל 1 *bal* 69x no, not, cannot, never [1077]

[1155] בֵּל *bēl* 3x Bel, "*Bel*" [1078]

[1158] בָּלַג *bālag* 4x [H] to flash (with a focus on suddenness); by extension: to smile, rejoice, gleam, have a cheerful attitude [1082]

[1161] בִּלְדַּד *bildad* 5x Bildad, "*Bel has loved*" [1085]

[1162] בָּלָה 1 *bālâ* 15x [Q] to wear out, waste away; [P] to enjoy, use to the full; to decay; to grow old; to oppress [1086]

[1165] בָּלֶה *bāleh* 5x old, worn-out [1087]

[1166] בַּלָּהָה *ballāhâ* 10x sudden terror, horrible end; in some contexts a horrible end refers to death [1091]

[1167] בִּלְהָה 1 *bilhâ* 10x Bilhah, "[perhaps] *simplicity* or *modesty* or *to be without concern*" [1090]

[1170] בְּלוֹי *b*e*lôy* 3x old, worn-out (things) [1094]

[1172] בְּלִי *b*e*lî* 57x lacking, without; nothing [1097]

[1173] בְּלִיל *b*e*lîl* 3x fodder, mash, fermented matter [1098]

[1175] בְּלִיַּעַל *b*e*liyya*ʿ*al* 27x wicked one, vile one, evil one, worthless one, transliterated "Belial"; a "son of Belial" or "man of Belial" is a troublemaker and scoundrel [1100]

[1176] בָּלַל 1 *bālal* 43x [Q] to confuse; feed; pour upon; [Qp] to mix (with);

[Htpolal] to be thrown about, shaken back and forth [1101]

[1179] בָּלַס *bālas* 1x [Q] to nip (scratch open) unripe sycamore-fig fruit, so as to promote ripening and make more palatable [1103]

[1180] 1 בָּלַע *bālaᶜ* 43x [Q] to swallow up; [N] to be swallowed; [P] to swallow up, gulp down, devour, consume; [Pu] be swallowed up, be devoured [1104]

[1182] 3 בָּלַע *bālaᶜ* 6x [N] be befuddled, confused; [P] to confuse, turn away; [Pu] to be led astray; [Ht] to be confused thoroughly [1104]

[1184] 2 בֶּלַע *belaᶜ* 1x harmful, with a likely focus on destruction, fig. of what is greedily swallowed up [1105]

[1185] 3 בֶּלַע *belaᶜ* 12x Bela, "*swallower, devourer*" [1106]

[1187] בַּלְעֲדֵי *balᶜadê* 17x apart from, except for, besides [1107]

[1189] 1 בִּלְעָם *bilᶜām* 60x Balaam, "[poss.] *Baal [lord] of the people;* [poss.] *the clan brings forth; devourer, glutton*" [1109]

[1191] בָּלַק *bālaq* 2x [Q] to devastate; [Pu] to be stripped, devastated [1110]

[1192] בָּלָק *bālāq* 43x Balak, "*devastator*" [1111]

[1194] בִּלְתִּי *biltî* 112x no, not, without; except for; besides [1115]

[1195] 1 בָּמָה *bāmâ* 106x high place, worship shrine (an elevated place, often artificial, for the worship of a god); heights [1116] See *high place.*

[1198] בְּמוֹ *bemô* 10x by, with, in [1119]

[1201] 1 בֵּן *bēn* 4,941x son, child (of either gender), descendant (in any generation), offspring (human or animal); by extension: a term of endearment; one of a class or kind or nation or family. A "son of man" is a "human being" (Nu 23:19), a term that often assumes messianic significance (Ps 8) [1121] See *child; grandchild; people; son.*

[1207] בֶּן־הֲדַד *ben-hadad* 25x Ben-Hadad, "*son of Hadad*" [1130]

[1208] בֶּן־הִנֹּם *ben-hinnōm* 10x Ben Hinnom, "*the son of Hinnom*" [2011*]

[1215] בָּנָה *bānâ* 377x [Q] to make, build, rebuild, establish; [Qp, N] to be built, established [1129] See *build, build up; fashion.*

[1224] בִּנְיָה *binyâ* 1x building, physical structure [1140]

[1226] בְּנָיָהוּ *benāyāhû* 31x Benaiah, "*Yahweh has built*" [1141]

[1227] בֵּנַיִם *bēnayim* 2x champion, single fighter [1143]

[1228] בִּנְיָמִין *binyāmîn* 166x Benjamin, "*son of [the] right hand; southerner*" [1144]

[1229] בֶּן־יְמִינִי *ben-yemînî* 9x Benjamite, of Benjamin, "*of Benjamin*" [1145]

[1230] בִּנְיָן *binyān* 7x building, structure; outer wall [1146]

[1235] בֹּסֶר *bōser* 5x unripe grapes, sour grapes [1154* & 1155]

[1237] 1 בַּעַד *baᶜad* 104x behind; through, over; around; from; on behalf of, for (benefit of) [1157*]

[1239] 1 בָּעָה *bāᶜâ* 3x [Q] to ask, inquire; [N] to be pillaged; other sources: searched out, with an implication that what is found would be taken and so ransacked [1158]

[1240] 2 בָּעָה *bāᶜâ* 2x [Q] to boil; [N] to bulge, be swollen [1158]

[1242] בְּעוֹר *beᶜôr* 10x Beor, "[perhaps] *a burning*" [1160]

[1243] בִּעוּת *biᶜût* 2x terror [1161*]

[1244] 1 בֹּעַז *bōᶜaz* 22x Boaz, "[prob.] *in him is strength*" [1162]

[1246] בָּעַט *bāʿaṭ* 2x [Q] to kick (in scorn) [1163]

[1248] בְּעִיר *beʿîr* 6x animals, livestock, cattle [1165]

[1249] 1 בָּעַל *bāʿal* 15x [Q] to rule over; to marry, be a husband; [Qp, N] to be married, have a husband [1166]

[1251] 1 בַּעַל *baʿal* 161x 1) Baal (pagan god); 2) husband, master, owner, citizen; used in many phrases to indicate mastery of an object: "lord of arrows" is a master archer; "lord of dreams" is an interpreter of dreams, etc., "*master, owner, lord*" [1167] See *Baal.*

[1256] בַּעַל זְבוּב *baʿal zebûb* 4x Baal-Zebub, "*Baal [lord] of the flies*" [1176]

[1266] 1 בַּעֲלָה *baʿalâ* 4x mistress (of sorceries); (female) owner [1172 & 1180*]

[1277] 1 בָּעַר *bāʿar* 60x [Q] to burn; [P] to light a fire, set a blaze; [Pu] to be burning; [Ht] to start a fire, consume with fire [1197] See *blaze; burn; flare up; light (a fire).*

[1278] 2 בָּעַר *bāʿar* 24x [N] to be purged; [P] to purge, remove, get rid of; [H] to graze [1197]

[1279] 3 בָּעַר *bāʿar* 7x [Q] to be senseless, to be brutal; [N] to behave senseless [1197]

[1280] בַּעַר *baʿar* 5x senselessness, stupidity, ignorance, comparable to an animal [1198]

[1282] בְּעֵרָה *beʿērâ* 1x fire [1200]

[1284] בַּעְשָׁא *baʿšāʾ* 28x Baasha, "*boldness*" [1201]

[1286] בָּעַת *bāʿat* 16x [N] to be afraid, be terrified; [P] to torment, terrify, overwhelm [1204]

[1287] בְּעָתָה *beʿātâ* 2x terror [1205]

[1288] בֹּץ *bōṣ* 1x mud, silt [1206]

[1289] בִּצָּה *biṣṣâ* 3x marsh, swamp, waterlogged ground [1207]

[1290] בָּצוּר *bāṣûr* 25x fortified [1208*]

[1292] 1 בָּצִיר *bāṣîr* 7x grape harvest; grapes; vineyard [1210]

[1293] 2 בָּצִיר *bāṣîr* 1x dense, inaccessible (forest) [1210]

[1294] בָּצָל *bāṣāl* 1x onion [1211*]

[1295] בְּצַלְאֵל *beṣalʾēl* 9x Bezalel, "*in the shadow of God [El]*" [1212]

[1298] בָּצַע *bāṣaʿ* 16x [Q] to cut off; to be greedy, make unjust gain; [P] to cut off; to finish; to make unjust gain [1214]

[1299] בֶּצַע *beṣaʿ* 23x ill-gotten gain, dishonest gain; cutting off [1215]

[1301] 1 בָּצֵק *bāṣēq* 2x [Q] to swell, become swollen [1216]

[1302] 2 בָּצֵק *bāṣēq* 5x dough made of flour, not yet leavened [1217]

[1305] 1 בָּצַר *bāṣar* 7x [Q] to harvest, gather grapes [1219]

[1306] 2 בָּצַר *bāṣar* 1x [Q] to humble, break (the spirit) [1219]

[1307] 3 בָּצַר *bāṣar* 4x [N] to be impossible, be thwarted; [P] to strengthen, fortify [1219]

[1309] 1 בֶּצֶר *beṣer* 2x gold ore [1220 & 1222*]

[1312] 1 בָּצְרָה *boṣrâ* 1x pen, sheep-fold [1223]

[1313] 2 בָּצְרָה *boṣrâ* 8x Bozrah, "*enclosure (for sheep), fortress*" [1224]

[1314] בַּצָּרָה *baṣṣārâ* 3x drought; trouble [1226]

[1315] בִּצָּרוֹן *biṣṣārôn* 1x fortress, stronghold [1225]

[1316] בַּצֹּרֶת *baṣṣōret* 1x drought [1226]

[1318] בַּקְבֻּק *baqbuq* 3x jar; in some contexts a flask [1228]

[1323] בָּקִיעַ *bāqiaʿ* 2x breach (in a defense); bits, debris [1233*]

[1324] בָּקַע *bāqaʿ* 51x [Q] to divide, split, tear open; [N] to be split, burst open; [P] to split open, burst forth; [Pu] to be cracked open, broken through, ripped open; [H] to break through, divide; [Ho] to be broken through; [Ht] to split apart [1234] See *divide; split; tear open.*

[1325] בֶּ֫קַע *beqaʿ* 2x beka (half-shekel, one-fifth of an ounce [five or six grams]) [1235]

[1326] בִּקְעָה *biqʿâ* 20x valley, plain [1237]

[1327] 1 בָּקַק *bāqaq* 8x [Q] to lay waste, ruin, destroy; [N] to be laid waste; [P] to devastate [1238]

[1328] 2 בָּקַק *bāqaq* 1x [Q] to grow abundantly, spread out [1238]

[1329] בָּקַר *bāqar* 7x [P] to inspect, seek; look after; consider [1239]

[1330] בָּקָר *bāqār* 183x animal, cow, bull; cattle, oxen, herd [1241] See *bull; cattle; cow; herds; oxen.*

[1332] 2 בֹּ֫קֶר *bōqer* 213x morning [1242] See *dawn; daybreak; morning.*

[1333] בַּקָּרָה *baqqārâ* 1x looking after, caring for [1243]

[1334] בִּקֹּ֫רֶת *biqqōret* 1x due punishment (after investigation) [1244]

[1335] בָּקַשׁ *bāqaš* 225x [P] to seek, search, look for, inquire about; [Pu] be sought, be investigated [1245] See *intend; look for; search; seek; strive.*

[1336] בַּקָּשָׁה *baqqāšâ* 8x request [1246]

[1337] 1 בַּר *bar* 4x son (exclusively male in the OT); the phrase translated "Kiss the Son" (Ps 2:12) is an act of homage to a king [1248]

[1338] 2 בַּר *bar* 7x pure; empty; favorite; radiant, bright [1249]

[1339] 3 בַּר *bar* 13x grain, wheat, that has been cleansed and threshed [1250]

[1340] 4 בַּר *bar* 1x wilds, in the open field [1250]

[1341] 1 בֹּר *bōr* 5x cleanness [1252]

[1342] 2 בֹּר *bōr* 2x soda, potash, lye, used in making soap [1253]

[1343] 1 בָּרָא *bārāʾ* 48x [Q] to create, Creator; [N] to be created; can refer to creating from nothing as well as to reforming existing materials, as in "create in me a pure heart" (Ps 51:10) [1254]

[1344] 2 בָּרָא *bārāʾ* 1x [H] to fatten [1254]

[1345] 3 בָּרָא *bārāʾ* 5x [P] to cut, cut down, clear (a forest) [1254]

[1350] בַּרְבֻּר *barbur* 1x fowl, bird (of various species) [1257]

[1351] בָּרַד *bārad* 1x [Q] to shower hail [1258]

[1352] בָּרָד *bārād* 28x hail, hailstones [1259]

[1353] בָּרֹד *bārōd* 4x spotted, dappled [1261]

[1356] 1 בָּרָה *bārâ* 6x [Q] to eat; [H] to give to eat, urge to eat [1262 & 1274*]

[1358] בָּרוּךְ *bārûk* 26x Baruch, "*be blessed*" [1263]

[1359] בָּרוּר *bārûr* 2x pure, sincere [1305*]

[1360] בְּרוֹשׁ *berôš* 19x pine tree; some sources: cypress or fir [1265]

[1361] בְּרוֹת *berôt* 1x fir tree; some sources: juniper or cypress [1266*]

[1362] בָּרוּת *bārût* 1x food [1267]

[1366] בַּרְזֶל *barzel* 76x iron, iron (implements) [1270] See *ax; iron; stubborn.*

[1367] בַּרְזִלַּי *barzillay* 12x Barzillai, "*[made of] iron*" [1271]

[1368] 1 בָּרַח *bāraḥ* 63x [Q] to flee, run away, escape; [H] to drive out, make flee [1272] See *escape; flee.*

[1371] בָּרִחַ *bāriaḥ* 4x gliding; fugitive [1281]

[1374] בָּרִיא *bārîʾ* 14x fat, choice, healthy [1277]

[1375] בְּרִיאָה *berî'â* 1x created thing, with a possible implication that it is something new [1278]

[1376] בִּרְיָה *biryâ* 3x food; in context it refers to food for sick people [1279]

[1378] בְּרִיחַ *berîaḥ* 40x bar, gate bar, crossbar [1280]

[1382] בְּרִית *berît* 287x covenant, treaty, compact, agreement, an association between two parties with various responsibilities, benefits, and penalties; "to cut a covenant" is "make a covenant," a figure of the act of ceremonially cutting an animal into two parts, with an implication of serious consequences for not fulfilling the covenant [1285] See *covenant; treaty.*

[1383] בֹּרִית *bōrît* 2x soap, made from soap plants or potash [1287]

[1384] 1 בָּרַךְ *bārak* 3x [Q] to kneel down; [H] to make kneel [1288]

[1385] 2 בָּרַךְ *bārak* 327x [P] to bless, pronounce blessings, give praise, give thanks, extol; [Qp, N, Pu] to be blessed, be praised; [Ht] to bless oneself, be blessed; this can mean to speak words invoking divine favor (bless), or speak of the excellence of someone (praise) [1288] See *bless; praise.*

[1386] בֶּרֶךְ *berek* 25x knee, the "buckling of the knees" means to falter, implying great fear or despair; "to bow the knee" means to be reverent or submissive [1290]

[1388] 1 בְּרָכָה *berākâ* 71x blessing; gift [1293] See *blessing; gift.*

[1391] בְּרֵכָה *berēkâ* 18x (man-made) pool, reservoir [1295]

[1394] בְּרֹמִים *berōmîm* 1x multicolored, a fabric of two-color webbing [1264]

[1397] בָּרַק *bāraq* 1x [Q] to flash lightning [1299]

[1398] 1 בָּרָק *bārāq* 21x lightning bolt, flash of lightning [1300]

[1399] 2 בָּרָק *bārāq* 14x Barak, "*lightning*" [1301]

[1402] בַּרְקָן *barqōn* 2x brier, a thorny plant [1303*]

[1403] בָּרֶקֶת *bāreqet* 2x beryl (a green stone, exact identification uncertain) [1304*]

[1404] בָּרְקַת *bārᵉqat* 1x beryl (a green stone, exact identification uncertain) [1304]

[1405] 1 בָּרַר *bārar* 15x [Q] to purge; [Qp] to be chosen, be choice; [N] to keep clean, be pure; [P] purify; [H] to cleanse; [Ht] to show oneself pure [1305]

[1406] 2 בָּרַר *bārar* 2x [Qp] to be sharpened, polished, [H] to sharpen [1305]

[1411] בֹּשֶׂם *bōśem* 30x spices, perfume, fragrance; this can refer to balsam oil or to perfume in general [1313* & 1314]

[1412] בָּשְׂמַת *bāśᵉmat* 7x Basemath, "*fragrant*" [1315]

[1413] בָּשַׂר *bāśar* 24x [P] to bring (good) news, proclaim (good) news; [Ht] to hear news [1319]

[1414] בָּשָׂר *bāśār* 270x flesh, the soft tissue mass of any animal; the whole body; particular parts of the body: meat, skin, genitals, etc.; by extension: humankind, living things [1320] See *flesh; meat.*

[1415] בְּשׂרָה *beśōrâ* 6x news, good news [1309]

[1418] בָּשַׁל *bāšal* 28x [Q] to ripen; boil; [P] to cook, boil, roast, bake; [Pu] to be cooked, be boiled; [H] ripen [1310]

[1419] בָּשֵׁל *bāšēl* 2x cooked, boiled [1311]

[1421] 1 בָּשָׁן *bāšān* 60x Bashan, "*fertile stoneless plain*" [1316]

[1423] בָּשְׁנָה *bošnâ* 1x disgrace, shame [1317]

[1424] בָּשַׁס *bāšas* 1x [Po] to trample [1318]

[1425] בֹּשֶׁת *bōšet* 30x shame, disgrace, humiliation [1322]

[1426] 1 בַּת *bat* 587x daughter, female child of any generation (granddaughter, etc.); by extension: any female, girl, woman; a term of endearment; fig., outlying village or settlement (of a "mother" city) [1323] See *daughter; girl; granddaughter; settlement; village.*

[1427] 2 בַּת *bat* 14x bath (liquid measure, equal to an ephah, about six gallons [about 22 liters]; some sources: eight to nine gallons) [1324]

[1428] 3 בַּת *bat* 1x woven garment [1004]

[1429] בָּתָה *bātâ* 1x wasteland [1326]

[1431] בַּתָּה *battâ* 1x steep ravine, face of a cliff [1327]

[1432] 1 בְּתוּאֵל *b^e^tûʾēl* 9x Bethuel, "*man of God [El]*" [1328]

[1435] בְּתוּלָה *b^e^tûlâ* 50x virgin, maiden; a marriageable woman who has never had sexual intercourse and still under the authority of her father; (unmarried) young woman [1330] See *virgin; young woman.*

[1436] בְּתוּלִים *b^e^tûlîm* 9x virginity; proof of virginity, referring to a cloth with blood from a virgin's first sexual encounter [1331]

[1438] בָּתַק *bātaq* 1x [P] to hack to pieces, slaughter [1333]

[1439] בָּתַר *bātar* 2x [Q, P] to cut in pieces [1334]

[1440] 1 בֶּתֶר *beter* 3x piece [1335]

[1441] 2 בֶּתֶר *beter* 1x ruggedness, referring to mountains with rugged ravines [1336]

[1444] בַּת־שֶׁבַע *bat-šebaʿ* 12x Bathsheba, "*seventh daughter* or *daughter of an oath*" [1339]

[1447] גֵּא *gēʾ* 1x proud, arrogant [1341]

[1448] גָּאָה *gāʾâ* 7x [Q] to grow tall, be high, to rise up; by extension: to be exalted [1342]

[1449] גֵּאָה *gēʾâ* 1x pride, arrogance [1344]

[1450] גֵּאֶה *gēʾeh* 8x proud, arrogant [1343]

[1452] גַּאֲוָה *gaʾ^a^wâ* 18x surging; majesty, glory, triumph; pride, arrogance, conceit [1346]

[1453] גְּאוּלִים *g^e^ʾûlîm* 1x redemption, with an implication that the redemption involves recompense [1350*]

[1454] גָּאוֹן *gāʾôn* 49x surging (waves), lush (high) thickets; majesty, splendor, glory; pride, arrogance [1347]

[1455] גֵּאוּת *gēʾût* 8x surging (sea), rising (smoke); majesty, glory; pride, arrogance [1348]

[1456] גַּאֲיוֹן *gaʾ^a^yôn* 1x arrogant, proud [1349]

[1457] 1 גָּאַל *gāʾal* 104x [Q] to redeem, deliver; (n.) avenger; kinsman-redeemer; [Qp] to be redeemed; [N] to be redeemed, redeem oneself; often this redemption is in the context of saving from danger or hostility, as a figure of purchasing a slave or indentured person. A "kinsman-redeemer" purchases a relative from slavery (actual or potential); a "kinsman-avenger" provides justice on behalf of a relative; both concepts are in the image of God as Redeemer [1350] See *avenge; ransom; redeem.*

[1458] 2 גָּאַל *gāʾal* 11x [N] to be stained, defiled; [P] to defile; [Pu] to be unclean, defiled; [H/Aphel] to stain; [Ht] to defile oneself [1351]

[1459] גֹּאַל *gōʾal* 1x defilement [1352]

[1460] גְּאֻלָּה *g^e^ʾullâ* 14x redemption (of a person or object); right of redemption; blood relatives; see also 1457 [1353]

[1461] 1 גַּב *gab* 10x eyebrow; rim (of a wheel); mound, back [1354]

[1462] 2 גַּב *gab* 2x defense [1354]

[1463] 1 גֵּב *gēb* 3x ditch; cistern [1356]

[1464] 2 גֵּב *gēb* 1x an architectural structure variously interpretated: beam, rafter, paneling [1356]

[1465] גֶּבֶא *gebe'* 2x cistern; marsh [1360]

[1466] גֵּבָה *gēbâ* 1x swarm (of locust) [1357*]

[1467] גָּבַהּ *gābah* 33x [Q] to be tall, tower high; to exalt; to be proud, haughty, arrogant; [H] to make high, grow tall; exalt; the attitude of pride or arrogance is a fig. extension the base meaning of being tall or high; something that is "too high" cannot be understood [1361]

[1468] גָּבֵהַּ *gābēah* 4x high, towered; proud, haughty; the attitude of pride or arrogance is a fig. extension the base meaning of being tall or high [1362 & 1364]

[1469] גָּבֹהַּ *gābōah* 38x high, tall; proud, haughty; the attitude of pride or arrogance is a fig. extension the base meaning of being tall or high [1364]

[1470] גֹּבַהּ *gōbah* 18x tallness, height; splendor, majesty; pride, haughtiness, conceit; the attitude of pride or arrogance is a fig. extension the base meaning of being tall or high [1363]

[1471] גַּבְהוּת *gabhût* 2x arrogance [1365]

[1473] גְּבוּל *g^ebûl* 241x territory, boundary, border [1366] See *border; boundary; coast; territory.*

[1474] גְּבוּלָה *g^ebûlâ* 2x boundary stone, border marker [1367]

[1475] גִּבּוֹר *gibbôr* 159x mighty one, mighty warrior, special guard [1368]

[1476] גְּבוּרָה *g^ebûrâ* 62x power, strength, might, achievement [1369] See *might; power; strength.*

[1477] גִּבֵּחַ *gibbēaḥ* 1x bald forehead [1371]

[1478] גַּבַּחַת *gabbaḥat* 4x bald spot on the forehead; bare spot on cloth [1372]

[1479] גֹּבַי *gōbay* 2x swarm of locust [1462*]

[1482] גְּבִינָה *g^ebînâ* 1x cheese [1385]

[1483] גָּבִיעַ *gābîaʿ* 14x cup, (drinking) bowl [1375]

[1484] גְּבִיר *g^ebîr* 2x lord, master [1376]

[1485] גְּבִירָה *g^ebîrâ* 13x mistress (female lord); queen [1377]

[1486] גָּבִישׁ *gābîš* 1x jasper [1378]

[1487] גָּבַל *gābal* 5x [Q] to set up a boundary; [H] to put limits around (a geographical area) [1379]

[1491] גַּבְלֻת *gablut* 2x braided (gold chain) [1383]

[1492] גִּבֵּן *gibbēn* 1x hunchbacked [1384]

[1493] גַּבְנֹן *gabnôn* 2x ruggedness; a many-peaked mountain range with an appearance that suggests wonder and majesty [1386]

[1494] גֶּבַע *gebaʿ* 15x Geba, "*hill*" [1387]

[1496] 1 גִּבְעָה *gibʿâ* 66x hill, hill top, height [1389] See *height; hill.*

[1497] 2 גִּבְעָה *gibʿâ* 49x Gibeah, "*mound, hill*" [1390]

[1498] גִּבְעוֹנִי *gibʿônî* 8x Gibeonite, of Gibeon, "*of Gibeon*" [1393]

[1499] גִּבְעֹל *gibʿōl* 1x bloom [1392]

[1500] גִּבְעוֹן *gibʿōn* 39x Gibeon, "*mound, hill*" [1391]

[1504] גָּבַר *gābar* 25x [Q] to rise, flood; to be greater, stronger; to prevail, overwhelm; [P] to strengthen; [H] to cause to triumph, confirm (a covenant); [Ht] to show oneself as a victor [1396 & 1399*]

[1505] 1 גֶּבֶר *geber* 66x (strong, young) man [1397] See *man.*

[1508] גַּבְרִיאֵל *gabrîʾēl* 2x Gabriel, "*[strong] man of God [El]*" [1403]

[1509] גְּבֶרֶת *g^eberet* 2x queen [1404]

[1511] גָּג *gāg* 30x roof, top [1406]

[1512] 1 גַּד *gad* 2x coriander [1407]

[1513] 2 גַּד *gad* 2x good fortune; (as a pagan god) Fortune [1408 & 1409*]

[1514] גָּד *gād* 70x Gad, "*fortune*" [1410]

[1517] 1 גָּדַד *gādad* 5x [Htpolal] to cut oneself, slash oneself [1413]

[1518] 2 גָּדַד *gādad* 3x [Q] to band together; [Htpolal] to band together against [1413]

[1521] 1 גְּדוּד *g^edûd* 1x ridge (of a furrow) [1417]

[1522] 2 גְּדוּד *g^edûd* 33x band of raiders; band of rebels; bandits; troops, divisions [1416]

[1523] גְּדוּדָה *g^edûdâ* 1x slash, cut (of the skin) [1418]

[1524] גָּדוֹל *gādôl* 527x great, large; much, more; this can refer to physical size, quantity, degree, and social status (great king, high priest) [1419] See *great; large.*

[1525] גְּדוּלָּה *g^edûllâ* 12x greatness, majesty, recognition, honor [1420]

[1526] גִּדּוּף *giddûp* 2x taunt, scorn, reviling [1421]

[1527] גְּדוּפָה *g^edûpâ* 1x taunt, scorn, reviling [1422]

[1528] גִּדּוּפָה *giddûpâ* 1x insult [1421]

[1531] גְּדִי *g^edî* 17x (male) young goat [1423]

[1532] 1 גָּדִי *gādî* 15x Gadite, of Gad, "*of Gad*" [1425]

[1536] גִּדְיָה *gidyâ* 4x bank (of a river) [1428]

[1537] גְּדִיָּה *g^ediyyâ* 1x (female) young goat [1429]

[1538] 1 גָּדִישׁ *gādîš* 3x shock of grain, sheaf of grain [1430]

[1539] 2 גָּדִישׁ *gādîš* 1x tomb [1430]

[1540] גָּדַל *gādal* 117x [Q] to grow up; be great, exalted; [P] to grow long, make great; to exalt, honor, glorify; [Pu] to be well-nurtured; [H] to make great, cause greatness; [Ht] to magnify oneself, show greatness; see also 1524 [1431] See *exalt; (be) great; magnify.*

[1541] גָּדֵל *gādēl* 4x great, powerful [1432]

[1542] גֹּדֶל *gōdel* 13x greatness, majesty, strength; pride, arrogance [1433]

[1544] גָּדִל *gādil* 2x tassel, festoon [1434]

[1546] גְּדַלְיָהוּ *g^edalyāhû* 26x Gedaliah, "*great is Yahweh*" [1436]

[1548] גָּדַע *gādaʿ* 23x [Q] to cut short, cut off, break; [P] to cut down, cut to pieces; [Qp, N, Pu] to be cut off, be cut down [1438]

[1549] גִּדְעוֹן *gidʿôn* 39x Gideon, "*one who cuts, hacks*" [1439]

[1552] גָּדַף *gādap* 7x [P] to blaspheme, revile [1442]

[1553] גָּדַר *gādar* 10x [Q] to build a stone wall, heap up stones for a wall [1443]

[1555] גָּדֵר *gādēr* 14x wall, fence, a wall made of loose stones from the field without mortar [1444* & 1447]

[1556] 1 גְּדֵרָה *g^edērâ* 9x wall, pen (for sheep) made of stone walls [1448]

[1564] גָּהָה *gāhâ* 1x [Q] to heal [1455]

[1565] גֵּהָה *gēhâ* 1x healing, cure; that which promotes healing: medicine [1456]

[1566] גָּהַר *gāhar* 3x [Q] to bow down; stretch out in prostration [1457]

[1567] גַּו *gaw* 3x back (of the body); "to thrust behind the back" means "to reject" [1458]

[1568] 1 גֵּו *gēw* 7x back (of the body); "to walk upon the back" is a sign of conquest and subjugation; "to send sin behind the back" is "to forgive" [1460]

[1569] 2 גֵּו *gēw* 1x fellow people, community [1460]

[1573] גּוֹג *gôg* 10x Gog, "*precious golden object*" [1463]

[1574] גּוּד *gûd* 3x [Q] to attack, invade [1464]

[1575] 1 גֵּוָה *gēwâ* 3x pride, lifting up [1467]

[1576] 2 גֵּוָה *gēwâ* 1x back (of the body) [1465 & 1466]

[1577] גּוּז *gûz* 2x [Q] to pass along, pass away [1468]

[1578] גּוֹזָל *gôzāl* 2x young bird, hatchling [1469]

[1580] גּוֹי *gôy* 567x people, nation; regularly in the OT, any people in contrast to Israel: the Gentiles, pagan, heathen, uncultured [1471] See *Gentile; nation; pagan.*

[1581] גְּוִיָּה *g^e^wiyyâ* 13x dead body, corpse; carcass [1472]

[1582] גּוֹיִם *gôyim* 3x Goiim, Goyim, "*nation, Gentiles*" [1471*]

[1583] גּוֹלָה *gôlâ* 41x exile, captive, people deported to another place [1473]

[1585] גּוּמָּץ *gûmmāṣ* 1x pit [1475]

[1588] גָּוַע *gāwaʿ* 24x [Q] to perish, die, breath one's last [1478]

[1589] גּוּף *gûp* 1x [H] to shut (a door) [1479]

[1590] גּוּפָה *gûpâ* 2x dead body, corpse [1480]

[1591] 1 גּוּר *gûr* 82x [Q] to live as an alien, dwell as a stranger, implying less social rights than a native; [Htpol] to stay, gather together [1481] See *dwell; live; settle; stay.*

[1592] 2 גּוּר *gûr* 6x [Q] to attack, stir up [1481]

[1593] 3 גּוּר *gûr* 10x [Q] to be terrified, be afraid, fear; to revere [1481]

[1594] 4 גּוּר *gûr* 7x cub (young of lions, jackals) [1482]

[1596] גּוֹר *gôr* 2x cub (of lion) [1484]

[1598] גּוֹרָל *gôrāl* 77x lot, device by which a decision was made, often a pebble, stick, or pottery shard either thrown or blindly pulled from a container; by extension: what is decided by lot, allotment (of land) [1486] See *lot.*

[1599] גּוּשׁ *gûš* 1x scab, something crusted [1487]

[1600] גֵּז *gēz* 4x fleece, sheared wool; grass mowed [1488]

[1601] גִּזְבָּר *gizbār* 1x treasurer [1489]

[1602] גָּזָה *gāzâ* 1x [Q] to bring forth, cut off (the umbilical cord) [1491]

[1603] גִּזָּה *gizzâ* 7x wool fleece [1492*]

[1605] גָּזַז *gāzaz* 15x [Q] to shear sheep; to shave one's head (in mourning) [1494]

[1607] גָּזִית *gāzît* 11x dressed stone, stone hewn or cut for masonry [1496]

[1608] גָּזַל *gāzal* 30x [Q] to rob, seize, snatch, take way; [Qp, N] to be robbed, be forcibly taken from [1497]

[1609] גֶּזֶל *gēzel* 2x denial of rights [1499]

[1610] גָּזֵל *gāzēl* 4x stealing, robbery, implying violence [1498]

[1611] גְּזֵלָה *g^e^zēlâ* 6x plunder, spoil, stolen things [1500]

[1612] גָּזָם *gāzām* 3x locust swarm; some sources: caterpillar or a specific state in the development of a locust [1501]

[1614] גֶּזַע *gezaʿ* 3x stump, root stock [1503]

[1615] 1 גָּזַר *gāzar* 12x [Q] to cut in two, divide, cut down; decide on; to disappear; [N] to be cut off, be excluded [1504]

[1616] 2 גָּזַר *gāzar* 1x [Q] to devour, eat, with a possible focus on carving or chewing up food [1504]

[1617] 1 גֶּזֶר *gezer* 2x pieces (something divided and cut up) [1506]

[1618] 2 גֶּזֶר *gezer* 5x Gezer, "[poss.] *pieces*" [1507]

[1619] גִּזְרָה *gizrâ* 8x courtyard; appearance [1508]

[1620] גְּזֵרָה *g^e^zērâ* 1x solitary place, unfertile land [1509]

[1623] גָּחוֹן *gāḥôn* 2x belly (of reptile) [1512]

[1624] גַּחַל *gaḥal* 15x burning coals, hot embers [1513*]

[1625] גַּחֶלֶת *gaḥelet* 2x burning coals [1513*]

[1628] גַּיְא *gay*ʾ 58x valley [1516]

[1630] גִּיד *gîd* 7x sinew, tendon [1517]

[1631] 1 גִּיחַ *gîaḥ* 6x [Q] to burst forth, surge, bring forth (a baby); [H] to charge; to thrash about [1518]

[1633] גִּיחוֹן *gîḥôn* 2x Gihon, "*to gush forth*" [1521]

[1634] גֵּיחֲזִי *gêḥ^a^zî* 11x Gehazi, "[poss.] *valley of vision*" [1522]

[1635] 1 גִּיל *gîl* 30x [Q] to rejoice, be glad, be joyful, the attitude and action of favorable circumstance, often expressed in shouts and song [1523]

[1636] 2 גִּיל *gîl* 1x age, stage in life [1524]

[1637] 3 גִּיל *gîl* 8x gladness, delight, jubilance; see also 1635 [1524]

[1638] גִּילָה *gîlâ* 2x rejoicing, delight [1525]

[1643] 1 גַּל *gal* 18x heap, pile (of rocks, rubble) [1530]

[1644] 2 גַּל *gal* 16x waves, breaker waves, surging waves; fountain [1530]

[1645] גֵּל *gēl* 3x dung, excrement, used for fuel in some contexts [1561*]

[1647] גַּלָּב *gallāb* 1x barber [1532]

[1648] גִּלְבֹּעַ *gilbōa*ʿ 8x Gilboa, "*bubbling*" [1533]

[1649] 1 גַּלְגַּל *galgal* 9x wheel; whirlwind [1534]

[1650] 2 גַּלְגַּל *galgal* 2x tumbleweed (a wheel-shaped plant) [1534]

[1651] 1 גִּלְגָּל *gilgāl* 1x wheel [1536]

[1652] 2 גִּלְגָּל *gilgāl* 40x Gilgal, "*circle of stones*" [1537]

[1653] גֻּלְגֹּלֶת *gulgōlet* 12x skull; individual, person [1538]

[1654] גֶּלֶד *gēled* 1x skin [1539*]

[1655] גָּלָה *gālâ* 187x [Q] to tell, uncover, reveal; depart, leave, be exiled, banished; [Qp] to be opened, unseal; be made known; [N] to be revealed, be exposed; [P] to reveal, expose (nakedness) = sexual relations; [Pu] to be opened, exiled; [H] to deport, exile [1540] See *depart; exile; expose; have sexual relations with; reveal.*

[1657] גֻּלָּה *gullâ* 15x spring (of water); bowl-shaped capital (of a pillar) [1543]

[1658] גִּלּוּלִים *gillûlîm* 48x (pl.) idols [1544*] See *idol.*

[1659] גְּלוֹם *g^e^lôm* 1x fabric [1545]

[1661] גָּלוּת *gālût* 15x exile, captive [1546]

[1662] גָּלַח *gālaḥ* 23x [P] to shave off, cut off; [Pu] be shaved off; [Ht] to have oneself shaven, shave oneself [1548]

[1663] גִּלָּיוֹן *gillāyôn* 2x scroll (some sources: wooden tablet with a wax cover); mirror [1549]

[1664] 1 גָּלִיל *gālîl* 4x turnable (door); rings; rods [1550]

[1665] 2 גָּלִיל *gālîl* 6x Galilee, "*ring, circle,* hence *region*" [1551]

[1666] גְּלִילָה *gelîlâ* 3x region, district [1552]

[1669] גָּלְיָת *golyāt* 6x Goliath, "*exile*" [1555]

[1670] 1 גָּלַל *gālal* 17x [Q] to roll down, roll away; to commit, turn over; [N] to be rolled; [P] to roll; [Polal] to be rolled; [Htpol] to roll about, wallow; "to commit, trust" is a figure of rolling care or responsibilty onto the Lord [1556]

[1672] 1 גָּלָל *gālāl* 2x dung, filth [1557]

[1673] 2 גָּלָל *gālāl* 10x because of, on account of, for the sake of [1558]

[1675] גִּלֲלַי *gilalay* 1x Gilalai [1562]

[1676] גָּלַם *gālam* 1x [Q] to roll up (clothing in a tight ball) [1563]

[1677] גֹּלֶם *gōlem* 1x unformed body, embryo [1564]

[1678] גַּלְמוּד *galmûd* 4x barren, haggard [1565]

[1679] גָּלַע *gālaʿ* 3x [Ht] to burst out (in quarrel); to defy [1566]

[1680] גִּלְעָד *gilʿād* 102x Gilead, "[perhaps] *monument of stones*" [1568]

[1682] גִּלְעָדִי *gilʿādî* 11x Gileadite, of Gilead, "*of Gilead*" [1569]

[1683] גָּלַשׁ *gālaš* 2x [Q] to descend; some sources: to leap, frisk [1570]

[1685] גַּם *gam* 769x also, surely, too; and, but, yet, even, moreover [1571]

[1686] גָּמָא *gāmāʾ* 2x [P] to eat up, swallow up; [H] to give water (to sip) [1572]

[1687] גֹּמֶא *gōmeʾ* 4x papyrus [1573]

[1688] גֹּמֶד *gōmed* 1x unit of measure: short cubit (the length from the elbow to the knuckles, about 12 to 18 inches) [1574]

[1691] גְּמוּל *gemûl* 19x what is done; benefit; what is deserved, recompense [1576]

[1692] גְּמוּלָה *gemûlâ* 3x what is done; retribution, recompense [1578]

[1694] גָּמַל *gāmal* 37x [Q] to do, produce, deal fully; to wean; to repay (what is deserved); [Qp, N] to be weaned [1580]

[1695] גָּמָל *gāmāl* 54x camel [1581] See *camel.*

[1698] גָּמַר *gāmar* 5x [Q] to bring to an end, fail; fulfill [1584]

[1699] 1 גֹּמֶר *gōmer* 5x Gomer, "*complete*" [1586]

[1703] גַּן *gan* 41x garden [1588]

[1704] גָּנַב *gānab* 40x [Q] to steal, be a thief, kidnap; to deceive; [Qp, N, Pu] to be stolen, forcibly carried off; [Ht] to steal oneself away, sneak in [1589]

[1705] גַּנָּב *gannāb* 17x thief; kidnapper [1590]

[1706] גְּנֵבָה *genēbâ* 2x stolen possession [1591]

[1708] גַּנָּה *gannâ* 16x garden, grove [1593 & 1594*]

[1709] 1 גֶּנֶז *genez* 2x (royal) treasury [1595]

[1710] 2 גֶּנֶז *genez* 1x rug [1595]

[1711] גַּנְזַךְ *ganzak* 1x (temple) storeroom, where treasures are kept [1597*]

[1713] גָּנַן *gānan* 8x [Q] to defend, shield, protect [1598]

[1716] גָּעָה *gāʿâ* 2x [Q] to bellow, low (of cattle) [1600]

[1718] גָּעַל *gāʿal* 10x [Q] to abhor, despise, loathe; [N] to be defiled; [H] to cause defiling = fail to impregnate [1602]

[1719] גֹּעַל *gōʿal* 1x despising, loathing [1604]

[1721] גָּעַר *gāʿar* 14x [Q] to rebuke, reprimand; prevent (insects) [1605]

[1722] גְּעָרָה *geʿārâ* 15x rebuke; threat [1606]

[1723] גָּעַשׁ *gāʿaš* 9x [Q] to shake, tremble; [Pu] to be shaken; [Ht] to shake back and forth, stagger, surge, tremble back and forth [1607]

[1726] 1 גַּף *gap* 1x height, elevation [1610]

[1727] 2 גַּף *gap* 3x body; by oneself [with 928] [1610]

[1728] גֶּפֶן *gepen* 55x vine, grapevine [1612] See *vine.*

[1729] גֹּפֶר *gōper* 1x cypress (wood); exact identity of the wood is uncertain; "gopher wood" is simply a transliteration of the Hebrew [1613]

[1730] גָּפְרִית *goprît* 7x sulfur; older versions: brimstone [1614]

[1731] גֵּר *gēr* 92x alien, stranger (in a foreign land) [1616] See *alien; sojourner; strange(r).*

[1732] גִּר *gir* 1x chalk [1615]

[1734] גָּרָב *gārāb* 3x festering sore [1618]

[1737] גַּרְגַּר *gargar* 1x ripe olives [1620]

[1738] גַּרְגְּרוֹת *gargerôt* 4x neck, throat [1621]

[1740] גָּרַד *gārad* 1x [Ht] to scrape oneself (with a broken piece of pottery) [1623]

[1741] גָּרָה *gārâ* 14x [P] to stir up (a dispute); [Ht] to provoke (to war), engage (to battle) [1624]

[1742] 1 גֵּרָה *gērâ* 11x cud [625]

[1743] 2 גֵּרָה *gērâ* 5x gerah (measure, one-twentieth of a shekel, about half a gram) [1626]

[1744] גָּרוֹן *gārôn* 8x throat, neck; by extension: mouth; an "outstretched neck" is a sign of arrogance and possibly of sexual misconduct [1627]

[1746] גָּרַז *gāraz* 1x [N] to be cut off, implying destruction [1629]

[1748] גְּרִזִים *gerizîm* 4x Gerizim [1630]

[1749] גַּרְזֶן *garzen* 4x ax, chisel [1631]

[1750] 1 גָּרַם *gāram* 1x [Q] to leave, reserve [1633]

[1751] 2 גָּרַם *gāram* 2x [P] to break, to break bones [1633]

[1752] גֶּרֶם *gerem* 5x bone, rawboned, bony; bareness [1634]

[1755] גֹּרֶן *gōren* 36x threshing floor [1637]

[1756] גָּרַס *gāras* 2x [Q] to be crushed; [H] to break, crush [1638]

[1757] 1 גָּרַע *gāraʿ* 21x [Q] to take away, reduce, hinder; [Qp] to be cut off (of a beard); [N] to be reduced, be taken away, to disappear [1639]

[1758] 2 גָּרַע *gāraʿ* 1x [P] to draw up (drops of water) [1639]

[1759] גָּרַף *gārap* 1x [Q] to sweep away (of a river) [1640]

[1760] גָּרַר *gārar* 5x [Q] to chew; to drag away; [Polal] to be sawn; [Htpol] to drive, swirl [1641]

[1761] גְּרָר *gerār* 10x Gerar, "*circle, region*" [1642]

[1762] גֶּרֶשׂ *gereś* 2x (coarse) crushed grain, grits, groats [1643]

[1763] 1 גָּרַשׁ *gāraš* 46x [Q] to drive out; [Qp] to be divorced; [N] to be banished; [P] to drive out, expel [Pu] to be banished [1644]

[1764] 2 גָּרַשׁ *gāraš* 3x [Q] to cast up, toss up; [N] to be tossed, be stirred up [1644]

[1765] גֶּרֶשׁ *gereš* 1x yield, produce [1645]

[1766] גְּרֻשָׁה *gerušâ* 1x dispossession [1646]

[1767] גֵּרְשׁוֹן *gēršôn* 17x Gershon, "*temporary resident there*" [1648]

[1768] גֵּרְשֹׁם *gēršōm* 14x Gershom, Gershon, "*temporary resident there*" [1647]

[1769] גֵּרְשֻׁנִּי *gēršunnî* 13x Gershonite, "*of Gershon*" [1649]

[1770] גְּשׁוּר *gᵉšûr* 9x Geshur, "*bridge*" [1650]

[1771] גְּשׁוּרִי *gᵉšûrî* 6x Geshurite, people of Geshur, "*of Geshur*" [1651]

[1772] גָּשַׁם *gāšam* 1x [H] to bring rain [1652]

[1773] 1 גֶּשֶׁם *gešem* 35x rain, shower, downpour [1653]

[1777] גֹּשֶׁן *gōšen* 15x Goshen, "*mound of earth*" [1657]

[1779] גָּשַׁשׁ *gāšaš* 2x [P] to grope along, feel one's way (as if blind) [1659]

[1780] 1 גַּת *gat* 5x winepress; also used as a hiding place [1660]

[1781] 2 גַּת *gat* 34x Gath, "*winepress*" [1661]

[1787] גִּתִּית *gittît* 3x gittith: unknown musical term, possibly the name of the tune, or the name of the instrument that played it, or even related in some way to ceremonies associated with the winepress [1665]

[1790] דָּאַב *dā'ab* 3x [Q] to be dim (of eyes); to sorrow [1669]

[1791] דְּאָבָה *dᵉ'ābâ* 1x dismay, despair [1670]

[1792] דְּאָבוֹן *dᵉ'ābôn* 1x despair [1671]

[1793] דָּאַג *dā'ag* 7x [Q] to worry, dread, be troubled, be afraid [1672]

[1794] דָּאג *dā'g* 1x fish [1709]

[1795] דֹּאֵג *dō'ēg* 6x Doeg, "*anxious*" [1673]

[1796] דְּאָגָה *dᵉ'āgâ* 6x fear, anxiety, restlessness [1674]

[1797] 1 דָּאָה *dā'â* 5x [Q] to swoop down, pounce; to soar [1675]

[1798] 2 דָּאָה *dā'â* 1x red kite (bird) [1676]

[1800] דֹּב *dōb* 12x bear (animal) [1677]

[1801] דֹּבֶא *dōbe'* 1x strength [1679]

[1803] דָּבַב *dābab* 1x [Q] to flow over gently [1680]

[1804] דִּבָּה *dibbâ* 9x bad report, slander, bad reputation, whisper [1681]

[1805] 1 דְּבוֹרָה *dᵉbôrâ* 4x wild honey bee; (pl.) swarm of bees [1682]

[1806] 2 דְּבוֹרָה *dᵉbôrâ* 10x Deborah, "*hornet, wasp, wild honey bee*" [1683]

[1807] דִּבְיֹנִים *dibyōnîm* 1x seed pods or doves' dung [1686*]

[1808] 1 דְּבִיר *dᵉbîr* 15x inner sanctuary, referring to the Most Holy Place [1687]

[1811] דְּבֵלָה *dᵉbēlâ* 5x pressed fig cakes; poultice of figs [1690]

[1815] דָּבַק *dābaq* 55x [Q] to be united, hold fast, keep, cling to; [H] to overtake, cause to cleave, press hard upon; [Pu] to be joined fast, be stuck together; [Ho] be made to cleave, stick to; from the base joining or fastening objects together comes the figure of close association of people [1692] See *overtake.*

[1816] דָּבֵק *dābēq* 3x holding fast, sticking to [1695]

[1817] דֶּבֶק *debeq* 3x welding; sections (of armor) [1694]

[1818] 1 דָּבַר *dābar* 5x [P] to depart; to destroy; [H] to subdue [1696]

[1819] 2 דָּבַר *dābar* 1,136x [Q, P, Ht] to say, speak, tell, command, promise; [Qp, Pu] to be spoken (of); [N] to speak together; a general term for verbal communication, note the specific contextual translations in the NIV [1696] See *speak; word.*

[1821] דָּבָר *dābār* 1,454x what is said, word (or any unit of speech such as a clause, or the whole of communication); matter (any event); thing (any object) [1697] See *affair; case; commandment; matter; report; word.*

[1822] 1 דֶּבֶר *deber* 49x plague, pestilence, disease, a pandemic occurrence of sickness and death; some sources identify specific diseases in specific contexts [1698]

[1824] דֹּבֶר *dōber* 2x pasture, in a remote place [1699]

[1825] דִּבֵּר *dibbēr* 1x word (of God) [1699]

[1826] דִּבְרָה *dibrâ* 5x cause; order; therefore, because [1700]

[1827] דֹּבְרוֹת *dōberôt* 1x raft, a collection of logs towed behind a ship [1702*]

[1830] דַּבֶּרֶת *dabberet* 1x instruction, word [1703*]

[1831] דְּבַשׁ *debaš* 54x honey [1706] See *honey.*

[1832] 1 דַּבֶּשֶׁת *dabbešet* 1x hump (of a camel) [1707]

[1834] דָּג *dāg* 18x fish [1709]

[1835] 1 דָּגָה *dāgâ* 1x [Q] to increase, multiply [1711]

[1836] 2 דָּגָה *dāgâ* 15x fish [1710]

[1837] דָּגוֹן *dāgôn* 13x Dagon (pagan god), "*[god of] grain; fish*" [1712]

[1838] 1 דָּגַל *dāgal* 1x [Qp] to be outstanding, be conspicuous [1713]

[1839] 2 דָּגַל *dāgal* 3x [Q] to lift a banner; [N] be gathered around the banner(s), organized as troops [1713]

[1840] דֶּגֶל *degel* 14x standard, banner [1714]

[1841] דָּגָן *dāgān* 40x grain [1715]

[1842] דָּגַר *dāgar* 2x [Q] to care for; hatch eggs [1716]

[1843] דַּד *dad* 4x bosom, breast [1717]

[1844] דָּדָה *dādâ* 2x [Ht] to walk, lead [1718]

[1850] דָּהַם *dāham* 1x [N] to be taken by surprise, be astounded [1724]

[1851] דָּהַר *dāhar* 1x [Q] to gallop [1725]

[1852] דַּהֲרָה *dahărâ* 2x galloping [1726]

[1853] דּוּב *dûb* 1x [H] to drain away, wear away; loss of life as a fig. extension of draining liquid out of a container [1727]

[1854] דַּוָּג *dawwāg* 1x fisherman [1728]

[1855] דּוּגָה *dûgâ* 1x fishing (hooks) [1729]

[1856] דּוֹד *dôd* 61x uncle, cousin, relative; beloved one, lover; a term of endearment ranging from friendship and familial affection to romantic love [1730] See *beloved; cousin; uncle.*

[1857] דּוּד *dûd* 8x basket; kettle, caldron, pot [1731]

[1858] דָּוִד *dāwid* 1,075x David, "*beloved one*" [1732]

[1859] דּוּדָאִים *dûdāʾîm* 6x mandrake plant, thought to be a fertility aid or aphrodisiac [1736*]

[1860] דּוֹדָה *dôdâ* 3x aunt (father's sister) [1733]

[1864] דָּוָה *dāwâ* 1x [Q] to have a monthly period, menstruate [1738]

[1865] דָּוֶה *dāweh* 5x pertaining to the menstrual cycle; fainting [1739]

[1866] דּוּחַ *dûaḥ* 3x [H] to rinse, wash, cleanse [1740]

[1867] דְּוַי *deway* 2x illness [1741]

[1868] דַּוָּי *dawwāy* 3x faint; afflicted [1742]

[1870] דּוּךְ *dûk* 1x [Q] to crush (in a mortar) [1743]

[1871] דּוּכִיפַת *dûkîpat* 2x hoopoe [1744]

[1872] 1 דּוּמָה *dûmâ* 2x silence [1745]

[1875] דּוּמִיָּה *dûmiyyâ* 4x silence, stillness; rest [1747]

[1876] דּוּמָם *dûmām* 3x in silence, quietly; lifeless [1748]

[1880] דּוֹנַג *dônag* 4x wax [1749]

[1881] דּוּץ *dûṣ* 1x [Q] to leap [1750]

[1883] 1 דּוּר *dûr* 1x [Q] to pile logs (around) [1752]

[1884] 2 דּוּר *dûr* 1x [Q] to dwell [1752]

[1885] 3 דּוּר *dûr* 2x all around, encircling; ball [1754]

[1886] 1 דּוֹר *dôr* 1x house, dwelling [1755]

[1887] 2 דּוֹר *dôr* 167x generation, generation to come; descendant [1755] See *generation.*

[1889] דּוּשׁ *dûš* 16x [Q] to tread, trample, thresh; [Qp, N, Ho] be trampled, be threshed [1758]

[1890] דָּחָה *dāḥâ* 7x [Q] to push, push away; trip up; [Qp] to totter; [N] to be brought down; [Pu] to be thrown down [1760]

[1892] דְּחִי *d*ᵉ*ḥî* 2x stumbling [1762]

[1893] דֹּחַן *dōḥan* 1x (sorghum) millet [1764]

[1894] דָּחַף *dāḥap* 4x [Qp] to be spurred on, be in haste; [N] to be eager, be rushed, hurry [1765]

[1895] דָּחַק *dāḥaq* 2x [Q] to afflict, oppress [1766]

[1896] דַּי *day* 39x enough, sufficient [1767]

[1897] דִּיבוֹן *dîbôn* 9x Dibon [1769]

[1899] דִּיג *dîg* 1x [Q] to catch fish [1770]

[1900] דַּיָּג *dayyāg* 2x fisherman [1771]

[1901] דַּיָּה *dayyâ* 2x falcon [1772]

[1902] דְּיוֹ *d*ᵉ*yô* 1x ink, a writing substance made of soot or metal shavings mixed with oil or resin [1773]

[1906] 1 דִּין *dîn* 24x [Q] to judge, punish; to plead, defend, vindicate, contend for; [N] to argue [1777]

[1907] 2 דִּין *dîn* 20x cause, legal case; judgment, justice [1779]

[1908] דַּיָּן *dayyān* 2x defender, judge [1781]

[1909] דִּינָה *dînâ* 8x Dinah, "*female judge*" [1783]

[1911] דָּיֵק *dāyēq* 6x siege works [1785]

[1912] דַּיִשׁ *dayiš* 1x threshing (season) [1786]

[1913] 1 דִּישׁוֹן *dîšôn* 1x ibex [1788]

[1916] דַּךְ *dak* 4x oppressed [1790]

[1917] דָּכָא *dākā*ʾ 18x [N] to be contrite; [P] to crush; [Pu] to be crushed, be dejected, be humbled; [Ht] to lie crushed [1792]

[1918] 1 דַּכָּא *dakkā*ʾ 3x crushed, contrite [1793]

[1919] 2 דַּכָּא *dakkā*ʾ 1x dust [1793]

[1920] דָּכָה *dākâ* 5x [Q, P] to crush; [N] to be crushed, contrite [1794]

[1922] דֳּכִי *d*ᵒ*kî* 1x pounding (waves) [1796]

[1923] 1 דַּל *dal* 1x door [1817*]

[1924] 2 דַּל *dal* 48x poor, needy, humble; weak, haggard, scrawny [1800]

[1925] דָּלַג *dālag* 5x [Q, P] to scale, ascend, leap up over [1801]

[1926] 1 דָּלָה *dālâ* 5x [Q, P] to draw up, draw water (from a well) [1802]

[1927] 2 דָּלָה *dālâ* 1x [Q] to hang limp, dangle [1802]

[1929] 1 דַּלָּה *dallâ* 2x threads remaining on the loom; flowing hair [1803]

[1930] 2 דַּלָּה *dallâ* 5x poor, a class of people with little status, influence, and social value [1803]

[1931] דָּלַח *dālaḥ* 3x [Q] to churn, stir up [1804]

[1932] דְּלִי *deli* 2x (water) bucket, possibly made of leather [1805]

[1935] דְּלִילָה *delîlâ* 6x Delilah, "*tease*" [1807]

[1936] דָּלִית *dālît* 8x branch, bough [1808*]

[1937] 1 דָּלַל *dālal* 7x [Q] to be in need, be weak, fade [1809]

[1938] 2 דָּלַל *dālal* 1x [Q] to dangle [1809]

[1940] 1 דָּלַף *dālap* 2x [Q] to leak; to pour out [1811]

[1941] 2 דָּלַף *dālap* 1x [Q] to be weary, be sleepless [1811]

[1942] דֶּלֶף *delep* 2x leaky roof [1812]

[1944] דָּלַק *dālaq* 9x [Q] to set on fire; to hunt, chase, pursue; [H] to inflame, kindle [1814]

[1945] דַּלֶּקֶת *dalleqet* 1x inflammation [1816]

[1946] דֶּלֶת *delet* 88x door, gate; column, lid, leaf (of a door) [1817] See *door; gate.*

[1947] דָּם *dām* 361x blood, lifeblood; by extension: bloodshed, death; blood-colored fluids: grape juice, wine; "to pour out blood" is "to kill" since life is in the blood [1818] See *blood.*

[1948] 1 דָּמָה *dāmâ* 29x [Q] to be like, liken, resemble; [N] to be like; [P] to think, plan, intend; to liken; [Ht] to consider oneself equal to [1819]

[1949] 2 דָּמָה *dāmâ* 4x [Q] to cease; to be silent; [N] to be silenced [1820]

[1950] 3 דָּמָה *dāmâ* 13x [Q] to destroy; [N] to perish, be ruined, be destroyed, be wiped out [1820]

[1951] דֻּמָה *dumâ* 1x one silenced [1822]

[1952] דְּמוּת *demût* 25x likeness, figure, image, form [1823] See *form; image; likeness; pattern; shape.*

[1953] דְּמִי *demî* 1x prime (of life), a fig. extension of being at a midway point in a journey [1824]

[1954] דֳּמִי *domî* 3x silence, rest [1824]

[1955] דִּמְיוֹן *dimyôn* 1x likeness [1825]

[1957] 1 דָּמַם *dāmam* 24x [Q] to be still, be silent, be quiet, rest; [N] to be silenced; [Po] to quiet [1826]

[1959] 3 דָּמַם *dāmam* 5x [Q] to perish; [N] to be laid waste, be silenced, be destroyed; [H] to doom to perish [1826]

[1960] דְּמָמָה *demāmâ* 3x hush, whisper [1827]

[1961] דֹּמֶן *dōmen* 6x refuse, dung [1828]

[1963] דָּמַע *dāmaʿ* 2x [Q] to weep [1830]

[1964] דֶּמַע *demaʿ* 1x juice [1831]

[1965] דִּמְעָה *dimʿâ* 23x tears, weeping [1832]

[1966] דַּמֶּשֶׂק *dammeśeq* 39x Damascus [1834]

[1968] 1 דָּן *dān* 50x Dan (person and tribe), "*judge*" [1835]

[1969] 2 דָּן *dān* 20x Dan (town), "*judge*" [1835]

[1975] דָּנִיֵּאל *dāniyyēʾl* 29x Daniel, "*God [El] is my judge*" [1840]

[1976] דֵּעַ *dēaʿ* 5x what is known, knowledge [1843]

[1978] דֵּעָה *dēʿâ* 6x knowledge [1844]

[1979] דְּעוּאֵל *deʿûʾēl* 5x Deuel, "*known of God [El]*" [1845]

[1980] דָּעַךְ *dāʿak* 9x [Q] to snuff out, extinguish; [N] to vanish; [Pu] to die out [1846]

[1981] 1 דַּעַת *daʿat* 88x knowledge; understanding, learning [1847] See *ability; knowledge.*

[1984] דֳּפִי *d^opî* 1x blemish, stain; slander [1848*]

[1985] דָּפַק *dāpaq* 3x [Q] to drive hard; to knock hard (= worry); [Ht] to pound (on a door) [1849]

[1987] דַּק *daq* 14x gaunt, thin, dwarfed; finely ground (incense), fine (dust) [1851]

[1988] דֹּק *dōq* 1x canopy, thin veil [1852]

[1990] דָּקַק *dāqaq* 13x [Q] to finely crush or grind; [H] to grind to powder, break to pieces; [Ho] to be ground (to make bread) [1854]

[1991] דָּקַר *dāqar* 11x [Q] to drive through, pierce, stab; [Qp, N, Pu] to be pierced [1856]

[1993] דַּר *dar* 1x mother-of-pearl [858]

[1994] דֵּרָאוֹן *dērāʾôn* 2x loathing, contempt, aversion [1860]

[1995] דָּרְבָן *dorbān* 1x (iron) goading stick [1861]

[1996] דָּרְבֹנָה *dorbōnâ* 1x (iron) goading stick [1861*]

[1998] דַּרְדַּר *dardar* 2x thistle [1863]

[1999] דָּרוֹם *dārôm* 19x south; south wind [1864]

[2000] 1 דְּרוֹר *d^erôr* 2x a kind of bird, perhaps swallow or dove [1866]

[2001] 2 דְּרוֹר *d^erôr* 1x oil of myrrh, stacte [1865]

[2002] 3 דְּרוֹר *d^erôr* 7x freedom, liberty; an event required every fifty years to restore Israelite slaves to freedom and Israelite land to tribal allotments [1865]

[2003] דָּרְיָוֶשׁ *dār^eyāweš* 10x Darius, "*he who upholds the good*" [1867]

[2005] דָּרַךְ *dārak* 63x [Q] to go out, set out, march on, walk upon, trample; to bend (a bow); [Qp] to string (a bow), be bent (of a bow); [H] to shoot (a bow); to cause to tread, to enable to go; to lead, guide [1869] See *bend; trample; tread; walk.*

[2006] דֶּרֶךְ *derek* 712x way, path, route, road, journey; by extension: conduct, way of life; a pagan god (Am 8:14) [1870] See *conduct; journey; path; road; way.*

[2007] דַּרְכְּמוֹנִים *dark^emônîm* 4x (pl.) drachmas (Persian: a unit of weight used as a money, the value of which is uncertain) [1871*]

[2008] דַּרְמֶשֶׂק *darmeśeq* 6x Damascus [1834]

[2011] דָּרַשׁ *dāraš* 165x [Q] to seek, inquire, consult; [Qp] to ponder, be sought after; [N] to let oneself be inquired of, to allow a search to be made [1875] See *care; inquire; require; search; seek.*

[2012] דָּשָׁא *dāšāʾ* 2x [Q] to become green (of pastures); [H] to produce, cause to shoot forth [1876]

[2013] דֶּשֶׁא *dešeʾ* 14x (new) green vegetation, (new) green grass [1877]

[2014] 1 דָּשֵׁן *dāšēn* 11x [Q] to thrive, grow fat; [P] to anoint, give health; to remove the (fat) ashes; [Pu] to prosper, be satisfied, be soaked (with fat); [Hotpaal] to be covered with fat [1878]

[2015] 2 דָּשֵׁן *dāšēn* 2x rich (pertaining to food which is fresh and possibly juicy), fresh [1879]

[2016] דֶּשֶׁן *dešen* 16x fat; ashes (the burned wood of the altar fire soaked with fat); by extension: abundance, riches, choice food; in the ancient Near East fatness was a positive, enviable state, though extreme obesity could be denounced or ridiculed [1880]

[2017] דָּת *dāt* 21x command (either written or oral), prescription, custom, edict, law [1881]

[2018] דָּתָן *dātān* 10x Dathan, "*strong*" [1885]

[2022] -הֲ *hᵃ*- 742x introduces a question; usually translated as a question mark [**]

[2026] הֵא *hēʾ* 2x surely! see!, a discourse marker of emphasis [1887]

[2027] הֶאָח *heʾāḥ* 12x Ah!, Aha! [1889]

[2035] 1 הַב *hab* 33x come!, give!, put!, ascribe! [3051*]

[2037] הַבְהַב *habhab* 1x gift [1890]

[2038] הָבַל *hābal* 5x [Q] to be worthless, meaningless; be proud, vain; [H] to fill with false hopes, cause to become vain [1891]

[2039] 1 הֶבֶל *hebel* 73x breath; by extension: something with no substance, meaninglessness, worthlessness, vanity, emptiness, futility; idol [1892] See *breath; futility; meaninglessness; temporality; vanity; worthless.*

[2040] 2 הֶבֶל *hebel* 8x Abel, "*morning mist*" [1893]

[2041] הָבְנִים *hobnîm* 1x ebony [1894*]

[2042] הָבַר *hābar* 1x [Q] (ptcp.) astrologer, one who divides (classifies) the night sky for the purpose of telling the future [1895]

[2047] 1 הָגָה *hāgâ* 25x [Q] to utter a sound, moan, meditate; [H] to mutter; from the base meaning of uttering a sound of any kind comes figure of meditation, the act of thoughtful deliberation with the implication of speaking to oneself [1897]

[2048] 2 הָגָה *hāgâ* 3x [Q] to expel, remove [1898]

[2049] הֶגֶה *hegeh* 3x moaning, mourning, rumbling [1899]

[2050] הָגוּת *hāgût* 1x utterance, meditation, which can include thinking and planning [1900]

[2052] הָגִיג *hāgîg* 2x sighing, meditation [1901]

[2053] הִגָּיוֹן *higgāyôn* 4x muttering (sounds spoken to no one in particular), meditation see also 2047; Higgaion, melody [1902]

[2054] הָגִין *hāgîn* 1x corresponding [1903]

[2057] הָגָר *hāgār* 12x Hagar, "*emigration, flight*" [1904]

[2059] הֵד *hēd* 1x joyous shout [1906]

[2060] הֲדַד *hᵃdad* 13x Hadad, "*thunderer*" [1908]

[2061] הֲדַדְעֶזֶר *hᵃdadʿezer* 21x Hadadezer, "*Hadad is a help*" [1909]

[2063] הָדָה *hādâ* 1x [Q] to put, stretch out [1911]

[2065] הֲדוּרִים *hᵃdûrîm* 1x mountains [1921*]

[2070] הָדַךְ *hādak* 1x [Q] to crush by treading upon [1915]

[2071] הֲדֹם *hᵃdōm* 6x footstool [1916]

[2072] הֲדַס *hᵃdas* 6x myrtle tree [1918]

[2073] הֲדַסָּה *hᵃdassâ* 1x Hadassah, "*myrtle;* [poss.] *bride* or *myrtle*" [1919]

[2074] הָדַף *hādap* 11x [Q] to shove, push, thrust, drive out [1920]

[2075] הָדַר *hādar* 6x [Q] to show favoritism; show respect; [Qp] to be in splendor; [N] to be shown respect; [Ht] to exalt oneself [1921]

[2077] הָדָר *hādār* 30x majesty, splendor, glory, nobility; often related to the appearance of an object that is beautiful and instills awe [1926]

[2078] הֶדֶר *heder* 1x splendor; "the royal splendor" may refer to the land of Israel, with the focus that this land is a valued ornament of the king [1925]

[2079] הֲדָרָה *hᵃdārâ* 5x splendor, glory [1927]

[2081] הָהּ *hāh* 1x Alas! [1929]

[2082] הוֹ *hô* 2x ah! (doubled for emphasis), with a strong implication of mourning or sorrow [1930]

[2083] הוּ *hû* 1x he, she, it; that, which [**]

[2086] 1 הוֹד *hôd* 24x splendor, majesty, glory, strength [1935]

[2092] 1 הָוָה *hāwâ* 1x [Q] to fall (on) [1933]

[2093] 2 הָוָה *hāwâ* 5x [Q] to be, become; to get, have [1933]

[2094] 1 הַוָּה *hawwâ* 3x (evil) desire, craving [1942]

[2095] 2 הַוָּה *hawwâ* 13x destruction, ruin, corruption [1942]

[2096] הֹוָה *hôwâ* 3x calamity, disaster [1943]

[2098] הוֹי *hôy* 51x woe!, ah!, oh!, alas!; (to invite) come! [1945] See *alas; woe.*

[2099] הוֹלֵלוֹת *hôlēlôt* 4x madness, delusion, folly [1947*]

[2100] הוֹלֵלוּת *hôlēlût* 1x madness, delusion, folly [1948]

[2101] הוּם *hûm* 4x [Q] to throw into confusion; [N] to be stirred up, be shook; [H] to be distraught; to throng [1949]

[2103] הוּן *hûn* 1x [H] to think it easy [1951]

[2104] הוֹן *hôn* 26x wealth, riches, possessions [1952]

[2107] הוֹשֵׁעַ *hôšēaʿ* 16x Hoshea; Joshua, "*salvation*" [1954]

[2109] הוּת *hût* 1x [Pol] to assault [2050*]

[2110] הוֹתִיר *hôtîr* 2x Hothir, "*one who remains*" [1956]

[2113] הִי *hî* 1x woe!, an exclamation of sorrow [1958]

[2116] הֵידָד *hêdād* 7x shout (of joy) [1959]

[2117] הֻיְּדוֹת *huyyᵉdôt* 1x (pl.) songs of thanksgiving [1960*]

[2118] הָיָה *hāyâ* 3,562x [Q] to be, become, happen; [N] to be done, happen; the common verb of being, referring to state of being, change of state, existence, and the occurring of events, or even possession [1961] See *be; become; come to pass.*

[2120] הֵיךְ *hêk* 2x how? [1963]

[2121] הֵיכָל *hêkāl* 80x a building of some kind: temple, sanctuary, palace; main hall [1964] See *palace; temple.*

[2122] הֵילֵל *hêlēl* 1x from the base meaning "shining one," this refers to an object in the night sky, often translated "morning star," and possibly referring to the planet Venus; fig. used as a title of the king of Babylon (Isa 14:12). The Latin "lucifer" also means "shining one," and has become a title of Satan due to a traditional equation of the king of Babylon with the devil [1966]

[2124] הֵימָן *hêmān* 17x Homam [1968]

[2125] הִין *hîn* 22x hin (liquid measure of volume, one-sixth of a bath, about one gallon [four liters]) [1969]

[2129] הַכָּרָה *hakkārâ* 1x look (on a face) as a non-verbal communication, which in context may refer to personal bias [1971]

[2133] הָלָא *hālāʾ* 1x [N] to be driven away, be removed [1972]

[2134] הָלְאָה *hālᵉʾâ* 16x beyond; far (and wide), some distance away; out of the way! [1973]

[2136] הִלּוּלִים *hillûlîm* 2x offering of praise; festival (related to a god) [1974*]

[2137] הַלָּז *hallāz* 7x this [1975]

[2138] הַלָּזֶה *hallāzeh* 3x this [1976]

[2141] הָלִיךְ *hālîk* 1x path, steps [1978]

[2142] הֲלִיכָה *hᵃlîkâ* 6x procession, way, walk; traveling merchants; affairs [1979]

[2143] הָלַךְ *hālak* 1,554x [Q] to walk, go, travel; [N] to fade away; [P] to walk about, go about; [H] to drive back, get rid of; enable to walk; to lead; bring; [Ht] to move to and fro, wander, walk about; by extension: to walk as a lifestyle, a pattern of conduct [1980 & 3212*] See *cease; come; follow; go.*

[2144] הֵלֶךְ *hēlek* 2x oozing, flowing; visitor [1982]

[2145] 1 הָלַל *hālal* 4x [H] to flash, radiate, shine [1984]

[2146] 2 הָלַל *hālal* 146x [P] to praise; give thanks; cheer, extol; [Pu] to be praised, be worthy of praise, be of renown; [Ht] to make one's boast in (the name of God); "Hallelujah" is a compound of the second person plural imperative and the personal name of God: hallelu-yah, praise Yah(weh); see 2149 [1984] See *boast; exult; praise.*

[2147] 3 הָלַל *hālal* 16x [Q] to be arrogant; [Po] to make a fool of, to mock, rail against; [Poal] to be foolish; [Htpo] to act like a madman; act furiously [1984]

[2150] הָלַם *hālam* 8x [Q] to strike, smash, beat, trample [1986]

[2151] הֲלֹם *hᵃlōm* 12x to here [1988]

[2153] הַלְמוּת *halmût* 1x hammer [1989]

[2155] 2 הָם *hām* 1x wealth [1991*]

[2159] הָמָה *hāmâ* 34x [Q] to make a noise, be tumultuous [1993]

[2161] הֵמָּה *hēmâ* 1x they, them [1992*]

[2162] הָמוֹן *hāmôn* 85x commotion, tumult, confusion; many, populace, hoards, army [1995] See *confusion; crowd; hordes; noise; tumult.*

[2166] הֶמְיָה *hemyâ* 1x noise, sound, tone [1998]

[2167] הֲמֻלָּה *hᵃmullâ* 2x tumult, sound, noise [1999]

[2169] 1 הָמַם *hāmam* 15x [Q] to throw into confusion; to rout [2000]

[2171] הָמַן *hāman* 1x [Q] to rage, be turbulent [1995*]

[2172] הָמָן *hāmān* 54x Haman [2001]

[2173] הֲמָסִים *hᵃmāsîm* 1x twigs, brushwood [2003*]

[2176] 1 הֵן *hēn* 107x see!, surely!; if, yet, but, then [2005 & 3860*] See *behold; look.*

[2178] 1 הֵנָּה *hēnnâ* 51x here, to here; on this side, on the opposite side [2008] See *here; now.*

[2179] 2 הֵנָּה *hēnnâ* 47x they, these, those [2007]

[2180] הִנֵּה *hinnēh* 1,061x look!, now!, here, there, a marker used to enliven a narrative, change a scene, emphasize an idea, or call attention to detail [2009] See *behold; look.*

[2182] הֲנָחָה *hᵃnāḥâ* 1x holiday, an official day of rest and celebration [2010]

[2187] הַס *has* 7x Silence!, Quiet!, Hush! [2013*]

[2188] הָסָה *hāsâ* 1x [H] to silence, cause to be still [2013]

[2198] הֲפֻגָה *hᵃpugâ* 1x relief, stopping [2014]

[2200] הָפַךְ *hāpak* 94x [Q] to overthrow, overturn, turn around, change; [Qp] to be turned over; [N] to be changed, transformed, turned into; [Ho] to be overwhelmed; [Ht] to tumble around, flash back and forth, swirl; from the base meaning of turning an object over comes the fig. extension of "changing one's mind" [2015] See *return; transform; turn.*

[2201] הֵפֶךְ *hēpek* 3x opposite, turning of things upside down, perversion [2016 & 2017*]

[2202] הֲפֵכָה *h^a pēkâ* 1x catastrophe, demolition [2018]

[2203] הֲפַכְפַּךְ *h^a pakpak* 1x devious, crooked [2019]

[2208] הַצָּלָה *hassālâ* 1x deliverance [2020]

[2210] הֹצֶן *hōsen* 1x weapon (variously interpreted) [2021]

[2215] הַר *har* 558x hill, mountain, range (of hills, mountains); referring to low hills as well as high mountains [2022 & 2042*] See *mountain.*

[2216] הֹר *hōr* 12x Hor, "[perhaps] *mountain*" [2023]

[2221] הַרְבֵּה *harbēh* 50x great (number), many, much, abundance [7235*]

[2222] הָרַג *hārag* 167x [Q] to kill, put to death, murder, slaughter; [Qp, N, Pu] to be slain, be put to death, be slaughtered [2026] See *kill; massacre; murder; slaughter.*

[2223] הֶרֶג *hereg* 5x slaughter, killing [2027]

[2224] הֲרֵגָה *h^a rēgâ* 5x slaughter [2028]

[2225] הָרָה *hārâ* 45x [Q] to conceive, become pregnant, be with child; [Gp; Pu] to be conceived, born [2029]

[2226] הָרֶה *hāreh* 12x pregnant, expecting (child) [2030]

[2228] הֵרוֹן *hērôn* 1x childbearing, pregnancy [2032]

[2230] הָרִיָּה *hāriyyâ* 1x pregnant, expecting [2030*]

[2231] הֵרָיוֹן *hērāyôn* 2x conception, pregnancy [2032]

[2232] הֲרִיסָה *h^a rîsâ* 1x ruin [2034]

[2233] הֲרִיסוּת *h^a rîsût* 1x waste, ruin, destruction [2035]

[2237] הָרָן *hārān* 7x Haran, "*mountaineer* [perhaps *sanctuary*" [2039]

[2238] הָרַס *hāras* 43x [Q] to tear down, break down, destroy; [Qp] to be in ruins; [N] to be destroyed, in ruins; [P] to destroy [2040]

[2239] הֶרֶס *heres* 1x destruction (= Heliopolis) [2041]

[2240] הֲרָרִי *h^a rārî* 5x Hararite [2043]

[2245] הַשְׁמָעוּת *hašmāʿût* 1x news, communication, information [2045]

[2247] הִתּוּךְ *hittûk* 1x melting [2046]

[2252] הָתַל *hātal* 1x [P] to taunt, mock [2048]

[2253] הֲתֻלִּים *h^a tulîm* 1x mockery [2049*]

[2256] -וְ *w^e*- 50,284x a marker showing the relationship between words, clauses, sentences, and sections; generally, coordinating: and, also; contrasting: but, yet, however; showing a logical relationship: because, so then; emphazing: even, indeed [**]

[2260] וָו *wāw* 13x hook, peg [2053]

[2261] וָזָר *wāzār* 1x guilty [2054]

[2263] וָלָד *wālād* 1x child [2056]

[2267] וַשְׁתִּי *waštî* 10x Vashti, "*one beautiful, desired*" [2060]

[2269] 1 זְאֵב *z^e ʾēb* 7x wolf [2061]

[2272] זָבַד *zābad* 1x [Q] to give (a gift), bestow [2064]

[2278] זְבַדְיָהוּ *z^e badyāhû* 3x Zebadiah, "*Yahweh bestows*" [2069]

[2279] זְבוּב *z^e bûb* 2x fly (insect) [2070]

[2282] זְבוּלוּן *z^e bûlûn* 45x Zebulun, "*honor Ge 30:20*" [2074]

[2284] זָבַח *zābah* 134x [Q, P] to offer a sacrifice; to slaughter, butcher [2076] See *sacrifice; slaughter.*

[2285] 1 זֶבַח *zebah* 162x sacrifice, offering [2077] See *sacrifice.*

[2290] זָבַל *zābal* 1x [Q] to honor, exalt; from the base meaning of lifting up or carrying an object, especially bringing presents, not found in the OT [2082]

[2292] 2 זְבֻל *zᵉbul* 5x magnificent dwelling, princely mansion, lofty dwelling [2073]

[2293] זָג *zāg* 1x skin, peel (of grape) [2085]

[2294] זֵד *zēd* 13x arrogant, proud, haughty [2086]

[2295] זָדוֹן *zādôn* 11x pride, arrogance, contempt, presumption [2087]

[2298] זָהָב *zāhāb* 392x gold, nugget of gold, gold piece or coin [2091] See *gold.*

[2299] זָהַם *zāham* 1x [P] to make repulsive, loathsome (to someone) [2092]

[2301] 1 זָהַר *zāhar* 1x [H] to shine [2094]

[2302] 2 זָהַר *zāhar* 21x [N] to be warned, take warning; [H] to give warning, dissuade [2094]

[2303] זֹהַר *zōhar* 2x brightness, shining [2096]

[2307] זוּב *zûb* 42x [Q] to flow, gush out; discharge (of body fluids); "flowing with milk and honey" is a figure of sweet abundance [2100]

[2308] זוֹב *zôb* 13x discharge (of body fluids) [2101]

[2312] זָוִית *zāwît* 2x corner (of a palace, altar), pillar [2106]

[2313] זוּל *zûl* 1x [Q] to pour out, weigh out [2107]

[2314] זוּלָה *zûlâ* 16x but, only, except; apart from, besides [2108]

[2316] זוּעַ *zûaᶜ* 3x [Q] to show fear, tremble; [Pil] to make tremble [2111]

[2317] זְוָעָה *zᵉwāᶜâ* 6x abhorrence, terror, object of dread [2113]

[2318] 1 זוּר *zûr* 4x [Q] to squeeze, press upon, crush [2115 & 2116*]

[2319] 2 זוּר *zûr* 6x [Q, N, Ho] to go astray, turn aside, be estranged [2114]

[2320] 3 זוּר *zûr* 1x [Q] to stink; by extension: to be offensive [2114]

[2322] זָחַח *zāḥaḥ* 2x [N] to swing out [2118]

[2323] 1 זָחַל *zāḥal* 2x [Q] to crawl, glide (of a snake) [2119]

[2324] 2 זָחַל *zāḥal* 1x [Q] to be afraid [2119]

[2326] זִיד *zîd* 10x [Q] to treat arrogantly, defy; [H] to cook; to act arrogantly, be contemptuous [2102]

[2327] זֵידוֹן *zêdôn* 1x raging (water), implying it is out of control [2121]

[2328] 1 זִיז *zîz* 2x creatures [2123]

[2329] 2 זִיז *zîz* 1x nipple (of a lactating breast) [2123]

[2338] זִיקוֹת *zîqôt* 2x flaming torch [2131*]

[2339] זַיִת *zayit* 38x olive (tree, grove, oil, leaf) [2132]

[2341] זַךְ *zak* 11x pure, clear; flawless, innocent, upright [2134]

[2342] זָכָה *zākâ* 8x [Q] to be pure; be justified, be acquitted; [P] to keep pure; [Ht] to make oneself clean, pure; usually referring to moral purity as a superior quality [2135]

[2343] זְכוֹכִית *zᵉkôkît* 1x crystal (referring to a transparent ornament) [2137]

[2344] זְכוּר *zᵉkûr* 4x male [2138]

[2348] זָכַךְ *zākak* 4x [Q] to be pure, bright, clean [2141]

[2349] 1 זָכַר *zākar* 235x [Q] to remember, commemorate, consider; [Qp] to remember; [N] to be remembered, be mentioned; [H] to bring to remembrance, remind, mention [2142] See *remember.*

[2350] 2 זָכַר *zākar* 1x [N] to be born male [2142]

[2351] זָכָר *zākār* 82x male, man [2145] See *male; man.*

[2352] זֵכֶר *zēker* 23x memory, remembrance (with an implication of honor, worship, and celebration); fame, renown [2143]

[2355] זִכָּרוֹן *zikkārôn* 24x memorial, remembrance (with an implication of honor, worship, and celebration), commemoration, reminder [2146]

[2357] זְכַרְיָה *zᵉkaryâ* 25x Zechariah, "*Yahweh remembers*" [2148]

[2358] זְכַרְיָהוּ *zᵉkaryāhû* 16x Zechariah, "*Yahweh remembers*" [2148]

[2359] זֻלּוּת *zullût* 1x vileness [2149]

[2360] זַלְזַל *zalzal* 1x shoots, sprigs, tendrils [2150]

[2361] 1 זָלַל *zālal* 7x [Q] to profligate, be a glutton, to gorge oneself; [H] to despise, treat contemptibly [2151]

[2362] 2 זָלַל *zālal* 2x [N] to tremble (of mountains) [2151]

[2363] זַלְעָפָה *zalᶜāpâ* 3x raging (wind); indignation; fits of hunger [2152]

[2364] זִלְפָּה *zilpâ* 7x Zilpah, "*short nosed person*" [2153]

[2365] 1 זִמָּה *zimmâ* 29x lewdness, shamelessness, evil [2154]

[2367] זְמוֹרָה *zᵉmôrâ* 5x vine branch [2156]

[2369] 1 זָמִיר *zāmîr* 7x song, music and song [2158]

[2372] זָמַם *zāmam* 13x [Q] to determine, plan, plot, intend, resolve [2161]

[2373] זָמָם *zāmām* 1x plan, plot [162]

[2374] זָמַן *zāman* 3x [Pu] to be set, be designated, appointed [2163]

[2375] זְמָן *zᵉmān* 4x time, appointed time [2165]

[2376] 1 זָמַר *zāmar* 45x [P] to sing, sing praises, to make music, to chant, sing, or play instruments to worship God and proclaim his excellence [2167]

[2377] 2 זָמַר *zāmar* 3x [Q] to prune (vines); [N] to be pruned [2168]

[2378] זֶמֶר *zemer* 1x mountain sheep; some sources: gazelle [2169]

[2379] 1 זִמְרָה *zimrâ* 7x singing, song, (instrumental) music [2172]

[2380] 2 זִמְרָה *zimrâ* 1x best product, having a high value [2173]

[2385] זַן *zan* 3x kind, sort [2177]

[2386] זָנַב *zānab* 2x [P] to cut off from the rear position, attack from the rear, as a fig. extension of the base meaning "to cut off a tail" [2179]

[2387] זָנָב *zānāb* 11x tail; stump [2180]

[2388] 1 זָנָה *zānâ* 60x [Q] to be, become a prostitute; to be sexually immoral, be promiscuous, commit adultery; [Pu] to be solicited for prostitution; [H] to make a prostitute, to turn to prostitution [2181] See *immorality; prostitute.*

[2390] זוֹנָה *zônâ* 33x prostitute, harlot [2181* & 2185*]

[2393] זְנוּנִים *zᵉnûnîm* 12x wanton lust, prostitution, adultery; by extension: idolatry, as unfaithfulness to God [2183*]

[2394] זְנוּת *zᵉnût* 9x prostitution, sexual immorality, unfaithfulness; by extension: idolatry, as unfaithfulness to God [2184]

[2395] 1 זָנַח *zānaḥ* 1x [H] to stink [2186]

[2396] 2 זָנַח *zānaḥ* 19x [Q] to reject, cast out; [H] to declare rejected; to remove [2186]

[2397] זָנַק *zānaq* 1x [P] to spring out [2187]

[2399] זֵעָה *zēᶜâ* 1x sweat; the "sweat of the brow" refers to doing heavy manual labor [2188]

[2400] זַעֲוָה *zaᶜᵃwâ* 2x thing of horror, terror [2189]

[2402] זְעֵיר *zᵉᶜêr* 5x little; a little longer [2191]

[2403] זָעַךְ *zāᶜak* 1x [N] to be extinguished [2193]

[2404] זָעַם *zāʿam* 12x [Q] to express wrath, show fury, denounce; [Qp] to be under wrath, be accursed; [N] to be scolded, be cursed [2194]

[2405] זַעַם *zaʿam* 22x wrath, anger, indignation, insolence [2195]

[2406] 1 זָעַף *zāʿap* 3x [Q] to rage against, become angry [2196]

[2407] 2 זָעַף *zāʿap* 2x [Q] to look dejected, look pitiful [2196]

[2408] זַעַף *zaʿap* 6x rage, wrath [2197]

[2409] זָעֵף *zāʿēp* 2x angry, raging [2198]

[2410] זָעַק *zāʿaq* 73x [Q] to cry out, call to, weep aloud, howl; [N] to be called, be summoned; be assembled; [H] to summon, cause to gather together, issue a proclamation [2199] See *call out; cry out; summon.*

[2411] זְעָקָה *zeʿāqâ* 18x outcry, shout, lament, wail [2201]

[2413] זֶפֶת *zepet* 3x pitch (resin) [2203]

[2414] 1 זֵק *zēq* 4x chains, fetters [2131]

[2415] 2 זֵק *zēq* 1x firebrands [2131]

[2416] 1 זָקֵן *zāqēn* 26x [Q] to be old; [H] to grow old; this can refer to maturity in contrast to youth or to advanced age [2204] See *elder; old.*

[2417] זָקָן *zāqān* 19x beard, whiskers (a sign of maturity or age); chin [2206]

[2418] 2 זָקֵן *zāqēn* 180x elder, old, aged, veteran; (n.) elder, leader, dignitary; "elder" can refer to a formal position as a community leader and arbiter [2205] See *elder; old.*

[2419] זֹקֶן *zōqen* 1x old age [2207]

[2420] זִקְנָה *ziqnâ* 6x old age, growing old [2209]

[2421] זְקֻנִים *zequnîm* 4x old age [2208*]

[2422] זָקַף *zāqap* 2x [Q] to lift up [2210]

[2423] זָקַק *zāqaq* 7x [Q] to refine, distill; [P] to refine; [Pu] to be refined, be purified [2212]

[2424] זָר *zār* 70x strange, foreign, alien, one of a different kind; unauthorized, illegitimate [2214*] See *foreign(er); strange(r); unauthorized.*

[2425] זֵר *zēr* 10x molding [2213]

[2426] זָרָא *zārāʾ* 1x loathsome thing [2214]

[2427] זָרַב *zārab* 1x [Pu] to become dry [2215]

[2428] זְרֻבָּבֶל *zerubbābel* 21x Zerubbabel, "*offspring [seed] of Babylon; scion* i.e., *one grafted into the [plant of] Babylon*" [2216]

[2430] 1 זָרָה *zārâ* 38x [Q, P] to scatter, spread out; winnow; [N, Pu] to be scattered, spread out [2219]

[2431] 2 זָרָה *zārâ* 1x [P] to measure off, discern [2219]

[2432] זְרוֹעַ *zerôaʿ* 91x arm, forearm, shoulder; power, strength, force [2220] See *arm; power; strength.*

[2433] זֵרוּעַ *zērûaʿ* 2x (plants from) seeds [2221]

[2435] זַרְזִיר *zarezîr* 1x a strutting animal, variously interpreted: rooster, horse, greyhound [2223]

[2436] זָרַח *zāraḥ* 18x [Q] to rise, dawn (of the sun); by extension: to appear bright red (as with a skin disorder) [2224]

[2437] 1 זֶרַח *zeraḥ* 1x dawning (of light) [2225]

[2438] 2 זֶרַח *zeraḥ* 21x Zerah, "*dawning, shining* or *flashing [red or scarlet] light*" [2226]

[2439] זַרְחִי *zarḥî* 6x Zerahite, "*of Zerah*" [2227]

[2440] זְרַחְיָה *zeraḥyâ* 5x Zerahiah, "*Yahweh shines brightly [red or scarlet]; Yahweh has risen [like the sun]*" [2228]

[2442] 2 זָרַם *zāram* 1x [Q] to sweep away (=2441?); [Po] to pour down [2229]

[2443] זֶרֶם *zerem* 9x rain, rainstorm, thunderstorm, torrent rains [2230]

[2444] זִרְמָה *zirmâ* 2x male genitals or emission [2231]

[2445] זָרַע *zāraʿ* 56x [Q] to sow seed, plant seed; [Qp] to be sown upon; [Pu] to be sown; [N] to be sown, be planted, to have children, have descendants; [H] to yield seed, to become pregnant; from the base meaning of scattering seed onto the ground comes the fig. extension "to have children" [2232] See *plant; sow.*

[2446] זֶרַע *zeraʿ* 229x seed, semen, that which propagates a species; by extension: that which is propagated, child, offspring, descendant, line, race [2233] See *descendant; offspring; seed.*

[2447] זֵרֹעִים *zērōʿîm* 1x vegetables [2235*]

[2448] זֵרְעֹנִים *zērʿōnîm* 1x vegetables [2235*]

[2449] זָרַף *zārap* 1x [Pil] to water, shower [2222*]

[2450] 1 זָרַק *zāraq* 35x [Q] to sprinkle, to scatter, to toss (in the air); [Pu] to be sprinkled [2236]

[2453] 2 זָרַר *zārar* 1x [Po] to sneeze [2237]

[2455] זֶרֶת *zeret* 7x handbreadth, span (of an open hand, a measure of about nine inches [23 cm]) [2239]

[2460] חֹב *ḥōb* 1x heart [2243]

[2461] חָבָא *ḥābāʾ* 36x [N] to be hidden, to hide oneself; [Pu] to keep oneself in hiding; [H] to hide (another); [Ho] to be hidden away; [Ht] to keep oneself hidden [2244]

[2462] חָבַב *ḥābab* 1x [Q] to love [2245]

[2464] חָבָה *ḥābâ* 2x [Q] to hide; [N] to conceal oneself [2247]

[2467] חַבּוּרָה *ḥabbûrâ* 7x bruise, welt, wound, injury [2250]

[2468] חָבַט *ḥābaṭ* 5x [Q] to thresh, beat out; [N] to be beaten [2251]

[2470] חֶבְיוֹן *ḥebyôn* 1x hiding, covering [2253]

[2471] 1 חָבַל *ḥābal* 12x [Q] to require a pledge, demand a security [2254]

[2472] 2 חָבַל *ḥābal* 12x [Q] to act wickedly, to offend; [P] to destroy, ruin, work havoc; [Pu] to be broken [2254]

[2473] 3 חָבַל *ḥābal* 3x [P] to conceive, be pregnant, to be in labor [2254]

[2474] 1 חֶבֶל *ḥebel* 2x procession, group [2256]

[2475] 2 חֶבֶל *ḥebel* 49x rope, cord, line, rigging; share, portion, region, district [2256]

[2476] 3 חֶבֶל *ḥebel* 1x destruction, ruin [2256]

[2477] חֵבֶל *ḥēbel* 8x labor pains, anguish of birth pangs [2256]

[2478] חֲבֹל *ḥᵃbōl* 3x pledge for a loan [2258]

[2479] חִבֵּל *ḥibbēl* 1x (ship's) rigging, mast [2260]

[2480] חֹבֵל *ḥōbēl* 5x seaman, sailor [2259]

[2481] חֲבֹלָה *ḥᵃbōlâ* 1x pledge for a loan [2258]

[2482] חֹבְלִים *ḥōbᵉlîm* 2x union [2256]

[2483] חֲבַצֶּלֶת *ḥᵃbaṣṣelet* 2x rose; crocus [2261]

[2485] חָבַק *ḥābaq* 13x [Q] to hold in one's arms, embrace; to fold one's hands; [P] to embrace, hug [2263]

[2486] חִבֻּק *ḥibbuq* 2x folding (of idle hands) [2264]

[2487] חֲבַקּוּק *ḥᵃbaqqûq* 2x Habakkuk, "*garden plant*" [2265]

[2488] 1 חָבַר *ḥābar* 1x [H] to make fine speeches [2266]

[2489] 2 חָבַר *ḥābar* 28x [Q] to join, unite, be attached, to be touching; to cast spells, to enchant; [Qp] to be joined; [P] to fasten, join; [Pu] to be fastened, be closely compacted; [Ht] to make an alliance, become allies [2266]

[2490] 1 חֶבֶר *ḥeber* 7x sharing; band, group; magic spell [2267]

[2492] חָבֵר *ḥābēr* 12x companion, associate, partner, friend [2270]

[2493] חַבָּר *ḥabbār* 1x (fellow) trader, one of a community of traders [2271]

[2494] חֲבַרְבֻּרוֹת *ḥ^a^barburôt* 1x spots (of a leopard) [2272*]

[2495] חֶבְרָה *ḥebrâ* 1x company, association [2274]

[2496] 1 חֶבְרוֹן *ḥebrôn* 63x Hebron, "*association*" [2275 & 5683*]

[2497] 2 חֶבְרוֹן *ḥebrôn* 10x Hebron, "*association*" [2275]

[2500] חֲבֶרֶת *ḥ^a^beret* 1x partner, (marriage) companion [2278]

[2501] חֹבֶרֶת *ḥōberet* 4x set (of curtains) [2279]

[2502] חָבַשׁ *ḥābaš* 32x [Q] to tie, bind, saddle; [Qp] to be saddled; to be twisted, wrapped around; [P] to bind up; [Pu] to be bound, bandaged [2280]

[2503] חֲבִתִּים *ḥ^a^bittîm* 1x offering bread (flat cakes, baked in a pan) [2281*]

[2504] חַג *ḥag* 62x religious feast, festival; festal procession [2282] See *feast; festival.*

[2505] חָגָּא *ḥoggāʾ* 1x terror; some sources: confusion [2283]

[2506] 1 חָגָב *ḥāgāb* 5x grasshopper, locust (in some cultures distinguished from a grasshopper and used as a food source) [2284]

[2510] חָגַג *ḥāgag* 16x [Q] to hold a festival, celebrate a festival; this can refer to a religious celebration or a revel [2287]

[2511] חָגוּ *ḥāgû* 3x clefts (of a rock) that can be used as a hiding place or retreat from danger [2288*]

[2512] חֲגוֹר *ḥ^a^gôr* 3x belt, sash [2290]

[2513] חָגוֹר *ḥāgôr* 1x belted (around the waist) [2289]

[2514] חֲגוֹרָה *ḥ^a^gôrâ* 5x covering; belt, sash [2290]

[2516] חַגַּי *ḥaggay* 9x Haggai, "*festal; born on the feast day*" [2292]

[2520] חָגַר *ḥāgar* 43x [Q] to tie, strap, fasten; to tuck (lower robe) into one's belt, gird; [Qp] to be tucked in, girded [2296]

[2521] 1 חַד *ḥad* 4x sharp (sword) [2299]

[2522] 2 חַד *ḥad* 1x one, each [2297]

[2523] חָדַד *ḥādad* 5x [Q] to be fierce, sharp; [Ho] to be sharpened; [Ht] to slash [2300]

[2525] 1 חָדָה *ḥādâ* 2x [Q] to be delighted; [P] to make glad [2302]

[2526] 2 חָדָה *ḥādâ* 1x [N] to be seen [2302]

[2529] חַדּוּד *ḥaddûd* 1x jagged, pointed [2303]

[2530] חֶדְוָה *ḥedwâ* 2x joy [2304]

[2532] 1 חָדַל *ḥādal* 55x [Q] to stop, cease, refrain, fail [2308] See *cease; fail; leave; refrain; stop.*

[2534] חָדֵל *ḥādēl* 3x refused, rejected, fleeting [2310]

[2537] חֵדֶק *ḥēdeq* 2x brier, thorn [2312]

[2539] חָדַר *ḥādar* 1x [Q] to close in on every side, surround [2314]

[2540] חֶדֶר *ḥeder* 38x room, chamber, bedroom; shrine; "the chambers of the belly" means "the most inner parts"; "the chambers of death" means "Sheol" [2315 & 2316*]

[2542] חָדַשׁ *ḥādaš* 10x [Q] to renew, restore, repair, reaffirm; [Ht] to renew oneself [2318]

[2543] חָדָשׁ *ḥādāš* 53x new, recent, fresh [2319] See *new.*

[2544] 1 חֹדֶשׁ *ḥōdeš* 283x month; new moon, new moon festival [2320] See *month; new moon.*

[2549] חוּב *ḥûb* 1x [P] to forfeit (one's head) [2325]

[2550] חוֹב *ḥôb* 1x loan, debt [2326]

[2552] 1 חוּג *ḥûg* 1x [Q] to encircle [2328]

[2553] 2 חוּג *ḥûg* 3x circle, horizon [2329]

[2554] חוּד *ḥûd* 4x [Q] to tell a riddle, set forth an allegory [2330]

[2555] 1 חָוָה *ḥāwâ* 6x [P] to tell, explain, show, display [2331]

[2556] 2 חָוָה *ḥāwâ* 173x [Hsh] to bow down low (in worship); prostrate oneself; pay one honor, homage [2331] See *bow down; worship.*

[2557] 1 חַוָּה *ḥawwâ* 3x settlement, camp; an unwalled village, a tent camp of nomadic peoples, more or less permanent [2333]

[2558] 2 חַוָּה *ḥawwâ* 2x Eve, "*life*" [2332]

[2560] 1 חוֹחַ *ḥôaḥ* 12x thicket, thistle, thornbush, bramble, briers; hook [2336]

[2562] חוּט *ḥûṭ* 7x line, cord, ribbon, thread [2339]

[2565] 1 חוּל *ḥûl* 10x [Q] to swirl, turn, fall, dance; [Pol] to wait; to dance (the round dance); [Htpol] to wait patiently; to swirl down; in some contexts this refers to a whirlwind [2342]

[2567] 1 חוֹל *ḥôl* 23x sand, grains of sand, with the associative meanings that the sands are vast and innumerable [2344]

[2569] חוּם *ḥûm* 4x dark-colored; some shade of gray [2345]

[2570] חוֹמָה *ḥômâ* 133x wall, with various associative meanings: protection, safety, or impenetrability [2346] See *wall.*

[2571] חוּס *ḥûs* 24x [Q] to show pity, mercy, have compassion, spare [347]

[2572] חוֹף *ḥôp* 7x coast, seashore, haven (for ships) [2348]

[2575] חוּץ *ḥûṣ* 164x out, outside; street, market area; countryside, fields, outdoors [2351] See *outside; street.*

[2578] 1 חָוַר *ḥāwar* 1x [Q] to grow pale [2357]

[2580] 1 חוּר *ḥûr* 2x white garments, white linen [2353]

[2581] 2 חוּר *ḥûr* 15x Hur, "[perhaps] *child*" [2354]

[2583] חוֹרָי *ḥôrāy* 1x fine linen [2355*]

[2590] 1 חוּשׁ *ḥûš* 17x [Q] to go quickly, hasten, rush upon; [Qp] to be ready; [H] to make hurry, hasten [2363 & 2439*]

[2591] 2 חוּשׁ *ḥûš* 3x [Q] to be greatly disturbed; to find enjoyment; [H] to be dismayed [2363]

[2593] חוּשַׁי *ḥûšay* 14x Hushai [2365]

[2597] 1 חוֹתָם *ḥôtām* 14x seal, signet ring [2368]

[2599] חֲזָאֵל *ḥ*^{a}*zāʾēl* 23x Hazael, "*God [El] sees*" [2371]

[2600] חָזָה *ḥāzâ* 55x [Q] to see, to look, observe, gaze; by extension: to choose (one thing over another); to have visions, to prophesy [2372] See *gaze; look; observe; see.*

[2601] חָזֶה *ḥāzeh* 13x breast (portion of sacrifice) [2373]

[2602] 1 חֹזֶה *ḥōzeh* 17x seer, one who receives a communication from God, with a possible focus that the message has a visual component [2374]

[2603] 2 חֹזֶה *ḥōzeh* 1x agreement [2374]

[2606] חָזוֹן *ḥāzôn* 35x vision, revelation, a message from God, with a possible focus on the visual aspects of the message [2377]

[2607] חָזוּת *ḥāzût* 5x vision; prominent appearance [2380]

[2608] חֲזוֹת *ḥazôt* 1x visions [2378*]

[2612] חִזָּיוֹן *ḥizzāyôn* 9x vision, dream, revelation [2384]

[2613] חֲזִיז *ḥazîz* 3x storm cloud, dark and producing lightning and thunder [2385]

[2614] חֲזִיר *ḥazîr* 7x pig, boar [2386]

[2616] חָזַק *ḥāzaq* 290x [Q] to be strong, hard, harsh, severe; [P] to harden (one's heart); to give strength, repair, encourage; [H] to grasp, seize, hold; to make repairs; [Ht] to establish oneself firmly; to encourage, to rally strength; from the base meaning of physical hardness come by extension: physical and internal strength of character; (negative) hardness of the heart, failure to respond to a person or message [2388] See *catch; courageous; grasp; harden; prevail; seize; strong.*

[2617] חָזָק *ḥāzāq* 57x mighty, powerful, strong, hard, severe; from the base meaning of physical hardness come by extension: physical and internal strength of character; (negative) hardness of the heart, failure to respond to a person or message [2389] See *mighty; obstinate; powerful; strong; stubborn; womb.*

[2618] חָזֵק *ḥāzēq* 2x strong, loud [2390]

[2619] חֵזֶק *ḥēzeq* 1x strength [2391]

[2620] חֹזֶק *ḥōzeq* 5x might, strength, power [2392]

[2621] חֶזְקָה *ḥezqâ* 4x strength, power [2393]

[2622] חָזְקָה *ḥozqâ* 5x force, harshness, urgency [2394]

[2624] חִזְקִיָּה *ḥizqiyyâ* 13x Hezekiah, "*Yahweh is [my] strength*" [2396]

[2625] חִזְקִיָּהוּ *ḥizqiyyāhû* 74x Hezekiah, "*Yahweh is [my] strength*" [2396]

[2626] חָח *ḥāḥ* 7x hook; brooch [2397]

[2627] חָטָא *ḥāṭāʾ* 240x [Q] to sin, do wrong, miss the way; [P] to purify, cleanse, to offer a sin offering; [H] to bring a sin upon, cause to commit a sin; [Ht] to purify oneself; "to sin," to willfully act contrary to the will and law of God, is a figure of missing or moving from a standard or mark [2398] See *(be) guilty; miss (the mark); sin.*

[2628] חֵטְא *ḥēṭʾ* 33x sin, action contrary to the will and law of God, with a strong implication that guilt follows, error; see also 2627 [2399]

[2629] חַטָּא *ḥaṭṭāʾ* 19x sinful, guilty; (n.) sinner, wicked one; see also 2627 [2400]

[2630] חֶטְאָה *ḥeṭʾâ* 1x sin; see also 2627 [2398]

[2631] חֲטָאָה *ḥaṭāʾâ* 8x sin, guilt, condemnation; sin offering; see also 2627 [2401]

[2632] חַטָּאָה *ḥaṭṭāʾâ* 2x sin, wickedness, fault; see also 2627 [2402]

[2633] חַטָּאת *ḥaṭṭāʾt* 298x sin, wrong, iniquity; sin offering, purification offering; see also 2627 [2403] See *sin; sin offering.*

[2634] חָטַב *ḥāṭab* 9x [Q] to cut, chop (wood); (n.) woodcutter, woodsman; [Pu] to carve [2404]

[2635] חֲטֻבוֹת *ḥaṭubôt* 1x colored, embroidered (fabric) [2405*]

[2636] חִטָּה *ḥiṭṭâ* 30x wheat [2406]

[2641] חָטַם *ḥāṭam* 1x [Q] to hold back, restrain [2413]

[2642] חָטַף *ḥāṭap* 3x [Q] to seize, carry off (by force) [2414]

[2643] חֹטֶר *ḥōṭer* 2x rod, switch; shoot, twig [2415]

[2644] 1 חַי *ḥay* 140x life, state of living (in contrast to death), lifetime; "as I live" is a formula for an oath, implying death should follow if what is sworn is not true [2416] See *life.*

[2646] 3 חַי *ḥay* 1x family, kin [2416]

[2648] חִידָה *ḥîdâ* 17x riddle, hard question, allegory; hidden things, intrigue; scorn (the asking of a riddle as a game could imply scorn and ridicule toward the person asked) [2420]

[2649] חָיָה *ḥāyâ* 283x [Q] to live; recover, revive; [P] to keep alive, preserve life; [H] to keep alive, save a life, spare a life, restore a life [2421 & 2425*] See *life; live; revive.*

[2650] חָיֶה *ḥāyeh* 1x vigorous [2422]

[2651] 1 חַיָּה *ḥayyâ* 96x animal, beast, livestock, living creature [2416*] See *animal; beast; living.*

[2652] 2 חַיָּה *ḥayyâ* 12x life, one's very being; hunger (of lions) [2416*]

[2653] 3 חַיָּה *ḥayyâ* 3x band, army; people, home [2416*]

[2654] חַיּוּת *ḥayyût* 1x lifetime [2424]

[2655] 1 חִיל *ḥîl* 46x [Q] to writhe, tremble, be in labor, give birth; [Pol] to give birth, bring forth; be in deep anguish, to twist; [Polal] to be brought forth, be given birth; [H] to shake; [Ho] to be born; [Htpalpal] be in distress; [Htpol] to be in torment [2342]

[2656] 2 חִיל *ḥîl* 2x [Q] to endure, prosper [2342]

[2657] חַיִל *ḥayil* 246x strength, capability, skill, valor, wealth; army, troop, warrior [2428] See *ability; army; capability; forces; power; rich, riches; strength; valiant; warriors; wealth.*

[2658] חֵיל *ḥêl* 7x ramparts, outer fortification, defense walls [2426 & 2430*]

[2659] 3 חִיל *ḥîl* 6x pain, anguish [2427]

[2660] חִילָה *ḥîlâ* 1x pain, any kind of physical trauma, as a fig. extension of the labor pains of birth [2427]

[2665] חִין *ḥîn* 1x gracefulness [2433]

[2666] חַיִץ *ḥayiṣ* 1x flimsy wall, inner wall [2434]

[2667] חִיצוֹן *ḥîṣôn* 25x outer, outside, exterior [2435]

[2668] חֵיק *ḥêq* 38x lap, bosom, the area to which one holds and cradles a loved one; by extension: the inner person, heart, seat of affection; fold of a cloak, gutter [2436]

[2669] חִירָה *ḥîrâ* 2x Hirah [2437]

[2670] חִירוֹם *ḥîrôm* 3x Hiram, "*[my] brother is elevated*" [2438]

[2671] חִירָם *ḥîrām* 20x Hiram, "*[my] brother is elevated*" [2438]

[2673] חִישׁ *ḥîš* 1x quickly, in haste [2440]

[2674] חֵךְ *ḥēk* 18x (area of the) mouth: lips, tongue (taste), roof of the mouth [2441]

[2675] חָכָה *ḥākâ* 14x [Q] to wait; [P] to lie in wait (ambush); hope for, long for [2442]

[2676] חַכָּה *ḥakkâ* 3x fishhook [2443]

[2677] חֲכִילָה *ḥ^a^kîlâ* 3x Hakilah [2444]

[2680] חַכְלִלוּת *ḥaklilût* 1x bloodshot (eyes); some sources: sparkling [2448]

[2681] חָכַם *ḥākam* 27x [Q] to be wise, be skillful, gain wisdom; [P] to make wiser, to teach wisdom; [Pu] to be skillful; [H] to make wise; [Ht] to deal shrewdly; to show oneself wise; to be wise implies understanding and acting in a manner that is effective and usually moral [2449]

[2682] חָכָם *ḥākām* 138x wise, skilled, shrewd, craftsman; (n.) wise person, sage, one who interprets divination or prophecy, one who has fear of the Lord and understanding that leads to effective (moral) action; see also 2681 [2450] See *wise, skillful.*

[2683] חָכְמָה *ḥokmâ* 153x wisdom, skill, learning; this can refer to skill in life, trade, war, or spiritual things; see also 2681 [2451] See *apptitude; experience; skill; wisdom.*

[2684] חָכְמוֹת *ḥākmôt* 4x wisdom; the plural form may imply its essential or supreme condition; see also 2681 [2454]

[2686] חָכַר *ḥākar* 1x [Q] to attack (vigorously) [1970*]

[2687] חֹל *ḥōl* 7x common use, not holy, ordinary [2455]

[2688] חָלָא *ḥālāʾ* 1x [Q] to be ill [2456]

[2689] 1 חֶלְאָה *ḥelʾâ* 5x deposit, encrustation, rust [2457]

[2692] חָלָב *ḥālāb* 44x milk [2461]

[2693] 1 חֵלֶב *ḥēleb* 92x fat, fat portions; by extension: finest, best part; callous (heart that is dull and unresponsive) [2459] See *best; fat.*

[2697] חֶלְבְּנָה *ḥelbᵉnâ* 1x galbanum (aromatic gum resin used to make incense) [2464]

[2698] חֶלֶד *ḥeled* 5x life, duration of life; this world [2465]

[2700] חֹלֶד *ḥōled* 1x weasel; some sources: rat or mole [2467]

[2703] 1 חָלָה *ḥālâ* 75x [Q] to be ill, be weak, be faint, become diseased, be wounded; [N] to be made sick, be incurable; [P] to afflict; [Pu] to become weak; [H] to make ill, to cause to suffer; [Ho] to be wounded; [Ht] to pretend to be ill, to feel sick [2470] See *diseased; ill; sick; weak; wounded.*

[2704] 2 חָלָה *ḥālâ* 17x [P] to entreat, implore, seek favor, intercede [2470]

[2705] חַלָּה *ḥallâ* 14x (ring-shaped) bread cakes [2471]

[2706] חֲלוֹם *ḥᵃlôm* 65x dream, dreamer; this can refer to a supernatural revelation by God by words and images [2472] See *dream.*

[2707] חַלּוֹן *ḥallôn* 31x window, narrow openings, parapet openings [2474]

[2710] חֲלוֹף *ḥᵃlôp* 1x destitute, vanishing [2475]

[2711] חֲלוּשָׁה *ḥᵃlûšâ* 1x defeat [2476]

[2714] חַלְחָלָה *ḥalḥālâ* 4x anguish, pain, trembling [2479]

[2715] חָלַט *ḥālaṭ* 1x [Q] to accept a statement [2480]

[2716] חֳלִי *ḥᵒlî* 24x illness, sickness, affliction; wound, injury [2483]

[2717] 1 חֲלִי *ḥᵃlî* 2x ornament, jewel [2481]

[2719] חֶלְיָה *ḥelyâ* 1x jewelry, ornament [2484]

[2720] 1 חָלִיל *ḥālîl* 6x flute [2485]

[2721] 2 חָלִיל *ḥālîl* 21x far be it!, never! [2486*]

[2722] חֲלִיפָה *ḥᵃlîpâ* 12x set, sequence, shift; renewal, relief [2487]

[2723] חֲלִיצָה *ḥᵃlîṣâ* 2x belongings, equipment [2488]

[2724] חֵלְכָה *ḥēlkâ* 3x victim [2489]

[2725] 1 חָלַל *ḥālal* 135x [N] to defile oneself, be profaned, be desecrated; [P] to defile, profane, desecrate; to enjoy; [Pu] to be defiled; [H] to begin, to proceed, launch; [Ho] to be begun [2490] See *begin; defile; desecrate; proceed; profane.*

[2726] 2 חָלַל *ḥālal* 8x [Q] to be wounded; [P] to pierce, wound; [Pu] to be killed; [Pol] to pierce, wound; [Polal] to be wounded [2490]

[2727] 3 חָלַל *ḥālal* 2x [Q, P] to play the flute [2490]

[2728] 1 חָלָל *ḥālāl* 94x dead, slain, casualty [2491] See *dead; killed; pierced; wounded.*

[2729] 2 חָלָל *ḥālāl* 3x defiled, profane (moral or ceremonial failure) [2491]

[2730] 1 חָלַם *ḥālam* 2x [Q] to grow strong; [H] to restore to health [2492]

[2731] 2 חָלַם *ḥālam* 27x [Q] to dream; [H] to encourage one to have dreams [2492]

[2733] חַלָּמוּת *ḥallāmût* 1x egg or mallow [2495]

[2734] חַלָּמִישׁ *ḥallāmîš* 5x flinty rock, hard rock [2496]

[2736] 1 חָלַף *ḥālap* 26x [Q] to go by, pass on, sweep by; to be new; [P] to change; [H] to change, exchange, replace, renew [2498]

[2737] 2 חָלַף *ḥālap* 2x [Q] to pierce, cut through [2498]

[2739] 2 חֵלֶף *ḥēlep* 2x in return for [2500]

[2740] 1 חָלַץ *ḥālaṣ* 23x [Q] to take off; [Qp] to be taken off; [N] to be delivered, be rescued; [P] to rescue, deliver; to tear out, rob [2502]

[2741] 2 חָלַץ *ḥālaṣ* 21x [Qp] to be armed (for battle); [N] to arm oneself; [H] to strengthen [2502]

[2743] חֲלָצַיִם *ḥ^alāṣayim* 10x waist, stomach, the area between the lowest ribs and the hip-bones; by extension: body, flesh; the inner person, heart [2504*]

[2744] 1 חָלַק *ḥālaq* 9x [Q] to be smooth, slippery; deceitful; [H] to speak deceit, flatter, be seductive [2505]

[2745] 2 חָלַק *ḥālaq* 55x [Q] to divide, apportion, assign; [N] to be divided, be dispersed, be distributed; [P] to divide, allot, apportion; [Pu] to be divided; [H] to get one's share; [Ht] to divide among themselves [2505] See *allot; apportion; divide; share.*

[2747] 1 חָלָק *ḥālāq* 9x smooth, slippery, pleasant, flattering [2509 & 2511*]

[2749] 1 חֵלֶק *ḥēleq* 1x smoothness [2506]

[2750] 2 חֵלֶק *ḥēleq* 66x share, portion, allotment, plot of ground [2506] See *lot; portion; share.*

[2752] חַלֻּק *ḥalluq* 1x smooth (stones) [2512]

[2753] 1 חֶלְקָה *ḥelqâ* 2x smoothness [2513]

[2754] 2 חֶלְקָה *ḥelqâ* 23x plot, field, tract [2513]

[2755] חֲלֻקָּה *ḥ^aluqqâ* 1x part, portion, division [2515]

[2759] חִלְקִיָּה *ḥilqiyyâ* 15x Hilkiah, "*Yahweh is [my] portion*" [2518]

[2760] חִלְקִיָּהוּ *ḥilqiyyāhû* 19x Hilkiah, "*Yahweh is [my] portion*" [2518]

[2761] חֲלַקְלַק *ḥ^alaqlaq* 4x slippery, slick and hard to walk on; by extension: slippery words, intrigue, insincere [2519]

[2764] 1 חָלַשׁ *ḥālaš* 1x [Q] to be laid low [2522]

[2765] 2 חָלַשׁ *ḥālaš* 2x [Q] to overcome, defeat [2522]

[2766] חַלָּשׁ *ḥallāš* 1x weak, weakling [2523]

[2767] 1 חָם *ḥām* 4x father-in-law [2524]

[2768] 2 חָם *ḥām* 2x hot, sweltering [2525]

[2769] 3 חָם *ḥām* 16x Ham [2526]

[2770] חֹם *ḥōm* 9x heat [2527]

[2772] חֶמְאָה *ḥemʾâ* 10x curds, curdled milk; butter, cream [2529]

[2773] חָמַד *ḥāmad* 21x [Q] to covet, lust, desire; delight in; [Qp] (n.) what is coveted: treasure, wealth; [N] to be pleasing, be desirable; [P] to delight; this can refer to proper delight and fondness, as well as to improper lust and desire [2530]

[2774] חֶמֶד *ḥemed* 6x fruitfulness, lushness; pleasantness; handsomeness [2531]

[2775] חֶמְדָּה *ḥemdâ* 16x desirable, pleasant, fine, valuable (things) [2532]

[2776] חֲמֻדוֹת *ḥ^{a}mudôt* 9x esteemed, precious, costly (things) [2530*]

[2778] חָמָה *ḥāmâ* 1x [Q] to watch, be careful [2534*]

[2779] חֵמָה *ḥēmâ* 125x anger, wrath, fury, rage, from the base meaning of heat (as in "hot-headed"); by extension: venom (poison that causes a burning sensation) [2534] See *anger; fury; poison; rage; venom; wrath.*

[2780] חַמָּה *ḥammâ* 6x heat (of the sun) [2535]

[2787] חָמוֹץ *ḥāmôṣ* 1x oppressor; oppressed [2541]

[2788] חַמּוּק *ḥammûq* 1x gracefulness, curve [2542]

[2789] 1 חֲמוֹר *ḥ^{a}môr* 96x donkey [2543] See *donkey.*

[2791] 3 חֲמוֹר *ḥ^{a}môr* 13x Hamor, "*male donkey*" [2544]

[2792] חָמוֹת *ḥāmôt* 1x mother-in-law [2545]

[2793] חֹמֶט *ḥōmeṭ* 1x skink (lizard) [2546]

[2796] חָמִיץ *ḥāmîṣ* 1x sour mash, sorrel-fodder [2548]

[2797] חֲמִישִׁי *ḥ^{a}mîšî* 45x fifth [2549]

[2798] חָמַל *ḥāmal* 41x [Q] to spare, take pity on, have mercy on [2550 & 2565*]

[2799] חֶמְלָה *ḥemlâ* 2x mercy [2551]

[2801] חָמַם *ḥāmam* 22x [Q] to be hot, be warm; by extension: to be aroused; be in a rage; [N] to burn with lust; [P] to let warm; [Ht] to warm oneself [2552]

[2802] חַמָּן *ḥammān* 8x incense altar [2553]

[2803] 1 חָמַס *ḥāmas* 8x [Q] to do violence, harm, to lay waste; to be stripped off; [N] to be mistreated [2554]

[2805] חָמָס *ḥāmās* 60x violence, destruction, malice, ruthlessness, fierceness [2555] See *badness; violence; wrong.*

[2806] 1 חָמֵץ *ḥāmēṣ* 4x [Q] to have yeast added, be leavened; by extension: [Ht] to be grieved, embittered [2556]

[2807] 2 חָמֵץ *ḥāmēṣ* 1x [Q] to be cruel, oppress [2556]

[2808] 3 חָמֵץ *ḥāmēṣ* 1x [Qp] to be stained crimson [2556]

[2809] 4 חָמֵץ *ḥāmēṣ* 11x something leavened, made with yeast [2557]

[2810] חֹמֶץ *ḥōmeṣ* 6x vinegar, wine vinegar [2558]

[2811] חָמַק *ḥāmaq* 2x [Q] to leave, turn away; [Ht] to wander, turn here and there [2559]

[2812] 1 חָמַר *ḥāmar* 2x [Q] to foam [2560]

[2813] 2 חָמַר *ḥāmar* 3x [Poalal] to be reddened, glow [2560]

[2814] 3 חָמַר *ḥāmar* 1x [Q] to coat, cover, to apply pitch as a sealant [2560]

[2815] חֶמֶר *ḥemer* 1x (foaming, fermenting) wine [2561]

[2816] 1 חֹמֶר *ḥōmer* 1x churning, storming (sea waters) [2563]

[2817] 2 חֹמֶר *ḥōmer* 17x clay, mortar, mud; "defenses of clay" are weak arguments [2563]

[2818] 3 חֹמֶר *ḥōmer* 13x homer (dry measure of volume, roughly the amount a donkey could carry, variously reckoned from six to eleven bushels [220 to 394 liters]) [2563]

[2819] חֵמָר *ḥēmār* 3x tar (used in waterproofing or mortar) [2564]

[2821] חָמַשׁ *ḥāmaš* 5x [Qp] to be organized for war; [P] to take a fifth [2567 & 2571*]

[2822] חָמֵשׁ *ḥāmēš* 508x five, (pl.) fifty [2568] See *fifth; fifty; five.*

[2823] 1 חֹמֶשׁ *ḥōmeš* 1x fifth [2569]

[2824] 2 חֹמֶשׁ *ḥōmeš* 4x stomach, belly [2570]

[2827] חֵמֶת *ḥēmet* 4x skin (for water or wine) [2573]

[2828] חֲמָת *ḥ^{a}māt* 24x Hamath, "*fortress*" [2574]

[2834] 1 חֵן *ḥēn* 69x favor, grace; charm; grace is the moral quality of kindness, displaying a favorable disposition; "to find grace in someone's eyes" means to be in a state of favor [2580] See *charm; favor; grace.*

[2837] 1 חָנָה *ḥānâ* 143x [Q] to set up camp, pitch camp, encamp [2583] See *camp; encamp.*

[2839] חַנָּה *ḥannâ* 13x Hannah, "*favor*" [2584]

[2840] 1 חֲנוֹךְ *ḥ^{a}nôk* 16x Enoch; Hanoch, "*initiated; follower*" [585]

[2842] חָנוּן *ḥānûn* 11x Hanun, "*favored*" [2586]

[2843] חַנּוּן *ḥannûn* 13x gracious, compassionate [2587]

[2844] חָנוּת *ḥānût* 1x vaulted cell [2588]

[2845] 1 חָנַט *ḥānaṭ* 1x [Q] to ripen [2590]

[2846] 2 חָנַט *ḥānaṭ* 3x [Q] to embalm [2590]

[2847] חֲנֻטִים *ḥ^{a}nuṭîm* 1x embalming [2590*]

[2849] חָנִיךְ *ḥānîk* 1x trained (and trusted person) [2593]

[2850] חֲנִינָה *ḥ^{a}nînâ* 1x favor, kindness [2594]

[2851] חֲנִית *ḥ^{a}nît* 48x spear [2595]

[2852] חָנַךְ *ḥānak* 5x [Q] to dedicate, to devote an object to deity; to train (morally and religiously) [2596]

[2853] חֲנֻכָּה *ḥ^{a}nukkâ* 8x dedication, offering for dedication [2598]

[2855] חִנָּם *ḥinnām* 32x without cause, for no reason; for nothing [2600]

[2857] חֲנָמַל *ḥ^{a}nāmal* 1x sleet [2602*]

[2858] 1 חָנַן *ḥānan* 77x [Q] to be gracious, to have mercy, to take pity, be kind; [Pol] to move to pity, be kind, be charming; [Ho] to be shown compassion, mercy; [Ht] to plead for grace, beg for mercy; this word implies acts of kindness, not simply feelings of pity [2603] See *forgive; show mercy, favor; to be gracious.*

[2859] 2 חָנַן *ḥānan* 1x [Q] to be loathsome [2603]

[2862] חֲנָנִי *ḥ^{a}nānî* 1x Hanani, "*gracious*" [2607]

[2863] חֲנַנְיָה *ḥ^{a}nanyâ* 25x Hananiah, "*Yahweh is gracious*" [2608]

[2866] 1 חָנֵף *ḥānēp* 11x [Q] to be desecrated, be defiled; [H] to corrupt, defile, pollute [2610]

[2868] 3 חָנֵף *ḥānēp* 13x godless, ungodly [2611]

[2869] חֹנֶף *ḥōnep* 1x ungodliness, godlessness [2612]

[2870] חֲנֻפָּה *ḥ^{a}nuppâ* 1x ungodliness, godlessness [2613]

[2871] חָנַק *ḥānaq* 2x [N] to hang oneself; [P] to strangle [2614]

[2873] 1 חָסַד *ḥāsad* 1x [P] to put to shame, reproach, with the strong implication of an insult [2616]

[2874] 2 חָסַד *ḥāsad* 2x [Ht] to conduct oneself as faithful [2616]

[2875] 1 חֶסֶד *ḥesed* 3x disgrace [2617]

[2876] 2 חֶסֶד *ḥesed* 249x unfailing love, loyal love, devotion, kindness, often based on a prior relationship, especially a covenant relationship [2617] See *kindness; love; loyalty; mercy.*

[2879] חָסָה *ḥāsâ* 37x [Q] to take refuge in, to trust in [2620]

[2883] חָסִיד *ḥāsîd* 33x godly, saints, the people of God with a focus on their faithfulness; this can refer to a prominent individual, with messianic significance (Ps 16:10) [2623]

[2884] חֲסִידָה *ḥ^a^sîdâ* 6x stork; some sources: heron [2624]

[2885] חָסִיל *ḥāsîl* 6x grasshoppers, locusts at a particular stage of development [2625]

[2886] חֲסִין *ḥ^a^sîn* 1x mighty, strong [2626]

[2887] חָסַל *ḥāsal* 1x [Q, H] to devour, consume [2628]

[2888] חָסַם *ḥāsam* 2x [Q] to muzzle (an animal); to block (the way) [2629]

[2889] חָסַן *ḥāsan* 1x [N] to be stored up [2630]

[2890] חֹסֶן *ḥōsen* 5x stored treasure, riches, wealth [2633]

[2891] חָסֹן *ḥāsōn* 2x mighty, strong [2634]

[2892] חַסְפַּס *ḥaspas* 1x [Pualal] to flake; some sources: to be scale-like, pertaining to the shape of an object; to crisp, crackle, pertaining to the brittleness of an object [2636]

[2893] 1 חָסֵר *ḥāsēr* 23x [Q] to lack; to have nothing; to go down, recede; [P] to make lower; to deprive; [H] to cause to lack, withhold [2637]

[2894] 2 חָסֵר *ḥāsēr* 17x lacking; wanting [2638]

[2895] חֶסֶר *ḥeser* 2x poverty, lack [2639]

[2896] חֹסֶר *ḥōser* 3x poverty, lack [2640]

[2898] חֶסְרוֹן *ḥesrôn* 1x what is lacking [2642]

[2899] 1 חַף *ḥap* 1x clean, pure [2643]

[2901] חָפָא *ḥāpā'* 1x [P] to do secretly [2644]

[2902] חָפָה *ḥāpâ* 12x [Q] to cover; [Qp] to be covered; [N] to be sheathed, be covered; [P] to panel, overlay, cover [2645]

[2903] 1 חֻפָּה *ḥuppâ* 3x canopy, shelter; chamber, pavilion (of marriage ceremony) [2646]

[2905] חָפַז *ḥāpaz* 9x [Q] to hurry away (in alarm or terror) [2648]

[2906] חִפָּזוֹן *ḥippāzôn* 3x haste [2649]

[2908] חֹפֶן *ḥōpen* 6x hollow of the hand, handful (sometimes as a measure of volume) [2651]

[2909] חָפְנִי *ḥopnî* 5x Hophni, "*tadpole*" [2652]

[2910] חָפַף *ḥāpap* 1x [Q] to shield, shelter [2653]

[2911] 1 חָפֵץ *ḥāpēṣ* 74x [Q] to desire, delight in, be pleased with, have pleasure [2654] See *delight; desire.*

[2912] 2 חָפֵץ *ḥāpaṣ* 1x [Q] to sway; some sources: to hang [2654]

[2913] 3 חָפֵץ *ḥāpēṣ* 12x desire, delight, pleasure [2655]

[2914] חֵפֶץ *ḥēpeṣ* 38x desire, delight, pleasure [2656]

[2916] 1 חָפַר *ḥāpar* 22x [Q] to dig, scoop, to paw, to make a hole of any depth in soil; by extension: to spy out, search for, look about, seek out [2658]

[2917] 2 חָפֵר *ḥāpar* 17x [Q] to feel dismay, be disgraced, be humiliated, be in confusion; [H] to bring disgrace, be ashamed, be humiliated [2659*]

[2924] חָפַשׂ *ḥāpaś* 24x [Q] to search for, examine, plot; [N] to be ransacked; [P] to search, look around, track down, hunt down; [Pu] to go into hiding, to devise; [Ht] to disguise oneself, become like [2664]

[2925] חֵ֫פֶשׂ *ḥēpeś* 1x plan, plot [2665]

[2926] חָפַשׁ *ḥāpaš* 1x [Pu] to be freed [2666]

[2927] חֹ֫פֶשׁ *ḥōpeš* 1x material (for saddle blanket) [2667]

[2928] חֻפְשָׁה *ḥupšâ* 1x freedom [2668]

[2930] חָפְשִׁי *ḥopšî* 17x free; set apart, exempt [2670]

[2931] חָפְשִׁית *ḥopšît* 2x separation, exemption (from duties) [2669]

[2932] חֵץ *ḥēṣ* 55x arrow; archer [2671] See *arrow.*

[2933] 1 חָצֵב *ḥāṣēb* 16x [Q] to dig; hew out, cut out; [Qp, N, Pu] to be dug, be engraved, be cut out; [H] to cut in pieces [2672]

[2934] 2 חָצַב *ḥāṣab* 1x [Q] to strike (with lightning) [2672]

[2935] חֹצֵב *ḥōṣēb* 85x stonecutter, mason [2672*]

[2936] חָצָה *ḥāṣâ* 15x [Q] to divide; set apart; to rise up to; [N] to be divided, be parceled out [2673]

[2937] 1 חָצוֹר *ḥāṣôr* 18x Hazor, "*enclosure*" [2674]

[2940] חֲצוֹת *ḥ^aṣôt* 3x middle (of the night), mid(night) [2676]

[2942] חֲצִי *ḥ^aṣî* 125x half, halfway, middle, midst [2677*] See *half; middle.*

[2943] 1 חֵצִי *ḥēṣî* 5x arrow [2678]

[2945] 1 חָצִיר *ḥāṣîr* 20x (green) grass; hay [2682]

[2946] 2 חָצִיר *ḥāṣîr* 1x leeks [2682]

[2948] 4 חָצִיר *ḥāṣîr* 1x home, abode, haunt [2681]

[2950] חֹ֫צֶן *ḥōṣen* 3x arms, folds of a robe [2684]

[2951] 1 חָצַץ *ḥāṣaṣ* 2x [Q] to be in order, in ranks; [P] to divide, share; [Pu] to come to an end [2686]

[2952] 2 חָצַץ *ḥāṣaṣ* 1x [P] to sing; some sources: to distribute water [2686]

[2953] חָצָץ *ḥāṣāṣ* 2x gravel [2687]

[2955] חֲצֹצֵר *ḥaṣṣar* 6x [P] to sound a trumpet, play a trumpet [2690*]

[2956] חֲצֹצְרָה *ḥ^aṣōṣ^erâ* 29x trumpet, a metal instrument used for signaling and music [2689]

[2958] 1 חָצֵר *ḥāṣēr* 192x courtyard, court of a house, enclosed areas; village, a permanent settlement but without walls [2691 & 2699*] See *court; village.*

[2976] חֹק *ḥōq* 131x decree, statute, prescription, a clear communication of what someone should do; allotment, share, portion, prescribed amount of something [2706] See *allotment; decree; limit; portion; quota; share; statute.*

[2977] חָקָה *ḥāqâ* 4x [Pu] to be carved, be portrayed; [Ht] mark for oneself; from the base meaning of carving or engraving is by extension of the act of writing; the communication itself, regulation [2707]

[2978] חֻקָּה *ḥuqqâ* 104x decree, ordinance, regulation, statute [2708] See *custom; decree; ordinance; regulations; statute.*

[2980] חָקַק *ḥāqaq* 19x [Q] to mark out, inscribe, chisel, engrave; [Qp] to be portrayed; [Po] to command, be a leader, ruler; staff (of a commander); [Pu] to be decreed; [Ho] to be written [2710]

[2983] חָקַר *ḥāqar* 27x [Q] to explore, search out, probe; [N] to be determined, be searched; [P] to search out [2713]

[2984] חֵ֫קֶר *ḥēqer* 13x searching, finding out, often negatively stated: what cannot be search thoroughly or found out [2714]

[2985] 1 חֹר *ḥōr* 13x noble, free person [2715]

[2986] 2 חֹר *ḥōr* 7x hole (in various forms) [2356]

[2987] חֻר *ḥur* 2x hole, pit [2352]

[2989] חֲרָאִים *ḥ^{a}rā'îm* 2x filth, excrement [2716*]

[2990] 1 חָרֵב *ḥārēb* 37x [Q] to be dried up, be parched; be desolate, lay in ruins; [N] to be ruined, be desolate; [Pu] to be dried up; [H] to lay waste, devastate, cause to dry up; [Ho] to lie in ruins [2717]

[2991] 2 חָרֵב *ḥārēb* 4x [Q] to kill; [N] to be slaughtered [2717]

[2992] 3 חָרֵב *ḥārēb* 10x dry, desolate, wasted, in ruins [2720]

[2995] חֶרֶב *hereb* 413x sword; dagger; knife; cutting tool; by extension: battle, war; used fig. of God's judgment [2719] See *dagger; knife; sword.*

[2996] 1 חֹרֶב *ḥōreb* 13x heat, dryness, drought, fever [2721]

[2997] 2 חֹרֶב *ḥōreb* 4x waste, rubble, object of horror, desolation [2721]

[2998] חֹרֵב *ḥōrēb* 17x Horeb, "*dry, desolate*" [2722]

[2999] חָרְבָּה *horbâ* 43x ruins, desolate place [2723]

[3000] חָרָבָה *hārābâ* 8x dry land, dry ground [2724]

[3001] חֲרָבוֹן *ḥ^{a}rābôn* 1x dry heat, implying a drought [2725]

[3004] חָרַג *ḥārag* 2x [Q] to come out trembling [2727]

[3005] חַרְגֹל *ḥargōl* 1x cricket; some sources: locust, grasshopper [2728]

[3006] חָרַד *ḥārad* 1x [Q] to tremble, quake, shudder, be startled; [H] to make afraid, frighten, make tremble [2729]

[3007] חָרֵד *ḥārēd* 39x trembling, fearful [2730]

[3010] 1 חֲרָדָה *ḥ^{a}rādâ* 9x panic, fear, terror, horror [2731]

[3013] 1 חָרָה *ḥārâ* 93x [Q] to be angry, be aroused; to burn with anger; [N] to rage; [H] to be jealous; [Tiphel] to compete, contend with; [Ht] to fret [2734 & 8474*] See *angry; burn.*

[3016] חֲרוּזִים *ḥ^{a}rûzîm* 1x string of jewels; some sources: string of beads or shells [2737*]

[3017] חָרוּל *hārûl* 3x weeds, undergrowth, variously identified [2738]

[3019] חָרוֹן *hārôn* 40x fierce (anger), burning (anger), wrath [2740]

[3021] 1 חָרוּץ *ḥārûṣ* 6x gold [2742]

[3022] 2 חָרוּץ *ḥārûṣ* 1x trench, ditch, moat, a military defense [2742]

[3023] 3 חָרוּץ *ḥārûṣ* 4x threshing sledge, sharp instrument for harvest [2742]

[3024] 4 חָרוּץ *ḥārûs* 1x maimed, mutilated, pertaining to what has been cut [2782*]

[3025] 5 חָרוּץ *ḥārûṣ* 2x decision [2742]

[3026] 6 חָרוּץ *ḥārûṣ* 5x diligent, industrious [2742]

[3031] חַרְחֻר *ḥarḥur* 1x scorching heat; some souces: fever [2746]

[3032] חֶרֶט *ḥereṭ* 2x pen; fashioning tool, stylus [2747]

[3033] חַרְטֹם *ḥarṭōm* 11x magician [2748]

[3034] חֳרִי *ḥ^{o}rî* 6x hot, burning, fierce (anger) [2750]

[3035] 1 חֹרִי *ḥōrî* 1x (white) bread or cake [2751]

[3038] חָרִיט *ḥāriṭ* 2x bag, purse [2754]

[3043] 1 חָרִיץ *ḥāriṣ* 1x portion, slice [2757]

[3044] 2 חָרִיץ *ḥāriṣ* 2x pick, hoe, an iron tool [2757]

[3045] חָרִישׁ *ḥārîš* 3x plowing, time of plowing [2758]

[3046] חֲרִישִׁי *ḥ^{a}rîšî* 1x scorching [2759]

[3047] חָרַךְ *ḥārak* 1x [Q] to roast; some sources: to capture [2760]

[3048] חֲרַכִּים *ḥ^{a}rakkîm* 1x lattice, a window covered by crossed strips of wood [2762*]

[3049] 1 חָרַם *ḥāram* 50x [H] to completely destroy, devote to destruction, exterminate, annihilate; [Ho] to be destroyed, be devoted to destruction; this can refer to anything which is under the ban from common use, some things are set apart for use by priests, other things are destroyed utterly as devoted to the LORD [2763] See *banish; destroy; devote to the ban.*

[3050] 2 חָרַם *ḥāram* 1x [Qp] to be disfigured, mutilated, any split portion of the face, possibly a cleft palate [2763]

[3051] 1 חֵרֶם *ḥērem* 29x devoted, set apart for destruction; this can refer to anything which is under the ban from common use, some things are set apart for use by priests, other things are destroyed utterly as devoted to the LORD [2764]

[3052] 2 חֵרֶם *ḥērem* 9x net, fishnet, trap [2764]

[3056] חֶרְמוֹן *ḥermôn* 14x Hermon, "*consecrated place*" [2768]

[3058] חֶרְמֵשׁ *ḥermēš* 3x sickle (for harvest of grain) [2770]

[3059] 1 חָרָן *ḥārān* 10x Haran, "*mountaineer* perhaps *sanctuary*" [2771]

[3063] 1 חֶרֶס *ḥeres* 1x itch, any eruptive skin rash [2775]

[3064] 2 חֶרֶס *ḥeres* 2x sun [2775]

[3068] חַרְסִית *ḥarsît* 1x potsherd [2777*]

[3069] 1 חָרַף *ḥārap* 1x [Q] (to spend the time of) winter [2778]

[3070] 2 חָרַף *ḥārap* 39x [Q] to treat with contempt, insult, reproach, taunt; [P] to defy, ridicule, taunt, mock, insult [2778]

[3072] 4 חָרַף *ḥārap* 1x [N] to be promised to a man, engaged [2778]

[3074] חֹרֶף *ḥōrep* 7x winter (the early time of the harvest cycle); prime (the early time of one's youth) [2779]

[3075] חֶרְפָּה *ḥerpâ* 73x disgrace, contempt, scorn, insult [2781] See *contempt; disgrace; insult; reproach.*

[3076] 1 חָרַץ *ḥāraṣ* 10x [Q] to pronounce, determine; [Qp, N] to be determined, be decreed [2782]

[3077] 2 חָרַץ *ḥāraṣ* 1x [Q] to pay attention, act quickly [2782]

[3078] חַרְצֹב *harṣōb* 2x struggle; chains [2784*]

[3079] חַרְצָן *harṣān* 1x seeds (of grapes); some sources: unripe fruit [2785*]

[3080] חָרַק *ḥāraq* 5x [Q] to gnash, grind (teeth) [2786]

[3081] 1 חָרַר *ḥārar* 9x [Q] to burn; (heated metal) glow; [N] be parched, burned, charred; [Pil] to kindle, cause to burn, glow; by extension: to have a fever [2787]

[3083] חֲרֵרִים *ḥ^a^rērîm* 1x parched place, a hot, lifeless desert place [2788*]

[3084] חֶרֶשׂ *ḥereś* 17x clay pot, earthenware; potsherd, fragment of pottery [2789]

[3086] 1 חָרַשׁ *ḥāraš* 27x [Q] to plow; engrave; plan, plot; [Qp] to be inscribed; [N] to be plowed; [H] to plot against [2790 & 2794*]

[3087] 2 חָרֵשׁ *ḥārēš* 47x [Q] to be silent, be quiet; to become deaf; [H] to be quiet, say nothing, be silent; [Ht] to make no moves, keep silent [2790]

[3089] 2 חֶרֶשׁ *hereš* 1x secretly, silently [2791]

[3091] 1 חֹרֶשׁ *ḥōreš* 3x wooded place, forest, thicket [2793]

[3093] חָרָשׁ *ḥārāš* 38x skilled craftsman: blacksmith, carpenter, stonemason, gemcutter, idol-maker, etc.; the ironic phrase "craftsman of destruction" means people who are very good at destroying things (Eze 21:31) [2796]

[3094] חֵרֵשׁ *ḥērēš* 9x deaf (one) [2795]

[3098] 1 חֲרֹשֶׁת *ḥ^arōšet* 4x cutting (stone), working (wood) [2799]

[3100] חָרַת *ḥārat* 1x [Qp] to be engraved [2801]

[3104] חָשַׂךְ *ḥāśak* 27x [Q] to keep back, to withhold, halt, spare; [N] to be spared, be relieved [2820]

[3105] חָשִׂף *ḥāśip* 1x small flock [2835]

[3106] 1 חָשַׂף *ḥāśap* 1x [Q] to strip bare, lay bare; to scoop out, draw out; [Qp] to be bared [2834]

[3108] חָשַׁב *ḥāšab* 124x [Q] to plan, plot, purpose, consider; to credit, account, impute; [N] to be thought, considered, regarded; be reckoned, accounted; [P] to determine, plan, plot; to compute, account; [Ht] to consider oneself [2803] See *calculate; count; plan; think; value.*

[3109] חֵשֶׁב *ḥēšeb* 8x waistband [2805]

[3110] חֹשֵׁב *ḥōšēb* 12x skilled craftsman, designer [2803*]

[3113] 1 חֶשְׁבּוֹן *ḥešbôn* 3x scheme, plan [2808]

[3114] 2 חֶשְׁבּוֹן *ḥešbôn* 38x Heshbon, "*reckoning*" [2809]

[3115] חִשָּׁבוֹן *ḥiššābôn* 2x catapult machine (for hurling against ramparts); scheme [2810]

[3120] חָשָׁה *ḥāšâ* 16x [Q] to be silent, be hushed; [H] to keep silent; to do nothing, hesitate [2814]

[3122] חָשׁוּק *ḥāšûq* 8x band, binding [2838]

[3124] חָשַׁךְ *ḥāšak* 17x [Q] to grow dark, be dim, be black; [H] to darken, make dark; often darkness has the associative meanings of gloom, despair, terror, ignorance, or hard to understand [2821]

[3125] חֹשֶׁךְ *ḥōšek* 80x darkness, dark; blackness, gloom; often darkness has the associative meanings of gloom, despair, terror, ignorance, or hard to understand [2822] See *darkness.*

[3126] חָשֹׁךְ *ḥāšōk* 1x obscure, dark, unknown [2823]

[3127] חָשְׁכָה *ḥoškâ* 1x darkness [2821*]

[3128] חֲשֵׁכָה *ḥ^ašēkâ* 7x darkness [2824* & 2825]

[3129] חָשַׁל *ḥāšal* 1x [N] to lag (behind), be worn out [2826]

[3133] חַשְׁמַל *ḥašmal* 3x glowing metal; some sources: electrum [2830]

[3134] חַשְׁמַן *ḥašman* 1x envoy [2831]

[3136] חֹשֶׁן *ḥōšen* 25x breastpiece [2833]

[3137] 1 חָשַׁק *ḥāšaq* 8x [Q] to set one's affection, desire, love, be attached to [2836]

[3138] 2 חָשַׁק *ḥāšaq* 3x [P] to make bands, make joints for binding; [Pu] to have bands [2836]

[3139] חֵשֶׁק *ḥēšeq* 4x thing desired, thing longed for [2837]

[3140] חִשֻּׁק *ḥiššuq* 1x spokes (of a wheel) [2839]

[3141] חִשֻּׁר *ḥiššur* 1x hub (of a wheel) [2840]

[3145] 1 חַת *ḥat* 2x fear, dread, terror [2844]

[3146] 2 חַת *ḥat* 2x terrified, broken [2844]

[3147] חֵת *ḥēt* 14x Hittite, "*descendants of Heth*" [2845]

[3149] חָתָה *ḥātâ* 4x [Q] to get, snatch, take away [2846]

[3150] חִתָּה *ḥittâ* 1x terror [2847]

[3151] חִתּוּל *ḥittûl* 1x splint, bandage [2848]

[3152] חַתְחַת *ḥatḥat* 1x horror, terror, danger [2849]

[3153] חִתִּי *ḥittî* 48x Hittite, "*descendants of Heth*" [2850]

[3154] חִתִּית *ḥittît* 8x terror [2851]

[3155] חָתַךְ *ḥātak* 1x [N] to be decreed [2852]

[3156] חָתַל *ḥātal* 2x [Pu, Ho] to be wrapped in strips of cloth [2853]

[3157] חֲתֻלָּה *ḥªtullâ* 1x band (of cloth) for wrapping [2854]

[3159] חָתַם *ḥātam* 25x [Q] to seal (with a signet ring); to seal up; by extension: to be a model; [Qp] to be sealed, be enclosed; [N] to be sealed; [P] to seal in; [H] to block, obstruct [2856]

[3160] חֹתֶמֶת *ḥōtemet* 1x signet ring seal [2858]

[3161] חָתַן *ḥātan* 11x [Q, Ht] to intermarry; to become a son-in-law [2859]

[3162] חֹתֵן *ḥōtēn* 21x father-in-law [2859*]

[3163] חָתָן *ḥātān* 20x son-in-law; bridegroom [2860]

[3164] חֲתֻנָּה *ḥªtunnâ* 1x wedding, marriage [2861]

[3165] חֹתֶנֶת *ḥōtenet* 1x mother-in-law (she who has a son-in-law) [2859*]

[3166] חָתַף *ḥātap* 1x [Q] to snatch away [2862]

[3167] חֶתֶף *ḥetep* 1x bandit, robber [2863]

[3168] חָתַר *ḥātar* 8x [Q] to dig, break into; row (in rough seas) [2864]

[3169] חָתַת *ḥātat* 55x [Q] to be shattered, dismayed, terrified; [N] to be discouraged, terrified; [P] to frighten; break; [H] to shatter, terrify [2865] See *afraid; (be) discouraged; (be) dismayed; (be) terrified.*

[3170] 1 חֲתַת *ḥªtat* 1x something dreadful, horrible [2866]

[3173] טֵאטֵא *ṭēʾṭēʾ* 1x [Pil] to sweep away [2894*]

[3178] טְבוּלִים *ṭᵉbûlîm* 1x turban [2871*]

[3179] טַבּוּר *ṭabbûr* 2x center (of the land), as a fig. extension of the navel of the body, not found in the OT [2872]

[3180] טָבַח *ṭābaḥ* 11x [Q] to slaughter, butcher; [Qp] to be slaughtered [2873]

[3181] 1 טֶבַח *ṭebaḥ* 12x slaughtering [2874]

[3184] טַבָּח *ṭabbāḥ* 32x cook, butcher; by extension: executioner; guard, imperial guard [2876]

[3185] טַבָּחָה *ṭabbāḥâ* 1x (female) cook (of meat) [2879]

[3186] טִבְחָה *ṭibḥâ* 3x slaughtered meat, butchered meat [2878]

[3188] טָבַל *ṭābal* 16x [Q] to dip, plunge; bathe, soak; [N] to be dipped [2881]

[3190] טָבַע *ṭābaʿ* 10x [Q] to sink down, to fall into; [Pu] to be drowned; [Ho] to be sunk, be settled into [2883]

[3192] טַבַּעַת *ṭabbaʿat* 50x ring; signet ring [2885] See *ring.*

[3196] טָהוֹר *ṭāhôr* 96x clean, pure, flawless, free from impurity; moral or ceremonial purity as a fig. extension of an object being free from defect or filth [2889 & 2890*] See *clean; pure.*

[3197] טָהֵר *ṭāhēr* 94x [Q] to be (ceremonially) clean, purified; [P] to pronounce clean, cleanse, make ceremonially clean, to purify; [Ht] to cleanse oneself, purify oneself; this can mean moral or ceremonial purity; see also 3196 [2891] See *cleanse; consecrate; purify.*

[3198] טֹהַר *ṭōhar* 4x purity; cleanness; clearness, brightness [2892]

[3199] טְהָר *ṭᵉhār* 1x splendor, purity [2892*]

[3200] טָהֳרָה *ṭohºrâ* 13x cleansing, purification; pronouncement of (ceremonial) cleansing [2893]

[3201] 1 טוֹב *ṭôb* 28x [Q] to be good, well, pleasing; [H] to do well, do good, prosper; this can refer to quality as well as to moral goodness [2896]

[3202] 2 טוֹב *ṭôb* 530x good, pleasing, desirable; goodness; this can refer to quality as well as to moral goodness [2896*] See *good; well.*

[3203] 3 טוֹב *ṭôb* 1x sweet(-smelling), perfume [2897]

[3204] 4 טוֹב *ṭôb* 4x Tob, "*good*" [2897]

[3206] טוּב *ṭûb* 32x good, best; goodness, prosperity; this can refer to quality as well as to moral goodness [2898]

[3208] טוֹבָה *ṭôbâ* 67x good, well-being; this can refer to quality as well as to moral goodness [2896*]

[3209] טוֹבִיָּה *ṭôbiyyâ* 17x Tobiah; Tobijah, "*Yahweh is good*" [2900]

[3211] טָוָה *ṭāwâ* 2x [Q] to spin (yarn) [2901]

[3212] טוּחַ *ṭûaḥ* 11x [Q] to cover with whitewash; overlay with plaster; [N] to be plastered, be coated [2902]

[3213] טוֹטָפֹת *ṭôṭāpōt* 3x symbol, sign (later, phylactery, a small box of Scripture verses worn as a sign of obedience to the covenant) [2903*]

[3214] טוּל *ṭûl* 14x [P] to hurl; [H] to thrown, hurl; [Ho] to be overpowered, be fallen, be hurled [2904]

[3215] טוּר *ṭûr* 26x row, course [2905]

[3216] טוּשׂ *ṭûś* 1x [Q] to swoop down; some sources: to flutter [2907]

[3217] טָחָה *ṭāḥâ* 1x [Pil] to shoot (an arrow the distance of a bowshot; the distance of a bowshot is still in sight, though it is out of hearing range) [2909]

[3218] טְחוֹן *ṭ^{e}ḥôn* 1x hand-mill, grinding-mill [2911]

[3219] טֻחוֹת *ṭuḥôt* 2x inner parts; heart, with a possible focus that this is a mysterious and unknowable part of a person [2910*]

[3220] טָחַח *ṭāḥaḥ* 1x [Q] to be smeared over [2902*]

[3221] טָחַן *ṭāḥan* 7x [Q] to grind to flour, crush to powder [2912]

[3222] טַחֲנָה *ṭaḥ^{a}nâ* 1x grinding-mill [2913]

[3223] טֹחֲנָה *ṭōḥ^{a}nâ* 1x grinder (= molar tooth) [2912*]

[3224] טְחֹרִים *ṭ^{e}ḥōrîm* 2x tumor, hemorrhoids [2914*]

[3225] טִיחַ *ṭîaḥ* 1x coating (of whitewash); some sources: coating of clay [2915]

[3226] טִיט *ṭîṭ* 13x mud, dirt, mire, clay [2916]

[3227] טִירָה *ṭîrâ* 7x camp (protected by stone walls); tower, battlement [2918]

[3228] טַל *ṭal* 31x dew, night mist [2919]

[3229] טָלָא *ṭālā'* 8x [Qp] to be spotted; be variegated; [Pu] to be patched [2921]

[3231] טָלֶה *ṭāleh* 3x lamb [2922* & 2924]

[3232] טַלְטֵלָה *ṭalṭēlâ* 1x hurling, throwing [2925]

[3233] טָלַל *ṭālal* 1x [P] to cover with a roof [2926]

[3237] 1 טָמֵא *ṭāmē'* 88x [Q] to be unclean, defiled; [N] to be made unclean, become defiled, impure; [P] to make unclean, defile, desecrate; [Pu] to become defiled; [Ht] to make oneself unclean, defiled; [Hotpaal] to be defiled; this can mean to be ceremonially impure or to be immoral in action [2930] See *defiled; impure; unclean.*

[3238] 2 טָמֵא *ṭāmē'* 162x unclean, defiled, impure; this can mean to be ceremonial impurity or active immorality [2931] See *defiled; impure; unclean.*

[3240] טֻמְאָה *ṭum'â* 36x uncleanness, impurity, filthiness; this can mean ceremonial impurity or a physical impurity on the body or in an object [2932]

[3241] טָמָה *ṭāmâ* 1x [N] to be considered stupid; some sources: to be regarded as unclean [2933]

[3243] טָמַן *ṭāman* 31x [Q] to hide; bury; [Qp] to be hidden; [N] to hide oneself; [H] to keep hidden [2934]

[3244] טֶנֶא *tene'* 4x basket [2935]

[3245] טָנַף *ṭānap* 1x [P] to soil, make dirty [2936]

[3246] טָעָה *ṭā'â* 1x [H] to lead astray [2937]

[3247] טָעַם *ṭā'am* 11x [Q] to taste; to see, discover by experience [2938]

[3248] טַעַם *ṭa'am* 13x taste; discretion; discernment; decree, judgment; "to turn from discernment" means "to pretend to be insane" (1Sa 21:13) [2940]

[3249] 1 טָעַן *ṭā'an* 1x [Pu] to be pierced [2944]

[3250] 2 טָעַן *ṭā'an* 1x [Q] to load [2943]

[3251] 1 טַף *ṭap* 42x (little) children, women and children, those (as a class) not able or barely able to march [2945]

[3253] 1 טָפַח *ṭāpaḥ* 1x [P] to spread out [2946]

[3254] 2 טָפַח *ṭāpaḥ* 1x [P] to care for; some sources: to bear healthy children [2946]

[3255] טֶפַח *ṭepaḥ* 2x span, handbreadth (the width of the hand at the base of the four fingers, about three inches (8 cm) [2947*]

[3256] טֹפַח *ṭōpaḥ* 5x handbreadth, span of the hand; see also 3255 [2948]

[3257] 1 טְפָחָה *ṭapḥâ* 1x handbreadth, a figure of a short unit of time, a few years; see also 3255 [2947*]

[3258] 2 טְפָחָה *ṭapḥâ* 1x eaves [2947*]

[3259] טִפֻּחִים *ṭippuḥîm* 1x caring for (children) [2949*]

[3260] טָפַל *ṭāpal* 3x [Q] to smear, cover [2950]

[3261] טִפְסָר *ṭipsār* 2x official, clerk [2951]

[3262] טָפַף *ṭāpap* 1x [Q] to take little steps, trip along [2952]

[3263] טָפַשׁ *ṭāpaš* 1x [Q] to be unfeeling, insensible [2954]

[3265] טָרַד *ṭārad* 2x [Q] to constantly drip [2956]

[3267] טָרַח *ṭāraḥ* 1x [H] to load down, burden with [2959]

[3268] טֹרַח *ṭōraḥ* 2x burden, problem, load [2960]

[3269] טָרִי *ṭārî* 2x fresh (bone); open, moist (sore) [2961]

[3270] טֶרֶם *ṭerem* 56x a marker of time: before; negative: not, not yet [2962]

[3271] טָרַף *ṭārap* 25x [Q] to tear, mangle; [Qp, N, Pu] to be torn (to pieces); [H] to provide (to enjoy) [2963]

[3272] טֶרֶף *ṭerep* 22x prey (food for wild animals) [2964]

[3273] טָרָף *ṭārāp* 2x fresh-picked (leaf or vegetation) [2965]

[3274] טְרֵפָה *ṭᵉrēpâ* 9x animal torn by wild beasts [2966]

[3277] יָאַב *yā'ab* 1x [Q] to long for [2968]

[3278] יָאָה *yā'â* 1x [Q] to be fitting, be proper [2969]

[3281] יָאִיר *yā'îr* 8x Jair, "*he gives light*" [2971]

[3282] 1 יָאַל *yā'al* 4x [N] to become foolish, act foolish [2973]

[3283] 2 יָאַל *yā'al* 19x [H] to begin; to determine; be intent upon; to agree to; to be content, be pleased; to be bold [2974]

[3284] יְאֹר *yᵉʾōr* 64x river, stream, the Nile river; likely the Tigris river in Daniel [2975] See *Nile; river; stream.*

[3286] יָאַשׁ *yāʾaš* 6x [N] to be despairing of, be without hope, give up; [P] to let despair [2976]

[3288] יֹאשִׁיָּהוּ *yōʾšiyyāhû* 52x Josiah, "*let* or *may Yahweh give*" [2977]

[3291] יָבַב *yābab* 12x [P] to cry out, lament [2980]

[3292] יְבוּל *yᵉbûl* 4x crops, produce, harvest [2981]

[3294] יְבוּסִי *yᵉbûsî* 41x Jebusite, "*of Jebus*" [2983]

[3297] יָבַל *yābal* 18x [H] to bring, take (a gift); [Ho] to be brought, be led, be carried off [2986]

[3298] 1 יָבָל *yābāl* 2x stream, watercourse [2988]

[3301] יַבֶּלֶת *yabbelet* 1x wart; some sources: running sore [2990*]

[3302] יָבַם *yābam* 3x [P] to fulfill the procreational duty of the brother-in-law [2992]

[3303] יָבָם *yābām* 2x husband's brother [2993]

[3304] יְבָמָה *yᵉbāmâ* 5x brother's widow; sister-in-law, husband's brother's widow [2994*]

[3309] יַבֹּק *yabbōq* 7x Jabbok, "*flowing* or *wrestling*" [2999]

[3312] 1 יָבֵשׁ *yābēš* 59x [Q] to dry up, be dry, be withered, be shriveled up; [P] to make wither, dry up; [H] to make wither, dry up [3001] See *dry up; wither.*

[3313] 2 יָבֵשׁ *yābēš* 10x dry, withered, by extension: a paralyzed person (whose limbs have a shriveled appearance) [3002]

[3315] 4 יָבֵשׁ *yābēš* 9x Jabesh, "*dry*" [3003]

[3316] יָבֵשׁ גִּלְעָד *yābēš gilʿād* 12x Jabesh Gilead, "*dry Gilead*" [3003*]

[3317] יַבָּשָׁה *yabbāšâ* 14x dry ground, dry land (in contrast to bodies of water) [3004]

[3318] יַבֶּשֶׁת *yabbešet* 2x dry ground, dry land [3006]

[3320] יָגַב *yāgab* 2x [Q] to work a field, do farm work [3009]

[3321] יָגֵב *yāgēb* 1x field [3010]

[3324] 1 יָגָה *yāgâ* 7x [N] to be grieved; [P] to bring grief; [H] to torment, bring grief [3013]

[3325] 2 יָגָה *yāgâ* 1x [H] to remove [3014]

[3326] יָגוֹן *yāgôn* 14x sorrow, anguish, grief [3015]

[3328] יָגוֹר *yāgôr* 2x fearing, filled with fear [3016]

[3329] יָגִיעַ *yāgîʿa* 1x weary, exhausted [3019]

[3330] יְגִיעַ *yᵉgîʿa* 16x labor, heavy work; the result of labor: produce, gain [3018]

[3331] יְגִיעָה *yᵉgîʿâ* 1x weariness [3024*]

[3333] יָגַע *yāgaʿ* 26x [Q] to labor, toil, be weary; [P] to make weary; [H] to make weary [3021]

[3334] יָגָע *yāgāʿ* 1x what is toiled for, the produce of labor [3022]

[3335] יָגֵעַ *yāgēaʿ* 3x worn out, weary, wearisome [3023]

[3336] יָגֹר *yāgōr* 5x [Q] to fear, dread [3025]

[3338] יָד *yād* 1,627x hand, by extension: arm, finger; fig. of control, power, strength, direction, care [3027] See *bank (of a river).* See *hand; memorial; monument.*

[3341] יָדַד *yādad* 3x [Q] to cast (lots for decision making) [3032]

[3342] יְדִדוּת *yᵉdidût* 1x loved one, beloved [3033]

[3343] 1 יָדָה *yādâ* 3x [Q] to shoot (a bow); [P] to throw (down) [3034]

[3344] 2 יָדָה *yādâ* 111x [H] to express praise, give thanks, extol, make a public confession, make an admission; to praise is to speak of the excellence of someone or something; to give thanks has a focus on the gratitude of the speaker [3034] See *confess; praise; (give) thanks.*

[3349] יְדוּתוּן *y^edûtûn* 16x Jeduthun [3038]

[3351] יָדִיד *yādîd* 8x lovely, beloved [3039]

[3353] יְדִידוֹת *y^edîdôt* 1x love (song, referring to a wedding song) [3038*]

[3359] יָדַע *yāda'* 956x [Q] to know, recognize, understand; to have sexual relations; [Qp] to be respected; [N] to be known, make oneself known; [P] to cause to know; [Pu] to be well known; [H] to show, teach, make known; [Ho] to be made aware; [Ht] to make oneself known; this can range in meaning from the mere acquisition and understanding of information to intimacy in relationship, including sexual relations [3045] See *acknowledge; know; understand.*

[3361] יְדַעְיָה *y^eda'yâ* 11x Jedaiah, "*Yahweh has favored* or *Yahweh knows*" [3048]

[3362] יִדְּעֹנִי *yidd^e'ōnî* 11x spiritist, soothsayer [3049]

[3363] יָהּ *yāh* 49x LORD (Yahweh) [3050] See LORD.

[3365] יְהָב *y^ehāb* 1x care, burden [3053]

[3366] יָהַד *yāhad* 1x [Ht] to become a Jew, this can mean to join the Jewish faith or simply to act like a Jew [3054]

[3369] יֵהוּא *yēhû'* 58x Jehu, "*Yahweh is he*" [3058]

[3370] יְהוֹאָחָז *y^ehô'āḥāz* 20x Jehoahaz, "*Yahweh holds*" [3059]

[3371] יְהוֹאָשׁ *y^ehô'āš* 17x Joash; Jehoash, "*Yahweh bestows; man of Yahweh*" [3060]

[3373] יְהוּדָה *y^ehûdâ* 819x Judah, of Judah, Judean, "*praised*" [3063]

[3374] 1 יְהוּדִי *y^ehûdî* 76x (person) of Judah, Judean, Jew, Jewish, "*of Judah*" [3064]

[3376] 1 יְהוּדִית *y^ehûdît* 6x in Hebrew (language), in the language of Judah [3066]

[3378] יהוה *yhwh* 6,829x LORD (Yahweh), the proper name of the one true God; knowledge and use of the name implies personal or covenant relationship; the name pictures God as the one who exists and/or causes existence [3068 & 3069] See *Lord; Yahweh.*

[3381] יְהוֹיָדָע *y^ehôyādā'* 51x Jehoiada, "*Yahweh has known*" [3077]

[3382] יְהוֹיָכִין *y^ehôyākîn* 10x Jehoiachin, "*Yahweh supports*" [3078]

[3383] יְהוֹיָקִים *y^ehôyāqîm* 36x Jehoiakim, "*Yahweh lifts up, establishes*" [3079]

[3386] יְהוֹנָדָב *y^ehônādāb* 8x Jonadab; Jehonadab, "*Yahweh is generous, noble*" [3082]

[3387] יְהוֹנָתָן *y^ehônātān* 82x Jonathan; Jehonathan, "*gift of Yahweh*" [3083]

[3393] יְהוֹרָם *y^ehôrām* 29x Joram; Jehoram, "*Yahweh exalts*" [3088]

[3397] יְהוֹשֻׁעַ *y^ehôšu'a* 218x Joshua, "*Yahweh saves*" [3091]

[3398] 1 יְהוֹשָׁפָט *y^ehôšāpāṭ* 82x Jehoshaphat, "*Yahweh has judged*" [3092]

[3400] יָהִיר *yāhîr* 2x arrogant, haughty [3093]

[3402] יַהֲלֹם *yāh^alōm* 3x emerald (precious stone, exact identification uncertain) [3095]

[3405] יוֹאָב *yô'āb* 145x Joab, "*Yahweh is father*" [3097]

[3408] יוֹאֵל *yôʾēl* 20x Joel, "*Yahweh is God [El]*" [3100]

[3409] יוֹאָשׁ *yôʾāš* 47x Joash; Jehoash [3101]

[3413] יוֹבֵל *yôbēl* 27x ram's horn; (blowing of ram's horn) jubilee, (Year of) Jubilee [3104]

[3414] 1 יוּבַל *yûbal* 1x stream, watercourse [3105]

[3419] יוֹחָנָן *yôḥānān* 24x Johanan, "*Yahweh is gracious*" [3110]

[3427] 1 יוֹם *yôm* 2,301x day (24 hours), daytime (in contrast to night); by extension: an indefinite period of time, an era with a certain characteristic, such as "the day of the LORD" and the prophetic "on that day" [3117] See *day; today; year.*

[3429] יוֹמָם *yômām* 53x day; in the daytime, by day [3119] See *daily; day.*

[3431] יָוֵן *yāwēn* 2x mire, mud, sediment [3121]

[3433] 1 יוֹנָה *yônâ* 32x dove; pigeon [3123]

[3434] 2 יוֹנָה *yônâ* 19x Jonah, "*dove*" [3124]

[3437] יוֹנֵק *yônēq* 12x infant, one nursing; tender shoot [3126]

[3438] יוֹנֶקֶת *yôneqet* 6x new shoot, young shoot (of a plant) [3127]

[3440] יוֹנָתָן *yônātān* 42x Jonathan, "*gift of Yahweh*" [3129]

[3441] יוֹסֵף *yôsēp* 213x Joseph, "*he will add*" [3130]

[3446] יוֹעֵץ *yôʿēṣ* 21x counselor, adviser, one who gives advice and direction, with the implication that the advice given is wise and valuable [3289*]

[3448] יוֹצֵאת *yôṣēʾt* 1x going into captivity, departure; some sources: miscarriage (of cattle) [3318*]

[3450] יוֹצֵר *yôṣēr* 20x potter [3335*]

[3452] 1 יוֹרֶה *yôreh* 2x archer [3384*]

[3453] 2 יוֹרֶה *yôreh* 2x autumn (i.e., the time of the early rains, from the end of October to the beginning of December) [3138]

[3456] יוֹרָם *yôrām* 20x Joram; Jehoram, "*Yahweh is exalted*" [3141]

[3462] יוֹתָם *yôtām* 24x Jotham, "*Yahweh will complete*" [3147]

[3463] יוֹתֵר *yôtēr* 10x the rest; gain, advantage, profit; more than [3148]

[3469] יָזַן *yāzan* 1x [Pu] to be lusty, be in the rut [2109*]

[3472] יֶזַע *yezaʿ* 1x perspiration, sweat [3154]

[3476] 2 יִזְרְעֶאל *yizrᵉʿeʾl* 34x Jezreel, "*God [El] will sow*" [3157]

[3477] יִזְרְעֵאלִי *yizrᵉʿēʾlî* 13x Jezreelite, of Jezreel, "*of Jezreel*" [3158 & 3159*]

[3479] יָחַד *yāḥad* 3x [Q] to join, be united; [P] to unite [3161]

[3480] יַחַד *yaḥad* 44x together, along with, in close proximity or concord either in space or time; by extension: close association in relationships, unity [3162]

[3481] יַחְדָּו *yaḥdāw* 96x together; altogether; at the same time [3162*] See *together.*

[3491] יְחִזְקִיָּהוּ *yᵉḥizqiyyāhû* 41x Hezekiah; Jehizkiah, "*Yahweh gives strength*" [3169]

[3495] יָחִיד *yāḥîd* 12x only son, only child (special and unique to the parents); precious life; alone, solitary [3173]

[3496] יְחִיָּה *yᵉḥiyyâ* 1x Jehiah, "*Yahweh lives*" [3174]

[3498] יָחַל *yāḥal* 43x [N] to wait; [P] to wait for, put hope in, expect; [H] to wait, put hope in [3176]

[3501] יָחַם *yāḥam* 6x [Q] to be in (breeding) heat, be in the rut; [P] to be in (breeding) heat, to mate, to conceive [3179]

[3502] יַחְמוּר *yaḥmûr* 2x roebuck, the roe deer [3180]

[3504] יָחֵף *yāḥēp* 5x barefoot [3182]

[3509] יָחַשׂ *yāhaś* 20x [Ht] to enroll oneself in a genealogical record, be in a family register [3187]

[3510] יַחַשׂ *yaḥaś* 1x (book of) genealogy [3188]

[3512] יָטַב *yāṭab* 117x [Q] to be good, go well; to be glad, pleased; [H] to do good, right; to make successful, cause to prosper; "to be good in the eyes" indicates pleasure in and acceptance of a person or situation [2895* & 3190] See *do good; go well; please; prosper.*

[3516] יַיִן *yayin* 141x wine, an alcoholic beverage made of naturally fermented fruit juice (usually grapes), usually diluted with water for general consumption [3196] See *wine.*

[3519] יָכַח *yākaḥ* 59x [N] to reason together (in a legal case); to be vindicated; [H] to rebuke, discipline, punish; decide, argue, defend, judge; [Ho] to be chastened; [Ht] to lodge a charge against [3198] See *argue; contend; judge; punish; rebuke.*

[3523] יָכֹל *yākōl* 193x [Q] to be able, capable; overcome, prevail, have victory [3201]

[3528] יָלַד *yālad* 499x [Q] to give birth to, have a child, become the father of; [Qp, N, Pu, Ho] to be born, be a descendant; [P] to assist in childbirth, be a midwife; [H] to become the father of, cause to come to birth [3205] See *bear a child; beget; born; give birth.*

[3529] יֶלֶד *yeled* 89x male child, young boy; this can refer to a wide range of ages, from infant to young adult [3206] See *boy; child; young man.*

[3530] יַלְדָּה *yaldâ* 3x female child, young girl; this can refer to a wide range of ages, from infant to young adult [3207]

[3531] יַלְדוּת *yaldût* 3x youth, childhood [3208]

[3532] יָלַהּ *yālah* 1x [Q] to waste away, languish, implying anxiety and consternation [3856*]

[3533] יִלּוֹד *yillôd* 5x born (children) [3209]

[3535] יָלִיד *yālîd* 13x born (child, slave child); (pl.) descendants, children [3211]

[3536] יָלַל *yālal* 29x [H] to wail, howl [3213]

[3537] יְלֵל *y^e^lēl* 1x howling, wailing-cry [3214]

[3538] יְלָלָה *y^e^lālâ* 5x wailing, lamentation, howling [3215]

[3539] יַלֶּפֶת *yallepet* 2x running sore; some sources: scab, ringworm [3217]

[3540] יֶלֶק *yeleq* 9x locust, grasshopper; young locust, possibly some stage in the development of the locust [3218]

[3541] יַלְקוּט *yalqûṭ* 1x pouch [3219]

[3542] יָם *yām* 396x sea; seashore; the west (the direction of the Mediterranean Sea relative to the Near East); by extension: a large container for holding water; the recurring image of the sea as a terrifying danger and opponent of the LORD has its source in the Sea (Yamm) as a hostile Canaanite god [3220] See *sea.*

[3545] 1 יָמִין *yāmîn* 141x (direction) right; south, southward (south is right when facing east, the direction of orientation in the ancient Near East); the right is considered culturally to be stronger and of greater prestige than the left; to be seated on the right side of a ruler is a greater position than on the left side [3225]

[3553] יֵמִם *yēmim* 1x hot springs; traditionally: mules; others: adders [3222*]

[3554] יָמַן *yāman* 5x [H] to go the right; (ptcp.) right-handed [3231]

[3556] יְמָנִי *yᵉmānî* 33x (direction) right [3233]

[3558] יָמַר *yāmar* 1x [H] to change, exchange [3235]

[3561] יָנָה *yānâ* 19x [Q] to oppress, to crush; [H] to mistreat, take advantage of, oppress [3238]

[3566] יְנִיקָה *yᵉnîqâ* 1x shoot (of a plant) [3242]

[3567] יָנַק *yānaq* 16x [Q] to suck, be nursing; [H] to give nourishment, nurse [3243 & 5134*]

[3568] יַנְשׁוּף *yanšûp* 3x great owl (an unclean bird, variously identified) [3244]

[3569] 1 יָסַד *yāsad* 41x [Q] to lay a foundation, establish, ordain; [N] to be founded; [P] to lay a foundation, establish; [Pu, Ho] to be founded, have a foundation laid [3245]

[3570] 2 יָסַד *yāsad* 2x [N] to associate, conspire (together) [3245]

[3572] יְסוֹד *yᵉsôd* 20x foundation; base (of an altar); foot (base of the body); by extension: what is firm or enduring [3247]

[3573] יְסוּדָה *yᵉsûdâ* 1x foundation [3248]

[3574] יִסּוֹר *yissôr* 1x corrector, fault-finder, reprover [3250]

[3578] יָסַף *yāsap* 213x [Q] to add to, to do once more, to do again; [N] to be added to, to gain more, to be joined; [H] to increase, to cause to add to, to continue on, to add to, to happen again [3254] See *add; do again; exceed; increase; surpass.*

[3579] 1 יָסַר *yāsar* 42x [Q] to correct, discipline; [N] to accept correction, be warned, be disciplined; [P] to punish, correct, discipline; to instruct, train, discipline; [H] to catch; [Nitpael] to let oneself take warning [3256]

[3582] יָע *yāʿ* 9x shovel (for altar fires) [3257]

[3584] 2 יַעְבֵּץ *yaʿbēṣ* 3x Jabez, "*to grieve*" [3258]

[3585] יָעַד *yāʿad* 28x [Q] to select, appoint, set out; [N] to meet with, assemble, band together, join forces; [H] to summon, challenge; [Ho] to be set, be ordered [3259]

[3589] יָעָה *yāʿâ* 1x [Q] to sweep away [3261]

[3594] יָעַז *yāʿaz* 1x [N] to be arrogant, be insolent [3267]

[3597] יַעְזֵיר *yaʿzēr* 13x Jazer, "*he helps*" [3270]

[3598] יָעַט *yāʿaṭ* 1x [Q] to array, cover [3271]

[3603] יָעַל *yāʿal* 23x [H] to have value, have use, have benefit [3276*]

[3604] 1 יָעֵל *yāʿēl* 3x mountain goat, wild goat [3277]

[3605] 2 יָעֵל *yāʿēl* 6x Jael, "*mountain goat*" [3278]

[3607] 1 יַעֲלָה *yaʿᵃlâ* 1x (female) mountain goat, ibex; deer [3280]

[3610] 1 יַעַן *yaʿan* 99x for, because, since [3282]

[3612] יָעֵן *yāʿēn* 1x (male) ostrich [3283]

[3613] יַעֲנָה *yaʿᵃnâ* 8x owl; horned owl [3284]

[3615] 1 יָעֵף *yāʿēp* 8x [Q] to grow tired, be faint, exhaust oneself [3286*]

[3616] 2 יָעֵף *yāʿēp* 1x [Ho] to be in swift flight [3288*]

[3617] 3 יָעֵף *yāʿēp* 3x weary, exhausted, fatigued [3287]

[3618] יְעָף *yᵉʿāp* 1x flight; some source: tiredness, weariness [3288]

[3619] יָעַץ *yāʿaṣ* 80x [Q] to give advice, give counsel; to purpose, plan, plot, determine; [Qp] to be determined; [N] to seek advice, consult; to confer, to plot (together); [Ht] to consult together, conspire against [3289] See *advise; consult; counsel; counselor; plan; purpose.*

[3620] יַעֲקֹב *ya^caqōb* 349x Jacob, "*follower, replacer, one who follows at the heel*" [3290]

[3623] 1 יַעַר *ya^car* 56x forest, woods, thicket; (cultivated) tree groves [3264* & 3293] See *forest; thicket; woods.*

[3624] 2 יַעַר *yaʿar* 1x honeycomb [3293]

[3626] 1 יַעֲרָה *yaʿarâ* 1x honeycomb [3295]

[3636] יָפָה *yāpâ* 8x [Q] to be beautiful, delightful; [P] to adorn, make beautiful; [Ht] to adorn oneself [3302]

[3637] יָפֶה *yāpeh* 42x beautiful, fair, lovely, handsome [3303]

[3640] יָפַח *yāpaḥ* 1x [Ht] to gasp for breath [3306]

[3641] יָפֵחַ *yāpēah* 1x breathing out, with a strong implication that this breath results in an action or communication [3307]

[3642] יֳפִי *yopî* 19x beauty [3308]

[3645] יְפֵפִיָּה *yepêpiyyâ* 1x beautiful [3304*]

[3648] יְפֻנֶּה *yepunneh* 16x Jephunneh, "[perhaps] *may he [God] turn* or *turned*" [3312]

[3649] יָפַע *yāpaʿ* 8x [H] to shine forth, flash; smile [3313]

[3650] יִפְעָה *yipʿâ* 2x shining splendor [3314]

[3651] יֶפֶת *yepet* 11x Japheth, "*enlarge*" [3315]

[3653] 2 יִפְתָּח *yiptāḥ* 29x Jephthah, "*Yahweh opens, frees*" [3316]

[3655] יָצָא *yāṣāʾ* 1,076x [Q] to go out, come out; [H] to bring out, lead forth; produce; [Ho] to be brought out; emptied; by extension: to grow (of plants), to have offspring [3318] See *bring out; come out; go out.*

[3656] יָצַב *yāṣab* 49x [Ht] to stand one's ground, confront; to stand before, present oneself, commit oneself [3320]

[3657] יָצַג *yāṣag* 16x [H] to set, place, present; touch; [Ho] to be left behind [3322]

[3658] 1 יִצְהָר *yiṣhār* 1x olive oil [3323]

[3661] 1 יָצוּעַ *yāṣûʿa* 5x bed, couch [3326]

[3663] יִצְחָק *yiṣḥāq* 110x Isaac, "*he laughs, he will laugh* or *mock*; *[God] laughs*" [3327]

[3665] יָצִיא *yāṣîʾ* 1x coming forth [3329]

[3666] יָצִיעַ *yāṣîaʿ* 3x structure, room, often referring to an annex, wing, or level of a building [3326*]

[3667] יָצַע *yāṣaʿ* 4x [H] to spread out bedding; [Ho] to be spread out [3331*]

[3668] יָצַק *yāṣaq* 53x [Q] to pour out, cast out; [Qp] be cast out, be poured out, be smelted; [H] to pour out, spread out; [Ho] to be poured out, be washed away; be anointed [3332] See *cast; pour out.*

[3669] יְצֻקָה *yeṣuqâ* 1x casting (of metal), with a focus that this is one piece [3333]

[3670] יָצַר *yāṣar* 63x [Q] to form, fashion, shape, create; (of God) the Maker, the Creator; [N] to be formed; [Pu] to be formed; [Ho] to be forged, be formed; usually from existing material; God as Creator or Maker, has its focus his planning and forming the creation as a skilled craftsman [3335] See *form; make; plan.*

[3671] 1 יֵצֶר *yēṣer* 9x something formed, creation; inclination, disposition, motivation [3336]

[3674] יְצֻרִים *yeṣurîm* 1x frame, body, limbs, that which gives visible form to a person [3338*]

[3675] יָצַת *yāṣat* 26x [Q] to set ablaze; [N] to burn, be burned; [H] to kindle, set on fire [3341]

[3676] יֶקֶב *yeqeb* 16x winepress; (wine or oil) vat [3342]

[3678] יָקַד *yāqad* 8x [Q] to burn; to kindle a fire; [Ho] to be burning, be kindled [3344]

[3679] יְקֹד *y^eqōd* 2x blazing, burning [3350*]

[3682] יְקָהָה *y^eqāhâ* 2x obedience [3349]

[3683] יָקוּד *yāqûd* 1x hearth (of a fireplace) [3344]

[3684] יָקוֹט *yāqôṭ* 1x fragile (thing); possibly referring to a spider's web [2901* & 6990*]

[3685] יְקוּם *y^eqûm* 3x living thing, living creature [3351]

[3687] יָקוּשׁ *yāqûš* 4x fowler, one who snares birds [3353]

[3689] יָקַח *yāqaḥ* 1x [H] to become insolent, have audacity [3947*]

[3692] יַקִּיר *yaqqîr* 1x dear, precious [3357]

[3697] יָקַע *yāqaʿ* 8x [Q] to turn (away), wrench; [H] to kill and expose; [Ho] to be killed and exposed [3363]

[3699] יָקַץ *yāqaṣ* 11x [Q] to wake up, awake [3364]

[3700] יָקַר *yāqar* 11x [Q] to be precious, be costly; become well known; [H] to make scarce [3365]

[3701] יָקָר *yāqār* 34x precious, valuable, quality, pertaining to items that are rare, beloved, or splendid [3368]

[3702] יְקָר *y^eqār* 17x honor, splendor, riches, valuable things [3366]

[3704] יָקֹשׁ *yāqaš* 9x [Q] to lay a bird snare, set a trap; [N, Pu] to be ensnared, trapped [3369*]

[3707] 1 יָרֵא *yārēʾ* 317x [Q] to be afraid, be frightened; to revere, respect; [N] to be awesome, be dreadful, be feared; [P] to frighten, terrify, intimidate; in some contexts fear relates to terror and fright, in other contexts fear relates to honor, respect and awe, as in "the fear of the LORD" [3372] See *(be) afraid; fear; worship.*

[3710] 4 יָרֵא *yārēʾ* 63x fear; worship; see also 3707 [3373] See *afraid; fear; reverent.*

[3711] יִרְאָה *yirʾâ* 45x fear, reverence, piety; see also 3707 [3374]

[3714] יָרֵב *yārēb* 2x great (king) [3377]

[3715] יְרֻבַּעַל *y^erubbaʿal* 14x Jerub-Baal, "*Baal contends*" [3378]

[3716] יָרָבְעָם *yārobʿām* 104x Jeroboam, "*the people increase*" [3379]

[3718] יָרַד *yārad* 382x [Q] to come down, go down, descend; [H] to bring down, lower; [Ho] to be brought down, be taken down [3381] See *go down.*

[3720] יַרְדֵּן *yardēn* 182x Jordan, "*descending*" [3383]

[3721] 1 יָרָה *yārâ* 26x [Q] to throw, cast; shoot; [N] to be shot through; [H] to shoot (an arrow), to hurl [3384]

[3722] 2 יָרָה *yārâ* 3x [H] to water upon, rain, shower; [Ho] to be refreshed [3384]

[3723] 3 יָרָה *yārâ* 45x [H] to teach, instruct, give guidance, in a formal or informal setting, with an implied authority for the teacher and the content of what is taught [3384]

[3724] יָרַהּ *yārah* 1x [Q] to be frozen in fear [7297*]

[3728] יָרוֹק *yārôq* 1x green plant [3387]

[3731] יְרוּשָׁלַםִ *y^erûšālaim* 643x Jerusalem, "*foundation of Shalem [peace]*" [3389]

[3732] 1 יֶרַח *yeraḥ* 12x moon; (lunar) month [3391]

[3734] יָרֵחַ *yārēaḥ* 27x moon [3394]

[3735] יְרִחוֹ *y^eriḥô* 57x Jericho, "*moon city*" [3405]

[3736] יְרֹחָם *y^erōḥām* 10x Jeroham, "*he will be compassionate*" [3395]

[3740] יָרַט *yāraṭ* 2x [Q] to throw (into someone's custody); to be reckless, a fig. extension of going down a steep ravine [3399]

[3742] 1 יָרִיב *yārîb* 3x contender, accuser, adversary, opponent [3401]

[3749] יְרִיעָה *y^erî^câ* 54x tent curtain; tent, shelter, dwelling [3407] See *curtain.*

[3751] יָרֵךְ *yārēk* 34x the area and components of the torso: thigh, hip, breast, leg, side; by extension: side, base, of any object [3409]

[3752] יְרֵכָה *y^erēkâ* 28x far end, ends (of the earth); remote area: heights, depths [3411]

[3758] יִרְמְיָה *yirm^eyâ* 18x Jeremiah, "*Yahweh loosens [the womb]; Yahweh lifts up;* [poss.] *Yahweh shoots, establishes*" [3414]

[3759] יִרְמְיָהוּ *yirm^eyāhû* 129x Jeremiah, "*Yahweh loosens [the womb]; Yahweh lifts up;* [poss.] *Yahweh shoots, establishes*" [3414]

[3760] יָרַע *yāra^c* 1x [Q] to tremble, be faint-hearted [3415]

[3762] יָרַק *yāraq* 3x [Q] to spit (in the face as an act of contempt) [3417*]

[3763] יָרָק *yārāq* 3x vegetables, vegetable greens [3419]

[3764] יֶרֶק *yereq* 8x green (of plants, foliage, shoots, grass) [3418]

[3766] יֵרָקוֹן *yērāqôn* 6x paleness (of face); mildew (of grain) [3420]

[3768] יְרַקְרַק *y^eraqraq* 3x yellowish-green, pale-green (mildew); shining-yellowish (gold) [3422]

[3769] 1 יָרַשׁ *yāraš* 232x [Q] to be an heir, gain an inheritance, have as a possession; [N] to become destitute, to be poor; [P] to take possession of; [H] to drive away, push out, destroy; to cause to inherit; many of these meanings have a common element of gaining (by right or violence) or losing possession (by force or circumstance) [3423] See *drive out; inherit; possess, possessions; take possession.*

[3771] יְרֵשָׁה *y^erēšâ* 2x possession conquered [3424]

[3772] יְרֻשָּׁה *y^eruššâ* 14x possession, inheritance [3425]

[3776] יִשְׂרָאֵל *yiśrā^ēl* 2,505x Israel, "*he struggles with God [El]*" [3478]

[3778] יִשְׂרְאֵלִי *yiśr^e^ēlî* 5x Israelite, "*of Israel*" [3481 & 3482*]

[3779] יִשָּׂשכָר *yiśśāśkār* 43x Issachar, "*there is reward* [Gen. 30:18]; *may [God] show mercy; hired hand*" [3485]

[3780] יֵשׁ *yēš* 138x there is, it exists [3426]

[3782] יָשַׁב *yāšab* 1,088x [Q] to live, inhabit, dwell, stay; [N] to be settled, be inhabited; [P] to set up; to cause to settle, make dwell, to cause to sit; by extension: to marry, with a focus that the spouses live together [3427] See *dwell; live; remain; settle; sit.*

[3800] 1 יֵשׁוּעַ *yēšû^ca* 28x Jeshua, "*Yahweh saves*" [3442]

[3802] יְשׁוּעָה *y^ešû^câ* 78x salvation, deliverance, help, rescue from a dangerous circumstance or harmful state by a savior; divine salvation usually has its focus on rescue from earthly enemies, occasionally referring to salvation from guilt, sin, and punishment [3444] See *deliverance; salvation; savior.*

[3803] יֶשַׁח *yešaḥ* 1x emptiness; some sources: filth, dung [3445]

[3804] יָשַׁט *yāšaṭ* 3x [H] to extend; hold out [3447]

[3805] יִשַׁי *yišay* 4x Jesse [3448]

[3810] יְשִׁימוֹן *yešîmôn* 13x Jeshimon; wasteland [3452]

[3813] יָשִׁישׁ *yāšîš* 4x old, aged [3453]

[3817] יִשְׁמָעֵאל *yišmāʿēʾl* 48x Ishmael, "*God [El] he heard*" [3458]

[3818] יִשְׁמְעֵאלִי *yišmeʿēʾlî* 8x Ishmaelite, "*of Ishmael*" [3459]

[3822] 1 יָשֵׁן *yāšēn* 18x [Q] to sleep, fall asleep; [P] to put to sleep [3462 & 8153*]

[3823] 2 יָשֵׁן *yāšēn* 3x [N] to live a long time, be old, chronic [3462]

[3824] יָשָׁן *yāšān* 6x old; pertaining to last year [3465]

[3825] 3 יָשֵׁן *yāšēn* 7x sleeping, pertaining to sleep [3463]

[3828] יָשַׁע *yāšaʿ* 205x [N] to be rescued, be delivered, be saved; [H] to save, rescue, deliver; divine salvation has its focus on rescue from earthly enemies, occasionally referring to salvation from guilt, sin, and punishment [3467] See *deliver; rescue; save.*

[3829] יֵשַׁע *yēšaʿ* 36x salvation, deliverance, protection, often implying a victory is at hand; (of God) Savior, a title of God that focuses on rescue from earthly enemies, occasionally referring to salvation from guilt, sin, and punishment [3468]

[3833] יְשַׁעְיָהוּ *yešaʿyāhû* 35x Isaiah; Jeshaiah, "*Yahweh saves*" [3470]

[3835] יָשְׁפֵה *yāšepēh* 3x jasper (exact identification uncertain) [3471]

[3837] יָשַׁר *yāšar* 25x [Q] to do good, do right, be straight; [P] to make straight, make smooth; [Pu] to be evenly hammered; [H] to make straight, gaze straight; from the base meaning of straightening out a crooked object comes the fig. extension of doing an act that is not perverse, but right or just [3474]

[3838] 1 יָשָׁר *yāšār* 119x straight (not crooked or twisted); by extension, being morally straight: right, upright, innocent; (n.) upright person [3477] See *straight; upright.*

[3841] יֹשֶׁר *yōšer* 14x uprightness, straightness, honesty, integrity [3476]

[3842] יִשְׁרָה *yišrâ* 1x uprightness [3483]

[3844] יָשֵׁשׁ *yāšēš* 1x aged, decrepit [3486]

[3845] יָתֵד *yātēd* 25x tent peg, stake, pin (of a loom); tool for digging [3489]

[3846] יָתוֹם *yātôm* 42x fatherless, orphan [3490]

[3855] יָתַר *yātar* 106x [N] to remain, be left over, the rest; [H] to have left over, spare, preserve [3498] See *(be) left; remain; survive.*

[3856] 1 יֶתֶר *yeter* 97x remainder, remnant, the rest, what is left over [3499] See *excess; remainder; remnant.*

[3857] 2 יֶתֶר *yeter* 6x thong, cord, bowstring [3499]

[3858] 3 יֶתֶר *yeter* 9x Jether; Jethro [3500]

[3860] יִתְרָה *yitrâ* 2x wealth, abundance [3502]

[3861] יִתְרוֹ *yitrô* 9x Jethro, "*remainder*" [3503]

[3862] יִתְרוֹן *yitrôn* 10x profit, gain, increase [3504]

[3866] יֹתֶרֶת *yōteret* 11x covering, lobe (of certain animal livers) [3508]

[3869] -כְּ *ke*- 2,908x marker of comparison: as, like; marker of similarity or correspondence: according to; marker of time: when, as soon as, about [**]

[3872] כָּאַב *kāʾab* 8x [Q] to feel pain, ache; [H] to bring pain [3510]

[3873] כְּאֵב *keʾēb* 6x pain, anguish, suffering [3511]

[3874] כָּאָה *kāʾâ* 3x [N] to be brokenhearted, lose heart; [H] to dishearten, cause to lose heart [3512]

[3877] 1 כָּבֵד *kābēd* 114x [Q] to be heavy; to be wealthy, honored, glorified; to be failing, dull; [N] to be glorified, honored, renowned; [P] to honor, glorify, reward; [Pu] to be honored; [H] to make heavy, make hard; [Ht] to make numerous; honor oneself. If the base meaning is "to be weighty or heavy," then by extension, negatively: hard, dull, stubborn, difficult in circumstance; positively: substantial, honored, glorious, wealthy [3513] See *(be, make) heavy; honor; (be) unresponsive.*

[3878] 2 כָּבֵד *kābēd* 40x heavy, severe, difficult, an extended degree or amount, positive or negative; see also 3877 [3515]

[3879] 3 כָּבֵד *kābēd* 14x liver; heart [3516]

[3880] כֹּבֶד *kōbed* 4x heaviness; heavy mass (density, piles) [3514]

[3881] כְּבֵדֻת *kᵉbēdut* 1x difficulty, awkwardness [3517]

[3882] כָּבָה *kābâ* 24x [Q] to be quenched, snuffed out; [P] to quench, put out, snuff out [3518]

[3883] 1 כָּבוֹד *kābôd* 200x glory, honor, splendor, wealth; while related words can be positive or negative in context, this word is almost exclusively positive in the OT; "the Glory" a title for God focuses on his splendor and high status; "my glory" means "myself" (Ge 49:8); see also 3879 [3519] See *glory; honor.*

[3884] 2 כָּבוֹד *kābôd* 2x glorious, elegant [3520*]

[3885] כְּבוּדָּה *kᵉbûddâ* 1x possession, valuable property [3520]

[3888] כַּבִּיר *kabbîr* 10x great, mighty (of God and humans), with a focus on potency or ability [3524]

[3889] כָּבִיר *kābîr* 2x something braided; in context referring to goat's hair [3523]

[3890] כֶּבֶל *kebel* 2x shackles, fetters [3525]

[3891] כָּבַס *kābas* 51x [Q] (ptcp.) washer, fuller; [P] to wash, launder; [Pu] to be washed; [Hotpael] to be washed off [3526] See *cleanse; wash.*

[3892] כָּבַר *kābar* 2x [H] to multiply; provide in abundance [3527 & 4342*]

[3893] 1 כְּבָר *kᵉbār* 9x already, before [3528]

[3894] 2 כְּבָר *kᵉbār* 8x Kebar [3529]

[3895] 1 כְּבָרָה *kᵉbārâ* 1x sieve [3531]

[3896] 2 כִּבְרָה *kᵉbārâ* 3x (a certain) distance; some sources: as far as a horse can run; as far as one can see; about seven miles [3530*]

[3897] כֶּבֶשׂ *kebeś* 107x ram-lamb, young ram sheep [3532] See *lamb; sheep.*

[3898] כִּבְשָׂה *kibśâ* 8x ewe-lamb, young female sheep [3535]

[3899] כָּבַשׁ *kābaš* 14x [Q] to subdue, overcome, enslave; [N] be subdued, be subject, be brought under control; [P] to subdue; [H] subdue, subjugate [3533]

[3900] כֶּבֶשׁ *kebeš* 1x footstool [3534]

[3901] כִּבְשָׁן *kibšān* 4x furnace, likely in context referring to a kiln or forge for making glass, pottery, smelting, etc. [3536]

[3902] כַּד *kad* 18x jar, pitcher (of the size that could by carried on the shoulder) [3537]

[3905] כַּדְכֹּד *kadkōd* 2x ruby (exact identification unknown) [3539]

[3908] 1 כָּהָה *kāhâ* 12x [Q] to grow dim, be weak; [P] to fade, become faint [3543]

[3909] 2 כָּהָה *kāhâ* 1x [P] to rebuke, set (someone) right, with an implication that future bad behavior is curtailed [3543]

[3910] כֵּהֶה *kēheh* 4x dull; weak; smoldering; despairing [3544]

[3911] כֵּהָה *kēhâ* 1x healing, relief [3545]

[3912] כָּהַן *kāhan* 23x [P] to serve as a priest; see also 3913 [3547]

[3913] כֹּהֵן *kōhēn* 750x priest, who not only had religious duties, but also examined persons and things for medical diagnosis, policed the unruly, and taught the word of God [3548] See *priest*.

[3914] כְּהֻנָּה *k^ehunnâ* 14x priesthood, priestly office; see also 3913 [3550]

[3916] כּוֹבַע *kôba^c* 6x helmet [3553]

[3917] כָּוָה *kāwâ* 2x [N] to be burned, be scorched [3554]

[3918] כְּוִיָּה *k^ewiyyâ* 2x burn spot, scar (of a burn) [3555]

[3919] כּוֹכָב *kôkāb* 37x star, planet, a luminary in the night sky; by extension: human power (such as a king), heavenly power (that serve God); stargazer, one who studies the movements of the stars to predict the future [3556]

[3920] כּוּל *kûl* 37x [Q] to hold, seize; [Pil] to hold; to provide, supply, sustain; [H] to hold; to bear, endure [3557]

[3921] כּוּמָז *kûmāz* 2x ornament, necklace [3558]

[3922] 1 כּוּן *kûn* 219x [N] to be established, be steadfast, be firm, be prepared; [Pol] to establish, set in place, make secure; [Polal] to be made firm, be prepared; [H] to establish, make preparations, provide; [Ho] to be made ready, be established, be attached [3559] See *establish; prepare; provide*.

[3924] כַּוָּן *kawwān* 2x cake of bread (presented as an offering) [3561]

[3926] 1 כּוֹס *kôs* 31x cup [3563]

[3927] 2 כּוֹס *kôs* 3x little owl [3563]

[3929] 2 כּוּר *kûr* 9x (little) furnace (for smelting metals); by extension: the testing and purification process [3564]

[3931] כּוֹרֶשׁ *kôreš* 15x Cyrus [3566]

1 כּוּשׁ *kûš* 29x Cush [3568]

[3934] 1 כּוּשִׁי *kûšî* 25x Cushite, "*of Cush*" [3569 & 3571*]

[3938] כּוֹשָׁרָה *kôšārâ* 1x singing or prosperity, fortune [3574]

[3941] כָּזַב *kāzab* 16x [Q] to lie; [N] to be proven a liar, be false; [P] to lie, deceive, prove false; to fail; [H] to prove someone a liar [3576]

[3942] כָּזָב *kāzāb* 31x lie, falsehood; by extension: delusion; false god (worshiped by a deluded person) [3577]

[3946] 1 כֹּחַ *kōaḥ* 126x strength, power, might, ability; often physical strength and the vigor of good health, sometimes simply ability to accomplish an action [3581] See *power*.

[3947] 2 כֹּחַ *kōaḥ* 1x monitor lizard; some sources: any kind of lizard [3581]

[3948] כָּחַד *kāḥad* 32x [N] to be hidden; be destroyed, perish; [P] to hide, conceal, keep from; [H] to hide; to destroy, annihilate, get rid of [3582]

[3949] כָּחַל *kāḥal* 1x [Q] to paint (eyes) [3583]

[3950] כָּחַשׁ *kāḥaš* 22x [Q] to be thin; [N] to cringe, feign obedience; [P] to lie, deceive; fail; to cringe, feign obedience; [Ht] to cringe, feign obedience [3584]

[3951] כַּחַשׁ *kaḥaš* 6x lie, deception; gauntness, thinness, leanness [3585]

[3952] כֶּחָשׁ *keḥāš* 1x deceitful, untruthful [3586]

[3953] 1 כִּי *kî* 1x branding [3587]

[3954] 2 כִּי *kî* 4,483x a marker that shows the relationship between clauses, sentences, or sections; logical: for, that, because; contrast: but, except; introducing a statement, often untranslated [3588]

[3957] כִּיד *kîd* 1x destruction [3589]

[3958] כִּידוֹד *kîdôd* 1x spark [3590]

[3959] כִּידוֹן *kîdôn* 9x javelin, lance, spear [3591]

[3960] כִּידוֹר *kîdôr* 1x attack, battle [3593]

[3962] כִּיּוּן *kiyyûn* 1x pedestal [3594]

[3963] כִּיּוֹר *kiyyôr* 23x basin, pan, firepot [3595]

[3964] כִּילַי *kîlay* 2x scoundrel [3596]

[3965] כֵּילַפּוֹת *kêlappôt* 1x an iron-tipped tool: ax, crowbar, pickax, etc [3597*]

[3966] כִּימָה *kîmâ* 3x Pleiades (a constellation) [3598]

[3967] כִּיס *kîs* 5x bag, purse [3599]

[3968] כִּיר *kîr* 1x cooking pot, stove, a small portable cooking hearth, the form of the word suggesting it is large enough for a pair of pots [3600]

[3969] כִּישׁוֹר *kîšôr* 1x distaff, spindle, whorl, the small disk at the bottom of a distaff to promote turning [3601] See *vision.*

[3970] כָּכָה *kākâ* 37x this is what, this is how, thus [3602]

[3971] כִּכָּר *kikkār* 68x plain (geographical area); loaf of bread; cover (of lead); talent (unit of weight or value, about 75 pounds [34 kg]) [3603] See *loaf; plain; talent.*

[3972] כֹּל *kōl* 5,415x all, everyone, everything, totality of a mass or collective; every, any, a particular of a totality [3605] See *all; complete; each; every; everything; whole.*

[3973] 1 כָּלָא *kālāʾ* 17x [Q] to stop, withhold, contain; [Qp] to be confined; [N] to be restrained [3607]

[3974] 2 כָּלָא *kālāʾ* 1x [P] to finish [3607]

[3975] כֶּלֶא *keleʾ* 10x prison, (house of) imprisonment [3608]

[3977] כִּלְאַיִם *kilʾayim* 32x (things of) two kinds [3610]

[3978] כֶּלֶב *keleb* 35x dog; by extension of a person of low status: a dead dog; an immoral person: male prostitute [3611]

[3979] כָּלֵב *kālēb* 1x Caleb, "*dog; snappish, warding off*" [3612]

[3983] 1 כָּלָה *kālâ* 207x [Q] to finish, fulfill, complete; to fail, cease, perish; [P] to finish, complete, fulfill; to destroy, end, wipe out; [Pu] to be completed, be concluded [3615] See *complete; consume; destroy; finish.*

[3986] 3 כָּלָה *kālâ* 21x destruction, complete destruction [3617]

[3987] כַּלָּה *kallâ* 34x (before marriage) bride; daughter-in-law [3618]

[3989] כְּלוּא *kᵉlûʾ* 2x imprisonment [3628]

[3990] 1 כְּלוּב *kᵉlûb* 3x (fruit) basket; (bird) cage [3619]

[3994] כְּלוּלֹת *kᵉlûlōt* 1x time of betrothal, state of betrothal [3623*]

[3995] 1 כֶּלַח *kelaḥ* 2x full vigor [3624]

[3998] כְּלִי *kᵉlî* 325x article, utensil, thing; a general term that can be used of any object [3627] See *armor; article; furnishing; instrument; object; thing; utensil; vessel.*

[4000] כִּלְיָה *kilyâ* 31x kidney; by extension: inmost being: heart, mind, spirit, the seat of thought and emotion of the inner person; kernel (of wheat) [3629]

[4001] כִּלָּיוֹן *killāyôn* 2x destruction, annihilation; weariness, failure (of the eyes) [3631]

[4003] כָּלִיל *kālîl* 15x entire, whole, perfect; whole burnt offering [3632]

[4005] כָּלַל *kālal* 2x [Q] to bring to perfection, make complete [3634]

[4007] כָּלַם *kālam* 38x [N] to be disgraced, be humiliated, be put to shame; [H] to disgrace, humble, bring to shame; [Ho] to be mistreated, be despairing [3637]

[4009] כְּלִמָּה *k^e limmâ* 30x disgrace, shame, scorn [3639]

[4010] כְּלִמּוּת *k^e limmût* 1x shame, disgrace, insult [3640]

[4014] כָּמַהּ *kāmah* 1x [Q] to long for, yearn for [3642]

[4017] כְּמוֹ *k^e mô* 141x like, as; for, with, when [3644]

[4019] כְּמוֹשׁ *k^e môš* 8x Chemosh (pagan god) [3645]

[4021] כַּמֹּן *kammōn* 3x cummin (a small, flavorful seed of the carrot family) [3646]

[4022] כָּמַס *kāmas* 1x [Qp] to be kept in reserve [3647]

[4023] כָּמַר *kāmar* 4x [N] to become hot; become aroused, be excited (with compassion) [3648]

[4024] כֹּמֶר *kōmer* 3x priest, in the OT always one who serves a foreign god, with a possible focus on manic rituals and altered states of awareness [3649*]

[4025] כִּמְרִיר *kamrîr* 1x blackness, deep gloom [3650*]

[4026] 1 כֵּן *kēn* 20x honest; right, correct, orderly [3651]

[4027] 2 כֵּן *kēn* 752x marker to show sequence of logic: so, thus, therefore; marker to show sequence of events: so, then [3651]

[4029] 4 כֵּן *kēn* 10x stand (of a basin) [3653]

[4030] 5 כֵּן *kēn* 6x position; place [3653]

[4031] 6 כֵּן *kēn* 5x gnats, flies [3654]

[4033] כָּנָה *kānâ* 4x [P] to bestow a title or name of honor; to flatter by giving a name of honor [3655]

[4035] כַּנָּה *kannâ* 1x root [3657]

[4036] כִּנּוֹר *kinnôr* 42x a stringed instrument: harp, lyre, lute, zither [3658]

[4038] כִּנָּם *kinnām* 2x gnats [3654*]

[4043] כָּנַס *kānas* 11x [Q, P] to assemble, gather, store up; [Ht] to wrap around [3664]

[4044] כָּנַע *kānaʿ* 35x [N] to be humbled, be subdued, be subjected; [H] to subdue, humble, subject [3665]

[4045] כִּנְעָה *kinʿâ* 1x bundle of belongings [666]

[4046] 1 כְּנַעַן *k^e naʿan* 89x Canaan; Canaanite, "*land of purple,* hence *merchant, trader*" [3667]

[4047] 2 כְּנַעַן *k^e naʿan* 4x merchant, trader [3667]

[4048] כִּנְעָן *kinʿān* 1x trader, merchant [3669*]

[4050] 1 כְּנַעֲנִי *k^e naʿ^a nî* 71x Canaanite, of Canaan, in Canaan, "*of Canaan*" [3669]

[4051] 2 כְּנַעֲנִי *k^e naʿ^a nî* 2x merchant, trader [3669]

[4052] כָּנַף *kānap* 1x [N] to hide oneself, be hidden [3670]

[4053] כָּנָף *kānāp* 111x extreme part: wing (of creatures that fly); corner, hem (of garment); ends (of the earth) [3671] See *corner; edge; hem; skirt; species; wing.*

[4056] כְּנָת *k^e nāt* 1x associate, companion [3674]

[4057] כֶּסֶא *kese*ʾ 3x full moon [3677]

[4058] כִּסֵּא *kissē*ʾ 135x seat, chair; in a public or civic setting: place of authority, seat of honor; of royalty or deity: throne [3676* & 3678] See *kingdom; throne.*

[4059] כָּסָה *kāsâ* 153x [Qp] to be covered; [N] to be covered; [P] to cover, conceal; to decorate; to overwhelm; [Pu] to be covered, be shrouded; [Ht] to cover oneself, put on clothing [3680] See *conceal; cover; forgive; hide.*

[4062] כָּסוּי *kāsûy* 2x covering [3681]

[4064] כְּסוּת *k^e sût* 8x covering, cloak, clothing [3682]

[4065] כָּסַח *kāsaḥ* 2x [Qp] to be cut down (of brush) [3683]

[4067] 1 כְּסִיל *k^esîl* 70x foolish, stupid, insolent; (n.) fool, insolent person [3684] See *fool; shameless; stupid.*

[4068] 2 כְּסִיל *k^esîl* 4x Orion (and its adjoining constellations) [3685]

[4070] כְּסִילוּת *k^esîlût* 1x folly, stupidity, insolence, with a possible implication of rebellion [3687]

[4071] כָּסַל *kāsal* 1x [Q] to be foolish, be stupid [3688]

[4072] 1 כֶּסֶל *kesel* 7x waist, back; (pl.) loins [3689]

[4073] 2 כֶּסֶל *kesel* 6x trust, confidence; stupidity [3689]

[4074] כִּסְלָה *kislâ* 2x confidence; folly [3690*]

[4080] כָּסַם *kāsam* 2x [Q] to trip, clip (hair) [3697]

[4081] כֻּסֶּמֶת *kussemet* 3x spelt, emmer wheat [3698]

[4082] כָּסַס *kāsas* 1x [Q] to determine, reckon, compute [3699]

[4083] כָּסַף *kāsap* 6x [Q] to long for; be hungry; [N] to long for, yearn for; to be ashamed [3700]

[4084] כֶּסֶף *kesep* 403x silver, silver piece = money [3701] See *money; silver.*

[4086] כֶּסֶת *keset* 2x magic charm band [3704]

[4087] כָּעַס *kāʿas* 55x [Q] to be angry, be vexed, be incensed; [P] to anger, provoke; [H] to provoke to anger [3707] See *anger; irritate; provoke to anger.*

[4088] כַּעַס *kaʿas* 22x sorrow, grief, anxiety; anger, displeasure, annoyance [3708]

[4089] כַּעַשׂ *kaʿaś* 4x general uneasiness and anxiety, inwardly focused: anguish, grief; focused toward an object: anger, resentment [3708]

[4090] כַּף *kap* 195x hand (of a person), palm of the hand, sole of the foot, paw (of an animal); by extension: power, strength; something hollowed: socket, (shallow) dish; a measure of quantity: handful [3709] See *dish.*

[4091] כֵּף *kēp* 2x rock [3710]

[4092] כָּפָה *kāpâ* 1x [Q] to soothe, avert (anger) [3711]

[4093] כִּפָּה *kippâ* 4x palm branch, palm frond [3712]

[4094] 1 כְּפוֹר *k^epôr* 9x bowl, dish (made of gold or silver) [3713]

[4095] 2 כְּפוֹר *k^epôr* 3x frost [3713]

[4096] כָּפִיס *kāpîs* 10x beam (of woodwork); some sources: rafter [3714]

[4097] כְּפִיר *k^epîr* 30x young lion [3715]

[4099] כְּפִירִים *k^epîrîm* 2x villages [3715*]

[4100] כָּפַל *kāpal* 5x [Q] to fold double; [Qp] to be folded double; [N] to be doubled [3717]

[4101] כֶּפֶל *kepel* 3x double; two sides [3718]

[4102] כָּפַן *kāpan* 1x [Q] to hunger, send out roots in hunger [3719]

[4103] כָּפָן *kāpān* 2x hunger, famine [3720]

[4104] כָּפַף *kāpap* 5x [Q] to bow down in distress; [Qp] be bowed down; [N] bow down (before) [3721]

[4105] 1 כָּפַר *kāpar* 102x [Nitpael] to be atoned (for); [P] to make atonement; make amends, pardon, release, appease, forgive; [Pu] to be atoned for, be annulled; [Ht] to allow for atonement; atonement may be a figure of covering over and therefore forgetting (forgiving) sin [3722] See *appease; atone; wipe clean.*

[4106] 2 כָּפַר *kāpar* 1x [Q] to coat, cover (with pitch) [3722]

[4107] כָּפָר *kāpār* 2x (unwalled) village [3723]

[4108] 1 כֹּפֶר *kōper* 1x (unwalled) village [3724]

[4109] 2 כֹּפֶר *kōper* 1x pitch (used to cover and seal the ark of Noah) [3724]

[4110] 3 כֹּפֶר *kōper* 2x henna, henna blossom [3724]

[4111] 4 כֹּפֶר *kōper* 13x ransom, compensation, payment; bribe [3724]

[4113] כִּפֻּרִים *kippurîm* 8x atonement; atonement may be a figure of covering over and therefore forgetting (forgiving) sin; "day of Atonement" is an annual day of rest and with ceremonies accomplishing full atonement for the nation of Israel [3725*]

[4114] כַּפֹּרֶת *kappōret* 27x atonement cover (traditionally: mercy seat); the golden cover on the ark of the covenant, the place where atonement is made; see also 4113 [3727] See *atonement cover; mercy seat.*

[4115] כָּפַשׁ *kāpaš* 1x [H] to trample down [3728]

[4117] 2 כַּפְתּוֹר *kaptôr* 18x bud; top of a pillar or column [3730]

[4119] 1 כַּר *kar* 12x ram-lamb, (young) ram; battering ram [3733]

[4120] 2 כַּר *kar* 3x meadow, pastureland [3733]

[4121] 3 כַּר *kar* 1x saddle, saddle-bag [3733]

[4123] כֹּר *kōr* 7x cor (measure of dry or liquid volume, about 60 gallons [220 liters]) [3734]

[4124] כִּרְבֵּל *kirbēl* 1x [Pu] to be clothed, be wrapped [3736]

[4125] 1 כָּרָה *kārâ* 15x [Q] to dig; to hew (stone); to hollow out [3738]

[4126] 2 כָּרָה *kārâ* 4x [Q] to barter; purchase [3739]

[4127] 3 כָּרָה *kārâ* 1x [Q] to prepare a feast [3738]

[4130] כֵּרָה *kērâ* 1x feast, banquet [3740]

[4131] 1 כְּרוּב *k^e^rûb* 91x cherub, (pl.) cherubim, a class of supernatural beings that serve in the presence of God; used as ornamental figures on the atonement cover of the ark of the covenant and in the temple as well as on the walls and doors of the temple [3742] See *cherub, cherubim.*

[4135] כְּרִיתוּת *k^e^rîtût* 4x divorce [3748]

[4136] כַּרְכֹּב *karkōb* 2x ledge, rim, edge [3749]

[4137] כַּרְכֹּם *karkōm* 1x saffron (plant) [3750]

[4140] כִּרְכָּרָה *kirkārâ* 1x (fast running) female camel [3753]

[4142] 1 כֶּרֶם *kerem* 94x vineyard [3754] See *vineyard.*

[4144] כֹּרֵם *kōrēm* 5x worker in the vineyard, vine growers, vinedressers [3755]

[4147] כַּרְמִיל *karmîl* 3x crimson (yarn) [3758]

[4149] 1 כַּרְמֶל *karmel* 14x fertile land, fruitful land; this can refer to an orchard or plantation [3759]

[4150] 2 כַּרְמֶל *karmel* 7x Carmel (city), "*orchard planted with vine and fruit trees*" [3760]

[4151] 3 כַּרְמֶל *karmel* 5x Carmel (hill), "*orchard planted with vine and fruit trees*" [3760]

[4152] 4 כַּרְמֶל *karmel* 3x new grain, newly ripe grain [3759]

[4155] כִּרְסֵם *kirsēm* 1x [P] to ravage, eat away [3765]

[4156] כָּרַע *kāra*ᶜ 36x [Q] to kneel down, crouch, often with the associative meaning of respect and honor or of readiness for action; [H] to make bow down, make kneel (an act of oppression), make miserable [3766]

[4157] כֶּרַע *kera*ʿ 9x leg bone (the shank bone, between the knee and ankle) [3767*]

[4158] כַּרְפַּס *karpas* 1x (fine) linen [3768]

[4159] כָּרַר *kārar* 2x [Pil] to dance [3769]

[4160] כָּרֵשׂ *kārēś* 1x stomach, belly [3770*]

[4162] כָּרַת *kārat* 289x [Q] to cut off, cut down; to make (a covenant, agreement); [Qp] to be cut off, broken off; [N] to be cut off, be destroyed; [Pu] to be cut down; [H] to cut off, get rid of, destroy, kill; [Ho] to be cut off; "to cut a covenant" is "make a covenant," a figure of the act of ceremonially cutting an animal into two parts, with an implication of serious consequences for not fulfilling the covenant [3772] See *(make a) covenant; cut; destroy; exclude.*

[4164] כְּרֻתוֹת *kᵉrutôt* 3x beams (trimmed and cut) [3773*]

[4165] כְּרֵתִי *kᵉrētî* 11x Kerethite [3774]

[4166] כֶּשֶׂב *keśeb* 13x ram-lamb, young sheep [3775]

[4167] כִּשְׂבָּה *kiśbâ* 1x ewe-lamb, young sheep [3776]

[4169] כַּשְׂדִּים *kaśdîm* 80x Chaldean, Babylonian, astrologers [3778*]

[4170] כָּשָׂה *kāśâ* 1x [Q] to become sleek, heavy; stubborn, headstrong [3780]

[4172] כַּשִּׁיל *kaššîl* 1x axe [3781]

[4173] כָּשַׁל *kāšal* 65x [Q] to stumble, falter, fail; [N] be caused to stumble, be brought down; [H] to cause to stumble, overthrow, bring to ruin; [Ho] to be overthrown [3782] See *fall; stumble.*

[4174] כִּשָּׁלוֹן *kiššālôn* 1x falling down, stumbling [3783]

[4175] כָּשַׁף *kāšap* 6x [P] to engage in witchcraft, be a sorcerer [3784]

[4176] כֶּשֶׁף *kešep* 6x witchcraft, sorcery, often with the associative meanings of rebellion and seduction into false religion [3785]

[4177] כַּשָּׁף *kaššāp* 1x sorcerer [3786]

[4178] כָּשֵׁר *kāšēr* 3x [Q] to be right, successful; [H] to bring success [3787]

[4179] כִּשְׁרוֹן *kišrôn* 3x skill, achievement; benefit [3788]

[4180] כָּתַב *kātab* 225x [Q] to write, engrave (on stone tablets); [Qp] to be written, be inscribed; [N] to be written down, be listed, be recorded; [P] to issue a written statement; writing can refer to ink on leather or papyrus, stylus on wax or clay, or carving in stone [3789] See *write, writing.*

[4181] כְּתָב *kᵉtāb* 17x written communication in various forms: script, text, record, book (as a scroll or tablet) [3791*]

[4182] כְּתֹבֶת *kᵉtōbet* 1x tattoo mark [3793]

[4183] כִּתִּיִּים *kittiyyîm* 8x Kittim, Cyprus; western coastlands [3794*]

[4184] כָּתִית *kātît* 5x beaten or pressed olives; in some contexts this refers to virgin olive oil [3795]

[4185] כֹּתֶל *kōtel* 1x wall (of a house) [3796]

[4187] כָּתַם *kātam* 1x [N] be stained, be defiled [3799]

[4188] כֶּתֶם *ketem* 9x gold, pure gold [3800]

[4189] כֻּתֹּנֶת *kuttōnet* 29x garment, robe, tunic [3801]

[4190] כָּתֵף *kātēp* 67x shoulder, the part an animal or human that carries a load; by extension: shoulder piece; slope (of a hill), side, wall (of a building) [3802] See *shoulder; side.*

[4192] 1 כָּתַר *kātar* 1x [P] to bear with, have patience with [3803]

[4193] 2 כָּתַר *kātar* 4x [P] to surround, encircle; [H] to gather about; hem in [3803]

[4194] 3 כָּתַר *kātar* 1x [H] to crown, wear as a headdress [3803]

[4195] כֶּתֶר *keter* 3x crown (probably not jeweled), royal headdress, crest, high turban [3804]

[4196] כֹּתֶרֶת *kōteret* 24x capital (of a pillar or column) [3805]

[4197] כָּתַשׁ *kātaš* 1x [Q] to grind, pound (in a mortar) [3806]

[4198] כָּתַת *kātat* 16x [Q] to crush, beat; [Qp] to be crushed, be shattered; [P] to beat, crush, break to pieces; [Pu] to be crushed; [H] to beat down; [Ho] to be battered to pieces [3807]

[4200] לְ- *l^e-* 20,705x to, toward; in, through; before, at, with; temporally: before, until, when; logically: so that, in order to; agency: by means of [**]

[4202] לֹא *lō'* 5,172x no, not [3808]

[4206] לָאָה *lā'â* 19x [Q] to be weary; [N] to wear oneself out, be weary; [H] to wear someone out, try one's patience, frustrate [3811]

[4207] לֵאָה *lē'â* 34x Leah, "[poss.] *wild-cow; wild cow, gazelle; cow*" [3812]

[4211] לְאֹם *l^e'ōm* 35x people, nation [3816]

[4213] לֵב *lēb* 854x heart; by extension: the inner person, self, the seat of thought and emotion: conscience, courage, mind, understanding [3820] See *heart; mind; think.*

[4216] לָבֶא *lebe'* 1x lion [3833*]

[4218] לִבְאָה *lib'â* 1x lioness [3833*]

[4220] 1 לָבַב *lābab* 3x [N] to be made wise, be made intelligent; [P] to steal one's heart (from a lover's glance) [3823]

[4221] 2 לָבַב *lābab* 2x [P] to make special bread or pastry (heart-shaped?) [3823]

[4222] לֵבָב *lēbāb* 252x heart; by extension: the inner person, self, the seat of thought and emotion: conscience, courage, mind, understanding [3824]

[4223] לְבִבָה *l^ebibâ* 3x special bread (heart-shaped?) [3834]

[4225] לַבָּה *labbâ* 1x flame [3827]

[4226] לִבָּה *libbâ* 1x rage [3826]

[4229] לָבוּשׁ *lābûš* 1x clothing, garments [3830*]

[4230] לְבוּשׁ *l^ebûš* 31x clothing, garment, robe [3830]

[4231] לָבַט *lābaṭ* 3x [N] to come to ruin, be trampled [3832]

[4233] לָבִיא *lābî'* 11x lion, lioness [3833]

[4234] לְבִיָּא *l^ebiyyā'* 1x lioness [3833]

[4235] 1 לָבַן *lāban* 5x [H] to make white, be whitened; [Ht] to show oneself spotless, purified [3835]

[4236] 2 לָבַן *lāban* 3x [Q] to make bricks [3835]

[4237] 1 לָבָן *lābān* 29x white [3836]

[4238] 2 לָבָן *lābān* 54x Laban, "*white*" [3837]

[4242] לִבְנֶה *libneh* 2x poplar tree; some sources: storax tree [3839]

[4243] לִבְנָה *libnâ* 18x Libnah, "*white*" [3841]

[4244] 1 לְבָנָה *l^ebānâ* 3x bright (full) moon [3842]

[4247] לְבֹנָה *l^ebōnâ* 21x frankincense (a fragrant, resinous gum) [3828]

[4248] לְבָנוֹן *l^ebānôn* 71x Lebanon, "*white, snow*" [3844]

[4252] לָבַשׁ *lābaš* 112x [Q] to put on clothing, dress, clothe; [Qp] to be dressed; [Pu] to be dressed; [H] to dress another, clothe someone [3847] See *clothe; put on.*

[4253] לֹג *lōg* 5x log (liquid measure, about a third of a quart or liter) [3849]

[4256] לֵדָה *lēdâ* 4x delivery (of birth) [3205*]

[4258] לַהַב *lahab* 12x flame of fire; by extension: flash (of a blade), blade of a sword [3851]

[4259] לֶהָבָה *lehābâ* 19x flame, blaze, flash; (iron) point (of a blade) [3852]

[4261] לַהַג *lahag* 1x study, devotion to books [3854]

[4263] לָהַהּ *lāhah* 1x [Ht] to behave like a madman [3856]

[4265] 1 לָהַט *lāhaṭ* 10x [Q] to burn, flame; [P] to set afire, set ablaze, consume [3857]

[4266] 2 לָהַט *lāhaṭ* 1x [Q] to devour; (n.) ravenous beast [3857]

[4267] לַהַט *lahaṭ* 1x flame; referring to the supernatural blade of a sword [3858]

[4268] לְהָטִים *lᵉhāṭîm* 1x secret arts, sorceries [3858*]

[4269] לָהַם *lāham* 2x [Ht] to let oneself swallow greedily; (ptcp.) choice morsels [3859]

[4272] לַהֲקָה *lahᵃqâ* 1x group, community [3862]

[4273] לוּ *lû* 25x if! if only!; O that! [3863]

[4277] 1 לָוָה *lāwâ* 12x [Q] to accompany; [N] to be joined, be attached, be bound to [3867]

[4278] 2 לָוָה *lāwâ* 14x [Q] to borrow; [H] to lend [3867]

[4279] 1 לוּז *lûz* 6x [Q] to depart (from one's sight); [N] to be devious, be perverse, be deceitful; [H] to depart (from one's sight) [3868]

[4280] 2 לוּז *lûz* 1x almond tree (branch) [3869]

[4281] 3 לוּז *lûz* 8x Luz, "*almond tree*" [3870]

[4283] לוּחַ *lûaḥ* 43x tablets (of stone); board, panel (of wood); plate (metal) [3871]

[4286] לוּט *lûṭ* 4x [Q] to cover, enfold; [Qp] to be wrapped up; [H] to cover, wrap up [3874]

[4287] 1 לוֹט *lôṭ* 1x shroud, covering [3875]

[4288] 2 לוֹט *lôṭ* 33x Lot [3876]

[4290] 1 לֵוִי *lēwî* 62x Levi; Levite, "*of Levi*" [3878]

[4291] 2 לֵוִי *lēwî* 288x Levite, of Levi, "*of Levi*" [3878 & 3881*]

[4292] לִוְיָה *liwyâ* 2x garland, wreath [3880]

[4293] לִוְיָתָן *liwyātān* 6x Leviathan, sea-monster; this refers both to a serpent-like sea creature and to a mythological monster of chaos opposed to the true God [3882]

[4294] לוּל *lûl* 1x stairway; some sources: trap door [3883]

[4295] לוּלֵא *lûlēʾ* 14x if not, unless [3884]

[4296] לוּן *lûn* 15x [N] to grumble against, blame; [H] to grumble against, blame [3885]

[4297] לוּשׁ *lûš* 5x [Q] to knead (bread dough) [3888]

[4299] לָזוּת *lāzût* 1x crookedness, perversity, referring to a kind of speech [3891*]

[4300] לַח *laḥ* 6x fresh, fresh-cut, still moist [3892]

[4301] לֵחַ *lēaḥ* 1x strength [3893]

[4302] 1 לְחוּם *lᵉḥûm* 1x entrails [3894*]

[4303] 2 לְחוּם *lᵉḥûm* 1x blow, wound [3894*]

[4305] 1 לְחִי *lᵉḥî* 20x jaw, jawbone; by extension: cheek, jowl [3895]

[4308] לָחַךְ *lāḥak* 6x [Q] to lick up; [P] to lick up, subdue [3897]

[4309] 1 לָחַם *lāḥam* 171x [Q] to fight against, attack; [N] to fight against, attack [3898] See *attack; battle; fight.*

[4310] 2 לָחַם *lāḥam* 6x [Q] to eat, dine; [Qp] to be consumed [3898]

[4311] לָחֵם *lāḥem* 1x war; other sources vary [3901]

[4312] לֶחֶם *leḥem* 340x bread, bread loaf; any kind of food; time or act of eating, meal; "bread of the Presence" is a regular offering to the LORD presented on a designated table in the tabernacle and temple [3899] See *bread; food.*

[4315] לָחַץ *lāḥas* 19x [Q] to oppress, crush, confine; [N] to be pressed close [3905]

[4316] לַחַץ *laḥas* 12x oppression, affliction; short ration (of bread or water) [3906]

[4317] לָחַשׁ *lāḥaš* 3x [P] to charm, enchant (i.e., whisper); [Ht] to whisper together [3907]

[4318] לַחַשׁ *laḥaš* 5x charming, whispering; charm, enchanter [3908]

[4319] לָט *lāṭ* 7x quietly, privately, secretly, a fig. extension of the base meaning "no physical sound"; (pl.) secret arts, with a focus on mysterious and hidden elements of this magic [3814* & 3909]

[4320] לֹט *lōṭ* 2x myrrh (a resinous, fragrant and slightly bitter to the taste); some sources: mastic bark (a resinous gum of the rockrose plant) [3910]

[4321] לְטָאָה *lᵉṭāʾâ* 1x wall lizard; some sources: gecko [3911]

[4323] לָטַשׁ *lāṭaš* 5x [Q] to sharpen; to forge, hammer; to pierce (with the eyes); [Pu] to be sharpened [3913]

[4324] לֹיָה *lōyâ* 3x wreath, garland; some translate as a technical architectural term: border, rim [3914]

[4325] לַיִל *layil* 6x night [3915]

[4326] לַיְלָה *laylâ* 234x night; sometimes with the implication that it is the time of illicit, illegal, or immoral activity [3915] See *night.*

[4327] לִילִית *lîlît* 1x night creature; Lilith, a female demon of the night [3917]

[4328] לִין *lîn* 71x [Q] to spend the night, stay the night; [H] to hold back overnight, leave overnight; [Htpolal] to stay for the night; by extension: to stay, dwell an indeterminate amount of time [3885] See *remain; spend the night; stay.*

[4329] לִיץ *lîs* 6x [Q] to mock, scorn, talk big; [H] to mock; [Htpolal] to show oneself a mocker [3887*]

[4330] 1 לַיִשׁ *layiš* 3x lion [3918]

[4334] לָכַד *lākad* 121x [Q] to capture, seize, take as a possession; [N] to be taken captive, be seized, be taken [3920] See *capture; cling; seize; take captive.*

[4335] לֶכֶד *leked* 1x snaring, capturing [3921]

[4337] לָכִישׁ *lākîš* 24x Lachish [3923]

[4339] לֻלָאֹת *lulāʾōt* 13x (pl.) loops [3924*]

[4340] לָמַד *lāmad* 87x [Q] to learn, train for; [Qp] to be trained; [P] to teach, instruct, cause to learn; [Pu] to be trained; with implication that the learning will be put to use [3925] See *instruct; learn; teach; train.*

[4341] לִמֻּד *limmud* 6x accustomed to; (n.) a disciple, one who is taught, a follower [3928]

[4344] לְמוֹ *lᵉmô* 4x for, in, over [3926]

[4347] לֶמֶךְ *lemek* 11x Lamech [3929]

[4350] לֹעַ *lōʿa* 1x throat [3930]

[4351] לָעַב *lāʿab* 1x [H] to mock, make sport of (someone), make a game of (someone) [3931]

[4352] לָעַג *lāʿag* 21x [Q] to mock, scoff, ridicule; [N] to stammer, speak as a foreigner; [H] to mock, ridicule [3932]

[4353] לַעַג *laʿag* 7x scorn, ridicule, derision [3933]

[4357] לָעַז *lāʿaz* 1x [Q] to speak a foreign tongue, speak an unintelligible language [3937]

[4358] לָעַט *lāʿaṭ* 1x [H] to let (someone) gulp down [3938]

[4361] לְעַנּוֹת *leʿannôt* 1x leannoth [t.t. in Psalms] [6030*]

[4363] לָעַע 2 *lāʿaʿ* 1x [Q] to sip, lap, slurp [3216*]

[4365] לַפִּיד *lappîd* 13x torch, firebrand; by extension: lightning [3940]

[4369] לָפַת *lāpat* 3x [Q] to reach toward; [N] be turned aside; in some contexts there is an implication of touching or grasping the object reached toward [3943]

[4370] לֵץ *lēṣ* 16x mocker, babbler, scoffer [3887*]

[4371] לָצוֹן *lāṣôn* 3x mockery, scoffing, hostile speech of fools [3944]

[4372] לָצַץ *lāṣaṣ* 1x mocker, scoffer, with an implication that this class of person is foolish and rebellious [3945]

[4374] לָקַח *lāqaḥ* 967x [Q] to take, receive; [Qp] to be led away; [N] to be captured, taken away; [Pu] to be taken away, brought; [Ht] to flash back and forth; by extension: to gain possession, exercise authority; "to take a woman" means "to marry a wife" [3947] See *accept; capture; choose; deprive; get; grasp; marry; receive; seize; take.*

[4375] לֶקַח *leqaḥ* 9x teaching, instruction, learning [3948]

[4377] לָקַט *lāqaṭ* 37x [Q] to gather; [P] to gather, pick up, glean; [Pu] to be gathered up; [Ht] to gather oneself about; this act of gathering is general, and can refer to the second or final gleanings of the field or orchard [3950]

[4378] לֶקֶט *leqeṭ* 2x gleanings (of a harvest) [3951]

[4379] לָקַק *lāqaq* 7x [Q, P] to lap up, lick up [3952]

[4380] לָקַשׁ *lāqaš* 1x [P] to glean [3953]

[4381] לֶקֶשׁ *leqeš* 2x second crop, late grass at spring time [3954]

[4382] לָשָׁד *lāšād* 2x moist (food), strength [3955*]

[4383] לָשׁוֹן *lāšôn* 117x tongue; by extension: language, speech, noise (of an animal); something tongue-shaped: wedge (of precious metal), bay, gulf, flame of fire [3956] See *language; speech; tongue.*

[4384] לִשְׁכָּה *liškâ* 46x room, chamber; hall; storeroom [3957]

[4385] לֶשֶׁם 1 *lešem* 2x jacinth (exact identification is uncertain) [3958]

[4387] לָשַׁן *lāšan* 2x [Po] to slander; [H] to slander [3960]

[4390] לֶתֶךְ *lētek* 1x lethek (a dry measure, half a cor, about 6 bushels [220 liters]) [3963*]

[4393] מַאֲבוּס *maʾabûs* 1x granary [3965]

[4394] מְאֹד *meʾōd* 300x a marker of great degree or quanity: very, greatly, exceedingly, much [3966] See *exceedingly; greatly; strength; very.*

[4395] מֵאָה 1 *mēʾâ* 583x hundred [3967] See *hundred.*

[4397] מַאֲוַיִּים *maʾawiyyîm* 1x desires [3970*]

[4399] מְאוּמָה *meʾûmâ* 32x something, anything; (with negation) nothing [3972]

[4400] מָאוֹס *māʾôs* 1x refuse, trash [3973]

[4401] מָאוֹר *māʾôr* 19x light source, luminary, light-bearer [3974]

[4402] מְאוּרָה *meʾûrâ* 1x nest hole (of a viper) [3975]

[4404] מֹאזְנַיִם *mōʾznayim* 15x set of scales, (two) balance pans for weight measurement, with an emphasis on honesty and standardized measurements; by extension: righteous evaluation of motives and actions [3976*]

[4407] מַאֲכָל *maʾ ᵃkāl* 30x food, supplies, something to eat [3978]

[4408] מַאֲכֶלֶת *maʾ ᵃkelet* 4x (butcher) knife, sometimes with a ceremonial or sacrificial focus [3979]

[4409] מַאֲכֹלֶת *maʾ ᵃkōlet* 2x fuel (for a fire); a fig. extension of food that is consumed [3980]

[4410] מַאֲמָץ *maʾ ᵃmāṣ* 1x effort, exertion [3981]

[4411] מַאֲמָר *maʾ ᵃmār* 3x command, decree, instruction [3982*]

[4412] מָאֵן *māʾ an* 46x [P] to refuse, reject [3985*]

[4415] 1 מָאַס *māʾ as* 74x [Q] to reject, despise, spurn, disdain; [N] to be rejected, become vile [3988] See *despise; reject.*

[4416] 2 מָאַס *māʾ as* 2x [N] to be festering, be dissolving; be vanishing [3988]

[4418] מַאֲפֶה *maʾ ᵃpeh* 1x something baked [3989]

[4419] מַאֲפֵל *maʾ ᵃpēl* 1x darkness [3990]

[4420] מַאְפֵּלְיָה *maʾ pēlyâ* 1x great darkness [3991]

[4421] מָאַר *māʾ ar* 4x [H] to be destructive; to be painful [3992]

[4422] מַאֲרָב *maʾ ᵃrāb* 5x ambush; troops in an ambush [3993]

[4423] מְאֵרָה *meʾ ērâ* 5x curse [3994]

[4426] מִבְדָּלוֹת *mibdālôt* 1x set aside, selected, singled out [3995*]

[4427] מָבוֹא *mābôʾ* 24x entrance, entryway, gateway; "the place where the sun goes (sets)" is the direction west [3996 & 3997*]

[4428] מְבוּכָה *mebûkâ* 2x confusion, confused terror [3998]

[4429] מַבּוּל *mabbûl* 14x flood (waters) [3999]

[4431] מְבוּסָה *mebûsâ* 3x trampling down, implying subjugation [4001]

[4432] מַבּוּעַ *mabbûaʿ* 3x (a bubbling) spring (of water) [4002]

[4433] מְבוּקָה *mebûqâ* 1x plundering, devastation, desertion [4003]

[4434] מְבוּשִׁים *mebûšîm* 1x private parts, (male) genitals, with a possible focus on shame if exposed [4016*]

[4435] מִבְחוֹר *mibḥôr* 2x choicest (trees); major (towns) [4004]

[4436] 1 מִבְחָר *mibḥār* 12x choicest, best, elite, finest (persons or things) [4005]

[4438] מַבָּט *mabbāṭ* 3x hope, trust in, relying on [4007]

[4439] מִבְטָא *mibṭāʾ* 2x rash promise, rashness [4008]

[4440] מִבְטָח *mibṭāḥ* 15x security, trust, confidence [4009]

[4443] מַבְלִיגִית *mablîgît* 1x comfort, smile, cheerfulness [4010]

[4445] מִבְנֶה *mibneh* 1x building, structure [4011]

[4448] 1 מִבְצָר *mibṣār* 36x fortress, fortification, stronghold [4013]

[4450] 3 מִבְצָר *mibṣār* 1x ore [4013]

[4451] מִבְרָח *mibrāḥ* 1x fleeing, refugee [4015]

[4453] מְבַשְּׁלוֹת *mebaššelôt* 1x places for fire, cooking-places [4018*]

[4454] מָג *māg* 2x official (used with 8042) [7248*]

[4456] מִגְבָּלוֹת *migbālôt* 1x (braided) chains, (twisted) cords [4020*]

[4457] מִגְבָּעָה *migbāʿâ* 4x headband [4021]

[4458] מֶגֶד *meged* 12x choice things, best gifts [4022 & 4030*]

[4459] מְגִדּוֹ *m^e^giddô* 11x Megiddo, "*place of troops*" [4023]

[4463] 1 מִגְדָּל *migdāl* 48x tower, watchtower, usually a tall, narrow building used for defense; high platform (made of wood and used for public speaking to crowds); an elevated area such as a garden with mounds, terraces [4026]

[4470] מָגוֹג *māgôg* 4x Magog, "[perhaps] *land of Gog*" [4031]

[4471] 1 מָגוֹר *māgôr* 8x terror, horror [4032]

[4472] 2 מָגוֹר *māgôr* 11x to live as an alien, stay as a stranger; place to live, place to lodge [4033*]

[4475] מְגוֹרָה *m^e^gôrâ* 3x dread, fear [4034]

[4476] מְגוּרָה *m^e^gûrâ* 1x barn, grain-pit, storage chamber [4035]

[4477] מַגְזֵרָה *magzērâ* 1x ax [4037]

[4478] מַגָּל *maggāl* 2x sickle [4038]

[4479] מְגִלָּה *m^e^gillâ* 21x scroll (a rolled up document made of leather or papyrus) [4039]

[4480] מְגַמָּה *m^e^gammâ* 1x horde [4041]

[4481] מָגַן *māgan* 3x [P] to hand over, deliver to, present with [4042]

[4482] 1 מָגֵן *māgēn* 63x (small) shield used for defense, usually of oiled leather; by extension: ruler, a leader who protects; fig. of the impregnable scales of leviathan [4043] See *shield.*

[4485] מְגִנָּה *m^e^ginnâ* 1x veil, covering [4044]

[4486] מִגְעֶרֶת *mig*ʿ*eret* 1x rebuke, reproach [4045]

[4487] מַגֵּפָה *maggēpâ* 26x plague; blow, strike, slaughter [4046]

[4489] מָגַר *māgar* 2x [Qp] to be thrown; [P] to cast, throw down [4048]

[4490] מְגֵרָה *m^e^gērâ* 4x saw (stone-cutting tool) [4050]

[4492] מִגְרָעוֹת *migrā*ʿ*ôt* 1x offset ledge, recess, rebatement (of a wall) [4052*]

[4493] מֶגְרָפָה *megrāpâ* 1x clods (of earth) or a digging instrument: hoe, spade, shovel [4053]

[4494] מִגְרָשׁ *migrāš* 114x pastureland, untilled open land (belonging to a town) [4054] See *pastureland; space; suburbs.*

[4496] מַד *mad* 11x clothing, garment; measure, decree [4055]

[4497] 1 מִדְבָּר *midbār* 269x desert, wasteland, barren wilderness, desolate land that supports little life; open country, suitable for grazing [4057] See *desert; wasteland; wilderness.*

[4498] 2 מִדְבָּר *midbār* 1x mouth, instrument of speech [4057]

[4499] מָדַד *mādad* 52x [Q] to measure a distance; consider a plan; [N] to be measured; [P] to measure off; [Htpol] to stretch oneself out [4058 & 4059*] See *measure.*

[4500] 1 מִדָּה *middâ* 55x measurement, size, length; section (of a wall), length of life [4060] See *measurement; section; size.*

[4501] 2 מִדָּה *middâ* 1x tax [4060]

[4503] מָדוּ *mādû* 2x garment [4063*]

[4504] 2 מַדְוֶה *madweh* 2x disease, sickness [4064]

[4505] מַדּוּחִים *maddûḥîm* 1x misleading, able to deceive [4065*]

[4506] 1 מָדוֹן *mādôn* 22x dissension, quarrel, strife, contention [4066 & 4079* & 4090*]

[4508] מַדּוּעַ *maddûa*ʿ 72x Why?, What is the meaning? [4069]

[4509] מְדוּרָה *m^e^dûrâ* 2x (circular) pile of wood, fire pit [4071]

[4510] מִדְחֶה *midḥeh* 1x ruin, downfall [4072]

[4511] מַדְחֵפָה *madhēpâ* 1x blow, thrust; (pl.) blow after blow [4073*]

[4512] מָדַי *māday* 16x Madai; Media, Medes [4074]

[4518] 2 מִדְיָן *midyān* 59x Midian, Midianite [4080]

[4519] מְדִינָה *m^edînâ* 53x province, district, region [4082] See *district; province.*

[4521] מְדֹכָה *m^edōkâ* 1x mortar [4085]

[4523] 1 מַדְמֵנָה *madmēnâ* 1x manure-pile, dung-heap [4087]

[4529] מַדָּע *maddāʿ* 6x knowledge [4093]

[4530] מֹדָע *mōdāʿ* 2x (distant) relative, kinsman [4129]

[4531] מֹדַעַת *mōdaʿat* 1x (distant) kinsman [4130]

[4532] מַדְקֵרָה *madqērâ* 1x piercing (of a sword) [4094*]

[4533] מַדְרֵגָה *madrēgâ* 2x cliff, (steep) mountainside (with footholds and hiding places) [4095]

[4534] מִדְרָךְ *midrāk* 1x foot-width, footprint [4096]

[4535] מִדְרָשׁ *midrāš* 2x annotation, study, writing, exposition [4097]

[4536] מְדֻשָׁה *m^edušâ* 1x that which is crushed (by trampling on a threshing floor) [4098]

[4537] מָה *mâ* 752x why?, what?, how?; O!, who, whoever, whatever [4100]

[4538] מָהַהּ *māhah* 8x [Htpal] to wait, delay, linger, hesitate [4102]

[4539] מְהוּמָה *m^ehûmâ* 12x turmoil, confusion, panic, discomfiture [4103]

[4542] מָהִיר *māhîr* 4x skilled, well versed, experienced; speedy, prompt [4106]

[4543] מָהַל *māhal* 1x [Qp] to be diluted, changed to an adulterated state; referring to dilution by water [4107]

[4544] מַהֲלָךְ *mah^alāk* 5x passageway; journey [4108* & 4109]

[4545] מַהֲלָל *mah^alāl* 1x praise, good reputation [4110]

[4547] מַהֲלֻמוֹת *mah^alumôt* 2x (pl.) beating, thrashing, repeated blows to the body [4112*]

[4549] מַהֲמֹרוֹת *mah^amōrôt* 1x miry pits, pits filled with rain water [4113*]

[4550] מַהְפֵּכָה *mahpēkâ* 6x overthrow, destruction, demolishing [4114]

[4551] מַהְפֶּכֶת *mahpeket* 4x stocks (confining a prisoner, suggesting a crooked posture or distortion) [4115]

[4554] 1 מָהַר *māhar* 81x [N] to be swept away; to be impetuous, rash, disturbed; [P] to be quick, hasten, hurry, do at once [4116] See *hasten; hurry; procrastinate.*

[4555] 2 מָהַר *māhar* 2x [Q] to pay the purchase price for a bride [4117]

[4558] מֹהַר *mōhar* 3x bride-price, compensation to the father of the bride [4119]

[4559] מְהֵרָה *m^ehērâ* 20x haste, quickness, speed; (adv.) quickly, swiftly, soon, at once [4120]

[4562] מַהֲתַלָּה *mah^atallâ* 1x illusion, deception [4123]

[4566] 2 מוֹאָב *môʾāb* 179x Moab, Moabite [4124]

[4567] מוֹאָבִי *môʾābî* 16x Moabite, from Moab, "*of Moab*" [4125]

[4569] מוֹבָא *môbāʾ* 2x coming in; entrance (way) [4126]

[4570] מוּג *mûg* 17x [Q] to melt, waste away; [N] to melt away (in fear), be disheartened; to collapse; [Pol] to soften; to toss about; [Htpol] to melt away, flow from; from the base meaning the melting of a substance is the fig. extension of the inner person melting in fear [4127]

[4571] מוּד *môd* 1x [Pol] to shake, convulse, set into motion [4128*]

[4572] 1 מוֹט *môṭ* 40x [Q] to slip, fall, totter, stagger; [N] to be shaken, be caused to move, be toppled; [H] to bring down, to cause to fall; [Htpol] to be thoroughly shaken, be continually shaken [4131]

[4573] 2 מוֹט *môṭ* 4x carrying frame; pole; yoke bar [4132]

[4574] מוֹטָה *môṭâ* 12x yoke bar, pole, bar; by extension: oppression of subjected people [4133]

[4575] מוּךְ *mûk* 5x [Q] to become poor [4134]

[4576] 1 מוּל *mûl* 31x [Q] to circumcise; [Qp] to be circumcised; [N] to be circumcised, undergo circumcision, circumcise oneself; "to circumcise the heart" means to commit to covenant obedience from within, not only formally [4135] See *circumcise.*

[4577] 2 מוּל *mûl* 3x [H] to cut off, ward off [4135]

[4578] 3 מוּל *mûl* 35x before, opposite, in front of [4136]

[4580] מוֹלֶדֶת *môledet* 22x family, relatives, children; (land of) birth, native (land) [4138]

[4581] מוּלָה *mûlâ* 1x circumcision [4139]

[4583] מוּם *mûm* 21x defect, blemish, flaw, injury; by extension: shame, defilement [3971]

[4586] מוּסָד *mûsād* 2x foundation, laying the foundation stone [4143]

[4587] מוֹסָד *môsād* 8x foundation [4144]

[4589] מוֹסָדָה *môsādâ* 5x foundation [4146]

[4590] מוּסָךְ *mûsāk* 1x canopy [4329*]

[4591] מוֹסֵר *môsēr* 5x chains, shackles, fetters [4147]

[4592] מוּסָר *mûsār* 50x discipline, instruction, correction; wisdom and teaching that imply correcting errant behavior [4148] See *correction; discipline; instruction.*

[4593] 1 מוֹסֵרָה *môsērâ* 8x bonds, shackles, straps, chains, fetters [4147]

[4595] מוֹעֵד *môʿēd* 223x (Tent of) Meeting; appointed time, designated time, season [4150] See *appointed time; meeting; season.*

[4596] מוֹעָד *môʿād* 1x ranks, appointed place of a soldier [4151]

[4597] מוּעָדָה *mûʿādâ* 1x designation, appointment [4152]

[4599] מוּעָף *mûʿāp* 1x gloom, darkness; fig. of the emotional state of sadness and despondency [4155]

[4600] מוֹעֵצָה *môʿēṣâ* 7x plan, scheme, device, intrigue [4156]

[4601] מוּעָקָה *mûʿāqâ* 1x burden, misery, hardship [4157]

[4603] מוֹפֵת *môpēt* 36x wonder, sign, miracle, portent; symbol [4159]

[4604] 1 מוֹצָא *môṣāʾ* 27x act of going out, springing out, exiting, moving on; by extension, (n.) what goes out: spring (of water), mine shaft, sunrise, east [4161]

[4606] מוֹצָאָה *môṣāʾâ* 1x origin, coming out; latrine [4163]

[4607] 1 מוּצָק *mûṣāq* 2x casting (of metal) [4164]

[4608] 2 מוּצָק *mûṣāq* 2x restriction, constraint; distress, hardship [4165]

[4609] מוּצָקָה *mûṣāqâ* 1x casting (into one piece); channel, spout or lip (of a lamp) [4166]

[4610] מוּק *mûq* 2x [H] to scoff [4167]

[4611] מוֹקֵד *môqēd* 1x hearth, (place of) glowing embers, burning embers [4168]

[4612] מוֹקְדָה *môqᵉdâ* 1x hearth, place of burning [4169]

[4613] מוֹקֵשׁ *môqēš* 27x snare, trap, that which captures prey; by extension: ensnarement, entrapment (of a person) [4170]

[4614] 1 מוּר *mûr* 14x [N] to be changed; [H] to exchange, substitute, change [4171]

[4616] מוֹרָא *môrāʾ* 12x fear, terror, respect, reverence; awesome deed [4172]

[4617] מוֹרַג *môrag* 3x threshing sledge [4173]

[4618] מוֹרָד *môrād* 5x slope, road going down; something hammered down [4174]

[4619] 1 מוֹרֶה *môreh* 4x archer [4175]

[4620] 2 מוֹרֶה *môreh* 3x autumn rains [4175]

[4621] 3 מוֹרֶה *môreh* 4x teacher [4175]

[4623] 1 מוֹרָה *môrâ* 3x razor [4177]

[4625] 1 מוֹרָשׁ *môrāš* 2x possession, inheritance [4180]

[4626] 2 מוֹרָשׁ *môrāš* 1x desire [4180]

[4627] מוֹרָשָׁה *môrāšâ* 9x possession [4181]

[4629] מוֹרַשְׁתִּי *môraštî* 2x of Moresheth [4183]

[4630] 1 מוּשׁ *mûš* 3x [Q] to touch, feel; [H] be able to feel, touch [4184]

[4631] 2 מוּשׁ *mûš* 20x [Q] to depart, leave, move away, vanish; [H] to remove [4185]

[4632] מוֹשָׁב *môšāb* 43x dwelling, settlement, place to live, place [4186]

[4635] מוֹשִׁיעַ *môšîʿa* 21x savior, deliverer, rescuer; the OT concept of God as Savior has its focus on rescue from earthly enemies, occasionally referring to salvation from guilt, sin, and punishment [3467*]

[4636] מוֹשָׁעָה *môšāʿâ* 1x act of salvation, act of helping; see also 4635 [4190]

[4637] מוּת *mût* 854x [Q] to die, be killed, be dead; [Pol] to kill, slay, put to death; [H] to kill, make die, put to death, assassinate; [Ho] to be put to death, be murdered [4191 & 4192] See *die; kill; put to death.*

[4638] מָוֶת *māwet* 153x death, dying [4194] See *death.*

[4639] מוֹתָר *môtār* 3x profit, advantage [4195]

[4640] מִזְבֵּחַ *mizbēaḥ* 403x altar [4196] See *altar.*

[4641] מֶזֶג *mezeg* 1x blended wine, mixed wine (likely spiced) [4197]

[4642] מָזֶה *māzeh* 1x empty (from hunger), implying an unhealthy loss of weight and breakdown in health [4198]

[4646] מָזוּ *māzû* 1x barn, granary [4200*]

[4647] מְזוּזָה *mᵉzûzâ* 19x doorframe, doorpost, doorjamb [4201]

[4648] מָזוֹן *māzôn* 2x provisions, food [4202]

[4649] 1 מָזוֹר *māzôr* 3x sore, boil, ulcer [4205]

[4650] 2 מָזוֹר *māzôr* 1x trap, ambush [4204]

[4651] 1 מֵזַח *mēzaḥ* 1x harbor; an area in which wind and wave are restricted as a fig. extension of a girdle or belt that restrains [4206]

[4652] 2 מֵזַח *mēzaḥ* 1x belt, leather girdle worn next to the skin [4206]

[4653] מָזִיחַ *māzîḥa* 1x belt, girdle [4206]

[4654] מַזְכִּיר *mazkîr* 9x recorder, clerk, secretary [2142*]

[4655] מַזָּל *mazzāl* 1x constellation (possibly of the zodiac signs) [4208*]

[4657] מִזְלֵג *mazlēg* 7x (three-tined) meat fork [4207]

[4659] מְזִמָּה *m^ezimmâ* 19x discretion; scheme, plan, purpose, intent [4209]

[4660] מִזְמוֹר *mizmôr* 57x psalm, melody [4210] See *psalm.*

[4661] מַזְמֵרָה *mazmērâ* 4x pruning hook, pruning knife, vine-knife [4211]

[4662] מְזַמֶּרֶת *m^ezammeret* 5x wick trimmer (scissors, possibly also used as a snuffer) [4212*]

[4663] מִזְעָר *miz^cār* 4x small matter, few [4213]

[4665] מִזְרֶה *mizreh* 2x winnowing fork, shovel [4214]

[4666] מַזָּרוֹת *mazzārôt* 1x constellations, variously specified [4216*]

[4667] מִזְרָח *mizrāḥ* 74x direction of the sunrise, east, eastern; the east was the direction of orientation in the ancient Near East [4217] See *east.*

[4668] מְזָרִים *m^ezārîm* 1x driving (north) winds [2219* & 4215*]

[4669] מִזְרָע *mizrā^c* 1x seeded field, land sown [4218]

[4670] מִזְרָק *mizrāq* 32x sacred bowl used for sprinkling (the altar) [4219]

[4671] מֵחַ *mēaḥ* 2x fat sheep; (representing) the rich [4220]

[4672] מֹחַ *mōaḥ* 1x marrow (of the bones) [4221]

[4673] 1 מָחָא *māḥā^ɔ* 3x [Q] to clap (hands in joy) [4222]

[4675] מַחֲבֵא *maḥ^abē^ɔ* 1x shelter, hiding place (from wind) [4224]

[4676] מַחֲבֹא *maḥ^abō^ɔ* 1x hiding place [4224]

[4677] מְחַבְּרוֹת *m^eḥabb^erôt* 2x fittings, braces (of iron), joists, truss (of timber) [4226*]

[4678] מַחְבֶּרֶת *maḥberet* 8x place of joining, seam, set (of curtains) [4225]

[4679] מַחֲבַת *maḥ^abat* 5x (metal) griddle or baking pan [4227]

[4680] מַחֲגֹרֶת *maḥ^agōret* 1x girding (of sackcloth wrapped around the body) [4228]

[4681] 1 מָחָה *māḥâ* 34x [Q] to wash off, wipe out, blot out, destroy; [N] be blotted out, be wiped out, be exterminated; [H] to cause to blot out [4229]

[4682] 2 מָחָה *māḥâ* 1x [Q] to continue along, stretch along [4229]

[4683] 3 מָחָה *māḥâ* 1x [Pu] (choice food-dishes) to be filled with marrow [4229]

[4684] מְחוּגָה *m^eḥûgâ* 1x compass (for making circles) [4230]

[4685] מָחוֹז *māḥôz* 1x haven, harbor, which might include a population center like a repair yard and city [4231]

[4688] 1 מָחוֹל *māḥôl* 6x circle-dancing, round-dancing [4234]

[4690] מַחֲזֶה *maḥ^azeh* 4x vision [4236]

[4691] מֶחֱזָה *meḥ^ezâ* 4x light, place of seeing, in some contexts referring to a window [4237]

[4693] מְחִי *m^eḥî* 1x blow (of a battering ram) [4239]

[4695] מִחְיָה *miḥyâ* 8x saving of a life; raw flesh; food, sustenance; relief, recovering [4241]

[4697] 1 מְחִיר *m^eḥîr* 15x price, cost, money [4242]

[4700] מַחֲלֶה *maḥ^aleh* 2x sickness, disease [4245]

[4701] מַחֲלָה *maḥ^alâ* 4x disease, sickness [4245]

[4703] מְחֹלָה *m^eḥōlâ* 8x circle-dance, round-dance [4246]

[4704] מְחִלָּה *m^eḥillâ* 1x hole [4247]

[4708] מַחֲלֻיִים *maḥ^aluyîm* 1x sickness (caused by wounding) [4251*]

[4709] מַחֲלָף *maḥ^alāp* 1x utensil, perhaps a pan [4252]

[4710] מַחֲלָפָה *maḥᵃlāpâ* 3x braids (of hair) [4253]

[4711] מַחֲלָצוֹת *maḥᵃlāṣôt* 2x fine robes, fine, white, festival garments [4254*]

[4713] מַחֲלֹקֶת *maḥᵃlōqet* 42x portion, share (of land); division, group (of people) [4256]

[4714] 1 מָחֲלַת *māḥᵃlat* 2x mahalath (t.t. in the Psalms) [4257]

[4715] 2 מָחֲלַת *māḥᵃlat* 2x Mahalath, "*suffering of affliction NIV; sickness or suffering poem JB*" [4258]

[4716] מְחֹלָתִי *mᵉḥōlātî* 2x Meholathite, of Meholah, "*of Meholah*" [4259]

[4717] מַחְמָאֹת *maḥmāʾōt* 1x butter; some sources: curds, yogurt [4260*]

[4718] מַחְמָד *maḥmād* 13x thing of value, something of delight, treasure; "the delight of the eyes" is someone or something especially cherished [4261]

[4719] מַחְמֹד *maḥmōd* 1x treasure, something precious [4262*]

[4720] מַחְמָל *maḥmāl* 1x yearning [4263]

[4721] מַחְמֶצֶת *maḥmeṣet* 2x something made with yeast, with a sour taste [2557]

[4722] מַחֲנֶה *maḥᵃneh* 215x camp, group (military or civilian) [4264] See *camp.*

[4724] מַחֲנַיִם *maḥᵃnayim* 4x Mahanaim, "*double camp*" [4266]

[4725] מַחֲנָק *maḥᵃnāq* 1x strangling, suffocation [4267]

[4726] מַחְסֶה *maḥseh* 20x refuge, shelter [4268]

[4727] מַחְסוֹם *maḥsôm* 1x muzzle, a covering for the mouth to keep silence [4269]

[4728] מַחְסוֹר *maḥsôr* 13x need, lack of, scarcity, hence poverty [4270]

[4730] מָחַץ *māḥaṣ* 13x [Q] to beat to pieces, crush, shatter [4272]

[4731] מַחַץ *maḥaṣ* 1x wound (from a blow) [4273]

[4732] מַחְצֵב *maḥṣēb* 3x dressed (stone), hewn (stone) [4274]

[4733] מֶחֱצָה *meḥᵉṣâ* 2x half [4275]

[4734] מַחֲצִית *maḥᵃṣît* 16x half; noon, middle of the day [4276]

[4735] מָחַק *māḥaq* 1x [Q] to crush, smash, pierce [4277]

[4736] מֶחְקָר *meḥqār* 1x (unexplored) depths (of the earth) [4278]

[4737] מָחָר *māḥār* 52x tomorrow, the next day, in the future [4279] See *time to come; tomorrow.*

[4738] מַחֲרָאָה *maḥᵃrāʾâ* 1x latrine [4280]

[4739] מַחֲרֵשָׁה *maḥᵃrēšâ* 2x plowshare [4281 & 4282*]

[4740] מָחֳרָת *māḥᵒrāt* 32x the next day, the day after [4283]

[4741] מַחְשֹׂף *maḥśōp* 1x exposing, laying bare (of wood) [4286]

[4742] מַחֲשָׁבָה *maḥᵃšābâ* 56x thought, plan, scheme, plot, design [4284] See *mind; plan; thought.*

[4743] מַחְשָׁךְ *maḥšāk* 7x place of darkness, hiding place [4285]

[4745] מְחִתָּה *mᵉḥittâ* 11x ruin, undoing; terror, horror [4288]

[4746] מַחְתָּה *maḥtâ* 22x censer, firepan, tray [4289]

[4747] מַחְתֶּרֶת *maḥteret* 2x (the act of) breaking into (a house) and so trespassing [4290]

[4748] מַטְאֲטֵא *maṭʾᵃṭēʾ* 1x broom [4292]

[4749] מַטְבֵּחַ *maṭbēaḥ* 1x place of slaughter, slaughter yard [4293]

[4751] מַטֶּה *maṭṭeh* 252x staff, rod, club, a stick used to assist in walking, discipline, and guidance, often highly individualized and used for identification; of royalty: scepter; by extension: tribe, as a major unit of national group or clan (fig. identified with or under authority of a leader's staff) [4294] See *rod; staff; tribe.*

[4752] מַ֫טָּה *maṭṭâ* 19x below, beneath, lower, bottom [4295]

[4753] מִטָּה *miṭṭâ* 28x bed, couch, a piece of furniture on which one reclines for rest or sleep; by extension: bier, to carry the dead; carriage or palanquin (a vehicle carried on poles by porters) [4296]

[4754] מֻטֶּה *muṭṭeh* 1x injustice, warping (of justice), crookedness (of law) [4297]

[4757] מַטְוֶה *maṭweh* 1x that which is spun, yarn [4299]

[4758] מָטִיל *māṭîl* 1x (iron) rod [4300*]

[4759] מַטְמוֹן *maṭmôn* 5x (hidden) treasure, (hidden) riches [4301]

[4760] מַטָּע *maṭṭāʿ* 6x (the act or place of) planting [4302]

[4761] מַטְעָם *maṭʿām* 8x tasty food, delicacy [4303*]

[4762] מִטְפַּחַת *miṭpaḥat* 2x cloak, shawl [4304]

[4763] מָטַר *māṭar* 18x [N] to be rained upon; [H] to send rain down on; [Ho] to be rained upon; rain has a generally positive association of growth and refreshment, though excessive or ill-timed rain is potentially destructive to crops and even life-threatening [4305]

[4764] מָטָר *māṭār* 38x rain, rain shower; see also 4763 [4306]

[4766] מַטָּרָה *maṭṭārâ* 16x (the court of the) guard, i.e., place of confinement; (the Gate of the) Guard (a place); target [4307]

[4769] מִי *mî* 422x who?, what?, which?; anyone, whoever [4310]

[4774] מֵיטָב *mêṭāb* 6x best (part of something) [4315]

[4776] מִיכָאֵל *mîkāʾēl* 13x Michael, "*Who is like God [El]?*" [4317]

[4777] מִיכָה *mîkâ* 33x Micah; Mica; Micaiah, "*Who is like Yahweh?*" [4318]

[4781] מִיכָיְהוּ *mîkāyᵉhû* 21x Micaiah; Micah, "*Who is like Yahweh?*" [4321]

[4782] מִיכָל *mîkāl* 1x brook, stream; some sources: pool, reservoir [4323]

[4783] מִיכַל *mîkal* 17x Michal, "*Who is like God [El]?*" [4324*]

[4784] מַ֫יִם *mayim* 585x water; in nature: ocean, lake, flood, river; from the body: tears, urine [4325] See *water.*

[4786] מִין *mîn* 31x kind: genus or species [4327]

[4787] מֵינֶקֶת *mêneqet* 6x nursing woman, wet-nurse [3243*]

[4788] מֵיסָךְ *mêsāk* 0x see 4590 [4329]

[4790] מִיץ *mîṣ* 4x pressing, squeezing [4330]

[4793] מִישׁוֹר *mîšôr* 7x (geographical) plateau, plain, level ground; (of ruling and right living) uprightness, justice, straightness [4334]

[4797] מֵישָׁרִים *mêšārîm* 19x uprightness, fairness, equity, justice; moral uprightness and justice are fig. extensions of an object that is straight rather than crooked [4339*]

[4798] מֵיתָר *mêtār* 9x rope, cord; bow-string [4340]

[4799] מַכְאֹב *makʾōb* 16x pain, grief, sorrow, suffering [4341]

[4802] מַכְבֵּר *makbēr* 1x thick cloth, with a focus that it is twisted, braided, or woven [4346*]

[4803] מִכְבָּר *mikbār* 6x grating, lattice-work [4345*]

[4804] מַכָּה *makkâ* 48x wound, injury, physical damage to the body; by extension: plague, affliction, calamity, disaster [4347]

[4805] מִכְוָה *mikwâ* 5x burn (on the skin), scar; in context this is not an intentional mark or tattoo [4348]

[4806] מָכוֹן *mākôn* 17x (established) place, site; foundation (of earth or throne) [4349]

[4807] מְכוֹנָה *m^e^kônâ* 25x movable stand; (established) place, foundation [4350 & 4369*]

[4808] מְכוּרָה *m^e^kûrâ* 3x ancestry, origin, parentage [4351]

[4812] מָכַךְ *mākak* 3x [Q] to sink, go down, waste away; [N] to sag, be sunk down; [Ho] to be brought low [4355]

[4813] מִכְלָא *miklā᾿* 3x pen, fold (for sheep or goats) [4356*]

[4814] מִכְלוֹל *miklôl* 2x fullness, completeness, perfection [4358]

[4815] מַכְלוּל *maklûl* 1x beautiful garment, finery, with a focus the excellence of the item [4360*]

[4816] מִכְלוֹת *miklôt* 1x solid (gold), purest (gold) [4357*]

[4817] מִכְלָל *miklāl* 1x perfection [4359]

[4818] מַכֹּלֶת *makkōlet* 1x food [4361]

[4819] מִכְמָן *mikmān* 1x (hidden) treasure [4362]

[4821] מִכְמָר *mikmār* 2x net, snare (for capture of game) [4364]

[4823] מִכְמֶרֶת *mikmeret* 3x fishing net, dragnet (for fish) [4365]

[4829] מִכְנָס *miknās* 5x undergarment, some kind of shorts or trousers [4370]

[4830] מֶכֶס *mekes* 6x tribute, cultic dues or taxes [4371]

[4831] מִכְסָה *miksâ* 2x number (of persons); amount, valuation (of a thing) [4373]

[4832] מִכְסֶה *mikseh* 16x covering [4372]

[4833] מְכַסֶּה *m^e^kasseh* 4x covering (of a body or building); layer of fat (on the kidneys) [4374]

[4834] מַכְפֵּלָה *makpēlâ* 6x Machpelah, "*double [cave]*" [4375]

[4835] מָכַר *mākar* 80x [Q] to sell; [N] to be sold; [Ht] to sell oneself [4376] See *sell.*

[4836] מֶכֶר *meker* 3x worth, value; merchandise [4377]

[4837] מַכָּר *makkār* 2x treasurer [4378]

[4838] מִכְרֶה *mikreh* 1x (salt) pit [4379]

[4839] מְכֵרָה *m^e^kērâ* 1x sword, weapon [4380]

[4843] מַכְשֵׁלָה *makšēlâ* 2x heap of ruins, heap of rubble [4384]

[4844] מִכְתָּב *miktāb* 9x writing, inscription, letter [4385]

[4845] מְכִתָּה *m^e^kittâ* 1x pieces, crushed fragments [4386]

[4846] מִכְתָּם *miktām* 6x miktam (t.t. in the Psalms, of uncertain meaning) [4387]

[4847] מַכְתֵּשׁ *maktēš* 3x hollow place; mortar; market district (at a hollow place in the city?) [4388 & 4389]

[4848] מָלֵא 1 *mālē᾿* 252x [Q] to fill up, be full; [Qp] to be ordained, fulfilled; [N] to be filled, become filled up; [P] to fill up, satisfy; ordain, consecrate; [Pu] to be set; [Ht] to unite together; "to fill the hand" means to ordain or consecrate for service to God [4390] See *fill; fulfill.*

[4849] מָלֵא 2 *mālē᾿* 61x filled, full; "full of days" means "very old" [4392] See *full.*

[4850] מְלֹא *m^e^lō᾿* 38x what fills, what makes something full; fullness, everything [4393]

[4852] מְלֵאָה *m^e^lē᾿â* 3x full yield (of crops) [4395]

[4853] מִלֻּאָה *millu᾿â* 4x mounting (of jewels), setting (of jewels) [4396]

[4854] מִלֻּאִים *millu᾿îm* 14x ordination, consecration (of a priest); mounting, setting (of gem stones) [4394*]

[4855] מַלְאָךְ *mal᾿āk* 213x messenger, a human representative; angel, a supernatural representative of God, sometimes delivering messages, sometimes protecting God's people; the "angel of the LORD" sometimes shares divine characteristics and is sometimes thought to be a manifestation of God himself, or of the preincarnate Christ [4397] See *angel; messenger.*

[4856] מְלָאכָה *mᵉlāʾkâ* 167x work, deed, duty, craft, service; thing, something [4399] See *duty; work.*

[4857] מַלְאָכוּת *malʾākût* 1x message (from a commissioned messenger) [4400*]

[4858] מַלְאָכִי *malʾākî* 1x Malachi, "*my messenger* or *messenger of Yahweh*" [4401]

[4859] מִלֵּאת *millēʾt* 1x setting, mounting, the solid base in which a gem is set [4402]

[4860] מַלְבּוּשׁ *malbûš* 8x clothing, robe, attire, garment [4403]

[4861] מַלְבֵּן *malbēn* 3x brickwork, brick pavement; (the act of) brickmaking [4404]

[4863] מִלָּה *millâ* 38x word, what is said; the act of speaking, speech [4405]

[4864] מִלּוֹא *millôʾ* 6x supporting terrace (cf. Beth Millo) [4407]

[4865] מַלּוּחַ *mallûaḥ* 1x salt herb (collected by the destitute and banished) [4408]

[4867] מְלוּכָה *mᵉlûkâ* 25x kingship, rulership, royalty [4410]

[4869] מָלוֹן *mālôn* 8x place of overnight lodging, place where one spends the night [4411]

[4870] מְלוּנָה *mᵉlûnâ* 2x hut, structure (of a watchman in the field) [4412]

[4872] 1 מָלַח *mālaḥ* 1x [N] to vanish, be dispersed [4414]

[4873] 2 מָלַח *mālaḥ* 4x [Q] to season with salt; [Pu] to be salted; [Ho] to be rubbed with salt [4414]

[4874] 1 מֶלַח *melaḥ* 2x worn-out clothes, rags [4418*]

[4875] 2 מֶלַח *melaḥ* 29x salt, a staple of the ancient world; positively: for flavoring, as a nutrient, as a food preservative; as a medicine; for curing animal skins; negatively: used on fields to prevent or inhibit productive plant growth [4417]

[4876] מַלָּח *mallāḥ* 4x sailor, mariner [4419]

[4877] מְלֵחָה *mᵉlēḥâ* 3x salt flat, salt waste-lands, barren country [4420]

[4878] מִלְחָמָה *milḥāmâ* 319x fighting, battle (a particular engagement), war (as an ongoing event) [4421] See *battle; fighting; war.*

[4879] מֶלֶט *meleṭ* 1x clay flooring [4423]

[4880] 1 מָלַט *mālaṭ* 94x [N] to deliver oneself, escape, flee; [P] to save, deliver, rescue; [H] to rescue; to deliver (a child); [Ht] to shoot out (of sparks); to escape [4422] See *deliver; escape; rescue; save.*

[4884] מְלִילָה *mᵉlîlâ* 1x (rubbed) kernels (of grain) [4425]

[4885] מֵלִיץ *mēlîṣ* 5x intercessor, mediator (in various capacities); this can refer both to human and heavenly beings [3887* & 3945*]

[4886] מְלִיצָה *mᵉlîṣâ* 2x allusive saying, parable; ridicule [4426]

[4887] 1 מָלַךְ *mālak* 350x [Q] to reign as king; [H] to make one a king, have a coronation; [Ho] be made a king [4427] See *reign; rule.*

[4888] 2 מָלַךְ *mālak* 1x [N] to ponder, consider carefully within oneself [4427]

[4889] 1 מֶלֶךְ *melek* 2,530x king, royal ruler, human and divine; "the great king" is the more prominent of the leaders in a convenant agreement and is used of God (Ps 48:2); the "king of kings" is the supreme sovereign and is not used of God in the OT [4428 & 4429] See *king; leader.*

[4891] מֹ֫לֶךְ *mōlek* 9x Molech (pagan god), "*(shameful) king*" [4432]

[4892] מַלְכֹּ֫דֶת *malkōdet* 1x trap, snare [4434]

[4893] מַלְכָּה *malkâ* 35x queen (outside Israel), a female ruler of a kingdom; wife of a king, royalty but without much actual governmental power [4436]

[4895] מַלְכוּת *malkût* 91x kingdom, empire, realm; reign, royal power, position as a king [4438] See *dominion; kingdom; kingship; power.*

[4906] מְלֶ֫כֶת *m*[e]*leket* 5x Queen (of Heaven) [4446]

[4908] 1 מָלַל *mālal* 5x [Q] to wither away; [Pol] to wither; [Htpol] be blunted (of arrows) [5243*]

[4909] 2 מָלַל *mālal* 2x [Q] to circumcise; [N] to be cut off [5243*]

[4910] 3 מָלַל *mālal* 1x [P] to say, speak, proclaim [4448]

[4911] 4 מָלַל *mālal* 4x [Q] to signal by rubbing or scraping [4448]

[4913] מַלְמָד *malmād* 1x oxgoad, cattle prod, a (metal-tipped) poker used to guide animals, which could also be used as a weapon [4451]

[4914] מָלַץ *mālaṣ* 1x [N] to be smooth, pleasant, palatable, sweet [4452]

[4915] מֶלְצַר *melṣar* 1x guard, guardian, official [4453]

[4916] מָלַק *mālaq* 2x [Q] to wring off, pinch off (the head of a bird) [4454]

[4917] מַלְקוֹחַ *malqôaḥ* 7x spoils of war, plunder, war-booty [4455]

[4918] מַלְקוֹחַיִם *malqôḥayim* 1x roof of the mouth, palate [4455*]

[4919] מַלְקוֹשׁ *malqôš* 8x spring rains, latter rains of March-April [4456]

[4920] מֶלְקָחַיִם *melqāḥayim* 6x (pair of) wick trimmers; (pair of) tongs [4457*]

[4921] מֶלְתָּחָה *meltāḥâ* 1x wardrobe [4458]

[4922] מַלְתָּעוֹת *maltāʿôt* 1x fangs, teeth; some sources: jawbone [4459*]

[4923] מַמְּגוּרָה *mamm*[e]*gûrâ* 1x granary, grain-pit [4460]

[4924] מֵמַד *mēmād* 1x dimensions, measurement [4461*]

[4926] מָמוֹת *māmôt* 2x death [4463]

[4927] מַמְזֵר *mamzēr* 2x one born of a forbidden marriage; foreigner; this can have the associative meaning of being an unprivileged or despised class [4464]

[4928] מִמְכָּר *mimkār* 10x what is sold, goods, merchandise [4465]

[4929] מִמְכֶּ֫רֶת *mimkeret* 1x selling, sale [4466]

[4930] מַמְלָכָה *mamlākâ* 117x kingdom, royal dominion, reign [4467] See *dominion; kingdom; kingship.*

[4931] מַמְלָכוּת *mamlākût* 9x kingdom, realm, royal dominion [4468]

[4932] מִמְסָךְ *mimsāk* 2x bowl of mixed wine, with a focus on the wine [4469]

[4933] מֶ֫מֶר *memer* 1x bitterness, annoyance [4470]

[4934] 1 מַמְרֵא *mamrēʾ* 8x Mamre, "*strength*" [4471]

[4936] מַמְּרֹרִים *mamm*[e]*rōrîm* 1x misery, bitterness [4472*]

[4937] מִמְשַׁח *mimšaḥ* 1x anointing [4473]

[4938] מִמְשָׁל *mimšāl* 3x leader, ruler; power, dominion, sovereign authority [4474]

[4939] מֶמְשָׁלָה *memšālâ* 17x dominion, power to govern, authority to rule [4475]

[4940] מִמְשָׁק *mimšāq* 1x place, ground (overgrown with weeds) [4476]

[4941] מַמְתַקִּים *mamtaqqîm* 2x sweetness, sweet things [4477*]

[4942] 1 מָן *mān* 13x manna, a food given by God to the generation of the Exodus: "the grain of heaven" [4478]

[4943] 2 מָן *mān* 1x what? [4478]

[4944] 1 מֵן *mēn* 2x (music of) stringed instruments [4482]

[4945] 2 מֵן *mēn* 1x share, portion [4482]

[4946] מִן *min* 7,521x marker of a source or extension from a source: from, out of, of; temporary: since, after; logically: because of; of degree: more than [4480]

[4947] מַנְגִּינָה *mangînâ* 1x mocking song [4485]

[4948] 1 מָנָה *mānâ* 28x [Q] to count, number, take a census; [N] to be counted, be numbered; [P] to assign, appoint, provide; [Pu] to be assigned, be appointed [4487]

[4949] מָנֶה *māneh* 5x mina (unit of weight, about 1.25 pounds [0.6 kg]) [4488]

[4950] 2 מָנָה *mānâ* 12x share, portion, piece [4490]

[4951] מֹנֶה *mōneh* 2x time, occurrence [4489]

[4952] מִנְהָג *minhāg* 2x driving (of a chariot) [4491]

[4953] מִנְהָרָה *minhārâ* 1x shelter, hole, cave (in mountain clefts) [4492]

[4954] מָנוֹד *mānôd* 1x shaking of the head (in scorn or derision) [4493]

[4955] 1 מָנוֹחַ *mānôaḥ* 7x resting place; the home of a person or the lair of an animal, with the focus that this is a place of rest, satisfaction, and contentment [4494]

[4957] מְנוּחָה *menûḥâ* 21x resting place; see also 4955 [4496]

[4959] מָנוֹן *mānôn* 1x grief [4497]

[4960] מָנוֹס *mānôs* 8x place to flee, place of escape, refuge [4498]

[4961] מְנוּסָה *menûsâ* 2x flight, fleeing [4499]

[4962] מָנוֹר *mānôr* 4x (weaver's) rod, beam (of weavers) [4500]

[4963] מְנוֹרָה *menôrâ* 42x lampstand (holding an oil lamp; not a candlestick, holding a wax candle) [4501]

[4964] מִנְּזָר *minnezār* 1x guard, watchman, with a possible implication of status and rank [4502]

[4965] מֻנָּח *munnāḥ* 3x open area [3240* & 5117*]

[4966] מִנְחָה *minḥâ* 211x grain offering; animal offering or sacrifice; gift, tribute, present [4503] See *gift; grain offering; offering.*

[4972] מְנִי *meni* 1x Destiny (pagan god) [4507]

[4974] 2 מִנִּי *minnî* 34x from, out of; more than [4480]

[4978] מִנְלֶה *minleh* 1x possession, acquisition [4512]

[4979] מָנַע *māna*ʿ 29x [Q] to keep from, withhold, deny, refuse; [N] to be kept from, be withheld, be denied [4513]

[4980] מַנְעוּל *man*ʿ*ûl* 6x bolt, lock (of a door) [4514]

[4981] מִנְעָל *min*ʿ*āl* 1x bolt (on a gate) [4515]

[4982] מַנְעַמִּים *man*ʿ*ammîm* 1x (edible) delicacies [4516*]

[4983] מְנַעַנְעִים *mena*ʿ*an*ʿ*îm* 1x sistrum, rattle, percussion instrument not precisely identified [4517*]

[4984] מְנַקִּית *menaqqît* 4x bowl (used for drink offering) [4518]

[4985] מְנַשֶּׁה *menaššeh* 145x Manasseh, "*one that makes to forget*" [4519]

[4987] מְנָת *menāt* 9x portion, lot, assigned share [4521]

[4988] מָס *mās* 1x despairing (man) [4523]

[4989] מַס *mas* 23x forced labor, slave labor [4522]

[4990] מֵסַב *mēsab* 4x surrounding; round table, circle of feasters; (adv.) around, round about [4524]

[4991] מְסִבָּה *m*ᵉ*sibbâ* 1x (adv.) around, round about [4524*]

[4993] 1 מַסְגֵּר *masgēr* 3x prison, dungeon [4525]

[4994] 2 מַסְגֵּר *masgēr* 4x artisan, craftsman; some sources: metalworker, locksmith [4525]

[4995] מִסְגֶּרֶת *misgeret* 17x side panels (of a building); rim (of a table and base); stronghold; den [4526]

[4996] מַסַּד *massad* 1x foundation [4527]

[4997] מִסְדְּרוֹן *misd*ᵉ*rôn* 1x porch, vestibule [4528]

[4998] מָסָה *māsâ* 4x [H] to melt, dissolve; to consume; to drench (with tears) [4529]

[4999] 1 מַסָּה *massâ* 3x trial, test, temptation [531]

[5000] 2 מַסָּה *massâ* 1x despair [4531]

[5001] 3 מַסָּה *massâ* 5x Massah, "*test, try*" [4532]

[5002] מִסָּה *missâ* 1x proportion, measure [4530]

[5003] מַסְוֶה *masweh* 3x veil, covering [4533]

[5004] מְסוּכָה *m*ᵉ*sûkâ* 1x thorn hedge [4534]

[5005] מַסָּח *massāḥ* 1x in turn, taking turns [4535]

[5006] מִסְחָר *misḥār* 1x revenue [4536*]

[5007] מָסַךְ *māsak* 5x [Q] to mingle, mix (substances into drinks) [4537]

[5008] מֶסֶךְ *mesek* 1x mixture (of spices) [4538]

[5009] מָסָךְ *māsāk* 25x curtain, covering; by extension: shield, defense [4539]

[5010] מְסֻכָּה *m*ᵉ*sukâ* 1x (woven) covering [4540]

[5011] 1 מַסֵּכָה *massēkâ* 26x image, idol (of cast metal) [4541]

[5012] 2 מַסֵּכָה *massēkâ* 2x (woven) blanket, (interwoven) covering [4541]

[5014] מִסְכֵּן *miskēn* 4x poor, needy (one) [4542]

[5016] מִסְכְּנוֹת *misk*ᵉ*nôt* 7x storage places, warehouses [4543*]

[5017] מִסְכֵּנֻת *miskēnut* 1x scarcity, poverty [4544]

[5018] מַסֶּכֶת *masseket* 3x warp-threads (the lengthwise threads of a loom) [4545]

[5019] מְסִלָּה *m*ᵉ*sillâ* 27x main road; (raised) highway, ramp, stairs; by extension: lifestyle, conduct in life [4546]

[5020] מַסְלוּל *maslûl* 1x highway [4547]

[5021] מַסְמֵר *masmēr* 4x nail [4548]

[5022] מָסַס *māsas* 21x [Q] to waste away, dissolve; [N] to be melted, dissolved; [H] to cause to melt [4549]

[5023] מַסַּע *massaʿ* 12x journey, travels from place to place [4550]

[5024] 1 מַסָּע *massāʿ* 1x quarry [4551]

[5025] 2 מַסָּע *massāʿ* 1x a weapon probably thrown like a spear or javelin; dart [4551]

[5026] מִסְעָד *misʿād* 1x supports (for a building) [4552]

[5027] מִסְפֵּד *mispēd* 16x wailing, howling, weeping, mourning [4553]

[5028] מִסְפּוֹא *mispôʾ* 5x fodder, animal feed [4554]

[5029] מִסְפָּחָה *mispāḥâ* 2x veil, (head) covering [4555]

[5030] מִסְפַּחַת *mispaḥat* 3x (uninfectious) breaking out of skin, rash or scab; referring to something relatively harmless [4556]

[5031] 1 מִסְפָּר *mispār* 134x number, quantity; listing, inventory, census [4557] See *count; listed; number.*

[5034] מָסַר *māsar* 2x [Q] to supply, deliver; [N] to be supplied [4560]

[5037] מָסֹרֶת *māsōret* 1x bond, obligation, duty [4562]

[5039] מִסְתּוֹר *mistôr* 1x hiding place, shelter (from the elements) [4563]

[5040] מַסְתֵּר *mastēr* 1x (the act of) hiding [4564]

[5041] מִסְתָּר *mistār* 10x hiding place, covered place (from which to ambush) [4565]

[5042] מַעֲבָד *maᶜᵃbād* 1x deed, action [4566*]

[5043] מַעֲבֶה *maᶜᵃbeh* 1x mold, foundry [4568]

[5044] מַעֲבָר *maᶜᵃbār* 3x stroke (of a rod); (geographical) pass; ford (of a river) [4569]

[5045] מַעְבָּרָה *maᶜbārâ* 8x ford, river crossing; (geographical) pass [4569*]

[5046] 1 מַעְגָּל *maᶜgāl* 3x (circled) camp, encampment [4570]

[5047] 2 מַעְגָּל *maᶜgāl* 13x (rutted) path (of a cart or wagon) [4570]

[5048] מָעַד *māᶜad* 8x [Q] to slip, waver, wobble; [Pu] to become lame; [H] cause to wobble, to bend, wrench (one's back) [4154* & 4571 & 5976*]

[5051] מַעֲדַנּוֹת *maᶜᵃdannôt* 2x beautiful; some sources: bands, cords used for binding; (adv.) confidently [4575*]

[5052] מַעֲדַנִּים *maᶜᵃdannîm* 3x delicacy; delight [4574*]

[5053] מַעְדֵּר *maᶜdēr* 1x hoe (to cultivate ground) [4576]

[5054] מָעָה *māᶜâ* 1x grain (of sand) [4579*]

[5055] מֵעֶה *mēᶜeh* 33x viscera: stomach, heart, bowels, womb; (body as a whole); by extension: of the inner person, the seat of emotions: anguish, tenderness [4578]

[5056] מָעוֹג *māᶜôg* 1x provision, supply; some sources: flat bread [4580]

[5057] מָעוֹז *māᶜôz* 35x refuge, stronghold, fortress, place of protection; (used with "head") helmet [4581]

[5058] מָעֹוזֶן *māᶜôzen* 1x fortress, refuge [4581*]

[5061] 2 מָעוֹן *māᶜôn* 18x dwelling place [4583]

[5065] מְעוֹנֹתַי *meᶜônōtay* 2x Meonothai, "*my dwellings*" [4587]

[5066] מָעוּף *māᶜûp* 1x gloom, darkness [4588]

[5067] מָעוֹר *māᶜôr* 1x exposed genitals, nakedness [4589]

[5070] מָעַט *māᶜaṭ* 22x [Q] to dwindle, decrease, become few; [P] to become few; [H] to let reduce, make diminish, make collect little [4591]

[5071] מְעַט *meᶜaṭ* 101x little (of size), few (of quantity), short (of time) [4592] See *few; little.*

[5073] מַעֲטֶה *maᶜᵃṭeh* 1x garment, mantle, wrap [4594]

[5074] מַעֲטֶפֶת *maᶜᵃṭepet* 1x cape, outer garment [4595*]

[5075] מְעִי *meᶜî* 1x heap (of ruins) [4596]

[5077] מְעִיל *meᶜîl* 28x robe, cloak [4598]

[5078] מַעְיָן *maᶜyān* 23x spring, fountain, well; by extension: source of life (satisfaction, blessing) [4599]

[5080] מָעַךְ *māᶜak* 4x [Qp] be pressed (into the ground), be crushed, be bruised; [Pu] be fondled [4600]

[5083] מַעֲכָת *maᶜᵃkāt* 1x Maacah [4601]

[5085] מָעַל *māʿal* 35x [Q] to act unfaithfully, break faith, commit a violation [4603]

[5086] 1 מַעַל *maʿal* 29x unfaithfulness [4604]

[5087] 2 מַעַל *maʿal* 140x above, beyond; this refers to spatial position, to degree, and to time (afterward) [4605]

[5089] מֹעַל *mōʿal* 1x lifting (of hands) [4607]

[5090] מַעֲלֶה *maʿaleh* 16x and ascent: hill, mount, (geographical) pass; stairs [4608]

[5091] 1 מַעֲלָה *maʿalâ* 1x what goes through (or rises into) one's mind [4609]

[5092] 2 מַעֲלָה *maʿalâ* 46x ascent: steps, stairway, paces [4609]

[5095] מַעֲלָל *maʿalāl* 45x deeds, actions, practices, what is done [4611]

[5096] מַעֲמָד *maʿamād* 5x attendance, serving; position of attendant [4612]

[5097] מָעֳמָד *moʿomād* 1x foothold, firm ground [4613]

[5098] מַעֲמָסָה *maʿamāsâ* 1x heavy stone, hard-to-lift rock [4614]

[5099] מַעֲמַקִּים *maʿamaqqîm* 5x depths (of waters or seas) [4615*]

[5100] מַעַן *maʿan* 271x for the sake of, on account of, because; therefore, so that [4616]

[5101] 1 מַעֲנֶה *maʿaneh* 7x reply, answer, response [4617]

[5102] 2 מַעֲנֶה *maʿaneh* 1x purpose [4617]

[5103] מַעֲנָה *maʿanâ* 2x furrow, plow path [4618]

[5104] מְעֹנָה *meʿōnâ* 9x hiding place, refuge; dwelling place, (animal) den [4585]

[5107] מַעֲצֵבָה *maʿaṣēbâ* 1x place of torment, place of pain [4620]

[5108] מַעֲצָד *maʿaṣād* 2x chiseling tool (for wood carving); some sources: ax, adze [4621]

[5109] מַעְצוֹר *maʿṣôr* 1x hindrance [4622*]

[5110] מַעְצָר *maʿṣār* 1x self-control [4623]

[5111] מַעֲקֶה *maʿaqeh* 1x parapet, a short wall around the upper level of a house [4624]

[5112] מַעֲקַשִּׁים *maʿaqaššîm* 1x rough places, uneven terrain, rugged country [4625*]

[5113] מַעַר *maʿar* 2x nakedness; available space [4626]

[5114] 1 מַעֲרָב *maʿarāb* 9x wares, goods (for trade, exchange, or barter) [4627]

[5115] 2 מַעֲרָב *maʿarāb* 15x west (the place of the sunset) [4628]

[5117] 1 מְעָרָה *meʿārâ* 38x cave [4631]

[5118] 2 מְעָרָה *meʿārâ* 1x wasteland, bare field [4632]

[5119] מַעֲרָךְ *maʿarāk* 1x plan, consideration, arrangement [4633]

[5120] מַעֲרָכָה *maʿarākâ* 19x things arranged in a row: battle line, row of army ranks; row, layer (of things); by extension: proper arrangement of something fitting and suitable [4630* & 4634]

[5121] מַעֲרֶכֶת *maʿareket* 10x (consecrated) bread set in rows; see also 5120 [4635]

[5122] מַעֲרֹם *maʿarōm* 1x nakedness, naked person [4636]

[5124] מַעֲרָצָה *maʿarāṣâ* 1x terrifying power [4637]

[5126] מַעֲשֶׂה *maʿaśeh* 235x work, labor, deed; something made, something done [4639] See *deed; work.*

[5130] מַעֲשֵׂר *maʿaśēr* 32x tithe, setting aside a tenth [4643]

[5131] מַעֲשַׁקּוֹת *maʿašaqqôt* 2x (col.pl) extortion [4642*]

[5133] מִפְגָּע *mipgāʿ* 1x target [4645]

[5134] מַפָּח *mappāḥ* 1x (a dying) gasp, exhaling (of soul), with an implication of despair and affliction [4646]

[5135] מַפֻּחַ *mappuaḥ* 1x bellows [4647]

[5137] מֻפִּים *muppîm* 1x Muppim [4649]

[5138] מֵפִיץ *mēpîṣ* 1x war club [4650]

[5139] מַפָּל *mappāl* 2x sweepings, waste, refuse (of wheat); (fleshy) folds (of the leviathan) [4651]

[5140] מִפְלָאוֹת *miplāʾôt* 1x wonders, marvelous works [4652*]

[5141] מִפְלַגָּה *miplaggâ* 1x division (of family groups), subgroup of a clan [4653]

[5142] מַפָּלָה *mappālâ* 1x ruin, heap of rubble [4654]

[5143] מַפֵּלָה *mappēlâ* 2x ruin, heap of rubble [4654]

[5144] מִפְלָט *miplāṭ* 1x place of shelter, refuge, escape [4655]

[5145] מִפְלֶצֶת *mipleṣet* 4x repulsive image, disgraceful (idol) [4656]

[5146] מִפְלָשׂ *miplāś* 1x floating, hovering (clouds) [4657]

[5147] מַפֶּלֶת *mappelet* 8x downfall, collapse; (something downfallen) a shipwreck; carcass [4658]

[5148] מִפְעָל *mipʿāl* 1x deed, work [4659]

[5149] מִפְעָלָה *mipʿālâ* 2x deed, work [4659]

[5150] מַפָּץ *mappāṣ* 1x shattering, wrecking (weapon), implying death will follow its effective use [4660]

[5151] מַפֵּץ *mappēṣ* 1x war club [4661]

[5152] מִפְקָד *mipqād* 5x appointment (by a king); number, counting (of the people); Inspection (Gate) [4662 & 4663]

[5153] מִפְרָץ *miprāṣ* 1x cove, inlet, landing-place [4664]

[5154] מַפְרֶקֶת *mapreqet* 1x neck [4665*]

[5155] מִפְרָשׂ *miprāś* 2x spreading (used of clouds and canvas sail) [4666]

[5156] מִפְשָׂעָה *mipśāʿâ* 1x buttocks, posterior area [4667]

[5157] מִפְתָּח *miptāḥ* 1x opening (of lips) [4669]

[5158] מַפְתֵּחַ *maptēaḥ* 3x key [4668]

[5159] מִפְתָּן *miptān* 8x threshold [4670]

[5160] מֵץ *mēṣ* 1x oppressor [4160*]

[5161] מֹץ *mōṣ* 8x chaff [4671]

[5162] מָצָא *māṣāʾ* 457x [Q] to find, find out, discover, uncover; [N] to be found out; be caught; [H] to hand over, present; to bring upon, cause to encounter; "to find favor in the eyes" means "to be pleased" [4672] See *find; meet; reach.*

[5163] מַצָּב *maṣṣāb* 10x standing place; office; outpost, garrison [4673]

[5164] מֻצָּב *muṣṣāb* 2x pillar, tower [4674]

[5165] מַצָּבָה *maṣṣābâ* 1x outpost, garrison of soldiers on the perimeter of a guarded area [4675]

[5167] מַצֵּבָה *maṣṣēbâ* 34x sacred (upright) stone, stone pillar [4676]

[5169] 1 מַצֶּבֶת *maṣṣebet* 2x (tree) stump [4678]

[5170] 2 מַצֶּבֶת *maṣṣebet* 2x sacred (upright) stone, stone pillar [4678]

[5171] מְצָד *meṣād* 11x stronghold, fortress (with difficult access) [4679]

[5172] מָצָה *māṣâ* 7x [Q] to squeeze out; to drain dry; [N] to be drained out [4680]

[5174] 1 מַצָּה *maṣṣâ* 53x unleavened bread, bread made without yeast; bread quickly made, without waiting for the dough to rise [4682] See *bread, unleavened; unleavened bread.*

[5175] 2 מַצָּה *maṣṣâ* 3x quarrel, strife [4683]

[5177] מִצְהָלוֹת *miṣhālôt* 2x neighing [4684*]

[5178] 1 מָצוֹד *māṣôd* 2x (hunting) snare, net [4685]

[5180] 1 מְצוּדָה *m^{e}ṣûdâ* 3x (hunting) snare, net; prey [4686]

[5181] 2 מְצוּדָה *m^{e}ṣûdâ* 18x stronghold, fortress, prison (a place difficult to access) [4686]

[5182] 1 מְצוֹדָה *m^{e}ṣôdâ* 1x net [4685]

[5183] 2 מְצוֹדָה *m^{e}ṣôdâ* 2x fortress, prison (a place difficult to access) [4685]

[5184] מִצְוָה *miṣwâ* 184x command, order, prescription, instruction [4687] See *commandment; order.*

[5185] מְצוֹלָה *m^{e}ṣôlâ* 2x depths, the deep [4688 & 4699*]

[5186] מָצוֹק *māṣôq* 6x distress, suffering, stress, hardship [4689]

[5187] מָצוּק *māṣûq* 2x foundation, pillar, support [4690]

[5188] מְצוּקָה *m^{e}ṣûqâ* 7x distress, anguish, stress, affliction [4691]

[5189] 1 מָצוֹר *māṣôr* 22x siege; siege works, ramparts [4692]

[5190] 2 מָצוֹר *māṣôr* 4x stronghold, fortification, defense [4692]

[5193] מְצוּרָה *m^{e}ṣûrâ* 8x fortification, defense, fortress [4694]

[5194] מַצּוּת *maṣṣût* 1x enemy, person of strife [4695]

[5195] מֵצַח *mēṣaḥ* 13x forehead [4696]

[5196] מִצְחָה *miṣḥâ* 1x greaves (armor for the front or back of leg from ankle to knee) [4697]

[5197] מְצִלָּה *m^{e}ṣillâ* 1x (small) bell (on a horse) [4698]

[5199] מְצִלְתַּיִם *m^{e}ṣiltayim* 13x (pair of) cymbals [4700*]

[5200] מִצְנֶפֶת *miṣnepet* 12x turban, headband [4701]

[5201] מַצָּע *maṣṣāʿ* 1x bed, couch [4702]

[5202] מִצְעָד *miṣʿād* 3x step; (position of submission in a) train [703]

[5203] 1 מִצְעָר *miṣʿār* 5x small quantity, few [4705]

[5205] 1 מִצְפֶּה *miṣpeh* 2x watchtower (used for military defense and surveillance), any place that overlooks [4707]

[5207] מִצְפָּה *miṣpâ* 4x Mizpah, "*lookout point*" [4709]

[5208] מַצְפּוֹן *maṣpôn* 1x hidden treasure, hiding place [4710*]

[5209] מָצַץ *māṣaṣ* 1x [Q] to drink deeply, quaff [4711]

[5210] מֵצַר *mēṣar* 3x anguish, distress, hardship [4712]

[5212] מִצְרִי *miṣrî* 24x Egyptian [4713]

[5213] מִצְרַיִם *miṣrayim* 687x Mizraim; Egypt, Egyptian [4714]

[5214] מַצְרֵף *maṣrēp* 2x crucible, melting pot for metal [4715*]

[5215] מַק *maq* 2x stench, smell of decay [4716]

[5216] 1 מַקֶּבֶת *maqqebet* 4x hammer [4717* & 4718]

[5217] 2 מַקֶּבֶת *maqqebet* 1x quarry [4718]

[5219] מִקְדָּשׁ *miqdāš* 75x holy place, sanctuary, shrine [4720] See *holy place; sanctuary.*

[5220] מַקְהֵל *maqhēl* 2x assembly, congregation [4721]

[5223] 1 מִקְוֶה *miqweh* 5x hope [4723]

[5224] 2 מִקְוֶה *miqweh* 3x collection (of water), reservoir [4723]

[5225] מִקְוָה *miqwâ* 1x reservoir [4724]

[5226] מָקוֹם *māqôm* 401x place, site [4725] See *place.*

[5227] מָקוֹר *māqôr* 18x fountain, spring, source (of a flow), often with an implication of abundance or freshness [4726]

[5228] מִקָּח *miqqāḥ* 1x taking, accepting (a bribe) [4727]

[5229] מַקָּחוֹת *maqqāḥôt* 1x (pl.) merchandise, wares [4728*]

[5230] מִקְטָר *miqṭār* 1x burning [4729]

[5231] מֻקְטָר *muqṭār* 1x incense [6999*]

[5232] מְקַטֶּרֶת *meqaṭeret* 1x incense altar [6999*]

[5233] מִקְטֶרֶת *miqṭeret* 2x censer, incense burner [4730]

[5234] מַקֵּל *maqqēl* 18x branch, stick; staff, a stick used to assist in walking, discipline, and guidance; war club [4731]

[5236] מִקְלָט *miqlāṭ* 20x refuge, place of protection [4733]

[5237] מִקְלַעַת *miqlaʿat* 4x carving, engraving (on wood) [4734]

[5238] מִקְנֶה *miqneh* 76x livestock, (animals from) herds and flocks [4735] See *cattle; flock; livestock.*

[5239] מִקְנָה *miqnâ* 15x something bought, purchased, acquisition [4736]

[5241] מִקְסָם *miqsām* 2x divination [4738]

[5243] מִקְצוֹעַ *miqṣôᶜa* 12x corner (of a base); angle of a wall [4740]

[5244] מַקְצֻעָה *maqṣuᶜâ* 1x (wood) chisel [4741]

[5245] מָקַק *māqaq* 10x [N] to rot, waste away, fester; dissolve; [H] to cause to rot [4743]

[5246] מִקְרָא *miqrāʾ* 23x assembly, calling the community together, usually for a religious ceremony [4744]

[5247] מִקְרֶה *miqreh* 10x happening by chance; fate, destiny [4745]

[5248] מְקָרֶה *meqāreh* 1x rafters, roof beams [4746]

[5249] מְקֵרָה *meqērâ* 2x coolness; cool room, summer home [4747]

[5250] מִקְשֶׁה *miqšeh* 1x well-dressed hair [4748]

[5251] 1 מִקְשָׁה *miqšâ* 9x hammered work; some sources: embossed metal work [4749]

[5252] 2 מִקְשָׁה *miqšâ* 2x melon field, cucumber field [4750]

[5253] 1 מַר *mar* 4x bitter; bitterness, ranging from being merely disagreeable to the taste to being poisonous; by extension: anxiety, despair [4751]

[5254] 2 מַר *mar* 1x drop (in a bucket) [4752]

[5255] מֹר *mōr* 12x myrrh [4753]

[5257] 2 מָרָא *mārāʾ* 1x [Q] to flap, spread the feathers as it runs; this can also refer to the feet kicking up dirt [4754]

[5260] מַרְאֶה *marʾeh* 103x what is seen with the eye, appearance; by extension: vision, supernatural revelation with a focus on visual communication, but can include verbal content [4758] See *appearance; vision.*

[5261] 1 מַרְאָה *marʾâ* 11x vision [4759]

[5263] מֻרְאָה *murʾâ* 1x crop (of a bird) [4760]

[5265] מְרַאֲשׁוֹת *meraʾašôt* 10x head rest, place near the head [4761* & 4763*]

[5266] מֵרַב *mērab* 4x Merab, "*abundant*" [4764*]

[5267] מַרְבַד *marbad* 2x covering [4765]

[5268] מִרְבָּה *mirbâ* 1x so much [4767]

[5269] מַרְבֶּה *marbeh* 2x abundance, increase [4766]

[5270] מַרְבִּית *marbît* 5x great number; most, majority; profit [4768]

[5271] מַרְבֵּץ *marbēṣ* 2x lair, resting place, place to lie down [4769]

[5272] מַרְבֵּק *marbēq* 4x fattening (of a calf) [4770]

[5273] מַרְגּוֹעַ *margôaʿ* 1x resting place [4771]

[5274] מַרְגְּלוֹת *margᵉlôt* 5x (place of) the feet [4772*]

[5275] מַרְגֵּמָה *margēmâ* 1x sling [4773]

[5276] מַרְגֵּעָה *margēʿâ* 1x place of repose, resting-place [4774]

[5277] מָרַד *mārad* 25x [Q] to rebel, revolt [4775]

[5278] 1 מֶרֶד *mered* 1x rebellion [4777]

[5280] מַרְדּוּת *mardût* 1x rebellion, revolt [4780]

[5283] מָרְדֳּכַי *mordᵒkay* 60x Mordecai, "*Marduk*" [4782*]

[5284] מֻרְדָּף *murdāp* 1x aggression [4783]

[5286] 1 מָרָה *mārâ* 44x [Q] to rebel, defy, become disobedient; [H] to act as a rebel, defy by one's action [4784]

[5288] 3 מָרָה *mārâ* 5x Marah, "*bitter*" [4785]

[5289] מֹרָה *mōrâ* 2x bitterness, grief [4786]

[5291] מָרוּד *mārûd* 3x wandering; wanderer; homeless, with a focus on poverty [4788]

[5293] מָרוֹחַ *mārôaḥ* 1x damaged (by pounding or grinding) [4790*]

[5294] מָרוֹם *mārôm* 54x heights, (place) on high, being in an elevated position; by extension: pride, haughtiness, arrogance, an improperly high opinion of oneself; exaltation, high in honor and status [4791] See *heights; high; pride.*

[5296] מֵרוֹץ *mērôṣ* 1x foot race, running [4793]

[5297] 1 מְרוּצָה *mᵉrûṣâ* 4x manner or mode of running; course of a race [4794]

[5298] 2 מְרוּצָה *mᵉrûṣâ* 1x extortion [4835]

[5299] מְרוּקִים *mᵉrûqîm* 1x beauty treatments (including massage and ointments) [4795*]

[5301] מַרְזֵחַ *marzēaḥ* 2x funeral meal; cultic feast [4797* & 4798]

[5302] מָרַח *māraḥ* 1x [Q] to apply by spreading on or rubbing in [4799]

[5303] מֶרְחָב *merḥāb* 6x spaciousness, wideness, with the associative meaning that such a wide area is comfortable, and possibly safe and free [4800]

[5305] מֶרְחָק *merḥāq* 18x distance, far away [4801]

[5306] מַרְחֶשֶׁת *marḥešet* 2x cooking pan (with a lid) [4802]

[5307] מָרַט *mārat* 14x [Q] to pull out (hair); [Qp] to be polished, rubbed; [N] to lose one's hair, become bald; [Pu] to be polished, burnished, smooth (skinned) [4178* & 4803]

[5308] מְרִי *mᵉrî* 23x rebellion [4805]

[5309] מְרִיא *mᵉrîʾ* 8x fattened animal (choice for consumption) [4806]

[5312] 1 מְרִיבָה *mᵉrîbâ* 2x quarreling, strife; rebellion, with a focus on the feelings of enmity [4808]

[5313] 2 מְרִיבָה *mᵉrîbâ* 7x Meribah [4809]

[5319] מִרְיָם *miryām* 15x Miriam, "[variously] *bitterness; plump one; wished-for child; one who loves or is loved*" [4813]

[5320] מְרִירוּת *mᵉrîrût* 1x bitterness [4814]

[5321] מְרִירִי *mᵉrîrî* 1x bitter, in context referring to something deadly [4815]

[5322] מֹרֶךְ *mōrek* 1x fearfulness, despondency [4816]

[5323] מֶרְכָּב *merkāb* 3x seat, saddle, chariot [4817]

[5324] מֶרְכָּבָה *merkābâ* 44x chariot [4818]

[5326] מַרְכֹּלֶת *markōlet* 1x marketplace, place of merchandising [4819]

[5327] 1 מִרְמָה *mirmâ* 39x deceit, deception, dishonesty, treachery [4820]

[5330] מִרְמָס *mirmās* 7x trampling down, running over [4823]

[5334] מֵרַע *mēraʿ* 1x evil, atrocity [4827]

[5335] 1 מֵרֵעַ *mērēaʿ* 8x close friend, companion, personal adviser [4828]

[5337] מִרְעֶה *mirʿeh* 13x pasture, grazing place [4829]

[5338] מַרְעִית *marʿît* 10x pasture, place of grazing [4830*]

[5340] 1 מַרְפֵּא *marpēʾ* 14x healing, remedy [4832]

[5341] 2 מַרְפֵּא *marpēʾ* 2x calmness, composure [4832]

[5343] מִרְפָּשׂ *mirpāś* 1x what is muddy, fouled (by trampling) [4833]

[5344] מָרַץ *māraṣ* 4x [N] to be painful, hurtful; [H] to provoke, irritate [4834]

[5345] מַרְצֵעַ *marṣēaʿ* 2x awl (piercing tool) [4836]

[5346] מַרְצֶפֶת *marṣepet* 1x (stone) base, stone-layer [4837]

[5347] מָרַק *māraq* 4x [Q] to polish; [Qp] to be polished; [Pu] to be thoroughly scoured; [H] to cleanse [4838]

[5348] מָרָק *mārāq* 3x broth (juice stewed out of meat) [4839]

[5349] מֶרְקָח *merqāḥ* 1x aromatic herb, scented spice, perfume [4840]

[5350] מֶרְקָחָה *merqāḥâ* 2x ointment jar, spice-pot [4841]

[5351] מִרְקַחַת *mirqaḥat* 3x mixture of fragrant spices, blend of perfumes [4842]

[5352] מָרַר *mārar* 14x [Q] to be bitter; suffer anguish; [P] to make bitter, weep bitterly; [H] to make bitter; to grieve bitterly; [Htpal] to enrage oneself, be furious; from the base meaning "to taste bitter" come extensions of bitter feelings: anger, fury, anguish, rebellion [4843]

[5353] מָרֹר *mārōr* 5x bitter things [4844]

[5354] מְרֵרָה *merērâ* 1x gall (bitter fluid from the gall bladder) [4845]

[5355] מְרֹרָה *merōrâ* 2x gall bladder; venom, poison (of snakes) [4846]

[5356] 1 מְרָרִי *merārî* 39x Merari; Merarite, "*bitter*" [4847]

[5360] מִרְשַׁעַת *miršaʿat* 1x wickedness, of a person (that) wicked woman [4849]

[5362] 1 מַשָּׂא *maśśāʾ* 36x burden, load, what is lifted and carried; by extension: oppression; singing (lifting the voice) [4853]

[5363] 2 מַשָּׂא *maśśāʾ* 30x oracle, prophetic utterance, pronouncement, with the focus on the content of the message [4853]

[5365] מַשֹּׂא *maśśōʾ* 1x partiality [4856]

[5366] מַשָּׂאָה *maśśāʾâ* 1x uplifted (clouds of smoke) [4858]

[5368] מַשְׂאֵת *maśʾēt* 15x what is lifted up: portion (of food), tax, tribute, gift, burden [4864]

[5369] 1 מִשְׂגָּב *miśgāb* 17x fortress, refuge, stronghold [4869]

[5372] מְשׂוּכָּה *meśûkkâ* 1x thorn-hedge [4881]

[5373] מַשּׂוֹר *maśśôr* 1x saw (cutting tool) [4883]

[5374] מְשׂוּרָה *meśûrâ* 46x (liquid) measure of quantity, measure of capacity [4884]

[5375] 1 מָשׂוֹשׂ *māśôś* 16x joy, delight, celebration [4885]

[5376] 2 מָשׂוֹשׂ *māśôś* 1x wasting away, rotting away [4885]

[5377] מִשְׂחָק *miśḥāq* 1x (scoffing) laughter [4890]

[5378] מַשְׂטֵמָה *maśṭēmâ* 2x hostility, animosity, enmity [4895]

[5379] מְשֻׂכָה *m^e^śukâ* 1x (thorn) hedge (which impedes movement) [4881]

[5380] מַשְׂכִּיל *maśkîl* 14x maskil (t.t. in the Psalms, perhaps "wisdom song") [4905]

[5381] מַשְׂכִּית *maśkît* 6x carved image, sculpture, figurine; what is imagined, imagination [4906]

[5382] מַשְׂכֹּרֶת *maśkōret* 4x wage [4909]

[5383] מַשְׂמֵרָה *maśmērâ* 1x nail (on the end of a goad) [4930*]

[5384] מִשְׂפָּח *miśpāḥ* 1x bloodshed, with a focus on violence [4939]

[5385] מִשְׂרָה *miśrâ* 2x dominion, rule [4951]

[5386] מִשְׂרָפוֹת *miśrāpôt* 2x (complete) burning, funeral fire [4955*]

[5389] מַשְׂרֵת *maśrēt* 1x cooking pan [4958]

[5391] מַשָּׁא *maššāʾ* 4x debt; exacting of usury [4855]

[5393] מַשְׁאָב *mašʾāb* 1x watering channel, place to draw water [4857]

[5394] מַשָּׁאָה *maššāʾâ* 1x (secured) loan [4859]

[5396] מַשָּׁאוֹן *maššāʾôn* 1x deception [4860]

[5397] מַשֻּׁאוֹת *maššuʾôt* 2x ruin, rubble, desolation [4876*]

[5399] מִשְׁאָלָה *mišʾālâ* 2x desire [4862]

[5400] מִשְׁאֶרֶת *mišʾeret* 4x kneading trough [4863]

[5401] מִשְׁבְּצוֹת *mišb^e^ṣôt* 9x filigree settings (ornamental work with fine gold wire usually for setting jewels) [4865*]

[5402] מַשְׁבֵּר *mašbēr* 3x opening of the womb, the point where birth first occurs [4866*]

[5403] מִשְׁבָּר *mišbār* 5x breakers, waves [4867]

[5404] מִשְׁבָּת *mišbāt* 1x destruction, cessation, finish [4868]

[5405] מִשְׁגֶּה *mišgeh* 1x inadvertent mistake, oversight [4870]

[5406] מָשָׁה *māšâ* 3x [Q] to draw out; [H] to cause to draw out [4871]

[5407] מֹשֶׁה *mōšeh* 767x Moses, "*drawn out* [Ex 2:10]; Egyptian for *child*" [4872]

[5408] מַשֶּׁה *maššeh* 1x credit, loan; "the lord of the loan" is a "creditor" [4874]

[5409] מְשׁוֹאָה *m^e^šōʾâ* 3x wasteland, desolate land [4875]

[5412] מְשׁוּבָה *m^e^šûbâ* 14x waywardness, backsliding, faithlessness, apostasy [4878]

[5413] מְשׁוּגָה *m^e^šûgâ* 1x error [4879]

[5414] מָשׁוֹט *māšôṭ* 1x oar [4880]

[5415] מִשּׁוֹט *miššmôṭ* 1x oar [4880]

[5417] מָשַׁח *māšaḥ* 70x [Q] to anoint; [Qp] to be spread, be anointed; [N] to be anointed; usually referring to pouring or smearing sacred oil on a person in a ceremony of dedication, possibly symbolizing divine empowering to accomplish the task or office [4886] See *anoint; rub.*

[5418] מִשְׁחָה 1 *mišḥāh* 21x anointing (oil), anointment; usually referring to pouring or smearing sacred oil on a person in a ceremony of dedication, possibly symbolizing divine empowering to accomplish the task or office [4888]

[5419] מִשְׁחָה 2 *mišḥāh* 2x portion [4888]

[5420] מָשְׁחָה 1 *māšḥāh* 1x anointing, see 5417 [4888]

[5421] מָשְׁחָה 2 *mošḥâ* 1x portion [4888]

[5422] מַשְׁחִית *mašḥît* 16x destroyer, one who destroys; destruction, corruption; bird trap [4889]

[5423] מִשְׁחָר *mišḥār* 1x dawn, early morning light [4891]

[5424] מַשְׁחֵת *mašḥēt* 1x destruction, annihilation [4892]

[5425] מִשְׁחַת *mišḥat* 1x disfigurement, implying ugliness and repulsion [4893*]

[5426] מָשְׁחָת *mošḥāt* 1x deformity, defect, corruption [4893]

[5427] מִשְׁטוֹחַ *mišṭôaḥ* 3x place for spreading out nets, drying yard for nets [4894]

[5428] מִשְׁטָר *mišṭār* 1x dominion, rule; some sources: heavenly writing (the starry sky as God's communication) [4896]

[5429] מֶשִׁי *mešî* 2x costly fabric for garments; possibly referring to silk [4897]

[5431] מָשִׁיחַ *māšîaḥ* 38x anointed (one), usually refers to pouring or smearing sacred oil on a person in a ceremony of dedication, possibly symbolizing divine empowering to accomplish the task or office; the Anointed One, the Messiah, God's ultimate chosen one, identified in the NT as Jesus [4899]

[5432] מָשַׁךְ *māšak* 36x [Q] to draw up, drag; to extend, spread out; [N] to be prolonged, delayed; [Pu] to be deferred; to be tall [4900]

[5433] 1 מֶשֶׁךְ *mešek* 2x (leather) bag, pouch (= price) [4901]

[5434] 2 מֶשֶׁךְ *mešek* 10x Meshech [4902]

[5435] מִשְׁכָּב *miškāb* 46x bed, couch, used as a place for sleep, meditation, convalescence, marital relations, and worship [4904]

[5436] מֹשְׁכוֹת *mōšekôt* 1x cords, chains, fetters [4189*]

[5438] מִשְׁכָּן *miškān* 139x dwelling place, habitat, tent, tabernacle, the tent used as the central place of worship before the temple [4908] See *tabernacle.*

[5439] 1 מָשַׁל *māšal* 17x [Q] to quote (a proverb or saying), to make up a proverb; [N] to liken, be like; [P] to tell a proverb; [H] to liken, compare to; [Ht] to show oneself like [4911] See *compare; (be) like; liken; quote.*

[5440] 2 מָשַׁל *māšal* 80x [Q] to rule, govern, control; [H] make one a ruler, (n.) dominion [4910]

[5442] 1 מָשָׁל *māšāl* 40x wisdom sayings of various types: proverb, a short, pithy saying, easy to remember; parable, a brief story with a symbolic meaning; oracle, a discourse type of prophecy; taunt, ridicule, a stylized form for mocking an enemy [4912]

[5444] 1 מֹשֶׁל *mōšel* 1x likeness, similarity [4915]

[5445] 2 מֹשֶׁל *mōšel* 2x power, dominion [4915]

[5447] מִשְׁלוֹחַ *mišlôaḥ* 3x giving, sending (presents); laying on (hands) [4916]

[5448] מִשְׁלָח *mišlāḥ* 7x stretching out (of the hand) [4916]

[5449] מִשְׁלַחַת *mišlaḥat* 21x discharge (from military); band, company (of angels) [4917]

[5450] מְשֻׁלָּם *mešullām* 25x Meshullam, "*restitution*" [4918]

[5457] מְשַׁמָּה *mešammâ* 7x object of horror, desolate waste, dried up place [4923]

[5458] מִשְׁמָן *mišmān* 5x fatness; by extension: sturdiness, stoutness; richness, fertility, abundance, prosperity [4924*]

[5460] מַשְׁמַנִּים *mašmannîm* 1x choice food, festive food, rich with oil or fat (rare and valued in the ancient Near East) [4924*]

[5461] 1 מִשְׁמָע *mišmāʿ* 1x what one hears, rumor, hearsay [4926]

[5463] מִשְׁמַעַת *mišmaʿat* 4x bodyguard; subject, one obligated to allegiance [4928]

[5464] 1 מִשְׁמָר *mišmār* 22x guard or guarding, custody, imprisonment [4929]

[5466] מִשְׁמֶרֶת *mišmeret* 78x responsibility, duty, service; requirement, obligation; guard, watch, what is cared for [4931] See *care; duty; guard; responsibility.*

[5467] מִשְׁנֶה *mišneh* 34x second, next (in a series); twice, double [4932]

[5468] מְשִׁסָּה *mešissâ* 6x plunder, loot, booty [4933]

[5469] מִשְׁעוֹל *mišʿôl* 1x narrow path [4934]

[5470] מִשְׁעִי *mišʿî* 1x cleansing, implying cleansing by washing and rubbing [4935]

[5471] מִשְׁעָם *mišʿām* 1x Misham [4936]

[5472] מִשְׁעָן *mišʿān* 4x support, supplies [4937]

[5473] מַשְׁעֵן *mašʿēn* 1x support, supply [4937]

[5474] מַשְׁעֵנָה *mašʿēnâ* 1x support, supply [4938]

[5475] מִשְׁעֶנֶת *mišʿenet* 11x staff, stick [4938]

[5476] מִשְׁפָּחָה *mišpāḥâ* 304x clan, family, people [4940] See *clan; family; kind(s); kindred; nations; people(s).*

[5477] מִשְׁפָּט *mišpāṭ* 425x justice, judgment; law, regulation, prescription, specification [4941] See *decree; judgment; justice.*

[5478] מִשְׁפְּתַיִם *mišpetayim* 2x (dual) campfires or two saddlebags [4942*]

[5479] מֶשֶׁק *mešeq* 1x inheritance, possession [4943]

[5480] מַשָּׁק *maššāq* 1x onslaught, assault; formally "rushing," this is the sudden, aggressive movement of a swarm [4944]

[5481] מְשֻׁקָּד *mešuqqād* 6x shape of almond flowers [8246]

[5482] 1 מַשְׁקֶה *mašqeh* 19x cupbearer; drink (liquid); drinking vessel [4945]

[5484] מִשְׁקוֹל *mišqôl* 1x weight [4946]

[5485] מַשְׁקוֹף *mašqôp* 3x top (upper crosspiece of a door), lintel [4947]

[5486] מִשְׁקָל *mišqāl* 49x weight [4948]

[5487] מִשְׁקֶלֶת *mišqelet* 2x plumb line, leveling instrument [4949]

[5488] מִשְׁקָע *mišqāʿ* 1x clear (settled) water [4950]

[5489] מִשְׁרָה *mišrâ* 1x (grape) juice [4952]

[5491] מָשַׁשׁ *māšaš* 9x [Q] to touch, feel; [P] to grope, search thoroughly; [H] to let one feel [4959]

[5492] מִשְׁתֶּה *mišteh* 46x feast, banquet, dinner, with an focus on drinking [4960]

[5493] 1 מֹת *mōt* 20x men; few (people) [4962*]

[5495] מַתְבֵּן *matbēn* 1x heap of straw [4963]

[5497] מֶתֶג הָאַמָּה *meteg hāʾammâ* 1x Metheg Ammah [4965]

[5500] מְתוּשֶׁלַח *metûselaḥ* 6x Methuselah, "*man of the javelin*" [4968]

[5503] מָתַי *mātay* 43x How long?; When? [4970]

[5504] מַתְכֹּנֶת *matkōnet* 5x measure, formula [4971]

[5506] מְתַלְּעוֹת *metalleʿôt* 3x jaw; teeth [4973*]

[5507] מְתֹם *metōm* 4x health, soundness [4974]

[5508] 1 מַתָּן *mattān* 5x gift, present [4976]

[5510] 1 מַתָּנָה *mattānâ* 17x gift, something given, such as an offering to deity or a bribe [4979]

[5516] מָתְנַיִם *motnayim* 47x (dual) waist, lower back (lumbar region), loins; "girding the loins" involves tucking the skirt of a tunic or robe into the belt, thus preparing for action: running, working, fighting, etc [4975*]

[5517] מָתַק *mātaq* 6x [Q] to be, become sweet; [H] to taste sweet, enjoy sweetness [4985 & 4988*]

[5518] מָתֵק *mātēq* 2x sweetness; by extension: pleasantness [4986*]

[5519] מֹתֶק *mōteq* 1x sweetness [4987]

[5522] מַתַּת *mattat* 6x gift, something given [4991*]

[5529] 2 נָא *nāʾ* 1x raw (meat) [4995]

[5530] נֹא *nōʾ* 4x No = Thebes [4996]

[5532] נֹאד *nōʾd* 7x skin vessel (skinned in one piece, the appendages tied or sewn, the neck the funnel, used to hold liquid) [4997]

[5533] נָאָה *nāʾâ* 3x [Pilel] to be beautiful, adorn [4998]

[5534] נָאוֶה *nāʾweh* 10x lovely, fitting, suited [5000]

[5535] נָאַם *nāʾam* 1x [Q] to declare as a prophet [5001]

[5536] נְאֻם *neʾum* 5,002x declaration, oracle, utterance; often a marker introducing or punctuating prophetic discourse [5002] See *declaration; oracle; parable; revelation; utterance; word.*

[5537] נָאַף *nāʾap* 31x [Q, P] to commit adultery; [ptcp.] adulterer, adulteress; by extension: to be unfaithful to God (by having illicit relations with other gods) [5003]

[5538] נַאֲפוּפִים *naʾapûpîm* 1x (marks of) unfaithfulness, adultery; such marks might refer to jewelry or adornments which signal that a woman is available for illicit sex [5005*]

[5539] נִאֻפִים *niʾupîm* 2x adultery [5004*]

[5540] נָאַץ *nāʾaṣ* 24x [Q] to spurn, despise, reject; [P] to treat with contempt, revile, despise; [Htpo] be blasphemed, be reviled [5006]

[5541] נְאָצָה *neʾāṣâ* 2x disgrace, shame [5007]

[5542] נֶאָצָה *neʾāṣâ* 3x contemptible things, blasphemies [5007]

[5543] נָאַק *nāʾaq* 2x [Q] to groan [5008]

[5544] נְאָקָה *neʾāqâ* 4x groaning [5009]

[5545] נֵאַר *nāʾar* 2x [P] to renounce, abandon [5010]

[5547] נָבָא *nābāʾ* 115x [N, Ht] to prophesy, speak as a prophet; prophecy has its focus on encouraging or restoring covenant faithfulness, the telling of future events encourages obedience or warns against disobedience [5012] See *prophesy.*

[5549] 1 נְבוֹ *nebô* 11x Nebo, "*height* or *Mount of Nabu [Nebo]*" [5015]

[5553] נְבוּאָה *nebûʾâ* 3x prophecy, the word of the prophet; prophecy has its focus on encouraging or restoring covenant faithfulness, the telling of future events encourages obedience or warns against disobedience [5016]

[5554] נָבוּב *nābûb* 4x hollow thing; witless person [5014*]

[5555] נְבוּזַרְאֲדָן *nebûzarʾadān* 15x Nebuzaradan, "*Nebo [Nabu] has given seed [offspring]*" [5018]

[5557] נְבוּכַדְרֶאצַּר *nebûkadreʾṣṣar* 31x Nebuchadnezzar, "*Nebo protect my boundary stone; Nebo protect my son!*" [5019]

[5559] נָבוֹת *nābôt* 1x Naboth, "*sprout*" [5022]

[5560] נָבַח *nābaḥ* 1x [Q] to bark [5024]

[5564] נָבַט *nābaṭ* 70x [P] to look at; [H] to look at, gaze at, consider [5027] See *consider; look; see.*

[5565] נְבָט *nebāṭ* 25x Nebat, "*look to, regard [approvingly]*" [5028]

[5566] נָבִיא *nābîʾ* 317x prophet (true or false), see also 5547 [5030] See *prophet.*

[5567] נְבִיאָה *nᵉbîʾâ* 6x prophetess (true or false), see also 5547 [5031]

[5569] נֵבֶךְ *nēbek* 1x source springs (of the sea) [5033]

[5570] 1 נָבֵל *nābēl* 20x [Q] to wither, shrivel, fade, decay [5034]

[5571] 2 נָבַל *nābal* 5x [Q] to play the fool, act disdainfully; [P] to treat with contempt, dishonor, reject [5034]

[5572] 1 נָבָל *nābāl* 19x foolish, lacking understanding, (n.) fool; often pertaining to insolence, pride, and disobedience to God [5036]

[5573] 2 נָבָל *nābāl* 21x Nabal, *"fool"* [5037]

[5574] 1 נֵבֶל *nēbel* 11x (wine) skin; water jar, jug, pot (of clay) [[5035]]

[5575] 2 נֵבֶל *nēbel* 27x lyre, harp (stringed instrument) [5035]

[5576] נְבָלָה *nᵉbālâ* 13x (very) wicked thing, disgraceful thing; vileness, something a fool would do [5039]

[5577] נְבֵלָה *nᵉbēlâ* 48x dead body, carcass [5038]

[5578] נַבְלוּת *nablût* 1x (female) genitals [5040]

[5580] נָבַע *nābaʿ* 11x [H] to gush forth, bubble out, spew forth [5042]

[5582] נֶגֶב *negeb* 111x south, the Negev [5045]

[5583] נָגַד *nāgad* 371x [H] to tell, report, inform; [Ho] to be told, have reported to [5046] See *declare; report; tell.*

[5584] נֶגֶד *neged* 151x before, in front of, opposite of, beyond [5048]

[5585] נָגַהּ *nāgah* 6x [Q] to shine; [H] to cause to shine, give light [5050]

[5586] 1 נֹגַהּ *nōgah* 19x brightness, radiance, splendor, brilliance [5051]

[5588] נְגֹהָה *nᵉgōhâ* 1x brightness, luster [5054]

[5590] נָגַח *nāgaḥ* 11x [Q] to gore (a bull into a person); [P] to gore, push back, butt; to engage in pushing back, butting, thrusting [5055]

[5591] נַגָּח *naggāḥ* 2x (the act of) goring (a bull into a person) [5056]

[5592] נָגִיד *nāgîd* 44x leader, ruler, official, officer [5057]

[5593] נְגִינָה *nᵉgînâ* 14x stringed instrument; song that mocks, taunts [5058]

[5594] נָגַן *nāgan* 15x [Q] to play a stringed instrument, (n.) musician; [P] to play a stringed instrument [5059]

[5595] נָגַע *nāgaʿ* 150x [Q] to touch; to strike; [Qp] to be plagued, be stricken; [N] to let oneself be driven back (in a battle); [P] to inflict, afflict; [Pu] to be plagued; [H] to extend, reach out, cause to touch; ranging in meaning from simple contact to violence [5060] See *arrive; harm; reach; strike; touch.*

[5596] נֶגַע *negaʿ* 78x plague, blow (of various kinds): mildew, infection, sores, scourge, disaster [5061] See *disease; plague.*

[5597] נָגַף *nāgap* 49x [Q] to strike, afflict (with a plague); [N] to be defeated [5062]

[5598] נֶגֶף *negep* 7x plague; stumbling (caused by a stone) [5063]

[5599] נָגַר *nāgar* 10x [N] to be spilled, flow; [H] to pour out, hand over, deliver over; [Ho] to be poured down (a slope) [5064]

[5601] נָגַשׂ *nāgaś* 23x [Q] to oppress, exploit, (n.) a slave driver; [N] to be oppressed, be hard pressed [5065]

[5602] נָגַשׁ *nāgaš* 125x [Q] to come near, approach; [N] to come near, approach; [H] to bring forth, present; [Ho] to be brought, be presented; [Ht] to draw near, assemble [5066] See *approach; bring; near.*

[5603] נֵד *nēd* 4x heap, wall, barrier, dam [5067]

[5605] נָדַב *nādab* 17x [Q] to be willing; to prompt, incite; [Ht] to willingly offer oneself, volunteer, give a freewill offering [5068]

[5606] נָדָב *nādāb* 20x Nadab, "*volunteer, free will offering*" [5070]

[5607] נְדָבָה *n^e^dābâ* 26x free, voluntary; freewill offering [5071]

[5610] נָדַד *nādad* 28x [Q] to flee, be a fugitive; to wander, stray; [Pol] to flee away; [H] to banish, put to flight; [Ho] to be banished, be cast aside [5074]

[5611] נְדֻדִים *n^e^dudîm* 1x tossing and turning, restlessness (in bed in the night) [5076*]

[5612] נָדָה *nādâ* 2x [P] to exclude; to put off thoughts, suppose to be far off [5077]

[5613] נֵדֶה *nēdeh* 1x gift, reward; likely referring to a fee for service [5078]

[5614] נִדָּה *niddâ* 29x period of menstruation; (water used in) cleansing, "unclean" water; (act of) impurity, corruption, defilement [5079]

[5615] 1 נָדַח *nādaḥ* 51x [N] to be scattered, be exiled, be outcast; [Pu] be thrust into; [H] to cause to scatter, banish, drive out; [Ho] to be driven, be hunted [5080] See *banish; cast out; stray; turn away.*

[5616] 2 נָדַח *nādaḥ* 3x [Q] to wield (an ax); (to have hand) be put (to the ax); [H] to bring [5080]

[5618] נָדִיב *nādîb* 27x willing, generous; prince, noble, ruler, official [5081]

[5619] נְדִיבָה *n^e^dîbâ* 3x something noble; dignity, nobility [5082]

[5620] 1 נָדָן *nādān* 1x sheath (of a sword) [5084]

[5621] 2 נָדָן *nādān* 1x gift, wages of illicit sexual favors [5083]

[5622] נָדַף *nādap* 9x [Q] to blow away, scatter; [N] to be windblown, be fleeting [5086]

[5623] נָדַר *nādar* 31x [Q] to make a vow [5087]

[5624] נֶדֶר *nēder* 60x vow [5088] See *vow.*

[5625] נֹהַּ *nōah* 1x value, distinction [5089]

[5627] 1 נָהַג *nāhag* 30x [Q] to drive, lead, guide; [Qp] to be led; [P] to drive, lead forth, guide [5090]

[5628] 2 נָהַג *nāhag* 1x [P] to moan, sob, lament [5090]

[5629] 1 נָהָה *nāhâ* 3x [Q] to mourn, wail; [N] to be taunted (with a mournful song) [5091]

[5631] נְהִי *n^e^hî* 7x wailing, mourning, often related to mournful songs: lamentation [5092]

[5633] נָהַל *nāhal* 10x [P] guide, bring along, lead; [Ht] to move along [5095]

[5635] 1 נַהֲלֹל *nah^a^lōl* 1x watering hole [5097]

[5637] נָהַם *nāham* 5x [Q] to growl, roar; to groan [5098]

[5638] נַהַם *naham* 2x roaring, growling [5099]

[5639] נְהָמָה *n^e^hāmâ* 2x roaring, growling; anguish, groaning [5100]

[5640] נָהַק *nāhaq* 2x [Q] to bray (of a donkey) [5101]

[5641] 1 נָהַר *nāhar* 3x [Q] to stream to (like a river flow) [5102]

[5642] 2 נָהַר *nāhar* 3x [Q] to be radiant (with joy), beam (with joy) [5102]

[5643] נָהָר *nāhār* 119x river, stream, canal; the River, which can refer to the Euphrates, Tigris, or Nile [5104] See *river.*

[5644] נְהָרָה *n^e hārâ* 1x (beaming) light [5105]

[5646] 1 נוּ *nû* 1,647x us, our [**]

[5647] 2 נוּ *nû* 512x him, his; it, its [**]

[5648] נוא *nû'* 8x [Q] to hinder; [H] to forbid, thwart, discourage [5106]

[5649] נוב *nûb* 4x [Q] to bring forth, bear fruit, increase; [Pol] to make thrive [5107]

[5652] נוּג *nûg* 1x sorrow [3013*]

[5653] נוּד *nûd* 25x [Q] to sway, wander, be aimless, become homeless; to mourn, express sympathy (by shaking the head) [5110]

[5654] 1 נוֹד *nôd* 1x lament; some sources: wandering, homelessness [5112]

[5657] 1 נָוָה *nāwâ* 1x [Q] to be at rest, reach one's aim [5115]

[5658] 2 נָוָה *nāwâ* 1x [H] to praise [5115]

[5659] 1 נָוֶה *nāweh* 32x pasture, pastureland, with a possible focus that this is a place of rest and peace; (generally) abode, dwelling, house [5116]

[5661] 3 נָוָה *nāwâ* 15x pasture, pastureland; (generally) abode, dwelling, camp, place [4999]

[5663] 1 נוּחַ *nûaḥ* 140x [Q] to settle, rest, wait; [H] to put, keep, settle, rest; to leave, allow; [Ho] to be placed, find rest [5117] See *leave; place; put; rest; set; settle.*

[5665] נוֹחַ *nôaḥ* 1x resting place [5118]

[5667] נוּט *nûṭ* 1x [Q] to shake, quake [5120]

[5670] נוּם *nûm* 6x [Q] to sleep, slumber, implying detachment from activities and others; by extension: to be dead [5123]

[5671] נוּמָה *nûmâ* 1x drowsiness [5124]

[5672] 1 נוּן *nûn* 1x [N] to propagate, increase [5125]

[5673] 2 נוּן *nûn* 30x Nun, "*fish* hence *fertile, productive*" [5126]

[5674] נוּס *nûs* 160x [Q] to flee away, escape; [Pol] to drive along; [H] to put to flight, get to safety [5127] See *escape; flee.*

[5675] נוּעַ *nûa'* 40x [Q] to shake, sway, swagger, wander; [N] to be shaken; [H] to make wander, to set trembling, shake, toss [5128]

[5677] 1 נוּף *nûp* 35x [Pol] to wave (the fist) threateningly; [H] to wave, present (an offering) by waving; to shake, wield, sweep; [Ho] to be waved [5130]

[5678] 2 נוּף *nûp* 2x [Q] to sprinkle with myrrh (a bed); [H] to cause (rain) to fall [5130]

[5679] נוֹף *nôp* 1x loftiness, elevation, height [5131]

[5680] נוּץ *nûṣ* 1x [Q] to leave, go away [5132]

[5681] נוֹצָה *nôṣâ* 3x plumage, feathers [5133]

[5683] נוּשׁ *nûš* 1x [Q] to be sick [5136]

[5684] 1 נָזָה *nāzâ* 24x [Q] to spatter; [H] to sprinkle [5137]

[5686] נָזִיד *nāzîd* 6x stew, thick boiled food [5138]

[5687] נָזִיר *nāzîr* 6x Nazirite, with the designated meaning of separation; a class of people dedicated to God; untended vine, dedicated to God in the sabbatical year of rest [5139]

[5688] נָזַל *nāzal* 11x [Q] to flow down, pour down, stream down; [H] to make flow [5140]

[5689] נֹזֵל *nōzēl* 5x streams; surging waters [5140*]

[5690] נֶזֶם *nezem* 17x ring (in the nose or ear of male or female) [5141]

[5691] נֵזֶק *nēzeq* 1x burden, trouble [5143]

[5692] 1 נָזַר *nāzar* 5x [N] to separate oneself, consecrate oneself; [H] to keep separate [5144]

[5693] 2 נָזַר *nāzar* 5x [H] to abstain, separate as a Nazirite; see also 5687 [5144]

[5694] נֵזֶר *nēzer* 25x separation, dedication (to God); diadem, crown (as a sign of consecration); Nazirite, a class of people dedicated to God [5145]

[5695] נֹחַ *nōaḥ* 47x Noah, "*rest, comfort*" [5146]

[5697] 1 נָחָה *nāḥâ* 35x [Q, H] to lead, guide [5148]

[5701] נָחוֹר *nāḥôr* 18x Nahor, "*the mound of Nahuru*" [5152]

[5702] נָחוּשׁ *nāḥûš* 1x (made) of bronze [5153]

[5703] נְחוּשָׁה *n^{e}ḥûšâ* 10x copper, bronze [5154]

[5704] נְחִילוֹת *n^{e}ḥîlôt* 1x flutes (a t.t. in Ps 5) [5155*]

[5705] נָחִיר *nāḥîr* 1x (dual) nostrils [5156]

[5706] נָחַל *nāḥal* 59x [Q] to take as an appearance, take possession; [P] to assign an inheritance, allot; [H] to cause to inherit, give an inheritance; [Ho] to be allotted; [Ht] to obtain an inheritance for oneself; to distribute an inheritance [5157] See *get; inherit; possess, possessions; take possession.*

[5707] 1 נַחַל *naḥal* 137x river, stream, brook, wadi torrent; ravine, gorge, valley [5158] See *brook; gorge; ravine; river; stream; torrent; valley.*

[5709] 1 נַחֲלָה *naḥ^{a}lâ* 222x inheritance, property [5159] See *heritage; inheritance; possess, possessions.*

[5710] 2 נַחֲלָה *naḥ^{a}lâ* 1x disease [**]

[5711] 3 נַחֲלָה *naḥ^{a}lâ* 2x wadi (of Egypt) [5158]

[5714] נָחַם *nāḥam* 108x [N] to relent, repent, change one's mind; be grieved; [P] to comfort, console, express sympathy; [Pu] to be comforted, be consoled; [Ht] to console oneself; to change one's mind; avenge oneself [5162] See *change one's mind; comfort; grieve; relent; repent, repentance.*

[5716] נֹחַם *nōḥam* 1x compassion, pity [5164]

[5717] נֶחָמָה *neḥāmâ* 2x comfort, consolation [5165]

[5718] נְחֶמְיָה *n^{e}ḥemyâ* 8x Nehemiah, "*Yahweh has comforted*" [5166]

[5719] נִחֻמִים *niḥumîm* 3x comfort, compassion [5150*]

[5722] נָחַץ *nāḥaṣ* 1x [Qp] to be urgent [5169]

[5723] נָחַר *nāḥar* 2x [Q] to blow; [P] to snort [2734* & 2787*]

[5724] נַחַר *naḥar* 1x snorting (of a horse) [5170]

[5725] נַחֲרָה *naḥ^{a}râ* 1x snorting (of a horse) [5170]

[5727] נָחַשׁ *nāḥaš* 11x [P] to practice divination, interpret omens and signs [5172]

[5728] נַחַשׁ *naḥaš* 2x sorcery, magic curse, spell [5173]

[5729] 1 נָחָשׁ *nāḥāš* 31x snake, serpent; by extension: a mythological creature of chaos opposed to God [5175]

[5733] 1 נְחֹשֶׁת *n^{e}ḥōšet* 139x copper, bronze; this can refer to bronze as a medium of exchange [5178] See *brass; brazen; bronze; copper.*

[5737] נָחַת *nāḥat* 10x [Q] to descend, go down; [N] to be pierced, penetrate; [P] to bend (a bow); to level off; [H] to bring down [5181]

[5738] 1 נַ֫חַת *naḥat* 1x coming down, descending [5183]

[5739] 2 נַ֫חַת *naḥat* 6x rest, peace, tranquillity [5183]

[5741] נָחֵת *nāḥēt* 1x going down, descending [5185]

[5742] נָטָה *nāṭâ* 216x [Q] to spread out, stretch out; [Qp] to be outstretched, be spread out, be extended; [N] to be spread out, be stretched out; [H] to turn aside, pervert, lead astray; [Ho] to be outspread [5186] See *pitch (a tent); spread out; stretch out; turn.*

[5744] נָטִיל *nāṭîl* 1x weighing (of precious metals); by extension, trading: buying, selling, and bartering [5187]

[5745] נָטִיעַ *nāṭîʿa* 1x shoot (of a young plant) [5195]

[5746] נְטִישׁוֹת *n^eṭîšôt* 3x spreading branches, tendrils [5189*]

[5747] נָטַל *nāṭal* 4x [Q] to lay upon; to weigh; [P] to lift [5190]

[5748] נֵ֫טֶל *nēṭel* 1x burden, load [5192]

[5749] נָטַע *nāṭaʿ* 59x [Q] to plant (seed or stock); by extension: to place, set, set up (any object on any surface) [5193] See *establish; plant; sow.*

[5750] נֶ֫טַע *neṭaʿ* 4x garden, plants; young plant [5194]

[5752] נָטַף *nāṭap* 18x [Q] to pour down; gently fall, drip; [H] to (drip words) preach, prophesy [5197]

[5753] נָטָף *nāṭāp* 1x gum resin, drops of stacte (the resin of a shrub) [5198]

[5754] נֶ֫טֶף *neṭep* 1x drop (of water) [5198*]

[5755] נְטִפָה *n^eṭipâ* 2x pendant, a drop-shaped ornament [5188]

[5757] 1 נָטַר *nāṭar* 9x [Q] to care for, tend; to be angry, harbor a grudge [5201]

[5759] נָטַשׁ *nāṭaš* 40x [Q] to abandon, forsake, reject; [Qp] to be scattered; [N] to spread out; to be deserted; [Pu] to be abandoned [5203]

[5760] נִי *nî* 1x wailing [5204]

[5762] נִיב *nîb* 2x fruit; "fruit of the lips" is praise [5108*]

[5764] נִיד *nîd* 1x comfort [5205]

[5765] נִידָה *nîdâ* 1x uncleanness, impurity [5206]

[5767] נִיחֹחַ *nîḥōaḥ* 43x pleasing, soothing, appeasing [5207]

[5769] 2 נִין *nîn* 3x offspring, children, posterity [5209]

[5770] נִינְוֵה *nîn^ewēh* 17x Nineveh [5210]

[5773] נִיצוֹץ *nîṣôṣ* 1x spark [5213]

[5774] 1 נִיר *nîr* 2x [Q] to break up, bring into cultivation [5214]

[5775] 2 נִיר *nîr* 5x lamp; by extension: descendant (continuing of a line as the burning of a lamp) [5216]

[5776] 3 נִיר *nîr* 3x unplowed ground, likely referring to ground not plowed for the current season [5215]

[5777] 1 נָכָא *nākāʾ* 1x [N] to be driven out (by whipping or scourging) [5217]

[5778] 2 נָכָא *nākāʾ* 1x grieving (as one unmercifully beaten) [5218]

[5779] נָכֵא *nākēʾ* 3x crushed, beaten, broken [5218]

[5780] נְכֹאת *n^ekōʾt* 2x spices, resin [5219]

[5781] נֶ֫כֶד *neked* 3x descendant, progeny [5220]

[5782] נָכָה *nākâ* 501x [N] to be struck; [Pu] to be destroyed; [H] to kill, slaughter, destroy, defeat; [Ho] to be beat, be struck, be wounded, be killed [5221] See *beat; destroy; hit; kill; strike.*

[5783] נָכֶה *nākeh* 3x lame, crippled; contrite [5223]

[5787] 1 נָכוֹן *nākôn* 1x strike, blow [3559*]

[5790] נֹכַח *nōkaḥ* 25x opposite, before, in front of [5226* & 5227]

[5791] נָכֹחַ *nākōaḥ* 8x proper, right, honest, what is straight [5228 & 5229*]

[5792] נָכַל *nākal* 4x [Q, P] to cheat, treat cunningly; [Ht] to conspire, plot [5230]

[5793] נֵכֶל *nēkel* 1x deception, cunning [5231]

[5794] נְכָסִים *n^{e}kāsîm* 5x riches, wealth, possessions [5233*]

[5795] 1 נָכַר *nākar* 50x [N] to disguise oneself, be not recognized; [P] to regard, consider; to favor; to misunderstand; [H] to recognize, acknowledge; [Ht] to make known [5234] See *acknowledge; disguise; distinguish; notice; recognize.*

[5796] 2 נָכַר *nākar* 5x [P] to treat as foreign; [Ht] to pretend to be a stranger [5234]

[5797] נֵכָר *nēkār* 36x (one from a foreign land) foreigner, alien, stranger [5236]

[5798] נֵכֶר *nēker* 2x misfortune, disaster [5235*]

[5799] נָכְרִי *nākrî* 45x foreign, alien; (n.) foreigner [5237]

[5800] נְכֹת *n^{e}kōt* 2x treasure, storage [5238]

[5801] נָלָה *nālâ* 1x [H] to stop [5239]

[5805] נְמָלָה *n^{e}mālâ* 2x ant [5244]

[5807] נָמֵר *nāmēr* 6x leopard [5246]

[5811] נִמְשִׁי *nimšî* 5x Nimshi [5250]

[5813] נְסִבָּה *n^{e}sibbâ* 1x turn of events [5252]

[5814] נָסָה *nāsâ* 36x [P] to test (usually to prove character or faithfulness), to attempt; to test God implies a lack of confidence in his revealed character, thus is wicked [5254] See *prove; test; try.*

[5815] נָסַח *nāsaḥ* 4x [Q] to tear down; [N] to be uprooted, be torn down [5255]

[5816] 1 נָסִיךְ *nāsîk* 2x drink offering; metal image, idol [5257]

[5817] 2 נָסִיךְ *nāsîk* 4x prince, leader [5257]

[5818] 1 נָסַךְ *nāsak* 23x [Q] to pour out; [N] to be poured out; [P] to pour out; [H] to pour out; [Ho] to be poured out; usually of pouring out a drink offering to deity [5258]

[5819] 2 נָסַךְ *nāsak* 1x [Qp] to be woven [5259]

[5820] 3 נָסַךְ *nāsak* 2x [Q] to install, set; [N] to be appointed [5258]

[5821] 1 נֶסֶךְ *nesek* 60x drink offering [5262]

[5822] 2 נֶסֶךְ *nesek* 4x metal image, idol [5262]

[5823] 1 נָסַס *nāsas* 1x [Q] to falter [5263]

[5824] 2 נָסַס *nāsas* 2x [Htpol] to unfurl; to sparkle [5264]

[5825] נָסַע *nāsaʿ* 146x [Q] to set out, move on, leave, travel on; [N] to be pulled up; [H] to lead, bring out; to pull out [5265] See *depart; journey; leave; move; set out; travel.*

[5830] נְעוּרִים *n^{e}ʿûrîm* 46x youth, childhood, boyhood [5271*]

[5831] נְעוּרוֹת *n^{e}ʿûrôt* 1x youth [5271*]

[5833] 1 נָעִים *nāʿîm* 11x pleasant, charming [5273]

[5834] 2 נָעִים *nāʿîm* 2x singing, sweetly sounding, musical [5273]

[5835] 1 נָעַל *nāʿal* 6x [Q] to lock up, bolt; [Qp] to be locked up, be sealed [5274]

[5836] 2 נָעַל *nāʿal* 2x [Q] to put on a sandal; [H] to provide with sandals [5274]

[5837] נַעַל *naʿal* 22x sandal (normal footware); not to wear sandals could have the associative meaning of being in poverty, misery, or disgrace [5275]

[5838] נָעֵם *nāʿēm* 8x [Q] to be pleasant, be dear, be favored [5276]

[5840] נֹעַם *nōʿam* 7x pleasantness, favor [5278]

[5843] נָעֳמִי *nāʿomî* 21x Naomi, "*my joy*" [5281]

[5845] נַעֲמָן *naʿamān* 16x Naaman, "*pleasantness*" [5283]

[5846] נַעֲמָנִים *naʿamānîm* 1x finest (of Adonis [?]) [5282*]

[5848] נַעֲצוּץ *naʿaṣûṣ* 2x thornbush [5285]

[5849] 1 נָעַר *nāʿar* 1x [Q] to growl [5286]

[5850] 2 נָעַר *nāʿar* 11x [Q] to shake off; to refuse; [Qp] be shaken out; [N] to shake oneself free, be shaken off; [P] to shake off, sweep away; [Ht] to shake oneself free [5287]

[5853] 2 נַעַר *naʿar* 240x young man, boy, child, ranging in age from infancy to young adulthood; by extension: servant, attendant, steward, with a possible focus on lower social status [5288] See *boy; child; servant; young man; youth.*

[5854] נֹעַר *nōʿar* 4x youth [5290]

[5855] 1 נַעֲרָה *naʿarâ* 76x young woman, girl, ranging in age from infancy to young adulthood; by extension: servant, maid, with a possible focus on lower social status [5291] See *girl; maid; young woman.*

[5861] נְעֹרֶת *neʿōret* 7x tinder (broken fibers shaken off flax) [5296]

[5864] 1 נָפָה *nāpâ* 1x sieve (winnowing device) [5299]

[5870] נָפַח *nāpaḥ* 11x [Q] to blow upon, breathe upon; [Qp, Pu] to be blown upon; [H] to sniff out; to cause to breathe out [5301]

[5872] נְפִילִים *nepîlîm* 3x Nephilim [5303*]

[5876] נֹפֶךְ *nōpek* 4x turquoise (green semi-precious stone) [5306]

[5877] נָפַל *nāpal* 435x [Q] to fall, fail; [Pilal?] to fall; [H] to cause to fall, to cast down, drop; (used of casting lots) to allocate; [Ht] to fall prostrate (to worship); to fall upon (to attack); by extension: to happen (of circumstance falling on a person) [5307] See *allocate; bow down; die; fall.*

[5878] נֵפֶל *nēpel* 3x stillborn child, miscarriage [5309]

[5879] 1 נָפַץ *nāpaṣ* 17x [Q] to shatter; [P] to shatter; (of log raft) to separate; [Pu] to be crushed [5310]

[5880] 2 נָפַץ *nāpaṣ* 3x [Q] to scatter [5310]

[5881] נֶפֶץ *nepeṣ* 1x bursting, pelting (of rain) [5311]

[5882] נָפַשׁ *nāpaš* 3x [N] to be refreshed, refresh oneself [5314]

[5883] נֶפֶשׁ *nepeš* 757x breath; by extension: life, life force, soul, an immaterial part of a person, the seat of emotion and desire; a creature or person as a whole: self, body, even corpse [5315] See *being; breath; person; soul.*

[5885] נֹפֶת *nōpet* 5x honey of the honeycomb [5317]

[5887] נַפְתּוּלִים *naptûlîm* 1x struggles, wrestlings [5319*]

[5889] נַפְתָּלִי *naptālî* 51x Naphtali, "*wrestling*" [5321]

[5890] 1 נֵץ *nēṣ* 2x blossom [5322]

[5891] 2 נֵץ *nēṣ* 3x hawk or falcon (bird of prey) [5322]

[5893] 1 נָצַב *nāṣab* 74x [N] to stand oneself before; (n.) officer, official; [H] to station, set up, establish; [Ho] to be set up, be decreed [5324] See *establish; officer; set; stand.*

[5896] 2 נִצָּב *niṣṣāb* 1x handle, hilt (of sword, dagger or knife) [5325]

[5897] 1 נָצָה *nāṣâ* 8x [N] to fight (quarreling that can come to blows and struggles); [H] to rebel, engage in a struggle [5327]

[5898] 2 נָצָה *nāṣâ* 8x [Q] to lie in ruins; [N] to be laid waste, be desolate [5327]

[5900] נִצָּה *niṣṣâ* 2x blossom [5328]

[5901] 1 נֹצָה *nōṣâ* 1x contents (of a bird's crop) [5133]

[5904] נָצַח *nāṣaḥ* 65x [N] to be enduring, lasting; [P] to direct, supervise; (n.) director (of music, 55 times in the Psalms), supervisor [5329] See *director of music; supervisor.*

[5905] 1 נֵצַח *nēsaḥ* 43x glory, majesty, splendor; forever, unending, everlasting, always; "the Glory of Israel" as a title of God probably emphasizes both glory and eternity [5331]

[5906] 2 נֵצַח *nēsaḥ* 2x juice (= blood) [5332]

[5907] 1 נְצִיב *n^eṣîb* 11x garrison, outpost; pillar [5333]

[5911] נָצַל *nāṣal* 213x [N] to be saved, be delivered, be spared; [P] to plunder, take away, tear away; [H] to deliver, save, rescue; [Ho] to be snatched; [Ht] to strip off oneself [5337] See *deliver; rescue; save; take away.*

[5913] 1 נָצַץ *nāṣaṣ* 1x [Q] to gleam, sparkle [5340]

[5914] 2 נָצַץ *nāṣaṣ* 3x [H] to bloom, blossom [5006* & 5132*]

[5915] נָצַר *nāṣar* 63x [Q] to guard, watch, protect, keep, preserve; [Qp] to be kept secret, be hidden [5341] See *guard; keep; tend; watch.*

[5916] נֵצֶר *nēṣer* 4x branch, shoot (of a plant) [5342]

[5917] נִצְּרָה *niṣṣ^erâ* 1x watching, guarding [5341*]

[5918] 1 נָקַב *nāqab* 16x [Q] to bore (a hole), pierce; to designate, bestow; [Qp] to have a hole; to be notable; [N] to be designated, be registered [5344]

[5919] 2 נָקַב *nāqab* 3x [Q] to blaspheme, with a focus on marring someone's reputation [5918 & 7686]

[5920] 1 נֶקֶב *neqeb* 1x mounting (used in gold jewelry) [5345]

[5922] נְקֵבָה *n^eqēbâ* 22x female, woman [5347]

[5923] נָקֹד *nāqōd* 9x speckled, spotted [5348]

[5924] נֹקֵד *nōqēd* 2x shepherd, one who raises sheep [5349]

[5925] נְקֻדָּה *n^equddâ* 1x point, drops (of silver on a gold earring) [5351]

[5926] נִקֻּדִים *niqqudîm* 3x (small) cakes; crumbling (food supplies) [5350*]

[5927] נָקָה *nāqâ* 44x [Q] to go unpunished; [N] be innocent, be released, go unpunished; [P] to leave unpunished, consider innocent, pardon [5352]

[5929] נָקִי *nāqî* 43x innocent, free of blame, not guilty [5355]

[5931] נִקָּיוֹן *niqqāyôn* 5x cleanness, purity; by extension: moral or ceremonial innocence, purity, cleanness; "cleanness of teeth" is a sign of lack of food in famine [5356]

[5932] נָקִיק *nāqîq* 3x crevice, cleft, crack [5357]

[5933] נָקַם *nāqam* 35x [Q] to seek vengeance, avenge; [N] to be avenged, avenge oneself; [P] to avenge; [Ho or Qp] to be avenged; [Ht] to take one's own vengeance [5358] See *avenge; punish, punishment.*

[5934] נָקָם *nāqām* 17x vengeance, revenge [5359] See *avenge; punish, punishment; vengeance.*

[5935] נְקָמָה *n^eqāmâ* 27x vengeance, revenge [5360] See *avenge; punish, punishment; vengeance.*

[5936] נָקַע *nāqaʿ* 3x [Q] to turn away in disgust [5361]

[5937] 1 נָקַף *nāqap* 2x [P] to cut down; to be destroyed [5362]

[5938] 2 נָקַף *nāqap* 17x [Q] to go through a yearly cycle; [H] to surround, encircle, engulf [5362]

[5939] נֹקֶף *nōqep* 2x beating (fruit off olive tree in harvest) [5363]

[5940] נִקְפָּה *niqpâ* 1x rope (around waist) [5364]

[5941] נָקַר *nāqar* 6x [Q] to gouge out, peck out (an eye); [P] to gouge out; to pierce; [Pu] to be hewn out (of quarry rock) [5365]

[5942] נְקָרָה *n^eqārâ* 2x cleft; cavern [5366]

[5943] נָקַשׁ *nāqaš* 4x [N] to be ensnared; [P] to lay out snares; [Ht] to lay out traps, set a trap [5367]

[5944] 1 נֵר *nēr* 44x lamp (fueled by olive oil); by extension: life (as a burning lamp); light (showing the way of truth) [5216]

[5948] נֵרְדְּ *nērd* 3x nard (aromatic ointment) [5373]

[5951] נָשָׂא *nāśāʾ* 659x [Q] to bear, carry, lift up; forgive; [Qp] to be forgiven, honored, carried; [N] to be carried off, lifted up; [P] to elevate, carry along; [H] to cause to carry, to bring; [Ht] to exalt oneself, lift up oneself; from the base meaning of rise in elevation come fig. extensions "to exalt, honor," as the lifting up of a person in status, and "to forgive," as the removal of guilt and its penalties; "to lift up the eyes" means "to look up" [4984* & 5375 & 5379* & 7721*] See *bear; carry; forgive; lift.*

[5952] נָשַׂג *nāśag* 50x [H] to overtake, catch up, attain; to reach, to be able to afford [5381] See *afford; overtake.*

[5953] נְשׂוּאָה *n^eśûʾâ* 1x burden, load (of images that are carried about) [5385]

[5954] 1 נָשִׂיא *nāśîʾ* 130x leader, ruler, chief, prince [5387] See *chief; leader; official.*

[5955] 2 נָשִׂיא *nāśîʾ* 4x cloud, rising mist, damp fog [5387]

[5956] נָשַׂק *nāśaq* 3x [N] to be kindled; [H] to kindle a fire, burn [5400]

[5957] 1 נָשָׁא *nāšāʾ* 18x [Q] to give a loan, be a creditor; [H] to make a loan; to subject one to tribute [5378 & 5383]

[5958] 2 נָשָׁא *nāšāʾ* 15x [N] to be deceived; [H] to deceive [5377]

[5959] נָשַׁב *nāšab* 3x [Q] to blow; [H] to cause to blow; to drive away [5380]

[5960] 1 נָשָׁה *nāšâ* 9x [Q] to forget; [N] to be forgotten; [P] to make forget; [H] to make one forget; to allow one to forget [5382]

[5962] נָשֶׁה *nāšeh* 2x tendon (attached to the hip), perhaps the sciatic nerve [5384]

[5963] נְשִׁי *n^ešî* 1x debt [5386]

[5964] נְשִׁיָּה *n^ešiyyâ* 1x oblivion, place forgotten (by the LORD) [5388]

[5965] נְשִׁיקָה *n^ešîqâ* 2x kiss [5390]

[5966] 1 נָשַׁךְ *nāšak* 11x [Q] to bite; [Qp] to be bitten; [P] to bite [5391]

[5967] 2 נָשַׁךְ *nāšak* 5x [Q] to earn interest; to claim interest against one; [H] to charge interest [5391]

[5968] נֶשֶׁךְ *nešek* 12x interest, usury [5392]

[5969] נִשְׁכָּה *niškâ* 3x room (for various uses: living, storage, etc.) [5393]

[5970] נָשַׁל *nāšal* 7x [Q] to take off, come off; to drive out [5394]

[5971] נָשַׁם *nāšam* 1x [Q] to gasp, pant [5395]

[5972] נְשָׁמָה *n^e^šāmâ* 24x breath, blast of breath; by extension: life, life force, spirit [5397]

[5973] נָשַׁף *nāšap* 2x [Q] to blow [5398]

[5974] נֶשֶׁף *nešep* 12x dusk, dawn (of morning); twilight (of evening) [5399]

[5975] 1 נָשַׁק *nāšaq* 30x [Q] to kiss; [P] to kiss (repeatedly or intensely); a kiss can show familial or romantic affection, as well as homage and submission [5401]

[5976] 2 נָשַׁק *nāšaq* 5x [Q] to be equipped, arm oneself; [H] to brush against, touch up against [5401]

[5977] 1 נֶשֶׁק *nešeq* 10x weapon; armory [5402]

[5979] נֶשֶׁר *nešer* 26x eagle; vulture [5404]

[5980] נָשַׁת *nāšat* 4x [Q] to be dry, be parched; [N] to be dried up [5405]

[5981] נִשְׁתְּוָן *ništ^e^wān* 2x letter, writing, see 10496 [5406]

[5983] נָתַח *nātaḥ* 9x [P] to cut into pieces [5408]

[5984] נֵתַח *nētaḥ* 13x piece (of butchered things or persons) [5409]

[5985] נָתִיב *nātîb* 5x path [5410]

[5986] נְתִיבָה *n^e^tîbâ* 21x path, way, road; by extension: behavior, lifestyle [5410]

[5987] נָתִין *nātîn* 17x servant [5411]

[5988] נָתַךְ *nātak* 21x [Q] to pour out; [N] to be poured out, be melted; [H] to pour out (liquid or money); to melt; [Ho] to be melted [5413]

[5989] נָתַן *nātan* 2,014x [Q] to give, put; [Qp] to be given, dedicated; [N] to be given; [Ho or Qp] to be given; note the many contextual translations in the NIV [5414] See *bestow; give; make; place; set; yield.*

[5990] נָתָן *nātān* 42x Nathan, "*gift*" [5416]

[5993] נְתַנְיָהוּ *n^e^tanyāhû* 5x Nethaniah, "*Yahweh has given*" [5418]

[5994] נְתַן־מֶלֶךְ *n^e^tan-melek* 1x Nathan-Melech, "*gift of king* or *gift of Melek, Molech, Malk*" [5419]

[5995] נָתַס *nātas* 1x [Q] to break up, tear up [5420]

[5996] נָתַע *nātaʿ* 1x [N] to be broken down, be knocked out (of teeth) [5421]

[5997] נָתַץ *nātaṣ* 42x [Q] to break down, tear down, demolish; [Qp] to be broken down; [N] to be shattered, lay in ruins; [P] to tear down, break down, shatter, destroy; [Pu] to be demolished; [Ho] to be broken up [5422]

[5998] נָתַק *nātaq* 27x [Q] to draw away, pull off; [Qp] to be torn; [N] to be lured away, be shattered, be torn, be broken; [P] to break, tear; [H] to lure away, drag off; [Ho] to be drawn away [5423]

[5999] נֶתֶק *neteq* 14x diseased area of skin: itch; some sources: ringworm, eczema [5424]

[6000] 1 נָתַר *nātar* 1x [H] to let loose, withdraw [5425]

[6001] 2 נָתַר *nātar* 3x [Q] to leap up; [P] to hop up; [H] to make leap up, jump up [5425]

[6002] 3 נָתַר *nātar* 3x [H] to set free, release, untie [5425]

[6003] נֶתֶר *neter* 2x natron (a sodium carbonate for washing) [5427]

[6004] נָתַשׁ *nātaš* 20x [Q] to uproot; [N] to be uprooted; [Ho] to be uprooted [5428]

[6006] סְאָה *s^eʾ^â* 9x seah (dry measure, one-third of an ephah, about seven quarts or liters) [5429]

[6007] סְאוֹן *s^eʾ^ôn* 1x boot [5430]

[6008] סָאַן *sāʾan* 1x [Q] to tramp along in boots [5431]

[6009] סַאסְּאָה *saʾssᵉʾâ* 1x warfare, chasing away [5432*]

[6010] 1 סָבָא *sābāʾ* 5x [Q] to be a drunkard, drink too much; [Qp] to be drunk [5433]

[6011] סֹבֶא *sōbeʾ* 3x wine, drink, implying drunkenness [5435]

[6015] סָבַב *sābab* 163x [Q] to go around, surround, encircle, engulf; [N] to change direction; to be surrounded; [P] to change; [Pol] to surround, shield, go about; [H] to turn about, circle around; [Ho] to be set, mounted, surrounded; to be changed [4141* & 4142* & 5437] See *go around; surround; turn.*

[6016] סִבָּה *sibbâ* 1x turning, arrangement (of events) [5438]

[6017] סָבִיב *sābîb* 334x all around, on all sides, surrounding, encircling [5439]

[6018] סָבַךְ *sābak* 2x [Qp, Pu] to be entangled, entwined [5440]

[6019] סְבַךְ *sᵉbak* 3x thicket, underbrush [5442*]

[6020] סְבֹךְ *sᵉbōk* 2x thicket, underbrush (where animals can live or hide) [5441*]

[6022] סָבַל *sābal* 13x [Q] to bear, carry, sustain; [Pu] to be (heavy) laden; [Ht] to drag oneself along [5445]

[6023] סֵבֶל *sēbel* 3x burden; forced labor [5447]

[6024] סֹבֶל *sōbel* 3x burden [5448]

[6025] סַבָּל *sabbāl* 5x carrier, burden-bearer [5449]

[6026] סִבְלוֹת *siblôt* 6x forced labor, burden-bearer [5450*]

[6027] סִבֹּלֶת *sibbōlet* 1x Sibboleth, "*ear of grain* or *torrent of water*" [5451]

[6032] סָגַד *sāgad* 4x [Q] to bow down (in worship) [5456]

[6033] סְגוֹר *sᵉgôr* 1x enclosure, closing (of the heart) [5458]

[6034] סָגוּר *sāgûr* 9x purity (of gold) [5462*]

[6035] סְגֻלָּה *sᵉgullâ* 8x treasured possession, personal property [5459]

[6036] סֶגֶן *segen* 17x official, officer, commander [5461*]

[6037] סָגַר *sāgar* 91x [Q] to shut, close; [Qp] to be shut; [N] to be confined, to be shut up, be imprisoned; [P] to deliver; [Pu] to be shut up, be barred, be closed; [H] to surrender, give over, deliver up; to put in isolation [5462] See *hand over; shut.*

[6038] סָגָר *sāgār* 1x javelin, (battle) ax [5462*]

[6039] סַגְרִיר *sagrîr* 1x heavy rain, downpour of rain [5464]

[6040] סַד *sad* 2x shackles [5465]

[6041] סָדִין *sādîn* 4x linen garment [5466]

[6042] סְדֹם *sᵉdōm* 39x Sodom [5467]

[6043] סֵדֶר *sēder* 1x order, arrangement; "the land of disorder" refers to the Underworld, the region of darkness and chaos [5468*]

[6044] סַהַר *sahar* 1x roundness; referring to the shape of a bowl [5469]

[6046] סוֹא *sôʾ* 1x So [5471]

[6047] 1 סוּג *sûg* 24x [Q] to turn away, be faithless, be disloyal; [N] to be turned back, be disloyal, be faithless; [H] to move, displace; [Ho] to be driven back [5472 & 7734*]

[6048] 2 סוּג *sûg* 1x [Qp] to be encircled, be bordered (by lilies) [5473]

[6050] סוּגַר *sûgar* 1x cage; some sources: neck-stock (of iron or wood) [5474]

[6051] סוֹד *sôd* 21x confidential talk, conspiracy; council, confidant [5475]

[6054] סוּחָה *sûḥâ* 1x refuse, garbage, offal [5478]

[6056] 1 סוּךְ *sûk* 2x [Pil] to spur on, stir up [5526*]

[6057] 2 סוּךְ *sûk* 10x [Q] to anoint, to use oils or perfumes or lotions; [H] to put on lotions; [Ho] to be poured on; this can refer to the application of oils, perfumes, lotions, or resins to the body [5480]

[6061] 1 סוּס *sûs* 138x (male) horse, stallion [5483] See *horse*.

[6063] סוּסָה *sûsâ* 1x (female) horse, mare [5484]

[6066] 1 סוּף *sûp* 6x [Q] to come to an end; demolish; die; [H] to sweep away [5486]

[6067] סוֹף *sôp* 5x end, conclusion, destiny; rear guard [5490]

[6068] 2 סוּף *sûp* 28x reed; Reed Sea (traditionally, Red Sea) [5488]

[6070] 1 סוּפָה *sûpāh* 15x storm wind, whirlwind, tempest, gale [5492]

[6073] 1 סוּר *sûr* 298x [Q] to turn away, depart, leave; [Qp] to be rejected; [Pol] to drag from, turn aside; [H] to remove, get rid of, take off; [Ho] to be removed, be abolished; by extension: to forsake, reject [3249* & 5493]

[6074] 2 סוּר *sûr* 1x corrupt [5494]

[6077] 1 סוּת *sût* 18x [H] to incite, entice, urge, mislead [5496]

[6078] 2 סוּת *sût* 1x robe, garment [5497]

[6079] סָחַב *sāḥab* 5x [Q] to drag down [5498]

[6080] סְחָבָה *s^e^ḥābâ* 2x rag [5499]

[6081] סָחָה *sāḥâ* 1x [P] to scrape away [5500]

[6082] סְחִי *s^e^ḥî* 1x scum, refuse [5501]

[6084] סָחִישׁ *sāḥîš* 1x grain that shoots up on its own (in the second year) [7823]

[6085] סָחַף *sāḥap* 2x [Q] to wash away (of rain); [N] to be washed away, be laid low [5502]

[6086] סָחַר *sāḥar* 21x [Q] to be a trader, a merchant; [Pealal] to pound, throb (of the heart) [5503 & 5505]

[6087] סַ֫חַר *saḥar* 7x profit (from merchandising in the marketplace) [5504]

[6088] סְחֹרָה *s^e^ḥōrâ* 1x customer [5506]

[6089] סֹחֵרָה *sōḥērâ* 1x rampart, wall [5507]

[6090] סֹחֶ֫רֶת *sōḥeret* 1x costly stone (not specifically defined) [5508]

[6091] סֵט *sēṭ* 1x faithlessness, transgression [7750*]

[6092] סִיג *sig* 7x dross (usually of silver) [5509]

[6095] סִיחוֹן *sîḥôn* 37x Sihon [5511]

[6099] סִינַי *sînay* 35x Sinai, "*Sin; glare [from white chalk]*" [5514]

[6101] סִיס *sîs* 2x swift, swallow [5483*]

[6102] סִיסְרָא *sîs^e^rā'* 21x Sisera [5516]

[6105] סִיר *sîr* 29x pot, pan, caldron, washbasin [5518]

[6106] סִירָה *sîrâ* 5x thorn, thornbush; fishhook, barb [5518]

[6107] סָךְ *sāk* 1x multitude, throng [5519]

[6108] סֹךְ *sōk* 4x covering, dwelling (of human or lion) [5520]

[6109] סֻכָּה *sukkâ* 32x tabernacle, shrine; booth, shelter, dwelling, tent [5521]

[6111] סֻכּוֹת *sukkôt* 18x Succoth, "*booths*" [5523]

[6114] 1 סָכַךְ *sākak* 18x [Q] to cover, conceal, overshadow, shield; [H] to cover, shield; to relieve oneself [5526]

[6115] 2 סָכַךְ *sākak* 2x [Q] to knit together; [Pol] to knit together [5526]

[6116] סֹכֵךְ *sōkēk* 1x protective shield (a portable roof) [5526*]

[6117] סְכָכָה *s^e^kākâ* 1x Secacah, "*thicket, cover*" [5527]

[6118] סָכַל *sākal* 8x [N] to do a foolish thing; [P] to turn into foolishness; [H] to act like a fool [5528]

[6119] סָכָל *sākāl* 7x foolish (one), senseless, stupid [5530]

[6120] סֶ֫כֶל *sekel* 1x foolishness, fool [5529]

[6121] סִכְלוּת *siklût* 6x folly [5531]

[6122] 1 סָכַן *sākan* 9x [Q] to be of use, benefit, profit; [H] to be in the habit; be familiar with; to get along well with [5532]

[6123] 2 סָכַן *sākan* 1x [Pu] to be poor [5533]

[6124] 3 סָכַן *sākan* 1x [N] to be endangered [5533]

[6125] סֹכֵן *sōkēn* 3x steward, nurse, attendant [5532*]

[6126] 1 סָכַר *sākar* 2x [N] to be closed; be silent [5534]

[6127] 2 סָכַר *sākar* 1x [P] to hand over, deliver [5534]

[6128] 3 סָכַר *sākar* 1x [Q] to hire [7936*]

[6129] סָכַת *sākat* 1x [H] to be silent, be still [5535]

[6130] סַל *sal* 15x basket [5536]

[6131] סָלָא *sālā'* 1x [Pu] to be weighed (in correlation to gold) [5537]

[6134] סָלַד *sālad* 1x [P] to skip (for joy) [5539]

[6136] 1 סָלָה *sālâ* 2x [Q] to reject, toss aside; [P] to reject [5541]

[6137] 2 סָלָה *sālâ* 2x [Pu] to be bought, be paid for [5541]

[6138] סֶ֫לָה *selâ* 74x selah (t.t. in the Psalms) [5542] See *selah.*

[6141] סִלּוֹן *sillôn* 2x thorn, brier [5544]

[6142] סָלַח *sālaḥ* 46x [Q] to forgive, release, pardon; [N] to be forgiven [5545]

[6143] סַלָּח *sallāḥ* 1x forgiving [5546]

[6145] סְלִיחָה *selîḥâ* 3x forgiveness, pardon [5547]

[6147] 1 סָלַל *sālal* 2x [Pil] to esteem, cherish; [Htpol] to behave haughtily, insolently [5549]

[6148] 2 סָלַל *sālal* 10x [Q] to build up, heap up (a highway), extol; to pile up [5549]

[6149] סֹלְלָה *sōlelâ* 11x siege ramp, siege mound [5550]

[6150] סֻלָּם *sullām* 1x stairway; some sources: ladder [5551]

[6151] סַלְסִלָּה *salsillâ* 1x branch, shoot; some sources: basket [5552]

[6152] 1 סֶלַע *selaʿ* 58x rock, stone; rock formation: cliff, crag; by extension: stronghold, fortress; God as a "Rock" focuses on stability, faithfulness, and protection [5553] See *cliff; rock.*

[6155] סָלְעָם *solʿām* 1x edible locust or katydid [5556]

[6156] סָלַף *sālap* 7x [P] to twist; to overthrow; to frustrate [5557]

[6157] סֶ֫לֶף *selep* 2x duplicity, perversity, deceit [5558]

[6158] סָלַק *sālaq* 1x [Q] to go up, ascend, climb up [5927*]

[6159] סֹלֶת *sōlet* 53x fine flour (likely wheat flour) [5560] See *fine flour; flour.*

[6160] סַם *sam* 16x fragrant perfume [5561]

[6163] סְמָדַר *semādar* 3x blossom (of a vine) [5563]

[6164] סָמַךְ *sāmak* 48x [Q] to sustain, uphold; to lay (one's hand upon); [Qp] to be braced, be steadfast; [N] to lean upon, rely upon, gain confidence; [P] to strengthen, refresh [5564]

[6166] סֶ֫מֶל *semel* 5x image, idol [5566]

[6168] סָמַן *sāman* 1x [N] to be appointed, apportioned [5567]

[6169] סָמַר *sāmar* 2x [Q] to tremble, shudder (i.e., to have goose bumps, gooseflesh); [P] to bristle, stand on end (of hair) [5568]

[6170] סָמָר *sāmār* 1x bristling (locust) [5569]

[6174] סְנֶה *s^eneh* 6x bush, thorny shrub [5572*]

[6177] סַנְוֵרִים *sanwērîm* 3x blindness [5575*]

[6178] סַנְחֵרִיב *sanḥērîb* 13x Sennacherib, "*Sin has increased the brothers; Sin replace the [lost] brothers!*" [5576]

[6180] סַנְסִנָּה *sansinnâ* 1x fruit cluster (of date tree) [5577*]

[6181] סְנַפִּיר *s^enappîr* 5x fin [5579]

[6182] סָס *sās* 1x (garment) moth; some sources: worm [5580]

[6184] סָעַד *sāʿad* 12x [Q] to sustain, support, refresh [5582]

[6185] סָעָה *sāʿâ* 1x [Q] to slander, defame, speak with malice [5584]

[6186] 1 סָעִיף *sāʿîp* 4x cleft, crag [5585]

[6187] 2 סָעִיף *sāʿîp* 2x bough, branch [5585]

[6188] סָעַף *sāʿap* 1x [P] to lop off, trim down [5586]

[6189] סֵעֵף *sēʿēp* 1x double-minded, divided in heart [5588]

[6190] סְעַפָּה *s^eʿappâ* 2x bough [5589]

[6191] סְעִפִּים *s^eʿippîm* 1x division, divided opinion, a fig. extension of hobbling on crutches made of boughs [5587*]

[6192] סָעַר *sāʿar* 7x [Q] to grow stormier, rougher; [N] to be enraged; [P] to scatter in a wind; [Po] to scatter, swirl; [Pu] to be lashed by storms [5590]

[6193] סַעַר *saʿar* 8x windstorm, tempest, gale [5591]

[6194] סְעָרָה *s^eʿārâ* 16x windstorm, tempest, gale [5591]

[6195] 1 סַף *sap* 7x basin, bowl [5592]

[6197] 3 סַף *sap* 24x threshold, door frame, entrance, doorway; doorkeeper [5592]

[6199] סָפַד *sāpad* 30x [Q] to beat the breast, mourn, lament, weep; [N] to be mourned [5594]

[6200] סָפָה *sāpâ* 16x [Q] to sweep away; take away; bring disaster; [N] to be swept away; be destroyed [5595]

[6202] 1 סָפַח *sāpaḥ* 4x [Q] to associate, attach to; [N] to be attached, be united; [Pu] be joined together; [Ht] to feel oneself attached to [5596]

[6203] 2 סָפַח *sāpaḥ* 1x [P] to pour out [5596]

[6204] סַפַּחַת *sappaḥat* 2x rash, skin eruption [5597]

[6206] 1 סָפִיחַ *sāpîaḥ* 4x what grows on its own, after-growth in a fallow year [5599]

[6207] 2 סָפִיחַ *sāpîaḥ* 1x torrent, downpour [5599]

[6208] סְפִינָה *s^epînâ* 1x ship (with a covering or deck) [5600]

[6209] סַפִּיר *sappîr* 1x sapphire; some sources: lapis lazuli [5601]

[6210] סֵפֶל *sēpel* 2x bowl (for water or curdled milk) [5602]

[6211] סָפַן *sāpan* 6x [Q] to cover; [Qp] to be roofed, be paneled, be roofed [5603]

[6212] סִפֻּן *sippun* 2x ceiling [5604]

[6213] סַפְסִיג *sapsîg* 1x glaze [5509*]

[6214] סָפַף *sāpap* 1x [Htpol] to stand at the threshold [5605]

[6215] 1 סָפַק *sāpaq* 6x [Q] to clap hands; beat one's breast; to punish, slap [5606]

[6216] 2 סָפַק *sāpaq* 1x [Q] to wallow, splash [5606]

[6217] סֶפֶק *sepeq* 1x riches, abundance [5607]

[6218] סָפַר *sāpar* 107x [Q] to count, number, take a census; [N] to be counted, be recorded; by extension: [P] to tell, proclaim, recount (an event or principle); [Pu] to be told [5608] See *declare; tell.*

[6219] 1 סֵפֶר *sēper* 191x book (as a scroll or tablet), scroll, letter, certificate, deed, dispatch [5612] See *book; scroll.*

[6221] סֹפֵר *sōpēr* 54x learned writer, scribe, secretary [5608*] See *scribe; secretary.*

[6222] 1 סְפָר *sᵉpār* 0x census [5610]

[6225] סִפְרָה *siprâ* 1x record, writing, scroll [5612]

[6228] סְפֹרוֹת *sᵉpōrôt* 1x measure, number; some sources: art of writing [5615*]

[6233] סָר *sār* 1x captain [8269*]

[6234] סַר *sar* 3x sullen, dejected, discouraged [5620]

[6235] סָרָב *sārāb* 1x briers [5621]

[6239] 1 סָרָה *sārâ* 1x ceasing, stopping [5627]

[6240] 2 סָרָה *sārâ* 7x rebellion, revolt [5627]

[6242] סָרוּחַ *sārûaḥ* 3x flowing, lounging [5628*]

[6243] 1 סָרַח *sāraḥ* 3x [Q] to hang down, overhang, spread over; [Qp] to be overhanged [5628]

[6244] 2 סָרַח *sāraḥ* 1x [N] to be decayed, be spoiled, become stinking [5628]

[6245] סֶרַח *seraḥ* 1x overhang, what projects over [5629]

[6246] סִרְיוֹן *siryôn* 2x (scale) armor, coat of mail [5630*]

[6247] סָרִיס *sārîs* 45x court official, palace officer, eunuch [5631]

[6248] 1 סֶרֶן *seren* 1x axle [5633]

[6249] 2 סֶרֶן *seren* 21x ruler, prince [5633]

[6250] סַרְעַפָּה *sarʿappâ* 1x bough [5634]

[6251] סָרַף *sārap* 1x [P] to burn [5635]

[6252] סִרְפָּד *sirpād* 1x briers, stinging nettles [5636]

[6253] 1 סָרַר *sārar* 17x [Q] to be stubborn, be obstinate, be rebellious [5637]

[6254] 2 סָרַר *sārar* 1x [Q] to be in charge, superintend [8269*]

[6255] סְתָו *sᵉtāw* 1x winter, rainy season [5638]

[6258] סָתַם *sātam* 12x [Q] to stop up, block off, seal; [Qp] to be closed up; by extension: to be in a secret place; [N] to be closed; [P] to stop up [5640]

[6259] סָתַר *sātar* 82x [Q] to be hidden, be concealed, have a refuge; [P] to hide; [Pu] to be hidden; [H] to hide, conceal; [Ht] to hide oneself, keep oneself hidden [5641] See *conceal; hide; secret.*

[6260] סֵתֶר *sēter* 35x hiding place, secret place, shelter; covering, veil; (adv.) secretly, in secret [5643]

[6261] סִתְרָה *sitrâ* 1x shelter, hiding-place, refuge [5643]

[6264] 1 עָב *ʿāb* 3x overhang, overhanging roof [5646]

[6265] 2 עָב *ʿāb* 30x clouds [5645]

[6266] 3 עָב *ʿāb* 1x thicket [5645]

[6268] עָבַד *ʿābad* 290x [Q] to work, serve, labor, do; to worship, minister, work in ministry; [N] to be plowed, be cultivated; [Pu] to be worked; [H] to reduce to servitude, enslave, cause to serve; [Ho] to be caused to serve, worship (a god) [5647] See *serve; worship.*

[6269] 1 עֶבֶד *ʿebed* 803x servant, slave, attendant; indentured servants and owned slaves had varying levels of status and responsibilities; according to the OT Law, a Hebrew slave could be sold to a Hebrew master for only six years, but there was no time limit for Gentile slaves [5650] See *servant.*

[6272] עַבְדָּא *ʿabdāʾ* 2x Abda, "*servant of Yahweh*" [5653]

[6273] עֹבֵד־אֱדוֹם *ʿōbēd-ᵉdôm* 20x Obed-Edom, "*servant [worshiper] of Edom*" [5654*]

[6275] עֲבֹדָה *ʿᵃbōdâ* 145x work, service, labor, task, duty, job; special work and service to God: service, ministry; forced labor: slavery [5656] See *labor; service.*

[6276] עֲבֻדָּה *ʿᵃbuddâ* 2x servant, slave [5657]

[6282] עֹבַדְיָהוּ *ʿōbadyāhû* 9x Obadiah, "*servant [worshiper] of Yahweh*" [5662]

[6285] עַבְדֻת *ʿabdut* 3x slavery, servitude [5659]

[6286] עָבָה *ʿābâ* 3x [Q] to be thick [5666]

[6287] עֲבוֹט *ʿᵃbôṭ* 4x pledge, (garment) security (for a loan) [5667]

[6288] 1 עֲבוּר *ʿᵃbûr* 49x marker of cause or reason: for, because; marker of purpose or intent: on account of; in order to; a marker of result: then; benefit: for [5668]

[6289] 2 עֲבוּר *ʿᵃbûr* 2x produce, yield [5669]

[6290] 1 עָבוֹת *ʿābôt* 4x leafy, dense, interwoven foliage [5687]

[6291] 2 עָבוֹת *ʿābôt* 5x thick foliage [5688*]

[6292] 1 עָבַט *ʿābaṭ* 5x [Q] to borrow, i.e., take or receive a pledge; [H] to lend on a pledge [5670]

[6293] 2 עָבַט *ʿābaṭ* 1x [P] to swerve, change (a course), implying a lack of purpose [5670]

[6294] עַבְטִיט *ʿabṭîṭ* 1x heavy pledges, excessive mortgage for a debt; there may be an implication of undue force being used to keep the pledge [5671]

[6295] עֳבִי *ʿᵃbî* 6x thickness, density, mold [5672]

[6296] 1 עָבַר *ʿābar* 553x [Q] to pass over, cross over, travel through; [N] to be crossed; [P] to extend; to breed; [H] to make pass through, let pass over, send over; by extension: to forgive, as the passing over of guilt [5674] See *cross over; pass by, through.*

[6297] 2 עָבַר *ʿābar* 8x [Ht] to be very angry, show oneself angry [5674]

[6298] 1 עֵבֶר *ʿēber* 90x what is on the other side, what is beyond, across; i.e., east or west; Trans-Euphrates [5676]

[6301] עֶבְרָה *ʿebrâ* 34x wrath, anger, fury, rage; insolence [5678]

[6302] עֲבָרָה *ʿᵃbārâ* 3x ford, crossing [5679]

[6303] 1 עִבְרִי *ʿibrî* 34x Hebrew [5680]

[6308] עָבַשׁ *ʿābaš* 1x [Q] to shrivel, wither, dry up [5685]

[6309] עָבַת *ʿābat* 1x [P] to conspire, twist [5686]

[6310] עֲבֹת *ʿᵃbōt* 19x rope, cord, chains, ties; fetters, harness [5688]

[6311] עָגַב *ʿāgab* 7x [Q] to lust, have sensual desire for [5689]

[6312] עֲגָבָה *ʿᵃgābâ* 2x lust, sensual desire [5691]

[6313] עֲגָבִים *ʿᵃgābîm* 1x devotion, love [5690*]

[6314] עֻגָה *ʿugâ* 7x (round, flat) bread cakes [5692]

[6315] עָגוּר *ʿāgûr* 2x (short footed) thrush (a bird) [5693]

[6316] עָגִיל *ʿāgîl* 2x earring [5694]

[6317] עֲגִילָה *ʿᵃgîlâ* 1x circular shield [5699*]

[6318] עָגֹל *ʿāgōl* 6x circular, round [5696]

[6319] עֵגֶל *ʿēgel* 36x bull-calf; calf-shaped idol [5695]

[6320] 1 עֶגְלָה *ʿeglâ* 11x heifer-calf, young cow [5697]

[6322] עֲגָלָה *ʿagālâ* 24x cart [5699]

[6327] עָגַם *ʿāgam* 1x [Q] to grieve for, have pity on [5701]

[6328] עָגַן *ʿāgan* 1x [N] to keep withdrawn (from marital relations) [5702]

[6329] 1 עַד *ʿad* 48x a unit of time, referring to the past: old, ancient; without limit: forever, eternal, for ever and ever; continual, always [5703]

[6330] 2 עַד *ʿad* 126x until, up to, as far as [5704]

[6331] 3 עַד *ʿad* 1x prey, plunder [5706]

[6332] עֵד *ʿēd* 69x witness, testimony; an object that serves as a memorial or a person giving of legal evidence [5707] See *witness.*

[6334] 1 עָדָה *ʿādâ* 2x [Q] to prowl; [H] to take away, remove [5710]

[6335] 2 עָדָה *ʿādâ* 8x [Q] to adorn oneself, put on jewelry [5710]

[6337] 1 עֵדָה *ʿēdâ* 171x community, assembly, with a possible focus on the unity of the congregation; this can refer to good or evil groups; human or animal groups [5712] See *assembly; community; herd; swarm.*

[6338] 2 עֵדָה *ʿēdâ* 5x witness [5713]

[6340] עִדָּה *ʿiddâ* 1x menstruation [5708]

[6343] עֵדוּת *ʿēdût* 61x testimony, statute, stipulation, regulation; this can also mean "the Testimony" as a formal written copy of the precepts and stipulations of a covenant [5715] See *decree; regulations; requirement; statute; testimony; warning.*

[6344] עֲדִי *ʿadî* 14x ornament, beautiful jewelry [5716]

[6349] 1 עָדִין *ʿādîn* 1x voluptuous, wantonness [5719]

[6357] עָדַן *ʿādan* 1x [Ht] to revel in the good life, luxuriate [5727]

[6358] 1 עֵדֶן *ʿēden* 3x delight, delicacy; finery [5730]

[6359] 2 עֵדֶן *ʿēden* 4x Eden, "*paradise, delight,* [poss.] *flat land*" [5731]

[6362] עֲדֶן *ʿaden* 1x yet [5728]

[6364] עֲדֶנָה *ʿadenâ* 1x still [5728]

[6366] עֶדְנָה *ʿednâ* 1x (sexual) pleasure, delight [5730]

[6369] עָדַף *ʿādap* 9x [Q] (ptcp.) what is left over, what is additional; [H] to have a surplus [5736]

[6370] 1 עָדַר *ʿādar* 2x [Q] to help, serve; referring to a fighting unit that acts as a group [5737]

[6371] 2 עָדַר *ʿādar* 2x [N] to be cultivated, be weeded [5737]

[6372] 3 עָדַר *ʿādar* 7x [N] to be missing; be lacking; [P] to let be lacking [5737]

[6373] 1 עֵדֶר *ʿēder* 39x flock, herd [5739]

[6378] עֲדָשִׁים *ʿadāšîm* 4x lentils [5742*]

[6380] עוּב *ʿûb* 1x [H] to cover with a cloud [5743]

[6381] עוֹבֵד *ʿôbēd* 10x Obed, "*servant [worshiper]*" [5744]

[6383] עוּג *ʿûg* 1x [Q] to bake a (round, flat) cake of bread [5746]

[6384] עוֹג *ʿôg* 22x Og [5747]

[6385] עוּגָב *ʿûgāb* 4x flute [5748]

[6386] 1 עוּד *ʿûd* 44x [P] to surround (with ropes); [Pil] to sustain, relieve; [H] to admonish, warn, charge, declare; to testify, to call on a witness; [Ho] to be warned; [Htpol] to hold each other up; from the base meaning of binding (with ropes) come the fig. extensions of "to warn, charge, testify" (bind with words) and "to help, sustain" (bind oneself to another in aid and comfort) [5749]

[6388] עוֹד *ʿôd* 490x longer, again, still, more [5750]

[6390] עָוָה 1 *ʿāwâ* 17x [Q] to do wrong; [N] to be perverse, be warped; [P] to ruin, make crooked; [H] to do wrong, pervert; from the base meaning of twisting an object comes the fig. extension of twisting morality: to be perverse, to do wrong [5753]

[6392] עַוָּה 1 *ʿawwâ* 3x ruin, wreckage, rubble [5754]

[6396] עֲוִיל 1 *ʿᵃwîl* 2x little boys [5759]

[6397] עֲוִיל 2 *ʿᵃwîl* 1x evil one, unjust one [5760]

[6400] עֲוִית *ʿᵃwît* 2x Avith [5762]

[6401] עָוַל 1 *ʿāwal* 2x [P] to do evil, act wrong [5765]

[6402] עוּל 2 *ʿûl* 5x [Q] to nurse, suckle [5763]

[6403] עוּל 3 *ʿûl* 3x nursing infant, baby [5764]

[6404] עָוֶל *ʿāwel* 22x wrong, evil, sin, injustice, what is morally perverted, warped, and twisted, an extension of the base meaning of a physically twisted, crooked object (not found in the OT) [5766]

[6405] עַוָּל *ʿawwāl* 5x wicked one, evil one, unjust one [5767]

[6406] עַוְלָה *ʿawlâ* 32x wickedness, evil, injustice [5766]

[6407] עוֹלֵל *ʿôlēl* 11x child, little one [5768]

[6408] עוֹלָל *ʿôlāl* 9x child, little one [5768*]

[6409] עוֹלָם *ʿôlām* 439x everlasting, forever, eternity; from of old, ancient, lasting, for a duration [5769] See *ancient; eternal; everlasting; forever.*

[6411] עָוֹן *ʿāwōn* 233x sin, wickedness, iniquity, often with a focus on the guilt or liability incurred, and the punishment to follow [5771] See *guilt; iniquity; sin; wicked, wickedness.*

[6413] עִוְעִים *ʿiwʿîm* 1x (col. pl.) dizziness, staggering, frenzy [5773*]

[6414] עוּף 1 *ʿûp* 24x [Q] to fly; [Pol] to dart about (of a flying bird or a snake); [H] to let (eyes) glance; [Ht] to fly away [5774]

[6416] עוֹף *ʿôp* 71x bird, winged creatures, flying creatures [5775] See *bird; insect.*

[6418] עוּץ 1 *ʿûṣ* 2x [Q] to consider, devise, plan [5779]

[6421] עוּק *ʿûq* 2x [Q] to crush, totter; [H] to crush, cause to totter [5781]

[6422] עָוַר 1 *ʿāwar* 5x [P] to make blind [5786]

[6423] עוּר 2 *ʿûr* 1x [N] to be uncovered, be laid bare [5783]

[6424] עוּר 3 *ʿûr* 80x [Q] to awake; [N] to be aroused, stirred up, wakened; [Pol] to awaken, arouse, raise up; [Pil] to raise, keep up; [H] to stir up, rouse, waken; [Htpol] to rouse oneself [5782] See *arouse; awake; incite; stir up; wake, wake up.*

[6425] עוֹר *ʿôr* 99x skin, hide, leather [5785] See *hide; leather; skin.*

[6426] עִוֵּר *ʿiwwēr* 26x blind [5787]

[6427] עִוָּרוֹן *ʿiwwārôn* 2x blindness, blinding [5788]

[6428] עַוֶּרֶת *ʿawweret* 1x blindness [5788]

[6429] עוּשׁ *ʿûš* 1x [Q] to be quick or to help [5789]

[6430] עָוַת *ʿāwat* 11x [P] to make crooked, pervert; [Pu] to be twisted, be made crooked; [Ht] to stoop down, bend over; from the base meaning of twisting an object comes the fig. extension of twisting morality: to pervert [5791]

[6431] עוּת ʿût 1x [Q] to sustain, help [5790]

[6432] עַוָּתָה ʿawwātâ 1x wrong [5792]

[6434] עַז ʿaz 23x strong, mighty, powerful, fierce [5794]

[6435] עָז ʿāz 1x power, strength [5794]

[6436] עֵז ʿēz 74x goat; goat hair [5795] See *goat; goat hair.*

[6437] עֹז ʿōz 76x strength, power, might; stronghold, fortification; strong-willed, stubborn; [5797] See *power; refuge; strength.*

[6438] עֻזָּא ʿuzzāʾ 11x Uzza, Uzzah, "*strong, fierce one*" [5798]

[6439] עֲזָאזֵל ʿ^{a}zāʾzēl 4x scapegoat, a goat sent into the wilderness of the Day of Atonement, symbolically carrying away the sin of the community; some see this word as the name of the desert spirit (Azazel) to whom the goat is sent [5799]

[6440] עָזַב 1 ʿāzab 214x [Q] to leave, abandon, reject, desert; [Qp] be left, be abandoned, be freed; [N] be abandoned, be forsaken, be neglected; [Pu] be deserted, be abandoned [5800] See *abandon; forsake; leave; set free.*

[6441] עָזַב 2 ʿāzab 4x [Q] to restore, help [5800]

[6442] עִזְבוֹנִים ʿizbônîm 7x merchandise, goods [5801*]

[6449] עֱזוּז ʿ^{e}zûz 3x power, strength [5807]

[6450] עִזּוּז ʿizzûz 2x strong, powerful [5808]

[6451] עָזַז ʿāzaz 10x [Q] to be strong, overpower; [H] to put on a bold face, be brazen [5810]

[6460] עֻזִּיָּהוּ ʿuzziyyāhû 19x Uzziah, "*Yahweh is [my] strength*" [5818]

[6465] עָזְנִיָּה ʿozniyyâ 2x black vulture [5822]

[6466] עָזַק ʿāzaq 1x [P] to dig [5823]

[6468] עָזַר ʿāzar 82x [Q] to help, support; [Qp] to be helped; [N] to be helped [5826] See *help.*

[6469] עֵזֶר 1 ʿēzer 22x help, helper [5828] See *helper.*

[6474] עֶזְרָא ʿezrāʾ 22x Ezra, "*help*" [5830]

[6476] עֶזְרָה 1 ʿezrâ 26x help, aid, support; helper, ally [5833]

[6478] עֲזָרָה ʿ^{a}zārâ 9x court, enclosure; ledge, barrier [5835]

[6481] עֲזַרְיָה ʿ^{a}zaryâ 32x Azariah, "*Yahweh has helped*" [5838]

[6482] עֲזַרְיָהוּ ʿ^{a}zaryāhû 16x Azariah; Azariahu, "*Yahweh has helped*" [5838]

[6485] עֵט ʿēṭ 4x (iron) engraving tool, stylus; (reed) pen [5842]

[6486] עָטָה 1 ʿāṭâ 15x [Q] to cover, wrap oneself; [H] cover, wrap another (thing) [5844]

[6487] עָטָה 2 ʿāṭâ 3x [Q] to grasp; [Pu] to be grasped [4593* & 5844]

[6488] עָטוּף ʿāṭûp 2x weak, faint [5848*]

[6489] עֲטִין ʿ^{a}ṭîn 1x body, part of body; or pail, bucket [5845]

[6490] עֲטִישָׁה ʿ^{a}ṭîšâ 1x snorting, sneezing [5846]

[6491] עֲטַלֵּף ʿ^{a}ṭallēp 3x bat (animal) [5847]

[6493] עָטַף 1 ʿāṭap 3x [Q] to clothe, mantle; to turn aside [5848]

[6494] עָטַף 2 ʿāṭap 11x [Q] to grow faint; [N] to be faint; [H] to be feeble; [Ht] to ebb away, grow faint [5848]

[6496] עָטַר 1 ʿāṭar 2x [Q] to surround, close in upon [5849]

[6497] עָטַר 2 ʿāṭar 5x [P] to crown, place a wreath (on the head); [H] to bestow a crown [5849]

[6498] עֲטָרָה 1 ʿ^{a}ṭārâ 23x crown, wreath, placed on the head as a symbol of celebration or status; can be made of plants or precious metals [5850]

[6504] עַי ʿay 38x Ai, *"ruin, the heap"* [5857]

[6505] עִי ʿî 5x heap of rubble; (of a person) a broken man [5856]

[6506] 1 עֵיבָל ʿêbāl 4x Ebal [5858]

[6512] 1 עִיט ʿîṭ 1x [Q] to hurl insults [5860]

[6513] 2 עִיט ʿîṭ 2x [Q] to pounce upon (with shrieks and screams) [5860]

[6514] עַיִט ʿayiṭ 8x (coll) birds of prey, carrion birds [5861]

[6522] עְיָם ʿ[a]yām 1x scorching (of wind) [5868]

[6523] עָיַן ʿāyan 1x [Q] to keep an eye on, look at (with suspicion or jealousy) [5770*]

[6524] 1 עַיִן ʿayin 889x eye; by extension: sight; spring, fountain; to be "evil of eye" is to be displeased; to be "good of eye" is to be pleased; to be "good in one's eyes" is to be pleasing; "right in one's eyes" means acceptable by one's personal standards [5869] See *eyes; sight.*

[6545] עִיף ʿîp 5x [Q] to be faint, be exhausted [5774* & 5888*]

[6546] עָיֵף ʿāyēp 18x weary, faint; famished, parched [5889]

[6547] 1 עֵיפָה ʿêpāh 2x darkness [5890]

[6551] 1 עִיר ʿîr 1,087x city, town, village, a general term for a population center [5892] See *city; town.*

[6552] 2 עִיר ʿîr 2x anguish, terror, wrath [5892]

[6554] 4 עִיר ʿîr 1x (male) donkey (young and robust) [5895*]

[6555] עַיִר ʿayir 7x (male) donkey [5895*]

[6567] עֵירֹם ʿêrōm 10x naked; nakedness [5903]

[6568] עַיִשׁ ʿayiš 1x constellation: the Bear or the Lion, or some other constellation [5906]

[6571] עַכָּבִישׁ ʿakkābîš 2x spider [5908]

[6572] עַכְבָּר ʿakbār 6x (jumping) rat, jerboa [5909]

[6576] עָכַס ʿākas 1x [P] to jingle, rattle (of ankle ornaments) [5913]

[6577] עֶכֶס ʿekes 2x bangle, ankle ornament [5914]

[6579] עָכַר ʿākar 14x [Q] to bring trouble, make trouble; [N] to be troubled, be anguished [5916]

[6582] עַכְשׁוּב ʿakšûb 1x (horned) viper; other sources: asp [5919]

[6583] 1 עַל ʿal 4x (the) Most High [5920]

[6584] 2 עַל ʿal 5,771x marker of relationship: spatial: on, upon, over, against, toward; logical: because of, according to; temporal: on, when, during [5921]

[6585] עֹל ʿōl 40x yoke, placed on draft animals; by extension: a figure of oppression or of proper training [5923]

[6589] עִלֵּג ʿillēg 1x speaking inarticulately; (pl.n.) stammerers [5926]

[6590] עָלָה ʿālâ 894x [Q] to go up, ascend, rise; [N] to be lifted up, withdraw, be exalted; [H] to take up, set up, offer a sacrifice; [Ho] to be offered up, be carried away, be recorded; [Ht] to raise oneself up; from the base meaning of rise in elevation comes the fig. extension "to exalt, honor," as the lifting up of a person in status [5927] See *ascend; bring up; exalt; go up.*

[6591] עָלֶה ʿāleh 18x leaves, foliage [5929]

[6592] 1 עֹלָה ʿōlâ 286x burnt offering, wholly dedicated to God [5930] See *burnt offering.*

[6594] 1 עַלְוָה ʿalwâ 1x evil, wickedness [5932]

[6596] עֲלוּמִים ʿ*a*lûmîm 4x (abst.pl.) youthfulness, (the vigor of) youth [5934*]

[6598] עֲלוּקָה ʿ*a*lûqâ 1x leech [5936]

[6600] עָלַז ʿālaz 16x [Q] to rejoice, be jubilant [5937]

[6601] עָלֵז ʿālēz 1x reveling, exultant; (n.) reveler [5938]

[6602] עֲלָטָה ʿ*a*lāṭâ 4x darkness, dusk [5939]

[6603] 1 עֵלִי ʿēlî 33x Eli, "*Yahweh is exalted; God [El] is exalted*" [5941]

[6604] 2 עֵלִי ʿēlî 1x Most High [5942*]

[6605] עֱלִי ʿ*e*lî 1x pestle (of a mortar) [5940]

[6606] עִלִּי ʿillî 2x upper [5942]

[6608] עֲלִיָּה ʿ*a*liyyâ 19x upper room, upper parts [5944]

[6609] 1 עֶלְיוֹן ʿelyôn 22x upper, also used in place names [5945]

[6610] 2 עֶלְיוֹן ʿelyôn 31x (the) Most High, a title of God with a focus on supremacy in status and power [5945]

[6611] עַלִּיז ʿallîz 7x rejoicing, exulting; reveling, wild [5947]

[6612] עֲלִיל ʿ*a*lîl 1x furnace [5948]

[6613] עֲלִילָה ʿ*a*lîlâ 24x what is done, deed, action [5949]

[6614] עֲלִילִיָּה ʿ*a*lîliyyâ 1x deed [5950]

[6617] עֲלִיצֻת ʿ*a*lîṣut 1x rejoicing, exaltation, including verbal expressions of joy and praise; from a negative perspective: haughtiness, presumption, gloating [5951]

[6618] 1 עָלַל ʿālal 18x [Po] to deal with; to glean, go over a second time; [Poal] to be dealt with (in a way that causes suffering); [Ht] to deal harshly, abuse, mistreat; [Htpo] to take part in (wickedness) [5953]

[6619] 2 עָלַל ʿālal 1x [Po] to thrust (in) [5953]

[6620] 3 עָלַל ʿālal 1x [Po] to act or play the child; (n.) youths [5953]

[6622] עֹלֵלוֹת ʿōlēlôt 6x gleanings [5955*]

[6623] עָלַם ʿālam 29x [Qp] to be in secret; [N] to be concealed, be hidden, be unaware; [H] to hide, shut off, conceal; [Ht] to hide oneself from, ignore [5956]

[6624] עֶלֶם ʿelem 2x boy, young man [5958]

[6625] עַלְמָה ʿalmâ 7x girl, young woman, (in certain contexts) virgin [5959]

[6628] עֲלָמוֹת ʿ*a*lāmôt 2x alamoth (t.t. in the Psalms) [5961]

[6632] עָלַס ʿālas 3x [Q] to enjoy; [N] to appear glad; [Ht] to enjoy one another [5965]

[6633] עָלַע ʿālaʿ 1x [Palpal] to drink, feast on [5966]

[6634] עָלַף ʿālap 6x [Pu] to faint; to be withered; be decorated, covered; [Ht] to disguise oneself; to grow faint [5968]

[6636] עָלַץ ʿālaṣ 8x [Q] to rejoice, be jubilant [5970]

[6637] עֹלָתָה ʿōlātâ 1x injustice [5766*]

[6638] 1 עַם ʿam 32x father's relatives, one's people [5971]

[6639] 2 עַם ʿam 1,869x people, nation, countrymen; army, troop [5971] See *assembly; nation; people; troops.*

[6640] עִם ʿim 1,049x marker of association or proximity: to, toward; with, among [5973]

[6641] עָמַד ʿāmad 524x [Q] to stand, stand up, stand still; [H] to cause to stand, present; to appoint, assign; [Ho] to be presented, be caused to stand [5975] See *appoint; endurance, endure; stand.*

[6642] עֹמֶד ʿōmed 8x standing-place (a position, station, or post) [5977]

[6643] עִמָּד *ʿimmād* 45x with [5978]

[6644] עֶמְדָּה *ʿemdâ* 1x place to stand, protection [5979]

[6645] 1 עֻמָּה *ʿummâ* 32x close by; alongside; adjoining [5980]

[6647] עַמּוּד *ʿammûd* 112x pillar, post, column; used fig. of the pillar-shaped cloud of God's presence [5982] See *column; pillar; post.*

[6648] עַמּוֹן *ʿammôn* 106x Ammonite; Ammon, "*my people [Ge 19:38]*" [5983]

[6649] עַמּוֹנִי *ʿammônî* 20x Ammonite, from Ammon, "*of Ammon*" [5984 & 5985*]

[6650] עָמוֹס *ʿāmôs* 7x Amos, "*burden bearer*" [5986]

[6658] עָמִיר *ʿāmîr* 4x (newly) cut grain [5995]

[6660] עָמִית *ʿāmît* 12x neighbor, countryman, associate (one in close, united relation) [5997]

[6661] עָמַל *ʿāmal* 11x [Q] to labor, toil, pour forth effort [5998]

[6662] 1 עָמָל *ʿāmāl* 54x trouble, work, labor, toil [5999] See *trouble; work.*

[6664] 1 עָמֵל *ʿāmēl* 4x misery; workman, laborer [6001]

[6665] 2 עָמֵל *ʿāmēl* 5x toiling, laboring [6001]

[6667] עֲמָלֵק *ʿ^{a}mālēq* 39x Amalek; Amalekite [6002]

[6668] עֲמָלֵקִי *ʿ^{a}mālēqî* 12x Amalekite, "*of Amalek*" [6003]

[6669] 1 עָמַם *ʿāmam* 1x [Q] to be rival to, be equal to [6004]

[6670] 2 עָמַם *ʿāmam* 2x [Q] to grow dark; [Ho] to lose luster, grow dark [6004]

[6672] עִמָּנוּ אֵל *ʿimmānû ʾēl* 2x Immanuel, "*God with us*" [6005]

[6673] עָמַס *ʿāmas* 9x [Q] to load a burden, carry a burden; [Qp] to be burdensome, be upheld; [H] to lay a burden upon [6006]

[6676] עָמַק *ʿāmaq* 9x [Q] to be profound; [H] to make deep (in various senses) [6009]

[6677] עֵמֶק *ʿēmeq* 65x valley; (low-lying) plain [6010] See *plain; valley.*

[6678] עָמֹק *ʿāmōq* 17x deep; profound [6013]

[6679] עֹמֶק *ʿōmeq* 2x depth [6011]

[6680] עָמֵק *ʿāmēq* 3x obscure, unintelligible, by extension of what is physically deep (not found in the OT) [6012]

[6682] 1 עָמַר *ʿāmar* 1x [P] to bind sheaves (of newly cut grain) [6014]

[6683] 2 עָמַר *ʿāmar* 2x [Ht] to treat brutally, deal tyrannically with [6014]

[6684] 1 עֹמֶר *ʿōmer* 8x sheaf of grain [6016]

[6685] 2 עֹמֶר *ʿōmer* 6x omer (dry measure, one-tenth of an ephah, about two quarts or liters) [6016]

[6686] עֲמֹרָה *ʿ^{a}mōrâ* 19x Gomorrah, "*to overwhelm with water*" [6017]

[6687] עָמְרִי *ʿomrî* 18x Omri, "*thrive, live long*" [6018]

[6690] עֲמָשָׂא *ʿ^{a}māśāʾ* 16x Amasa, "*[my] people are from Jesse*" [6021]

[6694] עֵנָב *ʿēnāb* 19x cluster of grapes [6025]

[6695] עָנַג *ʿānag* 10x [Pu] to be delicate; [Ht] to delight oneself, enjoy, to mock [6026]

[6696] עֹנֶג *ʿōneg* 2x delight, luxury, enjoyment [6027]

[6697] עָנֹג *ʿānōg* 3x sensitive, delicate [6028]

[6698] עָנַד *ʿānad* 2x [Q] to bind around, bind upon [6029]

[6699] 1 עָנָה *ʿānâ* 316x [Q] to answer, reply, respond; [N] to be answered; usually verbal, the response can involve action [6030] See *answer; reply; respond.*

[6700] 2 עָנָה ʿānâ 79x [Q] to be afflicted; to stoop down; [N] to be afflicted, humbled, oppressed; [P] to afflict, oppress, subdue, humble, mistreat; [Pu] to be afflicted, deny oneself; [H] to afflict another, oppress; [Ht] to humble oneself; humbling by force implies dishonor [6031] See *afflict; contrition; humble; oppress; repent, repentance.*

[6701] 3 עָנָה ʿānâ 3x [Q] to be concerned about, be worried about; [H] to keep occupied, keep oneself busy [6031]

[6702] 4 עָנָה ʿānâ 15x [Q] to sing; [P] to sing to or sing about [6030]

[6703] עֹנָה ʿōnâ 1x marital rights (of intercourse) [5772*]

[6705] עָנָו ʿānāw 22x humble, afflicted, poor, oppressed [6035]

[6708] עֲנָוָה ʿ^{a}nāwâ 6x humility [6038]

[6711] עֲנוּשִׁים ʿ^{a}nûšîm 1x (punishing) fines [6064*]

[6713] עֱנוּת ʿ^{e}nût 1x suffering, affliction [6039]

[6714] עָנִי ʿānî 80x needy, poor, afflicted, oppressed, often referring to a class of persons of low status and lacking resources [6041] See *afflicted; humble; needy; oppressed; poor.*

[6715] עֳנִי ʿ^{o}nî 37x affliction, suffering, misery [6040]

[6721] עִנְיָן ʿinyān 8x task, work, labor; misfortune, cares, troubles [6045]

[6725] 1 עָנַן ʿānan 1x [P] to bring clouds [6049]

[6726] 2 עָנַן ʿānan 10x [Po] to practice sorcery, practice divination, cast spells [6049]

[6727] 1 עָנָן ʿānān 87x cloud, of moisture or smoke, natural or supernatural [6051] See *cloud; mist.*

[6729] עֲנָנָה ʿ^{a}nānâ 1x cloud, likely referring to a dense rain cloud [6053]

[6733] עָנָף ʿānāp 7x branches [6057]

[6734] עָנֵף ʿānēp 1x full of branches [6058]

[6735] עָנַק ʿānaq 3x [Q] to put on (as a necklace); [H] to supply, a fig. extension of putting an adornment around the neck [6059]

[6736] 1 עֲנָק ʿ^{a}nāq 3x necklace chain [6060*]

[6740] עָנַשׁ ʿānaš 8x [Q] to levy a fine (as a punishment or recompense); [N] to be fined, be punished [6064]

[6741] עֹנֶשׁ ʿōneš 2x levy, penalty, fine [6066]

[6747] עָסִיס ʿāsîs 5x new wine (relatively sweet); nectar [6071]

[6748] עָסַס ʿāsas 1x [Q] to trample down [6072]

[6751] עֳפִי ʿ^{o}pî 1x branch [6073*]

[6752] 1 עָפַל ʿāpal 1x [Pu] to be puffed up, be swelled [6075]

[6753] 2 עָפַל ʿāpal 1x [H] to have presumption, to have the audacity to [6075]

[6754] 1 עֹפֶל ʿōpel 6x tumor, hemorrhoid, abscess [6076]

[6755] 2 עֹפֶל ʿōpel 8x hill; (as a proper name) the hill of Ophel [6077]

[6757] עַפְעַפַּיִם ʿapʿappayim 10x flashing rays (of dawn); glances or flitting of eyes or eyelids [6079*]

[6758] עָפַף ʿāpap 1x [Po] to brandish, cause to fly to and fro [5774*]

[6759] עָפַר ʿāpar 1x [P] to shower (with dust or dirt) [6080]

[6760] עָפָר ʿāpār 110x dust, earth, soil in any form; used as a figure of something that cannot be counted [6083]

[6762] עֹפֶר ʿōper 5x fawn (of a deer or gazelle) [6082]

[6769] עֹפֶרֶת ʿōperet 90x lead (a mineral) [5777]

[6770] עֵץ ʿēṣ 330x tree; by extension, the product of the tree: wood, any wooden object [6086] See *timber; tree; wood.*

[6771] 1 עָצַב ʿāṣab 2x [P] to shape; [H] to make an image (of the Queen of Heaven) [6087]

[6772] 2 עָצַב ʿāṣab 14x [Q] to interfere with; [Qp] to be distressed; [N] to be grieved, be distressed; [P] to grieve; [H] to grieve; [Ht] to be filled with grief, be filled with pain [6087]

[6773] עָצָב ʿāṣāb 17x idol, image, a crafted object believed to represent or even possess a spirit or god [6091]

[6774] עַצָּב ʿaṣṣāb 1x (hard) worker, toiler [6092*]

[6775] 1 עֶצֶב ʿeṣeb 1x pot, vessel [6089]

[6776] 2 עֶצֶב ʿeṣeb 6x pain, toil, hard work [6089]

[6777] 1 עֹצֶב ʿōṣeb 1x idol [6090]

[6778] 2 עֹצֶב ʿōṣeb 4x pain, toil [6090]

[6779] עִצָּבוֹן ʿiṣṣābôn 3x pain, hardship, distress [6093]

[6780] עַצֶּבֶת ʿaṣṣebet 5x pain, sorrow, grief [6094]

[6781] עָצָה ʿāṣâ 1x [Q] to wink (the eye), as a non-verbal communication of what is evil, malicious, or lurid [6095]

[6782] עָצֶה ʿāṣeh 1x backbone, tailbone [6096]

[6783] 1 עֵצָה ʿēṣâ 87x advice, counsel, plan, purpose, scheme [6098] See *advice; counsel; plan; purpose.*

[6785] 3 עֵצָה ʿēṣâ 2x (coll.) wood; this can refer to wooden idols [6097]

[6786] עָצוּם ʿāṣûm 31x strong, mighty, powerful [6099]

[6788] עָצַל ʿāṣal 1x [N] to hesitate, be sluggish, be slow [6101]

[6789] עָצֵל ʿāṣēl 14x sluggish, slow, lazy; (n.) sluggard, one with no discipline or motivation, a moral failure [6102]

[6790] עַצְלָה ʿaṣlâ 1x laziness, slowness, sluggishness [6103]

[6791] עַצְלוּת ʿaṣlût 1x idleness, sluggishness, laziness [6104]

[6792] עֲצַלְתַּיִם ʿ^{a}ṣaltayim 1x extreme laziness, indolence [6103*]

[6793] 1 עָצַם ʿāṣam 18x [Q] to be vast, powerful, numerous; [P] to crush his bone; [H] to make numerous, make powerful, make vast [6105]

[6794] 2 עָצַם ʿāṣam 2x [Q] to close (the eyes); [P] to tightly shut (the eyes) [6105]

[6795] 1 עֶצֶם ʿeṣem 126x bone; by extension: the whole body, any part of the body, limb; strength of the body, vigor; (adv.) that very (day); "one's bone and flesh" is a close relative [6106] See *bones.*

[6797] 1 עֹצֶם ʿōṣem 3x might, strength [6108]

[6798] 2 עֹצֶם ʿōṣem 1x framework (of bones of the human body) [6108]

[6800] עָצְמָה ʿoṣmâ 20x power, potency, might [6109]

[6802] עֲצֻמוֹת ʿ^{a}ṣumôt 1x defensive arguments, strong words [6110*]

[6804] עֶצְנִי ʿeṣnî 1x Eznite, see 2851 [6112]

[6806] עָצַר ʿāṣar 46x [Q] to refrain, hold back, restrain; [Qp] to be enslaved, be constrained; [N] to be stopped, be detained [6113*]

[6807] עֶצֶר ʿeṣer 1x restraint, oppression [6114]

[6808] עֹצֶר ʿōṣer 3x oppression; barrenness [6115]

[6809] עֲצָרָה ʿ^{a}ṣārâ 11x assembly, usually on a festive day [6116]

[6810] עָקַב ʿāqab 5x [Q] to deceive; to grasp at the heel; [P] to hold the heel, to hold back [6117]

[6811] 1 עָקֵב ʿāqēb 13x heel, hoof; footstep, footprint; by extension:

rear guard of a military formation; a euphemism for private parts [6119]

[6812] 2 עָקֵב *ʿāqēb* 1x deceiver [6120]

[6813] עֵקֶב *ʿēqeb* 15x (c.) because; (n.) a reward; unto the end [6118]

[6814] 1 עָקֹב *ʿāqōb* 1x footprint [6121]

[6815] 2 עָקֹב *ʿāqōb* 2x deceitful; rough, bumpy [6121]

[6817] עָקְבָה *ʿōqbâ* 1x deceptiveness, cunning, craftiness [6122*]

[6818] עָקַד *ʿāqad* 1x [Q] to bind (feet) [6123]

[6819] עָקֹד *ʿāqōd* 7x streaked, striped [6124]

[6821] עָקָה *ʿāqâ* 1x pressure; oppressive look, stare, or actions [6125]

[6823] עָקַל *ʿāqal* 1x [Pu] to be perverted, be distorted, be crooked [6127]

[6824] עֲקַלְקַל *ʿ^{a}qalqāl* 2x crooked, winding [6128]

[6825] עֲקַלָּתוֹן *ʿ^{a}qallātôn* 1x coiling (serpent) [6129]

[6827] 1 עָקַר *ʿāqar* 2x [Q] to root up; [N] to be uprooted [6131]

[6828] 2 עָקַר *ʿāqar* 5x [P] to hamstring (to cut the tendon and render helpless or useless) [6131]

[6829] עָקָר *ʿāqār* 12x barren, sterile, without children [6135]

[6830] 1 עֵקֶר *ʿēqer* 1x offspring, as the fig. extension of a plant that grows up from a root [6133]

[6832] עַקְרָב *ʿaqrāb* 9x scorpion [6137]

[6833] עֶקְרוֹן *ʿeqrôn* 22x Ekron, "[perhaps] *barren place* or *fertile place*" [6138]

[6835] עָקַשׁ *ʿāqaš* 5x [N] to be perverse, be crooked; [P] to take crooked paths; to distort; [H] to pronounce guilty [6140]

[6836] 1 עִקֵּשׁ *ʿiqqēš* 11x perverse, crooked, warped [6141]

[6838] עִקְּשׁוּת *ʿiqq^{e}šût* 2x perversion, corruption, crookedness [6143]

[6839] 1 עָר *ʿār* 2x enemy, adversary [6145]

[6842] 1 עָרַב *ʿārab* 17x [Q] to put up a security, make a guarantee, give a pledge; [Ht] to make a bargain, make a wager [6148]

[6843] 2 עָרַב *ʿārab* 5x [Ht] to mingle, join in with, share with [6148]

[6844] 3 עָרַב *ʿārab* 85x [Q] to be pleasing, be pleasant, be acceptable [6149*]

[6845] 4 עָרַב *ʿārab* 3x [Q] to become evening; (opposite of joy) turn to gloom; [H] to do something in the evening [6150]

[6847] 2 עֶרֶב *ʿereb* 134x evening, twilight, dusk, the fading of the day; twilight can extend into the dark of the night [6153] See *evening; twilight.*

[6849] 1 עֵרֶב *ʿēreb* 9x knitted or woven material [6154]

[6850] 2 עֵרֶב *ʿēreb* 5x foreign people [6154]

[6851] 1 עֲרַב *ʿ^{a}rab* 7x Arabia, Arab [6152]

[6853] עָרֵב *ʿārēb* 2x pleasant, sweet (voice) [6156]

[6854] 1 עֹרֵב *ʿōrēb* 10x raven [6158]

[6856] עָרֹב *ʿārōb* 9x swarms of flies [6157]

[6857] 1 עֲרָבָה *ʿ^{a}rābâ* 5x poplar tree [6155*]

[6858] 2 עֲרָבָה *ʿ^{a}rābâ* 60x plains (a geographical region of desert, wilderness or wasteland); (pr.n.) Arabah [6160] See *Arabah; desert; plain; wilderness.*

[6859] עֲרֻבָּה *ʿ^{a}rubbâ* 2x security, pledge; assurance [6161]

[6860] עֵרָבוֹן *ʿērābôn* 3x pledge, security [6162*] See *pledge.*

[6861] עַרְבִי *ʿarbî* 7x Arab, of Arabia; may also refer to bedouin in general [6163]

[6864] עָרַג *ʿārag* 3x [Q] to pant for, long for (as a thirsty animal) [6165]

[6867] 1 עָרָה *ʿārâ* 14x [N] to be poured; [P] to lay bare, empty, expose, strip; [H] to make exposed; to cause to pour out; to dishonor; [Ht] to show oneself naked [6168]

[6868] 2 עָרָה *ʿārâ* 1x plants, bulrushes [6169]

[6870] עֲרוּגָה *ʿ^a^rûgâ* 4x garden bed, garden plot [6170]

[6871] עָרוֹד *ʿārôd* 1x wild donkey [6171]

[6872] עֶרְוָה *ʿerwâ* 54x nakedness (indecent or shameful in certain situations); "to expose the nakedness" is to have sexual relations [6172] See *naked; sexual relationships; shame.*

[6873] עָרוֹם *ʿārôm* 16x naked, stripped [6174]

[6874] עָרוּם *ʿārûm* 11x wise and understanding; with a positive connotation: prudent, clever; with a negative connotation: crafty [6175]

[6877] עָרוּץ *ʿārûṣ* 1x dry or dreadful [6178]

[6880] עֶרְיָה *ʿeryâ* 6x bareness, nakedness, the state of being uncovered [6181]

[6881] עֲרִיסָה *ʿ^a^rîsâ* 4x ground meal (dough in the first phase of bread making) [6182]

[6882] עֲרִיפִים *ʿ^a^rîpîm* 1x cloud [6183*]

[6883] עָרִיץ *ʿārîṣ* 21x ruthless, cruel, fierce [6184]

[6884] עֲרִירִי *ʿ^a^rîrî* 4x childless, very undesireable and even shameful in the ancient Near East [6185]

[6885] עָרַךְ *ʿārak* 75x [Q] to arrange in rows; put in order, take up (battle) positions; [Qp] to be arranged, be put in order, be put in formation; [H] to set a value [6186] See *arrange; deploy; draw up; prepare; set; spread; take up.*

[6886] עֵרֶךְ *ʿērek* 33x proper estimated value [6187]

[6887] עָרֵל *ʿāral* 2x [Q] to regard as forbidden, leave unharvested [6188*]

[6888] עָרֵל *ʿārēl* 35x uncircumcised (i.e., having a foreskin of the penis) [6189]

[6889] עָרְלָה *ʿorlâ* 15x foreskin (of the penis) [6190]

[6890] 1 עָרַם *ʿāram* 1x [N] to be piled up, be dammed up [6192]

[6891] 2 עָרַם *ʿāram* 6x [Q] to be crafty, show prudence; [H] to initiate cunning plans [6191]

[6893] עָרְמָה *ʿormâ* 5x prudence, cunning [6195]

[6894] עֲרֵמָה *ʿ^a^rēmâ* 11x heap, mound (of grain) [6194]

[6895] עֶרְמוֹן *ʿermôn* 2x plane tree [6196*]

[6899] עַרְעָר *ʿarʿār* 3x destitute, naked, stripped; (juniper) bush [6199]

[6902] עֹרֶף *ʿōrep* 33x neck; to be "stiff of neck" is to be obstinate, stubborn, implying rebellion [6203]

[6903] 1 עָרַף *ʿārap* 2x [Q] to trickle, drip [6201]

[6904] 2 עָרַף *ʿārap* 6x [Q] to break; [Qp] be broken [6202]

[6906] עֲרָפֶל *ʿ^a^rāpel* 15x dark or thick clouds; deep gloom [6205]

[6907] עָרַץ *ʿāraṣ* 15x [Q] to shake, to shake in terror; [N] to be feared; [H] to dread, stand in awe [6206]

[6908] עָרַק *ʿāraq* 2x [Q] to gnaw [6207]

[6910] עָרַר *ʿārar* 4x [Q] to strip off; [Po] to strip; [Pil] to level, demolish; [Htpal] to be laid utterly bare [6209]

[6911] עֶרֶשׂ *ʿereś* 10x bed, couch [6210]

[6912] עֵשֶׂב *ʿēśeb* 33x green plant, vegetation, grass [6212]

[6913] 1 עָשָׂה *ʿāśâ* 2,632x [Q] to do, make; [Qp] to be done; [N] to be done, be made; [Pu] to be made; a generic of action, seen in the many contextual translations of the NIV [6213] See *acquire; do; make; perform.*

[6914] 2 עָשָׂה *ʿāśâ* 3x [P] to caress, squeeze [6213]

[6916] עֵשָׂו *ʿēśāw* 97x Esau, "*hairy*" [6215]

[6917] עָשׂוֹר *ʿāśôr* 16x (group of) ten [6218]

[6920] עֲשִׂירִי *ʿaśîrî* 29x tenth [6224]

[6921] עָשַׂק *ʿāśaq* 1x [Ht] to dispute, quarrel [6229]

[6923] עָשַׂר *ʿāśar* 9x [Q] to take a tenth; [P] to give a tenth, set aside a tenth; [H] to give or receive a tenth [6237]

[6924] עֶשֶׂר *ʿeśer* 56x ten [6235] See *ten.*

[6925] עָשָׂר *ʿāśār* 205x ten (always used in combined numbers) [6240] See *twelve.*

[6926] עֶשְׂרֵה *ʿeśrēh* 136x ten (used in compound numbers) [6240*] See *twelve.*

[6927] עֲשָׂרָה *ʿaśārâ* 65x ten [6235] See *ten.*

[6928] עִשָּׂרוֹן *ʿiśśārôn* 33x tenth part [6241]

[6929] עֶשְׂרִים *ʿeśrîm* 316x twenty (pl. of "ten" [6924]) [6242] See *twenty.*

[6930] עֲשֶׂרֶת *ʿaśeret* 52x (group of) ten [6240*] See *ten.*

[6931] 1 עָשׁ *ʿāš* 7x moth, which consumes some natural fabrics [6211]

[6934] עָשׁוֹק *ʿāšôq* 1x oppressor [6216]

[6935] עֲשׁוּקִים *ʿašûqîm* 3x oppression [6217*]

[6936] עָשׁוֹת *ʿāšôt* 1x wrought, fashioned (iron) [6219]

[6938] עָשִׁיר *ʿāšîr* 23x rich, wealthy; (n.) the rich, rich person [6223]

[6939] עָשַׁן *ʿāšan* 6x [Q] to envelope in smoke, smolder [6225]

[6940] 1 עָשָׁן *ʿāšān* 25x smoke (billowing, ascending, blowing) [6227]

[6941] 2 עָשָׁן *ʿāšān* 4x Ashan, "*smoke*" [6228]

[6942] עָשֵׁן *ʿāšēn* 2x smoking, smoldering [6226]

[6943] עָשַׁק *ʿāšaq* 37x [Q] to oppress, mistreat; to defraud, extort; [Qp] to be oppressed, be tormented; [Pu] to be crushed [6231]

[6945] עֹשֶׁק *ʿōšeq* 15x oppression, tyranny; extortion [6233]

[6946] עָשְׁקָה *ʿošqâ* 1x trouble, oppression [6234]

[6947] עָשַׁר *ʿāšar* 17x [Q] to be, become rich; [H] to make rich, bring wealth [6238]

[6948] עֹשֶׁר *ʿōšer* 37x wealth, riches [6239]

[6949] עָשַׁשׁ *ʿāšaš* 3x [Q] to grow weak [6244*]

[6950] 1 עָשַׁת *ʿāšat* 1x [Q] to grow sleek (i.e., smooth or shiny) [6245]

[6951] 2 עָשַׁת *ʿāšat* 1x [Ht] to take notice [6245]

[6952] עֶשֶׁת *ʿešet* 1x polished piece, slab, plate [6247]

[6953] עַשְׁתּוּת *ʿaštût* 1x thought [6248]

[6954] עַשְׁתֵּי *ʿaštê* 18x eleven, eleventh [6249]

[6955] עֶשְׁתֹּנֶת *ʿeštōnet* 1x plan, thought [6250*]

[6956] עַשְׁתֹּרֶת *ʿaštōret* 9x Ashtoreth (pagan god) [6253]

[6957] עַשְׁתֶּרֶת *ʿašteret* 4x lamb or ewe [6251*]

[6958] עַשְׁתָּרֹת *ʿaštārōt* 6x Ashtaroth [6252*]

[6961] עֵת *ʿēt* 296x time (in general); a unit of time (of various lengths), season [6256] See *season; time.*

[6963] עָתַד *ʿātad* 2x [P] to make ready; [Ht] to be destined [6257]

[6964] עַתָּה *ʿattâ* 432x now [6258]

[6965] עָתוּד *ʿātûd* 1x supply, treasure [6259]

[6966] עַתּוּד *ʿattûd* 29x male goat; (of humans) a leader [6260]

[6967] עִתִּי *ʿittî* 1x available [6261]

[6969] עָתִיד *ʿātîd* 5x ready, prepared [6264]

[6971] עָתִיק *ʿātîq* 1x fine, choice, select [6266]

[6972] עַתִּיק *ʿattîq* 2x taken, removed (from place or time) [6267]

[6977] עָתַם *ʿātam* 1x [N] to be destroyed; in context, to be scorched [6272]

[6980] עָתַק *ʿātaq* 9x [Q] to move; to grow old, grow weak; [H] to move on; to fail; to copy [6275]

[6981] עָתָק *ʿātāq* 4x arrogant, insolent, outstretched [6277]

[6982] עָתֵק *ʿātēq* 1x enduring (wealth) [6276]

[6983] 1 עָתַר *ʿātar* 20x [Q] to pray; [N] to respond to prayer, be moved by an entreaty; [H] to pray, make entreaty [6279]

[6984] 2 עָתַר *ʿātar* 2x [N] to be multiplied; [H] to multiply [6280]

[6985] 1 עָתָר *ʿātār* 1x worshiper [6282]

[6986] 2 עָתָר *ʿātār* 1x fragrance, perfume [6282]

[6988] עֲתֶרֶת *ʿaᵃteret* 1x abundance [6283]

[6990] פָּאָה *pāʾâ* 1x [H] to split into pieces, scatter [6284]

[6991] 1 פֵּאָה *pēʾâ* 86x side, edge, boundary; forehead or crown of the head [6285] See *border; boundary; edge; side.*

[6992] 2 פֵּאָה *pēʾâ* 1x piece, part; possibly the same as 6991 [6285]

[6994] 1 פָּאַר *pāʾar* 1x [P] to knock down olives a second time [6286]

[6995] 2 פָּאַר *pāʾar* 13x [P] to honor, adorn, endow with splendor; [Ht] to glorify oneself, display one's splendor; (negatively) to boast [6286]

[6996] פְּאֵר *pᵉʾēr* 7x turban, headdress [6287]

[6997] פֹּארָה *pōʾrâ* 6x branch, leafy bough [6288]

[6998] פֻּארָה *puʾrâ* 1x bough [6288]

[6999] פָּארוּר *pāʾrûr* 2x growing pale, turning pale; some sources: to burn, glow [6289]

[7000] פָּארָן *pāʾrān* 10x Paran, "*plain*" [6290]

[7001] פַּג *pag* 1x early fruit, in context, unripe fig buds [6291]

[7002] פִּגּוּל *piggûl* 4x (ceremonially) unclean meat, kept too long after a sacrifice [6292]

[7003] פָּגַע *pāgaʿ* 46x to strike, touch; intercede for, plead with; [H] to make intercession, intervene; strike; cause to encounter [6293]

[7004] פֶּגַע *pegaʿ* 2x chance, occurrence [6294]

[7006] פָּגַר *pāgar* 2x [P] to be exhausted [6296]

[7007] פֶּגֶר *peger* 2x dead body, corpse; carcass; by extension: lifeless idol, with a focus that it is unclean and impotent [6297]

[7008] פָּגַשׁ *pāgaš* 14x [Q] to meet; to attack; [N] to have in common, to meet together; [P] to come upon, encounter [6298]

[7009] פָּדָה *pādâ* 60x [Q] to redeem, ransom, deliver, rescue, buy; [Qp] to be redeemed, be ransomed; [N] to be ransomed, be redeemed; [H] to let be ransomed; [Ho] to be brought to be ransomed; this can mean to purchase a devoted animal from sacrifice or to purchase a person from slavery to freedom or new ownership; by extension: divine salvation from oppression, death, or sin [6299] See *ransom; redeem.*

[7012] פְּדוּיִם *p^edûyim* 3x redemption, ransom, paid to purchase firstborn Israelites from dedication to God [6302*]

[7014] פְּדוּת *p^edût* 3x redemption, ransom, always of divine action [6304]

[7017] פִּדְיוֹם *pidyôm* 1x redemption, ransom [6306]

[7018] פִּדְיוֹן *pidyôn* 2x redemption money, ransom payment [6306]

[7021] פָּדַע *pādaʿ* 1x [Q] to spare, deliver [6308]

[7022] פֶּדֶר *peder* 3x suet (the hard fat about kidney's and loins of animals) [6309]

[7023] פֶּה *peh* 498x mouth (human or animal); by extension: speech, command, testimony; any opening; edge (of a sword) [6310 & 6366*] See *edge; mouth; opening.*

[7024] פֹּה *pōh* 82x here [6311]

[7028] פּוּג *pûg* 4x [Q] to grow numb, be feeble; [N] to be benumbed, be feeble [6313]

[7029] פּוּגָה *pûgâ* 1x relief, relaxation [6314]

[7031] 1 פּוּחַ *pûaḥ* 3x [Q] to blow, become dawn (of the day); [H] to blow (of wind) [6315]

[7032] 2 פּוּחַ *pûaḥ* 12x [Q] to breathe out; [H] to breathe out, sneer, malign [6315]

[7037] פּוּךְ *pûk* 4x turquoise (stone); (eye) paint, possibly derived from turquoise [6320]

[7038] פּוֹל *pôl* 2x beans [6321]

[7041] פּוּן *pûn* 1x [Q] to be in despair [6323]

[7046] 1 פּוּץ *pûṣ* 65x [Q] to be scattered; [Qp] to be scattered; [N] to be scattered; [H] to cause to scatter [6327] See *disperse; scatter.*

[7048] 1 פּוּק *pûq* 2x [Q] to stumble, totter; [H] to totter [6328 & 6329]

[7049] 2 פּוּק *pûq* 7x [H] to bring out, furnish, promote [6329]

[7050] פּוּקָה *pûqâ* 1x staggering, stumbling [6330]

[7052] 2 פּוּר *pûr* 8x pur (the lot), pebbles, sticks, or pottery shards that were thrown to make decisions; (pl.) Purim, a Jewish festival celebrating God's control over the casting of lots [6332]

[7053] פּוּרָה *pûrâ* 2x trough of the winepress; measure (equal to the filling of the winepress) [6333]

[7054] פּוֹרָתָא *pôrātāʾ* 1x Poratha [6334]

[7055] 1 פּוּשׁ *pûš* 3x [Q] to leap, frolic, gallop; this may refer to the playful pawing action of a young animal [6335]

[7056] 2 פּוּשׁ *pûš* 1x [N] to be scattered [6335]

[7058] פַּז *paz* 9x pure gold [6337*]

[7059] 1 פָּזַז *pāzaz* 1x [Ho] to be set with pure gold [6338]

[7060] 2 פָּזַז *pāzaz* 2x [Q] to be limber; [P] to leap [6339]

[7061] פָּזַר *pāzar* 10x [Qp] to be scattered; [P] to scatter; [N] to be scattered; [Pu] to be dispersed [6340]

[7062] 1 פַּח *paḥ* 24x snare, bird-trap [6341]

[7063] 2 פַּח *paḥ* 2x thin sheets (of hammered metal) [6341]

[7064] פָּחַד *pāḥad* 25x [Q] to tremble, be afraid; [P] to live in terror, fear; [H] to make shake, make tremble [6342]

[7065] 1 פַּ֫חַד *paḥad* 49x fear, terror, dread [6343]

[7066] 2 פַּ֫חַד *paḥad* 1x thigh [6344]

[7067] פַּחְדָּה *paḥdâ* 1x awe, dread [6345]

[7068] פֶּחָה *peḥâ* 28x governor, officer [6346]

[7069] פָּחַז *pāḥaz* 2x [Q] to be arrogant, be insolent [6348]

[7070] פַּ֫חַז *paḥaz* 1x turbulence, recklessness [6349]

[7071] פַּחֲזוּת *paḥᵃzût* 1x insolence, arrogance, with an implication of recklessness [6350]

[7072] פָּחַח *pāḥaḥ* 1x [H] to trap; [Ho] to be entrapped [6351]

[7073] פֶּחָם *peḥām* 4x coal, charcoal [6352]

[7074] פַּ֫חַת *paḥat* 10x pit, cave [6354]

[7076] פְּחֶ֫תֶת *pᵉḥetet* 1x mildew (that eats away at a garment) [6356]

[7077] פִּטְדָה *piṭdâ* 4x topaz; some sources: chrysolite [6357]

[7079] פַּטִּישׁ *paṭîš* 3x (sledge-)hammer [6360]

[7080] פָּטַר *pāṭar* 9x [Q] to elude, escape, release; [Qp] to be opened; [H] to open wide the mouth (as an insult) [6358* & 6362]

[7081] פֶּ֫טֶר *peṭer* 11x first offspring, firstborn [6363]

[7082] פִּטְרָה *piṭrâ* 1x firstborn [6363]

[7085] פִּיד *pîd* 4x misfortune, distress, calamity [6365]

[7086] פִּיחַ *pîaḥ* 2x soot (from a furnace) [6368]

[7088] פִּים *pîm* 1x pim (two-thirds of a shekel, about one-third of an ounce [7.6 grams]) [**]

[7089] פִּימָה *pîmâ* 1x fat, referring to an abundant life [6371]

[7090] פִּינְחָס *pînᵉḥās* 25x Phinehas, "*the black man*" [6372]

[7092] פִּיפִיּוֹת *pîpiyyôt* 2x double-edged, with many teeth [6374*]

[7094] פִּיתוֹן *pîtôn* 2x Pithon [6377]

[7095] פַּךְ *pak* 3x flask, (small) jug [6378]

[7096] פָּכָה *pākâ* 1x [P] to trickle [6379]

[7098] פָּלָא *pālāʾ* 71x [N] to be wonderful, be marvelous, be amazing; to be hard; [P] to fulfill; [H] to show a wonder, to cause to astound; [Ht] to show oneself marvelous [6381] See *difficult; miracle; wonderful; wonders.*

[7099] פֶּ֫לֶא *peleʾ* 13x wonder, miracle, astounding thing [6382]

[7100] פִּלְאִי *pilʾî* 2x wonderful, beyond understanding [6383]

[7103] פָּלַג *pālag* 4x [N] to be divided; [P] to cut open, divide [6385]

[7104] 1 פֶּ֫לֶג *peleg* 10x stream, artificial irrigation canal [6388]

[7106] פְּלַגָּה *pᵉlaggâ* 3x district, division; stream [6390]

[7107] פְּלֻגָּה *pᵉluggâ* 1x division (of a clan or family) [6391]

[7108] פִּלֶ֫גֶשׁ *pilegeš* 37x concubine, a female consort generally with lower status and fewer rights than a wife, with the function of giving social status or pleasure to the husband; once this refers to a woman's male consorts (Eze 23:20) [6370]

[7110] פְּלָדֹת *pᵉlādōt* 1x (polished) metal [6393*]

[7111] פָּלָה *pālâ* 5x [N] to be distinguished; [H] to deal differently, make a distinction [6395]

[7114] פָּלַח *pālaḥ* 5x [Q] to plow; [P] to cut up, pierce; to bring forth (from the womb) [6398]

[7115] פֶּלַח *pelaḥ* 6x millstone; half (of a pomegranate); slice (of a cake) [6400]

[7117] פָּלַט *pālaṭ* 26x [Q] to escape; [P] to rescue, deliver; [H] to bring to safety [6403]

[7119] פַּלֵּט *pallēṭ* 1x deliverance [6405]

[7127] פָּלִיט *pālîṭ* 18x fugitive, one who escapes [6412]

[7128] פָּלֵיט *pālêṭ* 4x fugitive, one who escapes [6412]

[7129] פְּלֵיטָה *p^elêṭâ* 30x fugitive, one who escapes, survivors, remnant [6413]

[7130] פָּלִיל *pālîl* 2x judge [6414]

[7131] פְּלִילָה *p^elîlâ* 1x decision [6415]

[7132] פְּלִילִי *p^elîlî* 2x for a judge, calling for judgment [6416]

[7133] פְּלִילִיָּה *p^elîliyyâ* 1x rendering of a decision, the calling for a judgment [6417]

[7134] 1 פֶּלֶךְ *pelek* 2x spindle-whorl, which could be used as a crutch [6418]

[7135] 2 פֶּלֶךְ *pelek* 8x district [6418]

[7136] 1 פָּלַל *pālal* 4x [P] to mediate, intervene; to expect; to furnish justification [6419]

[7137] 2 פָּלַל *pālal* 84x [Ht] to pray [6419] See *intercede; pray.*

[7140] פַּלְמֹנִי *palmōnî* 1x certain one [6422]

[7141] פְּלֹנִי *p^elōnî* 3x certain one [6423]

[7142] 1 פָּלַס *pālas* 4x [P] to make level, make smooth, prepare [6424]

[7143] 2 פָּלַס *pālas* 2x [P] to examine, observe [6424]

[7144] פֶּלֶס *peles* 2x balance, scale [6425]

[7145] פָּלַץ *pālaṣ* 1x [Ht] to tremble, shake [6426]

[7146] פַּלָּצוּת *pallāṣût* 4x trembling, shuddering, shaking [6427]

[7147] פָּלַשׁ *pālaš* 4x [Ht] to roll oneself (in the dust or ash) [6428]

[7148] פְּלֶשֶׁת *p^elešet* 9x Philistia; Philistine [6429]

[7149] פְּלִשְׁתִּי *p^elištî* 287x Philistine [6430]

[7151] פְּלֻת *p^elut* 1x distinction [6304*]

[7153] פֶּן *pen* 133x lest, not [6435*]

[7154] פַּנַּג *pannag* 1x food, confection [6436]

[7155] פָּנָה *pānâ* 134x [Q] to turn (in various senses); [P] to prepare; to turn away; [H] to turn; [Ho] to be caused to turn [6437] See *turn.*

[7156] פָּנֶה *pāneh* 2,126x face; by extension: appearance, presence; (pp.) before, in front of, in the presence of; to "show one's face" is a sign of favor; to "turn" or "hide one's face" is a sign of rejection [3942* & 6440] See *countenance; face; head; presence.*

[7157] פִּנָּה *pinnâ* 31x corner (of a structure), cornerstone (as a crucial element); stronghold; by extension: leader [6434* & 6438]

[7163] פְּנִימָה *p^enîmâ* 13x inner, inside, within [6441]

[7164] פְּנִימִי *p^enîmî* 31x inner [6442]

[7165] פְּנִינִים *p^enînîm* 6x rubies or corals [6443*]

[7167] פָּנַק *pānaq* 1x [P] to pamper [6445]

[7168] פַּס *pas* 5x ornamentation, many-colored or long-sleeved garment [6446]

[7170] פָּסַג *pāsag* 1x [P] to look over or to walk among [6448]

[7171] פִּסְגָּה *pisgâ* 8x Pisgah [6449]

[7172] פִּסָּה *pissâ* 1x abundance, plenty [6451]

[7173] 1 פָּסַח *pāsaḥ* 4x [Q] to pass over [6452]

[7174] 2 פָּסַח *pāsaḥ* 3x [Q] to be limp; [N] to become crippled; to worship in a limping dance [6452]

[7175] פֶּסַח *pesaḥ* 49x Passover; this can refer to the festival, the meal, or the lamb sacrificed at the festival [6453]

[7177] פִּסֵּחַ *pisseēaḥ* 14x lame, crippled [6455]

[7178] פָּסִיל *pāsîl* 23x idol, carved image [6456]

[7180] פָּסַל *pāsal* 6x [Q] to chisel out, carve (stone or wood) [6458]

[7181] פֶּסֶל *pesel* 31x idol, usually an image carved of wood or stone [6459]

[7182] פָּסַס *pāsas* 1x [Q] to vanish [6461]

[7184] פָּעָה *pāʿâ* 2x [Q] to cry out, groan (in childbirth) [6463]

[7188] פָּעַל *pāʿal* 58x [Q] to do, make [6466] See *do; make.*

[7189] פֹּעַל *pōʿal* 37x work, deed, labor [6467]

[7190] פְּעֻלָּה *p^e^ʿullâ* 14x work, deed, recompense [6468]

[7192] פָּעַם *pāʿam* 5x [Q] to push, impel; [N] to be troubled; [Ht] to be troubled [6470]

[7193] פַּעַם *paʿam* 118x step, foot; time, occurrence [6471] See *foot; time.*

[7194] פַּעֲמֹן *paʿ^a^môn* 7x bell (on a robe) [6472*]

[7196] פָּעַר *pāʿar* 4x [Q] to open wide (mouth) [6473]

[7198] פָּצָה *pāṣâ* 15x [Q] to open (mouth); to deliver, set free [6475]

[7200] 2 פָּצַח *pāṣaḥ* 8x [Q] to break forth, burst forth; [P] to break (in pieces) [6476]

[7201] פְּצִירָה *p^e^ṣîrâ* 1x sharpening (of plowshare) [6477]

[7202] פָּצַל *pāṣal* 2x [P] to peel (bark off boughs) [6478]

[7203] פְּצָלוֹת *p^e^ṣālôt* 1x stripes (made by peeling bark) [6479*]

[7204] פָּצַם *pāṣam* 1x [Q] to tear open [6480]

[7205] פָּצַע *pāṣaʿ* 3x [Q] to bruise, wound; [Qp] to be emasculated (by crushing) [6481]

[7206] פֶּצַע *peṣaʿ* 8x wound, bruise [6482]

[7207] פָּצַץ *pāṣaṣ* 3x [Pol] to break to pieces, shatter; [Pil] to crush, smash; [Htpol] to be crumbled, be shattered [6327*]

[7210] פָּצַר *pāṣar* 7x [Q] to insist on, bring pressure, persuade; [H] to be arrogant [6484]

[7211] פִּק *piq* 1x giving way, shaking (of knees) [6375*]

[7212] פָּקַד *pāqad* 304x [Q] to pay attention, care for; to count, number; to punish; [Qp] to be counted, listed; [N] to be missing, empty; [P] to muster; [Pu] to be robbed; to be recorded; [H] to appoint, give a charge; [Ho] to be appointed; [Ht] be mustered, counted; [Hotpaal] to be counted [6485] See *appoint; attend to; care; count; muster; number; punish; visit.*

[7213] פְּקֻדָּה *p^e^quddâ* 32x positive: appointment, charge, visitation; negative: punishment [6486]

[7214] פִּקָּדוֹן *piqqādôn* 3x something entrusted, something in reserve [6487]

[7215] פְּקִדֻת *p^e^qidut* 1x (captain of the) guard [6488]

[7217] פְּקוּדִים p^e*qûdîm* 1x accounting (of materials) [6485*]

[7218] פִּקּוּדִים *piqqûdîm* 24x precepts, directions, orders [6490*]

[7219] פָּקַח *pāqaḥ* 19x [Q] to open; [Qp] to be opened; [N] to be opened [6491]

[7221] פִּקֵּחַ *piqqēaḥ* 2x (normal) sighted [6493]

[7223] פְּקַח־קוֹחַ p^e*qaḥ-qôaḥ* 1x opening (of eyesight); some sources: opening a prison house to release prisoners [6495]

[7224] פָּקִיד *pāqîd* 13x chief officer, supervisor, commissioner [6496]

[7225] פְּקָעִים p^e*qāʿîm* 3x gourds [6497*]

[7226] פַּקֻּעֹת *paqquʿōt* 1x gourds [6498*]

[7228] פַּר *par* 133x bull [6499] See *bull.*

[7229] פָּרָא *pārāʾ* 1x [H] to thrive in fruitfulness [6500]

[7230] פֶּרֶא *pereʾ* 9x wild donkey; some sources: zebra, onager [6501]

[7232] פַּרְבָּר *parbār* 2x court (of the temple) [6503]

[7233] פָּרַד *pārad* 26x [Qp] to be spread out; [N] to be separated, be parted; [P] to consort with; [Pu] to be scattered; [H] to set apart, divide, separate; [Ht] to be scattered, be parted [6504]

[7234] פֶּרֶד *pered* 14x mule [6505]

[7235] פִּרְדָּה *pirdâ* 3x (female) mule [6506]

[7236] פַּרְדֵּס *pardēs* 3x park, forest, orchard [6508]

[7237] פְּרֻדֹת p^e*rudōt* 1x grain (of seed); some sources: dried fig [6507*]

[7238] פָּרָה 1 *pārâ* 29x [Q] to be fruitful, flourish; [H] to make fruitful [6509]

[7239] פָּרָה 2 *pārâ* 26x cow, heifer [6510]

[7241] פֶּרֶה *pereh* 1x wild donkey [6501]

[7247] פַּרְוָר *parwār* 1x court [6503]

[7248] פָּרוּר *pārûr* 3x cooking pot [6517]

[7250] פָּרָז *pārāz* 1x warrior [6518]

[7251] פְּרָזוֹן p^e*rāzôn* 2x dwellers in the open country; warriors [6520]

[7252] פְּרָזוֹת p^e*rāzôt* 2x rural, open country [6519*]

[7253] פְּרָזִי p^e*rāzî* 4x rural, open country [6521]

[7254] פְּרִזִּי p^e*rizzî* 23x Perizzite [6522]

[7255] פָּרַח 1 *pāraḥ* 34x [Q] to sprout, blossom; break out, flourish; [H] to make flourish, bring to bud [6524]

[7256] פָּרַח 2 *pāraḥ* 2x [Q] to fly; (n.) a bird [6524]

[7258] פֶּרַח *peraḥ* 17x blossom, bud; floral work [6525]

[7259] פִּרְחַח *pirḥaḥ* 1x offspring, brood, tribe, with a focus on energetic behavior [6526]

[7260] פָּרַט *pāraṭ* 1x [Q] to strum, improvise (on a musical instrument) [6527]

[7261] פֶּרֶט *pereṭ* 1x fallen grapes [6528]

[7262] פְּרִי p^e*rî* 119x fruit, produce, crops; by extension: offspring of any creature; result of any action; "fruit of the lips" is speech, praise; "fruit of the hand" is something earned [6529] See *crops; fruit; produce.*

[7264] פָּרִיץ 1 *pārîṣ* 1x ferocious (animal) [6530]

[7265] פָּרִיץ 2 *pārîṣ* 5x robber; violent one [6530]

[7266] פֶּרֶךְ *perek* 6x ruthlessness, brutality, violence [6531]

[7267] פָּרֹכֶת *pārōket* 25x curtain [6532*] See *curtain; veil.*

[7268] פָּרַם *pāram* 3x [Q] to tear; [Qp] to be torn [6533]

[7271] 1 פָּרַס *pāras* 14x [Q] to offer food, share food; [H] to have a divided hoof [6536]

[7272] פֶּרֶס *peres* 2x vulture [6538]

[7273] 2 פָּרַס *pāras* 28x Persia; Persian [6539]

[7274] פַּרְסָה *parsâ* 21x hoof [6541]

[7276] 1 פָּרַע *pāraʿ* 1x [Q] to take the lead [6544]

[7277] 2 פָּרַע *pāraʿ* 15x [Q] to be out of control, be unkempt; to ignore, avoid; [Qp] to be unkempt, be running wild; [N] be unrestrained; [H] to let neglect; to promote wickedness [6544]

[7278] 1 פֶּרַע *peraʿ* 2x leader, prince [6546*]

[7279] 2 פֶּרַע *peraʿ* 2x long hair of head [6545]

[7281] פַּרְעֹה *parʿōh* 274x Pharaoh [6547]

[7282] 1 פַּרְעֹשׁ *parʿōš* 2x flea [6550]

[7287] פָּרַץ *pāraṣ* 49x [Q] to break out, burst forth; [Qp] to be broken through; [N] to be spread abroad; [Pu] to be broken down; [Ht] to break oneself away [6555]

[7288] 1 פֶּרֶץ *pereṣ* 19x breech, break, gap caused by something breaking through; by extension: outburst of anger [6556]

[7293] פָּרַק *pāraq* 10x [Q] to rip to pieces; to free (by tearing away); [P] to take off, tear off; [Ht] to take off from oneself, tear off from oneself [6561]

[7294] פֶּרֶק *pereq* 2x crossroad; plunder [6563]

[7296] 1 פָּרַר *pārar* 49x [H] to break, violate, nullify; [Ho] to be broken, revoked, thwarted [6565]

[7297] 2 פָּרַר *pārar* 4x [Q] to split asunder; [Pil] to shatter; [Pol] to split open; [Htpol] to split asunder [6565]

[7298] פָּרַשׂ *pāraś* 67x [Q] to spread out, scatter; [Qp] to be spread out; [N] to be scattered; [P] to scatter, spread out [6566] See *scatter; spread.*

[7300] 1 פָּרַשׁ *pāraš* 3x [Q] to make clear; [N] to be given; [Pu] to be made clear [6567]

[7301] 2 פָּרַשׁ *pāraš* 1x [H] to secrete poison [6567]

[7302] 1 פֶּרֶשׁ *pereš* 7x offal, dung or intestinal contents of a butchered animal [6569]

[7304] 1 פָּרָשׁ *pārāš* 18x horse [6571]

[7305] 2 פָּרָשׁ *pārāš* 38x horseman [6571]

[7306] פַּרְשֶׁגֶן *paršegen* 1x copy [6572]

[7307] פַּרְשְׁדֹן *parš^{e}dōn* 1x back (of a person), back door [?] [6574]

[7308] פָּרָשָׁה *pārāšâ* 2x exact amount, exact statement [6575]

[7310] פְּרָת *p^{e}rāt* 19x Euphrates (mighty river of Mesopotamia); Perath (small river or valley in the book of Jeremiah) [6578]

[7312] פַּרְתְּמִים *part^{e}mîm* 3x nobles, princes [6579*]

[7313] פָּשָׂה *pāśâ* 22x [Q] to spread [6581]

[7314] פָּשַׂע *pāśaʿ* 1x [Q] to march, step forth [6585]

[7315] פֶּשַׂע *peśaʿ* 1x step [6587]

[7316] פָּשַׂק *pāśaq* 2x [Q] to open wide (the lips in talking or smirking); [P] to spread the feet or legs (in immorality) [6589]

[7317] פַּשׁ *paš* 1x wickedness or weakness, foolishness [6580]

[7318] פָּשַׁח *pāšaḥ* 1x [P] to mangle [6582]

[7320] פָּשַׁט *pāšaṭ* 43x [Q] to take off, strip; to make a sudden dash, raid; [P] to strip; [H] to take off, strip off; [Ht] to strip oneself [6584]

[7321] פָּשַׁע *pāšaʿ* 41x [Q] to rebel, revolt (against human or divine authority) [6586]

[7322] פֶּשַׁע *pešaʿ* 93x rebellion, revolt, sin, transgression (against human or divine authority) [6588] See *offense; rebellion; sin; transgression.*

[7323] פֵּשֶׁר *pēšer* 1x explanation, interpretation [6592]

[7324] פֵּשֶׁת *pēšet* 16x flax, linen (made of flax) [6593*]

[7325] פִּשְׁתָּה *pištâ* 4x flax, wick (made of flax) [6594]

[7326] פַּת *pat* 14x little piece, morsel (of food) [6595]

[7327] פֹּת *pōt* 2x scalp, forehead; socket (for doors) [6596]

[7328] פִּתְאֹם *pitʾōm* 25x suddenly, unexpectedly, all at once, in an instant [6597]

[7329] פַּת־בַּג *pat-bag* 6x (fine) food, choice provisions [6598]

[7330] פִּתְגָם *pitgām* 2x edict, decree; sentence (for a crime) [6599]

[7331] 1 פָּתָה *pātâ* 27x [Q] to be simple, easily deceived, enticed; [P] to seduce, entice, deceive, allure; [N] to be enticed, deceived; [Pu] to be deceived, enticed, persuaded [6601]

[7332] 2 פָּתָה *pātâ* 1x [H] to provide ample space, make spacious [6601]

[7333] פְּתוּאֵל *pᵉtûʾēl* 1x Pethuel, "*God's opening*" [6602]

[7335] פְּתוֹר *pᵉtôr* 2x Pethor [6604]

[7337] 1 פָּתַח *pātaḥ* 136x [Q] to open; [Qp] to be opened; [N] to be opened; [P] to loosen, release, take off; [Ht] to free oneself [6605] See *open; release; set free.*

[7338] 2 פָּתַח *pātaḥ* 9x [P] to engrave, carve; [Pu] to be engraved [6605]

[7339] פֶּתַח *petaḥ* 164x entrance, opening; of a building or city: door, gate [6607] See *entrance.*

[7340] פֵּתַח *pētaḥ* 1x revelation, disclosure, an extension opening a door or gate [6608]

[7341] פִּתָּחוֹן *pittāḥôn* 2x opening (of mouth for communication) [6610]

[7343] 1 פֶּתִי *petî* 16x simple, naive, someone easily deceived or persuaded [6612]

[7344] 2 פֶּתִי *petî* 3x simple ways, simplemindedness [6612]

[7345] פְּתִיגִיל *pᵉtîgîl* 1x fine clothing [6614]

[7346] פְּתַיּוּת *pᵉtayyût* 1x undisciplined, deceptive [6615]

[7347] פְּתִיחָה *pᵉtîḥâ* 2x drawn sword [6609*]

[7348] פָּתִיל *pātîl* 11x cord, strands, string [6616]

[7349] פָּתַל *pātal* 5x [N] to have a struggle; to be wily, be crooked; [Ht] to show oneself shrewd [6617]

[7350] פְּתַלְתֹּל *pᵉtaltōl* 1x crooked, perverse [6618]

[7352] פֶּתֶן *peten* 6x cobra, serpent; some sources: viper [6620]

[7353] פֶּתַע *petaʿ* 7x instant; (adv.) suddenly, in an instant [6621]

[7354] פָּתַר *pātar* 9x [Q] to interpret, give the meaning (of a dream) [6622]

[7355] פִּתְרוֹן *pittārôn* 5x interpretation, meaning [6623*]

[7358] פַּתְשֶׁגֶן *patšegen* 3x copy (of a text) [6572]

[7359] פָּתַת *pātat* 1x [Q] to crumble [6626]

[7362] צֵאָה *ṣēʾâ* 0x excrement, dung [6627]

[7363] צֹאָה *ṣōʾâ* 0x filth, excrement, dung; by extension: moral filth [6675]

[7364] צֹאִי *ṣōʾî* 3x filthy, befouled (with excrement) [6674*]

[7365] צֶאֱלִים *ṣeʾelîm* 2x lotus plant [6628*]

[7366] צֹאן *ṣōʾn* 274x flock, sheep, goats (in contrast to larger mammals: cattle, donkeys, camels, etc.) [6629] See *flock; goat; lamb; sheep.*

[7368] צֶאֱצָאִים *ṣeʾeṣāʾîm* 11x offspring, descendant [6631*]

[7369] צָב 1 *ṣāb* 2x (covered) wagon; some sources: litter without wheels [6632]

[7370] צָב 2 *ṣāb* 1x lizard (of unspecified species) [6632]

[7371] צָבָא 1 *ṣābāʾ* 14x [Q] to fight, do battle; to serve in (temple) corps [6633]

[7372] צָבָא 2 *ṣābāʾ* 487x army, host, divisions (of an army); as a title of God: of Hosts (the heavenly armies), the Almighty, with a focus on great power to conquer or rule, a fig. extension of the leader of an great army [6635] See *Almighty; army; host.*

[7373] צָבָא 3 *ṣābāʾ* 1x gazelle [6643*]

[7374] צְבָאָה *ṣebāʾâ* 2x (female) gazelle [6643*]

[7377] צָבָה *ṣābâ* 2x [Q] to swell; [H] to cause to swell [6638]

[7379] צָבֶה *ṣābeh* 1x swollen [6639]

[7380] צָבוּעַ *ṣābûʿa* 1x speckled, variegated, pertaining to the pattern on a winged creature [6641]

[7381] צָבַט *ṣābaṭ* 1x [Q] to offer (food to another person) [6642]

[7382] צְבִי 1 *ṣebî* 18x ornament, beautiful (thing), glory [6643]

[7383] צְבִי 2 *ṣebî* 11x gazelle [6643]

[7386] צְבִיָּה *ṣebiyyâ* 2x (female) gazelle [6646]

[7389] צֶבַע *ṣebaʿ* 3x colorful (dyed) garment [6648]

[7392] צָבַר *ṣābar* 7x [Q] to store up, heap up, pile up [6651]

[7393] צִבֻּר *ṣibbur* 1x pile, heap [6652]

[7395] צֶבֶת *ṣebet* 1x bundle (of grain with the stalk) [6653]

[7396] צַד 1 *ṣad* 34x side (of something) [6654]

[7399] צָדָה 1 *ṣādâ* 2x [Q] to lie in wait, hunt down a person [6658]

[7400] צָדָה 2 *ṣādâ* 1x [N] to be destroyed, be laid waste [6658]

[7401] צָדוֹק *ṣādôq* 53x Zadok, "*righteous one*" [6659]

[7402] צְדִיָּה *ṣediyyâ* 2x ambush, lying-in-wait (with malicious intent) [6660]

[7404] צַדִּיק *ṣaddîq* 206x righteous, upright, just, innocent; in accordance with a proper (God's) standard, and so implying innocence [6662] See *innocent; just; righteous, righteousness.*

[7405] צָדַק *ṣādaq* 40x [Q] to be righteous, be innocent, be vindicated; in accordance with a proper (God's) standard, and so implying innocence [6663]

[7406] צֶדֶק *ṣedeq* 123x righteousness, justice, rightness, acting according to a proper (God's) standard, doing what is right, being in the right [6664] See *justice; righteous, righteousness; rightness.*

[7407] צְדָקָה *ṣedāqâ* 159x righteousness, acting according to a proper (God's) standard, doing what is right, being in the right [6666] See *innocence; justice; rightetous, righteousness.*

[7409] צִדְקִיָּהוּ *ṣidqiyyāhû* 57x Zedekiah, "*Yahweh is [my] righteousness*" [6667]

[7410] צָהַב *ṣāhab* 1x [Ho] to be polished, gleaming copper color [6668]

[7411] צָהֹב *ṣāhōb* 3x yellow, blond; some sources: gleaming red [6669]

[7412] 1 צָהַל *ṣāhal* 8x [Q] to shout out, celebrate; to neigh (of a horse) [6670]

[7413] 2 צָהַל *ṣāhal* 1x [H] to make shine [6670]

[7414] צָהַר *ṣāhar* 1x [H] to press olives; some sources relate to 7416 and translate "to spend the noontime" [6671]

[7415] צֹהַר *ṣōhar* 1x roof, covering (for the ark of Noah) [6672]

[7416] צָהֳרַיִם *ṣohᵒrayim* 23x noon, noonday, midday [6672*]

[7417] צַו *ṣaw* 1x worthless thing, an idol or utterance (perhaps a nonsense syllable, a mocking sound) [6673]

[7418] צַוָּאר *ṣawwāʾr* 41x (back of) neck [6677]

[7421] צוּד *ṣûd* 17x [Q] to hunt, stalk; [Pil] to ensnare; by extension to stalk people for capture or oppression [6679]

[7422] צָוָה *ṣāwâ* 496x [P] to command, order, instruct, give direction; [Pu] to be commanded, be directed, be ordered [6680] See *command; forbid; order.*

[7423] צָוַח *ṣāwaḥ* 1x [Q] to shout, cry aloud [6681]

[7424] צְוָחָה *ṣᵉwāḥâ* 4x cry of distress, wail [6682]

[7425] צוּלָה *ṣûlâ* 1x the watery deep, the ocean abyss [6683]

[7426] צוּם *ṣûm* 21x [Q] to fast, to voluntarily abstain from food as dedication to deity, as a sign of mourning, or possibly as a medical treatment [6684]

[7427] צוֹם *ṣôm* 26x fast, time of fasting, act of fasting; see also 7426 [6685]

[7429] 1 צוּף *ṣûp* 3x [Q] to flow; [H] to make float; to overwhelm (with water) [6687]

[7430] 2 צוּף *ṣûp* 2x honeycomb (dripping with honey) [6688]

[7437] 1 צוּץ *ṣûṣ* 8x [Q] to bud, blossom; [H] to put forth blossoms; to cause to flourish [6692]

[7438] 2 צוּץ *ṣûṣ* 1x [H] to peer at, look at [6692]

[7439] 1 צוּק *ṣûq* 11x [H] to oppress, compel, nag, inflict [6693]

[7440] 2 צוּק *ṣûq* 1x [Q] to pour out [6694]

[7441] צוֹק *ṣôq* 1x trouble, oppression [6695]

[7442] צוּקָה *ṣûqâ* 3x trouble, distress, oppression [6695]

[7443] 1 צוּר *ṣûr* 35x [Q] to siege, besiege, enclose [6696]

[7444] 2 צוּר *ṣûr* 4x [Q] to oppose, harass [6696]

[7445] 3 צוּר *ṣûr* 2x [Q] to fashion, shape [6697]

[7446] 4 צוּר *ṣûr* 73x rock; stone mass, rocky crag; a title of God, with a focus of stability, and possibly as a place of security and safety [6697] See *rock.*

[7450] צוֹר *ṣôr* 42x Tyre, "*rocky place*" [6865]

[7451] צוּרָה *ṣûrâ* 4x design, form [6699]

[7452] צוּרִיאֵל *ṣûrîʾēl* 1x Zuriel, "*God [El] is [my] rock*" [6700]

[7454] צַוְּרֹנִים *ṣawwᵉrōnîm* 1x necklace [6677*]

[7455] צוּת *ṣût* 1x [H] to set on fire [6702]

[7456] צַח *ṣaḥ* 4x radiant, shimmering, scorching, clear [6703]

[7457] צִחֶה *ṣiḥeh* 1x parched [6704]

[7458] צָחַח *ṣāḥaḥ* 1x [Q] to be white [6705]

[7460] צָחִיחַ *ṣāḥiaḥ* 5x bare (rock or place in a wall) [6706]

[7461] צְחִיחָה *ṣᵉḥîḥâ* 1x bare, (sun-)scorched land [6707]

[7462] צַחֲנָה *ṣaḥ^{a}nâ* 1x putrid smell, stench [6709]

[7463] צַחְצָחוֹת *ṣaḥṣāḥôt* 1x bare, (sun-)scorched land [6710*]

[7464] צָחַק *ṣāḥaq* 13x [Q] to laugh; [P] to mock, make sport, caress; this can mean to laugh with delight or in scorn [6711]

[7465] צְחֹק *ṣ^{e}ḥōq* 2x laughter, scorn [6712]

[7467] צָחֹר *ṣāḥōr* 1x white, yellowish red, tawny [6715]

[7469] 1 צִי *ṣî* 4x ship [6716]

[7470] 2 צִי *ṣî* 6x desert creature, referring to known animals or presumed spirits or demons; tribe of the desert [6728*]

[7472] צִיד *ṣîd* 1x [Ht] to pack provisions for oneself [6679*]

[7473] 1 צַיִד *ṣayid* 14x (hunting) game; hunter [6718]

[7474] 2 צַיִד *ṣayid* 5x food supply, provision [6718]

[7475] צַיָּד *ṣayyād* 1x hunter [6719]

[7476] צֵידָה *ṣêdâ* 9x food, provisions, supplies [6720]

[7477] צִידוֹן *ṣîdôn* 20x Sidon, "*fishery*" [6721]

[7480] צִיָּה *ṣiyyâ* 16x desert, parched land, dry land, waterless region [6723]

[7481] צָיוֹן *ṣāyôn* 2x desert, waterless country [6724]

[7482] צִיּוֹן *ṣiyyôn* 154x Zion, "*citadel*" [6726]

[7483] צִיּוּן *ṣiyyûn* 3x sign, stone marker [6725]

[7485] צִינֹק *ṣînōq* 1x neck-iron, iron collar [6729]

[7488] 1 צִיץ *ṣîṣ* 14x flower, blossom; (ornamental) plate [6731]

[7490] 3 צִיץ *ṣîṣ* 1x salt [6731]

[7491] צִיצָה *ṣîṣâ* 1x flower [6733]

[7492] צִיצִת *ṣîṣit* 4x tassel of threads; tuft of hair [6734]

[7493] 1 צִיר *ṣîr* 1x [Ht] to act as a delegation [6735 & 6737*]

[7494] 2 צִיר *ṣîr* 1x hinge, (door-)pivot [6735 & 6737*]

[7495] 3 צִיר *ṣîr* 6x envoy, messenger [6735 & 6737*]

[7496] 4 צִיר *ṣîr* 5x pains, pangs, anguish [6735 & 6737*]

[7497] 5 צִיר *ṣîr* 2x idol [6736]

[7498] צֵל *ṣēl* 53x shadow, shade, protection [6738 & 6752*] See *protection; shade; shadow; shelter; transitoriness.*

[7499] צָלָה *ṣālâ* 3x [Q] to roast (meat) [6740]

[7501] צְלוּל *ṣ^{e}lûl* 1x round loaf [6742]

[7502] 1 צָלַח *ṣālaḥ* 10x [Q] to be powerful, come forcefully; to rush [6743]

[7503] 2 צָלַח *ṣālaḥ* 55x [Q] to prosper, prevail, succeed, avail; [H] to make a success, grant prosperity, make victorious [6743]

[7504] צְלֹחִית *ṣ^{e}lōḥît* 1x (shallow) bowl; some sources: pan, cruse, dish [6746]

[7505] צַלַּחַת *ṣallaḥat* 4x dish, pan [6745* & 6747]

[7507] צָלִי *ṣālî* 3x roasted (meat) [6748]

[7509] 1 צָלַל *ṣālal* 4x [Q] to tingle; to quiver [6750]

[7510] 2 צָלַל *ṣālal* 1x [Q] to sink down [6749]

[7511] 3 צָלַל *ṣālal* 2x [Q] to grow dark; [H] to give shade [6751]

[7512] 1 צֶלֶם *ṣelem* 15x image (usually referring to an object of worship), idol [6754] See *idol; image.*

[7513] 2 צֶלֶם *ṣelem* 2x phantom, fantasy, shadowy thing [6754]

[7516] צַלְמָוֶת *ṣalmāwet* 18x shadow, darkness, gloom, blackness [6757]

[7519] צָלַע *ṣālaʿ* 4x [Q] to be lame, limp [6760]

[7520] צֶלַע *ṣelaʿ* 4x stumbling, falling, slipping [6761]

[7521] צֵלָע 1 *ṣēlāʿ* 41x side [6763]

[7526] צְלָצַל *ṣᵉlāṣal* 1x (swarm of) locust; some sources: cricket [6767]

[7527] צִלְצָל 1 *ṣilṣāl* 1x whirring, buzzing [6767*]

[7528] צִלְצָל 2 *ṣilṣāl* 1x (fishing) spear [6767*]

[7529] צֶלְצְלִים *ṣelṣelîm* 3x cymbals [6767*]

[7532] צָמֵא 1 *ṣāmēʾ* 1x [Q] to thirst, be thirsty [6770]

[7533] צָמָא *ṣāmāʾ* 17x thirst (of humans and animals); used fig. of parched ground [6772]

[7534] צָמֵא 2 *ṣāmēʾ* 9x thirsty, used of humans and animals; used fig. of parched ground [6771]

[7535] צִמְאָה *ṣimʾâ* 1x thirst [6773]

[7536] צִמָּאוֹן *ṣimmāʾôn* 3x thirsty ground [6774]

[7537] צָמַד *ṣāmad* 5x [N] to be joined together; [Pu] to be strapped on; [H] to harness, attach to [6775]

[7538] צֶמֶד *ṣemed* 15x yoke, team of two, pair; this can refer to a measurement of land, as the acreage a team of animals can plow [6776]

[7539] צַמָּה *ṣammâ* 4x veil [6777]

[7540] צִמּוּקִים *ṣimmûqîm* 4x raisin cakes [6778*]

[7541] צָמַח *ṣāmaḥ* 33x [Q] to sprout up, spring up; [P] to grow; [H] to cause to grow, bring to fruition [6779]

[7542] צֶמַח *ṣemaḥ* 12x growth (which sprouts); (as a messianic title) the Branch [6780]

[7543] צָמִיד 1 *ṣāmîd* 6x bracelet [6781]

[7544] צָמִיד 2 *ṣāmîd* 1x lid, cover [6781]

[7545] צַמִּים *ṣammîm* 1x snare [6782]

[7546] צָמַק *ṣāmaq* 1x [Q] to be dry, shriveled (of breasts) [6784]

[7547] צֶמֶר *ṣemer* 16x wool [6785]

[7550] צַמֶּרֶת *ṣammeret* 5x top (of a tree) [6788]

[7551] צָמַת *ṣāmat* 15x [Q] to silence; [N] to be silenced; [Pil] to destroy; [P] to wear out; [H] to put to silence, destroy [6789]

[7552] צְמִתֻת *ṣᵉmitut* 2x permanence, finality [6783]

[7553] צֵן *ṣēn* 3x thorn; hook [6791]

[7554] צִן *ṣin* 10x Zin [6790]

[7556] צֹנֶה *ṣōneh* 1x flocks (of sheep and goats) [6792]

[7557] צִנָּה 1 *ṣinnâ* 1x coolness [6793]

[7558] צִנָּה 2 *ṣinnâ* 20x (large) shield [6793]

[7560] צָנוּעַ *ṣānûʿa* 1x humble, modest [6800*]

[7562] צִנּוֹר *ṣinnôr* 2x water shaft; waterfall [6794*]

[7563] צָנַח *ṣānaḥ* 3x [Q] to get down; to go down [6795]

[7564] צְנִינִים *ṣᵉnînîm* 2x thorns [6796*]

[7565] צָנִיף *ṣānîp* 4x turban [6797]

[7566] צְנִיפָה *ṣᵉnîpâ* 1x turban (of woman), an ornamental head wrap [6797]

[7568] צָנֻם *ṣānum* 1x withered [6798*]

[7570] צָנַע *ṣānaʿ* 1x [H] to show a humble (walk with God), as an extension of acting in a cautious manner [6800]

[7571] צָנַף *ṣānap* 3x [Q] to wrap around, wind around [6801]

[7572] צְנֵפָה *ṣᵉnēpâ* 1x winding, wrapping [6802]

[7573] צִנְצֶנֶת *ṣinṣenet* 1x vessel, receptacle, likely referring to a jar [6803]

[7574] צַנְתָּרוֹת *ṣantārôt* 1x pipes [6804*]

[7575] צָעַד *ṣāᶜad* 8x [Q] to step, march; [H] to make march [6805]

[7576] צַעַד *ṣaᶜad* 14x step, stride [6806]

[7577] 1 צְעָדָה *ṣᵉᶜādāh* 2x marching [6807]

[7578] 2 צְעָדָה *ṣᵉᶜādāh* 1x ankle chains [6807]

[7579] צָעָה *ṣāᶜâ* 5x [Q] to lay down, stoop, incline; [P] to tip, pour out [6808]

[7581] צָעִיף *ṣāᶜip* 3x veil [6809]

[7582] 1 צָעִיר *ṣāᶜîr* 23x younger, small, little, lowly [4704* & 6810]

[7584] צְעִירָה *ṣᵉᶜîrâ* 1x youth, youngest (offspring) [6812]

[7585] צָעַן *ṣāᶜan* 1x [Q] to pack up, move (a tent) [6813]

[7589] צַעֲצֻעִים *saᶜᵃsuᶜîm* 1x sculptured work (by metal casting) [6816*]

[7590] צָעַק *ṣāᶜaq* 55x [Q] to cry; [N] to be called out, be summoned; [P] to keep crying; [H] to call together, summon [6817] See *cry out.*

[7591] צְעָקָה *ṣᵉᶜāqâ* 21x cry of distress, outcry, wailing [6818*]

[7592] צָעַר *ṣāᶜar* 3x [Q] to be trivial, insignificant, little [6819]

[7594] צָפַד *ṣāpad* 1x [Q] to shrivel [6821]

[7595] 1 צָפָה *ṣāpâ* 36x [Q] to keep watch, be a lookout; [Qp] to be spied out; [P] to watch, lookout [6822]

[7596] 2 צָפָה *ṣāpâ* 47x [Q] to arrange; [P] to overlay, cover, adorn; [Pu] to be overlaid, be coated [6823]

[7597] 3 צָפָה *ṣāpâ* 1x out-flow, discharge [6824]

[7599] צִפּוּי *ṣippûy* 5x overlaying, (metal) plating [6826]

[7600] 1 צָפוֹן *ṣāpôn* 153x north, northern [6828] See *north.*

[7603] 1 צְפוֹנִי *ṣᵉpônî* 1x northern; (n.) northerner [6830]

[7606] 1 צִפּוֹר *ṣippôr* 40x bird (individual and collective) [6833]

[7608] צַפַּחַת *ṣappaḥat* 7x jug, jar (for liquid), a portable convex or spherical shape, with a lid or plug for transport [6835]

[7610] צִפִּיָּה *ṣippiyyâ* 1x watchtower, lookout [6836]

[7613] צַפִּיחִת *ṣappîḥit* 1x wafer, flat-cake [6838]

[7616] צָפִיעַ *ṣāpîᶜa* 1x manure, dung [6832*]

[7617] צְפִיעָה *ṣᵉpîᶜâ* 1x offshoots, leaf [6849*]

[7618] צָפִיר *ṣāpîr* 6x (male) goat [6842]

[7619] צְפִירָה *ṣᵉpîrâ* 3x crown, wreath; doom [6843]

[7620] צָפִית *ṣāpît* 1x rug, carpet [6844]

[7621] צָפַן *ṣāpan* 32x [Q] to hide, conceal, store up; [Qp] to be treasured, be cherished; [N] to be stored up, be concealed; [H] to hide [6845]

[7622] צְפַנְיָה *ṣᵉpanyâ* 8x Zephaniah, "*Yahweh has hidden [to shelter]* or *Yahweh has hidden [as a treasure]*" [6846]

[7625] צֶפַע *sepaᶜ* 1x viper, serpent [6848]

[7626] צִפְעֹנִי *ṣipᶜōnî* 4x viper [6848]

[7627] צָפַף *ṣāpap* 4x [Pil] to chirp; to whisper [6850]

[7628] צַפְצָפָה *ṣapṣāpâ* 1x willow [6851]

[7629] צָפַר *ṣāpar* 1x [Q] to leave, depart [6852]

[7630] צְפַרְדֵּעַ *ṣᵉpardēᶜa* 13x frogs [6854]

[7632] צִפֹּרֶן *ṣippōren* 2x nail (of finger or toe); (flint or hard stone) point (of a stylus) [6856]

[7633] צֶפֶת *ṣepet* 1x capital (of a pillar) [6858]

[7639] 1 צַר *ṣar* 47x (n.) trouble, distress, anguish; (a.) narrow [6862]

[7640] 2 צַר *ṣar* 433x enemy, foe, adversary, opponent [6862] See *adversary; enemy; foe.*

[7641] 3 צַר *ṣar* 1x flint, known for its hardness [6862]

[7644] 1 צֹר *ṣōr* 5x flint knife [6864]

[7646] צָרַב *ṣārab* 1x [N] to be scorched [6866]

[7647] צָרָב *ṣārāb* 1x scorching [6867*]

[7648] צָרֶבֶת *ṣārebet* 2x scar [6867]

[7650] 1 צָרָה *ṣārâ* 70x trouble, distress, calamity, anguish [6869] See *distress; tribulation; trouble.*

[7651] 2 צָרָה *ṣārâ* 1x rival-wife [6869]

[7655] 1 צְרוֹר *ṣ^e^rôr* 7x pouch, purse, sachet, bag [6872]

[7656] 2 צְרוֹר *ṣ^e^rôr* 2x pebble [6872]

[7658] צָרַח *ṣāraḥ* 2x [Q] to shout, cry out; [H] to raise the battle cry [6873]

[7661] צֳרִי *ṣ^o^rî* 6x balm, mastic (resin), usually obtained from processing from the bark of a tree [6875]

[7663] צְרִיחַ *ṣ^e^rîaḥ* 4x pit, (underground) stronghold, likely referring to a man-made pit [6877]

[7664] צֹרֶךְ *ṣōrek* 1x need [6878]

[7665] צָרַע *ṣāraʿ* 20x [Qp, Pu] to be leprous, afflicted with an infectious skin disease [6879]

[7667] צִרְעָה *ṣirʿâ* 3x hornets or discouragement [6880]

[7669] צָרַעַת *ṣāraʿat* 35x infectious skin disease; (of clothing) mildew [6883]

[7671] צָרַף *ṣārap* 34x [Q] to smelt, refine (metals); (n.) (gold- or silver-)smith [6884] See *refine; smelt; test.*

[7672] צֹרְפִי *ṣōr^e^pî* 1x (member of the) goldsmiths [6885]

[7674] 1 צָרַר *ṣārar* 30x [Q] to bind up, wrap up, tie up; to hamper, oppress, be in distress; [Qp] be bound, be confined; [Pu] to be mended; [H] to bring trouble, distress, oppress [3334* & 6887]

[7675] 2 צָרַר *ṣārar* 26x [Q] to be a rival-wife; to be an enemy, adversary [6887]

[7683] קֵא *qēʾ* 1x vomit [6892]

[7684] קָאַת *qāʾat* 5x desert owl [6893]

[7685] קַב *qab* 1x cab (dry measure, one-eighteenth of an ephah, about one quart or liter) [6894]

[7686] קָבַב *qābab* 14x [Q] to curse [6895]

[7687] קֵבָה *qēbâ* 2x maw (4th stomach of cud-chewing animals); (of humans) belly, stomach area [6896 & 6897*]

[7688] קֻבָּה *qubbâ* 1x woman's section (of a tent) [6898]

[7689] קִבּוּץ *qibbûṣ* 1x collection (of idols) [6899]

[7690] קְבוּרָה *q^e^bûrâ* 14x tomb, grave, burial [6900]

[7691] קָבַל *qābal* 13x [P] to receive, take; [H] to match, correspond [6901]

[7692] קְבֹל *q^e^bōl* 2x (something) in front of, battering ram [6904* & 6905*]

[7693] קָבַע *qābaʿ* 6x [Q] to rob, plunder [6906]

[7694] קֻבַּעַת *qubbaʿat* 2x cup, goblet [6907]

[7695] קָבַץ *qābaṣ* 127x [Q] to collect, gather, assemble; [Qp] to be assembled; [N] to be gathered, be assembled, be joined; [P] to gather, assemble; [Pu] to be gathered; [Ht] to gather (themselves) together [6908] See *gather.*

[7697] קְבֻצָה *qᵉbuṣâ* 1x gathering [6910]

[7699] קָבַר *qābar* 133x [Q] to store up, pile up, heap up [6912] See *bury.*

[7700] קֶבֶר *qeber* 67x burial site, tomb, grave [6913] See *grave; tomb.*

[7702] קָדַד *qādad* 15x [Q] to bow low, bow down [6915]

[7703] קִדָּה *qiddâ* 2x cassia (a spice) [6916]

[7704] קְדוּמִים *qᵉdûmîm* 1x age-old, ancient [6917*]

[7705] קָדוֹשׁ *qādôš* 117x holy, sacred, consecrated, set apart as dedicated to God; by extension: pure, innocent, free from impurity; (n.) holy people of God, saints; as a title of God, "the Holy One" focuses on God as unique, wholly other [6918] See *holy; pure; sacred; saint.*

[7706] קָדַח *qādaḥ* 5x [Q] to kindle, light (a fire) [6919]

[7707] קַדַּחַת *qaddaḥat* 2x fever, inflammation [6920]

[7708] קָדִים *qādîm* 69x east, eastern, the direction of orientation in the ancient Near East (facing the sunrise); east is also the direction of the great desert, thus an east or desert wind is particularly hot [6921] See *east.*

[7709] קָדַם *qādam* 26x [P] to be in front of, meet, confront [6923]

[7710] קֶדֶם *qedem* 61x (as a direction) east, eastern; the direction of orientation in the ancient Near East (facing the sunrise); (used of time) ancient, eternal, long ago, possibly relating to east as the direction of origin (as the sunrise) [6924] See *ancient; east; long ago.*

[7711] קֵדְמָה *qēdem* 26x eastern, (toward the) east; see also 7710 [6924*]

[7712] קַדְמָה *qadmâ* 6x past, antiquity; ancient (city); see also 7710 [6927]

[7713] קִדְמָה *qidmâ* 4x east; see also 7710 [6926]

[7716] קַדְמוֹן *qadmôn* 1x eastern; see also 7710 [6930]

[7719] 1 קַדְמֹנִי *qadmōnî* 10x (of a direction) eastern; (of time) old, former, past; see also 7710 [6931]

[7721] קָדְקֹד *qodqōd* 12x top or crown of the head [6936]

[7722] קָדַר *qādar* 17x [Q] to grow dark, be black; to mourn, wail, grieve; [H] to make dark, bring gloom; [Ht] to grow dark [6937]

[7724] קִדְרוֹן *qidrôn* 11x Kidron [6939]

[7725] קַדְרוּת *qadrût* 1x darkness, blackness [6940]

[7726] קְדֹרַנִּית *qᵉdōrannît* 1x in mourner's attire, in an unkempt manner [6941]

[7727] קָדַשׁ *qādaš* 171x [Q] to be holy, sacred, consecrated; [N] to show oneself holy, be consecrated; [P] to consecrate, make holy; [Pu] to be dedicated, consecrated; [Ht] to consecrate oneself; [H] to set apart, consecrate, dedicate, regard as holy; to set apart as dedicated to God; by extension: pure, innocent, free from impurity [6942] See *consecrate; dedicate; make holy; sanctify; set apart.*

[7728] 1 קָדֵשׁ *qādēš* 11x (male or female) shrine prostitute [6945 & 6948*]

[7729] 2 קָדֵשׁ *qādēš* 14x Kadesh, "*sacred place*" [6946]

[7731] קֹדֶשׁ *qōdeš* 470x holy or sacred thing, holy or sacred place, sanctuary; holiness, set apart as dedicated to God; the "holy of holies" is the most holy place, set apart exclusively for the Presence of God, with very limited high priestly access; see also 7727 [6944] See *holiness; purity; sacredness.*

[7732] קָדֵשׁ בַּרְנֵעַ *qādēš barnēaʿ* 10x Kadesh Barnea, "*sacred place of Barnea*" [6947]

[7733] קָהָה *qāhâ* 4x [Q] to be dull, blunt (of teeth); [P] to be dull [6949]

[7735] קָהַל *qāhal* 39x [N] to be gathered, be assembled; [H] to summon, call together, cause to assemble [6950]

[7736] קָהָל *qāhāl* 123x assembly, community, often of Israel assembled for religious ceremony [6951] See *community; mob.*

[7737] קְהִלָּה *qᵉhillâ* 2x assembly, meeting [6952]

[7738] קֹהֶלֶת *qōhelet* 7x (as a title or name) the Teacher, one who calls together and instructs the assembly [6953]

[7740] קְהָת *qᵉhāt* 32x Kohath, Kohathite [6955]

[7742] קָו 1 *qāw* 20x measuring line, ruler [6957]

[7743] קָו 2 *qāw* 4x strange speech [6978*]

[7746] קֹובַע *qôbaʿ* 2x helmet [6959]

[7747] קָוָה 1 *qāwâ* 47x [Q] to hope in; [P] to hope for, wait for, look for [6960]

[7748] קָוָה 2 *qāwâ* 2x [N] to be gathered [6960]

[7752] קוּט *qûṭ* 7x [Q] to feel anger, loathing; [N] to feel loathing; [Htpolal] to loathe, abhor [5354* & 6962]

[7754] קוֹל *qôl* 505x sound, voice, noise [6963] See *noise; sound; voice.*

[7756] קוּם *qûm* 627x [Q] to get up, arise, stand, establish; [P] to establish, confirm, restore; [Pol] to raise up; [H] to set up, establish, restore; [Ho] to be set up, be raised up; [Htpol] to raise up against [6965] See *arise; establish; get up; raise up; rise; stand.*

[7757] קוֹמָה *qômâ* 45x height [6967]

[7758] קוֹמְמִיּוּת *qômᵉmiyyût* 1x (adv.) with head held high [6968]

[7761] קוֹף *qôp* 2x ape [6971]

[7762] קוּץ 1 *qûṣ* 8x [Q] to detest, be disgusted, loathe [6973]

[7763] קוּץ 2 *qûṣ* 1x [H] to tear apart [6972 & 6974]

[7764] קוֹץ 1 *qôṣ* 12x thorns, thornbush [6975]

[7767] קְוֻצּוֹת *qᵉwuṣṣôt* 2x (locks) of hair [6977*]

[7769] קוּר 1 *qûr* 2x [Q] to dig (a well or water hole) [6979]

[7770] קוּר 2 *qûr* 2x thread (of a spider cobweb) [6980]

[7771] קוֹרָה *qôrâ* 5x beam, pole, roof beams, tree [6982]

[7772] קוּשׁ *qûš* 1x [Q] to set a snare [6983*]

[7775] קַט *qaṭ* 1x little; soon (with 3869 & 5071) [6985*]

[7776] קֶטֶב *qeṭeb* 4x plague, destruction [6986 & 6987*]

[7778] קְטוּרָה *qᵉṭûrâ* 4x Keturah, "*incense, scented one*" [6989]

[7779] קָטַל *qāṭal* 3x [Q] to slay, kill [6991]

[7780] קֶטֶל *qeṭel* 1x slaughter [6993]

[7781] קָטֹן 1 *qāṭōn* 4x [Q] to be unworthy, not enough, trifling; [H] to make a (measure) small [6994]

[7782] קֹטֶן *qōṭen* 2x little finger; possibly a euphemism for penis [6995]

[7783] קָטָן 1 *qāṭān* 47x small (in size); few (in quantity); by extension, of status: lesser, insignificant; of age: young(est) [6996]

[7785] קָטֹן 2 *qāṭōn* 74x small (in size); by extension, of status: least, insignificant; of age: young(est) [6996] See *small; young.*

[7786] קָטַף *qāṭap* 5x [Q] to pick off (grain), break off (twigs); [N] to be picked off [6998]

[7787] קָטַר 1 *qāṭar* 115x [P] to burn an offering (of incense smoke); [Pu] to be perfumed; [H] to make a burned smoking offering; [Ho] to be burned as an offering [6999] See *burn.*

[7788] 2 קָטַר *qāṭar* 1x [Qp] to be enclosed [7000]

[7789] קִטֵּר *qiṭṭēr* 1x incense, often as or accompanying an offering to God [7002]

[7792] קְטֹרֶת *qᵉṭōret* 60x incense, smoke offering, its pleasant fragrance symbolic of God's acceptance [7004] See *incense.*

[7794] 1 קִיא *qîʾ* 9x [Q] to vomit; [H] to vomit out, spit out [6958 & 7006*]

[7795] 2 קִיא *qîʾ* 3x vomit [6892]

[7798] קִיטוֹר *qîṭôr* 4x smoke [7008]

[7799] קִים *qîm* 1x foe, adversary [7009]

[7800] קִימָה *qîmâ* 1x standing up [7012]

[7801] קִין *qîn* 8x [Pol] to chant a lament, sing a dirge [6969]

[7802] 1 קַיִן *qayin* 1x spearhead, spear [7013]

[7803] 2 קַיִן *qayin* 16x Cain, "*metal worker; brought forth, acquired Ge 4:1*" [7014]

[7806] 1 קִינָה *qînâ* 18x lament, mourning song, dirge [7015]

[7810] קִיץ *qîṣ* 23x [Q] to pass the summer; [H] to rouse, awaken [6974*]

[7811] קַיִץ *qayiṣ* 20x summer; by extension, summer fruit, ripe fruit [7019]

[7812] קִיצוֹן *qîṣôn* 4x end, outermost [7020]

[7813] קִיקָיוֹן *qîqāyôn* 5x caster-oil vine; some sources: cucumber plant [7021]

[7814] קִיקָלוֹן *qîqālôn* 1x disgrace [7022]

[7815] 1 קִיר *qîr* 73x wall (of a building or city); by extension, any surface of a construction: side, ceiling, surface; one who "urinates on a wall" is male [7023] See *wall.*

[7824] קַל *qal* 13x fleet-footed, swift, speedy [7031]

[7825] 1 קֹל *qōl* 1x lightness, (i.e., frivolity or light-heartedness) [6963]

[7828] 1 קָלָה *qālâ* 4x [Q] to burn; [Qp] to be roasted; [N] to have a burning sensation [7033]

[7829] 2 קָלָה *qālâ* 7x [N] to be lightly esteemed, to be a nobody, be degraded; [H] to dishonor, treat with contempt [7034]

[7830] קָלוֹן *qālôn* 17x shame, disgrace, dishonor [7036]

[7831] קַלַּחַת *qallaḥat* 2x caldron, (cooking) pot [7037]

[7832] קָלַט *qālaṭ* 1x [Qp] to be stunted [7038]

[7833] קָלִי *qālî* 5x roasted grain, parched grain [7039]

[7837] קָלַל *qālal* 82x [Q] to recede, grow smaller; to be vile, to disdain, despise; to be swift; [N] to be trivial, insignificant; to be swift; [P] to curse, blaspheme, revile; [Pu] to be accursed; [H] to lighten; to humble; to treat with contempt; [Htpal] to be shaken [7043] See *curse; despise; lighten; recede.*

[7838] קָלָל *qālāl* 1x burnished, polished [7044]

[7839] קְלָלָה *qᵉlālâ* 2x curse, condemnation [7045]

[7840] קָלַס *qālas* 33x [P] to scorn; [Ht] to make fun of [7046]

[7841] קֶלֶס *qeles* 4x derision, reproach [7047]

[7842] קַלָּסָה *qallāsâ* 3x laughingstock, object of derision [7048]

[7843] 1 קָלַע *qālaʿ* 1x [Q, P] to hurl a stone (from a sling) [7049]

[7844] 2 קָלַע *qālaʿ* 4x [Q] to carve [7049]

[7845] 1 קֶלַע *qelaʿ* 3x sling (a weapon) [7050]

[7846] 2 קֶלַע *qela*ʿ 6x curtains [7050]

[7847] קַלָּע *qallā*ʿ 15x slinger (one who uses a sling) [7051]

[7848] קְלֹקֵל *q*ᵉ*lōqēl* 1x miserable (food), starvation (rations) [7052]

[7849] קִלְּשׁוֹן *qill*ᵉ*šôn* 1x (sharp pointed, three-pronged) fork [7053]

[7850] קָמָה *qāmâ* 8x standing grain [7054]

[7853] קִמּוֹשׂ *qimmôś* 3x thorns, nettles, briers (weeds of all kinds) [7057* & 7063*]

[7854] קֶמַח *qemaḥ* 14x flour [7058]

[7855] קָמַט *qāmaṭ* 2x [Q] to seize; [Pu] to be seized [7059]

[7857] קָמַל *qāmal* 2x [Q] to wither [7060]

[7858] קָמַץ *qāmaṣ* 3x [Q] to take a handful [7061]

[7859] קֹמֶץ *qōmeṣ* 4x handful; (pl.) abundance [7062]

[7860] קֵן *qēn* 13x nest [7064]

[7861] קָנָא *qānā*ʾ 34x [P] (of negative attitude) to be jealous, be envious; (of positive attitude) to be zealous [7065]

[7862] קַנָּא *qannā*ʾ 6x jealous; an adjective or title used exclusively of God, focusing on his desire for exclusive relationships [7067]

[7863] קִנְאָה *qin*ᵉʾ*â* 43x jealousy, envy, zeal [7068]

[7864] 1 קָנָה *qānâ* 85x [Q] to buy, acquire, get; [N] to be bought [7069] See *buy; create; purchase; redeem.*

[7865] 2 קָנָה *qānâ* 6x [Q] to create, bring forth; (as a title of God) Creator [7069] See *buy; create; redeem.*

[7866] קָנֶה *qāneh* 62x branch, rod; (calamus) reed, stalk, shaft, cane; by extension: a measure of length, variously reckoned [7070] See *branch; reed; rod.*

[7868] קַנּוֹא *qannô*ʾ 2x jealous [7072]

[7871] קִנְיָן *qinyān* 11x goods, property, possessions [7075]

[7872] קִנָּמוֹן *qinnāmôn* 3x cinnamon (a spice from the far east) [7076]

[7873] קָנַן *qānan* 5x [P] to make a nest; [Pu] to be nestled, nested [7077]

[7874] קֶנֶץ *qeneṣ* 1x end, an extension of a snare or net that captures or restrains (not found in the OT) [7078]

[7876] קָסַם *qāsam* 20x [Q] to practice divination, be a soothsayer, seek an omen [7080]

[7877] קֶסֶם *qesem* 11x divination: pagan practice of determining the future by examining the position of stars, communication with the dead or with spirits, examining animal organs, or casting lots [7081]

[7878] קָסַס *qāsas* 1x [Pol] to strip off [7082]

[7879] קֶסֶת *qeset* 3x writing kit, writing-case [7083]

[7882] קַעֲקַע *qaʿ*ᵃ*qa*ʿ 1x tattoo [7085]

[7883] קְעָרָה *q*ᵉʿ*ārâ* 17x plate, dish [7086]

[7884] קָפָא *qāpā*ʾ 31x [Q, N] to congeal, thicken; [H] to curdle [7087]

[7885] קִפָּאוֹן *qippā*ʾ*ôn* 1x frost [7087*]

[7886] קָפַד *qāpad* 1x [P] to roll up [7088]

[7887] קִפֹּד *qippōd* 3x screech owl; some sources: hedgehog [7090]

[7888] קְפָדָה *q*ᵉ*pādâ* 1x terror, anguish [7089]

[7889] קִפּוֹז *qippôz* 1x owl; some sources: tree snake [7091]

[7890] קָפַץ *qāpaṣ* 7x [Q] to draw together, shut; [N] to be gathered up; [P] to bound, leap [7092]

[7891] קֵץ *qēṣ* 67x end, limit, boundary [7093] See *end; limit.*

[7892] קָצַב *qāṣab* 2x [Q] to cut off; [Qp] to be shorn, be cut off [7094]

[7893] קֶצֶב *qeṣeb* 3x shape, foundation [7095]

[7894] 1 קָצָה *qāṣâ* 4x [P] to cut off, reduce; [H] to scrape off [7096]

[7895] קָצֶה *qāṣeh* 92x end, limit, outskirts, edge [7097] See *edge; end; shore; uttermost.*

[7896] 2 קָצָה *qāṣâ* 35x end, fringe, edge [7098]

[7897] קֵצֶה *qēṣeh* 5x end, boundary, limit [7097]

[7898] קָצוּ *qāṣû* 3x ends, borders (of the earth) [7099*]

[7900] קָצוּר *qāṣûr* 1x narrow, short [7114*]

[7902] קֶצַח *qeṣaḥ* 3x caraway, cummin [7100]

[7903] קָצִין *qāṣîn* 12x commander, ruler, leader [7101]

[7904] 1 קְצִיעָה *qᵉṣîʿāh* 1x cassia [7102]

[7907] 1 קָצִיר *qāṣîr* 49x harvest, time of reaping [7105]

[7908] 2 קָצִיר *qāṣîr* 5x branch, bough, twig, shoot [7105]

[7909] 1 קָצַע *qāṣaʿ* 1x [H] to scrape off [7106]

[7910] 2 קָצַע *qāṣaʿ* 3x [Pu, Ho] to be made with corners [4742* & 7106]

[7911] קָצַף *qāṣap* 34x [Q] to be angry; [H] to provoke to anger; [Ht] to be enraged [7107]

[7912] 1 קֶצֶף *qeṣep* 28x wrath, anger, fury [7110]

[7913] 2 קֶצֶף *qeṣep* 1x twig (snapped off) [7110]

[7914] קְצָפָה *qᵉṣāpâ* 1x stump, splintering [7111]

[7917] 1 קָצַר *qāṣar* 34x [Q] to reap, harvest, gather [7114]

[7918] 2 קָצַר *qāṣar* 14x [Q] to be short; (by extension) to be impatient, angry; [P] to cut short; [H] to shorten, cut short [7114]

[7919] קֹצֶר *qōṣer* 1x discouragement, despondency, an extension of shortness or lack (of spirit) [7115]

[7920] קָצֵר *qāṣēr* 5x shortened: quick-tempered, impatient [7116]

[7921] קְצָת *qᵉṣāt* 7x end, extremity [7117]

[7922] קַר *qar* 3x cool, cold (water); cool-headed, even-tempered (of one's spirit) [7119]

[7923] קֹר *qōr* 1x cold [7120]

[7924] 1 קָרָא *qārāʾ* 739x [Q] to call, summon, announce, proclaim; [Qp] to be invited as a guest, be appointed; [N] to be called, be summoned; [Pu] to be called; "to call on the name of the LORD" means to proclaim or praise the excellence of Yahweh, to worship Yahweh, or to summon Yahweh by name for help [7121] See *call; proclaim; summon.*

[7925] 2 קָרָא *qārāʾ* 136x [Q] to meet, encounter, happen; [N] to have met, have happened; [H] to cause to happen [7122 & 7125*] See *against; deploy; encounter; happen; meet; toward.*

[7926] 1 קֹרֵא *qōrēʾ* 2x partridge [7124]

[7928] קָרַב *qārab* 280x [Q] to come near, approach; [N] to present oneself, be brought near; [P] to bring near, approach; [H] to bring near, offer, present [7126] See *approach; bring near; come near; draw near; offer; present.*

[7929] קָרֵב *qārēb* 12x approaching, coming near [7131]

[7930] קְרָב *qᵉrāb* 9x war, battle [7128]

[7931] קֶרֶב *qereb* 227x inner parts; by extension: heart or mind as the seat of thought and emotion; interior, midst; (pp.) among, in the midst of [7130] See *inmost being; inner parts; midst; within.*

[7932] קִרְבָה *qirbâ* 2x nearness, approach [7132*]

[7933] קָרְבָּן *qorbān* 80x gift, offering, sacrifice [7133] See *gift; offering.*

[7934] קֻרְבָּן *qurbān* 2x contribution, supply (of wood) [7133]

[7935] קַרְדֹּם *qardōm* 5x ax; some sources: adze [7134]

[7936] 1 קָרָה *qārâ* 27x [Q] to happen, meet, encounter; [N] to meet with, have happen; [P] to make beams, build beams; [H] to give success, to select oneself [7136]

[7937] קָרֶה *qāreh* 1x emission (at night) [7137]

[7938] 2 קָרָה *qārâ* 6x cold [7135]

[7940] קָרוֹב *qārôb* 75x near, close [7138] See *near.*

[7942] קָרַח *qāraḥ* 5x [Q] to shave, make bald; [N] to shave oneself, make oneself bald; [H] to shave another, make bald; [Ho] to be rubbed bare, be make bald [7139 & 7144*]

[7943] קֶרַח *qeraḥ* 7x ice, frost, hail [7140]

[7944] קֵרֵחַ *qērēaḥ* 3x bald, bald-headed [7142]

[7946] קֹרַח *qōraḥ* 37x Korah, "*shaven, bald*" [7141]

[7947] קָרְחָה *qorḥâ* 11x baldness, shaving the head [7146*]

[7949] קָרַחַת *qāraḥat* 4x bald spot (not the forehead area); bare spot (of articles) [7146]

[7950] קְרִי *qᵉrî* 7x hostile encounter, hostility [7147]

[7951] קָרִיא *qārîʾ* 2x summoned, called [7148]

[7952] קְרִיאָה *qᵉrîʾâ* 1x message, appeal [7150]

[7953] קִרְיָה *qiryâ* 29x city, town [7151]

[7961] קִרְיַת יְעָרִים *qiryat yᵉʿārîm* 19x Kiriath Jearim, "*city of timberlands*" [7157]

[7965] קָרַם *qāram* 2x [Q] to cover with, spread; [N] to be spread over [7159]

[7966] קָרַן *qāran* 4x [Q] to be radiant; [H] to be with horns [7160]

[7967] קֶרֶן *qeren* 76x horn, (pair) of horns; something made of horns: wind instrument, container; horn often symbolizes strength and status, as in "horn of salvation" [7161] See *corner; horn; point.*

[7970] קָרַס *qāras* 2x [Q] to stoop low, bend down [7164]

[7971] קֶרֶס *qeres* 10x clasp, hook (of curtains) [7165]

[7972] קַרְסֹל *qarsōl* 2x (dual) ankles [7166]

[7973] קָרַע *qāraʿ* 63x [Q] to tear, rend, rip; [Qp] to be torn; [N] to be torn to pieces, be split apart [7167] See *rend; rip; tear.*

[7974] קְרָעִים *qᵉrāʿîm* 0x torn pieces (of a garment), rags [7168*]

[7975] קָרַץ *qāraṣ* 4x [Q] to maliciously wink, purse (the lips); [Pu] to be shaped [7169]

[7976] קֶרֶץ *qereṣ* 5x gadfly; some sources: mosquito [7171]

[7977] 1 קַרְקַע *qarqaʿ* 1x floor [7172]

[7981] 1 קָרַר *qārar* 2x [H] to pour out or to keep cool [6979*]

[7982] 2 קָרַר *qārar* 1x [Pil] to tear down [6979*]

[7983] קֶרֶשׁ *qereš* 51x frame [7175] See *board; frame.*

[7984] קֶרֶת *qeret* 5x city, town [7176]

[7987] קַשְׂוָה *qaśwâ* 4x pitcher, jar [7184]

[7988] קְשִׂיטָה *qᵉśîṭâ* 3x piece of silver (unknown unit of weight or value) [7192]

[7989] קַשְׂקֶשֶׂת *qaśqeśet* 8x scales (as on skin of marine creatures); scale armor [7193]

[7990] קַשׁ *qaš* 16x stubble, chaff, straw [7179]

[7991] קִשֻּׁאָה *qiššuʾâ* 1x cucumber [7180*]

[7992] קָשַׁב *qāšab* 46x [Q] to listen; [H] to pay attention, give heed, listen [7181]

[7993] קֶשֶׁב *qešeb* 4x paying attention, responding [7182]

[7994] קַשָּׁב *qaššāb* 2x attentive [7183]

[7995] קַשֻּׁב *qaššub* 3x attentive [7183]

[7996] קָשָׁה *qāšâ* 29x [Q] to be hard, harsh, cruel; [N] to be distressed; [P] to have great difficulty (in labor); [H] to make stiff, harden, be difficult [7185]

[7997] קָשֶׁה *qāšeh* 36x hard, harsh, difficult, fierce; stubborn, stiff(-necked), obstinate [7186]

[7998] קָשַׁח *qāšaḥ* 1x [H] to harden [7188]

[7999] קֹשְׁטְ *qōšṭ* 1x true [7189]

[8000] קֹשֶׁט *qōšeṭ* 1x bow (weapon) [7189]

[8001] קְשִׁי *qᵉšî* 1x stubbornness [7190]

[8003] קָשַׁר *qāšar* 44x [Q] to tie, bind; to plot, conspire; [Qp] to be bound up; be strong; [N] to be joined with; [P] to bind; [Pu] to be strong; [Ht] to conspire together [7194]

[8004] קֶשֶׁר *qešer* 16x conspiracy, treason [7195]

[8005] קִשֻּׁרִים *qiššurîm* 2x sashes, wedding ornaments [7196*]

[8006] 1 קָשַׁשׁ *qāšaš* 8x [Q] to gather together; [Pol] to gather; [Htpol] to gather together [7197]

[8008] קֶשֶׁת *qešet* 76x bow (weapon); by extension, something bow shaped: rainbow [7198] See *bow.*

[8009] קַשָּׁת *qaššāt* 1x archer [7199]

[8011] 1 רָאָה *rāʾâ* 1,311x [Q] to see, look, view; to realize, know, consider; [Qp] to be selected; [N] to become visible, appear, show oneself; [Pu] to be seen; [H] to cause to see, show; [Ho] to be shown; [Ht] to look at each other, meet with; a general word for visual perception; note the many contextual translations in the NIV [7200 & 7202*] See *appear; consider; look; perceive; see.*

[8012] 2 רָאָה *rāʾâ* 1x red kite [7201]

[8014] 1 רֹאֶה *rōʾeh* 12x seer [7203]

[8015] 2 רֹאֶה *rōʾeh* 1x vision [7203]

[8017] רְאוּבֵן *rᵉʾûbēn* 72x Reuben, "*see, a son! [Ge 29:32]; substitute a son*" [7205]

[8018] רְאוּבֵנִי *rᵉʾûbēnî* 18x Reubenite, of Reuben, "*of Reuben*" [7206]

[8019] רַאֲוָה *raʾᵃwâ* 1x spectacle, sight [7207]

[8021] רְאוּת *rᵉʾût* 1x look [7200*]

[8023] רְאִי *rᵉʾî* 1x mirror [7209]

[8024] רֳאִי *rᵒʾî* 4x appearance, spectacle [7210]

[8027] רָאַם *rāʾam* 1x [Q] to rise up high [7213]

[8028] רְאֵם *rᵉʾēm* 9x wild oxen [7214]

[8029] 1 רָאמוֹת *rāʾmôt* 2x coral [7215*]

[8031] 1 רֹאשׁ *rōʾš* 600x head (of the body); by extension: top (of an object); high in status or authority: leader, chief; source or origin: first, beginning; "to lift up the head" can mean to take a census, to behead, or to restore to a position [7218 & 7226*] See *beginning; chief; company; division; head; headwater; leader; top.*

[8032] 2 רֹאשׁ *rōʾš* 12x poison; gall; bitterness [7219]

[8033] 3 רֹאשׁ *rōʾš* 1x Rosh, "*head, leader*" [7220]

[8036] רֹאשָׁה *rōʾšâ* 1x uppermost, cap[stone] [7222]

[8037] רִאשׁוֹן *riʾšôn* 182x (of position) first, foremost; (of time) former, beginning, earlier [7223] See *before; beginning; early; first; former; previous.*

[8038] רִאשֹׁנִי *riʾšōnî* 1x first [7224]

[8040] רֵאשִׁית *rēʾšît* 51x what is first; beginning [7225] See *beginning; firstfruits.*

[8041] 1 רַב *rab* 419x many, much; great, abundant, numerous [7227]

[8042] 2 רַב *rab* 33x commander, chief officer, high official [7227]

[8043] 3 רַב *rab* 3x archer [7228]

[8044] רֹב *rōb* 150x greatness, abundance; multitude [7230] See *abundance; great; many; multitude; numerous.*

[8045] 1 רָבַב *rābab* 20x [Q] to abound, increase, be great; [Pu] to increase by tens of thousands [7231]

[8046] 2 רָבַב *rābab* 1x [Q] to shoot (an arrow) [7232]

[8047] רְבָבָה *rᵉbābâ* 16x ten thousand, myriad; (virtually) countless number [7233]

[8048] רָבַד *rābad* 1x [Q] to cover [7234]

[8049] 1 רָבָה *rābâ* 229x [Q] to increase in number, multiply, grow large; [P] to rear (offspring); to gain; make numerous; [H] to cause to increase, make numerous, enlarge [7235] See *increase; multiply.*

[8050] 2 רָבָה *rābâ* 1x [Q] to shoot; (ptcp.) archer [7235]

[8052] רִבּוֹא *ribbôʾ* 10x ten thousand; myriad, (virtually) countless number [7239]

[8053] רְבִיבִים *rᵉbîbîm* 6x rain shower, abundant rain, gentle rain [7241*]

[8054] רָבִיד *rābîd* 3x necklace, ornamental chain [7242]

[8055] רְבִיעִי *rᵉbîʿî* 55x fourth [7243] See *fourth; quarter.*

[8057] רָבַךְ *rābak* 3x [Ho] to be kneaded, mixed (of dough) [7246]

[8061] 1 רָבַע *rābaʿ* 4x [Q] to lie down with, have sexual relations with; [H] to mate, cross-breed [7250 & 7252* & 7254*]

[8062] 2 רָבַע *rābaʿ* 12x [Qp, P] to be squared, have four corners [7251]

[8063] 1 רֶבַע *rebaʿ* 7x fourth-part, quarter; side (of a square thing) [7253]

[8065] 1 רֹבַע *rōbaʿ* 2x fourth-part, quarter [7255]

[8067] רִבֵּעַ *ribbēaʿ* 4x fourth; (n.) the fourth generation [7256]

[8069] רָבַץ *rābaṣ* 30x [Q] to lie down; [H] to make lie down; to cause to rest [7257]

[8070] רֵבֶץ *rēbeṣ* 4x resting place [7258]

[8071] רִבְקָה *ribqâ* 30x Rebekah, "[poss.] *choice calf*" [7259]

[8072] רַב־שָׁקֵה *rab-šāqēh* 6x Assyrian officer: (field) commander, cupbearer [7262*]

[8073] רֶגֶב *regeb* 2x clod of dirt [7263]

[8074] רָגַז *rāgaz* 41x [Q] to quake, shake, tremble; to be angry, be in anguish; [H] to cause to shake, make tremble, cause a disturbance; [Ht] to enrage oneself (against) [7264]

[8075] רֹגֶז *rōgez* 7x turmoil, excitement, tumult [7267]

[8076] רַגָּז *raggāz* 11x anxious, trembling [7268]

[8077] רָגְזָה *rogzâ* 1x shuddering, agitation [7269]

[8078] רָגַל *rāgal* 26x [Q] to slander; [P] to spy, explore [7270 & 8637*]

[8079] רֶגֶל *regel* 251x foot; by extension, body parts associated with the foot: sole, legs, big toe, ankle; a euphemism for the genitals; footing or base of an object; footstep, as a measure of length [7272] See *foot; leg.*

[8081] רַגְלִי *raglî* 12x (persons) on foot (i.e., not riding) [7273]

[8083] רָגַם *rāgam* 16x [Q] to execute by hurling stones [7275]

[8086] רִגְמָה *rigmâ* 1x great throng, crowd, a bustling, noisy group [7277]

[8087] רָגַן *rāgan* 7x [Q] to complain; [N] to be grumbling, be gossiping [5372* & 7279]

[8088] 1 רָגַע *rāgaʿ* 7x [Q] to stir up, churn up; [H] to do something in an instant [7280]

[8089] 2 רָגַע *rāgaʿ* 5x [N] to cease; [H] to find repose, bring rest [7280]

[8090] 3 רָגַע *rāgaʿ* 1x [Q] to harden, crust over [7280]

[8091] רָגֵעַ *rāgēaʿ* 1x quiet, resting [7282]

[8092] רֶגַע *regaʿ* 22x moment, instant; peace, tranquillity [7281]

[8093] רָגַשׁ *rāgaš* 1x [Q] to be restless, be in tumult, likely referring to a rebellious conspiracy [7283]

[8094] רֶגֶשׁ *regeš* 1x throng [7285]

[8095] רִגְשָׁה *rigšâ* 1x crowd, throng [7285]

[8096] רָדַד *rādad* 2x [Q] to subdue, beat down; [H] to hammer out flat [7286]

[8097] 1 רָדָה *rādâ* 23x [Q] to rule over; [H] to cause to dominate [7287]

[8098] 2 רָדָה *rādâ* 2x [Q] to scoop out, scrape out [7287]

[8100] רְדִיד *r^edîd* 2x cloak, shawl, something wrapped around [7289]

[8101] רָדַם *rādam* 7x [N] to be in a heavy sleep [7290]

[8103] רָדַף *rādap* 144x [Q] to pursue, chase, persecute; [N] to be pursued, be hounded; [P] to pursue, chase; [Pu] to be chased; [H] to chase [7291] See *follow after; persecute; pursue.*

[8104] רָהַב *rāhab* 4x [Q] to rise up against; press one's plea; [H] to overwhelm; make bold [7292]

[8105] רַהַב *rahab* 6x Rahab, a sea monster of chaos that opposes God; used of the land of Egypt, with a focus on affliction or arrogance [7293 & 7294]

[8107] רָהָב *rāhāb* 1x proud, defiant [7295]

[8110] 1 רַהַט *rahaṭ* 3x watering trough [7298]

[8111] 2 רַהַט *rahaṭ* 1x truss, rafter [7298]

[8112] רָהִיט *rāhîṭ* 1x rafters [7351*]

[8113] רוּד *rûd* 4x [Q] to roam; [H] to grow restless, cause restlessness [7300]

[8115] רָוָה *rāwâ* 14x [Q] to drink to satisfaction, quench the thirst; [P] to drench, refresh, satisfy; [H] to lavish upon, cause to refresh; from the base meaning of quenching thirst come the fig. extensions of refreshment, satisfaction, and fulfillment [7301]

[8116] רָוֶה *rāweh* 4x well-watered, drenched [7302]

[8118] רָוַח *rāwaḥ* 3x [Q] to feel relief; [Pu] to be spacious [7304]

[8119] רֶוַח *rewaḥ* 2x relief; space [7305]

[8120] רוּחַ *rûaḥ* 378x breath, wind; by extension: spirit, mind, heart, as the immaterial part of a person that can respond to God, the seat of life; spirit being, especially the Spirit of God [7307] See *breath; life; patience, (be) patient; spirit; wind.*

[8121] רְוָחָה *r^ewāḥâ* 2x relief, respite [7309]

[8122] רְוָיָה *r^ewāyâ* 2x place of abundance, overflowing [7310]

[8123] 1 רוּם *rûm* 197x [Q] to be high, raise up; to be proud, haughty; [Pol] to exalt, lift high; [Polal] to be exalted, be lifted up; [H] to cause to lift up, present (an offering); to raise up against, rebel; [Ho] to be presented, be taken away; to exalt oneself; from the base meaning of being high in spatial position come the fig. extensions of being high in status: exalted, and high in attitude: proud, arrogant [7311] See *exalt; lift up.*

[8124] 2 רוּם *rûm* 6x height; haughtiness, pride [7312]

[8125] רוֹם *rôm* 1x on high [7315]

[8127] רוֹמָה *rômâ* 1x proudly, haughtily [7317]

[8128] רוֹמָם *rômām* 2x praise, exaltation [7318]

[8129] רוֹמֵמֻת *rômēmut* 1x rising up, lifting up [7319* & 7427*]

[8130] רוּן *rûn* 1x [Htpol] to awake from a stupor, become sober [7442*]

[8131] רוּעַ *rûa*ᶜ 45x [H] to raise a battle cry; sound a trumpet blast; shout in triumph or exaltation [7321]

[8132] רוּץ *rûṣ* 104x [Q] to run, hurry, be a messenger; [Pol] to dart about, run to and fro; [H] to chase; to bring quickly [7323] See *run; rush.*

[8133] רוּשׁ *rûš* 23x [Q] to be poor, be in poverty, be oppressed; [Htpol] to pretend to be poor [7326]

[8134] רוּת *rût* 12x Ruth, "*friendship; refreshed [as with water]*; [poss.] *comrade, companion*" [7327]

[8135] רָזָה *rāzâ* 2x [Q] to destroy; [N] to waste away [7329]

[8136] רָזֶה *rāzeh* 2x lean; barren [7330]

[8137] 1 רָזוֹן *rāzôn* 3x wasting disease; short, scrimped (ephah) [7332]

[8138] 2 רָזוֹן *rāzôn* 1x prince, dignitary [7333]

[8140] רָזִי *rāzî* 2x wasting away, leanness [7334]

[8141] רָזַם *rāzam* 1x [Q] to wink, flash the eyes [7335]

[8142] רָזַן *rāzan* 6x [Q] to be a ruler; (ptcp.) a prince, ruler [7336]

[8143] רָחַב *rāḥab* 25x [Q] to be wide; to swell (with joy); to boast; [N] to be roomy, be broad; [H] to enlarge, broaden, make wide [7337]

[8144] רַ֫חַב *raḥab* 2x spacious place, vast expanse [7338]

[8145] רֹ֫חַב *rōḥab* 103x breadth, width [7341] See *breadth; broad; wide, width.*

[8146] 1 רָחָב *rāḥāb* 21x spacious, broad, roomy [7342]

[8148] 1 רְחֹב *r*ᵉ*ḥōb* 43x public square, open street [7339]

[8154] רְחַבְעָם *r*ᵉ*ḥab*ᶜ*ām* 50x Rehoboam, "*[my] people will enlarge, expand*" [7346]

[8157] רַחוּם *raḥûm* 13x compassionate, merciful [7349]

[8158] רָחוֹק *rāḥôq* 84x far, distant; (n.) distance, afar [7350] See *distant; far.*

[8160] רֵחַיִם *rēḥayim* 5x handmill; pair of mill stones [7347*]

[8161] 1 רָחֵל *rāḥēl* 4x ewe-sheep [7353]

[8162] 2 רָחֵל *rāḥēl* 47x Rachel, "*ewe*" [7354]

[8163] רָחַם *rāḥam* 47x [Q] to love; [P] to have compassion on, show mercy, take pity on; [Pu] to find compassion, be loved; feelings of compassion are usually accompanied by acts of compassion [7355]

[8164] רָחָם *rāḥām* 1x carrion-vulture; some sources: osprey [7360]

[8167] רֶ֫חֶם *reḥem* 31x womb; by extension: mother, any female, birth; an "open womb" is able to conceive; a "closed womb" cannot conceive [7358]

[8168] רָחָמָה *rāḥāmâ* 1x carrion-vulture; some sources: osprey [7360]

[8169] רַחֲמָה *raḥ*ᵃ*mâ* 1x womb; slang for woman [7361]

[8172] רַחֲמָנִי *raḥ^{a}mānî* 1x compassionate [7362]

[8173] 1 רָחַף *rāḥap* 3x [Q] to tremble, shake; [P] to hover [7363]

[8175] רָחַץ *rāḥaṣ* 72x [Q] to wash, bathe; [Pu] to be cleansed; [Ht] to wash oneself [7364] See *bathe; cleanse.*

[8176] רַחַץ *raḥaṣ* 2x washing [7366]

[8177] רַחְצָה *raḥṣâ* 2x washing [7367]

[8178] רָחַק *rāḥaq* 59x [Q] to be far off; to avoid, stand aloof; [P] to send far away, extend; [H] to remove far away, drive far off, go very far [7368] See *distant; far; remove.*

[8179] רָחֵק *rāḥēq* 1x one who is far away [7369]

[8180] רָחַשׁ *rāḥaš* 1x [Q] to be stirred up (one's heart) [7370]

[8181] רַחַת *raḥat* 1x winnowing fork, shovel [7371]

[8182] רָטַב *rāṭab* 1x [Q] to be drenched, be wet [7372]

[8183] רָטֹב *rāṭōb* 1x well-watered (plant) [7373]

[8185] רֶטֶט *reṭeṭ* 1x panic [7374]

[8186] רֻטֲפַשׁ *ruṭ^{a}paš* 1x [Qp] to be renewed [7375]

[8187] רָטַשׁ *rāṭaš* 6x [P] to dash to pieces; [Pu] to be dashed to pieces [7376*]

[8188] רִי *ri* 1x moisture [7377]

[8189] 1 רִיב *rîb* 72x [Q] to quarrel, contend, plead for [7378] See *contend; defend; plead; present; quarrel; take up.*

[8190] 2 רִיב *rîb* 62x contention, grievance, strife, legal dispute [7379] See *case; cause; dispute; lawsuit; strife.*

[8191] רִיבָה *rîbâ* 2x legal plea [7379*]

[8193] רִיחַ *rîaḥ* 11x [H] to smell (an aroma or odor) [7306*]

[8194] רֵיחַ *rêaḥ* 58x aroma; pleasing and acceptable: fragrance; unpleasing and unacceptable: stench; both connotations are used of sacrifices as accepted or rejected by God [7381] See *aroma; fragrance; odor; smell.*

[8195] רִיפוֹת *rîpôt* 2x grain [7383*]

[8197] 1 רִיק *riq* 19x [H] to pour forth, empty out; to draw (a sword) [7324*]

[8198] 2 רִיק *rîq* 12x emptiness, nothingness, vanity [7385]

[8199] רֵיק *rêq* 14x empty; idle, worthless [7386]

[8200] רֵיקָם *rêqām* 16x empty-handed, without cause or satisfaction [7387]

[8201] 1 רִיר *rîr* 1x [Q] to flow [7325*]

[8202] 2 רִיר *rîr* 2x saliva; white (of an egg); some sources: a kind of plant juice [7388]

[8203] רֵישׁ *rêš* 7x poverty [7389]

[8204] רֹךְ *rōk* 1x gentleness, tenderness, softness [7391]

[8205] רַךְ *rak* 18x gentle, tender, weak, soft [7390]

[8206] רָכַב *rākab* 78x [Q] to ride or mount a riding animal [7392] See *drive; mount; ride.*

[8207] רֶכֶב *rekeb* 120x chariot; large upper mill stone [7393] See *chariot; millstone.*

[8208] רַכָּב *rakkāb* 3x chariot driver, horseman [7395]

[8210] רִכְבָּה *rikbâ* 1x act of riding [7396]

[8213] רְכוּב *r^{e}kûb* 1x chariot [7398]

[8214] רְכוּשׁ *r^{e}kûš* 28x possessions, property, goods, equipment [7399]

[8215] רָכִיל *rākîl* 6x slanderer, gossip [7400]

[8216] רָכַךְ *rākak* 6x [Q] to be soft, faint-hearted; [Pu] to be soothed; [H] to make faint [7401]

[8217] רָכַל *rākal* 17x [Q] to do trade, act as a merchant; (n.) trader, merchant [7402]

[8219] רְכֻלָּה *rekullâ* 4x trading of merchandise [7404]

[8220] רָכַס *rākas* 2x [Q] to tie, bind [7405]

[8221] רֶכֶס *rekes* 1x rugged place [7406]

[8222] רֹכֶס *rōkes* 1x intrigue, plot, conspiracy [7407]

[8223] רָכַשׁ *rākaš* 5x [Q] to tie, bind [7408]

[8224] רֶכֶשׁ *rekeš* 4x team of horses; fast horses (for couriers) [7409]

[8227] 1 רָמָה *rāmâ* 4x [Q] to hurl (horse and rider); to shoot (arrows) [7411]

[8228] 2 רָמָה *rāmâ* 8x [P] to deceive, betray [7411]

[8229] 3 רָמָה *rāmâ* 5x lofty shrine; height [7413]

[8230] 4 רָמָה *rāmâ* 36x Ramah; Ramoth, "*elevated spot, height*" [7414]

[8231] רִמָּה *rimmâ* 7x worm, maggot [7415]

[8232] 1 רִמּוֹן *rimmôn* 32x pomegranate: the tree, its fruit, or decorative objects shaped like the fruit [7416]

[8239] רָמוּת *rāmût* 1x remains, refuse, rubbish [7419]

[8240] רָמוֹת גִּלְעָד *rāmôt gilʿād* 20x Ramoth Gilead, "*heights in Gilead*" [7433]

[8242] רֹמַח *rōmaḥ* 15x spear [7420]

[8244] 1 רְמִיָּה *remiyyâ* 7x laziness, laxness, slackness [7423]

[8245] 2 רְמִיָּה *remiyyâ* 8x deceit [7423]

[8247] רַמָּכָה *rammākâ* 1x fast mare [7424*]

[8249] 1 רָמַם *rāmam* 1x [Q] to be full of maggots, be wormy [7311*]

[8250] 2 רָמַם *rāmam* 5x [Q] to be exalted; [N] to rise upward; to get away [7426]

[8252] רָמַס *rāmas* 19x [Q] to trample, tread upon; [N] to be trampled [7429]

[8253] רָמַשׂ *rāmaś* 17x [Q] to move along (ground or in the water) [7430]

[8254] רֶמֶשׂ *remeś* 17x creatures that move along (ground or sea) [7431]

[8260] רֹן *rōn* 1x (joyful) song [7438]

[8261] רָנָה *rānâ* 1x [Q] to rattle [7439]

[8262] 1 רִנָּה *rinnâ* 33x shout of joy, song of joy; cry of pleading [7440]

[8264] רָנַן *rānan* 53x [Q] to shout for joy, sing for joy; to cry, plead; [P] to sing for joy; [Polal] to sing for joy; [H] to make sing, call for songs of joy [7442 & 7444*] See *cry out; shout; sing.*

[8265] רְנָנָה *renānâ* 4x shout of joy, joyful song [7445]

[8266] רְנָנִים *renānîm* 1x female ostrich [7443*]

[8268] 1 רָסִיס *rāsîs* 1x drop (of moisture) [7447]

[8269] 2 רָסִיס *rāsîs* 1x broken piece (of rubble) [7447]

[8270] 1 רֶסֶן *resen* 4x bridle [7448]

[8272] רָסַס *rāsas* 1x [Q] to moisten, sprinkle [7450]

[8273] 1 רַע *raʿ* 312x bad, disagreeable, inferior in quality; by extension: evil, wicked in ethical quality; what is disagreeable to God is ethically evil; God's actions of judgment are disagreeable to the wicked (Eze 14:21), but are not ethically evil [7451] See *bad; corrupt; destruction; disaster; evil; ugly; wicked, wickedness.*

[8275] 1 רֵעַ *rēaʿ* 3x shouting, roar [7452]

[8276] 2 רֵעַ *rēaʿ* 188x neighbor; friend, companion, associate [7453] See *friend; neighbor; other.*

[8277] 3 רֵעַ *rēaʿ* 2x thought, intention [7454]

[8278] רֹעַ *rōaʿ* 19x bad, disagreeable, inferior in quality; by extension: evil, wicked in ethical quality [7455]

[8279] 1 רָעֵב *rāʿēb* 13x [Q] to be hungry, be famished, be starving [7456]

[8280] רָעָב *rāʿāb* 101x hunger, famine, starvation [7457* & 7458] See *famine; hunger; starvation.*

[8281] 2 רָעֵב *rāʿēb* 20x hungry [7456]

[8282] רְעָבוֹן *reʿābôn* 3x hunger, famine, starvation [7459]

[8283] רָעַד *rāʿad* 3x [Q, H] to tremble [7460]

[8284] רַעַד *raʿad* 2x trembling [7461]

[8285] רְעָדָה *reʿādâ* 4x trembling [7461]

[8286] 1 רָעָה *rāʿâ* 167x [Q] to be a shepherd, to care for flocks, graze; by extension: to rule, with a focus on care and concern [7473*] See *feed; graze; shepherd; tend.*

[8287] 2 רָעָה *rāʿâ* 5x [Q] to be a companion, be a friend; [P] to be an attendant of the groom (of a wedding) [7462]

[8288] 3 רָעָה *rāʿâ* 354x bad, disaster, harm, trouble; by extension: ethical evil, wickedness; what is "bad" to God is ethically evil; God's actions of judgment are "bad" to the wicked (Jer 18:8), but are not ethically evil [7465*] See *calamity; disaster; evil; trouble; wicked, wickedness; wrongdoing.*

[8291] רֵעֶה *rēʿeh* 4x friend, personal advisor [7463]

[8292] רֵעָה *rēʿâ* 3x companion, friend [7464]

[8295] 1 רְעוּת *reʿût* 6x (female) neighbor; fellow (female) [7468]

[8296] 2 רְעוּת *reʿût* 7x chasing after [7469]

[8297] רְעִי *reʿî* 1x pastured (cattle) [7471]

[8299] רַעְיָה *raʿyâ* 9x darling, beloved, formally, companion, a woman who is the object of a man's love and affection [7474]

[8301] רַעְיוֹן *raʿyôn* 3x chasing after, striving for [7475]

[8302] רָעַל *rāʿal* 2x [Ho] to be made to quiver [7477]

[8303] רַעַל *raʿal* 1x reeling [7478]

[8304] רְעָלָה *reʿālâ* 1x veil [7479*]

[8306] 1 רָעַם *rāʿam* 11x [Q] to storm, thunder; [H] to make thunder, make storm [7481]

[8307] 2 רָעַם *rāʿam* 2x [Q] to be confused, distorted; [H] to irritate, agitate [7481]

[8308] רַעַם *raʿam* 6x thunder; thunderous shout [7482]

[8310] 1 רַעְמָה *raʿmâ* 1x mane (of a horse) [7483]

[8315] רָעַן *rāʿan* 1x [Palel] to flourish [7488*]

[8316] רַעֲנָן *raʿanān* 19x spreading (tree), verdant, luxuriant [7488]

[8317] 1 רָעַע *rāʿaʿ* 95x [Q] to be distressed, be displeased; (by extension) to be bad, be evil; [N] to suffer harm; [H] to do wickedness; bring trouble, mistreat; this refers to what is displeasing from a personal perspective; what is displeasing to God is ethically evil [7489] See *afflict; bad; evil.*

[8318] 2 רָעַע *rāʿaʿ* 6x [Q] to break, shatter; [Htpol] to come to ruin [7489]

[8319] רָעַף *rāʿap* 5x [Q] to drop, fall, overflow; [H] to cause to rain [7491]

[8320] רָעַץ *rāʿaṣ* 2x [Q] to shatter [7492]

[8321] 1 רָעַשׁ *rāʿaš* 30x [Q] to shake, quake, tremble; [N] to be made to quake; [H] to cause to shake, make to tremble [7493]

[8323] רַ֫עַשׁ *raʿaš* 17x commotion, rattling, earthquake; this can mean a quaking motion and the sounds from a quaking motion; by extension: any clamor, discord, or frenzy [7494]

[8324] 1 רָפָא *rāpāʾ* 69x [Q] to heal; [N] to be healed, be cured; [P] to heal, repair; [Ht] to recover [7495] See *cure; heal; restore.*

[8326] רִפְאוּת *ripʾût* 1x health, healing [7500]

[8327] 1 רְפָאִים *rᵉpāʾîm* 8x dead, the spirits of the departed [7496*]

[8331] רָפַד *rāpad* 3x [Q] to spread (mud, so as to leave a trail); [P] to spread out; to refresh [7502]

[8332] 1 רָפָה *rāpâ* 46x [Q] to hang limp, sink down, be feeble; [N] to be lazy; [P] to lower; discourage; [H] to leave alone, abandon, withdraw; [Ht] to show oneself slack [7503]

[8333] רָפֶה *rāpeh* 4x weak, feeble [7504]

[8337] רְפוּאָה *rᵉpûʾâ* 3x healing [7499]

[8339] רְפִידָה *rᵉpîdâ* 1x base (of a royal carriage); some sources: seat cover [7507]

[8342] רִפָּיוֹן *rippāyôn* 1x hanging limp, possibly referring to despair [7510]

[8343] רַפְסֹדוֹת *rapsōdôt* 1x (log) rafts [7513*]

[8344] רָפַף *rāpap* 1x [Poal] to quake, shake [7322*]

[8345] רָפַק *rāpaq* 1x [Ht] to lean oneself (upon) [7514]

[8346] רָפַשׂ *rāpaś* 5x [Q] to muddy (a stream by trampling through); [N] to be muddied; [Ht] to be humbled, humble oneself [7511* & 7515]

[8347] רֶ֫פֶשׁ *repeš* 1x mire (of the sea) [7516]

[8348] רֶ֫פֶת *repet* 1x stall, enclosure for cattle [7517]

[8349] רַץ *raṣ* 1x bar (of silver) [7518]

[8351] 1 רָצָא *rāṣāʾ* 1x [Q] to run forth [7519]

[8353] רָצַד *rāṣad* 1x [P] to gaze in hostility [7520]

[8354] 1 רָצָה *rāṣâ* 52x [Q] to be pleased, delight in, accept; [Qp] to be favored, be esteemed; [N] to be accepted; [H] to enjoy; [Ht] to regain favor [7521]

[8355] 2 רָצָה *rāṣâ* 4x [Q] to pay for (sin); [N] to be paid for; [P] to make amends [7521]

[8356] רָצוֹן *rāṣôn* 56x pleasure, acceptance, favor, will [7522] See *acceptable, accepted; delight; desire; favor; goodwill; please; pleasing; pleasure; will; wish.*

[8357] רָצַח *rāṣaḥ* 47x [Q] to murder, kill; [N] to be murdered, killed; [P] to murder, kill [7523]

[8358] רֶ֫צַח *reṣaḥ* 1x slaughter, murder, agony of death [7524]

[8361] רָצַע *rāṣaʿ* 11x [Q] to pierce (ear) [7527]

[8362] רָצַף *rāṣap* 1x [Qp] to be inlaid, be fitted [7528]

[8363] 1 רֶ֫צֶף *reṣep* 1x hot coals, live coals [7529]

[8365] 1 רִצְפָּה *riṣpâ* 2x live coal, hot coal [7531]

[8367] רִצְפָה *riṣᵉpâ* 4x (stone) pavement [7531]

[8368] רָצַץ *rāṣaṣ* 7x [Q] break, smash, oppress; [Qp] to be smashed, broken, splintered, oppressed; [N] to be broken, splintered; [P] to oppress, crush; [H] to crush to pieces; [Htpol] to jostle each other [7533]

[8369] 1 רַק *raq* 20x lean, thin, lank [7534]

[8370] 2 רַק *raq* 3x only, but, however, except [7535]

[8371] רֹק *rōq* 109x spit, saliva; "to swallow one's spit" means a very brief time [7536]

[8372] רָקַב *rāqab* 3x [Q] to rot, become worm-eaten [7537]

[8373] רָקָב *rāqāb* 2x rottenness, decay [7538]

[8376] רָקַד *rāqad* 9x [Q] to skip, dance; [P] to leap about, dance; [H] to make skip [7540]

[8377] רַקָּה *raqqâ* 5x temple (of the head) [7541]

[8379] רָקַח *rāqaḥ* 8x [Q] to make perfume, mix spices; [Pu] to be blended (of perfume); [H] to mix spices [7543]

[8380] רֶקַח *reqaḥ* 1x (powdered) spice [7544]

[8381] רֹקַח *rōqaḥ* 2x fragrant blend, spice-blend [7545]

[8382] רַקָּח *raqqāḥ* 1x perfume-maker, ointment-mixer [7546]

[8383] רִקֻּחַ *riqquaḥ* 1x perfume, ointment [7547]

[8384] רַקָּחָה *raqqāḥâ* 1x perfume-maker, ointment-mixer [7548]

[8385] רָקִיעַ *rāqîaʿ* 17x expanse (of the sky or heaven); the space above the earth that holds visible objects: clouds, planets, stars [7549]

[8386] רָקִיק *rāqîq* 8x wafer, (thin, flat) cake [7550]

[8387] רָקַם *rāqam* 9x [Q] to embroider, weave colored thread; [Pu] to be woven together [7551]

[8391] רִקְמָה *riqmâ* 12x embroidered work; varied colored things [7553]

[8392] רָקַע *rāqaʿ* 11x [Q] to spread out; stamp upon, trample; [P] to hammer out thin, overlay (with precious metal); [Pu] to be hammered, be beaten thin; [H] to cause to spread out, make into plated metal [7554]

[8393] רִקֻּעַ *riqquaʿ* 1x sheet, something beaten thin [7555]

[8394] רָקַק *rāqaq* 1x [Q] to spit saliva [7556]

[8397] רִשְׁיוֹן *rišyôn* 1x authorization, permission [7558]

[8398] רָשַׁם *rāšam* 1x [Qp] to be written, be inscribed [7559]

[8399] רָשַׁע *rāšaʿ* 34x [Q] to do evil, act wickedly; to be guilty; [H] to declare guilty, condemn, inflict punishment; to do wrong [7561]

[8400] רֶשַׁע *rešaʿ* 30x evil, wickedness, wrongdoing [7562]

[8401] רָשָׁע *rāšāʿ* 264x wicked, evil, guilty [7563] See *evil; guilty; wicked, wickedness.*

[8402] רִשְׁעָה *rišʿâ* 15x wickedness [7564]

[8404] רֶשֶׁף 1 *rešep* 7x flame [7565]

[8406] רָשַׁשׁ *rāšaš* 2x [Pol] to destroy, shatter; [Pu] to be crushed, shattered [7567]

[8407] רֶשֶׁת *rešet* 22x net, snare, trap (for catching game); network (net-like metal grating) [7568]

[8408] רַתּוֹק *rattôq* 1x chain [7569]

[8409] רָתַח *rātaḥ* 3x [P] to bring to a boil; [Pu] to be caused to churn; [H] to make to churn [7570]

[8410] רֶתַח *retaḥ* 1x boiling [7571]

[8411] רַתִּיקָה *rattîqâ* 1x chain [7572]

[8412] רָתַם *rātam* 1x [Q] to tie up, harness (horse team) [7573]

[8413] רֹתֶם *rōtem* 4x broom tree [7574]

[8415] רָתַק *rātaq* 1x [Pu] to be bound with chains [7576]

[8416] רְתֻקוֹת r^e*tuqôt* 1x chains [7577*]

[8417] רְתֵת r^e*tēt* 1x trembling, fright [7578]

[8419] שְׂאֹר *śᵉʾōr* 5x yeast, leaven [7603]

[8420] 1 שְׂאֵת *śᵉʾēt* 7x splendor, honor, loftiness, acceptance [7613]

[8421] 2 שְׂאֵת *śᵉʾēt* 7x swelling [7613]

[8422] שְׂבָכָה *śᵉbākâ* 16x network, lattice, interwoven mesh [7638 & 7639]

[8425] שָׂבַע *śābaʿ* 97x [Q] to be satisfied, have enough, be satiated; the filling and even overfilling of appetites and desires [7646] See *(have) enough; (be) filled; (be) satisfied.*

[8426] שָׂבָע *śābāʿ* 8x abundance, overflowing [7647]

[8427] שֹׂבַע *śōbaʿ* 7x one's fill to contentment, all one wants [7648]

[8428] שָׂבֵעַ *śābēaʿ* 10x full, abounding [7649]

[8429] שָׂבְעָה *śābʿâ* 4x abundance, satisfaction, enough [7654]

[8430] שִׂבְעָה *śibʿâ* 1x abundance, plenty [7653]

[8431] 1 שָׂבַר *śābar* 2x [Q] to examine [7663]

[8432] 2 שָׂבַר *śābar* 6x [P] to wait for, hope for [7663]

[8433] שֵׂבֶר *śēber* 2x hope [7664]

[8434] שָׂגָא *śāgāʾ* 2x [H] to make great, extol [7679]

[8435] שָׂגַב *śāgab* 20x [Q] to be too strong for; [N] to be lofty, be exalted; [P] to lift high; to protect; [Pu] to be kept safe; [H] to act exalted [7682]

[8436] שָׂגָה *śāgâ* 4x [Q] to be prosperous, thrive, grow; [H] to increase (in wealth) [7685]

[8438] שַׂגִּיא *śaggîʾ* 2x exalted [7689]

[8440] שָׂדַד *śādad* 3x [P] to till, harrow, break up the ground [7702]

[8441] שָׂדֶה *śādeh* 329x area of land, usually cultivated: field, open country, countryside [7704] See *field; land; wild.*

[8442] שָׂדַי *śāday* 13x field; see also 8441 [7704]

[8444] שְׂדֵרָה *śᵉdērâ* 4x ranks, rows; planks (architectural term) [7713]

[8445] שֶׂה *śeh* 47x sheep, lamb [7716 & 2089*]

[8446] שָׂהֵד *śāhēd* 1x witness [7717]

[8448] שַׂהֲרֹנִים *śahᵃrōnîm* 3x ornamental crescent (or moon shaped) necklace [7720]

[8449] שׂוֹבֶךְ *śôbek* 1x tangle of branches [7730]

[8451] 2 שׂוּג *śûg* 1x [Pil] to cause growth, raise [7735]

[8452] שׂוּחַ *śûaḥ* 1x [Q] to meditate [7742]

[8453] שַׂוְחָט *śawḥāṭ* 1x see 8821 [**]

[8455] שׂוּךְ *śûk* 2x [Q] to block with thorn hedges [7753]

[8456] שׂוֹךְ *śôk* 1x branch or brushwood [7754]

[8457] שׂוֹכָה *śôkâ* 1x branch or brushwood [7754]

[8461] שׂוּמָה *śûmâ* 1x intention [7760*]

[8464] שׂוּשׂ *śûś* 1x [Q] to rejoice, be pleased, be delighted [7797]

[8465] שֵׂחַ *śēaḥ* 27x thoughts [7808]

[8466] שָׂחָה *śāḥâ* 3x [Q] to swim; [H] to make swim, flood [7811]

[8467] שָׂחוּ *śāḥû* 1x water deep enough to swim in [7813]

[8468] שְׂחוֹק *śᵉḥôq* 15x laughter, which can communicate joy or ridicule; object of ridicule: laughingstock [7814]

[8469] שָׂחַט *śāḥaṭ* 1x [Q] to squeeze out (juice from grapes) [7818]

[8470] שָׂחִיף *śāḥîp* 1x covered, paneled [7824]

[8471] שָׂחַק *śāḥaq* 36x [Q] to laugh, be amused; to laugh at, mock, scoff; [P] to celebrate, rejoice, frolic; [H] to scorn; this can communicate joy or ridicule [7832]

[8473] שֵׂט *śēṭ* 1x rebel [7846]

[8474] שָׂטָה *śāṭâ* 6x [Q] to go astray [7847]

[8475] שָׂטַם *śāṭam* 6x [Q] to hold a grudge, hold hostility toward [7852]

[8476] שָׂטַן *śāṭan* 6x [Q] to accuse, slander [7853]

[8477] שָׂטָן *śāṭān* 27x (human) adversary, accuser, one who opposes, slanderer; (as a proper name) Satan, the spirit being who is an opponent of God and slanderer of his creation [7854]

[8478] 1 שִׂטְנָה *śiṭnâ* 1x accusation [7855]

[8480] שִׂיא *śîʾ* 1x height [7863]

[8482] שִׂיב *śîb* 2x [Q] to be gray(-haired); hence, old [7867]

[8483] שֵׂיב *śêb* 1x gray-headedness, old age [7869]

[8484] שֵׂיבָה *śêbâ* 19x gray-haired (person), old age [7872]

[8485] שִׂיג *śîg* 1x busyness; perhaps: bowel movement [7873]

[8486] 1 שִׂיד *śîd* 2x [Q] to coat with (a whitewash) plaster [7874]

[8487] 2 שִׂיד *śîd* 4x lime, plaster (used as a whitewash) [7875]

[8488] 1 שִׂיחַ *śîaḥ* 21x [Q] to meditate, muse on, consider, think on [7878]

[8489] 2 שִׂיחַ *śîaḥ* 4x bush, shrub [7880]

[8490] 3 שִׂיחַ *śîaḥ* 13x complaint, lament [7879]

[8491] שִׂיחָה *śîḥâ* 3x meditation [7881]

[8492] שִׂים *śîm* 588x [Q] to place, put, establish, appoint; [Qp] to be placed, set upon; [H] to cause to place, put; [Ho] to be set [7760 & 7787*] See *make; place; put; set; take; turn.*

[8493] שֵׂךְ *śēk* 1x barb, splinter, thorn [7899]

[8494] שֹׂךְ *śōk* 1x dwelling place [7900]

[8496] שֻׂכָּה *śukkâ* 1x harpoon [7905]

[8498] שֶׂכְוִי *śekwî* 1x mind; some sources: mist [7907]

[8500] שְׂכִיָּה *śᵉkiyyâ* 1x marine vessel, ship [7914]

[8501] שַׂכִּין *śakkîn* 1x knife [7915]

[8502] שָׂכִיר *śākîr* 18x hired worker, servant under contract [7916 & 7917*]

[8503] 1 שָׂכַךְ *śākak* 2x [Q] to cover (with the purpose to hide or screen) [5526*]

[8505] 1 שָׂכַל *śākal* 60x [Q] to have success; [H] to have insight, wisdom, understanding; to prosper, successful; the potent capacity to understand and so exercise skill in life, a state caused by proper training and teaching, enhanced by careful observation [7919] See *prosper; understand; (be) wise.*

[8506] 2 שָׂכַל *śākal* 1x [P] to cross (the hands and arms in an extended motion) [7919]

[8507] שֶׂכֶל *śekel* 16x understanding, wisdom, discretion; see also 8505 [7922]

[8508] שִׂכְלוּת *śiklût* 1x folly [5531]

[8509] שָׂכַר *śākar* 20x [Q] to hire; [Qp] to be hired; [N] to hire oneself; [Ht] to earn wages for oneself [7936]

[8510] 1 שָׂכָר *śākār* 28x wage, reward [7939]

[8512] שֶׂכֶר *śeker* 2x wage, reward [7938]

[8513] שְׂלָו *śᵉlāw* 4x quail [7958]

[8515] 1 שַׂלְמָה *śalmâ* 16x clothing, garment, cloak, robe [8008]

[8520] שְׂמֹאל *śᵉmōʾl* 54x left (opposite of right); north [8040 & 8041*] See *left; north.*

[8521] שִׂמְאֵל *śimʾēl* 5x [H] to go to the left; be left-handed [8041*]

[8522] שְׂמָאלִי *śᵉmāʾlî* 9x on the left; northern [8042]

[8523] שָׂמַח *śāmaḥ* 156x [Q] to rejoice, be glad, delight in [8055] See *delight; gladden; gloat; joy; rejoice.*

[8524] שָׂמֵחַ *śāmēaḥ* 20x rejoicing, gladness, delight [8056]

[8525] שִׂמְחָה *śimḥâ* 94x joy, gladness, pleasure, delight [8057] See *gladness; happiness; joy; pleasure; rejoicing.*

[8526] שְׂמִיכָה *śᵉmîkâ* 1x covering [8063]

[8529] שִׂמְלָה *śimlâ* 29x clothing, garment, cloak [8071]

[8531] שָׂמַם *śāmam* 1x [H] to paint or perfume [**]

[8532] שְׂמָמִית *śᵉmāmît* 1x lizard; some sources: gecko [8079]

[8533] שָׂנֵא *śānēʾ* 148x [Q] to hate, be an enemy; [Qp] to be unloved; [N] to be hated, be shunned; [P] to be an adversary, be a foe; "hate" can be active, as an enemy or adversary; or passive, as someone unloved or shunned [8130] See *abhor; despise; dislike; hate.*

[8534] שִׂנְאָה *śinʾâ* 17x hatred, malice [8135]

[8535] שָׂנִיא *śānîʾ* 1x not loved, disdained [8146]

[8537] 1 שָׂעִיר *śāʿîr* 3x hairy, shaggy [8163] See *hairy.*

[8538] 2 שָׂעִיר *śāʿîr* 52x male goat [8163] See *goat.*

[8539] 3 שָׂעִיר *śāʿîr* 2x goat idol [8163] See *goat.*

[8540] 4 שָׂעִיר *śāʿîr* 1x rain shower [8164]

[8541] 1 שֵׂעִיר *śēʿîr* 35x Seir, "*hairy, shaggy, covered with trees;* [poss.] *the place of the goats* or *the place of Esau [Ge 25:25 BDB]; small forest, rich forest*" [8165]

[8544] 1 שְׂעִירָה *śᵉʿîrâ* 2x female goat [8166]

[8546] שְׂעִפִּים *śᵉʿippîm* 2x disquieted thoughts, troubled thoughts [5587*]

[8547] 1 שָׂעַר *śāʿar* 3x [Q] to shudder, bristle with horror [8175]

[8548] 2 שָׂעַר *śāʿar* 4x [Q] to sweep away (by the wind); [N] to be in a storm; [P] to sweep away (by a wind); [Ht] to storm against [8175]

[8549] 3 שָׂעַר *śāʿar* 1x [Q] to know about, be acquainted with [8175]

[8550] 1 שַׂעַר *śaʿar* 3x horror, shudder, an extension of the bristling of hair (in excitement or fear) [8178]

[8551] 2 שַׂעַר *śaʿar* 1x wind storm, gale [8178]

[8552] שֵׂעָר *śēʿār* 28x hair [8181]

[8553] שַׂעֲרָה *śaʿᵃrâ* 7x hair [8185]

[8554] שְׂעָרָה *śᵉʿārâ* 2x storm, gale [8183]

[8556] שְׂעֹרִים *śᵉʿōrîm* 1x Seorim, "*one born at the time of the barley [harvest]*" [8188]

[8557] שָׂפָה *śāpâ* 178x lips (of the mouth); by extension: speech, language; edge of an object, rim, border; the "lip of the sea" is the seashore [8193] See *bank (of a river); edge; language; lip; shore; speech.*

[8558] שָׂפַח *śāpaḥ* 1x [P] to bring sores, make scabby [5596]

[8559] שָׂפָם *śāpām* 5x (the area of the) mustache; lower part of the face [8222]

[8561] שָׂפַן *śāpan* 1x [Qp] to be hidden [8226]

[8562] 1 שָׂפַק *śāpaq* 2x [Q] to clap one's hands (in derision); [H] to clasp hands [5606]

[8563] 2 שָׂפַק *śāpaq* 1x [Q] to be enough [5606]

[8565] שֵׂפֶק *śēpeq* 1x plenty, sufficiency [5607]

[8566] שַׂק *śaq* 48x sackcloth; sack [8242]

[8567] שָׂקַד *śāqad* 1x [N] to be bound [8244]

[8568] שָׂקַר *śāqar* 1x [P] to flirt, ogle (with the eyes) [8265]

[8569] שַׂר *śar* 421x ruler of various spheres (military, religious, governmental): commander, official, prince, chief, leader; "Prince of Peace" is a title of the child who would rule on David's throne, referring to the Messiah [8269] See *chief; leader; official; prince.*

[8571] שָׂרַג *śārag* 2x [Pu] to be close-knit, be intertwined; [Ht] to be woven together [8276]

[8572] שָׂרַד *śārad* 1x [Q] to run away, escape [8277]

[8573] שְׂרָד *śᵉrād* 4x woven material (with some kind of braiding woven in it) [8278]

[8574] שֶׂרֶד *śered* 1x marker (for wood chiseling) [8279]

[8575] 1 שָׂרָה *śārâ* 3x [Q] to struggle, contend [8280]

[8576] 2 שָׂרָה *śārâ* 5x woman of nobility, lady of royal birth, queen [8282]

[8577] 3 שָׂרָה *śārâ* 38x Sarah, "*princess*" [8283]

[8579] שְׂרוֹךְ *śᵉrôk* 2x thong (of a sandal) [8288]

[8581] שָׂרַט *śāraṭ* 3x [Q] to make a cut, incise the skin; [N] to make oneself incised, cut oneself [8295]

[8582] שֶׂרֶט *śereṭ* 1x cut, incision [8296]

[8583] שָׂרֶטֶת *śāreṭet* 1x cut, incision; this may refer to a tattoo [8296]

[8584] שָׂרַי *śāray* 17x Sarai, "*princess*" [8297]

[8585] שָׂרִיג *śārîg* 3x branch, tendril (of grape vines and fig trees) [8299]

[8586] 1 שָׂרִיד *śārîd* 28x survivor; those left [8300]

[8591] שָׂרִיק *śārîq* 1x combed (flax, as a first step for making linen) [8305*]

[8592] שָׂרַךְ *śārak* 1x [P] to run here and there (aimlessly) [8308]

[8594] שָׂרַע *śāraʿ* 3x [Qp] to be deformed; [Ht] to stretch oneself [8311]

[8595] שַׂרְעַפִּים *śarʿappîm* 2x anxiety, anxious thoughts [8312]

[8596] שָׂרַף *śārap* 117x [Q] to burn, set a fire; [Qp, N, Pu] to be burned up [8313]

[8597] 1 שָׂרָף *śārāp* 7x venomous snake; seraph (six-winged being) [8314]

[8599] שְׂרֵפָה *śᵉrēpâ* 13x burning [8316]

[8601] 1 שָׂרֹק *śārōq* 1x brown, dark red (color of grapes) [8320*]

[8602] 2 שָׂרֹק *śārōq* 1x choice vines [8291*]

[8603] 1 שֹׂרֵק *śōrēq* 2x choice vines [8321]

[8605] שְׂרֵקָה *śᵉrēqâ* 1x choice vine [8322]

[8606] שָׂרַר *śārar* 7x [Q] to rule, govern; [H] to choose a prince; [Ht] to act out as a ruler [7786* & 8323]

[8607] שָׂשׂוֹן *śāśôn* 22x joy, gladness [8342]

[8608] שָׂתַם *śātam* 1x [Q] to shut out, obstruct [5640]

[8609] שָׂתַר *śātar* 1x [N] to be broken out (with tumors) [8368]

[8611] -שֶׁ *ša-* 140x who, that, because [7945*]

[8612] שָׁאַב *šāʾab* 19x [Q] to draw and carry water [7579]

[8613] שָׁאַג *šāʾag* 20x [Q] to roar [7580]

[8614] שְׁאָגָה *šᵉʾāgâ* 7x roar, groan [7581]

[8615] 1 שָׁאָה *šā'â* 4x [Q] to lie wasted; [N] to be ruined; [H] to turn into desolation [7582]

[8616] 2 שָׁאָה *šā'â* 2x [N] to roar [7582]

[8617] 3 שָׁאָה *šā'â* 1x [Ht] to watch closely, gaze at [7583]

[8619] שְׁאוֹל *š^e'ôl* 65x grave; by extension, realm of death, deepest depths, transliterated "Sheol" [7585] See *netherworld; Sheol.*

[8620] שָׁאוּל *šā'ûl* 406x Saul, Shaul, "*asked,* [poss.] *dedicated to God*" [7586]

[8622] 1 שָׁאוֹן *šā'ôn* 1x waste, desolation; a slime pit that may refer to Sheol (8619) [7588]

[8623] 2 שָׁאוֹן *šā'ôn* 17x roar, uproar, tumult, loud noise [7588]

[8624] שְׁאָט *š^e'āṭ* 3x malice [7589]

[8625] שְׁאִיָּה *š^e'iyyâ* 1x desolation, ruin [7591]

[8626] שָׁאַל *šā'al* 176x [Q] to ask, inquire, request; [Qp] to be given over; [N] to ask permission; [P] to ask intently, beg; [H] to give what is asked for [7592] See *ask; inquire.*

[8629] שְׁאֵלָה *š^e'ēlâ* 13x petition, request [7596]

[8631] שָׁאַן *šā'an* 5x [Palpal] to be at ease, be at rest, be secure [7599]

[8633] שַׁאֲנָן *ša'^anān* 10x at ease, complacent, secure; insolent, proud [7600]

[8634] 1 שָׁאַף *šā'ap* 11x [Q] to pant after, long for, pursue [7602]

[8635] 2 שָׁאַף *šā'ap* 3x [Q] to trample, crush [7602]

[8636] שָׁאַר *šā'ar* 133x [Q] to remain; [N] to be left, remain; [H] to leave, spare [7604] See *left; remain; survive.*

[8637] שְׁאָר *š^e'ār* 25x remainder, remnant, the rest [7605]

[8638] שְׁאֵר *š^e'ēr* 18x flesh, meat; by extension: the body as a whole; blood relative, as one's "flesh and blood" [7607]

[8642] שְׁאֵרִית *š^e'ērît* 66x remnant, remainder, the rest [7611] See *remainder; remnant.*

[8643] שֵׁאת *šē't* 1x ruin, desolation [7612]

[8646] שְׁבָבִים *š^ebābîm* 1x broken pieces, splinters [7616]

[8647] שָׁבָה *šābâ* 46x [Q] to take captive; [Qp, N] to be taken captive [7617]

[8648] שְׁבוֹ *š^ebô* 2x agate (exact identification is uncertain) [7618]

[8651] שָׁבוּעַ *šābûʿa* 20x week (a time period of seven); Feast of Weeks, a festival celebrating the first produce of the harvest; a unit of time used in the book of Daniel, possibly a "week" of seven years [7620]

[8652] שְׁבוּעָה *š^ebûʿâ* 29x sworn oath [7621]

[8653] שָׁבוּר *šābûr* 1x injury (by fracture) [7665*]

[8654] שְׁבוּת *š^ebût* 24x captivity, exile; fortunes [7622]

[8655] 1 שָׁבַח *šābah* 9x [P] to glorify, commend, extol; [Ht] to glory in [7623]

[8656] 2 שָׁבַח *šābaḥ* 3x [P] to keep still; [H] to cause stillness [7623]

[8657] שֵׁבֶט *šēbeṭ* 190x rod, staff, a stick used to assist in walking, discipline, and guidance, often highly individualized and used for identification; of royalty: scepter; by extension: tribe, as a major unit of national group or clan (fig. identified with or under authority of a leader's staff), people, clan, family [7626] See *rod; scepter; tribe.*

[8660] שְׁבִי *š^ebî* 48x captivity, exile; captive, prisoner [7628]

[8663] שָׁבִיב *šābîb* 1x flame; some sources: spark [7632]

[8664] שִׁבְיָה *šibyâ* 9x captive, prisoner; captivity [7633]

[8665] שְׁבִיָּה *šᵉbiyyâ* 1x captive [7628*]

[8666] שְׁבִיל *šᵉbîl* 2x way, path [7635*]

[8667] שָׁבִיס *šābîs* 1x headband [7636]

[8668] שְׁבִיעִי *šᵉbîʿî* 98x seventh [7637] See *seven; seventh.*

[8669] שְׁבִית *šᵉbît* 8x captivity; fortune [7622]

[8670] שֹׁבֶל *šōbel* 1x skirt, hem of skirt [7640]

[8671] שַׁבְּלוּל *šabbᵉlûl* 1x slug, snail; some sources: miscarriage [7642]

[8672] 1 שִׁבֹּלֶת *šibbōlet* 16x head of grain [7641]

[8673] 2 שִׁבֹּלֶת *šibbōlet* 3x flood, torrent, flow [7641]

[8678] שָׁבַע *šābaʿ* 186x [N] to swear an oath, make a sworn promise; [H] to make one swear an oath, give a charge [7650] See *swear; take an oath.*

[8679] 1 שֶׁבַע *šebaʿ* 490x seven; (pl.) seventy [7651] See *seven; seventy.*

[8685] שִׁבְעָנָה *šibʿānâ* 1x seven [7658]

[8687] שָׁבַץ *šābaṣ* 2x [P] to weave; [Pu] to be woven (of fine metal), (n.) a filigree setting [7660]

[8688] שָׁבָץ *šābāṣ* 1x seizure, cramp, referring to death throes [7661]

[8689] 1 שָׁבַר *šābar* 148x [Q] to break, destroy, crush; [Qp] to be broken; [N] to be destroyed, be smashed, be broken; [P] to break, smash, shatter; [H] to bring to break through (of birth); [Ho] to be crushed [7665] See *break.*

[8690] 2 שָׁבַר *šābar* 21x [Q] to buy grain or food; [H] to sell, allow to buy grain [7666]

[8691] 1 שֶׁבֶר *šeber* 44x destruction, brokenness, injury; "destruction of spirit" is discouragement, and so lacking motivation and being faint-hearted [7667]

[8692] 2 שֶׁבֶר *šeber* 9x grain [7668]

[8694] שֶׁבֶר *šeber* 1x interpretation (of a dream) [7667]

[8695] שִׁבָּרוֹן *šibbārôn* 2x destruction, brokenness [7670*]

[8696] שְׁבָרִים *šᵉbārîm* 1x stone quarry [7671]

[8697] 1 שָׁבַת *šābat* 71x [Q] to rest, observe the Sabbath; [N] to come to an end, disappear; [H] to put to an end, stop [7673] See *cease; end; rest; stop.*

[8699] 1 שֶׁבֶת *šebet* 6x place of sitting or settling, site, seat [7675]

[8700] 2 שֶׁבֶת *šebet* 2x cessation, doing-nothing [7674]

[8701] שַׁבָּת *šabbāt* 111x Sabbath, the seventh day of the week in the Hebrew calendar (modern Saturday) with a focus of this day as a day of rest and worship; by extension: sabbath, any day or year or period of rest [7676] See *Sabbath.*

[8702] שַׁבָּתוֹן *šabbātôn* 11x (day of) rest [7677]

[8704] שָׁגַג *šāgag* 4x [Q] to err unintentionally, go astray [7683]

[8705] שְׁגָגָה *šᵉgāgâ* 19x unintentional wrong, accidental error [7684]

[8706] שָׁגָה *šāgâ* 21x [Q] to sin unintentionally, go astray, wander [7686]

[8708] שָׁגַח *šāgaḥ* 3x [H] to gaze, stare [7688]

[8709] שְׁגִיאָה *šᵉgîʾâ* 1x error, mistake [7691]

[8711] שָׁגַל *šāgal* 4x [Q] to ravish, sexually violate; [Qp, N, Pu] to be ravished, be raped [7693]

[8712] שֵׁגַל *šēgal* 2x queen, royal bride [7694]

[8713] שָׁגַע *šāgaʿ* 7x [Pu] to be mad, act like a maniac; [Ht] to carry on like a madman [7696]

[8714] שִׁגָּעוֹן *šiggāʿôn* 3x madness [7697]

[8715] שֶׁגֶר *šeger* 5x calf, offspring (of cattle) [7698]

[8716] שַׁד *šad* 21x (female) breast [7699]

[8717] שֵׁד *šēd* 2x demon, evil spirit [7700]

[8718] 1 שֹׁד *šōd* 3x (female) breast [7699]

[8719] 2 שֹׁד *šōd* 24x destruction, ruin, violence [7701]

[8720] שָׁדַד *šādad* 59x [Q] to devastate, devastate; [Qp] to be destroyed; [H] to be ruined; [P, Pol] to ravage, destroy; [Pu] to be destroyed, be ruined; [Ho] to be ruined [7703 & 7736*] See *destroy; devastate.*

[8721] שִׁדָּה *šiddâ* 2x lady, concubine; (pl.) harem [7705]

[8724] שַׁדַּי *šadday* 48x Almighty [7706] See *Almighty.*

[8727] שְׁדֵמָה *š^e^dēmâ* 5x (cultivated) field; terrace [7709]

[8728] שָׁדַף *šādap* 3x [Qp] to be scorched [7710]

[8729] שְׁדֵפָה *š^e^dēpâ* 2x scorching [7711]

[8730] שִׁדָּפוֹן *šiddāpôn* 5x blight [7711]

[8732] 1 שֹׁהַם *šōham* 1x onyx (exact identification is uncertain) [7718]

[8736] שָׁוְא *šāwʾ* 54x worthlessness, vanity, falseness [7723] See *falseness; futility; vain; worthless.*

[8738] שׁוֹא *šôʾ* 1x ravage [7722]

[8739] שׁוֹאָה *šôʾâ* 12x trouble, ruin, disaster, desolation [7722]

[8740] 1 שׁוּב *šûb* 1,075x [Q] to turn back, turn to, return; [Qp] to return; [Pol] to restore, bring back; [Polal] to be recovered; [H] to restore, recover, bring back; [Ho] to be returned, be brought back; from the base meaning of turning back comes the fig. extension of restoration of relationship, as when one returns in repentance to God [7725] See *repent, repentance; restore; return; turn.*

[8743] 1 שׁוֹבָב *šôbāb* 3x faithless, rebellious, apostate [7726]

[8745] שׁוֹבֵב *šôbēb* 3x unfaithful, traitorous, apostate [7728]

[8746] שׁוּבָה *šûbâ* 1x returning, i.e., repentance [7729]

[8750] 1 שָׁוָה *šāwâ* 14x [Q] to be like, be equal; to be appropriate, be deserved; [N] to be like; [P] to make smooth; [H] to liken; to count as equal [7737]

[8751] 2 שָׁוָה *šāwâ* 7x [P] to set, place, bestow [7737]

[8755] 1 שׁוּחַ *šûaḥ* 1x [Q] sink down [7743]

[8757] 1 שׁוּחָה *šûḥâ* 5x pit, rift [7745]

[8763] 1 שׁוּט *šûṭ* 13x [Q] to roam, go about; to oar (a boat); [Pol] to wander, go here and there; [Htpol] to rush here and there [7751]

[8764] 2 שׁוּט *šûṭ* 3x [Q] to malign, act malicious [7590*]

[8765] 1 שׁוֹט *šôṭ* 11x whip, lash [7752]

[8767] שׁוּל *šûl* 11x hem (of a robe); skirt [7757]

[8768] שׁוֹלָל *šôlāl* 3x barefoot, stripped [7758*]

[8770] שׁוּמִים *šûmîm* 12x garlic [7762]

[8775] שָׁוַע *šāwaʿ* 22x [P] to cry for help, plead [7768]

[8776] שֶׁוַע *šewaʿ* 1x cry for help [7773]

[8777] 1 שׁוֹעַ *šôʿa* 2x highly respected, noble; (n.) the rich [7771]

[8779] 3 שׁוֹעַ *šôʿa* 1x crying out [7771]

[8780] 1 שׁוּעַ *šûʿa* 1x cry for help [7769]

[8782] 3 שׁוּעַ *šûʿa* 1x wealth [7769]

[8784] שַׁוְעָה *šawʿâ* 11x cry for help [7775]

[8785] 1 שׁוּעָל *šûʿāl* 7x fox; jackal [7776]

[8788] שׁוֹעֵר *šôʿēr* 37x gatekeeper, doorkeeper [7778]

[8789] 1 שׁוּף *šûp* 2x [Q] to crush; some sources: bruise, a wound that is not fatal [7779]

[8790] 2 שׁוּף *šûp* 1x [Q] to strike [7779]

[8795] שׁוֹפָר *šôpār* 72x trumpet, ram's horn [7782] See *trumpet.*

[8796] 1 שׁוּק *šûq* 3x [H] to prove narrow, overflow; [Polel] to water abundantly [7783]

[8797] שׁוֹק *šôq* 19x (lower) thigh; leg [7785]

[8798] 2 שׁוּק *šûq* 4x street [7784]

[8799] שֹׁקֵק *šôqēq* 4x thirsty, unquenched [8264*]

[8800] 1 שׁוּר *šûr* 2x [Q] to see, look, view [7789]

[8801] 2 שׁוּר *šûr* 14x [Q] to travel, descend [7788]

[8802] שׁוֹר *šôr* 79x bull, ox [7794] See *bull; ox.*

[8803] 3 שׁוּר *šûr* 3x wall [7791]

[8805] שׁוּרָה *šûrâ* 1x supporting wall (of a terrace) [7791*]

[8806] שׁוֹרֵר *šôrēr* 6x enemy, adversary [8324*]

[8808] 1 שׁוּשַׁן *šûšan* 17x lily plant; some sources: lotus plant [7799]

[8809] 2 שׁוּשַׁן *šûšan* 21x Susa [7800]

[8812] שָׁזַף *šāzap* 3x [Q] to see; to be darkened [7805]

[8813] שָׁזַר *šāzar* 21x [Ho] to be finely twisted [7806]

[8814] שַׁח *šaḥ* 1x downward, bent, low [7807]

[8815] שָׁחַד *šāḥad* 2x [Q] to give a gift; pay a bribe; pay a ransom [7809]

[8816] שֹׁחַד *šōḥad* 23x bribe, gift [7810*]

[8817] שָׁחָה *šāḥâ* 2x [Q] to bow down; [H] to weigh down, cause to bow [7812]

[8818] שְׁחוֹר *šeḥôr* 1x soot [7815]

[8819] שְׁחוּת *šeḥût* 1x trap, pit [7816]

[8820] שָׁחַח *šāḥaḥ* 18x [Q] to bow down, bend low; [N] to be brought low; [H] to humble, bring low [7817]

[8821] 1 שָׁחַט *šāḥaṭ* 81x [Q] to slaughter, kill; [Qp, N] to be killed, be slaughtered [7819] See *kill; slaughter.*

[8822] 2 שָׁחַט *šāḥaṭ* 5x [Qp] to be hammered, beaten; some sources: to be alloyed, blended, referring to the mixing of metals [7819 & 7820]

[8823] שַׁחֲטָה *šaḥăṭâ* 1x slaughter [7819*]

[8824] שְׁחִיטָה *šeḥîṭâ* 1x killing, slaughter [7821]

[8825] שְׁחִין *šeḥîn* 13x boils, skin sores [7822]

[8826] שָׁחִיס *šāḥîs* 1x growth, what springs up [7823]

[8827] שְׁחִית *šeḥît* 2x pit, trap, grave [7825]

[8828] שַׁחַל *šaḥal* 7x lion [7826]

[8829] שְׁחֵלֶת *šeḥēlet* 1x onycha (a fragrant spice) [7827]

[8830] שַׁחַף *šaḥap* 2x gull or possibly bat [7828]

[8831] שַׁחֶפֶת *šaḥepet* 2x wasting disease, consumption [7829]

[8832] שַׁחַץ *šaḥaṣ* 2x pride, dignity [7830]

[8835] שָׁחַק *šāḥaq* 4x [Q] to grind, wear away [7833]

[8836] שַׁחַק *šaḥaq* 21x clouds, skies [7834]

[8837] 1 שָׁחַר *šāḥar* 1x [Q] to become black [7835]

[8838] 2 שָׁחַר *šāḥar* 13x [Q] to seek, look; [P] to earnestly seek, search for [7836]

[8839] שָׁחֹר *šāḥōr* 6x black, dark [7838]

[8840] שַׁחַר *šaḥar* 23x dawn, daybreak [7837]

[8841] שַׁחֲרוּת *šaḥ^{a}rût* 1x vigor, prime of youth, an extension of dark hair color (or perhaps of the dawn) [7839]

[8842] שְׁחַרְחֹר *š^{e}ḥarḥōr* 1x dark, swarthy (complexion) [7840*]

[8845] שָׁחַת *šāḥat* 152x [N] to be corrupt, be ruined, be marred; [P] to corrupt, destroy, ruin; [H] to destroy, corrupt, bring to ruin [516* & 7843] See *corrupt; destroy; ruin; spoil.*

[8846] שַׁחַת *šaḥat* 23x pit, dungeon; corruption, decay [7845]

[8847] שִׁטָּה *šiṭâ* 29x acacia wood [7848]

[8848] שָׁטַח *šāṭaḥ* 6x [Q] to spread out, enlarge, scatter; [P] to spread out [7849]

[8849] שֹׁטֵט *šōṭēṭ* 1x whip, scourge [7850]

[8851] שָׁטַף *šāṭap* 31x [Q] to overflow, flood, wash away; [N] to be rinsed, be swept away; [Pu] to be rinsed [7857]

[8852] שֶׁטֶף *šeṭep* 6x flood, torrents (of rain) [7858]

[8853] שֹׁטֵר *šāṭar* 25x [Q] to keep a record; (n.) official, officer, foreman [7860*]

[8856] שַׁי *šay* 3x gift [7862]

[8859] 1 שִׁיבָה *šîbâ* 1x stay [7871]

[8860] 2 שִׁיבָה *šîbâ* 1x captives [7870]

[8861] שָׁיָה *šāyâ* 1x [Q] to desert, forget [7876]

[8863] שִׂיחַ *šîḥa* 5x [Q] to disintegrate away (to dust) [7817*]

[8864] שִׁיחָה *šîḥâ* 2x pit, pitfall [7882]

[8872] שִׁילֹנִי *šîlōnî* 6x Shilonite, of Shiloh, "*of Shiloh*" [7888*]

[8875] שַׁיִן *šayin* 2x urine [7890]

[8876] 1 שִׁיר *šîr* 87x [Q] to sing; [P ptcp.] singer, musician [7891] See *sing; singer.*

[8877] 2 שִׁיר *šîr* 78x song, music [7892]

[8878] שִׁירָה *šîrâ* 13x song [7892]

[8880] שַׁיִשׁ *šayiš* 1x alabaster [7893]

[8883] 1 שִׁית *šît* 86x [Q] to place, put, set; [Ho] to be demanded [7896] See *make; place; put; set.*

[8884] 2 שִׁית *šît* 2x garment [7897]

[8885] שַׁיִת *šayit* 7x thorns, thorn-bushes [7898]

[8886] שָׁכַב *šākab* 213x [Q] to lie down, rest; sleep with; (as a euphemism of sexual intercourse) to lie with, sleep with; [H] to make lie down; [Ho] to be laid down [7901] See *lie down; rest; (have) sexual relations; sleep.*

[8887] שִׁכְבָה *šikbâ* 9x emission, discharge [7902*]

[8888] שְׁכֹבֶת *š^{e}kōbet* 4x sexual relations, sexual intercourse [7903]

[8889] שָׁכָה *šākâ* 1x [H] to be well-fed; lusting [7904]

[8890] שְׁכוֹל *š^{e}kôl* 3x forlornness, loss of children [7908]

[8891] שַׁכּוּל *šakkûl* 6x pertaining to the loss of offspring [7909]

[8892] שְׁכוּלָה *š^{e}kûlâ* 1x bereaved (of children) [7909*]

[8893] שִׁכּוֹר *šikkôr* 13x drunk, drunkenness; (n.) a drunkard [7910]

[8894] שָׁכַח *šākaḥ* 102x [Q] to forget; [N] to be forgotten; [P] to make forget; [H] to make forget; [Ht] to be forgotten [7911] See *forget.*

[8895] שָׁכֵחַ *šākēaḥ* 2x forgetting [7913]

[8896] שָׁכַךְ *šākak* 5x [Q] to recede, reside; [H] to get rid of [7918]

[8897] שָׁכֹל *šākal* 23x [Q] to be bereaved (of children); [P] to make childless, bring bereavement, suffer miscarriage; [H] to miscarry [7921*]

[8898] שִׁכֻּלִים *šikkulîm* 1x (state of) bereavement (of children) [7923]

[8899] שָׁכַם *šākam* 65x [H] to do early in the morning; to do again and again [7925] See *do again; (be) eager; repeat; rise early.*

[8900] 1 שְׁכֶם *šᵉkem* 22x shoulder (upper part of the back); by extension: ridge of land [7926 & 7929*]

[8901] 2 שְׁכֶם *šᵉkem* 48x Shechem (town), "*shoulders [and upper part of the back];* [poss.] *shoulder [saddle of a hill]*" [7927]

[8902] 3 שְׁכֶם *šᵉkem* 15x Shechem (person), "*shoulders [and upper part of the back];* [poss.] *shoulder [saddle of a hill]*" [7927]

[8905] שָׁכַן *šākan* 130x [Q] to dwell, abide, live among, stay; [P] to make to dwell, make a home; [H] to cause to dwell, settle in, set up a dwelling [7931 & 7933*] See *dwell; live; rest; settle; stay.*

[8907] שָׁכֵן *šākēn* 20x neighbor; inhabitant [7934]

[8910] שָׁכַר *šākar* 18x [Q] to become drunk, drink to one's fill; [P] to make drunk; [H] to make drunk; [Ht] to behave drunken [7937]

[8911] שֵׁכָר *šēkār* 23x fermented drink, beer [7941]

[8912] שָׁכֻר *šākur* 1x drunken [7937*]

[8913] 1 שִׁכָּרוֹן *šikkārôn* 3x drunkenness [7943]

[8915] שַׁל *šal* 1x irreverent act [7944]

[8916] שַׁלְאֲנַן *šalʾanan* 1x secure [7946*]

[8917] שָׁלַב *šālab* 2x [Pu] to be joined, set parallel, dovetailed [7947]

[8918] שָׁלָב *šālāb* 3x upright, crossbar [7948]

[8919] שָׁלַג *šālag* 1x [H] to snow [7949]

[8920] 1 שֶׁלֶג *šeleg* 19x snow [7950]

[8921] 2 שֶׁלֶג *šeleg* 1x soap (processed from the soapwort plant) [7950]

[8922] 1 שָׁלָה *šālâ* 7x [Q] to be at ease, have peace; [N] to give oneself to rest; [H] to raise hopes [7951]

[8923] 2 שָׁלָה *šālâ* 1x [Q] to take away, extract [7952 & 7953]

[8924] 1 שֵׁלָה *šēlâ* 1x petition [7956]

[8926] שִׁלֹה *šilōh* 22x Shiloh [7887]

[8927] שַׁלְהֶבֶת *šalhebet* 2x flame [7957]

[8928] שַׁלְהֶבֶתְיָה *šalhebetyâ* 1x mighty flame (or 8927 + 3363) [7957*]

[8929] שָׁלֵו *šālēw* 8x quiet, at ease, carefree [7961]

[8930] שָׁלוּ *šālû* 1x secure feeling, ease [7959*]

[8932] שַׁלְוָה *šalwâ* 8x security, ease [7962]

[8933] שִׁלּוּחִים *šillûḥîm* 3x parting gifts; sending away [7964*]

[8934] שָׁלוֹם *šālôm* 237x peace, safety, prosperity, well-being; intactness, wholeness; peace can have a focus of security, safety which can bring feelings of satisfaction, well-being, and contentment [7965] See *completeness; health; peace; prosperity; safety; well-being.*

[8936] שִׁלּוּם *šillûm* 4x retribution, reckoning; bribe, gift [7966]

[8938] שָׁלַח *šālaḥ* 847x [Q] to send out; [Qp] to be sent away; [N] to be sent; [P] to send away, let go, release; [Pu] to be sent away, thrust out; [H] to send out; "to let go" from a marriage relationship is to divorce [7971] See *banish; divorce; send.*

[8939] 1 שֶׁלַח *šelaḥ* 7x weapon, sword, javelin [7973]

[8943] שְׁלֻחוֹת *šᵉluḥôt* 1x shoot (of a vine) [7976*]

[8945] שְׁלָחִים *šᵉlāḥîm* 1x shoots, sprouts of a plant (in a closed, private garden) [7973*]

[8947] שֻׁלְחָן *šulᵉḥān* 71x table [7979] See *table.*

[8948] שָׁלַט *šālaṭ* 8x [Q] to control, lord over; [H] to let rule, enable [7980]

[8949] שֶׁלֶט *šeleṭ* 7x small (round) shield [7982]

[8950] שִׁלְטוֹן *šilṭôn* 2x supremacy [7983]

[8951] שַׁלֶּטֶת *šalleṭet* 1x brazen, domineering [7986]

[8952] שְׁלִי *šᵉlî* 1x privateness, uninterruptedness [7987]

[8953] שִׁלְיָה *šilyâ* 1x afterbirth [7988]

[8954] שַׁלִּיט *šallîṭ* 4x ruler, governor [7989]

[8955] 1 שָׁלִישׁ *šālîš* 2x bowlful, basketful (a unit of measure, probably of one-third of something) [7991]

[8956] 2 שָׁלִישׁ *šālîš* 1x lute [7991]

[8957] 3 שָׁלִישׁ *šālîš* 14x officer [7991]

[8958] שְׁלִישִׁי *šᵉlîšî* 71x third [7992] See *third; three.*

[8959] שָׁלַךְ *šālak* 125x [H] to throw, hurl, scatter; [Ho] to be thrown, be cast [7993] See *throw.*

[8960] שָׁלָךְ *šālāk* 2x cormorant [7994]

[8961] 1 שַׁלֶּכֶת *šalleket* 1x cutting down [7995]

[8963] 1 שָׁלַל *šālal* 2x [Q] to pull out [7997]

[8964] 2 שָׁלַל *šālal* 14x [Q] to plunder, loot; [Htpol] to be plundered [7997]

[8965] שָׁלָל *šālāl* 74x plunder, spoil, loot [7998] See *booty; plunder.*

[8966] 1 שָׁלֵם *šālēm* 116x [Q] to be finished, be completed; be at peace; [Qp] to be at peace; [P] to repay, make restitution, fulfill (a vow); [Pu] be repaid, be fulfilled; [H] to make peace; cause to fulfill; [Ho] to be brought into peace [7999*] See *fulfill; (be at) peace; repay; reward.*

[8968] שֶׁלֶם *šelem* 87x fellowship (offering) [8002] See *fellowship offering; peace offering.*

[8969] 2 שָׁלֵם *šālēm* 27x safe, complete, whole [8003]

[8974] שִׁלֻּמָה *šillumâ* 1x punishment, retribution [8011]

[8976] שְׁלֹמֹה *šᵉlōmōh* 293x Solomon, "*peace, well-being*" [8010]

[8988] שַׁלְמֹנִים *šalmōnîm* 1x gifts [8021*]

[8990] שָׁלַף *šālap* 25x [Q] to draw out (a sword); remove (a sandal); [Qp] to be drawn (sword) [8025]

[8992] שָׁלַשׁ *šālaš* 10x [P] to do a third time, on the third day; [Pu] to be three years old, in three parts [8027]

[8993] שָׁלֹשׁ *šālōš* 606x three; (pl.) thirty [7969] See *thirty; three.*

[8997] שִׁלְשׁוֹם *šilšôm* 24x formally, three days ago; used with 9453, "yesterday and three days ago," as an adverb of time: formerly, previously [8032]

[8998] שָׁלִשִׁי *šālišî* 2x [the] Three [7991*]

[9000] שִׁלֵּשִׁים *šillēšîm* 5x third (generation) [8029*]

[9004] שָׁם *šām* 864x there, where [8033]

[9005] 1 שֵׁם *šēm* 864x name, a proper designation of a person, place, or thing; by extension: renown, fame; "to call on the name of the LORD" means to proclaim or praise the excellence of Yahweh, to worship Yahweh, or to summon Yahweh by name for help [8034] See *fame; name.*

[9006] 2 שֵׁם *šēm* 17x Shem, "*name, fame*" [8035]

[9012] שָׁמַד *šāmad* 90x [N] to be destroyed; [H] to destroy, demolish, annihilate [8045] See *annihilate; destroy; exterminate.*

[9014] 1 שַׁמָּה *šammâ* 40x thing of horror; desolation, devastation, what is laid waste [8047]

[9017] שְׁמוּאֵל *šᵉmûʾēl* 141x Samuel; Shemuel, "*his name is God [El]; heard of God; the unnamed god is El*" [8050]

[9019] שְׁמוּעָה *šᵉmûʿâ* 27x message, rumor, report [8052]

[9023] שָׁמַט *šāmaṭ* 9x [Q] to drop down, stumble; to lie unplowed; [N] to be thrown down; [H] to cancel a debt [8058]

[9024] שְׁמִטָּה *šᵉmiṭṭâ* 5x canceling of debt [8059]

[9028] שָׁמַיִם *šāmayim* 421x region above the earth: the heavens: place of the stars, sky, air; heaven: the invisible realm of God [8064] See *air; heaven, heavens; sky.*

[9029] שְׁמִינִי *šᵉmînî* 28x eighth [8066]

[9030] שְׁמִינִית *šᵉmînît* 3x sheminith [8067]

[9031] 1 שָׁמִיר *šāmîr* 8x briers [8068]

[9032] 2 שָׁמִיר *šāmîr* 3x hardest stone; (other contexts) flint or emery [8068]

[9037] 1 שָׁמֵם *šāmēm* 92x [Q] to be desolate, be appalled; [N] to become desolate, be appalled; [Pol] to cause desolation, be appalled; [H] to bring to devastation, cause to be appalled; [Ho] to lie desolate; [Htpol] to destroy oneself, be appalled [8074] See *(be) appalled; deserted; (be) desolate; horrified; lay waste; shudder.*

[9038] 2 שָׁמֵם *šāmēm* 2x desolate, deserted [8076]

[9039] שְׁמָמָה *šᵉmāmâ* 56x desolation, ruin, wasteland [8077] See *desolation; wasteland.*

[9040] שִׁמְמָה *šimᵉmâ* 1x desolation [8077]

[9041] שִׁמָּמוֹן *šimmāmôn* 2x despair, which may border on feelings of horror and shuddering [8078]

[9042] 1 שָׁמֵן *šāmēn* 5x [Q] to grow fat; [H] to show as well-fed; by extension: to be calloused, unresponsive of heart [8080*]

[9043] שֶׁמֶן *šemen* 193x olive, the tree and its products: olive berry, olive oil, olive wood; olive oil was a staple of diet in biblical times, and was also used as a medicine, lamp fuel, and in religious offerings and ritual [8081] See *oil; olive oil.*

[9044] שָׁמָן *šāmān* 2x richness, fatness [4924*]

[9045] 2 שָׁמֵן *šāmēn* 10x rich, fertile [8082]

[9046] שְׁמֹנֶה *šᵉmōneh* 147x eight; (pl.) eighty [8083] See *eight; eighth; eighty.*

[9048] שָׁמַע *šāmaʿ* 1,165x [Q] to hear, listen, obey; [N] to be heard; [P] to summon, call together; [H] to proclaim, summon, make hear; from the base meaning of hearing come the extensions of understanding and obedience [8085] See *announce; hear; listen; obey; perceive; proclaim; understand.*

[9049] 1 שֶׁמַע *šemaʿ* 1x clash, sound [8085*]

[9051] שֵׁמַע *šēmaʿ* 17x what is heard, report, news, rumor [8088]

[9053] שֹׁמַע *šōmaʿ* 4x report; reputation [8089]

[9058] שִׁמְעוֹן *šimʿôn* 44x Simeon, Simeonite, "*he has heard* or *obedient one*" [8095]

[9059] 1 שִׁמְעִי *šimʿî* 44x Shimei, "*Yahweh has heard* or *famous*" [8096]

[9061] שְׁמַעְיָה *šᵉmaʿyâ* 34x Shemaiah, "*Yahweh hears*" [8098]

[9066] שֵׁמֶץ *šēmeṣ* 2x whisper [8102*]

[9067] שִׁמְצָה *šimṣâ* 1x laughingstock, derision [8103]

[9068] שָׁמַר *šāmar* 469x [Q] to keep, watch, observe, guard; [Qp] to be set aside, be secured; [N] to be careful, beware; [P] to cling to; [Ht] to keep oneself; to observe for oneself [8104] See *examine; guard; keep; obey; preserve; tend; watch.*

[9069] 1 שֶׁמֶר *šemer* 5x dregs (of wine); aged wine [8105]

[9072] שָׁמְרָה *šomrâ* 1x guard, watch [8108]

[9073] שְׁמֻרָה *š^{e}murâ* 1x eyelid (that covers and protects the eye) [8109]

[9076] שֹׁמְרוֹן *šōm^{e}rôn* 109x Samaria, the capital city of northern kingdom of Israel; by extension, the northern kingdom itself, "*belonging to the clan of Shemer [1Ki 16:24]*" [8111]

[9081] שִׁמֻּרִים *šimmurîm* 2x vigil, night-watch [8107*]

[9087] שֶׁמֶשׁ *šemeš* 134x sun [8121] See *sun.*

[9088] שִׁמְשׁוֹן *šimšôn* 38x Samson, "*little one of Shemesh* or *strong*" [8123]

[9094] 1 שֵׁן *šēn* 55x tooth (human or animal); by extension, anything tooth shaped: rocky crag; "cleanness of teeth" is a sign of lack of food in famine [8127] See *ivory; tooth.*

[9096] שָׁנָא *šānāʾ* 1x [Q] to become dull [8132]

[9097] שֵׁנָא *šēnāʾ* 1x sleep [8142]

[9099] שִׁנְאָן *šinʾān* 1x high in rank or number [8136]

[9101] 1 שָׁנָה *šānâ* 24x [Q] to repeat, do again; [N] to be repeated; [P] to change, alter; to pretend; [Pu] to be changed; [Ht] to disguise oneself [8132* & 8138]

[9102] 2 שָׁנָה *šānâ* 878x year [8141] See *year.*

[9104] שֵׁנָה *šēnâ* 23x sleep, with a focus of rest and inactivity, sometimes laziness; by extension: death [8142]

[9105] שֶׁנְהַבִּים *šenhabbîm* 2x ivory [8143]

[9106] 1 שָׁנִי *šānî* 42x scarlet, crimson (thread) [8144]

[9108] שֵׁנִי *šēnî* 156x second [8145] See *second; two.*

[9109] שְׁנַיִם *š^{e}nayim* 769x two [8147] See *two.*

[9110] שְׁנִינָה *š^{e}nînâ* 4x object of ridicule [8148]

[9111] 1 שָׁנַן *šānan* 8x [Q] to sharpen; [Qp] be sharpened; [Htpol] to be embittered [8150]

[9112] 2 שָׁנַן *šānan* 1x [P] to impress, repeat [8150]

[9113] שָׁנַס *šānas* 1x [P] to tuck up the cloak (into the belt) [8151]

[9115] שָׁסָה *šāsâ* 11x [Q] to raid, loot, plunder; [Qp] to be looted [8154]

[9116] שָׁסַס *šāsas* 6x [Q] to plunder, ransack; [N] to be looted, be ransacked [8155]

[9117] שָׁסַע *šāsaʿ* 9x [Q] to divide; [Qp] be divided; [P] to tear apart [8156]

[9118] שֶׁסַע *šesaʿ* 4x cleft (split hoof) [8157]

[9119] שָׁסַף *šāsap* 1x [P] to hack to pieces (for execution) [8158]

[9120] שָׁעָה *šāʿâ* 11x [Q] to look with favor, have regard for, pay attention to [8159]

[9121] שְׁעָטָה *š^{e}ʿāṭâ* 1x galloping, pounding (hooves) [8161]

[9122] שַׁעַטְנֵז *šaʿaṭnēz* 2x woven cloth; likely referring to a wide mesh [8162]

[9123] שֹׁעַל *šōʿal* 3x hollow of the hand; handful, a measure of volume [8168]

[9128] שָׁעַן *šāʿan* 22x [N] to lean oneself upon, rely on [8172]

[9129] 1 שָׁעַע *šāʿaʿ* 4x [Q] be blinded; [H] to make close the eyes; [Htpal] to blind oneself; a fig. extension of smearing over or pasting objects together [8173]

[9130] 2 שָׁעַע *šāʿaʿ* 6x [Pil] to take joy in, delight in; [Pulpal] to be dandled; [Htpal] to delight oneself in [8173]

[9132] שָׁעַר *šāʿar* 1x [Q] to think, estimate, calculate [8176]

[9133] 1 שַׁעַר *šaʿar* 373x gate, gateway; often referring to the entrance to a city, a key point of the city's defense and a place for public hearings and decisions [8179] See *gate.*

[9134] 2 שַׁעַר *šaʿar* 1x measure (of grain) [8180]

[9135] שֹׁעָר *šōʿār* 1x burst open, i.e., poor quality (figs) [8182]

[9136] שַׁעֲרוּר *šaʿarûr* 2x something horrible, shocking thing [8186*]

[9137] שַׁעֲרוּרִי *šaʿarûrî* 2x horrible thing [8187*]

[9141] שַׁעֲשׁוּעִים *šaʿašûʿîm* 9x delight [8191*]

[9142] שָׁפָה *šāpâ* 2x [N, Pu] to be swept bare [8192]

[9144] שְׁפוֹט *šᵉpôṭ* 2x judgment, punishment [8196]

[9147] שְׁפוֹת *šᵉpôt* 1x milk product: cream, curds, cheese, etc [8194*]

[9148] שִׁפְחָה *šipᵉḥâ* 63x maidservant, female slave [8198] See *maidservant; servant.*

[9149] שָׁפַט *šāpaṭ* 204x [Q] to judge, decide; lead, defend, vindicate; [N] to execute judgment, be brought to trial; to argue a matter; [Po] (ptcp.) judge [8199] See *govern; judge.*

[9150] שֶׁפֶט *šepeṭ* 16x judgment, punishment [8201]

[9155] 1 שְׁפִי *šᵉpî* 9x barren height [8205]

[9159] שְׁפִיפֹן *šᵉpîpōn* 1x viper [8207]

[9161] שָׁפַךְ *šāpak* 117x [Q] to pour out, shed, spill; [Qp, N, Pu] to be outpoured, be shed; [Ht] be scattered, ebb away; "to shed blood" means to kill [8210] See *pour out.*

[9162] שֶׁפֶךְ *šepek* 2x dump (for throwing out ash refuse) [8211]

[9163] שָׁפְכָה *šopkâ* 1x male organ (fluid duct) [8212]

[9164] 1 שָׁפֵל *šāpēl* 30x [Q] to be humbled, be brought low; [H] to humble, bring low [8213]

[9165] שֵׁפֶל *šēpel* 2x low estate, humble condition [8216*]

[9166] שָׁפָל *šāpāl* 18x low, deep [8217]

[9168] שִׁפְלָה *šiplâ* 1x state of lowliness, condition of humiliation [8218]

[9169] שְׁפֵלָה *šᵉpēlâ* 20x (western) foothills, Shephelah, a major buffer area between the (Philistine) coastal plain and the highlands of Judah [8219]

[9170] שִׁפְלוּת *šiplût* 1x idleness, inactivity, an extension of lowering the hands to a position of rest [8220]

[9176] 1 שָׁפָן *šāpān* 4x coney [8227]

[9179] שֶׁפַע *šepaʿ* 1x abundance [8228]

[9180] שִׁפְעָה *šipʿâ* 6x (of water) flood; mass (of humans or animals) [8229]

[9182] שָׁפַר *šāpar* 1x [Q] to be delightful, pleasing [8231]

[9183] 1 שֶׁפֶר *šeper* 1x beauty, loveliness [8233]

[9185] 1 שִׁפְרָה *šiprâ* 1x fairness, clearness (of skies) [8235]

[9189] שָׁפַת *šāpat* 5x [Q] to place, put [8239]

[9190] 1 שְׁפַתַּיִם *šᵉpattayim* 1x an area of inactivity: (place of the) fireplaces; some sources: saddlebags or sheepfolds [8240*]

[9191] 2 שְׁפַתַּיִם *šᵉpattayim* 1x double-pronged hooks [8240*]

[9192] שֶׁצֶף *šeṣep* 1x surging, flooding (of anger) [8241]

[9193] 1 שָׁקַד *šāqad* 12x [Q] to be awake, watch, stand guard [8245]

[9196] שָׁקֵד *šāqēd* 4x almond tree, almond nuts [8247]

[9197] שָׁקָה *šāqâ* 62x [N] to be given a drink; [Pu] to be moistened; [H] to give a drink to [8248] See *make to drink; water.*

[9198] שִׁקּוּי *šiqqûy* 3x drink; nourishing drink [8249* & 8250]

[9199] שִׁקּוּץ *šiqqûṣ* 28x detestable thing, vileness, abomination [8251]

[9200] שָׁקַט *šāqaṭ* 41x [Q] to be at rest, be at peace; [H] to keep silent, remain quiet, remain calm [8252]

[9201] שֶׁקֶט *šeqeṭ* 1x quietness [8253]

[9202] שָׁקַל *šāqal* 22x [Q] to weigh out, make payment; [N] to be weighed [8254]

[9203] שֶׁקֶל *šeqel* 88x shekel (a unit of weight and value, about two-fifths of an ounce [11.5 grams]) [8255] See *shekel.*

[9204] שִׁקְמָה *šiqmâ* 7x sycamore-fig tree [8256]

[9205] שָׁקַע *šāqaʿ* 6x [Q] to sink down; [N] to sink; [H] to make sink down, make settle [8257]

[9206] שְׁקַעֲרוּרָה *šᵉqaʿărûrâ* 1x depression, hollow [8258]

[9207] שָׁקַף *šāqap* 22x [N] to look down on, overlook; [H] to look down on [8259]

[9208] שֶׁקֶף *šāqep* 1x frame work (of a door) [8260*]

[9209] שְׁקֻפִים *šᵉqupîm* 2x clerestory window (a high place window) [8261*]

[9210] שָׁקַץ *šāqaṣ* 7x [P] to detest, abhor, defile [8262]

[9211] שֶׁקֶץ *šeqeṣ* 11x detestable thing [8263]

[9212] שָׁקַק *šāqaq* 24x [Q] to rush forth, charge forth; [Htpal] to rush back and forth [8264]

[9213] שָׁקַר *šāqar* 6x [Q] to deal falsely with; [P] to deceive, lie, betray [8266]

[9214] שֶׁקֶר *šeqer* 113x lie, falseness, deception; vanity [8267] See *deception; falseness; lie.*

[9216] שֹׁקֶת *šōqet* 2x watering-trough [8268]

[9217] 1 שֵׁר *šēr* 1x bracelet [8285*]

[9219] שֹׁר *šōr* 2x navel; umbilical cord [8270]

[9220] שָׁרָב *šārāb* 2x parching heat; burning hot sand [8273]

[9222] שַׁרְבִיט *šarbîṭ* 4x scepter, staff [8275]

[9223] 1 שָׁרָה *šārâ* 2x [Q] to unleash; to deliver, set free [3474* & 8281*]

[9224] 2 שָׁרָה *šārâ* 1x vineyard [8284 & 8281*]

[9233] שִׁרְיָה *širyâ* 1x a weapon that is thrown: javelin, lance, light spear; some sources: arrowhead [8302]

[9234] שִׁרְיוֹן *širyôn* 8x coat of scale armor [8302]

[9235] שָׁרִיר *šārîr* 1x muscle [8306]

[9237] שָׁרַץ *šāraṣ* 14x [Q] to teem, swarm, move about [8317]

[9238] שֶׁרֶץ *šereṣ* 15x creatures that teem, swarm, move about [8318]

[9239] שָׁרַק *šāraq* 12x [Q] to whistle, hiss, scoff [8319]

[9240] שְׁרֵקָה *šᵉrēqâ* 7x object of scorn, thing of derision, something held in contempt; an extension of the act of whistling or shrieking in derision [8322]

[9241] שְׁרִקָה *šᵉriqâ* 2x whistling; scorn; some sources: flute playing [8292*]

[9244] שְׁרִרוּת *šᵉrirût* 10x stubbornness [8307]

[9245] שָׁרַשׁ *šāraš* 8x [P] to uproot; [Poel/Poal] to take root; [Pu] to be uprooted; [H] to take root [8327]

[9247] שֹׁרֶשׁ *šōreš* 33x root of a plant; by extension: base or bottom of any object; source of a family line; "the Root of Jesse" is a messianic title, emphasizing Davidic origin [8326 & 8328*]

[9249] שַׁרְשְׁרָה *šaršᵉrâ* 8x chain [8333]

[9250] שָׁרַת *šārat* 98x [P] to minister, serve, attend [8334] See *minister; officiate; serve.*

[9251] שָׁרֵת *šārēt* 1x cultic service [8335]

[9252] 1 שֵׁשׁ *šēš* 274x six; (pl.) sixty [8337] See *six; sixth; sixty.*

[9253] 2 שֵׁשׁ *šēš* 3x alabaster [8336]

[9254] 3 שֵׁשׁ *šēš* 38x fine linen, byssus (processed from the flax plant) [8336]

[9255] שָׁשָׁא *šāšā᾽* 1x [P] to lead along [8338]

[9257] שָׁשָׁה *šāšâ* 1x [P] to give a sixth part [8341]

[9261] שִׁשִּׁי *šišî* 28x sixth [8345]

[9266] שָׁשַׁר *šāšar* 2x red color (from lead, iron rust, or insects) [8350]

[9268] 1 שֵׁת *šēt* 3x foundation; buttocks [8351 & 8352* & 8357*]

[9269] 2 שֵׁת *šēt* 9x Seth, "*determined, granted, Ge 4:25; restitution*" [8352]

[9271] 1 שָׁתָה *šātâ* 1x worker in weaving [8356]

[9272] 2 שָׁתָה *šātâ* 217x [Q] to drink; by extension: to be drunk; [N] to be drunken [8354] See *drink; give drink to; water.*

[9274] 1 שְׁתִי *šᵉtî* 9x woven material, made on a loom; some sources: warp, the vertical threads on a loom [8359]

[9275] 2 שְׁתִי *šᵉtî* 1x drunkenness, drinking [8358]

[9276] שְׁתִיָּה *šᵉtiyyâ* 1x (manner of) drinking [8360]

[9277] שָׁתִיל *šātîl* 1x slip, cutting (of a plant) [8363*]

[9278] שָׁתַל *šātal* 10x [Q] to plant; [Qp] to be planted [8362]

[9280] שָׁתַם *šātam* 2x [Qp] to be opened [8365]

[9283] שָׁתַע *šāta*ᶜ 2x [Q] to be dismayed [**]

[9284] שָׁתַק *šātaq* 4x [Q] to become calm, die down [8367]

[9286] שָׁתַת *šātat* 2x [Q] to be destined, appoint, lay claim [8371]

[9288] תָּא *tā᾽* 13x alcove for guards, guardroom [8372]

[9289] 1 תָּאַב *tā᾽ab* 2x [Q] to long for, desire [8373]

[9290] 2 תָּאַב *tā᾽ab* 1x [P] to abhor, loathe [8374]

[9291] תַּאֲבָה *ta᾽ᵃbâ* 1x longing, desiring [8375]

[9292] תָּאָה *tā᾽â* 2x [P] to draw a line, mark out (territory) [8376]

[9293] תְּאוֹ *tᵉ᾽ô* 2x antelope; some sources: wild ox or sheep [8377]

[9294] 1 תַּאֲוָה *ta᾽ᵃwāh* 21x longing, desire, craving [8378]

[9297] תַּאֲלָה *ta᾽ᵃlâ* 1x curse [8381]

[9298] תָּאַם *tā᾽am* 2x [H] to have twins [8382]

[9299] תַּאֲנָה *ta᾽ᵃnâ* 1x (time of) heat, rut [8385]

[9300] תְּאֵנָה *tᵉ᾽ēnâ* 39x fig; fig tree [8384]

[9301] תֹּאֲנָה *tō᾽ᵃnâ* 1x occasion, opportunity [8385]

[9302] תַּאֲנִיָּה *ta᾽ᵃniyyâ* 2x mourning [8386]

[9303] תְּאֻנִים *tᵉ᾽unîm* 1x efforts, toil [8383]

[9305] 1 תָּאַר *tā᾽ar* 6x [Q] to turn toward; [Pu] to be turned toward [8388]

[9306] 2 תָּאַר *tāʾar* 2x [P] to mark out a form, make an outline [8388]

[9307] תֹּאַר *tōʾar* 15x form, shape; beauty, fine-looking person [8389]

[9309] תְּאַשּׁוּר *teʾaššûr* 3x cypress tree, cypress wood [8391 & 839*]

[9310] תֵּבָה *tēbâ* 28x box-shaped thing: chest, ark, basket [8392]

[9311] תְּבוּאָה *tebûʾâ* 42x harvest, crops, produce [8393]

[9312] תְּבוּנָה *tebûnâ* 42x understanding, insight; ability, skill, wisdom [8394]

[9313] תְּבוּסָה *tebûsâ* 1x downfall, ruin [8395]

[9315] תֵּבֵל *tēbēl* 36x world, earth [8398]

[9316] תֶּבֶל *tebel* 2x perversion, abominable confusion [8397]

[9318] תַּבְלִית *tablît* 1x destruction [8399]

[9319] תְּבַלֻּל *teballul* 1x defect (obscuring vision); likely referring to a cataract [8400]

[9320] תֶּבֶן *teben* 17x straw [8401]

[9322] תַּבְנִית *tabnît* 20x image, form, shape [8403]

[9326] תַּגְמוּל *tagmûl* 1x benefit, gracious act [8408]

[9327] תִּגְרָה *tigrâ* 1x agitation, blow [8409]

[9329] תִּדְהָר *tidhār* 2x fir tree; some sources: elm or ash tree [8410]

[9332] תֹּהוּ *tōhû* 20x formless, waste, empty; (of speech) useless, confused, vain [8414]

[9333] תְּהוֹם *tehôm* 36x the deep, depths, with the associative meanings of darkness and secrecy, controlled or inhabited by mysterious powers; "the depths of the earth" is the abode of the dead [8415]

[9334] תָּהֳלָה *toholâ* 1x error [8417]

[9335] תְּהִלָּה *tehillâ* 58x praise, renown, glory; praise is proclaiming the excellence of a person or object [8416] See *praise.*

[9337] תַּהְפֻּכוֹת *tahpukôt* 10x perversity, confusing things [8419*]

[9338] תָּו *tāw* 3x mark (on the forehead); signing (a document) [8420]

[9339] תּוֹאֲמִים *tôʾamîm* 6x twins, (something) double [8380*]

[9340] תּוּבַל קַיִן *tûbal qayin* 2x Tubal-Cain [8423]

[9342] תּוּגָה *tûgâ* 4x grief, sorrow [8424]

[9343] תּוֹדָה *tôdâ* 32x thank offering; thanksgiving, confession of thankfulness; song of thanksgiving; thanks is the speaking of the excellence of a person or object, with a focus on the personal gratitude of the speaker [8426]

[9344] 1 תָּוָה *tāwâ* 2x [P] to put a mark, place a sign [8427]

[9345] 2 תָּוָה *tāwâ* 1x [H] to vex, bring pain [8428]

[9347] תּוֹחֶלֶת *tôḥelet* 5x hope, expectation [8431]

[9348] תָּוֶךְ *tāwek* 418x middle, midst, center, among, within [8432]

[9349] תּוֹכֵחָה *tôkēḥâ* 4x rebuke, punishment, correction [8433]

[9350] תּוֹכַחַת *tôkaḥat* 24x correction, rebuke, punishment [8433]

[9352] תּוֹלֵדוֹת *tôlēdôt* 39x account, record, genealogy, family line [8435*]

[9354] תּוֹלָל *tôlāl* 1x tormentor, oppressor [8437]

[9355] 1 תּוֹלָע *tôlāʿ* 2x (deep) red, purple [8438]

[9357] תּוֹלֵעָה *tôlēʿâ* 41x scarlet yarn, scarlet yarn; worm, maggot [8438]

[9359] תּוֹעֵבָה *tôʿēbâ* 118x detestable thing, loathsome thing, abomination [8441] See *abomination; detestable; repulsive.*

[9360] תּוֹעָה *tô*ʿ*â* 2x trouble, error [8442]

[9361] תּוֹעָפוֹת *tô*ʿ*āpôt* 4x best, choice; strength; some sources: horns [8443*]

[9362] תּוֹצָאוֹת *tôṣā*ʾ*ôt* 23x end, limit, starting point [8444*]

[9364] תּוֹקְעִים *tôqe*ʿ*îm* 1x striking of hands in pledge [8628*]

[9365] תּוּר *tûr* 24x [Q] to explore, investigate, search out; [H] to send out to spy [8446]

[9366] 1 תּוֹר *tôr* 15x turning; earring [8447 & 8448]

[9367] 2 תּוֹר *tôr* 14x dove [8449]

[9368] תּוֹרָה *tôrâ* 223x law, regulation, teaching, instruction; often referring to the five books of Moses in whole and in part [8451 & 8452*] See *instruction; law; regulations; teaching.*

[9369] תּוֹשָׁב *tôšāb* 13x temporary resident, stranger, alien [8453]

[9370] תּוּשִׁיָּה *tûšiyyâ* 11x success, victory; sound judgment, wisdom [8454]

[9371] תּוֹתָח *tôtāḥ* 1x (stout) club [8455]

[9372] תָּזַז *tāzaz* 1x [H] to cut down [8456]

[9373] תַּזְנוּת *taznût* 20x promiscuity, prostitution, act of lust [8457]

[9374] תַּחְבֻּלוֹת *taḥbulôt* 6x guidance, advice, giving direction [8458*]

[9377] תַּחֲלֻאִים *taḥ*^{a}*lu*ʾ*îm* 5x diseases [8463*]

[9378] תְּחִלָּה *t*^{e}*ḥillâ* 22x beginning, at first [8462]

[9379] תַּחְמָס *taḥmās* 2x screech owl [8464]

[9381] תַּחֲנָה *taḥ*^{a}*nâ* 1x encampment [8466]

[9382] 1 תְּחִנָּה *t*^{e}*ḥinnâ* 25x plea, petition, request, supplication [8467]

[9384] תַּחֲנוּן *taḥ*^{a}*nûn* 18x plea for mercy, petition, supplication [8469]

[9389] תַּחְרָא *taḥrā*ʾ 2x collar, edge around an opening in a garment [8473]

[9391] 1 תַּחַשׁ *taḥaš* 14x (leather of) a sea cow [8476]

[9393] 1 תַּחַת *taḥat* 505x under, in place of, succeeding (on a sequence) [8478]

[9396] תַּחְתּוֹן *taḥtôn* 14x lower [8481]

[9397] תַּחְתִּי *taḥtî* 19x lower; (n.) depths, below, sometimes referring to the underworld, the realm of the dead [8482]

[9399] תִּיכוֹן *tîkôn* 10x middle, center [8484]

[9401] תֵּימָא *têmā*ʾ 5x Tema, "*on the right [not left] side,* hence *south country*" [8485]

[9402] 1 תֵּימָן *têmān* 23x south, southward, south wind [8486]

[9406] תִּימָרָה *tîmārâ* 2x column (of smoke) [8490]

[9408] תִּירוֹשׁ *tîrôš* 38x new wine [8492]

[9411] תַּיִשׁ *tayiš* 4x male goat [8495]

[9412] תֹּךְ *tōk* 4x oppression, threat [8496 & 8501*]

[9413] תָּכָה *tākâ* 1x [Pu] to bow down [8497]

[9414] תְּכוּנָה *t*^{e}*kûnâ* 3x dwelling; arrangement, supply [8498 & 8499]

[9415] תֻּכִּיִּים *tukkiyyîm* 2x baboons; some sources: monkeys, peacocks, poultry [8500*]

[9416] תִּכְלָה *tiklâ* 1x perfection [8502]

[9417] תַּכְלִית *taklît* 5x end, limit, boundary [8503]

[9418] תְּכֵלֶת *t*^{e}*kēlet* 49x blue material [8504]

[9419] תָּכַן *tākan* 18x [Q] to weigh, estimate; [N] to be just, be weighted; [P] to hold firm, mark off, understand; [Pu] to be determined [8505]

[9420] 1 תֹּכֶן *tōken* 2x full quota, fixed measure; size, measurement [8506]

[9422] תָּכְנִית *toknît* 2x (perfect) example, design [8508]

[9423] תַּכְרִיךְ *takrîk* 1x robe, mantle [8509]

[9424] תֵּל *tēl* 5x mound, heap, ruin [8510]

[9428] תָּלָא *tālā'* 3x [Q] to hang; [Qp] to be suspended, be determined [8511]

[9429] תַּלְאֻבוֹת *tal'ubôt* 1x burning heat [8514*]

[9430] תְּלָאָה *t^elā'â* 5x hardship, burden [8513]

[9432] תִּלְבֹּשֶׁת *tilbōšet* 1x clothing, what is worn [8516]

[9434] תָּלָה *tālâ* 27x [Q, P] to hang, suspend; [Qp, N] to be hung [8518]

[9435] תָּלוּל *tālûl* 1x lofty, towering [8524*]

[9437] תְּלִי *t^elî* 1x quiver (case to hold arrows that hangs or dangles) [8522]

[9438] תָּלַל *tālal* 9x [H] to make a fool of, deceive, cheat; [Ho] to be deluded [2048*]

[9439] תֶּלֶם *telem* 5x furrow, plowed line [8525]

[9441] תַּלְמִיד *talmîd* 1x student, pupil [8527]

[9442] תְּלֻנּוֹת *t^elunnôt* 8x grumbling, complaint [8519*]

[9443] תָּלַע *tāla'* 1x [Pu] to be clad in scarlet material [8529]

[9444] תַּלְפִּיּוֹת *talpiyyôt* 1x elegance or courses of stones [8530*]

[9446] תַּלְתַּל *taltāl* 1x wavy [8534*]

[9447] תָּם *tām* 16x blameless, flawless, perfect [8535]

[9448] תֹּם *tōm* 25x blamelessness, integrity, innocence [8537]

[9449] תָּמַהּ *tāmah* 10x [Q] to be astonished, be astounded, be stunned; [Htpal] to be stunned in oneself [8539]

[9450] תֻּמָּה *tummâ* 5x integrity, blamelessness [8538]

[9451] תִּמָּהוֹן *timmāhôn* 2x confusion, panic [8541]

[9453] תְּמוֹל *t^emôl* 23x yesterday; (generally) before, in the past [8543]

[9454] תְּמוּנָה *t^emûnâ* 10x form, image, likeness [8544]

[9455] תְּמוּרָה *t^emûrâ* 6x substitution, transfer, exchange [8545]

[9456] תְּמוּתָה *t^emûtâ* 2x death [8546]

[9458] תָּמִיד *tāmîd* 104x (adv.) continually, constantly, regularly, daily [8548] See *always; constantly; continually; daily; ever; regular.*

[9459] תָּמִים *tāmîm* 91x without defect, blameless, perfect [8549] See *faithfulness; perfect; sincerity; unblemished; whole.*

[9460] תֻּמִּים *tummîm* 5x Thummim, formally "Perfections," devices used by the high priest to make God's will known, possibly related to the casting of lots [8550]

[9461] תָּמַךְ *tāmak* 21x [Q] to take hold of, grasp, hold secure; [N] to be seized [8551]

[9462] תָּמַם *tāmam* 64x [Q] to complete, finish, perfect; [H] to end, stop, complete; [Ht] to show oneself blameless [8552] See *complete; destroy; end; finish; perish.*

[9463] תִּמְנָה *timnâ* 12x Timnah, "*lot, portion*" [8553]

[9468] תֶּמֶס *temes* 1x melting away [8557]

[9469] 1 תָּמָר *tāmār* 12x palm tree [8558]

[9470] 2 תָּמָר *tāmār* 22x Tamar, "*date palm*" [8559]

[9473] 2 תֹּמֶר *tōmer* 1x scarecrow [8560]

[9474] תִּמֹרָה *timōrâ* 19x palm tree [8561]

[9475] תַּמְרוּק *tamrûq* 3x beauty treatment (including massages and cleansing rituals), cosmetics [8562*]

[9476] 1 תַּמְרוּרִים *tamrûrim* 3x bitterness [8563*]

[9477] 2 תַּמְרוּרִים *tamrûrim* 1x guidepost [8564*]

[9478] תַּן *tan* 14x jackal [8565 & 8568*]

[9479] 1 תָּנָה *tānâ* 2x [Q, H] to sell oneself as a prostitute [8566]

[9480] 2 תָּנָה *tānâ* 1x [P] to commemorate, recount [8567]

[9481] תְּנוּאָה *tᵉnûʾâ* 2x fault, opposition, what one has against another [8569]

[9482] תְּנוּבָה *tᵉnûbâ* 5x crop, produce [8570]

[9483] תְּנוּךְ *tᵉnûk* 8x lobe (of the ear) [8571]

[9484] תְּנוּמָה *tᵉnûmâ* 5x slumber, sleep [8572]

[9485] תְּנוּפָה *tᵉnûpâ* 30x wave offering, what it waved [8573]

[9486] תַּנּוּר *tannûr* 15x oven, furnace, firepot (a portable oven for cooking bread) [8574]

[9487] תַּנְחוּמוֹת *tanḥûmôt* 2x consolation [8575*]

[9488] תַּנְחוּמִים *tanḥûmîm* 3x consolation, comfort [8575*]

[9490] תַּנִּין *tannîn* 15x serpent, snake; monster of the deep; (pr.n.) Jackal (Well); can refer to large sea creatures as well as to mythological monsters of chaos opposed to God [8577]

[9491] 1 תִּנְשֶׁמֶת *tinšemet* 1x chameleon [8580]

[9492] 2 תִּנְשֶׁמֶת *tinšemet* 2x white owl [8580]

[9493] תָּעַב *tāʿab* 22x [N] to be repulsive, be vile, be rejected; [P] to detest, abhor, loathe, despise; [H] to behave in a vile manner [8581]

[9494] תָּעָה *tāʿâ* 51x [Q] to wander, go astray; [N] to deceive oneself; to stagger around (as a drunk); [H] to lead astray, make wander, mislead [8582] See *go astray; lead astray; stagger; stray; wander.*

[9496] תְּעוּדָה *tᵉʿûdâ* 3x testimony; method of legalizing transactions (sandal transaction) [8584]

[9498] 1 תְּעָלָה *tᵉʿālâ* 9x trench, channel, aqueduct [8585]

[9499] 2 תְּעָלָה *tᵉʿālâ* 2x healing [8585]

[9500] תַּעֲלוּלִים *taʿᵃlûlîm* 2x wantonness; harsh treatment, referring to impulsive people [8586*]

[9502] תַּעֲלֻמָה *taʿᵃlumâ* 3x secret; hidden thing [8587]

[9503] תַּעֲנוּג *taʿᵃnûg* 5x delight, pleasure; living in luxury [8588]

[9504] תַּעֲנִית *taʿᵃnît* 1x self-abasement, mortification [8589]

[9506] תָּעַע *tāʿaʿ* 2x [Pil] to mock; [Htpal] to scoff at [8591]

[9507] תְּעֻפָה *tᵉʿupâ* 1x darkness [5774*]

[9508] תַּעֲצֻמוֹת *taʿᵃsumôt* 1x strength, might [8592*]

[9509] תַּעַר *taʿar* 13x razor, knife, scabbard [8593]

[9510] תַּעֲרֻבוֹת *taʿᵃrûbôt* 2x hostage, formally "son of a pledge" [8594*]

[9511] תַּעְתֻּעִים *taʿtuʿîm* 2x mockery [8595*]

[9512] 1 תֹּף *tōp* 16x tambourine, timbrel [8596]

[9513] 2 תֹּף *tōp* 1x setting, jewelry; some sources uncertain in meaning [8596]

[9514] תִּפְאֶרֶת *tipʾeret* 51x glory, splendor, honor [8597]

[9515] 1 תַּפּוּחַ *tappûaḥ* 6x apple, apple tree [8598]

[9518] תְּפוּצָה *t^epûṣâ* 1x shattering, dispersing [8600*]

[9519] תֻּפִינִים *tupînîm* 1x broken into pieces [8601*]

[9521] 1 תָּפֵל *tāpēl* 5x whitewash [8602]

[9522] 2 תָּפֵל *tāpēl* 2x tasteless (food); worthless (prophetic visions) [8602]

[9524] תִּפְלָה *tiplâ* 3x repulsiveness, wrongdoing [8604]

[9525] תְּפִלָּה *t^epillâ* 77x prayer, plea, petition [8605] See *intercession; petition; prayer.*

[9526] תִּפְלֶצֶת *tipleṣet* 1x terror, horror, a state of great fear even to the point of shuddering [8606]

[9528] תָּפַף *tāpap* 2x [Q] to tap (play) a tambourine; [Pol] to beat (the breast) [8608]

[9529] תָּפַר *tāpar* 4x [Q] to sew, mend; [P] to sew (together) [8609]

[9530] תָּפַשׂ *tāpaś* 65x [Q] to take hold of, seize, capture; [Qp] to be covered; [N] to be seized, be caught, be captured; [P] to catch (a lizard) [8610] See *capture; grasp; take hold; seize.*

[9531] 1 תֹּפֶת *tōpet* 1x spitting [8611]

[9535] 1 תִּקְוָה *tiqwâ* 2x cord [8615]

[9536] 2 תִּקְוָה *tiqwâ* 32x hope, expectation [8615]

[9538] תְּקוּמָה *t^eqûmâ* 1x ability to stand [8617]

[9540] תָּקוֹעַ *tāqôa^c* 1x trumpet, for battle signals [8619]

[9543] תְּקוּפָה *t^eqûpâ* 4x turning, course [8622]

[9544] תַּקִּיף *taqqîp* 1x strong, mighty [8623]

[9545] תָּקַן *tāqan* 3x [Q] to be straight; [P] to straighten, set in order [8626]

[9546] תָּקַע *tāqa^c* 70x [Q] to sound (a trumpet); to pitch, camp; to strike, clap; [Qp] to be driven; [N] to be sounded (a trumpet); to put up a security [8628] See *blow; clap; thrust; sound (a trumpet).*

[9547] תֵּקַע *tēqa^c* 1x sounding, blast (of a trumpet) [8629]

[9548] תָּקַף *tāqap* 3x [Q] to overpower, overwhelm [8630]

[9549] תֹּקֶף *tōqep* 3x power, might, authority [8633]

[9551] תַּרְבּוּת *tarbût* 1x a group of the same kind, brood [8635]

[9552] תַּרְבִּית *tarbît* 6x excessive interest, exorbitant interest [8636]

[9553] תִּרְגֵּם *tirgēm* 1x [Pu] to be interpreted, be translated [8638*]

[9554] תַּרְדֵּמָה *tardēmâ* 7x deep (supernatural) sleep, often a state of divine revelation and activity [8639]

[9556] תְּרוּמָה *t^erûmâ* 76x offering, special gift, contribution [8641] See *contribution; gift; offering; portion.*

[9557] תְּרוּמִיָּה *t^erûmiyyâ* 1x special gift, tribute [8642]

[9558] תְּרוּעָה *t^erû^câ* 36x trumpet blast, battle cry [8643]

[9559] תְּרוּפָה *t^erûpâ* 1x healing [8644]

[9560] תִּרְזָה *tirzâ* 1x cypress tree [8645]

[9564] תָּרְמָה *tormâ* 1x (under) cover [8649]

[9567] תַּרְמִית *tarmît* 5x deceitfulness, delusion [8649]

[9568] תֹּרֶן *tōren* 3x (sailing) mast; flagstaff (on top of hill) [8650]

[9570] תַּרְעֵלָה *tar^cēlâ* 3x staggering, reeling [8653]

[9572] תְּרָפִים *t^erāpîm* 15x household god, idol [8655] See *household gods; idol.*

[9576] 1 תַּרְשִׁישׁ *taršîš* 25x Tarshish, ships of Tarshish = trading ships, "[poss.]

yellow jasper; [poss.] *greedy one; foundry, refinery*" [8659]

[9577] 2 תַּרְשִׁישׁ *tar^{e}šîš* 7x chrysolite [8658]

[9579] תִּרְשָׁתָא *tiršātāʾ* 5x governor [8660]

[9580] תַּרְתָּן *tartān* 2x supreme commander, second in command [8661]

[9582] תְּשׂוּמָה *t^{e}śûmâ* 1x pledge, security [8667*]

[9583] תְּשֻׁאָה *t^{e}šuʾâ* 5x shouting, commotion, thundering [8663]

[9587] תַּשְׁבֵּץ *tašbēṣ* 1x woven or checkered fabric [8665]

[9588] תְּשׁוּבָה *t^{e}šûbâ* 8x spring [time of year]; answer [8666]

[9591] תְּשׁוּעָה *t^{e}šûʿâ* 34x deliverance, salvation, victory; divine salvation has its focus on rescue from earthly enemies, occasionally referring to salvation from guilt, sin, and punishment [8668]

[9592] תְּשׁוּקָה *t^{e}šûqâ* 3x desire, longing [8669]

[9593] תְּשׁוּרָה *t^{e}šûrâ* 1x gift, present [8670]

[9595] תְּשִׁיעִי *t^{e}šîʿî* 8x ninth [8671]

[9596] תֵּשַׁע *tēšaʿ* 58x nine, (pl.) ninety [8672] See *nine, ninety, ninth.*

Greek-English Dictionary

The first number in bold brackets is the Goodrick-Kohlenberger number. Following it is the Greek word, its transliteration, frequency (i.e., the number of times it occurs in the New Testament) followed by an "x," and then its definition. The final smaller number in brackets is the corresponding Strong's number (e.g., [25]). If there is no corresponding Strong's number, then there are double asterisks ([**]). If the entry ends with an asterisk, then all occurrences of the word in the NT have been noted.

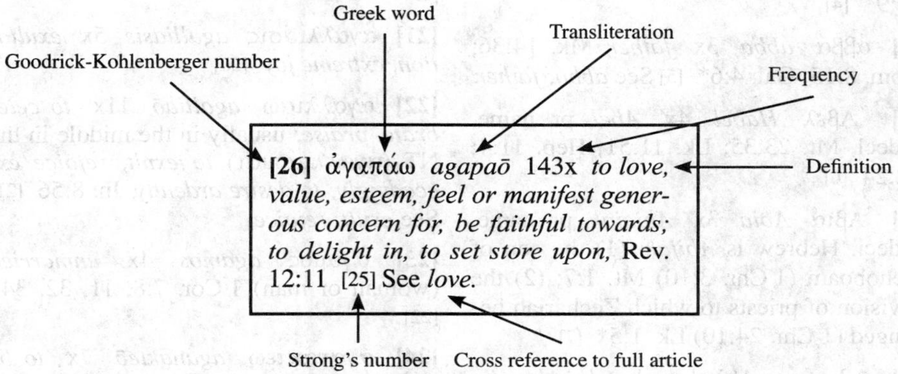

This dictionary includes all the Greek words that occur in the standard Greek NT. The frequencies are taken from the GNT-T database in the software program Accordance, which I helped develop.

This dictionary is not designed to replace a full dictionary (such as *A Greek-English Lexicon of the New Testament* by Frederick William Danker) or word study (such as *New International Dictionary of New Testament Theology: Abridged Edition* by Verlyn D. Verbrugge), but it will help for reference.

[2] ᾿Ααρών *Aarōn* 5x *Aaron,* pr. name, in decl, the brother of Moses (Exod. 4:14), Lk. 1:15; Acts 7:40; Heb. 5:4; 7:11; 9:4* [2]

[3] ᾿Αβαδδών *Abaddōn* 1x *Abaddon,* pr. name, indecl, alternate spelling: ᾿Αββαδων, the angel who rules in hell, Rev. 9:11* [3]

[4] ἀβαρής *abarēs* 1x literally: *weightless*; figurately: *not burdensome,* 2 Cor. 11:9* [4]

[5] ἀββά *abba* 3x *father,* Mk. 14:36; Rom. 8:15; Gal. 4:6* [5] See *abba; father.*

[6] ῞Αβελ *Habel* 4x *Abel,* pr. name, indecl, Mt. 23:35; Lk. 11:51; Heb. 11:4; 12:24 [6]

[7] ᾿Αβιά *Abia* 3x *Abiajah,* pr. name, indecl. Hebrew is *Abijah.* (1) the son of Rehoboam (1 Chr. 3:10) Mt. 1:7; (2) the division of priests to which Zechariah belonged (1 Chr. 24:10) Lk. 1:5* [7]

[8] ᾿Αβιαθάρ *Abiathar* 1x *Abiathar,* pr. name, indecl, Mk. 2:26* [8]

[9] ᾿Αβιληνή *Abilēnē* 1x *Abilene,* a district of the Syrian Decapolis; from *Abila,* the chief town, Lk. 3:1* [9]

[10] ᾿Αβιούδ *Abioud* 2x *Abihud,* pr. name, indecl [10]

[11] ᾿Αβραάμ *Abraam* 73x *Abraham,* pr. name indecl [11]

[12] ἄβυσσος *abyssos* 9x *bottomless; place of the dead,* Lk. 8:31; Rom. 10:7 [12]

[13] ῞Αγαβος *Hagabos* 2x *Agabus, pr. name,* Acts 11:28; 21:10* [13]

[14] ἀγαθοεργέω *agathoergeō* 2x *to do good, confer benefits,* Acts 14:17; 1 Tim. 6:18* [14]

[16] ἀγαθοποιέω *agathopoieō* 9x *to do good, do well; to do what is morally correct* (1 Pet. 2:15, 20) [15]

[17] ἀγαθοποιΐα *agathopoiia* 1x *well-doing,* 1 Pet. 4:19* [16]

[18] ἀγαθοποιός *agathopoios* 1x *doing good* or *right;* subst., *a well-doer,* 1 Pet. 2:14* [17]

[19] ἀγαθός *agathos* 102x *good, profitable, generous, upright, virtuous* [18] See *good.*

[20] ἀγαθωσύνη *agathōsynē* 4x *goodness, virtue, beneficence,* Rom. 5:14; Eph. 5:9; 2 Thess. 1:11; *generosity,* Gal. 5:22* [19]

[21] ἀγαλλίασις *agalliasis* 5x *exultation, extreme joy* [20]

[22] ἀγαλλιάω *agalliaō* 11x *to celebrate, praise;* usually in the middle in the NT (ἀγαλλιάομαι) *to exult, rejoice exceedingly; to desire ardently,* Jn. 8:56 [21] See *exult; rejoice.*

[23] ἄγαμος *agamos* 4x *unmarried* (woman or man) 1 Cor. 7:8, 11, 32, 34* [22]

[24] ἀγανακτέω *aganakteō* 7x *to be pained; to be angry, vexed, indignant; to manifest indignation,* Mk. 14:4; Lk. 13:14 [23]

[25] ἀγανάκτησις *aganaktēsis* 1x *indignation,* 2 Cor. 7:11* [24]

[26] ἀγαπάω *agapaō* 143x *to love, value, esteem, feel or manifest generous concern for, be faithful towards; to delight in, to set store upon,* Rev. 12:11 [25] See *love.*

[27] ἀγάπη *agapē* 116x *love, generosity, kindly concern, devotedness;* pl. *love-feasts,* Jude 12 [26] See *love.*

[28] ἀγαπητός *agapētos* 61x *beloved, dear; worthy of love* [27] See *beloved; dear.*

[29] ῾Αγάρ *Hagar* 2x pr. name, indecl, *Hagar* (Gen. 16), Gal. 4:24, 25* [28]

[30] ἀγγαρεύω *angareuō* 3x *to press,* or *compel* another to go somewhere, or carry some burden, Mt. 5:41; 27:32; Mk. 15:21* [29]

[31] ἀγγεῖον *angeion* 1x *a vessel, flask,* Mt. 25:4* [30]

[32] ἀγγελία *angelia* 2x *a messsage, doctrine,* or *precept,* delivered in the name of any one; *command,* 1 Jn. 1:5; 3:11* [31]

[33] ἀγγέλλω *angellō* 1x *to tell, to announce,* Jn. 20:18* [518]

[34] ἄγγελος *angelos* 175x *one sent, a messenger, angel* [32] See *angel; messenger.*

[35] ἄγγος *angos* 1x *vessel, container, basket,* Mt. 13:48* [30]

[36] ἀγέλη *agelē* 7x *flock, herd* [34]

[37] ἀγενεαλόγητος *agenealogētos* 1x *not included in a genealogy; independent of genealogy,* Heb. 7:3* [35]

[38] ἀγενής *agenēs* 1x lit., *without kin*; fig., *base, low, insignificant,* 1 Cor. 1:28* [36]

[39] ἁγιάζω *hagiazō* 28x *to separate, consecrate; cleanse, purify, sanctify; regard* or *reverence as holy* [37] See *consecrate; holy; make holy; sanctify.*

[40] ἁγιασμός *hagiasmos* 10x *sanctification, moral purity, sanctity* [38] See *holy.*

[41] ἅγιος *hagios* 233x *separate from common condition and use; dedicated.* Lk. 2:23; *hallowed;* used of things, τὰ ἅγια, *the sanctuary;* and of persons, *saints,* e.g., members of the first Christian communities; *pure, righteous,* ceremonially or morally; *holy* [39, 40] See *consecrate; holy; sacred; saint; sanctify.*

[42] ἁγιότης *hagiotēs* 1x *holiness, sanctity,* Heb. 12:10* [41]

[43] ἁγιωσύνη *hagiōsynē* 3x *sanctification, sanctity, holiness,* Rom. 1:4; 2 Cor. 7:1; 1 Thess. 3:13* [42]

[44] ἀγκάλη *ankalē* 1x *the arm,* Lk. 2:28* [43]

[45] ἄγκιστρον *ankistron* 1x *a hook, fish-hook,* Mt. 17:27* [44]

[46] ἄγκυρα *ankyra* 4x *an anchor,* Acts 27:29, 30, 40; Heb. 6:19* [45]

[47] ἄγναφος *agnaphos* 2x *unshrunken; new,* Mt. 9:16; Mk. 2:21* [46]

[48] ἁγνεία *hagneia* 2x *purity, chastity,* 1 Tim. 4:12; 5:2* [47] See *innocent.*

[49] ἁγνίζω *hagnizō* 7x *to purify; to purify morally, reform, to live like one under a vow of abstinence,* as the Nazarites [48] See *purify.*

[50] ἁγνισμός *hagnismos* 1x *purification, abstinence,* Acts 21:26* [49]

[51] ἀγνοέω *agnoeō* 22x *to be ignorant; not to understand; sin through ignorance* [50] See *(be) ignorant; not know; not understand.*

[52] ἀγνόημα *agnoēma* 1x *error, sin of ignorance,* Heb. 9:7* [51]

[53] ἄγνοια *agnoia* 4x *ignorance, willfulness,* Acts 3:17; 17:30; Eph. 4:18; 1 Pet. 1:14* [52]

[54] ἁγνός *hagnos* 8x *pure, chaste, modest, innocent, blameless* [53] See *innocent; pure, purity.*

[55] ἁγνότης *hagnotēs* 2x *purity, life of purity,* 2 Cor. 6:6; 11:3* [54] See *pure, purity.*

[56] ἁγνῶς *hagnōs* 1x *purely, with sincerity,* Phil. 1:17* [55]

[57] ἀγνωσια *agnōsia* 2x *ignorance,* 1 Cor. 15:34; 1 Pet. 2:15* [56]

[58] ἄγνωστος *agnōstos* 1x *unknown,* Acts 17:23* [57]

[59] ἀγορά *agora* 11x *a place of public concourse, forum, market-place; things said in the market, provision* [58] See *marketplace.*

[60] ἀγοράζω *agorazō* 30x *to buy; redeem, acquire* by a ransom or price paid [59] See *buy; purchase.*

[61] ἀγοραῖος *agoraios* 2x *one who visits the forum; a lounger, one who idles away his time in public places, a low fellow,* Acts 17:5; *pertaining to the forum, ju-*

dicial; ἀγόραιοι, *court days,* Acts 19:38* [60]

[62] ἄγρα *agra* 2x *a catching, thing taken, draught* of fishes, Lk. 5:4, 9* [61]

[63] ἀγράμματος *agrammatos* 1x *illiterate, unlearned,* Acts 4:13* [62]

[64] ἀγραυλέω *agrauleō* 1x *to remain in the open air, to live outside,* especially *by night,* Lk. 2:8* [63]

[65] ἀγρεύω *agreuō* 1x *to take in hunting, catch,* Mk. 12:13* [64]

[66] ἀγριέλαιος *agrielaios* 2x *a wild olive-tree, oleaster,* Rom. 11:17, 24* [65]

[67] ἄγριος *agrios* 3x *belonging to the field, wild; fierce, raging,* Mt. 3:4; Mk. 1:6; Jude 13* [66]

[68] Ἀγρίππας *Agrippas* 11x *Agrippa,* pr. name [67]

[69] ἀγρός *agros* 36x *a field,* especially *a cultivated field;* pl. *the country; lands, farms, villages* [68] See *countryside; field.*

[70] ἀγρυπνέω *agrypneō* 4x *to be awake, watch; to be watchful, vigilant* [69]

[71] ἀγρυπνία *agrypnia* 2x *want of sleep, watching,* 2 Cor. 6:5; 11:27* [70]

[72] ἄγω *agō* 67x *to lead. bring; lead away, drive off,* as a booty of cattle; *conduct, accompany; lead out, produce; conduct with force, drag, hurry away; guide, incite, entice; convey one's self, go, go away; pass* or *spend* as *time; celebrate* [33, 71] See *bring; go; lead.*

[73] ἀγωγή *agōgē* 1x *guidance, mode of instruction, discipline, course of life,* 2 Tim. 3:10* [72]

[74] ἀγών *agōn* 6x *place of contest, race-course, stadium; a contest, strife, contention; peril, toil* [73]

[75] ἀγωνία *agōnia* 1x *contest, violent struggle; agony, anguish,* Lk. 22:44* [74]

[76] ἀγωνίζομαι *agōnizomai* 8x *to be a combatant in the public games; to contend, fight, strive earnestly* [75]

[77] Ἀδάμ *Adam* 9x *Adam,* pr. name, indecl [76] See *Adam.*

[78] ἀδάπανος *adapanos* 1x *without expense, gratuitous,* 1 Cor. 9:18* [77]

[79] Ἀδδί *Addi* 1x *Addi,* pr. name, indecl Lk. 3:28* [78]

[80] ἀδελφή *adelphē* 26x *a sister; near kinswoman,* or *female relative, a female member of the Christian community* [79] See *sister.*

[81] ἀδελφός *adelphos* 343x *a brother, near kinsman* or *relative; one of the same nation* or *nature; one of equal rank and dignity; an associate, a member of the Christian community* [80] See *brother.*

[82] ἀδελφότης *adelphotēs* 2x *brotherhood, the body of the Christian brotherhood,* 1 Pet. 2:17; 5:9* [81]

[83] ἄδηλος *adēlos* 2x *not apparent* or *obvious; uncertain, not distinct,* Lk. 11:44; 1 Cor. 14:8* [82]

[84] ἀδηλότης *adēlotēs* 1x *uncertainty,* 1 Tim. 6:17* [83]

[85] ἀδήλως *adēlōs* 1x *not manifestly, uncertainly, dubiously,* 1 Cor. 9:26* [84]

[86] ἀδημονέω *adēmoneō* 3x *to be depressed* or *dejected, full of anguish* or *sorrow,* Mt. 26:37; Mk. 14:33; Phil. 2:26* [85]

[87] ᾅδης *hadēs* 10x *the invisible abode* or *mansion of the dead; the place of punishment, hell; the lowest place* or *condition,* Mt. 11:23; Lk. 10:15 [86] See *grave; hades; hell.*

[88] ἀδιάκριτος *adiakritos* 1x *undistinguishing, impartial,* Jas. 3:17* [87]

[89] ἀδιάλειπτος *adialeiptos* 2x *unceasing, constant, settled,* Rom. 9:2; 2 Tim. 1:3* [88]

[90] ἀδιαλείπτως *adialeiptōs* 4x *unceasingly, by an unvarying practice,* Rom. 1:9; 1 Thess. 1:2; 2:13; 5:17* [89]

[92] ἀδικέω *adikeō* 28x *to act unjustly; wrong; injure; violate a law* [91] See *do wrong; harm; mistreat.*

[93] ἀδίκημα *adikēma* 3x *an act of injustice, crime,* Acts 18:14; 24:20; Rev. 18:5* [92]

[94] ἀδικία *adikia* 25x *injustice, wrong; iniquity, falsehood, deceitfulness* [93] See *evil; unrighteousness; wicked, wickedness; wrongdoing.*

[96] ἄδικος *adikos* 12x *unjust, unrighteous, iniquitous, vicious; deceitful, fallacious* [94] See *evildoer; unjust; unrighteous; wicked, wickedness.*

[97] ἀδίκως *adikōs* 1x *unjustly, undeservedly,* 1 Pet. 2:19* [95]

[98] Ἀδμίν *Admin* 1x *Admin,* pr. name, indecl, Lk. 3:33* [689]

[99] ἀδόκιμος *adokimos* 8x *unable to stand test, rejected, refuse, worthless* [96]

[100] ἄδολος *adolos* 1x *without deceit, sincere,* 1 Pet. 2:2* [97]

[101] Ἀδραμυττηνός *Adramyttēnos* 1x *of Adramyttium,* a Greek city on the coast of Aeolia, in Asia Minor, Acts 27:2* [98]

[102] Ἀδρίας *Adrias* 1x *the Adriatic sea,* Acts 27:27* [99]

[103] ἁδρότης *hadrotēs* 1x *abundance,* 2 Cor. 8:20* [100]

[104] ἀδυνατέω *adynateō* 2x *not to be able; to be impossible,* Mt. 17:20; Lk. 1:37* [101]

[105] ἀδύνατος *adynatos* 10x *impotent, weak; impossible* [102] See *crippled; impossible.*

[106] ᾄδω *adō* 5x *to sing,* Eph. 5:19; Col. 3:16; Rev. 5:9; 14:3; 15:3* [103] See *sing.*

[107] ἀεί *aei* 7x *always, for ever, constantly* [104]

[108] ἀετός *aetos* 5x *an eagle,* Rev. 12:14; or *vulture,* Lk. 17:37 [105]

[109] ἄζυμος *azymos* 9x *unleavened;* τὰ ἄζυμα, *the feast of unleavened bread;* met. *pure from foreign matter, unadulterated, genuine;* τὸ ἄζυμον, *genuineness,* 1 Cor. 5:7, 8 [106]

[110] Ἀζώρ *Azōr* 2x *Azor,* pr. name, indecl, Mt. 1:13f.* [107]

[111] Ἄζωτος *Azōtos* 1x *Azotus, Ashdod,* a seaport in Palestine, Acts 8:40* [108]

[113] ἀήρ *aēr* 7x *air, atmosphere* [109]

[114] ἀθανασία *athanasia* 3x *immortality,* 1 Cor. 15:53, 54; 1 Tim. 6:16* [110]

[116] ἀθέμιτος *athemitos* 2x *unlawful, criminal, wicked,* Acts 10:28; 1 Pet. 4:3* [111]

[117] ἄθεος *atheos* 1x *an atheist; godless, estranged from the knowledge and worship of the true God,* Eph. 2:12* [112]

[118] ἄθεσμος *athesmos* 2x *lawless, unrestrained, licentious,* 2 Pet. 2:7; 3:17* [113]

[119] ἀθετέω *atheteō* 16x pr. *to displace, set aside; to abrogate, annul, violate, swerve from; reject, condemn* [114] See *annul; nullify; reject; set aside.*

[120] ἀθέτησις *athetēsis* 2x *abrogation, annulling,* Heb. 7:18; 9:26* [115]

[122] Ἀθηναῖος *Athēnaios* 2x *Athenian, inhabiting* or *belonging to Athens,* Acts 17:21, 22* [117]

[123] ἀθλέω *athleō* 2x *to strive, contend, be a champion in the public games,* 2 Tim. 2:5* [118]

[124] ἄθλησις *athlēsis* 1x *contest, combat, struggle, conflict,* Heb. 10:32* [119]

[125] ἀθροίζω *athroizō* 1x *to collect, gather,* Lk. 24:33* [4867]

[126] ἀθυμέω *athumeō* 1x *to be discouraged, lose heart,* Col. 3:21* [120]

[127] ἀθῷος *athōos* 2x *unpunished;* metaph. *innocent,* Mt. 27:4, 24* [121]

[128] αἴγειος *aigeios* 1x *belonging to a goat,* Heb. 11:37* [122]

[129] αἰγιαλός *aigialos* 6x *seashore, beach,* Mt. 13:2, 48; Jn. 21:4; Acts 21:5; 27:39f.* [123]

[130] Αἰγύπτιος *Aigyptios* 5x *Egyptian* [124]

[131] Αἴγυπτος *Aigyptos* 25x *Egypt* [125]

[132] ἀΐδιος *aidios* 2x *always existing, eternal,* Rom. 1:20; Jude 6 [126]

[133] αἰδώς *aidōs* 1x *modesty, reverence,* 1 Tim. 2:9* [127]

[134] Αἰθίοψ *Aithiops* 2x *an Ethiopian,* Acts 8:27* [128]

[135] αἷμα *haima* 97x *blood; of the color of blood; bloodshed; blood-guiltiness; natural descent* [129] See *blood; death; killing.*

[136] αἱματεκχυσία *haimatekchusia* 1x *an effusion* or *shedding of blood,* Heb. 9:22* [130]

[137] αἱμορροέω *haimorroeō* 1x *to have a flow of blood,* Mt. 9:20* [131]

[138] Αἰνέας *Aineas* 2x *Aeneas,* pr. name, Acts 9:33f.* [132]

[139] αἴνεσις *ainesis* 1x *praise,* Heb. 13:15* [133]

[140] αἰνέω *aineō* 8x *to praise, celebrate* [134]

[141] αἴνιγμα *ainigma* 1x *an enigma, riddle, any thing obscurely expressed* or *intimated,* 1 Cor. 13:12* [135]

[142] αἶνος *ainos* 2x *praise,* Mt. 21:16; Lk. 18:43* [136]

[143] Αἰνών *Ainōn* 1x *Enon,* pr. name, indecl, where Jn. was baptizing, Jn. 3:23* [137]

[145] αἱρέω *haireō* 3x some list as deponent αἱρέομαι, *to take;* mid. *to choose* [138]

[146] αἵρεσις *hairesis* 9x strictly, *a choice* or *option;* hence, *a religious sect, faction;* by implication, *discord, contention* [139]

[147] αἱρετίζω *hairetizō* 1x *to choose, choose with delight* or *love,* Mt. 12:18* [140]

[148] αἱρετικός *hairetikos* 1x *one who creates* or *fosters factions,* Tit. 3:10* [141]

[149] αἴρω *airō* 101x *to take up, lift, raise; bear, carry; take away, remove; destroy, kill* [142] See *carry off; lift up; remove; take up.*

[150] αἰσθάνομαι *aisthanomai* 1x *to perceive, understand,* Lk. 9:45* [143]

[151] αἴσθησις *aisthēsis* 1x *perception, understanding,* Phil. 1:9* [144]

[152] αἰσθητήριον *aisthētērion* 1x *an organ of perception; internal sense,* Heb. 5:14* [145]

[153] αἰσχροκερδής *aischrokerdēs* 2x *eager for dishonorable gain, greedy,* 1 Tim. 3:8; Tit. 1:7* [146]

[154] αἰσχροκερδῶς *aischrokerdōs* 1x *for the sake of base gain, greedily,* 1 Pet. 5:2* [147]

[155] αἰσχρολογία *aischrologia* 1x *vile* or *obscene language, foul talk,* Col. 3:8* [148]

[156] αἰσχρός *aischros* 4x strictly, *deformed,* opposed to καλός; metaph. *shameful, indecent, dishonorable, vile,* 1 Cor. 11:6; 14:35; Eph. 5:12; Tit. 1:11* [149, 150]

[157] αἰσχρότης *aischrotēs* 1x *obscenity, indecency,* Eph. 5:4* [151]

[158] αἰσχύνη *aischunē* 6x *shame, disgrace; cause of shame, dishonorable conduct* [152]

[160] αἰτέω *aiteō* 70x *to ask, request; demand; desire,* Acts 7:46 [154] See *ask; demand; request.*

[161] αἴτημα *aitēma* 3x *a thing asked* or *sought for; petition, request,* Lk. 23:24; Phil. 4:6; 1 Jn. 5:15* [155]

[162] αἰτία *aitia* 20x *cause, motive, incitement; accusation, crime, case* [156] See *basis; cause; charge; reason.*

[165] αἴτιος *aitios* 5x *causative;* αἴτιος, *an author* or *causer,* Heb. 5:9; τὸ αἴτιον, equivalent to αἰτία [158, 159]

[166] αἰτίωμα *aitiōma* 1x *charge, accusation,* Acts 25:7* [157]

[167] αἰφνίδιος *aiphnidios* 2x *unforeseen, unexpected, sudden,* Lk. 21:34; 1 Thess. 5:3* [160]

[168] αἰχμαλωσία *aichmalōsia* 3x *captivity, state of captivity; captive multitude,* Eph. 4:8; Rev. 13:10* [161]

[169] αἰχμαλωτεύω *aichmalōteuō* 1x *to lead captive;* met. *to captivate,* Eph. 4:8* [162]

[170] αἰχμαλωτίζω *aichmalōtizō* 4x *to lead captive;* by impl. *to subject,* Lk. 21:24; Rom. 7:23; 2 Cor. 10:5; 2 Tim. 3:6* [163]

[171] αἰχμάλωτος *aichmalōtos* 1x *a captive,* Lk. 4:18* [164]

[172] αἰών *aiōn* 122x pr. *a period of time of significant character; life; an era; an age:* hence, *a state of things marking an age* or *era; the present order of nature; the natural condition of man, the world;* ὁ αἰών, *illimitable duration, eternity;* as also, οἱ αἰῶνες, ὁ αἰῶν τῶν αἰώνων, οἱ αἰῶνες τῶν αἰώνων; by an Aramaism οἱ αἰῶνες, *the material universe,* Heb. 1:2 [165] See *age; eternity; time.*

[173] αἰώνιος *aiōnios* 71x *indeterminate as to duration, eternal, everlasting* [166] See *eternal.*

[174] ἀκαθαρσία *akatharsia* 10x *uncleanness; lewdness; impurity* of motive, 1 Thess. 2:3 [167] See *impure; unclean.*

[176] ἀκάθαρτος *akathartos* 32x *impure, unclean; lewd; foul* [169] See *defiled; evil; impure; unclean.*

[177] ἀκαιρέομαι *akaireomai* 1x *to be without opportunity* or *occasion,* Phil. 4:10* [170]

[178] ἀκαίρως *akairōs* 1x *unseasonably,* 2 Tim. 4:2* [171]

[179] ἄκακος *akakos* 2x *free from evil, innocent, blameless; simple,* Rom. 16:18; Heb. 7:26* [172]

[180] ἄκανθα *akantha* 14x *a thorn, thornbush,* Mt. 7:16; 13:7; 27:29 [173] See *thorn.*

[181] ἀκάνθινος *akanthinos* 2x *thorny, made of thorns,* Mk. 15:17; Jn. 19:5* [174]

[182] ἄκαρπος *akarpos* 7x *without fruit, unfruitful, barren;* by impl. *noxious* [175]

[183] ἀκατάγνωστος *akatagnōstos* 1x pr. *not worthy of condemnation* by a judge; hence, *irreprehensible,* Tit. 2:8* [176]

[184] ἀκατακάλυπτος *akatakalyptos* 2x *uncovered, unveiled,* 1 Cor. 11:5, 13* [177]

[185] ἀκατάκριτος *akatakritos* 2x *uncondemned* in a public trial, Acts 16:37; 22:25* [178]

[186] ἀκατάλυτος *akatalytos* 1x *incapable of dissolution, indissoluble;* hence, *enduring, everlasting,* Heb. 7:16* [179]

[188] ἀκατάπαυστος *akatapaustos* 1x also spelled ἀκατάπαστος, *which cannot be restrained* from a thing, *unceasing,* 2 Pet. 2:14* [180]

[189] ἀκαταστασία *akatastasia* 5x pr. *instability;* hence, *an unsettled state; disorder, commotion, tumult, sedition,* Lk. 21:9; 1 Cor. 14:33; 2 Cor. 6:5; 12:20; Jas. 3:16* [181]

[190] ἀκατάστατος *akatastatos* 2x *unstable, inconstant; unquiet, turbulent,* Jas. 1:8; 3:8* [182]

[193] ἀκέραιος *akeraios* 3x pr. *unmixed:* hence, *without mixture of vice* or *deceit, sincere, blameless,* Mt. 10:16; Rom. 16:19; Phil. 2:15* [185]

[195] ἀκλινής *aklinēs* 1x *not declining, unwavering, steady,* Heb. 10:23* [186]

[196] ἀκμάζω *akmazō* 1x *to flourish, ripen, be in one's prime,* Rev. 14:18* [187]

[197] ἀκμήν *akmēn* 1x pr. *the point of a weapon; point of time:* ἀκμήν, for κατὰκμήν, adv., *yet, still, even now,* Mt. 15:16* [188]

[198] ἀκοή *akoē* 24x *hearing; the act* or *sense of hearing,* 1 Cor. 12:17; 2 Pet. 2:8; *the instrument of hearing, the ear,* Mk. 7:35; *a thing heard;* announcement, *instruction, doctrine,* Jn. 12:38; Rom. 10:16; *report,* Mt. 4:24, et al [189] See *ear; hearing; message.*

[199] ἀκολουθέω *akoloutheō* 90x *to follow; follow* as a disciple; *imitate* [190] See *accompany; follow.*

[201] ἀκούω *akouō* 428x some list the future active as a middle deponent, ἀκούσομαι, *to hear; to hearken, listen to,* Mk. 4:3; Lk. 19:48; *to heed, obey,* Mt. 18:15; Acts 4:19; *to understand,* 1 Cor. 14:2; *to take in* or *admit* to mental acceptance, Mk. 4:33; Jn. 8:43, 47 [191] See *hear.*

[202] ἀκρασία *akrasia* 2x *intemperance, self-indulgence,* Mt. 23:25; *unruly appetite, lustfulness,* 1 Cor. 7:5* [192]

[203] ἀκρατής *akratēs* 1x *without self-control, intemperate,* 2 Tim. 3:3 [193]

[204] ἄκρατος *akratos* 1x *unmixed, unmingled* wine, Rev. 14:10* [194]

[205] ἀκρίβεια *akribeia* 1x *accuracy, exactness; preciseness,* or *rigor, severe discipline,* Acts 22:3* [195]

[207] ἀκριβής *akribēs* 1x *exact, strict,* Acts 26:5* [**]

[208] ἀκριβόω *akriboō* 2x *to inquire accurately* or *diligently,* Mt. 2:7, 16 (see v. 8)* [198]

[209] ἀκριβῶς *akribōs* 9x *accurately, diligently,* Mt. 2:8; Lk. 1:3; Acts 18:25; *circumspectly, strictly,* Eph. 5:15; *precisely, distinctly,* 1 Thess. 5:2 [199, 197]

[210] ἀκρίς *akris* 4x *a locust,* Mt. 3:4; Mk. 1:6; Rev. 9:3, 7* [200]

[211] ἀκροατήριον *akroatērion* 1x *a place of audience,* Acts 25:23* [201]

[212] ἀκροατής *akroatēs* 4x *a hearer,* Rom. 2:13; Jas. 1:22, 23, 25* [202]

[213] ἀκροβυστία *akrobystia* 20x *foreskin; uncircumcision, the state of being uncircumcised,* Rom. 4:10; the abstract being put for the concrete, *uncircumcised men,* i.e., *Gentiles,* Rom. 4:9, et al [203] See *uncircumcised, uncircumcision.*

[214] ἀκρογωνιαῖος *akrogōniaios* 2x literally: *lying at the extreme corner*; with λίθος, *corner* or *foundation stone,* Eph. 2:20; 1 Pet. 2:6* [204]

[215] ἀκροθίνιον *akrothinion* 1x *the first-fruits* of the produce of the ground, which were taken from the top of the heap and offered to the gods; *the best and choicest of the spoils* of war, usually collected in a heap, Heb. 7:4* [205]

[216] ἄκρον *akron* 6x *the top, tip, end, extremity,* Mk. 13:27; Lk. 16:24; Heb. 11:21 [206]

[217] Ἀκύλας *Akylas* 6x *Aquila,* pr. name, Paul's friend and Priscilla's husband, Acts 18:2, 18, 26; Rom. 16:3; 1 Cor. 16:19; 2 Tim. 4:19* [207]

[218] ἀκυρόω *akyroō* 3x *to deprive of authority, annul, cancel,* Mt. 15:6; Mk. 7:13; Gal. 3:17* [208]

[219] ἀκωλύτως *akōlytōs* 1x *without hindrance, freely,* Acts 28:31* [209]

[220] ἄκων *akōn* 1x *unwilling,* 1 Cor. 9:17* [210]

[223] ἀλάβαστρος *alabastros* 4x can be masculine, feminine (2x), or neuter (ἀλάβαστρον, 2x), *an alabaster vase,* Mk. 14:3 (2x); 26:7; Lk. 7:37* [211]

[224] ἀλαζονεία *alazoneia* 2x *arrogance; presumptuous speech,* Jas. 4:16; *haughtiness,* 1 Jn. 2:16* [212]

[225] ἀλαζών *alazōn* 2x *prideful, arrogant, boasting,* Rom. 1:30; 2 Tim. 3:2* [213]

[226] ἀλαλάζω *alalazō* 2x pr. *to raise the war-cry,* ἀλαλά: hence, *to utter* other *loud sounds; to wail,* Mk. 5:38; *to tinkle, ring,* 1 Cor. 13:1* [214]

[227] ἀλάλητος *alalētos* 1x *unutterable,* or, *unexpressed,* Rom. 8:26* [215]

[228] ἄλαλος *alalos* 3x *unable to speak* or *artilculate,* Mk. 7:37; 9:17, 25* [216]

[229] ἅλας *halas* 8x variant spellings of ἅλα and ἁλός, *salt,* Mt. 5:13; Mk. 9:50; met. *the salt* of wisdom and prudence, Col. 4:6 [217] See *salt.*

[230] ἀλείφω *aleiphō* 9x *to anoint* with oil or ointment [218] See *anoint.*

[231] ἀλεκτοροφωνία *alektorophōnia* 1x *the cock-crowing, the third watch of the night,* intermediate to mid-night and daybreak, and termed *cock-crow,* Mk. 13:35* [219]

[232] ἀλέκτωρ *alektōr* 12x *a cock, rooster,* Mt. 26:34; Mk. 14:30; Lk. 22:34; Jn. 13:38 [220] See *cock, rooster.*

[233] Ἀλεξανδρεύς *Alexandreus* 2x *a native of Alexandria, an Alexandrine,* Acts 6:9; 18:24 [221]

[234] Ἀλεξανδρῖνος *Alexandrinos* 2x *Alexandrian,* Acts 27:6; 28:11* [222]

[235] Ἀλέξανδρος *Alexandros* 6x *Alexander,* pr. name. (1) *The High Priest's kinsman,* Acts 4:6. (2) *A Jew of Ephesus,* Acts 19:33. (3) *The coppersmith,* 1 Tim. 1:20; 2 Tim. 4:14. (4) *Son of Simon of Cyrene,* Mk. 15:21* [223]

[236] ἄλευρον *aleuron* 2x *meal, flour,* Mt. 13:33; Lk. 13:21* [224]

[237] ἀλήθεια *alētheia* 109x *truth,* Mk. 5:33; *love of truth, sincerity,* 1 Cor. 5:8; divine *truth* revealed to man, Jn. 1:17; *practice in accordance with* Gospel *truth,* Jn. 3:21; 2 Jn. 4 [225] See *truth.*

[238] ἀληθεύω *alētheuō* 2x *to speak* or *maintain the truth; to act truly* or *sincerely,* Gal. 4:16; Eph. 4:15* [226]

[239] ἀληθής *alēthēs* 26x *true,* Jn. 4:18; *worthy of credit,* Jn. 5:31; *truthful,* Jn. 7:18 [227] See *truth.*

[240] ἀληθινός *alēthinos* 28x *sterling,* Lk. 16:11; *real,* Jn. 6:32; 1 Thess. 1:9; *unfeigned, trustworthy, true,* Jn. 19:35 [228] See *truth.*

[241] ἀλήθω *alēthō* 2x *to grind,* Mt. 24:41; Lk. 17:35* [229]

[242] ἀληθῶς *alēthōs* 18x *truly, really,* Mt. 14:33; *certainly, of a truth,* Jn. 17:8; Acts 12:11: *truly, actually,* Jn. 4:18 [230] See *really; surely; truly.*

[243] ἁλιεύς *halieus* 5x *a fisherman,* Mt. 4:18, 19; Mk. 1:16, 17; Lk. 5:2 [231]

[244] ἁλιεύω *halieuō* 1x *to fish,* Jn. 21:3* [232]

[245] ἁλίζω *halizō* 2x *to salt, season with salt, preserve by salting,* Mt. 5:13; Mk. 9:49* [233]

[246] ἀλίσγημα *alisgēma* 1x *pollution, defilement,* Acts 15:20* [234]

[247] ἀλλά *alla* 638x *but; however; but still more;* ἀλλάγε, *at all events;* ἀλλη, *unless, except.* Ἀλλά also serves to introduce a sentence with keenness and emphasis, Jn. 16:2; Rom. 6:5; 7:7; Phil. 3:8 [235]

[248] ἀλλάσσω *allassō* 6x *to change, alter, transform,* Acts 6:14; Rom. 1:23; 1 Cor. 15:51, 52; Gal. 4:20; Heb. 1:12 [236]

[249] ἀλλαχόθεν *allachothen* 1x *from another place* or *elsewhere,* Jn. 10:1* [237]

[250] ἀλλαχοῦ *allachou* 1x *elsewhere,* Mk. 1:38* [**]

[251] ἀλληγορέω *allēgoreō* 1x *to say what is either designed* or *fitted to convey a meaning other than the literal one, to allegorize;* ἀλληγορούμενος, *adapted to an-*

other meaning, otherwise significant, Gal. 4:24* [238]

[252] ἀλληλουϊά *hallēlouia* 4x (Hebrew) *hallelujah, praise Yahweh* or *the Lord,* Rev. 19:1, 3, 4, 6* [239] See *alleluia; hallelujah.*

[253] ἀλλήλων *allēlōn* 100x *one another, each other* [240] See *each other; one another.*

[254] ἀλλογενής *allogenēs* 1x *of another race* or *nation,* i.e., not a Jew; *a stranger, foreigner,* Lk. 17:18* [241]

[256] ἅλλομαι *hallomai* 3x *to leap, jump, leap up,* Acts 3:8; 14:10; *to spring,* as water, Jn. 4:14* [242]

[257] ἄλλος *allos* 155x *another, some other;* ὁ ἄλλος, *the other;* οἱ ἄλλοι, *the others, the rest* [243] See *another; other.*

[258] ἀλλοτριεπίσκοπος *allotriepiskopos* 1x pr. *one who meddles with the affairs of others, a busybody in other men's matters; factious,* 1 Pet. 4:15* [244]

[259] ἀλλότριος *allotrios* 14x *belonging to another,* Lk. 16:12; *foreign,* Acts 7:6; Heb. 11:9; *a foreigner, alien,* Mt. 17:25 [245] See *foreign(er); other; someone else; strange(r).*

[260] ἀλλόφυλος *allophylos* 1x *of another race* or *nation,* i.e., not a Jew, *a foreigner,* Acts 10:28* [246]

[261] ἄλλως *allōs* 1x *otherwise,* 1 Tim. 5:25* [247]

[262] ἀλοάω *aloaō* 3x *to thresh; to tread,* 1 Cor. 9:9, 10; 1 Tim. 5:18* [248]

[263] ἄλογος *alogos* 3x *without speech* or *reason, irrational, brute,* 2 Pet. 2:12; Jude 10; *unreasonable, absurd,* Acts 25:27* [249]

[264] ἀλόη *aloē* 1x *aloe, lign-aloe,* a tree which grows in India and Cochin-China, the wood of which is soft and bitter, though highly aromatic. It is used by the Orientals as a perfume; and employed for the purposes of embalming, Jn. 19:39* [250]

[266] ἁλυκός *halykos* 1x *brackish, bitter, salt,* Jas. 3:12* [252]

[267] ἄλυπος *alypos* 1x *free from grief* or *sorrow,* Phil. 2:28* [253]

[268] ἅλυσις *halysis* 11x *a chain,* Mk. 5:3, 4 [254] See *chain.*

[269] ἀλυσιτελής *alysitelēs* 1x pr. *bringing in no revenue* or *profit;* hence, *unprofitable, useless; detrimental; ruinous, disastrous,* Heb. 13:17* [255]

[270] ἄλφα *alpha* 3x first letter of Greek alphabet, *Alpha,* Rev. 1:8.; 21:6; 22:13* [1] See *Alpha.*

[271] Ἁλφαῖος *Halphaios* 5x *Alphaeus,* pr. name (1) *Father of Jas. the less,* Mt. 10:3; Mk. 3:18; Lk. 6:15; Acts 1:13. (2) *Father of Levi,* (or Matthew) Mk. 2:14* [256]

[272] ἅλων *halōn* 2x *a threshing-floor, a place where corn is trodden out;* meton. *the corn which is trodden out,* Mt. 3:12; Lk. 3:17* [257]

[273] ἀλώπηξ *alōpēx* 3x *a fox,* Mt. 8:20; Lk. 9:58; met. *a fox-like, crafty man,* Lk. 13:32* [258]

[274] ἅλωσις *halōsis* 1x *a taking, catching, capture,* 2 Pet. 2:12* [259]

[275] ἅμα *hama* 10x also functions as an improper preposition with the genitive (2x), *with, together with; at the same time* [260]

[276] ἀμαθής *amathēs* 1x *unlearned, uninstructed, rude,* 2 Pet. 3:16* [261]

[277] ἀμαράντινος *amarantinos* 1x *unfading;* hence, *enduring,* 1 Pet. 5:4* [262]

[278] ἀμάραντος *amarantos* 1x *unfading;* hence, *enduring,* 1 Pet. 1:4* [263]

[279] ἁμαρτάνω *hamartanō* 43x pr. *to miss a mark; to be in error,* 1 Cor. 15:34; Tit. 3:11; *to sin,* Jn. 5:14; *to be guilty of wrong,* Mt. 18:15 [264] See *sin.*

[280] ἁμάρτημα *hamartēma* 4x *an error; sin, offence,* Mk. 3:28; 4:12; Rom. 3:25; 1 Cor. 6:18 [265]

[281] ἁμαρτία *hamartia* 173x *error; offence, sin,* Mt. 1:21; *a principle* or *cause of sin,* Rom. 7:7; *proneness to sin, sinful propensity,* Rom. 7:17, 20; *guilt* or *imputation of sin,* Jn. 9:41; Heb. 9:26; *a guilty subject, sin-offering, expiatory victim,* 2 Cor. 5:21 [266] See *sin.*

[282] ἀμάρτυρος *amartyros* 1x *without testimony* or *witness, without evidence,* Acts 14:17* [267]

[283] ἁμαρτωλός *hamartōlos* 47x *one who deviates from the path of virtue, a sinner,* Mk. 2:17; *depraved,* Mk. 8:38; *sinful, detestable,* Rom. 7:13 [268] See *sinful; sinner.*

[285] ἄμαχος *amachos* 2x *not disposed to fight; not quarrelsome* or *contentious,* 1 Tim. 3:3; Tit. 3:2* [269]

[286] ἀμάω *amaō* 1x *to collect; to reap, mow* or *cut down,* Jas. 5:4* [270]

[287] ἀμέθυστος *amethustos* 1x *an amethyst,* a gem of a deep purple or violet color, so called from its supposed efficacy in keeping off drunkenness, Rev. 21:20* [271]

[288] ἀμελέω *ameleō* 4x *not to care for, to neglect, disregard,* Mt. 22:5; 1 Tim. 4:14; Heb. 2:3; 8:9* [272]

[289] ἄμεμπτος *amemptos* 5x *blameless, irreprehensible, without defect,* Lk. 1:6; Phil. 2:15; 3:6; 1 Thess. 3:13; Heb. 8:7* [273]

[290] ἀμέμπτως *amemptōs* 2x *blamelessly, unblamably, unexceptionably,* 1 Thess. 2:10; 5:23* [274]

[291] ἀμέριμνος *amerimnos* 2x *free from care* or *solicitude,* Mt. 28:14; 1 Cor. 7:32* [275]

[292] ἀμετάθετος *ametathetos* 2x *unchangeable,* Heb. 6:17, 18* [276]

[293] ἀμετακίνητος *ametakinētos* 1x *immovable, firm,* 1 Cor. 15:58* [277]

[294] ἀμεταμέλητος *ametamelētos* 2x *not to be repented of;* by impl. *irrevocable, enduring,* Rom. 11:29; 2 Cor. 7:10* [278]

[296] ἄμετρος *ametros* 2x *without* or *beyond measure, regardless of measure,* 2 Cor. 10:13, 15* [280]

[297] ἀμήν *amēn* 129x *in truth, most certainly; so be it;* ὁ ἀμήν, *the faithful and true one,* Rev. 3:14 [281] See *amen; truly.*

[298] ἀμήτωρ *amētōr* 1x pr. *without mother; independent of maternal descent,* Heb. 7:3* [282]

[299] ἀμίαντος *amiantos* 4x pr. *unstained, unsoiled;* met. *undefiled, chaste,* Heb. 7:26; 13:4; *pure, sincere,* Jas. 1:27; *undefiled, unimpaired,* 1 Pet. 1:4* [283]

[300] Ἀμιναδάβ *Aminadab* 3x *Aminadab,* pr. name, indecl, Mt. 1:4; Lk. 3:33* [284]

[302] ἄμμος *ammos* 5x *sand,* Mt. 7:26; Rom. 9:27; Heb. 11:12; Rev. 12:18, 20* [285]

[303] ἀμνός *amnos* 4x *a lamb,* Jn. 1:29, 36; Acts 8:32; 1 Pet. 1:19* [286]

[304] ἀμοιβή *amoibē* 1x (adequate) *return, recompense,* 1 Tim. 5:4* [287]

[306] ἄμπελος *ampelos* 9x *a vine, grapevine* [288] See *vine.*

[307] ἀμπελουργός *ampelourgos* 1x *a vine-dresser, gardner,* Lk. 13:7* [289]

[308] ἀμπελών *ampelōn* 23x *a vineyard* [290] See *vineyard.*

[309] Ἀμπλιᾶτος *Ampliatos* 1x *Ampliatus,* pr. name, Rom. 16:8* [291]

[310] ἀμύνομαι *amynomai* 1x *to ward off; to help, assist; to repel from oneself, resist, make a defence; to assume the office of protector and avenger,* Acts 7:24* [292]

[311] ἀμφιβάλλω *amphiballō* 1x *to throw around; to cast* a net, Mk. 1:16* [906 + 293]

[312] ἀμφίβληστρον *amphiblēstron* 1x pr. *what is thrown around,* e.g., a garment; *a large kind of fishnet,* Mt. 4:18* [293]

[313] ἀμφιέζω *amphiezō* 1x *to clothe,* Lk. 12:28* [294]

[314] ἀμφιέννυμι *amphiennymi* 3x also spelled ἀμφιέζω and ἀμφιέννυμι, *to clothe, invest,* Mt. 6:30; 11:8; Lk. 7:25* [294]

[315] Ἀμφίπολις *Amphipolis* 1x *Amphipolis,* a city of Thrace, on the river Strymon, Acts 17:1* [295]

[316] ἄμφοδον *amphodon* 1x pr. *a road leading round a town* or *village; the street of a village,* Mk. 11:4* [296]

[317] ἀμφότεροι *amphoteroi* 14x *both.* Only plural in the NT. [297] See *both.*

[318] ἀμώμητος *amōmētos* 1x *blameless, unblemished,* 2 Pet. 3:14* [298]

[319] ἄμωμον *amōmon* 1x *amomum,* an odoriferous shrub, from which a precious ointment was prepared, Rev. 18:13* [**]

[322] Ἀμώς *Amōs* 3x *Amos,* pr. name, indecl, Mt. 1:10; Lk. 3:25* [301]

[323] ἄν *an* 166x For the various constructions of this particle, and their significance, consult a grammar. At the beginning of a clause, it is another form of ἐάν, *if,* Jn. 20:23 [302]

[324] ἀνά *ana* 13x prep. used in the NT only in certain forms. ἀνὰ μέρος, *in turn;* ἀνὰ μέσον, *through the midst, between;* ἀνὰ δηνάριον, *at the rate of a denarius;* with numerals, ἀνὰ ἑκατόν, *in parties of a hundred.* In composition, *step by step, up, back, again* [303]

[325] ἀναβαθμός *anabathmos* 2x *the act of ascending; means of ascent, steps, stairs,* Acts 21:35, 40* [304]

[326] ἀναβαίνω *anabainō* 82x *to go up, ascend,* Mt. 5:1; *to climb,* Lk. 19:4; *to go on board,* Mk. 6:51; *to rise, mount upwards,* as smoke, Rev. 8:4; *to grow* or *spring up,* as plants, Mt. 13:7; *to spring up, arise,* as thoughts, Lk. 24:38 [305] See *ascend; go up.*

[327] ἀναβάλλω *anaballō* 1x *to throw back;* mid. *to put off, defer, adjourn,* Acts 24:22* [306]

[328] ἀναβιβάζω *anabibazō* 1x *to cause to come up* or *ascend, draw* or *bring up,* Mt. 13:48* [307]

[329] ἀναβλέπω *anablepō* 25x *to look upwards,* Mt. 14:19; *to see again, recover sight,* Mt. 11:5 [308] See *look up.*

[330] ἀνάβλεψις *anablepsis* 1x *recovery of sight,* Lk. 4:18* [309]

[331] ἀναβοάω *anaboaō* 1x *to cry out* or *aloud, exclaim,* Mt. 27:46* [310]

[332] ἀναβολή *anabolē* 1x *delay,* Acts 25:17* [311]

[333] ἀνάγαιον *anagaion* 2x *an upper room,* Mk. 14:15; Lk. 22:12* [508]

[334] ἀναγγέλλω *anangellō* 14x *to bring back word, announce, report,* Mk. 5:14; *to declare, set forth, teach,* Jn. 5:24 [312] See *report; tell.*

[335] ἀναγεννάω *anagennaō* 2x *to beget* or *bring forth again; to regenerate,* 1 Pet. 1:3, 23* [313]

[336] ἀναγινώσκω *anaginōskō* 32x *to gather exact knowledge of, recognize, discern;* especially, *to read* [314] See *read.*

[337] ἀναγκάζω *anankazō* 9x *to force, compel,* Acts 28:19; *to constrain, urge,* Lk. 14:23 [315] See *compel, compelled.*

[338] ἀναγκαῖος *anankaios* 8x *necessary, indispensable,* 1 Cor. 12:22; *necessary, needful, right, proper,* Acts 13:46; 2 Cor. 9:5; Phil. 1:24; 2:25; Heb. 8:3; *near, intimate, closely connected,* as friends, Acts 10:24 [316]

[339] ἀναγκαστῶς *anankastōs* 1x *by constraint* or *compulsion, unwillingly,* opposite to ἑκουσίως, 1 Pet. 5:2* [317]

[340] ἀνάγκη *anankē* 17x *necessity,* Mt. 18:7; *constraint, compulsion,* 2 Cor.

9:7; *obligation of duty,* moral or spiritual *necessity,* Rom. 13:5; *distress, trial, affliction,* Lk. 21:23; 1 Cor. 7:26; 2 Cor. 6:4; 12:10; 1 Thess. 3:7 [318] See *compelled; distress; must; necessary.*

[341] ἀναγνωρίζω *anagnōrizō* 1x *to recognize;* pass. *to be made known,* or *to cause one's self to be recognized,* Acts 7:13* [319]

[342] ἀνάγνωσις *anagnōsis* 3x *reading,* Acts 13:15; 2 Cor. 3:14; 1 Tim. 4:13* [320]

[343] ἀνάγω *anagō* 23x *to conduct; to lead* or *convey* up from a lower place to a higher, Lk. 4:5; *to offer up,* as a sacrifice, Acts 7:41; *to lead out, produce,* Acts 12:4; as a nautical term (in the middle or passive), *to set sail, put to sea,* Lk. 8:22 [321] See *bring up; lead up; put out to sea; sail.*

[344] ἀναδείκνυμι *anadeiknymi* 2x pr. *to show anything by raising it aloft,* as a torch; *to display, manifest, show plainly* or *openly,* Acts 1:24; *to mark out, constitute, appoint* by some outward sign, Lk. 10:1* [322]

[345] ἀνάδειξις *anadeixis* 1x *a showing forth, manifestation; public entrance upon the duty* or *office to which one is consecrated,* Lk. 1:80* [323]

[346] ἀναδέχομαι *anadechomai* 2x *to receive,* as opposed to shunning or refusing; *to receive* with hospitality, Acts 28:7; *to embrace* a proffer or promise, Heb. 11:17* [324]

[347] ἀναδίδωμι *anadidōmi* 1x *to give forth, up,* or *back; to deliver, present,* Acts 23:33* [325]

[348] ἀναζάω *anazaō* 3x *to live again, recover life, revive,* Rom. 7:9; met. *to live a new and reformed life,* Lk. 15:24, 32* [326]

[349] ἀναζητέω *anazēteō* 3x *to track; to seek diligently, inquire after, search for,* Lk. 2:44, 45; Acts 11:25* [327]

[350] ἀναζώννυμι *anazōnnymi* 1x *to gird* with a belt or girdle; *to gird one's self,* 1 Pet. 1:13* [328]

[351] ἀναζωπυρέω *anazōpyreō* 1x pr. *to kindle up a dormant fire;* met. *to revive, excite; to stir up, quicken* one's powers, 2 Tim. 1:6* [329]

[352] ἀναθάλλω *anathallō* 1x *to grow* or *bloom again*; *to renew*, Phil. 4:10* [330]

[353] ἀνάθεμα *anathema* 6x *a devoted thing,* ordinarily in a bad sense, *a person* or *thing accursed,* Rom. 9:3; 1 Cor. 12:3; 16:22; Gal. 1:8, 9; *a curse, execration, anathema,* Acts 23:14* [331] See *accursed; condemned; curse.*

[354] ἀναθεματίζω *anathematizō* 4x *to declare* any one *to be* ἀνάθεμα; *to curse, bind by a curse,* Mk. 14:71; Acts 23:12, 14, 21* [332]

[355] ἀναθεωρέω *anatheōreō* 2x *to view, behold attentively, contemplate,* Acts 17:23; Heb. 13:7* [333]

[356] ἀνάθημα *anathēma* 1x *a gift* or *offering consecrated to God,* Lk. 21:5* [334]

[357] ἀναίδεια *anaideia* 1x pr. *shamelessness;* hence, *persistence,* without regard to time, place, or person, Lk. 11:8* [335]

[358] ἀναίρεσις *anairesis* 1x *a taking up* or *away; a putting to death, murder,* Acts 8:1* [336]

[359] ἀναιρέω *anaireō* 24x pr. *to take up, lift,* as from the ground; *to take off, put to death, kill, murder,* Mt. 2:16; *to take away, abolish, abrogate,* Heb. 10:9; mid. *to take up* infants in order to bring them up, Acts 7:21 [337] See *abolish; kill; put to death; take away.*

[360] ἀναίτιος *anaitios* 2x *guiltless, innocent,* Mt. 12:5, 7* [338]

[361] ἀνακαθίζω *anakathizō* 2x *to set up;* intrans. *to sit up,* Lk. 7:15; Acts 9:40* [339]

[362] ἀνακαινίζω *anakainizō* 1x *to renovate, renew,* Heb. 6:6* [340] See *renew, renewal.*

[363] ἀνακαινόω *anakainoō* 2x *to invigorate, renew,* 2 Cor. 4:16; Col. 3:10* [341] See *renew, renewal.*

[364] ἀνακαίνωσις *anakainōsis* 2x *renovation, renewal,* Rom. 12:2; Tit. 3:5* [342] See *renew, renewal.*

[365] ἀνακαλύπτω *anakalyptō* 2x *to unveil, uncover;* pass. *to be unveiled,* 2 Cor. 3:18; met. *to be disclosed* in true character and condition, 2 Cor. 3:14* [343]

[366] ἀνακάμπτω *anakamptō* 4x pr. *to reflect, bend back;* hence, *to bend back* one's course, *return,* Mt. 2:12; Lk. 10:6; Acts 18:21; Heb. 11:15* [344]

[367] ἀνάκειμαι *anakeimai* 14x *to be laid up,* as offerings; later, *to lie, recline* at table, Mt. 9:10 [345] See *guest; recline.*

[368] ἀνακεφαλαιόω *anakephalaioō* 2x *to bring together several things under one, reduce under one head; to comprise,* Rom. 13:9; Eph. 1:10* [346]

[369] ἀνακλίνω *anaklinō* 6x *to lay down,* Lk. 2:7; *to cause to recline* at table, etc. Mk. 6:39; Lk. 9:15; 12:37; *to recline at table,* Mt. 8:11 [347]

[371] ἀνακράζω *anakrazō* 5x *to cry aloud, exclaim, shout,* Mk. 1:23; 6:49; Lk. 4:33; 8:28; 23:18* [349]

[373] ἀνακρίνω *anakrinō* 16x *to sift; to examine closely,* Acts 17:11; *to scrutinize, scan,* 1 Cor. 2:14, 15; 9:3; *to try* judicially, Lk. 23:14; *to judge, give judgment upon,* 1 Cor. 4:3, 4; *to put questions, be inquisitive,* 1 Cor. 10:25, 27; Acts 11:12 v.l [350] See *examine; investigate; judge.*

[374] ἀνάκρισις *anakrisis* 1x *investigation, judicial examination, hearing of a cause,* Acts 25:26* [351]

[376] ἀνακύπτω *anakyptō* 4x pr. *to raise up one's self, look up,* Lk. 13:11; Jn. 8:7, 10; met. *to look up* cheerily, *to be cheered,* Lk. 21:28* [352]

[377] ἀναλαμβάνω *analambanō* 13x *to take up, receive up,* Mk. 16:19; *to take up, carry,* Acts 7:43; *to take on board,* Acts 20:13, 14; *to take* in company, Acts 23:31; 2 Tim. 4:11 [353] See *lift up; take up.*

[378] ἀνάλημψις *analēmpsis* 1x *a taking up, receiving up,* Lk. 9:51* [354]

[381] ἀναλογία *analogia* 1x *analogy, ratio, proportion,* Rom. 12:6* [356]

[382] ἀναλογίζομαι *analogizomai* 1x *to consider attentively,* Heb. 12:3* [357]

[383] ἄναλος *analos* 1x *without saltness, without the taste and pungency of salt, insipid,* Mk. 9:50 [358]

[384] ἀναλόω *analoō* 2x *to destroy,* Luke 9:54; Gal. 5:15 [355]

[385] ἀνάλυσις *analysis* 1x pr. *dissolution;* met. *departure, death,* 2 Tim. 4:6* [359]

[386] ἀναλύω *analyō* 2x pr. *to loose, dissolve;* intrans. *to loose* in order to departure; *to depart,* Lk. 12:36; *to depart* from life, Phil. 1:23* [360]

[387] ἀναμάρτητος *anamartētos* 1x *without sin, guiltless,* Jn. 8:7* [361]

[388] ἀναμένω *anamenō* 1x *to await, wait for, expect,* 1 Thess. 1:10* [362]

[389] ἀναμιμνῄσκω *anamimnēskō* 6x *to remind, cause to remember,* 1 Cor. 4:17; *to exhort,* 2 Tim. 1:6; *to call to mind, recollect, remember,* Mk. 11:21; 14:72; 2 Cor. 7:15; Heb. 10:32* [363]

[390] ἀνάμνησις *anamnēsis* 4x *remembrance; a commemoration, memorial,* Lk. 22:19; 1 Cor. 11:24, 25; Heb. 10:3* [364]

[391] ἀνανεόω *ananeoō* 1x also spelled ἀνανεόομαι, *to renew;* pass. *to be renewed, be renovated,* by inward reformation, Eph. 4:23* [365]

[392] ἀνανήφω *ananēphō* 1x *to become sober;* met. *to recover sobriety* of mind, 2 Tim. 2:26* [366]

[393] Ἁνανίας *Hananias* 11x *Ananias,* pr. name I. *A Christian of Jerusalem,* Acts 5:1, etc. II. *A Christian of Damascus,* Acts 9:12, etc. III. *High Priest,* Acts 23:2; 24:1 [367]

[394] ἀναντίρρητος *anantirrētos* 1x *not to be contradicted, indisputable,* Acts 19:36* [368]

[395] ἀναντιρρήτως *anantirrētōs* 1x pr. *without contradiction* or *gainsaying; without hesitation, promptly,* Acts 10:29* [369]

[396] ἀνάξιος *anaxios* 1x *inadequate, unworthy,* 1 Cor. 6:2* [370]

[397] ἀναξίως *anaxiōs* 1x *unworthily, in an improper manner,* 1 Cor. 11:27* [371]

[398] ἀνάπαυσις *anapausis* 5x *rest, intermission,* Mt. 11:29; Rev. 4:8; 14:11; meton. *place of rest, fixed habitation,* Mt. 12:43; Lk. 11:24* [372]

[399] ἀναπαύω *anapauō* 12x *to cause to rest, to soothe, refresh,* Mt. 11:28; mid. *to take rest, repose, refreshment,* Mt. 26:45; *to have a fixed place of rest, abide, dwell,* 1 Pet. 4:14 [373] See *refresh; rest.*

[400] ἀναπείθω *anapeithō* 1x *to persuade* to a different opinion, *to seduce,* Acts 18:13* [374]

[401] ἀνάπειρος *anapeiros* 2x also spelled ἀνάπηρος, *maimed, deprived of some member of the body,* or *at least of its use,* Lk. 14:13, 21 [376]

[402] ἀναπέμπω *anapempō* 5x *to send back,* Phlm. 12; *to send up, remit* to a tribunal, Lk. 23:7, 11, 15; Acts 25:21* [375]

[403] ἀναπηδάω *anapēdaō* 1x *to leap up, stand up,* Mk. 10:50* [450]

[404] ἀναπίπτω *anapiptō* 12x *to fall* or *recline backwards; to recline* at table, etc., Lk. 11:37; *to throw one's self back,* Jn. 21:20 [377] See *recline; sit down.*

[405] ἀναπληρόω *anaplēroō* 6x *to fill up, complete,* 1 Thess. 2:16; *to fulfil, confirm,* as a prophecy by the event, Mt. 13:14; *to fill* the place of any one, 1 Cor. 14:16; *to supply, make good,* 1 Cor. 16:17; Phil. 2:30; *to observe fully, keep* the law, Gal. 6:2* [378]

[406] ἀναπολόγητος *anapologētos* 2x *inexcusable,* Rom. 1:20; 2:1* [379]

[408] ἀναπτύσσω *anaptyssō* 1x *to roll back, unroll, unfold,* Lk. 4:17* [380]

[409] ἀνάπτω *anaptō* 2x *to light, kindle, set on fire,* Lk. 12:49; Jas. 3:5* [381]

[410] ἀναρίθμητος *anarithmētos* 1x *innumerable,* Heb. 11:12* [382]

[411] ἀνασείω *anaseiō* 2x pr. *to shake up;* met. *to stir up, instigate,* Mk. 15:11; Lk. 23:5* [383]

[412] ἀνασκευάζω *anaskeuazō* 1x pr. *to collect one's effects* or *baggage* (σκευή) in order to remove; *to lay waste by carrying off* or *destroying* every thing; met. *to unsettle, pervert, subvert,* Acts 15:24* [384]

[413] ἀνασπάω *anaspaō* 2x *to draw up, to draw out,* Lk. 14:5; Acts 11:10* [385]

[414] ἀνάστασις *anastasis* 42x *a raising* or *rising up; resurrection,* Mt. 22:23; meton. *the author of resurrection,* Jn. 11:25; met. *an uprising* into a state of higher advancement and blessedness, Lk. 2:34 [386] See *resurrection.*

[415] ἀναστατόω *anastatoō* 3x *to lay waste, destroy; to disturb, throw into commotion,* Acts 17:6; *to excite to sedition and tumult,* Acts 21:38; *to disturb* the mind of any one by doubts, etc.; *to subvert, unsettle,* Gal. 5:12* [387]

[416] ἀνασταυρόω *anastauroō* 1x *to crucify again,* Heb. 6:6* [388]

[417] ἀναστενάζω *anastenazō* 1x *to sigh, groan deeply,* Mk. 8:12* [389]

[418] ἀναστρέφω *anastrephō* 9x *to overturn, throw down, to turn back, return,* Acts 5:22; 15:16; *to live, to conduct one's self,* 2 Cor. 1:12; Eph. 2:3; 1 Tim. 3:15; Heb. 13:18; 1 Pet. 1:17; 2 Pet. 2:18; *to* *gaze,* Heb. 10:33* [390] See *behave; conduct; live; turn back.*

[419] ἀναστροφή *anastrophē* 13x *conversation, mode of life, conduct, deportment,* Gal. 1:13 [391] See *conduct; life; way of life.*

[421] ἀνατάσσομαι *anatassomai* 1x pr. *to arrange;* hence, *to compose,* Lk. 1:1* [392]

[422] ἀνατέλλω *anatellō* 9x *to cause to rise,* Mt. 5:45; intrans. *to rise,* as the sun, stars, etc., Mt. 4:16; *to spring* by birth, Heb. 7:14 [393]

[423] ἀνατίθημι *anatithēmi* 2x in NT only mid., *to submit to* a person's *consideration, statement,* or *report* of matters, Acts 25:14; Gal. 2:2* [394]

[424] ἀνατολή *anatolē* 11x pr. *a rising* of the sun, etc.; *the place of rising, the east,* as also pl. ἀνατολαί, Mt. 2:1, 2; met. *the dawn* or *day-spring,* Lk. 1:78 [395] See *east; rising.*

[426] ἀνατρέπω *anatrepō* 3x pr. *to overturn, overthrow;* met. *to subvert, corrupt,* 2 Tim. 2:18; Tit. 1:11; Jn. 2:15* [396]

[427] ἀνατρέφω *anatrephō* 3x *to nurse,* as an infant, Acts 7:20; *to bring up, educate,* Acts 7:21; 22:3* [397]

[428] ἀναφαίνω *anaphainō* 2x *to bring to light, display;* mid. and pass. *to appear,* Lk. 19:11; a nautical term, *to come in sight of,* Acts 21:3* [398]

[429] ἀναφέρω *anapherō* 10x *to bear* or *carry upwards, lead up,* Mt. 17:1; *to offer* sacrifices, Heb. 7:27; *to bear aloft* or *sustain* a burden, as sins, 1 Pet. 2:24; Heb. 9:28 [399] See *bear (sins); lead up; offer up; take up.*

[430] ἀναφωνέω *anaphōneō* 1x *to exclaim, cry out,* Lk. 1:42* [400]

[431] ἀνάχυσις *anachusis* 1x *a pouring out;* met. *excess, stream, flood,* 1 Pet. 4:4* [401]

[432] ἀναχωρέω *anachōreō* 14x *to go backward; to depart, go away,* Mt. 2:12; *to withdraw, retire,* Mt. 9:24; Acts 23:19; 26:31 [402] See *depart; return.*

[433] ἀνάψυξις *anapsyxis* 1x pr. *a refreshing coolness* after heat; met. *refreshing, recreation, rest,* Acts 3:20* [403]

[434] ἀναψύχω *anapsychō* 1x *to recreate by fresh air; to refresh, cheer,* 2 Tim. 1:16* [404]

[435] ἀνδραποδιστής *andrapodistēs* 1x *a man-stealer, kidnapper,* 1 Tim. 1:10* [405]

[436] Ἀνδρέας *Andreas* 13x *Andrew,* pr. name [406]

[437] ἀνδρίζομαι *andrizomai* 1x *to render brave* or *manly;* mid. *to show* or *behave one's self like a man,* 1 Cor. 16:13* [407]

[438] Ἀνδρόνικος *Andronikos* 1x *Andronicus,* pr. name, Rom. 16:7* [408]

[439] ἀνδροφόνος *androphonos* 1x *a homicide, man-slayer, murderer,* 1 Tim. 1:9* [409]

[441] ἀνέγκλητος *anenklētos* 5x *unblamable, irreproachable,* 1 Cor. 1:8; Col. 1:22; 1 Tim. 3:10; Tit. 1:6, 7* [410]

[442] ἀνεκδιήγητος *anekdiēgētos* 1x *which cannot be related, inexpressible, unutterable, indescribable,* 2 Cor. 9:15* [411]

[443] ἀνεκλάλητος *aneklalētos* 1x *unspeakable, ineffable,* 1 Pet. 1:8* [412]

[444] ἀνέκλειπτος *anekleiptos* 1x *unfailing, exhaustless,* Lk. 12:33* [413]

[445] ἀνεκτός *anektos* 5x *tolerable, supportable,* Mt. 10:15; 11:22, 24; Lk. 10:12, 14* [414]

[446] ἀνελεήμων *aneleēmōn* 1x *unmerciful, uncompassionate, cruel,* Rom. 1:31* [415]

[447] ἀνέλεος *aneleos* 1x *merciless,* Jas. 2:13* [448]

[448] ἀνεμίζω *anemizō* 1x *to agitate with the wind;* pass. *to be agitated* or *driven by the wind,* Jas. 1:6* [416]

[449] ἄνεμος *anemos* 31x *the wind;* met. *a wind* of shifting doctrine, Eph. 4:14 [417] See *wind.*

[450] ἀνένδεκτος *anendektos* 1x *impossible, what cannot be,* Lk. 17:1* [418]

[451] ἀνεξεραύνητος *anexeraunētos* 1x also spelled ἀνεξερεύνητος, *unfathomable, incapable of human explanation,* Rom. 11:33* [419]

[452] ἀνεξίκακος *anexikakos* 1x *enduring* or *patient under evils and injuries,* 2 Tim. 2:24* [420]

[453] ἀνεξιχνίαστος *anexichniastos* 2x *to track out,* ἴχνος, *a track which cannot be explored, inscrutable, incomprehensible,* Rom. 11:33; Eph. 3:8* [421]

[454] ἀνεπαίσχυντος *anepaischuntos* 1x *without cause of shame, irreproachable,* 2 Tim. 2:15* [422]

[455] ἀνεπίλημπτος *anepilēmptos* 3x also spelled ἀνεπίληπρος. pr. *not to be laid hold of;* met. *beyond reproach, unblamable,* 1 Tim. 3:2; 5:7; 6:14* [423]

[456] ἀνέρχομαι *anerchomai* 3x *to ascend, go up,* Jn. 6:3; Gal. 1:17, 18* [424]

[457] ἄνεσις *anesis* 5x pr. *the relaxing* of a state of constraint; *relaxation* of rigor of confinement, Acts 24:23; met. *ease, rest, peace, tranquility,* 2 Cor. 2:13; 7:5; 8:13; 2 Thess. 1:7* [425]

[458] ἀνετάζω *anetazō* 2x *to examine thoroughly; to examine* by torture, Acts 22:24, 29* [426]

[459] ἄνευ *aneu* 3x some classify as an improper preposition, *without,* Mt. 10:29; 1 Pet. 3:1; 4:9* [427]

[460] ἀνεύθετος *aneuthetos* 1x *unfavorably situated, inconvenient,* Acts 27:12* [428]

[461] ἀνευρίσκω *aneuriskō* 2x *to find by diligent search,* Lk. 2:16; Acts 21:4* [429]

[462] ἀνέχομαι *anechōmai* 15x also listed as ἀνέχω, but it is always in the middle in our literature, *to endure patiently*, 1 Cor. 4:12; 2 Cor. 11:20; 2 Thess. 1:4; *to bear with*, Matt 17:7; *to suffer, admit, permit*, Acts 18:14; 2 Cor. 11:4; 2 Tim. 4:3; Heb. 13:22 [430] See *bear with; endurance, endure; tolerate.*

[463] ἀνεψιός *anepsios* 1x *a nephew, cousin,* Col. 4:10* [431]

[464] ἄνηθον *anēthon* 1x *dill,* an aromatic plant, Mt. 23:23* [432]

[465] ἀνήκω *anēkō* 3x *to come up to, to pertain to;* ἀνήκει, impers. *it is fit, proper, becoming,* Col. 3:18; Eph. 5:4; Phlm. 8* [433]

[466] ἀνήμερος *anēmeros* 1x *savage, fierce, ferocious,* 2 Tim. 3:3* [434]

[467] ἀνήρ *anēr* 216x *a male person of full age and stature,* as opposed to a child or female, 1 Cor. 13:11; *a husband,* Mt. 1:16; *a man, human being, individual,* Lk. 11:31; used also pleonastically with other nouns and adjectives, Lk. 5:8; Acts 1:16 [435] See *husband; man.*

[468] ἀνθίστημι *anthistēmi* 14x *to oppose, resist, stand out against* [436] See *oppose; resist.*

[469] ἀνθομολογέομαι *anthomologeomai* 1x pr. *to come to an agreement;* hence, *to confess openly what is due; to confess, give thanks, render praise,* Lk. 2:38* [437]

[470] ἄνθος *anthos* 4x *a flower,* Jas. 1:10, 11; 1 Pet. 1:24 (2x)* [438]

[471] ἀνθρακιά *anthrakia* 2x *a mass* or *heap of live coals,* Jn. 18:18; 21:9 [439]

[472] ἄνθραξ *anthrax* 1x *a coal, burning coal,* Rom. 12:20* [440]

[473] ἀνθρωπάρεσκος *anthrōpareskos* 2x *desirous of pleasing men,* Eph. 6:6; Col. 3:22* [441]

[474] ἀνθρώπινος *anthrōpinos* 7x *human, belonging to man,* 1 Cor. 2:4, 13; 4:3; 10:13; Jas. 3:7; 1 Pet. 2:13; *suited to man,* Rom. 6:19* [442]

[475] ἀνθρωποκτόνος *anthrōpoktonos* 3x *a homicide, murderer,* Jn. 8:44; 1 Jn. 3:15* [443]

[476] ἄνθρωπος *anthrōpos* 550x *a human being,* Jn. 16:21; Phil. 2:7; *an individual,* Rom. 3:28, et al. freq.; used also pleonastically with other words, Mt. 11:19; et al.; met. *the* spiritual frame of the inner *man,* Rom. 7:22; Eph. 3:16; 1 Pet. 3:4 [444] See *human being; humankind; man; mankind; person.*

[478] ἀνθύπατος *anthupatos* 5x *a proconsul,* Acts 13:7, 8, 12; 19:38 [446]

[479] ἀνίημι *aniēmi* 4x (1) *to loose, slacken,* Acts 27:40; *to unbind, unfasten,* Acts 16:26; (2) *to omit, dispense with,* Eph. 6:9; (3) *to leave* or *neglect,* Heb. 13:5* [447]

[481] ἄνιπτος *aniptos* 2x literally: *unwashed*; figuratively: *ceremonially unclean* Mt. 15:20; Mk. 7:2* [449]

[482] ἀνίστημι *anistēmi* 108x trans. *to cause to stand up* or *rise,* Acts 9:41; *to raise up,* as the dead, Jn. 6:39; *to raise up* into existence, Mt. 22:24; intrans. and mid., *to rise up,* Mt. 9:9; *to rise up* into existence, Acts 7:18; 20:30 [450] See *get up; raise up; stand up.*

[483] Ἅννα *Hanna* 1x *Anna,* pr. name, Lk. 2:26* [451]

[484] Ἅννας *Hannas* 4x *Annas,* pr. name, short version of Ἅνανος, Lk. 3:2; Jn. 18:13, 24; Acts 4:6* [452]

[485] ἀνόητος *anoētos* 6x *inconsiderate, unintelligent, unwise;* Lk. 24:25; Rom. 1:14; Gal. 3:1, 3; Tit. 3:3; *brutish,* 1 Tim. 6:9 [453]

[486] ἄνοια *anoia* 2x *want of understanding; folly, rashness, madness,* Lk. 6:11; 2 Tim. 3:9* [454]

[487] ἀνοίγω *anoigō* 77x trans. *to open,* Mt. 2:11; intrans. *to be opened, to be open,* Mt. 3:16; Jn. 1:52 [455] See *open; reveal; speak.*

[488] ἀνοικοδομέω *anoikodomeō* 2x *to rebuild,* Acts 15:16 (2x)* [456]

[489] ἄνοιξις *anoixis* 1x *an opening, act of opening,* Eph. 6:19* [457]

[490] ἀνομία *anomia* 15x *lawlessness; violation of law,* 1 Jn. 3:4; *iniquity, sin,* Mt. 7:23 [458] See *lawless, lawlessness; wicked, wickedness.*

[491] ἄνομος *anomos* 9x *lawless, without law, not subject to law,* 1 Cor. 9:21; *lawless, violating law, wicked, impious,* Acts 2:23; *a transgressor,* Mk. 15:28; Lk. 22:37 [459] See *lawless, lawlessness; wicked, wickedness.*

[492] ἀνόμως *anomōs* 2x *without* the intervention of *law,* Rom. 2:12 (2x) [460]

[494] ἀνορθόω *anorthoō* 3x *to restore to straightness* or *erectness,* Lk. 13:13; *to re-invigorate,* Heb. 12:12; *to re-erect,* Acts 15:16* [461]

[495] ἀνόσιος *anosios* 2x *impious, unholy,* 1 Tim. 1:9; 2 Tim. 3:2* [462]

[496] ἀνοχή *anochē* 2x *forbearance, patience,* Rom. 2:4; 3:26* [463]

[497] ἀνταγωνίζομαι *antagōnizomai* 1x *to contend, strive against,* Heb. 12:4* [464]

[498] ἀντάλλαγμα *antallagma* 2x *a price paid in exchange* for a thing; *compensation, equivalent ransom,* Mt. 16:26; Mk. 8:37* [465]

[499] ἀνταναπληρόω *antanaplēroō* 1x *to fill up, complete, supply,* Col. 1:24* [466]

[500] ἀνταποδίδωμι *antapodidōmi* 7x *to repay, give back, return, recompense,* Lk. 14:14 (2x); Rom. 11:35; 12:19; 1 Thess. 3:9; 2 Thess. 1:6; Heb. 10:30 [467]

[501] ἀνταπόδομα *antapodoma* 2x *repayment, recompense, retribution,* Lk. 14:12; Rom. 11:9* [468]

[502] ἀνταπόδοσις *antapodosis* 1x *recompense, reward,* Col. 3:24* [469]

[503] ἀνταποκρίνομαι *antapokrinomai* 2x occurs in the NT only in the middle, *to answer, speak in answer,* Lk. 14:6; *to reply against, contradict, dispute,* Rom. 9:20* [470]

[504] ἀντέχω *antechō* 4x *to hold firmly, cling* or *adhere to; to be devoted to* any one, Lk. 16:13; Tit. 1:9; *to exercise a zealous care for* any one, 1 Thess. 5:14; Mk. 6:24* [472]

[505] ἀντί *anti* 22x *over against;* hence, *in correspondence to, answering to,* Jn. 1:16; *in place of,* Mt. 2:22; *in retribution* or *return for,* Mt. 5:38; *in consideration of,* Heb. 12:2, 16; *on account of,* Mt. 17:27; ἀνθ᾽ ὧν, *because,* Lk. 1:20 [473]

[506] ἀντιβάλλω *antiballō* 1x pr. *to throw* or *toss from one to another;* met. *to agitate, to converse* or *discourse about,* Lk. 24:17* [474]

[507] ἀντιδιατίθημι *antidiatithēmi* 1x *to set opposite;* mid. (only in the NT) *to be of an opposite opinion, to be adverse; opponent,* 2 Tim. 2:25* [475]

[508] ἀντίδικος *antidikos* 5x *an opponent in a lawsuit,* Mt. 5:25 (2x); Lk. 12:58; 18:3; *an adversary,* 1 Pet. 5:8* [476]

[509] ἀντίθεσις *antithesis* 1x pr. *opposition;* hence, *a question proposed for dispute, disputation,* 1 Tim. 6:20* [477]

[510] ἀντικαθίστημι *antikathistēmi* 1x trans. *to set in opposition;* intrans. *to withstand, resist,* Heb. 12:4* [478]

[511] ἀντικαλέω *antikaleō* 1x *to invite in return,* Lk. 14:12* [479]

[512] ἀντίκειμαι *antikeimai* 8x pr. *occupy an opposite position;* met. *to oppose, be adverse to,* Gal. 5:17; 1 Tim. 1:10; *opponent, hostile,* Lk. 13:7 [480]

[513] ἄντικρυς *antikrys* 1x can function as an improper preposition with the gen., also spelled ἀντικρύ, *opposite to, over against,* Acts 20:15* [481]

[514] ἀντιλαμβάνω *antilambanō* 3x *to aid, assist, help,* Lk. 1:54; Acts 20:35; *to be a recipient,* 1 Tim. 6:2* [482]

[515] ἀντιλέγω *antilegō* 11x *to speak against, contradict; to gainsay, deny,* Lk. 20:27; *to oppose,* Jn. 19:12; Acts 13:45; 28:19; Rom. 10:21; Tit. 1:9; 2:9; pass. *to be spoken against, decried,* Lk. 2:34; Acts 28:22* [471, 483] See *contradict; rebel; speak against.*

[516] ἀντίλημψις *antilēmpsis* 1x *aid, assistance;* meton, *one who aids* or *assists, a help,* 1 Cor. 12:28* [484]

[517] ἀντιλογία *antilogia* 4x *contradiction, question,* Heb. 6:16; 7:7; *opposition, rebellion,* Jude 11; *hostility,* Heb. 12:3* [485]

[518] ἀντιλοιδορέω *antiloidoreō* 1x *to reproach* or *revile again* or *in return,* 1 Pet. 2:23* [486]

[519] ἀντίλυτρον *antilytron* 1x *a ransom,* 1 Tim. 2:6* [487]

[520] ἀντιμετρέω *antimetreō* 1x *to measure in return,* Lk. 6:38* [488]

[521] ἀντιμισθία *antimisthia* 2x *a retribution, recompense,* Rom. 1:27; 2 Cor. 6:13* [489]

[522] Ἀντιόχεια *Antiocheia* 18x *Antioch,* pr. name I. *Antioch,* the metropolis of Syria, where the disciples first received the name of Christians II. *Antioch,* a city of Pisidia, Acts 13:14; 14:19; 2 Tim. 3:11 [490]

[523] Ἀντιοχεύς *Antiocheus* 1x *an inhabitant of Antioch,* Acts 6:5* [491]

[524] ἀντιπαρέρχομαι *antiparerchomai* 2x *to pass over against, to pass along* without noticing, Lk. 10:31, 32* [492]

[525] Ἀντιπᾶς *Antipas* 1x *Antipas,* pr. name, Rev. 2:13* [493]

[526] Ἀντιπατρίς *Antipatris* 1x *Antipatris,* pr. name, Acts 23:31* [494]

[527] ἀντιπέρα *antipera* 1x can function as an improper preposition with the gen., *opposite,* Lk. 8:26* [495]

[528] ἀντιπίπτω *antipiptō* 1x pr. *to fall upon, rush upon* any one; hence, *to resist by force, oppose, strive against,* Acts 7:51* [496]

[529] ἀντιστρατεύομαι *antistrateuomai* 1x *to war against; to contravene, oppose,* Rom. 7:23* [497]

[530] ἀντιτάσσω *antitassō* 5x *to post in adverse array,* as an army; mid. *to set oneself in opposition, resist,* Acts 18:6; Rom. 13:2; Jas. 5:6; *to be averse,* Jas. 4:6; 1 Pet. 5:5* [498]

[531] ἀντίτυπος *antitypos* 2x *of correspondent stamp* or *form; corresponding, in correspondent fashion,* 1 Pet. 3:21; τὸ ἀντίτυπον, *a copy, representation,* Heb. 9:24* [499]

[532] ἀντίχριστος *antichristos* 5x *antichrist, an opposer of Christ,* 1 Jn. 2:18, 22; 4:3; 2 Jn. 7; plural in 1 Jn. 2:18* [500] See *antichrist.*

[533] ἀντλέω *antleō* 4x *to draw,* e.g., wine, water, etc.; Jn. 2:8, 9; 4:7, 15* [501]

[534] ἄντλημα *antlēma* 1x pr. *that which is drawn; a bucket, vessel for drawing water,* Jn. 4:11* [502]

[535] ἀντοφθαλμέω *antophthalmeō* 1x pr. *to look in the face,* met. a nautical term, *to bear up against* the wind, Acts 27:15* [503]

[536] ἄνυδρος *anydros* 4x *without water, dry,* 2 Pet. 2:17; Jude 12; τόποι ἄνυδροι, *dry places,* and therefore, in the East, *barren, desert,* Mt. 12:43; Lk. 11:24* [504]

[537] ἀνυπόκριτος *anypokritos* 6x *unfeigned, real, sincere,* Rom. 12:9 [505]

[538] ἀνυπότακτος *anypotaktos* 4x *not subjected, not made subordinate,* Heb. 2:8; *insubordinate, refractory, disorderly, contumacious, lawless,* 1 Tim. 1:9; Tit. 1:6, 10 [506]

[539] ἄνω *anō* 9x *above,* Acts 2:19; Gal. 4:26; Col. 3:1; *up, upwards,* Jn. 11:41; ὁ, ἡ, τό, ἄνω, *that which is above,* Jn. 8:23; ἕως ἄνω, *to the top* [507]

[540] ἄνωθεν *anōthen* 13x *from above, from a higher place,* Jn. 3:31; of time, *from the first* or *beginning,* Acts 26:5; *from the source,* Lk. 1:33; *again, anew,* Jn. 3:3, 7; Gal. 4:9; with a prep., *the top* or *upper part,* Mt. 27:51 [509] See *again; from above.*

[541] ἀνωτερικός *anōterikos* 1x *upper, higher, inland,* Acts 19:1* [510]

[543] ἀνωφελής *anōphelēs* 2x *useless, unprofitable,* Tit. 3:9; Heb. 7:18* [512]

[544] ἀξίνη *axinē* 2x *an axe,* Mt. 3:10; Lk. 3:9* [513]

[545] ἄξιος *axios* 41x pr. *of equal value; worthy, estimable,* Mt. 10:11, 13; *worthy of, deserving,* either good or evil, Mt. 10:10; *correspondent to,* Mt. 3:8; Lk. 3:8; Acts 26:20; *comparable, countervailing,* Rom. 8:18; *suitable, due,* Lk. 23:41 [514] See *deserving; worthy.*

[546] ἀξιόω *axioō* 7x *to judge* or *esteem worthy* or *deserving; to deem fitting, to require,* Acts 15:38; 28:22 [515] See *worthy.*

[547] ἀξίως *axiōs* 6x *worthily,* Col. 1:10; *suitably, in a manner becoming,* Rom. 16:2 [516]

[548] ἀόρατος *aoratos* 5x *invisible,* Rom. 1:20; Col. 1:15, 16; 1 Tim. 1:17; Heb. 11:27 [517]

[550] ἀπαγγέλλω *apangellō* 45x *to announce that with which a person is charged,* or *which is called for by circumstances; to carry back word,* Mt. 2:8; *to report,* Mt. 8:33; *to declare plainly,* Heb. 2:12; *to announce* formally, 1 Jn. 1:2, 3 [518] See *report; tell.*

[551] ἀπάγχω *apanchō* 1x *to strangle;* mid. *to choke* or *strangle one's self, hang one's self,* Mt. 27:5* [519]

[552] ἀπάγω *apagō* 15x *to lead away,* Mt. 26:57; *to conduct,* Mt. 7:13, 14; pass. *to be led off* to execution, Acts 12:19; met. *to be led astray, seduced,* 1 Cor. 12:1 [520] See *lead away.*

[553] ἀπαίδευτος *apaideutos* 1x *uninstructed, ignorant; silly, unprofitable,* 2 Tim. 2:23* [521]

[554] ἀπαίρω *apairō* 3x *to take away;* pass. *to be taken away; to be withdrawn,* Mt. 9:15; Mk. 2:20; Lk. 5:35* [522]

[555] ἀπαιτέω *apaiteō* 2x *to demand, require,* Lk. 12:20; *to demand back,* Lk. 6:30* [523]

[556] ἀπαλγέω *apalgeō* 1x pr. *to desist from grief;* hence, *to become insensible* or *callous,* Eph. 4:19* [524]

[557] ἀπαλλάσσω *apallassō* 3x *to set free, deliver, set at liberty,* Heb. 2:15; *to rid* judicially, Lk. 12:58; mid. *to depart, remove,* Acts 19:12* [525]

[558] ἀπαλλοτριόω *apallotrioō* 3x pass. *to be alienated from, be a stranger to; alien,* Eph. 2:12; 4:18; Col. 1:21* [526]

[559] ἁπαλός *hapalos* 2x *soft, tender,* Mt. 24:32; Mk. 13:28* [527]

[560] ἀπαντάω *apantaō* 2x *to meet, encounter,* Mk. 14:13; Lk. 17:12* [528]

[561] ἀπάντησις *apantēsis* 3x *a meeting, encounter;* εἰς ἀπάντησιν, *to meet,* Mt. 25:6; Acts 28:15; 1 Thess. 4:17* [529]

[562] ἅπαξ *hapax* 14x *once,* 2 Cor. 11:25; *once for all,* Heb. 6:4; 9:26, 28; 10:2; 1 Pet. 3:18, 20; Jude 3; εἰδὼς ἅπαξ, *knowing once for ever, unfailingly, constantly,* Jude 5 [530] See *once; once for all.*

[563] ἀπαράβατος *aparabatos* 1x *not transient; not to be superseded, unchangeable,* Heb. 7:24* [531]

[564] ἀπαρασκεύαστος *aparaskeuastos* 1x *unprepared,* 2 Cor. 9:4* [532]

[565] ἀπαρνέομαι *aparneomai* 11x *to deny, disown,* Mt. 26:34; *to renounce, disregard,* Mt. 16:24 [533] See *deny; disown; reject.*

[568] ἀπαρτισμός *apartismos* 1x *completion, perfection,* Lk. 14:28* [535]

[569] ἀπαρχή *aparchē* 9x pr. *the first act of a sacrifice;* hence, *the firstfruits, first portion, firstling,* Rom. 8:23 [536] See *firstfruits.*

[570] ἅπας *hapas* 34x *all, the whole* [537] See *all; everyone.*

[571] ἀπασπάζομαι *apaspazomai* 1x *to take leave of, say farwell to,* Acts 21:6* [782]

[572] ἀπατάω *apataō* 3x *to deceive, seduce into error,* Eph. 5:6; 1 Tim. 2:14; Jas. 1:26* [538]

[573] ἀπάτη *apatē* 7x *deceit, deception, delusion* [539]

[574] ἀπάτωρ *apatōr* 1x pr. *without a father, fatherless;* hence, *independent of paternal descent,* Heb. 7:3* [540]

[575] ἀπαύγασμα *apaugasma* 1x *a radiance,* Heb. 1:3* [541]

[577] ἀπείθεια *apeitheia* 7x *an uncompliant disposition; obstinacy, disobedience, unbelief,* Rom. 11:30, 32; Eph. 2:2; 5:6; Heb. 4:6, 11; Col. 3:6* [543]

[578] ἀπειθέω *apeitheō* 14x *to be uncompliant; to refuse belief, disbelieve,* Jn. 3:36; *to refuse belief and obedience,* Rom. 10:21; 1 Pet. 3:20; *to refuse conformity,* Rom. 2:8 [544] See *disobey; refuse to believe; reject.*

[579] ἀπειθής *apeithēs* 6x *who will not be persuaded, uncompliant; disobedient,* Lk. 1:17; Acts 26:19; Rom. 1:30; 2 Tim. 3:2; Tit. 1:16; 3:3 [545]

[580] ἀπειλέω *apeileō* 2x *to threaten, menace, rebuke,* Acts 4:17; 1 Pet. 2:23* [546]

[581] ἀπειλή *apeilē* 3x *threat, commination,* Acts 4:29; 9:1; *harshness of language,* Eph. 6:9* [547]

[582] ἄπειμι *apeimi* 7x *to be absent, away* 1 Cor. 5:3; 2 Cor. 10:1, 11; 13:2, 10; Phil. 1:27; Col. 2:5* [548]

[583] ἄπειμι *apeimi* 1x *to go away, depart, come* Acts 17:10* [549]

[584] ἀπεῖπον *apeipon* 1x *to refuse, forbid, to renounce, disclaim,* 2 Cor. 4:2* [550, 561]

[585] ἀπείραστος *apeirastos* 1x *inexperienced, untempted, incapable of being tempted,* Jas. 1:13* [551]

[586] ἄπειρος *apeiros* 1x *inexperienced, unskillful, ignorant,* Heb. 5:13* [552]

[587] ἀπεκδέχομαι *apekdechomai* 8x *to expect, wait* or *look for,* Rom. 8:19, 23, 25; 1 Cor. 1:7; Gal. 5:5; Phil. 3:20; Heb. 9:28 [553]

[588] ἀπεκδύομαι *apekdyomai* 2x *to put off, renounce,* Col. 3:9; *to despoil* a rival, Col. 2:15* [554]

[589] ἀπέκδυσις *apekdysis* 1x *a putting* or *stripping off, renunciation,* Col. 2:11* [555]

[590] ἀπελαύνω *apelaunō* 1x *to drive away,* Acts 18:16* [556]

[591] ἀπελεγμός *apelegmos* 1x pr. *refutation;* by impl. *disrepute. contempt,* Acts 19:27* [557]

[592] ἀπελεύθερος *apeleutheros* 1x *a freed-man,* 1 Cor. 7:22* [558]

[593] Ἀπελλῆς *Apellēs* 1x *Apelles,* proper name, Rom. 16:10* [559]

[594] ἀπελπίζω *apelpizō* 1x *to lay aside hope, despond, despair;* also, *to hope for* something *in return,* Lk. 6:35* [560]

[595] ἀπέναντι *apenanti* 5x some classify as an improper preposition, *opposite to, over against,* Mt. 27:61; *contrary to, in opposititition to, against,* Acts 17:7; *before, in the presence of,* Mt. 27:24; Rom. 3:18; Acts 3:16* [561]

[596] ἀπέραντος *aperantos* 1x *unlimited, interminable, endless,* 1 Tim. 1:4* [562]

[597] ἀπερισπάστως *aperispastōs* 1x *without distraction, without care* or *solicitude,* 1 Cor. 7:35* [563]

[598] ἀπερίτμητος *aperitmētos* 1x pr. *uncircumcised;* met. *uncircumcised* in respect of untowardness and obduracy, Acts 7:51* [564]

[599] ἀπέρχομαι *aperchomai* 117x *to go away, depart,* Mt. 8:18; *to go forth, pervade,* as a rumor, Mt. 4:24; *to arrive at* a destination, Lk. 23:33; *to pass away, disappear,* Rev. 21:4; ἀπέρχομαι ὀπίσω, *to follow,* Mk. 1:20 [565] See *go; go away; withdraw.*

[600] ἀπέχω *apechō* 19x trans. *to have in full* what is due or is sought, Mt. 6:2, 5, 16; Lk. 6:24; Phil. 4:18; *to have altogether,* Phlm. 15; hence, *it is enough,* Mk. 14:41; intrans. *to be distant,* Lk. 7:6; *to be estranged,* Mt. 15:8; Mk. 7:6, mid. *to abstain from,* Acts 14:20 [566, 567, 568] See *abstain from; (be) far; receive in full.*

[601] ἀπιστέω *apisteō* 8x *to refuse belief, be incredulous, disbelieve,* Mk. 16:11, 16; Lk. 24:11, 41; Acts 28:24; *to prove false, violate one's faith, be unfaithful,* Rom. 3:3; 2 Tim. 2:13 [569]

[602] ἀπιστία *apistia* 11x *unbelief, want of trust and confidence; a state of unbelief,* 1 Tim. 1:13; *violation of faith, faithlessness,* Rom. 3:3; Heb. 3:12, 19 [570] See *lack of faith; unbelief.*

[603] ἄπιστος *apistos* 23x *unbelieving, without confidence* in any one, Mt. 17:17; *violating one's faith, unfaithful, false, treacherous,* Lk. 12:46; *an unbeliever, infidel, pagan,* 1 Cor. 6:6; pass. *incredible,* Acts 26:8 [571] See *unbelieving, unbeliever.*

[605] ἁπλότης *haplotēs* 8x *simplicity, sincerity, purity* of mind, Rom. 12:8; 11:3; Eph. 6:5; Col. 3:22; *liberality,* as arising from simplicity and frankness of character, 2 Cor. 8:2; 9:11, 13; 11:3* [572]

[606] ἁπλοῦς *haplous* 2x pr. *single;* hence, *simple, uncompounded; sound, perfect,* Mt. 6:22; Lk. 11:34* [573]

[607] ἁπλῶς *haplōs* 1x *in simplicity; sincerely, really,* or, *liberally, bountifully,* Jas. 1:5* [574]

[608] ἀπό *apo* 646x pr. *forth, from, away from;* hence, it variously signifies *departure; distance of time* or *place; avoidance; riddance; derivation from a quarter, source,* or *material; origination from agency* or *instrumentality* [575]

[609] ἀποβαίνω *apobainō* 4x *to step off; to disembark* from a ship, Lk. 5:2; Jn. 21:9; *to become, result, happen,* Lk. 21:13; Phil. 1:19* [576]

[610] ἀποβάλλω *apoballō* 2x *to cast* or *throw off, cast aside,* Mk. 10:50; Heb. 10:35* [577]

[611] ἀποβλέπω *apoblepō* 1x pr. *to look off from all other objects and at a single one;* hence, *to turn a steady gaze, to look with fixed and earnest attention,* Heb. 11:26* [578]

[612] ἀπόβλητος *apoblētos* 1x pr. *to be cast away;* met. *to be condemned, regarded as vile,* 1 Tim. 4:4* [579]

[613] ἀποβολή *apobolē* 2x *a casting off; rejection, reprobation,* Rom. 11:15; *loss, deprivation,* of life, etc., Acts 27:22* [580]

[614] ἀπογίνομαι *apoginomai* 1x *to be away from, unconnected with; to die;* met. *to die* to a thing by renouncing it, 1 Pet. 2:24* [581]

[615] ἀπογραφή *apographē* 2x *a register, inventory; registration, enrollment,* Lk. 2:2; Acts 5:37* [582]

[616] ἀπογράφω *apographō* 4x pr. *to copy;* hence, *to register, enrol,* Lk. 2:1; Heb. 12:23; mid. *to procure the registration of one's name, to give in one's name for registration,* Lk. 2:3, 5* [583]

[617] ἀποδείκνυμι *apodeiknymi* 4x *to point out, display; to prove, evince, demonstrate,* Acts 25:7; *to designate, proclaim, hold forth,* 2 Thess. 2:4; *to constitute, appoint,* Acts 2:22; 1 Cor. 4:9* [584]

[618] ἀπόδειξις *apodeixis* 1x *manifestation, demonstration, indubitable proof,* 1 Cor. 2:4* [585]

[620] ἀποδεκατόω *apodekatoō* 4x *to pay* or *give tithes of,* Mt. 23:23; Lk. 11:42; 18:12; *to tithe, levy tithes upon,* Heb. 7:5* [586]

[621] ἀπόδεκτος *apodektos* 2x *acceptable, pleasant,* 1 Tim. 2:3; 5:4* [587]

[622] ἀποδέχομαι *apodechomai* 7x *to receive* kindly or heartily, *welcome,* Lk. 8:40; 9:11; Acts 18:27; 28:30; *to receive* with hearty assent, *embrace,* Acts 2:41; *to accept* with satisfaction, Acts 24:3* [588]

[623] ἀποδημέω *apodēmeō* 6x *to be absent from one's home* or *country; to go on travel,* Mt. 21:33; 25:14, 15; Mk. 12:1; Lk. 15:13; 20:9* [589]

[624] ἀπόδημος *apodēmos* 1x *absent* in foreign countries, Mk. 13:34* [590]

[625] ἀποδίδωμι *apodidōmi* 48x *to give in answer to a claim* or *expectation; to render* a due, Mt. 12:36; 16:27; 21:41; 22:21; *to recompense,* Mt. 6:4, 6, 18; *to discharge* an obligation, Mt. 5:33; *to pay* a debt, Mt. 5:26; *to render back, requite,* Rom. 12:17; *to give back, restore,* Lk. 4:20; 9:42; *to refund,* Lk. 10:35; 19:8; mid., *to sell,* Acts 5:8; 7:9; Heb. 12:16; pass., *to be sold,* Mt. 18:25; *to be given up* at a request, Mt. 27:58 [591] See *deliver; give (back); hand over; produce; reimburse; repay; reward; sell.*

[626] ἀποδιορίζω *apodiorizō* 1x pr. *to separate by intervening boundaries; to separate* or *divide,* Jude 19* [592]

[627] ἀποδοκιμάζω *apodokimazō* 9x *to reject upon trial; to reject,* Mt. 21:42; Mk. 12:10; Lk. 20:17; 1 Pet. 2:4, 7; pass., *to be disallowed* a claim, *declared useless,* Lk. 9:22; 17:25; Heb. 12:17 [593]

[628] ἀποδοχή *apodochē* 2x pr. *reception, welcome;* met. *reception* of hearty assent, 1 Tim. 1:15; 4:9* [594]

[629] ἀπόθεσις *apothesis* 2x *a putting off* or *away, laying aside,* a euphemism for death, 1 Pet. 3:21; 2 Pet. 1:14* [595]

[630] ἀποθήκη *apothēkē* 6x *a place where anything is laid up for preservation, repository, granary, storehouse, barn,* Mt. 3:12; 6:26; 13:30; Lk. 3:17; 12:18, 24 [596]

[631] ἀποθησαυρίζω *apothēsaurizō* 1x pr. *to lay up in store, hoard;* met. *to treasure up, secure,* 1 Tim. 6:19* [597]

[632] ἀποθλίβω *apothlibō* 1x pr. *to press out; to press close, press upon, crowd,* Lk. 8:45* [598]

[633] ἀποθνήσκω *apothnēskō* 111x *to die,* Mt. 8:32; *to decay, rot,* as seeds, Jn. 12:24; 1 Cor. 15:36; *to wither, become dry,* as a tree, Jude 12; met. *to die* the death of final condemnation and misery, Jn. 6:50; 8:21, 24; *to die* to a thing by renunciation or utter separation, Rom. 6:2; 1 Cor. 15:31; Gal. 2;19; Col. 3:3 [599] See *die.*

[635] ἀποκαθίστημι *apokathistēmi* 8x also spelled ἀποκαθιστάνω, *to restore* a thing to its former place or state, Mt. 12:13; 17:11; Mk. 3:5; 8:25 [600] See *restore, restoration.*

[636] ἀποκαλύπτω *apokalyptō* 26x pr. *uncover; to reveal,* Mt. 11:25; pass. *to be disclosed,* Lk. 2:35; Eph. 3:5; *to be plainly signified, distinctly declared,* Rom. 1:17, 18; *to be set forth, announced,* Gal. 3:23; *to be discovered* in true character, 1 Cor. 3:13; *to be manifested, appear,* Jn. 12:38;Rom. 8:18; 2 Thess. 2:3, 6, 8; 1 Pet. 1:5; 5:1 [601] See *disclose; reveal.*

[637] ἀποκάλυψις *apokalypsis* 18x *a disclosure, revelation,* Rom. 2:5; *manifestation, appearance,* Rom. 8:19; 1 Cor. 1:7; 2 Thess. 1:7; 1 Pet. 1:7, 13; 4:13; met. spiritual *enlightenment,* Lk. 2:32 [602] See *revelation.*

[638] ἀποκαραδοκία *apokaradokia* 2x *earnest expectation, eager hope,* Rom. 8:19; Phil. 1:20* [603]

[639] ἀποκαταλλάσσω *apokatallassō* 3x *to transfer from a certain state to another which is quite different;* hence, *to reconcile, restore to favor,* Eph. 2:16; Col. 1:20, 22* [604] See *reconcile.*

[640] ἀποκατάστασις *apokatastasis* 1x pr. *a restitution* or *restoration of* a thing to its former state; hence, *the renovation* of a new and better era, Acts 3:21* [605]

[641] ἀπόκειμαι *apokeimai* 4x *to be laid up, preserved,* Lk. 19:20; *to be in store, be reserved, await* any one, Col. 1:5; 2 Tim. 4:8; Heb. 9:27* [606]

[642] ἀποκεφαλίζω *apokephalizō* 4x *to behead,* Mt. 14:10; Mk. 6:16, 28; Lk. 9:9 [607]

[643] ἀποκλείω *apokleiō* 1x *to close, shut up,* Lk. 13:25* [608]

[644] ἀποκόπτω *apokoptō* 6x *to cut off,* Mk. 9:43, 45; Jn. 18:10, 26; Acts 27:32; *to castrate, make a eunich,* Gal. 5:12* [609]

[645] ἀπόκριμα *apokrima* 1x *a judicial sentence,* 2 Cor. 1:9* [610]

[646] ἀποκρίνομαι *apokrinomai* 231x *to answer,* Mt. 3:15; in NT *to respond* to certain present circumstances, *to avow,* Mt. 11:25 [611] See *answer; reply.*

[647] ἀπόκρισις *apokrisis* 4x *an answer, reply,* Lk. 2:47; 20:26; Jn. 1:22; 19:9 [612]

[648] ἀποκρύπτω *apokryptō* 4x *to hide away; to conceal, withhold from sight* or *knowledge,* Lk. 10:21; 1 Cor. 2:7; Eph. 3:9; Col. 1:26* [613]

[649] ἀπόκρυφος *apokryphos* 3x *hidden away; concealed,* Mk. 4:22; Lk. 8:17; *stored up,* Col. 2:3* [614]

[650] ἀποκτείνω *apokteinō* 74x also spelled ἀποκτέννω or ἀποκτένω, *to kill,* Mt. 14:5; *to destroy, annihilate,* Mt. 10:28; *to destroy* a hostile principle, Eph. 2:16; met. *to kill* by spiritual condemnation,

Rom. 7:11; 2 Cor. 3:6 [615] See *kill; put to death.*

[652] ἀποκυέω *apokyeō* 2x pr. *to bring forth,* as women; met. *to generate, produce,* Jas. 1:15; *to generate* by spiritual birth, Jas. 1:18* [616]

[653] ἀποκυλίω *apokyliō* 3x *to roll away,* Mt. 28:2; Mk. 16:3, 4; Lk. 24:2* [617]

[655] ἀπολαμβάνω *apolambanō* 10x *to receive* what is due, sought, or needed, Lk. 23:41; Rom. 1:27; Gal. 4:5; Col. 3:24; 2 Jn. 8; *to receive in full,* Lk. 16:25; *to receive back, recover,* Lk. 6:34; 15:27; 18:30; mid. *to take aside, lead away,* Mk. 7:33 [618] See *get back; receive; (be) repaid.*

[656] ἀπόλαυσις *apolausis* 2x *beneficial participation,* 1 Tim. 6:17; *enjoyment, pleasure,* Heb. 11:25* [619]

[657] ἀπολείπω *apoleipō* 7x *to leave, leave behind;* pass. *to be left, remain,* 2 Tim. 4:13, 20; Heb. 4:6, 9; 10:26; *to relinquish, forsake, desert,* Tit. 1:5; Jude 6* [620]

[660] ἀπόλλυμι *apollymi* 90x *to destroy utterly; to kill,* Mt. 2:13; *to bring to nought, make void,* 1 Cor. 1:19; *to lose, be deprived of,* Mt. 10:42; *to be destroyed, perish,* Mt. 9:17; *to be put to death, to die,* Mt. 26:52; *to be lost, to stray,* Mt. 10:6 [622] See *destroy; lose; perish.*

[661] Ἀπολλύων *Apollyōn* 1x *Apollyon, Destroyer,* i.q. Ἀβαδδών, Rev. 9:11* [623]

[662] Ἀπολλωνία *Apollōnia* 1x *Apollonia,* a city of Macedonia, Acts 17:1* [624]

[663] Ἀπολλῶς *Apollōs* 10x *Apollos,* pr. name, Acts 18:24; 19:1; 1 Cor. 1:12; 3:4-6, 22; 4:6; 16:12; Tit. 3:13* [625]

[664] ἀπολογέομαι *apologeomai* 10x *to defend one's self against a charge, to make a defence,* Lk. 12:11; 21:14 [626] See *defend.*

[665] ἀπολογία *apologia* 8x *a verbal defence,* Acts 22:1; 25:16 [627]

[666] ἀπολούω *apolouō* 2x *to cleanse by bathing;* mid. *to cleanse one's self; to procure one's self to be cleansed;* met., of sin, Acts 22:16; 1 Cor. 6:11* [628] See *wash, washing.*

[667] ἀπολύτρωσις *apolytrōsis* 10x *redemption, a deliverance, procured by the payment of a ransom;* meton. the author of *redemption,* 1 Cor. 1:30; *deliverance,* simply, the idea of a ransom being excluded, Lk. 21:28; Heb. 11:35 [629] See *ransom; redemption.*

[668] ἀπολύω *apolyō* 66x pr. *to loose; to release* from a tie or burden, Mt. 18:27; *to divorce,* Mt. 1:19; *to remit, forgive,* Lk. 6:37; *to liberate, discharge,* Mt. 27:15; *to dismiss,* Mt. 15:23; Acts 19:40; *to allow to depart, to send away,* Mt. 14:15; *to permit,* or, *signal departure* from life, Lk. 2:29; mid. *to depart,* Acts 28:25; pass. *to be rid,* Lk. 13:12 [630] See *divorce; release; send away.*

[669] ἀπομάσσω *apomassō* 1x *to wipe off;* mid. *to wipe off one's self,* Lk. 10:11* [631]

[671] ἀπονέμω *aponemō* 1x *to portion off; to assign, bestow,* 1 Pet. 3:7* [632]

[672] ἀπονίπτω *aponiptō* 1x *to cleanse* a part of the body *by washing;* mid., of one's self, Mt. 27:24* [633]

[674] ἀποπίπτω *apopiptō* 1x *to fall off* or *from,* Acts 9:18* [634]

[675] ἀποπλανάω *apoplanaō* 2x *to cause to wander;* met. *to deceive, pervert, seduce,* Mk. 13:22; pass. *to wander;* met. *to swerve from, apostatize,* 1 Tim. 6:10* [635]

[676] ἀποπλέω *apopleō* 4x *to depart by ship, sail away,* Acts 13:4; 14:26; 20:15; 27:1* [636]

[678] ἀποπνίγω *apopnigō* 2x *to choke, suffocate,* Lk. 8:7; *to drown,* Lk. 8:33* [638]

[679] ἀπορέω *aporeō* 6x also spelled ἀπορρίπτω, pr. *to be without means;* met.

to hesitate, be at a stand, be in doubt and perplexity, Jn. 13:22; Acts 25:20; 2 Cor. 4:8; Gal. 4:20 [639]

[680] ἀπορία *aporia* 1x *doubt, uncertainty, perplexity,* Lk. 21:25* [640]

[681] ἀπορίπτω *aporiptō* 1x *to throw off, throw down,* Acts 27:43* [641]

[682] ἀπορφανίζω *aporphanizō* 1x lit., *to make an orphan*; fig., *to deprive, bereave,* 1 Thess. 2:17* [642]

[684] ἀποσκίασμα *aposkiasma* 1x *a shadow cast;* met. *a shade, the slightest trace,* Jas. 1:17* [644]

[685] ἀποσπάω *apospaō* 4x *to draw away from; to draw out* or *forth,* Mt. 26:51; *to draw away, seduce,* Acts 20:30; *to separate one's self, to part,* Lk. 22:41; Acts 21:1* [645]

[686] ἀποστασία *apostasia* 2x *a falling away, a rebellion, apostasy,* Acts 21:21; 2 Thess. 2:3* [646]

[687] ἀποστάσιον *apostasion* 3x *defection, desertion,* as of a freedman from a patron; in NT *the act of putting away a wife, repudiation, divorce,* Mt. 19:7; Mk. 10:4; meton. *a bill of repudiation, deed of divorce,* Mt. 5:31* [647]

[689] ἀποστεγάζω *apostegazō* 1x *to remove* or *break through a covering* or *roof* of a place, Mk. 2:4* [648]

[690] ἀποστέλλω *apostellō* 132x *to send forth* a messenger, agent, message, or command, Mt. 2:16; 10:5; *to put forth into action,* Mk. 4:29; *to liberate, rid,* Lk. 4:19; *to dismiss, send away,* Mk. 12:3 [649] See *send.*

[691] ἀποστερέω *apostereō* 6x *to deprive, detach; to debar,* 1 Cor. 7:5; *to deprive* in a bad sense, *defraud,* Mk. 10:19; 1 Cor. 6:7; mid. *to suffer one's self to be deprived* or *defrauded,* 1 Cor. 6:8; pass. *to be destitute* or *devoid of,* 1 Tim. 6:5; *to be unjustly withheld,* Jas. 5:4* [650]

[692] ἀποστολή *apostolē* 4x *a sending, expedition; office* or *duty of one sent as a messenger* or *agent; office of an apostle, apostleship,* Acts 1:25; Rom. 1:5; 1 Cor. 9:2; Gal. 2:8* [651]

[693] ἀπόστολος *apostolos* 80x *one sent as a messenger* or *agent, the bearer of a commission, messenger,* Jn. 13:16; *an apostle,* Mt. 10:2 [652] See *apostle; delegate; messenger; send.*

[694] ἀποστοματίζω *apostomatizō* 1x pr. *to speak* or *repeat offhand;* also, *to require* or *lead* others *to speak without premeditation,* as by questions calculated to elicit unpremeditated answers, *to endeavor to entrap into unguarded language,* Lk. 11:53* [653]

[695] ἀποστρέφω *apostrephō* 9x *to turn away; to remove,* Acts 3:26; Rom. 11:26; 2 Tim. 4:4; *to turn* a people from their allegiance, to their sovereign, *pervert, incite to revolt,* Lk. 23:14; *to replace, restore,* Mt. 26:52; *to turn away from* any one, *to slight, reject, repulse,* Mt. 5:42; Tit. 1:14; Heb. 12:25; *to desert,* 2 Tim. 1:15 [654]

[696] ἀποστυγέω *apostygeō* 1x *to shrink from with abhorrence, detest,* Rom. 12:9* [655]

[697] ἀποσυνάγωγος *aposynagōgos* 3x *expelled* or *excluded from the synagogue, excommunicated, cut off from the rights and privileges of a Jew, excluded from society,* Jn. 9:22; 12:42; 16:2* [656]

[698] ἀποτάσσω *apotassō* 6x middle: *to take leave of, bid farewell to,* Lk. 9:61; Acts 18:18, 21; 2 Cor. 2:13; *to dismiss, send away,* Mk. 6:46; fig: *to renounce, forsake,* Lk. 14:33 [657]

[699] ἀποτελέω *apoteleō* 2x *to complete;* pass. *to be perfected, to arrive at full stature* or *measure,* Lk. 13:32; Jas. 1:15* [658]

[700] ἀποτίθημι *apotithēmi* 9x mid: *to lay off, lay down* or *aside,* as garments, Acts 7:58; me [659]

[701] ἀποτινάσσω *apotinassō* 2x *to shake off,* Lk. 9:5; Acts 28:5* [660]

[702] ἀποτίνω *apotinō* 1x *to pay off* what is claimed or due; *to repay, refund, make good,* Phlm. 19* [661]

[703] ἀποτολμάω *apotolmaō* 1x *to dare* or *risk outright; to speak outright, without reserve* or *restraint,* Rom. 10:20 [662]

[704] ἀποτομία *apotomia* 2x pr. *abruptness;* met. *severity, rigor,* Rom. 11:22 (2x)* [663]

[705] ἀποτόμως *apotomōs* 2x *sharply, severely,* 2 Cor. 13:10; Tit. 1:13* [664]

[706] ἀποτρέπω *apotrepō* 1x mid: *to turn* any one *away* from a thing; mid. *to turn one's self away* from any one; *to avoid, shun,* 2 Tim. 3:5* [665]

[707] ἀπουσία *apousia* 1x *absence,* Phil. 2:12* [666]

[708] ἀποφέρω *apopherō* 6x *to bear* or *carry away, conduct away,* Mk. 15:1; Lk. 16:22; Acts 19:12; 1 Cor. 16:3; Rev. 17:3; 21:10* [667]

[709] ἀποφεύγω *apopheugō* 3x *to flee from, escape;* met. *to be rid, be freed from,* 2 Pet. 1:4; 2:18, 20* [668]

[710] ἀποφθέγγομαι *apophthengomai* 3x *to speak out, declare,* particularly solemn, weighty, or pithy sayings, Acts 2:4, 14; 26:25* [669]

[711] ἀποφορτίζομαι *apophortizomai* 1x *to unload,* Acts 21:3* [670]

[712] ἀπόχρησις *apochrēsis* 1x *a using up,* or, *a discharge of an intended use,* Col. 2:22* [671]

[713] ἀποχωρέω *apochōreō* 3x *to go from* or *away, depart,* Mt. 7:23; Lk. 9:39; Acts 13:13* [672]

[714] ἀποχωρίζω *apochōrizō* 2x *to separate;* pass. *to be swept aside,* Rev. 6:14; mid. *to part,* Acts 15:39* [673]

[715] ἀποψύχω *apopsychō* 1x pr. *to breathe out, faint away, die;* met. *to faint at heart, be dismayed,* Lk. 21:26* [674]

[716] Ἄππιος *Appios* 1x *the forum* or *marketplace, of Appius;* a village on the Appian road, near Rome, Acts 28:15* [675]

[717] ἀπρόσιτος *aprositos* 1x *unapproached, unapproachable,* 1 Tim. 6:16* [676]

[718] ἀπρόσκοπος *aproskopos* 3x *not stumbling* or *jarring;* met. *not stumbling* or *jarring* against moral rule, *unblamable, clear,* Acts 24:16; Phil. 1:10; *free from offensiveness,* 1 Cor. 10:32* [677]

[719] ἀπροσωπολήμπτως *aprosōpolēmptōs* 1x *without respect of persons, impartially,* 1 Pet. 1:17* [678]

[720] ἄπταιστος *aptaistos* 1x *free from stumbling;* met. *free from* moral *stumbling, offence; irreprehensible,* Jude 24* [679]

[721] ἅπτω *haptō* 39x pr. *to bring in contact, fit, fasten; to light, kindle,* Mk. 4:21; Lk. 8:16; *to touch,* Mt. 8:3; *to meddle, venture to partake,* Col. 2:21; *to have intercourse with, to know carnally,* 1 Cor. 7:1; by impl. *to harm,* 1 Jn. 5:18 [680, 681] See *cling; light; take hold; touch.*

[722] Ἀπφία *Apphia* 1x *Apphia,* pr. name, Phlm. 2* [682]

[723] ἀπωθέω *apōtheō* 6x *to thrust away, repel from one's self, repulse,* Acts 7:27; *to refuse, reject, cast off,* Acts 7:39; 13:46; Rom. 11:1, 2; 1 Tim. 1:19* [683]

[724] ἀπώλεια *apōleia* 18x *consumption, destruction; waste, profusion,* Mt. 26:8; Mk. 14:4; *destruction, state of being destroyed,* Acts 25:6; eternal *ruin, perdition,* Mt. 7:13; Acts 8:20 [684] See *destruction; ruin; waste.*

[725] ἀρά *ara* 1x pr. *a prayer;* more commonly *a prayer for evil; curse, cursing, imprecation,* Rom. 3:14* [685]

[726] ἄρα *ara* 49x a particle which denotes, first, transition from one thing to another by natural sequence; secondly, logical inference; in which case the premises are either expressed, Mt. 12:28, or to be variously supplied, *therefore, then, consequently; as a result,* Acts 17:27 [686]

[727] ἆρα *ara* 3x inferential particle, used mainly in interrogations, Lk. 18:8; Acts 8:30; Gal. 2:17* [687]

[728] Ἀραβία *Arabia* 2x *Arabia,* Gal. 1:17; 4:25* [688]

[730] Ἀράμ *Aram* 2x *Aram,* pr. name, indecl, Mt. 1:3-4* [689]

[731] ἄραφος *araphos* 1x *not sewed, seamless,* Jn. 19:23* [729]

[732] Ἄραψ *Araps* 1x *an Arabian,* Acts 2:11* [690]

[733] ἀργέω *argeō* 1x pr. *to be unemployed; to be inoperative, to linger,* 2 Pet. 2:3* [691]

[734] ἀργός *argos* 8x pr. *inactive, unemployed,* Mt. 20:3, 6; *idle, averse from labor,* 1 Tim. 5:13; Tit. 1:12; met. 2 Pet. 1:8; *unprofitable, hollow,* or by impl., *injurious,* Mt. 12:36; Jas. 2:20* [692]

[736] ἀργύριον *argyrion* 20x *silver;* meton. *money,* Mt. 25:18, 27 [694] See *money; silver.*

[737] ἀργυροκόπος *argyrokopos* 1x *a forger of silver, silversmith,* Acts 19:24* [695]

[738] ἄργυρος *argyros* 5x *silver;* meton. *anything made of silver; money,* Jas. 5:3 [696]

[739] ἀργυροῦς *argyrous* 3x *made of silver,* Acts 19:24; 2 Tim. 2:20; Rev. 9:20* [693]

[741] Ἀρεοπαγίτης *Areopagitēs* 1x *a judge of the court of Areopagus,* Acts 17:34* [698]

[742] ἀρεσκεία *areskeia* 1x *a pleasing, desire of pleasing,* Col. 1:10* [699]

[743] ἀρέσκω *areskō* 17x *to please,* Mt. 14:6; *to be pleasing, acceptable,* Acts 6:5; *to consult the pleasure of* any one, Rom. 15:1, 2, 3; 1 Cor. 10:33; *to seek favor with,* Gal. 1:10; 1 Thess. 2:4 [700] See *please.*

[744] ἀρεστός *arestos* 4x *pleasing, acceptable,* Acts 12:3; 1 Jn. 3:22; 8:29, *deemed proper,* Acts 6:2 [701]

[745] Ἁρέτας *Haretas* 1x *Aretas,* pr. name, 2 Cor. 11:32* [702]

[746] ἀρετή *aretē* 5x *goodness, good quality* of any kind; *a gracious act* of God, 1 Pet. 2:9; 2 Pet. 1:3; *virtue, uprightness,* Phil. 4:8; 2 Pet. 1:5* [703]

[748] ἀρήν *arēn* 1x *a sheep, lamb,* Lk. 10:3* [704]

[749] ἀριθμέω *arithmeō* 3x *to count,* Mt. 10:30; Lk. 12:7; Rev. 7:9* [705]

[750] ἀριθμός *arithmos* 18x *a number,* Lk. 22:3; Jn. 6:10; Acts 4:4; Rev. 20:8; 13:18 [706] See *number.*

[751] Ἁριμαθαία *Harimathaia* 4x *Arimathea,* a town of Palestine, Mt. 27:57; Mk. 15:43; Lk. 23:51; Jn. 19:38* [707]

[752] Ἀρίσταρχος *Aristarchos* 5x *Aristarchus,* pr. name, Acts 19:29; 20:4; 27:2; Col. 4:10; Phlm. 24* [708]

[753] ἀριστάω *aristaō* 3x *to take the first meal, breakfast,* Jn. 21:12, 15; also, *to take a mid-day meal,* Lk. 11:37* [709]

[754] ἀριστερός *aristeros* 4x *the left hand,* Mt. 6:3; so ἐξ ἀριστερῶν, sc. μερῶν, Lk. 23:33; 2 Cor. 6:7; Mk. 10:37* [710]

[755] Ἀριστόβουλος *Aristoboulos* 1x *Aristobulus,* pr. name, Rom. 16:10* [711]

[756] ἄριστον *ariston* 3x pr. *the first meal, breakfast;* afterwards extended to signify also *a slight mid-day meal, luncheon,* Mt. 22:4; Lk. 11:38; 14:12* [712]

[757] ἀρκετός *arketos* 3x *sufficient, enough,* Mt. 6:34; 10:25; 1 Pet. 4:3* [713]

[758] ἀρκέω *arkeō* 8x pr. *to ward off;* thence; *to be of service, avail; to suffice, be enough,* Mt. 25:9; pass. *to be contented, satisfied,* Lk. 3:14; 1 Tim. 6:8; Heb. 13:5; 3 Jn. 10 [714]

[759] ἄρκος *arkos* 1x also spelled ἄρκτος, *a bear,* Rev. 13:2* [715]

[761] ἅρμα *harma* 4x *a chariot, vehicle,* Acts 8:28, 29, 38; Rev. 9:9* [716]

[762] Ἁρμαγεδών *Harmagedōn* 1x *Armageddon,* Rev. 16:16* [717]

[764] ἁρμόζω *harmozō* 1x *to fit together; to join, unite,* in marriage, *espouse, betroth,* 2 Cor. 11:2* [718]

[765] ἁρμός *harmos* 1x *a joint* or *articulation* of the bones, Heb. 4:12* [719]

[766] ἀρνέομαι *arneomai* 33x *to deny, disclaim, disown,* Mt. 10:33; *to renounce,* Tit. 2:12; *to decline, refuse,* Heb. 11:24; absol. *to deny, contradict,* Lk. 8:15 [720] See *deny; disown; reject; renounce.*

[767] Ἀρνί *Arni* 1x *Arni,* pr. name, Lk. 3:33* [**]

[768] ἀρνίον *arnion* 30x *a young lamb, lamb,* Jn. 21:15; Rev. 5:6, 8 [721] See *lamb.*

[769] ἀροτριάω *arotriaō* 3x *to plow,* Lk. 17:7; 1 Cor. 9:10* [722]

[770] ἄροτρον *arotron* 1x *a plow,* Lk. 9:62* [723]

[771] ἁρπαγή *harpagē* 3x *plunder, pillage; the act of plundering,* Heb. 10:34; *prey, spoil,* Mt. 23:25; Lk. 11:39* [724]

[772] ἁρπαγμός *harpagmos* 1x *eager seizure;* in NT, *a thing retained with an eager grasp,* or *eagerly claimed and conspicuously exercised,* Phil. 2:6* [725]

[773] ἁρπάζω *harpazō* 14x *to seize,* as a wild beast, Jn. 10:12; *take away by force, snatch away,* Mt. 13:19; Jn. 10:28, 29; Acts 23:10; Jude 23; met. *to seize on with avidity, eagerly, appropriate,* Mt. 11:12; *to convey away suddenly, transport hastily,* Jn. 6:15 [726] See *catch; snatch.*

[774] ἅρπαξ *harpax* 5x pr. *raveneous, ravening,* as a wild beast, Mt. 7:15; met. *rapacious, given to extortion and robbery, an extortioner,* Lk. 18:11; 1 Cor. 5:10, 11; 6:10* [727]

[775] ἀρραβών *arrabōn* 3x *a pledge, earnest,* 2 Cor. 1:22; 5:5; Eph. 1:14* [728] See *deposit; guarantee; pledge.*

[777] ἄρρητος *arrētos* 1x pr. *not spoken; what ought not to be spoken, secret; which cannot be spoken* or *uttered,* 2 Cor. 12:4* [731]

[779] ἄρρωστος *arrōstos* 5x *ill, sick, an invalid,* Mt. 14:14; Mk. 6:5, 13; 16:18; 1 Cor. 11:30 [732]

[780] ἀρσενοκοίτης *arsenokoitēs* 2x *a male engaging in same-gender sexual activity, a sodomite, pedarest,* 1 Cor. 6:9; 1 Tim. 1:10* [733]

[781] ἄρσην *arsēn* 9x *male, of the male sex,* Mt. 19:4; Mk. 10:6; Lk. 2:23; Rom. 1:27; Gal. 3:28; Rev. 12:5, 13* [730] See *male.*

[782] Ἀρτεμᾶς *Artemas* 1x *Artemas,* pr. name, Tit. 3:12* [734]

[783] Ἄρτεμις *Artemis* 5x *Artemis* or *Diana,* Acts 19:24, 27, 28, 34, 35* [735]

[784] ἀρτέμων *artemōn* 1x *a topsail, foresail;* or, according to others, *the dolon* of Pliny and Pollux, a small sail near the bow of the ship, which was hoisted when the wind was too strong to use the larger sails, Acts 27:40* [736]

[785] ἄρτι *arti* 36x pr. *at the present moment, close upon it* either before of after; *now, at the present juncture,* Mt. 3:15; *forthwith, presently; just now, recently,* 1 Thess. 3:6; ἕως ἄρτι, *until now, hitherto,* Mt. 11:12; Jn. 2:10; ἀπ᾽ ἄρτι, or ἀπάρτι, *from this time, henceforth,* Mt. 23:39 [737] See *now.*

[786] ἀρτιγέννητος *artigennētos* 1x *just born, new-born,* 1 Pet. 2:2* [738]

[787] ἄρτιος *artios* 1x *entirely suited; complete* in accomplishment, *ready,* 2 Tim. 3:17* [739]

[788] ἄρτος *artos* 97x *bread; a loaf* or *thin cake of bread,* Mt. 26:26; *food,* Mt. 15:2; Mk. 3:20; *bread, maintenance, liv-*

ing, necessaries of life, Mt. 6:11; Lk. 11:3; 2 Thess. 3:8 [740] See *bread; food; loaf.*

[789] ἀρτύω *artyō* 3x pr. *to fit, prepare; to season, make savoury,* Mk. 9:50; Lk. 14:34; Col. 4:6* [741]

[790] Ἀρφαξάδ *Arphaxad* 1x *Arphaxad,* pr. name, indecl, Lk. 3:36* [742]

[791] ἀρχάγγελος *archangelos* 2x *an archangel, chief angel,* 1 Thess. 4:16; Jude 9* [743]

[792] ἀρχαῖος *archaios* 11x *old, ancient, of former age,* Mt. 5:21, 33; *of long standing, old, veteran,* Acts 21:16; ἀφ᾽ ἡμερῶν ἀρχαίων, *from early days, from an early period,* of the Gospel, Acts 15:7 [744] See *ancient; old.*

[793] Ἀρχέλαος *Archelaos* 1x *Archelaus,* pr. name, Mt. 2:22* [745]

[794] ἀρχή *archē* 55x *a beginning,* Mt. 24:8; *an extremity, corner,* or, *an attached cord,* Acts 10:11; 11:5; *first place, headship; high estate, eminence,* Jude 6; *authority,* Lk. 20:20; *an authority, magistrate,* Lk. 12:11; *a principality, prince,* of spiritual existence, Eph. 3:10; 6:12; ἀπ᾽ ἀρχῆς, ἐξ ἀρχῆς, *from the first, originally,* Mt. 19:4, 8; Lk. 1:2; Jn. 6:64; 2 Thess. 2:13; 1 Jn. 1:1; 2:7; ἐν ἀρχῇ, κατ᾽ ἀρχάς, *in the beginning* of things, Jn. 1:1, 2; Heb. 1:10; ἐν ἀρχῇ, *at the first,* Acts 11:15; τὴν ἀρχήν, used adverbially, *wholly, altogether,* Jn. 8:25 [746] See *beginning; ruler.*

[795] ἀρχηγός *archēgos* 4x *a chief, leader, prince,* Acts 5:31; *a prime author,* Acts 3:15; Heb. 2:10; 12:2* [747]

[796] ἀρχιερατικός *archieratikos* 1x *belonging to* or *connected with the high-priest* or *his office,* Acts 4:6* [748]

[797] ἀρχιερεύς *archiereus* 122x *a high-priest, chief-priest* [749] See *chief priest; high priest.*

[799] ἀρχιποίμην *archipoimēn* 1x *chief shepherd,* 1 Pet. 5:4* [750]

[800] Ἄρχιππος *Archippos* 2x *Archippus,* pr. name, Col. 4:17; Phlm. 2, inscr. and subscr.* [751]

[801] ἀρχισυνάγωγος *archisynagōgos* 9x *a president* or *moderating elder of a synagogue,* Mk. 5:22, 35, 36, 38; Lk. 8:49 [752]

[802] ἀρχιτέκτων *architektōn* 1x *architect, head* or *master-builder,* 1 Cor. 3:10* [753]

[803] ἀρχιτελώνης *architelōnēs* 1x *a chief publican, chief collector of the customs* or *taxes,* Lk. 19:2* [754]

[804] ἀρχιτρίκλινος *architriklinos* 3x *director of a feast,* Jn. 2:8, 9* [755]

[806] ἄρχω *archō* 86x (1) pr. (act.) *to be first; to rule,* Mk. 10:42; Rom. 15:12 (2) mid. *to begin,* Mt. 4:17; *to take commencement,* Lk. 24:27; 1 Pet. 4:17 [756, 757] See *begin; rule.*

[807] ἄρχων *archōn* 37x *one invested with power and dignity, chief, ruler, prince, magistrate,* Mt. 9:23; 20:25 [758] See *leader; prince; ruler.*

[808] ἄρωμα *arōma* 4x *an aromatic substance, spice,* etc., Mk. 16:1; Lk. 23:56; 24:1; Jn. 19:40* [759]

[810] ἀσάλευτος *asaleutos* 2x *unshaken, immovable,* Acts 27:41; met. *firm, stable, enduring,* Heb. 12:28* [761]

[811] Ἀσάφ *Asaph* 2x *Asaph,* pr. name, indecl, Mt. 1:7, 8* [760]

[812] ἄσβεστος *asbestos* 3x *unquenched; inextinguishable, unquenchable,* Mt. 3:12; Mk. 9:43; Lk. 3:17* [762]

[813] ἀσέβεια *asebeia* 6x *impiety, ungodliness; dishonesty, wickedness,* Rom. 1:18; 11:26; 2 Tim. 2:16; Tit. 2:12; Jude 15, 18* [763]

[814] ἀσεβέω *asebeō* 1x *to be impious, to act impiously* or *wickedly, live an impious life,* 2 Pet. 2:6; Jude 15* [764]

[815] ἀσεβής *asebēs* 9x *impious, ungodly; wicked, sinful,* Rom. 4:5; 5:6 [765] See *godless; ungodly; wicked, wickedness.*

[816] ἀσέλγεια *aselgeia* 10x *intemperance; licentiousness, lasciviousness,* Rom. 13:13; *insolence, outrageous behavior,* Mk. 7:22 [766] See *debauchery; lewdness; sensuality.*

[817] ἄσημος *asēmos* 1x pr. *not marked;* met. *not noted, not remarkable, unknown to fame, ignoble, mean, inconsiderable,* Acts 21:39* [767]

[818] Ἀσήρ *Asēr* 2x *Asher,* pr. name, indecl (Gen. 30:13; 49:20; 2 Chr. 30:11) Lk. 2:36; Rev. 7:6* [768]

[819] ἀσθένεια *astheneia* 24x *want of strength, weakness, feebleness,* 1 Cor. 15:43; bodily *infirmity, state of ill health, sickness,* Mt. 8:17; Lk. 5:15; met. *infirmity, frailty, imperfection,* intellectual and moral, Rom. 6:19; 1 Cor. 2:3; Heb. 5:2; 7:28; *suffering, affliction, distress, calamity,* Rom. 8:26 [769] See *illness; sickness; weakness.*

[820] ἀσθενέω *astheneō* 33x *to be weak, infirm, deficient in strength; to be inefficient,* Rom. 8:3; 2 Cor. 13:3; *to be sick,* Mt. 25:36; met. *to be weak* in faith, *to doubt, hesitate, be unsettled, timid,* Rom. 14:1; 1 Cor. 8:9, 11, 12; 2 Cor. 11:29; *to be deficient in authority, dignity,* or *power, be contemptible,* 2 Cor. 11:21; 13:3, 9; *to be afflicted, distressed, needy,* Acts 20:35; 2 Cor. 12:10; 13:4, 9 [770] See *sick; weak.*

[821] ἀσθένημα *asthenēma* 1x pr. *weakness, infirmity,* met. *doubt, hesitation,* Rom. 15:1* [771]

[822] ἀσθενής *asthenēs* 26x *without strength, weak, infirm,* Mt. 26:41; Mk. 14:38; 1 Pet. 3:7; *helpless,* Rom. 5:6; *imperfect, inefficient,* Gal. 4:9; *feeble, without energy,* 2 Cor. 10:10; *infirm* in body, *sick, sickly,* Mt. 25:39, 43, 44; *weak,* mentally or spiritually, *dubious, hesitating,* 1 Cor. 8:7, 10; 9:22; 1 Thess. 5:14; *afflicted, distressed, oppressed with calamities,* 1 Cor. 4:10 [772] See *sick; weak.*

[823] Ἀσία *Asia* 18x *Asia,* the Roman province, Acts 19:27 [773]

[824] Ἀσιανός *Asianos* 1x *belonging to the Roman province of Asia,* Acts 20:4* [774]

[825] Ἀσιάρχης *Asiarchēs* 1x *an Asiarch,* an officer in the province of Asia, as in other eastern provinces of the Roman empire, selected, with others, from the more opulent citizens, to preside over the things pertaining to religious worship, and to exhibit annual public games at their own expense in honor of the gods, in the manner of the aediles at Rome, Acts 19:31* [775]

[826] ἀσιτία *asitia* 1x *abstinence from food, fasting,* Acts 27:21* [776]

[827] ἄσιτος *asitos* 1x *abstaining from food, fasting,* Acts 27:33* [777]

[828] ἀσκέω *askeō* 1x pr. *to work* materials; absol. *to train* or *exert one's self, make endeavor,* Acts 24:16* [778]

[829] ἀσκός *askos* 12x *a leather bag* or *bottle, bottle of skin,* Mt. 9:17; Mk. 2:22; Lk. 5:37, 38 [779] See *wineskin.*

[830] ἀσμένως *asmenōs* 1x *gladly, joyfully,* Acts 21:17* [780]

[831] ἄσοφος *asophos* 1x *unwise; destitute of* Christian *wisdom,* Eph. 5:15* [781]

[832] ἀσπάζομαι *aspazomai* 59x *to salute, greet, welcome, express good wishes, pay respects,* Mt. 10:12; Mk. 9:15, et al. freq.; *to bid farewell,* Acts 20:1; 21:6; *to treat with affection,* Mt. 5:47; met. *to embrace* mentally, *welcome* to the heart of understanding, Heb. 11:13 [782] See *greet; welcome.*

[833] ἀσπασμός *aspasmos* 10x *salutation, greeting,* Mt. 23:7; Mk. 12:38 [783] See *greeting.*

[834] ἄσπιλος *aspilos* 4x *spotless, unblemished, pure,* 1 Tim. 6:14; Jas. 1:27; 1 Pet. 1:19; 2 Pet. 3:14* [784]

[835] ἀσπίς *aspis* 1x *an asp,* a species of serpent of the most deadly venom, Rom. 3:13* [785]

[836] ἄσπονδος *aspondos* 1x pr. *unwilling to make a treaty;* hence, *implacable, irreconcilable,* 2 Tim. 3:3* [786]

[837] ἀσσάριον *assarion* 2x dimin. of the Latin, *as,* a Roman brass coin with the value of one-tenth of a denarius, or δραχμή, used to convey the idea of a trifle or very small sum, Mt. 10:29; Lk. 12:6* [787]

[839] ἆσσον *asson* 1x *nearer; very nigh, close;* used as the compar. of ἄγχι, Acts 27:13* [788]

[840] Ἆσσος *Assos* 2x *Assos,* a maritime city of Mysia, in Asia Minor, Acts 20:13-14* [789]

[841] ἀστατέω *astateō* 1x *to be unsettled, to be a wanderer, be homeless,* 1 Cor. 4:11* [790]

[842] ἀστεῖος *asteios* 2x pr. *belonging to a city; well bred, polite, polished;* hence, *elegant, fair, comely, beautiful,* Acts 7:20; Heb. 11:23* [791]

[843] ἀστήρ *astēr* 24x *a star, luminous body like a star, luminary,* Mt. 2:2, 7, 9, 10; Rev. 1:16 [792] See *star.*

[844] ἀστήρικτος *astēriktos* 2x *not made firm; unsettled, unstable, unsteady,* 2 Pet. 2:14; 3:16* [793]

[845] ἄστοργος *astorgos* 2x *devoid of natural* or *instinctive affection, without affection to kindred,* Rom. 1:31; 2 Tim. 3:3* [794]

[846] ἀστοχέω *astocheō* 3x pr. *to miss the mark;* met. *to err, deviate, swerve from,* 1 Tim. 1:6; 6:21; 2 Tim. 2:18* [795]

[847] ἀστραπή *astrapē* 9x *lightning,* Mt. 24:27; *brightness, lustre,* Lk. 11:36 [796]

[848] ἀστράπτω *astraptō* 2x *to lighten, flash as lightning,* Lk. 17:24; *to be bright, shining,* Lk. 24:4* [797]

[849] ἄστρον *astron* 4x *a constellation; a star,* Lk. 21:25; Acts 7:43; 27:20; Heb. 11:12* [798] See *star.*

[850] Ἀσύγκριτος *Asynkritos* 1x *Asyncritus,* pr. name, Rom. 16:14* [799]

[851] ἀσύμφωνος *asymphōnos* 1x *discordant in sound;* met. *discordant, at difference,* Acts 28:25* [800]

[852] ἀσύνετος *asynetos* 5x *unintelligent, dull,* Mt. 15:16; Mk. 7:18; *reckless, perverse,* Rom. 1:21, 31; *unenlightened, heathenish,* Rom. 10:19 [801]

[853] ἀσύνθετος *asynthetos* 1x *unable to be trusted, undutiful,* Rom. 1:31* [802]

[854] ἀσφάλεια *asphaleia* 3x pr. *state of security from falling, firmness; safety, security,* 1 Thess. 5:3; *certainty, truth,* Lk. 1:4; *means of security,* Acts 5:23* [803]

[855] ἀσφαλής *asphalēs* 5x pr. *firm, secure from falling; firm, sure, steady, immovable,* Heb. 6:19; met. *certain, sure,* Acts 21:34; 22:30; 25:26; *safe, making secure,* Phil. 3:1* [804]

[856] ἀσφαλίζω *asphalizō* 4x mid: *to make fast, safe,* or *secure,* Mt. 27:64, 65, 66; Acts 16:24* [805]

[857] ἀσφαλῶς *asphalōs* 3x *securely, safely; without fail, safely,* Mk. 14:44; Acts 16:23; *certainly, assuredly,* Acts 2:36* [806]

[858] ἀσχημονέω *aschēmoneō* 2x *to behave in an unbecoming manner* or *indecorously,* 1 Cor. 13:5; *to behave in a manner open to censure,* 1 Cor. 7:36* [807]

[859] ἀσχημοσύνη *aschēmosynē* 2x pr. *external indecorum; nakedness, shame, pudenda,* Rev. 16:15; *indecency, infamous lust* or *lewdness,* Rom. 1:27* [808]

[860] ἀσχήμων *aschēmōn* 1x *indecorous, uncomely, indecent,* 1 Cor. 12:23* [809]

[861] ἀσωτία *asōtia* 3x *dissoluteness, debauchery,* Eph. 5:18; Tit. 1:6; 1 Pet. 4:4* [810]

[862] ἀσώτως *asōtōs* 1x *dissolutely, loosely,* Lk. 15:13* [811]

[863] ἀτακτέω *atakteō* 1x pr. *to infringe* military *order;* met. *to be irregular, behave disorderly, to be lazy,* 2 Thess. 3:7* [812]

[864] ἄτακτος *ataktos* 1x pr. used of soldiers, *disorderly;* met. *irregular* in conduct, *disorderly, lazy,* 1 Thess. 5:14* [813]

[865] ἀτάκτως *ataktōs* 2x *disorderly, irresponsible,* 2 Thess. 3:6, 11* [814]

[866] ἄτεκνος *ateknos* 2x *childless,* Lk. 20:28, 29* [815]

[867] ἀτενίζω *atenizō* 14x *to fix one's eyes upon, look steadily, gaze intently,* Lk. 4:20 [816] See *gaze; look straight; stare.*

[868] ἄτερ *ater* 2x improper prep with the gen., *without,* Lk. 22:6, 35* [817]

[869] ἀτιμάζω *atimazō* 7x also spelled ἀτιμάω and ἀντιμόω, *to dishonor, slight,* Jn. 8:49; Rom. 2:23; Jas. 2:6; *to treat with indignity,* Mk. 12:4; Lk. 20:11; Acts 5:41; *to abuse, debase,* Rom. 1:24* [818]

[871] ἀτιμία *atimia* 7x *dishonor, infamy,* Rom. 1:26; *shame,* 1 Cor. 11:14; *meanness, vileness,* 1 Cor. 15:43; 2 Cor. 6:8; *a dishonorable use,* Rom. 9:21; 2 Tim. 2:20; κατὰ ἀτιμίαν, *slightingly, disparagingly,* 2 Cor. 11:21 [819]

[872] ἄτιμος *atimos* 4x *unhonored, without honor,* Mt. 13:57; Mk. 6:4; *despised,* 1 Cor. 4:10; 12:23* [820]

[874] ἀτμίς *atmis* 2x *an exhalation, vapor, smoke,* Acts 2:19; Jas. 4:14* [822]

[875] ἄτομος *atomos* 1x *indivisible,* and by impl. *exceedingly minute;* ἐν ἀτόμῳ, sc. χρόνῳ, *in an indivisible point of time, in an instant* or *moment,* 1 Cor. 15:52* [823]

[876] ἄτοπος *atopos* 4x pr. *out of place; inopportune, unsuitable, absurd; new, unusual, strange;* in NT *improper, amiss, wicked,* Lk. 23:41; Acts 25:5; 2 Thess. 3:2; *noxious, harmful,* Acts 28:6* [824]

[877] Ἀττάλεια *Attaleia* 1x *Attalia,* a city of Pamphylia, Acts 14:25* [825]

[878] αὐγάζω *augazō* 1x *to see distinctly, discern,* or possibly *to shine, give light* at 2 Cor. 4:4* [826]

[879] αὐγή *augē* 1x *radiance; daybreak, dawn,* Acts 20:11* [827]

[881] αὐθάδης *authadēs* 2x *one who pleases himself, willful, obstinate; arrogant, stubborn,* Tit. 1:7; 2 Pet. 2:10* [829]

[882] αὐθαίρετος *authairetos* 2x pr. *one who chooses his own course of action; acting spontaneously, of one's own accord,* 2 Cor. 8:3, 17* [830]

[883] αὐθεντέω *authenteō* 1x *to have authority over, domineer,* 1 Tim. 2:12* [831]

[884] αὐλέω *auleō* 3x *to play on a pipe* or *flute, pipe,* Mt. 11:17; Lk. 7:32; 1 Cor. 14:7* [832]

[885] αὐλή *aulē* 12x pr. *an unroofed enclosure; court-yard; sheepfold,* Jn. 10:1, 16; *an exterior court,* i.q. προαύλιον, an enclosed place between the door and the street, Rev. 11:2; *an interior court, quadrangle,* the open court in the middle of Oriental houses, which are commonly built in the form of a square enclosing this court, Mt. 26:58, 69; by synec. *a house, mansion, palace,* Mt. 26:3; Lk. 11:21 [833] See *courtyard; palace.*

[886] αὐλητής *aulētēs* 2x *a player on a pipe* or *flute,* Mt. 9:23; Rev. 18:22* [834]

[887] αὐλίζομαι *aulizomai* 2x pr. *to pass the time in a court-yard; to lodge;* hence, *to pass the night* in any place, *to lodge at night, pass* or *remain through the night,* Mt. 21:17; Lk. 21:37* [835]

[888] αὐλός *aulos* 1x *a pipe* or *flute,* 1 Cor. 14:7* [836]

[889] αὐξάνω *auxanō* 21x also spelled αὔξω, trans. *to cause to grow* or *increase;* pass. *to be increased, enlarged,* Mt. 13:32; 1 Cor. 3:6, 7; intrans. *to increase, grow,* Mt. 6:28; Mk. 4:8 [837] See *become greater; grow; increase.*

[890] αὔξησις *auxēsis* 2x *increase, growth,* Eph. 4:16; Col. 2:19* [838]

[891] αὔξω *auxō* 2x see αὐξάνω, Eph. 2:21; Col. 2:19* [837]

[892] αὔριον *aurion* 14x *tomorrow,* Mt. 6:30; ἡ αὔριον, sc. ἡμέρα, *the next day,* Mt. 6:34 [839] See *tomorrow.*

[893] αὐστηρός *austēros* 2x pr. *harsh, sour in flavor;* met. *harsh, rigid, ungenerous,* Lk. 19:21, 22* [840]

[894] αὐτάρκεια *autarkeia* 2x *a competence of the necessaries of life,* 2 Cor. 9:8; *a frame of mind viewing one's lot as sufficient, contentedness,* 1 Tim. 6:6* [841]

[895] αὐτάρκης *autarkēs* 1x pr. *sufficient* or *adequate in one's self; contented with one's lot,* Phil. 4:11* [842]

[896] αὐτοκατάκριτος *autokatakritos* 1x *self-condemned,* Tit. 3:11* [843]

[897] αὐτόματος *automatos* 2x *self-excited, acting spontaneously, spontaneous, of his own accord,* Mk. 4:8; Acts 12:10* [844]

[898] αὐτόπτης *autoptēs* 1x *an eye-witness,* Lk. 1:2* [845]

[899] αὐτός *autos* 5,597x *self, very; alone,* Mk. 6:31; 2 Cor. 12:13; *of one's self, of one's own motion,* Jn. 16:27; used also in the oblique cases independently as a personal pron. of the third person; ὁ αὐτός, *the same; unchangeable,* Heb. 1:12; κατὰ τὸ αὐτό, *at the same time, together,* Acts 14:1; ἐπὶ τὸ αὐτό, *in one and the same place,* Mt. 22:34; *at the same time, together,* Acts 3:1 [846, 847, 848]

[7000] αὐτοῦ *autou* 4x *here*, Mt. 26:36; Lk. 9:27; *there*, Acts 18:19; 21:4*

[900] αὐτόφωρος *autophōros* 1x pr. *caught in the act of theft,* Jn. 8:4* [1888]

[901] αὐτόχειρ *autocheir* 1x *acting* or *doing anything with one's own hands,* Acts 27:19* [849]

[902] αὐχέω *aucheō* 1x *to boast,* Jas. 3:5* [3166]

[903] αὐχμηρός *auchmēros* 1x *squalid, filthy;* by impl. *dark, obscure, murky,* 2 Pet. 1:19* [850]

[904] ἀφαιρέω *aphaireō* 10x *to take away, remove,* Lk. 1:25; 10:42; *to take off, cut off, remove by cutting off,* Mt. 26:15; Mk. 14:47; Lk. 22:50 [851] See *cut off; take away.*

[905] ἀφανής *aphanēs* 1x *out of sight; not manifest, hidden, concealed,* Heb. 4:13* [852]

[906] ἀφανίζω *aphanizō* 5x *to remove out of sight, cause to disappear;* pass. *to disappear, vanish,* Jas. 4:14; by impl. *to destroy, consume,* so that nothing shall be left visible, Mt. 6:19, 20; met. *to spoil, deform, disfigure,* Mt. 6:16; *to perish,* Acts 13:41* [853]

[907] ἀφανισμός *aphanismos* 1x *a disappearing, vanishing away;* met. *destruction, abolition, abrogation,* Heb. 8:13* [854]

[908] ἄφαντος *aphantos* 1x *not appearing, not seen, invisible;* hence, ἄφαντος γενέσθαι, *to disappear, vanish,* Lk. 24:31* [855]

[909] ἀφεδρών *aphedrōn* 2x *a latrine,* Mt. 15:17; Mk. 7:19* [856]

[910] ἀφειδία *apheidia* 1x pr. *the disposition of one who is* ἀφειδής, *unsparing;* hence, in NT *unsparingness* in the way of rigorous treatment, *non-indulgence,* Col. 2:23* [857]

[911] ἀφελότης *aphelotēs* 1x *sincerity, simplicity,* Acts 2:46 [858]

[912] ἄφεσις *aphesis* 17x *dismission, deliverance,* from captivity, Lk. 4:18 (2x); *remission, forgiveness, pardon,* Mt. 26:28 [859] See *forgiveness; freedom; release.*

[913] ἁφή *haphē* 2x *a fastening; a ligament,* by which the different members are connected, *commissure, joint,* Eph. 4:16; Col. 2:19* [860]

[914] ἀφθαρσία *aphtharsia* 7x *incorruptibility,* 1 Cor. 15:42, 53, 54; *immor-*

tality, Rom. 2:7; 2 Tim. 1:10; *soundness, purity;* ἐν ἀφθαρσίᾳ, *purely, sincerely* or *constantly, unfailingly,* Eph. 6:24 [861]

[915] ἄφθαρτος *aphthartos* 8x *incorruptible, immortal, imperishable, undying, enduring,* Rom. 1:23; 1 Cor. 9:25; 15:52 [862]

[917] ἀφθορία *aphthoria* 1x pr. *incapability of decay;* met. *incorruptness, integrity, genuineness, purity,* Tit. 2:7* [90]

[918] ἀφίημι *aphiēmi* 143x *to send away, dismiss, suffer to depart; to emit, send forth;* τὴν φωνήν, *the voice, to cry out, utter an exclamation,* Mk. 15:37; τὸ πνεῦμα, *the spirit, to expire,* Mt. 27:50; *to omit, pass over* or *by; to let alone, care not for,* Mt. 15:14; 23:23; Heb. 6:1; *to permit, suffer, let, forbid not; to give up, yield, resign,* Mt. 5:40; *to remit, forgive, pardon; to relax, suffer to become less intense,* Rev. 2:4; *to leave, depart from; to desert, forsake; to leave remaining* or *alone; to leave behind,* sc. at one's death, Mk. 12:19, 20, 21, 22; Jn. 14:27 [863] See *divorce; forgive; leave.*

[919] ἀφικνέομαι *aphikneomai* 1x *to come, arrive at; to reach* as a report, Rom. 16:19* [864]

[920] ἀφιλάγαθος *aphilagathos* 1x *not a lover of good* and *good men,* 2 Tim. 3:3* [865]

[921] ἀφιλάργυρος *aphilargyros* 2x *not fond of money, not covetous, generous,* 1 Tim. 3:3; Heb. 13:5* [866]

[922] ἄφιξις *aphixis* 1x *arrival; departure,* Acts 20:29* [867]

[923] ἀφίστημι *aphistēmi* 14x trans. *to put away, separate; to draw off* or *away, withdraw, induce to revolt,* Acts 5:37; intrans., and mid., *to depart, go away from,* Lk. 2:37; met. *to desist* or *refrain from, let alone,* Acts 5:38; 22:29; 2 Cor. 12:8; *to make defection, fall away, apostatize,* Lk. 8:13; 1 Tim. 4:1; Heb. 3:12; *to withdraw from, have no intercourse with,* 1 Tim. 6:5; *to abstain from,* 2 Tim. 2:19 [868] See *abandon; depart; fall away; leave; take away; turn away.*

[924] ἄφνω *aphnō* 3x *suddenly, unexpectedly,* Acts 2:2; 16:26; 28:6* [869]

[925] ἀφόβως *aphobōs* 4x *fearlessly, boldly, intrepidly,* Phil. 1:14; *securely, peacefully, tranquilly,* Lk. 1:74; 1 Cor. 16:10; *boldly, shamelessly,* Jude 12* [870]

[926] ἀφομοιόω *aphomoioō* 1x *to assimilate, cause to resemble,* Heb. 7:3* [871]

[927] ἀφοράω *aphoraō* 2x *to view with undivided attention* by looking away from every other object; *to regard fixedly and earnestly,* Heb. 12:2; *to see distinctly,* Phil. 2:23* [542, 872]

[928] ἀφορίζω *aphorizō* 10x *to limit off; to separate, sever* from the rest, Mt. 13:49; *to separate* from society, *cut off from all intercourse, excommunicate,* Lk. 6:22; *to set apart, select,* Acts 13:2; Rom. 1:1; Gal. 1:15 [873] See *exclude; separate; set apart.*

[929] ἀφορμή *aphormē* 7x pr. *a starting point; means* to accomplish an object; *occasion, opportunity,* Rom. 7:8, 11 [874]

[930] ἀφρίζω *aphrizō* 2x *to froth, foam,* Mk. 9:18, 20* [875]

[931] ἀφρός *aphros* 1x *froth, foam,* Lk. 9:39* [876]

[932] ἀφροσύνη *aphrosynē* 4x *inconsiderateness, folly;* boastful *folly,* 2 Cor. 11:1, 17, 21; in NT *foolishness, levity, wickedness, impiety,* Mk. 7:22* [877]

[933] ἄφρων *aphrōn* 11x *unwise, inconsiderate, simple, foolish,* Lk. 11:40; 12:20; 1 Cor. 15:36; *ignorant,* religiously *unenlightened,* Rom. 2:20; Eph. 5:17; 1 Pet. 2:15; boastfully *foolish, vain,* 2 Cor. 11:16, 19 [878] See *fool; foolish.*

[934] ἀφυπνόω *aphypnoō* 1x *to awake from sleep;* in NT *to go off into sleep, fall asleep,* Lk. 8:23* [879]

[936] ἄφωνος *aphōnos* 4x *dumb, destitute of the power of speech,* 1 Cor. 12:2;

2 Pet. 2:16; *silent, mute, uttering no voice,* Acts 8:32; *inarticulate, consisting of inarticulate sounds, unmeaning,* 1 Cor. 14:10* [880]

[937] Ἀχάζ *Achaz* 2x *Ahaz,* pr. name, indecl, Mt. 1:9* [881]

[938] Ἀχαΐα *Achaia* 10x *Achaia,* the Roman province, comprehending all Greece to the south of Thessaly [882]

[939] Ἀχαϊκός *Achaikos* 1x *Achaicus,* pr. name, 1 Cor. 16:17* [883]

[940] ἀχάριστος *acharistos* 2x *unthankful, ungrateful,* Lk. 6:35; 2 Tim. 3:2* [884]

[942] ἀχειροποίητος *acheiropoiētos* 3x *not made with hands,* Mk. 14:58; 2 Cor. 5:1; Col. 2:11* [886]

[943] Ἀχίμ *Achim* 2x *Achim,* pr. name, indecl, Mt. 1:14* [885]

[944] ἀχλύς *achlys* 1x *a mist; darkening, dimness,* of the sight, Acts 13:11* [887]

[945] ἀχρεῖος *achreios* 2x *useless, unprofitable, worthless,* Mt. 25:30; *unmeritorious,* Lk. 17:10* [888]

[946] ἀχρειόω *achreioō* 1x also ἀχρεόω, pas., *to render useless;* met., *to become corrupt, depraved,* Rom. 3:12* [889]

[947] ἄχρηστος *achrēstos* 1x *unuseful, useless, unprofitable,* and by impl. *detrimental, causing loss,* Phlm. 11* [890]

[948] ἄχρι *achri* 49x improper prep with the gen., also functioning as a conj, also spelled ἄχρις (Gal. 3:19; Heb. 3:13; Rev. 2:25), with respect to place, *as far as;* to time, *until, during*; as a conj., *until* [891]

[949] ἄχυρον *achuron* 2x *chaff, straw broken up* by treading out the grain, Mt. 3:12; Lk. 3:17* [892]

[950] ἀψευδής *apseudēs* 1x *free from falsehood; incapable of falsehood,* Tit. 1:2* [893]

[952] ἄψινθος *apsinthos* 2x see ἀψίνθιον [894]

[953] ἄψυχος *apsychos* 1x *void of life* or *sense, inanimate,* 1 Cor. 14:7* [895]

[955] Βάαλ *Baal* 1x *Baal,* (Hebrew for *Master*) pr. name, indecl., Rom. 11:4* [896]

[956] Βαβυλών *Babylōn* 12x *Babylon,* 1 Pet. 5:13 [897]

[957] βαθμός *bathmos* 1x pr. *a step, stair;* met. *grade* of dignity, *degree, rank, standing,* 1 Tim. 3:13* [898]

[958] βάθος *bathos* 8x *depth;* τὸ βάθος, *deep water,* Lk. 5:4; Mt. 13:5; met. *fullness, abundance, immensity,* Rom. 11:33; *an extreme degree,* 2 Cor. 8:2; pl. *profundities, deep-laid plans,* 1 Cor. 2:10; Rev. 2:24 [899]

[959] βαθύνω *bathunō* 1x *to deepen, excavate,* Lk. 6:48* [900]

[960] βαθύς *bathus* 4x *deep,* Jn. 4:11; met. *deep, profound,* Acts 20:9; Rev. 2:24; ὄρθρου βαθέος, lit. *at deep morning twilight, at the earliest dawn,* Lk. 24:1* [901]

[961] βάϊον *baion* 1x *a palm branch,* Jn. 12:13* [902]

[962] Βαλαάμ *Balaam* 3x *Balaam,* pr. name, indecl. [903]

[963] Βαλάκ *Balak* 1x *Balak,* pr. name, indecl., Rev. 2:14* [904]

[964] βαλλάντιον *ballantion* 4x also spelled βαλάντιον, *a bag, purse,* Lk. 10:4; 12:33; 22:35, 36* [905]

[965] βάλλω *ballō* 122x pluperfect, ἐβεβλήμην, *to throw, cast; to lay,* Rev. 2:22; Mt. 8:6, 14; *to put, place,* Jas. 3:3; *to place, deposit,* Mt. 27:6; Mk. 12:41-44; Lk. 21:1-4; Jn. 12:6; *to pour,* Jn. 13:5; *to thrust,* Jn. 18:11; 20:27; Mk. 7:33; Rev. 14:19; *to send forth,* Mt. 10:34; *to assault, strike,* Mk. 14:65; met. *to suggest,* Jn. 13:2; intrans. *to rush, beat,* as the wind, Acts 27:14 [906] See *throw.*

[966] βαπτίζω *baptizō* 77x pr. *to dip, immerse; to cleanse* or *purify by washing; to administer the rite of baptism, to* *baptize;* met. with various reference to the ideas associated with Christian baptism as an act of dedication, e.g. marked designation, devotion, trial, etc.; mid. *to procure baptism for one's self, to undergo baptism,* Acts 22:16 [907] See *baptize.*

[967] βάπτισμα *baptisma* 19x pr. *immersion; baptism, ordinance of baptism,* Mt. 3:7; Rom. 6:4; met. *baptism* in the trial of suffering, Mt. 20:22, 23; Mk. 10:38, 39 [908] See *baptism, baptist.*

[968] βαπτισμός *baptismos* 4x pr. *an act of dipping* or *immersion: a baptism,* Col. 2:12; Heb. 6:2; *an ablution,* Mk. 7:4; Heb. 9:10* [909] See *baptism; wash, washing.*

[969] βαπτιστής *baptistēs* 12x *one who baptizes, a baptist,* Mt. 3:1; 11:11, 12 [910] See *baptism, baptist.*

[970] βάπτω *baptō* 4x *to dip,* Jn. 13:26; Lk. 16:24; *to dye,* Rev. 19:13* [911]

[972] Βαραββᾶς *Barabbas* 11x *Barabbas,* pr. name [912]

[973] Βαράκ *Barak* 1x *Barak,* pr. name, indecl., Heb. 11:32* [913]

[974] Βαραχίας *Barachias* 1x *Barachias,* pr. name, Mt. 23:35 [914]

[975] βάρβαρος *barbaros* 6x pr. *one to whom a pure Greek dialect is not native; one who is not a proper Greek, a barbarian,* Rom. 1:14; Col. 3:11; Acts 28:2, 4; *a foreigner speaking a strange language,* 1 Cor. 14:11* [915]

[976] βαρέω *bareō* 6x *to be heavy upon, weigh down, burden, oppress,* as sleep, Mt. 26:43; Mk. 14:40; Lk. 9:32; *calamities,* 2 Cor. 1:8; 5:4; or, *trouble, care, expense,* etc. 1 Tim. 5:16* [916]

[977] βαρέως *bareōs* 2x *heavily;* met. *with difficulty, dully, stupidly,* Mt. 13:15; Acts 28:27* [917]

[978] Βαρθολομαῖος *Bartholomaios* 4x *Bartholomew,* pr. name [918]

[979] Βαριησοῦς *Bariēsous* 1x *Bar-jesus,* pr. name, Acts 13:6* [919]

[980] Βαριωνᾶ *Bariōna* 1x also Βὰρ Ἰωνᾶ or Βαριωνᾶς, *Bar-jona,* pr. name, Mt. 16:17* [920]

[982] Βαρναβᾶς *Barnabas* 28x *Barnabas,* pr. name, Acts 4:36; 13:1f.; 14:12; 15:2f.; 1 Cor. 9:6; Gal. 2:1, 9, 13; Col. 4:10 [921]

[983] βάρος *baros* 6x *weight, heaviness; a burden, anything grievous and hard to be borne,* Mt. 20:12; Acts 15:28; Gal. 6:2; Rev. 2:24; *burden, charge* or *weight, influence, dignity, honor,* 1 Thess. 2:7; with another noun in government, *fulness, abundance, excellence,* 2 Cor. 4:17* [922]

[984] Βαρσαββᾶς *Barsabbas* 2x *Bar-sabas,* pr. name (1) *Joseph, surnamed Justus,* Acts 1:23 (2) *Judas,* Acts 15:22* [923]

[985] Βαρτιμαῖος *Bartimaios* 1x *Bartimaeus,* pr. name, Mk. 10:46* [924]

[987] βαρύς *barys* 6x *heavy;* met. *burdensome, oppressive* or *difficult of observance,* as precepts, Mt. 23:4; 1 Jn. 5:3; *weighty, important, momentous,* Mt. 23:23; Acts 25:7; *grievous, oppressive, afflictive, violent,* Acts 20:29; *authoritative, strict, stern, severe,* 2 Cor. 10:10* [926]

[988] βαρύτιμος *barytimos* 1x *of great price, precious,* Mt. 26:7* [927]

[989] βασανίζω *basanizō* 12x pr. *to apply the lapis Lydius* or *touchstone;* met. *to examine, scrutinize, try,* either by words or torture; in NT *to afflict, torment;* pass. *to be afflicted, tormented, pained,* by diseases, Mt. 8:6, 29, 35; *to be tossed, agitated,* as by the waves, Mt. 14:24 [928] See *suffer; torment; torture.*

[990] βασανισμός *basanismos* 6x pr. *examination by torture; torment, torture,* Rev. 9:5; 14:11; 18:7, 10, 15* [929]

[991] βασανιστής *basanistēs* 1x pr. *an inquisitor, tormentor;* in NT *a keeper of a prison, jailer,* Mt. 18:34* [930]

[992] βάσανος *basanos* 3x pr. *lapis Lydius,* a species of stone from Lydia, which being applied to metals was thought to indicate any alloy which might be mixed with them, and therefore used in the trial of metals; hence, *examination* of a person, especially by torture; in NT *torture, torment, severe pain,* Mt. 4:24; Lk. 16:23, 28* [931]

[993] βασιλεία *basileia* 162x *a kingdom, realm,* the region or country governed by a king; *kingly power, authority, dominion, reign; royal dignity,* the title and honor of king; ἡ βασιλεία, Mt. 9:35, ἡ βασιλεία τοῦ θεοῦ or τοῦ Χριστου or τοῦ οὐρανοῦ or τῶν οὐρανῶν, *the reign* or *kingdom of the Messiah,* both in a false and true conception of it; used also with various limitation, of its administration and coming history, as in the parables; its distinctive nature, Rom. 14:17; its requirements, privileges, rewards, consummation [932] See *dominion; kingdom; reign; rule.*

[994] βασίλειος *basileios* 2x *royal, regal;* met. *possessed of high prerogatives and distinction,* 1 Pet. 2:9; τὰ βαείλεια, sc. δώματα, *regal mansion, palaces,* Lk. 7:25* [933, 934]

[995] βασιλεύς *basileus* 115x *a king, monarch, one possessing regal authority* [935] See *king; rule; ruler.*

[996] βασιλεύω *basileuō* 21x *to possess regal authority, be a king, reign; to rule, govern,* Mt. 2:22; met. *to be in force, predominate, prevail,* Rom. 5:14, 17, 21; met. *to be in kingly case, fare royally,* 1 Cor. 4:8 [936] See *reign; rule; ruler.*

[997] βασιλικός *basilikos* 5x *royal, regal,* Acts 12:20, 21; βασιλικός, used as a subst. *a person attached to the king, courtier,* Jn. 4:46, 49; met. *royal, of the highest excellence,* Jas. 2:8* [937]

[999] βασίλισσα *basilissa* 4x *a queen,* Mt. 12:42; Lk. 11:31; Acts 8:27; Rev. 18:7* [938]

[1000] βάσις *basis* 1x pr. *a step; the foot,* Acts 3:7* [939]

[1001] βασκαίνω *baskainō* 1x pr. *to slander;* thence, *to bewitch* by spells, or by any other means; *to delude,* Gal. 3:1* [940]

[1002] βαστάζω *bastazō* 27x pr. *to lift, raise, bear aloft; to bear, carry* in the hands or about the person; *carry* as a message, Acts 9:15; *to take away, remove,* Mt. 8:17; Jn. 20:15; *to take up,* Jn. 10:31; Lk. 14:27; *to bear* as a burden *endure, suffer; to sustain,* Rom. 11:18; *to bear with, tolerate; to sustain* mentally, *comprehend,* Jn. 16:12 [941] See *bear; carry.*

[1003] βάτος *batos* 5x *a thorn-bush,* Mk. 12:26; Lk. 6:44; 20:37; Acts 7:30, 35* [942]

[1004] βάτος *batos* 1x *a bath,* a measure for liquids, which is stated by Josephus (*Ant.* 8.57) to contain seventy-two sextarii, or about thirteen and one half gallons. Others estimate it to be nine gallons; and others, seven and one half gallons, Lk. 16:6* [943]

[1005] βάτραχος *batrachos* 1x *a frog,* Rev. 16:13 [944]

[1006] βατταλογέω *battalogeō* 1x also spelled βαττολογέω, pr. *to stammer;* hence, *to babble; to use vain repetitions,* Mt. 6:7* [945]

[1007] βδέλυγμα *bdelygma* 6x *an abomination, an abominable thing,* Mt. 24:15; Mk. 13:14; *idolatry with all its pollution,* Lk. 16:15; Rev. 17:4, 5; 21:27* [946]

[1008] βδελυκτός *bdelyktos* 1x *abominable, detestable,* Tit. 1:16* [947]

[1009] βδελύσσομαι *bdelyssomai* 2x *to abominate, loathe, detest, abhor,* Rom. 2:22; pass. *to be abominable, detestable,* Rev. 21:8* [948]

[1010] βέβαιος *bebaios* 8x *firm, stable, steadfast,* Heb. 3:14; 6:19; *sure, certain, established,* Rom. 4:16 [949]

[1011] βεβαιόω *bebaioō* 8x *to confirm, establish; to render constant and unwavering,* 1 Cor. 1:8; *to strengthen* or *establish* by arguments or proofs, *ratify,* Mk. 16:20; *to verify,* as promises, Rom. 15:8 [950]

[1012] βεβαίωσις *bebaiōsis* 2x *confirmation, firm establishment,* Phil. 1:7; Heb. 6:16* [951]

[1013] βέβηλος *bebēlos* 5x pr. *what is open and accessible to all;* hence, *profane, not religious, not connected with religion; unholy; a despiser, scorner,* 1 Tim. 1:9; 4:7 [952] See *profane.*

[1014] βεβηλόω *bebēloō* 2x *to profane, pollute, violate,* Mt. 12:5; Acts 24:6* [953]

[1015] Βεελζεβούλ *Beelzeboul* 7x variant spellings of Βεελζεβούβ and βεελζεβούλ, *Beelzeboul,* pr. name, indecl., Mt. 10:25 [954]

[1016] Βελιάρ *Beliar* 1x *Belial,* pr. name, indecl., 2 Cor. 6:15* [955]

[1017] βελόνη *belonē* 1x pr. *the point of a spear; a needle,* Lk. 18:25* [4476]

[1018] βέλος *belos* 1x *a missile weapon, dart, arrow,* Eph. 6:16* [956]

[1019] βελτίων *beltiōn* 1x *better;* βέλτιον, as an adv., *very well, too well to need informing,* 2 Tim. 1:18* [957]

[1021] Βενιαμίν *Beniamin* 4x *Benjamin,* pr. name, indecl. Acts 13:21; Rom. 11:1; Phil. 3:5; Rev. 7:8* [958]

[1022] Βερνίκη *Bernikē* 3x *Bernice,* pr. name, Acts 25:13, 23; 26:30* [959]

[1023] Βέροια *Beroia* 2x *Berea,* a town of Macedonia, Acts 17:10, 13* [960]

[1024] Βεροιαῖος *Beroiaios* 1x *belonging to Berea,* Acts 20:4* [961]

[1029] Βηθανία *Bēthania* 12x *Bethany* (1) A village near Jerusalem, at the Mount of Olives, Mt. 21:17; Mk. 11:1. (2) A village beyond the Jordan, Jn. 1:28 [963]

[1031] Βηθεσδά *Bēthesda* 1x *Bethesda,* indecl., Jn. 5:2* [964]

[1033] Βηθλέεμ *Bēthleem* 8x *Bethlehem,* indecl., a town in Palestine [965]

[1034] Βηθσαϊδά *Bēthsaida* 7x also spelled Βηθσαϊδάν (1035) *Bethsaida,* indecl. (1) A city of Galilee, Mt. 11:21; Mk. 6:45,. (2) A city of Lower Gaulanitis, near the Lake of Gennesareth, Lk. 9:10 [966]

[1036] Βηθφαγή *Bēthphagē* 3x *Bethphage,* indecl., a part of the Mount of Olives, Mt. 21:1; Mk. 11:1; Lk. 19:29* [967]

[1037] βῆμα *bēma* 12x *a step, footstep, foot-breadth, space to set the foot on,* Acts 7:5; *an elevated place ascended by steps, tribunal, throne,* Mt. 27:19; Acts 12:21 [968] See *court; judgment seat; throne.*

[1039] βήρυλλος *bēryllos* 1x *a beryl,* a precious stone of a sea-green color, found chiefly in India, Rev. 21:20* [969]

[1040] βία *bia* 3x *force, impetus, violence,* Acts 5:26; 21:35; 27:41* [970] See *violence.*

[1041] βιάζω *biazō* 2x also written as a middle deponent, βιάζομαι, *to urge, constrain, overpower by force; to press earnestly forward, to rush,* Lk. 16:16; pass. *to be an object of a forceful movement,* Mt. 11:12* [971]

[1042] βίαιος *biaios* 1x *violent, strong,* Acts 2:2* [972]

[1043] βιαστής *biastēs* 1x *one who uses violence,* or *is impetuous; one who is forceful* in eager pursuit, Mt. 11:12* [973]

[1044] βιβλαρίδιον *biblaridion* 3x *a small volume* or *scroll, a little book,* Rev. 10:2, 9, 10* [974]

[1046] βιβλίον *biblion* 34x *a written volule* or *roll, book,* Lk. 4:17, 20; *a scroll, bill, billet,* Mt. 19:7; Mk. 10:4 [975] See *book; scroll; write, writing.*

[1047] βίβλος *biblos* 10x pr. *the inner bark* or *rind of the papyrus,* which was anciently used instead of paper; hence, *a written volume* or *roll, book, catalogue, account,* Mt. 1:1; Mk. 12:26 [976] See *book; scroll; write, writing.*

[1048] βιβρώσκω *bibrōskō* 1x *to eat,* Jn. 6:13* [977]

[1049] Βιθυνία *Bithunia* 2x *Bithynia,* a province of Asia Minor, Acts 16:7; 1 Pet. 1:1* [978]

[1050] βίος *bios* 10x *life; means of living; sustenance, maintenance, substance, goods,* Mk. 12:44, Lk. 8:14, 43; 15:12, 30; 21:4; 1 Tim. 2:2; 2 Tim. 2:4; 1 Jn. 2:16; 3:17* [979] See *life; possess, possessions; property.*

[1051] βιόω *bioō* 1x *to live,* 1 Pet. 4:2* [980]

[1052] βίωσις *biōsis* 1x *manner of life,* Acts 26:4* [981]

[1053] βιωτικός *biōtikos* 3x *pertaining to this life* or *the things of this life,* Lk. 21:34; 1 Cor. 6:3, 4* [982]

[1054] βλαβερός *blaberos* 1x *hurtful,* 1 Tim. 6:9* [983]

[1055] βλάπτω *blaptō* 2x pr. *to weaken, hinder, disable; to hurt, harm, injure,* Mk. 16:18; Lk. 4:35* [984]

[1056] βλαστάνω *blastanō* 4x also spelled βλαστάω, intrans. *to germinate, bud, sprout, spring up,* Mt. 13:26; Mk. 4:27; Heb. 9:4; trans. and causative, *to cause to shoot, to produce, yield,* Jas. 5:18* [985]

[1058] Βλάστος *Blastos* 1x *Blastus,* pr. name, Acts 12:20* [986]

[1059] βλασφημέω *blasphēmeō* 34x *to defame, revile, slander,* Mt. 27:39; *to speak of God* or *divine things in terms of impious irreverence, to blaspheme,* Mt. 9:3; 26:65 [987] See *blaspheme; insult; revile; slander.*

[1060] βλασφημία *blasphēmia* 18x *slander, railing, reproach,* Mt. 15:19; Mk. 7:22; *blasphemy,* Mt. 12:31; 26:65 [988] See *blasphemy; mockery.*

[1061] βλάσφημος *blasphēmos* 4x *slanderous, railing, reproachful,* 2 Tim. 3:2; 2 Pet. 2:11; *blasphemous,* Acts 6:11, 13; 1 Tim. 1:13 [989]

[1062] βλέμμα *blemma* 1x *a look; the act of seeing, sight,* 2 Pet. 2:8* [990]

[1063] βλέπω *blepō* 133x *to have the faculty of sight, to see,* Mt. 12:22; *to exercise sight, to see,* Mt. 6:4; *to look* towards or at, Mt. 22:16; *to face,* Acts 27:12; *to take heed,* Mt. 24:4; in NT, βλέπειν ἀπό, *to beware of, shun,* Mk. 8:15; trans., *to cast a look on,* Mt. 5:28; *to see, behold,* Mt. 13:17; *to observe,* Mt. 7:3; *to have an eye to, see to,* Mk. 13:9; Col. 4:17; 2 Jn. 8; *to discern* mentally, *perceive,* Rom. 7:23; 2 Cor. 7:8; Jas. 2:22; *to guard against,* Phil. 3:2; pass., *to be an object of sight, be visible,* Rom. 8:24 [991] See *look at; see; watch.*

[1064] βλητέος *blēteos* 1x *requiring to be cast* or *put,* Lk. 5:38* [992]

[1065] Βοανηργές *Boanērges* 1x *Boanerges,* pr. name, indecl., Mk. 3:17* [993]

[1066] βοάω *boaō* 12x *to cry out; to exclaim, proclaim,* Mt. 3:3; 15:34; Acts 8:7; πρός τινα, *to invoke, implore the aid of any one,* Lk. 18:7 [994] See *call; cry out; shout.*

[1067] Βόες *Boes* 2x *Boaz,* pr. name, indecl., Mt. 1:5* [1003]

[1068] βοή *boē* 1x *a cry, outcry, exclamation,* Jas. 5:4* [995]

[1069] βοήθεια *boētheia* 2x *help, succor,* Heb. 4:16; meton. pl. *helps, contrivances for relief and safety,* Acts 27:17* [996]

[1070] βοηθέω *boētheō* 8x *to run to the aid of those who cry for help; to advance to the assistance of any one, help, aid, succor,* Mt. 15:25; Mk. 9:22, 24 [997]

[1071] βοηθός *boēthos* 1x *a helper,* Heb. 13:6* [998]

[1073] βόθυνος *bothunos* 3x *a pit, well* or *cistern,* Mt. 12:11; 15:14; Lk. 6:39* [999]

[1074] βολή *bolē* 1x *a cast, a throw; the distance to which a thing can be thrown,* Lk. 22:41* [1000]

[1075] βολίζω *bolizō* 2x *to take soundings, sound* Acts 27:28* [1001]

[1078] Βόος *Boos* 1x also spelled Βόοζ, *Boaz,* pr. name, indecl., Lk. 3:32* [1003]

[1079] βόρβορος *borboros* 1x *mud, mire, dung, filth,* 2 Pet. 2:22* [1004]

[1080] βορρᾶς *borras* 2x pr. *the north* or *N.N.E. wind;* meton. *the north,* Lk. 13:29; Rev. 21:13* [1005]

[1081] βόσκω *boskō* 9x *to feed, pasture, tend while grazing;* βόσκομαι, *to feed, be feeding,* Mt. 8:30, 33; Lk. 8:32, 34 [1006] See *feed.*

[1082] Βοσόρ *Bosor* 1x *Bosor,* pr. name, indecl., 2 Pet. 2:15* [1007]

[1083] βοτάνη *botanē* 1x *herb, herbage, produce of the earth,* Heb. 6:7* [1008]

[1084] βότρυς *botrys* 1x *a bunch* or *cluster of grapes,* Rev. 14:18* [1009]

[1085] βουλευτής *bouleutēs* 2x *a counsellor, senator; member of the Sanhedrin,* Mk. 15:43; Lk. 23:50* [1010]

[1086] βουλεύω *bouleuō* 6x mid., *to give counsel; to deliberate,* Lk. 14:31; Jn. 12:10; 11:53; *to purpose, determine,* Acts 27:39; 2 Cor. 1:17 (2x)* [1011]

[1087] βουλή *boulē* 12x *counsel, purpose, design, determination, decree,* Lk. 7:30; 23:51, et al. freq.; by impl. *secret thoughts, cogitations* of the mind, 1 Cor. 4:5 [1012] See *counsel; purpose.*

[1088] βούλημα *boulēma* 3x *purpose, will, determination,* Acts 27:43; Rom. 9:19; 1 Pet. 4:3* [1013]

[1089] βούλομαι *boulomai* 37x *to be willing, disposed,* Mk. 15:15; Acts 25:20; 28:18; *to intend,* Mt. 1:19; Acts 5:28; 12:4; 2 Cor. 1:15; *to desire,* 1 Tim. 6:9; *to choose, be pleased,* Jn. 18:39; Acts 18:15; Jas. 3:4; *to will, decree, appoint,* Lk. 22:42; Jas. 1:18; 1 Cor. 12:11; 1 Tim. 2:8; 5:14; ἐβουλόμην, *I could wish,* Acts 25:22 [1014] See *choose; desire; intend; plan; want; will.*

[1090] βουνός *bounos* 2x *a hill, rising ground,* Lk. 3:5; 23:30* [1015]

[1091] βοῦς *bous* 8x *an ox, a bull* or *cow,* an animal of the ox kind, Lk. 13:15 [1016]

[1092] βραβεῖον *brabeion* 2x *a prize* bestowed on victors in the public games, such as a crown, wreath, chaplet, garland, etc., 1 Cor. 9:24; Phil. 3:14* [1017]

[1093] βραβεύω *brabeuō* 1x pr. *to be a director* or *arbiter in the public games;* in NT *to preside, direct, rule, govern, be predominate,* Col. 3:15* [1018]

[1094] βραδύνω *bradynō* 2x *to be slow, to delay,* 1 Tim. 3:15; 2 Pet. 3:9* [1019]

[1095] βραδυπλοέω *bradyploeō* 1x *to sail slowly,* Acts 27:7* [1020]

[1096] βραδύς *bradys* 3x *slow, not hasty,* Jas. 1:19; *slow* of understanding, *heavy, stupid,* Lk. 24:25* [1021]

[1097] βραδύτης *bradytēs* 1x *slowness, tardiness, delay,* 2 Pet. 3:9* [1022]

[1098] βραχίων *brachiōn* 3x *the arm; the arm* as a symbol of power, Lk. 1:51; Jn. 12:38; Acts 13:17* [1023] See *arm.*

[1099] βραχύς *brachus* 7x *short, brief; few, small,* Lk. 22:58; Jn. 6:7; Acts 5:34; 27:28; Heb. 2:7, 9; 13:22* [1024]

[1100] βρέφος *brephos* 8x *a child;* whether unborn, *an embryo, fetus,* Lk. 1:41, 44; or just born, *an infant,* Lk. 2:12, 16; Acts 7:19; or partly grown, Lk. 18:15; 2 Tim. 3:15; met. *a babe* in simplicity of faith, 1 Pet. 2:2* [1025]

[1101] βρέχω *brechō* 7x *to wet, moisten,* Lk. 7:38; *to rain, cause* or *send rain,* Mt. 5:45; Lk. 17:29 [1026]

[1103] βροντή *brontē* 12x *thunder,* Mk. 3:17; Jn. 12:29 [1027] See *thunder.*

[1104] βροχή *brochē* 2x *rain,* Mt. 7:25, 27* [1028]

[1105] βρόχος *brochos* 1x *a cord, noose,* 1 Cor. 7:35* [1029]

[1106] βρυγμός *brygmos* 7x *gnashing* of teeth together, Mt. 8:12, 13, 42, 50; 22:13; 24:51; 25:30; Lk. 13:28* [1030]

[1107] βρύχω *brychō* 1x *to grate* or *gnash* the teeth, Acts 7:54* [1031]

[1108] βρύω *bryō* 1x pr. *to be full, to swell* with anything; *to emit, send forth,* Jas. 3:11* [1032]

[1109] βρῶμα *brōma* 17x *food,* Mt. 14:15; Mk. 7:19; *solid food,* 1 Cor. 3:2 [1033] See *food.*

[1110] βρώσιμος *brōsimos* 1x *eatable, that may be eaten,* Lk. 24:41* [1034]

[1111] βρῶσις *brōsis* 11x *eating, the act of eating,* Rom. 14:17; 1 Cor. 8:4; *meat, food,* Jn. 6:27; Heb. 12:16; *a canker* or *rust,* Mt. 6:19, 20 [1035] See *eating; food.*

[1112] βυθίζω *bythizō* 2x *to immerse, submerge, cause to sink,* Lk. 5:7; *to plunge deep, drown,* 1 Tim. 6:9* [1036]

[1113] βυθός *bythos* 1x *the bottom, lowest part; the deep, sea,* 2 Cor. 11:25* [1037]

[1114] βυρσεύς *byrseus* 3x *a tanner, leather-dresser,* Acts 9:43; 10:6, 32* [1038]

[1115] βύσσινος *byssinos* 5x *made of fine linen* or *fine cotton,* Rev. 18:16; 18:8 (2x), 14* [1039]

[1116] βύσσος *byssos* 1x *byssus,* a species of fine cotton highly prized by the ancients, Lk. 16:19* [1040]

[1117] βωμός *bōmos* 1x pr. *a slightly-elevated spot, base, pedestal;* hence, *an altar,* Acts 17:23* [1041]

[1119] Γαββαθᾶ *Gabbatha* 1x *Gabbatha,* pr. name, indecl., Jn. 19:13* [1042]

[1120] Γαβριήλ *Gabriēl* 2x *Gabriel,* pr. name, indecl., Lk. 1:19, 26* [1043]

[1121] γάγγραινα *gangraina* 1x *gangrene, mortification,* 2 Tim. 2:17* [1044]

[1122] Γάδ *Gad* 1x *Gad,* pr. name, indecl., Rev. 7:5* [1045]

[1123] Γαδαρηνός *Gadarēnos* 1x *an inhabitant of Gadara,* the chief city of Perea, Mt. 8:28* [1046]

[1124] Γάζα *Gaza* 1x *Gaza,* a strong city of Palestine, Acts 8:26* [1048]

[1125] γάζα *gaza* 1x *treasure, treasury,* Acts 8:27* [1047]

[1126] γαζοφυλάκιον *gazophylakion* 5x also spelled γαζοφυλακεῖον, *a treasury; the sacred treasure,* Mk. 12:41, 43; Lk. 21:1; Jn. 8:20* [1049]

[1127] Γάϊος *Gaios* 5x *Gaius,* pr. name. (1) Of Macedonia, Acts 19:29. (2) Of Corinth, 1 Cor. 1:14. (3) Of Derbe, Acts 20:4. (4) A Christian to whom John addressed his third Epistle, 3 Jn. 1; Rom. 16:23* [1050]

[1128] γάλα *gala* 5x *milk,* 1 Cor. 9:7; met. spiritual *milk,* consisting in the elements of Christian instruction, 1 Cor. 3:2; Heb. 5:12, 13; spiritual *nutriment,* 1 Pet. 2:2* [1051]

[1129] Γαλάτης *Galatēs* 1x *a Galatian, inhabitant of Galatia,* Gal. 3:1* [1052]

[1130] Γαλατία *Galatia* 4x *Galatia* or *Gallo-Graecia,* a province of Asia Minor, 1 Cor. 6:1; Gal. 1:2; 2 Tim. 4:10; 1 Pet. 1:1* [1053]

[1131] Γαλατικός *Galatikos* 2x *Galatian,* Acts 16:6; 18:23* [1054]

[1132] γαλήνη *galēnē* 3x *tranquillity of the sea, a calm,* Mt. 8:26; Mk. 4:39; Lk. 8:24* [1055]

[1133] Γαλιλαία *Galilaia* 61x *Galilee,* a district of Palestine north of Samaria, Mt. 4:15 [1056]

[1134] Γαλιλαῖος *Galilaios* 11x *a native of Galilee,* Mt. 26:69; Mk. 14:70; Lk. 13:1; Jn. 4:45; Acts 1:11 [1057]

[1136] Γαλλίων *Galliōn* 3x *Gallio,* pr. name, Acts 18:12, 14, 17* [1058]

[1137] Γαμαλιήλ *Gamaliēl* 2x *Gamaliel,* pr. name, indecl. [1059]

[1138] γαμέω *gameō* 28x *to marry,* Mt. 5:32, et al.; absol. *to marry, enter the marriage state,* Mt. 19:10, et al.; mid. *to marry, be married,* Mk. 10:12; 1 Cor. 7:39 [1060] See *marry, marriage; wedding.*

[1139] γαμίζω *gamizō* 7x also spelled γαμίσκω, *to give in marriage, permit to marry,* 1 Cor. 7:38 [1061]

[1140] γαμίσκω *gamiskō* 1x see γαμίζω [1061]

[1141] γάμος *gamos* 16x *a wedding; nuptial festivities, a marriage festival,* Mt. 22:2; 25:10; Jn. 2:1, 2; Rev. 19:7, 9; any *feast* or *banquet,* Lk. 12:36; 14:8; *the marriage state,* Heb. 13:4 [1062] See *marry, marriage; wedding.*

[1142] γάρ *gar* 1,041x *for;* it is, however, frequently used with an ellipsis of the clause to which it has reference, and its force must then be variously expressed: Mt. 15:27; 27:23, et al.; it is also sometimes epexegetic, or introductory of an intimated detail of circumstances, *now, then,* Mt. 1:18 [1063]

[1143] γαστήρ *gastēr* 9x *the belly, stomach; the womb,* Lk. 1:31; ἐν γαστρὶ ἔχειν, *to be with child,* Mt. 1:18, 23; 24:19, et al.; γαστέρες, *gluttons,* Tit. 1:12 [1064]

[1145] γε *ge* 24x an enclitic particle imparting emphasis; indicating that a particular regard is to be had to the term to which it is attached. Its force is to be conveyed, when this is possible, by various expression; *at least, indeed, even* [1065]

[1146] Γεδεών *Gedeōn* 1x *Gideon* (Judges 6-8), pr. name, indecl., Heb. 11:32* [1066]

[1147] γέεννα *geenna* 12x *Gehenna,* pr. *the valley of Hinnom,* south of Jerusalem, once celebrated for the horrid worship of Moloch, and afterwards polluted with every species of filth, as well as the carcasses of animals, and dead bodies of malefactors; to consume which, in order to avert the pestilence which such a mass of corruption would occasion, constant fires were kept burning; hence, *hell, the fires of Tartarus, the place of punishment in Hades,* Mt. 5:22, 29, 30; 10:28; 18:9, et al. [1067] See *hell.*

[1149] Γεθσημανί *Gethsēmani* 2x *Gethsemane,* pr. name, indecl., Mt. 26:36; Mk. 14:32* [1068]

[1150] γείτων *geitōn* 4x *a neighbor,* Lk. 14:12; 15:6, 9; Jn. 9:8* [1069]

[1151] γελάω *gelaō* 2x *to laugh, smile;* by impl. *to be merry, happy, to rejoice,* Lk. 6:21, 25* [1070]

[1152] γέλως *gelōs* 1x *laughter;* by impl. *mirth, joy, rejoicing,* Jas. 4:9* [1071]

[1153] γεμίζω *gemizō* 8x *to fill,* Mt. 4:37; 15:36, et al. [1072]

[1154] γέμω *gemō* 11x *to be full,* Mt. 23:27; Lk. 11:39, et al. [1073] See *(to be) covered; (to be) full.*

[1155] γενεά *genea* 43x pr. *birth;* hence, *progeny; a generation* of mankind, Mt. 11:16; 23:36, et al.; *a generation,* a step in a genealogy, Mt. 1:17; *a generation,* an interval of time, *an age;* in NT *course of life,* in respect of its events, interests, or character, Lk. 16:8; Acts 13:36 [1074] See *age; generation; race.*

[1156] γενεαλογέω *genealogeō* 1x *to reckon one's descent, derive one's origin,* Heb. 7:6* [1075]

[1157] γενεαλογία *genealogia* 2x *genealogy, catalogue of ancestors, history of descent,* 1 Tim. 1:4; Tit. 3:9* [1076]

[1160] γενέσια *genesia* 2x pr. *a day observed in memory of the dead;* in NT equivalent to γενέθλια, *celebration of one's birthday, birthday-festival,* Mt. 14:6; Mk. 6:21* [1077]

[1161] γένεσις *genesis* 5x *birth, nativity,* Mt. 1:18; Lk. 1:14; Jas. 1:23; *successive generation, descent, lineage,* Mt. 1:1; meton. *life,* Mt. 1:18; Jas. 3:6* [1078]

[1162] γενετή *genetē* 1x *birth,* Jn. 9:1* [1079]

[1163] γένημα *genēma* 4x *natural produce, fruit, increase,* Mt. 26:29; Mk. 14:25; Lk. 12:18; 22:18; 2 Cor. 9:10* [1081]

[1164] γεννάω *gennaō* 97x *to beget, generate,* Mt. 1:2-16, et al.; of women, *to bring forth, bear, give birth to,* Lk. 1:13, 57, et al.; pass. *to be born, produced,* Mt. 2:1, 4, et al.; met. *to produce, excite, give occasion to, effect,* 2 Tim. 2:23; from the Hebrew, *to constitute as son, to constitute as king,* or *as the representative* or *viceregent of God,* Acts 13:33; Heb. 1:5; 5:5; by impl. *to be a parent to* any one; pass. *to be a son* or *child to* any one, Jn. 1:13; 1 Cor. 4:15, et al. [1080] See *bear a child; born; father; give birth.*

[1165] γέννημα *gennēma* 4x *what is born* or *produced, offspring, progeny, brood,* Mt. 3:7; 12:34, et al.; *fruit, produce,* Mt. 26:29; Mk. 14:25, et al.; *fruit, increase,* Lk. 12:18; 2 Cor. 9:10 [1081]

[1166] Γεννησαρέτ *Gennēsaret* 3x *Gennesaret,* a lake of Palestine, called also the *Sea of Tiberias,* Mt. 14:34; Mk. 6:53; Lk. 5:1* [1082]

[1168] γεννητός *gennētos* 2x *born* or *produced of,* Mt. 11:11; Lk. 7:28* [1084]

[1169] γένος *genos* 20x *offspring, progeny,* Acts 17:28, 29; *family, kindred, lineage,* Acts 7:13, et al.; *race, nation, people,* Mk. 7:26; Acts 4:36, et al.; *kind, sort, species,* Mt. 13:47, et al. [1085] See *family; kind; offspring; people.*

[1170] Γερασηνός *Gerasēnos* 3x also spelled Γεργεσηνός, *from Gerasene,* belonging to the city of Gerasa, Mk. 5:1; Lk. 8:26, 37* [1086]

[1172] γερουσία *gerousia* 1x *a senate, assembly of elders; the elders* of Israel collectively, Acts 5:21* [1087]

[1173] γέρων *gerōn* 1x *an old man,* Jn. 3:4* [1088]

[1174] γεύομαι *geuomai* 15x *to taste,* Mt. 27:34; Jn. 2:9; absol. *to take food,* Acts 10:10, et al.; met. *to have perception of, experience,* Heb. 6:4, 5; 1 Pet. 2:3; θανάτου γεύεσθαι, *to experience death, to die,* Mt. 16:28, et al. [1089] See *eat; partake; taste.*

[1175] γεωργέω *geōrgeō* 1x *to cultivate, till the earth,* Heb. 6:7* [1090]

[1176] γεώργιον *geōrgion* 1x *cultivated field* or *ground, a farm,* 1 Cor. 3:9* [1091]

[1177] γεωργός *geōrgos* 19x *a farmer, one who tills the earth,* 2 Tim. 2:6; Jas. 5:7; in NT spc. *a vine-dresser, keeper of a vineyard,* i.q. ἀμπελουργός, Mt. 21:33, 34, et al. [1092] See *farmer; tenant farmer.*

[1178] γῆ *gē* 250x *earth, soil,* Mt. 13:5; Mk. 4:8, et al.; *the ground, surface of the earth,* Mt. 10:29; Lk. 6:49, et al.; *the land,* as opposed to the sea or a lake, Lk. 5:11; Jn. 21:8, 9, 11; *the earth, world,* Mt. 5:18, 35, et al.; by synec. *the inhabitants of the earth,* Mt. 5:13; 6:10; 10:34; *a land, region, tract, country, territory,* Mt. 2:20; 14:34;by way of eminence, *the* chosen *land,* Mt. 5:5; 24:30; 27:45; Eph. 6:3; *the inhabitants of a region* or *country,* Mt. 10:15; 11:24, et al. [1093] See *earth; ground; land; soil.*

[1179] γῆρας *gēras* 1x gen. *old age,* Lk. 1:36* [1094]

[1180] γηράσκω *gēraskō* 2x *to be* or *become old,* Jn. 21:18; Heb. 8:13* [1095]

[1181] γίνομαι *ginomai* 669x pluperfect, εγενόει (3rd sg), *to come into existence; to be created, exist by creation,* Jn. 1:3, 10; Heb. 11:3; Jas. 3:9; *to be born, produced, grow,* Mt. 21:19; Jn. 8:58, et al.; *to arise, come on, occur,* as the phenomena of nature, etc.; Mt. 8:24, 26; 9:16, et al.; *to come, approach,* as morning or evening, Mt. 8:16; 14:15, 23; *to be appointed, constituted, established,* Mk. 2:27; Gal. 3:17, et al.; *to take place, come to pass, happen, occur,* Mt. 1:22; 24:6, 20, 21, 34, et al. freq.; *to be done, performed, effected,* Mt. 21:42, et al.; *to be fulfilled, satisfied,* Mt. 6:10; 26:42, et al.; *to come into a particular state* or *condition; to become, assume the character and appearance* of anything, Mt. 5:45, et al.; *to become* or *be made* anything, *be changed* or *converted,* Mt. 4:3;

21:42; Mk. 1:17, et al.; *to be,* Mt. 11:26; 19:8; γίνεσθαι ὑπό τινα, *to be subject to,* Gal. 4:4; γίνεσθαι ἐν ἑαυτῷ, *to come to one's self, to recover from a trance* or *surprise,* Acts 12:11; μὴ γένοιτο, *let it not be, far be it from, God forbid,* Lk. 20:16; Rom. 3:4, 31, et al.; *to be kept, celebrated, solemnized,* as festivals, Mt. 26:2, et al.; *to be finished, completed,* Heb. 4:3 [1096] See *be; become.*

[1182] γινώσκω *ginōskō* 222x *to know,* whether the action be inceptive or complete and settled; *to perceive,* Mt. 22:18; Mk. 5:29; 8:17; 12:12; Lk. 8:46; *to mark, discern,* Mt. 25:24; Lk. 19:44; *to ascertain by examination,* Mk. 6:38; Jn. 7:51; Acts 23:28; *to understand,* Mk. 4:13; Lk. 18:34; Jn. 12:16; 13:7; Acts 8:30; 1 Cor. 14:7, 9; *to acknowledge,* Mt. 7:23; 2 Cor. 3:2; *to resolve, conclude,* Lk. 16:4; Jn. 7:26; 17:8; *to be assured,* Lk. 21:20; Jn. 6:69; 8:52; 2 Pet. 1:20; *to be skilled, to be master of* a thing, Mt. 16:3; Acts 21:37; *to know* carnally, Mt. 1:25; Lk. 1:34; from the Hebrew, *to view with favor,* 1 Cor. 8:3; Gal. 4:9 [1097] See *know; realize; understand.*

[1183] γλεῦκος *gleukos* 1x pr. *the unfermented juice of grapes;* hence, *sweet new wine,* Acts 2:13* [1098]

[1184] γλυκύς *glykys* 4x *sweet,* Jas. 3:11-12; Rev. 10:9, 10* [1099]

[1185] γλῶσσα *glōssa* 50x *the tongue,* Mk. 7:33, 35, et al.; meton. *speech, talk,* 1 Jn. 3:18; *a tongue, language,* Acts 2:11; 1 Cor. 13:1, et al.; meton. *a language not proper to a speaker, a gift* or *faculty of such language,* Mk. 16:17; 1 Cor. 14:13, 14, 26, et al.; from Hebrew, *a nation,* as defined by its language, Rev. 5:9, et al.; let. *a tongue-shaped flale,* Acts 2:3 [1100] See *language; tongue.*

[1186] γλωσσόκομον *glōssokomon* 2x pr. *a box for keeping the tongues, mouthpieces,* or *reeds* of musical instruments; hence, genr. *any box* or *receptacle;* in NT *a purse, money-bag,* Jn. 12:6; 13:29* [1101]

[1187] γναφεύς *gnapheus* 1x *a fuller, a bleacher,* Mk. 9:3* [1102]

[1188] γνήσιος *gnēsios* 4x *lawful, legitimate,* as children; *genuine,* in faith, etc.; 1 Tim. 1:2; Tit. 1:4; *true, sincere,* 2 Cor. 8:8; Phil. 4:3* [1103]

[1189] γνησίως *gnēsiōs* 1x *genuinely, sincerely,* Phil. 2:20* [1104]

[1190] γνόφος *gnophos* 1x *a thick cloud, darkness,* Heb. 12:18* [1105]

[1191] γνώμη *gnōmē* 9x *the mind,* as the means of knowing and judging; *assent,* Phlm. 14; *purpose, resolution,* Acts 20:3; *opinion, judgment,* 1 Cor. 1:10; 7:40; *suggestion, suggested advice,* as distinguished from positive injunction, Acts 20:3; 1 Cor. 7:25; 2 Cor. 8:10 [1106]

[1192] γνωρίζω *gnōrizō* 25x *to make known, reveal, declare,* Jn. 15:15; 17:26, et al.; *to know,* Phil. 1:22 [1107] See *make known; tell.*

[1194] γνῶσις *gnōsis* 29x *knowledge,* Lk. 1:77; *knowledge* of an especial kind and relatively high character, Lk. 11:52; Rom. 2:20; 1 Tim. 6:20; more particularly in respect of Christian enlightenment, Rom. 15:14; 1 Cor. 8:10; 12:8; 2 Cor. 11:6, et al. [1108] See *knowledge.*

[1195] γνώστης *gnōstēs* 1x *one acquainted with* a thing, *knowing, skilful,* Acts 26:3* [1109]

[1196] γνωστός *gnōstos* 15x *known,* Jn. 18:15, 16, et al.; *certain, incontrovertible,* Acts 4:16; τὸ γνωστόν, *that which is known* or *is cognizable, the unquestionable attributes,* Rom. 1:19; subst. *an acquaintance,* Lk. 2:44; 23:49 [1110] See *friend; known; outstanding.*

[1197] γογγύζω *gongyzō* 8x *to speak privately and in a low voice, mutter,* Jn. 7:32; *to utter secret and sullen discontent, express indignant complaint, murmur, grumble,* Mt. 20:11; Lk. 5:30; Jn. 6:41, 43, 61; 1 Cor. 10:10* [1111] See *grumble; murmur.*

[1198] γογγυσμός *gongysmos* 4x *a muttering, murmuring, low and suppressed discourse,* Jn. 7:12; *the expression of secret and sullen discontent, murmuring, complaint,* Acts 6:1; Phil. 2:14; 1 Pet. 4:9* [1112]

[1199] γογγυστής *gongystēs* 1x *a murmurer, grumbler,* Jude 16* [1113]

[1200] γόης *goēs* 1x *a juggler, diviner;* hence, by impl. *an impostor, cheat,* 2 Tim. 3:13* [1114]

[1201] Γολγοθᾶ *Golgotha* 3x *Golgotha,* pr. name, Mt. 27:33; Mk. 15:22; Jn. 19:17* [1115]

[1202] Γόμορρα *Gomorra* 4x *Gomorrha* (Gen. 19), pr. name, Mt. 10:15; Rom. 9:29; 2 Pet. 2:6; Jude 7* [1116]

[1203] γόμος *gomos* 3x *the cargo* of a ship, Acts 21:3; by impl. *merchandise,* Rev. 18:11, 12* [1117]

[1204] γονεύς *goneus* 20x *a father;* pl. in NT *parents,* Mt. 10:21; Lk. 2:27, 41; 2 Cor. 12:14 [1118] See *parents.*

[1205] γόνυ *gony* 12x *the knee,* Lk. 22:41; Heb. 12:12, et al. [1119] See *knee.*

[1206] γονυπετέω *gonypeteō* 4x *to fall upon one's knees, to kneel before,* Mt. 17:14; 27:29; Mk. 1:40; 10:17* [1120]

[1207] γράμμα *gramma* 14x pr. *that which is written* or *drawn; a letter, character of the alphabet, a writing, book,* Jn. 5:47; *an acknowledgment of debt, an account, a bill, note,* Lk. 16:6, 7; *an epistle, letter,* Acts 28:21; Gal. 6:11; ἱερὰ γράμματα, *the sacred books of the Old Testament, the Jewish Scriptures,* 2 Tim. 3:15; spc. *the letter* of the law of Moses, *the bare literal sense,* Rom. 2:27, 29; 7:6; 2 Cor. 3:6, 7; pl. *letters, learning,* Jn. 7:15; Acts 26:24* [1121] See *learning; letters; write, writing.*

[1208] γραμματεύς *grammateus* 63x *a scribe; a clerk, town-clerk, registrar, recorder,* Acts 19:35; *one skilled in the Jewish law, a teacher* or *interpreter of the law,* Mt. 2:4; 5:20, et al. freq.; genr. *a religious teacher,* Mt. 13:52; by synec. *any one distinguished for learning* or *wisdom,* 1 Cor. 1:20 [1122] See *scribe; teacher of the law.*

[1209] γραπτός *graptos* 1x *written,* Rom. 2:15* [1123]

[1210] γραφή *graphē* 50x *a writing;* in NT *the Holy Scriptures, the Jewish Scriptures,* or *Books of the Old Testament,* Mt. 21:42; Jn. 5:39, et al.; by synec. *doctrines, declarations, oracles,* or *promises* contained in the sacred books, Mt. 22:29; Mk. 12:24, et al.; spc. *a prophecy,* Mt. 26:54; Mk. 14:49; Lk. 4:21; 24:27, 32; with the addition of προφητική, Rom. 16:26; of τῶν προφητῶν, Mt. 26:56 [1124] See *Scripture.*

[1211] γράφω *graphō* 191x *to engrave, write,* according to the ancient method of writing on plates of metal, waxes tables, etc., Jn. 8:6, 8; *to write* on parchment, paper, etc., generally, Mt. 27:37, et al.; *to write letters to another,* Acts 23:25; 2 Cor. 2:9; 13:10, et al.; *to describe in writing,* Jn. 1:46; Rom. 10:5; *to inscribe* in a catalogue, etc., Lk. 10:20; Rev. 13:8; 17:8, et al.; *to write* a law, *command,* or *enact in writing,* Mk. 10:5; 12:19; Lk. 2:23, et al. [1125] See *Scripture; write, writing.*

[1212] γραώδης *graōdēs* 1x *old-womanish;* by impl. *silly, absurd,* 1 Tim. 4:7* [1126]

[1213] γρηγορέω *grēgoreō* 22x *to be awake, to watch,* Mt. 26:38, 40, 41; Mk. 14:34; 37, 38; *to be alive,* 1 Thess. 5:10; met. *to be watchful, attentive, vigilant, circumspect,* Mt. 25:13; Mk. 13:35, et al. [1127] See *guard; keep watch; wake, wake up; watch.*

[1214] γυμνάζω *gymnazō* 4x pr. *to train in gymnastic discipline;* hence, *to exercise* in anything, *train to use, discipline,* 1 Tim. 4:7; Heb. 5:14; 12:11; 2 Pet. 2:14* [1128]

[1215] γυμνασία *gymnasia* 1x pr. *gymnastic exercise;* hence, *bodily discipline* of any kind, 1 Tim. 4:8* [1129]

[1217] γυμνιτεύω *gymniteuō* 1x *to be poorly clad,* 1 Cor. 4:11* [1130]

[1218] γυμνός *gymnos* 15x *naked, without clothing,* Mk. 14:51, 52; *without the upper garment, and clad only with an inner garment* or *tunic,* Jn. 21:7; *poorly* or *meanly clad, destitute of proper and sufficient clothing,* Mt. 25:36, 38, 43, 44; Acts 19:16; Jas. 2:15; met. *unclothed* with a body, 2 Cor. 5:3; *not covered, uncovered, open, manifest,* Heb. 4:13; *bare, mere,* 1 Cor. 15:37; *naked of* spiritual *clothing,* Rev. 3:17; 16:15; 17:16 [1131] See *naked; unclothed.*

[1219] γυμνότης *gymnotēs* 3x *nakedness; want of proper and sufficient clothing,* Rom. 8:35; 2 Cor. 11:27; spiritual *nakedness, being destitute of* spiritual *clothing,* Rev. 3:18* [1132]

[1220] γυναικάριον *gynaikarion* 1x *a little woman; a trifling, weak, silly woman,* 2 Tim. 3:6* [1133]

[1221] γυναικεῖος *gynaikeios* 1x *pertaining to women, female,* 1 Pet. 3:7* [1134]

[1222] γυνή *gynē* 215x *a woman,* Mt. 5:28, et al.; *a* married *woman, wife,* Mt. 5:31, 32; 14:3, et al.; in the voc. ὦ γύναι, *O woman!* an ordinary mode of addressing females under every circumstance; met. used of the Church, as united to Christ, Rev. 19:7; 21:9 [1135] See *wife; woman.*

[1223] Γώγ *Gōg* 1x *Gog,* pr. name of a nation, indecl., Rev. 20:8* [1136]

[1224] γωνία *gōnia* 9x *an* exterior *angle, projecting corner,* Mt. 6:5; 21:42; *an* interior *angle;* by impl. *a* dark *corner, obscure place,* Acts 26:26; *corner, extremity,* or *quarter* of the earth, Rev. 7:1; 20:8 [1137] See *capstone; corner; cornerstone.*

[1227] δαιμονίζομαι *daimonizomai* 13x in NT *to be possessed, afflicted, vexed, by a demon* or *evil spirit,* i.q. δαιμόνιον ἔχειν, Mt. 4:24; 8:16, 28, 33 [1139] See *demon-possessed.*

[1228] δαιμόνιον *daimonion* 63x *a* heathen *god, deity,* Acts 17:18; 1 Cor. 10:20, 21; Rev. 9:20; in NT, *a demon, evil spirit,* Mt. 7:22; 9:33, 34; 10:8; 12:24 [1140] See *demon.*

[1229] δαιμονιώδης *daimoniōdēs* 1x *pertaining to* or *proceeding from demons; demonic, devilish,* Jas. 3:15* [1141]

[1230] δαίμων *daimōn* 1x *a god, a superior power;* in NT *a malignant demon, evil angel,* Mt. 8:31* [1142]

[1231] δάκνω *daknō* 1x *to bite, sting;* met. *to molest, vex, injure,* Gal. 5:15* [1143]

[1232] δάκρυον *dakryon* 10x also spelled δάκρυ, *a tear* [1144] See *tears.*

[1233] δακρύω *dakryō* 1x *to shed tears, weep,* Jn. 11:35* [1145]

[1234] δακτύλιος *daktylios* 1x *a ring for the finger,* Lk. 15:22* [1146]

[1235] δάκτυλος *daktylos* 8x *a finger,* Mt. 23:4; Mk. 7:33; from Hebrew, *power,* Lk. 11:20 [1147]

[1236] Δαλμανουθά *Dalmanoutha* 1x *Dalmanutha,* indecl., a small town on the shore of the Sea of Tiberias, Mk. 8:10* [1148]

[1237] Δαλματία *Dalmatia* 1x *Dalmatia,* 2 Tim. 4:10* [1149]

[1238] δαμάζω *damazō* 4x also spelled δανείζω, *to subdue, tame,* Mk. 5:4; Jas. 3:7; met. *to restrain within proper limits,* Jas. 3:8* [1150]

[1239] δάμαλις *damalis* 1x *a heifer, young cow,* Heb. 9:13* [1151]

[1240] Δάμαρις *Damaris* 1x *Damaris,* pr. name, Acts 17:34* [1152]

[1241] Δαμασκηνός *Damaskēnos* 1x *A Damascene, a native of Damascus,* 2 Cor. 11:32* [1153]

[1242] Δαμασκός *Damaskos* 15x *Damascus,* the capital city of Syria [1154]

[1244] δανείζω *daneizō* 4x see δανίζω [1155]

[1245] δάνειον *daneion* 1x *a loan, debt,* Mt. 18:27* [1156]

[1248] Δανιήλ *Daniēl* 1x *Daniel,* pr. name, indecl., Mt. 24:15* [1158]

[1250] δανιστής *danistēs* 1x *a money-lender, creditor,* Lk. 7:41* [1157]

[1251] δαπανάω *dapanaō* 5x *to expend, be at expense,* Mk. 5:26; Acts 21:24; 2 Cor. 12:15; *to spend, waste, consume by extravagance,* Lk. 15:14; Jas. 4:3* [1159]

[1252] δαπάνη *dapanē* 1x *expense, cost,* Lk. 14:28* [1160]

[1253] Δαυίδ *Dauid* 59x also spelled Δανείδ and Δαβίδ, *David,* pr. name, indecl., Mt. 1:6; Lk. 1:27; Acts 2:29; Rom. 1:3; 2 Tim. 2:28 [1138]

[1254] δέ *de* 2,792x a conjunctive particle, marking the superaddition of a clause, whether in opposition or in continuation, to what has preceded, and it may be variously rendered *but, on the other hand, and, also, now,* etc.; καὶ δέ, when there is a special superaddition in continuation, *too, yea,* etc. It sometimes is found at the commencement of the apodosis of a sentence, Acts 11:17. It serves also to mark the resumption of an interrupted discourse, 2 Cor. 2:10; Gal. 2:6 [1161]

[1255] δέησις *deēsis* 18x *entreaty; prayer, supplication,* Lk. 1:13; 2:37; 5:33 [1162] See *petition; prayer; request; supplication.*

[1256] δεῖ *dei* 101x *it is binding, it is necessary, it is proper; it is inevitable,* Acts 21:22 [1163] See *must; necessary; ought; should.*

[1257] δεῖγμα *deigma* 1x pr. *that which is shown, a specimen, sample;* met. *an example* by way of warning, Jude 7* [1164]

[1258] δειγματίζω *deigmatizō* 2x *to make a public show* or *spectacle of,* Mt. 1:19; Col. 2:15* [1165]

[1259] δείκνυμι *deiknymi* 30x also formed δεικνύω 3x, *to show, point out, present to the sight,* Mt. 4:8; 8:4; *to exhibit, permit to see, cause to be seen,* Jn. 2:18; 10:32; 1 Tim. 6:15; *to demonstrate, prove,* Jas. 2:18; 3:13; met. *to teach, make known, declare, announce,* Mt. 16:21; Jn. 5:20; Acts 10:28 [1166] See *demonstrate; show.*

[1260] δεικνύω *deiknyō* 3x see δείκνυμι, Mt. 16:21; Jn. 2:18; Rev. 22:8* [**]

[1261] δειλία *deilia* 1x *timidity,* 2 Tim. 1:7* [1167]

[1262] δειλιάω *deiliaō* 1x *to be timid, be in fear,* Jn. 14:27* [1168]

[1264] δειλός *deilos* 3x *timid, fearful, cowardly,* Mt. 8:26; Mk. 4:40; Rev. 21:8* [1169]

[1265] δεῖνα *deina* 1x *such a one, a certain one,* Mt. 26:18* [1170]

[1267] δεινῶς *deinōs* 2x *dreadfully, grievously, greatly, terribly,* Mt. 8:6; Lk. 11:53* [1171]

[1268] δειπνέω *deipneō* 4x *to eat* or *dine,* Lk. 17:8; 22:20; 1 Cor. 11:25; Rev. 3:20 [1172]

[1270] δεῖπνον *deipnon* 16x pr. *a meal; supper, the principal meal taken in the evening,* Lk. 14:12; Jn. 13:2, 4; meton. *food,* 1 Cor. 11:21; *a feast, banquet,* Mt. 23:6; Mk. 6:21; 12:39 [1173] See *banquet; feast; supper.*

[1272] δεισιδαιμονία *deisidaimonia* 1x *fear of the gods;* in a bad sense, *superstition; a form of religious belief,* Acts 25:19* [1175]

[1273] δεισιδαίμων *deisidaimōn* 1x *reverencing the gods and divine things, religious;* in a bad sense, *superstitious;* in NT *careful and precise in the discharge of religious services,* Acts 17:22* [1174]

[1274] δέκα *deka* 25x *ten,* Mt. 20:24; 25:1; ἡμερῶν δέκα, *ten days, a few days, a short time,* Rev. 2:10 [1176] See *ten.*

[1277] δεκαοκτώ *dekaoktō* 2x *eighteen,* Lk. 13:4, 11* [1176 + 2532 + 3638]

[1278] δεκαπέντε *dekapente* 3x *fifteen,* indecl., Jn. 11:18; Acts 27:28; Gal. 1:18* [1178]

[1279] Δεκάπολις *Dekapolis* 3x *Decapolis,* a district of Palestine beyond Jordan, Mk. 5:20; 7:31; Mt. 4:25* [1179]

[1280] δεκατέσσαρες *dekatessares* 5x *fourteen,* Mt. 1:17; 2 Cor. 12:2; Gal. 2:1* [1180]

[1281] δέκατος *dekatos* 7x *tenth,* Jn. 1:39; Rev. 11:13; 21:20; δεκάτη, sc. μερίς, *a tenth part, tithe,* Heb. 7:2, 4, 8, 9* [1181, 1182] See *tenth; tithe.*

[1282] δεκατόω *dekatoō* 2x *to cause to pay tithes;* pass. *to be tithed, pay tithes,* Heb. 7:6, 9* [1183]

[1283] δεκτός *dektos* 5x *accepted, acceptable, agreeable, approved,* Lk. 4:24; Acts 10:35; Phil. 4:18; by impl. when used of a certain time, *marked by* divine *acceptance, propitious,* Lk. 4:19; 2 Cor. 6:2* [1184]

[1284] δελεάζω *deleazō* 3x pr. *to entrap, take* or *catch* with a bait; met. *allure, entice,* Jas. 1:14; 2 Pet. 2:14, 18* [1185]

[1285] δένδρον *dendron* 25x *a tree,* Mt. 3:10; 7:17; 13:32 [1186] See *tree.*

[1287] δεξιολάβος *dexiolabos* 1x *one posted on the right hand; a flank guard; a light armed spearman,* Acts 23:23* [1187]

[1288] δεξιος *dexios* 54x *right,* as opposed to left, Mt. 5:29, 30; Lk. 6:6; ἡ δεξιά, sc. χείρ, *the right hand,* Mt. 6:3; 27:29; τα δεξια, sc. μέρη, *the parts towards the right hand, the right hand side;* καθίζειν, or, καθῆσθαι, or, ἑστάναι, ἐκ δεξιῶν [μερῶν] τινος, *to sit* or *stand at the right hand of any one,* as a mark of the highest honor and dignity which he can bestow, Mt. 20:20; 26:64; εἶνι ἐκ δεξιῶν [μερῶν] τινος, *to be at one's right hand,* as a helper, Acts 2:25; δεξιὰς (χεῖρας) διδόναι, *to give the right hand* to any one, as a pledge of sincerity in one's promises, Gal. 2:9 [1188] See *right; right hand; right side.*

[1289] δέομαι *deomai* 22x *to be in want, to need; to ask, request,* Mt. 9:38; Lk. 5:12; 8:28, 38; in NT absol. *to pray, offer prayer, beseech, supplicate,* Lk. 21:36; 22:32; Acts 4:31; 8:22, 24 [1189] See *ask; beg; beseech; plead; pray.*

[1290] δεος *deos* 1x *fear,* Heb. 12:28* [127]

[1291] Δερβαῖος *Derbaios* 1x *an inhabitant of Derbe,* Acts 20:4* [1190]

[1292] Δέρβη *Derbē* 3x *Derbe,* a city of Lycaonia, Acts 14:6, 20; 16:0* [1191]

[1293] δέρμα *derma* 1x *the skin* of an animal, Heb. 11:37* [1192]

[1294] δερμάτινος *dermatinos* 2x *made of skin, leathern,* Mt. 3:4; Mk. 1:6* [1193]

[1296] δέρω *derō* 15x *to skin, flay;* hence, *to eat, scourge, beat,* Mt. 21:35; Mk. 12:3, 5; 13:9 [1194] See *beat; strike.*

[1297] δεσμεύω *desmeuō* 3x *to bind, bind up,* as a bundle, Mt. 23:4; *to bind, confine,* Lk. 8:29; Acts 22:4* [1195]

[1299] δέσμη *desmē* 1x *a bundle,* as of tares, Mt. 13:30* [1197]

[1300] δέσμιος *desmios* 16x *one bound, a prisoner,* Mt. 27:15, 16; Mk. 15:6 [1198] See *prisoner.*

[1301] δεσμός *desmos* 18x *a bond, anything by which one is bound, a cord, chain, fetters,* etc.; and by meton. *imprisonment,* Lk. 8:29; Acts 16:26; 20:23; *a string* or *ligament,* as of the tongue, Mk. 7:35; met. *an impediment, infirmity,* Lk. 13:16 [1199] See *bond; chain; fetter.*

[1302] δεσμοφύλαξ *desmophylax* 3x *a keeper of a prison, jailer,* Acts 16:23, 27, 36* [1200]

[1303] δεσμωτήριον *desmōtērion* 4x *a prison,* Mt. 11:2; Acts 5:21, 23; 16:26* [1201]

[1304] δεσμώτης *desmōtēs* 2x *a prisoner,* i.q. δέσμιος, Acts 27:1, 42* [1202]

[1305] δεσπότης *despotēs* 10x *a lord, master,* especially of slaves, 1 Tim. 6:1, 2; 2 Tim. 2:21; Tit. 2:9; 1 Pet. 2:18; by impl. as denoting the possession of supreme authority, *Lord, sovereign,* used of God, Lk. 2:29; Acts 4:24; Rev. 6:10; and of Christ, 2 Pet. 2:1; Jude 4 [1203] See *lord; master.*

[1306] δεῦρο *deuro* 9x *here;* used also as a sort of imperative, *come, Come here!* Mt. 19:21; Mk. 10:21; used of time, ἄχρι τοῦ δεῦρο, sc. χρόνου, *to the present time,* Rom. 1:13 [1204]

[1307] δεῦτε *deute* 12x *come,* Mt. 4:19; 11:28; as a particle of exhortation, incitement, etc., and followed by an imperative, *come now,* etc., Mt. 21:38; 28:6 [1205] See *come.*

[1308] δευτεραῖος *deuteraios* 1x *on the second day* of a certain state or process, and used as an epithet of the subject or agent, Acts 28:13* [1206]

[1311] δεύτερος *deuteros* 43x *second,* Mt. 22:26; τὸ δεύτερον, *again, the second time, another time,* Jude 5; so ἐκ δευτέρου, Mt. 26:42; and ἐν τῷ δευτέρῳ, Acts 7:13 [1208] See *second.*

[1312] δέχομαι *dechomai* 56x *to take* into one's hands, etc., Lk. 2:28; 16:6, 7; *to receive,* Acts 22:5; 28:21; Phil. 4:18; *to receive into and retain, contain,* Acts 3:21; met. *to receive* by the hearing, *learn, acquire a knowledge of,* 2 Cor. 11:4; Jas. 1:21; *to receive, admit, grant access to, receive kindly, welcome,* Mt. 10:40, 41; 18:5; *to receive* in hospitality, *entertain,* Lk. 9:53; Heb. 11:31; *to bear with, bear patiently,* 2 Cor. 11:16; met. *to receive, approve, assent to,* Mt. 11:14; Lk. 8:13; Acts 8:14; 11:1; *to admit,* and by impl. *to embrace, follow,* 1 Cor. 2:14; 2 Cor. 8:17 [1209] See *receive; welcome.*

[1313] δέω *deō* 43x *to bind, tie,* Mt. 13:30; 21:2; *to bind, confine,* Mt. 27:2; 14:3; *to impede, hinder,* 2 Tim. 2:9; *to bind* with infirmity, Lk. 13:16; *to bind* by a legal or moral tie, as marriage, Rom. 7:2; 1 Cor. 7:27, 39; by impl. *to impel, compel,* Acts 20:22; in NT *to pronounce* or *declare to be binding* or *obligatory,* or, *to declare to be prohibited and unlawful,* Mt. 16:19; 18:18 [1210] See *bind; tie, tie up.*

[1314] δή *dē* 5x a particle that adds an intensity of expression to a term or clause. Its simplest and most ordinary uses are when it gives impressiveness to an affirmation, *indeed, really, doubtless,* Mt. 13:23; or earnestness to a call, injunction, or entreaty, Lk. 2:15; Acts 13:2; 15:36; 1 Cor. 16:20* [1211]

[1316] δῆλος *dēlos* 3x pr. *clearly visible; plain, manifest, evident,* Mt. 26:73; 1 Cor. 15:27; Gal. 3:11* [1212]

[1317] δηλόω *dēloō* 7x *to render manifest* or *evident; to make known, to tell, relate, declare,* 1 Cor. 1:11; Col. 1:8; *to show, point out, bring to light,* 1 Cor. 3:13; *to indicate, signify,* Heb. 9:8; 12:27; 1 Pet. 1:11 [1213]

[1318] Δημᾶς *Dēmas* 3x *Demas,* pr. name, Col. 4:14; 2 Tim. 4:10; Phlm. 24* [1214]

[1319] δημηγορέω *dēmēgoreō* 1x *to address a public assembly, to deliver a public oration,* Acts 12:21* [1215]

[1320] Δημήτριος *Dēmētrios* 3x *Demetrius,* pr. name (1) *The Ephesian silversmith,* Acts 19:24, 38 (2) *A certain Christian,* 3 Jn. 12* [1216]

[1321] δημιουργός *dēmiourgos* 1x pr. *one who labors for the public,* or, *exercises some public calling; an architect,* especially, the Divine *Architect* of the universe, Heb. 11:10 [1217]

[1322] δῆμος *dēmos* 4x *the people,* Acts 12:22; 17:5; 19:30, 33* [1218]

[1323] δημόσιος *dēmosios* 4x *public, belonging to the public,* Acts 5:18; δημοσίᾳ, *publicly,* Acts 16:37; 18:28; 20:20* [1219]

[1324] δηνάριον *dēnarion* 16x Latin *denarius,* a Roman silver coin; the name originally meant *ten asses,* Mt. 18:28; Mk. 6:37; Rev. 6:6 [1220] See *coin; days wage; denarius.*

[1327] δήπου *dēpou* 1x *now in some way, surely,* Heb. 2:16* [1222]

[1328] διά *dia* 667x (1) gen., *through,* used of place or medium, Mt. 7:13; Lk. 6:1; 2 Cor. 11:33; *through,* of time, *during, in the course of,* Heb. 2:15; Acts 5:19; *through,* of immediate agency, causation, instrumentality, *by means of, by,* Jn. 1:3; Acts 3:18; of means or manner, *through, by, with,* Lk. 8:4; 2 Cor. 5:7; 8:8; of state or condition, *in a state of,* Rom. 4:11; (2) acc., used of causation which is not direct and immediate in the production of a result, *on account of, because of, for the sake of, with a view to,* Mk. 2:27; Jn. 1:31; rarely, *through, while subject to* a state of untoward circumstances, Gal. 4:13 [1223]

[1329] διαβαίνω *diabainō* 3x *to pass through* or *over,* Lk. 16:26; Acts 16:9; Heb. 11:29* [1224]

[1330] διαβάλλω *diaballō* 1x *to throw* or *convey through* or *over; to thrust through; to defame, inform against,* Lk. 16:1* [1225]

[1331] διαβεβαιόομαι *diabebaioomai* 2x *to assert strongly, insist,* 1 Tim. 1:7; Tit. 3:8* [1226]

[1332] διαβλέπω *diablepō* 3x *to look through; to view steadily,* Mk. 8:25; *to see clearly* or *steadily,* Mt. 7:5; Lk. 6:42* [1227]

[1333] διάβολος *diabolos* 37x *slanderer,* 1 Tim. 3:11; 2 Tim. 3:3; Tit. 2:3; *a treacherous informer, traitor,* Jn. 6:70; ὁ διάβολος, *the devil* [1228] See *devil.*

[1334] διαγγέλλω *diangellō* 3x *to publish abroad,* Lk. 9:60; Rom. 9:17; *to certify* to the public, Acts 21:26* [1229]

[1335] διαγίνομαι *diaginomai* 3x pas., *to continue through; to intervene, elapse* of time, Mk. 16:1; Acts 25:13; 27:9* [1230]

[1336] διαγινώσκω *diaginōskō* 2x pr. *to distinguish; to resolve determinately; to examine, inquire into,* judicially, Acts 23:15; 24:22* [1231]

[1338] διάγνωσις *diagnōsis* 1x pr. *an act of distinguishing* or *discernment; a determination; examination* judicially, *hearing, trial,* Acts 25:21* [1233]

[1339] διαγογγύζω *diagongyzō* 2x *to murmur, mutter,* Lk. 15:2; 19:7* [1234]

[1340] διαγρηγορέω *diagrēgoreō* 1x *to remain awake; to wake thoroughly,* Lk. 9:32* [1235]

[1341] διάγω *diagō* 2x *to conduct* or *carry through* or *over; to pass* or *spend* time, *live,* 1 Tim. 2:2; Tit. 3:3* [1236]

[1342] διαδέχομαι *diadechomai* 1x *to receive by transmission; to receive in return,* Acts 7:45* [1237]

[1343] διάδημα *diadēma* 3x pr. *a band* or *fillet; a diadem,* the badge of a sovereign, Rev. 12:3; 13:1; 19:12* [1238]

[1344] διαδίδωμι *diadidōmi* 4x *to deliver from hand to hand; to distribute, divide,* Lk. 11:22; 18:22; Jn. 6:11; Acts 4:35* [1239]

[1345] διάδοχος *diadochos* 1x *a successor,* Acts 24:27* [1240]

[1346] διαζώννυμι *diazōnnymi* 3x *to gird firmly round,* Jn. 13:4, 5; mid. *to gird round one's self,* Jn. 21:7* [1241]

[1347] διαθήκη *diathēkē* 33x *a testamentary disposition, will; a covenant,* Heb. 9:16, 17; Gal. 3:15; in NT, *a covenant* of God with men, Gal. 3:17; 4:24; Heb. 9:4; Mt. 26:28; *the writings of the old covenant,* 2 Cor. 3:14 [1242] See *covenant; testament; will.*

[1348] διαίρεσις *diairesis* 3x *a division; a distinction, difference, diversity,* 1 Cor. 12:4, 5, 6* [1243]

[1349] διαιρέω *diaireō* 2x *to divide, to divide out, distribute,* Lk. 15:12; 1 Cor. 12:11* [1244]

[1350] διακαθαίρω *diakathairō* 1x *to cleanse thoroughly,* Lk. 3:17* [1245]

[1351] διακαθαρίζω *diakatharizō* 1x *to cleanse thoroughly,* Mt. 3:12 [1245]

[1352] διακατελέγχομαι *diakatelenchomai* 1x *to maintain discussion strenuously and thoroughly, to totally refute,* Acts 18:28* [1246]

[1354] διακονέω *diakoneō* 37x *to wait, attend upon, serve,* Mt. 8:15; Mk. 1:31; Lk. 4:39; *to be an attendant* or *assistant,* Acts 19:22; *to minister to, relieve, assist,* or *supply with the necessaries of life, provide the means of living,* Mt. 4:11; 27:55; Mk. 1:13; 15:41; Lk. 8:3; *to fill the office of* διάκονος, *deacon, perform the duties of deacon,* 1 Tim. 3:10, 13; 1 Pet. 4:11; *to convey in charge, administer,* 2 Cor. 3:3; 8:19, 20; 1 Pet. 1:12; 4:10; pass. *to receive service,* Mt. 20:28; Mk. 10:45 [1247] See *serve.*

[1355] διακονία *diakonia* 34x *serving, service, waiting, attendance, the act of rendering friendly offices,* Lk. 10:40; 2 Tim. 4:11; Heb. 1:14; *relief, aid,* Acts 6:1; 11:29; 2 Cor. 8:4; 9:1, 12, 13; *a commission,* Acts 12:25; Rom. 15:31; *a commission* or *ministry* in the service of the Gospel, Acts 1:17, 25; 20:24; Rom. 11:13; 2 Cor. 4:1; 5:18; 1 Tim. 1:12; *service* in the Gospel, Acts 6:4; 21:19; 1 Cor. 16:15; 2 Cor. 6:3; 11:8; Eph. 4:12; Rev. 2:19; *a function, ministry,* or *office* in the Church, Rom. 12:7; 1 Cor. 12:5; Col. 4:17; 2 Tim. 4:5; *a ministering* in the conveyance of a revelation from God, 2 Cor. 3:7, 8, 9 [1248] See *ministry; service.*

[1356] διάκονος *diakonos* 29x *one who renders service* to another; *an attendant, servant,* Mt. 20:26; 22:13; Jn. 2:5, 9; *one who executes a commission, a deputy,* Rom. 13:4; Χριστοῦ, Θεοῦ, ἐν κυρίῳ, etc. *a* commissioned *minister* or *preacher* of the Gospel, 1 Cor. 3:5; 2 Cor. 6:4; *a minister* charged with an announcement or sentence, 2 Cor. 3:6; Gal. 2:17; Col. 1:23; *a minister* charged with a significant characteristic, Rom. 15:8; *a servitor, devoted follower,* Jn. 12:26; *a deacon* or *deaconess,* whose official duty was to superintend the alms of the Church, with other kindred services, Rom. 16:1; Phil. 1:1; 1 Tim. 3:8, 12 [1249] See *deacon; minister; servant.*

[1357] διακόσιοι *diakosioi* 8x *two hundred,* Mk. 6:37; Jn. 6:7; 21:8; Acts 23:23f.* [1250]

[1358] διακούω *diakouō* 1x *to hear* a thing *through; to hear* judicially, Acts 23:35* [1251]

[1359] διακρίνω *diakrinō* 19x *to separate, sever; to make a distinction* or *difference,* Acts 15:9; 1 Cor. 11:29; *to make to differ, distinguish, prefer, confer a superiority,* 1 Cor. 4:7; *to examine, scrutinize, estimate,* 1 Cor. 11:31; 14:29; *to discern, discriminate,* Mt. 16:3; *to judge, to decide a cause,* 1 Cor. 6:5; *to dispute, contend,* Acts 11:2; Jude 9; *to make a distinction* mentally, Jas. 2:4; Jude 22; in NT *to hesitate, be in doubt, doubt,* Mt. 21:21; Mk. 11:23 [1252] See *distinguish; doubt; evaluate; judge; waver.*

[1360] διάκρισις *diakrisis* 3x *a separation; a distinction,* or, *doubt,* Rom. 14:1; *a discerning, the act of discerning* or *distinguishing,* Heb. 5:14; *the faculty of distinguishing and estimating,* 1 Cor. 12:10* [1253]

[1361] διακωλύω *diakōlyō* 1x *to hinder, restrain, prohibit,* Mt. 3:14* [1254]

[1362] διαλαλέω *dialaleō* 2x *to talk with;* by impl. *to consult, deliberate,* Lk. 6:11; *to divulge, publish, spread by rumor,* Lk. 1:65* [1255]

[1363] διαλέγομαι *dialegomai* 13x *to discourse, argue, reason,* Acts 17:2, 17; 24:12; *to address, speak to,* Heb. 12:5; *to contend, dispute,* Mk. 9:34; Jude 9 [1256] See *argue; persuade; prove; reason.*

[1364] διαλείπω *dialeipō* 1x *to leave an interval; to intermit, cease,* Lk. 7:45* [1257]

[1365] διάλεκτος *dialektos* 6x *speech; manner of speaking; peculiar language* of a nation, *dialect, vernacular idiom,* Acts 1:19; 2:6, 8; 21:40; 22:2; 26:14 [1258]

[1367] διαλλάσσομαι *diallassomai* 1x *to be reconciled* to another, Mt. 5:24* [1259]

[1368] διαλογίζομαι *dialogizomai* 16x pr. *to make a settlement of accounts; to reason, deliberate, ponder, consider,* Mt. 16:7, 8; Mk. 2:6, 8; Jn. 11:50; *to dispute, contend,* Mk. 9:33 [1260] See *argue; consider; discuss; wonder.*

[1369] διαλογισμός *dialogismos* 14x *reasoning, thought, cogitation, purpose,* Mt. 15:19; Mk. 7:21; *discourse, dispute, disputation, contention,* Lk. 9:46; *doubt, hesitation, scruple,* Lk. 24:38 [1261] See *argument; discussion; thought.*

[1370] διαλύω *dialyō* 1x *to dissolve, dissipate, disperse,* Acts 5:36* [1262]

[1371] διαμαρτύρομαι *diamartyromai* 15x *to make solemn affirmation, protest; to make a solemn and earnest charge,* Lk. 16:28; Acts 2:40; *to declare solemnly and earnestly,* Acts 8:25; 18:5 [1263] See *testify; warn.*

[1372] διαμάχομαι *diamachomai* 1x *to fight out, to fight resolutely;* met. *to contend vehemently, insist,* Acts 23:9* [1264]

[1373] διαμένω *diamenō* 5x *to continue throughout; to continue, be permanent* or *unchanged,* Lk. 1:22; Gal. 2:5; Heb. 1:11; 2 Pet. 3:4; *to continue, remain constant,* Lk. 22:28 [1265]

[1374] διαμερίζω *diamerizō* 11x *to divide into parts and distribute,* Mt. 27:35; Mk. 15:24; Acts 2:3; pass. in NT *to be in a state of dissension,* Lk. 11:17, 18; 12:52, 53 [1266] See *divide; part.*

[1375] διαμερισμός *diamerismos* 1x *division;* met. in NT *disunion, dissension,* Lk. 12:51* [1267]

[1376] διανέμω *dianemō* 1x *to distribute; to divulge, spread abroad,* Acts 4:17* [1268]

[1377] διανεύω *dianeuō* 1x *to signify by a nod, beckon, make signs,* Lk. 1:22* [1269]

[1378] διανόημα *dianoēma* 1x *thought,* Lk. 11:17* [1270]

[1379] διάνοια *dianoia* 12x pr. *thought, intention; the mind, intellect, understanding,* Mt. 22:37; Mk. 12:30; Lk. 10:27; *an operation of the understanding, thought, imagination,* Lk. 1:51; *insight, comprehension,* 1 Jn. 5:20; *mode of thinking and feeling, disposition of mind and heart, the affection,* Eph. 2:3; Col. 1:21 [1271] See *mind; thought; understanding.*

[1380] διανοίγω *dianoigō* 8x *to open,* Mk. 7:34, 35; Lk. 2:23; 24:31; Acts 7:56; met. *to open* the sense of a thing, *explain, expound,* Lk. 24:32; Acts 17:3; διανοίγειν τὸν νοῦν, τὴν καρδίαν, *to open the mind, the heart,* so as to understand and receive, Lk. 24:45; Acts 16:14* [1272]

[1381] διανυκτερεύω *dianyktereuō* 1x *to pass the night, spend the whole night,* Lk. 6:12* [1273]

[1382] διανύω *dianyō* 1x *to complete, finish,* Acts 21:7* [1274]

[1384] διαπαρατριβή *diaparatribē* 1x *constant disputation,* 1 Tim. 6:5* [3859]

[1385] διαπεράω *diaperaō* 6x *to pass through* or *over,* Mt. 9:1; 14:34; Mk. 5:21; 6:53; Lk. 16:26; Acts 21:2* [1276]

[1386] διαπλέω *diapleō* 1x *to sail through* or *over,* Acts 27:5* [1277]

[1387] διαπονέομαι *diaponeomai* 2x pr. *to be thoroughly exercised with labor; to be wearied; to be vexed,* Acts 4:2; 16:18* [1278]

[1388] διαπορεύομαι *diaporeuomai* 5x *to go* or *pass through,* Lk. 6:1; 13:22; Acts 16:4; *to pass by,* Lk. 18:36 [1279]

[1389] διαπορέω *diaporeō* 4x *to be utterly at a loss; to be in doubt and perplexity,* Lk. 9:7; Acts 2:12; 5:24; 10:17 [1280]

[1390] διαπραγματεύομαι *diapragmateuomai* 1x *to despatch a matter thoroughly; to make profit in business, gain in trade,* Lk. 19:15* [1281]

[1391] διαπρίω *diapriō* 2x *to divide with a saw, saw asunder; to grate* the teeth in a rage; pass. met. *to be cut* to the heart, *to be enraged,* Acts 5:33; 7:54* [1282]

[1395] διαρπάζω *diarpazō* 3x *to plunder, spoil, pillage,* Mt. 12:29; Mk. 3:27 (2x)* [1283]

[1397] διασαφέω *diasapheō* 2x *to make known, declare, tell plainly,* or *fully,* Mt. 13:36; 18:31* [1285]

[1398] διασείω *diaseiō* 1x pr. *to shake thoroughly* or *violently; to harass, intimidate, extort from,* Lk. 3:14* [1286]

[1399] διασκορπίζω *diaskorpizō* 9x *to disperse, scatter,* Mt. 26:31; Mk. 14:27; *to dissipate, waste,* Lk. 15:13; 16:1; *to winnow,* or, *to strew,* Mt. 25:24, 26 [1287] See *scatter.*

[1400] διασπάω *diaspaō* 2x *to pull* or *tear asunder* or *in pieces, burst,* Mk. 5:4; Acts 23:10* [1288]

[1401] διασπείρω *diaspeirō* 3x *to scatter abroad* or *in every direction,* as seen; *to disperse,* Acts 8:1, 4; 11:19* [1289] See *scatter.*

[1402] διασπορά *diaspora* 3x pr. *a scattering,* as of seed; *dispersion;* in NT meton. *the dispersed portion* of the Jews, specially termed *the dispersion,* Jn. 7:35; Jas. 1:1; 1 Pet. 1:1* [1290]

[1403] διαστέλλω *diastellō* 8x *to determine, issue a decision; to state* or *explain distinctly and accurately;* hence, *to admonish, direct, charge, command,* Acts 15:24; Heb. 12:20; when followed by a negative clause, *to interdict, prohibit,* Mt. 16:30; Mk. 5:43 [1291] See *command; order; warn.*

[1404] διάστημα *diastēma* 1x *interval, space, distance,* Acts 5:7 [1292]

[1405] διαστολή *diastolē* 3x *distinction, difference,* Rom. 3:22; 10:12; 1 Cor. 14:7* [1293]

[1406] διαστρέφω *diastrephō* 7x *to distort, turn away;* met. *to pervert, corrupt,* Mt. 17:17; Lk. 9:41; *to turn out of the way, cause to make defection,* Lk. 23:2; Acts 13:8; διεστραμμένος, *perverse, corrupt, erroneous* [1294]

[1407] διασῴζω *diasōzō* 8x *to bring safely through; to convey in safety,* Acts 23:24; pass. *to reach a place* or *state of safety,* Acts 27:43, 44; 28:1, 4; 1 Pet. 3:20; *to heal, to restore to health,* Mt. 14:36; Lk. 7:3* [1295]

[1408] διαταγή *diatagē* 2x *an injunction, institute, ordinance,* Rom. 13:2; Acts 7:53* [1296]

[1409] διάταγμα *diatagma* 1x *a mandate, commandment, ordinance,* Heb. 11:23* [1297] See *commandment.*

[1410] διαταράσσω *diatarassō* 1x *to throw into a state of perturbation, to move* or *trouble greatly,* Lk. 1:29* [1298]

[1411] διατάσσω *diatassō* 16x pr. *to arrange, make a precise arrangement; to prescribe,* 1 Cor. 11:34; 16:1; Tit. 1:5; *to direct,* Lk. 8:55; Acts 20:13; *to charge,* Mt. 11:1; *to command,* Acts 18:2; *to ordain,* Gal. 3:19 [1299] See *command; direct; instruct; order.*

[1412] διατελέω *diateleō* 1x *to complete, finish;* intrans. *to continue, persevere,* in a certain state or course of action, Acts 27:33* [1300]

[1413] διατηρέω *diatēreō* 2x *to watch carefully, guard with vigilance; to treasure up,* Lk. 2:51; ἑαυτὸν ἐκ, *to keep one's self from, to abstain wholly from,* Acts 15:29* [1301]

[1416] διατίθημι *diatithēmi* 7x in NT only mid., so some list as διατίθεμαι, *to arrange; to arrange according to one's own mind; to make a disposition, to make a will; to settle the terms of a covenant, to* *ratify,* Acts 3:25; Heb. 8:10; 10:16; *to assign,* Lk. 22:29 [1303]

[1417] διατρίβω *diatribō* 9x pr. *to rub, wear away by friction;* met. *to pass* or *spend* time, *to remain, stay, tarry, continue,* Jn. 3:22; 11:54; Acts 12:19; 14:3, 28 [1304]

[1418] διατροφή *diatrophē* 1x *food, sustenance,* 1 Tim. 6:8* [1305]

[1419] διαυγάζω *diaugazō* 1x *to shine through, shine out, dawn,* 2 Pet. 1:19* [1306]

[1420] διαυγής *diaugēs* 1x *translucent, transparent,* Rev. 21:21* [1307]

[1422] διαφέρω *diapherō* 13x *to convey through, across,* Mk. 11:16; *to carry different ways* or *into different parts, separate;* pass. *to be borne, driven,* or *tossed hither and thither,* Acts 27:27; *to be proclaimed, published,* Acts 13:49; intrans. met. *to differ,* 1 Cor. 15:41; *to excel, be better* or *of greater value, be superior,* Mt. 6:26; 10:31; impers. διαφέρει, *it makes a difference, it is of consequence;* with οὐδέν, *it makes no difference, it is nothing,* Gal. 2:6 [1308] See *carry through; differ; spread out; valuable; (have) value.*

[1423] διαφεύγω *diapheugō* 1x *to flee through, escape by flight,* Acts 27:42* [1309]

[1424] διαφημίζω *diaphēmizō* 3x *to report, proclaim, publish, spread abroad,* Mt. 9:31; 28:15; Mk. 1:45* [1310]

[1425] διαφθείρω *diaphtheirō* 6x *to corrupt* or *destroy utterly; to waste, bring to decay,* Lk. 12:33; 2 Cor. 4:16; *to destroy,* Rev. 8:9; 11:18 (2x); met. *to corrupt, pervert utterly,* 1 Tim. 6:5* [1311] See *corrupt, corruption; destroy.*

[1426] διαφθορά *diaphthora* 6x *corruption, dissolution,* Acts 2:27, 31; 13:34, 35, 36, 37* [1312]

[1427] διάφορος *diaphoros* 4x *different, diverse, of different kinds,* Rom. 12:6; Heb. 9:10; *excellent, superior,* Heb. 1:4; 8:6* [1313]

[1428] διαφυλάσσω *diaphylassō* 1x *to keep* or *guard carefully* or *with vigilance; to guard, protect,* Lk. 4:10* [1314]

[1429] διαχειρίζω *diacheirizō* 2x pr. *to have in the hands, to manage;* mid. later, *to kill,* Acts 5:30; 26:21* [1315]

[1430] διαχλευάζω *diachleuazō* 1x *to jeer outright, deride,* Acts 2:13* [5512]

[1431] διαχωρίζω *diachōrizō* 1x *to depart, go away,* Lk. 9:33* [1316]

[1434] διδακτικός *didaktikos* 2x *apt* or *qualified to teach,* 1 Tim. 3:2; 2 Tim. 2:24* [1317]

[1435] διδακτός *didaktos* 3x pr. *taught, teachable,* of things; in NT *taught,* of person, Jn. 6:45; 1 Cor. 2:13* [1318]

[1436] διδασκαλία *didaskalia* 21x *the act* or *occupation of teaching,* Rom. 12:7; 1 Tim. 4:13; *information, instruction,* Rom. 15:4; 2 Tim. 3:16; *matter taught, precept, doctrine,* Mt. 15:9; 1 Tim. 1:10 [1319] See *doctrine; teaching.*

[1437] διδάσκαλος *didaskalos* 59x *a teacher, master,* Rom. 2:20; in NT as an equivalent, to ῥαββί, Jn. 1:39 [1320] See *rabbi; teacher.*

[1438] διδάσκω *didaskō* 97x *to teach,* Mt. 4:23; 22:16; *to teach* or *speak in a public assembly,* 1 Tim. 2:12; *to direct, admonish,* Mt. 28:15; Rom. 2:21 [1321] See *instruct; teach.*

[1439] διδαχή *didachē* 30x *instruction, the giving of instruction, teaching,* Mk. 4:2; 12:38; *instruction, what is taught, doctrine,* Mt. 16:12; Jn. 7:16, 17; meton. *mode of teaching and kind of doctrine taught,* Mt. 7:28; Mk. 1:27 [1322] See *doctrine; instruction; teaching.*

[1440] δίδραχμον *didrachmon* 2x *a didrachmon* or *double drachma,* a silver coin equal to the drachma of Alexandria, to two Attic drachmas, to two Roman denarii, and to the half-shekel of the Jews, Mt. 17:24 (2x)* [1323]

[1441] Δίδυμος *Didymos* 3x *a twin; Didymus,* the Greek equivalent to the name Thomas, Jn. 11:16; 20:24; 21:2* [1324]

[1443] δίδωμι *didōmi* 415x pluperfect, ἐδεδώκειν, *to give, bestow, present,* Mt. 4:9; 6:11; Jn. 3:16; 17:2, et al. freq.; *to give, cast, throw,* Mt. 7:6; *to supply, suggest,* Mt. 10:19; Mk. 13:11; *to distribute* alms, Mt. 19:21; Lk. 11:41; *to pay* tribute, etc., Mt. 22:17; Mk. 12:14; Lk. 20:22; *to be the author* or *source* of a thing, Lk. 12:51; Rom. 11:8; *to grant, permit, allow,* Acts 2:27; 13:35; Mt. 13:11; 19:11; *to deliver to, entrust, commit to the charge* of anyone, Mt. 25:15; Mk. 12:9; *to give* or *deliver up,* Lk. 22:19; Jn. 6:51; *to reveal, teach,* Acts 7:38; *to appoint, constitute,* Eph. 1:22; 4:11; *to consecrate, devote, offer in sacrifice,* 2 Cor. 8:5; Gal. 1:4; Rev. 8:3; *to present, expose* one's self in a place, Acts 19:31; *to recompense,* Rev. 2:23; *to attribute, ascribe,* Jn. 9:24; Rev. 11:13; from the Hebrew, *to place, put, fix, inscribe,* Heb. 8:10; 10:16; *to infix, impress,* 2 Cor. 12:7; Rev. 13:16; *to inflict,* Jn. 18:22; 19:3; 2 Thess. 1:8; *to give in charge, assign,* Jn. 5:36; 17:4; Rev. 9:5; *to exhibit, put forth,* Mt. 24:24; Acts 2:19; *to yield, bear* fruit, Mt. 13:8; διδόναι ἐργασίαν, *to endeavor, strive,* Lk. 12:58; διδόναι ἀπόκρισιν, *to answer, reply,* Jn. 1:22; διδόναι τόπον, *to give place, yield,* Lk. 14:9; Rom. 12:19 [1325] See *give; grasp; permit; yield.*

[1444] διεγείρω *diegeirō* 6x *to arouse* or *awake thoroughly,* Mt. 1:24; Mk. 4:38, 39; Lk. 8:24; pass. *to be raised, excited, agitated,* as a sea, Jn. 6:18; met. *to stir up, arouse, animate,* 2 Pet. 1:13; 3:1 [1326]

[1445] διενθυμέομαι *dienthumeomai* 1x *to revolve thoroughly in the mind, consider carefully, ponder, reflect,* Acts 10:19* [1760]

[1447] διέξοδος *diexodos* 1x *a passage throughout; a line of road, a thoroughfare,* Mt. 22:9* [1327]

[1449] διερμηνευτής *diermēneutēs* 1x *an interpreter,* 1 Cor. 14:28* [1328]

[1450] διερμηνεύω *diermēneuō* 6x *to explain, interpret, translate,* Lk. 24:27; Acts 9:36; 1 Cor. 14:5, 13, 27; *to be able to interpret,* 1 Cor. 12:30* [1329]

[1451] διέρχομαι *dierchomai* 43x *to pass through,* Mk. 10:25; Lk. 4:30; *to pass over, cross,* Mk. 4:35; Lk. 8:22; *to pass along,* Lk. 19:4; *to proceed,* Lk. 2:15; Acts 9:38; *to travel through* or *over* a country, *wander about,* Mt. 12:43; Lk. 9:6; *to transfix, pierce,* Lk. 2:35; *to spread abroad, be prevalent,* as a rumor, Lk. 5:15; met. *to extend to,* Rom. 5:12 [1330] See *come through; go through; pass through.*

[1452] διερωτάω *dierōtaō* 1x *to sift by questioning,* of persons; in NT, of things, *to ascertain by inquiry,* Acts 10:17* [1331]

[1453] διετής *dietēs* 1x *of two years; of the age of two years,* Mt. 2:16* [1332]

[1454] διετία *dietia* 2x *the space of two years,* Acts 24:27; 28:30* [1333]

[1455] διηγέομαι *diēgeomai* 8x pr. *to lead throughout; to declare thoroughly, detail, recount, relate, tell,* Mk. 5:16; 9:9; Lk. 8:39; Acts 8:33; Heb. 11:32 [1334]

[1456] διήγησις *diēgēsis* 1x *a narration, relation, history,* Lk. 1:1* [1335]

[1457] διηνεκής *diēnekēs* 4x *continuous, uninterrupted;* εἰς τὸ διηνεκές, *perpetually,* Heb. 7:3; 10:1, 12, 14* [1336]

[1458] διθάλασσος *dithalassos* 1x *surrounded on both sides by the sea;* τόπος διθάλασσος, *a shoal* or *sand-bank formed by the confluence of opposite currents,* Acts 27:41* [1337]

[1459] διϊκνέομαι *diikneomai* 1x *to go* or *pass through; to penetrate,* Heb. 4:12* [1338]

[1460] διΐστημι *diistēmi* 3x *to set at an interval, apart; to station at an interval* from a former position, Acts 27:28; intrans. *to stand apart; to depart, be parted,*

Lk. 24:51; of time, *to intervene, be interposed,* Lk. 22:59* [1339]

[1462] διϊσχυρίζομαι *diischurizomai* 2x *to feel* or *express reliance; to affirm confidently, insist,* Lk. 22:59; Acts 12:15* [1340]

[1464] δικαιοκρισία *dikaiokrisia* 1x *just* or *righteous judgment,* Rom. 2:5* [1341]

[1465] δίκαιος *dikaios* 79x *just, equitable, fair,* Mt. 20:4; Lk. 12:57; Jn. 5:30; Col. 4:1; of persons, *just, righteous,* absolutely, Jn. 17:25; Rom. 3:10, 26; 2 Tim. 4:8; 1 Pet. 3:18; 1 Jn. 1:9; 2:1, 29; Rev. 16:5; *righteous* by account and acceptance, Rom. 2:13; 5:19; in ordinary usage, *just, upright, innocent, pious,* Mt. 5:45; 9:13, et al. freq.; ὁ δίκαιος, *the Just One,* one of the distinctive titles of the Messiah, Acts 3:14; 7:52; 22:14 [1342] See *innocent; just; righteous, righteousness; upright.*

[1466] δικαιοσύνη *dikaiosynē* 92x *fair and equitable dealing, justice,* Acts 17:31; Heb. 11:33; Rom. 9:28; *integrity, virtue,* Lk. 1:75; Eph. 5:9; in NT *generosity, alms,* 2 Cor. 9:10, v.r.; Mt. 6:1; *piety, godliness,* Rom. 6:13; *investiture with the attribute of righteousness, acceptance as righteous, justification,* Rom. 4:11; 10:4, et al. freq.; *a provision* or *mean for justification,* Rom. 1:17; 2 Cor. 3:9; *an instance of justification,* 2 Cor. 5:21 [1343] See *innocence; justice; justification; righteous, righteousness.*

[1467] δικαιόω *dikaioō* 39x pr. *to make* or *render right* or *just;* mid. *to act with justice,* Rev. 22:11; *to avouch to be good and true, to vindicate,* Mt. 11:19; Lk. 7:29; *to set forth as good and just,* Lk. 10:29; 16:15; in NT *to hold as guiltless, to accept as righteous, to justify,* Rom. 3:26, 30; 4:5; 8:30, 33; pass. *to be held acquitted, to be cleared,* Acts 13:39; Rom. 3:24; 6:7; *to be approved, to stand approved, to stand accepted,* Rom. 2:13; 3:20, 28 [1344] See *justify; righteous, righteousness.*

[1468] δικαίωμα *dikaiōma* 10x pr. *a rightful act, act of justice, equity; a sentence,* of condemnation, Rev. 15:4; in NT, of acquittal, *justification,* Rom. 5:16; *a decree, law, ordinance,* Lk. 1:6; Rom. 1:32; 2:26; 8:4; Heb. 9:1, 10; *a meritorious act, an instance of perfect righteousness,* Rom. 5:18; Rev. 19:8* [1345] See *regulations; righteous, righteousness; righteous deeds.*

[1469] δικαίως *dikaiōs* 5x *justly, with strict justice,* 1 Pet. 2:23; *deservedly,* Lk. 23:41; *as it is right, fit* or *proper,* 1 Cor. 15:34; *uprightly, honestly, piously, religiously,* 1 Thess. 2:10; Tit. 2:12* [1346]

[1470] δικαίωσις *dikaiōsis* 2x pr. *a making right* or *just; a declaration of right* or *justice; a judicial sentence;* in NT, *acquittal, acceptance, justification,* Rom. 4:25; 5:18* [1347]

[1471] δικαστής *dikastēs* 2x *a judge,* Acts 7:27, 35* [1348]

[1472] δίκη *dikē* 3x *right, justice;* in NT *judicial punishment, vengeance,* 2 Thess. 1:9; Jude 7; *sentence of punishment, judgment,* Acts 25:15; personified, *the goddess of justice* or *vengeance, Nemesis, Paena,* Acts 28:4 [1349]

[1473] δίκτυον *diktyon* 12x *a net, fishing-net,* Mt. 4:20, 21 [1350] See *net.*

[1474] δίλογος *dilogos* 1x pr. *saying the same thing twice;* in NT *double-tongued, speaking one thing and meaning another, deceitful in words,* 1 Tim. 3:8* [1351]

[1475] διό *dio* 53x inferential conj., *on which account, wherefore, therefore,* Mt. 27:8; 1 Cor. 12:3 [1352]

[1476] διοδεύω *diodeuō* 2x *to travel through* a place, *traverse,* Lk. 8:1; Acts 17:1 [1353]

[1477] Διονύσιος *Dionysios* 1x *Dionysius,* pr. name, Acts 17:34* [1354]

[1478] διόπερ *dioper* 2x inferential conj., *on this very account, for this very reason, wherefore,* 1 Cor. 8:13; 10:14* [1355]

[1479] διοπετής *diopetēs* 1x *which fell from Jupiter,* or *heaven;* τοῦ διοπετοῦς, sc. ἀγάλματος, *image* or *statue*; for discussion of ellipsis see grammars, Acts 19:35* [1356]

[1480] διόρθωμα *diorthōma* 1x *correction, emendation, reformation,* Acts 24:2* [2735]

[1481] διόρθωσις *diorthōsis* 1x *a complete rectification, reformation,* Heb. 9:10 [1357]

[1482] διορύσσω *dioryssō* 4x *to dig* or *break through,* Mt. 6:19, 20; 24:43; Lk. 12:39* [1358]

[1483] Διόσκουροι *Dioskouroi* 1x *the Dioscuri, Castor and Pollux,* sons of Jupiter by Leda, and patrons of sailors, Acts 28:11* [1359]

[1484] διότι *dioti* 23x *on the account that, because,* Lk. 2:7; 21:28; *in as much as,* Lk. 1:13; Acts 18:10 [1360]

[1485] Διοτρέφης *Diotrephēs* 1x *Diotrephes,* pr. name, 3 Jn. 9* [1361]

[1487] διπλοῦς *diplous* 4x *double,* Mt. 23:15; 1 Tim. 5:17; Rev. 18:6 [1362]

[1488] διπλόω *diploō* 1x *to double; to render back double,* Rev. 18:6* [1363]

[1489] δίς *dis* 6x *twice,* Mk. 14:30, 72; in the sense of *entirely, utterly,* Jude 12; ἅπαξ καὶ δίς, *once and again, repeatedly,* Phil. 4:16 [1364]

[1490] δισμυριάς *dismyrias* 1x *twice ten thousand, two myriads,* Rev. 9:16* [1417 + 3461]

[1491] διστάζω *distazō* 2x *to doubt, waver, hesitate,* Mt. 14:31; 28:17* [1365]

[1492] δίστομος *distomos* 3x pr. *having two mouths; two-edged,* Heb. 4:12; Rev. 1:16; 2:12* [1366]

[1493] δισχίλιοι *dischilioi* 1x *two thousand,* Mk. 5:13* [1367]

[1494] διϋλίζω *diylizō* 1x *to strain, filter thoroughly; to strain out* or *off,* Mt. 23:24* [1368]

[1495] διχάζω *dichazō* 1x *to cut asunder, disunite;* met. *to cause to disagree, set at variance,* Mt. 10:35* [1369]

[1496] διχοστασία *dichostasia* 2x *a standing apart; a division, dissension,* Rom. 16:17; Gal. 5:20* [1370]

[1497] διχοτομέω *dichotomeō* 2x pr. *to cut into two parts, cut asunder;* in NT *to inflict a punishment of extreme severity,* Mt. 24:51; Lk. 12:46* [1371]

[1498] διψάω *dipsaō* 16x *to thirst, be thirsty,* Mt. 25:35, 37, 42, 44; met. *to thirst after* in spirit, *to desire* or *long for ardently,* Mt. 5:6; Jn. 4:14; 6:35 [1372] See *thirst.*

[1499] δίψος *dipsos* 1x *thirst,* 2 Cor. 11:27* [1373]

[1500] δίψυχος *dipsychos* 2x *double-minded, inconstant, fickle,* Jas. 1:8; 4:8* [1374]

[1501] διωγμός *diōgmos* 10x pr. *chase, pursuit; persecution* (specifically for religious reasons), Mt. 13:21; Mk. 4:17; 10:30 [1375] See *persecution.*

[1502] διώκτης *diōktēs* 1x *a persecutor,* 1 Tim. 1:13* [1376]

[1503] διώκω *diōkō* 45x *to put in rapid motion; to pursue; to follow, pursue the direction of,* Lk. 17:23; *to follow eagerly, endeavor earnestly to acquire,* Rom. 9:30, 31; 12:13; *to press forwards,* Phil. 3:12, 14; *to pursue* with malignity, *persecute,* Mt. 5:10, 11, 12, 44 [1377] See *persecute; pursue.*

[1504] δόγμα *dogma* 5x *a decree, statute, ordinance,* Lk. 2:1; Acts 16:4; 17:7; Eph. 2:15; Col. 2:14* [1378]

[1505] δογματίζω *dogmatizō* 1x *to decree, prescribe an ordinance;* mid. *to suffer laws to be imposed on one's self, to submit to, bind one's self by, ordinances,* Col. 2:20* [1379]

[1506] δοκέω *dokeō* 62x *to think, imagine, suppose, presume,* Mt. 3:9; 6:7; *to seem, appear,* Lk. 10:36; Acts 17:18; *it seems; it seems good, best,* or *right, it* *pleases,* Lk. 1:3; Acts 15:22, 25 [1380] See *believe; suppose; think.*

[1507] δοκιμάζω *dokimazō* 22x *to test, assay* metals, 1 Pet. 1:7; *to prove, try, examine, scrutinize,* Lk. 14:19; Rom. 12:2; *to put to the proof, tempt,* Heb. 3:9; *to approve* after trial, *judge worthy, choose,* Rom. 14:22; 1 Cor. 16:3; 2 Cor. 8:22; *to decide upon* after examination, *judge of, distinguish, discern,* Lk. 12:56; Rom. 2:18; Phil. 1:10 [1381] See *approve; discern; test.*

[1508] δοκιμασία *dokimasia* 1x *proof, probation, testing, examination,* Heb. 3:9* [1381]

[1509] δοκιμή *dokimē* 7x *trial, proof by trial,* 2 Cor. 8:2; *the state* or *disposition of that which has been tried and approved, approved character* or *temper,* Rom. 5:4; 2 Cor. 2:9; Phil. 2:22; *proof, document, evidence,* 2 Cor. 8:2; 13:3* [1382]

[1510] δοκίμιον *dokimion* 2x *that by means of which anything is tried, proof, criterion, test; trial, the act of trying* or *putting to proof,* Jas. 1:3; *approved character,* 1 Pet. 1:7* [1383]

[1511] δόκιμος *dokimos* 7x *proved, tried; approved* after examination and trial, Rom. 16:10; Jas. 1:12; by impl. *acceptable,* Rom. 14:18 [1384]

[1512] δοκός *dokos* 6x *a beam* or *spar* of timber, Mt. 7:3, 4, 5; Lk. 6:41, 42* [1385]

[1513] δόλιος *dolios* 1x *fraudulent, deceitful,* 2 Cor. 11:13* [1386]

[1514] δολιόω *dolioō* 1x *to deceive, use fraud* or *deceit,* Rom. 3:13* [1387]

[1515] δόλος *dolos* 11x pr. *a bait* or *contrivance for entrapping, fraud, deceit, cunning, guile,* Mt. 26:4; Mk. 7:22; 14:1 [1388] See *deceit.*

[1516] δολόω *doloō* 1x pr. *to entrap, beguile; to adulterate, corrupt, falsify,* 2 Cor. 4:2* [1389]

[1517] δόμα *doma* 4x *a gift, present,* Mt. 7:11; Lk. 11:13; Eph. 4:8; Phil. 4:17* [1390]

[1518] δόξα *doxa* 166x pr. *a seeming; appearance; a notion, imagination, opinion; the opinion which obtains respecting one; reputation, credit, honor, glory;* in NT *honorable consideration,* Lk. 14:10; *praise, glorification, honor,* Jn. 5:41, 44; Rom. 4:20; 15:7; *dignity, majesty,* Rom. 1:23; 2 Cor. 3:7; *a glorious manifestation, glorious working,* Jn. 11:40; 2 Pet. 1:3; pl. *dignitaries,* 2 Pet. 2:10; Jude 8; *glorification in a future state of bliss,* 2 Cor. 4:17; 2 Tim. 2:10; *pride, ornament,* 1 Cor. 11:15; 1 Thess. 2:20; *splendid array, pomp, magnificence,* Mt. 6:29; 19:28; *radiance, dazzling lustre,* Lk. 2:9; Acts 22:11 [1391] See *glory; honor; splendor.*

[1519] δοξάζω *doxazō* 61x *to think, suppose, judge; to extol, magnify,* Mt. 6:2; Lk. 4:15; in NT *to adore, worship,* Rom. 1:21; *to invest with dignity* or *majesty,* 2 Cor. 3:10; Heb. 5:5; *to signalize with a manifestation of dignity, excellence,* or *majesty,* Jn. 12:28; 13:32; *to glorify* by admission to a state of bliss, *to beatify,* Rom. 8:30 [1392] See *give honor; glorify; praise.*

[1520] Δορκάς *Dorkas* 2x *Dorcas,* pr. name, signifying a *gazelle* or *antelope,* Acts 9:36, 39* [1393]

[1521] δόσις *dosis* 2x pr. *giving, outlay;* Phil. 4:15; *a donation, gift,* Jas. 1:17* [1394]

[1522] δότης *dotēs* 1x *a giver,* 2 Cor. 9:7* [1395]

[1524] δουλαγωγέω *doulagōgeō* 1x pr. *to bring into slavery; to treat as a slave; to discipline into subjection,* 1 Cor. 9:27* [1396]

[1525] δουλεία *douleia* 5x *slavery, bondage, servile condition;* in NT met. with reference to degradation and unhappiness, Rom. 8:15, 21; Gal. 4:24; 5:1; Heb. 2:15* [1397]

[1526] δουλεύω *douleuō* 25x *to be a slave* or *servant; to be in slavery* or *subjection,* Jn. 8:33; Acts 7:7; Rom. 9:12; *to discharge the duties of a slave* or *servant,* Eph. 6:7; 1 Tim. 6:2; *to serve, be occupied in the service of, be devoted, subservient,* Mt. 6:24; Lk. 15:29; Acts 20:19; Rom. 14:18; 16:18; met. *to be enthralled, involved in a slavish service,* spiritually or morally, Gal. 4:9, 25; Tit. 3:3 [1398] See *(be) enslaved; serve.*

[1527] δούλη *doulē* 3x *female slave, bondmaid,* Lk. 1:38, 48; Acts 2:18* [1399]

[1528] δοῦλος *doulos* 126x *a male slave,* or *servant,* of various degrees, Mt. 8:9, et al. freq.; *a servitor, person of mean condition,* Phil. 2:7; fem. δούλη, *a female slave; a handmaiden,* Lk. 1:38, 48; Acts 2:18; δοῦλος, used figuratively, in a bad sense, *one involved in* moral or spiritual *thraldom,* Jn. 8:34; Rom. 6:17, 20; 1 Cor. 7:23; 2 Pet. 2:19; in a good sense, *a* devoted *servant* or *minister,* Acts 16:17; Rom. 1:1; *one pledged* or *bound to serve,* 1 Cor. 7:22; 2 Cor. 4:5 [1400, 1401] See *servant; slave.*

[1530] δουλόω *douloō* 8x *to reduce to servitude, enslave, oppress by retaining in servitude,* Acts 7:6; 2 Pet. 2:19; met. *to render subservient,* 1 Cor. 9:19; pass. *to be under restraint,* 1 Cor. 7:15; *to be in bondage,* spiritually or morally, Gal. 4:3; Tit. 2:3; *to become devoted to the service of,* Rom. 6:18, 22* [1402]

[1531] δοχή *dochē* 2x pr. *reception* of guests; in NT *a banquet, feast,* Lk. 5:29; 14:13 [1403]

[1532] δράκων *drakōn* 13x *a dragon* or *large serpent;* met. *the devil* or *Satan,* Rev. 12:3, 4, 7, 9, 13, 16, 17; 13:2, 4, 11; 16:13; 20:2 [1404] See *dragon.*

[1533] δράσσομαι *drassomai* 1x pr. *to grasp with the hand, clutch; to lay hold of, seize, take, catch,* 1 Cor. 3:19* [1405]

[1534] δραχμή *drachmē* 3x *a drachma,* an Attic silver coin of nearly the same value as the Roman *denarius,* Lk. 15:8, 9* [1406]

[1535] δρέπανον *drepanon* 8x *an instrument with a curved blade,* as *a sickle,* Mk. 4:29; Rev. 14:14, 15, 16, 17, 18, 19* [1407]

[1536] δρόμος *dromos* 3x *a course, race, race-course;* met. *course* of life or ministry, *career,* Acts 13:25; 20:24; 2 Tim. 4:7* [1408]

[1537] Δρούσιλλα *Drousilla* 1x *Drusilla,* pr. name, Acts 24:24* [1409]

[1538] δύναμαι *dynamai* 210x *to be able,* either intrinsically and absolutely, which is the ordinary signification; or, for specific reasons, Mt. 9:15; Lk. 16:2 [1410] See *ability; (be) able; can.*

[1539] δύναμις *dynamis* 119x *power; strength, ability,* Mt. 25:15; Heb. 11:11; *efficacy,* 1 Cor. 4:19, 20; Phil. 3:10; 1 Thess. 1:5; 2 Tim. 3:5; *energy,* Col. 1:29; 2 Tim. 1:7; *meaning, purport* of language, 1 Cor. 14:11; *authority,* Lk. 4:36; 9:1; *might, power, majesty,* Mt. 22:29; 24:30; Acts 3:12; Rom. 9:17; 2 Thess. 1:7; 2 Pet. 1:16; in NT *a manifestation* or *instance of power, mighty means,* Acts 8:10; Rom. 1:16; 1 Cor. 1:18, 24; ἡ δύναμις, *omnipotence,* Mt. 26:64; Lk. 22:69; Mt. 14:62; pl. *authorities,* Rom. 8:38; Eph. 1:21; 1 Pet. 3:22; *miraculous power,* Mk. 5:30; Lk. 1:35; 5:17; 6:19; 8:46; 24:49; 1 Cor. 2:4; *a miracle,* Mt. 11:20, 21, et al. freq.; *a worker of miracles,* 1 Cor. 12:28, 29; from the Hebrew αἱ δυνάμεις τῶν οὐρανῶν, *the heavenly luminaries,* Mt. 24:29; Mk. 13:25; Lk. 21:26; αἱ δυνάμεις, *the* spiritual *powers,* Mt. 14:2; Mk. 6:14 [1411] See *ability; miracle; power.*

[1540] δυναμόω *dynamoō* 2x *to strengthen, confirm,* Col. 1:11; Heb. 11:34* [1412]

[1541] δυνάστης *dynastēs* 3x *a potentate, sovereign; prince,* Lk. 1:52; 1 Tim. 6:15; *a person of rank and authority,* Acts 8:27* [1413]

[1542] δυνατέω *dynateō* 3x *to be powerful, mighty, to show one's self powerful,* 2 Cor. 9:8; 13:3; Rom. 14:4* [1414]

[1543] δυνατός *dynatos* 32x *able, having power, powerful, mighty;* δυνατὸς εἶναι, *to be able,* i.q. δύνασθαι, Lk. 14:31; Acts 11:17; ὁ δυνατός, *the Mighty One, God,* Lk. 1:49; τὸ δυνατόν, *power,* i.q. δύναμις, Rom. 9:22; *valid, powerful, efficacious,* 2 Cor. 10:4; *distinguished for rank, authority,* or *influence,* Acts 25:5; 1 Cor. 1:26; *distinguished for skill* or *excellence,* Lk. 24:19; Acts 7:22; Rom. 15:1; δυνατόν and δυνατά, *possible, capable of being done,* Mt. 19:26; 24:24 [1415] See *ability; mighty; possible.*

[1544] δύνω *dynō* 2x *to sink, go down, set* as the sun, Mk. 1:32; Lk. 4:40* [1416]

[1545] δύο *dyo* 135x *two,* Mt. 6:24; 21:38, 31, et al. freq.; οἱ δύο, *both,* Jn. 20:4; δύο ἢ τρεῖς, *two* or *three, some, a few,* Mt. 18:20; from the Hebrew, δύο δύο, *two and two,* Mk. 6:7, i.q. ἀνὰ δύο, Lk. 10:1, and κατὰ δύο, 1 Cor. 14:27 [1417] See *two.*

[1546] δυσβάστακτος *dysbastaktos* 1x *difficult* or *grievous to be borne, oppressive,* Lk. 11:46 [1419]

[1548] δυσεντέριον *dysenterion* 1x *dysentery,* Acts 28:8* [1420]

[1549] δυσερμήνευτος *dysermēneutos* 1x *difficult to be explained, hard to be understood,* Heb. 5:11* [1421]

[1550] δύσις *dysis* 1x *west,* Mk. 16:8 (shorter ending) [**]

[1551] δύσκολος *dyskolos* 1x pr. *peevish about food; hard to please, disagreeable;* in NT, *difficult,* Mk. 10:24* [1422]

[1552] δυσκόλως *dyskolōs* 3x *with difficulty, hardly,* Mt. 19:23; Mk. 10:23; Lk. 18:24* [1423]

[1553] δυσμή *dysmē* 5x *a sinking* or *setting;* pl. δυσμαί, *the setting of the sun;* hence, *the west,* Mt. 8:11; 24:27 [1424]

[1554] δυσνόητος *dysnoētos* 1x *hard to be understood,* 2 Pet. 3:16* [1425]

[1555] δυσφημέω *dysphēmeō* 1x pr. *to use ill words; to reproach, revile,* 1 Cor. 4:13* [987]

[1556] δυσφημία *dysphēmia* 1x *ill words; words of ill omen; reproach, contumely,* 2 Cor. 6:8* [1426]

[1557] δώδεκα *dōdeka* 75x *twelve,* Mt. 9:20; 10:1; οἱ δώδεκα, *the twelve* apostles, Mt. 26:14, 20 [1427] See *twelve.*

[1558] δωδέκατος *dōdekatos* 1x *the twelfth,* Rev. 21:20* [1428]

[1559] δωδεκάφυλον *dōdekaphylon* 1x *twelve tribes,* Acts 26:7* [1429]

[1560] δῶμα *dōma* 7x pr. *a house;* synec. *a roof,* Mt. 10:27; 24:17 [1430]

[1561] δωρεά *dōrea* 11x *a gift, free gift, benefit,* Jn. 4:10; Acts 2:38 [1431] See *gift.*

[1562] δωρεάν *dōrean* 9x *gratis, gratuitously, freely,* Mt. 10:8; Rom. 3:24; in NT *undeservedly, without cause,* Jn. 15:25; *in vain,* Gal. 2:21 [1432]

[1563] δωρέομαι *dōreomai* 3x *to give freely, grant,* Mk. 15:45; 2 Pet. 1:3, 4* [1433]

[1564] δώρημα *dōrēma* 2x *a gift, free gift,* Rom. 5:16; Jas. 1:17* [1434]

[1565] δῶρον *dōron* 19x *a gift, present,* Mt. 2:11; Eph. 2:8; Rev. 11:10; *an offering, sacrifice,* Mt. 5:23, 24; 8:4; δῶρον, σχ. ἐστι[ν], *it is consecrated to God,* Mt. 15:5; Mk. 7:11; *contribution* to the temple, Lk. 21:1, 4 [1435] See *gift; offering; present.*

[1568] ἔα *ea* 1x *Ha!* an expression of surprise or displeasure, Lk. 4:34* [1436]

[1569] ἐάν *ean* 350x *if,* ἐὰν μή, *except, unless;* also equivalent to ἀλλά, Gal. 2:16. Ἐάν, in NT as in the later Greek, is substituted for ἄν after relative words, Mt. 5:19. Tends to be an indicator for the subjunctive mood. [1437]

[1570] ἐάνπερ *eanper* 3x *if it be that, if indeed, if at all events,* Heb. 3:6, 14; 6:3 [1437 + 4007]

[1571] ἑαυτοῦ *heautou* 319x *himself, herself, itself,* Mt. 8:22; 12:26; 9:21; also used for the first and second persons, Rom. 8:23; Mt. 23:31; also equivalent to ἀλλήλων, Mk. 10:26; Jn. 12:19; ἀφ᾽ ἑαυτοῦ, ἀφ᾽ ἑαυτῶν, *of himself, themselves, voluntarily, spontaneously,* Lk. 12:57; 21:30; *of one's own will merely,* Jn. 5:19; δι᾽ ἑαυτοῦ, *of itself, in its own nature,* Rom. 14:14; ἐξ ἑαυτῶν, *of one's own self,* 2 Cor. 3:5; καθ᾽ ἑαυτόν, *by one's self, alone,* Acts 28:16; Jas. 2:17; παρ᾽ ἑαυτῷ, *with one's self, at home,* 1 Cor. 16:2; πρὸς ἑαυτόν, *to one's self, to one's home,* Lk. 24:12; Jn. 20:10; or, *with one's self,* Lk. 18:11 [1438]

[1572] ἐάω *eaō* 11x *to let, allow, permit, suffer to be done,* Mt. 24:43; Lk. 4:41; *to let be, let alone, desist from, stop,* Lk. 22:51; *to commit* a ship to the sea, *let* her *drive,* Acts 27:40 [1439] See *allow; let.*

[1573] ἑβδομήκοντα *hebdomēkonta* 5x *seventy,* indecl., Acts 7:14; οἱ ἑβδομήκοντα, *the seventy* disciples, Lk. 10:1, 17; Acts 23:23* [1440]

[1574] ἑβδομηκοντάκις *hebdomēkontakis* 1x indecl, *seventy times,* Mt. 18:22* [1441]

[1575] ἕβδομος *hebdomos* 9x *seventh,* Jn. 4:52; Heb. 4:4; Jude 14; Rev. 8:1 [1442]

[1576] Ἔβερ *Eber* 1x *Heber,* pr. name, indecl., Lk. 3:35* [1443]

[1578] Ἑβραῖος *Hebraios* 4x *a Hebrew, one descended from Abraham the Hebrew,* 2 Cor. 11:22; Phil. 3:5; in NT, *a Jew of Palestine, one speaking Aramaic,* opp. to Ἑλληνιστής, Acts 6:1* [1445]

[1579] Ἑβραΐς *Hebrais* 3x *the Hebrew* dialect, i.e., the Hebrew-Aramaic dialect of Palestine, Acts 21:40; 22:2; 26:14* [1446]

[1580] Ἑβραϊστί *Hebraisti* 7x *in Hebrew* or *Aramaic,* Jn. 5:2; 19:13, 17, 20; 20:16; Rev. 9:11; 16:16* [1447]

[1581] ἐγγίζω *engizō* 42x pr. *to cause to approach;* in NT intrans. *to approach, draw near,* Mt. 21:1; Lk. 18:35; met. *to be at hand,* Mt. 3:2; 4:17; μέχρι θανάτου ἐγγίζειν, *to be at the point of death,* Phil. 2:30; from Hebrew *to draw near* to God, *to offer* Him *reverence and worship,* Mt. 15:8; Heb. 7:19; Jas. 4:8; used of God, *to draw near* to men, *assist* them, *bestow favors* on them, Jas. 4:8 [1448] See *approach; come near; draw near.*

[1582] ἐγγράφω *engraphō* 3x *to engrave, inscribe,* Lk. 10:20; met. ἐγγεγραμμένος, *imprinted,* 2 Cor. 3:2, 3* [1449]

[1583] ἔγγυος *engyos* 1x *a guarantee, sponsor,* Heb. 7:22* [1450]

[1584] ἐγγύς *engys* 31x some view as an improper prep., followed by gen. or dat., *near,* as to place, Lk. 19:11; *close at hand,* Rom. 10:8; *near,* in respect of ready interposition, Phil. 4:5; *near,* as to time, Mt. 24:32, 33; *near* to God, as being in covenant with him, Eph. 2:13; οἱ ἐγγύς, *the people near* to God, the Jews, Eph. 2:17 [1451] See *near; nigh.*

[1586] ἐγείρω *egeirō* 144x *to excite, arouse, awaken,* Mt. 8:25; mid. *to awake,* Mt. 2:13, 20, 21; met. mid. *to rouse one's self* to a better course of conduct, Rom. 13:11; Eph. 5:14; *to raise* from the dead, Jn. 12:1; and mid. *to rise* from the dead, Mt. 27:52; Jn. 5:21; met. *to raise* as it were from the dead, 2 Cor. 4:14; *to raise up, cause to rise up* from a prone posture, Acts 3:7; and mid. *to rise up,* Mt. 17:7; *to restore to health,* Jas. 5:15; met. et seq. ἐπή, *to excite* to war; mid. *to rise up against,* Mt. 24:7; *to raise up again, rebuild,* Jn. 2:19, 20; *to raise up* from a lower place, *to draw up* or *out of* a ditch, Mt. 12:10; from Hebrew, *to raise up, to cause to arise* or *exist,* Acts 13:22, 23; mid. *to arise, exist, appear,* Mt. 3:9; 11:11 [1453] See *raise; rise up; waken.*

[1587] ἔγερσις *egersis* 1x pr. *the act of waking* or *rising up; resurrection resuscitation,* Mt. 27:53* [1454]

[1589] ἐγκαίνια *enkainia* 1x *initiation, consecration;* in NT *the feast of rededication,* an annual festival of eight days in the month Kislev, Jn. 10:22* [1456]

[1590] ἐγκαινίζω *enkainizō* 2x *to initiate, consecrate, dedicate, renovate; to institute,* Heb. 9:18; 10:20* [1457]

[1592] ἐγκαλέω *enkaleō* 7x can be followed by a dative, *to bring a charge against, accuse; to institute judicial proceedings,* Acts 19:38, 40; 23:28, 29; 26:2, 7; Rom. 8:33 [1458] See *accuse.*

[1593] ἐγκαταλείπω *enkataleipō* 10x *to leave, leave behind; to forsake, abandon,* Mt. 27:46; Mk. 15:34; Acts 2:27, 30; Rom. 9:29; 2 Cor. 4:9; 2 Tim. 4:10, 16; Heb. 10:25; 13:5* [1459] See *abandon; desert; forsake.*

[1594] ἐγκατοικέω *enkatoikeō* 1x *to dwell in,* or *among,* 2 Pet. 2:8* [1460]

[1595] ἐγκαυχάομαι *enkauchaomai* 1x *to boast in,* or *of,* 2 Thess. 1:4* [2620]

[1596] ἐγκεντρίζω *enkentrizō* 6x *to ingraft;* met. Rom. 11:17, 19, 23, 24* [1461]

[1598] ἔγκλημα *enklēma* 2x *an accusation, charge, crimination,* Acts 23:29; 25:16* [1462]

[1599] ἐγκομβόομαι *enkomboomai* 1x pr. *to put on a garment which is to be tied;* in NT *to put on, clothe one's self with;* met. 1 Pet. 5:5* [1463]

[1600] ἐγκοπή *enkopē* 1x alsn spelled ἐκκοπη, pr. *an incision,* e.g. a trench, etc., cut in the way of an enemy; *an impediment, hindrance,* 1 Cor. 9:12* [1464]

[1601] ἐγκόπτω *enkoptō* 5x pr. *to cut* or *strike in;* hence, *to impede, interrupt, hinder,* Rom. 15:22; 1 Thess. 2:18; 1 Pet. 3:7; Gal. 5:7; Acts 24:4* [1465]

[1602] ἐγκράτεια *enkrateia* 4x *self-control, continence, temperance,* Acts 24:25; Gal. 4:23; 2 Pet. 1:6* [1466]

[1603] ἐγκρατεύομαι *enkrateuomai* 2x *to possess the power of self-control* or *continence,* 1 Cor. 7:9; *to practise abstinence,* 1 Cor. 9:25* [1467]

[1604] ἐγκρατής *enkratēs* 1x *strong, stout; possessed of mastery; master of self,* Tit. 1:8* [1468]

[1605] ἐγκρίνω *enkrinō* 1x *to judge* or *reckon among, consider as belonging to, adjudge to the number of; class with, place in the same rank,* 2 Cor. 10:12* [1469]

[1606] ἐγκρύπτω *enkryptō* 2x *to conceal in* anything; *to mix, intermix,* Mt. 13:33; Lk. 13:21* [1470]

[1608] ἐγχρίω *enchriō* 1x *to rub in, anoint,* Rev. 3:18* [1472]

[1609] ἐγώ *egō* 2,666x *I,* gen., ἐμοῦ [μου], dat., ἐμοί [μοι], acc., ἐμέ [με] [1473, 1691, 1698, 1700, 2248, 2249, 2254, 2257, 3165, 3427, 3450] See *I.*

[1610] ἐδαφίζω *edaphizō* 1x pr. *to form a level and firm surface; to level with the ground, overthrow, raze, destroy,* Lk. 19:44* [1474]

[1611] ἔδαφος *edaphos* 1x pr. *a bottom, base;* hence, *the ground,* Acts 22:7* [1475]

[1612] ἑδραῖος *hedraios* 3x *sedentary;* met. *settled, steady, firm, steadfast, constant,* 1 Cor. 7:37; 15:58; Col. 1:23* [1476]

[1613] ἑδραίωμα *hedraiōma* 1x *a basis, foundation,* 1 Tim. 3:15* [1477]

[1614] Ἑζεκίας *Hezekias* 2x *Hezekiah,* pr. name, Mt. 1:9f.* [1478]

[1615] ἐθελοθρησκία *ethelothrēskia* 1x also spelled ἐθελοθρησκεια, *self-made religion,* Col. 2:23* [1479]

[1616] ἐθίζω *ethizō* 1x *to accustom;* pass. *to be customary,* Lk. 2:27* [1480]

[1617] ἐθνάρχης *ethnarchēs* 1x *a governor, chief* of any tribe or nation, 2 Cor. 11:32* [1481]

[1618] ἐθνικός *ethnikos* 4x *national;* in NT *Gentile, heathen, not Israelites,* Mt. 5:47; 6:7; 18:17; 3 Jn. 7* [1482]

[1619] ἐθνικῶς *ethnikōs* 1x *like a Gentile,* Gal. 2:14* [1483]

[1620] ἔθνος *ethnos* 162x *a multitude, company,* Acts 17:26; 1 Pet. 2:9; Rev. 21:24; *a nation, people,* Mt. 20:25; 21:43; pl. ἔθνη, from the Hebrew, *nations* or *people* as distinguished from the Jews, *the heathen, Gentiles,* Mt. 4:15; 10:5; Lk. 2:32 [1484] See *Gentile; nation.*

[1621] ἔθος *ethos* 12x *a custom, usage, habit,* Lk. 2:42; 22:39; *an institute, rite,* Lk. 1:9; Acts 6:14; 15:1 [1485] See *custom; habit.*

[1623] εἰ *ei* 502x *if,* Mt. 4:3, 6; 12:7; Acts 27:39, freq.; *since,* Acts 4:9; *whether,* Mk. 9:23; Acts 17:11; *that,* in certain expressions, Acts 26:8, 23; Heb. 7:15; by a suppression of the apodosis of a sentence, εἰ serves to express a wish; *O if! O that!* Lk. 19:42; 22:42; also a strong negation, Mk. 8:12; Heb. 3:11; 4:3; εἰ καί, *if even, though, although,* Lk. 18:4; εἰ μή, *unless, except,* Mt. 11:27; also equivalent to ἀλλά, *but,* Mt. 12:4; Mk. 13:32; Lk. 4:26, 27; εἰ μήτι, *unless perhaps, unless it be,* Lk. 9:13; εἴ τις, εἴ τι, pr. *if any one; whosoever, whatsoever,* Mt. 18:28. The syntax of this particle must be learned from the grammars. As an interrogative particle, *whether,* Acts 17:11; in NT as a mere note of interrogation, Lk. 22:49 [1487]

[1624] εἰδέα *eidea* 1x *appearance, face,* Mt. 28:3* [2397]

[1626] εἶδος *eidos* 5x *form, external appearance,* Lk. 3:22; 9:29; Jn. 5:37; *kind, species,* 1 Thess. 5:22; *sight, perception,* 2 Cor. 5:7* [1491]

[1627] εἰδωλεῖον *eidōleion* 1x *a heathen temple,* 1 Cor. 8:10* [1493]

[1628] εἰδωλόθυτος *eidōlothutos* 9x as a noun *meat offered to an idol,* Acts 15:29; 21:25; 1 Cor. 8:1, 4, 7, 10; 10:19; Rev. 2:14, 20* [1494]

[1629] εἰδωλολάτρης *eidōlolatrēs* 7x *an idolater, worshipper of idols,* 1 Cor. 5:10, 11; 6:9; 10:7; Eph. 5:5; Rev. 21:8; 22:15* [1496] See *idolater, idolatry.*

[1630] εἰδωλολατρία *eidōlolatria* 4x *idolatry, worship of idols,* 1 Cor. 10:14; Gal. 5:20; Col. 3:5; 1 Pet. 4:3* [1495] See *idolater, idolatry.*

[1631] εἴδωλον *eidōlon* 11x pr. *a form, shape, figure; image* or *statue;* hence, *an idol, image of a god,* Acts 7:41; *a heathen god,* 1 Cor. 8:4, 7; for εἰδωλόθυτον, *the flesh of victims sacrificed to idols,* Acts 15:20; Rom. 2:22; 1 Cor. 10:19; 12:12; 2 Cor. 6:16; 1 Thess. 1:9; 1 Jn. 5:21; Rev. 9:20* [1497] See *idol; image.*

[1632] εἰκῇ *eikē* 6x *without plan* or *system; without cause, rashly,* Col. 2:18; *to no purpose, in vain,* Rom. 13:4; 1 Cor. 15:2; Gal. 3:4 (2x); 4:11* [1500]

[1633] εἴκοσι *eikosi* 11x *twenty,* Lk. 14:31; Acts 27:28 [1501] See *twenty.*

[1634] εἴκω *eikō* 1x (1) *to yield, give place, submit,* Gal. 2:5. (2) the perfect form ἔοικα (2036) is from this same root and functions as a present, Jm 1:6, 23 (ἔοικεν, 3 sg). Some list it as a separate word, but see the discussion in Liddell and Scott* [1502]

[1635] εἰκών *eikōn* 23x *a material image, likeness, effigy,* Mt. 22:20; Mk. 12:16; *a representation, exact image,* 1 Cor. 11:7; 15:49; Rev. 13:14f.; *resemblance,* Rom. 1:23; 8:29; Col. 3:10; Heb. 10:1 [1504] See *image; liken.*

[1636] εἰλικρίνεια *eilikrineia* 3x *clearness, purity;* met. *sincerity, integrity, ingenuousness,* 1 Cor. 5:8; 2 Cor. 1:12; 2:17* [1505]

[1637] εἰλικρινής *eilikrinēs* 2x pr. *that which being viewed in the sunshine is found clear and pure;* met. *spotless, sincere, ingenuous,* Phil. 1:10; 2 Pet. 3:1* [1506]

[1639] εἰμί *eimi* 2,462x *to be, to exist,* Jn. 1:1; 17:5; Mt. 6:30; Lk. 4:25, freq.; ἐστί[ν], *it is possible, proper,* Heb. 9:5; a simple linking verb ("copula") to the subject and predicate, and therefore in itself affecting the force of the sentence only by its tense, mood, etc., Jn. 1:1; 15:1, freq.; it also forms a frequent circumlocution with the participles of the present and perfect of other verbs, Mt. 19:22; Mk. 2:6 [1488, 1498, 1510, 1511, 1526, 2070, 2071, 2252, 2258, 2277, 2468, 5600, 5607] See *be.*

[1641] εἵνεκεν *heineken* 2x see ἕνεκα, *on account of,* Lk. 4:18; Acts 28:20; 2 Cor. 3:10* [1752]

[1642] εἴπερ *eiper* 6x *if indeed, if it be so that, granted,* Rom. 8:9; 1 Cor. 15:15; *since indeed, since,* 2 Thess. 1:6; 1 Pet. 2:3; *although indeed,* 1 Cor. 8:5 [1512]

[1644] εἰρηνεύω *eirēneuō* 4x *to be at peace; to cultivate peace, concord,* or *harmony,* Mt. 9:50; Rom. 12:18; 2 Cor. 13:11; 1 Thess. 5:13* [1514]

[1645] εἰρήνη *eirēnē* 92x *peace,* Lk. 14:32; Acts 12:20; *tranquillity,* Lk. 11:21; Jn. 16:33; 1 Thess. 5:3; *concord, unity, love of peace,* Mt. 10:34; Lk. 12:51; meton. *the author of peace,* Eph. 2:14; from the Hebrew *every kind of blessing and good,* Lk. 1:79; 2:14, 29; meton. *a salutation expressive of good wishes, a benediction, blessing,* Mt. 10:13 [1515] See *peace.*

[1646] εἰρηνικός *eirēnikos* 2x *pertaining to peace; peaceable, disposed to peace,* Jas. 3:17; from the Hebrew, *profitable, blissful,* Heb. 12:11* [1516]

[1647] εἰρηνοποιέω *eirēnopoieō* 1x *to make peace,* Col. 1:20* [1517]

[1648] εἰρηνοποιός *eirēnopoios* 1x *a peace-maker, one who cultivates peace and concord,* Mt. 5:9* [1518]

[1650] εἰς *eis* 1,767x *to, as far as, to the extent of,* Mt. 2:23; 4:24; *until,* Jn. 13:1; *against,* Mt. 18:15; Lk. 12:10; *before, in the presence of,* Acts 22:30; *in order to, for, with a view to,* Mk. 1:38; *for the use* or *service of,* Jn. 6:9; Lk. 9:13; 1 Cor. 16:1; *with reference to,* 2 Cor. 10:13, 16; *in accordance with,* Mt. 12:41; Lk. 11:32; 2 Tim. 2:26; also equivalent to ἐν, Jn. 1:18; *by,* in forms of swearing, Mt. 5:35; from the Hebrew, εἶναι, γίνεσθαι εἰς, *to become, result in, amount to,* Mt. 19:5; 1 Cor. 4:3; εἰς τί, *why, wherefore,* Mt. 26:8 [1519]

[1651] εἷς *heis* 345x numeral *one,* Mt. 10:29, freq.; *only,* Mk. 12:6; *one* virtually by union, Mt. 19:5, 6; Jn. 10:30; *one and the same,* Lk. 12:52; Rom. 3:30; *one* in respect of office and standing, 1 Cor. 3:8; equivalent to τις, *a certain one,* Mt. 8:19; 16:14; *a, an,* Mt. 21:19; Jas. 4:13; εἷς ἕκαστος, *each one, every one,* Lk. 4:40; Acts 2:3; εἷς τὸν ἕνα, *one another,* 1 Thess. 5:11; εἷς καὶ εἷς, *the one- and the other,* Mt. 20:21; εἷς καθ᾽ εἷς and ὁδὲ καθ᾽ εἷς, *one by one, one after another, in succession,* Mk. 14:19; Jn. 8:9; as an ordinal, *first,* Mt. 28:1 [1520, 3391] See *one.*

[1652] εἰσάγω *eisagō* 11x *to lead* or *bring in, introduce, conduct* or *usher in* or *to* a place or person, Lk. 2:27; 14:21; 22:54; Jn. 18:16; Acts 9:8; 21:28f., 37; Heb. 1:6 [1521] See *bring in.*

[1653] εἰσακούω *eisakouō* 5x *to hear* or *hearken to, to heed,* 1 Cor. 14:21; *to listen to* the prayers of any one, *accept one's petition,* Mt. 6:7; Lk. 1:13; Acts 10:31; Heb. 5:7* [1522]

[1654] εἰσδέχομαι *eisdechomai* 1x *to admit; to receive into favor, receive kindly, accept with favor,* 2 Cor. 6:17* [1523]

[1655] εἴσειμι *eiseimi* 4x *to go in, enter,* Acts 3:3; 21:18, 26; Heb. 9:6* [1524]

[1656] εἰσέρχομαι *eiserchomai* 194x *to go* or *come in, enter,* Mt. 7:13; 8:5, 8; spc. *to enter* by force, *break in,* Mk. 3:27; Acts 20:29; met. with εἰς κόσμον, *to begin to exist, come into existence,* Rom. 5:12; 2 Jn. 7; or, *to make one's appearance on earth,* Heb. 10:5; *to enter into* or *take possession of,* Lk. 22:3; Jn. 13:27; *to enter into, enjoy, partake of,* Mt. 19:23, 24; *to enter into* any one's labor, *be* his *successor,* Jn. 4:38; *to fall into, be placed in* certain circumstances, Mt. 26:41; *to be put into,* Mt. 15:11; Acts 11:8; *to present* *one's self before,* Acts 19:30; met. *to arise, spring up,* Lk. 9:46; from the Hebrew, εἰσέρχεσθαι καὶ ἐξέρχεσθαι, *to go in and out, to live, discharge the ordinary functions of life,* Acts 1:21 [1525] See *enter.*

[1657] εἰσκαλέομαι *eiskaleomai* 1x *to call in; to invite in,* Acts 10:23* [1528]

[1658] εἴσοδος *eisodos* 5x *a place of entrance; the act of entrance,* Heb. 10:19; *admission, reception,* 1 Thess. 1:9; 2 Pet. 1:11; *a coming, approach, access,* 1 Thess. 2:1; *entrance* upon office, *commencement* or *beginning* of ministry, Acts 13:24* [1529]

[1659] εἰσπηδάω *eispēdaō* 1x *to leap* or *spring in, rush in eagerly,* Acts 16:29* [1530]

[1660] εἰσπορεύομαι *eisporeuomai* 18x *to go* or *come in, enter,* Mk. 1:21; 5:40; *to come to, visit,* Acts 28:30; *to be put in,* Mt. 15:17; Mk. 7:15, 18, 19; *to intervene,* Mk. 4:19 [1531] See *enter; go in.*

[1661] εἰστρέχω *eistrechō* 1x *to run in,* Acts 12:14* [1532]

[1662] εἰσφέρω *eispherō* 8x *to bring in* or *into,* Lk. 5:18, 19; 1 Tim. 6:7; Heb. 13:11; *to bring to* the ears of any one, *to announce,* Acts 17:20; *to lead into,* Mt. 6:13; Lk. 11:4; *drag in,* Lk. 12:11* [1533]

[1663] εἶτα *eita* 15x *then, afterwards,* Mk. 4:17, 28; Lk. 8:12; *in the next place,* 1 Cor. 12:28; *besides, furthermore,* Heb. 12:9 [1534]

[1664] εἴτε *eite* 65x *whether,* Rom. 12:6, 7, 8; 1 Cor. 3:22; 2 Cor. 1:6; 1 Thess. 5:10 [1535]

[1665] εἴωθα *eiōtha* 4x perfect of an obsolete present ἔθω, pluperfect is εἰώθειν, *to be accustomed, to be usual,* Mt. 27:15; Mk. 10:1; Lk. 4:16; Acts 17:2* [1486]

[1666] ἐκ *ek* 915x ἐξ before vowels, with genitive, *from, out of,* a place, Mt. 2:15; 3:17; *of, from, out of,* denoting origin or source, Mt. 1:3; 21:19; *of, from* some material, Mt. 3:9; Rom. 9:21; *of, from, among,* partitively, Mt. 6:27; 21:31; Mk. 9:17; *from,* denoting cause, Rev. 8:11; 17:6; means or instrument, Mt. 12:33, 37; *by, through,* denoting the author or efficient cause, Mt. 1:18; Jn. 10:32; *of,* denoting the distinguishing mark of a class, Rom. 2:8; Gal. 3:7; of time, *after,* 2 Cor. 4:6; Rev. 17:11; *from, after, since,* Mt. 19:12; Lk. 8:27; *for, with,* denoting a rate of payment, price, Mt. 20:2; 27:7; *at,* denoting position, Mt. 20:21, 23; after passive verbs, *by, of, from,* marking the agent, Mt. 15:5; Mk. 7:11; forming with certain words a periphrasis for an adverb, Mt. 26:42, 44; Mk. 6:51; Lk. 23:8; put after words of freeing, Rom. 7:24; 2 Cor. 1:10; used partitively after verbs of eating, drinking, etc., Jn. 6:26; 1 Cor. 9:7 [1537]

[1667] ἕκαστος *hekastos* 82x *each (one), every (one) separately,* Mt. 16:27; Lk. 13:15 [1538] See *each; every.*

[1668] ἑκάστοτε *hekastote* 1x *always,* 2 Pet. 1:15* [1539]

[1669] ἑκατόν *hekaton* 17x *one hundred,* Mt. 13:8; Mk. 4:8 [1540] See *hundred.*

[1670] ἑκατονταετής *hekatontaetēs* 1x *a hundred years old,* Rom. 4:19* [1541]

[1671] ἑκατονταπλασίων *hekatontaplasiōn* 3x *a hundredfold,* Mt. 19:29; Mk. 10:30; Lk. 8:8* [1542]

[1672] ἑκατοντάρχης *hekatontarchēs* 20x the text varies between this form and ἑκατόνταρχος, *commander of a hundred men, a centurion,* Lk. 23:47; Acts 10:1; 27:1ff. [1543] See *centurion.*

[1674] ἐκβαίνω *ekbainō* 1x *to go forth, go out of,* Heb. 11:15* [1831]

[1675] ἐκβάλλω *ekballō* 81x pluperfect, ἐκβεβλήκειν, *to cast out, eject by force,* Mt. 15:17; Acts 27:38; *to expel, force away,* Lk. 4:29; Acts 7:58; *to refuse,* Jn. 6:37; *to extract,* Mt. 7:4; *to reject with contempt, despise, contemn,* Lk. 6:22; in NT *to send forth, send out,* Mt. 9:38; Lk. 10:2; *to send away, dismiss,* Mt. 9:25; Mk. 1:12; met. *to spread abroad,* Mt. 12:20; *to bring out,* *produce,* Mt. 12:35; 13:52 [1544] See *drive out; eject; expel.*

[1676] ἔκβασις *ekbasis* 2x *a way out, egress;* hence, *result, issue,* Heb. 13:7; *means of clearance* or *successful endurance,* 1 Cor. 10:13* [1545]

[1678] ἐκβολή *ekbolē* 1x *a casting out;* especially, *a throwing overboard* of a cargo, Acts 27:18* [1546]

[1681] ἔκγονος *ekgonos* 1x *born of, descended from;* as a noun ἔκγονα, *descendants, grandchildren,* 1 Tim. 5:4* [1549]

[1682] ἐκδαπανάω *ekdapanaō* 1x *to expend, consume, exhaust,* 2 Cor. 12:15* [1550]

[1683] ἐκδέχομαι *ekdechomai* 6x pr. *to receive from* another; *to expect, look for,* Acts 17:16; *to wait for, to wait,* 1 Cor. 11:33; 16:11; Heb. 11:10; 10:13; Jas. 5:7* [1551]

[1684] ἔκδηλος *ekdēlos* 1x *clearly manifest, evident,* 2 Tim. 3:9* [1552]

[1685] ἐκδημέω *ekdēmeō* 3x pr. *to be absent from home, go abroad, travel;* hence, *to be absent from* any place or person, 2 Cor. 5:6, 8, 9* [1553]

[1686] ἐκδίδωμι *ekdidōmi* 4x middle, *to give out, to give up; to put out* at interest; in NT *to let out* to tenants, Mt. 21:33, 41; Lark 12:1; Lk. 20:9* [1554]

[1687] ἐκδιηγέομαι *ekdiēgeomai* 2x *to narrate fully, detail,* Acts 13:14; 15:3* [1555]

[1688] ἐκδικέω *ekdikeō* 6x pr. *to execute right and justice; to punish,* 2 Cor. 10:6; Rev. 6:10; 19:2; in NT *to right, avenge* a person, Lk. 18:3, 5; Rom. 12:9* [1556] See *avenge; punish, punishment; seek justice; vengeance.*

[1689] ἐκδίκησις *ekdikēsis* 9x *vengeance, punishment, retributive justice,* Lk. 21:22; Rom. 12:19; 2 Cor. 7:11; 1 Pet. 2:14; ἐκδίκησιν ποιεῖν, *to vindicate, avenge,* Lk. 18:7, 8; διδόναι ἐκδίκησιν, *to inflict vengeance,* Acts 7:24; 2 Thess. 1:8; Heb. 10:30* [1557]

[1690] ἔκδικος *ekdikos* 2x *an avenger, one who inflicts punishment,* Rom. 13:4; 1 Thess. 4:6* [1558]

[1691] ἐκδιώκω *ekdiōkō* 1x pr. *to chase away, drive out;* in NT *to persecute, vex, harass,* 1 Thess. 2:15* [1559]

[1692] ἔκδοτος *ekdotos* 1x *delivered up,* Acts 2:23* [1560]

[1693] ἐκδοχή *ekdochē* 1x *a looking for, expectation,* Heb. 10:27* [1561]

[1694] ἐκδύω *ekdyō* 6x pr. *to go out from; to take off, strip, unclothe,* Mt. 27:28, 31; mid. *to lay aside, to put off,* Mk. 15:20; Lk. 10:30; 2 Cor. 5:3f.* [1562]

[1695] ἐκεῖ *ekei* 105x *there, in that place,* Mt. 2:13, 15; *to that place,* Mt. 2:22; 17:20 [1563]

[1696] ἐκεῖθεν *ekeithen* 37x *from there,* Mt. 4:21; 5:26 [1564]

[1697] ἐκεῖνος *ekeinos* 265x demonstrative adjective or noun, *that, this, he,* etc., Mt. 17:27; 10:14; 2 Tim. 4:8; in contrast with οὗτος, referring to the former of two things previously mentioned, Lk. 18:14 [1565]

[1698] ἐκεῖσε *ekeise* 2x *there, at that place,* Acts 21:3; 22:5* [1566]

[1699] ἐκζητέω *ekzēteō* 7x *to seek out, investigate diligently, scrutinize,* 1 Pet. 1:10; *to ask for, beseech earnestly,* Heb. 12:17; *to seek diligently* or *earnestly after,* Acts 15:17; Rom. 3:11; Heb. 10:6; from the Hebrew, *to require, exact, demand,* Lk. 11:50, 51; Heb. 12:07* [1567]

[1700] ἐκζήτησις *ekzētēsis* 1x *useless speculation,* 1 Tim. 1:4* [2214]

[1701] ἐκθαμβέω *ekthambeō* 4x pas., *to be amazed, astonished, awe-struck,* Mk. 9:15; 14:33; 16:5, 6* [1568]

[1703] ἐκθαυμάζω *ekthaumazō* 1x *to wonder at, wonder greatly,* Mk. 12:17* [2296]

[1704] ἔκθετος *ekthetos* 1x *exposed, cast out, abandoned,* Acts 7:18* [1570]

[1705] ἐκκαθαίρω *ekkathairō* 2x *to cleanse thoroughly, purify,* 2 Tim. 2:21; *to purge out, eliminate,* 1 Cor. 5:7* [1571]

[1706] ἐκκαίω *ekkaiō* 1x pas., *to blaze out, to be inflamed,* Rom. 1:27* [1572]

[1708] ἐκκεντέω *ekkenteō* 2x *to stab, pierce deeply,* Jn. 19:37; Rev. 1:7* [1574]

[1709] ἐκκλάω *ekklaō* 3x *to break off,* pas., *be broken,* Rom. 11:17, 19, 20* [1575]

[1710] ἐκκλείω *ekkleiō* 2x *to shut out, exclude; to shut of, separate, insulate;* Gal. 4:17; *to leave no place for, eliminate,* Rom. 3:27* [1576]

[1711] ἐκκλησία *ekklēsia* 114x *a popular assembly,* Acts 19:32, 39, 41; in NT *the congregation* of the children of Israel, Acts 7:38; transferred to the Christian body, of which the congregation of Israel was a figure, *the Church,* 1 Cor. 12:28; Col. 1:18; a local portion of the *Church,* a local *church,* Rom. 16:1; *a* Christian *congregation,* 1 Cor. 14:4 [1577] See *church.*

[1712] ἐκκλίνω *ekklinō* 3x *to deflect, deviate,* Rom. 3:12; *to decline* or *turn away from, avoid,* Rom. 16:17; 1 Pet. 3:11 [1578]

[1713] ἐκκολυμβάω *ekkolymbaō* 1x *to swim out* to land, Acts 27:42* [1579]

[1714] ἐκκομίζω *ekkomizō* 1x *to carry out, bring out;* especially, *to carry out* a corpse for burial, Lk. 7:12* [1580]

[1716] ἐκκόπτω *ekkoptō* 10x *to cut out; to cut off,* Mt. 3:10; 5:30; met. *to cut off* an occasion, *remove, prevent,* 2 Cor. 11:12; *to render ineffectual,* Mt. 7:19; 18:8; Lk. 3:9; 12:7, 9; Rom. 11:22, 24; 1 Pet. 3:7* [1581] See *cut.*

[1717] ἐκκρεμάννυμι *ekkremannymi* 1x mid., *to hang upon* a speaker, *fondly listen to, be earnestly attentive,* Lk. 19:48* [1582]

[1718] ἐκλαλέω *eklaleō* 1x *to speak out; to tell, utter, divulge,* Acts 23:22* [1583]

[1719] ἐκλάμπω *eklampō* 1x *to shine out* or *forth,* Mt. 13:43* [1584]

[1720] ἐκλανθάνομαι *eklanthanomai* 1x *to make to forget; to forget entirely,* Heb. 12:5* [1585]

[1721] ἐκλέγομαι *eklegomai* 22x *to pick out;* in NT *to choose, select,* Lk. 6:13; 10:42; in NT *to choose out* as the recipients of special favor and privilege, Acts 13:17; 1 Cor. 1:27 [1586] See *choose; elect; set apart.*

[1722] ἐκλείπω *ekleipō* 4x *to fail, die out,* Lk. 22:32; *to come to an end,* Heb. 1:12; *to be defunct,* Lk. 16:9; 23:45* [1587]

[1723] ἐκλεκτός *eklektos* 22x *chosen out, selected;* in NT *chosen* as a recipient of special privilege, *elect,* Col. 3:12; *specially beloved,* Lk. 23:35; *possessed of prime excellence, exalted,* 1 Tim. 5:21; *choice, precious,* 1 Pet. 2:4, 6 [1588] See *chosen; elect; set apart.*

[1724] ἐκλογή *eklogē* 7x *the act of choosing out, election;* in NT *election* to privilege by divine grace, Rom. 9:11; 11:5, 28; 1 Thess. 1:4; 2 Pet. 1:10; ἡ ἐκλογή, *the elect,* Rom. 11:7; ἐκλογῆς, equivalent to ἐκλεκτόν, by Hebraism, Acts 9:15* [1589]

[1725] ἐκλύω *eklyō* 5x *to be weary, exhausted, faint,* Mt. 15:32; Mk. 8:3; Gal. 6:9; *to lose courage, to faint,* Heb. 12:3, 5* [1590]

[1726] ἐκμάσσω *ekmassō* 5x *to wipe off; to wipe dry,* Lk. 7:38, 44; Jn. 11:2; 12:3; 13:5* [1591]

[1727] ἐκμυκτηρίζω *ekmyktērizō* 2x *to mock, deride, scoff at,* Lk. 16:14; 23:35* [1592]

[1728] ἐκνεύω *ekneuō* 1x pr. *to swim out, to escape by swimming;* hence, generally, *to escape, get clear of* a place, Jn. 5:13; though ἐκνεύσας, in this place, may be referred to ἐκνεύω, *to deviate, withdraw** [1593]

[1729] ἐκνήφω *eknēphō* 1x pr. *to awake sober after intoxication;* met. *to shake off mental bewilderment, to wake up* from delusion and folly, 1 Cor. 15:34* [1594]

[1730] ἑκούσιος *hekousios* 1x *voluntary, spontaneous,* Phlm. 14* [1595]

[1731] ἑκουσίως *hekousiōs* 2x *voluntarily, spontaneously,* Heb. 10:26; 1 Pet. 5:2* [1596]

[1732] ἔκπαλαι *ekpalai* 2x *of old, long since,* 2 Pet. 2:3; 3:5* [1597]

[1733] ἐκπειράζω *ekpeirazō* 4x *to tempt, put to the test,* Mt. 4:7; Lk. 4:12; 1 Cor. 10:9; *to try, sound,* Lk. 10:25* [1598]

[1734] ἐκπέμπω *ekpempō* 2x *to send out,* or *away,* Acts 13:4; 17:10* [1599]

[1735] ἐκπερισσῶς *ekperissōs* 1x *exceedingly, vehemently,* Mk. 14:31* [1537 + 4053]

[1736] ἐκπετάννυμι *ekpetannymi* 1x pluperfect, ἐκπεπετάκειν, *to stretch forth, expand, extend,* Rom. 10:21* [1600]

[1737] ἐκπηδάω *ekpēdaō* 1x *to leap forth, rush out,* Acts 14:14* [1530]

[1738] ἐκπίπτω *ekpiptō* 10x *to fall off* or *from,* Acts 12:7; 27:32; met. *to fall from, forfeit, lose,* Gal. 5:4; 2 Pet. 3:17; *to be cast ashore,* Acts 27:17, 26, 29; *to fall to the ground, be fruitless, ineffectual,* Rom. 9:6; *to cease, come to an end,* Jas. 1:11; 1 Pet. 1:24* [1601] See *fail; fall; fall away.*

[1739] ἐκπλέω *ekpleō* 3x *to sail out of* or *from a place,* Acts 15:39; 18:18; 20:6* [1602]

[1740] ἐκπληρόω *ekplēroō* 1x *to fill out, complete, fill up;* met. *to fulfil, perform, accomplish,* Acts 13:33* [1603]

[1741] ἐκπλήρωσις *ekplērōsis* 1x pr. *a filling up, completion;* hence, *a fulfilling, accomplishment,* Acts 21:26* [1604]

[1742] ἐκπλήσσω *ekplēssō* 13x pr. *to strike out of;* hence, *to strike out of* one's wits, *to astound, amaze;* pass., *overwhelmed,* Mt. 7:28; 13:54 [1605] See *(be) amazed; astonish; astound.*

[1743] ἐκπνέω *ekpneō* 3x *to breathe out; to expire, die,* Mk. 15:37, 39; Lk. 23:46* [1606]

[1744] ἐκπορεύομαι *ekporeuomai* 33x *to go from* or *out of* a place, *depart from,* Mk. 11:19; 13:1; *to be voided,* Mk. 7:19; *to be cast out,* Mt. 17:21; *to proceed from, be spoken,* Mt. 4:4; 15:11; *to burst forth,* Rev. 4:5; *to be spread abroad,* Lk. 4:37; *to flow out,* Rev. 22:1; from the Hebrew, ἐκπορεύομαι καὶ εἰσπορεύομαι. see εἰσέρχομαι, Acts 9:28 [1607] See *come out; go out.*

[1745] ἐκπορνεύω *ekporneuō* 1x *to be given to fornication, indulge in immorality,* Jude 7* [1608]

[1746] ἐκπτύω *ekptyō* 1x lit., *to spit out*; met. *to reject,* Gal. 4:14* [1609]

[1748] ἐκριζόω *ekrizoō* 4x *to root up, eradicate, pull out by the roots,* Mt. 13:29; 15:13; Lk. 17:6; Jude 12* [1610]

[1749] ἔκστασις *ekstasis* 7x pr. *a displacement;* hence, *a displacement of the mind from its ordinary state and self-possession; amazement, astonishment,* Mk. 5:42; *excess of fear; fear, terror,* Mk. 16:8; Lk. 5:26; Acts 3:10; in NT *an ecstasy, a trance,* Acts 10:10; 11:5; 22:17* [1611]

[1750] ἐκστρέφω *ekstrephō* 1x pr. *to turn out of, to turn inside out;* hence, *to change entirely;* in NT pass. *to be perverted,* Tit. 3:11* [1612]

[1752] ἐκταράσσω *ektarassō* 1x *to disturb, disquiet, throw into confusion,* Acts 16:20* [1613]

[1753] ἐκτείνω *ekteinō* 16x *to stretch out,* Mt. 8:3; 12:13; *to lay* hands on any one, Lk. 22:53; *to exert* power and energy, Acts 4:30; *to cast out, let down* an anchor, Acts 27:30 [1614] See *stretch out.*

[1754] ἐκτελέω *ekteleō* 2x *to bring to an end, to finish, complete,* Lk. 14:29, 30* [1615]

[1755] ἐκτένεια *ekteneia* 1x pr. *extension;* in NT *intenseness, intentness;* ἐν ἐκτενείᾳ, *intently, perseverance, earnestness,* Acts 26:7* [1616]

[1756] ἐκτενής *ektenēs* 1x pr. *extended;* met. *intense, earnest, fervent, eager,* 1 Pet. 4:8* [1618]

[1757] ἐκτενῶς *ektenōs* 3x *intensely, fervently, earnestly,* Lk. 22:44; Acts 12:5; 1 Pet. 1:22* [1617, 1619]

[1758] ἐκτίθημι *ektithēmi* 4x pr. *to place outside, put forth; to expose* an infant, Acts 7:21; met. *to set forth, declare, explain,* Acts 11:4; 18:26; 28:23* [1620]

[1759] ἐκτινάσσω *ektinassō* 4x *to shake out, shake off,* Mt. 10:14; Mk. 6:11; Acts 13:51; 18:6* [1621]

[1760] ἐκτός *ektos* 8x also functions as an improper prep. (4x), *without, on the outside;* τὸ ἐκτός, *the exterior, outside,* Mt. 23:26; met. *besides,* Acts 26:22; 1 Cor. 15:27; ἐκτὸς εἰ μή, *unless, except,* 1 Cor. 14:5 [1622]

[1761] ἕκτος *hektos* 14x *sixth,* Mt. 20:5; 27:45 [1623] See *sixth.*

[1762] ἐκτρέπω *ektrepō* 5x mid. and pas., *to turn out* or *aside,* Heb. 12:13; *to turn aside* or *away, swerve,* 1 Tim. 1:6; 5:15; 2 Tim. 4:4; *to turn from, avoid,* 1 Tim. 6:20* [1624]

[1763] ἐκτρέφω *ektrephō* 2x *to nourish, promote health and strength,* Eph. 5:29; *to bring up, educate,* Eph. 6:4* [1625]

[1765] ἔκτρωμα *ektrōma* 1x *an abortion, baby prematurely born,* 1 Cor. 15:8* [1626]

[1766] ἐκφέρω *ekpherō* 8x *to bring forth, carry out,* Lk. 15:22; Acts 5:15; 1 Tim. 6:7; *to carry out* for burial, Acts 5:6, 9, 10; *to produce, yield,* Mk. 8:23; Heb. 6:8* [1627]

[1767] ἐκφεύγω *ekpheugō* 8x intrans. *to flee out, to make an escape,* Acts 16:27; 19:16; trans. *to escape, avoid,* Lk. 21:36; Rom. 2:3 [1628]

[1768] ἐκφοβέω *ekphobeō* 1x *to terrify,* 2 Cor. 10:9* [1629]

[1769] ἔκφοβος *ekphobos* 2x *frightened, horrified,* Mk. 9:6; Heb. 12:21* [1630]

[1770] ἐκφύω *ekphyō* 2x lit. *to cause to grow, to generate; to put forth, shoot,* Mt. 24:32; Mk. 13:28* [1631]

[1772] ἐκχέω *ekcheō* 16x also formed as ἐκχύννομαι (11x), *to pour out,* Rev. 16:1, 2, 3; *to shed* blood, Mt. 26:28; Mk. 14:24; pass. *to gush out,* Acts 1:18; *to spill, scatter,* Mt. 9:17; Jn. 2:15; met. *to give largely, bestow liberally,* Acts 2:17, 18, 33; 10:45; pass. *to rush headlong* into anything, *be abandoned to,* Jude 11 [1632] See *pour out; shed.*

[1773] ἐκχύννομαι *ekchunnomai* 11x some list as the active ἐκχύννω; see ἐκχέω (*1772*) [1632] See *pour out; shed.*

[1774] ἐκχωρέω *ekchōreō* 1x *to go out, depart from, flee,* Lk. 21:21* [1633]

[1775] ἐκψύχω *ekpsychō* 3x *to expire, give up one's spirit,* Acts 5:5, 10; 12:23* [1634]

[1776] ἑκών *hekōn* 2x *willing, voluntary,* Rom. 8:20; 1 Cor. 9:17* [1635]

[1777] ἐλαία *elaia* 15x *an olive tree,* Mt. 21:1; 24:3; *an olive, fruit of the olive tree,* Jas. 3:12, ὄρος τῶν ἐλαιῶν, *the Mount of Olives,* Mt. 21:1 [1636] See *olive.*

[1778] ἔλαιον *elaion* 11x *olive oil, oil,* Mt. 25:3, 4, 8; Mk. 6:13 [1637] See *oil; olive oil.*

[1779] ἐλαιών *elaiōn* 1x *an olive garden;* in NT the mount *Olivet,* Lk. 19:29; 21:37; Acts 1:12* [1638]

[1780] Ἐλαμίτης *Elamitēs* 1x *an Elamite; an inhabitant of Elam,* a province of Persia, Acts 2:9* [1639]

[1781] ἐλάσσων *elassōn* 4x ἐλάττων (1784) is the Attic form of this word. Twice it is used with σσ (Jn. 2:10; Rom. 9:12) and twice with ττ (1 Tim. 5:9; Heb. 7:7). It is used as the comparative of μικρός, *less; less* in age, *younger,* Rom. 9:12; *less* in dignity, *inferior,* Heb. 7:7; *less* in quality, *inferior; worse,* Jn. 2:10; 1 Tim. 5:9* [1640]

[1782] ἐλαττονέω *elattoneō* 1x trans. *to make less;* intrans. *to be less, inferior; to have too little, want, lack,* 2 Cor. 8:15* [1641]

[1783] ἐλαττόω *elattoō* 3x *to make less* or *inferior,* Heb. 2:7; pass. *to be made less* or *inferior,* Heb. 2:9; *to decline* in importance, Jn. 3:30* [1642]

[1785] ἐλαύνω *elaunō* 5x *to drive, urge forward, spur on,* Lk. 8:29; Jas. 3:4; 2 Pet. 2:17; *to impel* a vessel by oars, *to row,* Mk. 6:48; Jn. 6:19* [1643]

[1786] ἐλαφρία *elaphria* 1x *lightness* in weight; hence, *lightness of mind, levity,* 2 Cor. 1:17* [1644]

[1787] ἐλαφρός *elaphros* 2x *light, not heavy,* Mt. 11:30; 2 Cor. 4:17* [1645]

[1788] ἐλάχιστος *elachistos* 14x used as the superlative of μικρός, *smallest, least,* Mt. 2:6; 5:19 [1646, 1647] See *least.*

[1789] Ἐλεάζαρ *Eleazar* 2x *Eleazar,* pr. name, indecl., Mt. 1:15* [1648]

[1790] ἐλεάω *eleaō* 4x see ἐλεέω, *have mercy on,* Rom. 9:16; 12:8; Jude 22, 23* [1653]

[1791] ἐλεγμός *elegmos* 1x *reproof,* 2 Tim. 3:16, a later equivalent to ἔλεγχος* [1650]

[1792] ἔλεγξις *elenxis* 1x *reproof, rebuke,* 2 Pet. 2:16* [1649]

[1793] ἔλεγχος *elenchos* 1x pr. *a trial in order to proof, a proof;* meton. *a certain persuasion,* Heb. 11:1* [1650]

[1794] ἐλέγχω *elenchō* 17x *to put to proof, to test; to convict,* Jn. 8:46; Jas. 2:9; *to refute, confute,* 1 Cor. 14:24; Tit. 1:9; *to detect, lay bare, expose,* Jn. 3:20; Eph. 5:11, 13; *to reprove, rebuke,* Mt. 18:15; Lk. 3:19; 1 Tim. 5:20; *to discipline, chastise,* Heb. 12:5; Rev. 3:19; pass. *to experience conviction,* Jn. 3:20; 1 Cor. 14:24 [1651] See *rebuke; refute.*

[1795] ἐλεεινός *eleeinos* 2x *pitiable, wretched, miserable,* 1 Cor. 15:19; Rev. 3:17* [1652]

[1796] ἐλεέω *eleeō* 28x also formed as ἐλεάω 4x, *to pity, have compassion on;* pass. *to receive pity, experience compassion,* Mt. 5:7; 9:27; 15:22; *to be gracious to* any one, *show gracious favor and saving mercy towards;* pass. *to be an object of gracious favor and saving mercy,* Rom. 11:30, 31; spc. *to obtain pardon and forgiveness,* 1 Tim. 1:13, 16 [1653] See *mercy; pity.*

[1797] ἐλεημοσύνη *eleēmosynē* 13x *pity, compassion;* in NT *an act of kindness, alms, almsgiving,* Mt. 6:2, 3, 4; Lk. 11:41 [1654] See *alms; gift.*

[1798] ἐλεήμων *eleēmōn* 2x *merciful, pitiful, compassionate,* Mt. 5:7; Heb. 2:17* [1655]

[1799] ἔλεος *eleos* 27x *pity, mercy, compassion,* Mt. 9:13; 12:7; Lk. 1:50, 78; meton. *benefit* which results from compassion, *kindness, mercies, blessing,* Lk. 1:54, 58, 72; 10:37; Rom. 9:23 [1656] See *compassion; mercy.*

[1800] ἐλευθερία *eleutheria* 11x *liberty, freedom,* 1 Cor. 10:29; Gal. 2:4 [1657] See *freedom.*

[1801] ἐλεύθερος *eleutheros* 23x *free, in a state of freedom* as opposed to slavery, 1 Cor. 12:13; Gal. 3:28; *free, exempt,* Mt. 17:26; 1 Cor. 7:39; *unrestricted, unfettered,* 1 Cor. 9:1; *free* from the dominion of sin, etc., Jn. 8:36; Rom. 6:20; *free* in the possession of Gospel privileges, 1 Pet. 2:16 [1658] See *free; freedom; independent.*

[1802] ἐλευθερόω *eleutheroō* 7x *to free, set free,* Jn. 8:32, 36; Rom. 6:18, 22; 8:2, 21; Gal. 5:1* [1659]

[1803] ἔλευσις *eleusis* 1x *a coming, advent,* Acts 7:52* [1660]

[1804] ἐλεφάντινος *elephantinos* 1x *ivory, made of ivory,* Rev. 18:12* [1661]

[1806] Ἐλιακίμ *Eliakim* 3x also spelled Ἐλιακείμ, *Eliakim,* pr. name, indecl., Mt. 1:13; Lk. 3:30* [1662]

[1808] Ἐλιέζερ *Eliezer* 1x *Eliezer,* pr. name, indecl., Lk. 3:29* [1663]

[1809] Ἐλιούδ *Elioud* 2x *Eliud,* the father of Eleazar, Mt. 1:14, 15* [1664]

[1810] Ἐλισάβετ *Elisabet* 9x *Elizabeth,* the wife of Zechariah and mother of John the Baptist, Lk. 1:5, 13, 24, 36, 57 [1665]

[1811] Ἐλισαῖος *Elisaios* 1x also spelled Ἐλισσαῖος, *Elisha,* pr. name, Lk. 4:27* [1666]

[1813] ἑλίσσω *helissō* 2x *to roll, fold up,* as garments, Heb. 1:12; Rev. 6:14* [1507, 1667]

[1814] ἕλκος *helkos* 3x pr. *a wound;* hence, *an ulcer, sore,* Lk. 16:21; Rev. 16:2, 11* [1668]

[1815] ἑλκόω *helkoō* 1x pass. *to be afflicted with ulcers,* Lk. 16:20* [1669]

[1817] Ἑλλάς *Hellas* 1x *Hellas, Greece;* in NT *the southern portion of Greece* as distinguished from Macedonia, Acts 20:2* [1671]

[1818] Ἕλλην *Hellēn* 25x *a Greek,* Acts 18:17; Rom. 1:14; *one not a Jew, a Gentile,* Acts 14:1; 16:1, 3 [1672] See *Greeks.*

[1819] Ἑλληνικός *Hellēnikos* 1x *Greek, Grecian,* Rev. 9:11* [1673]

[1820] Ἑλληνίς *Hellēnis* 2x *a female Greek,* Mk. 7:26; Acts 17:12* [1674]

[1821] Ἑλληνιστής *Hellēnistēs* 3x pr. *one who uses the language and follows the customs of the Greeks;* in NT *a Jew by blood, but a native of a Greek-speaking country, Hellenist,* Acts 6:1; 9:29; 11:20* [1675]

[1822] Ἑλληνιστί *Hellēnisti* 2x *in the Greek language,* Jn. 19:20; Acts 21:37* [1676]

[1824] ἐλλογέω *ellogeō* 2x *to enter in an account, to put* or *charge to one's account,* Phlm. 18; in NT *to impute,* Rom. 5:13* [1677]

[1825] Ἐλμαδάμ *Elmadam* 1x also spelled Ἐλμωδάμ, *Elmadam,* pr. name, indecl., Lk. 3:28* [1678]

[1827] ἐλπίζω *elpizō* 31x *to hope, expect,* Lk. 23:8; 24:21; *to repose hope and confidence in, trust, confide,* Mt. 12:21; Jn. 5:45 [1679] See *desire; hope; wish.*

[1828] ἐλπίς *elpis* 53x pr. *expectation; hope,* Acts 24:15; Rom. 5:4; meton. *the object of hope, thing hoped for,* Rom. 8:24; Gal. 5:5; *the author* or *source of hope,* Col. 1:27; 1 Tim. 1:1; *trust, confidence,* 1 Pet. 1:21; ἐπ᾽ ἐλπίδι, *in security, with a guarantee,* Acts 2:26; Rom. 8:20 [1680] See *confident expectation; desire; hope; wish.*

[1829] Ἐλύμας *Elymas* 1x *Elymas,* pr. name, Acts 13:8* [1681]

[1830] ἐλωΐ *elōi* 2x Aramaic for, *my God,* Mk. 15:34* [1682]

[1831] ἐμαυτοῦ *emautou* 37x *myself, my own,* Lk. 7:7; Jn. 5:31 [1683]

[1832] ἐμβαίνω *embainō* 16x *to step in; to go on board* a ship, *embark,* Mt. 8:23; 9:1; 13:2 [1684] See *get into (a boat).*

[1833] ἐμβάλλω *emballō* 1x *to cast into,* Lk. 12:5* [1685]

[1835] ἐμβάπτω *embaptō* 2x *to dip in,* Mt. 26:23; *to dip* for food in a dish, Mk. 14:20* [1686]

[1836] ἐμβατεύω *embateuō* 1x pr. *to step into* or *upon;* met. *to search into, investigate; to pry into intrusively,* Col. 2:18* [1687]

[1837] ἐμβιβάζω *embibazō* 1x *to cause to step into* or *upon; to set in* or *upon;* especially, *to put on board,* Acts 27:6* [1688]

[1838] ἐμβλέπω *emblepō* 11x *to look attentively, gaze earnestly,* at an object, followed by εἰς, Mk. 6:26; Acts 1:11; *to direct a glance, to look searchingly* or *significantly,* at a person, followed by the dat., Mk. 10:21; 14:67; Lk. 22:61; absol.

to see clearly, Mk. 8:25; Acts 22:11 [1689] See *look at.*

[1839] ἐμβριμάομαι *embrimaomai* 5x Attic spelling, ejmbrimovomai, *to be greatly agitated,* Jn. 11:33, 38; *to charge* or *forbid sternly* or *vehemently,* Mt. 9:30; Mk. 1:43; *to express indignation, to censure,* Mk. 14:5* [1690]

[1840] ἐμέω *emeō* 1x *to vomit,* Rev. 3:16* [1692]

[1841] ἐμμαίνομαι *emmainomai* 1x *to be mad against, be furious toward,* Acts 26:11* [1693]

[1842] Ἐμμανουήλ *Emmanouēl* 1x *Emmanuel,* pr. name, indecl., Mt. 1:23* [1694] See *Immanuel.*

[1843] Ἐμμαοῦς *Emmaous* 1x *Emmaus,* pr. name, indecl., of a village near Jerusalem, Lk. 24:13* [1695]

[1844] ἐμμένω *emmenō* 4x pr. *to remain in* a place; met. *to abide by, to continue firm in, persevere in,* Acts 14:22; 28:30; Gal. 3:10; Heb. 8:9* [1696]

[1846] Ἑμμώρ *Hemmōr* 1x also spelled Ἑμμόρ, *Hamor,* pr. name, indecl., Acts 7:16 [1697]

[1847] ἐμός *emos* 76x *my, mine,* Jn. 7:16; 8:37 [1699]

[1848] ἐμπαιγμονή *empaigmonē* 1x *mocking, scoffing, derision,* 2 Pet. 3:3* [**]

[1849] ἐμπαιγμός *empaigmos* 1x *mocking, scoffing, scorn,* Heb. 11:36* [1701]

[1850] ἐμπαίζω *empaizō* 13x *to play upon, deride, mock, treat with scorn, ridicule,* Mt. 20:19; 27:29; by impl. *to delude, deceive,* Mt. 2:16 [1702] See *deceive; mock.*

[1851] ἐμπαίκτης *empaiktēs* 2x *a mocker, derider, scoffer,* 2 Pet. 3:3; Jude 18* [1703]

[1853] ἐμπεριπατέω *emperipateō* 1x pr. *to walk about in* a place; met. in NT *to live among, be conversant with,* 2 Cor. 6:16* [1704]

[1858] ἐμπίπλημι *empiplēmi* 5x also spelled ἐμπίμπλημι (1855) and ἐμπιμπλάω (1857), *to fill,* Acts 14:17; pass. *to be satisfied, satiated, full,* Lk. 1:53; 6:25; Jn. 6:12; met. *to have the full enjoyment of,* Rom. 15:24* [1705]

[1859] ἐμπίμπρημι *empimprēmi* 1x also spelled ἐμπίπρημι and ἐμπρηθω, *to set on fire, burn down,* Mt. 22:7* [1714]

[1860] ἐμπίπτω *empiptō* 7x *to fall into,* Mt. 12:11; Lk. 14:5; *to encounter,* Lk. 10:36; *to be involved in,* 1 Tim. 3:6, 7; 6:9; εἰς χεῖρας, *to fall under the chastisement of,* Heb. 10:31 [1706]

[1861] ἐμπλέκω *emplekō* 2x pr. *to intertwine;* met. *to implicate, entangle, involve;* pass. *to be implicated, involved,* or *to entangle one's self in,* 2 Tim. 2:4; 2 Pet. 2:20* [1707]

[1862] ἐμπλοκή *emplokē* 1x *braiding* or *plaiting* of hair, 1 Pet. 3:3* [1708]

[1863] ἐμπνέω *empneō* 1x gen., *to breathe into* or *upon; to respire, breathe;* met. *to breathe of, be animated with the spirit of,* Acts 9:1* [1709]

[1864] ἐμπορεύομαι *emporeuomai* 2x *to travel; to travel for business' sake; to trade, traffic,* Jas. 4:13; by impl., trans., *to make a gain of, deceive for one's own advantage,* 2 Pet. 2:3* [1710]

[1865] ἐμπορία *emporia* 1x *business, trade,* Mt. 22:5* [1711]

[1866] ἐμπόριον *emporion* 1x *a mart, marketplace, emporium;* met. *traffic,* Jn. 2:16* [1712]

[1867] ἔμπορος *emporos* 5x pr. *a passenger by sea; a traveller; one who travels about for traffic, a merchant,* Mt. 13:45; Rev. 18:3, 11, 15, 23* [1713]

[1869] ἔμπροσθεν *emprosthen* 48x also an improper prep., *before, in front of,* Lk. 19:4; Phil. 3:14; *before, in the presence of, in the face of,* Mt. 5:24; 23:14; *before, pre-*

vious to, Jn. 1:15, 27, 30; from the Hebrew, *in the sight* or *estimation of,* Mt. 11:26; 18:14 [1715]

[1870] ἐμπτύω *emptyō* 6x followed by the dat., or εἰς and the acc., *to spit upon,* Mt. 26:67; 27:30 [1716]

[1871] ἐμφανής *emphanēs* 2x *apparent, conspicuous, obvious to the sight,* Acts 10:40; met. *manifest, known, comprehended,* Rom. 10:20* [1717]

[1872] ἐμφανίζω *emphanizō* 10x *to cause to appear clearly; to communicate, report,* Acts 23:15, 22; *to bring charges against,* Acts 24:1; 25:2, 15, *to manifest, intimate plainly,* Heb. 11:14; *to reveal, make known,* Jn. 14:21, 22; pass. *to appear, be visible,* Mt. 27:53; *to present one's self,* Heb. 9:24* [1718] See *disclose; show.*

[1873] ἔμφοβος *emphobos* 5x *terrible;* in NT *terrified,* Lk. 24:5, 37; Acts 10:4; 24:25; Rev. 11:13* [1719]

[1874] ἐμφυσάω *emphysaō* 1x *to blow* or *breathe into, inflate;* in NT *to breathe upon,* Jn. 20:22* [1720]

[1875] ἔμφυτος *emphytos* 1x *implanted, ingrafted, infixed,* Jas. 1:21* [1721]

[1877] ἐν *en* 2,752x followed by the dat., *in,* Mt. 8:6; Mk. 12:26; Rev. 6:6,; *upon,* Lk. 8:32; *among,* Mt. 11:11; *before, in the presence of,* Mk. 8:38; *in the sight, estimation of,* 1 Cor. 14:11; *before,* judicially, 1 Cor. 6:2; *in,* of state, occupation, habit, Mt. 21:22; Lk. 7:25; Rom. 4:10; *in the case of,* Mt. 17:12; *in respect of,* Lk. 1:7; 1 Cor. 1:7; *on occasion of, on the ground of,* Mt. 6:7; Lk. 1:21; used of the thing by which an oath is made, Mt. 5:34; of the instrument, means, efficient cause, Rom. 12:21; Acts 4:12; *equipped with, furnished with,* 1 Cor. 4:21; Heb. 9:25; *arrayed with, accompanied by,* Lk. 14:31; Jude 14; of time, *during, in the course of,* Mt. 2:1; in NT of demoniacal possession, *possessed by,* Mk. 5:2 [1722]

[1878] ἐναγκαλίζομαι *enankalizomai* 2x *to take into* or *embrace in one's arms,* Mk. 9:36; 10:16* [1723]

[1879] ἐνάλιος *enalios* 1x *marine, living in the sea,* Jas. 3:7* [1724]

[1882] ἔναντι *enanti* 2x also an improper prep, *over against, in the presence of,* Lk. 1:8; Acts 8:21* [1725]

[1883] ἐναντίον *enantion* 8x acc sg neut of ἐναντίος used adverbially; the adj. does not appear in the NT, improper prep., *before, in the presence of,* Lk. 1:6; 20:26; Acts 8:32; 2 Cor. 2:7; Gal. 2:7; 1 Pet. 3:9; from the Hebrew, *in the sight* or *estimation of,* Acts 7:10; with τοῦ θεοῦ, an intensive expression, Lk. 24:19* [1726]

[1885] ἐναντίος *enantios* 8x *opposite to, over against,* Mk. 15:39; *contrary,* as the wind, Mt. 14:24; Acts 26:9; 28:17; ὁ ἐξ ἐναντίας, *an adverse party, enemy,* Tit. 2:8; *adverse, hostile, counter,* 1 Thess. 2:15 [1727]

[1887] ἐνάρχομαι *enarchomai* 2x *to begin, commence,* Gal. 3:3; Phil. 1:6* [1728]

[1888] ἔνατος *enatos* 10x *the ninth,* Mt. 20:5; 27:45f.; Mk. 15:33f.; Lk. 23:44; Acts 3:1; 10:3, 30; Rev. 21:20* [1766] See *ninth.*

[1890] ἐνδεής *endeēs* 1x *indigent, poor, needy,* Acts 4:34* [1729]

[1891] ἔνδειγμα *endeigma* 1x *a token, evidence, proof,* 2 Thess. 1:5* [1730]

[1892] ἐνδείκνυμι *endeiknymi* 11x *to manifest, display,* Rom. 9:17, 22; Heb. 6:10; *to give outward proof of,* Rom. 2:15; *to display* a certain bearing towards a person; hence, *to perpetrate openly,* 2 Tim. 4:14* [1731] See *demonstrate; show.*

[1893] ἔνδειξις *endeixis* 4x *a pointing out;* met. *manifestation, public declaration,* Rom. 3:25, 26; *a token, sign, proof,* i.q. ἔνδειγμα, 2 Cor. 8:24; Phil. 1:28* [1732]

[1894] ἕνδεκα *hendeka* 6x *eleven,* indecl. numeral, Mt. 28:16; Mk. 16:14; Lk. 24:9, 33; Acts 1:26; 2:14* [1733]

[1895] ἑνδέκατος *hendekatos* 3x *eleventh,* Mt. 20:6, 9; Rev. 21:20* [1734]

[1896] ἐνδέχομαι *endechomai* 1x *to admit, approve; to be possible,* impersonal, *it is possible,* Lk. 13:33* [1735]

[1897] ἐνδημέω *endēmeō* 3x *to dwell in* a place, *be at home,* 2 Cor. 5:6, 8, 9* [1736]

[1898] ἐνδιδύσκω *endidyskō* 2x a later form, equivalent to ἐνδύω, *to dress (oneself),* Mark 15:17; 16:19* [1737]

[1899] ἔνδικος *endikos* 2x *fair, just,* Rom. 3:8; Heb. 2:2* [1738]

[1901] ἐνδοξάζομαι *endoxazomai* 2x *to invest with glory;* pass. *to be glorified, to be made a subject of glorification,* 2 Thess. 1:10, 12* [1740]

[1902] ἔνδοξος *endoxos* 4x *honored,* 1 Cor. 4:10; *notable, memorable,* Lk. 13:17; *splendid, gorgeous,* Lk. 7:25; *in unsullied array,* Eph. 5:27* [1741]

[1903] ἔνδυμα *endyma* 8x *clothing, a garment,* Mt. 6:25, 28; 22:11, 12; in particular, *an outer garment, cloak, mantle,* Mt. 3:4; 7:15; 28:3; Lk. 12:23* [1742]

[1904] ἐνδυναμόω *endynamoō* 7x *to empower, invigorate,* Phil. 4:13; 1 Tim. 1:12; 2 Tim. 4:17; mid. *to summon up vigor, put forth energy,* Eph. 6:10; 2 Tim. 2:1; pass. *to acquire strength, be invigorated, be strong,* Acts 9:22; Rom. 4:20* [1743]

[1905] ἐνδύνω *endynō* 1x *enter, creep in,* 2 Tim. 3:6* [1744]

[1906] ἔνδυσις *endysis* 1x *a putting on,* or *wearing* of clothes, 1 Pet. 3:3* [1745]

[1907] ἐνδύω *endyō* 27x *to enter,* 2 Tim. 3:6; *to put on, clothe, invest, array,* Mt. 27:31; Mk. 15:17, 20; mid. *clothe one's self, be clothed,* Mt. 22:11, 27, 31; trop. *to be clothed* with spiritual gifts, graces, or character, Lk. 24:49; Rom. 13:14 [1746] See *clothe; put on; wear.*

[1908] ἐνδώμησις *endōmēsis* 1x *construction, material,* Rev. 21:18* [1739]

[1909] ἐνέδρα *enedra* 2x pr. *a sitting in* or *on a* spot; *an ambush,* or *lying in wait,* Acts 23:16; 25:3* [1747]

[1910] ἐνεδρεύω *enedreuō* 2x *to lie in wait* or *ambush for,* Acts 23:21; *to endeavor to entrap,* Lk. 11:54* [1748]

[1912] ἐνειλέω *eneileō* 1x *to envelope,* Mk. 15:46* [1750]

[1913] ἔνειμι *eneimi* 7x *to be in* or *within;* τὰ ἐνόντα, *those things which are within,* Lk. 11:41* [1751]

[1915] ἕνεκεν *heneken* 24x also spelled ἕνεκα, with the genitive, *on account of, for the sake of, by reason of.* Our text has ἕνεκεν 20x, ἕνεκα 4x (Mt. 19:5; Lk. 6:2; Acts 19:32; 26:21)* [1752]

[1916] ἐνενήκοντα *enenēkonta* 4x indecl, *ninety,* Mt. 18:12, 13; Lk. 15:4, 7* [1768]

[1917] ἐνεός *eneos* 1x *dumb, speechless,* Acts 9:7* [1769]

[1918] ἐνέργεια *energeia* 8x *energy, efficacy, power,* Phil. 3:21; Col. 2:12; *active energy, operation,* Eph. 1:19; 3:7; 4:16; Col. 1:29; 2 Thess. 2:9, 11* [1753]

[1919] ἐνεργέω *energeō* 21x *to effect,* 1 Cor. 12:6, 11; Gal. 3:5; Eph. 1:11; Phil. 2:13; *to put into operation,* Eph. 1:20; absol. *to be active,* Mt. 14:2; Mk. 6:14; Eph. 2:2; in NT *to communicate energy and efficiency,* Gal. 2:8; pass. or mid. *to come into activity, be actively developed; to be active, be in operation,* towards a result, 2 Cor. 4:12; 2 Thess. 2:7; *to be an active power* or *principle,* Rom. 7:5; 1 Thess. 2:12; *instinct with activity; in action, operative,* 2 Cor. 1:6; Gal. 5:6; Eph. 3:20; Col. 1:29; *earnest,* Jas. 5:16 [1754] See *operate; work.*

[1920] ἐνέργημα *energēma* 2x *an effect, thing effected, activity,* 1 Cor. 12:6; *operation, working,* 1 Cor. 12:10* [1755]

[1921] ἐνεργής *energēs* 3x *active,* Phlm. 6; *efficient, energetic,* Heb. 4:12; *adapted to accomplish* a thing, *effectual,* 1 Cor. 16:9* [1756]

[1922] ἐνευλογέω *eneulogeō* 2x *to bless in respect of,* or *by means of,* Acts 3:25; Gal. 3:8* [1757]

[1923] ἐνέχω *enechō* 3x *to hold within; to fix upon;* in NT intrans. (sc. χόλον) *to entertain a grudge against,* Mk. 6:19; *to be exasperated against,* Lk. 11:53; pass. *to be entangled, held fast in,* Gal. 5:1* [1758]

[1924] ἐνθάδε *enthade* 8x pr. *to this place,* Jn. 4:15, 16; also, *here, in this place,* Lk. 24:41; Acts 10:8; 16:28; 17:6; 25:17, 24* [1759]

[1925] ἔνθεν *enthen* 2x *from this place,* Mt. 17:20; Lk. 16:26* [1782]

[1926] ἐνθυμέομαι *enthumeomai* 2x *to ponder in one's mind, think of, meditate on,* Mt. 1:20; 9:4* [1760]

[1927] ἐνθύμησις *enthumēsis* 4x *the act of thought, reflection,* Mt. 9:4; 12:25; Heb. 4:12; *the result of thought, invention, device,* Acts 17:29* [1761]

[1929] ἐνιαυτός *eniautos* 14x *a year,* more particularly as being a cycle of seasons, and in respect of its revolution, Jn. 11:49, 51; 18:13; in NT *an era,* Lk. 4:19 [1763] See *year.*

[1931] ἐνίστημι *enistēmi* 7x *to place in* or *upon;* intrans., *to stand close upon; to be at hand, impend, to be present,* Rom. 8:38; 2 Thess. 2:2; Heb. 9:9 [1764] See *present.*

[1932] ἐνισχύω *enischuō* 2x *to strengthen, impart strength and vigor,* Lk. 22:43; intrans. *to gain, acquire,* or *recover strength and vigor, be strengthened,* Acts 9:19* [1765]

[1933] ἐννέα *ennea* 5x indecl, *nine,* Mt. 18:12f.; Lk. 15:4, 7; 17:17* [1767]

[1935] ἐννεύω *enneuō* 1x *to nod at, signify by a nod; to make signs; to intimate by signs,* Lk. 1:62* [1770]

[1936] ἔννοια *ennoia* 2x *notion, idea; thought, purpose, intention,* Heb. 4:12; 1 Pet. 4:1* [1771]

[1937] ἔννομος *ennomos* 2x *within law; lawful, legal,* Acts 19:39; in NT *subject* or *under a law, obedient to a law,* 1 Cor. 9:21* [1772]

[1939] ἔννυχος *ennychos* 1x *nocturnal, while still dark,* Mk. 1:35* [1773]

[1940] ἐνοικέω *enoikeō* 5x *to dwell in, inhabit;* in NT met. *to be indwelling* spiritually, Rom. 8:11; Col. 3:16; 2 Tim. 1:14; *to be infixed* mentally, 2 Tim. 1:5; of the Deity, *to indwell,* by special presence, 2 Cor. 6:16* [1774]

[1941] ἐνορκίζω *enorkizō* 1x *to adjure,* 1 Thess. 5:27* [3726]

[1942] ἑνότης *henotēs* 2x *oneness, unity,* Eph. 4:3, 13* [1775]

[1943] ἐνοχλέω *enochleō* 2x *to trouble, annoy; to be a trouble,* Lk. 6:18; Heb. 12:15* [1776]

[1944] ἔνοχος *enochos* 10x *held in* or *by; subjected to,* Heb. 2:15; *subject to, liable to, guilty, deserving,* Mt. 5:21, 22; 26:66; Mk. 3:29; 14:64; *an offender against,* 1 Cor. 11:27; Jas. 2:10* [1777] See *guilty; liable; subject to; worthy.*

[1945] ἔνταλμα *entalma* 3x *a precept, commandment, ordinance,* Mt. 15:9; Mk. 7:7; Col. 2:22* [1778]

[1946] ἐνταφιάζω *entaphiazō* 2x *to prepare* a body *for burial,* Mt. 26:12; absol. *to make the ordinary preparations for burial,* Jn. 19:40* [1779]

[1947] ἐνταφιασμός *entaphiasmos* 2x *preparation* of a corpse *for burial, burial* itself, Mk. 14:8; Jn. 12:7* [1780]

[1948] ἐντέλλω *entellō* 15x some list as ἐντέλλομαι, mid., *to enjoin, charge, command,* Mt. 4:6; 15:4; 17:9; *to direct,* Mt.

19:7; Mk. 10:3 [1781] See *command; instruct; order.*

[1949] ἐντεῦθεν *enteuthen* 10x *hence, from this place,* Mt. 17:20; Lk. 4:9; ἐντεῦθεν καὶ ἐντεῦθεν, *on each side,* Rev. 22:2; *hence, from this cause,* Jas. 4:1 [1782]

[1950] ἔντευξις *enteuxis* 2x pr. *a meeting with;* hence *address; prayer, supplication, intercession,* 1 Tim. 2:1; 4:5* [1783]

[1952] ἔντιμος *entimos* 5x *honored, estimable, dear,* Lk. 7:2; 14:8; Phil. 2:29; *highly-valued, precious, costly,* 1 Pet. 2:4, 6* [1784]

[1953] ἐντολή *entolē* 67x *an injunction; a precept, commandment, law,* Mt. 5:19; 15:3, 6; *an order, direction,* Acts 17:15; *an edict,* Jn. 11:57; *a direction,* Mk. 10:5; *a commission,* Jn. 10:18, *a charge* of matters to be proclaimed or received, Jn. 12:49, 50; 1 Tim. 6:14; 2 Pet. 2:21 [1785] See *commandment; order.*

[1954] ἐντόπιος *entopios* 1x *in* or *of a place; an inhabitant, citizen,* Acts 21:12* [1786]

[1955] ἐντός *entos* 2x improper prep., gen., *inside, within,* Lk. 17:21; τὸ ἐντός, *the interior, inside,* Mt. 23:26* [1787]

[1956] ἐντρέπω *entrepō* 9x mid., *to revere, reverence, regard,* Mt. 21:37; Mk. 12:6; absol. *to feel shame, be put to shame,* 2 Thess. 3:14; Tit. 2:8; pass., *be put to shame,* 2 Thess. 3:14; Tit. 3:8 [1788]

[1957] ἐντρέφω *entrephō* 1x *to nourish in, bring up* or *educate in,* 1 Tim. 4:6* [1789]

[1958] ἔντρομος *entromos* 3x *trembling, terrified,* Acts 7:32; 16:29; Heb. 12:21* [1790]

[1959] ἐντροπή *entropē* 2x *humiliation;* in NT *shame,* 1 Cor. 6:5; 15:34* [1791]

[1960] ἐντρυφάω *entryphaō* 1x *to live luxuriously, riot, revel,* 2 Pet. 2:13* [1792]

[1961] ἐντυγχάνω *entynchanō* 5x *to fill in with, meet; to have conversation with, address; to address* or *apply to* any one, Acts 25:24; ὑπέρ τινος, *to intercede for any one, plead the cause of,* Rom. 8:27, 34; Heb. 7:25; κατά τινος, *to address a representation* or *suit against any one, to accuse, complain of,* Rom. 11:2* [1793]

[1962] ἐντυλίσσω *entylissō* 3x *to wrap up in, inwrap, envelope,* Mt. 27:59; Lk. 23:53; *to wrap up, roll* or *fold together,* Jn. 20:7* [1794]

[1963] ἐντυπόω *entypoō* 1x *to impress a figure, instamp, engrave,* 2 Cor. 3:7* [1795]

[1964] ἐνυβρίζω *enybrizō* 1x *to insult, outrage,* Heb. 10:29* [1796]

[1965] ἐνυπνιάζομαι *enypniazomai* 2x *to dream,* in NT *to dream* under supernatural impression, Acts 2:17; *to dream* delusion, *have visions,* Jude 8* [1797]

[1966] ἐνύπνιον *enypnion* 1x *a dream;* in NT *a supernatural suggestion* or *impression received during sleep, a sleep-vision,* Acts 2:17* [1798]

[1967] ἐνώπιον *enōpion* 94x gen., *before, in the presence of,* Lk. 5:25; 8:47; *in front of,* Rev. 4:5, 6; *immediately preceding* as a forerunner, Lk. 1:17; Rev. 16:19; from the Hebrew, *in the presence of,* metaphysically, *i.e.* in the sphere of sensation or thought, Lk. 12:9; 15:10; Acts 10:31; *in the eyes of, in the judgment of,* Lk. 16:15; 24:11; Acts 4:19 [1799]

[1968] Ἐνώς *Enōs* 1x *Enos,* pr. name, indecl., Lk. 3:38* [1800]

[1969] ἐνωτίζομαι *enōtizomai* 1x *to give ear, listen, pay attention to,* Acts 2:14* [1801]

[1970] Ἑνώχ *Henōch* 3x *Enoch,* pr. name, indecl., Lk. 3:37; Heb. 11:5; 1 Pet. 3:19; Jude 14* [1802]

[1971] ἕξ *hex* 13x *six,* indecl., Mt. 17:1; Mk. 9:2 [1803] See *six.*

[1972] ἐξαγγέλλω *exangellō* 2x *to tell forth, divulge, publish; to declare abroad, celebrate,* 1 Pet. 2:9, shorter ending of Mark* [1804]

[1973] ἐξαγοράζω *exagorazō* 4x *to buy out* of the hands of a person; *to redeem, set free,* Gal. 3:13; 4:5; mid. *to redeem, buy off, to secure for one's self* or *one's own use; to rescue* from loss or misapplication, Eph. 5:16; Col. 4:5* [1805] See *redeem.*

[1974] ἐξάγω *exagō* 12x *to bring* or *lead out, conduct out of,* Mk. 8:23; 15:20; Lk. 24:50 [1806] See *lead out.*

[1975] ἐξαιρέω *exaireō* 8x *to take out of; to pluck out, tear out,* Mt. 5:29; 18:9; mid. *to take out of, select, choose,* Acts 26:17; *to rescue, deliver,* Acts 7:10, 34; 12:11; 23:27; Gal. 1:4* [1807]

[1976] ἐξαίρω *exairō* 1x pr. *to lift up out of;* in NT *to remove, eject,* 1 Cor. 5:13* [1808]

[1977] ἐξαιτέω *exaiteō* 1x *to ask for; to demand;* mid. *to demand for one's self,* Lk. 22:31; also, *to obtain by asking** [1809]

[1978] ἐξαίφνης *exaiphnēs* 5x *suddenly, unexpectedly,* Mk. 13:36; Lk. 2:13; 9:39; Acts 9:3; 22:6* [1810]

[1979] ἐξακολουθέω *exakoloutheō* 3x *to follow out; to imitate,* 2 Pet. 2:2, 15; *to observe as a guide,* 2 Pet. 1:16* [1811]

[1980] ἑξακόσιοι *hexakosioi* 2x *six hundred,* Rev. 13:18; 14:20* [1812]

[1981] ἐξαλείφω *exaleiphō* 5x pr. *to anoint* or *smear over;* hence, *to wipe off* or *away,* Rev. 7:17; 21:4; *to blot out, obliterate,* Col. 2:14; Rev. 3:5; met. *to wipe out* guilt, Acts 3:19* [1813] See *blot out; wipe out.*

[1982] ἐξάλλομαι *exallomai* 1x *to leap* or *spring up* or *forth,* Acts 3:8* [1814]

[1983] ἐξανάστασις *exanastasis* 1x *a raising up; a dislodgment; a rising up; a resurrection from* the dead, Phil. 3:11* [1815]

[1984] ἐξανατέλλω *exanatellō* 2x *to raise up, make to spring up;* intrans. *to rise up, sprout, spring up* or *forth,* Mt. 13:5; Mk. 4:5* [1816]

[1985] ἐξανίστημι *exanistēmi* 3x *to cause to rise up, raise up;* from the Hebrew, *to raise up* into existence, Mk. 12:19; Lk. 20:28; intrans. *to rise up from, stand forth,* Acts 15:5* [1817]

[1987] ἐξαπατάω *exapataō* 6x pr. *to deceive thoroughly; to deceive, delude,* Rom. 7:11; 16:18; 1 2 Cor. 3:18; 11:3; 2 Thess. 2:3; 1 Tim. 2:14* [1818]

[1988] ἐξάπινα *exapina* 1x *suddenly, immediately, unexpectedly,* Mk. 9:8* [1819]

[1989] ἐξαπορέω *exaporeō* 2x some list as a deponent ἐξαπορέομαι, pas., *to be in the utmost perplexity* or *despair,* 2 Cor. 1:8; 4:8* [1820]

[1990] ἐξαποστέλλω *exapostellō* 13x *to send out* or *forth; to send away, dismiss,* Lk. 1:53; *to dispatch* on a service or agency, Acts 7:12; *to send forth* as a pervading influence, Gal. 4:6 [1821] See *send.*

[1992] ἐξαρτίζω *exartizō* 2x *to equip* or *furnish completely,* 2 Tim. 3:17; *to complete* time, Acts 21:5* [1822]

[1993] ἐξαστράπτω *exastraptō* 1x pr. *to flash forth;* hence, *to glisten as lightning,* Lk. 9:29* [1823]

[1994] ἐξαυτῆς *exautēs* 6x *at the very time; presently, instantly, immediately,* Mk. 6:25; Acts 10:33; 11:11 [1824]

[1995] ἐξεγείρω *exegeirō* 2x *to raise up* from the dead, 1 Cor. 6:14; *to raise up* into existence, or into a certain condition, Rom. 9:17* [1825]

[1996] ἔξειμι *exeimi* 4x *to go out* or *forth,* Acts 13:42; *to depart,* Acts 17:15; 20:7; ἐπὶ τὴν γῆν, *to get to land,* from the water, Acts 27:43 [1826]

[1999] ἐξέλκω *exelkō* 1x *to draw* or *drag out;* met. *to withdraw, allure, hurry away,* Jas. 1:14* [1828]

[2000] ἐξέραμα *exerama* 1x *vomit,* 2 Pet. 2:22* [1829]

[2001] ἐξεραυνάω *exeraunaō* 1x *to search out, to examine closely,* 1 Pet. 1:10* [1830]

[2002] ἐξέρχομαι *exerchomai* 218x *to go* or *come out of; to come out,* Mt. 5:26; 8:34; *to proceed, emanate, take rise from,* Mt. 2:6; 15:18; 1 Cor. 14:36; *to come abroad,* 1 Jn. 4:1; *to go forth, go away, depart,* Mt. 9:31; Lk. 5:8; *to escape,* Jn. 10:39; *to pass away, come to an end,* Acts 16:19 [1831] See *come out; go out.*

[2003] ἔξεστιν *exestin* 31x 3rd person sing of the unused ἔξειμι (#1997) used impersonally, *it is possible; it is permitted, it is lawful,* Mt. 12:2, 4; Mk. 3:4; Lk. 6:9; Acts 22:25; 1 Cor. 6:12 [1832] See *lawful; (to be) permitted.*

[2004] ἐξετάζω *exetazō* 3x *to search out; to inquire by interrogation, examine strictly,* Mt. 2:8; 10:11; *to interrogate,* Jn. 21:12* [1833]

[2007] ἐξηγέομαι *exēgeomai* 6x *to be a leader; to detail, to set forth in language; to tell, narrate, recount,* Lk. 24:35; Acts 10:8; *to make known, reveal,* Jn. 1:18; Acts 15:12, 14; 21:19* [1834]

[2008] ἑξήκοντα *hexēkonta* 9x indecl, *sixty,* Mt. 13:8, 23 [1835]

[2009] ἑξῆς *hexēs* 5x *successively, in order;* in NT with the article ὁ, ἡ, τό, ἑξῆς, *next,* Lk. 7:11; 9:37; Acts 21:1; 25:17; 27:18* [1836]

[2010] ἐξηχέω *exēcheō* 1x act., *to make to sound forth;* pas., *to sound forth,* 1 Thess. 1:8* [1837]

[2011] ἕξις *hexis* 1x *a condition of body* or *mind,* strictly, as resulting from practice; *habit,* Heb. 5:14* [1838]

[2014] ἐξίστημι *existēmi* 17x pr. *to put out of its place; to astonish, amaze,* Lk. 24:22; Acts 8:9, 11; intrans. *to be astonished,* Mt. 12:23; *to be beside one's self,* Mk. 3:21; 2 Cor. 5:13 [1839] See *(be) amazed; astonish; astound; terrify.*

[2015] ἐξισχύω *exischuō* 1x *to be fully able, be strong,* Eph. 3:18* [1840]

[2016] ἔξοδος *exodos* 3x *a way out, a going out; a going out, departure, the exodus,* Heb. 11:22; met. *a departure* from life, *decease, death,* Lk. 9:31; 2 Pet. 1:15* [1841]

[2017] ἐξολεθρεύω *exolethreuō* 1x *to destroy utterly, root out,* Acts 3:23* [1842]

[2018] ἐξομολογέομαι *exomologeomai* 10x *to agree, bind one's self, promise,* Lk. 22:6; mid. *to confess,* Mt. 3:6; *to profess openly,* Phil. 2:11; Rev. 3:5; *to make open avowal* of benefits; *to praise, celebrate,* Mt. 11:25; Lk. 10:21 [1843] See *confess; praise; profess.*

[2019] ἐξορκίζω *exorkizō* 1x *to put an oath* to a person, *to adjure,* Mt. 26:63* [1844]

[2020] ἐξορκιστής *exorkistēs* 1x pr. *one who puts an oath;* in NT *an exorcist, one who by various kinds of incantations,* etc., *pretended to expel demons,* Acts 19:13* [1845]

[2021] ἐξορύσσω *exoryssō* 2x *to dig out* or *through, force up,* Mk. 2:4; *to pluck out* the eyes, Gal. 4:15* [1846]

[2022] ἐξουδενέω *exoudeneō* 1x also spelled ἐξουδενόω, *to treat with contempt,* Mk. 9:12* [1847]

[2024] ἐξουθενέω *exoutheneō* 11x also spelled ἐξουθενόω, *to make light of, set at naught, despise, treat with contempt and scorn,* Lk. 18:9; *to neglect, disregard,* 1 Thess. 5:20; ἐξουθενημένος, *contemptible,* 2 Cor. 10:10; *of small account,* 1 Cor. 1:28; 6:4; by impl. *to reject with contempt,* Acts 4:11 [1848] See *despise; hold in contempt; look down on; ridicule.*

[2026] ἐξουσία *exousia* 102x *power, ability, faculty,* Mt. 9:8; 10:1; *efficiency, energy,* Lk. 4:32; *liberty, licence,* Jn. 10:18; Acts 5:4; *authority, rule, dominion,* *jurisdiction,* Mt. 8:9; 28:18; meton. pl. *authorities, potentates, powers,* Lk. 12:11; 1 Cor. 15:24; Eph. 1:21; *right, authority, full power,* Mt. 9:6; 21:23; *privilege, prerogative,* Jn. 1:12; perhaps, *a veil,* 1 Cor. 11:10 [1849] See *authority; power; right.*

[2027] ἐξουσιάζω *exousiazō* 4x *to have* or *exercise power* or *authority over* anyone, Lk. 22:25; *to possess independent control over,* 1 Cor. 7:4 (2x); pass. *to be subject to, under the power* or *influence of,* 1 Cor. 6:12* [1850]

[2029] ἐξοχή *exochē* 1x pr. *prominence, anything prominent;* in NT *eminence, distinction,* Acts 25:23* [1851]

[2030] ἐξυπνίζω *exypnizō* 1x *to awake, arouse* from sleep, Jn. 11:11* [1852]

[2031] ἔξυπνος *exypnos* 1x *awake, aroused from sleep,* Acts 16:27* [1853]

[2032] ἔξω *exō* 63x can function as an improper prep., *without, out of doors;* Mt. 12:46, 47; ὁ, ἡ, τὸ ἔξω, *outer, external, foreign,* Acts 26:11; 2 Cor. 4:16; met. *not belonging to one's community,* Mk. 4:11; 1 Cor. 5:12, 13; *out, away,* from a place or person, Mt. 5:13; 13:48; as a prep., *out of,* Mk. 5:10 [1854] See *outdoors; outside.*

[2033] ἔξωθεν *exōthen* 13x can function as an improper prep., *outwardly, externally,* Mt. 23:27, 28; Mk. 7:15; ὁ, ἡ, τὸ ἔξωθεν, *outer, external,* Mt. 23:25; Lk. 11:39; τὸ ἔξωθεν, *the exterior,* Lk. 11:40; οἱ ἔξωθεν, *those who are without* the Christian community, 1 Tim. 3:7 [1855]

[2034] ἐξωθέω *exōtheō* 2x *to expel, drive out,* Acts 7:45; *to propel, urge forward,* Acts 27:39* [1856]

[2035] ἐξώτερος *exōteros* 3x comparative in form but used as a superlative, *outer, exterior, external,* Mt. 8:12; 22:13; 25:30* [1857]

[2036] ἔοικα *eoika* 2x see εἴκω (1634a), dat., *to be like,* Jas. 1:6, 23* [1503]

[2037] ἑορτάζω *heortazō* 1x *to keep a feast, celebrate a festival,* 1 Cor. 5:8* [1858]

[2038] ἑορτή *heortē* 25x *a solemn feast, public festival,* Lk. 2:41; 22:1; Jn. 13:1; spc. used of *the passover,* Mt. 26:5; 27:15 [1859] See *feast.*

[2039] ἐπαγγελία *epangelia* 52x *annunciation,* 2 Tim. 1:1; *a promise, act of promising,* Acts 13:23, 32; 23:21; meton. *the thing promised, promised favor and blessing,* Lk. 24:49; Acts 1:4 [1860] See *promise.*

[2040] ἐπαγγέλλομαι *epangellomai* 15x *to declare, to promise, undertake,* Mk. 14:11; Rom. 4:21; *to profess,* 1 Tim. 2:10 [1861] See *profess; promise.*

[2041] ἐπάγγελμα *epangelma* 2x *a promise,* 2 Pet. 3:13; meton. *promised favor* or *blessing,* 2 Pet. 1:4* [1862]

[2042] ἐπάγω *epagō* 3x *to bring upon, cause to come upon,* 2 Pet. 2:1, 5; met. *to cause to be imputed* or *attributed to, to bring* guilt *upon,* Acts 5:28* [1863]

[2043] ἐπαγωνίζομαι *epagōnizomai* 1x *to contend strenuously in defence of,* Jude 3* [1864]

[2044] ἐπαθροίζω *epathroizō* 1x act., *to gather together, to collect close upon,* or *beside*; pas., *to crowd upon,* Lk. 11:29* [1865]

[2045] Ἐπαίνετος *Epainetos* 1x *Epaenetus,* pr. name, Rom. 16:5* [1866]

[2046] ἐπαινέω *epaineō* 6x *to praise, commend, applaud,* Lk. 16:8; Rom. 15:11; 1 Cor. 11:2, 17, 22 (2x)* [1867]

[2047] ἔπαινος *epainos* 11x *praise, applause, honor paid,* Rom. 2:29; 2 Cor. 8:18; meton. *ground* or *reason of praise* or *commendation,* Phil. 4:8; *approval,* Rom. 13:3; 1 Pet. 2:14; 1 Cor. 4:5 [1868] See *commendation; praise.*

[2048] ἐπαίρω *epairō* 19x *to lift up, raise, elevate; to hoist,* Acts 27:40; τὴν φωνήν, *to lift up the voice, to speak in* *a loud voice,* Lk. 11:27; τὰς χεῖρας, *to lift up the hands* in prayer, Lk. 24:50; 1 Tim. 2:8; τοὺς ὀφθαλμούς, *to lift up the eyes, to look,* Mt. 17:8; τὴν κεφαλήν, *to lift up the head, to be encouraged, animated,* Lk. 21:28; τὴν πτέρναν, *to lift up the heel, to attack, assault;* or, *to seek one's overthrow* or *destruction,* Jn. 13:18; pass. *to be borne upwards,* Acts 1:9; met. mid. *to exalt one's self, assume consequence, be elated,* 2 Cor. 10:5 [1869] See *lift up; look up.*

[2049] ἐπαισχύνομαι *epaischunomai* 11x *to be ashamed of,* Mk. 8:38; Lk. 9:26; Rom. 1:16; 6:21; 2 Tim. 1:8, 12, 16; Heb. 2:11; 11:16* [1870] See *ashamed; embarrass, (be) embarrassed; (be) fearful.*

[2050] ἐπαιτέω *epaiteō* 2x *to prefer a suit* or *request in respect of certain circumstances; to ask alms, beg,* Lk. 16:3; 18:35* [1871]

[2051] ἐπακολουθέω *epakoloutheō* 4x *to follow upon; to accompany, be attendant,* Mk. 16:20; *to appear later,* 1 Tim. 5:24; met. *to follow* one's steps, *to imitate,* 1 Pet. 2:21; *to follow* a work, *pursue, prosecute, be studious of, devoted to,* 1 Tim. 5:10* [1872]

[2052] ἐπακούω *epakouō* 1x gen., *to listen* or *hearken to; to hear with favor,* 2 Cor. 6:2* [1873]

[2053] ἐπακροάομαι *epakroaomai* 1x gen., *to hear, hearken, listen to,* Acts 16:25* [1874]

[2054] ἐπάν *epan* 3x with subj., *whenever, as soon as,* Mt. 2:8; Lk. 11:22, 34* [1875]

[2055] ἐπάναγκες *epanankes* 1x *of necessity, necessarily;* τὰ ἐπάναγκες, *necessary things,* Acts 15:28* [1876]

[2056] ἐπανάγω *epanagō* 3x *to bring up* or *back;* intrans. *to return,* Mt. 21:18; a nautical term, *to put off from shore,* Lk. 5:3, 4* [1877]

[2057] ἐπαναμιμνῄσκω *epanamimnēskō* 1x *to remind, put in remembrance,* Rom. 15:15* [1878]

[2058] ἐπαναπαύομαι *epanapauomai* 2x pr. *to make to rest upon;* mid. *to rest upon; to abide with,* Lk. 10:6; *to rely on, confide in, abide by confidingly,* Rom. 2:17* [1879]

[2059] ἐπανέρχομαι *epanerchomai* 2x *to come back, return,* Lk. 10:35; 19:15* [1880]

[2060] ἐπανίστημι *epanistēmi* 2x *to raise up against;* mid. *to rise up against in rebellion,* Mt. 10:21; Mk. 13:12* [1881]

[2061] ἐπανόρθωσις *epanorthōsis* 1x *correction, reformation, improvement,* 2 Tim. 3:16* [1882]

[2062] ἐπάνω *epanō* 19x can function as an improper prep., *above, over, upon,* of place, Mt. 2:9; 5:14; *over,* of authority, Lk. 19:17, 19; *above, more than,* Mk. 14:5 [1883]

[2063] ἐπάρατος *eparatos* 1x *accursed,* Jn. 7:49* [1944]

[2064] ἐπαρκέω *eparkeō* 3x dat., pr. *to ward off; to assist, relieve, succor;* 1 Tim. 5:10, 16 (2x)* [1884]

[2065] ἐπαρχεία *eparcheia* 2x *province,* Acts 23:34; 25:1* [1885]

[2068] ἔπαυλις *epaulis* 1x pr. *a place to pass the night in; cottage, farm;* in NT *a dwelling, habitation, farm,* Acts 1:20* [1886]

[2069] ἐπαύριον *epaurion* 17x *tomorrow;* ἡ ἐπαύριον, sc. ἡμέρα, *the next* or *following day,* Mt. 27:62; Mk. 11:12 [1887]

[2071] Ἐπαφρᾶς *Epaphras* 3x *Epaphras,* pr. name, Col. 1:7; 4:12; Phlm. 23* [1889]

[2072] ἐπαφρίζω *epaphrizō* 1x *to foam out; to pour out like foam, vomit forth,* Jude 13* [1890]

[2073] Ἐπαφρόδιτος *Epaphroditos* 2x *Epaphroditus,* pr. name, Phil. 2:25; 4:18* [1891]

[2074] ἐπεγείρω *epegeirō* 2x *to raise* or *stir up against, excite* or *instigate against,* Acts 13:50; 14:2* [1892]

[2075] ἐπεί *epei* 26x *when, after, since, because, in as much as,* Mt. 18:32; 27:6; *for, for then, for else, since in that case,* Rom. 3:6; 11:6 [1893]

[2076] ἐπειδή *epeidē* 10x *since, because, in as much as,* Mt. 21:46; Lk. 11:6; Acts 13:46 [1894]

[2077] ἐπειδήπερ *epeidēper* 1x *since now, since indeed, considering that,* Lk. 1:1* [1895]

[2079] ἔπειμι *epeimi* 5x *to come upon; to come after; to succeed immediately,* Acts 7:26; 16:11; 20:15; 21:18; 23:11* [1966]

[2081] ἐπεισαγωγή *epeisagōgē* 1x *a superinduction, a further introduction,* whether by way of addition or substitution, Heb. 7:19* [1898]

[2082] ἐπεισέρχομαι *epeiserchomai* 1x *to come in upon, invade, surprise,* Lk. 21:35* [1904]

[2083] ἔπειτα *epeita* 16x *thereupon, then, after that, in the next place, afterwards,* Mk. 7:5; Lk. 16:7 [1899]

[2084] ἐπέκεινα *epekeina* 1x *BAGD* say it is an adverb with the gen.; others classify it as an improper prep., gen., *on yonder side, beyond,* Acts 7:43* [1900]

[2085] ἐπεκτείνομαι *epekteinomai* 1x pr. *to stretch out farther;* in NT mid. *to reach out towards, strain for,* Phil. 3:13* [1901]

[2086] ἐπενδύομαι *ependyomai* 2x *to put on over* or *in addition to;* mid. *to put on one's self in addition; to be further invested,* 2 Cor. 5:2, 4* [1902]

[2087] ἐπενδύτης *ependytēs* 1x *the outer* or *upper tunic,* worn between the inner tunic and the external garments, Jn. 21:7* [1903]

[2088] ἐπέρχομαι *eperchomai* 9x *to come to,* Acts 14:19; *to come upon,* Lk. 1:35; 21:26; Acts 1:8; Jas. 5:1; *to be coming on, to succeed,* Eph. 2:7; *to occur, happen to,* Acts 8:24; 13:40; *to come against, attack,* Lk. 11:22* [1904]

[2089] ἐπερωτάω *eperōtaō* 56x *to interrogate, question, ask,* Mt. 12:10; 17:10; in NT *to request, require,* Mt. 16:1; from the Hebrew, ἐπερωτᾶν τὸν θεόν, *to seek after, desire an acquaintance with God,* Rom. 10:20 [1905] See *ask; interrogate; question.*

[2090] ἐπερώτημα *eperōtēma* 1x pr. *an interrogation, question;* in NT *profession, pledge,* 1 Pet. 3:21* [1906]

[2091] ἐπέχω *epechō* 5x trans. *to hold out, present, exhibit, display,* Phil. 2:16; intrans. *to observe, take heed to, attend to,* Lk. 14:7; Acts 3:5; 1 Tim. 4:16; *to stay, delay,* Acts 19:22* [1907]

[2092] ἐπηρεάζω *epēreazō* 2x *to harass, insult,* Lk. 6:28; *to mistreat, abuse,* 1 Pet. 3:16* [1908]

[2093] ἐπί *epi* 890x (1) with the gen., *upon, on,* Mt. 4:6; 9:2; 27:19; *in,* of locality, Mk. 8:4; *near upon, by, at,* Mt. 21:19; Jn. 21:1; *upon, over,* of authority, Mt. 2:22; Acts 8:27; *in the presence of,* especially in a judicial sense, 2 Cor. 7:14; Acts 25:9; *in the case of, in respect of,* Jn. 6:2; Gal. 3:16; *in the time of, at the time of,* Acts 11:28; Rom. 1:10; ἐπ' ἀληθείας, *really, bona fide,* Mk. 12:32; (2) with the dat., *upon, on,* Mt. 14:8; Mk. 2:21; Lk. 12:44; *close upon, by,* Mt. 24:33; Jn. 4:6; *in the neighborhood* or *society of,* Acts 28:14; *over,* of authority, Mt. 24:47; *to,* of addition, *besides,* Mt. 25:20; Eph. 6:16; Col. 3:14; supervening *upon, after,* 2 Cor. 1:4; 7:4; *immediately upon,* Jn. 4:27; *upon,* of the object of an act, *towards, to,* Mk. 5:33; Lk. 18:7; Acts 5:35; *against,* of hostile posture or disposition, Lk. 12:52; *in dependence upon,* Mt. 4:4; Lk. 5:5; Acts 14:3; *upon the ground of,* Mt. 19:9; Lk. 1:59; Phil. 1:3; Heb. 7:11; 8:6; 9:17; *with a view to,* Gal. 5:13; 1 Thess. 4:7; (3) with the acc., *upon,* with the idea of previous or present motion, Mt. 4:5; 14:19, 26; *towards,* of place, *to,* Mt. 3:13; 22:34; *towards,* of the object of an action, Lk. 6:35; 9:38; *against,* of hostile movement, Mt. 10:21; *over,* of authority, Lk. 1:33; *to the extent of,* both of place and time, Rev. 21:16; Rom. 7:1; *near, by,* Mt. 9:9; *about, at, of time,* Acts 3:1; *in order to, with a view to, for the purpose of,* Mt. 3:7; Lk. 7:44 [1909]

[2094] ἐπιβαίνω *epibainō* 6x pr. *to step upon; to mount,* Mt. 21:5; *to go on board,* Acts 21:2; 27:2, *to enter,* Acts 20:18; *to enter upon,* Acts 21:4; 25:1* [1910]

[2095] ἐπιβάλλω *epiballō* 18x *to cast* or *throw upon,* Mk. 11:7; 1 Cor. 7:35; *to lay on, apply to,* Lk. 9:62; *to put on, sew on,* Mt. 9:16; Lk. 5:36; τὰς χεῖρας, *to lay hands on, offer violence to, seize,* Mt. 26:50; also, *to lay hand to, undertake, commence,* Acts 12:1; intrans. *to rush, dash, beat into,* Mk. 4:37; *to ponder, reflect on,* Mk. 14:72; *to fall to one's share, pertain to,* Lk. 15:12 [1911] See *arrest; break; lay on; sew on.*

[2096] ἐπιβαρέω *epibareō* 3x *to burden;* met. *to be burdensome, chargeable to,* 1 Thess. 2:9; 2 Thess. 3:8; *to bear hard upon, overcharge,* 2 Cor. 2:5* [1912]

[2097] ἐπιβιβάζω *epibibazō* 3x *to cause to ascend* or *mount, to set upon,* Lk. 10:34; 19:35; Acts 23:24* [1913]

[2098] ἐπιβλέπω *epiblepō* 3x *to look upon; to regard* with partiality, Jas. 2:3; *to regard* with kindness and favor, Lk. 1:48; 9:38* [1914]

[2099] ἐπίβλημα *epiblēma* 4x *that which is put over* or *upon;* in NT *a patch,* Mt. 9:16; Mk. 2:21; Lk. 5:36 (2x)* [1915]

[2101] ἐπιβουλή *epiboulē* 4x *a purpose* or *design against* any one; *conspiracy, plot,* Acts 9:24; 20:3, 19; 23:30* [1917]

[2102] ἐπιγαμβρεύω *epigambreuō* 1x *to marry* a wife *by the law of affinity,* Mt. 22:24* [1918]

[2103] ἐπίγειος *epigeios* 7x pr. *on the earth,* Phil. 2:10; *earthly, terrestrial,* Jn. 3:12; 1 Cor. 15:40; 2 Cor. 5:1; Phil. 3:19; *earthly, low, grovelling,* Jas. 3:15* [1919]

[2104] ἐπιγίνομαι *epiginomai* 1x *to come on, spring up,* as the wind, Acts 28:13* [1920]

[2105] ἐπιγινώσκω *epiginōskō* 44x pr. *to make* a thing *a subject of observation;* hence, *to arrive at knowledge from preliminaries; to attain to a knowledge of,* Mt. 11:27; *to ascertain,* Lk. 7:37; 23:7; *to perceive,* Mk. 2:8; 5:30; *to discern, detect,* Mt. 7:16, 20; *to recognize,* Mk. 6:33; Lk. 24:16, 31; Acts 3:10; *to acknowledge, admit,* 1 Cor. 14:37; 1 Tim. 4:3; pass. *to have one's character discerned and acknowledged,* 2 Cor. 6:9; from the Hebrew, *to regard* with favor and kindness, 1 Cor. 16:18 [1921] See *know; perceive; recognize; understand.*

[2106] ἐπίγνωσις *epignōsis* 20x *the coming at the knowledge* of a thing, *ascertainment,* Rom. 3:20; *a distance perception* or *impression, acknowledgment, insight,* Col. 2:2 [1922] See *knowledge; understanding.*

[2107] ἐπιγραφή *epigraphē* 5x *an inscription; a legend* of a coin, Mt. 22:20; Mk. 12:16; Lk. 20:24; *a label* of a criminal's name and offence, Mk. 15:26; Lk. 23:38* [1923]

[2108] ἐπιγράφω *epigraphō* 5x pluperfect pass., ἐπεγεγράμμην, *to imprint a mark on; to inscribe, engrave, write on,* Mk. 15:26; Acts 17:23; Rev. 21:12; met. *to imprint, impress deeply on,* Heb. 8:10; 10:16* [1924]

[2109] ἐπιδείκνυμι *epideiknymi* 7x *to exhibit,* Mt. 16:1; Acts 9:39; *to show,* Mt. 22:19; Lk. 17:14; *to point out,* Mt. 24:1; *to demonstrate, prove,* Acts 18:28; Heb. 6:17* [1925]

[2110] ἐπιδέχομαι *epidechomai* 2x *to admit; to receive kindly, welcome, entertain,* 3 Jn. 10; met. *to admit, approve, assent to,* 3 Jn. 9* [1926]

[2111] ἐπιδημέω *epidēmeō* 2x *to dwell among a people; to be at home among one's own people;* and in NT *to sojourn as a stranger among another people,* Acts 2:10; 17:21* [1927]

[2112] ἐπιδιατάσσομαι *epidiatassomai* 1x *to enjoin* anything *additional, superadd an injunction,* Gal. 3:15* [1928]

[2113] ἐπιδίδωμι *epididōmi* 9x *to give in addition;* also, *to give to, deliver to, give into one's hands,* Mt. 7:9, 10; Lk. 4:17; 11:11f.; 24:30, 42; Acts 15:30; intrans. probably a nautical term, *to commit a ship to the wind, let her drive,* Acts 27:15* [1929]

[2114] ἐπιδιορθόω *epidiorthoō* 1x *to set further to rights, to carry on an amendment, correct,* Tit. 1:5* [1930]

[2115] ἐπιδύω *epidyō* 1x *to set upon, to set during,* Eph. 4:26* [1931]

[2116] ἐπιείκεια *epieikeia* 2x also spelled ἐπιεικία, *reasonableness, equity;* in NT *gentleness, mildness,* 2 Cor. 10:1; *clemency,* Acts 24:4* [1932]

[2117] ἐπιεικής *epieikēs* 5x pr. *suitable; fair, reasonable; gentle, mild, patient,* 1 Tim. 3:3; Tit. 3:2; Jas. 3:17; 1 Pet. 2:18; τὸ ἐπιεικες, *mildness, gentleness,* Phil. 4:5* [1933]

[2118] ἐπιζητέω *epizēteō* 13x *to seek for, make search for,* Acts 12:19; *to require, demand,* Mt. 12:39; 16:4; Acts 19:39; *to desire, endeavor to obtain,* Rom. 11:7; Heb. 11:14; *to seek with care and anxiety,* Mt. 6:32 [1934] See *desire; look for; strive for.*

[2119] ἐπιθανάτιος *epithanatios* 1x *condemned to death, under sentence of death,* 1 Cor. 4:9* [1935]

[2120] ἐπίθεσις *epithesis* 4x *the act of placing upon, imposition* of hands, Acts 8:18; 1 Tim. 4:14; 2 Tim. 1:6; Heb. 6:2* [1936]

[2121] ἐπιθυμέω *epithumeō* 16x with the gen. or acc., *to set the heart upon; to desire, long for, have earnest desire,* Mt. 13:17; Lk. 15:16; *to lust after,* Mt. 5:28; spc. *to covet,* Rom. 13:9 [1937] See *covet; desire; lust.*

[2122] ἐπιθυμητής *epithumētēs* 1x *one who has an ardent desire for* anything, 1 Cor. 10:6* [1938]

[2123] ἐπιθυμία *epithumia* 38x *earnest desire,* Lk. 22:15; *irregular* or *violent desire,* Mk. 4:19; spc. impure *desire, lust,* Rom. 1:24; met. *the object of desire, what enkindles desire,* 1 Jn. 2:16, 17 [1939] See *desire; lust.*

[2125] ἐπικαθίζω *epikathizō* 1x *to cause to sit upon, seat upon,* Mt. 21:7 (where some mss read ἐπεκάθισεν, intrans. *to sit upon*)* [1940]

[2126] ἐπικαλέω *epikaleō* 30x pluperfect, ἐπεκέκλητο (3 sg), *to call on; to attach* or *connect a name,* Acts 15:17; Jas. 2:7; *to attach an additional name, to surname,* Mt. 10:3; pass. *to receive an appellation* or *surname,* Heb. 11:16; mid. *to call upon, invoke,* 2 Cor. 1:23; *to appeal to,* Acts 25:11, 12, 21 [1941] See *appeal; call; call on.*

[2127] ἐπικάλυμμα *epikalymma* 1x *a covering, veil;* met. *a cloak,* 1 Pet. 2:16* [1942]

[2128] ἐπικαλύπτω *epikalyptō* 1x *to cover over;* met. *to cover* or *veil* by a pardon, Rom. 4:7* [1943]

[2129] ἐπικατάρατος *epikataratos* 2x *cursed, accursed; subject to the curse* of condemnation, Gal. 3:10; *infamous,* Gal. 3:13* [1944]

[2130] ἐπίκειμαι *epikeimai* 7x *to lie upon, be placed upon,* Jn. 11:38; 21:9; *to press, urge upon,* Lk. 5:1; Acts 27:20; *be urgent, importunate upon,* Lk. 23:23; *to be imposed upon, be imposed* by law, Heb. 9:10; by necessity, 1 Cor. 9:16 [1945]

[2131] ἐπικέλλω *epikellō* 1x *to push* a ship *to shore,* Acts 27:41* [2027]

[2134] Ἐπικούρειος *Epikoureios* 1x *an Epicurean, follower of the philosophy of Epicurus,* Acts 17:18* [1946]

[2135] ἐπικουρία *epikouria* 1x *help, assistance,* Acts 26:22* [1947]

[2137] ἐπικρίνω *epikrinō* 1x *to decide; to decree,* Lk. 23:24* [1948]

[2138] ἐπιλαμβάνομαι *epilambanomai* 19x *to take hold of,* Mt. 14:31; Mk. 8:23; *to lay hold of, seize,* Lk. 23:26; Acts 16:19; met. *to seize on* as a ground of accusation, Lk. 20:20, 26; *to grasp, obtain* as if by seizure, 1 Tim. 6:12, 19; *to assume a portion of, to assume the nature of,* or, *to attach* or *ally one's self to,* Heb. 2:16 [1949] See *arrest; seize; take hold.*

[2140] ἐπιλανθάνομαι *epilanthanomai* 8x *to forget,* Mt. 16:5; *to be forgetful, neglectful of, to disregard,* Phil. 3:13; Heb. 6:10; in NT in a passive sense, *forgotten,* Lk. 12:6 [1950] See *forget.*

[2141] ἐπιλέγω *epilegō* 2x *to call,* Jn. 5:2; mid. *to select for one's self, choose,* Acts 15:40* [1951]

[2142] ἐπιλείπω *epileipō* 1x *to be insufficient, to run short, to fail,* Heb. 11:32* [1952]

[2143] ἐπιλείχω *epileichō* 1x *to lick,* Lk. 16:21* [621]

[2144] ἐπιλησμονή *epilēsmonē* 1x *forgetfulness, oblivion,* Jas. 1:25* [1953]

[2145] ἐπίλοιπος *epiloipos* 1x *remaining, still left,* 1 Pet. 4:2* [1954]

[2146] ἐπίλυσις *epilysis* 1x *a loosing, liberation;* met. *interpretation of* what is enigmatical and obscure, 2 Pet. 1:20* [1955]

[2147] ἐπιλύω *epilyō* 2x *to loose* what has previously been fastened or entangled, as a knot; met. *to solve, to explain,* what is enigmatical, as a parable, Mk. 4:34; *to settle, put an end to* a matter of debate, Acts 19:39* [1956]

[2148] ἐπιμαρτυρέω *epimartyreō* 1x *to bear testimony to; to testify solemnly,* 1 Pet. 5:12* [1957]

[2149] ἐπιμέλεια *epimeleia* 1x *care, attention,* Acts 27:3* [1958]

[2150] ἐπιμελέομαι *epimeleomai* 3x gen., *to take care of,* Lk. 10:34f.; 1 Tim. 3:5* [1959]

[2151] ἐπιμελῶς *epimelōs* 1x *carefully, diligently,* Lk. 15:8* [1960]

[2152] ἐπιμένω *epimenō* 16x *to stay longer, prolong a stay, remain on,* Acts 10:48; 15:34; *to continue, persevere,* Jn. 8:7; Acts 12:16; *to adhere to, continue to embrace,* Acts 13:43; Rom. 11:22; *to persist in,* Rom. 6:1; 1 Cor. 16:8 [1961] See *continue; remain; stay.*

[2153] ἐπινεύω *epineuō* 1x *to nod to;* met. *to assent to, consent,* Acts 18:20* [1962]

[2154] ἐπίνοια *epinoia* 1x *thought, purpose, device, intent,* Acts 8:22* [1963]

[2155] ἐπιορκέω *epiorkeō* 1x *to forswear one's self, to fail of observing one's oath,* Mt. 5:33* [1964]

[2156] ἐπίορκος *epiorkos* 1x *one who violates his oath, perjured,* 1 Tim. 1:10* [1965]

[2157] ἐπιούσιος *epiousios* 2x This word occurs nowhere else in Greek literature except in the context of the Lord's prayer. Guesses include, *necessary for today, necessary for tomorrow, daily, sufficient,* Mt. 6:11; Lk. 11:3* [1967]

[2158] ἐπιπίπτω *epipiptō* 11x *to fall upon; to throw one's self upon,* Lk. 15:20; Jn. 13:25; Acts 20:10, 37; *to press, urge upon,* Mk. 3:10; *to light upon,* Rom. 15:3; *to come over,* Acts 13:11; *to come upon, fall upon* mentally or spiritually, Lk. 1:12; Acts 8:16; 10:10, 44; 11:15; 19:17 [1968] See *come upon; embrace; fall upon.*

[2159] ἐπιπλήσσω *epiplēssō* 1x pr. *to inflict blows upon;* met. *to chide, reprove,* 1 Tim. 5:1* [1969]

[2160] ἐπιποθέω *epipotheō* 9x *to desire besides;* also, *to desire earnestly, long for,* 2 Cor. 5:2; *to have a strong bent,* Jas. 4:5; by impl. *to love, have affection for,* 2 Cor. 9:14 [1971]

[2161] ἐπιπόθησις *epipothēsis* 2x *earnest desire, strong affection,* 2 Cor. 7:7, 11* [1972]

[2162] ἐπιπόθητος *epipothētos* 1x *earnestly desired, longed for,* Phil. 4:1* [1973]

[2163] ἐπιποθία *epipothia* 1x *earnest desire,* Rom. 15:23* [1974]

[2164] ἐπιπορεύομαι *epiporeuomai* 1x *to travel to; to come to,* Lk. 8:4* [1975]

[2165] ἐπιράπτω *epiraptō* 1x also ἐπιρράπτω, *to sew on,* Mk. 2:21* [1976]

[2166] ἐπιρίπτω *epiriptō* 2x *to throw upon, cast upon,* Lk. 19:35; 1 Pet. 5:7* [1977]

[2168] ἐπίσημος *episēmos* 2x pr. *bearing a distinctive mark* or *device; noted, eminent,* Rom. 16:7; *notorious,* Mt. 27:16* [1978]

[2169] ἐπισιτισμός *episitismos* 1x *supply of food, provisions,* Lk. 9:12* [1979]

[2170] ἐπισκέπτομαι *episkeptomai* 11x *to look at observantly, to inspect; to look out, select,* Acts 6:3; *to go see, visit,* Acts 7:23; 15:36; *to visit* for the purpose of comfort and relief, Mt. 25:36, 43; Jas. 1:27; from the Hebrew, of God, *to visit,* Lk. 1:68, 78 [1980] See *look after; take care of; visit.*

[2171] ἐπισκευάζομαι *episkeuazomai* 1x *to prepare for a journey,* Acts 21:15* [643]

[2172] ἐπισκηνόω *episkēnoō* 1x *to quarter in* or *at;* met. *to abide upon,* 2 Cor. 12:9* [1981]

[2173] ἐπισκιάζω *episkiazō* 5x *to overshadow,* Mt. 17:5; met. *to shed influence upon,* Lk. 1:35 [1982]

[2174] ἐπισκοπέω *episkopeō* 2x *to look at, inspect;* met. *to be circumspect, heedful,* Heb. 12:15; *to oversee, to exercise the office of* ἐπίσκοπος, 1 Pet. 5:2* [1983]

[2175] ἐπισκοπή *episkopē* 4x *inspection, oversight, visitation;* of God, *visitation, interposition,* whether in mercy or judgment, Lk. 19:44; 1 Pet. 2:12; *the office of an ecclesiastical overseer,* 1 Tim. 3:1; from the Hebrew, *charge, function,* Acts 1:20* [1984]

[2176] ἐπίσκοπος *episkopos* 5x pr. *an inspector, overseer; a watcher, guardian,* 1 Pet. 2:25; in NT *an* ecclesiastical *overseer,* Acts 20:28; Phil. 1:1; 1 Tim. 3:2; Tit. 1:7* [1985] See *bishop; overseer.*

[2177] ἐπισπάομαι *epispaomai* 1x *to draw upon* or *after;* in NT mid. *to obliterate circumcision* by artificial extension of the foreskin, 1 Cor. 7:18* [1986]

[2178] ἐπισπείρω *epispeirō* 1x *to sow in* or *among,* Mt. 13:25* [4687]

[2179] ἐπίσταμαι *epistamai* 14x *to be versed in, to be master of,* 1 Tim. 6:4; *to be acquainted with,* Acts 18:25; 19:15; Jude 10: *to know,* Acts 10:28; *to remember, comprehend, understand,* Mk. 14:68 [1987] See *know; understand.*

[2180] ἐπίστασις *epistasis* 2x pr. *care of, attention to,* 2 Cor. 11:28 [1999]

[2181] ἐπιστάτης *epistatēs* 7x pr. *one who stands by; one who is set over;* in NT in voc., equivalent to διδάσκαλε, or ῥαββί, *master, doctor,* Lk. 5:5; 8:24, 45; 9:33, 49; 17:13* [1988]

[2182] ἐπιστέλλω *epistellō* 3x *to send word to, to send injunctions,* Acts 15:20; 21:25; *to write to, write* a letter, Heb. 13:22* [1989]

[2184] ἐπιστήμων *epistēmōn* 1x *knowing, discreet, understanding,* Jas. 3:13* [1990]

[2185] ἐπιστηρίζω *epistērizō* 4x pr. *to cause to rest* or *lean on, to settle upon;* met. *to conform, strengthen, establish,* 14:22; 15:32, 41; 18:23* [1991]

[2186] ἐπιστολή *epistolē* 24x *word sent; an order, command; an epistle, letter,* Acts 9:2; 15:30 [1992] See *epistle; letter.*

[2187] ἐπιστομίζω *epistomizō* 1x *to apply a curb* or *muzzle;* met. *to put to silence,* Tit. 1:11* [1993]

[2188] ἐπιστρέφω *epistrephō* 36x trans. *to turn towards; to turn round; to bring back, convert,* Lk. 1:16, 17; Jas. 5:19, 20; intrans. and mid. *to turn one's self upon* or *towards,* Acts 9:40; Rev. 1:12; *to turn about,* Mt. 9:22; *to turn back, return,* Mt. 12:44; met. *to be converted,* Acts 28:27 [1994] See *return; turn.*

[2189] ἐπιστροφή *epistrophē* 1x *a turning towards, a turning about;* in NT met. *conversion,* Acts 15:3* [1995]

[2190] ἐπισυνάγω *episynagō* 8x *to gather to* a place; *to gather together, assemble, convene,* Mt. 23:37; 24:31; Lk. 17:37 [1996]

[2191] ἐπισυναγωγή *episynagōgē* 2x *the act of being gathered together* or *assembled,* 2 Thess. 2:1; *an assembling together,* Heb. 10:25* [1997]

[2192] ἐπισυντρέχω *episyntrechō* 1x *to run together* to a place, Mk. 9:25* [1998]

[2195] ἐπισφαλής *episphalēs* 1x *on the verge of falling, unsteady;* met. *insecure, hazardous, dangerous,* Acts 27:9* [2000]

[2196] ἐπισχύω *epischuō* 1x *to strengthen;* intrans. *to gather strength;* met. *to be urgent, to press on* a point, *insist,* Lk. 23:5* [2001]

[2197] ἐπισωρεύω *episōreuō* 1x *to heap up, accumulate largely;* met. *to procure in abundance,* 2 Tim. 4:3* [2002]

[2198] ἐπιταγή *epitagē* 7x *injunction,* 1 Cor. 7:6, 25; 2 Cor. 8:8; *a decree,* Rom. 16:26; 1 Tim. 1:1; Tit. 1:3; *authoritativeness, strictness,* Tit. 2:15* [2003]

[2199] ἐπιτάσσω *epitassō* 10x with dat., *to set over* or *upon; to enjoin, charge,* Mk. 1:27; 6:39; Lk. 4:36 [2004] See *command; order.*

[2200] ἐπιτελέω *epiteleō* 10x *to bring to an end; to finish, complete, perfect,* Rom. 15:28; 2 Cor. 8:6, 11; *to perform,* Lk. 13:32; *to carry into practice, to realize,* 2 Cor. 7:1; *to discharge,* Heb. 9:6; *to execute,* Heb. 8:5; *to carry out to completion,* Phil. 1:6; mid. *to end, make an end,* Gal. 3:3; pass. *to be fully undergone, endured,* 1 Pet. 5:9 [2005] See *complete.*

[2201] ἐπιτήδειος *epitēdeios* 1x *fit, suitable, necessary,* Jas. 2:16* [2006]

[2202] ἐπιτίθημι *epitithēmi* 39x *to put, place,* or *lay upon,* Mt. 9:18; Lk. 4:40; *to impose* a name, Mk. 3:16, 17; *to inflict,* Acts 16:23; Lk. 10:30; Rev. 22:18; mid. *to impose* with authority, Acts 15:28; 28:10; *to set* or *fall upon, assail, assault, attack,* Acts 18:10 [2007] See *put on.*

[2203] ἐπιτιμάω *epitimaō* 29x pr. *to set a value upon; to assess a penalty; to allege as a crimination;* hence, *to reprove, chide, censure, rebuke, reprimand,* Mt. 19:13; Lk. 23:40; in NT *to admonish strongly, enjoin strictly,* Mt. 12:16; Lk. 17:3 [2008] See *rebuke.*

[2204] ἐπιτιμία *epitimia* 1x *a punishment, penalty,* 2 Cor. 2:6* [2009]

[2205] ἐπιτρέπω *epitrepō* 18x *to give over, to leave to the entire trust* or *management of* any one; hence, *to permit, allow, suffer,* Mt. 8:21; Mk. 5:13 [2010] See *allow; let; permit; suffer.*

[2207] ἐπιτροπή *epitropē* 1x *a trust; a commission, permission,* Acts 26:12* [2011]

[2208] ἐπίτροπος *epitropos* 3x *one to whose charge* or *control a thing is left; a steward, bailiff, agent, manager,* Mt. 20:8; *steward* or *overseer* of the revenue, *treasurer,* Lk. 8:3; *a guardian* of children, Gal. 4:2* [2012]

[2209] ἐπιτυγχάνω *epitynchanō* 5x *to light upon, find; to hit, reach; to acquire, obtain, attain,* Rom. 11:7 (2x); Heb. 6:15; 11:33; Jas. 4:2* [2013]

[2210] ἐπιφαίνω *epiphainō* 4x *to make to appear, to display;* pass. *to be manifested, revealed,* Tit. 2:11; 3:4; intrans. *to give light, shine,* Lk. 1:79; Acts 27:20* [2014]

[2211] ἐπιφάνεια *epiphaneia* 6x *appearance, manifestation,* 1 Tim. 6:14; 2 Tim. 1:10; *glorious display,* 2 Thess. 2:8; 2 Tim. 4:1, 8; Tit. 2:13* [2015]

[2213] ἐπιφαύσκω *epiphauskō* 1x *to shine upon, give light to, enlighten,* Eph. 5:14* [2017]

[2214] ἐπιφέρω *epipherō* 2x *to bring upon* or *against,* Jude 9; *to inflict,* Rom. 3:5* [2018]

[2215] ἐπιφωνέω *epiphōneō* 4x *to cry aloud, raise a shout* at a speaker, whether applaudingly, Acts 12:22; or the contrary, *to clamor at,* Lk. 23:21; Acts 21:34; 22:24* [2019]

[2216] ἐπιφώσκω *epiphōskō* 2x *to dawn,* Mt. 28:1; hence, used of the reckoned commencement of the day, *to be near commencing, to dawn on,* Lk. 23:54* [2020]

[2217] ἐπιχειρέω *epicheireō* 3x *to put hand to* a thing; *to undertake, attempt,* Lk. 1:1; Acts 9:29; 19:13* [2021]

[2219] ἐπιχέω *epicheō* 1x *to pour upon,* Lk. 10:34* [2022]

[2220] ἐπιχορηγέω *epichorēgeō* 5x *to supply further; to superadd,* 2 Pet. 1:5; *to supply, furnish, give,* 2 Cor. 9:10; Gal. 3:5; 2 Pet. 1:11; pass. *to gather vigor,* Col. 2:19* [2023]

[2221] ἐπιχορηγία *epichorēgia* 2x *supply, aid, support,* Eph. 4:16; Phil. 1:19* [2024]

[2222] ἐπιχρίω *epichriō* 2x *to smear upon, to anoint,* Jn. 9:6, 11* [2025]

[2224] ἐποικοδομέω *epoikodomeō* 7x *to build upon,* 1 Cor. 3:10, 12, 14; pass. met. *to be built upon* as parts of a spiritual structure, Eph. 2:20; *to build up, carry up a building;* met. *to build up in spiritual advancement,*Col. 2:7; Jude 20* [2026]

[2226] ἐπονομάζω *eponomazō* 1x *to attach a name to;* pass. *to be named,* Rom. 2:17* [2028]

[2227] ἐποπτεύω *epopteuō* 2x *to look upon, observe, watch; to witness, be an eye-witness of,* 1 Pet. 2:12; 3:2* [2029]

[2228] ἐπόπτης *epoptēs* 1x *a looker-on, eye-witness,* 2 Pet. 1:16* [2030]

[2229] ἔπος *epos* 1x *a word, that which is expressed by words;* ὡς ἔπος εἰπεῖν, *so to say, if the expression may be allowed,* Heb. 7:9* [2031]

[2230] ἐπουράνιος *epouranios* 19x *heavenly,* in respect of locality, Eph. 1:20; Phil. 2:10; τὰ ἐπουράνια, *the upper regions* of the air, Eph. 6:12; *heavenly,* in respect of essence and character, *unearthly,* 1 Cor. 15:48, 49; met. *divine, spiritual,* Jn. 3:12 [2032] See *heavenly.*

[2231] ἑπτά *hepta* 88x *seven,* indecl. numeral, Mt. 15:34, 37; by Jewish usage for a round number, Mt. 12:45; Lk. 11:26 [2033] See *seven.*

[2232] ἑπτάκις *heptakis* 4x *seven times,* Mt. 18:21, 22; Lk. 17:4 (2x)* [2034]

[2233] ἑπτακισχίλιοι *heptakischilioi* 1x *seven thousand,* Rom. 11:4* [2035]

[2235] Ἔραστος *Erastos* 3x *Erastus,* pr. name, Acts 19:22; Rom. 16:23; 2 Tim. 4:20* [2037]

[2236] ἐραυνάω *eraunaō* 6x *to search, examine, investigate,* Jn. 5:39; 7:52; Rom. 8:27; 1 Cor. 2:10; 1 Pet. 1:11; Rev. 2:23* [2045]

[2237] ἐργάζομαι *ergazomai* 41x intrans. *to work, labor,* Mt. 21:28; Lk. 13:14; *to trade, traffic, do business,* Mt. 25:16; Rev. 18:17; *to act, exert one's power, be active,* Jn. 5:17; trans. *to do, perform, commit,* Mt. 26:10; Jn. 6:28; *to be engaged in, occupied upon,* 1 Cor. 9:13; Rev. 18:17; *to acquire, gain by one's labor,* Jn. 6:27 [2038] See *do; perform; produce; work.*

[2238] ἐργασία *ergasia* 6x *work, labor;* in NT ἐργασίαν διδόναι, *to endeavor, strive,* Lk. 12:58; *performance, practice,* Eph. 4:19; *a trade, business, craft,* Acts

19:25, *gain* acquired by labor or trade, *profit,* Acts 16:16, 19; 19:24* [2039]

[2239] ἐργάτης *ergatēs* 16x *a workman, laborer,* Mt. 9:37, 38; 20:1, 2, 8; met. *a* spiritual *workman* or *laborer,* 2 Cor. 11:13; *an artisan, artificer,* Acts 19:25; *a worker, practicer,* Lk. 13:27 [2040] See *laborer; worker.*

[2240] ἔργον *ergon* 169x *anything done* or *to be done; a deed, work, action,* Jn. 3:21; Eph. 2:10; 2 Cor. 9:8, et al. freq.; *duty enjoined, office, charge, business,* Mk. 13:34; Jn. 4:34, et al. freq.; *a process, course of action,* Jas. 1:4; *a work, product of an action* or *process,* Acts 7:41; Heb. 1:10; *substance in effect,* Rom. 2:15 [2041] See *work.*

[2241] ἐρεθίζω *erethizō* 2x *to provoke, to irritate, exasperate,* Col. 3:21; *to incite, stimulate,* 2 Cor. 9:2* [2042]

[2242] ἐρείδω *ereidō* 1x *to make to lean upon; to fix firmly;* intrans. *to become firmly fixed, stick fast,* Acts 27:41* [2043]

[2243] ἐρεύγομαι *ereugomai* 1x *to vomit;* met. *to utter, declare openly,* Mt. 13:35* [2044]

[2244] ἐρημία *erēmia* 4x *a solitude, uninhabited region, waste, desert,* Mt. 15:33; Mk. 8:4; 2 Cor. 11:26; Heb. 11:38* [2047]

[2245] ἔρημος *erēmos* 48x *lone, desert, waste, uninhabited,* Mt. 14:13, 15; Mk. 6:31, 32, 35; *lone, abandoned* to ruin, Mt. 23:38; Lk. 13:35; met. *lone, unmarried,* Gal. 4:27; as a subst. *a desert, uninhabited region, waste,* Mt. 3:1; 24:26; Acts 7:36 [2048] See *barren; desert; desolate; secluded; wilderness.*

[2246] ἐρημόω *erēmoō* 5x *to lay waste, make desolate, bring to ruin,* Mt. 12:25; Lk. 11:17; Rev. 17:16; 18:17, 19* [2049]

[2247] ἐρήμωσις *erēmōsis* 3x *desolation, devastation,* Mt. 24:15; Mk. 13:14; Lk. 21:20* [2050]

[2248] ἐρίζω *erizō* 1x *to quarrel; to wrangle; to use the harsh tone of a wrangler* or *brawler, to grate,* Mt. 12:19* [2051]

[2249] ἐριθεία *eritheia* 7x *the service of a party, party spirit; feud, faction,* 2 Cor. 12:20; *contentious disposition, selfish ambition,* Gal. 5:20; Phil. 1:17; 2:3; Jas. 3:14; by impl. *untowardness, disobedience,* Rom. 2:8; Jas. 3:16* [2052] See *ambition.*

[2250] ἔριον *erion* 2x *wool,* Heb. 9:19; Rev. 1:14* [2053]

[2251] ἔρις *eris* 9x *altercation, strife,* Rom. 13:13; *contentious disposition,* Rom. 1:29; Phil. 1:15 [2054] See *strife.*

[2252] ἐρίφιον *eriphion* 1x *a goat, kid,* Mt. 25:33* [2055]

[2253] ἔριφος *eriphos* 2x *a goat, kid,* Mt. 25:32; Lk. 15:29* [2056]

[2254] Ἑρμᾶς *Hermas* 1x *Hermas,* pr. name, Rom. 16:14* [2057]

[2255] ἑρμηνεία *hermēneia* 2x *interpretation, explanation,* 1 Cor. 14:26; meton. *the power* or *faculty of interpreting,* 1 Cor. 12:10* [2058]

[2257] ἑρμηνεύω *hermēneuō* 3x *to explain, interpret, translate,* Jn. 1:42; 9:7; Heb. 7:2* [2059]

[2258] Ἑρμῆς *Hermēs* 2x *Hermes* or *Mercury,* son of Jupiter and Maia, the messenger and interpreter of the gods, and the patron of eloquence, learning, etc., Acts 14:12; Rom. 16:14* [2060]

[2259] Ἑρμογένης *Hermogenēs* 1x *Hermogenes,* pr. name, 2 Tim. 1:15* [2061]

[2260] ἑρπετόν *herpeton* 4x *a creeping animal, a reptile,* Acts 10:12; 11:6; Rom. 1:23; Jas. 3:7* [2062]

[2261] ἐρυθρός *erythros* 2x *red,* Acts 7:36; Heb. 11:29* [2063]

[2262] ἔρχομαι *erchomai* 632x *to come, to go, to pass.* By the combination of this verb with other terms, a variety of meaning results, which, however, is due, not to a change of meaning in the verb, but to the adjuncts. Ὁ ἐρχόμενος, *He who is coming, the expected Messiah,* Mt. 11:3 [2064] See *arrive; come; go.*

[2263] ἐρωτάω *erōtaō* 63x *to ask, interrogate, inquire of,* Mt. 21:24; Lk. 20:3; in NT *to ask, request, beg, beseech,* Mt. 15:23; Lk. 4:38; Jn. 14:16 [2065] See *ask; inquire; request.*

[2264] ἐσθής *esthēs* 8x also spelled ἔσθησις, *a robe, vestment, raiment, garment,* Lk. 23:11; 24:4; Acts 1:10; 10:30; 12:21; Jas. 2:2, 3* [2066]

[2266] ἐσθίω *esthiō* 158x *to eat,* Mt. 12:1; 15:27; ἐσθίειν καὶ πίνειν, *to eat and drink, to eat and drink* in the usual manner, *follow the common mode of living,* Mt. 11:18; also with the associated notion of supposed security, Lk. 17:27; *to feast, banquet,* Mt. 24:49; met. *to devour, consume,* Heb. 10:27; Jas. 5:3; from the Hebrew, ἄρτον ἐσθίειν, *to eat bread, to take food, take the usual meals,* Mt. 15:2 [2068, 5315] See *eat.*

[2268] Ἑσλί *Hesli* 1x *Esli,* pr. name, indecl., Lk. 3:25* [2069]

[2269] ἔσοπτρον *esoptron* 2x *mirror,* Jas. 1:23; 1 Cor. 13:12* [2072]

[2270] ἑσπέρα *hespera* 3x *evening,* Lk. 24:29; Acts 4:3; 28:23* [2073]

[2272] Ἑσρώμ *Hesrōm* 3x *Hezron,* pr. name, indecl., Mt. 1:3; Lk. 3:33* [2074]

[2274] ἔσχατος *eschatos* 52x *farthest; last, latest,* Mt. 12:45; Mk. 12:6; *lowest,* Mt. 19:30; 20:16; *in the lowest plight,* 1 Cor. 4:9 [2078] See *last.*

[2275] ἐσχάτως *eschatōs* 1x *to be in the last extremity,* Mk. 5:23* [2079]

[2276] ἔσω *esō* 9x can function as an improper prep., *in, within, in the interior of,* Mt. 26:58; Jn. 20:26; ὁ, ἡ, τὸ ἔσω, *inner, interior, internal;* met. *within* the pale of community, 1 Cor. 5:12; ὁ ἔσω ἄνθρωπος, *the inner man, the mind, soul,* Rom. 7:22 [2080]

[2277] ἔσωθεν *esōthen* 12x *from within, from the interior,* Mk. 7:21, 23; *within, in the internal parts,* Mt. 7:15; ὁ, ἡ, τὸ ἔσωθεν, *interior, internal,* Lk. 11:39, 40; ὁ ἔσωθεν ἄνθρωπος, *the mind, soul,* 2 Cor. 4:16 [2081]

[2278] ἐσώτερος *esōteros* 2x *inner, interior,* Acts 16:24; Heb. 6:19* [2082]

[2279] ἑταῖρος *hetairos* 3x *a companion, associate, fellow-comrade, friend,* Mt. 20:13; 22:12; 26:50* [2083]

[2280] ἑτερόγλωσσος *heteroglōssos* 1x *one who speaks another* or *foreign language,* 1 Cor. 14:21* [2084]

[2281] ἑτεροδιδασκαλέω *heterodidaskaleō* 2x *to teach other* or *different doctrine,* and spc. *what is foreign to the Christian religion,* 1 Tim. 1:3; 6:3* [2085]

[2282] ἑτεροζυγέω *heterozygeō* 1x *to be unequally yoked* or *matched,* 2 Cor. 6:14* [2086]

[2283] ἕτερος *heteros* 98x *other,* Mt. 12:45; *another, some other,* Mt. 8:21; *besides,* Lk. 23:32; ὁ ἕτερος, *the other* of two, Mt. 6:24; τῇ ἑτέρᾳ, *on the next* day, Acts 20:15; 27:3; ὁ ἕτερος, *one's neighbor,* Rom. 13:8; *different,* Lk. 9:29; *foreign, strange,* Acts 2:4; 1 Cor. 14:21; *illicit,* Jude 7 [2087] See *another; other.*

[2284] ἑτέρως *heterōs* 1x *otherwise, differently,* Phil. 3:15* [2088]

[2285] ἔτι *eti* 93x *yet, still,* Mt. 12:46; *still, further, longer,* Lk. 16:2; *further, besides, in addition,* Mt. 18:16; with a compar. *yet, still,* Phil. 1:9 [2089]

[2286] ἑτοιμάζω *hetoimazō* 40x *to make ready, prepare,* Mt. 22:4; 26:17 [2090] See *prepare.*

[2288] ἑτοιμασία *hetoimasia* 1x *preparation; preparedness, readiness,* Eph. 6:15* [2091]

[2289] ἕτοιμος *hetoimos* 17x *ready, prepared,* Mt. 22:4, 8; Mk. 14:15 [2092] See *ready.*

[2290] ἑτοίμως *hetoimōs* 3x *in readiness, preparedly,* Acts 21:13; 2 Cor. 2:14; 1 Pet. 4:5* [2093]

[2291] ἔτος *etos* 49x *a year,* Lk. 2:41; 3:23 [2094] See *year.*

[2293] Εὕα *heua* 2x *Eve,* pr. name, 2 Cor. 11:3; 1 Tim. 2:13* [2096]

[2294] εὐαγγελίζω *euangelizō* 54x *to address with good tidings,* Rev. 10:7; 14:6; but elsewhere *to proclaim as good tidings, to announce good tidings of,* Lk. 1:19; *to address with good tidings,* Acts 13:32; 14:15; *to address with the Gospel teaching, evangelize,* Acts 16:10; Gal. 1:9; absol. *to announce the good tidings* of the Gospel, Lk. 4:18; 9:6; pass. *to be announced as good tidings,* Lk. 16:16; *to be addressed with good tidings,* Mt. 11:5; Lk. 7:22; Heb. 4:2 [2097] See *evangelize; preach.*

[2295] εὐαγγέλιον *euangelion* 76x *glad tidings, good* or *joyful news,* Mt. 4:23; 9:35; *the Gospel; doctrines of the Gospel,* Mt. 26:13; Mk. 8:35; meton. *the preaching of,* or *instruction in, the Gospel,* 1 Cor. 4:15; 9:14 [2098] See *good news; Gospel.*

[2296] εὐαγγελιστής *euangelistēs* 3x pr. *one who announces glad tidings; an evangelist, preacher of the Gospel, teacher of the Christian religion,* Acts 21:8; Eph. 4:11; 2 Tim. 4:5* [2099] See *evangelist.*

[2297] εὐαρεστέω *euaresteō* 3x *to please,* Heb. 11:5, 6; pass. *to take pleasure in, be well pleased with,* Heb. 13:16* [2100]

[2298] εὐάρεστος *euarestos* 9x *well-pleasing, acceptable, grateful,* Rom. 12:1, 2 [2101] See *acceptable; pleasing.*

[2299] εὐαρέστως *euarestōs* 1x *acceptably,* Heb. 12:28 [2102]

[2300] Εὔβουλος *euboulos* 1x *Eubulus,* pr. name, 2 Tim. 4:21* [2103]

[2301] εὖγε *euge* 1x *Well done!* Lk. 19:17* [2095]

[2302] εὐγενής *eugenēs* 3x *well-born, of high rank, honorable,* Lk. 19:12; 1 Cor. 1:26; *generous, candid,* Acts 17:11* [2104]

[2304] εὐδία *eudia* 1x *serenity of the heavens, a cloudless sky, fair* or *fine weather,* Mt. 16:2* [2105]

[2305] εὐδοκέω *eudokeō* 21x *to think well, approve, consent, take delight* or *pleasure,* Mt. 3:17; 17:5; Mk. 1:11; Lk. 3:22; 12:32 [2106] See *(be) pleased; prefer; well pleased.*

[2306] εὐδοκία *eudokia* 9x *good will, favor,* Lk. 2:14; *good pleasure, purpose, intention,* Mt. 11:26; Lk. 10:21; Eph. 1:5, 9; Phil. 2:13; by impl. *desire,* Rom. 10:1; Phil. 1:15; 2 Thess. 1:11* [2107] See *desire; pleasure; purpose.*

[2307] εὐεργεσία *euergesia* 2x *well-doing, a good deed, benefit conferred,* Acts 4:9; *duty, good offices,* 1 Tim. 6:2* [2108]

[2308] εὐεργετέω *euergeteō* 1x *to do good, exercise beneficence,* Acts 10:38* [2109]

[2309] εὐεργέτης *euergetēs* 1x *a well-doer; a benefactor,* Lk. 22:25* [2110]

[2310] εὔθετος *euthetos* 3x pr. *well arranged, rightly disposed; fit, proper, adapted,* Lk. 9:62; 14:35; *useful,* Heb. 6:7* [2111]

[2311] εὐθέως *eutheōs* 36x *immediately, instantly, at once,* Mt. 8:3; 13:5 [2112] See *immediately.*

[2312] εὐθυδρομέω *euthudromeō* 2x *to run on a straight course; to sail on a direct course,* Acts 16:11; 21:1* [2113]

[2313] εὐθυμέω *euthumeō* 3x *to be cheerful, be in good spirits, take courage,* Acts 27:22, 25; Jas. 5:13* [2114]

[2314] εὔθυμος *euthumos* 1x *good cheer* or *courage, cheerful,* Acts 27:36* [2115]

[2315] εὐθύμως *euthumōs* 1x *cheerfully,* Acts 24:10* [2115]

[2316] εὐθύνω *euthunō* 2x *to guide straight; to direct, guide, steer* a ship, Jas. 3:4; *to make straight,* Jn. 1:23* [2116]

[2317] εὐθύς *euthus* 59x *straight forwards; directly, immediately, instantly,* Mt. 3:16; 13:20, 21 [2117] See *immediately.*

[2319] εὐθύτης *euthutēs* 1x *righteousness, uprightness, equity,* Heb. 1:8* [2118]

[2320] εὐκαιρέω *eukaireō* 3x *to have convenient time* or *opportunity, have leisure,* Mk. 6:31; 1 Cor. 16:12; *to be at leisure* for a thing, *to be disposed to attend, to give time,* Acts 17:21* [2119]

[2321] εὐκαιρία *eukairia* 2x *convenient opportunity, favorable occasion,* Mt. 26:16; Lk. 22:6* [2120]

[2322] εὔκαιρος *eukairos* 2x *timely, opportune, seasonable, convenient,* Mk. 6:21; Heb. 4:16* [2121]

[2323] εὐκαίρως *eukairōs* 2x *opportunely, seasonable, conveniently,* Mk. 14:11; 2 Tim. 4:2* [2122]

[2324] εὔκοπος *eukopos* 7x *easy,* Mt. 9:5; 19:24; Mk. 2:9; 10:25; Lk. 5:3; 16:17; 18:25 [2123]

[2325] εὐλάβεια *eulabeia* 2x *the disposition of one who is* εὐλαβής, *caution, circumspection;* in NT *reverence* to God, *piety,* Heb. 5:7; 12:28* [2124]

[2326] εὐλαβέομαι *eulabeomai* 1x *to fear, be afraid* or *apprehensive;* in NT absol. *to reverence* God, *to be influenced by pious awe,* Heb. 11:7* [2125]

[2327] εὐλαβής *eulabēs* 4x pr. *taking hold of well,* i.e., *warily;* hence, *cautious, circumspect; full of reverence* towards God, *devout, pious, religious,* Lk. 2:25; Acts 2:5; 8:2; 22:12* [2126]

[2328] εὐλογέω *eulogeō* 41x pr. *to speak well of,* in NT *to bless, ascribe praise and glorification,* Lk. 1:64; *to bless, invoke a blessing upon,* Mt. 5:44; *to bless, confer a favor* or *blessing upon,* Eph. 1:3; Heb. 6:14; pass. *to be blessed, to be an object of favor* or *blessing,* Lk. 1:28 [2127] See *bless; praise; thank.*

[2329] εὐλογητός *eulogētos* 8x *worthy of praise* or *blessing, blessed,* Mk. 14:61; Lk. 1:68 [2128] See *blessed; praise, praised.*

[2330] εὐλογία *eulogia* 16x pr. *good speaking; fair speech, flattery,* Rom. 16:18; in NT *blessing, praise, celebration,* 1 Cor. 10:16; Rev. 5:12, 13; *invocation of good, benediction,* Jas. 3:10; *a divine blessing,* Rom. 15:29; *a gift, benevolence,* 2 Cor. 9:5; *a frank gift,* as opposed to πλεονεξία, 2 Cor. 9:5; ἐπ᾽ εὐλογίαις, *liberally,* 2 Cor. 9:6 [2129] See *blessing; gift; praise.*

[2331] εὐμετάδοτος *eumetadotos* 1x *liberal, bountiful, generous,* 1 Tim. 6:18* [2130]

[2332] Εὐνίκη *eunikē* 1x *Eunice,* pr. name, 2 Tim. 1:5* [2131]

[2333] εὐνοέω *eunoeō* 1x *to have kind thoughts, be well affected* or *kindly disposed* towards, *make friends,* Mt. 5:25* [2132]

[2334] εὔνοια *eunoia* 1x *good will, kindliness; heartiness, enthusiasm,* Eph. 6:7* [2133]

[2336] εὐνοῦχος *eunouchos* 8x pr. *one who has charge of the bedchamber;* hence, *a eunuch, one emasculated,* Mt. 19:12; as eunuchs in the East often rose to places of power and trust, hence, *a minister of a court,* Acts 8:27, 34, 36, 38f.* [2135]

[2337] Εὐοδία *euodia* 1x *Euodia,* pr. name, Phil. 4:2* [2136]

[2338] εὐοδόω *euodoō* 4x *to give a prosperous journey; cause to prosper* or *be successful;* pass. *to have a prosperous journey, to succeed in a journey,* Rom. 1:10; met. *to be furthered, to prosper,* temporally or spiritually, 1 Cor. 16:2; 3 Jn. 2 (2x)* [2137]

[2339] εὐπάρεδρος *euparedros* 1x *constantly attending; devoted to;* τὸ εὐπάρεδρον, *devotedness,* 1 Cor. 7:35* [2145]

[2340] εὐπειθής *eupeithēs* 1x *easily persuaded, compliant,* Jas. 3:17* [2138]

[2342] εὐπερίστατος *euperistatos* 1x *easily* or *constantly distracted,* Heb. 12:1* [2139]

[2343] εὐποιΐα *eupoiia* 1x *doing good, beneficence,* Heb. 13:16* [2140]

[2344] εὐπορέω *euporeō* 1x *to be in prosperous circumstances, enjoy plenty,* Acts 11:29* [2141]

[2345] εὐπορία *euporia* 1x *wealth, abundance,* Acts 19:25* [2142]

[2346] εὐπρέπεια *euprepeia* 1x *grace, beauty,* Jas. 1:11* [2143]

[2347] εὐπρόσδεκτος *euprosdektos* 5x *acceptable, grateful, pleasing,* Rom. 15:16, 31; 2 Cor. 6:2; 8:12; 1 Pet. 2:5; in NT *gracious** [2144]

[2349] εὐπροσωπέω *euprosōpeō* 1x *to carry* or *make a fair appearance,* Gal. 6:12* [2146]

[2350] εὐρακύλων *eurakylōn* 1x *the northeaster,* Acts 27:14* [2148]

[2351] εὑρίσκω *heuriskō* 176x *to find, to meet with;* Mt. 18:28; 20:6; *to find out, to detect, discover,* Lk. 23:2, 4, 14; *to acquire, obtain, win, gain,* Lk. 1:30; 9:12; *to find* mentally, *to comprehend, recognize,* Acts 17:27; Rom. 7:21; *to find* by experience, *observe, gather,* Rom. 7:18; *to devise* as feasible, Lk. 5:19; 19:48 [2147] See *discover; find; obtain.*

[2352] εὐρακύλων *eurakylōn* 1x also spelled εὐρυκλύδων and εὐροκλύδων, which *BAGD* says was probably due to scribal error, *euracylon,* the name of a tempestuous southeast wind, Acts 27:14* [2148]

[2353] εὐρύχωρος *eurychōros* 1x *spacious; broad, wide,* Mt. 7:13* [2149]

[2354] εὐσέβεια *eusebeia* 15x *reverential feeling; piety, devotion, godliness,* Acts 3:12; 1 Tim. 2:2; 4:7, 8; *religion, the* Christian *religion,* 1 Tim. 3:16 [2150] See *devotion; godliness.*

[2355] εὐσεβέω *eusebeō* 2x *to exercise piety;* towards a deity, *to worship,* Acts 17:23; towards relatives, *to be dutiful towards,* 1 Tim. 5:4* [2151]

[2356] εὐσεβής *eusebēs* 3x *reverent; pious, devout, religious,* Acts 10:2, 7; 2 Pet. 2:9* [2152]

[2357] εὐσεβῶς *eusebōs* 2x *piously, religiously,* 2 Tim. 3:12; Tit. 2:12* [2153]

[2358] εὔσημος *eusēmos* 1x pr. *well marked, strongly marked;* met. *significant, intelligible,* 1 Cor. 14:9* [2154]

[2359] εὔσπλαγχνος *eusplanchnos* 2x *tender-hearted, compassionate,* Eph. 4:32; 1 Pet. 3:8* [2155]

[2361] εὐσχημόνως *euschēmonōs* 3x *in a becoming manner, with propriety, decently, gracefully,* Rom. 13:13; 1 Cor. 14:40; 1 Thess. 4:12* [2156]

[2362] εὐσχημοσύνη *euschēmosynē* 1x *comeliness, gracefulness;* artificial *comeliness, ornamental array, embellishment,* 1 Cor. 12:23* [2157]

[2363] εὐσχήμων *euschēmōn* 5x *of good appearance, pleasing to look upon, comely,* 1 Cor. 12:24; met. *becoming, decent,* τὸ εὔσχημον, *decorum, propriety,* 1 Cor. 7:35; *honorable, reputable, of high standing and influence,* Mk. 15:43; Acts 13:50; 17:12* [2158]

[2364] εὐτόνως *eutonōs* 2x *intensely, vehemently, strenuously,* Lk. 23:10; Acts 18:28* [2159]

[2365] εὐτραπελία *eutrapelia* 1x *facetiousness, pleasantry;* hence, *buffoonery, coarse laughter,* Eph. 5:4* [2160]

[2366] Εὔτυχος *eutychos* 1x *Eutychus,* pr. name, Acts 20:9* [2161]

[2367] εὐφημία *euphēmia* 1x pr. *use of words of good omen;* hence, *favorable expression, praise, commendation,* 2 Cor. 6:8* [2162]

[2368] εὔφημος *euphēmos* 1x pr. *of good omen, auspicious;* hence, *of good report,* *commendable, laudable, reputable,* Phil. 4:8* [2163]

[2369] εὐφορέω *euphoreō* 1x *to bear* or *bring forth well* or *plentifully, yield abundantly,* Lk. 12:16* [2164]

[2370] εὐφραίνω *euphrainō* 14x *to gladden,* 2 Cor. 2:2; pass. *to be glad, exult, rejoice,* Lk. 12:19; Acts 2:26; mid. *to feast in token of joy, keep a day of rejoicing,* Lk. 15:23, 24, 29, 32 [2165] See *celebrate; gladden; rejoice.*

[2371] Εὐφράτης *euphratēs* 2x the river *Euphrates,* Rev. 9:14; 16:12* [2166]

[2372] εὐφροσύνη *euphrosynē* 2x *joy, gladness, rejoicing,* Acts 2:28; 14:17* [2167]

[2373] εὐχαριστέω *eucharisteō* 38x *to thank,* Lk. 17:16; absol. *to give thanks,* Mt. 15:36; 26:27; pass. *to be made a matter of thankfulness,* 2 Cor. 1:11 [2168] See *give thanks; thanks.*

[2374] εὐχαριστία *eucharistia* 15x *gratitude, thankfulness,* Acts 24:3; *thanks, the act of giving thanks, thanksgiving,* 1 Cor. 14:16; *conversation marked by the gentle cheerfulness of a grateful heart,* as contrasted with the unseemly mirth of εὐτραπελία, Eph. 5:4 [2169] See *thanksgiving.*

[2375] εὐχάριστος *eucharistos* 1x *grateful, pleasing; mindful of benefits, thankful,* Col. 3:15* [2170]

[2376] εὐχή *euchē* 3x *a wish, prayer,* Jas. 5:15; *a vow,* Acts 21:23; Acts 18:18* [2171]

[2377] εὔχομαι *euchomai* 7x *to pray, offer prayer,* Acts 26:29; 2 Cor. 13:7, 9; Jas. 5:16; *to wish, desire,* Acts 27:29; Rom. 9:3; 3 Jn. 2* [2172]

[2378] εὔχρηστος *euchrēstos* 3x *highly useful, very profitable,* 2 Tim. 2:21; 4:11; Phlm. 11* [2173]

[2379] εὐψυχέω *eupsycheō* 1x *to be animated, encouraged, in good spirits,* Phil. 2:19* [2174]

[2380] εὐωδία *euōdia* 3x *a sweet smell, grateful odor, fragrance,* 2 Cor. 2:15; Eph. 5:2; Phil. 4:18* [2175] See *aroma.*

[2381] εὐώνυμος *euōnymos* 9x *of good name* or *omen;* used also as an euphemism by the Greeks instead of ἀριστερός, which was a word of bad import, as all omens on the left denoted misfortune; *the left,* Mt. 20:21, 23; 25:33, 41 [2176]

[2383] ἐφάλλομαι *ephallomai* 1x *to leap* or *spring upon, assault,* Acts 19:16* [2177]

[2384] ἐφάπαξ *ephapax* 5x *once for all,* Rom. 6:10; Heb. 7:27; 9:12; 10:10; *at once,* 1 Cor. 15:6* [2178]

[2386] Ἐφέσιος *Ephesios* 5x *Ephesian,* belonging to Ephesus, Acts 19:28, 34, 35; 21:29* [2180]

[2387] Ἔφεσος *Ephesos* 16x *Ephesus,* a celebrated city of Asia Minor, Acts 18:19, 21, 24; 1 Cor. 15:32* [2181]

[2388] ἐφευρετής *epheuretēs* 1x *an inventor, deviser,* Rom. 1:30* [2182]

[2389] ἐφημερία *ephēmeria* 2x pr. *daily course; the daily service* of the temple; *a class* of priests to which the daily service for a week was allotted in rotation, Lk. 1:5, 8* [2183]

[2390] ἐφήμερος *ephēmeros* 1x *lasting for a day; daily sufficient for a day, necessary for every day,* Jas. 2:15* [2184]

[2391] ἐφικνέομαι *ephikneomai* 2x *to come* or *reach to, to reach* a certain point or end; *to reach, arrive at,* 2 Cor. 10:13, 14* [2185]

[2392] ἐφίστημι *ephistēmi* 21x trans. *to place upon, over, close by;* intrans. *to stand by* or *near,* Lk. 2:38; 4:39; *to come suddenly upon,* Lk. 2:9; 24:4; *to come upon, assault,* Acts 6:12; 17:5; *to come near, approach,* Lk. 10:40; *to impend, be instant, to be at hand,* 1 Thess. 5:3; *to be present,* Acts 28:2; *to be pressing, urgent, earnest,* 2 Tim. 4:2 [2186] See *appear.*

[2393] ἐφοράω *ephoraō* 2x a proposed lexical form for the second aorist ἐπεῖδον [1896]

[2394] Ἐφραίμ *Ephraim* 1x *Ephraim,* pr. name, indecl. Jn. 11:54* [2187]

[2395] ἐφφαθά *ephphatha* 1x Aramaic, *be thou opened,* Mk. 7:34* [2188]

[2396] ἐχθές *echthes* 3x *yesterday,* Jn. 4:52; Acts 7:28; Heb. 13:8* [5504]

[2397] ἔχθρα *echthra* 6x *enmity, discord, feud,* Lk. 23:12; Gal. 5:20; *alienation,* Eph. 2:14, 16; *a principle* or *state of enmity,* Rom. 8:7; Jas. 4:4* [2189]

[2398] ἐχθρός *echthros* 32x *hated, under disfavor,* Rom. 11:28; *inimical, hostile,* Mt. 13:28; Col. 1:21; as a subst., *an enemy, adversary,* Mt. 5:43, 44; 10:36; Lk. 27:35 [2190] See *enemy.*

[2399] ἔχιδνα *echidna* 5x *a viper, poisonous serpent,* Acts 28:3; used also fig. of persons, Mt. 3:7; 12:34; 23:33; Lk. 3:7* [2191]

[2400] ἔχω *echō* 708x pluperfect., ἐσχήκειν, *to hold,* Rev. 1:16; *to seize, possess* a person, Mk. 16:8; *to have, possess,* Mt. 7:29, et al. freq.; *to have, have ready, be furnished with,* Mt. 5:23; Jn. 5:36; 6:68; *to have* as a matter of crimination, Mt. 5:23; Mk. 11:25; *to have* at command, Mt. 27:65; *to have* the power, *be able,* Mt. 18:25; Lk. 14:14; Acts 4:14; *to have* in marriage, Mt. 14:4; *to have, be affected by, subjected to,* Mt. 3:14; 12:10; Mk. 3:10; Jn. 12:48; 15:22, 24; 16:21, 22; Acts 23:29; 1 Tim. 5:12; Heb. 7:28; 1 Jn. 1:8; 4:18; χάραν ἔχειν, *to feel gratitude, be thankful,* 1 Tim. 1:12; 2 Tim. 1:3; Phlm. 7; *to hold, esteem, regard,* Mt. 14:5; Lk. 14:18, 19; *to have* or *hold* as an object of knowledge, faith, or practice, Jn. 5:38, 42; 14:21; 1 Jn. 5:12; 2 Jn. 9; *to hold on* in entire possession, *to retain,* Rom. 15:4; 2 Tim. 1:13; Heb. 12:28; intrans. with adverbs or adverbial expression, *to be, to fare,* Mt. 9:12; Mk. 2:17; 5:23; Lk. 5:31; Jn. 4:52; Acts 7:1; 12:15; 15:36; 21:13; 2 Cor. 10:6; 12:14; 1 Tim. 5:25; 1 Pet. 4:5; τὸ νῦν ἔχον, *for the present;* in NT ἔχειν ἐν γαστρί, *to be pregnant,* Mt. 1:18; as also ἔχειν κοίτην, Rom. 9:10; ἔχειν δαιμόνιον, *to be possessed,* Mt. 11:18; of time, *to have continued, to have lived,* Jn. 5:5, 6; 8:57; of space, *to embrace, be distant,* Acts 1:12; mid. pr. *to hold by, cling to;* hence, *to border upon, be next,* Mk. 1:38; Lk. 13:33; Acts 20:15; 21:26; *to tend immediately to,* Heb. 6:9 [2192] See *have; possess, possessions.*

[2401] ἕως *heōs* 146x can function as an improper prep., *while, as long as,* Jn. 9:4; *until,* Mt. 2:9; Lk. 15:4; as also in NT ἕως οὗ, ἕως ὅτου, Mt. 5:18, 26; ἕως ἄρτι, *until now,* Mt. 11:12; ἕως πότε, *until when, how long,* Mt. 17:17; ἕως σήμερον, *until this day, to this time,* 2 Cor. 3:15; as a prep. of time, *until,* Mt. 24:21; of place, *unto, even to,* Mt. 11:23; Lk. 2:15; ἕως ἄνω, *to the brim,* Jn. 2:7; ἕως εἰς, *even to, as far as,* Lk. 24:50; ἕως κάτω, *to the bottom;* ἕως ὧδε, *to this place,* Lk. 23:5; of state, *unto, even to,* Mt. 26:38; of number, *even, so much as,* Rom. 3:12, et al. freq. [2193]

[2404] Ζαβουλών *Zaboulōn* 3x *Zebulun,* pr. name, indecl., an Israelite tribe, Mt. 4:13, 15; Rev. 7:8* [2194]

[2405] Ζακχαῖος *Zakchaios* 3x *Zaccheus,* pr. name, Lk. 19:2, 5, 8* [2195]

[2406] Ζάρα *Zara* 1x *Zerah,* pr. name, indecl., Mt. 1:3* [2196]

[2408] Ζαχαρίας *Zacharias* 11x *Zacharias,* pr. name. (1) *Son of Barachias,* Mt. 23:35; Lk. 11:51. (2) *Father of Jn. the Baptist,* Lk. 1:5 [2197]

[2409] ζάω *zaō* 140x *to live, to be possessed of vitality, to exercise the functions of life,* Mt. 27:63; Acts 17:28; τὸ ζῆν, *life,* Heb. 2:15; *to have means of subsistence,* 1 Cor. 9:14; *to live, to pass existence* in a specific manner, Lk. 2:36; 15:13; *to be instinct with life and vigor;* hence, ζῶν, *living,* an epithet of God, in a sense peculiar to Himself; ἐλπὶς ζῶσα, *a living hope* in respect of vigor and constancy, 1 Pet. 1:3; ὕδωρ ζῶν, *living water* in respect of a full and unfailing flow, Jn. 4:10, 11; *to be alive* with cheered and hopeful feelings, 1 Thess. 3:8; *to be alive* in a state of salvation from spiritual death, 1 Jn. 4:9 [2198] See *alive; live.*

[2411] Ζεβεδαῖος *Zebedaios* 12x *Zebedee,* pr. name, the father of Jas. and John, Mt. 4:21; Mk. 10:35; Lk. 5:10; Jn. 21:1* [2199]

[2412] ζεστός *zestos* 3x pr. *boiled; boiling, boiling hot;* met. *glowing with zeal, fervent,* Rev. 3:15, 16* [2200]

[2414] ζεῦγος *zeugos* 2x *a yoke* of animals; *a pair, couple,* Lk. 2:24; 14:19* [2201]

[2415] ζευκτηρία *zeuktēria* 1x *a fastening, band,* Acts 27:40* [2202]

[2416] Ζεύς *Zeus* 2x the supreme god of the Greeks answering to the *Jupiter* of the Romans, Acts 14:12, 13* [2203]

[2417] ζέω *zeō* 2x *to boil, to be hot,* in NT met. *to be fervent, ardent, zealous,* Acts 18:25; Rom. 12:11* [2204]

[2418] ζηλεύω *zēleuō* 1x *to be zealous, earnest, eager,* Rev. 3:19* [2206]

[2419] ζῆλος *zēlos* 16x *generous rivalry; noble aspiration;* in NT *zeal, ardor in behalf of, ardent affection,* Jn. 2:17; Rom. 10:2; in a bad sense, *jealousy, envy, malice,* Acts 13:45; Rom. 13:13; *indignation, wrath,* Acts 5:17 [2205] See *earnestness; envy; jealousy; zeal.*

[2420] ζηλόω *zēloō* 11x *to have strong affection towards, be ardently devoted to,* 2 Cor. 11:2; *to make a show of affection and devotion towards,* Gal. 4:17; *to desire earnestly, aspire eagerly after,* 1 Cor. 12:31; 14:1, 39; absol. *to be fervent, to be zealous,* Rev. 3:19; *to be jealous, envious, spiteful,* Acts 7:9; 17:5; 1 Cor. 13:4; Jas. 4:2; pass. *to be an object of warm regard and devotion,* Gal. 4:18 [2206] See *desire eagerly; envy; jealous; zealous.*

[2421] ζηλωτής *zēlōtēs* 8x pr. *a generous rival, an imitator;* in NT *an aspirant,* 1 Cor. 14:12; Tit. 2:14; *a devoted adherent, a zealot,* Acts 21:20; 22:3; Gal. 1:14 [2207, 2208]

[2422] ζημία *zēmia* 4x *damage, loss, detriment,* Acts 27:10, 21; Phil. 3:7, 8* [2209]

[2424] Ζηνᾶς *Zēnas* 1x *Zenas,* pr. name, Tit. 3:13* [2211]

[2426] ζητέω *zēteō* 117x *to seek, look for,* Mt. 18:12; Lk. 2:48, 49; *to search after,* Mt. 13:45; *to be on the watch for,* Mt. 26:16; *to pursue, endeavor to obtain,* Rom. 2:7; 1 Pet. 3:11; *to desire, wish, want,* Mt. 12:47; *to seek, strive for,* Mt. 6:33; *to endeavor,* Mt. 21:46; *to require, demand, ask for,* Mk. 8:11; Lk. 11:16; 12:48; *to inquire* or *ask questions, question,* Jn. 16:19; *to deliberate,* Mk. 11:18; Lk. 12:29; in NT from Hebrew, ζητεῖν τὴν ψυχήν, *to seek the life* of any one, *to seek to kill,* Mt. 2:20 [2212] See *search; seek.*

[2427] ζήτημα *zētēma* 5x *a question; a subject of debate* or *controversy,* Acts 15:2; 18:15; 23:29; 25:19; 26:3* [2213]

[2428] ζήτησις *zētēsis* 7x *a seeking; an inquiry, a question; a dispute, debate, discussion,* Jn. 3:25; 1 Tim. 6:4; *a subject of dispute* or *controversy,* Acts 15:2, 7; 25:20; 2 Tim. 2:23; Tit. 3:9 [2214]

[2429] ζιζάνιον *zizanion* 8x *zizanium, darnel, spurious wheat,* a plant found in Palestine, which resembles wheat both in its stalk and grain, but is worthless, Mt. 13:25, 26, 27, 29, 30, 36, 38, 40* [2215]

[2431] Ζοροβαβέλ *Zorobabel* 3x *Zorobabel,* pr. name, indecl. (Ezra 2:2; 3:8), Mt. 1:12, 13; Lk. 3:27* [2216]

[2432] ζόφος *zophos* 5x *gloom, thick darkness,* Heb. 12:18; 2 Pet. 2:4, 17; Jude 6, 13* [2217]

[2433] ζυγός *zygos* 6x also spelled zugovn, ou, tov (n-2c), pr. *a cross bar* or *band; a yoke;* met. *a yoke* of servile condition, 1 Tim. 6:1; *a yoke* of service or obligation, Mt. 11:29, 30; Acts 15:10; Gal.

5:1; *the beam* of a balance; *a balance,* Rev. 6:5* [2218]

[2434] ζύμη *zymē* 13x *leaven, yeast,* Mt. 16:12; 13:33; met. *leaven* of the mind and conduct, by a system of doctrine or morals, used in a bad sense, Mt. 16:6, 11; 1 Cor. 5:6 [2219] See *leaven; yeast.*

[2435] ζυμόω *zymoō* 4x *to leaven, cause to ferment,* Mt. 13:33; Lk. 13:21; 1 Cor. 5:6; Gal. 5:9* [2220]

[2436] ζωγρέω *zōgreō* 2x pr. *to take alive, take prisoner in war* instead of killing; *to take captive, enthral,* 2 Tim. 2:26; also, *to catch* animals, as fish; in which sense it is used figuratively, Lk. 5:10* [2221]

[2437] ζωή *zōē* 135x *life, living existence,* Lk. 16:25; Acts 17:25; in NT spiritual *life* of deliverance from the proper penalty of sin, which is expressed by θάνατος, Jn. 6:51; Rom. 5:18; 6:4; the final *life* of the redeemed, Mt. 25:46; *life, source of* spiritual *life,* Jn. 5:39; 11:25; Col. 3:4 [2222] See *life.*

[2438] ζώνη *zōnē* 8x *a zone, belt, girdle,* Mt. 3:4; 10:9; Mk. 1:6; 6:8; Acts 21:11; Rev. 1:13; 15:6* [2223]

[2439] ζώννυμι *zōnnymi* 3x also spelled ζωννύω, *to gird, gird on, put on one's girdle,* Jn. 21:18 (2x), Acts 12:8* [2224]

[2441] ζῳογονέω *zōiogoneō* 3x pr. *to bring forth living creatures;* in NT *to preserve alive, save,* Lk. 17:33; Acts 7:19; 1 Tim. 6:13* [2225]

[2442] ζῷον *zōon* 23x *a living creature, animal,* Heb. 13:11; 2 Pet. 2:12 [2226] See *living creature.*

[2443] ζῳοποιέω *zōiopoieō* 11x pr. *to engender living creatures; to quicken, make alive,* Rom. 4:17; 8:11; 1 Cor. 15:36; in NT met. *to quicken* with the life of salvation, Jn. 6:63; 2 Cor. 3:6 [2227] See *give life.*

[2445] ἤ *ē* 343x can function as a conj (298t), *either, or,* Mt. 6:24; after comparatives, and ἄλλος, ἕτερος, expressed or implied, *than,* Mt. 10:15; 18:8; Acts 17:21; 24:21; intensive after ἀλλά and πρίν, Lk. 12:51; Mt. 1:18; it also serves to point an interrogation, Rom. 3:29 [2228]

[2448] ἡγεμονεύω *hēgemoneuō* 2x *to be a guide, leader, chief;* in NT *to hold the office of a Roman provincial governor,* Lk. 2:2; 3:1* [2230]

[2449] ἡγεμονία *hēgemonia* 1x *leadership, sovereignty;* in NT *a reign,* Lk. 3:1* [2231]

[2450] ἡγεμών *hēgemōn* 20x *a guide; a leader; a chieftain, prince,* Mt. 2:6; *a Roman provincial governor,* under whatever title, Mt. 10:18; 27:2; Lk. 20:20; Acts 23:24 [2232] See *governor; leader; ruler.*

[2451] ἡγέομαι *hēgeomai* 28x *to lead the way; to take the lead,* Acts 14:12; *to be chief, to preside, govern, rule,* Mt. 2:6; Acts 7:10; ἡγούμενος, *a chief officer* in the church, Heb. 13:7, 17, 24; also, *to think, consider, count, esteem, regard,* Acts 26:2; 2 Cor. 9:5 [2233] See *consider; regard; think.*

[2452] ἡδέως *hēdeōs* 5x *with pleasure, gladly, willingly,* Mk. 6:20; 12:37; 2 Cor. 11:19 [2234, 2236]

[2453] ἤδη *ēdē* 62x *before now, now, already,* Mt. 3:10; 5:28; ἤδη ποτέ, *at length,* Rom. 1:10; Phil. 4:10 [2235]

[2454] ἡδονή *hēdonē* 5x *pleasure, gratification;* esp. *sensual pleasure,* Lk. 8:14; Tit. 3:3; Jas. 4:3; 2 Pet. 2:13; *a passion,* Jas. 4:1* [2237]

[2455] ἡδύοσμον *hēdyosmon* 2x *garden mint,* Mt. 23:23; Lk. 11:42* [2238]

[2456] ἦθος *ēthos* 1x pr. *a place of customary resort;* hence, *a settled habit of mind and manners,* 1 Cor. 15:33* [2239]

[2457] ἥκω *hēkō* 26x *to become, have arrived,* Mt. 8:11; Mk. 8:3; Lk. 15:27; Rev. 15:4* [2240] See *come.*

[2458] ἠλί *ēli* 2x Aramaic for *My God!,* Mt. 27:46 (2x)* [2241]

[2459] Ἡλί *ēli* 1x *Heli,* the father of Joseph, Lk. 3:23* [2242]

[2460] Ἡλίας *ēlias* 29x *Elijah,* pr name, (1 Ki. 17-20), Mt. 11:14; 17:3f.; Mk. 15:35f.; Lk. 1:7; Jn. 1:21; Jas. 5:17 [2243]

[2461] ἡλικία *hēlikia* 8x *a particular period of life; the period fitted for a particular function, prime,* Heb. 11:11; *full age, years of discretion,* Jn. 9:21, 23; perhaps, *the whole duration of life,* Mt. 6:27; Lk. 12:25; otherwise, *stature,* Lk. 2:52; 19:3; Eph. 4:13* [2244]

[2462] ἡλίκος *hēlikos* 3x *as great as; how great,* Col. 2:1; Jas. 3:5 (2x)* [2245]

[2463] ἥλιος *hēlios* 32x *the sun,* Mt. 13:43; 17:2; Mk. 1:32; meton. *light of the sun, light,* Acts 13:11 [2246] See *sun.*

[2464] ἧλος *hēlos* 2x *a nail,* Jn. 20:25 (2x)* [2247]

[7005] ἡμεῖς *hēmeis* 864x see ἐγώ

[2465] ἡμέρα *hēmera* 389x *day, a day, the interval from sunrise to sunset,* opp. to νύξ, Mt. 4:2; 12:40; Lk. 2:44; *the interval of twenty-four hours,* comprehending day and night, Mt. 6:34; 15:32; from the Hebrew, ἡμέρᾳ καὶ ἡμέρᾳ, *day by day, every day,* 2 Cor. 4:16; ἡμέραν ἐξ ἡμέρας, *from day to day, continually,* 2 Pet. 2:8; καθ᾽ ἡμέραν, *every day, daily,* Acts 17:17; Heb. 3:13; *a point* or *period of time,* Lk. 19:42; Acts 15:7; Eph. 6:13; *a judgement, trial,* 1 Cor. 4:3 [2250] See *day.*

[2466] ἡμέτερος *hēmeteros* 7x *our,* Lk. 16:12; Acts 2:11; 24:6; 26:5; Rom. 15:4; 2 Tim. 4:15; Tit. 3:14; 1 Jn. 1:3; 2:2* [2251]

[2467] ἡμιθανής *hēmithanēs* 1x *half dead,* Lk. 10:30* [2253]

[2468] ἥμισυς *hēmisys* 5x *half,* Mk. 6:23; Lk. 19:8; Rev. 11:9, 11; 12:14* [2255]

[2469] ἡμιώριον *hēmiōrion* 1x also spelled ἡμίωρον, *half an hour,* Rev. 8:1* [2256]

[2471] ἡνίκα *hēnika* 2x *when,* 2 Cor. 3:15, 16* [2259]

[2472] ἤπερ *ēper* 1x strengthened form of ἤ, *than,* Jn. 12:43* [2260]

[2473] ἤπιος *ēpios* 2x *mild, gentle, kind,* 2 Tim. 2:24; 1 Thess. 2:7* [2261]

[2474] Ἤρ *ēr* 1x *Er,* pr. name, indecl., Lk. 3:28* [2262]

[2475] ἤρεμος *ēremos* 1x *tranquil, quiet,* 1 Tim. 2:2* [2263]

[2476] Ἡρῴδης *hērōdēs* 43x *Herod,* pr. name. (1) *Herod the Great,* Mt. 2:1. (2) *Herod Antipas,* tetrarch of Galilee and Peraea, Mt. 14:1. (3) *Herod Agrippa,* Acts 12:1 [2264]

[2477] Ἡρῳδιανοί *hērōidianoi* 3x *Herodians,* partisans of Ἡρῴδης, *Herod Antipas,* Mt. 22:16; Mk. 3:6; 12:13* [2265]

[2478] Ἡρῳδιάς *hērōidias* 6x *Herodias,* pr. name, the wife of Herod Antipas, Mt. 14:3, 6; Mk. 6:17, 19, 22; Lk. 3:19* [2266]

[2479] Ἡρῳδίων *hērōidiōn* 1x *Herodian,* pr. name, Rom. 16:11* [2267]

[2480] Ἠσαΐας *ēsaias* 22x *Isaiah,* pr. name, Mt. 3:3; 13:14; Mk. 1:2; Lk. 4:17; Jn. 1:23; 12:38, 39, 41; Acts 8:28; Rom. 9:27, 29 [2268]

[2481] Ἠσαῦ *ēsau* 3x *Esau,* pr. name, indecl. (Gen. 27-28), Rom. 9:13; Heb. 11:20; 12:16* [2269]

[2482] ἥσσων *hēssōn* 2x *lesser, inferior, weaker,* 1 Cor. 11:17; 2 Cor. 12:15* [2276]

[2483] ἡσυχάζω *hēsychazō* 5x *to be still, at rest; to live peaceably, be quiet,* 1 Thess. 4:11; *to rest* from labor, Lk. 23:56; *to be silent* or *quiet, acquiesce, to desist* from discussion, Lk. 14:4; Acts 11:18; 21:14* [2270]

[2484] ἡσυχία *hēsychia* 4x *rest, quiet, tranquillity; a quiet, tranquil life,* 2 Thess. 3:12; *silence, silent attention,* Acts 22:2; 1 Tim. 2:11, 12* [2271]

[2485] ἡσύχιος *hēsychios* 2x *quiet, tranquil, peaceful,* 1 Tim. 2:2; 1 Pet. 3:4* [2272]

[2486] ἤτοι *ētoi* 1x *whether,* with an elevated tone, Rom. 6:16* [2273]

[2487] ἡττάομαι *hēttaomai* 2x *to be less, inferior to; to fare worse*; by impl. *to be overcome, vanquished,* 2 Pet. 2:19, 20* [2274]

[2488] ἥττημα *hēttēma* 2x *an inferiority,* to a particular standard; *default, defeat, failure, shortcoming,* Rom. 11:12; 1 Cor. 6:7* [2275]

[2490] ἠχέω *ēcheō* 1x *to sound, ring,* 1 Cor. 13:1* [2278]

[2491] ἦχος *ēchos* 3x *roar, sound, noise,*, Heb. 12:19; *report,* Lk. 4:37; Acts 2:2* [2279]

[2492] ἦχος *ēchos* 1x *sound, noise,* Lk. 21:25* [2279]

[2497] Θαδδαῖος *Thaddaios* 2x *Thaddaeus,* pr. name, Mt. 10:3; Mk. 3:18* [2280]

[2498] θάλασσα *thalassa* 91x *the sea,* Mt. 23:15, Mk. 9:42; *a sea,* Acts 7:36; *an inland sea, lake,* Mt. 8:24 [2281] See *sea.*

[2499] θάλπω *thalpō* 2x *to impart warmth;* met. *to cherish, nurse, foster, comfort,* Eph. 5:29; 1 Thess. 2:7* [2282]

[2500] Θαμάρ *Thamar* 1x *Tamar,* (Gen. 38), pr. name, indecl., Mt. 1:3* [2283]

[2501] θαμβέω *thambeō* 3x *to be astonished, amazed, awestruck* Mt. 1:27; 10:24, 32* [2284]

[2502] θάμβος *thambos* 3x *astonishment, amazement, awe,* Lk. 4:36; 5:9; Acts 3:10* [2285]

[2503] θανάσιμος *thanasimos* 1x *deadly, mortal, fatal,* Mk. 16:18* [2286]

[2504] θανατηφόρος *thanatēphoros* 1x *bringing* or *causing death, deadly, fatal,* Jas. 3:8* [2287]

[2505] θάνατος *thanatos* 120x *death, the extinction of life,* whether naturally, Lk. 2:26; Mk. 9:1; or violently, Mt. 10:21; 15:4; *imminent danger of death,* 2 Cor. 4:11, 12; 11:23; in NT spiritual *death,* as opposed to ζωή in its spiritual sense, in respect of a forfeiture of salvation, Jn. 8:51; Rom. 6:16 [2288] See *death.*

[2506] θανατόω *thanatoō* 11x *to put to death, deliver to death,* Mt. 10:21; 26:59; Mk. 13:12; pass. *to be exposed to imminent danger of death,* Rom. 8:36; in NT met. *to subdue,* Rom. 8:13; pass. *to be dead to, to be rid, parted from,* as if by the intervention of death, Rom. 7:4 [2289] See *kill; put to death.*

[2507] θάπτω *thaptō* 11x *to bury,* Mt. 8:21, 22; 14:12 [2290] See *bury.*

[2508] Θάρα *Thara* 1x *Terah,* Abraham's father, pr. name, indecl., Lk. 3:34* [2291]

[2509] θαρρέω *tharreō* 6x *to be confident, courageous,* 2 Cor. 5:6, 8; 7:16; 10:1, 2; Heb. 13:6* [2292]

[2510] θαρσέω *tharseō* 7x *to be of good courage, be of good cheer,* Mt. 9:2; *to be confident, hopeful*; *to be bold, maintain a bold bearing,* Mt. 9:22; 14:27; Mk. 6:50; 10:49; Jn. 16:33; Acts 23:11* [2293]

[2511] θάρσος *tharsos* 1x *courage, confidence,* Acts 28:15* [2294]

[2512] θαῦμα *thauma* 2x *a wonder; wonder, admiration, astonishment,* 2 Cor. 11:14; Rev. 17:6* [2295]

[2513] θαυμάζω *thaumazō* 43x *to admire, regard with admiration, wonder at,* Lk. 7:9; Acts 7:31; *to reverence, adore,* 2 Thess. 1:10; absol. *to wonder, be filled with wonder, admiration,* or *astonishment,* Mt. 8:10; Lk. 4:22 [2296] See *(be) amazed; astound; marvel; wonder.*

[2514] θαυμάσιος *thaumasios* 1x *wonderful, admirable, marvellous;* τὸ θαυμάσιον, *a wonder, wonderful work,* Mt. 21:15* [2297]

[2515] θαυμαστός *thaumastos* 6x *wondrous, glorious,* 1 Pet. 2:9; Rev. 15:1; *marvellous, strange, uncommon,* Mt. 21:42; Mk. 12:11; Jn. 9:30; Rev. 15:3* [2298]

[2516] θεά *thea* 1x *a goddess,* Acts 19:27* [2299]

[2517] θεάομαι *theaomai* 22x *to gaze upon,* Mt. 6:1; 23:5; Lk. 7:24; *to see, discern with the eyes,* Mk. 16:11, 14; Lk. 5:27; Jn. 1:14, 32, 38; *to see, visit,* Rom. 15:24 [2300] See *behold; observe; see.*

[2518] θεατρίζω *theatrizō* 1x *to be exposed as in a theater, to be made a gazing-stock, object of scorn,* Heb. 10:33* [2301]

[2519] θέατρον *theatron* 3x *a theater, a place where public games and spectacles are exhibited,* Acts 19:29, 31; meton. *a show, gazing-stock,* 1 Cor. 4:9* [2302]

[2520] θεῖον *theion* 7x *brimstone, sulphur,* Lk. 17:29; Rev. 9:17; 14:10; 19:20; 20:10; 21:8* [2303]

[2521] θεῖος *theios* 3x *divine, pertaining to God,* 2 Pet. 1:3, 4; τὸ θεῖον, *the divine nature, divinity,* Acts 17:29* [2304]

[2522] θειότης *theiotēs* 1x *divinity, deity, godhead, divine majesty,* Rom. 1:20* [2305]

[2523] θειώδης *theiōdēs* 1x *of brimstone, sulphurous,* Rev. 9:17* [2306]

[2525] θέλημα *thelēma* 62x *will, bent, inclination,* 1 Cor. 16:12; Eph. 2:3; 1 Pet. 4:3; *resolve,* 1 Cor. 7:37; *will, purpose, design,* 2 Tim. 2:26; 2 Pet. 1:21; *will, sovereign pleasure, behest,* Mt. 18:14; Lk. 12:47; Acts 13:22, et al. freq.; ἐν τῷ θελήματι θεοῦ, *Deo permittente, if God please* or *permit,* Rom. 1:10 [2307] See *will.*

[2526] θέλησις *thelēsis* 1x *will, pleasure,* Heb. 2:4* [2308]

[2527] θέλω *thelō* 208x *to exercise the will,* properly by an unimpassioned operation; *to be willing,* Mt. 17:4; *to be inclined, disposed,* Rom. 13:3; *to choose,* Lk. 1:62; *to intend, design,* Lk. 14:28; *to will,* Jn. 5:21; 21:22; ἤθελον, *I could wish,* Gal. 4:20 [2309] See *desire; want; will.*

[2528] θεμέλιον *themelion* 1x in Acts 16:26 *themelion* is used as a neuter noun from *themelios* (*2529*), *foundation* such as the foundation of a prison* [2310] See *foundation.*

[2529] θεμέλιος *themelios* 15x see θεμέλιον (*2528*) *a foundation,* Lk. 6:48, 49; Heb. 11:10; met. *a foundation* laid in elementary instruction, Heb. 6:1; *a foundation* of a superstructure of faith, doctrine, or hope, 1 Cor. 3:10, 11, 12; Eph. 2:20; 1 Tim. 6:19; *a foundation* laid in the commencement of the preaching of the Gospel, Rom. 15:20* [2310] See *foundation.*

[2530] θεμελιόω *themelioō* 5x *to found, lay the foundation of,* Mt. 7:25; Heb. 1:10; met. *to ground, establish, render firm and unwavering,* Eph. 3:17; Col. 1:23; 1 Pet. 5:10* [2311]

[2531] θεοδίδακτος *theodidaktos* 1x *taught of God, divinely instructed,* 1 Thess. 4:9* [2312]

[2534] θεομάχος *theomachos* 1x *fighting against God, in conflict with God,* Acts 5:39* [2314]

[2535] θεόπνευστος *theopneustos* 1x *divinely inspired,* 2 Tim. 3:16* [2315]

[2536] θεός *theos* 1,317x *a deity,* Acts 7:43; 1 Cor. 8:5; *an idol,* Acts 7:40; *God, the true God,* Mt. 3:9, et al. freq.; *God, possessed of true godhead,* Jn. 1:1; Rom. 9:5; from the Hebrew, applied to potentates, Jn. 10:34, 35; τῷ θεῷ, an intensive term, from the Hebrew, *exceedingly,* Acts 7:20, and, perhaps, 2 Cor. 10:4 [2316] See *God.*

[2537] θεοσέβεια *theosebeia* 1x *worshipping of God, reverence towards God, piety,* 1 Tim. 2:10* [2317]

[2538] θεοσεβής *theosebēs* 1x *reverencing God, pious, godly, devout, a sincere worshipper of God,* Jn. 9:31* [2318]

[2539] θεοστυγής *theostygēs* 1x *God-hated;* in NT *a hater and despiser of God,* Rom. 1:30* [2319]

[2540] θεότης *theotēs* 1x *divinity, deity, godhead,* Col. 2:9* [2320]

[2541] Θεόφιλος *Theophilos* 2x *Theophilus,* pr. name, Lk. 1:3; Acts 1:1* [2321]

[2542] θεραπεία *therapeia* 3x *service, attendance; healing, cure,* Lk. 9:11; Rev. 22:2; meton. *those who render service, servants, domestics, family household,* Lk. 12:42* [2322]

[2543] θεραπεύω *therapeuō* 43x *to heal, cure,* Mt. 4:23, 24; 8:16; pass. *to receive service,* Acts 17:25; *to serve, minister to, render service and attendance; to render* divine *service, worship,* Acts 17:25 [2323] See *cure; heal.*

[2544] θεράπων *therapōn* 1x *an attendant, a servant; a minister,* Heb. 3:5* [2324]

[2545] θερίζω *therizō* 21x *to gather in harvest, reap,* Mt. 6:26; 25:24, 26; met. *to reap* the reward of labor, 1 Cor. 9:11; 2 Cor. 9:6; *to reap* the harvest of vengeance, Rev. 14:15, 16 [2325] See *harvest; reap.*

[2546] θερισμός *therismos* 13x *a harvest, the act of gathering in the harvest, reaping,* Jn. 4:35; met. *the harvest* of the Gospel, Mt. 9:37, 38; Lk. 10:2; *a crop;* met. *the crop* of vengeance, Rev. 14:15 [2326] See *harvest.*

[2547] θεριστής *theristēs* 2x *one who gathers in the harvest, a reaper,* Mt. 13:30, 39* [2327]

[2548] θερμαίνω *thermainō* 6x *to warm;* mid. *to warm one's self,* Mt. 14:54, 67; Jn. 18:18, 25; Jas. 2:16* [2328]

[2549] θέρμη *thermē* 1x also formed as θέρμα, *heat, warmth,* Acts 28:3* [2327]

[2550] θέρος *theros* 3x *the warm season of the year, summer,* Mt. 24:32; Mk. 13:28; Lk. 21:30* [2330]

[2552] Θεσσαλονικεύς *Thessalonikeus* 4x *Thessalonian, of Thessalonica,* Acts 20:4; 27:2; inscription to 1 and 2 Thess.* [2331]

[2553] Θεσσαλονίκη *Thessalonikē* 5x *Thessalonica,* a city of Macedonia, Acts 17:1, 11, 13; Phil. 4:16; 2 Tim. 4:10* [2332]

[2554] Θευδᾶς *Theudas* 1x *Theudas,* pr. name, Acts 5:36* [2333]

[2555] θεωρέω *theōreō* 58x *to be a spectator, to gaze on, contemplate; to behold, view* with interest and attention, Mt. 27:55; 28:1; *to contemplate* mentally, *consider,* Heb. 7:4; in NT *to see, perceive,* Mk. 3:11; *to come to a knowledge of,* Jn. 6:40; from the Hebrew, *to experience, undergo,* Jn. 8:51 [2334] See *perceive; see; watch.*

[2556] θεωρία *theōria* 1x *a beholding; a sight, spectacle,* Lk. 23:48* [2335]

[2557] θήκη *thēkē* 1x *a repository, receptacle; a case, sheath, scabbard,* Jn. 18:11* [2336]

[2558] θηλάζω *thēlazō* 5x *to suckle, give suck,* Mt. 24:19; Mk. 13:17; Lk. 21:23; *to suck,* Mt. 21:16; Lk. 11:27* [2337]

[2559] θῆλυς *thēlys* 5x *female;* τὸ θῆλυ, σχ. γένος, *a female,* Mt. 19:4; Mk. 10:6; Gal. 3:28; ἡ θήλεια, *woman,* Rom. 1:26, 27* [2338]

[2560] θήρα *thēra* 1x *hunting, the chase;* met. *means of capture, a cause of destruction,* Rom. 11:9* [2339]

[2561] θηρεύω *thēreuō* 1x *to hunt, catch;* met. *to seize on, lay hold of,* Lk. 11:54* [2340]

[2562] θηριομαχέω *thēriomacheō* 1x *to fight with wild beasts;* met. *to be exposed to furious hostility,* 1 Cor. 15:32* [2341]

[2563] θηρίον *thērion* 46x *a beast, wild animal,* Mk. 1:13; Acts 10:12; met. *a brute, brutish man,* Tit. 1:12 [2342] See *beast.*

[2564] θησαυρίζω *thēsaurizō* 8x *to collect and lay up stores* or *wealth, treasure,*

Mt. 6:19, 20; Lk. 12:21; 2 Cor. 12:14; Jas. 5:3; *to heap up, accumulate,* Rom. 2:5; 1 Cor. 16:2; *to reserve, keep in store,* 2 Pet. 3:7 [2343]

[2565] θησαυρός *thēsauros* 17x *a treasury, a store, treasure, precious deposit,* Mt. 6:19, 20, 21; *a receptacle in which precious articles are kept, a casket,* Mt. 2:11; *a storehouse,* Mt. 12:35 [2344] See *storeroom; treasure.*

[2566] θιγγάνω *thinganō* 3x *to touch,* Col. 2:21; Heb. 12:20; *to harm,* Heb. 11:28* [2345]

[2567] θλίβω *thlibō* 10x *to squeeze, press; to press upon, encumber, throng, crowd,* Mk. 3:9; met. *to distress, afflict,* 2 Cor. 1:6; 4:8; pass. *to be compressed, narrow,* Mt. 7:14 [2346] See *persecute; press; trouble.*

[2568] θλῖψις *thlipsis* 45x pr. *pressure, compression;* met. *affliction, distress* of mind, 2 Cor. 2:4; *distressing circumstances, trial, affliction,* Mt. 25:9 [2347] See *affliction; distress; tribulation; trouble.*

[2569] θνῄσκω *thnēskō* 9x *to die;* in NT *to be dead,* Mt. 2:20; Mk. 15:44 [2348]

[2570] θνητός *thnētos* 6x *mortal, subject to death,* Rom. 6:12; 8:11; 2 Cor. 4:11; τὸ θνητόν, *mortality,* 1 Cor. 15:53, 54; 2 Cor. 5:4* [2349] See *mortal.*

[2571] θορυβάζω *thorybazō* 1x *to be troubled, disturbed,* Lk. 10:41* [5182]

[2572] θορυβέω *thorybeō* 4x *to make a din, uproar;* trans. *to disturb, throw into commotion,* Acts 17:5; in NT mid. *to manifest agitation of mind, to raise a lament,* Mt. 9:23; Mk. 5:39; Acts 20:10* [2350]

[2573] θόρυβος *thorybos* 7x *an uproar, din; an outward expression of mental agitation, outcry,* Mk. 5:38; *a tumult, commotion,* Mt. 26:5 [2351]

[2575] θραύω *thrauō* 1x *to break, shiver;* met., *shattered, crushed* by cruel oppression, Lk. 4:18* [2352]

[2576] θρέμμα *thremma* 1x *that which is reared* (especially sheep and goats); pl. *cattle,* Jn. 4:12* [2353]

[2577] θρηνέω *thrēneō* 4x *to lament, bewail,* Mt. 11:17; Lk. 7:32; 23:27; Jn. 16:20* [2354]

[2579] θρησκεία *thrēskeia* 4x *religious worship,* Col. 2:18; *religion, a religious system,* Acts 26:5; *religion, piety,* Jas. 1:26, 27* [2356]

[2581] θριαμβεύω *thriambeuō* 2x pr. *to celebrate a triumph;* trans. *to lead in triumph, celebrate a triumph over,* Col. 2:15; in NT *to cause to triumph,* or, *to render conspicuous,* 2 Cor. 2:14* [2358]

[2582] θρίξ *thrix* 15x *a hair; the hair* of the head, Mt. 5:36; 10:30; of an animal, Mt. 3:4; Mk. 1:6 [2359] See *hair.*

[2583] θροέω *throeō* 3x *to cry aloud;* in NT pass., *to be disturbed, disquieted, alarmed, terrified,* Mt. 24:6; Mk. 13:7; 2 Thess. 2:2* [2360]

[2584] θρόμβος *thrombos* 1x *a lump;* espec. *a clot* of blood, *drop,* Lk. 22:44* [2361]

[2585] θρόνος *thronos* 62x *a seat, a throne,* Mt. 5:34; 19:28; Lk. 1:52; meton. *power, dominion,* Lk. 1:32; Heb. 1:8; *a potentate,* Col. 1:16 [2362] See *throne.*

[2587] Θυάτειρα *Thuateira* 4x *Thyatira,* a city of Lydia, Acts 16:14; Rev. 1:11; 2:18, 24* [2363]

[2588] θυγάτηρ *thugatēr* 28x *a daughter,* Mt. 9:18; 10:35, 37; in the vocative, an expression of affection and kindness, Mt. 9:22; from the Hebrew, *one of the female posterity* of any one, Lk. 1:5; met. *a city,* Mt. 21:5; Jn. 12:15; pl. *female inhabitants,* Lk. 23:28 [2364] See *daughter.*

[2589] θυγάτριον *thugatrion* 2x *a little daughter, female child,* Mk. 5:23; 7:25* [2365]

[2590] θύελλα *thuella* 1x *a tempest, whirlwind, hurricane,* Heb. 12:18* [2366]

[2591] θύϊνος *thuinos* 1x *thyme,* of θυΐα, *thya,* an aromatic evergreen tree, arbor vitae, resembling the cedar, and found in Libya, Rev. 18:12* [2367]

[2592] θυμίαμα *thumiama* 6x *incense, any odoriferous substance burnt in religious worship,* Rev. 5:8; 8:3, 4; 18:13; or, *the act of burning incense,* Lk. 1:10, 11* [2368]

[2593] θυμιατήριον *thumiatērion* 1x *an altar* of burning incense, Heb. 9:4* [2369]

[2594] θυμιάω *thumiaō* 1x *to burn incense,* Lk. 1:9* [2370]

[2595] θυμομαχέω *thumomacheō* 1x *to wage war fiercely; to be warmly hostile to, be enraged against,* Acts 12:20* [2371]

[2596] θυμός *thumos* 18x pr. *the soul, mind;* hence, *a strong passion* or *emotion of the mind; anger, wrath,* Lk. 4:28; Acts 19:28; pl. *swellings of anger,* 2 Cor. 12:20; Gal. 5:20 [2372] See *anger; fury; rage; wrath.*

[2597] θυμόω *thumoō* 1x *to provoke to anger;* pass. *to be angered, enraged,* Mt. 2:16* [2373]

[2598] θύρα *thura* 39x *a door, gate,* Mt. 6:6; Mk. 1:33; *an entrance,* Mt. 27:60; in NT met. *an opening, occasion, opportunity,* Acts 14:27; 1 Cor. 16:9; meton. *a medium* or *means of entrance,* Jn. 10:7, 9 [2374] See *door.*

[2599] θυρεός *thureos* 1x *a stone* or *other material employed to close a doorway;* later, *a large oblong shield,* Eph. 6:16* [2375]

[2600] θυρίς *thuris* 2x *a small opening; a window,* Acts 20:9; 2 Cor. 11:33* [2376]

[2601] θυρωρός *thurōros* 4x *a doorkeeper, porter,* Mk. 13:34; Jn. 10:3; 18:16, 17* [2377]

[2602] θυσία *thusia* 28x *sacrifice, the act of sacrificing,* Heb. 9:26; *the thing sacrificed, a victim,* Mt. 9:13; 12:7; *the flesh of victims* eaten by the sacrificers, 1 Cor. 10:18; in NT *an offering* or *service* to God, Phil. 4:18 [2378] See *offering; sacrifice.*

[2603] θυσιαστήριον *thusiastērion* 23x *an altar,* Mt. 5:23, 24; Lk. 1:11; spc. *the altar of burnt-offering,* Mt. 23:35; Lk. 11:51; meton. *a class of sacrifices,* Heb. 13:10 [2379] See *altar.*

[2604] θύω *thuō* 14x *to offer; to kill in sacrifice, sacrifice, immolate,* Acts 14:13, 18; in NT *to slaughter* for food, Mt. 22:4 [2380] See *kill; sacrifice.*

[2605] Θωμᾶς *Thōmas* 11x *Thomas,* pr. name, Mt. 10:3; Mk. 3:18; Lk. 6:15; Jn. 11:16; 14:5; 20:24, 26, 27, 28; 21:2; Acts 1:13* [2381]

[2606] θώραξ *thōrax* 5x *a breast-plate, armor for the body,* consisting of two parts, one covering the breast and the other the back, Eph. 6:14; 1 Thess. 5:8; Rev. 9:9, 17* [2382]

[2608] Ἰάϊρος *Iairos* 2x also spelled Ἰάειρος, *Jairus,* pr. name, Mk. 5:22; Lk. 8:41* [2383]

[2609] Ἰακώβ *Iakōb* 27x *Jacob,* pr. name, indecl. (1) Son of Issac, Matt 1:2. (2) Father of Joseph, Mary's husband, Matt 1:15, 16 [2384]

[2610] Ἰάκωβος *Iakōbos* 42x *James,* pr. name (1) *Son of Zebedee,* Mt. 4:21. (2) *Son of Alphaeus and Mary, brother of Jude,* Mt. 10:3. (3) *James the less, brother of Jesus,* Gal. 1:19 [2385]

[2611] ἴαμα *iama* 3x *healing, cure,* 1 Cor. 12:9, 28, 30* [2386]

[2612] Ἰαμβρῆς *Iambrēs* 1x *Jambres,* pr. name, 2 Tim. 3:8* [2387]

[2613] Ἰανναί *Iannai* 1x *Jannai,* pr. name, indecl., Lk. 3:24* [2388]

[2614] Ἰάννης *Iannēs* 1x *Jannes,* pr. name, 2 Tim. 3:8* [2389]

[2615] ἰάομαι *iaomai* 26x *to heal, cure,* Mt. 8:8; Lk. 9:2; met. *to heal,* spiritually, *restore from a state of sin and condem-*

nation, Mt. 13:15; Heb. 12:13 [2390] See *cure; heal.*

[2616] Ἰάρετ *Iaret* 1x *Jared,* pr. name, indecl., Lk. 3:37* [2391]

[2617] ἴασις *iasis* 3x *healing, cure,* Lk. 13:32; Acts 4:22, 30* [2392]

[2618] ἴασπις *iaspis* 4x *jasper,* a precious stone of various colors, as purple, cerulian green, etc. Rev. 4:3; 21:11, 18, 19* [2393]

[2619] Ἰάσων *Iasōn* 5x *Jason*, Acts 17:5-7 (3x), 9; Rom. 16:21* [2394]

[2620] ἰατρός *iatros* 7x *physician,* Mt. 9:12; Mk. 2:17; 5:26; Lk. 4:23; 5:31; 8:43; Col. 4:14* [2395]

[2623] ἴδε *ide* 29x the imperative of εἶδον used as a particle, *Lo! Behold!* Jn. 16:29; 19:4, 5 [2396] See *look.*

[2625] ἴδιος *idios* 114x *one's own,* Mk. 15:20; Jn. 7:18; *due, proper, specially assigned,* Gal. 6:9; 1 Tim. 2:6; 6:15; Tit. 1:3; also used in NT as a simple possessive, Eph. 5:22; τὰ ἴδια, *one's home, household, people,* Jn. 1:11; 16:32; 19:17; οἱ ἴδιοι, *members of one's own household, friends,* Jn.1:11; Acts 24:23; ἰδίᾳ, adverbially, *respectively,* 1 Cor. 12:11; κατ᾽ ἰδίαν, adv., *privately, aside, by one's self, alone,* Mt. 14:13, 23 [2398] See *one's own.*

[2626] ἰδιώτης *idiōtēs* 5x pr. *one in private life, one devoid of special learning* or *gifts, a plain person,* Acts 4:13; 2 Cor. 11:6; *ungifted,* 1 Cor. 14:16, 23, 24* [2399]

[2627] ἰδού *idou* 200x aorist middle imperative of εἶδον used as an interjection, *Look! See! Lo!* Mt. 1:23; Lk. 1:38; Acts 8:36 [2400] See *behold; look.*

[2628] Ἰδουμαία *Idoumaia* 1x *Idumaea,* a country south of Judea, Mk. 3:8* [2401]

[2629] ἱδρώς *hidrōs* 1x *sweat,* Lk. 22:44* [2402]

[2630] Ἰεζάβελ *Iezabel* 1x *Jezebel,* (1 Ki. 16:31), pr. name, indecl., Rev. 2:20* [2403]

[2631] Ἱεράπολις *Hierapolis* 1x *Hierapolis,* a city of Phrygia, Col. 4:13* [2404]

[2632] ἱερατεία *hierateia* 2x *priesthood, sacerdotal office,* Lk. 1:9; Heb. 7:5* [2405]

[2633] ἱεράτευμα *hierateuma* 2x *a priesthood;* meton. *a body of priests,* 1 Pet. 2:5, 9* [2406]

[2634] ἱερατεύω *hierateuō* 1x *to officiate as a priest, perform sacred rites,* Lk. 1:8* [2407]

[2635] Ἰερεμίας *Ieremias* 3x *Jeremiah,* pr. name, Mt. 2:17; 16:14; 27:9* [2408]

[2636] ἱερεύς *hiereus* 31x *a priest, one who performs sacrificial rites,* Mt. 8:4; Lk. 1:5; Jn. 1:19 [2409] See *priest.*

[2637] Ἰεριχώ *Ierichō* 7x *Jericho,* a city of Palestine, Mt. 20:29; Mk. 10:46; Lk. 10:30; 18:35; 19:1; Heb. 11:30* [2410]

[2638] ἱερόθυτος *hierothutos* 1x *offered in sacrifice,* 1 Cor. 10:28* [1494]

[2639] ἱερόν *hieron* 72x *temple, sanctuary,* Mt. 4:5; Lk. 4:9; Acts 19:27 [2411] See *temple.*

[2640] ἱεροπρεπής *hieroprepēs* 1x *reverent*, Tit. 2:13* [2412]

[2641] ἱερός *hieros* 2x *holy, divine, set apart,* 2 Tim. 3:15; τὰ ἱερά, *sacred rites,* 1 Cor. 9:13* [2413]

[2642] Ἱεροσόλυμα *Hierosolyma* 62x see Ἰερουσαλήμ [2414]

[2643] Ἱεροσολυμίτης *Hierosolymitēs* 2x *a native of Jerusalem,* Mk. 1:5; Jn. 7:25* [2415]

[2644] ἱεροσυλέω *hierosyleō* 1x *to despoil temples, commit sacrilege,* Rom. 2:22* [2416]

[2645] ἱερόσυλος *hierosylos* 1x *one who despoils temples, commits sacrilege,* Acts 19:37* [2417]

[2646] ἱερουργέω *hierourgeō* 1x *to officiate as priest, perform sacred rites;* in NT *to minister* in a divine commission, Rom. 15:16* [2418]

[2647] Ἰερουσαλήμ *Ierousalēm* 77x *Jerusalem,* pr. name, indecl., also spelled Ἱεροσόλυμα 62x in our text [2419]

[2648] ἱερωσύνη *hierōsynē* 3x *a priesthood, sacerdotal office,* Heb. 7:11, 12, 24* [2420]

[2649] Ἰεσσαί *Iessai* 5x *Jesse,* father of David (1 Sam. 16), pr. name, indecl., Mt. 1:5f.; Lk. 3:32; Acts 13:22; Rom. 15:12* [2421]

[2650] Ἰεφθάε *Iephthae* 1x *Jephthah,* (Jdg. 11f.), pr. name, indecl., Heb. 11:32* [2422]

[2651] Ἰεχονίας *Iechonias* 2x *Jechoniah,* pr. name, Mt. 1:11, 12; Lk. 3:23ff.* [2423]

[2652] Ἰησοῦς *Iēsous* 917x *a Savior, Jesus,* Mt. 1:21, 25; 2:1, et al. freq.; *Joshua,* Acts 7:45; Heb. 4:8; *Jesus,* a Jewish Christian, Col. 4:11 [2424] See *Jesus.*

[2653] ἱκανός *hikanos* 39x *befitting; sufficient, enough,* Lk. 22:38; ἱκανὸν ποιεῖν τινί, *to satisfy, gratify,* Mk. 15:15; τὸ ἱκανὸν λαμβάνειν, *to take security* or *bail* of any one, Acts 17:9; or persons, *adequate, competent, qualified,* 2 Cor. 2:16; *fit, worthy,* Mt. 3:11; 8:8; of number or quantity, *considerable, large, great, much,* and pl. *many,* Mt. 28:12; Mk. 10:46 [2425] See *adequate; deserve; sufficient.*

[2654] ἱκανότης *hikanotēs* 1x *sufficiency, ability, fitness, qualification,* 2 Cor. 3:5* [2426]

[2655] ἱκανόω *hikanoō* 2x *to make sufficient* or *competent, qualify,* 2 Cor. 3:6; Col. 1:12* [2427]

[2656] ἱκετηρία *hiketēria* 1x pr. *an olive branch* borne by suppliants in their hands; *prayer, supplication,* Heb. 5:7* [2428]

[2657] ἰκμάς *ikmas* 1x *moisture,* Lk. 8:6* [2429]

[2658] Ἰκόνιον *Ikonion* 6x *Iconium,* a city of Lycaonia, in Asia Minor, Acts 13:51; 14:1, 19, 21; 16:2; 2 Tim. 3:11* [2430]

[2659] ἱλαρός *hilaros* 1x *cheerful, not grudging,* 2 Cor. 9:7* [2431]

[2660] ἱλαρότης *hilarotēs* 1x *cheerfulness, graciousness,* Rom. 12:8* [2432]

[2661] ἱλάσκομαι *hilaskomai* 2x *to appease, render propitious;* in NT *to expiate, make an atonement* or *expiation for,* Heb. 2:17; ἱλάσθητι, *be gracious, show mercy, pardon,* Lk. 18:13* [2433] See *atone; (have) mercy; propitiate, propitiation,*

[2662] ἱλασμός *hilasmos* 2x *atoning sacrifice, sin offering, propitiation, expiation; one who makes propitiation/expiation,* 1 Jn. 2:2; 4:10* [2434] See *atonement, atoning sacrifice; propitiate, propitiation.*

[2663] ἱλαστήριον *hilastērion* 2x *the cover of the ark of the covenant, the mercy-seat, the place of propitiation,* Rom. 3:25; Heb. 9:5* [2435] See *atonement, atoning sacrifice; propitiate, propitiation.*

[2664] ἵλεως *hileōs* 2x *propitious, favorable, merciful, gracious,* Heb. 8:12; from the Hebrew, ἵλεως σοι (ὁ θεός) *God have mercy on thee, God forbid, far be it from thee,* Mt. 16:22* [2436]

[2665] Ἰλλυρικόν *Illyrikon* 1x *Illyricum,* a country between the Adriatic and the Danube, Rom. 15:19* [2437]

[2666] ἱμάς *himas* 4x *a strap* or *thong of leather,* Acts 22:25; *a shoe-latchet,* Mk. 1:7; Lk. 3:16; Jn. 1:27* [2438]

[2667] ἱματίζω *himatizō* 2x *to clothe;* pass. *to be clothed,* Mk. 5:15; Lk. 8:35* [2439]

[2668] ἱμάτιον *himation* 60x *a garment; the upper garment, mantle,* Mt. 5:40; 9:16, 20, 21; pl. *the mantle and tunic together,* Mt. 26:65; pl. genr. *garments, raiment,* Mt. 11:8; 24:18 [2440] See *cloak; clothes; robe.*

[2669] ἱματισμός *himatismos* 5x *garment; raiment, apparel, clothing,* Lk. 7:25; 9:29; Jn. 19:24; Acts 20:33; 1 Tim. 2:9* [2441]

[2671] ἵνα *hina* 663x *that, in order that,* Mt. 19:13; Mk. 1:38; Jn. 1:22; 3:15; 17:1; ἵνα μή, *that not, lest,* Mt. 7:1; in NT equivalent to ὥστε, *so that, so as that,* Jn. 9:2; also, marking a simple circumstance, *the circumstance that,* Mt. 10:25; Jn. 4:34; 6:29; 1 Jn. 4:17; 5:3 [2443]

[2672] ἱνατί *hinati* 6x *Why is it that? For what reason? Why?* Mt. 9:4; 27:46; Lk. 13:7; Acts 4:25; 7:26; 1 Cor. 10:29* [2444]

[2673] Ἰόππη *Ioppē* 10x *Joppa,* a city of Palestine, Acts 9:36, 38, 42f.; 10:5, 8, 23, 32; 11:5, 13* [2445]

[2674] Ἰορδάνης *Iordanēs* 15x *the river Jordan,* Mt. 3:5; Mk. 10:1; Lk. 4:1; Jn. 3:26 [2446]

[2675] ἰός *ios* 3x *a missile weapon, arrow, dart; venom, poison,* Rom. 3:13; Jas. 3:8; *rust,* Jas. 5:3* [2447]

[2677] Ἰουδαία *Ioudaia* 44x *Judea,* the southern party of the country, below Samaria, Mt. 2:1, 5, 22; 3:1; meton. *the inhabitants of Judea* [2449]

[2679] Ἰουδαϊκός *Ioudaikos* 1x *Jewish, current among the Jews,* Tit. 1:14* [2451]

[2680] Ἰουδαϊκῶς *Ioudaikōs* 1x *in the manner of Jews, according to Jewish custom,* Gal. 2:14* [2452]

[2681] Ἰουδαῖος *Ioudaios* 194x *Jewish,* Mk. 1:5; Jn. 3:22; Acts 16:1; 24:24; pr. *one sprung from the tribe of Judah,* or *a subject of the kingdom of Judah;* in NT *a descendant of Jacob, a Jew,* Mt. 28:15; Mk. 7:3; Acts 19:34; Rom. 2:28, 29 [2453] See *Jews.*

[2682] Ἰουδαϊσμός *Ioudaismos* 2x *Judaism, the character and condition of a Jew; practice of the Jewish religion,* Gal. 1:13, 14* [2454]

[2683] Ἰούδας *Ioudas* 44x *Judas, Jude,* pr. name. (1) *Judah, son of Jacob; the tribe of Judah,* Mt. 1:2; Lk. 1:39. (2) *Juda, son of Joseph, of the ancestry of Jesus,* Lk. 3:30. (3) *Juda, son of Joanna, of the ancestry of Jesus,* Lk. 3:26. (4) *Judas, brother of James, Jude,* Lk. 6:16; Jude 1. (5) *Judas Iscariot, son of Simon,* Mt. 10:4; Jn. 6:71. (6) *Judas, brother of Jesus,* Mt. 13:55; Mk. 6:3. (7) *Judas of Galilee,* Acts 5:37 . (8) *Judas, surnamed Barsabas,* Acts 15:22. (9) *Judas of Damascus,* Acts 9:11 [2455]

[2684] Ἰουλία *Ioulia* 1x *Julia,* pr. name, Rom. 16:15* [2456]

[2685] Ἰούλιος *Ioulios* 2x *Julius,* pr. name, Acts 27:1, 3* [2457]

[2687] Ἰουνιᾶς *Iounias* 1x *Junia,* pr. name, Rom. 16:7* [2458]

[2688] Ἰοῦστος *Ioustos* 3x *Justus,* pr. name (1) *Joseph Barsabas,* Acts 1:23 (2) *Justus of Corinth,* Acts 18:7 (3) *Jesus, called Justus,* Col. 4:11* [2459]

[2689] ἱππεύς *hippeus* 2x *a horseman;* pl. ἱππεῖς, *horsemen, cavalry,* Acts 23:23, 32* [2460]

[2690] ἱππικός *hippikos* 1x *equestrian;* τὸ ἱππικόν, *cavalry, horse,* Rev. 9:16* [2461]

[2691] ἵππος *hippos* 17x *a horse,* Jas. 3:3; Rev. 6:2, 4, 5, 8; 9:7, 17; 18:13; 19:11, 14 [2462] See *horse.*

[2692] ἶρις *iris* 2x *a rainbow, iris,* Rev. 4:3; 10:1* [2463]

[2693] Ἰσαάκ *Isaak* 20x *Isaac,* pr. name, indecl., Mt. 1:2; 8:11; 23:32; Acts 3:13;. Rom. 9:7f.; Gal. 4:28; Heb. 11:9ff.; Jas. 2:21 [2464]

[2694] ἰσάγγελος *isangelos* 1x *equal* or *similar to angels,* Lk. 20:36* [2465]

[2696] Ἰσκαριώθ *Iskariōth* 3x see Ἰσκαριώτης [2469]

[2697] Ἰσκαριώτης *Iskariōtēs* 8x *Iscariot,* surname of Judas, Mt. 10:4; 26:14; Lk.

22:3; Jn. 6:71; Jn. 12:4; 13:2, 26; 14:22. Also spelled Ἰσκαριώθ in our text 3x (Mk. 3:19; 14:10; Lk. 6:16), which is indeclinable.* [2469]

[2698] ἴσος *isos* 8x *equal, like,* Mt. 20:12; Lk. 6:34; *on an equality,* Phil. 2:6; met. *correspondent, consistent,* Mk. 14:56, 59 [2470]

[2699] ἰσότης *isotēs* 3x *equality, equal proportion,* 2 Cor. 8:13, 14; *fairness, equity, what is equitable,* Col. 4:1* [2471]

[2700] ἰσότιμος *isotimos* 1x *of equal price, equally precious* or *valuable,* 2 Pet. 1:1* [2472]

[2701] ἰσόψυχος *isopsychos* 1x *like-minded, of the same mind and spirit,* Phil. 2:20* [2473]

[2702] Ἰσραήλ *Israēl* 68x *Israel,* pr. name, indecl. [2474] See *Israel.*

[2703] Ἰσραηλίτης *Israēlitēs* 9x *an Israelite, a descendant of* Ἰσραήλ, *Israel* or *Jacob,* Jn. 1:47; Acts 2:22 [2475]

[2704] Ἰσσαχάρ *Issachar* 1x *Issachar,* pr. name, indecl., Rev. 7:7* [2466]

[2705] ἵστημι *histēmi* 154x pluperfect, ἑστάμην, also formed as στήκω 10x, trans. *to make to stand, set, place,* Mt. 4:5; *to set forth, appoint,* Acts 1:23; *to fix, appoint,* Acts 17:31; *to establish, confirm,* Rom. 10:3; Heb. 10:9; *to set down, impute,* Acts 7:60; *to weigh out, pay,* Mt. 26:15; intrans. *to stand,* Mt. 12:46; *to stand fast, be firm, be permanent, endure,* Mt. 12:25; Eph. 6:13; *to be confirmed, proved,* Mt. 18:16; 2 Cor. 13:1; *to stop,* Lk. 7:14; 8:44; Acts 8:38 [2476] See *appear; establish; place; propose; set; stand.*

[2707] ἱστορέω *historeō* 1x *to ascertain by inquiry and examination; to inquire of;* in NT *to visit* in order to become acquainted with, Gal. 1:18* [2477]

[2708] ἰσχυρός *ischuros* 29x *strong, mighty, robust,* Mt. 12:29; Lk. 11:21; *powerful, mighty,* 1 Cor. 1:27; 4:10; 1 Jn. 2:14; *strong, fortified,* Rev. 18:10; *vehement,* Mt. 14:20; *energetic,* 2 Cor. 10:10; *sure, firm,* Heb. 6:18 [2478] See *mighty; powerful; strong.*

[2709] ἰσχύς *ischus* 10x *strength, might, power,* Rev. 18:2; Eph. 1:19; *faculty, ability,* 1 Pet. 4:11; Mk. 12:30, 33; Lk. 10:27 [2479] See *might; power; strength.*

[2710] ἰσχύω *ischuō* 28x *to be strong, be well, be in good health,* Mt. 9:12; *to have power, be able,* Mt. 8:28; 26:40; *to have power* or *efficiency, avail, be valid,* Gal. 5:6; Heb. 9:17; *to be of service, be serviceable,* Mt. 5:13; meton. *to prevail,* Acts 19:16; Rev. 12:8 [2480] See *(be) able; overpower; prevail; (be) strong.*

[2711] ἴσως *isōs* 1x *equally; perhaps, it may be that,* Lk. 20:13* [2481]

[2712] Ἰταλία *Italia* 4x *Italy,* Acts 18:2; 27:1, 6; Heb. 13:24* [2482]

[2713] Ἰταλικός *Italikos* 1x *Italian,* Acts 10:1* [2483]

[2714] Ἰτουραῖος *Itouraios* 1x *Ituraea,* a district of Palestine beyond Jordan, Lk. 3:1* [2484]

[2715] ἰχθύδιον *ichthudion* 2x *a small fish,* Mt. 15:34; Mk. 8:7* [2485]

[2716] ἰχθύς *ichthus* 20x *a fish,* Mt. 15:36; 17:27; Lk. 5:6 [2486] See *fish.*

[2717] ἴχνος *ichnos* 3x *a footstep, track;* in NT pl. *footsteps, line of conduct,* Rom. 4:12; 2 Cor. 12:18; 1 Pet. 2:21* [2487]

[2718] Ἰωαθάμ *Iōatham* 2x *Joatham,* pr. name, indecl., Mt. 1:9* [2488]

[2720] Ἰωανάν *Iōanan* 1x *Joanan,* pr. name, indecl., Lk. 3:27* [2489]

[2721] Ἰωάννα *Iōanna* 2x also spelled Ἰωάνα, *Joanna,* pr. name, Lk. 8:3; 24:10* [2489, 2490]

[2722] Ἰωάννης *Iōannēs* 135x also spelled Ἰωάνης, *Joannes, John,* pr. name (1) *John the Baptist,* Mt. 3:1, et al. (2) *John, son of Zebedee, the apostle,* Mt. 4:21, et al. (3) *John, surnamed Mark,* Acts

12:12, et al. (4) *John, the high-priest,* Acts 4:6 [2491]

[2724] Ἰώβ *Iōb* 1x *Job,* pr. name, indecl., Jas. 5:11* [2492]

[2725] Ἰωβήδ *Iōbēd* 3x *Obed,* David's grandfather, pr. name, indecl., Mt. 1:5; Lk. 3:32* [5601]

[2726] Ἰωδά *Iōda* 1x *Joda,* pr. name, indecl., Lk. 3:26* [2455]

[2727] Ἰωήλ *Iōēl* 1x *Joel,* an Old Testament prophet, pr. name, indecl., Acts 2:16* [2493]

[2729] Ἰωνάμ *Iōnam* 1x *Jonam,* pr. name, indecl., Lk. 3:30* [2494]

[2731] Ἰωνᾶς *Iōnas* 9x *Jonas,* pr. name *Jonah, the prophet,* Mt. 12:39; Lk. 11:29 [2495]

[2732] Ἰωράμ *Iōram* 2x *Joram,* king of Judah (2 Ki. 8:16ff.), pr. name, indecl., Mt. 1:8* [2496]

[2733] Ἰωρίμ *Iōrim* 1x *Jorim,* pr. name, indecl., Lk. 3:29* [2497]

[2734] Ἰωσαφάτ *Iōsaphat* 2x *Josaphat,* king of Judah (1 Ki. 22:41), pr. name, indecl., Mt. 1:8* [2498]

[2736] Ἰωσῆς *Iōsēs* 4x *Joses, Joseph* pr. name Mt. 27:56; Mk. 6:3; 15:40, 47* [2500]

[2737] Ἰωσήφ *Iōsēph* 35x *Joseph,* pr. name, indecl. (1) *Joseph, son of Jacob,* Jn. 4:5. (2) *Joseph, son of Jonan,* Lk. 3:30. (3) *Joseph, son of Judas,* Lk. 3:26. (4) *Joseph, son of Mattathias,* Lk. 3:24. (5) *Joseph, the husband of Mary,* Mt. 1:16. (6) *Joseph of Arimathea,* Mt. 27:57. (7) *Joseph Barsabas,* Acts 1:23. (8) *Joseph Barnabas,* Acts 4:36 [2501]

[2738] Ἰωσήχ *Iōsēch* 1x *Josech,* pr. name, indecl., Lk. 3:26* [2501]

[2739] Ἰωσίας *Iōsias* 2x *Josiah,* king of Judah (2 Ki. 22), Mt. 1:10, 11* [2502]

[2740] ἰῶτα *iōta* 1x *iota;* in NT used like the Hebrew/Aramaic *yod*, the smallest letter in the Hebrew/Aramaic alphabet, as an expression for *the least* or *minutest part; a jot,* Mt. 5:18* [2503]

[2743] κἀγώ *kagō* 84x *and I, I also, but I,* a crasis of καί and ἐγώ, dat., κἀμοί, acc., κἀμέ [2504]

[2745] καθά *katha* 1x can function as an adverb, *just as,* Mt. 27:10* [2505]

[2746] καθαίρεσις *kathairesis* 3x *tearing down, destruction,* 2 Cor. 10:4, 8; 13:10* [2506]

[2747] καθαιρέω *kathaireō* 9x *take* or *bring down,* Mk. 15:36, 46; Lk. 1:52; 23:53; Acts 13:29; *tear down, destroy,* Lk. 12:18; Acts 13:19; 19:27; 2 Cor. 10:4* [2507]

[2748] καθαίρω *kathairō* 1x *to cleanse* from filth; *to clear* by pruning, *prune,* Jn. 15:2; met. *to cleanse* from sin, *make expiation* [2508]

[2749] καθάπερ *kathaper* 13x can function as an adverb, *even as, just as,* Rom. 3:4; 4:6; 9:13; 10:15; 11:8; 12:4; 1 Cor. 10:10; 12:12; 2 Cor. 1:14; 3:13, 18; 8:11; 1 Thess. 2:11; 3:6, 12; 4:5; Heb. 4:2* [2509]

[2750] καθάπτω *kathaptō* 1x trans. *to fasten* or *fit to;* in NT equivalent to καθάπτομαι, *to fix one's self upon, fasten upon, take hold of, seize,* Acts 28:3* [2510]

[2751] καθαρίζω *katharizō* 31x *to cleanse, render pure, purify,* Mt. 23:25; Lk. 11:39; *to cleanse* from leprosy, Mt. 8:2, 3; 10:8; met. *to cleanse* from sin, *purify by an expiatory offering, make expiation for,* Heb. 9:22, 23; 1 Jn. 1:7; *to cleanse* from sin, *free from the influence of error and sin,* Acts 15:9; 2 Cor. 7:1; *to pronounce* ceremonially *clean,* Acts 10:15; 11:9 [2511] See *cleanse; make clean.*

[2752] καθαρισμός *katharismos* 7x ceremonial *cleansing, purification,* Lk. 2:22; 5:14; *mode of purification,* Jn. 2:6; 3:25; *cleansing* of lepers, Mk. 1:44; met. *expiation,* Heb. 1:3; 2 Pet. 1:9* [2512]

[2754] καθαρός *katharos* 27x *clean, pure, unsoiled,* Mt. 23:26; 27:59; met. *clean* from guilt, *guiltless, innocent,* Acts 18:6; 20:26; *sincere, upright, virtuous, void of evil,* Mt. 5:8; Jn. 15:3; *clean* ceremonially and morally, Lk. 11:41 [2513] See *clean.*

[2755] καθαρότης *katharotēs* 1x *cleanness;* ceremonial *purity,* Heb. 9:13* [2514]

[2756] καθέδρα *kathedra* 3x *chair, seat,* Mt. 21:12; 23:2; Mk. 11:15* [2515]

[2757] καθέζομαι *kathezomai* 7x *to seat one's self, sit down,* Mt. 26:55; Lk. 2:46; Jn. 4:6; 1:20; 20:12; Acts 6:15; 20:9* [2516]

[2759] καθεξῆς *kathexēs* 5x *in a continual order* or *series, successively, consecutively,* Lk. 1:3; Acts 11:4; 18:23; ὁ, ἡ, καθεξῆς, *succeeding, subsequent,* Lk. 8:1; Acts 3:24* [2517]

[2761] καθεύδω *katheudō* 22x *to sleep, be fast asleep,* Mt. 8:24; 9:24; met. *to sleep* in spiritual sloth, Eph. 5:14; 1 Thess. 5:6; *to sleep* the sleep of death, *to die,* 1 Thess. 5:10 [2518] See *sleep.*

[2762] καθηγητής *kathēgētēs* 2x pr. *a guide, leader;* in NT *a teacher, instructor,* Mt. 23:10* [2519]

[2763] καθήκω *kathēkō* 2x *to reach, extend to;* καθήκει, impers. *it is fitting, meet,* Acts 22:22; τὸ καθῆκον, *what is fit, right, duty*; τὰ μὴ καθήκοντα, by litotes for *what is abominable* or *detestable,* Rom. 1:28* [2520]

[2764] κάθημαι *kathēmai* 91x *to sit, be sitting,* Mt. 9:9; Lk. 10:13; *to be seated,* 1 Cor. 14:30; *to be enthroned,* Rev. 18:7; *to dwell, reside,* Mt. 4:16; Lk. 1:79; 21:35 [2521] See *reside; seated; sit.*

[2766] καθημερινός *kathēmerinos* 1x *daily, day by day,* Acts 6:1* [2522]

[2767] καθίζω *kathizō* 46x (1) trans. *to cause to sit, place;* καθίζομαι, *to be seated, sit,* Mt. 19:28; Lk. 22:30; *to cause to sit* as judges, *place, appoint,* 1 Cor. 6:4; (2) intrans. *to sit, sit down,* Mt. 13:48; 26:36; *to remain, settle, stay, continue, live,* Lk. 24:49 [2523] See *sit.*

[2768] καθίημι *kathiēmi* 4x *to let down, lower,* Lk. 5:19; Acts 9:25; 10:11; 11:5* [2524]

[2770] καθίστημι *kathistēmi* 21x also formed as καθιστάνω, *to place, set,* Jas. 3:6; *to set, constitute, appoint,* Mt. 24:45, 47; Lk. 12:14; *to set down* in a place, *conduct,* Acts 17:15; *to make, render,* or *cause to be,* 2 Pet. 1:8; pass. *to be rendered,* Rom. 5:19 [2525] See *appoint; become; escort; put in charge.*

[2771] καθό *katho* 4x *as,* Rom. 8:26; *according as, in proportion as, to the degree that,* 2 Cor. 8:12; 1 Pet. 4:13* [2526]

[2773] καθόλου *katholou* 1x *on the whole, entirely, in general, altogether, completely;* with a negative, *not at all,* Acts 4:18* [2527]

[2774] καθοπλίζω *kathoplizō* 1x middle, *to arm oneself (completely),* Lk. 11:21* [2528]

[2775] καθοράω *kathoraō* 1x pr. *to look down upon,* in the NT *to mark, perceive, discern,* Rom. 1:20* [2529]

[2776] καθότι *kathoti* 6x *as, just as, according as, in proportion as,* Acts 2:45; 4:35; *inasmuch as,* Lk. 1:7; 19:9; Acts 2:24; 17:31* [2530]

[2777] καθώς *kathōs* 182x *as, just as, in the manner that,* Mt. 21:6; 26:24; *how, in what manner,* Acts 15:14; *according as,* Mk. 4:33; *inasmuch as,* Jn. 17:2; of time, *when,* Acts 7:17 [2531]

[2778] καθώσπερ *kathōsper* 1x *just as, exactly as,* Heb. 5:4* [2509]

[2779] καί *kai* 9,160x (1) *and,* Mt. 2:2, 3, 11; 4:22; (2) καί ... καί, *both ... and;* (3) as a cumulative particle, *also, too,* Mt. 5:39; Jn. 8:19; 1 Cor. 11:6; (4) emphatic, *even, also,* Mt. 10:30; 1 Cor. 2:10; in NT adversative, *but,* Mt. 11:19; also introductory of the apodosis of a sentence, Gal. 3:28; Jas. 2:4 [2532]

[2780] Καϊάφας *Kaiaphas* 9x *Caiaphas,* pr. name, the high priest from A.D. 18-36, Mt. 26:3, 57; Lk. 3:2; Jn. 11:49; 18:13f., 24, 28; Acts 4:6* [2533]

[2782] Κάϊν *Kain* 3x *Cain,* pr. name, indecl., Heb. 11:4; 1 Jn. 3:12; Jude 11* [2535]

[2783] Καϊνάμ *Kainam* 2x *Cainan,* pr. name, indecl., Lk. 3:36, 37* [2536]

[2785] καινός *kainos* 41x *new, recently made,* Mt. 9:17; Mk. 2:22; *new* in species, character, or mode, Mt. 26:28, 29; Mk. 14:24, 25; Lk. 22:20; Jn. 13:34; 2 Cor. 5:17; Gal. 6:15; Eph. 2:15; 4:24; 1 Jn. 2:7; Rev. 3:12; *novel, strange,* Mk. 1:27; Acts 17:19; *new* to the possessor, Mk. 16:17; *unheard of, unusual,* Mk. 1:27; Acts 17:19; met. *renovated, better, of higher excellence,* 2 Cor. 5:17; Rev. 5:9 [2537] See *new.*

[2786] καινότης *kainotēs* 2x *newness,* Rom. 6:4; 7:6* [2538]

[2788] καίπερ *kaiper* 5x *though, although;* Phil. 3:4; Heb. 5:8; 7:5; 12:17; 2 Pet. 1:12* [2539]

[2789] καιρός *kairos* 85x pr. *fitness, proportion, suitableness; a fitting situation, suitable place,* 1 Pet. 4:17; *a limited period of time marked by a suitableness of circumstances, a fitting season,* 1 Cor. 4:5; 1 Tim. 2:6; 6:15; Tit. 1:3; *opportunity,* Acts 24:25; Gal. 6:10; Heb. 11:15; *a limited period of time marked by characteristic circumstances, a signal juncture, a marked season,* Mt. 16:3; Lk. 12:56; 21:8; 1 Pet. 1:11; *a destined time,* Mt. 8:29; 26:18; Mk. 1:15; Lk. 21:24; 1 Thess. 5:1; *a season* in ordinary succession, equivalent to ὥρα, Mt. 13:30; Acts 14:17; in NT *a limited time, a short season,* Lk. 4:13; simply, *a point of time,* Mt. 11:25; Lk. 13:1 [2540] See *season; time.*

[2790] Καῖσαρ *Kaisar* 29x *Caesar,* pr. name [2541]

[2791] Καισάρεια *Kaisareia* 17x *Caesarea* (1) *Caesarea Philippi,* Mt. 16:13; Mk. 8:27; (2) *Caesarea Augusta,* Acts 8:40 [2542]

[2792] καίτοι *kaitoi* 2x *and yet, though, although,* Acts 14:17; Heb. 4:3* [2543]

[2793] καίτοιγε *kaitoige* 1x *although indeed, and yet,* Jn. 4:2* [2544]

[2794] καίω *kaiō* 11x *to cause to burn, kindle, light,* Mt. 5:15; pass. *to be kindled, burn, flame,* Lk. 12:35; met. *to be kindled* into emotion, Lk. 24:32; *to consume with fire,* Jn. 15:6; 1 Cor. 13:3 [2545] See *burn.*

[2795] κἀκεῖ *kakei* 10x crasis, *and there,* Mt. 5:23; 10:11; *there also,* Acts 17:13 [2546]

[2796] κἀκεῖθεν *kakeithen* 10x crasis, *and there,* Mk. 10:1; Acts 7:4; 14:26; 20:15; 21:1; 27:4, 12; 28:15; *and then, afterwards,* Acts 13:21 [2547]

[2797] κἀκεῖνος *kakeinos* 22x crasis, *and he, she, it; and this, and that,* Mt. 15:18; 23:23; *he, she, it also; this also, that also,* Mt. 20:4 [2548]

[2798] κακία *kakia* 11x *malice, malignity,* Rom. 1:29; Eph. 4:31; *wickedness, depravity,* Acts 8:22; 1 Cor. 5:8; in NT *evil, trouble, calamity, misfortune,* Mt. 6:34 [2549] See *evil; malice; wicked, wickedness.*

[2799] κακοήθεια *kakoētheia* 1x *disposition for mischief, misfortune, malignity,* Rom. 1:29* [2550]

[2800] κακολογέω *kakologeō* 4x *to speak evil of, revile, abuse, insult,* Mk. 9:39; Acts 19:9; *to address with offensive language, to treat with disrespect,* Matt, 15:4; Mk. 7:10* [2551]

[2801] κακοπάθεια *kakopatheia* 1x *a state of suffering, affliction, trouble,* in NT *endurance in affliction, perseverance,* Jas. 5:10* [2552]

[2802] κακοπαθέω *kakopatheō* 3x *to suffer evil* or *afflictions,* 2 Tim. 2:9; *to be afflicted, troubled, dejected,* Jas. 5:13; in NT *to show endurance in trials and afflictions,* 2 Tim. 4:5* [2553]

[2803] κακοποιέω *kakopoieō* 4x *to cause evil, injure, do harm,* Mk. 3:4; Lk. 6:9; *to do evil, commit sin,* 1 Pet. 3:17; 3 Jn. 11* [2554]

[2804] κακοποιός *kakopoios* 3x *an evil-doer,* 1 Pet. 2:12, 14; 4:15* [2555]

[2805] κακός *kakos* 50x *bad, of a bad quality* or *disposition, worthless, corrupt, depraved,* Mt. 21:41; 24:48; Mk. 7:21; *wicked, criminal, morally bad;* τὸ κακόν, *evil, wickedness, crime,* Mt. 27:23; Acts 23:9; *deceitful,* 1 Pet. 3:10; *mischievous, harmful, destructive;* τὸ κακόν, *evil mischief, harm, injury,* Tit. 1:12; *afflictive;* τὸ κακόν, *evil, misery, affliction, suffering,* Lk. 16;25 [2556] See *bad; evil; wicked, wickedness; wrong.*

[2806] κακοῦργος *kakourgos* 4x *an evil-doer, malefactor, criminal,* Lk. 23:32, 33, 39; 2 Tim. 2:9* [2557]

[2807] κακουχέω *kakoucheō* 2x *to torment, afflict, harass;* pass. *to be afflicted, be oppressed with evils,* Heb. 11:37 13:3* [2558]

[2808] κακόω *kakoō* 6x *to harm, mistreat, cause evil to, oppress,* Acts 7:6, 19; 12:1; 18:10; 1 Pet. 3:13; in NT *to make angry, embitter,* Acts 14:2* [2559]

[2809] κακῶς *kakōs* 16x *ill, badly;* physically *ill, sick,* Mt. 4:24; 8:16; *grievously, vehemently,* Mt. 15:22; *wretchedly, miserably,* Mt. 21:41; *wickedly, reproachfully,* Acts 23:5; *wrongly, criminally,* Jn. 18:23; *amiss,* Jas. 4:3 [2560] See *evil; sick; wrong.*

[2810] κάκωσις *kakōsis* 1x *ill treatment, affliction, oppression, misery,* Acts 7:34* [2561]

[2811] καλάμη *kalamē* 1x *the stalk* of grain, *straw, stubble,* 1 Cor. 3:12* [2562]

[2812] κάλαμος *kalamos* 12x *a reed, cane,* Mt. 11:7; 12:20; Lk. 7:24; *a reed* in its various appliances, as, a wand, a staff, Mt. 27:29, 30, 48; Mk. 15:19, 36; *a measuring-rod,* Rev. 11:1; 21:15f.; a writer's *reed,* 3 Jn. 13* [2563] See *reed.*

[2813] καλέω *kaleō* 148x *to call, call to,* Jn. 10:3; *to call* into one's presence, *send for* a person, Mt. 2:7; *to summon,* Mt. 2:15; 25:14; *to invite,* Mt. 22:9; *to call* to the performance of a certain thing, Mt. 9:13; Heb. 11:8; *to call* to a participation in the privileges of the Gospel, Rom. 8:30; 9:24; 1 Cor. 1:9; 7:18; *to call* to an office or dignity, Heb. 5:4; *to name, style,* Mt. 1:21; pass. *to be styled, regarded,* Mt. 5:9, 19 [2564] See *call; invite; summon.*

[2814] καλλιέλαιος *kallielaios* 1x pr. adj. *productive of good oil;* as subst. *a cultivated olive tree,* Rom. 11:24* [2565]

[2815] καλοδιδάσκαλος *kalodidaskalos* 1x *teaching what is good; a teacher of good,* Tit. 2:3* [2567]

[2818] καλοποιέω *kalopoieō* 1x *to do well, do good, do what is right,* 2 Thess. 3:13* [2569]

[2819] καλός *kalos* 101x pr. *beautiful; good, of good quality* or *disposition; fertile, rich,* Mt. 13:8, 23; *useful, profitable,* Lk. 14:34; καλόν ἐστι[ν], *it is profitable, it is well,* Mt. 18:8, 9; *excellent, choice, select, goodly,* Mt. 7:17, 19; καλόν ἐστι[ν], *it is pleasant, delightful,* Mt. 17:4; *just, full* measure, Lk. 6:38; *honorable, distinguished,* Jas. 2:7; *good, possessing moral excellence, worthy, upright, virtuous,* Jn. 10:11, 14; 1 Tim. 4:6; τὸ καλόν, and τὸ καλόν ἔργον, *what is good and right, a good deed, rectitude, virtue,* Mt. 5:16; Rom. 7:18, 21; *right, duty, propriety,* Mt. 15:26; *benefit, favor,* Jn. 10:32, 33 [2566, 2570] See *beautiful; good.*

[2820] κάλυμμα *kalymma* 4x *a covering; a veil,* 2 Cor. 3:13; met. *a veil, a blind* to spiritual vision, 2 Cor. 3:14, 15, 16* [2571]

[2821] καλύπτω *kalyptō* 8x *to cover,* Mt. 8:24; Lk. 8:16; 23:30; *to hide, conceal,* Mt. 10:26; 2 Cor. 4:3; met. *to cover, throw a veil* of oblivion *over,* Jas. 5:20; 1 Pet. 4:8 [2572]

[2822] καλῶς *kalōs* 37x *well, rightly, suitable, with propriety, becomingly,*

1 Cor. 7:37; 14:17; Gal. 4:17; 5:7; *truly, justly, correctly,* Mk. 12:32; Lk. 20:39; Jn. 4:17; *appositely,* Mt. 15:7; Mk. 7:6; *becomingly, honorably,* Jas. 2:3; *well, effectually,* Mk. 7:9, 37; καλῶς εἰπεῖν, *to speak well, praise, applaud,* Lk. 6:26; καλῶς ἔχειν, *to be convalescent,* Mk. 16:18; καλῶς ποιεῖν, *to do good, confer benefits,* Mt. 5:44; 12:12; *to do well, act virtuously,* Phil. 4:14 [2573] See *good; right; well.*

[2823] κάμηλος *kamēlos* 6x *a camel,* Mt. 3:4; 23:24 [2574] See *camel.*

[2825] κάμινος *kaminos* 4x *a furnace, oven, kiln,* Mt. 13:42, 50; Rev. 1:15; 9:2* [2575]

[2826] καμμύω *kammyō* 2x *to shut, close* the eyes, Mt. 13:15; Acts 28:27* [2576]

[2827] κάμνω *kamnō* 2x *to tire with exertion, labor to weariness; to be wearied, tired out, exhausted, be discouraged,* Heb. 12:3; *to labor* under disease, *be sick,* Jas. 5:15* [2577]

[2828] κάμπτω *kamptō* 4x trans. *to bend, inflect* the knee, Rom. 11:4; Eph. 3:14 intrans. *to bend, bow,* Rom. 14:11; Phil. 2:10* [2578]

[2829] κἄν *kan* 17x crasis, *and if,* Mk. 16:18; *also if,* Mt. 21:21; *even if, if even, although,* Jn. 10:38; *if so much as,* Heb. 12:20; also in NT simply equivalent to καί, as a particle of emphasis, by a pleonasm of ἄν, *at least, at all events,* Mk. 6:56; Acts 5:15; 2 Cor. 11:16 [2579]

[2830] Κανά *Kana* 4x indecl. *Cana,* a town in Galilee, Jn. 2:1, 11; 4:46; 21:2* [2580]

[2831] Καναναῖος *Kananaios* 2x *a Canaanite,* Mt. 10:4; Mk. 3:18* [2581]

[2833] Κανδάκη *Kandakē* 1x *Candace,* pr. name, Acts 8:27* [2582]

[2834] κανών *kanōn* 4x *a measure, rule;* in NT *prescribed range* of action or duty, 2 Cor. 10:13, 15, 16; met. *rule* of conduct or doctrine, Gal. 6:16* [2583]

[2836] καπηλεύω *kapēleuō* 1x pr. *to be* κάπηλος, *a retailer; to peddle with; to corrupt, adulterate,* 2 Cor. 2:17* [2585]

[2837] καπνός *kapnos* 13x *smoke,* Acts 2:19; Rev. 8:4 [2586] See *smoke.*

[2838] Καππαδοκία *Kappadokia* 2x *Cappadocia,* a district of Asia Minor, Acts 2:9; 1 Pet. 1:1* [2587]

[2840] καρδία *kardia* 156x *the heart,* regarded as the seat of feeling, impulse, affection, desire, Mt. 6:21; 22:37; Phil. 1:7; *the heart,* as the seat of intellect, Mt. 13:15; Rom. 1:21; *the heart,* as the inner and mental frame, Mt. 5:8; Lk. 16:15; 1 Pet. 3:4; *the conscience,* 1 Jn. 3:20, 21; *the heart, the inner part, middle, center,* Mt. 12:40 [2588] See *heart.*

[2841] καρδιογνώστης *kardiognōstēs* 2x *heart-knower, searcher of hearts,* Acts 1:24; 15:8* [2589]

[2842] Κάρπος *Karpos* 1x *Carpus,* pr. name, 2 Tim. 4:13* [2591]

[2843] καρπός *karpos* 66x *fruit,* Mt. 3:10; 21:19, 34; from the Hebrew, καρπὸς κοιλίας, *fruit of the womb, offspring,* Lk. 1:42; καρπὸς ὀσφύος, *fruit of the loins, offspring, posterity,* Acts 2:30; καρπὸς χειλέων, *fruit of the lips, praise,* Heb. 13:15; met. *conduct, actions,* Mt. 3:8; 7:16; Rom. 6:22; *benefit, profit,* Rom. 1:13; 6:21; *reward,* Phil. 4:17 [2590] See *crop; fruit.*

[2844] καρποφορέω *karpophoreō* 8x *to bear fruit, yield,* Mk. 4:28; met, *to bring forth the fruit* of action or conduct, Mt. 13:23; Rom. 7:5; mid. *to expand by fruitfulness, to develop itself by success,* Col. 1:6, 10 [2592]

[2845] καρποφόρος *karpophoros* 1x *fruitful, adapted to bring forth fruit,* Acts 14:17* [2593]

[2846] καρτερέω *kartereō* 1x *to be stout; to endure patiently, persevere, bear up with fortitude,* Heb. 11:27* [2594]

[2847] κάρφος *karphos* 6x *any small dry thing,* as *chaff, stubble, splinter*; Mt. 7:3, 4, 5; Lk. 6:41, 42* [2595]

[2848] κατά *kata* 473x *down from,* Mt. 8:32; *down upon, upon,* Mk. 14:3; Acts 27:14; *down into;* κατὰ βάθους, *profound, deepest,* 2 Cor. 8:2; *down over, throughout* a space, Lk. 4:14; 23:5; *concerning,* in cases of pointed allegation, 1 Cor. 15:15; *against,* Mt. 12:30; *by,* in oaths, Mt. 26:63; with an acc. of place, *in the quarter of, about, near, at,* Lk. 10;32; Acts 2:10; *throughout,* Lk. 8:39; *in,* Rom. 16:5; *among,* Acts 21:21; *in the presence of,* Lk. 2:31; *in the direction of, towards,* Acts 8:26; Phil. 3:14; of time, *within the range of; during, in the course of, at, about,* Acts 12:1; 27:27; distributively, κατ᾽ οἶκον, *by houses, from house to house,* Acts 2:46; kata; duvo, *two and two,* 1 Cor. 14:27; καθ᾽ ἡμέραν, *daily,* Mt. 26:55; trop., *according to, conformable to, in proportion to,* Mt. 9:29; 25:15; *after the fashion* or *likeness of.* Heb. 5:6; *in virtue of,* Mt. 19:3; *as respects,* Rom. 11:3; Acts 25;14; Heb. 9:9 [2596]

[2849] καταβαίνω *katabainō* 81x *to come* or *go down, descend,* Mt. 8:1; 17:9; *to lead down,* Acts 8:26; *to come down, fall,* Mt. 7:25, 27; *to be let down,* Acts 10:11; 11:5 [2597] See *come down; descend; go down.*

[2850] καταβάλλω *kataballō* 2x *to cast down,* 2 Cor. 4:9; mid. *to lay down, lay* a foundation, Heb. 6:1* [2598]

[2851] καταβαρέω *katabareō* 1x pr. *to weigh down,* met. *to burden, be burdensome to,* 2 Cor. 12:16* [2599]

[2852] καταβαρύνω *katabarynō* 1x *to weigh down, depress,* pass., *be heavy,* Mk. 14:40* [925]

[2853] κατάβασις *katabasis* 1x *the act of descending; a way down, descent,* Lk. 19:37* [2600]

[2856] καταβολή *katabolē* 11x pr. *a casting down; laying the foundation, foundation; beginning, commencement,* Mt. 13:35; 25:34; *conception* in the womb, Heb. 11:11 [2602] See *creation; foundation.*

[2857] καταβραβεύω *katabrabeuō* 1x pr. *to give an unfavorable decision as respects a prize;* hence, *to decide against,* Col. 2:18* [2603]

[2858] καταγγελεύς *katangeleus* 1x *one who announces* anything, *a proclaimer, publisher,* Acts 17:18* [2604]

[2859] καταγγέλλω *katangellō* 18x *to announce, proclaim,* Acts 13:38; in NT *to laud, celebrate,* Rom. 1:8 [2605] See *announce; make public; proclaim.*

[2860] καταγελάω *katagelaō* 3x *to deride, laugh at, jeer,* Mt. 9:24; Mk. 5:40; Lk. 8:53* [2606]

[2861] καταγινώσκω *kataginōskō* 3x *to determine against, condemn, blame, reprehend,* Gal. 2:11; 1 Jn. 3:20, 21 [2607]

[2862] κατάγνυμι *katagnymi* 4x *to break in pieces, crush, break in two,* Mt. 12:20; Jn. 19:31, 32, 33* [2608]

[2863] καταγράφω *katagraphō* 1x *to trace, draw in outline, write,* Jn. 8:6* [1125]

[2864] κατάγω *katagō* 9x *to lead, bring,* or *conduct down,* Acts 9:30; 22:30; 23:15, 20, 28; *to bring* a ship *to land;* pass. κατάγομαι, aor. κατήχθην, *to come to land, land, touch,* Lk. 5:11 [2609]

[2865] καταγωνίζομαι *katagōnizomai* 1x *to subdue, vanquish, overcome, conquer,* Heb. 11:33* [2610]

[2866] καταδέω *katadeō* 1x *to bind up; to bandage* a wound, Lk. 10:34* [2611]

[2867] κατάδηλος *katadēlos* 1x *quite clear* or *evident,* Heb. 7:15* [2612]

[2868] καταδικάζω *katadikazō* 5x *to give judgment against, condemn,* Mt. 12:7, 37; Lk. 6:37; Jas. 5:6* [2613]

[2869] καταδίκη *katadikē* 1x *condemnation, sentence of condemnation,* Acts 25:15* [1349]

[2870] καταδιώκω *katadiōkō* 1x *to follow hard upon; to track, search for, follow perseveringly,* Mk. 1:36* [2614]

[2871] καταδουλόω *katadouloō* 2x *to reduce to absolute servitude, make a slave of,* 2 Cor. 11:20; Gal. 2:4* [2615]

[2872] καταδυναστεύω *katadynasteuō* 2x *to tyrannize over, oppress, exploit,* Acts 10:38; Jas. 2:6* [2616]

[2873] κατάθεμα *katathema* 1x *an execration, curse;* by meton. *what is worthy of cursing* or *condemnation,* Rev. 22:3* [2652]

[2874] καταθεματίζω *katathematizō* 1x *to curse,* Mt. 26:74* [2653]

[2875] καταισχύνω *kataischunō* 13x *to humiliate, shame, put to shame,* 1 Cor. 1:27; pass. *to be ashamed, be put to shame,* Lk. 13:17; *to dishonor, disgrace,* 1 Cor. 11:4, 5; from the Hebrew, *to frustrate, disappoint,* Rom. 5:5; 9:33; 1 Pet. 2:6 [2617] See *ashamed; disappoint; embarrass, (be) embarrassed; humiliate.*

[2876] κατακαίω *katakaiō* 12x *to burn up, consume with fire,* Mt. 3:12; 13:30, 40 [2618] See *burn.*

[2877] κατακαλύπτω *katakalyptō* 3x *to veil;* mid. *to veil one's self, be veiled* or *covered,* 1 Cor. 11:6, 7. In the pres act ind., 2nd sg, the personal ending σαι does not simplify as normal, κατακαυχᾶσαι* [2619]

[2878] κατακαυχάομαι *katakauchaomai* 4x *to boast, glory over, assume superiority over,* Rom. 11:18 (2x); Jas. 2:13; 3:14* [2620]

[2879] κατάκειμαι *katakeimai* 12x *to lie, be in a recumbent position, be laid down,* Mk. 1:30; 2:4; Lk. 5:25; Jn. 5:3, 6; Acts 9:33; 28:8; *to recline* at table, Mk. 2:15; 14:3; Lk. 5:29; 7:37; 1 Cor. 8:10* [2621] See *lie down; recline.*

[2880] κατακλάω *kataklaō* 2x *to break, break in pieces,* Mk. 6:41; Lk. 9:16* [2622]

[2881] κατακλείω *katakleiō* 2x *to close, shut fast; to shut up, confine,* Lk. 3:20; Acts 26:10* [2623]

[2883] κατακληρονομέω *kataklēronomeō* 1x *to give as inheritance,* Acts 13:19* [2624]

[2884] κατακλίνω *kataklinō* 5x *to cause to lie down, cause to recline* at table, Lk. 9:14, 15; mid. *to lie down, recline,* Lk. 7:36; 14:8; 24:30* [2625]

[2885] κατακλύζω *kataklyzō* 1x *to inundate, flood, deluge,* 2 Pet. 3:6* [2626]

[2886] κατακλυσμός *kataklysmos* 4x *flood, deluge,* Mt. 24:38, 39; Lk. 17:27; 2 Pet. 2:5* [2627]

[2887] κατακολουθέω *katakoloutheō* 2x *to follow closely* or *earnestly,* Lk. 23:55; Acts 16:17* [2628]

[2888] κατακόπτω *katakoptō* 1x *to cut* or *dash in pieces; to mangle, wound,* Mk. 5:5* [2629]

[2889] κατακρημνίζω *katakrēmnizō* 1x *to cast down headlong,* Lk. 4:29* [2630]

[2890] κατάκριμα *katakrima* 3x *punishment, condemnation, condemning sentence,* Rom. 5:16, 18; 8:1* [2631]

[2891] κατακρίνω *katakrinō* 18x *to give judgment against, condemn,* Mt. 27:3; Jn. 8:10, 11; *to condemn, to place in a guilty light* by contrast, Mt. 12:41, 42; Lk. 11:31, 32; Heb. 11:7 [2632] See *condemn; judge guilty.*

[2892] κατάκρισις *katakrisis* 2x *condemnation,* 2 Cor. 3:9; *censure,* 2 Cor. 7:3* [2633]

[2893] κατακύπτω *katakyptō* 1x *to bend down,* Jn. 8:8* [2596 + 2955]

[2894] κατακυριεύω *katakyrieuō* 4x *to get into one's power;* in NT *to bring under, master, overcome,* Acts 19:16; *to domineer over,* Mt. 20:25; Mk. 10:42; 1 Pet. 5:3* [2634]

[2895] καταλαλέω *katalaleō* 5x *to blab out; to speak against, slander,* Jas. 4:11; 1 Pet. 2:12; 3:16* [2635]

[2896] καταλαλιά *katalalia* 2x *evil-speaking, detraction, backbiting, slandering,* 2 Cor. 12:20; 1 Pet. 2:1* [2636]

[2897] κατάλαλος *katalalos* 1x *slanderous; a detractor, slanderer,* Rom. 1:30* [2637]

[2898] καταλαμβάνω *katalambanō* 15x *to lay hold of, grasp; to obtain, attain,* Rom. 9:30; 1 Cor. 9:24; Phil. 3:12, 13; *to seize, to take possession of,* Mk. 9:18; *to come suddenly upon; overtake, surprise,* Jn. 12:35; 1 Thess. 5:4; *to detect in the act, seize,* Jn. 8:3, 4; met. *to comprehend, apprehend,* Jn. 1:5; mid. *to understand, perceive,* Acts 4:13; 10:34; 25:25; Eph. 3:18* [2638] See *catch; grasp; obtain; seize; understand.*

[2899] καταλέγω *katalegō* 1x *to select, enter in a list* or *catalog, enroll,* 1 Tim. 5:9* [2639]

[2901] καταλείπω *kataleipō* 24x *to leave behind; to leave behind* at death, Mk. 12:19; *to relinquish, let remain,* Mk. 14:52; *to quit, depart from, forsake,* Mt. 4:13; 16:4; *to neglect,* Acts 6:2; *to leave alone,* or *without assistance,* Lk. 10:40; *to reserve,* Rom. 11:4 [2641] See *depart; leave behind.*

[2902] καταλιθάζω *katalithazō* 1x *to stone, kill by stoning,* Lk. 20:6* [2642]

[2903] καταλλαγή *katallagē* 4x pr. *an exchange; reconciliation, restoration to favor,* Rom. 5:11; 11:15; 2 Cor. 5:18, 19* [2643] See *reconciliation.*

[2904] καταλλάσσω *katallassō* 6x *to change, exchange; to reconcile;* pass. *to be reconciled,* Rom. 5:10 (2x); 1 Cor. 7:11; 2 Cor. 5:18, 19, 20* [2644] See *reconcile.*

[2905] κατάλοιπος *kataloipos* 1x *remaining;* οἱ κατάλοιποι, *the rest,* Acts 15:17* [2645]

[2906] κατάλυμα *katalyma* 3x *lodging, inn,* Lk. 2:7; *a guest-chamber,* Mk. 14:14; Lk. 22:11* [2646]

[2907] καταλύω *katalyō* 17x *to dissolve; to destroy, demolish, overthrow, throw down,* Mt. 24:2; 26:61; met. *to nullify, abrogate,* Mt. 5:17; Acts 5:38, 39; absol. *to unloose* harness, etc., *to halt, to stop for the night, lodge,* Lk. 9:12 [2647] See *destroy.*

[2908] καταμανθάνω *katamanthanō* 1x *to learn* or *observe thoroughly; to consider accurately and diligently, contemplate,* Mt. 6:28* [2648]

[2909] καταμαρτυρέω *katamartyreō* 3x *to witness* or *testify against,* Mt. 26:62; 27:13; Mk. 14:60* [2649]

[2910] καταμένω *katamenō* 1x *to remain; to abide, dwell,* Acts 1:13* [2650]

[2914] καταναλίσκω *katanaliskō* 1x *to consume,* as fire, Heb. 12:29* [2654]

[2915] καταναρκάω *katanarkaō* 3x in NT *to be burdensome to the disadvantage of* any one, *to be a dead weight upon;* by impl. *to be troublesome, burdensome to,* in respect of maintenance, 2 Cor. 11:9; 12:13, 14* [2655]

[2916] κατανεύω *kataneuō* 1x pr. *to nod, signify assent by a nod;* genr. *to make signs, beckon,* Lk. 5:7* [2656]

[2917] κατανοέω *katanoeō* 14x *to perceive, understand, apprehend,* Lk. 20:23; *to observe, consider, contemplate,* Lk. 12:24, 27; *to discern, detect,* Mt. 7:3; *to have regard to, make account of,* Rom. 4:19 [2657] See *consider; look; perceive.*

[2918] καταντάω *katantaō* 13x *to come to, arrive at,* Acts 16:1; 20:15; of an epoch, *to come upon,* 1 Cor. 10:11; met. *to reach, attain to,* Acts 26:7 [2658] See *arrive.*

[2919] κατάνυξις *katanyxis* 1x in NT *deep sleep, stupor, dullness,* Rom. 11:8* [2659]

[2920] κατανύσσομαι *katanyssomai* 1x *to pierce through; to pierce* with compunction and pain of heart, Acts 2:37* [2660]

[2921] καταξιόω *kataxioō* 3x *to consider worthy of,* Lk. 20:35; Acts 5:41; 2 Thess. 1:5* [2661]

[2922] καταπατέω *katapateō* 5x *to trample upon, tread down* or *under feet,* Mt. 5:13; 7:6; Lk. 8:5; 12:1; met. *to trample on* by indignity, *spurn,* Heb. 10:29* [2662]

[2923] κατάπαυσις *katapausis* 9x pr. *the act of giving rest; a state of settled* or *final rest,* Heb. 3:11, 18; 4:1, 3, 4, 5, 11; *a place of rest, place of abode, dwelling, habitation,* Acts 7:49* [2663]

[2924] καταπαύω *katapauō* 4x *to cause to cease, restrain,* Acts 14:18; *to cause to rest, give final rest to, settle finally,* Heb. 4:8; intrans. *to rest, desist from,* Heb. 4:4, 10* [2664]

[2925] καταπέτασμα *katapetasma* 6x *a veil, curtain,* Mt. 27:51; Mk. 15:38; Lk. 23:45; Heb. 6:19; 9:3; 10:20* [2665] See *veil.*

[2927] καταπίνω *katapinō* 7x *to drink, swallow, gulp down,* Mt. 23:24; *to swallow up, absorb,* Rev. 12:16; 2 Cor. 5:4; *to engulf, submerge, overwhelm,* Heb. 11:29; *to swallow greedily, devour,* 1 Pet. 5:8; *to destroy, annihilate,* 1 Cor. 15:54; 2 Cor. 2:7* [2666]

[2928] καταπίπτω *katapiptō* 3x *to fall down, fall prostrate,* Lk. 8:6; Acts 26:14; 28:6* [2667]

[2929] καταπλέω *katapleō* 1x *to sail towards land, to come to land,* Lk. 8:26* [2668]

[2930] καταπονέω *kataponeō* 2x *to exhaust by labor* or *suffering; to wear out,* 2 Pet. 2:7; *to overpower, oppress,* Acts 7:24* [2669]

[2931] καταποντίζω *katapontizō* 2x *to sink in the sea;* pass. *to sink,* Mt. 14:30; *to be plunged, submerged, drowned,* Mt. 18:6* [2670]

[2932] κατάρα *katara* 6x *a cursing, execration, imprecation,* Jas. 3:10; from the Hebrew, *condemnation, doom,* Gal. 3:10; Heb. 6:8; 2 Pet. 2:14; meton., *a doomed one, one on whom condemnation falls,* Gal. 3:13* [2671]

[2933] καταράομαι *kataraomai* 5x *to curse, to wish evil to, imprecate evil upon,* Mk. 11:21; Lk. 6:28; Rom. 12:14; Jas. 3:9; in NT pass. *to be cursed,* Mt. 25:41* [2672]

[2934] καταργέω *katargeō* 27x *to render useless* or *unproductive, occupy unprofitable,* Lk. 13:7; *to render powerless,* Rom. 6:6; *to make empty and unmeaning,* Rom. 4:14; *to render null, to abrogate, cancel,* Rom. 3:3, 31; Eph. 2:15; *to bring to an end,* 1 Cor. 2:6; 13:8; 15:24, 26; 2 Cor. 3:7; *to destroy, annihilate,* 2 Thess. 2:8; Heb. 2:14; *to free from, dissever from,* Rom. 7:2, 6; Gal. 5:4 [2673] See *destroy; nullify; release.*

[2935] καταριθμέω *katarithmeō* 1x *to enumerate, number with, count with,* Acts 1:17* [2674]

[2936] καταρτίζω *katartizō* 13x *to adjust thoroughly; to knit together, unite completely,* 1 Cor. 1:10; *to frame,* Heb. 11:3; *to prepare, provide,* Mt. 21:16; Heb. 10:5; *to qualify fully, to complete* in character, Lk. 6:40; Heb. 13:21; 1 Pet. 5:10; perf. pass. κατηρτισμένα, *fit, ripe,* Rom. 9:22; *to repair, refit,* Mt. 4:21; Mk. 1:19; *to supply, make good,* 1 Thess. 3:10; *to restore* to a forfeited condition, *to reinstate,* Gal. 6:1; 2 Cor. 13:11* [2675] See *prepare; put in order; restore.*

[2937] κατάρτισις *katartisis* 1x pr. *a complete adjustment; completeness* of character, *perfection,* 2 Cor. 13:9* [2676]

[2938] καταρτισμός *katartismos* 1x *a perfectly adjusted adaptation; complete qualification* for a specific purpose, Eph. 4:12* [2677]

[2939] κατασείω *kataseiō* 4x *to shake down* or *violently,* Acts 19:33; τὴν χεῖρα, or τῇ χειρί, *to wave the hand, beckon; to* *signal silence by waving the hand,* Acts 12:17; 13:16; 21:40* [2678]

[2940] κατασκάπτω *kataskaptō* 2x pr. *to dig down under, undermine;* by impl. *to overthrow; demolish, raze,* Rom. 11:3; τὰ κατεσκαμμένα, *ruins,* Acts 15:16* [2679]

[2941] κατασκευάζω *kataskeuazō* 11x *to prepare, put in readiness,* Mt. 11:10; Mk. 1:2; Lk. 1:17; 7:27; *to construct, form, build,* Heb. 3:3, 4; 9:2, 6; 11:7; 1 Pet. 3:20* [2680] See *build, build up; prepare.*

[2942] κατασκηνόω *kataskēnoō* 4x *to pitch one's tent;* in NT *to rest in* a place, *settle, abide,* Acts 2:26; *to haunt, roost,* Mt. 13:32; Mk. 4:32; Lk. 13:19* [2681]

[2943] κατασκήνωσις *kataskēnōsis* 2x pr. *the pitching a tent; a tent;* in NT *a dwelling place,* Mt. 8:20; Lk. 9:58* [2682]

[2944] κατασκιάζω *kataskiazō* 1x *to overshadow,* Heb. 9:5* [2683]

[2945] κατασκοπέω *kataskopeō* 1x *to view closely and accurately; to spy out,* Gal. 2:4* [2684]

[2946] κατάσκοπος *kataskopos* 1x *a scout, spy,* Heb. 11:31* [2685]

[2947] κατασοφίζομαι *katasophizomai* 1x *to exercise cleverness to the detriment of* any one, *to outwit; to make a victim of subtlety, to practice on the insidious dealing,* Acts 7:19* [2686]

[2948] καταστέλλω *katastellō* 2x *to arrange, dispose in regular order; to appease, quiet, pacify,* Acts 19:35, 36* [2687]

[2949] κατάστημα *katastēma* 1x *determinate state, behavior, condition; personal appearance,* Tit. 2:3* [2688]

[2950] καταστολή *katastolē* 1x pr. *an arranging in order; adjustment of dress;* in NT *apparel, dress,* 1 Tim. 2:9* [2689]

[2951] καταστρέφω *katastrephō* 2x *to invert; to overturn, upset, overthrow, throw down,* Mt. 21:12; Mk. 11:15* [2690]

[2952] καταστρηνιάω *katastrēniaō* 1x *to be headstrong* or *wanton towards,* 1 Tim. 5:11* [2691]

[2953] καταστροφή *katastrophē* 2x *an overthrow, destruction,* 2 Pet. 2:6; met. *overthrow* of right principle or faith, *utter detriment, perversion,* 2 Tim. 2:14* [2692]

[2954] καταστρώννυμι *katastrōnnymi* 1x *to lay flat;* pass. *to be laid prostrate* in death, 1 Cor. 10:5* [2693]

[2955] κατασύρω *katasyrō* 1x *to drag down, to drag away* by force, Lk. 12:58* [2694]

[2956] κατασφάζω *katasphazō* 1x also spelled κατασφάττω, *to slaughter, slay,* Lk. 19:27* [2695]

[2958] κατασφραγίζω *katasphragizō* 1x *to seal up,* Rev. 5:1* [2696]

[2959] κατάσχεσις *kataschesis* 2x *a possession, thing possessed,* Acts 7:5, 45* [2697]

[2960] κατατίθημι *katatithēmi* 2x mid. *to ay up for one's self;* χάριν, or χάριτας, *to lay up a store of favor for one's self, earn a title to favor* at the hands of a person, *to curry favor with,* Acts 24:27; 25:9* [2698]

[2961] κατατομή *katatomē* 1x *mutilation,* Phil. 3:2* [2699]

[2963] κατατρέχω *katatrechō* 1x *to run down,* Acts 21:32* [2701]

[2965] καταφέρω *katapherō* 4x *to bear down; to overpower,* as sleep, Acts 20:9; καταφέρειν ψῆφον, *to give a vote* or *verdict,* Acts 26:10; *to bring charges,* Acts 25:7* [2702]

[2966] καταφεύγω *katapheugō* 2x *to flee to* for refuge, Acts 14:6; Heb. 6:18* [2703]

[2967] καταφθείρω *kataphtheirō* 1x *to destroy, corrupt, deprave,* 2 Tim. 3:8* [2704]

[2968] καταφιλέω *kataphileō* 6x *to kiss affectionately* or *with a semblance of affection, to kiss with earnest gesture,* Mt.

26:49; Mk. 14:45; Lk. 7:38, 45; 15:20; Acts 20:37* [2705]

[2969] καταφρονέω *kataphroneō* 9x pr. *to look down on; to scorn, despise,* Mt. 18:10; Rom. 2:4; *to slight,* Mt. 6:24; Lk. 16:13; 1 Cor. 11:22; 1 Tim. 4:12; 6:2; 2 Pet. 2:10; *to disregard,* Heb. 12:2* [2706]

[2970] καταφρονητής *kataphronētēs* 1x *despiser, scorner,* Acts 13:41* [2707]

[2972] καταχέω *katacheō* 2x *to pour out* or *down upon,* Mt. 26:7; Mk. 14:3* [2708]

[2973] καταχθόνιος *katachthonios* 1x *under the earth, subterranean, infernal,* Phil. 2:10* [2709]

[2974] καταχράομαι *katachraomai* 2x *to use downright; to use up, consume; to make an unrestrained use of, use eagerly,* 1 Cor. 7:31; *to use to the full, stretch to the utmost, exploit,* 1 Cor. 9:18* [2710]

[2976] καταψύχω *katapsychō* 1x *to cool, refresh,* Lk. 16:24* [2711]

[2977] κατείδωλος *kateidōlos* 1x *rife with idols, sunk in idolatry, grossly idolatrous,* Acts 17:16* [2712]

[2978] κατέναντι *katenanti* 8x can function as an improper prep., *over against, opposite to,* Mk. 11:2; 12:41; 13:3; ὁ, ἡ, τό, κατέναντι, *opposite,* Lk. 19:30; *before, in the presence of, in the sight of,* Rom. 4:17 [2713]

[2979] κατενώπιον *katenōpion* 3x can function as an improper prep., *in the presence of, in the sight of, before*; Eph. 1:4; Col. 1:22; Jude 24* [2714]

[2980] κατεξουσιάζω *katexousiazō* 2x *to exercise lordship* or *authority over, domineer over,* Mt. 20:25; Mk. 10:42* [2715]

[2981] κατεργάζομαι *katergazomai* 22x *to work out; to effect, produce, bring out as a result,* Rom. 4:15; 5:3; 7:13; 2 Cor. 4:17; 7:10; Phil. 2:12; 1 Pet. 4:3; Jas. 1:3; *to work, practice, realize in practice,* Rom. 1:27; 2:9; *to work* or *mould into fitness,* 2 Cor. 5:5, *despatch,* Eph. 6:13 [2716] See *bring about; do; produce.*

[2982] κατέρχομαι *katerchomai* 16x *to come* or *go down,* Lk. 4:31; 9:37; Acts 8:5; 9:32; *to land at, touch at,* Acts 18:22; 27:5 [2718] See *come down, go down; land.*

[2983] κατεσθίω *katesthiō* 14x also spelled κατέσθω, *to eat up, devour,* Mt. 13:4; *to consume,* Rev. 11:5, *to expend, squander,* Lk. 15:30; met. *to make a prey of, plunder,* Mt. 23:13; Mk. 12:40; Lk. 20:47; 2 Cor. 11:20; *to annoy, injure,* Gal. 5:15 [2719] See *devour; eat.*

[2985] κατευθύνω *kateuthunō* 3x optative, κατευθύναι (3rd sg), *to make straight; to direct, guide aright,* Lk. 1:79; 1 Thess. 3:11; 2 Thess. 3:5* [2720]

[2986] κατευλογέω *kateulogeō* 1x *to bless,* Mk. 10:16* [2127]

[2987] κατεφίσταμαι *katephistamai* 1x *to come upon suddenly, rush upon, assault,* Acts 18:12* [2721]

[2988] κατέχω *katechō* 17x (1) transitive, *to hold down; to detain, retain,* Lk. 4:42; Rom. 1:18; Phlm. 13; *to hinder, restrain,* 2 Thess. 2:6, 7; *to hold downright, hold in a firm grasp, to have in full and secure possession,* 1 Cor. 7:30; 2 Cor. 6:10; *to come into full possession of, seize upon*; *to keep, retain,* 1 Thess. 5:21; *to occupy,* Lk. 14:9; met. *to hold fast* mentally, *retain,* Lk. 8:15; 1 Cor. 11:2; 15:2; *to maintain,* Heb. 3:6, 14; 10:23; (2) intransitive, a nautical term, *to land, touch,* Acts 27:40; pass. *to be in the grasp of, to be bound by,* Rom. 7:6* [2722] See *hold; restrain.*

[2989] κατηγορέω *katēgoreō* 23x *to speak against, accuse,* Mt. 12:10; 27:12; Jn. 5:45 [2723] See *accuse.*

[2990] κατηγορία *katēgoria* 3x *an accusation, crimination,* Jn. 18:29; 1 Tim. 5:19; Tit. 1:6* [2724]

[2991] κατήγορος *katēgoros* 4x *an accuser,* Acts 23:30, 35; Acts 25:16, 18* [2725]

[2992] κατήγωρ *katēgōr* 1x *an accuser,* Rev. 12:10, a barbarous form for κατήγορος* [2725]

[2993] κατήφεια *katēpheia* 1x *dejection, sorrow,* Jas. 4:9* [2726]

[2994] κατηχέω *katēcheō* 8x pr. *to sound in the ears, make the ears ring; to instruct orally, to instruct, inform,* 1 Cor. 14:19; pass. *to be taught, be instructed,* Lk. 1:4; Rom. 2:18; Gal. 6:6; *to be made acquainted,* Acts 18:25; *to receive information, hear report,* Acts 21:21, 24* [2727] See *inform; instruct; teach.*

[2995] κατιόω *katioō* 1x *to cover with rust;* pass. *to rust, become rusty* or *tarnished,* Jas. 5:3* [2728]

[2996] κατισχύω *katischuō* 3x *to overpower,* Mt. 16:18; absol. *to predominate, get the upper hand,* Lk. 21:36; 23:23* [2729]

[2997] κατοικέω *katoikeō* 44x trans. *to inhabit,* Acts 1:19; absol. *to have an abode, dwell,* Lk. 13:4; Acts 11:29; *to take up* or *find an abode,* Acts 7:2; *to indwell,* Eph. 3:17; Jas. 4:5 [2730] See *dwell; live.*

[2998] κατοίκησις *katoikēsis* 1x *an abode, dwelling, habitation,* Mk. 5:3* [2731]

[2999] κατοικητήριον *katoikētērion* 2x *an abode, dwelling, habitation,* the same as κατοίκησις, Eph. 2:22; Rev. 18:2* [2732]

[3000] κατοικία *katoikia* 1x *habitation,* i.q. κατοίκησις, Acts 17:26* [2733]

[3001] κατοικίζω *katoikizō* 1x *to cause to dwell,* Jas. 4:5* [2730]

[3002] κατοπτρίζω *katoptrizō* 1x *to show in a mirror; to present a clear and correct image of* a thing, mid. *to have presented in a mirror, to have a clear image presented,* or, *to reflect,* 2 Cor. 3:18* [2734]

[3004] κάτω *katō* 9x (1) *down, downwards,* Mt. 4:6; Lk. 4:9; Jn. 8:6; Acts 20:9; (2) *beneath, below, under,* Mt. 27:51; Mk. 14:66; 15:38; Acts 2:19; ὁ, ἡ, τό, κάτω, *what is below, earthly,* Jn. 8:23* [2736]

[3005] κατώτερος *katōteros* 1x *lower,* Eph. 4:9* [2737]

[3006] κατωτέρω *katōterō* 1x *lower, farther down;* of time, *under,* Mt. 2:16* [2736]

[3007] Καῦδα *Kauda* 1x also spelled Κλαῦδα (3084) and Κλαῦδη (3085), *Cauda,* indecl. prop. name of an island, Acts 27:16* [2802]

[3008] καῦμα *kauma* 2x *heat, scorching* or *burning heat,* Rev. 7:16; 16:9* [2738]

[3009] καυματίζω *kaumatizō* 4x *to scorch, burn,* Mt. 13:6; Mk. 4:6; Rev. 16:8, 9* [2739]

[3011] καῦσις *kausis* 1x *burning, being burned,* Heb. 6:8* [2740]

[3012] καυσόω *kausoō* 2x *to be on fire, burn intensely,* 2 Pet. 3:10, 12* [2741]

[3013] καυστηριάζω *kaustēriazō* 1x also spelled καυτηριάζω, *to cauterize, brand;* pass. met. *to be branded* with marks of guilt, or, *to be seared* into insensibility, 1 Tim. 4:2* [2743]

[3014] καύσων *kausōn* 3x *fervent scorching heat; the scorching* of the sun, Mt. 20:12; *hot weather, a hot time,* Lk. 12:55; *the scorching wind of the East, Eurus,* Jas. 1:11* [2742]

[3016] καυχάομαι *kauchaomai* 37x *to glory, boast,* Rom. 2:17, 23; ὑπέρ τινος, *to boast of* a person or thing, *to undertake a complimentary testimony to,* 2 Cor. 12:5; *to rejoice, exult,* Rom. 5:2, 3, 11 [2744] See *boast; brag; rejoice.*

[3017] καύχημα *kauchēma* 11x *a glorying, boasting,* 1 Cor. 5:6; *a ground* or *matter of glorying* or *boasting,* Rom. 4:2; *joy, exultation,* Phil. 1:26; *complimentary testimony,* 1 Cor. 9:15, 16; 2 Cor. 9:3 [2745] See *boast; pride.*

[3018] καύχησις *kauchēsis* 11x *boasting, pride,* a later equivalent to καύχημαι, Rom. 3:27; 2 Cor. 7:4, 14; 11:10 [2746] See *boast; glory; pride.*

[3019] Καφαρναούμ *Kapharnaoum* 16x indecl. pr. name, *Capernaum* [2584]

[3020] Κεγχρεαί *Kenchreai* 2x *Cenchreae,* the port of Corinth on the Saronic Gulf; Acts 18:18; Rom. 16:1* [2747]

[3022] Κεδρών *Kedrōn* 1x indecl. pr. name, *Kidron,* a valley near Jerusalem, Jn. 18:1* [2748]

[3023] κεῖμαι *keimai* 24x *to lie, to be laid; to recline, to be lying, to have been laid down,* Mt. 28:6; Lk. 2:12; *to have been laid, placed, set,* Mt. 3:10; Lk. 3:9; Jn. 2:6; *to be situated,* as a city, Mt. 5:14; Rev. 21:16; *to be in store,* Lk. 12:19; met. *to be constituted, established* as a law, 1 Tim. 1:9; in NT of persons, *to be specially set, solemnly appointed, destined,* Lk. 2:34; Phil. 1:16; 1 Thess. 3:3; *to lie* under an influence, *to be involved in,* 1 Jn. 5:19 [2749] See *lie down.*

[3024] κειρία *keiria* 1x *a bandage, swath,* in NT pl. *graveclothes,* Jn. 11:44* [2750]

[3025] κείρω *keirō* 4x *to cut off* the hair, *shear, shave,* Acts 8:32; 18:18; 1 Cor. 11:6 (2x)* [2751]

[3026] κέλευσμα *keleusma* 1x *a word of command; a mutual cheer;* hence, in NT *a loud shout, an arousing outcry,* 1 Thess. 4:16* [2752]

[3027] κελεύω *keleuō* 25x *to order, command, direct, bid,* Mt. 8:18; 14:19, 28 [2753] See *command; order.*

[3029] κενοδοξία *kenodoxia* 1x *empty conceit,* Phil. 2:3* [2754]

[3030] κενόδοξος *kenodoxos* 1x *boastful,* Gal. 5:26* [2755]

[3031] κενός *kenos* 18x *empty; having nothing, empty-handed,* Mk. 12:3; met. *vain, fruitless, void of effect,* Acts 4:25; 1 Cor. 15:10; εἰς κενόν, *in vain, to no purpose,* 2 Cor. 6:1; *hollow, fallacious, false,* Eph. 5:6; Col. 2:8; *inconsiderate, foolish,* 1 Thess. 3:5; Jas. 2:20 [2756] See *empty; empty-handed; futile; useless; vain.*

[3032] κενοφωνία *kenophōnia* 2x *vain, empty babbling, vain disputation, fruitless discussion,* 1 Tim. 6:20; 2 Tim. 2:16* [2757]

[3033] κενόω *kenoō* 5x *to empty, evacuate;* ἑαυτόν, *to divest one's self of one's prerogatives, abase one's self,* Phil. 2:7; *to deprive a thing* of its proper functions, Rom. 4:14; 1 Cor. 1:17; *to show to be without foundation, falsify,* 1 Cor. 9:15; 2 Cor. 9:3* [2758]

[3034] κέντρον *kentron* 4x *a sharp point; a sting* of an animal, Rev. 9:10; *a prick, stimulus, goad,* Acts 26:14; met. of death, *destructive power, deadly venom,* 1 Cor. 15:55, 56* [2759]

[3035] κεντυρίων *kentyriōn* 3x in its original signification, *a commander of a hundred* foot-soldiers, *a centurion,* Mk. 15:39, 44, 45* [2760]

[3036] κενῶς *kenōs* 1x *in vain, to no purpose, unmeaning,* Jas. 4:5* [2761]

[3037] κεραία *keraia* 2x pr. *a horn-like projection, a point, extremity;* in NT *an apex,* or *fine point;* as of letters, used for *the minutest part, a tittle,* Mt. 5:18; Lk. 16:17* [2762]

[3038] κεραμεύς *kerameus* 3x *a potter,* Mt. 27:7, 10; Rom. 9:21* [2763]

[3039] κεραμικός *keramikos* 1x *made by a potter, earthen,* Rev. 2:27* [2764]

[3040] κεράμιον *keramion* 2x *an earthenware vessel, a pitcher, jar,* Mk. 14:13; Lk. 22;10* [2765]

[3041] κέραμος *keramos* 1x *potter's clay; earthenware; a roof, tile, tiling,* Lk. 5:19* [2766]

[3042] κεράννυμι *kerannymi* 3x *to mix, mingle,* drink; *to prepare* for drinking, Rev. 14:10; 18:6 (2x)* [2767]

[3043] κέρας *keras* 11x *a horn,* Rev. 5:6; 12:3; *a horn-like projection* at the corners of an altar, Rev. 9:13; from the Hebrew, *a horn* as a symbol of power, Lk. 1:69 [2768] See *horn.*

[3044] κεράτιον *keration* 1x pr. *a little horn;* in NT *a pod, the pod of the carob tree,* or *Ceratonia siliqua* of Linnaeus, a common tree in the East and the south of Europe, growing to a considerable size, and producing long slender pods, with a pulp of a sweetish taste, and several brown shining seeds like beans, sometimes eaten by the poorer people in Syria and Palestine, and commonly used for fattening swine, Lk. 15:16* [2769]

[3045] κερδαίνω *kerdainō* 17x *to gain* as a matter of profit, Mt. 25:17; *to win, acquire possession of,* Mt. 16:26; *to profit in the avoidance of, to avoid,* Acts 27:21; in NT Χριστόν, *to win* Christ, *to become possessed of* the privileges of the Gospel, Phil. 3:8; *to win over* from estrangement, Mt. 18:15; *to win over* to embrace the Gospel, 1 Cor. 9:19, 20, 21, 22; 1 Pet. 3:1; absol. *to make gain,* Jas. 4:13 [2770] See *gain; win.*

[3046] κέρδος *kerdos* 3x *gain, profit,* Phil. 1:21; 3:7; Tit. 1:11* [2771]

[3047] κέρμα *kerma* 1x *something clipped small; small change, small pieces of money, coin,* Jn. 2:15* [2772]

[3048] κερματιστής *kermatistēs* 1x *a money changer,* Jn. 2:14* [2773]

[3049] κεφάλαιον *kephalaion* 2x *a sum total; a sum of money, capital,* Acts 22:28; *the crowning* or *ultimate point* to preliminary matters, Heb. 8:1* [2774]

[3051] κεφαλή *kephalē* 75x *the head,* Mt. 5:36; 6:17; *the head, top;* κεφαλὴ γωνίας, *the head of the corner, the chief cornerstone,* Mt. 21:42; Lk. 20:17; met. *the head, superior, chief, principal, one to whom others are subordinate,* 1 Cor. 11:3; Eph. 1:22 [2776] See *head.*

[3052] κεφαλιόω *kephalioō* 1x *to hit the head,* Mk. 12:4* [2775]

[3053] κεφαλίς *kephalis* 1x in NT *a roll, volume, division* of a book, Heb. 10:7* [2777]

[3055] κημόω *kēmoō* 1x *to muzzle,* 1 Cor. 9:9* [5392]

[3056] κῆνσος *kēnsos* 4x *a census, assessment, enumeration of the people and a valuation of their property;* in NT *tribute, tax,* Mt. 17:25; *poll-tax,* Mt. 22:17, 19; Mk. 12:14* [2778]

[3057] κῆπος *kēpos* 5x *a garden, any place planted with trees and herbs,* Lk. 13:19; Jn. 18:1, 26; 19:41* [2779]

[3058] κηπουρός *kēpouros* 1x *a garden-keeper, gardener,* Jn. 20:15* [2780]

[3060] κήρυγμα *kērygma* 9x *proclamation, proclaiming, public annunciation,* Mt. 12:41; *public inculcation, preaching,* 1 Cor. 2:4; 15:14; meton. *what is publicly inculcated, doctrine,* Rom. 16:25; Tit. 1:3* [2782]

[3061] κῆρυξ *kēryx* 3x *a herald, public messenger;* in NT *a proclaimer, publisher, preacher,* 1 Tim. 2:7; 2 Tim. 1:11; 2 Pet. 2:5* [2783]

[3062] κηρύσσω *kēryssō* 61x *to publish, proclaim,* as a herald, 1 Cor. 9:27; *to announce openly and publicly,* Mk. 1:4; Lk. 4:18; *to noise abroad,* Mk. 1:45; 7:36; *to announce* as a matter of doctrine, *inculcate, preach,* Mt. 24:14; Mk. 1:38; 13:10; Acts 15:21; Rom. 2:21 [2784] See *preach; proclaim; tell.*

[3063] κῆτος *kētos* 1x *a large fish, sea monster, whale,* Mt. 12:40* [2785]

[3064] Κηφᾶς *Kēphas* 9x *Cephas, Rock,* rendered into Greek by Πέτρος, Jn. 1:42; 1 Cor. 1:12; 3:22; 9:5; 15:5; Gal. 1:18; 2:9, 11, 14* [2786]

[3066] κιβωτός *kibōtos* 6x *a chest, coffer; the ark* of the covenant, Heb. 9:4; Rev. 11:19; *the ark* of Noah, Mt. 24:38; Lk. 17:27; Heb. 11:7; 1 Pet. 3:20* [2787]

[3067] κιθάρα *kithara* 4x *a lyre, harp,* 1 Cor. 14:7; Rev. 5:8; 14:2; 15:2* [2788]

[3068] κιθαρίζω *kitharizō* 2x *to play on a lyre* or *harp,* 1 Cor. 14:7; Rev. 14:2* [2789]

[3069] κιθαρῳδός *kitharōidos* 2x *one who plays on the lyre and accompanies it with his voice,* Rev. 14:2; 18:22* [2790]

[3070] Κιλικία *Kilikia* 8x *Cilicia,* a province of Asia Minor, Gal. 1:21 [2791]

[3073] κινδυνεύω *kindyneuō* 4x *to be in danger* or *peril,* Lk. 8:23; Acts 19:27, 40; 1 Cor. 15:30* [2793]

[3074] κίνδυνος *kindynos* 9x *danger, peril,* Rom. 8:35; 2 Cor. 11:26* [2794]

[3075] κινέω *kineō* 8x *to move,* Mt. 23:4; *to excite, agitate,* Acts 21:30; 24:5; *to remove,* Rev. 2:5; 6:14; in NT κεφαλὴν, *to shake the head* in derision, Mt. 27:39; Mk. 15:29; mid., *to move, possess the faculty of motion, exercise the functions of life,* Acts 17:28* [2795] See *arouse; move; stir.*

[3077] κιννάμωμον *kinnamōmon* 1x *cinnamon,* Rev. 18:13* [2792]

[3078] Κίς *Kis* 1x *Kish,* the father of Saul, pr. name, indecl., Acts 13:21* [2797]

[3079] κίχρημι *kichrēmi* 1x *to lend,* Lk. 11:5* [5531]

[3080] κλάδος *klados* 11x *a bough, branch, shoot,* Mt. 13:32; 21:8; met. *a branch* of a family stock, Rom. 11:16, 21 [2798] See *branch.*

[3081] κλαίω *klaiō* 40x intrans. *to weep, shed tears,* Mt. 26:75; Mk. 5:38, 39; Lk. 19:41; 23:28; trans. *to weep for, bewail,* Mt. 2:18 [2799] See *cry; mourn; wail; weep.*

[3082] κλάσις *klasis* 2x *a breaking, the act of breaking,* Lk. 24:35; Acts 2:42 [2800]

[3083] κλάσμα *klasma* 9x *a piece broken off, fragment,* Mt. 14:20; 15:37; Mk. 6:43; 8:8, 19, 20; Lk. 9:17; Jn. 6:12f.* [2801]

[3086] Κλαυδία *Klaudia* 1x *Claudia,* pr. name, 2 Tim. 4:21* [2803]

[3087] Κλαύδιος *Klaudios* 3x *Claudius,* pr. name (1) *The fourth Roman Emperor,* Acts 11:28; 18:2. (2) *Claudius Lysias, a Roman captain,* Acts 23:26* [2804]

[3088] κλαυθμός *klauthmos* 9x *weeping, crying,* Mt. 2:18; 8:12 [2805]

[3089] κλάω *klaō* 14x *to break off;* in NT *to break* bread, Mt. 14:19; with figurative reference to the violent death of Christ, 1 Cor. 11:24 [2806] See *break.*

[3090] κλείς *kleis* 6x *a key,* used in NT as the symbol of power, authority, etc. Mt. 16:19; Rev. 1:18; 3:7; 9:1; 20:1; met. *the key* of entrance into knowledge, Lk. 11:52* [2807]

[3091] κλείω *kleiō* 16x *to close, shut,* Mt. 6:6; 25:10; *to shut up* a person, Rev. 20:3; met. of the heavens, Lk. 4:25; Rev. 11:6; κλεῖσαι τὰ σπλάγχνα, *to shut one's bowels, to be hard-hearted, void of compassion,* 1 Jn. 3:17; κλείειν τὴν βασιλεία τῶν οὐρανῶν, *to endeavor to prevent entrance into the kingdom of heaven,* Mt. 23:13 [2808] See *shut.*

[3092] κλέμμα *klemma* 1x *theft,* Rev. 9:21* [2809]

[3093] Κλεοπᾶς *Kleopas* 1x *Cleopas,* pr. name, Lk. 24:18* [2810]

[3094] κλέος *kleos* 1x pr. *rumor, report; good report, praise, credit,* 1 Pet. 2:20* [2811]

[3095] κλέπτης *kleptēs* 16x *a thief,* Mt. 6:19, 20; 24:43; trop. *a thief* by imposture, Jn. 10:8 [2812] See *thief.*

[3096] κλέπτω *kleptō* 13x *to steal,* Mt. 6:19, 20; 19:18; *to take away stealthily, remove secretly,* Mt. 27:64; 28:13 [2813] See *steal.*

[3097] κλῆμα *klēma* 4x *a branch, shoot, twig,* esp. of the vine, Jn. 15:2, 4-6* [2814]

[3098] Κλήμης *Klēmēs* 1x *Clemens, Clement,* pr. name, Latin, Phil. 4:3* [2815]

[3099] κληρονομέω *klēronomeō* 18x pr. *to acquire by lot; to inherit, obtain by inheritance;* in NT *to obtain, acquire, receive possession of,* Mt. 5:5; 19:29; absol. *to be heir,* Gal. 4:30 [2816] See *inherit.*

[3100] κληρονομία *klēronomia* 14x *an inheritance, patrimony,* Mt. 21:38; Mk. 12:7; *a possession, portion, property,* Acts 7:5; 20:32; in NT *a share, participation* in privileges, Acts 20:32; Eph. 1:14; 5:5 [2817] See *inheritance.*

[3101] κληρονόμος *klēronomos* 15x *an heir,* Mt. 21:38; Gal. 4:1; *a possessor,* Rom. 4:13; Heb. 11:7; Jas. 2:5 [2818] See *heir.*

[3102] κλῆρος *klēros* 11x *a lot, die, a thing used in determining chances,* Mt. 27:35; Mk. 15:24; Lk. 23:34; Jn. 19:24; Acts 1:26; *assignment, investiture,* Acts 1:17; *allotment, destination,* Col. 1:12; *a part, portion, share,* Acts 8:21; 26:18; *a* constituent *portion* of the Church, 1 Pet. 5:3* [2819] See *inheritance; lot; share.*

[3103] κληρόω *klēroō* 1x *to obtain by lot* or *assignment; to obtain a portion, receive a share,* Eph. 1:11* [2820]

[3104] κλῆσις *klēsis* 11x *a call, calling, invitation;* in NT *the call* or *invitation* to the privileges of the Gospel, Rom. 11:29; Eph. 1:18; *the favor and privilege of the invitation,* 2 Thess. 1:11; 2 Pet. 1:10; *the temporal condition in which the call found a person,* 1 Cor. 1:26; 7:20 [2821] See *calling.*

[3105] κλητός *klētos* 10x *called, invited,* in NT *called* to privileges or function, Mt. 20:16; 22:14; Rom. 1:1, 6, 7; 8:28; 1 Cor. 1:1, 2, 24; Jude 1; Rev. 17:14 [2822] See *called.*

[3106] κλίβανος *klibanos* 2x *an oven,* Mt. 6:30; Lk. 12:28* [2823]

[3107] κλίμα *klima* 3x pr. *a slope; a portion of the* ideal *slope* of the earth's surface; *a tract* or *region* of country, Rom. 15:23; 2 Cor. 11:10; Gal. 1:21* [2824]

[3108] κλινάριον *klinarion* 1x *a small bed* or *couch,* Acts 5:15* [2825]

[3109] κλίνη *klinē* 9x *a couch, bed,* Mt. 9:2, 6; Mk. 4:21; Rev. 2:22 [2825]

[3110] κλινίδιον *klinidion* 2x *a small couch* or *bed,* Lk. 5:19, 24* [2826]

[3111] κλίνω *klinō* 7x pr. trans. *to cause to slope* or *bend; to bow down,* Lk. 24:5; Jn. 19:30; *to lay down* to rest, Mt. 8:20; Lk. 9:58; *to put to flight* troops, Heb. 11:34; intrans. of the day, *to decline,* Lk. 9:12; 24:29* [2827]

[3112] κλισία *klisia* 1x pr. *a place for reclining; a tent, seat, couch;* in NT *a group of persons reclining* at a meal. Lk. 9:14* [2828]

[3113] κλοπή *klopē* 2x *theft,* Mt. 15:19; Mk. 7:21* [2829]

[3114] κλύδων *klydōn* 2x *a wave, billow, surge,* Lk. 8:24; Jas. 1:6* [2830]

[3115] κλυδωνίζομαι *klydōnizomai* 1x *to be tossed by waves;* met. *to fluctuate* in opinion, *be agitated, tossed to and fro,* Eph. 4:14* [2831]

[3116] Κλωπᾶς *Klōpas* 1x *Cleopas,* pr. name, Jn. 19:25* [2832]

[3117] κνήθω *knēthō* 1x *to scratch; to tickle, cause titillation;* in NT mid. met. *to procure pleasurable excitement for; to indulge an itching,* 2 Tim. 4:3* [2833]

[3118] Κνίδος *Knidos* 1x *Cnidus,* a city of Caria, in Asia Minor, Acts 27:7* [2834]

[3119] κοδράντης *kodrantēs* 2x *a Roman brass coin,* equivalent to the *fourth part* of an *as,* or ἀσσάριον, or to δύο λεπτά, Mt. 5:26; Mk. 12:42* [2835]

[3120] κοιλία *koilia* 22x *a cavity; the belly,* Mt. 15:17; Mk. 7:19; *the stomach,* Mt. 12:40; Lk. 15:16; *the womb,* Mt. 19:12; Lk. 1:15; from the Hebrew, *the inner self,* Jn. 7:38 [2836] See *appetite; belly; stomach; womb.*

[3121] κοιμάω *koimaō* 18x *to lull to sleep;* pass. *to fall asleep, be asleep,* Mt. 28:13; Lk. 22:45; met. *to sleep* in death, Acts 7:60; 13:36; 2 Pet. 3:4 [2837] See *asleep; fall asleep.*

[3122] κοίμησις *koimēsis* 1x *sleep;* meton. *rest, repose,* Jn. 11:13* [2838]

[3123] κοινός *koinos* 14x *common, belonging equally to several,* Acts 2:44; 4:32; in NT *common, profane,* Heb. 10:29; Rev. 21:27; ceremonially *unclean,* Mk. 7:2; Acts 10:14 [2839] See *common; impure; profane.*

[3124] κοινόω *koinoō* 14x *to make common,* in NT *to profane, desecrate,* Acts 21:28; *to render* ceremonially *unclean, defile, pollute,* Mt. 15:11, 18, 20; 7:15, 18, 20, 23; Heb. 9:13; *to pronounce unclean* ceremonially, Acts 10:15; 11:9* [2840] See *defile; make impure.*

[3125] κοινωνέω *koinōneō* 8x *to have in common, share,* Heb. 2:14; *to be associated in, to become a sharer in,* Rom. 15:27; 1 Pet. 4:13; *to become implicated in, be a party to,* 1 Tim. 5:22; 2 Jn. 11; *to associate one's self with* by sympathy and assistance, *to communicate with* in the way of aid and relief, Rom. 12:13; Gal. 6:6; Phil. 4:15* [2841] See *participate in; share.*

[3126] κοινωνία *koinōnia* 19x *fellowship, partnership,* Acts 2:42; 2 Cor. 6:14; 13:13; Gal. 2:9; Phil. 3:10; 1 Jn. 1:3; *participation, communion,* 1 Cor. 10:16; *aid, relief,* Heb. 13:16; *contribution in aid,* Rom. 15:26 [2842] See *communion; fellowship; participation; sharing.*

[3127] κοινωνικός *koinōnikos* 1x *social;* in NT *generous, liberal, beneficent,* 1 Tim. 6:18* [2843]

[3128] κοινωνός *koinōnos* 10x *a fellow, partner, companion,* Mt. 23:30; Lk. 5:10; 1 Cor. 10:18, 20; 2 Cor. 8:23; Phlm. 17; Heb. 10:33; *a sharer, partaker,* 2 Cor. 1:7; 1 Pet. 5:1; 2 Pet. 1:4* [2844] See *participant; partner.*

[3130] κοίτη *koitē* 4x *a bed,* Lk. 11:7; *the* conjugal *bed,* Heb. 13:4; meton. *sexual intercourse, concubitus;* hence, *lewdness, whoredom, chambering,* Rom. 13:13; in NT *conception,* Rom. 9:10* [2845]

[3131] κοιτών *koitōn* 1x *a bed-chamber,* Acts 12:20* [2846]

[3132] κόκκινος *kokkinos* 6x *dyed with coccus, crimson, scarlet,* Mt. 27:28; Heb. 9:19; Rev. 17:3, 4; 18:12, 16* [2847]

[3133] κόκκος *kokkos* 7x *a kernel, grain, seed,* Mt. 13:31; 17:20; Mk. 4:31; Lk. 13:19; 17:6; Jn. 12:24; 1 Cor. 15:37* [2848]

[3134] κολάζω *kolazō* 2x pr. *to curtail, to coerce; to chastise, punish,* Acts 4:21; 2 Pet. 2:9* [2849]

[3135] κολακεία *kolakeia* 1x *flattery, adulation, obsequiousness,* 1 Thess. 2:5* [2850]

[3136] κόλασις *kolasis* 2x *chastisement, punishment,* Mt. 25:46; *painful disquietude, torment,* 1 Jn. 4:18* [2851]

[3139] κολαφίζω *kolaphizō* 5x *to beat with the fist, buffet,* Mt. 26:67; Mk. 14:65; met. *to maltreat, treat with excessive force,* 1 Cor. 4:11; *to punish,* 1 Pet. 2:20; *to buffet, fret, afflict,* 2 Cor. 12:7* [2852]

[3140] κολλάω *kollaō* 12x *to glue* or *weld together;* mid. *to adhere to,* Lk. 10:11; met. *to attach one's self to, unite with, associate with,* Lk. 15:15; Acts 5:13; Rev. 18:5 [2853] See *cling; join; unite.*

[3141] κολλούριον *kollourion* 1x also spelled κολλύριον, *collyrium, eye-salve,* Rev. 3:18* [2854]

[3142] κολλυβιστής *kollybistēs* 3x *a money-changer,* Mt. 21:12; Mk. 11:15; Jn. 2:15* [2855]

[3143] κολοβόω *koloboō* 4x in NT of time, *to cut short, shorten,* Mt. 24:22; Mk. 13:20* [2856]

[3145] Κολοσσαί *Kolossai* 1x also spelled Κολασσαεύς, *Colossae,* a city of Phrygia, Col. 1:2* [2857]

[3146] κόλπος *kolpos* 6x *the bosom,* Lk. 16:22, 23; Jn. 1:18; 13:23; *the bosom of a garment,* Lk. 6:38; *a bay, creek, inlet,* Acts 27:39* [2859]

[3147] κολυμβάω *kolymbaō* 1x *to dive;* in NT *to swim,* Acts 27:43* [2860]

[3148] κολυμβήθρα *kolymbēthra* 3x *a place where any one may swim; a pond, pool,* Jn. 5:2, 4, 7; 9:7* [2861]

[3149] κολωνία *kolōnia* 1x *a Roman colony,* Acts 16:12* [2862]

[3150] κομάω *komaō* 2x *to have long hair, wear the hair long,* 1 Cor. 11:14, 15* [2863]

[3151] κόμη *komē* 1x *the hair; a head of long hair,* 1 Cor. 11:15* [2864]

[3152] κομίζω *komizō* 10x pr. *to take into kindly keeping, to provide for; to convey, bring,* Lk. 7:37; mid. *to bring for one's self; to receive, obtain,* 2 Cor. 5:10; Eph. 6:8; *to receive again, recover,* Mt. 25:27; Heb. 11:19 [2865] See *pay back; receive.*

[3153] κομψότερον *kompsoteron* 1x in NT *in better health,* Jn. 4:52* [2866]

[3154] κονιάω *koniaō* 2x *to whitewash,* or, *plaster,* Mt. 23:27; Acts 23:3* [2867]

[3155] κονιορτός *koniortos* 5x *dust,* Mt. 10:14; Lk. 9:5; 10:11; Acts 13:51; 22:23* [2868]

[3156] κοπάζω *kopazō* 3x pr. *to grow weary, suffer exhaustion; to abate, be stilled,* Mt. 14:32; Mk. 4:39; 6:51* [2869]

[3157] κοπετός *kopetos* 1x pr. *a beating* of the breast, etc., in token of grief; *a wailing, lamentation,* Acts 8:2* [2870]

[3158] κοπή *kopē* 1x *a stroke, smiting;* in NT *slaughter,* Heb. 7:1* [2871]

[3159] κοπιάω *kopiaō* 23x *to be wearied* or *spent with labor, faint from weariness,* Mt. 11:28; Jn. 4:6; in NT *to labor hard, to toil,* Lk. 5:5; Jn. 4:38 [2872] See *labor; toil.*

[3160] κόπος *kopos* 18x *trouble, difficulty, uneasiness,* Mt. 26:10; Mk. 14:6; *labor, wearisome labor, travail, toil,* 1 Cor. 3:8; 15:58; meton. *the fruit* or *consequence of labor,* Jn. 4:38; 2 Cor. 10:15 [2873] See *labor; toil.*

[3161] κοπρία *kopria* 1x *dung, manure,* Lk. 14:35* [2874]

[3162] κόπριον *koprion* 1x *dung, manure,* Lk. 13:8* [2874]

[3164] κόπτω *koptō* 8x *to smite, cut; to cut off* or *down,* Mt. 21:8; Mk. 11:8; mid. *to beat one's self* in mourning, *lament, bewail,* Mt. 11:17; 24:30; Lk. 8:52; 23:27; Rev. 1:7; 18:9* [2875]

[3165] κόραξ *korax* 1x *a raven, crow,* Lk. 12:24* [2876]

[3166] κοράσιον *korasion* 8x *a girl, damsel, maiden,* Mt. 9:24, 25; 14:11; Mk. 5:41, 42; 6:22, 28* [2877]

[3167] κορβᾶν *korban* 1x *corban, a gift, offering, oblation, anything consecrated to God,* Mk. 7:11* [2878]

[3168] κορβανᾶς *korbanas* 1x *temple treasury, the sacred treasury,* Mt. 27:6* [2878]

[3169] Κόρε *Kore* 1x *Korah,* Jude 11* [2879]

[3170] κορέννυμι *korennymi* 2x *to satisfy,* Acts 27:38; 1 Cor. 4:8* [2880]

[3171] Κορίνθιος *Korinthios* 2x *Corinthian; an inhabitant of* Κόρινθος, *Corinth,* Acts 18:8; 2 Cor. 6:11* [2881]

[3172] Κόρινθος *Korinthos* 6x *Corinth,* a celebrated city of Greece, Acts 18:1; 19:1: 1 Cor. 1:2; 2 Cor. 1:1, 23; 2 Tim. 4:20* [2882]

[3173] Κορνήλιος *Kornēlios* 8x *Cornelius,* a Latin pr. name, Acts 10:1, 3, 17, 22, 24f., 30f.* [2883]

[3174] κόρος *koros* 1x *a cor,* the largest Jewish measure for things dry, equal to the homer, and about fifteen bushels English, according to Josephus, Lk. 16:7* [2884]

[3175] κοσμέω *kosmeō* 10x pluperfect, ἐκεκόσμητο (3 sg), *to arrange, set in order; to adorn, decorate, embellish,* Mt. 12:44; 23:29; *to prepare, put in readiness, trim,* Mt. 25:7; met. *to honor, dignify,* Tit. 2:10 [2885] See *adorn; decorate; make attractive; put in order; trim.*

[3176] κοσμικός *kosmikos* 2x pr. *belonging to the universe,* in NT *accommodated to the present state of things, adapted to this world, worldly,* Tit. 2:12; τὸ κοσμικόν, as a subst. *the apparatus* for the service of the tabernacle, Heb. 9:1* [2886]

[3177] κόσμιος *kosmios* 2x *decorous, respectable, well-ordered,* 1 Tim. 2:9; 3:2* [2887]

[3179] κοσμοκράτωρ *kosmokratōr* 1x pr. *monarch of the world;* in NT *a worldly prince, a power paramount in the world* of the unbelieving and ungodly, Eph. 6:12* [2888]

[3180] κόσμος *kosmos* 186x (1) pr. *order, regular disposition; ornament, decoration, embellishment,* 1 Pet. 3:3; (2) *the world, the material universe,* Mt. 13:35; *the world, the aggregate of sensitive existence,* 1 Cor. 4:9; *the* lower *world, the earth,* Mk. 16:15; *the world, the aggregate of mankind,* Mt. 5:14; *the world, the public,* Jn. 7:4; in NT *the present order of things, the* secular *world,* Jn. 18:36; *the human race* external to the Jewish nation, *the* heathen *world,* Rom. 11:12, 15; *the world* external to the Christian body, 1 Jn. 3:1, 13; *the world* or *material system* of the Mosaic covenant, Gal. 4:3; Col. 2:8, 20 [2889] See *universe; world.*

[3181] Κούαρτος *Kouartos* 1x *Quartus,* a Latin pr. name, Rom. 16:23* [2890]

[3182] κοῦμ *koum* 1x an Aramaic imperative, also spelled κοῦμι, *stand up,* Mk. 5:41* [2891]

[3184] κουστωδία *koustōdia* 3x *a watch, guard,* Mt. 27:65, 66; 28:11* [2892]

[3185] κουφίζω *kouphizō* 1x *to lighten, make light* or *less heavy,* Acts 27:38* [2893]

[3186] κόφινος *kophinos* 6x *a large basket,* Mt. 14:20; 16:9; Mk. 6:43; 8:19; Lk. 9:17; Jn. 6:13* [2894]

[3187] κράβαττος *krabattos* 11x also spelled κράββατος, *mattress, pallet, bed,* Mk. 2:4, 9, 11f.; 6:55; Jn. 5:8-11; Acts 5:15; 9:33* [2895] See *bed; cot; mat.*

[3189] κράζω *krazō* 55x *to utter a cry,* Mt. 14:26; *to exclaim, cry out,* Mt. 9:27; Jn. 1:15; *to cry* for vengeance, Jas. 5:4; *to cry* in supplication, Rom. 8:15; Gal. 4:6 [2896] See *cry out; shout.*

[3190] κραιπάλη *kraipalē* 1x also spelled κρεπάλη, *drunken dissipation,* Lk. 21:34* [2897]

[3191] κρανίον *kranion* 4x *a skull,* Mt. 27:33; Mk. 15:22; Lk. 23:33; Jn. 19:17* [2898] See *Calvary*; *Golgatha*; *skull.*

[3192] κράσπεδον *kraspedon* 5x *a margin, border, edge,* in NT *a fringe, tuft, tassel,* Mt. 9:20; 14:36; 23:5; Mk. 6:56; Lk. 8:44* [2899]

[3193] κραταιός *krataios* 1x *strong, mighty, powerful,* 1 Pet. 5:6* [2900]

[3194] κραταιόω *krataioō* 4x *to strengthen, render strong, corroborate, confirm;* pass. *to grow strong, acquire strength,* Lk. 1:80; 2:40; Eph. 3:16; *to be firm, resolute,* 1 Cor. 16:13* [2901]

[3195] κρατέω *krateō* 47x pr. *to be strong; to be superior* to any one, *subdue, vanquish,* Acts 2:24; *to get into one's power, lay hold of, seize, apprehend,* Mt. 14:3; 18:28; 21:46; *to gain, compass, attain,* Acts 27:13; in NT *to lay hold of, grasp, clasp,* Mt. 9:25; Mk. 1:31; 5:41; *to retain, keep under reserve,* Mk. 9:10; met, *to hold fast, observe,* Mk. 7:3, 8; 2 Thess. 2:15; *to hold to, adhere to,* Acts 3:11; Col. 2:19; *to restrain, hinder, repress,* Lk. 24:16; Rev. 7:1; *to retain, not to remit,* sins, Jn. 20:23 [2902] See *arrest; grasp; hold; seize.*

[3196] κράτιστος *kratistos* 4x *strongest;* in NT κράτιστε, a term of respect, *most excellent, noble,* or *illustrious,* Lk. 1:3; Acts 23:26; 24:3; 26:25* [2903]

[3197] κράτος *kratos* 12x *strength, power, might, force,* Acts 19:20; Eph. 1:19; meton. *a display of might,* Lk. 1:51; *power, sway, dominion,* Heb. 2:14; 1 Pet. 4:11; 5:11 [2904] See *might; power; strength.*

[3198] κραυγάζω *kraugazō* 9x *to cry out, exclaim, shout,* Mt. 12:19; Acts 22:23 [2905]

[3199] κραυγή *kraugē* 6x *a cry, outcry, clamor, shouting,* Mt. 25:6; Lk. 1:42; Acts 23:9; Eph. 4:31; *a cry* of sorrow, *wailing, lamentation,* Rev. 21:4; *a cry* for help, *earnest supplication,* Heb. 5:7* [2906]

[3200] κρέας *kreas* 2x *flesh, meat,* a later form of κρέατος, Rom. 14:21; 1 Cor. 8:13* [2907]

[3202] κρείττων *kreittōn* 19x can also be spelled κρείσσων, *better, more useful* or *profitable, more conducive to good,* 1 Cor. 7:8, 38; *superior, more excellent, of a higher nature, more valuable,* Heb. 1:4; 6:9; 7:7, 19, 22 [2908, 2909] See *better.*

[3203] κρεμάννυμι *kremannymi* 7x also spelled κρέμαμαι and κρεμάζω, *to hang, suspend,* Acts 5:30; 10:39; pass. *to be hung, suspended,* Mt. 18:6; Lk. 23:39; mid. κρέμαμαι, *to hang, be suspended,* Acts 28:4; Gal. 3:13; met. κρέμαμαι ἐν, *to hang upon, to be referable to* as an ultimate principle, Mt. 22:40 [2910]

[3204] κρημνός *krēmnos* 3x *a hanging steep, precipice, a steep bank,* Mt. 8:32; Mk. 5:13; Lk. 8:33* [2911]

[3205] Κρής *Krēs* 2x *a Cretan, an inhabitant of* Κρήτη, Acts 2:11; Tit. 1:12* [2912]

[3206] Κρήσκης *Krēskēs* 1x *Crescens,* a Latin pr. name, 2 Tim. 4:10* [2913]

[3207] Κρήτη *Krētē* 5x *Crete,* a large island in the eastern part of the Mediterranean, Acts 27:7, 12f., 21, Tit. 1:5* [2914]

[3208] κριθή *krithē* 1x *barley,* Rev. 6:6* [2915]

[3209] κρίθινος *krithinos* 2x *made of barley,* Jn. 6:9, 13* [2916]

[3210] κρίμα *krima* 27x *judgment; a sentence, award,* Mt. 7:2; *a judicial sentence,* Lk. 23:40; 24:20; Rom. 2:2; 5:16; *an* adverse *sentence,* Mt. 23:14; Rom. 13:2; 1 Tim. 5:12; Jas. 3:1; *judgment, administration of justice,* Jn. 9:39; Acts 24:25; *execution of justice,* 1 Pet. 4:17; *a lawsuit;* 1 Cor. 6:7; in NT *judicial visitation,* 1 Cor. 11:29; 2 Pet. 2:3; *an* administrative *decree,* Rom. 11:33 [2917] See *condemnation; judgment; punishment.*

[3211] κρίνον *krinon* 2x *a lily,* Mt. 6:28; Lk. 12:27* [2918]

[3212] κρίνω *krinō* 114x pluperfect, κεκρίκει (3 sg), pr. *to separate; to make a distinction between; to exercise judgment upon; to estimate,* Rom. 14:5; *to judge, to assume censorial power over, to call to account,* Mt. 7:1; Lk. 6:37; Rom. 2:1, 3; 14:3, 4, 10, 13; Col. 2:16; Jas. 4:11, 12; *to bring under question,* Rom. 14:22; *to judge* judicially, *to try* as a judge, Jn. 18:31; *to bring to trial,* Acts 13:27; *to sentence,* Lk. 19:22; Jn. 7:51; *to resolve on, decree,* Acts 16:4; Rev. 16:5; absol. *to decide, determine, resolve,* Acts 3:13; 15:19; 27:1; *to deem,* Acts 13:46; *to form a judgment, pass judgment,* Jn. 8:15; pass. *to be brought to trial,* Acts 25:10, 20; Rom. 3:4; *to be brought to account, to incur arraignment, be arraigned,* 1 Cor. 10:29; mid. *to go to law, litigate,* Mt. 5:40; in NT *to judge, to visit judicially,* Acts 7:7; 1 Cor. 11:31, 32; 1 Pet. 4:6; *to judge, to right, to vindicate,* Heb. 10:30; *to administer government over, to govern,* Mt. 19:28; Lk. 22:30 [2919] See *consider; decide; judge.*

[3213] κρίσις *krisis* 47x pr. *distinction; discrimination; judgment, decision, award,* Jn. 5:30; 7:24; 8:16; *a* judicial *sentence,* Jn. 3:19; Jas. 2:13; *an* adverse *sentence,* Mt. 23:33; Mk. 3:29; *judgment, judicial process, trial,* Mt. 10:15; Jn. 5:24; 12:31; 16:8; *judgment, administration of justice,* Jn. 5:22, 27; in NT *a court of justice, tribunal,* Mt. 5:21, 22; *an impeachment,* 2 Pet. 2:11; Jude 9; from the Hebrew, *justice, equity,* Mt. 12:18, 20; 23:23; Lk. 11:42 [2920] See *condemnation; judgment; justice.*

[3214] Κρίσπος *Krispos* 2x *Crispus,* a Latin pr. name, Acts 18:8; 1 Cor. 1:14* [2921]

[3215] κριτήριον *kritērion* 3x pr. *a standard* or *means by which to judge, criterion; a court of justice, tribunal,* Jas. 2:6; *a cause, controversy,* 1 Cor. 6:2, 4* [2922]

[3216] κριτής *kritēs* 19x *a judge,* Mt. 5:25; from the Hebrew, *a magistrate, ruler,* Acts 13:20; 24:10 [2923] See *judge.*

[3217] κριτικός *kritikos* 1x *able* or *quick to discern* or *judge,* Heb. 4:12* [2924]

[3218] κρούω *krouō* 9x *to knock* at a door, Mt. 7:7, 8; Lk. 11:9, 10; 12:36; 13:25; Acts 12:13, 16; Rev. 3:20* [2925]

[3219] κρύπτη *kryptē* 1x *a vault* or *closet, a cell* for storage, *dark secret place,* Lk. 11:33* [2926]

[3220] κρυπτός *kryptos* 17x *hidden, concealed, secret, clandestine,* Mt. 6:4, 6; τὰ κρυπτά, *secrets,* Rom. 2:16; 1 Cor. 14:25 [2927] See *hidden; secret.*

[3221] κρύπτω *kryptō* 18x *to hide, conceal,* Mt. 5:14; in NT *to lay up in store,* Col. 3:3; Rev. 2:17; κεκρυμμένος, *concealed, secret,* Jn. 19:38 [2928] See *conceal; hide.*

[3222] κρυσταλλίζω *krystallizō* 1x *to be clear, brilliant like crystal,* Rev. 21:11* [2929]

[3223] κρύσταλλος *krystallos* 2x pr. *clear ice; crystal,* Rev. 4:6; 22:1* [2930]

[3224] κρυφαῖος *kryphaios* 2x *secret, hidden,* Mt. 6:18* [2927]

[3225] κρυφῇ *kryphē* 1x *in secret, secretly, not openly,* Eph. 5:12* [2931]

[3227] κτάομαι *ktaomai* 7x *to get, procure, provide,* Mt. 10:9; *to make gain, gain,* Lk. 18:12; *to purchase,* Acts 8:20; 22:28; *to be the cause* or *occasion of purchasing,* Acts 1:18; *to preserve, save,* Lk. 21:19; *to get under control, to be winning the mastery over,* 1 Thess. 4:4; perf. κέκτημαι, *to possess** [2932]

[3228] κτῆμα *ktēma* 4x *a possession, property, field,* Mt. 19:22; Mk. 10:22; Acts 2:45; 5:1* [2933]

[3229] κτῆνος *ktēnos* 4x pr. *property,* generally used in the plural, τὰ κτήνη; *property* in animals; *a beast of burden, domesticated animal,* Lk. 10:34; Acts 23:24; *beasts, cattle,* 1 Cor. 15:39; Rev. 18:13* [2934]

[3230] κτήτωρ *ktētōr* 1x *a possessor, owner,* Acts 4:34* [2935]

[3231] κτίζω *ktizō* 15x pr. *to reduce from a state of disorder and wildness;* in NT *to call into being, to create,* Mk. 13:19; *to call into individual existence, to frame,* Eph. 2:15; *to create* spiritually, *to invest with a* spiritual *frame,* Eph. 2:10; 4:24 [2936] See *create.*

[3232] κτίσις *ktisis* 19x (1) pr. *a framing, founding;* (2) in NT *creation, the act of creating,* Rom. 1:20; *creation, the material universe,* Mk. 10:6; 13:19; Heb. 9:11; 2 Pet. 3:4; *a created thing, a creature,* Rom. 1:25; 8:39; Col. 1:15; Heb. 4:13; *the* human *creation,* Mk. 16:15; Rom. 8:19, 20, 21, 22; Col. 1:23; *a* spiritual *creation,* 2 Cor. 5:17; Gal. 6:15; (3) *an institution, ordinance,* 1 Pet. 2:13 [2937] See *creation.*

[3233] κτίσμα *ktisma* 4x pr. *a thing founded;* in NT *a created being, creature,* 1 Tim. 4:4; Jas. 1:18; Rev. 5:13; 8:9* [2938]

[3234] κτίστης *ktistēs* 1x *a founder;* in NT *a creator,* 1 Pet. 4:19* [2939]

[3235] κυβεία *kybeia* 1x also spelled κυβία, pr. *dice playing;* met. *craftiness, trickery,* Eph. 4:14* [2940]

[3236] κυβέρνησις *kybernēsis* 1x *government, office of a governor* or *director;* meton. *a director,* 1 Cor. 12:28* [2941]

[3237] κυβερνήτης *kybernētēs* 2x *a pilot, helmsman,* Acts 27:11; Rev. 18:17* [2942]

[3238] κυκλεύω *kykleuō* 1x *to encircle, surround, encompass,* Rev. 20:9* [2944]

[3239] κυκλόθεν *kyklothen* 3x *all around, round about,* Rev. 4:3, 4, 8* [2943]

[3240] κυκλόω *kykloō* 4x *to encircle, surround, encompass, come around.* Jn. 10:24; Acts 14:20; spc. *to lay siege to,* Lk. 21:20; *to march round,* Heb. 11:30* [2944]

[3241] κύκλῳ *kyklōi* 8x from κύκλος, functions in the NT only as an improper prep., *a circle;* in NT κύκλῳ functions adverbially, *round, round about, around,* Mk. 3:34; 6:6, 36 [2945]

[3243] κυλισμός *kylismos* 1x also spelled κύλισμα, a rolling, wallowing, 2 Pet. 2:22* [2946]

[3244] κυλίω *kyliō* 1x *to roll*; mid. *to roll one's self, to wallow,* Mk. 9:20 [2947]

[3245] κυλλός *kyllos* 4x pr. *crooked, bent, maimed, lame, crippled,* Mt. 18:8; Mk. 9:43, used as a noun meaning *cripple,* Mt. 15:30ff.* [2948]

[3246] κῦμα *kyma* 5x *a wave, surge, billow,* Mt. 8:24; 14:24; Mk. 4:37; Acts 27:41; Jude 13* [2949]

[3247] κύμβαλον *kymbalon* 1x *a cymbal,* 1 Cor. 13:1* [2950]

[3248] κύμινον *kyminon* 1x *cumin, cuminum salivum* of Linnaeus, a plant, a native of Egypt and Syria, whose seeds are of an aromatic, warm, bitterish taste, with a strong but not disagreeable smell, and used by the ancients as a condiment, Mt. 23:23* [2951]

[3249] κυνάριον *kynarion* 4x *a little* or *worthless dog,* Mt. 15:26, 27; Mk. 7:27, 28* [2952]

[3250] Κύπριος *Kyprios* 3x *a Cypriot, an inhabitant of Cyprus,* Acts 4:36; 11:20; 21:16* [2953]

[3251] Κύπρος *Kypros* 5x *Cyprus,* an island in the eastern part of the Mediterranean, Acts 11:19; 13:4; 15:39; 21:3; 27:4* [2954]

[3252] κύπτω *kyptō* 2x *to bend forwards, stoop down,* Mk. 1:7; Jn. 8:6* [2955]

[3254] Κυρηναῖος *Kyrēnaios* 6x *a Cyrenian, an inhabitant of Cyrene,* Mt. 27:32; Mk. 15:21; Lk. 23:26; Acts 6:9; 11:20; 13:1* [2956]

[3255] Κυρήνη *Kyrēnē* 1x *Cyrene,* a city founded by a colony of Greeks, in Northern Africa, Acts 2:10* [2957]

[3256] Κυρήνιος *Kyrēnios* 1x *Cyrenius* (perhaps *Quirinus*) pr. name, the governor of Syria, Lk. 2:2* [2958]

[3257] κυρία *kyria* 2x *a lady,* 2 Jn. 1:1, 5* [2959]

[3258] κυριακός *kyriakos* 2x *pertaining to the Lord Jesus Christ, the Lord's,* 1 Cor. 11:20; Rev. 1:10* [2960]

[3259] κυριεύω *kyrieuō* 7x *to be lord over, to be possessed of, mastery over,* Rom. 6:9, 14; 7:1; 14:9; 2 Cor. 1:24; 1 Tim. 6:15; *to exercise control over,* Lk. 22:25* [2961]

[3261] κύριος *kyrios* 717x *a lord, master,* Mt. 12:8; *an owner, possessor,* Mt. 20:8; *a potentate, sovereign,* Acts 25:26; *a power, deity,* 1 Cor. 8:5; *the Lord, Jehovah,* Mt. 1:22; *the Lord* Jesus Christ, Mt. 24:42; Mk. 16:19; Lk. 10:1; Jn. 4:1; 1 Cor. 4:5; freq.; κύριε, a term of respect of various force, *Sir, Lord,* Mt. 13:27; Acts 9:6, et al. freq. [2962] See *lord; master; sir.*

[3262] κυριότης *kyriotēs* 4x *lordship; constituted authority,* Eph. 1:21; 2 Pet. 2:10; Jude 8; pl. *authorities, potentates,* Col. 1:16. The Ephesian and Colossian passage could also be speaking about angelic powers.* [2963]

[3263] κυρόω *kyroō* 2x *to confirm, ratify,* Gal. 3:15; *to reaffirm, assure,* 2 Cor. 2:8* [2964]

[3264] κύων *kyōn* 5x *a dog,* Mt. 7:6; Lk. 16:21; 2 Pet. 2:22; met. *a dog, a religious corrupter,* Phil. 3:2; *miscreant,* Rev. 22:15* [2965]

[3265] κῶλον *kōlon* 1x lit., *a member* or *limb of the body,* fig., *dead body, corpse,* Heb. 3:17* [2966]

[3266] κωλύω *kōlyō* 23x *to hinder, restrain, prevent,* Mt. 19:14; Acts 8:36; Rom. 1:13 [2967] See *forbid; hinder; oppose; stop.*

[3267] κώμη *kōmē* 27x *a village, a country town,* Mt. 9:35; 10:11; Lk. 8:1 [2968] See *village.*

[3268] κωμόπολις *kōmopolis* 1x *a large village, market town,* Mk. 1:38* [2969]

[3269] κῶμος *kōmos* 3x pr. *a festive procession, a merry-making;* in NT *a revel, lewd, immoral feasting,* Rom. 13:13; Gal. 5:21; 1 Pet. 4:3* [2970]

[3270] κώνωψ *kōnōps* 1x *a gnat, mosquito,* which is found in wine when becoming sour, Mt. 23:24* [2971]

[3272] Κωσάμ *Kōsam* 1x *Cosam,* pr. name, indecl., Lk. 3:28* [2973]

[3273] κωφός *kōphos* 14x pr. *blunt, dull,* as a weapon; *dull* of hearing, *deaf,* Mt. 11:5; Mk. 7:32, 37; 9:25; Lk. 7:22; *dumb, mute,* Mt. 9:32, 33; 12:22; 15:30, 31; Lk. 1:22; meton. *making dumb, causing dumbness,* Lk. 11:14* [2974] See *deaf; mute.*

[3275] λαγχάνω *lanchanō* 4x *to have assigned to one, to obtain, receive,* Acts 1:17; 2 Pet. 1:1; *to have fall to one by lot,* Lk. 1:9; absol. *to cast lots,* Jn. 19:24* [2975]

[3276] Λάζαρος *Lazaros* 15x *Lazarus,* pr. name [2976]

[3277] λάθρα *lathrai* 4x *secretly, privately,* Mt. 1:19; 2:7; Jn. 11:28; Acts 16:37* [2977]

[3278] λαῖλαψ *lailaps* 3x *a squall of wind, a hurricane,* Mk. 4:37; Lk. 8:23; 2 Pet. 2:17* [2978]

[3279] λακάω *lakaō* 1x *burst open,* Acts 1:18* [2997]

[3280] λακτίζω *laktizō* 1x *to kick,* Acts 26:14* [2979]

[3281] λαλέω *laleō* 296x *to make vocal utterance; to babble, to talk;* in NT absol. *to exercise the faculty of speech,* Mt. 9:33; *to speak,* Mt. 10:20; *to hold converse with, to talk with,* Mt. 12:46; Mk. 6:50; Rev. 1:12; *to discourse, to make an address,* Lk. 11:37; Acts 11:20; 21:39; *to make announcement, to make a declaration,* Lk. 1:55; *to make mention,* Jn. 12:41; Acts 2:31; Heb. 4:8; 2 Pet. 3:16; trans. *to speak, address, preach,* Mt. 9:18; Jn. 3:11; Tit. 2:1; *to give utterance to, utter,* Mk. 2:7; Jn. 3:34; *to declare, announce, reveal,* Lk. 24:25 et al.; *to disclose,* 2 Cor. 12:4 [2980] See *say; speak.*

[3282] λαλιά *lalia* 3x *talk, speech;* in NT *matter of discourse,* Jn. 4:42; 8:43; *language, dialect,* Mt. 26:73* [2981]

[3284] λαμβάνω *lambanō* 258x *to take, take up, take in the hand,* Mt. 10:38; 13:31, 33; *to take on one's self, sustain,* Mt. 8:17; *to take, seize, seize upon,* Mt. 5:40; 21:34; Lk. 5:26; 1 Cor. 10:13; *to catch,* Lk. 5:5; 2 Cor. 12:16; *to assume, put on,* Phil. 2:7; *to make a rightful* or *successful assumption of,* Jn. 3:27; *to conceive,* Acts 28:15; *to take* by way of provision, Mt. 16:5; *to get, get together,* Mt. 16:9; *to receive* as payment, Mt. 17:24; Heb. 7:8; *to take* to wife, Mk. 12:19; *to admit, give reception to,* Jn. 6:21; 2 Jn. 10; met. *to give* mental *reception to,* Jn. 3:11; *to be* simply *recipient of, to receive,* Mt. 7:8; Jn. 7:23, 39; 19:30; Acts 10:43; in NT λαμβάνειν πεῖραν, *to make encounter of* a matter of difficulty or trial, Heb. 11:29, 36; λαμβάνειν ἀρχήν, *to begin,* Heb. 2:3; λαμβάνειν συμβούλιον, *to take counsel, consult,* Mt. 12:14; λαμβάνειν λήθην, *to forget,* 2 Pet. 1:9; λαμβάνειν ὑπόμνησιν, *to recollect, call to mind,* 2 Tim. 1:5; λαμβάειν περιτομήν, *to receive circumcision, be circumcised,* Jn. 7:23; λαμβάνειν καταλλαγήν, *to be reconciled,* Rom. 5:11; λαμβάνειν κρίμα, *to receive condemnation* or *punishment, be punished,* Mk. 12:40; from the Hebrew, πρόσωπον λαμβάνειν, *to accept the person* of any one, *show partiality towards,* Lk. 20:21 [2983] See *get; receive; seize; take.*

[3285] Λάμεχ *Lamech* 1x *Lamech,* pr. name, indecl., Lk. 3:36* [2984]

[3286] λαμπάς *lampas* 9x *a light,* Acts 20:8; *a lamp,* Rev. 4:5; 8:10, *a* portable *lamp, lantern, torch,* Mt. 25:1, 3, 4, 7, 8; Jn. 18:3* [2985]

[3287] λαμπρός *lampros* 9x *bright, resplendent, shining,* Rev. 22:16; *clear, transparent,* Rev. 22:1; *white, glistening,* Acts 10:30; Rev. 15:6; Rev. 19:8; *of a bright color, gaudy,* Lk. 23:11; by impl. *splendid, magnificent, sumptuous,* Jas. 2:2, 3; Rev. 18:14* [2986]

[3288] λαμπρότης *lamprotēs* 1x *brightness, splendor,* Acts 26:13* [2987]

[3289] λαμπρῶς *lamprōs* 1x *splendidly; magnificently, sumptuously,* Lk. 16:19* [2988]

[3290] λάμπω *lampō* 7x *to shine, give light,* Mt. 5:15, 16; 17:2; *to flash, shine,* Lk. 17:24; Acts 12:7; 2 Cor. 4:6* [2989]

[3291] λανθάνω *lanthanō* 6x *to be unnoticed; to escape the knowledge* or *observation of* a person, Acts 26:26; 2 Pet. 3:5, 8; absol. *to be concealed* or *hidden, escape detection,* Mk. 7:24; Lk. 8:47; with a participle of another verb, *to be unconscious* of an action while being the subject or object of it, Heb. 13:2* [2990]

[3292] λαξευτός *laxeutos* 1x *cut in stone, hewn out of stone* or *rock,* Lk. 23:53* [2991]

[3293] Λαοδίκεια *Laodikeia* 6x *Laodicea,* a city of Phrygia in Asia Minor, Rev. 3:14* [2993]

[3294] Λαοδικεύς *Laodikeus* 1x *a Laodicean, an inhabitant of Laodicea,* Col. 4:16* [2994]

[3295] λαός *laos* 142x *a body of people; a concourse of people, a multitude,* Mt. 27:25; Lk. 8:47; *the common people,* Mt. 26:5; *a people, nation,* Mt. 2:4; Lk. 2:32; Tit. 2:14; ὁ λαός, *the people* of Israel, Lk. 2:10 [2992] See *people.*

[3296] λάρυγξ *larynx* 1x *the throat, gullet,* Rom. 3:13* [2995]

[3297] Λασαία *Lasaia* 1x *Lasaea,* also spelled Λασέα, a maritime town in Crete, Acts 27:8 [2996]

[3300] λατομέω *latomeō* 2x *to hew stones; to cut out of stone, hew from stone,* Mt. 27:60; Mk. 15:46; Lk. 23:53* [2998]

[3301] λατρεία *latreia* 5x *service, servitude; religious service, worship,* Jn. 16:2; Rom. 9:4; 12:1; Heb. 9:1, 6* [2999]

[3302] λατρεύω *latreuō* 21x *to be a servant, to serve,* Acts 27:23; *to render religious service and homage, worship,* Mt. 4:10; Lk. 1:74; spc. *to offer sacrifices, present offerings,* Heb. 8:5; 9:9 [3000] See *serve; worship.*

[3303] λάχανον *lachanon* 4x *a garden herb, vegetable,* Mt. 13:32; Mk. 4:32; Lk. 11:42; Rom. 14:2* [3001]

[3305] λεγιών *legiōn* 4x also spelled λεγεών, *a* Roman *legion;* in NT used indefinitely for a great number, Mt. 26:53; Mk. 5:9, 15, Lk. 8:30* [3003]

[3306] λέγω *legō* 2,353x *to lay, to arrange, to gather; to say,* Mt. 1:20; *to speak, make an address* or *speech,* Acts 26:1; *to say* mentally, in thought, Mt. 3:9; Lk. 3:8; *to say* in written language, Mk. 15:28; Lk. 1:63; Jn. 19:37; *to say,* as distinguished from acting, Mt. 23:3; *to mention, speak of,* Mk. 14:71; Lk. 9:31; Jn. 8:27; *to tell, declare, narrate,* Mt. 21:27; Mk. 10:32; *to express,* Heb. 5:11; *to put forth, propound,* Lk. 5:36; 13:6; Jn. 16:29; *to mean, to intend to signify,* 1 Cor. 1:12; 10:29; *to say, declare, affirm, maintain,* Mt. 3:9; 5:18; Mk. 12:18; Acts 17:7; 26:22; 1 Cor. 1:10; *to enjoin,* Acts 15:24; 21:21; Rom. 2:22; *to term, designate, cull,* Mt. 19:17; Mk. 12:37; Lk. 20:37; 23:2; 1 Cor. 8:5; *to call* by a name, Mt. 2:23; pass. *to be further named, to be surnamed,* Mt. 1:16; *to be explained, interpreted,* Jn. 4:25; 20:16, 24; in NT σὺ λέγεις, *you say,* a form of affirmative answer to a question Mt. 27:11; Mk.

15:2; Jn. 18:37 [2036, 2046, 3004, 4483] See *call; name; say; speak; talk; tell.*

[3307] λεῖμμα *leimma* 1x pr. *a remnant;* in NT *a small residue,* Rom. 11:5* [3005] See *remnant.*

[3308] λεῖος *leios* 1x *smooth, level, plain,* Lk. 3:5* [3006]

[3309] λείπω *leipō* 6x trans. *to leave, forsake;* pass. *to be left, deserted;* by impl. *to be destitute of, deficient in,* Jas. 1:4, 5; 2:15; intrans. *to fail, be wanting, be deficient,* Lk. 18:22; Tit. 1:5; 3:13* [3007]

[3310] λειτουργέω *leitourgeō* 3x pr. *to perform some public service at one's own expense;* in NT *to officiate* as a priest, Heb. 10:11; *to minister* in the Christian Church, Acts 13:2; *to minister to, assist, succor,* Rom. 15:27* [3008]

[3311] λειτουργία *leitourgia* 6x pr. *a public service discharged by a citizen at his own expense;* in NT *a* sacred *ministration,* Lk. 1:23; Phil. 2:17; Heb. 8:6; 9:21; *a kind office, aid, relief,* 2 Cor. 9:12; Phil. 2:30* [3009]

[3312] λειτουργικός *leitourgikos* 1x *ministering; engaged in holy service,* Heb. 1:14* [3010]

[3313] λειτουργός *leitourgos* 5x pr. *a person of property who performed a public duty* or *service to the state at his own expense;* in NT *a minister* or *servant,* Rom. 13:6; 15:16; Heb. 1:7; 8:2; *one who ministers relief,* Phil. 2:25* [3011]

[3316] λεμά *lema* 2x Aramaic for *Why? Wherefore?* Mt. 27:46; Mk. 15:34* [2982]

[3317] λέντιον *lention* 2x *a coarse cloth,* with which servants were girded, *a towel, napkin, apron,* Jn. 13:4, 5* [3012]

[3318] λεπίς *lepis* 1x *a scale, shell, rind, crust, incrustation,* Acts 9:18* [3013]

[3319] λέπρα *lepra* 4x *the leprosy,* Mt. 8:3; Mk. 1:42; Lk. 5:12, 13* [3014]

[3320] λεπρός *lepros* 9x *leprous; a leper,* Mt. 8:2; 10:8 [3015]

[3322] Λευί *Leui* 8x *Levi,* also spelled Λευίς (3323), pr. name. When the NT refers to the Λευί of the OT, the word is indecl. (n-3g[2]); when it refers to a NT person, it is partially declined (n-3g[1]): Λευίς (nom); Λευὶν (acc). (1) *Levi, son of Jacob,* Heb. 7:5, 9; Rev. 7:7. (2) *Levi, son of Symeon,* Lk. 3:29 (3) *Levi, son of Melchi,* Lk. 3:24 [3017]

[3324] Λευίτης *Leuitēs* 3x *a Levite, one of the posterity of Levi,* Jn. 1:19; Lk. 10:32; Acts 4:36* [3019]

[3325] Λευιτικός *Leuitikos* 1x *Levitical, pertaining to the Levites,* Heb. 7:11* [3020]

[3326] λευκαίνω *leukainō* 2x *to brighten, to make white,* Mk. 9:3; Rev. 7:14* [3021]

[3328] λευκός *leukos* 25x pr. *light, bright; white,* Mt. 5:36; 17:2; *whitening, growing white,* Jn. 4:35 [3022] See *white.*

[3329] λέων *leōn* 9x *a lion,* Heb. 11:33; 1 Pet. 5:8; Rev. 4:7; 9:8, 17; 10:3; 13:2; met. *a lion, cruel adversary, tyrant,* 2 Tim. 4:17; *a lion, a hero, deliverer,* Rev. 5:5* [3023]

[3330] λήθη *lēthē* 1x *forgetfulness, oblivion,* 2 Pet. 1:9* [3024]

[3331] λῆμψις *lēmpsis* 1x also spelled λῆψις, *taking, receiving,* Phil. 4:15* [3028]

[3332] ληνός *lēnos* 5x pr. *a tub. trough; a wine-press,* into which grapes were cast and trodden, Rev. 14:19, 20; 19:15; *a wine-vat,* i.q. ὑπολήνιον, the lower vat into which the juice of the trodden grapes flowed, Mt. 21:33* [3025]

[3333] λῆρος *lēros* 1x *idle talk; an empty tale, nonsense,* Lk. 24:11* [3026]

[3334] λῃστής *lēstēs* 15x *a plunderer, robber, highwayman,* Mt. 21:13; 26:55; Mk. 11:17; Lk. 10:30; 2 Cor. 11:26; *a bandit, brigand,* Mt. 27:38, 44; Mk. 15:27; Jn. 18:40; trop. *a robber, rapacious imposter,*

Jn. 10:1, 8 [3027] See *bandit; insurrectionist; robber.*

[3336] λίαν *lian* 12x *much, greatly, exceedingly,* Mt. 2:16; 4:8; 8:28 [3029]

[3337] λίβανος *libanos* 2x *arbor thurifera,* the tree producing frankincense, growing in Arabia and Mount Lebanon; in NT *frankincense,* the transparent gum that distils from incisions in the tree, Mt. 2:11; Rev. 18:13* [3030]

[3338] λιβανωτός *libanōtos* 2x *frankincense;* in NT *a censer,* Rev. 8:3, 5* [3031]

[3339] Λιβερτῖνος *Libertinos* 1x *a freedman, one who having been a slave has obtained his freedom,* or *whose father was a freed-man;* in NT the λιβερτῖνοι probably denote Jews who had been carried captive to Rome, and subsequently manumitted, Acts 6:9* [3032]

[3340] Λιβύη *Libyē* 1x *Libya,* a part of Africa, bordering on the west of Egypt, Acts 2:10* [3033]

[3342] λιθάζω *lithazō* 9x *to stone, pelt* or *kill with stones,* Jn. 8:5; 10:31, 32, 33; 11:8; Acts 5:26; 14:19; 2 Cor. 11:25; Heb. 11:37* [3034]

[3343] λίθινος *lithinos* 3x *made of stone,* Jn. 2:6; 2 Cor. 3:3; Rev. 9:20* [3035]

[3344] λιθοβολέω *lithoboleō* 7x *to stone, pelt with stones,* in order to kill, Mt. 21:35; 23:37 [3036]

[3345] λίθος *lithos* 59x *a stone,* Mt. 3:9; 4:3, 6; used figuratively, of Christ, Eph. 2:20; 1 Pet. 2:6; of believers, 1 Pet. 2:5; meton. *a tablet of stone,* 2 Cor. 3:7; *a precious stone,* Rev. 4:3 [3037] See *rock; stone.*

[3346] λιθόστρωτος *lithostrōtos* 1x *a pavement made of blocks of stone,* Jn. 19:13* [3038]

[3347] λικμάω *likmaō* 2x pr. *to winnow grain;* in NT *to scatter like chaff, crush,* Mt. 21:44; Lk. 20:18* [3039]

[3348] λιμήν *limēn* 3x *a port, haven, harbor,* Καλὰ Λιμένες, Acts 27:8, 12* [3040]

[3349] λίμνη *limnē* 11x *a tract of standing water; a lake,* Lk. 5:1; Rev. 20:14 [3041] See *lake; pond.*

[3350] λιμός *limos* 12x *famine, scarcity of food, want of grain,* Mt. 24:7; *famine, hunger, famishment,* Lk. 15:17; Rom. 8:35 [3042] See *famine; hunger.*

[3351] λίνον *linon* 2x *flax;* by meton. *a flaxen wick,* Mt. 12:20; *linen,* Rev. 15:6* [3043]

[3352] Λίνος *Linos* 1x some accent as Λῖνος, *Linus,* pr. name, 2 Tim. 4:21* [3044]

[3353] λιπαρός *liparos* 1x lit., *fat;* fig., *rich, sumptuous,* Rev. 18:14* [3045]

[3354] λίτρα *litra* 2x *a pound, libra,* equivalent to about twelve ounces (American), Jn. 12:3; 19:39* [3046]

[3355] λίψ *lips* 1x pr. *the south-west wind;* meton. *the south-west quarter of the heavens,* Acts 27:12* [3047]

[3356] λογεία *logeia* 2x *collection* of money, 1 Cor. 16:1f.* [3048]

[3357] λογίζομαι *logizomai* 40x (1) pr. *to count, calculate; to count, enumerate,* Mk. 15:28; Lk. 22:37; *to set down* as a matter of account, 1 Cor. 13:5; 2 Cor. 3:5; 12:6; *to impute,* Rom. 4:3; 2 Cor. 5:19; 2 Tim. 4:16; *to account,* Rom. 2:26; 8:36; εἰς οὐδὲν λογισθῆναι, *to be set at nought, despised,* Acts 19:27; *to regard, deem, consider,* Rom. 6:11; 14:14; 1 Cor. 4:1; 2 Cor. 10:2; Phil. 3:13; (2) *to infer, conclude, presume,* Rom. 2:3; 3:28; 8:18; 2 Cor. 10:2, 7, 11; Heb. 11:19; 1 Pet. 5:12; (3) *to think upon, ponder,* Phil. 4:8; absol. *to reason,* Mk. 11:31; 1 Cor. 13:11 [3049] See *consider; credit; regard; think.*

[3358] λογικός *logikos* 2x *pertaining to speech; pertaining to reason;* in NT *rational, spiritual, pertaining to the mind and soul,* Rom. 12:1; 1 Pet. 2:2* [3050]

[3359] λόγιον *logion* 4x *an oracle, a divine communication* or *revelation,* Acts 7:38; Rom. 3:2; Heb. 5:12; 1 Pet. 4:11* [3051] See *oracle.*

[3360] λόγιος *logios* 1x *gifted with learning* or *eloquence,* Acts 18:24* [3052]

[3361] λογισμός *logismos* 2x pr. *a computation, act of computing; a thought, cogitation,* Rom. 2:15; *a conception, device,* 2 Cor. 10:4* [3053]

[3362] λογομαχέω *logomacheō* 1x *to contend about words;* by impl. *to dispute about trivial things,* 2 Tim. 2:14* [3054]

[3363] λογομαχία *logomachia* 1x *contention* or *strife about words;* by impl. *a dispute about trivial things, unprofitable controversy,* 1 Tim. 6:4* [3055]

[3364] λόγος *logos* 330x *a word, a thing uttered,* Mt. 12:32, 37; 1 Cor. 14:19; *speech, language, talk,* Mt. 22:15; Lk. 20:20; 2 Cor. 10:10; Jas. 3:2; *converse,* Lk. 24:17; mere *talk, wordy show,* 1 Cor. 4:19, 20; Col. 2:23; 1 Jn. 3:18; *language, mode of discourse, style of speaking,* Mt. 5:37; 1 Cor. 1:17; 1 Thess. 2:5; *a saying, a speech,* Mk. 7:29; Eph. 4:29; *an expression, form of words, formula,* Mt. 26:44; Rom. 13:9; Gal. 5:14; *a saying, a thing propounded in discourse,* Mt. 7:24; 19:11; Jn. 4:37; 6:60; 1 Tim. 1:15; *a message, announcement,* 2 Cor. 5:19; *a* prophetic *announcement,* Jn. 12:38; *an account, statement,* 1 Pet. 3:15; *a story, report,* Mt. 28:15; Jn. 4:39; 21:23; 2 Thess. 2:2; *a* written *narrative, a treatise,* Acts 1:1; *a set discourse,* Acts 20:7; *doctrine,* Jn. 8:31, 37; 2 Tim. 2:17; *subject-matter,* Acts 15:6; *reckoning, account,* Mt. 12:36; 18:23; 25:19; Lk. 16:2; Acts 19:40; 20:24; Rom. 9:28; Phil. 4:15, 17; Heb. 4:13; *a plea,* Mt. 5:32; Acts 19:38; *a motive,* Acts 10:29; *reason,* Acts 18:14; ὁ λόγος, *the word* of God, especially in the Gospel, Mt. 13:21, 22; Mk. 16:20; Lk. 1:2; Acts 6:4; ὁ λόγος, *the* divine *WORD,* or *Logos,* Jn. 1:1 [3056] See *message; report; word.*

[3365] λόγχη *lonchē* 1x pr. *the head of a javelin; a spear, lance,* Jn. 19:34* [3057]

[3366] λοιδορέω *loidoreō* 4x *to revile, rail at, abuse,* Jn. 9:28; Acts 23:4; 1 Cor. 4:12; 1 Pet. 2:23* [3058]

[3367] λοιδορία *loidoria* 3x *reviling, railing, verbal abuse,* 1 Tim. 5:14; 1 Pet. 3:9* [3059]

[3368] λοίδορος *loidoros* 2x *reviling, railing;* as a subst. *a reviler, railer,* 1 Cor. 5:11; 6:10* [3060]

[3369] λοιμός *loimos* 2x *a pestilence, plague,* Lk. 21:11; met. *a pest, pestilent fellow,* Acts 24:5* [3061]

[3370] λοιπός *loipos* 55x *remaining; the rest, remainder,* Mt. 22:6; as an adv., οὗ λοιποῦ, *henceforth,* Gal. 6:17; τὸ λοιπόν, or λοιπόν, *henceforward,* Mt. 26:45; 2 Tim. 4:8; Acts 27:20; *as to the rest, besides,* 1 Cor. 1:16; *finally,* Eph. 6:10; ὃ δὲ λοιπόν, *but, now, furthermore,* 1 Cor. 4:2 [3062, 3063, 3064] See *left over; remaining.*

[3371] Λουκᾶς *Loukas* 3x *Luke,* pr. name [3065]

[3372] Λούκιος *Loukios* 2x *Lucius,* pr. name, (1) a person from Cyrene of Antioch, Acts 13:1. (2) a person who sends his greeting with Paul, Rom. 16:21* [3066]

[3373] λουτρόν *loutron* 2x *a bath, water for bathing; a bathing, washing, ablution,* Eph. 5:26; Tit. 3:5* [3067] See *wash, washing.*

[3374] λούω *louō* 5x pr. *to bathe the body,* as distinguished from washing only the extremities, Jn. 13:10; *to bathe, wash,* Acts 9:37; 16:33; Heb. 10:22; 2 Pet. 2:22* [3068] See *wash, washing.*

[3375] Λύδδα *Lydda* 3x *Lydda,* a town in Palestine, Acts 9:32, 35, 38* [3069]

[3376] Λυδία *Lydia* 2x *Lydia,* pr. name of a woman, Acts 16:14, 40* [3070]

[3377] Λυκαονία *Lykaonia* 1x *Lycaonia,* a province of Asia Minor, Acts 14:6* [3071]

[3378] Λυκαονιστί *Lykaonisti* 1x *in the dialect of Lycaonia,* Acts 14:11* [3072]

[3379] Λυκία *Lykia* 1x *Lycia,* a province of Asia Minor, Acts 27:5* [3073]

[3380] λύκος *lykos* 6x *a wolf,* Mt. 10:16; Lk. 10:3; Jn. 10:12; met. *a person of wolf-like character,* Mt. 7:15; Acts 20:29* [3074]

[3381] λυμαίνω *lymainō* 1x some list as a deponent, λυμαίνομαι, *to outrage, harm, violently maltreat;* in NT *to make havoc of, ruin,* Acts 8:3* [3075]

[3382] λυπέω *lypeō* 26x *to occasion grief* or *sorrow to, to distress,* 2 Cor. 2:2, 5; 7:8; pass. *to be grieved, pained, distressed, sorrowful,* Mt. 17:23; 19:22; *to aggrieve, cross, vex,* Eph. 4:30; pass. *to feel pained,* Rom. 14:15 [3076] See *sorrow.*

[3383] λύπη *lypē* 16x *pain, distress,* Jn. 16:21; *grief, sorrow,* Jn. 16:6, 20, 22; meton. *cause of grief, trouble, affliction,* 1 Pet. 2:19 [3077] See *grief; pain; sorrow.*

[3384] Λυσανίας *Lysanias* 1x *Lyssanias,* pr. name, Lk. 3:1* [3078]

[3385] Λυσίας *Lysias* 2x *Lysias,* pr. name, Acts 23:26; 24:7, 22* [3079]

[3386] λύσις *lysis* 1x *a loosing;* in NT *a release* from the marriage bond, *a divorce,* 1 Cor. 7:27* [3080]

[3387] λυσιτελέω *lysiteleō* 1x pr. *to compensate for incurred expense;* by impl. *to be advantageous to, to profit, advantage;* impers. Lk. 17:2* [3081]

[3388] Λύστρα *Lystra* 6x *Lystra,* a city of Lycaonia, in Asia Minor, Acts 14:6, 8, 21; 16:1f.; 2 Tim. 3:11* [3082]

[3389] λύτρον *lytron* 2x pr. *price paid; a ransom,* Mt. 20:28; Mk. 10:45* [3083] See *ransom.*

[3390] λυτρόω *lytroō* 3x *to release for a ransom;* mid, *to ransom, redeem, deliver, liberate,* Lk. 24:21; Tit. 2:14; 1 Pet. 1:18* [3084] See *redeem.*

[3391] λύτρωσις *lytrōsis* 3x *redemption,* Heb. 9:12; *liberation, deliverance,* Lk. 1:68; 2:38* [3085] See *redemption.*

[3392] λυτρωτής *lytrōtēs* 1x *a redeemer; a deliverer,* Acts 7:35* [3086]

[3393] λυχνία *lychnia* 12x *a candlestick, lampstand,* Mt. 5:15; met. *a candlestick,* as a figure of a Christian church, Rev. 1:12, 13, 20; of a teacher or prophet, Rev. 11:4 [3087] See *candle, candlestick; lamp, lampstand.*

[3394] λύχνος *lychnos* 14x *a light, lamp, candle,* etc., Mt. 5:15; Mk. 4:21; met. *a lamp,* as a figure of a distinguished teacher, Jn. 5:35 [3088] See *candle, candlestick; lamp, lampstand.*

[3395] λύω *lyō* 42x *to loosen, unbind, unfasten,* Mk. 1:7; *to loose, untie,* Mt. 21:2; Jn. 11:44; *to disengage,* 1 Cor. 7:27; *to set free, set at liberty, deliver,* Lk. 13:16; *to break,* Acts 27:41; Rev. 5:2, 5; *to break up, dismiss,* Acts 13:43; *to destroy, demolish,* Jn. 2:19; Eph. 2:14; met *to infringe,* Mt. 5:19; Jn. 5:18; 7:23; *to make void, nullify,* Jn. 10:35; in NT *to declare free,* of privileges, or, in respect of lawfulness, Mt. 16:19 [3089] See *break; destroy; free; loose; untie.*

[3396] Λωΐς *Lōis* 1x *Lois,* pr. name of a woman, 2 Tim. 1:5* [3090]

[3397] Λώτ *Lōt* 4x *Lot,* pr. name, indecl., Lk. 17:28, 29, 32; 2 Pet. 2:7* [3091]

[3399] Μάαθ *Maath* 1x *Maath,* pr. name, indecl., Lk. 3:26* [3092]

[3400] Μαγαδάν *Magadan* 1x *Magadan,* pr. name, indecl., Mt. 15:39* [3093]

[3402] Μαγδαληνή *Magdalēnē* 12x *Magdalene,* pr. name (*of Magdala*), Jn. 20:18 [3094]

[3404] μαγεία *mageia* 1x pr. *the system of the magians; magic,* Acts 8:11* [3095]

[3405] μαγεύω *mageuō* 1x *to be a magician; to use magical arts, practise magic, sorcery,* Acts 8:9* [3096]

[3407] μάγος *magos* 6x (1) *a magus, sage of the magician religion, magician, astrologer, wise man,* Mt. 2:1, 7, 16; (2) *a magician, sorcerer,* Acts 13:6, 8* [3097]

[3408] Μαγώγ *Magōg* 1x *Magog,* pr. name, indecl., Rev. 20:8* [3098]

[3409] Μαδιάμ *Madiam* 1x *Madian,* a district of Arabia Petra, Acts 7:29* [3099]

[3411] μαθητεύω *mathēteuō* 4x intrans. *to be a disciple, follow as a disciple,* Mt. 27:57; in NT trans. *to make a disciple of, to train in discipleship,* Mt. 28:19; Acts 14:21; pass. *to be trained, disciplined, instructed,* Mt. 13:52* [3100]

[3412] μαθητής *mathētēs* 261x *a disciple,* Mt. 10:24, 42, et al. [3101] See *disciple.*

[3413] μαθήτρια *mathētria* 1x *a female disciple; a female Christian,* Acts 9:36* [3102]

[3415] Μαθθάτ *Maththat* 2x also spelled Ματθάτ, *Mathat,* pr. name, indecl., Lk. 3:24, 29* [3158]

[3416] Μαθθίας *Maththias* 2x also spelled Ματθίας, *BAGD* suggest it is a shortened form of Ματταθίας, *Matthias,* pr. name, Acts 1:23, 26* [3159]

[3419] μαίνομαι *mainomai* 5x *to be disordered in mind, mad,* Jn. 10:20; Acts 12:15; 26:24, 25; 1 Cor. 14:23* [3105]

[3420] μακαρίζω *makarizō* 2x *to pronounce happy, fortunate,* Lk. 1:48; Jas. 5:11* [3106]

[3421] μακάριος *makarios* 50x *happy, blessed,* as a noun it can depict someone who receives divine favor, Mt. 5:3, 4, 5, 7; Lk. 1: 45 [3107] See *blessed; favored; fortunate; happy; privileged.*

[3422] μακαρισμός *makarismos* 3x *a happy calling, the act of pronouncing happy,* Rom. 4:6, 9; *self-congratulation,* Gal. 4:15* [3108]

[3423] Μακεδονία *Makedonia* 22x *Macedonia,* Acts 16:9; Rom. 15:26; 1 Cor. 16:5; 1 Thess. 1:7; 1 Tim. 1:3 [3109]

[3424] Μακεδών *Makedōn* 5x *a native of Macedonia,* Acts 16:9; 19:29; 27:2; 2 Cor. 9:2, 4* [3110]

[3425] μάκελλον *makellon* 1x *meat market, marketplace, slaughter house,* 1 Cor. 10:25* [3111]

[3426] μακράν *makran* 10x *far, far off, at a distance, far distant,* Mt. 8:30; Mk. 12:34; met. οἱ μακράν, *remote, alien,* Eph. 2:13, 17; so οἱ εἰς μακράν, Acts 2:39 [3112] See *distant; far.*

[3427] μακρόθεν *makrothen* 14x *far off, at a distance, from afar, from a distance,* Mk. 8:3; 11:13; preceded by ἀπό, in the same sense, Mt. 26:58 [3113]

[3428] μακροθυμέω *makrothumeō* 10x *to be slow towards, be long-enduring; to exercise patience, be long-suffering, clement,* or *indulgent, to forbear,* Mt. 18:26, 29; 1 Cor. 13:4; 1 Thess. 5:14; 2 Pet. 3:9; *to have patience, endure patiently, wait with patient expectation,* Heb. 6:15; Jas. 5:7, 8; *to bear long* with entreaties for deliverance and avengement, Lk. 18:7* [3114] See *endurance, endure; patience, (be) patient; slow to anger.*

[3429] μακροθυμία *makrothumia* 14x *patience; patient enduring of evil, fortitude,* Col. 1:11; Col. 3:12; 1 Tim. 1:16; 1 Pet. 3:20; *slowness of avenging injuries, long-suffering, forbearance, clemency,* Rom. 2:4; 9:22; 2 Cor. 6:6; Gal. 5:22; Eph. 4:2; 2 Tim. 4:2; Jas. 5:10; *patient expectation,* 2 Tim. 3:10; Heb. 6:12; 2 Pet. 3:15* [3115] See *endurance, endure; patience, (be) patient; slow to anger.*

[3430] μακροθύμως *makrothumōs* 1x *patiently,* Acts 26:3* [3116]

[3431] μακρός *makros* 4x *long;* of space, *far, distant, remote,* Lk. 15:13; 19:12; of time, *of long duration,* Mk. 12:40; Lk. 20:47* [3117]

[3432] μακροχρόνιος *makrochronios* 1x *of long duration; long-lived,* Eph. 6:3* [3118]

[3433] μαλακία *malakia* 3x *softness; listlessness, indisposition, weakness, infirmity of body,* Mt. 4:23; 9:35; 10:1* [3119]

[3434] μαλακός *malakos* 4x *soft; soft to the touch, delicate,* Mt. 11:8; Lk. 7:25; met. *an instrument of unnatural lust, effeminate,* 1 Cor. 6:9* [3120]

[3435] Μαλελεήλ *Maleleēl* 1x *Maleleel,* pr. name, indecl., Lk. 3:37* [3121]

[3436] μάλιστα *malista* 12x *most, most of all, chiefly, especially,* Acts 20:38; 25:26 [3122]

[3437] μᾶλλον *mallon* 81x *more, to a greater extent, in a higher degree,* Mt. 18:13; 27:24; Jn. 5:18; 1 Cor. 14:18; *rather, in preference,* Mt. 10:6; Eph. 4:28; used in a periphrasis for the comparative, Acts 20:35; as an intensive with a comparative term, Mt. 6:26; Mk. 7:36; 2 Cor. 7:13; Phil. 1:23; μᾶλλον δέ, *yea rather,* or, *more properly speaking,* Rom. 8:34; Gal. 4:9; Eph. 5:11 [3123] See *instead; more; rather.*

[3438] Μάλχος *Malchos* 1x *Malchus,* pr. name, Jn. 18:10* [3124]

[3439] μάμμη *mammē* 1x *a mother;* later, *a grandmother,* 2 Tim. 1:5* [3125]

[3440] μαμωνᾶς *mamōnas* 4x *wealth, riches,* Lk. 16:9, 11; personified, like the Greek Πλοῦτος, *Mammon,* Mt. 6:24; Lk. 16:13* [3126]

[3441] Μαναήν *Manaēn* 1x *Manaen,* pr. name, indecl., Acts 13:1* [3127]

[3442] Μανασσῆς *Manassēs* 3x *Manasses,* pr. name (1) *the tribe of Manasseh,* Rev. 7:6 (2) *Manasseh, king of Judah,* Mt. 1:10* [3128]

[3443] μανθάνω *manthanō* 25x *to learn, be taught,* Mt. 9:13; 11:29; 24:32; *to learn* by practice or experience, *acquire a custom* or *habit,* Phil. 4:11; 1 Tim. 5:4, 13; *to ascertain, be informed,* Acts 23:27; *to understand, comprehend,* Rev. 14:3 [3129] See *learn.*

[3444] μανία *mania* 1x *madness, insanity,* Acts 26:24* [3130]

[3445] μάννα *manna* 4x *manna,* the miraculous food of the Israelites while in the desert, Jn. 6:31, 49; Heb. 9:4; Rev. 2:17* [3131] See *manna.*

[3446] μαντεύομαι *manteuomai* 1x *to speak oracles, to divine,* Acts 16:16* [3132]

[3447] μαραίνω *marainō* 1x *to quench, cause to decay, fade,* or *wither;* pass. *to wither, waste away,* met. *to fade away, disappear, perish,* Jas. 1:11* [3133]

[3449] μαργαρίτης *margaritēs* 9x *a pearl,* Mt. 7:6; 13:45, 46; 1 Tim. 2:9; Rev. 17:4; 18:12, 16; 21:21* [3135]

[3450] Μάρθα *Martha* 13x *Martha,* pr. name, Jn. 12:2 [3136]

[3451] Μαρια *Maria* 27x *Mary,* pr. name (1) The mother of Jesus, Mt. 1:16; Acts 1:14. (2) *Mary,* wife of Clopas, mother of James, Mk. 15:40; Lk. 24:10; Jn. 19:25. (3) *Mary Magdalene,* Mt. 27:56; Lk. 20:18. (4) Sister of Martha and Lazarus, Lk. 10:39; Jn. 11:1; 12:3. (5) Mother of Jn. surnamed Mark, Acts 12:12 (6) A Christian at Rome, Rom. 16:6 [3137]

[3452] Μαριάμ *Mariam* 27x the indeclinable form of Μαρία [3137]

[3453] Μᾶρκος *Markos* 8x *Mark,* pr. name [3138]

[3454] μάρμαρος *marmaros* 1x *a white glistening stone; marble,* Rev. 18:12* [3139]

[3455] μαρτυρέω *martyreō* 76x trans. *to testify, depose,* Jn. 3:11, 32; 1 Jn. 1:2; Rev. 1:2; 22:20; absol. *to give evidence,* Jn. 18:23; *to bear testimony, testify,* Lk. 4:22; Jn. 1:7, 8; *to bear testimony* in confirmation, Acts 14:3; *to declare* distinctly and formally, Jn. 4:44; pass. *to be the subject of testimony, to obtain attestation* to character, Acts 6:3; 10:22; 1 Tim. 5:10; Heb. 11:2, 4; mid. equivalent to μαρτύρομαι, *to make a solemn appeal,* Acts 26:22; 1 Thess. 2:12 [3140] See *confirm; testify; witness.*

[3456] μαρτυρία *martyria* 37x judicial *evidence,* Mk. 14:55, 56, 59; Lk. 22:71; *testimony* in general, Tit. 1:13; 1 Jn. 5:9 *testimony, declaration* in a matter of fact or doctrine, Jn. 1:19; 3:11; Acts 22:18; *attestation* to character, Jn. 5:34, 36; *reputation,* 1 Tim. 3:7 [3141] See *testimony; witness.*

[3457] μαρτύριον *martyrion* 19x *testimony, evidence,* Acts 4:33; 2 Cor. 1:12; Jas. 5:3; in NT *testimony, mode of solemn declaration,* Mt. 8:4; Lk. 9:5; *testimony, matter of solemn declaration,* 1 Cor. 1:6; 2:1; 1 Tim. 2:6; σκηνὴ τοῦ μαρτυρίου, a title of the Mosaic tabernacle, Acts 7:44; Rev. 15:5 [3142] See *testimony; witness.*

[3458] μαρτύρομαι *martyromai* 5x *to call to witness;* intrans. *to make a solemn affirmation* or *declaration,* Acts 20:26; 26:22; Gal. 5:3; *to make a solemn appeal,* Eph. 4:17; 1 Thess. 2:12* [3143]

[3459] μάρτυς *martys* 35x (1) a judicial *witness, deponent,* Mt. 18:16; Heb. 10:28; (2) generally, *a witness* to a circumstance, Lk. 24:48; Acts 10:41; in NT *a witness, a testifier,* of a doctrine, Rev. 1:5; 3:14; 11:3; (3) *a martyr,* Acts 22:20; Rev. 2:13 [3144] See *witness.*

[3460] μασάομαι *masaomai* 1x *to chew, masticate,* in NT *to gnaw,* Rev. 16:10* [3145]

[3463] μαστιγόω *mastigoō* 7x *to scourge, whip,* Mt. 10:17; 20:19; 23:34; Mk. 10:34; Lk. 18:33; Jn. 19:1; met. *to chastise,* Heb. 12:6* [3146]

[3464] μαστίζω *mastizō* 1x *to scourge,* Acts 22:25* [3147]

[3465] μάστιξ *mastix* 6x *a scourge, whip,* Acts 22:24; Heb. 11:36; met. *a scourge* of disease, Mk. 3:10; 5:29, 34; Lk. 7:21* [3148]

[3466] μαστός *mastos* 3x *the breast, pap,* Lk. 11:27; 23:29; Rev. 1:13* [3149]

[3467] ματαιολογία *mataiologia* 1x *vain talking, idle disputation,* 1 Tim. 1:6* [3150]

[3468] ματαιολόγος *mataiologos* 1x *a vain talker, given to vain talking* or *trivial disputation,* Tit. 1:10* [3151]

[3469] μάταιος *mataios* 6x *idle, ineffective, worthless,* 1 Cor. 3:20; *groundless, deceptive, fallacious,* 1 Cor. 15:17; *useless, fruitless, unprofitable,* Tit. 3:9; Jas. 1:26; from the Hebrew, *erroneous* in principle, *corrupt, perverted,* 1 Pet. 1:18; τὰ μάταια, *superstition, idolatry,* Acts 14:15* [3152]

[3470] ματαιότης *mataiotēs* 3x *vanity, folly, futility,* from the Hebrew, religious *error,* Eph. 4:17; 2 Pet. 2:18; *false religion,* Rom. 8:20* [3153]

[3471] ματαιόω *mataioō* 1x *to make vain;* from the Hebrew, pass. *to fall into religious error, to be perverted,* Rom. 1:21* [3154]

[3472] μάτην *matēn* 2x *in vain, fruitlessly, without profit,* Mt. 15:9; Mk. 7:7* [3155]

[3474] Ματθάν *Matthan* 2x *Matthan,* pr. name, indecl., Mt. 1:15 (2x)* [3157]

[3477] Ματταθά *Mattatha* 1x *Mattatha,* pr. name, indecl.; Lk. 3:31* [3160]

[3478] Ματταθίας *Mattathias* 2x see also Μαθθίας, *Mattathias,* pr. name, Lk. 3:25, 26* [3161]

[3479] μάχαιρα *machaira* 29x *a large knife, dagger; a sword,* Mt. 26:47, 51; *the sword* of the executioner, Acts 12:2; Rom. 8:35; Heb. 11:37; hence, φορεῖν μάχαιραν, *to bear the sword, to have the power of life and death,* Rom. 13:4; meton. *war,* Mt. 10:34 [3162] See *sword.*

[3480] μάχη *machē* 4x *a fight, battle, conflict;* in NT *contention, dispute, strife, controversy,* 2 Cor. 7:5; 2 Tim. 2:23; Tit. 3:9; Jas. 4:1* [3163]

[3481] μάχομαι *machomai* 4x *to fight; to quarrel,* Acts 7:26; 2 Tim. 2:24; *to contend, dispute,* Jn. 6:52; Jas. 4:2* [3164]

[3483] μεγαλεῖος *megaleios* 1x *magnificent, splendid;* τὰ μεγαλεῖα, *great things, wonderful works,* Acts 2:11* [3167]

[3484] μεγαλειότης *megaleiotēs* 3x *majesty, magnificence, glory,* Lk. 9:43; Acts 19:27; 2 Pet. 1:16* [3168]

[3485] μεγαλοπρεπής *megaloprepēs* 1x pr. *becoming a great man; magnificent, glorious, most splendid,* 2 Pet. 1:17* [3169]

[3486] μεγαλύνω *megalynō* 8x lit., *to enlarge, amplify,* Mt. 23:5; 2 Cor. 10:15; *to manifest in an extraordinary degree,* Lk. 1:58; fig., *to magnify, exalt, extol,* Lk. 1:46; Acts 5:13; Acts 10:46; 19:17; Phil. 1:20* [3170] See *exalt; magnify.*

[3487] μεγάλως *megalōs* 1x *greatly, very much, vehemently,* Phil. 4:10* [3171]

[3488] μεγαλωσύνη *megalōsynē* 3x *greatness, majesty,* Heb. 1:3; 8:1; ascribed *majesty,* Jude 25* [3172]

[3489] μέγας *megas* 243x *great, large in size,* Mt. 27:60; Mk. 4:32; *great, much, numerous,* Mk. 5:11; Heb. 11:26; *great, grown up, adult,* Heb. 11:24; *great, vehement, intense,* Mt. 2:10; 28:8; *great, sumptuous,* Lk. 5:29; *great, important, weighty, of high importance,* 1 Cor. 9:11; 13:13; *great, splendid, magnificent,* Rev. 15:3; *extraordinary, wonderful,* 2 Cor. 11:15; *great, solemn,* Jn. 7:37; 19:31; *great* in rank, *noble,* Rev. 11:18; 13:16; *great* in dignity, *distinguished, eminent, illustrious, powerful,* Mt. 5:19; 18:1, 4; *great, arrogant, boastful,* Rev. 13:5 [3173] See *great; large; loud.*

[3490] μέγεθος *megethos* 1x *greatness, vastness,* Eph. 1:19* [3174]

[3491] μεγιστάν *megistan* 3x *great men, lords, chiefs, nobles, princes,* Mk. 6:21; Rev. 6:15; 18:23* [3175]

[3493] μεθερμηνεύω *methermēneuō* 8x *to translate, interpret,* Mt. 1:23; Mk. 5:41; 15:22, 34; Jn. 1:38, 41; Acts 4:36; 13:8* [3177]

[3494] μέθη *methē* 3x *strong drink; drunkenness,* Lk. 21:34; *an indulgence in drinking,* Rom. 13:13; Gal. 5:21* [3178]

[3496] μεθίστημι *methistēmi* 5x *to cause a change of position; to remove, transport,* 1 Cor. 13:2; *to transfer,* Col. 1:13; met. *to cause to change sides;* by impl. *to pervert, mislead,* Acts 19:26; *to remove* from office, *dismiss, discard,* Lk. 16:4; Acts 13:22* [3179]

[3497] μεθοδεία *methodeia* 2x *wile, scheme, scheming, craftiness,* Eph. 4:14; 6:11* [3180]

[3499] μεθύσκω *methuskō* 5x *to inebriate, make drunk;* pass. *to be intoxicated, to be drunk,* Lk. 12:45; Eph. 5:18; 1 Thess. 5:7; Rev. 17:2; *to drink freely,* Jn. 2:10* [3182]

[3500] μέθυσος *methusos* 2x *drunken; a drunkard,* 1 Cor. 5:11; 6:10* [3183]

[3501] μεθύω *methuō* 5x *to be intoxicated, be drunk,* Mt. 24:49; Acts 2:15; 1 Cor. 11:21; 1 Thess. 5:7; Rev. 17:6* [3184]

[3505] μείζων *meizōn* 48x *greater,* comparative of μέγας [3185, 3187] See *greater; greatest.*

[3506] μέλας *melas* 6x *black,* Mt. 5:36; Rev. 6:5, 12, the form μέλαν means *ink,* 2 Cor. 3:3; 2 Jn. 12; 3 Jn. 13 [3188, 3189]

[3507] Μελεά *Melea* 1x *Melea,* indecl. pr. name, Lk. 3:31* [3190]

[3508] μέλει *melei* 10x *there is a care, it concerns,* Mt. 22:16; Acts 18:17; 1 Cor. 7:21; 9:9 [3199] See *care about; concerned.*

[3509] μελετάω *meletaō* 2x *to care for; to bestow careful thought upon, to give* *painful attention to, be earnest in,* 1 Tim. 4:15; *to devise,* Acts 4:25* [3191]

[3510] μέλι *meli* 4x *honey,* Mt. 3:4; Mk. 1:6; Rev. 10:9, 10* [3192]

[3514] Μελίτη *Melitē* 1x also spelled Μελιτήνη, *Malta,* an island in the Mediterranean, Acts 28:1* [3194]

[3516] μέλλω *mellō* 109x *to be about to, be on the point of,* Mt. 2:13; Jn. 4:47; it serves to express in general a settled futurity, Mt. 11:14; Lk. 9:31; Jn. 11:51; *to intend,* Lk. 10:1; participle μέλλων, μέλλουσα, μέλλον, *future* as distinguished from past and present, Mt. 12:32; Lk. 13:9; *to be always, as it were, about to do, to delay, linger,* Acts 22:16 [3195] See *about to; going to; intend to.*

[3517] μέλος *melos* 34x *a member, limb, any part of the body,* Mt. 5:29, 30; Rom. 12:4; 1 Cor. 6:15; 12:12 [3196] See *member; part.*

[3518] Μελχί *Melchi* 2x *Melchi,* pr. name, indecl., Lk. 3:24, 28* [3197]

[3519] Μελχισέδεκ *Melchisedek* 8x *Melchisedek,* pr. name, indecl., Heb. 5:6, 10; 6:20; 7:1, 10f., 15, 17* [3198]

[3521] μεμβράνα *membrana* 1x *parchment, vellum,* 2 Tim. 4:13* [3200]

[3522] μέμφομαι *memphomai* 2x *to find fault with, blame, censure; to intimate dissatisfaction with,* Heb. 8:8; absol. *to find fault,* Rom. 9:19* [3201]

[3523] μεμψίμοιρος *mempsimoiros* 1x *finding fault* or *being discontented with one's lot, querulous; a discontented, querulous person, a complainer,* Jude 16* [3202]

[3525] μέν *men* 179x a particle serving to indicate that the term or clause with which it is used stands distinguished from another, usually in the sequel, and then mostly with δέ correspondent, Mt. 3:11; 9:39; Acts 1:1; ὁ μὲν ... ὁ δέ, *this ... that, the one ... the other*, Phil. 1:16, 17; *one ... another*, οἱ μὲν ... οἱ δέ, *some ... others*, Matt 22:5; ὅλλος μὲν ... ὅλλος δέ, *one ... another*, pl. *some ... others*, Matt 13:8; 21:35; ὅλλος μὲν ... ὅλλος δέ, *one ... another*, 1 Cor. 15:39; ὧδε μὲν ... ἐκεῖ δέ, *here ... there*, Heb. 7:8; τοῦτο μὲν ... τοῦτο δέ, *partly ... partly*, Heb. 10:33 [3303]

[3527] Μεννά *Menna* 1x *Menna,* pr. name, indecl., Lk. 3:31* [**]

[3528] μενοῦν *menoun* 1x see μενοῦνγε [3304]

[3529] μενοῦνγε *menounge* 3x also spelled as two words, μενοῦν γε (Lk. 11:28), a combination of particles serving to take up what has just preceded, with either emphasize or to correct; *indeed, really, truly, rather,* Rom. 9:20; 10:18; Phil. 3:8* [3304]

[3530] μέντοι *mentoi* 8x *truly, certainly, sure,* Jn. 4:27; Jude 8 [3305]

[3531] μένω *menō* 118x pluperfect, memenhvkein, *to stay,* Mt. 26:38; Acts 27:31; *to continue;* 1 Cor. 7:11; 2 Tim. 2:13; *to dwell, lodge, sojourn,* Jn. 1:39; Acts 9:43; *to remain,* Jn. 9:41; *to rest, settle,* Jn. 1:32, 33; 3:36; *to last, endure,* Mt. 11:23; Jn. 6:27; 1 Cor. 3:14; *to survive,* 1 Cor. 15:6; *to be existent,* 1 Cor. 13:13; *to continue unchanged,* Rom. 9:11; *to be permanent,* Jn. 15:16; 2 Cor. 3:11; Heb. 10:34; 13:14; 1 Pet. 1:23; *to persevere, be constant, be steadfast,* 1 Tim. 2:15; 2 Tim. 3:14; *to abide, to be in close and settled union,* Jn. 6:56; 14:10; 15:4; *to indwell,* Jn. 5:38; 1 Jn. 2:14; trans. *to wait for,* Acts 20:5, 23 [3306] See *abide; await; remain; stay; wait for.*

[3532] μερίζω *merizō* 14x *to divide; to divide out, distribute,* Mk. 6:41; *to assign, bestow,* Rom. 12:3; 1 Cor. 7:17; 2 Cor. 10:13; Heb. 7:2; mid. *to share,* Lk. 12:13; pass. *to be subdivided, to admit distinctions,* Mk. 3:24-26; 1 Cor. 1:13; *to be severed* by discord, *be at variance,* Mt. 12:25, 26; *to differ,* 1 Cor. 7:34* [3307] See *assign; divide.*

[3533] μέριμνα *merimna* 6x *care,* Mt. 13:22; Mk. 4:19; Lk. 8:14; 21:34; *anxiety,* *anxious interest,* 2 Cor. 11:28; 1 Pet. 5:7* [3308] See *anxiety; concern; worry.*

[3534] μεριμνάω *merimnaō* 19x *to be anxious,* or *solicitous,* Phil. 4:6; *to expend careful thought,* Mt. 6:27, 28, 31, 34a; 10:19; Lk. 10:41; 12:11, 22, 25, 26; *to concern one's self,* Mt. 6:25; 1 Cor. 12:25; *to have the thoughts occupied with,* 1 Cor. 7:32, 33, 34; *to feel an interest in,* Phil. 2:20* [3309] See *concerned; worry.*

[3535] μερίς *meris* 5x *a part; a division* of a country, *district, region, tract,* Acts 16:12; *a portion,* Lk. 10:42; *an* allotted *portion,* Col. 1:12; *a portion* in common, *share,* Acts 8:21; 2 Cor. 6:15* [3310]

[3536] μερισμός *merismos* 2x *a dividing, act of dividing,* Heb. 4:12; *distribution, gifts distributed,* Heb. 2:4* [3311]

[3537] μεριστής *meristēs* 1x *a divider, arbitrator,* Lk. 12:14* [3312]

[3538] μέρος *meros* 42x *a part, portion, division,* of a whole, Lk. 11:36; 15:12; Acts 5:2; Eph. 4:16; *a piece, fragment,* Lk. 24:42; Jn. 19:23; *a party, faction,* Acts 23:9; allotted *portion, lot, destiny,* Mt. 24:51; Lk. 12:46; *a calling, craft,* Acts 19:27; *a* partner's *portion, partnership, fellowship,* Jn. 13:8; pl. μέρη, a local *quarter, district, region,* Mt. 2:22; 16:13; Acts 19:1; Eph. 4:9; *side* of a ship, Jn. 21:6; ἐν μέρει, *in respect,* 2 Cor. 3:10; 9:3; Col. 2:16; 1 Pet. 4:16; μέρος τι, *partly, in some part,* 1 Cor. 11:18; ἀνὰ μέρος, *alternately, one after another,* 1 Cor. 14:27; ἀπὸ μέρους, *partly, in some part* or *measure,* 2 Cor. 1:14; ἐκ μέρους, *individually,* 1 Cor. 12:27; *partly, imperfectly,* 1 Cor. 13:9; κατὰ μέρος, *particularly, in detail,* Heb. 9:5 [3313] See *place; region; share.*

[3540] μεσημβρία *mesēmbria* 2x *midday, noon,* Acts 22:6; meton. *the south,* Acts 8:26* [3314]

[3541] μεσιτεύω *mesiteuō* 1x *to perform offices between two parties; to intervene, interpose,* Heb. 6:17* [3315]

[3542] μεσίτης *mesitēs* 6x *one that acts between two parties; a mediator, one who interposes to reconcile two adverse parties,* 1 Tim. 2:5; *an arbitrator, one who is the medium of communication between two parties, a mid-party,* Gal. 3:19, 20; Heb. 8:6; 9:15; 12:24* [3316] See *mediator.*

[3543] μεσονύκτιον *mesonyktion* 4x *midnight,* Lk. 11:5, Mk. 13:35; Acts 16:25; 20:7* [3317]

[3544] Μεσοποταμία *Mesopotamia* 2x *Mesopotamia,* the country lying between the rivers Tigris and Euphrates, Acts 2:9; 7:2* [3318]

[3545] μέσος *mesos* 58x *mid, middle,* Mt. 25:6; Acts 26:13; ἀνὰ μέσον, *in the midst;* from the Hebrew, *in, among,* Mt. 13:25; *between,* 1 Cor. 6:5; διὰ μέσου, *through the midst of,* Lk. 4:30; εἰς τὸ μέσον, *into,* or *in the midst,* Mk. 3:3; Lk. 6:8; ἐκ μέσου, *from the midst, out of the way,* Col. 2:14; 2 Thess. 2:7; from the Hebrew, *from, from among,* Mt. 13:49; ἐν τῷ μέσῳ, *in the midst,* Mt. 10:16; *in the midst, in public, publicly,* Mt. 14:6 ἐν μέσῳ, *in the midst of; among,* Mt. 18:20; κατὰ μέσον τῆς νυκτός, *about midnight,* Acts 27:27 [3319] See *among; middle.*

[3546] μεσότοιχον *mesotoichon* 1x *a middle wall; a partition wall, a barrier,* Eph. 2:14* [3320]

[3547] μεσουράνημα *mesouranēma* 3x *the mid-heaven, mid-air,* Rev. 8:13; 14:6; 19:17* [3321]

[3548] μεσόω *mesoō* 1x *to be in the middle* or *midst; to be advanced midway,* Jn. 7:14* [3322]

[3549] Μεσσίας *Messias* 2x *the Messiah, the Anointed One,* i.q. ὁ Χριστός, Jn. 1:42, 4:25* [3323]

[3550] μεστός *mestos* 9x *full, full of, filled with,* Jn. 19:29; 21:11; *replete,* Mt. 23:28; Rom. 1:29; 15:14; Jas. 3:8, 17; 2 Pet. 2:14* [3324]

[3551] μεστόω *mestoō* 1x *to fill;* pass. *to be filled, be full,* Acts 2:13* [3325]

[3552] μετά *meta* 469x (1) gen., *with, together with,* Mt. 16:27; 12:41; 26:55; *with, on the same side* or *party with, in aid of,* Mt. 12:30; 20:20; *with, by means of,* Acts 13:17; *with,* of conflict, Rev. 11:7; *with, among,* Lk. 24:5; *with, to, towards,* Lk. 1:58, 72; (2) acc., *after,* of place, *behind,* Heb. 9:3; of time, *after,* Mt. 17:1; 24:29; followed by an infin. with the neut. article, *after, after that,* Mt. 26:32; Lk. 22:20 [3326]

[3553] μεταβαίνω *metabainō* 12x *to go* or *pass from one place to another,* Jn. 5:24; *to pass away, be removed,* Mt. 17:20; *to go away, depart,* Mt. 8:34 [3327] See *depart; leave; pass on.*

[3554] μεταβάλλω *metaballō* 1x *to change;* mid. *to change one's mind,* Acts 28:6* [3328]

[3555] μετάγω *metagō* 2x *to lead* or *move from one place to another; to change direction, turn about,* Jas. 3:3, 4* [3329]

[3556] μεταδίδωμι *metadidōmi* 5x *to give a part, to share,* Lk. 3:11; *to impart, bestow,* Rom. 1:11; 12:8; Eph. 4:28; 1 Thess. 2:8* [3330]

[3557] μετάθεσις *metathesis* 3x *a removal, translation,* Heb. 11:5; 12:27; *a transmutation, change by the abolition of one thing, and the substitution of another,* Heb. 7:12* [3331]

[3558] μεταίρω *metairō* 2x *to remove, transfer;* in NT intrans. *to go away, depart,* Mt. 13:53; 19:1* [3332]

[3559] μετακαλέω *metakaleō* 4x *to call from one place into another;* mid. *to call* or *send for, invite to come to oneself,* Acts 7:14; 10:32; 20:17; 24:25* [3333]

[3560] μετακινέω *metakineō* 1x *to move away, remove;* pass. met. *to stir away from, to swerve,* Col. 1:23* [3334]

[3561] μεταλαμβάνω *metalambanō* 7x *to partake of, share in,* Acts 2:46; 27:33f.; 2 Tim. 2:6; Heb. 6:7; 12:10; *to get, obtain, find,* Acts 24:25* [3335]

[3562] μετάλημψις *metalēmpsis* 1x *a partaking of, a being partaken of,* 1 Tim. 4:3* [3336]

[3563] μεταλλάσσω *metallassō* 2x *to exchange, change for* or *into, transmute,* Rom. 1:25, 26* [3337]

[3564] μεταμέλομαι *metamelomai* 6x *to change one's judgment on past points of conduct; to change one's mind and purpose,* Heb. 7:21; *to repent, regret,* Mt. 21:29, 32; 27:3; 2 Cor. 7:8* [3338]

[3565] μεταμορφόω *metamorphoō* 4x *to change the external form, transfigure;* mid. *to change one's form, be transfigured,* Mt. 17:2; Mk. 9:2; *to undergo a* spiritual *transformation* Rom. 12:2; 2 Cor. 3:18* [3339] See *transfigure; transform.*

[3566] μετανοέω *metanoeō* 34x *to undergo a change in frame of mind and feeling, to repent,* Lk. 17:3, 4; *to make a change of principle and practice, to reform,* Mt. 3:2 [3340] See *repent, repentance; turn.*

[3567] μετάνοια *metanoia* 22x *a change of mode of thought and feeling, repentance,* Mt. 3:8; Acts 20:21; 2 Tim. 2:25; practical *reformation,* Lk. 15:7; *reversal* of the past, Heb. 12:17 [3341] See *repent, repentance; turn.*

[3568] μεταξύ *metaxy* 9x can function as an improper prep., *between,* Mt. 23:35; Lk. 11:51; 16:26; Acts 15:9; ἐν τῷ μεταξύ, sc. χρόνῳ, *in the meantime, meanwhile,* Jn. 4:31; in NT ὁ μεταξύ, *following, succeeding,* Acts 13:42 [3342]

[3569] μεταπέμπω *metapempō* 9x *to send after;* mid. *to send after* or *for* any one, *invite to come to one's self,* Acts 10:5, 22, 29; 11:13; 20:1; 24:24, 26; 25:3* [3343]

[3570] μεταστρέφω *metastrephō* 2x *to turn about; convert* into something else, *change,* Acts 2:20; by impl. *to pervert,* Gal. 1:7* [3344]

[3571] μετασχηματίζω *metaschēmatizō* 5x *to remodel, transfigure,* Phil. 3:21; mid. *to transform one's self,* 2 Cor. 11:13,

14, 15; *to transfer* an imagination, 1 Cor. 4:6* [3345]

[3572] μετατίθημι *metatithēmi* 6x *to transport,* Acts 7:16; *to transfer,* Heb. 7:12; *to translate* out of the world, Heb. 11:5; met. *to transfer* to other purposes, *to pervert,* Jude 4; mid. *to transfer one's self, to change over,* Gal. 1:6* [3346]

[3573] μετατρέπω *metatrepō* 1x *to turn around, change, alter,* Jas. 4:9* [3344]

[3575] μετέπειτα *metepeita* 1x *afterwards,* Heb. 12:17* [3347]

[3576] μετέχω *metechō* 8x *to share in, partake,* 1 Cor. 9:10, 12; 10:17, 21; 1 Cor. 10:30; Heb. 2:14; 5:13; *to be a member of,* Heb. 7:13* [3348] See *partake; share.*

[3577] μετεωρίζομαι *meteōrizomai* 1x *to raise aloft;* met. *to unsettle in mind;* pass. *to be excited with anxiety, be in anxious suspense,* Lk. 12:29* [3349]

[3578] μετοικεσία *metoikesia* 4x *change of abode* or *country, migration,* Mt. 1:11, 12, 17* [3350]

[3579] μετοικίζω *metoikizō* 2x *to cause to change abode, cause to emigrate,* Acts 7:4, 43* [3351]

[3580] μετοχή *metochē* 1x *a sharing, partaking; communion, fellowship,* 2 Cor. 6:14* [3352]

[3581] μέτοχος *metochos* 6x *a partaker,* Heb. 3:1, 14; 6:4; 12:8; *an associate, partner, fellow,* Lk. 5:7; Heb. 1:9* [3353]

[3582] μετρέω *metreō* 11x *to allot, measure,* Mt. 7:2; Mk. 4:24; Lk. 6:38; Rev. 11:1, 2; 21:15-17; met. *to estimate,* 2 Cor. 10:12* [3354] See *measure.*

[3583] μετρητής *metrētēs* 1x pr. *a measurer;* also, *metretes,* Latin *metreta,* equivalent to the Attic ἀμφορεύς, i.e., three-fourths of the Attic μέδιμνος, and therefore equal to about nine gallons, Jn. 2:6* [3355]

[3584] μετριοπαθέω *metriopatheō* 1x *to moderate one's passions; to be gentle, compassionate,* Heb. 5:2* [3356]

[3585] μετρίως *metriōs* 1x *moderately; slightly;* οὐ μετρίως *no little, not a little, much, greatly,* Acts 20:12* [3357]

[3586] μέτρον *metron* 14x *measure,* Mt. 7:2; Mk. 4:24; Lk. 6:38; Rev. 21:17; *measure, standard,* Eph. 4:13; *extent, compass,* 2 Cor. 10:13; allotted *measure, specific portion,* Rom. 12:3; Eph. 4:7, 16; ἐκ μέτρον, *by measure, with definite limitation,* Jn. 3:34 [3358] See *measure.*

[3587] μέτωπον *metōpon* 8x *forehead, front,* Rev. 7:3; 9:4; 13:16; 14:1, 9; 17:5; 20:4; 22:4* [3359]

[3588] μέχρι *mechri* 17x improper prep. and a conj (*until*), can also spelled μέχρις, *unto, even to,* Rom. 15:19; of time, *until, till,* Mt. 11:23; Mk. 13:30 [3360]

[3590] μή *mē* 1,042x a negative particle, can function as a conj, *not,* for the particulars of its usage, especially as distinguished from that of οὐ, consult a grammar; as a conj., *lest, that not,* Mt. 5:29, 30; 18:10; 24:6; Mk. 13:36; μή, or μήτι, or μήποτε, when prefixed to an interrogative clause, it expresses an intimation either of the reality of the matters respecting which the question is asked, Mt. 12:23; or the contrary, Jn. 4:12 [3361]

[3592] μηδαμῶς *mēdamōs* 2x *by no means,* Acts 10:14; 11:8* [3365]

[3593] μηδέ *mēde* 56x negative disjunctive particle, can function as an adverb and a conj, *neither,* and repeated, *neither-nor,* Mt. 6:25; 7:6; 10:9, 10; *not even, not so much as,* Mk. 2:2 [3366]

[3594] μηδείς *mēdeis* 90x *not one, none, no one,* Mt. 8:4 [3367]

[3595] μηδέποτε *mēdepote* 1x *not at any time, never,* 2 Tim. 3:7* [3368]

[3596] μηδέπω *mēdepō* 1x *not yet, not as yet,* Heb. 11:7* [3369]

[3597] Μῆδος *Mēdos* 1x *a Mede, a native of Media* in Asia, Acts 2:9* [3370]

[3600] μηκέτι *mēketi* 22x *no more, no longer,* Mk. 1:45; 2:2 [3371]

[3601] μῆκος *mēkos* 2x *length,* Eph. 3:18; Rev. 21:16* [3372]

[3602] μηκύνω *mēkynō* 1x *to lengthen, prolong;* mid. *to grow up,* as plants, Mk. 4:27* [3373]

[3603] μηλωτή *mēlōtē* 1x *a sheepskin,* Heb. 11:37* [3374]

[3604] μήν *mēn* 18x *a month,* Lk. 1:24, 26, 36, 56; in NT *the new moon, the day of the new moon,* Gal. 4:10 [3375] See *month.*

[3606] μηνύω *mēnyō* 4x *to disclose* what is secret, Jn. 11:57; Acts 23:30; 1 Cor. 10:28; *to declare, indicate,* Lk. 20:37* [3377]

[3607] μήποτε *mēpote* 25x can function as an adverb, *BAGD* lists it as a negative part., conj., and interrogative part., same signif. and usage as μη, Mt. 4:6; 13:15; Heb. 9:17; also, *whether,* Lk. 3:15 [3379]

[3609] μήπω *mēpō* 2x *not yet, not as yet,* Rom. 9:11; Heb. 9:8* [3380]

[3611] μηρός *mēros* 1x *the thigh,* Rev. 19:16* [3382]

[3612] μήτε *mēte* 34x *neither;* μήτε ... μήτε, or μὴ ... μήτε, or μηδὲ ... μητέ, *neither ... nor,* Mt. 5:34, 35, 36; Acts 23:8; 2 Thess. 2:2; in NT also equivalent to μηδέ, *not even, not so much as,* Mk. 3:20 [3383]

[3613] μήτηρ *mētēr* 83x *a mother,* Mt. 1:18; 12:49, 50, et al. freq.; *a parent* city, Gal. 4:26; Rev. 17:5 [3384] See *mother.*

[3614] μήτι *mēti* 18x interrogative particle, used in questions expecting a negative answer; has the same use as μή in the form εἰ μήτε, Lk. 9:3; also when prefixed to an interrogative clause, Mt. 7:16; Jn. 4:29 [3385, 3387]

[3616] μήτρα *mētra* 2x *the womb,* Lk. 2:23; Rom. 4:19* [3388]

[3618] μητρολῴας *mētrolōas* 1x *one who murders* or *strikes his mother, matricide,* 1 Tim. 1:9* [3389]

[3620] μιαίνω *miainō* 5x pr. *to tinge, dye, stain; to pollute, defile,* ceremonially, Jn. 18:28; *to corrupt, deprave,* Tit. 1:15 (2x); Heb. 12:15; Jude 8* [3392]

[3621] μίασμα *miasma* 1x *pollution,* moral *defilement, corruption, 2 Pet. 2:20** [3393]

[3622] μιασμός *miasmos* 1x *pollution, corruption, defiling,* 2 Pet. 2:10* [3394]

[3623] μίγμα *migma* 1x *a mixture,* Jn. 19:39* [3395]

[3624] μίγνυμι *mignymi* 4x also spelled μειγνυμι, *to mix, mingle,* Mt. 27:34; Lk. 13:1; Rev. 8:7 [3396]

[3625] μικρός *mikros* 46x *little, small* in size quantity, etc. Mt. 13:32; Lk. 12:32; Rev. 3:8; *small, little* in age, *young, not adult,* Mk. 15:40; *little, short* in time, Jn. 7:33; μικρόν, sc. χρόνον, *a little while, a short time,* Jn. 13:33; μετὰ μικρόν, *after a little while, a little while afterwards,* Mt. 26:73; *little* in number, Lk. 12:32; *small, little in dignity, low, humble,* Mt. 10:42; 11:11; μικρόν, as an adv., *little, a little,* Mt. 26:39 [3397, 3398] See *insignificant; little; small.*

[3626] Μίλητος *Milētos* 3x *Miletus,* a seaport city of Caria, on the west coast of Asia Minor, Acts 20:15, 17; 2 Tim. 4:20* [3399]

[3627] μίλιον *milion* 1x *a Roman mile,* which contained *mille passuum,* 1000 paces, or 8 stadia, 4,854 feet, Mt. 5:41* [3400]

[3628] μιμέομαι *mimeomai* 4x *to imitate, follow* as an example, *strive to resemble,* 2 Thess. 3:7, 9; Heb. 13:7; 3 Jn. 11* [3401] See *imitate, imitator.*

[3629] μιμητής *mimētēs* 6x *an imitator, follower,* 1 Cor. 4:16; 11:1; Eph. 5:1; 1 Thess. 1:6; 2:14; Heb. 6:12* [3402] See *imitate, imitator.*

[3630] μιμνῄσκομαι *mimnēskomai* 23x *to remember, recollect, call to mind,* Mt. 26:75; Lk. 1:54, 72; 16:25; in NT, in a passive sense, *to be called to mind, be borne in mind,* Acts 10:31; Rev. 16:19 [3403] See *remember.*

[3631] μισέω *miseō* 40x *to hate, regard with ill-will,* Mt. 5:43, 44; 10:22; *to detest, abhor,* Jn. 3:20; Rom. 7:15; in NT *to regard with less affection, love less, esteem less,* Mt. 6:24; Lk. 14:26 [3404] See *hate.*

[3632] μισθαποδοσία *misthapodosia* 3x pr. *the discharge of wages; requital; reward,* Heb. 10:35; 11:26; *punishment,* Heb. 2:2* [3405]

[3633] μισθαποδότης *misthapodotēs* 1x *a bestower of remuneration; recompenser, rewarder,* Heb. 11:6* [3406]

[3634] μίσθιος *misthios* 2x *hired;* as a subst., *a hired servant, hireling,* Lk. 15:17, 19* [3407]

[3635] μισθός *misthos* 29x *hire, wages,* Mt. 20:8; Jas. 5:4; *reward,* Mt. 5:12, 46; 6:1, 2, 5, 16; *punishment,* 2 Pet. 2:13 [3408] See *reward; wage.*

[3636] μισθόω *misthoō* 2x *to hire out, let out to hire;* mid. *to hire,* Mt. 20:1, 7* [3409]

[3637] μίσθωμα *misthōma* 1x *hire, rent;* in NT *a hired dwelling,* Acts 28:30* [3410]

[3638] μισθωτός *misthōtos* 3x *a hireling,* Mk. 1:20; Jn. 10:12, 13* [3411]

[3639] Μιτυλήνη *Mitylēnē* 1x *Mitylene,* the capital city of Lesbos, in the Aegean sea, Acts 20:14* [3412]

[3640] Μιχαήλ *Michaēl* 2x *Michael, the archangel,* indecl., Jude 9; Rev. 12:7* [3413]

[3641] μνᾶ *mna* 9x Latin *mina; a weight,* equivalent to 100 drachmas; also *a sum,* equivalent to 100 drachmas and the sixtieth part of a talent, Lk. 19:13, 16, 18, 20, 24f.* [3414]

[3643] Μνάσων *Mnasōn* 1x *Mnason,* pr. name, Acts 21:16* [3416]

[3644] μνεία *mneia* 7x *remembrance, recollection,* Phil. 1:3; 1 Thess. 3:6; 2 Tim. 1:3; *mention;* μνείαν ποιεῖσθαι, *to make mention,* Rom. 1:9; Eph. 1:16; 1 Thess. 1:2; Phlm. 4* [3417]

[3645] μνῆμα *mnēma* 8x pr. *a memorial, monument; a tomb, sepulchre,* Mk. 5:3, 5; Lk. 8:27; 23:53; 24:1; Acts 2:29; 7:16; Rev. 11:9* [3418]

[3646] μνημεῖον *mnēmeion* 40x *monument, memorial,* Lk. 11:47; *grave, tomb,* Mt. 23:39; Mk. 5:2; Lk. 11:44; Jn. 11:17, 31, 38; Acts 13:29 [3419] See *grave; tomb.*

[3647] μνήμη *mnēmē* 1x *remembrance, recollection, memory;* μνήμην ποιεῖσθαι, *to make mention,* 2 Pet. 1:15* [3420]

[3648] μνημονεύω *mnēmoneuō* 21x *to remember, recollect, call to mind,* Mt. 16:9; Lk. 17:32; Acts 20:31; *to be mindful of, to fix the thoughts upon,* Heb. 11:15; *to make mention, mention, speak of,* Heb. 11:22 [3421] See *remember.*

[3649] μνημόσυνον *mnēmosynon* 3x *a record, memorial,* Acts 10:4; honorable *remembrance,* Mt. 26:13; Mk. 14:9* [3422]

[3650] μνηστεύω *mnēsteuō* 3x *to ask in marriage; to betroth;* pass. *to be betrothed, engaged,* Mt. 1:18; Lk. 1:27; 2:5* [3423]

[3652] μογιλάλος *mogilalos* 1x *having an impediment in one's speech, speaking with difficulty, a stammerer,* Mk. 7:32* [3424]

[3653] μόγις *mogis* 1x *with difficulty, scarcely, hardly,* Lk. 9:39* [3425]

[3654] μόδιος *modios* 3x *a modius,* a Roman measure for things dry, containing 16 sextarii, and equivalent to about *a peck* (8.75 liters); in NT *a corn measure,* Mt. 5:15; Mk. 4:21; Lk. 11:33* [3426]

[3655] μοιχαλίς *moichalis* 7x *an adulteress,* Rom. 7:3; Jas. 4:4; by meton., *an adulterous appearance, lustful significance,* 2 Pet. 2:14; from the Hebrew, spiritually *adulterous, faithless, ungodly,* Mt. 12:39; 16:4; Mk. 8:38* [3428]

[3656] μοιχάω *moichaō* 4x act., *to cause to commit adultery,* pass., *to commit* or *be guilty of adultery,* Mt. 5:32; 19:9; Mk. 10:11f.* [3429]

[3657] μοιχεία *moicheia* 3x *adultery,* Mt. 15:19; Mk. 7:22; Jn. 8:3* [3430]

[3658] μοιχεύω *moicheuō* 15x trans. *to commit adultery with, debauch,* Mt. 5:28; absol. and mid. *to commit adultery,* Mt. 5:27; Jn. 8:4; *to commit* spiritual *adultery, be guilty of idolatry,* Rev. 2:22 [3431] See *adultery; commit adultery.*

[3659] μοιχός *moichos* 3x *an adulterer,* Lk. 18:11; 1 Cor. 6:9; Heb. 13:4* [3432]

[3660] μόλις *molis* 6x *with difficulty, scarcely, hardly,* Acts 14:18; 27:7, 8, 16; Rom. 5:7; 1 Pet. 4:18* [3433]

[3661] Μολόχ *Moloch* 1x *Moloch,* pr. name, indecl., Acts 7:43* [3434]

[3662] μολύνω *molynō* 3x pr. *to stain, sully; to defile, contaminate* morally, 1 Cor. 8:7; Rev. 14:4; *to soil,* Rev. 3:4* [3435]

[3663] μολυσμός *molysmos* 1x *pollution, defilement,* 2 Cor. 7:1* [3436]

[3664] μομφή *momphē* 1x *a complaint, cause* or *ground of complaint,* Col. 3:13* [3437]

[3665] μονή *monē* 2x *a stay in any place; an abode, dwelling, mansion,* Jn. 14:2, 23* [3438]

[3666] μονογενής *monogenēs* 9x *only-begotten, only-born,* Lk. 7:12; 8:42; 9:38; Heb. 11:17; *only-begotten* in respect of peculiar generation, *unique,* Jn. 1:14, 18; 3:16, 18; 1 Jn. 4:9* [3439]

[3667] μόνον *monon* 70x the accusative singular form of *monos* (*3668*) used as an adverb meaning *only, alone* [3331] See *only.*

[3668] μόνος *monos* 44x *without accompaniment, alone,* Mt. 14:23; 18:15; Lk. 10:40; *singly existent, sole, only,* Jn. 17:3; *lone solitary,* Jn. 8:29; 16:32; *alone* in respect of restriction, *only,* Mt. 4:4; 12:4; *alone* in respect of circumstances, *only,* Lk. 24:18; *not multiplied by reproduction, lone, barren,* Jn. 12:24 [3332] See *alone; only.*

[3669] μονόφθαλμος *monophthalmos* 2x *one-eyed; deprived of an eye,* Mt. 18:9; Mk. 9:47* [3442]

[3670] μονόω *monoō* 1x *to leave alone;* pass. *to be left alone, be lone,* 1 Tim. 5:5* [3443]

[3671] μορφή *morphē* 3x *form, outward appearance,* Mk. 16:12; Phil. 2:6, 7* [3444] See *form; nature.*

[3672] μορφόω *morphoō* 1x *to give shape to, mold, fashion,* Gal. 4:19* [3445]

[3673] μόρφωσις *morphōsis* 2x pr. *a shaping, moulding;* in NT *external form, appearance,* 2 Tim. 3:5; a settled *form.* prescribed *system,* Rom. 2:20* [3446]

[3674] μοσχοποιέω *moschopoieō* 1x *to form an image of a calf,* Acts 7:41* [3447]

[3675] μόσχος *moschos* 6x pr. *a tender branch, shoot; a young animal; a calf, young bull,* Lk. 15:23, 27, 30; Heb. 12:19; Rev. 4:7* [3448]

[3676] μουσικός *mousikos* 1x pr. *devoted to the arts of the Muses; a musician;* in NT, perhaps, *a singer,* Rev. 18:22* [3451]

[3677] μόχθος *mochthos* 3x *wearisome labor, toil, travail,* 2 Cor. 11:27; 1 Thess. 2:9; 2 Thess. 3:8* [3449]

[3678] μυελός *myelos* 1x *marrow,* Heb. 4:12* [3452]

[3679] μυέω *myeō* 1x *to initiate, instruct* in the sacred mysteries; in NT pass. *to be disciplined* in a practical lesson, *to learn* a lesson, Phil. 4:12* [3453]

[3680] μῦθος *mythos* 5x *a word, speech, a tale; a fable, figment,* 1 Tim. 1:4; 4:7; 2 Tim. 4:4; Tit. 1:14; 2 Pet. 1:16* [3454] See *myth.*

[3681] μυκάομαι *mykaomai* 1x *to low, bellow,* as a bull; also, *to roar,* as a lion, Rev. 10:3* [3455]

[3682] μυκτηρίζω *myktērizō* 1x *to contract the nose in contempt and derision, toss up the nose; to mock, deride,* Gal. 6:7* [3456]

[3683] μυλικός *mylikos* 1x *of a mill, belonging to a mill,* Lk. 17:2* [3457]

[3684] μύλινος *mylinos* 1x *belonging to a mill,* Rev. 18:21* [3458]

[3685] μύλος *mylos* 4x *a millstone,* Mt. 18:6; 24:41; Mk. 9:42; Rev. 18:22* [3458]

[3688] Μύρα *Myra* 1x neuter plural, *Myra,* a city of Lycia, Acts 27:5* [3460]

[3689] μυριάς *myrias* 8x *a myriad, ten thousand,* Acts 19:19; indefinitely, *a vast multitude,* Lk. 12:1; Acts 21:20; Heb. 12:22; Jude 14; Rev. 5:11; 9:16* [3461]

[3690] μυρίζω *myrizō* 1x *to anoint,* Mk. 14:8* [3462]

[3691] μύριοι *myrioi* 1x indefinitely, *a great number*; specifically, μύριοι, *a myriad, ten thousand,* Mt. 18:24* [3463]

[3692] μυρίος *myrios* 2x *innumerable,* 1 Cor. 4:15; 14:19* [3463]

[3693] μύρον *myron* 14x pr. *aromatic juice which distills from trees; ointment, unguent,* usually perfumed, Mt. 26:7, 12; Mk. 14:3, 4 [3464] See *ointment; perfume.*

[3695] Μυσία *Mysia* 2x *Mysia,* a province of Asia Minor, Acts 16:7f.* [3465]

[3696] μυστήριον *mystērion* 28x *a matter to the knowledge of which initiation is necessary; a secret* which would remain such but for revelation, Mt. 3:11; Rom. 11:25; Col. 1:26; *a concealed power* or *principle,* 2 Thess. 2:7; *a hidden meaning* of a symbol, Rev. 1:20: 17:7 [3466] See *mystery; secret.*

[3697] μυωπάζω *myōpazō* 1x pr. *to close the eyes, contract the eyelids, wink; to be nearsighted, partially blinded, slow to understand,* 2 Pet. 1:9* [3467]

[3698] μώλωψ *mōlōps* 1x *the mark of a blow; a stripe, a wound,* 1 Pet. 2:24* [3468]

[3699] μωμάομαι *mōmaomai* 2x *to find fault with, censure, blame,* 2 Cor. 8:20; passively, 2 Cor. 6:3* [3469]

[3700] μῶμος *mōmos* 1x *blame, ridicule; a disgrace* to society, *a stain,* 2 Pet. 2:13* [3470]

[3701] μωραίνω *mōrainō* 4x *to be foolish, to play the fool;* in NT trans. *to make foolish, convict of folly,* 1 Cor. 1:20; pass. *to be convicted of folly, to incur the character of folly,* Rom. 1:22; *to be rendered insipid,* Mt. 5:13; Lk. 14:34* [3471]

[3702] μωρία *mōria* 5x *foolishness,* 1 Cor. 1:18, 21, 23; 2:14; 3:19* [3472]

[3703] μωρολογία *mōrologia* 1x *foolish talk,* Eph. 5:4* [3473]

[3704] μωρός *mōros* 12x pr. *dull; foolish,* Mt. 7:26; 23:17; 25:2f., 8; 1 Cor. 1:25, 27; 3:18; 4:10; 2 Tim. 2:23; Tit. 3:9; from the Hebrew, *a fool* in senseless wickedness, Mt. 5:22* [3474] See *fool; foolish.*

[3707] Μωϋσῆς *Mōysēs* 80x also spelled Μωσῆς, *Moses,* pr. name, Mt. 8:4; Jn. 1:17; Rom. 5:14 [3475]

[3709] Ναασσών *Naassōn* 3x *Naasson,* pr. name, indecl., Mt. 1:4; Lk. 3:32* [3476]

[3710] Ναγγαί *Nangai* 1x *Naggai, Nagge,* pr. name, indecl., Lk. 3:25* [3477]

[3711] Ναζαρά *Nazara* 2x see Ναζαρέθ, Mt. 4:13; Lk. 4:16* [3478]

[3714] Ναζαρέθ *Nazareth* 6x an indeclinable form, *Nazareth,* is spelled Ναζαρέτ (4x) and Ναζαρά (2x) [3478]

[3715] Ναζαρέτ *Nazaret* 4x see Ναζαρέθ, Mt. 2:23; Mk. 1:9; Jn. 1:45, 46* [3478]

[3716] Ναζαρηνός *Nazarēnos* 6x *an inhabitant of Nazareth,* Mk. 1:24; 10:47; 4:67; 16:6; Lk. 4:34; 24:19* [3479]

[3717] Ναζωραῖος *Nazōraios* 13x also spelled Ναζαρηνός, *a Nazarite; an inhabitant of Nazareth,* Mt. 2:23; 26:71; Lk. 18:37; Jn. 18:5, 7; 19:19; Acts 2:22; 3:6; 4:10; 6:14; 22:8; 24:5; 26:9* [3480]

[3718] Ναθάμ *Natham* 1x also spelled Ναθάν, *Nathan,* pr. name, indecl., Lk. 3:31* [3481]

[3720] Ναθαναήλ *Nathanaēl* 6x *Nathanael,* pr. name, indecl., Jn. 1:45-49; 21:2 [3482]

[3721] ναί *nai* 33x a particle, used to strengthen an affirmation, *certainly,* Rev. 22:20; to make an affirmation, or express an assent, *yea, yes,* Mt. 5:37; Acts 5:8 [3483]

[3722] Ναιμάν *Naiman* 1x also spelled Νεεμάν, *Naaman,* pr. name, indecl., Lk. 4:27* [3497]

[3723] Ναΐν *Nain* 1x *Nain,* a town of Palestine, indecl., Lk. 7:11* [3484]

[3724] ναός *naos* 45x pr. *a dwelling; the dwelling* of a deity, *a temple,* Mt. 26:61; Acts 7:48; used figuratively of individuals, Jn. 2:19; 1 Cor. 3:16; spc. *the cell of a temple;* hence, *the Holy Place* of the Temple of Jerusalem, Mt. 23:35; Lk. 1:9; *a model of a temple, a shrine,* Acts 19:24 [3485] See *temple.*

[3725] Ναούμ *Naoum* 1x *Naum,* pr. name, indecl., Lk. 3:25* [3486]

[3726] νάρδος *nardos* 2x *spikenard,* a species of aromatic plant with grassy leaves and a fibrous root, of which the best and strongest grows in India; in NT *oil of spikenard,* an oil extracted from the plant, which was highly prized and used as an ointment either pure or mixed with other substances, Mk. 14:3; Jn. 12:3* [3487]

[3727] Νάρκισσος *Narkissos* 1x *Narcissus,* pr. name, Rom. 16:11* [3488]

[3728] ναυαγέω *nauageō* 2x *to make shipwreck, be shipwrecked,* 2 Cor. 11:25; 1 Tim. 1:19* [3489]

[3729] ναύκληρος *nauklēros* 1x *the master* or *owner of a ship,* Acts 27:11* [3490]

[3730] ναῦς *naus* 1x *a ship, vessel,* Acts 27:41* [3491]

[3731] ναύτης *nautēs* 3x *sailor, seaman,* Acts 27:27, 30; Rev. 18:17* [3492]

[3732] Ναχώρ *Nachōr* 1x *Nachor,* pr. name, indecl., Lk. 3:34* [3493]

[3733] νεανίας *neanias* 3x *a young man, youth,* Acts 20:9; 23:17; used of *one who is in the prime of life,* Acts 7:58* [3494]

[3734] νεανίσκος *neaniskos* 11x *a young man, youth,* Mk. 14:51; 16:5; used of *one in the prime of life,* Mt. 19:20, 22; νεανίσκοι, *soldiers,* Mk. 14:51 [3495] See *young man.*

[3735] Νέα πόλις *Neapolis* 1x *Neapolis,* a city of Thrace on the Strymonic gulf, Acts 16:11* [3496]

[3738] νεκρός *nekros* 128x *dead, without life,* Mt. 11:5; 22:31; met. νεκρός τινι, *dead to a thing, no longer devoted to,* or *under the influence of a thing,* Rom. 6:11; *dead* in respect of fruitlessness, Jas. 2:17, 20, 26; morally or spiritually *dead,* Rom. 6:13; Eph. 5:14; *dead* in alienation from God, Eph. 2:1, 5; Col. 2:13; *subject to death, mortal,* Rom. 8:10; *causing death and misery, fatal, having a destructive power,* Heb. 6:1; 9:14 [3498] See *dead.*

[3739] νεκρόω *nekroō* 3x pr. *to put to death, kill;* in NT met. *to deaden, mortify,* Col. 3:5; pass. *to be rendered impotent,* Rom. 4:19; Heb. 11:12* [3499]

[3740] νέκρωσις *nekrōsis* 2x pr. *a putting to death; dying, abandonment to death,* 2 Cor. 4:10; *deadness, impotency,* Rom. 4:19* [3500]

[3741] νεομηνία *neomēnia* 1x *new moon, first of the month,* Col. 2:16* [3561]

[3742] νέος *neos* 24x *recent, new, fresh,* Mt. 9:17; 1 Cor. 5:7; Col. 3:10; Heb. 12:24; *young, youthful,* Tit. 2:4. In Acts 16:11 is used in the name Νέαν πόλις, which some lexicons list as its own lexical form. This occurrence is not included in the word's frequency count. [3501] See *young.*

[3744] νεότης *neotēs* 4x *youth,* Mt. 19:20 [3503]

[3745] νεόφυτος *neophytos* 1x *newly* or *recently planted* met. *a neophyte, one newly implanted* into the Christian Church, *a new convert,* 1 Tim. 3:6* [3504]

[3748] νεύω *neuō* 2x *to nod; to intimate by a nod* or *significant gesture,* Jn. 13:24; Acts 24:10* [3506]

[3749] νεφέλη *nephelē* 25x *a cloud,* Mt. 17:5; 24:30; 26:64 [3507] See *cloud.*

[3750] Νεφθαλίμ *Nephthalim* 3x *Nephthalim,* pr. name, indecl., Mt. 4:13, 15; Rev. 5:6* [3508]

[3751] νέφος *nephos* 1x *a cloud;* trop. *a cloud, a throng* of persons, Heb. 12:1* [3509]

[3752] νεφρός *nephros* 1x *a kidney;* pl. νεφροί, *the kidneys, reins;* from the Hebrew *the reins* regarded as a seat of desire and affection, Rev. 2:23* [3510]

[3753] νεωκόρος *neōkoros* 1x pr. *one who sweeps* or *cleanses a temple;* generally, *one who has the charge of a temple;* in NT *a devotee* city, as having specially dedicated a temple to some deity, Acts 19:35* [3511]

[3754] νεωτερικός *neōterikos* 1x *juvenile, natural to youth, youthful,* 2 Tim. 2:22* [3512]

[3755] νή *nē* 1x *by, BAGD* calls it a "particle of strong affirmation," and is followed by the person or thing (in the acc) by which the person swears, 1 Cor. 15:31* [3513]

[3756] νήθω *nēthō* 2x *to spin,* Mt. 6:28; Lk. 12:27* [3514]

[3757] νηπιάζω *nēpiazō* 1x *to be childlike,* 1 Cor. 14:20* [3515]

[3758] νήπιος *nēpios* 15x pr. *not speaking,* Latin *infans; an infant, babe, child,* Mt. 21:16; 1 Cor. 13:11; *one below the age of manhood, a minor,* Gal. 4:1; met. *a babe* in knowledge, *unlearned, simple,* Mt. 11:25; Rom. 2:20 [3516] See *child; infant.*

[3759] Νηρεύς *Nēreus* 1x *Nereus,* pr. name, Rom. 16:15* [3517]

[3760] Νηρί *Nēri* 1x *Neri,* pr. name, indecl., Lk. 3:27* [3518]

[3761] νησίον *nēsion* 1x *a small island,* Acts 27:16* [3519]

[3762] νῆσος *nēsos* 9x *an island,* Acts 13:6; 27:26 [3520]

[3763] νηστεία *nēsteia* 5x *fasting, want of food,* 2 Cor. 6:5; 11:27; *a fast,* religious *abstinence from food,* Mt. 17:21; Lk. 2:37; spc. *the annual public fast of the Jews, the great day of atonement,* occurring in the month Tisri, corresponding to the new moon of October, Acts 27:9* [3521]

[3764] νηστεύω *nēsteuō* 20x *to fast,* Mt. 4:2; 6:16, 17, 18; 9:15 [3522] See *fast.*

[3765] νῆστις *nēstis* 2x can also be masc. with a gen. in ιδος (n-3c[2]), *fasting, hungry,* Mt. 15:32; Mk. 8:3* [3523]

[3767] νηφάλιος *nēphalios* 3x *somber, temperate, abstinent in respect to wine,* etc.; in NT met., *vigilant, circumspect, self-controlled,* 1 Tim. 3:2, 11; Tit. 2:2* [3524]

[3768] νήφω *nēphō* 6x *to be sober, not intoxicated;* in NT met., *to be vigilant, circumspect,* 1 Thess. 5:6, 8 [3525]

[3769] Νίγερ *Niger* 1x *Niger,* pr. name, probably not declined, Acts 13:1* [3526]

[3770] Νικάνωρ *Nikanōr* 1x *Nicanor,* pr. name, Acts 6:5* [3527]

[3771] νικάω *nikaō* 28x *to conquer, overcome, vanquish, subdue,* Lk. 1:22; Jn. 16:33; absol. *to overcome, prevail,* Rev. 5:5; *to come off superior* in a judicial cause, Rom. 3:4 [3528] See *overcome; (be) victorious.*

[3772] νίκη *nikē* 1x *victory;* meton. *a victorious principle,* 1 Jn. 5:4* [3529]

[3773] Νικόδημος *Nikodēmos* 5x *Nicodemus,* pr. name, Jn. 3:1, 4, 9; 7:50; 19:39* [3530]

[3774] Νικολαΐτης *Nikolaitēs* 2x *a Nicolaitan,* or follower of Nicolaus, a heresy of the Apostolic age, Rev. 2:6, 15* [3531]

[3775] Νικόλαος *Nikolaos* 1x *Nicolaus,* pr. name, Acts 6:5* [3532]

[3776] Νικόπολις *Nikopolis* 1x *Nicopolis,* a city of Macedonia, Tit. 3:12* [3533]

[3777] νῖκος *nikos* 4x *victory,* Mt. 12:20; 1 Cor. 15:54, 55, 57* [3534]

[3780] Νινευίτης *Nineuitēs* 3x *a Ninevite, an inhabitant of Nineveh,* Mt. 12:41; Lk. 11:30, 32* [3536]

[3781] νιπτήρ *niptēr* 1x *a basin* for washing some part of the person, Jn. 13:5* [3537]

[3782] νίπτω *niptō* 17x *to wash;* spc. *to wash* some part of the person, as distinguished from λούω, Mt. 6:17; Jn. 13:8 [3538] See *wash.*

[3783] νοέω *noeō* 14x *to perceive, observe; to mark* attentively, Mt. 24:15; Mk. 13:14; 2 Tim. 2:7; *to understand, comprehend,* Mt. 15:17; *to conceive,* Eph. 3:20 [3539] See *reflect on; see; understand.*

[3784] νόημα *noēma* 6x *the mind, the understanding, intellect,* 2 Cor. 3:14; 4:4; Phil. 4:7; *the heart, soul, affections, feelings, disposition,* 2 Cor. 11:3; *a conception of the mind, thought, purpose, device,* 2 Cor. 2:11; 10:5* [3540]

[3785] νόθος *nothos* 1x *spurious, bastard,* Heb. 12:8* [3541]

[3786] νομή *nomē* 2x *pasture, pasturage,* Jn. 10:9; ἔχειν νομήν, *to eat its way, spread corrosion,* 2 Tim. 2:17* [3542]

[3787] νομίζω *nomizō* 15x *to own as settled and established; to deem,* 1 Cor. 7:26; 1 Tim. 6:5; *to suppose, presume,* Mt. 5:17; 20:10; Lk. 2:44; *to be usual, customary,* Acts 16:13 [3543] See *think; suppose.*

[3788] νομικός *nomikos* 9x *pertaining to law; relating to the* Mosaic *law,* Tit. 3:9; as a subst., *one skilled in law, a jurist, lawyer,* Tit. 3:13; spc. *an interpreter and teacher of the* Mosaic *law,* Mt. 22:35 [3544]

[3789] νομίμως *nomimōs* 2x *lawfully, agreeably to law* or *custom, rightfully,* 1 Tim. 1:8; 2 Tim. 2:5* [3545]

[3790] νόμισμα *nomisma* 1x pr. *a thing sanctioned by law* or *custom; lawful money, coin,* Mt. 22:19* [3546]

[3791] νομοδιδάσκαλος *nomodidaskalos* 3x *a teacher and interpreter of the* Mosaic *law,* Lk. 5:17; Acts 5:34; 1 Tim. 1:7 [3547]

[3792] νομοθεσία *nomothesia* 1x *legislation;* ἡ νομοθεσία, *the gift of the* Divine *law,* or *the* Mosaic *law* itself, Rom. 9:4* [3548]

[3793] νομοθετέω *nomotheteō* 2x *to impose a law, give laws;* in NT pass., *to have a law imposed on one's self, receive a law,* Heb. 7:11; *to be enacted, constituted,* Heb. 8:6* [3549]

[3794] νομοθέτης *nomothetēs* 1x *a legislator, lawgiver,* Jas. 4:12* [3550]

[3795] νόμος *nomos* 194x *a law,* Rom. 4:15; 1 Tim. 1:9; *the* Mosaic *law,* Mt. 5:17, et al. freq.; *the Old Testament Scripture,* Jn. 10:34; *a legal tie,* Rom. 7:2, 3; *a law, a rule, standard,* Rom. 3:27; *a rule* of life and conduct, Gal. 6:2, Jas. 1:25 [3551] See *law.*

[3796] νοσέω *noseō* 1x *to be sick;* met. *to have a diseased appetite* or *craving for* a thing, *have an excessive and vicious fondness for* a thing, 1 Tim. 6:4* [3552]

[3798] νόσος *nosos* 11x *a disease, sickness, distemper,* Mt. 4:23, 24; 8:17; 9:35 [3554] See *illness; sickness.*

[3799] νοσσιά *nossia* 1x *a brood* of young birds, Lk. 13:34* [3555]

[3800] νοσσίον *nossion* 1x *the young of birds, a chick;* pl. *a brood* of young birds, Mt. 23:37* [3556]

[3801] νοσσός *nossos* 1x also spelled νεοσσός, *the young of birds, a young bird, chick,* Lk. 2:24* [3502]

[3802] νοσφίζω *nosphizō* 3x *to deprive, rob;* mid. *to misappropriate; to make secret reservation,* Acts 5:2, 3; *to purloin,* Tit. 2:10* [3557]

[3803] νότος *notos* 7x *the south wind,* Lk. 12:55; Acts 27:13; 28:13; meton. *the south, the southern quarter of the heavens,* Mt. 12:42; Lk. 11:31; 13:29; Rev. 21:13* [3558]

[3804] νουθεσία *nouthesia* 3x *warning, admonition,* 1 Cor. 10:11; Eph. 6:4; Tit. 3:10* [3559]

[3805] νουθετέω *noutheteō* 8x pr. *to put in mind; to admonish, warn,* Acts 20:31; Rom. 15:14 [3560] See *admonish; warn.*

[3807] νουνεχῶς *nounechōs* 1x *understandingly, sensibly, discreetly,* Mk. 12:34* [3562]

[3808] νοῦς *nous* 24x *the mind, intellect,* 1 Cor. 14:15, 19; *understanding, intelligent faculty,* Lk. 24:45; *intellect, judgment,* Rom. 7:23, 25; *opinion, sentiment,* Rom. 14:5; 1 Cor. 1:10; *mind, thought, conception,* Rom. 11:34; 1 Cor. 2:16; Phil. 4:7; *settled state of mind,* 2 Thess. 2:2; *frame of mind,* Rom. 1:28; 12:2; Col. 2:18; Eph. 4:23; 1 Tim. 6:5; 2 Tim. 3:8; Tit. 1:15 [3563] See *intellect; mind; understanding.*

[3811] νύμφη *nymphē* 8x *a bride,* Jn. 3:29; Rev. 18:23; 21:2, 9; 22:17; opposed to πενθερά, *a daughter-in-law,* Mt. 10:35; Lk. 12:53* [3565] See *bride.*

[3812] νυμφίος *nymphios* 16x *a bridegroom,* Mt. 9:15; 25:1, 5, 6, 10 [3566] See *bridegroom.*

[3813] νυμφών *nymphōn* 3x *a bridal-chamber;* in NT υἱοὶ τοῦ νυμφῶνος, *sons of the bridal-chamber, the bridegroom's attendant friends, groomsmen,* Mt. 9:15; Mk. 2:19; Lk. 5:34* [3567]

[3814] νῦν *nyn* 147x *now, at the present time,* Mk. 10:30; Lk. 6:21, et al. freq.; *just now,* Jn. 11:8; *forthwith,* Jn. 12:31; καὶ νῦν, *even now, as matters stand,* Jn. 11:22; *now,* expressive of a marked tone of address, Acts 7:34; 13:11; Jas. 4:13; 5:1; τὸ νῦν, *the present time,* Lk. 1:48; τανῦν, or τὰ νῦν, *now,* Acts 4:29 [3568] See *now; present time.*

[3815] νυνί *nyni* 20x of time, *now, at this very moment,* an emphatic form of νῦν although it now carries the same meaning [3570] See *now.*

[3816] νύξ *nyx* 61x *night,* Mt. 2:14; 28:13; Jn. 3:2; met. spiritual *night,* moral *darkness,* Rom. 13:12; 1 Thess. 5:5 [3571] See *night.*

[3817] νύσσω *nyssō* 1x *to prick* or *pierce,* Jn. 19:34* [3572] See *pierce.*

[3818] νυστάζω *nystazō* 2x *to nod; to nod in sleep; to sink into a sleep,* Mt. 25:5; *to slumber* in inactivity, 2 Pet. 2:3* [3573]

[3819] νυχθήμερον *nychthēmeron* 1x *a day and night, twenty-four hours,* 2 Cor. 11:25* [3574]

[3820] Νῶε *Nōe* 8x *Noah,* pr. name, indecl., Mt. 24:37ff; Lk. 3:36; 17:26f.; Heb. 11:7; 1 Pet. 3:20; 2 Pet. 2:25* [3575]

[3821] νωθρός *nōthros* 2x *slow, sluggish, lazy,* Heb. 5:11; 6:12* [3576]

[3822] νῶτος *nōtos* 1x *the back* of men or animals, Rom. 11:10* [3577]

[3825] ξενία *xenia* 2x pr. *state of being a guest;* then, *the reception of a guest* or *stranger, hospitality,* in NT *a lodging,* Acts 28:23; Phlm. 22* [3578]

[3826] ξενίζω *xenizō* 10x *to receive as a guest, entertain,* Acts 10:23; 28:7; Heb. 13:2; pass. *to be entertained as a guest, to lodge* or *reside with,* Acts 10:6, 18, 32; 21:16; *to strike with a feeling of strangeness, to surprise;* pass. or mid. *to be struck with surprise, be staggered, be amazed,* 1 Pet. 4:4, 12; intrans. *to be strange;* ξενίζοντα, *strange matters, novelties,* Acts 17:20* [3579] See *entertain; show hospitality; strange(r); (be) surprised.*

[3827] ξενοδοχέω *xenodocheō* 1x *to receive and entertain strangers, exercise hospitality,* 1 Tim. 5:10* [3580]

[3828] ξένος *xenos* 14x *strange, foreign, alien,* Eph. 2:12, 19; *strange, unexpected, surprising,* 1 Pet. 4:12; *novel,* Heb. 13:9; subst. *a stranger,* Mt. 25:35, et al.; *a host,* Rom. 16:23 [3581] See *alien; foreign(er); host; strange(r).*

[3829] ξέστης *xestēs* 1x *a sextarius,* a Roman measure, containing about one pint English; in NT used for *a small vessel, cup, pot,* Mk. 7:4* [3582]

[3830] ξηραίνω *xērainō* 15x *to dry up, parch,* Jas. 1:11; pass. *to be parched,* Mt. 13:6, et al.; *to be ripened* as corn, Rev. 14:15; *to be withered, to wither,* Mk. 11:20; of parts of the body, *to be withered,* Mk. 3:1, 3; *to pine,* Mk. 9:18 [3583] See *dry up; scorch; wither.*

[3831] ξηρός *xēros* 8x *dry, withered,* Lk. 23:31; ἡ ξηρά, sc. γῆ, *the dry land, land,* Mt. 23:15; Heb. 11:29; of parts of the body, *withered,* Mt. 12:10 [3584]

[3832] ξύλινος *xylinos* 2x *wooden, of wood, made of wood,* 2 Tim. 2:20; Rev. 9:20* [3585]

[3833] ξύλον *xylon* 20x *wood, timber,* 1 Cor. 3:12; Rev. 18:12; *stocks,* Acts 16:24; *a club,* Mt. 26:47, 55; *a post, cross, gibbet,* Acts 5:30; 10:29; 13:29; *a tree,* Lk. 23:31; Rev. 2:7 [3586] See *club; stocks; tree; wood.*

[3834] ξυράω *xyraō* 3x *to cut off the hair, shear, shave,* Acts 21:24; 1 Cor. 11:5, 6* [3587]

[3836] ὁ *ho* 19,867x the prepositive article, answering, to a considerable extent, to the English definite article; but, for the principle and facts of its usage, consult a grammar; ὁ μὲν ... ὁ δέ, *the one ... the other,* Phil. 1:16, 17; Heb. 7:5, 6, 20, 21, 23, 24; pl. *some ... others,* Mt. 13:23; 22:5, 6; ὁ δέ, *but he,* Mt. 4:4; 12:48; οἱ δέ, *but others,* Mt. 28:17; used, in a poetic quotation, for a personal pronoun, Acts 17:28 [3588, 5120]

[3837] ὀγδοήκοντα *ogdoēkonta* 2x indecl. numeral, *eighty,* Lk. 2:37; 16:7* [3589]

[3838] ὄγδοος *ogdoos* 5x *the eighth,* Lk. 1:59; Acts 7:8; 2 Pet. 2:5; Rev. 17:11; 21:20* [3590]

[3839] ὄγκος *onkos* 1x pr. *bulk, weight; a burden, impediment,* Heb. 12:1* [3591]

[3840] ὅδε *hode* 10x *this, that, he, she, it,* Lk. 10:39; 16:25; Acts 15:23 [3592]

[3841] ὁδεύω *hodeuō* 1x *to journey, travel,* Lk. 10:33* [3593]

[3842] ὁδηγέω *hodēgeō* 5x *to lead, guide,* Mt. 15:14; Lk. 6:39; Rev. 7:17; met. *to instruct, teach,* Jn. 16:13; Acts 8:31* [3594]

[3843] ὁδηγός *hodēgos* 5x *a guide, leader,* Acts 1:16; met. *an instructor, teacher,* Mt. 15:14; 23:16, 24; Rom. 2:19* [3595]

[3844] ὁδοιπορέω *hodoiporeō* 1x *to journey, travel,* Acts 10:9* [3596]

[3845] ὁδοιπορία *hodoiporia* 2x *to journey, journeying, travel,* Jn. 4:6; 2 Cor. 11:26* [3597]

[3847] ὁδός *hodos* 101x *a way, road,* Mt. 2:12; 7:13, 14; 8:28; 22:9, 10; *means of access, approach, entrance,* Jn. 14:6; Heb. 9:8; *direction, quarter, region,* Mt. 4:15; 10:5 *the act of journeying, a journey, way, course,* Mt. 10:10; Mk. 2:23; 1 Thess. 3:11; *a journey,* as regards extent, Acts 1:12; met. *a way,* systematic *course* of pursuit, Lk. 1:79; Acts 2:28; 16:17; *a way,* systematic *course* of action or conduct, Mt. 21:32; Rom. 11:33; 1 Cor. 4:17; *a way, system of doctrine,* Acts 18:26; ἡ ὁδός, *the way of the Christian faith,* Acts 19:9, 23, 24:22 [3598] See *journey; path; road; way.*

[3848] ὀδούς *odous* 12x *a tooth,* Mt. 5:38; 8:12 [3599] See *tooth.*

[3849] ὀδυνάω *odynaō* 4x *to pain* either bodily or mentally; pass. *to be in an agony,* *be tormented,* Lk. 2:48; 16:24, 25; *to be distressed, grieved,* Acts 20:38* [3600]

[3850] ὀδύνη *odynē* 2x *pain* of body of mind; *sorrow, grief,* Rom. 9:2; 1 Tim. 6:10* [3601]

[3851] ὀδυρμός *odyrmos* 2x *bitter lamentation, wailing,* Mt. 2:18; meton. *sorrow, mourning,* 2 Cor. 7:7* [3602]

[3852] Ὀζίας *Ozias* 2x *Uzziah,* pr. name, indeclinable, Lk. 3:23ff.* [3604]

[3853] ὄζω *ozō* 1x *to smell, emit an odor; to have an offensive smell, stink,* Jn. 11:39* [3605]

[3854] ὅθεν *hothen* 15x *whence,* Mt. 12:44; Acts 14:26; *from the place where,* Mt. 25:24, 26; *whence, from which circumstance,* 1 Jn. 2:18; *wherefore, whereupon,* Mt. 14:7 [3606]

[3855] ὀθόνη *othonē* 2x pr. *fine linen; a linen cloth; a sheet,* Acts 10:11; 11:5* [3607]

[3856] ὀθόνιον *othonion* 5x *a linen cloth;* in NT *a swath, bandage* for a corpse, Lk. 24:12 [3608]

[3857] οἶδα *oida* 318x *to know,* Mt. 6:8; *to know how,* Mt. 7:11; from the Hebrew, *to regard with favor,* 1 Thess. 5:12. οἶδα is actually a perfect form functioning as a present, and ᾔδειν is actually a pluperfect form functioning as an aorist. [1492] See *understand.*

[3858] οἰκεῖος *oikeios* 3x *belonging to a house, domestic;* pl. *members of a family, immediate kin,* 1 Tim. 5:8; *members of* a spiritual *family,* Eph. 2:19; *members of a* spiritual *brotherhood,* Gal. 6:10* [3609]

[3859] οἰκετεία *oiketeia* 1x *the members, of a household,* Mt. 24:45* [2322]

[3860] οἰκέτης *oiketēs* 4x pr. *an inmate of a house; a domestic servant, household slave,* Lk. 16:13; Acts 10:7; Rom. 14:4; 1 Pet. 2:18* [3610]

[3861] οἰκέω *oikeō* 9x *to dwell in, inhabit,* 1 Tim. 6:16; intrans. *to dwell, live; to cohabit,* 1 Cor. 7:12, 13; *to be indwelling, indwell,* Rom. 7:17, 18, 20; 8:9, 11; 1 Cor. 3:16* [3611]

[3862] οἴκημα *oikēma* 1x *a dwelling;* used in various conventional senses, and among them, *a prison, cell,* Acts 12:7* [3612]

[3863] οἰκητήριον *oikētērion* 2x *a habitation, dwelling, an abode,* Jude 6; trop. *the* personal *abode* of the soul, 2 Cor. 5:2* [3613]

[3864] οἰκία *oikia* 93x *a house, dwelling, an abode,* Mt. 2:11; 7:24, 27; trop. *the* bodily *abode* of the soul, 2 Cor. 5:1; meton. *a household, family,* Mt. 10:13; 12:25; meton. *goods, property, means,* Mt. 23:13 [3614] See *house.*

[3865] οἰκιακός *oikiakos* 2x *belonging to a house;* pl. *the members of a household* or *family, kindred,* Mt. 10:25, 36* [3615]

[3866] οἰκοδεσποτέω *oikodespoteō* 1x pr. *to be master of a household; to occupy one's self in the management of a household,* 1 Tim. 5:14* [3616]

[3867] οἰκοδεσπότης *oikodespotēs* 12x *the master* or *head of a house* or *family,* Mt. 10:25; 13:27, 52 [3617] See *landowner; master; owner.*

[3868] οἰκοδομέω *oikodomeō* 40x pluperfect, ᾠκοδόμητο (3 sg), *to build a house; to build,* Mt. 7:24; *to repair, embellish, and amplify* a building, Mt. 23:29; *to construct, establish,* Mt. 16:18; met. *to contribute to advancement* in religious knowledge, *to edify,* 1 Cor. 14:4, 17; *to advance* a person's spiritual condition, *to edify,* 1 Cor. 8:1; pass. *to make spiritual* advancement, *be edified,* Acts 9:31; *to advance* in presumption, 1 Cor. 8:10 [3618] See *edify; strengthen.*

[3869] οἰκοδομή *oikodomē* 18x pr. *the act of building; a building, structure,* Mt. 24:1; in NT *a* spiritual *structure,* as instanced in the Christian body, 1 Cor. 3:9; Eph. 2:21; religious *advancement, edifica-*

tion, Rom. 14:19; 1 Cor. 14:3 [3619] See *building, building up; edification.*

[3871] οἰκοδόμος *oikodomos* 1x *a builder, architect,* Acts 4:11* [3618]

[3872] οἰκονομέω *oikonomeō* 1x *to manage a household; to manage the affairs* of any one, *be steward,* Lk. 16:2* [3621]

[3873] οἰκονομία *oikonomia* 9x pr. *the management of a household; a stewardship,* Lk. 16:2, 3, 4; in NT *an* apostolic *stewardship, a* ministerial *commission* in the publication and furtherance of the Gospel, 1 Cor. 9:17; 3:2; Col. 1:25; or, *an arranged plan, a scheme,* Eph. 1:10; *a due discharge of a commission,* 1 Tim. 1:4, Eph. 3:9* [3622]

[3874] οἰκονόμος *oikonomos* 10x *the manager of a household; a steward,* Lk. 12:42; 16:1, 3, 8; 1 Cor. 4:2; *a manager, trustee,* Gal. 4:2; *a* public *steward, treasurer,* Rom. 16:23; *a* spiritual *steward, the holder of a commission* in the service of the Gospel, 1 Cor. 4:1; Tit. 1:7; 1 Pet. 4:10* [3623] See *manager; steward.*

[3875] οἶκος *oikos* 114x *a house, dwelling,* Mt. 9:6, 7; Mk. 2:1, 11; 3:20; *place of abode, seat, site,* Mt. 23:38; Lk. 13:35; met. *a* spiritual *house* or *structure,* 1 Pet. 2:5; meton. *a household, family,* Lk. 10:5; 11:17; *a* spiritual *household,* 1 Tim. 3:15; Heb. 3:6; *family, lineage,* Lk. 1:27, 69; 2:4; from the Hebrew, *a people, nation,* Mt. 10:6; 15:24 [3624] See *family; house; temple.*

[3876] οἰκουμένη *oikoumenē* 15x some list as a participle, *the habitable earth, world, M*att 24:14; Rom. 10:18; Heb. 1:6; used, however, with various restrictions of meaning, according to the context, Lk. 2:1; Acts 17:6; meton. *the inhabitants of the earth, the whole human race, mankind,* Acts 17:31; 19:27; Rev. 3:10. Some view this word as a participial form of οἰκέω. [3625] See *humankind; inhabited earth.*

[3877] οἰκουργός *oikourgos* 1x *one who is occupied in domestic affairs,* Tit. 2:5* [3626]

[3880] οἰκτιρμός *oiktirmos* 5x *compassion; kindness,* in relieving sorrow and want, Phil. 2:1; Col. 3:12; Heb. 10:28; *favor, grace, mercy,* Rom. 12:1; 2 Cor. 1:3* [3628]

[3881] οἰκτίρμων *oiktirmōn* 3x *compassionate, merciful,* Lk. 6:36; Jas. 5:11* [3629]

[3882] οἰκτίρω *oiktirō* 2x also spelled οἰκτείρω, *to have compassion on, exercise grace* or *favor towards,* Rom. 9:15* [3627]

[3884] οἰνοπότης *oinopotēs* 2x *wine-drinking;* in a bad sense, *a wine-bibber, tippler,* Mt. 11:19; Lk. 7:34* [3630]

[3885] οἶνος *oinos* 34x *wine,* Mt. 9:17; Mk. 2:22; meton. *the vine and its clusters,* Rev. 6:6 met. οἶνος, *a potion,* οἶνος τοῦ θυμοῦ, *a furious potion,* Rev. 14:8, 10; 16:19; 17:2, 18:3 [3631] See *wine.*

[3886] οἰνοφλυγία *oinophlygia* 1x *drunkenness,* 1 Pet. 4:3* [3632]

[3887] οἴομαι *oiomai* 3x *to think, suppose, imagine, presume,* Jn. 21:25; Phil. 1:17. οἰέσθω in Jas. 1:7 formed from the contracted form οἶμαι* [3633]

[3888] οἷος *hoios* 14x *what, of what kind* or *sort, as,* Mt. 24:21; Mk. 9:3; οὐχ, οἷον, *not so as, not as implying,* Rom. 9:6 [3634]

[3890] ὀκνέω *okneō* 1x *to be slow; to delay, hesitate,* Acts 9:38* [3635]

[3891] ὀκνηρός *oknēros* 3x *slow; slothful, indolent, idle,* Mt. 25:26; Rom. 12:11; *tedious, troublesome,* Phil. 3:1* [3636]

[3892] ὀκταήμερος *oktaēmeros* 1x *on the eighth day,* Phil. 3:5* [3637]

[3893] ὀκτώ *oktō* 8x *eight,* Lk. 2:21; 9:28 [3638]

[3897] ὄλεθρος *olethros* 4x *perdition, destruction,* 1 Cor. 5:5, 1 Thess. 5:3; 2 Thess. 1:9; 1 Tim. 6:9* [3639]

[3898] ὀλιγοπιστία *oligopistia* 1x *littleness* or *imperfectness of faith,* Mt. 17:20* [570]

[3899] ὀλιγόπιστος *oligopistos* 5x *scant of faith, of little faith, one whose faith is small and weak,* Mt. 6:30; 8:26; 14:31; 16:18; Lk. 12:28* [3640]

[3900] ὀλίγος *oligos* 40x *little, small,* in number, etc.; pl. *few,* Mt. 7:14; 9:37; 20:16; Lk. 13:23; δἰ ὀλίγων, sc. λόγων, *in a few words, briefly,* 1 Pet. 5:12; *little* in time, *short, brief,* Acts 14:28; Rev. 12:12; πρὸς ὀλίγον, sc. χρόνον, *for a short time, for a little while,* Jas. 4:14; *little, small, light,* etc., in magnitude, amount, etc., Lk. 7:47; Acts 12:18; 15:2; ἐν ὀλίγῳ, *concisely, briefly,* Eph. 3:3; *almost,* Acts 26:28, 29 [3641] See *few; little; short; small.*

[3901] ὀλιγόψυχος *oligopsychos* 1x *fainthearted,* 1 Tim. 5:14* [3642]

[3902] ὀλιγωρέω *oligōreō* 1x *to neglect, regard slightly, make light of, despise,* Heb. 12:5* [3643]

[3903] ὀλίγως *oligōs* 1x *little, scarcely,* 2 Pet. 2:18* [3689]

[3904] ὀλοθρευτής *olothreutēs* 1x *a destroyer,* 1 Cor. 10:10* [3644]

[3905] ὀλοθρεύω *olothreuō* 1x also spelled ὀλεθρεύω, *to destroy, cause to perish,* Heb. 11:28* [3645]

[3906] ὁλοκαύτωμα *holokautōma* 3x *a holocaust, whole burnt-offering,* Mk. 12:33; Heb. 10:6, 8* [3646]

[3907] ὁλοκληρία *holoklēria* 1x *perfect soundness,* Acts 3:16* [3647]

[3908] ὁλόκληρος *holoklēros* 2x *whole, having all its parts, sound, perfect, complete in every part;* in NT *the whole,* 1 Thess. 5:23; morally, *perfect, faultless, blameless,* Jas. 1:4* [3648]

[3909] ὀλολύζω *ololyzō* 1x pr. *to cry aloud in invocation; to howl, utter cries of distress, lament, bewail,* Jas. 5:1* [3649]

[3910] ὅλος *holos* 109x *all, whole, entire,* Mt. 1:22; 4:23, 24 [3650] See *all; whole.*

[3911] ὁλοτελής *holotelēs* 1x *complete; all, the whole,* 1 Thess. 5:23* [3651]

[3912] Ὀλυμπᾶς *Olympas* 1x *Olympas,* pr. name, Rom. 16:15* [3652]

[3913] ὄλυνθος *olynthos* 1x *an unripe* or *unseasonable fig,* such as, shaded by the foliage, does not ripen at the usual season, but hangs on the trees during winter, Rev. 6:13* [3653]

[3914] ὅλως *holōs* 4x *wholly, altogether; actually, really,* 1 Cor. 5:1; 6:7; 15:29; with a negative, *at all,* Mt. 5:34* [3654]

[3915] ὄμβρος *ombros* 1x *rain, a storm of rain,* Lk. 12:54* [3655]

[3916] ὁμείρομαι *homeiromai* 1x also spelled ἱμείρομαι, *to desire earnestly, have a strong affection for,* 1 Thess. 2:8* [2442]

[3917] ὁμιλέω *homileō* 4x *to be in company with, associate with; to converse with, talk with,* Lk. 24:14, 15; Acts 20:11; 24:26* [3656]

[3918] ὁμιλία *homilia* 1x *intercourse, communication, converse,* 1 Cor. 15:33* [3657]

[3920] ὁμίχλη *homichlē* 1x *a mist, fog, a cloud,* 2 Pet. 2:17* [**]

[3921] ὄμμα *omma* 2x *the eye,* Mt. 20:34; Mk. 8:23* [3659]

[3923] ὀμνύω *omnyō* 26x *to swear,* Mt. 5:34; *to promise with an oath,* Mk. 6:23; Acts 2:30; 7:17 [3660] See *swear.*

[3924] ὁμοθυμαδόν *homothumadon* 11x *with one mind, with one accord, unanimously,* Acts 1:14; Rom. 15:6; *together, at once, at the same time,* Acts 2:1, 46; 4:24 [3661] See *together; unanimous.*

[3926] ὁμοιοπαθής *homoiopathēs* 2x *being affected in the same way* as another, *subject to the same incidents, of like infirmities, subject to the same frailties and evils,* Acts 14:15; Jas. 5:17* [3663]

[3927] ὅμοιος *homoios* 45x *like, similar, resembling,* Mt. 11:16; 13:31, 33, 44, 45, 47, 52; Jn. 8:55, et al. freq.; *like, of similar drift and force,* Mt. 22:39 [3664] See *like, liken; similar.*

[3928] ὁμοιότης *homoiotēs* 2x *likeness, similitude,* Heb. 4:15; 7:15* [3665]

[3929] ὁμοιόω *homoioō* 15x *to make like, cause to be like* or *resemble, assimilate;* pass. *to be made like, become like, resemble,* Mt. 6:8; 13:24; 18:23; *to liken, compare,* Mt. 7:24, 26; 11:16 [3666] See *compare; like, liken; similar.*

[3930] ὁμοίωμα *homoiōma* 6x pr. *that which is conformed* or *assimilated; form, shape, figure,* Rev. 9:7; *likeness, resemblance, similitude,* Rom. 1:23; 5:14; 6:5; 8:3; Phil. 2:7* [3667] See *image; liken; similarity.*

[3931] ὁμοίως *homoiōs* 30x *likewise, in a similar manner,* Mt. 22:26; 27:41 [3668] See *likewise; similar.*

[3932] ὁμοίωσις *homoiōsis* 1x pr. *assimilation; likeness, resemblance,* Jas. 3:9* [3669]

[3933] ὁμολογέω *homologeō* 26x *to speak in accordance, adopt the same terms of language; to engage, promise,* Mt. 14:7; *to admit, avow frankly,* Jn. 1:20; Acts 24:14; *to confess,* 1 Jn. 1:9; *to profess, confess,* Jn. 9:22; 12:42; Acts 23:8; *to avouch, declare openly and solemnly,* Mt. 7:23; in NT ὁμολογεῖν ἐν, *to accord belief,* Mt. 10:32; Lk. 12:8; *to accord approbation,* Lk. 12:8; from the Hebrew, *to accord praise,* Heb. 13:15 [3670] See *acknowledge; confess; promise.*

[3934] ὁμολογία *homologia* 6x *assent, consent; profession,* 2 Cor. 9:13; 1 Tim. 6:12, 13; Heb. 3:1; 4:14; 10:23* [3671]

[3935] ὁμολογουμένως *homologoumenōs* 1x *confessedly, avowedly, without controversy,* 1 Tim. 3:16* [3672]

[3937] ὁμότεχνος *homotechnos* 1x *to the same trade* or *occupation,* Acts 18:3* [3673]

[3938] ὁμοῦ *homou* 4x *together; in the same place,* Jn. 21:2; *together at the same time,* Jn. 4:36; 20:4; Acts 2:1* [3674]

[3939] ὁμόφρων *homophrōn* 1x *of like mind, of the same mind, like-minded,* 1 Pet. 3:8* [3675]

[3940] ὅμως *homōs* 3x *yet, nevertheless;* with μέντοι, *but nevertheless, but for all that,* Jn. 12:42; *even, though it be but,* 1 Cor. 14:7; Gal. 3:15* [3676]

[3941] ὄναρ *onar* 6x *a dream,* Mt. 1:20; 2:12, 13, 19, 22; 27:19* [3677]

[3942] ὀνάριον *onarion* 1x *a young donkey, a donkey's colt,* Jn. 12:14* [3678]

[3943] ὀνειδίζω *oneidizō* 9x *to censure, inveigh against,* Mt. 11:20; Mk. 16:14; *to reproach* or *revile,* Jas. 1:5; *to revile, insult with insulting language,* Mt. 5:11 [3679] See *insult; reproach.*

[3944] ὀνειδισμός *oneidismos* 5x *censure,* 1 Tim. 3:7; *reproach, reviling,* Rom. 15:3 [3680] See *insult; reproach.*

[3945] ὄνειδος *oneidos* 1x pr. *fame, report, character;* usually, *reproach, disgrace,* Lk. 1:25* [3681]

[3946] Ὀνήσιμος *Onēsimos* 2x *Onesimus,* pr. name, Col. 4:9; Phlm. 10* [3682]

[3947] Ὀνησίφορος *Onēsiphoros* 2x *Onesiphorus,* pr. name, 2 Tim. 1:16; 4:19* [3683]

[3948] ὀνικός *onikos* 2x *pertaining to a donkey;* μύλος ὀνικός, *a millstone turned by a donkey, a large* or *an upper millstone,* Mt. 18:6; Mk. 9:42* [3684]

[3949] ὀνίνημι *oninēmi* 1x optative, ὀναίμην, *to receive profit, pleasure,* etc.; with a gen., *to have joy of,* Phlm. 20* [3685]

[3950] ὄνομα *onoma* 231x *a name; the proper name* of a person, etc., Mt. 1:23, 25; 10:2; 27:32; *a* mere *name* or *reputation,* Rev. 3:1; in NT *a name* as the representative of a person, Mt. 6:9; Lk. 6:22; 11:2; *the name* of the author of a commission, delegated authority, or religious profession, Mt. 7:22; 10:22; 12:21; 18:5, 20; 19:29; 21:9; 28:19; Acts 3:16; 4:7, 12; εἰς ὄνομα, ἐν ὀνόματι, *on the score of being* possessor of a certain character, Mt. 10:41, 42; Mk. 9:41 [3686] See *name.*

[3951] ὀνομάζω *onomazō* 10x *to name,* Lk. 6:14; *to style, entitle,* Lk. 6:13; 1 Cor. 5:11; *to make mention of,* Eph. 5:3; *to make known,* Rom. 15:20; *to pronounce* in exorcism, Acts 19:13; in NT *to profess,* 2 Tim. 2:19 [3687] See *designate; name.*

[3952] ὄνος *onos* 5x *donkey, ass,* male or female, Mt. 21:2, 5, 7 [3688]

[3953] ὄντως *ontōs* 10x *really, in truth, truly,* Mk. 11:32; Lk. 23:47. [3689]

[3954] ὄξος *oxos* 6x *vinegar; a wine of sharp flavor, posca,* which was an ordinary beverage, and was often mixed with bitter herbs, etc., and this given to the condemned criminals in order to stupefy them, and lessen their sufferings, Mt. 27:48; Mk. 15:36; Lk. 23:36; Jn. 19:29, 30 [3690]

[3955] ὀξύς *oxys* 8x *sharp, keen,* Rev. 1:16; 2:12; 14:14, 17, 18; 19:15; *swift, nimble,* Rom. 3:15* [3691]

[3956] ὀπή *opē* 2x *a hole; a hole, vent, opening,* Jas. 3:11; *a hole, cavern,* Heb. 11:38* [3692]

[3957] ὄπισθεν *opisthen* 7x can function as an improper prep., *from behind, behind, after, at the back of,* Mt. 9:20; 15:23 [3693]

[3958] ὀπίσω *opisō* 35x can function as an improper prep., *behind, after, at one's back,* Mt. 4:10; Lk. 7:38; Rev. 1:10; τὰ ὀπίσω, *the things which are behind,* Phil. 3:13; ὀπίσω and εἰς τὰ ὀπίσω, *back, backwards,* Mt. 24:18; Mk. 13:16; Lk. 9:62, when an improper prep., takes the gen. [3694]

[3959] ὁπλίζω *hoplizō* 1x *to arm, equip;* mid. *to arm one's self, equip one's self,* 1 Pet. 4:1* [3695]

[3960] ὅπλον *hoplon* 6x *an implement,* Rom. 6:13; pl. τὰ ὅπλα, *arms, armor, weapons,* whether offensive or defensive, Jn. 18:3; Rom. 13:12; 2 Cor. 6:7; 10:4* [3696]

[3961] ὁποῖος *hopoios* 5x *what, of what sort* or *manner,* 1 Cor. 3:13; Gal. 2:6; 1 Thess. 1:9; Jas. 1:24; after τοιοῦτος, *as,* Acts 26:29* [3697]

[3963] ὅπου *hopou* 82x *where, in which place, in what place,* Mt. 6:19, 20, 21; Rev. 2:13; *whither, to what place,* Jn. 8:21; 14:4; ὅπου ἄν, or ἐάν, *wherever, in whatever place,* Mt. 24:28; *whithersoever,* Mt. 8:19; Jas. 3:4; met. *where, in which thing, state,* etc., Col. 3:11; *whereas,* 1 Cor. 3:3; 2 Pet. 2:11 [3699]

[3964] ὀπτάνομαι *optanomai* 1x *to be seen, appear,* Acts 1:3* [3700]

[3965] ὀπτασία *optasia* 4x *a vision, apparition,* Lk. 1:22; 24:23; Acts 26:19; 2 Cor. 12:1* [3701]

[3966] ὀπτός *optos* 1x *dressed by fire, roasted, broiled,* etc., Lk. 24:42* [3702]

[3967] ὀπώρα *opōra* 1x *autumn; the fruit season;* meton. *fruits,* Rev. 18:14* [3703]

[3968] ὅπως *hopōs* 53x can function as a conj., *how, in what way* or *manner, by what means,* Mt. 22:5; Lk. 24:20; conj. *that, in order that,* and ὅπως μή, *that not, lest,* Mt. 6:2, 4, 5, 16, 18; Acts 9:2, et al. freq. [3704]

[3969] ὅραμα *horama* 12x *a thing seen, sight, appearance,* Acts 7:31; *a vision,* Mt. 17:9; Acts 9:10, 12 [3705] See *vision.*

[3970] ὅρασις *horasis* 4x *seeing, sight; appearance, aspect, a vision,* Acts 2:17; Rev. 9:17; 4:3* [3706]

[3971] ὁρατός *horatos* 1x *visible,* Col. 1:16* [3707]

[3972] ὁράω *horaō* 454x pluperfect, ἑωράκειν, some list εἶδον as the second aorist of ὁράω, *to see, behold,* Mt. 2:2, et al. freq.; *to look,* Jn. 19:37; *to visit,* Jn.

16:22; Heb. 13:23; *to mark, observe,* Acts 8:23; Jas. 2:24; *to be admitted to witness,* Lk. 17:22; Jn. 3:36; Col. 2:18; with θεόν, *to be admitted into the more immediate presence of God,* Mt. 5:8; Heb. 12:14; *to attain to a true knowledge of God,* 3 Jn. 11; *to see to* a thing, Mt. 27:4; Acts 18:15; ὅρα, *see, take care,* Mt. 8:4; Heb. 8:5; pass. *to appear,* Lk. 1:11; Acts 2:3; *to reveal one's self,* Acts 26:16; *to present one's self,* Acts 7:26 [3708] See *appear; consider; perceive; see.*

[3973] ὀργή *orgē* 36x pr. *mental bent, impulse; anger, indignation, wrath,* Eph. 4:31; Col. 3:8; μετ᾽ ὀργῆς, *indignantly,* Mk. 3:5; *vengeance, punishment,* Mt. 3:7; Lk. 3:7; 21:23; Rom. 13:4, 5 [3709] See *anger; wrath.*

[3974] ὀργίζω *orgizō* 8x some list as deponent, ὀργίζομαι, *to provoke to anger, irritate;* pass. *to be angry, indignant, enraged,* Mt. 5:22; 18:34 [3710]

[3975] ὀργίλος *orgilos* 1x *prone to anger, irascible, passionate,* Tit. 1:7* [3711]

[3976] ὀργυιά *orgyuia* 2x *the space measured by the arms outstretched; a fathom,* Acts 27:28 (2x)* [3712]

[3977] ὀρέγω *oregō* 3x *to extend, stretch out;* mid. *to stretch one's self out, to reach forward to,* met. *to desire earnestly, long after,* 1 Tim. 3:1; Heb. 11:16; by impl. *to indulge in, be devoted to,* 1 Tim. 6:10* [3713]

[3978] ὀρεινός *oreinos* 2x *mountainous, hilly,* Lk. 1:39, 65* [3714]

[3979] ὄρεξις *orexis* 1x *desire, longing; lust, concupiscence,* Rom. 1:27* [3715]

[3980] ὀρθοποδέω *orthopodeō* 1x *to walk in a straight course; to be straightforward* in moral conduct, Gal. 2:14* [3716]

[3981] ὀρθός *orthos* 2x *erect, upright,* Acts 14:10; *plain, level, straight,* Heb. 12:13* [3717]

[3982] ὀρθοτομέω *orthotomeō* 1x *to cut straight; to set forth truthfully, without perversion* or *distortion,* 2 Tim. 2:15* [3718]

[3983] ὀρθρίζω *orthrizō* 1x *to rise early in the morning; to come with the dawn,* Lk. 21:38* [3719]

[3984] ὀρθρινός *orthrinos* 1x a later form of ὄρθριος, *of* or *belonging to the morning, morning,* Lk. 24:22* [3720]

[3986] ὄρθρος *orthros* 3x *the dawn; the morning,* Jn. 8:2; Acts 5:21; ὄρθος βαθύς, *the first streak of dawn, the early dawn,* Lk. 24:1* [3722]

[3987] ὀρθῶς *orthōs* 4x *straightly; rightly, correctly,* Mk. 7:35; Lk. 7:43; 10:28; 20:21* [3723]

[3988] ὁρίζω *horizō* 8x *to set bounds to, to bound; to restrict,* Heb. 4:7; *to settle, appoint definitively,* Acts 17:26; *to fix determinately,* Acts 2:23; *to decree, destine,* Lk. 22:22; *to constitute, appoint,* Acts 10:42; 17:31; *to characterize with precision, to set forth distinctively,* Rom. 1:4; absol. *to resolve,* Acts 11:29* [3724] See *appoint; decide; determine; set.*

[3990] ὅριον *horion* 12x *a limit, bound, border of a territory* or *country;* pl. τὰ ὅρια, *region, territory, district,* Mt. 2:16; 4:13; 8:34 [3725] See *region; vicinity.*

[3991] ὁρκίζω *horkizō* 2x *to put to an oath; to obtest, adjure, conjure,* Mk. 5:7; Acts 19:13* [3726]

[3992] ὅρκος *horkos* 10x *an oath,* Mt. 14:7, 9; 26:72; meton. *that which is solemnly promised, a vow,* Mt. 5:33 [3727] See *oath.*

[3993] ὁρκωμοσία *horkōmosia* 4x *the act of taking an oath; an oath,* Heb. 7:20, 21, 28* [3728]

[3994] ὁρμάω *hormaō* 5x pr. trans. *to put in motion, incite;* intrans. *to rush,* Mt. 8:32; Mk. 5:13; Lk. 8:33 [3729]

[3995] ὁρμή *hormē* 2x *impetus, impulse; assault, violent attempt,* Acts 14:5; met.

impulse of mind, purpose, will, Jas. 3:4 [3730]

[3996] ὅρμημα *hormēma* 1x *violent* or *impetuous motion; violence,* Rev. 18:21* [3731]

[3997] ὄρνεον *orneon* 3x *a bird, fowl,* Rev. 18:2; 19:17, 21* [3732]

[3998] ὄρνις *ornis* 2x *bird, fowl;* domestic *hen,* Mt. 23:37; Lk. 13:34* [3733]

[3999] ὁροθεσία *horothesia* 1x pr. *the act of fixing boundaries; a bound set, certain bound, fixed limit,* Acts 17:26* [3734]

[4001] ὄρος *oros* 63x *a mountain, hill,* Mt. 5:1, 14; 8:1; 17:20 [3735] See *hill; mountain.*

[4002] ὀρύσσω *oryssō* 3x *to dig, excavate,* Mt. 21:33; 25:18; Mk. 12:1* [3736]

[4003] ὀρφανός *orphanos* 2x *bereaved* of parents, *orphan,* Jas. 1:27; *bereaved, desolate,* Jn. 14:18 [3737]

[4004] ὀρχέομαι *orcheomai* 4x *to dance,* Mt. 11:6, 17; Mk. 6:22; Lk. 7:32* [3738]

[4005] ὅς *hos* 1,407x *who, which, what, that,* Mt. 1:16, 23, 25; in NT interrog. ἐφ᾽ ὅ, *wherefore, why,* Mt. 26:50; in NT ὅς μὲν ... ὅς δέ, for ὁ μὲν ... ὁ δέ, Mt. 21:35; 2 Cor. 2:16 [3739]

[4006] ὁσάκις *hosakis* 3x *as often as,* 1 Cor. 11:25, 26; Rev. 11:6* [3740]

[4008] ὅσιος *hosios* 8x pr. *sanctioned by the supreme law of God, and nature; pious, devout,* Tit. 1:8; *pure,* 1 Tim. 2:8; supremely *holy,* Acts 2:27; 13:35; Heb. 7:26; Rev. 15:4; 16:5; τὰ ὅσια, *pledged bounties, mercies,* Acts 13:34* [3741] See *holy.*

[4009] ὁσιότης *hosiotēs* 2x *piety, sacred observance of all duties towards God, holiness,* Lk. 1:75; Eph. 4:24* [3742]

[4010] ὁσίως *hosiōs* 1x *piously,* 1 Thess. 2:10* [3743]

[4011] ὀσμή *osmē* 6x *smell, odor; fragrant odor,* Jn. 12:3; Eph. 5:2; Phil. 4:18; met. 2 Cor. 2:14, 16* [3744] See *aroma; odor.*

[4012] ὅσος *hosos* 110x *as great, as much,* Mk. 7:36; Jn. 6:11; Heb. 1:4; 8:6; 10:25; ἐφ᾽ ὅσον χρόνον, *for how long a time, while, as long as,* Rom. 7:1; so, ἐφ᾽ ὅσον, sc. χρόνον, Mt. 9:15; ὅσον χρόνον, *how long,* Mk. 2:19; neut. ὅσον repeated, ὅσον ὅσον, used to give intensity to other qualifying words, e.g., μικρόν, *the very least, a very little while,* Heb. 10:37; ἐφ᾽ ὅσον, *in as much as,* Mt. 25:40, 45; καθ᾽ ὅσον, *by how much, so far as,* Heb. 3:3; or, *in as much as, as, so,* Heb. 7:20; 9:27; pl. ὅσα, *so far as, as much as,* Rev. 1:2; 18:7; *how great, how much, how many, what,* Mk. 3:8; 5:19, 20; *how many, as many as, all who,* 2 Cor. 1:20; Phil. 3:15; 1 Tim. 6:1; ὅσος ἄν, or ἐάν, *whoever, whatsoever,* Mt. 7:12; 18:18 [3745]

[4014] ὀστέον *osteon* 4x contracted form, ὀστοῦν, οῦ, τό, *a bone,* Mt. 23:27; Lk. 24:39; Jn. 19:36; Heb. 11:22* [3747]

[4015] ὅστις *hostis* 144x *whoever, whatever; whosoever, whatsoever,* Mt. 5:39, 41; 13:12; 18:4; its use in place of the simple relative is also required in various cases, which may be learned from the grammars; ἕως ὅτου, sc. χρόνου, *until,* Lk. 13:8; *while,* Mt. 5:25 [3748, 3755]

[4017] ὀστράκινος *ostrakinos* 2x *earthen, of earthenware,* 2 Cor. 4:7; 2 Tim. 2:20* [3749]

[4018] ὄσφρησις *osphrēsis* 1x *smell, the sense of smelling,* 1 Cor. 12:17* [3750]

[4019] ὀσφῦς *osphys* 8x *the loins,* Mt. 3:4; Mk. 1:6. On the accent see BDF, 13. [3751]

[4020] ὅταν *hotan* 123x *when, whenever,* Mt. 5:11; 6:2; Mk. 3:11; Rev. 4:9, et al. freq.; in NT *in case of, on occasion of,* Jn. 9:5; 1 Cor. 15:27; Heb. 1:6 [3752]

[4021] ὅτε *hote* 103x *when, at the time that, at what time,* Mt. 7:28; 9:25; Lk. 13:35, et al. freq. [3753]

[4022] ὅτι *hoti* 1,296x originally was the neuter of ὅστις, *that,* Mt. 2:16, 22, 23; 6:5, 16; often used pleonastically in reciting another's words, Mt. 9:18; Lk. 19:42; Acts 5:23; as a causal particle, *for that, for, because,* Mt. 2:18; 5:3, 4, 5; 13:13; *because, seeing that, since,* Lk. 23:40; Acts 1:17 [3754]

[4023] οὗ *hou* 24x *where, in what place,* Mt. 2:9; 18:20; *whither, to what place,* Lk. 10:1; 22:10; 24:28; οὗ ἐάν, *whithersoever,* 1 Cor. 16:6 [3757]

[4024] οὐ *ou* 1,623x negative adverb, originally the gen. of ὅς, spelled οὐκ if followed by a word beginning with a vowel and a smooth breathing, οὐχ if followed by a vowel and rough breathing, *not, no,* Mt. 5:37; 12:43; 23:37; for the peculiarities of its usage (especially as distinct from μή) consult a grammar [3756]

[4025] οὐά *oua* 1x expressive of insult and derision, *Ah! Ah!,* Mk. 15:29* [3758]

[4026] οὐαί *ouai* 46x *Wo! Alas!* Mt. 11:21; 18:7; 23:13, 14, 15, 16; ἡ οὐαί, subst., *a woe, calamity,* Rev. 9:12; 11:14 [3759] See *alas; woe.*

[4027] οὐδαμῶς *oudamōs* 1x *by no means,* Mt. 2:6* [3760]

[4028] οὐδέ *oude* 143x negative conj., *neither, nor, and not, also not,* Mt. 5:15; 6:15, 20, 26, 28; when single, *not even* Mt. 6:29; 8:10 [3761]

[4029] οὐδείς *oudeis* 227x latter form, οὐθείς (4032), *not one, no one, none, nothing,* Mt. 5:13; 6:24; 19:17; met. οὐδέν, *nothing, of no account, naught,* Jn. 8:54; Acts 21:24 [3762]

[4030] οὐδέποτε *oudepote* 16x *never,* Mt. 7:23; 21:16, 42, et al. freq. [3763]

[4031] οὐδέπω *oudepō* 4x *not yet, never yet, never,* Jn. 7:39; 19:41; 20:9; Acts 8:16* [3764]

[4032] οὐθείς *outheis* 7x see οὐδείς [3762]

[4033] οὐκέτι *ouketi* 47x *no longer, no more,* Mt. 22:46 [3765]

[4034] οὐκοῦν *oukoun* 1x *then, therefore;* used interrogatively, Jn. 18:37* [3766]

[4036] οὖν *oun* 499x *then, now then,* Mt. 13:18; Jn. 19:29; *then, thereupon,* Lk. 15:28; Jn. 6:14; *therefore, consequently,* Mt. 5:48: Mk. 10:9; it also serves to mark the resumption of discourse after an interruption by a parenthesis, 1 Cor. 8:4. Sometimes it is not translated. [3767]

[4037] οὔπω *oupō* 26x *not yet,* Mt. 15:17; 16:9; 24:6 Jn. 2:4 [3768]

[4038] οὐρά *oura* 5x *a tail,* Rev. 9:10 (2x), 19 (2x); 12:4* [3769]

[4039] οὐράνιος *ouranios* 9x *heavenly, celestial,* Mt. 6:14, 26, 32; 15:13 [3770] See *heaven, heavens; heavenly.*

[4040] οὐρανόθεν *ouranothen* 2x *from heaven,* Acts 14:17; 26:13* [3771]

[4041] οὐρανός *ouranos* 273x *heaven, the heavens, the visible heavens and all their phenomena,* Mt. 5:18; 16:1; 24:29, et al. freq.; *the air, atmosphere,* in which the clouds and tempests gather, the birds fly, etc., Mt. 6:26; 16:2, 3; *heaven* as the peculiar seat and abode of God, of angels, of glorified spirits, etc., Mt. 5:34, 45, 48; 6:1, 9, 10; 12:50; Jn. 3:13, 31; 6:32, 38, 41, 42, 50, 51, 58; in NT *heaven* as a term expressive of the Divine Being, His administration, etc., Mt. 19:14; 21:25; Lk. 20:4, 5; Jn. 3:27 [3772] See *heaven, heavens; sky.*

[4042] Οὐρβανός *ourbanos* 1x *Urbanus, Urban,* pr. name, Rom. 16:9* [3773]

[4043] Οὐρίας *ourias* 1x *Urias, Uriah,* pr. name (2 Sam. 11; 12:24), Mt. 1:6* [3774]

[4044] οὖς *ous* 36x *the ear,* Mt. 10:27; Mk. 7:33; Lk. 22:50; Acts 7:57 [3775] See *ear.*

[4045] οὐσία *ousia* 2x *substance, property, goods, fortune,* Lk. 15:12, 13* [3776]

[4046] οὔτε *oute* 87x *neither, nor,* Lk. 20:36; οὔτε ... οὔτε, or οὐτὲ ... οὔτε, *neither ... nor,* Lk. 20:35; Gal. 1:12; in NT also used singly in the sense of οὐδέ, *not even,* Mk. 5:3; Lk. 12:26; 1 Cor. 3:2 [3777]

[4047] οὗτος *houtos* 1,387x *this, this* person or thing, Mt. 3:3, 9, 17; 8:9; 10:2; 24:34, et al. freq.; used by way of contempt, *this fellow,* Mt. 13:55; 27:47; αὐτὸ τοῦτο, *this very thing, this same thing,* 2 Cor. 2:3; 7:11; εἰς αὐτὸ τοῦτο, and elliptically, αὐτὸ τοῦτο, *for this same purpose, on this account,* Eph. 6:18, 22; 2 Pet. 1:5; καὶ οὗτος, *and moreover,* Lk. 7:12; 16:1; 20:30; καὶ τοῦτο, *and that too,* 1 Cor. 6:6, 8; τοῦτο μὲν ... τοῦτο δέ, *partly ... partly,* Heb. 10:33 [3778, 5023, 5025, 5026, 5123, 5124, 5125, 5126, 5127, 5128, 5129, 5130]

[4048] οὕτως *houtōs* 208x *thus, in this way,* Mt. 1:18; 2:5; 5:16; et al. freq.; ὃς μὲν οὕτως, ὃς δὲ οὕτως, *one so, and another so, one in one way, and another in another,* 1 Cor. 7:7; *so,* Mt. 7:12; 12:40; 24:27, 37, et al. freq.; *thus, under such circumstances,* Acts 20:11; *in such a condition,* viz., one previously mentioned, Acts 27:17; 1 Cor. 7:26, 40; and, perhaps, Jn. 4:6; *in an ordinary way, at ease,* like Latin *sic,* perhaps, Jn. 4:6 [3779]

[4049] οὐχί *ouchi* 54x a strengthened form of οὐ, *not,* Jn. 13:10, 11; when followed by ἀλλά, *nay, not so, by no means,* Lk. 1:60; 12:51; used also in negative interrogations, Mt. 5:46, 47; 6:25 [3780]

[4050] ὀφειλέτης *opheiletēs* 7x *a debtor, one who owes,* Mt. 18:24; met. *one who is in any way bound,* or *under obligation* to perform any duty, Rom. 1:14; 8:12; 15:27; Gal. 5:3; in NT *one who fails in duty, a delinquent, offender,* Mt. 6:12; *a sinner,* Lk. 13:4, cf. v. 2* [3781] See *debtor; obligation.*

[4051] ὀφειλή *opheilē* 3x *a debt,* Mt. 18:32; met. *a duty, due,* Rom. 13:7; 1 Cor. 7:3* [3782]

[4052] ὀφείλημα *opheilēma* 2x *a debt; a due,* Rom. 4:4, in NT *a delinquency, offence, fault, sin,* Mt. 6:12, cf. v. 14* [3783]

[4053] ὀφείλω *opheilō* 35x *to owe, be indebted,* Mt. 18:28, 30, 34; *to incur a bond, to be bound to make discharge,* Mt. 23:16, 18; *to be bound* or *obliged* by what is due or fitting or consequently necessary, Lk. 17:10; Jn. 13:14; *to incur desert, to deserve,* Jn. 19:7; *to be due* or *fitting,* 1 Cor. 7:3, 36; from the Aramaic, *to be delinquent,* Lk. 11:4 [3784] See *ought; owe.*

[4054] ὄφελον *ophelon* 4x originally a ptcp (aor act ptcp nom sg neut) from ὀφείλω, used in NT as an interj. to introduce a wish that cannot be attained, *O that! Would that!* 1 Cor. 4:8; 2 Cor. 11:1; Gal. 5:12; Rev. 3:15* [3785]

[4055] ὄφελος *ophelos* 3x *profit, benefit, advantage,* 1 Cor. 15:32; Jas. 2:14, 16* [3786]

[4056] ὀφθαλμοδουλία *ophthalmodoulia* 2x also written ὀφθαλμοδουλεία, *eye-service, service rendered only while under inspection,* Eph. 6:6; Col. 3:22* [3787]

[4057] ὀφθαλμός *ophthalmos* 100x *an eye,* Mt. 5:29, 38; 6:23; 7:3, 4, 5; ὀφθαλμὸς πονηρός, *an evil eye, an envious eye, envy,* Mt. 20:15; Mk. 7:22; met. *the* intellectual *eye,* Mt. 13:15; Mk. 8:18; Jn. 12:40; Acts 26:18 [3788] See *eye.*

[4058] ὄφις *ophis* 14x *a serpent,* Mt. 7:10; 10:16; *an* artificial *serpent,* Jn. 3:14; used of *the devil* or *Satan,* Rev. 12:9, 14, 15; 20:2; met. *a man of serpentine character,* Mt. 23:33 [3789] See *serpent; snake.*

[4059] ὀφρῦς *ophrys* 1x *a brow, eyebrow; the brow* of a mountain, *edge* of a precipice, Lk. 4:29* [3790]

[4061] ὀχλέω *ochleō* 1x pr. *to mob; to disturb, trouble,* Acts 5:16* [3791]

[4062] ὀχλοποιέω *ochlopoieō* 1x *to collect a mob, create a tumult,* Acts 17:5* [3792]

[4063] ὄχλος *ochlos* 175x *a crowd, a confused multitude of people,* Mt. 4:25; 5:1; 7:28; spc. *the common people,* Jn. 7:49; *a multitude, great number,* Lk. 5:29; 6:17; Acts 1:15; by impl. *tumult, uproar,* Lk. 22:6; Acts 24:18 [3793] See *crowd; mob; multitude; number.*

[4065] ὀχύρωμα *ochurōma* 1x *a stronghold;* met. *an* opposing *bulwark* of error or vice, 2 Cor. 10:4* [3794]

[4066] ὀψάριον *opsarion* 5x *a little fish,* Jn. 6:9, 11; 21:9, 10, 13* [3795]

[4067] ὀψέ *opse* 3x can function as an improper prep., *late;* put for *the first watch, at evening,* Mk. 11:19; 13:35; ὀψὲ σαββάτων, *after the close of the Sabbath,* Mt. 28:1 [3796]

[4068] ὀψία *opsia* 15x *evening,* either before or after sundown [3798]

[4069] ὄψιμος *opsimos* 1x *late; latter,* Jas. 5:7; poetic and later prose for ὄψιος* [3797] See *evening.*

[4071] ὄψις *opsis* 3x *a sight; the face, countenance,* Jn. 11:44; Rev. 1:16; *external appearance,* Jn. 7:24* [3799]

[4072] ὀψώνιον *opsōnion* 4x *provisions; a stipend* or *pay* of soldiers, Lk. 3:14; 1 Cor. 9:7; *wages* of any kind, 2 Cor. 11:8; due *wages, a* stated *recompense,* Rom. 6:23* [3800]

[4074] παγιδεύω *pagideuō* 1x *to ensnare, entrap, entangle,* Mt. 22:15* [3802]

[4075] παγίς *pagis* 5x *a snare, trap,* Lk. 21:35; met. *device, wile,* 1 Tim. 3:7; 6:9; 2 Tim. 2:26; met. *a trap* of ruin, Rom. 11:9* [3803]

[4076] πάγος *pagos* 2x *a hill,* Ἄρειος πάγος, *Areopagus, the hill of Mars,* at Athens, Acts 17:19, 22 [697]

[4077] πάθημα *pathēma* 16x *what is suffered; suffering, affliction,* Rom. 8:18; 2 Cor. 1:5, 6, 7; Phil. 3:10; *emotion, passion,* Rom. 7:5; Gal. 5:24 [3804] See *suffering.*

[4078] παθητός *pathētos* 1x *passible, capable of suffering, liable to suffer;* in NT *destined to suffer,* Acts 26:23* [3805]

[4079] πάθος *pathos* 3x *suffering; an affection, passion,* especially sexual, Rom. 1:26 [3806]

[4080] παιδαγωγός *paidagōgos* 3x *a pedagogue, childtender,* a person, usually a slave or freedman, to whom the care of the boys of a family was committed, whose duty it was to attend them at their play, lead them to and from the public school, and exercise a constant superintendence over their conduct and safety; in NT an ordinary *director* or *minister* contrasted with an Apostle, as a pedagogue occupies an inferior position to a parent, 1 Cor. 4:15; a term applied to the Mosaic law, as dealing with men as in a state of mere childhood and tutelage, Gal. 3:24, 25* [3807]

[4081] παιδάριον *paidarion* 1x *a little boy, child; a boy, lad,* Jn. 6:9* [3808]

[4082] παιδεία *paideia* 6x *education, training up, nurture* of children, Eph. 6:4; *instruction, discipline,* 2 Tim. 3:16; in NT *correction, chastisement,* Heb. 12:5, 7, 8, 11* [3809]

[4083] παιδευτής *paideutēs* 2x *a preceptor, instructor, teacher,* pr. of boys; gener. Rom. 2:20; in NT *a chastiser,* Heb. 12:9* [3810]

[4084] παιδεύω *paideuō* 13x *to educate, instruct* children, Acts 7:22; 22:3; genr. παιδεύομαι, *to be taught, learn,* 1 Tim. 1:20; *to admonish, instruct by admonition,* 2 Tim. 2:25; Tit. 2:12; in NT *to chastise, chasten,* 1 Cor. 11:32; 2 Cor. 6:9; Heb. 12:6, 7, 10; Rev. 3:19; of criminals, *to scourge,* Lk. 23:16, 22* [3811] See *discipline; educate; punish; teach.*

[4085] παιδιόθεν *paidiothen* 1x *from childhood, from a child,* Mk. 9:21* [3812]

[4086] παιδίον *paidion* 52x *an infant, babe,* Mt. 2:8; but usually in NT as equiv. to παῖς, Mt. 14:21; Mk. 7:28, et al. freq.; pl. voc. used by way of endearment, *my* *dear children,* 1 Jn. 2:18; also as a term of familiar address, *children, my lads,* Jn. 21:5 [3813] See *child; little child.*

[4087] παιδίσκη *paidiskē* 13x *a girl, damsel, maiden; a female slave* or *servant,* Mt. 26:69; Mk. 14:66, 69 [3814] See *girl; servant girl.*

[4089] παίζω *paizō* 1x *to play in the manner of children; to sport, to practise the festive gestures* of idolatrous worship, 1 Cor. 10:7* [3815]

[4090] παῖς *pais* 24x *a child* in relation to parents, of either sex, Jn. 4:51; *a child* in respect of age, either male or female, and of all ages from infancy up to manhood, *a boy, youth, girl, maiden,* Mt. 2:16; 17:18; Lk. 2:43; 8:54; *a servant, slave,* Mt. 8:6, 8, 13, cf. v. 9; Lk. 7:7, cf. v. 3, 10; *an attendant, minister,* Mt. 14:2; Lk. 1:69; Acts 4:25; also, Lk. 1:54; or, perhaps, *a child* in respect of fatherly regard [3816] See *child.*

[4091] παίω *paiō* 5x *to strike, smite,* with the fist, Mt. 26:68; Lk. 22:64; with a sword, Mk. 14:47; Jn. 18:10; *to strike* as a scorpion, *to sting,* Rev. 9:5* [3817]

[4093] πάλαι *palai* 6x *of old, long ago,* Mt. 11:21; Lk. 10:13; Heb. 1:1; Jude 4; οἱ πάλαι, *old, former,* 2 Pet. 1:9; *some time since, already,* Mk. 15:44 [3819]

[4094] παλαιός *palaios* 19x *old, not new* or *recent,* Mt. 9:16, 17; 13:52; Lk. 5:36 [3820] See *old.*

[4095] παλαιότης *palaiotēs* 1x *oldness, obsoleteness,* Rom. 7:6* [3821]

[4096] παλαιόω *palaioō* 4x *to make old;* pass. *to grow old, to become worn,* Lk. 12:33; Heb. 1:11; met. *to treat as antiquated, to abrogate, supersede,* Heb. 8:13* [3822]

[4097] πάλη *palē* 1x *wrestling; struggle, contest,* Eph. 6:12* [3823]

[4098] παλιγγενεσία *palingenesia* 2x *a new birth; regeneration, renovation,* Mt. 19:28; Tit. 3:5. See unpublished Ph.D. dissertation, William D. Mounce, *The Origin of the New Testament Metaphor of Rebirth,* University of Aberdeen, Scotland* [3824] See *regeneration.*

[4099] πάλιν *palin* 141x pr. *back; again, back again,* Jn. 10:17; Acts 10:16; 11:10; *again* by repetition, Mt. 26:43; *again* in continuation, *further,* Mt. 5:33; 13:44, 45, 47, 18:19; *again, on the other hand,* 1 Jn. 2:8 [3825]

[4101] παμπληθεί *pamplēthei* 1x *the whole multitude together, all at once,* Lk. 23:18* [3826]

[4103] Παμφυλία *Pamphylia* 5x *Pamphylia,* a country of Asia Minor, Acts 2:10; 13:13; 14:24; 15:38; 27:5* [3828]

[4106] πανδοχεῖον *pandocheion* 1x *a public inn, place where travelers may lodge,* called in the East by the name of *menzil, khan, caravanserai,* Lk. 10:34* [3829]

[4107] πανδοχεύς *pandocheus* 1x *the keeper of a public inn* or *caravanserai, a host,* Lk. 10:35* [3830]

[4108] πανήγυρις *panēgyris* 1x pr. *an assembly of an entire people; a solemn gathering at a festival; a festive convocation,* Heb. 12:22* [3831]

[4109] πανοικεί *panoikei* 1x also spelled πανοικί, *with one's whole household* or *family,* Acts 16:34* [3832]

[4110] πανοπλία *panoplia* 3x *panoply, complete armor, a complete suit of armor,* both offensive and defensive, as the shield, sword, spear, helmet, breastplate, etc., Lk. 11:22; Eph. 6:11, 13* [3833]

[4111] πανουργία *panourgia* 5x *craft, cunning,* Lk. 20:23; 1 Cor. 3:19 [3834]

[4112] πανοῦργος *panourgos* 1x pr. *ready to do anything;* hence, *crafty, cunning, artful, wily,* 2 Cor. 12:16* [3835]

[4114] πανταχῇ *pantachē* 1x *everywhere,* Acts 21:28* [3837]

[4116] πανταχοῦ *pantachou* 7x *in all places, everywhere,* Mk. 16:20; Lk. 9:6 [3837]

[4117] παντελής *pantelēs* 2x *perfect, complete;* εἰς τὸ παντελές, adverbially, *throughout, through all time, ever,* Heb. 7:25; with a negative, *at all,* Lk. 13:11* [3838]

[4118] πάντῃ *pantē* 1x *everywhere; in every way, in every instance,* Acts 24:3* [3839]

[4119] πάντοθεν *pantothen* 3x *from every place, from all parts, on all sides, on every side, round about,* Mk. 1:45; Lk. 19:43; Heb. 9:4* [3840]

[4120] παντοκράτωρ *pantokratōr* 10x *almighty, omnipotent,* 2 Cor. 6:18; Rev. 1:8; 4:8 [3841] See *almighty.*

[4121] πάντοτε *pantote* 41x *always, at all times, ever,* Mt. 26:11; Mk. 14:7; Lk. 15:31; 18:1 [3842]

[4122] πάντως *pantōs* 8x *wholly, altogether; at any rate, by all means,* 1 Cor. 9:22; by impl. *surely, assuredly, certainly,* Lk. 4:23; Acts 21:22; 28:4; 1 Cor. 9:10; οὐ πάντως, *in nowise, not in the least,* Rom. 3:9; 1 Cor. 5:10; 16:12* [3843]

[4123] παρά *para* 194x (1) gen., *from,* indicating source or origin, Mt. 2:4, 7; Mk. 8:11; Lk. 2:1; οἱ παρ᾽ αὐτοῦ, *his relatives* or *kinsmen,* Mk. 3:21; τὰ παρ᾽ αὐτῆς πάντα, *all her substance, property,* etc., Mk. 5:26. (2) dat., *with, in, among,* etc., Mt. 6:1; 19:26; 21:25; 22:25; παρ᾽ ἑαυτῷ, a*t home,* 1 Cor. 16:2; *in the sight of, in the judgment* or *estimation of,* 1 Cor. 3:19; 2 Pet. 2:11; 3:8. (3) acc., motion, *by, near to, along,* Mt. 4:18; motion, *towards, to, at,* Mt. 15:30; Mk. 2:13; motion terminating in rest, *at, by, near, by the side of,* Mk. 4:1, 4; Lk. 5:1; 8:5; *in deviation from, in violation of, inconsistently with,* Acts 18:13; Rom. 1:26; 11:24; *above, more than,* Lk. 13:2, 4; Rom. 1:25. (4) Misc., after comparatives, Lk. 3:13; 1 Cor. 3:11; *except, save,* 2 Cor. 11:24; *beyond, past,* Heb. 11:11; *in respect of, on the score of,* 1 Cor. 12:15, 16 [3844]

[4124] παραβαίνω *parabainō* 3x pr. *to step by the side of; to deviate;* met. *to transgress, violate,* Mt. 15:2, 3; *to incur forfeiture,* Acts 1:25* [3845]

[4125] παραβάλλω *paraballō* 1x *to cast* or *throw by the side of;* absol., a nautical term, *to bring to, land,* Acts 20:15* [3846]

[4126] παράβασις *parabasis* 7x *a stepping by the side, deviation; a transgression, violation of law,* Rom. 2:23; 4:15 [3847] See *transgression.*

[4127] παραβάτης *parabatēs* 5x *transgressor, violator of law,* Rom. 2:25, 27; Gal. 2:18; Jas. 2:9, 11* [3848]

[4128] παραβιάζομαι *parabiazomai* 2x *to force; to constrain press* with urgent entreaties, Lk. 24:29; Acts 16:15* [3849]

[4129] παραβολεύομαι *paraboleuomai* 1x also spelled παραβουλεύομαι, *to stake* or *risk one's self,* Phil. 2:30* [3851]

[4130] παραβολή *parabolē* 50x *a placing one thing by the side of another; a comparing; a parallel case cited in illustration; a comparison, simile, similitude,* Mk. 4:30; Heb. 11:19; *a parable,* a short relation under which something else is figured, or in which that which is fictitious is employed to represent that which is real, Mt. 13:3, 10, 13, 18, 24, 31, 33, 34, 36, 53; 21:33, 45; 22:1; 24:32; in NT *a type, pattern, emblem,* Heb. 9:9; *a sentiment, grave and significant precept, maxim,* Lk. 14:7; *an obscure and enigmatical saying, anything expressed in remote and ambiguous terms,* Mt. 13:35; Mk. 7:17; *a proverb, adage,* Lk. 4:23 [3850] See *illustration; parable; proverb.*

[4132] παραγγελία *parangelia* 5x *a command, order, charge,* Acts 5:28; 16:24; *direction, precept,* 1 Thess. 4:2; 1 Tim. 1:5, 18* [3852]

[4133] παραγγέλλω *parangellō* 32x *to announce, notify; to command, direct, charge,* Mt. 10:5; Mk. 6:8, 8:6; Lk. 9:21; *to charge, entreat solemnly,* 1 Tim. 6:13 [3853] See *command; instruct; order.*

[4134] παραγίνομαι *paraginomai* 37x pluperfect, παραγεγόνει (3 sg), *to be by the side of; to come, approach, arrive,* Mt. 2:1; 3:13; Mk. 14:43; Lk. 7:4; seq. ἐπί, *to come upon* in order to seize, Lk. 22:52; *to come forth in public, make appearance,* Mt. 3:1; Heb. 9:11 [3854] See *arrive; come.*

[4135] παράγω *paragō* 10x *to lead beside;* intrans. *to pass along* or *by,* Mt. 20:30; Jn. 9:1; *to pass on,* Mt. 9:9, 27; intrans. and mid. *to pass away, be in a state of transition,* 1 Cor. 7:31; 1 Jn. 2:8, 17 [3855] See *pass.*

[4136] παραδειγματίζω *paradeigmatizō* 1x *to make an example of; to expose to ignominy and shame,* Heb. 6:6* [3856]

[4137] παράδεισος *paradeisos* 3x *a park, a forest where wild beasts were kept for hunting; a pleasure-park, a garden of trees of various kinds;* used in the LXX for *the Garden of Eden;* in NT the celestial *paradise,* Lk. 23:43; 2 Cor. 12:4; Rev. 2:7* [3857]

[4138] παραδέχομαι *paradechomai* 6x *to accept, receive,* met. *to receive, admit, yield assent to,* Mk. 4:20; Acts 15:4; 16:21; 22:18; 1 Tim. 5:19; in NT *to receive* or *embrace with favor, approve, love,* Heb. 12:6* [3858]

[4140] παραδίδωμι *paradidōmi* 119x pluperfect, παραδεδώκεισαν (3 pl), *to give over, hand over, deliver up,* Mt. 4:12; 5:25; 10:4, 17; *to commit, intrust,* Mt. 11:27; 25:14; *to commit, commend,* Acts 14:26; 15:40; *to yield up,* Jn. 19:30; 1 Cor. 15:24; *to abandon,* Acts 7:42; Eph. 4:19; *to stake, hazard,* Acts 15:26; *to deliver* as a matter of injunction, instruction, etc., Mk. 7:13; Lk. 1:2; Acts 6:14; absol. *to render a yield, to be matured,* Mk. 4:29 [3860] See *betray; hand over; pass down.*

[4141] παράδοξος *paradoxos* 1x *unexpected; strange, wonderful, astonishing,* Lk. 5:26* [3861]

[4142] παράδοσις *paradosis* 13x *delivery, handing over, transmission;* in NT *what is transmitted* in the way of teaching, *precept, doctrine,* 1 Cor. 11:2; 2 Thess. 2:15; 3:6; *tradition, traditionary law,* handed down from age to age, Mt. 15:2, 3, 6 [3862] See *tradition.*

[4143] παραζηλόω *parazēloō* 4x *to provoke to jealousy,* Rom. 10:19; *to excite to emulation,* Rom. 11:11, 14; *to provoke to indignation,* 1 Cor. 10:22* [3863]

[4144] παραθαλάσσιος *parathalassios* 1x *by the sea-side, situated on the seacoast, maritime,* Mt. 4:13* [3864]

[4145] παραθεωρέω *paratheōreō* 1x *to look at things placed side by side,* as in comparison, *to compare in thus looking, to regard less in comparison, overlook, neglect,* Acts 6:1* [3865]

[4146] παραθήκη *parathēkē* 3x *a deposit, a thing committed to one's charge, a trust,* 1 Tim. 6:20; 2 Tim. 1:12; 2 Tim. 1:14* [3866]

[4147] παραινέω *paraineō* 2x *to advise, exhort,* Acts 27:9, 22* [3867]

[4148] παραιτέομαι *paraiteomai* 12x *to entreat; to beg off, excuse one's self,* Lk. 14:18, 19; *to deprecate, entreat against,* Acts 25:11; Heb. 12:19; *to decline receiving, refuse, reject,* 1 Tim. 4:7; 5:11; Tit. 3:10; Heb. 12:25; *to decline, avoid, shun,* 2 Tim. 2:23 [3868] See *make excuses; reject; request.*

[4149] παρακαθέζομαι *parakathezomai* 1x *to sit down by,* Lk. 10:39* [3869]

[4151] παρακαλέω *parakaleō* 109x *to call for, invite to come, send for,* Acts 28:20; *to call upon, exhort, admonish, persuade,* Lk. 3:18; Acts 2:40; 11:23; *to beg, beseech, entreat, implore,* Mt. 8:5, 31; 18:29; Mk. 1:40; *to animate, encourage, comfort, console,* Mt. 2:18; 5:4; 2 Cor. 1:4, 6; pass. *to be cheered, comforted,* Lk. 16:25; Acts 20:12; 2 Cor. 7:13 [3870] See *ask; comfort; exhort; implore; summon.*

[4152] παρακαλύπτω *parakalyptō* 1x *to cover over, veil;* met. pass. *to be veiled* from comprehension, Lk. 9:45* [3871]

[4154] παράκειμαι *parakeimai* 2x *to lie near, be adjacent;* met. *to be at hand, be present,* Rom. 7:18, 21* [3873]

[4155] παράκλησις *paraklēsis* 29x *a calling upon, exhortation, incitement, persuasion,* Rom. 12:8; 1 Cor. 14:3; *hortatory instruction,* Acts 13:15; 15:31; *entreaty, importunity, earnest supplication,* 2 Cor. 8:4; *solace, consolation,* Lk. 2:25; Rom. 15:4, 5; 2 Cor. 1:3, 4, 5, 6, 7; *cheering and supporting influence,* Acts 9:31; *joy, gladness, rejoicing,* 2 Cor. 7:13; *cheer, joy, enjoyment,* Lk. 6:24 [3874] See *comfort; consolation; encouragement.*

[4156] παράκλητος *paraklētos* 5x *one called* or *sent for to assist another; an advocate, one who pleads the cause of another,* 1 Jn. 2:1; genr. *one present to render various beneficial service,* and thus *the Paraclete,* whose influence and operation were to compensate for the departure of Christ himself, Jn. 14:16, 26; 15:26; 16:7* [3875] See *advocate; counselor; helper.*

[4157] παρακοή *parakoē* 3x *an erroneous* or *imperfect hearing; disobedience,* Rom. 5:19; *a deviation from obedience,* 2 Cor. 10:6; Heb. 2:2* [3876]

[4158] παρακολουθέω *parakoloutheō* 3x *to follow* or *accompany closely; to accompany, attend, characterize,* Mk. 16:17; *to follow* with the thoughts, *trace,* Lk. 1:3; *to conform to,* 1 Tim. 4:6; 2 Tim. 3:10* [3877]

[4159] παρακούω *parakouō* 3x *to overhear,* Mk. 5:36; *to hear amiss, to fail to listen, neglect to obey, disregard,* Mt. 18:17 (2x)* [3878]

[4160] παρακύπτω *parakyptō* 5x *to stoop beside; to stoop down* in order to take a view, Lk. 24:12; Jn. 20:5, 11; *to bestow a close and attentive look, to look intently, to penetrate,* Jas. 1:25; 1 Pet. 1:12* [3879]

[4161] παραλαμβάνω *paralambanō* 49x pr. *to take to one's side; to take, receive to one's self,* Mt. 1:20; Jn. 14:3; *to take* with one's self, Mt. 2:13, 14, 20, 21; 4:5, 8; *to receive* in charge or possession, Col. 4:17; Heb. 12:28; *to receive* as a matter of instruction, Mk. 7:4; 1 Cor. 11:23; 15:3; *to receive, admit, acknowledge,* Jn. 1:11; 1 Cor. 15:1; Col. 2:6; pass. *to be carried off,* Mt. 24:40, 41; Lk. 17:34, 35, 36 [3880] See *accept; receive.*

[4162] παραλέγομαι *paralegomai* 2x *to gather* a course *along; to sail by, coast along,* Acts 27:8, 13* [3881]

[4163] παράλιος *paralios* 1x *adjacent to the sea, maritime;* ἡ παράλιος, sc. χώρα, *the sea coast,* Lk. 6:17* [3882]

[4164] παραλλαγή *parallagē* 1x *a shifting, mutation, change,* Jas. 1:17* [3883]

[4165] παραλογίζομαι *paralogizomai* 2x *to misreckon, make a false reckoning; to impose upon, deceive, delude, circumvent,* Col. 2:4; Jas. 1:22* [3884]

[4166] παραλυτικός *paralytikos* 10x *lame, palsied,* used only as a noun in NT, *paralytic,* Mt. 4:24; 8:6; 9:2, 6 [3885] See *lame; paralytic.*

[4168] παραλύω *paralyō* 5x *to unloose from proper fixity* or *consistency of substance; to enervate* or *paralyze* the body or limbs; pass. *to be enervated* or *enfeebled,* Heb. 12:12; pass. perf. part. παραλελυμένος, *paralytic,* Lk. 5:18, 24 [3886]

[4169] παραμένω *paramenō* 4x *to stay beside; to continue, stay, abide,* 1 Cor. 16:6; Heb. 7:23; met. *to remain constant in, persevere in,* Phil. 1:25; Jas. 1:25* [3887]

[4170] παραμυθέομαι *paramytheomai* 4x *to exercise a gentle influence by words; to soothe, comfort, console,* Jn. 11:19, 31; 1 Thess. 5:14; *to cheer, exhort,* 1 Thess. 2:12* [3888]

[4171] παραμυθία *paramythia* 1x *comfort, encouragement,* 1 Cor. 14:3* [3889]

[4172] παραμύθιον *paramythion* 1x *gentle cheering, encouragement,* Phil. 2:1* [3890]

[4174] παρανομέω *paranomeō* 1x *to violate* or *transgress the law,* Acts 23:3* [3891]

[4175] παρανομία *paranomia* 1x *violation of the law, transgression,* 2 Pet. 2:16* [3892]

[4176] παραπικραίνω *parapikrainō* 1x pr. *to incite to bitter feelings; to provoke;* absol. *to act provokingly, be rebellious,* Heb. 3:16* [3893]

[4177] παραπικρασμός *parapikrasmos* 2x *exasperation, provocation; rebellion,* Heb. 3:8, 15* [3894]

[4178] παραπίπτω *parapiptō* 1x pr. *to fall by the side of;* met. *to fall off* or *away from, make defection from,* Heb. 6:6* [3895]

[4179] παραπλέω *parapleō* 1x *to sail by* or *past* a place, Acts 20:16* [3896]

[4180] παραπλήσιος *paraplēsios* 1x pr. *near alongside;* met. *like, similar;* neut. παραπλήσιον, adverbially, *near to, nearly, with a near approach to,* Phil. 2:27* [3897]

[4181] παραπλησίως *paraplēsiōs* 1x *like, in the same* or *like manner,* Heb. 2:14* [3898]

[4182] παραπορεύομαι *paraporeuomai* 5x *to pass by the side of; to pass along,* Mt. 27:39; Mk. 2:23; 9:30; 11:20; 15:29* [3899]

[4183] παράπτωμα *paraptōma* 19x pr. *a stumbling aside, a false step;* in NT *a trespass, fault, offence, transgression,* Mt. 6:14, 15; Mk. 11:25, 26; Rom. 4:25; *a fall* in faith, Rom. 11:11, 12 [3900] See *sin; transgression; trespass.*

[4184] παραρρέω *pararreō* 1x *to flow beside; to glide aside from; to fall off* from profession, *decline* from steadfastness, *make forfeit* of faith, Heb. 2:1* [3901]

[4185] παράσημος *parasēmos* 1x *a distinguishing mark; an ensign* of a ship, Acts 28:11* [3902]

[4186] παρασκευάζω *paraskeuazō* 4x *to prepare, make ready,* 2 Cor. 9:2, 3; mid. *to prepare one's self, put one's self in readiness,* Acts 10:10; 1 Cor. 14:8* [3903]

[4187] παρασκευή *paraskeuē* 6x *a getting ready, preparation,* in NT *preparation* for a feast, *day of preparation,* Mt. 27:62; Mk. 15:42 [3904]

[4189] παρατείνω *parateinō* 1x *to extend, stretch out; to prolong, continue,* Acts 20:7* [3905]

[4190] παρατηρέω *paratēreō* 6x *to watch narrowly,* Acts 9:24; *to observe* or *watch insidiously,* Mk. 3:2; Lk. 6:7; 14:1; 20:20; *to observe scrupulously,* Gal. 4:10* [3906]

[4191] παρατήρησις *paratērēsis* 1x *careful watching, intent observation,* Lk. 17:20* [3907]

[4192] παρατίθημι *paratithēmi* 19x *to place by the side of,* or *near; to set before,* Mk. 6:41; 8:6, 7; Lk. 9:16; met. *to set* or *lay before, propound,* Mt. 13:24, 31; *to inculcate,* Acts 17:3; *to deposit, commit to the charge of, entrust,* Lk. 12:48; 23:46; *to commend,* Acts 14:23 [3908] See *commit; set before.*

[4193] παρατυγχάνω *paratynchanō* 1x *to happen, to chance upon, chance to meet,* Acts 17:17* [3909]

[4194] παραυτίκα *parautika* 1x *instantly, immediately;* ὁ, ἡ, τό, παραυτίκα, *momentary, transient,* 2 Cor. 4:17* [3910]

[4195] παραφέρω *parapherō* 4x *to carry past; to cause to pass away,* Mk. 14:36; Lk. 22:42; pass. *to be swept along,* Jude 12; *to be led away, misled, seduced,* Heb. 13:9* [3911]

[4196] παραφρονέω *paraphroneō* 1x *to be beside one's wits;* παραφρονῶν, *in foolish style,* 2 Cor. 11:23* [3912]

[4197] παραφρονία *paraphronia* 1x *madness, folly,* 2 Pet. 2:16* [3913]

[4199] παραχειμάζω *paracheimazō* 4x *to winter, spend the winter,* Acts 27:12; 28:11; 1 Cor. 16:6; Tit. 3:12* [3914]

[4200] παραχειμασία *paracheimasia* 1x *a wintering* in a place, Acts 27:12* [3915]

[4202] παραχρῆμα *parachrēma* 18x *at once, immediately,* Mt. 21:19, 20; Lk. 1:64 [3916] See *immediately.*

[4203] πάρδαλις *pardalis* 1x *a leopard* or *panther,* Rev. 13:2* [3917]

[4204] παρεδρεύω *paredreuō* 1x *to sit near; to attend, serve,* 1 Cor. 9:13* [4332]

[4205] πάρειμι *pareimi* 24x *to be beside; to be present,* Lk. 13:1; *to have come,* Mt. 26:50; Jn. 7:6; 11:28; Col. 1:6; *to be in possession,* Heb. 13:5; 2 Pet. 1:9, 12; part. παρών, οὖσα, όν, *present,* 1 Cor. 5:3; τὸ παρόν, *the present time, the present,* Heb. 12:11 [3918] See *(be) present.*

[4206] παρεισάγω *pareisagō* 1x *to introduce stealthily,* 2 Pet. 2:1* [3919]

[4207] παρείσακτος *pareisaktos* 1x *secretly introduced, brought in stealthily,* Gal. 2:4* [3920]

[4209] παρεισέρχομαι *pareiserchomai* 2x *to supervene,* Rom. 5:20; *to steal in,* Gal. 2:4* [3922]

[4210] παρεισφέρω *pareispherō* 1x *to bring in beside; to bring into play, exhibit in addition,* 2 Pet. 1:5* [3923]

[4211] παρεκτός *parektos* 3x can function as an improper prep., *without, on the outside; except,* Mt. 5:32; Acts 26:29; τὰ παρεκτός, *other matters,* 2 Cor. 11:28 [3924]

[4212] παρεμβάλλω *paremballō* 1x *to cast up, set up, throw up* a palisade, Lk. 19:43* [4016]

[4213] παρεμβολή *parembolē* 10x *an insertion besides;* later, *a marshalling* of an army; *an array* of battle, *army,* Heb. 11:34; *a camp,* Heb. 13:11, 13; Rev. 20:9; *a standing camp, fortress, citadel, castle,* Acts 21:34, 37; 22:24; 23:10, 16, 32* [3925] See *barracks; camp.*

[4214] παρενοχλέω *parenochleō* 1x *to trouble, harass,* Acts 15:19* [3926]

[4215] παρεπίδημος *parepidēmos* 3x *residing in a country not one's own, a sojourner, stranger,* Heb. 11:13; 1 Pet. 1:1; 2:11* [3927] See *alien; strange(r).*

[4216] παρέρχομαι *parerchomai* 29x *to pass beside, pass along, pass by,* Mt. 8:28; Mk. 6:48; *to pass, elapse,* as time, Mt. 14:15; Acts 27:19; *to pass away, be removed,* Mt. 26:39, 42; Mk. 14:35; met. *to pass away, disappear, vanish, perish,* Mt. 5:18; 24:34, 35; *to become vain, be rendered void,* Mt. 5:18; Mk. 13:31; trans. *to pass by, disregard, neglect,* Lk. 11:42; 15:29; *to come to the side of, come to,* Lk. 12:37; 17:7 [3928] See *disappear; pass away; pass by.*

[4217] πάρεσις *paresis* 1x *a letting pass; a passing over,* Rom. 3:25* [3929]

[4218] παρέχω *parechō* 16x *to hold beside; to hold out to, offer, present,* Lk. 6:29; *to confer, render,* Lk. 7:4; Acts 22:2; 28:2; Col. 4:1; *to afford, furnish,* Acts 16:16; 17:31; 19:24; 1 Tim. 6:17; *to exhibit,* Tit. 2:7; *to be the cause of, occasion,* Mt. 26:10; Mk. 14:6; Lk. 11:7 [3930] See *bother; provide.*

[4219] παρηγορία *parēgoria* 1x *exhortation; comfort, solace, consolation,* Col. 4:11* [3931]

[4220] παρθενία *parthenia* 1x *virginity,* Lk. 2:36* [3932]

[4221] παρθένος *parthenos* 15x *a virgin, maid,* Mt. 1:23; 25:1, 7, 11; Acts 21:9; in NT also masc., *chaste,* Rev. 14:4 [3933] See *virgin.*

[4222] Πάρθοι *Parthoi* 1x *a Parthian, a native of Parthia, in central Asia,* Acts 2:9 [3934]

[4223] παρίημι *pariēmi* 2x *to let pass beside, let fall beside; to relax,* Lk. 11:42; perf. pass. part. παρειμένος, *hanging down* *helplessly, unstrung, feeble,* Heb. 12:12* [3935]

[4225] παρίστημι *paristēmi* 41x pluperfect, παρειστήκειν, also formed as παριστάνω, trans. *to place beside; to have in readiness, provide,* Acts 23:24; *to range beside, to place at the disposal of,* Mt. 26:53; Acts 9:41; *to present* to God, *dedicate, consecrate, devote,* Lk. 2:22; Rom. 6:13, 19; *to prove, demonstrate, show,* Acts 1:3; 24:13; *to commend, recommend,* 1 Cor. 8:8; intrans. perf. παρέστηκα, part. παρεστώς, pluperf. παρειστήκειν, 2 aor. παρέστην, and mid., *to stand by* or *before,* Acts 27:24; Rom. 14:10; *to stand by, to be present,* Mk. 14:47, 69, 70; *to stand in attendance, attend,* Lk. 1:19; 1:24; of time, *to be present, have come,* Mk. 4:29; *to stand by* in aid, *assist, support,* Rom. 16:2 [3936] See *offer; place; present; stand.*

[4226] Παρμενᾶς *Parmenas* 1x *Parmenas,* pr. name, Acts 6:5* [3937]

[4227] πάροδος *parodos* 1x *a way by; a passing by;* ἐν παρόδῳ, *in passing, by the way,* 1 Cor. 16:7* [3938]

[4228] παροικέω *paroikeō* 2x *to dwell beside;* later, *to reside in a place as a stranger, sojourn, be a stranger* or *sojourner,* Lk. 24:18; Heb. 11:9* [3939]

[4229] παροικία *paroikia* 2x *a sojourning, temporary residence in a foreign land,* Acts 13:17; 1 Pet. 1:17* [3940]

[4230] πάροικος *paroikos* 4x *a neighbor;* later, *a sojourner, temporary resident, stranger,* Acts 7:6, 29; Eph. 2:19; 1 Pet. 2:11* [3941] See *alien; foreign(er); strange(r).*

[4231] παροιμία *paroimia* 5x *a byword, proverb, adage,* 2 Pet. 2:22; in NT *an obscure saying, enigma,* Jn. 16:25, 29; *a parable, similitude, figurative discourse,* Jn. 10:6* [3942]

[4232] πάροινος *paroinos* 2x pr. *pertaining to wine, drunken;* hence, *quarrelsome, insolent, overbearing,* 1 Tim. 3:3; Tit. 1:7* [3943]

[4233] παροίχομαι *paroichomai* 1x *to have gone by;* perf. part. παρῳχημένος, *by-gone,* Acts 14:16* [3944]

[4234] παρομοιάζω *paromoiazō* 1x *to be like, to resemble,* Mt. 23:27* [3945]

[4235] παρόμοιος *paromoios* 1x *nearly resembling, similar, like,* Mk. 7:13* [3946]

[4236] παροξύνω *paroxynō* 2x *to sharpen;* met. *to incite, stir up,* Acts 17:16; *to irritate, provoke,* 1 Cor. 13:5* [3947]

[4237] παροξυσμός *paroxysmos* 2x *an inciting, incitement,* Heb. 10:24; *a sharp fit of anger, sharp contention, angry dispute,* Acts 15:39* [3948]

[4239] παροργίζω *parorgizō* 2x *to provoke to anger, irritate, exasperate,* Rom. 10:19; Eph. 6:4* [3949]

[4240] παροργισμός *parorgismos* 1x *provocation to anger; anger excited, indignation, wrath,* Eph. 4:26* [3950]

[4241] παροτρύνω *parotrynō* 1x *to stir up, incite, instigate,* Acts 13:50* [3951]

[4242] παρουσία *parousia* 24x *presence,* 2 Cor. 10:10; Phil. 2:12; *a coming, arrival, advent,* Phil. 1:26; Mt. 24:3, 27, 37, 39; 1 Cor. 15:23 [3952] See *coming; presence.*

[4243] παροψίς *paropsis* 1x pr. *a dainty side dish;* meton. *a plate, platter,* Mt. 23:25* [3953]

[4244] παρρησία *parrēsia* 31x *freedom in speaking, boldness of speech,* Acts 4:13; παρρησίᾳ, as an adv., *freely, boldly,* Jn. 7:13, 26; so μετὰ παρρησίας, Acts 2:29; 4:29, 31; *license, authority,* Phlm. 8; *confidence, assurance,* 2 Cor. 7:4; Eph. 3:12; Heb. 3:6; 10:19; *openness, frankness,* 2 Cor. 3:12; παρρησίᾳ, and ἐν παρρησίᾳ, adverbially, *openly, plainly, perspicuously, unambiguously,* Mk. 8:32; Jn. 10:24; *publicly, before all,* Jn. 7:4 [3954] See *assurance; boldness; certainty; confidence.*

[4245] παρρησιάζομαι *parrēsiazomai* 9x *to speak plainly, freely, boldly, and confidently,* Acts 13:46; 14:3 [3955]

[4246] πᾶς *pas* 1,243x *all;* in the sg. *the whole, entire,* usually when the substantive has the article, Mt. 6:29; 8:32; Acts 19:26; *every,* only with an anarthrous subst., Mt. 3:10; 4:4; pl. *all,* Mt. 1:17, et al. freq.; πάντα, *in all respects,* Acts 20:35; 1 Cor. 9:25; 10:33; 11:2; by a Hebraism, a negative with πᾶς is sometimes equivalent to οὐδείς or μηδείς, Mt. 24:22; Lk. 1:37; Acts 10:14; Rom. 3:20; 1 Cor. 1:29; Eph. 4:29 [3956] See *all; each; every.*

[4247] πάσχα *pascha* 29x *the passover, the paschal lamb,* Mt. 26:17; Mk. 14:12; met. used of Christ, the true *paschal lamb,* 1 Cor. 5:7; *the feast of the passover, the day on which the paschal lamb was slain and eaten,* the 14th of Nisan, Mt. 26:18; Mk. 14:1; Heb. 11:28; more genr. *the whole paschal festival,* including the seven days of *the feast of unleavened bread,* Mt. 26:2; Lk. 2:41; Jn. 2:13 [3957] See *passover.*

[4248] πάσχω *paschō* 42x *to be affected by* a thing, whether good or bad, *to suffer, endure* evil, Mt. 16:21; 17:12, 15; 27:19; absol. *to suffer* death, Lk. 22:15; 24:26 [3958] See *suffer.*

[4249] Πάταρα *Patara* 1x *Patara,* a city on the seacoast of Lycia, in Asia Minor, Acts 21:1* [3959]

[4250] πατάσσω *patassō* 10x *to strike, beat upon; to smite, wound,* Mt. 26:51; Lk. 22:49, 50; by impl. *to kill, slay,* Mt. 26:31; Mk. 14:27; Acts 7:24; *to strike gently,* Acts 12:7; from the Hebrew, *to smite* with disease, plagues, etc., Acts 12:23; Rev. 11:6; 19:15* [3960] See *hit; strike.*

[4251] πατέω *pateō* 5x intrans. *to tread,* Lk. 10:19; trans. *to tread* the winepress, Rev. 14:20; 19:15; *to trample,* Lk. 21:24; Rev. 11:2* [3961]

[4252] πατήρ *patēr* 413x *a father,* Mt. 2:22; 4:21, 22; spc. used of God, as the *Father* of man by creation, preservation, etc., Mt. 5:16, 45, 48; and peculiarly as the *Father* of our Lord Jesus Christ, Mt. 7:21; 2 Cor. 1:3; *the founder of a race, remote progenitor, forefather, ancestor,* Mt. 3:9; 23:30, 32; *an elder, senior, father* in age, 1 Jn. 2:13, 14; *a* spiritual *father,* 1 Cor. 4:15; *father* by origination, Jn. 8:44; Heb. 12:9; used as an appellation of honor, Mt. 23:9; Acts 7:2 [3962] See *ancestor; father.*

[4253] Πάτμος *Patmos* 1x *Patmos,* an island in the Aegean sea, Rev. 1:9* [3963]

[4255] πατριά *patria* 3x *descent, lineage; a family, tribe, race,* Lk. 2:4; Acts 3:25; Eph. 3:15* [3965]

[4256] πατριάρχης *patriarchēs* 4x *a patriarch, head* or *founder of a family,* Acts 2:29; 7:8, 9; Heb. 7:4* [3966]

[4257] πατρικός *patrikos* 1x *from fathers* or *ancestors, ancestral, paternal,* Gal. 1:14* [3967]

[4258] πατρίς *patris* 8x *one's native place, country,* or *city,* Mt. 13:54, 57; Mk. 6:1, 4; Lk. 4:23, 24; Jn. 4:44; *a* heavenly *country,* Heb. 11:14* [3968]

[4259] Πατροβᾶς *Patrobas* 1x *Patrobas,* pr. name, Rom. 16:14* [3969]

[4260] πατρολῴας *patrolōas* 1x also spelled πατραλῴας, *one who kills one's father, a patricide,* 1 Tim. 1:9* [3964]

[4261] πατροπαράδοτος *patroparadotos* 1x *handed down* or *received by tradition from one's fathers* or *ancestors,* 1 Pet. 1:18* [3970]

[4262] πατρῷος *patrōos* 3x *received from one's ancestors, paternal, ancestral,* Acts 22:3; 24:14; 28:17* [3971]

[4263] Παῦλος *Paulos* 158x *Paulus, Paul,* pr. name. (1) *Paul, the Apostle,* Acts 13:9, et al. freq. (2) *Sergius Paulus, the deputy* or *proconsul of Cyprus,* Acts 13:7 [3972]

[4264] παύω *pauō* 15x *to cause to pause* or *cease, restrain, prohibit,* 1 Pet. 3:10; mid. perf. πέπαυται, *to cease, stop, leave off, desist, refrain,* 1 Pet. 4:1 [3973] See *finish; stop.*

[4265] Πάφος *Paphos* 2x *Paphos,* the chief city in the island of Cyprus [3974]

[4266] παχύνω *pachunō* 2x *to fatten, make gross;* met. pass. *to be rendered gross, dull, unfeeling,* Mt. 13:15; Acts 28:27* [3975]

[4267] πέδη *pedē* 3x *a fetter, shackle,* Mk. 5:4; Lk. 8:29* [3976]

[4268] πεδινός *pedinos* 1x *level, flat,* Lk. 6:17* [3977]

[4269] πεζεύω *pezeuō* 1x pr. *to travel on foot; to travel by land,* Acts 20:13* [3978]

[4270] πεζῇ *pezē* 2x *on foot,* or, *by land,* Mt. 14:13; Mk. 6:33 [3979]

[4272] πειθαρχέω *peitharcheō* 4x *to obey* one *in authority,* Acts 5:29, 32; Tit. 3:1; genr. *to obey, follow,* or *conform to advice,* Acts 27:21* [3980]

[4273] πειθός *peithos* 1x also spelled πιθός, *persuasive, skillful,* 1 Cor. 2:4* [3981]

[4275] πείθω *peithō* 52x pluperfect, ἐπεποίθειν, *to persuade, seek to persuade, endeavor to convince,* Acts 18:4; 19:8, 26; 28:23; *to persuade, influence by persuasion,* Mt. 27:20; Acts 13:43; 26:28; *to incite, instigate,* Acts 14:19; *to appease, render tranquil, to quiet,* 1 Jn. 3:19; *to strive to conciliate, aspire to the favor of,* Gal. 1:10; *to pacify, conciliate, win over,* Mt. 28:14; Acts 12:20; pass. and mid. *to be persuaded of, be confident of,* Lk. 20:6; Rom. 8:38; Heb. 6:9; *to suffer one's self to be persuaded, yield to persuasion, to be induced,* Acts 21:14; *to be convinced, to believe, yield belief,* Lk. 16:31; Acts 17:4; *to assent, listen to, obey, follow,* Acts 5:36, 37, 40; 2 perf. πέποιθα, to *be assured, be confident,* 2 Cor. 2:3; Phil. 1:6; Heb. 13:18; *to confide in, trust, rely on, place hope and confidence in,* Mt. 27:43; Mk. 10:24; Rom. 2:19 [3982] See *convince; persuade.*

[4277] πεινάω *peinaō* 23x *to hunger, be hungry,* Mt. 4:2; Mk. 11:12; *to be exposed to hunger, be famished,* 1 Cor. 4:11; Phil. 4:12; met. *to hunger after, desire earnestly, long for,* Mt. 5:6 [3983] See *hungry.*

[4278] πεῖρα *peira* 2x *a trial, attempt, endeavor;* λαμβάνειν πεῖραν, *to attempt,* Heb. 11:29; also, *to experience,* Heb. 11:36* [3984]

[4279] πειράζω *peirazō* 38x *to make proof* or *trial of, put to the proof,* whether with good or mischievous intent, Mt. 16:1; 22:35; absol. *to attempt,* Acts 16:7; 24:6; in NT *to tempt,* Mt. 4:1; *to try, subject to trial,* 1 Cor. 10:13 [3985] See *attempt; tempt; test; try.*

[4280] πειρασμός *peirasmos* 21x *a putting to the proof, proof, trial,* 1 Pet. 4:12; Heb. 3:8; direct *temptation* to sin, Lk. 4:13; *trial, temptation,* Mt. 6:13; 26:41; 1 Cor. 10:13; *trial, calamity, affliction,* Lk. 22:28 [3986] See *temptation; trial.*

[4281] πειράω *peiraō* 1x *to try, attempt, essay, endeavor,* Acts 26:21* [3987]

[4282] πεισμονή *peismonē* 1x *a yielding to persuasion, assent,* Gal. 5:8* [3988]

[4283] πέλαγος *pelagos* 2x *the deep, the open sea,* Mt. 18:6; *a sea,* distinguished from the sea in general, and named from an adjacent country, Acts 27:5* [3989]

[4284] πελεκίζω *pelekizō* 1x *to strike* or *cut with an axe; to behead,* Rev. 20:4* [3990]

[4286] πέμπτος *pemptos* 4x *fifth,* Rev. 6:9; 9:1; 16:10; 21:20* [3991]

[4287] πέμπω *pempō* 79x *to send, to despatch on any message, embassy, business,* etc., Mt. 2:8; 11:2; 14:10; *to transmit,* Acts 11:29; Rev. 1:11; *to dismiss, permit to go,* Mk. 5:12; *to send in* or *among,* 2 Thess. 2:11; *to thrust in,* or *put forth,* Rev. 14:15, 18 [3992] See *send.*

[4288] πένης *penēs* 1x pr. *one who labors for his bread; poor, needy,* 2 Cor. 9:9* [3993]

[4289] πενθερά *penthera* 6x *a mother-in-law,* Mt. 8:14; 10:35; Mk. 1:30; Lk. 4:38; 12:53* [3994]

[4290] πενθερός *pentheros* 1x *a father-in-law,* Jn. 18:13* [3995]

[4291] πενθέω *pentheō* 10x trans. *to lament over,* 2 Cor. 12:21; absol. *to lament, be sad, mourn,* Mt. 5:4; 9:15; Mk. 16:10; mid. *to bewail one's self, to feel guilt,* 1 Cor. 5:2 [3996] See *bewail; mourn.*

[4292] πένθος *penthos* 5x *mourning, sorrow, sadness, grief,* Jas. 4:9 [3997]

[4293] πενιχρός *penichros* 1x *poor, needy,* Lk. 21:2* [3998]

[4294] πεντάκις *pentakis* 1x *five times,* 2 Cor. 11:24* [3999]

[4295] πεντακισχίλιοι *pentakischilioi* 6x *five times one thousand, five thousand,* Mt. 14:21; 16:9 [4000]

[4296] πεντακόσιοι *pentakosioi* 2x *five hundred,* Lk. 7:41; 1 Cor. 15:6* [4001]

[4297] πέντε *pente* 38x *five,* Mt. 14:17, 19; 16:9 [4002] See *five.*

[4298] πεντεκαιδέκατος *pentekaidekatos* 1x *fifteenth,* Lk. 3:1* [4003]

[4299] πεντήκοντα *pentēkonta* 7x *fifty,* Mk. 6:40; Lk. 7:41 [4004]

[4300] πεντηκοστή *pentēkostē* 3x *Pentecost,* or *the Feast of Weeks;* one of the three great Jewish festivals, so called because it was celebrated on the *fiftieth* day, reckoning from the second day of the feast of unleavened bread, i.e., from the 16th day of Nisan, Acts 2:1; 20:16; 1 Cor. 16:8* [4005] See *Pentecost.*

[4301] πεποίθησις *pepoithēsis* 6x *trust, confidence, reliance,* 2 Cor. 1:15 [4006]

[4304] περαιτέρω *peraiterō* 1x compar. adv. of πέραν, Acts 19:39* [4012 + 2087]

[4305] πέραν *peran* 23x can function as an improper prep., *across, beyond, over, on the other side,* Mt. 4:15, 25; 19:1; Jn. 6:1, 17; ὁ, ἡ, τό, πέραν, *farther, on the farther side,* and τὸ πέραν, *the farther side, the other side,* Mt. 8:18, 28; 14:22 [4008]

[4306] πέρας *peras* 4x *an extremity, end,* Mt. 12:42; Lk. 11:31; Rom. 10:18; *an end, conclusion, termination,* Heb. 6:16* [4009]

[4307] Πέργαμος *Pergamos* 2x *Pergamus,* a city of Mysia, in Asia Minor, Rev. 1:11; 2:12* [4010]

[4308] Πέργη *Pergē* 3x *Perga,* the chief city of Pamphylia, in Asia Minor, Acts 13:13f.; 14:25 [4011]

[4309] περί *peri* 333x pr. of place, (1) gen., *about, around; about, concerning, respecting,* Mt. 2:8; 11:10; 22:31; Jn. 8:18; Rom. 8:3, et al. freq.; (2) acc., of place, *about, around, round about,* Mt. 3:4; Mk. 3:34; Lk. 13:8; οἱ περί τινα, *the companions* of a person, Lk. 22:49; *a person and his companions,* Acts 13:13; simply *a person,* Jn. 11:19; τὰ περί τινα, *the condition, circumstances of* any one, Phil. 2:23; of time, *about,* Mt. 20:3, 5, 6, 9; *about, concerning, respecting, touching,* Lk. 10:40; 1 Tim. 1:19; 6:21; Tit. 2:7 [4012]

[4310] περιάγω *periagō* 6x *to lead around, carry about* Acts 13:11 in one's company, 1 Cor. 9:5; *to traverse,* Mt. 4:23; 9:35; 23:15; Mk. 6:6 [4013]

[4311] περιαιρέω *periaireō* 5x *to take off, lift off, remove,* 2 Cor. 3:16; *to cast off,* Acts 27:40; met. *to cut off* hope, Acts 27:20; met. *to take away* sin, *remove the guilt* of sin, *make expiation for* sin, Heb. 10:11 [4014]

[4312] περιάπτω *periaptō* 1x *to light a fire, kindle,* Lk. 22:55* [681]

[4313] περιαστράπτω *periastraptō* 2x *to lighten around, shine like lightning around,* Acts 9:3; 22:6* [4015]

[4314] περιβάλλω *periballō* 23x *to cast around; to clothe,* Mt. 25:36, 38, 43; mid. *to clothe one's self, to be clothed,* Mt. 6:29, 31; Lk. 23:11; Jn. 19:2; Acts 12:8; Rev. 4:4 [4016] See *clothe; dress; wear.*

[4315] περιβλέπω *periblepō* 7x trans. *to look around upon,* Mk. 3:5, 34; 11:11; Lk. 6:10; absol. *to look around,* Mk. 5:32; 9:8; 10:23* [4017]

[4316] περιβόλαιον *peribolaion* 2x *that which is thrown around* any one, *clothing,* covering; *a cloak,* Heb. 1:12; *a covering,* 1 Cor. 11:15* [4018]

[4317] περιδέω *perideō* 1x pluperfect, περιεδέδετο (pass., 3 sg), *to bind round about;* pass. *to be bound around, be bound up,* Jn. 11:44* [4019]

[4318] περιεργάζομαι *periergazomai* 1x *to do a thing with excessive* or *superfluous care; to be a busybody,* 2 Thess. 3:11* [4020]

[4319] περίεργος *periergos* 2x *over careful; officious, a busybody,* 1 Tim. 5:13; in NT περίεργα, *magic arts, sorcery,* Acts 19:19* [4021]

[4320] περιέρχομαι *perierchomai* 3x *to go about, wander about, rove,* Acts 19:13; Heb. 11:37; *to go about, visit* from house to house, 1 Tim. 5:13* [4022]

[4321] περιέχω *periechō* 2x *to encompass, enclose;* met. *to encompass, seize on* the mind, Lk. 5:9; περιέχει, impers. *it is contained, it is among the contents* of a writing, 1 Pet. 2:6* [4023]

[4322] περιζώννυμι *perizōnnymi* 6x also spelled περιζωννύω, *to bind around with a girdle, gird;* in NT mid. *to gird one's self* in preparation for bodily motion and exertion, Lk. 12:37; 17:8; *to wear a girdle,* Rev. 1:13; 15:6 [4024]

[4324] περίθεσις *perithesis* 1x *a putting on, wearing* of dress, etc., 1 Pet. 3:3* [4025]

[4325] περιΐστημι *periistēmi* 4x *to place around;* intrans. 2 aor. περιέστην, perf. part. περιεστώς, *to stand around,* Jn. 11:42; Acts 25:7; mid. *to keep aloof from, avoid, shun,* 2 Tim. 2:16; Tit. 3:9* [4026]

[4326] περικάθαρμα *perikatharma* 1x pr. *filth;* met. *refuse, outcast,* 1 Cor. 4:13* [4027]

[4328] περικαλύπτω *perikalyptō* 3x *to cover round about, cover over; to cover* the face, Mk. 14:65; *to blindfold,* Lk. 22:64; pass. *to be overlaid,* Heb. 9:4* [4028]

[4329] περίκειμαι *perikeimai* 5x *to lie around, be surround,* Heb. 12:1; *to be hung around,* Mk. 9:42; Lk. 17:2; *to have around one's self, to wear,* Acts 28:20; *to be in submission to,* Heb. 5:2* [4029]

[4330] περικεφαλαία *perikephalaia* 2x *a helmet,* Eph. 6:17; 1 Thess. 5:8* [4030]

[4331] περικρατής *perikratēs* 1x *overpowering;* περικρατὴς γενέσθαι, *to become master of, to secure,* Acts 27:16* [4031]

[4332] περικρύβω *perikrybō* 1x also spelled περικρύπτω, *to hide* or *keep from sight, to conceal by envelopment; to conceal,* Lk. 1:24* [4032]

[4333] περικυκλόω *perikykloō* 1x *to encircle, surround,* Lk. 19:43* [4033]

[4334] περιλάμπω *perilampō* 2x *to shine around,* Lk. 2:9; Acts 26:13* [4034]

[4335] περιλείπομαι *perileipomai* 2x *to leave remaining;* pass. *to remain, survive,* 1 Thess. 4:15, 17* [4035]

[4337] περίλυπος *perilypos* 5x *greatly grieved, exceedingly sorrowful,* Mt. 26:38; Mk. 14:34 [4036]

[4338] περιμένω *perimenō* 1x *to await, wait for,* Acts 1:4* [4037]

[4339] πέριξ *perix* 1x *neighboring,* Acts 5:16* [4038]

[4340] περιοικέω *perioikeō* 1x *to dwell around,* or *in the vicinity; to be a neighbor,* Lk. 1:65* [4039]

[4341] περίοικος *perioikos* 1x *one who dwells in the vicinity, a neighbor,* Lk. 1:58* [4040]

[4342] περιούσιος *periousios* 1x *chosen; peculiar, special,* Tit. 2:14* [4041]

[4343] περιοχή *periochē* 1x lit., *a compass, circumference, contents;* fig., *a section, a portion* of Scripture, Acts 8:32* [4042]

[4344] περιπατέω *peripateō* 95x pluperfect, περι[ε]πεπατήκει (3 sg), *to walk,*

walk about, Mt. 9:5; 11:5; 14:25, 26, 29; *to rove, roam,* 1 Pet. 5:8; with μετά, *to accompany, follow*, Jn. 6:66; Rev. 3:4; *to walk, frequent* a locality, Jn. 7:1; 11:54; from the Hebrew, *to maintain a* certain *walk* of life and conduct, Gal. 5:16; Eph. 2:10 [4043] See *behave; live; walk.*

[4345] περιπείρω *peripeirō* 1x *to put on a spit, transfix;* met. *to pierce, wound deeply,* 1 Tim. 6:10* [4044]

[4346] περιπίπτω *peripiptō* 3x *to fall around* or *upon, to fall in with,* Lk. 10:30; *to fall into, light upon,* Acts 27:41; *to be involved in,* Jas. 1:2* [4045]

[4347] περιποιέω *peripoieō* 3x *to cause to remain over and above, to reserve, save,* Lk. 17:33; mid. *to acquire, gain, earn,* 1 Tim. 3:13; *to purchase,* Acts 20:28* [4046]

[4348] περιποίησις *peripoiēsis* 5x *a laying up, keeping; an acquiring* or *obtaining, acquisition,* 1 Thess. 5:9; 2 Thess. 2:14; *a saving, preservation,* Heb. 10:39; *a peculiar possession, specialty,* Eph. 1:14; 1 Pet. 2:9* [4047]

[4351] περιρήγνυμι *perirēgnymi* 1x also spelled περιρρήγνυμι, *to break* or *tear all around; to strip off,* Acts 16:22* [4048]

[4352] περισπάω *perispaō* 1x *to draw off from around; to wheel about; to distract;* pass. *to be distracted, over busied,* Lk. 10:40* [4049]

[4353] περισσεία *perisseia* 4x *superabundance,* Rom. 5:17; 2 Cor. 8:2; 10:15; Jas. 1:21* [4050]

[4354] περίσσευμα *perisseuma* 5x *more than enough, residue over and above,* Mk. 8:8; *abundance, exuberance,* Mt. 12:34; Lk. 6:45; *superabundance, affluence,* 2 Cor. 8:14* [4051]

[4355] περισσεύω *perisseuō* 39x *to be over and above, to be superfluous,* Mt. 14:20; Mk. 12:44; Lk. 21:4; *to exist in full quantity, to abound, be abundant,* Rom. 5:15; 2 Cor. 1:5; *to increase, be augmented,* Acts 16:5; *to be advanced, be rendered more prominent,* Rom. 3:7; of persons, *to be abundantly gifted, richly furnished, abound,* Lk. 15:17; Rom. 15:13; 1 Cor. 14:12; 2 Cor. 8:7; *to be possessed of a full sufficiency,* Phil. 4:12, 18; *to abound* in performance, 1 Cor. 15:58; *to be a gainer,* 1 Cor. 8:8; in NT trans., *to cause to be abundant,* 2 Cor. 4:15; 9:8; Eph. 1:8; *to cause to be abundantly furnished, cause to abound,* 1 Thess. 3:12; pass. *to be gifted with abundance,* Mt. 13:12; 25:29 [4052] See *abound; exceed; left over; overflow.*

[4356] περισσός *perissos* 6x *over and above,* Mt. 5:37; *superfluous,* 2 Cor. 9:1; *extraordinary,* Mt. 5:47; compar. *more, greater,* Mt. 11:9; 23:14; *excessive,* 2 Cor. 2:7; adverbially, περισσόν, *in full abundance,* Jn. 10:10; περισσότερον, and ἐκ περισσοῦ, *exceedingly, vehemently,* Mk. 6:51; 7:36; 1 Cor. 15:10; Eph. 3:20; τὸ περισσόν, *preeminence, advantage,* Rom. 3:1 [4053]

[4358] περισσότερος *perissoteros* 16x comparative adj. from περισσός, *greater, more,* Mk. 12:40; Lk. 20:47; *even more,* Lk. 12:48; 1 Cor. 15:10; *even more, so much more,* Mk. 7:36 [4055] See *greater; more.*

[4359] περισσοτέρως *perissoterōs* 12x *more, more abundantly, more earnestly, more vehemently,* 2 Cor. 7:13; *exceedingly,* Gal. 1:14 [4056] See *beyond measure; exceedlingly.*

[4360] περισσῶς *perissōs* 4x *much, abundantly, vehemently,* Acts 26:11; *more, more abundantly,* Mt. 27:23; Mk. 10:26; 15:14* [4057]

[4361] περιστερά *peristera* 10x *a dove, pigeon,* Mt. 3:16; 10:16 [4058] See *dove; pigeon.*

[4362] περιτέμνω *peritemnō* 17x *to cut around; to circumcise, remove the prepuce,* Lk. 1:59; 2:21; met. Col. 2:11; mid. *to submit to circumcision,* Acts 15:1 [4059] See *circumcise.*

[4363] περιτίθημι *peritithēmi* 8x *to place around, put about* or *around,* Mt.

21:33; 27:28; met. *to attach, bestow,* 1 Cor. 12:23 [4060]

[4364] περιτομή *peritomē* 36x *circumcision, the act* or *custom of circumcision,* Jn. 7:22, 23; Acts 7:8; *the state of being circumcised, the being circumcised,* Rom. 2:25, 26, 27; 4:10; meton. *the circumcision, those who are circumcised,* Rom. 3:30; 4:9 met. spiritual *circumcision* of the heart and affection, Rom. 2:29; Col. 2:11; meton. *persons* spiritually *circumcised,* Phil. 3:3 [4061] See *circumcision.*

[4365] περιτρέπω *peritrepō* 1x *to turn about; to bring round* into any state, Acts 26:24* [4062]

[4366] περιτρέχω *peritrechō* 1x *to run about, run up and down,* Mk. 6:55* [4063]

[4367] περιφέρω *peripherō* 3x *to bear* or *carry about,* Mk. 6:55; 2 Cor. 4:10; pass. *to be borne about hither and thither, driven to and fro,* Eph. 4:14* [4064]

[4368] περιφρονέω *periphroneō* 1x *to contemplate, reflect on; to despise, disregard,* Tit. 2:15* [4065]

[4369] περίχωρος *perichōros* 9x *neighboring;* ἡ περίχωρος, sc. γῆ, *an adjacent region, country round about,* Mt. 14:35; Mk. 1:28; meton. *inhabitants of the region round about,* Mt. 3:5 [4066]

[4370] περίψημα *peripsēma* 1x *filth which is wiped off;* met. 1 Cor. 4:13* [4067]

[4371] περπερεύομαι *perpereuomai* 1x *to vaunt one's self,* 1 Cor. 13:4* [4068]

[4372] Περσίς *Persis* 1x *Persis,* pr. name, Rom. 16:12* [4069]

[4373] πέρυσι *perysi* 2x *last year, a year ago,* 2 Cor. 8:10; 9:2* [4070]

[4374] πετεινόν *peteinon* 14x *a bird, fowl,* Mt. 6:26; 8:20 [4071] See *bird.*

[4375] πέτομαι *petomai* 5x also spelled πετάομαι, *to fly,* Rev. 4:7; 8:13; 12:14; 14:6; 19:17* [4072]

[4376] πέτρα *petra* 15x *a rock,* Mt. 7:24, 25; met. Rom. 9:33; 1 Pet. 2:8; *crags, clefts,* Rev. 6:15, 16; *stony ground,* Lk. 8:6, 13 [4073] See *rock.*

[4377] Πέτρος *Petros* 156x *a stone;* in NT the Greek rendering of the surname Cephas, given to the Apostle Simon, and having, therefore, the same sense as πέτρα, *Peter,* Mt. 4:18; 8:14 [4074]

[4378] πετρώδης *petrōdēs* 4x *like rock; stony, rocky,* Mt. 13:5, 20; Mk. 4:5, 16* [4075]

[4379] πήγανον *pēganon* 1x *rue,* a plant, *ruta graveolens* of Linnaeus, Lk. 11:42* [4076]

[4380] πηγή *pēgē* 11x *a source, spring, fountain,* Jas. 3:11, 12; *a well,* Jn. 4:6; *an issue, flux, flow,* Mk. 5:29; met. Jn. 4:14 [4077] See *fountain; spring; well.*

[4381] πήγνυμι *pēgnymi* 1x *to fasten; to pitch* a tent, Heb. 8:2* [4078]

[4382] πηδάλιον *pēdalion* 2x *a rudder,* Acts 27:40; Jas. 3:4* [4079]

[4383] πηλίκος *pēlikos* 2x *how large,* Gal. 6:11; *how great* in dignity, Heb. 7:4* [4080]

[4384] πηλός *pēlos* 6x *moist earth, mud, slime,* Jn. 9:6, 11, 14, 15; *clay,* potter's *clay,* Rom. 9:21* [4081]

[4385] πήρα *pēra* 6x *a leather bag* or *sack* for provisions, *wallet,* Mt. 10:10; Mk. 6:8 [4082]

[4388] πῆχυς *pēchus* 4x pr. *cubitus, the forearm;* hence, *a cubit,* a measure of length, equal to the distance from the elbow to the extremity of the middle finger, usually considered as equivalent to a foot and one half, or 17 inches and one half, Jn. 21:8; Rev. 21:17; met. of time, *a span,* Mt. 6:27; Lk. 12:25* [4083]

[4389] πιάζω *piazō* 12x *to press;* in NT *to take* or *lay hold of,* Acts 3:7; *to take, catch* fish, etc., Jn. 21:3, 10; Rev. 19:20; *to take, seize, apprehend, arrest,* Jn. 7:30, 32, 44 [4084] See *arrest; catch.*

[4390] πιέζω *piezō* 1x *to press, to press* or *squeeze down, make compact by pressure,* Lk. 6:38* [4085]

[4391] πιθανολογία *pithanologia* 1x *persuasive speech, plausible discourse,* Col. 2:4* [4086]

[4393] πικραίνω *pikrainō* 4x *to embitter, render bitter,* Rev. 10:9; pass. *to be embittered, be made bitter,* Rev. 8:11; 10:10; met. pass. *to be embittered, to grow angry, harsh,* Col. 3:19* [4087]

[4394] πικρία *pikria* 4x *bitterness,* Acts 8:23; Heb. 12:15; met. *bitterness* of spirit and language, *harshness,* Rom. 3:14; Eph. 4:31* [4088]

[4395] πικρός *pikros* 2x *bitter,* Jas. 3:11; met. *bitter, harsh,* Jas. 3:14* [4089]

[4396] πικρῶς *pikrōs* 2x *bitterly,* Mt. 26:75; Lk. 22:62* [4090]

[4397] Πιλᾶτος *Pilatos* 55x *Pilate,* pr. name [4091]

[4398] πίμπλημι *pimplēmi* 24x *to fill,* Mt. 27:48; pass. *to be filled* mentally, *be under full influence,* Lk. 1:15; 4:28; *to be fulfilled,* Lk. 21:22; of stated time, *to be brought to a close, arrive at its close,* Lk. 1:23, 57; 2:6, 21, 22 [4130] See *complete; fill; fulfill.*

[4399] πίμπρημι *pimprēmi* 1x *to set on fire, burn, inflame;* in NT pass., *to swell from inflamation,* Acts 28:6* [4092]

[4400] πινακίδιον *pinakidion* 1x *a small tablet* for writing, Lk. 1:63* [4093]

[4402] πίναξ *pinax* 5x pr. *a board* or *plank;* in NT *a plate, platter, dish* on which food was served, Mk. 14:8, 11 [4094]

[4403] πίνω *pinō* 73x *to drink,* Mt. 6:25, 31; 26:27, 29, et al. freq.; trop. of the earth, *to drink in, imbibe,* Heb. 6:7 [4095] See *drink.*

[4404] πιότης *piotēs* 1x *fatness, richness,* Rom. 11:17* [4096]

[4405] πιπράσκω *pipraskō* 9x *to sell,* Mt. 13:46; 18:25; met. with ὑπό, pass. *to be sold under, to be a slave to, be devoted to,* Rom. 7:14 [4097]

[4406] πίπτω *piptō* 90x *to fall,* Mt. 15:27; Lk. 10:18; *to fall, fall prostrate, fall down,* Mt. 17:6; 18:29; Lk. 17:16; *to fall down* dead, Lk. 21:24; *to fall, fall in ruins,* Mt. 7:25, 27; Lk. 11:17; met. *to fall, come by chance,* as a lot, Acts 1:26; *to fall, to fail, become null and void, fall to the ground,* Lk. 16:17; *to fall* into a worse state, Rev. 2:5; *to come to ruin,* Rom. 11:11; Heb. 4:11; *to fall* into sin, Rom. 11:22; 1 Cor. 10:2; *to fall* in judgment, by condemnation, Rev. 14:8; *to fall* upon, *seize,* Rev. 11:11; *to light* upon, Rev. 7:16; *to fall* under, *incur,* Jas. 5:12 [4098] See *bow down; collapse; fall.*

[4407] Πισιδία *Pisidia* 1x *Pisidia,* a country of Asia Minor, Acts 14:24* [4099]

[4409] πιστεύω *pisteuō* 241x pluperfect, πεπιστεύκειν, *to believe, give credit to,* Mk. 1:15; 16:13; Lk. 24:25; intrans. *to believe, have a mental persuasion,* Mt. 8:13; 9:28; Jas. 2:19; *to believe, be of opinion,* Rom. 14:2; in NT πιστεύειν ἐν, εἰς, ἐπί, *to believe in* or *on,* Mt. 18:6; 27:42; Jn. 3:15, 16, 18; absol. *to believe, be a believer,* Acts 2:44; 4:4, 32; 13:48; trans. *to intrust, commit to the charge* or *power of,* Lk. 16:11; Jn. 2:24; pass. *to be intrusted with,* Rom. 3:2; 1 Cor. 9:17 [4100] See *believe; convince; entrust; trust.*

[4410] πιστικός *pistikos* 2x *genuine, unadulterated, pure,* Mk. 14:3; Jn. 12:3* [4101]

[4411] πίστις *pistis* 243x *faith, belief, firm persuasion,* 2 Cor. 5:7; Heb. 11:1; *assurance, firm conviction,* Rom. 14:23; *ground of belief, guarantee, assurance,* Acts 17:31; *good faith, honesty, integrity,* Mt. 23:23; Gal. 5:22; Tit. 2:10; *faithfulness, truthfulness,* Rom. 3:3; in NT *faith* in God and Christ, Mt. 8:10; Acts 3:16, et al. freq.; ἡ πίστις, *the* matter of Gospel *faith,* Acts 6:7; Jude 3 [4102] See *faith; faithfulness; trustworthiness.*

[4412] πιστός *pistos* 67x *faithful, true, trusty,* Mt. 24:45; 25:21, 23; Lk. 12:42; 2 Tim. 2:2; *put in trust,* 1 Cor. 7:25; *true, veracious,* Rev. 1:5; 2:13; *credible, sure, certain, indubitable,* Acts 13:34; 1 Tim. 1:15; *believing, yielding belief and confidence,* Jn. 20:27; Gal. 3:9; spc. *a* Christian *believer,* Acts 10:45; 16:1, 15; 2 Cor. 6:15; πιστόν, *in a true-hearted manner, right-mindedly,* 3 Jn. 5 [4103] See *dependable; faithful; reliable; trustworthy.*

[4413] πιστόω *pistoō* 1x *to make trustworthy;* pass. *to be assured, feel sure belief,* 2 Tim. 3:14* [4104]

[4414] πλανάω *planaō* 39x *to lead astray, cause to wander;* pass. *to go astray, wander about, stray,* Mt. 18:12, 13; 1 Pet. 2:25; met. *to mislead, deceive,* Mt. 24:4, 5, 11, 24; pass. *to be deceived, err, mistake,* Mt. 22:29; *to seduce, delude,* Jn. 7:12; pass. *to be seduced* or *wander* from the path of virtue, *to sin, transgress,* Tit. 3:3; Heb. 5:2; Jas. 5:19 [4105] See *deceive; go astray; lead astray; wander.*

[4415] πλάνη *planē* 10x *a wandering; deceit, deception, delusion, imposture, fraud,* Mt. 27:64; 1 Thess. 2:3; *seduction, deceiving,* Eph. 4:14; 2 Thess. 2:11; 1 Jn. 4:6; *error, false opinion,* 2 Pet. 3:17; *wandering* from the path of truth and virtue, *perverseness, wickedness, sin,* Rom. 1:27; Jas. 5:20; 2 Pet. 2:18; Jude 11* [4106] See *deceit; deception; error.*

[4417] πλανήτης *planētēs* 1x *a rover, roving, a wanderer, wandering;* ἀστὴρ πλανήτης, *a wandering star,* Jude 13* [4107]

[4418] πλάνος *planos* 5x *a wanderer, vagabond;* also act. *deceiving, seducing; a deceiver, impostor,* Mt. 27:63; 2 Cor. 6:8; 1 Tim. 4:1; 2 Jn. 7* [4108]

[4419] πλάξ *plax* 3x *a flat broad surface;* a *table, tablet,* 2 Cor. 3:3; Heb. 9:4* [4109]

[4420] πλάσμα *plasma* 1x *a thing formed* or *fashioned;* spc. *a potter's vessel,* Rom. 9:20* [4110]

[4421] πλάσσω *plassō* 2x *to form, fashion, mould,* Rom. 9:20; 1 Tim. 2:13* [4111]

[4422] πλαστός *plastos* 1x *formed, fashioned, moulded;* met. *fabricated, counterfeit, delusive,* 2 Pet. 2:3* [4112]

[4423] πλατεῖα *plateia* 9x *a street, broad way,* Mt. 6:5; 12:19; Lk. 10:10 [4113] See *street.*

[4424] πλάτος *platos* 4x *breadth,* Eph. 3:18; Rev. 20:9; 21:16* [4114]

[4425] πλατύνω *platynō* 3x *to make broad, widen, enlarge,* Mt. 23:5; pass. met. of the heart, from the Hebrew, *to be expanded* with kindly and genial feelings, 2 Cor. 6:11, 13* [4115]

[4426] πλατύς *platys* 1x *broad, wide,* Mt. 7:13* [4116]

[4427] πλέγμα *plegma* 1x *anything plaited* or *intertwined; a braid* of hair, 1 Tim. 2:9* [4117]

[4428] πλέκω *plekō* 3x *to interweave, weave, braid, plait,* Mt. 27:29; Mk. 15:17; Jn. 19:2* [4120]

[4429] πλεονάζω *pleonazō* 9x *to be more than enough; to have more than enough, to have in abundance,* 2 Cor. 8:15; *to abound, be abundant,* 2 Thess. 1:3; 2 Pet. 1:8; *to increase, be augmented,* Rom. 5:20; *to come into wider action, be more widely spread,* Rom. 6:1; 2 Cor. 4:15; in NT trans. *to cause to abound* or *increase, to augment,* 1 Thess. 3:12 [4121]

[4430] πλεονεκτέω *pleonekteō* 5x *to have more* than another; *to take advantage of; to overreach, make gain of,* 2 Cor. 7:2; 12:17, 18; *to wrong,* 1 Thess. 4:6; *to get the better,* or *an advantage of,* 2 Cor. 2:11* [4122]

[4431] πλεονέκτης *pleonektēs* 4x *one who has* or *claims to have more than his share; a covetous, avaricious person, one who defrauds for the sake of gain,* 1 Cor. 5:10, 11; 6:10; Eph. 5:5* [4123]

[4432] πλεονεξία *pleonexia* 10x *some advantage which one possesses over another; an inordinate desire of riches, covetousness,* Lk. 12:15; *grasping, overreaching, extortion,* Rom. 1:29; 1 Thess. 2:5; *a gift exacted by importunity and conferred with grudging, a hard-wrung gift,* 2 Cor. 9:5; *a scheme of extortion,* Mk. 7:22 [4124] See *covetousness; greed.*

[4433] πλευρά *pleura* 5x pr. *a rib; the side* of the body, Jn. 19:34; 20:20, 25, 27; Acts 12:7* [4125]

[4434] πλέω *pleō* 6x *to sail,* Lk. 8:23; Acts 21:3; 27:2, 6, 24; Rev. 18:17* [4126]

[4435] πληγή *plēgē* 22x *a blow, stroke, stripe,* Lk. 10:30; 12:48; meton. *a wound,* Acts 16:33; Rev. 13:3, 12, 14; from the Hebrew, *a plague, affliction, calamity,* Rev. 9:20; 11:6 [4127] See *beating; plague; wound.*

[4436] πλῆθος *plēthos* 31x *fullness, amplitude, magnitude; a multitude, a great number,* Lk. 1:10; 2:13; 5:6; *a multitude, a crowd, throng,* Mk. 3:7, 8; Lk. 6:17 [4128] See *crowd; multitude; number.*

[4437] πληθύνω *plēthunō* 12x optative, πληθύναι (3 sg), trans. *to multiply, cause to increase, augment,* 2 Cor. 9:10; Heb. 6:14; pass. *to be multiplied, increase, be accumulated,* Mt. 24:12; Acts 6:7; 7:17; intrans. *to multiply, increase, be augmented,* Acts 6:1 [4129] See *grow; increase; multiply.*

[4438] πλήκτης *plēktēs* 2x *a striker, one apt to strike; a quarrelsome, violent person,* 1 Tim. 3:3; Tit. 1:7* [4131]

[4439] πλήμμυρα *plēmmyra* 1x *the flood-tide; a flood,* Lk. 6:48* [4132]

[4440] πλήν *plēn* 31x can function as an improper prep., *besides, except,* Mk. 12:32; Acts 8:1; 20:23; as a conj. *but, however, nevertheless,* Mt. 18:7; Lk. 19:27; Eph. 5:33; equivalent to ἀλλά, Lk. 6:35; 12:31; Acts 27:22 [4133]

[4441] πλήρης *plērēs* 16x *full, filled,* Mt. 14:20; 15:37; *full* of disease, Lk. 5:12; met. *full of, abounding in, wholly occupied with, completely under the influence of,* or *affected by,* Lk. 4:1; Jn. 1:14; Acts 9:36; *full, complete, perfect,* Mk. 4:28 [4134] See *filled; full.*

[4442] πληροφορέω *plērophoreō* 6x *to bring full measure, to give in full; to carry out fully, to discharge completely,* 2 Tim. 4:5, 17; pass. of things, *to be fully established* as a matter of certainty, Lk. 1:1; of persons, *to be fully convinced, assured,* Rom. 4:21; 14:15; Col. 4:12* [4135]

[4443] πληροφορία *plērophoria* 4x *full conviction, firm persuasion, assurance,* 1 Thess. 1:5; Col. 2:2 [4136]

[4444] πληρόω *plēroō* 86x pluperf., πεπληρώκει (3 sg), *to fill, make full, fill up,* Mt. 13:48; 23:32; Lk. 3:5; *to fill up* a deficiency, Phil. 4:18, 19; *to pervade,* Jn. 12:3; Acts 2:2; *to pervade* with an influence, *to influence fully, possess fully,* Jn. 16:6; Acts 2:28; 5:3; Rom. 1:29; Eph. 5:18; *to complete, perfect,* Jn. 3:29; Eph. 3:19; *to bring to an end,* Lk. 7:1; *to perform fully, discharge,* Mt. 3:15; Acts 12:25; 13:25; 14:26; Rom. 13:8; Col. 4:17; *to consummate,* Mt. 5:17; *to realize, accomplish, fulfil,* Lk. 1:20; 9:31; Acts 3:18; 13:27; from the Hebrew; *to set forth fully,* Rom. 15:19; Col. 1:25; pass. of time, *to be fulfilled, come to an end, be fully arrived,* Mk. 1:15; Lk. 21:24; Jn. 7:8; of prophecy, *to receive fulfillment,* Mt. 1:22, et al. freq. [4137] See *fill; fulfill.*

[4445] πλήρωμα *plērōma* 17x *that which fills up; full measure, entire content,* Mk. 8:20; 1 Cor. 10:26, 28; *complement, full extent, full number,* Gal. 4:4; Eph. 1:10; *that which fills up a deficiency, a supplement, a patch,* Mt. 9:16; *fulness, abundance,* Jn. 1:16; *full measure,* Rom. 15:29; *a fulfilling, perfect performance,* Rom. 13:10; *complete attainment* of entire belief, *full acceptance,* Rom. 11:12; *full development, plenitude,* Eph. 4:13; Col. 1:19; 2:9 [4138] See *fulfillment; fullness.*

[4446] πλησίον *plēsion* 17x can function as an improper prep., *near, near by,*

Jn. 4:5; ὁ πλησίον, *a neighbor,* Mt. 19:19; Rom. 15:2; a friendly *neighbor,* Mt. 5:43 [4139] See *near; neighbor.*

[4447] πλησμονή *plēsmonē* 1x *a filling up;* met. *gratification, satisfaction,* Col. 2:23* [4140]

[4448] πλήσσω *plēssō* 1x also spelled πλήττω, *to strike, smite;* from the Hebrew, *to smite, to plague, blast,* Rev. 8:12 [4141]

[4449] πλοιάριον *ploiarion* 5x *a small vessel, boat,* Mk. 3:9; Jn. 6:22, 23, 24 [4142]

[4450] πλοῖον *ploion* 67x *a vessel, ship, bark,* whether large or small, Mt. 4:21, 22; Acts 21:2, 3 [4143] See *boat; ship.*

[4454] πλούσιος *plousios* 28x *rich, opulent, wealthy;* and pl. οἱ πλούσιοι, *the rich,* Mt. 19:23, 24; 27:57; met. *rich, abounding in, distinguished for,* Eph. 2:4; Jas. 2:5; Rev. 2:9; 3:17; *rich* in glory, dignity, bliss, etc., 2 Cor. 8:9 [4145] See *rich, riches; wealth.*

[4455] πλουσίως *plousiōs* 4x *rich, largely, abundantly,* Col. 3:16 [4146]

[4456] πλουτέω *plouteō* 12x *to be* or *become rich,* Lk. 1:25; 1 Tim. 6:9; trop. Lk. 12:21; met. *to abound in, be abundantly furnished with,* 1 Tim. 6:18; *to be* spiritually *enriched,* 2 Cor. 8:9 [4147] See *rich, riches; wealth.*

[4457] πλουτίζω *ploutizō* 3x *to make rich, enrich;* met. *to enrich* spiritually, 1 Cor. 1:5; 2 Cor. 6:10; 9:11* [4148]

[4458] πλοῦτος *ploutos* 22x *riches, wealth, opulence,* Mt. 13:22; Lk. 8:14; in NT, πλοῦτος τοῦ Θεοῦ, or Χριστοῦ, *those rich benefits, those abundant blessings which flow from God* or *Christ,* Eph. 3:8; Phil. 4:19; meton. *richness, abundance,* Rom. 2:4; 11:33; 2 Cor. 8:2; meton. *a* spiritual *enriching,* Rom. 11:12 [4149] See *rich, riches; wealth.*

[4459] πλύνω *plynō* 3x *to wash* garments, Lk. 5:1; Rev. 7:14; 22:14* [4150]

[4460] πνεῦμα *pneuma* 379x *wind, air in motion,* Jn. 3:8; *breath,* 2 Thess. 2:8; the substance *spirit,* Jn. 3:6; *a spirit, spiritual being,* Jn. 4:24; Acts 23:8, 9; Heb. 1:14; *a* bodiless *spirit, specter,* Lk. 24:37; *a* foul *spirit,* δαιμόνιον, Mt. 8:16; Lk. 10:20; *spirit,* as a vital principle, Jn. 6:63; 1 Cor. 15:45; *the* human *spirit, the soul,* Mt. 26:41; 27:50; Acts 7:59; 1 Cor. 7:34; Jas. 2:26; *the spirit* as the seat of thought and feeling, *the mind,* Mk. 8:12; Acts 19:21; *spirit, mental frame,* 1 Cor. 4:21; 1 Pet. 3:4; *a* characteristic *spirit, an influential principle,* Lk. 9:55; 1 Cor. 2:12; 2 Tim. 1:7; *a pervading influence,* Rom. 11:8; *spirit, frame of mind,* as distinguished from outward circumstances and action, Mt. 5:3; *spirit* as distinguished from outward show and form. Jn. 4:23; *spirit, a* divinely bestowed *spiritual frame,* characteristic of true believers, Rom. 8:4; Jude 19; *spirit,* latent *spiritual import, spiritual significance,* as distinguished from the mere letter, Rom. 2:29; 7:6; 2 Cor. 3:6, 17; *spirit,* as a term for a process superior to a merely natural or carnal course of things, by the operation of the Divine Spirit, Rom. 8:4; Gal. 4:29; *a spiritual dispensation,* or *a* sealing energy of the Holy *Spirit,* Heb. 9:14; the Holy Spirit, Mt. 3:16; 12:31; Jn. 1:32, 33; *a gift of the Holy Spirit,* Jn. 7:39; Acts 19:2; 1 Cor. 14:12; *an operation* or *influence of the Holy Spirit,* 1 Cor. 12:3; *a spiritual influence, an inspiration,* Mt. 22:43; Lk. 2:27; Eph. 1:17; *a professedly divine communication,* or, *a professed possessor of a spiritual communication,* 1 Cor. 12:10; 2 Thess. 2:2; 1 Jn. 4:1, 2, 3 [4151] See *spirit.*

[4461] πνευματικός *pneumatikos* 26x *spiritual, pertaining to the soul,* as distinguished from what concerns the body, Rom. 15:27; 1 Cor. 9:11; *spiritual, pertaining to the nature of spirits,* 1 Cor. 15:44; τὰ πνευματικα; τῆς πονηρίας, i.q. τὰ πνεύματα τὰ πονηρά, *evil spirits,* Eph. 6:12; *spiritual, pertaining* or *relating to the influences of the Holy Spirit,* of things, Rom. 1:11; 7:14; τὰ πνευματικά, *spiritual gifts,* 1 Cor. 12:1; 14:1; *superior in process to the natural course of things, miraculous,* 1 Cor. 10:3; of persons, *gifted with a spiritual frame of mind, spiritually affected,* 1 Cor. 2:13, 15; *endowed with spiritual gifts, inspired,* 1 Cor. 14:37 [4152] See *spiritual.*

[4462] πνευματικῶς *pneumatikōs* 2x *spiritually, through spiritual views and affections,* 1 Cor. 2:14; *spiritually, in a spiritual sense, allegorically,* Rev. 11:8* [4153]

[4463] πνέω *pneō* 7x *to breathe; to blow,* as the wind, Mt. 7:25, 27 [4154]

[4464] πνίγω *pnigō* 3x *to stifle, suffocate, choke,* Mk. 5:13; *to seize by the throat,* Mk. 13:17; 18:28* [4155]

[4465] πνικτός *pniktos* 3x *strangled, suffocated;* in NT τὸ πνικτόν, *the flesh of animals killed by strangulation* or *suffocation,* Acts 15:20, 29; 21:25* [4156]

[4466] πνοή *pnoē* 2x *breath, respiration,* Acts 17:25; *a wind, a blast of wind, breeze,* Acts 2:2* [4157]

[4468] ποδήρης *podērēs* 1x *reaching to the feet;* as subst. sc. ἐσθής, *a long, flowing robe reaching down to the feet,* Rev. 1:13* [4158]

[4470] πόθεν *pothen* 29x *whence? from where,* used of place, etc., Mt. 15:33; met. of a state of dignity, Rev. 2:5; used of origin, Mt. 21:25; of cause, source, author, etc., Mt. 13:27, 54, 56; Lk. 1:43; *how? in what way?* Mk. 8:4; 12:37 [4159]

[4472] ποιέω *poieō* 568x pluperf., πεποιήκειν, *to make, form, construct,* Mt. 17:4; Mk. 9:5; Jn. 2:15; of God, *to create,* Mt. 19:4; Acts 4:24; *to make, prepare* a feast, etc., Mt. 22:2; Mk. 6:21; met. *to make, establish, ratify,* a covenant, Heb. 8:9; *to make, assume, consider, regard,* Mt. 12:33; *to make, effect, bring to pass, cause to take place, do, accomplish,* Mt. 7:22; 21:21; Mk. 3:8; 6:5; 7:37; met. *to perfect, accomplish, fulfil, put in execution* a purpose, promise, etc., Lk. 16:4; 19:48; *to cause, make,* Mt. 5:32; Jn. 11:37; Acts 24:12; *to make* gain, *gain, acquire,* Mt. 25:16; Lk. 19:18; *to get, procure,* Lk. 12:33; *to make, to cause to be* or *become* a thing, Mt. 21:13; 23:15; *to use, treat,* Lk. 15:19; *to make, constitute, appoint* to some office, Mt. 4:19; Mk. 3:14; *to make, declare to be,* 1 Jn. 1:10; 5:10; *to do, to perform, execute, practise, act,* Mt. 5:46, 47, 6:2, 3; *to commit* evil, Mt. 13:41; 27:23; *to be devoted to, follow, practise,* Jn. 3:21; 5:29; Rom. 3:12; *to do, execute, fulfil, keep, observe, obey,* precepts, etc., Mt. 1:24; 5:19; 7:21, 24, 26; *to bring* evil *upon, inflict,* Acts 9:13; *to keep, celebrate* a festival, Mt. 26:18; *to institute the celebration of* a festival, Heb. 11:28; ποιεῖν τινα ἔξω, *to cause to leave* a place, i.q. ἔξω ἄγειν, *to lead* or *conduct out,* Acts 5:34; *to pass, spend* time, *continue for* a time, Mt. 20:12; Acts 15:33; 18:23; Jas. 4:13; *to bear,* as trees, *yield, produce,* Mt. 3:8, 10; 7:17, 18, 19; with a substantive or adjective it forms a periphrasis for the verb corresponding to the noun or adjective, e.g. δῆλον ποιεῖν, i.q. δηλοῦν, *to make manifest, betray,* Mt. 26:73; ἐκδίκησιν ποιεῖν, i.q. ἐδικεῖν, *to vindicate, avenge,* Lk. 18:7, 8; ἔκθετον ποιεῖν, i.q. ἐκτιθέναι, *to expose* infants, Acts 7:19; ἐνέδραν ποιεῖν, i.q. ἐνεδρεύειν, *to lie in wait,* Acts 25:3; ἐξουσίαν ποιεῖν, i.q. ἐξουσιάζειν, *to exercise power* or *authority,* Rev. 13:12; κρίσιν ποιεῖν, i.q. κρίνειν, *to judge, act as judge,* Jn. 5:27; λύτρωσιν ποιεῖν, i.q. λυτροῦν, *to deliver, set free,* Lk. 1:68; μονὴν ποιεῖν, i.q. μένειν, *to remain, dwell,* Jn. 14:23; πόλεμον ποιεῖν, i.q. πολεμεῖν, *to make* or *wage war, fight,* Rev. 11:7; συμβούλιον ποιεῖν, i.q. συμβουλεύεσθαι, *to consult together, deliberate,* Mk. 3:6; συνωμοσίαν ποιεῖν, i.q. συνομνύναι, and συστροφὴν ποιεῖν, i.q. συστρέφεσθαι, *to conspire together, form a conspiracy,* Acts 23:12, 13; φανερὸν ποιεῖν, i.q. φανεροῦν, *to make known, betray,* Mt. 12:16; ἀναβολὴν ποιέσθαι, i.q. ἀναβάλλεσθαι, *to delay, procrastinate,* Acts 25:17; βέβαιον ποιεῖσθαι, i.q. βεβαιοῦν, *to confirm, render firm and sure,* 2 Pet. 1:10; δεήσεις ποιεῖσθαι, i.q.

δεῖσθαι, *to pray, offer prayer*, Lk. 5:33; ἐκβολὴν ποιεῖσθαι, i.q. ἐκβάλλειν, *to cast out, throw overboard*, Acts 27:18; καθαρισμὸν ποιεῖσθαι, i.q. καθαρίζειν, *to cleanse* from sin, Heb. 1:3; κοινωνίαν ποιεῖσθαι, i.q. κοινωνεῖν, *to communicate in liberality, bestow alms*, Rom. 15:26; κοπετὸν ποιεῖν, i.q. κόπτεσθαι, *to lament, bewail*, Acts 8:2; λόγον ποιεῖσθαι, *to regard, make account of*, Acts 20:24; μνείαν ποιεῖσθαι, i.q. μνησθῆναι, *to call to mind*, Rom. 1:9; μνήμην ποιεῖσθαι, *to remember, retain in memory*, 2 Pet. 1:15; πορείαν ποιεῖσθαι, i.q. πορεύεσθαι, *to go, journey, travel*, Lk. 13:22; πρόνοιαν ποιεῖσθαι, i.q. προνοεῖσθαι, *to take care of, provide for*, Rom. 13:14; σπουδὴν ποιεῖσθαι, *to act with diligence and earnestness*, Jude 3 [4160] See *accomplish; appoint; create; do; make.*

[4473] ποίημα *poiēma* 2x *that which is made* or *done; a work, workmanship, creation,* Rom. 1:20; met. Eph. 2:10* [4161]

[4474] ποίησις *poiēsis* 1x *a making; an acting, doing, performance; observance* of a law, Jas. 1:25* [4162]

[4475] ποιητής *poiētēs* 6x *a maker; the maker* or *author* of a song or poem, *a poet,* Acts 17:28; *a doer; a performer* of the enactments of a law, Rom. 2:13 [4163]

[4476] ποικίλος *poikilos* 10x *of various colors, variegated, checkered; various, diverse, manifold,* Mt. 4:24 [4164] See *various.*

[4477] ποιμαίνω *poimainō* 11x *to feed, pasture, tend a flock,* Lk. 17:7; 1 Cor. 9:7; trop. *to feed* with selfish indulgence, *to pamper,* Jude 12; met. *to tend, direct, superintend,* Mt. 2:6; Jn. 21:16; *to rule,* Rev. 2:27 [4165] See *shepherd.*

[4478] ποιμήν *poimēn* 18x *one who tends flocks* or *herds, a shepherd, herdsman,* Mt. 9:36; 25:32; met. *a pastor, superintendent, guardian,* Jn. 10:11, 14, 16 [4166] See *pastor; shepherd.*

[4479] ποίμνη *poimnē* 5x *a flock* of sheep, Lk. 2:8; 1 Cor. 9:7; meton. *a flock* of disciples, Mt. 26:31; Jn. 10:16* [4167]

[4480] ποίμνιον *poimnion* 5x *a flock;* met. *a flock* of Christian disciples, Lk. 12:32; Acts 20:28, 29; 1 Pet. 5:2, 3* [4168]

[4481] ποῖος *poios* 33x *of what kind, sort* or *species,* Jn. 12:33; 21:19; *what? which?* Mt. 19:18; 21:23, 24, 27 [4169]

[4482] πολεμέω *polemeō* 7x *to make* or *wage war, fight,* Rev. 2:16; 12:7; *to battle, quarrel,* Jas. 4:2 [4170]

[4483] πόλεμος *polemos* 18x *war,* Mt. 24:6; Mk. 13:7; *battle, engagement, combat,* 1 Cor. 14:8; Heb. 11:34; *battling, strife,* Jas. 4:1 [4171] See *battle; fight; war.*

[4484] πόλις *polis* 162x *a city, an enclosed and walled town,* Mt. 10:5, 11; 11:1; meton. *the inhabitants of a city,* Mt. 8:34; 10:15; with a gen. of person, or a personal pronoun, *the city* of any one, *the city* of one's birth or residence, Mt. 9:1; Lk. 2:4, 11; ἡ πόλις, *the city,* κατ᾽ ἐξοχήν, *Jerusalem,* Mt. 21:18; 28:11; met. *a place of permanent residence, abode, home,* Heb. 11:10, 16; 13:14. The frequency count does not include its occurrence in the name Νέαν πόλιν in Acts 16:11 [4172] See *city; town; village.*

[4485] πολιτάρχης *politarchēs* 2x *a ruler* or *prefect of a city, city magistrate,* Acts 17:6, 8* [4173]

[4486] πολιτεία *politeia* 2x *the state of being a citizen; citizenship, the right* or *privilege of being a citizen, freedom of a city* or *state,* Acts 22:28; *a commonwealth, community,* Eph. 2:12* [4174]

[4487] πολίτευμα *politeuma* 1x *the administration of a commonwealth;* in NT equivalent to πολιτεία, *a community, commonwealth,* Phil. 3:20* [4175]

[4488] πολιτεύομαι *politeuomai* 2x intrans. *to be a citizen;* trans. *to govern a city* or *state, administer the affairs of a state;*

pass. *to be governed;* in NT *to order one's life and conduct, converse, live,* in a certain manner as to habits and principles, Acts 23:1; Phil. 1:27* [4176]

[4489] πολίτης *politēs* 4x *a citizen,* Lk. 15:15; 19:14; Acts 21:39; Heb. 8:11* [4177]

[4490] πολλάκις *pollakis* 18x *many times, often, frequently,* Mt. 17:15; Mk. 5:4; 9:22 [4178] See *often.*

[4491] πολλαπλασίων *pollaplasiōn* 1x *manifold, many times more,* Lk. 18:30* [4179]

[4494] πολυλογία *polylogia* 1x *wordiness, loquacity,* Mt. 6:7* [4180]

[4495] πολυμερῶς *polymerōs* 1x *in many parts* or *ways,* Heb. 1:1* [4181]

[4497] πολυποίκιλος *polypoikilos* 1x *exceedingly various, multiform, manifold;* by impl. *immense, infinite,* Eph. 3:10* [4182]

[4498] πολύς *polys* 416x *great* in magnitude or quantity, *much, large,* Mt. 13:5; Jn. 3:23; 15:8; pl. *many,* Mt. 3:7; in time, *long,* Mt. 25:19; Mk. 6:35; Jn. 5:6; οἱ πολλοί, *the many, the mass,* Rom. 5:15; 12:5; 1 Cor. 10:33; τὸ πολύ, *much,* 2 Cor. 8:15; πολύ, as an adv., *much, greatly,* Mk. 12:27; Lk. 7:47; of time, ἐπὶ πολύ, *a long time,* Acts 28:6; μετ᾽ οὐ πολὺ, *not long after,* Acts 27:14; followed by a compar., *much,* 2 Cor. 8:22; πολλῷ, *much, by much,* Mt. 6:30; Mk. 10:48; τὰ πολλά, as an adv., *most frequently, generally,* Rom. 15:22; πολλά, as an adv., *much, greatly, vehemently,* Mk. 1:45; 3:12; of time, *many times, frequently, often,* Mt. 9:14 [4118, 4119, 4183] See *great; large; many.*

[4499] πολύσπλαγχνος *polysplanchnos* 1x *very merciful, very compassionate,* Jas. 5:11* [4184]

[4500] πολυτελής *polytelēs* 3x *expensive, costly,* Mk. 14:3; 1 Tim. 2:9; *of great value, very precious,* 1 Pet. 3:4* [4185]

[4501] πολύτιμος *polytimos* 3x *of great price, costly, precious,* Mt. 13:46; Jn. 12:3; 1 Pet. 1:7* [4186]

[4502] πολυτρόπως *polytropōs* 1x *in many ways, in various modes,* Heb. 1:1* [4187]

[4503] πόμα *poma* 2x *drink,* 1 Cor. 10:4; Heb. 9:10* [4188]

[4504] πονηρία *ponēria* 7x pr. *badness, bad condition;* in NT *evil disposition* of mind, *wickedness, mischief, malignity,* Mt. 22:18; pl. πονηρίαι, *wicked deeds, villanies,* Mk. 7:23; Acts 3:26 [4189]

[4505] πονηρός *ponēros* 78x *bad, unsound,* Mt. 6:23; 7:17, 18; *evil, afflictive,* Eph. 5:16; 6:13; Rev. 16:2; *evil, wrongful, malignant, malevolent,* Mt. 5:11, 39; Acts 28:21; *evil, wicked, impious,* and τὸ πονηρόν, *evil, wrong, wickedness,* Mt. 5:37, 45; 9:4; *slothful, inactive,* Mt. 25:26; Lk. 19:22; ὁ πονηρός, *the evil one, the devil,* Mt. 13:19, 38; Jn. 17:15; *evil* eye, i.q. φθονερός *envious,* Mt. 20:15; Mk. 7:22; impl. *covetous,* Mt. 7:11 [4190, 4191] See *bad; evil; wicked, wickedness.*

[4506] πόνος *ponos* 4x *labor, travail; pain, misery, anguish,* Col. 4:13; Rev. 16:10, 11; 21:4* [4192]

[4507] Ποντικός *Pontikos* 1x *belonging to* or *an inhabitant of Pontus,* Acts 18:2* [4193]

[4508] Πόντιος *Pontios* 3x *Pontius,* pr. name, Acts 4:27 [4194]

[4509] Πόντος *Pontos* 1x *Pontus,* country of Asia Minor, Acts 2:9; 1 Pet. 1:1* [5117]

[4511] Πόπλιος *Poplios* 2x *Publius,* pr. name, Acts 28:7, 8* [4196]

[4512] πορεία *poreia* 2x *a going, progress; a journey, travel,* Lk. 13:22; from the Hebrew, *way* of life, *business, occupation,* Jas. 1:11* [4197]

[4513] πορεύω *poreuō* 153x also listed as a deponent, πορεύομαι, *to go, pass from one place to another,* Mt. 17:27; 18:12; *to* *go away, depart,* Mt. 24:1; 25:41; Jn. 14:2, 3; trop. *to go away, depart,* from life, *to die,* Lk. 22:22; *to go, pass on one's way, journey, travel,* Mt. 2:8, 9; Lk. 1:39; 2:41; πορεύομαι ὀπίσω, *to go after, to become a follower* or *partisan,* Lk. 21:8; or, *to pursue after, be devoted to,* 2 Pet. 2:10; from the Hebrew, *to go* or *proceed* in any way or course of life, *live* in any manner, Lk. 1:6; 8:14; Acts 9:31 [4198] See *go; travel; walk.*

[4514] πορθέω *portheō* 3x *to lay waste, destroy;* impl. *to harass, ravage,* Acts 9:21; Gal. 1:13, 23* [4199]

[4516] πορισμός *porismos* 2x *a providing, procuring;* meton. *source of gain,* 1 Tim. 6:5, 6* [4200]

[4517] Πόρκιος *Porkios* 1x *Porcius,* pr. name, Acts 24:27* [4201]

[4518] πορνεία *porneia* 25x *fornication, whoredom,* Mt. 15:19; Mk. 7:21; Acts 15:20, 29; *concubinage,* Jn. 8:41; *adultery,* Mt. 5:32; 19:9; *incest,* 1 Cor. 5:1; *lewdness, uncleanness,* genr., Rom. 1:29; from the Hebrew, put symbolically for *idolatry,* Rev. 2:21; 14:8 [4202] See *fornication; sexual immorality.*

[4519] πορνεύω *porneuō* 8x *to commit fornication,* 1 Cor. 6:18; 10:8; Rev. 2:14, 20; from the Hebrew, *to commit* spiritual *fornication, practise idolatry,* Rev. 17:2; 18:3, 9* [4203] See *commit sexual immorality; fornication; sexual immorality.*

[4520] πόρνη *pornē* 12x *a prostitute, a whore, harlot, an unchaste female,* Mt. 21:31, 32; from the Hebrew, a*n idolatress,* Rev. 17:1, 5, 15 [4204] See *harlot; prostitute.*

[4521] πόρνος *pornos* 10x *a catamite;* in NT *a fornicator, impure person,* 1 Cor. 5:9, 10, 11; 6:9 [4205] See *fornicator; sexual immorality.*

[4522] πόρρω *porrō* 4x *in advance, far advanced; far, far off, at a distance,* Mt. 15:8; Mk. 7:6; Lk. 14:32, can be an improper prep. with the gen. The comparative form of the adverb appears as πορρώτερον at Lk. 24:28.* [4206]

[4523] πόρρωθεν *porrōthen* 2x *from a distance, from afar,* Heb. 11:13; *at a distance, far, far off,* Lk. 17:12* [4207]

[4525] πορφύρα *porphyra* 4x *purpura, murex,* a species of shellfish that yielded the purple dye, highly esteemed by the ancients, its tint being a bright crimson; in NT *a purple garment, robe of purple,* Lk. 16:19; Rev. 18:12 [4209]

[4527] πορφυρόπωλις *porphyropōlis* 1x *a female seller of purple cloths,* Acts 16:4* [4211]

[4528] πορφυροῦς *porphyrous* 4x contracted form is πορφύρεος, *purple,* Jn. 19:2, 5; *purple clothing,* Rev. 17:4; 18:16* [4210]

[4529] ποσάκις *posakis* 3x *How many times? How often?* Mt. 18:21; 23:37; Lk. 13:34* [4212]

[4530] πόσις *posis* 3x *drinking; drink, beverage,* Jn. 6:55; Rom. 14:17; Col. 2:16* [4213]

[4531] πόσος *posos* 27x *How great? How much?* Mt. 6:23; Lk. 16:5, 7; 2 Cor. 7:11; πόσῳ, adverbially before a comparative, *How much? By how much?* Mt. 7:11; 10:25; Heb. 10:29; of time, *How long?* Mk. 9:21; of number, pl. *How many?* Mt. 15:34; 16:9, 10 [4214]

[4532] ποταμός *potamos* 17x *a river, stream,* Mk. 1:5; Acts 16:13; met. and allegor. Jn. 7:38; Rev. 22:1, 2; *a flood, winter torrent,* for χείμαρρος ποταμός, Mt. 7:25, 27 [4215] See *river; stream.*

[4533] ποταμοφόρητος *potamophorētos* 1x *borne along* or *carried away by a flood* or *torrent,* Rev. 12:15* [4216]

[4534] ποταπός *potapos* 7x *Of what country?* in NT equivalent to ποῖος, *What? Of what manner? Of what kind* or *sort?* Lk. 1:29; 7:37; denoting admiration, *What? What kind of? How great?* Mt. 8:27; Mk. 13:1 [4217]

[4536] πότε *pote* 19x interrogative adverb, *When? At what time?* Mt. 24:3; 25:37, 38, 39, 44; ἕως πότε, *until when? how long?* Mt. 17:17 [4219]

[4537] ποτε *pote* 29x enclitic particle, *once, some time* or *other,* either past or future; *formerly,* Jn. 9:13; *at length,* Lk. 22:32; *at any time, ever,* Eph. 5:29; Heb. 2:1; intensive after interrogatives, *ever,* 1 Cor. 9:7; Heb. 1:5 [4218]

[4538] πότερον *poteron* 1x interrogative of πότερος, α, ον, which never occurs in NT other than in this form, *whether?,* Jn. 7:17* [4220]

[4539] ποτήριον *potērion* 31x *a vessel for drinking, cup,* Mt. 10:42; 23:25, 26; meton. *the contents of a cup, liquor contained in a cup,* Lk. 22:20; 1 Cor. 10:16; from the Hebrew, *the cup* or *potion* of what God's administration deals out, Mt. 20:22, 23; Rev. 14:10 [4221] See *cup.*

[4540] ποτίζω *potizō* 15x *to cause to drink, give drink to,* Mt. 10:42; met. 1 Cor. 3:2; Rev. 14:8; *to water, irrigate,* met. 1 Cor. 3:6, 7, 8 [4222] See *give to drink; water.*

[4541] Ποτίολοι *Potioloi* 1x *Puteoli,* a town of Italy, Acts 28:13* [4223]

[4542] πότος *potos* 1x *a drinking; a drinking together, drinking bout,* 1 Pet. 4:3* [4224]

[4543] που *pou* 4x enclitic, *somewhere, in a certain place,* Heb. 2:6; 4:4; with numerals, *thereabout,* Rom. 4:19* [4225]

[4544] ποῦ *pou* 48x interrogative, *where? In what place?* direct, Mt. 2:2; Lk. 8:25; Jn. 1:39; indirect, Mt. 2:4; Jn. 1:40; *whither,* Jn. 3:8; 7:35; 13:36 [4226]

[4545] Πούδης *Poudēs* 1x *Pudens,* pr. name, Latin, 2 Tim. 4:21* [4227]

[4546] πούς *pous* 93x *the foot,* Mt. 4:6; 5:35; 7:6; 22:44; 28:9; Lk. 1:79; Acts 5:9; Rom. 3:15 [4228] See *feet; foot.*

[4547] πρᾶγμα *pragma* 11x *a thing done, fact, deed, work, transaction,* Lk. 1:1; Jas. 3:16; *a matter, affair,* Mt. 18:19; Rom. 16:2; *a matter* of dispute, 1 Cor. 6:1; *a thing,* genr., Heb. 10:1; 11:1; τὸ πρᾶγμα, a euphemism for *unlawful sexual conduct,* perhaps, 1 Thess. 4:6 [4229] See *matter; thing.*

[4548] πραγματεία *pragmateia* 1x *an application to a matter of business;* in NT *business, affair, transaction,* 2 Tim. 2:4* [4230]

[4549] πραγματεύομαι *pragmateuomai* 1x *to be occupied with* or *employed in any business, do business; to trade traffic,* Lk. 19:13* [4231]

[4550] πραιτώριον *praitōrion* 8x when used in reference to a camp, *the tent of the general* or *commander-in-chief;* hence, in reference to a province, *the palace in which the governor of the province resided,* Mt. 27:27; Mk. 15:16; Acts 23:35; *the camp occupied by the praetorian cohorts at Rome, the praetorian camp,* or, *the Roman emperor's palace,* Phil. 1:13 [4232] See *palace.*

[4551] πράκτωρ *praktōr* 2x *an exactor of dues* or *penalties; an officer* who enforced payment of debts by imprisonment, Lk. 12:58* [4233]

[4552] πρᾶξις *praxis* 6x *operation, business, office,* Rom. 12:4; πρᾶξις, and πραξεις, *actions, mode of acting, ways, deeds, practice, behavior,* Mt. 16:27; Lk. 23:51 [4234]

[4555] πρασιά *prasia* 2x *a small area* or *bed in a garden;* trop. *a company of persons disposed in squares;* from the Hebrew, πρασιαὶ πρασιαί, *by areas, by squares,* like beds in a garden, Mk. 6:40* [4237]

[4556] πράσσω *prassō* 39x *to do, execute, perform, practise, act, transact,* and of evil, *to commit,* Lk. 22:23; 23:15; Jn. 3:20; Acts 26:9, 20, 26, 31; *to fulfil, obey, observe* a law, Rom. 2:25; *to do to* any one, Acts 16:28; 5:35; *to occupy one's self with, be engaged in, busy one's self about,* Acts 19:19; 1 Thess. 4:11; absol. *to fare,* Acts

15:29; Eph. 6:21; *to exact, require, collect* tribute, money lent, etc., Lk. 3:13; 19:23 [4238] See *act; do; practice.*

[4557] πραϋπάθεια *praupatheia* 1x *meekness, gentleness of mind, kindness,* 1 Tim. 6:11* [4236]

[4558] πραΰς *praus* 4x also spelled πρᾶος, *meek, gentle, kind, forgiving,* Mt. 5:5; *mild, benevolent, humane,* Mt. 11:29; 21:5; 1 Pet. 3:4* [4239]

[4559] πραΰτης *prautēs* 11x also spelled πραότης, ητος, ἡ, *meekness, mildness, forbearance,* 1 Pet. 3:15; *gentleness, kindness,* Jas. 1:21; 3:13; Gal. 5:23 [4240] See *gentleness; humility*

[4560] πρέπω *prepō* 7x *it becomes, it is fitting, it is proper, it is right,* etc., and part. πρέπον, *becoming, suitable, decorous,* etc., Mt. 3:15; 1 Cor. 11:13; Eph. 5:3; 1 Tim. 2:10 [4241]

[4561] πρεσβεία *presbeia* 2x *eldership, seniority; an embassy, legation; a body of ambassadors, legates,* Lk. 14:32; 19:14* [4242]

[4563] πρεσβεύω *presbeuō* 2x *to be elder; to be an ambassador, perform the duties of an ambassador,* 2 Cor. 5:20; Eph. 6:20* [4243]

[4564] πρεσβυτέριον *presbyterion* 3x *a body of old men, an assembly of elders; the Jewish Sanhedrin,* Lk. 22:66; Acts 22:5; *a body of elders* in the Christian church, *a presbytery,* 1 Tim. 4:14* [4244]

[4565] πρεσβύτερος *presbyteros* 66x *elder, senior; older, more advanced in years,* Lk. 15:25; Jn. 8:9; Acts 2:17; *an elder* in respect of age, *person advanced in years,* 1 Tim. 5:1, 2; pl. spc. *ancients, ancestors, fathers,* Mt. 15:2; Heb. 11:2; as an appellation of dignity, *an elder,* local *dignitary,* Lk. 7:3; *an elder, member of the Jewish Sanhedrin,* Mt. 16:21; 21:23; 26:3, 47, 57, 59; *an elder* or *presbyter* of the Christian church, Acts 11:30; 14:23, et al. freq. [4245] See *elder; older.*

[4566] πρεσβύτης *presbytēs* 3x *an old man, aged person,* Lk. 1:18; Tit. 2:2; Phlm. 9* [4246]

[4567] πρεσβῦτις *presbytis* 1x *an aged woman,* Tit. 2:3* [4247]

[4568] πρηνής *prēnēs* 1x *prone, headforemost;* πρηνὴς γενόμενος, *falling headlong,* Acts 1:18* [4248]

[4569] πρίζω *prizō* 1x also spelled πρίω, *to saw, saw in two,* Heb. 11:37* [4249]

[4570] πρίν *prin* 13x can function as a temporal conj. and an improper prep., *before,* of time, Mt. 26:34, 75; Mk. 14:72; πρὶν ἤ, *sooner than, before,* Mt. 1:18; Lk. 2:26 [4250]

[4571] Πρίσκα *Priska* 3x see also Πρόσκιλλα, *Prisca,* pr. name, Rom. 16:3; 1 Cor. 16:19; 2 Tim. 4:19* [4251]

[4572] Πρίσκιλλα *Priskilla* 3x *Priscilla,* pr. name, the diminutive form of Πρίσκα, the wife of Apollos, Acts 18:2, 18, 26* [4252]

[4574] πρό *pro* 47x *before,* of place, *in front of, in advance of,* Mt. 11:10; Lk. 1:76; Acts 5:23; *before,* of time, Mt. 5:12; Lk. 11:38; before an infin. with the gen. of the article, *before, before that,* Mt. 6:8; Lk. 2:21; *before, above, in preference,* Jas. 5:12; 1 Pet. 4:8 [4253]

[4575] προάγω *proagō* 20x *to lead, bring,* or *conduct forth, produce,* Acts 12:6; 16:30; 25:26; intrans. *to go before, to go first,* Mt. 2:9; 21:9; Mk. 6:45; 1 Tim. 5:24; part. προάγων, ουσα, ον, *preceding, previous, antecedent,* 1 Tim. 1:18; Heb. 7:18; hence, in NT, trans. *to precede,* Mt. 14:22; *to be in advance of,* Mt. 21:31 [4254] See *go ahead.*

[4576] προαιρέω *proaireō* 1x *to prefer, choose;* met. *to purpose, intend considerately,* 2 Cor. 9:7* [4255]

[4577] προαιτιάομαι *proaitiaomai* 1x pr. *to charge beforehand; to convince beforehand,* Rom. 3:9, since the charges in the case in question were drawn from Scripture.* [4256]

[4578] προακούω *proakouō* 1x *to hear beforehand* or *already,* Col. 1:5* [4257]

[4579] προαμαρτάνω *proamartanō* 2x *to sin before;* perf., *to have already sinned, have sinned heretofore,* 2 Cor. 12:21; 13:2* [4258]

[4580] προαύλιον *proaulion* 1x *the exterior court* before an edifice, Mk. 14:68* [4259]

[4581] προβαίνω *probainō* 5x *to go forward, advance,* Mt. 4:21; Mk. 1:19; *to advance* in life, Lk. 1:7, 18; 2:36* [4260]

[4582] προβάλλω *proballō* 2x *to cast before, project; to put* or *urge forward,* Acts 19:33; *to put forth,* as a tree its blossoms, etc., Lk. 21:30* [4261]

[4583] προβατικός *probatikos* 1x *belonging* or *pertaining to sheep;* ἡ προβατική, (πύλη) *the sheep gate,* Jn. 5:2* [4262]

[4585] πρόβατον *probaton* 39x *a sheep,* Mt. 7:15; 9:36; 10:16; met. Mt. 10:6; 15:24 [4263] See *sheep.*

[4586] προβιβάζω *probibazō* 1x *to cause* any one *to advance, to lead forward;* met. *to incite, instigate,* Mt. 14:8* [4264]

[4587] προβλέπω *problepō* 1x *to foresee;* mid. *to provide beforehand,* Heb. 11:40* [4265]

[4588] προγίνομαι *proginomai* 1x *to be* or *happen before, be previously done* or *committed;* προγεγονώς, *bygone, previous,* Rom. 3:25 [4266]

[4589] προγινώσκω *proginōskō* 5x *to know beforehand, to be previously acquainted with,* Acts 26:5; 2 Pet. 3:17; *to determine on beforehand, to foreordain,* 1 Pet. 1:20; in NT, from the Hebrew, *to foreknow, to appoint as the subject of future privileges,* Rom. 8:29; 11:2* [4267] See *foreknow, foreknowledge.*

[4590] πρόγνωσις *prognōsis* 2x *foreknowledge;* in NT *previous determination, purpose,* Acts 2:23; 1 Pet. 1:2* [4268] See *foreknow, foreknowledge.*

[4591] πρόγονος *progonos* 2x *born earlier, elder; a progenitor,* pl. *progenitors; parents,* 1 Tim. 5:4; *forefathers, ancestors,* 2 Tim. 1:3* [4269]

[4592] προγράφω *prographō* 4x *to write before,* Rom. 15:4; Eph. 3:3; *to make a subject of public notice; to set forth unreservedly and distinctly,* Gal. 3:1; *to designate clearly,* Jude 4* [4270]

[4593] πρόδηλος *prodēlos* 3x *previously manifest, before known; plainly manifest, very clear, prominently conspicuous,* 1 Tim. 5:24, 25; Heb. 7:14* [4271]

[4594] προδίδωμι *prodidōmi* 1x *to give before, precede in giving;* Rom. 11:35* [4272]

[4595] προδότης *prodotēs* 3x *a betrayer, traitor,* Lk. 6:16; Acts 7:52; 2 Tim. 3:4* [4273]

[4596] πρόδρομος *prodromos* 1x *a precursor, forerunner, one who advances to explore and prepare the way,* Heb. 6:20* [4274]

[4598] προελπίζω *proelpizō* 1x *to have hope and confidence* in a person or thing *beforehand,* Eph. 1:12* [4276]

[4599] προενάρχομαι *proenarchomai* 2x *to begin before* a particular time, 2 Cor. 8:6, 10* [4278]

[4601] προέρχομαι *proerchomai* 9x *to go forwards, advance, proceed,* Mt. 26:39; Mk. 14:35; Acts 12:10; *to precede, go before* any one, Lk. 22:47; *to precede* in time, *be a forerunner* or *precursor,* Lk. 1:17; *to outgo, outstrip in going,* Mk. 6:33; *to travel in advance of* any one, *precede,* 20:5, 13; 2 Cor. 9:5* [4281]

[4602] προετοιμάζω *proetoimazō* 2x *to prepare beforehand;* in NT *to appoint beforehand,* Rom. 9:23; Eph. 2:10* [4282]

[4603] προευαγγελίζομαι *proeuangelizomai* 1x *to announce joyful tidings beforehand,* Gal. 3:8* [4283]

[4604] προέχω *proechō* 1x *to have* or *hold before;* intrans. and mid. *to excel, surpass, have advantage* or *preeminence,* Rom. 3:9* [4284]

[4605] προηγέομαι *proēgeomai* 1x *to go before, precede, lead onward;* met. *to endeavor to take the lead of, vie with,* or, *to give precedence to, to prefer,* Rom. 12:10* [4285]

[4606] πρόθεσις *prothesis* 12x *a setting forth* or *before;* οἱ ἄρτοι τῆς προθέσεως, and ἡ πρόθεσις τῶν ἄρτων, *the shewbread,* the twelve loaves of bread, corresponding to the twelve tribes, which were *set out* in two rows upon the golden table in the sanctuary, Mt. 12:4; Mk. 2:26; Lk. 6:4; Heb. 9:2; *predetermination, purpose,* Acts 11:23; 27:13; Rom. 8:28; 2 Tim. 3:10 [4286] See *purpose.*

[4607] προθεσμία *prothesmia* 1x *a time before appointed, set* or *appointed time,* Gal. 4:2* [4287]

[4608] προθυμία *prothumia* 5x *promptness, readiness, eagerness of mind, willingness,* Acts 17:11; 2 Cor. 8:11, 12, 19; 9:2* [4288]

[4609] πρόθυμος *prothumos* 3x *ready in mind, prepared, prompt, willing,* Mt. 26:41; Mk. 14:38; τὸ πρόθυμον, i.q. ἡ προθυμία, *readiness, eagerness of mind,* Rom. 1:15* [4289]

[4610] προθύμως *prothumōs* 1x *promptly, readily, willingly, heartily, cheerfully,* 1 Pet. 5:2* [4290]

[4611] πρόϊμος *proimos* 1x also spelled πρώϊμος, *early,* Jas. 5:7* [4406]

[4613] προΐστημι *proistēmi* 8x *to set before;* met. *to set over, appoint with authority;* intrans. 2 aor. προὔστην, perf. προέστηκα, part. προεστώς, and mid. προΐσταμαι, *to preside, govern, superintend,* Rom. 12:8; 1 Thess. 5:12; 1 Tim. 3:4, 5, 12; 5:17; mid. *to undertake resolutely, to practise diligently, to maintain the practice of,* Tit. 3:8, 14* [4291]

[4614] προκαλέω *prokaleō* 1x *to call out, challenge to fight; to provoke, irritate, with feelings of ungenerous rivalry,* Gal. 5:26* [4292]

[4615] προκαταγγέλλω *prokatangellō* 2x *to declare* or *announce beforehand, foretell, predict,* Acts 3:18; 7:52* [4293]

[4616] προκαταρτίζω *prokatartizō* 1x *to make ready, prepare,* or *complete beforehand,* 2 Cor. 9:5* [4294]

[4618] πρόκειμαι *prokeimai* 5x *to lie* or *be placed before;* met. *to be proposed* or *set before,* as a duty, example, reward, etc., Heb. 6:18; 12:1, 2; Jude 7; *to be at hand, be present,* 2 Cor. 8:12* [4295]

[4619] προκηρύσσω *prokēryssō* 1x *to announce publicly;* in NT *to announce before,* Acts 13:24* [4296]

[4620] προκοπή *prokopē* 3x *advance upon a way;* met. *progress, advancement, furtherance,* Phil. 1:12, 25; 1 Tim. 4:15* [4297]

[4621] προκόπτω *prokoptō* 6x pr. *to cut* a passage *forward; to advance, make progress; to advance,* as time, *to be far spent,* Rom. 13:12; met. *to advance* in wisdom, age, or stature, Lk. 2:52; seq. ejn, *to make progress* or *proficiency in,* Gal. 1:14; προκόπτω ἐπὶ πλεῖον, *to proceed* or *advance* further, 2 Tim. 2:16; 3:9; προκόπτω ἐπὶ τὸ χεῖρον, *to grow* worse and worse, 2 Tim. 3:13* [4298]

[4622] πρόκριμα *prokrima* 1x *previous judgment, prejudice,* or, *preference, partiality,* 1 Tim. 5:21* [4299]

[4623] προκυρόω *prokyroō* 1x *to sanction and establish previously, ratify and confirm before,* Gal. 3:17* [4300]

[4624] προλαμβάνω *prolambanō* 3x *to take before* another, 1 Cor. 11:21; trop. *to anticipate, do beforehand,* Mk. 14:8; *to take by surprise;* pass. *be taken unexpectedly, be overtaken, be taken by surprise,* Gal. 6:1* [4301]

[4625] προλέγω *prolegō* 15x *to tell beforehand, to foretell,* Mt. 24:25; Acts 1:16; Rom. 9:29; 2 Cor. 13:2; Gal. 5:21; 1 Thess. 3:4 [4302, 4277, 4280] See *say before; warn.*

[4626] προμαρτύρομαι *promartyromai* 1x pr. *to witness* or *testify beforehand; to declare beforehand, predict,* 1 Pet. 1:11* [4303]

[4627] προμελετάω *promeletaō* 1x *to practise beforehand; to premeditate,* Lk. 21:14* [4304]

[4628] προμεριμνάω *promerimnaō* 1x *to be anxious* or *solicitous beforehand, to ponder beforehand,* Mk. 13:11* [4305]

[4629] προνοέω *pronoeō* 3x *to perceive beforehand, foresee; to provide for,* 1 Tim. 5:8; mid. *to provide for one's self;* by impl. *to apply one's self to* a thing, *practice, strive to exhibit,* Rom. 12:17; 2 Cor. 8:21* [4306]

[4630] πρόνοια *pronoia* 2x *forethought; providence, provident care,* Acts 24:2; *provision,* Rom. 13:14* [4307]

[4632] προοράω *prooraō* 4x *to foresee,* Acts 2:31; Gal. 3:8; *to see before,* Acts 21:29; in NT *to have vividly present to the mind, to be mindful of,* Acts 2:25* [4275, 4308]

[4633] προορίζω *proorizō* 6x *to limit* or *mark out beforehand; to design definitely beforehand, ordain beforehand, predestine,* Acts 4:28; Rom. 8:29, 30 [4309] See *predestine.*

[4634] προπάσχω *propaschō* 1x *to experience previously,* of ill treatment, 1 Thess. 2:2* [4310]

[4635] προπάτωρ *propatōr* 1x *a grandfather; a progenitor,* or *ancestor,* Rom. 4:1* [3962]

[4636] προπέμπω *propempō* 9x *to send on before; to accompany* or *attend out of respect, escort, accompany for a certain distance on setting out on a journey,* Acts 15:3; 20:38; 21:5; *to furnish with things necessary for a journey,* Tit. 3:13; 3 Jn. 6 [4311]

[4637] προπετής *propetēs* 2x *falling forwards;* meton. *precipitate, rash,* Acts 19:36; 2 Tim. 3:4* [4312]

[4638] προπορεύομαι *proporeuomai* 2x *to precede, go before,* Acts 7:40; Lk. 1:76* [4313]

[4639] πρός *pros* 700x *from;* met. *for the benefit of,* Acts 27:34; with a dative, *near, by, at, by the side of, in the vicinity of,* Mk. 5:11; Lk. 19:37; with an accusative, used of the place to which anything tends, *to, unto, towards,* Mt. 2:12; 3:5, 13; *at, close upon,* Mt. 3:10; Mk. 5:22; *near to, in the vicinity of,* Mk. 6:45; after verbs of speaking, praying, answering to a charge, etc., *to,* Mt. 3:15; 27:14; of place where, *with, in, among, by, at,* etc., Mt. 26:55; Mk. 11:4; Lk. 1:80; of time, *for, during,* Lk. 8:13; 1 Cor. 7:5; *near, towards,* Lk. 24:29; of the end, object, purpose for which an action is exerted, or to which any quality, etc., has reference, *to,* Jn. 4:35; Acts 3:10; 27:12; before an infin. with τό, *in order to, that, in order that,* Mt. 6:1; 13:30; 26:12; *so as to, so that,* Mt. 5:28; of the relation which any action, state, quality, etc., bears to any person or thing, *in relation to, of, concerning, in respect to, with reference to,* Mt. 19:8; Lk. 12:41; 18:1; 20:19; *as it respects, as it concerns, with relation to,* Mt. 27:4; Jn. 21:22, 23; *according to, in conformity with,* Lk. 12:47; 2 Cor. 5:10; *in comparison with,* Rom. 8:18; *in attention to,* Eph. 3:4; of the actions, dispositions, etc., exhibited with respect to any one, whether friendly, *towards,* Gal. 6:10; Eph. 6:9; or unfriendly, *with, against,* Lk. 23:12; Acts 23:30; after verbs signifying to converse, dispute, make a covenant, etc., *with,* Lk. 24:14; Acts 2:7; 3:25 [4314]

[4640] προσάββατον *prosabbaton* 1x *the day before the sabbath, sabbath-eve,* Mk. 15:42* [4315]

[4641] προσαγορεύω *prosagoreuō* 1x *to speak to, accost, to name, declare,* Heb. 5:10* [4316]

[4642] προσάγω *prosagō* 4x *to lead* or *conduct to, bring,* Lk. 9:41; Acts 16:20; *to conduct to the presence of, to procure access for,* 1 Pet. 3:18; *to bring near; to near,* in a nautical sense, Acts 27:27* [4317]

[4643] προσαγωγή *prosagōgē* 3x *approach; access, admission,* to the presence of any one, Rom. 5:2; Eph. 2:18; 3:12* [4318] See *access.*

[4644] προσαιτέω *prosaiteō* 1x *to ask for in addition; to ask earnestly, beg; to beg* alms, Jn. 9:8* [4319]

[4645] προσαίτης *prosaitēs* 2x *a beggar, mendicant,* Mk. 10:46; Jn. 9:8* [4319]

[4646] προσαναβαίνω *prosanabainō* 1x *to go up further,* Lk. 14:10* [4320]

[4649] προσαναλόω *prosanaloō* 1x *to spend,* Lk. 8:43* [4321]

[4650] προσαναπληρόω *prosanaplēroō* 2x *to fill up by addition; to supply* deficiencies, 2 Cor. 9:12; 11:9* [4322]

[4651] προσανατίθημι *prosanatithēmi* 2x occurs in the NT only as a middle, *to lay upon over and above;* mid. *to put one's self in free communication with, to confer with,* Gal. 1:16; *to confer upon, to propound as a matter of consideration,* Gal. 2:6* [4323]

[4653] προσαπειλέω *prosapeileō* 1x *to threaten in addition, utter additional threats,* Acts 4:21* [4324]

[4655] προσδαπανάω *prosdapanaō* 1x *to spend besides, expend over and above,* Lk. 10:35* [4325]

[4656] προσδέομαι *prosdeomai* 1x *to want besides* or *in addition, need,* Acts 17:25* [4326]

[4657] προσδέχομαι *prosdechomai* 14x *to receive, accept; to receive, admit, grant access to,* Lk. 15:2; *to receive, admit, accept,* and with οὐ, *to reject,* Heb. 11:35; *to submit to,* Heb. 10:34; *to receive kindly,* as a guest, *entertain,* Rom. 16:2; *to receive, admit,* as a hope, Acts 24:15; *to look* or *wait for, expect, await,* Mk. 15:43; Lk. 2:25 [4327] See *await; expect; receive; wait for; welcome.*

[4659] προσδοκάω *prosdokaō* 16x *to look for, be expectant of,* Mt. 11:3; Lk. 7:19, 20; Acts 3:5; 2 Pet. 3:12, 13, 14; *to expect,* Acts 28:6; *to wait for,* Lk. 1:21; 8:40; Acts 10:24; 27:33; absol. *to think, anticipate,* Mt. 24:50; Lk. 12:46 [4328] See *expect; look for; wait for.*

[4660] προσδοκία *prosdokia* 2x *a looking for, expectation, anticipation,* Lk. 21:26; meton. *expectation, what is expected* or *anticipated,* Acts 12:11* [4329]

[4661] προσεάω *proseaō* 1x *to permit an approach,* Acts 27:7* [4330]

[4664] προσεργάζομαι *prosergazomai* 1x pr. *to work in addition; to gain in addition* in trade, Lk. 19:16* [4333]

[4665] προσέρχομαι *proserchomai* 86x *to come* or *go to* any one, *approach,* Mt. 4:3, 11; 5:1; 8:19, 25, et al. freq.; trop. *to come* or *go to, approach, draw near,* spiritually, Heb. 7:25; 11:6; 4:16; 1 Pet. 2:4; met. *to assent to, accede to, concur in,* 1 Tim. 6:3 [4334] See *approach; come to.*

[4666] προσευχή *proseuchē* 36x *prayer,* Mt. 17:21; 21:13, 22; Lk. 6:12; Acts 1:14; meton. *a place where prayer is offered, an oratory,* perhaps, Acts 16:13, 16 [4335] See *prayer.*

[4667] προσεύχομαι *proseuchomai* 85x *to pray, offer prayer,* Mt. 5:44; 6:5, 6 [4336] See *pray.*

[4668] προσέχω *prosechō* 24x *to have in addition; to hold to, bring near;* absol. *to apply* the mind to a thing, *to give heed to, attend to, observe, consider,* Acts 5:35; Heb. 2:1; 2 Pet. 1:19; *to take care of, provide for,* Acts 20:28; when followed by ἀπό, μή, or μήποτε, *to beware of, take heed of, guard against,* Mt. 6:1; 7:15; *to assent to, yield credence to, follow, adhere* or *be attached to,* Acts 8:6, 10, 11; 16:14; *to give one's self up to, be addicted to, engage in, be occupied with,* 1 Tim. 1:4, 3:8 [4337] See *guard; pay attention; watch out.*

[4669] προσηλόω *prosēloō* 1x *to nail to, affix with nails,* Col. 2:14* [4338]

[4670] προσήλυτος *prosēlytos* 4x pr. *a newcomer, a stranger;* in NT *a proselyte, convert from paganism to Judaism,* Mt. 23:15; Acts 2:11; 6:5; 13:43* [4339]

[4672] πρόσκαιρος *proskairos* 4x *opportune,* in NT *continuing for a limited time, temporary, transient,* Mt. 13:21; Mk. 4:17; 2 Cor. 4:18; Heb. 11:25* [4340]

[4673] προσκαλέω *proskaleō* 29x *to call to one's self, summon,* Mt. 10:1; 15:10, 32; 18:2; *to invite,* Acts 2:39; *to call* to the performance of a thing, *appoint,* Acts 13:2; 16:10 [4341] See *summon.*

[4674] προσκαρτερέω *proskartereō* 10x *to persist in adherence to* a thing; *to be intently engaged in, attend constantly to,* Acts 1:14; 2:42; Rom. 13:6; *to remain constantly* in a place, Acts 2:46; *to constantly attend upon, continue near to, be at hand,* Mk. 3:9; Acts 8:13; 10:7 [4342] See *attend to; (be) devoted to.*

[4675] προσκαρτέρησις *proskarterēsis* 1x *perseverance, unremitting continuance in* a thing, Eph. 6:18* [4343]

[4676] προσκεφάλαιον *proskephalaion* 1x pr. *a cushion for the head, pillow;* also, *a boat cushion,* Mk. 4:38* [4344]

[4677] προσκληρόω *prosklēroō* 1x pr. *to assign by lot;* in NT, *to adjoin one's self to, associate with, follow as a disciple,* Acts 17:4* [4345]

[4679] προσκλίνω *prosklinō* 1x pr. *to make to lean upon* or *against* a thing; met., to *join one's self to, follow as an adherent,* Acts 5:36* [4347]

[4680] πρόσκλισις *prosklisis* 1x pr. *a leaning upon* or *towards* a thing; met. *a leaning towards* any one, *inclination* of mind *towards, partiality,* 1 Tim. 5:21* [4346]

[4681] προσκολλάω *proskollaō* 2x pr. *to glue to; to cleave closely to,* Mk. 10:7; Eph. 5:31* [4347]

[4682] πρόσκομμα *proskomma* 6x *a stumbling,* Rom. 9:32, 33; 1 Pet. 2:8; met. *a stumbling block, an occasion of sinning, means of inducing to sin,* Rom. 14:13; 1 Cor. 8:9; met. *a* moral *stumbling, a shock* to the moral or religious sense, *a* moral *embarrassment,* Rom. 14:20* [4348] See *offense; stumbling block.*

[4683] προσκοπή *proskopē* 1x pr. *a stumbling; offense;* in NT *an offense, shock, ground of exception,* 2 Cor. 6:3* [4349]

[4684] προσκόπτω *proskoptō* 8x *to dash against, to beat upon,* Mt. 7:27; *to strike* the foot *against,* Mt. 4:6; Lk. 4:11; *to stumble,* Jn. 11:9, 10; met. *to stumble at, to take offense at,* Rom. 9:32; 14:21; 1 Pet. 2:8* [4350]

[4685] προσκυλίω *proskyliō* 2x *to roll to* or *against,* Mt. 27:60; Mk. 15:46* [4351]

[4686] προσκυνέω *proskyneō* 60x *to do reverence* or *homage by kissing the hand;* in NT *to do reverence* or *homage by prostration,* Mt. 2:2, 8, 11; 20:20; Lk. 4:7; 24:52; *to pay* divine *homage, worship, adore,* Mt. 4:10; Jn. 4:20, 21; Heb. 1:6; *to bow one's self in adoration,* Heb. 11:21 [4352] See *fall down before; worship.*

[4687] προσκυνητής *proskynētēs* 1x *a worshiper,* Jn. 4:23* [4353]

[4688] προσλαλέω *proslaleō* 2x *to speak to, converse with,* Acts 13:43; 28:20* [4354]

[4689] προσλαμβάνω *proslambanō* 12x *to take to one's self, assume, take as a companion* or *associate,* Acts 17:5; 18:26; *to take,* as food, Acts 27:33, 36; *to receive kindly* or *hospitably, admit to one's society and friendship, treat with kindness,* Acts 28:2; Rom. 14:1, 3; 15:7; Phlm. 17; *to take* or *draw to one's self* as a preliminary to an address of admonition, Mt. 16:22; Mk. 8:32* [4355] See *accept; take aside; welcome.*

[4691] πρόσλημψις *proslēmpsis* 1x also spelled πρόσληψις, *acceptance,* Rom. 11:15* [4356]

[4693] προσμένω *prosmenō* 7x *to continue, remain, stay* in a place, 1 Tim. 1:3; *to remain* or *continue with* any one, Mt. 15:32; Mk. 8:2; Acts 18:18; *to adhere to,* Acts 11:23; met. *to remain constant in, persevere in,* Acts 13:43; 1 Tim. 5:5* [4357]

[4694] προσορμίζω *prosormizō* 1x *to bring a ship to its station* or *to land;* mid. *to come to the land,* Mk. 6:53* [4358]

[4695] προσοφείλω *prosopheilō* 1x *to owe besides* or *in addition,* Phlm. 19* [4359]

[4696] προσοχθίζω *prosochthizō* 2x *to be vexed* or *angry at,* Heb. 3:10, 17* [4360]

[4698] πρόσπεινος *prospeinos* 1x *very hungry,* Acts 10:10* [4361]

[4699] προσπήγνυμι *prospēgnymi* 1x *to fix to, affix to,* Acts 2:23* [4362]

[4700] προσπίπτω *prospiptō* 8x *to fall* or *impinge upon* or *against* a thing; *to fall down to* any one, Mk. 3:11; 7:25; *to rush violently upon, beat against,* Mt. 7:25 [4363]

[4701] προσποιέω *prospoieō* 1x *to add* or *attach;* mid. *to attach to one's self; to claim* or *arrogate to one's self; to assume the appearance of, make a show of, pretend,* Lk. 24:28* [4364]

[4702] προσπορεύομαι *prosporeuomai* 1x *to go* or *come to* any one, Mk. 10:35* [4365]

[4704] προσρήσσω *prosrēssō* 2x also spelled προσρήγνυμι, *to break* or *burst upon, dash against,* Lk. 6:48, 49* [4366]

[4705] προστάσσω *prostassō* 7x pr. *to place* or *station at* or *against; to enjoin, command, direct,* Mt. 1:24; 8:4; Mk. 1:44; *to assign, constitute, appoint,* Acts 17:26 [4367] See *command; instruct.*

[4706] προστάτις *prostatis* 1x *a patroness, protectress,* Rom. 16:2* [4368]

[4707] προστίθημι *prostithēmi* 18x *to put to* or *near; to lay with* or *by the side of,* Acts 13:36; *to add, adjoin,* Mt. 6:27, 33; Lk. 3:20; Acts 2:41; from the Hebrew, denote *continuation,* or *repetition,* Lk. 19:11; 20:11, 12; Acts 12:3 [4369] See *add; increase.*

[4708] προστρέχω *prostrechō* 3x *to run to,* or *up,* Mk. 9:15; 10:17; Acts 8:30* [4370]

[4709] προσφάγιον *prosphagion* 1x *what is eaten besides;* hence, genr. *victuals, food,* Jn. 21:5* [4371]

[4710] πρόσφατος *prosphatos* 1x pr. *recently killed;* hence, genr. *recent, new, newly* or *lately made,* Heb. 10:20* [4372]

[4711] προσφάτως *prosphatōs* 1x *newly, recently, lately,* Acts 18:2* [4373]

[4712] προσφέρω *prospherō* 47x *to bear* or *bring to,* Mt. 4:24; 25:20; *to bring to* or *before* magistrates, Lk. 12:11; 23:14; *to bring near to, apply to,* Jn. 19:29; *to offer, tender, proffer,* as money, Acts 8:18; *to offer, present,* as gifts, oblations, etc., Mt. 2:11; 5:23; Heb. 5:7; *to offer* in sacrifice, Mk. 1:44; Lk. 5:14; *to offer up* any one as a sacrifice to God, Heb. 9:25, 28; 11:17; mid. *to bear one's self towards, behave* or *conduct one's self towards, to deal with, treat* any one, Heb. 12:7 [4374] See *bring; offer.*

[4713] προσφιλής *prosphilēs* 1x *friendly, grateful, acceptable,* Phil. 4:8* [4375]

[4714] προσφορά *prosphora* 9x pr. *a bringing to;* in NT *an offering, an act of offering up* or *sacrificing,* Heb. 10:10, 14, 18; trop. Rom. 15:16; *an offering, oblation, a thing offered,* Eph. 5:2; Heb. 10:5, 8; *a sacrifice, victim offered,* Acts 21:26; 24:17* [4376]

[4715] προσφωνέω *prosphōneō* 7x *to speak to, address,* Mt. 11:16; Lk. 7:32; 13:12; *to address, harangue,* Acts 22:2; *to call* to one's self, Lk. 6:13 [4377]

[4717] πρόσχυσις *proschusis* 1x *an effusion, sprinkling,* Heb. 11:28* [4378]

[4718] προσψαύω *prospsauō* 1x *to touch upon, touch lightly,* with the dative, Lk. 11:46* [4379]

[4719] προσωπολημπτέω *prosōpolēmpteō* 1x *show partiality,* Jas. 2:9* [4380]

[4720] προσωπολήμπτης *prosōpolēmptēs* 1x *one who shows partiality,* Acts 10:34* [4381]

[4721] προσωποληµψία *prosōpolēmpsia* 4x *respect of persons, partiality,* Rom. 2:11; Eph. 6:9; Col. 3:25; Jas. 2:1* [4382]

[4725] πρόσωπον *prosōpon* 76x *the face, countenance, visage,* Mt. 6:16, 17; 17:2, 6; according to late usage, *a person, individual,* 2 Cor. 1:11; hence, *a personal presence,* 1 Thess. 2:17; from the Hebrew, πρόσωπον πρὸς πρόσωπον, *face to face, clearly, perfectly,* 1 Cor. 13:12; *face, surface, external form, figure, appearance,* Mt. 16:3; Lk. 12:56; *external circumstances,* or *condition* of any one, Mt. 22:16; Mk. 12:14; πρόσωπον λαμβάνειν, *to have respect to the external circumstances* of any one, Lk. 20:21; Gal. 2:6; ἐν προσώπῳ, *in presence of,* 2 Cor. 2:10; ἀπὸ προσώπου, *from the presence of, from,* Acts 3:19; also, *from before,* Acts 7:45; εἰς πρόσωπον, and κατὰ πρόσωπον, *in the presence of, before,* Acts 3:13; 2 Cor. 8:24; also, *openly,* Gal. 2:11; κατὰ πρόσωπον, ἔχειν, *to have before one's face, to have* any one *present,* Acts 25:16; ἀπὸ προσώπου, *from,* Rev. 12:14; πρὸ προσώπου, *before,* Acts 13:24 [4383] See *countenance; face.*

[4727] προτείνω *proteinō* 1x *to extend before; to stretch out,* Acts 22:25* [4385]

[4728] πρότερος *proteros* 11x *former, prior,* Eph. 4:22; *before, formerly,* Jn. 6:62 [4386, 4387] See *earlier; former.*

[4729] προτίθημι *protithēmi* 3x *to place before; to set forth, propose publicly,* Rom. 3:25; mid. προτίθεμαι, *to purpose, determine, design beforehand,* Rom. 1:13; Eph. 1:9* [4388] See *plan; present.*

[4730] προτρέπω *protrepō* 1x *to turn forwards; to impel; to excite, urge, exhort,* Acts 18:27* [4389]

[4731] προτρέχω *protrechō* 2x *to run before,* or *in advance,* Lk. 19:4; Jn. 20:4* [4390]

[4732] προϋπάρχω *prouparchō* 2x *to be before,* or *formerly,* Lk. 23:12; Acts 8:9* [4391]

[4733] πρόφασις *prophasis* 6x pr. *that which appears in front, that which is put forward to hide the true state of things; a fair show* or *pretext,* Acts 27:30; *a specious cloak,* Mt. 23:13; 1 Thess. 2:5; *an excuse,* Jn. 15:22 [4392]

[4734] προφέρω *propherō* 2x *to bring before, present; to bring forth* or *out, produce,* Lk. 6:45 (2x)* [4393]

[4735] προφητεία *prophēteia* 19x *prophecy, a prediction of future events,* Mt. 13:14; 2 Pet. 1:20, 21; *prophecy, a gifted faculty of setting forth and enforcing revealed truth,* 1 Cor. 12:10; 13:2; *prophecy, matter of divine teaching set forth by special gift,* 1 Tim. 1:18 [4394] See *prophecy.*

[4736] προφητεύω *prophēteuō* 28x *to exercise the function of a* προφήτης; *to prophesy, to foretell the future,* Mt. 11:13; *to divine,* Mt. 26:68; Mk. 14:65; Lk. 22:64; *to prophesy, to set forth matter of divine teaching by special faculty,* 1 Cor. 13:9; 14:1 [4395] See *prophesy.*

[4737] προφήτης *prophētēs* 144x pr. *a spokesman for* another; spc. *a spokesman* or *interpreter* for a deity; *a prophet, seer,* Tit. 1:12; in NT *a prophet, a divinely commissioned and inspired person,* Mt. 14:5; Lk. 7:16, 39; Jn. 9:17; *a prophet* in the Christian church, *a person gifted for the exposition of divine truth,* 1 Cor. 12:28, 29; *a prophet, a foreteller of the future,* Mt. 1:22, et al. freq.; οἱ προφῆται, *the prophetic scriptures of the Old Testament,* Lk. 16:29 [4396] See *prophet.*

[4738] προφητικός *prophētikos* 2x *prophetic, uttered by prophets,* Rom. 16:26; 2 Pet. 1:19* [4397]

[4739] προφῆτις *prophētis* 2x *a prophetess, a divinely gifted female teacher,* Lk. 2:36; Rev. 2:20* [4398]

[4740] προφθάνω *prophthanō* 1x *to outstrip, anticipate; to anticipate* any one in doing or saying a thing, *be beforehand with,* Mt. 17:25* [4399]

[4741] προχειρίζω *procheirizō* 3x also listed as a deponent, προχειρίζομαι, *to take into the hand, to make ready for use* or *action; to constitute, destine,* Acts 3:20; 22:14; 26:16* [4400] See *appoint; choose.*

[4742] προχειροτονέω *procheirotoneō* 1x pr. *to elect before* Acts 10:41* [4401]

[4743] Πρόχορος *Prochoros* 1x *Prochorus,* pr. name, Acts 6:5* [4402]

[4744] πρύμνα *prymna* 3x *the hinder part of a vessel, stern,* Mk. 4:38; Acts 27:29, 41* [4403]

[4745] πρωΐ *prōi* 12x *in the morning, early,* Mt. 16:3; 20:1; Mk. 15:1; Acts 28:23; *the morning watch,* which ushers in the dawn, Mk. 13:35 [4404] See *dawn; early; morning.*

[4746] πρωΐα *prōia* 2x *morning, the morning hour,* Mt. 27:1; Jn. 21:4* [4405]

[4748] πρωϊνός *prōinos* 2x *belonging to the morning, morning,* Rev. 2:28; 22:16* [4407]

[4749] πρῷρα *prōra* 2x *the forepart of a vessel, prow,* Acts 27:30, 41* [4408]

[4750] πρωτεύω *prōteuō* 1x *to be first, to hold the first rank* or *highest dignity, have the preeminence, be chief,* Col. 1:18* [4409]

[4751] πρωτοκαθεδρία *prōtokathedria* 4x *the first* or *uppermost seat, the most honorable seat,* Mt. 23:6; Mk. 12:39; Lk. 11:43; 20:46* [4410]

[4752] πρωτοκλισία *prōtoklisia* 5x *the first place of reclining* at table, *the most honorable place at table,* Mt. 23:6; Mk. 12:39; Lk. 14:7, 8; 20:46 [4411]

[4754] πρῶτον *prōton* 60x an accusative singular neuter form of πρῶτος (*4755*) that became solidified in function as an adverb, *first* in time, *in the first place,* Mk. 4:28; 16:9; τὸ πρῶτον, *at the first, formerly,* Jn. 12:16; 19:39; *first* in dignity, importance, etc., *before all things,* Mt. 6:33 [4412] See *first.*

[4755] πρῶτος *prōtos* 95x *first* in time, order, etc., Mt. 10:2; 26:17; *first* in dignity, importance, etc., *chief, principal, most important,* Mk. 6:21; Lk. 19:47; Acts 13:50; 16:12; as an equivalent to the compar. πρότερος (*4754*), *prior,* Jn. 1:5, 30; 15:18; Mt. 27:64; adverbially, *first,* Jn. 1:42; 5:4; 8:7 [4413] See *first.*

[4756] πρωτοστάτης *prōtostatēs* 1x pr. *one stationed in the first rank* of an army; *a leader; a chief, ringleader,* Acts 24:5* [4414]

[4757] πρωτοτόκια *prōtotokia* 1x *the rights of primogeniture, birthright,* Heb. 12:16 [4415]

[4758] πρωτότοκος *prōtotokos* 8x *firstborn,* Lk. 2:7; Heb. 11:28; in NT *prior in generation,* Col. 1:15; *a firstborn* head of a spiritual family, Rom. 8:29; Heb. 1:6; *firstborn,* as possessed of the peculiar privilege of spiritual generation, Heb. 12:23 [4416] See *firstborn.*

[4759] πρώτως *prōtōs* 1x *for the first time,* Acts 11:26* [4412]

[4760] πταίω *ptaiō* 5x *to cause to stumble;* intrans. *to stumble, stagger, fall; to make a false step;* met. *to err, transgress,* Rom. 11:11; Jas. 2:10; 3:2 (2x); met. *to fail* of an object, 2 Pet. 1:10* [4417]

[4761] πτέρνα *pterna* 1x *the heel,* Jn. 13:18* [4418]

[4762] πτερύγιον *pterygion* 2x *a little wing; the extremity, the extreme point* of a thing; *a pinnacle,* or *apex* of a building, Mt. 4:5; Lk. 4:9* [4419]

[4763] πτέρυξ *pteryx* 5x *a wing, pinion,* Mt. 23:37; Lk. 13:34 [4420]

[4764] πτηνός *ptēnos* 1x as adj., *winged, with feathers;* as noun, *a bird, fowl,* 1 Cor. 15:39* [4421]

[4765] πτοέω *ptoeō* 2x *to terrify, affright;* pass. *to be terrified,* Lk. 21:9; 24:37* [4422]

[4766] πτόησις *ptoēsis* 1x *consternation, dismay,* 1 Pet. 3:6* [4423]

[4767] Πτολεμαΐς *Ptolemais* 1x *Ptolemais,* a city on the seacoast of Galilee: the modern *Acre,* Acts 21:7* [4424]

[4768] πτύον *ptyon* 2x *a fan, winnowing fork,* Mt. 3:12; Lk. 3:17* [4425]

[4769] πτύρω *ptyrō* 1x *to scare, terrify;* pass. *to be terrified, be in consternation,* Phil. 1:28* [4426]

[4770] πτύσμα *ptysma* 1x *spittle, saliva,* Jn. 9:6* [4427]

[4771] πτύσσω *ptyssō* 1x *to fold; to roll up* a scroll, Lk. 4:20* [4428]

[4772] πτύω *ptyō* 3x *to spit, spit out,* Mk. 7:33; 8:23; Jn. 9:6 [4429]

[4773] πτῶμα *ptōma* 7x *a fall; a dead body, carcass, corpse,* Mt. 24:28; Mk. 6:29 [4430]

[4774] πτῶσις *ptōsis* 2x *a fall, crash, ruin,* Mt. 7:27; met. *downfall, ruin,* Lk. 2:34* [4431]

[4775] πτωχεία *ptōcheia* 3x *begging; beggary; poverty,* 2 Cor. 8:2, 9; Rev. 2:9* [4432]

[4776] πτωχεύω *ptōcheuō* 1x *to be a beggar; to be* or *become poor, be in poverty,* 2 Cor. 8:9* [4433]

[4777] πτωχός *ptōchos* 34x *reduced to beggary, mendicant; poor, indigent,* Mt. 19:21; 26:9, 11; met. spiritually *poor,* Rev. 3:17; by impl. *a person of low condition,* Mt. 11:4; Lk. 4:18; 7:22; met. *beggarly, sorry,* Gal. 4:9; met. *lowly,* Mt. 5:3; Lk. 6:20 [4434] See *poor.*

[4778] πυγμή *pygmē* 1x *together with the forearm,* or, *with care, carefully,* Mk. 7:3* [4435]

[4781] πυκνός *pyknos* 3x *dense, thick; frequent,* 1 Tim. 5:23; πυκνά, as an adverb, *frequently, often,* Lk. 5:33; so the compar. πυκνότερον, *very frequently,* Acts 24:26* [4437]

[4782] πυκτεύω *pykteuō* 1x *to box, fight as a boxer,* 1 Cor. 9:26* [4438]

[4783] πύλη *pylē* 10x *a gate,* Mt. 7:13, 14; Lk. 7:12; Acts 12:10; πύλαι ᾅδου, *the gates of hades, the nether world and its powers, the powers of destruction, dissolution,* Mt. 16:18 [4439] See *door; gate.*

[4784] πυλών *pylōn* 18x *a gateway, vestibule,* Mt. 26:71; Lk. 16:20; *a gate,* Acts 14:13; Rev. 21:12, 13, 15, 21, 25 [4440] See *gate.*

[4785] πυνθάνομαι *pynthanomai* 12x *to ask, inquire,* Mt. 2:4; Lk. 15:26; *to investigate, examine* judicially, Acts 23:20; *to ascertain by inquiry, understand,* Acts 23:34 [4441] See *ask.*

[4786] πῦρ *pyr* 71x *fire,* Mt. 3:10; 7:19; 13:40, et al. freq.; πυρός, used by Hebraism with the force of an adjective, *fiery, fierce,* Heb. 10:27; *fire* used figuratively to express various circumstances of severe trial, Lk. 12:49; 1 Cor. 3:13; Jude 23 [4442] See *fire.*

[4787] πυρά *pyra* 2x *a fire, heap of combustibles,* Acts 28:2, 3* [4443]

[4788] πύργος *pyrgos* 4x *a tower,* Mt. 21:33; Mk. 12:1; Lk. 13:4; genr. *a castle, palace,* Lk. 14:28* [4444]

[4789] πυρέσσω *pyressō* 2x *to be feverish, be sick of a fever,* Mt. 8:14; Mk. 1:30* [4445]

[4790] πυρετός *pyretos* 6x *scorching and noxious heat; a fever,* Mt. 8:15; Mk. 1:31 [4446]

[4791] πύρινος *pyrinos* 1x pr. *of fire, fiery, burning; shining, glittering,* Rev. 9:17* [4447]

[4792] πυρόω *pyroō* 6x *to set on fire, burn;* pass. *to be kindled, be on fire, burn, flame,* Eph. 6:16; 2 Pet. 3:12; Rev. 1:15; met. *to fire* with distressful feelings, 2 Cor. 11:29; of lust, *to be inflamed, burn,* 1 Cor. 7:9; *to be tried with fire,* as metals, Rev. 3:18* [4448]

[4793] πυρράζω *pyrrazō* 2x *to be fiery red,* Mt. 16:2, 3* [4449]

[4794] πυρρός *pyrros* 2x *of the color of fire, fiery red,* Rev. 6:4; 12:3* [4450]

[4795] Πύρρος *Pyrros* 1x *Pyrrhus,* pr. name, Acts 20:4* [**]

[4796] πύρωσις *pyrōsis* 3x *a burning, conflagration,* Rev. 18:9, 18; met. *a fiery test* of trying circumstances, 1 Pet. 4:12* [4451]

[4797] πωλέω *pōleō* 22x *to sell,* Mt. 10:29; 13:44 [4453] See *sell.*

[4798] πῶλος *pōlos* 12x *a youngling; a foal* or *colt,* Mt. 21:2, 5, 7; Mk. 11:2 [4454] See *colt.*

[4799] πώποτε *pōpote* 6x *ever yet, ever, at any time,* Lk. 19:30; Jn. 1:18 [4455]

[4800] πωρόω *pōroō* 5x *to petrify; to harden;* in NT *to harden* the feelings, Jn. 12:40; pass. *to become callous, unimpressible,* Mk. 6:52; 8:17; Rom. 11:7; 2 Cor. 3:14* [4456]

[4801] πώρωσις *pōrōsis* 3x *a hardening;* met. *hardness* of heart, *callousness, insensibility,* Mk. 3:5; Rom. 11:25; Eph. 4:18* [4457]

[4802] πῶς *pōs* 103x interrogative particle, *How? In what manner? By what means?* Mt. 7:4; 22:12; Jn. 6:52; used in interrogations which imply a negative, Mt. 12:26, 29, 34; 22:45; 23:33; Acts 8:31; put concisely for *How is it that? How does it come to pass that?* Mt. 16:11; 22:43; Mk. 4:40; Jn. 7:15; with an indirect interrogation, *how, in what manner,* Mt. 6:28; 10:19; Mk. 11:18; put for τί, *What?* Lk. 10:26; put for ὡς, as a particle of exclamation, *how, how much, how greatly,* Mk. 10:23, 24 [4459]

[4803] πως *pōs* 15x enclitic particle, *in any way, by any means,* Acts 27:12; Rom. 1:10 [4452, 4458]

[4805] Ῥαάβ *Rhaab* 2x *Rahab,* pr. name, indecl (Jsh. 2; 6:17, 25) Heb. 11:31; Jas. 2:25* [4460]

[4806] ῥαββί *rhabbi* 15x also spelled ῥαββεί, *rabbi, my master, teacher,* Mt. 23:7, 8; 26:25, 49 [4461] See *master; rabbi; sir.*

[4808] ῥαββουνί *rhabbouni* 2x a form of ῥαββί, *my teacher,* Mk. 10:51; Jn. 20:16 [4462]

[4810] ῥαβδίζω *rhabdizō* 2x *to beat with rods,* Acts 16:22; 2 Cor. 11:25* [4463]

[4811] ῥάβδος *rhabdos* 12x *a rod, wand,* Heb. 9:4; Rev. 11:1; *a rod* of correction, 1 Cor. 4:21; *a staff,* Mt. 10:10; Heb. 11:21; *a scepter,* Heb. 1:8; Rev. 2:27 [4464] See *rod; scepter; staff.*

[4812] ῥαβδοῦχος *rhabdouchos* 2x *the bearer of a wand* of office; *a lictor, sergeant,* a public servant who bore a bundle or rods before the magistrates as insignia of their office, and carried into execution the sentences they pronounced, Acts 16:35, 38* [4465]

[4814] Ῥαγαύ *Rhagau* 1x *Ragau,* pr. name, indecl. Lk. 3:35* [4466]

[4815] ῥᾳδιούργημα *rhadiourgēma* 1x pr. *anything done lightly, levity; reckless conduct, crime,* Acts 18:14* [4467]

[4816] ῥᾳδιουργία *rhadiourgia* 1x *facility of doing* anything; *levity in doing; recklessness, wickedness,* Acts 13:10* [4468]

[4818] Ῥαιφάν *Rhaiphan* 1x pr. name., *Rephan,* Acts 7:43* [4481]

[4819] ῥακά *rhaka* 1x *raca,* an Aramaic term of bitter contempt, *worthless fellow, fool,* Mt. 5:22* [4469]

[4820] ῥάκος *rhakos* 2x *a piece torn off; a bit of cloth, cloth,* Mt. 9:16; Mk. 2:21* [4470]

[4821] Ῥαμά *Rhama* 1x *Rama,* a city of Judea [4471]

[4822] ῥαντίζω *rhantizō* 4x *to sprinkle,* Heb. 9:13, 19, 21; met. and by impl. *to cleanse by sprinkling, purify, free from pollution,* Heb. 10:22* [4472]

[4823] ῥαντισμός *rhantismos* 2x pr. *a sprinkling;* met. *a cleansing, purification,* Heb. 12:24; 1 Pet. 1:2* [4473]

[4824] ῥαπίζω *rhapizō* 2x *to beat with rods; to strike with the palm of the hand, cuff, clap,* Mt. 5:39; 26:67* [4474]

[4825] ῥάπισμα *rhapisma* 3x *a blow with the palm of the hand, cuff, slap,* Mk. 14:65; Jn. 18:22; 19:3* [4475]

[4827] ῥαφίς *rhaphis* 2x *a needle,* Mt. 19:24; Mk. 10:25* [4476]

[4829] Ῥαχάβ *Rhachab* 1x *Rachab,* pr. name, indecl., Mt. 1:5* [4477]

[4830] Ῥαχήλ *Rhachēl* 1x *Rachel,* pr. name, indecl., Mt. 2:18* [4478]

[4831] Ῥεβέκκα *Rhebekka* 1x *Rebecca,* pr. name, Rom. 9:10* [4479]

[4832] ῥέδη *rhedē* 1x *a carriage with four wheels* for travelling, *a chariot,* Rev. 18:13* [4480]

[4835] ῥέω *rheō* 1x *flow, overflow with,* Jn. 7:38* [4482]

[4836] Ῥήγιον *Rhēgion* 1x *Rhegium,* a city at the southwestern extremity of Italy, Acts 28:13* [4484]

[4837] ῥῆγμα *rhēgma* 1x *a rent; a crash, ruin,* Lk. 6:49* [4485]

[4838] ῥήγνυμι *rhēgnymi* 1x see ῥήσσω [4486]

[4839] ῥῆμα *rhēma* 68x *that which is spoken; declaration, saying, speech, word,* Mt. 12:36; 26:75; Mk. 9:32; 14:72; *a command, mandate, direction,* Lk. 3:2; 5:5; *a promise,* Lk. 1:38; 2:29; *a prediction, prophecy,* 2 Pet. 3:2; *a doctrine* of God or Christ, Jn. 3:34; 5:47; 6:63, 68; Acts 5:20; *an accusation, charge, crimination,* Mt. 5:11; 27:14; from the Hebrew, *a thing,* Mt. 4:4; Lk. 4:4; *a matter, affair, transaction, business,* Mt. 18:16; Lk. 1:65; 2 Cor. 13:1 [4487] See *event; matter; word.*

[4840] Ῥησά *Rhēsa* 1x *Rhesa,* pr. name, indecl., Lk. 3:27* [4488]

[4841] ῥήσσω *rhēssō* 6x also spelled ῥήγνυμι 1x in our text (Mt. 9:17). *to rend, shatter; to break* or *burst in pieces* Mt. 9:17; Mk. 2:22; Lk. 5:37; *to rend, lacerate,* Mt. 7:6; *to cast* or *dash* upon the ground, *convulse,* Mk. 9:18; Lk. 9:42; absol. *to break forth* into exclamation, Gal. 4:27 [4486]

[4842] ῥήτωρ *rhētōr* 1x *an orator, advocate,* Acts 24:1* [4489]

[4843] ῥητῶς *rhētōs* 1x *in express words, expressly,* 1 Tim. 4:1* [4490]

[4844] ῥίζα *rhiza* 17x *a root* of a tree, Mt. 3:10; 13:6; met. ἔχειν ῥίζαν, or ἔχειν ῥίζαν ἐν ἑαυτῷ, *to be rooted* in faith, Mt. 13:21; Mk. 4:17; Lk. 8:13; met. *cause, source, origin,* 1 Tim. 6:10; Heb. 12:15; by synec. *the trunk, stock* of a tree, met. Rom. 11:16, 17, 18; met. *offspring, progeny, a descendant,* Rom. 15:12; Rev. 5:5; 22:16 [4491] See *root.*

[4845] ῥιζόω *rhizoō* 2x *to root, cause to take root; firmly rooted, strengthened with roots;* met. *firm, constant, firmly fixed,* Eph. 3:17; Col. 2:7* [4492]

[4846] ῥιπή *rhipē* 1x pr. *a rapid sweep, jerk; a wink, twinkling* of the eye, 1 Cor. 15:52* [4493]

[4847] ῥιπίζω *rhipizō* 1x *to fan, blow, ventilate; to toss, agitate,* e.g. the ocean by the wind, Jas. 1:6* [4494]

[4848] ῥιπτέω *rhipteō* 1x also spelled ῥίπτω, frequent and repeated action, *to toss repeatedly, toss up* with violent gesture, Acts 22:23 (ῥιπτούντων)* [4495]

[4849] ῥίπτω *rhiptō* 7x also spelled ῥιπτέω, *to hurl, throw, cast; to throw* or *cast down,* Mt. 27:5; Lk. 4:35; 17:2; *to throw* or *cast* out, Acts 27:19, 29; *to lay down, set down,* Mt. 15:30; pass. *to be dispersed, scattered,* Mt. 9:36* [4496]

[4850] Ῥοβοάμ *Rhoboam* 2x *Roboam,* pr. name, indecl., Mt. 1:7* [4497]

[4851] Ῥόδη *Rhodē* 1x *Rhoda,* pr. name, Acts 12:13* [4498]

[4852] Ῥόδος *Rhodos* 1x *Rhodes,* an island in the Mediterranean, south of Caria, Acts 21:1* [4499]

[4853] ῥοιζηδόν *rhoizēdon* 1x *with a noise, with a crash,* etc., 2 Pet. 3:10* [4500]

[4855] ῥομφαία *rhomphaia* 7x pr. *a* Thracian *broad-sword; a sword,* Rev. 1:16; 2:12; by meton. *war,* Rev. 6:8; met. *a thrill of anguish,* Lk. 2:35 [4501]

[4857] Ῥουβήν *Rhoubēn* 1x *Reuben,* pr. name, indecl., Rev. 7:5* [4502]

[4858] Ῥούθ *Rhouth* 1x *Ruth,* pr. name, indecl., Mt. 1:5* [4503]

[4859] Ῥοῦφος *Rhouphos* 2x *Rufus,* pr. name, Mk. 15:21; Rom. 16:13* [4504]

[4860] ῥύμη *rhymē* 4x pr. *a rush* or *sweep* of a body in motion; *a street,* Acts 9:11; 12:10; *a narrow street, lane, alley,* as distinguished from πλατεῖα, Mt. 6:2; Lk. 14:21* [4505]

[4861] ῥύομαι *rhyomai* 17x *to drag* out of danger, *to rescue, save,* Mt. 6:13; 27:43; *to be rescued, delivered,* Lk. 1:74; Rom. 15:31; 2 Thess. 3:2; 2 Tim. 4:17 [4506] See *deliver; rescue.*

[4862] ῥυπαίνω *rhypainō* 1x *to make filthy, defile,* Rev. 22:11* [4510]

[4864] ῥυπαρία *rhyparia* 1x *filth;* met. moral *filthiness, uncleanness, pollution,* Jas. 1:21* [4507]

[4865] ῥυπαρός *rhyparos* 2x *filthy, squalid, sordid, dirty,* Jas. 2:2; met. *defiled, polluted,* Rev. 22:11* [4508]

[4866] ῥύπος *rhypos* 1x *filth, squalor,* 1 Pet. 3:21* [4509]

[4868] ῥύσις *rhysis* 3x *a flowing; a* morbid *flux,* Mk. 5:25; Lk. 8:43, 44* [4511]

[4869] ῥυτίς *rhytis* 1x *a wrinkle;* met. *a* disfiguring *wrinkle, flaw, blemish,* Eph. 5:27* [4512]

[4871] Ῥωμαῖος *Rhōmaios* 12x *Roman; a Roman citizen,* Jn. 11:48; Acts 2:10; 16:21 [4514]

[4872] Ῥωμαϊστί *Rhōmaisti* 1x *in the Roman language, in Latin,* Jn. 19:20* [4515]

[4873] Ῥώμη *Rhōmē* 8x *Rome,* Acts 18:2; 19:21; 23:11; 28:14, 16; Rom. 1:7, 15; 2 Tim. 1:17* [4516]

[4874] ῥώννυμι *rhōnnymi* 1x *to strengthen, render firm; to be well, enjoy firm health;* at the end of letters, like the Latin *vale, farewell,* Acts 15:29* [4517]

[4876] σαβαχθάνι *sabachthani* 2x (Aramaic) *sabacthani, you have forsaken me;* interrogatively, *have you forsaken me?* preceded with λαμᾶ, *Why?* Mt. 27:46; Mk. 15:34* [4518]

[4877] Σαβαώθ *Sabaōth* 2x (Hebrew) *hosts, armies,* indecl., Rom. 9:29; Jas. 5:4* [4519]

[4878] σαββατισμός *sabbatismos* 1x pr. *a keeping of a sabbath; a state of rest, a sabbath-state,* Heb. 4:9* [4520]

[4879] σάββατον *sabbaton* 68x pr. *cessation from labor, rest; the* Jewish *sabbath,* both in the sg. and pl., Mt. 12:2, 5, 8; 28:1; Lk. 4:16; *a week,* sg. and pl., Mt. 28:1; Mk. 16:9; pl. *sabbaths,* or *times of sacred rest,* Col. 2:16 [4521] See *sabbath.*

[4880] σαγήνη *sagēnē* 1x *a large net,* Mt. 13:47* [4522]

[4881] Σαδδουκαῖος *Saddoukaios* 14x *a Sadducee, one belonging to the sect of the Sadducees,* which, according to the Talmudists, was founded by one, *Sadoc,* about three centuries before the Christian era: they were directly opposed in sentiments to the Pharisees, Mt. 3:7; 16:1, 6, 11, 12; 22:23, 34; Mk. 12:18; Lk. 20:27; Acts 4:1; 5:17; 23:6-8* [4523]

[4882] Σαδώκ *Sadōk* 2x *Zadok,* pr. name, indecl., Mt. 1:14* [4524]

[4883] σαίνω *sainō* 1x pr. *to wag* the tail; *to fawn, flatter, cajole;* pass. *to be cajoled; to be wrought upon, to be perturbed,* 1 Thess. 3:3* [4525]

[4884] σάκκος *sakkos* 4x *sackcloth,* a coarse black cloth made of hair (goat or camel), Rev. 6:12; a mourning garment of *sackcloth,* Mt. 11:21; Lk. 10:13; Rev. 11:3* [4526]

[4885] Σαλά *Sala* 2x *Sala,* pr. name, indecl., Lk. 3:32, 35* [4527]

[4886] Σαλαθιήλ *Salathiēl* 3x *Shealtiel,* pr. name, indecl., Mt. 1:12; Lk. 3:27* [4528]

[4887] Σαλαμίς *Salamis* 1x *Salamis,* a city in the island of Cyprus, Acts 13:5* [4529]

[4887.5] Σαλείμ *Saleim* 1x *Saleim,* also formed as Σαλίμ (*4890*). John was baptizing at Aenon near Saleim, Jn. 3:26* [4529]

[4888] σαλεύω *saleuō* 15x *to make to rock, to shake,* Mt. 11:7; 24:29; Mk. 13:25; Lk. 6:38, 48; 7:24; 21:26; Acts 4:31; 16:26; Heb. 12:26; met. *to stir up, excite* the people, Acts 17:13; *to agitate, disturb* mentally, Acts 2:25; 2 Thess. 2:2; pass. impl. *to totter, be ready to fall, be near to ruin,* met. Heb. 12:36, 27* [4531] See *agitate; shake.*

[4889] Σαλήμ *Salēm* 2x (Hebrew, meaning *peace*), *Salem,* pr. name, indecl., Heb. 7:1f.* [4532]

[4891] Σαλμών *Salmōn* 2x *Salmon,* pr. name, indecl., Mt. 1:4f.* [4533]

[4892] Σαλμώνη *Salmōnē* 1x *Salmone,* a promontory, the eastern extremity of Crete, Acts 27:7* [4534]

[4893] σάλος *salos* 1x *agitation, tossing, rolling,* spc. of the sea, Lk. 21:25* [4535]

[4894] σάλπιγξ *salpinx* 11x *trumpet,* 1 Cor. 14:8; Heb. 12:19; Rev. 1:10; 4:1; 8:2, 6; 13:9; 1 Thess. 4:16; *sound of the trumpet,* Mt. 24:31; 1 Cor. 15:52; 1 Thess. 4:16* [4536] See *trumpet.*

[4895] σαλπίζω *salpizō* 12x *to sound a trumpet,* Mt. 6:2; 1 Cor. 5:52; Rev. 8:6, 7, 8, 10, 12, 13; 9:1, 13; 10:7; 11:15* [4537] See *sound (a trumpet).*

[4896] σαλπιστής *salpistēs* 1x *a trumpeter,* Rev. 18:22* [4538]

[4897] Σαλώμη *Salōmē* 2x *Salome,* pr. name, a Galilean woman who followed Jesus, Mt. 27:56; Mk. 15:40; 16:1* [4539]

[4899] Σαμάρεια *Samareia* 11x *Samaria,* the city and region so called, Acts 8:14 [4540]

[4901] Σαμαρίτης *Samaritēs* 9x *a Samaritan, an inhabitant of the city* or *region of Samaria,* applied by the Jews as a term of reproach and contempt, Mt. 10:5; Jn. 4:9, 39f.; 8:48; Lk. 9:52; 10:33; 17:16; Acts 8:25* [4541]

[4902] Σαμαρῖτις *Samaritis* 2x *a Samaritan woman,* Jn. 4:9* [4542]

[4903] Σαμοθρᾴκη *Samothrakē* 1x *Samothrace,* an island in the northern part of the Aegean sea, Acts 16:11* [4543]

[4904] Σάμος *Samos* 1x *Samos,* a celebrated island, in the Aegean sea, Acts 20:15* [4544]

[4905] Σαμουήλ *Samouēl* 3x (1 Sam. 1:1-25:1), *Samuel,* pr. name, indecl., Acts 3:24; 13:20; Heb. 11:32* [4545]

[4907] Σαμψών *Sampsōn* 1x (Jdg. 13-16), *Samson,* pr. name, indecl., Heb. 11:32* [4546]

[4908] σανδάλιον *sandalion* 2x *a sandal,* a sole of wood or hide, covering the bottom of the foot, and bound on with leathern thongs, Mk. 6:9, Acts 12:8* [4547]

[4909] σανίς *sanis* 1x *a board, plank,* Acts 27:44* [4548]

[4910] Σαούλ *Saoul* 9x *Saul,* pr. name, indecl. I. *Saul, king of Israel,* Acts 13:21; II. *The Apostle Paul,* Acts 9:4, 17; 22:7, 13; 26:14* [4549]

[4911] σαπρός *sapros* 8x pr. *rotten, putrid;* hence, *bad, of a bad quality,* Mt. 7:17, 18; 12:33; Lk. 6:43; *refuse,* Mt. 13:48; met. *corrupt, depraved, vicious, foul, impure,* Eph. 4:29* [4550]

[4912] Σάπφιρα *Sapphira* 1x *Sapphira,* wife of Ananias and a member of the Jerusalem church, Acts 5:1* [4551]

[4913] σάπφιρος *sapphiros* 1x *a sapphire,* a precious stone of a blue color in various shades, next in hardness and value to the diamond, Rev. 21:19 [4552]

[4914] σαργάνη *sarganē* 1x *twisted* or *plaited work; a netword of cords like a basket, basket of ropes,* etc. 2 Cor. 11:33* [4553]

[4915] Σάρδεις *Sardeis* 3x *Sardis,* the capital city of Lydia, in Asia Minor Rev. 1:11; 3:1, 4* [4554]

[4917] σάρδιον *sardion* 2x *carnelian,* a reddish precious stone, Rev. 4:3; 21:20* [4556]

[4918] σαρδόνυξ *sardonyx* 1x *sardonyx,* a gem exhibiting the color of the carnelian and the white of the calcedony, intermingled in alternate layers, Rev. 21:20* [4557]

[4919] Σάρεπτα *Sarepta* 1x *Sarepta,* a city of Phoenicia, between Tyre and Sidon, Lk. 4:26* [4558]

[4920] σαρκικός *sarkikos* 7x *fleshly; pertaining to the body, corporeal, physical,* Rom. 15:27; 1 Cor. 9:11; *carnal, pertaining to the flesh,* 1 Pet. 2:11; *carnal, low in spiritual knowledge and frame,* 1 Cor. 3:3 (2x); *carnal, human* as opposed to divine, 2 Cor. 1:12; 10:4* [4559] See *fleshly; worldly;*

[4921] σάρκινος *sarkinos* 4x *of flesh, fleshly,* 2 Cor. 3:3; Rom. 7:14; 1 Cor. 3:1; Heb. 7:16* [4560]

[4922] σάρξ *sarx* 147x *flesh,* Lk. 24:39; Jn. 3:6; *the* human *body,* 2 Cor. 7:5; *flesh, human nature, human frame,* Jn. 1:13, 14; 1 Pet. 4:1; 1 Jn. 4:2; *kindred,* Rom. 11:14; *lineage,* Rom. 1:3; 9:3; *flesh, humanity, human beings,* Mt. 24:22; Lk. 3:6; Jn. 17:2; *the circumstances of the body, material condition,* 1 Cor. 5:5; 7:28; Phlm. 16; *flesh, mere humanity, human fashion,* 1 Cor. 1:26; 2 Cor. 1:17; *flesh* as the seat of passion and frailty, Rom. 8:1, 3, 5; *carnality,* Gal. 5:24; *materiality, material circumstance,* as opposed to the spiritual, Phil. 3:3, 4; Col. 2:18; *a material system* or *mode,* Gal. 3:3; Heb. 9:10 [4561] See *body; flesh; sinful nature.*

[4924] σαρόω *saroō* 3x *to sweep, to clean with a broom,* Mt. 12:44; Lk. 11:25; 15:8* [4563]

[4925] Σάρρα *Sarra* 4x *Sara, Sarah,* pr. name, the wife of Abraham, Rom. 4:19; 9:9; Heb. 11:11; 1 Pet. 3:6* [4564]

[4926] Σαρών *Sarōn* 1x *Saron,* a level tract of Palestine, between Caesarea and Joppa, Acts 9:35* [4565]

[4928] Σατανᾶς *Satanas* 36x *an adversary, opponent, enemy,* perhaps, Mt. 16:23; Mk. 8:33; Lk. 4:8; elsewhere, *Satan, the devil,* Mt. 4:10; Mk. 1:13 [4567] See *Satan.*

[4929] σάτον *saton* 2x *a satum* or *seah,* a Hebrew measure for things dry, containing, as Josephus testifies, (*Ant.* 9.85) an Italian modius and one half, or 24 sextarii, and therefore equivalent to somewhat less than three gallons English, Mt. 13:33; Lk. 13:21* [4568]

[4930] Σαῦλος *Saulos* 15x *Saul,* the Hebrew name of the Apostle Paul, Σαούλ with a Greek termination, Acts 7:58; 8:1, 3; 9:1 [4569]

[4931] σβέννυμι *sbennymi* 6x *to extinguish, quench,* Mt. 12:20; 25:8; Mk.

9:44, 46, 48; Eph. 6:16; Heb. 11:34; met. *to quench, damp, hinder, thwart,* 1 Thess. 5:19* [4570] See *quench.*

[4932] σεαυτοῦ *seautou* 43x *of yourself, to yourself,* etc. Mt. 4:6; 8:4; 19:19 [4572]

[4933] σεβάζομαι *sebazomai* 1x *to feel dread of* a thing; *to venerate, adore, worship,* Rom. 1:25* [4573]

[4934] σέβασμα *sebasma* 2x *an object of religious veneration and worship,* Acts 17:23; 2 Thess. 2:4* [4574]

[4935] σεβαστός *sebastos* 3x pr. *venerable, august;* ὁ Σεβαστός, i.q. Latin *Augustus,* Acts 25:21, 25; *Augustan,* or, *Sebastan,* named from the city Sebaste, Acts 27:1* [4575]

[4936] σέβω *sebō* 10x mid., *to stand in awe; to venerate, reverence, worship, adore,* Mt. 15:9; Mk. 7:7; Acts 18:13; 19:27; part. σεβόμενος, η, ον, *worshiping, devout, pious,* a term applied to proselytes to Judaism, Acts 13:43; 16:14; 18:7; 13:50; 17:4, 17* [4576] See *worship.*

[4937] σειρά *seira* 1x *a cord, rope, band;* in NT *a chain,* 2 Pet. 2:4* [4577]

[4939] σεισμός *seismos* 14x pr. *a shaking, agitation, concussion; an earthquake,* Mt. 24:7; 27:54; *a tempest,* Mt. 8:24 [4578] See *earthquake; storm.*

[4940] σείω *seiō* 5x *to shake, agitate,* Heb. 12:26; pass. *to quake,* Mt. 27:51; 28:4; Rev. 6:13; met. *to put in commotion, agitate,* Mt. 21:10 [4579]

[4941] Σεκοῦνδος *Sekoundos* 1x *Secundus,* pr. name, Acts 20:4* [4580]

[4942] Σελεύκεια *Seleukeia* 1x *Seleucia,* a city of Syria, west of Antioch, on the Orontes, Acts 13:4* [4581]

[4943] σελήνη *selēnē* 9x *the moon,* Mt. 24:29; Mk. 13:24 [4582] See *moon.*

[4944] σεληνιάζομαι *selēniazomai* 2x *to be a lunatic,* Mt. 4:24; 17:15* [4583]

[4946] Σεμεΐν *Semein* 1x *Semei,* pr. name, indecl., Lk. 3:26* [4584]

[4947] σεμίδαλις *semidalis* 1x *the finest flour,* Rev. 18:13* [4585]

[4948] σεμνός *semnos* 4x *august, venerable; honorable, reputable,* Phil. 4:8; *grave, serious, dignified,* 1 Tim. 3:8, 11; Tit. 2:2* [4586]

[4949] σεμνότης *semnotēs* 3x pr. *majesty; gravity, dignity, dignified seriousness,* 1 Tim. 2:2; 3:4; Tit. 2:7* [4587]

[4950] Σέργιος *Sergios* 1x *Sergius,* pr. name, Acts 13:7* [4588]

[4952] Σερούχ *Serouch* 1x *Serug,* proper name, Lk. 3:35* [4562]

[4953] Σήθ *Sēth* 1x *Seth,* (Gen. 4:25f.) pr. name, indecl., Lk. 3:38* [4589]

[4954] Σήμ *Sēm* 1x *Shem,* (Gen. 5:32) pr. name, indecl., Lk. 3:36* [4590]

[4955] σημαίνω *sēmainō* 6x *to indicate by a sign, to signal; to indicate, intimate,* Jn. 12:33; 18:32; 21:19; *to make known, communicate,* Acts 11:28; Rev. 1:1; *to specify,* Acts 25:27* [4591]

[4956] σημεῖον *sēmeion* 77x *a sign, a mark, token,* by which anything is known or distinguished, Mt. 16:3; 24:3; 2 Thess. 3:17; *a token, pledge, assurance,* Lk. 2:12; *a proof, evidence, convincing token,* Mt. 12:38; 16:1; Jn. 2:18; in NT *a sign, wonder, remarkable event, wonderful appearance, extraordinary phenomenon,* 1 Cor. 14:22; Rev. 12:1, 3; 15:1; *a portent, prodigy,* Mt. 24:30; Acts 2:19; *a wonderful work, miraculous operation, miracle,* Mt. 24:24; Mk. 16:17, 20; meton. *a sign, a signal character,* Lk. 2:34 [4592] See *miracle; sign.*

[4957] σημειόω *sēmeioō* 1x mid., *to mark, inscribe marks upon;* mid. *to mark for one's self, note,* 2 Thess. 3:14* [4593]

[4958] σήμερον *sēmeron* 41x *today, this day,* Mt. 6:11, 30; 16:3; 21:28; *now, at present,* Heb. 13:8; 2 Cor. 3:15; ἡ σήμερον, sc. ἡμέρα, sometimes expressed, *this day, the present day,* Acts 20:26; ἕως or ἄχρι τῆς σήμερον, *until this day, until our times,* Mt. 11:23; 27:8 [4594] See *today.*

[4960] σήπω *sēpō* 1x *to cause to putrify, rot, be corrupted* or *rotten,* Jas. 5:2* [4595]

[4962] σής *sēs* 3x *a moth,* Lk. 12:33; Mt. 6:19f.* [4597]

[4963] σητόβρωτος *sētobrōtos* 1x *moth-eaten,* Jas. 5:2* [4598]

[4964] σθενόω *sthenoō* 1x *to strengthen, impart strength,* 1 Pet. 5:10* [4599]

[4965] σιαγών *siagōn* 2x *the jawbone;* in NT *the cheek,* Mt. 5:39; Lk. 6:29* [4600]

[4967] σιγάω *sigaō* 10x *to be silent, keep silence,* Lk. 9:36; 20:26; Acts 15:12f.; 1 Cor. 14:28, 30, 34; Lk. 18:39; trans. *to keep in silence, not to reveal, to conceal;* pass. *to be concealed, not to be revealed,* Rom. 16:25* [4601] See *quiet; silent.*

[4968] σιγή *sigē* 2x *silence,* Acts 21:40; Rev. 8:1* [4602]

[4970] σίδηρος *sidēros* 1x *iron,* Rev. 18:12* [4604]

[4971] σιδηροῦς *sidērous* 5x *made of iron,* Acts 12:10; Rev. 2:27; 9:9; 12:5; 19:15* [4603]

[4972] Σιδών *Sidōn* 9x *Sidon,* a celebrated city of Phoenicia, Mt. 11:21f.; Mk. 3:8; 7:31; Lk. 6:17; Acts 27:3 [4605]

[4973] Σιδώνιος *Sidōnios* 2x *Sidonian; an inhabitant of* Σιδών, *Sidon,* Acts 12:20; Lk. 4:26* [4606]

[4974] σικάριος *sikarios* 1x *an assassin, bandit, robber,* Acts 21:38* [4607]

[4975] σίκερα *sikera* 1x *strong* or *inebriating drink,* Lk. 1:15* [4608]

[4976] Σίλας *Silas* 12x *Silas,* pr. name, in Luke, Acts 15:22; see Σιλουανός [4609]

[4977] Σιλουανός *Silouanos* 4x *Silvanus,* pr. name, 2 Cor. 1:19; 1 Thess. 1:1; 2 Thess. 1:1; 1 Pet. 5:12, see Σίλας* [4610]

[4978] Σιλωάμ *Silōam* 3x *Siloam,* a pool or fountain near Jerusalem, Lk. 13:4; Jn. 9:7, 11* [4611]

[4980] σιμικίνθιον *simikinthion* 1x *an apron,* Acts 19:12* [4612]

[4981] Σίμων *Simōn* 75x *Simon,* pr. name. (1) *Simon Peter,* Mt. 4:18. (2) *Simon (the Canaanite) the Zealot,* Mt. 10:4; Acts 1:13 . (3) *Simon, brother of Jesus,* Mt. 13:55; Mk. 6:3. (4) *Simon, the leper,* Mt. 26:6; Mk. 14:3. (5) *Simon, the Pharisee,* Lk. 7:40. (6) *Simon of Cyrene,* Mt. 27:32. (7) *Simon, father of Judas Iscariot,* Jn. 6:71. (8) *Simon, the sorcerer,* Acts 8:9. (9) *Simon, the tanner, of Joppa,* Acts 9:43; 10:6 [4613]

[4982] Σινά *Sina* 4x *Mount Sinai,* in Arabia, Acts 7:30, 38; Gal. 4:24, 25* [4614]

[4983] σίναπι *sinapi* 5x *mustard;* in NT probably the shrub, not the herb, *Khardal, Salvadora Persica L.,* the fruit of which possesses the pungency of mustard, Mt. 13:31; 17:20; Mk. 4:31; Lk. 13:19; 17:6* [4615]

[4984] σινδών *sindōn* 6x *sindon;* pr. *fine Indian cloth; fine linen;* in NT *a linen garment, an upper garment* or *wrapper of fine linen,* worn in summer by night, and used to envelope dead bodies, Mt. 27:59; Mk. 14:51, 52; 15:46; Lk. 23:53* [4616]

[4985] σινιάζω *siniazō* 1x *to sift;* met. *to sift* by trials and temptations, Lk. 22:31* [4617]

[4986] σιρικός *sirikos* 1x see also σηρικός, *silk, of silk, silken;* τὸ σηρικόν, *silken stuff,* Rev. 18:12* [4596]

[4988] σιτευτός *siteutos* 3x *fed, fatted,* Lk. 15:23, 27, 30* [4618]

[4989] σιτίον *sition* 1x *provision of corn, food,* Acts 7:12* [4621]

[4990] σιτιστός *sitistos* 1x *fatted, a fatling, cattle,* Mt. 22:4* [4619]

[4991] σιτομέτριον *sitometrion* 1x *a certain measure of grain* distributed for food at set times to the slaves of a family, *a ration,* Lk. 12:42* [4620]

[4992] σῖτος *sitos* 14x *corn, grain, wheat,* Mt. 3:12; 13:25, 29, 30; Mk. 4:28 [4621] See *grain; wheat.*

[4994] Σιών *Siōn* 7x *Zion, Mt. Zion, a hill within the city of Jerusalem,* indecl., Heb. 12:22; Rev. 14:1; *poetic use,* Mt. 21:5; Jn. 12:15; *people of Israel,* Rom. 9:33; 11:26; *new Jerusalem of Christianity,* 1 Pet. 2:6* [4622]

[4995] σιωπάω *siōpaō* 10x *to be silent, keep silence, hold one's peace,* Mt. 20:31; 26:63; Mk. 3:4; 9:34; 10:48; 14:61; Lk. 19:40; Acts 18:9; σιωπῶν, *silent, dumb,* Lk. 1:20; met. *to be silent, still, hushed, calm,* as the sea, Mk. 4:39* [4623] See *quiet; silent.*

[4997] σκανδαλίζω *skandalizō* 29x pr. *to cause to stumble;* met. *offend,* Mt. 17:27; *to offend, shock, excite feeling of repugnance,* Jn. 6:61; 1 Cor. 8:13; pass. *to be offended, shocked, pained,* Mt. 15:12; Rom. 14:21; 2 Cor. 11:29; σκανδαλίζεσθαι ἔν τινι, *to be affected with scruples of repugnance towards any one* as respects his claims or pretensions, Mt. 11:6; 13:57; met. *to cause to stumble* morally, *to cause to falter* or *err,* Mt. 5:29; 18:6; pass. *to falter, fall away,* Mt. 13:21 [4624] See *cause to sin; offend.*

[4998] σκάνδαλον *skandalon* 15x pr. *a trap-spring;* also genr. *a stumbling block, anything against which one stumbles, an impediment;* met. *a cause of ruin, destruction, misery,* etc., Rom. 9:33; 11:9; 1 Pet. 2:8; *a cause* or *occasion of sinning,* Mt. 16:23; 18:7 (3x); Lk. 17:1; Rom. 14:13; 16:17; Rev. 2:14; *scandal, offense, cause of indignation,* Mt. 13:41; 1 Cor. 1:23; Gal. 5:11; 1 Jn. 2:10* [4625] See *cause of sin; obstacle; offense; stumbling block.*

[4999] σκάπτω *skaptō* 3x *to dig, excavate,* Lk. 6:48; 13:8; 16:3* [4626]

[5002] σκάφη *skaphē* 3x pr. *anything excavated* or *hollowed; a boat, skiff,* Acts 27:16, 30, 32* [4627]

[5003] σκέλος *skelos* 3x *the leg,* Jn. 19:31, 32, 33* [4628]

[5004] σκέπασμα *skepasma* 1x *covering; clothing, raiment,* 1 Tim. 6:8* [4629]

[5005] Σκευᾶς *Skeuas* 1x *Sceva,* pr. name, Acts 19:14* [4630]

[5006] σκευή *skeuē* 1x *apparatus; tackle,* Acts 27:19* [4631]

[5007] σκεῦος *skeuos* 23x *a vessel, utensil* for containing anything, Mk. 11:16; Lk. 8:16; Rom. 9:21; *any utensil, instrument;* σκεύη, *household stuff, furniture, goods,* etc., Mt. 12:29; Mk. 3:27; *the mast of a ship,* or, *the sail,* Acts 27:17; met. *an instrument, means, organ, minister,* Acts 9:15; σκεύη ὀργῆς and σκεύη ἐλέους, *vessels of wrath,* or, *of mercy, persons visited by punishment,* or, *the divine favor,* Rom. 9:22, 23; *the vessel* or *frame* of the human individual, 1 Thess. 4:4; 1 Pet. 3:7 [4632] See *container; instrument; jar.*

[5008] σκηνή *skēnē* 20x *a tent, tabernacle;* genr. *any temporary dwelling; a tent, booth,* Mt. 17:4; Heb. 11:9; *the tabernacle* of the covenant, Heb. 8:5; 9:1, 21; 13:10; allegor. *the* celestial or true *tabernacle,* Heb. 8:2; 9:11; *a division* or *compartment of the tabernacle,* Heb. 9:2, 3, 6; *a* small portable *tent* or *shrine,* Acts 7:43; *an abode* or *seat* of a lineage, Acts 15:16; *a mansion, habitation, abode, dwelling,* Lk. 16:9; Rev. 13:6 [4633] See *tabernacle; tent.*

[5009] σκηνοπηγία *skēnopēgia* 1x pr. *a pitching of tents* or *booths;* hence, *the feast of tabernacles* or *booths,* instituted in memory of the forty years' wandering of the Israelites in the desert, and as a season of gratitude for the ingathering of harvest, celebrated for eight days, commencing on the 15th of Tisri, Jn. 7:2* [4634]

[5010] σκηνοποιός *skēnopoios* 1x *a tent-maker,* Acts 18:3* [4635]

[5011] σκῆνος *skēnos* 2x *a tent, tabernacle, lodging;* met. *the* corporeal *tabernacle,* 2 Cor. 5:1, 4* [4636]

[5012] σκηνόω *skēnoō* 5x *to pitch tent, encamp; to tabernacle, dwell in a tent; to dwell, have one's abode,* Jn. 1:14; Rev. 7:15; 12:12; 13:6; 21:3* [4637] See *dwell; live; pitch (a tent).*

[5013] σκήνωμα *skēnōma* 3x *a habitation, abode, dwelling,* Acts 7:46; *the* corporeal *tabernacle* of the soul, 2 Pet. 1:13, 14* [4638]

[5014] σκιά *skia* 7x *a shade, shadow,* Mk. 4:32; Acts 5:15; met. *a shadow, a foreshadowing, a vague outline,* in distinction from ἡ εἰκών, the perfect image or delineation, and τὸ σῶμα, the reality, Col. 2:17; Heb. 8:5; 10:1; *gloom;* σκιὰ θανάτου, *death shade, the thickest darkness,* Mt. 4:16; Lk. 1:79* [4639]

[5015] σκιρτάω *skirtaō* 3x *to leap,* Lk. 1:41, 44; *to leap, skip, bound* for joy, Lk. 6:23* [4640]

[5016] σκληροκαρδία *sklērokardia* 3x *hardness of heart, obstinacy, perverseness,* Mt. 19:8; Mk. 10:5; 16:14* [4641]

[5017] σκληρός *sklēros* 5x *dry, hard* to the touch; met. *harsh, severe, stern,* Mt. 25:24; *vehement, violent, fierce,* Jas. 3:4; *grievous, painful,* Acts 26:14; *grating* to the mind, *repulsive, offensive,* Jn. 6:60; *stubborn, resistance to authority,* Jude 15* [4642]

[5018] σκληρότης *sklērotēs* 1x *hardness;* met. σκληρότης τῆς καρδίας, *hardness of heart, obstinacy, perverseness,* Rom. 2:5* [4643]

[5019] σκληροτράχηλος *sklērotrachēlos* 1x *stiff-necked, obstinate,* Acts 7:51* [4644]

[5020] σκληρύνω *sklērynō* 6x *to harden;* met. *to harden* morally, *to make stubborn,* Heb. 3:8, 15; 4:7; as a negation of ἐλεεῖν, *to leave to stubbornness and contumacy,* Rom. 9:18; mid. and pass. *to put on a stubborn frame,* Acts 19:9; Heb. 3:13* [4645]

[5021] σκολιός *skolios* 4x *crooked, tortuous,* Lk. 3:5; met. *perverse, wicked,* Acts 2:40; Phil. 2:15; *crooked, peevish, morose,* 1 Pet. 2:18* [4646]

[5022] σκόλοψ *skolops* 1x *anything pointed;* met. *a thorn, a plague,* 2 Cor. 12:7* [4647]

[5023] σκοπέω *skopeō* 6x *to view attentively, watch; to see, observe, take care, beware,* Lk. 11:35; Gal. 6:1; *to regard, have respect to,* 2 Cor. 4:18; Phil. 2:4; *to mark, note,* Rom. 16:17; Phil. 3:17* [4648]

[5024] σκοπός *skopos* 1x *a watcher;* also, *a distant object on which the eye is kept fixed; a mark, goal,* Phil. 3:14* [4649]

[5026] σκορπίος *skorpios* 5x *a scorpion,* a large insect, sometimes several inches in length, shaped somewhat like a crab and furnished with a tail terminating in a stinger from which it emits a dangerous poison, Lk. 10:19; 11:12; Rev. 9:3, 5, 10* [4651]

[5027] σκοτεινός *skoteinos* 3x *dark,* Mt. 6:23; Lk. 11:34, 36* [4652]

[5028] σκοτία *skotia* 16x *darkness,* Jn. 6:17; 20:1; *privacy,* Mt. 10:27; Lk. 12:3; met. moral or spiritual *darkness,* Jn. 1:5 (2x); 8:12; 12:35, 46; 1 Jn. 1:5; 2:8, 9, 11* [4653] See *darkenss.*

[5030] σκότος *skotos* 31x *darkness,* Mt. 27:45; Acts 2:20; *gloom* of punishment and misery, Mt. 8:12; 2 Pet. 2:17; met. moral or spiritual *darkness,* Mt. 4:16; Jn. 3:19; Eph. 5:11; *a realm of* moral *darkness,* Eph. 5:8; 6:12 [4655] See *darkness.*

[5031] σκοτόω *skotoō* 3x *to darken, shroud in darkness,* Eph. 4:18; Rev. 9:2; 16:10 [4656]

[5032] σκύβαλον *skybalon* 1x *dung, sweepings, refuse, rubbish,* Phil. 3:8* [4657]

[5033] Σκύθης *Skythēs* 1x *A Scythian, a native of Scythia,* the modern Mongolia and Tartary, Col. 3:11* [4658]

[5034] σκυθρωπός *skythrōpos* 2x *of a stern, morose, sour, gloomy,* or *dejected countenance,* Mt. 6:16; Lk. 24:17* [4659]

[5035] σκύλλω *skyllō* 4x *to flay, lacerate;* met. *to vex, trouble, annoy,* Mk. 5:35; Lk. 7:6; 8:49; pass. met. ἐσκυλμένοι, *in sorry plight,* Mt. 9:36* [4660]

[5036] σκῦλον *skylon* 1x *spoils stripped off an enemy;* σκῦλα, *spoil, plunder, booty,* Lk. 11:22* [4661]

[5037] σκωληκόβρωτος *skōlēkobrōtos* 1x *eaten of worms, consumed by worms,* Acts 12:23* [4662]

[5038] σκώληξ *skōlēx* 1x *a worm;* met. *gnawing anguish,* Mk. 9:48* [4663]

[5039] σμαράγδινος *smaragdinos* 1x *of smaragdus* or *emerald,* Rev. 4:3* [4664]

[5040] σμάραγδος *smaragdos* 1x *smaragdus, the emerald,* a gem of a pure green color; but under this name the ancients probably comprised all stones of a fine green color, Rev. 21:19* [4665]

[5043] σμύρνα *smyrna* 2x *myrrh,* an aromatic bitter resin, or gum, issuing by incision, and sometimes spontaneously, from the trunk and larger branches of a small thorny tree growing in Egypt, Arabia, and Abyssinia, much used by the ancients in unguents, Mt. 2:11; Jn. 19:39* [4666]

[5044] Σμύρνα *Smyrna* 2x *Smyrna,* a maritime city of Ionia, in Asia Minor, Rev. 1:11; 2:8* [4667]

[5046] σμυρνίζω *smyrnizō* 1x *to mingle* or *flavor with myrrh,* Mk. 15:23* [4669]

[5047] Σόδομα *Sodoma* 9x *Sodom,* (Gen. 19:24) one of the four cities of the vale of Siddim, now covered by the Dead sea, Mt. 11:23f.; Lk. 17:29; Rom. 9:29; 2 Pet. 2:6; Rev. 11:8 [4670]

[5048] Σολομών *Solomōn* 12x *Solomon,* also spelled Σολομῶν, pr. name, son and successor of David, Mt. 1:6f.; 6:29; Lk. 11:31; Jn. 10:23; Acts 3:11; 7:47 [4672]

[5049] σορός *soros* 1x *a coffer; an urn for receiving the ashes of the dead; a coffin;* in NT *a bier,* Lk. 7:14* [4673]

[5050] σός *sos* 26x *yours,* Mt. 7:3, 22; οἱ σοί, *your kindred, friends,* etc., Mk. 5:19; τὸ σόν and τὰ σά, *what is yours, your property, goods,* etc., Mt. 20:14; 25:25; Lk. 6:30 [4674]

[5051] σουδάριον *soudarion* 4x *a handkerchief, napkin,* etc., Lk. 19:20; Jn. 11:44; 20:7; Acts 19:12* [4676]

[5052] Σουσάννα *Sousanna* 1x *Susanna,* pr. name, Lk. 8:3* [4677]

[5053] σοφία *sophia* 51x *wisdom* in general, *knowledge,* Mt. 12:42; Lk. 2:40, 52; 11:31; Acts 7:10; *ability,* Lk. 21:15; Acts 6:3, 10; practical *wisdom, prudence,* Col. 4:5; *learning, science,* Mt. 13:54; Mk. 6:2; Acts 7:22; scientific *skill,* 1 Cor. 1:17; 2:1; professed *wisdom,* human *philosophy,* 1 Cor. 1:19, 20, 22; 2:4, 5, 6; superior *knowledge and enlightenment,* Col. 2:23; in NT divine *wisdom,* Rom. 11:33; Eph. 3:10; Col. 2:3; revealed *wisdom,* Mt. 11:19; Lk. 11:49; 1 Cor. 1:24, 30; 2:7; Christian *enlightenment,* 1 Cor. 12:8; Eph. 1:8, 17; Col. 1:9, 28, 3:16; Jas. 1:5; 3:13 [4678] See *wisdom.*

[5054] σοφίζω *sophizō* 2x *to make wise, enlighten,* 2 Tim. 3:15; mid. *to invent skilfully, devise artfully,* pass. 2 Pet. 1:16* [4679]

[5055] σοφός *sophos* 20x *wise* generally, 1 Cor. 1:25; *shrewd, clever,* Rom. 16:19; 1 Cor. 3:10; 6:5; *learned, intelligent,* Mt. 11:25; Rom. 1:14, 22; 1 Cor. 1:19, 20, 26, 27; 3:18; in NT divinely *instructed,* Mt. 23:34; *furnished with* Christian *wisdom,* spiritually *enlightened,* Jas. 3:13; *all wise,* Rom. 16:27; 1 Tim. 1:17; Jude 25 [4680] See *wisdom.*

[5056] Σπανία *Spania* 2x *Spain,* Rom. 15:24, 28* [4681]

[5057] σπαράσσω *sparassō* 3x pr. *to tear, lacerate;* by impl. *to agitate greatly,* *convulse, distort by convulsion,* Mk. 1:26; 9:26; Lk. 9:39* [4682]

[5058] σπαργανόω *sparganoō* 2x *to swathe, wrap in swaddling cloths,* Lk. 2:7, 12* [4683]

[5059] σπαταλάω *spatalaō* 2x *to live luxuriously, voluptuously, wantonly,* 1 Tim. 5:6; Jas. 5:5* [4684]

[5060] σπάω *spaō* 2x *to draw, pull; to draw* a sword, Mk. 14:47; Acts 16:27* [4685]

[5061] σπεῖρα *speira* 7x *anything twisted* or *wreathed, a cord, coil, band,* etc.; *a band of soldiers, company, troop;* used for a Roman *cohort,* about 600 soldiers, Mt. 27:27; Acts 10:1; *the* temple *guard,* Mk. 15:16; Jn. 18:3, 12; Acts 21:31; 27:1* [4686]

[5062] σπείρω *speirō* 52x *to sow* seed, Mt. 6:26; 13:3, 4, 18, 24, 25, 27, 37, 3 [4687] See *sow.*

[5063] σπεκουλάτωρ *spekoulatōr* 1x *a sentinel, life-guardsman,* a kind of soldiers who formed the body-guard of princes, etc., one of whose duties was to put criminals to death, Mk. 6:27* [4688]

[5064] σπένδω *spendō* 2x *to pour out a libation* or *drink-offering;* in NT mid. *to make a libation of one's self* by expending energy and life in the service of the Gospel, Phil. 2:17; pass. *to be in the act of being sacrificed* in the cause of the Gospel, 2 Tim. 4:6* [4689]

[5065] σπέρμα *sperma* 43x *seed,* Mt. 13:24, 27, 37, 38; *semen virile,* Heb. 11:11; *offspring, posterity,* Mt. 22:24, 25; Jn. 7:42; *a seed* of future generations, Rom. 9:29; in NT met. *a seed* or *principle* of spiritual life, 1 Jn. 3:9 [4690] See *descendant; seed.*

[5066] σπερμολόγος *spermologos* 1x pr. *seed-picking; one who picks up and retails scraps of information; a gossip; a babbler,* Acts 17:18* [4691]

[5067] σπεύδω *speudō* 6x trans. *to urge on, impel, quicken; to quicken* in idea, *to be eager for the arrival of,* 2 Pet. 3:12; intrans. *to hasten, make haste,* Acts 20:16; 22:18; the part. has the force of an adverb, *quickly, hastily,* Lk. 2:16; 19:5, 6* [4692]

[5068] σπήλαιον *spēlaion* 6x *a cave, cavern, den, hideout,* Mt. 21:13; Mk. 11:17; Lk. 19:46; Jn. 11:38; Heb. 11:38; Rev. 6:5* [4693]

[5069] σπιλάς *spilas* 1x *a sharply-cleft portion of rock;* in NT *a flaw, stigma,* Jude 12* [4694]

[5070] σπίλος *spilos* 2x *a spot, stain, blot;* a moral *blemish,* Eph. 5:27; 2 Pet. 2:13* [4696]

[5071] σπιλόω *spiloō* 2x *to spot, soil; to contaminate, defile,* Jas. 3:6; Jude 23* [4695]

[5072] σπλαγχνίζομαι *splanchnizomai* 12x *to be moved with pity* or *compassion,* Mt. 9:36; 14:14; 20:34; Lk. 7:13; *to be compassionate,* Mt. 18:27 [4697] See *(have) compassion; show compassion.*

[5073] σπλάγχνον *splanchnon* 11x *the chief intestines, viscera; the entrails, bowels,* Acts 1:18; met. *the heart, the affections of the heart, the tender affections,* Lk. 1:78; 2 Cor. 6:12; 7:15; Phil. 1:8, 2:1; Col. 3:12; Phlm. 7, 20; 1 Jn. 3:17; meton. *a cherished one, dear as one's self,* Phlm. 12* [4698] See *affection; compassion; pity; tenderness.*

[5074] σπόγγος *spongos* 3x *a sponge,* Mt. 27:48; Mk. 15:36; Jn. 19:29* [4699]

[5075] σποδός *spodos* 3x *ashes,* Mt. 11:21; Lk. 10:13; Heb. 9:13* [4700]

[5076] σπορά *spora* 1x *a sowing; seed sown;* met. generative *seed, generation,* 1 Pet. 1:23* [4701]

[5077] σπόριμος *sporimos* 3x *sown, fit to be sown;* in NT τὰ σπόριμα, *fields which are sown, fields of grain, cornfields,* Mt. 12:1; Mk. 2:23; Lk. 6:1* [4702]

[5078] σπόρος *sporos* 6x *a sowing;* in NT *seed, that which is sown,* Mk. 4:26, 27;

Lk. 8:5, 11; met. *the seed sown* in almsgiving, 2 Cor. 9:10* [4703]

[5079] σπουδάζω *spoudazō* 11x *to hurry; be bent upon,* Gal. 2:10; *to endeavor earnestly, strive,* Eph. 4:3 [4704] See *make effort; strive.*

[5080] σπουδαῖος *spoudaios* 3x *earnest, eager, forward, zealous,* 2 Cor. 8:17, 22 (2x)* [4705, 4706, 4707]

[5081] σπουδαίως *spoudaiōs* 4x *earnestly, eagerly, diligently,* Lk. 7:4; 2 Tim. 1:17; Tit. 3:13; compar. σπουδαιοτέρως, *more earnestly, with special urgency,* Phil. 2:28 [4708, 4709]

[5082] σπουδή *spoudē* 12x *haste;* μετὰ σπουδῆς, *with haste, hastily, quickly,* Mk. 6:25; Lk. 1:39; *earnestness, earnest application, diligence, enthusiasm,* Rom. 12:8, 11; 2 Cor. 7:11, 12; 8:16; 8:7f. [4710] See *concern; eagerness; earnestness.*

[5083] σπυρίς *spyris* 5x also spelled σφυρίς, *a basket, handbasket* for provision, Mt. 15:37; 16:10; Mk. 8:8, 20; Acts 9:25* [4711]

[5084] στάδιον *stadion* 7x pr. *a fixed standard of measure; a stadium,* the eighth part of a Roman mile, and nearly equal to a furlong, containing 201.45 yards, *about 192 meters,* Lk. 24:13; Mt. 14:24; Jn. 6:19; 11:18; Rev. 14:20; 21:16; *a race-course, a race,* 1 Cor. 9:24* [4712]

[5085] στάμνος *stamnos* 1x can be masculine, but not in the NT, *a wine jar; a pot, jar, urn, vase,* Heb. 9:4* [4713]

[5086] στασιαστής *stasiastēs* 1x *a partisan, rebel, revolutionary,* Mt. 15:7* [4955]

[5087] στάσις *stasis* 9x *a setting; a standing; an* effective *position, an* unimpaired *standing* or *dignity,* Heb. 9:8; *a gathered party, a group;* hence, *a tumultuous assemblage, popular outbreak,* Mk. 15:7; Acts 19:40; Lk. 23:19, 25; *seditious movement,* Acts 24:5; *discord, dispute, dissension,* Acts 15:2; 23:7, 10* [4714]

[5088] στατήρ *statēr* 1x pr. *a weight; a stater,* an Attic silver coin, equal in value to the Jewish shekel, or to four Attic or two Alexandrian drachmas, Mt. 17:27* [4715]

[5089] σταυρός *stauros* 27x *a stake; a cross,* Mt. 27:32, 40, 42; Phil. 2:8; by impl. *the punishment of the cross, crucifixion,* Eph. 2:16; Heb. 12:2; meton. *the crucifixion* of Christ in respect of its import, *the doctrine of the cross,* 1 Cor. 17:18; Gal. 5:11; 6:12, 14; met. *to take up,* or *bear one's cross, to be ready to encounter any extremity,* Mt. 10:38; 16:24 [4716] See *cross.*

[5090] σταυρόω *stauroō* 46x *to fix stakes;* later, *to crucify, affix to the cross,* Mt. 20:19; 23:34; met. *to crucify, to mortify, to deaden, to make a sacrifice of,* Gal. 5:24; pass. *to be cut off* from a thing, as by a violent death, *to be come dead to,* Gal. 6:14 [4717] See *crucify.*

[5091] σταφυλή *staphylē* 3x *a cluster* or *bunch of grapes,* Mt. 7:16; Lk. 6:44, Rev. 14:18* [4718]

[5092] στάχυς *stachus* 5x *an ear of corn, head of grain,* Mt. 12:1; Mk. 2:23; 4:28; Lk. 6:1* [4719]

[5093] Στάχυς *Stachus* 1x *Stachys,* pr. name, Rom. 16:9* [4720]

[5094] στέγη *stegē* 3x *a roof, flat roof* of a house, Mt. 8:8; Mk. 2:4; Lk. 7:6* [4721]

[5095] στέγω *stegō* 4x *to cover; to hold off, to hold in;* hence, *to hold out against, to endure patiently,* 1 Cor. 9:12; 13:7; absol. *to contain one's self,* 1 Thess. 3:1, 5* [4722]

[5096] στεῖρα *steira* 5x *barren, incapable of bearing children,* Lk. 1:7, 36; 23:29; Gal. 4:27; Heb. 11:11* [4723]

[5097] στέλλω *stellō* 2x pr. *to place in set order, to arrange; to equip; to despatch; to stow;* mid. *to contract one's self, to shrink; to withdraw from, avoid, shun,* 2 Cor. 8:20; 2 Thess. 3:6* [4724]

[5098] στέμμα *stemma* 1x *a crown, wreath,* Acts 14:13* [4725]

[5099] στεναγμός *stenagmos* 2x *a sighing, groaning, groan,* Acts 7:34; an inward *sighing,* Rom. 8:26* [4726]

[5100] στενάζω *stenazō* 6x *to groan, sigh,* Rom. 8:23; 2 Cor. 5:2, 4; Heb. 13:17; *to sigh* inwardly, Mk. 7:34; *to give vent to querulous* or *censorious feelings,* Jas. 5:9* [4727]

[5101] στενός *stenos* 3x *narrow, strait,* Mt. 7:13, 14; Lk. 13:24* [4728]

[5102] στενοχωρέω *stenochōreō* 3x *to crowd together into a narrow place, straiten;* pass. met. *to be in straits, to be cooped up, to be cramped* from action, 2 Cor. 4:8; *to be cramped* in feeling, 2 Cor. 6:12* [4729]

[5103] στενοχωρία *stenochōria* 4x pr. *narrowness of place, a narrow place;* met. *straits, distress, anguish,* Rom. 2:9; 8:35; 2 Cor. 6:4; 12:10* [4730]

[5104] στερεός *stereos* 4x *stiff, hard;* of food, *solid,* as opposed to what is liquid and light, Heb. 5:12, 14; *firm, steadfast,* 2 Tim. 2:19; 1 Pet. 5:9* [4731]

[5105] στερεόω *stereoō* 3x *to make firm; to strengthen,* Acts 3:7, 16; *to settle,* Acts 16:5* [4732]

[5106] στερέωμα *stereōma* 1x pr. *what is solid and firm;* met. *firmness, steadfastness, constancy,* Col. 2:5* [4733]

[5107] Στεφανᾶς *Stephanas* 3x *Stephanas,* pr. name, 1 Cor. 1:16; 16:15, 17* [4734]

[5108] Στέφανος *Stephanos* 7x *Stephen,* pr. name, Acts 6:5, 8f.; 7:59; 8:2; 11:19; 22:20* [4736]

[5109] στέφανος *stephanos* 18x *that which forms an encirclement; a crown,* Mt. 27:29; Rev. 4:4, 10; *wreath,* conferred on a victor in the public games, 1 Cor. 9:25; met. *a crown, reward, prize,* 2 Tim. 4:8; Jas. 1:12; *a crown, ornament, honor, glory* [4735] See *crown; wreath.*

[5110] στεφανόω *stephanoō* 3x *to crown; to crown* as victor in the games, [4737]

[5111] στῆθος *stēthos* 5x *the breast, chest,* Lk. 18:13; 23:48; Jn. 13:25; 21:20; Rev. 15:6* [4738]

[5112] στήκω *stēkō* 9x *to stand,* Mk. 3:31; 11:25; met. *to stand* when under judgment, *to be approved,* Rom. 14:4; *to stand firm, be constant, persevere,* 1 Cor. 16:13; Gal. 5:1; Phil. 1:27; 4:1; 1 Thess. 3:8; 2 Thess. 2:15* [4739] See *stand firm.*

[5113] στηριγμός *stērigmos* 1x pr. *a fixing, settling; a state of firmness, fixedness;* met. *firmness* of belief, *settle frame* of mind, 2 Pet. 3:17* [4740]

[5114] στηρίζω *stērizō* 13x *to set fast; to set* in a certain position or direction, Lk. 9:51; met. *to render* mentally *steadfast, to settle, confirm,* Lk. 22:32; Rom. 1:11; *to stand immovable,* Lk. 16:26; met. *to be* mentally *settled,* 2 Pet. 1:12 [4741] See *establish; fix; strengthen.*

[5115] στιβάς *stibas* 1x *a stuffing of leaves, boughs,* etc., meton. *a bough, branch,* Mk. 11:8* [4746]

[5116] στίγμα *stigma* 1x *a mark, brand,* Gal. 6:17* [4742]

[5117] στιγμή *stigmē* 1x pr. *a point;* met. *a point* of time, *moment, instant,* Lk. 4:5* [4743]

[5118] στίλβω *stilbō* 1x *to shine, glisten, be radiant,* Mk. 9:3* [4744]

[5119] στοά *stoa* 4x *a colonnade, cloister, covered walk supported by columns,* Jn. 5:2; 10:23; Acts 3:11; 5:12* [4745] See *porch.*

[5121] Στοϊκός *Stoikos* 1x *Stoic,* Acts 17:18* [4770]

[5122] στοιχεῖον *stoicheion* 7x *an element; an element* of the natural universe, 2 Pet. 3:10, 12; *an element* or *rudiment* of any intellectual or religious system, Gal. 4:3, 9; Col. 2:8, 20; Heb. 5:12* [4747]

[5123] στοιχέω *stoicheō* 5x pr. *to advance in a line;* met. *to frame one's conduct* by a certain rule, Acts 21:24; Rom. 4:12; Gal. 5:25; 6:16; Phil. 3:16* [4748]

[5124] στολή *stolē* 9x *equipment; dress; a long garment, flowing robe,* worn by priests, kings, and persons of distinction, Mt. 12:38; 16:5; Lk. 15:22; Rev. 6:11 [4749]

[5125] στόμα *stoma* 78x *the mouth,* Mt. 12:34; 15:11, 17, 18; 21:16; *speech, words,* Mt. 18:16; 2 Cor. 13:1; *command of speech, facility of language,* Lk. 21:15; from the Hebrew, ἀνοίγειν τὸ στόμα, *to utter, to speak,* Mt. 5:2, 13:35; also, used of the earth, *to rend, yawn,* Rev. 12:16; στόμα πρὸς στόμα λαλεῖν, *to speak mouth to mouth, face to face,* 2 Jn. 12; 3 Jn. 14; *the edge* or *point* of a weapon, Lk. 21:24; Heb. 11:34 [4750] See *edge; mouth; testimony.*

[5126] στόμαχος *stomachos* 1x pr. *the gullet* leading to the stomach; hence, later, *the stomach* itself, 1 Tim. 5:23* [4751]

[5127] στρατεία *strateia* 2x *a military expedition, campaign;* and genr. *military service, warfare;* met. *the* Christian *warfare,* 2 Cor. 10:4; *fight,* 1 Tim. 1:18* [4752]

[5128] στράτευμα *strateuma* 8x *an army,* Mt. 22:7; Rev. 19:14, 19; *an armed force, corps,* Acts 23:10, 27; *troops, guards,* Lk. 23:11; Rev. 9:16* [4753] See *army.*

[5130] στρατηγός *stratēgos* 10x *a leader* or *commander of an army, general; a* Roman *praetor, provincial magistrate,* Acts 16:20, 22, 35, 36, 38; στρατηγός τοῦ ἱεροῦ, *the captain* or *prefect of the temple,* the chief of the Levites who kept guard in and around the temple, Lk. 22:4, 52; Acts 4:1; 5:24, 26* [4755] See *magistrate.*

[5131] στρατιά *stratia* 2x *an army, host;* from the Hebrew, στρατιὰ οὐράνιος, or τοῦ οὐρανοῦ, *the heavenly host, the host of heaven, the hosts of angels,* Lk. 2:13; *the stars,* Acts 7:42* [4756]

[5132] στρατιώτης *stratiōtēs* 26x *a soldier,* Mt. 8:9; 27:27; met. *a soldier* of Christ, 2 Tim. 2:3 [4757] See *soldier.*

[5133] στρατολογέω *stratologeō* 1x *to collect* or *gather an army, enlist troops,* 2 Tim. 2:4* [4758]

[5136] στρατόπεδον *stratopedon* 1x pr. *the site of an encampment; an encampment;* meton. *an army,* Lk. 21:20* [4760]

[5137] στρεβλόω *strebloō* 1x pr. *to distort* the limbs *on a rack;* met. *to wrench, distort, pervert,* 2 Pet. 3:16* [4761]

[5138] στρέφω *strephō* 21x *to twist; to turn,* Mt. 5:39; *to make a change* of substance, *to change,* Rev. 11:6; absol. *to change* or *turn* one's course of dealing, Acts 7:42; mid. *to turn one's self about,* Mt. 16:23; Lk. 7:9; *to turn back,* Acts 7:39; *to change one's direction, to turn* elsewhere, Acts 13:46; *to change one's course of principle and conduct, to be converted,* Mt. 18:3 [4762] See *change; return; turn.*

[5139] στρηνιάω *strēniaō* 2x *to be wanton, to revel, riot,* Rev. 18:7, 9* [4763]

[5140] στρῆνος *strēnos* 1x *luxury, sensuality,* Rev. 18:3* [4764]

[5141] στρουθίον *strouthion* 4x *any small bird,* spc. *a sparrow,* Mt. 10:29, 31; Lk. 12:6, 7* [4765]

[5143] στρωννύω *strōnnyō* 6x the thematic form of στρώννυμι, the μι form never being visible in the NT, *to spread, to strew,* Mt. 21:8; Mk. 11:8; *to spread* a couch, *make your own bed,* Acts 9:34; used of a supper-chamber, pass. *to have the couches spread, to be prepared, furnished,* Mk. 14:15; Lk. 22:12* [4766]

[5144] στυγητός *stygētos* 1x *hateful, disgusting, detested,* Tit. 3:3* [4767]

[5145] στυγνάζω *stygnazō* 2x *to put on a gloomy and downcast look, to be shocked, appalled,* Mk. 10:22; of the sky, *to lower,* Mt. 16:3* [4768]

[5146] στῦλος *stylos* 4x *a pillar, column,* Rev. 10:1; used of persons of authority, influence, etc., *a support* or *pillar* of the Church, Gal. 2:9; Rev. 3:12; *a support* of true doctrine, 1 Tim. 3:15* [4769] See *pillar.*

[5148] σύ *sy* 2,906x *you,* gen., σοῦ, dat., σοί, acc., σε, Mt. 1:20; 2:6 [4571, 4671, 4675, 4771, 5209, 5210, 5213, 5216]

[5149] συγγένεια *syngeneia* 3x *kindred; kinsfolk, kinsmen, relatives,* Lk. 1:61; Acts 7:3, 14* [4772]

[5150] συγγενής *syngenēs* 11x *kindred, akin;* as a subst. *a kinsman* or *kinswoman, relative;* Mk. 6:4; Lk. 1:58; 2:44; 14:12; 21:16; Jn. 18:26; Acts 10:24; *one* nationally *akin, a fellow countryman,* Rom. 9:3; 16:7, 11, 21* [4773] See *relative.*

[5151] συγγενίς *syngenis* 1x *a kinswoman, female relative,* Lk. 1:36* [4773]

[5152] συγγνώμη *syngnōmē* 1x *pardon; concession, leave, permission,* 1 Cor. 7:6* [4774]

[5153] συγκάθημαι *synkathēmai* 2x *to sit in company with,* Mk. 14:54; Acts 26:30* [4775]

[5154] συγκαθίζω *synkathizō* 2x trans. *to cause to sit down with, seat in company with,* Eph. 2:6; intrans. *to sit in company with; to sit down together,* Lk. 22:55* [4776]

[5155] συγκακοπαθέω *synkakopatheō* 2x *to suffer evils along with* someone; *to be enduringly adherent,* 2 Tim. 1:8; 2:3* [4777]

[5156] συγκακουχέομαι *synkakoucheomai* 1x *to encounter adversity along with* any one, Heb. 11:25* [4778]

[5157] συγκαλέω *synkaleō* 8x *to call together,* Mk. 15:16; Lk. 15:6, 9; Acts 5:21; mid. *to call around one's self,* Lk. 9:1; 23:13; Acts 10:24; 28:17* [4779]

[5158] συγκαλύπτω *synkalyptō* 1x *to cover completely, to cover up;* met. *to conceal,* Lk. 12:2* [4780]

[5159] συγκάμπτω *synkamptō* 1x *to bend* or *bow together; to bow down* the back of any one afflictively, Rom. 11:10* [4781]

[5160] συγκαταβαίνω *synkatabainō* 1x *to go down with* anyone, Acts 25:5* [4782]

[5161] συγκατάθεσις *synkatathesis* 1x *assent;* in NT *accord, alliance, agreement,* 2 Cor. 6:16* [4783]

[5163] συγκατατίθημι *synkatatithēmi* 1x *to set down together with;* mid. *to agree, accord,* Lk. 23:51* [4784]

[5164] συγκαταψηφίζομαι *synkatapsēphizomai* 1x *to count, number with, be chosen together with,* Acts 1:26* [4785]

[5166] συγκεράννυμι *synkerannymi* 2x pluperf., συνεκέκρατο (3 sg), *to mix with, mingle together; to blend,* 1 Cor. 12:24; pass. *to be combined, united,* Heb. 4:2* [4786]

[5167] συγκινέω *synkineō* 1x *to agitate, put in turmoil; to excite,* Acts 6:12* [4787]

[5168] συγκλείω *synkleiō* 4x *to shut up together, to hem in; to enclose,* Lk. 5:6; met. *to band* under a sweeping sentence, Rom. 11:32; Gal. 3:22; pass. *to be banded* under a bar of disability, Gal. 3:23* [4788]

[5169] συγκληρονόμος *synklēronomos* 4x pr. *a coheir,* Rom. 8:17; *a fellow participant,* Eph. 3:6; Heb. 11:9; 1 Pet. 3:7* [4789]

[5170] συγκοινωνέω *synkoinōneō* 3x *to be a joint partaker, participate with* a person; in NT *to mix one's self up* in a thing, *to involve one's self, be an accomplice in,* Eph. 5:11; Rev. 18:4; *to sympathize actively in, to relieve,* Phil. 4:14* [4790]

[5171] συγκοινωνός *synkoinōnos* 4x *one who partakes jointly; a coparticipant,* Rom. 11:17; *a copartner* in service, *fellow,* 1 Cor. 9:23; Phil. 1:7; *a sharer,* 1 Cor. 9:23; Rev. 1:9* [4791]

[5172] συγκομίζω *synkomizō* 1x *to prepare for burial, take charge of the funeral* of any one, *bury,* Acts 8:2* [4792]

[5173] συγκρίνω *synkrinō* 3x *to combine, compound; to compare, to estimate by comparing with* something else, or, *to match,* 2 Cor. 10:12 (2x); *to explain, to illustrate,* or, *to suit,* 1 Cor. 2:13* [4793]

[5174] συγκύπτω *synkyptō* 1x *to bend* or *bow together; to be bowed together, bent over,* Lk. 13:11* [4794]

[5175] συγκυρία *synkyria* 1x *concurrence, coincidence, chance, accident;* κατὰ συγκρυίαν, *by chance, accidentally,* Lk. 10:31* [4795]

[5176] συγχαίρω *synchairō* 7x *to rejoice with* any one, *sympathize in joy,* Lk. 1:58; 15:6, 9; Phil. 2:17, 18; met. 1 Cor. 12:26; *to sympathize in the advancement of, congratulate,* 1 Cor. 13:6* [4796]

[5177] συγχέω *syncheō* 5x *to pour together, mingle by pouring together;* hence, *to confound, perplex, amaze,* Acts 2:6; *to confound* in dispute, Acts 9:22; *to throw into confusion, fill with uproar,* Acts 19:32; 21:27, 31* [4797]

[5178] συγχράομαι *synchraomai* 1x *use in common; associate with, have dealings with,* Jn. 4:9* [4798]

[5180] σύγχυσις *synchusis* 1x pr. *a pouring together;* hence, *confusion, commotion, tumult, uproar,* Acts 19:29* [4799]

[5182] συζάω *syzaō* 3x *to live with; to continue in life with* someone, 2 Cor. 7:3; *to coexist in life with* another, Rom. 6:8; 2 Tim. 2:11* [4800]

[5183] συζεύγνυμι *syzeugnymi* 2x *to join together;* trop. *join together, unite,* Mt. 19:6; Mk. 10:9* [4801]

[5184] συζητέω *syzēteō* 10x *to seek, ask,* or *inquire with* another; *to deliberate, debate,* Mk. 1:27; 9:10; Lk. 24:15; *to hold discourse with, argue, reason,* Mk. 8:11; 12:28; Lk. 22:23; Acts 6:9; 9:29; *to question, dispute, quibble,* Mk. 9:14, 16* [4802] See *debate; discuss.*

[5186] συζητητής *syzētētēs* 1x *a disputant, controversial reasoner, sophist,* 1 Cor. 1:20* [4804]

[5187] σύζυγος *syzygos* 1x *an associate, comrade, fellow laborer,* or it could be the person's name, Phil. 4:3* [4805]

[5188] συζωοποιέω *syzōopoieō* 2x *to make alive together with another; to make a sharer in the quickening of another,* Eph. 2:5; Col. 2:13* [4806]

[5189] συκάμινος *sykaminos* 1x *a sycamore tree, mulberry tree,* i.q. συκομοραία, q.v., Lk. 17:6* [4807]

[5190] συκῆ *sykē* 16x *a fig tree,* Mt. 21:19 [4808] See *fig tree.*

[5191] συκομορέα *sykomorea* 1x *the fig mulberry tree, sycamore fig,* Lk. 19:4* [4809]

[5192] σῦκον *sykon* 4x *a fig, a ripe fig,* Mt. 7:16; Mk. 11:13; Lk. 6:44; Jas. 3:12* [4810]

[5193] συκοφαντέω *sykophanteō* 2x *to inform against; to accuse falsely;* by impl. *to wrong by false accusations; to extort* money *by false informations,* Lk. 3:14; 19:8* [4811]

[5194] συλαγωγέω *sylagōgeō* 1x *to carry off as a prey* or *booty;* met. *to make victims of fraud,* Col. 2:8* [4812]

[5195] συλάω *sylaō* 1x *to strip; to rob,* 2 Cor. 11:8* [4813]

[5196] συλλαλέω *syllaleō* 6x *to talk, converse,* or *discuss with,* Mt. 17:3; Mk. 9:4; Lk. 4:36; 9:30; 22:4; Acts 25:12* [4814]

[5197] συλλαμβάνω *syllambanō* 16x *to catch; to seize, apprehend,* Mt. 26:55; Acts 1:16; *to catch,* as prey, Lk. 5:9; *to conceive, become pregnant,* Lk. 1:24, 31, 36; 2:21; met. Jas. 1:15; mid. *to help, aid, assist,* Lk. 5:7; Phil. 4:3 [4815] See *arrest; catch; conceive; seize.*

[5198] συλλέγω *syllegō* 8x *to collect, gather,* Mt. 7:16, 13:28-30, 40f., 48; Lk. 6:44* [4816]

[5199] συλλογίζομαι *syllogizomai* 1x *to reason together; to consider, deliberate, reason,* Lk. 20:5* [4817]

[5200] συλλυπέω *syllypeō* 1x *to be grieved together with; to be grieved,* Mk. 3:5* [4818]

[5201] συμβαίνω *symbainō* 8x *to step* or *come together; to happen, meet, fall out,* Mk. 10:32; Lk. 24:14 ; Acts 3:10; 20:19; 21:35; 1 Cor. 10:11; 1 Pet. 4:12; 2 Pet. 2:22* [4819]

[5202] συμβάλλω *symballō* 6x pr. *to throw together;* absol. *to meet and join,* Acts 20:14; *to meet* in war, *to encounter, engage with,* Lk. 14:31; *to encounter* in discourse or dispute, Acts 17:18; *to consult together,* Acts 4:15; mid. *to contribute, be of service to, to aid,* Acts 18:27; συμβάλλειν ἐν τῇ καρδίᾳ, *to revolve in mind, ponder upon,* Lk. 2:19* [4820]

[5203] συμβασιλεύω *symbasileuō* 2x *to reign with;* met. *to enjoy honor with,* 1 Cor. 4:8; 2 Tim. 2:12* [4821]

[5204] συμβιβάζω *symbibazō* 7x pr. *to cause to come together; to unite, knit together,* Eph. 4:16; Col. 2:2, 19; *to infer, conclude,* Acts 16:10; by impl. *to prove, demonstrate,* Acts 9:22; in NT *to teach, instruct,* Acts 19:33; 1 Cor. 2:16* [4822]

[5205] συμβουλεύω *symbouleuō* 4x *to counsel, advise, exhort,* Jn. 18:14; Rev. 3:18; mid. *to consult together, plot,* Mt. 26:4; Acts 9:23* [4823]

[5206] συμβούλιον *symboulion* 8x *counsel, consultation, mutual consultation,* Mt. 12:14; 22:15; 27:1, 7; 28:12; Mk. 3:6; Acts 27:1, 7; 28:12; *a council of counsellors,* Acts 25:12* [4824]

[5207] σύμβουλος *symboulos* 1x *a counsellor; advisor, one who shares one's counsel,* Rom. 11:34* [4825]

[5208] Συμεών *Symeōn* 7x *Symeon, Simeon,* pr. name. indecl. (1) *Simeon,* son of Juda, Lk. 3:30. (2) *Simeon,* son of Jacob, Rev. 7:7. (3) *Simeon,* a prophet of Jerusalem, Lk. 2:25, 34. (4) *Simeon,* or *Simon Peter,* Acts 15:14; 2 Pet. 1:1. (5) *Simeon,* called Niger, Acts 13:1* [4826]

[5209] συμμαθητής *symmathētēs* 1x *a fellow disciple,* Jn. 11:16* [4827]

[5210] συμμαρτυρέω *symmartyreō* 3x *to testify* or *bear witness together with* another, *confirm, add testimony,* Rom. 2:15; 8:16; 9:1* [4828]

[5211] συμμερίζω *symmerizō* 1x *to divide with* another so as to receive a part to one's self, *share with, partake with,* 1 Cor. 9:13* [4829]

[5212] συμμέτοχος *symmetochos* 2x *a partaker with* any one, *a joint partaker,* Eph. 3:6; 5:7* [4830]

[5213] συμμιμητής *symmimētēs* 1x *an imitator together with* any one, *a joint imitator,* Phil. 3:17* [4831]

[5214] συμμορφίζω *symmorphizō* 1x *to conform to, take on the same form as,* Phil. 3:10* [4833]

[5215] σύμμορφος *symmorphos* 2x *of like form, assimilated, conformed, similar in form,* Rom. 8:29; Phil. 3:21* [4832]

[5217] συμπαθέω *sympatheō* 2x *to sympathize with,* Heb. 4:15; *to be compassionate,* Heb. 10:34* [4834]

[5218] συμπαθής *sympathēs* 1x *sympathizing, compassionate,* 1 Pet. 3:8* [4835]

[5219] συμπαραγίνομαι *symparaginomai* 1x *to be present together with; to come together, convene,* Lk. 23:48* [4836]

[5220] συμπαρακαλέω *symparakaleō* 1x *to invite, exhort* along with others; pass. *to share in mutual encouragement,* Rom. 1:12* [4837]

[5221] συμπαραλαμβάνω *symparalambanō* 4x *to take along with, take as a com-*

panion, Acts 12:25; 15:37, 38; Gal. 2:1* [4838]

[5223] συμπάρειμι *sympareimi* 1x *to be present with* any one, Acts 25:24* [4840]

[5224] συμπάσχω *sympaschō* 2x *to suffer with, sympathize,* 1 Cor. 12:26; *to suffer as* another, *endure corresponding sufferings,* Rom. 8:17* [4841]

[5225] συμπέμπω *sympempō* 2x *to send with* any one, 2 Cor. 8:18, 22* [4842]

[5227] συμπεριλαμβάνω *symperilambanō* 1x *to embrace together; to embrace,* Acts 20:10* [4843]

[5228] συμπίνω *sympinō* 1x *to drink with* any one, Acts 10:41* [4844]

[5229] συμπίπτω *sympiptō* 1x *fall together, collapse,* Lk. 6: 49* [4098]

[5230] συμπληρόω *symplēroō* 3x *to fill, fill up,* Lk. 8:23; pass., of time, *to be completed, have fully come,* Lk. 9:51; Acts 2:1* [4845]

[5231] συμπνίγω *sympnigō* 5x *to throttle, choke;* trop. *to choke* the growth or increase of seed or plants, Mt. 13:22; Mk. 4:7, 19; Lk. 8:14; *to press upon, crowd,* Lk. 8:42* [4846]

[5232] συμπολίτης *sympolitēs* 1x *a fellow citizen,* met. Eph. 2:19* [4847]

[5233] συμπορεύομαι *symporeuomai* 4x *to go with, accompany,* Lk. 7:11; 14:25; 24:15; *to come together, assemble,* Mk. 10:1* [4848]

[5235] συμπόσιον *symposion* 2x *a drinking together; a feast, banquet; a festive company;* in NT, pl. συμπόσια, *eating party,* Mk. 6:39 (2x)* [4849]

[5236] συμπρεσβύτερος *sympresbyteros* 1x *a fellow elder, fellow presbyter,* 1 Pet. 5:1* [4850]

[5237] συμφέρω *spherō* 15x *to bring together, collect,* Acts 19:19; absol. *be for the benefit* of any one, *be profitable, advantageous, expedient,* 1 Cor. 6:12; *to suit best, be appropriate,* 2 Cor. 8:10; *good, benefit, profit, advantage,* Acts 20:20; 1 Cor. 7:35; *it is profitable, advantageous, expedient,* Mt. 5:29, 30; 19:10 [4851] See *(be) beneficial.*

[5238] σύμφημι *symphēmi* 1x pr. *to agree with,* Rom. 7:16* [4852]

[5239] σύμφορος *symphoros* 2x *profitable, expedient,* 1 Cor. 7:35; 10:33* [4851]

[5241] συμφυλέτης *symphyletēs* 1x pr. *one of the same tribe; a fellow citizen, fellow countryman,* 1 Thess. 2:14* [4853]

[5242] σύμφυτος *symphytos* 1x pr. *planted together, grown together;* in NT met. *grown together, closely entwined* or *united with,* Rom. 6:5* [4854]

[5243] συμφύω *symphyō* 1x *to make to grow together;* pass. *to grow* or *spring up with,* Lk. 8:7* [4855]

[5244] συμφωνέω *symphōneō* 6x *to sound together, to be in unison, be in accord;* trop. *to agree with, accord with* in purport, Acts 15:15; *to harmonize with, suit with,* Lk. 5:36; *to agree with, make an agreement,* Mt. 18:19; 20:2, 13; Acts 5:9* [4856] See *agree.*

[5245] συμφώνησις *symphōnēsis* 1x *unison, accord; agreement,* 2 Cor. 6:15* [4857]

[5246] συμφωνία *symphōnia* 1x *symphony, harmony of sounds, concert of instruments, music,* Lk. 15:25* [4858]

[5247] σύμφωνος *symphōnos* 1x *agreeing in sound;* met. *harmonious, agreeing, accord, agreement,* 1 Cor. 7:5* [4859]

[5248] συμψηφίζω *sympsēphizō* 1x *to calculate together, compute, reckon up,* Acts 19:19* [4860]

[5249] σύμψυχος *sympsychos* 1x *united in mind, at unity,* Phil. 2:2 [4861]

[5250] σύν *syn* 128x *with, together with,* Mt. 25:27; 26:35; 27:38; *attendant on,* 1 Cor. 15:10; *besides,* Lk. 24:21; *with, with the assistance of,* 1 Cor. 5:4; *with, in the same manner as,* Gal. 3:9; εἶναι σύν τινι, *to be with any one, to be in company with, accompany,* Lk. 2:13; 8:38; *to be on the side of, be a partisan of any one,* Acts 4:13; 14:4; οἱ σύν τινι, *those with any one, the companions of any one,* Mk. 2:26; Acts 22:9; *the colleagues, associates of any one,* Acts 5:17, 21 [4862]

[5251] συνάγω *synagō* 59x *to bring together, collect, gather,* as grain, fruits, etc., Mt. 3:12 6:26; 13:30, 47; *to collect* an assembly; pass. *to convene, come together, meet,* Mt. 2:4; 13:2; 18:20; 22:10; in NT *to receive with kindness and hospitality, to entertain,* Mt. 25:35, 38, 43 [4863] See *gather; harvest.*

[5252] συναγωγή *synagōgē* 56x *a collecting, gathering; a* Christian *assembly* or *congregation,* Jas. 2:2; *the congregation* of a synagogue, Acts 9:2; hence, the place itself, *a synagogue,* Lk. 7:5 [4864] See *assembly; congregation; synagogue.*

[5253] συναγωνίζομαι *synagōnizomai* 1x *to combat in company with* any one; *to exert one's strength with, to be earnest in aiding, help,* Rom. 15:30* [4865]

[5254] συναθλέω *synathleō* 2x pr. *to fight* or *work on the side of* any one; in NT *to cooperate vigorously with* a person, Phil. 4:3; *to make effort in the cause of, in support of* a thing, Phil. 1:27* [4866]

[5255] συναθροίζω *synathroizō* 2x *to gather; to bring together,* Acts 19:25; pass. *to come together, convene,* Acts 12:12* [4867]

[5256] συναίρω *synairō* 3x *to take up* a thing *with* any one; in NT συναίρειν λόγον, *to settle accounts, reckon* in order to payment, Mt. 18:23, 24; 25:19* [4868]

[5257] συναιχμάλωτος *synaichmalōtos* 3x *a fellow captive,* Rom. 16:7; Col. 4:10; Phlm. 23* [4869]

[5258] συνακολουθέω *synakoloutheō* 3x *to follow in company with, accompany,* Mk. 5:37; 14:51; Lk. 23:49* [4870]

[5259] συναλίζω *synalizō* 1x *to cause to come together, collect, assemble, congregate;* mid. *to convene to one's self,* Acts 1:4* [4871]

[5261] συναλλάσσω *synallassō* 1x *to negotiate* or *bargain with* someone; *to reconcile,* Acts 7:26* [4900]

[5262] συναναβαίνω *synanabainō* 2x *to go up, ascend with* someone, Mk. 15:41; Acts 13:31* [4872]

[5263] συνανάκειμαι *synanakeimai* 7x *to recline with* someone at table, Mt. 9:10; 14:9; Mk. 2:15; 6:22; Lk. 7:49; 14:10, 15* [4873]

[5265] συναναπαύομαι *synanapauomai* 1x *to experience refreshment* or *rest in company with* someone, Rom. 15:32* [4875]

[5267] συναντάω *synantaō* 6x *to meet with, fall in with, encounter,* Lk. 9:37; 22:10; Acts 10:25; Heb. 7:1, 10; *to occur, happen to, befall,* Acts 20:22* [4876]

[5269] συναντιλαμβάνομαι *synantilambanomai* 2x pr. *to take hold of with* someone; *to support, help, aid,* Lk. 10:40; Rom. 8:26* [4878]

[5270] συναπάγω *synapagō* 3x *to lead* or *carry away with; to seduce;* pass. *to be led away* [4879]

[5271] συναποθνήσκω *synapothnēskō* 3x *to die together with* any one, Mk. 14:31; 2 Cor. 7:3; met. *to die with,* in respect of a spiritual likeness, 2 Tim. 2:11* [4880]

[5272] συναπόλλυμι *synapollymi* 1x *to destroy together with* others; mid. *to perish* or *be destroyed with* others, Heb. 11:31* [4881]

[5273] συναποστέλλω *synapostellō* 1x *to send forth together with* someone, 2 Cor. 12:18* [4882]

[5274] συναρμολογέω *synarmologeō* 2x *to join together fitly, fit* or *frame together, compact,* Eph. 2:21; 4:16* [4883]

[5275] συναρπάζω *synarpazō* 4x pluperf., συνηρπάκειν, *to snatch up, clutch; to seize and carry off suddenly,* Acts 6:12;

to seize with force and violence, Lk. 8:29; Acts 19:29; pass. of a ship, *to be caught and swept on* by the wind, Acts 27:15* [4884]

[5277] συναυξάνω *synauxanō* 1x pas., *to grow together* in company, Mt. 13:30* [4885]

[5278] σύνδεσμος *syndesmos* 4x *that which binds together,* Col. 2:19; *a band* of union, Eph. 4:3; Col. 3:14; *a bundle,* or, *bond,* Acts 8:23* [4886]

[5279] συνδέω *syndeō* 1x *to bind together;* in NT pass. *to be in bonds together,* Heb. 13:3* [4887]

[5280] συνδοξάζω *syndoxazō* 1x in NT *to glorify together with, to exalt to a state of dignity and happiness in company with, to make to partake in the glorification* of another, Rom. 8:17* [4888]

[5281] σύνδουλος *syndoulos* 10x *a fellow-slave, fellow-servant,* Mt. 24:49; 18:28f., 31, 33; Col. 4:7; Rev. 6:11; 19:10; 22:9; *a fellow-minister* of Christ, Col. 1:7* [4889] See *fellow servant; fellow slave.*

[5282] συνδρομή *syndromē* 1x *a running together, forming a mob,* Acts 21:30* [4890]

[5283] συνεγείρω *synegeirō* 3x *to raise up with* any one; *to raise up with* Christ by spiritual resemblance of His resurrection, Eph. 2:6; Col. 2:12; 3:1* [4891]

[5284] συνέδριον *synedrion* 22x pr. *a sitting together, assembly,* etc., in NT *the Sanhedrin,* the supreme council of the Jewish nation, Mt. 5:22; 26:59; meton. *the Sanhedrin,* as including the members and place of meeting, Lk. 22:66; Acts 4:15; genr. *a* judicial *council, tribunal,* Mt. 10:17; Mk. 13:9 [4892] See *council; Sanhedrin.*

[5287] συνείδησις *syneidēsis* 30x *consciousness,* Heb. 10:2; *a present idea, persisting notion, impression of reality,* 1 Pet. 2:19; *conscience,* as an inward moral impression of one's actions and principles, Acts 23:1; 24:16; Rom. 9:1; 2 Cor. 1:12; *conscience,* as the inward faculty of moral judgment, Rom. 2:15; 13:5; 1 Cor. 8:7b, 10, 12; 10:25, 27, 28, 29; 2 Cor. 4:2; 5:11; 1 Tim. 1:5, 19; 3:9; 4:2; 2 Tim. 1:3; *conscience,* as the inward moral and spiritual frame, Tit. 1:15; Heb. 9:9, 14; 10:22; 13:18; 1 Pet. 3:16, 21* [4893] See *conscience, consciousness.*

[5289] σύνειμι *syneimi* 2x from εἰμί, *to be with, be in company with,* Lk. 9:18; Acts 22:11* [4895]

[5290] σύνειμι *syneimi* 1x from εἶμι, *to come together,* Lk. 8:4* [4896]

[5291] συνεισέρχομαι *syneiserchomai* 2x *to enter with* someone, Jn. 18:15; *to embark with,* Jn. 6:22* [4897]

[5292] συνέκδημος *synekdēmos* 2x *one who accompanies* another *to foreign countries, fellow traveller,* Acts 19:29; 2 Cor. 8:19* [4898]

[5293] συνεκλεκτός *syneklektos* 1x *chosen along with* others; *elected* to Gospel privileges *along with,* 1 Pet. 5:13* [4899]

[5296] συνεπιμαρτυρέω *synepimartyreō* 1x *to join in according testimony; to support by testimony, to confirm, sanction,* Heb. 2:4* [4901]

[5298] συνεπιτίθημι *synepitithēmi* 1x can also be spelled συνεπιτίθεμαι, mid., *to set upon along with, join with others* in an attack; *to unite in impeaching,* Acts 24:9* [4934]

[5299] συνέπομαι *synepomai* 1x *to follow with, attend, accompany,* Acts 20:4* [4902]

[5300] συνεργέω *synergeō* 5x *to work together with, to cooperate,* etc., 1 Cor. 16:16; 2 Cor. 6:1; *to assist, afford aid to,* Mk. 16:20; Jas. 2:22; absol. *to conspire actively* to a result, Rom. 8:28* [4903]

[5301] συνεργός *synergos* 13x *a fellow laborer, associate, helper,* Rom. 16:3, 9, 21; 2 Cor. 1:24 [4904] See *coworker; fellow worker.*

[5302] συνέρχομαι *synerchomai* 30x pluperf., συνεληλύθεισάν (3 pl), *to come together; to assemble,* Mk. 3:20; 6:33; 14:53; *to cohabit* matrimonially, Mt. 1:18; 1 Cor. 7:5; *to go* or *come with* any one, *to accompany,* Lk. 23:55; Acts 9:39; *to company with, associate with,* Acts 1:21 [4905] See *assemble; come together; gather.*

[5303] συνεσθίω *synesthiō* 5x *to eat with,* Acts 10:41; 11:3; 1 Cor. 5:11; by impl. *to associate with, live on familiar terms with,* Lk. 15:2; Gal. 2:12* [4906]

[5304] σύνεσις *synesis* 7x pr. *a sending together, a junction,* as of streams; met. *understanding, intelligence, discernment,* Lk. 2:47; 1 Cor. 1:19; meton. *the understanding, intellect, mind,* Mk. 12:33; Eph. 3:4; Col. 1:9; 2:2; 2 Tim. 2:7* [4907] See *insight; understanding.*

[5305] συνετός *synetos* 4x *intelligent, discerning, wise, prudent,* Mt. 11:25; Lk. 10:21; Acts 13:7; 1 Cor. 1:19* [4908]

[5306] συνευδοκέω *syneudokeō* 6x *to approve with* another; *to agree with in principle,* Rom. 1:32; *to stamp approval,* Lk. 11:48; Acts 8:1; 22:20; *to be willing, agreeable,* 1 Cor. 7:12, 13* [4909]

[5307] συνευωχέομαι *syneuōcheomai* 2x *to feast together with,* 2 Pet. 2:13; Jude 12* [4910]

[5308] συνεφίστημι *synephistēmi* 1x *to set together upon, join in an attack,* Acts 16:22* [4911]

[5309] συνέχω *synechō* 12x pr. *to hold together; to confine, shut up, close;* τὰ ωτα, *to stop the ears,* Acts 7:57; *to confine,* as a besieged city, Lk. 19:43; *to hold, hold fast, have the custody of* any one, Lk. 22:63; *to hem in, urge, press upon,* Lk. 8:45; *to exercise a constraining influence on,* 2 Cor. 5:14; pass. *to be seized with, be affected with,* as fear, disease, etc., Mt. 4:24; Lk. 4:38; 8:37; Acts 28:8; *to be in a state of* mental *constriction, to be hard pressed* by urgency of circumstances, Lk. 12:50; Acts 18:5; Phil. 1:23* [4912] See *compel; suffer.*

[5310] συνήδομαι *synēdomai* 1x *to be pleased along with* others; *to congratulate; to delight in, approve cordially,* Rom. 7:22* [4913]

[5311] συνήθεια *synētheia* 3x *use, custom; an established custom, practice,* Jn. 18:39; 1 Cor. 8:7; 11:16* [4914]

[5312] συνηλικιώτης *synēlikiōtēs* 1x *one of the same age, an equal in age,* Gal. 1:14* [4915]

[5313] συνθάπτω *synthaptō* 2x *to bury with;* pass. in NT *to be buried with* Christ symbolically, Rom. 6:4; Col. 2:12* [4916]

[5314] συνθλάω *synthlaō* 2x *to crush together; to break in pieces, shatter,* Mt. 21:44; Lk. 20:18* [4917]

[5315] συνθλίβω *synthlibō* 2x *to press together; to press upon, crowd,* Mk. 5:24, 31* [4918]

[5316] συνθρύπτω *synthryptō* 1x *to crush to pieces;* met. *to break* the heart of any one, *to make to recoil in fear,* Acts 21:13* [4919]

[5317] συνίημι *syniēmi* 26x also συνίω, see *BAGD* for a discussion, pr. *to send together;* met. *to understand, comprehend thoroughly,* Mt. 13:51; Lk. 2:50; 18:34; 24:45; *to perceive clearly,* Mt. 16:12; 17:13; Acts 7:25; Rom. 15:21; Eph. 5:17; absol. *to be well judging, sensible,* 2 Cor. 10:12; *to be* spiritually *intelligent,* Mt. 13:13, 14, 15; Acts 28:26, 27; *to be* religiously *wise,* Rom. 3:11 [4920] See *realize; understand.*

[5319] συνίστημι *synistēmi* 16x also spelled συνιστάνω and συνιστάω, *to place together; to recommend to favorable attention,* Rom. 16:1; 2 Cor. 3:1; 10:18; *to place in a striking point of view,* Rom. 3:5; 5:8; Gal. 2:18; *to stand beside,* Lk. 9:32; *to have been permanently framed,* Col. 1:17; *to possess consistence,* 2 Pet. 3:5 [4921] See *commend; hold together.*

[5321] συνοδεύω *synodeuō* 1x *to journey* or *travel with, accompany on a journey,* Acts 9:7* [4922]

[5322] συνοδία *synodia* 1x pr. *a journeying together;* meton. *a company of fellow travellers, caravan,* Lk. 2:44* [4923]

[5323] σύνοιδα *synoida* 2x a defective verb that is actually perfect in form but present in meaning, *to share in the knowledge of* a thing; *to be privy to,* Acts 5:2; *to be conscious;* οὐδέν σύνοιδα, *to have a clear conscience,* 1 Cor. 4:4* [4894]

[5324] συνοικέω *synoikeō* 1x *to dwell with; to live* or *cohabit with,* 1 Pet. 3:7* [4924]

[5325] συνοικοδομέω *synoikodomeō* 1x *to build in company with* someone; pass. *to be built up, form a constituent part of a structure,* Eph. 2:22* [4925]

[5326] συνομιλέω *synomileō* 1x pr. *to be in company with; to talk* or *converse with,* Acts 10:27* [4926]

[5327] συνομορέω *synomoreō* 1x *to be next to, be next door,* Acts 18:7* [4927]

[5328] συνοράω *synoraō* 2x *perceive, become aware of, realize,* Acts 12:12; 14:6* [4894]

[5330] συνοχή *synochē* 2x pr. *a being held together; compression;* in NT met. *distress of mind, anxiety,* Lk. 21:25; 2 Cor. 2:4 [4928]

[5332] συντάσσω *syntassō* 3x pr. *to arrange* or *place in order together;* in NT *to order, charge, direct,* Mt. 21:6, 26:19; 27:10* [4929] See *command; instruct.*

[5333] συντέλεια *synteleia* 6x *a complete combination, a completion, consummation, end,* Mt. 13:39, 40, 49; 24:3; 28:20; Heb. 9:26* [4930]

[5334] συντελέω *synteleō* 6x pr. *to bring to an end altogether; to finish, end,* Lk. 4:13; *to consummate,* Rom. 9:28; *to ratify* a covenant, Heb. 8:8; pass. *to be terminated,* Lk. 4:2; Acts 21:27; *to be fully realized,* Mk. 13:4* [4931]

[5335] συντέμνω *syntemnō* 1x pr. *to cut short, contract by cutting off;* met. *to execute speedily,* or from the Hebrew, *to determine, decide, decree,* Rom. 9:28 (2x)* [4932]

[5337] συντηρέω *syntēreō* 3x *to keep safe and sound,* Mt. 9:17; *to observe strictly,* or, *to secure from harm, protect,* Mk. 6:20; *to preserve in memory, keep carefully in mind,* Lk. 2:19* [4933]

[5338] συντίθημι *syntithēmi* 3x *to agree together, come to a mutual understanding,* Jn. 9:22; Acts 23:20; *to bargain, to pledge one's self,* Lk. 22:5* [4934]

[5339] συντόμως *syntomōs* 1x *concisely, briefly,* Acts 24:4* [4935]

[5340] συντρέχω *syntrechō* 3x *to run together, flock together,* Mk. 6:33; Acts 3:11; *to run in company with* others, met. 1 Pet. 4:4* [4936]

[5341] συντρίβω *syntribō* 7x *to rub together; to shiver,* Mk. 14:3; Rev. 2:27; *to break, break in pieces,* Mk. 5:4; Jn. 19:36; *to break down, crush, bruise,* Mt. 12:20; met. *to break the power of* any one, *deprive of strength, debilitate,* Lk. 9:39; Rom. 16:20* [4937]

[5342] σύντριμμα *syntrimma* 1x *a breaking, bruising;* in NT *destruction, ruin,* Rom. 3:16* [4938]

[5343] σύντροφος *syntrophos* 1x *nursed with* another; *one brought up* (*NIV*) or *educated with* another, *intimate friend, friend of the court* (*RSV*) Acts 13:1* [4939]

[5344] συντυγχάνω *syntynchanō* 1x *to meet* or *fall in with; join,* in NT *to get to, approach,* Lk. 8:19* [4940]

[5345] Συντύχη *Syntychē* 1x *Syntyche,* pr. name, Phil. 4:2* [4941]

[5347] συνυποκρίνομαι *synypokrinomai* 1x *to dissemble, feign with,* or *in the same manner as* another, *join in the playing of the hypocrite,* Gal. 2:13* [4942]

[5348] συνυπουργέω *synypourgeō* 1x *to aid along with* another, *help together,* 2 Cor. 1:11* [4943]

[5349] συνωδίνω *synōdinō* 1x pr. *to travail at the same time with;* trop. *suffer together,* Rom. 8:22* [4944]

[5350] συνωμοσία *synōmosia* 1x *a banding by oath; a combination, conspiracy,* Acts 23:13* [4945]

[5352] Συράκουσαι *Syrakousai* 1x *Syracuse,* a celebrated city of Sicily, Acts 28:12* [4946]

[5353] Συρία *Syria* 8x *Syria,* an extensive country of Asia, Mt. 4:24; Lk. 2:2; Acts 15:23 [4947]

[5354] Σύρος *Syros* 1x *a Syrian,* Lk. 4:27* [4948]

[5355] Συροφοινίκισσα *Syrophoinikissa* 1x *a Syrophoenician woman,* Phoenicia being included in Syria, Mk. 7:26* [4949]

[5358] Σύρτις *Syrtis* 1x *a shoal, sandbank, a place dangerous on account of shoals,* two of which were particularly famous on the northern coast of Africa, one lying near Carthage, and the other, *the syrtis major,* lying between Cyrene and Leptis, which is probably referred to in Acts 27:17* [4950]

[5359] σύρω *syrō* 5x *to draw, drag,* Jn. 21:8; Rev. 12:4; *to force away, hale* before magistrates, etc., Acts 8:3; 14:19; 17:6* [4951]

[5360] συσπαράσσω *sysparassō* 2x *to tear to pieces; to convulse altogether,* Mk. 9:20; Lk. 9:42* [4952]

[5361] σύσσημον *syssēmon* 1x *a signal,* Mk. 14:44* [4953]

[5362] σύσσωμος *syssōmos* 1x *united in the same body;* met. pl. *joint members* in a spiritual body, Eph. 3:6* [4954]

[5364] συστατικός *systatikos* 1x *commendatory, recommendatory,* 2 Cor. 3:1* [4956]

[5365] συσταυρόω *systauroō* 5x *to crucify with* another, Mt. 27:44; Mk. 15:32; Jn. 19:32; pass. met. *to be crucified with* another in a spiritual resemblance, Rom. 6:6; Gal. 2:20* [4957]

[5366] συστέλλω *systellō* 2x *to draw together, contract, straiten; to enwrap;* hence, i.q. περιστέλλω, *to lay out, prepare for burial,* Acts 5:6; pass. *to be shortened,* 1 Cor. 7:29* [4958]

[5367] συστενάζω *systenazō* 1x *to groan* or *lament together,* Rom. 8:22* [4959]

[5368] συστοιχέω *systoicheō* 1x pr. *to be in the same row with;* met. *to correspond to,* Gal. 4:25* [4960]

[5369] συστρατιώτης *systratiōtēs* 2x *a fellow soldier, co-militant,* in the service of Christ, Phil. 2:25; Phlm. 2* [4961]

[5370] συστρέφω *systrephō* 2x *to turn* or *roll together; to collect, gather,* Acts 28:3; Mt. 17:22* [4962]

[5371] συστροφή *systrophē* 2x *a gathering, tumultuous assembly,* Acts 19:40; *a combination, conspiracy,* Acts 23:12* [4963]

[5372] συσχηματίζω *syschēmatizō* 2x *to fashion in accordance with;* mid/pass. *to conform* or *assimilate one's self to,* met. Rom. 12:2; 1 Pet. 1:14* [4964]

[5373] Συχάρ *Sychar* 1x *Sychar,* indecl., a city of Samaria, Jn. 4:5* [4965]

[5374] Συχέμ *Sychem* 2x *Shechem,* indecl., fem., a city of Samaria, Acts 7:16* [4966]

[5375] σφαγή *sphagē* 3x *slaughter,* Acts 8:32; Rom. 8:36; Jas. 5:5* [4967]

[5376] σφάγιον *sphagion* 1x *a victim* slaughtered in sacrifice, *offering,* Acts 7:42* [4968]

[5377] σφάζω *sphazō* 10x also spelled σφάττω, *to slaughter, kill, slay;* pr. used of animals killed in sacrifice, etc., Rev. 5:6, 9, 12; 13:8; of persons, etc., 1 Jn. 3:12; Rev. 6:4, 9; 18:24; *to wound mortally,* Rev. 13:3* [4969] See *slay.*

[5379] σφόδρα *sphodra* 11x *much, greatly, exceedingly,* Mt. 2:10; 17:6; Mk. 16:4; Lk. 18:23; Acts 6:7 [4970] See *greatly.*

[5380] σφοδρῶς *sphodrōs* 1x *exceedingly, vehemently,* Acts 27:18* [4971]

[5381] σφραγίζω *sphragizō* 15x *to seal, stamp with a seal,* Mt. 27:66; Rev. 20:3; *to seal up, to close up, conceal,* Rev. 10:4; 22:10; *to set a mark upon, distinguish by a mark,* Eph. 1:13; 4:30; Rev. 7:3, 4, 5, 8; *to seal, to mark distinctively* as invested with a certain character, Jn. 6:27; mid. *to set one's own mark upon, seal as one's own, to impress with a mark of acceptance,* 2 Cor. 1:22; *to deliver over safely to* someone, Rom. 15:28; absol. *to set to one's seal, to make a solemn declaration,* Jn. 3:33* [4972] See *seal.*

[5382] σφραγίς *sphragis* 16x *a seal, a signet ring,* Rev. 7:2; *an inscription on a seal, motto,* 2 Tim. 2:19; *a seal, the impression of a seal,* Rev. 5:1, 2, 5, 9, 6:1, 3, 5, 7, 9, 12; 8:1; *a seal, a distinctive mark,* Rev. 9:4; *a seal, a token, proof,* 1 Cor. 9:2; *a token* of guarantee, Rom. 4:11* [4973] See *seal.*

[5383] σφυδρόν *sphydron* 1x *ankle,* Acts 3:7* [4974]

[5385] σχεδόν *schedon* 3x pr. *near,* of place; hence, *nearly, almost,* Acts 13:44; 19:26; Heb. 9:22* [4975]

[5386] σχῆμα *schēma* 2x *fashion, form; fashion, external show,* 1 Cor. 7:31; Phil. 2:7* [4976] See *appearance; figure; form.*

[5387] σχίζω *schizō* 11x *to split,* Mt. 27:51; Mk. 15:38; *to rend, tear asunder,* Mt. 27:51; Lk. 5:36; 23:45; Jn. 19:24; 21:11); mid. *to open* or *unfold* with a chasm, Mk. 1:10; pass. met. *to be divided* into parties or factions, Acts 14:4; 23:7* [4977] See *divide; split; tear.*

[5388] σχίσμα *schisma* 8x *a split,* Mt. 9:16; Mk. 2:21; met. *a division* into parties, *schism,* Jn. 7:43; 9:16; 10:19; 1 Cor. 1:10; 11:18; 12:25* [4978] See *division.*

[5389] σχοινίον *schoinion* 2x pr. *a cord made of rushes;* genr. *a rope, cord,* Jn. 2:15; Acts 27:32* [4979]

[5390] σχολάζω *scholazō* 2x *to be unemployed, to be at leisure; to be at leisure* for a thing, *to devote one's self entirely* to a thing, 1 Cor. 7:5; *to be unoccupied, empty,* Mt. 12:44* [4980]

[5391] σχολή *scholē* 1x *freedom from occupation;* later, *ease, leisure; a school,* Acts 19:9* [4981]

[5392] σῴζω *sōzō* 106x *to save, rescue; to preserve safe and unharmed,* Mark. 8:25; 10:22; 24:22; 27:40, 42, 49; 1 Tim. 2:15; σῴζειν εἰς, *to bring safely to,* 2 Tim. 4:18; *to cure, heal, restore to health,* Mt. 9:21, 22; Mk. 5:23, 28, 34; 6:56; *to save, preserve* from being lost, Mt. 16:25; Mk. 3:4; 8:35; σῴζειν ἀπό, *to deliver from, set free from,* Mt. 1:21; Jn. 12:27; Acts 2:40; in NT *to rescue* from unbelief, *convert,* Rom. 11:14; 1 Cor. 1:21; 7:16; *to bring within the pale of saving privilege,* Tit. 3:5; 1 Pet. 3:21; *to save* from final ruin, 1 Tim. 1:15; pass. *to be brought within the pale of saving privilege,* Acts 2:47; Eph. 2:5, 8; *to be in the way of salvation,* 1 Cor. 15:2; 2 Cor. 2:15 [4982] See *heal; rescue; save.*

[5393] σῶμα *sōma* 142x *the body* of an animal; *a* living *body,* Mt. 5:29, 30; 6:22, 23, 25; Jas. 3:3; *a person, individual,* 1 Cor. 6:16; *a* dead *body; corpse, carcass,* Mt. 14:12; 27:52, 58; Heb. 13:11; *the* human *body* considered as the seat and occasion of moral imperfection, as inducing to sin through its appetites and passions, Rom. 7:24; 8:13; genr. *a body, a material substance,* 1 Cor. 15:37, 38, 40; *the substance, reality,* as opposed to ἡ σκιά, Col. 2:17; in NT met., *the* aggregate *body* of believers, *the body* of the Church, Rom. 12:5; Col. 1:18 [4983] See *body.*

[5394] σωματικός *sōmatikos* 2x *bodily, of* or *belonging to the body,* 1 Tim. 4:8; *corporeal, material,* Lk. 3:22* [4984]

[5395] σωματικῶς *sōmatikōs* 1x *bodily, in a bodily frame,* Col. 2:9* [4985]

[5396] Σώπατρος *Sōpatros* 1x *Sopater,* pr. name, Acts 20:4* [4986]

[5397] σωρεύω *sōreuō* 2x *to heap* or *pile up,* Rom. 12:20; met. pass. *to be filled* with sins, 2 Tim. 3:6* [4987]

[5398] Σωσθένης *Sōsthenēs* 2x *Sosthenes,* pr. name, Acts 18:17; 1 Cor. 1:1* [4988]

[5399] Σωσίπατρος *Sōsipatros* 1x *Sosipater,* pr. name, Rom. 16:21* [4989]

[5400] σωτήρ *sōtēr* 24x *a savior, preserver, deliverer,* Lk. 1:47; 2:11; Acts 5:31 [4990] See *savior.*

[5401] σωτηρία *sōtēria* 46x *a saving, preservation,* Acts 27:34; Heb. 11:7; *deliverance,* Lk. 1:69, 71; Acts 7:25; *salvation,* spiritual and eternal, Lk. 1:77; 19:9; Acts 4:12; Rev. 7:10; *a being placed in a condition of salvation* by an embracing of the Gospel, Rom. 10:1, 10; 2 Tim. 3:15; *means* or *opportunity of salvation,* Acts 13:26; Rom. 11:11; Heb. 2:3; ἡ σωτηρία, *the* promised *deliverance* by the Messiah, Jn. 4:22 [4991] See *salvation.*

[5403] σωτήριος *sōtērios* 1x *imparting salvation, saving,* Lk. 2:30; 3:6; Acts 28:28; Eph. 6:17; Tit. 2:11* [4992]

[5404] σωφρονέω *sōphroneō* 6x *to be of a sound mind, be in one's right mind, be sane,* Mk. 5:15; Lk. 8:35; *to be calm,* 2 Cor. 5:13; *to be sober-minded, sedate,* Tit. 2:6; 1 Pet. 4:7; *to be of a modest, humble mind,* Rom. 12:3* [4993]

[5405] σωφρονίζω *sōphronizō* 1x *encourage, to restore to a right mind; to make sober-minded, to steady* by exhortation and guidance, Tit. 2:4* [4994]

[5406] σωφρονισμός *sōphronismos* 1x *self discipline, prudence,* 2 Tim. 1:7* [4995]

[5407] σωφρόνως *sōphronōs* 1x *in the manner of a person in his right mind; soberly, temperately,* Tit. 2:12* [4996]

[5408] σωφροσύνη *sōphrosynē* 3x *sanity, soundness of mind, a sane mind,* Acts 26:25; female *modesty,* 1 Tim. 2:9, 15* [4997]

[5409] σώφρων *sōphrōn* 4x *of a sound mind, sane; temperate, discreet,* 1 Tim. 3:2; Tit. 1:8; 2:2; *modest, chaste,* Tit. 2:5* [4998]

[5411] ταβέρναι *tabernai* 1x *taverns,* used in the NT only in the transliterated Latin name of "Three Taverns" (Τριῶν ταβερνῶν), see 5553, Acts 28:15* [4999]

[5412] Ταβιθά *Tabitha* 2x *antelope, Tabitha,* pr. name, Acts 9:36, 40* [5000]

[5413] τάγμα *tagma* 1x pr. *anything placed in order;* in NT *order of* succession, *class, group,* 1 Cor. 15:23* [5001]

[5414] τακτός *taktos* 1x pr. *arranged; fixed, appointed, set,* Acts 12:21* [5002]

[5415] ταλαιπωρέω *talaipōreō* 1x *to endure severe labor and hardship; to be harassed; complain,* Jas. 4:9* [5003]

[5416] ταλαιπωρία *talaipōria* 2x *toil, difficulty, hardship; calamity, misery, distress,* Rom. 3:16; Jas. 5:1* [5004]

[5417] ταλαίπωρος *talaipōros* 2x pr. *enduring severe effort and hardship;* hence, *wretched, miserable, afflicted,* Rom. 7:24; Rev. 3:17* [5005]

[5418] ταλαντιαῖος *talantiaios* 1x *of a talent weight, weighing a talent,* Rev. 16:21* [5006]

[5419] τάλαντον *talanton* 14x *the scale of a balance; a talent,* which as a weight was among the Jews equivalent to 3000 shekels, i.e., as usually estimated, 114 lbs. 15 dwts. Troy; while the Attic talent, on the usual estimate, was only equal to 56 lbs. 11 oz. Troy, Mt. 18:24; 25:15, 16, 20, 22, 24, 25, 28* [5007] See *talent.*

[5420] ταλιθά *talitha* 1x Aramaic, *(little) girl,* Mk. 5:41* [5008]

[5421] ταμεῖον *tameion* 4x *a storehouse, granary, barn,* Lk. 12:24; *a chamber, clos-*

et, place of retirement and privacy, Mt. 6:6; 24:26; Lk. 12:3* [5009]

[5423] τάξις *taxis* 9x *order, regular disposition, arrangement; order, series, succession,* Lk. 1:8; *an order, distinctive class,* as of priests, Heb. 5:6, 10; 6:20; 7:11(2x), 17; *order, good order,* 1 Cor. 14:40; *orderliness, well-regulated conduct,* Col. 2:5* [5010]

[5424] ταπεινός *tapeinos* 8x *low* in situation; of condition, *humble, poor, mean, depressed,* Lk. 1:52; 2 Cor. 7:6; Jas. 1:9; met. of the mind, *humble, lowly, modest,* Mt. 11:29; Rom. 12:16; 2 Cor. 10:1; Jas. 4:6; 1 Pet. 5:5* [5011]

[5425] ταπεινοφροσύνη *tapeinophrosynē* 7x *lowliness* or *humility of mind, modesty,* Acts 20:19; Eph. 4:2; Phil. 2:3; Col. 2:18, 23; 3:12; 1 Pet. 5:5* [5012]

[5426] ταπεινόφρων *tapeinophrōn* 1x *humble-minded,* 1 Pet. 3:8* [5391]

[5427] ταπεινόω *tapeinoō* 14x *to bring low, depress, level,* Lk. 3:5; met. *to humble, abase,* Phil. 2:8; mid. *to descend to,* or *live in, a humble condition,* 2 Cor. 11:7; Phil. 4:12; *to humble, depress the pride of,* any one, Mt. 18:4; mid. *to humble one's self, exhibit humility and contrition,* Jas. 4:10; 1 Pet. 5:6; *to humble* with respect to hopes and expectations, *to depress* with disappointment, Mt. 23:12; Lk. 14:11; 18:14; 2 Cor. 12:21* [5013] See *humble; humiliate; make low.*

[5428] ταπείνωσις *tapeinōsis* 4x *depression; low estate, abject condition,* Lk. 1:48; Acts 8:33; Phil. 3:21; Jas. 1:10* [5014]

[5429] ταράσσω *tarassō* 17x *to agitate, trouble,* as water, Jn. 5:7; met. *to agitate, trouble* the mind; with fear, *to terrify, put in consternation,* Mt. 2:3; 14:26; with grief, etc., *affect with grief, anxiety,* etc., Jn. 12:27; 13:21; with doubt, etc., *to unsettle, perplex,* Acts 15:24; Gal. 1:7 [5015] See *distress; disturb; trouble.*

[5431] τάραχος *tarachos* 2x *agitation, commotion; consternation, terror,* Acts 12:18; *excitement, tumult, public contention,* Acts 19:23* [5017]

[5432] Ταρσεύς *Tarseus* 2x *of,* or *a native of* Ταρσός, *Tarsus,* the metropolis of Cilicia, Acts 9:11; 21:39* [5018]

[5433] Ταρσός *Tarsos* 3x *Tarsus,* the chief city of Cilicia, and birth-place of the Apostle Paul, Acts 9:30; 11:25; 22:3* [5019]

[5434] ταρταρόω *tartaroō* 1x *to cast* or *thrust down to Tartarus* or *Gehenna,* 2 Pet. 2:4* [5020]

[5435] τάσσω *tassō* 8x *to arrange; to set, appoint,* in a certain station, Lk. 7:8; Rom. 13:1; *to set, devote,* to a pursuit, 1 Cor. 16:15; *to dispose, frame,* for an object, Acts 13:48; *to arrange, appoint,* place or time, Mt. 28:16; Acts 28:23; *to allot, assign,* Acts 22:10; *to settle, decide,* Acts 15:2* [5021]

[5436] ταῦρος *tauros* 4x *a bull, ox,* Mt. 22:4; Acts 14:13; Heb. 9:13; 10:4* [5022]

[5438] ταφή *taphē* 1x *burial, the act of burying, burial place,* Mt. 27:7* [5027]

[5439] τάφος *taphos* 7x *a sepulchre, grave, tomb,* Mt. 23:27, 29; 27:61, 64, 66; 28:1; met. Rom. 3:13* [5028]

[5440] τάχα *tacha* 2x pr. *quickly, soon; perhaps, possibly,* Rom. 5:7; Phlm. 15* [5029]

[5441] ταχέως *tacheōs* 15x adverb of ταχύς, *quickly, speedily; soon, shortly,* 1 Cor. 4:19; Gal. 1:6; *hastily,* Lk. 14:21; 16:6; *with inconsiderate haste,* 1 Tim. 5:22 [5030, 5032, 5033] See *quickly; soon.*

[5442] ταχινός *tachinos* 2x *swift, speedy,* 2 Pet. 2:1; *near at hand, impending,* 2 Pet. 1:14* [5031]

[5443] τάχος *tachos* 8x *swiftness, speed, quickness;* ἐν τάχει, *with speed, quickly, speedily; soon, shortly,* Lk. 18:8; Acts 25:4; *hastily, immediately,* Acts 12:7;

22:18; Rom. 16:20; 1 Tim. 3:14; Rev. 1:1; 22:6* [5034]

[5444] ταχύς *tachus* 13x *swift, fleet, quick;* met. *ready, prompt,* Jas. 1:19; Mt. 28:7f.; Mk. 9:39; Lk. 15:22; Jn. 11:29 [5035, 5036] See *quickly; soon.*

[5445] τε *te* 215x enclitic, can function as a conj., serving either as a lightly-appending link, Acts 1:15; *and,* Acts 2:3; or as an inclusive prefix, Lk. 12:45; *both,* Lk. 24:20; Acts 26:16 [5037]

[5446] τεῖχος *teichos* 9x *a wall* of a city, Acts 9:25; 2 Cor. 11:33; Heb. 11:30; Rev. 21:12, 14f., 17-19* [5038]

[5447] τεκμήριον *tekmērion* 1x *a sign, indubitable token, clear proof,* Acts 1:3* [5039]

[5448] τεκνίον *teknion* 8x *a little child;* τεκνία, an endearing appellation, *my dear children,* Jn. 13:33; 1 Jn. 2:1, 12, 28; 3:7, 18; 4:4; 5:21* [5040]

[5449] τεκνογονέω *teknogoneō* 1x *to bear children, to rear a family,* 1 Tim. 5:14* [5041]

[5450] τεκνογονία *teknogonia* 1x *the bearing of children, the rearing of a family,* 1 Tim. 2:15* [5042]

[5451] τέκνον *teknon* 99x *a child, a son* or *daughter,* Mt. 2:18; Lk. 1:7; pl. *descendants, posterity,* Mt. 3:9; Acts 2:39; *child, son,* as a term of endearment, Mt. 9:2; Mk. 2:5; 10:24; pl. *children, inhabitants, people,* of a city, Mt. 23:37; Lk. 19:44; from the Hebrew, met. *a child* or *son* in virtue of discipleship, 1 Cor. 4:17; 1 Tim. 1:2; 2 Tim. 1:2; Tit. 1:4; Phlm. 10; 3 Jn. 4; *a child* in virtue of gracious acceptance, Jn. 1:12; 11:52; Rom. 8:16, 21; 1 Jn. 3:1; *a child* in virtue of spiritual conformity, Jn. 8:39; Phil. 2:15; 1 Jn. 3:10; *a child of, one characterized by* some condition or quality, Mt. 11:19; Eph. 2:3; 5:8; 1 Pet. 1:14; 2 Pet. 2:14 [5043] See *children.*

[5452] τεκνοτροφέω *teknotropheō* 1x *to rear a family,* 1 Tim. 5:10* [5044]

[5454] τέκτων *tektōn* 2x *an artisan;* and spc. *one who works with wood, a carpenter,* Mt. 13:55; Mk. 6:3* [5045]

[5455] τέλειος *teleios* 19x *brought to completion; fully accomplished, fully developed,* Jas. 1:4a; *fully realized, thorough,* 1 Jn. 4:18; *complete, entire,* as opposed to what is partial and limited, 1 Cor. 13:10; *full grown of ripe age,* 1 Cor. 14:20; Eph. 4:13; Heb. 5:14; *fully accomplished* in Christian enlightenment, 1 Cor. 2:6; Phil. 3:15; Col. 1:28; *perfect* in some point of character, *without shortcoming* in respect of a certain standard, Mt. 5:48; 19:21; Col. 4:12; Jas. 1:4b; 3:2; *perfect, consummate,* Rom. 12:2; Jas. 1:17, 25; compar. *of higher excellence and efficiency,* Heb. 9:11* [5046] See *end; mature; perfect.*

[5456] τελειότης *teleiotēs* 2x *completeness, perfectness,* Col. 3:14; *ripeness* of knowledge or practice, *maturity,* Heb. 6:1* [5047]

[5457] τελειόω *teleioō* 23x *to execute fully, discharge,* Jn. 4:34; 5:36; 17:4; *to reach the end of, run through, finish,* Lk. 2:43; Acts 20:24; *to consummate, place in a condition of finality,* Heb. 7:19; *to perfect* a person, *advance* a person *to final completeness* of character, Heb. 2:10; 5:9; 7:28; *to perfect* a person, *advance* a person *to a completeness* of its kind, which needs no further provision, Heb. 9:9; 10:1, 14; pass. *to receive fulfillment,* Jn. 19:28; *to be brought to the goal, to reach the end of one's course,* Lk. 13:32; Phil. 3:12; Heb. 11:40; 12:23; *to be fully developed,* 2 Cor. 12:9; Jas. 2:22; 1 Jn. 2:5; 4:12, 17; *to be completely organized, to be closely embodied,* Jn. 17:23 [5048] See *complete; end; fulfill; perfect.*

[5458] τελείως *teleiōs* 1x *perfectly, completely,* 1 Pet. 1:13* [5049]

[5459] τελείωσις *teleiōsis* 2x *a completing; a fulfillment, an accomplishment* of predictions, promised, etc., Lk. 1:45; *finality* of function, *completeness* of operation and effect, Heb. 7:11* [5050]

[5460] τελειωτής *teleiōtēs* 1x *a finisher, one who completes and perfects* a thing; *one who brings through to final attainment, perfecter,* Heb. 12:2* [5051]

[5461] τελεσφορέω *telesphoreō* 1x *to bring to maturity,* as fruits, etc.; met. Lk. 8:14* [5052]

[5462] τελευτάω *teleutaō* 11x *to end, finish, complete;* absol. *to end* [5053] See *die.*

[5463] τελευτή *teleutē* 1x *a finishing, end;* hence, *end* of life, *death, decease,* Mt. 2:15* [5054]

[5464] τελέω *teleō* 28x *to finish, complete, conclude,* an operation, Mt. 11:1; 13:53; 19:1; *to finish* a circuit, Mt. 10:23; *to fulfil, to carry out into full operation,* Rom. 2:27; Gal. 5:16; Jas. 2:8; *to pay* dues, Mt. 17:24; pass. *to be fulfilled, realized,* Lk. 12:50; 18:31; of time, *to be ended, elapse,* Rom. 15:8; 20:3, 5, 7 [5055] See *complete; end.*

[5465] τέλος *telos* 40x *an end attained, consummation; an end, closing act,* Mt. 24:6, 14; 1 Cor. 15:24; *full performance, perfect discharge,* Rom. 10:4; *fulfillment, realization,* Lk. 22:37; *final dealing,* developed *issue,* Jas. 5:11; *issue, final stage,* 1 Cor. 10:11; *issue, result,* Mt. 26:58; Rom. 6:21, 22; 1 Pet. 1:9; antitypical *issue,* 2 Cor. 3:13; practical *issue,* 1 Tim. 1:5; *ultimate destiny,* Phil. 3:19; Heb. 6:8; 1 Pet. 4:17; *a tax* or *dues,* Mt. 17:25; Rom. 13:7; εἰς τέλος, *to the full,* 1 Thess. 2:16; εἰς τέλος, *continually,* Lk. 18:5; εἰς τέλος, μέχρι, ἄχρι τέλους, *throughout,* Mt. 10:22; Mk. 13:13; Jn. 13:1; Heb. 3:6, 14; 6:11; Rev. 2:26 [5056] See *end.*

[5467] τελώνης *telōnēs* 21x *one who farms the public revenues;* in NT *a publican, collector of imposts, revenue officer, tax gatherer,* Mt. 5:46; 9:10, 11; 10:3; Mk. 2:15f.; Lk. 3:12 [5057] See *tax collector.*

[5468] τελώνιον *telōnion* 3x *a customhouse, toll house; collector's office,* Mt. 9:9; Mk. 2:14; Lk. 5:27* [5058]

[5469] τέρας *teras* 16x *a prodigy, portent,* Acts 2:19; *a signal act, wonder, miracle,* Mt. 13:22; Jn. 4:48; Acts 2:43 [5059] See *miracle; wonders.*

[5470] Τέρτιος *Tertios* 1x *Tertius,* pr. name, a helper of Paul, Rom. 16:22* [5060]

[5472] Τέρτυλλος *Tertyllos* 2x *Tertullus,* pr. name, an attorney, Acts 24:1f.* [5061]

[5475] τέσσαρες *tessares* 41x *four,* Mt. 24:31; Mk. 2:3 [5064] See *four.*

[5476] τεσσαρεσκαιδέκατος *tessareskaidekatos* 2x *the fourteenth,* Acts 27:27, 33* [5065]

[5477] τεσσεράκοντα *tesserakonta* 22x *forty,* indecl., Mt. 4:2; Jn. 2:20; Acts 1:3; 23:13, 21; Heb. 3:9; Rev. 11:2; 21:17 [5062] See *forty.*

[5478] τεσσερακονταετής *tesserakontaetēs* 2x *forty years,* Acts 7:23; 13:18* [5063]

[5479] τεταρταῖος *tetartaios* 1x *on the fourth day,* Jn. 11:39* [5066]

[5480] τέταρτος *tetartos* 10x *fourth,* Mt. 14:25; *the fourth part, quarter,* Rev. 6:8 [5067] See *fourth.*

[5481] τετράγωνος *tetragōnos* 1x *four-angled, quadrangular, square,* Rev. 21:16* [5068]

[5482] τετράδιον *tetradion* 1x *a set of four; a detachment of four* men, Acts 12:4* [5069]

[5483] τετρακισχίλιοι *tetrakischilioi* 5x *four thousand,* Mt. 15:38; 16:10; Mk. 8:9, 20; Acts 21:38* [5070]

[5484] τετρακόσιοι *tetrakosioi* 4x *four hundred,* Acts 5:36; 7:6; 13:20; Gal. 3:17* [5071]

[5485] τετράμηνος *tetramēnos* 1x *of four months, four months in duration,* Jn. 4:35* [5072]

[5487] τετραπλοῦς *tetraplous* 1x contracted form of τετραπλόος, *four times* *(as much), fourfold, quadruple,* Lk. 19:8* [5073]

[5488] τετράπους *tetrapous* 3x *four-footed; quadrupeds,* Acts 10:12; 11:6; Rom. 1:23* [5074]

[5489] τετρααρχέω *tetraarcheō* 3x also spelled τετραρχέω, *be tetrarch,* Lk. 3:1 (3x)* [5075]

[5490] τετραάρχης *tetraarchēs* 4x also spelled τετράρχης, *a tetrarch,* title of a prince, whose rank was lower than a king, Mt. 14:1; Lk. 3:19; 9:7; Acts 13:1* [5076]

[5491] τεφρόω *tephroō* 1x *to reduce to ashes, to consume, destroy,* 2 Pet. 2:6* [5077]

[5492] τέχνη *technē* 3x *art, skill,* Acts 17:29; *an art, trade, craft,* Acts 18:3; Rev. 18:22* [5078]

[5493] τεχνίτης *technitēs* 4x *an artisan; workman, mechanic,* Acts 19:24, 38; Rev. 18:22; *an architect, builder,* Heb. 11:10* [5079]

[5494] τήκω *tēkō* 1x *to dissolve;* pass. *to melt,* 2 Pet. 3:12* [5080]

[5495] τηλαυγῶς *tēlaugōs* 1x *clearly, plainly, distinctly,* Mk. 8:25* [5081]

[5496] τηλικοῦτος *tēlikoutos* 4x *so great, large, important,* 2 Cor. 1:10; Heb. 2:3; Jas. 3:4; Rev. 16:18* [5082]

[5498] τηρέω *tēreō* 70x *to keep watch upon, guard,* Mt. 27:36, 54; 28:4; Acts 12:6; *to watch over* protectively, *guard,* 1 Jn. 5:18; Rev. 16:15; *to mark attentively, to heed,* Rev. 1:3; *to observe* practically, *keep strictly,* Mt. 19:17; 23:3; 28:20; Mk. 7:9; Jn. 8:51; *to preserve, shield,* Jn. 17:15; *to store up, reserve,* Jn. 2:10; 12:7; 1 Pet. 1:4; 2 Pet. 2:4, 9, 17; *to keep in custody,* Acts 12:5; 16:23; *to maintain,* Eph. 4:3; 2 Tim. 4:7; *to keep* in a condition, Jn. 17:11, 12; 1 Cor. 7:37; 2 Cor. 11:9; 1 Tim. 5:22; Jas. 1:27 [5083] See *keep; obey.*

[5499] τήρησις *tērēsis* 3x *a keeping, custody;* meton. *a place of custody, prison, ward,* Acts 4:3; 5:18; met. practical *observance, strict performance,* 1 Cor. 7:19* [5084]

[5500] Τιβεριάς *Tiberias* 3x *Tiberias,* a city of Galilee, built by Herod Antipas, and named in honor of Tiberius, Jn. 6:1, 23; 21:1* [5085]

[5501] Τιβέριος *Tiberios* 1x *Tiberius,* the third Roman emperor, *14-37 A.D.,* Lk. 3:1* [5086]

[5502] τίθημι *tithēmi* 100x by-form of τιθέω, *to place, set, lay,* Mt. 5:15; Mk. 6:56; Lk. 6:48; *to produce* at table, Jn. 2:10; *to deposit, lay,* Mt. 27:60; Lk. 23:53; Acts 3:2; *to lay down,* Lk. 19:21, 22; Jn. 10:11, 15, 17, 18; 1 Jn. 3:16; *to lay aside, put off,* Jn. 13:4; *to allocate, assign,* Mt. 24:51; Lk. 12:46; *to set, appoint,* Jn. 15:16; Acts 13:47; Heb. 1:2; *to render, make,* Mt. 22:44; Rom. 4:17; 1 Cor. 9:18; mid. *to put* in custody, Mt. 14:3; Acts 4:3; *to reserve,* Acts 1:7; *to commit* as a matter of charge, 2 Cor. 5:19; *to set,* with design, in a certain arrangement or position, Acts 20:28; 1 Cor. 12:18, 28; 1 Thess. 5:9; 1 Tim. 1:12; pass. 1 Tim. 2:7; 2 Tim. 1:11; 1 Pet. 2:8; τιθέναι τὰ γόνατα, *to kneel down,* Mk. 15:19; Lk. 22:41; Acts 7:60; 9:40; 20:36; 21:5; τίθεσθαι ἐν τῇ καρδίᾳ, *to lay to heart, ponder,* Lk. 1:66; also, εἰς τὰς καρδίας, Lk. 21:14; *to design, resolve,* Acts 5:4; also, ἐν πνεύματι, Acts 19:21; also, βουλήν, Acts 17:12; τίθεσθαι εἰς τὰ ὦτα, *to give attentive audience to, to listen to retentively,* Lk. 9:44 [5087] See *appoint; lay down; place; put.*

[5503] τίκτω *tiktō* 18x *to bear, bring forth* children, Mt. 1:21, 23; trop. *to bear, produce,* as the earth, *yield,* Heb. 6:7; met. *to give birth to,* Jas. 1:15 [5088] See *bring forth; give birth; produce.*

[5504] τίλλω *tillō* 3x *to pull, pluck off,* Mt. 12:1; Mk. 2:23; Lk. 6:1* [5089]

[5505] Τιμαῖος *Timaios* 1x *Timaeus,* pr. name, Mk. 10:46* [5090]

[5506] τιμάω *timaō* 21x *to estimate in respect of worth; to hold in estimation, respect, honor, reverence,* Mt. 15:4, 5, 8;

19:19; Mk. 7:10; *to honor* with reverent service, Jn. 5:23 (4x); 8:49; *to treat with honor, manifest consideration towards,* Acts 28:10; *to treat graciously, visit with marks of favor,* Jn. 12:26; mid. *to price,* Mt. 27:9 [5091] See *honor; value.*

[5507] τιμή *timē* 41x *a pricing, estimate of worth; price, value,* Mt. 27:9; *price* paid, Mt. 27:6; meton. *a thing of price,* and collectively, *precious things,* Rev. 21:24, 26; *preciousness,* 1 Pet. 2:7; substantial *value,* real *worth,* Col. 2:23; *careful regard, honor, state of honor, dignity,* Rom. 9:21; Heb. 5:4; *honor* conferred, *observance, veneration,* Rom. 2:7, 10; 12:10; *mark of favor and consideration,* Acts 28:10, *honorarium, compensation,* 1 Tim. 5:7 [5092] See *honor; price; respect; value.*

[5508] τίμιος *timios* 13x *precious, costly, of great price,* 1 Cor. 3:12; Rev. 18:12; *precious, dear, valuable,* Acts 20:24; 1 Pet. 1:7, 19; *honored, esteemed, respected,* Acts 5:34; Heb. 13:4 [5093] See *honorable; precious; valuable.*

[5509] τιμιότης *timiotēs* 1x *preciousness, costliness;* meton. *precious things, valuable merchandise,* Rev. 18:19* [5094]

[5510] Τιμόθεος *Timotheos* 24x *Timotheus, Timothy,* pr. name, *son of Eunice, traveling companion of Paul,* Acts 16:1; Rom. 16:21; 1 Cor. 4:17; 2 Cor. 1:1; Phil. 1:1; Col. 1:1; 1 Thess. 1:1; 1 Tim. 1:2, 18; 6:20; 2 Tim. 1:2 [5095]

[5511] Τίμων *Timōn* 1x *Timon,* pr. name, Acts 6:5* [5096]

[5512] τιμωρέω *timōreō* 2x *to avenge,* someone; in NT *to punish,* Acts 22:5; 26:11* [5097]

[5513] τιμωρία *timōria* 1x *punishment,* Heb. 10:29* [5098]

[5514] τίνω *tinō* 1x *to pay; to pay* a penalty, *incur* punishment, 2 Thess. 1:9* [5099]

[5515] τίς *tis* 555x *Who? What?* Mt. 3:7; 5:13; 19:27; equivalent to πότερος, *Whether? which* of two things? Mt. 9:5; Mk. 2:9; Phil. 1:22; *Why?* Mt. 8:26; 9:11, 14; τί ὅτι, *Why is it that?* Mk. 2:16; Jn. 14:22; *What?* as an emphatic interrogative, Acts 26:8; τί, *How very!* Mt. 7:14; in indirect question, Mt. 10:11 [5101]

[5516] τις *tis* 534x enclitic, indefinite pronoun, *a certain one, someone,* Mt. 12:47; pl. *some, certain, several,* Lk. 8:2; Acts 9:19; 2 Pet. 3:16; *one, a person,* Mt. 12:29; Lk. 14:8; Jn. 6:50; combined with the name of an individual, *one,* Mk. 15:21; *as it were in a manner, a kind of,* Heb. 10:27; Jas. 1:18; *any* whatever, Mt. 8:28; Lk. 11:36; Rom. 8:39; τις, *somebody* of consequence, Acts 5:36; τι, *something* of consequence, Gal. 2:6; 6:3; τι, *anything* at all, *anything* worth account, 1 Cor. 3:7; 10:19; τι *at all,* Phil. 3:15; Phlm. 18 [5100]

[5517] Τίτιος *Titios* 1x *Titius,* pr. name, Acts 18:7* [2459]

[5518] τίτλος *titlos* 2x *an inscribed roll, superscription,* Jn. 19:19, 20* [5102]

[5519] Τίτος *Titos* 13x *Titus,* pr. name, friend and helper of Paul, 2 Cor. 2:13; 7:6; Gal. 2:1; 2 Tim. 4:10; Tit. 1:4 [5103]

[5521] τοιγαροῦν *toigaroun* 2x *well then, so then, wherefore, for that reason,* 1 Thess. 4:8; Heb. 12:1* [5105]

[5524] τοιόσδε *toiosde* 1x *such as this; such as follows,* 2 Pet. 1:17* [5107]

[5525] τοιοῦτος *toioutos* 57x *such, such like, of this kind* or *sort,* Mt. 18:5; 19:14; *such, so great,* Mt. 9:8; Mk. 6:2; ὁ τοιοῦτος, *such a fellow,* Acts 22:22; also, *the one alluded to,* 1 Cor. 1:5; 2 Cor. 2:6, 7; 12:2, 3, 5 [5108]

[5526] τοῖχος *toichos* 1x *a wall* of a building, as distinct from a city wall or fortification (τεῖχος) Acts 23:3* [5109]

[5527] τόκος *tokos* 2x *a bringing forth; offspring;* met. *produce* of money lent, *interest, usury,* Mt. 25:27; Lk. 19:23* [5110]

[5528] τολμάω *tolmaō* 16x *to assume resolution* to do a thing, Mk. 15:43; Rom.

5:7; Phil. 1:14; *to make up the mind,* 2 Cor. 10:12; *to dare,* Acts 5:13; 7:32; *to presume,* Mt. 22:46; Mk. 12:34; Lk. 20:40; Jn. 21:12; Rom. 15:18; Jude 9; *to have the face,* 1 Cor. 6:1; absol. *to assume a bold bearing, courageous,* 2 Cor. 10:2; 11:21* [5111] See *(have) courage; dare.*

[5529] τολμηρός *tolmēros* 1x *bold, daring,* Rom. 15:15* [5112]

[5532] τολμητής *tolmētēs* 1x *one who is bold;* in a bad sense, *a presumptuous, audacious person,* 2 Pet. 2:10* [5113]

[5533] τομός *tomos* 1x *cutting, sharp, sharper,* Heb. 4:12* [5114]

[5534] τόξον *toxon* 1x *a bow,* Rev. 6:2* [5115]

[5535] τοπάζιον *topazion* 1x *a topaz,* a gem of a yellowish color, different from the modern topaz, Rev. 21:20* [5116]

[5536] τόπος *topos* 94x *a place, locality,* Mt. 12:43; Lk. 6:17; *a* limited *spot* or *ground,* Mt. 24:15; 27:33; Jn. 4:20; Acts 6:13; *a* precise *spot* or *situation,* Mt. 28:6; Mk. 16:6; Lk. 14:9; *a dwelling place, abode, mansion, dwelling, seat,* Jn. 14:2, 3; Acts 4:31; *a place* of ordinary deposit, Mt. 26:52; *a place, passage* in a book, Lk. 4:17; *place* occupied, *room, space,* Lk. 2:7; 14:9, 22; *place, opportunity,* Acts 25:16; Heb. 12:17; *place, condition, position,* 1 Cor. 14:16 [5117] See *district; place; region.*

[5537] τοσοῦτος *tosoutos* 20x *so great, so much,* Mt. 8:10; 15:33; *so long,* of time, Jn. 14:9; pl. *so many,* Mt. 15:33 [5118]

[5538] τότε *tote* 160x *then, at that time,* Mt. 2:17; 3:5; 11:20; *then,* Mt. 12:29; 13:26; 25:31; ἀπὸ τότε, *from that time,* Mt. 4:17; 16:21; ὁ τότε, *which then was,* 2 Pet. 3:6 [5119]

[5543] τράγος *tragos* 4x *a male goat,* Heb. 9:12, 13, 19; 10:4* [5131]

[5544] τράπεζα *trapeza* 15x *a table, an eating table,* Mt. 15:27; Mk. 7:28; Heb. 9:2; by impl. *a meal, feast,* Rom. 11:9; 1 Cor. 10:21; *a table* or *counter* of a money changer, Mt. 21:12; *a bank,* Lk. 19:23; by impl. pl. *money matters,* Acts 6:2 [5132] See *table.*

[5545] τραπεζίτης *trapezitēs* 1x *a money changer, broker, banker,* who exchanges or loans money for a premium, Mt. 25:27* [5133]

[5546] τραῦμα *trauma* 1x *a wound,* Lk. 10:34* [5134]

[5547] τραυματίζω *traumatizō* 2x *to wound,* Lk. 20:12; Acts 19:16* [5135]

[5548] τραχηλίζω *trachēlizō* 1x pr. *to grip the neck; to bend the neck back,* so as to make bare or expose the throat, as in slaughtering animals, etc.; met. *to lay bare in view,* Heb. 4:13* [5136]

[5549] τράχηλος *trachēlos* 7x *the neck,* Mt. 18:6; Mk. 9:42; Lk. 15:20; 17:2; ἐπιθεῖναι ζυγὸν ἐπὶ τὸν τράχηλον, *to put a yoke upon the neck* of someone, met. *to bind to a burdensome observance,* Acts 15:10; 20:37; ὑποτιθέναι τὸν τράχηλον, *to lay down one's neck* under the axe of the executioner, *to imperil one's life,* Rom. 16:4* [5137]

[5550] τραχύς *trachus* 2x *rough, rugged, uneven,* Lk. 3:5; εἰς τραχεῖς τόπους, *on a rocky shore,* Acts 27:29* [5138]

[5551] Τραχωνῖτις *Trachōnitis* 1x *Trachonitis,* part of the tetrarchy of Herod Antipas, the north-easternmost habitable district east of the Jordan, Lk. 3:1* [5139]

[5552] τρεῖς *treis* 68x *three,* Mt. 12:40. The frequency count does not include its occurrence in the name Τριῶν ταβερνῶν in Acts 28:15 (5553) [5140] See *three.*

[5553] Τρεῖς ταβέρναι *treis tabernai* 1x *Three Taverns,* the name of a station on the Appian Way in Acts 28:15 (Τριῶν ταβερνῶν). The Latin *taberna* is an inn or shop [5992]

[5554] τρέμω *tremō* 3x *to tremble, be agitated from fear,* Mk. 5:33; Lk. 8:47; by impl. *to fear, be afraid,* 2 Pet. 2:10* [5141]

[5555] τρέφω *trephō* 9x *to nourish; to feed, support, cherish, provide for,* [5142]

[5556] τρέχω *trechō* 20x *to run,* Mt. 27:48; 28:8; *to run a race,* 1 Cor. 9:24; met. 1 Cor. 9:24, 26; Heb. 12:1; in NT *to run* a certain course of conduct, Gal. 5:7; *to run* a course of exertion, Rom. 9:16; Gal. 2:2; Phil. 2:16; *to run, to progress freely, to advance rapidly,* 2 Thess. 3:1 [5143] See *run.*

[5557] τρῆμα *trēma* 1x *an aperture, hole, eye of a needle,* Lk. 18:25* [5169]

[5558] τριάκοντα *triakonta* 11x *thirty,* indecl., Mt. 13:8, 23; Mk. 4:8; Lk. 3:23 [5144] See *thirty.*

[5559] τριακόσιοι *triakosioi* 2x *three hundred,* Mk. 14:5; Jn. 12:5* [5145]

[5560] τρίβολος *tribolos* 2x pr. *three-pronged; a thistle, thorn,* Mt. 7:16; Heb. 6:8* [5146]

[5561] τρίβος *tribos* 3x *a beaten track; a road, highway,* Mt. 3:3; Mk. 1:3; Lk. 3:4* [5147]

[5562] τριετία *trietia* 1x *the space of three years,* Acts 20:31* [5148]

[5563] τρίζω *trizō* 1x *to creak, grating sound; to gnash, grind* the teeth, Mk. 9:18* [5149]

[5564] τρίμηνος *trimēnos* 1x *the space of three months,* Heb. 11:23* [5150]

[5565] τρίς *tris* 12x *three times, thrice,* Mt. 26:34, 75; ἐπὶ τρίς, *to the extent of thrice, as many as three times,* Acts 10:16; 11:10 [5151] See *three times.*

[5566] τρίστεγον *tristegon* 1x *the third floor, third story,* Acts 20:9* [5152]

[5567] τρισχίλιοι *trischilioi* 1x *three thousand,* Acts 2:41* [5153]

[5568] τρίτον *triton* 8x the accusative singular neuter form of *tritos* (*5569*) used adverbially *the third time, for the third time,* Mk. 14:41; Lk. 23:22 [5154] See *third.*

[5569] τρίτος *tritos* 48x *third,* Mt. 20:3; 27:64; ἐκ τρίτου, *the third time, for the third time,* Mt. 26:44; τὸ τρίτον, sc. μέρος, *the third part,* Rev. 8:7, 12; [5154] See *third.*

[5570] τρίχινος *trichinos* 1x *of hair, made of hair,* Rev. 6:12* [5155]

[5571] τρόμος *tromos* 5x pr. *a trembling, quaking; trembling* from fear, *fear, terror, agitation of mind,* Mk. 16:8; *anxious,* under solemn responsibility, 1 Cor. 2:3; *reverence, veneration, awe,* 2 Cor. 7:15; Eph. 6:5; Phil. 2:12* [5156]

[5572] τροπή *tropē* 1x *a turning round; a turning back, change, mutation,* Jas. 1:17* [5157]

[5573] τρόπος *tropos* 13x *a turn; mode, manner, way,* Jude 7; ὃν τρόπον, + καθ᾽ ὃν τρόπον, *in which manner, as, even as,* Mt. 23:37; Acts 15:11; κατὰ μηδένα τρόπον, *in no way, by no means,* 2 Thess. 2:3; ἐν παντὶ τρόπῳ, and παντὶ τρόπῳ *in every way, by every means,* Phil. 1:18; 2 Thess. 3:16; *turn* of mind or action, *habit, disposition,* Heb. 13:5 [5158]

[5574] τροποφορέω *tropophoreō* 1x *to bear with the disposition, manners, and conduct of* any one, *to put up with,* Acts 13:18* [5159]

[5575] τροφή *trophē* 16x *nourishment, food,* Mt. 3:4; Lk. 12:23; Jn. 4:8; Acts 9:19; Jas. 2:15; *provision,* Mt. 24:45; *sustenance, maintenance,* Mt. 10:10; met. *nourishment* of the mind, *of spiritual nourishment,* Heb. 5:12, 14 [5160] See *food.*

[5576] Τρόφιμος *Trophimos* 3x *Trophimus,* pr. name, of Ephesus, a friend of Paul, Acts 20:4; 21:29; 2 Tim. 4:20* [5161]

[5577] τροφός *trophos* 1x *a nurse,* 1 Thess. 2:7* [5162]

[5579] τροχιά *trochia* 1x *a track, way, path,* met. Heb. 12:13* [5163]

[5580] τροχός *trochos* 1x pr. *a runner; anything spherical, a wheel; drift, course,* with which signification the word is usually written τρόχος, Jas. 3:6* [5164]

[5581] τρύβλιον *tryblion* 2x *a bowl, dish,* Mt. 26:23; Mk. 14:20* [5165]

[5582] τρυγάω *trygaō* 3x *to harvest, gather,* fruits, and spc. grapes, Lk. 6:44; Rev. 14:18, 19* [5166]

[5583] τρυγών *trygōn* 1x *a turtledove,* Lk. 2:24* [5167]

[5584] τρυμαλιά *trymalia* 1x *a hole, perforation; eye* of a needle, Mk. 10:25* [5168]

[5585] τρύπημα *trypēma* 1x *a hole; eye* of a needle, Mt. 19:24* [5169]

[5586] Τρύφαινα *Tryphaina* 1x *Tryphaena,* pr. name, Rom. 16:12* [5170]

[5587] τρυφάω *tryphaō* 1x *to live self-indulgently, luxuriously,* Jas. 5:5* [5171]

[5588] τρυφή *tryphē* 2x *indulgent living, luxury,* Lk. 7:25; 2 Pet. 2:13* [5172]

[5589] Τρυφῶσα *Tryphōsa* 1x *Tryphosa,* pr. name, Rom. 16:12* [5173]

[5590] Τρῳάς *Trōias* 6x *Troas,* a city on the coast of Phrygia, near the site of ancient Troy, Acts 16:8, 11; 20:5f.; 2 Cor. 2:12; 2 Tim. 4:13* [5174]

[5592] τρώγω *trōgō* 6x pr. *to crunch; to eat,* Mt. 24:38; from the Hebrew, ἄρτον τρώγειν, *to take food, partake of a meal,* Jn. 6:54, 56-58; 13:18* [5176]

[5593] τυγχάνω *tynchanō* 12x *to hit* an object; *to attain to, to obtain, acquire, enjoy,* Lk. 20:35; Acts 24:2; 26:22; 27:3; 2 Tim. 2:10; Heb. 8:6; 11:35; intrans. *to happen, fall out, chance; common, ordinary,* Acts 19:11; 28:2; as an adv., *it may be, perchance, perhaps,* 1 Cor. 16:6; εἰ τύχοι, *as it so happens, as the case may be,* 1 Cor. 14:10; 15:37* [5177] See *happen; turn out.*

[5594] τυμπανίζω *tympanizō* 1x pr. *to beat a drum; to drum upon;* in NT *to torture, beat to death with rods and clubs,* Heb. 11:35* [5178]

[5595] τυπικῶς *typikōs* 1x *figuratively, typically,* 1 Cor. 10:11* [5179]

[5596] τύπος *typos* 15x pr. *an impress; a print, mark,* of a wound inflicted, Jn. 20:25; *a delineation; an image, statue,* Acts 7:43; *a formula, scheme,* Rom. 6:17; *form,* Acts 23:25; *a figure, counterpart,* 1 Cor. 10:6; *an* anticipative *figure, type,* Rom. 5:14; *a model pattern,* Acts 7:44; Heb. 8:5; *a* moral *pattern,* Phil. 3:17; 1 Thess. 1:7; 2 Thess. 3:9; 1 Tim. 4:12; Tit. 2:7; 1 Pet. 5:3* [5179] See *example; model; pattern.*

[5597] τύπτω *typtō* 13x *to beat, strike, smite,* Mt. 24:49; 27:30; *to beat* the breast, as expressive of grief or strong emotion, Lk. 18:13; 23:48; in NT met. *to wound* or *shock* the conscience of any one, 1 Cor. 8:12; from the Hebrew, *to smite* with evil, *punish,* Acts 23:3 [5180] See *beat; strike.*

[5598] Τύραννος *Tyrannos* 1x *Tyrannus,* an Ephesian, Acts 19:9* [5181]

[5601] Τύριος *Tyrios* 1x *a Tyrian, an inhabitant of Tyre,* Acts 12:20* [5183]

[5602] Τύρος *Tyros* 11x *Tyre,* a celebrated and wealthy commercial city of Phoenicia, Mt. 11:21; 15:21; Mk. 7:24; Acts 21:3, 7 [5184]

[5603] τυφλός *typhlos* 50x *blind,* Mt. 9:27, 28; 11:5; 12:22; met. mentally *blind,* Mt. 15:14; 23:16 [5185] See *blind.*

[5604] τυφλόω *typhloō* 3x *to blind, render blind;* met. Jn. 12:40; 2 Cor. 4:4; 1 Jn. 2:11* [5186]

[5605] τυφόω *typhoō* 3x *to besmoke;* met. *to possess with the fumes* of conceit; pass. *to be demented with conceit, puffed up,* 1 Tim. 3:6; 6:4; 2 Tim. 3:4; 1 Tim. 6:4* [5187]

[5606] τύφω *typhō* 1x *to raise a smoke;* pass. *to emit smoke, smoke, smoulder,* Mt. 12:20* [5188]

[5607] τυφωνικός *typhōnikos* 1x *stormy, tempestuous;* with ἄνεμος it means *hurricane, typhoon, whirlwind,* Acts 27:14* [5189]

[5608] Τυχικός *Tychikos* 5x *Tychicus,* pr. name, a friend or companion of Paul, Acts 20:4; Eph. 6:21; Col. 4:7; 2 Tim. 4:12; Tit. 3:12; Eph. subscr.; Col. subscr.* [5190]

[5610] ὑακίνθινος *hyakinthinos* 1x *hyacinthine, resembling the hyacinth in color, dark blue,* Rev. 9:17* [5191]

[5611] ὑάκινθος *hyakinthos* 1x *a hyacinth,* a gem resembling the color of the *hyacinth flower, dark blue,* Rev. 21:20* [5192]

[5612] ὑάλινος *hyalinos* 3x *made of glass; glassy, translucent,* Rev. 4:6; 15:2* [5193]

[5613] ὕαλος *hyalos* 2x *a transparent stone, crystal;* also, *glass,* Rev. 21:18, 21* [5194]

[5614] ὑβρίζω *hybrizō* 5x *to run riot;* trans. *to outrage, to treat in an arrogant* or *spiteful manner,* Mt. 22:6; Lk. 11:45; 18:32; Acts 14:5; 1 Thess. 2:2* [5195]

[5615] ὕβρις *hybris* 3x *insolence; shame, insult, outrage,* 2 Cor. 12:10; *damage* by sea, Acts 27:10, 21* [5196]

[5616] ὑβριστής *hybristēs* 2x *an overbearing, violent person,* Rom. 1:30; 1 Tim. 1:13* [5197]

[5617] ὑγιαίνω *hygiainō* 12x *to be sound, in health,* Lk. 5:31; 7:10; *to be safe and sound,* Lk. 15:27; 3 Jn. 2; met. *to be healthful* or *sound* in faith, doctrine, etc., Tit. 1:9, 13; 2:1, 2; *sound, pure, uncorrupted,* 1 Tim. 1:10; 6:3; 2 Tim. 1:13; 4:3* [5198] See *(be) healthy; (be) sound.*

[5618] ὑγιής *hygiēs* 11x *sound, in health,* Mt. 12:13; 15:31; met. of doctrine, *sound, pure, wholesome,* Tit. 2:8 [5199] See *well; whole.*

[5619] ὑγρός *hygros* 1x pr. *wet, moist, humid;* used of a tree, *full of sap, fresh, green,* Lk. 23:31* [5200]

[5620] ὑδρία *hydria* 3x *a water pot pitcher,* Jn. 2:6, 7; *a bucket, pail,* Jn. 4:28* [5201]

[5621] ὑδροποτέω *hydropoteō* 1x *to be only a water drinker,* 1 Tim. 5:23* [5202]

[5622] ὑδρωπικός *hydrōpikos* 1x *dropsical, suffering from dropsey,* Lk. 14:2* [5203]

[5623] ὕδωρ *hydōr* 76x *water,* Mt. 3:11, 16; 14:28, 29; 17:15; Jn. 5:3, 4, 7; *watery fluid,* Jn. 19:34; ὕδωρ ζῶν, *living water, fresh flowing water,* Jn. 4:11; met. of spiritual refreshment, Jn. 4:10; 7:38 [5204] See *water.*

[5624] ὑετός *hyetos* 5x *rain,* Acts 14:17; 28:2; Heb. 6:7; Jas. 5:18; Rev. 11:6* [5205]

[5625] υἱοθεσία *hyiothesia* 5x *adoption, a placing in the condition of a son,* Rom. 8:15, 23; 9:4; Gal. 4:5; Eph. 1:5* [5206] See *adoption.*

[5626] υἱός *hyios* 377x *a son,* Mt. 1:21, 25; 7:9; 13:55 freq.; *a* legitimate *son,* Heb. 12:8; *a son* artificially constituted, Acts 7:21; Heb. 11:24; *a descendant,* Mt. 1:1, 20; Mk. 12:35; in NT *the young* of an animal, Mt. 21:5; *a* spiritual *son* in respect of conversion or discipleship, 1 Pet. 5:13; from the Hebrew, *a disciple,* perhaps, Mt. 12:27; *a son* as implying connection in respect of membership, service, resemblance, manifestation, destiny, etc., Mt. 8:12; 9:15; 13:38; 23:15; Mk. 2:29; 3:17; Lk. 5:34; 10:6; 16:8; 20:34, 36; Jn. 17:12; Acts 2:25; 4:36; 13:10; Eph. 2:2; 5:6; Col. 3:6; 1 Thess. 5:5; 2 Thess. 2:3; υἱὸς θεοῦ, κ.τ.λ., *son of God* in respect of divinity, Mt. 4:3, 6; 14:33; Rom. 1:4; also, in respect of privilege and character, Mt. 5:9, 45; Lk. 6:35; Rom. 8:14, 19; 9:26; Gal. 3:26; ὁ υἱὸς τοῦ θεοῦ, κ.τ.λ., a title of the Messiah, Mt. 26:63; Mk. 3:11; 14:61; Jn. 1:34, 50; 20:31; υἱὸς ἀνθρώπου, *a son of man, a man,* Mk. 3:28; Eph. 3:5; Heb. 2:6; ὁ υἱὸς τοῦ ἀνθρώπου, a title of the Messiah, Mt. 8:20 freq.; as also, ὁ υἱὸς Δαβίδ, (Δαυίδ) Mt. 12:23 [5207] See *child; son.*

[5627] ὕλη *hylē* 1x *wood, a forest;* in NT *firewood, a mass of fuel,* Jas. 3:5* [5208]

[7007] ὑμεῖς *hymeis* 1,840x see σύ

[5628] Ὑμέναιος *Hymenaios* 2x *Hymenaeus,* pr. name, 1 Tim. 1:20; 2 Tim. 2:17* [5211]

[5629] ὑμέτερος *hymeteros* 11x *your, yours,* Lk. 6:20; Jn. 7:6; 15:20 [5212]

[5630] ὑμνέω *hymneō* 4x *to hymn, praise, celebrate* or *worship with hymns,* Acts 16:25; Heb. 2:12; absol. *to sing a hymn,* Mt. 26:30; Mk. 14:26* [5214]

[5631] ὕμνος *hymnos* 2x *a song; a hymn, song of praise* to God, Eph. 5:19; Col. 3:16* [5215]

[5632] ὑπάγω *hypagō* 79x *to lead* or *bring under; to lead* or *bring from under; draw on* or *away;* in NT intrans. *to go away, depart,* Mt. 8:4, 13; 9:6; ὕπαγε ὀπίσω μου, *Get behind me! Away! Begone!* Mt. 4:10; 16:23; *to go,* Mt. 5:41; Lk. 12:58; *to depart* life, Mt. 26:24 [5217] See *depart; go.*

[5633] ὑπακοή *hypakoē* 15x *a hearkening to; obedience,* Rom. 5:19; 6:16; 1 Pet. 1:14; *submissiveness,* Rom. 16:19; 2 Cor. 7:15; *submission,* Rom. 1:5; 15:18; 16:26; 2 Cor. 10:5; Heb. 5:8; 1 Pet. 1:2, 22; *compliance,* Phlm. 21 [5218] See *obedience.*

[5634] ὑπακούω *hypakouō* 21x *to give ear; to listen,* Acts 12:13; *to obey,* Mt. 8:27; Mk. 1:27; in NT *to render submissive acceptance,* Acts 6:7; Rom. 6:17; 2 Thess. 1:8; Heb. 5:9; absol. *to be submissive,* Phil. 2:12 [5219] See *obey.*

[5635] ὕπανδρος *hypandros* 1x *bound to a man, married,* Rom. 7:2* [5220]

[5636] ὑπαντάω *hypantaō* 10x *to meet,* Mt. 8:28; Lk. 8:27; Jn. 11:20, 30; 12:18 [5221] See *oppose.*

[5637] ὑπάντησις *hypantēsis* 3x *a meeting, act of meeting,* Mt. 8:34; 25:1; Jn. 12:13* [5222]

[5638] ὕπαρξις *hyparxis* 2x *goods possessed, substance, property,* Acts 2:45; Heb. 10:34* [5223]

[5639] ὑπάρχω *hyparchō* 60x *to begin; to come into existence; to exist; to be, subsist,* Acts 19:40; 28:18; *to be in possession, to belong,* Acts 3:6; 4:37; *goods, possessions, property,* Mt. 19:21; Lk. 8:3; *to be,* Lk. 7:25; 8:41 [5224, 5225] See *be; exist; possess, possessions.*

[5640] ὑπείκω *hypeikō* 1x *to yield, give way;* absol. *to be submissive,* Heb. 13:17* [5226]

[5641] ὑπεναντίος *hypenantios* 2x *over against; contrast, adverse,* Col. 2:14; ὁ ὑπεναντίος, *an opponent, adversary,* Heb. 10:27* [5227]

[5642] ὑπέρ *hyper* 150x (1) gen., *above, over;* met. *in behalf of,* Mt. 5:44; Mk. 9:40; Jn. 17:19; *instead of* beneficially, Phlm. 13; *in maintenance of,* Rom. 15:8; *for the furtherance of,* Jn. 11:4; 2 Cor. 1:6, 8; *for the realization of,* Phil. 2:13; equivalent to περί, *about, concerning,* with the further signification of interest or concern in the subject, Acts 5:41; Rom. 9:27; 2 Cor. 5:12; 8:23; 2 Thess. 2:1. (2) acc., *over, beyond;* met. *beyond, more than,* Mt. 10:37; 2 Cor. 1:8; used after comparative terms, Lk. 16:8; 2 Cor. 12:13; Heb. 4:12. (3) in NT as an adv., *in a higher degree, in fuller measure,* 2 Cor. 11:23 [5228]

[5643] ὑπεραίρω *hyperairō* 3x *to raise* or *lift up above* or *over;* mid. *to lift up one's self;* met. *to be over-elated,* 2 Cor. 12:7 (2x); *to bear one's self arrogantly, to rear a haughty front,* 2 Thess. 2:4* [5229]

[5644] ὑπέρακμος *hyperakmos* 1x *past the bloom of life, past one's prime,* 1 Cor. 7:36* [5230]

[5645] ὑπεράνω *hyperanō* 3x can function as an improper prep., *above, over, far above;* of place, Eph. 4:10; Heb. 9:5; of rank, dignity, Eph. 1:21* [5231]

[5647] ὑπεραυξάνω *hyperauxanō* 1x *to increase exceedingly,* 2 Thess. 1:3* [5232]

[5648] ὑπερβαίνω *hyperbainō* 1x *to overstep; to wrong, transgress,* 1 Thess. 4:6* [5233]

[5649] ὑπερβαλλόντως *hyperballontōs* 1x *exceedingly, above measure,* 2 Cor. 11:23* [5234]

[5650] ὑπερβάλλω *hyperballō* 5x pr. *to cast* or *throw over* or *beyond, to overshoot;* met. *to surpass, excel; surpassing,* 2 Cor. 3:10; 9:14; Eph. 1:19; 2:7; 3:19* [5235]

[5651] ὑπερβολή *hyperbolē* 8x pr. *a throwing beyond, an overshooting; extraordinary amount* or *character, transcendency,* 2 Cor. 12:7; 4:7; καθ᾽ ὑπερβολήν, adverbially, *exceedingly, extremely,* Rom. 7:13; 2 Cor. 1:8; Gal. 1:13; *a far better way,* 1 Cor. 12:31; *beyond all measure,* 2 Cor. 4:17* [5236]

[5654] ὑπερέκεινα *hyperekeina* 1x *BAGD* list as an adverb used with the gen., others list as an improper prep., *beyond,* 2 Cor. 10:16* [5238]

[5655] ὑπερεκπερισσοῦ *hyperekperissou* 3x *in over abundance; beyond all measure, superabundantly,* Eph. 3:20; 1 Thess. 3:10; 5:13* [5240]

[5657] ὑπερεκτείνω *hyperekteinō* 1x *to overextend, overstretch,* 2 Cor. 10:14* [5239]

[5658] ὑπερεκχύννω *hyperekchunnō* 1x *to pour out above measure* or *in excess;* pass. *to run over, overflow,* Lk. 6:38* [5240]

[5659] ὑπερεντυγχάνω *hyperentynchanō* 1x *to intercede for,* Rom. 8:26* [5241]

[5660] ὑπερέχω *hyperechō* 5x *to hold above;* intrans. *to stand out above, to overtop;* met. *to surpass, excel,* Phil. 2:3; 4:7; τὸ ὑπερέχον, *excellence, preeminence,* Phil. 3:8; *to be higher, superior,* Rom. 13:1; 1 Pet. 2:13* [5242]

[5661] ὑπερηφανία *hyperēphania* 1x *haughtiness, arrogance,* Mk. 7:22* [5243]

[5662] ὑπερήφανος *hyperēphanos* 5x *assuming, haughty, arrogant,* Lk. 1:51; Rom. 1:30; 2 Tim. 3:2; Jas. 4:6; 1 Pet. 5:5* [5244]

[5663] ὑπερλίαν *hyperlian* 2x *in the highest degree, preeminently, especially, superlatively,* 2 Cor. 11:5; 12:11* [5244]

[5664] ὑπερνικάω *hypernikaō* 1x *to overpower in victory; to be abundantly victorious, prevail mightily,* Rom. 8:37* [5245]

[5665] ὑπέρογκος *hyperonkos* 2x pr. *swollen, overgrown;* of language, *swelling, pompous, boastful,* 2 Pet. 2:18; Jude 16* [5246]

[5666] ὑπεροράω *hyperoraō* 1x *overlook, disregard,* Acts 17:30* [5237]

[5667] ὑπεροχή *hyperochē* 2x *prominence;* met., *excellence, rare quality,* 1 Cor. 2:1; *eminent station, authority,* 1 Tim. 2:2* [5247]

[5668] ὑπερπερισσεύω *hyperperisseuō* 2x *to superabound; to abound still more,* Rom. 5:20; mid. *to be abundantly filled, overflow,* 2 Cor. 7:4* [5248]

[5669] ὑπερπερισσῶς *hyperperissōs* 1x *superabundantly, most vehemently, above all measure,* Mk. 7:37* [5249]

[5670] ὑπερπλεονάζω *hyperpleonazō* 1x *to superabound, be in exceeding abundance, over exceed,* 1 Tim. 1:14* [5250]

[5671] ὑπερυψόω *hyperypsoō* 1x *to exalt supremely,* Phil. 2:9* [5251]

[5672] ὑπερφρονέω *hyperphroneō* 1x *to have lofty thoughts, be elated, haughty,* Rom. 12:3* [5252]

[5673] ὑπερῷον *hyperōon* 4x *the upper part of a house, upper room,* or *chamber,* Acts 1:13; 9:37, 39; 20:8* [5253]

[5674] ὑπέχω *hypechō* 1x pr. *to hold under; to render, undergo, suffer,* Jude 7* [5254]

[5675] ὑπήκοος *hypēkoos* 3x *giving ear; obedient, submissive,* Acts 7:39; 2 Cor. 2:9; Phil. 2:8* [5255]

[5676] ὑπηρετέω *hypēreteō* 3x *to subserve,* Acts 13:36; *to relieve, supply,* Acts

20:34; *to render kind offices,* Acts 24:23* [5256]

[5677] ὑπηρέτης *hypēretēs* 20x pr. *an under-rower, a rower, one of a ship's crew; a minister, attendant, servant; an attendant* on a magistrate, *officer,* Mt. 5:25; *an attendant* or *officer* of the Sanhedrin, Mt. 26:58; *an attendant,* or *servant* of a synagogue, Lk. 4:20; *a minister, attendant, assistant* in any work, Lk. 1:2; Jn. 18:36 [5257] See *guard; minister; official.*

[5678] ὕπνος *hypnos* 6x *sleep,* Mt. 1:24; Lk. 9:32; Jn. 11:13; Acts 20:9; met. spiritual *sleep,* religious *slumber,* Rom. 13:11* [5258]

[5679] ὑπό *hypo* 220x (1) gen., *under;* hence, used to express influence, causation, agency; *by,* Mt. 1:22 freq.; *by the agency of, at the hands of,* 2 Cor. 11:24; Heb. 12:3. (2) acc., *under,* with the idea of motion associated, Mt. 5:15; *under,* Jn. 1:49; 1 Cor. 10:1; *under* subjection to, Rom. 6:14; 1 Tim. 6:1; of time, *at, about,* Acts 5:21 [5259]

[5680] ὑποβάλλω *hypoballō* 1x *to cast under;* met. *to suggest, instigate,* Acts 6:11* [5260]

[5681] ὑπογραμμός *hypogrammos* 1x pr. *a copy to write after;* met. *an example for imitation, pattern,* 1 Pet. 2:21* [5261]

[5682] ὑπόδειγμα *hypodeigma* 6x *a token, intimation; an example, model,* proposed for imitation or admonition, Jn. 13:15; Heb. 4:11; Jas. 5:10; 2 Pet. 2:6; *a copy,* Heb. 8:5; 9:23* [5262] See *copy; example.*

[5683] ὑποδείκνυμι *hypodeiknymi* 6x also spelled ὑποδεικνύω, *to indicate,* Acts 20:35; *to intimate, suggest, show, prove,* Mt. 3:7; Lk. 3:7; 6:47; 12:5; Acts 9:16* [5263]

[5685] ὑποδέχομαι *hypodechomai* 4x *to give reception to; to receive as a guest, welcome, entertain,* Lk. 10:38; 19:6; Acts 17:7; Jas. 2:25* [5264]

[5686] ὑποδέω *hypodeō* 3x *to bind under,* mid. *to bind under one's self, put on one's own feet,* Acts 12:8; *to shoe,* Eph. 6:15; pass. *to be shod,* Mk. 6:9* [5265]

[5687] ὑπόδημα *hypodēma* 10x *anything bound under; a sandal,* Mt. 3:11; 10:10 [5266] See *sandal.*

[5688] ὑπόδικος *hypodikos* 1x *under a legal process;* also, *under a judicial sentence; under verdict* to an opposed party in a suit, *liable to penalty,* Rom. 3:19* [5267]

[5689] ὑποζύγιον *hypozygion* 2x *an animal subject to the yoke, a beast of burden;* in NT spc. *an ass, donkey,* Mt. 21:5; 2 Pet. 2:16* [5268]

[5690] ὑποζώννυμι *hypozōnnymi* 1x *to gird under,* of persons; *to undergird* a ship with cables, chains, etc., Acts 27:17* [5269]

[5691] ὑποκάτω *hypokatō* 11x can function as an improper prep., *under, beneath, underneath,* Mk. 6:11; 7:28; met. Heb. 2:8 [5270]

[5693] ὑποκρίνομαι *hypokrinomai* 1x *to answer, respond; to act a part* upon the stage; hence, *to assume a counterfeit character; to pretend, feign,* Lk. 20:20* [5271]

[5694] ὑπόκρισις *hypokrisis* 6x *a response, answer; an over-acting personification, acting; hypocrisy, simulation,* Mt. 23:28; Mk. 12:15; Lk. 12:1; Gal. 2:13; 1 Tim. 4:2; 1 Pet. 2:1* [5272] See *hypocrisy.*

[5695] ὑποκριτής *hypokritēs* 17x *the giver of an answer* or *response; a stage-player, actor;* in NT *a* moral or religious *counterfeit, a hypocrite,* Mt. 6:2, 5, 16; 7:5 [5273] See *hypocrite.*

[5696] ὑπολαμβάνω *hypolambanō* 5x *to take up,* by placing one's self underneath what is taken up; *to catch away, withdraw,* Acts 1:9; *to take up* discourse by continuation; hence, *to answer,* Lk. 10:30; *to take up* a notion, *to think, suppose,* Lk. 7:43; Acts 2:15; *receive as a guest,* 3 Jn. 8* [5274]

[5698] ὑπόλειμμα *hypoleimma* 1x *a remnant,* Rom. 9:27* [2640] See *remnant.*

[5699] ὑπολείπω *hypoleipō* 1x *to leave remaining, leave behind;* pass. *to be left surviving,* Rom. 11:3* [5275]

[5700] ὑπολήνιον *hypolēnion* 1x *a vat,* placed under the press, ληνός, to receive the juice, Mk. 12:1* [5276]

[5701] ὑπολιμπάνω *hypolimpanō* 1x *to leave behind,* 1 Pet. 2:21* [5277]

[5702] ὑπομένω *hypomenō* 17x intrans. *to remain* or *stay behind,* when others have departed, Lk. 2:43; trans. *to bear up under, endure, suffer patiently,* 1 Cor. 13:7; Heb. 10:32; absol. *to continue firmly, hold out, remain constant, persevere,* Mt. 10:22; 24:13 [5278] See *endurance, endure; persevere; stand firm; stay.*

[5703] ὑπομιμνῄσκω *hypomimnēskō* 7x *remember, remind,* Jn. 14:26; Tit. 3:1; 2 Pet. 1:12; Jude 5; *to suggest recollection of, remind* others *of,* 2 Tim. 2:14; 3 Jn. 10; *to call to mind, recollect, remember,* Lk. 22:61* [5279]

[5704] ὑπόμνησις *hypomnēsis* 3x *a putting in mind, act of reminding,* 2 Pet. 1:13; 3:1; *remembrance, recollection,* 2 Tim. 1:5* [5280]

[5705] ὑπομονή *hypomonē* 32x *patient endurance,* 2 Cor. 12:12; Col. 1:11; *patient awaiting,* Lk. 21:19; *a patient frame of mind, patience,* Rom. 5:3, 4; 15:4, 5; Jas. 1:3; *perseverance,* Rom. 2:7; *endurance* in adherence to an object, 1 Thess. 1:3; 2 Thess. 3:5; Rev. 1:9; ἐν ὑπομονῇ and δι᾽ ὑπομονῆς, *constantly, perseveringly,* Lk. 8:15; Rom. 8:25; Heb. 12:1; *an enduring* of affliction, etc., *the act of suffering, undergoing,* etc., 2 Cor. 1:6; 6:4 [5281] See *endurance, endure; perseverance.*

[5706] ὑπονοέω *hyponoeō* 3x *to suspect; to suppose, deem,* Acts 13:25; 25:18; 27:27* [5282]

[5707] ὑπόνοια *hyponoia* 1x *suspicion, surmise,* 1 Tim. 6:4* [5283]

[5709] ὑποπλέω *hypopleō* 2x *to sail under; to sail under* the lee, or, *to the south of,* an island, etc., Acts 27:4, 7* [5284]

[5710] ὑποπνέω *hypopneō* 1x *to blow gently,* as the wind, Acts 27:13* [5285]

[5711] ὑποπόδιον *hypopodion* 7x *a footstool,* Jas. 2:3 [5286] See *footstool.*

[5712] ὑπόστασις *hypostasis* 5x pr. *a standing under; a taking* of a thing *upon one's self; an assumed position, an assumption* of a specific character, 2 Cor. 11:17; *an engagement undertaken* with regard to the conduct of others, *a vouching,* 2 Cor. 9:4; or of one's self, *a pledged profession,* Heb. 3:14; *an assured impression, a mental realizing,* Heb. 11:1; *a substructure, basis; subsistence, essence,* Heb. 1:3* [5287]

[5713] ὑποστέλλω *hypostellō* 4x pr. *to let down, to stow away; to draw back, withdraw,* Gal. 2:12; mid. *to shrink back, recoil,* Heb. 10:38; *to keep back, suppress, conceal,* Acts 20:20, 27* [5288]

[5714] ὑποστολή *hypostolē* 1x *a shrinking back,* Heb. 10:39* [5289]

[5715] ὑποστρέφω *hypostrephō* 35x *to turn back, return,* Mk. 14:40; Lk. 1:56; 2:39, 43, 45 [5290] See *return.*

[5716] ὑποστρωννύω *hypostrōnnyō* 1x *to stow under, spread underneath,* Lk. 19:36* [5291]

[5717] ὑποταγή *hypotagē* 4x *subordination,* 1 Tim. 3:4; *submissiveness, obedience,* 2 Cor. 9:13; Gal. 2:5; 1 Tim. 2:11* [5292]

[5718] ὑποτάσσω *hypotassō* 38x *to place* or *arrange under; to subordinate,* 1 Cor. 15:27; *to bring under influence,* Rom. 8:20; pass. *to be subordinated,* 1 Cor. 14:32; *to be brought under a state* or *influence,* Rom. 8:20; mid. *to submit one's self, render obedience, be submissive,* Lk. 2:51; 10:17 [5293] See *(be) subject; submit.*

[5719] ὑποτίθημι *hypotithēmi* 2x *to place under; to lay down* the neck beneath the sword of the executioner, *to set on imminent risk,* Rom. 16:4; mid. *to suggest, recommend to attention,* 1 Tim. 4:6* [5294]

[5720] ὑποτρέχω *hypotrechō* 1x *to run under;* as a nautical term, *to sail under* the lee of, Acts 27:16* [5295]

[5721] ὑποτύπωσις *hypotypōsis* 2x *a sketch, delineation; a form, formula, presentment, sample,* 2 Tim. 1:13; *a pattern, a model representation,* 1 Tim. 1:16* [5296]

[5722] ὑποφέρω *hypopherō* 3x *to bear under; to bear up under, support, sustain,* 1 Cor. 10:13; *to endure patiently,* 1 Pet. 2:19; *to undergo,* 2 Tim. 3:11* [5297]

[5723] ὑποχωρέω *hypochōreō* 2x *to withdraw, retire, retreat,* Lk. 5:16; 9:10* [5298]

[5724] ὑπωπιάζω *hypōpiazō* 2x pr. *to strike one upon the parts beneath the eye; to beat black and blue;* hence, *to discipline by hardship, coerce,* 1 Cor. 9:27; met. *to weary* by continual importunities, *pester,* Lk. 18:5* [5299]

[5725] ὗς *hys* 1x *a hog, swine, boar, sow,* 2 Pet. 2:22* [5300]

[5727] ὕσσωπος *hyssōpos* 2x *hyssop,* in NT, however, not the plant usually so named, but probably the caper plant; *a bunch of hyssop,* Heb. 9:19; *a hyssop stalk,* Jn. 19:29* [5301]

[5728] ὑστερέω *hystereō* 16x *to be behind* in place or time, *to be in the rear; to fall short of, be inferior to,* 2 Cor. 11:5; 12:11; *to fail of, fail to attain,* Heb. 4:1; *to be in want of, lack,* Lk. 22:35; *to be wanting,* Mk. 10:21; absol. *to be defective, in default,* Mt. 19:20; 1 Cor. 12:24; *to run short,* Jn. 2:3; mid. *to come short of* a privilege or standard, *to miss,* Rom. 3:23; absol. *to come short, be below standard,* 1 Cor. 1:7; *to come short* of sufficiency, *to be in need, want,* Lk. 15:14; 2 Cor. 11:9; Phil. 4:12; Heb. 11:37; *to be a loser, suffer detriment,* 1 Cor. 8:8; in NT ὑστερεῖν ἀπό, *to be backwards with respect to, to slight,* Heb. 12:15* [5302] See *fall short; lack.*

[5729] ὑστέρημα *hysterēma* 9x *a shortcoming, defect;* personal *shortcoming,* 1 Cor. 16:17; Phil. 2:30; Col. 1:24; 1 Thess. 3:10; *want, need, poverty, penury,* Lk. 21:4; 2 Cor. 8:14; 9:12; 11:9* [5303] See *lacking.*

[5730] ὑστέρησις *hysterēsis* 2x *want, need,* Mk. 12:44; Phil. 4:11* [5304]

[5731] ὕστερος *hysteros* 12x *posterior* in place or time; *subsequent, later, last, finally,* Mt. 21:31; 1 Tim. 4:1 [5305, 5306] See *afterward; finally; later.*

[5733] ὑφαντός *hyphantos* 1x *woven,* Jn. 19:23* [5307]

[5734] ὑψηλός *hypsēlos* 11x *high, lofty, elevated,* Mt. 4:8; 17:1; τὰ ὑψηλά, *the highest* heaven, Heb. 1:3; *upraised,* Acts 13:17; met. *highly esteemed,* Lk. 16:15; φρονεῖν τὰ ὑψηλά, *to have lofty thoughts, be proud, arrogant,* Rom. 12:16 [5308] See *exalted; high; proud.*

[5735] ὑψηλοφρονέω *hypsēlophroneō* 1x *to have lofty thoughts, be proud, haughty,* 1 Tim. 6:17* [5309]

[5736] ὕψιστος *hypsistos* 13x *highest, loftiest, most elevated;* τὰ ὕψιστα, from the Hebrew, *the highest* heaven, Mt. 21:9; Mk. 11:10; met. ὁ ὕψιστος, *the Most High,* Mk. 5:7 [5310] See *high; most high.*

[5737] ὕψος *hypsos* 6x *height,* Eph. 3:18; Rev. 21:16; met. *exaltation, dignity, eminence,* Jas. 1:9; from the Hebrew, *the height* of heaven, Lk. 1:78; 24:49; Eph. 4:8* [5311] See *exalted; high.*

[5738] ὑψόω *hypsoō* 20x *to raise aloft, lift up,* Jn. 3:14; 8:28; met. *to elevate* in condition, *uplift, exalt,* Mt. 11:23; 23:12; Lk. 1:52 [5312] See *exalt; lift up.*

[5739] ὕψωμα *hypsōma* 2x *height,* Rom. 8:39; *a towering* of self-conceit, *presumption,* 2 Cor. 10:5* [5313]

[5741] φάγος *phagos* 2x *a glutton,* Mt. 11:19; Lk. 7:34* [5314]

[5742] φαιλόνης *phailonēs* 1x *a thick cloak* for travelling, with a hood, 2 Tim. 4:13* [5341]

[5743] φαίνω *phainō* 31x *to cause to appear, bring to light;* absol. *to shine,* Jn. 1:5; 5:35; 2 Pet. 1:19; 1 Jn. 2:8; Rev. 1:16; 8:12; 21:23; mid./pass. *to be seen, appear, be visible,* Mt. 1:20; 2:7, 13, 19; τὰ φαινόμενα, *things visible, things obvious to the senses,* Heb. 11:3; φαίνομαι, *to appear, seen, be in appearance,* Mt. 23:27; Lk. 24:11; *to appear* in thought, *seen* in idea, *be a notion,* Mk. 14:64 [5316] See *appear; shine.*

[5744] Φάλεκ *Phalek* 1x *Peleg,* also spelled Φάλεγ, pr. name, indecl., Lk. 3:35* [5317]

[5745] φανερός *phaneros* 18x *apparent, manifest, clear, known, well-known,* Mk. 4:22; 6:14; Gal. 5:19; *in outward guise, externally,* Rom. 2:28 [5318] See *known; obvious; plain.*

[5746] φανερόω *phaneroō* 49x *to bring to light, to set in a clear light; to manifest, display,* Jn. 2:11; 7:4; 9:3; *to show,* Rom. 1:19; 2 Cor. 7:12; *to declare, make known,* Jn. 17:6; *to disclose,* Mk. 4:22; 1 Cor. 4:5; Col. 4:4; *to reveal,* Rom. 3:21; 16:26; Col. 1:26; *to present to view,* Jn. 21:1, 14; pass. *to make an appearance,* Mk. 16:12, 14; spc. of Christ, *to be* personally *manifested,* Jn. 1:31; Col. 3:4; 1 Pet. 1:20; 5:4; 1 Jn. 3:5; *to be laid bare, appear in true character,* 2 Cor. 5:10, 11 [5319] See *appear; disclose; reveal.*

[5747] φανερῶς *phanerōs* 3x *manifestly; clearly, plainly, distinctly,* Acts 10:3; *openly, publicly,* Mk. 1:45; Jn. 7:10* [5320] See *openly; publicly.*

[5748] φανέρωσις *phanerōsis* 2x *a disclosure, clear display,* 2 Cor. 4:2; *an* outward *evidencing* of a latent principle, active *exhibition,* 1 Cor. 12:7* [5321]

[5749] φανός *phanos* 1x *a torch, lantern, light,* Jn. 18:3* [5322]

[5750] Φανουήλ *Phanouēl* 1x *Phanuel,* pr. name, indecl., Lk. 2:36* [5323]

[5751] φαντάζω *phantazō* 1x *to render visible, cause to appear;* pass. *to appear, be seen;* τὸ φανταζόμενον, *the sight, spectacle,* Heb. 12:21* [5324]

[5752] φαντασία *phantasia* 1x pr. *a rendering visible; a display; pomp, parade,* Acts 25:23* [5325]

[5753] φάντασμα *phantasma* 2x *a phantom, specter,* Mt. 14:26; Mk. 6:49* [5326]

[5754] φάραγξ *pharanx* 1x *a cleft, ravine, valley,* Lk. 3:5* [5327]

[5755] Φαραώ *Pharaō* 5x *Pharaoh,* pr. name, indecl., Acts 7:10, 13, 21; Rom. 9:17; Heb. 11:24* [5328]

[5756] Φαρές *Phares* 3x *Perezs,* pr. name, indecl., Mt. 1:3; Lk. 3:33* [5329]

[5757] Φαρισαῖος *Pharisaios* 98x *a Pharisee, a follower of the sect of the Pharisees,* a numerous and powerful sect of the Jews, distinguished for their ceremonial observances, and apparent sanctity of life, and for being rigid interpreters of the Mosaic law; but who frequently violated its spirit by their traditional interpretations and precepts, to which they ascribed nearly an equal authority with the OT Scriptures, Mt. 5:20; 12:2; 23:14 [5330] See *Pharisee.*

[5758] φαρμακεία *pharmakeia* 2x *employment of drugs* for any purpose; *sorcery, magic, enchantment,* Rev. 18:23; Gal. 5:20* [5331]

[5760] φάρμακον *pharmakon* 1x *a drug; an enchantment; magic potion, charm,* Rev. 9:21* [5331]

[5761] φάρμακος *pharmakos* 2x *a sorcerer, magician,* Rev. 21:8; 22:15* [5333]

[5762] φάσις *phasis* 1x *report, information,* Acts 21:31* [5334]

[5763] φάσκω *phaskō* 3x *to assert, affirm,* Acts 24:9; 25:19; Rom. 1:22* [5335]

[5764] φάτνη *phatnē* 4x *a manger, stall,* Lk. 2:7, 12, 16; 13:15* [5336]

[5765] φαῦλος *phaulos* 6x *vile, refuse; evil, wicked;* Jn. 3:20; 5:29; Rom. 9:11; 2 Cor. 5:10; Tit. 2:8; Jas. 3:16* [5337]

[5766] φέγγος *phengos* 2x *light, splendor, radiance,* Mt. 24:29; Mk. 13:24* [5338]

[5767] φείδομαι *pheidomai* 10x *to spare; to be tender of,* Rom. 8:32; *to spare,* in respect of hard dealing, Acts 20:29; Rom. 11:21; 1 Cor. 7:28; 2 Cor. 1:23; 13:2; 2 Pet. 2:4, 5; absol. *to forbear, abstain,* 2 Cor. 12:6* [5339] See *spare.*

[5768] φειδομένως *pheidomenōs* 2x *sparingly,* 2 Cor. 9:6 (2x)* [5340]

[5770] φέρω *pherō* 66x *to bear, carry,* Mk. 2:3; *to bring,* Mt. 14:11, 18; *to conduct,* Mt. 17:17; Jn. 21:18; *to bear, endure,* Rom. 9:22; Heb. 12:20; 13:13; *to uphold, maintain, conserve,* Heb. 1:3; *to bear, bring forth, produce,* Mk. 4:8; Jn. 12:24; 15:2; *to bring forward, advance, allege,* Jn. 18:29; Acts 25:7; 2 Pet. 2:11; *to offer, ascribe,* Rev. 21:24, 26; absol. used of a gate, *to lead,* Acts 12:10; pass. *to be brought* within reach, *offered,* 1 Pet. 1:13; *to be brought in, to enter,* Heb. 9:16; *to be under a moving influence, to be moved,* 2 Pet. 1:21; mid. *to rush, sweep,* Acts 2:2; *to proceed, come forth, have utterance,* 2 Pet. 1:17, 18, 21; *to proceed, make progress,* Heb. 6:1; used of a ship, *to drive* before the wind, Acts 27:15, 17 [5342] See *bring; carry; endurance, endure; present; sustain.*

[5771] φεύγω *pheugō* 29x absol. *to flee, take to flight,* Mt. 2:13; 8:33; *to shrink, stand fearfully aloof,* 1 Cor. 10:14; *to make escape,* Mt. 23:33; trans. *to shun,* 1 Cor. 6:18; 1 Tim. 6:11; 2 Tim. 2:22; *to escape,* Heb. 11:34 [5343] See *escape; flee; run away.*

[5772] Φῆλιξ *Phēlix* 9x *Felix,* pr. name, Acts 23:24, 26; 24:3, 22, 24f., 27; 25:14* [5344]

[5773] φήμη *phēmē* 2x pr. *a celestial* or *oracular utterance; an utterance; fame, rumor, report,* Mt. 9:26; Lk. 4:14* [5345]

[5774] φημί *phēmi* 66x *to utter; to say, speak,* Mt. 8:8; 14:8; 26:34, 61; *to say, allege, affirm,* Rom. 3:8 [5346] See *answer; declare; reply; say.*

[5776] Φῆστος *Phēstos* 13x *Festus,* pr. name, Acts 24:27; 25:1, 4, 12ff., 22ff.; 26:24f., 32* [5347]

[5777] φθάνω *phthanō* 7x *come before, precede,* 1 Thess. 4:15; absol. *to advance, make progress,* 2 Cor. 10:14; Phil. 3:16; *to come up* with, *come* upon, *be close at hand,* Mt. 12:28; Lk. 11:20; 1 Thess. 2:16; *to attain* an object of pursuit, Rom. 9:31* [5348]

[5778] φθαρτός *phthartos* 6x *corruptible, perishable,* Rom. 1:23; 1 Cor. 9:25; 15:53f.; 1 Pet. 1:18, 23* [5349] See *corrupt; corruption.*

[5779] φθέγγομαι *phthengomai* 3x *to emit a sound; to speak,* Acts 4:18; 2 Pet. 2:16, 18* [5350]

[5780] φθείρω *phtheirō* 9x *to spoil, ruin,* 1 Cor. 3:17; 2 Cor. 7:2; *to corrupt,* morally *deprave,* 1 Cor. 15:33; 2 Cor. 11:3 [5351] See *corrupt, corruption; destroy.*

[5781] φθινοπωρινός *phthinopōrinos* 1x *autumnal, bare,* Jude 12* [5352]

[5782] φθόγγος *phthongos* 2x *a* vocal *sound,* Rom. 10:18; 1 Cor. 14:7* [5353]

[5783] φθονέω *phthoneō* 1x *to envy,* Gal. 5:26* [5354]

[5784] φθόνος *phthonos* 9x *envy, jealously, spite,* Mt. 27:18; Mk. 15:10; Rom. 1:29; Gal. 5:21; Phil. 1:15; 1 Tim. 6:4; Tit. 3:3; Jas. 4:5; 1 Pet. 2:1* [5355] See *envy.*

[5785] φθορά *phthora* 9x *corruption, decay, ruin, corruptibility, mortality,* Rom. 8:21; 1 Cor. 15:42; meton. *corruptible, perishable substance,* 1 Cor. 15:50; *killing, slaughter,* 2 Pet. 2:12; spiritual *ruin,* Gal. 6:8; Col. 2:22; met. moral *corruption, depravity,* 2 Pet. 1:4; 2:19* [5356] See *corrupt, corruption; destruction.*

[5786] φιάλη *phialē* 12x *a bowl, shallow cup,* Rev. 5:8; 15:7; 16:1, 2, 3, 4 [5357] See *bowl.*

[5787] φιλάγαθος *philagathos* 1x *a lover of goodness,* or, *of the good, a fosterer of virtue,* Tit. 1:8* [5358]

[5788] Φιλαδέλφεια *Philadelpheia* 2x *Philadelphia,* a city of Lydia, near Mount Tmolus, Rev. 1:11; 3:7* [5359]

[5789] φιλαδελφία *philadelphia* 6x *brotherly love;* in NT *love of the* Christian *brotherhood,* Rom. 12:10; 1 Thess. 4:9; Heb. 13:1; 1 Pet. 1:22; 2 Pet. 1:7* [5360]

[5790] φιλάδελφος *philadelphos* 1x *brother-loving;* in NT *loving the members of the* Christian *brotherhood,* 1 Pet. 3:8* [5361]

[5791] φίλανδρος *philandros* 1x *husband-loving; conjugal,* Tit. 2:4* [5362]

[5792] φιλανθρωπία *philanthrōpia* 2x *philanthropy, love of mankind,* Tit. 3:4; *benevolence, humanity,* Acts 28:2* [5363]

[5793] φιλανθρώπως *philanthrōpōs* 1x *humanely, benevolently, kindly,* Acts 27:3* [5364]

[5794] φιλαργυρία *philargyria* 1x *love of money, covetousness,* 1 Tim. 6:10* [5365]

[5795] φιλάργυρος *philargyros* 2x *money-loving, covetous,* Lk. 16:14; 2 Tim. 3:2* [5366]

[5796] φίλαυτος *philautos* 1x *self-loving; selfish,* 2 Tim. 3:2* [5367]

[5797] φιλέω *phileō* 25x pr. *to manifest some act* or *token of kindness* or *affection; to kiss,* Mt. 26:48; Mk. 14:44; Lk. 22:47; *to love, regard with affection, have affection for,* Mt. 10:37; Jn. 5:20; *to like, be fond of, delight in* a thing, Mt. 23:6; Rev. 22:15; *to cherish inordinately, set store by,* Jn. 12:25 [5368] See *love.*

[5798] φιλήδονος *philēdonos* 1x *pleasure-loving; a lover of pleasure,* 2 Tim. 3:4* [5369]

[5799] φίλημα *philēma* 7x *a kiss,* Lk. 7:45; 22:48; Rom. 16:16; 1 Cor. 16:20; 2 Cor. 13:12; 1 Thess. 5:26; 1 Pet. 5:14* [5370]

[5800] Φιλήμων *Philēmōn* 1x *Philemon,* pr. name, Phlm. 1; subscr. and title* [5371]

[5801] Φίλητος *Philētos* 1x *Philetus,* pr. name, 2 Tim. 2:17* [5372]

[5802] φιλία *philia* 1x *affection, fondness, love,* Jas. 4:4* [5373]

[5803] Φιλιππήσιος *Philippēsios* 1x *a Philippian, a citizen of* Φίλιπποι, *Philippi,* Phil. 4:15; title* [5374]

[5804] Φίλιπποι *Philippoi* 4x *Philippi,* a considerable city of Macedonia, east of Amphipolis, Acts 16:12; 20:6; Phil. 1:1; 1 Thess. 2:2; 1 & 2 Cor. subscr.* [5375]

[5805] Φίλιππος *Philippos* 36x *Philip,* pr. name . (1) *Philip, the Apostle,* Mt. 10:3. (2) *Philip, the Evangelist,* Acts 6:5. (3) *Philip, son of Herod the Great and Mariamne,* Mt. 14:3 . (4) *Philip, son of Herod the Great and Cleopatra,* Mt. 16:13; Lk. 3:1 [5376]

[5806] φιλόθεος *philotheos* 1x *God-loving, pious; a lover of God,* 2 Tim. 3:4* [5377]

[5807] Φιλόλογος *Philologos* 1x *Philologus,* pr. name, Rom. 16:15* [5378]

[5808] φιλονεικία *philoneikia* 1x *a love of contention; rivalry, contention,* Lk. 22:24* [5379]

[5809] φιλόνεικος *philoneikos* 1x *fond of contention; contentious, disputatious,* 1 Cor. 11:16* [5380]

[5810] φιλοξενία *philoxenia* 2x *kindness to strangers, hospitality,* Rom. 12:13; Heb. 13:2* [5381]

[5811] φιλόξενος *philoxenos* 3x *kind to strangers, hospitable,* 1 Tim. 3:2; Tit. 1:8; 1 Pet. 4:9* [5382]

[5812] φιλοπρωτεύω *philoprōteuō* 1x *to love* or *desire to be first* or *chief, affect preeminence,* 3 Jn. 9* [5383]

[5813] φίλος *philos* 29x *loved, dear; devoted;* Acts 19:31; as a subst., *a friend,* Lk. 7:6; 11:5, 6, 8; *a congenial associate,* Mt. 11:19; Lk. 7:34; Jas. 4:4; used as a word of courteous appellation, Lk. 14:10 [5384] See *friend.*

[5814] φιλοσοφία *philosophia* 1x *a love of science;* systematic *philosophy;* in NT *the philosophy* of the Jewish gnosis, Col. 2:8* [5385]

[5815] φιλόσοφος *philosophos* 1x pr. *a lover of science, a* systematic *philosopher,* Acts 17:18* [5386]

[5816] φιλόστοργος *philostorgos* 1x *tenderly affectionate,* Rom. 12:10* [5387]

[5817] φιλότεκνος *philoteknos* 1x *loving one's children, duly parental,* Tit. 2:4* [5388]

[5818] φιλοτιμέομαι *philotimeomai* 3x pr. *to be ambitious of honor;* by impl. *to exert one's self* to accomplish a thing, *use one's utmost efforts, endeavor earnestly,* Rom. 15:20; 2 Cor. 5:9; 1 Thess. 4:11* [5389]

[5819] φιλοφρόνως *philophronōs* 1x *with kindly feeling* or *manner, courteously,* Acts 28:7* [5390]

[5821] φιμόω *phimoō* 7x *to muzzle,* 1 Tim. 5:18; met. and by impl. *to silence, put to silence;* pass. *to be silent, speechless,* Mt. 22:12, 34; 1 Pet. 2:15; Mk. 1:25; trop. pass. *to be hushed,* as winds and waves, Mk. 4:39; Lk. 4:35* [5392] See *muzzle; quiet; speechless.*

[5823] Φλέγων *Phlegōn* 1x *Phlegon,* pr. name, Rom. 16:14* [5393]

[5824] φλογίζω *phlogizō* 2x *to set in a flame, kindle, inflame,* Jas. 3:6 (2x)* [5394]

[5825] φλόξ *phlox* 7x *a flame,* Lk. 16:24; Acts 7:30 [5395]

[5826] φλυαρέω *phlyareō* 1x *to talk folly* or *nonsense;* in NT trans., *bring unjustified charges against,* 3 Jn. 10* [5396]

[5827] φλύαρος *phlyaros* 1x *a gossip, tattler,* 1 Tim. 5:13* [5397]

[5828] φοβέομαι *phobeomai* 95x has an active form, φοβέω (5828), but only occurs as a passive (deponent) in our literature, *to fear, dread,* Mt. 10:26; 14:5; *to fear reverentially, to reverence,* Mk. 6:20; Lk. 1:50; Acts 10:2; Eph. 5:33; Rev. 11:18; *to be afraid* to do a thing, Mt. 2:22; Mk. 9:32; *to be reluctant, to scruple,* Mt. 1:20; *to fear, be apprehensive,* Acts 27:17; 2 Cor. 11:3; 12:20; *to be fearfully anxious,* Heb. 4:1; absol. *to be fearful, afraid, alarmed,* Mt. 14:27; 17:6, 7; Mk. 16:8; *to be fearfully impressed,* Rom. 11:20 [5399] See *(be) afraid; fear; respect; stand in awe.*

[5829] φοβερός *phoberos* 3x *fearful; terrible,* Heb. 10:27, 31; 12:21* [5398]

[5831] φόβητρον *phobētron* 1x *something which inspires terror; terrible sight* or *event,* Lk. 21:11* [5400]

[5832] φόβος *phobos* 47x *fear, terror, affright,* Mt. 14:26; Lk. 1:12; *astonishment, amazement,* Mt. 28:8; Mk. 4:41; *trembling concern,* 1 Cor. 2:3; 2 Cor. 7:15; meton. *a terror, an object* or *cause of terror,* Rom. 13:5; *reverential fear, awe,* Acts 9:31; Rom. 3:18; *respect, deference,* Rom. 13:7; 1 Pet. 2:18 [5401] See *alarm; awe; fear; fright; respect.*

[5833] Φοίβη *Phoibē* 1x *Phoebe,* pr. name, Rom. 16:1* [5402]

[5834] Φοινίκη *Phoinikē* 3x *Phoenice, Phoenicia,* a country on the east of the Mediterranean, between Palestine and Syria, anciently celebrated for commerce, Acts 11:19; 15:3; 21:2* [5403]

[5836] φοῖνιξ *phoinix* 2x *the palm tree, the date palm,* Jn. 12:13; Rev. 7:9. Identical in form to the word meaning *phoenix,* the Egyptian bird.* [5404]

[5837] Φοῖνιξ *Phoinix* 1x *Phoenix, Phoenice,* a city, with a harbor, on the southeast coast of Crete, Acts 27:12* [5405]

[5838] φονεύς *phoneus* 7x *a homicide, murderer,* Mt. 22:7; Acts 3:14; 7:52; 28:4; 1 Pet. 4:15; Rev. 21: 8; 22:15* [5406]

[5839] φονεύω *phoneuō* 12x *to put to death, kill, stay,* Mt. 23:31, 35; absol. *to commit murder,* Mt. 5:21 [5407] See *murder.*

[5840] φόνος *phonos* 9x *a killing, slaughter, murder,* Mt. 15:19; Mk. 7:21; 15:7 [5408]

[5841] φορέω *phoreō* 6x *to bear; to wear,* Mt. 11:8; Jn. 19:5; Rom. 13:4; 1 Cor. 15:49; Jas. 2:3 [5409]

[5842] φόρον *phoron* 1x *a forum, marketplace;* Φόρον Ἀππίου, *Forum Appii,* the name of a small town on the Appian way, according to Antoninus, forty-three Roman miles from Rome, or about forty English miles, Acts 28:15* [5410]

[5843] φόρος *phoros* 5x *tribute, tax,* strictly such as is laid on dependent and subject people, Lk. 20:22; 23:2; Rom. 13:6, 7* [5411]

[5844] φορτίζω *phortizō* 2x *to load, burden;* met. Mt. 11:28; Lk. 11:46* [5412]

[5845] φορτίον *phortion* 6x *a load, burden;* of a ship, *freight, cargo,* Acts 27:10; met. *a burden* of imposed precepts, etc., Mt. 11:30; 23:4; Lk. 11:46 (2x); of faults, sins, etc., Gal. 6:5* [5413]

[5847] Φορτουνᾶτος *Phortounatos* 1x *Fortunatus,* pr. name, 1 Cor. 16:17* [5415]

[5848] φραγέλλιον *phragellion* 1x *a whip, scourge,* Jn. 2:15* [5416]

[5849] φραγελλόω *phragelloō* 2x *to scourge,* Mt. 27:26; Mk. 15:15* [5417]

[5850] φραγμός *phragmos* 4x *a fence, hedge; a hedgeside path,* Mt. 21:33; Mk. 12:1; Lk. 14:23; met. *a* parting *fence,* Eph. 2:14* [5418]

[5851] φράζω *phrazō* 1x pr. *to propound in distinct terms, to tell;* in NT *to explain, interpret, expound,* Mt. 15:15* [5419]

[5852] φράσσω *phrassō* 3x *to fence in;* by impl. *to obstruct, stop, close up,* Heb. 11:33; met. *to silence, put to silence,* Rom. 3:19; 2 Cor. 11:10* [5420]

[5853] φρέαρ *phrear* 7x *a well, cistern,* Lk. 14:5; Jn. 4:11, 12; *a pit,* Rev. 9:1, 2* [5421] See *pit.*

[5854] φρεναπατάω *phrenapataō* 1x *to deceive the mind; to deceive, impose on,* Gal. 6:3* [5422]

[5855] φρεναπάτης *phrenapatēs* 1x *a deceiver, seducer,* Tit. 1:10* [5423]

[5856] φρήν *phrēn* 2x pr. *the diaphragm, midriff; the mind, intellect, understanding,* 1 Cor. 14:20 (2x)* [5424]

[5857] φρίσσω *phrissō* 1x *to be ruffled, to bristle; to shiver, shudder* from fear, Jas. 2:19* [5425]

[5858] φρονέω *phroneō* 26x *to think, to mind; to be of opinion,* Acts 28:22; Phil. 1:7; *to take thought, be considerate,* Phil. 4:10; *to entertain sentiments* or *inclinations* of a specific kind, *to be minded,* Rom. 12:16; 15:5; 1 Cor. 13:11; 2 Cor. 13:11; Gal. 5:10; Phil. 2:2; 3:16; 4:2; *to be in a* certain *frame of mind,* Rom. 12:3; Phil. 2:5; *to imagine, entertain conceit,* 1 Cor. 4:6; *to heed, pay regard to,* Rom. 14:6; *to incline to, be set upon, mind,* Mt. 16:23; Mk. 8:33; Rom. 8:5; Phil. 3:15, 19; Col. 3:2 [5426] See *set the mind on; think.*

[5859] φρόνημα *phronēma* 4x *frame of thought, will, aspirations,* Rom. 8:6, 7, 27* [5427]

[5860] φρόνησις *phronēsis* 2x *a thoughtful frame, sense, rightmindedness,* Lk. 1:17; *intelligence,* Eph. 1:8* [5428]

[5861] φρόνιμος *phronimos* 14x *considerate, thoughtful, prudent, discreet,* Mt. 7:24; 10:16; 24:45; 25:2, 4, 8, 9; Lk. 12:42; *sensible, wise,* Rom. 11:25; 12:16; 1 Cor. 4:10; 10:15; 2 Cor. 11:19* [5429] See *intelligent; prudent; shrewd; wise, skillful.*

[5862] φρονίμως *phronimōs* 1x *considerately, providently,* Lk. 16:8* [5430]

[5863] φροντίζω *phrontizō* 1x *to be considerate, be careful,* Tit. 3:8* [5431]

[5864] φρουρέω *phroureō* 4x *to keep watch;* trans. *to guard, watch,* with a military guard, 2 Cor. 11:32; *to keep* in a condition of restraint, Gal. 3:23; *to keep* in a state of settlement or security, Phil. 4:7; 1 Pet. 1:5* [5432]

[5865] φρυάσσω *phryassō* 1x pr. *to snort, neigh, stamp,* etc.; as a high-spirited horse; hence, *to be noisy, fierce, insolent, and tumultuous, to rage, tumultuate,* Acts 4:25* [5433]

[5866] φρύγανον *phryganon* 1x *a dry twig, branch,* etc., Acts 28:3* [5434]

[5867] Φρυγία *Phrygia* 3x *Phrygia,* an inland province of Asia Minor, Acts 2:10; 16:6; 18:23; 1 Tim. subscr.* [5435]

[5869] Φύγελος *Phygelos* 1x *Phygellus,* pr. name, 2 Tim. 1:15* [5436]

[5870] φυγή *phygē* 1x *a fleeing, flight,* Mt. 24:20* [5437]

[5871] φυλακή *phylakē* 47x *a keeping watch, ward, guard,* Lk. 2:8; *a place of watch,* Rev. 18:2; *a watch, guard, body of guards,* Acts 12:10; *ward, custody, imprisonment,* 2 Cor. 6:5; 11:23; Heb. 11:36; *prison,* 1 Pet. 3:19; *a place of custody, prison,* Mt. 14:10; 25:39, 44; *a watch* or *division,* of the night, which in the time of our Savior was divided into watches of three hours each, called ὀψέ, μεσονύκτιον, ἀλεκτοροψωνία and πρωΐα, or πρωΐ, Mt. 14:25; 24:43; Mk. 6:48; Lk. 12:38 (2x) [5438] See *jail; prison; watch.*

[5872] φυλακίζω *phylakizō* 1x *to deliver into custody, put in prison, imprison,* Acts 22:19* [5439]

[5873] φυλακτήριον *phylaktērion* 1x *the station of a guard* or *watch; a preservative, safeguard;* hence, *a phylactery* or *amulet,* worn about the person; from which circumstance the word is used in the NT as a term for the Jewish *Tephillin* or *prayer-case,* which took their rise from the injunction in Deut. 6:8; 11:18; Mt. 23:5* [5440]

[5874] φύλαξ *phylax* 3x *a watchman, guard, sentinel,* Acts 5:23; 12:6, 19* [5441]

[5875] φυλάσσω *phylassō* 31x *to be on watch, keep* watch, Lk. 2:8; *to have in keeping,* Acts 20:20; *to have in custody,* Acts 28:16; *to keep* under restraint, *confine,* Lk. 8:29; Acts 12:4; 23:35; *to guard, defend,* Lk. 11:21; *to keep safe, preserve,* Jn. 12:25; 17:12; 2 Thess. 3:3; 2 Pet. 2:5; Jude 24; *to keep* in abstinence, Acts 21:25; 1 Jn. 5:21; *to observe* a matter of injunction or duty, Mk. 10:20; Lk. 11:28; Acts 7:53; 16:4; 21:24; mid. *to be on one's guard, beware,* Lk. 12:15; 2 Tim. 4:15; 2 Pet. 3:17 [5442] See *beware; guard; keep; obey; observe.*

[5876] φυλή *phylē* 31x *a tribe,* Mt. 19:28; 24:30; Lk. 2:36; *a people, nation,* Rev. 1:7; 5:9 [5443] See *people; tribe.*

[5877] φύλλον *phyllon* 6x *a leaf,* Mt. 21:19 [5444]

[5878] φύραμα *phyrama* 5x *that which is mingled and reduced to a uniform consistence, by kneading, beating, treading,* etc.; *a mass* of potter's clay, Rom. 9:21; of dough, 1 Cor. 5:6, 7; Gal. 5:9; met. Rom. 11:16* [5445]

[5879] φυσικός *physikos* 3x *natural, agreeable to nature,* Rom. 1:26, 27; *following the instinct of nature,* as animals, 2 Pet. 2:12* [5446]

[5880] φυσικῶς *physikōs* 1x *naturally, by natural instinct,* Jude 10* [5447]

[5881] φυσιόω *physioō* 7x *to inflate puff up;* met. *to inflate* with pride and vanity, 1 Cor. 8:1; pass. *to be inflated* with pride, *to be proud, vain, arrogant,* 1 Cor. 4:6, 18, 19; 5:2; 13:4; Col. 2:18* [5448]

[5882] φύσις *physis* 14x *essence,* Gal. 4:8; *native condition, birth,* Rom. 2:27; 11:21, 24; Gal. 2:15; Eph. 2:3; *native species, kind,* Jas. 3:7; *nature, natural frame,* 2 Pet. 1:4; *nature, native instinct,* Rom.

2:14; 1 Cor. 11:14; *nature, prescribed course of nature,* Rom. 1:26* [5449] See *kind; natural condition; nature.*

[5883] φυσίωσις *physiōsis* 1x pr. *inflation;* met. *inflation* of mind, *pride,* 2 Cor. 12:20* [5450]

[5884] φυτεία *phyteia* 1x *plantation, the act of planting; a plant,* met. Mt. 15:13* [5451]

[5885] φυτεύω *phyteuō* 11x *to plant, set,* Mt. 21:33; Lk. 13:6; 17:6, 28; 20:9; met. Mt. 15:13; Mk. 12:1; *to plant* the Gospel, 1 Cor. 3:6, 7, 8; 9:7* [5452] See *plant.*

[5886] φύω *phyō* 3x *to generate, produce;* pass. *to be generated, produced;* of plants, *to germinate, sprout,* Lk. 8:6, 8; intrans. *to germinate, spring* or *grow up,* Heb. 12:15* [5453]

[5887] φωλεός *phōleos* 2x *a den, lair, burrow,* Mt. 8:20; Lk. 9:58* [5454]

[5888] φωνέω *phōneō* 43x *to sound, utter a sound;* of the cock, *to crow,* Mt. 26:34, 74, 75; *to call,* or *cry out, exclaim,* Lk. 8:8, 54; 16:24; 23:46; *to call to,* Mt. 27:47; Mk. 3:31; *to call,* Jn. 13:13; *to call, summon,* Mt. 20:32; *to invite* to a feast, Lk. 14:12 [5455] See *call; crow; invite; make a noise; summon.*

[5889] φωνή *phōnē* 139x *a sound,* Mt. 24:31; Jn. 3:8; Rev. 4:5; 8:5; *a cry,* Mt. 2:18; *an* articulate *sound, voice,* Mt. 3:3, 17; 17:5; 27:46, 50; *voice, speech, discourse,* Jn. 10:16, 27; Acts 7:31; 12:22; 13:27; Heb. 3:7, 15; *tone* of address, Gal. 4:20; *language, tongue, dialect,* 1 Cor. 14:10 [5456] See *language; sound; speech; voice.*

[5890] φῶς *phōs* 73x *light,* Mt. 17:2; 2 Cor. 4:6; *daylight, broad day,* Mt. 10:27; Lk. 12:3; *radiance, blaze of light,* Mt. 4:16; Acts 9:3; 12:7; *an instrument* or *means of light, a light,* Mt. 6:23; Acts 16:29; *a fire,* Mk. 14:54; Lk. 22:56; from the Hebrew, *the light* of God's presence, 2 Cor. 11:14; 1 Tim. 6:16; met. *the light* of Divine truth, spiritual *illumination,* Lk. 16:8; Jn. 3:19; Rom. 13:12; Eph. 5:8; 1 Pet. 2:9; 1 Jn. 1:7; 2:8, 9, 10; *a source* or *dispenser of* spiritual *light,* Mt. 5:14; Jn. 1:4, 5, 7, 8, 9; 8:12; 9:5; pure *radiance,* perfect *brightness,* 1 Jn. 1:5 [5457] See *light.*

[5891] φωστήρ *phōstēr* 2x *a cause of light, illuminator; a light, luminary, star,* Phil. 2:15; *radiance,* or, *luminary,* Rev. 21:11* [5458]

[5892] φωσφόρος *phōsphoros* 1x *light-bringing;* sc. ἀστήρ, *Lucifer, the morning star,* met. 2 Pet. 1:19* [5459]

[5893] φωτεινός *phōteinos* 5x *radiant, lustrous,* Mt. 17:5; *enlightened, illuminated,* Mt. 6:22; Lk. 11:34, 36 (2x)* [5460]

[5894] φωτίζω *phōtizō* 11x *to light, give light to, illuminate, shine upon,* Lk. 11:36; Rev. 18:1; 21:23; met. *to enlighten* spiritually, Jn. 1:9; Eph. 1:18; 3:9; Heb. 6:4; 10:32; *to reveal, to bring to light, make known,* 1 Cor. 4:5; 2 Tim. 1:10; intrans. *shine,* Rev. 22:5* [5461] See *enlighten; (give) light.*

[5895] φωτισμός *phōtismos* 2x *illumination; a shining forth, bringing to light, enlightenment,* 2 Cor. 4:4, 6* [5462]

[5897] χαίρω *chairō* 74x *to rejoice, be glad, be joyful, be full of joy,* Mt. 2:10; 5:12; 18:13; Mk. 14:11; Rom. 12:12; 2 Cor. 2:3; a term of salutation, *Hail!* Mt. 26:49; λεγω χαίρειν, *to greet,* 2 Jn. 10:11; an epistolary forth, *Health!* Acts 15:23 [5463] See *rejoice.*

[5898] χάλαζα *chalaza* 4x *hail,* Rev. 8:7; 11:19; 16:21 (2x)* [5464]

[5899] χαλάω *chalaō* 7x *to slacken; to let down, lower,* Mk. 2:4; Lk. 5:4, 5; Acts 9:25; 27:17, 30; 1 Cor. 11:33* [5465]

[5900] Χαλδαῖος *Chaldaios* 1x *a Chaldean, a native of Chaldea,* a country of central Asia, which seems to have included Mesopotamia, Acts 7:4* [5466]

[5901] χαλεπός *chalepos* 2x *hard, rugged; furious, ferocious,* Mt. 8:28; *difficult, trying,* 2 Tim. 3:1* [5467]

[5902] χαλιναγωγέω *chalinagōgeō* 2x pr. *to guide with a bridle;* met. *to bridle, control, sway,* Jas. 1:26; 3:2* [5468]

[5903] χαλινός *chalinos* 2x *a bridle, bit,* Jas. 3:3; Rev. 14:20* [5469]

[5906] χαλκεύς *chalkeus* 1x pr. *a coppersmith;* hence, genr. *a worker in metals, smith,* 2 Tim. 4:14* [5471]

[5907] χαλκηδών *chalkēdōn* 1x *chalcedony,* the name of a gem, generally of a whitish, bluish, or gray color, susceptible of a high and beautiful polish, and of which there are several varieties, as the onyx, modern carnelian, etc., Rev. 21:19* [5472]

[5908] χαλκίον *chalkion* 1x *a vessel, copper, brazen utensil,* Mk. 7:4* [5473]

[5909] χαλκολίβανον *chalkolibanon* 2x *orichalcum, fine bronze,* a factitious metal of which there were several varieties, the white being of the highest repute, or, *deep-tinted frankincense,* Rev. 1:15; 2:18* [5474]

[5910] χαλκός *chalkos* 5x *copper,* also, *bronze,* Rev. 18:12; *a brazen musical instrument,* 1 Cor. 13:1; *copper money,* Mt. 10:9; *money* in general, Mk. 6:8; 12:41* [5475]

[5911] χαλκοῦς *chalkous* 1x contracted form of χάλκεος, *made of copper, brass,* or *bronze,* Rev. 9:20* [5470]

[5912] χαμαί *chamai* 2x *on the ground, to the earth,* Jn. 9:6; 18:6* [5476]

[5913] Χανάαν *Chanaan* 2x *Canaan,* the ancient name of Palestine, Acts 7:11; 13:19 [5477]

[5914] Χαναναῖος *Chananaios* 1x *Canaanitish, of Canaan,* Mt. 15:22* [5478]

[5915] χαρά *chara* 59x *joy, gladness, rejoicing,* Mt. 2:10; 13:20, 44; 28:8; meton, *joy, cause of joy, occasion of rejoicing,* Lk. 2:10; Phil. 4:1; 1 Thess. 2:19, 20; *bliss,* Mt. 25:21, 23 [5479] See *gladness; happiness; joy.*

[5916] χάραγμα *charagma* 8x *an imprinted mark,* Rev. 13:16, 17; 14:9, 11; 16:2; 19:20; 20:4; *sculpture,* Acts 17:29* [5480]

[5917] χαρακτήρ *charaktēr* 1x *an impress, exact expression,* Heb. 1:3* [5481]

[5918] χάραξ *charax* 1x *a stake; a* military *palisade, rampart,* formed from the earth thrown out of the ditch, and stuck with sharp stakes or palisades, Lk. 19:43* [5482]

[5919] χαρίζομαι *charizomai* 23x *to gratify; to bestow* in kindness, *grant* as a free favor, Lk. 7:21; Rom. 8:32; *to grant the deliverance* of a person in favor to the desire of others, Acts 3:14; 27:24; Phlm. 22; *to sacrifice* a person to the demand of enemies, Acts 25:11; *to remit, forgive,* Lk. 7:42; 2 Cor. 2:7, 10 [5483] See *forgive; give.*

[5920] χάριν *charin* 9x the acc. sg form of the noun χάριν which can be used as an improper prep., *on account of,* Lk. 7:47; Eph. 3:1, 14; 1 Jn. 3:12; *for the sake of, in order to,* Gal. 3:19; Tit. 1:5, 11; Jude 16; *on the score of,* 1 Tim. 5:14* [5484]

[5921] χάρις *charis* 155x *pleasing show, charm; beauty, gracefulness; a pleasing circumstance, matter of approval,* 1 Pet. 2:19, 20; *kindly bearing, graciousness,* Lk. 4:22; *a beneficial opportunity, benefit,* 2 Cor. 1:15; Eph. 4:29; *a charitable act, generous gift,* 1 Cor. 16:3; 2 Cor. 8:4, 6; *an act of favor,* Acts 25:3; *favor, acceptance,* Lk. 1:30, 52; Acts 2:47; 7:10, 46; *free favor, free gift, grace,* Jn. 1:14, 16, 17; Rom. 4:4, 16; 11:5, 6; Eph. 2:5, 8; 1 Pet. 3:7; *free favor* specially manifested by God towards man in the Gospel scheme, *grace,* Acts 15:11; Rom. 3:24; 5:15, 17, 20, 21; 6:1; 2 Cor. 4:15; *a gracious provision, gracious scheme, grace,* Rom. 6:14, 15; Heb. 2:9; 12:28; 13:9; *gracious dealing* from God, *grace,* Acts 14:26; 15:40; Rom. 1:7; 1 Cor. 1:4; 15:10; Gal. 1:15; *a commission graciously devolved* by God upon a human agent, Rom. 1:5; 12:3; 15:15; 1 Cor. 3:10; 2 Cor. 1:12; Gal. 2:9; Eph. 3:8; *grace, gra-*

ciously bestowed divine *endowment* or *influence,* Lk. 2:40; Acts 4:33; 11:23; Rom. 12:6; 2 Cor. 12:9; *grace,* Acts 11:43; Rom. 5:2; Gal. 5:4; 2 Pet. 3:18; *an emotion correspondent to what is pleasing* or *kindly; sense of obligation,* Lk. 17:9; *a grateful frame of mind,* 1 Cor. 10:30; *thanks,* Lk. 6:32, 33, 34; Rom. 6:17; 1 Cor. 15:57; χάριν or χάριτας καταθέσθαι, *to oblige, gratify,* Acts 24:27; 25:9 [5485] See *favor; grace.*

[5922] χάρισμα *charisma* 17x *a free favor, free gift,* Rom. 5:15, 16; 6:23; 2 Cor. 1:11; *benefit,* Rom. 1:11; a divinely conferred *endowment,* 1 Cor. 12:4, 9, 28, 30, 31 [5486] See *gift; spiritual endowment.*

[5923] χαριτόω *charitoō* 2x *to favor, visit with favor, to make an object of favor, to gift,* Eph. 1:6; pass. *to be visited with free favor, be an object of gracious visitation,* Lk. 1:28* [5487]

[5924] Χαρράν *Charran* 2x *Charran,* a city in the northern part of Mesopotamia, Acts 7:2, 4* [5488]

[5925] χάρτης *chartēs* 1x *paper,* 2 Jn. 12* [5489]

[5926] χάσμα *chasma* 1x *a chasm, gulf,* Lk. 16:26* [5490]

[5927] χεῖλος *cheilos* 7x *a lip,* and pl. τὰ χείλη, *the lips,* Mt. 15:8; Mk. 7:6; Rom. 3:13; Heb. 13:15; 1 Pet. 3:10; trop. χεῖλος τῆς θαλάσσης, *the seashore,* Heb. 11:12; meton. *language, dialect,* 1 Cor. 14:21* [5491]

[5928] χειμάζω *cheimazō* 1x *to excite a tempest, toss with a tempest;* pass. *to be storm-tossed,* Acts 27:18* [5492]

[5930] χειμών *cheimōn* 6x *stormy weather,* Mt. 16:3; *a storm, tempest,* Acts 27:20; *winter,* Mt. 24:20; Mk. 13:18; Jn. 10:22; 2 Tim. 4:21* [5494]

[5931] χείρ *cheir* 177x *a hand,* Mt. 3:12; 4:6; 8:15 freq.; from the Hebrew, χεὶρ Κυρίου, *a* special *operation of God,* Acts 11:21; 13:3; ἐν χειρί, *by agency,* Acts 7:35; Gal. 3:19 [5495] See *hand.*

[5932] χειραγωγέω *cheiragōgeō* 2x *to lead by the hand,* Acts 9:8; 22:11* [5496]

[5933] χειραγωγός *cheiragōgos* 1x *one who leads another by the hand,* Acts 13:11* [5497]

[5934] χειρόγραφον *cheirographon* 1x *handwriting; a written form, literal instrument,* as distinguished from a spiritual dispensation, Col. 2:14* [5498]

[5935] χειροποίητος *cheiropoiētos* 6x *made by hand, artificial, material,* Mk. 14:58; Acts 7:48; 17:24; Eph. 2:11; Heb. 9:11, 24* [5499]

[5936] χειροτονέω *cheirotoneō* 2x *to stretch out the hand; to constitute by voting; to appoint, constitute,* Acts 14:23; 2 Cor. 8:19* [5500]

[5937] χείρων *cheirōn* 11x *worse,* Mt. 9:16; *more severe,* Jn. 5:14; Heb. 10:29 [5501] See *worse.*

[5938] Χερούβ *Cheroub* 1x also spelled Χερουβείν and Χερουβίμ, indecl. *cherub, a two-winged figure over the ark of the covenant,* Heb. 9:5* [5502]

[5939] χήρα *chēra* 26x *a widow,* Mt. 23:14; Lk. 4:26 [5503] See *widow.*

[5941] χιλίαρχος *chiliarchos* 21x *commander of a thousand men;* hence, genr. *a commander, military chief,* Mk. 6:21; Rev. 6:15; 19:18; spc. *a* legionary *tribune,* Acts 21:31, 32, 33, 37; *the prefect* of the temple, Jn. 18:12 [5506] See *commander.*

[5942] χιλιάς *chilias* 23x the number *one thousand, a thousand,* Lk. 14:31; Acts 4:4 [5505] See *thousand.*

[5943] χίλιοι *chilioi* 11x *a thousand,* 2 Pet. 3:8; Rev. 11:3; 12:6; 14:20; 20:2-7* [5507] See *thousand.*

[5945] χιτών *chitōn* 11x *a tunic, vest,* the inner garment which fitted close to the body, having armholes, and sometimes sleeves, and reaching below the knees, worn by both sexes, Mt. 5:40; 10:10; pl. χιτῶνες, *clothes, garments* in general, Mk. 14:63 [5509] See *garment; tunic.*

[5946] χιών *chiōn* 2x *snow,* Mt. 28:3; Rev. 1:14* [5510]

[5948] χλαμύς *chlamys* 2x *chlamys,* a type of *cloak;* a Roman military commander's *cloak,* Mt. 27:28, 31* [5511]

[5949] χλευάζω *chleuazō* 1x *to jeer, scoff,* Acts 17:32* [5512]

[5950] χλιαρός *chliaros* 1x *warm, tepid; lukewarm,* Rev. 3:16* [5513]

[5952] χλωρός *chlōros* 4x *pale green; green, verdent,* Mk. 6:39; Rev. 8:7; 9:4; *pale, sallow,* Rev. 6:8* [5515]

[5954] χοϊκός *choikos* 4x *of earth, earthy,* 1 Cor. 15:47, 48, 49* [5517]

[5955] χοῖνιξ *choinix* 2x *a choenix,* an Attic measure for things dry, being the 48th part of a medimnus, consequently equal to the 8th part of the Roman modius, and nearly equivalent to about one quart, being considered a sufficient daily allowance for the sustenance of one man, Rev. 6:6 (2x)* [5518]

[5956] χοῖρος *choiros* 12x pr. *a young swine; a swine, hog,* or *sow,* Mt. 8:30, 31, 32 [5519] See *pig.*

[5957] χολάω *cholaō* 1x pr. *to be melancholy;* used later as an equivalent to χολοῦμαι, *to be angry, incensed,* Jn. 7:23* [5520]

[5958] χολή *cholē* 2x *the bile, gall;* in NT *a bitter ingredient,* as *wormwood,* Mt. 27:34; χολὴ πικρίας, *intense bitterness,* met. *thorough disaffection* to divine truth, *utter estrangement,* Acts 8:23* [5521]

[5960] Χοραζίν *Chorazin* 2x also spelled Χωραζίν and Χοραζείν, *Chorazin,* a town of Galilee, probably near Bethsaida and Capernaum, indecl., Mt. 11:21; Lk. 10:13* [5523]

[5961] χορηγέω *chorēgeō* 2x *to lead a chorus;* at Athens, *to defray the cost of a chorus;* hence, *to supply funds; to supply, furnish,* 2 Cor. 9:10; 1 Pet. 4:11* [5524]

[5962] χορός *choros* 1x *dancing* with music, Lk. 15:25* [5525]

[5963] χορτάζω *chortazō* 16x pr. *to feed* or *fill with grass, herbage,* etc., *to fatten;* used of animals of prey, *to satiate, gorge,* Rev. 19:21; of persons, *to satisfy with food,* Mt. 14:20; 15:33, 37; met. *to satisfy* the desire of any one, Mt. 5:6 [5526] See *satisfy.*

[5964] χόρτασμα *chortasma* 1x *pasture, provender* for cattle; *food, provision, sustenance,* for men, Acts 7:11* [5527]

[5965] χόρτος *chortos* 15x *an enclosure; pasture ground; fodder* for beasts; in NT *herbage, grass,* Mt. 6:30; 14:19; *a plant* of corn, Mt. 13:26; Mk. 4:28 [5528] See *grass.*

[5967] χοῦς *chous* 2x uncontracted form χόος, *dust,* acc., χοῦν, Mk. 6:11; Rev. 18:19* [5522]

[5968] χράομαι *chraomai* 11x *to use, make use of, employ,* Acts 27:17; 1 Cor. 7:31; *to take advantage of,* 1 Cor. 7:21; 9:12, 15; *to use, to treat, behave towards,* Acts 27:3; 2 Cor. 13:10 [5530] See *use.*

[5970] χρεία *chreia* 49x *use; need, necessity, requisiteness,* Eph. 4:29; Heb. 7:11; personal *need, an* individual *want,* Acts 20:34; Rom. 12:13; Phil. 2:25; 4:16, 19; χρείαν ἔχω, *to need, require, want,* Mt. 6:8; 14:16; Mk. 2:25; Jn. 2:25; ἐστὶ χρεία, *there is need,* Lk. 10:42; τὰ πρὸς τὴν χρείαν, *necessary things,* Acts 28:10; *a necessary business, affair,* Acts 6:3 [5532] See *need.*

[5971] χρεοφειλέτης *chreopheiletēs* 2x *debtor,* Lk. 7:41; 16:5* [5533]

[5973] χρή *chrē* 1x impersonal verb, *there is need* or *occasion, it is necessary, it is requisite; it becomes, it is proper,* Jas. 3:10* [5534]

[5974] χρῄζω *chrēzō* 5x *to need, want, desire,* Mt. 6:32; Lk. 11:8; 12:30; Rom. 16:2; 2 Cor. 3:1* [5535]

[5975] χρῆμα *chrēma* 6x *anything useful,* or *needful;* pl. *wealth, riches,* Mk. 10:23; Lk. 18:24; *money,* Acts 8:18, 20; 24:26; sg. *price,* Acts 4:37* [5536]

[5976] χρηματίζω *chrēmatizō* 9x *to have dealings, transact business; to negotiate; to give answer on deliberation;* in NT *to utter a divine communication,* Heb. 12:25; pass. *to be divinely instructed, receive a revelation* or *warning from God,* Mt. 2:12, 22; Lk. 2:26; Acts 10:22; Heb. 8:5; 11:7; intrans. *to receive an appellation,* Acts 11:26; Rom. 7:3* [5537]

[5977] χρηματισμός *chrēmatismos* 1x in NT *a response from God, a divine communication, oracle,* Rom. 11:4* [5538]

[5978] χρήσιμος *chrēsimos* 1x *useful, profitable,* 2 Tim. 2:14* [5539]

[5979] χρῆσις *chrēsis* 2x *use, employment; manner of using,* Rom. 1:26, 27* [5540]

[5980] χρηστεύομαι *chrēsteuomai* 1x *to be gentle, benign, kind,* 1 Cor. 13:4* [5541]

[5981] χρηστολογία *chrēstologia* 1x *bland address, fair speaking,* Rom. 16:18* [5542]

[5982] χρηστός *chrēstos* 7x *useful, profitable; good, agreeable,* Lk. 5:39; *easy,* as a yoke, Mt. 11:30; *gentle, benign, kind, obliging, gracious,* Lk. 6:35; Eph. 4:32; Rom. 2:4; 1 Pet. 2:3; *good* in character, disposition, etc., *virtuous,* 1 Cor. 15:33* [5543] See *kind.*

[5983] χρηστότης *chrēstotēs* 10x pr. *goodness, kindness, gentleness,* Rom. 2:4; 11:22(3x); 2 Cor. 6:6; Gal. 5:22; Col. 3:12; Tit. 3:4; *kindness* shown, *beneficence,* Eph. 2:7; *goodness, virtue,* Rom. 3:12* [5544] See *goodness; kindness.*

[5984] χρῖσμα *chrisma* 3x pr. *anything which is applied by smearing; ointment;* in NT *an anointing,* in the reception of spiritual privileges, 1 Jn. 2:20, 27* [5545]

[5985] Χριστιανός *Christianos* 3x *a Christian, follower of Christ,* Acts 11:26; 26:28; 1 Pet. 4:16* [5546] See *Christian.*

[5986] Χριστός *Christos* 529x pr. *anointed;* ὁ Χριστός, *the Christ, the Anointed One,* i.q. Μεσσίας, *the Messiah,* Mt. 1:16, 17; Jn. 1:20, 25, 42; meton. *Christ, the word* or *doctrine of Christ,* 2 Cor. 1:19; 21; Eph. 4:20; *Christ, a* truly *Christian frame* of doctrine and affection, Rom. 8:10; Gal. 4:19; *Christ, the Church of Christ,* 1 Cor. 12:12; *Christ the* distinctive *privileges of the Gospel of Christ,* Gal. 3:27; Phil. 3:8; Heb. 3:14 [5547] See *anointed one; Christ; Messiah.*

[5987] χρίω *chriō* 5x *to anoint;* in NT *to anoint,* by way of instituting to a dignity, function, or privilege, Lk. 4:18; Acts 4:27; 10:38; 2 Cor. 1:21; Heb. 1:9* [5548] See *anoint.*

[5988] χρονίζω *chronizō* 5x *to spend time; to linger, delay, be long,* Mt. 24:48; 25:5; Lk. 1:21; 12:45; Heb. 10:37* [5549]

[5989] χρόνος *chronos* 54x *time,* whether in respect of duration or a definite point of its lapse, Mt. 2:7; 25:19 freq.; *an epoch, era,* marked *duration,* Acts 1:7; 1 Thess. 5:1 [5550] See *time.*

[5990] χρονοτριβέω *chronotribeō* 1x *to spend time, waste time, linger, delay,* Acts 20:16* [5551]

[5992] χρυσίον *chrysion* 12x *gold,* Heb. 9:4; 1 Pet. 1:7; Rev. 3:18; 21:18, 21; spc. *gold when coined* or *manufactured; golden ornaments,* 1 Tim. 2:9; 1 Pet. 3:3; Rev. 17:4; 18:16; *gold coin, money,* Acts 3:6; 20:33; 1 Pet. 1:18* [5553] See *gold.*

[5993] χρυσοδακτύλιος *chrysodaktylios* 1x *having rings of gold on the fingers,* Jas. 2:2* [5554]

[5994] χρυσόλιθος *chrysolithos* 1x *chrysolite,* a name applied by the ancients to all gems of a gold color; spc. the modern *topaz,* Rev. 21:10* [5555]

[5995] χρυσόπρασος *chrysoprasos* 1x *a chrysoprase,* a species of gem of a golden green color like that of a leek, Rev. 21:20* [5556]

[5996] χρυσός *chrysos* 10x *gold,* Mt. 2:11; 23:16, 17; meton. *gold ornaments,* 1 Tim. 2:9; *gold coin, money,* Mt. 10:9 [5557] See *gold.*

[5997] χρυσοῦς *chrysous* 18x *golden, made of* or *adorned with gold,* 2 Tim. 2:20; Heb. 9:4; Rev. 1:12, 13, 20; 9:13, 20, 21:15 [5552] See *gold.*

[5998] χρυσόω *chrysoō* 2x *to gild, overlay with gold, adorn* or *deck with gold,* Rev. 17:4; 18:16* [5558]

[5999] χρώς *chrōs* 1x *the skin; the body surface;* Acts 19:12* [5559]

[6000] χωλός *chōlos* 14x *crippled in the feet, limping, halting, lame,* Mt. 11:5; 15:30, 31; met. *limping, weak,* spiritually, Heb. 12:13; *maimed, deprived of a foot,* for ἀναπηρός, Mk. 9:45 [5560] See *crippled; lame.*

[6001] χώρα *chōra* 28x *space, room; a country, region, tract, province,* Mk. 5:10; Lk. 2:8; *a district, territory, suburbs,* Mt. 8:28; meton. *the inhabitants of a country, region,* etc., Mk. 1:5; Acts 12:20; *the country,* as opposed to the city or town, Lk. 21:21; *a field, farm,* Lk. 12:16; Jn. 4:35 [5561] See *country; field; region.*

[6003] χωρέω *chōreō* 10x *to make room,* either by motion or capacity; *to move, pass,* Mt. 15:17; *to proceed, go on,* 2 Pet. 3:9; *to progress, make way,* Jn. 8:37; trans. *to hold* as contents, *contain, afford room for,* Mk. 2:2; Jn. 2:6; 21:25; met. *to give* mental *admittance to, to yield accordance,* Mt. 19:11, 12; *to admit* to approbation and esteem, *to regard cordially,* 2 Cor. 7:2* [5562] See *accept; hold; (have) room for.*

[6004] χωρίζω *chōrizō* 13x *to divide, separate,* Mt. 19:6; Mk. 10:9; Rom. 8:35, 39; *to dissociate one's self, to part,* 1 Cor. 7:10, 11, 15; *to withdraw, depart,* Acts 1:4; 18:1, 2; Phlm. 15; *to be aloof,* Heb. 7:26* [5563] See *divorce; separate.*

[6005] χωρίον *chōrion* 10x *a place, spot;* Mt. 26:36; Mk. 14:32; *a field, farm, estate, domain,* Jn. 4:5; Acts 1:18, 19(2x); 4:34; 5:3, 8; 28:7* [5564] See *field; place.*

[6006] χωρίς *chōris* 41x can function as an improper prep., *apart,* Jn. 20:7; *apart from, parted from,* Jn. 15:5; Jas. 2:18, 20, 26; *alien from,* Eph. 2:12; *apart from, on a distinct footing from,* 1 Cor. 11:11; *apart from, distinct from, without the intervention of,* Rom. 3:21, 28; 4:6; *apart from* the company of, *independently of,* 1 Cor. 4:8; Heb. 11:40 *without* the presence of, Heb. 9:28; *without* the agency of, Jn. 1:3; Rom. 10:14; *without* the employment of, Mt. 13:34; Mk. 4:34; Heb. 7:20, 21; 9:7, 18, 22; *without,* Lk. 6:49; Phil. 2:14; 1 Tim. 2:8; 5:21; Phlm. 14; Heb. 10:28; 11:6; 12:8, 14; *clear from,* Heb. 7:7; *irrespectively of,* Rom. 7:8, 9; *without reckoning, besides,* Mt. 14:21; 15:38; 2 Cor. 11:28; *with the exception of,* Heb. 4:15 [5565]

[6008] χῶρος *chōros* 1x *Corus,* or *Caurus, the northwest wind;* meton, *the northwest* quarter of the heavens, Acts 27:12* [5566]

[6010] ψάλλω *psallō* 5x *to move by a touch, to twitch; to touch, strike* the strings or chords of an instrument; absol. *to play on a stringed instrument; to sing to music;* in NT *to sing praises,* Rom. 15:9; 1 Cor. 14:15; Eph. 5:19; Jas. 5:13* [5567] See *sing.*

[6011] ψαλμός *psalmos* 7x *impulse, touch* of the chords of a stringed instrument; in NT *a sacred song, psalm,* Lk. 20:42; 24:44; Acts 1:20; 13:33; 1 Cor. 14:26; Eph. 5:19; Col. 3:16* [5568] See *psalm.*

[6012] ψευδάδελφος *pseudadelphos* 2x *a false brother, a pretend Christian,* 2 Cor. 11:26; Gal. 2:4* [5569]

[6013] ψευδαπόστολος *pseudapostolos* 1x *a false apostle, pretend minister of Christ,* 2 Cor. 11:13* [5570]

[6014] ψευδης *pseudēs* 3x *false, lying,* Acts 6:13; Rev. 2:2; in NT pl. *maintainers* *of* religious *falsehood, corrupters of the truth* of God, Rev. 21:8* [5571]

[6015] ψευδοδιδάσκαλος *pseudodidaskalos* 1x *a false teacher, one who teaches false doctrines,* 2 Pet. 2:1* [5572]

[6016] ψευδολόγος *pseudologos* 1x *false-speaking,* 1 Tim. 4:2* [5573]

[6017] ψεύδομαι *pseudomai* 12x *lie,* Mt. 5:11; Acts 5:4; Rom. 9:1; 2 Cor. 11:31 [5574] See *lie.*

[6018] ψευδομαρτυρέω *pseudomartyreō* 5x *to bear false witness, give false testimony,* Mt. 19:18; Mk. 10:19; 14:56, 57; Lk. 18:20* [5576]

[6019] ψευδομαρτυρία *pseudomartyria* 2x *false witness, false testimony,* Mt. 15:19; 26:59* [5577]

[6020] ψευδόμαρτυς *pseudomartys* 2x *a false witness,* Mt. 26:60 (2x); 1 Cor. 15:15* [5575]

[6021] ψευδοπροφήτης *pseudoprophētēs* 11x *a false prophet, one who falsely claims to speak by divine inspiration,* whether as a foreteller of future events, or as a teacher of doctrines, Mt. 7:15; 24:24; Mk. 13:22; Acts 13:6; 1 Jn. 4:1; Rev. 16:13 [5578] See *false prophet.*

[6022] ψεῦδος *pseudos* 10x *falsehood,* Jn. 8:44; Eph. 4:25; 2 Thess. 2:9, 11; 1 Jn. 2:21, 27; in NT religious *falsehood, perversion* of religious truth, *false religion,* Rom. 1:25; *the practices of false religion,* Rev. 14:15; 21:27; 22:15* [5579] See *deception; falsehood; lie.*

[6023] ψευδόχριστος *pseudochristos* 2x *a false Christ, pretend Messiah,* Mt. 24:24; Mk. 13:22* [5580]

[6024] ψευδώνυμος *pseudōnymos* 1x *falsely named, falsely called,* 1 Tim. 6:20* [5581]

[6025] ψεῦσμα *pseusma* 1x *a falsehood, lie;* in NT *untruthfulness,* Rom. 3:7* [5582]

[6026] ψεύστης *pseustēs* 10x *one who utters a falsehood, a liar,* Jn. 8:44, 55; Rom. 3:4; 1 Tim. 1:10; Tit. 1:12; 1 Jn. 1:10; 2:4, 22; 4:20; 5:10* [5583] See *liar.*

[6027] ψηλαφάω *psēlaphaō* 4x *to feel, handle,* Lk. 24:39; *to feel* or *grope for* or *after,* as persons in the dark, Acts 17:27; Heb. 12:18; 1 Jn. 1:1* [5584]

[6028] ψηφίζω *psēphizō* 2x *to reckon by means of pebbles, compute by counters;* hence genr. *to compute, reckon, calculate,* Lk. 14:28; Rev. 13:18* [5585]

[6029] ψῆφος *psēphos* 3x *a small stone, pebble; a pebble* variously employed, especially in a ballot; hence, *a vote, suffrage,* Acts 26:10; *a pebble* or *stone;* probably given as a token, Rev. 2:17 (2x)* [5586]

[6030] ψιθυρισμός *psithurismos* 1x *a whispering; a* calumnious *whispering, gossip,* 2 Cor. 12:20* [5587]

[6031] ψιθυριστής *psithuristēs* 1x *a whisperer; a whisperer, gossip,* Rom. 1:29* [5588]

[6033] ψιχίον *psichion* 2x *a morsel, crumb, bit,* Mt. 15:27; Mk. 7:28* [5589]

[6034] ψυχή *psychē* 103x *breath; the principle of animal life; the life,* Mt. 2:20; 6:25; Mk. 3:4; Lk. 21:19; Jn. 10:11; *an inanimate being,* 1 Cor. 15:45; *a* human *individual, soul,* Acts 2:41; 3:23; 7:14; 27:37; Rom. 13:1; 1 Pet. 3:20; *the* immaterial *soul,* Mt. 10:28; 1 Pet. 1:9; 2:11, 25; 4:19; *the soul* as the seat of religious and moral sentiment, Mt. 11:29; Acts 14:2, 22; 15:24; Eph. 6:6; *the soul,* as a seat of feeling, Mt. 12:18; 26:38; *the soul, the* inner *self,* Lk. 12:19 [5590] See *life; mind; person; soul.*

[6035] ψυχικός *psychikos* 6x *pertaining to the life* or *soul;* in NT *animal,* as distinguished from spiritual subsistence, 1 Cor. 15:44, 46; *occupied with mere animal things, animal, sensual,* 1 Cor. 2:14; Jas. 3:15; Jude 19* [5591]

[6036] ψῦχος *psychos* 3x *cold,* Jn. 18:18; Acts 28:2; 2 Cor. 11:27* [5592]

[6037] ψυχρός *psychros* 4x *cool, cold,* Mt. 10:42; met. Rev. 3:15, 16* [5593]

[6038] ψύχω *psychō* 1x *to breathe; to cool;* pass. *to be cooled;* met. of affection, Mt. 24:12* [5594]

[6039] ψωμίζω *psōmizō* 2x pr. *to feed by morsels;* hence, genr. *to feed, supply with food,* Rom. 12:20; *to bestow in supplying food,* 1 Cor. 13:3* [5595]

[6040] ψωμίον *psōmion* 4x *a bit, morsel, mouthful,* Jn. 13:26, 27, 30* [5596]

[6041] ψώχω *psōchō* 1x *to rub in pieces,* as the ears of grain, Lk. 6:1* [5597]

[6042] Ὦ *ō* 3x *Omega,* the last letter of the Greek alphabet, hence, met. τὸ Ω, *the last,* Rev. 1:8; 21:6; 22:13* [5598] See *Alpha; Omega.*

[6043] ὦ *ō* 17x *O!,* Mt. 15:28; Mk. 9:19; Acts 1:1; Rom. 2:1, 3; 11:33 [5599]

[6045] ὧδε *hōde* 61x *here, in this place,* Mt. 12:6, 41; ὧδε ἢ ὧδε, *here* or *there,* Mt. 24:23; τὰ ὧδε, *the state of things here,* Col. 4:9; met. *herein, in this thing,* Rev. 13:10, 18; *to this place,* Mt. 8:29; 14:18 [5602]

[6046] ᾠδή *ōdē* 7x *an ode, song, hymn,* Eph. 5:19; Col. 3:16; Rev. 5:9; 14:3; 15:3* [5603]

[6047] ὠδίν *ōdin* 4x *the spasms* or *pains,* of a woman in travail, *a birth pang,* 1 Thess. 5:3; pl. met. *birth throes, preliminary troubles* to the development of a catastrophe, Mt. 24:8; Mk. 13:8; from the Hebrew, *a stringent band, a snare, noose,* Acts 2:24* [5604]

[6048] ὠδίνω *ōdinō* 3x *to be in travail,* Gal. 4:27; Rev. 12:2; met. *to travail with, suffer birth pangs, to make effort to bring to* spiritual birth, Gal. 4:19* [5605] See *birth pangs; travail.*

[6049] ὦμος *ōmos* 2x *the shoulder,* Mt. 23:4; Lk. 15:5* [5606]

[6050] ὠνέομαι *ōneomai* 1x *to buy, purchase,* Acts 7:16* [5608]

[6051] ᾠόν *ōon* 1x *an egg,* Lk. 11:12* [5609]

[6052] ὥρα *hōra* 106x *a limited portion of time,* marked out by part of a settled routine or train of circumstances; *a season of the year; time of day,* Mt. 14:15; Mk. 6:35; 11:11; *an hour,* Mt. 20:3; Jn. 11:9; in NT *an* eventful *season,* 1 Jn. 2:18 (2x); Rev. 3:10; 14:7; *due time,* Jn. 16:21; Rom. 13:11; *a* destined *period, hour,* Mt. 26:45; Mk. 14:35; Jn. 2:4; 7:30; *a short period,* Mt. 26:40; Jn. 5:35; 2 Cor. 7:8; Gal. 2:5; 1 Thess. 2:17; Phlm. 15; *a point of time, time,* Mt. 8:13; 24:42; Lk. 2:38 [5610] See *hour.*

[6053] ὡραῖος *hōraios* 4x *timely, seasonable; in prime, blooming;* in NT *beautiful,* Mt. 23:27; Acts 3:2, 10; Rom. 10:15* [5611]

[6054] ὠρύομαι *ōryomai* 1x *to howl; to roar,* as a lion, 1 Pet. 5:8* [5612]

[6055] ὡς *hōs* 504x conjunction formed from the relative pronoun ὅς, used as a comparative part. and conj., *as,* correlatively, Mk. 4:26; Jn. 7:46; Rom. 5:15; *as, like as,* Mt. 10:16; Eph. 5:8; *according as,* Gal. 6:10; *as, as it were,* Rev. 8:8; *as,* Lk. 16:1; Acts 3:12; before numerals, *about,* Mk. 5:13; conj. *that,* Acts 10:28; *how,* Rom. 11:2; *when,* Mt. 28:9; Phil. 2:23; as an exclamatory particle, *how,* Rom. 10:15; equivalent to ὥστε, *accordingly,* Heb. 3:11; also, *on condition that, provided that,* Acts 20:24; ὡς εἰπεῖν, *so to speak,* Heb. 7:9 [5613]

[6057] ὡσαννά *hōsanna* 6x *Hosanna! save now, help now,* Mt. 21:9, 15; Mk. 11:9, 10; Jn. 12:13* [5614] See *hosanna.*

[6058] ὡσαύτως *hōsautōs* 17x *just so, in just the same way* or *manner, likewise,* Mt. 20:5; 21:30 [5615]

[6059] ὡσεί *hōsei* 21[illegible] *...t were,* ...ms of num- *as, like,* Mt. 3:16 [illegible] 14:21; Lk. 1:56; ber or qu[illegible]

[6060] Ὡσηέ *hōsēe* 1x *Hosea,* pr. name, indecl., Rom. 9:25* [5617]

[6061] ὥσπερ *hōsper* 36x *just as, as,* Mt. 6:2; 24:37; 1 Thess. 5:3 [5618]

[6062] ὡσπερεί *hōsperei* 1x *just as if; as it were,* 1 Cor. 15:8* [5619]

[6063] ὥστε *hōste* 83x *so that, so as that, so as to,* Mt. 8:24; Mk. 2:12; Acts 14:1; Gal. 2:13; as an illative particle, *therefore, consequently,* Mt. 12:12; 23:31 [5620]

[6064] ὠτάριον *ōtarion* 2x *an ear,* Mt. 14:47; Jn. 18:10* [5621]

[6065] ὠτίον *ōtion* 3x in NT simply equivalent to οὖς, *an ear,* Mt. 26:51; Lk. 22:51; Jn. 18:26* [5621]

[6066] ὠφέλεια *ōpheleia* 2x *help; profit, gain, advantage, benefit,* Rom. 3:1; Jude 16* [5622]

[6067] ὠφελέω *ōpheleō* 15x *to help, profit, benefit, accomplish,* Mt. 27:24; Mk. 7:11; Rom. 2:25; *be of value,* Jn. 6:63 [5623] See *gain; profit; value.*

[6068] ὠφέλιμος *ōphelimos* 4x *profitable, useful, beneficial; serviceable,* 1 Tim. 4:8 (2x); 2 Tim. 3:16; Tit. 3:8* [5624]